Marguerite Gastin

P9-BHY-267

COLUMBIA
DICTIONARY
OF MODERN
EUROPEAN
LITERATURE

COLUMBIA

DICTIONARY

OF MODERN

EUROPEAN

LITERATURE

SECOND EDITION,
FULLY REVISED
AND ENLARGED

JEAN-ALBERT BÉDÉ AND
WILLIAM B. EDGERTON
GENERAL
EDITORS

COLUMBIA UNIVERSITY PRESS
NEW YORK
1980

"The Magpie," by Artur Lundkvist, translated by W. H. Auden and Leif Sjöberg, © 1974 by New Directions Corp.

"We Are Many" from *Antiworlds and the Fifth Ace*, by Andrei Voznesensky, edited by Patricia Blake and Max Hayward, © 1966, 1967 by Basic Books, © 1963 by Encounter.

The First Edition of the *Columbia Dictionary of Modern European Literature*, Horatio Smith, General Editor, was published in 1947.

Library of Congress Cataloging in Publication Data
Main entry under title:

Columbia dictionary of modern European literature.

    1.   European literature—20th century—Dictionaries.
2.   European literature—20th century—Bio-bibliography.
3.   Authors European—20th century—Biography.
I. Bédé, Jean-Albert. II. Edgerton, William Benbow, 1914-
PN771.C575   1980   803   80-17082
ISBN 0-231-03717-1

Columbia University Press
New York   Guildford, Surrey
Copyright © 1980 Columbia University Press
All rights reserved
Printed in the United States of America

Dedicated to the memory of
Jean-Albert Bédé (1903–1977),
Ernest J. Simmons (1903–1972),
and
Horatio Smith (1886–1946)

PREFACE

The map of the Western world is fragmented by a double network of linguistic and national boundaries, but there can be no doubt whatever that the literary map of the West—for all its fruitful diversity—is one variegated whole. Sharing common cultural roots in Greek and Roman antiquity and the Judeo-Christian heritage, Europe and its cultural progeny in the New World have engaged for centuries in a continual literary traffic in ideas, themes, plots, and movements. The Italian Renaissance, the Spanish baroque, 17th-century French classicism, English preromanticism, German romanticism, all are examples of the multifarious strands woven into the fabric of European literature, as are the contributions not only of great writers from large nations—Dante, Shakespeare, Molière—but also of those from small countries, such as Erasmus of Holland, Rousseau of Switzerland, and Ibsen of Norway. Spain has contributed two great themes, Don Juan and Don Quixote, and at least one fictional genre—the picaresque novel— that can be traced all over Europe. In the early 18th century, Addison and Steele in their *Spectator* provided the model and the name for a new kind of literary journal that was imitated from France and Spain in the West to Poland, Russia, and Romania in the East. The great Russian poet Pushkin took the theme of "The Golden Cockerel" from the American Washington Irving, who had acquired it in Spain and used it in one of his tales in *The Alhambra*. As René Wellek and Austin Warren rightly observed many years ago in their *Theory of Literature,* the idea of a self-contained national literature is obviously false.

For this reason the *Columbia Dictionary of Modern European Literature* (Second Edition) has an obvious value for students and scholars in the growing field of comparative literature. But it is equally useful to specialists in a single national literature who are aware of the need to see their specialty within its larger context, and will serve the throng of serious readers all over the English-speaking world who have helped to provide such writers as Camus and Sartre, Günter Grass and Heinrich Böll, Pasternak and Solzhenitsyn, with larger audiences in translation than in their native language. For the scholarly specialist in English, or French, or any of the other European literatures, the *Dictionary* will serve as an indispensable supplement to the narrower but more detailed body of information available in reference works confined to a single national literature.

This Second Edition of the *Dictionary* is a fully revised and enlarged version of the work that was first published in 1947 under the general editorship of Horatio Smith, then chairman of the French Department at Columbia University. Twenty-five years later, encouraged by the favorable reception of the First Edition and the continuing demand for it, the Columbia University Press undertook a search for a suitable general editor to plan and supervise the creation of a Second Edition. This search culminated in 1972 with the appointment of Jean-Albert Bédé, then Blanche W. Knopf Professor Emeritus of French Literature at Columbia University, who immediately set about reviewing the First Edition, producing new tentative lists of articles for each national literature on the basis of subsequent developments, and selecting an editorial staff of 28 scholars to take responsibility for the 36 European literatures exclusive of English that were to be represented. The present volume is essentially a monument to the vision, energy, and combination of diplomacy and firmness, that were the hallmark of Professor Bédé. Manuscript for the new edition of the *Dictionary* had started coming in when Professor Bédé—apparently in the best of health and vigorously engaged in his editorial duties—died suddenly in January 1977.

In the emergency caused by this tragic loss, the Columbia University Press turned for a successor as general editor to the Second Edition's associate editor for the Slavic literatures, whom Professor Bédé had chosen in consultation with the late Ernest J. Simmons, then Professor Emeritus of Russian Literature at Columbia University. The new general editor was almost immediately confronted with the task of finding replacements for three key positions on the editorial staff. Professor Bédé himself had been in charge of French literature and thus left this section without an editor; and a combination of emergencies, including illness, cut short the work of Professor Joseph Bauke of Columbia University as editor for German, and of Professor Germán Bleiberg then of Vassar College as editor for Spanish. A special word of grateful acknowledgment is extended here to the three scholars who took over responsibility for these crucially important sections on short notice and at a late hour: Professors Douglas W. Alden of the University of Virginia, for French; Harold L. Boudreau of the University of Massachusetts, for Spanish; and A. Leslie Willson of the University of Texas, for German.

The Second Edition of the *Dictionary* takes as its starting point the period toward the end of the 19th century when Europe was swept by a wave of new literary movements, which were largely inspired by the French symbolists and were known by various names in different countries—symbolism, decadence, and modernism being among the most widely used. Nevertheless, writers were selected for inclusion in the *Dictionary* on the basis of their relevance to 20th-century literature. Baudelaire and Bécquer are included even though they died in 1867 and 1870 respectively, because French symbolism and Spanish poetry of the 20th century can scarcely be imagined without their seminal influence. Dostoyevsky, who died in 1881, is included; but Turgenev, who died in 1883, is omitted; this because Turgenev is a great Russian writer of the past, but Dostoyevsky is a vital force in Western literature to this day.

In selecting writers as subjects for inclusion in this volume we were committed above all to seeking out the best in each literature—but the best according to whose standards? Those of the country that produced literature? Those of the English-speaking countries for which this *Dictionary* is published? Those of the scholars (in most cases, American) who have prepared the *Dictionary*? There are no simple answers to such questions. The Anglo-Saxon world has never properly appreciated Racine; Edgar Allan Poe tends to be more highly regarded in France than in his homeland; and the latest Soviet literary encyclopedia gives more space to Jack London and the now forgotten Mayne Reid than to Emerson, Hawthorne, Melville, or Henry James—while omitting its own Solzhenitsyn entirely. In the end the choices made here could only reflect the best judgment of the editors themselves; and if, when another quarter-century has passed, some new group of editors review our work in preparation for a Third Edition, those of us who are still around will no doubt be highly curious to see how well our present judgment has been vindicated.

The relative allocation of space among individual writers and national literatures has required literally hundreds of value judgments on the part of the editorial staff. Confident as we are about the validity of our collective decisions, we are even more confident that all our scholarly colleagues will be able here to find something somewhere on which to disagree with us. Such disagreements are evidence of the fallibility that Providence has distributed with such even-handed justice among editors and their critics, but such disagreements are also testimony to the strength of free and unfettered scholarship.

The approximately 500 contributors to this volume (more than twice as many as in the First Edition) represent a distinguished array of scholars not only from the United States and Canada but also from several countries in Europe. In general, the scholars of foreign background have been encouraged to write in the language in which they felt the most comfortable, and the editors have made the necessary English translations. For example, the Slavic section alone includes articles originally written in French, German, Polish, Russian, and Serbo-Croatian. Initials at the end of each article identify the author or authors, as well as the revisors of articles reprinted from the First Edition in updated form. Immediately following this preface is a complete list of editors and contributors, with a key to the initials identifying them.

Basically, this new edition of the *Dictionary* follows the pattern of the first. The number of authors treated in individual articles has almost doubled, rising from 1,167 to 1,853; but each article continues to provide basic biographical information about the writer, a critical discussion of the writer's principal works, and a brief bibliography compiled especially with a view to meeting the needs of readers who may not be specialists in the literature to which the writer belongs. Each survey article on a national literature contains cross-references (indicated by small capitals) to individual articles on the principal authors in that literature, and similar cross-references within the articles on individual authors provide assistance to the reader in seeing the patterns of influence and relationship that run through the whole of Western literature. For all except the most obvious foreign titles, English translations have been provided. If a work has been translated into English, the title and publication date of the translation are given. Unless otherwise indicated, the dates listed after plays refer to first publication rather than first performance. The place of publication for works is given only in some cases (notably with émigré writers) where it is not within the country to whose national literature the work in question belongs. Names and titles in Bulgarian, Russian, and Ukrainian are spelled in a transliteration system designed to facilitate their pronunciation by English-speakers. Unfortunately, it has proved impossible to present any simple guide to the pronunciation of names that are all written in the same 26 letters of the Latin alphabet but according to more than 20 different systems of orthography. In the bibliographies, many periodicals are abbreviated according to a system based on that used in the annual *MLA International Bibliography*; a list of these abbreviations, with their apposite periodical titles, follows the list of contributors (in the periodical list, capitalization of foreign periodical titles also follows the style of the *MLA International Bibliography*).

For me personally as general editor, the experience of sharing in the preparation of the *Columbia Dictionary of Modern European Literature* with this group of prominent scholars has been strenuous, time-consuming, and immensely rewarding. In the process of reading through the hundreds of pages of the book in typescript, this armchair Columbus has discovered enough Americas to keep him busy with literary explorations for the rest of his lifetime; and he offers the hope that the *Dictionary* may give all its readers the same experience.

I cannot conclude this preface without a word of warm appreciation to the staff of the Columbia University Press, and particularly to Agnes Greenhall, that model editor in charge of the *Dictionary,* who along with her associates revealed an uncanny talent for taking each contributor's words (including my own) and making them say more clearly and effectively what we had intended them to say in the first place.

WILLIAM B. EDGERTON
Indiana University
March
1980

CONTRIBUTORS

Names are arranged alphabetically according to the initials that
appear at the conclusion of each article. Some articles published in
the First Edition of the *Dictionary* have been retained in the Second
Edition; the authors of these articles are identified only by the term
"First Edition" after their names. An asterisk* after the name of a contributor to the Second Edition indicates that the contributor is deceased.

A.A. Anthony Adamovich, New York City
A.A.C. António A. Cirugião, University of
    Connecticut
A.Am. Alba Amoia, Hunter College, City
    University of New York
A.Ar. Artine Artinian, Bard College
A.As. Andrés Amorós, Complutense University of
    Madrid
A.B. Anna Balakian, New York University
A.Bo. André Bourgeois, Rice University
A.C. Anthony Caprio, American University
A.Ch. Albert Chesneau, University of Lyon
A.C.L. André C. Lévêque, First Edition
A.D. Andonis Decavalles, Fairleigh Dickinson
    University
A. del R. Angel del Río, First Edition
A.E. Alvin Eustis, University of California,
    Berkeley
A.E.S. Armand E. Singer, West Virginia University
A.F. Albert Feuillerat, First Edition
A.G. Alrik Gustafson, First Edition
A.G.A. A. Gerald Anderson, University of
    Washington
A.G.B. Allan G. Blunden, Cornwall, England
A.H.G. Anne Hyde Greet, University of California,
    Santa Barbara
A.I. Antonio Illiano, University of North
    Carolina, Chapel Hill
A.Id. Andrés Iduarte, First Edition
A.J.B. Adriaan J. Barnouw, First Edition
A.J.K. Arthur J. Knodel, University of Southern
    California
A.J.W. Archibald J. Welton, College of Staten
    Island, City University of New York
A.K. Ante Kadić, Indiana University
A.Ka. Alexander Kaun, First Edition
A.L. Asmund Lien, University of Trondheim
A.L.M. Anne L. Martin, Flinders University of
    South Australia
A.L.W. A. Leslie Willson, University of Texas,
    Austin
A.M. André Marissel, Noisy-le-Sec, France
A.McV. Albert McVitty, First Edition
A.M.G. Anthony M. Gisolfi, State University of
    New York, Albany
A.M.S. Alex M. Shane, State University of New
    York, Albany
A.P. Arshi Pipa, University of Minnesota

A.Pal. Augustus Pallotta, Syracuse University
A.Pao. Anne Paolucci, Saint John's University
A.P.B. Angelo P. Bertocci, Wolcott, Vermont
A.P.C. Arthur P. Coleman, First Edition
A.P.D. Andrew P. Debicki, University of Kansas
A.P.O. Anna P. Otten, Antioch College
A.R. Anna Raitière, York College, City
    University of New York
A.Re. Alojz Rebula, Trieste
A.R.T. Anthony R. Terrizzi, University of
    Massachusetts
A.Ruf. Antonio Rufino, Rutgers University
A.Rus. Adelaide Russo, Barnard College
A.S. Arlette Shenkan, Middlesex County College
A.S.-B. Antonio Sánchez-Barbudo, University of
    Wisconsin, Madison
A.Sc. Albert Schinz, First Edition
A.Si. Alain Silvera, Bryn Mawr College
A.Sp. Aleksandar Spasov, Skopje, Yugoslavia
A.Sz. Alex Szogyi, Hunter College, City
    University of New York
A.T. Alberto Traldi, City College, City University
    of New York
A.V. Antanas Vaičiulaitis, Bethesda, Maryland
A. van E. A. van Elslander, State University of Ghent
A.V.R. Alphonse V. Roche, Northwestern
    University
A.W. Andrzej Wirth, Lehman College, City
    University of New York
A.Z. Alicja Zadroźna, Bloomington, Indiana
B.B. Bruno Braunrot, Georgia State University
B.C. Biruta Cap, Easton, Pennsylvania
B.Ci. Birutė Ciplijauskaité, University of
    Wisconsin, Madison
B.Co. Beatrice Corrigan,* Toronto, Canada
B.Cz. Bogdan Czaykowski, University of British
    Columbia
B.G. Bernard Guyon,* University of Provence,
    France
B.K. Bettina Knapp, Hunter College, City
    University of New York
B.Ko. Blaže Koneski, Skopje, Yugoslavia
B.K.S. Brita K. Stendahl, Radcliffe Institute
B.M. Bruce Merry, University College, Dublin
B.M.W. Benjamin M. Woodbridge, First Edition
B.N.W. Betty Nance Weber,* University of Texas,
    Austin
B.P.S. Barry P. Scherr, Dartmouth College

B.Q.M. Bayard Q. Morgan, First Edition
B.R.L. Bluma Renée Lang, First Edition
B.S. Birgitta Steene, University of Washington
B.Su. Benjamin Suhl, Fairleigh Dickinson University
B.Sw. Brian Swann, Cooper Union
B.V. Bronius Vaskelis, Lafayette College
B.W. Brita Wigforss, University of Göteborg
C.A. Christos Alexiou, University of Birmingham, England
C.A.M. Charles A. Moser, George Washington University
C.A.Ma. Clarence A. Manning, First Edition
C.A.Me. Carmine A. Mezzacappa, Rutgers University
C.As. Claudette Asselin, Rome, Italy
C.B. Clarence Brown, Princeton University
C.Ba. César Barja, First Edition
C.C. C. Choquet, New York City
C.C.Z. Cecile C. Zorach, University of Michigan
C.E.F. Charlotte E. Forsyth, First Edition
C.E.F.S. Claire E. F. Schub, Princeton University
C.H.B. C. H. Bedford, University of Toronto
C.J. Claudia Johnson, University of Texas, Austin
C.K. Charles Klopp, Ohio State University
C.L. Carlos Lynes, University of Pennsylvania
C.L.B. Claude L. Bourcier, First Edition
C.L.H. Claire L. Huffman, Brooklyn College, City University of New York
C.M. Christopher Middleton, University of Texas, Austin
C.M.A. Ciriaco Morón Arroyo, Cornell University
C.Mi. Czesław Miłosz, University of California, Berkeley
C.M.P. Costas M. Proussis, Hellenic College
C.P. Claude Pichois, Vanderbilt University
C.S. Christiane Seiler, Indiana University, Purdue University
C.S.B. Catharine S. Brosman, Tulane University
C.W. Charles Weir, Jr., First Edition
D.A.L. David A. Lowe, Vanderbilt University
D.B. Dagmar Barnouw, University of Pittsburgh
D.Ba. Dominique Baudouin, University of British Columbia
D.Be. Dominique Bertin, Free University of Brussels
D.Br. Dorothy Brodin, Lehman College, City University of New York
D.B.R. Donald B. Rice, Hamline University
D.C. Dana Carton, Cedar Crest College
D.C.G. Daniel C. Gerould, Graduate Center, City University of New York
D.C.H. David C. Hoy, Barnard College
D.F. Donald Fanger, Harvard University
D.Fi. Donald Fiene, University of Tennessee
D.H.C. David H. Chisholm, University of Arizona
D.H.S. David H. Stewart, Texas Agricultural and Mechanical University
D.J.P. David J. Parent, Illinois State University
D.J.W. David J. Ward, Frankfurt am Main, West Germany
D.K. Dodona Kiziria, Indiana University
D.K.A. Doris King Arjona, First Edition
D.M. Dante Matelli, Rome, Italy
D.N. David Noakes, New York University
D.O'C. David O'Connell, University of Illinois, Chicago Circle
D.R.McK. Douglas R. McKay, University of Colorado

D.S. Dina Sherzer, University of Texas, Austin
D.T.W. Daniel T. Weissbort, University of Iowa
D.V. Darío Villanueva, University of Santiago de Compostela
D. van B. Dina van Berlaer-Hellemans, Free University of Brussels
D.W. David Welsh, University of Michigan
D.W.A. Douglas W. Alden, University of Virginia
E.B. Erhard Bahr, University of California, Los Angeles
E.B.N. Elizabeth B. Neatrour, James Madison University
E.D.C. Earle D. Clowney, Atlanta University
E.F. Ernst Feise, First Edition
E.F.H. Edith F. Helman, First Edition
E.G.-L. Emilio González-López, First Edition
E.H. Einar Haugen, Harvard University
E.Ha. Elfi Hahn, Stanford University
E.Har. Edward Harvey, Kenyon College
E.H.H. E. Herman Hespelt, First Edition
E.H.L. Edgar H. Lehrman, Washington University
E.Ho. Erich Hofacker, First Edition
E.H.S. Edna H. Spitz, Stanford University
E.I.F. E. Inman Fox, Knox College
E.J. Ernst Jockers, First Edition
E.J.C. Edward J. Czerwinski, State University of New York, Stony Brook
E.K. Edmund Keeley, Princeton University
E.Kr. Egbert Krispyn, University of Georgia
E.L. Emanuele Licastro, State University of New York, Buffalo
E.M. Elaine Marks, University of Wisconsin, Madison
E.M.D. Eduardo Moyone Dias, University of California, Los Angeles
E.M.F. E. M. Fleissner, First Edition
E.Mo. Ernst Morwitz, First Edition
E.M.-S. Edouard Morot-Sir, University of North Carolina, Chapel Hill
E.M.T. Ewa M. Thompson, Rice University
E.O. Erika Ostrovsky, New York University
E.R. Ernst Rose, First Edition
E.S.B. Ethel S. Brook, New York City
E.W. Edward Wasiolek, University of Chicago
F.B. Fernand Baldensperger, First Edition
F.Br. Friedrich Bruns, First Edition
F. de O. Federico de Onís, First Edition
F. de P. Ferran de Pol, First Edition
F.F.-T. Francisco Fernández-Turienzo, University of Massachusetts
F.G.L. Francisco Garcia Lorca, First Edition
F.G.P. Frederick G. Peters, Barnard College
F.H.M. Franz H. Mautner, First Edition
F.J.J. Frederic J. Jones, University College, Cardiff
F.M.B. Fedor M. Ballo, Boulogne-Billancourt, France
F.R.-R. Francisco Ruis-Ramón, Purdue University
F.S. Franz Schneider, Gonzaga University
F.Sp. Frank Spiecker, First Edition
F.V. Fernand Vial, Fordham University
F.Ve. Fernand Verhesen, Royal Academy of French Language and Literature, Brussels
F.Vi. Fred Viebahn, Oberlin College
F.W.J.H. Frederick W. J. Heuser, First Edition
G.B. Gunilla Bergsten, University of Uppsala
G.Bi. Gloria Bien, Connecticut College
G.Bl. Germán Bleiberg, State University of New York, Albany
G.Br. Germaine Brée, Wake Forest University
G.C. Glauco Cambon, University of Connecticut

G.Ca. Giovanni Carsaniga, University of Sussex, England

G.Ce. Giovanni Cecchetti, University of California, Los Angeles

G.C.S. George C. Schoolfield, Yale University

G.D.K. Gary D. Keller, Eastern Michigan University

G.E.K. Grant E. Kaiser, Emory University

G.E.W. George E. Wellwarth, State University of New York, Binghamton

G.G. George Gömöri, University of Cambridge

G.Gi. George Gibian, Cornell University

G.G.S. Gisela G. Strand, Hope College

G.Gu. Germán Gullón, University of Pennsylvania

G.H. Geoffrey Hosking, University of Essex, England

G.K. George Kline, Bryn Mawr College

G.Ke. Günther Keil, First Edition

G.L. Georges Lefranc, Antony, France

G.M. Gita May, Columbia University

G.M.M. Gerald M. Moser, Pennsylvania State University

G.O. Gavin Orton, The University, Hull

G.P.B. Gian Paolo Biasin, University of Texas, Austin

G.P.O. Gifford P. Orwen, State University College, Geneseo

G.R.B. Gretchen R. Besser, South Orange, New Jersey

G.R.Bl. Gerda R. Blumenthal, Catholic University of America

G.S. G. Singh, Queen's University, Belfast

G.Sh. Gennady Shmakov, New York City

G.Si. Georges Sion, Royal Academy of French Language and Literature, Brussels

G.S.N.L. George S. N. Luckyj, University of Toronto

G.St. Gleb Struve, University of California, Berkeley

G.W.R. George W. Reinhardt, University of Connecticut

G.Z. George Zayed, Boston College

H.A.G. Howard A. Goldman, Tel Aviv University

H.A.L. Hanna Astrup Larsen, First Edition

H.A.S. Heinrich A. Stammler, University of Kansas

H.B. Hillel Barzel, Bar Ilan University, Israel

H.Bä. Hans Bänziger, Bryn Mawr College

H.Bf. Hermann Barnstorff, First Edition

H.-B.M. Hans-Bernhard Moeller, University of Texas, Austin

H.Bo. Hermann Boechenstein, First Edition

H.C. Halina Chybowska, First Edition

H.C.B. H. Chonon Berkowitz, First Edition

H.E. Herman Ermolaev, Princeton University

H.E.P. Helmut E. Pfanner, University of New Hampshire

H.F. Harold Fisch, Bar Ilan University, Israel

H.I. Hans Isaksson, University of Stockholm

H.K. Halvdan Koht, First Edition

H.K.M. Heinz K. Meier, Old Dominion University

H.L. Harry Lawton, University of California, Santa Barbara

H.L.B. Harold L. Boudreau, University of Massachusetts

H.L.K. Herbert L. Kaufman, Alabama School of Fine Arts

H.McL. Hugh McLean, University of California, Berkeley

H.P. Henri Peyre, Graduate Center, City University of New York

H.P.S. Hartmut P. Schnell, University of California, Irvine

H.R. Harold Raley, University of Houston

H.Re. Helmut Rehder, First Edition

H.Res. H. Reshetar, University of Washington

H.S. Helene Scher, Amherst College

H.Sc. Heinrich Schneider, First Edition

H.Se. Henning Sehmsdorf, University of Washington

H.Sm. Horatio Smith, General Editor, First Edition

H.S.N. Harald S. Naess, University of Wisconsin, Madison

H.St. Herbert Steiner, First Edition

H.T.N. Helen T. Naughton, College of Notre Dame, Belmont, California

H.T.Y. Howard T. Young, Pomona College

H.W.H. Hermann W. Haller, Queens College, City University of New York

H.W.P. Hugh W. Puckett, First Edition

H.W.T. H. W. Tjalsma, Leverett, Massachusetts

I.B. Irma Brandeis, Bard College

I.C. Izidor Cankar, First Edition

I. de W. Isabelle de Wyzewa, First Edition

I.H. Inge Halpert, Columbia University

I.H.C. Irina H. Corten, University of Minnesota

I.I. Ivar Ivask, *World Literature Today,* University of Oklahoma

I.S. Ivan Sanders, Suffolk County Community College

I.Si. István Siklós, London, England

I.Sk. Ian Skelton, Manchester, England

I.W. Irwin Weil, Northwestern University

J.-A.B. Jean-Albert Bédé,* First Edition

J.-A.G. Jean-Albert Goris, First Edition

J.B. Jacques Barchilon, University of Colorado

J.B.-N. Jean Bellemin-Noël, University of Paris

J.C. Joseph Cary, University of Connecticut

J.Ca. Jean Cathala, Paris, France

J.Ch. Jon Cherubini, Fort Lee, New Jersey

J.-C.M. Jean-Claude Martin, Brooklyn College, City University of New York

J.Cr. John Crispin, Vanderbilt University

J. de S. Jorge de Sena,* University of California, Santa Barbara

J.D.G. J. D. Gauthier, S. J., Boston College

J.D.Gr. Joan Delaney Grossman, University of California, Berkeley

J.D.H. J. D. Hubert, University of California, Irvine

J.E.M. John E. Malmstad, Columbia University

J.F.C. Jaume Ferran Camps, Syracuse University

J.F.E. John F. Erwin, Mount Holyoke College

J.F.G. Jane F. Goodloe, First Edition

J.G. Jerry Glenn, University of Cincinnati

J.H. Javier Herrero, University of Pittsburgh

J.Ho. Johannes Holthusen, University of Munich

J.Hy. Jean Hytier, Columbia University

J.K. Jack Kolbert, The Monterey Institute of International Studies

J.K.H. Juergen K. Hoegl, University of Illinois, Urbana

J.L. James Lawler, Dalhousie University

J.Le. Jacqueline Leiner, University of Washington

J.L.G.-M. J. L. Gómez-Martínez, University of Georgia

J.L.S. James L. Stark, Seattle University

J.Me. John Meyer, First Edition

J.M.K. Janice M. Kozma, University of Kansas

J.-M.K. Jean-Marie Klinkenberg, University of Liège

J.M.L. June M. Legge, Atlanta University

J.M.M.i V. J. M. Miguel i Vergés, First Edition

J.M.P. Joy M. Potter, University of Texas, Austin

J.O. José Ortega, University of Wisconsin, Parkside

J.O'B. Justin O'Brien, First Edition

J.O.J. José Olivio Jiménez, Hunter College, City University of New York

J.P. Jože Pogačnik, University of Novi Sad, Yugoslavia

J.-P.C. Jean-Pierre Cap, Lafayette College

J.-P.Ca. Jean-Pierre Cauvin, University of Texas, Austin

J.-P. de N. Jean-Paul de Nola, University of Palermo

J.R. Joseph Reményi, First Edition

J.R.K. Jerzy R. Krzyzanowski, Ohio State University

J.S. Jean Sareil, Columbia University

J.Sa. Joan Sales, First Edition

J.S.B. J. S. Bernstein, University of California, Los Angeles

J.Sw. Janet Swaffar, University of Texas, Austin

J.T.B. Joachim T. Baer, University of North Carolina, Greensboro

J.T.S.W. James T. S. Wheelock, University of Colorado

J.V.A. Jean V. Alter, University of Pennsylvania

J. van S. J. van Schoor, State University of Ghent

J.W. Jean Weisgerber, Free University of Brussels

J.W.D. Janet W. Díaz, Texas Technological University

J.W.S. Joe W. Shepard, Carleton College

K.A.F. Kjetil A. Flatin, University of Oslo

K.C. Kenneth Chapman, University of California, Los Angeles

K.Co. Kenneth Cornell,* Yale University

K.H. Kornel Huvos, University of Cincinnati

K.L. Kai Laitinen, University of Helsinki

K.P. Karin Petherick, University College, London

K.Pi. Kurt Pinthus, First Edition

K.R.W. Katherine R. Whitmore, First Edition

K.S.M. Kurt S. Maier, Library of Congress

L.A. Louis Adamic, First Edition

L.B. LeRoy Breunig, Barnard College

L.G.-del-V. Luis González-del-Valle, University of Nebraska

L.G.S. Leonard G. Sbrocchi, University of Ottawa

L.G.Sc. Leonard G. Schulze, University of Texas, Austin

L.K. Louis Kibler, Wayne State University

L.Ko. Leon Kochnitzky, First Edition

L.LeS. Laurent LeSage, Pennsylvania State University

L.N. Lowry Nelson, Jr., Yale University

L.R. Luciano Rebay, Columbia University

L.R.S. Louise R. Schub, Brooklyn College

L.S. Leif Sjöberg, State University of New York, Stony Brook

L.S.P. de L. Luis S. Ponce de León, California State University

L.S.R. Leon S. Roudiez, Columbia University

L.St. Leon Stilman, First Edition

L.T. Leon Twarog, Ohio State University

L.V. Lynn Visson, Hunter College, City University of New York

L.W.C. Laurence W. Cor, University of Wyoming

M.A.C. Mary Ann Caws, Graduate Center, City University of New York

M.B. Michel Bartosik, Free University of Brussels

M.Br. Micheline Braun, Graduate Center, City University of New York

M.B.-C. Micheline Besnard-Coursodon, New York City

M.Bu. Marianne Burkhard, University of Illinois, Urbana

M.C. Maurice Cagnon, Montclair State College

M.D. Mathurin Dondo, First Edition

M.E.B. Merle E. Brown, University of Iowa

M.E.C. Maurice Edgar Coindreau, First Edition

M.E.W. Margaret E. Ward, Wellesley College

M.E.W.J. Margaret E. W. Jones, University of Kentucky

M.F. Max Fischer, First Edition

M.G. Mieczysław Giergielewicz, Philadelphia, Pennsylvania

M.G.C. Maxine G. Cutler, Harrison, New York

M.Gi. Margaret Gilman, First Edition

M.G.L. Madeline G. Levine, University of North Carolina, Chapel Hill

M.H. Marc Hanrez, University of Wisconsin, Madison

M.Ha. Max Hayward,* Saint Antony's College, Oxford

M.I.M. Marilyn I. Madden, Bowling Green State University

M.J.B. M. J. Benardete, First Edition

M.J.C. Mary Jane Ciccarello, Columbia University

M.J.F. Melvin J. Friedman, University of Wisconsin, Milwaukee

M.L.C.-M. Maria Luise Caputo-Mayr, Temple University

M.L.H. Marjorie L. Hoover, New York City

M.M. Mateja Matejić, Ohio State University

M.M.C. Marion M. Coleman, First Edition

M.M.G. Mark M. Grimshaw, University of Kent, England

M.P. Marian Pankowski, Free University of Brussels

M.P.M. Mildred P. Mortimer, Haverford College

M.R. Marc Richir, Free University of Brussels

M.R.C. Michael R. Campo, Trinity College, Hartford

M.Ri. Michele Ricciardelli, State University of New York, Buffalo

M.-R.L. Marie-Rose Logan, Columbia University

M.S. Murray Sachs, Brandeis University

M.Sa. Micheline Sakharoff, California State University, Northridge

M.Sc. Marilyn Schneider, University of Minnesota

M.Sl. Marc Slonim, First Edition

M.S.M. Margaret S. Maurin, Bryn Mawr College

M. van P. Monika van Paemel, Brussels, Belgium

N.Å.S. Nils Åke Sjöstedt, University of Göteborg

N.B.A. Nicholson B. Adams, First Edition

N.L.G. Norma Lorre Goodrich, Scripps College

N.M. Nicholas Moravcevich, University of Illinois, Chicago Circle

N.R. Neal Rendleman, New York City

O.F. Otis Fellowes, Columbia University

O.F.B. Otto F. Best, University of Maryland

O.M. Olga Matich, University of Southern California

O.P.G. Ole Paus Grundt, First Edition

O.R. Olga Ragusa, Columbia University

O.Re. Otto Reinert, University of Washington

O.S.F. O. S. Fleissner, First Edition

O.W.T. Otto W. Tetzlaff, Angelo State University

P.A.C. Pierre A. Clamens, First Edition
P.-A.H. Per-Arne Henricson, Askim, Sweden
P.A.M. Paul A. Moylan, Emerson College
P.A.P. Peter A. Pertzoff, First Edition
P.B. Peter Bien, Dartmouth College
P.Bl. Patricia Blake, New York City
P.Br. Pierre Brodin, Lycée Français de New York
P.C. Patricia Carden, Cornell University
P.Ca. Peter Caws, Hunter College, City University of New York
P. de W. Paul de Wispeleare, University of Antwerp
P.D.W. Philip D. Walker, University of California, Santa Barbara
P.F. Pietro Ferrua, Lewis and Clark College
P.Fr. Pia Friedrich, University of Washington
P.G.C. Pablo Gil Casado, University of North Carolina, Chapel Hill
P.G.T. Paul G. Teodorescu, Romanian Studies Association of America
P.H. Paul Hadermann, Free University of Brussels
P.K. Philip Kolb, University of Illinois, Urbana
P.-O.W. Pierre-Olivier Walzer, University of Berne
P.R. Paul Reigstad, Pacific Lutheran University
P.R.P. Paul R. Pope, First Edition
P.S. Paul Stewart, Southern Connecticut State College
P.So. Philippe Sollers, Paris, France
P.V. Paul Várnai, Carleton University
P. van A. Paul van Aken, Steenhuize-Wijnhuize, Belgium
P.W.O'C. Patricia W. O'Connor, University of Cincinnati
P.W.S. Philip W. Silver, Columbia University
R.A. Robert Abirached, University of Caen
R.A.M. Robert A. Maguire, Columbia University
R.A.Me. Regula A. Meier, Old Dominion University
R.A.P.-R. Richard A. Preto-Rodas, University of Illinois, Urbana
R.A.Z. Richard A. Zipser, Oberlin College
R.B. Reinhard Becker, New York University
R.Bu. Robert Burniaux, Overÿsse, Belgium
R.By. Roland Beyen, Catholic University of Leuven
R.C. Rodolfo Cardona, Boston University
R.C.L. Rosette C. Lamont, Graduate Center, City University of New York
R.D.B.T. R. D. B. Thomson, University of Toronto
R. de C.S. Rafael de Cózar Sievert, University of Seville
R.D.S. Robert D. Spector, Long Island University
R.E.H. Ruth E. Hager, College of New Rochelle
R.E.J. Robert Emmet Jones, Massachusetts Institute of Technology
R.F. Robert Frickx, Free University of Brussels
R.Fu. Robin Fulton, Stavanger, Norway
R.G. Ricardo Guillón, University of Chicago
R.G.H. Russell G. Hamilton, University of Minnesota
R.G.M. Robert G. Marshall, Sweet Briar College
R.H. Renée Hubert, University of California, Irvine
R.J. Robert Jackson, Yale University
R.J.N. R. J. Niess, First Edition
R.J.R. Robert J. Rodini, University of Wisconsin, Madison
R.J.T. Remo J. Trivelli, University of Rhode Island
R.K. Rolf Kieser, Queens College, City University of New York
R.L. Ricardo Landeira, University of Wyoming

R.Lo. Richard Lourie, Newton, Massachusetts
R.M. Richard Mills, Austin, Texas
R.M.-L. Ramón Martínez-López, Santiago de Compostela, Spain
R.Mo. Roland Mortier, Free University of Brussels
R.P.H. Robert P. Hughes, University of California, Berkeley
R.Q.-W. Rita Quercia-Wilson, University of Witwatersrand
R.R.R. Ralph R. Read, III, University of Texas, Austin
R.Š. Rimvydas Šilbajoris, Ohio State University
R.Sc. Rainer Schulte, University of Texas, Dallas
R.S.D. Robert S. Dombroski, University of Connecticut
R.S.S. Raymond S. Sayers, Queens College, City University of New York
R.T. R. Trousson, Brussels, Belgium
R.T.D. Robert T. Denommé, University of Virginia
R.V. Richard Vernier, Wayne State University
R.W. René Wellek, Yale University
R.Wa. Rosemarie Waldrop, Providence, Rhode Island
R.Z. Richard Ziegfeld, University of South Carolina
S.A. Sverre Arestad, University of Washington
S.A.B. Sven Arne Bergmann, Göteborg, Sweden
S.Ac. Skip Acuff, University of Texas, Austin
S.A.R. S. A. Rhodes, First Edition
S.B. Staffan Bergsten, University of Uppsala
S.D.B. Sidney D. Braun, Lehman College, City University of New York
S.D.-T. Santiago Daydí-Tolson, University of Virginia
S.E. Stefán Einarsson, First Edition
S.E.R. Spencer E. Roberts, Brooklyn College, City University of New York
S.F. Samuel Fiszman, Indiana University
S.G. Sol Gittlemann, Tufts University
S.H. Sharon Harwood, Memphis State University
S.H.C. Samuel H. Cross, First Edition
S.H.R. Sven H. Rossel, University of Washington
S.J. Sharon Jackiw, Wheaton College
S.K. Simon Karlinsky, University of California, Berkeley
S.L. Sol Liptzin, University of Jerusalem
S.Lé. Sydney Lévy, University of Wisconsin
S.L.F. Seymour L. Flaxman, Graduate Center, City University of New York
S.M. Siegfried Mews, University of North Carolina, Chapel Hill
S.M.G. Sumner M. Greenfield, University of Massachusetts
S.M.L. Sonia M. Lee, Trinity College, Hartford
S.N. Suzanne Nalbantian, New York University
S.N.D. Sam N. Driver, Brown University
S.Ni. Samuel Niger, First Edition
S.P. Sergio Pacifici, Queens College, City University of New York
S.Pa. Sybille Pantazzi, Art Gallery of Toronto
S.S. Samuel Sandler, University of Chicago
S.Sc. Sydney Schultze, University of Louisville
S.Sk. Sigmund Skard, University of Oslo
S.S.H. Sveinn Skorri Höskuldsson, University of Iceland
S.S.M. Solita S. Marichal, Simmons College
S.W. Seymour Weiner, University of Massachusetts
T.A.P. Thomas A. Perry, East Texas State University

T.B. Teodolinda Barolini, University of California, Berkeley
T.Br. Timothy Brown,* University of Arizona
T.D. Thomas Doulis, Portland State University
T. de L. Teresa de Lauretis, University of Wisconsin, Milwaukee
T. Di N. Thomas Di Napoli, Louisiana State University
T.F.S. Thomas F. Staley, University of Tulsa
T.G.B. Thomas G. Bergin, Yale University
T.H.G. Thomas H. Goetz, State University College, Fredonia
T.L. Torborg Lundell, University of California, Santa Barbara
T.M. Thanasis Maskaleris, San Francisco State College
T.M.C. T. M. Campbell, First Edition
T.Me. Thomas Mermall, Brooklyn College
T.O'N. Tom O'Neill, Trinity College, Dublin
T.P.F. Thomas P. Freeman, State University of New York, Brockport
T.S. Thérèse Spire, Paris, France
T.S.H. Talat S. Halman, Princeton University
T.T. Tymon Terlecki, University of Illinois, Chicago Circle
T.W. Tibor Wlassics, University of Pittsburgh
T.W.G. Titiana W. Greene, Barnard College
U.M. Ursula Mahlendorf, University of California, Santa Barbara
U.S. Ursula Schoeni, Queens College, City University of New York
V.A. Victor Angelescu, Lawrence Institute of Technology
V.C. Vicente Cabrera, Colorado State University
V.D.M. Vasa D. Mihailovich, University of North Carolina, Chapel Hill
V.E. Victor Erlich, Yale University

V.G. Vincent Guilloton, First Edition
V.L. Vadim Liapunov, Indiana University
V.La. Victor Lange, First Edition
V.M. Vladimir Markov, University of California, Los Angeles
V.N. Valters Nollendorfs, University of Wisconsin, Madison
V.S. Volkmar Sander, New York University
V.T. Victor Terras, Brown University
W.A.R. Walter A. Reichart, First Edition
W.B.E. William B. Edgerton, Indiana University
W. De S. William De Sua, Michigan State University
W.E.H. William E. Harkins, Columbia University
W.H. Wolfgang Heuss, Munich, Germany
W.Ho. Werner Hoffmeister, Dartmouth College
W.H.R. William H. Roberts, University of New Mexico
W.H.Ro. Winthrop H. Root, First Edition
W.K.C. William K. Cook, New Rochelle, New York
W.K.Co. W. K. Cornell, First Edition
W.K.P. William K. Pfeiler, First Edition
W.L. Wolfgang Leiner, University of Washington
W.M.F. Wilbur M. Frohock, Harvard University
W.N. Werner Neuse, First Edition
W.P. Wolfgang Paulsen, First Edition
W.R.G. William R. Gaede, First Edition
W.T. Walter Theurer, New York City
W.T.S. William T. Starr, Northwestern University
W.V.B. W. V. Blomster, University of Colorado
W.W. Wiktor Weintraub, Harvard University
Y.G. Yvette Gindine, Queens College, City University of New York
Y.L.S. Yvonne L. Sandstrom, Southeastern Massachusetts University
Z.F. Zbigniew Folejewski, University of Ottawa
Z.T. Zina Tillona, University of Massachusetts
Z.V. Zolita Vella, New York City
Z.Y. Zoya Yurieff, New York University

PERIODICAL AND SERIES
ABBREVIATIONS

AGald Anales Galdosianos
AGR American-German Review
Alföld Alföld: Irodalmi és Művelődési Folyóirat
AnBret Annales de Bretagne et des Pays de l'Ouest
Anhembi Anhembi
ANP Anales de la Novela de Posguerra
APR American Poetry Review
Arbor Arbor: Revista General de Investigación y Cultura
L'Arc L'Arc: Cahiers Méditerranéens
Arena Arena
ASEER American Slavic and East European Review
ASoc Arts in Society
ASR The American-Scandinavian Review
AUS Annales Universitatis Saraviensis
Aut Aut Aut Aut
BA Books Abroad
BARLLF Bulletin de l'Académie Royale de Langue et de Littérature Françaises
Basis Basis: Jahrbuch für Deutsche Gegenwartsliteratur
BCR British-Croatian Review
Belfagor Belfagor: Rassegna di Varia Umanità
BHTP Bulletin d'Histoire du Théâtre Portugais
BIEC Bulletin, Institut d'Estudis Catalans
Birtingur Birtingur
BJR Bulletin des Jeunes Romanistes
BLM Bonniers Litterära Magasin
BR Belorussian Review
BulSS Bulletin of Spanish Studies
CA Cuadernos Americanos
CahiersVS Cahiers du Vingtième Siècle
CASS Canadian-American Slavic Studies
CAT Cahiers d'Analyse Textuelle
CdR Cahiers du Rhône
CdT Corriere del Ticino
CduS Cahiers du Sud
CFr Culture Française
CHA Cuadernos Hispanoamericanos: Revista Mensual de Cultura Hispanica
CLIT Contemporary Literature in Translation
CLS Comparative Literature Studies
Colóquio Colóquio/Letras
ConL Contemporary Literature
Convivium Convivium (São Paulo)
Correspondant Correspondant
CQ The Cambridge Quarterly
CRI Cau`dernos de Ruedo Ibérico
Crit Critique: Studies in Modern Fiction

Criticism Criticism: A Quarterly for Literature and the Arts
CS Cahiers des Saisons
Csillag Csillag
CVL Cahiers des Amis de Valery Larbaud
Delo Delo
Diacritics Diacritics: A Review of Contemporary Criticism
Dialoghi Dialoghi: Revista Bimestrale di Letteratura Arti Scienze
DialogW Dialog: Miesięcznik Poswięcony Dramaturgii Współczesnej: Teatralnej, Filmowej, Radiowej, Telewizyjnej
Divan Divan
DJ Danish Journal
DN Disraeli Newsletter
DnL Die Neue Literatur
Don Don
Dryade Dryade
DT Der Turmer
Dunátùl Dunátùl
ECr L'Esprit Créateur
Encounter Encounter
Escolios Escolios
ESl Etudes Slaves et Est-Européennes
Espresso Espresso
Esprit Esprit
EstLit La Estafeta Literaria: Revista Quincenal de Libros, Artes y Espetáculos
Estreno Estreno: Cuadernos del Teatro Español Contemporáneo
Ethnica Ethnica
Europe Europe: Revue Littéraire Mensuelle
EV Encres Vives
The Falcon The Falcon
Félagsbréf AB Félagsbréf AB
FI Forum Italicum
Filologia Filologia
FLe Fiera Letteraria
FMLS Forum for Modern Language Studies
ForumZ Forum (Zagreb)
FR French Review: Journal of the American Association of Teachers of French
Galleria Galleria: Rassegna Bimestrale di Cultura
GL&L German Life and Letters
GQ German Quarterly
GR Germanic Review
Gramma Gramma
Grande Revue Grande Revue
Grani Grani: Zhurnal Literatury, Iskusstva

Nauki i Obshchestvenno-politicheskoy Mysti

Hermes Hermes: Zeitschrift für Klassische Philologie

L'Herne Cahiers de l'Herne

Herse Herse

Híd Híd

Hispania Hispania: A Journal Devoted to the Interests of the Teaching of Spanish and Portuguese

Hispano Hispanófila

Hora de España Hora de España

Horisont Horisont

Horizon Horizon

HR Hispanic Review

IISS Harvard Slavic Studies

HungQ Hungarian Quarterly

Iðunn Iðunn

IFR International Fiction Review

IL L'Information Littéraire

Insula Insula: Revista Bibliográfica de Ciencias y Letras

IOC Index on Censorship

IQ Italian Quarterly

IRHS International Review for Social History

Irodalomtörténet Irodalomtörténet: History of Literature

IS Italian Studies

Italica Italica

Itk Itk

JByelS Journal of Byelorussian Studies

JCS Journal of Croatian Studies

JH Jewish Heritage

JSSTC Journal of Spanish Studies: Twentieth Century

KFLQ Kentucky Foreign Language Quarterly

Kontinent Kontinent

Kortárs Irodalmi és Kritikai Folyóirat

Kritik Kritik: Tidsskrift for Litteratur, Forskning, Undervisning

Kritika Kritika (Budapest)

KRQ Kentucky Romance Quarterly

KulturaP Kultura (Paris)

Lang&S Language and Style: An International Journal

Le Feu Le Feu

LEL La Estafeta Literaria

Letture Letture: Libro e Spettacolo/Mensile di Studi e Rassegne

Letteratura Letteratura

LE&W Literature East and West

LFL Les Feuilles Libres

LiF Livres de France

Lit Littérature

Lituanus Lituanus: Lithuanian Quarterly

LMS Letopis Matice Srpske

LuK Literatur und Kritik

Magyar Csillag Magyar Csillag

Magyarok Magyarok

MAL Modern Austrian Literature: Journal of the International Arthur Schnitzler Research Association

Marges Marges

MArt Mundus Artium: A Journal of International Literature and the Arts

MD Modern Drama

MdeF Mercure de France

Merkur Merkur

Mester Mester

Mímir Mímir

MLQ Modern Language Quarterly

MLR Modern Language Review

Mogućnosti Mogućnosti: Književnost, Umjetnost, Kulturni Problemi

Monatshefte Monatshefte: A Journal Devoted to the Study of German Language and Literature/für Deutschen Unterricht, Deutsche Sprache und Literatur

Mosaic Mosaic: A Journal for the Comparative Study of Literature and Ideas

MPT Modern Poetry in Translation

MQR Michigan Quarterly Review

MR Massachusetts Review: A Quarterly of Literature, the Arts and Public Affairs

NA Nuova Antologia

NAR North American Review

NHQ New Hungarian Quarterly

NLittH Norsk Litteratur Historie

NO Nouvel Observateur

NovM Novy Mir

NovZ Novy Zhurnal (New York)

NRF Nouvelle Revue Française

NVT Nieuw Vlaams Tijdschrift

NY The New Yorker

NYRB The New York Review of Books

NYTBR New York Times Book Review

Nyugat Nyugat

Obliques Obliques

Ocidente Ocidente

OL Orbis Litterarum: International Review of Literary Studies

Opyty Opyty

OSP Oxford Slavonic Papers

Osteuropa Osteuropa: Zeitschrift für Gegenwartsfragen des Ostens

O Tempo O Tempo e o Modo

Paragone Paragone: Rivista Mensile de Arte Figurativa e Letteratura

PCP Pacific Coast Philology

PFr Présence Francophone: Revue Littéraire

Plural Plural: Crítica, Arte, Literatura

PMLA PMLA Publications of the Modern Language Association of America

Poésie Poési

Poétique Poétique: Revue de Théorie et d'Analyse Littéraires

PolR Polish Review

PQ Philological Quarterly

Preuves Preuves: Les Idees Qui Changent le Monde

PrP Premier Plan

PSA Papeles de Son Armadans

PTh Paris Théâtre

QL La Quinzaine Littéraire

Rad Rad Jugoslavenske Akademije Znanosti i Umjetnosti

RBl Revue Bleu

RdDM Revue des Deux Mondes

RdF Revue de France

RdP Revue de Paris

Rep Republika

RevPh Revue Philosophique

RevS Revue Socialiste

RH Revue Hebdomadaire

RHM Revista Hispánica Moderna: Columbia University Hispanic Studies

RIFD Revista Internazionale di Filosofie del Diritto

Rinascita Rinascita
RL Revista de Literatura
RLC Revue de Littérature Comparée
RLit Russkaya Literatura
RLMC Revista di Letterature Moderne Comparate
RLT Russian Literature Triquarterly
RNL Review of National Literatures
RP Río Piedras
RR Romanic Review
RUB Revue de l'Université de Bruxelles
RusR Russian Review: An American Quarterly Devoted to Russia Past and Present
Saggi Saggi e Ricerche di Letteratura Francese
Samtiden Samtiden: Tidsskrift for Politikk, Litteratur og Samfunnssporsmal
SAQ South Atlantic Quarterly
SatR Saturday Review
Savremenik Savremenik: Mesečni Književni Časopis
Scan Scandinavica: An International Journal of Scandinavian Studies
SchM Schweizer Monatshefte: Zeitschrift für Politik, Wirtschaft, Kultur
SEEJ Slavic and East European Journal
SEER Slavonic and East European Review
Seminar Seminar: A Journal of Germanic Studies
SFr Studi Francesi
Skírnir Skírnir
SlavR Slavic Review: American Quarterly of Soviet and East European Studies
SLT Svensk Litteraturtidskrift: Utgiven av Samfundet De Nio
Sodobnost Sodobnost
SovStudies Soviet Studies
SR Sewanee Review
SS Scandinavian Studies
Sub-stance Sub-stance: A Review of Theory and Literary Criticism
SuF Sinn und Form: Beiträge zur Literatur

Survey Survey: A Journal of East & West Studies
Symposium Symposium
Synthèses Synthèses
TDR The Drama Review
TelQ Tel Quel
Thespis Thespis
TLR The Literary Review
TLS Times Literary Supplement
TMEJ The Middle East Journal
TriQ Tri-Quarterly
TRSLUK Transactions of the Royal Society of Literature of the United Kingdom
TSLL Texas Studies in Literature and Language: A Journal of the Humanities
TuDR Tulane Drama Review
Tw Twórczość
TWA Transactions of the Wisconsin Academy of Sciences, Arts, and Letters
TWAS Twayne's World Authors Series
UCPMP University of California Publications in Modern Philology
UDR University of Dayton Review
ÚÍ Új Írás: Irodalmi, Művészeti és Kritikai Folyóirat
Ujhold Ujhold
Új Látóhatár Új Látóhatár
Umanesimo Umanesimo
UR Ulbandus Review
Vestnik Vestnik
VLit Voprosy Literatury
Wiadomości Wiadomości
WLT World Literature Today: A Literary Quarterly of the University of Oklahoma
WR Western Review
YFS Yale French Studies
YaIS Yale Italian Studies
Y/T Yale/Theatre
Znamya Znamya: Literaturno-Khudozhestvenny i Obshchestvenno-politicheskiy Zhurnal
ZSP Zeitschrift für Slavische Philologie

COLUMBIA
DICTIONARY
OF MODERN
EUROPEAN
LITERATURE

A

Aakjær, Jeppe (1866–1930), Danish novelist, playwright, and poet, son of a poor peasant from Jutland, was born in the village of Aakjar. For several years he made his living as a lecturer and teacher, after which he studied history in Copenhagen, returning to Jutland in 1907. In Copenhagen, Aakjær was attracted by Georg BRANDES's radicalism while simultaneously longing for the old peasant culture. This conflict dominates his books, where nostalgia runs parallel to social agitation. Aakjær's most important novel, *Vredens Børn* (1904; Children of Wrath), indignantly attacks the abuse of the farm worker by the well-to-do farmer, while his dramas and the novel *Arbejdets Glæde* (1914; Joy of Work) defend peasant society against industrialization. As literary works, these books are problematic: agitation dominates, and the character drawing is rather sketchy. Aakjær was, however, an important writer of popular and melodious verses (he was an excellent translator of Robert Burns), his most important collection being *Rugens Sange* (1906; Songs of the Rye). The motifs in his poems—often treated idyllically and sentimentally—originate in the people and nature of his native region and in personal childhood memories. They are penetrated by a mystical feeling of solidarity with family and soil.

See: W. Westergaard, "Jeppe Aakjær," *ASR* 12 (1924): 665–69.   S.H.R.

Aanrud, Hans (1863–1953), Norwegian short-story writer and dramatist, was born to a peasant family in Gausdal in central Norway. Most of his active years as a critic and writer were spent in Oslo. Aanrud wrote harsh modern comedies on lower-middle-class life in the capital, but his fame rests on short stories and children's books picturing the peasants of his home valley before the coming of industrialization.

Aanrud's horizon is that of his farmers. His conception of society is static, and his psychology may be a touch conventional, but within his narrow field he is a master: love of his subject gives him vision. Although he is a realist, he approaches his subject with a respectful devotion that links him to other contemporary regionalists (*see* NORWEGIAN LITERATURE). Aanrud's style springs from that of the popular tradition—terse, restrained, and suggestive—and it is he who has set the tone for the short story of Norwegian farm life. In his stories, his native valley is recreated with intimate preciseness of detail; landscape, climate, and atmosphere, work and play, characters and situations are portrayed with striking clarity.

Aanrud has little interest in the somber and complicated aspects of life, yet his chef d'oeuvre, "En vinternatt" (1896; Eng. tr., "A Winter Night," 1928), is a drama of passion and tragedy compressed into a few pages of terrifying reticence. His charming children's books, on the other hand, are pure idylls. *Sidsel Sidsærk* (1903) and *Sølve Solfeng* (1910) have been translated into English as *Sidsel Longskirt and Solve Suntrap: Two Children of Norway* (1935).

See: P. Hallberg, *Harmonisk realism* (1965).   S.Sk.

Abell, Kjeld (1901–61), Danish dramatist, was born in the southern Jutland town of Ribe. He gave up a career as a political scientist in favor of the theater and made his living as a stage and costume designer and supernumerary. Owing to his knowledge of modern dramatists like Bertolt BRECHT and Jean GIRAUDOUX and directors like Max Reinhardt, Abell revitalized the Danish theater and broke the prevailing naturalistic tradition. Like Brecht, he wished to raise the social and political consciousness of his audience. His first play, *Melodien, der blev væk* (1935; Eng. tr., *The Melody That Got Lost,* 1939), experimentally utilizing all the resources of the theater, is a delightful socialistic satire on the petit bourgeois, who lack the melody, that is, the rhythm of life. The same point of view is found in *Eva aftjener sin Barnepligt* (1936; Eva Does Her Duty), a defense of the freedom of the individual against the conventions of society. *Anna Sophie Hedvig* (1939; Eng. tr. in *Scandinavian Plays of the 20th Century,* series 2, 1944) is a drama about an insignificant teacher who kills a colleague in order to protect her own world against injustice. It is a direct attack upon the passivity of the bourgeoisie in the presence of totalitarianism. The struggle against evil is a theme that is treated in different ways in two plays published during World War II as well as in *Silkeborg* (1946), a tribute to the Danish Resistance and an attack upon the collaborators during the German occupation of 1940–45. The humanist's dilemma in a postwar world threatened by violence and destruction is analyzed in Abell's last plays, *Vetsera blomstrer ikke for enhver* (1956; Vetsera Doesn't Bloom for Everybody), *Den blå Pekingeser* (1954; The Blue Pekingese), and *Skriget* (1961; The Cry). These are symbolic and philosophical plays, experimentally mingling drama and reality, past and present, in their protest against destructive isolation.

See: A. Gustafson, Introduction, in *Scandinavian Plays of the 20th Century,* series 2 (1944), pp. 17–20; F. Schyberg, *Kjeld Abell* (1947); F. J. Marker, *Kjeld Abell, TWAS* 394 (1976).   S.H.R.

Abramov, Fyodor Aleksandrovich (1920–), Russian novelist, was born in Verkola. He first attracted attention in 1954 when, as a young critic, he wrote an article attacking the "varnishing of reality" practised in most post-World War I fiction about life on collective farms. Drawing on his deep knowledge of the Arkhangelsk region where he was born, Abramov has spent most of his creative life writing novels and short stories about life in its villages from World War II to the present: the novels and some of the stories in the collection *Izbrannoye* (2 vols., 1975). In them he shows how peasant life and culture, sapped by the manner in which collectivization was carried out, is further threatened by the war, which draws off all the able-bodied men and demands huge quantities of produce and timber. In the fatherless Pryaslin family (whose name forms the title of his principal trilogy), Abramov summarizes the mutual solidarity that binds the poverty-stricken peasants together, even when individual members rebel against the privations imposed. Abramov's narrative language is closely modeled on peasant speech, and shows a strong awareness of the history, culture, and dialect of the European Far North.

See: I. Ignatyeva, "Fyodor Abramov—letopisets kolkhoznoy zhizni," *Radio Liberty Research Bulletin,* no. 281/73; F. Abramov, "Koye-chto o pisatelskom trude (intervyu)," *VLit* 3 (1974): 180–95.   G.H.

Achard, Marcel (1899–1974), French playwright and screenwriter, was born in Sainte-Foy-lès-Lyon, near Lyon, into an old agricultural family. At the age of 20 he went to Paris, where he was successively a paper salesman, a prompter at the Théâtre du Vieux-Colombier, and a journalist. Achard wrote his first play at 23, but his first success came with *Voulez-vous jouer avec moâ?* (1924; Will You Play with Me?), staged by Charles DULLIN, and his second with *Jean de la lune* (1929; John of the Moon). Then, for nearly half a century, he delighted the audiences of Paris boulevard theaters with his comedies. His other most successful plays were *Malbrough s'en va-t-en guerre* (1924; Marlborough Goes to War), *Mistigri* (1930), *Domino* (1932; Eng. tr., 1932), and *Noix de coco* (1936; Cocoanut). *Auprès de ma blonde* (1946; Next to My Blonde) gained him an international reputation and was produced on Broadway in S. N. Behrman's English version *I Know My Love*. Another New York and London hit was *A Shot in the Dark* (1961), adapted from *L'idiote* (1960). *Patate* (1957) ran successfully for years.

Achard's plays treat love with fantasy, humor, and a gaiety tempered with melancholy; they are amusing and moving without being disturbing. Among his predecessors, Achard most admired Pierre Marivaux (1688–1763), Pierre-Augustin Beaumarchais (1732–99), Georges FEYDEAU, and Sacha GUITRY. In addition to his plays, Achard wrote a dozen film scenarios, including *Jean de la lune*, *L'Etrange Monsieur Victor*, *Mayerling*, *Gribouille*, and *L'Alibi*. A figure of the "Tout-Paris," the social set of celebrities, he was president of the International Festival of Cannes (1958–59) and of the Festival of Venice (1960). Achard was elected to the Académie Française in 1959.

See: D. Knowles, *French Drama of the Inter-War Years* (1967), pp. 183–87. A.R.

Achterberg, Gerrit (1905–62), Dutch poet, was born in Langbroek, near Utrecht. He became a teacher but then devoted himself completely to poetry, never working in any other literary genre. His first volume, *Afvaart* (1931; Setting Sail), showed his independence from his like-minded colleagues at the literary magazine *Opwaartsche Wegen* and already contained elements that are characteristic of his poetry as a whole. The voyage is an attempt to go to another part of the world and to find the dead beloved and be reunited with her. Although the real relationship between man and woman is over, the emotional and psychological one remains. This transcendental longing becomes all-consuming and is painful because it cannot be fulfilled. Love has become an absolute, for death is irrevocable. It is striking that all this is evident in a volume of poetry published several years before the poet murdered his landlady's 16-year-old daughter, with whom he was having an affair. He was then confined to a mental institution for a time. The connection between love and death dominates a large part of his work. A new and very productive period began with *Eiland der ziel* (1939; Island of the Soul). Many volumes of poetry belong to this period, for example, *Thebe* (1941), *Schaatsenrijder* (1944; Ice Skater), *Sintels* (1944; Cinders), *Limiet* (1946; Limit), *Radar* (1946), *Energie* (1946), *En Jezus schreef in 't zand* (1947; And Jesus Wrote in the Sand), *Doornroosje* (1947; Sleeping Beauty), and *Sneeuwwitje* (1949; Snow White). In his poetry, Achterberg often attempted to make the past a reality, and he hoped to restore the dead beloved to life through the power of the poetic word. He wants a combination of "you and death and I" and a restoration of the unity that existed "in the beginning." Achterberg was a metaphysical poet and also a Christian poet, whose work reflects Calvinist thought. The anthologies *Oude cryptogamen* (1951; Old Cryptograms), *Cryptogamen* (1953), *Cryptogamen III* (1954), and *Cryptogamen 4* (1961) give a good view of his poetic development; and his poetry has also been collected in *Verzamelde ge-*

dichten (1963). Although Achterberg has been linked with romanticism and with expressionism, he is preeminently a poet of the word. His imagery is unusual, and he often coined new words of his own. As the titles of such volumes as *Ballade van de gasfitter* (1953) and *Autodroom* (1954) show, he drew widely on modern science and technology for his vocabulary, often choosing words that suggest several interpretations. Achterberg was one of the greatest poets of his generation and in 1950 became the first one to win the P. C. Hooft Prize.

See: A. de Longie, *Gerrit Achterberg* (1970); R. Houwink, *Het raadsel "Achterberg"* (1973). S.L.F.

Adama van Scheltema, Carel Steven (1877–1924), Dutch poet, was born in Amsterdam. After studying medicine for a while, he turned to literature, launching his career with a volume of sonnets, *Een weg van verzen* (1900; A Path of Verses). He adhered mainly to the traditional form, and another volume of sonnets soon followed, *Uit den dool* (1901; From Rambles). In *Van zon en zomer* (1902; Of Sun and Summer), he used the lyric stanza. He reinforced the structure and meter of his poetry by the use of repetition and the refrain, which sometimes became rather obvious. His poetry had a simple, even homely style. It won him great popularity, and many of his poems were set to music. He expressed the humanitarian ideals that were widely held at the turn of the century, but some critics have questioned whether he was really a socialist. His best work is contained in such later volumes of poetry as *Zwervers Verzen* (1904; A Wanderer's Verses), *Eenzame liedjes* (1906; Solitary Songs), *Zingende stemmen* (1916; Singing Voices), and *De keerende kudde* (1920; The Turning Herd). The disillusionment he felt in World War I is evident in his later work. Larger efforts, *Levende steden* (1903–04; Living Cities) and *De Tors* (1924; The Torso), were less successful. He also wrote a controversial book on literary theory, in which he turned against the "Men of the Eighties," whom he had once admired, *De grondslagen eener nieuwe poëzie: Proeve van een maatschappelijk kunstleer tegenover het naturalisme en anarchisme, de Tachtigers en hun decadenten* (1907; The Foundations of a New Poetry: An Attempt at a Social Theory of Art, as against Naturalism and Anarchism, the Men of the Eighties and Their Decadents). Although he possessed humor and wit among his poetic gifts, he lacked a sure grasp of poetic language and was often weak in his use of imagery.

See: F. Drost, *Carel Steven Adama van Scheltema* (1952). S.L.F.

Adamov, Arthur (1908–70), French dramatist, was born in Kislovodsk, Russia, the son of a wealthy owner of oil wells in Baku, on the Caspian Sea. At the outbreak of World War I the Adamovs were vacationing in Germany, and they narrowly escaped internment as enemy aliens by fleeing to Switzerland, where they stayed from 1914 to 1922. Among the Russian expatriates they knew in Geneva were Georges and Ludmilla PITOËFF, the famous director and his actress wife, whose production of Shakespeare's *Macbeth* inspired Adamov with an early passion for the theater. The family fortune was lost in the Russian Revolution (1917), and in 1922 the Adamovs returned to Germany. Young Adamov was enrolled in the French lycée of Mainz, where he met Victor A., the prototype of Victor in *Le Ping-Pong* (1955; Eng. tr., 1959) and of Viktor in *Si l'été revenait* (1970; If Summer Should Return). At this time, Adamov wrote a story of adolescent love in which a boy wounds himself with branches to attract the attention of a girl. The theme anticipates Adamov's typical association of eroticism and masochism, a reflection of his own psyche and of his sexual impotence. The latter is revealed in his haunting confessional work *L'Aveu* (1946; The Confession), a journal that together with *L'Homme et l'enfant* (1968; Man and Child) may outlast his plays. Both the journals and the plays reveal Adamov's subconscious feelings of guilt in regard to his self-induced failure.

In 1924, the Adamov family moved to France. Around this time, he joined a demonstration calling for the freedom of Sacco and Vanzetti, an act that anticipated Adamov's lifelong struggle against social injustice. It was in Paris that young Arthur came in contact with Paul ELUARD and the surrealists, Georges Neveux, Jacques PRÉVERT, the director Roger Blin (who was later to play an important role in staging his early plays), the sculptor Albert Giacometti, and Antonin ARTAUD (who influenced Adamov's concept of the theater).

In 1928, Adamov fell in love with Irène, a Russian girl living in Paris with her family. It was she who gave the writer the nickname by which he is best known, Ern, an echo of her own name. The girl's family was opposed to the relationship with a penniless would-be writer, favoring marriage to a successful German businessman instead. When the latter appeared in Paris, Adamov staged a mock-suicide, only one of a series of such attempts.

As a dramatist, Adamov's work belongs to the 1950s, when Eugène IONESCO, Samuel BECKETT, Boris VIAN, and Jean GENET were creating what have come to be known as metaphysical farces. Adamov himself despised the term "theater of the absurd," feeling that life is not absurd but deeply sad and comic at the same time. Nor did he feel that the well-made play could be the vehicle for the ironic vision of the post-Auschwitz, post–World War II world. A specific incident provided him with the inspiration for his first play, *La Parodie* (1950; The Parody): at a subway entrance, a blind beggar is jostled by two working girls who keep on humming a familiar refrain ("I closed my eyes, it was wonderful!"). The unconscious cruelty of the girls, the irony of the whole encounter moved Adamov to seek to concretize upon the stage the image of human solitude. In a series of 12 tableaux, the drama presents the parallel adventures of two men, N. and The Employee, both scorned by Lili, both destroyed by life in the hostile environment of a metropolis. The protagonist of this expressionist drama is the city itself, an urban jungle in which both pessimists and optimists are doomed to lose their freedom. Other plays that can be said to belong to Adamov's first manner—Kafkaesque, oneiric, and darkly cruel—are *L'Invasion* (1950; Eng. tr., *The Invasion,* 1968), *La Grande et la Petite Manoeuvre* (1950; The Great and the Small Maneuver), *Le Sens de la marche* (1953; The Direction of the March), *Tous contre tous* (1953; Each against All), *Les Retrouvailles* (1955; The Reunions) and, above all, his short masterpiece *Le Professeur Taranne* (1953; Eng. tr., *Professor Taranne,* 1960). The latter, which is almost a transcription of a dream, focuses on the concept of identity. A distinguished professor is accused by children of indecent exposure on a beach. The more he proclaims his innocence, the less believable he sounds. Acquaintances, including a former colleague, fail to recognize him. Handed a notebook that is allegedly his, Taranne is unable to read his own writing. A letter from the rector of the university where he was teaching informs him that he will not be rehired because he plagiarized his lectures. At the end of the play, Taranne begins to strip, performing the very act of which he was initially accused. The play dramatizes the erosion of self-confidence, the onslaught of madness when what we consider our identity is questioned and denied.

Adamov's most successful play is *Le Ping-Pong,* a work of transition between his early metaphysical plays and the political, Marxist dramas of his second phase. *Le Ping-Pong* blends the personal and the public worlds. Despite the title (taken from the last ironic scene in which the two protagonists, now aged, are seen playing at ping-pong, the final game of their wasted lives), the dramatis personae of the play revolve around a pinball machine. At once a symbol and a reality, it suggests the capitalist system of the United States. Each character is defined only in its relation to the functioning of the machine. At the same time, the machine has a hypnotic presence on the stage. *Le Ping-Pong* is the perfect example of the new theater where objects can have greater reality than people, and where human beings are automatons. The language spoken by the characters is a tapestry of clichés, not unlike those used by Ionesco. Images and language mirror the dehumanized society Adamov is satirizing.

The Brechtian plays (see Bertolt BRECHT) of Adamov's second phase belong to the tradition of epic theater: *Paolo Paoli* (1957; Eng. tr., 1959), concerning the socioeconomic relationship between a feather merchant and an entomologist trading in butterflies caught by prisoners serving life sentences in French Guiana; *Le Printemps 71* (1960; Spring 71), a portrayal of the uprising of the Paris Commune; *La Politique des restes* (1967; The Politics of Waste), a play based on the clinical observations of Doctor Minkowski concerning a psychosis based on the proliferation of objects; and *Off Limits* (1969), Adamov's satire of the United States at the time of the Vietnam War.

Adamov was also a theoretician of his craft. In 1955 he published a study of August STRINDBERG, and his *Ici et maintenant* (1964; Here and Now) remains an important contribution to dramaturgy. He also worked as a translator, producing French versions of *Danton's Death* and *Woyzeck* by Georg Büchner, Strindberg's *The Pelican*, Maksim GORKY's *Enemies,* Anton CHEKHOV's *The Wood Demon,* and Nikolay Gogol's *The Inspector General.* He also adapted Gogol's *Dead Souls* for the stage.

In 1947, Adamov met Jacqueline Trehet, née Autrusseau (whom he nicknamed "Le Bison"); they were married in 1961. Yet even his profound love for Jacqueline could not save him from despair. Adamov longed for success, became an alcoholic, and finally succeeded in taking his own life, as his father had done before him. Although Adamov does not rank with Beckett and Ionesco, with whom he has been compared, he is still one of the major figures among French dramatists of the second half of the 20th century. A greater writer than his contemporaries had recognized, he was an oblique, divided man, a passionate, ethical human being, and a modest innovator.

See: E. Jacquart, *Le Théâtre de dérision* (1974); J. H. Reilly, *Arthur Adamov* (1974).   R.C.L.

Adamovich, Georgy Viktorovich (1894–1972), Russian poet and critic, was born in Moscow. He began his career as an associate of Nikolay GUMILYOV and the acmeists. In the early 1920s he left Russia and settled in Paris (*see* RUSSIAN LITERATURE). He published very little poetry altogether, and included the best of all his verse in his slender last volume, *Yedinstvo* (1967; Unity).

In the émigré life of Paris, Adamovich became a respected and very influential critic. He advocated a sparse style in poetry, the most direct and unadorned means of expressing the reality of the Russian poet living in emigration. This plain verse, often on existential themes, became known as the "Parisian Note," and is associated with a number of younger poets, including Igor CHINNOV and Anatoly STEIGER although Adamovich himself never spoke of the "Parisian Note" as a school or movement.

His own verse is perhaps too musical to fit the stylistic prescription of his "Note." Its themes, however, are quite in keeping with the kind of poetry Adamovich was advising the younger poets to write. Adamovich selected much of his key critical prose for the collection *Kommentarii* (1967; Commentaries), in which he took a somewhat skeptical view of modernism, attacked the merely fashionable, and advocated the kind of truth-saying that he saw especially in Lev TOLSTOY. In his numerous essays, Adamovich has provided a controversial but penetrating and valuable reappraisal of much of Russian literature.

See: R. Hagglund, "Adamovich as a Literary Critic," Ph.D. Dissertation, University of Washington (1967); I. Chinnov, "Vspominaya Adamovicha," *NovZ* 109 (1972): 136–47.   H.W.T.

Ady, Endre (1877–1919), Hungarian poet, was born in Érmindszent, a small village between Hungary proper and Transylvania, into a family of impoverished country gentry and Protestant ministers. Ady was the greatest and most influential Hungarian poet of his generation. After some half-hearted attempts to study law in Debrecen, where he published his first, very weak book of poetry, *Versek* (1899; Poems), and in Budapest, Ady embarked upon a career as a journalist in Nagyvárad. At the time, Nagyvárad (now Oradea, Romania) was an important center of intellectual life, and its atmosphere of inquiry had a liberating effect upon the young Ady. Although most of his Nagyvárad poems, collected in *Még egyszer* (1903; Once More), still belong to Ady's formative period, some newspaper articles written at the time point to the radicalization of his political thought and to his interest in modern literature. In 1903 he met Adél Brüll, the "Leda" of his passionate love poems. The cultured, sensitive wife of a lawyer, she induced Ady to visit Paris in 1904. Influenced by Charles BAUDELAIRE, Paul VERLAINE, and "the poet of beggars," Jehan Rictus, Ady broke a late-Victorian taboo still prevalent in Hungarian literature by producing daring, outspoken poems on sensual love. Moreover, his newly found symbolism began to embrace subjects such as the power of money and political stagnation. In this the Russian Revolution of 1905 may have played the role of a catalyst. Ady's articles for *Budapesti Napló* show the impact of the 1905 Revolution on him, and his verse collection *Uj versek* (1906; New Poems) testifies to his success in translating the shock waves of history and the rise of a new sensibility into the language of poetry. *Uj versek* is the most important single volume of poetry in modern Hungarian literature. It represented a challenge to half-feudal, "historical" Hungary, striking at its delusions, prejudices, and inertia and sounding like a bugle call over what Ady called the sleepy "Hungarian Fallow." Ady's haughty self-stylization— "Fear not, my ship, Tomorrow's hero is aboard" (Eng. tr. by A. N. Nyerges)—made it even harder for the conservatives to accept him; he was rejected on both the grounds of social radicalism and provocative "modernism."

In 1906–07, Ady again stayed in Paris, and his next book of poetry, *Vér és arany* (1907; Blood and Gold), definitively established him as the leading symbolist poet in Hungary. In 1908 the literary review *Nyugat* was launched, and Ady—in spite of periodic quarrels with his allies and supporters—soon became its permanent contributor and star poet. Between 1908 and 1914, Ady had no permanent home. Travels in Italy and France and visits to his native village alternated with spells in hospitals and rest homes where he sought a cure for his bouts of nervous depression and for the syphylis contracted in his youth. In 1912 his long relationship with "Leda" came to an end. Three years later he married a young girl, Berta Boncza ("Csinszka"), the Muse of his last, melancholy love poems. Between 1908 and the time of his marriage, Ady published six books of poetry and contributed to two anthologies of new authors entitled *Holnap* (1908, 1909; Tomorrow). During these years, he wrote an increasing number of both religious and revolutionary poems, often invoking revolution in a "religious" language (for example, he sends his heart—the "ark of the covenant"—to the Hungarian proletariat). This trend in his poetry paralleled the political struggle that culminated in the suffrage reform of 1912. After this date, and increasingly during World War I, Ady felt depressed, isolated, and cheated by his fellowmen. He saw the war as a senseless massacre and chose to live in semiseclusion. His pacifist and antiwar poems were collected in *A halottak élén* (1918; Leading the Dead), a moving book reflecting his determination to remain "a man in inhumanity." In early 1919, Ady died of pneumonia. His funeral was a national event and marked the end of an epoch.

Although for several decades Ady's legend obscured the measure of his real achievement, it is now possible to appraise his work unemotionally. Ady's poetic world is erected upon metaphysical antinomies such as life-death, past-future, ego-nonego. The hierarchical principle of this world is vitality; anything that leads to a fuller life is "sacred." The celebration of life, however, often hides a death wish, resulting in what has been called Ady's "haunted and haunting symbolism." Money appears in his imagination as a monstrous swine-headed creature locked in a fight with him, as in the poem "Harc a Nagyúrral" (1905; Eng. tr., *Lord Swine-Head*, 1969); his fear of death becomes the "Good Prince of Silence" and the spirit of prerevolutionary Hungary the "Lost Horseman." In addition to its dramatic symbolism, Ady's work reveals immense claims for leadership and an unquenchable thirst for success. The line "I came to be not just a conjurer but Everything" best sums up his position. While Friedrich NIETZSCHE's ideas help to articulate Ady's programmatic self-centeredness, there were also objective reasons to explain his sense of mission and the validity of his role as "the conscience of the Hungarian nation" and the apostle of a coming revolution. He appeared at a juncture of Hungarian history when certain unsolved national and social questions were emerging with particular force, threatening the survival of the Austro-Hungarian monarchy. Ady expressed the political dilemmas of his epoch with much sincerity and great moral passion but was unable to foresee their eventual solution. He hoped for a democratic revolution and a spiritual rebirth involving a reconciliation with the non-Hungarian minorities, a desire expressed in the poem "Magyar jakobinus dala" (1908; Song of a Hungarian Jacobin). Yet he also feared the destruction of his nation, which, if it resisted progress, would "fall through the huge sieve of Time." Ady's revolutionary expectations are often couched in biological or even sexual terms, and there is an intricate relationship between sex, politics, and religion in his poetry. His almost blasphemous, "God-probing" poems constitute an important part of a diverse and rich poetic output, although the symbol of God or Christ stands for a variety of things, such as hope in the future or human brotherhood. Ady's religious language is biblical and recalls the style of 16th-century Protestant preachers, whereas his grimly ironic *kuruc* poems imitate the speech of the anti-Hapsburg peasant-soldiers of the 17th and 18th centuries. The result is, in fact, a unique blend of archaic and new expressions. Ady's prosody broke the stifling hegemony of iambic verse and opened up new possibilities for syllabic as well as mixed metric verse forms. His complete poems, *Összes versei,* were first published in 1930.

See: M. Babits, "Tanulmány Adyról," *Nyugat* 13 (1920): 128–47; Gy. Földessy, *Ady Endre tanulmányok* (1921); Gy. Bölöni, *Az igazi Ady* (1934); J. Révai, *Ady* (1945); L. Hatvany, *Ady,* 2 vols. (1959); J. Reményi, *Hungarian Writers and Literature* (1964), pp. 193–212; A. Nyerges, Introduction to *Poems of Endre Ady* (1969), pp. 13–56; I. Király, *Ady Endre* (1973).   G.G.

Afinogenov, Aleksandr Nikolayevich (1904–41), Russian dramatist, was born in Skopin. He began his career as a journalist but from 1926 on devoted himself completely to the theater. Expelled from the Communist Party in 1937 for "ties with enemies of the people," he was later reinstated when the charges were proved false. He died in an air raid on Moscow. Lyrical and psychological, Afinogenov's plays show the influence of Anton CHEKHOV and Maksim GORKY. Despite weaknesses, *Strakh* (1930; Eng. tr., *Fear,* 1934), about an intellectual who insists that science must be apolitical and that the Soviet system is wrong because it is founded on fear, remains one of the better Soviet plays. Less good is *Dalyokoye* (1935; Eng. tr., *Far Taiga,* 1946), which glorifies the heroism of everyday work on an isolated railroad siding in Siberia and proclaims the victory of a true Bolshevik life over death. Despite a Chekhovian mood and well-drawn characters, the bombast of the play's dialogue destroys its credibility. Afinogenov's most popular play was his comedy *Mashenka* (1940; Eng. tr., *Listen, Professor!,* 1944), where, without intrusive ideology, he shows how the moral purity and beauty of the new Soviet youth wins a hostile intellectual over to the side of Revolutionary Russia.

Afinogenov's overall success came from choosing plots that reflected important processes taking place in Soviet life at the time, from probing his characters' inner lives, and from making his negative characters believable human beings.

See: A. Karaganov, *Aleksandr Afinogenov* (1957).
                                                      S.E.R.

Agârbiceanu, Ion (1882–1963), Romanian novelist, short-story writer, and essayist, was born in Cenade (Sibiu). After seminary training in Budapest, he became an Orthodox priest, serving in the Apuseni Mountains (1904–10), the setting for his first sketches and stories, and for his first novel, *Arhanghelii* (1914; The Archangels). He also served in Orlat (1910–06; 1918–09) and in Cluj. After Adolf Hitler's annexation of Austria and the Vienna Diktat (1940), he left for Sibiu, but returned to Cluj in 1945.

Agârbiceanu was a prolific contributor to the journals *Familia, Sămănătorul,* and *Viaţa românească,* but his work was uneven. His best stories are "Fefeleaga" (an onomatopeic word suggesting slow movement of man or beast; 1906; Eng. tr., 1966) and "Popa Vasile" (1905; The Priest Man). Collections of his sketches and stories include *De la ţară* (1905; From the Countryside), *În clasa cultă* (1909; Among the Cultured Classes), *Două iubiri* (1910; Two Loves), *În întuneric* (1910; In the Darkness), *Luncuşoara din Paresimi* (1920; Luncuşoara in Lent), *Chipuri de ceară* (1921; Wax Figures), and *Trăsurica verde* (1921; The Green Gig). His novellas include *Spaima* (1922; Fear), *Dezamăgire* (1925; Disappointment), and *Stafia* (1934; The Phantom). Of his novels, the masterpiece is *Legea trupului* (1912; The Law of the Flesh). Others are *Legea minţii* (1927; The Law of Reason), *Biruinta* (1931; Victory), *Sectarii* (1938; The Sectarians), and *Vîltoarea* (1941–43; Vortices). Agârbiceanu's last

works—his memoirs and reminiscenses—were among his best: *Amintirlei* (1940; Recollections); *În pragul vieţii:* vol. 1, *Acasă*; vol. 2, *Pe drumuri*; vol. 3, *Lume nouă* (1940–45; On the Threshhold of Life: vol. 1, At Home; vol. 2, On the Way; vol. 3, New World); *Din copilărie* (1956; Childhood); *Din munţi şi din cîmpii* (1957; From the Mountains and the Plains); *File din cartea naturii* (1959; Pages from the Book of Nature); and *Fricosul* (1960; The Coward). He left several unpublished manuscripts, later included in his collected works *Opere* (9 vols., 1962–76). Writing in the tradition of Ioan Slavici (1848–1924), Agârbiceanu created objective and analytic, yet sympathetic descriptions of Transylvanian life before and during World War I.

See: M. Zaciu, *Ion Agârbiceanu* (1964); J. Steinberg, *Introduction to Romanian Literature* (1966), pp. 195–201; D. Vatamaniuc, *Ion Agârbiceanu* (1970, 1974); C. Regman, *Agârbiceanu şi demonii* (1973).   T.A.P.

Agnon, Shmuel Yosef, pseud. of Shmuel Yosef Czaczkes (1888–1970), Israeli novelist, was born in Buczacz, now in the USSR. He received a traditional education, and occupied himself in his youth with Hebrew and Yiddish journalism. In 1907 he moved to Jaffa, Palestine. A year later, he published the story "Agunot" (Deserted Wives) and adopted the name of Agnon—an anagram of that title—suggesting that his writing would be concerned, among other matters, with alienation, loss, and the search for identity. Agnon earned fame with his early work, written in a somewhat heavily brocaded Hebrew style with much rabbinic allusion and Hassidic fantasy. He left Palestine for Germany in 1913, where he moved in literary and scholarly circles, and met the publisher S. Zalman Schocken, whose patronage he enjoyed until his death in 1970. Here Agnon also met and married his wife, Esther Marx. On his return to Palestine in 1924, Agnon settled in Jerusalem, remaining there for the rest of his life.

In his first full-length novel, *Hakhnasat Kala* (1931; Eng. tr., *The Bridal Canopy,* 1937), Agnon describes the picaresque adventures of Reb Yudel, a Hassidic, East European Don Quixote of the early 19th century. The hero inhabits an inner world of joy and holiness that is ironically at odds with his situation as a mendicant and with the harsh reality of the world through which he moves. Agnon's second major novel, and undoubtedly his masterpiece, is *Oreah Nata Lalun* (1935; Eng. tr., *A Guest for the Night,* 1968). The work was inspired by a brief sentimental journey Agnon made to his birthplace (termed "Shebush" in the novel) in 1930. The narrator recalls his early years in the shtetl, with its warmth, humanity, and spiritual consolations, but he sees this period through the perspective of the intervening war years that ravaged the life of the community. The narrator then describes the new Jewish life in Palestine for his friends in Shebush. The total effect of *Oreah Nata Lalun* is of an epic vision of the shtetl in decline and of modern Jewish history at the crossroads. All of this is further enhanced by an intensity of personal reminiscence and observation suggestive of Marcel PROUST. The combination of realism and symbolism in this novel is typical of Agnon's mature writing. Particularly memorable is the symbol of the great brass key to the *Bet-Midrash* (House of Study), which serves to unify the vision of past, present, and future.

Agnon shifts locales in *Temol Shilshom* (1945; The Day Before Yesterday). In this novel, Yitzhak Kummer, a descendant of Reb Yudel of *The Bridal Canopy,* makes the journey from Europe to Palestine where he becomes involved in the frustrations and difficulties of the incipient Jewish nation. He dies of rabies after being bitten by a mad dog named Balak who, grotesquely, becomes a major character in the novel.

The work by means of which Agnon has had the greatest influence on his younger contemporaries is probably *Sefer HaMaasim* (1951; Book of Fables), a collection of 21 short stories marked by a surrealistic abandonment of normal continuity and by a technique akin to stream of consciousness. As in a dream, time and place are confused; the symbolic and everyday worlds are yoked together as in Franz KAFKA, although perhaps with greater violence. It has been suggested that Agnon and Kafka have much in common, since both shared the same cultural background (that of the Austro-Hungarian Empire at the beginning of the 20th century), and both were acutely aware of modern man's spiritual crisis and frustrated search for salvation. Unlike Kafka, however, Agnon preserves some sense of the persisting value of the Jewish tradition.

Agnon was a remarkably prolific writer. His bibliography of some 250 works of fiction includes a fascinating variety of short stories and novellas. Specific mention should be made of the hauntingly beautiful *Betrothed* (Eng. tr., 1966) and "The Doctor's Divorce" (Eng. tr., 1965). Of the vast amount of unpublished material he left at his death, seven volumes have since appeared. These include the unfinished novel *Shira,* whose central female character displays the power of physical love with a frankness not encountered elsewhere in his fiction. Agnon was awarded the Israel Prize in 1954 and again in 1958. He shared the Nobel Prize for Literature with Nelly SACHS in 1966.

See: A. J. Band, *Nostalgia and Nightmare: A Study in the Fiction of S. Y. Agnon* (1968); B. Hochman, *The Fiction of S. Y. Agnon* (1970); H. Fisch, *S. Y. Agnon* (1975); R. Alter, "Agnon's Mediterranean Fable," in his *Defenses of the Imagination: Jewish Writers and Modern Historical Crisis* (1977), pp. 187–198.   H.F.

Agustí, Ignacio (1913–74), Spanish novelist, journalist, essayist, and poet, was born in Llisá del Vall, Barcelona, of an upper-middle-class family. He received his secondary schooling with the Jesuits (1923–29) and earned a degree from the School of Law of the University of Barcelona in 1934. His brief dedication to the legal profession was interrupted by the Spanish Civil War, following which he became a professional newspaperman. Agustí served as correspondent for *La Vanguardia* in Zurich and Bern (1942–44), was associated with *L'Instant* and *La Veu de Catalunya,* and worked for 14 years as founder and director of the weekly *Destino* (1944–58). He held similar posts with *El Español* and *Tele Exprés.* Agustí wrote both in his native Catalan and in Castilian, producing solid novels noted more for their historical testimony than for their artistic content. Considered innovative in his day, he was a relatively traditional narrator in the classic realist vein of Benito PÉREZ GALDÓS, Charles Dickens, and the Catalans, Narcís OLLER and Victor CATALÀ. *Los surcos* (1942; The Furrows) is his "poematic" first effort. The cycle "La ceniza fue árbol" (The Ashes Were Once a Tree) appeared over some three decades and includes *Mariona Rebull* (1944), *El viudo Rius* (1945; Widower Rius), *Desiderio* (1957), *19 de julio* (1966), and *Guerra civil* (1972; Civil War). His most significant literary achievement, this pentalogy covers the period from 1865 to the Spanish Civil War and reflects life in Barcelona as that city was becoming the industrial and commercial center of Spain, with the bloody class struggle that accompanied the socioeconomic process. The series studies the lives of two families, the industrial Rius clan and the merchant Rebulls, united by marriage, and their

struggle against the working class in defense of inherited privilege. Agustí's later, generally inferior, works follow the fortunes of their descendants. Also of some importance as a poet in Catalan, Agustí was included by Felix Ros in his *Antología poética de la lengua catalana, puesta en versos castellanos* (1965; Anthology of Catalan Poetry, in Castilian verse). His first publication was an adolescent collection of Catalan lyrics, *El veler* (1932; The Sailboat). His youthful interest in the theater produced *La coronela* (1932; The Colonel's Lady) and several other titles during the 1930s.

See: E. G. de Nora, *La novela española contemporánea,* vol. 3 (1967), pp. 130–9; A. Valbuena Prat, *Historia de la literatura española,* vol. 4 (1968), p. 10; J. Manegat, "En la muerte . . . de Ignacio Agustí," *EstLit* 536 (March 15, 1974): 4–7.   J.W.D.

Ahlin, Lars (1915–), Swedish author of novels and short stories, was born in Sundsvall. With his first novel, *Tåbb med Manifestet* (1943; Tåbb and the Manifesto), he achieved recognition as an important writer. In his novels, which are mostly set in Sundsvall, the characters suffer from a dichotomy between the ideal and reality and its effect upon their concept of self. Survival is possible only through compromise, but this is not always accomplished. In *Fromma mord* (1952; Pious Murders) idealism leads to murder. Although Ahlin's characters often belong to the lower social classes, he is not a proletarian writer in the traditional sense. He is more interested in spiritual distress than in social misery, and his characters' social rank is subordinate to their classless spiritual torments: Ahlin stresses human equality, which he believes lies in spiritual identity independent of social position.

In 1933, following five years in a Communist youth organization, Ahlin became interested in theology and began to study Martin Luther, Søren KIERKEGAARD, Karl Barth, and Anders Nygren's *Agape and Eros* (Eng. tr., 1932). Ahlin's concept of equality emanates from his readings of Luther, whose statement that people are simultaneously sinners and saints seems to explain Ahlin's own experience of a world full of sacred and profane elements inexplicably mixed. Like Pär LAGERKVIST, Ahlin is interested in questions about man's relation to good and evil, which he often presents in grotesque scenes, as in *Min död är min* (1945; My Death Is Mine). He is also influenced by Fyodor DOSTOYEVSKY's concept of all-embracing love. Such love and honest execution of one's work, even if tedious and trivial, provide balance and satisfaction for Ahlin's protagonists. In *Stora glömskan* (1954; The Great Forgetter), happiness comes by forgetting timebound values, and love is the guiding principle for human relations. *Kvinna kvinna* (1955; Woman Woman) is a passionate story about judgment in love. The famous short story "Kommer hem och är snäll" (1944; Coming Home to be Nice) describes awkward and often unsuccessful ways to communicate love. In *Natt i marknadstället* (1957; Night in the Booth), a woman murders her husband rather than see him punished when he commits a crime that was motivated only by his desire to feel successful and be deserving of her love, which he cannot accept unconditionally.

In his attempt to renew the form of the novel, Ahlin often breaks his narrative flow with stories, discussions, and other distracting devices. His technically most advanced novels are *Om* (1946; If) and *Bark och löv* (1961; Bark and Leaves). His experiments with form have not always been well received, but Ahlin is unquestionably regarded an outstanding storyteller and lauded for his profound insight into the psychology of human relations.

See: E. H. Linder, *Ny Illustrerad Svensk Litteraturhis-*

toria, vol. 5 (1966); L. Furuland, ed., *Synpunkter på Lars Ahlin* (1971); A. Melberg, *På väg från realismen* (1973); T. Lundell, *Lars Ahlin, TWAS* 430 (1977).   T.L.

Ahmet Haşim (1885-1933), Turkish poet and essayist, was born in Baghdad. He moved to Istanbul in 1896 and graduated from the Galatasaray Lycée in 1907. He attended law school in Istanbul, but left to become a teacher of French in Smyrna (1908-11). Until his death, he taught at various academic institutions, among which were the Academy of Fine Arts, Military Academy, and Civil Service School.

Ahmet Haşim, who was the earliest major symbolist in Turkish poetry, published his first poem in 1901 and joined the "Fecr-i Ati" (Dawn of the Future) group in 1909, although his subjective aesthetics and complex style stood in contrast to the social concerns and the simpler language of his fellow members. He published two collections of poems: *Göl Saatleri* (1921; Hours by the Lake) and *Piyale* (1926; The Cup). His essays and newspaper articles were collected in the volumes *Bize Göre* (1928; According to Us) and *Gurabahane-i Laklakan* (1928; Nursing Home for Indigent Storks). *Frankfurt Seyahatnamesi* (1933; Frankfurt Travelogue) is regarded as one of the best books of travel impressions in Turkish.

Haşim's earlier poems, written in strict stanzaic form and classical meters, express the poet's suffering and malaise in somber tones and through grim depictions of nature. His later poems, considerably freer in form although still in conventional prosody, are notable for rich and fresh metaphors, an intricate rhythmic system attuned to symbols and emotions, and themes of love and anguish expressed in striking images. Haşim's symbolism served as a potent force in the modernization of Turkish poetry.   T.S.H.

Aichinger, Ilse (1921-), Austrian short-story writer, novelist, and radio playwright, was born in Vienna. She studied medicine for over two years before turning to writing. In 1949 and 1950, she was a publisher's reader and subsequently collaborated in founding the Hochschule für Gestaltung in Ulm. She is the widow of the German poet Günter EICH, whom she married in 1953, and lives in Bayrisch Gmain, Upper Bavaria.

Representative of the post-World War II writers associated with the "Gruppe 47" (*see* GERMAN LITERATURE), Aichinger has won several literary prizes and is particularly recognized for her short stories. Her first work of fiction, the novel *Die größere Hoffnung* (1948; Eng. tr., *Herod's Children*, 1963), was set against the gloomy background of Germany under Adolf Hitler. Its protagonist Ellen, a young Jewish girl, suffers anguish and persecution in a way that Aichinger herself experienced. But the novel's importance does not rest on autobiography or on contemporary events; rather, using a loose structure in which dialogue, dream, monologue, and lyricism interrupt epic narrative, the author brings into relief underlying parabolic meaning. Opposite forces strive against one another: light and darkness, good and evil, life and death. Only by accepting death can the individual fulfill himself or herself and give meaning to his or her life.

This thought also underlies the collection of short stories *Der Gefesselte* (1953; Eng. tr., *The Bound Man*, 1956). The chief character of the title story, although visibly bound in chains, has renounced free movement and learned to live with his fetters. Renunciation and acceptance of human bondage are present in several other stories.

The short-story collection *Eliza, Eliza* (1965) contains familiar themes but adds a greater variety of vantage points. Assuming various identities, the narrator explores a spectrum of sense perceptions and states of mind. There is, for instance, a mouse whose great happiness is that "she cannot be found"; someone watches a green donkey cross a bridge daily but does not want to encounter it for fear of getting too attached to it and hence missing it too much when it dies. In another story a straw man, bearing the human traits of an old, retired railroad man, "reeks of mildew like old uniforms" and passes his days sitting around, pitiful, congenial, humble, but already dead.

Franz KAFKA and the surrealists influenced Aichinger; much of her work is obscure in meaning but written in a style that is masterly in its clarity. With empathy she describes the human struggle in an incomprehensible and alienated world, elevating concrete reality into symbolic event through surprising flights of imagery to create a fictional world unmistakably her own.

Other works by Aichinger include *Knopfe* (1953; Buttons), *Zu keiner Stunde* (1957; At No Hour), *Besuch im Pfarrhaus* (1961; Visit at the Parsonage), *Wo ich wohne* (1963; Where I Live), *Auckland* (1969), *Nachricht vom Tag* (1970; News of the Day), and *Dialoge, Erzählungen, Gedichte* (1970; Dialogues, Stories, Poems), ed. by H. F. Schafroth.

See: C. E. Bedwell, "Who Is the Bound Man? Towards an Interpretation of Ilse Aichinger's *Der Gefesselte*," *GQ* 38 (1965): 30-37; E. Oldemeyer, "Zeitlichkeit und Glück: Gedanken zu Texten von Ilse Aichinger," in *Geistesgeschichtliche Perspektiven: Festgabe für Rudolf Fahrner,* ed. by G. Grossklaus (1969), pp. 281-305.   A.P.O.

Aistis, Jonas, pseud. of Jonas Aleksandravičius (1904-73), Lithuanian poet, was born in Kampiškes near Kaunas. He studied literature at the University of Kaunas and later philology and medieval French literature at the University of Grenoble, where he received his doctorate in 1944. In 1946, Aistis emigrated to the United States, where he taught high school in Connecticut and later worked for Radio Free Europe. From 1958 to his death he worked for the Library of Congress.

His first book, *Eiléraščiai* (1932; Poems), established Aistis as one of the finest lyric voices in Lithuanian literature. It was followed by *Imago mortis* (1933; Image of Death), *Intymios giesmes* (1935; Intimate Songs), and *Užgese chimeros akys* (1937; Chimera's Burned-Out Eyes). The volume *Poezija* (1961; Poetry) contains all of Aistis's verse published up to 1961. He also wrote several books of essays on a variety of topics, mostly literary.

Aistis's work is elegiac in tone, with a touch of humor and satire. He molded into an intensely personal idiom a vast cultural heritage, ranging from Lithuanian folk songs and tales to the great masterworks of world literature. In a language of subtle nuance and sparkling imagery, he created intimate lyrics dealing with the heart's response to nature, with the creative process itself, with religious experience, and with the historical destiny of his nation. Traces of his style can be seen in the work of some Lithuanian poets of the younger generation. Aistis also wrote under the pseudonyms Jonas Kossu-Aleksandravičius and Jonas Kuosa-Aleksandriškis.

See: A. Vaičiulaitis, "Jonas Aistis," *Encyclopedia Lituanica,* vol. 1 (1970), pp. 43-45; R. Šilbajoris, "Aspects of Poetic Imagery in the Work of Jonas Aistis," in his *Perfection of Exile: Fourteen Contemporary Lithuanian Writers* (1970), pp. 77-93.   A.V.

Aken, Piet van (1920-), Belgian (Flemish) novelist, was born in Terhagen, a small industrial village nested along the Rupel River where the brick factories are located. This environment plays an important role in his novels and short stories. In his early novels, *De falende god* (1942; The Failing God) and *Het hart en de klok* (1944; The Heart and the Clock), he attempted to endow his native land with mythic dimensions. *Het hart* is the result of this attempt: through the conflict between the old generation of rulers, Steenklamp, and the new conqueror, Heylen, van Aken sketches out the strife between the life led by the course of the seasons and instinctive impulses on the one hand, and the imperturbable workings of the spirit and of time on the other hand. In *De Duivel vaart in ons* (1946; The Devil Thrives in Us) and especially in *Het Begeren* (1952; Desire), this strife is more explicitly related to the rise of the workers' movement and socialist ideas. Yet both novels tend to show that the inexplicable and often contradictory forces at work in people severely limit their actions. In *Het Begeren*, the passionate relationship between man and wife plays a central role. The main character falls in love with his sister-in-law; as his tumultuous sentimental life unfolds, so does the social fight of the workers against the capitalists. Stylistically, this novel represents an innovation in the works of van Aken. His hazy, evocative descriptions here give place to a more realistic and direct narrative style, to a more contained tone, and to a language based on everyday reality. The short story "Klinkaart" (1954; Clay) constitutes a high point in van Aken's series of social stories. This short story concerns the initiation of a young girl to the hard world of brickworkers and capitalist exploiters. On her first day at work, she is not only baptized by the older workers but also raped by the foreman. After those novels, van Aken abandoned the theme of the Rupel region and used it only as a backdrop against which he placed the sentimental evolution of his characters. *De wilde jaren* (1958; The Wild Years) deals with the milieu of crime. A handful of young people have ransacked a jewelry store and killed the owner. They hide in an abandoned villa. In their isolation, they discover their own vulnerability and undergo a real purification. Similarly, inspired by current events, this time the colonial question that Belgium confronted at the end of 50 years of rule over what is today an independent Zaire, van Aken wrote *De nikkers* (1959; The Niggers).

With *De verraders* (1962; The Traitors), he turned again to the topic with which he had already dealt in *Alleen de doden ontkomen* (1947; Only the Dead Escape). This novel evokes the political frictions that took place after World War II and especially the problems of collaboration and repression. The subsequent novels of van Aken were a surprise and, after the previous books, become the high point of his work. *De jager, niet de prooi* (1965; The Hunter, Not the Prey) and *Slapende honden* (1966; Sleeping Dogs) are developed as a quest toward an entangled (confused) past that the respective main characters want to organize and justify. Louis in *De jager* returns mutilated from the Korean War in order to uncover why and how his unfaithful wife died, but all he finds with certitude is an image of himself. Such is also the case in *Slapende honden* with Absilis, who, 25 years after World War II, wants to know who has betrayed his Resistance group and has also murdered his friend, his conscience. Van Aken's last novel, *Dood getij* (1979; Near Tide) appeared after a long period of silence.

See: E. Popelier, *Piet van Aken* (1972); F. Auwera, *Piet van Aken* (1974).   P. van A.

Akhmadulina, Bella Akhatovna (1937–), Russian poet, was born in Moscow, into a family of mixed Russian-Italian-Tartar origin. She completed her education in 1960 at the Gorky Literary Institute in Moscow. Her first published poems appeared at the end of the 1950s, coinciding in time with the period of political "thaw" in the Soviet Union. This created a favorable atmosphere for the development of Akhmadulina's poetic personality in close association with the outlook of the writers who represented the independent liberal movement of that time in Soviet literature.

The most characteristic traits in Akhmadulina's poetry are a distinctive lyricism, a provocative frankness in confession, and an emotional intensity that are reminiscent of Marina TSVETAYEVA. Akhmadulina's poetry is exclusively urban in theme and is characterized by everyday images of contemporary city life, such as streets, crowds, cars, and airplanes. These prosaic objects, however, take on whimsical traits, and their ordinary meaning is transformed when they reflect the lyric persona's acutely subjective view of the world and his appraisal of that world. An important place in Akhmadulina's work is devoted to the theme of poetry as such and to the poet's relation to his own creative work as well as to the work of his fellow poets. This theme is linked to moral and ethical problems, thus making Akhmadulina a continuer of the classical Russian literary tradition in which ethical obligations are closely united with the obligation of loyalty to humanistic ideals.

Akhmadulina's activity as a translator also links her to the classical tradition of Russian poetry. She has translated especially from contemporary Georgian poets. Her translations, like those of Boris PASTERNAK, are distinguished by her introduction into the original of personal, individual feelings and moods characteristic of her own poetry.

Akhmadulina's works are notable for the sincerity, freshness, and independence of her views. Most of her poems are written in the traditional Russian iambic tetrameter, but she also uses *dolniki*, the Russian meter based purely on a fixed number of accented syllables. She does not hesitate to include technical terminology and conversational expressions in her poetic vocabulary, along with a broad range of material drawn from the contemporary literary language. The syntax of her poetry, however, is characterized by a literary refinement and at times by a structural complexity that are reminiscent of Tsvetayeva and Pasternak.

See: A. Rzhevsky, "Zvuk struny (o tvorchestve Belly Akhmadulinoy)," in *Vozdushnye puti* 5 (New York, 1967): 257–78; C. Rydel, "The Metaphysical World of Bella Akhmadulina," *RLT* 1 (1971): 326–41; C. Rydel, "A Bibliography of Works by and about Bella Akhmadulina," *RLT* 1 (1971), 434–41; P. Antokolsky, Introduction to B. Akhmadulina, *Stikhi* (1975); D. Brown, *Soviet Russian Literature since Stalin* (1978), pp. 116–21.
                                                                D.K.

Akhmatova, Anna, pseud. of Anna Andreyevna Gorenko (1889–1966), Russian poet, was born near Odessa but grew up in Tsarskoye Selo. She began her education there at the girls' gymnasium and studied also at the famous Smolny Institute in Petersburg, before finally graduating from the Fundukleyev Gymnasium in Kiev. After a brief period in law school in Kiev, she returned to Petersburg for advanced courses in literature, where she came under the influence of one of her teachers, the poet Innokenty ANNENSKY. In 1910, she married the acmeist poet Nikolay GUMILYOV, also a friend of Annensky and also from Tsarskoye Selo. The association with Gumilyov proved important to Akhmatova's early literary development. They visited Europe twice before World War I; after war broke out, however, Gumilyov enlisted in the cavalry. The apparently stormy marriage did not survive the strain of the long wartime separation, and they were divorced in 1918. Their son Lev, born in 1912, remained with Akhmatova.

The troubled years following the October Revolution (1917) were difficult ones for both poets. Akhmatova, although essentially apolitical, suffered from political attacks as well as from material deprivation. In 1921, Gumilyov was executed as an alleged counterrevolutionary. Akhmatova, who was one of the outstanding and widely read poets of the period, was unable to publish her poetry for almost two decades, although her work was often central in the critical literary studies and disputes of the 1920s.

Following the complete regimentation of literature under Iosif Stalin, Akhmatova suffered greatly from the repressions of the 1930s; and as part of the terroristic campaign against her, her son Lev was repeatedly imprisoned. Only in the relative relaxation of controls during World War II was Akhmatova's situation improved for a time. She endured the bombardment preceding the siege of Leningrad and was ultimately evacuated to Tashkent, where she spent the war years, often gravely ill. In 1942, her poem "Courage" was printed in *Pravda*, and her war poems received wide circulation. Finally "rehabilitated," Akhmatova was, for the moment, publicly recognized among the first of Russia's poets.

In 1946, with the reimposition of complete regimentation and the beginning of the Zhdanov era, Akhmatova, along with Mikhail ZOSHCHENKO, was singled out to bear the brunt of the new attack against artists and intellectuals. As a culmination of the campaign against Akhmatova, her son, who had been released from prison and had subsequently given distinguished service in the air force, was arrested again in 1949 and sentenced to 15 years of exile at hard labor. He was freed only in 1956.

During the early 1950s, Akhmatova was permitted to publish translations of poetry from other languages, but it was not until the "thaw" following the death of Stalin that she was able to publish her own work. In 1958, her first volume since 1922 was published without restraint, and gradually rehabilitation was made complete. In 1964, Akhmatova was permitted to travel to Italy for an international poetry award and to Oxford for an honorary degree. In 1966, a book-length study was published about her, the first in the Soviet Union since the 1920s. She died that same year, having spent her last years honored both at home and abroad.

In the decade from 1912 to 1922, Akhmatova achieved immense critical and popular success with several small volumes of love lyrics characterized by their controlled passion. She was early associated with the acmeist group of poets, whose claim for simplicity and clarity (in contradistinction to the grandiloquence and the mystical turn of much of the earlier symbolist poetry) coincided with Akhmatova's practice. The volumes from this period are *Vecher* (1912; Evening), *Chotki* (1914; Rosary), *Belaya staya* (1917; The White Flock), *Podorozhnik* (1921; The Buckthorn), and *Anno Domini MCMXXI* (1922).

Although Akhmatova deliberately limits herself to the primary theme of woman's love, her secondary thematic material is rich and varied, deriving largely from the cultural, religious, and national history and tradition of Russia. The relatively few poems in which the love theme is not dominant or at least present draw also on this material: historical figures, Russia's cities and towns, the wealth of Russian folk tradition and oral poetry, the ancient churches, and the forms of Russian Orthodoxy.

During this early period in her work, Akhmatova's innovations in traditional versification were generally recognized, but in retrospect her accomplishment in an age characterized by radical innovation seems to lie rather in

her ingenious reworking and renewing of established forms. As a consequence, Akhmatova's early work does not appear dated, as does the poetry of some of her more radically innovative contemporaries.

Akhmatova continued to write during the years when she could not publish, and around 1940 her poetry underwent an immense burst of creative activity and redirection. In that year, she effectively completed *Requiem*, an epic cry for her people in the grip of the Stalinist terror, and began her other long masterwork *Poema bez geroya* (finished in 1962; Eng. tr., "Poem without a Hero," 1971).

Akhmatova's sense of history, so important to the background of many of her early poems, becomes a dominant theme in the later works. Whereas in her earlier works cultural-historical impressions fuse with the intensity of the lyrical moment, in later works the historical moment itself often becomes the very source of the lyrical emotion. The poet's past and Russia's past, both present already in Akhmatova's early poems, become the subjects of many of the more successful later works.

In style as well as theme, her poetry also shows a marked consistency. There is, of course, a shift in emphasis and further experimentation, but it is difficult to find a poem from the later years that is not in some important way prefigured by the poetry of 1912–22. Where there is change—as is expected in a talented poet of over 55 years of creativity—it occurs in the order of development, the broadening of theme, the deepening of intellectual content. Oddly enough, it is in "Poem without a Hero" and the works of the later period that Akhmatova reflects Osip MANDELSHTAM's retroflective characterization of the early acmeism: "a longing after world culture."

Neither of the magnificent long poems *Requiem* (Munich, 1963; Eng. tr., 1964) or *Poema bez geroya* have yet been published in the Soviet Union, and the last Soviet collection published in her lifetime, *Beg Vremeni* (1965; The Course of Time), suffers from their exclusion. It does, however, include selections from the period of enforced silence (1922–40); and while there are indications that the Akhmatova archive is still far from complete, there is now a fairly comprehensive picture of one of the most arresting Russian poets of the 20th century. English translations of her poems are in the collection *Selected Poems* (1969; tr. by R. McKane).

Anna Akhmatova became a legend in her own time, a symbol of uncompromising artistic integrity in the face of repression and regimentation. The last link with the "Silver Age" of Russian poetry before and just after the October Revolution, she was a formative influence on a whole new generation of poets.

See: B. Eikhenbaum, *Anna Akhmatova: opyt analiza* (1923); E. Dobin, *Poeziya Anny Akhmatovoy* (1968); G. Struve and B. Filippov, eds., *Sochineniya* (1968); K. Verheul, *The Theme of Time in the Poetry of Anna Akhmatova* (1971); S. Driver, *Anna Akhmatova* (1972).   S.N.D.

Aksyonov, Vasily Pavlovich (1932–), Russian writer, was born in Kazan, the son of a Communist Party functionary. His mother, Yevgeniya Ginzburg, is the author of *Journey into the Whirlwind* (1967), an autobiographical account of her life in a concentration camp, which was widely publicized in the West (*see* RUSSIAN LITERATURE).

In 1959, Aksyonov abandoned his career as a physician to devote himself to writing. His first significant work was the novella *Kollegi* (1960; Eng. tr., *Colleagues*, 1962) about young doctors. In 1961 he published *Zvyozdny bilet* (Eng. tr., *A Starry Ticket*, 1962), a novel that won him a reputation as an avant-garde writer and the "Soviet Salinger." It portrays several Moscow teenagers who, after graduating from high school, decide not to study for college entrance examinations and instead take off for the Baltic Coast to have a good time and to "find themselves." Their summer is filled with funny incidents, conflicts, disappointments, and the discovery of sex and love. They are immature and naive but touching in their attempt to rebel against the establishment and against what they consider false values. A striking feature of the novel is its teenage slang, which is delightfully true to life. Conservative critics have attacked Aksyonov for "condoning amorality among the Soviet youth."

Aksyonov subsequently wrote several volumes of stories, a play, and two novels: *Pora, moy drug, pora* (1964; Eng. tr., *It's Time, My Friend, It's Time,* 1969) and *Lyubov k elektrichestvu* (1971; Love for Electricity). The former depicts the lives and problems of young intellectuals; the latter is a biography of Leonid Krasin, a Russian revolutionary. Of Aksyonov's short stories "Na polputi k lune" (1962; Eng. tr., "Halfway to the Moon," 1964) is the best. It describes with zestful humor and a touch of sadness a truck driver's unrequited infatuation with an airline hostess.

Aksyonov's works are characterized by a dynamic pace, in which action predominates over description. His language is colloquial and punctuated with startling turns of phrase. On the whole, his style is refreshingly original.

I.H.C.

Alain, pseud. of Emile Chartier (1868–1951), French essayist and philosopher, was born in Mortagne. He was known as Chartier—just plain Chartier—to countless students in the lycées of Lorient, Rouen, and Henri IV in Paris, as well as to his fellow alumni of the Ecole Normale Supérieure. But to the general public he was the Alain of thousands and thousands of "Propos" that he contributed, beginning in 1906, first to the *Dépêche de Rouen* (1906-14), then to such publications as the *Libres Propos* (a weekly edited by himself, 1921-24), the *Revue des vivants, Revue européenne, Europe, Alsace française, Navire d'argent,* and the *Nouvelle Revue française.* The typical *propos* is a short, aphoristic piece of 50 or 60 lines, strewn with concrete or poetical images, pointing, like a fable or parable, to a practical lesson. Although the *propos* as a genre belongs to the art of the "columnist," Alain's essays constitute definitely superior journalism, and through them he entered the long line of French moralists who for centuries meted out to the reader pleasant and digestible pills of worldly wisdom. Roughly one-fourth of these sketches were collected in volume form, sometimes under loose titles—such as *Les Cent et un Propos d'Alain* (5 vols., 1908-29; The 101 Words of Alain), *Les Propos d'Alain* (2 vols., 1920; Words by Alain), *Propos sur l'esthétique* (1923; Words on Aesthetics), *Propos sur le christianisme* (1924; Words on Christianity), *Propos sur le bonheur* (1925; Eng. tr., *Alain on Happiness,* 1973), *Propos sur l'éducation* (1932; Words on Education), *Propos de littérature* (1934; Words on Literature), *Propos de politique* (1934; Words on Politics), and *Propos d'économique* (1935; Words on Economics)—sometimes under a more significant heading, indicative of a system. Thus a glance at the remainder of Alain's lengthy bibliography reveals his sustained interest in militant pacifism—*Mars, ou la guerre jugée* (1921; Eng. tr., *Mars; or, The Truth about War,* 1930), followed in 1939 by *Convulsion de la force* (Convulsion of Force) and *Echec à la force* (Defeat of Force); in democracy and politics—*Eléments d'une doctrine radicale* (1925; Elements of a Radical Doctrine), *Le Citoyen contre les pouvoirs* (1925; The Citizen against the Powers that Be); in aesthetics—*Système des beaux-arts* (1920; System of the Fine Arts, completed by *Vingt Leçons sur les beaux-arts*

[1931; 20 Lessons on the Fine Arts]), *La Visite au musicien* (1927; Visit to the Musician), and *Entretiens chez le sculpteur* (1937; Conversations at the Sculptor's); in psychology and philosophy proper—*Quatre-vingt-un Chapitres sur l'esprit et les passions* (1915; 81 Chapters on the Mind and the Passions), *Lettres au Docteur Mondor* (1924; Letters to Dr. Mondor), *Sentiments, passions et signes* (1926; Sentiments, Passions, and Signs), *Esquisses de l'homme* (1927; Sketches of Man), *Entretiens au bord de la mer* (1931; Conversations at the Seashore), *Les Dieux* (1934; Eng. tr., *The Gods,* 1975), *Les Saisons de l'esprit* (1937; The Seasons of the Mind), *Minerve, ou de la sagesse* (1939; Minerva, or Concerning Wisdom); in philosophical exegesis and literary criticism—*Les Idées et les âges* (2 vols., 1927; Ideas and Ages), *Introduction aux Passions de l'âme de Descartes* (1928; Descarte's Introduction to the Passions of the Soul), *Idées. Platon, Descartes, Hegel* (1932; Ideas: Plato, Descartes, Hegel; reprinted in 1939 with an additional study on Auguste Comte), *Stendhal* (1935), *Avec Balzac* (1937; With Balzac), commentary (1929) on *Charmes* by Paul VALÉRY, and another (1936 on Valéry's *La Jeune Parque.* In a class by themselves stand *Histoire de mes pensées* (1936; History of My Thoughts) and *Souvenirs de guerre* (1937; Memories of War).

There is no mystery to the selection of Chartier's pen name. It was chosen in obvious remembrance of his 15th-century homonym, the famous poet Alain Chartier. From one Norman to another, the greeting appears natural enough. One wonders, however, whether the medieval Alain, polished courtier and much traveled diplomat that he was, would have thought of writing: "I do not just happen to be from Normandy. I am Normandy itself." Such is Alain's boast—and a fair one indeed. Around Mortagne, his native town, among the hedgerows and the bushes, he found the old "Chouan" spirit still intact and took it as his own. It is an earthy spirit, intent upon real things, sober, unafraid, diffident. With Alain it becomes the "radical" spirit or the faculty, rooted in one's conscience, to resist power—outwardly if power is illegal, inwardly (with due physical obeisance) if power is legal, but to resist in both cases—for all power, according to Alain, is arbitrary in character, and it is the essence of any power, political or not, to be "regal," to overreach itself, to corrupt and be corrupted. If democracy, for instance, commands his stout respect, it is not that democracy is good government (there are no good governments as such); it is because democracy devised the best means of curbing the excesses of government and setting up the citizen against the powers that be.

A fitting epigraph to Alain's creed would be found in the sentence, "The minute we think, we should learn how not to die." To live, then, is to be awake. To be awake is to react. Acceptance of ready-made ideas means surrender; total conformity means death. Is it at all surprising that youth responded to such a stirring call? In fact, Alain's prestige radiated far into academic and literary circles. He was revered and heeded by his disciples as few lycée professors have ever been. To be sure, a few older students, such as André MAUROIS and Henri MASSIS, were stimulated rather than deeply marked; but Jean PRÉVOST, some 15 years their junior, was fated to represent the Alain tradition at its sturdiest. This gifted writer joined the French Forces of the Interior during World War II and perished in 1944 at the hands of the Germans, thus demonstrating in exemplary fashion that "resistance" in the Alain sense is something other—and something more—than "conscientious objection."

See: J. Prévost, A. Thibaudet, R. Fernandez, J. Schlumberger, and P. Bost, "L'Œuvre d'Alain," in *Europe* 16 (1928): 129–52; Anon., *Alain, professeur* (1932);

D. Saurat, "Alain," in *NRF* 39 (1932): 760–66; J. O. Robinson, *Alain: lecteur de Balzac et de Stendhal* (1958); O. Reboul, *L'Homme et ses passions d'après Alain*, 2 vols. (1968); H. Giraud, *La Morale d'Alain* (1970); G. Pascal, *L'Idée de philosophie chez Alain* (1970); S. Vayssac, *La Lecture en marge d'Alain* (1977).

J.-A.B. rev. D.W.A.

Alain-Fournier, pseud. of Henri-Alban Fournier (1886–1914), French novelist, was born in La Chapelle d'Angillon, the son of schoolteachers. He spent an unusually happy childhood in villages of central France (Bas-Berry, Sologne) familiar to readers of his one masterpiece, *Le Grand Meaulnes* (1913; Eng. trs., *The Wanderer*, 1928; *The Lost Domain*, 1959). For a time, he lived in Brest, where he had gone in hopes of a naval career. He then completed his secondary education at the lycée in Bourges now named for him. Alain-Fournier then spent three years in Paris at the lycées Lakanal and Louis-le-Grand preparing for the Ecole Normale Supérieure. In the former he met his lifelong friend and future brother-in-law, the critic Jacques RIVIÈRE. Their extensive correspondence (4 vols., 1926–28) is essential reading not only as personal revelation but also as testimony to their changing aesthetic ideals in art, music, the dance, and literature.

Following two unsuccessful attempts to enter the Ecole Normale and two years of military service, Alain-Fournier turned to literary journalism. Yet his cherished ambition was to convey poetically his intense devotion to the landscape and atmosphere of his childhood. Soon he was to create, in *Le Grand Meaulnes*, a mysterious domain whose chatelaine, the blond Yvonne de Q., was modeled on a woman with whom he had had only one lengthy conversation in 1905 in Paris. Perhaps because she was the incarnation of his adolescent dreams, perhaps because she was as inaccessible as happiness, this love was to affect deeply his emotional life and his demands on women.

Although Alain-Fournier was certain of the subject matter of his fiction, he struggled for eight years to develop a suitable form. After his early enthusiasm for the minor symbolists (Jules Laforgue and Francis JAMMES, in particular), idealism, Claude Debussy's *Pelléas et Mélisande*, and the English Pre-Raphaelites, he sensed affinities in the work of Arthur RIMBAUD, Fyodor Dostoyevsky, Paul CLAUDEL, Thomas Hardy, and his friend Charles PÉGUY. Alain-Fournier's early poems and poetic stories, published later as *Miracles* (1924), reveal a slow trend away from the ineffable towards the concrete, the renunciation of pure lyricism for narrative directness. The result is the poetic realism of *Le Grand Meaulnes*.

Critics agree that the three heroes of the novel represent different facets of the author's personality. Yet interpretations of these figures as well as of the contrasting female characters have differed sufficiently to provoke fruitful controversy. The very theme of the novel remains ambiguous. Some critics see it as the rejection of adulthood or the glorification of purity, while others stress the polarity between the oneiric sequence of the *fête étrange* and the succeeding disillusionment. Still others sense that the Lost Domain is the incarnation of childhood's capacity for belief, acceptance, and wonder. Throughout the novel, Alain-Fournier illustrates the immanence of magic and marvel in daily life. By an immediate automatic sublimation, reality is perceived simultaneously as precise and mysterious, particular and ideal. The artist's task is to render palpable this "latent dose of wonder."

Early criticism of Alain-Fournier and his work leaned heavily towards hagiographic enthusiasm and biographical detail. Within the last 10 years, however, studies of the structures, themes, imagery, and archetypal elements in the novel have made increasingly apparent its careful craftsmanship, psychological interest, and stylistic excellence. Nevertheless, no recent commentary surpasses Jacques Rivière's introduction to *Miracles*.

Alain-Fournier was working on a play and a second novel, *Colombe Blanchet* (fragments published in the *Nouvelle Revue française*, 1922), when he disappeared in combat in September 1914. Perhaps, as this intransigent dreamer had foreseen, death proved the greatest adventure of all.

See: J. Rivière, Introduction to Alain-Fournier, *Miracles* (1924); R. Gibson, *The Quest of Alain-Fournier* (1953); R. Champigny, *Portrait of a Symbolist Hero* (1954); M. Guiomar, *Inconscient et imaginaire dans Le Grand Meaulnes* (1964).   H.T.N.

Alas, Leopoldo, pseud. Clarín (1852–1901), Spanish novelist, short-story writer, essayist, and literary critic, was born in Zamora although usually associated with Asturias, where his family came from and where he spent most of his adult life as a professor of law at the University of Oviedo. As a student in Madrid (1871–78), he lived through the aftermath of the liberal revolution of 1868 and the restoration, which shaped his Republican political beliefs. In the capital he studied with the *krausistas*, followers of the German philosopher Karl Krause who were reformers of the philosophical and pedagogical trends of the time in Spain. Krausism greatly influenced Clarín's idealistic inclination towards a permanent spiritual and metaphysical search, and it is this aspect of his intellectual profile that makes him a predecessor of the turn-of-the-century writers who tried to change the mental habits and styles then prevalent in Spain. To grasp his literary personality we must consider his inquisitive, critical spirit together with the tenets of positivism and naturalism, the movements whose methods he absorbed not as philosophies but as techniques for studying the world. The romantic undertones of his sensibilities show in his patent dissatisfaction with his times. This dissatisfaction compelled him to study the cultural manifestations of society while developing a perspective for his supreme ideals of justice and truth, and marks his works with a profoundly moralistic tone.

A poignant and ever-active pen in newspapers and magazines made Clarín famous as the foremost literary critic of his time. His journalistic pieces exude satire and irony as they needle the ignorant and the perpetrators of bad taste. Of no less importance is his more serious criticism. Although it lacks critical apparatus, it reveals his ample cultural background, his fine interpretative powers, and his subtle literary perceptions, especially of the novel. His works provided a tonic and stimulus to the flat literary atmosphere of the late 19th century in Spain. Examples of his criticism are: *Solos de Clarín* (1881), *La literatura en 1881* (1882), *Sermón perdido* (1885; Lost Sermon), *Nueva campaña* (1887; New Campaign), *Mezclilla* (1897; Miscellany), *Ensayos y revistas* (1892; Essays and Reviews), *Palique* (1893; Small Talk), and eight *Folletos literarios* (1886–91; Literary Feuilletons).

In contrast to his bold career as a literary critic, Clarín's fictional writing was extremely cautious. He began with short stories, mostly in a humorous, satirical vein. Then came *Pipá* (1879), a short novel in which naturalistic techniques appear in his work for the first time. His masterpiece, and one of the most significant fictional works of the 19th century, is *La Regenta* (1885; The Regent's Wife). Clarín's inspiration to write a long novel came from two different sources; the first was a resurgence of the novel in Spain, with the appearance in five years of no less than a dozen important works; the second was a lively polemic about naturalism, in which Clarín was a protagonist as well as a proponent. But to frame Clarín as a pure naturalist would be to underestimate his intellectual personality, which absorbed naturalism and put it to the test of seeking moral truth. Ana Ozores, the protagonist of *La Regenta*, a beautiful, sensitive young married woman, is besieged by the boredom and alienation of the traditional ways of life in the provincial town where she lives. When her restless spirit reaches out, looking for self-fulfillment, it finds few options beyond the limits set by domestic activities. She finally accepts the love of one of her two suitors, a Don Juan figure named Alvaro Mesía (the other is a priest, Fermín de Pas). Ana soon discovers the Don Juanism of her lover and his materialistic motives. This coincides with her husband's discovery of the adultery, followed by his death in the defense of his honor. The naturalism of the novel resides in the attention given to detail and the detached presentation of the problem of the possibilities life offers to Ana. Clarín's own contribution is his moralistic judgment of society, which before the scandal does not offer Ana a way to fulfill her longing honestly, and which turns against her after the scandal, condemning her to a life of isolation.

Although it lacks the inspirational breadth of *La Regenta*, his only other novel, *Su único hijo* (1890; His Only Child) is exemplary in its condensation. Clarín the craftsman creates a showcase of the fictional techniques of the 19th-century novel in which, beneath the naturalistic lines, it is possible to discern a more dramatic novel and the direct, intense presentation of reality. The protagonist, Bonifacio Reyes, is torn by two opposing loves, the one for his mistress and the other for an unborn child whom he wishes to disassociate from her. His confused state of mind is revealed through direct narration, indirect style, and dialogues that at crucial moments are replaced by monologues. In *La Regenta* Clarín accepts the traditional modes of realistic narration, whereas in *Su único hijo* he takes a step into the 20th century. In this novel the idealistic inclination latent in earlier works surfaces with a distinctly religious and spiritual meaning, as it does in his later short stories and his last works. Among these the most remarkable collections are *Doña Berta, Cuervo* (Crow), and *Superchería* (Superstition), all published in 1892, and the short stories contained in *El Señor y lo demás son cuentos* (1892; The Lord and Other Stories), *Cuentos morales* (1896; Moral Stories), and *El gallo de Sócrates* (1901; Socrates' Rooster).

See: S. Beser, *Leopoldo Alas, crítico literario* (1970); J. Rutherford, *La Regenta* (1974).   G.Gu.

Albanian literature. Albanian literature is nearly coextensive with Albanian nationalism. This became an organized movement after the Congress of Berlin in 1878 and culminated in Albania's independence in 1912. The country's occupation by the troops of Benito Mussolini in 1939 gave rise to another movement of national liberation that brought a Communist government to power in 1944. Far from discouraging nationalism, Albanian communism has supported it vigorously, partly as an act of self-defense after Albania's break first with Yugoslavia (1948) and then with the Soviet Union (1960).

A convenient date for marking the beginning of Albanian modern literature is 1912, the year of the nation's independence. Until 1836, when Girolamo de Rada published his *Milosao*, which marks the birth of artistic literature, the literature of the diaspora far outweighed that of the mother country. The Italo-Albanians Girolamo de Rada, Gabriele Dara, Giuseppe Serembe, and Giuseppe Schirò were the forerunners of Albanian literature, producing works that combined Byzantine and Roman elements. The major native writers of the preindependence ("awakening") period were expatriates: the Frashëri brothers, Naim and Sami, living in Constantinople; Pashko Vassa in Lebanon; Çajupi, pseud. of Andon Chako (1866–1930) in Egypt; Asdren (Aleks Sotir Drenova) in Romania; and Faik Konitza and Fan Noli in the United States. Literature in the mother country centered in Scutari, where Ndre Mjeda, Ndoc Nikaj, Gjergj FISHTA, Vinçenc Prennushi, and Luigj Gurakuqi were engaged in intense activity. The literature of the preindependence period is both militantly patriotic and romantic, nostalgically rooted in folklore and national history. The dominant genre of this romantic literature was the epic, while narrative writing was limited to the historical novel and, to a still lesser extent, to the short story.

Modern literature is for the most part the continuation and aftermath of the romantic movement. An interim period of Westernized democracy (1920–24) was succeeded by a Byzantine-like autocracy that left the socioeconomic structure inherited from the Turkish domination basically unchanged. The younger representatives of the romantic movement, of whom Gjergj Fishta is the most important, produced their main works during the independence period. Opposed to Fishta, and in many respects his rival, was Ndre Mjeda (1866–1937), a Jesuit who was both a lyrical poet and a linguist. Mjeda's romanticism in *Juvenilia* (1917) is tempered with classicism in a way reminiscent of Giosuè Carducci, while his feeling for the idyllic countryside brings him close to Giovanni PASCOLI. Mjeda was a perfectionist who published little, a master of the sonnet, as in *Lissus* (1921) and *Scodra* (1932), and an inspiring example of an uncompromising poet possessed with the dignity of his vocation. Another learned poet of the period was Asdren—Aleksander Drenova (1872–1947)—whose several collections of poems, especially *Psalme murgu* (1930; A Poor Man's Psalms), are remarkable for their range of motifs and metrical variety. Çajupi, a democratic writer combining lyricism with satire, is the author of *Baba Tomorri* (1902, Father Tomor).

The Tosk (southern) counterpart of Fishta is Fan Noli (1880–1965). Educated in the United States and ordained an Orthodox priest to serve the interests of the Albanian immigrants, Noli went back to his country to take part in politics and in 1924 became premier of the short-lived, only truly democratic Albanian government. After that disastrous experiment, the agnostic and leftist bishop returned to the United States where he headed the Albanian Orthodox Church in America. Here Noli earned his Ph.D. with a thesis (published in 1950) entitled *George Castrioti Scanderbeg*. He also published many works of liturgy and catechism in both Albanian and English, including a *Byzantine Hymnal* (1959), as well as a collection of satirical poems, *Albumi* (1948; Album). His introductory essays to his own translations of Omar Khayyam, Shakespeare, Cervantes, and Henrik IBSEN made him a pioneer of Albanian literary criticism. A brilliant essayist and publicist was Faik Konitza (1875–1943), editor of the scholarly journal *Albania* from 1897 to 1910. In *Dielli*, an Albanian-American journal of which he was twice director, Konitza published a satirical novel, *Dr. Gjilpëra* (1925; Dr. Needle), in which he ridicules the autocratic Albanian government whose minister plenipotentiary in Washington he eventually became. His unfinished *Albania: The Rock Garden of Southeastern Europe* (1957) is an essay in English.

During the period of independence (1912–44), a new generation of writers emerged, trying, under the influence of modern European trends, to break loose from the bonds of tradition. The leading poets of this period were

Lasgush Poradeci (1899-) and MIGJENI. Poradeci studied in Bucharest and Graz, falling under the spell of Mihail Eminescu (*see* ROMANIAN LITERATURE) and Hindu pantheism. His *Vallja e yjve* (1933; The Dance of the Stars) contains poems that interiorize landscapes or celebrate the divine spirit whose vocal instrument the poet is. Poradeci exhibits a meditative mind in search of transcendental meanings to soothe his own melancholy, and he achieves musical modulations that charm the reader. Migjeni's *Vargjet e lira* (1936; Free Verse) is, on the contrary, meant to dispel the magic of "old tales," to free the mind from the bonds of the past and awaken it to the injustice of the social order.

The independence period witnessed the development of the short story and the birth of the Albanian drama. The first collection of Albanian short stories ever published is *Hi dhe shpuzë* (1915; Ashes and Embers) by Midhat Frashëri (1880- 1949), a publicist and ideologist of Albanian nationalism. Ernest Koliqi (1903- 75) produced two volumes of short stories. The second, *Tregtarë flamujsh* (1935; Merchants of Flags), deals with bourgeois psychology in his native town, Scutari. The stories in *Netë shqipëtare* (1937; Albanian Nights) by Mitrush Kuteli, pseud. of Dhimitër Pasko (1907-), an Albanian-Romanian, are lyrical evocations of scenes and customs of his own native town, Pogradeci. Among other significant narrative writers, Sterjo Spasse deals with contemporary problems, Anton Logoreci depicts scenes of everyday life, and Vedat Kokona experiments with French narrative techniques. A prolific but uneven playwright was Kristo Floqi (1873- 194?), author of 5 plays and more than 15 comedies and one-act sketches. The playwright Etëhem Haxhiademi (1907-) wrote classical verse tragedies.

The occupation of Albania by Italy in 1939 was facilitated by the collaboration of various intellectuals, including writers. Koliqi, who was minister of education and president of the Albanian Fascist Grand Council, is a case of a writer lost to politics. As the major exponent of Albanian fascism, both in his country and later as an exile in Italy, Koliqi has been advocating, through magazines and books, a return to tradition and to a language including many archaic features.

The best of the exiled writers is the poet Martin Camaj, a former editor of the Italo-Albanian magazine *Shêjzat/Le Pleiadi* and now a professor of Albanian at the University of Munich. Camaj is divided between an allegiance to tradition conditioned by his Gheg highland origin and an eagerness for innovation prompted by his contacts with various cultural climates. His most recent volume of poetry, *Lyrika mes dy moteve* (1967; Middle-Age Poems), marks a departure from the traditional motifs and style of his youth as found in *Nji fyell ndër male* (1953; A Flute in the Mountains).

Contemporary literature in the mother country includes very few works that are artistically relevant. The Communist takeover resulted in the confinement and execution of many nationalistic and nonconformist writers and intellectuals, including Communist dissenters such as Sejfullah Malëshova, the author of *Vjersha* (1945; Poems) and the minister of culture and foremost Communist Party ideologist in the period 1944- 47. While the regime has eliminated many literary professionals, it has, on the other hand, imposed the official doctrine of socialist realism, whose function it is to advertise political slogans and to extol Party leaders. This doctrine has made it impossible for young Communists and fellow travelers to develop their literary talents. The most promising of the recent poets, Llazar Siliqi, author of *Prishtina* (1949), has undergone a steady involution. The title of one novel, *Këneta*

(1959; The Bog), by Fatmir Gjata, a winner of the Prize of the Republic, epitomizes the situation in the narrative. The most ambitious novel so far, Jakov Xoxa's *Lumi i vdekur* (1967; The Dead River) draws upon Mikhail SHOLOKHOV's *And Quiet Flows the Don*. Contemporary Albanian drama is less than mediocre, while comedy, hardly thinkable in such a climate, is indeed nonexistent. Literary criticism is irrelevant.

On such a gray horizon, Ismail Kadare (1936-) is a lonely star. A writer whose communism does not coincide with the official ideology, Kadare has been tolerated mostly on account of his success abroad, where he has been greeted as an Albanian Yevgeny YEVTUSHENKO. His *Vjersha e poema* (1969; Short and Long Poems) combines epic and lyrical elements, a narrative verve, and a rich metaphoric vein. His narrative style includes daring imaginative and innovative techniques. The controversial *Gjenerali i ushtërisë së vdekur* (1963; The General of the Dead Army), translated and published in some 15 countries, is the first Albanian novel worthy of the name. Since 1963, Kadare has published three other novels, none of which can compete with his first one.

The burgeoning literature of the Albanians in Yugoslavia is a recent phenomenon. In 1956, there appeared a collective volume of poems and short stories, *Shkëndijat e para* (First Sparks). Many volumes of poetry and prose have since followed, a phenomenon due in part to the considerable freedom of expression in literature and the arts allowed by the Yugoslav government. Apart from the nationalistic concern underlying the writing of the Albanians in Yugoslavia, their styles differ widely. Noteworthy among these writers are the dramatist Josip V. Rela, the novelists Tajar Hatibi and Ramiz Kelmendi, the poets Enver Gjergjeku and Muhamet Kërveshi, and the essayist Rexhep Qosja.

See: A. Logoreci, "The Dialogue of Modern Albanian Writing," *BA* 1 (1956): 155- 59; G. Schirò, *Storia della letteratura albanese* (1959); T. Zavalani, "P.E.N. in Exile: Albanians," *Arena* (March 1964): 9- 18; A. Pipa, *Albanian Literature: Social Perspectives* (1978).   A.P.

Albert-Birot, Pierre (1876- 1967), French poet, was born in Angoulême. He belonged to the generation between Guillaume APOLLINAIRE and the dada and surrealism movements that helped delineate a new poetic spirit deriving from futurism (*see* ITALIAN LITERATURE). His magazine *SIC* (1916- 19; reprinted 1973) regrouped the avant-garde trends of 1916- 19. He staged Apollinaire's play *Les Mamelles de Tirésias* (The Breasts of Tiresias) in 1917, and with him Albert-Birot coined the word "surrealism." His own experiments in the theater between 1919 and 1924, such as the comic drama *Les Femmes pliantes* (perf. 1919, pub. 1923; Flexible Women), foreshadowed the new theater of the 1950s. He also wrote more than 15 volumes of poetry, the early ones being republished in 1967 as *Poésie 1916- 1924* (Poetry 1916- 1924).

Albert-Birot first exalted the joy of living, "La Joie des sept couleurs" (The joy of seven colors), in down-to-earth poetry in which humor and a sense of the marvelous or the absurd combine with ingenuousness. His poetry then broadened to encompass philosophical and cosmic dimensions in *Poèmes à l'autre moi* (1927; Poems to the Other Self); *La Panthère noire* (1938; The Black Panther), his best volume; *Dix poèmes à la mer* (1954; 10 Poems to the Sea); and *Aux trente-deux vents* (1970; To the 32 Winds). In the work of Albert-Birot, poetry becomes the avenue of communication between the indifference of the world and the aspirations of the self, which is invited to a transcendent, Adamic existence. This primitivist vein inspired the prose *Mémoires d'Adam* (1948; Adam's

Diary). Albert-Birot's linguistic diversity was also demonstrated in *Grabinoulor* (1933, 1964), an immense prose narrative, defying literary categories, that concerns the adventures of a little man who becomes a superman. This epic of the modern imagination, transgressing limits of time and space, is written in unpunctuated movements of great power and verbal creativity.

See: J. Follain, *Pierre Albert-Birot* (1967); special issue of *F* 2–3 (1973). D.Ba.

Alberti, Rafael (1902–), Spanish poet, was born at Puerto de Santa María, near Cádiz. His poetic trajectory is a continuous search for lost paradises, with three distinct phases. In the first, represented by *Marinero en tierra* (1925; Inland Sailor), Alberti attempted a lyrical recovery of the lost paradise of childhood. The second, represented by *Sobre los ángeles* (1929; Eng. tr., *Concerning the Angels*, 1967) portrays the budding of a paradise that withers before it has a chance to bloom. The third phase, the poet's writings in exile (1939–75), brings the promise of a paradise still lost in the distant future. In his first book, *Marinero en tierra* (awarded the National Prize for Literature), Alberti expressed the sorrow of a child who has lost his seaside paradise. The child engages in a downward search, because for him paradise is a lost orchard sunk in the depths of the sea. Most dreamers have looked for paradise on earth or above it, and although Alberti's downward search reflects many traits of these traditional paradises, it also reveals his originality. The young sailor-poet and his mermaid companion merrily hawk oranges and seaweeds from a toy cart pulled by a salmon in the depths of the sea. *Marinero en tierra* is a song of happiness without precedent in Spanish poetry. Like an adolescent Odysseus, the young poet created a paradise for two, although the book ends on a note of self-questioning. Alberti's masterpiece, *Sobre los ángeles*, chronicles the poet's attempt to recover his identity after a frightening inner crisis. There is an infinite variety of angels in this book. Some correspond to traditional angelology, but many are entirely Alberti's own: the Dumb Angel, the Ugly Angel, the Angel of Numbers, the angels of coal, ashes, and mildew. Most of them seem to be fallen angels who represent different stages of anguish and inner crisis. They fight among themselves in a crumbling though expanding cosmic space, or they descend swiftly on the helpless poet. Man's task in *Sobre los ángeles*, as the author points out in the first poem ("Paradise Lost"), is to remember and to recapture the vision of a lost paradise. What Alberti describes again and again in the poems that follow, however, is a chaotic, abysmal, and cruel world. Nevertheless, Alberti's second poetic phase did not end on a note of doom. The poet's endurance resulted in a work of disturbing beauty.

In 1933, Alberti surprised most of his readers by stating that he would henceforth be a spokesman for the Communist Party and for revolution in Spain. From 1933 to 1939 much of his poetry focused on political and social issues, as in *Consignas* (1933; Party Lines) and *De un momento a otro: poesía e historia* (1937; From One Moment to the Next: Poetry and History), which includes the Civil War poem "Capital of Glory." After the defeat of the Spanish Republic in 1939, Alberti settled in Argentina and produced some of the best poetry of exile ever written in Spanish. The earth, which in his first book was a negative element, became an object of love. *Retornos de lo vivo lejano* (1952; Returns of Distant Life) is the best expression of Alberti's longing for the Spain of his childhood and youth. But *Baladas y canciones del Paraná* (1954; Paraná Ballads and Songs) is perhaps Alberti's most nostalgic book, because the present is seen as if it were already a lost paradise. *Baladas* describes the poet's summers on the banks of the Paraná River in South America. There man stands alone and motionless on his balcony, looking at the river but thinking of the lost land of his earlier years. The horses and the river are also motionless. Only a boat passes from time to time on its way to the sea, toward the lost paradise. Alberti's poetic trajectory thus comes full circle. In his search for paradise, he began by rejecting inland life and plunging into an underwater orchard that symbolized happy, early days. From that garden he entered the nightmare of *Sobre los ángeles*. Later, from South America, he made the imaginary voyage back to the southern Spain of his birth. That is why the memory of things past plays such a fundamental role in the poetry of Alberti, and not only in his poetry: his longing, while in exile, for the Spain of his youth led him to write an exceptional book of autobiographical recollection, *La arboleda perdida* (2 vols., 1942, 1959; Eng. tr., *The Lost Grove*, 1978).

Alberti left Argentina and settled in Rome, where he still lives, in 1963. In 1965 the Soviet Union awarded him the Lenin Prize for his writings as a Communist poet. Alberti returned to Spain on April 27, 1977, after 38 years of exile, to run for Congress at the head of the Communist Party ticket for his native province of Cádiz. His electoral campaign was probably the only one in Spanish history in which the candidate did not make speeches but recited poetry from his books and new works written as he campaigned. The latter were published with the title *Alberti tal cual* (1978; Alberti as Himself). After three months in the reborn Spanish Cortes he resigned from his seat in order to be replaced by another member of the Communist Party and to be able to continue his creative work as a poet and as a painter. Alberti began his artistic activity as a painter during his Rome years and has had many exhibitions of his paintings and graphic works.

Rafael Alberti is the outstanding example in Spain of the committed poet, but his political verses are more a testimony to his ideological fidelity than to his art. Alberti's poetic world, one of the richest in Spanish poetry of the 20th century, expresses, in a highly singular fusion of traditional and modern elements, the anxiety of the times and man's perennial search for a better world. He is a poet of nostalgia but also of faith in the human condition. A volume of *Selected Poems*, edited and translated by Ben Belitt, was published in 1966.

See: C. B. Morris, *Rafael Alberti's "Sobre los Angeles"* (1966); S. Salinas de Marichal, *El mundo poético de Rafael Alberti* (1968); *The Malahat Review* [Alberti Issue] 47 (July 1978). S.S.M.

Alcover i Maspons, Joan (1854–1926), Catalan poet, was born in Palma de Majorca, where he grew up and devoted himself to the practice of law. He did not start to write in Catalan until about 1900. Apparently this particular medium was precisely what he needed to produce a truly vigorous literary work. Poems like "La creu" (The Cross), "Mallorca" (Majorca), "La serra" (The Sierra), "Ramon Llull," "Beethoven," and "Cançó de la balanguera" (Song of the Spinning Girl) attracted the attention of critics, and the society Rat Penat of Valencia, devoted to the cultivation of literature in the native tongue, made him an honorary member. Like other poets of Majorca, Alcover had a true gift of form. Indeed it is curious that poets so dissimilar in regard to themes as Alcover, Miguel COSTA I LLOBERA, and Gabriel ALOMAR should all show an instinctive Parnassianism. Alcover expressed a deeply felt personal bereavement in elegies of consummate beauty. Manuel de Montoliu has asserted that he is the most profoundly human poet of the Catalan Renaissance.

In 1921 Alcover's poems were collected in a slender volume, *Poesies*. More recently, the Illustració Catalana has published the complete works of Alcover in three volumes, the first devoted to his poetry, the second to literary-biographical sketches, and the third to his speeches and articles. His *Obres Completes* was published in 1951.

See: M. De Montoliu, *Estudis de literatura catalana* (1912); C. Riba, *Escolis* (1921); R. Crossmann, *Katalanische Lyrik der Gegenwart* (1923); A. Schneeberger, *Anthologie des poètes catalans contemporains* (1923); C. Giardini, *Antologia dei poeti catalani contemporanei, 1845–1925* (1926).   F. de P.

Aldanov, Mark Aleksandrovich, pseud. of M. A. Landau (1886–1957), Russian novelist, biographer, and essayist, was born in Kiev, the son of a well-to-do Austrian industrialist and a Russian mother. Educated at Kiev University in the faculties of both science and law, he published numerous scientific works in Russia before the 1917 Revolution as well as two books in France on chemistry long after he had achieved prominence as a novelist. He left Russia in 1919 and spent the rest of his life in France except for the years 1941–47, which he spent in the United States.

Aldanov is best known for his historical novels, beginning with a tetralogy on the French Revolution and its aftermath, as if to illustrate his later statement that "in modern Europe only people who have lived through the Bolshevik Revolution can properly understand the French Revolution." Entitled *Myslitel* (The Thinker), this work comprises the novels *Devyatoye termidora* (1923; Eng. tr., *The Ninth Thermidor*, 1926); *Svyataya Yelena, malenkiy ostrov* (1923; Eng. tr., *Saint Helena, Little Island*, 1924); *Chortov most* (1925; Eng. tr., *The Devil's Bridge*, 1928); and *Zagovor* (1927; The Conspiracy). It was followed by a trilogy on the October Revolution of 1917: *Klyuch* (1930; Eng. tr., *The Key*, 1931); *Begstvo* (1932; Eng. tr., with *Klyuch* as *The Escape*, books 1 and 2, 1950); and *Peshchera* (2 vols., 1934, 1936; The Cave). Aldanov's best-known novel, although scarcely his most distinguished, is *Nachalo kontsa* (1939; Eng. tr., *The Fifth Seal*, 1943), a satirical and highly involved account of confrontations in Western Europe on the eve of World War II between members of the new Soviet upper class and various representatives of Western European society. *Istoki* (1950; Eng. tr., *Before the Deluge*, 1947), a panoramic view of Russia in the years leading up to the assassination of Tsar Alexander II in 1881, is generally ranked along with *The Ninth Thermidor* as Aldanov's two best novels.

Even though Aldanov's achievement as a historical novelist gives him a claim to recognition among the best 20th-century Russian practitioners of that genre, there are critics who hold in higher esteem his works as a biographer, essayist, and social critic, and his three short philosophical tales, *Desyataya simfoniya* (1931; Eng. tr., *The Tenth Symphony*, 1948), *Punshevaya vodka* (1940; Punch Vodka); and *Mogila voina* (1940; A Soldier's Grave; Eng. tr., *For Thee the Best*, 1945). His works have been published in 24 languages, but they are still almost unknown and largely unavailable in his native land. Combining his inborn gift as a writer with the rigorous training of a scientist, the critical mind of a historian, and the generous liberal outlook of a highly cultivated Russian European, Aldanov achieved a prominence second only to that of Ivan BUNIN among Russian émigré writers of the period between the two world wars.

See: G. Struve, *Russkaya literatura v izgnanii* (1956), pp. 115–18, 268–72; C. N. Lee, *The Novels of Mark Aleksandrovič Aldanov* (1969), and "Mark Aleksandrovich Aldanov: zhizn i tvorchestvo," *Russkaya literatura v emigratsii*, ed. N. Poltoratsky (1972), pp. 95–104, 370–71; D. and H. Cristesco, *Bibliographie des œuvres de Marc Aldanov* (1976).   W.B.E.

Aldecoa, Ignacio (1925–69), Spanish novelist and short-story writer, was born in Victoria, in the province of Álava, and studied philosophy and letters at the universities of Madrid and Salamanca. His first stories appeared in such literary journals as *Juventud*, *La Hora*, *Clavileño*, *Ateneo*, and *Correo Literario*. His finely elaborated novels, *El fulgor y la sangre* (1954; The Brightness and the Blood) and *Con el viento solano* (1956; With the Easterly Wind), recount daily, and sometimes tragic, events in the lives of ordinary people, such as fishermen, gypsies, and civil guards. *Gran Sol* (1957; Great Sole), the first part of an unfinished trilogy, chronicles the voyage of 13 fishermen and their struggle with the sea. Intensity, precision, and technical virtuosity characterize Aldecoa's prose, especially his excellent short stories: *Vísperas del silencio* (1955; On the Verge of Silence); *Espera de tercera clase* (1955; Third-Class Waiting Room); *El corazón y otros frutos amargos* (1959; The Heart and Other Bitter Fruits); *Caballo de pica* (1961; Picador's Horse); *Arqueología* (1961; Archaeology) and *Cuaderno de Godo* (1961; A Gothic Notebook). Aldecoa is basically a social-realist writer, but without moral or political overtones. His stylistic expertise is especially evident in the scientific precision of his language.

See: E. González López, "Las novelas de I. Aldecoa," *RHM* 26 (1960): 112–3; R. Senabre, "La obra narrativa de Ignacio Aldecoa," *PSA* 166 (1970):5–24; James H. Abbot et al., *Ignacio Aldecoa: A Collection of Critical Essays* (1977).   J.O.

Aleixandre, Vicente (1898–), Spanish poet, was born in Seville and grew up in Málaga. He received the National Prize for Literature in 1933 and the Critics Prize in 1963, 1969, and 1975. Since 1949 he has been a member of the Royal Spanish Academy of the Language in Madrid, where he has spent most of his adult life. His importance as one of the major figures of contemporary European poetry was recognized in 1977, when he was awarded the Nobel Prize for Literature.

His first book, *Ámbito* (1928; Scope), is still associated with the concept of pure poetry that was prevalent in the 1920s, although it also contains the most significant elements of the author's own poetic world. The other collections that Aleixandre wrote prior to the Civil War are *Pasión de la tierra* (1928–29; Passion of the Earth), *Espadas como labios* (1930–31; Swords Like Lips), *La destrucción o el amor* (1933; Destruction or Love), and *Mundo a solas* (1934–36; World Alone), some of which were published after the dates given here, which are those of their composition. In these books the poet reveals his free and very personal assimilation of the most advanced techniques of contemporary irrational expression, especially surrealism, although Aleixandre has never considered himself an orthodox surrealist. The central vision of this poetry, in the author's words, is that of "the amorous unity of the universe," and from it arise his major themes: love and passion conceived as the destruction of the reductive limits of man, the impulse toward human identification or communion with the physical cosmos, and the song of the primal forces of creation. A grand, cosmic vision, an exalted neoromantic tone, and extreme complexity of imaginative and linguistic resources—with the resulting difficulties for the reader—characterize Aleixandre's first period. The culminating work of this period is *La destrucción o el amor*, one of the most intense works of all 20th-century Hispanic poetry. The author himself has recognized how much his early poetry owed to his reading Sigmund Freud.

The first book Aleixandre published after the Spanish Civil War, *Sombra del paraíso* (1944; Shadow of Paradise), continues the theme of the poet's nostalgia for total identification with the innocent reality of nature. But this nostalgia is now felt from the limited perspective of the historically situated man, thus heralding the second phase of Aleixandre's work. Henceforth his great central theme is human life itself in its strict temporality. Aleixandre's point of view now highlights specifically existential questions, and although this visionary poet previously longed for fusion with physical matter, in his second phase he identifies himself by his contact with and knowledge of others, that is, of humanity. *Historia del corazón* (1954; History of the Heart) and *En un vasto dominio* (1962; In a Vast Domain) are the definitive books of this period. Their poetic subjects are time and death, matter seen as history, love understood as companionship or support, and solidarity among men—themes common to realist and historicist tendencies of so much of Western literature in the aftermath of World War II. Aleixandre has defined his poetic evolution as "aspiring to the light," and this second plateau of his work is also characterized by a growing clarity of language, which does not, however, become prosaic or lose its natural stylistic vigor.

Like *Sombra del paraíso, En un vasto dominio* is another key transitional work that reveals the coherence and organic evolution of Aleixandre's poetic thought. On the one hand, *En un vasto dominio* synthesizes the great conflicts of his earlier poetry (the mythic vision and historical awareness), while on the other it opens the way for a rigorous intellectual poetry rooted in the specific problem of knowledge and in an agonized confrontation with the ultimate realities of man. The subject matter of Aleixandre's most recent books, the product of his vital and astonishingly creative old age, is basically epistemological and metaphysical. In *Poemas de la consumación* (1968) and *Diálogos del conocimento* (1974; Dialogues of Knowledge), the poet asks several questions. Where is truth? Can one reach it? Which path to it is more viable: the solipsistic adventure of pure thought or the way of the heart, which leads to the reality of life and the senses? The answer would seem to be more closed and nihilistic in *Poemas de la consumación*, the most lyric and tragic of his books, and more open, relative, and integrating in *Diálogos*. As befits a poetry of thought, Aleixandre's style in these books becomes sententious and self-contained, and he employs numerous aphorisms, contradictions, and paradoxes. Aleixandre's work as a whole, then, deals in poetic terms with the drama of man on earth, from the dream of cosmic and historical transcendence to an uncompromising inquiry into man's possibilities and limitations. His poetic idiom is vigorous, luminous, very original, and always new.

In prose he has written *Los encuentros* (1958; Encounters), a collection of lyrical portraits of Spanish and Spanish-American writers of the present and the past. His many essays, articles, and notes on poetic subjects and literary criticism appear in his *Obras completas* (1977). Aleixandre's penetrating comments on his own poetry are available in *Mis poemas mejores* (1976; My Best Poems), and a broad bilingual sampling of his poetry may be found in Lewis Hyde's collection, *A Longing for the Light: Selected Poems of Vicente Aleixandre* (1979).

When the Civil War ended in 1939, most of the great figures of Aleixandre's group (the Generation of 1927) had left Spain. Because of a chronic kidney disease, which has immobilized him from his youth, Aleixandre had to remain in Madrid. His presence there, together with his warm, friendly, and stimulating disposition, has been a decisive factor in the development of succeeding generations of poets who sought and received advice and support from the master. Throughout the difficult postwar years, Aleixandre maintained a position of strict ideological and political independence from the official regime. At the same time, through his presence, friendship, and example to younger poets—as well as his very personal evolution—he has provided for Spanish poetry half a century of continuity.

See: K. Schwartz, *Vicente Aleixandre* (1970); J. O. Jiménez, *Cinco Poetas del Tiempo* (1972), pp. 42–122; D. Puccini, *La parola poetica di Vicente Aleixandre* (1976); C. Bousono, *La poesía de Vicente Aleixandre* (1977).

J.O.J.

Aleramo, Sibilla, pseud. of Rina Faccio (1876–1960), Italian novelist and poet, was born in Alessandria. She spent her childhood in Milan, where she attended elementary school, her only formal education. Her father took a position as director of a glassworks in a small town in southern Italy, and here Aleramo spent her adolescence. She was married at 16. After nine years of an unhappy marriage, she left her husband and son. She wrote articles on social and feminist issues for numerous women's magazines and cultural journals and was editor of the Milanese weekly *Italia femminile* for several months in 1899.

Aleramo's first novel, *Una donna* (1906; Eng. tr., *A Woman at Bay*, 1908), is, to a great extent, her autobiography up to the time of her separation from her husband. The novel is a powerful analysis of the position of women in Italy and depicts the struggle of one woman for an independent and active role within society. *Una donna* was a great success in Italy and was soon translated into several European languages. It is still considered her most significant work; having been recently rediscovered by Italian and European feminists, the novel has been reprinted (1973).

Before settling in Rome in 1919, Aleramo traveled throughout Italy and France and founded and directed, along with the poet Giovanni Cena, schools for the illiterate peasants of the Roman countryside. Her second novel, *Il passaggio* (1919; The Passage), is a lyrical work that intertwines present impressions with past memories and is directly related to the events of *Una donna*. This autobiographical narration continues in her other novels, *Transfigurazione* (1922; Transfiguration) and *Amo, dunque sono* (1927; I Love, Therefore I Am), an attempt in epistolary form to define what the author considered to be the true essence of women, love, and feeling. *Il frustino* (1932; The Whip), Aleramo's only novel written in the third person, is the confession of a love affair, as well as a further attempt to portray the soul of a woman artist trying to develop her own spirituality. This theme is dealt with more fully in her essay "Apologia dello spirito femminile" (Defense of the Feminine Spirit), available in her collection of prose writings *Andando e stando* (1921; Going and Staying), in which she argues that women artists must reject the mere imitation of male creativity in order to develop their own powers and, finally, their own literature. This prose collection, along with *Gioie d'occasione* (1930; Joys on Sale), which won the Prix de la Latinité in Paris in 1933, and *Orsa minore* (1938), contain critical essays and memoirs. Later prose collections are *Dal mio diario: 1940–1944* (1945), excerpts from her still unpublished diaries of the war years: *Il mondo è adolescente* (1949; The World Is Adolescent); and *Russia alto paese* (1953; Russia, Lofty Country).

Aleramo's poetry is written in free verse and consists primarily of brief lyrical expressions of her search for spiritual perfection through love. Her volumes of poetry include *Momenti* (1920; Moments), *Poesie* (1929; Poems), and *Si alla terra* (1935; Yes to the Earth). Almost all of these works are contained in *Selva d'amore* (1947; Forest of Love), which won the Versilia Prize in 1948. Aleramo's later collections of poetry, *Aiutatemi a dire* (1951; Help Me to Say) and *Luci della mia sera* (1956; Lights of My Evening), appeared after she joined the Italian Communist Party in 1946. These volumes mark a shift from her earlier strong personal expression and almost overwhelming sensuality to an attempt at creating a choral voice that would speak for the masses of the Italian working people. From 1946 until her death, Aleramo was an active Party member, giving poetry readings and talks to groups of workers and farmers throughout Italy and Europe.

Aleramo's other writings include two dramas, *Endimione* (1923) and "Francesca Diamante" (unpublished); *Dino Campana–Sibilla Aleramo: Lettere* (1952), the love letters written during her affair with the poet Dino CAMPANA; and her translations of *Le Pèlerin* by Charles VILDRAC (1925), *La Princesse de Clèves* by Mme de Lafayette (1934), and the love letters of Georges Sand and Alfred de Musset (1945).

See: R. S. Phelps, "Sibilla Aleramo," *Italian Silhouettes* (1924), pp. 198–212; R. Guerricchio, *Storia di Sibilla* (1974); A. Mazzotti, "Sibilla Aleramo," in *Letteratura italiana: i contemporanei*, vol. 1 (1975), pp. 211–34.

M.J.C.

Aliger, Margarita Iosifovna (1915–), Russian poet, was born in Odessa and educated at the Gorky Institute of World Literature. She published her first collection of verse in 1938. During World War II, she became famous as a war correspondent, in particular through her poems *Vesna v Leningrade* (1942; Spring in Leningrad), concerning the blockade of Leningrad by the Germans, and *Zoya* (1942), a long work dedicated to Zoya Kosmodemyanskaya, a Moscow schoolgirl tortured and hanged by the Germans. Her postwar works include the play *Skazka o pravde* (1945; A Fairy Tale about the Truth), the dramatic poem *Pervy grom* (1947; The First Thunderclap), and the verse collection *Orliny zalyot* (1948–52; The Eagle's Flight). Her cycle *Leninskiye gory* (1953; Lenin Hills) describes the construction of Moscow State University. Aliger's poetry is characterized by a highly personal, emotional tone as well as by political and philosophical concerns. She has also translated poetry from Ukrainian, Azerbaydzhanian, and Uzbek.

See: K. Simonov, "Zametki pisatelya," *NovM* 1 (1947): 165–70; I. Grinberg, *Puti sovetskoy poezii* (1968), pp. 233–38.

L.V.

Almada-Negreiros, José de (1893–1970), Portuguese poet and prose writer, born on São Tomé Island, near the west coast of Africa. He lived most of his life in Lisbon, except for youthful sojourns in Paris and Spain. Almada, who was very young when he began his career as a caricaturist, in time became the finest Portuguese painter of the first half of the 20th century. He was also one of the most important members of the generation of writers (Fernando PESSOA, Mário de SÁ-CARNEIRO, and others) who launched the literary avant-garde in Portugal in 1915. His verse and prose poems, novels, plays, essays, and other literary works are among the most innovative texts in Portuguese; and some of them, like those published in *Portugal Futurista* (1917), anticipate many devices made famous by James Joyce and the French surrealists. Among these works, the prose poems of *A invenção do*

dia claro (1921; The Invention of Clear Day) and the novel *Nome de guerra* (written in 1925, published in 1938; Pseudonym) are outstanding. Intellectual abstractionism, a deliriously ironic rationalism, traditional sentimentality, direct realism, calculated expressionism, automatic writing, and a very graphic imagination are all the driving forces behind a very rich style, which ranges from stentorian invective (Almada wrote some of the more violent texts in favor of modern art and literature, attacking established values) to childlike simplicity and from aesthetical charm to brutal primitivism. But his writing always teems with a visually intense love of life and external reality. Nothing summarizes Almada's stand better than the old saying he made his own: "Joy is the most serious thing in life." Publication of his complete works began in 1970, the year of his death in Lisbon.

See: Various, "Homenagem a Almada-Negreiros," *Colóquio* 60 (October 1970): 3–47; J. de Sena, "Almada-Negreiros," *Grande dicionário da literatura portuguesa* pt. 4 (1972), pp. 145–48.

J. de S.

Alomar, Gabriel (1873–1941), Spanish poet and essayist, was born in Palma de Majorca and died in Cairo, where he had served as Spanish ambassador to Egypt. He preferred the Catalan language for his poetry and Spanish for his prose. As a poet he showed constant concern for form and style. Although Alomar was one of the first and most enthusiastic Spanish proponents of futurism, he represents nevertheless a moment of transition between Parnassianism and modernism. In his essays he manifests an ideology akin to the critical and renovating spirit of the Generation of 1898 (*see* SPANISH LITERATURE). He was influential in the intellectual circles of the eastern regions of the Spanish Mediterranean (the Balearic Islands, Catalonia, and Valencia), which saw in Alomar the standard-bearer of the new literary and political faith of contemporary Europe. Some of his essays were collected in a volume entitled *Verba* (1917). His book of Catalan poetry is entitled *La columna de foc* (1911; The Column of Fire).

See: J. Mascaró, "Gabriel Alomar," *BulSS* 20 (1943): 48–54.

E.G.-L. rev. H.L.B.

Alonso, Dámaso (1898–), Spanish poet, critic, philologist, and literary historian, was born in Madrid. A student of Ramón MENÉNDEZ PIDAL, he was trained at the University of Madrid and the Centro de Estudios Históricos. Alonso is professor emeritus of philology at the University of Madrid and president of the Royal Spanish Academy of the Language. He holds honorary doctorates from many universities, including Oxford, Rome, and Freiburg, and has taught at many major institutions in Europe and North America.

Alonso's writings have had a profound influence on the course of Spanish criticism. His book *La lengua poética de Góngora* (1935; Góngora's Poetic Language) initiated a reappraisal of Golden Age literature that has fundamentally altered the perception of Spanish literary history. *Poesía española* (1950) and *Seis calas en la expresión literaria española* (1951; Six Studies of Spanish Literary Expression) mark the beginning of Spanish stylistic criticism and anticipate many discoveries of structuralist criticism. Alonso has also written books on contemporary Spanish poetry, on Menéndez Pidal, on Saint John of the Cross, and on Lope de Vega, in addition to several volumes of collected essays and editions of the works of Luis de Góngora, Saint John, Francisco de Medrano, and others. His complete works, now in the process of publication, will comprise 10 volumes averaging around 1,000 pages each. Most of the leading critics in Spain have been his disciples and have been profoundly influenced by the way in which his work combines perceptive intuitions with systematic stylistic study.

Alonso's work has also contributed to the basic knowledge of Spanish literature and language. He participated in the discovery and identification of the Judeo-Arabic *jarchas* and unearthed several important medieval works. He also edited documents that cast new light on Góngora and his work. His philological studies include a monograph on Andalusian speech and a fundamental book on peninsular phonetic fragmentation, as well as numerous articles that have significantly influenced the course of Spanish linguistics.

In addition to being an outstanding scholar, Alonso is a major poet. His earliest book, *Poemas puros, poemillas de la ciudad* (1921; Pure Poems, Little Poems of the City) reveals a highly original use of language and perspective to embody the conflict between prosaic and idealistic visions. This theme continues in *Oscura noticia* (1944; Dark News), which collects poems written after 1918. But Alonso's major impact on Spanish poetry came with the publication of *Hijos de la ira* (1944; Eng. tr., *Children of Wrath*, 1970). Written in free verse and making use of everyday vocabulary, this book consists of the monologue of a modern speaker in anguish over the meaninglessness of his surroundings, who questions the value of existence and seeks an answer in love. The book signals a reaction against the neoclassical poetry of the immediate post-Civil War period. It served as an example and a model to younger poets, marking the beginning of a new era of philosophically and socially involved verse. Ten years later, Alonso published *Hombre y Dios* (1955; Man and God). This work also focuses on the search for the meaning of life. The structure can be seen in dramatic terms, whereby different poems present different attitudes ranging from naive complacency to anguished desperation. A complex unity, centered on the protagonist's acceptance of man's values and limitations, emerges from the poems as a whole. Alonso is also the author of *Gozos de la vista* (1955–56; The Joys of Sight), published only in sections appearing in different places, and of other works appearing in magazines and anthologies.

Mention should also be made of Alonso's work as a translator. His versions of the poetry of T. S. Eliot, Gerard Manley Hopkins, William Butler Yeats, and D. H. Lawrence made these authors available to the Spanish reader. They also found an echo in Alonso's creative work. One feels the presence of Hopkins, for instance, in *Hijos de la ira*. Alonso also translated James Joyce's *Portrait of the Artist as a Young Man* and works by Hilaire Belloc and Gil Vicente. He is the author of several short stories and works of creative prose, most of them written in the 1920s, of a radio play written in 1955, and of many essays and public letters.

Alonso's work places him at the forefront of 20th-century Spanish letters, not only because of its considerable intrinsic value, but because of its role in setting new trends and in determining the direction of later works in both criticism and poetry.

See: C. Bousoño, "La poesía de Dámaso Alonso," *PSA* 11 (1958): 231–85; M. J. Flys, *La poesía existencial de Dámaso Alonso* (1968); A. P. Debicki, *Dámaso Alonso* (1974).   A.P.D.

Althusser, Louis (1918–), French Marxist philosopher, was born in Birmandreïs, Algeria. He entered the Ecole Normale Supérieure in 1939, and in 1948, spurred on by "an interest in philosophy and a passion for politics," he became a philosophy professor and joined the French Communist Party. Since then, Althusser has become increasingly influential and controversial. Through his teaching at the Ecole Normale and, since the early 1960s through his books, he has emerged as a central figure in French philosophy and an internationally recognized authority on Karl Marx. He has remained a member of the Communist Party, although he is sometimes in disagreement with its leaders.

Althusser's philosophy begins with the injunction that Marx must be reread and rediscovered, an urgent and difficult task—urgent because of the scientific value of his philosophy ("a *new* science, the science of history"), difficult because, "it is not enough to have a book before one's eyes, one must *know* how to read it." This rediscovery implies, on the one hand, the rejection of Marx's early works (written before what Althusser calls an "epistemological rupture" around 1845–46), and on the other, the rejection of false, bourgeois, and humanistic interpretations. Indeed, of prime importance for Althusser is his provocative interpretation of Marx's philosophy as "antihumanist." This antihumanism has led in recent years to widespread discussion and criticism of Althusser, who explains at length that such antihumanism is theoretical, meaning that in Marx's materialistic perspective, man is never considered the "center of his own world, the original essence or goal of his world." The rediscovery of authentic Marxism, says Althusser, must entail the recognition of "the revolutionary nature of Marx's thought." The class struggle remains the key concept in Marx's philosophy. Because of its political dimension, Marxist theory is even more important than earlier discoveries in mathematics and physics, for in alliance with the working-class movement, it becomes a weapon to transform the world.

Althusser's most important works are: *Montesquieu, la politique et l'histoire* (1959; Eng. tr., *Politics and History: Montesquieu, Rousseau, Hegel and Marx*, 1972), *Pour Marx* (1965; For Marx), *Lire le Capital* (1965; Reading Capital), *Présentation du Livre I du Capital* (1969; Presentation of Book 1 of *Capital*), *Réponse à John Lewis* (1972), and *Positions* (1976).

See: R. Aron, *D'une sainte famille à l'autre* (1969).
                                                                    C.C.

Altolaguirre, Manuel (1905–59), Spanish poet, publisher, and filmmaker, was born in Málaga. The youngest member of the Generation of 1927, in the 1920s he printed his own work as well as first editions of work by Federico GARCÍA LORCA, Luis CERNUDA, Rafael ALBERTI, and others. With Emilio PRADOS he edited *Litoral*, which Paul VALÉRY called the best poetry review in Europe. Several of García Lorca's *romances gitanos* (gypsy ballads) first appeared in its pages. In the 1930s, Altolaguirre lectured on Spanish literature in Paris and London. Wherever he went, he took with him his portable printing press. While in England, he published *1616*, a journal dedicated to bilingual versions of Spanish and English romantic and modern poetry—the title refers to the common death date of Cervantes and Shakespeare.

In 1935, Altolaguirre returned to Madrid, where he published Alberti and Pablo Neruda's *Caballo verde para la poesía*, a review concerned with the "rehumanization" of literature (*see* José ORTEGA Y GASSET). As supplements of his review *Héroe*, he published the first edition of García Lorca's *Primeras canciones* and Miguel HERNÁNDEZ's *El rayo que no cesa*. During the Civil War, he printed war ballads at the Republican front. The paper for Neruda's *España en el corazón* was made from enemy flags and uniforms.

Altolaguirre's best-known volume of poetry is *Las islas invitadas* (1926, 1936; The Invited Islands). His *Poesías completas* (1960) contains all but 30 of the approximately

300 poems he wrote between 1926 and 1959. In his early work he describes nature in a subjective and extremely Gongoristic style, using some of the most daring metaphors of his generation. Later, he concentrated on three themes: solitude, love as a means of temporarily transcending this solitude by becoming one with the universe, and death as a sad but natural reintegration with the earth.

After the Spanish Civil War, Altolaguirre lived in Cuba and Mexico, where he dedicated himself primarily to filmmaking. He wrote the scripts of 20 feature-length films based on classic Spanish novels and plays, of which the most famous is Luis Buñuel's *Subida al cielo* (Flight to Heaven). He also produced the majority of his films.

Altolaguirre wrote plays, criticism, and translations in addition to poetry. He died in an automobile crash near Burgos, on his way back to Madrid from the San Sebastián film festival, where his film *Cantar de los cantares* (Song of Songs) had received an honorable mention.

See: C. B. Morris, *A Generation of Spanish Poets: 1920–1925* (1969); M. S. Altolaguirre, Introduction to a critical edition of *Las islas invitadas* (1973); C. D. Hernandez de Telles, *Manuel Altolaguirre: vida y literatura* (1974).   J.Cr.

Álvarez Quintero, Serafín (1871–1938) and **Joaquín** (1873–1944), Spanish dramatists, were born in Utrera in the province of Seville. They began to write and enact plays in their home while still in their teens, and in 1888 they presented a farce entitled *Esgrima y amor* (Love and Fencing) in Seville's Teatro Cervantes. The following year, they moved to Madrid where, prior to their literary recognition, they held minor government posts in the Treasury Department. The success of a musical comedy (zarzuela), *La buena sombra* (1898; Charm), established their career. From then on, a half dozen new plays produced in a single year was not unusual for them, and they continued to publish somewhat less insistently well into the 1930s. In all, they wrote some 228 theatrical works of various kinds, of which all but a very few were staged. Their brief and colorful skits (*sainetes*) with Andalusian settings, types, and dialect of the so-called *género chico* (one-act comedy), are exemplified by such works as *La reja* (1897) and *El patio* (1900). Among the most successful of these are *Hablando se entiende la gente* (1913; Eng. tr., *By their Words Ye Shall Know Them*, 1917) and the less typical *Mañana de sol* (1905; Eng. tr., *A Sunny Morning*, 1914), a charming curtain raiser based on a *dolora* by Ramón de Campoamor about a man and a woman who meet again in old age and renew a youthful love, each pretending unsuccessfully to be someone else. Among the Quinteros' best-known longer plays are *Las de Caín* (1908; The Cain Girls), whose punning title also refers to the trials of a father saddled with the task of marrying off five daughters; *Doña Clarines* (1909; Eng. tr., 1932), a more serious work about an excessive devotion to truthtelling; and *Puebla de las mujeres* (1912; Eng. tr., *The Women Have Their Way*, 1928).

The Quinteros' *sainetes* are in the tradition of Lope de Rueda's 16th-century curtain raisers (*pasos*), the interludes (*entremeses*) of Cervantes, and the 18th-century *sainetes* of Ramón de la Cruz. Their work also owes something to the romantic 19th-century local colorists or *costumbristas*. Andalusia is the setting of most of their plays, but it is a picturesque Andalusia of charm, sentiment, and humor, not a realistically portrayed one. The authors were interested in amusing an audience, not in studying social or psychological problems. The plays were often inspired by popular phenomena such as a folk song, a colloquial expression, or a poem familiar to everyone. The Quintero brothers were not innovators, but

during their lifetime they were among the most popular of playwrights with the Spanish public and were also well known in other countries. More than 100 of their plays were translated into a variety of languages. In recent decades, however, interest has declined, and their work has dated markedly. It now seems more insubstantial, sentimental, and formula-ridden than it did to earlier audiences.

See: J. M. Alonso, "Prólogo-estudio" to S. y J. Álvarez Quintero, *Teatro selecto* (1971).   H.L.B.

Alvaro, Corrado (1895–1956), Italian novelist and essayist, was born in San Luca (Reggio di Calabria). His family, although not wealthy, belonged to the landholding class; his father was an elementary school teacher. Alvaro's education was interrupted by World War I, during which he served as an artillery officer and was wounded in action. He began his career in journalism in the immediate postwar period, writing for *Il resto del carlino* and *Il corriere della sera*. In 1920 he took his doctorate in letters at the University of Milan. Shortly thereafter he left for Rome (with his wife, Laura Babini, also a writer) to become editor of *Il mondo*, the organ of the Liberal-Democratic leader Giovanni Amendola. In 1926 the paper was suppressed by the Fascists. Alvaro suffered personal molestation and was obliged to abandon journalism except for a few special assignments given him by *La stampa*. After spending some time in Berlin and Paris, he returned to Italy to devote himself to his own writing. Upon the fall of Mussolini he became editor of *Il popolo di Roma*, but the German occupation of the capital forced him to go into hiding. After the war he worked for a year as editor of the Neapolitan journal *Il Risorgimento*. The remaining years of his life were spent in Rome.

Alvaro's first publication was a volume of poetry, *Poesie in grigioverde* (1917; Poems in Uniform), but his major contributions to Italian letters are in the areas of prose narrative and the social documentary essay. Ricardo Scrivano finds the titles of two of Alvaro's early works, *La siepe e l'orto* (1920; The Hedge and the Garden) and *L'uomo nel labirinto* (1926; Man in the Labyrinth), suggestive of the two poles of the writer's inspiration: the garden symbolizing his native Calabria, the labyrinth symbolizing the big city that at once attracted and dismayed him. *L'uomo nel labirinto*, although a slight work, has a paradigmatic significance, dealing with the frustrations and disillusionment of a transplanted provincial in a great metropolis. The same motif appears in *Gente in Aspromonte* (1930; Eng. tr., *Revolt in Aspromonte*, 1962). Perhaps Alvaro's best creative effort, it is the account of an exploited and exasperated peasant driven to banditry by the harsh conditions of the feudal world in which he lives. In its atmosphere and realistic depiction of the lives of the humble, *Gente* echoes Giovanni VERGA. *Vent'anni* (1930; 20 Years Old) tells the story of the war's corrosive effect on a simple Calabrian soldier. This pattern of the individual versus society takes on an even sharper political significance in *L'uomo è forte* (1938; Eng. tr., *Man Is Strong*, 1948), a story of life in a totalitarian country, unnamed and politely assumed to be the Soviet Union (where Alvaro had spent some time as a special correspondent) but equally identifiable with Fascist Italy. The novel has the air of a fable (perhaps owing something to Tommaso Campanella [1568–1639], whose works Alvaro edited in 1935); and its composition during the high tide of the Fascist dictatorship can be considered an act of courageous affirmation. Alvaro's other works of importance include *L'età breve* (1946; The Transient Age), at once a portrayal of a lonely adolescent and an exploration of the conservative mores of the south; its companion piece, *Mastrangelina* (1960); and the short-story collection *75 racconti* (1955; 75 Stories).

It may be that Alvaro's best works are those not strictly "creative," those that combine his personal memories with perceptive comments on his country and his times. Such books as *Quasi una vita* (1950; Almost a Lifetime), *Il nostro tempo e la speranza* (1952; Our Times and Hope), and *Ultimo diario (1948–1956)* (1959; Last Diary) are written with appealing sincerity and reveal a wise, warm, and responsive personality. Alvaro also wrote plays, of which *La lunga notte di Medea* (1949; Eng. tr., *The Long Night of Medea*, 1966) was the most successful.

In his last years, Alvaro held a position of unique prestige among Italian writers. Both the tenor of his life and the quality of his works had created a universal recognition of his integrity. Indeed, although a few of his novels will undoubtedly survive, the image and example of this thoughtful, generous man may prove to be even greater than his works.

See: F. Virdia, *Dizionario biografico degli italiani*, vol. 2 (1960), pp. 581–86; M. A. Tancredi, *Corrado Alvaro* (1969); L. Reina, *Cultura e storia di Alvaro* (1973); V. Paladino, *Itinerari alvariani* (1974).   T.G.B.

Amalrik, Andrey Alekseyevich (1938–), Russian prose-writer, journalist, and playwright, born in Moscow, is one of the most independent and original political and social critics to have emerged in the post-Stalinist Soviet Union. The son of a historian, Amalrik himself studied history at Moscow University but was expelled in 1963 after writing a controversial essay. His nonconformist life-style led to his arrest in 1965 on a charge of "parasitism." Accused of disseminating pornographic and anti-Soviet works, he was exiled to Siberia, where he worked on a collective farm, an experience he later described in *Nezhelannoye puteshestviye v Sibir* (1970; Eng. tr., *An Involuntary Journey to Siberia,* 1970). He was permitted to return to Moscow in 1966 and worked there as a journalist until KGB pressure brought about his dismissal in 1968. He nevertheless continued to pursue an independent course, especially in his essay *Prosushchestvuyet li Sovetskiy Soyuz do 1984 goda?* (1969; Eng. tr., *Will the Soviet Union Survive until 1984?* 1969), which predicts the disintegration of the Soviet Union. Arrested again in 1970, he was sentenced to hard labor, but in 1976 he and his wife were permitted to leave the Soviet Union, going first to Holland and subsequently to the United States. A dogged individualist in a strict, conformist society, Amalrik has depicted in his writings a striking picture of totalitarianism near the end of its tether. In his play *Nos!Nos?No-s!* (1970; Eng. tr., *Nose! Nose? No-se! and other Plays,* 1970), he employs the techniques of the theater of the absurd to comment on a world where the wholesale application of a devitalized Marxism has resulted in linguistic and philosophical impoverishment. Amalrik has persisted in defending the right to think independently and to present his own conclusions, however unwelcome they may be to either Right or Left.   D.T.W.

Amiel, Denys, pseud. of Guillaume Roche (1884–), French playwright, began his career as secretary to Henry BATAILLE. Amiel's works were performed almost without interruption between 1932 and 1937 at the Théâtre Saint-Georges. His tragicomedies, representative of his time, used commonplace themes already thoroughly explored by dramatists who preceded him. They usually focus on the psychological and emotional conflicts of women in the throes of adultery, liaisons, divorce, or other matrimonial problems.

Although Amiel's works continue the tradition of Georges de PORTO-RICHE and Henry Bataille, they are also distinguished by his use of the intimist techniques found in the works of Jean-Marc BERNARD and "the school of silence."

Amiel's most successful play, written in collaboration with André OBEY, was *La Souriante Madame Beudet* (1922; The Smiling Madame Beudet), which portrays a sensitive woman married to a boor. Her smile, taken by others to be a sign of happiness, masks her desperate dissatisfaction, which eventually leads to an attempt on her husband's life.   E.D.C. and J.M.L.

Anday, Melih Cevdet (1915–), Turkish poet, playwright, essayist, novelist, and translator, was born in Istanbul. He studied law for a short time at the University of Ankara and sociology in Belgium (1937–38). Later he worked for the publications division of the Ministry of Public Education and for the Ankara Library. From 1951 on, he was associated with several major Istanbul dailies, principally *Cumhuriyet,* for which he has been an important columnist. From 1954 to the late 1970s, he served as a teacher of diction and dramatic literature at the Istanbul Conservatory.

In the 1940s, together with Orhan Veli KANIK and Oktay Rifat (1914–), he initiated the "Garip" (Strange) movement, which purged Turkish poetry of formal structure, rhyme, meters, and conventional themes; stressed the colloquial language; and lionized the common people. From the late 1950s on, Anday's poetry evolved in the direction of intellectual complexity and philosophical exploration. In the 1970s he undertook a systematic effort to create a synthesis of diverse cultures and mythologies. His collections of poetry are *Garip* (1941; Strange), with O. V. Kanik and O. Rifat; *Rahati Kaçan Ağaç* (1946; The Restless Tree); *Telgrafhane* (1952; Telegraph Office); *Yanyana* (1956; Side by Side); *Kolları Bağlı Odiseus* (1962; Odysseus Bound); *Göçebe Denizin Üstünde* (1970; Eng. tr., *On the Nomad Sea,* 1974); and *Teknenin Ölümü* (1975; Death of the Vessel). Anday's other works include the major plays *İçerdekiler* (1965; Those Inside) and *Mikado'nun Çöpleri* (Mikado's Rubbish); the novels *Aylaklar* (1965; The Loafers); *Gizli Emir* (1970; Secret Command), and *İsa'nin Güncesi* (1974; Isa's Diary); and the collections of essays *Doğu-Batı* (1961; East-West), *Konuşarak* (1964; Talking), and *Yeni Tanrılar* (1974; New Gods). Anday has won numerous awards for his plays, fiction, and translations.

See: M. C. Anday, *Ulyssé bras attachés* (1971).
                                        T.S.H.

Andersch, Alfred (1914–), German writer, was born in Munich. He turned to radical politics under the influence of chaotic conditions in Weimar Germany. At the age of 18 he assumed leadership of Bavarian Communist Youth, which resulted in his imprisonment in Dachau for six months in 1933. Later drafted into the Nazi army, he deserted in Italy in 1944, voluntarily becoming an American prisoner of war. Upon his return to Germany he launched, together with Hans Werner RICHTER, the aggressively critical periodical *Der Ruf,* which was forbidden by the U.S. military government. A new journal, *Texte und Zeichen,* begun in 1955, was devoted to the new literary generation. Still another periodical, *studio frankfurt,* resulted from Andersch's interest in radio experimentation, a field to which he contributed numerous radio plays.

Andersch associated with "Gruppe 47" (*see* GERMAN LITERATURE). *Die Kirschen der Freiheit* (1952; Cherries of Freedom) is a critical examination of his life prior to 1944, while confrontation with his leftist past is the subject of the stories in *Geister und Leute* (1958; Ghosts and People). Extreme disillusionment, resulting in the shift from revolutionary politics to aesthetic concern, became a major theme of his work. Andersch's major novels include *Sansibar, oder, der letzte Grund* (1957; Eng. tr., *Flight to Afar*, 1958), which secured his literary position and remains his most highly regarded work; *Die Rote* (1960; Eng. tr., *The Redhead*, 1961), also successful as a film; *Efraim* (1967; Eng. tr., *Efraim's Book*, 1970), a projection of events from the Nazi era upon the Germany of the 1960s; and *Winterspelt* (1974; Eng. tr., 1978), a story from the Franco-German front of 1944. This effort is counterpointed by continuous production of short stories, collected in *In der Nacht der Giraffe* (1960; Eng. tr., *The Night of the Giraffe*, 1964) and *Mein Verschwinden in Providence* (1971; Eng. tr., *My Disappearance in Providence*, 1978). Andersch's entire work is haunted by the loneliness of the individual within modern society: the individual must remove himself from all false relations and obligations in favor of a free but necessarily lonely existence. A paperback edition of Andersch's complete work, *Werkausgabe*, appeared in 1979.   W.V.B.

Andersen, Benny (1929–), Danish poet and writer of fiction, was born in Copenhagen. He made his living in an advertising agency and as a bar pianist. Andersen first achieved recognition with the collection of poems *Den musikalske ål* (1960; The Musical Eel), which, despite a humorous tone, treats an existential problem: the condition of man in modern society. Andersen proves to be a masterful stylist in the collections *Kamera med køkkenadgang* (1962; Camera with Kitchen Access) and *Den indre bowlerhat* (1964; The Inner Bowler Hat), which were followed by the short-story collections *Puderne* (1965; The Cushions) and *Tykke-Olsen m.fl.* (1968; Fat Olsen and Others). The ironical but good-natured tone of the earlier poems is continued in a later series of collections, all of which primarily focus attention on everyday annoyances of the common man, a tendency that culminates in *Svantes viser* (1972; Svante's Songs), the text and music of which (both by Andersen) have become extremely popular. Andersen has a strong predilection for the lyrical portrait. In the volume *Personlige papirer* (1974; Personal Papers) he analyzes the role of the poet, and this personal element is also predominant in *Nomade med noder* (1976; Nomad with Notes), a collection of poetic and documentary texts from Andersen's life as a traveling musician during the 1950s and in his latest poetry collection *Under begge øjne* (1978; Under Both Eyes).

See: L. Marx, "Exercises in Living: Benny Andersen's Literary Perspective," *WLT* 52, no. 4 (1978): 550–54.
                                                                                             S.H.R.

Andersen, Tryggve (1866–1920), Norwegian novelist, was born in eastern Norway. His father was a government official and his mother the daughter of a farmer. Andersen thus united in himself the two cultural and literary currents whose interplay and occasional conflict have been central to modern Norwegian development. At the University of Christiania he received a good education in philology and history. He became a fastidious stylist, carefully adapting vernacular words and expressions for the use of the traditional literary language.

From about 1890 on, Andersen was one of the leaders of the neoromantic group (*see* NORWEGIAN LITERATURE), and his stylistic ideals of conciseness and lucidity influenced many young authors. His own first work, the historical novel *I cancelliraadens dage* (1897; Eng. tr., *In the Days of the Councillor*, 1969), is a profound study of the milieu, psychology, and conflicts of Norwegian society at the end of Danish domination, during the early years of the 19th century. His second novel, *Mot kveld* (1900; Towards Night), is filled with apprehensions of

death and apocalyptical forebodings. The novels were followed by a number of short stories that established Andersen as the master of this literary genre in Norway. His short stories, which show the influence of Edgar Allan Poe, were brought together in *Samlede fortællinger* (3 vols., 1916; Collected Stories).

See: A. Villum, *Trygve Andersen og I cancelliraadens dage* (1932); T. H. Schiff, "Tryggve Andersen's Novel *Mot kveld* and its Motto," *SS* 48, no. 2: 146–55.   H.K.

Andersen Nexø, Martin: *see* NEXØ, MARTIN ANDERSEN.

Andersson, Dan (1888–1920), Swedish poet, short-story writer, and novelist, was born in an isolated district of Dalecarlia. He is the greatest poet and one of the most gifted writers of prose fiction among modern Swedish proletarian authors. His life was short and tragic, extreme poverty dogging his every step from childhood to the grave. The son of a poor folk school teacher, he spent, at the age of 14, some 8 months visiting relatives in Minnesota. Upon his return to Sweden, he became a forest laborer and charcoal burner, at which occupations, except for a short period at Brunnsvik Folk High School, he spent the remainder of his life. His literary work was reasonably prolific, considering the vicissitudes of his life. The best of his poetry was published in two volumes, *Kolvaktarens visor* (1915; The Charcoal Burner's Songs) and *Svarta ballader* (1917; Black Ballads). A collection of short stories, *Kolarhistorier* (1914; Charcoal Burner's Tales), and two novels, *De tre hemlösa* (1918; Three Homeless Ones) and *David Ramms arv* (1919; David Ramm's Heritage), constitute the best of his prose. A selection from his poetry has been translated into English by Caroline Schleef under the title *Charcoal-Burner's Ballad & Other Poems* (1943). Andersson's poetry was strongly influenced on its formal side by Rudyard Kipling and Robert William Service and perhaps to a lesser extent by his countrymen Gustav FRÖDING and Erik Axel KARLFELDT, and his prose in both its spirit and its form owes much to Fyodor DOSTOYEVSKY and the Knut HAMSUN of *Hunger* and *Mysteries*. Though his work everywhere reveals a strong sense of solidarity with the lower working classes, he does not directly attack the existing economic and social order and scarcely seems conscious of any sharp class conflicts. His heavy, brooding temperament was concerned primarily with religious and metaphysical problems, although he was never able to resolve the somber disharmonies of the life that was the object of his brooding. He approached these problems with a fierce primitive intensity, and whatever stray flashes of light he found in the awesome gloom of human existence become a part of the primitive wilderness mysticism that was essential to him. "His view of life," wrote a Swedish critic, "is a grim fatalism, and his whole work is a fragmentary theodicy, occasionally lighted by flashes from his innermost soul . . ." His poetry is marked by rich, buoyant rhythms, on occasion softened and subdued, and by a bold, sharp, achingly haunting figurative language, eminently appropriate to his somber, restless, ceaselessly searching poetic temperament.

See: T. Fogelqvist, Introduction to D. Andersson, *Samlade skrifter*, I (1934), viii–lxxvi; W. Bernhard, *En bok om Dan Andersson* (1941, 4th ed., 1966); A.-M. Odstedt, *Dan Andersson: en levnadsteckning* (1941); E. R. Gummerus, *Den hemlöse: Dan Andersson—studier* (1965) and *En bilderbok om Dan Andersson* (1969).   A.G.

Andrade, Eugénio de (1923–), Portuguese poet and translator, born in Póvoa da Atalaia, near Castelo Branco. He spent his childhood in Lisbon and received his secondary education in Coimbra. Since then he has lived in Oporto, where he is a civil servant. Andrade's first volume of poetry, *Narciso* (Narcissus), appeared in 1940, and he has since published 14 or more slim books of verse, including *Adolescente* (1942), *As mãos e os frutos* (1948; Hands and Fruits), *Coração do dia* (1958; Heart of Day), *Obscuro domínio* (1971; Dark Domain), as well as translations of Federico GARCÍA LORCA and of the anonymous 17th-century *Lettres portugaises* in 1968 and 1969 respectively. In his early volumes especially, Andrade's poetry remains within the Portuguese lyrical tradition, but it reveals as well the influence of the all-pervading surrealism of the 20th century through its profusion of imagery and metaphors; these also indicate his deep interest in García Lorca. Andrade is the poet of the brief lyric that captures sharply the experience of a moment, whether it be the instant of love, an April morning, the pain of sudden separation, the realization of loneliness, or the awakening of nostalgia. He relies on delicate sense impressions, usually of external nature or natural objects. The images are sensuous and sparsely delineated, and the symbols and metaphors are commonly springs, rivers, and the sea. Andrade's writing is deeply personal, and although it contains no note of social protest, it conveys a strong feeling of human solidarity.

See: E. Lourenço, "Eugénio de Andrade ou o Paraiso sem mediação," *Antologia (1945–1961) de E. de A.* (1961); various authors, *21 ensaios sobre Eugénio de Andrade* (1973); J. de Sena, "Eugénio de Andrade," *Grande dicionário da literatura portuguesa*, pt. 6 (n.d., ca. 1973), pp. 273–74. R.S.S.

Andreas-Salomé, Lou (1861–1937), German novelist, essayist, and confidante of Friedrich NIETZSCHE, Rainer Maria RILKE, and Sigmund Freud, was born in Petersburg, Russia. She met Nietzsche in 1882, and, after separating from him and his friend Paul Ree, published an account of his thought, *Friedrich Nietzsche in seinen Werken* (1894; Friedrich Nietzsche in His Works). Though she was married to the Orientalist Friedrich Carl Andreas in 1887, she continued to pursue her travels across Europe, often in the company of men intensely engaged in shaping their own thought. *Hendrik Ibsens Frauengestalten* (1892; Henrik Ibsen's Women Figures) was followed by a series of psychological and religious novels. In 1897, Andreas-Salomé met Rilke, with whom she made two visits to her homeland, where they met Lev TOLSTOY and the folk poet Drozhzin. She had published her analysis of sexual love, *Die Erotik* (1910; Eroticism), before she met Freud in 1911. Although she turned to an earlier chapter of her life in *Rainer Maria Rilke* (1928), she was now publishing mainly psychological studies and writing her memoirs, published as *Lebensrückblick* (1951; Backward Glance at Life). Although her relationships with Nietzsche, Rilke, Freud, and others (including Gerhart HAUPTMANN and Frank WEDEKIND) remain fascinating, she was an important thinker in her own right.

See: H. F. Peters, *My Sister, My Spouse* (1962); R. Binion, *Frau Lou* (1968). L.G.Sc.

Andresen, Sophia de Mello Breyner (1919–), Portuguese poet and author of short stories and children's books, was born in Oporto. She studied classical philology at the University of Lisbon, and is the mother of five children. Andresen has contributed to many literary magazines, among them *Cadernos de Poesia* and *Unicórnio*. Her first book of verse, *Poesia* (1944), had been followed by 11 others up to 1972, including *Dia do mar* (1947; Ocean Day), *No tempo dividido* (1954; In Divided Time), *Livro*

sexto (1962; Sixth Book), and *Dual* (1972), as well as an *Antologia* (1968). Her short stories are represented by *Contos exemplares* (1962; Exemplary Tales). She has translated Shakespeare and other poets and written critical essays, including one on the Brazilian poet she resembles, Cecília Meireles. Although her poetry at first showed the influence of Fernando PESSOA and to a certain extent that of the 16th-century Portuguese lyricists and although like Cecília Meireles she is a postsymbolist, she cannot easily be classified as a member of any definite literary group of her time. Her lyrics, which are abstract both spatially and temporally, are obsessively concerned with the substance of existence and the presence of death. A deeply religious woman, she exhibits in both her writing and her life her indignation about social injustice and human callousness. Her themes are frequently the eternal ones of man's solitariness and the brevity of human affections and relations. To a large extent, the symbols in her poetry seem to be taken from her garden and a favorite beach. The metaphors that she likes to use are the sea, the wind, air, night, and distant horizons. Her abstract world is an intense, organic one. Andresen's verse, whether free or traditional, is couched in simple, almost brutally direct language, and through the years it has become increasingly concise.

See: D. Mourão-Ferreira, *Vinte poetas contemporâneos* (1960), pp. 131–35; F. Guimarães, "A poesia de Ruy Cinatti, Jorge de Sena, Sophia Andresen, e Eugénio de Andrade," *Estrada larga*, vol. 3 (1962), pp. 332–43; J. Sena, "Sophia de Mello Breyner Andresen," *Grande dicionário da literatura portuguesa*, pt. 6 (n.d., ca. 1973), pp. 280–81. R.S.S.

Andreyev, Leonid Nikolayevich (1871–1919), Russian prose writer, dramatist, and publicist, was born in Orel, a Russian provincial capital. At the age of 16 he survived a suicide attempt (out of a lifetime total of 3) with Dostoyevskian overtones: he lay between the rails of a railroad track while a train rolled over him.

In addition to early attempts at literature and painting, Andreyev finished a law program in 1897. When he was a young court reporter, he started writing journalistic satires, and this led him into a career as a short-story writer.

Andreyev made his métier the expression of extreme emotions akin to madness, and in 1902 he achieved national fame, or perhaps notoriety, with the publication of two stories: "Bezdna" (Eng. tr., "The Abyss," 1924) and "V tumane" (In the Fog). They deal with the themes of rape, necrophilia, and venereal disease, and they caused a great scandal. Among others, Sofia Tolstoy, the wife of Lev TOLSTOY, publicly denounced Andreyev.

Andreyev subsequently turned his attention to two topical themes: war and political repression. *Krasny smekhi* (Eng. tr., *The Red Laugh*, 1905), written in 1904, during the Russo-Japanese War, deals with the "horror and madness" (an opening phrase constantly repeated) of modern military conflict. It ends, typically for Andreyev, with death by insanity. *The Red Laugh* is unrestrained in its imaginings—Andreyev never experienced war personally.

In 1908, Andreyev wrote his most famous story, "Rasskaz o semi poveshannykh" (Eng. tr., "The Seven That Were Hanged," 1909). Set in a time of political repression and executions in Russia, the story describes the lives of five convicted terrorists, during the last weeks before their actual executions. He contrasts their experience to the terror and heart attack endured by their intended victim, a government minister, as well as to the suffering of two common criminals hanged along with them. The tension in the story is unusually well controlled by the author, and the reader is even captivated by Andreyev's uncommonly effective language.

Andreyev's most famous play is "Tot kto poluchayet poshchochiny" (1915; Eng. tr., "He Who Gets Slapped," 1921), which is set in a circus and is permeated with his usual themes of thwarted love, masked identity, enforced pretense, murder, and suicide. He also achieves, however, some uncharacteristically humorous touches.

In 1919, Andreyev wrote *Spasite! (S.O.S.)* (Eng. tr., *Russia's Call to Humanity, "Save Our Souls,"* 1919), an extreme and impassioned anti-Bolshevik tract, a kind of death wail for the author and his Russia. The resonance from this work made it difficult to establish him in the Soviet literary canon, but his friend Maksim GORKY succeeded in this difficult task. Andreyev himself had opposed the 1917 October Revolution, and he died in exile in Finland.

In spite of Andreyev's obvious bombast and mostly superficial language, he is eminently readable as the unconcealed manipulator of the literary horror machine. His perception of the world's madness and evil leaves a definite imprint on the reader's imagination.

See: A. Kaun, *Leonid Andreyev: A Critical Study* (1924, repr. 1969); M. Gorky, "Leonid Andreyev," in *Reminiscences of Tolstoy, Chekhov, and Andreyev* (1959); J. B. Woodward, *Leonid Andreyev: A Study* (1969).   I.W.

Andrić, Ivo (1892–1974), Serbian novelist, short-story writer and essayist, was born in Dolac, near Travnik in Bosnia, into a middle-class family. He was the most distinguished Serbian prose writer of the post-World War II era and the only Yugoslav writer to receive the Nobel Prize for Literature (1961). Andrić completed secondary school in Sarajevo and studied Slavic philology at the universities of Zagreb, Cracow, and Vienna. During World War I, he was imprisoned by the Austrians as a member of the "Young Bosnia" revolutionary organization. He subsequently completed his university studies at Graz and entered the Yugoslav diplomatic service, in which he remained until the start of World War II. He spent the war years writing in occupied Belgrade, and in the postwar, socialist era he concentrated entirely on his literary endeavor.

Andrić's earliest literary efforts were several poems published in an anthology, translations of August STRINDBERG and Walt Whitman, and two collections of lyrical, deeply introspective prose poems, *Ex Ponto* (1918) and *Nemiri* 1920; Restlessness). Beginning with the story "Put Alije Djerzeleza" (1920; The Journey of Alija Djerzelez), Andrić turned his attention to prose. In the two following decades, he produced three collections of short stories (1924, 1931, and 1936) inspired by the life and traditions of his native Bosnia, a land in which centuries of struggle among the Orthodox, Catholic, and Muslim forces and heritages created a milieu of rare complexity and striking contrasts. Many of these stories, as well as those that appeared after World War II either individually or in the collection *Nove Pripovetke* (1948; New Stories), are clustered in several large cycles. In each of these, the central characters are shown in a number of distinct situations designed to capture such inner and outer changes of personalities and milieu as are insinuated by the passing of time.

Both stylistically and thematically, Andrić's tales of the Bosnian past heralded his two great novel-chronicles *Na Drini ćuprija* (1945; Eng. tr., *The Bridge on the Drina,* 1959) and *Travnička hronika* (1945; Eng. trs., *Bosnian Story,* 1958, and *Bosnian Chronicle,* 1963), which he published simultaneously at the end of World War II. *Na Drini ćuprija* is by far Andrić's most famous work. This monumental chronicle focuses on a Bosnian microcosm, the town of Višegrad and its ancient bridge across the river Drina. The work covers centuries, observing generations of townsfolk locked in ceaseless struggle against the ravages of natural forces and human destructiveness. *Travnička hronika* is an equally penetrating psychological study of the Bosnian milieu, although it is conceived on a smaller scale. Set in the turbulent decade of the Napoleonic wars, the novel depicts the town of Travnik and the destinies of its inhabitants, both domestic and foreign, as perceived by the newly arrived French consul. Both novels are particularly notable for their subtle contrast of Western and Oriental atmosphere and values within Bosnia and for their superb portrayal of numerous characters belonging to the feuding but coexisting Christian, Muslim, and Jewish communities.

After World War II, Andrić also published several short stories on contemporary subjects and themes, some travel memoirs, and a number of essays on Yugoslav authors—Petar Kočić, Isak Samokovlija, (*see* SERBIAN LITERATURE), Petor Njegoš, Vuk Karadžić, Simo Matavulh—and both Yugoslav and foreign painters—Bijelić, Džumhur, and Francisco Goya. He also published two short novels. The first of these, *Gospodjica* (1945; Eng. tr., *The Woman from Sarajevo,* 1966) concerns a well-to-do old maid who is gradually destroyed by her insecurity and miserliness. The second work, *Prokleta avlija* (1954; Eng. tr., *Devil's Yard,* 1962), is set in the Ottoman past and depicts the notorious Istanbul prison yard. Here guilty and innocent inmates from all over the Ottoman Empire languish in an endless morass of pain, deprivation, and misery.

Although Andrić's work frequently betrays his profound sadness over the misery and waste inherent in the passing of time, it still contains some heartening messages of faith in man's struggle against evil as well as sympathy for his pains. Andrić is also an exemplary stylist, with an impeccable feeling for clear and measured expression. The plasticity of his narrative, the depth of his psychological insight, and the universality of his symbolism remain unsurpassed in all of Serbian literature.

See: P. Džadžić, *Ivo Andrić* (1957); R. Minde, *Ivo Andrić: Studien über seine Erzählkunst* (1962); *Ivo Andrić: zbornik radova u izdanju Instituta za teoriju književnosti* (1962); M. J. Bandić, *Ivo Andrić: zagonetka vedrine* (1963).   N.M.

Andrzejewski, Jerzy (1909–), Polish novelist, was born in Warsaw and studied Polish philology at Warsaw University. In 1936 he published his first volume of short stories, *Drogi nieuniknione* (Unavoidable Roads), and in 1938, his first novel, *Ład serca* (Mode of the Heart), for which he received national recognition and which revealed him as a writer sensitive to moral problems, to the dramatic struggle of the human soul, thus linking him with such novelists as Joseph Conrad, Georges BERNANOS, and François MAURIAC. During World War II he was active in the literary resistance movement in Warsaw. His collection of short stories *Noc* (1945; The Night), devoted to the writer's war experiences, was followed by a novel, *Popiół i diament* (1948; Eng. tr., *Ashes and Diamonds,* 1962), which discussed the most important political, moral, and psychological problems in the period immediately following the war in Poland. For a short period, Andrzejewski embraced the Communist ideology, but in 1955 he published a collection of short stories, *Złoty lis* (The Golden Fox), which marked his departure from political dogma, and in 1957 he published a novel *Ciemności kryją ziemie* (Eng. tr., *The Inquisitors,* 1960), a philosophical parable on the autocratic rule of a totalitarian ideology. His historical-philosophical novel about the Children's Crusade of 1212, *Bramy raju* (1960; Eng. tr., *The Gates of Paradise*, 1962), was followed by a contemporary novel, *Idzie skacząc po górach,* (1963; Eng. tr., *A Sitter for a Satyr*, 1965), a satirical parodistic story about the life of a contemporary artist. In the short novel *Apelacja* (1968, Eng. tr., *The Appeal*, 1971), published abroad, Andrzejewski made a direct attack on the totalitarian methods of the Communist regime, pointing out its corruption and inhumane methods of breaking human minds. He is also the author of several volumes of short stories and short fiction. The most important problem to which Andrzejewski returns again and again is the role of ideas and morals in the life of the individual and in history.

See: M. J. Kryński, "The Metamorphoses of Jerzy Andrzejewski: The Road From Belief to Skepticism," *PolR* 6 (1961): 111–16; *Słownik współczesnych pisarzy polskich,* vol. 1 (1963), pp. 127–32; J. R. Krzyżanowski, "On the History of *Ashes and Diamond*," *SEEJ* 16, no. 3 (1971): 324–31.   J.R.K.

Andújar, Manuel (1913–), Spanish novelist and dramatist, was born in La Carolina in the province of Jaén and studied in Málaga. He worked as a civil servant until the Spanish Civil War, when he fled to France and was imprisoned in the concentration camp of Saint Ciprien. Exiled to Mexico, he founded *Las Españas,* one of the most prestigious Spanish literary publications in Mexico City, with J. R. Arana. Since his return to Madrid he has worked in the publishing industry.

His most important literary work is the trilogy *Vísperas* (1970; Eves), which includes *Llanura* (1947; The Plain), *El vencido* (1949; The Defeated), and *El destino de Lázaro* (1959; The Fate of Lazarus). These novels deal with the geographical and historical reality of Spain's peasants, its miners and the inhabitants of the port city of Málaga. The social and psychological conflicts in Andújar's writings are expressed in colloquial and popular language with a technique rooted in 19th-century Spanish realism. Because of the importance given to the causes and effects of the Spanish Civil War, Andújar's works can be categorized as "literature of exile."

See: J. R. Marra López, *Narrativa española fuera de España* (1963), pp. 443–75; R. Conte, "El realismo simbólico de Manuel Andújar," Introduction to *Vísperas* (1970), pp. 9–19.   J.O.

Annensky, Innokenty Fyodorovich (1856–1909), Russian poet, dramatist, translator, essayist, and classical scholar, was born in Omsk. He combined his writing with a successful career as a teacher and a district inspector of schools. His first book of verse, *Tikhiye pesni* (1904; Quiet Songs), was ignored or patronized by critics. Nevertheless, he soon became prominent in Petersburg literary circles and influential among the young poets there, notably Anna AKHMATOVA and Nikolay GUMILYOV, who later took the name acmeists and called Annensky their teacher. Annensky died suddenly on the day his application for retirement from the civil service was accepted, before he could assume the active role in literature he had long desired. His two other verse collections, *Kiparisovy larets* (1910; The Cypress Chest) and *Posmertnye stikhi* (1923; Posthumous Verse), were edited after his death by his son. He remains insufficiently appreciated and studied in his homeland. No satisfactory edition of his complete works exists.

Annensky often criticized the Russian symbolist movement and intensely disliked its religious, mystical, and nationalistic orientation. Indeed, he is the only major Russian poet who can be called a "symbolist" or "decadent" in the French sense. The decadent spirit dominating European letters at the end of the 19th century permeates his highly original and intimate verse. Poems like "Sentyabr" (September) recall Paul VERLAINE's statement, "I like the word 'decadence' with its reflections of purple and gold," and a feeling of anxiety or *toska* pervades everything he wrote. His constant themes of death (even spring is a "black" time of decay), the inevitability of time's passing, the ephemeral, mysterious nature of life, and the poet's own tormented awareness of beauty's fragile impermanence make clear why this aesthetic skeptic, ironical but compassionate, could never share the confidence of Russia's "younger symbolists" (such as Andrey BELY and Vyacheslav IVANOV) in the poet's power to transform man's tragic condition. Annensky expressed his bleak vision in the indirect and suggestive discourse of symbols, fusing this with a clarity of detail, an exceptional feeling for the objects of daily life, and an acuteness of psychological observation that have led some commentators to compare his poetry to the works of Anton CHEKHOV.

Besides translations from Latin, French, German, and English he put all of Euripides into Russian. His own four original verse tragedies—*Melanippa-filosof* (1901; Melanippe the Philosopher), *Tsar Iksion* (1902; King Ixion), *Laodamiya* (1906; Laodamia), and *Famira-kifared* (1913; Thamyris Cytharoed)—depict spiritual conflicts and a nihilistic vision through classical symbols and myths in a thoroughly modern fashion. His very personal, often whimsical criticism on both European and Russian literature is collected in two volumes: *Kniga otrazheniy* (1906; Book of Reflections) and *Vtoraya kniga otrazheniy* (1909; Second Book of Reflections).

See: A. V. Fyodorov, Introduction to I. Annensky, *Stikhotvoreniya i tragedii* (1959); V. Setchkarev, *Studies in the Life and Works of Innokenty Annensky* (1963); translations in V. Markov and M. Sparks, *Modern Russian Poetry* (1967), pp. 112–29.   J.E.M.

Anouilh, Jean (1910–), French playwright, was born in Cérisole (Bordeaux). He is the author of at least 40 dramatic works, most of which he has grouped under adjectives descriptive of their dominant tone: "black," "pink," "brilliant," "jarring," "costumed," and "baroque" (the adjectives occurring in the titles of each of his collections of plays). Anouilh treats an assortment of themes ranging from the heroism of the individual to the mediocrity of the masses, from the profoundly sincere search for love to the painful recognition of human selfishness. The essence of his early plays is the hero's insistence on remaining pure and intransigent in the midst of corruption and compromise; in the later works, he focuses on resignation, disillusionment, and bitterness in the face of contemporary materialism and spiritual aridity.

Anouilh belongs to the generation raised during World War I who grew up despising middle-class moral traditions. Typical bourgeois families are the butt of ridicule in many of Anouilh's plays, and he excels in pouring out his contempt and scorn for their vulgarity and hypocrisy. Although he knew poverty in his childhood—a poverty that probably inspired his early, bitter "black" plays—Anouilh today lives in elegant seclusion in his various Parisian and Neuilly dwellings.

A fellow student of Jean-Louis BARRAULT in 1927 and secretary to Louis JOUVET at the Comédie des Champs-Elysées in 1931–32, Anouilh had his first plays produced by Aurélien LUGNÉ-POE and the Pitoëffs (*see* Georges PITOËFF) in the 1930s. During the occupation of Paris by the Nazis, he remained immersed in his work and aloof from politics, but in the late 1950s he clashed with General de Gaulle, beginning a feud that was to find literary expression in *L'Hurluberlu* (1958; Eng. tr., *The Fighting Cock*, 1960) and *Le Songe du critique* (1960; The Critic's Dream).

The typical conflict in the "black" plays—*L'Hermine* (1931; Eng. tr., *The Ermine*, 1955), *Jézabel* (1932), *La Sauvage* (1934), *Le Voyageur sans bagage* (1937; Eng. tr., *Traveller without Luggage*, 1959), *Eurydice* (1942; Eng. tr., 1948), *Antigone* (1942; Eng. tr., 1946), *Roméo et Jeannette* (1945; Eng. tr., 1958), and *Médée* (1946; Eng. tr., *Medea*, 1972)—is the conflict between the "pure" individual in search of an ideal, and a corrupt, triumphant society that forces the hero to compromise his or her integrity. The only recourse is a tragic escape from reality, either through solitude and isolation, or through actual or symbolic death. In the "pink" plays—*Le Bal des voleurs* (1938; Eng. tr., *Thieves' Carnival*, 1952), *Le Rendez-vous de Senlis* (1937), and *Léocadia* (1939)—Anouilh's characters "escape" black reality through fantasy, illusion, and changing personality. The first two "brilliant" plays, *L'Invitation au château* (1947; Eng. tr., *Ring 'round the Moon*, 1950) and *Cécile* (1949; Eng. tr., *Cecile, or the School for Fathers*, 1967), maintain the overall levity of the "pink" plays, whereas the last two, *La Répétition* (1950; Eng. tr., *The Rehearsal*, 1961) and *Colombe* (1950; Eng. tr., 1959), are fashioned around the "black" theme of the destruction of a pure love.

In some ways similar to the "black" plays, the "jarring" plays see Anouilh's attention shift from the "heroic" race to the "mediocre" race and its compromise with life. The effect of these plays is "jarring" because two irreconcilables—comedy and tragedy—clash on a battlefield strewn with the cast-off armor of men's defense mechanisms. Although Anouilh's cynicism dominates *Ardèle* (1948; Eng. tr., 1959), *La Valse des toréadors* (1951; Eng. tr., *The Waltz of the Toreadors*, 1956), *Ornifle* (1955; Eng. tr., 1970), and *Pauvre Bitos* (1956; Eng. tr., *Poor Bitos*, 1964), one can nevertheless read into them a certain tolerance of the unsuccessful hero. The rigidity of the earlier plays yields to the mellowing influence of maturity, and Anouilh seems resigned to the inevitability of love's impurity and the evanescence of ideals. The central figure in these plays is a middle-aged man, who seems to represent a stage in Anouilh's own life and conscience. Striving to remain young, blossoming every spring like an old tree (but a tree whose trunk is rotting), his life is absurd and his ideas are reactionary. Plagued by conscience, he recognizes the purity and beauty of intransigence when he sees it, but he is incapable of correcting his own loose morals and weaknesses. A similar central character, now middle-aged, dominates *Les Poissons rouges* (1970; Goldfish) and the "baroque" plays—*Cher Antoine* (1969; Eng. tr., *Dear Antoine*, 1971), *Ne réveillez pas Madame* (1970; Don't Awaken Madame), and *Le Directeur de l'Opéra* (1972)—as well as the more recent and as yet unlabeled plays, *Monsieur Barnett* (1975) and *Chers Zoiseaux* (1977; Dear Birds). Most of these plays have as their hallmark tragicomic bourgeois family scenes. They express Anouilh's love for the theater (or literature) as a form of escape, as well as his marked conservatism regarding such themes as "man's honor," permissiveness towards children, divorce, abortion, and labor unions. The principal character in these plays indulges in blatant nostalgia for the past and is proud to refer to himself as a "fachiste"—a play on the French words for *Fascist* and *angry*.

A series of Anouilh plays that includes *Pauvre Bitos* and the "costumed" plays—*L'Alouette* (1952; Eng. tr., *The Lark*, 1955), *Becket ou l'honneur de Dieu* (1959; Eng.

tr., *Becket, or, The Honour of God*, 1962), and *La Foire d'empoigne* (1962; Eng. tr., *Catch as Catch Can*, 1967)—deals with historical figures: Robespierre, Joan of Arc, Henry Plantagenet and Becket, Napoleon and Louis XVIII, respectively. Most of these plays are presented as improvisations, with characters fitting into their historical roles on stage, mixing reality with illusion, and changing the sequence and accuracy of history for the desired dramatic effects. Similarly, in his plays revolving around mythological and legendary heroes (Eurydice, Antigone, Orestes, and Medea), Anouilh reinterprets myth in accordance with a general post–World War I movement away from realism and toward stylization, fantasy, and symbolism. It is probably on the best of his mythical and historical plays—*Antigone, Becket, The Lark*—that Anouilh's reputation will most solidly rest.

Most recently, Anouilh has brought three controversial plays to the Parisian stage: *Le Scénario* (1976), a cynical attack on the movie world; *Vive Henri IV* (1977), a series of historical flashbacks played out by 18 actors interpreting 64 different roles; and *La Culotte* (1978), a comic fantasy on the theme of women's liberation.

See: A. della Fazia, *Jean Anouilh* (1969); K. W. Kelly, *Jean Anouilh: An Annotated Bibliography* (1973); L. W. Falb, *Jean Anouilh* (1977).   A.Am.

Antoine, André (1858–1943), French actor, theater director and producer, and drama critic, was born in Limoges but went to Paris while very young. He was the first and, in many ways, the most important of the reformers of the modern theater in France and Western Europe. An avid reader driven by an early passion for the theater, Antoine educated himself, frequented theaters, attended a school of diction, and acquired a solid, although unacademic, histrionic training. While still a clerk for the Paris Gas Company, he joined a group of amateur players and finally, in the face of every kind of difficulty, succeeded in starting his own independent theater, the Théâtre Libre (1887–94). As director of this avant-garde group, he launched the attack against the established theater, which by then had fallen into a state of sterile self-perpetuation and, reduced to a commercial venture, was content to bring light, reassuring entertainment to a bourgeois public. Free from censorship and open only to a sophisticated audience, the Théâtre Libre served as a laboratory where authors, directors, and actors alike could experiment with new forms of drama. To break away from the artificial playmaking of his contemporaries, Antoine advocated greater realism and the *tranche de vie* ("slice of life") as opposed to well-constructed plays. He stressed verisimilitude in stage setting, proposed a new lighting system doing away with footlights, and experimented with more realistic scenery. He advocated new methods of acting far removed from the grandiloquent manner of the conservatoire and stressed naturalness of voice and gesture.

Besides producing new plays by unknown dramatists, Antoine helped to revitalize native drama by importing foreign masterpieces by Lev TOLSTOY, Henrik IBSEN, August STRINDBERG, Gerhart HAUPTMANN, and Bjørnstjerne BJØRNSON. As director of his own regular playhouse, the Théâtre Antoine (1896–1906), he sought to win over the general public and continued his work of renovation, a task he expanded further while director of the Odéon (1906–14), by applying his ideas to the production of great classics, particularly Shakespeare. By the time he left the theater in 1914 to become a drama critic, Antoine had paved the way for much of the significant theatrical activity of the 20th century. His *Memories of the Théâtre Libre*, tr. by M. A. Carlson, was published in 1964.

See: M. Roussou, *André Antoine* (1954); F. Pruner, *Les*

Luttes d'Antoine au Théâtre Libre (1964); S. M. Waxman, *Antoine and the Théâtre Libre* (1964). M.Sa.

Antokolsky, Pavel Grigoryevich (1896–1978), Russian poet, was born in Petersburg, the son of a Jewish attorney and the grandson of a famous sculptor. He studied law at Moscow University and acting with Yevgeny Vakhtangov, and as a young actor he traveled in the West. Drama and Western culture provided the themes of such early romantic verse collections as *Zapad* (1926; The West), *Tretya kniga* (1927; Third Book), and the narrative poems "Robespyer i Gorgona" (1928; Robespierre and Gorgon) and "Kommuna 71 goda" (1933; The Commune of '71). A long poem, "Fransua Viyon" (1934; François Villon), depicts the medieval French vagabond poet against a historical panorama, a technique characteristic of Antokolsky's work in general; "Fransua Viyon" also attacks contemporary France as bourgeois.

For two decades after the publication of the collection *Deystvuyushchiye litsa* (Dramatis Personae) in 1932, Antokolsky lauded Soviet industrial development over Western culture. He joined the Communist Party in 1943. During World War II his own front-line theater group produced his dramatic poem "Chkalov" (1942). His long poem "Syn" (1943; Son), which won a Stalin Prize in 1946, contrasts the Communist upbringing of his only son, who died at the front, with the miseducation of German youth. The "thaw" after Iosif Stalin's death led to the collection *Masterskaya* (1958; Workshop), which praises freedom, and *Chetvyortoye izmereniye* (1964; The Fourth Dimension), and the very fine *Povest vremennykh let* (1964; Tale of Bygone Years), both of which experiment with lyrical construction in their exploration of the nature of time and the nature of Antokolsky's silent age. After the thaw he returned to approved themes. He has written interesting criticism of many Russian poets, especially Aleksandr Pushkin, who is also the subject of his collections *Pushkinskiy god* (1938; Pushkin's [Centennial] Year) and *O Pushkine* (1960; On Pushkin). Like *Sila Vetnama* (1960; The Strength of Vietnam), *O Pushkine* mixes verse with essays. Antokolsky has translated French, Bulgarian, Azerbaijani, and Georgian verse into Russian, and his own verse has been translated into many languages.

H.A.G.

Antonych, Bohdan Ihor (1909–37), Ukrainian poet, was born in the Lemky region. His poetry represents the highest literary achievement of the western Ukraine during the period between the two world wars. Essentially an imagist, Antonych excelled in lyrical and contemplative verse. His main collections are *Try persteni* (1934; Three Rings), *Knyha leva* (1936; The Book of the Lion), and *Zelena evanheliya* (1938; The Green Gospels). His collected works have been published in Prešov (1966), Kiev (1967), and New York (1967). A selection of his poems has appeared in English under the title *Square of Angels* (1977). G.S.N.L.

Apollinaire, Guillaume, pseud. of Guillaume Apollinaris de Kostrowitzky (1880–1918), French poet, art critic, impresario, and leader of the avant-garde in Paris during the first two decades of the 20th century, was born in Rome of an unwed Polish mother and an unknown father, probably an Italian army officer. Apollinaire received a French education in schools in Monte Carlo, Cannes, and Nice. Much of his poetic imagery was inspired by two sojourns, one in the Ardennes region of Belgium (during the summer of 1899) and particularly the year he spent as a tutor in the Rhineland (1901–02), which included considerable travel in Central Europe.

Establishing himself in Paris, Apollinaire was soon contributing poems and short stories to the periodicals founded during the symbolist movement: *La Revue blanche, La Plume, Le Mercure de France*. In 1903 he launched his own magazine, *Le Festin d'Esope*, followed after nine issues by *La Revue immoraliste* (one issue). It was here that for the first time (1905) he printed the name of Pablo Picasso, whose most ardent champion he was to remain until his death. In fact, until World War I, Apollinaire was less well known as a poet than as the defender of modern painting. It was he who brought Picasso and Georges Braque together in 1907, helped organize the cubist room 41 at the Salon des Indépendants in 1911, lectured at the important Section d'Or exhibit in 1912, baptized orphism and proclaimed it at a Robert Delaunay show in Berlin, issued a manifesto for futurism (*see* ITALIAN LITERATURE), and founded and edited the influential *Soirées de Paris*. His magnetism, his all-embracing enthusiasms, and his very ubiquity made him a prime mover of the avant-garde in prewar Paris. During his life, Apollinaire published only one slim volume on painting: *Méditations esthétiques: les peintres cubistes* (1913; annotated ed., 1965; Eng. tr., *The Cubist Painters, Aesthetic Meditations 1913*, 1949), and it was only with the posthumous publication in 1960 of his widely scattered writings under the title *Chroniques d'art* (Eng. tr., *Apollinaire on Art*, 1972) that the breadth and importance of his written criticism became fully known.

In 1913, Apollinaire published the volume that has come to be recognized as his masterpiece, *Alcools* (annotated ed., 1953; Eng. trs., 1964, 1965, 1966), a selection of some 50 poems composed over the previous 15 years and reflecting his development from the symbolist to the so-called cubist style, as exemplified in particular by the liminary poem "Zone." Thereafter he continued to experiment with new forms of verse, such as the "poème-conversation," the "poème-promenade," poems on painters (Delaunay, Marc Chagall, Henri Rousseau), and the "calligrammes" or poems arranged typographically in the actual shape of the object evoked.

With the outbreak of World War I, Apollinaire enlisted and fought on the front in Champagne until receiving a head wound in March 1916. During and after his convalescence in Paris, he again frequented the Left Bank cafés, arranged new exhibits, lectured on "l'esprit nouveau," coined the word "surrealism" (apropos of Jean Cocteau's ballet *Parade* in 1917), staged his play *Les Mamelles de Tirésias* (1918; The Breasts of Tiresias) in 1917, and published *Calligrammes* (1918; annotated ed., 1955), a selection of prewar (1913–14) and war poems. The latter have caused a good deal of controversy, since they seem to stress the beauty and enchantment of trench warfare with a kind of detachment that could be called callous if one did not know that the author was himself sitting in the trench under fire. Two days before the armistice, Apollinaire died in his apartment on the Boulevard Saint-Germain after a brief illness, the victim of the influenza epidemic of that winter.

Apollinaire's other works include *L'Enchanteur pourrissant* (The Rotting Enchanter), published in 1909 (annotated ed., 1972) with woodcuts by André Derain, a reworking in poetic prose dialogue of the medieval legend of Merlin and Viviane; *L'Hérésiarque et cie* (1910; annotated ed., 1954; Heresiarch and Co.), a collection of short stories in which the fusion of fantasy, eeriness, erudition, and irony is distinctly Apollinairian; *Le Bestiaire* (1911, published with woodcuts by Raoul Dufy), a series of highly polished poems, a number of which were later set to music by Francis Poulenc; *Le Poète assassiné* (1916, 1959; The Poet Assassinated), a loosely knit novel on the life and death of Croniamantal, a larger-than-life alter ego of the author; *Il y a* (1925; There Is), poems and essays published by the poet's widow; and various erotica including *Les Onze Mille Verges* (1973; Eng. tr., 1979), a parody of the Marquis de Sade and the pornographic genre.

Apollinaire was, above all, a lyric poet. As his contemporaries recognized, some of the poems in *Alcools* were inspired by the painter Marie Laurencin, and those at the end of *Calligrammes*—especially the final poem, "La Jolie Rousse" (The Pretty Red-Head), Apollinaire's poetic "testament"—by Jacqueline Kolb, whom he married in 1918. It was not until after World War II, however, with the discovery of his relationships with three other women, that the extent of the love poetry became clear. Annie Playden, an English governess, was found to have inspired many of the Rhineland pieces, particularly the masterpiece "La Chanson du mal-aimé" (The Song of the Ill-Beloved) in *Alcools*. Louise de Coligny-Châtillon and Madeleine Pagès authorized the publication of the often intimate lines addressed to them by the soldier-poet during the war. The volumes are entitled *Poèmes à Lou* (1955; Poems to Lou) and *Tendre comme le souvenir* (1952; Tender as Memory).

Apollinaire's style ranges from the most elegiac to the most dithyrambic. He foresaw constantly widening frontiers for the poetry of the new century, and his efforts to explore the depths of the unconscious, to introduce the imagery of the modern city, to create a more direct, conversational language and more pliable poetic structures based on discontinuity and "simultaneity" were all to have a direct influence on the surrealist generation (*see* FRENCH LITERATURE). Today his rank as a major poet derives rather from the charm and authenticity of a very personal voice expressing the endless probing of an ever-elusive self, a voice that seems to speak even more distinctly to the last than to the first half of the 20th century.

See: F. Steegmuller, *Apollinaire: Poet among Painters* (1963, 1971, 1973); M. Davies, *Apollinaire* (1964); S. Bates, *Guillaume Apollinaire* (1967); P. Adéma, *Guillaume Apollinaire* (1968); L. Breunig, *Guillaume Apollinaire* (1969).

L.B.

Aragon, Louis (1897–), French poet, critic, journalist, novelist, short-story writer, and translator, was born in Paris. His vast production includes more than 80 volumes. With André BRETON and Philippe SOUPAULT, he launched the review *Littérature* (1919–21), an anarchic, subversive enterprise of dadaist (*see* FRENCH LITERATURE) persuasion, given to provocative press campaigns. His first collection of poems, *Feu de joie* (1920; Bonfire), was written in this vein, as were *Anicet* (1921) and *Les Aventures de Télémaque* (1922; The Adventures of Telemachus), both ironical accounts of spiritual itineraries and early examples of antinovels. To this phase also belong the sardonic short stories of *Le Libertinage* (1924) and the verse (written 1920–24) published in *Le Mouvement perpétuel* (1926; Perpetual Motion), a systematic derision of poetic language. The dadaist program of negativism soon gave way to a new formulation. Together with Breton, Aragon founded *La Révolution surréaliste* (1924–29), and became a leading exponent of surrealism (*see* FRENCH LITERATURE), whose constructive tenets he advocated in the brilliant manifesto *Une Vague de rêves* (1924; A Wave of Dreams), a homage to dreams and the power of the unconscious. His remarkable prose poem *Le Paysan de Paris* (1926; Eng. trs., *Nightwalker*, 1970, *Paris Peasant*, 1971) created "a modern mythology," revealing the everyday wonders of city life and celebrat-

ing the fusion of imagination and reality in a virtuoso style characteristic of the author.

Aragon's career took a different orientation when he joined the Communist Party (1927)—a lifelong commitment—and in 1928 met the Russian-born writer Elsa TRIOLET, who became his wife and exerted a profound and acknowledged influence on his work. His *Traité du style* (1928; Treatise on Style) already signals the defusing process by which surrealism was stripped of its revolutionary implications and made safe for bourgeois consumption. During his first visit to the USSR (1930), Aragon participated in the Kharkov Writers Conference and was deeply impressed by the massive industrial effort then under way. Back in Paris, he published *Persécuté Persécuteur* (1931; Persecuted Persecutor), a call to political violence that was taken literally by the French authorities, who threatened him with repression. There followed a period of intense activity as journalist and editor for Communist newspapers (*L'Humanité, Commune, Ce Soir*). His volume of poetry *Hourra l'Oural* (1934) and his essay *Pour un réalisme socialiste* (1935; For a Socialist Realism) reflect the Marxist approach, as does in a freer vein the four-novel cycle entitled *Le Monde réel* (1934–46; The Real World): *Les Cloches de Bâle* (1934; Eng. tr., *The Bells of Basel*, 1936), *Les Beaux Quartiers* (1936; Eng. tr., *Residential Quarter*, 1938), *Les Voyageurs de l'impériale* (1947; Eng. trs., *The Century Was Young*, 1941, *Passengers of Destiny*, 1947), and *Aurélien* (1944; Eng. tr., 1946). This vast social fresco depicts the erosion of the French bourgeoisie during the Third Republic.

During the German occupation of France, Aragon was the most popular poet of the French Resistance. Using traditional themes and simple imagery, *Le Crève-coeur* (1941; Heartbreak), *Le Musée Grévin* (1943; The Grévin Museum), and *La Diane française* (1945; The French Diana) sang the past glories of the motherland, its present suffering, and the hopes for liberation. These poems were immediately acclaimed and later set to music, as were also numerous love poems from the long cycle dedicated to Elsa, stretching from *Les Yeux d'Elsa* (1942; The Eyes of Elsa) to *Les Chambres* (1969; The Rooms), and including two verse autobiographies, *Les Yeux et la mémoire* (1954; Eyes and Memory) and *Le Roman inachevé* (1956; The Unfinished Novel).

Beginning with *Les Communistes* (5 vols., 1949–51), a series of novels supposed to cover the German occupation but left incomplete (although revised in 1966), Aragon's fiction dispenses with orthodox social realism and linear development. *La Semaine sainte* (1958; Eng. tr., *Holy Week*, 1961), concerning King Louis XVIII's unheroic flight to Brussels in 1815, offers subjective comments on history and politics as well as a sustained reflection on the role of art in its relationship to life. The interplay between creator and creation functions as a leitmotiv in *La Mise à mort* (1965; The Kill), while *Blanche ou l'oubli* (1967; Blanche or Forgetfulness) combines an anguished monologue on solitude with a theory of the novel as a lie revealing the truth. *Théâtre/Roman* (1974; Theater/Novel) continues to blend personal confidences and theoretical reflections, as does *Henri Matisse, roman* (1971; Eng. tr., *Henri Matisse: A Novel*, 1972), which celebrates, under the label of fiction, the art of a painter to whom Aragon dedicated *L'Apologie du luxe* (1947; In Defense of Luxury). A fraction of Aragon's extensive literary criticism has been collected in *Chroniques du Bel Canto* (1947; Chronicles of the Bel Canto), *La Lumière de Stendhal* (1954; The Light of Stendhal), *Littératures soviétiques* (1955; Soviet Literatures), and *J'abats mon jeu* (1959; I Put My Cards on the Table).

By virtue of the wealth and variety of his œuvre, Aragon is unquestionably a major 20th-century French man of letters. He is a supreme example of the committed writer who found his creative freedom through both personal lyricism and social responsibility.

See: R. Garaudy, *L'Itinéraire d'Aragon* (1961); M. Adereth, *Commitment in Modern French Literature* (1967); G. Sadoul, *Aragon* (1967); L. Becker, *Louis Aragon* (1971); B. Lecherbonnier, *Aragon* (1971); P. Daix, *Aragon: une vie à changer* (1975).   Y.G.

Aranguren, José Luis L. (1909–), Spanish philosopher, essayist, and literary critic, was born in Ávila. He began his literary career with an excellent monograph, *La filosofía de Eugenio D'Ors* (1945), whose philosophy of forms, together with the innovative ideas of José ORTEGA Y GASSET, Martin Heidegger, Otto Friedrich Bollnow, and others, provided the point of departure for another of Aranguren's most important and original works, *Protestantismo y catolicismo como formas de existencia* (1954). In this work he studied the way the great reformers lived their Christianity. He focused on Martin Luther, whose tragic, agonized Christianity of inner contradiction—*simul justus et peccator*—reappears, secularized, in the existentialism of Heidegger. In *La crisis del catolicismo* (1969), Aranguren analyzed the church's response to the crises of organization, of theology, of authority, and finally of faith, which have resulted in the modernization of its institutions, crises that in the last analysis have their roots in the Protestant Reformation. The self-annulment of protestant theology in the radical theology of Paul Tillich and the Godless theology of Dietrich Bonhoeffer prepares the way for the advent of "Protestant Catholicism," a phenomenon already hinted at by contemporary American theologians like Michael Novak and Daniel J. Callahan. But the problem of how to be a Christian in our times is for Aranguren also an ethical problem. He deals with this in his *Ética* (1958). Man cannot deny his ethical and moral nature, the reality of which is found precisely in his carrying out the projects that he shapes for himself. There is certainly no longer any place for a normative ethic; neither is Immanuel Kant's ethics of duty acceptable. But there is an ethics of content, or rather a moral content in ethics: there are virtues that, recalling Aristotle's *Nichomachean Ethics*, are given to us so that we can fulfill ourselves on earth and achieve happiness. A dialogue is therefore possible with Marxism, which attempts to improve the physical conditions of life and to improve man's social reality with a concern that is moral in nature, as Aranguren tried to prove in *El marxismo como moral* (1968). The very proposition "It is just to carry out the establishment of socialism" is a moral statement in agreement with the most orthodox analytical philosophy. The form of life that technological societies attempt to create is also based on a moral decision, even though it may be only a morality of well-being. Aranguren explained these points convincingly in *Moralidades de hoy y de mañana* (1973; Moralities of Today and Tomorrow) and *Human Communication* (1967). Finally, since poets and novelists are part of this natural ethical preoccupation of man, literature—especially Spanish literature—commands Aranguren's attention in two freshly conceived books: *Crítica y meditación* (1957) and *Estudios literarios* (1976). His work as a whole is an impressive attempt to establish a dialogue with modern thought, both technological and literary.

See: H. Carpintero, "La visión de un moralista: José Luis Aranguren," in *Cinco aventuras españolas* (1967), pp. 109–54.   F.F.-T.

Arbasino, Alberto (1930–), Italian novelist, theater critic, and literary journalist, was born in Voghera. He was the enfant terrible of Italian literature during the 1950s and early 1960s. His demanding style is witty, flamboyant, and intellectual. Arbasino's connection with "Gruppo 63," the most important avant-garde movement in Italy since futurism (*see* ITALIAN LITERATURE), is apparent in *L'anonimo lombardo* (1959; The Anonymous Lombard) and *Parigi o cara* (1961; Paris, My Dear). His novel *Super Eliogabalo* (1969) was an immediate best-seller, despite its linguistic pyrotechnics and its kaleidoscopic compression of historical events. In this work, Arbasino draws upon Albert CAMUS's *Caligula* and Antonin ARTAUD's *Héliogabale* to create a wide-ranging exploration of self-destructive power and of anarchic rebellion as a response to tyranny. *Fratelli d'Italia* (1969; enlarged ed., 1976; Brothers of Italy), another novel, combines the style of a mature travel diary with the *roman-vérité* (documentary novel) in order to tell the story of a group of eccentric young travelers and their frenetic encounters with chic women and aristocratic society.

Arbasino's criticism is, like his fiction, self-consciously sophisticated and intellectual. *Grazie per le magnifiche rose* (1965; Thank You for the Magnificent Roses), which has been criticized as a summa of name-dropping, is a work of over 500 pages of concentrated invective against a national theater that can no longer excite or arouse. Another volume of theater criticism, *La maleducazione teatrale* (1966; Bad Theatrical Upbringing), is a self-confident comparison of Italian drama with English and American productions, laced throughout with acerbic bits of salon gossip. The 60 essays and reviews collected in *Sessanta posizioni* (1971; 60 Positions) display the sustained irony typical of Arbasino's literary journalism. He is more relaxed and less polemical in the brief, witty novel *La bella di Lodi* (1972; The Beautiful Girl from Lodi), a series of pungent vignettes of contemporary life. Other works by Arbasino are *Il principe costante* (1972; The Constant Prince), based on a play by Calderón, and *Amate sponde* (1974; Beloved Shores), a musical written with M. Monicelli. The volume of essays entitled *Fantasmi italiani* (1977; Italian Ghosts) contains a fierce attack on contemporary Italian culture and the language of engagé discussion.

See: G. Bàrberi-Squarotti, in *Poesia e narrativa nel secondo Novecento* (1971); G. Pullini, in *Il romanzo italiano del dopoguerra* (1972).   R.Q.-W.

Arbaud, Joseph d' (1871–1950), Provençal poet and novelist, was born at Meyrargues in Provence. His mother, herself the daughter of a poet, had written a book of Provençal verse long before marrying Count d'Arbaud. She had joined the "Félibrige" (*see* PROVENÇAL LITERATURE) and acquired a good reputation under the pen name La Felibresso dóu Cauloun. Thus d'Arbaud was raised in a milieu where poetry and love for the home speech were long-standing traditions. Furthermore, he was encouraged by Frédéric MISTRAL, who considered him as being far above the other poets of the younger generation. Time has not belied this judgment.

After finishing a law course at the University of Aix-en-Provence, d'Arbaud remained for some time in the old capital enjoying society life. He then decided to leave it for the remote and solitary Camargue, one of the rare places where the language and traditions were still unimpaired. For several years he lived the life of a *gardian* or cowboy. To this long and direct contact with primitive nature and rustic people he owed the best part of his work. In Aix, where he had to return because of his health, he became an active champion of Provençal regionalism. He contributed articles to both French and

Provençal reviews and devoted much of his time to *Le Feu, organe du régionalisme méditerranéen*, of which he was editor and coeditor at various periods between 1917 and 1937.

D'Arbaud produced five books in the vernacular with accompanying French translations. *Lou Lausié d'Arle* (1913; The Laurel of Arles) is a volume of verse replete with fine poetry, remarkable for its power of suggestion, clothed in admirable form, written in a refined and at the same time rich, racy, and colorful language. The Laurel of Arles, the Provençal tree that must ever root deeper in order to grow higher, is symbolic of the poet's own conception of life. Among his poems published only in periodicals or in the form of short pamphlets are a few that must be considered among his best: *La Coumbo* (The Dell), *Li Cant palustre* (1919; Songs of the Marshes), *Li Rampau d'aram* (1920; The Brazen Boughs), and *La Visioun de l'Uba* (1921; Vision of the North). D'Arbaud's philosophy is further developed in *La Bestio dóu Vacarès* (1924; The Beast of the Vaccarès), the story of a *gardian* with his horse, and also that of the "beast," a fantastic being, half human, half animal, a voice of the past, the qualified interpreter of Provençal traditions. This work transcends the limits of regional literature. The next two books, *La Caraco* (1926; The Gypsy) and *La Souvagino* (1929; Wild Animals), are collections of short stories likewise carrying a philosophical and social meaning.

D'Arbaud confined himself to the expression of his deepest feelings, and this with the utmost precision, constraint, and sobriety. The classical and somewhat aristocratic quality of his work makes it more appealing to the elite than to the common folk of Provence who speak the language. It is not characterized by the joyous spirit and optimism of the other Félibres, and there is no Rabelaisian laughter—hardly a smile—in his stories. The "most worthy successor of Mistral" is undoubtedly a genuine Provençal and one who has drawn most of his inspiration from the soil of Provence, but he belongs to the serious, reserved and meditative type that he has sketched in *La Provence, types et coutumes* (1939; Provence: Types and Customs). It is to this book, the only one he wrote in French, that d'Arbaud owed the crowning of his complete works by the French Academy (1939). His last novel, *L'Antifo* (1969; On the Loose), published posthumously, did not add to his reputation, already confirmed as one of the greatest enjoyed by a modern Provençal poet. The centenary of his birth was splendidly commemorated in 1974.

See: C. P. Julian and P. Fontan, *Anthologie du Félibrige provençal, 1850 à nos jours* (1924); E. Chauffard, "Un grand poète provençal: Joseph d'Arbaud," *RdF*, année 10 (1930): 717–38; B. Durand, *Joseph d'Arbaud* (1974).   A.V.R.

Arbó, Sebastià Juan (1902–) Catalan novelist and biographer, was born at Sant Carles de la Ràpita in Tarragona. He moved to Amposta in 1910 at the age of eight and in 1927 to Barcelona, where he has resided ever since. His talents first came to light with *L'inútil combat* (1931; Futile Combat) and became even more apparent in *Terres de l'Edre* (1932). The Castilian version of this novel received the Fastenrath Prize of the Royal Spanish Academy of the Language. Other early works are *Notes d'un estudiant que va morir boig* (1933; Notes of a Student Who Died Mad), *Camins de nit* (1935; Paths of the Nights), and *Tino Costa* (1946), all of which reflect his love for the land where he was born. In Castilian he has written *Sobre las piedras grises* (On Gray Stones), awarded the Nadal Prize in 1948; *María Molinari* (1951); *Nocturno de Alarmas* (1957; A Nocturn of Alarms);

Martín de Caretas, a modern picaresque; and *Entre la tierra y el mar* (Between Land and Sea), awarded the Vicente Blasco Ibáñez Prize in 1966. Among his other books in Catalan are *L'Hora negra* (1961; The Dark Hour) and *L'espera* (1967; The Wait). As a biographer, Arbó's most outstanding works are the widely translated *Cervantes* (1946), *Verdaguer, el poeta, el sacerdote i el mon* (1952; Verdaguer: the Poet, the Priest, and the World), *Oscar Wilde* (1960), and *Don Pío Baroja y su Tiempo* (1963; Pío Baroja and His Period), for which he received the National Prize for Literature. His other works include *Los hombres de la tierra y el mar* (1962; Men of the Land and the Sea), *Narraciones del Delta* (1965; Tales from the Delta), and *Hechos y figuras* (1968; Facts and Figures). Arbó's rural world is one of the most solid and comprehensive of those created by Catalan novelists.

See: S. Beser, Prologue to S. J. Arbó, *Obra catalana completa I—Novel·les de l'Ebre* (1966).   J.F.C.

Arbuzov, Aleksey Nikolayevich (1908–), Russian playwright, born in Moscow, is at his best when portraying youth. His plays are lyrical and psychological, and they have sometimes placed him in conflict with the Soviet critics because of their muted ideology, experimental form, and lack of negative characters. Although his characters are Russian, their problems are universal, hence Arbuzov's popularity abroad. *Tanya* (1939), *Irkutskaya istoriya* (1959; Eng. tr., *It Happened in Irkutsk*, 1962), and *Moy bedny Marat* (1965; Eng. tr., *The Promise*, 1967), Arbuzov's best works, all deal in very different ways—dramatically, not didactically—with the spiritual development of young men and women. More recent plays, in which he focuses on middle-aged characters, are less successful. But in *Zhestokiye igry* (1978; Cruel Games), he is again back on familiar territory, portraying sympathetically a group of young Russians whose lives have been warped by indifferent, misunderstanding, or egotistic parents.

See: I. Vishnevskaya, *Aleksey Arbuzov* (1971). S.E.R.

Arghezi, Tudor, pseud. of Ion N. Theodorescu (1880–1967), Romanian poet, prose writer, and translator, was born in Bucharest. At the age of 16 he made his official poetic debut in Alexandru MACEDONSKI's journal *Ligă ortodoxă*. At various times he was a monk, a deacon, and a laborer, and for several years he lived in France and Switzerland. During the 1930s, Arghezi wrote several novels and contributed translations and essays to numerous journals. It was as a poet, however, that he was destined to leave his mark. Although his first volumes of poems, *Cuvînte potrivite* (1927; Matched Words), followed by *Flori de mucigai* (1931; Flowers of Mold), were not instant successes with the critics and public, his reputation grew. Arghezi's fame reached its zenith in the last decade of his life with *Poeme noi* (1963; New Poems), *Cadenţe* (1965; Cadences), *Ritmuri* (1966; Rhythms), and *Litanii* (1967; Litanies). He was elected to the Romanian Academy in 1956 and received the Viennese Herder Prize in 1965.

Arghezi created a poetic style that is widely imitated. Through his rich vocabulary, new syntactic and morphological patterns, and the extraordinary plasticity of his images, he provided Romania with a new literary language.

See: E. Manu, *Prolegomene Argheziene* (1968); Ş. Cioculescu, *Introducere în poezia lui Tudor Arghezi* (1971); A. Bojin, *Fenomenul Arghezian* (1976).   V.A.

Arland, Marcel (1899–), French critic, novelist, and short-story writer, was born in Varennes-sur-Amance. He is a

member of the Académie Française and has been associated during his entire career with the *Nouvelle Revue
française*, either as a member of the editorial committee
or as director. His criticism reflects the journal's combining of keen aesthetic appreciation with ethical concerns.
A disciple of André GIDE, Arland has attempted to re-
define or enlarge traditional aesthetic and moral positions
and has called for a modern form of classical art.

Secondary in his criticism, but strongly felt in his fiction, are a romantic fervor and a metaphysical disquiet,
traits that led to his clash in 1924 with Jacques RIVIÈRE
over Arland's celebrated article "Sur un nouveau mal du
siècle." Fervor and disquiet impart depth and resonance
to his fiction's basic themes: the individual's rebellion
against traditional values, and the torments that lovers
cannot help inflicting on each other. The first theme is
best embodied in his novel *L'Order* (1929; Order), which
won the Goncourt Prize; the second, by his short novel
La Vigie (1935; The Lookout).

Arland has used memories of his native village to create
his most satisfying works, partly autobiographical short
stories in which an adolescent narrator observes, in his
own intensified and distorted fashion, the dramas of
adults. These include *Les Vivants* (1934; The Living), *Les
Plus Beaux de nos jours* (1937; Our Finest Days), and *Il
faut de tout pour faire un monde* (1946; It Takes Everything to Make a World).

See: A. Eustis, *Trois Critiques de "La Nouvelle Revue
française"* (1961), pp. 23–70.   A.E.

Arniches y Barrera, Carlos (1866–1943), Spanish playwright, was born in Alicante. He grew up in the midst of
economic privation and social unrest. His family moved
to Barcelona when Carlos was 14. From there he journeyed to Madrid to resolve immediate financial hardships
by writing humorous pieces for the local press. With the
premiere in 1888 of the first in a long series of musical
satires, Arniches embarked on a steady ascent towards
material comfort and prosperity. He was a key figure in
the rise and splendor of the *género chico*, that festive
satellite of stage drama that delighted audiences for over
30 years with comical portrayals, usually in one act, of
the language, customs, and sentiments of everyday life.
By 1895, he had emerged as one of Spain's most celebrated purveyors of light musical revues. In the course of
forging a distinctly personal style, Arniches wrote over
60 percent of his 191 plays in collaboration with more
than 20 playwrights. The coauthor from whom he gained
his most constructive insights into the development of
ingenious plots and the intelligent use of dialogue was his
gifted friend Enrique García Álvarez (1873–1931). Between them they produced 25 plays in the popular tradition of one-act *comediettas*, zarzuelas, *sainetes*, revues,
pasillos, entremeses, and comic sketches, each designed
to emphasize the cares and struggles of the common people of a given locality.

Early in his career, Arniches perfected the classical
Spanish *sainete* and became its most distinguished architect. Such plays as *El santo de la Isidra* (1898; Isidra's
Saint) and *Las estrellas* (1904; The Stars) brought him
fame and fortune as Spain's "Illustrious Sainetero."
Gradually he shifted away from lighthearted short plays
featuring local color, or *costumbrismo* (*see* SPANISH LIT-
ERATURE), into the domain of a more serious concern for
the moral and social conscience of humanity. This pre-
ceptive leaning produced several protest plays dealing
with such problems as the misuse of idleness—*La
Señorita de Trevélez* (1916), political tyranny—*Los ca-
ciques* (1920; The Bosses), and provincial hypocrisy—*La
heroica villa* (1921; The Heroic Town). Yet even at this

most incisively didactic stage, Arniches never forsook his
characteristic benevolent humor.

Late in life he added a new and exciting genre to his
repertory of full-length drama: the grotesque tragedy. The
term refers to the use of caricature, exaggeration, and
heightened improbability to produce a tragicomic effect.
Some of his most engaging works belong to this mature
period, notably *Es mi hombre* (1921; That's My Man) and
La locura de Don Juan (1923; Don Juan's Madness).

The principal source of Arniches's vision of the joys
and sorrows of common people was the simple lives of
his fellow citizens of Madrid, whose speech habits and
customs provided the background, dialogue, warmth, and
color for most of his writings. In a strictly literary sense,
Arniches paved the way for such playwrights as Enrique
JARDIEL PONCELA, Miguel MIHURA, and Alfonso PASO to
realize many of their stage successes within the current
of the Spanish theater of humor.

See: V. Ramos, *Vida y teatro de Carlos Arniches*
(1966); D. R. McKay, *Carlos Arniches* (1972).

D.R.McK.

Aron, Raymond (1905–), French sociologist and journalist, was born in Paris and studied at the Ecole Normale
Supérieure. Aron has taught in various French universities and in 1957 became professor of sociology at the
Sorbonne. He began his intellectual career with a study
of the German sociologist Max Weber and of the epistemological problem of objectivity in human sciences. This
is the concern of his *Introduction à la philosophie de
l'histoire: essai sur les limites de l'objectivité historique*
(1938; Eng. tr., *Introduction to the Philosophy of History:
An Essay on the Limits of Historical Objectivity*, 1961),
in which he attacked the then dominant dogma of historical objectivity. His main interests have been in the economics and political life of modern society. He has promoted what he called an "analytical and scientific
rationalism" that rejects the principles and methodologies
of the great 19th-century philosophers of history, especially
those that are Hegelian and Marxist.

Aron's writings are numerous and diverse. They range
from scientific or philosophical essays, such as *La Sociologie allemande contemporaine* (1949–50; Eng. tr.,
German Sociology, 1957), *La Philosophie critique de
l'histoire* (1951; The Critical Philosophy of History), and
Les Etapes de la pensée sociologique (1967; The Stages
of Sociological Thought), to studies devoted to the political problems of his generation such as *L'Opium des
intellectuels* (1955; Eng. tr., *The Opium of the Intellectuals*, 1957), *L'Algérie et la république* (1958; Algeria and
the Republic), and *Paix et guerre des nations* (1962; Eng.
tr., *Peace and War: A Theory of International Relations*,
1966). Aron has also written regular editorials for daily
and weekly Parisian magazines and newspapers. He has
always remained halfway between pure scientific research
and committed or polemic writings, justifying by this attitude a radical skepticism toward the possibility of objective knowledge in the history and sociology of the
present and the past. Aron has promoted a sort of political
rationalism in action, based upon the intellectual and
moral values of the liberalism that began with the French
philosophers of the 18th century and Alexis de Tocque-
ville.   E.M.-S.

Arpino, Giovanni (1927–), Italian novelist, was born in
Pola (now Pula, Yugoslavia). He received his doctorate
from the University of Turin and has done editorial work
for various publishing houses. Arpino's novels are concerned with man's relationship to an ever-changing society. They often focus on the self-analysis and growing

self-awareness of the narrator-protagonist. *Gli anni del giudizio* (1958; Years of Decision), *Una nuvola d'ira* (1962; A Cloud of Anger), and *L'ombra delle colline* (1964; Shadow on the Hills) are set in the Langhe Hills of Piedmont in the post–World War II period. In these works, the tension between passion and ideology, between individual and society emerges without any facile solution or abstract conciliation. In *Gli anni* and *Una nuvola*, Arpino suggests that no ideology can resolve human problems and that humanity realizes itself only through love, defined as solidarity. In *L'ombra*, the protagonist returns to the Langhe Hills where he had participated in the Resistance as a youth; now an adult, he sees the hopes and dreams of that "heroic" time collapse. In this sense, Arpino is rooted in a terrain similar to that of Cesare PAVESE, and like Pavese he depicts the conflict between myth and history, between individual dreams and aspirations and the demands of political "engagement."

In other works, Arpino transcends the boundaries of the Piedmont countryside. In *Un delitto d'onore* (1961; Eng. tr., *A Crime of Honor*, 1963), he focuses on southern Italy during the 1920s, condemning its past and present prejudices and absurdities. *Un'anima persa* (1966; A Lost Soul) is the story of a rural student who, living with wealthy relatives in Turin, witnesses the subterfuges, corruption, and hypocrisies of contemporary society.

Arpino's later books, *Randagio è l'eroe* (1972; The Hero Is Straying), *Domingo il favoloso* (1975; Domingo the Fabulous), and *Il primo quarto di luna* (1976; The First Quarter of the Moon), abandon realistic subject matter for a vision of a changed, spiritualized world in which ordinary events have allegorical meanings and transmit a message of Christian love and hope. A dominant theme of his short stories, collected under the title *Racconti di vent'anni* (1974; 20 Years' Worth of Stories), is man's solitude, both as a psychological phenomenon and as the result of dehumanized contemporary society. Arpino has also written three books for children: *Rafè e Micropiede* (1959; Rafè and Tiny Foot), *Le mille e una Italia* (1960; 1001 Italys), and *L'assalto al treno* (1966; Attack on the Train). He is one of the more interesting contemporary Italian writers, combining readability with just enough linguistic and formal experimentation to be intellectually challenging.

See: G. Pullini, in *Letteratura italiana: i contemporanei*, vol. 6 (1974), pp. 1813–34; M. Romano, *Giovanni Arpino* (1974).   A.R.T.

Arrabal, Fernando (1932–), Spanish dramatist, novelist, and filmmaker, now living in France and writing in French, was born in Melilla, Spanish Morocco. His father was an army officer of Republican sympathies, while his mother came from a pious, conservative bourgeois background. Arrabal's father was arrested in July 1936; his death sentence was later commuted to 30 years in jail. Transferred to various prisons, he allegedly lost his mind and was confined to a psychiatric ward, from which he escaped in January 1942 wearing only his pajamas. The disappearance left no trace, and the family assumed that he perished of the cold. Fernando was brought up by his mother's parents, the Terans, who conspired with their daughter to obliterate all memories of the children's father. At the age of 17, Fernando discovered some letters and documents in a trunk. His private mythology still feeds on the shock of that discovery and on his unfounded suspicions that his mother denounced her husband. Images of betrayal, prison torture, and executions fill the baroque theater of the avant-garde dramatist.

The cloistered atmosphere of his mother's house, the subtly cruel treatment he received at the hands of the priests who were his teachers at the parochial school of Getafe, the mockery of classmates who found him dwarf-like with his big head and fragile body, conspired to foster in the boy that mixture of sadomasochistic sensuality and spirit of rebellion that characterizes every aspect of his work. Nor did he fare any better at the Military Academy. Arrabal preferred to spend his days at the movies, seeing the Marx Brothers and Charlie Chaplin, whose tragic humor was to leave a mark on his dramaturgy. He also read voraciously: Franz KAFKA, Fyodor DOSTOYEVSKY, Marcel PROUST, Albert CAMUS, William Faulkner, and John Steinbeck. His favorite writer, however, was Lewis Carroll. Arrabal's childlike dialogue and mixture of terror and humor are derived from *Alice in Wonderland*. The latter is also the source for Arrabal's *Jeunes Barbares d'aujourd'hui* (1975; Today's Young Barbarians).

Arrabal left the Academy for the Escuela Teórico-Práctica de la Industria del Papel in Valencia, where he passed his baccalaureate. Shortly afterward, he wrote his first play, *Los Soldados*, better known in its French version, *Pique-nique en campagne* (1952; Eng. tr., *Picnic on the Battlefield*, 1967). This Chaplinesque black-humor farce is an indictment of all wars. Arrabal's next play, *Los Hombres del triciclo, Le Tricycle* (1953; Eng. tr., *The Tricycle*, 1967), won second prize in the annual Barcelona competition. Arrabal was amazed when the critics accused him of imitating Samuel BECKETT, whose work he did not know. In the same year he saw for the first time Eugène IONESCO's *La Cantatrice chauve* (1953; Eng. tr., *The Bald Soprano*, 1958) and Beckett's *En attendant Godot* (1952; Eng. tr., *Waiting for Godot*, 1954), performed by the Dido Pequeño Theatro, and realized that these were indeed his literary ancestors. Still in pursuit of self-discovery and self-definition, a penniless Arrabal hitchhiked to Paris to see the Berliner Ensemble's production of Bertolt BRECHT's *Mother Courage*. Although he was at first attracted to it, Arrabal later rejected Brecht's alienation effect and the whole notion of didactic theater.

In the summer of 1954, Arrabal met Luce Moreau, a French student of Spanish literature. The couple waited four years to marry (1958), doing so only after the young dramatist recovered from a bout with tuberculosis. It was in the sanatorium of Bouffémont, and shortly after leaving it, that Arrabal wrote his oneiric plays: *Cérémonie pour un noir assassiné* (1956; Ceremony for a Black Victim), *Le Labyrinthe* (1956; Eng. tr., *The Labyrinth*, 1967), *Les Deux Bourreaux* (1956; Eng. tr., *The Two Executioners*, 1962), and *Fando et Lis* (1955; Eng. tr., 1962), a drama about the love of a paralyzed young woman and the young man who wheels her around in a baby carriage. The masterpiece of Arrabal's first phase is *Cimetière des voitures* (1957; Eng. tr., *The Car Cemetery*, 1962), a metaphor for the human and mechanical wreckage of our civilization, and a charade Passion play. In a dumping ground where human refuse inhabits the rusted shells of abandoned cars, three jazz musicians, vagabond clowns patterned on the Marx Brothers, reenact the last days of Christ. Emanou, the 33-year-old trumpet player who admits to occasional murders, is a fallen Christ accompanied by the mute saxophonist Fodère (Peter), a Harpo figure, and betrayed to the police by the clarinetist Tope (Judas). Victor Garcia's 1966 production of the play made theater history and established Arrabal's international reputation. This period of Arrabal's work concluded with *Guernica* (1959; Eng. tr., 1967) and *La Bicyclette du condamné* (1959; Eng. tr., *The Condemned Man's Bicycle*, 1967). The first is typical Arrabal in that it brings the epic tale of devastation down to the intimate level of personal tragedy. An aged, humble, married couple, Fanchou and Lira, live out the sorrow of separation and death. The dialogue between husband and wife is tender and child-like. Lira remains invisible, having been trapped by the raid in the tiny toilet of the farmhouse. These are the innocent victims of war.

In 1962, Arrabal met with the Mexican director Alexandro Jodorowsky and with Roland Topor and Jacques Sternberg at the Café de la Paix, where they decided to found the "Panic Group" in order to stress the unique quality of their aesthetic. The term "Pan" suggests an all-embracing, cosmic, grotesquely beautiful form, as comic and terrifying as the Greek deity. Jodorowsky had experimented with happenings, and was at that time involved in creating "panic ephemerals," scenarios open to improvisations, particularly of a violent character. Arrabal was particularly interested in returning to the ritual roots of drama and in fashioning modern baroque plays, avant-garde *auto-sacramentales*. In February of the same year, he was introduced to André BRETON, who helped him publish the first panic manifestos in the surrealist (*see* FRENCH LITERATURE) review *La Brèche*. Arrabal's first panic drama, and perhaps his most important play, is *L'Architecte et l'Empereur d'Assyrie* (1966; Eng. tr., *The Architect and the Emperor of Assyria*, 1969). The play dramatizes the confrontation on a Robinson Crusoe island of two men who represent humanity: a noble savage, the Architect; and the survivor of a plane crash, the Emperor. The latter proceeds to teach history and civilization to his Good Man Friday, whose ability to command the elements testifies to his superiority. In a series of plays within the play, the two men reenact the totality of the human experience.

In the summer of 1967, while working on his play *Le Jardin des délices* (1969; Eng. tr., *Garden of Delights*, 1974), Arrabal was again in Spain. At a Madrid department store, while helping promote the Spanish edition of his book *Fêtes et rites de la confusion* (1967; Festivals and Rituals of Confusion), he autographed a copy for an "admirer" who turned out to be a police agent provocateur. Arrabal's panic inscription was, in true surrealist tradition, scatological, blasphemous, and antinationalist. This prank landed the writer in jail, where he might still be languishing were it not for the intervention of a group of intellectuals led by Beckett, Ionesco, and Jean-Paul SARTRE. The trial took place in September, and Arrabal was acquitted, but the months in jail revived the writer's memories of his father's suffering and brought him to an even greater consciousness of political repression in Franco's Spain. Two plays bear the imprint of this experience: the final version of *Garden of Delights*, and his guerrilla play *Et ils passèrent des menottes aux fleurs* (1969; Eng. tr., *And They Put Handcuffs on the Flowers*, 1974). The latter dramatizes the dreams, fears, and tortures of Spanish prisoners. One of them dies by garrot in a kind of crucifixion that sheds a light of love and hope in the inferno of the prison.

Arrabal's recent *La Ballade du train fantôme* (1974; The Ballad of the Ghost Train) is set in Madrid, New Mexico—a ghost town. Behind the abandoned mining town, haunted by memories of past glory, we perceive the other Madrid, the decaying capital of Spain. His latest play, *Baal Babylone*, was premiered in January 1980. In addition to writing plays, Arrabal directs a theater review, commissions paintings of himself in various surrealist states, composes manifestos, and gives lectures. He has also written the screenplays for *Viva la meurte, The Tricycle, I Will Go Like a Mad Horse*, and *Guernica*.

See: A. Schifres, *Entretiens avec Arrabal* (1969); B. Gille, *Arrabal* (1970); R. L. Farmer, "Fernando Arrabal's Guerrilla Theatre," *YFS* 46 (1971); F. Raymond-Munschau, *Arrabal* (1972); D. Mendelson, "Arrabal et le jeu dramatique des échecs," *Lit* 9 (February 1973): 101–17.

R.C.L.

Artaud, Antonin (1896–1948), French dramatic theorist, theater director, and playwright, was born in Marseille. He became an actor and designer with Charles DULLIN's company at the Théâtre de l'Atelier in Paris in 1921 and later with the Pitoëff company (*see* Georges PITOËFF) at the Comédie des Champs-Elysées. After a brief flirtation with André BRETON's surrealism movement (*see* FRENCH LITERATURE), from which he picked up influences that were later to appear in his own plays, Artaud organized the Théâtre Alfred Jarry (*see* Alfred JARRY), which operated from 1927 to 1929. His only other attempt at theatrical production occurred in 1935, when he established the Théâtre de la Cruauté (theater of cruelty) and staged *Les Cenci*, which he had adapted from Percy Bysshe Shelley and Stendhal.

Artaud's interest in primitive theater led him to Mexico, where he witnessed some of the mysterious rituals of the Tarahumara Indians, and to the Aran Islands off western Ireland. During this latter trip, Artaud was overcome by paranoid delusions that had been troubling him since the age of 19, and for most of the rest of his life he was confined to mental institutions. Nevertheless, he continued to write prolifically, if intermittently, throughout his life.

Artaud's reputation rests largely on his theoretical essays, collected under the title *Le Théâtre et son double* (1938; Eng. tr., *The Theatre and Its Double*, 1958). In these writings, Artaud expanded on his basic theory that the purpose of drama, as well as of all the other arts, was to bring human beings back to a consciousness of their primal nature, by which he meant human nature before it had been corrupted and metamorphosed by arbitrarily imposed behavior patterns. The function of art was to strip away the layers of artificiality accumulated through the ages in the name of culture and to bring audiences to the realization that their personae were composed of anger, hate, longing, physical desire, and other instinctual feelings. In order to accomplish this end, Artaud devised his much misunderstood and misinterpreted theory of a "theater of cruelty." This does not mean the realistic depiction of acts that might be considered cruel in the colloquial sense, but the transmission of a sense of the cosmic, mindless—and therefore implacable—cruelty to which all men are subject. In short, Artaud attempted to evolve a system that would arouse a consciousness in the spectator of the contrast between the violence dormant within the self and the omnipotence of the forces outside it. What he actually evolved was a theater that was spontaneous, inspired only by the emotion of the moment and free of all literary preconceptions. With his new concept of theater, perhaps best exemplified in *Le jet du sang* (1925; Eng. tr., *The Spurt of Blood* in *Evergreen Review*, 1963), Artaud hoped to become the catalytic agent for an entirely new kind of drama, one that used the complex resources of the modern theater to express the age-old cry of fear and protest, the most elemental human impulse.

See: G. Charbonnier, *Essai sur Antonin Artaud* (1959); E. Sellin, *The Dramatic Concepts of Antonin Artaud* (1968); G. E. Wellwarth, *The Theatre of Protest and Paradox* (1971), pp. 15–27.

G.E.W.

Artmann, Hans Carl (1921–), Austrian poet, prose writer, and translator, was born and grew up in Breitensee, a suburb of Vienna. Drafted into the army during World War II, he held various jobs before becoming a free-lance writer in 1950. Traveling widely, he resided for the most part in Berlin and in Malmö, Sweden, and now lives in Salzburg.

At first a nature poet, Artmann soon turned to surrealist, dadaist, and lettrist traditions. In the Vienna of the early 1950s he joined a group of avant-garde poets, became instrumental in the formation of the "Wiener Gruppe" (see GERMAN LITERATURE), and assumed leadership of it until 1958. His knowledge of over 20 languages, and his extensive reading in German as well as in foreign literatures, brought new ideas to the group. Together the poets experimented with new modes of writing, such as Wortmontage and Textmontage, imitating differing styles and cultivating the Viennese dialect. Artmann's sparkling, eccentric personality encouraged debate and collective work, but the diverse interests within the group led to his eventual withdrawal.

A polyglot in language and protean in nature, Artmann has adhered to nothing for long, whether principle, style, or philosophy. Chameleon-like, he becomes surrealist or folk poet, tramp or bourgeois, dadaist or nature poet, dreamer or pop artist, clown or baroque bard, tragedian or comedian according to his interest of the moment. His models have been François Villon, Rabelais, Francisco Quevedo, Paul ELUARD, Isou, Federico GARCÍA LORCA, Pablo Neruda, Gertrude Stein, Hugo Ball, Dylan Thomas, among others. Children's rhymes, horror stories, commedia dell'arte, comics, picaresque novels, baroque and 18th-century literature, Celtic myths, pop art, fairy tales, and the poetry of several modern lyric poets have influenced his work. At home in many styles, languages, historical periods, and geographical locations, he often combines them or moves from one to another. Fascinated with languages and words, he puts them in unusual contexts, lets them "do their own choreography." In the poetry collection med ana schwoazzn dintn (1958; With Black Ink), he wrote his own phonetic transcription of the Viennese dialect, combined with surrealist elements; Grünverschlossene Botschaft (1966; Message Locked in Green) contains 90 dreams fashioned after baroque lyrics, comic strips, dadaism, and the work of Federico García Lorca; Fleiß und Industrie (1967; Diligence and Industry) portrays 30 crafts practiced in preindustrial Vienna in the style of public school textbooks of the time; Die Fahrt zur Insel Nantucket (1969; The Voyage to Nantucket Island), a collection of plays, borrows the models of Punch and Judy shows and soap opera. Die Jagd nach Dr. Unspeakable (1971; The Hunt for Dr. Unspeakable) is a novel about the poet's search for identity, oscillating between the two poles of reason and fantasy; his search winds through caverns and over high mountains, in and out of Celtic and Eskimo tales, until finally reason kills fantasy. But in his next novel, Nachrichten aus Nord und Süd (1978; News of North and South), fantasy breaks loose again to reign supreme: memories, sweeping associations, and autobiographical and literary references, inextricably interlinked, form a network of relationships that provokes in the reader verbal and stylistic combinations and associations. Artmann is also known as a translator of works from Spanish, French, English, Swedish, and other literatures.

His further works include: Von denen Husaren und anderen Seiltänzern (1959; On Those Hussars and Other Tightrope Walkers), a volume of stories; Das suchen nach dem gestrigen tag (1964; Looking for Yesterday); Verbarium (1966), poetry; Der Landgraf zu Camprodon (1966; The Count of Camprodon); Ein lilienweißer Brief aus Lincolnshire (collected poetry, 1945–1966, 1969; A Lilywhite Letter from Lincolnshire); and The Best of H. C. Artmann (1970).

See: G. Bisinger, ed., Über Hans Carl Artmann (1972).

A.P.O.

Artsybashev, Mikhail Petrovich (1878–1927), Russian novelist, short-story writer, and dramatist, was born in Kharkov province and got his start writing for provincial newspapers. He achieved real recognition, however, with the novella Smert' Lande (1904; Eng. tr., Ivan Lande, 1916). This book established a kind of hero that figured prominently in his later work: the "utterly sincere man," whose unshakable convictions collide with conventional morality. The most notorious example of the "utterly sincere man" is Sanin, in the novel of the same name (1907; Eng. tr., Sanine, 1917), whose mockery of current intellectual fads and celebration of sexual gratification created a scandal that landed the author in court for having written "pornography." Another such figure, Naumov, in U posledney cherty (1910–12; Eng. tr., The Breaking Point, 1915) advocates self-destruction as the worthiest defiance of the shameful inevitability of death. In general, Artsybashev saw sex and death as the only realities, hereby reflecting the disillusionment with civilization and the fascination with primitivism that were so widespread in his time. He also wrote about another kind of hero who cannot cope with these realities, and instead reacts with resigned despair or with a mindless violence, which for a time won the author a "radical" reputation. Artsybashev also wrote a number of plays. After the Bolshevik Revolution (1917) he emigrated to Warsaw. For today's reader, his work is mainly of topical interest. R.A.M.

Asch, Sholem (1880–1957), Yiddish novelist and dramatist, was born in Kutno, Poland. He inherited from his mother a delicate romanticism, and from his father self-confidence and a healthy aggressiveness. His schooling consisted of little more than a limited training in the Hebrew language and its literature, both ancient and modern. At the age of 19, he went to Warsaw, taking with him sketches he had written about small-town life. A year later, these sketches appeared in the Yiddish press. In Warsaw, Asch came under the influence of Yitzkhok Leibush PERETZ. His first novel, Dos Shtetl (1905; The Shtetl), presents in lyric prose a semi-idyllic, quietly humorous picture of Jewish small towns. Asch's romantic realism was a departure from the pure naturalism of MENDELE MOCHER SFORIM, and his idealization of the shtetl contrasted sharply with the sober, pointed satire practiced by all his predecessors except SHOLOM ALEICHEM. His lyric dramas Moshiakhs Tsaytn (1906; The Days of the Messiah) and Der Got fun Nekome (1907; Eng. tr., The God of Vengeance, 1918) were performed not only in the Yiddish theaters of Europe and the United States, but also on the Russian and Polish stages and in Max Reinhardt's Deutsches Theater in Berlin.

Asch's novels, too, were international successes and were translated into many languages. Their fascination stemmed from the freshness of his approach, his intimate humor, and the restrained but warm lyricism with which he depicted the mundane experiences of ordinary people. Asch's early novels are drawn on an epic scale and span the social ladder, from thieves, brothel inmates, and other underworld characters to revolutionary leaders, martyrs, and saints. His central figures are generally striving to free themselves from inner conflicts. Almost all of them suffer from a sense of guilt and seek security in faith in a God who will purify them, granting them vigor, wholeness, and inner peace. Asch's most impressive novels are his trilogy, *Farn Mabl* (1927–32; Eng. tr., *Three Cities,* 1933), in which the romantic attitudes of the hero are accentuated by the novels' realistically portrayed social backdrop; *Der Tilim Yid* (1934; Eng. tr., *Salvation,* 1934), a summing up of the basic themes to be found in his earlier novels and a most lucid expression of his innermost beliefs; *Der Man fun Notseres* (1939; Eng. tr., *The Nazarene,* 1939), which describes the historical Jewish background of the founder of Christianity; and *The Apostle* (Eng. tr., 1943, not published in the original Yiddish), based on the life of Saint Paul. The author's colorful and meticulous descriptions of the beginning of the Christian era attempt to bridge the tragic barrier between Judaism and Christianity.

In 1954, Asch, who had lived in the United States for many years and who had become a U. S. citizen, settled in Bat Yam, Israel, where he wrote his last novel, *Der Novi* (1955; Eng. tr., *The Prophet,* 1955), about Deutero-Isaiah, the author of the second part of the Book of Isaiah. His home in Israel is now the Sholem Asch Museum.

See: S. Niger, *Sholem Asch* (1950); E. H. Jeshurin, *Sholem Asch Bibliographie* (1958).　　　　　S.Ni.

Aseyev, Nikolay Nikolayevich (1889–1963), Russian poet, born in Kursk province to middle-class parents, launched his literary career in 1911 while a student in Moscow. In his first collection, *Nochnaya fleyta* (1914; Nocturnal Flute), symbolist influence prevails. In 1914, after a brief association with the "Tsentrifuga" group, Aseyev embraced the poetics of cubo-futurism (*see* RUSSIAN LITERATURE). He soon retreated from the extreme formalism advocated in the preface to *Letorey* (1915), but futurist traits such as "metaphysical" and "realized" metaphors, etymologism, and even verbal cubism remained prominent in his poetry, as did a preference for accentual verse, assonance-consonance rhyme, and strident consonantal sound patterns.

After some years in the Far East (1916–21), Aseyev returned to Moscow and in 1922 joined the periodical *Lef,* whose utilitarian aesthetics he enthusiastically accepted, as evidenced in *Stalnoy solovey* (1922; The Steel Nightingale). From then on, much of his work was versified journalism. Some of his poems became popular songs: "Marsh Budyonnogo" (The Budyonny March), "Vintovochka" (My Rifle), "Pyatikontsovaya" (Five-Pointed Star). The "revolutionary romanticism" of his verse epics, such as *Budyonny* (1923), *Dvadtsat shest* (1925; Twenty-Six), and *Semyon Proskakov* (1928), also appealed to unsophisticated readers.

Aseyev's later years were marked by his devotion to the memory of Vladimir MAYAKOVSKY, and his lengthy poetic biography of his friend, *Mayakovsky nachinayetsya* (1937–50; Incipit Mayakovsky), is done in Mayakovsky's manner and contains many echoes of his poetry. Toward the end of his life Aseyev wrote some unpretentious *Gelegenheitsdichtung* (occasional poetry) in which he all but abandoned his Mayakovskian mannerisms.

See: V. Markov, *Russian Futurism* (1968); V. Milkov, *Nikolay Aseyev: literaturny portret* (1973).　　　V.T.

Asnyk, Adam (1838–1897), Polish poet and playwright, was born in Kalisz and died in Cracow. He studied at the Medical Academy in Warsaw, and as a student he was imprisoned in the Warsaw Citadel in 1860 for his involvement in a patriotic clandestine organization. Later he participated in the 1863 uprising and even served as a member of the National Council. After the collapse of the uprising, Asnyk left the country and went first to Italy and then to Germany. In Heidelberg he received his doctoral degree in philosophy. Because he was not allowed

to return to his native region in Poland, which was under Russian occupation, he settled in Lvov and later in Cracow, which were under Austrian rule. There he was involved in much social and political action. In 1882–94 he was coeditor of the newspaper *Nowa Reforma.*

Asnyk wrote several plays—*Przyjaciele Hioba* (1879; Friends of Job), *Cola Rienzi* (1873), *Kiejstut* (1878)—as well as novels. He is best known, however, for his lyrics. Asnyk belonged to the generation who watched the decline of their hopes with the failure of the 1863 uprising, and he built his poetic personality upon a certain kind of stoicism. Asnyk continued the poetic tradition of romanticism. His poetry was often modeled after Słowacki but he preferred smaller forms. Yet Asnyk's concern with intellectual problems, scientific evolutionism, and moderation in expression of feelings connect him with positivism, and he is considered a leading poet of this period. Asnyk's love lyrics, some of them written in an ironical tone, are pleasant and graceful. Asnyk also wrote satirical and political poems, philosophical lyrics, and a cycle of sonnets, "Nad głębiami" ("Over the Depths"), in which he meditates on the unity of nature and human fate and the inevitability of change. He was also one of the first poets to express the beauty of the Tatra Mountains. Asnyk published several volumes of poetry under the title *Poezje* (1869, 1872, 1880, 1894; Poems). Some of his lyrics were set to music by such composers as Mieczysław Karłowicz, Władysław Żeleński, and Ignacy Paderewski.

See: J. Krzyżanowski, "Adam Asnyk poeta czasów niepoetyckich," in *W kręgu wielkich realistów* (1962), pp. 247–62; M. Szypowska, *Asnyk znany i nieznany* (1971).　　　　　　　　　　　　　　　A.Z.

Aspenström, Werner (1918–), Swedish poet, dramatist, and essayist, reveals a great deal about his background in a single sentence in his autobiography, *Bäcken* (1958; The Brook): "The forest village in Dalecarlia where I was born and within the confines of which I stayed during my first eighteen years was five miles from the center of the parish, a town with a couple of tall chimneys but an even higher church spire." Aspenström traveled a long and arduous route to the university, having first worked in various menial capacities, including that of a gravedigger, before he received his B.A. at the age of 26, by which time he had already published *Förberedelse* (1943; Preparation), a collection of poetry exhibiting youthful idealism. In *Skriket och tystnaden* (1946; The Scream and the Silence), his style had been liberated from traditionalism, owing partly to the influence of Karl VENNBERG. His three collections of poetry—*Snölegend* (1949; Snow Legend), which was Aspenström's breakthrough; *Litania* (1952; Litany); and *Hundarna* (1954; The Dogs)— are, according to his introduction to *Dikter 1946–54* (1955; Selected Poems), regarded by him as a unity. Often in miniature poems he presents objects or animals in an anthropomorphized form, so that we recognize the human in them.

Aspenström's dependence on myth and popular tales (usually reflecting highly topical and controversial problems) became particularly pronounced in *Dikter under träden* (1956; Poems beneath the Trees), *Om dagen om natten* (1961; By Day by Night), *Trappan* (1964; The Staircase), *66 Dikter* (1964; 66 Poems), *Inre* (1969; Inward), *Under tiden* (1972; Meanwhile, or Miracle Time), *Jordvagga-Himmelstak* (1973; Earth Cradle–Celestial Ceiling), with the poet's valuable commentaries, pp. 62–87, and *Ordbok* (1976; Dictionary). His *Dikter* (Selected Poems) appeared in 1977 and 1978. Aspenström favors "timeless" poetry, which at best is universal and at worst is so personal that it may be banal, exclusive, or even somewhat morbid. But he has also written engagé works. Since the late 1940s he has most effectively stressed one message: Stop the bomb! Immediately after World War II he was one of the leading proponents and ideologists of Sweden's nonalignment policy, arguing that being located between superpowers, Sweden might serve better ends (such as Finland's security) by staying neutral. On conservation, Aspenström has also taken a strong stand. In one passage he expresses his philosophy, his commitment to a reverence for life: "Each treetop constitutes a densely populated micro-society of spiders, ladybugs, and beetles, and cutting down the tree means a catastrophe comparable to the destruction of an average-sized Swedish city. Many of these insects were born there, they have adapted themselves and made arrangements for themselves for generations, but deprived of the treetop they die!"

Most of Aspenström's 40 plays are short curtain-raisers. Some are poetic whereas others are hard to define; still others are comedies. In addition to these, he has produced the full-length plays *Mattan* (perf. 1964; The Carpet); *Spindlarna* (perf. 1966; The Spiders), about the first astronaut landing on the moon; *Job* (perf. 1969), dealing with the prophet in a modern setting; and *Jag måste till Berlin* (perf. 1968; I Must Go to Berlin), referring to a line by Sergey Yesenin—a good play about Isadora Duncan, although its ending is weak and insufficiently dramatic. In an attempt to shift the time of this last drama from the present to the past, Aspenström cuts off the action just before the curtain falls. He appears at the end as a narrator, the storyteller, who calmly informs the audience of what has happened. *Det eviga* (1959; Eng. tr., "The Apes Shall Inherit the Earth," in *TDR* 6, no. 2, 1961: 92–97) alludes to Bishop Tegnér's famous poem "The Eternal" and is close to the absurd theater of Samuel BECKETT and Eugène IONESCO. "The Apes Shall Inherit the Earth" is by far Aspenström's most theatrical play. In 1976, Aspenström's play *Väntarna* (Those Who Wait), a child-adult play, enjoyed great success at the Stockholm City Theater. Selections of his dramatic works appeared in *Teater I* (1959); *II* (1963); *III* (1966); and *IV* (1978).

Aspenström's first public statements were anticlerical, but generally, as Carl Fehrman has pointed out, Aspenström oscillates between trust and distrust. It can be argued that everything Aspenström wrote contains poetry. If his defense of poetry takes the form of a life mysticism, perhaps with some Oriental and Jungian overtones, it is clearly related to his belief that "reality" consists above all of contradictions and conflicts; one of his books of essays is *Motsägelser* (1961, 1968; Contradictions), "the title of which covers the contents," the author maintains. Accordingly, he perceives the "I" as a kind of magnetic field, that is, something presupposing two poles. "He who seeks a meaning finds two meanings," he says in one poem. In "Bondestudentens sista Brev" (1961; "The Last Letter of the Peasant Student," tr. by W. H. Auden), these lines are to be found indicating his view of life as an arena of conflicting forces: "Contradictions, muffled tumult/better I did not find the world./ Ganglia, germ-cells, outgrowths,/each striving in its own direction." Werner Aspenström, who has been called a "modern Thoreau," has admitted that his copy of Walden (in Swedish translation) is heavily annotated. A typical poem by Aspenström is "The Clenched Fist Does Not Win All Bouts":

How muscular the little fly feels
in the hand closed around it.
How it buzzes and butts
like a motor lawn-mower.

How its wings get bigger and bigger
till they force the hand to open
and make an air strip
and the fly, though slightly damaged,
takes off.

Tr. by W. H. Auden and Leif Sjöberg

Aspenström's collections of essays *Bäcken* (The Brook), a charming book of childhood memories and fantasies from his native Dalecarlia, has appeared in three different editions: 1958, 1965, and 1973. Among other collections of his essays are *Sommar* (1968; Summer), *Skäl* (1970; Reasons), and *Blåvalen* (1975; The Blue Whale), and *Vissa sidor och ovissa* (1979), a selection of essays.

See: G. Printz-Påhlson, *Solen i spegeln* (1958), pp. 152–84; E. Törnqvist, "Poet in the Space Age: A Theme in Aspenström's Plays," *SS* 39, no. 1 (1967): 1–15; L. Sjöberg, "Werner Aspenström: A Writer for All Seasons," *ASR* (December 1969): 385–92; R. Goodman, *Drama on Stage* (1971), pp. 575–600.   L.S.

Aub, Max (1903–72), Spanish novelist, playwright, and critic, was born in Paris of a German father and a French mother and moved to Spain with his family at the age of 11. This foreign-born youth was later to become one of the most prolific contemporary writers in the Spanish language. The Spanish Civil War of 1936–39 had a tremendous influence on both his life and his work. He wrote several short novels, in reality poetic narratives, before 1936: *Geografía* (1921), *Fábula verde* (1932; Green Fable), and *Luis Alvarez Petreña* (1934), an epistolary novel of individual frustration ending in suicide. A collection of unperformed plays entitled *Teatro incompleto* (1931) and some poems were a clear indication of Aub's promise.

The Civil War caused him to go into exile, first in France, then in North Africa, and finally in Mexico, where he remained until his death. He returned to Spain briefly in 1968.

Aub's novels of the Civil War are a mural or gallery containing innumerable characters. Through them, Aub depicts the chaos, the struggle, and the defeat of the Republic. The years that preceded the Civil War are described in *Campo cerrado* (1943; Closed Field), which ends with the fighting in the streets of Barcelona during the first tragic days of civil strife. The battlefields and life in the cities, on both sides of the front, appear in *Campo de sangre* (1945; Bloody Field) and *Campo abierto* (1951; Open Field). The last days of the defense of Madrid are the subject of *Campo del Moro* (1963). This title is in reality a play on words, since Moors fought in Francisco Franco's army, and Campo del Moro (The Moor's Field) is also the name of a park in Madrid. The bitter first weeks of exile in a French refugee camp are the subject of *Campo francés* (1965; French Field) and the tragedy of the last hours of Republican leaders, soldiers, and civilians waiting in the harbor of Alicante for ships that never came is narrated in *Campo de los Almendros* (1968; Field of Almond Trees). Although the cycle was completed, the same themes return again and again in Aub's short stories, collected in *No son cuentos (cuentos)* (1944; These Are Not Stories [Stories]), *Historias de mala muerte* (1965; Stories of Mean Deaths), and *Ultimos cuentos de la guerra de España* (1969; Last Stories of the Spanish War).

His other novels either depict the lives of Spanish Republicans in exile, sometimes with a certain humor, as in *La verdadera historia de la muerte de Francisco Franco y otros cuentos* (1960; The True Story of the Death of Francisco Franco and Other Tales), or else they recreate the author's past. *Las buenas intenciones* (1954; Good

Intentions) and *La calle de Valverde* (1961; Valverde Street) are exercises in nostalgia, loving recollections of life in Spain before the Civil War, when the author was young and unsuspecting of what destiny had in store for him and for many other Spaniards of his generation.

Although he never became a successful playwright, Aub also wrote for the theater. His first play dates from 1928, and in 1968 his *Teatro completo* was published in Mexico. As a critic he studied contemporary Spanish literature in *Discurso de la novela española contemporánea* (1945) and *La poesía española contemporánea* (1954). Aub was a master of his adopted language, and he rejoiced in the subtleties, richness, and ambiguities of Spanish. His complex prose makes him a difficult writer to translate, although there are some French, German, and Dutch translations of his novels.

See: I. Soldevila Durante, *La obra narrativa de Max Aub* (1973).   L.S.P. de L.

Aubanel, Théodore (1829–86), Provençal poet, was born in Avignon. He belonged to a family of printers. He began writing poetry in French, which was the language spoken in his home. His shift to Provençal, not an imperative urge, was due principally to the influence of Joseph ROU-MANILLE. Having realized that the local speech was a rich, poetical language, closer than French to Provençal reality, he joined the group of young poets who were to be the founders of the "Félibrige" (*see* PROVENÇAL LITERATURE).

Aubanel's literary production was relatively small. He is known above all as the author of *La Miougrano entre-duberto* (1860; The Split Pomegranate) and of *Li Fiho d'Avignoun* (1885; The Young Ladies of Avignon), two collections of lyrics, published with accompanying French translation. The former appeared at a very opportune moment, one year after the epoch-making publication of *Mirèio,* by Frédéric MISTRAL. It added much to the fast-growing prestige of the Félibrige school. It brought a new element to Provençal lyricism, that of pure passion. Here was found a bold, direct, and realistic expression of intense human suffering caused by frustrated love, the anguish experienced by the author himself after his sweetheart had entered a convent to become a nun. Critics acclaimed Aubanel as having won a place between Mistral and Roumanille.

Li Fiho d'Avignoun has been interpreted as a confession of the author's mature age. Here again poetry has its source in the violent conflict between flesh and spirit, Christian principles winning over passion and desire. Although a zealous Catholic and a highly honorable husband and family head, the author had to suffer persecution from the pens of unenlightened censors who accused him of being an impious renegade. It is generally believed that the ordeals he had to undergo in his various attempts to publish the book actually shortened his life. A pure hymn to beauty, *Li Fiho d'Avignoun* contains very fine verse on almost every page. A few of its poems, such as "Lou Bal," "La Venus d'Avignoun," and, above all, "La Venus d'Arle," are little masterpieces by themselves, any one of which would have been sufficient to bring his name to posterity. Aubanel wrote three five-act plays in verse. He published one, *Lou Pan dou pecat* (1882; The Bread of Sin), which was produced in the original text and in a French version by Paul Arène. It is a powerful, violent, grim drama of rustic love. A posthumous collection of poems, *Lou Reire soulèu* (1899; From behind the Sun), does not give anything essentially new about the author or his art. More important from the standpoint of biography is the correspondence with one of his feminine inspirers, *Lettres à Mignon* (1899).

Aubanel was a great lyric poet, second in Provençal literature only to Mistral. His work has not reached a very large public but has been appreciated by those for whom it was written, the select few. His plea, "Luse tout ço qu'es bèu, tout ço qu'es laid s'escounde" (Let beauty shine and ugliness hide), is that of a great artist whose main object has always been to find love and beauty, whether moral or physical, Christian or pagan.

See: L. Legré, *Théodore Aubanel, par un témoin de sa vie* (1894); N. Welter, *Théodore Aubanel, un chantre provençal de la beauté* (1902); J. Vincent, *Théodore Aubanel, la vie et l'homme* (1924); Léo Larguier, *Théodore Aubanel* (1946); C. Liprandi, *Théodore Aubanel, œuvres choisies* (1952).   A.V.R.

Audiberti, Jacques (1899–1965), French poet, novelist, and playwright, was born in Antibes. He made his mark as a poet in the late 1930s after moving to Paris, where he joined the currently fashionable literary circles and collaborated on the journal *Petit Parisien*. During his lifetime, Audiberti published 15 novels, the first of them being *Abraxas* (1938), *Septième* (1939; Seventh), and *Urujac* (1941). It is, however, as a dramatist that he will be remembered most clearly.

Audiberti was profoundly impressed by the theories of Antonin ARTAUD, on whom he published an essay in 1948, the year Audiberti's first volume of plays appeared. From Artaud, Audiberti derived two principal themes: the conflict between paganism and Christianity, and the presence of a primordial spirit of evil in human affairs. In such plays as *Quoat-Quoat* (1946) and *Opera parlé* (1956; Spoken Opera), Audiberti wrote of the power latent in the primeval myths that formed the human character and of their superiority to what he considered the artificially superimposed pseudomyths by which we now live. *Le Mal court* (1947; The Evil Runs) and *La Fête noire* (1948; The Black Feast) illustrate Audiberti's absorption with the problem of evil. He felt that the more men drift away from their atavistic origins, the more they become overpowered by evil, until, in the more complex types of society, they cease to be human at all. Audiberti's plays tend to be characterized by an overemphasis on philosophical speculation at the expense of stagecraft and by a richly symbolic poetic language peppered with surrealistic effects.

See: M. Giroud, *Jacques Audiberti* (1967); G. E. Wellwarth, *The Theatre of Protest and Paradox* (1971), pp. 85–96.   G.E.W.

Aukrust, Olav (1883–1929), Norwegian poet, was born in the mountain valley of Gudbrandsdal, the center of the ancestral folk culture of Norway. The influences of his home, surroundings, and extensive studies soon imbued him with a sense of the country's national heritage; its literary traditions, going back to ballads and the Eddas; its *nynorsk* language (*see* NORWEGIAN LITERATURE); its folk art and culture; and the whole of popular Norwegian philosophy. Under the influence of the folk high school movement, Aukrust espoused a religious nationalism in which mystic and realistic elements were curiously mingled, as indeed they were in his own mind. His literary work is an attempt to show in poetic images the spiritual growth and destiny of the Norwegian people within an eternal framework.

In two large volumes of loosely connected lyrical poems, *Himmelvarden* (1916; The Mountain Cairn) and *Solrenning* (1930; Sunrise), Aukrust used his own struggle against the primitive powers of darkness and his redemption through Christianity to symbolize the development of the Norwegian nation. In a remarkable way, the psychological interpretation of Norway and her people is made to emanate from the landscape, pictured with overwhelming power of visualization. These two collections, containing striking pictures of folk life as well as some of the greatest love lyrics in Norwegian literature, show a profundity of thought and feeling, orchestral mastery of the language, and an amazing rhythmical inventiveness. Aukrust's other books, *Hamar i hellom* (1926; Spirit from the Mountains) and the unfinished *Norske terningar* (1931; Norwegian Dice), are fragments of a large cycle that was intended in a similar way to depict the nation's spiritual development from the local beginnings of culture through the development of national self-assertion into a realm of universal ideas. These two works, again showing Aukrust's poetic power and astounding knowledge of all manifestations of Norwegian character and life, move freely from sublime spirituality to broad realism and baroque humor.

In spite of its fragmentary character, Aukrust's poetic work is one of the most original interpretations of the spiritual history of his nation and one of the strongest expressions of poetic genius in modern Norwegian literature.

See: I. Krokann, *Olav Aukrust* (1933); L. Mæhle, *Vegen til varden* (1968).   S.Sk.

Austrian literature: *see* GERMAN LITERATURE.

Averchenko, Arkady Timofeyevich (1881–1925), Russian humorist, was born in Sevastopol, and at 15 began to work as an office clerk in Kharkov and to write humorous stories. He went to Petersburg in 1908 and joined the staff of *Strekoza*, later reorganized as *Satirikon*. This humorous journal established Averchenko's career. From 1908 to 1913, under his editorship, it was the most popular satirical journal in Russia. The *Satirikon* period marked the zenith of Averchenko's career. His short stories and one-act plays were immensely popular. After the Russian Revolution (1917), Averchenko fled to Constantinople, finally settling in Prague.

Based on coarse farcical situations and verbal quips, Averchenko's immensely popular stories depict the banality of middle-class life and often involve grotesque figures. *Vesyolye ustritsy* (1910; The Gay Oysters) and *Otdykh na krapive* (1922; Resting on a Nettle) are two well-known collections.

See: D. A. Levitsky, *Arkady Averchenko: zhiznenny put* (Washington, 1973).   E.B.N.

Ayala, Francisco (1906–), Spanish novelist, critic, and sociologist, was born in Granada. A professor of political science at the University of Madrid, he cultivated his academic and literary interests both in Spain and in several American countries after he went into exile in 1939, at the end of the Spanish Civil War. He returned to Spain in the 1960s. His first novels, *El boxeador y un ángel* (1929; The Boxer and an Angel) and *Cazador en el alba* (1930; Hunter at Dawn), followed the literary fashion of the time. Both are written in a highly polished prose style in which metaphor is paramount. European political events of the 1930s, particularly in Spain, had a pronounced influence on his writings. In the 1940s, Ayala denounced his former approach to fiction and began to deal instead with contemporary events, although in an indirect way. *La cabeza del cordero* (1949; The Lamb's Head) is a collection of short stories revolving around the Spanish Civil War. The discord in the hearts of many Spaniards even before the Civil War is the subject of "El mensaje" (The Message), the first story of this collection. In the second story, "El Tajo" (a play on words, as *Tajo*

means both the Tagus River, which runs through central Spain, and "cut" or "trench"), the difficulty of overcoming the divisive consequences of the Civil War is expressed in a stark plot of death, fear, and mistrust. Other stories point out the rootlessness of the lives of Republican exiles who, like Ayala, had to abandon their native land in 1939. *Los usurpadores* (1949; The Usurpers) is still another collection of short stories based on historical events and legends of Spain's past, reaching as far back as the Middle Ages. Whoever has power over other human beings, says Ayala, is a usurper. *Historia de macacos* (1955; Story About Monkeys) is a humorous presentation in six short stories of human weaknesses and foibles.

Muertes de perro (1958; Eng. tr., *Death as a Way of Life*, 1964) and its sequel, *El fondo del vaso* (1962; The Dregs), two novels set in an imaginary but all too believable small Latin American republic, are stories of corruption and what happens when absolute power falls into the hands of a single ruler.

Like many other Spanish Republican exiles, Ayala was able to overcome the brutal separation from his native country and people, finding in Latin America new sources of inspiration for his fiction. These two novels were not published in Spain until 1968 and 1970, respectively, when official censorship had relaxed. *El as de bastos* (1963; The Ace of Clubs) and *El rapto* (1965; The Elopement) are collections of short stories. In the latter, Ayala dealt for the first time with contemporary Spanish society as he found it after his return from exile. Other short stories followed in *El jardín de las delicias* (1971; The Garden of Delights).

His numerous books of literary theory and criticism include an investigation of the role of the writer in modern society, in *El escritor en la sociedad de masas* (1956; The Writer in Mass Society); essays on Cervantes and other classical Spanish writers, in *Experiencia e invención* (1960); and studies in baroque literature, in *Realidad y ensueño* (1963; Dream and Reality).

Ayala is a master of prose style and subtle humor. He understands human nature and smiles with tolerance at human weakness.

See: K. Ellis, *El arte narrativo de Francisco Ayala* (1964); A. Amorós, *Bibliografía de Francisco Ayala* (1973).   L.S.P. de L.

Aygi, Gennady (1934–), Soviet poet of Chuvash nationality, wrote his first works in the Chuvash language but since 1960 has written his poetry in Russian. He was born in the village of Shaymurino, in the Chuvash Autonomous Republic of the USSR, and completed his education at the Gorky Literary Institute in Moscow, where he was a pupil of Mikhail Svetlov. Within the Soviet Union only his Chuvash poetry has been published, both in the original and in Russian translation; but his original Russian poetry has circulated in *samizdat* (*see* RUSSIAN LITERATURE) and has attracted considerable attention abroad, notably in Czechoslovakia and Poland. Two volumes of his Russian poems have been published in Czech translation, two in German, and one in Polish; and individual poems have been published abroad in Czech, German, Polish, Serbian, French, and Portuguese in numerous periodicals. Aygi himself is a distinguished translator, having published Chuvash translations of Russian, Hungarian, and Polish poetry and a large anthology of French poetry from the 15th to the 20th century.

In theme and style as well as in his cultural origin Aygi stands apart in contemporary Russian poetry. His break with traditional poetic forms is reminiscent of Viktor KHLEBNIKOV and Vladimir MAYAKOVSKY, and he himself has also acknowledged the influence of the Czech poet Jiří WOLKER. His poetry reflects his preoccupation with cultural and philosophical values, somewhat in the spirit of his mentor Boris PASTERNAK; and he has paid tribute to the Bible and to the Danish philosopher Søren KIERKEGAARD as influences upon his poetry in recent years.

The only edition of Aygi's poems in the original Russian is *Stikhi 1954–1971* (Munich, 1975; Poems 1954–1971), edited by Wolfgang Kasack, with notes by the poet himself and with an extensive bibliography of works by and about Aygi in Chuvash, Russian, and other European languages.   W.B.E.

Ayguesparse, Albert (1900–), Belgian poet, novelist, critic, and essayist who writes in French, was born in Brussels. He first wrote poetry of deep protest against social injustices, or *engagement*. His subsequent poetic work, however, has evolved toward the more personal lyricism of *Vin noir de Cahors* (1957; Dark Wine of Cahors), a long amorous reflection of a very poetic nature in which existential anguish and bewilderment with life join together in a lucidly conquered serenity. As a prose writer, Ayguesparse is the author of short stories and novellas characterized by a certain magic realism (*Selon toute vraisemblance*, 1961; In All Likelihood) and novels marked by a deliberate faithfulness to an objective aesthetic. A keen observer of the working class and provincial bourgeoisie between the two world wars—whether in a story about a strike (*La Main morte*, 1938; The Dead Hand), bankruptcy (*L'Heure de la vérité*, 1947; The Hour of Truth), the evocation of Provence in a Mauritanian climate (*Notre Ombre nous précède*, 1953; Our Shadow Precedes Us), or a psychological portrait of a commonplace character (*Simon-la-bonté*, 1965; Simon-the-Good)— this lucid idealist always suggests, behind the implacable cause-and-effect logic, what happiness in justice there should be in this world. "Even if I no longer hope," he writes, "I fight for the real world as opposed to the promised land, for love as opposed to imposture." As editor of the review *Marginales*, Albert Ayguesparse has also pursued a career as critic and essayist. He received the Prix Triennal du Roman in 1955 and became a member of the Royal Academy of French Language and Literature of Belgium in 1962.

See: J. Rousselot, *Albert Ayguesparse ou la leçon du réel* (1965); J. Belmans, *Albert Ayguesparse* (1967); J. Crickillon, *L'Œuvre romanesque d'Albert Ayguesparse* (1970).   R.Bu.

Aymé, Marcel (1902–67), French novelist, essayist, and playwright, was born in Joigny. Unlike most of his fellow-writers, he was not shaped by the classical and humanist disciplines of the usual university mold. After trying many different types of work, including bricklaying and journalism, he turned to writing in 1926, during his convalescence from a long illness. His early novels, largely based on childhood memories, were about small towns, such as *Brûlebois* (1926), or the country, such as *La Table-aux-Crevés* (1929). From then on, Aymé published a novel or a collection of short stories almost every year. His novels include *La Rue sans nom* (1930; Street without a Name); *Le Vaurien* (1931; The Good-for-nothing); *La Jument verte* (1933; The Green Mare), which made him famous; *Maison basse* (1935; Low House); *Le Moulin de la Sourdine* (1936; The Mill of the Sourdine); *Gustalin* (1937); *Le Boeuf clandestin* (1939; The Clandestine Ox); *La Belle Image* (1941; The Beautiful Image); *Travelingue* (1941; Traveling); *La Vouivre* (1943); *Le Chemin des écoliers* (1946; Long Way Around); *Uranus* (1948); and *Les Tiroirs de l'inconnu* (1960; Drawers of the Unknown). His collections of short stories include *Le Puits aux im-*

ages (1932; Picture Well), *Le Nain* (1934; The Dwarf), *Derrière chez Martin* (1938; Behind Martin's), *Le Passe-Muraille* (1943; Wall-Jumper), *Le Vin de Paris* (1947; The Wine of Paris), and *En Arrière* (1950; To the Rear). Three collections of charming tales, *Les Contes du Chat perché* (1939; Tales of the Perched Cat), awarded the Chantecler Prize, *Autres contes du Chat perché* (1950; Other Tales of the Perched Cat), and *Derniers contes du Chat perché* (1950; Last Tales of the Perched Cat), were ostensibly written for children, but they appeal to everyone.

In 1944, Aymé produced his first play, *Vogue la galère* (Come What May), followed by a series of more or less successful, but always interesting and frequently amusing offerings, among them *Clérembard* (1950), his most famous play; *La Tête des autres* (1954; Other People's Heads); *Louisiana* (1961); *Les Maxibules* (1962); *Le Minotaure* (1967); and *La Convention Belzébir* (1967). *Silhouette du scandale* (1938; Silhouette of Scandal) and *Le Confort intellectuel* (1949; Intellectual Comfort) might be called satirical essays. These works reflect Aymé's critical appraisal of the contemporary scene.

Aymé does not fit into any given category or literary trend. A vigorously individual style, a vivid imagination, and an extraordinary sense of the tragicomic world about him make him one of the most readable and fascinating writers of his day. He is a fabulist, a teller of tall tales, often wildly burlesque, but above all a meticulous observer with an uncanny ability to portray the real world in precise, incisive detail. Many works, especially *La Jument verte*, a bawdy story of peasant and small-town life, are in the best Rabelaisian tradition. Others, like *Le Chemin des écoliers* and *Uranus*, are bitter portraits of society. The writings of this protean author contain a wealth of vigorous satire, imagination, and gaiety that places him among the most original writers France has produced.

See: J. Cathelin, *Marcel Aymé ou le paysan de Paris* (1958); P. Vandromme, *Aymé* (1960); D. Brodin, *The Comic World of Marcel Aymé* (1964).   D.Br.

Aytmatov, Chingiz (1928–), Kirghiz short-story writer, novelist, and playwright, is the Soviet Union's most distinguished non-Russian author writing in Russian. Kirghizia, a Central Asian Soviet republic, provides the language of his early works and the setting for all his compositions. Aytmatov's civic themes are Kirghizia's growing pains, female emancipation, and destalinization, while his lyric concerns are man in nature and history.

The issues of Kirghizia's breaking away from its past and the new, emancipated role for women overlap in such a story as "Dzhamilya" (1958), one of the four early, optimistic tales gathered together in the collection *Povesti gor i stepey* (1962; Eng. tr., *Novellas of Mountains and Steppes*, 1973), which won a Lenin Prize.

Aytmatov's mature, more pessimistic work begins with the novel *Proshchay, Gulsary!* (1966; Eng. tr., *Farewell, Gulsary!*, 1970), his first work written in Russian. The history of a man, his horse, and a collective farm, *Proshchay* is a stark indictment of the darker deeds of the Iosif Stalin regime. *Bely parokhod* (1970; Eng. tr., *The White Steamship*, 1972), is the tragic story of a young Kirghiz boy who, disgusted by the ugliness of the adult world, drowns himself. Aytmatov was severely criticized for the tragic world view implicit in this work. Aytmatov's later story "Ranniye zhuravli" (1975; Eng. tr., "The Early Cranes," 1976) is a dark-toned study of a group of teenage boys during World War II.   D.A.L.

Azaña, Manuel (1880–1940), Spanish statesman, essayist, critic, orator, dramatist, and novelist, was born in Alcalá de Henares. He recived his secondary education at the

Augustinian school in the Escorial and was trained as a lawyer at the University of Madrid. Employed as a civil servant, he frequented the Madrid Ateneo from about 1900, serving as its secretary from 1913 to 1920. He lectured, wrote for newspapers and periodicals, and ran unsuccessfully in 1913 and 1923 as Reformist Party candidate for the Cortes. His first book grew out of a year's scholarship in Paris and studies of the French and Spanish military. Entitled *Estudios de política francesa contemporánea* (1919; Studies of Contemporary French Politics), it was the first of a projected three-volume study. He also published several translations from French and English, notably the Protestant George Borrow's *The Bible in Spain* (1921). From 1920 to 1923, Azaña and his future brother-in-law, Cipriano Rivas Cherif, edited the monthly *La Pluma,* publishing early works of Jorge GUILLÉN, Pedro SALINAS, and José MORENO VILLA. In 1923–24 they edited the political journal *España,* founded by José ORTEGA Y GASSET. In 1926, Azaña's "Vida de don Juan Valera" (Life of Don Juan Valera) won the National Prize for Literature. Although it was not published, much of its substance appeared in the introduction to his edition of *Pepita Jiménez* (1927) and other studies of Juan VALERA.

Azaña felt a kinship with Valera because of his dual vocation as writer and statesman. He identified and defined his own literary Generation of 1914, which included Ortega, Américo CASTRO, Salvador de MADARIAGA, and Ramón PÉREZ DE AYALA. They differed from the illustrious Generation of 1898 in their characteristic intellectual precision stemming from their university educations. Azaña's "El *Idearium* de Ganivet" in *Plumas y palabras* (1930; Words and Sketches) is a direct challenge to the Generation of 1898, and his essay on Don Quixote in *La invención del Quijote y otros ensayos* (1934; The Invention of *Don Quixote* and Other Essays) picks up where Miguel de UNAMUNO left off. *El jardín de los frailes* (1927; The Monks' Garden) portrays a boy's life in the Escorial school. Avowedly not autobiographical, its vivid picture of a society and a real life experience brought Azaña literary recognition. His play *La Corona* (1930; The Crown) has two heroes, an idealistic ex-seminarian and a realist who is a successful revolutionary. Audiences in 1932, after the advent of the Republic, saw it as an allegory. An unfinished novel, *Fresdeval,* dates from this period. The essay "Tres generaciones del Ateneo" (Three Generations of the Ateneo), in *La invención del Quijote,* remains invaluable.

Azaña came to political prominence as president of the Ateneo, spokesman for Madrid's intelligentsia, and head of his own Republican Action Party, founded in 1926. During the 1930s he played a major political role as minister of war, as premier (1931–33, 1936), and as opposition leader in the intervening years. As president of the Republic during the Civil War (1936–39) he failed to secure the unifying role he sought and instead played only a secondary part, although he led the Cortes with eloquence and reason. His carefully wrought speeches of this period were met with enormous popular admiration, far greater than his earlier writings had received. On one occasion in 1935 he addressed a crowd of half a million people. His memoirs have the utmost historical importance but vary considerably in literary quality. At least *Mi rebelión en Barcelona* (1935) can stand with his orations. *La velada en Benicarló* (1939; Vigil in Benicarló), a dialogue, presents Spain's agonizing Civil War in all of its frustrating complexity more brilliantly than any other literary treatment. Azaña died in exile in France.

The statesman Azaña has overshadowed Azaña the writer. Scurrilous attacks from the Left and the Right have further obscured his commanding position in the 1930s. Nevertheless, the careful, colorful quality of his best prose, the depth of his learning, and the subtlety of his thought guarantee the survival of his work. His vision of belles-lettres which have historical, even utilitarian validity replaced the approach of the earlier generation. His full historical and intellectual importance will eventually, and inevitably, be recognized, and some of his prose—essays, speeches, the *Velada en Benicarló,* and the *Jardín de los frailes*—may well be counted among Spain's classics.

See: J. Marichal, *La vocación de Manuel Azaña* (1960); C. Rivas Cherif, *Retrato de un desconocido* (1960); F. Sedwick, *The Tragedy of Manuel Azaña and the Fate of the Spanish Republic* (1963).   P.S.

Azorín, pseud. of José Martínez Ruiz (1873–1967), Spanish essayist, novelist, and playwright, was born in Monóvar, a town in the province of Alicante. He studied law in Valencia, where he began his career as a writer. His first books were either collections of articles in which he often satirically attacked the writers of his time or theoretical pamphlets on literary criticism and sociology. Martínez Ruiz was first recognized, however, for his radical social articles, influenced by anarchist thought and published in the best leftist newspapers and reviews of Madrid, where he lived from 1896 on.

Toward the end of the 19th century, Spain was suffering from a confused sense of national identity caused by rapid industrialization, which resulted in shifting social classes and values, and by the loss of its last overseas colonies in 1898. Some writers called for the "Europeanization" of Spain so that it could participate in democratic capitalism, while others turned either to an examination of the distinguishing characteristics of Spanish culture or to pessimistic meditations on the human condition. The writers of the Generation of 1898, of which Martínez Ruiz was an important figure and which owed its definition in part to him, were pervaded by this tension between action and contemplation.

Martínez Ruiz's first novels, *Diario de un enfermo* (1901; Diary of a Sick Person), *La voluntad* (1902; Will), *Antonio Azorín* (1903), and *Las confesiones de un pequeño filósofo* (1904; Confessions of a Little Philosopher), describe the ambivalent reactions of an autobiographical protagonist named Antonio Azorín (Martínez Ruiz adopted the surname as his pseudonym in 1905) toward his historical circumstances and his sensations and thoughts while contemplating the life, customs, and landscape of his country. His perspective on reality is both that of a social reformer and that of a skeptic who broods over the destruction of time and the transcendence of art. The novels are in the form of vignettes with little narrative structure. They challenge the aesthetics of the traditional novel by reducing external reality to disconnected impressions which reveal the author's sensibility, thus pointing to the chasm between life and the contemplation of life. In these works we can already detect the makings of Azorín's impressionistic style, with cubist overtones, which stood in marked contrast to the prose of his contemporaries. He wrote short, simple sentences in which he eschewed the potentialities of the verb, emphasized the noun, and changed the value of adverbs and adjectives.

From 1905 on, the works of Azorín are characterized by a vision of the artist as the "little philosopher" who focuses on apparently unimportant or commonplace events and makes them transcendent. He comes to see the past and the countryside of Spain through the eyes of other written texts, in the process reevaluating almost the entire body of Spanish literature. Most of what Azorín wrote between 1905 and 1925 falls into the category of vignettes and essays published first in newspapers (mainly in *ABC*, the most widely circulated daily in Spain) and then collected in volumes: *La ruta de Don Quijote* (1905), *Los pueblos* (1905; Towns), *España* (1909), *Castilla* (1912), *Lecturas españolas* (1912; Spanish Readings), and *Clásicos y modernos* (1913). Exceptions like the novels *El licenciado Vidriera* (1915; Graduate Glass; changed later to *Tomás Rueda*), *Don Juan* (1922; Eng. tr., 1923), and *Doña Inés* (1925) share the same intentions.

In these works, his influence on how the contemporary Spaniard views his history and traditions is inestimable. Azorín defines Spanish sensibility as a painful awareness of time and change, tempered by the Spaniard's ability to transcend historical and material reality by grasping the eternal or mystical. His effort to find continuity and coherence in Spanish history was undoubtedly due to the influence of two of Spain's most notable conservatives. Between 1907 and 1919, Azorín was elected five different times as a deputy to the Spanish Parliament from the Conservative Party and twice served as undersecretary for public instruction.

Azorín's novels *Félix Vargas* (1928; changed later to *El caballero inactual*, The Non-Present Gentleman), *Superrealismo* (1929; changed later to *El libro de Levante*), *Pueblo* (1930), and his short stories, *Blanco en azul* (1929; Eng. tr., *The Sirens and Other Stories*, 1931), are experimental fiction written under the aegis of surrealism and expressionism. In them he sought to describe, through attention to affective memory and evocative imagination, a strange form of existence beyond the ordinary bounds of time and space, with particular interest in the act of creation and the splitting of the personality as states of mind that radically change one's perspectives on reality.

During the 1920s and 1930s, Azorín was also active as a drama critic. He introduced the Spaniards to the avant-garde theater in Europe and wrote several experimental plays, mostly farces and fantasies: *Old Spain!* (1926), *Brandy, mucho Brandy* (1927), *Comedia del arte* (1927), *Lo invisible* (1927), *Angelita* (1930), and *Cervantes o la casa encantada* (1931; Cervantes or the Enchanted House).

During the Spanish Republic (1931–36) Azorín returned to social and political journalism, supporting liberal reform, but he spent the entire Civil War (1936–39) uncommited in Paris. Upon his return to Madrid, he quietly accommodated to Francisco Franco's regime and wrote what were to be his last novels: *El escritor* (1942; The Writer), *El enfermo* (1943; The Sick Person), *Capricho* (1943; Caprice), *La isla sin aurora* (1943; Island without Dawn), *María Fontán* (1944), and *Salvadora de Olbena* (1944). The first two are autobiographical in nature and reveal Azorín's state of mind and some of his ideas on writing. The others are humorous, ironic fantasies in which the author attempts to remove all allusions to external reality as normally perceived. When these last efforts at experimenting with the art of the novel failed, Azorín devoted the rest of his life to writing memoirs and contributing to newspapers. The only edition of his complete works was published in 1953, but since then more than 20 volumes of articles not previously collected have followed.

See: E. I. Fox, *Azorín as a Literary Critic* (1962); L. Livingstone, *Tema y forma en las novelas de Azorín* (1970); J. M. Valverde, *Azorín* (1971).   E.I.F.

B

Babel, Isaak Emmanuilovich (1894–1941), Russian writer of short stories and plays, emerged on the Russian literary scene with dazzling effect in 1924 with the publication of two stories from his cycle *Konarmiya* (1926; Eng. tr., *Red Cavalry*, 1929) in Vladimir MAYAKOVSKY's magazine *Lef*. These shocking vignettes of war, written in a bravura style full of color and brutal detail, were the fruits of Babel's own participation in the Civil War as a correspondent and propagandist in the First Cavalry's Polish campaign during the summer and fall of 1920. In this campaign the Cossack cavalry, led by Semyon Budyonny, extended the struggle between the Reds (revolutionary government) and Whites (supporters of the old order) onto Polish soil. The Reds penetrated almost to Warsaw but were driven back, and Poland was lost. *Konarmiya*, written in 1923–25, but based on notes taken by Babel during the 1920 campaign, is not a chronicle. It is a series of short fictions in which violence and brutality are submitted to rigorous examination. Some stories are narrated in a stylized form of the Cossacks' own language and attempt to penetrate the mentality that can kill without qualm. Others show Babel's concern with the poverty-stricken and demoralized Jews of the shtetlach, the little towns of Poland and Galicia. A few create saintly men of peace who serve as a counterweight to the violent Cossacks. Throughout the stories the narrator, a Jew and intellectual, Babel's fictionalized alter ego, observes and attempts to understand what he has witnessed. The cycle is unified by the narrator's quest to achieve a comprehension of human nature in which these seemingly irreconcilable aspects—violence and peacefulness—can be unified. From the vantage point of the present day, Babel

takes his place among the great modern stylists who turned their sense of an unprecedented break with the presuppositions of the past into new literary forms; but to his contemporaries, Russian and non-Russian, *Konarmiya* had the immediacy of firsthand observation of current history. It was translated into more than 20 foreign languages and brought its author international fame.

Raised in the Black Sea port of Odessa, the son of a Jewish small businessman, Babel was among those writers from provincial or marginal areas of Russian cultural life who entered into the mainstream after the turn of the century, altering profoundly the tone of literary discourse. The first major Russian Jewish writer to write in Russian, he incorporated the life and experience of the ghetto and shtetl into his stories and plays, often preserving the intonations and verbal gestures of Yiddish in the Russian speech of his characters. In addition, Babel combined the theme of ghetto life with the rich cosmopolitanism and color of lower-class Odessa life to create a style striking in its supple, imaginative use of language. His cycle *Odesskiye rasskazy* (1924; Eng. tr., *Tales of Odessa* in *The Collected Stories*, 1955) is a mythical recreation of the marginal figures of ghetto life: the small merchants, middlemen, and entrepreneurs; the petty criminals and "hit men"; the saloon keepers and brawlers; even the Odessa rabbis and the various hangers-on at the synagogue, figures as colorful as the gangsters. The "king" of the gangsters is Benya Krik, who bests the forces of respectability with elegance and wit while manifesting the ability to "spend the night with a Russian woman and satisfy her." Lyubka Schneeweis, the proprietor of the tavern, is called "The Cossack" because of her size and strength. Thus

Babel renders the oppressed Jews of the ghetto magically potent.

Babel's third major cycle of stories is also set in Odessa but presents life there in a different tonality. Written between 1925 and 1930, these stories were not published in a separate volume but form a clearly independent work in theme and style. (See the English translations in *The Collected Stories*, 1955.) Beginning with "Istoriya moyey golubyatni" (1925; "The Story of My Dovecote") and continuing through seven stories, Babel wrote a series of fictionalized accounts of his childhood and young manhood, centering upon his struggle to break out of the confines of his Jewish upbringing and realize his vocation as an artist. In "Istoriya moyey golubyatni" and "Pervaya lyubov" (1925; "First Love") the child protagonist observes a pogrom and is subjected to the violence of the larger world in which he must live. In other stories he discovers aspects of the reality that he must know to become a writer.

Babel also wrote two plays, "Zakat" and "Maria," as well as a number of film scenarios. "Zakat" (1928; Eng. tr., "Sunset" in *Noonday 3*, 1960) returns to the Odessa gangster world of Benya Krik, but treats it in a much darker vein. The play's chief figure is Benya's father, Mendel Krik, a brawling giant of an old man who wants to sell the family carting business and run away to Bessarabia with his young mistress. His sons brutally suppress him, keeping the family intact and restoring order to domestic and community life. The somber power of the play comes from its portrait of Mendel, who wages a fierce struggle against age, loss of vitality, and decline. The production of the play by the Moscow Art Theater was not a success and it never entered the repertory. "Maria" (1935; Eng. tr., "Marya" in *Three Soviet Plays*, 1966), which returns to the 1917 October Revolution as theme, is a weaker effort and has attracted little attention.

Mention must be made of the political vicissitudes of Babel's career. As a young man, Babel came to Petersburg with the hope of making a literary career for himself and had the good fortune to attract the notice of Maksim GORKY, who published two of his stories in his magazine *Khronika*. Gorky, who liked to develop and encourage younger writers, became Babel's lifelong friend and protector. The publication of the *Red Cavalry* stories in the mid-1920s not only brought Babel fame, but also plunged him into a political controversy that cast a shadow upon his career. The commander of the First Cavalry, Semyon Budyonny, attacked Babel's depiction of the campaign for its emphasis on brutal acts and accused him of failing to grasp the meaning of the Revolution. Babel was defended by Gorky and continued to publish and enjoy the perquisites granted to successful writers. In the flexible cultural life of the 1920s, with its tolerance of "fellow travelers," Babel's general sympathy with the spirit and prrinciples of the Revolution was an acceptable if controversial political position. With the bureaucratization of all literary culture in the 1930s and the demand for conformity to socialist realism, however, little room was left for works of moral complexity. In the 1930s, Babel revised his stories for the two editions of his collected works that appeared in his lifetime (1932, 1936), deleting a few passages that were too politically ambiguous or too erotic for the stricter standards. He published less, and "Babel's silence" became a topic of Soviet literary journalism. Nevertheless, Babel survived the early stages of the purges, perhaps owing to the protection of Gorky. In 1939 he was arrested at his cottage in Peredelkino, the writers' colony. The Soviet government has announced that he died in 1941. He was "rehabilitated," along with other noted victims of the purges, after the death of Iosif Stalin in 1953. His collected works (*Izbrannoye*), based on the 1936 edition but including new materials, were republished in 1957 and 1966.

See: P. Carden, *The Art of Isaac Babel* (1972); J. E. Falen, *Isaac Babel, Russian Master of the Short Story* (1974).   P.C.

Babits, Mihály (1883–1941), Hungarian poet, critic, novelist, and short-story writer, was born in Szekszárd and died in Budapest. Babits's parents were middle-class intellectuals, and he grew up in a rich cultural environment. He was educated at the Cistercian secondary school in Pécs and at the University of Budapest. As a school teacher, he taught in such provincial towns as Baja, Szeged, Fogaras, and Újpest, but in his moments of real freedom he was a poet, and gradually his poetic self demanded complete attention. When his first poems appeared in *Nyugat* (*see* HUNGARIAN LITERATURE), they immediately impressed discriminating readers with their great erudition. This first impression was so strong that later it was difficult for readers and critics to recognize his vehemence, emotional restlessness, fantastic vision, and crucified spirit.

Babits never sided with dogmas nor did he ever subordinate the principle of artistic integrity to didacticism or propaganda. By nature he was a contemplative person rather than a man of action; he had the intelligence of a creator and not of a pamphleteer. His neurotic sensitiveness sometimes seemed to be in need of humanization, but in truth he was never so removed from life as to be fairly called an ivory-tower poet. While he was influenced by the psychology of Sigmund Freud, by the philosophy of Henri BERGSON, and by certain critical norms of Julien BENDA, the catholicity of Babits's taste was always such that he could absorb many ideas without paying the tribute of mere resemblance or imitation. He believed in values, not slogans.

Babits was not only one of the most gifted poets and writers of modern Hungary, but one of the most erudite and versatile as well. He made the discursive essay popular in his native country, and he produced Hungarian translations of Sophocles' *Oedipus Rex*, Dante's *Divine Comedy*, Shakespeare's *The Tempest*, medieval Latin hymns, and the works of many French, German, English, and American poets and writers. His *Az európai irodalom története* (1934; History of European Literature) is an independent spirit's interpretation of great writers and poets. His plays are book-dramas. After World War I, Babits became one of the editors of *Nyugat*. He was less radical than his predecessors, but not less strict in his standard of criticism. Despite increased political nationalism he was unwilling to compromise his aesthetic doctrines and remained the standard-bearer of an enlightened liberalism and humanism. His passion for creative integrity was so honest that his pragmatic compromises were merely matters of inevitable policy and they were not the betrayal of the spirit.

Babits's early poems showed an affinity with poetic symbolism. He was always very fond of Edgar Allan Poe and of certain French and English symbolic poets and emphasized images and workmanship in their fashion. Like so many other symbolic poets, he was a master of onomatopoeia. When he reached maturity, however, he rejected modern terminologies and poetic fashions and became introspective. A comparison of his early poems with those of the later period reveal a broader conception of the good life and a deeper understanding of life's experiences. The somewhat "decadent" Babits is best represented by the following volumes of poetry: *Herceg, hátha megjön a tél is* (1911; But Prince, if Winter Should

Come), *Recitativ* (1911; Recitative), *Nyugtalanság völgye* (1917; The Valley of Restlessness), and *Sziget és tenger* (1925; Island and Sea). A later, mellow Babits found his voice in *Versenyt az esztendőkkel* (1928; Racing the Years) and in *Jónás könyve* (1939; The Book of Jonah). *Haláfinai* (1926; The Sons of Death), his most ambitious novel, is a large, compassionate work about the dying gentry and middle class. Babits's other stories and novels, including *Karácsonyi Madonna* (1920; Christmas Madonna), *Timár Virgil fia* (1922; The Son of Vergil Timar), and *Kártyavár* (1924; House of Cards), reflect a mind inclined to be fantastic in its psychological orientation and positive in its refusal of the obvious. *Irodalmi problémák* (1917; Literary Problems) shows Babits at his very best as an essayist.

See: A. Schöpflin, *Irók, könyvek, emlékek* (1925); D. Keresztúry, Introduction to M. Babits, *Válogatott müvei* (1959); J. Reményi, *Hungarian Writers and Literature* (1964), pp. 306–25.   J.R. rev. G.G.

Bacchelli, Riccardo (1891–), Italian poet, novelist, dramatist, and essayist, was born in Bologna. His father was a prominent citizen of the town and his mother was German. Bacchelli began but never finished his university studies. Precociously attracted to a literary career, he produced his first novel at the age of 20 and his first book of verse three years later. Bacchelli served in combat in World War I. He has been an active, articulate, and uniquely versatile writer, achieving distinction in many fields.

Bacchelli's novels have been remarkably varied. *Lo sa il tonno* (1923; The Tunny Knows) is a delicious political satire, aimed at the pretensions of fascism; *Il diavolo al Pontelungo* (1927; Eng. tr., *The Devil at Long Bridge*, 1929) combines satire, history, and psychological insight; the trilogy *Il mulino del Po* (1938, 1939, 1940; Eng. tr., [parts 1 and 2] *The Mill on the Po*, 1950; [part 3] *Nothing New under the Sun*, 1955) is a historical saga of Tolstoyan proportions. Bacchelli is also adept at depicting the psychology of intimate personal relations, as evidenced by *Una passione coniugale* (1930; A Conjugal Passion) and *Tre giorni di passione* (1955; Three Days of Passion), among other works. His restless inspiration has also produced such books as the Utopian *La città degli amanti* (1929; Eng. tr., *Love Town*, 1930), the lyric *Iride* (1937), the mischievous *La Cometa* (1951; The Comet), and such historical novels as *Il pianto del figlio di Lais* (1945; The Tears of the Son of Lais), *Il figlio di Stalin* (1953; Eng. tr., *Son of Stalin*, 1956), and *Non ti chiamerò più padre* (1959; No Longer Shall I Call You Father), an imaginative account of the life of Saint Francis. Nor is the end in sight, for Bacchelli's nimble pen continues to follow the quirks of contemporary society and to chronicle events and personae of the past. *Il progresso è un razzo* (1975; Progress Is a Rocket) and *Il sommergibile* (1978; The Submarine) testify to the enduring vigor of his inspiration.

As a poet, Bacchelli strives for a classical restraint and a nonrhetorical sobriety, avoiding both the sentimentalism of the *crepuscolari* and the self-conscious austerity of the *ermetici* (*see* ITALIAN LITERATURE). He is a defender of the hendecasyllable. His *Parole d'amore* (1935; Words of Love) contains some fine and characteristic pages, whereas his drama *Amleto* (1919) is a refreshing attempt at interpreting Shakespeare's *Hamlet* in a new light.

Bacchelli is also an engaging essayist and a persuasive literary critic. In his youth, he was associated with *La voce*, and during his lifetime he has been a regular contributor to many journals; his name, however, is linked mainly with *La ronda* (*see* ITALIAN LITERATURE), which

in the 1920s proclaimed itself the defender of traditional literary values. Bacchelli's evocation of his own country in *Bella Italia* (1928; Beautiful Italy) is warm and perceptive. *Nel fiume della storia* (1955; In the River of History) is representative of his critical approach. Bacchelli has also written many purely historical studies, including a biography of Gioacchino Rossini (1954). Indeed, his cultural arsenal is so richly stocked and his talent so exuberant that many of his creative works contain incidental essays—on customs, morals, politics, or on words themselves, for Bacchelli loves words and their ways. Although he describes himself as *apolitico*, Bacchelli is by temperament a conservative. Critics find in his pages affinities with 18th-century French writers and with both French and Italian 19th-century masters. The influence of Alessandro Manzoni (1785–1873) is immediately recognizable in *Il mulino del Po*. Bacchelli is a deliberate stylist and a humanist; he likes the large canvas with room for digressions and homilies. This characteristic sets Bacchelli apart from the mainstream of Italian letters today. To some readers his work seems a little too self-consciously elegant; Giuseppe PREZZOLINI found him "ponderous" and "mannered." And it is true that, as Giulio Marzot suggests, Bacchelli demands of his readers not only a certain cultural preparation but considerable patience as well. Yet Ernest Hatch Wilkins applauds "his serenity, his humor and his strong stylistic conscience." Of *Il mulino del Po* Luigi Russo said simply, "It will last," and one may expect that the verdict will apply to Bacchelli's work as a whole.

See: G. Marzot, in *Letteratura italiana: i contemporanei*, vol. 2 (1975); A. Dosi Barsizza, *Invito alla lettura di Riccardo Bacchelli* (1971); C. Gargiulo, *Riccardo Bacchelli: letterato e storico* (1974).   T.G.B.

Bachelard, Gaston (1884–1962), French philosopher, was born in Hyères. As an epistemologist and critic, his influence on recent developments in literary criticism has been decisive. A professor of the history and philosophy of sciences at the University of Dijon and later at the Sorbonne, he began his intellectual career with research on the newest aspects of sciences, Einstein's physics of relativity, and wave mechanics. Following and then going beyond the rationalist epistemology of Léon Brunschvicg, Bachelard proposed new interpretations and visions of the scientific mind in essays such as *La Valeur inductive de la relativité* (1929; The Inductive Value of Relativity), *Le Nouvel Esprit scientifique* (1934; The New Scientific Spirit), *La Formation de l'esprit scientifique* (1938; The Formation of the Scientific Spirit), and *Le Rationalisme appliqué* (1949; Applied Rationalism). In addition to critical reflection describing the most important theoretical innovations of our time, Bachelard became gradually involved in studies on poetic creation. In opposition to the psychoanalytic hermeneutics of human languages and cultures, he proposed and applied a phenomenological methodology that also differs from Edmund Husserl's phenomenology.

Bachelard was searching for the unconscious and empirical forms of the artistic activities of mankind. His main interest was in the different universal images that organize space and time through art and poetry. His essays such as *La Psychanalyse du feu* (1938; Eng. tr., *The Psychoanalysis of Fire*, 1964), *L'Eau et les rêves* (1942; Eng. tr., *Water and Dreams*, 1965), and *La Poétique de l'espace* (1958; Eng. tr., *The Poetics of Space*, 1965) had a decisive influence on the "new critics" after 1960, to whom he offered new instruments for the exploration of the imaginary world of poets and artists. His analysis insisted on the originality of the "poetic image" as an incipient dream or reverie. Bachelard opened up a new field in the understanding of man, an epistemological and critical domain covering the sciences of poetry, the knowledge of which can be termed the "ontology of imagination." E.M.-S.

Bachmann, Ingeborg (1926–73), Austrian poet, essayist, librettist, novelist, and author of short stories and radio plays, was born in Klagenfurt, the capital of Carinthia. After World War II she studied jurisprudence and philosophy at Innsbruck, Graz, and Vienna. Awarded a doctorate in 1950 for a dissertation on the critical reception of the existentialist philosophy of Martin HEIDEGGER, she was deeply influenced by the works of other language philosophers as well, notably Ludwig Wittgenstein. Her concern with the limits of the expressible struck responsive chords in postwar German letters, and she was awarded the prize of the "Gruppe 47" (*see* GERMAN LITERATURE) in 1953, the year of the publication of her first collection of poetry, *Die gestundete Zeit* (Time Suspended). She was invited to lecture at Harvard University in 1955, and in 1959 she was the first holder of the newly created chair for poetics at the University of Frankfurt, where she lectured on "Literature as Utopia." Public adulation continued. In 1959 she was awarded the Prize of the War Blind for *Der gute Gott von Manhattan* (1958; The Good Lord of Manhattan), a radio play. For her collection of stories *Das dreißigste Jahr* (1961; Eng. tr., *The Thirtieth Year*, 1964) she was awarded the Berlin Critics Prize, and she was inducted into the West Berlin Academy of Arts in the same year. The Büchner Prize followed in 1965, and the Austrian National Medal in 1968. Although there were critics who labeled her work "Kitsch"—she was reclusive, although not haughty, and some critics resented her aversion to epistolary communication—Bachmann was widely recognized as a legitimate master at a time when German literature was trying to come to terms with its own legitimacy. After almost two decades of poetry and short prose, she published her first novel, *Malina*, in 1971. A complete edition of her works appear in 1978, five years after her untimely death in Rome, where she had increasingly spent her time and where she perished as the result of a fire in her apartment.

See: I. Bachmann, *Eine Einführung* (1963; contributions by various critics); H. Pausch, *Ingeborg Bachmann* (1975). L.G.Sc.

Bacovia, George, pseud. of George Vasiliu (1884–1957), Romanian poet, was born in Bacău, from which he took the pen name Bacovia. He studied law at Iaşi and Bucharest but never practiced. After holding a series of minor positions as copyist, bookkeeper, and art teacher, Bacovia spent much of his life in sanatoriums because of mental illness. Early in his career, he came under the influence of Alexandru MACEDONSKI, whose journal *Literatorul* published some of his early poems. His first volume of collected poems was *Plumb* (1916; Lead), followed at long intervals by *Scîntei galben* (1926; Yellow Sparks), *Cu voi* (1930; With You) and *Stanţe burgheze* (1946; Middle-Class Attitudes).

Between the ages of 18 and 20, Bacovia fully developed his lyrical style, strongly influenced by French symbolism. The poems in *Plumb*, written in 1900, display this perfected technique, with its impeccable rhythms and orchestrated sounds. In this volume, Bacovia uses the metaphor of lead to suggest both weight and inertia, something earthly and yet overwhelming. Bacovia's lyricism is characterized by a continual restlessness, a sublime fear. Man lives in a world of potential disaster and is unable to extricate himself from his tragedy. As Romania's most important symbolist poet, Bacovia has had a great influence on younger writers.

See: M. Petroveanu, *George Bacovia* (1970). V.A.

Baczyński, Krzysztof Kamil (1921–44), Polish poet, was born in Warsaw and died as a soldier during the Warsaw uprising. The son of a literary critic, Stanisław Baczyński, he started to write poetry before World War II as a high school student, but his great lyrical talent developed and reached maturity during the war. Baczyński belonged to the first generation of youth born and raised in independent Poland, and his poems depicting the tragic fate of this generation during the war are the most dramatic. At the beginning he was close to the poetry of Józef CZECHOWICZ and the so-called catastrophists; later he turned to the great romantic poets, especially to Juliusz Słowacki and Cyprian NORWID. His patriotism, present in all of his poetry, underwent transformations that arose from the conflict between his desire for personal and artistic independence and the moral duty to participate in the fight against the Nazi occupation. Baczyński was co-editor of the clandestine literary monthly *Droga*; in 1942 he enrolled in the clandestine Warsaw University, and in 1943 he joined the Home Army. Baczyński's poetic output includes lyric poems, fantastic narrative poems, reflective religious lyrics, and love poems. Some of his poems were published in the clandestine press: *Zamknięty echem* (1940; Closed in an Echo), *Dwie miłości* (1940; Two Loves), *Wiersze wybrane* (1942; Selected Poems), *Arkusz poetycki* (1943; Poetic Sheet), as well as in clandestine anthologies. After the war his works were published in the volume *Śpiew z pożogi* (1947; Singing from Ravages of War) and in 1961 *Utwory zebrane* (Collected Works).

See: K. Wyka, "Wstęp," in *Utwory zebrane* (1961), pp. 5–64. A.Z.

Bagritsky, Eduard Georgievich, pseud. of Eduard Dzyubin, (1985–1934) Russian poet, was born in Odessa, of a poor Jewish family. He graduated from a technical school as land surveyor, but never practiced his profession. Bagritsky took part in the civil war as a member of a guerrilla detachment and as a poet attached to the "propaganda train" that was sent to the front by proletarian organizations. Bagritsky started to produce poetry in 1915–16, but his mature works were written after 1924. In 1926 he joined the "Pereval" group and in the following year went over to the constructivists whose leaders were his personal friends, but his poetry is by no means an expression of this particular school (*see* RUSSIAN LITERATURE). Eclectic in scope, it impresses by its romanticism and passionate sense of life. The romantic trend is strongly felt in Bagritsky's imagery and his visions of the far distant past. It was not by mere chance that one of his first collections of poems bore an Albrecht Dürer drawing on the cover. In "Ptitselov" (The Bird Catcher) Bagritsky proclaimed his utter love for "nature, wind, songs, and freedom." One of his preferred heroes was the exuberant Till Eulenspiegel. He made excellent translations of various poets, especially of Robert Burns and Walter Scott. He also devoted many of his poems to contemporary themes, always choosing colorful scenes and dramatic episodes. Soviet critics praise highly his "Duma pro Opanasa" (Ballad of Opanas), a narrative poem of civil war in which motives of Ukrainian folklore are skillfully merged into modern rhythms. In spite of its great metric variety and the trace of many conflicting influences, ranging from the classics to Vladimir MAYAKOVSKY's futurism, Bagritsky's poetry has a fundamental unity revealed by the dynamism of its images, the tense rapidity of its rhythms, the sensuous strength of its descriptions, and the general feeling of optimism and vitality. After his death his works were published in *Sobraniye sochineniy v dvukh tomakh* (1938; Collected Works in Two Volumes).

See: A. Sinyavsky, "E. G. Bagritsky," in *Istoriya russkoy sovetskoy literatury*, vol. 1 (1958), pp. 397–420.

M.Sl. rev. W.B.E.

Bahr, Hermann (1863–1934), Austrian critic, novelist, and dramatist, was born in Linz and died in Munich. His closest association was with "Jungwien," a group of writers he claimed to have founded or discovered in 1891, which dominated Austrian literature during the quarter of a century preceding World War I. This group included Arthur SCHNITZLER, Hugo von HOFMANNSTHAL, Richard BEER-HOFFMANN, Peter Altenberg, and Felix Salten. Bahr was its most prolific and versatile member. As a critic he anticipated the reaction against naturalism, just as this movement was attaining supremacy, and as early as 1891 he espoused the cause of the emerging neoromanticists, symbolists, and decadents in his volume *Die Überwindung des Naturalismus* (Overcoming Naturalism). When these trends finally triumphed, he became the spokesman of the new expressionistic youth, and in his book *Expressionismus* (1916; Eng. tr., *Expressionism*, 1925) he helped define the characteristics of this literary tendency. As a novelist, as in *Theater* (1897), he was a superb and witty narrator of the charm and folly of Vienna, the overrefined capital of a dying empire. As a dramatist he is best remembered for *Das Konzert* (1909; Eng. tr., *The Concert*, 1910), a sophisticated comedy of Vienna, which was successfully produced on both European and American stages.

See: H. Kindermann, *Hermann Bahr, ein Leben für das europäische Theater* (1954).   S.L. rev. A.L.W.

Baillon, André (1875–1932), Belgian novelist, was born in Antwerp. He came from a liberal-minded, rich, bourgeois family. Having lost his mother when he was five years old, he was at first raised by an aunt in Termonde in a climate of devotion and tyrannical authority, which he was later to evoke in *Le Neveu de Mademoiselle Autorité* (1932; The Nephew of Miss Authority). As a child, Baillon was very withdrawn, and his solitude increased even more when he became a boarding student at the Collège Saint Joseph at Turnhout. There, the red-haired, frail, poorly dressed youth aroused the derision of his classmates.

Baillon settled in Brussels and published his first texts in Belgian reviews. The idea of suicide already obsessed him when he met a common girl, a servant fallen into prostitution for a time. She cared for him and gave him a zest for life, and he was later to recount her story in his most famous work, *Histoire d'une Marie* (1921; The Story of a Girl Named Mary).

Disgusted with city life, he moved with Marie to Westmalle, in Campine, where he raised chickens while continuing to write. There he received his friends, both writers and painters, and refined and polished his style with a touch of the self-critical irony that characterizes all his writing. From this experience came the story first entitled *Moi quelque part* (1920; Me, Somewhere), later rebaptized *En Sabots* (1922; In Wooden Shoes).

When he returned to Brussels, Baillon worked as a night editor for the daily newspaper *La Dernière Heure*. Once again he garnered from this experience the basis for his next novel, *Par Fil spécial* (1924; By Special Cable). World War I represented for Baillon a digression that spurred him on to an intense literary outpouring, encouraged by his second wife, the pianist Germaine Lievens.

Baillon's true literary debut came when he was 47, upon the Parisian publication of *En Sabots* (In Wooden Shoes) in 1922. Acclaimed by Charles VILDRAC and Jean-Richard BLOCH, he moved to Paris and signed a contract with Rider publishers. Cut off from his native surroundings and obliged to maintain an intense literary output, Baillon did not adapt well to the life of a professional writer. Overworked and bothered by neurasthenia, he underwent several successive cures, one being at La Salpêtrière. While bedridden, he wrote some astonishing books, which depict his suffering and reflect the progression of an interior malady that leaves him without hope: *Un homme si simple* (1925; Such a Simple Man), *Chalet I* (1926), *Le Perce-oreille du Luxembourg* (1928; The Earwig of the Luxembourg), and, above all, the admirable collection entitled *Délires* (1927; Deliriums). A final passion was to illuminate his life—his liaison with Marie de Vivier, told by her in *L'Homme pointu* (1942; The Sharp Man). Baillon, however, believed himself to be medically and intellectually lost. In April 1932, he took an overdose of sleeping pills and died at the hospital at St. Germain-en-Laye.

His own hangman, a cruel analyst, a maniac of public confession, Baillon was also an ironic storyteller and a thorough observer of life and human misery. Ill at ease in long works, he excelled in sketches, in concrete evocations, with the cold detachment of a Jules RENARD. Baillon's writing veered away from lyricism, preferring instead an extreme truthfulness, which relied on both the technique and subject in question. Baillon will also be remembered for his incursions into the world of the mentally ill, for his fraternal sympathy for all those who refused to become a part of the social machine, and for the mixture of humor and realism in his tone. The first piece of news of *Délires* is that of an unappreciated masterpiece. He analyzes in it the devastating effects of madness on the creator devoured by the words that he liberated. As rhythmic as a logical hallucination, this strange prose poem is the summit of an art founded on concision and the ultimate limit of an experience.

Baillon represents an important watershed in Belgian literature of French expression, which, before him, was consecrated to a coruscating style and unrestricted lyricism (Camille LEMONNIER, Eekhoud, and so on). His mystique of simplicity inaugurated a new manner and rejected the old regionalist habits of the realist and naturalist era.

See: R. de Lannay, *Un bien pauvre homme: André Baillon* (1945); J. Stevo, "André Baillon," *Synthèses* 4, no. 47 (1950): 196–208; M. de Vivier, *Introduction à l'œuvre d'André Baillon* (1950); P. Bay, *Le suicide de Baillon* (1964).   R.Mo.

Baklanov, Grigory Yákovlevich, pseud. of Grigory Yakovlevich Fridman (1923–), Russian novelist, was born in Voronezh. After serving throughout World War II as an officer in combat units, he entered the Gorky Literary Institute in Moscow and began to publish even before completing his course in 1951. The success of *Yuzhneye glavnogo udara* (1958; South of the Main Attack) assured his reputation as a war novelist. This was followed by *Pyad zemli* (1959; A Few Inches of Ground), *Myortvye sramu ne imut* (1961; No Shame Lies upon the Dead), *Iul 41-go goda* (1965; July 1941), and *Karpukhin* (1966), all on the theme of war. Baklanov's recent novel, *Druzya* (Friends) was published in the periodical *Novy mir* in 1975.

One of the best representatives of the second flowering of the war novel in the Soviet Union, Baklanov replaces the exaltation of heroism with descriptions of the human suffering experienced in the course of military operations that is generally overlooked by historians. In *Iul 41-go goda* he presents an excellent analysis of the paralyzing fear inculcated in the military cadres by the Stalinist terror.   J.Ca.

Baldini, Antonio (1889–1962), Italian essayist and critic, was born in Rome. He wrote for several newspapers and magazines, including *La tribuna, Corriere della sera,* and *La voce.* From 1931 until his death he was chief editor of *Nuova antologia.* Many of his books, beginning with *Umori di gioventù* (1919; Youthful Moods), are collections of articles. Baldini was a master of the literary genre *prosa d'arte* (artistic prose) (*see* ITALIAN LITERATURE), which flourished in Italy between the two world wars. During this period, the political situation in Italy made writing style more important than content. One of the most influential representatives of this trend was *La ronda,* a literary review Baldini helped to found. In *La ronda* the powerful ideological pressures for a "return to law and order," which culminated in fascism, were transformed into a plea for a return to tradition and classicism in literature, a rejection of realism, and a cultivation of form.

Baldini excelled in descriptive essays so polished and stylistically perfect as to make up for their lack of any real content. People, landscapes, and fragments of experience are used as a pretext for extended literary divertissements, stylistic exercises, and amusing meanderings of the imagination. It is as if Baldini liked to take pictures through a pinhole and blow them up to let his audience admire his technical skill and the quality of the enlargement, without really caring whether there was anything worthwhile to see. In *Nostro Purgatorio* (1918; This Purgatory of Ours), for example, war is purified of all horror and unpleasantness. Italy, and Rome in particular, appear in *Rugantino* (1942) and *Italia di Bonincontro* (1940) as a series of fascinating but idealized landscape paintings. The literary portraits in *Salti di gomitolo* (1920; The Jumping Skein) and *Amici allo spiedo* (1932; Friends on the Spit) are full of sympathetic humor and are often very perceptive, but they never seem to overcome the limitations of a world view in which life acquires meaning and substance only when transmuted into literature, and where moralism tends to replace knowledge and insight.

Perhaps Baldini's best books are those praising easygoing indulgence and idleness, although not without a corrective dose of irony and self-deprecation. Notable among these are *Michelaccio* (1924), *Melafumo* (1950), and *Il doppio Melafumo* (1955). His works of literary criticism, such as *Lodovico della tranquillità* (1933; Lodovico the Quiet Man) or *Cattedra d'occasione* (1941; Occasional Lectures), reveal his own literary idiosyncrasies more than those of the authors he writes about.

See: C. Varese, *Cultura letteraria contemporanea* (1951); R. Sgroi, "Antonio Baldini," in *Letteratura italiana: i contemporanei,* vol. 2 (1975), pp. 923–40.   G.Ca.

Baliński, Stanisław (1899–), Polish poet, short-story writer, essayist, and translator, was born in Warsaw. After studying law and literature at Warsaw University, he entered the Ministry of Foreign Affairs and held various positions in Brazil, Persia, Manchuria, and Denmark. In 1924 he published a volume of short stories, *Miasto księżyców* (City of the Moons). Close to the "Skamander" group, he published a volume of mature verse *Wieczór na Wschodzie* (1928; Evening in the Orient). During World War II he worked for the Polish exile government in London, where he printed three volumes of lyrical verse: *Wielka podróż* (1941; The Great Journey), *Rzecz*

sumienia (1942; A Matter of Conscience), and *Tamten brzeg nocy* (1943; The Other Shore of the Night). In 1945 his *Trzy poematy o Warszawie* (Three Poems of Warsaw) appeared in print. He also published essays, reviews, and translations from English, Italian, and Russian, including the *Odes* of John Keats (1951). He was a convincing example of the doom and nostalgic anguish of exile, and he was haunted by remorse over parting with his country in the midst of its struggle. His concern for frankness led him to avoid experimentation and to rely on traditional, neoclassic means of expression.

See: T. Terlecki, ed., *Literatura polska na obczyźnie 1940–1960,* vol. 1 (1964), pp. 101–03; M. Danilewicz Zielińska, *Szkice o literaturze emigracyjnej* (1978), pp. 179–82.   M.G.

Ball, Hugo (1886–1927), German poet, playwright, and novelist, was born in Pirmasens, the son of a shoe manufacturer. He studied philosophy and sociology at Munich, Heidelberg, and Basel, without finishing, then turned to dramaturgy. An early expressionist who shared with his peers an abhorrence of authoritarianism and the bourgeosie, Ball became a pacifist through his experiences of World War I and emigrated to Switzerland in 1915, where he cofounded the early dadaist movement. He became a journalist, then suddenly turned his back on the experimental, language-shaping style of his early works and converted to Catholicism.

Ball's works include the early expressionistic tragicomedy *Die Nase des Michelangelo* (1911; Michelangelo's Nose) and the drama *Der Henker von Brescia* (1914; The Executioner of Brescia), which were followed by the novels *Flametti oder vom Dandysmus der Armen* (1918; Flametti, or the Dandyism of the Poor) and *Tenderenda der Phantast* (written 1920, first pub. 1967; Tenderenda the Dreamer), a mixture of prose and poetry, quite in the tradition of his activist literary persona.

Ball's collection of essays *Zur Kritik der deutschen Intelligenz* (1919; A Critique of the German Intelligentsia) was reissued in 1924 under the title *Die Folgen der Reformation* (The Consequences of the Reformation). His diary of 1927 bore the title *Die Flucht aus der Zeit* (Eng. tr., *Flight out of Time,* 1974). A friend of Hermann HESSE, who held him in high esteem, Ball wrote a biography of Hesse in 1927. His letters from the years 1911–27 were published in 1957. He was married in 1920 to Emmy Ball-Hennings (1885–1948), herself a writer, who wrote much about her husband after his death.

Ball's late period has drawn most commentary, though his early period is more significant for German letters.

See: G. E. Steinke, *The Life and Work of Hugo Ball, Founder of Dadaism* (1967).   A.L.W.

Ballester i Moragues, Alexandre (1934–), Catalan dramatist, was born in Gavà on the outskirts of Barcelona and moved with his family to Majorca, his father's birthplace, when he was one year old. In Majorca he studied to become a teacher but dedicated himself instead to freelance journalism. His first play, *Foc colgat* (Buried Fire), won the Carlos Lemos Prize. It was written in 1964 but not performed until 1968. Subsequent works are *Jo i l'absent* (1965; The Absentee and I); *Siau benvingut* (1966; Welcome, Siau); *Un baül groc p'en Nofre Taylor* (1966; A Golden Trunk for Nofre Taylor); *Dins un gruix de vellut* (1957; Inside a Thickness of Velvet), for which he received the Josep Maria de Sagarra Prize; *La tragedia del tres i no res* (1967; The Tragedy of Three and Nothing); *Massa temps sense piano* (1968; A Long Time without a Piano), awarded a prize by the newspaper *Ultima*

Hora; and *Fins al darrer mot* (1969; Until the Last Word), winner of the Santamaria Prize.

Ballester has also written books of poems and stories, and his novel *La servitud* (Servility) won the City of Palma Prize in 1965. He won the City of Palma Prize for Theater in 1964 and the Cova del Drach Prize in Barcelona in 1968. A wide knowledge of foreign dramatic literature has expanded the range of Ballester's work and contributed to its great originality. The expressionism of his work is quite uncommon in Catalan literature.

See: X. Fàbregas, "El teatro d'Alexandre Ballester," *Serra d'Or* (July 1968); F. Roda, Prologue to A. Ballester i Moragues, *Siau benvingut* (1968).   J.F.C.

Balmont, Konstantin Dmitriyevich (1867–1942), Russian poet, translator, essayist, and novelist, was born on an estate near Shuya. He eventually became one of the pioneers of the "symbolist-decadent" movement and the greatest poetical success of the first years of the 20th century (*see* RUSSIAN LITERATURE). Balmont made an unspectacular literary debut with *Sbornik stikhotvoreniy* (1890; Book of Poems), but his next three books, *Pod severnym nebom* (1894; Under Northern Skies), *V bezbrezhnosti* (1895; In Boundlessness), and *Tishina* (1898; Silence), established him as a leading Russian decadent and a "musical" poet. This musicality, reminiscent of Edgar Allan Poe and frequently mentioned by critics, amounts to metrical and stanzaic variety and a stress on alliteration. This early period of neoromantic, melancholy poetry, in which the influence of Percy Bysshe Shelley, Walt Whitman, and Charles BAUDELAIRE is also noticeable, was followed by a period of Nietzschean self-affirmation (*see* Friedrich NIETZSCHE) as evidenced in *Goryashchiye zdaniya* (1900; Burning Buildings), *Budem kak solntse* (1903; Let Us Be Like the Sun)—his greatest success—and *Tolko lyubov* (1903; Love Alone). Although loud colors, passion, violence, eroticism, and the grotesque distinguish these poems from the earlier, more quiet, impressionistic, and often pantheistic landscapes, the typical Balmont poem remains a symbolic picture, a hymn of praise, a vision or an exhortation, often marked by thematic contrasts and categorical declarations, but also by a childlike purity of spirit. Technically, they employ strong caesuras, long, flowing lines, and repeated phrases. Certain themes remained constant with Balmont: childhood, nature, sorcery, boundlessness, beauty, and the "moment."

Balmont, who looked, spoke, and behaved like a poet, was a legendary figure, and his public recitations drew large audiences. His love affairs were notorious (and invariably material for his poetry), he drank heavily, and he was often in political trouble with the authorities. The years 1905–12 he spent in Europe in voluntary political exile, making a return impossible by publishing poetry abusing the Russian monarchs and the army. Few Russian poets traveled as extensively as Balmont or wrote so profusely of his travels, discovering for Russian literature such neglected areas as Spain, England, Scandinavia, Mexico, Egypt, and Oceania.

Balmont had become acquainted with theosophy in the late 1890s, and this subsequently turned him to Indian esoteric thought. Beginning with *Liturgiya krasoty* (1905; Liturgy of Beauty), his writings deal increasingly with the basic elements of the universe (fire, water, air, earth), mythologies, cosmogonies, and occult subjects. Paradoxically, this enrichment coincided with an artistic crisis and decline apparent, but not pervasive, in such books as *Zlye chary* (1906; Evil Spells); *Zhar-ptitsa* (1907; The Firebird), based on Slavic folklore; and *Ptitsy v vozdukhe* (1908; Birds in the Air). The critics, already annoyed with the steady flood of his poetry in print, declared him a

"has been." Balmont's name continued to be a household word, but he was not read and seldom taken seriously by the literary establishment. Ironically, during the years 1914–17 he published perhaps his best books of verse: *Bely Zodchiy* (1914; White Architect), *Yasen* (1916; The Ash), and especially *Sonety solntsa, myoda i luny* (1917; Sonnets of Son, Honey, and Moon), of whose form he was a virtuoso.

In 1917, after enthusiastically greeting the February Revolution, Balmont was disgusted and depressed by the October Revolution. He left Russia in 1920 for health reasons, soon burning his bridges behind him with anti-Soviet statements and poems. His poems about the nightmare of revolution were collected in *Marevo* (1922; Mirage). The best poetry of his final exile (often nostalgic and patriotic) is to be found in *V razdvinutoy dali* (Belgrade, 1930; Distances Drawn Apart) and *Severnoye siyaniye* (Paris, 1931; Northern Lights). Younger émigré poets ignored Balmont. He lived in bitter isolation and, for the last years of his life, mentally ill in a Russian old people's home near Paris. Much fascinating material and many clues to his work can be found in his books of essays, particularly in *Gornye vershiny* (1904; Mountain Peaks), where, incidentally, he tries to establish the native roots of Russian symbolism; *Zmeinye tsvety* (1910; Snakelike Flowers); and *Poeziya kak volshebstvo* (1915; Poetry as Magic). Among Balmont's numerous translations—often criticized but occasionally admired—those from Shelley, Whitman, and Pedro Calderón de la Barca, and *Zovy drevnosti* (1908; Calls of Antiquity), filled with free adaptations of the poetry of ancient civilizations, should be mentioned.

Although uneven, Balmont's poetry, in addition to developing a new kind of verse "musicality" and otherwise enriching modern Russian poetry (themes, techniques), and collectively helping to create Russian symbolism, is also a magnificent, individual, gigantic enlargement of the frontiers of Russian poetry—geographically, historically, and spiritually.

See: R. Poggioli, *The Poets of Russia* (1960), pp. 89–96; V. Markov, "Balmont: A Reappraisal," *SlavR* 28, no. 2 (June 1969): 221–64; R. L. Patterson, "Balmont: In Search of Sun and Shadow," with trs. of Balmont poems, *RLT* 4 (1972): 51–59, 241–64.   V.M.

Bałucki, Michał, pseuds. Elpidon and Załega (1837–1901), Polish dramatist, the father of Polish bourgeois comedy, was born and died in Cracow, and there he spent most of his life. His early writings, poems of love and death in the mood of Słowacki, are all forgotten except for the lyric "Góralu, czy ci nie żal?" (Oh, mountaineer, dost thou not grieve?), which is sung to a popular folk melody. In the 1870s, Bałucki turned from poetry to the novel, using this form as an instrument of protest against the clergy and aristocracy, whose form of conservatism he hated, against, on the other hand, the growing trend to naturalism in life and literature, and especially against the new freedom accorded women and the mounting popularity of Henrik IBSEN. Bałucki did not find his proper medium until he began to write plays, and even then, although the successful *Radcy pana radcy* (The Counselors of Mr. Councilor) appeared in 1869, it was not until the 1880s that he can be said to have mastered that medium. With *Krewniaki* (1879; Kinfolk), the still popular *Grube ryby* (1881; Big Fish), *Dom otwarty* (1883; Open House), and *Klub kawalerów* (1890; Bachelors' Club), he provided the Polish theater of the future with a rich repertory of satirical bourgeois comedy. Bałucki was a man out of tune with his times, his gift of comedy being largely unappreciated by contemporary theatergoers who sought in the drama not amusement, but sublimity and emotional exaltation. Bałucki died a suicide, unable to survive the storm of disapproval that greeted his play *Blagierzy* (1900; The Imposters).

See: J. Maciejewski, "Michał Bałucki," in *Obraz literatury polskiej XlX i XX wieku. Literatura polska w okresie realizmu i naturalizmu*, vol. 3 (1969), pp. 175–212.

A.P.C.

Bang, Herman (1857–1912), Danish novelist and short-story writer, was born on the island of Als. Following his unsuccessful attempt to be an actor in Copenhagen, Ban became an influential journalist and critic in opposition to Georg BRANDES. Beginning in 1884, Bang constantly traveled throughout Europe. He was a stage director in Norway and Paris during the 1890s and in Copenhagen from 1900 on. He died during a recital tour in the United States.

Bang's first novel, *Haabløse Slægter* (1880; Generations without Hope), is written in the spirit of naturalism, but the belief in the victory of progress is here replaced by a pessimistic view of life (*see* DANISH LITERATURE). The book is partly an autobiographical account of the degeneration of an old family and of the downfall of the decadent main character (a type brought into Danish literature by Bang and like him a homosexual) behind whose mask the author hid his own suffering and despair. Bang's main motifs are found here: the disappointed expectations of life, loneliness, and the transformation of love from tenderness to destructive desire. The same motifs are also present in *Excentriske Noveller* (1885; Eccentric Short Stories), about poeple outside of society like Bang himself, and in *Stille Existenser* (1886; Quiet Existences), a series of tragic idylls, among which "Ved Vejen" (By the Wayside) is regarded as Bang's masterpiece; "Ved Vejen" is both a cinematic picture of Danish provincial life and a subtle portrait of a gentle woman consumed in a marriage without love, and longing for tenderness. This motif is continued in the ironical but also tragic short stories collected in *Under Aaget* (1890; Under the Yoke) as well as in the two novels *Tine* (1889) and *Ludvigsbakke* (1896). In the former, the theme of destruction is found both in the fate of the main character and in the defeat of Denmark by Prussia in 1864. In the latter, Bang, like August STRINDBERG, describes the relationship between man and woman as a torment leading to destruction.

The period picture of *Haabløse Slægter* is continued in *Stuk* (1887; Stucco), the first Danish collective novel, depicting the spiritual hollowness and economic swindle behind the miscalculated attempt to transform provincial Copenhagen into a European metropolis. Autobiographical traits are disguised in Bang's two novels set in artistic circles, *Mikaël* (1904) and *De unden Fædreland* (1906; Eng. tr., *Denied a Country*, 1927), dealing with the isolation and homelessness of the artist. *De unden Fædreland* most consistently illustrates Bang's impressionistic technique: nothing is described or analysed; everything is situation, motion, or direct speech, a scenic technique influenced by Jonas LIE and the novels of Hans Christian Andersen. Bang's "quiet existences" are described without social or ideological polemics, but exclusively through his original artistry, the elements of which—sensitivity, observation, and flexible intelligence—made him one of the foremost Danish masters of impressionism.

See: T. Nilsson *Impressionisten Herman Bang* (1965); K. P. Mortensen, *Sonderinger i Herman Bang's romaner* (1973).

S.H.R.

Banti, Anna, pseud. of Lucia Lopresti Longhi (1895–1978), Italian fiction writer and critic, was born in Florence. She married Roberto Longhi, the art critic, and directed the literature section of the Florentine journal *Paragone,* which she founded with him in 1950. Banti was trained in art history, and her writing accentuates the visual. Among her works of nonfiction are studies of Lorenzo Lotto (1953) and Matilde SERAO (1965), a collection of essays entitled *Opinioni* (1961; Opinions), and a translation of the celebrated *L'Art italien* by André Chastel (1957–58). Her fiction, in addition to using art as subject matter, appeals in an imaginative way to the reader's sense of sight. Banti's most widely acclaimed works are the novel *Artemisia* (1947), also published in *Due storie* (1969; Two Stories), and the story "Lavinia fuggita" (Lavinia Has Run Away) of *Le donne muoiono* (1951; Women Die), also published in *Campi elisi* (1963; Elysian Fields). Both depict earlier historical periods and have a psychological focus, in contrast to the typical patterns of contemporary Italian neorealism.

In *Artemisia,* Banti employs the Olympian authorial view of 19th-century prose as well as the Italian *prosa d'arte* style (*see* ITALIAN LITERATURE). The narrative sweeps across time and space, following the life of Artemisia Gentileschi, successful 17th-century artist and teacher, an impassioned lonely woman. At the same time, Banti's novel tells of the loss of the original manuscript during World War II, Banti's own absorption in her full-scale but stillborn heroine, and the recreated story that was finally reborn in print.

"Lavinia" develops like a photograph, its details slowly emerging. What eventually defines itself is a tale of a woman's thwarted human potential. The setting is 18th-century Venice, famous for its musical life; the chief representative of that life, "Don Antonio" Vivaldi, enters the plot briefly but critically.

Other historical works are *Il bastardo* (1953; The Bastard), *Noi credevamo* (1967; We Once Believed), and *La camicia bruciata* (1973; The Burned Shirt), the story of Margaret Louise, cousin to Louis XIV and wife of the Medici ruler Cosimo III. The futuristic title story of the collection *Je vous écris d'un pays lointain* (1971; I Write to You from a Distant Land) is an uncharacteristic effort and less successful. Banti also translated William Thackeray's *Vanity Fair* (1948) and Virginia Woolf's *Jacob's Room* (1950).

See: G. A. Peritore, "Anna Banti," in *Letteratura italiana: i contemporanei*, vol. 3 (1969), pp. 211–34; E. B. Sabelli, "Il 'romanzo' di Marguerite Louise: Perchè?" *Paragone* 280 (1973): 118–26.

M.Sc.

Barac, Antun (1894–1955), Croatian critic, was born near Crikvenica. He studied Slavic literatures in Zagreb, and taught in secondary schools until 1930, when he became professor of Yugoslav literatures at Zagreb University. As a gymnasium student in Sušak, Barac espoused a pro-Yugoslav ideology and was active in political organizations; during World War II, he spent six months in concentration camps, an experience that he describes in his posthumous collection of essays and reminiscences, *Bijeg od knjige* (1965; Escape from the Book).

Barac produced a series of monographs dealing with significant Croatian writers of the 19th and 20th centuries: *Vladimir Nazor* (1918), *August Šenoa* (1926), *Vidrić* (1940), and *Mažuranić* (1945). He was equally interested in basic questions on literature, which he dealt with in numerous studies collected in *Knjiga eseja* (1924; A Book of Essays); *Članci o književnosti* (1935; Articles about Literature); *Književnost i narod* (1941; Literature and the People), and *Veličina malenih* (1947; The Greatness of Minor Writers).

In *Jugoslavenska književnost* (1954; Eng. tr., *A History of Yugoslav literature*, 1955 [1973]), Barac is at his best when he speaks about the 19th century; he is less successful when dealing with the earlier period, and he abstains almost entirely from discussing literature since World War II. In *Hrvatska književna kritika* (1938; Croatian Literary Criticism), Barac covers the period 1842–1914 and stresses the interaction between the development of literature itself and the development of literary criticism. In his monograph *Književnost Ilirizma* (1954; Illyrian Literature), he presented both the Illyrian movement as a whole and those individuals who played significant roles in it.

See: S. Lasić, "O literarno-historijskom metodu u djelima Barca," *Pogledi* 55 (1956), 3–69; I. Frangeš, "Djelo Antuna Barca," *Umjetnost riječi* 3 (1962): 139–159; V. Antić, "Antun Barac u ogledalu zavičaja," *Riječka revija* 7 (1964): 499–558. A.K.

Barbosa, Jorge (1902–71), Portuguese poet from the Cape Verde Islands, was born on São Tiago Island in this south Atlantic archipelago. He participated in the decisive moments of Cape Verde's search for identity when he and other intellectuals formed the *Claridade* movement in the 1930s. Barbosa personifies the regionalist fervor that gave rise to the slogan "Let's sink our feet into the soil of Cape Verde."

Virtually all of Barbosa's poems deal with typical Cape Verdean themes: the sea, drought, loneliness, wanderlust, and emigration. Most were published in three collections, *Arquipélago* (1935; Archipelago), *Ambiente* (1941; The Air We Breathe), and *Caderno de um ilhéu* (1956; An Islander's Notebook). "Panorama," *Arquipélago*'s introductory poem, sets a tone of desolation and humility as Barbosa resignedly terms his islands the forgotten remnants of a continent in a lonely corner of the world. Loneliness constantly accompanies the islanders, who savor the nostalgia born of fleeting moments of communal melancholy. The arrival of a German freighter, a native son's return from America, even an object washed ashore break the monotony and transport the Cape Verdean to some distant, more exciting land. Brazil captured Barbosa's imagination. In several poems he recreates a Utopia in its image, a sisterland that embodies, on a mammoth scale, the Creole world of his tiny islands. From the lonely, desolate island of Sal, where he served as a customs official, Barbosa made imaginary, lyrical voyages in such fanciful poems as "Você, Brasil" (You, Brazil); but he spent the rest of his life in the customs administration of another island, São Vicente.

A few months prior to Barbosa's death, a Lisbon critic hailed him as one of the greatest poets in the Portuguese language. Jorge de Sena had already called him "a simple lyric poet, . . . uncommon through the restraint of his tone and the directness of his unadorned expression."

See: J. de Figueiredo, ed., *Modernos poetas cabo-verdianos* (1961); G. Mariano, *Uma introdução à poesia de Jorge Barbosa* (1964); N. Araujo, *A Study of Cape Verdean Literature* (1966), pp. 99–110. R.G.H.

Barbu, Ion, pseud. of Dan Barbilian, (1895–1961), Romanian poet, was born in Cîmpulung. He was educated at the universities of Bucharest, Göttingen, and Berlin, and in 1924 he joined the Faculty of Mathematics at the University of Bucharest.

Barbu's interest in poetry dates from 1912, when his poem "Elan" was published in *Sburătorul*. The best of his early poems is "După melci" (1921; Looking for Snails). Although he was initially influenced by the French Parnassians and symbolists (*see* FRENCH LITERATURE), Barbu's exotic landscapes gave way to Romanian settings with a bizarre Oriental and Balkan coloration in a strange folk verse: the Isarlîk cycle. In 1927 he began

to articulate theories concerning a compact poetry of "essences" comparable to the "abstractions [and] associations of mathematics." He reached his poetic maturity with *Joc secund* (1930; Mirrored Play), a work whose imagery springs not from immediate realities but from their reflections.

Barbu's reputation rests upon his original poetics, which exerted a great influence upon poets writing between the world wars. He is also known for his craftsmanship, employing verbal music, compact imagery, and provocative symbols, and for his intellectualizing of the concrete and transfiguration of the commonplace through "poetically descriptive incantations." The posthumous volume *Ochian* (1964; The Spy Glass) contains most of his poetry. Some of Barbu's poems have been translated into English and are available in *Modern Romanian Poetry* (1973).

See: T. Vianu, *Ion Barbu* (1935, 1970); B. Nicolescu, *Ion Barbu: Cosmologia "Jocului secund"* (1968); D. Pillot, *Ion Barbu* (1969). T.A.P.

Barbusse, Henri (1873–1935), French novelist, journalist, political writer, and activist, was born in Asnières. During seven years as a journalist, he wrote the poems published in *Les Pleureuses* (1895; The Weepers), his first creative work. A first novel in 1903 was followed by *L'Enfer* (1908; Eng. tr., *The Inferno*, 1918), the relentless observation of two people seen through a hole in their hotel room wall. This novel prefigured Barbusse's determination never to compromise his vision of truth. *L'Enfer* became famous only after the sensational success in France of *Le Feu* (1916; Eng. tr., *Under Fire*, 1917), which won the Goncourt Prize. Barbusse's depiction of his war experiences in *Le Feu* made him many enemies, but within five years, over half a million copies of the novel were sold. *Le Feu* showed the common soldiers' immeasurable resources of strength, courage, and brotherhood despite the dehumanization of warfare. This antiwar work published in the very midst of the war won Barbusse worldwide fame. It was called "not only a novel but an act of courage," particularly because of a scene of fraternization between French and German infantrymen "among the thirty million men who fought this war without wanting to." Translated into 51 languages, *Le Feu* galvanized international antiwar sentiment and infuriated superpatriots.

A volunteer on the day that France declared war in August 1914, Barbusse was demobilized a year later because of broken health. He labored tirelessly to produce scores of novels, all didactic. *Clarté* (1919; Clarity) further explores war's evils and hypocrisies on the "home front," showing workers' lives disrupted and families deprived. In the wake of *Le Feu*, *Clarté* was inevitably successful and became the basis for an international antiwar organization called "Clarté." In 1923, Barbusse publicly joined the young French Communist Party, and two years later he published *Les Enchaînements* (Eng. tr., *Chains*, 1925), a Marxist "epic vision of the terrible homogeneity of history."

There followed many short stories and novels, as well as *Jésus* (1927), a biography in which Jesus is shown as a revolutionary worker and a carpenter for brotherhood. Barbusse joined with Romain ROLLAND in leading the Amsterdam World Congress against War and Fascism in 1932, for the threat of Hitlerism was already obvious. The same year, he completed the unconventional biography *Zola* (Eng. tr., 1932) and went to the United States to help found the American League against War and Fascism. Exhausted and tubercular, he accepted the USSR's invitation for care in a sunlit sanatorium, but it was too late. He died in Moscow in 1935 and was buried in Paris.

Over 250,000 people accompanied his bier to Père Lachaise Cemetery.

See: A. Vidal, *Henri Barbusse: soldat de la paix* (1953); V. Brett, *Henri Barbusse: sa marche vers la clarté, son mouvement Clarté* (1963); special nos. of *Europe* (November 1955, January 1969, September 1974).   E.S.B.

Bardèche, Maurice (1909–), French essayist and literary historian, was born in Bourges. He studied at the Ecole Normale Supérieure and went on to receive a *doctorat ès lettres* and the *agrégation* in literature. He taught at the Sorbonne and at the University of Lille, leaving his post there in 1944. Robert BRASILLACH, a rightist who was executed after the liberation of France, was his close friend at the Ecole Normale and later his brother-in-law. Together they wrote *Histoire du cinéma* (1935; Eng. tr., *History of Motion Pictures,* 1938); Bardèche has since edited Brasillach's posthumous works.

Bardèche's right-wing political philosophy makes him a controversial figure; he has spoken out in several strongly worded pamphlets, such as *Sparte et les sudistes* (1969; Sparta and the Southernists). Although he is no longer teaching, Bardèche has continued his scholarly work in literature. He has devoted himself to the giants of modern fiction—Honoré de Balzac, Stendhal, Marcel PROUST and, most recently, Gustave Flaubert in *L'Œuvre de Flaubert* (1974). His approach is academic, working from the author's life, his manuscripts, and from the social history of the times. In another field and in quite a different mood (although just as thoroughly documented) is his study of women throughout the ages, *Histoire de la femme* (1969).   L.LeS.

Barea, Arturo (1897–1957), Spanish novelist and critic, was born in Madrid. He began his literary career at the age of 42 with a collection of short stories, some not more than three pages in length, about the Spanish Civil War. This book, *Valor y miedo* (1938; Courage and Fear), appeared in the midst of the war. Barea's talent was to be recognized following the war, when he was living in England as an exile. His trilogy *The Forging of a Rebel* (1946), first published in English, was an instant success. Later printed in Spanish as *La forja de un rebelde* (1951), this autobiographical narrative became one of the best-known novels of the Spanish Civil War written by a Spanish national. The first volume, *La forja* (The Forge), narrates Barea's impoverished childhood in Madrid during the reign of Alfonso XIII. His experiences as a young boy in the poor section of the capital convinced him that radical changes were necessary in Spain. The second volume of the trilogy, *La ruta* (The Route), narrates Barea's stint with the army in the Moroccan campaign that ended in the military disaster of 1921, an episode that confirmed the social convictions of his youth. This tale of corruption and incompetence is similar to Ramon José SENDER's novel *Imán* (1930). The third volume, *La llama* (The Flame), is the story of the seige of Madrid during the Civil War of 1936–39. The popular reaction to the Fascist revolt, the chaos, heroism, and violence of those first days, are depicted with stark realism in this novel.

After the success of his trilogy, Barea wrote only one more novel, *La raíz rota* (1955; Eng. tr., *The Broken Root,* 1952), which deals with the difficult years of postwar Spain. A collection of short stories, *El centro de la pista* (1960; The Middle of the Road), was published posthumously. Two books of literary criticism complete his work: *Lorca, el poeta y su pueblo* (1956; Eng. tr., *Lorca: The Poet and his People,* 1944), and *Unamuno* (1952). Barea's reputation as a novelist rests mainly on *The Forging of a Rebel,* although the Spanish version is marred by

the fact that it was poorly retranslated into Spanish from the English edition. The freshness of his prose, the credibility that results from the author's descriptions of personal experiences, and the "confessional" tone of the narrative all contribute to the strong impact of *La forja de un rebelde.*   L.S. P. de L.

Barlach, Ernst (1870–1938), German dramatist, sculptor, and designer, was born in Wedel, Holstein, the son of a country physician. Because of the early death of his father, Barlach's education was somewhat irregular, but in 1891 he succeeded in being admitted to the Academy of Arts in Dresden to study sculpture and design. For 15 years after 1895 he traveled extensively; lived in Hamburg, Berlin, and many other German cities; and visited Russia and Italy. Among these trips the stay in Russia in 1906 was decisive, for there Barlach learned "a Christian humility toward all things." In 1910 he settled permanently at Güstrow, an old Mecklenburg town famous for its magnificent cathedral. There he lived in solitude and almost complete seclusion until his death.

To speak of Barlach the dramatist is to speak of Barlach the sculptor and designer as well. His characters and statues alike bring to mind the great figures of the Romanesque and early Gothic period. In the lithographic illustrations he made for some of his plays, he achieved an almost perfect unity of the two arts.

Although many literary critics see a representative of expressionism in him, Barlach himself wanted his dramatic characters interpreted as real people, not as visions or reflections of his own condition. It remains true, however, that when he wrote for the theater he often tried to push into metaphysics. The old Faustian tradition emerges here against a Mecklenburg background. Barlach's first drama, *Der tote Tag* (1912; The Dead Day), is an allegory of a son who tries unsuccessfully to break away from his mother because he perceives the creative paternal spirit in the world outside. The same tension between the world and God, the maternal and paternal powers, is repeated in the plays that followed. His strongest drama, *Der arme Vetter* (1918; The Poor Cousin), reflects this contrast, and the same theme can be found in *Die echten Sedemunds* (1920; Eng. tr., *The Genuine Sedemunds,* 1964), *Der Findling* (1922; The Foundling), and *Der blaue Boll* (1926; Eng. tr., *The Blue Boll,* 1964). In *Die Sündflut* (1924; Eng. tr., *The Flood,* 1964) the contrast is expressed in biblical terms: the pious Noah and the refractory Calan contend for God. Some of these plays, with their mixture of mysticism, realism, and grotesque humor, are surprisingly effective. Barlach himself was a Faustian seeker who was always driven by his longing for God. Although tied to the earth, he wanted to share in infinity in order to save himself from resignation or despair.

See: E. Barlach, *Ein selbsterzähltes Leben* (1930); W. Muschg, *Der Dichter Ernst Barlach* (1958); E. M. Chick, *Ernst Barlach* (1967); C. D. Carls, *Ernst Barlach* (Eng. tr., 1969).   H.Sc. rev. A.L.W.

Baroja y Nessi, Pío (1872–1956), Spanish novelist, was born in San Sebastián. After practising medicine for some years and acting as manager of his aunt's bakery, he devoted himself exclusively to writing. In 1934 he became a member of the Royal Spanish Academy of the Language. He is the outstanding novelist of the Generation of 1898 (*see* SPANISH LITERATURE), sharing with its members a deep preoccupation with Spain, an interest in history and philosophy (especially the works of Arthur Schopenhauer and Friedrich NIETZSCHE), and a great attention to the Spanish landscape. Like them, he was in search of

Spain's essence. His work is a combination of realistic "slices of life" and existentialist anguish. His greatest contribution to the Spanish novel is his introduction of contemporary colloquial discourse, devoid of rhetoricism or pathos, in short, simple sentences or paragraphs. The fragmented structure of his nearly 100 books reflects 20th-century haste and restlessness. He did not create extraordinary heroes or plots that adhere to strict chronology, nor did he explain everything to the reader. Rather, by employing a technique of giving scattered impressions, he created the vision of a society of stubborn individuals. Although he at first presented only the negative aspects of the church and state, his faith in science eventually vanished as well, just as humor gradually gave way to sarcasm and irony. A taste for determinism was counterbalanced by Baroja's inextinguishable spirit of adventure and invention.

Baroja's first book, a collection of short sketches entitled *Vidas sombrías* (1900; Somber Lives), contains in undeveloped form all the characteristics of his later fiction: a profound knowledge of his Basque homeland, lyric interludes (less common in his more mature work), vivid portraits created with a few vigorous brush strokes, interest in the lot of the poor, loose structure, and true-to-life dialogue. *Camino de perfección* (1902; The Way to Perfection) describes the protagonist's quasi-mystical journey across Spain in search of his own self and of Spain's eternal tradition, in the sense of Miguel de Un-amuno's *intrahistoria*. Baroja won universal acclaim with the trilogy *La lucha por la vida* (1904; Eng. tr., *The Quest*, 1922; *Weeds*, 1923; *Red Dawn*, 1924), a stark portrayal of life in Madrid's lowest quarters, where the theme of anarchism—quite popular among his peers—is introduced. When he rewrote these novels in book form (they were originally published as serials), Baroja with amazing skill created a new protagonist embodying Nietzschean will power. *El árbol de la ciencia* (1911; Eng. tr., *The Tree of Knowledge*, 1928) is considered the most representative novel of the generation. The academic and intellectual circles of Madrid are here described and criticized, and a small provincial town is realistically sketched with all of its vices.

In 1913, Baroja embarked on his 22-volume *Memorias de un hombre de acción*, concluded in 1934. This series of historical novels in the manner of Benito Pérez Galdós's "Episodios nacionales" deals with 19th century Spain by centering on one character. The outstanding characteristics of the series are its antiheroicism, demythification, and lack of narrative unity except for one continuous character and one general theme: the absurdity of all wars and political affiliations, which inevitably lead to ruin and destruction. The fast-changing scenes, the unending arrivals and departures of new characters, the focus on everyday happenings and behind the scenes or backstage intrigues in Madrid, produce a surprisingly complete and vivid portrait of Spanish society. Baroja employed various narrators as "objective" witnesses, each with a different interpretation of the events. As in his contemporary novels, life is seen as a carnival or "bloody masquerade." Human destinies are eclipsed by the briskly revolving wheel of fortune: a man's life is vain gesticulation in a world gone crazy. This pessimistic attitude is evident also in the novels of contemporary setting *César o nada* (1910; Eng. tr., *Caesar or Nothing*, 1919), *El mundo es ansí* (1912; The Way of the World), and *El gran torbellino del mundo* (1926; The Great Whirlwind of Life). The spirit of adventure gives birth to *Paradox, Rey* (1906; Eng. tr., *Paradox, King*, 1931) and *Las inquietudes de Shanti Andía* (1911; Eng. tr., *The Restlessness of Shanti Andia*, 1959). The post-Civil War novels explore oneiric devices and fantasy. None equals the earlier works.

A third facet of Baroja's writings is his essays and autobiographical works such as *Juventud, egolatría* (1917; Eng. tr., *Youth, Egolatry*, 1920) and his multivolume *Memorias* begun in 1941 and continued until 1955, a retrospective evaluation of his life, works, and contemporaries, presenting glimpses of the changing Spanish scene throughout the years. *La caverna del humorismo* (1919; The Grotto of Humor) opens insights into his concept of art. He expounded his ideas on the novel in the prologue to *La nave de los locos* (1925; The Ship of Fools), defining the genre as "an open sack which can hold anything." He also tried his hand at poetry and drama.

Baroja's novels have been criticized for their lack of structure, their failure to create an autonomous fictional world, and an excess of characters lacking psychological depth. Some critics have called them hasty patchworks and blamed Baroja's consistent repudiation of rhetorical devices, artificially contrived unity of plot, and polished expression. Although Baroja wrote at the rate of one novel or more per year, all of his books underwent several revisions, as is manifest from extant manuscripts. His historical novels rest on thorough documentation. Borrowing from Stendhal and César Saint-Réal, he defined the novel as a mirror held up to reflect the happenings on the road, a conception that stresses movement and rejects the tight "frame." While composing, he freely juggled different parts, frequently incorporating earlier sketches or fragments. A characteristic of his technique is the interruption into the narration of divagations and generalizations. Baroja tends to predispose the reader by offering opinions about new characters before introducing them. Although there is a tremendous amount of action in his books, it is seldom generated by great passion or commitment to firm ideals. Rather, skepticism is the predominant attitude. He captivates the reader by the directness of his approach, his savory language, and the pulsation of life in his novels. His own detachment from the characters is that of a dispassionate and sometimes cynical observer, and it prefigures the authorial attitude of younger novelists like Camilo José Cela, who has hailed Baroja as "the father of all novels posterior to him."

See: L. L. Barrow, *Negation in Baroja: A Key to his Novelistic Creativity* (1971); B. P. Patt, *Pío Baroja* (1971); J. Martínez Palacio, ed., *Pío Baroja* (1974). B.Ci.

Barolini, Antonio (1910–71), Italian poet, novelist, and journalist, was born in Vicenza. Here he published several slim volumes of poetry, including the collection *La gaia gioventù* (1938, 1953; Glad Youth). This was followed by *Il meraviglioso giardino* (1941; The Marvelous Garden), whose favorable notice from the critic Pietro Pancrazi established Barolini as a poet. In 1951, Barolini moved to New York as foreign correspondent for the Turin daily *La stampa*. His book of verse *Elegie di Croton* (1959; Croton Elegies) reflects his American experiences. This volume won the Bagutta Prize in 1960. He returned to Italy in 1965. The definitive collection of Barolini's poetry is *L'angelo attento* (1968; The Watchful Angel), which contains previously unpublished poems as well as consolidating the material in the earlier volumes.

During his years in New York, Barolini developed his talents as a raconteur in nostalgic stories about the rapidly disappearing provincial Italian life of his youth. In his short fiction, Barolini strikes a note between melancholy and humor; one of these stories, "La grande schidionata del cugino Canal" (The Great Bird Barbecue of Cousin Canal), is considered by Eugenio Montale to be his masterpiece. Many of Barolini's stories first appeared in the *New Yorker* and the *Reporter,* translated into English by the author's wife, Helen. In 1960 his collected short stories appeared in English as *Our Last Family Countess*; the enlarged Italian version, *L'ultima contessa di famiglia,* was published in 1968.

In 1962, Barolini published his first novel, *Una lunga pazzia* (Eng. tr., *A Long Madness,* 1964), a work concerned with religious bigotry. It has the traditional form of the 19th-century realistic novel, including an omniscient narrator. Barolini's other novels are *Le notti della paura* (1967; The Nights of Fear), describing the underground life of a young man in Venice during the Nazi occupation, and *La memoria di Stefano* (1970; Stephen's Memory).

A book of essays, *Il paradiso che verrà* (The Paradise That Will Come), published posthumously in 1972, demonstrates the concern with spiritual issues that came to dominate Barolini's work. It is, however, in his poetry that Barolini's love for the real, his fascination with the earthly garden, is best integrated with his faith in the divine. Indeed, Barolini stands out among the Italian poets of his generation for his aloofness from the themes of our times; instead of alienation, one finds in his work an almost naive commitment to life.

See: E. Montale, "Poeta sperso fra gli uomini," *Corriere della sera* (Apr. 20, 1968); G. Pampaloni, in *Letteratura italiana: i contemporanei,* vol. 5 (1974), pp. 709–26.   T.B.

Barrault, Jean-Louis (1910–), French actor, director, producer, mime, lecturer, and writer, was born in Le Vésinet. He first performed on stage in 1931 (on his 21st birthday) in a small role in Charles DULLIN's production of *Volpone.* His first experience as a director was with *Autour d'une mère* (1935), an adaptation of William Faulkner, at the Atelier. During the 1930s, Barrault met the great mime Etienne Decroux, Antonin ARTAUD, and the actress Madeleine Renaud, whom he married in 1940. Barrault was introduced to Paul CLAUDEL in 1937, and the two formed one of the major author-director relationships of the contemporary theater. In 1939, Barrault, Jean ANOUILH, and others founded the review *La Nouvelle Saison.* The next year, at the behest of Jacques COPEAU, Barrault joined the Comédie-Française, where he excelled in the role of Corneille's Le Cid.

The high point of Barrault's theatrical career may have been his 1943 adaptation of Claudel's *Le Soulier de satin* (1929; Eng. tr., *The Satin Slipper,* 1931). Buoyed by his success, Barrault adapted a number of other Claudel works. He also worked with André GIDE on adaptations of Shakespeare's *Hamlet* and *Antony and Cleopatra* and Franz KAFKA's *The Trial.* In 1946, Barrault and Renaud left the Comédie-Française to found their own company, the Théâtre Madeleine Renaud–Jean-Louis Barrault at the Théâtre Marigny. Here he produced Claudel's *Partage de Midi* (1905; Eng. tr., *Break of Noon,* 1960), as well as plays by and based on Gide, Kafka, and Armand SALACROU. In 1957 he became director of the Théâtre Sarah-Bernhardt, and in 1959 André MALRAUX appointed him director of the Odéon-Théâtre de France. Barrault directed his famous productions of Eugène IONESCO's *Rhinocéros* (1959; Eng. tr., 1960) in 1960 and, in 1963, of Ionesco's *Le Piéton de l'air* (1963; Eng. tr., *A Stroller in the Air,* 1968) and Samuel BECKETT's *Happy Days* (1961). Over the course of his career, Barrault has also been responsible for important theatrical innovations in collaboration with the playwrights Jean COCTEAU and Christopher Fry, directors such as Louis JOUVET and Christian Bérard, and the composers Arthur Honegger, Darius Milhaud, and Pierre Boulez. During recent years, Barrault's most famous production has perhaps been his montage of Rabelais's life and work. In addition to his extensive theatrical work throughout the world with the Compagnie Renault-Barrault, he has worked in films, notably *Les Enfants du Paradis* (1945). In 1968, Barrault risked his theater and his career by his deep involvement with the student uprising in Paris.

Although there are those who consider Barrault a second-rate actor with a rasping voice as well as an unsuccessful theater and opera director, none would deny his knowledge and feeling for the theater and his charismatic presence, which he has perhaps best used to advantage in his many poetry readings and public lectures. His writings have appeared mainly in his own publication, *Les Cahiers de la Compagnie Madeleine Renaud–Jean-Louis Barrault.* His numerous essays and books include *Réflexions sur le théâtre* (1949; Eng. tr., *Reflections on the Theatre,* 1951), *Une Troupe et ses auteurs* (1950; A Company and Its Authors), *Je suis homme de théâtre* (1961; I Am a Man of the Theater), and *Nouvelles Réflexions sur le théâtre* (1959; Eng. tr., *The Theatre of Jean-Louis Barrault,* 1961). His edition of Racine's *Phèdre* (1946) is among the outstanding modern editions of a classical play.

See: A. Frank, *Jean-Louis Barrault* (1970).   A.Sz.

Barrès, Maurice (1862–1923), French novelist, essayist, journalist, and politician, was born at Charmes-sur-Moselle and died at Neuilly-sur-Seine. He published his first article in a Nancy newspaper in 1881. Soon thereafter, Barrès moved to Paris, where he was to spend the major part of his life. He contributed to several Parisian reviews and founded one himself, *Les Taches d'encre* (November 1884–February 1885), but it was through his humorous pamphlet *Huit jours chez M. Renan* (1885; A Week at Mr. Renan's), that Barrès finally attracted the attention of the Paris literary circles. The success of his first novel, *Sous l'œil des barbares* (1888; Under the Eye of the Barbarians), was partly due to a favorable review by Paul BOURGET, who sensed the budding genius of the young author. Along with *Un Homme libre* (1889; A Free Man) and *Le Jardin de Bérénice* (1891; The Garden of Berenice), this novel was part of the trilogy entitled *Le Culte du moi* (The Cult of the Ego). These three books, of unequal value, contain a number of passages with deep and clear insight into human psychology, cast in a graceful, fluid, and musical language. Their subject is the fascinating investigation of the inner life of a young man who admits but one reality, his own self. This egotist begins to meditate on society, however, when he realizes that he cannot cultivate and enrich his personality without communing with his fellow men, whom he professes to despise. Barrès's next book was *L'Ennemi des lois* (1893; The Enemy of the Laws), which registers an evolution towards greater moral responsibility.

Having discovered that his "individual soul" was dependent on the "collective soul," Barrès was led first to accept his own limitations, next to convince himself of the predominance of instinct over reason, and finally to believe that French energies would be best revived through the cult of provincial and national traditions and reverence for the soil and the dead. Hence his passage from dream to action, his evolution from pure egotism to regionalism and nationalism. This new aspect of his philosophy is illustrated and dramatized in a second trilogy, *Le Roman de l'énergie nationale* (The Novel of National Energy), which includes *Les Déracinés* (1897; The Uprooted), *L'Appel au soldat* (1900; The Call to the Soldier), and *Leurs Figures* (1903; Their Faces). *Les Déracinés* is the story of seven Lorrainers whose lives turn out to be failures because, says the author, they have been "uprooted" by college education. The book, packed with social and philosophical digressions, has been one of the most influential, and also most discussed, works of modern French literature. *L'Appel au soldat* and *Leurs Figures* were directly inspired by the author's personal experiences in public life. He had been elected deputy for Nancy in 1889 and had already played an important role in national politics.

Barrès also sought inspiration in foreign lands. Two collections of short stories and essays, *Du sang, de la volupté, de la mort* (1894; Blood, Voluptuousness, and Death), and *Amori et dolori sacrum* (1903), the morbid and sensual character of which is accurately suggested by the titles, are the results of travels in Spain and Italy. In these books, the author again emerges as a peerless artist, a dilettante, and a romantic seeker of violent sensations. His now well-developed ego, immensely enriched, remains the real subject matter of these as well as some subsequent works. Also inspired by travels abroad are his *Le Voyage de Sparte* (1905; The Trip to Sparta), *Greco, ou le Secret de Tolède* (1912; El Greco, or the Secret of Toledo), the delightful short novel *Un Jardin sur l'Oronte* (1922; A Garden on the Oronte), and *Une Enquête aux pays du levant* (1923; A Commission of Inquiry in the Countries of the Near East). His third trilogy, *Les Bastions de l'est* (Bastions of the East), consisting of *Au service de l'Allemagne* (1905; In the Service of Germany); *Colette Baudoche: histoire d'une jeune fille de Metz* (1909; Eng. tr., *Colette Baudoche: The Story of a Young Girl of Metz,* 1918), and *Le Génie du Rhin* (1921; The Genius of the Rhine), is a logical sequence to the novel of national energy. Maurice Barrès, who at the age of eight had seen his father and his grandfather taken as hostages, devoted the greater part of his life to the building of those "bastions" or intellectual fortresses meant to protect French civilization from any threatening foreign influences or armed forces. The essays collected in *Les Amitiés françaises* (1903; French Friendships), as well as numerous speeches and articles, had similar aims.

Among Barrès's other important works are *La Colline inspirée* (1913; Eng. tr., *The Sacred Hill,* 1929), a fascinating lyrical and symbolical novel; *La Grande Pitié des églises de France* (1914; The Great Pity of the Churches of France), a collection of speeches in Parliament; and *Le Mystère en pleine lumière* (1924; Mystery in Full Light), a posthumous collection of short stories. Barrès himself, and some critics with him, regarded his *Chronique de la grande guerre* (1920–24; Chronicle of the Great War) as the most deserving of his works. In consists of 14 volumes of collected articles dealing with events from 1914 to 1918. Finally, 11 volumes of *Mes Cahiers* (1929–38; My Notebooks), his journal from 1896 to 1918, are essential for a full understanding and appreciation of his life and work.

Barrès must be considered primarily as an original writer who created a style of his own and whose influence has been both literary and ideological. He endowed words and ideas with such an intense life, marking them with such a personal stamp, that some soon became as inseparable from his name as they were to be from the history of modern thought and literature in France. This applies particularly to *le culte du moi,* that is, the best expression of rugged individualism; *les barbares* (other people); the theme of *les déracinés* and that of *la terre et les morts,* which are fundamental elements of regionalism; and *le nationalisme,* which became the rallying doctrine of all reactionary forces during the last decade of the 19th century. In the field of politics, Barrès devoted himself to the issues of the return of Alsace-Lorraine to France and German expansion. Toward the end of his life, he was widely respected as a sincere and great patriot. Even his political opponents admired the man who had tempered his traditionalism and finally given up polemics in an effort to further national unity.

See: E. R. Curtius, *Maurice Barrès und die geistigen Grundlagen des französischen Nationalismus* (1921); A. Thibaudet, *La Vie de Maurice Barrès* (1921); P. Moreau, *Maurice Barrès* (1946); R. Lalou, *Maurice Barrès* (1950); J.-M. Domenach, *Barrès par lui-même* (1960); P. de Boisdeffre, *Barrès* (1962); E. Carassus, *Barrès et sa fortune littéraire* (1970).   A.V.R.

Barthes, Roland (1915–80), French critic, was born in Cherbourg. He attracted much attention with *Le Degré zéro de l'écriture* (1953; Eng. tr., *Writing Degree Zero,* 1968), which introduced the concept of *écriture* ("scription") as distinguished from style, language, and writing. In *Mythologies* (1957; Eng. tr., 1972), Barthes examined manifestations of French bourgeois ideology in newspapers, magazines, films and other forms of entertainment. In *Sur Racine* (1963; Eng., tr., *On Racine,* 1964), he posited Racine's work as being both transparent and questioning, enabling each reader to provide a different answer in keeping with his or her own history, language, and freedom. The ensuing controversy enabled Barthes to define his positions in *Critique et vérité* (1966; Criticism and Truth), where he showed the extent to which critical terms and approaches previously taken for granted were a function of dominant-class ideology. To replace this, Barthes called for a science of literature based on a linguistic model.

In *Eléments de sémiologie* (1964; Eng. tr., *Elements of Semiology,* 1968), Barthes provided a basis for the "science of signs" that Ferdinand de Saussure (1857–1913) had envisaged. In *Système de la mode* (1967; System of Fashion) he tested the semiotic approach by studying descriptions of women's apparel in fashion magazines. *S/Z* (1970; Eng. tr., 1974), an analysis of Honoré de Balzac's *Sarrasine,* revealed the text's plural nature and the several networks of codes that inform it. Barthes's method often involves a sensuous manhandling of the text; appropriately, a later essay is called *Le Plaisir du texte* (1973; Eng. tr., *The Pleasure of the Text,* 1975). *L'Empire des signes* (1970; The Empire of Signs), written after a visit to Japan, is a euphoric counterpart to *Mythologies,* a sympathetic shaping of a country's myth seen from abroad, on the basis of signs perceived within. How signs make up various language systems within that of natural language became a major object of Barthes's concern with *Sade, Fourier, Loyola* (1971; Eng. tr., 1976), a description of three such language systems as seen in the writings of three "founders of language." In *Fragments d'un discours amoureux* (1977; Eng. tr., *A Lover's Discourse: Fragments,* 1978), he studied clichés of erotic discourse (as opposed to sexual practice). *Image, Music, Text* (1977) and *The Eiffel Tower and Other Mythologies* (1979) bring together essays translated into English but not collected in book form in the original French. Barthes discusses himself in *Barthes par lui-même* (1975; Eng. tr., *Roland Barthes,* 1976).

Barthes was elected to the Collège de France in 1976. The papers from a colloquium on his critical methods were published as *Prétexte: Roland Barthes* (1978), acknowledging him as the leading critic of his generation.

See: special issues of *TelQ* 47 (1971) and *L'Arc* 56 (1974); G. de Mallac and M. Eberbach, *Barthes* (1971); S. Heath, *Vertige du déplacement: lecture de Barthes* (1974).   L.S.R.

Bassani, Giorgio (1916-), Italian novelist, poet, and essayist, was born in Bologna. He lived in Ferrara until 1943, when he took part in the anti-Fascist Resistance and moved to Rome. There he edited the international review *Botteghe oscure* and was an editor for the publisher Feltrinelli. (His name is tied to the discovery of Giuseppe TOMASI DI LAMPEDUSA's *Il Gattopardo* in 1958.) For a while Bassani was a director of the Italian radio-television network. He is an editor of *Paragone* and the president of "Italia Nostra."

Because of the Fascist "racist laws" against Jews, Bassani published his first collection of short prose pieces, *Una città di pianura* (1940; A City in the Plain), under the pseudonym Giacomo Marchi. After World War II, he published three collections of poetry: *Storie dei poveri amanti e altre poesie* (1945-46; Stories of Poor Lovers and Other Poems), *Te lucis ante* (1947), and *Un'altra libertà* (1952; Another Freedom); they were collected in *L'alba ai vetri: poesie 1942-50* (1963; Dawn at the Windowpanes: Poems 1942-50).

In the 1950s, Bassani published two stories: *La passeggiata prima di cena* (1953; Eng. tr., "The Walk Before Supper," 1962) and *Gli ultimi anni di Clelia Trotti* (1955; Eng. tr., "The Last Years of Clelia Trotti," 1962), winner of the Veillon Prize. These were included in *Cinque storie ferraresi* (1956; Eng. tr., *Five stories of Ferrara*, 1971), winner of the Strega Prize, and later in *Le storie ferraresi* (1960; Eng. tr., *A Prospect of Ferrara*, 1962), which then became *Dentro le mura* (1973; Inside the Walls). His later works are: *Gli occhiali d'oro* (1958; Eng. tr., *The Gold-Rimmed Spectacles*, 1960), also included in *Le storie ferraresi*; *Il giardino dei Finzi-Contini* (1962; Eng. tr., *The Garden of the Finzi-Continis*, 1965), winner of the Viareggio Prize; *Dietro la porta* (1964; Eng. tr., *Behind the Door*, 1972); *Due novelle* (1965; partial Eng. tr., "The Snows of Yesteryears," 1967); *Le parole preparate e altri saggi di letteratura* (1966; The Prepared Words and Other Essays on Literature); *L'airone* (1968; Eng. tr., *The Heron*, 1970), winner of the Campiello Prize; *L'odore del fieno* (1972; The Odor of Hay); and *Epitaffio* (1974; Epitaph), a collection of poems. The whole of Bassani's narrative oeuvre has been entirely rewritten and is now incorporated in *Il romanzo di Ferrara* (1974; The Novel of Ferrara).

Bassani's work began with lyric prose pieces and poems in a "low key" with religious overtones, and continued in an increasingly expanded, self-conscious effort to combine his inner lyricism with an objective rendering of historical and social reality. Narrative prose, rather than poetry, became his natural way of expressing his *vision du monde*.

The ever-present background for Bassani's stories is the city of Ferrara (the "city in the plain" of the Po Valley), with its Christian and Jewish elements, the habits, manners, and idiosyncrasies of its inhabitants, and the perspectives of its landscapes. While relating a personal experience (usually that of a "Proustian" narrator in search of his lost time), Bassani is able to create the portrait of a city, indeed of a whole society, in the years immediately preceding World War II. *Cinque storie ferraresi*, with its impeccable balance between judgment and representation, between the elegiac and the historical, leads to the perfect results of the novella *Gli occhiali d'oro* and of the novel *Il giardino dei Finzi-Contini*, perhaps Bassani's finest achievements.

In *Gli occhiali d'oro*, Bassani presents the admirably drawn figure of Dr. Fadigati, a homosexual cast aside by the moralistic society of Ferrara, isolated from it just as the Jewish narrator is on the eve of the "racist laws"— an isolation later developed in *Dietro la porta*. *Il giardino*

is a delicate portrait of the narrator and Micòl—an unreachable, unforgettable feminine figure—and provides formidable documentation of the condition of Italian Jews under fascism. At the same time it is a melancholy meditation on death, a theme that is then carried further in *L'airone*.

Bassani's work deals with the difficulty of finding truth in memory, of organizing straight historical information into the chronological confusion of a story, and of providing a moral judgment about fleeting facts and their subtle, inner motivations. His style is polished and "classic," slow-flowing and pausing, a perfect tool (fashioned after Alessandro Manzoni [1785-1873], Giacomo Leopardi [1798-1837], and Giovanni VERGA) with which to follow the meanderings of memory and moral conscience. In it the lyrical, introverted inspiration of the poet is fused with the broad, objective vision of the novelist of manners.

See: G. Varanini, *Bassani* (1970); Massimo Grillandi, *Invito alla lettura di Giorgio Bassani* (1972).   G.P.B.

Basterra, Ramón de (1888-1928), Spanish poet and essayist, was born in Bilbao. He was concerned with both the past and the future of things Hispanic, and he wrote with equal fervor about Basque and Catholic tradition and about the novelties of the machine age. The scion of a wealthy Bilbao family, he studied in Germany and held diplomatic posts in Romania, Rome, and Venezuela. He died in Madrid. His prose studies, *La obra de Trajano* (1921; The Works of Trajan) and *Una empresa del siglo XVIII: Los navíos de la ilustración* (1925; An 18th-Century Undertaking: The Ships of the Enlightenment), demonstrate his constant attempt to define the centrifugal culture of Spain.

In successive books, Basterra's vision became more inclusive, turning westward beneath the dome of Greater Spain which, for him, arches over the Occident from Rome to Manila. *Las ubres luminosas* (1923; The Shining Udders) records a pilgrimage to Rome. It is a paean of praise to the Mother City ("most illustrious of wolves") from whom Spain inherited much of her culture. *La sencillez de los seres* (1923; The Simplicity of Beings) is a tribute to the people of northern Spain, especially the Basques. *Los labios del monte* (1924; The Lips of the Mountain) is a panoramic glorification of the Basques' defense of the Catholic faith, from the reconquest to the present.

The "Vírulo" of Basterra's last two books represents the peripatetic poet himself. In the morning of *Vírulo, mocedades* (1924; Vírulo, Youth) he starts west toward the mechanized world of the Hispanic present and future. *Vírulo, mediodía* (1927; Vírulo, Noon) finds him in the heart of modernity. His poetry no longer has the classicism or the romanticism of earlier works. It is now charged with neobaroque imagery, and the poet has become "the Aesop of the Machine." Basterra remains a minor poet, but his use of imagery and metaphor reveals an inventiveness that allies him with the avant-garde poets of his day.

See: G. Díaz Plaja, *La poesía y el pensamiento de Ramón de Basterra* (1941); G. Allegra, "Tradizione e avanguardia in Basterra," *Dialoghi* 18 (1970): 31-41.   D.K.A. rev. H.L.B.

Bataille, Georges (1897-1962), French essayist and novelist, was born in Billom. He has only recently been recognized as a major writer. His importance stems from his dealing with basic drives that govern human behavior and a concomitant need to "tell everything." His writings convey the experience of man's limits, that is, according to Maurice BLANCHOT, "what man undergoes when he has decided to challenge himself radically." Among notions that inform Bataille's works are the mutually dependent ideas of interdict and transgression. Interdict is tied to the anguish that emerges as one uncovers the realities of sexuality and death; transgression is to be understood in the light of religious ceremony and sacrifice. In *Lascaux ou la naissance de l'art* (1955; Lascaux or the Birth of Art), Bataille refers to the "crime of the sacrificer who, to the accompaniment of anguished silence of participants, fully cognizant of what was at stake, himself in a state of anguish, killed the victim, thereby violating the interdict against murder." In the same essay he depicted art as being born out of such a moment of religious transgression and tied both art and transgression to the domain of the sacred.

Bataille was a learned man and a graduate of the Ecole des Chartes. For many years he worked in the numismatics section of the Bibliothèque Nationale. Although he contributed to many reviews, the obscurity in which he worked was ended only with publication of his essays *L'Expérience intérieure* (1943; Interior Experience), *Le Coupable* (1944; The Guilty One), and *Sur Nietzsche* (1945; On Nietzsche). The best access to his work, however, is through *La Part maudite* (1949; The Accursed Part) and *L'Erotisme* (1957). In the background of his texts loom the writings of G. W. F. Hegel, Karl Marx, Friedrich NIETZSCHE, and Marcel Mauss, in addition to a large body of literature that includes surrealism, of which he called himself the "enemy from within." With some qualifications this phrase could also describe Bataille's stance toward much of Western culture (including theology and mysticism). From within the ideology in which he lived, he sought to transgress the interdicts that insured its homogeneity and to lay the basis for what might be called heterogeneous thought.

Bataille's fiction, such as *Histoire de l'œil* (1928; Story of the Eye), *Madama Edwarda* (1941), or *L'Abbé C...* (1950), does not fall into the reassuring categories of the erotic or obscene as commonly understood. He wrote that the secret of eroticism was in the power it afforded one to face death squarely and see in it an opening into an unintelligible and unknowable continuity of being. This relates to his definition of literary creation, a "sovereign operation," as he wrote in *La Littérature et le mal* (1957; Literature and Evil), a form of communing in which both writer's and reader's isolated beings are negated through the literary text. Bataille's fiction does not titillate; more likely it will produce a sense of horror—perhaps not unlike the fear aroused by tragedy but accomplishing, instead of a catharsis, a break with what one fantasizes oneself to be.

See: special issues of *Crit* 195-96 (1963), *L'Arc* 32 (1967), and *Gramma* 1 (1974); P. Sollers, *Logiques* (1968), pp. 291-97, and *Bataille* (1973); D. Hollier, *La Prise de la Concorde* (1974); C. Limousin, *Bataille* (1974); J. Durançon, *Georges Bataille* (1976); A. Arnaud and G. Excoffon-Lafarge, *Bataille* (1978).   L.S.R.

Bataille, Henry (1872-1922), French playwright and poet, was born in Nîmes. He entered the Ecole des Beaux Arts in 1890 to study painting. Four years later, influenced by Robert d'Humières, with whom he had written *La Belle au bois dormant* (1894; Sleeping Beauty), he made his debut as a dramatist. From 1900 to 1914, Henry Bataille was the most celebrated French playwright. Both the public and the critics praised *L'Enchantement* (1900; The Enchantment), *Le Masque* (1902; The Mask), *Maman Colibri* (1905; Mother Hummingbird), *Poliche* (1906), *La Femme nue* (1908; The Naked Woman), *Le Scandale*

(1909; The Scandal), *La Vierge folle* (1910; The Mad Virgin), *L'Enfant de l'amour* (1911; Love Child), and *Les Flambeaux* (1912; The Torches). In 1913 *Le Phalène* (The Moth), too obviously inspired by the life of Marie Bashkirtseff, was violently discussed. Three plays, *L'Amazone* (1916), *L'Animateur* (1920; The Animator), and *La Chair humaine* (1922; Human Flesh), mark an evolution towards the theater of ideas. *L'Homme à la rose* (1920; The Man with the Rose) offered variations on the theme of Don Juan. *La Tendresse* (1921; Tenderness) and *La Possession* (1921) are the last manifestations of a great talent that had gradually degenerated.

The weakness of Bataille's theater is partly due to the fact that it is the reflection of a period already belonging to the past. Many of his plays were inspired directly and exclusively by contemporary events and became dated very rapidly. A romanticist by nature, Bataille felt, moreover, a morbid attraction for exceptional and often repulsive characters. His best dramas are excellent psychological studies of irrepressible passions. They contain powerful scenes but suffer from an excess of lyricism and from artificialities of style, factors contributing in no small measure to the partial oblivion into which they have fallen. As a poet, Bataille wrote *La Chambre blanche* (1895; The White Chamber), *Le Beau Voyage* (1905; The Beautiful Trip), *La Divine Tragédie* (1917; The Divine Tragedy), and *La Quadrature de l'amour* (1920; The Squaring of Love). Some of his opinions on dramatic art can be found in *Ecrits sur le théâtre* (1917; Writings on the Theater). *L'Enfance éternelle* (1922; Eternal Childhood) contains autobiographical data.

See: D. Amiel, *Henry Bataille* (1912) and *Le Règne intérieur* (1912); P. Lièvre, "Henry Bataille," *Marges* 15 (1918): 203-12; special no. of *Herse* (May-June 1921); P. Blanchart, *Henry Bataille: son œuvre* (1922); L. Lemonnier, "Le Théâtre d'Henry Bataille," *Grande Revue* 108 (1922): 244-62; G. de Catalogne, *Henry Bataille, ou le romantisme de l'instinct* (1925); E. Seillière, *L'Evolution morale dans le théâtre d'Henry Bataille* (1936).
                                    M.E.C. rev. D.W.A.

Baty, Gaston (1885-1952), French theatrical director and producer, was born in Pélussin. He advocated an alliance of all the arts in the theater. Baty's fundamental ideas derive from his attempt to fill what he considered a void in the theater created by the insufficiency of dialogue. According to his theory, the printed text is only a partial reproduction of the author's state of mind while writing the play. The words represent only a residue of all that nourished the emotions of the playwright and, therefore, the task of the director is to restore what has vanished after the author's transmission of his vision into written symbols. By resorting to nonverbal means, the director adds to words what they are unable to express. The director is called upon to "orchestrate" the dialogue with all the elements of stagecraft at his command; indeed, for Baty, the written text is like an orchestral composition reduced to a piano score, while a play performed on the stage can be compared to a score performed by a symphony. Thus only the intimate fusion of light, color, gesture, movement, sound, and silence can enrich and strengthen the drama and create "the supreme art, the theater."

Unlike Charles DULLIN and Louis JOUVET, Baty was exclusively a director, not an actor. He formed his first company, "Les Compagnons de la Chimère," in 1922. This troupe produced plays at the Studio des Champs-Elysées in 1924, and in 1930 the company moved to the Théâtre Montparnasse. Baty's interpretations of Racine's *Phèdre* and *Bérénice* and Alfred de Musset's *Les Caprices de Marianne* and *Lorenzaccio* provoked notable interest. He also produced Jean-Jacques BERNARD's *Martine,* Jean Victor PELLERIN's *Têtes de Rechange,* and Henri LEN-ORMAND's *Le Simoun,* plays written in conformity with Baty's idea of the theater.

See: M. Brillant, *Préface au masque et l'encensoir par Gaston Baty* (1926); J. Hort, *Les Théâtres du cartel et leurs animateurs: Pitoëff, Baty, Jouvet, Dullin* (1944).

L.W.C.

Baudelaire, Charles Pierre (1821–67), French poet and critic, was born in Paris, where he spent most of his life. Soon after his elderly father's death in 1827, his mother married Major Aupick. Although until 1839 he and Charles were on good terms, Baudelaire was to find him a difficult and unsympathetic stepfather. After his school years at Lyon and then at the Collège Louis-le-Grand in Paris, Baudelaire enjoyed a brief period of independence and began his literary career. In 1841 his family sent him off on a long sea voyage; he returned, however, in less than a year, after short stays on the islands of Mauritius and Bourbon (Réunion). Upon coming of age he inherited his father's fortune, and for a time he lived the life of a rich young dandy. During this period, he contracted syphilis, which was eventually to consume him. His family, alarmed by the rapidity with which his fortune was disappearing, assigned him a financial guardianship in 1844. He was continually burdened with debts, in constant difficulties with publishers and printers, forever moving from one miserable lodging to another. Yet he still retained the needs and tastes of a dandy, much like those of his character Samuel Cramer in the short story "La Fanfarlo" (1847). His life was further complicated by his liaison with the mulatto Jeanne Duval, to whom he remained attached, often in a chivalrous manner, for many years. Many of his poems were inspired by her; others belong to a period of idealized devotion to Mme Sabatier, and still others to a brief liaison with the actress Marie Daubrun.

During the unrest of 1848, Baudelaire was a republican and a socialist, probably as a result of the philosophical theories to which he had previously adhered and perhaps out of compassion for the poor working classes. But disillusionment with these theories followed; Baudelaire discovered the ideas of Joseph de Maistre, from which he adopted his philosophy of providentialism and a keen awareness of original sin. Gustave Flaubert wondered whether Baudelaire had not insisted too strongly, in *Les Paradis artificiels,* on the existence of an "Evil Spirit." Baudelaire replied that "after examining scrupulously the depths of my past reveries, I realized that I have always been obsessed by the impossibility of understanding some of man's actions or thoughts save by the hypothesis of the intervention of some exterior evil force." In the middle of the 19th century, no one believed more in Satan's existence than Baudelaire, and no one rejected more firmly than he the illusion that material progress would lead to moral progress.

Baudelaire's stepfather, who had become a senator of the Second Empire, died in 1857. Subsequently, Baudelaire drew closer to his mother and spent an artistically productive time with her at Honfleur in 1859. In 1861 he made a defiant although unsuccessful application for admission to the Académie Française. By 1864, France had become unbearable to Baudelaire, and he set out for Belgium, supposedly on a lecture tour and to visit private art collections. He was to experience only new defeat. This time, he turned his hatred against the Belgians and furiously took notes for a pamphlet entitled *Pauvre Belgique!* (Poor Belgium!), which he never finished. Struck down there by paralysis in 1866, he was brought back to Paris, where he died on August 31, 1867.

In *Les Fleurs du mal* (1857; Eng. tr., *Flowers of Evil,* 1909), Baudelaire brought together poems on which he had been at work for years, many of which had already appeared in periodicals. The publication of the volume provoked a trial that resulted in Baudelaire's condemnation for offense against public morals and the suppression of 6 of the 100 poems. The second edition (1861) added more than 35 new poems; the posthumous edition of 1868, more than 25. In *Le Spleen de Paris* (Eng. tr., *Paris Spleen,* 1869, 1947), 50 prose poems first published as a volume in 1869 (most had been published in Baudelaire's lifetime), he developed a new form that allowed more freedom and more realistic detail than the versification of his time permitted. Ranging from the short story ("Une Mort héroïque") to the lyrical prose poem ("L'Invitation au voyage") and the whimsical anecdote ("Le Miroir," "La Soupe et les nuages"), this work must be considered as Baudelaire's most modern poetic laboratory.

Baudelaire's affiliation with his predecessors, with the 16th-century Pléiade and Racine as well as with the romantics, is apparent on the surface, and his passion for perfection of form seems to ally him with the Parnassian poets. But his poetry is intensely personal, marked with a desperate sincerity. The struggle between good and evil, the efforts and failures of the faltering will, the dark and devious attempts to escape from spleen and despair, the passionate devotion to beauty, cry out from the depths of this poetry. Baudelaire's external world is as distinctive as his inner one—the great city with its sordid streets and crowded houses, the vast expanses of sea and sky, the tropical sights and sounds and smells of his early voyage. For him nature is a great storehouse of images; the outer and inner worlds are bound together by mysterious correspondences, not merely between the different senses, but between the visible and invisible worlds. His images are not developed in splendid isolation, like those of the romantic poets, but are symbols in which image and meaning are fused into one by his visionary genius. His poetry has a perfection of form and music that at times gives it classic simplicity, at times a distantly echoing intensity. Baudelaire brought to French poetry a dark splendor, a magic density that it had not yet known. Unlike Victor Hugo (1802–85), Baudelaire experienced difficulty in creating. His inspiration was slight, which could be explained by psychophysiological and sociological reasons, but he created out of these difficulties a new set of values. Beginning with Baudelaire, poetry ceases to be a discourse on nature, God, death, or love. The object of poetry is itself. It becomes a meditation on poetic creation, on the nature of poetry: the first 20 poems of *Les Fleurs du mal,* "La Musique" (Music), "La Mort des artistes" (The Death of Artists), and several prose poems are devoted to this search. Consequently, even before encountering Edgar Allan Poe's precepts concerning the length of a poem, Baudelaire preferred the short poem that strikes the reader and captures his attention: the sonnet.

Baudelaire himself said that he considered the poet the best of critics. His own criticism, collected in the two posthumous volumes *Curiosités esthétiques* (1868; Aesthetic Curiosities) and *L'Art romantique* (1869; Romantic Art), is almost entirely of his contemporaries, whom he judged with amazing sureness (see *The Mirror of Art: Critical Studies,* 1955). His art criticism, centered on Delacroix, covers the Salons of 1845, 1846, and 1859 and the Exposition of 1855; it includes three articles on the essence of laughter and caricature (1855–57) as well as *Le Peintre de la vie moderne* (1863; The Painter of Modern

Life) and *L'Œuvre et la vie d'Eugène Delacroix* (1863; The Work and Life of Eugène Delacroix). Baudelaire's literary criticism includes one article on and two prefaces to Poe (1852, 1856, and 1857), one essay on Théophile Gautier (1859), and the commentaries written on his contemporaries—Hugo, Gautier, Théodore de Banville, Leconte de Lisle, Marceline Desbordes-Valmore, and others—for an anthology directed by Eugène Crépet, *Les Poëtes français* (1861-63; French Poets), and a number of shorter articles, including one on *Madame Bovary* (1857). In 1861, Baudelaire made his one excursion into musical criticism with *Richard Wagner et Tannhäuser à Paris*. For him criticism is first of all poetic, the translation of an experience, a reflection of the work of art. Then the intelligence comes into play, and he goes on to "transform delight into knowledge" (*transformer ma volupté en connaissance*), to deduce from experience the laws of art, crystallized in his great all-embracing conception of the imagination.

About 1847, Baudelaire discovered Poe, with whom he felt from the first a fraternal affinity. A large part of his literary effort was devoted to his admirable translation of Poe's tales and other works, *Histoires extraordinaires* (1856; Extraordinary Stories), *Nouvelles Histoires extraordinaires* (1857; New Extraordinary Stories), *Aventures d'Arthur Gordon Pym* (1858), *Eureka* (1864), and *Histoires grotesques et sérieuses* (1864; Grotesque and Serious Stories). *Les Paradis artificiels* (1860; Artificial Paradises) comprises an original work, "Poëme du haschisch" (Poem of Hashish), and "Un mangeur d'opium" (An Opium Eater), a subtle adaptation of Thomas De Quincey's work. After Baudelaire's death, the *Oeuvres posthumes* (1887-1908; Posthumous Works) gathered together early poems, scattered articles, and unfinished sketches, as well as *Fusées* and *Mon Coeur mis à nu* (Eng. tr., *My Heart Laid Bare*, 1950), the so-called *Journaux intimes* (Eng. tr., *Intimate Journals*, 1930). The publication of his letters, *Correspondance* (2 vols., 1973), has added much to our knowledge of Baudelaire the man. An English selection, *Letters of Baudelaire*, was published in 1927. Baudelaire's *Œuvres complètes* (Complete Works) were published in two volumes in 1975-76.

Although he died in 1867, one has only to think of Stéphane MALLARMÉ and Arthur RIMBAUD, Paul CLAUDEL and Paul VALÉRY, André GIDE and Marcel PROUST, Pierre-Jean JOUVE, Pierre EMMANUEL, and Yves BONNEFOY, of Charles Algernon Swinburne and William Butler Yeats, Ezra Pound and T. S. Eliot, of Stefan GEORGE and Rainer Maria RILKE to realize how truly Baudelaire belongs with the moderns.

See: A. Cassagne, *Versification et métrique de Charles Baudelaire* (1906); J. Pommier, *La Mystique de Baudelaire* (1932) and *Dans les chemins de Baudelaire* (1945); L. J. Austin, *L'Univers poétique de Baudelaire* (1939); G. Blin, *Baudelaire* (1939) and *Le Sadisme de Baudelaire* (1948); M. Gilman, *Baudelaire the Critic* (1943, repr. 1971); B. Fondane, *Baudelaire et l'expérience du gouffre* (1947); H. Peyre, *Connaissance de Baudelaire* (1951); J. Prévost, *Baudelaire: essai sur l'inspiration et la création poétique* (1953); R. Vivier, *L'Originalité de Baudelaire* (1965); C. Mauron, *Le Dernier Baudelaire* (1966); M. Milner, *Baudelaire: enfer ou ciel qu'importe!* (1967); F. W. Leakey, *Baudelaire and Nature* (1969).

M.Gi. rev. C.P.

Bauer, Wolfgang (1941-), Austrian playwright, was born in Graz, where "Forum Stadtpark" produced his first one-act plays in 1962. His breakthrough came with *Magic Afternoon*, which, in 1968 and 1969, played on 60 stages in Germany. His first publication, *Mikrodramen* (1962;

Microdramas), with its spoofing of theater conventions, seemed to put him in the lineage of dada and the "Wiener Gruppe" (*see* GERMAN LITERATURE), as do his "bad masterpiece," *Das Stille Schilf* (1969; Silent Reeds), poems, and his novel, *Der Fieberkopf* (1967; The Fever Head). The longer plays, *Magic Afternoon, Change, Party for Six* (Eng. titles for German originals; 1969) deal with adaptation to lives felt to be meaningless, where experience is secondhand (drugs, rock music, movie talk, literary references) and where attempts to break out of routine only double society's lethal game of manipulation. The small talk of insiders (in dialect) gives way to eruptions of violence in Bauer's loosely strung sequences of scenes. *Gespenster* (1974; Ghosts), *Silvester oder Das Massaker im Hotel Sacher* (1974; Silvester or the Massacre in Hotel Sacher), and *Film und Frau* (1974; Film and Women) turn again to ritualized parody of media conventions, for example, the reception of sadistic Western scenes in *Film und Frau*. A collected volume of his work, *Die Sumpftänzer* (The Swamp Dancers), appeared in 1978.

See: *Text & Kritik* 59 (1978). R.Wa.

Bazhan, Mykola (1904-), Ukrainian poet, was born in Kamyanets-Podilsky (Kamenets-Podolski). In the 1920s he worked for the All-Ukrainian Film Administration (VUFKU). According to the critic Lavrinenko, his best poetry shows his "own expressionist-Baroque-Romantic style." Bazhan started to write under the influence of futurism, as evidenced in the volume *Simnadtsyaty patrul* (1926; The 17th Patrol). His greatest achievement was reached in the collections *Rizblena tin* (1927; The Sculpted Shadow), *Budivli* (1929; Buildings), and the unfinished poem *Sliptsi* (1930; The Blind Men). His poetic power lies in a mingling of lyrical and intellectual expression. During the 1930s and 1940s, Bazhan became a faithful follower of socialist realism and joined the Communist Party. After Iosif Stalin's death in 1953, he recovered some of his earlier vigor, notably in "Opovidannya pro nadiyu: varyatsiyi na temu R. M. Rilke" (1966; A Tale about Hope: Variations on a Theme by R. M. Rilke). Bazhan is a talented translator from the Georgian, notably from the poetry of Shota Rustaveli. He has also been the editor-in-chief of the multivolume Soviet Ukrainian encyclopedia. G.S.N.L.

Bazin, Hervé pseud. of Jean-Pierre-Marie Hervé-Bazin (1911-), French novelist, was born in Angers. He spent his youth with his two brothers on Patys, his family's nearby country estate, which later provided the setting for several of his novels. His mother's domineering nature and lack of affection, the frequent changes of tutors and schools, and the family's persistence in stifling his natural inclination toward literature while forcing him in other directions built up an insufferable psychological climate that was prolonged by years of disoriented efforts to make a living, to write, and to establish his own family.

The frustrations of his youth were vented in Bazin's first published novel, *Vipère au poing* (1948; Eng. tr., *Viper in the Fist*, 1951), and to a lesser degree in *La Tête contre les murs* (1949; Eng. tr., *Head against the Wall*, 1952) and *Qui j'ose aimer* (1956; Eng. tr., *A Tribe of Women*, 1958). In his subsequent novels, Bazin showed more restraint in treating family relationships. His autobiographical trilogy of the Rézeau family examines patiently won mutual affection between a father and an illegitimate son, in *Au nom du fils* (1960; Eng. tr., *In the Name of the Son*, 1962), and a husband's perception of the gnawing routine preoccupations of a typical household, in *Le Matrimoine* (1967; Matrimony). *Le Cri de la chouette* (1972; The Screech of the Owl) completed the trilogy.

Some of Bazin's novels are based on an exceptional character or event: the extraordinary willpower of Janie Kofman in *Lève-toi et marche* (1952; Eng. tr., *Constance,* 1955), or the exodus and repatriation of the inhabitants of Tristan da Cunha after the island's 1961 volcanic eruption in *Les Bienheureux de la désolation* (1970; Eng. tr., *Tristan,* 1971). *Un feu dévore un autre feu* (1978; A Fire Consumes Another Fire) has a political theme and is quite different from any novel he has written previously.

Although Bazin has also written short stories, essays, criticism, and several volumes of poetry, he is essentially a novelist. Both his bold, often caricatural style, likened to Francisco Goya's painting, and his sarcasm are tempered by his characters' more nuanced feelings and his own attachment to nature, which are expressed in his longer narratives. Bazin's inspiration and style are personal. No literary influence is discernible, except that of François MAURIAC whom he "read in his father's library" and whose preoccupations with and perception of the family he shared. Yet the anticlerical Bazin is totally unlike Mauriac in style, beliefs, and outlook. Denouncing bourgeois values, his works radiate a positive, rational, and vital force, and his protagonists shun or try to overcome that which is physically and spiritually sick and deformed.

A member of the Académie Goncourt since 1958, Hervé Bazin has won many prizes. His works have been translated into at least 22 languages. His major novels, particularly *Viper in the Fist,* have appeared in English and have had numerous French editions. Like *Head against the Wall* and *L'Huile sur le feu* (Oil on the Fire), *Viper* has been made into a film. Although he is one of the most widely read French post–World War II authors, Bazin has not been the object of many critical studies.

See: R. Moustiers, *Hervé Bazin ou le romancier en mouvement* (1973).   B.C.

Bazin, René (1853–1932), French novelist, was born and brought up in Angers. As a boy he was very fond of country life and read many novels of adventures by Mayne Reid and tales of American Indians. He attended the Catholic University of Angers and in 1875 was appointed professor of law at that institution.

His first novel, *Stéphanette* (1884), was published under the pseudonym Bernard Seigny. Many other novels followed, published under his own name, most of which dealt with country life in Anjou, Poitou, and Vendée. The list includes *Une Tache d'encre* (1888; Eng. trs., *A Blot of Ink,* 1892, *Ink Stain,* 1905), *Les Noellet* (1890; Eng. tr., *This, My Son,* 1909), *La Sarcelle bleue* (1892; The Blue Teal), *Madame Corentine* (1893; Eng. tr., *Those of His Own Household,* 1914), *Humble Amour* (1894), and *De toute son âme* (1897; Eng. tr., *Redemption,* 1897). Particularly successful was a series dealing with the then acute problem of the threatened desertion of the land for the industrial cities: *La Terre qui meurt* (1899; Eng. tr., *Autumn Glory,* 1901; stage version in 1913), *Donatienne* (1903; Eng. tr., *The Penitent,* 1912), *Le Blé qui lève* (1907; Eng. tr., *The Coming Harvest,* 1908), and *La Closerie de Champdolent* (1917; The Enclosed Garden of Champdolent). Another capital problem that challenged the attention of Bazin was the question of Alsace-Lorraine, treated in *Les Oberlé* (1901; stage version in 1912; Eng. tr., *The Children of Alsace,* 1912), *Les Nouveaux Oberlé* (1919; The New Oberlés), and *Baltus le Lorrain* (1926; Baltus from Lorraine). This patriotic note was never dissociated from the religious, Roman Catholic note, as well illus-trated in the author's last story, *Magnificat* (1931; Eng. tr., 1932).

Bazin also wrote books in various other fields: *La Douce France* (1911; Eng. tr., *Gentle France,* 1913), *Charles de Foucauld, explorateur du Maroc, ermite au Sahara* (1921; Eng. tr., *Charles de Foucauld, Hermit and Explorer,* 1923), several collections of short stories, and several accounts of travels in Italy, Spain, and the provinces of France. *Etapes de ma vie* (1936; Stages of My Life) was published posthumously.

Bazin was an urbane writer, more serious than brilliant, a conscientious and orthodox workman. He was elected to the Académie Française in 1903.

See: A. de Bersaucourt, *René Bazin* (1906); C. Bauman, *René Bazin* (1924); F. Mauriac, *René Bazin* (1931).

           A.Sc. rev. D.W.A.

Beauvoir, Simone de (1908–), French moralist, feminist, autobiographer, essayist, and novelist, was born in Paris into an upper middle-class family whose religious and social values she rejected early. A brilliant student, she received her *agrégation de philosophie* in 1929 and taught philosophy in French lycées from 1931 to 1943. She became the best-known woman writer of her generation and one of the outspoken atheistic, left-wing intellectuals who exerted a strong influence on the beliefs and opinions of readers both in France and abroad in the years following World War II. Throughout her life she has maintained a passionate, rigorous dialogue with Jean-Paul SARTRE, whose existentialism provides the philosophical categories for her writings.

Simone de Beauvoir's 22 published texts—novels and short stories, a play, essays, documentary studies, autobiography—are unified by her persistent desire to reveal to her characters and to her readers the falsity and the dangers inherent in certain philosophical, political, social, and psychological presuppositions and the inauthentic attitudes and behavior these presuppositions determine. Her aim is always to recreate her own experience for herself and to communicate it to others and, in so doing, to teach her readers how to reevaluate their own experience in relation to the proposed model.

The dichotomy between ambiguity—in the novels and short stories from *L'Invitée* (1943; Eng. tr., *She Came to Stay,* 1949) to *La Femme rompue* (1967; Eng. tr., *The Woman Destroyed,* 1968)—and affirmation—in the essays and documentary studies from *Pyrrhus et Cinéas* (1944) to *La Vieillesse* (1970; Eng. tr., *The Coming of Age,* 1972)—represents the two thematic axes of her work: the sense of the absurd and the need for commitment. The sense of the absurd is made explicit in the novels through the problems of the female protagonist: Françoise in *L'Invitée,* Hélène in *Le Sang des autres* (1945; Eng. tr., *The Blood of Others,* 1948), Régine in *Tous les hommes sont mortels* (1946; Eng. tr., *All Men Are Mortal,* 1955), Anne in *Les Mandarins* (1954; Eng. tr., *The Mandarins,* 1956), Laurence in *Les Belles Images* (1966; Eng. tr., 1968), the three successive protagonists in *La Femme rompue.* In both their private and professional lives, these women experience a dread of nothingness, a feeling of impotence and failure that is often related to their dependence on a man whom they consider to be superior.

The need for commitment is in part the consequence of Beauvoir's need to escape from the sense of the absurd and in part the consequence of her desire to alter radically human consciousness and human society. Her commitment is predicated on a conviction about what is wrong with prevalent right-wing ideologies and political systems, as in *Pyrrhus et Cinéas, Pour une morale de l'ambiguïté* (1947; Eng. tr., *The Ethics of Ambiguity,* 1948),

L'Amérique au jour le jour (1948; Eng. tr., *America Day by Day*, 1953), *L'Existentialisme et la sagesse des nations* (1948; Existentialism and the Wisdom of Nations), and *Privilèges* (1955); what is oppressive and inaccurate in traditional attitudes towards women, as in *Le Deuxième Sexe* (1949; Eng. tr., *The Second Sex*, 1953), and towards the elderly, as in *La Vieillesse*; and the confidence that these ideologies, systems, and attitudes can be changed by women and men who understand what is evil and are willing to speak out aggressively for what is good.

These contradictory, perhaps romantic, conceptions of the human condition embodied in the novels and essays coalesce in the four volumes of Beauvoir's autobiography: *Mémoires d'une jeune fille rangée* (1954; Eng. tr., *Memoirs of a Dutiful Daughter*, 1959), *La Force de l'âge* (1960; Eng. tr., *The Prime of Life*, 1962), *La Force des choses* (1963; Eng. tr., *Force of Circumstance*, 1964), and *Tout compte fait* (1972; Eng. tr., *All Said and Done*, 1974). In these volumes, Beauvoir chronicles the development of her affective and intellectual life and provides an invaluable document on the formation of antiestablishment, antibourgeois French intellectuals in the period between 1929 and 1970 and their evolution from an ethics of individualism to an ethics of commitment. The vacillation between the sense of the absurd and the need for commitment becomes more coherent as the reader follows Beauvoir in her attempts to deal with the absence of God, the beauties of nature, her feelings of affection and love, and the inhumanity of man to man. The relation of private to public events, of a happy childhood, for example, to the years of German occupation, explain the constant movement between optimism and despair, between the joy she experiences during celebrations and the horror she feels at times in the solitude of her bed. What appeared to be irreconcilable statements are, in fact, one long statement about the complexities of living and of attempting to understand the human, and particularly the female, adventure.

Simone de Beauvoir's major contribution consists in her capacity to raise fundamental questions about life and death, good and evil, women and men, and to discuss them in a specific context using both her own experience and the accumulated experience contained in libraries. Her best books are never academic exercises but polemical works that portray the creation of an emergent atheistic ideology and feminist sensibility.

See: F. Jeanson, *Simone de Beauvoir ou l'Entreprise de vivre* (1966); R. D. Cottrell, *Simone de Beauvoir* (1975).

E.M.

Becher, Johannes Robert (1891–1958), German poet and novelist, was born in Munich, the son of a judge. He studied philosophy and medicine and started his literary career with radically expressionistic poetry. His first collection of poems and prose, *Verfall und Triumph* (1914; Decline and Triumph), is typical of the explosive and chaotic early expressionism that destroyed traditional language and syntax as a gesture symbolic of the intellectual destruction of the traditional world. With the critical vehemence of his attitude, Becher soon turned to radical politics. As a pacifist he became involved with the left-wing Spartacists (splintered from the Social Democrats) during the World War I and soon joined the Communist Party. During years of great lyric activity he became head of the Union of Proletarian-Revolutionary Writers. Publication of the collection of verse entitled *Der Leichnam auf dem Thron* (1925; The Corpse on the Throne) and the novel *Levisite oder der einzig gerechte Krieg* (1926; The Only Just War) resulted in charges of preparatory steps toward treason.

Becher escaped arrest on the night of the Reichstag fire (1933), fled from Germany, and settled in Moscow in 1935, where he edited the periodical *Internationale Literatur*. Upon his return to Berlin in 1945, he headed the Cultural Union for Democratic Renewal of Germany. Together with Paul Wiegler, he launched the literary periodical *Sinn und Form*. He became president of the East German Academy of Arts and in 1954 cultural minister of the German Democratic Republic (GDR). He received many honors, including the Lenin Peace Prize (1952). In his postwar creative work, he attempted to define a new literary humanism within socialist realism but never again equaled the product of his early years. Verse such as the paean to Walter Ulbricht stands as a sad echo of his greatness. Most significant of his late works are the autobiographical novel *Abschied* (1941; Eng. tr., *Farewell*, 1970) and the diaries that record his experiences as writer and state functionary: *Poetische Konfession* (1954), *Macht der Poesie* (1955; Power of Poetry), and *Das poetische Prinzip* (1957). Conflict between his position as official spokesman for GDR cultural policy and his close association with progressive artists such as Bertolt BRECHT and Hanns Eisler—near whom he is buried in the Dorotheenstädtische Friedhof in Berlin—is registered in his comment of 1955: "So greatly have I loved poetry that I did not refuse things which at bottom were deeply repulsive to me; I undertook all sorts of things which not only dirtied my hands, but which also caused damage to my soul and . . . to my love of poetry as well."

K.Pi rev. W.V.B.

Beck, Béatrix (1914–), Belgian novelist born in Villard-sur-Ollon, Switzerland, is the daughter of the Belgian novelist Christian Beck. She received her education in France at the University of Grenoble and was for a time secretary to André GIDE. In 1936 she married Naum Szapiro. Her realistic novels are characterized by their humor, economy of description, and dialogue, as well as by a preoccupation with childhood and the finding or creating of God. In *Barny* (1948), Beck introduced a semiautobiographical character who was to become the central figure in subsequent works. The young narrator speaks naturally of unprecedented events, and the bizarre nature of the tale is enhanced by the narrator's seeing everything through the eyes of her mother, Aldeveen, who is mad. This odd narration, which Georges BATAILLE described as enchanting rather than exasperating (*Critique*, August 1949), is also a story of friendship and death. Barny spends hours talking with her friend, Donique, about God. Barny's religious despair leads her to an abortive attempt at suicide: she cannot manage to drown herself in the bath tub. *Une Mort irrégulière* (1951; An Irregular Death) recounts the story of Barny's husband, a stateless Jew caught in the events of World War II. In 1952, Beck won the Goncourt Prize for *Léon Morin, Prêtre* (1952; Eng. tr., *The Priest*, 1953; American ed., *The Passionate Heart*, 1953). According to Brendan Gill, this work treats a religious dilemma much in the manner of François MAURIAC, but without Mauriac's characteristic despair. A young French woman lives with her child, France, after the death of her Jewish husband in German-occupied France. She suffers deprivation, worries about the fate of her Jewish friends, and becomes embittered by her disbelief in institutions. One day she enters a church with the intention of taunting the priest in the confessional. Things do not, however, go as planned. She is converted to Catholicism by the priest, who shares her leftist political views, and falls in love with him. Beck's other works include *Des Accommodements avec le ciel*

(1954; Working Things Out with Heaven), in which the convert has difficulty accepting the religious establishment, and *Le Muet* (1963; The Mute), which finds Barny in England with rich relatives during the post-World War II period. Children's language and their confrontations with the adult world are further explored in later works such as *Noli* (1978) and *La Décharge* (1979; The Discharge), which was awarded the Prix du Livre Inter '79.

See: H. J. G. Godin, *The Creative Process in French Literature* (1974). A.Rus.

Becker, Jurek (1937–), East German novelist, was born in Łódź, Poland, the son of Jewish parents. After the German invasion in 1939, he lived in the Łódź ghetto; from 1943 to 1945 he was in concentration camps at Ravensbrück and Sachsenhausen. At the end of World War II, he moved with his father to Berlin, where he attended school and completed his *Abitur* in 1955. Following military service, he studied philosophy in Berlin until 1960, when he was expelled from the university for political reasons. He has since worked as a free-lance writer and is known as one of the most original and talented novelists writing in German today. International recognition came to Becker after the publication of his first novel, *Jakob der Lügner* (1969; Eng. tr., *Jacob the Liar*, 1975), the moving story of a middle-aged Jew in a Polish ghetto during the Occupation, whom fate and circumstances force to become a "liar"—also a notable film. In *Irreführung der Behörden* (1973; Confounding the Authorities), Becker depicts the career of an opportunistic young writer who makes compromises as an artist in order to become successful. *Der Boxer* (1975), the most autobiographical of his novels, deals with the problems confronting a concentration camp survivor living in postwar Germany. A later book, *Schlaflose Tage* (1978; Sleepless Days), is about a school teacher whose determination to stop being an opportunist leads him to sacrifice his job and comfortable bourgeois existence. This novel's rejection for publication in East Germany was a major factor in Becker's decision to move to West Berlin late in 1977. R.A.Z.

Becker, Jürgen (1932–), German poet, playwright, and prose writer, was born in Cologne. He achieved his first success with *Felder* (1964; Fields). The 101 short texts of this collection, which presents perspectives of daily life in Cologne, consist of fragmentary descriptive and reflective passages; pure narration is scrupulously avoided. Disillusionment with modern society is often expressed by means of irony and subtle humor. Becker was awarded the prestigious prize of the "Gruppe 47" for a reading from *Ränder* (1968; Margins), a book similar to, but more tightly constructed than, *Felder*. The points of departure for these texts are the Mediterranean region and the Rhineland; the fragmentation of modern society is again the principal focal point. An increasing concern with the relation between language and reality is seen here. In the three radio plays of *Bilder, Häuser, Hausfreunde* (1969; Images, Houses, Friends of the Family), idle chatter by for the most part nameless characters alternates with comments about serious matters. Becker's poetry, collected in *Schnee* (1971; Snow), *Das Ende der Landschaftsmalerei* (1974; The End of Landscape Painting), and *Erzähl mir nichts vom Krieg* (1977; Don't Talk to Me about War), similarly dwells on the arbitrary nature of modern life. Other works include *Umgebungen* (1970; Surroundings); a third collection of prose texts, with photographs, in *Eine Zeit ohne Wörter* (1971; A Time without Words); and the drama *Die Zeit nach Harriman* (1971;

The Time after Harriman). *Uber Jürgen Becker*, ed. by L. Kreutzer, was published in 1972. J.G.

Becker, Knuth (1891–1974), Danish novelist, was born in the northern Jutland town of Hjørring. As a boy, Becker spent some time in a reform school. Later he worked as a mechanic until he won recognition with the autobiographical novel *Det daglige Brød* (1932; The Daily Bread). This is the first volume of Becker's major work, an extensive cycle about a boy, Kai Gøtsche, who is beset by a series of conflicts because he is unable to find understanding in his environment. *Verden venter* (1934; The World is Waiting) describes Kai's years in a reform school while *Uroligt Foraar* (1938–39; Uneasy Spring) and *Naar Toget Kører* (1944; When the Train Starts) tell about his difficulties as an adult. *Marianne* (1956) and *Huset* (1962; The House) depict Kai's involvement with war and love and display a more optimistic tone. Personal experiences are the central points of Becker's works, which, in addition to providing broad descriptions of the contemporary scene, also contain critical analyses of the relationship between the individual and society.

See: E. Frederiksen, *Knuth Becker* (1970); K. Birket-Smith, "Knuth Becker," *ASR* 62 (1974): 285–90.

S.H.R.

Beckett, Samuel (1906–), Irish novelist, playwright, and poet, famous for his writings in French, was born in Foxrock, near Dublin, on Good Friday, April 13. He was awarded the Nobel Prize for Literature in 1969 to the accompaniment of such empty and meaningless rhetoric as "from that position, in the realms of annihilation, the writing of Samuel Beckett rises like a miserere from all mankind . . . ." Indeed, Beckett has always honored Paul VERLAINE's wise suggestion, "prends l'éloquence et tords-lui son cou!" ("Take eloquence and wring its neck!") and his work has increasingly moved toward a spare, accentless prose. Beckett was educated at Portora Royal School and Trinity College, Dublin (B.A. 1927, M.A. 1931, Hon. Doctor of Letters, 1959) and then served as a *lecteur d'anglais* (English reader) at the Ecole Normale Supérieure in Paris. He taught French at Trinity followed his return to Ireland, only to give up the academic life irrevocably in 1932. After what critics call his *Wanderjahre* (1932–37), he settled permanently in Paris.

Beckett, who belongs in a unique way to both Irish and French literature, began his career under the shadow of James Joyce. He wrote the opening essay "Dante . . . Bruno. Vico . . . Joyce" for a collection extravagantly entitled *Our Examination round His Factification for Incamination of Work in Progress* (1929), devoted to what was later to be called *Finnegans Wake*. He assisted in the translation into French of the "Anna Livia Plurabelle" section of Joyce's last book, published in the May 1931 *Nouvelle Revue française*. The poems in *Echo's Bones and Other Precipitates* (1935), especially "Enueg I" and "Enueg II," abound in Joycean reverberations. The 10 stories in *More Pricks than Kicks* (1934) seem closely associated with Joyce's *Dubliners*, which they echo and occasionally parody. Beckett's acrostic "Home Olga" (1934) was written for James Joyce, whose name was spelled out by the first letters of the 10 lines of the poem. Even *Murphy* (1938), Beckett's first novel, has its Joycean moments; it was no accident that Joyce, who was personally associated with Beckett for some time, committed parts of the book to memory. *Murphy* probably marks the end of Beckett's apprenticeship. It is the work of a writer who places a premium on clever and suggestive word plays. One sentence from this work, "In the beginning was the pun," succinctly accounts for Beckett's verbal habits up through *Murphy*.

The novel *Watt* (finished by 1945 but not published until 1953) represents the darker, brooding side of the Irish writer and begins to suggest the direction Beckett's mature fiction was to take. Murphy's inquiries into the nature of self turn into Watt's elaborate epistemological gestures. While Murphy ends up as an attendant in an insane asylum, Watt becomes an inmate in a similar institution. The "Addenda" to *Watt* has as its final words: "no symbols where none intended"—a warning perhaps to those who try to reduce Beckett to inflexible emblematic terms.

Between 1937 and 1939, Beckett wrote some early poems in French, but he only turned to that language with a vengeance during his most productive period: the five years following World War II. French was to be the language of virtually all his subsequent fiction and much of his best drama. It has been Beckett's habit to turn his French oeuvre into English himself—often taking astonishing liberties with his text—so that we seem to have what amounts to "original" versions in two languages. These "self-translations," as they have been called, operate both ways as Beckett continues, with the help of occasional collaborators, to turn the English works into French. (He also works closely with his German translator, Elmar Tophoven, who lives in Paris, and he has overseen the German production of several of his plays in Berlin.) The French novels written after World War II include *Mercier et Camier* (1970; Eng. tr., *Mercier and Camier*, 1974) and the trilogy *Molloy, Malone meurt*, and *L'Innommable* (1951–53; Eng. tr., *Molloy* [1955], *Malone Dies* [1956], *The Unnamable* [1958]). *Mercier et Camier* is a transitional work, having elements of both the early and later manner. Watt appears as a character toward the end of this novel, and Murphy's name is mentioned on one occasion—thus anticipating a practice Beckett was to use in works like *Malone meurt* and *L'Innommable*, in which there are catalogues of names drawn from Beckett's previous fiction. Some of the objects that figure prominently in *Mercier et Camier*, like bicycles, umbrellas, and sacks, were to reappear, and the stichomythic exchanges between the protagonists often make us think ahead to the dialogue between Estragon and Vladimir in *En attendant Godot* (1952, first performed on January 5, 1953; Eng. tr., *Waiting for Godot*, 1954). The "old young" Mercier and Camier prepare us for the monologists of the trilogy.

The narrative of *Molloy* is told in two parts by Molloy and Moran respectively. Molloy's search for his mother in part one and Moran's search for Molloy in part two result in two elaborate mock-quests. What at first seem to be separate stories gradually merge, and the seemingly worldly Moran comes more and more to resemble—and even to become one with—the crippled and inept Molloy. Malone, the narrator of *Malone meurt*, confined to his bed, occupies his time by telling stories and by threatening to inventory his possessions; his search for a lost pencil stub is as demanding an activity as any he engages in. The unnamed monologist of *L'Innommable* seems even less in control of things than Malone. His soliloquy has an otherworldly quality that he characterizes as "a step towards silence and the end of madness, the madness of having to speak and not being able to."

Beckett's last full-length novel, *Comment c'est* (1961; Eng. tr., *How It Is*, 1964), seems even more appreciative than *L'Innommable* of the spaces between words and silences. This three-part work, "before Pim with Pim after Pim," is divided into unpunctuated units that seem to act as breath groups and look something like stanzas

of poetry on the page. Phrases like "vast stretch of time," "murmur in the mud," "quaqua on all sides" recur with the frequency and insistency of leitmotivs.

The brief texts that Beckett wrote in the mid-1960s, such as *Imagination morte imaginez* (1965; Eng. tr., *Imagination Dead Imagine*, 1965), *Assez* (1966; Eng. tr., *Enough*, 1967), *Bing* (1966; Eng. tr., *Ping*, 1967), and the collection *Pour finir encore et autres foirades* (1976; Eng. tr., *Fizzles*, 1976), reveal an even more drastic reduction of language than *Comment c'est*. They appear to come out of a condition that Beckett first suggested in "Three Dialogues" (1949): "there is nothing to express, nothing with which to express, nothing from which to express."

Beckett began to write plays in the years following World War II. His first play of this period, "Eleutheria," remains unperformed and unpublished, but his second one, *En attendant Godot*, brought him international recognition. The interminable waiting of the two tramps, Estragon and Vladimir, and the failure of Godot to arrive have occasioned more commentary and controversy than anything of a literary nature within recent memory. *Fin de partie* (1957; Eng. tr., *Endgame*, 1958) has a more hermetic, claustrophobic quality than *Godot*, and the movements of the characters are even more restricted than those of the participants in the earlier play. Critics have pointed to a variety of Shakespearean and biblical echoes and allusions in this work.

Most of Beckett's remaining plays were written originally in English. *Krapp's Last Tape* (1958) finds a 69-year-old man alone on stage with his tape recorder, trying to recapture a period of his life 30 years earlier. *Happy Days* (1961) has two acts like *Godot* but no more movement than either *Fin de partie* or *Krapp's Last Tape*. Winnie, who is covered up to her waist in earth in the first act and up to her neck in the second, does most of the talking, although she does manage to elicit an occasional response from Willie, her husband. Winnie goes to great lengths to explain the importance of "things" and to inventory her possessions, much like the narrators of the trilogy. The radio piece *All That Fall* (done for the BBC on Jan. 13, 1957) is the most Irish of the plays and dramatically the most fleshed out. The language lacks the harshness and austerity of that of *Godot* and *Fin de partie*. The remaining plays in the canon are relatively brief and, like the recent fiction, increasingly reveal a distrust of language and a commitment to silence.

See: J. Fletcher, *The Novels of Samuel Beckett* (1964; rev. 1970); M. Esslin, ed., *Samuel Beckett: A Collection of Critical Essays* (1965); R. Federman and J. Fletcher, *Samuel Beckett: His Works and His Critics* (1970); M. J. Friedman, ed., *Samuel Beckett Now* (1970; rev. ed. 1975); L. Harvey, *Samuel Beckett Poet and Critic* (1970); H. Kenner, *A Reader's Guide to Samuel Beckett* (1973); A. Alvarez, *Samuel Beckett* (1973); R. Cohn, *Back to Beckett* (1973); V. Mercier, *Beckett/Beckett* (1977); D. Bair, *Samuel Beckett: A Biography* (1978). M.J.F.

Bécquer, Gustavo Adolfo (1836–70), Spanish poet and author of romantic prose legends, was born in Seville with the surname Domínguez Insausti y Bastida. His father, a painter of Andalusian scenes, was known as Bécquer, a name derived from the Flemish Vequer and belonging to the family's ancestors, who had settled in the south of Spain at the close of the 16th century. At the age of five, Bécquer saw his father die. Six years later came the death of his mother. The orphan attended the naval school of San Telmo and in 1854, full of literary illusions, went to Madrid to support himself as a writer. Teetering constantly on the brink of financial ruin, he managed to keep alive by writing zarzuelas and, in 1864, accepting the post of censor of novels. His older brother Valeriano continued in their father's footsteps as a painter and had a great influence on Gustavo. An unhappy love life left its mark on the poet. He was attracted to Julia and Josefina Espín, nieces of the composer Gioacchino Rossini, and attended their musical soirées without ever declaring his intentions. A shadowy aristocratic woman, tentatively identified as Elisa Guillén, supposedly inspired some of his poems. In 1861 he married Casta Esteban Navarro from Soria. Evidently unsuited for each other, they separated after seven years and two children, and Gustavo went to live in Toledo with his brother. In 1867 he began to edit his *Rimas* for publication, but the manuscript was lost during the revolution of 1868. Bécquer's always precarious health did not survive the rigors of the Madrid winter of 1870, and he died in December, just three months after the death of his brother.

Bécquer belongs to a tradition of delicate and symbolic Spanish lyric poetry that goes back to Saint John of the Cross and was continued in the 20th century by Juan Ramón JIMÉNEZ. Deeply reflective, tormented by his imagination, full of religious longings, and fascinated by the ideal of love, Bécquer was a full-fledged romantic poet. At the same time, his work comes historically late enough to reveal some of the compressions of style and tone that were taking place in symbolism. To Antonio MACHADO Y RUIZ and Juan Ramón Jiménez at the turn of the century, Bécquer summarized all that was worthwhile in 19th century poetry, and suggested a viable model. He is, thus, a point of departure for the important flowering of Spanish poetry in the 20th century.

Bécquer's ideas on poetry may be found in various sources. The popular *Rimas* (1871; Rhymes), the prologue to Augusto Ferrán's *La soledad* (1860; Solitude), and the *Cartas literarias a una mujer* (1860–61; Literary Letters to a Woman) chart the preoccupations of European romantics and suggest the course that much modern Spanish verse would take. Poetry was a spiritual exercise of the highest order, and its chief inspiration was woman. Like William Wordsworth, Bécquer wrote his poetry in the afterglow of recollected emotions, but these were so strong that they dictated to his pen. He was reflective about the creative process in a way that cannot be found among his contemporaries but that was common in English and German romanticism. He called his ideas the insane children of his fancy and confessed difficulty in discerning the difference between reality and imagination. As it had for Percy Bysshe Shelley, love offered Bécquer transcendental possibilities. Finally, in a way that links him with the French symbolists, he was acutely aware of the wretched inability of words to express adequately the noble, delicate, and complicated feelings that thronged his mind.

Everything he wrote betrays these convictions. The first volume of *Historia de los templos de España* (1857; History of Spanish Temples) records the intense reactions of his imagination to the church of San Juan de los Reyes in Toledo. The *Leyendas* (Legends), published in journals and collected after his death, celebrate the inaccessibility and the aura of danger associated with nymphs, goddesses, and female spirits of the dead. Based on folk tales and influenced by writers like E. T. A. Hoffmann, the *Leyendas* offer a supple, rich, and poetic prose that still has numerous admirers. In the Monasterio de Veruela, located between Soria and Aragón, Bécquer wrote *Cartas desde mi celda* (1863–64; Letters from my Cell). This work continues to explore the workings of the creative mind and contains some of the finest 19th century Spanish descriptions of landscape. The *Rimas* have provided Spanish poetry with many set pieces and have gone through numerous editions. They chronicle the happiness and agony of love, and confusion and despair in the face of death. Some of the experimental metrical combinations prepare the way for similar efforts in *modernismo* (*see* SPANISH LITERATURE).

See E. L. King, *Gustavo Adolfo Bécquer from Painter to Poet* (1953); J. Guillén, *Language and Poetry* (1961); R. Brown, *Gustavo Adolfo Bécquer en dos tiempos* (1963).   H.T.Y.

Beer-Hofmann, Richard (1866–1945), Austrian poet, novelist, and dramatist, was born in Vienna. He first attracted public notice in 1893 with a slender volume of stories entitled *Novellen*. These tales betray the influence of Guy de Maupassant in subject matter and of Gustav Flaubert in style. Beer-Hofmann's earliest lyric, *Schlaflied für Miriam* (1898; Lullaby for Miriam), is the finest philosophic lullaby in German. In it, eternal chords are touched—the dark origin of life and its unknown end, the impossibility of communicating our deepest experiences even to those nearest to us, and the tragic necessity for each generation to recapitulate the past with all its errors and suffering. Yet behind the apparent chaotic structure of the universe, the poet recognizes a mysterious purpose and a certain continuity of existence. In Beer-Hofmann's only novel, *Der Tod Georgs* (1900; George's Death), the realization of this purpose comes to the hero as, in the presence of death, he broods on the meaning of life; he is wrested from his self-centered existence as an aesthetic epicurean and whirled into the midst of his people's struggle for justice.

In *Der Graf von Charolais* (1904; The Count of Charolais), Beer-Hofmann's first and best-known play, the hero, who sees the brittleness of all human relations and the instability of all human emotions, retains to the end his unshakable faith in the bonds linking parents and children. Beer-Hofmann was of Jewish origin, and his approach to eternal problems is essentially biblical; his visions are reminiscent of those of prophets of the Old Testament. In a biblical trilogy he seeks to restate for modern man the Hebraic position on fundamental questions. The first part of the trilogy, *Jakobs Traum* (Eng. tr., *Jacob's Dream*, 1946), depicts the inner crisis of Jacob, the legendary ancestor of the Jews, during the memorable night at Bethel. The second part of the trilogy, *Der junge David* (1933; Young David), deals with the testing of David, the descendant of Jacob. Completed shortly before Adolf Hitler's rise to power, this play gives the Hebraic answer to Nazi ideology: just as it does not pay for an individual to live solely for himself, so too it does not pay for a people to think primarily in terms of its own aggrandizement. A people is important only in so far as it confers its creative gifts upon others, coordinating its own welfare with that of humanity at large.

In 1939, Beer-Hofmann emigrated to New York. In his 75th year the poet collected in a slender volume, *Verse*, all his lyric production that he cared to see preserved. In his impressionistic sketches *Aus dem Fragment Paula: Herbstmorgen in Österreich* (1944; From the Fragment "Paula": Autumnal Morning in Austria), he attempted to recapture the autumnal mood of Austria as it penetrated his own life and shaped his own personality.

See: S. Liptzin, *Richard Beer-Hofmann* (1936).
                                                          S.L. rev. A.L.W.

Begović, Milan (1876–1948), Croatian poet, dramatist, novelist, and short-story writer, was born in the Dalmatian town of Vrlika. From 1908 to 1915, he worked as a stage director in Hamburg and Vienna, and in 1920 he was appointed professor at the Actor's School in Zagreb.

In 1927 he became the director of the Zagreb Theater, but the royal government soon forced him into retirement.

In his collection of poems, *Knjiga Boccadoro* (1900; The Book of Bocca d'Oro), Begović sang about young, beautiful, and lascivious women, and the pleasures of the flesh. Novelty, boldness, richness of vocabulary, smoothness of verse—all these made Begović very popular among younger readers and critics, while older ones condemned his book as "scandalous pornography." From poetry, Begović gradually moved to writing for the stage. He was quite successful in this field, particularly during the years between the two world wars. Well acquainted with contemporary European drama, especially with light French comedies, Begović was at his best when describing the romantic triangle, the unhappy marriage, and the passionate entanglement. Begović's superbly written short stories, such as those collected in *Quartet* (1936) and *Puste želje* (1942; Vain Wishes) also abound in erotic episodes.

Begović's first novel, *Dunja u kovčegu* (1921; The Quince in the Valise) is one of the most elaborate works ever written in Croatian. His second novel, *Giga Barićeva* (1940), is impressive as a whole, not only for its rich language, but also for its endearing, humorous characterizations.

See: A. G. Matoš, "Knjiga Boccadoro," *LMS* 6 (1901): 86–95; A. Barac, "Giga Barićeva," *Savremenik* 2 (1941): 53–57; B. Hećimović, "Dramski rad Milan Begovića." *Rad* 326 (1962): 195–221.   A.K.

Béguin, Albert (1901–57), Swiss critic, translator, and editor, was born into a family of agnostic educators in La Chaux-de-Fonds, in the Neuchâtel canton. In his formative years, Béguin was attracted to the nonorthodox spiritual quality of such Catholic writers as Charles PÉGUY and Paul CLAUDEL. Although Béguin eventually became a socialist dedicated to humanitarian concerns, his critical works usually emphasize the mystical aspects of literature. Béguin received his *licence* in literature at the University of Geneva, and in 1925 he moved to Paris, where he was exposed to the ideological ferment of the era but was personally unable to adopt a single political platform. During this time he began to study German romanticism, a subject of seminal importance to him. He also began translating into French works by such German writers as E. T. A. Hoffmann, Edvard Mörike, Jean Paul, Goethe, Ludwig Tieck, and Georg Büchner.

In his many critical works, written after 1936, Béguin studied 19th- and 20th-century French and German literature. His most important critical work is his doctoral dissertation, presented at the University of Geneva. *L'Ame romantique et le rêve, essai sur le romantisme allemand et la poésie française* (1937; The Romantic Soul and the Dream, Essays on German Romanticism and French Poetry). In *L'Ame,* Béguin shed a new light on romanticism by establishing a link between a group of German mystic romantic poets and several latter-day French poets. He traced the evolution of modern poetry from its origins in the works of such writers as Jean Paul, Novalis, and E. T. A. Hoffmann to its culmination in the works of such select French poets as Gérard de Nerval, Charles BAUDELAIRE, Victor Hugo, and, most importantly, Stéphane MALLARMÉ and Arthur RIMBAUD. Concerned with the mystical and metaphysical bases of romanticism, Béguin focused on the dream motif as the common denominator of all the poets studied. Differing from the usual evaluation of the romantics as effete escapists, Béguin characterized them as Promethean adventurers who treated the dream not as an ornamental device but as a gateway to the infinite.

Béguin's faith in Germany was shaken during World War II. In order to find refuge from his disillusion, he converted to Catholicism in 1940. His *Faiblesse de l'Allemagne* (1945; Germany's Weakness) attributes Germany's weaknesses to that nation's inability to transform its ideals into a collective social reality.

In addition to teaching at the university of Halle and Basel, Béguin appealed to a wider public during and after the war as the founder and director of the journal *Les Cahiers du Rhône* and as editor of *Esprit,* a Paris journal oriented toward Catholic writers, but in the context of universal literature. Béguin's works include studies of individual writers, such as *Gérard de Nerval* (1936), *Léon Bloy l'impatient* (1944), *Balzac Visionnaire* (1946), *L'Ève de Péguy* (1948; Péguy's Eve), and *Patience de Ramuz* (1950), and annotated editions of works by Georges BERNANOS and Blaise Pascal.

See: "Albert Béguin: Etapes d'une Pensée," *CdR* 96, no. 30 (December 1957); P. Grotzer, *Les Ecrits d'Albert Beguin: essai de bibliographie* (1967).   S.N.

Belgian literature in Flemish. When the southern Netherlands were separated from the northern provinces at the end of the 16th century, the intellectual as well as the economic center of the Lowlands moved to the north. For 200 years Flemish literature was reduced to Pietist writings of sometimes inane sentimentality and ridiculously detailed symbolism. Literary expression died out. Immediately after the creation of an independent Belgium in 1830, it was revived by the prolific novelist Hendrik CONSCIENCE. His sentimental nationalism, based on what Flanders had achieved in the Middle Ages and on the story of its revolt against tyranny in the 16th century, brought about a renaissance of literary activity. About 1860 his work was well under way, and a number of writers had sprung up who created a literary "climate" in which the fundamental trends of Flemish letters were already plainly visible—a constant tendency toward cozy provincialism, which finds its expression in the peasant novel, and, on the other hand, a definite longing for universality, which uses social and psychological elements. At times these two tendencies intermingle.

About 1880 the majority of the reading public in Flanders belonged to the rural Catholic population. In their struggle for linguistic equality in the new state and as a means of self-defense, they took comfort in their local characteristics, their picturesque way of life, their verbal particularities, all of which were employed to prove that Flanders and the Flemish language had a right to exist. Therefore, it was quite natural as well as fashionable for the writers of the second half of the 19th century to depict the amenities of life on the farm and in the country in the most lively colors, to exalt the virtues of the rustics, to underlie their habits, their wit, and their customs; and to represent them as a touchstone to guarantee the language and personality of the Flemish people. The cult of local expression and idiosyncrasy led to an acute provincialism, which manifested itself in the use of dialectal forms and in an opposition to the generally accepted medium of a standard Netherlandish language.

All these handicaps, however, were brilliantly overcome by the one poet of universal stature whom Flanders produced in the 19th century, the priest Guido Gezelle (1830–99). He embodied the pure Gothic spirit. He looked at nature and its botanic details as the miniaturists of the Middle Ages did; with absolute faith in his metaphysical certainties, he attained to a mystical familiarity with the Creator that made his art appear as the last flowering of medieval devotion. His verse is purely lyrical, although he seldom referred to his personal life, which was at bottom difficult and not devoid of the tragic. Most of his poems deal with the feasts and ceremonies of the church or with the rural Flemish landscape. They have a charming simplicity and directness and a warmth that was never equaled in Dutch letters except in the 14th century. Nevertheless, he wrote his best poetry on those occasions when he broke the restraint his clerical functions imposed upon him—his verse is then of a very high lyrical quality. It has the unerring musical perfection of the best lieder. Gezelle was, indeed, the perfect example of the Franciscan poet, for never was so much joy derived from nature without evident sensuality; never was there in Dutch literature a character as simple in its unity, as forceful in its lyrical power. Reacting against verbose pomposity and pedantic metrical rules, Gezelle adopted an extremely versatile meter, for which he found inspiration in the English and Scottish poets. His poems abound in subtle, elegant onomatopoeia and graceful alliterations, and they follow a strictly personal rhythm. Many of them would fit the later formula of la poésie pure.

A great linguist, he made such an excellent translation (1886) of Henry Wadsworth Longfellow's Hiawatha that it became familiar to all Flemish readers. It took his countrymen and the Dutch some time to recognize his significance, to find out his exceptional stature. His localisms had constituted a barrier for both groups, his uncompromising and enthusiastic Catholicism was another. When, about 1880, he was introduced to the general public in Holland, his plea for a predominance of the West Flanders tongue was already lost, but he had become the outstanding example of a writer who by the mere contemplation and idealistic description of rural beauties had achieved greatness and even universal recognition. Although some of his poems, for example, "Dien Avond en die Rooze" (That Evening and That Rose) and "O 't ruischen van het Ranke Riet" (O Rustling of the Rushes' Throng), have been translated carefully into English, like all great lyrical work, they remain essentially unrenderable.

Parallel to Conscience's enthusiastic prose was the sudden romantic burst of national feeling expressed in the poems of Albrecht Rodenbach (1856–80). He was the herald of the Flemish political revival. His turbulent, ebullient inspiration was a combination of classicism and Germanic lyricism. Having produced a number of songs and recitation pieces on historical themes and an unfinished drama in verse, Gudrun (1882), he died very young, a great promise, a symbol of idealistic youth.

Against the rural idealism of Conscience and Gezelle there reacted a few minor realists like August Snieders (1825–1904) and Domien Sleeckx (1818–1901); a charming essayist, Anton Bergmann (1835–74); and the interesting novelist Virginie Loveling (1836–1923). Except for the last-named, their writings had little power in their realism, and their style was conservative and often dull.

It took the revival of Dutch letters, about 1880, to provoke a definite emancipation of Flemish literature. This renewal was prepared by a transitional writer of great dynamism, Pol de Mont (1857–1931), a moderately sensual, highly lyrical, and musical poet, who was a true internationalist in his thoughts and a genuine symbolist in his expression. He was the first writer in many decades to feel and speak with the freedom of a well-educated heathen, but this attitude, although closer than that of anybody else in Flanders to the main currents of European thought and sensibility, was never expressed in an aggressive fashion. He discovered and heralded Gezelle's poetry in Holland and in Flanders. His own writings include Rijzende Sterren (1879; Rising Stars) and Lentesotternijen (1881; Spring Follies).

In the 1890s a new generation of writers came to the fore. They rallied around a monthly called Van Nu en Straks (Today and Tomorrow), which was definitely internationalist and liberal in its program. The driving spirit, the philosopher of the movement, was August VERMEYLEN, a forceful critic with generous views; the literary theoretician of the movement was Prosper van Langendonck (1862–1920), a somber, weak, romantic poet; but its real creative geniuses were Cyriel BUYSSE, Herman TEIRLINCK, Stijn STREUVELS, and, above all, Karel van de WOESTIJNE.

Buysse was a born narrator of the school of Guy de Maupassant, whom Maurice MAETERLINCK used to count "among the three or four great rural raconteurs of the these last fifty years." He wrote a faithful chronicle of life in the Flemish villages as it evolved rapidly in the last decades.

Undoubtedly, the country baker Stijn Streuvels, a nephew of Guido Gezelle, was the most gifted of the prose writers of that period. There exists an evident synchronism between his early books and the vogue of luminist painting, for example, Lenteleven (1899; Spring Life). Except when he portrayed children, as in Prutske (1922), his psychology appeared rather simple, but his gift for plastic detail and minute yet lyrical description was impressive. In his writings the physical environment, the atmosphere, absorbs people or, rather, reduces them to a secondary, even minor role. People to Streuvels were not the measure of things, but their playthings. Several of his longer novels, including De Vlaschgaard (1907; The Flax Field) and Werkmenschen (1927; Working People), have an epic quality that is very much akin to that found in Scandinavian and Russian literature. In his later work, for example, Alma met de vlassen haren (1930; Alma with the Flaxen Hair), the analysis of devotional life was his preoccupation, and he began also to give more attention to the sexual relations and problems of his personages. The exclusive love for the native soil and its inhabitants, which hampered many of his colleagues on their path to greatness and condemned them to provincialism, turned out in his case to be an asset and a starting point for truly universal expression.

All the writers grouped around Van Nu en Straks were decided individualists. Like their Dutch colleagues of the 1880s, they wanted "to give the most individual expression to their most individual emotions." The outstanding poet of the group, Karel van de Woestijne, succeeded in doing this to such an extent that, had he been writing in one of the major world languages, he could hardly have failed to be universally recognized as one of the greatest lyric poets of his time.

He had no other theme but himself; no other drama to tell but the eternal conflict between mind and matter. His extensive poetical work is little else but a symbolic autobiography. He was as responsive as Gezelle to nature and its thousand details, but his life was dominated by a pendulum movement of attraction and repulsion of the eternal feminine, as in Het Vaderhuis (1903; The Father House) and De gulden schaduw (1910; The Golden Shadow). In one of his long poems he sees with Adam "that Eve, in her wickedness, was beautiful." The drama of his life, as expressed in his writings, lies there as well as in a deep conviction of the sinfulness of his spontaneous reactions. He sang his joys and pains with such refined analytic preciseness, such exceptional warmth and tenseness, that there is scarcely anything that approaches his work in European literature. He had the burning heat of the great mystics like Saint John of the Cross or Saint Theresa, but always, like Paul VERLAINE, he went to the extreme in the humiliating confession of his weakness and frailty. Never in Flemish or Dutch literature had such a great heart witnessed and interpreted the constant conflict between a lucid intelligence and a hypersensitive nature. A good deal of his poetical work exists in a brooding atmosphere in which sensations and thoughts bloom like hothouse flowers of rare and slightly terrifying beauty. Life to him, who harbored a Gothic heart in a Renaissance body, is but a long conflict between his brilliant intelligence and the toll inevitably exacted by his senses. Woman, who had appeared until then in Flemish poetry and prose either as the devoted mother or the idealized Dulcinea, was to him full of mystery, of charm, of menace, a messenger of destruction and death. The leitmotivs of love and death run through his poems as if they were a verbal transcription of Isolde's *Liebestod*.

Van de Woestijne was a profound humanist. The rare poems that do not refer to his personal life deal with heroes of antiquity, for example, *Interludiën* (2 vols., 1912; Interludes), especially with Hercules, whom he made the symbol of disenchanted grandeur. His goddesses, heroes, and heroines, in their Greek disguise, reveal the split personality, the melancholy, the doubt, and the longing for serene beauty that were characteristic of the atmosphere and literature of the turn of the century. These are decorative poems of moving beauty. In the second period of his life, van de Woestijne became a poet of great metaphysical depth; often his verse had a strange, wry sarcasm: *De modderen Man* (1920; The Man of Mud), *God aan Zee* (1926; God at the Sea), and *Het Bergmeer* (1928; The Mountain Lake). To such an extent did van de Woestijne interpret the lyrical sensuality of Peter Paul Rubens, as well as Bruegel's irony and keen observation, that his influence dominated Flemish letters over two decades. Many poets were under his spell and, lacking his subtle balance and genius, devoted themselves to a decadent kind of writing, which, by its extremely personal character, provoked a strong reaction in the generation of writers that spoke out during and after World War I.

The writers of the generation that sprang up between 1917 and 1921 were greatly impressed by social and political problems. Although they recognized the eminence of authors like van de Woestijne and others, they objected to an ivory-tower attitude, which they condemned as irresponsible and antisocial. They wanted poetry not to be a lyrical confession: they felt that the poet should be the conscience of the world, a seer and prophet like Walt Whitman, always busy drawing the moral of events and—in a broad sense—guiding public opinion. The external elements of the modern world should be incorporated into the poetical vocabulary; no conservative rules of prosody should hamper free expression. They used vers libre, or they resorted to the psalmodic rhythm so successfully used by Paul CLAUDEL. For a brief period they indeed succeeded in interpreting the spirit of their time; their expressionist experiments exploded the calm impressionist atmosphere; literature became unthinkable without humanitarian declamations and modernistic bric-a-brac. Their organ, *Ruimte* (Space), which rallied Paul van OSTAYEN, Wies MOENS, Achilles Mussche (1896–), Gaston BURSSENS, Jan-Albert Goris, Victor Brunclair (1899–1945), and others, was short-lived; but their influence was decisive for a considerable period.

They were essentially poets. The leader and most versatile of them all, Paul van Ostayen, started out as a young literary dandy, following the footsteps of the *Jungwien* poets. Soon he turned to the political, prophetic genre, in the manner of the German expressionists Franz WERFEL, Georg TRAKL, and Johannes BECHER, in *Het Sienjaal* (1918; The Signal). Later on he became a dadaist for a brief period—*Bezette Stad* (1921; The City Occu-

pied)—and concluded his short life by writing extremely suggestive, highly musical poetry of great refinement and purity. His short stories, burlesque adventures (*Self Defense*, 1933), told with a keenly analytic sarcasm, were a very effective antidote against rhetoric and pomposity. Moens and Mussche, both generous, ardent, lyrical natures, used a biblical and slightly Oriental style to express their vivid social reactions, whereas Goris, after writing a spectacular modernistic baroque piece on Saint Francis in *Lof-Litanie vam Sint Franciscus van Assisi* (1919; Litany in Praise of Saint Francis of Assisi), evolved a style that has been considered a reconciliation of expressionism and classic simplicity; in his apparently free verse the discipline is as severe as in the classical meter, as in *Het Huis* (1925; The House). Other poets were given to cosmic jugglery, sometimes really impressive. Others still, like Paul Verbruggen (1891–), attained a great purity of expression.

However, this revolt against tradition did not change the aspect of Flemish letters: the cozy, rural, and small-town novel received a new and powerful endorsement in Felix TIMMERMANS, a most prolific novelist who expressed a kind of reserved pantheistic joy of life in a very fresh and lyrical book, *Pallieter* (1916; Eng. tr., 1924). This Dionysian paean was followed by a number of books that were amusing transcriptions of old Flemish paintings and that were sometimes as charming as the products of these *petits maîtres*. Timmermans enjoyed a tremendous popularity in Germany, where he was considered a Low German author. Notwithstanding very humorous, although unorthodox, stylistic gifts, he remained a popular author, and one of his later novels, *Boerenpsalm* (1935; Peasant Psalm), is a remarkably adult and sanguine book. Other authors like Teirlinck, Maurits Sabbe (1873–1938), Ernest Claes (1889–), and Lode Baekelmans (1879–) continued the solidly established tradition of charming provincial writing.

Besides the *Ruimte* group, a number of poets gathered around a tiny review called *Het Fonteintje* (The Little Fountain). They were not humanitarians but humanists, classicists; and they tried to disengage themselves from van de Woestijne's grip. They resorted to a humoristic style, inspired by Paul Jean TOULET, a wise, melancholic poet, who wrote fluent, charming verse in which he told people that the world was not exactly "cosmic," but seriously personal. Among them, Raymond Herreman (1896–) was the most outstanding and the most versatile.

The novelist Alfons de Ridder, whose writings through their merciless humor and grim moral courage are unique in Flemish letters, can also be considered as belonging to this school. He writes in *Villa des Roses* (1913) and *Tsjip* (1934; Cheep) of middle-class people with deep sarcastic anger and a chastely hidden feeling for human misery. Although he wrote only a few poems, he is also a very remarkable poet.

When the conflict and discussions between the two groups, the humanitarians and the cozy moralists, had subsided, when principles and theories no longer determined literary activity, and when the eternal problems of existence had again taken the place of temporary political and social issues, a number of young novelists appeared who brought a new accent into Flemish letters. They had found out that the one and only subject of the novel is human beings, not the climate or the fauna and flora that surround them. This discovery was responsible for an increase in tempo and a better psychological insight. Among these writers, the most classical-minded is Maurice ROELANTS. His novels go back to the great tradition of Benjamin Constant's *Adolphe* and to the works of other keen analysts of the human soul. With less technical perfection, but extreme generosity, Lode Zielens (1901-44) devotes attention to the Flemish proletariat. He overflows with the milk of human kindness. But the most powerful and productive of them all is Gerard WALSCHAP. Using all the resources of rhetoric, his story rushes down like a mountain stream. His search is essentially along psychopathological lines. Although his characters often border on the abnormal, the moral of his work is always a belief in the profound goodness and greatness of life and of people. Aside from his torrential tempo, which comes close to the tornado pace that James Cain used in *The Postman Always Rings Twice,* the European author he may best be compared with is François MAURIAC.

The great influence of Herman Teirlinck on the Flemish theater between the two wars should be mentioned. He introduced the modernistic theatrical conceptions with great success.

One of the most remarkable literary facts after World War I in Flanders was that the influence of Flemish letters on Dutch writing augmented considerably. Most of the young Flemish writers, by increasing the distance between their work and the folklore novelistics of their elders, came close enough to Dutch literature to make their works indistinguishable from Dutch publications.

During and immediately after World War II, a number of young Flemish writers completely changed the literary scene of Flanders. They did away with the descriptive, impressionistic style of their predecessors and were absorbed by social problems. Outstanding among them is Louis-Paul BOON (*Chapel Road*). He is a true proletarian. His style goes back to that of Emile ZOLA, with a strong flowering of local sentimentality. Hugo CLAUS, strongly influenced by American writers, published a few good novels but devotes his time now to rewriting such classics as Sophocles, Seneca, Pedro Calderón, and others. He also dabbled in cinema and produced a five-and-a-half-hour movie on Peter Paul Rubens. It was not a success. On the other hand, his poetry is remarkable. Johan DAISNE and his pupil Hubert LAMPO are analysts of the magic-realistic school. Among the younger writers, Jef Geeraerts (Gangen *I* published in New York) is a unique phenomenon. His work—Gangen *I, II, III, IV*—is based on his experiences as a territorial Belgian agent in the then Congo (now Zaire). His work is powerful and colorful. He was the first Flemish writer to use complete frankness in sexual matters. His only resemblance to Henry Miller's oeuvre is that Geeraerts's books are emphatically autobiographical and dominated by the spirit of his sexual materialism and hedonism. Ward RUYSLINCK is the best promise for the future, as Paul SNOEK is for poetry. The author of this essay published about 20 novels and many short stories. The first novel, *The Book of Joachim of Babylon,* appeared in 14 foreign translations. There is no doubt that modern Flemish authors have become mature.

The 1950s constitute an important period in the development of Flemish literature, especially in the domain of poetry. Although a number of poets like Jos de Haes, Hubert van Herreweghen, and Christine D'HAEN continued traditional poetic forms, an avant-garde movement emerged in magazines such as *Tijd en Mens* (1949-55), *De (Kunst-)meridiaan* (1951-60), and *De Tafelronde* (1953-). Many in this so-called preexperimentalist generation confronted what Jan WALRAVENS described as the "paradox of '53," that is, with the opposition between the necessity of activism and the pursuit of purer poetic experimentation. Important figures of this generation include Remy C. van de Kerckhove, Ben Cami, and Albert Bontridder, as well as theoreticians such as Clara Haesaert, Marcel Wauters, and Erik van Ruysbeek. The next

generation of experimentalists, which gathered around the magazine *Gard-Sivik* (1955-63), set itself up against the prevailing social activism. According to the poet and critic Paul de Vrees, these "Vijftigers" (writers of the 1950s) "inscribed the conscientious objection of poetry on their shield." De Vrees here referred to the perennial recognition of poetry as an autonomous activity which cannot and should not be subordinated to the propaganda of activism. Yet it still must be noted that experimentalist poets like Gust Gils, Paul Snoek, and Hugues Pernath, although not activists, did protest against a materialistic world full of absurdity, violence, brutality, and suffering. These experimentalists, among whom are Jan van der Hoeven as well as Jaak Brouwers, Adriaan de Roover, Adriaan Peel, Rudo Durant, and Hedwig Speliers, developed in different directions. The neoexperimentalists of the 1960s looked to jazz in the creation of a wild, impulsive poetry. A concern with social and political reality appears in the works of Lucienne Stassaert, Max Kazan and, especially, Marcel van Maele. The mannerists constitute a separate group favoring a highly aesthetic conception of poetry; best known among them are the Antwerp figures Patrick Conrad, Nic van Bruggen, and Leonard Nolens, who celebrates fundamental themes in an almost liturgical style.

At the end of the 1960s, a new realism came to the forefront in opposition to unnatural poetic language and to romantic conceptions of the writer's task. The most representative members of this movement are Roland Jooris, Daniel van Ryssel, Patricia Lasoen, and, above all, the journalist Herman de Coninckx, who has sought a compromise between poetic and romantic aestheticism and new realistic portrayals of everyday reality. Current poets hover between poles of romanticism and disillusion; freed from the mundane world, they long for truth and authenticity. This form of sensitivity is perhaps best represented in the work of Eddy van Vliet and of the late Jotie T'Hooft.

World War II and its impact on social and political life has received extensive treatment in Flemish prose. The concerns evidenced in the novels of Boon, Claus, Daisne, and van Aken are continued by Maurice D'Haese, Georges Hebbelinck, Frank Liedel, Libera Carlier, and Prosper de Smet. Whether or not they deal specifically with the war, such writers reflect a sense of despair and a feeling that the world is hopelessly doomed. The existentialist approach emerges in the works of Frans de Bruyn, Bert van Aerschot, and Jos VANDELOO. In the 1960s, the Flemish novel underwent many transformations: the classical novel gave way to the *nouveau roman.* For many authors, the text acquires a therapeutic value: they search for their inner selves and put life in order through writing. Such is the case with Willy Spillebeen, Clem Schouwenaars, Fernand Auwera, and, especially, Jef Geeraerts, whose best works were inspired by his years in the Congo.

The magazine *Komma* (1965-69) constituted a milestone in the development of modern Flemish prose. The editors of this progressive magazine—Rene Gysen, Willy Roggeman, Julien Wevergergh, and Paul de Wispelaere—attempted to confront a rapidly changing world. Abolishing artificial boundaries between literary genres, they presented prismatic structures in which images, autobiographical fragments, and critical insights combine. Their work made major contributions to the renewal of the novel. Experimentation with the novel form was undertaken by writers such as Ivo Michiels, C. C. Krijgelmans, Mark Insingel, Marc Andries, Laurent Veydt, and Daniel Robberechts. The 1960s also witnessed a stream of critical and polemical writings which often led to satirical forms.

These "angry young men" included Julien Wevergergh, Herwig Leus, Herman J. Claeys, and Jan Emiel Daele. Viewing society from a critical perspective, they season their approach with an appropriate dose of irony. Walter van den Broeck, one of the few contemporary Flemish authors to write plays, fits well within this category. Among the most promising of recent Flemish talents are Walter van den Broeck and Claude van de Berge, who succeeds in creating a highly original musical prose.

See: G. Kalff *Geschiedenis der Nederlandsche Letterkunde* 6 vols. (1906–10); P. Hamelius, *Introduction à la littérature flamande de Belgique* (1921); A. de Ridder, *La littérature flamande contemporaine* (1923); F. de Backer, *Contemporary Flemish Literature* (1934); A. Vermeylen, *De Vlaamsche letteren van Gezelle tot heden* (1949); M. Gijsen, *De literatuur in Zuid-Nederland sedert 1830* (1951); B. Kemp, *De Vlaamse letteren tussen gisteren en morgen 1930–1960* (1963); J. Weisgerber, *Aspecten van de Vlaamse roman 1927–1960* (1964); R. F. Lissens, *De Vlaamse letterkunde van 1780 tot heden* (1967); B. F. van Vlierden, *Van In't Wonderjaer tot De verwondering* (1969); H. Bousset, *Schreien, schrijven, schreeuwen* (1973) and *Woord en schroom* (1977); P. van Aken, *Letterwijs, letterwijzer* (1979); O. Rens, *Acht Eeuwen Nederlandse Letteren* (1979).

J.-A.G. and P. van A.

Belgian literature in French. The 20th century has witnessed the blossoming of a prolific and varied literary culture in Belgium, where nearly half of the population claims French as its native language. This culture, which has produced what is probably the richest and most vigorous French language literature outside of France, has emerged from the nation's peculiar historical background. Although the creation of Belgium as a specific political entity dates only from 1830, monuments of French literature such as the *Cantilène Sainte Eulalie* and the commentaries of Jean Froissart and Philippe de Commynes were written in the milieu of powerful states centered within the present geographical boundaries of Belgium: the affluent, influential Burgundian states and the court of the counts of Flanders. This historical element is not without significance, since, from Charles De Coster to Michel de GHELDERODE, many Belgian writers have drawn their inspiration from the glorious medieval and Renaissance past of a Flanders that often assumes a legendary and even mythical dimension. The late medieval and Renaissance periods also evidenced the development of a Walloon and Picard literature represented by the chronicles of a Jean d'Outremeuse, Jacques de Hemricourt, and Georges Chastellain, a literature whose heritage has been continued in southern Belgium. Later, in the midst of the 18th-century Hapsburg hegemony, the *Mélanges militaires, littéraires et sentimentaires* (1795–1811; Miscellaneous Military, Literary, and Personal Reminescences) of Prince Charles-Joseph de Ligne reflected the cosmopolitan aspirations to which today's Belgian literary community has remained faithful. An assessment of modern Belgian literature thus must take into account the historical impact of a Flemish tradition expressed in French, of a vigorous Walloon and Picard heritage, and of continuing affinities with French and other European literatures.

The specific relationship between Belgian literature and that of France appears particularly difficult to delineate. The geographic and cultural closeness to France has led someone like Géo NORGE to declare that "A distinction based upon nationality seems ridiculous. French literature in Belgium is but a category of French literature in general." On the other hand, the eminent critic Gustave Charlier claimed that Belgian literature, "although it does not constitute a national literature in the strict sense of the term, still has its own genuine unity which does not allow for a full association to the literature of the France of Louis XIV, of Napoleon III, or of Albert Lebrun." The common denominator of the French language inevitably conditions Belgian literature of French expression and obliges this literature to transcend national borders, but this common denominator has also served as a medium for a literature with specific, unique characteristics.

In the late 19th century, an awareness of a specifically Belgian literary culture crystallized around the review *La Jeune Belgique* (1881–97). The writers associated with this review, whose impact was to be felt in the 20th century, not only promoted the ideals associated with Parnassian and symbolist esthetics, but also recognized Octave Pirmez (1832–84) and Charles De Coster (1827–79) as their forerunners in the forging of a Belgian literature. Pirmez and De Coster epitomize, each in his own right, different aspects of the Belgian temper. A true Walloon born in Hainaut, where he spent most of his life, Pirmez was viewed by the "Jeune Belgique" group as a writer sensitive to formal artistic criteria. Although Pirmez, who has been called an "unrecognized Vauvenargues," has not exercised a great influence on subsequent generations, his melancholic romanticism, his love of nature, and his meditative tone illustrate certain typical aspects of the Walloon spirit, aspects that appear in the poetry and short stories of writers like Jean Tousseul—*Les Cahiers de Jean Stienon* (1936; The Notebooks of Jean Stienon), Roger FOULON—*Prières pour un vivant* (1950, Prayers for the Living), and Marcel THIRY—*Vie poésie* (1961, Life Poetry) and *Songes et Spélonques* (1973; Dreams and Retreats). At the other end of the spectrum, the celebrated masterpiece of Charles De Coster, *Les Aventures de Tyl Ulenspiegel et de Lamme Goedzak* (1867; The Adventures of Tyl Ulenspiegel and Lamme Goedzak), constitutes one of the most innovative manifestations of the picaresque novel. The account of the wanderings of the roguish Tyl and his friend Lamme presents, in a blend of epic and folk tale, a vision of the political and religious life of the people of the southern Low Countries in the 16th century and of their struggle against the Spanish invaders. De Coster himself asserted that the adventures of Tyl and Lamme "are made of a blend of Latin spirit and Germanic feeling." In an appealing and slightly archaic French, De Coster managed to render the essence of a certain ebullient and pugnacious Flemish temperament. Soon translated into several languages, including Russian, *Les Aventures de Tyl Ulenspiegel et Lamme Goedzak* is, however, seldom read in its full original version. Nonetheless, influential Belgian authors from Emile VERHAEREN to Franz HELLENS and Michel de Ghelderode have relished the colorful style of De Coster and the picturesque character of Tyl. De Ghelderode, for instance, in an interview with his friend Jean STEVO, went so far as to say, "It was after reading De Coster's *Ulenspiegel* in 1915–1916 that I decided to write. This influence was, for me, determinative." Just as Pirmez symbolized a certain Walloon inspiration, De Coster illustrated aspects of Flemish character and tradition.

Belgian literature is characterized not only by the country's bicultural heritage, but also by strong individual talents whose work tends to escape rigid categorizations by movements or schools. In the various literary genres—poetry, prose, and theater—writers such as Fernand CROMMELYNCK, Michel de Ghelderode, and Henri MICHAUX cannot easily be classified. Nonetheless, Belgian writers have played significant roles in the emergence and development of symbolism and surrealism. As it happens, most of poets who have looked to a symbolist aesthetics have a Flemish background, whereas the irreverent spirit of surrealism has drawn particularly authors from a Walloon tradition. A friend of Stéphane MALLARMÉ and the author of an important study of the French symbolists, Albert MOCKEL became the theorist of what could be termed the Belgian counterpart of the symbolist movement. Indeed, Mockel's aesthetics might be linked to that of symbolism insofar as it envisages free verse based on accentuation and uninterrupted concordance of sounds. Along with this impassioned poet and advocate of Wagnerian music must be counted Charles van Lerberghe, Georges RODENBACH, and Max ELSKAMP, who bring to poetic creation a specific originality characterized by the discrete use of the symbol, by a vibrant sensuality, and, particularly in the case of Elskamp, by a mystical impulse. If *La Chanson d'Eve* (1904; Eve's Song) belongs to one of the most melodious registers of the French language, the metaphysical meditations of Georges Rodenbach's *Bruges la morte* (1892), a work for which the philosopher Gaston BACHELARD had a special predilection, reveal a harmonious blending of visions of canals, belltowers, and beguines with a keen exploration of the unconscious. Perhaps less marked by the symbolist impulse, Max Elskamp expressed his own mystical anguish in *La Louange de la vie* (1898; Praise of Life); his taste for popular culture appears in works like *La Chanson de la rue Saint Paul* (1922; Song of Saint Paul Street), a collection in which he evokes his childhood in Antwerp. Often compared to Jules Laforgue, with whom he shared a sense of popular poetic rhythms and of irony, Elskamp holds a special place in the history of Belgian literature through his syntactic and metric innovations as well as through the evocative power which earned him the title "imagier de la Flandre."

In the wake of symbolism, Emile Verhaeren and Maurice MAETERLINCK occupy positions that also transcend the Belgian borders and, at the same time, their attachment to their native country remained strong. Dominated by a lyrical power and a stentorian vitality, the work of Verhaeren expanded through a wide register encompassing the realm of legends, the opposition between city and country, and the energy and squalor of "tentacular" cities. Few poets have so forcefully explored the world of labor and the miseries of the worker caught up in the ascendance of the international socialism that swept through Belgium in the last part of the 19th century. Works like *Les Visages de la Vie* (1899; The Faces of Life) present a stormy vision encompassing the coal mines of the Hainaut region as well as the mills of the plains; yet in other collections, like *Les Heures* (1905; The Hours), the tone becomes softer in celebration of a joyful love.

In contrast to the work of Verhaeren, that of Maeterlinck opens on to a universe of mystery and uneasiness permeated by a rhythmic, musical sense. As the eminent critic Michael Riffaterre has quite rightly pointed out in regard to *Serres chaudes* (1899; Warm Hothouses), by far Maeterlinck's masterpiece, a kind of pointillism frequently found in the decadent school emerges, with sensorial notations following one after another, but the lexicon remains very simple and avoids unusual words favored by strict symbolists.

While Rodenbach, Verhaeren, and Maeterlinck spent much time in Paris and kept close ties with French writers, most Belgian surrealists never settled in Paris and rarely had more than sporadic contact with André BRETON. Surrealism's precursor, the dada movement launched by Tristan Tzara in 1919, found a sympathetic response in the poetic work of Clément Pansaers and Paul Neuhuys. A friend of Louis ARAGON, Pansaers published in 1920 a dadaist poem, "Le Pan-pan au cul nu du Nègre" (Spanking the Naked Bottom of the Negro), which enjoyed a certain success in Paris. The most eminent representative of Belgian surrealism, the painter and writer René Magritte, whose *Ecrits* (Writings) was published in 1979, returned to live in Belgium after a stay in France for several years, during which time he encountered Aragon, Max Ernst, Marcel Duchamp, Paul ELUARD, Salvador Dali, Man Ray, and Breton. In Belgium, Magritte became associated with a considerable number of writers and artists whose preoccupations paralleled those of the surrealists in France. Belgian surrealism may not have produced major literary works, but it did promote a rejection of conventionality and of habits of language in the light and "black" humor of writers like Achille CHAVÉE, Louis Scutenaire, Paul Nougé, Marcel Lecomte, Paul Colinet, Marcel Marien, and E. L. T. Mesens. Bussy's *Anthologie du Surréalisme en Belgique* (1972) presents a careful choice of texts that are often inaccessible and that attest to the intense climate of literary experimentation and creativity engendered during nearly half a century.

Outside of movements and schools, the work of Henri Michaux reveals a questioning of the creative process through poetic writing and through the well-known "mescaline" drawings. Born in Namur in 1899, Michaux soon severed all ties with Belgium and retired into solitude in Paris. His work, from *Voyage en grande Carabagne* (1936; Trip to the Grand Carabagne) to *Façons d'endormi, Façons d'éveillé* (1969; Sleepy Attitudes, Awake Attitudes), has evolved outside Belgium. Yet, the cautious, exploratory process through which Michaux reinvents syntax, words, and things finds an echo in the poetic thrust of Christian Dotrémont (1922–79) and of Max Loreau.

Belgian poetry since World War II has also witnessed the continuation of a more classical tradition illustrated early in the 20th century by O. J. Périer and manifested more recently in the remarkable works of Marcel Thiry, Robert MONTAL, Albert AYGUESPARSE, Jean MUNO, and Robert GOFFIN. In these poets' works, their personal lyricism renders, in traditional schemes of free-flowing verse, such perennial poetic themes as the fragility of happiness and new imagery emerging in the contemporary world. Goffin, for instance, adjusts his poetic repertoire to the modern phenomena of cycle races, the cinema, and the music hall. In a different range, close to that of Jules SUPERVIELLE and of Jacques PRÉVERT, the work of Maurice CARÊME reflects a deep understanding of the world of children. Far from being naive, his work illustrates Sigmund Freud's statement that the poet, like a child at play, creates a world of fantasy, which he takes seriously. Both joy and a sense of irony dominate in most of his poems, revealing a truly unique creator.

Although poetry has achieved a special place in Belgian literature, Belgium has not failed to produce a number of distinguished novelists. With Charles Plisnier and Alexis Curvers, the Walloon region has contributed two great prose writers. Plisnier, whose masterpiece *Faux-Passeports* (Eng. tr., *Memoirs of a Secret Revolutionary*) won the Goncourt Prize in 1937, has created carefully structured novels centered on such themes as political militancy, social conformity, and sexual conflict. Curvers, who gained wide public recognition for *Tempo di Roma* (1957; Eng. tr., 1960), portrays the difficulties of adolescence and the world of sophisticated dillettantes. Georges SIMENON, like Curvers a Liégois, has earned an unequaled reputation in the world of the detective novel. Translated and read throughout the world, the adventures of Inspector Maigret reveal the talent of a great story-teller who understands human motivation. Simenon sets his intrigues in countries where he has traveled as, for instance, in *Trois Chambres à Manhattan* (1946; Eng. tr., *Three Beds in Manhattan*).

Since World War II, several women of Belgian origin have emerged as first-rate novelists, including Françoise MALLET-JORIS, Béatrix BECK, and Dominique ROLIN. The daughter of the essayist and playwright Suzanne LILAR, Mallet-Joris was a literary child prodigy. At the age of nine, she wrote her first novel; several years later, Fernand CROMMELYNCK and Marie GEVERS read her poetry with enthusiasm. Her first published novel, *Le Rempart des Béguines* (1951; Eng. tr., *The Illusionist*, 1952), surprised the public with its precociousness and its clear, cool vision of hypocritical bourgeois society. In 1958, her novel *L'Empire céleste* (1958; Eng. tr., *Café Céleste*, 1959) won France's prestigious Femina Prize. Originally a novelist of social commentary, she has progressively moved in the direction of autobiography and historical fiction.

In 1952, Béatrix Beck received the Goncourt Prize for *Léon Morin, Prêtre* (1952; Eng. tr., *The Priest*, 1953), a work that reflected the religious obsession haunting Beck's earlier works such as *Barny* (1948) and *Une Mort irrégulière* (1951; An Irregular Death). While Mallet-Joris and Beck masterfully explore the resources of the traditional novel, Dominique Rolin engages in an avant-garde handling of style and form that has won the praise of Philippe SOLLERS and the *Tel Quel* group.

In the multifaceted development of Belgian prose, the novels and short stories of André BAILLON, Franz HELLENS, Marcel MOREAU, Jean Ray, and Marcel Thiry deserve a special mention for their insights into the uncanny and the bizarre.

In the course of the 19th century, such Belgian writers as Charles van LERBERGHE, Georges Rodenbach, Emile Verhaeren, and Albert GIRAUD produced dramatic works that received relatively little attention and acclaim. But the Belgian theater attained sudden recognition with the success of Maurice Maeterlinck's *La Princesse Maleine* (1889; Eng. tr., *Princess Maleine*, 1911). This dramatist's subsequent works, such as *L'Intruse* (1890; Eng. tr., *The Intruder*, 1918) and *Pelléas et Mélisande* (1892; Eng. tr., 1920), vividly brought to the stage the ideals of symbolist aesthetics. In the years following Maeterlinck's successes, Belgian playwrights achieved international prominence. The Parisian performance of Fernand Crommelynck's *Le Cocu magnifique* (1921; Eng. tr., *The Magnificent Cuckold*, 1966), which has been called "truly the greatest play Belgian literature has produced," signaled the appearance of a major European talent. The son of a Belgian father and a French mother, Crommelynck undoubtedly stands out as one of the major playwrights of the period between the two world wars. Centering on the themes of love and jealousy, his plays are written in a flamboyant and ornate language that is truly original and that, as Georges SION has written, evidences a "baroque vitality." Following World War II, another Belgian writer produced plays of baroque dimensions: the performance of Michel de Ghelderode's *Fastes d'Enfer* (1943; Eng. tr., *Chronicles of Hell*, 1960) in 1952 provoked a literary sensation in Paris at the time when the theater of the absurd was achieving notoriety. As Roland Beyen has pointed out, it is unclear whether Ghelderode actually influenced writers like Eugène Ionesco, Samuel BECKETT, Jean GENET, and Fernando ARRABAL, but it is certain that many of their "innovations" were already present in his work and that this work contributed to the acceptance of such innovations.

In *Fastes d'Enfer,* as in some 20 other plays, Ghelderode created a peculiar atmosphere in which cruelty and lust triumph.

In addition to the tendencies illustrated by Maeterlinck, Crommelynck, and Ghelderode, the Belgian theater since World War II has directed its attention to the exploration of psychological analysis and of historical themes. In 1946, Suzanne Lilar's *Le Burlador* (1946; Eng. tr., *The Burlador,* 1966) was widely acclaimed in Paris. This play's hero is a deceiver and a seducer, incapable of experiencing love as a lasting sentiment, a figure who moves to the limits of passion and feeling. This treatment of the Don Juan theme by a woman was considered particularly powerful and ambitious. This same theme appeared in the *Don Juan* (1948) of Charles BERTIN, where a tortured, satanic Don Juan emerges in a work of remarkable theatrical sensitivity and forceful dialogue. In the works of Jean MOGIN and Georges SION, psychological exploration is linked to the quest for the absolute. Mogin's characters pursue purity and austerity; those of Sion struggle as well with the complex problems of faith and grace. Among the Belgian writers who have brought historical figures to the stage are Herman CLOSSON, author of *Godefroid de Bouillon* (1935) and *Sire Halewijn* (1954), and Charles Bertin, in his *Christophe Colomb* (1958). Recent Belgian theater has also witnessed the successful exploration of lighter subjects, as in Edmond Kinds's *Le Valet des songes* (1953; The Knave of Dreams), Sion's *La Malle de Paméla* (1955; Pamela's Trunk), and Paul WILLEMS's *Il pleut dans ma maison* (1961; It's Raining in My House).

No panorama of Belgian literature would be complete if it were not to take into account the important role played by a number of periodicals in grouping young writers sharing similar ideals and tendencies. As early as the end of the 19th century, Edmond Picard's *L'Art moderne* sought to promote a specifically Belgian literature and, in contrast to the group around *La Jeune Belgique*, to foster a socially oriented literature set apart from symbolist aesthetics. At the same time, *La Wallonie* (1886–92), directed by the Liége poet and critic Albert MOCKEL, published such important works as *Les Flaireurs* of Charles van Lerberghe and *L'Intruse* of Maurice Maeterlinck. Emile Verhaeren's experiments with free verse appeared in another short-lived review, *Le Coq rouge*. Another journal, founded by Franz Hellens and published from 1920 to 1941, first under the title *Signaux de France et de Belgique* and then as *Le Disque vert*, widened the horizons of Belgian literary life by publishing not only works of authors of Belgian origin (such as Henri Michaux) but also those of Blaise CENDRARS, André MALRAUX, André GIDE, Pierre MacORLAN, and Vladimir MAYAKOVSKY.

In the period between the world wars, such reviews continued to provide a forum for Belgian letters. Associated with *Le Journal des poètes*, for instance, were such writers as Pierre Bourgeois, Fernand Verhesen, Arthur Haulot, and Maurice Carême. An eloquent witness to the poetic productivity of Belgium, this review contributed, under the guidance of Haulot, to the formation of the celebrated "Biennale de Poésie" at Knokke, drawing celebrated poets (such as Léopold SENGHOR) from the entire French-speaking world. In the same period, such avant-garde periodicals as *Le Rouge et le noir, Phantomas,* and *Le Thyrse* contributed to cultural life and, in particular, gave a forum of expression to such Belgian surrealists as Marcel Lecomte, Achille Chavée, Colinet, and Nougé. Other magazines, such as *Synthèses* (1946–72), *La revue nationale* (1928–74), and *La revue générale* (1873–), have offered a panorama of literary and political works by a wide variety of authors, foreign as well as

Belgian. Such reviews, based in Brussels, attest to the vital role played by the capital as the "mirror of Belgian letters."

The Royal Academy of French Language and Literature, founded in Brussels on the eve of World War I by the minister of science and art, Jules DESTRÉE, has increasingly become a center of active literary life through its meetings and its financial support, as has the Center for Belgian Authors at the Maison Camille Lemonnier inaugurated by Queen Elizabeth in 1946. Because of such support Belgian writers are able to have their works appear in print without having to pass through the complex publishing machinery of Belgium's imposing neighbor to the south. The Royal Academy elects 30 Belgian members—20 creative writers and 10 philologists—as well as 10 foreign members, among whom have been such eminent French authors as COLETTE and Jean COCTEAU. Like the Académie Française, the Belgian Academy counts scholars, essayists, and philologists among its members. Roland Mortier, the distinguished Enlightenment scholar, Joseph Hanse, the literary historian, Emilie Noulet, the scholar of Paul Valéry and Stéphane Mallarmé, Claire Preaux, the classical philologist, and Raymond Trousson, the comparatist, have continued in the traditions established by Georges Rency, Gustave Charlier, and Henry Gregóire and have brought Belgium to a place of eminence in the world of literary scholarship. Moreover, such critics of Belgian origin as Georges Poulet and Paul de Man (*Blindness and Insight*, 1971; *Allegories of Reading*, 1979) have brought a truly innovative dimension to the philosophical and theoretical study of literature.

Belgian writers have also benefited from their associations with the plastic arts. The American critic B. M. Woodbridge has underlined the close relationship that has existed in Belgium between literature and the arts since the 19th century. The critical works of writers like Camille Lemonnier and the impact of innovative artists from James Ensor to René Magritte, Paul Delvaux, and, most recently, Pierre Aléchinsky reveal the important place that art and artists hold in Belgian cultural life. The contributions of such art historians and critics as Philippe Roberts-Jones, Robert Delevoy, Emile Langui, Paul Caso, and the brothers Luc and Paul Haesarts have underlined the links between literature and art and have illustrated the importance of the essay as a literary form. Finally, if Henri Pirenne's magisterial *Histoire de Belgique* (7 vols., 1900–32) brought new respect and attention to historical writing, his task has been ably continued by such creative scholar-writers as Luc Hommel (*Marie de Bourgogne ou le grand heritage* [1945]), Carlo BRONNE (*Leopold premier et son temps* [1942; Leopold I and His Times]), and Georges-Henri Dumont (*Histoire de la Belgique* [1977]). It might be said that, in the 20th century, Belgian writers of French expression have heard the slogan of the *Jeune Belgique* group: "Soyons-nous!"—"Let us be ourselves!"

See: B. M. Woodbridge, *Le Roman belge contemporain* (1930); R. Guiette, *Poètes français de Belgique de Verhaeren au surréalisme* (1948); S. Lilar, *Soixante ans de théâtre belge* (1952); G. Charlier and J. Hanse, *Histoire illustrée des lettres françaises de Belgique* (1958); A. Mor and J. Weisgerber, *Storia delle letterature del Belgio* (1958); *Bibliographie des écrivains français de Belgique*, vols. 1–4, through letter "N" (1958–72); J. Rousselot, *Dictionnaire de la poésie française contemporaine* (1968); M. Piron, "Les Lettres françaises de Belgique," in *Littérature française*, vol. 2 (1968); R. Bodart, *La Poésie française de Belgique, 1942–1968* (1968); C. Bussy, *Anthologie du surréalisme en Belgique* (1972); R. Burniaux and R. Frickx, *La Littérature belge d'expression française* (1974); A. Jans, *Lettres vivantes: deux générations d'écrivains français en Belgique 1945–1975*, (1975); L. Wouters, *Panorama de la poésie française de Belgique* (1976); G. H. Dumont, *Histoire de la Belgique* (1977).
M.-R.L.

Bellido, José María (1922–), Spanish playwright, was born in San Sebastián. A well-traveled, multilingual Basque with deep roots in his native province of Guipúzcoa, Bellido began writing plays in the late 1940s. His work is probably the most extensive and varied of the so-called underground theater of the Franco era. Bellido is a highly imaginative iconoclast who calls into ironic question any and all aspects of the human condition, be they traditional, contemporary, or futuristic. *Tren a F...* (1960; Eng. tr., *Train to H...*, 1970), for example, is a bizarre allegory of the stagnation and inconsistencies of traditionalist religion. *El pan y el arroz o Geometría en amarillo* (1966; Eng. tr., *Bread and Rice, or Geometry in Yellow*, 1970) is a mordant satire of how a complete takeover of society by an archetypal power elite is thwarted by the passive resistance of Oriental children who multiply in geometric progression. Bellido himself divides his theater into two chronological periods, before 1959 and after 1959 when he read the complete works of Bertolt BRECHT and underwent a crisis of political conscience and weathered the throes of the question of authorial purpose. Rather than an ideologue, Bellido is a profound humanist. He considers the most typical and meaningful part of his theater to be a series of 23 short plays which span his entire career and which he grouped together in the early 1970s under the general title *La suite fantástica*. He refers to these as "temblores" (quiverings), that is, spontaneous works conceived and developed without limitations of form and dominated by paradox and fantasy. Published up to now only in isolated segments, the *temblores* will eventually have to be counted among the most original works of the modern European theater.

See: G. E. Wellwarth, *Spanish Underground Drama* (1972).
S.M.G.

Belorussian literature. Modern Belorussian literature began to take shape during a period of Russian suppression of the Belorussian language. In the second half of the 19th century a series of administrative acts prohibited publication in Belorussian. The first of these acts took place in 1859 and was later reinforced following the 1863 Belorussian uprising against Russian rule. When the ban on publication in Belorussian was partly (and only temporarily) lifted in 1889–93, the poet Ivan Niasłuchoŭski (1851–97) managed to publish several of his Belorussian poems in the local Russian publications. In 1891–96, the "father of modern Belorussian literature," Frańcišak Bahuševič (1840–1900) succeeded in publishing his poems abroad. Thus was modern Belorussian literature founded. Until the 1920s, Belorussian writers were influenced by romantic humanitarianism and romantic realism, as well as by a national democratic stance with a tradition of dramatized social criticism.

After the Russian Revolution of 1905, the ban on publishing in Belorussian was lifted, and the literary movement "Našaniŭstva" was founded. The movement took its name from the journal *Naša Niva* (1906–15; Our Soil), which had succeeded the short-lived *Naša Dola* (1906; Our Fate). During the years 1906 to 1908, the two periodicals had introduced a dozen successors to Bahuševič and Niasłuchoŭski, including the movement's two leading poets, Jakub Kołas, pseud. of Kanstantyn Mickievič

(1882–1956) and Janka Kupała, pseud. of Ivan Łucevič (1882–1942).

In 1909, Belorussian literature began to move beyond popular and national levels and to reach the standards and forms of a major European literature. This advance came with a new group of writers and poets, especially Maksim Bahdanovič (1891–1917), who supported the idea of a national renaissance or *adradžeńnie*. "Našaniŭstva" thus developed into "Adradženstva" (Renaissance), which remained the dominant school until the 1920s.

Bahdanovič described "Adradženstva" as "a recapitulative course on European literary schools of the modern period." Bahdanovič himself recapitulated and thus introduced neoclassicism, impressionism, and symbolism into Belorussian poetry, while at the same time paying tribute to the traditional romantic realism. In addition to Bahdanovič, Kupała, and Kołas, major writers of "Adradženstva" included Aleś Harun, pseud. of Aleksandar Prušynski (1887–1920), and Maksim Harecki (1893–1939).

In 1921–22, signs of a profound internal crisis appeared within "Aradženstva." Revolutionary elements challenged both the foundation of the movement and its leading exponents, demanding a rejuvenation and updating of ideology, themes, and artistic techniques. In 1923 these revolutionaries founded the new journal *Mał, adniak* (Saplings), gathering around it an organization of aspiring writers. To the predominant romantic humanitarianism and national democracy of "Adradženstva," they offered revolutionary romanticism and national communism, together with an imitation of Soviet Russian proletarian poetry, imaginism, and futurism (*see* RUSSIAN LITERATURE).

In 1926 a group of "Mał. adniak" members set up a new organization and journal, *Uzvyšša* (Excelsior). The new movement, "Uzvyšenstva" (Excelsiorism), aimed to create a literature of "excelsior heights that will be seen by centuries and nations." This movement renounced both recapitulation and the imitation of any established literary school, and espoused the idea of national progress and the development of an original Belorussian school based on Belorussian folk poetry. *Uzvyšša* brought to literature Uładzimier Duboŭka (1900–) and Jazep Pušča, pseud. of Jazep Płaščynski (1902–64), the finest lyricists in Belorussian poetry; Kuźma Čorny, pseud. of Mikałaj Ramanoŭski (1900–44), a superb fiction writer; Kandrat Krapiva, pseud. of Kandrat Atrachovič (1896–), the wittiest Belorussian satirist; and Adam Babareka (1899–1937), the most profound and subtle Belorussian critic.

During the 1930s all original literary movements were suppressed and all literary organizations were disbanded. Many writers lost their freedom, their talents, and often their lives. Only 4 of the 16 members of "Uzvyšša" were able to write and publish after 1937.

In contemporary Belorussian literature Duboŭka and Krapiva are the most outstanding writers, largely preserving the tenets of the "Uzvyšša" school while paying the necessary tribute to official socialist realism. Other important writers include Maksim Tank, pseud. of Aŭhien Skurka, and Uładzimier Karatkievič, and the fiction writers Vasil Bykaŭ (who also publishes in Russian as Vasil BYKOV) and Janka Bryl.

See: A. Adamovich, *Opposition to Sovietization in Belorussian Literature, 1917–1957* (1958) and "Forty Years of Belorussian Literature in the BSSR: A Review of Events," *BR* 7 (1959): 51–65; A McMillin, "A Conspectus and Bibliography of Byelorussian Literature in the Nineteenth Century," *JByelS* 2, no. 3 (1971): 271–88; V. Rich, tr., *Like Water, Like Fire: An Anthology of Byelorussian Poetry from 1828 to the Present Day* (1971); T. Bird, ed.,

"Modern Byelorussian Literature: Articles and Documents," *Queens Slavic Papers,* vol. 3 (1975). A.A.

Belov, Vasily Ivanovich (1932–), Russian novelist and short-story writer, was born in Timonikha, a village in the Vologda region, to a family of farmers. He worked for a time on a collective farm and as a rural schoolteacher, and he joined the Communist Party in 1956. Following the publication of several collections of poems and short stories, he published the novel *Privychnoye delo* (1968; The Usual Affair). By a rare coincidence, this peasant novel about love and misery was greeted with enthusiasm by the critics, the intelligentsia, and the general public. It was followed by a series of works also set in the northern Russian countryside: *Plotnitskiye rasskazy* (1968; Carpenter Stories); *Bukhtiny vologodskiye* (1969; Vologda Coves); *Malchiki* (1973; Boys); *Tseluyutsya zori* (1975; The Dawns Kiss); and *Kanuny* (1976; Eves). The novel *Kanuny,* Belov's most outstanding work since *Privychnoye delo,* is a portrayal of the damage wrought by collectivization; its published version, however, was heavily censored.

Solidly rooted in his native Vologda, Belov has a keen sense of the uniqueness of that region, which has never been invaded and thus is preeminently Russian. It is an area with age-old traditions that even forced collectivization has not been able completely to destroy. Belov's work, which belongs to the new school of peasant literature, advocates a return to the sources and upholds the moral values of the Russian peasant. His writing is distinguished by language that is authentically redolent of the soil, by an almost pantheistic poetry of nature, and by an infinitely tender compassion for the unfortunate fate of the peasant. J.Ca.

Bely, Andrey, pseud. of Boris Nikolayevich Bugayev (1880–1934), Russian novelist and poet, was a leading theoretician of the Russian symbolist movement. Born in Moscow, he took his pen name to avoid embarrassing his father, a noted mathematician who considered Bely's interests in Oriental mysticism, Arthur Schopenhauer, and Friedrich NIETZSCHE a betrayal of the positivist traditions of the Russian intelligentsia. Other formative influences were Bely's studies of physics, biology, music, and especially, as was the case with other "junior symbolists" (such as Alexsandr BLOK and Vyacheslav IVANOV), the philosophy and poetry of Vladimir SOLOVYOV. Bely's classically Oedipal conflict with his father provided a major theme for his fiction and poetry. In his first four fictional narratives, all subtitled "Symphony," he experimented with forms derived from music (the sonata-allegro structure and the four-movement symphonic cycle). The "Third Symphony," *Vozvrat* (1905; The Return), a fantasy about a student of chemistry who is actually an exile from another universe, applied these musical principles most successfully and logically. The four "Symphonies" inaugurated the system of refrains and leitmotifs and the blend of poetic lyricism and satirical comedy that are typical of Bely's major novels.

Bely's first collection of verse, *Zoloto v lazuri* (1904; Gold in the Azure), projects the poet's joyous, pantheistic personal cosmogony in vivid imagery and displays a virtuoso verbal texture that strongly affected such later poets as Boris PASTERNAK and Vladimir MAYAKOVSKY. Even more masterful verbally, his second collection, *Pepel* (1909; Ashes), turns to themes of social concern and is far more pessimistic in outlook, reflecting the poet's disillusionment after the failure of the 1905 Revolution. *Urna* (1909; The Urn) is a volume of love lyrics, inspired by Bely's complicated love affair with the wife of Aleksandr

Blok, and consisting of stylized evocations of 18th- and early 19th-century Russian poets. Bely's critical and theoretical essays, collected in *Simvolizm* and *Lug zelyony* (both 1910; Symbolism; The Green Meadow), contain a thorough, if subjective, outline of symbolist aesthetics; they also present pioneer methods of studying Russian metrics and versification, which have given rise to an entirely new scholarly discipline still thriving today.

Bely's first three novels can now be seen as his most durable and influential contribution. *Serebryany golub* (1909; Eng. tr., *The Silver Dove,* 1974) concerns a young intellectual's involvement with a peasant eschatological religious sect. *Peterburg* (1916, with three subsequent revisions; truncated Eng. tr., *St. Petersburg,* 1959; Eng. tr. of complete text, *Petersburg,* 1978) is a feverish comedy of revolutionary conspiracy and betrayal, part delirium, part carnival, played out against the geometrically austere backdrop of the capital of tsarist Russia. *Kotik Letayev* (1916; Eng. tr., 1971) traces a child's incipient consciousness as it emerges from an undifferentiated chaos and becomes aware of the outside world. These three novels, with their emancipated syntax, wide use of diverse kinds of diction, puns, and neologisms, and surprising twists of plot, were basic to the literary origins of such Soviet writers as Boris PILNYAK, Yevgeny ZAMYATIN, Isaak BABEL, and Andrey PLATONOV and of the more innovative émigré novelists, such as Vladimir NABOKOV and Vasily Yanovsky. They also map out and prefigure the sensibility and structural devices of later Western novelists, such as James Joyce, Alain ROBBE-GRILLET, and Thomas Pynchon.

All Bely's work after *Peterburg* is affected by his conversion to anthroposophy (he spent several years in Dornach, Switzerland, as Rudolf Steiner's disciple). The impact of this conversion is particularly evident in his book of confessions, *Zapiski chudaka* (1921; Diary of an Eccentric), and in *Glossolalia* (1922), subtitled "A Poem on Sonority," a set of meditations on the nature of human speech. Bely's greatest achievements as a poet are his autobiographical narrative poem "Pervoe svidanye" (1921; The First Rendezvous), his most organic use of the four-movement symphonic structure for literary purposes, and his collection *Posle razluki* (1922; After Separation). As revealed in these works, Bely's poetic manner had been changed and revitalized by his close study of such postsymbolist poets as Viktor KHLEBNIKOV and Marina TSVETAYEVA. His later novels, *Kreshchony kitayets* (1927; The Baptized Chinaman), which is a sequel to *Kotik Letayev,* the two-volume *Moskva* (1926; Moscow), and *Maski* (1932; Masks), elaborate the themes and techniques of his earlier novels without adding anything of substance to their achievement.

Bely's memoir *Vospominaniya o Bloke* (1923; Reminiscences About Blok) is a splendidly written, highly personal account of the star-crossed friendship of two major poets. His later trilogy of memoirs, consisting of *Na rubezhe dvukh stoletiy* (1930; On the Boundary between Two Centuries), *Nachalo veka* (1933; The Beginning of the Century), and *Mezhdu dvukh revolyutsiy* (1934; Between Two Revolutions), written, like his later novels, in a kind of metrical prose, is a wide-ranging panorama of Russian cultural history. But in trying to accommodate himself to the Soviet establishment's evergrowing hostility to the modernism of the early 20th century, Bely often rewrote history and slandered both his own past and the symbolist movement to which he so richly contributed. His last book, *Masterstvo Gogolya* (1934; Gogol's Mastery) is a ground-breaking stylistic study of Nikolay Gogol, whose heir and follower Bely considered himself to be. Despite his repeated protestations of loyalty to the Soviet regime,

Bely's own work and writings about him were banned in the Soviet Union after 1940. The ban has been partially lifted since 1965, but Bely is still denied his rightful recognition as a major, seminal figure in 20th-century Russian literature.

See: O. A. Maslenikov, *The Frenzied Poets: Andrei Biely and the Russian Symbolists* (1952); J. D. Elsworth, *Andrey Bely* (London, 1972); G. Janecek, ed., *Andrey Bely: A Critical Review* (1978). · S.K.

Benavente, Jacinto (1866–1954), Spanish playwright, was born and lived all his life in Madrid. He premiered more than 170 plays and was awarded the Nobel Prize for Literature in 1922. In his early years, when he wrote *El nido ajeno* (1894; The Alien Nest), *Gente conocida* (1896; Well-Known People), and *La comida de las fieras* (1898; The Banquet of the Beasts), Benavente set out to create a theater that would expose the contradictions of bourgeois society, typified by the conflicts between theory and practice, between system and individual, in the Madrid bourgeoisie. He addressed himself to the problem of finding the theatrical form best suited to this purpose. The first step, from which all subsequent steps follow, was the removal of rhetoric from theatrical language, not only from verbal language but from all the signs characteristic of dramatic structure, from the configuration of situations and patterns of conduct to the visual elements that define the setting and the general tonality of gesture. This language was completely new and revolutionary on the Spanish stage at the end of the 19th and beginning of the 20th centuries. It signified a definitive break with the romantic heritage, which had become a conventional formula still dominant in the works of José ECHEGARAY and his disciples. This new way of speaking and acting on stage introduced to Spain a new theatrical realism in which the characters, their passions, conflicts, and confrontations, were the least important elements, while the dramatic chronicle of the vices and virtues—generally petty vices and petty virtues—of the bourgeoisie assumed primary importance. This antirhetorical theatrical language is the foundation of Benavente's dramatic art. Due to its influence over all contemporary theater, Benavente's art was destined to become the official dramatic art, that is, to become publicly accepted as the dominant pattern and archetype of Spanish theater in the first 30 years of the 20th century.

All of the so-called defects of Benavente's style—dialogue without dialects, evasion of truly dramatic situations, absence of tension, and psychological schematism—as well as its so-called virtues—literary quality of the dialogue, finesse, elegance, critical mordacity, delicacy, naturalness, technical mastery, and, above all, the perfect and complex theatrical rhythm of the dialogue—give to each of his works a characteristic and unmistakable dramatic style that does not vary substantially throughout his prolific and uninterrupted production.

Benavente gathered his characters in four fundamental stage settings: bourgeois, urban interiors (salons and parlors); cosmopolitan interiors (luxurious salons at an elegant winter resort, in a yacht, or in a palace); provincial interiors typified by Moraleda, a symbol of the provincial city; rural interiors (wealthy peasant kitchens, dining rooms, or living rooms). In these same settings, although poetically transfigured, the action of his "fantastic" or "children's" theater, for which Benavente's imagination was so poorly endowed, also takes place. Only his masterwork, *Los intereses creados* (1907; Eng. tr., *The Bonds of Interest,* 1915), transcends these four settings.

The bourgeois, urban interiors were the focus of the greater part of Benavente's works, from the early plays

El nido ajeno and *Gente conocida* to post-Civil War works like *Al fin, mujer* (1942; At Last, Woman) or *Su amante esposa* (1950; His Loving Wife). In this category are such representative titles as *Lo cursi* (1901; Bad Taste), *Campo de armiño* (1916; Eng. tr., *Field of Ermine*, 1935), and *Titania* (1945). These plays reveal the narrow but coherent repertory of public attitudes of the upper middle class. Locked into its prejudices, this class judges reality according to standards that are in manifest contradiction with reality, as if the class were incapable of overcoming it, thus condemning itself to experience the permanent and stultifying disjunction of its moral and ideological code and individual modes of conduct and behavior. Benavente attacked the falseness of social convention, hypocrisy, phariseeism, and the tyranny of appearances, malice, and stupidity, but without seriously questioning the principles underlying the ideology of the criticized social class.

The first work that situates its characters in a cosmopolitan setting is *La noche del sábado* (1903; Eng. tr., *Saturday Night*, 1918). Another is *La princesa Bebé* (1904; Eng. tr., *Princess Bebé*, 1919). Both have themes reminiscent of novels of romance. Other sentimental chronicles of the duties and aspirations of a morally bankrupt aristocracy are *La mariposa que voló sobre el mar* (1926; The Butterfly that Flew over the Sea) and *Mater Imperatrix* (1950). These works have a double intention: they are both elegiac (the swan songs of a society that is fatally wounded but beautiful, like a useless luxury item) and critical (society is dying because of its inability to make real its ideals, to adapt them to the new times instead of taking refuge in its dreams). Benavente portrayed, although in an abstract and sentimental way, the last hour of a beautiful phantom world that, not knowing how to live in a real sense, limited itself to conversing in brilliant hollow phrases.

The most representative works set in an old provincial city and characterized by an atmosphere of moral suffocation and intolerance, spiritual atrophy, intellectual poverty, and political corruption, are *La gobernadora* (1901; Eng. tr., *The Governor's Wife*, 1918), *Los malhechores del bien* (1905; Eng. tr., *The Evildoers of Good*, 1917), and *Pepa Doncel* (1928). Benavente's criticism of this ultraconservative society lacks social significance in general, as his intention is limited to reflecting a moral environment. The plays are no more than simple "mirrors of customs," alternately sly or sentimental in their resolutions.

The most prominent work in the group with rural settings is *La malquerida* (1913; Eng. tr., 1917), a powerful drama of incestuous passion. The vigorously individualized characters enter into conflict in a dramatic universe that still retains all of its validity.

Benavente's most valuable contribution to the repertory of masterpieces of contemporary Western theater is *Los intereses creados,* in which he created a new and original commedia dell'arte whose puppet master, Crispín, manipulates the secret and invisible strings that move each of the figures on his universal stage. The Leandro/Crispín pair embodies an archetypal and mythical idea, in which the author synthesizes the eternal human dialect of the real and the ideal, truth and dreams.

It would be an error of historical appraisal to forget the innovative role that Benavente's theater played in the last years of the 19th century and in the first years of the 20th by breaking definitively with melodramatic and declamatory theatrical tradition based on vicissitude and pathos. Nor should we fail to recognize his originality in the use of the most modern theatrical forms of his time. But it would be equally inaccurate not to recognize Benavente's persistent use of a single dramatic formula, thus failing to renew his art after having once established his ascendancy.

See: M. C. Peñuelas, *Jacinto Benavente* (1968); J. Ortiz Griffin, *Drama y sociedad en la obra de Benavente (1894–1914)* (1974); R. L. Sheehan, *Benavente and the Spanish Panorama, 1894–1954* (1976).   F.R.-R.

Benda, Julien (1867–1956), French polemicist and essayist, was born in Paris, where he spent his entire life in close contact with the intellectual events of the capital. From his earliest essays, which appeared in 1900, Benda's position remained the same—a vehement defense of reason, intellectualism, and classicism, and an attack on the contemporary indifference to these values. At first, Benda's target was the anti-Dreyfus faction, then Henri BERGSON and Charles PÉGUY. He took all the modernists to task in *Belphégor* (1919) and even more strongly in the celebrated *La Trahison des clercs* (1927; The Betrayal of the Intellectuals). The "clercs" are the intellectuals, who, Benda declares, have betrayed their trust by abandoning traditional values in favor of relativism, utilitarianism, and pragmatism. His attack continued in subsequent works, the most notable perhaps being *La France byzantine* (1945). Benda may sound like the voice of a lone prophet, but he must really be heard against the background of the political battles between Left and Right during the first several decades of the 20th century. He was not alone in wanting to turn back the clock, but this does not mean that he may be easily identified with a group. Among more recent thinkers, Roger Caillois might be closest to his position.

Benda's concept of literary criticism, as expressed in an article in *La Nouvelle Revue française* (May 1954), is in line with his thinking in general. For him, criticism left the straight path with Charles Sainte-Beuve (1804–69) and has gone completely astray with the modern impressionistic critics Charles Du Bos, Gabriel MARCEL, and Albert THIBAUDET. Benda's notion of criticism harks back to classic criticism, which took as its task the judgment of a work by objective standards and rules and was concerned with permanent, universal qualities rather than the temporary impact of the work or the idiosyncrasies of the author. One cannot help thinking how great Benda's dismay would have been at Georges Poulet and his school or at the semiotic critics of today like Julia KRISTEVA.

Since Claude MAURIAC's retort to Benda in *La Trahison d'un clerc* (1945), little attention seems to have been paid to this once very controversial figure. A new printing of *La Trahison des clercs* has not stimulated noticeable critical reaction.

See: R. J. Niess, *Julien Benda* (1956).   L.LeS.

Bender, Hans (1919–), German poet, short-story writer, novelist, anthologist, and editor, was born in Mühlhausen, south of Heidelberg, the son of a family of farmers and craftsmen. He received his secondary school degree in 1939 and went on to study German literature and art history in Erlangen and Heidelberg, until his studies were interrupted by World War II. He was a soldier in the German army from 1940 to 1945, when he was taken captive by Russian troops; he then spent four years as a prisoner of war, returning to West Germany in 1949 and resuming his studies. Early on, Bender became a passionate although restrained and sober practitioner and advocate of literature, first as the editor of *Konturen* (1951–52), as a coeditor of the yearbook of art and literature *Jahresring,* and for a time as the editor of the cultural monthly *Magnum.* Since 1954, when he became the cofounder and coeditor of *Akzente,* he has dedicated his energies to German writing in that pace-setting literary magazine (edited from 1954 to 1967 with the cofounder Walter Höllerer, edited by Bender alone from 1968 to 1976, and since 1977 edited with Michael Krüger). A reprint of issues of the first 20 years, in 5 volumes, sold an astonishing 100,000 copies in 1977.

A gentle man, Bender belies that gentleness and selfless involvement with literature through a strength of character and a severity of judgment that makes him the most awesome and respected of literary editors. The pages of *Akzente* are themselves a history of German literature after 1945, containing the first publication of many authors who have since become leaders in German letters. It has been said that Bender's postbox is the fullest and most sought-after in West Germany. His friend, the critic Robert Stauffer, claims that Bender's cats, Crazy and Ben, mind the pile of manuscripts and letters during their master's frequent lecture trips.

In his writing, in poems, stories, essays, Bender has a laconic, realistic style bare of self-depiction and full of direct, unadorned things and people. Unsentimental, even when concerned with the inhumane horrors of war and captivity, as in the novel *Wunschkost* (1959; Last Meal) and in the exemplary story "Die Wölfe kommen zurück" (The Wolves Return), his prose grips and fascinates the reader; he lets language loose but keeps a firm hand on the reins of words and emotions. He has been anthologized frequently as a master storyteller.

Among his works are the volume of early poems *Fremde soll vorüber sein* (1951; What's Foreign is Past); the novel *Eine Sache wie die Liebe* (1954; Something like Love); the volume of poems *Lyrische Biographie* (1957; Lyrical Biography); the collection of stories *Wölfe und Tauben* (1957; Wolves and Doves); and *Mit dem Postschiff* (1962; With the Mail Steamer), a collection of 24 stories. The volume *Die halbe Sonne* (1968; The Half Sun) is a collection of stories and travel impressions. He has collected notebook entries and aphorisms in two small volumes, in *Aufzeichnungen einiger Tage* (1971; Notes on Random Days) and *Einer von ihnen* (1979; One of Them). On the occasion of his 50th birthday, the Hanser Verlag published a collection of his writings under the title *Worte, Bilder, Menschen* (1969; Words, Images, People). His works have been translated into Greek, Japanese, and Turkish.

Bender is an indefatigable and sought-after anthologist, most notably in *Mein Gedicht ist mein Messer* (1955; My Poem is My Blade), a volume that contains poets' own comments about specific poems; in the collection *Widerspiel: Deutsche Lyrik seit 1945* (1961; Counterplay: German Lyrics Since 1945); and in the best-selling *In diesem Lande leben wir* (1979; This is the Land We Live in). He writes critical essays for newspapers, magazines, and radio. In the fall of 1968 and again in 1979 he was writer-in-residence at The University of Texas at Austin. He is the advisory editor of the bilingual literary magazine *Dimension,* published in Austin since 1968.

Bender's literary glance transforms things memorably and compassionately, and his editorial choices have become legendary in contemporary German writing for their aptness and validity.

See: H. B. J. Ueda, "Hans Benders Kurzgeschichten," Ph.D. Dissertation, University of Texas (1974).

A.L.W.

Benediktsson, Einar (1864–1940), Icelandic poet, was born at Elliðavatn near Reykjavik, but he grew up in the north of Iceland. His father was a judge of the superior court, a district magistrate, and a political leader. Emulating the father, the son studied law in Copenhagen, graduating in 1892, and became a political editor for *Dagskrá* (1896–98), an attorney, and a district magistrate (1904–07). After that he lived abroad, often in England, dividing his time between promotion of Icelandic natural resources and writing poetry, until he returned to his homeland shortly before 1930, his health broken. There he stayed in seclusion until his death.

Benediktsson's criticism of the older poets, especially the realists, in *Dagskrá* marks the turning point to a new national romanticism, with renewed stress on the national heritage and an insisting on a new capitalistic development of Iceland's natural resources. To begin with, he experimented with impressionistic prose sketches, but later he concentrated on poetry, producing the volumes *Sögur og kvæði* (1897; Stories and Poems), *Hafblik* (1906; Smooth Seas), *Hrannir* (1913; Waves), *Vogar* (1921; Inlets), and *Hvammar* (1930; Hollows). He made a translation (1901) of Henrik IBSEN's *Peer Gynt*.

Benediktsson towered over his contemporaries. He was a great idealist aspiring to material as well as spiritual progress for his nation. His mind was occupied with the science and philosophy of the times, but it was also furnished with an abundance of images and patterns drawn from the native word-stock, and his power over the Icelandic language has become proverbial. His style is aristocratic and ornate, and there is hardly a slipshod note in the whole of his production. His poems are at times hard reading because of the unusually heavy burden of thought that they carry. Like Matthías Jochumsson, Benediktsson is both broad and profound; but while Jochumsson centered his thought on God and man, Benediktsson started with nature, whose outer form, land, sea, and sky, he described with unequaled mastery and whose inner structure, from the electron to the galaxy, he seemed to sense in a mystic communion. Indeed this mystic communion with the whole world, this pantheistic feeling, is evident in most of his poetry, whether about the virgin nature of his homeland or the works of man in civilized countries—the forges of Newcastle upon Tyne, an evening in Rome, Stockholm, Fifth Avenue. He has tried to formulate his pantheistic religion in the essay "Alhygð" in *Eimreiðin* (1926).

In the beginning, Benediktsson was a progressive national romanticist urging his compatriots not only to conserve the precious part of their heritage, their language and literature, but also to throw off their political yoke and even more so the sloth of centuries in order to join in the rapid progress of industrialization. What he preached he tried to carry out in practice, but without much success. In his later years his philosophical and mystic bent came more to the fore, but he never lost his dream of progress and expansion. In his poetry he roamed vikinglike over many lands in search of subjects, but no amount of foreign influence ever brought him to forget his beloved homeland.

See: K. Andrésson, *Einar Benediktsson sjötugur* (1934); R. Beck, "Iceland's 'Poet Laureate,'" *BA* 10 (1936): 270–71; S. Nordal, "Einar Benediktsson," *Skírnir* 64 (1940): 5–23.

S.E.

Benelli, Sem (1877–1949), Italian playwright, was born in Filettole (Prato) of humble stock. His formal education was interrupted by his father's death and he turned to journalism and writing. His verse drama *La cena delle beffe* (1909; Eng. trs., *The Jester's Supper,* 1924–25, *The Jest,* 1949) brought him international renown. In 1919 the play received a famous New York production starring the Barrymores. Benelli served in World War I and became a Fascist deputy in 1921. He broke with the party after the killing of Giacomo Matteotti in 1924 but volunteered for the Ethiopian campaign, only to return to an anti-Fascist position and self-imposed exile in Switzerland during World War II. He wrote a number of plays in prose and a few works of social and political commentary, but he is chiefly remembered for his romantic verse dramas, which include *La cena, La maschera di Bruto* (1908; The Mask of Brutus), and *L'amore dei tre re* (1910; The Love of the Three Kings).

See: D. Spoleti, *Sem Benelli e il suo teatro* (1956).

T.G.B.

Benet, Juan (1927–), Spanish prose writer and dramatist, was born in Madrid, where he works as a civil engineer. Benet's prolific literary career encompasses many genres. His volumes of short stories include *Nunca llegarás a nada* (1968; You'll Never Amount to Anything), *Cinco narraciones y dos fábulas* (1972; Five Narrations and Two Fables), *Sub Rosa* (1973), *Cuentos* (1977; Stories), and *Del Pozo y del Numa* (1978; Of Pozo and Numa). His plays are collected in *Teatro* (1970) and his essays in *La inspiración y el estilo* (1966; Inspiration and Style), *Puerta de tierra* (1970; Earth's Door), and *En ciernes* (1976; Latency). His most acclaimed work is the trilogy composed of the novels *Volverás a Región* (1967; You Will Return to Región), *Una meditación* (1970; A Meditation), and *Un viaje de invierno* (1972; A Winter Journey). Reminiscent of William Faulkner, Benet's works, including his recent novel, *En el estado* (1977; In the State), are characterized by temporal complexity, intricate structures, and a labyrinthine mythical setting symbolizing the moral and physical ruin of Spain. His rich, original, hermetic, and experimental prose requires the reader's active participation. The highly intellectual and avant-garde features of Benet's style also make it difficult to place him within any stylistic trend of postwar Spain.

See: P. Gimferrer, "Sobre Juan Benet," *Plural* 17 (1973): 13–16; J. Ortega, "Estudios sobre la obra de Juan Benet," *CHA* 282 (1974): 229–59; D. K. Herzberger, *The Novelistic World of Juan Benet* (1977). J.O.

Benguerel i Llobet, Xavier (1905–), Catalan novelist, was born in Barcelona. He had achieved celebrity before the Spanish Civil War with *Pàgines d'un adolescent* (1929; Writings of an Adolescent), awarded the Ales Esteses Prize, *La Vida d'Olga* (1934; Olga's Life), *El teu secret* (1934; Your Secret), *Suburbi* (1936; Suburbs), *L'home i el sue àngel* (1937; Man and His Angel), and *Sense retorn* (1939; No Return). His subsequent years of exile in France and Chile are portrayed in *La màscara* (1947; The Mask), *L'home dins el mirall* (1951; The Man inside the Mirror), and *La família Roquier* (1953; The Roquier Family). After returning to Catalonia, Benguerel wrote *El desapregut* (1955; The Missing Person), *El testament* (1955; The Will), *Els fugitius* (1956; The Fugitives), *Soc un assassí* (1957; I Am an Assassin), *El viatge* (1957; The Journey), *L'intrús* (1960; The Intruder), *El pobre senyor Font* (1964; Poor Mr. Font), *Gorra de plat* (1967; The Silver Cap), *La veritat del foc* (1966; The Truth about the Fire), *Els vençuts* (1969; The Vanquished), *1939* (1973), and *Icària* (1974). His 1974 translation of *Icària* into Castilian received the Planeta Prize and drew attention to him in Spain, where some of his books had already been translated. His novel *Llibre del retorn* (Book of the Return) won the Critics Prize for Catalan Fiction of 1977. In addition to his narrative works, he has written outstanding poetry in *Poemes* (1934), and drama, including *El casament de la Xela* (perf. 1937; The Marriage of Xela), *Fira de desenganys* (1941; The Fair of Disillusion), and *El testament* (1960; The Will). Other prizes received by Benguerel are the Premi dels Novelistes in 1936 and the Premi Ignasi Iglesias. He has also done excellent translations of Edgar Allan Poe and of Paul VALÉRY.

See: J. Ferrater i Mora, Epistolary Prologue to *Obres Completes* of X. Benguerel (1967); D. Guanse, Prologue to *Xavier Benguerel es confessa de las seves relacions amb La Fontaine, Edgar Allan Poe, Paul Valery* (1947). J. Marco, "Una cronica barcelonina de Xavier Benguerel" in *Sobre literatura catalana i altres assaigs* (1968). J.F.C.

Benjamin, Walter (1892–1940), German philosopher, essayist, and critic, was born in Berlin and studied at Freiburg, Munich, Berlin, and Bern, where he received his Ph.D. After several unsuccessful attempts to embark upon a university career he settled in Berlin as a free-lance writer and translator. In 1933 he emigrated to Paris, where he became a member of the Frankfurt Institute of Social Research. Just before he was to emigrate to America, after the German occupation of France, he took his life at the Franco-Spanish border.

Benjamin wrote a great number of literary and critical essays, book reviews, and commentaries, but besides his dissertation, *Der Begriff der Kunstkritik in der deutschen Romantik* (1920; The Concept of Art Criticism in German Romanticism), only two books appeared during his lifetime: *Der Ursprung des deutschen Trauerspiels* (1928; The Origin of German Tragedy), and *Einbahnstrasse* (1928; One-Way Street). Several of his major critical essays appeared in instalments, such as *Goethes Wahlverwandtschaften* (1924–25; Goethe's "Elective Affinities"), or abroad and in French, such as *Das Kunstwerk im Zeitalter seiner technischen Reproduzierbarkeit* (1936; Eng. tr., *The Work of Art in the Age of Mechanical Reproduction*, 1969) and attracted little attention.

Although many of Benjamin's acquaintances, including Hugo von HOFMANNSTHAL, Ernst Bloch, Bertolt BRECHT, and Hannah Arendt very early recognized him as a radical thinker, his writings received little notice. It was not until the reestablishment of the Frankfurt School in 1949 and the subsequent gradual publication of his works by his colleague Theodor W. Adorno and his lifelong friend Gershom Scholem that his stature as a critic became known. Benjamin's observation of the loss of authenticity (aura) and the irreversible break with tradition in art articulated the way perception is changed by and dependent upon technology and mass culture. His claim that art "instead of being based on ritual" is beginning to be based on another practice—politics" and his challenge to investigate its changed social function have had especially great influence on post-World War II theory of literary criticism from Marxist aestheticism to the theory of literary reception. A selection of Benjamin's work in English translation can be found in *Reflections: Essays, Aphorisms, Autobiographical Writings*, ed. by P. Demetz (1978).

See: R. Tiedemann, H. Schweppenhäuser, eds., *Walter Benjamin: Gesammelte Schriften*, 6 vols. (1974); *Über Walter Benjamin* (1968); H. Arendt, ed., *W. Benjamin, Illuminations*, (1969); S. Unseld, *Zur Aktualität Walter Benjamins* (1972). V.S.

Benn, Gottfried (1886–1956), German poet and essayist, grew up in a village parsonage in an area now part of Poland. After completing his studies at the humanistic gymnasium in Frankfurt an der Oder, Benn, at his father's wish, studied theology and philosophy for two years in Marburg before entering the Kaiser Wilhelm Academy for the Education of Military Physicians in Berlin, where he completed his medical training in 1910. He served as a military physician in both world wars and practiced medicine as a civilian in Berlin, specializing in dermatology and venereology and contributing to medical journals in those fields.

Benn's first poetry, a small volume entitled *Morgue*, appeared in 1912. Arising from the young medical student's reactions to anatomical dissections, these poems—of which "Schöne Jugend" (Lovely Youth) and "Kleine Aster" (Little Aster) are particularly well known—unmask brutally yet laconically the physical decay underlying human life. Although denounced by the press as "disgusting," *Morgue* was met with enthusiasm among the younger expressionist writers, some of whom Benn was getting to know in Berlin. During this period, Benn also began a liaison with the expressionist poet Else LAS-KER-SCHÜLER, to whom he dedicated his second volume of poetry, *Söhne* (1913; Sons).

During World War I, Benn was stationed for three years in Brussels, where he served as attending physician at the execution of Edith Cavell, an event that he related in detail in an essay published in 1928. His schedule in Brussels, where he was physician at an army brothel, left him free time for writing. In addition to poetry, Benn here wrote five semiautobiographical short stories around the young doctor Rönne, *Gehirne* (1917; Brains). Rönne introduces a theme recurrent in Benn's work: the dissolution of individual identity, the self as a transitory composite of momentary reflections and impressions, devoid of continuity and of a fixed orientation. Echoing expressionist values, Rönne himself views his own rational scientific milieu with contempt and longs for the return to a mythic, primal world. In this period, Benn also attempted several dramas, only two of which he allowed to be republished later in a volume of early poems and dramas, *Der Vermessungsdirigent* (1919; The Survey Director) and *Etappe* (1919; Eng. tr., *Home Front*, 1958).

Returning to Berlin in 1917, Benn established his own medical practice, which he continued until 1935. More volumes of poetry came out in subsequent years: *Schutt* (1924; Rubble), *Betäubung* (1925; Narcosis), and *Spaltung* (1925; Split). They reveal a further development of many motifs from earlier work, such as the rhapsodic longing for an archaic, prerational world—often in a luxuriant southerly milieu—and the lament over the modern cleavage between reason and emotion. At the same time they show a movement toward less shocking imagery and toward more rigorous form, with extensive use of end rhyme and meter in conventional strophic composition.

During the interwar period, Benn published essays on such diverse subjects as the psychology of artistic creation, Goethe and the natural sciences, expressionism, Stefan GEORGE, Filippo MARINETTI, and Heinrich MANN. He also collaborated with the composer Paul Hindemith on an oratorio, *Das Unaufhörliche* (The Unceasing), which was first performed in 1931 with Otto Klemperer conducting the Berlin Philharmonic.

In 1929 Benn became embroiled with two leftist intellectuals, the poet Johannes R. BECHER (later minister of culture of the German Democratic Republic) and the journalist Egon Erwin Kisch, in a debate about the social and political functions of art. The discussions revealed Benn's antipathy toward leftist ideologies, his view of history as the chaotic product of irrational, elemental forces, and his cynical dismissal of individualism. When Adolf Hitler seized power, Benn welcomed Naziism as a vitalistic attack on European intellectualism and on the effete civilization rooted in it. Several essays in his collections *Der neue Staat und die Intellektuellen* (1933; The New State and the Intellectuals) and *Kunst und Macht* (1934; Art and Power) document his infatuation with the rhetoric of the new ideology and his disdain for self-exiled intellec-

tuals. Disenchantment came soon, however, and by 1936, Benn was being publicly attacked by the Nazi Party. As an army doctor from 1935 to 1945 he nevertheless continued to write in private.

Benn's *Statische Gedichte* (Static Poems) appeared in Zürich in 1948 and initiated his rise to fame in the postwar era. Like the poems of the middle years, these reflect attention to strict form; the lines and strophes are longer here, and the tone is more sober. Among these poems is the one that is possibly Benn's most famous, "Verlorenes Ich" (Eng. tr., "The Lost I," 1972), a postmortem on modern consciousness, characterized by the pithy formulation, "Die Welt zerdacht" ("the world thought to pieces").

Other publications of Benn's later years include more poetry—*Destillationen* (1953; Distillations), *Fragmente* (1953; Fragments), *Aprèslude* (1953)—essays, autobiographical prose—*Doppelleben* (1950; Double Life)—and fiction—*Der Ptolemäer* (1949; The Ptolemean). In 1951 at Marburg, Benn presented the lecture *Probleme der Lyrik* (Problems of Lyric Poetry), a manifesto of his philosophy of poetry and artistic creation that, along with his poems themselves, was to exercise great influence on postwar German poets. At his death in 1956, Benn was regarded in Germany as one of the 20th century's most important poets.

Benn's reputation abroad never approached his fame in Germany, in part because of the difficulty his work poses to translators. Even in Germany, as an exponent of Friedrich NIETZSCHE's assertion that art is the only metaphysical activity open to modern man, Benn was hailed by some as a radical modernist and decried by others as a decadent nihilist withdrawing from social responsibility into a doctrine of *l'art pour l'art*. Though incontestably one of Germany's major modern poets, Benn continues to be an object of controversy.

Benn's poetry is available to English-speaking readers through translations in C. Middleton and M. Hamburger, *Modern German Poetry, 1910–1960* (1963), E. B. Ashton, *Primal Vision* (1958), J. M. Ritchie, *Gottfried Benn, the Unreconstructed Expressionist* (1972), and in *Metamorphosis* 3 (1962); *Gottfried Benn: Selected Poems* (1970), ed. by F. W. Wodtke, presents the poems in German but with extensive annotations for the English-speaking reader.

See: E. Lohner, *Passion und Intellekt: die Lyrik Gottfried Benn* (1961); F. W. Wodtke, *Gottfried Benn* (1970); R. Alter, *Gottfried Benn: The Artist and Politics (1910–1934)* (1976); the following anthologies also contain introductions in English: E. B. Ashton, ed., *Primal Vision: Selected Writings of Gottfried Benn* (1958); F. W. Wodtke, ed., *Gottfried Benn: Selected Poems* (1970); J. M. Ritchie, *Gottfried Benn, The Unreconstructed Expressionist* (1972).   C.C.Z.

Benoit, Pierre (1886–1962), French novelist, was born in Albi, Tarn. His childhood was spent in Tunisia and Algeria in the various garrisons to which his father, an army officer, was assigned. This background partly explains his love of travel and his inappeasable curiosity concerning picturesque places and exotic countries. In 1910, having started the study of law in Algiers, completed his military service in a regiment of Zouaves, and obtained his degree in literature in Montpellier, he went to Paris to prepare for a degree in history. His preparation was not, however, of a very serious nature. He much preferred the society of his friends, many of whom were also to make a name for themselves in the world of letters, such as Francis CARCO, Pierre MACORLAN, and Roland DORGELÈS. Benoit failed to receive his degree but later, having passed an examination for a position in the Ministry of Public Instruction, became a government employee. During World War I he served as a lieutenant and was wounded.

At the time of his arrival in Paris, Benoit had already written a play, which has never been published, and several poems, which appeared in 1914 under the title *Diadumène*. His first novel, *Koenigsmark* (1918; Eng. tr., *The Secret Spring*, 1920), enjoyed great success and revealed its author to be a talented novelist. Conceived during the war, it is natural that it should deal with Germany. *L'Atlantide* (1919; Eng. tr., *The Queen of Atlantis*, 1920), one of the first best-sellers of the postwar period, was a very well done adventure story. The scene of *Pour Don Carlos* (1920; For Don Carlos) is Spain, of *Le Lac salé* (1921; Eng. tr., *Salt Lake*, 1922) Utah, of *La Chaussée des géants* (1922; The Giants' Causeway) the Ireland of the Sinn Feiners. *Mlle de la Ferté* (1923) takes place in France, as does *Le Roman des quatre* (The Novel of the Four), published in the same year and written in collaboration with Paul BOURGET, Gérard d'Houville, and Henri Duvernois.

Because his duties with the Ministry of Public Instruction did not leave him sufficient leisure, Benoit resigned and in 1923 left for a 22-month tour through Turkey and Syria, from which he brought back *La Châtelaine du Liban* (1924; The Lady of the Manor from Lebanon) and *Le Puits de Jacob* (1925; Eng. tr., *Jacob's Well*, 1926). A trip to the Far East furnished him with the inspiration for *Le Roi lépreux* (1927; The Leper King). There but remained for him to take a trip around the world, and this he proceeded to do. From Suez he went to Ceylon, Australia, New Caledonia, the New Hebrides, Tahiti, Panama, and the Antilles. Upon his return he wrote *Erromango* (1929), the locale of which is the New Hebrides. The heroine of *Le Soleil de minuit* (1930; Midnight Sun) is called Amide, and like all the author's heroines her name begins with the letter A. His *Axelle* (1928) conforms to this rule, and in it he once again treats of Germany and of the camps of war prisoners there. For many years, Benoit annually composed a love and adventure story, usually cleverly done and easy to read. He was elected to the Académie Française in 1931 but resigned in 1959. In 1958 he gave a series of radio interviews published the same year as *De Koenigsmark à Montsalvat*.

See: R. Aigrain, "L'Art et l'érudition de M. Pierre Benoit," *Correspondant* 278 (1920): 701–19; A. Praviel, "Un Romancier de Gascogne: M. Pierre Benoit," *Correspondant* 287 (1922): 835–47; C. Garnier, "Pierre Benoit," in *RdDM* 7 (1955): 451–61; J. Daisne, *Pierre Benoit ou l'éloge du roman romanesque* (1964).

P.Br. rev. D.W.A.

Berdyayev, Nikolay Aleksandrovich (1874–1948), Russian philosopher, was born in Kiev to an aristocratic family. A Marxist in his youth, he came under the influence of Immanuel Kant, Friedrich von Schelling, Jacob Boehme, Vladimir SOLOVYOV, and Friedrich NIETZSCHE around the turn of the century and moved in the direction of neo-idealism and an ethics and metaphysics inspired by Christian thought. On the eve of World War I, Berdyayev was harassed by the tsarist government for his criticism of the Russian church, which he said had ossified under the bureaucratized Holy Synod. Nevertheless, he belonged to the "Vekhi" group, which had resolutely broken with the traditional radicalism and materialism of the Russian Revolutionary intelligentsia. He was forced by the Bolshevik government to leave Russia. He settled in Clamart, near Paris. He died there in 1948, having played a prominent, though occasionally controversial, role in Russian intellectual and spiritual life abroad for more than a quarter of a century (*see* RUSSIAN LITERATURE). Most of his writings are translated into French, German, and English. Berdyayev is the only philosopher from the "Russian renaissance of religious philosophy" that took place in the first half of this century whose works have enjoyed a modicum of success in the English-speaking world.

Berdyayev's basic intuition was an ontologism of freedom in which freedom is primordial and uncreated. He believed that man is endowed with creative freedom to assist God in the process of continuing creation. The spiritual and moral dynamism implied here leads Berdyayev to the negation of all objectification and crystallization in the personal life of man, state, society, culture, and religion—in opposition, for example, to Georg Hegel's concept of the "objective spirit."

In his social philosophy, Berdyayev attempted to combine a strongly accented personalism with a heightened awareness of the importance of the community. He was doubtlessly influenced by the Orthodox Christian concept of "Sobornost" that was developed by, among others, Aleksey Khomyakov. In 1912, Berdyayev published an interesting monograph about Khomyakov. The literary figure who most concerned him was Fyodor DOSTOYEVSKY, and he wrote a sympathetic study about Dostoyevsky's thought, interpreting him in terms of his own spiritual dynamism.

See: V. Zenkovsky, *History of Russian Philosophy* (1953); F. Stepun, *Mystische Weltschau* (1964); M. Broński, "O filozofii Bierdiajewa," *KulturaP* 1/328–2/329 (1975): 185–95.

H.A.S.

Berent, Wacław (1873–1940), Polish novelist and essayist of the "Młoda Polska" (Young Poland) tradition, was born and died in Warsaw. He began to write during the period of transition from Polish positivism to symbolism. His early short stories, "Nauczyciel" (1894; The Teacher) and "Przy niedzieli" (1894; On a Sunday) and *Fachowiec* (1895; The Specialist), the author's first novel, illustrate Berent's debt to the positivist tradition and his attempt (in *Fachowiec*) to free himself from it. His next work, "W puszczy" (1896; In the Wilderness), clearly reflects an effort to interpret reality symbolically. Berent's novel *Próchno* (1903; Rotten Wood) established his fame as a writer. In its analysis of the fin-de-siècle mood among artists and intellectuals (no precise national setting), it has become recognized as a classic. In it, Berent incorporated ideas from Arthur Schopenhauer, Friedrich NIETZSCHE, and the Hindu holy books and reached his own synthesis. His highly developed feeling for style and his poetic gift (a number of his own poems are included) found full display for the first time in this work. A serious student of Nietzsche, he became not only a foremost translator into Polish of the German philosopher's writings, but also an equally perceptive commentator on Nietzsche's thoughts in a number of essays: "Fryderyk Nietzsche, Z psychologii sztuki" (1902; Friedrich Nietzsche, On the Psychology of Art) and "Źródła i ujścia Nietzscheanizmu" (1906; Sources and Outlets of Nietzscheanism).

Berent's second novel, *Ozimina* (1911: Winter Wheat), raises questions about Poland's relation to its past at the beginning of the 20th century. His third novel, a kind of medieval ballad, *Żywe kamienie* (1918; Living Stones), develops in a highly stylized prose the question of art and the special role of the artist in life. Artistic creativity is presented as a profoundly religious activity answering a human need and essential to man's spiritual well-being. *Żywe kamienie* is considered Berent's masterpiece.

After nearly 15 years as an editor of literary periodicals and a translator, Berent returned to artistic writing in the

1930s with biographical sketches: *Nurt* (1934; Current), *Diogenes w kontuszu* (1937; A Diogenes in Polish Garb), and *Zmierzch wodzów* (1939; Twilight of the Leaders). In these works, questions of style are subordinated to a concern with the revitalization of ethical values that the author discerned in the lives of Polish statesmen, artists, and other public figures in the late 18th and early 19th centuries.

See: W. Studencki, *O Wacławie Berencie,* vols. 1 and 2 (1968-69); P. Hultberg, *Styl wczesnej prozy fabularnej Wacława Berenta* (1969); J. T. Baer, *Wacław Berent, His Life and Work* (1974).   J.T.B.

Bergamín, José (1897-), Spanish essayist and poet, was born in Madrid. He was one of the most significant writers of the Pombo Club presided over by Ramón GÓMEZ DE LA SERNA. Chronologically he belongs to the generation of Rafael ALBERTI, Vincente ALEIXANDRE, Federico GARCÍA LORCA, and Jorge GUILLÉN. Influenced by the then current literary taste, Bergamín tended to adopt shorter forms of prose expression. The most consummate examples of this fragmentation of the literary unit are seen in the "glosses" of Eugenio D'ORS, in the *greguerías* of Ramón Gómez de la Serna, and in the "aphorisms" of Bergamín. His first book, *El cohete y la estrella* (1922; The Skyrocket and the Star), and some of his delightful later works, like *La cabeza a pájaros* (1934; Castles in the Air), are in this manner. He was the founder of *Cruz y Raya* (1933-36), a journal that, besides collecting the finest Spanish literature produced during the years of its publication, reflected the liberal Catholic religious and ideological position of Bergamín, who had close connections with the French and Belgian group of the journal *Esprit.* After the Spanish Civil War (1936-39) he went into exile, first in Mexico, then in Venezuela, Uruguay, and, finally, France. In 1958 he returned to Spain but soon after, in 1963, he had to seek asylum at the embassy of Uruguay and leave the country again. In Mexico he published *Detrás de la cruz* (1941; Behind the Cross), devoted to the spiritual drama of the Spanish people. Among his books of essays the following stand out: *Disparadero español* (1936-40; From a Spanish Perspective); *La voz apagada* (1945; The Subdued Voice); *Fronteras infernales de la poesía* (1959; Poetry's Frontier with Hell); *Al volver* (1962; After Coming Back), the second edition of which was published under the title of *Antes de ayer y pasado mañana* (1974; Day Before Yesterday and the Day after Tomorrow); and *La importancia del demonio y otras cosas sin importancia* (1974; The Importance of the Devil and Other Unimportant Matters). Notwithstanding his very modern sensibility, Bergamín has pronounced Spanish roots, particularly in the Generation of 1898. He took a number of themes from Miguel de UNAMUNO and at times is closer to the literary currents emanating from that movement than to the tastes that prevailed after World War I. His group posited a whole series of ideological and stylistic problems. As it sought a new linguistic flexibility, it rejuvenated words by giving them new yet pristine meanings, evolving in certain sectors of Spanish prose a rhetoric that in successive stages led to the linguistic "wit" or modern "conceptism" of Bergamín. He himself offers us a sagacious interpretation of the related spirit of the 17th century in his work *Mangas y capirotes* (1933; Personal Views).

Even though Bergamín wrote sonnets in the decade of the 1920s—Aleixandre and Antonio MACHADO remember him with admiration—not until 1962 did he introduce himself to the public as a poet with his *Rimas y sonetos rezagados* (Postponed Rhymes and Sonnets). This book of verse was followed by others that established him decisively as a poet: *Duendecitos y coplas* (1963; Little Goblins and Couplets), *La claridad desierta* (1973; The Lonely Light), *Del otoño y los mirlos* (1975; Autumn and Blackbirds), and *Apartada orilla* (1976; Distant Shore). His poetry is usually written in simple forms typical of the popular tradition: rhymes, couplets, and ballads.

See: C. Alonso, "José Bergamín: Utopía y popularismo: anotaciones a unos textos de encrucijada 1936-1939," *RL* 13 (1974): 10-16; N. Dennis, "José Bergamín y la exaltación del disparate," *CHA* 288 (1974): 539-56.
                                                            F.G.L. rev. J.L.G.-M.

Bergengruen, Werner (1892-1964), German novelist, novella-writer, poet, and essayist, was born in Riga, Latvia. The son of a physician, he emigrated to Germany with his family as a child; studied law, history, and literature at German universities; fought against the Red Army in the Baltic during World War I; and was expelled from the Academy of Writers by the Nazis in 1937. A convert to Catholicism, Bergengruen enjoyed considerable popularity after 1945, partly for his belief in an "integral world" at the core of reality despite all hardships and sufferings, an idea expressed by the title of his major collection of poems, *Die heile Welt* (1950; The Hale World). His major novels are *Der Grosstyrann und das Gericht* (1935; The Grand Tyrant and the Tribunal), which was interpreted as a roman à clef against the Third Reich, and *Am Himmel wie auf Erden* (1940; In Heaven as on Earth), a novel about mass hysteria and superstition. Bergengruen's best hope of survival rests, however, on his collections of novellas, especially *Der letzte Rittmeister* (1952; The Last Cavalier) and *Der Tod von Reval* (1939; The Reval Dance of Death), containing stories about his Baltic homeland, and a short novel, *Pelageja* (1947), about a Russian Alaskan expedition shipwrecked in the area of the present state of Washington. Bergengruen's basic literary goal was a mystical one based on the "analogy of being": to trace latent eternal structures by means of concrete images and characters. A selection of autobiographical writings, Bergengruen's *Dichtergehäuse,* was published in 1966.

See: H. Bänziger, *Werner Bergengruen: Weg und Werk* (1961); A. Soergel and C. Hohoff, *Dichtung und Dichter der Zeit* (1964), pp. 776-79.   D.J.P.

Berggolts, Olga Fyodorovna (1910-75), Russian poet, was born in Petersburg into a Russian intellectual family of remotely German origin. In 1934 she published her first book of poetry and in 1935 a series of stories, *Noch v novom mire* (Night in the New World), in both of which she celebrated the achievements of the first Five-Year Plans. Her husband, the poet Boris Kornilov, was executed in the Stalinist purges of 1937 and she herself was imprisoned for a time. She joined the Communist Party in 1940. During the siege of Leningrad (1941-44) she remained in the city, played an active role in organizing aid for the population, and became one of the symbolic figures of the resistance effort through her writing and her daily radio broadcasts. After the war she completed *Pervorossiysk* (1950), a poem about the first agricultural commune founded in the Altay region during Vladimir Lenin's time by workers from Petrograd, and published *Vernost* (1954; Loyalty), a tragedy in verse about the siege of Sevastopol in World War II. Hitherto guided by the events of the moment, this authentic poet did not reveal her full stature until the years of destalinization. *Dnevnye zvyozdy* (1959; Daytime Stars), an autobiographical meditation that is deeply moving in its truthful rendering of experience, its originality of composition, and its quality of style, is one of the highest achievements of what Soviet critics call "lyric prose." *Uzel* (1965; A Bundle), a selection of poems written during the Iosif Stalin period without any hope of publication, is of key importance for an understanding not only of one of the most attractive personalities in present-day Russian literature but also of the drama of a whole generation, torn as the author revealed herself to be between a total political commitment and an anguish that stubbornly insisted on believing in tomorrow.

J.Ca.

Bergh, Herman van den (1897–1967), Dutch poet and journalist, was born in Amsterdam. He studied law at the university there, and for some years was a violist in the Concertgebouw orchestra. Van den Bergh was the first to adapt expressionism to Dutch poetry. His volumes *De Boog* (1917; The Bow) and *De Spiegel* (1925; The Mirror) reveal a love of nature and a passionate expressionism. He insisted that when he wrote the poems in *De Boog*, he had never read a German expressionist poem; it must be remembered that the borders were closed during World War I because of Dutch neutrality. When he became the leading spirit at the magazine *Het Getij* (The Tide) and gathered a group of modern young disciples about him, it became the organ of expressionism. The new movement also made itself felt in painting and music. Van den Bergh argued for a new style in life and poetry. In *Nieuwe Tucht* (1928; New Discipline), a collection of criticism and essays from *Het Getij*, there is no mention of the word *expressionism*, nor any reference to the German poets. He published four essays on Guillaume APOLLINAIRE in the magazine *De Vrije Bladen* (The Free Pages) in 1924. Then, for 30 years, he published no poetry. With the publication of his *Verzamelde gedichten*, however, new work appeared. *Het litteken van Odysseus* (1956; The Scar of Odysseus), *Kansen op een wrak* (1957; Chances of a Wreck), and *Verstandhouding met de vijand* (1958; Collusion with the Enemy) reveal a deepening of his personality and his talent. In all these volumes of verse, his expressionistic style remains undiminished and is able to give effective voice to his deeper emotions.   S.L.F.

Bergman, Ernst Ingmar (1918–), Swedish filmmaker, theater director, and playwright, was born in Uppsala, the son of a Lutheran clergyman and chaplain to the Court of Sweden. Bergman was attracted to the stage and the screen at an early age. When he was 10 years old he received his most memorable toy, a magic lantern and puppet theater for which he made scenery and dolls, and wrote plays. Throughout his adolescence Bergman spent much of his pocket money on film for a *laterna magica* and film projector. He was an avid reader of August STRINDBERG and in 1935 saw his first theater production, Olof Molander's staging of Strindberg's *A Dream Play*, a production that was to leave a lasting impression on him.

Bergman wrote for the stage, most notably three dramas published in 1948 under the common title *Moraliteter* (Morality Plays). A radio play called *Staden* (The City), full of Strindberg reminiscences, followed in 1951, and in 1954 Bergman made his actual dramatic debut as a playwright with *Trämålning* (Eng. tr., *Wood Painting*, 1961), which became the basis for Bergman's first film to receive widespread international attention, *Det sjunde inseglet* (1956; Eng. tr., *The Seventh Seal*, 1960).

Although Bergman's earliest artistic ambitions had been those of a literary writer, he soon began to feel that his real talents were visual and auditory rather than purely verbal. He stopped writing plays for the stage but continued his work as a theater director and became the head of the Royal Dramatic Theater in 1963, a position he kept

for three years until he resigned in order to get away from administrative duties.

Bergman's first screenplay, *Hets* (1944; Torment), was made into a film by Swedish director Alf Sjöberg, with Bergman serving as his assistant. For several years following the successful release of *Hets*, Bergman worked as a director for Svensk Filmindustri (SF), turning other people's film scripts into movies. His apprenticeship years ended in 1948, when he moved temporarily to a different production company (Sandrews) and directed the first film based on his own script, *Fängelse* (Prison; American film title: *The Devil's Wanton*). Four years later Bergman achieved what many consider his first artistic success with the film *Gycklarnas afton* (1952, The Eve of the Clowns; American film title: *The Naked Night*).

Bergman's real breakthrough as a filmmaker came with the comedy *Sommarnattens leende* (1955; Eng. tr., *Smiles of a Summer Night*, 1960), which received the coveted jury prize at the Cannes Film Festival in 1956. *Sommarnattens'* success gave Bergman more freedom at Svensk Filmindustri and allowed him to make a group of serious films, which quickly solidified his position as one of the world's leading filmmakers and may in part have been responsible for the New Wave movement in the French cinema. In such films as *Sjunde inseglet* (1956; screenplay not published in Sweden; Eng. tr., *The Seventh Seal*, 1960), *Smultronstället* (1957; screenplay not published in Sweden; Eng. tr., *Wild Strawberries*, 1960), *Ansiktet* (1958; The Face; screenplay not published in Sweden; Eng. tr., *The Magician*, 1960), and *Nära livet* (1958; screenplay by Ingmar Bergman and Ulla ISAKSSON not published in Sweden or the United States), Bergman used the film medium to explore a highly personal, though culturally derivative, set of metaphysical motifs.

In the early 1960s, after making the film *Jungfrukällan*, based on a novel by Ulla Isaksson (1960; Eng. tr., *The Virgin Spring*, 1961), Bergman began to evolve—assisted by his new cameraman Sven Nykvist—a series of so-called chamber films, most notably: *En filmtrilogi* (1973; Eng. tr., *A Trilogy*, 1964), that is, the films: *Såsom i en spegel* (produced 1961; Eng. tr., *Through a Glass Darkly*); *Nattvardsgästerna* (produced 1963; The Communicants; Eng. tr., *Winter Light*, 1964), and *Tystnaden* (1963; Eng. tr., *The Silence*, 1964). These were followed by *Persona* (1966; Eng. tr., *Persona*, 1972); *Vargtimmen* (1968; The Hour of the Wolf); *Skammen* (1969; Eng. tr., *Shame*, 1973); *Passionen* (1970; The Passion of Anna); and *Viskningar och rop* (1972; Eng. tr., *Cries and Whispers*, 1973).

In his chamber films, Bergman attempts to emulate Strindberg's concept of the chamber play, that is, an intimate piece of theater covering short spans of time, employing only a few actors, and emphasizing a leitmotiv rather than conventional character conflict. All of the aforementioned chamber films except *Cries and Whispers* are set in contemporary time on a barren island in the Baltic. Here Bergman's mise-en-scène abandons the historical milieu of many of his films of the 1950s, and his camera style focuses more exclusively on the actors through long penetrating shots and close-ups.

In his television drama *Scener från ett äktenskap* (1973; Eng. tr., *Scenes from a Marriage*, 1974), Bergman attempts a realistic, psychological study of a middle-class married couple. Free from the visual symbolism of many of his earlier films and less directly concerned with metaphysical issues than such works as *En filmtrilogi*, *Persona*, and *Viskningar, Scener*, nevertheless, bears the highly personal Ingmar Bergman stamp, that is, superb acting performance, impeccable yet unobtrusive camera work, and a reiteration of perennial Bergman themes: the absolute loneliness of the individual and the "Strindbergian" tension between the sexes.

See: R. Wood, *Ingmar Bergman* (1969); P. Cowie, *Sweden,* vol. 2 (1970); J. Simon, *Ingmar Bergman Directs* (1972); B. Steene, *Ingmar Bergman* (1972).   B.S.

Bergman, Hjalmar (1883–1931), Swedish novelist and playwright, was born in Örebro. His status as one of the great Swedish writers of the 20th century has become increasingly obvious since his death, and he has latterly become the object of a number of scholarly studies. Moreover, a society, *Hjalmar Bergman Samfundet,* stimulates interest in his work. During the major part of his working life this extraordinarily sensitive artist, who frequently sought cover behind a mask of burlesque humor and parody, was not accorded the recognition he deserved. His work was considered strange, bizarre, and, in some senses, difficult and depressing. An unfortunate childhood relationship with his domineering father left lifelong scars; a fictional-autobiographical account of his Oedipal relationship to his parents is found in *Jan, Ljung och Medardus* (1923; I, Ljung and Medardus). His affluent, middle-class background in the provincial town of Örebro, a center of mining and forestry where his banker father had widespread connections, gave him unrivaled insight into the personalities and history of the area; and in this he resembles Thomas MANN, whose *Buddenbrooks* demonstrates a conflict between middle-class stability and individual artistic freedom—a theme that Bergman explored in *Loewenhistorier* (1913; Stories about Loewen), *Knutsmässomarknad* (1916; Saint Knut's Fair), and *Farmor och Vår Herre* (1921; Eng. tr., *Thy Rod and Thy Staff,* 1937).

Bergman's first novel, *Solivro* (1906), is a symbolist fantasy concerned with the clash between good and evil; his next novel, *Blåblommor* (1907; Blue Flowers), shows uncanny psychological insight into the mechanics of repressed passion reminiscent of Fyodor DOSTOYEVSKY. It is noteworthy that the moral issues raised by forbidden passion (Bergman himself struggled with homosexuality) are often in his books represented by incestuous relationships, most notably in *Mor i Sutre* (1917, Mother in Sutre), where a strong-willed mother centers her emotions upon a favorite son, who dies tragically, and in *Chefen fru Ingeborg* (1924; Eng. tr., *The Head of the Firm,* 1936), where a successful businesswoman falls unwillingly in love with her daughter's fiancé and finally commits suicide. *Savonarola* (1909), a study of the Florentine preacher, and a short-story collection, *Amourer* (1910), demonstrate Bergman's mastery of pastiche, his skillful archaisms, and his love of Italy, where he spent much time as a young man, both before and after his marriage to Stina Lindberg, daughter of actor-manager August Lindberg. *Hans nåds testamente* (1910; Eng. tr., *The Baron's Will,* in *Four Plays,* 1968), *Vi Bookar, Krokar och Rothar* (1912, We Books, Crooks and Rooths), and *Komedier i Bergslagen* (1914–16) establish his native province, Berslagen, and the fictive town of Wadköping (in reality Örebro) as the social, human, and geographical axis of the majority of his ensuing novels. Like Honoré de Balzac in *La Comédie humaine,* with which his novels have been compared, Bergman has a large cast list of characters who span several generations and reappear in a number of works. His gallery of eccentrics, drawn with great skill, and his lively narrative are reminiscent of Charles Dickens, whom he admired. Particularly *Vi Bookar* presents the expansion of capitalist industry, with attendant social misery for the workers. Bergman's sense of compassion is keen; however, his preoccupations were not overtly political but concerned with the individual's personal morality. *En döds memoarer* (1918; The Memoirs of One Dead) occupies a central place among his works; in it his hero learns to accept and to perceive the inevitability of his predestined fate. Bergman the determinist elaborates a quietistic ethic with skillful use of symbolism; the presentation of decadence and death has affinities with Mann's *Death in Venice.*

Up to 1917, Bergman had been regarded by critics and the reading public as an acquired taste. His plays *Maria, Jesu moder* (1905; Mary, Mother of Jesus), *Parisina* (1915), and *Marionettspel* (1917; Marionette Plays) had been performed without much success. Then with the novel *Markurells i Wadköping* (1919; Eng. tr., *God's Orchid,* 1924), which many regard as his undisputed masterpiece, he had his great breakthrough. In this supremely funny and simultaneously tragic book—later successfully dramatized—the aging and far-from-attractive hero is humbled and chastised by relentless fate, which reveals to him that the son on whom he had lavished all his egocentric affections is not, in fact, his child. The comic inventiveness of the scenes of provincial life in this novel is surpassed only by the tragic grandeur of the climax. This was the first of Bergman's *avskedsromaner* (novels of farewell), in which he said goodbye to love and family life, to ambition and dreams of grandeur, and to middle-class security, respectively; the other two are *Herr von Hancken* (1920) and *Farmor och Vår Herre* (1921; Eng. tr., *Thy Rod and Thy Staff,* 1937). The former is a farcical, early-19th-century pastiche in which the vainglorious aging hero is stripped of his pretensions; the latter, a subtle study of a domineering matriarch who in old age is forced to reappraise her actions and learn humility. Bergman's play *Dollar* (1926) is a lightweight satire on American values, but *Swedenhielms* (1926; Eng. tr., *The Swedenhielm Family*) was a far more successful comedy, a perennial box office draw featuring a fictive Swedish Nobel Prize winner and his family. Bergman's finest play is probably *Porten* (1923; The Doorway), in which the hero learns to walk out of the door leading to loneliness and death. *Four Plays (Markurells of Wadköping, The Baron's Will, Swedenhielms, Mr. Sleeman is Coming)* was published in New York in 1968.

Bergman's last years were fraught with personal problems. He alternated periods of reckless living with medical care for alcoholism. In spite of this strain, he was remarkably productive up to the end. His last novel, *Clownen Jac* (1930; Jac, the Clown), which in setting contrasts the heavily satirized superficiality of Hollywood with the serenity of a Swedish farm, is also his artistic testament. The clown (or artist) Jac, Bergman's alter ego, forces a confrontation with his public and accuses it of living parasitically on its entertainers and never exposing itself to the seriousness of their message. In private, Jac accuses himself of having failed in his own life on the plane of human relationships and resolves to make amends. This simplification of the theme does nothing to suggest the vitality and urgency of the writing. Bergman died alone in a hotel room in Berlin.

See: E. H. Linder, *Sju världars herre* (1962); S. E. Ek, *Verklighet och vision* (1964); M. B. Bergom Larson, *Diktarens demaskering. En monografi över Hjalmar Bergmans roman Herr von Hancken* (1970); A. Gustafson, *History of Swedish Literature* (1961); K. Petherick, *Stilimitation i tre av Hjalmar Bergmans romaner. En undersökning av den roll pastisch, parodi och citat spelar i Knutsmässo marknad, En döds memoarer och Herr von Hancken* (1971); T. Bonnier, *Längesen* (1972); E. H. Linder, *Kärlek och fadershus farväl. Hjalmar Bergmans liv och diktning från Markurells i Wadköping till Farmor och*

Vår Herre (1973); E. H. Linder, *Hjalmar Bergman, TWAS* 736 (1975). K.P.

Bergson, Henri (1859–1942), French philosopher, was born in Paris. His early childhood was spent in London, but when he was nine years old, his family moved to Paris, where he lived until his death. In 1878, Bergson entered the Ecole Normale Supérieure at the same time as Jean JAURÈS. He passed the doctorate in philosophy in 1889 and became professor of philosophy, first in secondary schools, then at the Ecole Normale, and finally at the Collège de France, where he taught from 1900 to 1924. He was elected a member of the Académie Française in 1914 and was awarded the Nobel Prize for Literature in 1927.

Very early in his academic career, Bergson became famous as the promoter of a new philosophy. From the beginning, he opposed the dominant philosophies of the 18th and 19th centuries, the criticism of Immanuel Kant, the positivism of Auguste Comte, the philosophies of history and evolution of G. W. F. Hegel and Herbert Spencer, and the English psychology of associationism that claimed to explain the human mind by a few basic laws of association. Bergsonism has been related to the religious revival of the beginning of the 20th century. It has been present in the great intellectual fights through which our era tried to build up new spiritual roads and new visions of man. Bergsonism was the model of a philosophy protesting against the artificiality of conceptual analysis and inviting concrete descriptions of spiritual experiences. In that perspective, it has been either an inspiring force or a model to be surpassed. As such it has been associated with the neo-Thomism of Jacques MARITAIN (a sort of brother-enemy), with surrealism (*see* FRENCH LITERATURE), with the "philosophie de l'esprit" movement, and with existentialism (*see* FRENCH LITERATURE).

In his doctoral dissertation, *Essai sur les données immédiates de la conscience* (1889; Eng. tr., *Time and Free Will: An Essay on the Immediate Data of Conscience,* 1910), Bergson attacked the principles and methodologies of scientific psychology, at the same time rejecting psychophysical and psychophysiological methodologies and associationism. He opposed the mathematical interpretation of time to the direct experience of duration as pure intuition of consciousness. Bergson then described psychological life as interior life, as qualitative, continuous, and free invention. He suggested this new approach to consciousness and its stream by use of poetic images that do not risk destroying the understanding of the human mind by itself, as do the usual concepts that imitate the spatial structures. Thus the recurrent image of water and flow (Bergson borrowed the image of the stream of consciousness from his friend William James). The first psychological analyses in the *Essai* were developed into a critique of the psychophysiological theories of memory in *Matière et mémoire* (1896; Eng. tr., *Matter and Memory,* 1910). Bergson opposed habit to pure memory and came to a new interpretation of the brain: it is not a place for the storage of remembrances, but the instrument thanks to which images can be recalled and made conscious again.

In a new phase, Bergson extended the preceding views to the expansion of life as a creative force in *L'Evolution créatrice* (1907; Eng. tr., *Creative Evolution,* 1911). According to this view, life invents its biological forms through the tools of instinct and intelligence. Bergson showed the theoretical weaknesses of the Darwinian and Lamarckian theories of transformisms. In their place, Bergson presents a grandiose vision of all biological forms, vegetal as well as animal, launched in an intense effort of creation and successive victories over inert matter. In 1919 the volume entitled *L'Energie spirituelle* (Eng. tr., *Mind-Energy,* 1920) gathered articles already published by Bergson since 1900 on such psychological or metaphysical problems as dreams, intellectual effort, life and consciousness, and metaphysical intuition. The last book published by Bergson, *La Pensée et le mouvant* (1934; Eng. tr., *The Creative Mind,* 1946), offered other very important studies, especially "Introduction à la métaphysique" (Introduction to Metaphysics), "L'Intuition philosophique" (Philosophical Intuition), and "Le Possible et le réel" (The Possible and the Actual). Two years earlier, Bergson had provided his ultimate vision of man, through the evolution of his societies and his histories, in *Les Deux Sources de la morale et de la religion* (1932; Eng. tr., *The Two Sources of Morality and Religion,* 1935). In this work, a final answer to the 19th century's philosophies of history and its positivist theories of sociology, Bergson followed the pattern of his earlier books. He contrasted closed and open societies, in a parallel to closed and open ethics: closed or static societies are dominated and unified by the categorical imperatives of moral and political laws; dynamic or open societies constitute a sort of human creation in evolution, animated by creators of all sorts, heroes, saints, and mystics who attract other men by inspiring their admiration. Again it is the eternal fight between matter, its inertia and determinism on the one hand, and on the other, spiritual freedom, its inventions, and its cultures. Bergson's thought will remain an act of faith in the constant power of creation found at the heart of reality, be it called God, Life, or Spirit.

See: J. Maritain, *La Philosophie bergsonienne: Etudes critiques* (1914; Eng. tr., *Bergsonian Philosophy and Thomism,* 1955, 1968); J. Chevalier, *Henri Bergson* (1926; Eng. tr., 1928); A. Robinet, *Bergson et les metámorphoses de la durée* (1965); M. Barthélemy-Madaule, *Bergson* (1967); G. Politzer, *La Fin d'une parade philosophique: le bergsonisme* (1967); I. J. Gallagher, *Morality in Evolution: The Moral Philosophy of Henri Bergson* (1970); G. Lafrance, *La Philosophie sociale de Bergson: sources et inspirations* (1974); G. Bretonneau, *Création et valeurs esthétiques chez Bergson* (1975); A. Pilkington, *Bergson and His Influence: A Reassessment* (1976). E.M.-S.

Berl, Emmanuel (1892–1976), French essayist, journalist, historian, and novelist, was born in the Paris suburb of Le Vésinet and lived in Paris the remainder of his life. Influenced during his early childhood by the intellectual atmosphere that he found especially in the company of his mother's relatives, Berl disdained the industrial and bourgeois values of his father. Before serving in the trenches during World War I, the memory of whose dead and suffering was to obsess him during his lifetime, he wrote a dissertation at the Sorbonne (1913) on François de Fénelon's (1651–1715) quietism, a form of religious mysticism, but he pursued his studies no further. Of an assimilated Jewish family that, however, looked with disfavor on conversion, Berl was always conscious of anti-Semitism. He was fascinated by the Zohar and the Cabala. The authors whom he admired most included Michel de Montaigne, Denis Diderot, Voltaire, and Friedrich NIETZSCHE, mostly because of their philosophy of tolerance.

Aware of the evils of war, Berl espoused pacifism and undertook a series of essays—*Mort de la pensée bourgeoise* (1929; Death of Bourgeois Thought), *Mort de la morale bourgeoise* (1930; Death of Bourgeois Morality), and *La Politique et les partis* (1932; Politics and Parties)—

in which he predicted the perils to civilization caused by existing bourgeois values. His social vision gained further dimensions when, with the encouragement of Gaston Gallimard, he assumed the direction of *Marianne* (1932–37), a left-wing weekly. During the 1930s he also edited, with his close friend Pierre DRIEU LA ROCHELLE, *Les Derniers Jours* (1937) and *Pavé de Paris* (1927). Distrusting capitalism, although not completely adhering to socialism, he adopted many of the ideas of Jean JAURÈS and Georges Clemenceau. It was also during the post–World War I period that Berl experimented with the novel, indulging in sentimental and psychological analyses such as *La Route No. 10* (1927), and *Méditation sur un amour défunt* (1926; Meditation on a Dead Love). His conception of love, quite different from that of his good friend Marcel PROUST, betrays a preoccupation with its relationship to middle-class thinking. In *Recherches sur la nature de l'amour* (1925; Research into the Nature of Love) and *Le Bourgeois et l'amour* (1931; The Bourgeois and Love), Berl concluded that it leaves in its wake nothing but the ashes of absence and disappearance.

Because of his advocacy of the Munich Peace Pact, Berl had to be hidden during the German occupation. After the liberation of France, his work developed and his reputation began to climb. With his third wife, the chanteuse Mireille, Berl finally found personal tranquillity. He now broadened his interests to include issues of history, culture, and civilization, writing such works as *Structure et destin de l'Europe* (1946; Structure and Destiny of Europe), a general history of the West; *Histoire de l'Europe* (1946–47; History of Europe); *La Fin de la Troisième République* (1968; The End of the Third Republic); *Europe et Asie* (1969); and *A contretemps* (1969; Out of Season). In search of a new definition of values, he became preoccupied with the importance of every human being, with sentiments as well as with ideas. While disclaiming any autobiographical intentions as well as the characterization of novelist, he conjures up, in *Présence des morts* (1956; Presence of the Dead), *Rachel et autres grâces* (1965; Rachel and Other Graces), and, especially, in *Sylvia* (1952), the phantom of his subterranean life, and he evokes his past and his Jewish background. If Berl, while alive, had few readers and did not fulfill his lifetime ambition to be a "grand esprit," he nevertheless was rewarded with the Grand Prix de Littérature of the Académie Française in 1967 and, in 1975, with the Marcel Proust Prize.

See: P. Modiano: *Interrogatoire suivi de Il fait beau, allons au cimetière* (1976); P. Nora, "Berl, Le Grand Rabbin Voltaire," *NO* 620 (July 27, 1976).   S.D.B.

Bernanos, Georges (1888–1948), French novelist and essayist, was born in Paris. One of the major novelists of his generation, he carried into the 20th century the fictional legacy of Honoré de Balzac and Fyodor DOSTOYEVSKY. Bernanos was 38 years old when he published his first and instantly acclaimed novel, *Sous le soleil de Satan* (1926; Eng. tr., *Under the Star of Satan*, 1940). This was followed by *L'Imposture* (1927) and its sequel, *La Joie* (1929; Eng. tr., *Joy*, 1946); *Un Mauvais Rêve* (1935; A Bad Dream); and *Un Crime* (1935; Eng. tr., *The Crime*, 1936). His masterpiece, *Journal d'un curé de campagne* (Eng. tr., *Diary of a Country Priest*, 1937), appeared in 1936. By the end of that year he had also completed *Nouvelle Histoire de Mouchette* (1937; New Story about Mouchette) and all but the final chapter of his last and most complex novel, *Monsieur Ouine* (1943; Eng. tr., *The Open Mind*, 1945). In the late 1930s, Bernanos, feeling compelled to speak out against ominous political events

in Europe, turned away from fiction, never to get back to it again.

Except for *Dialogues des Carmélites* (1947; Eng. tr., *The Fearless Heart*, 1952), the play he wrote shortly before his death and that became his spiritual and artistic testament, Bernanos devoted the last 12 years of his life to impassioned polemical essays and articles. In retrospect, these writings reveal how much more significant than their political differences at the time were the bonds that linked Bernanos, the Catholic monarchist and onetime disciple of Charles MAURRAS, to such left-wing fellow writers as André MALRAUX, Albert CAMUS, and Simone WEIL. If the latter did not share his mystical vision of an "ancienne France" of heroes and saints, they were joined in a common battle to defend what Malraux has called "la qualité humaine" against barbarism. With a sense of outrage bordering on despair, Bernanos denounced the Franco repressions in Spain, the appeasement at Munich, the French bourgeoisie's mindless surrender to technology and totalitarian violence, the shame of the armistice and collaboration and, finally, the cruel aftermath of the liberation of France. His best-known works of that period include *Les Grands Cimetières sous la lune* (1938; Eng. tr., *Diary of My Times*, 1938); *Lettre aux Anglais* (1942; Eng. tr., *Plea for Liberty*, 1944); and *Les Enfants humiliés* (1949; Eng. tr., *Tradition of Freedom*, 1950), which contains some of his most moving pages.

Yet, by and large, these volumes, in reflecting the contingencies of history, have paled next to his earlier fictional works, in which a great Christian imagination created a world that is both contemporary and timeless. In the tragic climate of a materialistic and disoriented society, his protagonists are seen struggling to realize a vision of human freedom and communion, first dreamed by them in childhood, only to be engulfed in the mirages held out to them by Satan, God's ape and rival. In its 20th-century rural and Parisian settings, the existence in which Bernanos's children, priests, writers, impostors, and madmen live is a perilous supernatural adventure: every move they make steers them closer to either the truth of their own being and to salvation, or to satanic delusion or nothingness. Theirs is a world in which all the signs are reversed, a world defying understanding. They are tossed back and forth between two powers that vie for their faith and yet whose solicitations they cannot clearly distinguish: on one side, divine grace, which denudes the soul, leaving it as if struck by a curse, and turning existence into a mysterious reenactment of Christ's agony in the Garden of Gethsemane; on the other, satanic hatred, which, having invaded the soul through the lesions caused by pride, fear, or simple weariness, lures it into a false paradise of peace and freedom. The supernatural dimension inherent in Bernanos's dramatic vision of human destiny is made tangible for the reader by the narrator's voice. Increasingly purified of an initial stridency reminiscent of Léon BLOY, and devoid of Balzacian omniscience, it is the voice of a poet and witness who accompanies his characters along their uncertain path and quietly intercedes for them in their anguish. In *Monsieur Ouine*, Bernanos succeeded by means of a complex narrative structure in transforming his vision of evil into a poetic myth. Absence and ambiguity are the work's dominant motifs, dissolving the specificity of events and universalizing the themes of exile, betrayal, violence, and death. Yet, although Satan's triumphs appear to be far more numerous than God's (he does indeed emerge as Prince of the World while the bulk of humanity appear as pitiful "stumps of men" who have missed their vocation), the novels of Georges Bernanos reflect the writer's lifelong, heroic battle against the temptation of despair. Underlying his somber vision there is a childlike faith. Indeed, it is expressed in the pivotal theme of childhood to which all other themes are intimately related. In the spiritual sense in which Bernanos conceived it, childhood is that state of integrity and trust in which man "faces up" to his authentic calling, namely, to become a saint in the total gift of his being to divine love. Although it may be submerged in the course of an increasingly perverse and self-deluded existence, that sense of childhood is never wholly lost. Hence its power to surge up at any one of the great Bernanosian moments of crisis and, in an instant, to redeem a life by reversing its direction.

See: M. Milner, *Georges Bernanos* (1967); B. T. Fitch, *Dimensions et structures chez Bernanos* (1969).

G.R.Bl.

Bernard, Jean-Jacques (1888-1972), French dramatist and novelist, was born in Enghien-les-Bains, the son of the playwright Tristan Bernard. Jean-Jacques Bernard was the outstanding exponent of the dramatic theory baptized the "school of silence." According to it, "the theater is first and foremost the art of expressing what is unspoken," that is to say, the inaudible but pregnant speech of the heart and soul, what lies inhibited or buried in the subconsciousness, what a pretentious rhetoric befogs or conceals behind a screen of words.

Bernard's talent, first revealed before World War I, came to flower in his postwar theater, in *La Maison épargnée* (1919; The Spared House) and especially in *Le Feu qui reprend mal* (1921; Eng. tr., *The Sulky Fire,* 1939), both dramas of soldiers who return from war, one to face an unsympathetic environment, the other to face love grown cold through absence and not readily rekindled. Bernard's art reached its peak in *Martine* (1922; Eng. tr., 1927), which tells the simple tale of a peasant girl's romance with a city charmer, a romance blighted all too soon. Here is pure drama in its essence, freed from all rhetoric, ideology, and dramatic trappings. The characters in it are transparent; the passion is both intense and diaphanous.

The same qualities characterize the rest of Bernard's delicately intimate dramas. He mirrored the illusions and deceptions of life, its pipe dreams, the rainbows of romance and highways of desire that the imagination builds from the horizon to one's door and that reality pricks like bubbles. In plays such as *L'Invitation au voyage* (1924; Eng. trs., *Glamour,* 1927, *Invitation to a Voyage,* 1939), *L'Ame en peine* (1926; Eng. tr., *The Unquiet Spirit,* 1932), *A la recherche des cœurs* (1934; In Search of Hearts), and *National 6* (1935), he painted the tragedies of love, of deep but smothered passion, of soul mates in distress and divided on earth, and the dramas of spiritual and social imperfections and even of industrial strife. He has rendered as with strings, and in a minor key, the themes and variations the postwar theater often played as though with wind instruments, sometimes off-key. With Bernard, poetry caught up with realism and psychology in the theater. He extracted beauty and pathos out of the most fugitive aspects of life—a look, a sign, a momentary silence. His insight into the heart was not marred by splashes of jarring passion. The quality of his analysis, the purity of his style, and the sensitiveness of his dramatic climate gave to his creations a classic ring. Bernard also wrote short stories, as well as such novels as *Le Roman de Martine* (1929; The Romance of Martine) and *Madeleine Landier* (1933). After the liberation of France, he published an account of the imprisonment of French Jews in a concentration camp, *Le Camp de la mort lente:*

Compiègne 1941-1942 (1945; The Camp of Slow Death: Compiègne 1941-1942).

See: M. Daniels, *French Drama of the Unspoken* (1953), pp. 172-237; D. Knowles, *French Drama of the Inter-War Years* (1968), pp. 113-19; K. A. Branford, *A Study of Jean-Jacques Bernard's Théâtre de l'Inexprime* (1977).

S.A.R.

Bernard, Jean-Marc (1881-1915), French poet and critic, was born in Valence. His early years were spent in Belgium, with a one-year sojourn in England and a few months in Germany. His interest in poetry appeared early, as did evidence of his keen search for a poetic "master." In this quest, Bernard came under the influence of Francis VIELÉ-GRIFFIN (later repudiated) and the poet-priest Louis Le CARDONNEL. Having settled in his mother's native Saint-Rambert-d'Albon, Bernard founded the satirical, neoclassicist periodical *Les Guêpes* (1909-12) with Raoul Monier, a Valentinois educated in law, who "converted" Bernard to the ideas of Charles MAURRAS and the royalist group Action Française. As a critic, Bernard generally allied himself with the *Revue critique des idées et des livres.* His poetic work, entitled *Sub tegmine fagi: amours, bergeries et jeux* (1913; In the Shade of the Beech Tree: Loves, Pastorals, Games), has been compared to that of Catullus and Tibullus, but he considered himself an epigone of François Villon, whose works he edited (published posthumously in 1918). Bernard also edited the *Rondeaux* of Charles d'Orléans (1391-1465) and a polemical choice of *Pages politiques de poètes français* (1912; Political Pages of French Poets). Bernard's most famous essay—considered an attack on Stéphane MALLARMÉ—was responsible for the suppression of the original first number of the *Nouvelle Revue française.* Numbered among the "poètes fantaisistes" (along with Francis CARCO, Tristan DERÈME, Robert de la Vaissière, Jean PELLERIN, and Léon Vérane), he wrote a "De Profundis" that is considered the best French poem to come out of World War I. Bernard was about to adopt a new literary manner when he volunteered for the war and died in battle at Souchez.

His *Œuvres* (Works), together with Raoul Monier's *Reliquiae* (Remains), were edited by Henri Clouard and Henri Martineau (2 vols., 1923). S.W.

Bernari, Carlo, pseud. of Carlo Bernard (1909-), Italian novelist and short-story writer, was born in Naples, a city that has served as the setting for much of his fiction. His first novel, *Tre operai* (1934; Three Factory Workers), now widely considered an important precursor of Italian neorealism, treats the urban proletariat of his native city with an unblinking realism that was unusual for its time and that contributed to the novel's suppression by the Fascist authorities. In *Prologo alle tenebre* (1947; Prologue to the Shadows) and then again in *Le radiose giornate* (1969; The Radiant Days), Bernari examined the problem of sincerity in human relations against the backdrop of the clandestine anti-Fascist struggle during the German occupation of Naples. *Speranzella* (1949), which won the Viareggio Prize in 1950, is a less intensely personal work. The title refers both to the book's setting, a street in one of Naples's most crowded and bustling neighborhoods, and to the "bit of hope" that animates the residents of this street in their constant struggle for survival. The real hero of the novel, however, is the Neapolitan popular language itself, whose lively and colorful cadences are vividly reproduced by the richly mimetic Italian of the narration. Naples and Neapolitan life are also the subject of *Napoli guerra e pace* (1945; Naples

War and Peace), *Vesuvio e pane* (1952; Bread and Mount Vesuvius), and *La Bibbia napoletana* (1961; The Neapolitan Bible). *Domani e poi domani* (1957; Tomorrow and Tomorrow), however, is set in Puglia and concerns an unconventional love affair and its impact on a provincial town, while *Era l'anno del sole quieto* (1964; The Year of the Silent Sun) is a study of the human and material obstacles to industrialization of the south during the *boom italiano*. This last work, which makes free use of the technological jargon of the 1960s, is further evidence of Bernari's interest in exploring different levels of linguistic experience. The failure of the novel's entrepeneur-hero, faced with archaic and recalcitrant southern social realities, ties the book thematically to *Tre operai*, another tale involving factory life and bitter disappointment in the south.

Throughout his career, Bernari's fiction has been marked by a restless experimentalism and a tenacious devotion to his native region and to human values. Bernari has also been a journalist; his essays, collected in *Non gettate via la scala* (1973; Don't Throw Away the Ladder), are also important for an understanding of his art.

See: special number of *La fiera letteraria*, (Feb. 2, 1958); E. Pesce, *Bernari* (1970).   C.K.

Bernhard, Thomas (1931–), Austrian novelist, dramatist, and poet, was born near Maastricht, in Holland, the son of Austrian parents. His maternal grandfather, Johannes Freumbichler, was himself a writer and figured significantly in Bernhard's youth, which was spent in rural Austria and Bavaria. After troubled years in a Salzburg boarding school and extensive musical training at the Mozarteum, Bernhard entered a commercial apprenticeship, which ended when he had to enter a tuberculosis sanatorium. After his recovery, Bernhard worked for several years as a court reporter before turning to literature.

Bernhard's first published work was rather imitative poetry that did not attract great critical attention: *Auf der Erde und in der Hölle* (1957; On Earth and in Hell), *Unter dem Eisen des Mondes* (1958; Under the Iron of the Moon), and *In hora mortis* (1958). His first two novels, however, *Frost* (1963) and *Amras* (1964), revealed a startling originality, anticipating his widely acclaimed 1967 novel, *Verstörung* (Eng. tr. *Gargoyles,* 1970). These works are set in bleak, craggy landscapes of rural Austria, populated by a brutal and stupid peasantry; the sensitive, intellectually or artistically inclined protagonists, often members of the local aristocracy, live in states of increasing isolation, ending in suicide or insanity. Narrated in the first person, the novels show Bernhard's tendencies toward monologue and toward monologues embedded in one another, a technique particularly striking in *Gehen* (1971; Walking).

In *Verstörung* the narrator, a mining student on a short visit home, accompanies his father, a country doctor, on one day's rounds and gives an account of the hopeless, sometimes gruesome cases, ending with the schizophrenic Prince Saurau. Earlier the narrator had written his father a letter about the unsatisfactory relationships within their own family. The father's insistence that his son accompany him is an indirect answer to this letter, an answer implying the brutality of human relationships, the illusoriness of love, and the futility of attempted communication. The latter half of the book consists of Prince Saurau's monologue as he walks with father and son around the grounds of his vast and remote alpine estate. This bizarre piece of prose reflects recurrent themes of Bernhard: life as a destructive process leading only to death;

despair as the only possible response to life; democratic social idealism as a false notion; and speech only as monologue, as a frenetic, temporary therapy for the individual. Bernhard's other fictional works include *Ungenach* (1968), *Watten* (1969), *Das Kalkwerk* (1970; Eng. tr., *The Lime Works,* 1973), *Korrektur* (1975; Revision), and short stories.

Turning to drama in the early 1970s, Bernhard wrote *Ein Fest für Boris* (1970; A Party for Boris), a macabre piece about a frenzied birthday party for a group of cripples, during which the guest of honor dies. Two of his dramas bear the subtitle "comedy": *Die Macht der Gewohnheit* (1974; Eng. tr., *The Force of Habit,* 1976) and *Immanuel Kant* (1978). The former is set in a third-rate circus, where the director has for years insisted on daily rehearsals of Franz Schubert's *Trout* Quintet. The indifference and aversion of all the players makes a satisfactory performance impossible. Art here is a means through which the director torments others, forcing them in turn to torment him; true, perfect art remains an illusion that, nevertheless, must be joylessly pursued. Several other of Bernhard's dramas deal with art and the artist, for example, *Der Ignorant und der Wahnsinnige* (1972; The Ignoramus and the Madman) and *Die Berühmten* (1976; The Famous Ones).

The autobiographical writings, *Die Ursache* (1975; The Cause), *Der Keller* (1976; The Cellar), and *Der Atem* (1978; Breath), disclose the personal traumas underlying the author's obsessions with violence, disease, suicide, and death.

Bernhard's strength lies in the intensity of his perceptions, the vehemence of his hatreds, and the originality with which he presents them. His language bursts with superlatives and hyperbole, the forceful articulation of negative absolutes. At the same time his writing sometimes becomes monochromatic, lacking in nuance. His wholesale condemnation of communism, socialism, and democracy, his disdain for the masses, and his refusal— springing from his essentially solipsistic perspective—to acknowledge the social and political dimensions of life have won him the favor of conservative critics and the enmity of leftist ones. His dramas, which lack the excessive verbiage of the narratives and which sometimes recall Samuel BECKETT, are more accessible than his fiction. His prose style, particularly his complex sentences with embedded series of subordinate clauses, are difficult to reproduce in English, and his work is little known in English-speaking countries.

Stylistically and thematically Bernhard owes much to German literary tradition, particularly to Heinrich von Kleist and Novalis. At the same time he is an undeniably Austrian writer, compelled by a problematic dependence on and yet an intense hatred toward the provincial landscapes that he describes and in which, despite broad travels, he continues to live. He has won numerous literary prizes in Austria and West Germany, including the Georg Büchner Prize (1970).

See: B. Sorg, *Thomas Bernhard* (1977).   C.C.Z.

Bernstein, Henry (1876–1953), French playwright, was born in Paris. He is generally thought of as a painter of heartless and brutal characters, hard businessmen, and cynical adventurers. This reputation is due to violent dramas such as *La Rafale* (1905; Eng. tr., *The Whirlwind,* 1906), *La Griffe* (1906; The Talon), and *Samson* (1907). Bernstein, however, had begun his dramatic career with comedies of a milder type, including *Le Marché* (1900; The Trading), *Le Détour* (1902), *Joujou* (1902; Plaything), *Frère Jacques* (1904; Eng. tr., *Brother Jacques,* 1904;

written with Pierre Veber), and *Le Bercail* (1904; Eng. tr., *The Redemption of Evelyn Vaudray*, 1911).

After 1913 he wrote a few plays where the emphasis is placed on the characters rather than on a tense, dynamic plot. *Le Secret* (1913), an analysis of a malicious woman who enjoys hurting those whom she pretends to love, and *La Galerie des glaces* (1924; Hall of Mirrors), built around a case of inferiority complex and retrospective jealousy, are among his best psychological dramas. Such subtle studies are the exception in Henry Bernstein's theater. As a rule his characters are dominated by violent passions, which they satisfy without any consideration for the usual codes of morality and decency. The public at times reacted unfavorably, as in the case of *Après moi* (1911; Eng. tr., *After Me*, 1911).

Bernstein was an expert technician who knew how to place his characters in the light that would best intensify the tragic elements of the plot. *Israël* (1908), based on a conflict between Jews and members of the French aristocracy, provides an excellent example of his talent in creating dramatic atmospheres. Aware of the changes in the public's taste, Bernstein, while keeping his main characteristics, treated with remarkable ease the most varied subjects. *Judith* (1922), *Mélo* (1929; Melodrama), and *Espoir* (1934; Eng. tr., *Promise*, 1936) are proofs of his versatility.

See: G. Rageot, "Un Nouveau Bernstein," in *RBl* (Nov. 15, 1924) and "La Nouvelle Esthétique d'Henry Bernstein," *RBl* (Apr. 3, 1926); L. Le Sidaner, *Henry Bernstein* (1931); R. Dornès, "Henry Bernstein, dramaturge et écrivain," in *PTh* 69 (1953): 7–13.

M.E.C. rev. D.W.A.

Bertin, Charles (1919–), Belgian poet, novelist, and playwright, was born in Mons. He is a member of the Royal Academy of French Language and Literature of Belgium. In poetry, Bertin has expressed the torments of disenchantment and lassitude, the uneasiness of a soul cut off from the appeasement of faith, as in *Psaumes sans la grâce* (1947; Psalms without Grace) and *Chant noir* (1949; Dark Song). His best-known novels include *Journal d'un crime* (1961; Diary of a Crime), a detective story with metaphysical concerns, and *Le Bel Age* (1964; A Mellow Age), a social portrait and psychological analysis with Balzacian overtones. As a playwright, Bertin has evoked solitary destinies: In *Don Juan* (1948), in the traits of a character who is both satanic and tortured; in *Christophe Colomb* (1958; Christopher Columbus), in which the hero fights to remain faithful to the meaning of his quest; and in *Je reviendrai à Badenburg* (1970; I Will Return to Badenburg), in which the passion for life confronts the obsession with death. *Roi Bonheur* (1966; King Happiness), a "philosophical farce" in the commedia dell'arte style, is a cry of revolt against the absurd, being very close to the *Caligula* of Albert CAMUS. A lucid analyst, a demanding writer, and a man of the theater gifted with sensitivity as well as an aptitude for reflection, Bertin is one of the most accomplished authors of his generation.

See: M. Aubrion, *Charles Bertin* (1968).   R.T.

Berto, Giuseppe (1914–78), Italian novelist, short-story writer, and dramatist, was born in Mogliano Veneto, just north of Venice. He received a degree in letters from the University of Padua and taught briefly. Soon after Italy entered World War II, Berto enlisted in the Voluntary Militia for National Security and was sent to North Africa. In May 1943, he was captured and eventually confined in an American prison camp in Hereford, Texas. His writing career began during his imprisonment with some short stories, the short novel *Le opere di Dio* (1948;

Eng. tr., *The Works of God*, 1950), and a novel later published as *Il cielo è rosso* (1947; Eng. tr., *The Sky Is Red*, 1948). *Il cielo è rosso*, a moving account of the recuperative powers of four young children forced to live in a bombed-out city, won critical acclaim both in Italy and abroad. Berto's early writings have a simple, solemn style that is often striking in its imagery. They reflect the tragedy of men dehumanized by war, oppressed by a sense of the ineluctability of events, and suffering under the recognition of a universal evil for which they share the guilt and which condemns them to a state of loneliness and frustration.

Berto's most significant literary achievements came after a long period of crisis, during which he suffered from a serious neurosis. He recorded his experiences in psychoanalysis in *Il male oscuro* (1964; Eng. tr., *Incubus*, 1966), an avant-garde novel that won two literary prizes and was acclaimed in Italy as one of the most significant prose works of the 1960s. In *Il male oscuro*, Berto's theme is the inner man, guilt-ridden and sexually inhibited. He is treated ironically by means of a narrative technique the author called "associative discourse," wherein—as in psychoanalytical free association—all traditional logical relationships are abandoned. The same technique was used in a later novel, *La cosa buffa* (1966; Eng. tr., *Antonio in Love*, 1968), in which the protagonist is an analogue of the neurotic central figure of *Il male oscuro*.

Among Berto's other works are a collection of 20 short stories, *Un po' di successo* (1963; A Bit of Success), which bridges the neorealism of the author's early work and the stylistic innovations of his later period; *Guerra in camicia nera* (1955; War in a Black Shirt), a diary of his months in North Africa with the Fascist militia; two dramas, *L'uomo e la sua morte* (1964; Man and His Death) and *La passione secondo noi stessi* (1972; The Passion According to Ourselves); and a romance-drama, *Anonimo veneziano* (1971; Eng. tr., *Anonymous Venetian*, 1973). His last novel, *La gloria* (1978; Glory), was published posthumously.

See: D. Heiney, *America in Modern Italian Literature* (1964); R. Esposito, "Rassegna di studi su Giuseppe Berto," in *Critica letteraria*, vol. 1 (1973), pp. 176–84; O. Lombardi, *Invito alla lettura di Berto* (1974).   R.J.R.

Bertrana, Prudenci (1867–1942), Catalan novelist, was born in the city of Torosa, received his education in Ampurdan, and spent much of his youth in Gerona, where he contemplated nature and developed his talent as a writer and painter. He originally intended to be a painter, but it was in the literary field that he attained real success. His first important work was *Nàufrags* (1907; The Shipwrecked). *Josafat* (1906) is characterized by a crude and savage realism that characterizes all of his subsequent work. *Jo* (1925) is a passionate and turbulent novel in which characters are observed with a stinging sharpness and one does not know where the fiction ends and libel begins. *Proses barbares* (1911) are wild stories written in a typically lively and colorful prose. Other works are *Herois* (1920; Heroes) and *El meu amic Pellini* (1923; My Friend Pellini). In 1931 his novel *L'hereu* (The Heir) won the coveted Crexells Prize, which the government of Catalonia awarded each year to the best novel. Full of biographical references, *L'hereu* reveals Bertrana's predilection for the vigorous portrayal of nature in terms of sharp contrasts brought out with the love of a landscape artist. A later novel was *El vagabund* (1933; The Vagabond). Bertrana's first theatrical works were *La dona neta* (The Tidy Lady) and *Tieta Claudina* (Dear Aunt Claudina). Gerona has honored his memory by creating the Prudenci

Bertrana Prize. Bertrana also did considerable work as a journalist.

In all of his literary work there is present Bertrana's dual identity as painter and writer. He brought to Catalan literature a pessimism perhaps less severe than that of Victor CATALÀ and cultivated a less bitter but nevertheless acrid ruralism. Some of his work has a warm and vital human quality.   F. de P.

Bessa-Luís, Agustina (1922–), Portuguese novelist and short-story writer, was born in Vila-Meã, near the town of Amarante in the north of Portugal, the rural world that serves as the background of most of her novels and stories. Her early works, such as *Mundo fechado* (1948; Closed World) and *Os super-homens* (1950; The Supermen), received little public notice and even less critical praise. With her third novel, *A sibila* (1953; The Sibyl), however, Bessa-Luís not only won two literary awards but also met with wide public acclaim and established a literary perspective and a distinctive style, both of which she has continued to cultivate ever since (*see* PORTUGUESE LITERATURE).

Far removed from the traditional novel's objectivity and penchant for plot, Bessa-Luís's works provide keen character portrayals delineated from a point of view that combines third-person narrative and frequent author's comments with the immediacy of monologue and stream of consciousness. Meditation weighs more heavily than events, and there is little dialogue and even less description or narrated action. The author's probing psychological analyses center upon the inadequacy of common sense and the need for intuition and a sense of the marvelous. Central characters are often depicted as repositories of detailed memories, whose painstaking introspection reveals multiple, even contradictory motivations. Bessa-Luís employs a richly suggestive vocabulary and a hypnotic rhythm, whose repetitive cadence is well suited to insinuate what logical analysis cannot wholly categorize. The labyrinth of human experience renders social relationships problematic, as we find in a trilogy devoted to family ties, *As relações humanas* (Human Relationships), comprising *Os quatro rios* (1964; The Four Rivers), *A dança das espadas* (1965; Sword Dance) and *Canção diante de uma porta fechada* (1966; Song in Front of a Closed Door). The same theme underlies another series, *A bíblia dos pobres* (The Bible of the Poor), which so far includes *Homens e mulheres* (1967; Men and Women) and *As categorias* (1970; The Categories). In all these novels, the mood is heightened by an undercurrent of suspense that occasionally leads to surprise, astonishment, or even fear. Bessa-Luís has written numerous other novels; a three-act play, *O inseparável, ou o amigo por testamento* (1958; Inseparable, or, The Bequeathed Friend); and a book of impressions of travels through Europe, *Embaixada a Caligula* (1960; On a Mission to Caligula). In all her works, critics often detect echoes of Marcel PROUST, Franz KAFKA, and Honoré de Balzac.

See: A. Quadros, *Crítica e verdade* (1964), pp. 168–76; J. Carvalho, "A. Bessa-Luís e o romance moderno," *Segundo Congresso Brasileiro de Língua e Literatura* (1971), pp. 257–70.   R.A.P.-R.

Betocchi, Carlo (1899–), Italian poet, was born in Turin. He moved to Florence when still a child. He studied civil engineering, but soon joined a Florentine group of poets and writers, later becoming an editor of the important Catholic literary journal *Il frontespizio* (1928–38), under whose auspices he published his first book of poetry, *Realtà vince il sogno* (1932; Reality Conquers Dreams). Other slim volumes followed, until he collected most of his poems in *Poesie 1930–1954* (1955), which was awarded the Viareggio Prize. A second collection, *L'estate di San Martino* (Indian Summer), appeared in 1961. This volume, especially the section entitled "Diaretto invecchiando" (Little Diary, as I Grow Old), represents Betocchi's most mature work. *Un passo, un altro passo* (A Step, Another Step), a third collection, appeared in 1967. In addition to these three volumes of poetry, Betocchi has produced many still uncollected prose writings.

Betocchi's poetry is filled with a deep sense of the transience of man on earth, and of an anguish to which it proposes the comfort of a vivid presence of God. This anguish is born of an intense metaphysical yearning, which springs from a constant need both to transcend and to give a meaning to sensuality. Faced with such a task, his poetry achieves valid results through a surprising amalgam of contemporary forms and a traditional literary vocabulary. While at times Betocchi may take on Dantesque tones or may pursue expressive patterns typical of poets such as Giovanni PASCOLI or Giosuè Carducci (1835–1907), he can immediately transform them into something entirely new and personal. Betocchi's poems sing of sun and shadows, of walls and roofs, of birds, of fields and country roads, simple things that become vehicles to express his complex needs and desires. His sense of universal anguish, intensified by the devastations of World War II, is evident in the poem "Lungo la via Casilina" (Along the Casilina Way). After the war, Betocchi's poetry became more introspective, but it did not abandon its clarity. He fashioned his words and images into crystalline expressions of an ancient wisdom, but one that he had totally reconquered and made his own. This type of poetry is very difficult, for it constantly threatens to sink to platitudinous levels, yet a highly personal use of language makes Betocchi's lines supple and rich. A selection of his poems was published in 1964, in an English translation by I. L. Salomon.

See: V. Volpini, in *Letteratura italiana: i contemporanei*, vol. 2 (1975), pp. 1281–97.   G.Ce.

Betti, Ugo (1892–1953), Italian playwright, poet, and short-story writer, was born in Camerino. In 1901 his family moved to Parma. After receiving a law degree, he volunteered to serve in the Italian army, won a decoration, and was captured at Caporetto (now in Yugoslavia) in 1917. While in a prison camp in Germany, he composed his first verses. After World War I, Betti, now a pacifist, returned to Parma. He began his career in the judiciary and wrote his first play in 1924. In 1930, the year of his marriage, he went to Rome as a judge, and in 1950 he was nominated to the Court of Appeals. With the Paris production of his masterpiece, *Delitto all'isola delle capre* (1950; Eng. tr., *Crime on Goat Island*, 1961), he achieved worldwide fame as a playwright only a few months before his death.

Betti's first volume of verse, *Il re pensieroso* (1922; The Thoughtful King), is an evocation of pain and evil, heavily influenced by the symbolists, the *crepuscolari* (*see* ITALIAN LITERATURE), Maurice MAETERLINCK, Giovanni PASCOLI, and others. *Canzonette—La morte* (1932; Little Songs—Death), his best volume of poems, expresses joy and solitude, and fear of both death and of a mute God. His third volume, *Uomo e donna* (1937; Man and Woman), is a touching but often sentimental view of nature, fraternal relations, love, and the Christian God.

Betti's short stories, written in a kind of symbolic realism, are collected in *Caino* (1928; Cain), *Le case* (1933; The Houses), and *Una strana serata* (1948; A Strange Evening). The power of some of them lies in their disconsolate rebellion against a joyless existence. Human beings, alienated by their monotonous lives from nature, society, and themselves, suffer an uncommunicable feeling of, and need for, compassion. Betti's only novel, *La piera alta* (1948; The High Mountain), is an unimportant work.

In the most successful of his 25 plays, Betti dramatizes a pitiless, relentless, Augustinian fathoming of the bottomless self in order "to understand the tremendous, bewildering incongruity that we see between our existence and what it ought to be according to the aspiration of our soul; to understand *why* life is the marvelously tranquil iniquity that it is." In his best work he reminds some critics of Henrik IBSEN, Luigi PIRANDELLO, and Franz KAFKA. Eight of Betti's dramas (his attempts at comedy are failures) take the form of a legal investigation, the most prominent among them being *Frana allo scalo nord* (1935; Eng. tr., *Landslide*, 1964), *Ispezione* (1947; Eng. tr., *The Inquiry*, 1966), and *Corruzione al palazzo di giustizia* (1949; Corruption at the Palace of Justice). In other plays, the investigation takes a nonlegal turn: the arrival of an individual from the protagonist's past, as in *Notte in casa del ricco* (1942; Night in the House of the Rich Man); the unsettling introduction of a stranger in *Delitto*; or the protagonist's quest for himself in *Lotta fino all'alba* (1949; Eng. tr., *Struggle till Dawn*, 1964).

In Betti's drama, the investigation is not a matter of uncovering facts but of excavating the individual psyche, of revealing, as in *Corruzione,* a collective consciousness of shared guilt. Sometimes it is a matter of shattering the most obvious social myths: respectability, success, familial and romantic love, as in *Ispezione.* At other times (as in *Delitto*), Betti's protagonist, confronted with instinctual forces, tries to "murder" and annihilate them but fails and is engulfed.

What, then, is Betti's answer? That salvation can be achieved only through pity (as in *Frana*) or the willingness to be punished for one's guilt (as in *Corruzione*). When despair is unbearable, some characters escape into the transcendental existence of a comprehending but unjudging God. Yet even this paradise does not lessen the hell of their earlier lives. For some, anguish remains. *Ispezione* offers gnawing routine; *Notte,* loneliness; *Irene innocente* (1950; Innocent Irene) ends in suicide.

See: G. Rizzo, "Regression-Progression in Ugo Betti's Drama," *TuDR* (Fall 1963); A. Di Pietro, *L'opera di Ugo Betti,* 2 vols. (1966–68). E.L.

Beyatlı, Yahya Kemal (1884–1958), Turkish poet and essayist, was born in Skopje (now in Yugoslavia). He completed his lycée education in Istanbul and studied in Paris, where he lived from 1903 to 1912. Between the years 1915 and 1923 he was a lecturer at the University of Istanbul. At different periods he served as a member of Parliament for a total of 13 years and held embassy posts in Warsaw, Madrid, and Karachi, retiring in 1949.

After achieving stature as a neoclassical poet in the late 1910s, he maintained a dominant position in Turkey's literary circles until his death in 1958. His funeral was probably the most tumultuous ever for a Turkish poet. His poems were collected posthumously by the Yahya Kemal Institute: *Kendi Gök Kubbemiz* (1961; Our Own Vault of Heaven), *Eski Şiirin Rüzgâriyle* (1962; With the Breeze of our Time-Honored Poetry), and *Rubâîler* (1963; Rubaiyyat), which includes his versions of Omar Khayyam's *Rubaiyat.* The institute, which also maintains a Beyatlı Museum in Istanbul, collected his articles, essays, and memoirs in several volumes: *Aziz Istanbul* (1964; Dear Istanbul), *Eğil Dağlar* (1966; Mountains, Bend Down), *Siyasî Hikâyeler* (1968; Political Anecdotes), *Siyasî ve Edebî Portreler* (1968; Political and Literary Portraits), *Edebiyata Dair* (1971; On Literature), and *Çocukluğum, Gençliğim ve Siyasî Hâtıralarım* (1973; My Childhood, Youth, and Political Recollections).

Beyatlı's aesthetics stressed the use of Ottoman-Turkish stanzaic forms and prosody, although his vocabulary was predominantly attuned to the living language of his own times. His main themes were the glories of the Ottoman past, the natural and architectural splendor of Istanbul, and Turkish heroics. Among his most successful poems are those that express romantic love, metaphysical concerns, and lyrical responses to music and the plastic arts. He is generally recognized as Turkey's best neoclassical poet.

See: A. Hamdi Tanpınar, *Yahya Kemal* (1962).

T.S.H.

Bezruč, Petr, pseud. of Vladimír Vašek (1867–1958), Czech poet, was born in Opava, in Austrian Silesia, where his father, Antonín Vašek, was a prominent Czech philologist and patriot. After studying classics at the University of Prague, Bezruč entered the postal service in Brno, Moravia, where he worked until 1927. During World War I, he was imprisoned for anti-Austrian journalistic writing. His voice subsequently was often raised in favor of an aggressive nationalism and a strong local Moravian patriotism.

Bezruč's fame derives mainly from a single collection of poems, *Slezské písně* (Silesian Songs), which first appeared in a small edition in 1903 as *Slezské číslo* (A Silesian Number) and then was successively enlarged. It is the most original, authentic, and powerful group of poems in modern Czech literature. As a poet, Bezruč eschewed all self-expression and created the figure of a popular bard and prophet, Petr Bezruč ("Peter Without Hands"), who sings the sorrows of his race. Petr speaks particularly for the Czechs in Silesia, where Austrian oppression was especially severe. While passionately accusing the German landlords and capitalists, Bezruč also pleads for his people, the miners and peasants of Silesia, whose fate meant little to their fellow Czechs in Bohemia and Moravia. His rhapsodies have a tragic dimension and succeed in transforming an apparently local topic into a universal outcry for justice, a cry of hatred and anger against all oppressors. Bezruč was the master of an austere rhetoric of grandiose visions and symbols, and of a monumental semifree type of verse that was not completely divorced from popular forms. Only in a few poems is there an occasional note of personal resignation and melancholy reminiscence; usually the seer's mask is preserved with dignity and pathos.

Bezruč seems almost without literary ancestors. He was familiar with the folk ballad and sometimes used it to great effect, as in the poem "Maryčka Magdónova," about a girl who drowns herself. He knew and admired Josef Svatopluk MACHAR, from whom he adopted some unnecessary classical conventions, and he must have read some of the social poetry of the later Heinrich Heine. But essentially he stands alone: the fiercest, finest voice raised against national and social oppression in all Czechoslovakia.

See: A. Veselý, *Petr Bezruč, básník a člověk* (1927); J. V. Sedlák, *Petr Bezruč* (1931); K. Rektorisová, *Bezručův verš* (1935); J. Janů, *Petr Bezruč* (1947); A. Králík, *Kapitoly o Slezských písních* (1957). R.W.

Białoszewski, Miron (1922–), Polish poet, playwright, and prosaist, was born in Warsaw. He represents the extreme of a tendency to reexamine the Polish language by breaking up the grammar and even words. When he was young, his poems on rusty pipes, dirty staircases, iron stoves, and kitchen utensils were rejected as politically offensive, and he succeeded in publishing his first volume, *Obroty rzeczy* (1956; Turns of Things), only after the "thaw." His poetry evolved towards exploration of everyday speech, especially that heard in the Warsaw street; it is built with fragments of sentences, mispronounced verbs, odd ends of declined nouns. This is especially marked in his volume *Mylne wzruszenia* (1961; Wrong Emotions). Białoszewski could be called a poet of approximative and lame existence. His reducing the language to a state of magma fulfills, of course, a special function in the service of his not very joyous philosophy. Some readers see in him and in similar poets a reaction to the language as used by mass media. He published two more volumes of poetry: *Rachunek zachciankowy* (1959; Calculus of Whims) and *Było i było* (1965; Were and Were). Białoszewski is also the author of plays resembling his poems, *Teatr osobny. Dramaty* (1971; The Theatre Apart), and of a book in prose, *Pamiętnik z Powstania Warszawskiego* (1970; Eng. tr., *A Memoir of the Warsaw Uprising,* 1977), where horrors of the 1944 battles in the city receive an antiheroic treatment and are described, in broken popular idioms, from the perspective of the civilian population, as well as of the prose works *Szumy, zlepy, ciągi* (1976; Noises, Clusters, Currents) and *Zawał,* (1977; Heart Attack).

See: S. Barańczak, *Jezyk poętycki Mirona Białoszewskiego* (1974). C.Mi.

Bianciardi, Luciano (1922–71), Italian novelist, translator, journalist, sportswriter, and social critic, was born in Grosseto. He took his degree in philosophy at the Scuola Normale di Pisa, writing a thesis on John Dewey. In Grosseto he taught *liceo* for three years and reorganized the city's library of materials on the Risorgimento. Bianciardi belonged to a generation of socially committed leftist intellectuals who worked in publishing and contributed to many progressive periodicals during the 1950s. He was a member of the original editorial staff of the Feltrinelli publishing house and also became associated with *Il contemporaneo* at its inception in 1954. From 1957 on he earned his living as a translator and columnist.

A brilliant, polemical, incisive chronicler of contemporary culture, Bianciardi was a literary maverick. His work is often autobiographical, and his eclectic, innovative, parajournalistic style is erudite and satirical. He wrote works of social inquiry, exemplified by *I minatori della Maremma* (1956; Maremma's Miners), coauthored with Carlo CASSOLA. Related works on industrial subjects include *Il lavoro culturale* (1957, 1964; Cultural Work), *L'integrazione* (1960; Integration), and *La vita agra* (1962; Eng. tr., *It's a Hard Life,* 1965). Works concerning the Risorgimento include *Da Quarto a Torino* (1960; From Quarto to Turin), *La battaglia soda* (1964; Real Battle), and *Daghela avanti un passo!* (1969; Step Lively). *Aprire il fuoco* (1969; Open Fire) synthesizes both industrial and historical themes. *Viaggio in Barberia* (1969; Travels in Barberia) is a travelogue. *La vita agra* and the short story "Il complesso di Loth" (Loth's Complex) were both made into films.

Bianciardi traced the mining industry in Tuscany from the 18th to the 20th century in *I minatori,* focusing on the Ribolla lignite mine near Grosseto, the site of the 1954 explosion that killed 43 miners. *Il lavoro culturale* is a satire concerning two leftist intellectual brothers who want to promote culture in the provinces. The humor in *L'integrazione* approaches the grotesque. This novel, a sequel to *Il lavoro culturale,* chronicles the brothers' migration to the city and derisively documents their experiences in the publishing world during the 1950s publishing boom. Their ensuing alienation provokes a schism: the narrator opts for integration with society, while his disillusioned brother prefers to drop out. *La vita agra,* Bianciardi's commercially most successful novel, is concerned with the further alienation of a once idealistic intellectual who goes to the city to dynamite the skyscraper offices of an industrial conglomerate. The industrialization of modern life frustrates his every endeavor, and he becomes angry, regimented, and isolated, suspended in a void of existential anxiety.

Giuseppe Garibaldi (1807–82) is the principal figure in Bianciardi's popular histories based on accounts of participants in the Risorgimento. *Da Quarto* is a history of the Mille expedition. *La battaglia soda,* a novel written in the style of the 19th-century Maremman patriot Giuseppe Bandi, begins with the taking of Capua (November 1860) and concludes with the disastrous second battle of Custoza (June 1866). *Daghela* discusses the most important moments and figures of Italian unification. The hermetic and complex *Aprire il fuoco* illustrates Bianciardi's fatalistically cyclical interpretation of history. Purposefully confusing events of the Risorgimento with the present, the novel traces the highly structured routine, fantasies, and reminiscences of a paranoid translator and political exile.

See: G. Bàrberi-Squarotti, in *La narrativa italiana del dopoguerra* (1965), pp. 198–200; G. Manacorda, *Storia della letteratura italiana contemporanea (1940–1965)* (1967), pp. 359–60; M. Terrosi, *Bianciardi com'era* (1974). Z.V.

Bichsel, Peter (1935–), Swiss writer and journalist, grew up in Olten, Solothurn canton, attended the teachers college in Solothurn, and taught at the elementary school in Bellach, where he eventually settled. He first came to the attention of the reading public in 1965, when he was awarded the prize of the prestigious German writers' association, "Gruppe 47."

Bichsel's fascination with words and sounds and with the differences between his spoken language, the Solothurn dialect, and his written language, standard German, accounts for his many stylistic experiments. His collection *Eigentlich möchte Frau Blum den Milchmann kennenlernen* (1964; Eng. tr., *And Really Frau Blum Would Very Much Like to Meet the Milkman,* 1969) contains 21 stories in a mere 88 pages. The words in these stories have been chosen with great care, even though they describe trivial scenes and ordinary people. The characters appear lonely as their dialogue indicates no depth of communication among them. Various stylistic devices, such as the frequent use of the subjunctive, invite the reader to participate in the stories. Bichsel's novel *Die Jahreszeiten* (1967; The Seasons) is a mosaic of facts. While the novel's language is precise and lucid, the story of its hero, Kieniger, remains obscure. The stories collected in *Kindergeschichten* (1969; Eng. tr., *There is No Such Place as America,* 1970) have such titles as "The Earth Is Round" and "A Table Is a Table." In the latter story, new names are given to old things, thus a "bed" is called a "picture." Everything appears simple but questions arise that put long-accepted facts in doubt. *Kindergeschichten* and *Frau Blum* have been translated into a dozen languages, making Bichsel internationally one of the best known of the younger Swiss writers. He has also written newspaper articles, many of them critical of his country. Two of Bichsel's articles have appeared as a booklet entitled *Des Schweizers Schweiz* (1969; The Switzerland of the Swiss). In 1979, after a hiatus of almost a decade, Bichsel published *Geschichten zur falschen Zeit* (1979; Stories at the Wrong Time). The main character bears a strong resemblance to the author. The "I" reflects on the thinking of those around him.

See: W. Bucher and G. Ammann, eds., *Schweizer Schriftsteller im Gespräch,* vol. 1 (1970), pp. 13–47.

R.A.Me.

Bieler, Manfred (1934–), German prose writer and radio and television playwright, was born in Zerbst, Anhalt, was educated in Dessau and Asch, and undertook German studies at Humboldt University, East Berlin, from 1953 to 1956. He held various jobs, one as a sailor on a fishing vessel, before becoming a free-lance writer in 1957. In 1966 he left East Germany for Prague, married the Czech Marcella Matejovská, and became a Czech citizen. After the Soviet invasion of 1968, Bieler moved to Munich, where he still lives.

A chronicler like Fontane, Bieler describes people in their environment at a particular point in time. Basically naturalistic, his analysis nevertheless exhibits romantic sensitivity, with parody, the grotesque, the surreal, and symbolic elements present. *Der Schuß auf die Kanzel* (1958; The Shot at the Pulpit), several radio plays, and the picaresque novel *Bonifaz oder der Matrose in der Flasche* (1963; Eng. tr., *The Sailor in the Bottle,* 1966) made the author known. His novel *Maria Morzeck oder das Kaninchen bin ich* (1965, 1969 in West Germany; Maria Morzeck, or I'm the Bunny) led to an official reprimand by the GDR authorities because the work criticizes hardships and the lack of freedom in East Germany. Relating the story of a high school girl who cannot go to the university because her family does not unconditionally support the Communist Party, Bieler focuses on negative aspects of life in East Germany, rather than stressing "the process of democratization." The book was forbidden, as was the film based on it.

The short-story collection *Der junge Roth* (1969; Young Roth) contains a variety of literary modes, from naturalism to realism and surrealism. In *Der Passagier* (1971; The Passenger), surrealism is present in various dreams and a midnight confession after a funeral. The novel *Der Mädchenkrieg* (1975; The Girls' War) takes place in Prague during the time of Adolf Hitler and traces the generational and social conflicts in an upper-class German family. Three daughters represent different vantage points, and references to the human environment give insight into the times. Even wealthier are the protagonists of the novel *Der Kanal* (1978; The Channel). The most important character, Karsta Lackner, never spends less than 100 marks, "except for tips." Bieler has come full circle: from the very poor and sociocritical writing to the very rich and sociohistorical observation.

Widely known for over 20 radio plays, among which *Drei Rosen aus Papier* (1969; Three Paper Roses) won particular acclaim, Bieler has also written half a dozen television plays. The volume *Märchen und Zeitungen* (1966; Fairy Tales and Gazettes) contains some of his stories.

See: F. Raddatz, *Traditionen und Tendenzen: Materialien zur Literatur der DDR* (1972). A.P.O.

Bienek, Horst (1930–), German novelist, poet, essayist, film producer, radio author, and editor, was born in Gleiwitz, Upper Silesia, in present-day Poland. He studied with Bertolt BRECHT in East Berlin. After his political arrest in 1951, he was interned in a prison camp at Vorkuta, Siberia, until the amnesty of 1956, after which he settled in West Germany, where he now lives as a free-lance writer in Munich. His works include *Traumbuch eines Gefangenen* (1957; A Prisoner's Dream Book), poems and essays; *Nachtstücke* (1959; Night Pieces), sto-

ries; *Werkstattgespräche mit Schriftstellern, 15 Interviews* (1962; Workshop Conversations with Authors); *Was war, was ist* (1966; What Was, What Is), poems; *Die Zelle* (1968; Eng. tr., *The Cell,* 1972), which shows an affinity with the new novel (*see* FRENCH LITERATURE) and which was filmed in 1970 and 1971; *Vorgefundene Gedichte* (1969; Poems at Hand); *Bakunin: Eine Invention* (1970; Eng. tr., 1977), a Borgeslike treatment of the life of the Russian anarchist Mikhail Bakunin; *Solschenizyn und andere Essays* (1972; Solzhenitsyn and Other Essays); *Die Zeit danach* (1974; The Time Afterward), poems; *Die Erste Polka* (1975; Eng. tr., *The First Polka,* 1978); *Gleiwitzer Kindheit* (1976; Gleiwitz Childhood), poems; and *Septemberlicht* (1977; September Light). *Die Erste Polka, Septemberlicht,* and *Zeit ohne Glocken* (1979; A Time without Bells), for which Bienek received the Wilhelm Raabe Prize, form part of a tetralogy projected for completion in 1981 about life in a small town on the German-Polish border in World War II. More traditional in style and format, the novels emphasize "lyric" and "meditative" passages along with action and dialogue. Other prizes Bienek has won include the Bremen Literary Prize (1969) and the Hermann Kesten Film Prize (1975). R.R.R.

Biermann, Wolf (1936–), East and West German poet and cabaret performer, was born in Hamburg of Jewish parents. His father, a Communist, died at Auschwitz. Biermann himself emigrated to East Germany in 1953, where in East Berlin he studied philosophy, economics, mathematics, and for a time taught aesthetics.

An acerbic, guitar-playing cabaret showman, Biermann was forbidden to make public appearances in 1962, having been charged with besmirching the party of the working classes (although he had himself been a candidate for membership in that party) and with singing obscene "sewer songs." The ban was lifted in 1963, and in 1964 Biermann toured West Germany, performing also in East Germany again. When the East German periodical *Neues Deutschland* again began a campaign against him in 1965, he was again forbidden to perform in public, but he sang at home and his songs and texts were circulated privately. In November 1976, Biermann was permitted to travel to Cologne to give a concert; during the performance the East German government announced he would not be permitted to return to East Berlin, which caused a furor among his friends and admirers there, resulting in the emigration to the West of dozens of writers, actors, artists, and other intellectuals, as well as the official censure of others for their publicly announced support of Biermann.

Biermann is the author of two stage works. "Köpenicker Brautgang," also called "Berliner Brautgang" (Köpenick Bridal Walk), written in 1964, has never been performed or published. His eight-act musical piece *Der Dra-Dra—die große Drachentöterschau* (The Dra-Dra—The Great Dragon-Slayer Show) was both published (1970) and performed (1971). In this song-filled play he attacks the dragons of the world, dragons being his metaphor for "parasitic power, exploitation, despotism, and counter-revolutionary terror." The Dra-Dra is one's own personal dragon, who is tamer and not as bestial as others. Other animals—pig, dog, donkey, cat—play social roles in the play, which features key political figures in thin disguise.

Biermann's first volume of poems (all to be sung) was *Die Drahtharfe* (1965; Eng. tr., *The Wire Harp,* 1968). It exemplifies the themes of his songs of protest and lament: the opposition of alienation (from one strongly alienated), excoriation of bureaucracy (a universal theme), criticism of witless proletarian goals, demanding self-analysis and self-criticism of the individual in a society filled with paradoxes. His own political stance has always been strongly Marxist, although he was ejected from the Communist Party for his strong individualistic views. His performances are in the tradition of Bertolt BRECHT and François Villon, vibrant voices against oppression and for freedom of opinion and expression. His texts are scornful, filled with puns and challenges, sung with dramatic effect and accompanied by now strident and now melodic chords on his guitar. They celebrate his favorite like-minded citizens of the world.

Mit Marx- und Engelszungen (1968; With Tongues of Marx and Engels [a pun on angels]) and *Für meine Genossen* (1972; For My Comrades), reveal a more bitter, isolated Biermann, with less irony than is customary. The effect of the denial of his citizenship in a land he loves with wrenching ambivalence is clear in his ironic *Nachlaß* (1977; Posthumous Works), emphasizing his solitary, outsider nature. Selected *Poems and Ballads* appeared in English translation in 1977.

See: P. Roos, ed., *Exil: Die Ausbürgerung Wolf Biermanns aus der DDR* (1977); *Über Wolf Biermann* (1977).

A.L.W.

Bigongiari, Piero (1914–), Italian critic, poet, and translator, was born in Navacchio (Pisa). He lives in Florence, where he is a professor of modern Italian literature. He is a leading exponent of hermeticism (*see* ITALIAN LITERATURE). In *L'elaborazione della lirica leopardiana* (1937; The Elaboration of Leopardi's Poetry, the latest ed. is *Leopardi*, 1962) and "Il critico come scrittore" (1938; The Critic as a Writer) in *Bargello*, he began to enunciate the premises of his poetically inspired but scientifically oriented criticism. He has elaborated on his hermetic poetics in works such as *Il senso della lirica italiana* (1952; The Meaning of Italian Lyric Poetry), *Poesia italiana del Novecento* (1965; Italian Poetry of the 20th Century), *Capitoli di una storia della poesia italiana* (1968; Chapters of a History of Italian Poetry), *Prosa per il Novecento* (1970; Prose for the 20th Century), and *La poesia come funzione simbolica del linguaggio* (1972; Poetry as a Symbolic Function of Language).

Calling his criticism "an art in its departure and a science in its arrival," Bigongiari insists on the relation between the creative and the critical acts. He stresses the interconnections of reason and fantasy, existence and essence, physics and metaphysics. In his poetry tangible things transcend themselves and are elevated to mythical dimensions. His volumes of poetry include *La figlia di Babilonia* (1942; The Daughter of Babylon), *Rogo* (1952; The Pyre), and *Il corvo bianco* (1955; The White Crow), now collected in *Stato di cose* (1968; State of Affairs), and *Le mura di Pistoia* (1958; The Walls of Pistoia), *Torre di Arnolfo* (1964; Arnolfo's Tower), and *Antimateria* (1972; Antimatter).

See: A. Noferi in *Letteratura italiana: i contemporanei*, vol. 3 (1975), pp. 763–79.

M.Ri.

Billetdoux, François (1927–), French playwright, was born in Paris. He studied at Charles DULLIN's Ecole d'Art Dramatique (1944) and the Institut des Hautes Etudes Cinématographiques (1945). In 1949 he became program director of the Radio-Télévision Française in Martinique. Billetdoux's success as a playwright was rapid, and his plays *Tchin-Tchin* (1959), *Le Comportement des époux Bredburry* (1960; The Behavior of the Bredburry Couple), *Va donc chez Törpe* (1961; Then Go to Törpe's), *Il faut passer par les nuages* (1966; You Must Pass through the Clouds), *Comment va le monde, Môssieu? Il tourne,*

Môssieu! (1972; How Goes the World, Mister? It Turns, Mister!), and *Les Veuves* (1972; The Widows) were well received. His more recent plays include *La Nostalgie, camarade* (1974; Nostalgia, Comrade).

A master of orthodox theatrical technique, Billetdoux fashions his plays with skill, leading us always forward to the climax and denouement. His style is taut and rapid; at once romantic and realistic; prosaic, yet with the counterforce of bold and tender images, frightening silences, and periods of delirium. Billetdoux never manipulates his creations; he lets them glide and talk willy-nilly, responding to their inner compulsions, revealing, as they converse, the grandeur and degradation of their personalities. He tries to remain objective, an outsider peering in, a doctor studying a patient through a microscope, or a botanist fascinated by the thousands of small lines and hollows in a piece of vegetable matter. Yet, in spite of his efforts at detachment, Billetdoux still looks upon his characters with humanity and compassion. *Tchin-Tchin* is a "love duet" that features two ordinary individuals who are unable to accept the reality of their situations. They indulge in a mirage that creates an atmosphere even more wretched than the reality they so desperately fear. *Va donc chez Törpe* brings to the stage characters who are not flesh-and-blood human beings, but shadows that hover about in a strange sensation-filled atmosphere. The plot is simple: in an unnamed country in central Europe, Mlle Törpe runs an inn where poets, artists, and businessmen seek refuge. Something strange occurs: five suicides take place within a period of several weeks. An inspector arrives to investigate, but the answers given him are bizarre and nebulous. He is unaware that the guests gather about Mlle Törpe, look up to her, confide in her, and love her. Each individual is a marked person, menaced, sensitive, and gracious, driven by longing and hopelessness as well as by feelings of revolt.

In *Il faut passer par les nuages* a rich old lady is pursued by her future inheritors. She decides to sell her possessions with the hope of creating a better relationship with her relatives. She fails and remains painfully alone. Her dreams of happiness have been transmuted into the cold, sharp, and hard diamonds she holds in her bag. This play, with a cast of 45 characters, "tells a whole life," declared Billetdoux, but it might also be considered an "analysis or balance-sheet of the Occidental bourgeoisie."

See: *Cahiers de la Compagnie Madeleine Renaud–Jean-Louis Barrault* 46 (1964); M. Corvin, *Théâtre nouveau* (1969); B. Knapp, *Off-Stage Voices* (1975), pp. 187–96.

B.K.

Binding, Rudolf Georg (1867–1938), German novelist and poet, was born at Basel, the son of the internationally famous jurist Karl Binding. He studied at Leipzig and Berlin, but instead of entering upon a professional career he devoted his time to horse racing and to travel, especially in Italy and Greece. A cavalry captain in World War I, he became mayor of a small town near Frankfurt am Main and died at Starnberg in Bavaria.

Binding was past the age of 40 when he began translating from Gabriele D'ANNUNZIO and cultivating the small genre (legends and short stories) in which he soon established himself as a master. Although there are traces of Goethe, Heinrich von Kleist, Gottfried Keller, and Stefan GEORGE in his works, he is essentially a literary self-made man, his real "educators" being his father, the Rhine, horses, the Hermes statue by Praxiteles, and nature itself. For Binding, writing combined romantic longing for the divine with the classical urge to embody the divine in human form. His small literary output excels in deep psychological insight, dramatic condensation, and musical language. Whether human or divine, his characters all have the same purity of soul, the same readiness for sacrifice, the same calmness in the presence of fate and death.

In the story collection *Legenden der Zeit* (1909; Legends of Time) inhabitants of heaven and earth meet in helpful understanding, as in "Coelestina," occasionally mocking each other about rigoristic dogmas, as in "St. Georgs Stellvertreter" (The Deputy of Saint George). The people in Binding's novellas live their religion through friendship, as in *Die Waffenbrüder* (1910; Comrades in Arms); love, as in *Die Vogelscheuche* (1910; The Scarecrow); and service, as in *Der Wingult* (1921). *Aus dem Kriege*, a diary written during World War I and published in 1925 (Eng. tr , *Fatalist at War*, 1929), is a courageous, realistic, prophetic, and chivalrous book. Binding's *Erlebtes Leben* (1928; A Life Lived), a classical autobiographical gem, is representative of a generation of writers in the search of the true meaning of their lives, who were tragically deceived by the "as if" values of the glittering but shallow Second Reich. In *Rufe und Reden* (1928; Summons and Speeches) Binding discussed the political and cultural problems resulting from World War I and warned the German people against increasing materialism, while in his *Antwort eines Deutschen an die Welt* (1933; Answer of a German to the World) he defended his people against foreign accusations. He achieved a lighter tone in the Apollonian lyric prose hymn *Reitvorschrift an eine Geliebte* (1924; Riding Instructions to a Beloved), the philosophical dialogues *Spiegelgespräche* (1933; Mirror Conversations), and the tragicomical anecdote *Wir fordern Reims zur Übergabe* (1935; We Demand Reims Surrender). In *Moselfahrt aus Liebeskummer* (1932; A Trip on the Mosel from Pangs of Love) he attempted a new form of the novella by embodying in a beautiful woman the character of a special landscape, thus making nature the real protagonist of the story. *Vom Leben der Plastik* (1933; On the Life of Sculpture) is a subtle interpretation of Georg Kolbe's sculptural work.

Although Binding wrote poetry, notably *Gedichte* (1914; Poems), *Stolz und Trauer* (1922; Pride and Sorrow), and *Sieg des Herzens* (1937; Triumph of the Heart), he earned his reputation through his legends, novellas, and autobiography.

See: L. F. Barthel, *Das war Binding: ein Buch der Erinnerung* (1955).   E.J. rev. A.L.W.

Bitov, Andrey Georgiyevich (1937–), Russian writer of fiction, was born in Leningrad, the son of an architect, and was educated there in the Institute of Mining Engineering. He began publishing at the end of the 1950s and attracted widespread critical attention with his first collection of short stories, *Bolshoy shar* (The Big Balloon), published in 1963. In this book, as in the short novels that are the title stories of his next two volumes, *Takoye dolgoye detstvo* (1965; Such a Long Childhood) and *Dachnaya mestnost* (1967; A Country Place), Bitov revealed the extraordinary talent for exploring the inner world of his characters that has led one American critic, Deming Brown, to call him "probably the most subtle psychologist among writers of his generation" in Russia.

Bitov's first full-length novel, *Pushkinskiy Dom* (Pushkin House) was finally published in the United States in 1978. It had been circulating at home in *samizdat* copies ever since 1970, when the author began trying vainly to have it printed by a Soviet press in complete and undistorted form. This brilliantly written, densely textured work is vibrant with echoes of the whole Russian literary and cultural heritage. In its broad philosophical treatment of basic human problems within the context of modern Russian culture, it marks the emergence of Bitov as a major figure among contemporary fiction writers of his generation in the Soviet Union.

See: D. Brown, *Soviet Russian Literature since Stalin* (1978), pp. 192–97; A. Gimeyn, "Nulevoy chas" [review of *Pushkinskiy Dom*], *Kontinent* 20 (1979): 369–73.
W.B.E.

Björling, Gunnar (1887–1960), Finland-Swedish poet, was born in Helsinki. He studied philosophy and was influenced by the ethical relativism of the Finnish sociologist Edward Westermarck. Later he drew some inspiration from the works of Friedrich NIETZSCHE, Henri BERGSON, and Bergson's contemporary Marie-Jean Guyon. Björling's first volume of poetry, *Vilande dag* (Restful Day), appeared in 1922. He published several subsequent books at his own expense, and not until the 1940s was he really noticed by the literary critics in Finland and Scandinavia.

Björling is the most complex and difficult of the Finland-Swedish modernists of the 1920s (*see* FINLAND-SWEDISH LITERATURE). He has some points of contact with contemporary Central European poetry—he once called his style "universalist dada-individualism"—and he averred interest in jazz and films. Crucial to his thinking was the idea of the endless flow of life. In his later poetry, this idea is also reflected in his style: the poet sometimes dismembers sentence after sentence so as to illustrate the unfinished or limitless nature of all being; the same words and phrases may be deliberately repeated, while some conjunctions may have no lexical function except to create a feeling of strangeness or to fill up space. To some extent, Björling could be compared with e. e. cummings, with whose poetry, however, he was not familiar when writing his poems between the wars.

Because of his continuous repetition of the same themes, Björling has no "principal" works in the accepted sense. A few of his numerous books may be mentioned—*Korset och löftet* (1925; The Cross and the Promise), *Solgrönt* (1933; Sungreen)—but he can best be studied in the selections he himself compiled before his death, such as *Du jord du dag* (1957; You Earth You Day), *En mun vid hand* (1958; A Mouth on a Hand), and *Hund skenar glad* (1959; Dog Bolts Gladly).

See: B. Holmqvist, *Modern finlandssvensk literatur* (1951); B. Carpelan, *Studier i Gunnar Björlings diktning 1922–1933* (1960); M. Enckell, *Det omvända anletet* (1969) and *Över stumhetens gräns* (1972).   K.L.

Bjørneboe, Jens (1920–76), Norwegian novelist, dramatist, and poet, was born in Kristiansand. He studied to be a painter, but for most of his life he lived near Oslo, working as a teacher and writer.

With the exception of four collections of traditional verse, which reveal a metaphysical, almost religious strain in his thinking, Bjørneboe's books bear witness to an intense social and political engagement. His first novel, *Før hanen galer* (1952; Before the Cock Crows), concerns two of the men engaged in the Nazi medical experiments in Germany during World War II. He describes with horrified fascination his characters' ability to combine the roles of loving father and husband with that of the cruel cynic in the laboratory. Man's capacity for cruelty continued to fascinate Bjørneboe, and he treats the theme with obsessive thoroughness in his trilogy on "the history of bestiality": *Frihetens øyeblikk* (1966; Eng. tr., *The Moment of Freedom*, 1975), *Kruttårnet* (1969; The Gunpowder Tower), and *Stillheten* (1973; The Silence). In these novels, Bjørneboe seeks to document man's history as an infinite process of cruelty; chilling accounts of atrocities are entered into the record kept by a court clerk whose own anguished reflections transform the novels into intensely human documents.

The years Bjørneboe had spent reading in preparation for his trilogy led him to accept an anarchistic view of the world: all institutions become tools in the hands of evil. In *Jonas* (1955; Eng. tr., *The Least of These,* 1960) and *Den onde hyrde* (1960; The Evil Shepherd), he seeks to show how institutional "care," in a boys' home and in a prison respectively, destroys defenseless young persons. In *Haiene* (1974; The Sharks), a novel about a sailing ship's last voyage, Bjørneboe again depicts the lurking brutality of man, but implicit in this account of a degrading life at sea is the faint hope that the destructiveness of Western individualism will be replaced by a new sense of common responsibility. Bjørneboe's dramas, such as *Til lykke med dagen* (1965; Many Happy Returns of the Day) and *Semmelweiss* (1969), are impassioned pleas for justice and compassion. In the play *Fugleelskerne* (1966; The Bird Lovers), he heaps scorching sarcasm on man's inability to commit himself to the truth.

Bjørneboe's role as a literary gadfly often embroiled him in controversies on moral and social issues, granting him a superficial celebrity that tended to overshadow his position as an artist. He was a writer of great skill, endowed with a poetic, if pessimistic, vision of human life.

See: J. M. Hoberman, "The Political Imagination of Jens Bjørneboe: A Study of *Under en hårdere himmel,*" *SS* 48, no. 1 (1976): 52–70; L. Mjøset, *Linjer i nordisk prosa—Norge 1965–1975* (1977), pp. 49–74.   K.A.F.

Bjørnson, Bjørnstjerne (1832–1910), Norwegian poet, novelist, and dramatist, was born in Kvikne and was raised in the Romsdal district. Of the "Big Four" Norwegian classic authors (Bjørnson, Henrik IBSEN, Jonas LIE, and Alexander KIELLAND), Bjørnson was the dominant voice during his lifetime. Since then, however, his fame has diminished in relation to the other three. Bjørnson made notable and original contributions in every literary genre, producing some 20 plays, 8 novels, numerous short stories, a volume of lyrical verse, and a cycle of epic poems. Besides his strictly literary output, he produced 2 volumes of articles, literary criticism, and political speeches, as well as some 17 volumes of letters. The sheer bulk of his nonliterary writings illustrates Bjørnson's commitment to the political and cultural development of his people. At times, his public involvement threatened to eclipse the artist within him, a fact that explains the uneven quality of his literary undertakings. At his best, Bjørnson created timeless works of immense vitality, with powerful imagery and vibrant poetry, but he also wrote banal exemplifications of moral and social teachings, works seriously flawed by his overriding concern with the instruction of the reader.

Those of Bjørnson's literary works that have become permanent classics include his incomparable peasant stories, some of his lyrical poetry, and a handful of superb plays. The peasant stories "Thrond" (1857), *Synnøve Solbakken* (1857; Eng. tr., *Trust and Trial,* 1858), *Arne* (1859), *En glad Gut* (1860; Eng. tr., *Ovind,* 1869), and "Faderen" (1860; The Father) derive from Bjørnson's intimate understanding of rural life dating from his childhood in western Norway. Combining features of the Bildingsroman, the pastoral, and the sentimental novel, these works generally deal with the problem of fusing instinct with self-mastery, and spontaneity with responsibility to the community. Akin to folk tale and medieval saga in language and style, they contributed immeasurably to the development of a uniquely Norwegian tradition of fiction. Alternating with fiction about peasant life,

Bjørnson penned a series of historical plays designed to show the cultural and spiritual continuity between the heroes of pre-Christian Norway and the people of the modern period. The best of these plays is the powerful trilogy *Sigurd Slembe* (1862; Eng. tr., 1888). Bjørnson's lyrics were published under the title *Digte og Sange* (1870; Eng. tr., *Poems and Songs,* 1915). A few of these are intimate and purely personal, while the bulk consists of songs and musical idylls (many have been set to music), romances built on saga motifs, occasional verse on domestic and public topics, as well as the national anthem. Some of Bjørnson's most enduring poetry may be found in the epic cycle *Arnljot Gelline* (1870).

From the start, Bjørnson made his public influence felt as a theater director, public speaker, and journalist, embracing aesthetic as well as most of the political, social, and moral questions of the day. But after 1863 this involvement became even more pronounced. His plays *En Fallit* (1875; Eng. tr., *The Bankrupt,* 1914), *Redaktøren* (1875; Eng. tr., *The Editor,* 1914), *Kongen* (1877; The King), and *En hanske* (1883; Eng. tr., *A Gauntlet,* 1886) proved controversial but highly effective in castigating the status quo. Bjørnson's reading of Hippolyte Taine, Ernest Renan, Charles Darwin, and others precipitated a religious crisis that caused him to reject Christian dogma. This crisis found expression in his greatest play, *Over Ævne* (1883; Eng. tr., *Pastor Sang,* 1893). Another dramatic masterpiece, *Paul Lange og Tora Parsberg* (1893; Eng. tr., 1899), which arose from Bjørnson's role in the political downfall and suicide of his one-time friend Ole Richter, is a scathing attack on political fanaticism and a plea for tolerance of the weak.

After 1890, Bjørnson was mostly concerned with the problems of industrialization, the search for international peace, and the defense of oppressed minorities and individuals, such as Alfred Dreyfus. Bjørnson received the Nobel Prize for Literature in 1903. His last notable play, the comedy *Når den ny vin blomstrer* (Eng. tr., *When the New Wine Blooms*) was published in 1909.

See: H. Noreng, *Bjørnsons dramatiske diktning* (1954); F. Bull, "Bjørnstjerne Bjørnson," *NLittH* 4, no. 2 (1963); H. Noreng, "Bjørnson Research: A Survey," *Scan* 4 (1965); P. Amdam, *Bjørnstjerne Bjørnson* (1978).

H.Se.

Bjørnvig, Thorkild (1918–), Danish poet and scholar, was born in the Jutland city of Århus. He has lectured at Danish universities. The chief motif of his first collection, *Stjærnen bag Gavlen* (1947; The Star behind the Gable), is Eros, described in the metamorphosis of young love: its rise, consummation, and destruction. In *Anubis* (1955), Bjørnvig explains that love is doomed because one's feelings are prevented by reflection from developing harmoniously. This tension between feeling and reflection dominates *Figur og Ild* (1959; Figure and Fire). The two collections prove Bjørnvig to be the foremost stylist of his generation, a classicist influenced by poets such as Helge RODE and Rainer RILKE. The next two volumes indicate an artistic development from the earlier prosodic tightness to a freer style, still unclarified in *Vibrationer* (1966; Vibrations) but brought to perfection in *Ravnen* (1968; The Raven). This last work is composed as a magnificent myth set in the region of the soul where the divided self reaches a momentary reconciliation and identity after experiencing crises of love and personality. In the 1970s, Bjørnvig came forth with a more timely production. The essay collection *Oprør mod neonguden* (1970; Revolt against the Neon God) is a critical analysis of trends within the rebellion of youth, whereas an increased interest in ecological problems is expressed in the poetry volume *Delfinen* (1975; The Dolphin). In a later collection, *Morgenmørke* (1977; Morning Darkness), Bjørnvig again turns inwards toward the sphere of his own personality, toward the identity theme as this is displayed in love and human interrelationship.

See: P. Dahl, *Thorkild Bjørnvig's tænkning* (1976).

S.H.R.

Blaga, Lucian (1895–1961), Romanian philosopher, poet, and dramatist, was born in Lancrăm, the ninth and last child of Isidore Blaga, a priest. He graduated from the Theological Faculty in Sibiu in 1917 and studied philosophy at the University of Vienna. In his first collection of poems, *Poemele Lumini* (1917; Poems of Light), Blaga uses light as a metaphor for an interior impulse, primary and divine. Blaga called his poetic technique "metaphysical traditionalism," a style in which images are synthesized by a mythological imagination. The gradual perfection of this technique can be seen in *Pasii profetului* (1921; In the Footsteps of the Prophet), *În marea trecere* (1924; The Great Passage), *Lauda somnului* (1929; In Praise of Sleep), *La cumpăna apelor* (1933; At the Water-Divide), and *La curţile dorului* (1938; In the Courts of Nostalgia). Beginning in 1921 he edited the journal *Gîndirea*, in which he published most of his philosophic work: *Trilogia cunoasterii* (3 vols., 1931–34; The Trilogy of Knowledge), *Trilogia culturii* (3 vols., 1935–37; The Trilogy of Culture); and *Trilogia valorilor* (3 vols., 1939–42; The Trilogy of Values). His most important dramas are *Zamolxe* (1921) and *Meşterul Manole* (1927; Master Manole). Like his poetry, Blaga's dramatic works purport to illustrate his philosophic system, which is, in essence, a type of intuitive, nonrational, spiritualistic agnosticism influenced by German inductive philosophy. Basically, however, this system is pure metaphor, poetry disguised as philosophy, and it is as such that it has become increasingly popular since his death.

See: C. S. Chrohmălniceanu, *Lucian Blaga* (1963); D. Micu, *Lirica lui Lucian Blaga* (1967); M. Bucur, *Blaga: dor şi eternitate* (1971).

V.A.

Blaman, Anna, pseud. of Johanna Petronella Vrugt (1905–60), Dutch novelist, short-story writer, and poet, was born in Rotterdam. She studied French and became a high school French teacher. Blaman began her literary career by publishing poetry in *Criterium* and *Helikon* but made her debut in the novel, the genre in which she was to become famous, with *Vrouw en vriend* (1941; Woman and Friend). This novel of love's disillusionment revealed the mastery of psychology that became characteristic of her work. It portrays the unsuccessful marriage of a writer, as does her second novel, *Eenzaam avontuur* (1948; Lonely Adventure). *Op leven en dood* (1954; Eng. tr., *A Matter of Life and Death,* 1974) is, to a certain extent, an autobiographical novel, but the author explores the relationships of the hero with his friends from an existential point of view, in a world flawed by loneliness and human inadequacy. In addition to two volumes of short stories, *Ram Horna* (1951) and *Overdag* (1957; During the Day), Blaman also published the novella *De kruisvaarder* (1950; The Crusader). *De Verliezers* (1960; The Losers) was her last, unfinished novel and reflects a fundamental attitude in her fiction, for she chose to be with Albert CAMUS's "victims." In 1957 she received the P. C. Hooft Prize.

See: C. Lührs, *Mijn zuster Anna Blaman* (1976).

S.L.F.

Blanchot, Maurice (1907–), French critic and novelist, was born in Quain. He is a contributor to the *Nouvelle*

Revue française and *Critique.* As a critic, Blanchot is less concerned with judging any particular book than with exploring the reasons that bring literature into being—its connection with the silence that precedes or even accompanies it. He conceives of literature as growing out of an "initial catastrophe" intimately affecting the world of the writer-to-be, an upheaval reflected in language itself as words lose their attributes as signs. While such a remark might have led to semiological investigations, Blanchot's reflections take a philosophical turn instead. He eventually recognizes criticism as a "modest activity; a useful accessory; sometimes a necessary betrayal." In his work, commonly accepted concepts such as hero, genius, masterwork, and even literature itself are stripped of their mystifying aura.

Blanchot's essays have been collected in *Faux-pas* (1943), *La Part du feu* (1949; Sacrifice to Save the Rest), *L'Espace littéraire* (1955; Literary Space), *Le Livre à venir* (1959; The Book to Come), *L'Entretien infini* (1969; The Infinite Conversation), and *L'Amitié* (1971; Friendship). *Comment la littérature est-elle possible?* (1942; How Is Literature Possible?) and *Lautréamont et Sade* (1949) are full-length essays.

Blanchot's fiction may be divided into two groups. The first, including *Thomas l'obscure* (1941; Thomas the Obscure), *Aminadab* (1942), *L'Arrêt de mort* (1948; The Sentence of Death), and *Le Très-haut* (1949; The Very High), shows surface resemblances to some of the works of Franz KAFKA and Samuel BECKETT. The second begins with a new, tightened version of *Thomas l'obscur* (1950), followed by *Au moment voulu* (1951; The Proper Moment), *Celui que ne m'accompagnait pas* (1952; He Who Did Not Accompany Me), *Le Dernier Homme* (1957; The Last Man), and *L'Attente l'oubli* (1962; Wait-Forgetfulness). Here stories have all but vanished, and the effect is similar to that produced by poetry. More and more, Blanchot uses what Emmanuel Levinas has called a "language of pure transcendence, without correlative," but one that cannot silence "the ancillary logos that follows its trail and never ceases to speak." Hence the tension and drama of the text. In a later work of fiction, *La Folie du jour* (1973; The Madness of the Day), he may be suggesting that only in madness can the logos be silenced. *Le Pas au-delà* (1973; The Step Beyond) brings together fiction and philosophical essay.

See: special issue of *Crit* 229 (1966); F. Collin, *Maurice Blanchot et la question de l'écriture* (1971); D. Wilhem, *Maurice Blanchot: la voix narrative* (1974).

L.S.R.

Blasco Ibáñez, Vicente (1867–1928), Spanish novelist, was born in Valencia, where his parents ran a corner grocery store. From modest beginnings he rose to the greatest international prominence known to any Spanish writer of his generation. The story of his life, as has often been suggested, reads like his best fiction. An ebullient man of action, he devoted his life to a diverse array of activities, writing and politics being his persistent and primary concerns. Restless even as a young man, he interrupted his study of law at the University of Valencia to go to Madrid in pursuit of his dream of becoming a writer. After several editors rejected his first manuscript, he settled for being secretary to Manuel Fernández y González, a famous author of serial novels whose rapid writing technique influenced Blasco's habits. While in Madrid, Blasco began his career as a political agitator by composing fiery speeches against the monarchy and the Roman Catholic Church and advocating the Republican cause. His political actions frequently landed him in jail and even caused him to be exiled to Paris in 1890. Upon returning to Valencia he founded a newspaper, *El Pueblo* (The People), a vehicle for his ideas into which he sank all his money. Again, the inflammatory tone of his articles created troubles for him: disputes, duels, jail, and another exile, this time to Italy. But along with the uninterrupted series of scandals, his popularity as a defender of the socially disadvantaged had grown tremendously, and it carried him to an elected seat in the Spanish Parliament in 1898.

The election did not slow his pace or prevent him from establishing a publishing house or meeting frequently with friends like the painter Joaquín Sorolla or the novelist Benito PÉREZ GALDÓS. He fought his duels and made the usual inflammatory speeches in Parliament. By the time he was reelected for the sixth time, in 1907, he had become disillusioned with politics. Looking for new horizons, he began to travel. He settled for a while in Argentina, where after giving some lectures he spent his energy on founding two cities, Cervantes and Nueva Valencia. Back in Europe at the outbreak of World War I, he defended the Allied cause with his characteristic ardor. His fiction also served the cause—in fact, these works catapulted him to international fame. His novels were translated in the United States, and after millions of copies had sold, the translations were adapted for the motion picture screen. In 1921, Blasco Ibáñez was the most famous writer in the world and also a millionaire. He moved finally to France, where he divided his time until his death between the so-called good life of traveling and gambling and his lifelong love of writing.

More than as a historian, essayist, playwright, or short-story writer, Blasco Ibáñez is remembered as a novelist. With a life as eventful as his, it is easy to see why his novels are notable not so much for their artistry or psychological finesse as for the mark of their author's passionate, restless spirit. His characters' personalities are often veiled by their actions or reflected by the individual's clash with his social milieu. It is this aspect, the creation of a social atmosphere, achieved with unparalled richness and vivacity, that makes him a master of description. Nor is it surprising that his social concerns surface in his novels, as he was the only Spanish writer who consistently and closely adhered to the deterministic philosophy of Emile ZOLA. This philosophy was rejected by the majority of his contemporaries, whose subscription to naturalism was usually confined to a greater or lesser use of its literary techniques. The novels of Blasco's first period exemplify his attitude. *Arroz y tartana* (1895; Eng. tr., *The Three Roses*, 1932), *Flor de mayo* (1896; Eng. tr., *The Mayflower*, 1921), *La barraca* (1898; Eng. tr., *The Cabin*, 1919), *Entre naranjos* (1900; Eng. tr., *The Torrent*, 1921), and *Cañas y barro* (1902; Eng. tr., *Reeds and Mud*, 1928) are all praiseworthy for their colorful and realistic depiction of his native Valencia, in its entirety: city, sea, and fertile countryside. The subsequent group of novels shows an evolution in Blasco's understanding of naturalism, for in them social aspects are emphasized more than determinism: *La catedral* (1903; Eng. tr., *The Shadow of the Cathedral*, 1919), *El intruso* (1904; Eng. tr., *The Intruder*, 1928), *La bodega* (1905; Eng. tr., *The Fruit of the Vine*, 1919), *La horda* (1905; Eng. tr., *The Mob*, 1929), and the best of the group, *Sangre y arena* (1908; Eng. tr., *Blood and Sand*, 1919), in which the colorful descriptions of his early works are retained and combined with a more poignant social message. These novels are extremely important in assessing Blasco's profile, for they display a novelist who has surpassed the 19th century and adopted the revolutionary attitude of 20th-century modernists such as the young Miguel de UNAMUNO or AZORÍN. Paradoxically, Blasco's late works—*Los cuatro jinetes del Apocalipsis* (1916; Eng. tr., *The Four Horsemen of the Apocalypse*, 1918) and *Mare Nostrum* (1918; Eng. tr.,

Our Sea, 1919)—although his most popular, are his weakest. They are a defense of the Allied cause in the form of war novels and have little literary value. Of even less interest are his last works, historical novels that attempt to underscore the contribution of Spanish culture to humanity. *El Papa del mar* (1925; Eng. tr., *The Pope of the Sea*, 1929) represents this type of fiction, which is quite alien to contemporary taste and sensibility.

See: J. L. León Roca, *Vicente Blasco Ibáñez* (1967); C. Blanco Aguinaga, *Juventud del 98* (1970); A. Grove Day and E. C. Knowlton, Jr., *V. Blasco Ibáñez* (1972).

G.Gu.

Bleiberg, Germán (1915-), Spanish poet and critic, was born and studied in Madrid. In 1961 he emigrated to the United States, where he currently teaches at the State University of New York.

His *Sonetos amorosos* (1936; Love Sonnets), written in the manner of Garcilaso de la Vega, the 16th-century poet, and acclaimed for their musicality and technical brilliance, established Bleiberg as a key figure of the Generation of 1936 and influenced the *garcilasista* movement of the early 1940s. In *Más allá de las ruinas* (1947; Beyond the Ruins), and later in *Selección de poemas, 1936-1973* (1975), he evolves into a poet who uses language in a manner similar to the surrealists but whose preoccupations are existentialist in nature. He has also written plays: *Sombras de héroes* (1937; Ghosts of Heroes), on the bombing of Guernica, and *La huída* (1938; The Escape), for which he shared the National Prize for Literature with Miguel HERNÁNDEZ.

Bleiberg's critical works range in subject from the picaresque novel to music and contemporary poetry. He has published several anthologies and has translated Novalis, Bjørnstjerne BJØRNSON, and Rainer Maria RILKE into Spanish. In addition, he is the editor of two standard reference works, *Diccionario de Literatura Española*, with J. Marías (1972), and *Diccionario de Historia de España* (3 vols., 1968-69).

See: C. D. Ley, *Spanish Poetry since 1939* (1962), pp. 31-34; E. I. Fox, "Germán Bleiberg: poeta de la existencia," *Symposium* (Summer 1968): 153-64.   E.I.F.

Blixen, Karen (1885-1962), pseuds. Isak Dinesen and Pierre Andrézel, Danish author, was born in northern Zealand. The daughter of the officer and writer Wilhelm Dinesen, she studied painting at the Copenhagen Academy of Fine Arts (1903-05) and made lengthy visits to Paris and Rome. From 1914 to 1931 she owned a coffee plantation in Kenya. Blixen became famous with *Seven Gothic Tales* (1934; Danish tr., *Syv fantastiske Fortællinger*, 1935), first published in the United States. It is a series of imaginative tales far removed from the social and critical realism of the Danish interwar period. Blixen was influenced by European and Oriental narrative art: the Bible, the *Arabian Nights*, the Icelandic sagas, the world classics, and the Danish romantics. Most of the tales have a cosmopolitan background or an aristocratic or historical milieu and are set in the 18th and 19th centuries, thus creating a fairy tale atmosphere that is combined with two main themes: Eros, in the descriptions of wistful but suppressed eroticism (for example, "The Monkey" and "The Supper at Elsinore") and the Dream, which is regarded as a pseudoexistence for people unable to realize their God-given role (for example, "The Dreamers"). After the autobiography *Den afrikanske Farm* (1937; Eng. tr., *Out of Africa*, 1938), describing her meeting with the nature and people of Africa, Blixen returned to her imaginative style with *Vinter-Eventyr* (1942; Eng. tr., *Winter's Tales*, 1942). Danish motifs are predominant in the stories, which are closer to modern times and more psychological; but Blixen's view of life remains the same. In her masterpiece, "Sorg-Agre" (Eng. tr., "Sorrow Acre, 1942), man is regarded as a marionette in the hands of God, subjected to his own personal destiny. After having published a thriller, *Gengædelsens Veje* (1944; Eng. trs., *The Angelic Avengers,* 1946, *Roads of Retribution,* 1947), Blixen reappeared in 1957 with a new impressive work, *Sidste Fortællinger* (Eng. tr., *Last Tales,* 1957), which, like "Sorg-Agre," deals with the necessity of accepting the rules of the human tragedy. This tragedy can be overcome through art, and both *Skæbne-Anekdoter* (1958; Eng. tr., *Anecdotes of Destiny,* 1958) and the posthumous story, *Ehrengard* (1963; Eng. tr., 1963), describe the relationship between life and art and the interference of fate.

While still living, Blixen received international recognition. She was outside of, or rather above, the main currents of contemporary literature; but she still influenced Danish and foreign writers, including Carson McCullers and Truman Capote. Technically, Blixen's stories are in part stylistic imitations, but her imagination is, nevertheless, modern: dreams are transformed into reality and vice versa, ideas are transposed into the paradoxical, and romanticism is destroyed by irony.

See: H. Brix, *Karen Blixen's Eventyr* (1949); R. Langbaum, *The Gayety of Vision* (1964); D. Hannah, *Isak Dinesen and Karen Blixen* (1971); T. R. Whissen, *Isak Dinesen's Aesthetics* (1973); N. M. Scholtz, "From Revenge to Reconciliation," *Scan* 12, no. 1 (1973): 27–36.

S.H.R.

Bloch, Jean-Richard (1886–1947), French writer and journalist, was born in Paris, where he also died after an eventful life. A historian by training, he soon turned to literature, contributing to the genres of novel, essay, drama, and poetry while pursuing pedagogical, journalistic, and political careers. A socialist during his youth and a Communist after 1921, Bloch constantly sought new trends that would lead literature away from formalism and "bourgeois refinements." In France he was one of the pioneers of "modern" realism and of art for the masses, which he defined as "the affirmation of a common thought of an entire people and of an entire class." Such art, he hoped, would help to eliminate oppression and promote the dignity of man.

Bloch's formative, socialist years are characterized by concern for social reality and a revolutionary optimism. These are reflected in his two volumes of stories, *Lévy* (1912) and *Les Chasses de Renaut* (1927; The Hunting Grounds of Renaut); in his essay *Carnaval est mort* (1921; Carnival Is Dead); in an exotic novel, *La Nuit kurde* (1925; Eng. tr., *A Night in Kurdistan,* 1931); and in his best-known novel, *. . . Et compagnie* (1918; Eng. tr., ". . . & Co.," 1930), which deals with the capitalist growth of a factory, the dehumanization of its owners, and the workers for whom the author foresees an optimistic future. World War I—in which he fought and was wounded three times—together with the Russian Revolution of 1917 mark the beginning of Bloch's second intellectual period. He experimented with various genres, dealing with colonial life in two travel accounts, *Sur un cargo* (1924; On a Tramp Steamer) and *Cacaouettes et bananes* (1928; Peanuts and Bananas); with new dramatic trends in the essay *Destin du théâtre* (1930; Destiny of the Theater); with problems of power, war, and revolution in the play *Le Dernier Empereur* (written 1919; The Last Emperor) and a collection of articles entitled *Espagne Espagne* (1936; Spain Spain); with the question of individual versus individualism in two essays, *Destin du*

siècle (1931; Destiny of the Century) and *Offrande à la politique* (1931; An Offering to Politics); with the masses and their uprisings in *Naissance d'une cité* (Birth of a City), staged as a mass spectacle in 1937; with the relationship between author and public in the essay *Naissance d'une culture* (1936; Birth of a Culture) and in the novel *Sybilla* (1932); and with the French Resistance in the play *Toulon* (1943).

In 1934, Bloch was a French delegate to the First Congress of Soviet Writers in Moscow, at which he was reprimanded for his "individualistic tendencies." Events after 1936 caused Bloch to intensify his political and journalistic activities. He worked and spoke against nonintervention, against fascism, and for Republican Spain; in 1937 he became codirector of the daily *Ce Soir,* and during the Nazi occupation he participated in the clandestine press. In 1941 Bloch left for the USSR, where he worked as a radio and newspaper journalist. In 1945 he returned to Paris, resumed codirectorship of *Ce Soir,* and was elected Conseiller de la République. Before his sudden death, he assembled his notes on the USSR into a book, *Moscou—Paris.* His posthumous publications include *De la France trahie à la France en armes* (1949; From France Betrayed to France in Arms), comprising his Radio Moscow reports, and an unfinished biography of Iosif Stalin. In 1950, Bloch was posthumously awarded the Gold Medal of France by the Communist-led World Peace Council.

See: special no. of *Europe* 446 (June 1966): 3–126.

J.Le. and H.Res.

Bloem, Jakobus Cornelis (1887–1966), Dutch poet and essayist, was born in Oudshoorn. He studied law at Utrecht, held a number of government positions, and was for a time an editor of *De Nieuwe Rotterdamse Courant,* one of the leading Dutch newspapers. He developed as a poet very slowly, and published his first poems in *De Beweging. Het verlangen* (1921; Longing) was his first volume of poetry, and remained the only one for some time. There is a note of longing in all his verse—for a vague happiness and love. Yet the failure to find fulfillment for this longing is not followed by despair, but by disillusionment and resignation. There are limits to life and to man's creative powers. While Bloem's early poetry was closely related to that of his contemporaries Gossaert and VAN EYCK, in *Media Vita* (1931; In the Middle of Life) and *De nederlaag* (1937; The Defeat), he moved away from neoclassicism and "inspired rhetoric," and came closer to Leopold than to Pieter BOUTENS. His poetry is autumnal and elegiac, and both volumes reveal a preoccupation with death. The poetic line is shorter, and the language is less classical and more direct. His skeptical attitude toward life is evident in the opening poem of *Sintels* (1945; Cinders), in which he asks whether "a handful of poems is enough to justify an existence." Bloem was influenced by both Charles BAUDELAIRE and Jean MORÉAS, as well as by A. E. Housman.

His later verse was more concise than his early poetry. Although Bloem was limited both in theme and in the volume of his work, he was a perfectionist, whose poems are always models of artistic technique. His poetry was published in a single volume as *Verzamelde gedichten* (1947; Collected Poems), which has been republished several times. In 1953, he won the P. C. Hooft Prize for *Avond* (1950; Evening). The last poem in *Afscheid* (1957; Farewell) speaks of a cyclical quality in life, in which things go on in the same way they always have, but there is still the awareness of mortality. Bloem was not a literary critic, but he has written some interesting essays about his own poetry and about other poets, whom he admired. Thus, his *Verzamelde beschouwingen* (1950; Collected Views) affords an insight into his own work and his literary credo.

See: J. Kamerbeek, *De poëzie van Jakobus Cornelis Bloem in Europees perspectief* (1967); A. L. Sötemann, *Over de dichter Jakobus Cornelis Bloem* (1974).

S.L.F.

Blok, Aleksandr Aleksandrovich (1880–1921), Russian poet, is considered the greatest of the Russian symbolists. He was the son of A. L. Blok, a professor of law at Warsaw University (a Russian, but with some German ancestors), and Aleksandra Beketova, daughter of the rector of Petersburg University. Blok's parents separated shortly after his birth, and he was brought up in the Beketov household until his mother's remarriage (when he was nine). Most of his life was spent in Petersburg, which later became the setting of his urban poetry, with summers on the Beketov estate called "Shakhmatovo," near Moscow, which inspired his nature lyrics. Blok attended a gymnasium in Petersburg and then matriculated at the university there, first studying law, then philology, and graduating in 1906. The great chemist Dmitry Mendeleyev had an estate near Shakhmatovo, and Blok had a childhood romance with his daughter, Lyubov, which eventually led to marriage (1903). The marriage, incidentally, was not a happy one.

Encouraged by his relatives (his grandmother, mother, and aunts were all writers or translators), Blok began writing verse very early—neoromantic lyrics inspired by such standard 19th-century authors as Vasily Zhukovsky, Afanasy Fet, Konstantin Sluchevsky, and Yakov Polonsky; "modernist" trends reached him only later. A profound influence was the poetry and other writings of Vladimir SOLOVYOV in which Blok found mystical revelation. Blok dated his serious career as a poet from 1897, but he began to publish only in 1903. His first volume of poetry, *Stikhi o prekrasnoy dame* (Verses About the Beautiful Lady) was published in 1904. (In his three-volume collected verse published in 1911–12, however, Blok placed before the poems of this collection a body of verse written earlier, given the title "Ante lucem.") In the "Beautiful Lady" cycle the poet represents himself as a humble "acolyte" or even "slave" in the service of an elusive female deity more or less identified with the "divine wisdom" celebrated by Solovyov. The relationship, although sometimes ecstatic, is often frustrating and humiliating, with threats of betrayal on both sides. A mood of disillusionment and mockery gains intensity in Blok's next period, 1902–04, in which the cycle of poems later given the title "Rasputya" (Crossroads) was written. Urban motifs also make an appearance in these poems which were partly influenced by Valery BRYUSOV's *Urbi et orbi*. Blok's ironic disillusionment reaches its peak in the play *Balaganchik* (1906; Eng. tr., *The Puppet Show*, 1963), a brilliant and poignant satire on "Petersburg mysticism." Earlier Blok had been cast by some younger poets, notably Andrey BELY, in the role of a prophet, and Blok's wife had been cast as a veritable incarnation of divinity. Thus to Bely, *Balaganchik* seemed a blasphemous betrayal—one of the many twists in the tortuous *odi-et-amo* relationship of these two extraordinarily gifted men.

Blok's next two volumes of verse were *Nechayannaya radost* (1907; Unexpected Joy) and *Zemlya v snegu* (1907; The Earth in Snow). The former includes the cycle "Puzyri zemli" (Bubbles of the Earth), in which quaint motifs from folk demonology were utilized, and the longer poem "Nochnaya fialka" (Night Violet), an evocative narration of an actual dream. Many of the poems in *Zemlya v snegu* (in the collected verse regrouped as the cycles "Snezh-naya maska" [Snow Mask] and "Faina") were inspired by Blok's whirlwind romance with the actress Natalya Volokhova.

In the field of drama, *Balaganchik* was followed by *Korol na ploshchadi* (1907; Eng. tr., *The King in the Square*, 1934), a not wholly successful attempt to deal symbolically with the theme of political power; *Neznakomka* (1907; The Stranger), which, like Blok's famous lyric of the same title (1906), evokes the goddesslike female presence in a debased setting of vulgarity and sexuality; and *Pesnya sudby* (1909; Eng. tr., *The Song of Fate*, 1938), in which the hero-poet is torn between his pure wife, associated with an ivory tower, and the cruel gypsy Faina, representing the real Russian world. Blok's most substantial, though not necessarily greatest, work for the theater is *Roza i krest* (1913; Eng. tr., *The Rose and the Cross*, 1936), in which his persistent themes of erotic ambivalence and mystical quest are realized in a medieval French setting.

During the years 1907 to 1916, Blok attained full maturity as a lyric poet. The mood of the dazzling and immensely powerful poems written in this period, however, is one of abysmal depression. Among the poem cycles are "Strashny mir" (A Frightful World), "Plyaski smerti" (Dances of Death), and "Chornaya krov" (Black Blood). In 1909, Blok and his wife traveled in Italy, a trip that evoked a fine cycle of culture poems; and in 1913, Blok's affair with the singer Lyubov Delmas inspired a new cycle of passionate lyrics ("Carmen"). In this period, the themes of history and national destiny also become prominent, both in verse, such as the cycle "Rodina" (Native Land), which includes "Na pole Kulikovom" (On the Field of Kulikovo), and in prose essays, such as "Narod i intelligentsiya" (1909; The People and the Intelligentsia) (*see* RUSSIAN LITERATURE). National destiny is also the subject of Blok's iambic epic *Vozmezdiye* (unfinished; written 1910–21; Retribution), in which, against a sharply etched historical background, he grappled with the subject of Russian guilt for the oppression of Poland. Another long poem of this period is the haunting fable *Soloviny sad* (1915; Nightingale Garden).

In 1916, Blok was called up for the army, but served only in civil defense forces near Pinsk. In March 1917, he returned to Petrograd and was appointed secretary of the provisional government's commission for interrogating the last tsarist ministers. Blok greeted both 1917 Revolutions apocalyptically, as the dawn of a new era in human history. His last burst of poetic inspiration came in the first months of 1918, when he wrote "Dvenadtsat" (Eng. tr., "The Twelve," 1920) and "Skify" (The Scythians). The former, his masterpiece, portrays 12 Red Guardsmen led by a symbolic Christ into scenes of revolutionary chaos and violence. "The Scythians" is an exercise in poetic rhetoric on the subject of Russia versus Europe, partly inspired by the ideas of the Left Socialist Revolutionaries.

In his last years, Blok wrote little. He served on various editing and theatrical commissions and as head of the Petrograd branch of the Union of Poets. But the light of inspiration had gone out; the "music" had ceased. Blok's health, both mental and physical, deteriorated; and on Aug. 7, 1921, he died of "psychesthenia" and heart disease. Besides his verse and plays, Blok left a considerable body of prose essays and reviews.

See: C. H. Kisch, *Alexander Blok, Prophet of Revolution* (1960); F. D. Reeve, *Alexander Blok: Between Image and Idea* (1962); R. Kemball, *Alexander Blok: A Study in Rhythm and Metre* (1965); L. E. Vogel, *Aleksandr Blok: The Journey to Italy* (1973); S. Hackel, *The Poet and the Revolution* (1975); A. Pyman, *The Life of*

Aleksandr Blok: A Biography, vol. 1, *The Distant Thunder (1880–1908)* (1979). H.McL.

Blondel, Maurice (1861–1949), French philosopher, was born in Dijon into a traditional Catholic family. He was educated at the local lycée and at the faculty of letters in his native city, obtaining his bachelor's degree as well as a licentiate in letters and law. Selected as one of the candidates for the Ecole Normale Supérieure, he went to Paris, where he studied under Léon Ollé-Laprune. Blondel's deep Catholic faith, stimulated and encouraged by Ollé-Laprune's equally intense faith, opened the line of philosophical investigation that was to become his life's work, namely, to revitalize Catholic thought by aligning it with the advances made since the early days of scholasticism. The result of his inquiry was to become an alternative to Thomism.

In 1893, Blondel presented his thesis at the University of Paris, entitled "L'Action: essai d'une critique de la vie et d'une science de la pratique" (Action: Toward a Critique of Life and a Science of Practice). As the title suggests, he proposed a philosophy of action that tended to reconcile intellectualism and pragmatism and to bridge the differences between science and religion. The term "action" is used here in a very broad sense. It does not mean simply the act itself but includes the entire existential, concrete, and human conditions surrounding the will and the accompanying opening of the will. By his very nature, man must act, and he does so constantly by making moral, political, social, and artistic choices. Man must also question his acts as to their meaning and responsibility in the face of life. Between the act and its fulfillment, however, there is always a gulf. In order to bridge this gulf, man by his voluntary action seeks fulfillment in the order of phenomena. This order does not contain sufficient values to satisfy the will. The result is a constant enlargement of action into other areas. Sooner or later, the imperatives of action will lead man beyond the order of phenomena to the discovery of the "supraphenomenal" or the transcendent, a discovery that must lead to the supernatural if man is truly consistent with himself. Action, then, becomes the basis of the moral ideal as well as of religious belief. The highest form of action, "penser à Dieu" (to contemplate God), includes and contains all others. Everything in the existential and concrete order calls for the supernatural and tends to it to such a degree that reason cannot dismiss it as a mere superfluity.

Blondel's thesis stirred up a great deal of controversy. Scientism, positivism, and conceptualistic rationalism dominated the field of philosophy, especially at the University of Paris. "L'Action," with its accent on the concrete, on commitment, on involvement, and on options following the study of personal action, constituted a serious attack on formalism. A practical result of his thesis was a delay in receiving an appointment to a teaching position in a state university. Normally, this would have been done immediately after the defense, but because of the nature of Blondel's thesis, it was not until 1895 that he was assigned to lecture at Lille. The following year, he received a professorship at Aix-en-Provence, where he taught until 1927. Plagued by fragile health and failing eyesight, Blondel went into active retirement in 1929. Yet although his brilliant teaching career was curtailed, he entered into an intensely active writing period that lasted for 20 years. During that time, he dictated 10 major volumes, including his trilogy: *La Pensée* (1934; Thought), *L'Etre et les êtres* (1935; Being and Beings), and *L'Action* (1937).

Blondel's orthodoxy was never really in question, even though he was accused of modernist leanings. In 1944 there appeared the first volume of *La Philosophie et l'esprit chrétien* (Philosophy and the Christian Spirit). The book came to the attention of Pope Pius XII, who sent him warm and encouraging praise in a message transmitted by the papal secretary, Msgr Montini, later Pope Paul VI. This accolade from Rome dispelled any doubt as to the philosopher's orthodoxy while also pointing out his contributions to 20th-century Catholic thought. Blondel died in 1949 in Aix-en-Provence just as he was preparing the third volume of *La Philosophie*.

See: H. Duméry, *Raison et religion dans la philosophie de Blondel* (1963); C. Tresmontant, *Introduction à la metaphysique de Maurice Blondel* (1963); J. M. Somerville, *Total Commitment: Blondel's "L'Action"* (1968).

J.D.G.

Bloy, Léon-Marie (1846–1917), French novelist and essayist, was born in Périgueux. An intransigent Catholic writer, he earned the reputation of a polemist with the publication of *Le Pal* (1885; The Stake), *Les Dernières Colonnes de l'église* (1903; The Last Pillars of the Church), and *Belluaires et Porchers* (1905; Beast-Tamers and Swineherds). With Charles PÉGUY, Paul CLAUDEL, and Georges BERNANOS, Bloy is one of the four prophetical writers who contributed to the flowering of a Catholic renewal in French letters.

Bloy's work cannot be understood apart from his life and personality. While still very young, he went to Paris to become a writer. Here years of poverty, hardship, and tragedy ensued, leaving indelible traces upon his mind and work. His two novels, *Le Désespéré* (1886; The Desperate Man) and *La Femme pauvre* (1887; Eng. tr., *The Woman Who Was Poor,* 1939), are essentially autobiographies, utilizing many details of his personal experiences. For example, Marchénoir's liaison with the visionary Véronique Cheminot reflects Bloy's own relationship with Anne-Marie Roulé, a young Bretonne whose last years were spent in an insane asylum, while Marchénoir's friendship with Clotilde Maréchal is modeled on Bloy's friendship with Berthe Dumont, who died of tetanus poisoning. In the later chapters of *La Femme pauvre,* the character Clotilde also incorporates aspects of Jeanne Molbech, Bloy's wife and the daughter of a Danish poet.

The journal of Léon Bloy, his running diary, comprising eight volumes, includes *Le Mendiant ingrat* (1898; The Ungrateful Beggar), *Le Pèlerin de l'absolu* (1914; Pilgrim of the Absolute), and *La Porte des humbles* (1920; Gateway of the Humble), the last published posthumously. His voluminous correspondence has been issued as *Lettres de jeunesse* (1920; Youthful Letters), *Lettres à sa fiancée* (1922; Eng. tr., *Letters to His Fiancée,* 1937), *Lettres à ses filleuls* (1928; Letters to his Godchildren), and *Lettres à Véronique* (1933). The best of Bloy is found in these volumes of correspondence, his two novels, and a small volume entitled *Le Salut par les Juifs* (1892; Salvation through the Jews), a meditation on the destiny of Israel in the divine plan.

In his revolt against the turpitude and injustice of the world, Bloy momentarily became an active atheist and socialist, but under the influence of Barbey d'Aurevilly, his friend and literary mentor, he returned to his faith. The vehemence, bitterness, and scorn so often condemned in his work are, in fact, the outcry of a man of sorrow overwhelmed by the spectacle of a society indifferent to its spiritual destiny. This outlook is evident in *Propos d'un entrepreneur de démolitions* (1884; Words of a House-Wrecker) and *Le Sang du pauvre* (1909; The Blood of the Poor). By nature a poet, totally oriented toward absolute values and intolerant of mediocrity, he sought through verbal violence to awaken his contemporaries to the reality of the supernatural combat in which their lives were involved. In his intemperate attacks on his fellow creatures, Bloy so antagonized both Catholics and non-Catholics that his work suffered from a conspiracy of silence. Yet many of his pages, for sheer power of language and poetic beauty, will always rank among the finest in French literature. Today, he has his admirers and might be considered to be the object of a cult.

See: J. Maritain, *Quelques Pages sur Léon Bloy* (1927); A. Béguin, *Léon Bloy l'impatient* (1944; Eng. tr., *Léon Bloy: A Study in Impatience,* 1947); J. Bollery, *Léon Bloy: essai de biographie,* 3 vols. (1947–54); J. Petit, *Léon Bloy* (1966); R. E. Hager, *Léon Bloy et l'évolution du conte cruel: ses "Histoires désobligeantes"* (1967).　　R.E.H.

Blum, Léon (1872–1950), French statesman and literary critic, was born in Paris into a Jewish family of Alsatian origin. He was the leading French socialist after Jean JAURÈS. Like Jaurès, Blum was originally a writer and identified with the "socialism of the intellectuals," often in opposition to the socialism of the working classes. Unlike Jaurès, however, Blum was cosmopolitan, trained in law, and a frequenter of artistic circles. Moreover, Blum experienced the extremes of supreme power and imprisonment—only to return to power and then find himself disowned by his own party.

Although he was admitted to the Ecole Normale Supérieure in 1890, Blum was expelled the next year because of two failures at the *licence* degree. At this time, his principal interest was literature, and he contributed poetry to several reviews, collaborating with André GIDE and Pierre LOUŸS on *La Conque* (1891); with Fernand Gregh, Daniel HALÉVY, and Marcel PROUST on *Le Banquet* (1892); and with Félix FÉNÉON, Octave MIRBEAU, Jules RENARD, Tristan Bernard, Alfred Capus, and the Natanson brothers on *La Revue blanche* (1894).

In 1895, Blum resumed his legal studies and entered the Conseil d'Etat. Under the influence of Lucien Herr, whom he had known at the Ecole Normale, Blum progressed from literary anarchism to militant socialism. It was the time of the Dreyfus Affair. In 1899, Blum represented the Groupe de l'Unité Socialiste at the Japy convention. At this point, Blum was not a Marxist; he criticized the "weak links" in Marx's economic doctrine and called his metaphysics "mediocre." In 1901, Blum published *Congrès ouvriers et socialistes français* (French Workers and Socialists Congresses).

Despite his political activities, Blum still devoted a large part of his time to literature. In 1902 he wrote a two-act play, *La Colère* (Anger). Less rationalistic than many of his friends, he appreciated both Paul CLAUDEL and Georges de PORTO-RICHE. He denounced the conformity of the Conservatoire d'Art Dramatique and of the Comédie-Française, and he approved the innovations of the younger theatrical producers. Blum wrote literary and dramatic columns for various newspapers, including *L'Humanité, Le Matin, L'Excelsior,* and *Comœdia.* In 1901 he anonymously published *Nouvelles Conversations de Goethe avec Eckermann* (New Conversations of Goethe with Eckermann), placing into Goethe's mouth opinions that were really his own. For example, *Nouvelles Conversations* stated that history is made by men who awaken the critical sense and provide syntheses for specialists (like Lucien Herr) who are themselves incapable of making them. Among Blum's other publications of this period is *Du mariage* (1907; Eng. tr., *Marriage,* 1950). Developing the idea that women and men pass through a period of polygamy before becoming ready for monogamy, Blum advised many experiments before entering into marriage; the work caused a scandal. In 1914

he published *Stendhal et le Beylisme,* in which he analyzed contradictions in Stendhal that perhaps also pertained to Blum himself: romanticism and the critical spirit, passion and objectivity. The work marks a kind of farewell to youth for this French critic.

World War I plunged Blum into political action and put a permanent end to his nonpolitical writing. From *chef de cabinet* of Marcel Sembat, the minister of public works (1914–16), Blum advanced to important positions in the Socialist Party, was elected deputy for Paris, became leader of the Socialist group in the Chamber of Deputies, and assumed the editorship of the Socialist daily *Le Populaire.* In 1936, he summarized his political experience in *La Réforme gouvernementale.* When the Popular Front was formed with Communist support that same year, he became prime minister. After the fall of the Popular Front, Blum remained in parliament and, at the defeat of France in 1940, voted against giving "full powers" to Marshal Pétain. Imprisoned, he was brought to trial in Riom for his alleged responsibility for the defeat, but he defended himself with such intelligence, skill, and courage that the trial was interrupted and never resumed.

While in prison, Blum wrote *A l'échelle humaine* (Eng. tr., *For All Mankind,* 1946), in which he called the Communist Party the "National Foreign Party." In March 1943, Blum was deported to Buchenwald, from which he was liberated in 1945. He returned to his position as editor of *Le Populaire,* but he was no longer in control of the Party, which was now suffering political defeat. In 1947, President Vincent Auriol invited Blum to form a cabinet to set up the Fourth Republic, but he failed to receive a majority in parliament. His career now over, Blum lived for three more years.

See: J. Colton, *Léon Blum* (1966); G. Ziebura, *Léon Blum et le parti socialiste: 1872–1966* (1967); special Blum no. of *RevS* (September 1975).　　G.L.

Bobrowski, Johannes (1917–65), East German poet and novelist, was born at Tilsit in East Prussia, the son of a railroad official. Raised close to the Lithuanian border with its mixed population of Germans, Poles, Lithuanians, and Jews, he was confronted early with concrete aspects of Germany's historical guilt toward her eastern neighbors. Acceptance of this guilt and atonement for it became his "theme," as were the pleas for communication and mutual respect for the other's humanity. His concept of tolerance was profoundly shaped by the intellectual tradition of Königsberg, the city of Immanuel Kant, Johann Gottfried Herder, and Friedrich Klopstock, where he moved with his family in 1928: it meant an active interest in the other's cultural-social existence, an informed appreciation of his "otherness." Learning to understand and use the complexity of his own cultural tradition—the discipline of classical prosody, the precise exuberance of baroque polyphony were to have marked influence on his poetry with its subtle and sophisticated use of the ode form and musical structures like counterpoint—proved to be excellent preparation for his understanding of the political and cultural necessity of coexistence.

A talented musician—Bobrowski had studied the organ, concentrating on the great masters of the baroque period—and interested in art and art history, which he studied at Berlin University before World War II, he started to write poetry under the influence of the experience of the Russian landscape in the winter of 1943–44, not because of the impact of an enormous elementary landscape alien and hostile to human beings but rather because it was a landscape expressive of the destruction people brought upon each other.

A prisoner of war until 1949, from 1952 on Bobrowski worked as an editor for East Berlin publishing houses, maturing as a writer. His poetry appeared first in journals, then in the collected volumes *Sarmatische Zeit* (1961; Sarmatian Time), *Schattenland Ströme* (1962; Eng. tr., *Shadow Land*, 1966), *Wetterzeichen* (1966; Sign of Storm), and *Im Windgesträuch* (1970; In the Tumbleweed of Wind)—the last two posthumously collected and published. The first two collections brought him immediate success: The unmistakably original poetic cosmos of Sarmatia, reconstruction of the country between the Vistula and Memel rivers, appeared highly controlled with its modified sapphic and alcaic ode forms and strikingly sensuous nature imagery, yet the poetry was curiously accessible. More than any other author of the German Democratic Republic (GDR), Bobrowski found an enthusiastic audience in the West. GDR criticism has stressed his involvement with the problem of people's social existence, the socialist quality of his humanistic Christianity, and his concern with Germany's guilt-ridden past. Both perspectives are needed to do justice to his achievement.

Bobrowski saw the poet as a potentially effective historiographer because of his special gift for the preservation of the particular. One cannot ask poetry to bring about change, "a time without fear," yet it is of the utmost importance that a poet's communication with his reader be a dialogue and that it be convincing. Creating the everyday language and gestures of the Sarmatian people interacting with the Sarmatian landscape, the poet is aware that he is dealing with human beings in the 10th millennium of their history, born with the same passions—leading to social guilt—as in a two-year-old. Like Herder, Bobrowski saw such guilt as a lack of understanding of the diversity of cultural achievement. His poetry was meant to create a willingness to undertake the adventure of diversity; verbal images, their systems and rhythms, cannot be self-sufficiently beautiful; their beauty has to be sustained by their elation to the world of experience shared by the poet and the reader.

The need to integrate mutuality in the basic structures of poetic language led Bobrowski to a medium that accommodates a variety of speakers with greater ease and precision, narrative prose. The novels *Levins Mühle* (1964; Eng. tr., *Levin's Mill*, 1970) and *Litauische Klaviere* (1966; Lithuanian Pianos) and the short stories collected in *Boehlendorff und Mäusefest* (1965; Boehlendorff and Feast of Mice) and *Der Mahner* (1967; Eng. tr., *I Taste Bitterness*, 1970) occupied his last years much more than lyric poetry. *Levins Mühle*, the best known of his prose texts, develops the social complexity and ambiguity of guilt—its clearly disastrous consequences for the social fabric. Turbulent and inconsistent, lucid in its concentration on the confused experience of social relations in inarticulate daily speech, the novel ends on a cautiously hopeful note, in contrast to the more pessimistic *Klaviere*, where the author despairs of bringing together Germans and Lithuanians in the face of the rising power of the Nazis.

See: B. Keith-Smith, *Johannes Bobrowski* (1970); G. Rostin, *Johannes Bobrowski: Selbstzeugnisse und neue Beiträge über sein Werk* (1975). D.B.

Bodelsen, Anders (1937–), Danish novelist, journalist, and critic, was born in Frederiksberg, near Copenhagen. His first important work, *Drivhuset* (1965; The Hothouse), with its 14 detective stories and precise pictures of the welfare state, contains those two elements that dominate his later production. In "Rama Sama" (1967; Eng. tr., 1973), Bodelsen penetrates the realistic milieu that forms the outer shell in his works and discovers a series of

dangerous forces that threaten human beings. The realistic novel is subtly combined with the thriller in two novels published in 1968, *Hændeligt uheld* (Eng. trs., *Hit and Run, Run, Run*, 1970; *One Down*, 1970) and *Tænk på et tal* (Eng. tr., *Think of a Number*, 1969), and with science fiction in *Frysepunktet* (1969; Eng. tr., *Freezing Point*, 1971). *Hjælp* (1971; Help) contains short stories about the condition of people in modern society, which in *Straus* (1971; Eng. tr., 1974) is depicted as competitive and success demanding, producing the ruin of a writer. In *Alt hvad du ønsker dig* (1974; All That You Desire), however, the main character tries to escape this society by using magic, but the concluding moral of this modern tale is that reality has to be accepted as it is. This is also demonstrated in *De gode tider* (1977; The Good Times) and its sequel *År tor år* (1979; Year by Year) which treat the economic boom of the 1960s, as well as the younger generation's increasingly radical discussions about politics and economic systems, in a rather didactic way. Because of his contemporary themes and fluent journalistic style, Bodelsen is one of the most widely read authors in Scandinavia. S.H.R.

Böðvarsson, Guðmundur (1904–74), Icelandic novelist, short-story writer, essayist, and poet, was born in the parish of Hvítársíða in the Borgarfjörður district of western Iceland, where his parents ran a farm. His father died while the boy was still young, and lack of means prevented Böðvarsson from receiving any formal education, but he was brought up by the local clergyman in a cultured home where he had the chance to read literature—and through his own efforts he became a well-educated man. Except for three years late in life, Böðvarsson always lived in the parish of his birth, long operating the farm where he had been born.

His first book was a collection of verse entitled *Kysstu mig sól* (1936; Kiss Me, Sun); it was to be followed by nine other volumes of poetry besides collected editions. He also published a novel, *Dyr í vegginn* (1958; Door in the Wall), and three collections of short stories and narratives, in addition to translating *Tólf kviður úr Divina Commedia* (1968; Twelve Cantos from Dante's *Divine Comedy*).

Böðvarsson's first few books of poetry are dominated by the light lyrical style that had come to the fore in Iceland after 1920. Although his earliest poems show the influence of such figures as Tómas GUÐMUNDSSON and Steinn STEINARR, Böðvarsson soon evolved his own distinctive voice, and his style developed towards freer, more concentrated modernistic forms.

Ideologically, he allied himself from the start with the generation of radical socialists among Icelandic poets who placed their mark on the 1930s, and he is in many ways an author reminiscent of Stephan G. STEPHANSSON, the Icelandic-Canadian who was also a lifelong farmer, poet, socialist, and pacifist.

Although Böðvarsson spent his life in the region of his birth, his works are international in outlook; events in the larger world—the Spanish Civil War, World War II, the use of the atomic bomb, and the Cold War—all left a deep impression on him. Still his poems are, above all, notable for the author's close communion with Icelandic nature—a subject he did not approach as a romantic visitor, but rather as he had experienced it within himself in his life as a farmer. The conflicting forces of nature—its life-giving elements and power of destruction—are revealed in simple, easily grasped pictures and given depth because of Böðvarsson's nearness to the subject. Caution and thoughtfulness—also the traits of a farmer—can also be perceived in his poetry, although sometimes in the guise of sorrow over lost opportunities. Always a skeptic at heart, he, nevertheless, typically resolved his doubts in the end through his unshakable faith in the power of life.

Böðvarsson composed many protest poems attacking war and power plays on the international scene. He was an adamant Icelandic nationalist and hence saw the presence of foreign troops in Iceland as a betrayal of the most sacred principles of Icelandic nationality.

Despite the fact that Böðvarsson's poetry grew more skeptical and pessimistic with the years, his stability and balance enabled him to avoid complete estrangement and despair; instead, he confronted the problems of life, as he saw them, uncomplainingly and thoughtfully, thus exhibiting a brave, yet modest, philosophy of life—a stance he gave expression to in poems of extraordinary rhythmic softness.

See: S. Hólmarsson, "Um Guðmund Böðvarsson og skáldskap hans," in G. Böðvarsson, *Ljóðasafn*, vol. 1 (1974), pp. 7–22.   S.S.H.

Bojer, Johan (1872–1959), Norwegian novelist, was born and raised in Rissa, near Trondheim. His first works were published in the 1890s, but he established himself as a writer only with *Troens magt* (1903; Eng. tr., *The Power of a Lie*, 1908), a work that received considerable attention both in Norway and France because it appeared at the time of the Dreyfus Affair. Bojer treated the theme of *Troens magt*, corruption and self-deception in political circles, in several other books as well.

It was with the novel *Fangen som sang* (1913; Eng. tr., *The Prisoner Who Sang*, 1924), that Bojer reached his full artistic maturity. With psychological insight and artistic abandon, he depicts the life of the gifted but spineless Andreas Berget, a man who squanders his life. Bojer's most significant novels, *Den siste viking* (1921; Eng. tr., *Last of the Vikings*, 1923) and *Folk ve sjøen* (1929; Eng. tr., *Folk by the Sea*, 1931; American title, *The Everlasting Struggle*, 1931), are accounts of the hard life of the common people on the coast of northern Norway. Although they are faced with poverty and catastrophes, the people of these barren lands never lose their humanity. In these novels, Bojer observes the perseverance of the human spirit, not with sentimentality, but rather with admiration and sometimes with awe.

Bojer acquired a large, admiring reading public abroad, not least in the United States, and his account of the Norwegian pioneer, *Vor egen stamme* (1924; Eng. tr., *The Emigrants*, 1925), belongs among the classics of European emigrant novels. He also produced two interesting autobiographical works, *Læregutt* (1924; Apprentice) and *Svenn* (1946; Journeyman).

See: C. Gad, *Johan Bojer: The Man and His Works* (1920; 1974); T. Ræder, *Johan Bojer og heimbygda Rissa* (1972).   K.A.F.

Böll, Heinrich (1917–), West German novelist and essayist, was born and raised in Cologne, the son of a cabinetmaker. On the paternal side descended from Catholics who had fled England rather than accept the state religion of Henry VIII, he grew up in an atmosphere of religious piety coupled with skepticism toward the institutional church. Successfully eluding membership in the Hitler Youth, Böll in 1938, after a short apprenticeship in a bookstore, was drafted into the compulsory work program (*Arbeitsdienst*) and shortly thereafter into the army. He fought on various fronts before being captured by the Americans in 1945. Returning to Cologne after a few months in captivity, the writer worked briefly in his father's shop and at the city's bureau of vital statistics. After 1951 writing became his sole profession. The winner

of numerous literary awards, Böll enjoys the most widespread reputation of any German writer in the postwar decades. From 1971 to 1974 he served as president of the International PEN Club. In 1972 he became the first German writer to receive the Nobel Prize for Literature since the naturalized Swiss citizen Hermann HESSE in 1946 and Thomas MANN in 1929. Böll's works, translated into nearly 40 languages, have met with success in both East and West. Although primarily a novelist, Böll has also written radio plays and in 1972 published a volume of poems. Together with his wife, Annemarie Böll, he has translated many English, Irish, and American works into German, among them the works of J. D. Salinger, John Millington Synge, and Brendan Behan.

Stark style and simple narrative structure characterize Böll's early works. The long story *Der Zug war pünktlich* (1949; Eng. tr., *The Train Was on Time*, 1956); the collection of stories *Wanderer, kommst du nach Spa . . .* (1950; Eng. tr., *Traveller, if You Come to Spa*, 1956); and the author's first novel, *Wo warst du Adam?* (1951; Eng. tr., *Adam, Where Art Thou?*, 1955), deal directly with the senseless evil of war and its crushing effect on individual victims. The novels that followed, *Und sagte kein einziges Wort* (1953; Eng. tr., *Acquainted with the Night*, 1954), *Haus ohne Hüter* (1954; Eng. tr., *Tomorrow and Yesterday*, 1957), and *Das Brot der frühen Jahre* (1955; Eng. tr., *The Bread of our Early Years*, 1957), turn more fully to contemporary society and confront the problems of reestablishing normal human relationships and family life in the wake of the war. These works show Böll emerging from the somber drabness of so-called rubble literature (*Trümmerliteratur*) and beginning to develop the humorous and satirical talent marking his mature works. His best purely satirical pieces also fall within this period: *Nicht nur zur Weihnachtszeit* (1952; Eng. tr., "Christmas Every Day," 1957), "Es wird etwas geschehen" (1954; Eng. tr., "Action Will Be Taken," 1966), "Doktor Murkes gesammeltes Schweigen" (1955; Eng. tr., "Murke's Collected Silences," 1966), and "Hauptstädtisches Journal" (1957; Eng. tr., "Bonn Diary," 1966). In the travel book *Irisches Tagebuch* (1957; Eng. tr., *Irish Journal*, 1967), Böll portrays a country that has attracted him for many years as a vacation spot, offering him refuge from the frenzied materialism he senses so acutely in his own country.

Böll's first major novel, *Billard um Halbzehn* (1959; Eng. tr., *Billiards at Half-past Nine*, 1961), reflects a new sophistication of narrative technique. Through continually shifting multiple perspectives with frequent retrospective glances, the novel focuses on three generations of a family within a 24-hour period. It is the day celebrating the dedication of a monastery designed by a young member of the Fähmel family on the site of an earlier monastery built by his grandfather, Heinrich, then destroyed by his father, Robert, during the war. The novel's central symbols, the buffaloes and the lambs, refer partly to the Nazis and those resisting them but designate more broadly those conforming to the herd and those accepting individual responsibility. The grotesque ending, in which the grandmother, Johanna—confined to a mental institution since 1942—attempts to assassinate a political figure, brings the question of personal responsibility and resistance to conformity back into the sphere of contemporary Germany.

The first-person novel *Ansichten eines Clowns* (1963; Eng. tr., *The Clown*, 1965), also covering a single day, portrays the alienation of a young mime, Hans Schnier, from his wealthy Protestant family and from his Catholic girlfriend, Marie, who has forsaken him for a conventional member of the church's establishment. A bitter attack on the church and its compromises with Germany and her past, the novel reflects Böll's problematic relationship to Catholicism.

Longer and more complex than any of his previous works, the novel *Gruppenbild mit Dame* (1971; Eng. tr., *Group Portrait with Lady,* 1973) sets out to recount the biography of Leni Pfeiffer, presented through the anonymous biographer's notes on interviews with the woman's countless friends and acquaintances. This structure permits a panoramic view of West German society and its history, as characters from diverse social, economic, and political backgrounds present their interpretations of events affecting Leni. The protagonist herself loses importance in the course of the rather unwieldy novel, which derives its strength instead from the depth and vitality of the group portrait. The diffuseness of *Gruppenbild* points out the limitations of Böll's talent, which excels in simpler, linear narrative but falters under a multiplicity of perspectives and temporal relationships.

After *Gruppenbild, Die verlorene Ehre der Katharina Blum* (1974; Eng. tr., *The Lost Honor of Katharina Blum,* 1975) returns to a simpler narrative mode. Subtitled "Oder wie Gewalt entstehen und wohin sie führen kann" ("How Violence Develops and Where It Can Lead"), the book describes the violent disruption of a young woman's life by sensational journalism. Her cold-blooded murder of a reporter at the end, echoing Johanna Fähmel's attempt in *Billard,* appears as a justified statement in defense of human dignity.

As an outspoken publicist, Böll has often elicited lively debate in West Germany through his stance on internal and international social and political questions, among them the treatment of the Baader-Meinhof terrorists by the conservative Springer Press syndicate (concerns that form the background of *Die verlorene Ehre*) and the plight of dissidents in the Soviet Union. Several collections of his essays have appeared: *Aufsätze, Kritiken, Reden* (1967; Essays, Critiques, Speeches), *Neue politische und literarische Schriften* (1973; New Political and Literary Writings), and *Einmischung erwünscht: Schriften zur Zeit* (1977; Intervention Desired: Writings for Our Times). Since 1976, together with Günter GRASS and Carola Stern, he has published the journal *L 76,* which strives to promote discussion of democratic socialism as an alternative to both capitalism and totalitarian Marxism. The author's public political comment and his fictional work derive from common concerns of Böll the Christian moralist: a denunciation of the perversion of human values through materialism, conformity, and hypocrisy in postwar Western culture and a compassion for the victims of such perversion. Bureaucracies—of church, business, and government—frequently embody these forces threatening the individual's integrity. In Böll's Germany such bureaucracies also provide an unwelcome continuity between the Nazi past and the present, thus serving the suppression of historical awareness so important to Böll. The author's attacks on the sources of social evils have become more militant from his early stories to his mature novels. In his fiction the militancy of the social criticism does not preclude occasional lapses into sentimentality. In general, however, Böll succeeds in averting such lapses through his richly imaginative sense of humor and sensitive exploitation of the grotesque.

See: T. Ziolkowski, "Heinrich Böll, Conscience and Craft," *BA* 34 (1960): 213–22; W. J. Schwarz, *Heinrich Böll, Teller of Tales* (1961); M. Reich-Ranicki, ed., *In Sachen Böll, Ansichten und Einsichten* (1970); J. H. Reid, *Heinrich Böll* (1973)   C.C.Z.

Bondarev, Yury Vasilyevich (1924–), Russian prose writer, was born in Orsk. He fought in World War II and graduated from the Gorky Literary Institute in 1951. He began writing short stories in 1949, but later switched to novels. His first novel was *Yunost komandirov* (1956; Youth of Commanders). Bondarev's dominant theme has been the moral image of his generation as reflected in its war experiences. Two short novels, *Batalyony prosyat ognya* (1957; Battalions Ask for Fire) and *Posledniye zalpy* (1959; Eng. tr., *The Last Shots,* 1961), and the novel *Goryachiy sneg* (1969; Eng. tr., *The Hot Snow,* 1971) all focus on intense moments in battle that require the utmost endurance and self-sacrifice. The novel *Tishina* (1962; Eng. tr., *Silence,* 1965), its sequel *Dvoye* (1964; Two People), and the short novel *Rodstvenniki* (1969; The Relatives) all give fairly realistic portrayals of postwar Soviet life during periods of political purges. The novel *Bereg* (1975; The Shore) explores the vagaries of life in the story of a young Soviet lieutenant's love for a German girl during the last days of World War II and their fateful encounter 26 years later. While Bondarev is strong in his presentation of detail, his interpretations always remain within official confines.   H.E.

Bonnefoy, Yves (1923–), French poet and essayist, was born in Tours. He studied mathematics and philosophy there and at the University of Poitiers. Bonnefoy went to Paris in 1944, where he frequented surrealist circles (*see* FRENCH LITERATURE) and, under their auspices, published his first literary work, *Traité du pianiste* (1946; Treatise of the Pianist). It was, however, with the publication of *Du mouvement et de l'immobilité de Douve* (1953; Eng. tr., *On the Motion and Immobility of Douve,* 1968) that Bonnefoy first received critical acclaim for the austere quality of his poetic idiom and for his integration of somber elemental images with formal restraints reminiscent of traditional French prosody. In this cycle of poems, the allegorical figure of Douve undergoes the ordeal of a journey through disintegration and death, while at the same time pursuing reintegration and hope. The work reflects Bonnefoy's concern with the relationship between poetry (and indeed all forms of art) and reality. As he stated in a 1969 interview, "the intention of poetry, which differs in this from all other preoccupations of consciousness, except the religious one, is to tear away beings and things from the definitions and descriptions that fragment them, in order to give them back their proper identity. Or, as Blake said, their unity, their own presence."

After *Douve,* Bonnefoy produced two books of poems, *Hier régnant désert* (1958; In Yesterday's Desert Dominion) and *Pierre écrite* (1965; Eng. tr., *Words in Stone,* 1976), as well as two collections of essays on art and poetry, *L'Improbable* (1959) and *Un rêve fait à Mantoue* (1967; A Dream in Mantua). These works continue Bonnefoy's search for a reconciliation, often symbolized by the motif of a "vrai lieu" (true place), standing for intellectual apprehension and immediate experience and for meaning and presence. His relentless denunciation of conceptual thought as a screen designed to protect a too complacent consciousness from reality, and his attention to the enduring quality of primeval elements (stone, tree, water) have sometimes led critics to characterize Bonnefoy as an "existentialist" poet. The label should, however, not refer to Sartrean existentialism (*see* Jean-Paul SARTRE) so much as to the influence of Lev SHESTOV and to a conscious kinship with Oriental modes of intuition.

In recent years, the tension in Bonnefoy's writings has subsided and given way to a more serene acceptance of the limitations of poetry. His poetic practice, with its muted imagery and its ever more pronounced avoidance of formal beauties, has become, in *Dans le leurre du seuil* (1975; In the Lure of the Threshold), even more illustrative of the adage proposed in *Hier régnant désert*: "Imperfection is the Peak." At the same time, the spiritual task of poetry, stated in *L'Improbable* as that of "reinventing a hope" and "rethinking the rapport between Man and things," is perceived in *Dans le leurre* and in the essay *Terre seconde* (1976; Another Earth) as an enterprise capable of success. In these works, human finitude is no longer treated as the limit of apprehension, but as its point of departure. Bonnefoy's collected *Poèmes* (1945-75) were published in 1978, shortly after the poet was awarded the Montaigne Prize.

Generally acknowledged as the most influential French poet of his generation, Bonnefoy has also gained recognition as an art critic for such studies as *Peintures murales de la France gothique* (1954; French Gothic Murals) and *Rome 1630: l'horizon du premier baroque* (1970; The Horizon of the First Baroque). His spiritual autobiography, entitled *L'Arrière-pays* (1972; The Country Beyond), combines a meditation on the visual arts with reflections on the intent and genesis of poetic creation. Several of the essays collected in *Le Nuage rouge* (1977; The Red Cloud) stress the parallels between the perceptions and responsibilities of art and poetry. This dual concern, as well as a more conscious affinity with the ethics and aesthetics emantating from Zen Buddhist thought, are further reflected in the short prose narratives of *Rue Traversière* (1977). Bonnefoy is also a noted translator of Shakespeare and William Butler Yeats.

See: J. E. Jackson, *Yves Bonnefoy* (1976).   R.V.

Bonsels, Waldemar (1881-1952), German novelist, poet, and playwright, was born near Hamburg and wandered over Europe, Egypt, India, and much more of the western hemisphere before finally settling in Ambach on Lake Starnberg, where he died. His *Indienfahrt* (written in 1912 but not published until 1916; Eng. tr., *An Indian Journey*, 1928) was a new kind of travel literature. In a few simple and lyrically conceived incidents he characterized India, the poverty of its humanity, and the lush extravagance of nature. Impressions of North and South America were set forth in two later books, *Brasilianische Tage und Nächte* (with A. von Dungern, 1931; Brazilian Days and Nights) and *Der Reiter in der Wüste: eine Amerikafahrt* (1935; The Rider in the Desert: A Journey to America).

Bonsels' popularity rests, however, upon one book in particular, *Die Biene Maja* (1912; Eng. tr., *The Adventures of Maya, the Bee*, 1922). This tale, in which the creatures of nature are disarmingly endowed with the most pleasing aspects of human intelligence and emotions, elaborates an incredibly sentimental gospel of love for nature, for a vaguely conceived God, and for one's fellow beings. Three further tales told in the same manner, *Das Anjekind* (1913; Eng. tr., *Angel-Child*, 1926), *Himmelsvolk* (1915; Eng. tr., *Heaven Folk*, 1924), *Mario und die Tiere* (1927; Eng. tr., *Adventures of Mario*, 1930), proved to be almost as popular. The struggle and search for God and pleasure are enlarged in Bonsels' vagabond trilogy, *Menschenwege* (1918; Human Paths), *Eros und die Evangelien* (1920; Eros and the Gospels), and *Narren und Helden* (1923; Eng. tr. of the trilogy, *Notes of a Vagabond*, 1931). His earliest books, *Der tiefste Traum* (1911; The Deepest Dream) and *Wartalun* (1911), happily fuse the supernatural and German folk themes. *Tage der Kindheit* (1931; Days of Childhood) is an autobiographical narrative.

See: F. Adler, *Waldemar Bonsels: sein Weltbild und seine Gestalten* (1925).   V.La. rev. A.L.W.

Bontempelli, Massimo (1878-1960), Italian novelist, short-story writer, dramatist, and journalist, was born in Como. His father was a civil engineer employed by the state railroads. During his youth, Bontempelli lived in various northern Italian cities. After taking a double degree in philosophy and letters at the University of Turin, he taught in secondary schools. In 1910 he left teaching to devote himself to journalism and literature. He was a propagandist for fascism, lecturing abroad on behalf of the regime and accepting nomination to the Italian Academy in 1930. Nevertheless, Bontempelli preserved a certain independence. He refused the chair of literature at the University of Florence, made vacant by the dismissal of Attilio Momigliano under the racial laws, and for two years he was suspended from the Fascist Party. After World War II, Bontempelli joined the Left. He was elected senator, but his election was invalidated because of his Fascist past.

Bontempelli's early works show the influence of Giosuè Carducci (1835-1907), and indeed, like Carducci he edited classical Italian authors for school use. Around 1910, Bontempelli turned to a new style of writing, attempting to create a truly "modern" literature. Although the example of futurism (*see* ITALIAN LITERATURE) influenced his decision, he was never a docile follower of that school. As Luigi Russo remarks, Bontempelli's mature work combines the humanism of Carducci, the logical severity of Benedetto CROCE, and the insouciance of the futurists. In his fondness for treating abnormal situations with calculated gravity he also has much in common with Luigi PIRANDELLO. His style is admirable for its clarity and sobriety. Among his best-known works are *Sette savi* (1909; Seven Sages), *La vita intensa* (1920; The Intense Life), and *La vita operosa* (1921; The Industrious Life). The short stories in these collections present unusual situations and have the impact of parables. Noteworthy among his novels are *Il figlio di due madri* (1929; The Son of Two Mothers) and *Vita e morte di Adria e dei suoi figli* (1930; Life and Death of Adria and Her Children). The latter, concerning a woman who withdraws from the world to preserve the legend of her beauty, is at once a study of solipsism and an ironic commentary on the contemporary world. All of these works exemplify the author's theory that "modern" creative art should combine invention—even to the point of fantasy—with scrupulous realism of detail. Bontempelli also wrote a number of plays, very similar in nature to those of Pirandello and the *grotteschi*. His most successful play is probably *Nostra Dea* (1925; Our Goddess), dealing with the concept of multiple personality.

Bontempelli was an active and articulate journalist all his life and contributed to practically every important review and newspaper of his time. The polemical essay *L'avventura novecentista* (1938; 20th-Century Adventure), written at the time he was founding, with Curzio MALAPARTE, his own review, *'900,* is not only a defense of his "magic realism" (as he defines his art) but also a thoughtful analysis of the aesthetic problems that the 20th-century artist must face. Giorgio Pullini hazards the opinion that *L'avventura* may be Bontempelli's most enduring work.

See: A. Asor Rosa, *Dizionario biografico degli italiani* (1970); F. Tempesti, *Bontempelli* (1974); G. Pullini, in *Letteratura italiana: i contemporanei*, vol. 1 (1975).
                                                                         T.G.B.

Boon, Louis Paul (1912-79), Belgian novelist, poet, critic, and journalist, was born in Aalst. The quantity, range and quality of Boon's work place him among the most important authors in modern Dutch literature. His first novel,

De voorstad groeit (1942; The Suburb Grows) deals with the origin and development of a proletarian district in the industrial city of Aalst. This book displays a number of characteristics that are present in Boon's later work: the highly fragmented structure, revealing the influence of John Dos Passos, and the colorful popular language in which the impact of Louis-Ferinand CELINE is apparent. In this novel, the life of the common man is presented through representative types who strike out as strong individuals even though described from the collectivist standpoint of rising socialism. Boon extended this theme further, broadened it historically, and mixed it with autobiographical elements in two masterpieces, *De Kapellekensbaan* (1953; Eng. tr., *Chapel Road*, 1972) and *Zomer te Ter-Muren* (1956; Summer in Ter-Muren). *De Kapellekensbaan* is in many ways an experimental novel that has significantly contributed to the renewal of Dutch prose. It consists of three novels that are closely interwoven: the novel of the working girl, Ondine; the topical novel in which the writer Boontje and his many friends distinguish between novel and commentary; and the novel of Reinart de Vos (later published separately as *Wapenbroeders*, 1955; Brothers in Arms), which is recounted by one of the friends, the alter ego of Boontje. Through a network of personal case histories, this complex work contains the story of the rise and fall of Belgian socialism as well as the universal history of the individual in his hopeless battle with social forces. It also constitutes a statement of Boon's own conception of the novel as genre. The bitter social vision that forms the basis of the novel is that of a dreamed for but doomed revolution. Boon has already treated this theme in an earlier work, *Vergeten Straat* (1946; Forgotten Street), a Utopia set in a neighborhood of Brussels. Novel and historical chronicle are also combined in later works, in which the chronicle plays an increasingly greater role. This trend appears in such monumental works as *Pieter Daens of hoe in de negentiende eeuw arbeiders vochten tegen armoede en onrecht* (1971; Pieter Daens or How in the Nineteenth Century the Workers Fought Against Poverty and Injustice), which deals with the history of the Christian-Democratic movement, Daenism; *De zwarte hand of het anarchisme in de negentiende eeuw in het industrielstadje Aalst* (1976; The Black Hand of Anarchy in the Nineteenth-Century Industrial City of Aalst); and *Het Geuzenboek* (1979; The Book of the Beggers) treating the social decline of Flanders during the Spanish wars of the 16th century. This last work is described by critics as a social and political couterpart of Charles de Coster's *Thijl Uilenspiegel*. Also noteworthy are *Mijn kleine oorlog* (1949; My Little War), an image of World War II as seen through the eyes of a common man, and *De Paradijsvogel* (1958; Bird of Paradise), a mythical and symbolic tale. A number of Boon's novels are more personal in nature: *Abel Gholaerts* (1944), a self protrait insppired by the life of Vincent van Gogh; *Menuet* (1955), the story of a triangular relationship set up as a triptych; and the autibiographical *Verscheurd jeugdportret* (1975; Shattered Youth Portrait).

See: J. Weverbergh snd J. Leus, *Boonboek* (1972); P. de Wispelaere, *Louis Paul Boon, tendere anarchist* (1976); G. J. van Bork and G. ten Houten-Biezeveld, *Over Boon* (1978). P. de W.

Borchardt, Rudolf (1877–1945), German poet, essayist, historian, was born in Königsberg of a Jewish family that had been Protestant for generations and had settled in East Prussia. He studied classics at Berlin, Bonn, and Göttingen. After 1904 he lived in Italy, with the exception of short periods in Germany and the years of World War I, a conflict in which he took part. His few publications before 1918 and the lectures he gave during later years aroused passionate interest and opposition.

Borchardt was a poet of high aims, a philologist and historian of genius gifted with the power of evoking the great past, a "revolutionary conservative," a violent fighter generous in love and hate, an artist of strongly nationalistic tendencies, and a volcanic personality. And such is his work—of lava and flame. His style, with its sharp outlines, its Latin periods, and its wide historical vistas, has a poetry of its own, heroic and scornful. His anthologies, *Deutsche Denkreden* (1925; German Memorial Speeches), *Ewiger Vorrat deutscher Poesie* (1926; Eternal Store of German Poetry), *Der Deutsche in der Landschaft* (1927; The German in the Landscape), form an integral part of his work. His translations were born of his vision of the past, of the medieval period as well as of the Greek middle ages. They range from Tacitus and Hartmann von Aue to Homer and Pindar; his translation of Pindar in 1930 is one of his supreme achievements. His translations also range in scope from Walter Savage Landor's prose and Algernon Charles Swinburne's verse to old Provençal and to Dante—his translation of the *Divine Comedy* (1930) was the work of decades. For Dante, Borchardt created a poetic language of his own, a historically unrealized stage between the German of the Middle Ages and the later language. Most of his translations, as well as the anthologies, were followed by essays that shed new light on their subjects.

One of Borchardt's tales, "Der Durant," published as a fragment, is perhaps the only legitimate continuation of the German medieval epic, remarkable for its somber force. On this tale and on some of his lyrics of love and despair, notably *Jugendgedichte* (1913; Poems of Youth), Borchardt's significance as a poet may be said to rest securely. An anthology of his verse and prose, *Ausgewählte Werke 1900–1918* (Selected Works), was published in 1925.

See: W. Kraft, *Rudolf Borchardt: Welt aus Poesie und Geschichte* (1961); H. Arbogast, ed., *Über Rudolf Borchardt* (1977). H.St. rev. A.L.W.

Borchert, Wolfgang (1921–47), German writer, playwright, and actor, was born in Hamburg. His father was a primary school teacher and his mother a writer. Borchert's life and work paralleled Nazi society, and conflict between this sensitive individual and the regime was inevitable. Although he survived the Third Reich, its malice finally claimed Borchert in an early death. Compelled by military service to forgo an acting career, Borchert criticized the state in open correspondence. His wounds on the Russian Front (1941) and imprisonment for antigovernment criticism (1942 and 1944) rendered him physically weak and precipitated his death.

Borchert dealt directly with the physical and psychological conditions of life in Nazi Germany: its totalitarianism and destruction. The intense condensed nature of his style is reminiscent of expressionistic writing. The haunting figure of Beckmann, the universal returning veteran, from *Draußen vor der Tür* (1947; Eng. tr., *The Man Outside*, 1952), indelibly etches a picture of Germany in ashes and rubble.

Borchert's mastery of narrative as shown in *An diesem Dienstag* (1947; This Tuesday), *Die Hundeblume* (1947; The Dandelion), and in the posthumously published *Die traurigen Geranien* (1962; The Mournful Geraniums), attains a high level of psychological intensity in such stories as "Das Brot" (The Bread), "Die Küchenuhr" (The Kitchen Clock), and "Die lange, lange Straße lang" (Along the Long, Long Road). Seeming to plumb the depths of despair, Borchert found hope, however small, in a flower in "Die Hundeblume" and in human contact in "Nachts schlafen die Ratten doch" (Rats Do Sleep at Night).

See: P. Rühmkorf, *Wolfgang Borchert* (1961).

J.L.S.

Bordeaux, Henry (1870–1963), French novelist and critic, was born in Thonon-les-Bains into a typically large, provincial bourgeois family. They were well off, his father having developed a successful legal practice. Between 1900 and 1939, Bordeaux's books were eagerly awaited and devoured by more Parisian and provincial bourgeois readers with a solid classical education than those written by any other novelist. This was due to the fact that his readers found in his novels all characteristics, values, and virtues that were the very essence of their own social milieux. Bordeaux satisfied this appetite by writing more than 50 novels, most of which are doomed to oblivion. Yet the better ones are still worth reading: *La Peur de vivre* (1902; Eng. tr., *The Fear of Living,* 1914), *Les Roquevillard* (1906; Eng. tr., *The Will to Live,* 1914); *La Croisée des chemins* (1909; Eng. tr., *The Parting of the Ways,* 1911), *La Robe de laine* (1910; Eng. tr., *The Woolen Dress,* 1913), *La Neige sur les pas* (1912; Eng. tr., *Footprints beneath the Snow,* 1914), and *La Maison* (1913; Eng. tr., *The House, 1916*).

Besides novels, Bordeaux wrote a large number of monographs and essays on various subjects. He was always interested in the theater, and the four volumes of his *La Vie au théâtre* contain the reviews he wrote between 1910 and 1921 while he was the drama critic for *La Revue hebdomadaire*. These essays reveal both his conservative preferences and his fairness in judging plays that did not appeal to his own taste. During World War I, in which he served as an army captain, he composed well-documented books based on his experiences.

Like Honoré de Balzac, Bordeaux was a traditionalist who saw in a solid, religious, patriotic, and hard-working family the basic social cell insuring the strength of the nation. Most of his characters are conformists who believe in respecting their parents, in the prestige of their elders, in the unity of the family, and even in the solidarity of generations. Yet many of his heroes and heroines are sinners who rebel against traditions. In the end, however, after Bordeaux has studied their motivation, his rebellious characters yield to bourgeois conformity, either because of their awareness of their duties to society as a whole or because of their religious faith. Traditional order triumphs.

Bordeaux is an excellent technician, and his plots are cleverly and solidly built. But he is also a realistic writer, which is a quality denied to him by his detractors, who see in him only "the novelist of the family and the soil." In 1919 the Académie Française awarded him the seat left vacant by the death of Jules LEMAÎTRE.

See: J. Bertaut, *Henry Bordeaux et son œuvre* (1924); E. Jaloux, *De Pascal à Barrès* (1927).   A.Bo.

Bordewijk, Ferdinand (1884–1965), Dutch novelist, short-story writer, and dramatist, was born in Amsterdam. After a brief period as a teacher, he turned to law and always maintained that this, and not literature, constituted his true professional interest. Under the pseudonym of Ton Ven, he made his literary debut with a volume of poetry, *Paddestoelen* (1916; Toadstools), which failed to attract a public. Between 1919 and 1924 he brought out three volumes of *Fantastische Vertellingen* (Tales of the Imagination), which reveal the influence of Edgar Allan Poe. He then won a reputation with three short novels:

Blokken (1931; Blocks), which depicts a nameless totalitarian society that dehumanizes its citizens; *Knorrende Beesten* (1933; Growling Beasts), a satire on automobiles and modern life: and *Bint* (1934), a portrait of a stern teacher, who drives his students on under iron discipline. By this time Bordewijk had developed a cool and sober style that heightened the effect of his objective attitude toward his characters. *Karakter* (1938; Eng. tr., *Character,* 1966), his greatest novel, portrays the relationship between a son, who eventually becomes a lawyer, and his father, who made him overcome obstacles to develop his character. Here, and in other novels, Bordewijk demonstrates a mastery of psychology in bringing out the relationships between his characters. Among his other important novels are *Rood Paleis* (1936; Red Palace), *Apollyon* (1941), *Eiken van Dodona* (1946; The Oaks of Dodona), *Noorderlicht* (1948; Aurora Borealis), *De Doopvont* (1952; The Baptismal Font), and *Bloesemtak* (1955; A Spray of Blossoms). Bordewijk has been awarded the P. C. Hooft Prize.

See: P. H. Dubois, *Over Ferdinand Bordewijk* (1953).

S.L.F.

Borgen, Johan (1902–79), Norwegian dramatist, novelist, and short-story writer, was born in Christiania (now Oslo), the son of a well-educated, artistically inclined mother and an attorney father. His upperclass background always marked Borgen; although always to the far left of the political spectrum, he remained conservative in life-style, and he was unsuccessful in expressing his political views in his literary production.

Borgen is recognized today as one of the leading Norwegian writers of the 20th century, but his success was slow in coming. After publishing his first book in 1925, a collection of short stories that attracted little notice, he traveled around Europe for several years before working as a journalist for the irreverent Oslo daily, *Dagbladet*. As a journalist, Borgen immediately won attention for his witty, ironic, and often sarcastic column, written under the signature Mumle Gåsegg. These writings later earned him a stay at a concentration camp outside Oslo during the Nazi occupation of Norway. Before that time, however, he had published short stories, plays, and a novel. The novel, *Når alt kommer til alt* (1934; Everything Considered), introduces the typical Borgen protagonist—a middle-aged intellectual in quest of an identity. The same character appears in *Mens vi venter* (1938; While We're Waiting), a Pirandello-inspired play (*see* Luigi PIRANDELLO) that has enjoyed considerable stage success.

After World War II, Borgen established himself as one of Norway's finest short-story writers. His first collection, *Hvetebrøds dager* (1948; Honeymoon), followed by others such as *Noveller om kjærlighet* (1952; Short Stories about Love) and *Nye noveller* (1965; New Short Stories), demonstrates Borgen's rare mastery of this genre. Within the brief scope of a story, he had the uncanny ability to catch a fleeting mood and to reveal latent poetic layers of the human psyche. The first novel of the *Lillelord* trilogy marked his international breakthrough. *Lillelord* (1955; Little Lord), *De mørke kilder* (1956; The Dark Springs), and *Vi har ham nå* (1957; We Have Him Now) treat the childhood and segments in the adult life of Wilfred Sagen, a Norwegian Little Lord Fauntleroy figure, who slowly degenerates into a state of schizoid languor and moral depravation. The trilogy provides an exceptional analysis of social and personal degeneration and final disintegration. Borgen's later novels, related in theme and execution to the works of Marcel PROUST and Franz KAFKA, are experimental and untraditional, but they are still marked by the same unparalleled sense of expression that characterized his earlier prose. *"Jeg"* (1959; "I") and *Den røde tåken* (1967; Eng. tr., *The Red Mist*, 1973) are outstanding examples of his ability to represent the inner conflicts that threaten the basis of the established personality.

In his novels, as in his most important play, *Frigjøringsdag* (1963; Day of Liberation), Borgen has continued to explore the existential void of modern man. He has no moral message to relate, but his works have a poetic dimension that places them among the important achievements in 20th-century Norwegian literature.

See: R. Birn, *Johan Borgen, TWAS* (1974).　　K.A.F.

Borgese, Giuseppe Antonio (1882–1952), Italian essayist, novelist, and journalist, was born near Palermo. He graduated from the University of Florence in 1903, and in 1905 he expanded his doctoral thesis into the highly praised *Storia della critica romantica in Italia* (History of Romantic Criticism in Italy). This book and other essays, which show the influence of Benedetto CROCE, earned him notoriety in literary circles. Engaged in fiery polemics with other young men of letters, Borgese proposed an ambitious but contradictory task for his country: the reestablishment of Italian cultural primacy and the modernization of Italian intellectual life.

While many young rebels joined the futurists (*see* ITALIAN LITERATURE), Borgese gradually retreated to more traditional ground. He was an early admirer of Gabriele D'ANNUNZIO, but in 1909 he repudiated the poet as well as the literary and ideological trend of *dannunzianesimo*. Concurrently, he divorced himself from Croce's aesthetics and from his critical methodology. Before World War I, Borgese produced a ponderous quantity of militant criticism for journals and the literary pages of newspapers. He had moderated his youthful views in favor of a reconciliation between serious books and a temperate life: he named a three-volume collection of his criticism *La vita e il libro* (1913; Life and Books). In 1909, after a two-year stay in Germany, Borgese was offered the chair of German literature at the University of Rome. His lectures and essays on Johann Wolfgang von Goethe revealed Borgese's inclination toward creative criticism. In a belatedly romantic fashion he seemed to maintain that critics had to compete with authors in inventiveness. He eventually grew weary of such competing, however, and after World War I turned to creative literature himself. His first and best novel was *Rubè* (1921; Eng. tr., 1923). In broodings reminiscent of Luigi PIRANDELLO, the novel's protagonist anticipates the anguish that was to pervade European literature for decades. In Italy, *Rubè* transfused some blood into the novel, a genre critics and poets had relegated to a literary no-man's-land. Borgese's second novel and several plays, written in the 1920s, were not as successful. He achieved excellence, however, in shorter pieces, notably his short stories and his brilliant feature articles for *Corriere della sera*.

Borgese found life under fascism insufferable. In 1931 he left Italy for the United States where he taught modern literature at Smith College and at the University of Chicago. In America he was active among European exiles. His *Goliath—The March of Fascism* (1937; Ital. tr., 1946) was a committed intellectual's passionate indictment of Benito Mussolini's tyranny. In 1947 Borgese returned to Italy and to his old chair of aesthetics at the University of Milan. He continued his criticism of Croce's monographical approach to literary history and his own plea for a return to Francesco De Sanctis's reading of poetry in the light of culture and history. And yet, while he was apparently correct as to the legitimacy of literary historiography, he could not convincingly refute Croce's aes-

thetic theory. Borgese's "Figurazione e trasfigurazione" (Figuration and Transfiguration) in *Poetica dell'unità* (1934) is exuberant with such definitions of poetry as "the symbolic representation of the absolute," yet his own theory has more to do with aesthetic transcendence than with De Sanctis's descent from the ideal into the real. Although he had sided with the classicists, Borgese continued to be an irrepressible romantic.

See: A. Rufino, *La critica letteraria di G. A. Borgese* (1969); G. A. Peritore, in *Letteratura italiana: i contemporanei*, vol. 1 (1975), pp. 449–68.　　A.Ruf.

Born, Nicholas (1937–79), German poet and novelist, was born in Duisburg. He apprenticed in chemigraphy in Essen, where he lived from 1957 to 1965, traveling during those years to the Balkans, Greece, and Turkey. After participating in the collective composition of an experimental novel, *Das Gästehaus* (The Guest House), with the Literarisches Coloquium Berlin in 1964–65, he spent the year 1969–70 as a fellow at the Writers Workshop at the University of Iowa. He was a member of the Mainz Academy of the Sciences and of Literature and was an editor of Rowohlt's *Literaturmagazin*.

A friendly loner, Born published his first novel, *Der zweite Tag* (The Second Day) in 1965; representative of the new realism promoted by Dieter WELLERSHOFF, it relates the incidents of the second day of a trip. Born's second novel, *Die erdabgewandte Seite der Geschichte* (1976; The Side of History Turned Away from the Earth), tells of a love affair and its disintegration during the student protest movements of the late 1960s. His last novel, *Die Fälschung* (1979; The Counterfeit), takes place in Beirut during the civil conflict of the 1970s.

As a poet Born worried about self-identity, criticized everyday political events, captured snapshots of everyday life, and reminisced about events gone by and persons dead. His volumes of poetry are *Marktlage* (1967; State of the Market), *Wo mir der Kopf steht* (1970; Which End Is Up), *Das Auge des Entdeckers* (1972; The Eye of the Explorer), and collected poems in *Gedichte 1967–1978* (1978). His long poem *Feriengedicht* (Eng. tr., *Vacation Poem*) appeared in 1971 in *Dimension*, vol. 4. Born was concerned with language, with the role of literature and the writer in contemporary society—he was an enemy of the cliché. He also wrote a "Utopian children's book," *Oton und Iton* (1974).　　A.L.W.

Borowski, Tadeusz (1922–51), Polish writer and publicist, was born in Zhitomir and died, committing suicide, in Warsaw. During World War II he studied Polish literature at the underground Warsaw University. His first collection of poems, *Gdziekolwiek ziemia* (1942; Wherever the Earth), appeared in clandestine press and is characterized by an apocalyptic and catastrophic tone. In 1943 he was arrested and sent to the concentration camps in Auschwitz and Dachau. After the war he published in Munich a collection of poetry written during the Occupation, *Imiona nurtu* (1945; The Names of the Current). In 1946 he returned to Poland. After an initial association with the Catholic press, Borowski underwent a significant ideological evolution. He became a Marxist and a propagator of socialist realism, and gradually his political interests predominated over his literary interests, making him into a kind of Communist Party journalist. His suicide was the result of a dramatic crisis, both ideological and personal in nature. His lasting contribution to Polish letters has to be seen in two collections of short stories concerned with his experience in Nazi concentration camps, *Kamienny świat* (1948; The World of Stone) and *Pożegnanie z Marią* (1948; Farewell to Maria). An English translation, *This*

Way for the Gas, Ladies and Gentlemen, and Other Stories (1967), contains some short stories from both volumes. The question evidently confronting Borowski was how to make the death of millions a tragedy in terms of literature. He was conscious of the inadequacy of the classical design of tragedy for expressing the tragedy of mass murder. This awareness led him to a momentous discovery, and made neither the victim nor the murderer the hero of his stories. The new conception of tragedy unfolding in a world of destroyed values was in a way the principle underlying Borowski's stories.

See: T. Drewnowski, *Ucieczka z kamiennego świata. (O Tadeuszu Borowskim)* (1962); A. Wirth, "A Discovery of Tragedy," *PolR* 12, no. 3 (1967): 43–52; J. Kott, Introduction to T. Borowski, *This Way for the Gas, Ladies and Gentlemen* (1976), pp. 11–26.   A.W.

Bosch, Andrés (1926–), Spanish novelist, was born in Palma de Mallorca. Since his childhood he has lived in Barcelona, where he studied law at the university. Today he devotes his time to literature and collaborative newspaper writing.

Bosch belongs to a small group of novelists known as "the metaphysicians," among whom figure García-Viñó, Antonio PRIETO, Manuel San Martín, and Carlos ROJAS. Chronologically, these authors belong to the Generation of 1954, but what separates them from the rest of the Generation is their rejection of social realism (the aesthetic stance adopted by most writers of the Generation) and their preference for an intellectual realism that has psychological and metaphysical implications.

All of Bosch's novels are concerned with the same problem: the individual's inability to fulfill the objectives he has formulated as the very goal of his existence. The author shows the inner conflict of the protagonist as well as his struggle with the society in which he lives until he arrives at an intimate understanding of himself. Bosch's first novel, *La noche* (1959; Night), tells the story of a boxer who painfully agonizes over who he really is and who he would like to be, until, in defeat, he discovers his true identity. *Homenaje privado* (1962; Private Homage), one of his best novels, portrays the life of a character who has died, showing how injustice frustrated and ruined his existence.

All of Bosch's novels are written in clear prose devoid of excess. His greatest success lies in his ability to present the "objective" alongside the "subjective," always changing the point of reference. The outer world is captured through attention to objects, details, and gestures, all of which contribute to defining the characters' environment and underscoring their way of life.

See: M. García-Viñó, *Novela española actual* (1967), pp. 175–99.   P.G.C.

Bosco, Henri (1888–1976), French novelist and poet, was born in Avignon. He was so closely identified with his native Provence and the Mediterranean world as to be appropriately classified as a regional writer. Bosco was inspired to pursue classical studies by his love of the region's cultural origins. For more than 30 years he was a teacher of Latin and Greek, holding positions in varied locations in the Mediterranean world: Italy, Algeria, Morocco, and Provence. In his literary career, which he launched relatively late in life, he also displayed a mind and an imagination steeped in the cultural traditions of his meridional environment.

Bosco's first publication, an awkward autobiographical novel entitled *Pierre Lampédouze*, appeared in 1924, when he was already approaching middle age. Over the next two decades Bosco occasionally published collections of poems or novels of life in the Midi, while continuing his full-time duties as a teacher. These years constituted Bosco's long, slow literary apprenticeship. Only one work during this period, *L'Ane Culotte* (1937; Culotte the Donkey), a tale of childhood and nature involving a young girl named Hyacinthe and a donkey, attracted serious attention.

In 1945, Bosco retired from active teaching. That same year, he experienced his first taste of national literary fame when his novel *Le Mas Théotime* (Eng. tr., *Farm in Provence,* 1947) won the Renaudot Prize and brought him readers in large numbers. The next 10 years constituted the most productive and distinguished decade of Bosco's life, during which he gave his increased public a new novel almost every year, brought out a consolidated collection of his best poems, and attained recognition as the foremost literary figure of his region. Much of his later work, especially since 1955, has shown a distinctly inward turn, an interest in the haunted, private thoughts of the lonely—particularly of lonely children. Significantly, the personal memoirs he published in the early 1960s focused almost exclusively on his childhood. Bosco's inward turn seems a natural development in a literary sensibility that had always been concerned with the dark and inarticulate sides of human nature and with the inhospitable and even violent aspects of the natural environment. Bosco's brooding introspectiveness, his preoccupation with loneliness and silence, and his vision of life as a conflict between the civilized and the primitive have indeed made him a unique figure among meridional authors, who tend usually to have the sunny and voluble disposition associated with the region's climate.

Bosco's novels tend to have few characters and a spare plot and to convey a poetic sense of life in a simple style of classic purity. His own favorite work, *Malicroix* (1948), which is in the critical consensus also his finest piece of writing, exemplifies his qualities at their best. The novel has almost no plot: to earn an inheritance the hero must spend a lonely winter on an isolated farm situated on a small island in the Rhône River, deep in the wild region known as the Camargue. In the course of his ordeal, he struggles both with the terrors of nature, including a flood, and with the terrors of loneliness and fear within himself. In the end, he arrives at a peaceful acceptance of his environment and of his heredity, that is, himself. *Malicroix* illustrates Bosco's uncanny ability to sustain a specific and intense regional emphasis in his writing while exploring themes of universal meaning and permanent human value.

Bosco's roots in his region and in the past enabled his work to remain almost eerily untouched by public events, such as wars and political upheavals, and by the changing fashions of literary taste. Steadfastly going his own way, he pursued a timeless, private vision of the world, one that he evoked in a simple, unmannered style.

See: R. T. Sussex, *Henri Bosco: Poet-Novelist* (1966); J. C. Godin, *Henri Bosco: une poétique du mystère* (1968).   M.S.

Bosshart, Jacob (1862–1924), Swiss novelist, short-story writer, and poet, was born in a lonely farm in Stürzikton near Zürich. He trained at a teachers college and later studied at the universities of Heidelberg, Paris, and Zürich, earning a Ph.D. degree at Zürich. An able educator, Bosshart served as rector of the cantonal gymnasium in Zürich for 17 years. Ill health forced him to resign, and he subsequently moved to Clavadel, where he worked at his writing and fought a losing battle against tuberculosis.

Bosshart produced nearly 40 short stories, 1 novel, and

a collection of poems. Many of his works are drawn from his childhood experiences, and he is at his best when describing the life, work, and customs of a farming community. Although Bosshart's subject matter resembles that of Jeremias Gotthelf, his portrayals are not as finely chiseled and his characters never lose their sternness. Indeed, Bosshart's view of mankind is extraordinarily bleak. The misery of Salome in "Die alte Salome" (The Old Salome) and of Lene in "Durch Schmerzen empor" (Upward through Grief) is brought about by human wrongdoing and heartlessness, which Bosshart exposed with biting realism. The collection *Erdschollen* (1913; Earth Clods) contains one of Bosshart's best-known stories, "Schweizer." His novel, *Ein Rufer in der Wüste* (1921; A Voice in the Wilderness), documents the turbulent period immediately preceding World War I. Its hero, Reinhart Stauffer, the son of a well-to-do manufacturer and army officer, leaves his father's factory to join the struggling workers. Unable to accept their revolutionary actions, Stauffer eventually dies, a thwarted idealist at the threshold of a new era. Bosshart's other works include the short-story collections *Im Nebel* (1898; In the Fog), *Die Barettlitochter* (1901; The Daughter of Barettli), *Gesammelte Erzählungen* (1921; Collected Short Stories), *Träume der Wüste* (1918; Dreams of the Desert), and *Gedichte* (1924; Poems), the latter a volume of posthumously published poetry.

See: M. Konzelmann, *Jakob Bosshart* (1929); W. Günther, *Dichter der neuren Schweiz*, vol. 1 (1963), pp. 281–330.   R.A.Me.

Botto, António (Tomás) (1900–59), Portuguese poet, was born in Concavada, near the town Abrantes. As a youth he entered the civil service and briefly occupied the position of district administrator in Angola. In 1947 he emigrated to Brazil, where he lived in poverty. In 1956 he suffered a serious and prolonged illness, and three years later he was killed by an automboile in Rio de Janeiro. His voluminous production includes poetry, drama, and short fiction. Botto's first collection of verse, *Trovas* (1917; Lays), was followed by *Cantigas de saudades* (1918; Nostalgic Airs) and *Cantares* (1919; Chants); but his first important book of poems was *Canções* (1921; Songs), whose second, enlarged edition (1922) was seized by the authorites because of its frank praise of male beauty and homosexual relations. Botto's aesthetic approach to what was then considered unorthodox was explained in essays by two great contemporary poets, José RÉGIO and Fernando PESSOA. Later editions of *Canções*, issued up to 1956, absorbed such volumes as *Curiosidades estéticas* (1924; Aesthetic Curiosities), *Dandismo* (1928; Dandyism), *Ciúme* (1934; Jealousy), and *Sonetos* (1938; Sonnets). Two other collections of poetry are *O livro do povo* (1944; The People's Book) and *Odio e amor* (1947; Hate and Love). A kind of novella, *Cartas que me foram devolvidas* (1932; Letters Returned to Me), was to be included in *Canções*. For children, Botto wrote *O livro das crianças* (1932; Eng. tr., *The Children's Book*, 1936). Of his three plays, one in three acts, *Alfama* (1933), is justly considered a masterpiece of the contemporary Portuguese theater. An expressionist drama, it presents a bitter picture of life in a Lisbon slum, Alfama, and a heroine who is a proletarian sister of Hedda Gabler (*see* Henrik IBSEN). Some of Botto's poems were also inspired by Lisbon's *basfonds* and *fado* songs, among them "Pequenas canções de cabaret" (Little Cabaret Songs) in *Baionetas da morte* (1936; Death's Bayonets) and also in *Canções*. However, his sophisticated musicality may best be appreciated in earlier verses, colloquial, spontaneous,

free in form, and more often than not unrhymed. Botto was a pagan and a sensualist who engaged in an unending quest for beauty, which was frequently symbolized for him in the figure of a handsome youth and an act of homosexual love.

See: J. Régio, *António Botto e o amor* (1937); F. Pessoa, *Páginas de doutrina estética* (1946), pp. 57–80, 91–97; J. P. de Andrade, "António Botto," *Dicionário das literaturas portuguesa, brasileira e galega*, vol. 1, 2d ed. (1969).   R.S.S.

Bourdet, Edouard (1887–1945), French dramatist, was born in Saint-Germain-en-Laye. He wrote comedies of manners and psychological plays. The first category includes *Le Rubicon* (1910), *L'Homme enchaîné* (1923; The Man in Chains), *Vient de paraître* (1927; Just Published), *Le Sexe faible* (1929; The Weaker Sex), *La Fleur des pois* (1932; The Dandy), *Les Temps difficiles* (1934; Difficult Times), *Fric-Frac* (1935; Burglary), and *Père* (1942; Father). In these works, Bourdet satirized the greed and lust of the middle class, of writers and publishers, and of the cosmopolitan set. Among his serious dramas are *La Cage ouverte* (1912; The Open Cage), *L'Heure du berger* (1922; The Shepherd's Hour), *La Prisonnière* (1926; The Prisoner), *Margot* (1935), and *Hyménée* (1941; Marriage), which deal with extramarital and premarital love, homosexuality, and incest. Such themes as the loss of masculinity, the importance of the mother figure, and the disintegration of the family unit are as relevant today as they were in the 1920s and 1930s.

Bourdet showed a preference for three-act plays, a disregard for the unities of time and place, a fondness for careful expositions, and a respect for verisimilitude and the proprieties, in spite of risqué subject matter. His style reflects natural speech and the argots of publishing, finance, and the underworld. A certain cynicism recalls Dancourt's (1661–1725) corrupt society, and his relentless depiction of bourgeois foibles is reminiscent of Octave MIRBEAU and Henri Becque (1837–99). Although Bourdet has left no legacy of original thought, style, or poetic vision, his plays offer the personal, disabused view of an *honnête homme* confronted with the spectacle of the human condition.

See: F. Porché, "Edouard Bourdet," *RdP* 44 (1937), vol. 5: 217–28; P. Surer, "Etudes sur le théâtre contemporain," *IL* 8, no. 5 (1956): 184–87.   A.J.W.

Bourges, Elémir (1852–1925), French novelist and playwright, was born in Manosque. After a period of relative neglect, he is now considered an important precursor as well as a master of symbolist prose. Bourges devoted his life almost exclusively to the kind of quasi-religious quest of art and beauty that his friend Stéphane MALLARMÉ was then pursuing with equally painstaking zeal in the field of poetry. Reacting strongly against what he saw as the naturalists' tendency to present a degraded and deformed image of man, Bourges sought a nobler, more heroic, and for him truer vision in the great literatures of the past. In the wake of such models as Aeschylus, the Elizabethan dramatists, Percy Bysshe Shelley, and Goethe, he made man's tragic struggle with fate the central theme of his own work. While this cultural debt accounts for the exceptionally broad range of Bourges's intellectual, ethical, and literary preoccupations, it also marks his artistic limits. Bourges's undeniable feeling for lyricism and dramatic tension is frequently subverted by the weight of his excessively self-conscious erudition and uncompromising ideology. This is most clearly noticeable in his two-part play *La Nef* (1904, 1922; The Ship), a reinterpretation of the Promethean myth, whose lengthy philosophical digressions and overly systematic allegorical plot are more likely to elicit respect than unqualified admiration.

As a novelist, however, Bourges's importance is no longer in question. If *Les Oiseaux s'envolent et les fleurs tombent* (1893; The Birds Take Flight and Flowers Fall) still disconcerts some readers with its operatic vehemence, *Le Crépuscule des dieux* (1884; The Twilight of the Gods), with its successful casting of irrational psychology into the classical mold of rigorous prose, asserts itself today as one of the few undisputed masterpieces of symbolist fiction.

See: H. Clouard, "Hardiesse et échec d'Elémir Bourges," in *Histoire de la littérature française du symbolisme à nos jours*, vol. 1 (1947), pp. 168–72; A. Lebois, *Les Tendances du symbolisme à travers l'œuvre d'Elémir Bourges* (1952). B.B.

Bourget, Paul (1852–1935), French novelist and critic, was born in Amiens. He received his principal education in Paris at the Lycée Louis-le-Grand and the Ecole des Hautes Etudes. Resisting his father's encouragement to become a teacher, he followed his childhood bent to write. His first article, on Baruch Spinoza, appeared in 1872 when he was barely 20. After publishing an important essay in the *Revue des deux mondes* (1873) on realistic and pietistic novels, Bourget turned to poetry. His first book of poems, *La Vie inquiète* (1875; The Restless Life), was followed by a verse novel, *Edel* (1877), and a volume of poetry, *Les Aveux* (1882; The Avowals). In 1883 he published *Essais de psychologie contemporaine* (Essays on Contemporary Psychology), a volume that included five essays on the mental and psychological characteristics of Stendhal, Hippolyte Taine, Ernest Renan, Gustave Flaubert, and Charles BAUDELAIRE (figures mainly from the generation just before his own), assessing their responsibility for the pessimism Bourget saw everywhere around him. These essays, and those in *Nouveaux Essais* (1885) on the Goncourts, Denys AMIEL, Dumas *fils*, Ivan Turgenev, and Leconte de Lisle, actually adopted Taine's own dictum that literature is a "living psychology," yet they were widely hailed as the most original and illuminating criticism since Charles-Augustin Sainte-Beuve (1804–69). Bourget thus became the spokesman for the intellectual French youth that had already warmly greeted his poetry.

Although Bourget continued to write criticism throughout his life, he preferred being a novelist, wisely choosing a form favoring his analytical gifts, the psychological novel. *L'Irréparable* appeared in 1884, *Cruelle énigme* in 1885 (Eng. trs., *A Cruel Enigma*, 1887, *Love's Cruel Enigma*, 1891), and *André Cornélis* (Eng. tr., *The Story of André Cornélis*, 1909) and *Mensonges* (Eng. trs., *Lies*, 1892, *A Living Lie*, 1893) in 1887. Bourget not only revived a kind of fiction that was specifically French, but gave it new form: a particularly minute analysis of human feelings, applying the precise investigative techniques of his *Essais*. He satisfied a generation reared under the unchallenged domination of realism. The world he chose to dissect—a world of wealthy parvenu waifs left behind by the Second Empire—was no place for presenting the innocent aspects of love. But behind the painter of rather objectionable situations lurked a stern moralist convinced that "psychology is to ethics what anatomy is to therapeutics." This moralism, denied by some of his Victorian critics, surfaced openly in *Le Disciple* (1889; Eng. tr., *The Disciple*, 1898), an earnest indictment of determinism. The preface spelled out his lesson; lauding spiritual values, he beseeched the youth of his time to shun sci-

entific epicurism, a sure road to immorality. Henceforth Bourget not only sounded the ethical note ever more distinctly, but further enlarged his scope when he discovered that he could not properly dissociate his characters from their social milieu. This approach appears first in *Cosmopolis* (1893; Eng. tr., *Cosmopolis: A Novel*, 1893), where the love interest is subservient to a denunciation of cosmopolitanism. The political discussions attendant upon the Dreyfus Affair accelerated Bourget's advance toward a social consciousness. He came to see the only remedy for the moral diseases of his country in a return to its ancient traditions. He therefore recommended the rehabilitation of an aristocracy, like England's, hereditary but open to any man of merit.

For some years, Bourget advocated a revival of France's pristine Catholicism, at least as a social and moral force. By 1901 he had overcome the last of his doctrinal doubts and accepted Catholic dogma in toto. Nearly all his novels after 1900—including *L'Etape* (1902; The Stage), *Un Divorce* (1904; Eng. trs., *A Divorce*, 1904, *Divorce: A Domestic Tragedy of Modern France*, 1904), and *L'Emigré* (1907; Eng. tr., *The Weight of the Name*, 1909)—present some aspect of these social and religious beliefs. In the novels *Le Sens de la mort* (1915; Eng. tr., *The Night Cometh*, 1916), *Cœur pensif ne sait où il va* (1924; Pensive Heart Knows Not Where It Goes), *Nos Actes nous suivent* (1927; Our Acts Follow Us), and others, Bourget turned to moral and social problems raised by World War I. Similar problems inform several of his polemical volumes as well, such as *Pages de critique et de doctrine* (1912; Pages of Criticism and Doctrine), *Nouvelles Pages* (1922), *Au service de l'ordre* (2 vols., 1929, 1933; In the Service of Order), and *Quelques témoignages* (2 vols., 1928, 1934; Some Testimony), collected from speeches and newspaper and magazine articles. The timid novelist even abandoned the solitude of his study for the rigors of the speaker's platform to defend such groups as the monarchic Action Française, although he was too cautious and rational ever to espouse their more radical aspects.

In addition to his other works, Bourget exhibited his amazing versatility in more than 20 volumes of novellas and short stories. He attempted everything from simple anecdotes to leisurely, complicated narratives, and in such collections as *Pastels: Dix Portraits de femmes* (1889; Ten Portraits of Women), *Nouveaux Pastels: Dix Portraits d'hommes* (1890; Eng. tr., *Pastels of Men*, 1891–92), *Complications sentimentales* (1898; Sentimental Complications), *Drames de famille* (1900; Family Dramas), *Les Détours du cœur* (1908; The Tricks of the Heart), and *Anomalies* (1920; Eng. tr., 1920)—in which he indulged his lasting fascination with psychiatric abnormalities—the variety defies classification. These stories probably represent his finest work, a few reaching a degree of excellence rarely surpassed.

Bourget also essayed drama, his interest in the stage dating back to 1879–1882, when he was drama critic for the *Globe*. The stagestruck Bourget was responsible, as author or collaborator, for 16 plays, some original, most adapted from his fiction, four in the mold of Alfred de Musset's *comédies-proverbes*. His most significant theatrical works are *La Barricade* (1910) and *Le Tribun* (1911; Eng. tr., *A Tribune of the People*, 1910?), which evoke the politicosocial atmosphere of that time.

Bourget's indefatigable globetrotting produced some charming travel books. *Sensations d'Italie* (1891; Eng. tr., *The Glamour of Italy*, 1923) evokes the beauties of his second fatherland, while *Etudes anglaises* (1889; English Studies) shows almost equal admiration for the British Isles. *Outre-mer: notes sur l'Amérique* (1895; Eng. tr.,

Outre-mer: Impressions of America, 1895) is an eminently perspicacious, readable account of his tour of the United States.

Few writers have successfully worn so many hats: excellent novelist, short-story writer, and literary critic; popular poet and dramatist; cogent polemist on religion, economics, and politics; delightful and sharp-eyed commentator on travel. Caught in the maelstrom of the political dissensions of the period 1894–1914, Bourget became a prophet to some, but others ridiculed him for his intransigent conservatism. Yet his keen intellect, his insight into the hidden motives of human actions, the lucidity of his reasoning, and his deft handling of the most complicated plots are generally recognized. He lacks the vital imagination of a Balzac, his chief model, and his style, at least to hypercritical French readers, is rather ordinary. But his minutely accurate observations and his sincerity as a social reporter make his works invaluable documents for students of French society between the War of 1870 and World War II.

See: V. Giraud, *Paul Bourget* (1934); A. Feuillerat, *Paul Bourget* (1937); A. E. Singer, *Paul Bourget* (1976).

A.F. rev. A.E.S.

Bousoño, Carlos (1923–), Spanish poet, critic, and theorist, was born in Boal (Asturias) and has been a professor at the University of Madrid since 1950. He received the Fastenrath Prize from the Royal Spanish Academy of the Language for his *Teoría de la expresión poética* (1952), the Critics' Prize for his last two books of poetry, and the National Prize for Literature in critical theory for *El ir-. racionalismo poético: El símbolo.*

Bousoño's first volume of poetry, *Subida al amor* (1945; Ascent to Love), was openly religious in tone, but his work soon reflected a profoundly existential vision of life as a luminous flowering out of the void. This view is clear in the title of his second book, *Primavera de la muerte* (1946; Springtime of Death). This intuition, corresponding to that of a "nothingness that is," and the movement between the poles of that dialectic, provide the subject of his next two works: the world as nothingness or death in *Noche del sentido* (1957; Night of the Senses) and the world as being, or the recovery of the world after doubt, in *Invasión de la realidad* (1962). His more recent poetry, in *Oda en la ceniza* (1968; Ode in the Ashes) and *Las monedas contra la losa* (1973; Coins Against the Gravestone), presents a new and complex style that in itself reflects the two faces of that dialectic, that is, the splendor and the emptiness of the world. Bousoño created the "expressive surprise" by using rhetorical devices of great effectiveness and originality, particularly paradox and detailed nonallegorical development of images, which he himself analyzed most lucidly in the introduction to his *Antología poética* (1976). Because of his continued intellectual and artistic evolution, Bousoño is today the most vital poet, and one of the most intense, of the first poetic generation of post-Civil War Spain.

His other important critical and theoretical works include *La poesía de Vicente Aleixandre* (1977), the most complete study to date of the 1977 Nobel laureate, and *Seis calas en la expresión literaria española* (1969; Six Approaches to Spanish Literary Expression). He has also written a great many essays and several substantive studies of other contemporary Spanish poets (Claudio RODRÍGUEZ, Francisco BRINES, and Guillermo CARNERO) which have served as prologues to anthologies of their works. Bousoño's *Teoría de la expresión poética* formulated at an early date positions that have taken on major importance in the field of literary interpretation in recent years, especially his concept of poetry as a modification of language or a departure from the linguistic norm. This study offers a lucid explication of the techniques of modern poetry. Markedly expanded and refined in later editions (the 6th, in two volumes, is from 1977), it is now almost a new work. Bousoño's theoretical system leads him to interpret artistic expression in general and contains the outlines of a personal treatise on aesthetics. The same can be said of his last two books in this field: *El irracionalismo poético: el símbolo* and *Superrealismo y simbolización poética* (1978), which are decisive contributions to the analysis of these subjects. Bousoño is today the most important Hispanic literary theorist.

See: F. Brines, "Carlos Bousoño: una poesía religiosa desde la incredulidad," *CHA* 320–21 (February-March 1977): 221–48; J. Olivio Jiménez, *Cinco poetas del tiempo* (1972), pp. 327–415; J. Olivio Jiménez, *Diez años de poesía española, 1960–1970* (1972), pp. 243–79.   J.O.J.

Bousquet, Joë (1897–1950), French poet and essayist, was born in Narbonne. He attended the lycée of Carcassonne, spent a few months in England in 1913, began to study at the Paris Commerce School, and enlisted during World War I. On May 27, 1918, he was severely wounded and remained paralyzed for the rest of his life. "Each day is the day of our death," he wrote. Yet if Bousquet could not discover the world, the world came to him. He had many friends in literary cir??? (Paul VALÉRY, André GIDE, Louis ARAGON, Paul ÉLUARD, Ferdinand Alquié, René Nelli) and in artistic circles (Max Ernst, Salvador Dali, Tal Coat, Paul Klee, André Masson). Bousquet survived his ordeal thanks to his interests in literature, philosophy, and language. Indeed, he was in touch with the whole French intelligentsia and his conversation was legendary. *François-Paul Alibert* (1925), his first published work, was a homage to his first literary master. Bousquet's other works are mostly extracts from the huge diary he kept all his life. *Il ne fait pas assez noir* (1931; It is Not Dark Enough), *La Tisane des sarments* (1936; The Infusion of Vine-Shoots), *Traduit du silence* (1941; Translated from Silence), and *La Connaissance du soir* (1945; Knowledge of the Evening) show the greatness and the originality of the poet. He left several essays unpublished at the time of his death.

Bousquet has been called a "Mediterranean Novalis." He was one of the masters of his generation, and his life remains an outstanding example of courage.

See: F. Alquié, *Philosophie du surréalisme* (1950); S. André, H. Juin, and G. Massat, *Joë Bousquet* (1958); R. Nelli, *Joë Bousquet: sa vie, son œuvre* (1975).

J.-C.M.

Boutens, Pieter Cornelis (1870–1943), Dutch poet, was born in Middelburg, on the island of Walcheren. He studied classics at Utrecht, and taught Latin and Greek in a secondary school in Voorschoten, but from 1904 on, he lived as a private citizen in The Hague. Boutens grew up in a devout home, and the language of the Bible is evident in his work. At the same time, he was the heir of the individualism, the subjectivisim, and the emotions of the "Men of the Eighties." Their influence is evident in his first volume of verse, *Verzen* (1898; Poems), for which Lodewijk VAN DEYSSEL wrote the introduction. His striving for individual expression sometimes led to obscurity, as is also evident in his *Praeludiën* (1902; Preludes). He did not have a spontaneous feeling for natural phenomena outside himself. Yet his own familiarity with the classics eventually made itself felt in the neoclassical simplicity of *Stemmen* (1907; Voices), *Vergeten liedjes* (1909; Forgotten Songs), and *Carmina* (1912; Songs). Boutens had an ear for melody, and he was a master of both the language and poetic form, who found just the right word to express every nuance perceived by his delicate senses. Although he never enjoyed fame, his modern adaptation of the medieval legend of Mary in *Beatrijs* (1908; Beatrice) brought him a popular reputation. He studied Platonism, but his belief in the force of love, the importance of beauty, and the inner reality behind the world of ideas goes back to German romanticism. These motifs appeared in such volumes of poetry as *Lentemaan* (1917; Spring Moon), *Sonnetten* (1920), and *Zomerwolken* (1922; Summer Clouds).

Boutens' poetry became more philosophical and cerebral, so that he has often been criticized for being cold and lacking genuine emotion. On the other hand, *Bezonnen verzen* (1931; Level-Headed Poems), *Hollandsche kwatrijnen* (1932; Dutch Quatrins), and *Tusschenspelen* (1942; Interludes) show the sincerity of his feelings as a Dutchman. Even at the age of 18, Boutens was at work turning Plato into Dutch, and during his life he produced a number of translations of high literary quality, such as Aeschylus' *Agamemnon* (1904), Goethe's *Tasso* (1919), Sophocles' *Electra* (1920), and Homer's *Odyssey* (1937). His work has been published as *Verzamelde Werken, I–VII* (1943–54; Collected Works), part of which he prepared himself, and *Verzamelde Lyriek* (1968; Collected Lyrics).

See: D. A. M. Binnendijk, *Een protest tegen den tijd: inleiding tot de poëzie van Boutens* (1945); Karel de Clerck, *Uit het leven van Pieter Cornelis Boutens* (1969).

S.L.F.

Boye, Karin (1900–41), Swedish poet, novelist, and short-story writer, was born in Göteborg and died, apparently a suicide, when she was just past 40. She was among the most original and arresting of modern Swedish authors. As a personality she was intent, moody, tautly emotional, rigorously honest; as an artist she was by instinct simple and direct, although her subtle analytical temperament led her not infrequently to employ literary-technical devices that suggest certain strong affinities with modern expressionistic trends in the graphic arts. It was perhaps the rare combination of deep emotionalism and sharp critical intelligence in the same artistic personality that brought about the inner crisis that resulted in her early death. Her last novel, *Kallocain* (1941), reveals clearly enough that she had come to look upon certain developments in modern life (particularly political developments) with such passionate disillusionment that she could not continue to live in a world that at so many essential points inevitably did violence to the deepest and most sensitive of individual values. Her earliest work, two volumes of poems entitled *Moln* (1922; Clouds) and *Gömda land* (1924; Hidden Lands), reveals a young poet of undeniable technical skill, but one who is inspired by what might seem to be a somewhat overstrained, youthful idealism. Her later poetry, contained in the volumes *Härdarna* (1927; Hearthstones) and *För trädets skull* (1935; For the Sake of the Tree), maintains with no essential change the austere, rigorous idealism of her earlier verse, though this later poetry has in it much more of the substance of an immediate actual life, and it is moved by a passionately warm feeling for mankind. That which is most characteristic of her best poetry is the note of a fine, dignified personal reserve giving way to a vigorous humanitarianism under the pressure of an overwhelming sense of responsibility to a suffering mankind.

Besides her verse, Boye wrote two volumes of short stories as well as five novels. The spirit of high seriousness characteristic of Boye's poetry is just as centrally present in her prose fiction and in the novels, in fact, her brooding analytical preoccupations come into even sharper relief than in most of her poetry. The novels of the early 1930s—*Astarte* (1931), *Merit vaknar* (1933; Merit Awakens), and *Kris* (1934; Crisis)—are strongly stylized and schematic in form, in part because of the sharp focus on particular moral and psychological problems typical of these stories, in part because of the author's conscious effort to employ contemporary expressionistic literary techniques. The two later novels, *För lite* (1936; Too Little) and *Kallocain,* manage more successfully to avoid the purely schematic and the abstract, telling the central tale more naturally and directly, though they, too, are concerned primarily with psychological and moral problems of a highly complex kind. *För lite* is a strangely gripping tale that illustrates with probing, moody power how a once promising literary figure lives a weary shadow life of evasiveness and frustration because of his inability to rise creatively above the petty domestic fate that is his. *Kallocain* is Boye's contribution to the literature of flaming protest against modern totalitarian politics, written at a time when totalitarianism was everywhere victorious in Europe. The posthumously published collection of poetry *De sju dödssynderna* (1941; The Seven Deadly Sins), about love and death, is generally considered to be her best work.

See: M. Abenius, *Drabbad av renhet: en bok om Karin Boye's liv och diktning* (1950; new ed. under the title *Karin Boye,* 1965); R. B. Vowes, Introduction to K. Boye, *Kallocain* (1966) pp. vii–xxv.   A.G.

Boylesve, René, pseud. of René Tardiveau (1867–1926), French novelist, was born and spent his childhood in La Haye-Descartes, where his father was a notary. His mother died when he was only four. The child spent his summer vacations with his mother's aunt (the Félicie Planté found in several of his novels) on a country estate a few miles from the town, acquiring there the deep love and understanding of nature that permeate his works.

Boylesve published books written in several very different veins. The best-known Boylesve is the author of libertine stories that remind one of such writers as Restif de la Bretonne (1734–1806) and André-Robert-Andréade Nerciat. He numbered among his friends the best of the sensuously pagan writers of his period—Henri de RÉGNIER, Pierre LOUŸS, and Hugues Rebell—whom he had met in connection with *L'Ermitage,* a small symbolist review in which he made his literary debut. All of these writers had a solid classical background and valued a beautiful style. This explains why Boylesve's most licentious novels—*Les Bains de Bade* (1896; The Baths of Baden), *La Leçon d'amour dans un parc* (1902; Lesson in Love in a Park), and *Les Nouvelles Leçons d'amour dans un parc* (1926; New Lessons in Love in a Park)—retain a flavor of aristocratic elegance and a finesse that one does not find in the libertine novels of the later 18th century.

One of Boylesve's best-known novels, *Le Parfum des Iles Borromées* (1898; The Perfume of the Borromée Isles), is like a hyphen between his libertine stories and a series of novels of psychological analysis that suggest a link with Pierre Chaderlos de Laclos (1741–1803). In these psychological novels, such as *Sainte-Marie-des-fleurs* (1897; Saint Mary of the Flowers), *Mon Amour* (1908; My Love), *Elise* (1921), and *Souvenirs du jardin détruit* (1934; Memories of a Destroyed Garden), there is the same lucid, cruel probing in throbbing flesh as well as in troubled spirits that one finds in Laclos, the same bitterness and cynicism resulting from a pessimistic outlook on love because of too tender a heart.

The most substantial of Boylesve's novels, however,

are those in which he studies bourgeois life in Paris and in Touraine, his native province. Like Honoré de Balzac (1799–1850), he defined the novelist's role as that of historian of the mores of his time. He is essentially a moralist in *Mademoiselle Cloque* (1899), *La Becquée* (1901; Eng. tr., *Daily Bread* in *Young Vigilance*, 1929) and its sequel, *L'Enfant à la balustrade* (1903; Eng. trs., *The House on the Hill*, 1904, *The Child at the Balustrade* in *Young Vigilance*, 1929), *La Jeune Fille bien élevée* (1909; The Well Brought-up Girl) and its sequel, *Madeleine jeune femme* (1912; Madeleine as a Young Woman; the two novels combined in Eng. tr. as *A Gentlewoman of France*, 1916), and *Le Bel Avenir* (1905; The Beautiful Future).

Boylesve's characters are the result of close observation. His works reveal the narrowness, the monotony, and the cruelty of life, as well as the pettiness, the indifference, and the vileness of human beings. Some powerfully drawn characters stand out: Mlle Cloque, who wages what she knows to be a lost war against the hypocrisy, vanity, envy, and covetousness of a sordid society backed by the power of the Church and the money of a Jew; Félicie Planté, who fights a bitter battle against her greedy relatives in order to protect the integrity of her estate, which she wants to save for her grandnephew (Boylesve).

In addition to his novels, Boylesve published several collections of short stories, which correspond in subject to his three types of novels. Of special importance for an understanding of Boylesve's permanent melancholy is one recurring theme: in love, as in every phase of life, mediocrity triumphs. Elevation of spirit, beauty of sentiments, and idealism no longer mean anything. This theme is exemplified in the story of Madeleine, whose mind and heart were permeated by idealistic concepts of the Absolute impressed upon her daily during her years in one of the best convent schools in France. After several disillusionments, she is forced by family circumstances to marry a worthless man. Disenchantment sets in immediately; she realizes that, in this world, there is no absolute, no idealism, no nobility, no beauty, and no great love—one has to accept compromises in everything. Beneath the magical style, each of Boylesve's works hides a cruel drama.

One should not overlook Boylesve's first novel, *Le Médecin des dames de Néans* (1896; The Doctor of the Ladies of Néans). Charles du Bos judged it a Proustian novel nearly 20 years before *A la recherche du temps perdu* (*see* Marcel PROUST). Boylesve would probably have kept on writing in that manner if the director of *La Revue de Paris* had not stupidly discouraged the timid novice when he brought in his manuscript of "Les Bonnets de dentelle," the first version of *La Becquée*. Later, after the success of Proust's literary revolution, Boylesve repented bitterly not having followed his intuition.

See: G. Truc, *Introduction à la lecture de René Boylesve* (1931); E. Gérard-Gailly, *René Boylesve: ennemi de l'amour* (1932); J. Ménard, *L'Œuvre de Boylesve* (1956); A. Bourgeois, *La Vie de Boylesve* (1958).   A.Bo.

Boyson, Emil (1897–), Norwegian poet and novelist, was born in Bergen. He attracted critical attention with his first book, *Sommertørst* (1927; Summer Thirst), a highly experimental, nonnaturalistic novel. This was followed by *Yngre herre på besøk* (1936; A Young Gentleman Visiting) and *Vandring mot havet* (1937; Journey toward the Sea). In these novels, Boyson gave free rein to his lyrical fantasy. Their refined stream-of-consciousness style makes these books important steps away from the then dominant naturalistic novel tradition in Norway (*see* NORWEGIAN LITERATURE).

Despite his innovative early novels, however, Boyson's main contribution lies in the field of poetry. His production is not large, but it contains memorable verse, some of the finest in Norwegian poetry of the 20th century. Although his approach is intellectual—inquisitive and philosophic—he has managed to blend his questions and reflections into sensual, almost mystical images of love and beauty. Boyson has been influenced by the French symbolists as well as by William Butler Yeats and T. S. Eliot, but he has remained a deeply original poet in his relentless pursuit of congruity of thought and expression. Among Boyson's finest poems are "Dryadens hind" (The Dryad and the Hind), published in *Gjemt i mørket* (1939; Hidden in the Darkness), and "Vindu i februar" (Window in February), published in *Gjenkjennelse* (1957; Recognition).

See: A. Aarnes, ed., *Poesi og virkelighet* (1967); A. Kittang and A. Aarseth, *Lyriske strukturer* (1968; rev. ed., 1976).   K.A.F.

Braak, Menno ter (1902–40), Dutch essayist, critic, and novelist, was born in Eibergen. He studied history and Dutch at the University of Amsterdam, and received his doctorate with a dissertation on Emperor Otto III. He had a thorough knowledge of cultural history and a rationalistic philosophy. He was influenced in his ideas by Friedrich NIETZSCHE, but in many aspects, he is related to Busken Huet, an affinity he denied. He was also an admirer of Multatuli. Passionate and polemical, ter Braak was the best critic in the group that gathered around *De Vrije Bladen* (The Free Pages) and *Forum*. When Binnendijk, one of the editors of *De Vrije Bladen* published *Prisma*, an anthology of modern poetry, ter Braak criticized the imitativeness of some of the poets, and demanded more originality and character, for he felt that beauty meant nothing in poetry if there were no character. A long and influential debate ensued, which the poet J. C. Bloem summarized in the telling contrast of the phrase *vorm of vent* (form or fellow). One important result of this literary conflict was that ter Braak left *De Vrije Bladen,* and with Charles Edgar du Perron and the Flemish novelist Maurice Roelants, founded *Forum,* a new magazine that was to be very important in the development of modern Dutch literature. They left no doubt that it was the personality of the creative writer, not form, that mattered. During this period, he wrote two novels, *Hampton Court* (1931) and *Dr. Dumay verliest* (1933; Dr. Dumay Loses). *Démasqué der schoonheid* (1932; Beauty Unmasked) is a continuation of the debate on aestheticism, while *Politicus zonder partij* (1934; Politician without a Party) demonstrates the influence of Nietzsche. In *Van oude en nieuwe christenen* (1937; Of Christians, Old and New), he discussed collective systems of government, such as socialism, fascism, national socialism, and communism, and decided that democracy had more to offer the individual than any of these systems. He became one of the most outspoken critics of the Nazis, and when they invaded the Netherlands in May 1940, he took his own life. Ter Braak also wrote on film, in which he saw new possibilities. His *Verzamelde Werken* (1950–52; Collected Works) were published in seven volumes. S.L.F.

Braaten, Oskar (1881–1939), Norwegian dramatist, novelist, and short-story writer, was born to poor parents in Oslo's East End. He became the first Norwegian writer of stature to use the working-class family as the subject for his writing. Braaten's social engagement, however, is rarely expressed explicitly in his literary production. He was often opposed to the radical elements in the workers' movement, and with his private, lyrical nature he was apt to call attention to the lighter side of the worker's family life. Although his social indignation is apparent in his two novels, *Ulvehiet* (1919; The Wolf's Lair) and *Matilde* (1920), both of which treat life in Oslo's East End, Braaten's real strength, even in these works, is his creation of atmosphere and his psychological realism. His writing bears witness to his admiration for the unsung heroes of the working class. Through his many novels and short stories, and through his immensely popular folk comedies, *Ungen* (1911; The Child) and *Den store barnedåpen* (1925; The Great Christening Ceremony), Braaten opened up a new world to the Norwegian reading public.

See: A. Lind, *Oskar Braaten* (1962).   K.A.F.

Bracco, Roberto (1862–1943), Italian playwright and short-story writer, was born in Naples. Between 1886 and 1922 he wrote 31 plays, ranging from frothy drawing-room comedies that mock aristocratic marital mores and poignant melodramas depicting Neapolitan low life to problem plays that explore psychological motivation and social issues. Bracco's theater reflects diverse literary and cultural influences: French Second Empire drama, in its stagecraft; *verismo* (*see* ITALIAN LITERATURE), in its social milieux and character types; Henrick IBSEN and the philosophical current of transcendental idealism, in its themes; and psychoanalysis, in its introspective characterization. A recurrent genre in Bracco's canon is the witty comedy, inspired by Parisian *pochades*; the finest of his comedies is *Infedele* (1894; Unfaithful), a paradoxical look at upper-class adultery. Verist influence is evident in his sentimental and polemical sketches of the victimized poor, such as *Don Pietro Caruso* (1895) and *Sperduti nel buio* (1901; Lost in the Dark), two of Bracco's best plays.

Bracco's originality lies in his drama of ideas and, more so, in his "intimist" theater of subtle psychological investigation. Conflicts between materialist and spiritual outlooks, the dilemma of contrary impulses toward freedom and duty, and the release of women from denigrating social conventions are concerns of the better problem plays: *Il trionfo* (1895; The Triumph), *Tragedie dell'anima* (1899; Tragedies of the Soul), *Maternità* (1903; Maternity), *I fantasmi* (1906; Eng. tr., *Phantasms*, 1908), and *La piccola fonte* (1905; Eng. tr., *The Hidden Spring*, 1907). Bracco's late plays are distinguished by character analysis that is suggestive of Freudian theory, intimating the subconscious through allusion and atmosphere. The outstanding example of this technique is his very best work, *Il piccolo santo* (1909; The Humble Saint), in which a saintly priest unconsciously harbors dark desires and unwittingly commits murder, actuating these desires through an external agent gifted with extrasensory perception.

Bracco's lesser writings include Neapolitan dialect verse, 200 short stories, and articles penned as journalist, drama critic, and music critic for several Neapolitan dailies. Bracco's plays enjoyed immense popularity in Italy, but with the advent of fascism, they were banned, for Bracco was an outspoken enemy of the regime. His plays were also staged and admired throughout Europe, and English versions appeared in London and New York.

See: R. Altrocchi, "Bracco and the Drama of the Subconscious," *NAR* 224 (1927): 151–62; A. Stäuble, *Il teatro di Roberto Bracco* (1959).   J.C.

Brancati, Vitaliano (1907–54), Italian novelist, dramatist, screenwriter, journalist, and essayist, was born in Pachino, Sicily. During his early years, Brancati upheld Gabriele D'ANNUNZIO as his literary model and fascism as his political ideal. These influences are evident in his plays *Fedor* (1928) and *Everest* (1931). In 1928 he moved to Rome and collaborated on the Fascist paper *Il Tevere*. Here he also wrote the play *Piave* and his first novel, *L'amico del vincitore* (1932; The Winner's Friend). In later years, Brancati claimed that in 1933 he privately threw over his early literary and political ideals. It was, however, only after his editorship of *Quadrivio* had immersed him in the cultural environment of fascism, and after his novel *Singolare avventura di viaggio* (1934; Strange Travel Adventure) had run into difficulties with the government, that he repudiated his early writings and broke openly with the Fascists. Disillusioned, he returned to Sicily and spent several years teaching, reading, and searching for new literary models. During this period he wrote *Gli anni perduti* (written 1934–36, published 1941; Lost Years) and *Questo matrimonio si deve fare* (1938; This Marriage Must Take Place).

Brancati achieved recognition with the novel *Don Giovanni in Sicilia* (1941; Don Giovanni in Sicily). He returned to Rome and wrote filmscripts as well as the play *Le trombe di Eustachio* (1942; Eustachian Tubes). Subsequent works include the collection *I piaceri, o parole all'orecchio* (1943; Pleasures, or Whispered Words), which combines narrative, memoirs, and critical analysis, and *I fascisti invecchiano* (1946; Fascists Grow Old), a volume of political notes and essays. Brancati considered his finest work to be the story "Il vecchio con gli stivali" (1944; The Old Man Wearing Boots), a critical success praised by Benedetto CROCE. In 1946 he was awarded the Vendemmia Prize for "Vecchio"; he married the actress Anna Proclemer the same year. *Diario romano* (Roman Diary), serialized during 1947, presents Brancati as a social commentator and a profoundly disillusioned man. His novel *Il bell'Antonio* (1949; Eng. tr., *Antonio, the Great Lover*, 1952), won the Bagutta Prize. His last years were marred by financial and personal difficulties.

Brancati's major work is shaped by a complex sensibility, at once satirical, ironic, and nostalgic. This sensibility is articulated most clearly in terms of a defective but fascinating Sicily. In *Gli anni perduti*, Brancati treats the physical and mental torpor of Sicily, but, despite occasionally successful satire and comedy, he has difficulty in reconciling political allegory with detached observation of Sicilian life. *Don Giovanni*, condemned by some critics for structural weaknesses and a one-dimensional treatment of character, has also been praised for its rigorous and complex style, its mixture of nostalgia and satire, and its analysis of the phenomenon of *gallismo*. This term refers to the frustrated (and, therefore, idealized) masculine sexual aggressiveness of the provincial south. Although *gallismo* may be analogous to Fascist political aggression, Brancati studies it as a psychological and social phenomenon that predates and transcends all temporal contingencies. In *Il bell'Antonio*, Brancati introduces the use of social environment as a kind of dramatic chorus, but again critics noted flaws in structure and tone, especially in the novel's tension between the psychological investigation of character and a satiric treatment of provincial realities. In *Paolo il caldo* (1955; Paul the Overheated), left unfinished at his death, Brancati expresses the tensions between reason and happiness, disquieting memory and detached observation, and between reasoned, personal moderation and the erotic impulse as an answer to death and decay. Although Brancati's life and works seem to fall into pro- and anti-Fascist periods, a sense of desolation underlies both attitudes. Even his later idealistic call for a moderate, reasoned society is undermined by the view that man is fundamentally unchangeable and a prey to demagoguery, whether from the political Left or the Right.

See: V. G. Stacchini, *La narrativa di Vitaliano Brancati* (1970) and *Il teatro di Vitaliano Brancati* (1972).

C.L.H.

Brandão, Raul (1867-1930), Portuguese novelist, dramatist, and essayist, was born in Foz do Douro near Oporto. He trained for a military career and advanced as far as the rank of captain before his retirement in 1912. Brandão's literary and journalistic career had begun earlier: his first major work, *Impressões e paisagens* (1890; Impressions and Landscapes), is a collection of stories about the tragic lives of the common people, a preoccupation that was to become central to his writing and make him of special interest to the later neorealists. In *História de um palhaço* (1896; A Clown's Story), his character K. Maurício seeks refuge from reality in dreams and imagination. Among the most important of Brandão's works are *A farsa* (1903; The Farce), *Os pobres* (1906; The Poor), *Húmus* (1917; Humus), and the late *Pobre de pedir* (1931; Reduced to Begging), in which he presents a world of pain, sorrow, and suffering. Again the only escape is into the world of dream and fantasy, as in the case of Gebo, an impoverished old man whose embittered wife tells him to go out and steal and whose daughter is the only one who speaks to him with love and understanding. After a lifetime of unremitting hardship, Gebo longs only for the sleep of death. The author's profound compassion permeates this nightmare world of injustice and helplessness. In *Pescadores* (1923; Fisherman) and *As ilhas desconhecidas* (1927; The Unknown Islands), the beauty of the Portuguese landscape helps to poeticize and lighten the tone. In his *Memórias* (3 vols., 1919, 1925, 1933; Memoir), Brandão reconstructs the last days of the Portuguese monarchy and the establishment and difficulties of the republic through vignettes, comments of participants, gossip, personal observations, documents, and newspaper interviews. He attempts to capture the spirit of the times as well as to sum up a lifetime of sympathy for the poor and humble and abhorrence of violence. For the theater Brandão wrote *O Gebo e a sombra* (1923; "Rags" and the Shadow), *O rei imaginário* (1923; The Imaginary King), and *O avejão* (1929; That Scarecrow of a Man).

See: M. A. Brandão, *Um coração e uma vontade: memórias* (1959); J. P. de Andrade, *Raul Brandão* (1963).

T.Br.

Brandes, Georg (1842-1927), Danish critic and literary historian, was born in Copenhagen. He came from an irreligious Jewish home and after a religious crisis of several years, caused by Søren KIERKEGAARD's uncompromising teaching, became (about 1863) a confirmed atheist. His university studies began in 1859, and he received his doctorate in 1870. From 1871 to 1887, Brandes was a lecturer at the University of Copenhagen, becoming a professor in 1902. He was schooled in the Hellenistic tradition and the Hegelian speculative didactic method, and only the introduction to the French critics Hippolyte Taine and Charles Sainte-Beuve after 1865 caused a gradual transition from an abstract to a concrete, historical view of literature. Brandes learned from Taine that race, milieu, and the moment are decisive factors for writers and their works; from Sainte-Beuve, that the literary work itself is a psychological document of the author. The literary and biographical discourse became Brandes's favorite genre, for example, in *Danske Digtere* (1877; Danish Authors).

His travels in England, Italy, and France (1870-71) made him aware of then current thoughts and changed his national complacency into ruthless criticism of Denmark's antiquated educational ideals and limited horizons. Upon his return, Brandes decided to "open the doors outward"; and his university lectures, begun in 1871, on *Hovedstrømninger i det nittende Aarhundredes Litteratur* (published 1872-90; Eng. tr., *Main Currents in Nineteenth Century Literature,* 1901-05) were a declaration of war on the established order. The descriptions of the romantic victory over the ideas of the French Revolution and the pursuant liberal change with Percy Bysshe Shelley and Lord Byron in England, Victor Hugo in France, and Heinrich Heine in Germany contained clear allusions to contemporary Denmark, which was, according to Brandes, 40 years behind the rest of Europe. His aim was to awaken the nation from its romantic dreams and proclaim "the faith in the right of free inquiry and the final victory of free thought." The series of lectures of 1871-87 aroused enthusiasm but also bitter resistance from the church, university, and the press. Equally controversial was Brandes's positive program, which, among other things, declared that a literature is only alive insofar as it "makes problems a matter of debate": marriage, religion, and social conditions.

The 1880s became a period of dissension for Brandes, who, in the meantime, had grown beyond the ideas of the 1870s. No longer did he pay attention to current popular ideas. In 1888 he was the first to direct attention to Friedrich NIETZSCHE, whose contempt for the average man contributed to Brandes's turning away from the polemic, naturalistic program of the university lectures. The earlier reformer had now become an aristocratic individualist. As early as in his *Hovedstrømninger,* Brandes had shown an interest in single individuals rather than in ideas or literary currents, and during his stay in Berlin (1877-82), he published a series of outstanding monographs, *Søren Kierkegaard* (1877), *Benjamin Disraëli* (1878; Eng. tr., *Lord Beaconsfield,* 1880), and *Ferdinand Lassalle* (1881; Eng. tr., 1911). In 1889 his new program was presented in *Aristokratisk Radikalisme* (Aristocratic Radicalism). The great personality, regarded as the source and object of culture, is contrasted with the materialistic naturalism. The Nietzsche-inspired hero worship is expressed in the brilliant work *William Shakespeare* (1895-96; Eng. tr., 1898), of dubious value as a scholarly study owing to the parallels drawn between the life and work of Shakespeare but exceptional as aesthetic analysis and literary psychology. Nietzschean ideas are equally evident in four extensive and popular biographies, *Goethe* (1914-15; Eng. tr., 1924), *Voltaire* (1916-17; Eng. tr., 1930), *Julius Caesar* (1918; Eng. tr., 1924), and *Michelangelo* (1921).

Brandes has, as nobody else, been a source of controversy in Scandinavia, but there is no doubt as to his great significance. His scholarship might lack method, but his biographies and essays are truly outstanding. Through his infallible intuition, Brandes discovered a whole generation of Danish writers (Jens Peter JACOBSEN, Holger DRACHMANN, Karl GJELLERUP), presented in *Det moderne Gjennembruds Mænd* (1883; Men of the Modern Breakthrough); and he influenced a number of important Scandinavian authors (Bjørnstjerne BJØRNSON, Henrik IBSEN, Knut HAMSUN, and August STRINDBERG). He introduced the newer Nordic literature to the rest of the world and focused attention on several great figures in European intellectual life such as Paul CLAUDEL, Ibsen, and Nietzsche.

See: J. Moritzen, *Georg Brandes in Life and Letters* (1922); H. Fenger, *Georg Brandes' Læreaar* (1955); B. Nolin, *Den gode europén* (1965), and *Georg Brandes, TWAS* 390 (1976).

S.H.R.

Brandt, Jørgen Gustava (1929–), Danish poet and novelist, was born in Copenhagen. The recipient of a business education, he has worked for the Danish Broadcasting Corporation since 1964. In his debut collection of poems, *Korn i Pelegs Mark* (1949; Grain in the Fields of Peleg), the moods of a young town dweller are surrealistically described with a mingling of spiritual and material realities. Following a series of stylistically perfect but impersonal collections published during the 1950s, Brandt's earlier introversion was transformed in *Fragment af imorgen* (1960; Fragment of Tomorrow) into an experience of harmony with the outer world. In *Ateliers* (1967), there are a number of mythical and religious symbols, which, in the collections *Vendinger* (1971; Turns) and *Her omkring* (1974; Around Here), are used to express Brandt's longing for a mystical rest in existence, a longing that explains the author's alternation between large and small texts, poetry and prose. This led in 1969 and 1973 respectively to the lyrical novels *Kvinden på Lüneburg Hede* (The Woman on the Luneburg Moors) and *Pink Champagne*. A temporary culmination was reached with the lyrical trilogy *Mit hjerte i København* (1975; My Heart in Copenhagen), *Jathåram* (1976), and *Regnansigt* (1976; Rain Face), an intensive acknowledgment of life, intermingling past and present in remembrances, moods, and portraits. Brandt's writing is subtle and intellectual without direct involvement in current ideological problems, which, however, is a mark not of aestheticism but rather of a philosophical point of view.   S.H.R.

Brandys, Kazimierz (1916–), Polish prose writer, playwright, and essayist, was born in Łódź and studied law at Warsaw University. Brandys's early novel *Miasto niepokonane* (1946; The Invincible City) presents the heroic struggle of the city of Warsaw during the German occupation in World War II. In his four-part cycle of novels, *Między wojnami* (1948–51; Between the Wars), Brandys portrayed the historically conditioned destinies of the heroes from the intelligentsia in the interwar period, during World War II, and in the first years after the war. In his collection of short stories *Czerwona czapeczka* (1956; The Red Cap), especially in the story "Obrona Grenady" (The Defense of the Grenada), as well as in the novel *Matka Królów* (1957; Eng. tr., *Sons and Comrades*, 1960), he presents the moral tragedies and conflicts during the Stalinist period. His *Listy do pani Z. Wspomnienia z teraźniejszości*, vols. 1–3 (1958–60; Letters to Mrs. Z. Recollections from the Present) consists of short essays that have the character of philosophical meditations about various phenomena of contemporary life, especially in Poland.
See: J. Ziomek, *Kazimierz Brandys* (1964).   J.T.B.

Branner, Hans Christian (1903–66), Danish novelist, short-story writer, and playwright, was born in the vicinity of Copenhagen. Following his failure as an actor in the provinces, Branner was employed in the publishing business from 1923 to 1933. He made his literary debut with the collective novel (*see* DANISH LITERATURE) *Legetøj* (1936; Toys), which describes the spread of lies and deceit throughout a commercial firm—a symbol of Europe at that time and the growing Nazism. Like Karen BLIXEN, Branner was skeptical about all ideological and social systems. In his works, people are placed in the center and examined from a psychoanalytical point of view. Later Branner was strongly influenced by existentialism, the fundamentals of which—despair, responsibility, and isolation—increasingly became the focal point of his attention. *Barnet leger ved Stranden* (1937; The Child

is Playing on the Beach) consists of psychological analyses of the importance of childhood experiences for the adult view of life. The short stories in *Om lidt er vi borte* (1939; In a Little While We Are Gone) reach an international level owing to Branner's ability to penetrate the world of the child and uncover an essential drama behind a seemingly trite incident. In *To Minutters Stilhed* (1944; Eng. tr., *Two Minutes of Silence*, 1966), the problems of puberty are described in three short stories, although the theme of love predominates, seen as the sole possibility of breaking human isolation. The novel *Drømmen om en Kvinde* (1941; The Dream of a Woman) consists of the stream of consciousness of 5 persons during a 24-hour period, concentrating on the 2 fundamental but most isolated situations in life—birth and death—while also demonstrating the necessity of human contact. The suggested humanistic point of view is fully developed in Branner's best-known novel, *Rytteren* (1949; Eng. trs., *The Riding Master*, 1951, *The Mistress*, 1953), depicting the attempt of people to free themselves from the past.

After 1939, World War II forms the gloomy background of Branner's entire production. *Ingen kender Natten* (1955; Eng. tr., *No Man Knows the Night*, 1958) impressively alternates between two milieus, that of the Resistance and that of the collaborators. The historical frame is, however, subordinate. The novel actually depicts the situation of a rootless human being dominated by nihilism and Freudianism.

Among Branner's finest achievements is a series of radio plays and his victory as a dramatist came with *Søskende* (1952; Eng. tr., "The Judge," in *Contemporary Danish Plays*, 1955), in which the woman, who (according to Branner) is closer to the source of life and able to submit to as well as save the man, takes up the fight against the decay of emotions. The religiously inspired ideological drama *Thermopylæ* (1958; Eng. tr., "Thermopylae," in *Modern Nordic Plays, Denmark*, 1973) analyzes, from Branner's pessimistic and moralistic point of view, the role of humanism in a world of violence and terror.
See: E. Frederiksen, *Hans Christian Branner* (1966); T. L. Markey, *Hans Christian Branner, TWAS* 245 (1973).   S.H.R.

Brasillach, Robert (1900–45), French novelist, pamphleteer, critic, journalist, and poet, was born in Perpignan, the son of an army officer. A precocious and gifted student, he took *licence* degrees in Latin, French, Greek, and philology and attended the Ecole Normale Supérieure. His classical interests are mirrored in his *Présence de Virgile* (1931), *Pierre Corneille* (1938), the posthumous *Anthologie de la poésie grecque* (1950; Anthology of Greek Poetry), and the play *Bérénice* (1954), which was driven from the Paris stage by police when produced under the title *La Reine de Césarée* (The Queen of Cesarea) in 1957. Charles MAURRAS appointed him literary critic of *Action française* in 1931, and throughout the 1930s Brasillach was associated with that paper and with the pro-Fascist weekly *Je suis partout*, of which he was an editor.

Captured in 1940 while serving in the French army, he returned to Paris and resumed work at the revitalized *Je suis partout* in May of that year. Arrested in September 1944, he was executed in February 1945, a victim of the political hysteria prevailing at the time.

Brasillach's *Histoire du cinéma* (1935; Eng. tr., *History of Motion Pictures*, 1938), written with his brother-in-law Maurice BARDÈCHE, remains an important book. Brasillach also wrote seven novels, *Le Voleur d'étincelles*

(1932; The Thief of Sparks), *L'Enfant de la nuit* (1934; The Child of Night), *Le Marchand d'oiseaux* (1936; The Bird Seller), *Comme le temps passe* (1937; Eng. tr., *Youth Goes Over*, 1938), *Les Sept Couleurs* (1939; The Seven Colors), *La Conquérante* (1942; The Conqueress), and *Six Heures à perdre* (1953; Six Hours to Lose), all of which display fine workmanship, but not greatness. His two volumes of poetry, *Poèmes* (1944) and *Poèmes de Fresnes* (1945), show the breadth of his literary talent. Among his many political works are *Histoire de la guerre d'Espagne* (1939; History of the War in Spain), *Notre avant-guerre* (1941; Our Prewar Period), and *Journal d'un homme occupé* (1955; Diary of a Busy Man). A fine edition of his *Œuvres complètes* was published in 1963-65.

See: P. Vandromme, *Robert Brasillach: l'homme et l'œuvre* (1956). D.O'C.

Bratny, Roman (1921-), Polish novelist, was born in Cracow. His former name was Roman Mularczyk. He represents a generation of writers who emerged just after World War II and whose works reflect the traumatic experiences of the war. Active in the Resistance movement, he tried to convey the spirit of the young freedom-fighters, first in poetry and later in numerous short stories and short novels. His most successful novel, *Kolumbowie. Rocznik 20* (1957; The Columbuses. Born in 1920), deals largely with problems of life and struggle under the Nazi occupation of Poland, culminating in the Warsaw uprising of 1944, and with the bitter disappointment brought about by the postwar period. In the 1960s and 1970s, Bratny published several more short novels depicting the social and political problems in a country ruled by a Communist regime: *Nauka chodzenia* (1967; Learning to Walk), *Życie raz jeszcze* (1967; Life Once Again), *Izba tonów i drwina* (1970; House of Tones and a Sneer), and *Trzej w linii prostej* (1970; Three in a Straight Line).

See: *Słownik współczesnych pisarzy polskich*, vol. 1 (1963), pp. 271-73. J.R.K.

Brecht, Bertolt (1898-1956), German dramatist, poet, theatrical theoretician, and producer, was born in Augsburg, Bavaria, and studied medicine and natural science at Munich (1917-21). He spent his military service as a medical orderly, in 1918. Brecht's first plays date from this time: *Baal* (1918-19; Eng. tr., 1964), *Trommeln in der Nacht* (1918-20; Eng. tr., *Drums in the Night*, 1966), *Im Dickicht der Städte* (1921-24; Eng. tr., *In the Jungle of Cities*, 1961), *Mann ist Mann* (1924-26; Eng. tr., *A Man's a Man*, 1961), *Die Dreigroschenoper* (1928; Eng. tr., *The Three-Penny Opera*, 1955), *Aufstieg und Fall der Stadt Mahagonny* (1928-29; Eng. tr., *Rise and Fall of the City of Mahagonny*, 1976), as well as the poems and songs collected as *Die Hauspostille* (1927; Eng. tr., *A Manual of Piety*, 1966). A selection of poems written between 1913 and 1956 were published in English translation as *Poems* in 1976.

Martin Esslin, who has divided Brecht's life and work into five major periods, describes the first period (1918–ca. 1927) as a time of cynicism and anarchic nihilism. The individual in Brecht's work is unable to control his fate: either he lives at the mercy of inner compulsions beyond conscious restraint or he is victimized in the jungle of the cities by incomprehensible social conditions. Thus the fundamental impulse that informs Brecht's pre-Marxist phase is an amoral yielding to powerful instinctual forces, a passive drifting in the stream of life.

Brecht's second period (ca. 1927–ca. 1934), which represents a dialectical reversal in his life and work, is an austere and didactic phase informed by a desperate quest for self-discipline. The major works are *Die heilige Johanna der Schlachthöfe* (1929-31; Eng. tr., *Saint Joan of the Stockyards*, 1956), *Die Maßnahme* (1930; Eng. tr., *The Measures Taken*, 1965), *Die Ausnahme und die Regel* (1930; Eng. tr., *The Exception and the Rule*, 1965), *Die Mutter* (1930-31; Eng. tr., *The Mother*, 1965), and a volume of poems, *Lieder, Gedichte, Chöre* (1934). Brecht's search to stem the dangers of man's irrational nature, which appeared to him to be threatening both the social order as well as the stability of the individual self, ended in his conversion to communism.

The initial sense of freedom and exhilaration in Germany following the collapse of the Wilhelmine society and its values at the end of World War I in 1918 soon gave way to a pervading sense of anxiety; the fear of total moral permissiveness, the mounting threat of social anarchy, and for the alienated individual the danger of ever-increasing psychological solipsism. Communist ideology provided Brecht with a rational form of salvation, for it indicated a clearly marked path leading out of social chaos and mass misery. At the same time Communist discipline provided Brecht's inner life with the moral straitjacket he desperately needed at this time. Brecht henceforth assumed a tough, objective, intellectual, antiromantic persona and from this viewpoint condemned as decadent and immoral such attitudes and psychological states as sentimentality, introspection, inspiration, subjectivity, genius, and individuality. The measure of artistic greatness for Brecht became not originality, intellectual profundity, and psychological depth but typicality, concreteness, directness, and social relevance.

Brecht's new political commitment, with its attendant effect upon his aesthetic theory and practice, received its starkest and most encompassing dramatic expression in the didactic play *Die Maßnahme*. This drama remains the classic statement of the Communist tragedy, which even the Communist Party was unable to stomach. In the play a young comrade is murdered by the Party for having been unable to resist acting upon his natural impulses, that is, his sympathy and compassion for the poor and the exploited. By immediately attempting to alleviate the desperate conditions of the poor and by refusing to compromise his personal moral standards, however, he has served only to postpone the day of the proletarian revolution. The lesson of this drama is that the freedom of the individual must be totally suppressed on behalf of Party discipline today so that mankind as a whole will be able to achieve freedom and full humanity in the future. Also, violence against the rich is justified because of the constant violence done to the poor by the laws of the rich.

The third phase of Brecht's life (ca. 1934-1938) contains works written in more conventional forms and with baldly propagandistic themes: *Der Dreigroschenroman* (1934; Eng. tr., *The Three-Penny Novel*, 1956), *Furcht und Elend des Dritten Reiches* (1935-38; Eng. tr., *The Private Life of the Master Race*, 1944), and *Die Gewehre der Frau Carrar* (1937; Eng. tr., *Señora Carrar's Rifles*, 1938). In these plays the style is direct and often journalistic and the themes are anti-Fascist.

Brecht's fourth period (1938-ca. 1947) is the phase of his greatest plays and poetry. *Leben des Galilei* (1938-39; Eng. tr., *The Life of Galileo*, 1947) treats both Galileo's recantation of the heliocentric theory of the universe as well as his own self-condemnation for having agreed to suppress the truth at the command of the Roman Catholic Church instead of having fearlessly and publicly declared it. *Mutter Courage und ihre Kinder* (1939; Eng. tr., *Mother Courage and Her Children*, 1941) demonstrates that it is the blind greed of the small entrepreneur that makes large wars possible. Mother Courage, seen by Brecht as a negative character, fails to comprehend that in her efforts to support her family by living off the war commercially she has actually caused the destruction of her children. *Der gute Mensch von Sezuan* (1938–40; Eng. tr., *The Good Woman of Setzuan,* 1961) demonstrates the tragic dilemma that man cannot be good and at the same time survive in a world based upon competition, greed, and self-aggrandizement. Therefore, all the natural feelings of love, sympathy, and compassion must be suppressed. The naturally generous good woman of Setzuan has to take on the persona of a cruel and calculating male in order to protect herself from exploitation and total ruin. The three silly and ineffectual gods can only recommend to all mankind the moral imperative "be good," without explaining how such behavior is feasible in a corrupt society. In the drama's epilogue, however, Brecht pleads with the audience to find a way to change a degraded and degrading world. *Der kaukasische Kreidekreis* (1944–45; Eng. tr., *The Caucasian Chalk Circle,* 1948) argues that ownership belongs to those who can use things in the best way. Children belong to those women who are the most motherly, and the land belongs to those who can best cultivate it. The poetry of this period, which includes satirical as well as narrative poems, appeared under the title *Svendborger Gedichte* (1939; Swendborg Poems).

Brecht's fifth period (1947–56) began with his appearance before the House Un-American Activities Committee in Washington, D.C., and his permanent departure shortly thereafter for Europe. On his arrival in East Berlin in 1949 he founded the "Berliner Ensemble." During this period he wrote two minor dramas: *Die Tage der Kommune* (1948–49; Eng. tr., *The Days of the Commune,* 1978) and *Turandot oder der Kongreß der Weißwäscher* (1953–54; Turandot or the Congress of Whitewashers). Brecht's most important dramatic productions at this time resulted in adaptations of works from a variety of sources: *Antigone* (1947) from Friedrich Hölderlin's translation of Sophocles' drama; *Der Hofmeister* (1950; The Private Tutor), from the play by J. M. R. Lenz; *Coriolan* (1951–53), based on Shakespeare's *Coriolanus*; *Don Juan* (1952) from the drama by Molière; *Der Prozeß der Jeanne d'Arc zu Rouen 1431* (1952; The Trial of Jeanne d'Arc at Rouen) from Anna Seghers's version; and *Paulsen und Trompeter,* based upon Farquhar's comedy. This was the period in which Brecht, now the possessor of his own theater, became a great stage director. He also wrote much poetry and published a volume of stories in the style of Heinrich von Kleist under the title of *Kalendergeschichten* (1948; Eng. tr., *Tales from the Calendar,* 1961).

Brecht's profound distrust of intuition and inspiration caused him to write several theoretical essays on the nature and function of his own "epic theater," in which he attempted to provide his art with a rational justification based on Marxist thought. Brecht's most comprehensive, lucid, and dogmatic formulation, presented in the form of 77 paragraphs, is found in his *Kleines Organon für das Theater* (1949; Eng. tr., *A Little Organon for the Theater,* 1951).

Brecht believed that the theater's primary function should be to teach about the exploitation and corruption endemic in capitalist society. It was his unwavering assumption that the audience, once roused to indignation, would necessarily embrace the Marxist program to restructure all social relationships.

Brecht's theater is extroverted, and thus the subject of his work is not the complex inner life of the single individual, rather, the smallest dramatic unit is formed by two individuals interacting amid social, economic, and historical forces. It was for this reason that Brecht felt that his "epic theater" was the single art form best able to comprehend and present the modern human condition in all its complexity.

Brecht argued that the modern theater should be more like the lecture hall than the traditional "Aristotelian theater," which strives to create the illusion of real events happening on the stage, to facilitate the spectator's identification with the protagonist to the point of self-oblivion, and to send him home refreshed and purged of all feelings of fear and pity. Brecht, on the other hand, wanted the spectator to remain wide awake, an emotionally uninvolved rational human being, whose cool and critical attitude toward the events and characters on the stage would allow him to understand the complex and political issues being illustrated.

Brecht believed that the creation of such a critical attitude could occur only if the spectator's natural tendency to identify with the protagonist was constantly counteracted. For only a spectator alienated from the drama would be able to see familiar things and events (the corruption and exploitation existing at every level of his society) in a new and strange way. (A corollary is Brecht's demand that the actor also remain alienated from his role: he must consider that he is merely demonstrating a possible way of behaving, merely "acting" in quotation marks. If the actor does not identify with his role, the audience will also be inhibited from identifying with that role.) The alienated spectator will come to realize that present-day social relations are not immutable or necessary but arbitrary and changeable. Therefore, Brecht's theatergoer is not meant to leave the theater feeling relieved, refreshed, ennobled, and uplifted by the spectacle of the profound spiritual nobility of a great tragic figure. Rather, he should feel indignant, tense, emotionally and intellectually aroused, and thus determined to change the world.

Brecht used other antirealistic techniques to promote and maintain alienation. For instance, if a tender love scene seemed likely to carry away an emotionally gripped spectator, Brecht would interrupt the lyrical mood with a strident song on a very unlovely subject. In this way the audience would be jolted back into a thoughtful attitude. Brecht further advised that the source of music should be exposed to full view rather than hidden in the orchestra pit. As in a boxing ring, lighting, too, should be visible. And the curtain should be dispensed with, for it preserves the illusion that between the acts wizards are secretly preparing magical effects for the delight of the spectators. The director must always strive consciously to oppose the Wagnerian concept of the *Gesamtkunstwerk* with its powerful narcotic effects, which traditional theater tends to create.

Brecht's dramatic theory also provides the playwright with new freedoms. Since the "epic theater" drops the pretense of presenting real events occurring in the present moment upon the stage, the playwright can drop the contrived and tedious ritual of naturalistic exposition in the first scene. Characters may now address the audience directly, provide the necessary background information, and even explain the purpose of the drama. The conclusion of the play may also be revealed so that the element of suspense will not distract the audience from critical thinking. Thus, the concept of the well-made play is rejected: Brecht's dramas tend to be episodic with scenes only very loosely knit together. The playwright's sole imperative (and consequent freedom) is that he structures the drama in whatever manner necessary to deliver best the message of the play.

By his rejection of the psychological mechanism of identification, Brecht was fighting against one of the most powerful elements not only of traditional drama but in the human psyche itself. Brecht's battle to attain a state of alienation in the spectator was a constant and never totally successful campaign. He felt both despair and indignation when the first-night audience of *Mutter Courage* in Zürich regarded the protagonist as a great tragic figure of suffering humanity. *Die Dreigroschenoper* ran for years in New York and had great success before the most bourgeois of audiences which, after the performance, felt not the slightest indignation or need to change the world. Only the already convinced become more convinced after experiencing Brecht's dramatic lessons.

Brecht's life mirrored the political, intellectual, and spiritual chaos of German life during its most tumultuous 50-year period. And his art represented for him a contribution toward hastening the Utopian day of man's secular redemption from this chaos as diagnosed and described by Karl Marx. In a world without God, it was Marx's vision that saved Brecht from nihilistic despair, for the flaw in life was not to be found in the psyche of man nor was it viewed as an inherent metaphysical flaw in nature. Suffering arose from social mismanagement, and what man had so irrationally created could also be recreated by him. Thus Brecht found a new hope anchored in the power of man's reason and given direction by the dogma of an authoritarian political system. A prerequisite condition, however, was that the individual had to subordinate himself to the group, and the artist had to place his art in the service of the proletarian revolution.

How, then, can it be explained that Brecht's drama has (with the exception of East Berlin) been almost unproduced in Communist countries? Communist officials and theoreticians believed that Brecht had quite specifically not written drama that would aid the revolution. Brecht, however, felt that he understood Marx better than the Marxists and that he possessed a greater faith in the ultimate triumph of communism than did Marxist politicians. Brecht's certainty was based upon a vision of human nature that he firmly believed could gain reality only in a Communist state; man was essentially compassionate and generous, but his nature had been perverted by capitalism, which had changed him into a solitary beast of prey, brutal, greedy, callous, and motivated only by a will to power over others. That Communist society would undo this pathology was clear to any rationally thinking man. Brecht soon realized, however, that the aesthetics of socialist realism promulgated by Iosif Stalin was not based on thinking at all. The Party preferred an attitude of irrational acceptance. Brecht experienced a further shock when the Party reinstated naturalism as the officially sanctioned style at the Moscow Art Theater and condemned as decadent everything that was abstract, experimental, and not immediately obvious.

Brecht resisted the suggestions of the Party that he make his message more obvious, less dependent upon critical thinking. He felt this was unnecessary, since as day must follow night he believed in the inevitable advent of communism. It was sufficient to reveal, criticize, and denounce the social evils of the capitalistic system without ever needing to present dramatically and concretely the positive world ahead.

Brecht's situation as a Communist artist is a highly peculiar one. The East applauds the production in the West of Brecht's dramas as a method of propaganda designed to undermine capitalistic self-confidence and also to show that the Communist world has been able to produce an artist of the first rank. But they protect their own citizens from exposure to his art. The West strives to ignore Brecht's communism and to praise him as an artist whose dramas as art works far transcend any particular political message.

See: M. Esslin, *Bertolt Brecht* (1959); P. Demetz, ed. *Brecht: A Collection of Critical Essays* (1962); J. Willett, *The Theater of Bertolt Brecht* (1968).   F.G.P.

Brekke, Paal (1923–), Norwegian poet, novelist, and literary critic, grew up and has lived most of his life in Oslo. He was the articulate center of the group of poets who, in the late 1940s and early 1950s, changed the climate of Norwegian poetry. Inspired by T. S. Eliot (Brekke translated *The Waste Land* into Norwegian), Ezra Pound, and the Swedish modernists (*see* SWEDISH LITERATURE), Brekke presents his view of the postwar world in fragmented, disjointed, and sometimes chaotic verse. His collections of poetry, such as *Skyggefektning* (1949; Shadow Fencing), contain visions of horror, but also original images of beauty and love. In his fourth and perhaps most important collection to date, *Roerne fra Itaka* (1960; The Oarsmen from Ithaca), Brekke mixes ancient myths with modern reality in new and original ways. The collection ends with a monumental song to love and beauty.

Brekke's later poetry is marked by his political radicalization, partly spurred by a visit to poverty-strriken districts in India. In his account of this trip, *En munnfull av Ganger* (1962; A Mouthful of Anger), he describes his political radicalization, and in his poetry there are no longer any visions of hope. *Det skjeve smil i rosa* (1965; The Wry Smile in Rosy Red) is filled with castigations of Western opportunism, brutality, and complacency, and in *Aftenen er stille* (1972; The Evening Is Quiet), Brekke comments, with Brechtian sarcasm and irony (*see* Bertolt BRECHT), on the treatment of old people in the modern welfare state.

In addition to his poetry, Brekke has published two important novels, *Aldrende Orfeus* (1951; Aging Orpheus) and *Og hekken vokste kjempehøy* (1953; And the Hedge Grew High). Written in a combination of traditional narrative and refined stream-of-consciousness style, both novels express the author's humanistic commitment to exploring the connection between man's instinct for isolation and his desire to destroy his surroundings.

See: J. E. Vold, "Et essay om Paal Brekke," *Samtiden,* no. 3 (1979): 27–38.   K.A.F.

Bremond, Henri (1865–1933), French historian of religious ideas, was born in Aix-en-Provence in a house of pious Roman Catholic traditions. Bremond entered the Society of Jesus, in which other members of his family were prominent. He spent nearly 10 years in England and Wales and came back to France with broader views. His retirement from his order in 1904 and his faithfulness to his modernist friend George Tyrrell in 1909 suggested, without casting any doubt upon Bremond's orthodoxy, his evolution from dogma to feeling and, so to speak, from Jacques-Bénigne Bossuet to François de Fénelon. Bremond had met Maurice BARRÈS in Athens and had also visited Antonio FOGAZZARO. Two collections of essays, both entitled *L'Inquiétude religieuse* (1901, 1909; Religious Anxiety), and numerous contributions to the *Etudes* and the *Correspondant* proved his definite interest in "choice souls," *Newman* (1905; Eng. tr., *The Mystery of Newman,* 1907) and *Fénelon* (1910) exemplifying the foremost among them.

When he was able to give up as a livelihood teaching in Jesuit schools, Bremond devoted most of his time—hampered, however, by poor health—to his lifework, the presentation of religious currents in French literature. He offered a unique blending of religious enthusiasm and of literary, nontheological affinities. No one in the long list of modern ecclesiastical authors has produced anything comparable to this erudite writer's unfinished *Histoire littéraire du sentiment religieux en France* (11 vols., 1916–33; Eng. tr., *A Literary History of Religious Thought,* 1928–36). In his view an element of mysticism, transcending the matter-of-factness of life, was the indispensable basis for rich, substantial, and vital feeling. It was this conviction that led this man of sunny Provence to take sides in favor of romanticism, in its spiritual sense, and to supplement his learned studies by works of contemporary interest such as *De la poésie pure* (1926; Concerning Pure Poetry), *Prière et poésie* (1926; Eng. tr., *Prayer and Poetry,* 1927), and *Racine et Valéry* (1930).

As a kind of spiritual adviser to young men of letters, his role during his brief stays in Paris and his contact with circles connected with the Académie Française (to which he was elected in 1923) made him for a certain time a well-known figure in the world of letters (see interviews and articles in *Nouvelles littéraires*). But he always went back with satisfaction to his winter quarters near Pau and to a life of meditation and research. This "Catholic Sainte-Beuve," as he was called, could not easily dispense with some kind of cell.

See: M. Martin du Gard, *De Sainte-Beuve à Fénelon: Henri Bremond* (1927); C. Moisan, *Henri Bremond et la poésie pure* (1967); M. Nédoncelle, ed., *Entretiens sur Henri Bremond* (1967); A. Blanchet, *Henri Bremond: 1865–1904* (1975).   F.B. rev. D.W.A.

Breton, André (1896–1966), French poet, essayist, and theoretician, was born in Tinchebray of Breton parents. He spent his childhood on the Brittany coast, whose luminous seascapes and coastlines were to spark his search for crystalline clarities both in life and in his own writings. A student of medicine, he served in World War I in the neurological wards for the war-injured in Nantes, where he was able to practice what he had learned about psychiatry in the works of Jean Charcot, Pierre Janet, and Sigmund Freud. There he also met Jacques Vaché, a wounded soldier whose rebellious behavior instilled in Breton the seeds of subversion and intensified his aversion to the absurdity of so-called rational civilization.

In Paris, Breton gravitated toward Guillaume APOLLINAIRE, the poetic adventurer of the cubist generation, and toward Francis Picabia, the Spanish avant-garde artist and friend of Tristan TZARA. Breton became part of the group that welcomed the dada movement (*see* FRENCH LITERATURE) to Paris in 1919. By the end of that year, he had turned toward another, more positive revolution in life-style and artistic communication, one for which he was to adopt the word "surrealism," previously used by Apollinaire and others of his elders, but to which he gave his own special definitions in his first Surrealist Manifesto in 1924. The doctrine was adopted by many erstwhile Dada followers, and for the next 15 years surrealist ranks remained in a state of flux, with joiners and dissenters including the poets Louis ARAGON, Paul ELUARD, Robert DESNOS, and Benjamin PÉRET, the dramatic theorist Antonin ARTAUD, and writers from other lands, all participating in the work of the two major periodicals that Breton controlled: *La Révolution surréaliste* (1924–30) and *Le Surréalisme au service de la révolution* (1930–33). An international coterie of artists joined these writers, among them Salvador Dali, Max Ernst, Yves Tanguy, René Magritte, Victor Brauner, Toyen, and Roberto Matta.

Breton defined surrealism as a state of being that utilizes the resources of the subconscious self through such liberating devices as psychic automatism, hypnosis, and the simulation of the verbal communication of the de-

ranged. Freeing the self from built-in prejudices and verbal inhibitions was expected to raise the poetic consciousness to a level of acuity where antinomies would be perceived in the manner of the alchemists' *conjunctio oppositorum*. In 1919, Breton and Philippe SOUPAULT coauthored *Les Champs magnétiques* (Magnetic Fields), the first experiment in automatic writing, presumably unleashing a flow of words attracted to each other like atoms in a magnetic field. In a later work, *Poisson soluble* (1924; Soluble Fish), the companion piece of the Manifesto, Breton demonstrated the use of free associations as the basis of a poetic narrative in which his experiences as a young poet in Paris and as a child in Lorient are intermingled, taking the form of dialogues with mythological beings and incorporating erotic adventures. In three other narratives, Breton explored the poetics of life in terms of a relationship with the irrational, as in *Nadja* (1928; Eng. tr., 1960); connections between the dream and the realities of the conscious state, as in *Les Vases communicants* (1932; Communicating Vases); and the mystique of random encounters, as in *L'Amour fou* (1937; Madly in Love). Although these works are in part philosophical essays, their fundamental mood is one of a quest for ideal love, finally attained within the structure of the Cinderella myth in *L'Amour fou*.

The setting of Breton's last prose narrative, *Arcane 17* (1945), is Canada during World War II. A parable of the poet's self-exile, this work derives its title from the emblem of the morning star that replaces Lucifer's destructiveness symbolized in the previous arcana. Hope restored in the darkness is identified with nature's cycle of death and resurrection and with the salutary power of a new love—in Breton's concept, always the same and only one, a love ever renewable: "the secret of loving you always for the first time," he wrote in *L'Air de l'eau*. In his prose as well as his poetry, Breton attributed to physical love a powerfully gnostic dynamism: the beloved is a conduit to the mysteries of natural forces, and her magical resources must be put to the service of a failed humanism. The figure of Melusine, evoked in *Arcane 17,* is part of the mythology of exile; she is the dispossessed, the mediator, the guardian of the imperiled. The third emblem involves the Percé Rock, at the tip of the Gaspé Peninsula, like a dark curtain shutting off the outside world. A monolith containing layers of geological strata, it corresponds to mankind's historical episodes, divided against itself yet a single emergence.

Breton's poetry, which is largely in free verse, has been collected under several headings. The first group, *Clair de terre* (1923; Earth Light), contains most of his automatically provoked poems of the early 1920s with their juxtaposition of distant realities. By the time of his Second Manifesto (1930), an essay strongly indicative of his preoccupation with the occult, a new technique emerges: "the one-in-the-other image" in a totally syncretic system. *Le Revolver à cheveux blancs* (1932; The White-haired Revolver) and *L'Air de l'eau* (1934; The Air in the Water) consist of poems based on this closely deliberated structure, projecting Breton's ontological visions and erotic experiences onto a chthonian world. In 1931 he wrote his most famous poem, "L'Union libre," which in its title comprises one of surrealism's most cherished notions: freedom with interdependence. By associating images drawn from the female anatomy, their correspondences in the animal, vegetable, and mineral kingdoms, and the powers of the four elements of air, water, fire, and earth, Breton evokes a generic portrait of the feminine and the sources of her power. In general, his poetry is dense and highly metonymic, employing a gothic succession of light and darkness. He also makes use of a bio-botanical lexicon previously lacking in poetic associations. For Breton, nature is an ignited matter, convulsive in its beauty under his vigilant eye; as he writes in *Nadja*, "Beauty will be convulsive or not at all."

During the 1920s, Breton's political involvements brought him briefly into the orbit of the French Communist Party, but he quickly rejected its Stalinist orientation. In 1935 his hopes for an association between surrealism and communism were completely shattered at the Congress of Writers for the Defense of Culture (see "Du temps où les surréalistes avaient raison" [When the Surrealists Were Right], 1935). Later, he sought out the exiled Leon Trotsky in Mexico, and the consequence of the visit was a position paper on the civil liberties of the artist, "Pour un art révolutionnaire indépendant" (1938; For an Independent Revolutionary Art). Breton's poetry, however, was never contaminated by his politics. During the World War II years, he produced three great modern poetic epics, placing on a metaphoric, mythological level themes of exile (*Fata Morgana*, 1941), liberty (*Les Etats-Généraux*, 1943), and the unity of the peoples of the world (*Ode à Charles Fourier*, 1947). These poems are intricately composed, and their hermetic nature is closer to Stéphane MALLARMÉ's elliptical structures than to automatism.

Another of Breton's major works, written between the wars and enlarged periodically, was *Le Surréalisme et la peinture* (1928; Eng. tr., *Surrealism and Painting*, 1972), which related the parallel questions of poetry and painting in terms of the analogical structure communicating psychic relationships; "Everything," Breton wrote, "is subject, nothing is object." An astute, sometimes brutal critic of literature, he situated surrealism in the lineage of Arthur RIMBAUD (the alchemy of the word) and of LAUTRÉAMONT (the power of rebellion). He compiled an anthology of black humor, using selections from the literature of the past to bring that distinctive element of modernism into focus.

Occupying the central position in the surrealism movement, Breton united aesthetic and ethical principles under the slogan "poetry, liberty, and love." His last poetic work, *Constellations* (1956), consists of a series of poems paralleling Joan Miro's 22 gouaches, created earlier (1940) under the same collective title. Here Breton synthesized the image of the poet as craftsman and magician, nurtured by earth and aiming at the stars.

See: J. Gracq, *André Breton* (1948); C. Mauriac, *André Breton* (1949); F. Alquié, *Philosophie du surréalisme* (1955); C. Browder, *André Breton: Arbiter of Surrealism* (1967; A. Balakian, *André Breton: Magus of Surrealism* (1971); M. Bonnet, *André Breton: naissance de l'aventure surréaliste* (1975).   A.B.

Breza, Tadeusz (1905-70), Polish novelist and essayist, was born in the manor Siekierzyńce, Volhynia, and died in Warsaw. He spent some time as a novice in a Benedictine monastery in Belgium, later studied philosophy at Warsaw and London universities, and served as a diplomat. During World War II he was active in the cultural underground movement, and after the war he was once again employed in diplomacy as cultural attaché in Rome and Paris. Breza began his literary career with a psychological novel, *Adam Grywałd* (1936). After World War II, he published a cycle of sociopolitical and psychological novels, *Mury Jerycha* (1946; The Walls of Jericho) and *Niebo i ziemia* (1949; The Sky and the Earth), in which he presented a broad panorama of Polish society and its political leadership just before World War II. His contemporary novel *Uczta Baltazara* (1952; Balthasar's Feast), as well as a collection of short stories, short novels, and

criticism, was followed by a highly successful collection of essays, *Spiżowa brama* (1960; A Bronze Gate), and a novel, *Urząd* (1960; The Office), which resulted from his experiences in Rome, both presenting the internal affairs and conflicts in the Vatican and revealing keen psychological observations of many aspects of the ideological and intellectual life of the Catholic Church at the close of the pontificate of Pius XII.

See: J. Pieszczachowicz, *Tadeusz Breza* (1973).

J.R.K.

Březina, Otokar, pseud. of Václav Jebavý, (1868-1929), Czech poet, was the leader of the Czech symbolist movement and one of the greatest lyric writers in Czech literature. The son of a poor shoemaker, he was born in Počátky in southern Bohemia, and taught school for much of his life in different towns in Moravia. His first collection of poetry, *Tajemné dálky* (Mysterious Distances), was published in 1895, when he was nearing 30, and within six years he had published four more small collections. After his volume of essays appeared in 1903, Brezina stopped writing. Late in his life he was interviewed by visitors and friends, and they, especially the Catholic poet Jakub Deml, gave accounts of his later views that excited much disappointment and controversy: the poet seemed to be consumed by a disgruntled and narrow provincial nationalism. But Březina's political views are relatively unimportant. He was a great poet who must be judged on the basis of his five small booklets of poetry.

Tajemné dálky is a work of youthful pessimism, only superficially touched by a still largely aesthetic mysticism. Its themes are fin de siècle: the bitterness of frustration, the constancy of guilt, the tragedy of love and friendship, and the attraction of death, which appears as a distant comforter and savior. In a few poems, personal sorrows, like the early death of the poet's parents, are hinted at, but the solemn tones of prayer generally prevail. Březina's use of intricate clusters of images—many of which are drawn from the Catholic liturgy—strangely farfetched yet extremely effective rhymes, and alexandrines (indicating a reading of Charles BAUDELAIRE) make even this first book unique in Czech poetry. But the truly great Březina began to emerge only in *Svítání na Západě* (1896; Dawn in the West), and this collection in turn represents a transition to *Větry od pólů* (1897; Polar Winds), which reveals Březina as a highly original symbolist poet. In *Větry*, the early pessimism has almost disappeared to be replaced by a cosmic optimism that contains nothing of the shallow belief in progress, but is rather the final insight of a mystic who has reached an acceptance of all existence as part of the divine pattern. God's mysterious will works through the striving and the evolution of all created things towards cooperation and unity with Him. In a highly personal way, Březina managed to combine the insight of all mystics, of whom he was an ardent student, with a monistic optimism that shows a knowledge of Ralph Waldo Emerson and even Friedrich NIETZSCHE. By *Větry*, Březina had also found his most personal style: free verse, with many dactyls and anapests, sometimes rhymed, of enormously long lines; clusters of magnificent metaphors that seem to ignite one from the other; hymns and dithyrambs that are sometimes put into the mouths of imaginary speakers, including the sun, the earth, the waters, and the mystery of fire. The images from the liturgy have disappeared, replaced by metaphors drawn from the sciences and such ordinary activities as winegrowing or farming.

Březina's next collection *Stavitelé chrámu* (1899; Builders of the Temple), represents a partial backsliding into pessimism. Doubts and uncertainties have again arisen in the poet's mind: the suffering of all creation, including inert matter, is voiced in curious poems. Symbolic types, such as "prophets," "martyrs," "blind men," "madmen," join in a stupendous oratorio of the whole universe. Březina's last and possibly greatest collection, *Ruce* (1901; Hands), represents a return to belief and certainty. The stress is stronger than before on the concept of man's cooperation with God and on the unity of humanity, conceived of as including the living, the dead, and the unborn. The innumerable visible and invisible hands of the title poem, like a magical chain, carry out the mysterious laws of God's eternal will. One poem sings the "roundelay of hearts," another foresees redeemed man for whose sake "it is joyous to live," and another evokes the time when the "delivered" earth will be extinguished and the mighty current of eternity will roll on. Some of the poems return to traditional stanzas and closed rhyme forms, a change continued in 13 later scattered poems in which Březina also returns to personal themes. Thus the cycle came to an end, and the poet imposed silence upon himself. His volume of essays, *Hudba pramenů* (1903; The Music of the Springs), planned as a commentary to his poetry, is rather a paraphrase, on a lower stylistic level, of his main ideas on art as service to God, on the hidden economy of the universe, and on justice and the masses. The highly ornate and metaphorical diction is not illuminated by the same glow of imagination and the same visionary power that uphold even the longest of his poems.

In Březina's work modern Czech poetry reached a peak where the air is rarified and sometimes difficult to breathe. Březina's contacts with ordinary reality are slight, and his social message has little in common with contemporary movements: it breathes the spirit of all mysticism.

See: M. Marten, *Otokar Březina* (1903); F. X. Šalda, *Duše a dílo* (1913); J. Staněk, *Otokar Březina* (1918); P. Selver, *Otokar Březina: A Study in Czech Literature* (1921); E. Saudek, *Pod oblohou Otokara Březiny* (1928); A. Veselý, *Otokar Březina* (1928); G. Picková-Saudková, *Hovory s Otokarem Březinou* (1929); J. Deml, *Mé svědectví o Otokaru Březinovi* (1931); A. Pospíšilová, *Otokar Březina* (1936); P. Fraenkel, *O. Březina: genese díla* (1937); O. Králík, *Otokar Březina* (1948).   R.W.

Brieux, Eugène (1858–1932), French dramatist, was born and reared in one of the working-class districts of Paris, where his father was a carpenter. His limited early education was later complemented with wide reading. Brieux was already interested in the theater at the time of his stay at Rouen as a journalist. His first plays worthy of attention were produced by André ANTOINE—*Ménages d'artistes* (1890; Eng. tr., *Artists' Families*, 1918) and *Blanchette* (1892; Eng. tr., 1913), the latter making him known to the public at large. From then on Brieux's literary production was regular and even more than plentiful; he wrote 40 plays. He was elected to the Académie Française in 1910.

If, like most of the playwrights of the Théâtre Libre where he made his début, Brieux had a tendency to unveil with a sometimes cruel realism selfishness and pettiness, particularly of the bourgeoisie, he did it without the bitter irony and pessimism of Henry Becque's disciples. Indeed Brieux was something of a missionary. He denounced tirelessly the moral degradation of the individual by other men, by institutions, or by social habits and prejudices, pointing out the ultimate disastrous consequences—and doing this in the mood of a reformer.

Blanchette is about popular education. *La Couvée* (1893; The Covey) presents a problem dear to Brieux,

that of the intervention of parents in the lives of their children. When these parents, influenced by a more or less disguised egoism, try to impose their will on their children, especially where it concerns marriage and the dowry, Brieux's indignation bursts forth. There are similar themes in *Les Trois Filles de M. Dupont* (1897; Eng. tr., *The Three Daughters of M. Dupont* in *Three Plays by Brieux*, 1911), one of his best plays, and in *La Petite Amie* (1902; The Sweetheart). In plays like *La Française* (1907; The Frenchwoman), *La Femme seule* (1913; Eng. tr., *Woman on Her Own*, 1916), and *Pierrette et Galaor* (1923) Brieux is an ardent defender of women and girls, and in his desire to protect their rights he may seem to go so far as to uphold free union and the illegitimate child. Yet Brieux is at heart a very conservative moralist: if he seems to favor antisocial solutions, it is because for him society as it exists now leaves us no alternative. In fact, it is the family he defends in *Le Berceau* (1898; The Cradle), in which he attacks divorce when there are children, and in *Les Remplaçantes* (1901; The Women Substitutes), in which he protests against the practice of wet-nursing. Brieux is somewhat in conflict with himself in *Maternité* (1913; Eng. tr., *Maternity*, 1907), divided between arguments about preventing the birth of unwanted children and the realization that abortion is an antisocial practice. *La Robe rouge* (1900; Eng. tr., *The Red Robe* in T. H. Dickinson, ed., *Chief Contemporary Dramatists*, 1915), another outstanding play, develops two themes, the crushing of the individual by the powerful machine of the law and the degradation caused by greed and ambition in a judge; the author demands reform in criminal legislation.

Brieux has been criticized for oversimplifying very complex social problems. He was no deep thinker, nor even always coherent. When he wanders into a world that he does not know very well, the world of science in *L'Evasion* (1896; Eng. tr., *The Escape*, 1913) or the gallant society of *La Régence* (1927; The Regency), his talent weakens; and when he studies the problem of religion in *La Foi* (1912; Eng. tr., *False Gods*, 1929), his views appear shallow. He did not always avoid rhetoric and melodrama. He sometimes excelled in the portrayal of humble folk, whom he may have had particularly in mind when he said, "I have wished that the amount of suffering upon this earth might be diminished a little because I have lived."

See: P. V. Thomas, *The Plays of Eugène Brieux* (1915); A. Presas, *Brieux: portrait littéraire* (1930).
                                                                A.C.L. rev. D.W.A.

Brines, Francisco (1932–), Spanish poet born in Oliva, in the province of Valencia, has taught at Oxford University and is a critic of both literature and art. He received the Adonais Prize in 1959 and the Critics Prize in 1966. Brines has played a very important role in returning intimacy and metaphysical meditation to the overly realistic Spanish poetry of the post-Civil War period. The titles of his books—*Las brasas* (1960; Burning Coals), *Palabras a la oscuridad* (1966; Words to the Darkness), *Aún no* (1971; Not Yet)—reveal his major theme: man and life condemned to dispossession, loss, darkness, and death. In contrast to this basic nihilist and elegiac tendency in his work, there are the more positive themes of love, youthful beauty, eroticism, and passion for life. Brines has declared his preference for poetry created as an act of affirmation of that passion as well as of an in-depth knowledge of personal lived reality. His art is therefore a poetry of experience and of deeply felt reflection on that experience. His language, natural and terse although highly symbolic, has evolved from a style of strong appeal to the senses to a more austere and pithy diction. His most recent book, *Insistencias en Luzbel* (1977), is more metaphysical and abstract, and contains a rigorous poetic study of the ultimate realities of oblivion and nothingness.

In 1973, Brines published *Ensayo de una despedida* (1960–71; Rehearsal for a Departure), which contains his complete poems to that date. Among the members of the second poetic generation of post-Civil War Spain, Brines is the poet of deepest introspection and lyricism as well as one of those of greatest universality.

See: J. O. Jiménez, *Cinco poetas del tiempo* (1972), pp. 417–75; J. O. Jiménez, *Diez años de poesía española, 1960–1970* (1972), pp. 175–204; C. Bousoño, "Prólogo" to F. Brines, *Ensayo de una despedida, 1960–1971* (1973), pp. 11–94.   J.O.J.

Brinkmann, Rolf Dieter (1940–75), German poet and prose writer, was born in Vechta, Lower Saxony. He later moved to Cologne to study education. Between 1965 and 1975 he made frequent trips to London. He spent the fall of 1971 in a hut in the Eifel Mountains, desperate to escape the suffocating atmosphere of Cologne. Brinkmann lived at the Villa Massimo in Rome under a grant from the German government in 1973 and the following year lectured as visiting writer at the University of Texas, Austin. He was killed by a hit-and-run driver on a London street in the spring of 1975.

Brinkmann was an outsider who, like the first-person narrator in his collected short stories *Die Umarmung* (1965; The Embrace) and *Raupenbahn* (1966; Tilt-a-Whirl), felt himself the victim of an oppressive reality where objects prevail. His novel *Keiner weiss mehr* (1968; No One Knows More) relates the protagonist's struggle with an environment created by movies, rock music, and advertising. Brinkmann insisted on looking at what is actually there and challenges our being at the mercy of made-up attractions. He was not out to create literature but saw his writings as a by-product of living. His poetry is antitheoretical and geared to the senses. His language is that of everyday speech, and his images show ordinary events, as in *Was fraglich ist wofür?!* (1967; Questionable What For) and in *Gras* (1970; Grass). In the late 1960s he translated and edited American postbeat-generation poets in *Acid* (1969) and *Silverscreen* (1969) and wrote poetry inspired by the images of pop art in *Die Piloten* (1969). The poems in his last book, *Westwärts 1 & 2* (1975), which won the Petrarca Lyric Prize, defy language and express his dreams, discontentments, and memories. They are violent, tender, and cursing and possess the spontaneity of life where everything is in motion at all times.   H.P.S.

Brion, Marcel (1895–), French biographer, novelist, and critic, was born in Marseille of a French mother and a father of Irish extraction. This double heritage may account for the remarkably diverse nature of his work.

After some years of study in Switzerland and service during World War I, Brion returned to Marseille to practice law. Disenchanted, he set out in 1925 on an odyssey that would lead him over a 15-year period to the major libraries and museums of Europe, as well as to the Near East. A Renaissance figure in the breadth and scope of his interests, Brion is a prolific writer whose scholarly works include studies of *Laurent le Magnifique* (1937; Lorenzo the Magnificent), *Michel-Ange* (1939; Michelangelo), *Rembrandt* (1940), *Charles le Téméraire* (1947; Charles the Bold), and *Machiavel* (1948); works on art and archaeology, such as *La Résurrection des villes mortes* (1937; The Resurrection of Dead Cities), *Art abstrait* (1956; Abstract Art), and *Art fantastique* (1961; Fantastic Art); and studies of various aspects of German civilization, such as *Frédéric II de Hohenstaufen* (1948), *Goethe* (1949), *Schumann* (1954), and *L'Allemagne romantique* (2 vols., 1962–63; Romantic Germany).

Indeed, it was in Germany that Brion found his spiritual and emotional roots, drawing him towards that "other world" whose pioneers had been the German romantics. Like them, Brion used the methods and motifs of the supernatural to express a metaphysical quest that became the guiding thread of his fictional work. His first major novel, *La Folie Céladon* (1935), a tale of forsaken ideals, of loss and despair, set in the decadent splendor of a rococo pavilion, remains one of his most accomplished works. A series of evocative novels, among them *Un enfant de la terre et du ciel* (1943; A Child of Earth and Heaven), *Château d'ombres* (1943; Castle of Shadows), *L'Enchanteur* (1947), *La Rose de cire* (1964; The Wax Rose), and two short-story collections, *Les Escales de la haute nuit* (1942; The Stages of High Night) and *La Chanson de l'oiseau étranger* (1958; The Song of the Foreign Bird), were written in rapid succession over the next decade, even though some remained unpublished for several years. In 1966, having abandoned fiction for some two decades, Brion returned to the novel with the publication of *De l'autre côté de la forêt* (On the Other Side of the Forest), a volume that heralded a group of sumptuously oneiric works, including *L'Ombre d'un arbre mort* (1970; Shade of a Dead Tree), *Nous avons traversé la montagne* (1972; We Have Crossed the Mountain), and, most recently, *La Fête de la tour des âmes* (1974; The Festival of the Tower of Souls). A recipient of various literary prizes, Brion has been a member of the Académie Française since 1964.   M.S.M.

Broch, Hermann (1886–1951), Austro-American novelist, philosopher, and poet, is remembered primarily for the triology *Die Schlafwandler* (1930–32; Eng. tr., *The Sleepwalkers*, 1932), which was his first major literary effort. His other novels are of some note, but the philosophy, political writings, and mass psychology to which he devoted the end of his life are forgotten.

Broch was born in Vienna, the son of a textile manufacturer. He was trained as an engineer in Vienna and abroad, studying in New Orleans in 1907, after which he managed his family's factory in Teesdorf, Lower Austria. During World War I he served as an administrator for the Austrian Red Cross until 1916, when he assumed control of the devasted textile firm. He reestablished the firm and improved working conditions in a way that served as a model for the industry. Between 1908 and 1928, Broch steadily increased his involvement in the intellectual life of Vienna. He was acquainted with and influenced by Mach, Ludwig Wittgenstein, Sigmund Freud, Franz Blei, Frank Thiess, Robert MUSIL, and Karl KRAUS. In 1928, beset by the Great Depression, Broch sold his textile concern and, at the age of 42, began his literary career.

Pasenow oder Die Romantik—1888 (Passenow, or the Romantic), the first volume of *Schlafwandler,* created a sensation when it was first published in 1930. It is a witty and penetrating representation of the stagnation, stratification, and emotional repression in Berlin society up to the turn of the century. Ostensibly the story of a romance between an officer and a young countess, it is in fact a tale of complete moral cripples. Despair and brutality among denizens of the Rhine are the themes of the second volume, *Esch oder Die Anarchie—1903* (Esch, or the Anarchist). Here the sordid love affair of a clerk and a barmaid serves as the framework for a tale that reveals the bankruptcy of the values of middle-class life. In the third volume, *Hugenau oder Die Sachlichkeit—1918* (Hugenau, or the Realist), the themes and characters of the first volumes confront World War I and the deserter Hugenau. The interwoven stories in this volume and the discursive, philosophical chapters entitled ''The Decline of Values'' give a final image of complete, amoral rot. The work was an unqualified success, which freed Broch to work on a series of diverse projects, including the interesting novella *Die unbekannte Größe* (1933; Eng. tr., *The Unknown Quantity*, 1935), which is about the vagaries and unpredictability of the family life of a statistician.

In 1938, Broch was detained briefly by the Nazis, not for his Jewish faith but for his subversive doctrine. He fled and ultimately settled in New York.

Broch was vigorously involved in refugee relief for some time. His next major work, *Der Tod des Vergil* (1945; Eng. tr., *The Death of Vergil*, 1945), is a moving stream-of-consciousness epic wherein the last hours of Vergil's life provide a forum to explore the value of art, the nature of perception, and the meaning of life. The work is an exceptionally fine web, which was somewhat frayed in translation. His last completed work, *Die Schuldlosen* (1950; Eng. tr., *The Guiltless*, 1974), is a compilation of stories—some of which were written as early as 1933 and some in 1950—that here form a novel. This is a subtle work that shares much of the form, concerns, and intent of *Schlafwandler*, except that the advent of fascism, rather than the effect of the war, is the subject of explanation.

After Broch's death, several manuscripts of a final novel were found. These have been published in various versions and selections, the most readable of which is *Demeter* (1967). This was intended to be another examination of the question of fascism and serves as an intense study of demonic personalities.

Throughout his life, Broch's restless thoughts found print in numerous essays covering many topics. Most are collected in two volumes, *Dichten und Erkennen* and *Erkennen und Handeln* (1955; Poetry and Perception, and Perception and Action). Noteworthy among them are the literary studies ''James Joyce und die Gegenwart'' (1931; Eng. tr., ''James Joyce and the Present Age,'' 1949) and ''The Style of the Mythical Age'' (1947), which reveal his notion of modernity. Broch was also one of the great correspondents; he wrote voluminously to friends, strangers, enemies, and authors. A selection of these letters, many in English, is available in *Briefe* (1957).

At his death, Broch was honorary lecturer in the German department at Yale University. Broch's charm, engaging intelligence, and humane concerns belied the often acerbic edge in his work. His novels present a many-faceted image of his age.

See: T. Ziolkowski, *Hermann Broch* (1964); M. Durzak, *Hermann Broch: der Dichter und seine Zeit* (1968).

N.R.

Brodsky, Iosif (1940–), Russian poet and critic, was born in Leningrad, and has lived in emigration since 1972. He began writing poetry in 1958 and soon exhibited outstanding gifts as a verse translator. He has brilliantly rendered John Donne and Andrew Marvell into Russian. In 1956, the year after he dropped out of Soviet secondary school, he had begun to study Polish and was deeply impressed by the poetry of Cyprian NORWID, Zbigniew HERBERT, and Czesław MIŁOSZ. He also read in Polish translation important Western writers otherwise unavailable to him, including Marcel PROUST, Franz KAFKA, William Faulkner, and Virginia Woolf. During February and March 1964, Brodsky was tried in a Leningrad court and sentenced, as a ''social parasite,'' to five years' exile at hard labor in the far northern Arkhangelsk region. He was

released after 20 months and returned to Leningrad in November 1965. During his exile an American publisher issued the first collection of his poems: *Stikhotvoreniya i poemy* (1965; Shorter and Longer Poems). Several of his verse translations, but only four of his own poems, have been published in the Soviet Union.

Between 1965 and mid-1972, Brodsky wrote most of the mature poems included in his second book, *Ostanovka v pustyne* (New York, 1970; A Halt in the Wilderness), as well as many of those in his third book *Konets prekrasnoy epokhi* (Ann Arbor, 1977; The End of a Wonderful Era), and the first eight poems in his fourth book *Chast rechi* (1977; A Part of Speech). Most of the poems in this last book were written during the period of exile which began for Brodsky in June 1972. He lives in the United States and has been a citizen since 1977. He is poet in residence at the University of Michigan and has taught Russian poetry and comparative poetry at several universities, including Queens College and Columbia University. Brodsky has given readings throughout North America and Western Europe; his poetry has been translated into at least a dozen languages. He has been a Guggenheim Fellow and is a member of the American Academy and Institute of Arts and Letters. He was awarded an honorary Doctor of Letters degree by Yale in 1978. In 1979, Brodsky was awarded the Mondello Literary Prize (Italy).

Both in his adherence to strict poetic forms—which he has developed with great originality and technical virtuosity—and in his attachment to the historical and mythological origins of basic cultural, moral, and religious values Brodsky is a traditionalist and a ''classicist.'' His poetic language, which can be at once controversial and learned, is uniformly robust, unsentimental, and ''aggressive.'' His irony, which is pervasive, tends to be gentle or playful rather than angry or bitter.

Among Russian poets, Gavrila Derzhavin, Yevgeny Baratynsky, Osip MANDELSHTAM, Marina TSVETAYEVA, and Boris PASTERNAK in his last period are closest to Brodsky in spirit and have influenced him most directly; but English and American poets, from Donne and Marvell to T. S. Eliot and W. H. Auden, have influenced him at least as much. Brodsky was personally close to Anna AKHMATOVA from 1960 until her death in 1966. More than her poetry, or her praise of his own work, it was Anna Akhmatova as an exemplar of both a great poet and a great human being, living with dignity in a time of terror, that inspired the younger poet.

Under the influence of Fyodor DOSTOYEVSKY and Lev SHESTOV, Brodsky has articulated, in a series of major poems written between 1967 and 1978, a disturbing ''existentialist'' and ''absurdist'' vision of the unbearable horrors of human life and the infernal nothingness of death. He sees poetry, which is a revelation of ''what time does to human beings''—in the modalities of loss, separation, deformity, madness, old age, and death—as a way, in the end perhaps the *only* way, of enduring these horrors. Yet for Brodsky absurdity infects poetry itself, in the perceived contrast between the painful yet exalted process of creation and its estranged thinglike product—the jumble of black marks on white paper.

Brodsky has experienced, and expressed in powerful, unself-pitying poetry—with conscious echoes of Martial, Ovid, Dante, and Mandelshtam—the suffering, loss, and separation that exile entails, whether it be temporary and within the borders of one's native country or permanent and beyond them. The latter holds for the poet the special threat of silence (*molchaniye*) as loss of language, inability to speak or to sing. But Brodsky is above all a moralist, for whom the absurd and the death-in-life of enforced silence are not the whole or final story. "[E]ven after the Absurd," he has written, "one has to live, to eat, drink, . . . betray or not betray one's neighbor."

For English translations of Brodsky's poetry, see *Joseph Brodsky: Selected Poems* (1973) and *A Part of Speech* (1979). Brodsky's critical prose is collected in *Less than One* (1980).

See: W. H. Auden, Foreword, and G. L. Kline, Introduction, to *Joseph Brodsky: Selected Poems* (1973), pp. 9–12, 13–23; R. D. Sylvester, "The Poem as Scapegoat; An Introduction to Joseph Brodsky's *Halt in the Wilderness*," *TSLL* 17 (1975): 303–325; A. Losev, "Niotkuda s lyubovyu: zametki o stikhakh Iosifa Brodskogo," *Kontinent* no. 14 (1977): 307–31; and "Iosif Brodsky: posvyashchaetsya logike," *Vestnik* no. 127 (1978): 124–30; G. L. Kline and R. D. Sylvester, "Iosif Aleksandrovich Brodskii," *Modern Encyclopedia of Russian and Soviet Literature*, vol. 3 (1979), pp. 129–37.　　　　G.K.

Bródy, Sándor (1863–1924), Hungarian novelist, short-story writer, and playwright, was born in Eger and died in Budapest. Although his education was superficial, his work attracted many readers and critics because, in the context of Hungarian literature, his voice sounded fresh and his manner of writing seemed new. In fact, Bródy was a romantic naturalist, influenced by both Emile ZOLA and Mór Jókai (*see* HUNGARIAN LITERATURE), who made the mistake of thinking that he was the protagonist of French realism in Hungary.

Bródy was prolific, and although he wrote carelessly, his spontaneity impressed even those who might have been in disagreement with his views or literary manners. In general, his work indicates an attempt to understand truth in its social and sensual implications. In a sentimental but outspoken manner, he wrote about the unfairness of the modern world. He liked to speak as an eyewitness, but his own bittersweet emotionalism frequently overpowered his objectivity. Bródy either did not know or did not care to know the difference between good and mediocre writing; consequently, his work was uneven and his promise was only partly fulfilled. Nevertheless, he is entitled to recognition—if only because the vitality of his personality made him an influential figure in Hungarian literature for many years and because his fiction paved the way for freedom of expression on subjects ignored by earlier writers.

Bródy's first important book of short stories, *Nyomor* (1884; Destitution), remained one of his significant works. *Az ezüst kecske* (1898; The Silver Goat) is considered his best novel, while *A dada* (1902; The Nurse) and *Tanítónő* (1908; The School Marm) are his best plays. His cycle of short stories about Rembrandt (1924) has been translated into English as *Rembrandt: A Romance of Divine Love and Art* (1928).

See: A. Németh, *Szép Szó* (1936); I. Sőtér et al., *A magyar irodalom története*, vol. 4 (1965), pp. 764–79; (1965), F. Juhász, *Bródy Sándor* (1971).

J.R. rev. G.G.

Broniewski, Władysław (1897–1962), Polish poet, was born in Płock and died in Warsaw. He began writing while still in school and edited a school magazine. Broniewski left school to join Józef Piłsudski's legion in 1915 and fought in the Polish-Soviet War in 1920. After the war, as a young student, he participated in the literary and political life of Poland, was involved in the leftist movement, and became the most outstanding representative of "proletarian poetry" in Poland, highly praised for his genuine talent by critics of both the Left and Right.

His first volumes—*Wiatraki* (1925; Windmills), *Dymy nad miastem* (1927; Smoke over the City), *Komuna Paryska* (1929; Paris Commune), *Troska i pieśń* (1932; Sorrow and Song), and *Krzyk ostateczny* (1938; The Ultimate Cry)—were generally acclaimed as significant events in the development of modern Polish poetry. Although rather traditional in form, reminiscent of the elevated romantic tone, these poems spoke of the burning social problems of misery and injustice and are couched in an easy, melodious style, which evoked an immediate and spontaneous response from the reading audience. In 1939, during the German invasion, Broniewski wrote his famous patriotic poem "Bagnet na broń" (Fix Bayonet), later included in a volume having the same title, which was published in 1943.

That a revolutionary poet should rot in a Soviet jail, where he was put in 1940, was one of the many strange twists of fate in the life of many Polish writers during World War II. Freed later after the Sikorski-Maysky agreement, the poet left the USSR with the Polish army and lived briefly in the Middle East, where some of his deeply nostalgic lyrics were written and published in the volume *Drzewo rozpaczające* (1945; Tree of Despair). In 1946, Broniewski returned to Poland, where he was celebrated as an old "revolutionary," but his poetry never reached its previous heights, especially because he attempted to write according to the prescription of socialist realism, including such themes as *Słowo o Stalinie* (1949; Stanzas about Stalin). In the last years before his death, Broniewski published short nostalgic lyrics on his native region, *Mazowsze* (1952; Mazovia), and on the death of his daughter, *Anka* (1956). Broniewski was also a translator of Russian poetry and prose.

See: Z. Folejewski, "A Proletarian Prometheus Bound (Władysław Broniewski)," in *Studies in Modern Slavic Poetry* (1955), pp. 22–41; R. Matuszewski, *O poezji Władysława Broniewskiego* (1955); T. Bujnicki, *Władysław Broniewski* (1972).　　　　Z.F.

Bronne, Carlo (1901–), Belgian poet and essayist, was born in Liège. He combined a literary vocation with a career as a magistrate. As early as 1929, he published poetry, *Les fruits de cendre* (1929; Fruits of Ash) and *Collines que j'aimais* (1930; Those Hills I Treasured). Bronne subsequently turned to historical narratives, in which he expressed his love for the past and for his native country. In essays such as *La Porte d'exil* (1937; The Door of Exile), *Les Abeilles du manteau* (1939; The Bees of the Coat), and *Hôtel de l'Aigle noire* (1954; The Hotel of the Black Eagle), he combined a delicate poetic charm with historical exactness. In *Un Américain en Ardennes* (1974; An American in Ardennes), Bronne followed the traces of Ernest Hemingway, who was sent to Ardennes in 1944 as a war correspondent. An ardent lover of the southwestern part of Belgium, Bronne produced moving pages in *Bleu d'Ardennes* (1956; Blue of the Ardennes). *Leopold Ier et son temps* (1942; Leopold I and His Time), *L'Amalgame* (1948; The Amalgam), and *Albert Ier, le roi sans terre* (1965; Albert I, the Lackland King) exalt the historic role of Belgium within the European context. These works deserve to be consulted for their scholarly rigor as well as for their aesthetic appeal. Since 1975, Bronne has undertaken the writing of his memoirs: *Compère, qu'as-tu vu* (1975; Friend, What Have You Seen?) and *Le Temps des vendanges* (1976; The Grape-Gathering Season). These memoirs evoke the experiences of a traveler who has promoted his country's culture and literature. A member of the Royal Academy of French Language and Literature of Belgium, Bronne is also a corresponding member of the Institut de France and vice-president of the Belgian (French) section of the PEN Club.   G.Si.

Bronnen, Arnolt (1895–1959), Austrian writer, was born in Vienna. He became a successful and controversial playwright in Berlin. After 1927 he supported the Nazis, but in 1943 he joined the anti-Fascist Resistance and turned to communism. Bronnen wrote 13 plays and 5 novels, as well as memoirs, stories, radio plays, and reviews. *Vatermord* (1920; Patricide), his first success, is an expressionistic play having an Oedipal plot with a petit-bourgeois setting. Other early plays intertwine individual passions and social forces in exploring the dichotomies of anarchy/order, reason/instinct, liberation/oppression. The best are *Anarchie in Sillian* (1924; Anarchy in Sillian) and *Rheinische Rebellen* (1925; Rhenish Rebels). The novel *O.S.* (1929) propagandizes the German nationalist cause against Poland. After 1933, Bronnen grew fearful of Nazism, isolated himself, and used the historic mode to attack illegitimate power in the plays *N* (1935–36) and *Gloriana* (1941), which were banned. The novel *Aisopos* (1956; Aesop), his masterpiece, presents a life struggling for freedom and justice. Bronnen's autobiography appeared in 1954; and a memoir of his friendship with Bertolt BRECHT, in 1960.

See: K. Schröter, "Arnolt Bronnen, Protokollant seiner Epoche," in his *Literatur und Zeitgeschichte* (1970).
                                                                    W.H.

Bruheim, Jan Magnus (1914–), Norwegian poet, was born and raised on a farm in Skjåk in the Gudbrandsdal valley, where he has also lived most of his adult life. As so often is the case with the poetry of the *nynorsk* writers (*see* NORWEGIAN LITERATURE), Bruheim's poetry is imbued with the ancient rural culture of Norway. Yet although filled with memorable images of nature and the people of his valley, his verse reaches beyond the provincial in its expression of fear, faith, loneliness, and the human community.

Bruheim's first collections of poetry, such as *Stengd dør* (1941; Closed Door), written during World War II, are filled with the anguish and fears of that period. In later works, beginning with *Yta og djupe* (1945; The Surface and the Depth), his poetry gains a tone of quiet optimism, a quality that his verse has never lost. The doubt and anguish that sometimes erupt in later collections, such as *Ord gjennom larm* (1954; Words through the Noise) and *Stråler over stup* (1963; Rays across the Abyss), are more than balanced by Bruheim's faith in simple, traditional virtues: the good forces will win. Bruheim's poetry, whether in rhymed or unrhymed verse, is characterized by simplicity and lucidity, qualities that have also endeared him to Norwegian children in his several collections of children's poetry.   K.A.F.

Brunetière, Ferdinand (1849–1906), French critic and educator, was born in Toulon. He became the best known of a generation of famous literary critics called *normaliens* (because they were professors at the Ecole Normale Supérieure). He was also editor-in-chief of the prestigious *Revue des deux mondes* from 1893 until his death. Despite lifelong illness, Brunetière published over 30 volumes of criticism and polemics, including *Etudes critiques sur l'histoire de la littérature française* (8 vols., 1880–1907; Eng. tr., *Essays in French Literature: A Selection*, 1892); *Le Roman naturaliste* (1883; The Naturalist Novel); the unfinished *Evolution des genres dans l'histoire de la littérature* (Evolution of the Genres in Literary History), vol. 1: *L'Evolution de la critique depuis la Renaissance jusqu'à nos jours* (1890; The Evolution of Criticism from the Renaissance to the Present), with the related *Epoques du théâtre français: 1636–1850* (1892; Epochs of the French Theater: 1636–1850) and the *Evolution de la poésie lyrique en France au dix-neuvième siècle* (1894; Evolution of Lyric Poetry in France in the 19th Century); *Histoire de la littérature française classique: 1515–1830* (uncompleted; 4 vols., 1904–; History of Classic French Literature); and three volumes of *Discours de combat* (1900, 1903, 1907; Combat Speeches).

Brunetière favored judicial criticism, fought Anatole FRANCE's impressionism, and sneered at Charles-Augustin Sainte-Beuve's dilettantism. He most admired the formalized order and clarity of French classicism. A Catholic convert, he saw his newfound faith as a necessary bulwark against the doubts and moral decay of his time. He urged a return to the rules and dogmas of the 17th century, indicted the 18th century for lacking them, and disliked the 19th century's doctrine of art for art's sake. He ridiculed the scientific determinism of the naturalists, particularly Emile ZOLA, coining in 1895 the famous phrase "the bankruptcy of science"; "Science has lost its prestige and Religion regained a part of its own," he exulted.

Yet Brunetière belonged particularly to his own day in adopting a sort of literary Darwinism, his theory of the evolution of the genres. According to his theory, Rousseau's lyrical, poetic prose, for example, evolved into romantic poetry. For Brunetière, literary genres almost become living organisms, developing through natural selection and subject to change and decay, much like Darwin's plants and animals. Brunetière's acceptance of change and his tendency to clothe his concepts in scientific dress make him a modern at the same time that his espousal of classic beauty and order locates his spiritual home in the age of Louis XIV. Indeed, Brunetière could never quite reconcile a belief in evolution with his inborn conservatism. Brunetière sometimes let his theories unduly shape his conclusions, but if his doctrinaire rigidity repels, his impressive erudition and fine taste act as saving graces. Even hostile readers can profit from his measured judgments.

Brunetière once defined drama as "the spectacle of a will striving toward a goal." His own life personifies that observation. He used criticism and, especially, religious and social polemics as ideological battlefields, literally killing himself by writing and speaking endlessly on controversial causes such as the Dreyfus Affair. But like his famous theory, he himself evolved. His last work is a volume on Honoré de Balzac (1799–1850), praising him unreservedly, now viewing his sometimes sordid realism as inevitable and setting him up in the same relationship to the modern novel as Molière occupied to classical comedy. He even came to fault some of his contemporaries for failing to keep up with the discoveries of science—this from its formerly virulent critic. Nor was Brunetière always as rigid as his usual image suggests, for he could argue on occasion almost as impressionistically as Anatole France. Even his demand for judgments in literary criticism may reflect no more than his belief that a reader always assesses the worth of what he reads, but that the critic goes about it with the advantage of the "armed vision."

See: E. Curtius, *Ferdinand Brunetière* (1914); L.-J. Bondy, *Le Classicisme de Ferdinand Brunetière* (1930); V. Giraud, *Brunetière* (1932); E. Hocking, *Ferdinand Brunetière* (1935); J. Clark, *La Pensée de Ferdinand Brunetière* (1954).   A.E.S.

Bryll, Ernest (1935–), Polish poet, novelist, and playwright, was born in Warsaw. He studied Polish philology at Warsaw University and film at the State Institute of Art. His first volume of poetry, *Wigilie wariata* (Madman's Eves) appeared in 1958 and was followed by *Autoportret z bykiem* (1960; Self-Portrait with a Bull), *Twarz nie odsłonięta* (1963; A Not Uncovered Face), *Sztuka stosowana* (1966; Applied Art), *Mazowsze* (1967; Mazovia), *Muszla* (1968; Shell), and *Piołunie, piołunie* (1973; Bitterness, Bitterness). Bryll's poetry, based on romantic and neoromantic tradition and on folk poetry, expresses his own reflections and experiences and those of his generation. In the 1960s Bryll also published several novels: *Studium* (1963; A Study), *Ciotka* (1964; Auntie), *Ojciec* (1964; Father), and *Jałowiec* (1965; Juniper). These works form a kind of family saga, set in the Podlasie region and reflecting the social and psychological changes of the last few decades. Bryll then turned to drama: *Rzecz listopadowa* (1968; The November Affair), *Po górach, po chmurach* (1969; Over the Mountains, Over the Clouds), *Na szkle malowane* (1970; Painted on the Glass), *Kto ty jesteś, czyli Małe oratorium na dzień dzisiejszy* (1971; Who Are You or a Small Oratory for the Present Day), *Życie—jawą* (1973; Life—A Reality). In his dramas, Bryll revives the tradition of poetic drama associated with the plays of Adam Mickiewicz and Stanisław Wyspiański. It is a continuation of the romantic tradition but also a confrontation, and it offers a new understanding of history and contemporary problems.

See: S.Melkowski, "Plebejusz pisze wiersze," in *Debiuty poetyckie 1944–1960,* ed. by J. Kajtoch and J. Skórnicki (1972), pp. 557–65; D. Bieńkowska, "Ernest Bryll i teatr romantyczny—kontynuacja, czy deformacja?" in *Canadian Contributions to the Seventh International Congress of Slavists* (1974), pp. 99–108.   A.Z.

Bryusov, Valery Yakovlevich (1873–1924), Russian poet, prose writer, dramatist, essayist, and critic, born in Moscow, was one of the earliest Russian symbolists. From 1892 to 1897 he followed the lead of the French symbolists toward a "decadent" poetry created primarily for the "initiated," in which language is held to be a magic ritual and the expression of transcendental experience (Paul VERLAINE, Stéphane MALLARMÉ, Maurice MAETERLINCK). The names of two of his earliest collections of poetry—*Chefs d'œuvre* (1895) and *Me eum esse* (1897)—indicate his personal myth as leader of the Russian symbolists (*see* RUSSIAN LITERATURE). Around the turn of the century, Bryusov gave up such overly bold experiments. After his graduation in philology from Moscow University, he began to use new themes and forms in his lyric poetry, revealing an indebtedness to classical and Oriental antiquity, to the poetic traditions of Italy and France, to Russian romanticism, and, above all, to Aleksandr Pushkin. In addition to history and mythology, he soon showed a special predilection for erotic themes, which he often developed allegorically. His erotic ballads, elegies, and terza rima in *Urbi et Orbi* (1903) and several poetic cycles in *Vse napevy* (1909; All Melodies) are especially famous. His cool, solemn language is refined in its vocabulary, although not devoid of traditional rhetorical embellishment. He favored abstraction over any overly public display of feelings. In his propensity for the exoticism of extinct civilizations, he was a follower of the French Parnassians, notably Charles Leconte de Lisle. Under the influence of Emile VERHAEREN, Bryusov also became the poet of the city and its cultural and social constraints. His uneasy premonitions found expression in the apocalyptic poem "Kon bled" (1904; Pale Horse), in which the "pale horse" of the Apocalypse gallops along the main artery of a great city "among buses, cabs, and automobiles."

Bryusov reacted to the Russo-Japanese War and the Russian Revolution of 1905 with several poems in allegorical and historical guise. *Zerkalo teney* (1912; Mirror of Shadows), although devoted in part to variations on earlier themes, includes descriptions of the Russian countryside—for example, the cycle "Rodnye stepi" (Native Steppes)—as well as many of his philosophical ideas. This collection reflects Bryusov's aesthetically grounded "amoralism" and his intellectual subjectivism. His later collections bearing the stamp of war and revolution show a noticeable confinement to the purely artisan and a lack of genuine poetic élan. Foremost among these are *Posledniye mechty* (1920; Latest Dreams), *V takiye dni* (1921; On Such Days), and *Mig* (1922; Instant). Although his hymns to proletarian labor and the new historical era won Bryusov recognition from the new regime, they turned his poetry into a sort of obstacle course thematically.

Bryusov's prose writing developed in two different directions, one represented by his two-volume collection of decadent, fantastic short stories, *Zemnaya os* (1907; Axis of the Earth) and *Nochi i dni* (1913; Nights and Days), and the other by his continuation and completion of the symbolist historical novel, a genre inspired by Dmitry MEREZHKOVSKY. Bryusov's variously stylized prose works reveal an outstanding knowledge of both ancient and modern literature, including the works of Edgar Allan Poe, Stanisław PRZYBYSZEWSKI and Anatole FRANCE in the story "V podzemnoy tyurme" (1906; In an Underground Prison), and of Georges RODENBACH in the story "V zerkale" (1914; In the Mirror). Many of his stories describe highly exciting conflicts that constantly border on crisis; these works represent an effort to make mysterious or morbid fantasies credible through rational analysis. The narrators of these stories are eye witnesses who themselves often stand on the brink of the pathological. Among such stories are "Teper, kogda ya prosnulsya" (1902; Now that I Have Awakened); "Posledniye mucheniki" (1907; The Last Martyrs); a Utopian drama about the end of the world, "Zemlya" (1905; The Earth); and the anti-Utopian "Respublika yuzhnogo kresta" (1905; Eng. tr., "The Republic of the Southern Cross," 1918).

Bryusov's masterpieces are considered to be the historical novels *Ognenny angel* (1907–08; Eng. tr., *The Fiery Angel,* 1930), which is set in 16th-century Cologne; and *Altar pobedy* (1911–12; The Altar of Victory), which is set in 4th-century Rome. Both novels show the development of unusual intellectual and erotic passions, which must be viewed in connection with the profound crises that marked the transitions from heathen antiquity to the age of Christianity and from the Middle Ages to modern times. Bryusov was sometimes remarkably successful at reflecting ironically the soul of modern man in the intellectual discussions and problems of bygone epochs. *Ognenny angel,* which plays upon the occult and the works of the devil, is likewise a roman à clef, in which some of Bryusov's own acquaintances, for example, Andrey BELY, can be recognized. The unfinished novel *Jupiter poverzhenny* (1934; Jupiter Overthrown), a sequel to *Altar pobedy* about the final Christianization of Rome, was discovered after Bryusov's death.

Bryusov's work as an essayist and literary critic deals with many subjects, the most important being his theory of lyric poetry, a defense of the symbolist concept of art, and a study of the significance of Pushkin. He was a founder of the famous "Skorpion" Press (*see* RUSSIAN LITERATURE).

See: D. Maksimov, *Poeziya Valeriya Bryusova* (1940);

V. Setchkareff, *The Narrative Prose of Brjusov* (1959); K. Mochulsky, *Valery Bryusov* (Paris, 1962); T. Binyon, "Bibliography of the Works of Valery Bryusov," *OSP* vol. 3 (1965), pp. 117–140; D. Maksimov, *Valery Bryusov: poeziya i pozitsiya* (1969).   J.Ho.

Brzękowski, Jan (1903–), Polish poet and novelist, was born in Wiśnicz Nowy near Bochnia, and studied at the University of Cracow, where he received his doctorate in Polish philology. In 1928 he settled in France, working as a journalist, attaché in the Polish embassy, and director of a spa.

His literary beginnings are linked with the Cracow avant-garde movement centering on T. Peiper's review *Zwrotnica*. The poems of his first volume, *Tętno* (1925; Pulse), are essentially odes celebrating modern civilization. By 1930 he developed his own style akin to surrealism, and the poems of his middle period, from *Na katodzie* (1928; On the Cathode) to *Odyseje* (1948), rely largely on the associative method. Their most striking feature is obsessive, sensuous, often erotic imagery. In his later volumes, *Przyszłość nieotwarta* (1959; Unopened Future), *Science Fiction* (1964), and *Styczeń* (1970; January), he experimented with prose poems, epigrammatic forms, ironic narratives, and the absurd. He has also published three volumes of verse in French.

Of his several novels, possibly the most successful is *Dwudziestu czterech kochanków Perdity Loost* (1961; The Twenty-Four Lovers of Perdita Loost). His theoretical writings include *Poezja integralna* (1933; Integral Poetry) and *Wyobraźnia wyzwolona* (1966; The Liberated Imagination).

See: *Słownik współczesnych pisarzy polskich,* vol. 1 (1963): 305–07.   B.Cz.

Brzozowski, Stanisław, pseud. Adam Czepiel (1878–1911), Polish philosopher, theoretician of culture, literary critic, novelist and playwright was born in Maziarnia, near Cełm, and died in Florence of tuberculosis. He studied natural history at Warsaw University, but he was suspended by the Russian authorities because of his political activities. Besides his illness and poverty, the most tragic event in the last years of his short life was the false rumor that he was an agent of the Russian secret police.

Brzozowski started his literary career in 1901 with popular philosophical sketches and polemical literary articles. In the following years he wrote many works on contemporary Polish literature and literary criticism: *Współczesna powieść polska* (1906; Contemporary Polish Novel), *Współczesna krytyka literacka w Polsce* (1907; Contemporary Literary Criticism in Poland), and his best-known large work *Legenda Młodej Polski* (1909; The Legend of Young Poland) in which he gave critical recapitulation of the whole literary movement. His most important philosophical essays as well as essays on Polish, French, English and Russian writers and on Polish and European culture were gathered in the books *Wstęp do filozofii* (1906; An Introduction to Philosophy), *Kultura i życie* (1907; Culture and Life), *Idee* (1910; Ideas), *Głosy wśród nocy, studia nad romantycznym przesileniem kultury europejskiej* (1912; Voices in the Night, Studies of the Romantic Crisis of European Culture), and *Filozofia romantyzmu polskiego* (written in 1905, pub. 1924; The Philosophy of Polish Romanticism). In his critical articles, written according to a method he labelled philosophical, Brzozowski presented an extensive analysis of the relationship of literature to the whole of culture and social life. Moral and ethical values played a basic role in his rapid intellectual evolution. In the changing of his ideas from what he called "philosophy of action" to "philos-

ophy of labor." Brzozowski became attracted by the philosophy of Polish romantic philosophers and poets, such as August Cieszkowski, Adam Mickiewicz, Cyprian NORWID, by the works of Friedrich NIETZSCHE, Richard Avenarius, Johann Fichte, later by the ideas of Karl Marx combined with Georges SOREL's syndicalism; in the last years of his life he was influenced by the thoughts of the Catholic modernists, and particularly by the works of Cardinal John Newman, and he came to the conclusion that Catholicism was of great importance for the fullest development of humanism. Along with his critical and philosophical works, Brzozowski wrote novels, which are exemplifications in fiction of his philosophical and moral ideas. This is noticeable already in his youthful novel *Wiry* (1904; Whirlpools) and above all in his mature novels. *Płomienie* (1908; Flames) portrays the revolt and moral conflict of Russian professional revolutionaries, of Sergey Nechaev's group and of the terrorist revolutionary organization Narodnaia Vola. The novel (similar to Fyodor DOSTOEVSKY's works which Brzozowski admired and about which he wrote many times) is a tragedy of ideas written in the form of the diary of a Pole who became fascinated by the ideas and heroism of the Russian revolutionaries and who later became involved in the revolutionary movement in Western Europe. The following novel *Sam wśród ludzi* (1911; Alone Among Men), is the first volume of what was intended to be a series of novels entitled "Dębina" (Oakwood) that would present according to Brzozowski, "The philosophical and political transformation of European consciousness" between the years 1830 and 1878, "the whole polymorphism of the truth," the whole dramatism of the changes in the intellectual life of Europe in the 19th century. *Sam wśród ludzi* includes a synthesis as well as criticism of the romantic epoch and presents a panorama of Polish and European culture in the years 1830 to 1848. It is a story about the maturing of a young Polish nobleman who left his sybaritic surroundings to become a man "of ideas" and who found himself in the circle of the Hegelian Left in Berlin. Similar to *Płomienie* it is a tragedy of ideas, a polyphonic novel of many layers. His last unfinished novel *Książka o starej kobiecie* (1914; A Book about an Old Woman) is centered around a revolutionary of 1905 killed by his own party. The hero is shown through controversial fragmentary opinions of others. Brzozowski also wrote plays: *Mocarz* (1903; The Potentate), *Milczenie* (1903; Silence), *Warszawa* (1905; Warsaw). Many of his philosophical reflections are included in his *Pamiętniki* (1913; Memoirs). Brzozowski translated Cardinal Newman's writings.

See: C. Miłosz, *Człowiek wśród skorpionów* (1962); C. Miłosz, "A Controversial Polish Writer Stanislaw Brzozowski," in *California Slavic Studies,* vol. 2(1963), pp. 53–95; J. Z. Maciejewski, *W kłębowisku przeciwieństw* (1974); A. Walicki, R. Zimand, ed., *Wokół myśli Stanisława Brzozowskiego* (1974); C. Rowiński, *Stanisława Brzozowskiego "Legenda Młodej Polski" na tle epoki* (1975); T. Burek, "Arcydzieło niedokończone," *Tw* 6 (1976): 73–96; S. A. Mencwel, *Stanisław Brzozowski, kształtowanie myśli krytycznej* (1976), A. Walicki, *Stanisław Brzozowski- drogi myśli* (1977); A. Werner, "Stanisław Brzozowski," in *Obraz literatury polskiej XIX i XX wieku. Literatura okresu Młodej Polski,* vol. 4 (1977), pp. 549–617.   S.F.

Buczkowski, Leopold (1905–), Polish novelist, was born in Nakwasza, in Podolia. He studied Polish literature and painting in Cracow and Warsaw. During World War II he fought in the army, in a Partisan unit, and in the Warsaw uprising, and he escaped three times from German camps. He acheived his first literary success with his novel *Wertepy* (1947; Impassable Roads), a dramatic psychological and moralistic account of life in the rural areas of Poland's eastern provinces presented in a naturalistic and expressionistic style. Life in the territories under the German occupation during World War II provided Buczkowski with the complicated and involved plots of his next two novels, *Czarny potok* (1954; Eng. tr., *Black Torrent*, 1969) and *Dorycki krużganek* (1957; A Doric Gallery), in which he depicted respectively the nightmare of the Nazi extermination of a ghetto in a small town and the dramatic fortunes of Poles, Jews, and Ukrainians fighting together for survival. The gradual departure from traditional forms of plot and narration that was apparent in those novels developed even more in his following work, *Pierwsza świetność* (1966; The First Splendor), in which the author described the destruction and agony of places, people, culture, and customs in his native Podolia during the Nazi horror. The flow of narration is constantly interrupted by insertions; many sentences are unrelated to one another; the order of events is reversed as if the text were reconstituted from fragments of memories about the apocalyptic vision of this vanishing world. It is a work of many layers, in which the real facts become symbolic and the words acquire many meanings. The discarding of almost all rules of fiction culminates in Buczkowski's plotless work *Uroda na czasie* (1970; Beauty on Time), made out of fragments of speech, impersonal dialogues, and seemingly unrelated utterances by nameless characters. He has also published *Kąpiele w Lucca* (1975; Spa Resort in Lucca) and *Kamień w pieluszkach* (1978; A Stone in Diapers).

See: S. Lichański, "Proza L. Buczkowskiego," in *Literatura i krytyka* (1957), pp. 299–315.   J.R.K. and S.F.

Buero Vallejo, Antonio (1916–), Spanish playwright, was born in Guadalajara. In 1934 he enrolled in the San Fernando School of Fine Arts in Madrid. A supporter of the Republic, he received a death sentence at the end of the Civil War but was exonerated in 1946. In that same year he received the Lope de Vega Prize for his play *Historia de una escalera* (1946; The Story of a Stairway). He was elected to the Royal Spanish Academy of the Language in 1971.

Historically, *Historia de una escalera* marks the resurgence of serious theater after the Spanish Civil War. A tragedy of three generations of Madrid tenement dwellers, *Historia* deals with the frustrations that accompany the pursuit of human happiness. The setting and language are realistic, and the style is sober.

Buero Vallejo's basic theme is man's quest for a meaningful world and a justification of his tragic yet hopeful search for truth. His treatment of this theme has been varied. It is metaphysical in *En la ardiente oscuridad* (1950; In the Burning Darkness), fantastic in *Irene o el tesoro* (1954; Irene or the Treasure), biblical in *Las palabras en la arena* (1949; The Words in the Sand), and mythical in *La tejedora de sueños* (1952; Eng. tr., *The Dream Weaver*, 1967). His historical plays—*Un soñador para el pueblo* (1958; A Dreamer for the People), *Las Meninas* (1960; The Ladies-in-Waiting), and *El concierto de San Ovidio* (1963; Eng. tr., *The Concert at Saint Ovide*, 1967)—are based on material taken from the historical past in order to illuminate the problems facing men in the present. *El tragaluz* (1967; The Basement Window), the first play to treat openly the experience of the Civil War, presents the conflict of man's tragic existence. Technically, it is a play within a play and contains a complicated temporal structure.

Buero Vallejo's plays involve a permanent questioning of the human condition within various historical contexts. They emphasize man's search for a radical salvation. He is considered Spain's leading contemporary dramatist.

See: R. L. Nicholas, *The Tragic Stages of Antonio Buero Vallejo* (1972); J. Cortina, *El arte dramático de Antonio Buero Vallejo* (1973); M. Halsey, *Antonio Buero Vallejo* (1973).   J.O.

Bulgakov, Mikhail Afanasyevich (1891–1940), Russian novelist, dramatist, and short-story writer, for many years known chiefly as the author of the play *Dni Turbinykh* (1926; Eng. tr., *Days of the Turbins*, 1934), achieved international fame when his hitherto unpublished novel *Master i Margarita* (Eng. tr., *The Master and Margarita*, 1967) appeared in censored form in the Soviet journal *Moskva* in 1966–67. Some Western editions, including Michael Glenny's English translation and the Possev Russian version (1969), restored most of the deletions, thus clarifying aspects of the novel. The appearance in a Soviet volume, *Romany* (1973; Novels) of a yet fuller text plus *Belaya Gvardiya* (Eng. tr., *The White Guard*, 1969) and *Teatralny roman* (A Theatrical Novel; Eng. tr., *Black Snow*, 1967) presumably completes the publication of his major works. Several pieces published abroad or known to exist have yet to appear in the USSR.

Born in Kiev, the son of a theology professor, Bulgakov practiced medicine briefly before turning to literature. In Moscow from 1921 on, he published feuilletons and short stories in various newspapers. The appearance of "Dyavoliyada" (1924; Eng. tr., 1972) and "Rokovye yaytsa" (1925; Eng. tr., "The Fatal Eggs," 1964), both included in the 1925 volume *Dyavoliyada*, launched Bulgakov as a writer. The great boost to his reputation came, also in 1925, with the publication of two parts of *White Guard* in the journal *Rossiya*. The journal was closed before the third part could appear, but adaptation of the novel for the Moscow Art Theater as *Days of the Turbins* set Bulgakov on temporarily firm footing as a playwright. Immensely popular with the public although not with the critics, *Days* portrays a White family in Kiev during the turbulent Civil War days. Its chief sin was to show these doomed sympathizers with the "wrong" cause as warmly human and even well-meaning. Banned in 1929, it was reinstated in 1932 but published only in 1955. *Days* was followed by *Zoykina kvartira* (1926; Eng. tr., *Zoya's Apartment*, 1972), *Bagrovy ostrov* (1928; Eng. tr., *The Crimson Island*, 1972), both controversial and soon banned, and *Beg* (1928; Eng. tr., *Flight*, 1972), banned before its premiere despite the efforts of Maksim GORKY. The publication of Bulgakov's work and the staging of his plays ceased in 1929 and with some exceptions was not resumed until the mid-1950s, when *Flight* was at last performed. In 1930, Bulgakov wrote to the government protesting his exclusion from artistic life. Iosif Stalin personally assured him of employment in the theater, and Bulgakov subsequently joined the Moscow Art Theater where for several years he adapted classics for the stage. He also wrote librettos for the Bolshoy Theater, several movie scripts, and five plays, meanwhile privately pursuing what would eventually be recognized as his major work.

Bulgakov's rehabilitation began on a very cautious scale in the mid-1950s. The 1960s saw the publication of *Pyesy* (1962; Plays), including *Days, Flight, Kabala svyatosh (Molyer)* (1936; Eng. tr., *A Cabal of Hypocrites*, 1972), *Posledniye dni (Pushkin)* (1936; The Last Days [Pushkin]), and *Don Quixote* (1938); *Zhizn Gospodina de Molyera* (1932–33, pub. 1962; Life of M. de Molière, 1970); several stories and a volume of *Izbrannaya proza* (1966; Selected Prose), containing *White Guard, Black*

Snow, the fictionalized life of Molière, and *Zapiski yunogo vracha* (Notes of a Young Doctor). The greatest achievement of the Commission on the Literary Legacy of Mikhail Bulgakov was the publication of *The Master and Margarita*.

Bulgakov's stories of the 1920s belong very much to the NEP literature—the New Economic Policy, 1921–28, involved a temporary return to private initiative in order to revive the country economically. Satire on criminal doings, high and low living, stupidity and cupidity of both the old and new ruling classes, provided some of the most pungent and diverting fiction of the period. Characteristically Bulgakov's tales have no real heroes. "Diaboliad" portrays a poor clerk in a gigantic bureaucracy where he loses his identity, his sanity, and finally his life. It inevitably recalls stories of Nikolay Gogal and Fyodor Dostoyevsky. In both "The Fatal Eggs" and "Sobachye serdtse" (Eng. tr., "The Heart of a Dog," 1968) an elderly professor who unwittingly releases chaos through scientific experiment is made just faintly more sympathetic than the bumbling proletarians of the new order. Both stories combine mordant humor with science-fiction motifs to suggest that doing too much too fast leads to disaster. Among the plays, *Apartment* also deals with the seamy side of contemporary life. The scene is an atelier-bordello and the characters range from the hard-working madam and her ex-noble husband through assorted NEP-types to a pair of cloddish secret policemen. *Island*, despite its partly exotic setting, offers sharp comment on the problem of censorship in contemporary Russia. *Flight*, on the other hand, deals with White fugitives fleeing Russia. More orthodox in content than *Days*, since the Whites are shown less positively, it is far less conventional in form. Subtitled "Eight Dreams," the play moves through a phantasmagoria suggesting the ephemeral existence and identity of those in flight. It returned to the stage in 1956 and was filmed, with heavy editing, in 1971. *Ivan Vasilyevich* (1935) turned again to satire on contemporary Soviet society with a time-machine caper involving a house chairman and Ivan the Terrible. It was produced in Moscow and filmed in the early 1970s. One other play, *A Cabal of Hypocrites*, saw the stage briefly during Bulgakov's lifetime under the title *Molière*, but was so altered by the director, Konstantin Stanislavsky, as to drive Bulgakov from the Moscow Art Theater. This experience suggested the main events and satirical thrust of *Black Snow*, on which Bulgakov worked in the mid-1930s. Another portrayal of an artist's conflict with despotism is *The Last Days*, performed first in 1943 under the title *Pushkin*.

The exuberant imagination, trenchant humor, and eye for moral grotesque marking Bulgakov's early work came into full play in *The Master and Margarita*, begun in 1928. Writing over the last decade and more of his life, Bulgakov obviously invested it with much of his thought and experience of that time. In artistic conception and philosophical reach it is by far his most ambitious work. Its structure—three interwoven narratives in strikingly different keys—has provoked much debate and analysis. Closest to his early fiction is the account of Satan's visit to Moscow, where the satanic cohort exposes human foibles and metes out comic justice. On the second level, Bulgakov dramatizes perhaps his most personal concern, the freedom of art and the artist's duty to follow his inspiration. Victim of a vicious critical campaign, the Master retires to a madhouse after burning his manuscript. Margarita, whose love for the Master and his novel drives her to a pact with Satan, accomplishes the deliverance of both. The Master's novel, an unorthodox account of Jesus and Pontius Pilate, projects the problem of human cowardice onto the universal level. Fantasy, philosophy, realism, and satire blend intricately, and the three narratives are linked not only through plot but through Bulgakov's original use of myth, including the Faust legend. Richness of meaning, structure, and style make this novel a continuing subject of critical study.

See: E. Stenbock-Fermor, "Bulgakov's *The Master and Margarita* and Goethe's *Faust*," *SEEJ* 13 (1969): 309–25; J. D. Grossman, "*The Master and Margarita*: The Reach Exceeds the Grasp," *SlavR* 31 (1972): 89–100; A. C. Wright, *Mikhail Bulgakov: Life and Interpretations* (1978); E. C. Haber, "The Mythic Structure of Bulgakov's *The Master and Margarita*," *RusR* 34 (1975): 382–409; R. W. F. Pope, "Ambiguity and Meaning in *The Master and Margarita*: The Role of Afranius," *SlavR* 36 (1977): 1–24; I. F. Belza, "Genealogiya Mastera i Margarita," *Kontekst-1978* (1978), pp. 156–248; E. Proffer, *Mikhail Bulgakov: Life and Work* (1980).　　J.D.Gr.

Bulgarian literature. In the period before 1880, the few Bulgarian writers there were wrote to stimulate the national consciousness in preparation for the country's political liberation after nearly five centuries of Turkish rule. Khristo Botev (1848–76), the greatest 19th-century Bulgarian poet, called for both national and social revolution in impassioned poetry, which also, however, displayed a tinge of philosophical nihilism.

When autonomy was achieved in the wake of the Russo-Turkish War of 1877–78, the immediate task for Bulgarian writers was the continued development of the national consciousness, although under different conditions. The role in their liberation played by the Bulgarians themselves was for a time the leitmotif of the national Bulgarian writer Ivan Vazov, who in his novel *Pod igoto* (1893; Eng. tr., *Under the Yoke*, 1893) described the abortive uprising of April 1876, in the aftermath of which Khristo Botev had been killed. Even before this novel, however, Vazov had in poetry and prose enshrined the memory of the heroes of his country's recent as well as more distant past, summoning his contemporaries to be worthy of their national heritage. But by the mid-1890s a considerable disillusionment had set in among the still not very numerous intelligentsia. It found expression in the writings of Vazov himself, and in those of Aleko Konstantinov (1863–97), author of the *Bay Ganyu* sketches (1894–95), which depict the "contemporary Bulgarian," Bay Ganyu, as a blundering clod wholly insensitive to other people's feelings, oblivious of civilized proprieties, and even potentially dangerous. Konstantinov had previously systematized his impressions of the United States of 1893 in *Do Chikago i nazad* (1894; To Chicago and Back). A few years later, after he had become involved in politics, Konstantinov was felled by an assassin.

The disillusionment in the potential of a politically liberated Bulgaria felt by such writers as Vazov and Konstantinov developed in the late 19th and early 20th centuries into a widespread philosophical nihilism. The poet Stoyan Mikhaylovski (1856–1927), an odd combination of religious believer and philosophical nihilist, produced such works as *Kniga za bulgarskiya narod* (1897; Book of the Bulgarian People), in which he set forth an extremely cynical view of society and its rulers. He held, among other things, that there was no middle ground between social anarchy and political enslavement. A representative of this cynicism in prose was Georgi Stamatov (1869–1942), who in numerous short stories found the chief motivation for men's actions to be mere egotism and physical instincts, particularly the drives for survival, crude sexuality, and creature comforts. He maintained that virtually any seemingly idealistic motive could be reduced to crass self-interest. The poet Peyo YAVOROV expressed the deepest metaphysical despair in powerful modernist verse, and ended his life in suicide.

Yavorov was also attached to a new and important group that appeared at the end of the 19th century, the "Misul" (Thought) circle, named for the title of its journal. The "Misul" group felt that the time was ripe for the conscious internationalization of Bulgarian culture, for combining the best of the national culture with the best of international thought and art. For the most part well educated in European universities and at odds with the more nationally oriented Vazov group, the "Misul" circle dominated Bulgarian intellectual life during the early part of the 20th century. A driving spirit behind it was the literary critic Dr. Krustyu Krustev (1866–1919), who defended the primacy of the aesthetic principle in art and provided personal and editorial guidance for the writers of his circle. One of these was Petko Todorov (1879–1916), the author of many sketches and plays, who made extensive use of folk motifs in his dreamy and not always clear writing, particularly in his prose *Idilii* (1908; Idylls). Probably the central figure of the "Misul" circle was the poet and critic Pencho Slaveykov (1866–1912), son of the eminent 19th-century writer Petko Slaveykov. Pencho Slaveykov could be intellectually arrogant, as when, in a famous article written in 1906, he dismissed most of his literary predecessors, including Vazov, as inferior. Art was his holy of holies, and he looked to the great writers, artists, and composers of ancient and modern times for guidance in the molding of Bulgarian culture. He dedicated individual poems in his *Epicheski pesni* (1896–98; rev. and coll. 1907; Epic Songs) to such men as Ludwig van Beethoven and Percy Bysshe Shelley; his curious *Na Ostrova na blazhenite* (1910; The Isle of the Blessed) is an anthology of works by nonexistent poets complete with fictional biographies. Further, having decided that, in order to memorialize the liberation of 1877–78, his country needed a national poem on the model of Adam Mickiewicz's Polish epic *Pan Tadeusz,* Slaveykov began the poem *Kurvava pesen* (Song of Blood) as early as 1893. He labored over it intermittently all his life, but the poem was left incomplete at his untimely death in political exile.

Although modernist and internationalist in outlook, the "Misul" circle was not particularly sympathetic to symbolism, whose first stirrings in Bulgaria date from about 1905. The Bulgarian symbolists became the major force in the national literature for a short period after the decline of the "Misul" group and before the outbreak of World War I. The outstanding symbolist poet was Teodor Trayanov (1882–1945), author of such early verse collections as *Regina mortua* (1908; The Dead Queen). He later managed to keep the symbolist movement artificially alive during the 1920s through his journal *Khiperion* (Hyperion). A poet of great native talent and a fellow traveler of the symbolist movement was Dimcho Debelyanov (1887–1916), who, like many Bulgarian poets, wrote very few lyric poems; but those he wrote are of intense beauty. Killed at the front in 1916, Debelyanov has remained the principal symbol of a generation of Bulgarian intellectuals and artists cut down prematurely in World War I.

The years after the war and during the first half of the 1920s constituted a period of political and literary instability in Bulgaria. Communist ideology proved attractive to some writers. The poet Geo Milev (pseud. of Georgi Kasabov, 1895–1925), before the war a dedicated modernist and after the war a dedicated expressionist, eventually gravitated to the Communist camp. His epic poem *Septemvri* (1924; September), clearly influenced by Vladimir MAYAKOVSKY, treats the events of the political uprising of September 1923. During a period of political

anarchy and repression shortly thereafter, Milev was arrested, and he disappeared. Another idealistic Communist poet was Khristo Smirnenski (pseud. of Khristo Izmirliev, 1898–1923), who died of tuberculosis. His principal collection of verse is *Da bude den!* (1922; Let the Day Dawn!).

During the confusion of the mid-1920s many writers drifted away from Marxism, and several found shelter in the circle around the journal *Zlatorog* (Golden Horn), published from 1920 to 1944 by the remarkable critic Vladimir Vasilev (1883–1963). This resolutely antiideological journal published nearly all the best Bulgarian writers of the period between the two world wars. Prominent among them were the short-story writer, novelist, and playwright Yordan YOVKOV; Elisaveta Bagryana (pseud. of Elisaveta Belcheva, 1893–), the best lyric poet of interwar Bulgaria, who gave a contemporary and feminine twist to modernist and internationalist themes; and Georgi Raychev (1882–1947), a short-story writer of some talent who, however, depended too much upon raw sex for his subject matter and who, in a sense, sustained the decadence of the early 20th century into the 1920s and even later.

An important writer who declined to ally himself with any group was Elin Pelin (pseud. of Dimitur Ivanov, 1877–1949), whose productive literary life, however, ended about 1922. He described the mores of a patriarchal agrarian society, not always sympathetically, in his short stories and such novellas as *Geratsite* (1911; The Gerak Family) and *Zemya* (1922; Land), the latter detailing a man's corruption through his unreasoning greed for more land.

Although Bulgaria was left relatively untouched by the destruction of World War II, the imposition of a Communist government upon the country in 1944 led to radical changes in Bulgarian intellectual life. Some writers were executed, some died of hardship or ceased to publish, and the straitjacket of socialist realism in its Stalinist variant was fastened upon the others. For some years even such masters as Vazov were attacked and maligned, and very little new literature of any worth appeared. But literature revived somewhat as the result of the destalinization campaign that culminated in 1956–57. During the 1960s and early 1970s a new generation of younger poets, taking their inspiration from such older poets as Atanas Dalchev (1904–), an unprolific but fine writer who refused to compromise during the Stalinist period, came upon the scene. These men and women possess a remarkable technical mastery of verse and are searching for new things to say and new ways to say them. They are keenly interested in cultural and literary developments abroad. The strong Bulgarian tradition of historical fiction has been reinforced by such men as Dimitur Talev (1898–1965), author of a trilogy treating Bulgarian life during the 19th and early 20th centuries; Emiliyan Stanev (1907–79), who has set some of his novels in medieval Bulgaria; and Anton Donchev (1930–), whose fascinating *Vreme razdelno* (1964; Eng. tr., *Time of Parting,* 1968) describes the forcible conversion to Islam of Bulgarians under the Turkish yoke. Among prose writers dealing with contemporary themes should be mentioned Pavel Vezhinov (1914–) and Nikolay Khaytov (1919–), the latter a critic of the bureaucratization and lack of spontaneity of Bulgarian life today. Thus, under difficult conditions, Bulgarian writers are striving to maintain and develop the best traditions of their national culture.

See: L. B. Picchio, *Storia della letteratura bulgara* (1961); J. F. Brown, *Bulgaria under Communist Rule* (1970), pp. 240–62; C. A. Moser, *A History of Bulgarian Literature 865–1944* (1972).   C.A.M.

Bull, Olaf (1883–1933), Norwegian lyric poet, was born in Christiania (now Oslo). Bull might justly be called the John Keats of Norway: he was a dreamer, a pure artist, a passionate lover of truth and beauty, a master of concrete imagery, and a matchless workman who patiently wrought into imperishable form the full wealth of a pensive, restless spirit. He is the one Norwegian poet who was at once (*Digte*, 1909; Poems) recognized as a genius. Bull's counterpart to Keat's "Ode on a Grecian Urn" is a poem called "Metope" (1927), wherein melancholy over the fragility of life is woven into a vivid setting. Bull's collections of poetry include *Nye digte* (1913; New Poems), *Digte og Noveller* (1916; Poems and Novellas); *Stjernene* (1924; The Stars); *Metope* (1927), and *Oinos og Eros* (1930; Oinos and Eros). His themes are those of great lyric writers—nature, love, beauty, death, and the poet's self. He sang of the nature of Christiania, particularly the northern spring in its earliest, most auspicious moments vivifying every nuance of color and light among the shadows. In his treatment of love he sought the ideal beauty that is glimpsed but never won, dwelling much on memory, in which he found the true eternity. His goal was to experience poetically the entire universe, and he pursued it by delving into history, biology, geology, and other branches of learning, as well as by direct, acute perception of the other world. Bull traveled extensively in France and Italy, but spent nearly all his life in Oslo where he lived the life of a bohemian: reading, writing, and existing on a subsistence level. The latter fact contributed to his poor health and early death. Bull is generally ranked with Norway's masters of lyric verse, Henrik Wergeland and Bjørnstjerne BJØRNSON (*see* NORWEGIAN LITERATURE). Although Bull lacks their social stature and their urge to action, he shares their cosmic feeling and daring imagery and exceeds them in the perfection of form. Some of his most unforgettable poems deal with the laws of fantasy and the poet's difficult art. His sense of form extended beyond rhyme and rhythm into the very aural textures of his lines, which he wove together into a rich but subtle assonance. The aristocratic character of Bull's poetry won him admirers among the fastidious rather than the multitude. In form and spirit he has much in common with the French symbolists, especially Paul VALÉRY, and he learned from Henri BERGSON, but Bull's own singular genius is apparent in every line he wrote.

See: T. Greiff, *Olaf Bull* (1952); E. H. Ofstad, *Olaf Bulls lyrikk* (1952); E. A. Wyller, *Tidsproblemet hos Olaf Bull* (1959).   E.H.

Bunin, Ivan Alekseyevich (1870–1933), Russian poet, short-story writer, and novelist, was born in the town of Voronezh but grew up on the family estate in Oryol province, an area that has been called the Russian Tuscany, since it has been the home of many of Russia's great writers. Bunin began publishing in 1887, and by the time of the October Revolution of 1917 his fame was secure as a poet and prose writer. He was an implacable foe of the Revolution and left Russia in 1920 on the last French ship to sail from Odessa, making his way first to Constantinople, then to Bulgaria, and eventually to France, where he settled in Grasse. Bunin wrote some of his most beautiful works as an émigré and became for many a visible link with the literary tradition of Old Russia. In 1933 he achieved international recognition on being the first Russian to receive the Nobel Prize for Literature. Bunin must be looked on as one of the last representatives of classic Russian realism; and his acknowledged literary ancestors are Ivan Turgenev, Lev TOLSTOY, and Anton CHEKHOV.

His creative work before emigration included a period of considerable experimentation. Although he participated in many of the literary movements, he was an advocate of none. In an era of emotional excess and some irrationality, Bunin personified both in his person and his writing a classical calm, precision, and measure. He began his literary career in 1887 with the publication of a poem, and he published his first story, "Derevenskiy eskiz" (Country Sketch), in 1891 in N. K. Mikhaylovsky's journal *Russkoye bogatstvo*. By the turn of the century he had published more than a dozen stories and over 100 poems. Some of the traits of the mature Bunin are already in evidence in the stories that he published in the 1890s: the tendency to describe objective reality with painstaking precision, to paint "still-lifes" with almost no movement in time and space and no complication of plot or intrigue, to record the elements of sensuous life in great detail but seldom if ever to describe the inner life of his characters. Man is already conceived of as part of nature and subject to its processes of growth and decay.

It is during the years between 1900 and the beginning of the Revolution in 1917 that Bunin's talents matured and his art took definite form. Important tales of this period are "Tuman" (1901; Fog); "Zolotoye dno" (1903; Rich Soil); "Schastye" (1903; Happiness); "U istoka dney" (1907; At the Well of Days); "Nochnoy razgovor" (1911; A Night Conversation); "Chasha zhizni" (1914; The Cup of Life); and "Bratya" (1914; Eng. tr., "Brethren," 1933). Special mention must be made, however, of *Derevnya* (1910; Eng. tr., *The Village*, 1923); *Sukhodol* (1911; Eng. tr., *Dry Valley*, 1935); and "Gospodin iz San Frantsisko" (1914; Eng. tr., "The Gentleman from San Francisco," 1922). *The Village* destroys definitively the idealization that had characterized the preceding half-century of writing on the peasant. Bunin's portrayal of village life is dark, desolate, and unrelieved in its pessimism. The peasant is pictured as slothful, cruel, insensitive, and filthy. *Dry Valley* is a lament for the passing of estate and gentry life and something of a mythic history of the beginning and end of that life. "The Gentleman from San Francisco" satirizes the crass materialism of an American businessman and his tawdry conception of leisure and pleasure.

Despite his bitter opposition to the Revolution and the Soviet regime, Bunin made reference to the Revolution only in the following four stories: "Nesrochnaya vesna" (1923; Timeless Spring); "Sosed" (1924; The Neighbor); "Tovarishch Dozorny" (1924; Comrade Dozorny); and "Obuza" (1925; The Burden). Other important works published in the 1920s include "Solnechny udar" (1925; Eng. tr., "Sunstroke," 1929); "Delo korneta Yelagina" (1925; Eng. tr., "The Elaghin Affair," 1935); "Kostsy" (1921; The Mowers); *Mitina Lyubov* (1925; Eng. tr., *Mitya's Love*, 1926); and *Zhizn Arsenyeva* (Paris, 1927; 1st complete ed., New York, 1952; The Life of Arsenyev; Eng. tr. of 1927 ed., *The Well of Days*, 1933). The most important short stories published in the 1930s were later gathered into a wartime volume entitled *Tyomnye allei* (1943; Eng. tr., *Dark Avenues*, 1949). Of the émigré works, *Mitya's Love*, *The Life of Arsenyev*, and "Sunstroke" stand out. *Mitya's Love* is the tale of a young man's love and his destruction of that love and of his eventual self-destruction. The novel is clearly indebted to Lev Tolstoy's *The Devil*, but it has none of the heavy moralism or self-analysis of Tolstoy's tale. *The Life of Arsenyev* is the first part of a projected autobiographical novel that recalls Tolstoy's *Childhood, Boyhood, and Youth*. Bunin seemed to experience difficulty continuing this fictional autobiography, not finishing the only sequel, *Lika*, until 1939. "Sunstroke" is a beautiful fragment about an intense and brief love affair in a provincial town on the Volga. It shows well Bunin's ability to create the sensuous texture of some particular fragment of experience. Bunin's realism is characterized by concern for the elemental process of love and death. His characters live in very personal universes. The world of ideas is foreign to them, but the life of the senses in all its wonder and beauty is not. Bunin's style is dry, restrained, precise; in his works the sensuous world is distilled and distanced by a controlled and classic manner.

Bunin's genealogy is inscribed in the oldest records of Russian nobility, and his literary lineage goes back to the golden age of Russian poetry. He was the last representative of the class of nobleman writer, and he was the last representative of the literature of Old Russia, which with the Revolution of October 1917 had been scattered to all parts of the world. He died at the age of 83 in a small apartment in Paris. A representative number of stories in English translation may be found in the following volumes: *The Gentleman from San Francisco and Other Stories*, tr. by G. Guerney (1923); *The Elaghin Affair and Other Stories*, tr. by G. Guerney (1935); and *Grammar of Love*, tr. by J. Cournos (1934).

See: V. Afanasyev, *I. A. Bunin, ocherk tvorchestva* (1966); A. Baboreko, *I. A. Bunin, materialy lya biografii* (1967); A. Volkov, *Proza Ivana Bunina* (1969). E.W.

Burkhart, Erika (1922–), Swiss poet and novelist, was born in Aarau. Her father was a well-known adventurer, hunter, and author. Although Erika Burkart was educated as a schoolteacher, she decided to write rather than teach and lives in the former residence of the abbots of Muri in Althäusern. She regards her self-sought isolation as an option for nature.

Burkart's mystical belief in the divinity of nature is strikingly evident in her poems, which are replete with nature images possessing archetypal and symbolic connotations. Her most important volumes of poetry are *Der dunkle Vogel* (1953; The Dark Bird), *Sterngefährten* (1955; Companions of the Stars), *Bann und Flug* (1956; Spell and Flight), *Geist der Fluren* (1958; Spirit of the Fields), *Die gerettete Erde* (1960; The Saved Earth), *Mit den Augen der Kore* (1963; With the Eyes of the Maiden), *Ich lebe* (1964; I Am Alive), *Die weichenden Ufer* (1967; The Receding Shores), and *Die Transparenz der Scherben* (1973; The Transparency of the Fragments). In 1970 Burkhart published her first novel, *Moräne* (Moraine), on which she had worked for 11 years. The book concerns a stepsister and stepbrother, Lilith and Laurin, who fall in love with each other. Burkart insists that the incestuous motif did not interest her as much as the elective affinity between the two characters. The novel contains clear references to the Jungian principles of animus and anima and to Marcel PROUST.

See: W. Bucher and G. Ammann, eds., *Schweizer Schriftsteller im Gespräch*, vol. 2 (1971), pp. 11–46.
R.K.

Burlyuk, David Davidovich (1882–1967), Russian poet and painter, was born near Kharkov and studied art in Russia and Europe. Through his organizing and publishing activities the cubo-futurists became the best known avant-garde group in Russia (*see* RUSSIAN LITERATURE). His miscellany *Sadok sudey* (1910; A Trap for Judges) is considered the beginning of Russian futurism; he also organized and participated in the famous futurist tour across Russia with Vladimir MAYAKOVSKY, and Vasily KAMENSKY in 1913–14. After lecturing, publishing, and exhibiting his paintings for some years in the Far East, Burlyuk settled in New York in 1922, where he continued to paint

and publish. His eclectic poetry, printed in pre-Revolutionary futurist miscellanies and in his own American publications, could—like all his art—be labeled primitivistic. Many of his poems emphasize violence and are deliberately "antiaesthetic" in the use of different typefaces, the omission of prepositions, and the creation of special consonantal effects. His journal was published under the title *Color and Rhyme*, nos. 1–60 (1930–66).

See: K. Dreier, *Burlyuk* (1944); V. Markov, *Russian Futurism* (1968). V.M.

Burniaux, Constant (1892–1975), Belgian novelist and poet, was born in Brussels. He is best known for *Les Temps inquiets* (1944–52; Times of Unrest), which stands at the center of his abundant literary output. This romantic sequence constitutes an evocation of the cruel uncertainties of the first half of the 20th century as seen through the individual fate of a volunteer. Around this important work and announcing and prolonging it are some 20 other volumes—novels, narrations, novellas not without originality and with outbursts of cruel irony and cautious bounds of tenderness—which present the commonplace romanticism of all sorts of lives as in *Une petite vie* (1929; A Quiet Life) and *Les Ages de la vie* (1960; The Ages of Life). No doubt, a lyrical sighing appears as the most obvious common denominator of a literary production that spans the engraved sketches of *La Bêtise* (1925), in which the disinherited childhood of large cities is evoked with an almost documentary realism, and the kaleidoscopic, somewhat surrealistic composition of *D'humour et d'amour* (1968; About Humor and Love). From 1918 to 1975, Burniaux also never ceased writing prose poems or free verse, for example, in *Ondes courtes* (1951; Short Waves), which, "in their ingenuity tempered with lucidity, espouse in a certain way the rhythm of breathing and heart-beats" (Yves Gandon). In 1949, Burniaux won the Prix Triennal Du Roman, and in 1945 he became a member of the Royal Academy of French Language and Literature of Belgium.

See: "Hommage à Constant Burniaux," *Marginales* (1954); G. Charlier and J. Hanse, eds., *Histoire illustrée des lettres françaises de Belgique* (1958); *Bibliographie des écrivains français de Belgique*, vol. 1 (1958); A. Ayguesparse, *Constant Burniaux* (1960); J.-G. Linze, *Mieux connaître Constant Burniaux* (1972); D. Scheinert, *Constant Burniaux ou la hantise du temps* (1973); A. Jans, ed. *Lettres vivantes 1945–1975* (1975). R.Bu.

Burssens, Gaston (1896–1965), Belgian (Flemish) writer, was born in Dendermonde. He spent his youth in Mechelen, where he attended secondary school and was a student of the writer M. Sabbe. He often vacationed with his uncle, L. Spanoghe, who was a member of the "School of Dendermonde" and who introduced the young Burssens to the artistic circle that was to play a role in his later writings. During World War I, his family settled in its small estate in Bonheiden where he became acquainted with his future wife, Madeleine de Hollander. He studied at the Dutch-language University of Ghent during the German Occupation and worked on magazines such as *Aula, Vlaamsch Leven*, and *De Godedndag*, which furthered the cause of Flemish expressionism. Like others of his generation, Burssens encountered German expressionism through books and periodicals. His first works, *Verzen* (1918; Verses) and *Liederen uit de Stad en uit de Sel* (1920; Songs from the City and from the Cell) bear the clear traces of a "humanitarian" tendency that also influenced Paul van OSTAIJEN. But Burssens's personal preferences drew him to a transitional figure like KLABUND, whose pessimism and sultry eroticism still reflected the fin-de-siècle period. In this vein, Burssens reworked poems of Li Tai Pe and other oriental writers under the title of *De Yadefluit* (1919; The Jade Flute). After a brief incarceration because of activist sympathies and after his military service, he worked as a clerk, a grain merchant, and a soap manufacturer. He established friendships with painters including F. Jespers. Another great friendship was that with Paul van Ostaijen, who had praised the volume of poetry *Piano* (1924), an avant-garde work in form and content, for its organic-expressionistic characteristics. After van Ostaijen's death in 1928, Burssens's defense of his friend against the misconceptions of contemporaries led to the unfair charge that Burssens had been but his friend's disciple.

In 1925, Burssens married Madeleine and established himself in Antwerp. Like *Piano*, his subsequent volumes witness to the formal experimentation in which dominates a cooly ironical game of words, images, and concepts: *Enzovoort* (1926; Et cetera), *Klemmen voor Zangvogels* (1930; Traps for Singing Birds) and, above all, *French en andere Cancan* (1935; French and Other Cancan). A more serious tone appears in *De eeuw van Perikles* (1941; The Century of Pericles), in which the melancholic nature of Burssens comes forth unmasked as it does in his unpublished diary from that time. After the death of his wife in 1941, he wrote *Elegie*, one of the most moving elegies written in the Dutch language. Subsequently, satirical trends dominated in *Fabula Rasa* (1945) and *12 Nigger-Songs* (1946).

After World War II, Burssens achieved widespread fame; he was considered by the new "experimentalists" as a forerunner. He contributed to several magazines: *Podium, Dietsche Warande en Belfort, De Vlaamsche Gids, Tijd en Mens,* and the *Nieuwe Vlaams Tijdschrift.* In 1952, he received the national Triennial Prize for Poetry for *Pegasos van Troja* (1952; Pegasus of Troy). He established and continued friendships with fellow writers. Having married Yvette Goubetto in 1949 and having settled in Sint Anneke-Strand near Antwerp with her, he dedicated to her his "happiest" volume, *Ode* (1954). His *Adrien* (1958) received another Triennial Prize.

In his last volumes, the confessional character of Burssens's poetry emerges. The formal experimentation becomes less aggressively emphasized and, thanks to a more classical structuring, a more sober imagery reigns. After the stunning, alternately playful and cynical masks that Burssens had worn through his long poetic journey, the same constant elements remain: a melancholic realization of the brevity of human existence, a relativistic scepticism, and a disillusioned vulnerability.

See: G. Burssens, *Het neusje van de inktvis,* ed. by K. Jonckheere and H. C. Kool (1956); J. Walravens, *Gaston Burssens* (1960); K. Jonckheere, *Sleutelbos op Gaston Burssens* (1972).   P.H.

Butor, Michel (1926–), French novelist, essayist, critic, and poet, was born in Mons-en-Barœul. He emerged as one of the leading figures in the so-called *nouveau roman* (new novel) group during the 1950s (*see* FRENCH LITERATURE). Although he had written much poetry before, Butor's first book was a novel, *Passage de Milan* (1954), followed by three others, *L'Emploi du temps* (1956; Eng. tr., *Passing Time*, 1960), *La Modification* (1957; Eng. tr., *A Change of Heart*, 1959), and *Degrés* (1960; Eng. tr., *Degrees*, 1961). These, the only works he has labeled "novels," reveal the gradual disintegration of elements traditionally associated with the genre, such as plot, point of view, characters, and linear development.

Butor considers the novel to be a species of narrative patterned upon those used in a society to convey values acceptable to it. As an indirect means of challenging such values, he felt a need to experiment with new narrative forms. The very history of the novel, however, is so closely tied to that of the dominant class in Western society that an attack on the means by which its values are produced, that is, the narrative, was bound to change the novel beyond recognition. This meant that experiments could not be contained within the novel form. For all its self-destructive potential, *Degrés* remains a masterful novel, enclosed within the system it negates.

The many quotations with which *Degrés* is studded call attention to intensified workings of intertextuality, to use the term later introduced in France by Julia KRISTEVA. Eschewing the novel, Butor now explored various possibilities of intertextuality in his effort to change his readers' views of reality. *Mobile* (1962; Eng. tr., 1963) calls on them to respond to cues provided by a meticulously organized collage of variegated texts: a road atlas, road signs, mail-order house catalogues, advertisements, Audubon prints, writings by Thomas Jefferson, Andrew Carnegie, and others. All this activity takes place within the framework of an imaginary survey of the United States in which the evocative power of words and their interaction take precedence over the reality for which they supposedly stand. A similar process is evident in *Description de San Marco* (1963), for which a visit to the Venetian basilica serves as pretext, and *6 810 000 litres d'eau par seconde* (1965; Eng. tr., *Niagara*, 1969), which, like the earlier *Réseau aérien* (1962; Aerial Network), was designed for radio broadcast.

A common characteristic of these four works is that in each the narrator has either been eliminated or pushed into the background. In the fiction that followed, the subject of discourse is no longer repressed. *Portrait de l'artiste en jeune singe* (1967; Portrait of the Artist as a Young Monkey), labeled "capriccio," displays explicitly autobiographical elements; a first-person narrative that fuses narrator and author alternates with the account of a dream based on a tale from the *Arabian Nights.* But the subject is no longer unitary: it is, albeit fictitiously, divided between conscious and unconscious subject, each in turn interacting with texts that are read in the fiction. As one reads on in Butor's works, it becomes clear that "reading" and "fiction" assume broader connotations. One reads not only books but paintings, monuments, landscapes, and precious stones—all become "texts." Distinctions between fiction, nonfiction, biography, and poetry are also blurred, and all that remains is heterogeneous text.

The concept of intertextuality now encroaches upon what used to be called description and illustration, and it also involves interplay between words and music. After working with the Belgian composer Henri Pousseur on *Votre Faust* (Your Faust; fragments pub. 1962–, one version recorded in 1973), an aleatory opera, Butor wrote *Paysage de répons* (1968; Landscape of Response). Conceived as a text to accompany Pousseur's "Répons pour 8 exécutants" (Response for 8 Performers), it then developed independently—only to provoke a new version of Pousseur's composition. *Dialogue avec 33 variations de Ludwig van Beethoven sur une valse de Diabelli* (1971; Dialogue with 33 Variations by Beethoven on a Waltz by Diabelli) originated as a series of texts read during a public performance of Beethoven's Diabelli Variations; it was then expanded into its final form, a combination of historical, descriptive, technical, and lyric texts.

Butor has also done much work in collaboration with artists such as Pierre Alechinsky, Alexander Calder, Jacques Hérold, Gregory Masurovsky, Roberto Matta, Victor Vasarely, and Marie Helena Vieira da Silva. Such collaboration, often begun at the conceptual stage of the work, might be termed artisanal. Butor later had his own contribution to these joint efforts reprinted in modified form, dismembered and reassembled, in a series called *Illustrations* (1964, 1969, 1973, 1976). Here one's reading habits are in for a jolt: some texts are linear, others not; some have the appearance of prose, others not; some are syntactically coherent, others not; in all cases, the typographical design of the page plays a signal role.

This technique has spread to Butor's other works. It is most apparent in *Où* (1971; Where), a text of considerable achievement combining nine units of varying length that are wrought into a complex architecture. The first-person pronoun affirms the presence of the writer, who has traveled to Korea, Cambodia, California, Utah, and the Indian pueblo of Zuni, but the unitary nature of the subject of discourse is called into question by the contradictory drives that surface throughout—as well as by the incursions of extraneous texts. *Travaux d'approche* (1972; Works for Approaching) brings together some of the earlier poetry, a reworking of *Paysage de répons*, and a personal, humorous piece in which the writer assumes an ironic stance toward himself. In *Intervalle* (1973), an idea for a movie develops into an intertextual affair, and the irony of the previous work is now directed at the writing itself as this work includes a "diary" of its own development. *Matière de rêves* (1975; Matter for Dreams) is presented as a narration of five dreams in which the humor seems pointed at the public image of Butor; two sequels have appeared, *Second Sous-sol* (Second Subbasement) in 1976 and *Troisième Dessous* (Third Below) in 1977. These works suggest a critical reassessment of the writer's function. *Boomerang* (1978), typographically conventional (although printed in inks of three different colors), deepens the introspective quest.

The abundance of Butor's writings should not obscure his work as critic, even though this category also tends to merge with the others. His essays embrace the entire scope of French literature from François Villon, Rabelais, and Montaigne to the contemporary scene. They have been collected in a series entitled *Répertoire* (1960, 1964, 1968, 1974; partial Eng. tr., *Inventory*, 1968).

See: G. Raillard, *Butor* (1968); F. Aubral, *Michel Butor* (1973); G. Raillard, ed., *Butor/Colloque de Cerisy* (1974); M. Spencer, *Butor* (1974); A. Helbo, *Michel Butor* (1975); special issue of *Obliques* (February 1976); J. Waelti-Walters, *Michel Butor* (1977); D. McWilliams, *The Narratives of Michel Butor* (1978).   L.S.R.

Buysse, Cyriel (1859–1932), Belgian (Flemish) novelist and dramatist born in Nevele, near Ghent, belonged to a prominent family of scholars and writers. The poets and prose writers Rosalie and Virginie Loveling were his mother's sisters. After commercial studies in Ghent, he was set to work in his father's chicory plant in Nevele. There he came in close contact with the workers and the rural population that was to be incisively and authentically portrayed in short stories and novels like the autobiographical *Zoals het was* (1921; Such As It Was). In the autumn of 1886 he visited the United States for four months. Four years later, he returned there to establish a business, which, however, he was obliged to close early in 1893. Some of his novels and short stories, including his last novel, *Twee werelden* (1931; Two Worlds), were inspired by his American experiences. After his marriage in 1896 to a Dutch widow, Nelly Dyserinck-Tromp, he settled in The Hague. But after 1899, he spent the spring and summer months in his native country, near the picturesque river Lys. Buysse was a sportsman and a frequent traveler. He often visited his great friend, Maurice

MAETERLINCK, in different regions of France; on some of his trips, Buysse was accompanied by the luminist painter E. Claus and the French critic Leon Bazalgette. After World War I, which affected him deeply, Buysse stayed more and more frequently in Flanders, where he met with increasing popularity. In 1930, he was elected a member of the Belgian Royal Academy. Shortly before his death, he was awarded the title of baron by the Belgian sovereign.

Buysse wrote prolifically in many different genres: over 20 novels, dozens of short stories, dramas, travel accounts, and numerous articles in newspapers and magazines. Although he began to write in about 1885, major works appeared with regularity after his American journeys. In 1889, Buysse made the acquaintance of E. de Bom and, in the winter of 1891–1892, he met Maeterlinck. The former introduced him into *Van Nu en Straks* (Now and Later), the literary magazine that was to bring about a renewal of Flemish literature after 1893. Maeterlinck also acquainted Buysse with the French language magazine *Le Réveil*, in which Buysse published "Trois petits contes" (1895; Three Short Stories). Maeterlinck later dissuaded his friend from pursuing a career as a French language author; fortunately, Buysse followed this advice, for his subsequent works, written solely in Flemish, were to become representative both of naturalism and of mild or romantic realism in Dutch literature at the turn of the century. His naturalistic debut, the remarkable short story "De biezenstekker" (1890; The Bastard), was published in the authoritative Dutch literary magazine *De Nieuwe Gids*. His first novel, *Het recht van de sterkste* (1893; The Law of the Strongest), written in the naturalistic vein of Emile ZOLA and Lemonnier, provides an unsentimental, even harsh portrayal of a farmer who fights for survival in a severe, Darwinian world. But in later, more mature works, naturalism and romanticism seem to be in concord, as in *Het leven van Roseke van Dalen* (1906; The Life of Rosy van Dalen), probably his best work. *Het gezin Van Paemel* (1903; The Van Paemel Family), his best-known drama, is a social document in which the exploitation of country people is reported with courage and with an open, sympathetic mind. It is representative of the social concern that is apparent in the whole of Buysse's work. After about 1905, however, his novels and short stories seem to reveal a less pessimistic vision; his realism is gradually mitigated by light humor and lively characterization. His mature novels, *t' Bolleken* (1906; The Little Ball), *Het Ezelken* (1910; The Little Ass), and *De nachtelijke aanranding* (1912; The Nocturnal Agression), as well as short stories like "Tussen Leie en Schelde" (1904; Between the Lys and the Scheldt), "Lente" (1909; Spring), and "'k Herinner mij" (1909; I Remember), give an authentic but good-natured picture of rural life. In the major novels written after World War I, *Tantes* (1924; Aunts), *Uleken* (1926), and *De Schandpaal* (1928; The Pillory), new psychological perspectives are opened; the older generation is opposed by the younger, postwar generation, standing for a new sense of freedom. The whole of Buysse's prose presents some manifest shortcomings: its intellectual scope is somewhat restricted, certain themes recur too often, and the narrative structure may be found wanting. But such failings are amply compensated for by the authenticity of Buysse's vision, by the simplicity and vividness of his dialogue, and by his remarkable qualities as a narrator. Other works of Buysse which deserve to be mentioned include *Mea culpa* (1896), *Uit Vlaanderen* (1899; From Flanders), *Van arme mensen* (1901; About Poor People), *Oorlogsvisioenen* (1915; Vision of the War), and *Zomerleven* (1915; Summer Life).

See: A. van Elslander, *Cyriel Buysse uit zijn leven en zijn werk* (1960–61); P. H. S. van Vreckem, *De invloed van het Franse naturalisme in het werk van Cyriel Buysse* (1968), and the Introductions to Buysse's *Verzameld werk*, ed. by A. van Elslander and A. M. Musschoot (1974–).   A. van E.

Buzzati, Dino (1906–72), Italian novelist, short-story writer, journalist, and painter, was born in Belluno. From 1928 until his death, he worked in Milan as editor and correspondent for *Corriere della sera*. As a fiction writer, Buzzati was a master at transforming the ordinary into the extraordinary, fusing the world of nightmare with that of objective reality, and thus creating an ominous universe of ambiguous, allegorial dimensions. His first novel, *Bárnabo delle montagne* (1933; Barnabo of the Mountains), was followed by *Il segreto del Bosco Vecchio* (1935; The Secret of the Old Woods) and the novel which won him European as well as Italian fame, *Il deserto dei Tartari* (1940; Eng. tr., *The Tartar Steppe*, 1952). In *Il deserto* he tells the story of a young officer whose aspiration of heroic combat against the legendary Tartars is proven vain as the years pass routinely in a decaying fort, bringing him only illness and a lonely death. Mountain and desert imagery dominate Buzzati's works, informing themes of travel, hope, loneliness, disillusion, fear, and death. A central character usually incarnates these themes. Buzzati preferred the general type to the individual personality; he shunned the psychological analysis of Henry James and aimed rather at portraying humankind's shared existential dilemmas. Neither literary realism nor the neorealism of the politically engaged Italian writers of his generation appealed to him. Instead, he took pleasure in creating bizarre events, natural calamities, and monsters with which to rattle the lives of his predominantly bourgeois characters. But whether the background is fanciful or somber, the mode ironic or serious, the tales point to a view of the human condition as absurd, sadistic, and despairing. For Buzzati, the best of man lies in his youth—in the green years of optimism and health, which the aging adult recalls bittersweetly. The decisive presence in Buzzati is time—archdestroyer and bearer of Death, to whom the ultimate, bankrupting payment must eventually be made. Not even God brings solace to Buzzati's antiheroes, for like lost youth itself, religious feeling seems only a memory, an unattainable ideal.

The wide range of Buzzati's inventiveness is particularly evident in his short stories, published in 1942, 1948, and 1954. and reprinted in part in *Sessanta racconti* (1958; partial Eng. tr., *Catastrophe*, 1966). A few of the latest stories in this collection focus on contemporary urban life: Milan provides the setting, and technology (especially the automobile) the villain. Such seriocomic "chronicles" of the absurd and the routine also appear,

along with Buzzati's more traditional surreal material, in the collections *Il colombre* (1966; The Sea-Monster) and *Le notti difficili* (1971; Difficult Nights). These volumes, as well as *In quel preciso momento* (1955; rev. 1963; At That Exact Moment), include brief autobiographical pieces. A rich assortment of Buzzati's newspaper articles is assembled in *Cronache terrestri* (1972; Earth Chronicles). This posthumous volume underscores the cohesiveness of the writer's singular literary-journalistic rendering of reality.

Among Buzzati's other works are plays, such as *Un caso clinico* (1953; A Clinical Case; Fr. tr. by Albert CAMUS, 1955), poems, librettos, a children's book, the science-fiction novel *Il grande ritratto* (1960; Eng. tr., *Larger than Life*, 1962), and the realistic novel *Un amore* (1963; Eng. tr., *A Love Affair*, 1964). His paintings, often erotic and ironic, sadistic and surreal, have been reproduced, accompanied by commentaries written by himself, in *Dino Buzzati, pittore* (1967; Dino Buzzati, Painter), *Poema a fumetti* (1969; Comic-Strip Poem), and *I miracoli di Val Morel* (1971; The Miracles of the Val Morel). A substantial collection of Buzzati's novels, short stories, and poems, which also includes a good introductory essay and bibliography, has been published under the title *Romanzi e racconti* (1975).

See: C. Marabini, "Dino Buzzati," in *Nuova antologia* (July 1967), pp. 357–77; A. V. Arslan, *Invito alla lettura di Dino Buzzati* (1974).   M.Sc.

Bykov, Vasil Vladimirovich, Russian form of Belorussian Býkaŭ, (1924–), Belorussian novelist, was born in the Vitebsk region of the Belorussian Soviet Republic. His experiences in World War II left a profound imprint upon him and have provided the themes of all his novels.

Discovered by Aleksandr TVARDOVSKY when still a regional author writing in his native Belorussian language, Bykov gained national attention with *Myortvym ne bolno* (1966; The Dead Feel No Pain), a novel whose unsparing truthfulness aroused a storm of official indignation. Without sacrificing any of his devotion to the truth, Bykov did round off the sharp edges in *Kruglyansky most* (1969; The Kruglyansky Bridge), *Sotnikov* (1970; Eng. tr. *The Ordeal*, 1972), *Obelisk* (1973), and *Volchya staya* (1975; The Wolf Pack), all published in the journal *Novy mir*; and in *Yego batalyon* (1976; His Battalion), published in *Nash sovremennik*.

One of the most courageous of the officially sanctioned novelists in the Brezhnev era, Bykov has provided a new vision of war. He remains impartial in his condemnation of cruelty, regardless of which side may commit it, and considers any transgression against man inexcusable. Bykov was probably the first to hint at a forbidden truth, namely, that in terms of human lives, the cost of victory on the Eastern Front in World War II was far too high.
                                                                J.Ca.

C

Caballero Bonald, José Manuel (1926–), Spanish poet, novelist, and essayist, was born in Jerez. He studied astronomy in Cádiz and letters in Madrid, where he presently is associated with the publishing industry. In the collection *Las adivinaciones* (1952; Prophecies), Caballero Bonald cultivates a subjective, pessimistic, and enigmatic poetry that in *Las hojas muertas* (1959; Dead Leaves), and especially in *Pliegos de cordel* (1963; Ballads) evolves into ideologically committed lyricism. Con-

ceptually serene and lexically rich and musical, his later poetry, collected in *Descrédito del héroe* (1977; Discredit of the Hero) continues to express man's alienation in a hostile world.

Caballero Bonald's novel *Dos días setiembre* (1962; Two Days in September) is a social testimony to the lives of vintagers in southern Spain. This work is not only a critical interpretation of Spanish reality, but it also marks the beginning of the author's linguistic exploration of the poetic possibilities of language. This poetic treatment of narrative material culminates in *Agata ojo de gato* (1974; Cat's Eye Agate), a mythological chronicle of annihilation in a mysterious and desolate setting identifiable as Spain. The destructive fatalism that permeates the geography, bodies, and minds of this novel is expressed in a baroque rhetoric and an exuberant, sensuous prose. Caballero Bonald's social commitment finds efficient expression in the precise and poetic language of both his poetry and his fiction.

See: J. S. Curutchet, "Caballero Bonald: un precursor," in *Cuatro ensayos sobre la nueva novela española* (1974), pp. 11–29; J. Ortega, "Nuevos rumbos en la novelística española de posguerra: *Agata ojo de gato*, de Caballero Bonald," *ANP* (1977): 19–31.   J.O.

Cabanis, José (1922–), French novelist, essayist, and historian, was born in Toulouse. After studying law and philosophy, he became a lawyer. The first part of his long novel *L'Age ingrat* (1966; The Awkward Age) was published in 1952. Its hero, Gilbert Samalagnou, is a young man living in Toulouse at the end of the 1930s. In 1955, Cabanis left the bar to devote himself completely to writing. In *Le Fils* (1956; The Son), Cabanis showed his obsession with the passing of time. *Le Bonheur du jour* (1960; Happiness of the Day), a meditation on death, received the Critics Prize, and *La Bataille de Toulouse* (1968; Eng. tr., *The Battle of Toulouse*), won the Théophraste Renaudot Prize. Cabanis's distinguished essays include *Jouhandeau* (1960) and *Plaisirs et Lectures* (1964, 1968; Pleasures and Readings), the latter a two-volume collection of essays on such figures as René Descartes, Victor Hugo, André GIDE, and Pierre Choderlos de Laclos.

Lately Cabanis has been more interested in history. *Le Sacre de Napoléon* (1970; Napoleon's Coronation), *Charles X* (1972), and *Saint-Simon l'admirable* (1975) have all been praised. He is preparing a book on Louis Philippe. His other works include a volume of memoirs entitled *Les Profondes années* (1976; The Deep Years) and a chronicle of life in southwestern France.

Cabanis is a cultured writer, a profound moralist, a subtle observer of people and things, and a great artist. For Cabanis, to write is to rescue the world from oblivion.

See: P. de Boisdeffre, *Dictionnaire de Littérature contemporaine* (1963); H. Peyre, *French Novelists of Today* (1967); *Littérature de notre temps*, vol. 3 (1971).
J.-C.M.

Cabral, Alexandre (1917–), Portuguese novelist and essayist, was born in Lisbon, and worked in business offices before writing news items and advertisements. From 1943 to 1946, he and the poet Sidónio Muralha tried their luck in the Congo and Angola. That experience led Cabral to write his best prose: *Terra quente* (1953; Hot Country), *Histórias do Zaire* (1956; Stories of the Congo); some already in *Contos da Europa e da Africa* (1947; Tales from Europe and Africa) and *A Fula* (1963; High-Yaller). He was among the first to write honestly of the black African's relations with Europeans. Although never denying his own socialism, he seems more interested in portraying ordinary human beings than in manufacturing proletarian fiction. In the wake of José Maria Ferreira de CASTRO, Cabral, as one of the early neorealists, published tales of frustrated lives culminating in *O sol nascerá um dia* (1942; Some Day the Sun Shall Rise). Several of his novels show greater skill: *Fonte da Telha* (1949; Shingle Spring) depicts life in a wretched fishing village near Lisbon; *Malta brava* (1955; Wild Gang) evokes bittersweet memories of a boarding school; *Margem Norte* (1961; Northside), presents the memories of a Lisbonese drifter,

whose inhibition symbolizes the rotting of manhood during the Salazar years of "abject normalcy." Cabral attempted drama, too, in *As duas faces* (1959; Both Sides). More recently, he has turned to editing works of Camilo Castelo Branco, the tragic genius of 19th-century Portugal, and to the writing of essays, for example, *Notas oitocentistas* (1973; 19th-Century Notes). His slightly fictionalized (the censor was watching) memories of the literary and political fight against fascism appeared as *Memórias de um resistente* (1970, Memories of a Resister).   G.M.M.

Cadou, René Guy (1920–51), French poet, was born in Sainte-Reine-de-Bretagne in the Brière region. His childhood and his youth are at the core of his poetry. In 1937 he published his first work, *Les Brancardiers de l'aube* (The Stretcher-Bearers of Dawn). Soon afterwards, Cadou became part of the "Ecole de Rochefort," with such poets as Michel Manoll, Jean Rousselot, and Jean FOLLAIN. The two poets who influenced him most were Max JACOB and Pierre REVERDY. Like his father, Cadou was a primary-school teacher. Until his death he taught in different villages and published a book of poetry almost every year. *La Maison d'été* (1955; The Summer House) was Cadou's only attempt at a novel. Seghers published his complete works in two volumes in 1973.

Cadou is the poet of simple life. Nature and love for mankind are predominant themes in his poetry. His poems are about animals, trees, and flowers, and the houses and schools where he lives and teaches. As a lyric poet, Cadou is in the tradition of Ronsard, Francis JAMMES, and Charles PÉGUY. Cadou's memoirs, *Mon Enfance est à tout le monde* (My Childhood Belongs to Everybody), written in 1947 and published in 1969, are a superbly lyrical evocation of his younger years in the country.

See: special no. of *L'Herne* (1961); M. Manoll, *René Guy Cadou* (1969); special no. of *Poésie 11* (1970).
J.-C.M.

Caillavet, Gaston Arman de (1870–1915), French dramatist), a Parisian by birth and, one might say, by estate, grew up in the charmed circle of his mother's salon, where Anatole FRANCE reigned supreme. There he met Robert de FLERS, with whom he was to form a literary partnership as close and fortunate as that of Meilhac and Halévy a generation before.

Begun under such auspices, the two authors' collaboration could not but retain a distinctively refined quality. Witty, urbane, and tolerant, mildly naughty, mildly romantic, and mildly ironical, their librettos (with musical scores by Claude Terrasse, André Messager, Gabriel Pierné) and such light comedies as *Les Sentiers de la vertu* (1903; The Paths of Virtue), *Miquette et sa mère* (1906; Eng. tr., *Jenny and Her Mother*, 1907), *L'Ane de Buridan* (1909; Eng. tr., *Inconstant George*, 1909), and *La Belle Aventure* (1913, in collaboration with Etienne Rey; Eng. tr., *The Beautiful Adventure*, 1914) recall the exquisite daintiness of a Parisian gown or a champagne supper at the Bois. *Primerose* (1911; Eng. tr., *Primrose*, 1911) borders more decidedly on the sentimental, whereas *Monsieur Brotonneau* (1914), their last play, seemed to presage an evolution toward deeper character study. Particularly outstanding, however, is the trilogy *Le Roi* (1908, in collaboration with Emmanuel Arène; The King), hilariously funny as it records the unedifying escapades of visiting royalty; *Le Bois sacré* (1910; Eng. tr., *Decorating Clementine*, 1910), a broadside directed at those who worship official titles; and *L'Habit vert* (1912; The Green Uniform), a humorous caricature of the Académie

Française. These three plays, more meaningly satirical, yet brimming with a joie de vivre that is no more, perhaps evoke best the brilliant and subtle atmosphere of the old Parisian boulevard in its twilight.

See: C. Levi, *Autori drammatici francesi* (1923), pp. 275–306; J. Maurice-Pouquet, *Le Salon de Mme Arman de Caillavet* (1926); F. de Croisset, *La Vie parisienne au théâtre* (1929).   J.-A.B. rev. D.W.A.

Čaks, Aleksandrs, pseud. of Aleksandrs Čadarainis (1901–50), Latvian poet, influenced the development of Latvian poetry with his thematic and formal innovations. He was born in Riga. After serving in the Latvian Red Guards during the revolutionary wars that followed the Russian Revolution of 1917, Čaks returned to independent Latvia in 1922 and settled in Riga. His first four collections of poetry, which show the influence of Vladimir MAYA-KOVSKY and Sergey YESENIN, appeared in 1928 and 1929. In contrast to the pastoral settings and moods prevalent in most Latvian lyric poetry, Čaks wrote about the contemporary city, especially its seedy aspects. His frequent allusions to sexuality and alcohol attracted criticism from both the literary Right and Left. Čaks's early style is theatrical, characterized by bold similes and metaphors bordering on the hyperbolic, by the frequent use of free rhythmic patterns that at times lengthen to proselike paragraphs, and by the innovative use of partial rhyme patterns, which since have become standard in contemporary Latvian poetry. His early collections were edited and consolidated into *Mana paradīze* (1932; My Paradise).

Čaks's poetry grew more introspective, formally more subdued, but at the same time more concentrated and intense in *Iedomu spoguli* (1938; The Mirrors of Fancy). His two-part verse epic, *Mūžības skartie* (1937, 1939; Touched by Eternity), celebrating the legendary Latvian guards of World War I, earned him a major national prize (the Soviet Latvian edition of Čaks's works prints only brief excerpts). He collaborated with the Soviet regime in 1940–41 but stayed in Latvia during the German Occupation. His next and final collection, *Zem cēlas zvaigznzes* (1948; Under the Noble Star), contains both verse celebrating the Soviet state and pure lyric poetry; the lyric poetry was published in exile as *Augstā krastā* (1950; On a High Shore). Some posthumous material was published in Latvia in *Cīņai un darbam* (1951; For Struggle and Work) and in a two-volume anthology (1961); another selection of his poetry, *Mana Rīga* (1961; My Riga), published abroad, also contained previously unpublished material. Although in life and death an object of political controversies, Čaks was above all a poet whose work was not so much inspired by an ideology as by life itself. As such he became a model for the succeeding generation of poets both within and outside Latvia.   V.N.

Călinescu, George (1899–1965), Romanian critic, literary historian, novelist, poet, and translator, was born in Bucharest, but he spent much of his boyhood in Botoşani and Iaşi. In 1919 he made his debut as a poet in the journal *Sburătorul*. He graduated from the University of Bucharest, and then spent a period in Italy as archivist, scholar, and translator. Upon his return to Romania, he published his poetry in the journal *Universul literar*. He also contributed critical and creative work to most of the important literary journals of the day. From 1952 until 1963, Călinescu was editor of *Studii de istorie literară şi folclor* (Studies in Literary History and Folklore).

As a literary historian and critic, Călinescu greatly enhanced the scope and the study of Romanian literature. His most important works in these areas include a mon-umental six-volume study of Mihail Eminescu (1934–36); monographs on Ion Creangă (1938), Nicolae Filimon (1959), Grigore Alexandrescu (1963), and Vasile Alecsandri (1965) (*see* ROMANIAN LITERATURE); *Principii de estetică* (1939; Principles of Aesthetics); and a history of Romanian literature from its origins to the present (1941).

Călinescu made his debut as a novelist with *Cartea Nunţii* (1933; The Wedding Book), followed by *Enigma Otiliei* (1938; Otilia's Enigma). *Bietul Ioanide* (1953; Poor Ioanide) and its sequel, *Scrinul negru* (1960; The Black Chest), present a picture of Romanian society during the period between the two world wars. A book of verse, *Lauda lucrurilor* (In Praise of Things), was published in 1963 and *Teatru* (Theater) in 1965.

See: I. Rotaru, *O istorie a literaturii române*, vol. 2, (1972), pp. 775–813; S. Damian, *George Călinescu, romancier: eseu despre măstile jocului* (1974).   V.A.

Calvino, Italo (1923–), Italian novelist and essayist, was born in Cuba of Italian parents and spent his childhood and youth in San Remo. During World War II, he fought in the Resistance movement—a vital experience from which he drew inspiration for his first stories and for his first novel, *Il sentiero dei nidi di ragno* (1947; Eng. tr., *The Path of the Nest of Spiders*, 1956), which portrays some aspects of the Resistance as seen through the eyes of a small boy. As Cesare PAVESE observed, it was in this work that Calvino first displayed his talent for relieving realistic portrayal with fablelike twists in the narrative. He also alternates neorealism with fantasy in the short stories collected in *Ultimo viene il corvo* (1949; partial Eng. tr., *Adam, One Afternoon and Other Stories*, 1957) and the comprehensive edition of *I racconti* (1958; partial Eng. tr., *The Watcher and Other Stories*, 1971). In his major novels, however, the fable generally gains the upper hand, becoming an integral component of the complex structure of such works as *Il visconte dimezzato* (1952; Eng. tr., *The Cloven Viscount*, 1962), *Il barone rampante* (1957; Eng. tr., *The Baron in the Trees*, 1959), and *Il cavaliere inesistente* (1959; Eng. tr., *The Non-Existent Knight*, 1962). These three novels were reissued in 1960 as a trilogy with the title *I nostri antenati* (Our Forefathers). In these works, Calvino successfully blends the fabulous and the surrealistic with spirited, polemical satire of the modern condition. Ideological commitment also characterizes the 20 fables of *Marcovaldo* (1963), in which Calvino satirizes the economic boom and denounces the violence that urban civilization perpetrates on nature.

It is, however, in *Le cosmicomiche* (1965; Eng. tr., *Cosmicomics*, 1968) and *Ti con zero* (1967; Eng. tr., *t zero*, 1969)—a stream-of-consciousness narrative of the creation and evolution of the universe through the eyes of a man-formula called Qfwfq who acts as a sort of cosmic voice—that Calvino has most completely dismantled the anthropocentric myth through which mankind is accustomed to look at reality and knowledge. In spite of various influences from a number of sources (Jorge Luis Borges, Ferdinand de Saussure, Lewis Carroll, Roland BARTHES, the cartoon strip, semiotics, Vladimir Propp, Claude LÉVI-STRAUSS, Alain ROBBE-GRILLET, algebra, formal logic, astronomy), the writing of the *Cosmicomiche* (or *comicosmiche* with convertible terms and parodic play of words—cosmic comics, comic cosmoses) is the expression of a new kind of cosmogonic humor that is unlike anything ever written before. The unifying element is the filtered voice-personality of Qfwfq, the epistemic cell that lives in the first protozoan and in all later stages and forms of evolution (from mollusk to dinosaur to moon farmer), the graph of all that man has been and will be.

In the episodes of *Ti con zero* the clever interplay of time-space-motion is at the core of a constantly changing frame of reference in which opposite ideas and values (unity and multiplicity, past and present, chaos and order, probability and certainty) are made to coexist or coincide.

Calvino's increasing relativism has led, on one hand, to *Il castello dei destini incrociati* (1969; Eng. tr., *The Castle of Crossed Destinies*, 1977), a complex narrative using tarot cards as both tools and emblems for a sort of structuralistic game on human destiny. On the other hand, it has produced *Le città invisibili* (1972; Eng. tr., *Invisible Cities*, 1974), a masterpiece of unprecedented rigor and symmetry, challenging all preconceived notions and conventions of fiction. In *Le città invisibili*, the reader is faced with an imaginary Marco Polo who describes to an imaginary Kublai Khan the "invisible" cities of his vast empire: nine chapters, each containing a number of short narratives symmetrically arranged, are each preceded and followed by brief commentaries based on imaginary dialogues and discussions between the great traveler and the great listener. The task of providing meaning(s) to the stories (cities) is given, through the listening and arguing function of the great Khan, to the reader himself.

See: G. P. Bottino, *Calvino* (1967); J. R. Woodhouse, *Italo Calvino: A Reappraisal and an Appreciation of the Trilogy* (1968); G. Bonura, *Invito alla lettura di Calvino* (1972); G. Vidal, "Fabulous Calvino," *NYRB* (May 30, 1974).   A.I.

Calvo-Sotelo, Joaquín (1905–), Spanish playwright, was born in La Coruña. He completed his education in Madrid and practiced law there before turning to the novelty and excitement of the theater at the age of 25. By the mid-1940s he was one of Spain's most prolific and popular interpreters of contemporary social and moral dilemmas. He is the author of approximately 50 plays, generally prescriptive dramas that favor traditional family and religious values, impart decisive moral pronouncements, and attempt to evaluate in both somber and humorous ways the multiple dimensions of the Spanish world. Calvo-Sotelo's eclectic interests in stagecraft have produced such a vast array of serious and comic plays, however, that no single category conveniently encompasses their diversity of subject matter, treatment, and tone. They vary, for instance, from sentimental, escapist farces on the order of *La visita que no tocó el timbre* (1950; The Caller Who Didn't Ring the Bell) to heavy dramas of social conscience, such as *El jefe* (1953; The Leader). His repertory also includes provocative thesis studies dealing with war, best illustrated by *Criminal de guerra* (1951; War Criminal) and *La herencia* (1957; The Inheritance); religion, as in *La ciudad sin Dios* (1957; The Godless City); and even historical topics, best exemplified by *El proceso del arzobispo Carranza* (1964; The Trial of Archbishop Carranza). While it has lost much of the polemical impact that brought Calvo-Sotelo unparalleled notoriety in the late 1950s, *La muralla* (1954; The Wall) still remains his most highly acclaimed production. It is a play about domestic conflicts in a post-Civil War milieu of personal remorse, social hypocrisy, and moral corruption. In artistic terms, however, this popular play is excelled by a more recent work, the brutal tragicomedy *El inocente* (1968), a brilliant satirical depiction of evil in the business world, considered by many critics to be his best dramatic effort.

See: M. B. Poyatos, "'La muralla' de Calvo Sotelo, Auto de psicología Freudiana," *Hispania* 57 (March 1964): 31–39; M. P. Holt, *The Contemporary Spanish Theater, 1940–1972* (1975), pp. 67–83.   D.R.McK.

Camba, Julio (1884–1962), Spanish humorist and essayist born in Villanueva de Arosa, Galicia, began to write for the Galician newspaper *Diario de Pontevedra* while still in his teens. In search of a better and more intellectual environment, he went to Madrid, where he began writing for *El País*. He was soon collaborating on *El Mundo, El Imparcial, La Voz, ABC,* and *La Correspondencia de España*. It was in fact while working for the last newspaper and working as a special correspondent in several European and American countries that Camba began the most brilliant and fruitful period of his literary career, as a foreign chronicler. In his works the life of the modern world is seen through the eyes of a typical Spaniard and a man of rare insight. Camba's literary merit rests on his great originality and his cool and sharp intelligence, which enabled him to perceive the contrasts between different countries and the ridiculous side of life in all of them. He is gifted with faultless logic in examining and showing the absurdity of all national or human prejudice. Although he was clearly a skeptic who often laughed at the useless worries of men, Camba nevertheless revealed in his writings a serious and uncompromising respect for real values. At times he dealt thoughtfully with fundamental Spanish problems. Like other contemporary writers, he tried to understand Spain through its similarities to and differences from modern Europe. The following collections of essays are among his best books: *Alemania; impresiones de un español* (1916; Germany, A Spaniard's Impressions); *Londres; impresiones de un español* (1916; London, A Spaniard's Impressions); *Playas, ciudades y montañas* (1916; Beaches, Cities, and Mountains); *Un año en el otro mundo* (1917; One Year in the Other World) and *La ciudad automática* (1932; The Automatic City), both about the United States; *La rana viajera* (1920; The Traveling Frog); *Aventuras de una peseta* (1923; Adventures of a Penny); *Sobre casi todo* and *Sobre casi nada* (1928; About Almost Everything and About Almost Nothing); *La casa de Lúculo* (1929; Luculus's House); *Haciendo de república* (1934; Performing as a Republic); *Etcétera, etcétera* (1945); *Millones al horno* (1958; Millions into the Oven). In 1948 he published a selection of his writings in the two volumes which he called his *Obras completas*.

See: F. de Onís, "El humorismo de Julio Camba," *Hispania* 10 (1927): 167–75; A. del Río and M. J. Benardete, *El concepto contemporáneo de España* (1962), pp. 401–10.   J.L.G.-M.

Campana, Dino (1885–1932), Italian poet, was born in Marradi, north of Florence. He attended school in his native town and at the universities of Bologna and Florence, but his education was irregular and remained incomplete. Extremely sensitive, he never found the attention and understanding he needed, and at an early age manifested signs of mental instability. He was briefly committed to a psychiatric hospital in Imola. Upon his release in 1905, Campana traveled through Europe and then to Argentina. In 1910 he left Buenos Aires for Odessa, where he joined a group of gypsies. During his travels he earned his living by taking various odd jobs, from blacksmith to fireman. He was jailed repeatedly for vagrancy. Capana returned to Italy and traveled throughout the peninsula. In 1913, during another stay in Marradi, he wrote his only book, *Canti orfici* (Eng. tr., *Orphic Songs*, 1968), which he submitted to Giovanni PAPINI, the most important literary figure in Florence and a primary representative of the new avant-garde movement, futurism. Papini passed the manuscript on to Ardengo Soffici, who lost it. After a brief depression caused by this loss, Campana rewrote the book from memory and had it printed in Marradi at his own expense (1914). The original manuscript was found in 1972 and published under the title *Il più lungo giorno* (1974; The Longest Day). After 1914, Campana published only a few poems, although many more, mostly unfinished and often only first drafts of compositions already in print, were discovered a number of years after his death. These are now all available in the single volume of his works under the general title *Canti orfici*. In 1918, Campana was again committed to a psychiatric hospital near Florence, where he remained until his death.

Campana's poetry, which reflects his personal restlessness, can be characterized as an unbridled explosion of blazing images. By means of visual and aural perceptions, he communicates images without concern for any rational order. The poem "Genova" (Genoa) is his most complex, most typical work. In an era when the *crepuscolari* were nursing their consumptions in half-lit corners and the futurists, making music on noise machines, were striving to kill the past without being able to see the present (*see* ITALIAN LITERATURE), Campana bridged past and future with his flaming, violent lines, creating a poetry so personal and so daring that even today the boldness of its expressive structures and the sequences of its images strike us as extraordinarily new. A volume of love letters documents his affair with Sibilla ALERAMO.

See: F. Ulivi, in *Letteratura italiana: i contemporanei*, vol. 1 (1975), pp. 669–90.   G.Ce.

Campanile, Achille (1899–1976), Italian novelist, dramatist, and journalist, was born in Rome, the son of the journalist and scenarist Gaetano Mancini Campanile. He began his career writing for the newspaper *L'idea nazionale*, and continued to write for periodicals throughout his life. His first and most popular novel, *Ma che cosa è quest'amore?* (What Is This Love?), appeared as a serial in 1924 and in book form in 1927. It won immediate success for the brilliant extravagance of its humor and went through 10 editions in 9 years. In the same vein are *Se la luna mi porta fortuna* (1928; If the Moon Brings Me Luck) and *Agosto, moglie mia non ti conosco* (1930; August, My Wife I Do Not Know You). *Cantilena all'angolo della strada* (1933; Street-Corner Refrain), a collection of short stories, won the Viareggio Prize. After the novel *Il povero Piero* (1959; Poor Peter, dramatized under the same name in 1961), Campanile wrote chiefly for the theater.

The first of his *Tragedie in due battute* (Tragedies in Two Quips) appeared in 1924. These ironic parodies—often in two words—of the futurist (*see* ITALIAN LITERATURE) demand for brevity in the theater anticipated the wordless play *Breath* by Samuel BECKETT. By the time of his death, Campanile had written more than 500 of these miniature dramas. Campanile's longer plays, such as *L'amore fa fare questo e altro* (1931; Love Makes Us Do This and More), owe debt both to futurism and to the commedia dell'arte. They were fiercely challenged at their first performances, but have had a continuing, although generally unacknowledged, influence on the theater of the absurd. Like his novels, his plays depend on paradox, a rapid string of anecdotal episodes, and impossible solutions to implausible situations. A collection of plays written between 1924 and 1939, *L'inventore del cavallo e altre quindici commedie* (The Inventor of the Horse and 15 More Comedies), appeared in 1971. Campanile also wrote many scripts for films, radio, and television.

A newspaper commission as special correspondent resulted in *Battista al Giro d'Italia* (1932), which describes the marathon bicycle race as seen by the faithful retainer of a loser. Campanile lectured in Italy and South America

on humor in the theater, and he wrote two books on French and English humorists between 1890 and 1960, *Umoristi francesi* (1967) and *Umoristi inglesi* (1969).

See: S. Guarieri, in *Leonardo*, vol. 4 (1932) and vol. 6 (1935); L. Tonelli, in *Italia che scrive*, vol. 17 (1934); R. Rebora, in *Sipario* 181 (1961); G. Calendoli, in *Letteratura italiana: i contemporanei*, vol. 4 (1974), pp. 399–413.

B.Co.

Camus, Albert (1913–60), French novelist, playwright, essayist, critic, and journalist, was born in Algeria in Mondovi, near Constantine, into an almost destitute immigrant family, of an Alsatian father and Spanish mother. His father died of wounds in 1914. The mother and two boys settled in the working-class section of Algiers. Camus lived in Algeria until 1940. He completed his secondary studies (1923–30), contracting at 17 the pulmonary tuberculosis that plagued him for the rest of his life, then worked at odd jobs while studying at the university under the aegis of the philosopher Jean Grenier. An essay on Plotinus and Saint Augustine (1936) indicated the young agnostic's interest in the nature of religious belief.

Camus's vigorous, many-faceted personality emerged in the 1930s. The year his first marriage (1933–35) ended in divorce, Camus briefly joined the Communist Party (1935–36) and took an active part in organizing the Kabyls (Berbers of Algeria), resigning when he observed the manipulatory tactics of the Kremlin. He started his career as a reporter on the liberal *Alger-Républicain,* publishing a memorable report on the harsh economic conditions in Kabylia. He founded an amateur theatrical group, "Le Théâtre du Travail," later "L'Equipe" (1934–39), for which he adapted varied works and wrote the greater part of a "collective" play on a contemporary political incident in Spain, *Révolte dans les Asturies* (1936; Revolt in the Asturias). He published two small volumes of essays, *L'Envers et l'endroit* (1937; Eng. tr., "The Wrong Side and the Right Side," in *Lyrical and Critical Essays,* 1968) and *Noces* (1939; Eng. tr., "Nuptials," also in *Lyrical and Critical Essays*). During this decade, Camus abandoned an almost completed novel, *La Mort heureuse* (1971; Eng. tr., *A Happy Death,* 1972), and started to write the three works that assured his early fame: a novel, *L'Etranger* (1942, rev. 1953; Eng. tr., *The Stranger,* 1946); a philosophical essay, *Le Mythe de Sisyphe* (1942; rev. 1948, 1957; Eng. tr., *The Myth of Sisyphus and Other Essays,* 1955); and a play, *Caligula* (1944; rev. 1947, 1958; first staged 1945; Eng. tr., *Caligula and Three Other Plays,* 1958).

The major themes of Camus's work as well as his basic symbols and settings are all present in his early writings: sensuous joy in the beauty of the Mediterranean world, the sun, sea, light, aromas of the Algerian land, the sharp contrasts between the fertile coastland, the arid plateaus, and the Sahara desert; a natural identification with and sympathy for the workers and artisans of North Africa that later encompassed all the destitute of the world; and a fierce hatred of injustice and senseless cruelty. Perhaps most characteristic is a sentiment born of personal experience: a deeply felt revolt at the brevity of human life. Contrasts and oppositions—joy and futility, revolt and acceptance, beauty and death, love and solitude—inspire a rhetoric of paradox, contrast, symmetry, and balance in all of Camus's work.

The next years were to be difficult ones as he rapidly rose to national, then international fame. A second marriage and a brief sojourn in Oran, Algeria, were followed by a return to nonoccupied France (1942), where Camus became involved in Resistance activities. He eventually moved to Paris, ostensibly as a reader for the Gallimard publishing firm, but in fact as one of the three editors of the underground paper *Combat*, which in 1943 published his *Lettres à un ami allemand* (1945; Eng. tr., *Letters to a German Friend*, in *Resistance, Rebellion and Death*, 1961), a passionate justification of Resistance activities.

In the later 1940s, Camus was, with Jean-Paul SARTRE, the most prestigious intellectual and literary figure to emerge in postliberation France. *The Stranger, The Myth of Sisyphus*, and *Caligula* were widely acclaimed. The incisive editorials that appeared daily, then more sporadically, in *Combat* testified to the independence of his political commitments. He had an enthusiastic following among young intellectuals in the universities of the Western world, including the United States, which he visited in 1946. A second novel, *La Peste* (1947; Eng. tr., *The Plague*, 1948), translated into a symbolic form the collective experience of the war years; this has remained the most widely read of his works.

In the following years, Camus was caught up in the political and ideological controversies of postwar France. His anti-Stalinist socialism and his refusal to side with the extremists on either side in the Algerian War made him a target of bitter criticism, temporarily obscuring the significance of his intellectual evolution and the literary output that accompanied it: a play, *Les Justes* (1950; first staged, 1949; Eng. tr., *The Just Assassins*, in *Caligula and Three Other Plays*, 1958); an essay that stirred up harsh controversy and caused him to break with Sartre, *L'Homme révolté* (1951; Eng. tr., *The Rebel*, 1954 [abridged], 1956 [complete]); and, after a five-year lapse, *La Chute* (1956; Eng. tr., *The Fall*, 1957) and *L'Exil et le royaume* (1957; Eng. tr., *Exile and the Kingdom*, 1958), a collection of six short stories. The activities of that decade were rounded out by a book of lyrical essays, *L'Eté* (1954; Eng. tr., "Summer," in *Lyrical and Critical Essays*, 1968), three volumes of collected topical articles entitled *Actuelles* (1950, 1953, 1958; partial Eng. tr. in *Resistance, Rebellion and Death*, 1961); the stage adaptation of five plays, notably *Requiem pour une nonne* (1956) from William Faulkner's *Requiem for a Nun*, and *Les Possédés* (1959; Eng. tr., *The Possessed*, 1960) from Fyodor DOSTOYEVSKY's novel; and various addresses, among them the *Discours de Suède* (1958; Eng. tr., "Speech of Acceptance upon the Award of the Nobel Prize in Literature," *Atlantic Monthly*, May 1958). When Camus died at 46 in an automobile accident, he had been working on directing an experimental theater and writing a new trilogy of works, *Le Premier Homme* (The First Man), as well as a play and an essay.

Camus arranged his work in three cycles, each subsumed in a single mythological figure: the cycle of Sisyphus or of the absurd; the cycle of Prometheus or of revolt, deeply influenced by the historical moment; and the cycle of Nemesis or measure (judgment), which was not completed. The "absurd" subsumes in one word the paradoxical nature of the human creature who, in a secularized world, can make no sense of his life. "Revolt" refers to his intellectual refusal to accept his limitations, either metaphysical (the injustice of death) or human (injustices of power and inequality). Nemesis seems to refer to the retribution that is inevitably attendant upon excess. The discursive mode of the essay form serves to isolate the theme and its logical implications; the dramatic mode puts it to the test of action and confrontation; the fictional mode fleshes it out through the narration of the series of events that shape the character's fate, which then takes on the coloring of myth. In his best fictional works, the main characters—the Stranger, Clamence of *La Chute*, and, in *L'Exil et le royaume*, the priest of "Le Rénégade," the schoolmaster of "L'Hôte," the engineer

of "La Pierre qui pousse"—are mythical incarnations, contemporary avatars of age-old human drives, fears, or dreams, hence their power of continued fascination.

By the 1970s, when political passions had abated, Camus had achieved the status of a classic, widely read in popular paperback editions. Interest in his personality was superseded by an ever-mounting flood of scholarly and critical work rich in a wide diversity of interpretations. The field of Camus criticism was further encouraged by the posthumous publication of his notebooks, *Carnets 1935–1942* and *Carnets 1942–1951* (1962, 1964; Eng. tr., *Notebooks*, 1967, 1970), his early novel, and some brief early texts. As in the case of his two contemporaries, Sartre and, to a lesser extent, Samuel BECKETT, the fact that his works transcended national and language barriers and achieved transnational significance almost instantaneously was itself a sociocultural phenomenon of interest. But it is as a major literary figure whose novel *The Stranger* is perhaps among the two or three most significant novels of mid-century that Camus most indubitably survives.

See: G. Brée, *Albert Camus* (1964); *Revue des lettres modernes*, series "Albert Camus," nos. 170/171 (1968) to date; R. Quilliot, *The Sea and Prisons* (rev. ed., 1970); E. Freeman, *The Theatre of Albert Camus* (1971); D. Lazère, *The Unique Creation of Albert Camus* (1973).

G.Br.

Canetti, Elias (1905–), German novelist, dramatist, and social philosopher, was born in Ruse, Bulgaria, as the child of Sephardic Jews. He grew up in London, Vienna, Zurich, and Frankfurt, speaking the Spanish of the 16th century, English, and German. In 1938 he left Vienna for London, where he has lived intermittently, although he has continued to write in German.

His precise and intense involvement with three languages corresponds to the locus of his writing: between the conventional literary genres as well as between the different social sciences. Deeply influenced by Karl KRAUS's moral philosophy of language, Canetti has worked for a verbal precision that makes possible sudden insights into the human condition. In his first and only novel, *Die Blendung* (1935; Eng. tr., *Auto-da-Fé*, 1946), and two early dramas, *Die Hochzeit* (1932; The Wedding) and *Komödie der Eitelkeit* (1934; Comedy of Vanity), he recorded a great variety of "acoustic masks"—a character's speech habits that outline his individual function in a group as definitely as would a visual mask—presenting the chaos of contemporary society. Since his emigration, Canetti has sought to understand and analyze death as a social phenomenon, his most important contribution to literature being the psychological-anthropological-poetic study of *Masse und Macht* (1960; Eng. tr., *Crowds and Power*, 1962), the drama *Die Befristeten* (1952; Their Days Are Numbered), about a disordered society where everyone is given a fixed date for his death at birth, and the collection of aphorisms *Die Provinz des Menschen. Aufzeichnungen 1942–1972* (1973; Eng. tr., *The Human Province*, 1978). Defying the construction of a system of thought, Canetti, in these texts, carries on an extraordinarily consistent fight against the human acceptance of death. The relation between power and death is also the topic of *Die Stimmen von Marrakesch: Aufzeichnungen nach einer Reise* (1967; Eng. tr., *The Voices of Marrakesh*, 1978) and the essay on Franz KAFKA *Der andere Prozess: Kafkas Briefe an Felice* (1969; The Other Trial: Kafka's Letters to Felice). Canetti's autobiography, *Die gerettete Zunge* (1977; The Tongue That Was Saved), tracing his childhood and adolescence, relates the child's traumatic experience of his adored father's early death, the boy's complex relationships with his mother, and his later preoccupation with language as a social medium and with power and death as social problems.

See: H. G. Göpfert, ed., *Canetti lesen: Erfahrungen mit seinen Büchern* (1975); D. Barnouw, *Elias Canetti* (1979). D.B.

Cankar, Ivan (1875–1918), Slovenian novelist, dramatist, and poet, was born near Ljubljana, the son of an impoverished tailor with a large family. Hardships at home, combined with many humiliations and the figure of his mother, whom he later called a saint and martyr, left deep impressions on the mind of the frail, sensitive child. After graduation in 1896 from a technical high school in Ljubljana, Cankar went to Vienna on a scholarship to study architecture. He soon gave up his studies and the scholarship to devote himself exclusively to literary work. After 13 years in Vienna, writing constantly, Cankar returned to Ljubljana in 1909, already recognized as a major Slovenian writer.

In his first book, and only volume of poetry, *Erotika* (1899), Cankar reveals his partial dependence on the older Slovenian literature; but in his first book of prose, *Vinjete* (1899; Vignettes), a collection of short stories, he had obviously found his own voice, which was ultimately to establish him as the greatest Slovenian prose writer. In the astonishingly fertile period of his life 1900–13, Cankar produced many books dealing with three principal themes, repeated almost to the point of monotony. The first theme concerns the Slovenian artist who is an outcast, a tramp, a nuisance among "decent people," and a foreigner in his own country; it can be found in such works as: *Tujci* (1902; Foreigners), *V mesečini* (1905; In the Moonshine), and the related play, *Pohujšanje v Dolini Šentflorjanski* (1908; Scandal in the Valley of Saint Florian). The second theme concerns souls yearning for happiness in their misery, for beauty in the squalor of their lives. This motif is represented in *Na klancu* (1902; On the Slope), in the short-story collections *Križ na gori* (1904; The Cross on the Hill) and *Hiša Marije Pomočnice* (1904; The House of Our Lady of Help), and in the play *Lepa Vida* (1912; The Beautiful Vida). Finally, Cankar wrote satires criticizing Slovenian politics, social organization, and literature: *Za narodov blagor* (1901; For the Nation's Welfare); *Martin Kačur* (1906); *Krpanova kobila* (1907; Krpan's Mare); *Hlapec Jernej in njegova pravica* (1907; Eng. tr., *Yerney's Justice*, 1926); and *Hlapci* (1910; Servants).

In the last years of his life, Cankar mainly wrote feuilletons, in which genre he reached the peak of his art. These feuilletons are studies in self-analysis, personal confessions, memoirs, scenes of animal life, and symbolic stories dealing with personal and national problems arising from the war—the latter were published as *Podobe iz sanj* (1917; Parables from My Dreams). In the same form there also appeared the charming fragment of his unfinished autobiography, *Moje življenje* (1914; My Life). Wise, serene, and very simple, the feuilletons often betray an awareness of approaching death. Here Cankar expresses himself in a remarkably pure and pregnant style.

Cankar's literary works, published posthumously in 20 volumes, are surprisingly extensive in view of the writer's short life. His output marks a historical epoch in Slovenian literature. In part as a result of his close contact with the lively idiom of his native village, Cankar created a new, expressive, and sonorous language and a new rhythmic style immediately accepted by the younger generation of writers. Through his work, Slovenian prose became genuine art, and the somewhat provincial literature of his country, which hitherto could boast of only one internationally prominent writer, France Prešeren (*see* SLOVENIAN LITERATURE), was lifted to a level meriting general European recognition.

See: W. Walder, *Ivan Cankar als Künstlerpersönlichkeit* (1926); B. Meriggi, *Storià della letteratura slovena* (1961); D. Pirjevec, *Ivan Cankar in evropska literatura* (1964). I.C. rev. W.B.E. and A.K.

Cansinos-Asséns, Rafael (1883–1964), Spanish critic and novelist, was born in Seville. After 1901 he lived in Madrid, where he founded such literary reviews as *Cervantes* and *Grecia* and wrote for *Correspondencia de España, Los lunes del Imparcial,* and *Libertad.* Reacting against the *modernista* poetic movement, which had become stagnant (*see* SPANISH LITERATURE), Cansinos-Asséns introduced and fomented the so-called *ultraísta* school between 1918 and 1923.

As a critic, Cansinos-Asséns displayed a prodigious knowledge of European and American literature. His translations range from the writings of the Roman Emperor Julian to the complete works of Fyodor DOSTOYEVSKY. He wrote with great authority, although he was sometimes excessively anecdotal, and his judgment often leaned toward indulgence and overgenerosity. Worthy of especial note are his relatively early assessment of both primary and secondary figures of Latin American literature and his deep appreciation of the cultural and literary contributions of the Sephardic Jews.

His best works of fiction are his short novels *La encantadora* (1916; The Enchantress) and *El eterno milagro* (1918; The Eternal Miracle). The self-conscious search for metaphor and for plots that are both richly introspective and conventionally structured, although often farfetched, are characteristic of these works and reminiscent of Ramón del VALLE-INCLÁN and Concha ESPINA, although inferior in quality.

A prolific writer who was highly regarded during his lifetime, Cansinos-Asséns has received little critical attention in recent decades. His novels have yet to be published in their entirety. His literary criticism is best represented by *La nueva literatura* (4 vols., 1917–27; The New Literature), *España y los judíos españoles* (1919; Spain and the Spanish Jews), and *Poetas y prosistas del novecientos* (1919; Poets and Prose Writers of the Nineteen Hundreds). M.J.B. rev. H.R.

Čapek, Josef (1887–1945), Czech painter, art critic, and novelist, the elder brother of Karel ČAPEK, was born in Hronov in northeastern Bohemia. He studied painting in Prague and Paris. After the German invasion of Czechoslovakia in 1939, he was sent to a concentration camp. He died at Belsen in April 1945. Josef Čapek has a considerable reputation as a painter; he first belonged to the cubist school, but later developed his own style of playful primitivism. As a writer, he collaborated with his brother in early collections of sketches and stories and in the two plays *Ze života hmyzu* (1921; Eng. tr., *The Insect Play,* 1923) and *Adam Stvořitel* (1927; Eng. tr., *Adam the Creator,* 1930). He himself wrote a Utopian play, *Země mnoha jmen* (1923; Eng. tr., *The Land of Many Names,* 1926), and several collections of short stories and sketches. He also published two short novels: *Stín kapradiny* (1930; The Shadow of the Fern), a story of poachers in a suggestive nature setting, and *Kulhavý poutník* (1936; The Limping Pilgrim), more a philosophical meditation than an actual novel. Čapek's prose has been hailed as an anticipation of surrealism, largely because of his preoccupation with the subconscious. Josef Čapek was also an art critic noted for books such as *Nej-*

skromnější uměni (1920; The Humblest Art) and *Uměni přirodních národů* (1938; The Art of Primitive Nations), which expound and defend the art of children, savages, and untrained people.

See. V. Nezval, *Josef Čapek* (1937); V. Havel, *Josef Čapek, dramatik a jevištni výtvarník* (1963).   R.W.

Čapek, Karel (1890–1938), Czech novelist, playwright, and essayist, was the best-known literary figure of liberated Czechoslovakia after 1918. The son of a doctor, Čapek was born in Malé Svatoňovice in northeastern Bohemia. He studied philosophy at the University of Prague and wrote a graduating thesis on aesthetics. After working as a journalist, he was for a time a stage director at the theater in Vinohrady. His wife was Olga Scheinpflugová, a prominent actress. He died of pneumonia in 1938.

Čapek is best known as a dramatist. *R. U. R.* (1921; Eng. tr., 1923) and *Ze života hmyzu* (1921; Eng. tr., *The Insect Play*, 1923), the latter written in collaboration with his brother, Josef ČAPEK, took the world by storm and were performed with great success in both London and New York. *R. U. R.* even introduced the word "robot" (from *Robotit*, to drudge) into the English language. The play's main idea—a warning against the dangers of a machine civilization—was very timely in the 1920s. Throughout *R. U. R.*, Čapek's sense of theater is vividly evident: the automatons move stiffly, like dolls, and their great revolt against man produces many tense moments. There is, however, a flaw in the play's structure that is easy to overlook—the robots are changed into men of flesh and blood by a sleight of hand. Although its construction is looser, *The Insect Play* (also known in the United States as *The World We Live In*) is possibly a better work. It is almost a ballet or revue. The idea of presenting butterflies as lovers, beetles rolling balls of dirt as capitalists, and ants as militaristic imperialists, is carried out with gusto. Several vivid scenes featuring the ants present a perfect prophecy of totalitarianism with its canting slogans. Equally ingenious and effective on the stage are two of Čapek's less well-known plays: *Věc Makropulos* (1922; Eng. tr., *The Makropoulos Secret*, 1925), which argues amusingly against the desire for immortality, and *Bílá nemoc* (1937; Eng. tr., *Power and Glory*, 1938), an indignant outcry against dictators. The first of these served as the dramatic subject of the well-known opera of the same name by Janáček (1926). Less successful are Čapek's other plays, which include two early comedies, and the dramas *Adam Stvořitel* (1927; Eng. tr., *Adam the Creator*, 1930), written in collaboration with Josef Čapek, and *Matka* (1938; Eng. tr., *The Mother*, 1939).

But Čapek was not merely a dramatist. He was also an extremely ambitious and subtle practitioner of the craft of fiction, a philosopher-poet passionately interested in the problems of truth and justice. His early collections of stories, most notably *Trapné povídky*, (1921; Eng. tr., *Money and Other Stories*, 1929), are still full of youthful pessimism. Life is depicted as arbitrary and disconnected, brutal and disconcertingly irrational. The stories are painful and curiously inconclusive. But this was only the first step in Čapek's varied writing career. Two fanciful romances followed, *Továrna na absoluto* (1922; Eng. tr., *The Absolute at Large*, 1927) and *Krakatit* (1924; Eng. tr., 1925). In the first, a weird invention liberates the Absolute like a gas, producing an opportunity for much hilarious satire on hypocrisy, while the leading theme of the second is "Krakatit," a deadly explosive that might destroy civilization. After these two Wellsian pieces,

Čapek published a number of pleasant, humorous collections of sketches and essays in addition to several travel books, which give voice to his belief in the ordinary man and to his sense of the bewildering variety and beauty of the world. His optimism sometimes seems a shade too cheerful, his ridicule of the abnormal and extravagant too complacent. But there is also much quiet fun and insight, especially in *Anglické listy* (1923; Eng. tr., *Letters from England*, 1925) as well as in similar books on Italy, Holland, Spain, and Scandinavia. In the late 1920s, Čapek's interests veered increasingly toward practical politics and popular art forms. His conversations with President Tomáš Garrique MASARYK, published as *Hovory s T. G. Masarykem* (3 vols., 1928–35; Eng. tr., *President Masaryk Tells His Story*, 1934, *Masaryk on Thought and Life*, 1938), constitute a minor classic of popular biography and political education, while his *Devatero pohádek* (1931; Eng. tr., *Fairy Tales*, 1933) is a veritable treasure house of pure storytelling. The stories collected in *Povídky z jedné kapsy* and *Povídky z druhé kapsy* (1929; Eng. tr., *Tales from Two Pockets*, 1932) represent an attempt to create semiphilosophical mystery stories rather on the lines of G. K. Chesterton's Father Brown stories. But Čapek the poet and writer of tragedy is evident again in his great trilogy of novels *Hordubal* (1933; Eng. tr., 1943), *Povětroň* (1934; Eng. tr., *Meteor*, 1935), and *Obyčejný život* (1935; Eng. tr., *An Ordinary Life*, 1936). Each of these works tells the same story from a special point of view in order to enhance the variety of the story's meanings and to suggest the utter mysteriousness of ultimate reality. On the surface, *Hordubal* is a story of crime: a peasant who has returned from the United States to his home in Carpathian Russia dies under mysterious circumstances. *Povětroň* is made up of speculative reconstructions by a nurse, a doctor, and a poet as to the early history of a pilot whose plane has crashed; the novel implies that the imagined account comes nearest to the truth. The last novel, *Obyčejný život*, is the fictional autobiography of a Czech railway clerk who discovers unexpected hidden selves in his own mind and past. After the trilogy, Čapek wrote only two books of any length, *Válka s mloky* (1936; Eng. tr., *War with the Newts*, 1937), a fanciful romance that satirizes modern science and pseudoscience as well as international politics, and *Prvni parta* (1937; Eng. tr., *The First Rescue Party*, 1939), a straightforward, almost balladlike story of a pit disaster. *Život a dílo skladatele Foltýna* (1939; Eng. tr., *The Cheat*, 1941), was published posthumously. The fragment of an unfinished novel, it concerns a young man who marries a rich woman and uses others to build up his fraudulent reputation as a composer.

Although Čapek is best known for his plays, romances, and travel books, his finest work is the great trilogy of novels, which, taken together, constitutes one of the most successful attempts at a philosophical novel in any language. Czech critics have frequently censured Čapek as having been too international, but a book like *Obyčejný život* gives a finely drawn picture of the Czech scene, and there is something very representative and national in Čapek's love of the common man and his genuine faith in democracy and humanity.

See: V. Černý, *Karel Čapek* (1936); W. E. Harkins, *Karel Čapek* (1962); R. Wellek, "Karel Čapek," in *Essays on Czech Literature* (1963), pp. 46–61; A. Matuška, *Karel Čapek; An Essay* (1964); O. Králík, *Prvni řada v díle K. Čapka* (1972); L. Doležel, "Karel Čapek and Vladislav Vančura," in *Narrative Modes in Czech Literature* (1973), pp. 91–111; F. Buriánek, *Karel Čapek* (1978).
                    R.W.

Čapek-Chod, Karel Matěj (1860–1927), Czech novelist, the most prominent representative of the Czech naturalist movements, was born in Domažlice in western Bohemia. He worked as a reporter and journalist in Prague, where he died. Čapek (who later adopted the name Čapek-Chod) was the Emile ZOLA of Prague—a chronicler of the city's decaying bourgeoisie. Like that of other naturalists, Čapek's outlook on life was materialistic and pessimistic. He was a determinist who believed that a malicious fate plays ugly tricks upon us, thwarting our finest aspirations. Although Čapek had the naturalist's thirst for facts and details, his method was less objective than that of his foreign models: he indulged in the grotesque, used caricature, and enjoyed stylistic juggleries that produce an almost Rabelaisian effect. Although not free from vulgarities and trivialities, he had a fantastic vision of the world's tragedy and a rough kind of pity and humor that make his loose composition and lapses of taste forgiveable. His vitality and scope put him into the first rank of Czech novelists.

Čapek's most important novels are: *Kašpar Lén, mstitel* (1908; Caspar Lén, the Avenger), a crime story set in the outskirts of Prague; *Turbina* (1916; The Turbine), a tragicomedy about the decay of an upper bourgeois Prague family; *Antonín Vondrejc* (2 vols., 1917–18), another story of decay, concerning a poet forced into the drudgery of journalism; and *Jindrové* (1921; The Jindras), a war novel that centers around a conflict between father and son. Čapek-Chod also published several volumes of short stories.

See: H. Jelínek, *Etudes tchécoslovaques* (1927), pp. 223–29; A. Novák, "K. Matěj Čapek-Chod," in *Almanach České Akademie*, vol. 38 (1928), pp. 178–200; F. Kovárna, *K. M. Čapek-Chod* (1936).   R.W.

Caragiale, Ion Luca (1852–1912), Romanian dramatist and prose writer, received his early schooling at Ploeşti, the city closest to his native village of Haimanale. Between 1868 and 1870 he studied at the Bucharest Conservatory, where his uncle Costache, a well-known actor, was teaching. In 1870, Caragiale worked as prompter at the National Theater. He made his debut as humorist in the satirical journal *Ghîmpele* in 1873, writing under the pseudonym Palicar, and about this time, his excellent verse translation of Dominique-Alexandre Parodi's *Rome Vaincue* (1876; Rome Vanquished) was performed in Bucharest. His first dramatic work, *O noapte furtunoasa* (A Stormy Night) was read to the "Junimea" literary circle and then performed, to a lukewarm reception, at the National Theater in 1879. The lively comedy *O scrisoare pierdută* (1884; A Lost Letter) met with greater success. *D'ale Carnavalului* (1885; Carnival Events), however, was received unfavorably, as was the tragic drama *Năpastă* (1890; False Accusation), performed while Caragiale was director of the National Theater. Caragiale's contemporaries did not always appreciate the strongest element in his work: his irony.

In the 1890s, Caragiale abandoned drama for fiction. Two collections of short stories, *Păcat* (Sin) and *Note şi schiţe* (Notes and Sketches), were published in 1892. A third collection, *Moftul român* (Romanian Nonsense), followed in 1893. The second series of *Moftul român* (1901) contained "La hanul lui Mînjoala" (At Minjoala's Inn), one of his finest short stories. The colorful *Kir Ianulea* (1909; Lord Ianulea), the adaptation of a Machiavellian theme (Belfagor) is the masterpiece of the last period. Legal controversies surrounding his play *Năpastă* embittered the restless, improvident Caragiale. In 1904 he and his family moved to Berlin, where he spent most of the rest of his life.

See: Ş. Cioculescu, *Viaţa lui I. L. Caragiale* (1969); E. D. Tappe, *Ion Luca Caragiale* (1974).   V.A.

Carco, Francis, pseud. of François Marie Alexandre Carcopino-Tusoli (1886–1958), French novelist, poet, and art critic, was born of Corsican parents in Nouméa, New Caledonia, where his father was superintendent of prisons. The violence of his surroundings—the passionate, pent-up emotions of criminals, his father's quick temper and ready hand, the exotic scenery, his nurse's gruesome tales—contributed to enrich an algolagnic penchant. When Carco was nine years old, the family moved to the south of France where the countryside developed his sensuous love of nature and delight in physical sensation. At 14, an indifferent student but an avid reader of the *poètes maudits,* he practiced the technique of versification under the tutelage of Charles de Pomairols. Francis JAMMES and Henry BATAILLE influenced his first poems. The lycée of Agen witnessed his cultivation of a bohemian personality. During his military service, Carco became organizer and theorist of the group of "fantasist poets" whose kinship was one of temperament and viewpoint rather than one of art and technique. He wrote *La Bohème et mon cœur* (1912; augmented eds., 1922, 1929; complete ed., 1939; Bohemia and My Heart) under the aegis of Villon, Charles BAUDELAIRE, and Paul VERLAINE. The tragedy of their destinies, their sordid existence (itself helping them to create beauty), and their grandeur rising above social opprobrium exemplified for Carco the individual unfettering himself from the bourgeois and fulfilling his innermost purity of heart. Both the feeling of spiritual affinity and the problem of environment versus artistic personality produced *Le Roman de Villon* (1926; Eng. tr., *The Romance of Villon,* 1927); *La Légende et la vie d'Utrillo* (1927; The Legend and the Life of Utrillo), in the series "La Vie de Bohème" directed by Carco; and *Verlaine* (1939). Chapters of *Nostalgie de Paris* (1941; Nostalgia for Paris) are devoted to Baudelaire.

Montmartre before World War I—with its bohemian life, its milieu of artists and criminals, of pimps and prostitutes and narcotic addicts—is his special province. An apprenticeship as art critic for the newspaper *Homme libre* preceded the publication of *Jésus-la-Caille* (1914), first of a series in which he defended and explained, sympathetically yet objectively, this marginal society. *Les Innocents* (1916), *Bob et Bobette s'amusent* (1919; Bob and Bobette Amuse Themselves), and *Paname* (1925; Panama) are novels of *mœurs* revealing the moral code of a social stratum whose principles, although different, are severe, the violation of whose tenets induces the chastisement of the offender. The climax, the result of moral disintegration, comes from within rather than from direct punitive efforts of the external world. Fate cannot be avoided. It is the phosphorescence illuminating the consciences of these elemental beings who, confused by their own murky sense of maladjustment, suddenly find their world made too complex by problems of the spirit. Instinct, clouded by fear (*Perversité,* 1925; Eng. tr., *Perversity,* 1928) or premonition of doom (*L'Equipe,* 1919; The Team]) or an obsession (*Rue Pigalle,* 1927), succumbs to destiny. Carco lacks the sentimentality of a Charles-Louis PHILIPPE; objective and dispassionate in his writing (his economy of structure and precise penetration are consistently termed "classical" by critics), yet fundamentally a moralist, he objects to society's habit of condemning men for its own faults (*L'Amour vénal* [1924; Venal Love]). Nevertheless their degradation aroused in him a feeling of voluptuousness (*La Rue,* 1930), sublimating his personal emotional complexities. Paul BOURGET's influence, inciting him to write *L'Homme traqué* (1922; Eng. trs., *The Noose of Sin,* 1923, *The Hounded Man,* 1924), which won the Grand Prix of the Académie Française, enlarged the scope of his subject matter to include the bourgeois and to emphasize the psychological situation. The essential problem remains one of moral collapse in an individual incapable of escaping his fate. Carco wrote about 30 books in this vein, the first few replete with argot.

The passing of his youth evoked in this member of the Goncourt Academy a nostalgia for his bohemian days. His memoirs, important documents for a consideration of French literary and artistic life since the halcyon days of the cabaret Lapin Agile, reveal intimately the nature and heart of this expressionistic painter in light and shadow of subtle moods. Of his work Carco said that were the atmosphere removed nothing would remain. *De Montmartre au Quartier latin* (1927; Eng. tr., *The Last Bohemia,* 1928), *A voix basse* (1938; In a Low Voice), *Bohème d'artiste* (1940; An Artist's Bohemia), and others show him restrained yet passionate, intelligent yet physical, fusing himself with and purging himself by the pain of his protagonists. Francis Carco, the poet vibrantly sensitive to rain and glistening streets, is known as the defender of the *voyou* and the biographer of the prostitute. A definitive edition of the *Mémoires d'une vie* (Memories of a Life) was published in 1942 in Geneva, near which city Carco resided during a part of World War II. Carco spent the rest of his life writing reminiscences: *L'Ami des peintres: souvenirs* (1944; The Friend of the Painters: Memories), *Ombres vivantes* (1948; Living Shadows), *La Belle Epoque au temps de Bruant* (1954; The Belle Epoque in the Time of Bruant), and *Rendez-vous avec moi-même* (1957; Rendezvous with Myself). In 1953 he submitted to an interview by the well-known interviewer Michel Manoll; this was published as *Francis Carco vous parle* (Francis Carco Speaking).

See: H. Martineau, "Francis Carco," *Divan* 13 (1921): 172–80; A. Thérive, *Opinions littéraires* (1925), pp. 113–29; M. Ormoy et al., "Francis Carco, poëte," *Divan* 21 (1929): 145–212; Y. Gandon, *Le Démon du style* (1938), pp. 159–68; A. Rousseaux, *Littérature du XXième siècle* (1939), vol. 1, pp. 21–32; P. Chabaneux, *Francis Carco* (1949); S. S. Weiner, *Francis Carco: The Career of a Literary Bohemian* (1952); A. Négis, *Mon Ami Carco* (1953).   S.W. with D.W.A.

Cardarelli, Vincenzo, pseud. of Nazareno Caldarelli (1887–1959), Italian poet, essayist, and critic, was born in Corneto Tarquinia (now Tarquinia). He served as coeditor of *La ronda* and later as editor of *La fiera letteraria.* His literary work aimed principally at the restoration of classical tastes in modern Italy as a counterweight to neodecadent aesthetics. His most extensive contribution was to the fields of criticism and *prosa d'arte, (see* ITALIAN LITERATURE), but he was also a considerable poet. His writings are marked by a deep sense of classical balance, an extraordinarily limpid style, and a vast lyrical perspective. He differed from the contemporary hermetic school (*see* ITALIAN LITERATURE), however, by insisting that content is more important than form. Indeed, he felt that if a writer had something important to say, he would always find the appropriate form in which to say it.

In his works, Cardarelli examines the period of human maturity or self-consciousness, which he regards as lying between two other limiting conditions: the unself-consciousness of childhood and the consciouslessness of death. He believed that decadent modern society has lost the vigor of Renaissance humanism, and that it reveals its feebleness through a form of parasitism frequently practiced by the individual human being in which others are reduced to mere objects for that individual's gratification. In Cardarelli's view, this explains modern man's alienation. He proposes to revert, both morally and aesthetically, from the "metaphysical" sentimentality of romanticism to the "ethical" values implicit in a regenerative classical outlook.

His first works, *Prologhi* (1916; Prologues), *Viaggi nel tempo* (1920; Travels in Time), and *Favole della genesi* (1925; Stories of Genesis), are largely, but not exclusively, prose meditations on life and mythology. These were later collected in one volume (1929). *Il sole a picco* (1920; The Sun Overhead) is a collection of miscellaneous writings with a strong autobiographical flavor. His *Poesie* (1942; Poems) and *Poesie nuove* (1947; New Poems) include both new compositions as well as lyrics drawn from most of the early works mentioned above. His poetic style is not analogical, after the manner of Giuseppe UNGARETTI, but is, instead, discursive, serene, and tonally integrated, following the tradition fashioned by Petrarch and Giacomo Leopardi (1798–1837), whom he considered his masters. Cardarelli's verse is consequently highly meditative and rational in its development; its ethical character may be summed up in the phrase *esprimere è restituirsi* ("to write is to reconstitute oneself"). Among his later works are *Il cielo sulle città* (1939; The Sky over the Cities) and *Solitario in Arcadia* (1948; Alone in Arcadia). Cardarelli's *Opere complete* (Complete Works), ed. by G. Raimondi, appeared in 1962.

See: G. Contini, in *Esercizi di lettura* (1939); M. Luzi, *L'inferno e il limbo* (1949); R. Risi, *Vincenzo Cardarelli, prosatore e poeta* (1951); P. Bigongiari, in *Poesia italiana del Novecento* (1960); C. Di Biase, *Invito alla lettura di Cardarelli* (1975); F. J. Jones, *La poesia italiana contemporanea* (1975); P. Fuselli, *Vincenzo Cardarelli* (1977).   F.J.J.

Carême, Maurice (1899–1977), Belgian poet, was born in Wavre. From 1918 to 1942 he taught school in the Brussels suburb of Anderlecht. He retired in 1943 in order to devote himself entirely to writing. From the publication of his first poems in the journal *Nos Jeunes* in 1919, his work reflected a deep understanding of the world of children. Far from being simply naive, his poetry might be viewed as an illustration of Sigmund Freud's statement that the poet, like a child at play, creates a world of fantasy that he takes seriously. A joy and a sense of irony tend to dominate in most of his poems. For instance, in the well-known poem "Le Cerisier" (The Cherry Tree), which appeared in *La Lanterne magique* (1947), the laughter of a cherry tree spreads all over the world and is so contagious that God himself has to hide his face so that the saints do not see Him laughing. In volumes such as *Volière* (1954; Pigeon Run), *Le Voleur d'étincelles* (1956; The Robber of Sparks), *Fleurs de Soleil* (1966; Flowers of Sun), and *Poèmes pour petits enfants* (1976; Poems for Little Children), Carême explores a dialogue involving humans, animals, and plants. In such works, the verses are attuned to the rhythm of daily life or to that of nursery rhymes; these verses have inspired composers such as Florent Schmitt, Darius Milhaud, Francis Poulenc, and Jean Absil. Next to the magic world of children, two other themes are dear to the poet who called himself "a sower of dreams": his mother and his native province of Brabant. Few poets have portrayed with as much sensitivity and tenderness the image of the mother;

it is hardly surprising that excerpts from *Mère* (1935; Mother) are often assigned to school children on Mother's Day. In *Brabant* (1967), Carême sings the natural beauty of this region and the simple happiness of its rural inhabitants. To his talents as a poet, Carême added those of a story teller and essayist, notably in *Le Royaume des fleurs* (1934; The Kingdom of the Flowers). Carême's work received numerous literary awards including the Verhaeren Prize (1927), the Victor Rossel Prize (1948), the Prize of the French Academy (1952), and the International Grand Prize in Poetry (1968). With the exception of Emile VERHAEREN, few Belgian poets have been as widely translated. His poems recall the humor of Jacques PRÉVERT, as well as the fragile simplicity of Jules SUPERVIELLE. Not without reason might Carême be called French literature's Robert Louis Stevenson.

See: J. Charles, *Maurice Carême* (1965); P. Coran, *Maurice Carême* (1966); G. Delahaye, *Maurice Carême* (1969).   M.-R.L.

Carling, Finn (1925-), Norwegian dramatist and novelist, was born in Oslo, where he has lived all his life. In his first novels, such as *Piken og fuglen* (1952; The Girl and the Bird), Carling plays with complicated narrative patterns, weaving dreamlike romantic tales. The underlying theme in all these novels, dream versus reality, led to a personal crisis; and in *Desertøren* (1956; The Deserter), half fiction, half autobiography, and *Kilden og muren* (1958; The Spring and the Wall), an autobiography, he presents his life as a physically handicapped person (he was crippled) to the reader, his desires to escape this existence, but also his resolution to accept the inevitable and to see life as it really is. The result is a turning toward documentary presentation. In his more recent works, he writes about society's outsiders—the blind and the homosexuals—and his fiction becomes realistic, as in *Kometene* (1964; The Comets), *Fiendene* (1974; The Enemies) and *Tårnseileren* (1979; Pilot in the Tower) in which he depicts human isolation and loneliness and warns against the rising violence and brutality in society. The semidocumentary novel *Resten er taushet* (1973; The Rest is Silence) in which death is treated as a social phenomenon, and the short-story collections *Marginalene* (1977; The Marginal Ones), treating life's marginal existences and hailed as Carling's most important work, are similarly marked by this realism. *Gitrene* (1966; The Cage Bars), the best of his plays, is a boldly experimental attempt at dramatizing the processes that limit human freedom and personal expression.

See: L. Longum, *Et speil jor oss selv* (1968), pp. 94–105.   K.A.F.

Carner, Josep (1884-1970), Catalan poet, was born in Barcelona, where he received his primary and secondary education in a private academy. He studied law as well as philosophy and letters at the University of Barcelona. He published his first poems when he was only 12, and at 15 the journal *Renaixença*, which had a great influence in the evolution of Catalan letters and in reviving the patriotic spirit, was regularly accepting his work. In this period he also wrote two books of prose, *L'idil li dels nanyos* (1904; The Idyl of the Dwarfs) and *Deu rondalles de Jesus infant* (1905; Ten Stories about the Child Jesus). In *Primer llibre de sonets* (1905; First Book of Sonnets) and *Fruits saborosos* (1906; Delicious Fruit) one sees Carner's great promise as an innovator. Other poetical works are *Segon llibre de sonets* (1907; Second Book of Sonnets), *La malvestat d'Oriana* (1910; Oriana's Evil), and *Verger de les galanies* (1911; The Garden of Gallantry). In the pages of the daily paper *Veu de Catalunya*

he was simultaneously creating a new style of political journalism. *Monjoies* (1912; My Jewels), which shows Carner as the fully matured artist, was followed by *Auques i ventalls* (1914; Easter Prints and Fans) and *La Paraula al vent* (1916; The Word in the Wind). In 1916 he was elected a member of the Institut d'Estudis Catalans, the highest cultural honor in Catalonia. At that time, in addition to composing poems, articles, and essays for numerous publications, he directed the journals *Empori* and *Catalunya* and translated *Prosa catalana* into Spanish. This volume included short stories by Ixart, Vilanove, Caselles, other masters of the *Renaixença*, as well as Joaquim RUYRA.

In 1921 Josep Carner embarked upon a diplomatic career. He continued nevertheless to maintain his place in the world of Catalan literature, publishing in Barcelona works written in the foreign countries to which his responsibilities as a diplomat took him. When the Spanish Civil War broke out, Carner was in Brussels. Faithful to the Spanish Republic, he resigned from the diplomatic service and went into exile in Paris, Mexico, and Brussels. He died in Brussels in 1970, after a brief return to Catalonia, where his ashes were transferred in 1978.

Carner's career sums up the nonconformity of the generation that, abandoning romantic and traditional literary forms, attempted to renovate Catalan poetry. With him Catalonian poetry attains the full flowering of the *Renaixença*, and it is he who effected the fusion between the literary language and the findings of the philological section of the Institut d'Estudis Catalans, until that time without benefit of the voice of an apostle. A language that has suffered the literary prostration of centuries does not recover without pain—as is evident in all the works of the *Renaixença*. But Carner was a very great artist in language as in other respects, and although in his poetry certain archaic forms are still perpetuated, his work represents, from a linguistic point of view, a most important revolution. Indeed the Catalan linguistic reintegration has been called a literary miracle. His complete works were published in 1968.

See: J. Folguera, *Les noves valors de la poesia catalana* (1919); J. M. Miguel i Verges, Prologue to J. Carner, *Nabi*.   J.M.M.iV.

Caro Baroja, Julio (1914-), Spanish essayist and scholar, was born in Madrid. He is the son of an Andalusian publisher of Genoese ancestry, Rafael Caro Raggio, and maternal nephew of the painter Ricardo Baroja and the writer Pío BAROJA, with whom he lived until the novelist's death. Caro Baroja is in charge of his uncle's manuscripts and library in the family home in Vera de Bidasoa, and his memoir *Los Baroja* (1972; The Barojas) contains interesting information not only about his own uniquely productive and independent personality, but also about his uncle's and Spanish intellectual life before and after the Spanish Civil War. He is a member of the Royal Spanish Academy of History and from 1944 to 1953 was director of the Museum of the Spanish People in Madrid. There he compiled several catalogues of rural technology (plows, water wheels, windmills, and the like), a subject on which he has continued to work. Works like *Los pueblos de España* (1946; The Peoples of Spain), *Los vascos* (1949; The Basques), *Etnografía histórica de Navarra* (1972), *Estudios saharianos* (1955), and *El carnaval* (1965) have made him a major authority on Spanish ethnography and folklore, but his interest also extends to history and philology, as in *Los moriscos del reino de Granada* (1957; The Christian Moors of Granada), *Los judíos en la España moderna y contemporánea* (3 vols., 1961-62; The Jews in Modern and Contemporary Spain), *El señor in-*

quisidor y otras vidas por oficio (1968; The Inquisitor and Other Professional Lives), *Materiales para una historia de la lengua vasca en su relación con la latina* (1945–46; Materials for a History of the Basque Language in Its Relationship with Latin), and *La escritura en la España prerromana* (1954; Writing in Pre-Roman Spain). Especially interesting are his analyses of differing forms of religious life: *Las brujas y su mundo* (1961; Eng. tr., *The World of the Witches*, 1964) and *De la superstición al ateísmo* (1974). Literary erudition is not lacking in his immense bibliography, either. He is the author of an indispensable *Ensayo sobre la literatura de cordel* (1969; Essay on Broadside Literature) and of *Teatro popular y magia* (1974; Popular Theater and Magic). He has also published numerous newspaper articles and other types of essays, such as *El mito del carácter nacional* (1970).

See: D. J. Greenwood, "Julio Caro Baroja: sus obras e ideas," *Ethnica* 2 (1971): 79–97; A. Carreira, "Julio Caro Baroja: bibliografía," in several authors, *Homenaje a Julio Caro Baroja* (1978), pp. 15–41.   D.V.

Carossa, Hans (1878–1956), German prose writer and poet, was born in Bad Tölz, Bavaria, the son and grandson of physicians. He himself became a doctor, practicing in Passau, Nuremberg, and Munich. He served in the German army from 1916 until the last year of World War I, when he was wounded and shipped home.

As a family doctor, Carossa profited in his writing because of the intimacy with human values that are involved with the function of literature. His prose work *Doktor Bürgers Ende* (1913; Dr. Bürger's End), in which a physician kills himself when he is unable to save the life of his fiancée, and the novel *Der Arzt Gion* (1931; Eng. tr., *Doctor Gion*, 1933), which reflects post-war Munich, are both written from the viewpoint of Carossa's own profession. A later novel, *Geheimnisse des reiferen Lebens* (1936; Secrets of a More Mature Life), is a weaker work. Autobiographical works include *Eine Kindheit* (1922; Eng. tr., *A Childhood*, 1930), *Rumänisches Tagebuch* (1924; Eng. tr., *A Roumanian Diary*, 1929), *Verwandlungen einer Jugend* (1928; Eng. tr., *Boyhood and Youth*, 1930), *Das Jahr der schönen Täuschung* (1951; The Year of Sweet Disillusionment), *Ungleiche Welten* (1951; Unequal Worlds), and *Der Tag des jungen Arztes* (1955; The Day of the Young Doctor). His play, *Der alte Taschenspieler* (The Old Juggler), was published in 1956. Carossa's collected poetry, which appeared in 1938, reveals surprising objectivity while still colored by symbolism of the invisible and imponderable in life.

See: M. Machate, *Hans Carossa* (1934); A. Langen, *Hans Carossa: Weltbild und Stil* (1955); M. P. Alter, *The Concept of Physician in the Writings of Hans Carossa and Arthur Schnitzler* (1971).   A.L.W.

Carvalho, Maria Judite de (1921–), Portuguese short-story writer, was born in Lisbon, where she studied philology at the university. Except for six years spent in France and Belgium, Carvalho has resided in her nation's capital. Her urban background and her acquaintance with the world beyond the Iberian Peninsula have left a mark: her decided preference for the theme of the alienation of human beings in modern times. There may be few examples in any language of such poignant accounts of the tragic inability to communicate. Carvalho's plots are almost invariably concerned with characters, especially women, whose longing for a kindred spirit is matched only by their stubborn refusal to appear pathetic. Beginning with her first collection, *Tanta gente, Mariana* (1959; So Many People, Mariana), we enter a world where occasional cruelty, albeit often unintentional, cowardice,

and selfishness are everywhere apparent but where, notwithstanding an abundance of victims, no one is really to blame. Transcending the tedious marriages, the generation gaps, the indifference to the needs of others, a baleful universe seems bent on tormenting its children with foredoomed illusions. Moreover, the author's detachment prevents even the possibility of self-pity, so that the mood alternates between stoic resignation and tight-lipped resentment, with an occasional flash of black humor. Aside from *Os idólatras* (1969; The Idolaters), where she delves into a macabre futuristic world of uncertain setting, Carvalho's stories are usually set in middle- or working-class Lisbon. She achieves remarkable concentration by limiting the narrative to the perspective of a single character, be it a subjective observer, as in her longest work, a novella entitled *Os armários vazios* (1966; The Empty Closets), or an omniscient narrator, as in most of her stories. Not surprisingly, dialogue more often gives way to monologue. Her style, reflecting a world bereft of illusion, is consistently simple and direct.

The author's talent won critical acclaim in 1961, when she was awarded the Camilo Castelo Branco Prize by a jury of fellow writers for *As palavras poupadas* (1961; Words Left Unsaid). Her other works include *Paisagem sem barcos* (1963; Scene without Boats), *O seu amor por Etel* (1967; His Love for Ethel), *Flores ao telefone* (1968; Ms. Flores Is on the Phone), and *Tempo de Mercês* (1973; Time of Favors).

See: M. L. Lepecki, "Sobre Maria Judite de Carvalho," *Minas Gerais, Suplemento Literário*, Feb. 16, Feb. 23, and March 2, 1974.   R.A.P.-R.

Casona, Alejandro, pseud. of Alejandro Rodríguez Alvarez (1903–65), Spanish dramatist, was born in Asturias. While teaching in a country school in the Catalonian Pyrenees, he founded, with his students, the theatrical group known as "El Pájaro Pinto." In 1931, Casona was appointed director of the "Teatro Ambulante" or "Teatro del Pueblo." In 1933 he was awarded the Lope de Vega Prize for his play *La sirena varada* (The Stranded Mermaid), which was first staged in Madrid the following year.

Before he left Spain in 1937, Casona was already known and highly regarded as the author of two successful plays, *Otra vez el diablo* (The Devil Again) and *Nuestra Natacha* (Our Natacha). Both were staged in 1935, although the first was written in 1927. The latter is a beautiful and refined pedagogic fable criticizing the inhumane teaching methods employed at that time in Spanish reformatories.

Casona lived in a number of Spanish American countries before establishing his residence in Buenos Aires, where he staged most of his works. His post-Civil War plays do not depart in style or theme from the norms of the theater he wrote before the war.

The most important theme in the theater of Casona is the conflict between reality and illusion, between fantasy and truth, or between illusion and life. Three of his best-known plays—*La sirena varada, Prohibido suicidarse en primavera* (1937; Suicide Prohibited in the Spring), and *Los árboles mueren de pie* (1949; Trees Die Standing Up)—form a trilogy that is homogeneous in terms of theme, dramatic structure, style, and meaning. In these plays, Casona resolves the conflict in favor of reality, truth, and life. Illusion, fantasy, and the unreal carry with them the prestige and brilliance of beauty, but it is only in reality that human beings can live truthfully. If man's flight from reality is dramatized in collection with his return to it, it is no less certain that the return involves an enriching experience, because in his escape man has known unreality. What Casona seems to say in these three plays is that total humanity consists precisely of the compromise between the unreal and the real dimensions of existence, rather than their opposition or the exclusion of one dimension or the other. To live only in the first dimension leads to dehumanization, while to live only in the second brings on an impoverishment of the spirit. It is the harmonious compromise of both dimensions of existence that imparts fullness to human lives and at the same time makes them true and beautiful.

In two other plays, *Otra vez el diablo* and *La barca sin pescador* (1945; Eng. tr., *The Boat Without a Fisherman*, 1970), Casona introduces the Devil, who is depicted with unusual sympathy, poetic humor, and irony. This is a delightfully human, sarcastic, witty Devil, who has his moments of melancholy. The creation in these works of a poetic atmosphere, achieved by a skillful juggling of fantasy and reality, and based on an ironic and affectionate view of humanity, succeeds in raising these two works to a high aesthetic level. Casona's work suffers, however, when he introduces at the end of the play moral or spiritual lessons intended to transcend the dramatic action by giving it a symbolic value. The insertion of this rather cheap didactic element detracts from the overall value of the plays.

The two outstanding plays of Casona's poetic theater are *La dama del alba* (1944; Eng. tr., *Lady of the Dawn*, 1972) and *La casa de los siete balcones* (1957; The House of the Seven Balconies). The major theme of *La dama del alba* is the benevolent intervention of Death, the main character, who is poetically humanized in the form of a beautiful and mysterious pilgrim. The outcome of this human drama is brought about by the workings of poetic justice. Its meaning and beauty reside in the intense poetic quality of the characters, their rural world, their language, and the action of the play. These poetic symbols create a unified and effective dramatic universe. Although *La casa de los siete balcones* is not as well known, on the grounds of the beauty of its theatrical expression and its profound dramatic poetry it deserves to be considered Casona's best work.

In 1962, Casona returned to Spain for the occasion of the first performance in Madrid of *La dama del alba*. Performances of his other plays followed. He wrote his last work in Spain and saw it performed there the year before his death. Entitled *El caballero de las espuelas de oro* (1964; The Knight of the Golden Spurs), its protagonist is one of the great writers of the Spanish Golden Age, Francisco de Quevedo y Villegas.

See: J. Rodríguez Richart, *Vida y teatro de Alejandro Casona* (1963); E. Gurza, *La realidad caleidoscópica de Alejandro Casona* (1968); H. K. Moon, *Alejandro Casona, Playwright* (1970); H. B. Labrador, *Símbolo, mito y leyenda en al teatro de Casona* (1972).   F.R.R.

Cassola, Carlo (1917–), Italian novelist and short-story writer, was born in Rome. He has usually chosen Tuscany, especially the area around Volterra and the coastal town of Cecina, as the setting of his works. His best-known narratives concern housemaids, seamstresses, small shopkeepers, woodcutters, alabaster workers, railroad employees, and peasants. His prose, often characterized as dry, is unusually restrained and severe, unadorned by metaphors or other rhetorical devices, and lacking irony.

In Cassola's works, the simple, uneventful lives of the characters are shown not only to contain quiet strength and dignity, but also to be subject to moments of lyrical transport occasioned by the simplest events of everyday life. This lyricization of the banal, in a deliberately flat style made up almost entirely of phrases from the every-

day conversation of the relatively uneducated classes, is present from the very beginning of Cassola's career in the collections *La visita* (The Visit) and *Alla periferia* (On the Outskirts) of 1942. In these brief early stories, often no more than a single paragraph, action is reduced to a minimum and characterization frequently to a single gesture or a few, short phrases. The narrow narrative scope of these stories shows both a kinship with the "crepuscular" poetry (*see* ITALIAN LITERATURE) of the period just before World War I and a reaction against the Fascist rhetoric of the 1930s, when most of these pieces were written. In the longer, postwar stories collected in *Il taglio del bosco* (1959; The Cutting of the Forest), the minimal motion of the earlier fiction has been replaced by a greater narrative movement and a new concern for the social and political problems brought about by the war. This social commitment is an attitude that Cassola shares with the neorealist novelists of the era, but he differs from them in his political agnosticism and his continuing distrust of rhetoric.

An important element in Cassola's works is a female character whose apparent passivity conceals great strength and a profound attachment to the elemental rhythms of life. Such a figure is present in Cassola's first two novels, *Fausto e Anna* (1952; rev. ed. 1958; Eng. tr., 1960) and *La ragazza di Bube* (1960; Eng. tr., *Bebo's Girl*, 1962), both of which deal with World War II and the social and moral confusion of the postwar period. In these books, Cassola expresses disillusionment with many of the hopes of the Resistance, in which he himself had participated. A version of the earlier female protagonist appears in *Un cuore arido* (1961; Eng. tr., *An Arid Heart*, 1964), an account of a brief love affair between a soldier and a seamstress, and again in such later works as *La maestra* (The Schoolmistress) and *Storia di Ada* (Ada's Story), published together in 1965, as well as in *Una relazione* (1969; The Affair). Cassola places less emphasis on the women of *Il cacciatore* (1964; The Hunter), *Tempi memorabili* (1966; Times to Remember), and *Ferrovia locale* (1968; Branch Line), but in *Paura e tristezza* (1970; Fear and Sadness) the action once again centers around a heroine whose ability to derive intense enjoyment from the simplest moments of her everyday life enables her to endure an otherwise bleak existence.

In more recent works, such as *Monte Mario* (1973), *Gisella* (1974), *Troppo tardi* (1975; Too Late), *L'antagonista* (1976; The Antagonist), and *La disavventura* (1977; The Misadventure), Cassola has widened his scope to consider more middle-class and often antipathetic or "antagonistic" characters and situations, even though his personal sympathies clearly lie with the subject matter of his earlier (and probably better) work.

See: A. Asor Rosa, in *Scrittori e popolo* (1965); R. Macchioni Jodi, *Cassola* (1967); G. Manacorda, *Invito alla lettura di Carlo Cassola* (1973).   C.K.

Cassou, Jean (1897–), French novelist, poet, essayist, historian, and art critic, was born in Bilbao, Spain. In France he became an interpreter of the Spanish genius but was also influenced by German romanticism. Cassou's unique neoromanticism has oriented his work from a vindication of irrationality to a social commitment emphasizing personal and poetic values. On the basis of his essay *Eloge de la folie* (1925; In Praise of Folly) and his novel *La Clef des songes* (1929; A Key to Dreams), he was considered a supporter of ironic fancy and magic realism. Then in the 1930s he stood out as a writer committed to the struggle for human freedom and dignity. Jailed for his active part in the French Resistance, he composed his remarkable sonnets, *Trente-trois sonnets composés au secret*

(1944; 33 Sonnets Composed in Secret). A dozen other narrative works include *Les Massacres de Paris* (1935), about the events of 1871, and classical psychological novels loaded with poetic symbolism. His best novels— *Comme une grande image* (1931; Like a Great Image), *Le Centre du monde* (1945; The Center of the World), and *Le Temps d'aimer* (1959; A Time for Love)—exalt the absolute of human love. In his poetry, Cassou's grave lyricism is combined with gracefulness and strength, as in *Suite* (1951; Continuation), and *La Rose et le vin* (1952; The Rose and the Wine). *Pour la poésie* (1935; In Favor of Poetry), a volume of criticism, remains a landmark of the poetic sensibility of the 1930s.

As an essayist and historian, Cassou has opposed totalitarian restraints, championing, in works ranging from *Grandeur et infamie de Tolstoï* (1932; Tolstoy's Greatness and Infamy) to *Quarante-huit* (1939; The 1848 French Revolt) and *Parti pris* (1964; Prejudices), his individualistic and humanitarian ethics of freedom. As curator of the Paris Museum of Modern Art, he has published various studies on painting and a *Panorama des arts plastiques contemporains* (1960; Panorama of the Contemporary Plastic Arts). In 1965 he submitted to a long interview published as *Entretiens avec Jean Rousselot* (Conversations with Jean Rousselot).

See: P. Georgel, *Jean Cassou* (1967).   D.Ba.

Castellet i Diaz de Cossio, Josep Maria (1926–), Catalan critic, was born in Barcelona to a Catalan father and a Mexican mother. He has dedicated himself to writing literary criticism ever since his university years, having been associated with literary magazines like *Cuadrante* and *Laya*. He wrote his first works in Castilian. *Notas sobre literatura española contemporánea* (1955; Notes on Contemporary Spanish Literature), *La hora del lector* (1957; The Reader's Hour), and *Veinte años de poesía española* (1960; Twenty Years of Spanish Poetry) are among his most outstanding works. He collaborated with Joaquim Molas in compiling the anthology *Ocho Siglos de poesia catalana* (Eight Centuries of Catalonian Poetry) and with Molas initiated his important publications in Catalan with *Poesia catalana del segle XX* (1963; 20th-Century Catalonian Poetry). Other works of his in Catalan include *Poesia, realisme, història* (1965; Poetry, Realism, and History) and a study that appears as prologue to the *Poesia* of Salvador ESPRIU, to whom he also dedicated an essay that won the Taurus Prize, "Iniciació a la poesia de Salvador Espriu" (1971). Other books are *Lectura de Marcuse* (1969; A Reading of Marcuse) and *Nueve novísimos poetas españoles* (1970; Nine Very Recent Spanish Poets). *Questions de literatura, política, i societat* (1975; Social, Political, and Literary Issues) is one of the best introductions to his repertory of ideas. His book *Josep Pla o la raó narrativa* (Josep Pla, or Narrative Motive) was awarded the Josep Pla prize for 1977.

At the present time, Castellet directs Edicions 62, one of the publishing houses that have done the most for contemporary Catalan literature, and its subsidiary, Ediciones Península. He has studied the work of Ernest Hemingway in *La evolución espiritual de Hemingway* (1958; Hemingway's Spiritual Evolution), John Steinbeck in his prologue to *Obras completas* (1957), György LUKÁCS, and Yevgeny YEVTUSHENKO, as well as the work of Spanish authors like Camilo José CELA, Juan GOYTISOLO, and Gabriel Ferrater.

See: F. Vallverdu, Prologue to J. M. Castellet, *Poesia, realisme, història* (1965).   J.F.C.

Castilla del Pino, Carlos (1922–), Spanish psychiatrist, sociologist, and essayist, was born in Córdoba, where

since 1949 he has been the director of a neuropsychiatric center.

Castilla's writings fall into two categories: works of popularization, and studies in psychiatric sociology and philosophical anthropology. His popular works are inspired by Karl Marx's early essays, especially the *Economic and Philosophical Manuscripts of 1844*. They serve the very specific and conscious purpose of acquainting the Spanish public with socialist thought. Two of the author's academic endeavors stand out: *Un estudio sobre la depresión: fundamentos de antropología dialéctica* (1966; A Study of Depression: Foundations of Dialectical Anthropology) and *La culpa* (1968; Guilt). The study of depression is the first work of its kind in Spain to make use of Marxist categories with the explicit aim of transcending what Castilla calls the limitations of a "personalistic" concept of medicine. A therapeutic method based on dialectical anthropology starts with the premise that neurotic behavior can be adequately explained only when considered within the social context in which it occurs. Likewise, Castilla offers a corrective to the existential and psychoanalytic views of such phenomena as alienation and guilt, which he claims do not have ontological status. Rather, guilt is always "before others" and thus sociogenic.

Other important works are *Psicoanálisis y marxismo* (1969) and the autobiographical novel *Discurso de Onofre* (1977).   T.Me.

Castillo Puche, José Luis (1919–), Spanish novelist, was born in Yecla in the province of Murcia. He gave up religious studies at the Pontifical University of Comillas to pursue journalism and to study philosophy and letters at the University of Madrid. He worked at the Instituto de Cultura Hispánica and has traveled throughout America. His works include articles, essays, biographies, and novels.

Castillo Puche began his literary career with a volume on Pío BAROJA, *Memorias íntimas de Aviraneta* (1952; Aviraneta's Intimate Memoirs) and has also published a biography of Ernest Hemingway. His novel *Con la muerte al hombro* (1954; With Death at Hand) is an existentialist study of a character haunted by death, while *Sin camino* (1956; Off the Track) deals with a conflict between religious and secular vocations similar to that experienced by the author. The torment of sexual repression suffered by a would-be priest during his ordination ceremony is the theme of one of his later novels, *Como ovejas al matadero* (1971; Like Sheep to the Slaughter), whereas *El vengador* (1956; The Avenger) concerns the vengeful plans of an army officer returning to his home town after the Spanish Civil War. *Paralelo 40* (1963; The 40th Parallel) presents a conflict of individual conscience at an American military base in Spain.

Castillo Puche is a continuer of traditional 19th-century Spanish realism. He employs a direct, simple, and vigorous style and certain artificial narrative devices successfully depicting the religious problems confronted by his characters.

See: M. García-Viño, *Novela española actual* (1967), pp. 49–73; A. Gómez Gil, "José Luis Castillo Puche," *CA* 177 (1971): 234–47; G. Sobejano, *Novela española de nuestro tiempo* (1975), pp. 258–75.   J.O.

Castro, José Maria Ferreira de (1898–1974), Portuguese novelist, was born in Oliveira de Azeméis, south of Oporto. At the age of 12, he emigrated to Belém (also called Pará), Brazil. From there he traveled up the Amazon and Madeira rivers to work for nearly four years among the rubber gatherers, learning at first hand of the perpetual indebtedness that kept most of the workers in a condition of semislavery. There also he wrote his first novel, *O criminoso por ambição* (1916; Criminal through Ambition). Returning to Belém, he made a precarious living working at various jobs until he succeeded in publishing his novel. He then became a journalist. After visiting a number of Brazilian cities, Ferreira de Castro returned to Portugal in 1919, settling in Lisbon to devote himself to journalism and letters and publishing a series of novellas, short stories, articles, and essays.

In 1928 his career as a socially conscious novelist began in earnest with *Emigrantes* (Eng. tr., *Emigrants,* 1962), a story of the Portuguese driven by poverty to seek their fortunes abroad, in this case in Brazil. Brazil as the promised land where a man might make a fortune was not a new theme in Portuguese literature. Ferreira de Castro drew on his own experience and sympathy for those who suffer to reveal a world in which the poor were bound to lose, both in Portugal and in Brazil. In 1930 appeared *A selva* (Eng. tr., *Jungle,* 1935), probably his greatest novel. Here the Portuguese emigrant, like the author himself, cannot find work in Belém and travels up the river to a *seringal* (rubber estate) ironically named *Paraíso* (Paradise). Ferreira de Castro's hero is put to work as a rubber tapper and later is employed in the store and accounting side of the establishment, giving the author the opportunity to describe its social structure from bottom to top. The reader learns with Alberto how to tap a rubber tree and becomes familiar with the exotic world of the forest, its beauty and its dangers. At times the forest takes on a personality of its own and becomes almost a character in the novel, implacably hostile to the human beings working there. The author describes the tragedy of the *cearenses* (migrants from Ceará), driven by drought from the northeastern backlands to seek work in the rubber forests and subsequently trapped in a system from which escape is almost impossible. Alberto is shocked most of all by the lack of solidarity among the oppressed themselves and by their cooperation with their masters against their own comrades. Emerging in *A selva* is the socialist orientation that would eventually make Ferreira de Castro a precursor of the Portuguese neorealists.

His later novels are *Eternidade* (1933; Eternity), *Terra fria* (1934; Cold Uplands), and *A tempestade* (1940; The Storm). *A lã e a neve* (1947; Wool and Snow) follows a poor shepherd from the north of Portugal to a new and no less grim life as a factory worker. In *A curva da estrada* (1950; The Turn in the Road), a Spanish socialist leader works out his struggle of conscience over whether or not to leave the party. *A missão* (1954; Eng. tr., *The Mission,* 1961) contains three novellas; the title story presents another case of conscience—whether to paint the word *mission* on the roof of a monastery to protect the community against German bombers in wartime France but at the same time facilitate bombardment of a nearby factory. *O instinto supremo* (1968; The Strongest Instinct) returns to the Brazilian scene, dramatizing the effort to pacify the dangerous Parintintins—the very Indians who were the silent menace to the rubber tappers of *A selva*—without violating General Rondon's precept not to kill, even in self-defense.

Ferreira de Castro's books, especially *A selva,* have been translated into numerous foreign languages, making him the best-known Portuguese novelist of the 20th century.

See: J. Navarro, *Ferreira de Castro e o Amazonas* (1958); J. Brasil, *Ferreira de Castro* (1961); A. Salema, ed., *Ferreira de Castro, a sua vida, a sua personalidade, a sua obra* (1974).   T.Br.

Castro Quesada, Américo (1885–1972), Spanish literary critic and historian, was born in Cantagalo, Brazil, of Spanish parents. He studied philology and literature at the University of Granada, spent three years doing research at the University of Paris, and returned to Spain in 1908. In Madrid he became associated with Francisco GINER DE LOS RÍOS, the famous educator of the Institución Libre de Enseñanza, with Ramón MENÉNDEZ PIDAL, and with José ORTEGA Y GASSET. Castro assimilated the best of this liberal milieu by trying to be a rigorous philologist like Pidal, a systematic thinker like Ortega, and a committed teacher like Giner. In the early years of the 20th century, the problem of education in Spain attracted the attention of both intellectuals and politicians. Ortega lectured on "Social Pedagogy" (1910) and had Paul Natorp's *Sozialpädagogik* translated into Spanish (1914). E. L. André published an important book on *La educación de la adolescencia* (1916; Education of Adolescents), and Santiago Alba, minister of finance, published *Un programa económico y financiero* (1916; An Economic and Financial Plan) in which education was of vital concern. Castro took an active role in these discussions and a few years later published a collection of articles on the subject: *Lengua, enseñanza y literatura* (1924; Language, Teaching, and Literature). A close associate of Menéndez Pidal at the Center for Historical Studies, he was the founder and first director of the Institute of Hispanic Philology in Buenos Aires (1923). In 1925 he published his epoch-making book, *El pensamiento de Cervantes* (Cervantes's Thought). Following the then prevalent view of the Renaissance as a movement of secularization in contrast to the Middle Ages, Castro portrays Cervantes as a representative of the emerging rationalism. In 1936, like many other Spanish intellectuals, he left Spain, wandered through several countries and universities, and settled at Princeton University, where he taught until his retirement. He returned to Spain in 1968.

The experience of the Spanish Civil War brought about a profound change in Castro's views of Spanish life, history, and literature. In abstract terms he maintained the same ideal of scholarly rigor, but the contents and the criteria of values present in his later books frequently run counter to those espoused before 1936. In the later works the structure of Spanish history is defined as a dynamic relationship of cooperation and conflict among Christians, Jews, and Muslims during the Middle Ages. When the Jews were expelled and the Muslims defeated in 1492, the Christian Spaniards shunned those activities that had traditionally been performed by the banned castes: the liberal and the mechanical arts—in other words, scientific and economic activities. The Christian caste saw in war and in the defense of religion the source of honor, hence its inadaptability to the values of modern bourgeois Europe.

Castro was probably the first historian to have applied existential hermeneutics to the study of the entire history of a country. Elaborating on ideas of Ortega y Gasset, and indirectly of Martin Heidegger, he saw the role of the historian as the attempt to define the "vital standpoint" (*morada vital*) of a society in a given historical period or in different periods. Vital standpoint includes the history of ideas and the structure and hierarchy of the values of a society. It is more encompassing than the structuralist or history of ideas approach. Beyond ideas, facts, causes, and effects, Castro tried to define the specific way of life from which the facts derive their meaning. Intermediate between the extremes of psychohistory and Marxism, the concept of *morada vital* describes both the objective socioeconomic conditions of a society and a given community's awareness of those conditions. In such a concept of history, the past ceases to be the main temporal reference, and a society is understood from the point of view of its collective ideals and projects, that is, from the point of view of its future. With this idea, Castro found himself in opposition to Miguel de UNAMUNO's concept of "intrahistory," Menéndez Pidal's traditionalism, and the Ortega y Gasset of *Invertebrate Spain.*

Castro's main works in this second period are: *España en su historia: cristianos, moros y judíos* (1948); *La realidad histórica de España* (1954), profoundly renovated in subsequent editions; *Cervantes y los casticismos españoles* (1966; Cervantes and the Essence of Spain); and *Sobre el nombre y el quién de los españoles* (1973; Concerning the Spaniards: Their Name and Their Identity), which includes two previous books and other pages, the last one written on July 25, 1972, the very day he died. The following titles in English are translations of *España en su historia* and *La realidad histórica de España,* but they contain material not available in the Spanish versions and revisions which make them independent books in English: *The Structure of Spanish History* (1954); *The Spaniards: An Introduction to Their History* (1971). A collection of articles is also available in English with the title: *An Idea of History: Selected Essays of Americo Castro* (1977).

See: M. P. Hornik, ed., *Collected Studies in Honour of Américo Castro's Eightieth Year* (1965); A. Peña, *Américo Castro y su visión de España y de Cervantes* (1975); J. L. Gómez-Martínez, *Américo Castro y el origen de los españoles: historia de una polémica* (1975).

C.M.A.

Català, Victor, pseud. of Catalina Albert i Paradis (1873–1966), Catalan novelist and short-story writer, was born in L'Escala. The dramatic landscape and rugged people of this small fishing village exerted a marked influence on Català's literary vocation. At first she took part in the Jocs Florals or poetic competitions held each year in Barcelona as part of a tradition dating from the Middle Ages. But although her poetry did not pass unnoticed, she triumphed in the narrative genre. Her best works are the *Drames rurals* (1902; Rural Dramas), a series of stories or short novels in which she depicted, with a marked predilection for the darker hues, different aspects of the simple folk of the countryside. The novel *Solitud* (1905; Solitude) was awarded the Fastenrath Prize in the Jocs Florals and immediately translated into French, Spanish, Portuguese, English, and German. The pattern of contrasts and the interplay of the most sublime and the most perverse instincts constitute the essence of this great realistic novel, which exerted considerable influence on a number of important later prose writers. *Caires Vius* (1907) demonstrated that Català's style was not a passing caprice or a literary pose, but was grounded in her thought and in her sensibility. Other of Català's works include *La mare balena* (1920; The Mother Whale), a collection of stories, and the three-volume *Un film* (1910; A Film).

Català's work shows great daring in both the choice and treatment of subject matter. The new realistic view of life—and the startling fact that the author was a woman—disconcerted the public. But her literary boldness prevailed and a whole group of Catalan novelists followed in her footsteps, creating a type of rural novel with robust figures and rugged scenes full of grandeur. Prudenci BERTRANA was one of her outstanding followers. Other writers exaggerated this wild depiction of rural life, and for some years Catalan literature was dominated by rustic novels in which the characters spoke in the manner of peasants, an effect sometimes obtained by the facile use of vulgarity. The devotees of *ruralismo* were legion, if not always distinguished. There has also been in some quarters vigorous resistance to this vogue, but in any event Victor Català gave a great lesson in sincerity. Whatever direction the Catalan novel may have taken in recent years, Català's presence has been felt as an example of ardent and deepfelt literary integrity.

See: T. Garcés, "Coversa amb Victor Català," *Revista de Catalunya* (1926); A. Schmecberger, *Conteurs catalans* (1926).

F. de P.

Catalan literature. After highly honorable achievements in the Middle Ages and especially in the 15th century, Catalan literature went through a long period of decadence related to Catalonia's loss of political independence. At the end of the 18th century, Antoni de Capmany declared the Catalan idiom "dead for the republic of letters." But precisely at this time was born Antoni Puiz i Blanch, called Puigblanch (1775–1842), now rightly considered the initiator of a revival of Catalan writing known as the "Renaixença," which had results continuing to the present day. Two epic poems that he probably wrote between 1815 and 1820 seem to have circulated in manuscript among the students of the University of Cervera, with copies of a *Gramática y apologia de la lengua cathalana* published in 1814 by De Josep Pau Ballott (1747–1821). These documents deeply influenced the young intellectuals of the period.

In 1815, Bonaventura Carles Aribau (1798–1862), a student, was already writing his first poetry in Catalan. Aribau's famous "Oda a la patria" (Ode to the Homeland), a solemn and noble poem of homesickness for the native land and melancholy recollections of her lost grandeur, was published in 1833. This poem inaugurated the first, or romantic, period of the "Renaixença." From 1833 to 1859 certain foreign influences were important (Scottish philosophy, the manner of Walter Scott, Manzoni, and the German romantics), although the poet Joaquim RUBIO I ORS proclaimed literary independence in the prologue of his book of verse, *Lo gayter del Llobregat* (1841; The Piper of Llobregat). Catalan poetry was at that time characterized by noble melancholy, profound idealism, and a restrained style. These characterstics, the source of its particular charm, are especially apparent in the poems of Manuel Milá y Fontanals and of Josep Lluis Ponç i Gallarça (1823–94).

Two important events then occurred, almost simultaneously. In 1858 the Majorcan Marian Aguilo (1825–97) took up residence in Valencia as the librarian of the university and, because of his faith in the united destiny of the Catalan-speaking countries, became a true apostle of cultural rebirth. His enthusiasm stirred two energetic disciples, Vicente Wenceslao Querol and Teodor Llorente (1836–1911). Aguilo was in favor of a profoundly national literature free of all foreign influence, neither classical nor romantic. Querol and Llorente laid the foundations of a truly Valencian literary school, distinguished by the autochthonous character of its themes and the noble simplicity of its style. At the same time, by calling his poetry "rimas catalanas," Querol acknowledged the literary unity of Catalonia, Valencia, and the Balearic Islands. Aguilo exercised a parallel influence in Majorca. Although there had been precursors in Valencia and in Majorca and the other Balearic Islands, Aguilo's crusading spirit provided the movement with its greatest impulse.

In 1859 the Jocs Florals of Barcelona, which had been founded by a Catalan monarch of the 14th century, were reestablished. These poetic competitions represented a tendency to perpetuate, in fixed forms, the subject matter of a somewhat stylized medievalism. They exerted enormous social influence, as their anachronistic pomp aroused the interest of "good society" in Catalan poetry. Most of the poets who began to write in the tradition of the Jocs Florals are now forgotten. Victor Balaguer (1824–1901) is one of the exceptions. He was a fiery and declamatory poet, fond of Victor Hugo and enamored of Italy. He had witnessed Italy's war of national unity, which he considered an object lesson for the Catalan-speaking countries. Just as the Lombards, the Tuscans, and other groups form the Italian nation, he argued, so the Catalonians, the Valencians, and the natives of the Balearic Islands form the *patria lemosina*.

The great figure of 19th-century Catalan poetry, Jacint VERDAGUER I SANTALÓ, the son of humble peasants, was still in many respects a romantic. The rich Catalonian countryside held no secrets for him: his excursions made him thoroughly familiar with the names of herbs, birds, and minerals in the Ampurdanian, Majorcan, Leridan, and Valencian dialects. Mountains and rivers became living beings to him and his genial intuition gave him a feeling for primitive periods, which he described as if he had lived in them and known their heroes. His genius was predominantly epic in character. His two epic poems, *La Atlàntida* (1877) and *Canigó* (1885), have been translated into almost all of the literary languages of Europe and some of Asia. His highly personal style is characterized by an almost savage energy, which admirably suggests the primitive and barbarous character of the prehistoric epoch of *L'Atlàntida* and the ninth century of *Canigó*. Verdaguer's work in general, and more especially *Canigó*, can be said to sum up Catalan romanticism.

Although in this period various writers cultivated the historical novel in the manner of Walter Scott, the only prose of that time which has really survived is the humorous *costumbrismo* of Robert Robert (1840–1905), whose talent, at once tender and ironical, is reminiscent, although in a more subdued tone, of Charles Dickens. The theater attained the dignity of true dramatic poetry with the dramas of Frederic Soler (Pitarra) (1839–95).

The work of Angel GUIMERÀ sounds a new note. His *tragedias* added another genre—the tragic poem—to a literature that already had, in Verdaguer, a great epic poet. Although by preference Guimerà, like the romantics, found his themes in the Middle Ages, he handled them in a realistic manner and in a very personal style, distinguished by a concision that often borders on brutality. He deliberately seeks the unadorned substantive. His sentences are disorderly, rough-hewn, and hesitating. At times they give the sensation of a mere rough draft, of something drawn with force but incomplete, like certain statues of Auguste Rodin. The social message of his prose drama *Terra Baixa* (1896), which was widely translated and produced (Eng. tr., *Marta of the Lowlands,* 1914), has made it popular with the proletarian wing of the Catalan theater. In his *Poesies* (1887) he frequently treats macabre themes with a horrifying exactitude of detail.

Despite his sophistication, Joan MARAGALL I GORINA became very popular in Catalonia as the author of landscape poetry. He contemplated nature as would a good bourgeois on vacation, and this is the secret of his great success. At times he interwove philosophical ideas (particularly those of Friedrich NIETZSCHE) into his verse. This is especially true of the hero of "Comte Arnau," whom he intended to present as an incarnation of the superman. This won him the admiration of Miguel de UNAMUNO, who was responsible for Maragall's renown in Castile and in the Spanish American countries. His very beautiful "Cant espiritual" is a sort of realistic credo in which he expressed his candid admiration for the uni-

verse as perceived by the senses and deplored the fact that death has to deprive us of them.

The seed sown by Marian Aguilo bore fruit in the above-mentioned Majorcan school, with its classical, Mediterranean style. Miguel COSTA I LLOBERA is the Majorcan poet par excellence—circumspect, sober, devoid of sentimentalism, impeccable, strong, serene, and an admirer of Horace. Even in poetic meter he followed the models of antiquity. Another poet of great talent belonging to this school is Joan ALCOVER I MASPONS, whose moving elegies are a model in the genre. With Verdaguer and Guimerà, they are the Majorcan poets who carried the Catalan language to its greatest literary heights.

The spirit of realism naturally favored the development of the novel. Narcis OLLER I MORAGUES is considered, more or less correctly, a disciple of Emile ZOLA. Other initiators of Catalonian realism are Josep Pin i Soler (1842–1927); Joaquim RUYRA I OMS, author of short stories and short novels, whose delightful style won him the admiration of classic writers; Prudenci BERTRANA; and Victor CATALÀ, whose novel *Solitud* (1905) is esteemed by the Catalonians as a masterpiece. Later dramatic authors, notably Santiago RUSIÑOL and Ignasi IGLESIES abandoned the verse drama and cultivated a type of prose comedy that enjoyed a great popular success. Exaggeration of realism even led to the belief that dramatic poetry had died, its place taken by a dialogued prose where the chief ambition was to reproduce, like a phonograph, the conversations of real life.

During this period the philologist Pompeu FABRA I POE, later exiled in France, carried out his labor of standardizing and purifying the Catalan language. His first grammatical studies appeared in the last quarter of the 19th century and his voluminous *Gramática de la lengua catalana* (Grammar of the Catalan Language) in 1913. His orthographic system was officially adopted by the Institut d'Estudis Catalans.

In 1914 the Spanish state granted a semblance of autonomy to Catalonia—considered in a strict geographical sense, without Valencia and the Balearic Islands—which was organized with the name *Mancomunitat* under the presidency of Enric PRAT DE LA RIBA. He showed himself to be a most devoted patron of Catalan culture, and with this official stimulus a new literary movement, headed by Eugenio D'ORS took over the directing role in the intellectual life of the country. But this movement, while characterized by a courageous intellectual spirit and by a devastating criticism of realism and all that had preceded it, scornfully rejected the national literature of the preceding century while almost slavishly admiring certain foreign schools, in particular French symbolism. The literature of that period consequently had scarcely any roots in the national soil. On the other hand it profited by Pompeu Fabra's judicious reform of the literary language, although it is questionable whether what was gained in the direction of purity of language was a sufficient compensation for what was sacrificed in native genius. There was even a loss in a territorial sense, as the new literature tended to limit itself to a geographically circumscribed Catalonia.

A multitude of lyric poets then made their appearance, two of whom, Josep CARNER and Carles RIBA, continue to be admired. Carner was the poet of the comfortable and elegant life of the bourgeoisie that lived in the beautiful environs of Barcelona. He was also the poet of coquettish modistes and pretty neighborhood girls. Carner died in Brussels in 1970, and his remains were brought to Catalonia in 1978, where he was buried in Barcelona. The Hellenist Riba was above all an intellectual, a university man, and his learning was often an impediment to his poetry. His *Estances,* however, is profound and subtle and continues to exert a great influence on the younger generation.

The reaction against the realistic prose theater was carried out by Josep Maria de SAGARRA I CASTELLAR-NAU. He was the most original and at the same time the most popular writer of his period. His highly nationalistic dramatic poems enjoyed a noisy triumph on the stage. Unquestionably endowed with genius in his own way, he even undertook an epic poem, *El Comte Arnau* (1928), the first six cantos of which show an astounding vigor and simplicity. Unfortunately the last four cantos drag painfully. He also wrote various novels in a charmingly impudent style. Sagarra's language is extremely rich in native idioms that lend it an inimitable flavor, and it often attains a spontaneous kind of beauty.

The novelist Joan Puig i Ferreter, later an exile in France, introduced to Catalonia the great Russian authors of the 19th century. His *Camins de França,* a collection of highly personal confessions, does not conform to any particular literary school.

In 1931, Catalonia, still without Valencia and the Balearic Islands, was organized into an autonomous Generalitat. In 1939 it was invaded by Francisco Franco's army. The post-Civil War decades have seen an implacable persecution of the national culture, to the point where aging writers were shot and depositories of Catalonian books were burned. The year 1939 can be said to mark the abrupt suspension of Catalonia's literary life. Writers were condemned to silence in their own country. One can deduce something of the spirit of the time from what was produced by that portion of the group that exiled itself voluntarily in free countries. These writers looked forward to another stirring revival of the national spirit, with unity for the Catalan-speaking countries.

This unity is coming about as a result of the general election of July 15, 1977, which reinstated Catalonia's governing body, the Generalitat. Tarradellas, who was elected president while in exile in Mexico in 1954, has returned to Catalonia. The process of normalizing Catalonian culture is also being completed, as evidenced by the Congress of Catalonian Culture that was held in 1976–77.

Under these circumstances Catalan letters are returning to normalcy. The members of the Generation of 1936 who did not die in exile, guided by a spirit of reconciliation, have reestablished their movement. Despite the circumstances of the last decade, younger writers are following a course similar to that of writers in the rest of the Iberian Peninsula. The statistics that speak for the gradual affirmation of Catalan literature in the postwar period are remarkably eloquent: in 1942, 4 books were published in Catalan; in 1944, 12; in 1947, 53; in 1948, 60. Twenty years later, in 1968, 500 were published. In 1976, 855 were published and in 1977, 1,015. Albert Manent has noted that until 1946 more Catalan books were published in exile than in Catalonia itself. The emergence of social and historical realism in Catalan literature has paralleled similar development in Castilian literature. According to the critics Josep Maria CASTELLET I DIAZ DE COSSIO and Molas, social realism began when poetry went into the streets. It immediately developed into a literature of protest and criticism of the deteriorating status quo. The silent but determined opposition of the intellectuals played an important role in this protest. At present there is a reaction on the part of the youngest writers in favor of greater imagination and more formal purity.

Having survived all attempts to silence it, Catalan literature is today beginning to recover the greatness of its glorious past and embark on a second "Renaixença."

See: M. de Montoliu, *Manual d'història crítica de la literatura catalana moderna* (1922); J. J. A. Bertrand, *La Littérature catalane contemporaine, 1833–1933* (1933); J. Ruiz i Calonja, *Historia de la literatura catalana* (1954); J. Fuster, *Literatura catalana contemporània* (1971); J. Castellanos, ed., *Guia de Literatura catalana contemporània* (1973); A. Manent, *Literatura catalana a l'exili* (1976).   J.Sa. rev. J.F.C.

Cavafy, Constantine (1863–1933), Greek poet, was born in Alexandria, Egypt. He spent his entire life in Alexandria, apart from seven childhood years in England, three crucial years (ages 19–22) in Constantinople, and several brief visits abroad. Cavafy's authorized oeuvre amounts to only 154 poems, all short. The only volumes he published in his lifetime were a brochure with 14 poems, issued privately in 1904, and its reissue in 1910 with 7 additional poems. From 1912 on, Cavafy personally distributed his work in printed broadsheets—often with handwritten corrections—to a select readership. A collected edition of the authorized poems appeared posthumously in 1935. In recent years, many "unfinished" or rejected poems have been discovered and published.

A poet of the Greek diaspora, Cavafy was not influenced by Kostis PALAMAS and the folkloristic and nationalistic orientations of the New Athenian School (*see* GREEK LITERATURE). He brought to Greek poetry an awareness of a wider European sensibility involving the decline of values, skepticism, and Oscar Wilde's amoral aestheticism. Cavafy's early work continued the romanticism and puristic language of the Old Athenian School, to which he added symbolic colorations. He achieved his unique voice only in middle age when he developed a nonlyrical, unornamented style, reminiscent of the Hellenistic epigram and mime, objective, terse, and prosaic, yet meticulously wrought. The Hellenistic and Greco-Roman periods (ca. 325 B.C.–A.D. 400), with their sense of decadent transience and their eventual antagonism between fading paganism and encroaching Christianity, provided Cavafy with a mythical-historical parallel to the decadent modern world. From those periods he drew historical, legendary, or even imaginary figures to serve as masks for his own philosophic, aesthetic, historical, or erotic concerns. Regret for old age and for pleasures missed is a prevalent motif in the poems; art is seen as the only solace, the social pressures that made him hide his homosexuality behind innuendo (although certain poems are shockingly frank) encouraging this valuation of art above nature. Yet beneath the splendor of its aesthetic façades, Cavafy's poetry reveals anxiety, inconsistency, cynicism, and tragic defeat.

The full quality of Cavafy's work is impossible to convey in translation. His personal language is a mixture of demotic (*see* GREEK LITERATURE), the puristic idiom of the diaspora, and elements drawn from Byzantine and Hellenistic Greek, all subtly juxtaposed to achieve effects that are primarily ironic. Nevertheless, he has been appreciated in the English-speaking world as a major European poet. In Greece, Cavafy was ignored or derided during his lifetime, but since the mid-1930s, he has been one of the most decisive forces in the development of modern Greek verse. His influence was particularly strong on George SEFERIS. English translations of Cavafy's poetry include *The Complete Poems of Cavafy,* tr. by R. Dalven (1966), and *Collected Poems,* tr. by E. Keeley and P. Sherrard (1974).

See: P. Bien, *Constantine Cavafy* (1964); R. Liddell, *Cavafy: A Critical Biography* (1974); E. Keeley, *Cavafy's Alexandria: Study of a Myth in Progress* (1976).   A.D.

Cayrol, Jean (1911-), French novelist, poet, and screenwriter, was born in Bordeaux. He studied law and was briefly a librarian. Cayrol's first publications were short volumes of verse, including *Le Hollandais volant* (1936; The Flying Dutchman), *Les Poèmes du Pasteur Grimm* (1936; The Poems of Pastor Grimm), and *Les Phénomènes célestes* (1939; Celestial Phenomena). After the defeat of France in 1940, he engaged in Resistance work with his brother; arrested in March 1942, he was freed, then rearrested in June, spent nine months in Fresnes, and was then sent to the concentration camp at Mauthausen, where he spent the remainder of the war.

Cayrol's first postwar works, perhaps his best, reveal subtly the influence of the concentration camp, showing especially the difficulty of readaptation to ordinary life. Although these works have much in common with existentialism, Cayrol's Catholic faith, without appearing in his fiction explicitly, underlies his understanding of the modern dilemma. *On vous parle* (1947; Someone Is Speaking to You), which won the Renaudot Prize, *Les Premiers Jours* (1947; The First Days), and *Le Feu qui prend* (1950; The Fire That Catches), forming a trilogy under the title *Je vivrai l'amour des autres* (I Shall Live the Love of Others), give a fictional expression of the re-creation of the self and its integration into the collectivity of life. This is accomplished chiefly by means of charity and hope; faith is not explicit. Several collections of poetry, including *Et nunc* (1944), *Miroir de la rédemption* (1944; Mirror of the Redemption), and *Poèmes de la nuit et du brouillard* (1946; Poems of Night and Fog), also reflect Cayrol's war experiences, patriotism, and religious belief. Two essays published as *Lazare parmi nous* (1950; Lazarus among Us) show his awareness of the specifically modern anxiety emerging from a sense of being uprooted and from a lack of identity and direction.

Cayrol's subsequent novels, numbering more than a dozen, usually have apparently normal characters and situations, but the sense of alienation, the search for an authentic self, based on an authentic past, and the difficulty of human relationships all remain central concerns. Memory is a nearly constant theme. *L'Espace d'une nuit* (1954; Eng. tr., *All in a Night*, 1957) portrays the search for a father. *Les Corps étrangers* (1959; Eng. tr., *Foreign Bodies*, 1960) takes up the themes of falsehood and discovery. As the title of *Je l'entends encore* (1968; I Still Hear It) suggests, the world of "night and fog" in the concentration camps does not disappear from Cayrol's later fiction. In this key novel, a journalist, searching for his past, must go back to the camp where his parents died. Because Cayrol's fictional assumptions and techniques are not traditional, and because he often shows awareness of the problematic aspect of fictional language as well as the connection between language and situation, he has often been associated with or considered a precursor of the "new novel" (*see* FRENCH LITERATURE). His approach to time and space is characteristically phenomenological. In collaboration with Alain Resnais, he produced a documentary film on prison camps, *Nuit et brouillard* (1956; Night and Fog), and *Muriel* (1963), a film on the theme of memory. Cayrol also wrote the script for Claude Durand's *Le Coup de grâce* (1965; The Final Blow), concerning an informer under the German occupation. Later fictional works, such as *Histoire de la mer* (1973; Story of the Sea), explore in a fanciful or realistic manner the opposition between being and having, and the impact of technology on nature and man's relationships with it. Critics both Catholic (Albert BÉGUIN, Pierre EMMANUEL) and radical (Roland BARTHES) have praised Cayrol's fiction and poetry.

See: R. Barthes, "Jean Cayrol et ses romans," *Esprit* 188 (March 1952): 482-99; C. Lynes, "Jean Cayrol," in *The Novelist as Philosopher*, ed. by John Cruickshank (1962), pp. 183-205; D. Oster, *Jean Cayrol et son œuvre* (1968).
                                                                                          C.S.B.

Cecchi, Emilio (1884-1966), Italian essayist and critic, was born in Florence. He was a member of the group of writers gathered around the review *La voce*. Cecchi began his career as a poet and short-story writer, publishing *Inno* (1910; Hymn), a collection of tenuous, pensive verses, as well as stories in the vein of Gabriele D'ANNUNZIO. In 1911 he became a book reviewer for a daily newspaper. Soon afterward, Cecchi published his first major critical studies, *Rudyard Kipling* (1911) and *La poesia di Giovanni Pascoli* (1912; Giovanni PASCOLI's Poetry), and a series of shorter essays on contemporary writing, *Studi critici* (1912; Critical Studies). Although Cecchi's name later became synonymous with literary "hedonism" and artistic "escapism," his first publications show a strong moralistic bent, dominated by the romantic concept of the poet as educator and of poetry itself as identical with the "replete flux of life." The historicist rigor of Cecchi's early writings appears to be on the wane in his *Storia della letteratura inglese nel secolo XIX* (1915; An Outline of 19th-Century English Literature). Here style becomes the focus of literary analysis; Charles Lamb and Thomas De Quincey, the two "true saints of prose," are his avowed models of critical writing. Cecchi's two-stage method of research—a close reading of the texts with an unsystematic gathering of virgin impressions and, secondarily, an overview of the historical, political, and ideological background—sets the foundation for his major undertakings as a "reviewer of things," of life and the cosmos.

In 1919, Cecchi joined friends in founding and editing the review *La ronda*, soon to become the sanctuary of Italian "artistic prose" (*see* ITALIAN LITERATURE), literary "fragmentism," and impressionism. His definition of William Wordsworth's poetry, "imagination implying the whole of life experience," applies to his own masterwork, *Pesci rossi* (1920; Goldfish), a collection of short essays, written (1916-20) for the literary page of a newspaper. The essays are small miracles of artful artlessness, of concentration and divagation, of precision and vagueness. Embodying the *Ronda* concepts of poetical sensibility, Cecchi's "goldfish" succeed in approximating the polyphonic essence of reality. Both the much attacked "superficiality" and the much acclaimed "speculative depth" of *Pesci rossi* appear, upon close inspection, to be illusory. Cecchi's prose has often been called a return to classicism after the avant-garde vagaries of Italian writing in the preceding decade, but today this work appears rather as an important milestone in the development of 20th-century "baroque" (or decadent) style (*see* ITALIAN LITERATURE). Its closest historical parallel is the polychromatic prose of Daniello Bartoli (1608-85).

The influence of *Pesci rossi* on Italian prose and verse has been vast and lasting, affecting even such literary adversaries as Elio VITTORINI, Cesare PAVESE, and Edoardo SANGUINETI. Cecchi's later works include the travel memoirs *Messico* (1932; Mexico); *America amara* (1940; Bitter America), a harsh attack on the "American way of life," unfortunate in its coincidence with official propaganda; and *Appunti per un periplo dell'Africa* (1954; Notes on an African Circumnavigation). He also produced important studies in the field of art criticism, such as *Pittura italiana dell'Ottocento* (1926; 19th-Century Italian Painting) and *Donatello* (1942); further collections of essays and critical studies, *Di giorno in giorno* (1954; Day by Day), *Ritratti e profili* (1957; Portraits and Sketches), and *Saggi e vagabondaggi* (1964; Essays and Wanderings); and important translations, including Gottfried von Leibniz's *Nuovi saggi sull'intelletto umano* (1909–11) and Italian versions of Shakespeare's *Merry Wives of Windsor* (1946) and *Othello* (1947).

See: G. Luti, "Emilio Cecchi," in *I critici*, ed. by G. Grana (1963), vol. 3, pp. 2363–94; G. Pampaloni, "Emilio Cecchi," in *Storia della letteratura italiana*, ed. by E. Cecchi and N. Sapegno (1969), vol. 9, pp. 731–48; A. Pellegrini, *Emilio Cecchi: il critico e il poeta* (1969).

T.W.

Cela, Camilo José (1916–), prolific Spanish novelist, short-story writer, and travel diarist, was born in the province of La Coruña but lived largely in Madrid until 1954, when he moved to Majorca, where he has since made his home. He became a member of the Royal Spanish Academy of the Language in 1957 and has now also entered political life as a senator. In 1956 he founded the well-known literary journal *Papeles de Son Armadans*. Although Cela came to literature first through poetry, his primary fame is as a novelist, due to the fact that early in his career he published two of the most esteemed Spanish novels of the postwar period. The first of these, *La familia de Pascual Duarte* (1942; Eng. tr., *Pascual Duarte's Family*, 1946), signals the rebirth of the novel in Spain after the hiatus of the Civil War. Pascual Duarte is a shocking mixture of bloody criminal and pathetic victim of an "evil star" or a destructive social environment. The novel makes this double identity convincing and disturbing through the traditional device of the discovered manuscript (Pascual's prison memoirs) and through a finely calibrated thematic impasse that permits the reader no possible judgmental resolution. The much-used but ill-defined and now dubious critical term "tremendismo" (anguish plus violence?) was coined to describe the impact of *Pascual Duarte*.

Other novels of the 1940s are *Pabellón de reposo* (1943; Eng. tr., *Rest Home*, 1961), a product of Cela's treatment at a tuberculosis sanatorium, and *Nuevas andanzas y desventuras de Lazarillo de Tormes* (1944; New Travels and Misadventures of Lazarillo de Tormes), a modern picaresque on the model of the classic 16th-century novel. Cela's second universally admired novel is *La colmena* (1951; Eng. tr., *The Hive*, 1953). Whereas *Pascual Duarte*'s modernity is thematic, *La colmena*'s is structural. Although it has an obvious antecedent in John Dos Passos's *Manhattan Transfer* (1925), it is a far more vital work than its forerunner. Its technical example brings Spain abreast of the novel of the contemporary world. Early commentators, at the urging of its author, took it to be an "objective" novel, when in fact there are few more subjective writers than Cela. The prominence it gives to social themes, its fragmented structure, the short time span of the action, and its collective protagonist are nevertheless characteristics it has in common with the Spanish "objective" novel of the 1950s. *La colmena* is a portrait of post-Civil War Madrid in 1942, but the reality presented is strongly colored by its author's perspective and his tendency toward caricature.

The 1950s saw a number of other novels, among them the strange *La catira* (1955; The Blonde), with its Venezuelan setting and dialect, and the even more perplexing *Mrs. Caldwell habla con su hijo* (1953; Eng. tr., *Mrs. Caldwell Speaks to Her Son*, 1968), written in the form of a madwoman's letters. In the 1940s and 1950s, Cela also published many volumes of short works that he calls *apuntes* (vignettes) and that focus on picturesque rural or lower-class characters. They tend to be of uneven quality. Among the best are *Esas nubes que pasan* (1945; Those

Clouds Passing By), *El gallego y su cuadrilla* (1951; The Galician and His Bullfight Team), and the four novellas in *El molino de viento* (1956; The Windmill). One of these, "Timoteo el incomprendido" (Eng. tr., "A Misunderstood Genius," 1962), concerns the naive vocation, a theme often parodied by Cela, and is one of his most effective works.

Cela has published a number of travel books based on walking trips through rural Spain. The finest and freshest of these is the first, *Viaje a la Alcarria* (1948; Eng. tr., *Journey to the Alcarria*, 1964). All of Cela's best works reveal a very original combination of documentary observation of lower-class reality, an authorial attitude that blends compassion with cruelty, interest in colloquial language, and a talent for creating vivid characters. No matter how repugnant the subject matter (and much of it is so), humor is a constant.

The decade of the 1960s marks the decline in quality, although certainly not in quantity, of Cela's work. The approaching sterility of content is perhaps signaled by the two volumes of *Los viejos amigos* (1960, 1961; Old Friends), in which for the first time Cela ceases to observe and re-create life around him, opting instead to resuscitate characters from his earlier works. By the time he wrote *Viaje al Pirineo de Lérida* (1965; Journey to the Pyrenees at Lérida), a book based upon notes of a trip taken seven years earlier, the travel books too had lost contact with an observed reality. The 1960s and 1970s have also been the era of Cela's many "documentary" picture-books, the most notorious of which is *Izas, rabizas y colipoterras* (1964; Chippies, Trollops and Trulls), photographs of grotesque but pathetic prostitutes, accompanied by comically inhumane commentary. In recent years Cela's creative gifts seem to have degenerated into mannerism. His language talents are devoted to such linguistic extravagances as *El solitario* (1963), a work totally divorced from life, or the successive volumes of the *Diccionario secreto* of sexual terminology and the *Rol de cornudos* (1976; List of Cuckolds), a dictionary of the uses of a single word. Only with *San Camilo, 1936* (1969), a novel set in a personally observed Madrid just prior to the Civil War, did it seem to some readers that Cela had again produced a work of some importance, but this initial positive reaction has now faded. The novel's techniques seem forced, the usual emphasis on things sexual is here difficult to defend, and the "reality" portrayed, despite the pre-Civil War setting, seems to be identical to that of *La colmena*.

Cela's genius has been for the character sketch. He has the creative gift of life and all of his works—be they travel books, novels, annotated photographs, or his particular type of short story—grow from a focus on a caricatured person. Such a talent lends itself exceedingly well to the travel book or the gallery of types, but less well to the novel. When a structuring device can be found to link the sketches meaningfully, as in the case of *La colmena*, the results are brilliant; when it cannot, as in *Tobogán de hambrientos* (1962; Toboggan of the Hungry), the work remains a string of externally and arbitrarily related vignettes. Cela's highly individual voice has been a major influence on Spanish writers, and although all of his own important work was produced early in life, its brilliance remains undiminished by that fact.

See: A. Zamora Vicente, *Camilo José Cela* (1962); Paul Ilie, *La novelística de Camilo José Cela* (1963); D. W. McPheeters, *Camilo José Cela* (1969). H.L.B.

Celan, Paul, pseud. of Paul Antschel (1920–70), Austrian poet, essayist, and translator, was born in Czernowitz, Bukovina. He lost his Jewish parents in the holocaust and barely managed to escape with his own life. He moved to Vienna in 1947 and in 1948 settled permanently in Paris. Throughout his life he was obsessed by terrifying visions of the holocaust. He eventually drowned himself in the Seine.

Celan's essay *Edgar Jené und der Traum vom Traume* (1948; Edgar Jené and the Dream of the Dream) and the verse of *Der Sand aus den Urnen* (1948; The Sand from the Urns; Eng. tr., part 1 "At the Gate," in *Dimension 7* [1974]) are indebted to surrealism. Many of his early poems were reprinted in *Mohn und Gedächtnis* (1952; Poppy and Memory), the collection that brought the poet fame. Among these is "Todesfuge" (Death Fugue), a visionary portrayal of a death camp from the perspective of the victims and perhaps the best-known postwar German poem. Long melodious lines, striking images, and a concern with the holocaust characterize this early poetry. In the new verse of *Mohn*, the language becomes more restrained; Celan abandons his former style and themes, and the poetic word assumes great significance. These trends continue in *Von Schwelle zu Schwelle* (1955; From Threshold to Threshold) and *Sprachgitter* (1959; Speech-Grille). *Die Niemandsrose* (1963; The No-One's-Rose) marks a return to Jewish themes. Some poems in *Atemwende* (1967; Breath-Turning) resemble those of *Niemandsrose*, but others point forward to the four late collections, the poems of which are short and seem to lack reference to external reality. *Speech-Grille* (1971) and *Selected Poems* (1972) contain translations. *Der Meridian* (1961; Eng. tr., "The Meridian," in *Chicago Review* 29 [Winter 1978]) is a major essay on poetry and poetics. Celan also translated several important poets, including Aleksandr BLOK, Osip E. MANDELSHTAM, Arthur RIMBAUD, and William Shakespeare.

Critics disagree about the underlying themes of Celan's enigmatic verse. Some stress his relationship to the French tradition and see the primacy of language as an all-pervasive theme. Others interpret Celan as a Jewish poet, either an heir of the mystical tradition or a victim of the holocaust.

See: J. Glenn, *Paul Celan* (1973); D. Meinecke, ed., *Über Paul Celan* (1973).   J.G.

Celaya, Gabriel, pseud. of Rafael Gabriel Mugica Celaya (1911–), Spanish poet, was born in the Basque region, where his family owned a business. His literary career was slow to develop because of the conflict between his desire to become a writer and his duties to the family firm. From 1927 to 1935, while studying in Madrid, he lived at the Residencia de Estudiantes. There he had the opportunity to meet the most renowned writers of the period and grow increasingly interested in literature. After finishing his engineering studies he dutifully went back to his home town of San Sebastián to work for his family's company. The personal difficulties that resulted from the publication of his first book, *Marea de silencio* (1935; Tide of Silence), and a literary prize awarded to a second, unpublished book, were factors which motivated him to leave his job in 1936 and move to Madrid, where he became a professional writer. The Civil War (1936–39) forced him to change his plans, and in 1938 he was again working for his family's firm. For several years he experienced the isolation of writing in an absolutely hostile environment and not being able to publish. This caused him to suffer a deep crisis which he overcame through his encounter in 1946 with Amparo Gastón, the woman who helped him change his pessimistic view of the world and begin a new career as a writer. Together they founded "Norte," a publishing house that had a certain influence on the evolution of post-Civil War Spanish poetry. *Tran-*

quilamente hablando (1947; Calmly Speaking), published by Norte, exemplifies Celaya's discovery of the emotions and values of everyday life and his experimentation with a new, realistic poetic language. In 1956 he broke away from his family. By then he had become politically active and had written several books prompted by his new belief in poetry as a means for social change. The main theme of *Paz y concierto* (1953; Peace and Concert) is the brotherhood of men anguished by their human destiny and by social injustice. The same concept is the inspiration behind several other books, including *Cantos iberos* (1955; Iberian Songs). By denying aestheticism in favor of a prosaic, more direct communication of readily available ideas and emotions, his style acquired a directness and simplicity akin to the common spoken language and very appropriate to protest and social testimony. This desire to make poetry work for a social cause was to slacken after a few years, but he is widely considered the most outspoken social poet of the 1950s. In later books the poet expresses his disillusion in poems of the absurd.

Celaya's work includes more than 50 books of poems, several long essays on poetry, innumerable articles, and a few translations of poems by William Blake, Rainer Maria RILKE, Arthur RIMBAUD, and Paul ELUARD.

See: S. Keefe Ugalde, *Gabriel Celaya* (1978).

S.D.-T.

Céline, Louis-Ferdinand, pseud. of Louis-Ferdinand Destouches (1894–1961), French novelist, was born in Courbevoie, a suburb of Paris. He spent his childhood in the city, where he attended public schools and worked as an apprentice. Having enlisted in the cavalry in 1912, he was severely wounded at Ypres in 1914, decorated for heroism, and retired, severely disabled. He studied medicine in Rouen and received his degree in 1924. His doctoral thesis, *La Vie et l'œuvre de Philippe-Ignace Semmelweiss*, is now considered to be the first of his literary works.

After extensive travel, mostly on medical missions for the League of Nations, to Africa, Cuba, and the United States (where he studied problems of social medicine at the Ford factories in Detroit), Destouches returned to Paris and became a practicing physician. In 1932, while working in a clinic at Clichy, he published his first novel, *Voyage au bout de la nuit* (Eng. tr., *Journey to the End of Night*, 1934), and assumed the pseudonym Céline. Awarded the Renaudot Prize and subsequently translated into 17 languages, the work brought instant fame and infamy to its author. Similar reactions of a divided nature greeted Céline's second work, *Mort à crédit* (1936; Eng. tr., *Death on the Installment Plan*, 1938), in which stylistic innovation and a blackened literary vision of life predominate to an even greater extent than in *Voyage*.

A trip to the USSR in 1936 and the menace of another major war are perhaps at the base of the works produced during the second stage of Céline's literary career: the notorious "pamphlets" *Mea Culpa* (1937; Eng. tr., 1937), *Bagatelles pour un massacre* (1937; Trifles for a Massacre), *L'Ecole des cadavres* (1938; The School of Cadavers), and *Les Beaux Draps* (1941; The Fine Mess). Violently racist, filled with diatribes against communism, Zionism, freemasonry, as well as with antiwar sentiments (while, paradoxically, Céline attempted to enlist in the army and became ship's doctor on the *Shella*, sunk by German torpedoes), these works contributed to the author's subsequent arrest and imprisonment on charges of collaboration, as did his trip to Germany (July 1944 or March 1945) and his stay at Sigmaringen, the seat of the exiled Vichy government.

Céline was arrested in Copenhagen in December 1945.

He spent more than a year at the Danish prison (Vesterfangsel) and another four years in exile at Korsør on the Baltic Sea. Exonerated in 1951 by the French, the author returned to his native country and spent the remaining decade of his life at Bellevue, on the outskirts of Paris. His last years were marked by extensive creativity and the publication of a series of important works: *Féerie pour une autre fois* (1952; Fairy Tale for Another Time), *Féerie pour une autre fois II. Normance* (1954), *Entretiens avec le Professeur Y* (1955; Conversations with Professor Y.), *D'un château l'autre* (1957; Eng. tr., *From Castle to Castle*, 1968), *Nord* (1960; Eng. tr., *North*, 1972), and *Rigodon* (1969). Céline's last three novels provide a unique depiction of World War II—the catastrophe as seen from within Germany—as well as being among the most innovative stylistic creations and the greatest visions of doom the author ever produced.

Céline remains one of the most controversial figures of contemporary French literature. His works have been ranked with those of Marcel PROUST, Franz KAFKA, and James Joyce, yet Céline himself has been disparaged as a misanthrope, a nihilist, and a criminal. His complex, adventurous life is frequently confused with the exploits of his antagonists—a confusion perhaps due to his use of first-person narrative and main characters who bear his own name (Ferdinand, Ferdine, Dr. Destouches, Céline). While critical opinion is divided, there is general agreement that Céline is among the greatest innovators in the history of French letters. Céline died on July 1, 1961 (the same day as Ernest Hemingway) and was buried in almost clandestine fashion in a small cemetery at Bas Meudon, yet his fame has continued to grow after his death, as numerous critical studies on him indicate.

See: M. Hanrez, *Céline* (1961); E. Ostrovsky, *Céline and His Vision* (1967); Y. de la Quérière, *Céline et les mots* (1973); F. Vitoux, *Louis-Ferdinand Céline: misère et parole* (1973) and *Bébert le chat de Louis-Ferdinand Céline* (1976); P. H. Day, *Le Miroir allégorique de L.-F. Céline* (1974); B. Knapp, *Céline: Man of Hate* (1974); P. McCarthy, *Céline: A Critical Biography* (1975); *Cahiers Céline I: Céline et l'actualité littéraire: 1932–1957* (1976); F. Gibault, *Céline: le temps des espérances: 1894–1932* (1977).   E.O.

Cendrars, Blaise, pseud. of Frederic-Louis Sauser (1887–1961), Swiss poet and novelist, was born in La Chaux-de-Fonds. The nomadic life imposed upon the Sauser family by the future writer's creative but impractical father permanently marked him. He continually yearned for space and travel; although he made Paris his headquarters and France his adopted country, he never stayed long in one place. A distaste for comformity, an insatiable curiosity, and a remarkable mobility of thought led Cendrars to diversify himself in a literary production overwhelming in its variety and abundance.

A lucid witness of his time, Cendrars was fascinated, in the Baudelairean sense of the term, by "modernity." Big cities, publicity slogans, jazz, and black art were among his favorite subjects. Cendrars's language parallels the restlessness of his travels: it is swift, lively, and seems to flow without effort, even in his very long, often dense, prose sentences. His influence on avant-garde poetry, notably on Guillaume APOLLINAIRE, was decisive. Yet, although Cendrars participated in the cubist and surrealist movements, he always maintained his independence.

Cendrars published chiefly poetry from 1912 to 1924. His best verse, all of which contains autobiographical elements, is found in such volumes as *Les Pâques à New York* (1912; Easter in New York), *Prose du Transsibérien et de la petite Jehanne de France* (1913; Prose of the

Transsiberian and of Little Jehanne of France), *Panama ou les aventures de mes sept oncles* (1918; Panama or the Adventures of My Seven Uncles), and *Dix-neuf poèmes élastiques* (1919; Nineteen Elastic Poems). There are also autobiographical aspects to his prose chronicles, which include *L'Homme foudroyé* (1945; Eng. tr., *The Astonished Man*, 1970), *La Main coupée* (1946; Eng. tr., *Lice*, 1973), *Bourlinguer* (1948; Eng. tr., *Planus*, 1972), and *Le Lotissement du ciel* (1949; The Allotment of Heaven). His three major novels, *L'Or* (1925; Eng. tr., *Sutter's Gold*, 1926), *Moravagine* (1926), and *Les Confessions de Dan Yack* (1929) best show the polarity of Cendrars's personality: behind the active and productive man was an individual both ascetic and contemplative.

See: J. C. Lovey, *Situation de Blaise Cendrars* (1965).
                                                      U.S.

Čep, Jan (1902–74), Czech short-story writer and novelist, was the most gifted of the Czech ruralists. He was born in Myslechovice, near Litovel, in northern Moravia. After studying English and French at the University of Prague, without taking a degree, he became a reader in a large publishing house, and did much translating from the works of writers such as Joseph Conrad, Georges BERNANOS, and Henri Pourrat. In 1948, after the Communist takeover of Czechoslovakia, Čep emigrated to France, where he worked as an active opponent of the Communist regime. He was married to the daughter of the French critic Charles DU BOS.

Unlike the other ruralists—Josef Knap, František Křelina, and F. V. Kříž—Čep was a spiritual person who struggled for religious certainty and peace. In his works he usually depicted the "return of the native" who, broken by urban civilization, goes back to his rural home, to the soil, and finally to religion, which often affords only a glimpse of "our second home." There is a strong individual tone in Čep's highly sensitive style—ranking with the best in modern Czech prose—in the magic of his lyrical metaphors, and in the refined melancholy that pervades all his stories, sketches, and fictitious diaries and journals. A certain monotony of theme and lack of invention prevented Čep from reaching a wide public, but he is considered one of the most cultivated and genuine of modern Czech writers.

Čep's collections of short stories include *Zeměžluč* (1931; Bitter Herb), *Letnice* (1932; Whitsuntide), *Děravý plášt'* (1934; The Tattered Coat), *Modrá a zlatá* (1938; Blue and Gold), *Tvář pod pavučinami* (1941; The Face under the Cobwebs), and *Polní tráva* (1947; Grass of the Field). He also published a novel, *Hranice stínu* (1935; The Boundary of the Shadow), as well as a shorter fictional work, *Příbuzenstvo* (1938; The Relatives). A final story, "Před zavřenými dveřmi" (1953; In Front of Closed Doors), treats the tragic fate of the emigrant.

See: K. Sezima, "Jan Čep," in *Mlází* (1936); B. Fučík, "Básník dvojího domova," in J. Čep, *Zeměžluč, Letnice, Děravý plášt'* (1969).   R.W.

Cerdà, Jordi-Pere, pseud. of Antoni Cayrol (1920–), French-Catalan writer, was born in Sallagosa in the French Cerdagne and has resided in Perpignan since 1960, where he is a book dealer. He is today the best-known of the Catalan writers in the Roussillon, the Catalonian region of France. His pseudonym originated by chance, when the director of the journal *Tramontane* changed his signature from "Un cerdà" (a Cerdagnian) to "Jordi-Pere Cerdà." With this name he wrote *La guatlla i la garba* (1951; The Quail and the Chaff), *Tota llengua fa foc* (1955; Every Tongue Makes Fire), and *Ocells per a Cristofol*

(1961; Birds for Christopher), collected in his *Obra Poètica*. Included in the same collection are: *Cerdaneses* (Cerdagnian Topics), *La pell de Narcis* (The Skin of Narcissus), *Dietari de l'alba* (Diary of the Dawn), *Un barc sense armes* (A Boat without Arms), and *L'agost de l'any* (The August of the Year).

Cerdà's *Contalles de Cerdanya* (1961; Old Tales from Cerdagne) and his theatrical works, *Angeleta* (1952), *La set de la terra* (1952; The Thirst of the Earth), *El sol de la Ginesta* (perf. 1964; Four Women and the Sun), and *Un dia com un altre* (A Day Like Any Other), are also of great literary interest.

Both in his poetry and in his theater Cerdà reveals his love of and poetically transforms the landscape of the High Cerdagne in the Roussillon. Jordi-Pere Cerdà is clearly mindful of the events and realities of the times without denying the rural essence of his land, which he experiences firsthand.

The work of writers from the Roussillon, including Josep Sebastià Pons, the most prominent member of this group, is not sufficiently esteemed within the domain of Catalan literature. Jordi-Pere Cerdà has done a great deal to publicize the problems of writers in France who express themselves in Catalan, even though many of the same writers also write in French. Cerdà is no exception: he prefers French for his ideological works, in which he defends the Catalan language and culture.

The renaissance of Occitania has drawn attention to the work of men like Cerdà in the south of France or in "Catalonia-North," as those who have recently rediscovered the concept of the "Paìssos Catalans" like to call it. Cerdà has deservedly received some of the attention recently given to writers from outside the "Principat." In all of his works, whether poetry or drama, Cerdà's voice keeps alive the flame of the Catalan language in the Catalonia across the Pyrenees.

See: F. de B. Moll, Prologue to J.-P. Cerdà, *La set de la terra* (1956); P. Verdaguer, Introduction to J.-P. Cerdà, *Obra poetica* (1966); A. Manent, "L'obra del rossellonés Jordi-Pere Cerdà" in *Literatura catalana en debat* (1969).

J.F.C.

Cernuda, Luis (1902–63), Spanish poet and essayist, was born in Seville and graduated from its university. He studied law, philosophy and letters from 1919 until 1925, and was fortunate enough to have Pedro SALINAS as professor of Spanish literature. The older poet took an interest in Cernuda's work, gave early encouragement, and arranged for him to publish his first poems in the prestigious Madrid journal *Revista de Occidente,* in December 1925. When his widowed mother died in 1928, Cernuda left Seville for Madrid. The following year he took a post as lecturer in Spanish at Toulouse, again with Salinas's intercession. He visited Paris and returned to earn an unsatisfactory living by working in a Madrid bookstore. During the years of the Spanish Republic he was especially close to Manuel ALTOLAGUIRRE and Concha Méndez. He also followed the political inclinations of surrealism and contributed to the Madrid journal *Octubre*. When the Civil War overtook Spain, Cernuda worked for the Republican cause in Spain (Madrid and Valencia), France, and England, where he arrived in February 1938 to begin his long exile. In England he first taught at a school in Surrey. In January 1939 he obtained the post of lecturer in Spanish at Glasgow University. He later taught at Cambridge and the Instituto Español in London. In 1947 he immigrated to the United States to assume a position as professor of Spanish at Mount Holyoke. He remained until 1952 when, following a vacation in Mexico, he decided to become a permanent resident there. Al-though he was obliged to earn his living by teaching for regular periods in California, in the last years of his life he spent as much time as possible in Mexico. These sojourns allowed him to return to a milieu like that of his youth in Seville. As a matter of principle, he never returned to Spain, although he maintained contact with his family there. He died suddenly of a heart attack in Concha Méndez's home in Mexico City.

Until the outbreak of the Civil War, the development of Cernuda's poetry followed a pattern typical for a young member of his generation. His first book, later drastically revised, was *Perfil del aire* (1927; The Air in Profile). It shows an originality of tone and persona that for many reviewers was obscured by the evidence of Cernuda's literary influences. In the main, critics found *Perfil* formally correct in the manner of Jorge GUILLÉN and vaguely symbolist, after Stéphane MALLARMÉ, whereas Madrid literary circles admired the influence of Góngora and the "dehumanized art" described by José ORTEGA Y GASSET. Then, with *Un río, un amor* (1929; A River, A Love) and *Los placeres prohibidos* (1931; Forbidden Pleasures), Cernuda moved, with other young members of his generation, into the sphere of French surrealism. Although to date no one has given an adequate account of surrealism in Spain, J. M. Hinojosa and Juan LARREA seem to have been important conduits. As the titles suggest, in these two books Cernuda also gives his first, oblique expression to an important theme of his mature poetry, homosexual love. *Donde habite el olvido* (1934; Where Forgetfulness Dwells), his next book, is a homage to Gustavo BÉCQUER and marks his accession to a new diaphaneity. But as Derek Harris remarks, what really sets this book apart, in addition to the profound spiritual affinity with Bécquer, is the fact that in the last poem in the collection Cernuda gives the first evidence of his encounter with Friedrich Hölderlin's poetry. Cernuda's formal and thematic range became enriched with the addition of long hymnlike, narrative poems, and a cast of divinities in human form inhabiting classical Mediterranean settings. The melancholy romantic consciousness that earlier spoke through the *Perfil* poems, through Golden Age stanzaic forms like the eclogue, and through the mask of surrealism, finds its adequate vehicle in the long cadences of a new, somewhat mannered style. Later, Cernuda's study and translation of English romantic poetry reaffirmed the unusually important place poems about nature have in his work. No other contemporary Spanish poet except Miguel de UNAMUNO is comparable in this regard. In sum, his collected poems, entitled *La realidad y el deseo* (1936; 1940; 1958; 1964; Reality and Desire), run the entire gamut of generational styles. Yet throughout his complete poems—successive books were added under the general title—there is an extraordinary consistency due to the development of a private mythology which is in perfect accord with a prevailing tone of melancholy, unsatisfied desire, and intermittent defiance. Repeatedly, Cernuda turned to a limited number of themes: love, desire, nature, art, the self and the other, social repression, exile and the homeland. This narrow range is more than compensated for, nevertheless, by his inventiveness at finding mythical, historical, and mundane embodiments for his themes.

When World War II was over, Cernuda had completed *Las Nubes* (1940; Clouds), *Como quien espera el alba* (1947; As One Awaiting Dawn), *Vivir sin estar viviendo* (1949; Living without Being Alive), and *Con las horas contadas* (1956; Time Meted Out). Cernuda's final book of poems, *Desolación de la quimera* (The Chimera's Despair) was first published in 1958 and subsequently incorporated into the final edition of *La realidad*.

In the middle 1950s interest in Cernuda quickened among young Spanish poets, making him one of the first members of the Generation of 1927 to be critically rehabilitated in Spain. Cernuda's frankness about his homosexuality, together with his rejection of marginality, gave his later work a strong ethical cast that was not lost on Spanish poets living in the Spain of Francisco Franco, or on other contemporary writers such as Octavio Paz and Juan Goytisolo. Today, Cernuda has moved, in the estimation of poets and critics, from a relatively minor position to being one of the five major poets of his generation, along with Federico García Lorca, Salinas, Guillén, and Vicente Aleixandre.

In addition to his poetry, Cernuda is the author of a translation of Shakespeare's *Troilus and Cressida,* two collections of prose poems, *Ocnos* (1942) and *Variaciones sobre tema mexicano* (1952; Variations on a Mexican Theme), as well as numerous perceptive essays.

See: O. Paz, *Cuadrivio* (1965); P. Silver, *Luis Cernuda: el poeta en su leyenda* (1972); D. Harris, *Luis Cernuda: A Study of His Poetry* (1973). P.S.

Césaire, Aimé (1913–), French Caribbean poet, dramatist, and essayist was born in Martinique and studied in Paris. With Léopold Sédar Senghor and Léon Damas, he founded the periodical *Etudiant noir* (1934; The Black Student). His bitter confrontation with the squalor of his homeland prompted *Cahier d'un retour au pays natal* (1939; Eng. tr., *Return to My Native Land*, 1968), an intense, often hermetic poem that links self-discovery with the revalorization of black consciousness and pride, here for the first time given the name "négritude." His review *Tropiques* (1941–43), launched in Martinique, advocated surrealism (*see* French literature) as a "miraculous weapon" of liberation. To this vein belongs the poetry collected in *Les Armes miraculeuses* (1946; abridged Eng. tr., in *State of the Union,* 1966), *Soleil cou coupé* (1948), *Corps perdu* (1950), *Ferrements* (1960; abridged Eng. tr., in *State of the Union,* 1966), and *Cadastre* (1961; Eng. tr., *Cadastre: Poems,* 1973).

Césaire's drama is more accessible, centering on the issue of decolonization, the point at which black progressive leaders face black reactionary opposition. The sacrificed rebel is an allegorical hero in *Et les chiens se taisaient* (1956; And the Dogs Became Silent); a historical Haitian king is the protagonist of *La Tragédie du roi Christophe* (1963; Eng. tr., *The Tragedy of King Christophe,* 1969); and *Une Saison au Congo* (1966; Eng. tr., *A Season in the Congo,* 1968) retraces Patrice Lumumba's rise and fall. Césaire's *La tempête* (1969), an adaptation of Shakespeare's *Tempest*, focuses on the relationship between Prospero, the white master, and his slaves, the black Caliban and the mulatto Ariel.

Césaire's active political career as Martinique's deputy in the French parliament and as mayor of Fort-de-France has also been marked by a continued reflection on the problems of leadership. *Discours sur le colonialisme* (1950; Eng. tr., *Discourse on Colonialism,* 1972) denounces Western greed masquerading as a civilizing mission. *Lettre à Maurice Thorez* (1956; Eng. tr., *Letter to Maurice Thorez,* 1957) explains Césaire's reasons for leaving the Communist Party and accuses the Party of using the struggle of the colonized peoples for its own ends. *Toussaint Louverture* (1960) analyzes that complex precursor of the movement of Haitian independence.

See: L. Kesteloot, *Aimé Césaire: l'homme et l'œuvre* (1973) and *Black Writers in French* (1974). Y.G.

Cesarić, Dobriša (1902–), Croatian poet, was born in Slavonska Požega. After studying in Osijek an Zagreb, he became active as a poet in the 1930s, issuing one of his best collections, *Lirika* (Lyrics), in 1931. In 1945 he was elected to the Yugoslav Academy in Zagreb. Cesarić's entire opus contains no more than 100 poems, mostly short, of which he published two collections in the 1960s under the title *Izabrane pjesme* (1960, 1964; Selected Poems). He is also known as a translator, mostly of Russian and German poetry. Through his translations and his study of such Croatian forerunners as Antun Gustav Matoš and Tin Ujević, Cesarić has absorbed certain features of other writers' works, but his own poetry is far from mere imitation. Those who are familiar with his harmonious, carefully chiseled verses could recognize his poems even if they did not bear his mane.

Cesarić writes about love, nature, and his native Slavonia. Avoiding bombastic language, he tends to choose as his subject a common natural phenomenon—a cloud, a waterfall—in which he discovers profound symbolic meaning. Cesarić's poetry also deals, however, with the ugly aspects of the modern city, giving a sympathetic portrayal of the victims of social injustice. Yet he is not a revolutionary, for he is skeptical of radical gestures. Cesarić has also written some patriotic poems, notably "Trubač sa Seine—Matoš u Parizu" (1938; The Trumpeter on the Seine—Matoš in Paris).

See: J. Kaštelan, "Doživljaj i riječ," *Rep* 4 (1953): 321–29; V. Pavletić, *Kako su stvarali književnici* (1956), pp. 303–11; D. Jeremić, *Prsti nevernog Tome* (1965), pp. 101–16. A.K.

Céspedes, Alba de (1911–), Italian novelist, was born in Rome. Her paternal grandfather was the first president of Cuba. Her father served as Cuban ambassador at various capitals, including Rome. Her mother was Italian. De Céspedes is herself an Italian citizen, married to Franco Bounous of the Italian foreign service. She has lived in Cuba, the United States, the Soviet Union, and Pakistan, among other places. She now divides her time between Paris and Rome. De Céspedes has had a long and active career as a journalist. In 1944 she founded the review *Mercurio,* which she edited for four years. She has also served on the staffs of *Epoca* (where she had her own column) and *La stampa*. During World War II, she crossed the lines to broadcast from Radio Partigiana in Bari.

De Céspedes was a precocious writer, writing poetry and plays even as a child. By 1935 her stories were appearing in Italian magazines. Her novel *Nessuno torna indietro* (1938; Eng. tr., *There's No Turning Back*, 1941) brought her worldwide recognition and has been translated into 24 languages. Her most characteristic and technically best works are *Dalla parte di lei* (1949; Eng. tr., *The Best of Husbands,* 1952), the story of a marriage eroded by poor communication between the spouses, and *Quaderno proibito* (1952; Eng. tr., *The Secret,* 1958), a woman's analysis of her needs and relationships. Other works include *Prima e dopo* (1955; Eng. tr., *Between Then and Now,* 1959), *Il rimorso* (1963; Eng. tr., *Remorse,* 1967), *La bambolona* (1967; Eng. tr., 1970), and *Nel buio della notte* (1976; In the Dark of the Night). *Chansons des filles de mai* (1969; Songs of the Maytime Girls) is a volume of poems written in French (later translated into Italian by the author) dealing with the 1968 student demonstrations in Paris.

De Céspedes is a feminist in the sense that the focus of her interest is the life of the woman of today under the tensions of both traditional responsibilities and the pressures born of emancipation. Doubtless because of her concerns, she has been somewhat slighted by Italian critics—most of whom are men—who either ignore her or dismiss her as facile and superficial. Yet the scope of her public testifies to the appeal of her work. Her books invariably sell well in Italy, and she has been more widely translated than any Italian novelist except Alberto Mo-RAVIA, with whose work her own has some recognizable affinities. If her characters are not especially complicated, they are well drawn and convincing, and she has the rare gift of being able to tell a story economically and effectively.

See: G. Pullini, in *Il romanzo italiano del dopoguerra* (1961), pp. 372–76. T.G.B.

Chacel, Rosa (1898–), Spanish novelist and poet, was born in Valladolid. Her years of artistic formation were spent in Madrid, where she came in contact with the community of writers who contributed to the *Revista de Occidente*. Except for the periods 1930–39, part of which she spent in Italy, and 1961–62, she has lived outside of Spain. In 1939, after the Civil War, she established her residence in Buenos Aires. Since 1962 she has lived in Rio de Janeiro.

Chacel made her debut as a novelist in 1930 with *Estación, ida·y vuelta* (Station, Round Trip). Like the rest of her work, this novel conforms to the aesthetic of the "dehumanized" novel peculiar to those writers of the Generation of 1927, such as Francisco AYALA, Antonio ESPINA, and Benjamín JARNÉS, who followed the novelistic theories of José ORTEGA Y GASSET.

Her novelistic production has a clearly defined intellectual character. What sets it apart is her incessant exploration of the inner depths of her characters and her analysis of their states of mind. This constant projection of the "internal," at the expense of the "external," produces abstract and purely cerebral characters. *Memorias de Leticia Valle* (1945) is an exploration of the inner history of a 12-year-old girl who experiences characteristically adult problems. Here, as in the rest of her novels, the main character's intimate problem (her sexual attraction to her teacher) captivates the reader. The presentation, in a fluid and well-modulated prose enlivened by the author's technical expertise, also helps to maintain the reader's attention. But in this and other of Chacel's novels, the external world in which the character moves is not clearly defined, so that the true implications of the character's action are not as comprehensible as could be desired.

Chacel's novels anticipate the "new novel" which Juan BENET introduced in Spain in 1967, with his *Volverás a Región*. The similarities between the writers of the "new novel" and Rosa Chacel stem from a common antirealistic view of the novel characterized by a preference for discourse over dialogue, the recourse to memory instead of direct action, a taste for ambiguity, and the use of periphrastic phrasing.

As is the case with other Spanish writers in exile, Chacel's novels were unknown in Spain for many years. During the final years of the regime of Francisco Franco, her books were published in Spain with success. Worthy of attention are: *Teresa* (1941), *La sinrazón* (1960; The Wrong), *Icada, Nevda, Diada* (1971), and *La confesión* (1971).

See: J. R. Marra-López, *Narrativa española fuera de España* (1963), pp. 135–47; E. G. de Nora, *La novela española contemporánea*, vol. 3 (1962), pp. 204–07.
P.G.C.

Chadourne, Marc (1895–), French novelist, was born in Brive-la-Gaillarde. He was the younger brother of Louis Chadourne (1891–1924), a well-known poet and novelist who wrote about adolescent psychology, as in *L'Inquiète*

adolescence (1920; Restless Adolescence), and adventure, as in *Le Pot au noir* (1923; The Blackman's Pot). Marc Chadourne was a colonial administrator who traveled and lived in countries that later served as settings for his books. After World War II, he came to the United States and started a second career as a university professor.

Chadourne's first, widely acclaimed novel, *Vasco* (1927), which has a South Sea Islands setting, is a poetic work that suggests the disenchantment of the Westerner in the face of a Tahiti invaded by tourists and merchants and riddled with sickness. Novels directly inspired by Chadourne's travels and cosmopolitan experiences are *Chine* (1932; China), *L'U.R.S.S. sans passion* (1933; The USSR without Passion), and *Extrême-Occident* (1935; Far East). Other works, such as *Cécile de la Folie* (1930), which was awarded the Femina Prize, *Absence* (1933), *Dieu créa d'abord Lilith* (1937; God First Created Lilith), *La clé perdue* (1947; The Lost Key), and *Gladys ou les artifices* (1950; Gladys or the Stratagems) continue, to some extent, his exotic vein, but become increasingly psychological in nature. Chadourne also became more interested in spiritual, philosophical, and religious problems. Among his works on these themes is *Quand Dieu se fit américain* (1950; When God Became an American), a historical tale of the Mormon epic. He also published a well-documented, vivid biography of the prose writer Restif de la Bretonne (1734–1806). P.Br.

Chamson, André (1900–), French novelist and essayist, was born in Nîmes and grew up in the Cévennes Mountains. The life and people of this region provide the subject of his fiction. In *Roux le bandit* (1925; Eng. tr., *Roux the Bandit*, 1929), *Les Hommes de la route* (1927; Eng. tr., *The Road*, 1929), and *Le Crime des justes* (1928; Eng. tr., *The Crime of the Just*, 1930), grouped under the title *Suite Cénévole* in 1948, Chamson depicted the nonconformity, independence, and moral strength of the mountain peasants. Yet except for dialogue, his language is literary, not regional. Chamson's characters struggle for survival against modern civilization and against a rugged natural environment that, in some respects, they themselves resemble. His is a silent, solitary hero, isolated through personal choice or by destiny. In subsequent novels, Chamson's view expands from the regional to the national level, and he examines the political and ethical problems of World War II and postwar years. In some of his later works, however, he returns to his heritage.

Chamson was elected president of PEN International in 1956. He has been a member of the Académie Française since 1957 and director of the French National Archives since 1960.

See: L. Rolfe, *The Novels of André Chamson* (1971).
M.I.M.

Chapygin, Aleksey Pavlovich (1870–1937), Russian writer, one of the founders of the Soviet historical novel, was born in the province of Olonets. His northern peasant origins are to a large extent reflected in his writings. He is best known for his two novels about peasant uprisings in the 17th century, *Gulyashchiye lyudi* (1934–37; Itinerant Folk) and *Razin Stepan* (1926–27; Eng. tr., *Stepan Razin*, 1946). *Razin Stepan* is now considered a classic. Chapygin drew upon folkloric sources for both the style of the novel and his positive and romanticized portrait of Razin. The Soviets excuse this modernization of history as a justifiable polemic against the negative portrayal of Razin by 19th-century writers.

See: B. S. Valbe, *Aleksey Pavlovich Chapygin: ocherk zhizni i tvorchestva* (2d ed., 1959). L.T.

Char, René (1907–), French poet, was born in L'Isle-sur-la-Sorgue. He has remained attached to his native Vaucluse. His poetry, while marked by a long communion with nature, is fired with a moral fervor. Instead of advocating pastoral retreat, it expresses Char's commitment to an age whose absurdity he acknowledges, like his friend Albert CAMUS, finding its sources of renewal in images of fields, rivers, and rocks.

A tense idealism places Char's work in the line of Arthur RIMBAUD, to whom he has paid explicit homage. The early collection *Les Cloches sur le cœur* (1928; Bells on the Heart), however, reveals a seminal reading of Pierre REVERDY, its lighting penumbral, its mood unquiet. One year after the publication of this volume, Char met Paul ELUARD, who became a close companion. From 1929 he allied himself with the surrealist group (*see* FRENCH LITERATURE), and in 1930 he, André BRETON, and Eluard cosigned the "poem" *Ralentir Travaux* (Slow Down, Road Work). Char participated actively in one of the liveliest periods of the movement, helped to found the review *Le Surréalisme au service de la révolution,* and wrote a collection of poems under the title *Le Marteau sans maître* (1934; The Hammer without a Master). This volume, alternately giving voice to suffering and love, is the record of an inner conflict exacerbated to the point of crisis.

As he matured, Char found an aesthetic distance from his subject and consolidated an attitude that went beyond tragedy. This new development is already apparent in the rejuvenated language of *Moulin premier* (1937; First Mill), and its splendid resolution appears in *Le Visage nuptial* (1938; The Nuptial Face). The following year, Char was mobilized and served in the artillery in Alsace. Having returned to Vaucluse after the French defeat, he was sought by the Vichy police for alleged Communist affiliations and was obliged to flee. He became a member of the Armée Secrète and head of a Resistance sector; later, from 1943 to 1945, he held the rank of captain in the Forces Françaises Combattantes in charge of a parachute reception unit. *Feuillets d'Hypnos* (1946; Leaves of Hypnos), his prose record of these war years, articulates with vigor the experience of comradeship in the face of imminent death. Yet Char's creative harvest is seen above all in the poems of *Fureur et mystère* (1948; Madness and Mystery), which convey the full intensity of the poet's self-qualifying polarities of harshness and temperance. One can understand why Camus hailed it as one of the most important books of French poetry since Rimbaud's *Les Illuminations.*

Having reached his artistic and moral maturity with *Fureur et mystère,* Char continued to evolve as a writer and to seek new modes of expression, including the theater. During this period, his work was acutely responsive to the perils of the time, while also bearing witness to his personal turmoil. One notable work is the volume of poems *Lettera amorosa* (1953; Love Letter), an anguished exploration of love's absence that nonetheless concludes on a hymn of thanksgiving to the enduring notion of love, envisioned as an image wrenched from pain or a godhead newly realized. Several subsequent collections of Char's work have been published, the most important of which are *Commune Présence* (1964; Common Presence), a kind of summa arranged in eight major clusters or verbal constellations signifying his unceasing conflict with lovelessness; *Le Nu perdu* (1971; The Lost Nude), austere in tone and language, which describes the self-discipline of the sensibility; and, finally, *Aromates chasseurs* (1976; Hunting Aromatics), in which the Orion myth, implicit in Char's earlier work, becomes the symbol of transcendent hope—"un oubli servant d'étoile."

See: G. Mounin, *Avez-vous lu Char?* (1947); V. A. La Charité, *The Poetics and the Poetry of René Char* (1968); *L'Herne* 15 (1971); M. A. Caws, *The Presence of René Char* (1976).   J.L.

Chardonne, Jacques, pseud. of Jacques Boutelleau (1884–1968), French novelist, was born in Barbezieux of a French father and an American mother, Anna Haviland. A sensitive, passionate child, he early showed a leaning toward writing, yet he did not start on a literary career until he was 35. His memories of the happy days of his childhood are related in two books of familiar essays, *Le Bonheur de Barbezieux* (1938; The Happiness of Barbezieux) and *Chronique privée* (1940; Private Chronicle). In 1910, he became a member of the P. V. Stock publishing firm, which he later headed (1921–43). In 1915, however, his health failing, he was sent to Chardonne, a village near Vevey, Switzerland, to recover. It was during this convalescence of five years that he began his first book, *L'Epithalame* (1921; Eng. tr., *Epithalamium,* 1923), a novel concerned with the spiritual problems of married love. Only in marriage, Chardonne thinks, do men and women reveal the secrets of their hearts and show their full, complex personalities. He deals with the same theme in *Eva* (1930; Eng. tr., *Eva; or, The Interrupted Diary,* 1930) and *Claire* (1931) and in most of his other works. Besides his exquisite short essays and reflections about love, collected in *L'Amour, c'est beaucoup plus que l'amour* (1937; Love Is Much More than Love), his outstanding achievement is probably the cyclical novel *Les Destinées sentimentales* (1934–35; Sentimental Destinies), in which he presents not only the sentimental problems of husband and wife, but also a faithful picture of French family and business life and of French provincial society. Chardonne has been widely admired for his fine portrayal of characters, for the restraint and beauty of his style, and for the moral worth of his message.

See: G. Guitard-Auviste, *La Vie de Jacques Chardonne et son art* (1953).   P.Br.

Chartier, Emile: *see* ALAIN.

Châteaubriant, Alphonse de (1877–1951), French novelist, was born in Rennes and spent most of his life at the Château de la Motte Saint-Sulpice in Vendée. A member of the country nobility, he approached literature with typical detachment and reserve, always preferring the studious and tranquil life of the provinces.

Châteaubriant was already in his thirties when, in 1911, his first novel, *Monsieur des Lourdines* (Eng. tr., *The Keynote,* 1912), received the Goncourt Prize. It related the moving story of an old country gentleman compelled to sell family estates to pay off debts contracted by a prodigal son. Poetic language, subdued emotion, and a good plot revealed the author of this book to be a writer of unusual talent. Unspoiled by success, Châteaubriant waited 12 years before offering the public his next novel, *La Brière* (1923; Eng. tr., *The Peat-Cutters,* 1927). This work sets forth a somber but powerful picture of the primitive life of the people of La Brière, a region of peat bogs situated in the most remote section of Brittany, near the mouth of the Loire. So convincingly has Châteaubriant analyzed the fears and superstitions of the Briérons and described their drab and gloomy countryside that one soon has the impression of reading about people and places long familiar. In *La Brière,* Châteaubriant's artistic temperament found its most perfect expression. *La Réponse du Seigneur* (1933; The Lord's Reply) is the story of a gentleman of the old school, a descendant of the Templars and the last of his family. This novel falls far below the standard set in *Monsieur des Lourdines* and

La Brière. Châteaubriant also produced two other novels, *La Meute* (1927; The Pack) and *Au pays de Brière* (1935; In the Land of Brière).

It is a cruel irony of fate that, as a result of a trip to Germany, such a great artist should have written in 1937 *La Gerbe des forces: nouvelle Allemagne* (The Sheaf of Forces: New Germany), an ill-timed, injudicious praise of Nazism. A director of the pro-German newspaper *La Gerbe* during World War II, Châteaubriant died in Germany, an exile during the last years of his life.   P.Br.

Chavée, Achille (1906–70), Belgian poet, was born in Charleroi in Hainaut, the industrial and revolutionary province that was one of the centers of Belgian surrealism. Although the relations between this surrealism and that of Paris remained loose, André BRETON had greeted with enthusiasm Chavée's first two volumes of poetry, *Pour cause déterminée* (1935; For a Determined Reason) and *Le Cendrier de chair* (1936; The Ashtray of Flesh). Chavée then left for Spain in order to fight in the ranks of the international brigades. *Une Fois pour toutes* (1938; Once and for All) reflects this experience. Returning home, sick, he soon confronted another test—his opposition to the Nazis condemned him to a clandestine existence. After 1945, Chavée's social activity was more closely linked to poetry, in which he saw the expression of liberty and of desire. Without overestimating the liberating function of the poet, he saw poetic activity as a destroying of myths, as a shattering of alienating languages. *D'ombre et de sang* (1946; Of Shadow and of Blood) was the first in a series of nearly 20 collections of poems and aphorisms, among which were *Ecrit sur un drapeau qui brûle* (1948; Written on a Burning Flag), *Catalogue du seul* (1956; Catalog of the One Alone), *l'Eléphant blanc* (1961; The White Elephant), *Décoctions* (1964), and especially *De vie et mort naturelles* (1965; On Natural Life and Natural Death) and *Le Grand Cardiaque* (1969; The Serious Cardiac Case). Although a surrealist, Chavée did not accept the total primacy of the unconscious. His strength lay in his faithfulness to the passing moment, a faithfulness that preserves a diversity of form. His caustic aphorisms are particularly striking.

See: A. Miguel, *Achille Chavée* (1969); J. Vovelle, *Le Surréalisme en Belgique: histoire du mouvement surréaliste en Belgique* (1969); C. Hubin and G. Legros, "Introduction à la lecture d'Achille Chavée," *CAT* 12 (1970): 7–30.   J.-M.K.

Chekhov, Anton Pavlovich (1860–1904), Russian playwright and short-story writer, was born in Taganrog, southern Russia, to parents of serf origin. Chekhov became independent at the age of 16, supporting himself when his father's bankruptcy stranded him alone in Taganrog and later paying his own way through medical school at Moscow University. To finance his education and help support his family, Chekhov published numerous satirical and topical pieces in humor journals between 1880 and 1885, including his two early full-length novels, *Nenuzhnaya pobeda* (1882; Useless Victory) and *Drama na okhote* (1884; Eng. tr., *The Shooting Party*, 1926). He completed his studies and began practicing medicine in country hospitals in 1884.

Chekhov matured as a literary artist in 1886–87, when he pioneered a new form of concise, compact, and seemingly plotless short story, written in accordance with the recipe outlined in a letter to his brother Aleksandr: "1. Absence of lengthy verbiage of political-social-economic nature; 2. total objectivity; 3. truthful descriptions of persons and objects; 4. extreme brevity; 5. audacity and originality: flee the stereotype; 6. compassion." These specifications well describe such innovative and masterful stories of that period as "Toska" (1886; Eng. tr., "Misery," 1915), "Panikhida" (1886; Eng. tr., "The Requiem," 1908), "Grisha" (1886; Eng. tr., 1915), "Anyuta" (1886; Eng. tr., 1915), "Khoristka" (1886; Eng. tr., "The Chorus Girl," 1915), and "Agafya" (1886; Eng. tr., 1914). By 1888–89, when Chekhov began publishing in the leading literary journals, he turned to larger narrative forms, producing long stories that experimented with a variety of diverse narrative vantage points. "Step" (1888; Eng. tr., "The Steppe," 1915) mingles the perceptions of a little boy with the hidden voice of an omniscient adult narrator; "Skuchnaya istoriya" (1899; Eng. tr., "A Boring Story," 1915) shows the world through the eyes of a dying aged intellectual; "Imeniny" (1888; Eng. tr., "The Name-Day Party," 1916) depicts the world through the eyes of a pregnant woman; and "Pripadok" (1888; Eng. tr., "An Attack of Nerves," 1916) examines brothels through the eyes of a sensitive and naive young student.

Chekhov's rejection of traditional narrative techniques and his refusal to indulge in obvious sociological preaching incurred the wrath of liberal and radical critics of the 1880s and 1890s, who repeatedly denounced him as uninvolved and amoral. He was championed, however, by such leading writers as Nikolay LESKOV, Lev TOLSTOY, and Vladimir KOROLENKO. Chekhov's plays *Ivanov* (1887, rev. 1889; Eng. tr., 1923) and *Leshy* (1889; Eng. tr., *The Wood Demon*, 1926) point out the absurdity of the stereotypes basic to the thinking of the Russian liberal intelligentsia and contrast the reality and value of constructive work and of nature conservation with the sterility of the abstract sociological theorizing that was typical of the age.

The failure of *The Wood Demon* and his inability to complete a projected long novel led Chekhov to withdraw from literature temporarily for the sake of a research trip to the penal colony on Sakhalin. In 1890 he conducted a medical-statistical census on that island, hoping to use the results for his doctoral dissertation. The trip resulted in a book on the penal colony (1894), which helped alleviate the conditions of the settlers, and in three important stories: "Gusev" (1890; Eng. tr., 1917), "V ssylke" (1892; Eng. tr., "In Exile," 1903), and "Ubiystvo" (1895; Eng. tr., "The Murder," 1916).

In 1892, Chekhov settled on his own estate at Melikhovo, where he lived until 1898. During that time he operated a free medical clinic for the neighboring peasants, participated in famine relief, worked as a medical inspector during cholera epidemics, and served as a volunteer census taker. His major long stories of the Melikhovo period are as dense with meaning as most complex novels of ideas. These stories include "Duel" (1891; Eng. tr., "The Duel," 1916); "Palata nomer 6" (1892; Eng. tr., "Ward Number Six," 1916) and "Chorny monakh" (1894; Eng. tr., "The Black Monk," 1903), both of which cast doubt on the usual division between sanity and madness; and "Rasskaz neizvestnogo cheloveka" (1893; Eng. tr., "An Anonymous Story," 1916), which confronts the issue of revolutionary violence. Other major works of this period are "Babye tsarstvo" (1894; Eng. tr., "A Woman's Kingdom," 1916), a delicately crafted study of a woman caught between two social strata; "Moya zhizn" (1896; Eng. tr., "My Life," 1917), a story of one man's rebellion against social institutions; and "Muzhiki" (1897; Eng. tr., "The Peasants," 1908), a shattering examination of rural poverty.

Chekhov's breakthrough as an innovative playwright came in his plays *Chayka* (1896; Eng. tr., *The Seagull*, 1923) and *Dyadya Vanya* (1899; Eng. tr., *Uncle Vanya*, 1923), the second being a reworking of *The Wood Demon*.

In these plays the predictable and clear-cut structure of the well-made 19th-century play is abandoned, dramatic developments and conflicts are internalized, and traditional theatrical collisions and conflicts are replaced by a drama of noncommunication and nonhappening. The resulting dramatic mode is more subtle and ultimately more realistic and affected the subsequent development of all 20th-century Western drama.

Because of tuberculosis, Chekhov's last years were spent in Nice and Yalta. It was there that he wrote his last great stories: the 1898 trilogy about voluntary self-domestication, "Chelovek v futlyare" (Eng. tr., "The Man in a Shell," 1914), "Kryzhovnik" (Eng. tr., "Gooseberries," 1915), and "O lyubvi" (1898; Eng. tr., "About Love," 1915); the exquisite love story "Dama s sobachkoy" (1899; Eng. tr., "The Lady with the Dog," 1917); "V ovrage" (1900; Eng. tr., "In the Ravine," 1914), which shows the helplessness of innocence and goodness in the face of greed and which is arguably Chekhov's finest achievement in prose fiction; "Arkhiyerey" (1902; Eng. tr., "The Bishop," 1915), Chekhov's serene final acceptance of the inevitabilities of life and death; and "Nevesta" (1903; Eng. tr., "The Betrothed," 1916), his last and most optimistic story, showing a young woman's escape from provincial drabness into personal freedom and fulfillment.

Chekhov's last two plays were written for the Moscow Art Theater, with which he became further allied by his marriage to its leading actress, Olga Knipper, in 1901. *Tri sestry* (1901; Eng. tr., *Three Sisters*, 1923), Chekhov's most perfectly realized play, depicts the frustrating lives of provincial educators and army officers in poetic and seemingly disjointed dialogue that is suffused with an undercurrent of inner meaning. *Vishnyovy sad* (1904; Eng. tr., *The Cherry Orchard*, 1912) indicates a definite turn to the symbolist mode in drama, with an aristocratic family's loss of its home reflecting in poetic terms the larger developments in Russian society of the period.

Chekhov's plays and stories marked both the culmination and the natural end of 19th-century Russian realism. His innovative literary techniques and his rejection of the sociological obsessions of the preceding period paved the way for and ushered in the remarkable achievements of Russian symbolist prose and drama.

See: R. Hingley, *Chekhov* (1950); E. Simmons, *Chekhov* (1962); S. Karlinsky and M. H. Heim, *Anton Chekhov's Life and Thought* (1975).   S.K.

Chervinskaya, Lidiya Davydovna (1907–), Russian poet, has lived as an émigré in Paris most of her life. She is one of the purest exponents of the "Parisian note" in Russian émigré poetry. Her style is marked by descriptions of Parisian scenery and by flower imagery. In her poetry time is perceived as time of day and season and is often seen through a dreamy haze. The mood of Chervinskaya's poems is one of lassitude and sadness. There are occasional variations on themes from Russian classics, especially from Aleksandr Pushkin and Aleksandr BLOK. Chervinskaya's melodious poems, written in conventional meters, are gracefully unstructured and seem deliberately to leave things unsaid. Her collections include *Priblizheniya* (Paris, 1934; Approaches); *Rassvety* (Paris, 1937; Daybreaks); and *Dvenadtsat mesyatsev* (Paris, 1956; Twelve Months).   V.T.

Chessex, Jacques (1934–), Swiss poet, essayist, and novelist, was born in Payerne, Vaud canton. He grew up in an atmosphere of Calvinistic severity, under the authority of a much-admired but overpowering father. Only after his father's suicide in 1956 did Chessex find his own identity as a writer. He began his literary career as a contemplative nature poet. In his first poetry collections, *Le Jour proche* (1954; Near Day), *Chant du printemps* (1955; Spring Song), *Une Voix la nuit* (1957; A Voice at Night), and *Bataille dans l'air* (1959; Battle in the Air), he is in search of his own style. He affirms himself, however, in *Le Jeûne de huit nuits* (1966; The Eight Nights' Fasting) and *L'Ouvert obscur* (1967; The Dim Gap). Chessex has also produced works of narrative prose. *La Tête ouverte* (1962; The Open Head) and *Reste avec nous* (1967; Stay with Us) prepare the way for *La Confession du Pasteur Burn* (1967; The Confession of Pastor Burn) and mark the end of Chessex's first period by taking leave of the past. Almost a novel, *La Confession* is a cool self-analysis reminiscent of Benjamin Constant. *Carabas* (1971), on the other hand, is a violent affirmation of the self, a bold acknowledgment of the repressed "baroque-Catholic" side of Chessex's nature, as opposed to his "Calvinistic-austere" side. In full control of his art, he makes a tribute of his talent and love to his country and its people in *Portrait des Vaudois* (1969; Portrait of the Vaud People), but although the work starts from a very personal vision, it develops into a meditation on man in general and his universal problems. The same can be said of Chessex's more recent novel, *L'Ogre* (1973; The Ogre), as well as of his critical essays on French Swiss literature, *Les Saintes Ecritures, critique* (1972; The Holy Scriptures, A Critique).

Chessex's work is largely autobiographical, replete with the theme of the defiance of death, marked by contradictions, and boldly stressing immoderate and violent feelings, and yet his language is almost classical in its restraint. In 1963 Chessex was awarded the Schiller Prize and in 1973 the Goncourt Prize.   U.S.

Chiarelli, Luigi (1880–1947), Italian journalist and playwright, was born in Trani (Bari). He became interested in writing at an early age, and after a sojourn in Paris joined the staff of the Milanese daily *Il secolo* in 1911. His first plays were in the style of Grand Guignol, but he achieved international success with *La maschera e il volto* (1916; Eng. tr., *The Mask and the Face*, 1927), a play that inaugurated a new dramatic genre, *il grottesco* or theater of the grotesque (*see* ITALIAN LITERATURE), later recognized as a forerunner of theater of the absurd. The plot of *La maschera* revolves about a case of adultery. But in that mingling of melancholy and laughter typical of *teatro del grottesco*, the play turns out to be not a traditional bourgeois comedy but something different. With a twist that became more familiar through such plays of Luigi PIRANDELLO as *Pensaci, Giacomino!*, *Ma non è una cosa seria*, and *Il piacere dell'onestà*, two situations develop in rapid succession: the husband's triumph in the eyes of his friends when it is thought that he had murdered his wife to defend his honor, and his disgrace when it is found out that he had instead simply said he had done so in order to save face. This brings husband and wife together in their isolation from the group about them and makes it impossible for them to continue to accept the conventional values and prejudices of their society. None of Chiarelli's later plays, *La scala di seta* (1917; The Silken Ladder), *Chimere* (1921; Chimeras), *La morte degli amanti* (1923; The Death of the Lovers), or *Fuochi d'artificio* (1923; Fireworks), repeated the success of *La maschera*.

See: W. Starkie, *Luigi Pirandello* (1926), pp. 8–17; L. Ferrante, *Teatro italiano del grottesco* (1964).   O.R.

Chiaromonte, Nicola (1905–72), Italian humanist and critic, was born in Rapolla (Potenza). He graduated from the University of Rome with a degree in law. In 1925 he began to write for *Il mondo* and *Conscientia*, but was silenced by the Fascist government because he was a nonsympathizer. He emerged again in 1931, writing film reviews for *Italia letteraria* and articles for *Scenario, Solaria*, and *Quaderni*, the Italian journal published in Paris. In 1934, Chiaromonte emigrated to Paris, where he was able to write freely on political as well as literary subjects, and in 1936 he joined André MALRAUX's air squadron in the Spanish Civil War. When France fell, he made his way to the United States via Morocco and Algeria. For the next nine years he lived in New York, writing regularly for *Partisan Review, The New Republic*, and *Politics*. During this period he also coedited *Italia libera* with Enzo Tagliacozzo and Gaetano Salvemini. He moved back to Paris in 1949, where he spent three years working for UNESCO, and then returned to Rome. He lived there until his death, continuing his drama criticism for *Il mondo*, writing, and lecturing. From 1956 to 1968 he coedited the monthly review *Tempo presente* with Ignazio SILONE. In 1966 he was invited to give the Gauss Lectures in literary criticism at Princeton University. From 1968 until 1972 he was drama critic for *L'espresso*.

Chiaromonte was most concerned with the relation between immediate reality and the enduring values: justice, freedom, truth. As a critic of the drama and the novel, he sought to identify the view of reality expressed in each work, and its moral scope. He saw the genuine work of art as deriving its character from an interplay between its "natural and historic context" and "the meaning of our being in the world." His two books take different approaches to this goal. In *La situazione drammatica* (1960; The Dramatic Situation), Chiaromonte turns a short, sharp beam of light on some 30 dramatic works ranging from Shakespeare to Jean GENET to discern how each shows "the reality of existence, of the world, and of the beliefs by which men live." On the other hand, *Credere e non credere* (1971; Eng. tr., *The Paradox of History*, 1971) is a work of great critical and philosophical concentration. Here Chiaromonte explores the relations between men and historical events in novels by Lev TOLSTOY, Stendhal, Malraux, Roger MARTIN DU GARD, and Boris PASTERNAK. Each chapter examines questions of belief and conduct as they emerge from and affect a given culture and age; in a final chapter, he reflects on our own age of "bad faith," its utilitarian values, moral emptiness, and social disaster. He concludes that recovery is unlikely as long as men allow the framework of their empiric knowledge to dictate the boundaries of their beliefs.

Chiaromonte's posthumously published works include *The Worm of Consciousness and Other Essays* (1976) and *Silenzio e parole* (1978).

See: G. Luti, in *Cronache letterarie fra le due guerre* (1966).   I.B.

Chiesa, Francesco (1871–1973), Swiss poet, short-story writer, and novelist, was born in Sagno in the canton of Ticino. He took a law degree at the University of Pavia, and from 1897 to 1943 taught Italian literature and art history at the canton *liceo* at Lugano, becoming director in 1914.

Chiesa's work falls into two periods: the output of the first can be characterized as intellectualistic and abstract, that of the second, intimate and serene. The first period includes the poetry volumes *Preludio* (1897; Prelude), *Calliope* (1907), *I viali d'oro* (1911; The Golden Ways), and the tales collected in *Istorie e favole* (1913; Tales and Fables). *Calliope*, a poem of classic inspiration in the tradition of Giosuè Carducci, consists of three parts, *La cattedrale* (1903; The Cathedral), *La reggia* (1904; The

Royal Palace), and *La città* (1907; The City). While *Calliope* glorifies man's cultural achievements from the Middle Ages to modern times, the poems in *Fuochi di primavera* (1919; Spring Fires) are inspired by Chiesa's love for nature and for life in its immediate reality; they also announce the beginning of his next period.

Works of the second period include the autobiographical stories collected in *Racconti puerili* (1921; Tales of Childhood) and the novel *Tempo di marzo* (1925; March Weather), both of which are among Chiesa's best prose efforts. A plotless novel, *Tempo di marzo* depicts and analyzes the author's passage from early childhood to adolescence. It is fresh, colorful, and often humorous, and received much critical acclaim. Chiesa's nonautobiographical novels, *Villadorna* (1928) and *Sant'Amarillide* (1938), a somewhat moralistic story of a brave girl who supports her ruined family, were received with less enthusiasm. Most of Chiesa's other prose works, notably *Scoperte nel mio mondo* (1934; Discoveries in My Own World), *La scatola di pergamena* (1960; The Parchment Box), and *L'occhio intermittente* (1971; The Intermittent Eye), reveal him as a careful observer of everyday events, living in a quiet, untroubled, and highly personal world. His later volumes of poetry include *La stellata sera* (1933; The Starry Evening), *Sonetti di San Silvestro* (1973; Sonnets of Saint Sylvester), and *L'artefice malcontento* (1950; The Unhappy Artisan), the last an anthology of previously published poems, some retouched, a few verses added. Throughout his extraordinarily long and productive life, Chiesa vigorously defended the Italian culture of his native Ticino.

See: M. Ferraris, *Francesco Chiesa* (1951); G. Calgari, *Storia delle quattro letterature della Svizzera* (1958); A. Jenni, "Un'opera all'insegna della saggezza," *CdT* (June 14, 1973): 3.   H.W.H.

Chinnov, Igor Vladimirovich (1909–), Russian poet, was born in Riga, the son of a judge. He holds a law degree from the University of Riga (1939) and a *licence-ès-lettres* from the Sorbonne (1947). After fleeing Latvia during World War II, Chinnov lived in Paris as a free-lance *littérateur* until 1953, and was senior news editor and critic for Radio Liberty in Munich (1953–62). He has lived in the United States since 1962 and has held successive professorships of Russian literature at the universities of Kansas and Pittsburgh, and at Vanderbilt University. Chinnov has published seven collections of poetry: *Monolog* (1950; Monologue), *Linii* (1960; Lines), *Metafory* (1969; Metaphors), *Partitura* (1970; Musical Score), *Kompozitsiya* (1972; Composition), *Pastorali* (1976; Pastorals), *Antitezy* (1979; Antithesis), and also some reviews and essays.

Chinnov's concrete imagery reflects the intellectual, emotional, and aesthetic experience of a well-traveled and well-read European. A skeptic with a deep affection for religion, Chinnov observes life soberly but remains eager to catch glimpses of another, mystic reality. His earlier poetry shows the influence of acmeism. Autumnally pessimistic, it is gnomic, precise in its imagery, and restrained in its formal devices. The poems in *Metafory* show a tendency toward freer rhythms, some mysticism, and a more optimistic outlook. Since *Partitura* he has shown a growing tendency toward a more grotesque imagery, mixing poetic and prosaic language, word play, free verse, and sound symbolism. While he has always cultivated the euphonic side of his poetry, Chinnov now develops sound patterns as outright subtexts and creates surrealistic trains of etymological and acoustic associations.

See: E. Rais, "Poeziya Igorya Chinnova," *Vozrozh-*

deniye no. 275 (1971): 131–45; R. Morrison, ed. and tr., *America's Russian Poets* (1975), pp. 24–32.   V.T.

Chorny, Sasha, pseud. of Aleksandr Mikhaylovich Glikberg (1880–1932), Russian poet and satirist, was born in Odessa and attended school in Zhitomir and began to work for a local newspaper. In 1905 he moved to Petersburg, where his parodies of the symbolist poets and his political verses appeared in various periodicals, including *Satirikon*, the most popular humorous journal of the time. These pieces established his reputation as a gifted satirist. After leaving Soviet Russia in 1920, Chorny published his works in émigré periodicals. In addition to collections of verses such as *Satiry i lirika* (1911; Satires and Lyrics) and *Zhazhda* (1923; Thirst), his works include two volumes of short stories and many volumes of children's literature. His prose, however, is considered much weaker than his poetry.

See: K. Chukovsky, "Sasha Chorny," in S. Chorny, *Stikhotvoreniya* (Moscow, 1962).   E.B.N.

Christensen, Inger (1935–), Danish novelist and poet, was born in the Jutland town of Vejle. She became a teacher in 1958. Although her novels *Evighedsmaskinen* (1964; The Eternity Machine) and *Adorno* (1967) might be said to reveal an artificial and impersonal modernism, Christensen is completely original as a poet. The collections *Lys* (1962; Light) and *Græs* (1963; Grass) focus on the disquieting world of writing, the fear of loss of the self during the creative act, and the function of the word. They paved the way for *Det* (1969; It), the major lyrical work in Denmark during the 1960s. The book is symmetrically structured (three by three by eight poems) and expresses in a series of lyrical forms—songs, rhymed stanzas, and prose poems—the creative writing process, which represents for Christensen a possibility of discovering the universe that is hidden by language itself. An infinite distance exists between language and experience; only the self unites objects with words and makes possible a development from chaos to a varied and rich existence. Christensen's more recent work, the prose story *Det malede værelse* (1976; The Painted Room) about the Italian Renaissance painter Mantegna, reaches the conclusion that our world constitutes a constant process of creation, in which art is a highly integrated part.   S.H.R.

Christiansen, Sigurd (1891–1947), Norwegian novelist and dramatist, was born in Drammen, where he lived all his undramatic life as an official of the local post office. Christiansen pursued a single theme—man's responsibility for his actions—with a tenacity unparalleled in Norwegian letters. Although his style is heavy and often unoriginal, he treated his theme with ethical fervor and a probing mind and demonstrated a consummate skill in creating believable and moving psychological portrayals of men and women.

Although he had written important books before, Christiansen's first major work was a trilogy—*Inngangen* (1925; The Threshold), *Sverdene* (1927; The Swords), and *Riket* (1929; The Kingdom)—about a craftsman and his four children, whose lives are torn apart by aspirations, guilt, and desires for atonement. After scoring a great success with the prize-winning (but much weaker) novel *To levende og en død* (1931; Eng. tr., *Two Living and One Dead*, 1932) and the later *Agner i stormen* (1933; Eng. tr., *Chaff before the Wind*, 1934), Christiansen again created a major trilogy: *Drømmen og livet* (1935; Dream and Life), *Det ensomme hjerte* (1938; The Lonely Heart), and *Menneskenes lodd* (1945; The Fate of Man). These three books treat the life of Jørgen Wendt who, through

crises marked by loneliness and guilt, progresses from childhood to an existence as a mature artist. No other work in Norwegian literature conveys the agony and joy of artistic creation as movingly as does this trilogy. Of Christiansen's several plays, the most noteworthy is *En reise i natten* (1931, A Journey through the Night), an intense study of erotic maladjustment and guilt.

See: E. Kielland, *Sigurd Christiansen* (1952).

K.A.F.

Chukovskaya, Lidiya Korneyevna (1907–), Russian literary scholar, editor, publicist, and novelist, was born in Helsinki, Finland, the daughter of the eminent man of letters Korney CHUKOVSKY. In the Soviet Union she has published studies of Aleksandr Herzen and the Decembrists, and a book based on her long experience as an editor, *V. laboratorii redaktora* (2d ed., 1963; In the Laboratory of an Editor). Her two semiautobiographical short novels have been published only abroad: *Sofia Petrovna* (New York, 1966; also under the incorrect title *Opustely dom*, Paris 1965; Eng. tr., *The Deserted House*, 1967) and *Spusk pod vodu* (New York, 1972; Eng. tr., *Going Under*, 1972). Both were written at the time of the events that inspired them and were kept by the author, at considerable personal risk, until their existence could be revealed some years after Iosif Stalin's death. The first, set in Leningrad in 1937, conveys with stark immediacy the atmosphere of Stalin's great purge, particularly as it affected the intelligentsia. The second deals with a similar period of terror at the end of the 1940s, and is a subtle study of the psychological and moral havoc wrought by the renewed postwar campaign of terror against writers and intellectuals. Since the middle 1960s, Chukovskaya has become known as an outspoken champion of human rights in the Soviet Union.   M.Ha.

Chukovsky, Korney Ivanovich, pseud. of Nikolay Vasilyevich Korneychuk (1882–1969), Russian writer, translator, and critic, was born in Petersburg, the son of a Ukrainian peasant woman and a Russian student. Soon abandoned by his father, his mother moved with her two children to Odessa, where they lived in extreme poverty. The gymnasium that he attended for a while gave him, he wrote, "nothing serious in the way of knowledge," a defect that the boy soon overcame by omnivorous reading. By 1901, Chukovsky had published his first literary articles in a local newspaper, and in 1903 he went as its correspondent to London. He spent his time there chiefly reading the English poets and historians, and acquired that firsthand knowledge of English life and customs that would make him a great rarity among Soviet literary figures. After being fired for the want of topicality in his dispatches, he was at once invited by Valery BRYUSOV to contribute to *Vesy*, a leading literary journal. He returned to Odessa in time to witness the mutiny of the battleship *Potyomkin* in 1905 but soon went to Petersburg as editor of the satirical journal *Signal*. After the fourth issue, he was jailed briefly on political charges, and it was while awaiting trial that he began translating Walt Whitman, a poet for whom he had lifelong enthusiasm.

Chukovsky's immense literary career, spanning some 68 years, can be divided into four parts. As literary critic, his major contribution was his edition of Nikolay Nekrasov and his studies of that poet, including *Masterstvo Nekrasova* (1952; Nekrasov's Literary Art), for which he was awarded a Lenin Prize in 1962. He also left memoirs and critical studies of Walt Whitman, Oscar Wilde, Maksim GORKY, Leonid ANDREYEV, Aleksandr BLOK, and Vladimir MAYAKOVSKY. As translator, Chukovsky was not only a practitioner—translating Daniel Defoe, Charles

Dickens, Walt Whitman, Mark Twain, Rudyard Kipling, G. K. Chesterton, and O. Henry—but, above all, a theoretician. In 1919, he issued *Printsipy khudozhestvennogo perevoda* (Principles of Artistic Translation), a pamphlet on translation theory that was revised and expanded over the years and reprinted many times, acquiring in 1941 the title by which it is now known, *Vysokoye iskusstvo* (1941; The Lofty Art). It was as a children's writer, however, that Chukovsky earned his widest and perhaps his most enduring fame, again both as practitioner—*Krokodil* (1916; The Crocodile) and innumerable other rhymes— and as theoretician. *Ot dvukh do pyati* (1933; Eng. tr., *From Two to Five*, 1963) is a work about the language of children. This book spans both the third and fourth parts of his literary career, for Chukovsky was throughout his life a fighter for authentic Russian against the encroachments of modern vulgarisms. His views about the Russian language are expressed in *Zhivoy kak zhizn* (1962; Alive as Life). His collected works, *Sobraniye sochineniy*, were published from 1965 to 1969.

See: M. Petrovsky, *Kniga o Korneye Chukovskom* (1966).   C.B.

Cicognani, Bruno (1879–1972), Italian novelist, short-story writer, and dramatist, was born in Florence, the son of a magistrate. His mother was the sister of Enrico Nencioni, a friend of Giosuè Carducci (1835–1907) and Gabriele D'ANNUNZIO. Cicognani took his degree in law at Urbino and was a practicing attorney in Florence until 1940. He was a lifelong friend of Giovanni PAPINI. His first work, *La crittogama* (1909; The Cryptogram), is a lyrical novel in the D'Annunzian manner. With the publication of *Sei storielle di novo conio* (1917; Six Stories of New Coinage), however, Cicognani revealed his own talent, which lay in the realistic depiction of the working class and bourgeoisie of Florence, set forth in a compact, "spoken" prose that often verges on the dialectal. Cicognani masterfully fused style and substance in *La Velia* (1922), a study of a sensuous, self-centered woman depicted with a kind of clinical understanding against a background of lower-middle-class Florence. In the opinion of many critics, there is a richer element of compassion in *Villa Beatrice* (1931), a portrait of another female figure, a woman who is cold and unresponsive but, as the story discloses, through no fault of her own. These two novels are Cicognani's masterpieces, although among his short stories there are also many perceptive and sharply focused observations, all set against convincingly realistic backgrounds. Particularly characteristic of Cicognani's work are the collections *Il figurinaio e le figurine* (1920; The Peddler and His Figurines), *Il museo delle figurine viventi* (1928; The Museum of Living Figurines), and *Barucca* (1948).

For many readers, Cicognani's memoirs are his finest legacy. The autobiographical *L'omino che a spento i fochi* (1937; The Little Man Who Has Put Out the Fires) and *L'età favolosa* (1940; The Fabulous Age) extend their scope to include events, figures, and customs of the author's youth. In a way, they are historical documents, humanized by a warm, somewhat melancholy sensitivity. Cicognani also wrote two plays, *Belinda e il mostro* (1927; Belinda and the Monster) and *Yo, el rey* (1949; I the King). *Yo, el rey* treats a theme handled by Vittorio Alfieri (1749–1803) that in Cicognani's hands becomes a vehicle for probing the meaning of human tragedy and revealing his own religious concerns.

See: L. Russo, in *I narratori* (1958), pp. 184–87; P. Rebora, in *Letteratura italiana: i contemporanei*, vol. 1 (1975), pp. 279–92.   T.G.B.

Čingo, Živko (1936–), Macedonian short-story writer, was born near Ohrid, Yugoslavia. He has published two volumes of short stories: *Paskvelija* (1963) and *Nova Paskvelija* (1965; New Paskvelija). Čingo uses a lively, fluent, and authentic folk idiom, distinguished by its candor and clarity, to describe episodes from the life of Macedonian peasants living in the fictional town of Paskvelija. His complex characters exhibit an enthusiasm for life and a capacity for great self-sacrifice, and a humanistic tone pervades his prose.

Čingo has also published two novels, *Srebreni snegovi* (1967; Silver Snows) and *Golemata voda* (1971; The Great Water), in which he continues his experimentation in both theme and expression. He is also the author of several dramas and screenplays.

See: V. Ognev, "Živko Čingo i ego geroi," Preface to Čingo's *Požar* (Moscow, 1973).   A.Sp.

Cioran, Emile-Marcel, pseud. of Emil Cioran (1911–), Romanian philosopher and essayist, writing in French since 1949, was born in Răsinari, Romania, but moved to Paris on the eve of World War II. At the age of 23, he attracted critical attention in Romania for his *Peculmile disperării* (1934; On the Peaks of Depair) and received his first literary prize, but he also drew upon himself the ostracism of "official" literary circles. Cioran's first essay situates him on the border line between literature and philosophy; its prose is not imaginative enough to belong to literature and not systematic enough to be a philosophical treatise. Although various predecessors like Friedrich NIETZSCHE and Marcus Aurelius are assigned to him, Cioran's aphorisms are unique and make him an innovator in the genre. With the publication of *Cartea Amăgirilor* (1936; The Book of Mistakes), Cioran became the butt of attacks both from the Right and the Left, and in *Schimbarea la faţa României* (1936; Transfiguration of Romania) he became an outright polemicist. With *Lacrimi şi sfinţi* (1937; Tears and Saints) he made an incursion into hagiography and undertook a psychological and philosophical study of the ascetic vocation. *Amurgul gândurilor* (1940; Crepuscular Thoughts) appeared after the author had voluntarily exiled himself to France.

After a silence of 10 years because of the war and because of the challenge of learning French, Cioran published his *Précis de décomposition* (1949; Eng. tr., *A Short History of Decay*, 1975). He immediately won the approval of critics, as well as the Rivarol Prize; stylists acclaimed him and thinkers saw him as the exponent of nihilism. *Les Syllogismes de l'amertume* (1952; Syllogisms of Bitterness) confirmed his talents. In these works, Cioran unhinged philosophy from rationalism and brought it down to the existential level. These aphorisms, which remind one of his earlier works in Romanian, are a condensation of wisdom concerning the human condition. In *La Tentation d'exister* (1956; Eng. tr., *The Temptation to Exist*, 1968), he gives an extraordinary lesson in philosophical *disponibilité* (an allusion to the Gidian doctrine of always being open to new ideas [*see* André GIDE]). According to Cioran, wisdom consists of rejecting any so-called truth that might engender fanaticism (thus he categorically rejects Voltaire's dogmatic attacks on metaphysics). Next came *Histoire et utopie* (1960; History and Utopia). Here the tone becomes grandiloquent as Cioran passes political regimes through the sieve of his virulent criticism. The only value remaining is the individual himself, skeptical and rebellious to all systems. *La Chute dans le temps* (1964; Eng. tr., *The Fall into Time*, 1970) preaches a sermon on antihistoricity. The only chance for man—that being who is "extraordinary even in his mediocrity"—to avoid sinking into decay is to abandon himself to a religion of doubt. In *Le Mauvais Démiurge* (1969; Eng. tr., *The New Gods*, 1974), Cioran analyzes the history of religious thought, proposing the idea that pagan deities are superior to monotheism, a source of tyranny. *Valéry face à ses idoles* (1970; Valéry Confronted by His Idols) is a demythifying of the poet Paul VALÉRY, in whom Cioran sees only exaggerated preciosity. In his latest book, *De l'inconvénient d'être né* (1973; Eng. tr., *The Trouble with Being Born*, 1976), his thought is even more decanted and his style more refined. Are there still some values that can be preserved? Cioran answers that "the surest way of not being mistaken is to undermine one certainty after another." Cioran addresses himself to those who reject deities and who find that everything is superstructure and alienation; for them, pessimism reduces itself to a lesson of lucidity and salutary discouragement.

See: *TriQ* 20 (Winter 1968): 5–20; C. Newman, "On Cioran," *TriQ* 20 (Winter 1971): 406–23; P. Ferrua, "Présence de Pascal dans l'œuvre de Cioran," *CFr* (Paris) 23 (Winter 1974): 6–16; F. Savater, *Ensayo sobre Cioran* (1974).   P.F.

Cixous, Hélène (1937–), French novelist and critic, was born in Oran, Algeria. Her intensely personal works are characterized by a masterful intertwining of language and content, resulting in a style that is, in essence, a mixture of poetry and philosophical reflection. This interdependence of language and subject matter is exemplified by linkages of concepts through phoneme relationships, by leitmotiv repetitions in which work and idea are intimately coordinated, and by the development of whole textual passages out of a series of brilliantly executed verbal acrobatics. The early influence of James Joyce on her work is seen in Cixous's striking linguistic freedom, typified by her adept utilization of wordplay. In *Dedans* (1969; Within), which received the Médicis Prize in 1969, the first-person narrator, triply emprisoned in house, body, and mind, turns inward in an effort to explore and resolve various conflicting internal forces. A similar sense of imprisonment and absence is evoked in *Le Prénom de Dieu* (1966; God's First Name), a collection of short stories.

Cixous's novels include *Les Commencements* (1970; Beginnings), *Un Vrai Jardin* (1971; A Real Garden), *Le Troisième Corps* (1970; The Third Body), *Neutre* (1972; Neuter), *Tombe* (1973), *Portrait du soleil* (1974; Portrait of the Sun), *Partie* (1975), and *Révolutions pour plus d'un Faust* (1975; Revolutions for More than One Faust). A professor of English literature, Cixous has published many works of literary scholarship.   D.C. and A.C.

Clarín: *see* ALAS, LEOPOLDO.

Claudel, Paul (1868–1955), French poet, dramatist, and religious thinker, was born in the village of Villeneuve-sur-Fère, on the fringe of the old province of Champagne, the son of a middle-class family close to the soil. He was a brilliant pupil at the Lycée Louis-le-Grand in Paris, where he acquired an excellent knowledge of Greek, Latin, and philosophy. He fell under the influence of his sister Camille, born in 1864, a woman of fiery temperament and a talented sculptor, then a determined unbeliever and the mistress of Auguste Rodin. Camille went insane, living on until 1943 in an asylum; the fear of a similar fate haunted her brother and contributed to his desire for a strong discipline that would curb his fierce independence and his imagination. Claudel soon found this discipline in Catholicism, which he rediscovered on Christmas Eve 1886, in the cathedral of Notre-Dame,

after having been prepared for it by an ardent reading of Arthur RIMBAUD's poetry. His official conversion followed a few years later, in December 1890.

In 1890, Claudel passed the competitive examination for the French diplomatic service. He had been an occasional visitor at the symbolist *Cénacles* (literary circles) and at Stéphane MALLARMÉ's, but he refused to divorce literature from life and to profess the cult of the book and of the beautiful as the sole absolute. Instead, Claudel was anxious to develop his own literary gifts in isolation and away from the Parisian poetical hothouses. His diplomatic career took him to the United States, China, Germany, Brazil, Japan, to Washington as French ambassador from 1926 to 1933, and finally to Brussels. He retired in 1935 to his estate in Brangues (Isère). That same year he was rejected by the Académie Française, which elected him only in 1946.

Claudel wrote extensive, highly unorthodox commentaries on several books of the Old Testament and on the Book of Revelation. During and especially since World War II, his dramas were acclaimed on the Paris stage and elsewhere, largely through the admiring devotion of the producer Jean-Louis BARRAULT. Both young and older scholars from Europe, the United States, and Japan praised his literary works at all levels and wrote extensively on them. Of all the French writers of his own age group, Claudel and Marcel PROUST seem most destined for lasting international fame.

Although he affected some dogmatism in his peremptory statements and frequently contradicted himself, Claudel was a man of wide culture, an expert translator of Aeschylus, and an extraordinarily perceptive interpreter of the cultures of China and Japan as well as a deep student of Christian philosophy, Virgil, Dante, Shakespeare, and the Spaniards of the Golden Age. His essay on topics as varied as Chinese sensibility, Japanese scenery, English mystics, and Dutch painting are profound and provoking. So are his many writings on poetry and religion, on French metrics, and on some of his predecessors (Mallarmé, Rimbaud). His primary concern, however, was not with literature in itself but with religious faith. He refused to examine that faith critically and to question the complex notions of original sin, of miracles, and of redemption. When he was 32, he had gone through a crisis of illicit love the violence of which had left him terrified: he dramatized and sublimated it in his most grandiose drama, *Partage de Midi* (1905; Eng. tr., *Break of Noon*, 1960). He also alluded to this crisis frequently in his poems and in his correspondence. Many volumes of Claudel's letters addressed to André GIDE, André SUARÈS, Jacques RIVIÈRE, and others have appeared posthumously. To the Catholic dramatist, the world appears as a concert with the divine presence everywhere, to be seen and heard by anyone who has eyes and ears. The poet's task is to interpret that divine order and to teach others how to perceive and laud the beauty of creation. At times, Claudel composed splendidly finished and impeccably wrought poems in prose, as in *Connaissance de l'est* (1901, 1907; Knowing the East). More often, however, he gave free rein to his rhetorical gifts, resorting to splendid imagery, repetitions, exclamations, and to a verse of poetic prose, varied and rich in comparisons and assonances, a style which he preferred to the traditional rigid alexandrine. In *Cinq Grandes Odes* (1910; Five Great Odes) and *Cette Heure qui est entre le printemps et l'été* (1913; This Hour That Is between Spring and Summer, reprinted as *La Cantate à troix vois* [The Cantata with Three Voices] 1931), Claudel reached the heights of French lyrical poetry. He often resembles and matches Victor Hugo (1802–85), whom he refused to acknowledge as a kindred spirit, however, since Hugo had rejected Catholic orthodoxy.

Claudel's powerful, comprehensive genius was naturally drawn to the dramatic form, in which his creative imagination, his architectonic gifts, and his profound sense of the inner conflict in man, torn between matter and spirit, were to find full play. Some of his dramas, such as *La Ville* (1890; Eng. tr., *The City*, 1917), *Le Repos du septième jour* (1901; Rest on the Seventh Day), and even *Le Livre de Christophe Colomb* (1929; Eng. tr., *The Book of Christopher Columbus*, 1930), suffer from a formless lack of discipline or from some monotonous abstraction. *L'Otage* (The Hostage) is a much better structured tragedy on a purely human plane, but too harsh in its rigorous logic. Two early dramas, *Tête d'or* (1889; Golden Head) and *L'Echange* (1893; The Exchange), the second laid in an imaginary American setting, contain flashes of strange lyricism and moments of sublime beauty. But Claudel's three masterpieces are *L'Annonce faite à Marie* (1910; originally written as *La Jeune Fille Violaine*, 1900; Eng. tr., *The Tidings Brought to Mary*, 1916), *Partage de Midi*, and *Le Soulier de satin* (1929; Eng. tr., *The Satin Slipper*, 1931). The first is a moving drama situated in a poeticized Middle Ages and depicting, in a beautiful poetic style, human conflicts that result from deep religious belief; it is one of the greatest works of the French theater. *Partage*, which has perhaps more admirers among devotees of Claudel than among the general public, is a contemporary account of psychological conflicts, set against the backdrop of contemporary China; it is the best of all of Claudel's "realistic" plays, if indeed the word "realistic" can be applied to a play written in the typical Claudelian *verset* (free verse with a distinct rhythm based on "breath groups"). *Le Soulier* is a baroque drama, complex because of the multiplicity of plots, which, somewhat like a picaresque novel, follow the various characters through their adventures and religious experiences over four continents. It is divided into four *journées* (days), which are also subdivided into numerous scenes, each involving a change of characters and settings. Because of its length, it was never presented in its entirety, although, in a series of memorable performances directed by Jean-Louis Barrault at the Comédie-Française in 1943, it was given in a truncated version lasting most of a day. In a sense, *Le Soulier*, which presents psychological conflict in a religious context and in a stylized setting derived from the history of Christendom in the 16th century, is Claudel's greatest poetic achievement. It is yet to be appreciated in Anglo-Saxon countries because its dramatic qualities are submerged in great outbursts of lyricism.

See: G. Gadoffre, *Claudel et l'univers chinois* (1968); *Les Critiques de notre temps et Claudel* (1970); M. Lioure, *L'Esthétique dramatique de Claudel* (1971); J. Petit, *Claudel on the Theatre* (1972); "The France of Claudel," *RNL* (1973). H.P.

Claus, Hugo Maurice Julien (1929–), Belgian (Flemish) poet, novelist, and playwright, was born in Bruges. A self-made man unable to adapt himself to the traditional education system or to home life, he lived as a youth in a carefree way and hesitated for quite a time between literature and painting. He published his first work, a collection of classical poems, in 1947: *Kleine Reeks* (Short Series); it soon was followed by modernistic productions, namely, *Registreren* (1948; Registering) and *De Metsiers* (1950; The Duck Hunt), the novel that made him famous. But he continued to show a lively interest in the fine arts, as appears from his films, his numerous paintings, and the essays he devoted to the Dutch painters Corneille and Karel Appel, *Over het werk van Corneille* (1951; About Corneille's Work) and *Appel* (1962; Karel Appel, Painter).

In 1950, Claus went to live in Paris, after which he spent some time in Italy. He did not settle down in Belgium until 1955, when he married Elly Overzier. His earlier work reflects the then prevailing existentialist climate—an atmosphere of nausea, an awareness of life's absurdity, and a longing for freedom, all of which are so typical of postwar European and American literature. Yet Claus was at the time one of the major representatives of the so-called neo-avant-garde, which gained ground in Dutch and Flemish literature as soon as 1948 with such periodicals as *Reflex* (1948–49), *Tijd en Mens* (1949–55), *Cobra* (1949–51), *Blurb* (1950–51), and *Braak* (1950–51). Influenced by Van Ostaijen, T. S. Eliot, Ezra Pound, and the French surrealists, Claus also took an active part in the experimental movement led by Dutch, Danish, and Belgian writers and painters (Appel, Corneille, Alechinsky, and others). Yet he did not carry their principles to the extremes of rejecting all artistic conventions and, in particular, of distinguishing between the inner and the outer world. To Claus, art is conceived as a game that is played without any preconceived idea and that depends on the handling of words. Poetry thus does not aim at imitating or at rendering ideas, feelings, and things—it invents, reveals the unknown, and is, in fact, a source of knowledge. According to Claus, things exist because the writer conjures them up by his or her words. Thus, literature allows the writer to explore his or her self or, rather, "situation," to identify the powers (time, fate, reason, the family, and so on) that crush him or her down, and to warn the reader against them. Beauty is a side issue, the main thing being to express the irrational, instinctive, and "animal" side of existence. Such are the ideas that underline Claus's earlier poems "*tancredo infrasonic*" (1952) and "*Een Huis dat tussen Nacht en Morgen staat*" (1953; A House between Night and Morning) and the novels *De Metsiers* and *De Hondsdagen* (1952; Dog Days).

De Oostakkerse Gedichten (1955; Oostakker Poems) is a turning point in Claus's career. It marks the end of the experimental period, foreshadows his evolution toward a more intellectual poetry, and stresses the importance of myth. Although experimentalism made the writer aware of his specific language and themes, a subtle manipulation of history and culture is now being substituted for the original "wordplay." From there on, the poet tends to rely on a montage of quotations borrowed from literary and pictorial sources. The use of such devices reflects a growing social commitment, a desire to communicate through the values of our cultural heritage. This trend is further exemplified by Claus's interest in the stage: *Een Bruid in the Morgen* (1955; A Bride in the Morning), *Suiker* (1958; Sugar), *Thyestes* (1966), *Vrijdag* (1970; Friday), and other plays. At the same time Claus turns to myth to account for the human condition—the disastrous consequences of initiation as shown by the story of Adam and Eve and the domestic and religious problems connected with Oedipus' destiny. *De Verwondering* (1962; Astonishment), Claus's best novel to date, is developed along these lines. Under the guise of a journey to a castle where the heroine holds sway over a circle of exquislings, it is an allegory of the contemporary world, an unforgettable image of its horror, and a denunciation of evil, based on more or less cryptic references to Dante, Sir James Frazer's *The Golden Bough*, and classical mythology. Claus has also written superb love poems pervaded with an acute sense of both the violence and the ecstasy of sexual intercourse.

See: J. De Decker, *Over Claus' Toneel* (1971); G. Wildemeersch, *Hugo Claus of Oedipus in het Paradijs* (1973); J. Weisgerber, *Hugo Claus, Experiment en Traditie* (1974).   J.W.

Claussen, Sophus (1865–1932), Danish poet, was born on the island of Langeland. After matriculating in 1884, he became a painter and a journalist. From 1892 to 1894 he lived in Paris and Italy. His elusive, erotic stories from the provinces, *Unge Bander* (1894; Young Gangs) and *Kitty* (1895), as well as two lively travel books, *Antonius i Paris* (1896; Antonius in Paris) and *Valfart* (1896; Pilgrimage), are predominantly lyrical. Belonging to the generation of symbolists of the 1890s, Claussen joined his fellow writers Johannes JØRGENSEN and Viggo STUCKENBERG in the struggle against naturalism. Claussen did not have his breakthrough until *Pilefløjter* (1899; Willow Pipes), which shows him as an idyllist praising woman and the Danish countryside, and *Djævlerier* (1904; Diableries), in which Italian and French motifs dominate; these are two collections indicating Claussen's artistic grandeur and wide scope. Inspired by Charles BAUDELAIRE, Claussen created an artistic diabolism in *Djævlerier,* the erotic motif being woman as a vampire. In addition, *Djævlerier* contains a series of deeply reflective poems concerning the possibilities and situation of the artist. Similar themes are found in *Danske Vers* (1912; Danish Verses), a disillusioned poet's commentary on life and fate.

Claussen's following work, *Fabler* (1917; Fables), consists of symbolic poetry elevated beyond reason and progress. Besides allegorical period poems, the collection contains obscure and magical stanzas concerning the relations among the writer, his art, and the modern materialistic world, a conflict reaching prophetic proportion in the last of Claussen's most important collections, *Heroica* (1925). Threatened by technological culture, his religious humanism reached an impressive height in *Heroica*'s pathetic final poem, "Atomernes Oprør" (The Revolt of the Atoms), in which the poet calls for peace and conciliation "in order to save our star." Claussen's production thus represents the protest of imagination and beauty against the narrow horizons of naturalism and materialism. Decisive influences upon his writing came from Lord Byron, Percy Bysshe Shelley, Heinrich Heine, and Holger DRACHMANN as well as from Danish romanticism. Furthermore, Claussen was the first among Danish poets to adhere consistently to the aesthetics of French symbolism. He expresses himself directly in symbols, whereby he served as a model for Danish modernistic poetry of the 1940s and 1960s.

See: E. Frandsen, *Sophus Claussen* (1950); G. Modvig, *Eros, Kunst og socialitet* (1974).   S.H.R.

Clavel, Maurice (1920–79), French essayist, playwright, and novelist, was born in Frontignan. He was an active member of the Resistance throughout the German occupation. He became a professor of philosophy and, in 1944, a journalist. As a journalist, Clavel wrote for *Combat* and the *Nouvel Observateur* and was a guest commentator on French television.

Clavel wrote a number of plays, beginning with *Les Incendiaires* (1946; The Firebrands), *La Terrasse du Midi* (1947; The Southern Terrace), *Balmaseda* (1954), and *Saint-Eulage de Cordoue* (1965). He also adapted foreign plays for the French stage: Shakespeare's *Julius Caesar* (1964) and *Antony and Cleopatra* (1965), and Henrik IBSEN's *When We Dead Awaken* (1978). Many of his numerous novels, such as *Une fille pour l'été* (1957; A Girl for Summer), *Le Temps de Chartres* (1960; When We Were in Chartres), and *Combat: de la Résistance à*

la révolution (1973; Struggle: From the Resistance to the Revolution), are largely autobiographical. His other novels include *Le Jardin de Djemila* (1958; The Garden of Djemila), *La Pourpre de Judée ou les délices du genre humain* (1967; The Purple of Judea or the Delights of the Human Species), *La Perte et le fracas* (1971; Loss and Destruction), and *Le Tiers des étoiles* (1972; A Third of the Stars), for which he received the Médicis Prize.

It was, however, through his essays that Clavel gained his widest audience and exerted his considerable influence. His first collection, *Combat de Franc-Tireur pour une libération* (1969; A Partisan's Struggle for Liberation), contains essays written during the May 1968 uprising, in which Clavel was one of the few major intellectuals of his generation to play an active role. *Les Paroissiens de Palente* (1974; The Parishioners of Palent) recalls the workers' occupation of the Lip factories in 1973–74. In *Ce que je crois* (1975; What I Believe) and *Dieu est Dieu, nom de Dieu* (1976; God Is God, God Damn It), he expressed his newly rekindled Christian faith and his exasperation with liberal or unconcerned Catholics. Clavel's new orientation also inspired him to become mentor to the New Philosophers who have been taking the Marxists to task since the mid-1970s. One of his last publications, *Nous l'avons tous tué, ou ce juif de Socrate* (1977; We Have All Killed Him, or This Jew of a Socrates), is an informal and polemical yet profound meditation on the modern reactions to the philosophical foundations of Western thought.   J.-P.C.

Closson, Herman (1901–), Belgian playwright, was born in Brussels. He started out, in *Sous-sol* (1925; Basement) and *Spectacle ou la comédie du public* (1928; Spectacle or the Comedy of the Audience), as a prisoner of flashes reminiscent of Luigi PIRANDELLO. Later, however, Closson discovered his ethic: human beings put to the double test of transcending themselves and searching for their authenticity. The experience of Closson's characters easily goes through demystification. In *Godefroid de Bouillon* (1935), a weak man comes to accept the high mission in which he did not believe and to walk finally into his own legend; in *William ou la comédie de l'aventure* (1938; William or the Comedy of Adventure)—a clever play, which utilizes the resources of a play-within-a-play and has a moral of renunciation, which alone leads to grandeur—a Shakespeare in love with a queen of the underworld renounces this profane love for a higher passion; in *L'Epreuve du feu* (1944; Ordeal by Fire), a false Joan of Arc clings to her role and desperately tries to live at a height that will be fatal to her. Still other legendary figures have haunted Closson, *Borgia* (1947) or *Sire Halewyn* (1954) for example. He loves what transcends human beings, whether it be their dreams or their always vain pursuit of the ideal, as in *La Passante illuminée* (1939; The Illuminated Passerby) and *Hélène ou la dissemblance* (1942; Helen or Dissemblance). Closson has also mastered the technique of the spectacular play, for example, *Les Quatre Fils Aymon* (1941; The Four Sons of Aymon), and outdoor theater, for example, *Le Jeu de Han,* (1948; The Drama of Han) and *Yolande de Beersel* (1949).

See: J. Burniaux and R. Frickx, *La Littérature belge d'expression française* (1973); A. Jans, *Lettres vivantes 1945–1975* (1975).   R.T.

Coccioli, Carlo (1920–), Italian novelist who has written both in Italian and French, was born in Livorno. He lived in Africa and took part in the Italian Resistance during World War II. Since then he has lived in Florence, Paris, and Mexico. Coccioli's work bears natural affinities with that of Alberto MORAVIA and Ignazio SILONE, and like Silone, his reputation is stronger outside his native country. Yet Coccioli is distinctly removed from the mainstream of Italian literature. Except for Fyodor DOSTOYEVSKY, the major influences on his fiction are almost all French.

Two subjects pervade Coccioli's fiction: homosexuality and religion. They vie with each other, both substantively and thematically, but religion is by far the stronger. Although his first novel, *Il migliore e l'ultimo* (1946; The Best and the Last), deals with his experience as a partisan, *Fabrizio Lupo* (1952) concerns his major preoccupations, homosexuality and faith. *Manuel le Mexicain* (1956; Eng. tr., *Manuel the Mexican*, 1958), written in French, considers the persistence of the Aztec gods in Christian Mexico as well as taking up Coccioli's essential themes. The denouement of the novel, however, is far too melodramatic. *Il cielo e la terra* (1950; Eng. tr., *Heaven and Earth*, 1952) develops from what is at first a rather trite display of philosophic and religious questions into a serious and honest probing of the spiritual life of man in the 20th century.

Coccioli's real talent emerges in his next novel, *La pietra bianca* (1959; Eng. tr., *The White Stone*, 1960). The protagonist of *Il cielo e la terra*, Don Ardito Piccardi, now appears as a modern man lost in the confusion of metaphysical absurdity and religious skepticism. His loss of faith, alienation, and eventual, ambiguous reconciliation are depicted with narrative skill and empathy.

The works that have followed *La pietra bianca* have not achieved its breadth of vision. Coccioli's later works include *Ambroise* (1961), *Omeyotl, diario messicano* (1962; Omeyotl, Mexican Diary), *L'erede di Montezuma* (1964; The Heir of Montezuma), *Le corde dell'arpa* (1967; The Strings of the Harp), and *Uomini in fuga* (1973; Men in Flight).

See: T. F. Staley, "Faith and the Absurd: The Post-Existential Vision of Carlo Coccioli," in *The Shapeless God*, ed. by H. J. Mooney, Jr., and T. F. Staley (1968).

                                                                                                                T.F.S.

Cocteau, Jean (1891-1963), French poet, dramatist, and novelist, was born in Maisons-Laffitte, a prosperous community near Paris, the prodigal son of a wealthy notary. At a tender age he absorbed the earlier teachings of André GIDE and spent his life "pursuing his own youth." Every conceivable mood or mixture of moods colored in turn this fervent quest. On many occasions there stands revealed a tormented Cocteau almost tragically aware of human weakness, groping for certainty, afraid of love, afraid of life, afraid of death. His emotional attachments were always directed towards members of his own sex. The great tragedy of his life was unquestionably the untimely death (1923) at the age of twenty of Raymond RADIQUET, who had been his protégé over a period of five years.

Cocteau's early *Le Potomak* (1919, rev. 1924), a fantastic medley of cartoons, prose, and verse composed in 1913, was an exploration of the subconscious, attended by gloomy forebodings. The haven of religion tempted him for a while but, after having secured the good office of that experienced savior of souls, Jacques MARITAIN (see *Lettre à Jacques Maritain*, Eng. tr., *Art and Faith* [1948] and the latter's *Réponse à Jean Cocteau* [1926]), the neophyte flippantly recanted, thumbing his nose at his spiritual director. As Cocteau attested in *Opium: journal d'une désintoxication* (1930; Eng. tr., *Opium: The Diary of an Addict*, 1932), drugs offered him no better escape. Thus, despite Cocteau's low critical opinion of his youthful indiscretion, he ultimately reverted to the inspiration of *Le Potomak*—in *La Fin du Potomak* (1940; The End of the Potomak)—to express a personal drama he felt to be "much closer to Kafka [*see* Franz KAFKA] than to Goethe."

It is the sophisticated and exuberant Cocteau, however, who is more readily remembered, the Prince Charming who, especially in his prime, so captured the fancy of Parisians that they felt powerless to resent his conceit and eccentricities. He became the astute magician and purveyor of his own publicity; his tricks were legion, whether he permitted an exclusive nightclub to use the name of one of his works (*Le Bœuf sur le toit*) or decided to refurbish Jules VERNE's old *Tour du monde en quatre-vingt jours* (1873) and translate it into action as *Mon Premier Voyage* (1937; Eng. tr., *Round the World Again in Eighty Days*, 1937).

Cocteau became the incomparable promoter of new styles and new fashions, whose word in matters of taste was almost law. He sponsored with equal ease the painting of Pablo Picasso and Giorgio de Chirico; the Ballet Russe; the music of Igor Stravinsky, Erik Satie, and the "Groupe des Six" (Georges Auric, Louis Durey, Arthur Honegger, Darius Milhaud, Francis Poulenc, Germaine Tailleferre); the first appearances of American jazz; the clown act of the Fratellini brothers; and the films of Chaplin. The story of Cocteau's own modernistic ballets—such as *Parade*, score by Erik Satie and scenery by Picasso (1917); *Le Bœuf sur le toit, ou The Nothing Happens Bar*, score by Darius Milhaud (1920); *Les Mariés de la Tour Eiffel* (The Bride and Groom of the Eiffel Tower), score by the entire "Groupe des Six" (1921)—and, later, of his theater is one of gradual progress and ultimate triumph built on a sure knowledge of how and how far the "strong honey" of novelty may be made palatable to the general public. In this, Cocteau was helped immeasurably by the fact that he himself was a product of the *bourgeoisie bourgeoisante*. With a nimble mind and an ample provision of atavistic shrewdness or even conservatism, he called, on aesthetic grounds, for "order through anarchy" and labeled himself a "member of the classical Left."

The definite pattern of Cocteau's arabesques emerges clearly from his poems—*Poésie 1916-1923* (1924); *Opéra: œuvres poétiques 1925-1927* (1927; Opera: Poetic Works); *Mythologie* (1934); *Allégories* (1941); *Le Chiffre* (1952; The Figure); *Appogiatures* (1953; Appoggiaturas); and *Clair-obscur* (1954; Chiaroscuro)—and his critical essays, such as those collected in *Le Rappel à l'ordre* (1926; Eng. tr., *A Call to Order*, 1926), *Essai de critique indirecte* (1932; Essay of Indirect Criticism), and *Poésie critique* (1960; Poetry Criticism). Cocteau is often ranked with the "literary cubists," that is to say, with a group of writers who, mostly through direct acquaintance, fell under the influence of Picasso, transferring to literature that artist's contempt for traditional rhetorics, perspective, and anthropomorphic reality. Cocteau relied upon this technique to shock himself into a brief mystical trance, one that would afford him a glimpse of Beauty asleep in the "meadows of inner silence." "Poetry," he wrote "is a religion without hope."

This *art poétique* was substantially that of Max JACOB, André SALMON, and Guillaume APOLLINAIRE, all three Cocteau's elders, all three authentic bohemians and far less hampered than he by artificial constrictions. In the last analysis, it was Cocteau's not inconsiderable role to exploit their ideas on a grand scale. Like Charles BAUDELAIRE, he conceived of all art as poetry and of verse as but one of the wires through which the mysterious "fluid" might pass. Thus he called his criticism "poésie critique" and his ballets "poésie chorégraphique." In addition to the works mentioned above, his "poésie autobiographique" includes *Portraits-Souvenir 1900–1914* (1935) and his brilliant *La Difficulté d'être* (1947; The Difficulty of Being). Cocteau's "poésie de roman" includes *Thomas l'imposteur* (1923; Eng. tr., *Thomas the Imposter*, 1925), *Le Grand Ecart* (1923; Eng. tr., *The Grand Ecart*, 1925), and *Les Enfants terribles* (1929; Eng. tr., 1930), a novel of troubled adolescence that many consider Cocteau's masterpiece. The "poésie de théâtre" includes adaptations of Sophocles—*Antigone*, with scenery by Picasso and Renaissance costumes by Jean Hugo (1922; Eng. tr., 1961), and *Oedipe-Roi* (1928); Shakespeare—*Roméo et Juliette* (1924); and Torquato Tasso—*Renaud et Armide* (1943). Cocteau also composed *Orphée* (1926; Eng. tr., 1933), an original, one-act tragedy; *La Voix humaine* (1930; The Human Voice), a one-character play consisting exclusively of a telephone conversation; *La Machine infernale* (1934; Eng. tr., *The Infernal Machine*, 1936); *Les Chevaliers de la Table Ronde* (1937; The Knights of the Round Table); *Les Parents terribles* (1938); *Les Monstres sacrés* (1940); *La Machine à écrire* (1941; The Typewriter); *L'Aigle à deux têtes* (1946; The Two-Headed Eagle); and *Bacchus* (1952). Finally, Cocteau's "poésie cinématographique"—*Le Sang d'un poète* (1933; The Blood of a Poet), *L'Eternel Retour* (1944; Eternal Return), *La Belle et la bête* (1945; Beauty and the Beast), *Les Parents terribles* (1948), *Orphée* (1950), *Les Enfants terribles* (1950), and *Le Testament d'Orphée* (1960; Orpheus's Will)—and his "poésie graphique"—*Dessins* (1923; Sketches), *Vingt-cinq Dessins d'un dormeur* (1928; 25 Sketches for a Sleeper), and *Soixante Dessins pour "Les Enfants terribles"* (1934; 60 Sketches for *Les Enfants terribles*)—complete the picture of an extremely versatile artist.

During World War II, the Vichy government had branded Cocteau as "decadent" and had forbidden the production of his plays. His later years were more serene, however, and in a way, he became respectable. He was elected to the Académie Française in 1955. At the age of 70, he painted the now celebrated frescos in the town hall of Menton and in the chapel of Saint-Pierre at Villefranche-sur-Mer.

See: N. Oxenhandler, *Scandal and Parade: The Theatre of Jean Cocteau* (1957); W. Fowlie, *Jean Cocteau: The History of a Poet's Age* (1966); F. Brown, *An Impersonation of Angels: A Biography of Jean Cocteau* (1968); F. Steigmuller, *Cocteau: A Biography* (1970).

J.-A.B. rev. J.L.

Colette, pseud. of Sidonie Gabrielle Colette (1873–1954), French novelist, short-story writer, and chronicler, was born in Saint-Sauveur-en-Puisaye and died in her Palais Royal apartment in Paris. She was the outstanding French woman of letters of the first half of the 20th century. Colette spent her first 20 years under the tutelage of her mother, Sido, learning about the rituals of family and village life and developing her own intimacy with nature. In 1893 she changed tutors, marrying Henri Gauthier-Villars (M. Willy), the music critic and colorful Parisian figure of the *belle époque*, and went to live with him in Paris. He initiated her unique literary career by obliging her to write novels, which he signed as his own.

After her divorce from M. Willy in 1906, Colette became a music-hall dancer and mime, lived on and off with the Marquise de Belbeuf (Missy), and continued to write. In 1912, a few months after the death of her mother, Colette married Henry de Jouvenel, editor-in-chief of a Parisian newspaper and the father of her only child. During the 13 years of this second marriage, and in the years following her second divorce, Colette established herself as a distinguished novelist and newspaper journalist. She also gave lectures, opened a beauty salon, and acted in a stage adaptation of her most famous novel, *Chéri* (1920; Eng. tr., 1953). In 1935, after a 10-year liaison, she married Maurice Goudeket, who was to be her companion until her death. During her lifetime, Colette received many official honors: in 1935 she was elected to the Belgian Royal Academy; in 1945 she was elected to the Académie Goncourt, and in 1953 she was named Grand Officer of the Legion of Honor. When she died, she was refused Catholic burial, but was given a state funeral. This unconventional woman writer had become both a national monument and a mythological female figure, a model for the personal and professional aspirations of many women.

Variety and vitality characterize both the events of Colette's life and her literary production. The 49 volumes that Colette published in the half century between *Claudine à l'école* (1900; Eng. tr., *Claudine at School*, 1956) and *Le Fanal bleu* (1949; Eng. tr., *The Blue Lantern*, 1963) are diverse in genre and contain obvious thematic polarizations. Most of the first- and third-person novels and short stories are urban, Parisian tales written in an ironic mode. They portray the impossibility of harmony between a woman and a man and suggest, given this impossibility, what a woman must do in order to survive. The shadow of M. Willy and the mores of the *belle époque* dominate these works, which include: *Claudine à l'école*, *Claudine à Paris* (1901; Eng. tr., *Claudine in Paris*, 1958), *Claudine en ménage* (1902; Eng. tr., *Claudine Married*, 1960), *Claudine s'en va* (1903; Eng. tr., *Claudine and Annie*, 1962), *La Vagabonde* (1911; Eng. tr., *The Vagabond*, 1955), *L'Entrave* (1913; Eng. tr., *The Shackle*, 1964), *Mitsou ou comment l'esprit vient aux filles* (1919; Eng. tr., *Mitsou*, 1958), *Chéri: la fin de Chéri* (1926, Eng. tr., *The Last of Chéri*, 1953), *La Seconde* (1929; Eng. tr., *The Other One*, 1931), *La Chatte* (1933; Eng. tr., *The Cat*, 1953), *Duo* (1934; Eng. tr., 1935), *Mes Apprentissages* (1936; Eng. tr., *My Apprenticeships*, 1957), *Julie de Carneilhan* (1941; Eng. tr., 1952), and *Le Képi* (1943; Eng. tr., *The Tender Shoot and Other Stories*, 1959).

Most of Colette's fictionalized reminiscences, reportages, animal dialogues, and flower portraits are situated in pastoral settings and written in a lyrical mode. They describe the attempts of a solitary woman to recover elements of a lost paradise through memory and the craft of fiction. The indispensable presence of her mother Sido dominates these works: *Dialogues de bêtes* (1904; Eng. tr., *Creatures Great and Small*, 1957), *La Retraite sentimentale* (1907; Eng. tr., *The Retreat from Love*, 1973), *Les Vrilles de la vigne* (1908; The Tendrils of the Vine), *La maison de Claudine* (1922; Eng. tr., *My Mother's House*, 1953), *La Naissance du jour* (1928; Eng. tr., *Break of Day*, 1961), *Sido* (1929; Eng. tr., 1953), *Le Pur et l'impur* (1932; Eng. tr., *The Pure and the Impure*, 1967), *Journal à rebours* (1941; Eng. tr., *Looking Backward*, 1975), *De ma fenêtre* (1942; From My Window), *L'Etoile vesper* (1946; Eng. tr., *The Evening Star*, 1973), *Journal intermittent* (1949), and *Le Fanal bleu*.

What is common to both categories is a specifically female universe, composed of women, adolescents, cats, and flowers, and ruled by powerful female characters—all described with ruthless but loving precision. The younger heroines—Claudine, Minne, Camille, and Gigi—derive their vigor and their eventual independence from an unabashed awareness and acceptance of their sexuality. The older heroines—Lea, "Sido," Mme Dalleray, Mme Alvarez, and "Colette"—function as the revered mother-teacher, the exotic and sensuous woman who presides over the sexual ritual. Colette organized her fictional world along matriarchal lines. The men are invariably weaker than the women and, in most cases, physically and morally inferior. This hierarchical arrangement seems to have originated in Colette's perception of the contrast between her mother and her father, and between herself and M. Willy. Men, with the exception of adolescents, become in Colette's texts what women were traditionally in literature: objects overtly desired and secretly despised. Her male characters are drones destined only to serve the queen whose sexuality is represented as more profound and more mysterious. The most original aspect of Colette's fiction is the central place occupied by female figures and the reiterated indications that their power is related to their capacity to survive, without men, in a woman's garden.

See: T. Maulnier, *Introduction à Colette* (1954); M. Goudeket, *Près de Colette* (1956; Eng. tr., *Close to Colette*, 1957); R. D. Cottrell, *Colette* (1974).   E.M.

Colinas, Antonio (1946–), Spanish poet, essayist, and literary critic, was born in León. He has taught Spanish in the universities of Milan and Bergamo and translated such Italian authors as Edoardo SANGUINETI and Pier Paolo PASOLINI. In 1974 he published a bilingual anthology of poems by Giacomo Leopardi, preceded by a long critical study. His book of poems *Preludios a una noche total* (1969; Preludes to a Total Night) reveals his roots in early German romanticism (Friedrich Hölderlin, Novalis) and his poetry's tendency to lyricism with metaphysical overtones—both of which confirm his understanding of the poetic act as an exercise in enlightenment and an exploration of the mystery of reality. *Truenos y flautas en un templo* (1972; Thunder and Flutes in a Temple) pays tribute to the aesthetic and cultural tendencies that are so strong in his literary generation, the third to appear in Spain since the Civil War. A synthesis of those elements and the revelation of his true poetic voice is found in *Sepulcro en Tarquinia* (1975), which won the Critics' Prize the year it was published. In this volume, certain constant concerns of his poetry—love, nature or landscape, history, culture merged with life, mystery, and death—are dominant. They are expressed in a personal poetic language that is emotionally expressive, highly imaginative, and indicative of a writer markedly concerned with verbal beauty. Reality and dream, experience and imagination, deep human truth, and a return to expressive beauty are all combined in the fine work of Antonio Colinas, the most lyrical of today's young Spanish poets.

See: J. Olivio Jiménez, "El lirismo total de Antonio Colinas," *Escolios* 1, no. 3 (1976): 82–97; L. A. de Villena, "Sobre *Sepulcro en Tarquinia* de Antonio Colinas," *Insula* 354 (May 1976): 5–6.   J.O.J.

Conde, Carmen (1907–), Spanish poet, novelist, essayist, and biographer, was born in Cartagena. She completed studies in pedagogy and also studied philosophy and letters, acquiring a broad cultural background. Active literarily during the "avant-garde" years after World War I, she collaborated with Miguel HERNÁNDEZ, Ramón Sijé, and Oliver Mas in founding the review *El Gallo Crisis*. *Brocal* (1929; The Mouth of the Well), her first volume of poetry, was followed by *Júbilos* (1934; Jubilation). The largest and most essential part of her production, however, belongs to the post-Civil War period, beginning with the poetry of *Pasión del Verbo* (1944; Passion for the Word). Since 1940 she has contributed to periodicals such as *Espadaña* and *La Estafeta Literaria* and produced over 30 books of poetry, essay, novels, and children's stories (sometimes under the pseudonym Florentina del Mar). In 1967 she received the National Prize for Literature for

her *Obra poética,* a collection of her lyrics written between 1929 and 1966. The strong sensual imagery of her poetry expresses an abiding preoccupation with contemporary reality and an urgent desire to grasp the totality of the universe. Her work offers a valuable testimony of her epoch. Among her most important volumes of poetry are: *Ansia de la gracia* (1945; Desire for Grace), *Mi fin en el viento* (1947; My Destiny in the Wind), and *En un mundo de fugitivos* (1960; In a World of Fugitives). Subsequent titles are *Cita con la vida* (1976; Date with Life), and an anthology, *Días por la tierra* (1977; Days on Earth).

Her tensely dramatic novels are written in a personal and lyric style. They include: *Vidas contra su espejo* (1944; Lives against Their Mirror), *Soplo que va y no vuelve* (1944; Breath Which Goes Not to Return), *En manos del silencio* (1950; In the Hands of Silence), and *Las oscuras raíces* (1953; Dark Roots)—in the opinion of many critics, her best narrative. *Cobre* (1954; Copper) incorporates short stories previously published in the collections *Destino hallado* (Encountered Destiny) and *Solamente un viaje* (Only a Journey). *Empezando la vida* (1955; Beginning Life) contains childhood memoirs.

Considered daring for her time, accused of crudeness and masculinity, Conde prefers arduous questions of conscience, spiritual dilemmas, and social issues. In 1978 she became the first woman to be elected to the Royal Spanish Academy of the Language since its foundation in 1714, an accolade reflecting the respect of fellow writers and critics in Spain.

See: F. C. Sainz de Robles, *La novela española en el siglo XX* (1957), pp. 221 and 265; E. G. de Nora, *La novela española contemporánea,* vol. 2 (1967), pp. 385–7; A. Valbuena Prat, *Historia de la literatura española,* vol. 4 (1968), pp. 788–90.   J.W.D.

Conscience, Hendrik (1812–83), Flemish novelist, was born in Antwerp, Belgium. The son of a Napoleonic official, he took a great interest at an early age in his native land and its past. His voluminous work soon attained popularity and gave a new impetus to a language that had suffered from disuse. Conscience is quite rightly considered the first modern Flemish novelist. Deeply influenced by Sir Walter Scott, Victor Hugo, and Lamennais, he wrote more than 100 novels and tales ranging from historical and social works to folk stories. A vigor and enthusiasm permeates his writing, at times eclipsing the psychological analysis of individual characters. Among his best historical novels are *In't Wonderjaer* (1837; During the Wonderyear), consisting of sketches from the 16th century, and, above all, *De Leeuw van Vlaanderen* (1838; Eng. tr., *The Lion of Flanders,* 1855–57), an epic account of the Battle of the Golden Spurs in which the Flemish municipal militia conquered the French army at Kortrijk in 1302. Novels of a social and moral character such as *Siska van Roosemael* (1844) contain a sharp appraisal of the Frenchified Flemish middle class; *De plaag der Dorpen* (1855; The Plague of the Villages) constitutes a warning against the evil of alcoholism. In short novels such as *De Loteling* (1850; Eng. tr., *The Conscript,* 1864), *Rikke-Tikke Tak* (1851; Eng. tr. *Ricketicke-tack,* 1856), and *Baes Gansendonck* (1850; Boss Gansendonck), Conscience combines the moral themes of earlier works with poetic descriptions of the landscape near Kempen, northeast of Antwerp. Although it has been pointed out that Conscience employed Gallicisms and lacked a certain linguistic subtlety, it should be remembered that the role of a precursor is not easy. Alexandre Dumas and Victor Hugo were among those to appreciate this thematically rich and dense work. The popularity of Conscience soon spread beyond Belgium through translations in many languages. Works of Conscience available in English include *Sketches from Flemish Life* (1840), *The Progress of a Painter* (1852), *The Good Mother* (1852), *Tales of Flemish Life* (1854), *Tales of Old Flanders* (1855), *Tales and Romances* (6 vols., 1857), *The Headman's Son* (1861), *The Village Innkeeper* (1867), *The Happiness of Being Rich* (1869), *Tales* (5 vols., 1889), and *Popular Tales* (6 vols., 1902–06). The continuing impact of Conscience's work is attested by a recent work of the major Flemish writer Hugo CLAUS, *Het Goudland Spel naar de rman van Hendrik Conscience* (1966: The Goldland Play After the Novel of Hendrik Conscience).

See: F. Smits, *Henri Conscience et le Romantisme flamand* (1943); A. Van Hageland, *H. Conscience en het Volksleven* (1953).   M.-R.L.

Copeau, Jacques (1877–1949), French stage director and writer, was born in Paris and died in Beaune. After serving as drama critic of *L'Ermitage* and then of the *Grande Revue*, he participated in 1909 in the founding of the *Nouvelle Revue française*. In his articles, Copeau appealed for a radical reform of the theater, which had been given over to commercial speculation, conformism, and to the star system. In 1913 he decided to address the problem himself by founding the Théâtre du Vieux-Colombier on the Left Bank. It was Copeau's goal to bring the intellectual elite back to the theater. He planned to revive long-neglected classics and to support new dramatic authors of high literary stature; to form a homogenous company whose members would be initiated into all the trades of the stage and protected from the routines then current; to give preeminence to the stage director, the essential interpreter of the work and the sole coordinator of the elements that express it; and to renew scenic architecture by bringing the stage close to the audience, while denying the importance of stage machinery and rejecting the stage embellishments of the Italians.

In eight months, from October 1913 to May 1914, Copeau staged 13 classical and modern plays, the last of which, Shakespeare's *Twelfth Night,* firmly established his fame in France and abroad. He kept his distance from both the realism of André ANTOINE and the aestheticism of Jacques Rouché, remaining closer to Gordon Craig than to Konstantin Stanislavsky. At the outset he found remarkable collaborators, such as Charles DULLIN and Louis JOUVET, and strong supporters among the writers of the *Nouvelle Revue*—André GIDE, Jean SCHLUMBERGER, and Roger MARTIN DU GARD.

Declared unfit for military service during World War I, Copeau was sent by the French government to New York where, with the financial backing of Otto Kahn, he performed at the Garrick Theater from 1917 to 1919. Having returned to France, he reopened the Vieux-Colombier, which had been renovated according to his plans (with a permanently installed architectural stage, prolonged by a proscenium). There followed a succession of superb presentations: *Le Misanthrope* and *Les Fourberies de Scapin* by Molière, *The Winter's Tale* by Shakespeare, *Le Carrosse du Saint-Sacrement* by Prosper Mérimée, and, among the contemporaries, *Cromedeyre-le-Vieil* by Jules ROMAINS, *Saül* by Gide, and *Le Paquebot Tenacity* by Charles VILDRAC. Dullin left the Vieux-Colombier in 1919 and Jouvet broke with the company in 1922, yet neither of these events affected the success of the theater; rather it was Copeau himself who, seized by a mystical crisis that brought him back to Catholicism, decided to break with the Parisian intelligentsia. He closed his theater, moved to Burgundy, and founded there the itinerant company of the Copiaux. From 1925 to 1929, this troupe went from village to village giving performances. Then after

four years, he once more put an end to his experiment and returned to Paris, where he gave lectures and staged a few plays (including Racine's *Bajazet* in 1937 at the Comédie-Française). Copeau was appointed administrator of this national theater, but he was forced to resign at the beginning of the German occupation.

When he died at 72, Copeau was considered to be the patron of most young French producers, who had read with keen interest his 1941 article on theater for the people. His sober aesthetic and the moral reform for which he had appealed were soon to triumph resoundingly, thanks to Jean VILAR and his comrades (Jean Dasté, Hubert Gignoux, Maurice Sarrazin), the heirs of the Copiaux adventure.

See: M. Kurtz, *Jacques Copeau: biographie d'un théâtre* (1950); G. Lerminier, *J. Copeau le réformateur* (1953).   R.A.

Coromines, Pere (1870–1939), Catalan prose writer, was born in Barcelona to a family from Ampurias. He obtained his secondary education and pursued studies in law in Barcelona, where he had his first contact with the common people. His desire to inculcate the people with his theories, a combination of romantic anarchism and an almost mystic goodness, led to a misunderstanding that brought upon him a death sentence from which he escaped almost miraculously. Upon leaving the prison of Montjuic, he produced his first book, *Les presons imaginàries* (1899; The Imaginary Prisons). The title is an indication of the author's idealism. He proclaimed the earnest desire for goodness that constituted the guiding star of his whole life in 1911 with the publication of *Vida austera* (Austere Life), a work that won him the acclaim of critics, who called it a kind of "modern effort in the search for saintliness."

Pere Coromines also played an active role in politics; he was one of the founders of the old *Esquerra catalana* (Catalonian Left), an organ of Catalonianism. His journalistic campaigns in the journal *Poble Català* are a model of enthusiasm although his grave errors of political tact resulted in many years of ostracism, during which he dedicated himself to law and writing. He returned to active political life with the establishment of the Spanish Republic in 1931. He was one of those who drew up the Catalan statute of autonomy and was among the first *consejeros* of the new government. All of his work is stamped with a deep Catalan spirit, and even in the philosophic themes he attained a popular tone always in good taste. Among his other works are *Les hores d'amor serenes* (1912; The Serene Hours of Love); *Les gràcies de l'Empordá* (1919; The Graces of Emporda); *Cartes d'un visionari* (1921; Letters of a Visionary); *Estudi sobre el pensament filòsofic dels jueus espanyols a l'Edat Mitjana* (1921; Studies concerning the Philosophical Thought of the Spanish Jews in the Middle Ages); *A recés dels Tamarius* (1925; In the Shadow of the Tamarind Tree); a trilogy, *En Tomàs de Bajalta—Silén* (1925), *Pigmalió* (1928; Pygmalion), and *Prometeu* (1934; Prometheus); and *Interpretació del vuit-cent català* (1937; Interpretation of the Catalonian Penny). Coromines was the first Catalan author to die in America after the exodus of 1939. In his last works, written in France and Argentina, Coromines saw in the Catalonian dispersion something similar to the Hebrew diaspora. His posthumous notes, unfinished and issued fragmentarily by the publishing branch of the journal *Catalunya* of Buenos Aires, are in fact entitled *Diari de la Diàspora* (Diary of the Diaspora). In addition to the *Diari de la Diàspora*, the Buenos Aires journal *Catalunya* also published, posthumously, a collection of short stories, *Gl perfecte dandi* (1940; The Perfect Dandy).

See: "Advertiment," in P. Coromines, *El perfecte dandi;* J. Pous i Pages, "Pere Coromines i el seu temps," *Revista de Catalunya,* no. 97 (March 1940).

J.M.M.iV.

Cortesão, Jaime (1884–1960), Portuguese historian, essayist, dramatist, and poet, was born near Coimbra. Like his father, he studied medicine, but his love belonged to Portuguese history. During his student days in Oporto, he began to write poetry and participate in republican politics. With the advent of the Portuguese Republic in 1910, he founded the *Renascença Portuguesa* (Portuguese Renascence) movement (1912), promoted popular education, and was tireless in writing for periodicals—*A Águia, Atlântida,* and, later on, *Seara Nova.* The military dictatorship of 1926 drove him into exile in Belgium (1927), France (1927), Spain (1931–39), and Brazil (from 1940 on). There he continued a brilliant career as a historian of the Portuguese voyages and colonial expansion. Even during his last years, having returned to Portugal in 1955, he bravely challenged the police regime and was jailed with Antonio SÉRGIO and other civic leaders.

Cortesão's poetry, notably *A Morte da águia* (1910; The Eagle's Death), exalted Nietzschean heroism (*see* Friedrich NIETZSCHE) combined with a Franciscan, active love for all nature, to him the essence of his nation's psyche; this combination is particularly evident in the verse of *Glória humilde* (1914; Humble Glory) and *Divina voluptuosidade* (1923; Divine Sensuousness), as well as in "O Franciscanismo e a mística dos descobrimentos" (1932; Franciscanism and the Mystique of the Voyages of Discovery). An ardent, quixotic patriotism led him to work with others of his generation for a moral and spiritual rebirth under a democratic republic, expressed in his plays *Infante de Sagres* (1913; Prince Henry at Sagres), *Egas Moniz* (1918), and *Adão e Eva* (1921; Adam and Eve). Handsome, tall, daring, brilliant, yet faithful to his principles, Cortesão was by far the most attractive and exemplary figure of his time. He will chiefly be remembered as a historian with stimulating theories and vast syntheses. He also ranks among the few who enriched the literature of both Brazil and Portugal.

See: O. Lopes, *Jaime Cortesão* (1962). G.M.M.

Cortez, Alfredo (1880–1946), Portuguese dramatist, was born in Estremoz and studied law in Coimbra. His profession as a judge opened his eyes to the defects of society. He served the law most of his life in Lisbon and briefly in Angola, an experience reflected in the short play *Moamba* (posthumously published in 1968). He began writing plays in his 40s, and his career was cut short by illness. Starting as a naturalist, he satirized a materialistic, sensual society in his first play, *Zilda* (performed 1921). Cortez returned to such satire in his last plays of 1939, *Bâton* (Lipstick) and *Lá-lás,* neither of which the censors allowed to be produced. During the 1930s he pioneered the expressionistic techniques of farce. His best-known works are *À la fé* (performed 1924; In Faith), a delightful verse drama on a historical theme, the loyalty of the castellan of Coimbra; *Gladiadores* (1934; The Gladiators), a "caricature in three acts" lampooning feminism, male arrogance, the news media, and the law by means of grotesque puppets, and *Tá-Mar* (1936; High Seas), a lyrical play about Portuguese fishermen, exalting the honest laboring population in contrast to the immoral elite. In vain, Cortez and a few other innovators such as Raul BRANDÃO and José RÉGIO battled against the growing timidity of the stage, evidenced by the scandals Cortez provoked with plays and manifestos in 1923 and 1934. Now, however, his place as a versatile pioneer is secure.

See: E. Lisboa Filho, "O Teatro de Alfredo Cortez," *BHTP* 4 (1953): 1–48. G.M.M.

Coşbuc, George (1866–1918), Romanian poet, was born in Hordou, near Năsăud, into a family of priests. He attended the lyceum at Năsăud, where his gifts as a poet were already apparent at an early age. He later studied at the Faculty of Philosophy at Cluj. During his career, Coşbuc was associated with many Transylvanian literary journals that published his poetry: *Tribuna; Vatra,* which he founded with Ioan Slavici and Ion CARAGIALE; *Albina; Sămănătorul;* and *Viaţa literară.*

Coşbuc's early poems were written in an anecdotal style, but he reached his poetical maturity by the time of Mihail Eminescu's death in 1889 (*see* ROMANIAN LITERATURE). Unlike many of his contemporaries, Coşbuc did not fall under the influence of Eminescu's pessimism, but advanced Romanian poetry in new directions. He was versatile and created a wide range of feeling in his poetry. Both *Nunta Zamfirei* (1889; Zamfira's Wedding), which captures the exuberance of youth through its cadenced dance rhythms, and *Moartea lui Fulger* (1893; The Death of Fulger), with its philosophic resignation of a soul facing death, reflect the Romanian spirit in its most traditional, poetic form. *Noi vrem pamînt* (1894; We Want Land), inspired by contemporary social conditions, is a dramatic monologue imbued with the furious spirit of revolt. Social protest is voiced even more clearly in *Cîntece de vitezie* (1904; Songs of Valor), a collection of poems about Romania's war of independence.

In addition to his poetry, Coşbuc produced numerous translations from Virgil, Friedrich Schiller, Lord Byron, and Dante. His translation of the *Divine Comedy* (1924–32), which imitated even the exact number of syllables of the original, has remained a classic. Coşbuc's commentaries on the *Divine Comedy,* written for his own edification and published posthumously between 1964 and 1966, are still valuable for scholars.

See: G. Scridon, *Pagini despre Coşbuc* (1957); D. Vatamaniuc, *George Coşbuc, o privire asupre operei literare* (1967). V.A.

Ćosić, Dobrica (1921–), Serbian novelist and essayist, was born in Velika Drenova, in central Serbia. After graduating from agriculture school, he participated in World War II as a political commissar with the Partisans. Later he occupied Communist Party, administrative, and cultural positions, was elected a representative to the Yugoslav Parliament, and became president of the prestigious "Srpska Književna Zadruga" (Society of Serbian Letters). When his political views began to deviate from the official line, however, he was relieved of his duties and posts. He subsequently lived a private life as a professional writer.

Ćosić's first novel, *Daleko je sunce* (1951; The Sun Is Far Away), was universally acclaimed as the best Serbian fictional treatment of the events of World War II, especially of the Partisan struggle against foreign and domestic enemies. A simple but mature realism and a pronounced objectivity made this novel almost a contemporary classic. His other novels—*Koreni* (1954; Roots), *Deobe* (1961; Divisions), *Bajka* (1966; A Fable), and *Vreme smrti* (1972, 1975; The Time of Death)—all treat a related subject matter. What seems to emerge from these works is the grand design of a series of novels examining the emergence of the peasant as the most vital social force in the last century of Serbian history, especially during the two world wars. When completed, Ćosić's opus should present a unique analysis in fictional form of the social fabric of an entire nation as unfolded through the most important events in its recent history. Ćosić has also written two books of essays, the second of which, *Akcija* (1965; Action), offers his views as a political activist.

Although Ćosić's approach is basically realistic, his works harbor much deeper meaning. As he follows the destinies of the little man, he often shows that great events are often made great by seemingly insignificant participants. When writing of war, Ćosić seems to be intrigued mostly by the motives that drive people to make war on each other. All of this is especially evident in his best work to date, *Vreme smrti*. His powers of synthesis, together with his attention to detail, have made him a leading Serbian writer and one whose works often transcend their purely literary framework.

See: I. Bandić, "Izmedju sunca i korena," *Vreme romana* (1958), pp. 84–102; D. M. Jeremić, "Dobrica Ćosić," *Prsti nevernog Tome* (1965), pp. 255–79.

V.D.M.

Costa, Joaquín (1846–1911), Spanish jurist, historian, and political philosopher born in Monzón, in the province of Huesca, was a precursor of the Generation of 1898. Famed for his powerful oratory, he made impassioned speeches after the disastrous Spanish-American War of 1898 in an effort to dispel national lethargy and promote reform. In his celebrated lectures at the Madrid Ateneo, later collected in *Oligarquía y caciquismo* (1901; Oligarchy and Bossism), he made a lucid and ruthless attack on the pseudoparliamentary regime, declaring that the entire oligarchical system must be extirpated by means of a rapid "surgical operation." His rallying cry, "Desafricanización y europeización de España" (A Less African, More European Spain), raised one of the central issues to be debated by thinkers like Miguel de UNAMUNO, Ramiro de MAEZTU, and José ORTEGA Y GASSET. Although his gift of speech was widely admired and even imitated by younger intellectuals, several of the latter, notably Unamuno and later Ortega, felt that his proposed solutions to national ills did not adequately define the real problems of Spain. Costa urged the swift technical and pedagogical modernization of Spain, succinctly expressed in phrases like "La escuela y la despensa" (School and Pantry), but most members of the Generation of 1898 preferred to seek the origin of these problems, along with their possible solutions, in the primal ethos of Spain, and several came to distrust the idea of compromise with contemporary European culture. There is no doubt, however, that Costa's pronouncements contributed to an intellectual and artistic reappraisal of Spanish institutions and national character.

Although Costa was the apostle of Europeanization, he was also an untiring investigator of Spain's most ancient traditions. Indeed, his political speeches and essays occupied but a small fraction of his life. He spent much of his time digging away at mountains of documents with diligence and tenacity and writing long erudite works on such varied topics as custom as the source of law, in *La vida del derecho* (1876; The Life of Law) and *El derecho consuetudinario de España* (1885; Customary Law of Spain). He examined the political ideals of the Spanish people in their popular poetry in *La poesía popular española y mitología y literatura celto-hispanas* (1881; Popular Spanish Poetry and Celto-Hispanic Mythology and Literature); the evolution of Spanish political institutions, in *Estudios jurídicos y políticos* (1884; Juridical and Political Studies); the origins of Spanish culture, in the highly original *Estudios ibéricos* (1891–94; Iberian

Studies); and agrarian problems, in *Colectivismo agrario en España* (1898; Agrarian Collectivism in Spain)—a work that, incidentally, remains of interest today.

See: E. Tierno Galván, *Costa y el regeneracionismo* (1961); R. Pérez de la Dehesa, *El pensamiento de Costa y su influencia en la generación del 98* (1966).

E.F.H. rev. H.R.

Costa i Llobera, Miquel (1854–1922), Catalan poet, prose writer, and orator, was born of a well-to-do family on the island of Majorca. He moved to Barcelona and then to Madrid to study law, a career which he abandoned for lack of true vocation. In 1874 he competed in the poetic contests, the Jocs Florals, in Barcelona. Later he retired to Majorca, where he devoted himself leisurely to literature. In 1885 his first volume of poems, *Poesies*, was issued. He then went to Rome to study in the Gregorian University, was ordained a priest in 1888, and the following year received the degree of doctor of sacred theology. Travels through Italy gave a permanent classical stamp to his tastes and manner of thinking. Returning to his native island, he again devoted himself to literature in his native tongue and again took part in the poetic contests of Barcelona. He was named *mestre en gai saber* (master troubadour) in 1902 for having won first prize in each of the three essential subjects in the celebration of the Jocs Florals—in songs to faith, to love, and to the homeland. In 1909 he was named canon of the cathedral of Palma de Mallorca. *De l'agre de la terra* (From the Bitterness of the Earth), *Tradicions i fantasies* (Traditions and Fantasies), and *Visions de Palestina* (Visions of Palestine) appeared in 1897, 1903, and 1908 respectively. His crowning work is, without doubt, the volume of poetry entitled *Horacianes* (1906; Poems in the Manner of Horace), in which formal perfection and inspiration are happily joined.

The work of Costa i Llobera, although not voluminous, has exerted a wide influence on Catalan literature in general and in the development of the so-called Majorcan school, which aimed at formal perfection and admired the most varied forms of classicism. Costa i Llobera gives himself over completely to the power of full-blown emotion. Indeed, there is scarcely a trace of humor or irony in his poetry. His songs seem to spring tirelessly from a soul full of serenity, as though lost in contemplation of the inexhaustible beauties of the Majorcan countryside. His work has been recognized all over Europe and translated into Czech, Hungarian, German, and Swedish. An edition of his complete works was published in 1924 by the Illustració Catalana in four volumes.

See: M. de Montoliu, *Estudis de literatura catalana* (1912); A. Plana, *Antologia de poetes catalans moderns* (1914); C. Giardini, *Antologia dei poeti catalani contemporanei, 1845–1925* (1926).

F. de P.

Couperus, Louis Marie Anne (1863–1923), Dutch novelist, poet, and journalist, was born in The Hague. He lived and traveled abroad for many years, especially in Indonesia and Italy. After completing his education as a teacher, he devoted himself completely to literature and began by writing poetry. His first poems appeared in *De Gids* and were later published as *Een Lent van vaerzen* (1884; A Springtide of Verse) and *Orchideën* (1886; Orchids). His reputation as a writer, however, rests on his novels. He established it with *Eline Vere* (1889; Eng. tr., 1892), a novel about the aristocratic society of The Hague, from which Couperus himself came. The novel portrays the disintegration of a sensitive young woman, who is destroyed by her own lassitude and inertia. These qualities are seen as hereditary character defects, which form the fate not only of Eline, but of many of Couperus's heroes and heroines. This idea appears again in *Noodlot* (1890; Eng. tr., *Footsteps of Fate*, 1891), in which two men and a woman, involved in a triangular relationship, are doomed by their own hereditary weaknesses. *Noodlot* and such other novels of this period as *Extaze* (1892; Eng. tr., *Ecstasy: A Study of Happiness*, 1892), *Majesteit* (1893; Eng. tr., *Majesty*, 1894), *Wereldvrede* (1895; World Peace), *Metamorfoze* (1897; Metamorphosis)—based on Couperus's own development as a novelist—*Psyche* (1898; Eng. tr., 1908), and *Fidessa* (1899) do not come up to the achievement of *Eline Vere*.

With *De stille kracht* (1900; Eng. tr., *The Hidden Force: A Story of Modern Java*, 1922), however, Couperus again demonstrated his mastery of the psychological novel and also captured the mysterious atmosphere of Indonesia. Like *Eline Vere*, the novel portrays the complete destruction of the main character. Decay and disintegration also form the main theme of the tetralogy *De boeken der kleine zielen* (1901–03; The Books of the Small Souls), which consists of *De kleine zielen* (1901; Eng. tr., *Small Souls*, 1914), *Het late leven* (1902; Eng. tr., *The Later Life*, 1915), *Zielenschemering* (1902; Eng. tr., *The Twilight of the Souls*, 1917), and *Het heilige weten* (1903; Eng. tr., *Dr. Adriaan*, 1918). Again Couperus displays his talent for both character and the social novel. As before, his characters are from the upper classes of The Hague, and they have years of experience in Indonesia behind them. *Van oude menschen, de dingen die voorbijgaan* (1906; Eng. tr., *Old People and the Things That Pass*, 1918, 1963) depicts the same people in the same milieu but is also an outstanding example of Couperus's skill in constructing a novel. He portrays the last 18 months in the lives of the main characters, a couple in their nineties, who have hidden, for 60 years, the secret that made their life together possible. He keeps the reader in a state of suspense, and it remains one of his best novels. During his stay in Italy, he became interested in antiquity and wrote several historical novels, including *Dionyzos* (1904; Dionysus); *De berg van licht* (1905–06; The Mountain of Light), which has as its hero the child-emperor Heliogabalus; and *Herakles* (1913; Hercules), a reworking of classical myths. During his life in The Hague, Couperus wrote *De komedianten* (1917; Eng. tr., *The Comedians: A Story of Ancient Rome*, 1926), about the actor's life in Rome; *Xerxes, of de hoogmoed* (1919; Eng. tr., *Arrogance: The Conquests of Xerxes*, 1930); and *Iskander* (1920), a novel based on the life of Alexander the Great. Couperus also had a gift for short fiction, and his stories were collected in such volumes as *Eene illuzie* (1892; Illusion and Other Stories) and *Hooge troeven* (1896; High Trumps). He wrote travel books, and he was a successful journalist. For some years, he wrote weekly feuilletons for *Het Vaderland*, a newspaper in The Hague, and these were collected in the series *Van en over mijzelf en anderen* (1911–18; Of and about Myself and Others), where he reveals himself with humor and irony.

Couperus stood completely apart from "De Beweging van Tachtig" (The Movement of the Eighties). He was a dandy and explored the theme of homosexuality. Although his style is ornate, he is linked to the naturalists, especially in his view of heredity. A master of character and narration, however, he remains one of the most important novelists of the modern period.

See: H. van Booven, *Leven en werken van Louis Couperus* (1933); H. W. van Tricht, *Louis Couperus: een verkenning* (1960); A. Vogel, *De man met de orchidee: het levensverhaal van Louis Couperus* (1973).   S.L.F.

Courteline, Georges, pseud. of Georges Moineaux (1858–

1929), French poet and novelist, was born in Tours. He is best remembered for his one-act comedies. His father, a court reporter, also wrote light comedies. Courteline served in the cavalry and then worked as an indolent civil servant until 1894, at which time he had achieved success with his novels of barracks life, *Les Gaîtés de l'escadron* (1886; The Gaieties of the Squadron) and *Le Train de 8 h. 47* (1891; The 8:47 Train), and of office life, *Messieurs les Ronds-de-cuir* (1893; Eng. tr., *The Bureaucrats*, 1930). His dramatization of *Les Gaîtés de l'escadron* in 1895 caused him to turn from the novel to the theater.

Many of Courteline's comedies were produced at the Théâtre Libre by André ANTOINE and at the Comédie-Française. A keen observer of Parisian life, he portrayed everyday scenes, many satirizing lawyers and police. These include *Un Client sérieux* (1896; A Serious Customer), *Le Commissaire est bon enfant* (1899; Eng. tr., *The Commissioner*, 1960), *Le Gendarme est sans pitié* (1899; Eng. tr., *The Pitiless Policeman*, 1916), and *L'Article 330* (1900; Eng. tr., *Article 330*, 1961). Courteline satirized average people in *Monsieur Badin* (1897; Eng. tr., *Badin the Bold*, 1961); *Boubouroche*, his masterpiece (1893; Eng. tr., 1961); and *La Paix chez soi* (1903; Eng. tr., *Peace at Home*, 1918). Between 1890 and 1914, Courteline was at the peak of his career. He was made an officer of the Legion of Honor and in 1926 was elected to the Académie Goncourt. Like Molière, with whom he is often compared, Courteline was a perceptive creator of true-to-life characters, whom he described in vivid, vigorous style. But in imagination, scope, and depth, Courteline demonstrates mere talent where Molière had genius.

See: A. Dubeux, *La Curieuse Vie de Georges Courteline* (1958); P. Bornecque, *Le Théâtre de Georges Courteline* (1959).   A.S.

Craveirinha, José (1922–), a Mozambican poet writing in Portuguese, was born of an African woman and a European father in Lourenço Marques. Most of his relatively small output of poems has appeared in two volumes of limited distribution, *Chigubo* (1964), named after a traditional African dance, and *Karinguana ua karinguana* (1974), a Ronga term meaning, roughly, "once upon a time." His limited output and the fact that he is outside the mainstream of Portuguese poetry have combined to deny Craveirinha the recognition he deserves. Even so, some have praised his craft and the creativeness of his imagery, and exponents of an African literature of European expression laud his social consciousness and his message of black defiance. Much of the effectiveness of Craveirinha's poetry results from his use of rhetorical devices that simulate an African oral tradition. When the poet sings of the "blood of names," in "Hino à minha terra" (Anthem to My Land), he approaches what the German Africanist Janheinz Jahn called the Bantu concept of the power of the word that encompasses water, seed, and blood. Craveirinha breathes life into his poem by repeatedly using African place names until he reaches a driving power that transcends the merely exotic.

Accusations of subversion led to the poet's three-year imprisonment and the temporary silencing of his powerful voice. When he resumed writing, under the watchful eye of the censor, he did so with a caution that produced cryptic, often surrealistic imagery, for example, in poems appearing in *Caliban*, a literary journal of Lourenço Marques (1971–72). With the installation, in 1974, of a provisional black liberation government, the way was open for the publication of *Karingana ua karingana*. For all their defiance, these poems conjure up incantatory and ritualistic sentiments in Craveirinha's typically strong images.

See: R. A. Preto-Rodas, *Negritude as a Theme in the Poetry of the Portuguese-Speaking World* (1970), pp. 73–76; E. Lisboa, "Algumas considerações em torno da poesia de José Craveirinha," *Crónicas dos anos da peste,* vol. 1 (1973), pp. 209–24; R. G. Hamilton, *Voices from an Empire* (1975), pp. 202–12.   R.G.H.

Crémieux, Benjamin (1888–1944), French critic, *docteur ès lettres,* was born in Narbonne. Crémieux served as a member of the editorial committee of the influential *Nouvelle Revue française.* Cosmopolitan in outlook, he was permanent secretary of the French PEN Club and a frequent contributor to foreign literary periodicals. A specialist in Italian literature, he introduced both Luigi PIRANDELLO and Italo SVEVO to the French public through numerous articles, translations, and adaptations. In *XXᵉ Siècle* (1924; 20th Century), a collection of essays, he combined genetic criticism and an evolutionary method of tracing a writer's internal aesthetic development. The 90-page introductory essay to this volume provides one of the earliest detailed analyses of Marcel PROUST's structure, themes, and style.

Crémieux's masterpiece is *Inquiétude et reconstruction* (1931; Unrest and Reconstruction), in which his university training, familiarity with literary history, and ability to synthesize large areas of knowledge led him to apply the evolutionary method to the whole decade following World War I. He identified and followed in detail the parallel currents of anarchy and reconstruction with remarkable objectivity and critical acumen. Faithful to the program of the *Nouvelle Revue,* he heralded a modern classicism and humanism as the new direction. Crémieux's optimism prevented him from realizing until very late the significance of political and social unrest in Europe. When the Germans occupied France, he joined the Resistance, was arrested, and deported to Buchenwald, where he died.

See: A. Eustis, *Trois Critiques de "La Nouvelle Revue française"* (1961), pp. 71–120.   A.E.

Crevel, René (1900–35), French essayist and novelist, was born in Paris. While researching a dissertation on Denis Diderot, Crevel met and joined the surrealists (*see* FRENCH LITERATURE). He participated in their experimentations with hypnosis, dream transcriptions, and the functioning of language and soon became involved in the philosophical implications of surrealism, publishing philosophical treatises and militant tracts in *La Revue surréaliste.* Crevel transferred spiritual questions from the context of 18th-century rationalism to 20th-century materialistic dynamism: "What do I care for an *elsewhere* that I cannot imagine different from the *here and now*?" he asked in *Etes-vous fou?* (1929; Are You Crazy?). In *L'Esprit contre la raison* (1928; Mind against Reason) and *Le Clavecin de Diderot* (1932; Diderot's Harpsichord), Crevel called for the liberation of the mind from the barriers of reason and the strictures of bourgeois society. On the eve of the Congrès des Ecrivains pour la Défense de la Culture he committed suicide, an act attributed to his futile effort to conciliate the surrealists and the Marxists.

Crevel's literary work was a form of self-immolation and redemption, somewhat as it had been for his models, Arthur RIMBAUD and LAUTRÉAMONT. Crevel posthumously emerged as an avant-garde novelist, possessing an emblematic realism that combines brutality and an evanescent beauty. The child-woman heroine of the last of his three novels, *Babylone* (1927; Babylonia), is a free spirit, like André BRETON's Nadja, but she is more aggressive in her confrontation of cosmic and human forces. Crevel's narrative form is free, his subjectivity dispersed.

His 10 published volumes contain only scattered critical writings. None of Crevel's works has been translated into English.   A.B.

Crnjanski, Miloš (1893–), Serbian poet, novelist, and playwright, was born in Csongrád, Hungary. An ardent nationalist, he was nevertheless compelled to serve in the Austro-Hungarian army at the Eastern Front in World War I. The horrors of war filled him with such loathing that he became a militant pacifist. After World War I, Crnjanski worked as a journalist and served as a diplomat. Because of his antileftist views, he refused to return to his country after World War II, living for many years in London and working at various menial jobs. He finally returned to Yugoslavia in 1965 and settled in Belgrade, revered as one of the greatest contemporary Serbian writers.

Crnjanski's first publications were a volume of poetry, *Lirika Itake* (1919; The Lyrics of Ithaca), followed by a short poetic novel, *Dnevnik o Čarnojeviću* (1921; Diary about Čarnojević). In both works he displayed an unusual talent and strength of conviction, an antiwar attitude, and modernist tendencies, all of which made him one of the leading avant-garde poets. His best work, the two-volume novel *Seobe* (1929, 1962; Migrations), depicts the fate of the Serbs in Vojvodina in the second half of the 18th century, fighting for their foreign rulers while constantly dreaming of the renaissance of their own nation or of migration to Russia. His more recent works include the hymnlike poem *Lament nad Beogradom* (1962; Lament over Belgrade), which reflects the poet's closeness to Serbia's largest city and also gives him an opportunity to express mature, melancholy sentiments about life in general. *Kod Hiperborejaca* (1966; With the Hyperboreans) is a mixture of memoirs and a narrative about the last prewar days in Rome, where Crnjanski served as a diplomat. *Kap španske krvi* (1970; A Drop of Spanish Blood) is a fictionalized biography of the 19th-century dancer and adventuress Lola Montez. His most ambitious work since *Seobe* is *Roman o Londonu* (1971; A Novel about London). This sympathetic depiction of the tragic fate of a Russian émigré is replete with philosophizing about the vagaries of human existence.

Whether he was advocating modernistic tendencies in poetry, championing rightist causes, or expressing tolerance and quiet resignation after a long, rich life, Crnjanski has always been in the middle of battle and controversy. Relying more on emotions than analysis, he helped bring a cosmopolitan outlook to Serbian literature between the two world wars. His powerful talent, vitality, boldness, and master of the language account for his considerable influence among younger Serbian poets.

See: M. Žeželj, "Miloš Crnjanski," *Srpski književni glasnik* 58 (1939): 208–17, 278–86; N. Milošević, *Roman Miloša Crnjanskog* (1970); A. Petrov, *Poezija Crnjanskog i srpsko pesništvo* (1971).   V.D.M.

Croatian literature. The Croatian Renaissance of the 15th and 16th centuries developed in the coastal towns and on the islands of Dalmatia, the narrow region that had escaped Turkish conquest. Croatian writers were inspired not only by humanistic classicism and Italian literature but also by medieval Croatian religious writings and South Slavic folk poetry, in both of which were preserved the national spirit and the purity of the mother tongue. Three writers from Dalmatia, Marko Marulić (1450–1524), Marin Držić (1508–67), and Ivan Gundulić (1589–1638), are usually regarded as the best examples of the Croatian cultural activity that lasted from the late 15th through the 17th centuries. Marulić's poem *Judith* was written to encourage his countrymen in their fight against the Turks; Držić's comedies depict the city of Dubrovnik in the period of its prosperity and decadence; Gundulić in his epic poem *Osman* expressed the hope that the Poles would free their South Slavic brethren. In *Razgovor ugodni naroda slovinskoga* (1756; A Pleasant Discourse of the Slavic People), Andrija Kačić-Miošić imitated folk poetry so that the common people might more easily accept his Slavic history. Some of his poems were translated by Alberto Fortis into Italian and by Goethe into German.

The "Illyrian movement" (1830–49) grew out of the Croatian struggle in the early 19th century for political, social, and cultural independence from the Austrians and Hungarians. Based on the mistaken assumption that the ancient Illyrians were the ancestors of all the Slavs in the Balkan Peninsula, the movement originally had as its aim the encouragement of linguistic and cultural solidarity among all the South Slavs; but the Bulgarians were scarcely touched by it and the Slovenes and Serbs rejected it; consequently the movement remained essentially a Croatian phenomenon. The most talented writers among the "Illyrians" were Ivan Mažuranic (1814–90), Stanko Vraz (1810–51), and Petar Preradović (1818–72). Both Vraz and Preradović created songs that have not yet lost their power, yet only Mažuranic produced a masterpiece, his epic poem *Smrt Smail-age Čengića* (1846; Death of Smail-Aga Čengić). In this work Mažuranic covered the whole history of the Croats and other South Slavs in their struggle with the Ottoman Empire.

The most famous Croatian author of the 1870s was August Šenoa (1838–81), whose novels *Zlatarevo zlato* (1871; The Goldsmith's Gold) and *Seljačka buna* (1877; The Peasant Rebellion) have remained popular to this day. In the 1880s, other novelists treated predominantly historical subjects. These writers who were ardent Croatian nationalists, included Ante Kovačić (1854–89), Eugen Kumičić (1850–1904), Ksaver Šandor Djalski (1854–1935), and Vjenceslav Novak (1859–1905). Silvije Strahimir KRANJČEVIĆ was the best Croatian poet at the end of the 19th century.

The history of 20th-century Croatian letters may be conveniently divided into the "Moderna" period, the period between the two world wars, and the postwar period. The Croatian "Moderna" (modernism) period (1895–1918) may be dated from the famous incident in which Zagreb University students burned the Hungarian flag in the presence of Emperor Franz Josef. The period extends to the creation of the first, royal, Yugoslav state in December 1918. These students, at first imprisoned and then expelled from Zagreb, were allowed to study at other universities within the Austro-Hungarian Empire. The largest group went to Prague, where they fell under the influence of Tomáš MASARYK. Masaryk taught them to abandon their romantic dreams of a national past and instead to work pragmatically and patiently for the political, social, and cultural awakening of the masses. Among those who returned home from Prague, there emerged many journalists, sociologists, and politicians (such as Stjepan Radić). Yet with the exception of the literary critic Milan Marjanović (1879–1955), this group produced no significant writer. The circle of Croatian students in Vienna, although much smaller than the Prague group, was more artistically inclined and from its ranks came several good writers. These writers were at first influenced by Hermann BAHR (from whom they borrowed the term "Moderna"), and later they became a part of the Viennese branch of the "Secession movement" in the arts.

Other Croatian writers absorbed different foreign influences. Antun Gustav MATOŠ, an outstanding literary figure at the turn of the century, became directly acquainted with French letters during a sojourn of several years in Paris. Vladimir NAZOR, Ivo VOJNOVIĆ, and Milan BEGOVIĆ, three important writers from Dalmatia, were mainly influenced by the Italians. Still other Croatian writers kept in touch with literary trends in Poland, the Scandinavian countries, England, and even the United States. All these often contradictory currents created in the minds of the younger generation of Croatian writers a somewhat confused idea about literature. As long as they felt united against traditional values, they considered themselves a single movement, and collectively they form a distinctive chapter in Croatian literature. But they soon went off in various directions, each relying on his individual creative instinct.

In addition to Kranjčević, Matoš, Nazor, Vojnović, and Milan Begović, the "Moderna" writers include Vladimir Vidrić (1875–1909), a discreet and evasive poet who took refuge in antiquity, hoping to convey his liberal views through historical sketches; Dragutin Domjanić (1875–1933), whose melodious poems written in the Kajkavian dialect prove how deeply he was grieved by the miseries of the peasants; Fran Galović (1887–1914), whose elegiac, musical poetry, also in Kajkavian, expresses his love for his native region and his fear of death; Milutin Cihlar-Nehajev (1880–1931), an original literary critic who also wrote the powerful novel *Vuci* (1928; Wolves); Dinko Šimunović (1893–1933), whose novels of bourgeois life are rather weak but whose short stories superbly depict the peasants of the Dalmatian hinterland; Milan Ogrizović (1877–1923), who is best known for two dramas—the anticlerical *Prokletstvo* (1907; A Curse), and his successful adaptation of a famous Muslim folk song, *Hasanaginica* (1909; The Wife of Hasan-aga); Josip Kosor (1879–1961), whose naturalistic plays, obsessed with man's hunger for the land and for women, were better known and appreciated abroad than at home; Ivana Brlić-Mažuranić (1874–1938), who wrote popular children's stories and was nicknamed "the Croatian Andersen"; and Branko Vodnik (1879–1926), who opened broad, new horizons in literary criticism before his early death.

The two decades (1918–41) between the two world wars each have distinct political and cultural features. The first decade ended with the assassination of the Croatian peasant leader Stjepan Radić (1928) and with the proclamation of a dictatorship by King Alexander (1929). This period was dominated by modernistic trends in literature—expressionism in Zagreb and surrealism in Belgrade—and was a period of remarkable productivity, during which several periodicals of high quality were published. The 1930s, however, were less occupied with literary theories than with nationalistic, social, and ideological issues. Although the leftists were interesting and stimulating, particularly through Krleža's revisionist journals *Danas* (Today) and *Pečat* (The Signet), the dominant force in Croatian letters was still provided by the non-Communists, writing mostly in the journals *Savremenik* (Contemporary Review), *Hrvatska prosvjeta* (Croatian Lore), and *Hrvatska revija* (Croatian Review). Bourgeois and liberal authors were overconfident, however, especially when compared with the Stalinist propagandists. During this period, German influence, formerly strong, was replaced by the influence of French culture. The Italians were disliked for their annexation of Istria, and interest in Italian literature went into sharp decline, even in Dalmatia. The 19th-century Russian authors continued to be admired, and Fyodor DOSTOYEVSKY's impact upon certain writers was particularly powerful. In leftist circles, the Soviet writers—good and bad—were read and translated.

Significant writers of the period between the two world wars include Tin UJEVIĆ, Miroslav KRLEŽA, Antun BARAC, Dobriša CESARIĆ, and Dragutin TADIJANOVIĆ. Mention should also be made, however, of the poets Antun Branko Šimić (1898–1925) and Ljubo Wiesner (1885–1951), who were considered talented disciples of Matoš; Gustav Krklec (1899–1978), whose luminous, silvery verses were unique; Djuro Sudeta (1903–27) and Nikola Šop (1904–), who were responsible for the high esteem in which Catholic poetry was held; Ilija Nametak (1906–), who introduced the Bosnian Muslim milieu in his stories; Djuro Vilović (1889–1958), who treated the Croatian north and south in his prose; Slavko Kolar (1891–1963), the best Croatian humorist; and Mile Budak (1889–1945), who became the dominant literary figure of the late 1930s, in particular because of his novel *Ognjište* (1938; The Hearth).

In spite of World War II and the totalitarian regime of Ante Pavelić (1941–45), cultural activity did not stop in Zagreb. Although no significant literary works were produced during these years, Croatia displayed astonishing energy in publishing. Such leftists as Miroslav Krleža, Petar ŠEGEDIN, and Marijan Matković (1915–) remained in Zagreb, but did not participate in cultural life; and the prominent literary critic Antun Barac succeeded in publishing a text in which he defended his "freedom to be silent." Two Croatian "nationalist" writers, Vladimir Nazor and Ivan Goran Kovačić (1913–43), left the Croatian capital at the end of 1942 and joined Marshal Tito's Partisans. In the Bosnian mountains, Kovačić composed his powerful poem *Jama* (1944; The Pit), and Nazor wrote his famous "Partisan poems" (1944; *Pjesme partizanke*).

In 1945, the victorious Partisans established the Yugoslav "federated" state, enlarged the Croatian national boundaries with the recovery of Istria, satisfied the Macedonians by granting them their own republic, and increased the mass media and the number of schools. However, they also introduced a Communist dictatorship that has mercilessly tried (especially in the early postwar years) to eliminate every possible opponent. This regime at first adhered strictly to the postwar Soviet precepts of socialist realism, but from the middle 1950s onward, and particularly during the 1960s, there was a trend toward liberalization in every area of Yugoslav life.

The gradual improvement in the intellectual climate began with Šegedin's 1949 attack on socialist realism, and with Krleža's famous talk in Ljubljana in 1952 demanding creative freedom. Western writers such as T. S. Eliot and Federico GARCÍA LORCA were influential through translations of their works. Some Yugoslav authors who had previously been proscribed, such as Ujević and Šimić, were admired by a steadily growing number of younger writers grouped around the periodical *Krugovi* (1952–58; Cycles), later succeeded by *Književnik* (1959–61; The Bookman). The great majority of present-day Croatian writers, including Jure KAŠTELAN, began or continued their literary activity in these two periodicals.

Toward the end of the 1960s, there was a general belief, particularly among Yugoslav intellectuals, that the country was moving toward decentralized, democratic institutions. Their faith was expressed in their writings. The same spirit was manifest in the pages of several first-rate journals: *Forum* (published since 1962), *Kolo* (1963–71), *Kritika* (1968–71), and *Umjetnost riječi* (published since 1957; The Art of the Word). Not a single major Croatian city lacked a literary magazine, and the number of published books increased greatly.

At the beginning of the 1970s, however, fearing that the Communist Party apparatus no longer controlled the intellectuals and large segments of the population, Marshal Tito and his old guard "centralists" began crushing all liberal voices and reintroducing dogmatic orthodoxy. In Croatia, as in the rest of Yugoslavia, writers were once more subjected to witch-hunts, to attacks for the slightest deviation from ideological purity, and in many cases to imprisonment. The prestigious Croatian literary association "Matica Hrvatska" (Croatian Literary Society) was brought to a standstill.

This turbulent, oscillating postwar period witnessed the emergence of several significant figures. Along with Petar Šegedin, Ranko MARINKOVIĆ, Jure Kaštelan, and Vesna PARUN, there were the prose writers Vjekoslav Kaleb (1905–), Vladan Desnica (1905–67), Mirko Božić (1919–), Ivan Raos (1921–), Slobodan Novak (1924–), and Antun Šoljan (1932–); the poets Drago Ivanišević (1907–), Ivan Slamnig (1930–), Slavko Mihalić (1928–), and Vlado Gotovac (1930–); the playwright Marijan Matković; and several erudite, energetic literary critics, such as Vlatko Pavletić (1930–) and Ivo Frangeš (1920–).

After 1945, dozens of non-Communist Croatian authors escaped abroad, settling mostly in Argentina, where some of their works were brought out by Vinko Nikolić (1912–), the poet and publisher of *Hrvatska revija* (1951–). Among the better Croatian émigré writers are Srećko Karaman (1909–64), Vinko Nikolić, Ante Nizeteo (1913–), Boris Maruna (1940–), and Mirko Vidović (1940–). The best poet among them was Viktor VIDA, who finally could endure no longer the painful life of an émigré, and committed suicide.

See: A. Barac, *Yugoslav Literature* (1955, 1973); A. Kadić, *Contemporary Croatian Literature* (1960); A. Kadić, *From Croatian Renaissance to Yugoslav Socialism* (1969); V. Mihailovich and M. Matejić, eds., *Yugoslav Literature in English: A Bibliography* (1976).

A.K.

Croce, Benedetto (1866–1952), Italian philosopher and critic, was born to a well-to-do family in Pescasseroli (Abruzzi). He lived most of his life in Naples as a scholar of independent means, pursuing wide-ranging historical, philosophical, and literary studies and participating in public life. He was made a senator in 1910 and served for a time (1920–21) as minister of public instruction. In 1943 he became minister without portfolio and played an important role in the transition of Italy from monarchy to republic.

In a commemorative article written on the 20th anniversary of Croce's death, the journalist and critic Pietro Citati called him "the most complex, difficult and misunderstood writer of our century," comparing him to Michel de Montaigne (1533–92) and Jorge Luis Borges (1899–), "writers who seek to gather into their pages the essence of all the books that have ever been written . . . and who, after a long sojourn in dusty libraries, acquire a truly rare comprehension of their meaning." In a more conventional vein, Cecil Sprigge (1952) summarized Croce's achievement thus: "No comparable attempt has been made in modern times to bring into a comprehensive and fully interconnected pattern the entire range of human intellectual, or, to use Croce's own term, spiritual activity: indeed, by inference, the whole range of human experience and behaviour." So strong was Croce's impact and so pervasive his activity that it is impossible to speak of a half century of Italian intellectual life without making reference to him.

In 1902, Croce founded *La critica*, a semimonthly review, which he continued to direct until 1951; in its last six years it was published less regularly under the title *Quaderni della critica*. *La critica* undertook two main tasks. First, to assess the literary and cultural achievements of the first 50 years of Italian independence. Second, to provide a counterbalance to what Croce felt was the confusion created by the eclecticism of other periodicals. This was to be done by reviewing new publications in philosophy and criticism from the standpoint of philosophical idealism. (Croce cited Francis Bacon in the Introduction to *La critica*: "The truth emerges sooner out of error than out of confusion.") As advisor to the publisher Laterza of Bari, whose series *Scrittori d'Italia* (Writers of Italy) and *Classici della filosofia moderna* (Classics of Modern Philosophy) he planned and directed, Croce was instrumental in making available hitherto unpublished or out-of-print texts and in setting standards of textual scholarship. As a literary critic, he dealt with writers belonging to the main linguistic areas of the West, ranging from Homer and Aristophanes to Rainer Maria RILKE, Marcel PROUST, and Luigi PIRANDELLO. Among the best of his critical essays are *Ariosto, Shakespeare e Corneille* (1920, 4th ed., 1950; Eng. tr., 1920), *La poesia di Dante* (1921, 6th ed., 1948; Eng. tr., *The Poetry of Dante*, 1922), *Goethe* (1919, 4th ed., 1946; Eng. tr., 1923), and *Poesia e non poesia* (1923, 6th ed., 1950; Eng. tr., *European Literature in the Nineteenth Century*, 1924). The last volume includes essays on Sir Walter Scott, Stendhal, Heinrich Heine, Honoré de Balzac, Charles BAUDELAIRE, Gustave Flaubert, and Henrik IBSEN, as well as Alessandro Manzoni (1785–1873), Giacomo Leopardi (1798–1837), Giosuè Carducci (1835–1907), and others. As can be seen from the publication dates, Croce revised and reworked his essays over a period of about 30 years.

Croce's critical theory and practical criticism are part of a comprehensive theory of knowledge that he elaborated in the four volumes of his *Filosofia dello spirito* (1902–17, with subsequent editions to 1958; Eng. tr., *Aesthetic*, 1902, *Logic*, 1909, *Philosophy of the Practical*, 1909, *Theory and History of Historiography*, 1921). The sharp distinction between cognition of the particular by intuition and cognition of the universal by logic underlies Croce's recognition of the autonomous nature of aesthetic activity and of his formulation of the doctrine of intuition as expression (see *Estetica come scienza dell'espressione e linguistica generale* (1902, 9th ed., 1950; Eng. tr., *Aesthetic as Science of Expression and General Linguistic*, 1909, rev. tr., 1922, paperback, 1953). In his 1908 Heidelberg lecture, *Intuizione pura e il carattere lirico dell'arte* (Eng. tr., in *Aesthetic . . .*, 1909), Croce expanded his idea of "intuition as expression" to include the concept of "true poetry" (*liricità*, i.e., the successful union of a poetic image with an emotion). He explored the relation between "personality" and the work of art in *Breviario d'estetica* (1913; Eng. tr., *The Breviary of Aesthetics*, 1912) and *Aestetica in nuce* (1929, originally written and translated for the 14th ed. of *Encyclopaedia Britannica*), in which he also defined the universal, "cosmic" character of artistic expression. In *La poesia* (1936, 5th ed., 1953; Poetry), Croce turned to literature (as distinguished from poetry), an area he had formerly neglected. Literature, he now declared, was "a high expression of civilization," not to be confused, however, with poetry, "the unscheduled, unprogrammatical, spontaneous creation of genius."

In his numerous essays, Croce dealt with all the major and many minor Italian writers, but he never attempted a history of Italian literature, convinced as he was that, as Orsini puts it, "the true history of literature is the history of poetic personalities, each of which is an individual study." Among his earliest essays on Italian writers are the 80 or so that appeared in *La critica* between 1903 and 1914 and that were later collected and added to

in the six volumes of *La letteratura della nuova Italia* (4 vols., 1914–15, 5th ed., 1947–49; vols. 5 and 6, 1939–40; 3d ed., 6 vols., 1950; The Literature of the New Italy). The new Italy of the title refers to the nation that had come into being through unification. Some of his characterizations and evaluations have been deemed exemplary: Giosuè Carducci (1835–1907), a great poet of history but a weak critic; Giovanni VERGA, a novelist capable of transfiguring even the dictates of naturalism into poetry; Gabriele D'ANNUNZIO, a "dilettante of sensations"; Giovanni PASCOLI, the poet of the fragment and of the episodic description; Antonio FOGAZZARO, a mystical sensualist. Each of these essays plays an important role in the history of criticism on the writer with which it deals. Yet Croce's fundamental rejection of all art that fails to achieve classic perfection and measured repose places him outside the mainstream of the characteristic avant-garde movements of modernism and the increasing "brutalism" of the postmodern age.

Croce's essays generally follow a pattern in which a brief review of existing criticism serves to clear the ground of unnecessary problems and actual errors. The critic then moves to his principal concern: the characterization and thereby the evaluation of the writer's imagination and of his work. Extremely important to Croce is the expository part of the essay, which reveals the critic's range of human and cultural experience. In both his critical essays and his theoretical writings on aesthetics, Croce carried on an overt and a latent polemic against the survivals of positivism (*see* ITALIAN LITERATURE) and the romantic view of the history of literature as an expression of the political history of a nation. But while Croce's criticism is aesthetic in its uncompromising emphasis on the aesthetic fact, it is also strongly ethical, even psychological, in its recognition of the "poetic personality" as the basis of art.

Through *La poesia di Dante*, Croce has earned a permanent place in Dante studies. This highly controversial work draws a sharp distinction between the "theological-political romance" (i.e., the structure of an abstract scheme) of the *Divine Comedy* and the poetry that grows around it like a luxuriant vegetation. This distinction attacked the emphasis placed by traditional Dante scholarship on allegorical interpretations and the "riddles" found in the poem. Croce's study seemed to question the unity of the *Divine Comedy*, sparking a debate that raged for over 20 years and that redirected Dante studies toward an "aesthetic" reading of the work.

Croce's important contributions in the field of history of ideas include his *Storia dell'età barocca in Italia* (1929, 2d ed., 1946; History of the Baroque Age in Italy). Although this work resembles a typical history of 17th-century literature in the context of intellectual and cultural manifestations, it is actually the history of what Croce considered an artistic aberration, the *baroque*. Romanticism was also an aberration for him, and he returned to the phenomenon repeatedly, making a detailed analysis of it in *Storia d'Europa nel secolo decimonono* (1932, 7th ed., 1947; Eng. trs., *History of Europe in the Nineteenth Century*, 1933, *History as the Story of Liberty*, 1941, paperback, 1955). Croce's interest in broad literary problems is also evident in his advocacy of comparative literature as a field of research. As early as 1902, he discussed the necessity of studying both literary themes and influences. In this connection, too, he dealt with problems that continue to be actual.

In the decades after World War II, and especially since his death, Croce's heritage has been rejected both by the Marxists (who in Italy returned to the critical methods of Francesco De Sanctis [1817–83], in which history and society play a predominant role) and by the various kinds of structuralists, to whom Croce's critical method of characterization through appropriate epithets has proved particularly unsatisfactory.

Croce's own anthology of his work, *Filosofia. Poesia. Storia* (1951), is available in English translation as *Philosophy, Poetry, and History: An Anthology of Essays* (1966).

See: C. Sprigge, *Benedetto Croce: Man and Thinker* (1952); G. N. G. Orsini, *Benedetto Croce: Philosopher of Art and Literary Critic* (1961); G. Contini, *L'influenza culturale di Benedetto Croce* (1967).   O.R.

Crommelynck, Fernand (1886–1970), one of the greatest dramatists of the Belgian theater and a widely acclaimed writer of the French theater of the first half of the 20th century, was born in Paris of a French mother and a Belgian father. It would be fruitless to forge a rigid distinction between the "French" and "Belgian" elements in the work of this writer, whose life was divided between these two countries: the same language, similar historical backgrounds, and geographical proximity (Brussels is closer to Paris than are Bordeaux, Lyons, Marseille, and Strasbourg) all would render such a distinction useless in the case of a writer not primarily preoccupied with his own background. Yet even if Crommelynck's great works were created in Paris, the Belgian element remains discernible—a baroque vitality that is not typically French, as well as an admirable poetic usage of certain names and places.

Crommelynck's first work was produced in Brussels. A one-act play in verse, *Nous n'irons plus au bois* (1906; We Won't Go Anymore to the Woods), was followed by the prose *Le Marchand de regrets* (1913; The Seller of Regrets). But in 1908 he published in Brussels a play written first in verse and then expanded in a prose version, *Le Sculpteur de masques* (1908; The Sculptor of Masks). For this play, produced in Paris in 1911, Emile VERHAEREN wrote a preface referring to the play's "original and violent beauty." World War I brought a halt to this promising beginning, and Crommelynck became active as an actor and a journalist. By 1920, Crommelynck was again writing for the theater. *Les Amants puérils* (1921; The Childish Lovers) expressed a nocturnal and poignant poetic vision. *Le Cocu magnifique* (1921; Eng. tr., *The Magnificent Cuckold*, 1966), produced by Aurélien-Marie Lugné-Poë in Paris in 1920, revealed a sunny, shattering lyricism that rose above its own excesses. With this play, Crommelynck achieved worldwide attention. It concerns Bruno, the young jealous husband who seeks to be certain of his own unhappiness. Vsevolod Meyerhold's Moscow production of *Le Cocu magnifique*, in April 1922, with a constructivist staging, constitutes an important event in modern theater. In 1925, at the Comédie des Champs-Elysées, Louis Jouvet produced *Tripes d'or* (1930; Golden Tripes). Crommelynck's vision of greed is more than a psychological study; it is a lyrical portrait, often disturbing and at times outrageous. In 1929, Crommelynck returned to the Maison de l'Oeuvre, directed by Lugné-Poë, with *Carine ou la jeune fille folle de son âme* (1930; Carine or the Girl Enraptured by Her Own Soul). Carine, the play's main character, represents the purity that the world is to destroy. Although this play is less well known than others by Crommelynck, it is perhaps his most eloquent.

The year 1934 was a successful one for Crommelynck. On January 15 the Maison de l'Œuvre produced *Une Femme qu'a le coeur trop petit* (1934; A Lady Whose Heart Is Too Small); on November 24, *Chaud et froid* (1936; Hot and Cold) appeared at the Comédie des Champs-Élysées. The first of these is the charming comedy of Babine, whose heart is so small that all around her lie to protect her sensitivity. In the second, a mixture of farce and drama, a widow learns that her recently departed husband loved another. She sets out to be a model widow in order to defeat her rival in love, but a sudden and overwhelming infatuation changes her life.

At the age of 48, at the height of his creative activity, Crommelynck nearly ceased to write. From 1934 until his death in 1970, he produced only minor works: several film dialogues, a work on Falstaff entitled *Le Chevalier de la lune* (1954; The Knight of the Moon), and a detective story, *M. Larose, est-il l'assassin?* (1950; Is Mr. Larose the Murderer?). Perhaps manuscripts were lost, or works were left unfinished. A certain mystery surrounds the silence of this great writer. Yet the six major works alone testify to an exceptional author, a great baroque writer, by his dramatic inventiveness, by the originality of his characters, and by the quality of his writing.

See: D. I. Grossvogel, *The Self-Conscious Stage in Modern French Drama* (1958); G. Féal, *Le Théâtre de Crommelynck* (1976); B. Knapp, *Fernand Crommelynck* (1978).   G.Si.

Cunqueiro, Alvaro (1911–), Spanish novelist and essayist, was born in Galicia, a region heavily imbued with a Celtic tradition that often appears in its literature. Cunqueiro's early work (three volumes of poetry) were written in Galician, but he is equally adept in Castilian, into which he has translated some of his Galician works.

In a period when critical realism and authorial objectivity were popular modes of writing, Cunqueiro chose to maintain a highly subjective, poetic approach to fiction. His unique style combines fantasy, magic, legend, myth, impressive erudition, and a boundless imagination. A certain air of timelessness in his works is reinforced by anachronisms and themes that transcend the period in which they are set. Representative titles are: *Merlín y familia* (1957; Merlin and Family), a translation from the Galician original, *Merlin e familia* (1955), and *Las mocedades de Ulises* (1960; The Youth of Ulysses). *Un hombre que se parecía a Orestes* (1969; A Man Who Looked Like Orestes) goes beyond myth to explore human nature and the idea of destiny, while at the same time playing literary games. It won a Nadal Prize.

Other of Cunqueiro's works examine folklore or explore unusual subjects: *Las crónicas del sochantre* (1959; Chronicles of the Subchanter), for example, treats village folklore, whereas *Tertulia de boticas prodigiosas y escuela de curanderos* (1976; Talking about Prodigious Drugstores and the School for Quack Healers) provides interesting facts on the subject of drugs and related matters.

Cunqueiro's rich, poetic prose, laced with literary references, realistic detail, and touches of humor, contributes to a uniquely personal type of literature.

See: M. García Viñó, *Novela española actual* (1967), pp. 115–28.   M.E.W.J.

Curel, François de (1854–1928), French dramatist, was born in Metz into an aristocratic family of industrialists with medieval origins. After publishing several works of fiction, he submitted three plays to André ANTOINE, who encouraged him to become a playwright. Curel's early output may be classified as intimate family drama, beginning with *L'Envers d'une sainte* (1892; The Reverse of a Saint), which introduces the theme of failure and reveals the dark underside of the human personality. In *Les Fossiles* (1892; The Fossils), a noble family, threatened with extinction, produces an heir by ruthless maneuvering and a will to survive. Determination also characterizes the heroine of *L'Invitée* (1895; The Guest) who, after a long absence from her family, wins over her children from their father. The bleak *L'Amour brode* (1893; Love Embroiders), the second version of *Sauvé des eaux* (1889; Saved from the Waters), offers a study of perversity. In this play, a woman attempts to trick an emotional cripple into marriage but ends by precipitating his suicide. Curel rendered the text more compact and sharply focused in yet another version entitled *La Danse devant le miroir* (1913; The Dance before the Mirror). In *La Figurante* (1896; The Stand-In), a scheming woman is displaced by her niece in her lover's affections, yet today the play's irony and psychology seem strained.

Curel's second phase, that of provocative social comment, begins with *La Nouvelle Idole* (1895; The New Idol). Inspired by Louis Pasteur's discoveries, the play dramatizes the victory of faith over reason in a doctor whose materialism is transformed into altruism. *Le Repas du lion* (1897; The Lion's Meal) opposes the concepts of tradition and progress, concepts stemming from two aspects of the playwright's family heritage. To atone for an accidental death, Jean de Miremont works toward improving the lot of the poor, a gesture that proves contrary to his true nature, requiring that he govern the masses. The struggle between faith and reason is repeated in *La Fille sauvage* (1902; The Wild Girl), where human progress is traced from barbarism through Christianity, skepticism, and a return to brute instinct. The theme of the good-evil component of personality is illustrated again in *Le Coup d'aile* (1906; The Stroke of the Wing), in which an explorer who had abandoned his family for military glory gains his daughter's affection after attempting to win the love of humanity. Curel's last play, *Orage mystique* (1927; Mystical Storm), presents once more the motifs of failure and of a positivistic science pitted against the poetic impulse. The character of Dr. Tubal, however, remains more humane and open-minded than his counterparts in *La Nouvelle Idole*.

In his final works, Curel mingled the light touch of his comedies of manners with the serious intent of the philosophical dramas. *L'Ame en folie* (1919; The Soul Become Mad) continues the theme of the divided self and tells of a philosopher, a professional and marital failure, who is redeemed by his careful upbringing of a niece. Another failure dominates *La Comédie du génie* (1921; The Comedy of Genius) in the character of the dramatist who finds himself competing with his son, a successful playwright, and who discovers that the secret of genius lies in a message of love and feeling. *L'Ivresse du sage* (1922; The Intoxication of the Wise Man) strains credibility in its account of a near misalliance between a student and her pedantic professor who withdraws from society after learning of his pupil's intended marriage to another.

Curel's war plays reflect the playwright's disenchantment with the German annexation of Lorraine. *Terre inhumaine* (1922; Inhuman Land) illustrates the subversion of human values within a French family. The instinct for survival overcomes physical desire, heroism is corrupted by death, and prewar morality yields to violence. The problem of the dual personality is shown in *La Viveuse et le moribond* (1925; The Gay Lady and the Moribund) as a veteran, half-civilized, half-brute, living in a worthless postwar society, feels responsible for the death of his cousin whom he had refused to marry.

The issues that concern Curel transcend period and social class: man's fear of facing reality and his need to atone for misdeeds, guilt, or inadequacy through religion, as in *L'Envers d'une sainte;* suicide, as in *L'Amour brode*; philanthropy, as in *Le Repas du lion*; the education of a loved one, as in *L'Ame en folie*; fatherhood, as in *La Comédie du génie*; and occultism, as in *Orage mystique*. His plays do not advance theses but record the effects of ideas on human consciousness. Faced with adversity, his characters possess a strength of will that confers a certain grandeur on their efforts to attain lofty ideals. They are aristocrats in the fullest sense, and their attempts to effect progress through science and find God through faith are couched in an elevated, poetic style that befits its subject.

See: E. Pronier, *La Vie et l'œuvre de François de Curel* (1934); E. Braunstein, *François de Curel et le théâtre d'idées* (1962).   A.J.W.

Curros Enríquez, Manuel (1851–1908), Spanish poet and journalist who wrote principally in Galician, was born in the town of Celanova. From an early age he took part in heated liberal and Republican campaigns. He studied law, and as a result of the September Revolution of 1868 he moved to Madrid, where he edited *Imparcial, Porvenir, País* and other literary and political newspapers and journals. With the publication of his first book, the bishop of Orense brought legal action against him. He was convicted of irreverent attacks on the Catholic religion and the ministers of the Roman Catholic Church. A higher court absolved him, but his personal popularity and the fame of his works were greatly increased by the incident, especially in America, where there was a series of editions and expressions of devotion and esteem in the colonies of Spanish emigrants. He became a Treasury official in Orense and in 1894 moved to Havana, Cuba, where he was editor of the *Diario de la marina*. After his death in Havana, his body was moved to Galicia, where monuments and statues have been raised in his honor.

Aires d'a miña terra (1879; Songs from My Country), his first book and the cause of his denunciation by the church, contains the best of his poetry. Three poems in particular were responsible for the official protest. In "Mirando o chau" (Looking at the Earth), God observes his work, the creation, with the just and liberal spirit of Curros himself. Admittedly an imitation of Pierre Jean de Béranger, the poem also attacks the degeneration of the church, venal administration of justice, social inequality, and hypocrisy. "A igrexa fria" (The Cold Church) depicts licentious ecclesiastical life within sight of the ruins of a monastery. "O divino sainete" (The Divine Farce) is a parody of Dante in the traditional tercets of the medieval Galician lyric, in which the poet, accompanied by priests, monks, and fanatics led by the poet Añon, visits the pope and urges him to return to the true Christian life, abandoning luxury and pomp. Outstanding in this and similar poetry by Curros are the extraordinary energy of his satire, the sense of civic virility, and the natural flow of the language.

Perhaps Curros's most intense lyricism, however, is found in another type of poetry included in *Aires d'a miña terra*. The beautiful Marian legend, "A Virge d'o Cristal" (The Virgin of the Crystal), could be taken for one of the *Cantigas de Santa Maria* (Songs to the Virgin) of Alfonso the Wise. Highly dramatic is "Nouturnio" (Nocturne), a dialogue between an old man and his companion, a croaking toad, which ends in an angry threat to heaven. Equally vivid are the poems about emigration and homesickness, and those that recall family tragedies. The "complaint" of Rosalía de Castro and Eduardo PONDAL's Celtic evocations in Curros become a violent revolutionary protest.

See: R. Carballo Calero, *Historia da literatura galega contemporánea* (1975), pp. 337–98.

R.M.-L. rev. H.L.B.

Curvers, Alexis (1906–), Belgian novelist, was born in Liége. From 1924 to 1933 he was active in the journal *Cahiers mosains,* which enlivened the literary life of Liége between the two world wars. This journal defended classical aesthetics (Curvers was highly critical of romanticism) and propounded an ethics not unlike that of Mauras. As a teacher, Curvers gained many disciples. His first novel, *Bourg le rond* (1937) was written with Jean Hubaux (1894–1959), a colleague of Curvers's wife, the Hellenist Marie Delcourt. This work reveals a spirit of sharp irony. Curvers's stylistic gifts were further developed in *Printemps chez les ombres* (1939; Springtime in the Shadows), a story of disturbed adolescence among the middle classes. The sensitivity of a dilettante appears in the classical verses of *Cahier de poésie* (1949; Poetry Notebook). But wide public recognition came only with *Tempo di Roma* (1957; Eng. tr., 1960), for which Curvers received the Sainte Beuve Prize. The setting of this novel is Rome in the period immediately following the war. It describes the sudden infatuation of the young Picaro from the north with the Eternal City.

See: L. Rouche, *"Tempo di Roma* et l'autre Alexis Curvers," *Dryade* 12 (Winter 1957): 49–64.   J.-M.K.

Czaykowski, Bogdan (1932–), Polish poet, essayist, and translator, was born in Równe, in Eastern Poland. After 1939 he was deported to the Soviet Union and later evacuated to India. After World War II he moved to Great Britain. Czaykowski studied history at Dublin University and Polish literature in London, and he became involved in editorial and cultural activities, contributing poems to Polish émigré periodicals. Some of his poems were translated into several languages. In 1962 he joined the faculty of the University of Vancouver in Canada. Czaykowski has published several volumes of poetry, including *Reductio ad Absurdum* (1958), *Sura* (1961), *Spór z granicami* (1964; Strife against the Frontiers), and *Point-no-Point* fold universal trends and the native tradition, combines blunt directness with a surrealist bias. His translations into English include a volume of verse by Miron Białoszewski, published jointly with Andrzej Busza in 1974.

See: *Słownik współczesnych pisarzy polskich,* series II, vol. 1 (1977), pp. 181–84.   M.G.

Czech literature. Czech literature has a relatively ancient tradition among the vernacular literatures of Europe. In the 14th century there was a great flowering of belles lettres in Czech, one that influenced such Eastern European literatures as Polish and Hungarian. But this rich tradition was broken early in the 15th century by the Hussite religious reformation, which isolated the Czech nation from the rest of Europe. The loss of national independence in the 17th century and the subsequent Counter-Reformation further impeded the cultivation of a vernacular literature. Only at the end of the 18th century did a national revival take place with political autonomy and a wider use of the national language as its goals. In accordance with these goals, creative literature was conceived as narrowly nationalist in function. Also restrictive of broad literary development was the fact that the Czech lands—Bohemia and Moravia—were provincial regions of the Austrian Empire and had little direct contact with Western literature and culture. The progress of the nationalist movement received a severe setback in 1848, when revolution was firmly crushed, and another in 1867, when Austria gave autonomy to the Hungarians but not to the other peoples of the Empire. Still, in the last quarter of the 19th century, the Czech Parnassian poets and the realist writers of criticism, poetry, and fiction did help to broaden their countrymen's conception of literature and inculcate a more cosmopolitan spirit within them. The development of fiction and drama lagged behind that of lyric poetry, which had a stronger tradition dating from the early part of the century. The only vigorous prose tradition was that of the tale of rural life, cultivated by the great woman writer Božena Němcová (1820–62); this form reached its culmination in the realistic novels of Josef HOLEČEK and Teréza NOVÁKOVÁ. In spite of the rapid growth of the cities, urban realist fiction was very weak, achieving adequate expression only in the work of the naturalist novelist Karel Matéj ČAPEK-CHOD.

The coming of the 20th century brought very rapid changes to the Czech lands of Bohemia and Moravia. The Czechs threw off the dominant German influence (German had been for them a second language) and discovered the literature, philosophy, and criticism of the West, especially of France and England. In place of the romantic dreams of a great national past, which had occupied people earlier, the Czech realist critics of the 1890s called for a pragmatic program of political, social, and economic reform on which a new nation could be built. During the two decades preceding World War I, the philosopher, critic, and statesman Tomáš Garrigue MASARYK played a leading role in this change of national orientation. So also did the poets Josef Svatopluk MACHAR and Petr BEZRUČ, who produced a notable indigenous realistic poetry, which competed with the contemporary symbolist movement. A transitional figure between the realists and symbolists was Viktor DYK, who, like Masaryk and Machar, helped debunk Czech national illusions.

The Czech symbolist movement in poetry had begun in the mid-1890s, based partly on new trends in France and Belgium, partly on native romantic models. The symbolist poets, notably Otokar BŘEZINA, Antonín SOVA, Karel Hlaváček, and Otakar THEER, raised the euphonic and technical level of Czech verse, already high, while striving for mystic visions and religious absolutes. Stanislav Kostka NEUMANN, on the other hand, called for the triumph of both sensual love and socialism. Symbolist and impressionist fiction was weaker, and only the novelists Růžena SVOBODOVÁ and Fráňa ŠRÁMEK merit consideration. The critic František Zaver ŠALDA called for the victory of the avant-garde (by which he meant symbolism and impressionsim) and for the establishment of Czech literature on a par with its European counterparts, while another critic, Otokar FISCHER, introduced a modern type of psychological criticism.

Still, the national problem was unresolved in the 1890s, and the symbolist poets' mystic dreams proved to be shattered bubbles. The literary beginnings of the postsymbolist generation lacked promise, and at first these writers seemed inferior to their elders. But a turn came with the end of World War I and the establishment of the independent Czechoslovak Republic in 1918, with Masaryk as president. An optimistic spirit reigned, and the Czechs suddenly regained that national confidence seemingly essential to the production of great art. The postwar Republic rapidly became a center of the varied modern currents of futurism, vitalism, expressionism, and literary cubism and of modern scientific and technological development. The younger generation of writers now flowered into a brilliant maturity. For the first time, the novel and short story were the dominant genres in Czech literature. Jaroslav HAŠEK's brilliant comic novel on the war, *Osudy dobrého vojáka Švejka za světové války* (4 vols., 1921–23; Eng. tr., *Good Soldier Schweik,* 1930), captured world attention, as did the Utopian plays and novels of Karel ČAPEK. But Čapek also had a metaphysical side, and his trilogy of novels on man's pluralistic nature deserves to be more widely known than it is at present. So also does the work of Ivan OLBRACHT, Jaroslav DURYCH, and Vladislav VANČURA. Olbracht, the most traditional of the three, specialized in complex psychological portraits, but was most successful with his balladlike depictions of the people of the Carpathian Mountains. Durych was a historical novelist, whose Catholic outlook helped to inspire striking, almost expressionistic portrayals of the horrors of earthly life and the glories of God's grace and redemption. Wholly expressionist was Vančura, who cultivated a complex, ornate, at times almost grotesque style.

In the 1920s, a strong Czech expressionist movement developed, parallel but not related to the work of the German writer living in Prague, Franz KAFKA. Expressionist writers worthy of mention are Richard WEINER and the defrocked Catholic priest Jakub Deml (1878–1961); their work manifests a keen sense of existential anxiety and estrangement. Deml also relates to a group of Catholic writers led by Durych, who likewise reveal a sense of alienation, at least from the things of this world: they include Jan ČEP and the younger poet Jan Zahradníček (1905–60).

Poetry in the early 1920s was dominated by the so-called proletarian poets, followers of Neumann. Although naively optimistic, their work was full of warmth and sincerity. Proletarian poetry soon gave way to "poetism" (*poetismus*), a school of "pure poetry" created by Vítězslav NEZVAL, whose verse is a brilliant improvisation of dazzling images and intoxicating words. Favorite themes in poeticist verse were sensualism, the joys of the child, the pleasures of modern urban life, and the charm of such lesser arts as the circus and the revue. In the 1930s "poetism" in turn changed into surrealism, impelled by its own internal development and by the impact of the international surrealist movement. From all these trends there developed four poets of striking originality: Josef HORA, František HALAS, Jaroslav SEIFERT, and Vladimír HOLAN. Seifert, who sang of erotic charms and the joys of love, has the simplest and most direct voice; Halas was a profoundly individual and tragic poet obsessed with death and decay, while Hora and Holan were more meditative and philosophic, preoccupied with time and individual existence.

During the interwar period, even drama finally came to fruition, and the plays of the brothers Josef ČAPEK and Karel ČAPEK became known all over the world, although more for their scientific and Utopian themes than for their technical aspects, which were sometimes weak. František LANGER, a more able craftsman, also achieved some success abroad. But it was actually in modernist stage technique, as practiced by experimentalists like Emil František Burian (1904–59), that the Czech theatrical spirit expressed itself most strongly. Finally, criticism also flourished, still led by Šalda. Other notable figures included the comparatist literary historian Arne NOVÁK and the Marxist critic Bedřich Václavek (1897–1942). The Prague Linguistic Circle, founded in the mid-1920s, became a center of modern structuralist linguistics, while its principal literary theoreticians, notably Roman Jakobson (1896–) and Jan Mukařovský (1891–1975), laid down a linguistic and philosophic basis for the development of a holistic, structuralist view of the work of literature, one that still influences contemporary French structuralism.

The flowering of Czech literature in the 1920s and 1930s was destined to be fleeting. By the end of the 1930s, ominous notes of the coming doom and holocaust had begun to sound, especially in the fiction of Karel Čapek and the poetry of Halas and Holan. The betrayal at Munich, World War II, and the turn to socialism in 1948 proved to constitute a major watershed in the develop-

ment of Czech literature, with precedents only in the period following the loss of Czech independence in 1620, and the suppression of the revolution in 1848 (after which came the institution of strict Austrian censorship). Many of the major creative talents of the interwar period, notably Karel Čapek, had died by the end of that period; some, like Čapek's brother Josef or Vladislav Vančura, were victims of the Nazis. Other Nazi victims included the Marxist critic Václavek and the Jewish writer Karel Poláček (1892–1944), a fine satirist, whose novels depict the contradictions and limitations of society under the bourgeois Republic. The Communist editor and critic Julius Fučík (1903–43) was tortured to death by the Gestapo. His *Reportáž psaná na oprátce* (1945; Eng. tr., *Notes from the Gallows*, 1948), about his experience of the Nazi terror, is sentimental but does at times strike a true, primitive note of pathos. It was extremely popular all over Europe and is perhaps the most notable of all such "martyrologies."

There was a strict censorship during the German occupation (1938–45), and expressions of nationalist sentiment were of course banned, as was the work of former anti-Nazi writers (such as the brothers Čapek) and Jewish writers (such as Egon HOSTOVSKÝ, or Poláček). Thus the work that appeared during wartime is mostly unideological. The only major talent to emerge during this period was Václav Řezáč (1901–56), whose novels, such as *Svědek* (1942; The Witness) and *Rozhraní* (1944; Eng. tr., *If the Mirror Breaks*, 1959), are concerned, in a somewhat Čapek-like manner, with the interrelations of art and morality. Eduard Bass's (1888–1946) novel of circus life, *Cirkus Humberto* (1941; Eng. tr., *Umberto's Circus*, 1950), represents something new in Czech literature: a good, lively, popular story, free of serious pretensions to greatness.

With the end of the war in 1945, literature returned to normal, and a wave of books that could not have been published under the Germans appeared. The harvest in fiction was disappointing, however, poetry was more promising, and Seifert, Hrubín, and Holan produced important new collections dealing with life during the war and with the fact of liberation. Meanwhile, the work of a younger group of poets came to the fore. Most popular was that of Jiří Orten (1919–41), who died tragically young, run over by a German ambulance. His *Čítanka jaro* (1939; Spring Considered as a Child's Reader) is alive and happy with sparkling, animistic imagery, but his subsequent poetry is more tragic. Orten's contemporaries were the poets of "Group 42" (named for the year of their formation), who sought to make poetry out of the daily life of the modern city. To their number belong the older poet Oldřich Mikulášek (1910–), as well as Jiřina Hauková (1919–) and Josef Kainer (1917–72). The influence of Halas was dominant on all of these poets. Hauková, a poet of extreme sensitivity, writes of spiritual isolation and Kainer writes with an intellectualized cynicism that verges on black humor. Of the three, only Mikulššek, who began as an individualist, was able after 1948 to adapt to the restrictive demands of socialist realism.

Nor did criticism flourish in this brief postwar period. The climate for it was propitious, with the influence of the native school of Prague structuralists combining with the new imported currents of existentialism and Anglo-American New Criticism. But the turn to socialism in 1948 sounded a death knell to these new trends. Ironically, many Czech writers were themselves socialists, and they had looked forward to the coming of socialism to Czechoslovakia. At first it seemed to some that the new economic and political system would favor the development of diversified literary and artistic tendencies. But very soon the cultural climate changed, and the narrow, prescriptive dogma of socialist realism was imported from the Soviet Union to harness literature and art to the task of building socialism. That dogma required writers to adopt a positive attitude toward socialism and to promote it actively in their works. The past as well as the present had to be treated in terms of stereotyped conflicts between progressive Communists and decadent bourgeois.

Under such conditions, the fiction and poetry that could be published were sterile indeed. Several important writers emigrated, among them Jan Čep and Egon Hostovský, but more important was the "internal emigration" of many writers who, unable to conform or achieve publication for their works, virtually withdrew from literature. These included the poets Halas, Hrubín, and Holan. The poet Konstantin Biebl (1898–1951) committed suicide after producing a pallid volume of prosocialist verse, while the Catholic poet Jan Zahradníček was sent to a labor camp. Only Nezval was able to ride out the tide of events, but he did so by writing propagandist doggerel. Things were no better among the prose writers. Even Communists, such as Olbracht and Marie Majerová, were silent or turned largely to children's literature or translations. Řezáč attempted to conform by writing novels on the topical theme of resettling the border lands vacated by the Sudeten Germans, but the results were poor.

Critics turned to the problem of reevaluating the past of Czech literature. Here the new tone was set by the Communist ministers of education, Zdeněk Nejedlý (1878–1962) and Ladislav Štoll (1902–). Nejedlý called for writers to develop a definite relation to society, to become realists and emphasize the popular side of their work. He found the historical novelist Alois Jirásek (1851–1930), a follower of Walter Scott, to be the paragon of all these qualities. Štoll reevaluated the poetry of the 1920s and 1930s; and although most of it had been produced by left-wing writers, he dismissed much of it as "decadent," in particular the work of Halas, whose obsession with death he found to have been a harmful influence on younger poets. Jiří Wolker emerged as the supreme model of a Communist poet, because of his popularity, simplicity, and directness, and in spite of (or again because of) his sentimentality, naiveté, and (paradoxically) his lack of realism.

While the ideological "thaw" that followed the death of Iosif Stalin in 1953 came to Soviet literature as early as the spring of 1954, and to Polish literature by the mid-1950s, Czech literature experienced a relaxation only in 1957, and then only for a short time. This brief period saw the publication of the novel Zbabělci (1958; Eng. tr., The Cowards, 1970) by the young writer Josef Škvorecký. This novel broke the taboos existing in Czech literature by its idealization of young pro-Western jazz musicians, its critical treatment of the Soviet liberators of Czechoslovakia in 1945, and, most of all, by its vigorous, direct, and frequently scatological speech. Zbabělci was soon withdrawn from circulation and did not reappear until 1964. One reason for the lag in liberalization in Czechoslovakia was the weakness of the intelligentsia, cowed by the purges that had followed the trials of Vlado Clementis, the minister of foreign affairs, and Rudolf Slánský, secretary of the Communist Party, in 1952. Another factor was doubtless the absence of any strong ideological counterforce, analogous to the Catholic Church in Poland. It is of interest to note that, when reform ultimately came to Czechoslovakia in the 1960s, the leaders were younger members of the Communist

Party itself. But in the 1950s, Communist Party discipline was too strong for such activity.

The 1960s brought a wave of struggle for reform in the Communist Party, as well as a wave of experimentation in the arts. Czech films, rather than literature, succeeded in capturing world attention because of their natural manner and offbeat humor; other Czech new wave films were made in a grotesque style that recalled surrealism. The Czech stage also flourished, and in the mid-1960s Prague became a place of pilgrimage for those interested in modern theater.

In literature, much of the struggle focused on the liberals' interest in Franz Kafka, whose work epitomized for them the absurdity of life and man's alienation from the world. Marxist revisionism, a school of thought represented in Bohemia by Karel Kosík (1926–), called attention to the rediscovered late writings of Karl Marx, which emphasized man's ethical concerns and the importance of individual happiness. At the same time the revisionists stressed the inevitability of the individual's alienation from society, even under socialism, and Kafka's writings served them as an example of that alienation in its most extreme forms. In May 1963, a conference on Kafka was held in Czechoslovakia, attended by representatives from most of the Eastern European countries. The struggle for reform came to a head in 1967 at the fourth congress of Czechoslavak writers, where demands for liberalization were voiced with such force and eloquence that the tottering regime of President Antonín Novotný could hardly ignore them.

A number of dramatic new trends accompanied the literary renaissance of the 1960s. Suddenly, various deficiencies of socialism in general and the Communist Party in particular were openly discussed. In his novel Pravděpodobní tvář (1963; The Look of Things) and in a touching memoir of concentration camp life, Půlnoční slunce (1968; Eng. tr., Living and Partly Living, 1968), Jiří Mucha (1915–) exposed the injustice of the Communists' treatment of their supposed enemies. Other fiction writers revealed the contradictions and excesses of the new socialism; in doing this, they often turned the formulas of socialist realism inside out. Novelists who followed this approach included Ludvík Vaculík and Ivan Klíma (1931–), whose novel Hodina ticha (1963; An Hour of Silence) underlined the hypocrisy of Communist Party policy with regard to the collectivized countryside. The writers who used humor to point up the excesses of the Stalinist system include Škvorecký, in his later works of the 1960s, and Milan Kundera, whose novel Žert (1967; Eng. tr., The Joke, 1969) focused attention on the humorlessness and inhumanity of the regime, as well as on its total lack of ideological consistency.

Another important new trend was the use of allegory. In his novel Tovaryšstvo Ježíšovo (1969; The Society of Jesus), Jiri Šotola (1924–) likened the ministrations of the Communists to the repressive activities of the Jesuits after the loss of Czech independence early in the 17th century. Another allegorical work, this time Kafka-like, is Vaculík's novel Morčata (Eng. tr., The Guinea Pigs, 1973), a work that to date has not appeared in Czechoslovakia. It compares the paternalism of the socialist state to the attitudes of an owner of pet guinea pigs, at first affectionate but subsequently tyrannical and sadistic. The title of Ivan Klíma's allegorical drama Zámek (1965; The Castle) deliberately underscores its relation to Kafka: the "castle" of this play is the fortress of privilege of the established order—a symbol clearly pointing to the chateau at Dobříš, which the Writers Union maintained as a comfortable retreat for those writers who catered to Community Party demands. The influence of Kafka, perhaps the strongest single threat in all this writing, is particularly marked in the works of Ladislav Fuks, who produced a series of grotesque novels demonstrating an obsession with death. A native grotesque tradition also stemmed from the work of Kafka's contemporary and fellow Prague resident, Jaroslav Hašek, and it is best represented in the earthy, humorous stories of Bohumil Hrabal. Finally, the Western current of the absurd drama came to Bohemia, superbly represented by the plays of Václav Havel, who, like his Polish counterpart Sławomir Mrożek emphasized the absurdity and contradictions of life under socialism.

A unique novelist is Vladimír Páral (1932-), who mixes liberal doses of eroticism, pathos, and black humor. Páral writes about the new class of engineers and industrial managers whose lives in the socialist society are purposeless and dull. His finest novel, *Katapult* (1967; The Catapult), depicts the self-destruction of a business traveler who, out of boredom, systematically wrecks his career and his marriage. Páral's later work seems weaker, as exemplified by *Milenci a vrazi* (1969; Lovers and Murders), a long novel that attempts a synthetic picture of the decadence of modern industrial society.

Czech poetry also flourished in the late 1950s and the 1960s. The "Květen" (May) group of younger poets, led by Šotola, included Miroslav Holub (1923-), whose poems on scientific themes have gained him popularity abroad. The older poet Vladimír Holan underwent a brilliant creative revival and produced many meditative lyrics and longer poems somewhat reminiscent of T. S. Eliot. Free verse, denounced in the 1950s as decadent, reappeared, becoming the dominant form of Czech verse. In this time of intellectual and creative ferment, criticism lagged behind, perhaps because the best energies of the intellectuals were turned to the struggle for liberalization itself.

This literary renaissance, part of the "Prague Spring," came to a sudden end in 1968 with the Soviet occupation of Czechoslovakia. A number of writers emigrated, notably Ludvík Aškenazy, Arnošt Lustig, and Škvorecký. The last named founded a publishing house in Canada for Czech writers of the emigration. Of those who remained at home, Havel, Hrabal, Klíma, Kundera, Šotola, and Vaculík have been largely unable to publish. Several of them, in particular the last three, have resorted to publishing abroad, a practice that is technically legal, although it subjects these writers to intense official criticism. Whether the relatively liberal creative atmosphere found today in Poland will return to Czech life remains a question.

See: F. X. Šalda, *Moderní literatura česká* (3d ed., 1929) and *Krásná literatura česká v prvním desitiletí republiky* (1930); H. Jelínek, *Histoire de la littérature tchèque,* 3 vols. (1930-35); B. Václavek, *Česká literatura XX. století* (1935); A. Novák, *Přehlndné dějiny literatury české* (4th ed., 1939); P. Selver, *Czechoslovak Literature: An Outline* (1942); E. Hostovský, "The Czech Novel between the Two World Wars," *SEER* 21, no. 2 (November 1943): 78-96; A. Novák, *Stručné dějiny literatury české* (1946); A. M. Ripellino, *Storia della poesia ceca contemporanea* (1950); M. Součková, *A Literature in Crisis: Czech Literature, 1938-1950* (1954); B. Meriggi, *Storia della letteratura ceca e slovacca* (1958); F. Buriánek, *Soucasna ceska literatura* (1960); J. Petrimichl, *Patnáctlet české literatury* (1962); R. Wellek, *Essays on Czech Literature* (1963); "Ustav pro českou literaturu CSAV," *Slovník českých spisovatelů* (1964); A. French, *The Poets of Prague* (1969); A. Novák, *Czech Literature,* tr.

P. Kussi, ed., W. E. Harkins (1976); P. I. Trensky, *Czech Drama since World War II* (1978); W. E. Harkins and P. I. Trensky, eds., *Czech Literature since 1956: A Symposium* (1980). W.E.H.

Czechowicz, Józef (1903-39), Polish poet, was born and educated in Lublin. After working as a teacher in provincial schools, he moved in 1933 to Warsaw, where he established a literary circle, edited various periodicals, and worked for the radio. He died in Lublin in a German air raid at the beginning of World War II.

The poetry of Czechowicz, although limited in range, is remarkable for its lyrical purity, as well as for a highly original fusion of traditional and avant-garde techniques. It is essentially a poetry of mood, elegaic in tone and characterized by a subtle blending of evocative imagery and singsong rhythms that echo in a sophisticated manner (as in the music of Frederick Chopin) the lilt of folk music. In his earlier volumes, some of the best poems are evocations of the atmosphere of provincial towns and countryside: *Kamień* (1927; Stone), *dzień jak codzień* (1930; a day like every day), *ballada z tamtej strony* (1932; ballad from beyond), and *Stare kamienie* (1934; Old Stones). In the later volumes, *w błyskawicy* (1934; in the lightning), *nic więcej* (1936; nothing more), and especially *nuta człowiecza* (1939; the human note), his intellectual profundity increased significantly in his treatment of philosophical and metaphysical problems. These poems are characterized by Czechowicz's extreme sensitivity and by his premonitions of impending universal catastrophe and his own death. His output includes also plays and translations of poetry (James Joyce, Osip Mandelshtam, T. S. Eliot).

See: *Słownik współczesnych pisarzy polskich,* vol. 1 (1963), pp. 383-85; T. Kłak, *Czechowicz mity e megic* (1973). B.Cz.

Czerniawski, Adam (1934-), Polish poet, prose writer, essayist and translator, was born in Warsaw. In 1941 he left Poland, spent some years in the Middle East and finally settled in England. He studied English philology in London and philosophy in Oxford and in 1970 joined the faculty of the College of Design in Rochester. He was editor of the journals *Merkuriusz Polski* and *Kontynenty.* His first volume of poetry, *Polowanie na jednorożca* (Unicorn Hunting) appeared in 1956, followed by *Topografia wnętrza* (1962; Topography of Interior), *Sen Cytadela Gaj* (1966; Dream Citadel Grove), and *Widok Delft* (1973; A View of Delft). Along with his poetry he also published two volumes in prose: *Części mniejszej całości* (1964; Parts of A Smaller Unit) and *Akt* (1975; Act). He is also editor of the poetic anthology *Ryby na piasku* (1965; Fish on the Sand), containing the poetry of a group of Polish poets of the younger generation then living in London who chose not to consider themselves as exiles and refused to give up their Polish heritage. Czerniawski's poetry reflects his ties with T. S. Eliot and Cyprian Norwid. His prose came out of the same tradition as Witold Gombrowicz's. Compactness, responsibility for the word, and *irony* characterize his poetry, which combines universal trends with native tradition. He is the author of the collections of essays *Liryka i druk* (1972; Lyric Poetry and the Press) and *Wiersz współczesny* (1977; Contemporary Poetry), and has translated poems and plays by Tadeusz Różewicz into English.

See: *Słownik współczesnych pisarzy polskich,* series 11, vol. 1 (1977), pp. 185-88; M. Danilewicz Zielińska, *Szkice o literaturze emigracyjnej* (1978), pp. 319-26. A.Z.

Czuchnowski, Marian (1909–), Polish poet and novelist, was born in Polna, near Cracow. After studying law and philosophy at the University of Cracow, he joined the poetic group "Awangarda" and the leftist political movement. His activity subjected him to several arrests, and his poem *Powódź i śmierć* (1936; The Flood and the Death) was confiscated. He published several volumes of poetry, beginning with *Poranek goryczy* (1930; The Morning of Bitterness), and three novels, *Cynk* (1937; Zink), *Pieniądz* (1938; Money), and *Ksawera* (1939). After spending two years in a Soviet labor camp, he reached the Middle East, where he joined the Polish army, ultimately settled in London, and there continued his creative writing. His changed political opinions found some reflection in the prose linked with his wartime experiences: *Cofnięty czas* (1945; Time Pulled Back), *Z Moskwy do . . . Moskwy* (1945; From Moscow to . . . Moscow), and *Tyfus, teraz słowiki,* a novel (1951; Typhus, now Nightingales). His recent verse, maintaining a mood of dignified simplicity, often points to the wonders and blessings of everyday existence, for example, *Motyl i zakonnica* (1953; The Butterfly and the Nun) and *Dama w jedwabnym płaszczu deszczowym* (1954; The Lady in the Silk Raincoat).

See: T. Terlecki, ed., "Czuchnowski Laureatus," *Wiadomości* 4 (1956) and ed. *Literatura polska na obczyźnie, 1940–1960,* vol. 1 (1964), pp. 104–06.   M.G.

D

Dabit, Eugène (1898–1936), French novelist, was born in Paris, the son of a laborer. He attended school only until he was 11 years old and then worked as an apprentice locksmith, an elevator operator at the Lamarck station of the Paris subway, and a house painter. At 18 he enlisted in the army and served at the front from December 1916 to November 1918. Upon his return, he completed his education by attending night school, taking courses in drawing and painting. At this point, he discovered Honoré de Balzac, Gustave Flaubert, Emile ZOLA, Guy de Maupassant, Joris-Karl HUYSMANS, Marcel PROUST, and André GIDE. The works of Jules Vallès in particular were a revelation to him, for he recognized in them the Paris he knew—its joys, it sorrows, its violence, and its strength. Huysmans instilled in him an admiration for a vigorous, precise style. In reading Charles-Louis PHILIPPE, Dabit felt as if he were meeting a friend and a guide who would help him clarify his desires and bring to light his weaknesses.

In the 1920s, Dabit's parents became the proprietors of a 50-room hotel. He wrote of the lives of those who frequented the place in *Hôtel du Nord* (1929; Eng. tr., 1931), a realistic novel awarded the Populist Prize in 1931. He became well known overnight. Advised and encouraged by Roger MARTIN DU GARD and Gide, he wrote a second book, the partly autobiographical *Petit-Louis* (1930). From then on, one or two books appeared every year, among them *Villa Oasis* (1932), *Faubourgs de Paris* (1933; Suburbs of Paris), *Un Mort tout neuf* (1934; A Brand New Dead Man), *L'Ile* (1934; The Island), *La Zone verte* (1935; The Green Zone), and *Trains de vie* (1936; Ways of Life). In 1936, Dabit accompanied Gide and Louis GUILLOUX on a two-month trip to the USSR to attend the funeral of Maksim GORKY. Dabit died of scarlet fever in a hospital in Sevastopol, after having been ill only four days.

Like many writers born of the masses, Dabit mistrusted—perhaps a little too strongly—those of his associates who wrote for the masses. He doubted the sincerity of the "populist" school of writers and disliked being classed as one of them. The preface to his last book is typical in this respect; in it he declares that literature should be employed as a weapon against a treacherous and cruel world, but that art must not sacrifice any of its own value in the process.   P.Br.

Dąbrowska, Maria (1889–1965), Polish novelist, was born Maria Szumska in Russów, near Kalisz, and died in Warsaw. She was educated in Poland, Switzerland, and Belgium, where she started writing articles on the cooperative movement and on social and economic problems and later published short stories in Polish journals, beginning in 1914 with "Janek" (Little John) in the prestigious weekly *Prawda* in Warsaw. Her stories have appeared in the collections *Gałąź czereśni* (1922; Branch of a Cherry Tree), *Uśmiech dzieciństwa* (1923; A Smile of Childhood), and *Ludzie stamtąd* (1926; Folks from Over Yonder), devoted to the Polish countryside. The work that established Dąbrowska as one of the leading writers in Poland was her novel in four volumes, *Noce i dnie* (1932–34; Nights and Days). It is a chronicle-type novel, generally ranked with Thomas MANN's *Buddenbrooks* and John Galsworthy's *The Forstye Saga*. The social issues are more important here, however, and are solved in a more radical way, and the solutions go far beyond the problem of material fortune and misfortune. "Modernized realism" was the term suggested for the artistic style of this "family saga," which has now been translated into many languages of the world (although not yet into English).

During World War II, Dąbrowska was very active in the underground cultural movement in occupied Warsaw. Her volume of stories *Gwiazda zaranna* (1955; Eng. tr., *A Village Wedding,* 1957) was greeted in Poland as the artistic and moral triumph of a writer who remained faithful to human ideals and commanded universal respect. Dąbrowska did not hesitate to take up the basic issues of individual freedom versus the collective, and she solved them according to her humanistic ideals. She also wrote two historical plays, *Geniusz sierocy* (1939; The Orphan Genius) and *Stanisław i Bogumił* (1948), and numerous critical essays, for example, *Szkice o Conradzie* (1959; Essays on Conrad), and she published translations from English (Samuel Pepys's Diary), Danish, and Russian. Her last unfinished novel, *Przygody człowieką myślacego* (The Adventures of a Thinking Man), was published posthumously in 1970.

See: A. Kijowski, *Maria Dąbrowska* (in Polish, 1964); Z. Folejewski, *Maria Dąbrowska* (in English, 1967); E. Korzeniewska, *Maria Dąbrowska. Kronika życia* (1971).   Z.F.

Dagerman, Stig (1923–54) Swedish novelist, short-story writer, playwright, and critic, was born in Älvkarleby. He lived at Älvkarleby, Uppland, with his paternal grandparents until the age of eight, when he moved to Stockholm to be with his father. In that city at the age of 21, he became the cultural editor of the syndicalist newspaper, *Arbetaren*.

Dagerman's first novel, *Ormen* (1945; The Serpent), dealing with anxiety and guilt, caught the prevalent mood of the time immediately after World War II. *Ormen* consists of two parts: "Irène," about a girl who pushes her mother off a train and has a chance meeting with an army private and his serpent, a symbol of anxiety; and "Vi kan inte sova" (We cannot sleep), about the many reasons for the soldiers' fears and anxieties. In "Vi kan inte sova,"

Dagerman's alter ego, Scriver, is a Utopian who dreams of "a new epoch of intellectualism making at least somebody bold enough to look anxiety in the face rather than retiring to the grottoes of infantile mysticism and bedrooms." Scriver advances the theory that it is "the tragedy of contemporary humans to have ceased to be afraid." Only by recognizing anxiety as a basic human ingredient can we conquer it. But when Scriver challenges his anxiety, he dies. *De dömdas ö* (1946; Isle of the Damned), about seven shipwrecked people, treats the same theme, anxiety.

Dagerman's style had been influenced by William Faulkner and Ernest Hemingway; his symbols had by and large been assimilated, in a personal way, from Franz KAFKA. In his brilliant reportage *Tysk höst* (1947; German Autumn), Dagerman expressed his views on guilt and suffering, which related well to his outlook in the short-story collection *Nattens lekar* (1947; Eng. tr., *The Games of Night*, 1961). The title story alludes to the pipe dreams of the son of an alcoholic. The boy dreams of being superior to his father but has to console himself with drink. The story "The Condemned One" is clearly influenced by Pär LAGERKVIST.

Dagerman's novel *Bränt barn* (1948; Eng. tr., *A Burnt Child*, 1950) explores the neurosis of 20-year-old Bengt, who is inconsolable after having lost his mother but turns his sorrow into indignation against his father. Although striving for "innocence," Bengt, in vengeance, sleeps with his father's mistress. Barely surviving the subsequent crisis, he reduces his demands from innocence to consciousness but before long enters again into conflict situations. In the dramatization of the novel under the title *Ingen går fri* (1949; No One Is Acquitted), the theme of innocence is shown clearly as a form of self-deception: to know oneself is to mature.

Bröllopsbesvär (1949; Wedding Worries), which was also filmed, is set in the Uppland countryside, where Dagerman lived as a child. It is a remarkable sequence of profiles of Swedish country folk on a chaotic wedding night, when all, confused or bewitched, follow their impulses and wind up in the wrong bed. There are moments of comedy, but the main mood of this drama of enchanting grotesques is one of resigned sympathy. Dagerman's drama *Den dödsdömde* (1947; Eng. tr., *The Condemned*; 1951) discusses ethical problems.

After Dagerman's suicide, there appeared several posthumous works including the first chapter of a novel about C. J. L. Almqvist, *Tusen år hos gud* (1954; A Thousand Years with the Lord), *Vårt behov av tröst* (1955; Our Need of Solace), poems, short stories, and an autobiographical sketch and *Dagsedlar* (1954; Duty Roster), a collection of topical verse from *Arbetaren*.

See: O. Lagercrantz, *Stig Dagerman* (1958); L. A. Thompson, "Stig Dagerman's 'Vår nattliga badort': An Interpretation," *SCAN* 13, no. 2 (1974): 117–27; H. Sandberg, *En Stig Dagerman Bibliografi* (1975) and *Den politiske Dagerman, Tre studier* (1979). L.S.

Dağlarca, Fazıl Hüsnü (1914–), Turkish poet, was born in Istanbul. He graduated from the Military Academy. Dağlarca published his first book of poems, *Havaya Çizilen Dünya* (A World Sketched on Air), on the day he became a career officer in 1935. He retired 15 years later from the army with the rank of captain. After working for the Ministry of Labor as an inspector from 1952 to 1960, he operated his own bookshop in Istanbul until 1973. By 1980 he had published more than 50 collections of poems.

Dağlarca was often referred to as Turkey's leading living poet in the 1960s and 1970s. In addition to the major awards of Turkey, he won the Turkish Award of the International Poetry Forum (Pittsburgh, Pa.) in 1968 and

Yugoslavia's Golden Wreath in 1974. He was the Poet of the Year at the Rotterdam Poetry International in 1977. His poems have been translated into many languages, including English (*Selected Poems of Fazıl Hüsnü Dağlarca*, 1969).

His second book, *Çocuk ve Allah* (1940; Child and God), an exploration into human innocence and metaphysical bewilderment, is one of the masterworks of Turkish poetry. In *Çakır'ın Destanı* (1945; The Epic of Çakır) and *Taş Devri* (1945; The Stone Age), Dağlarca endeavored to find the psychic reality and the ideals of the universal person. His *Toprak Ana* (Mother Earth) of 1950 is a poignant elegiac panorama of deprivation and suffering in Anatolian villages, and *Aç Yazı* (Hungry Writing) of 1951 pits the poet against the world's imponderables, which miraculously give him the architectonics of faith in mankind and in poetry itself. Dağlarca's universalist themes are counterpoised with his patriotic pride, which he expressed in many national epic cycles—*Üç Şehitler Destanı* (1949; The Epic of the Three Martyrs), *İstiklâl Savaşı* (1951; The War of Independence), *İstanbul Fetih Destanı* (1953; The Epic of the Conquest of Istanbul), *Anıtkabir* (1953; Mausoleum), *Delice Böcek* (1957; The Insane Insect), and many others.

Some of Dağlarca's best poems in a universal vein are in *Âsû* (1955), *Batı Acısı* (1958; The Agony of the West), *Hoo'lar* (1960; Ho-os), and other books. In *Aylam* (1962; Moon Life), he explored the human aspects of space. In the 1960s, Dağlarca wrote scores of poems of social protest. His *Vietnam Savaşımız* (1966; Our Vietnam War) and *Vietnam Körü* (1970; The Blind of Vietnam), followed by *Hiroshima* (1970), are strong indictments of the United States. One of his major works is *Haydi* (1968; Come on), which comprises 1,243 quatrains of imagism and quintessential perceptions. In the 1970s, Dağlarca published several collections of verses for children.

In Turkey Dağlarca's name is often mentioned as a Nobel Prize prospect. T.S.H.

Daisne, Johan, pseud. of Herman Thiery (1912–), Belgian novelist, poet, dramatist, and critic of Flemish extraction, was born in Ghent. After studying economics and Slavic languages at the University of Ghent, he received his doctorate in 1936. In 1940 he served with the heavy artillery and was later a member of the Resistance. He became head of the Ghent Public Library in 1945 and still holds this position. Daisne has traveled a great deal and has visited Eastern Europe. He claims to have received his inspiration to write from the cinema, and he has produced a considerable amount of film criticism. He began his literary career as a student by publishing poetry, but, with *De trap van steen en wolken* (1942; The Stairway of Stone and Clouds), he turned to the novel. Like many of his novels, it is also autobiographical, and he evokes the memories of his childhood. His most famous novel is *De man die zijn haar kort liet knippen* (1974; Eng. tr. *The Man Who Had His Hair Cut Short*, 1965). It is one long outpouring of the troubled, muddled mind of the antihero, written in the first person singular and without breaks for paragraphs. It is an excellent example of Daisne's "magic realism," through which he penetrates beyond the ideal and the illusory in order to reach the ultimate reality of life. Daisne was one of the founders of the poetry magazine *Klaver(en)drie*, and his *Ikonakind* (1946; Ikona Child) is a volume of poetry dedicated to the memory of his daughter, who died at the age of seven weeks. *De nacht komt gauw genoeg* (1961; Night Comes Soon Enough) is a selection of his poetry. Among his plays are *De Charade van Advent* (1942) and the trilogy *De liefde is een schepping van vergoding* (1946; Love Is a Creation of Idolization). *Baratzeartea* (1963) shows his admiration of Pierre BENOIT, whereas both *Als kantwerk aan de kim* (1964; Like Lace on the Horizon) and *Reveillon-Reveillon* (1966) reflect his love for his daughter. Other novels of importance by Daisne are *Lago Maggiore* (1957), *Hoe schoon was mijn school* (1961; How Beautiful Was My School), *De neusvleugel van de muze* (1965; The Nostril of the Muse), and *Ontmoeting in de zonnekeer* (1967; Meeting in the Tropics). He has also written extensively on Russian literature. Daisne has received the Belgian Driejaarlijkse Staats Prize and the Kogge Literature Prize from the city of Minden in the Federal Republic of Germany.

See: B. Kemp, *Johan Daisne* (1974).   S.L.F.

Dam, Niels Albert (1880–1972), Danish novelist and short-story writer, was born near the Jutland city of Århus. He first received recognition after about 50 years of literary production. Dam made his literary debut in 1906 with a psychological triangle story, *Mellem de to Søer* (Between the Two Seas), which ends with a rather dramatically described murder. The criminal theme is also found in *Saa kom det ny Brødkorn* (1934; Then the New Grain Came), on the surface a naturalistic, regional novel but, in reality, a symbolic treatment of the dualism between spirit and matter. Realism turns into the fantastic in *Morfars By* (1956; Grandfather's Town), which contains a series of mythical stories about a parish and its inhabitants. Such myths, stories without tangible time or place, where the action is concentrated in single situations from the past, present, and visionary future of mankind, are found in the short-story collections *Syv Skilderier* (1962; Seven Pictures) and *Menneskelinien* (1965; The Line of Man). The same cultural-historical and anthropological point of view characterizes Dam's last stories, collected in *Menneskekår* (1967; Human Conditions), *Elleve Rids* (1968; 11 Sketches), and *Min moder og hendes sønner* (1969; My Mother and Her Sons).   S.H.R.

Daniel, Yuly Markovich (1925–), Russian prose writer, poet, and translator, was born in Moscow. He was tried in 1966, together with Andrey SINYAVSKY, for publishing in the West a cycle of stories written under the pseudonym "Nikolay Arzhak." He was sentenced to five years' hard labor for "defaming" the Soviet social and political system. After his release in 1970, he was allowed to settle in Kaluga (a town south of Moscow), and has since made his living as a translator. The four "Arzhak" stories are: "Govorit Moskva," "Ruki," "Iskupleniye," "Chelovek iz Minapa" (pub. Washington, D.C., in one volume under the title *Govorit Moskva*, 1963; Eng. tr., *This is Moscow Speaking and Other Stories*, 1969). All of them are in one way or another concerned with the moral consequences of Stalinism. Like his friend and codefendant Sinyavsky, Daniel often achieves his effects by fantasy and hyperbole. In *Govorit Moskva*, for instance, he describes the reaction of the Soviet population to a government decree announcing a "Public Murder Day," during which all citizens will have the right to kill victims of their choice. His verse written in the forced labor camp has been published in the West, *Stikhi iz nevoli* (Amsterdam, 1971; Verse from Captivity).

See: *On Trial: The Soviet State versus "Abram Tertz" and "Nikolai Arzhak,"* tr. and ed. by M. Hayward (1967).
                                                        M. Ha.

Daniel-Rops, pseud. of Henry-Jules-Charles Petiot (1901–65), French novelist, short-story writer, literary critic, essayist, poet, and historian, was born in Epinal. Daniel-Rops studied geography, history, and law at the University of Grenoble and was *agrégé* in history from the University of Lyon in 1922. In 1944, after having taught for more than 20 years in Chambéry, Amiens, and at the Lycée Pasteur in Neuilly-sur-Seine, Daniel-Rops devoted himself to writing.

In his novels, short stories, and essays, Daniel-Rops portrays the anxiety, restlessness, and despair of the modern world. Sensing the Pascalian antithesis of man's misery and grandeur, this Catholic writer saw Christian faith and the hope of redemption as providing the only path to sanity and the only escape from anguish. Influenced by the works of such diverse minds as Arthur RIMBAUD, William Blake, Friedrich Hölderlin, Emily Brontë, Franz KAFKA, August STRINDBERG, Anton CHEKHOV, Miguel de UNAMUNO, Luigi PIRANDELLO, Charles PÉGUY, Blaise Pascal, and the Catholic mystics, Daniel-Rops's works examine one pervasive question: man's destiny in the modern world. His first essay, *Notre Inquiétude* (1925; Our Anxiety), relates the intellectual and spiritual confusion that was the aftermath of World War I; the highly autobiographical novel *L'Ame obscure* (1929; The Obscure Soul) treats the same theme. *Mort, où est ta victoire?* (1934; Death, Where Is Thy Victory?), considered his masterpiece, and *L'Epée de feu* (1939; The Fiery Sword) demonstrate Daniel-Rops's obsession with the tragic problem of evil. These novels are permeated by a somber atmosphere reminiscent of Henrik IBSEN, but at the same time, they are illumined by the power of grace and the hope of salvation. The Pirandellian theme of the doubling of personality is apparent in the short stories that comprise *Deux Hommes en moi* (1936; Two Men in Me), a work also influenced by Chekhov.

The year 1930 marked a spiritual turning point for Daniel-Rops. After having sought instruction in the Catholic faith of his childhood, which he had all but abandoned during the 1920s, he undertook an examination of the general *inquiétude* of the world and the digression from God in several works, beginning with *Le Monde sans âme* (1932; World without Soul) and ending with *Par delà notre nuit* (1943; Beyond Our Night).

In 1942, Daniel-Rops united his Christian fervor with his early interest in history to begin a series of ecclesiastical histories: *Saint Bernard et son message* (1942; Saint Bernard and His Message), *Histoire sainte: le peuple de la Bible* (1943; Sacred History: The Common People and the Bible), *Jésus en son temps* (1945; Jesus in His Time), *L'Eglise des Apôtres et des Martyrs* (1948; The Church of the Apostles and the Martyrs). As a literary critic, Daniel-Rops wrote essays on Henri LENORMAND, Edouard ESTAUNIÉ, Péguy, Rimbaud, Ernest PSICHARI, Patrice de LA TOUR DU PIN, Blake, Pascal, and Kafka. *Orphiques* (1947) is a collection of seven religious poems. Daniel-Rops was elected to the Académie Française in 1955. He died in Chambéry.

See: P. Dournes, *Daniel-Rops ou le réalisme de l'esprit* (1949); P. de Boisdeffre, "L'Œuvre de Daniel-Rops," *RdDM*, no. 21 (1965), pp. 41–59.   S.H.

Danish literature. In Denmark, the first years of the 19th century were marked by a nationalism of unequaled force caused by the heroic battle by the Danish fleet against the British fleet outside Copenhagen in 1801, one of the last incidents of the French Revolutionary Wars. The feelings of nationalism, however, later received a severe blow because of Denmark's subsequent defeat in that same war, which led to the loss of Norway to Sweden in 1814. There was a growing tendency to isolate Denmark from all foreign influence, and the Danes instead turned to their glorious past for solace. After the revolt in Schleswig-Holstein of 1848–50, which Denmark successfully suppressed with the participation of Norwegian and Swedish volunteers, a so-called Scandinavianism emerged in the face of the growing Prussian imperialism, but it proved a failure during the attack by Prussia and Austria in 1864, when Denmark lost northern Schleswig.

This failure of the national dream gave rise to heated debates about the relationship between the ideal and reality, between faith and knowledge: a threatening premonition of a change in Danish intellectual life. Simultaneously, the political consciousness of the people was aroused, and in literature a reaction was noticeable against romanticism, which had been strongly influenced by Germany. With the writings of Frederik Paludan-Müller (1809–76) and Søren KIERKEGAARD, aesthetic harmony was destroyed, the secularized state church was rejected in favor of personal, religious commitment, and social criticism began to appear. The subsequent literary realism had its major forerunners in the prose works of S. S. Blicher (1782–1848) and Meïr Aron Goldschmidt (1819–87); and the modern psychological novel, in Hans Egede SCHACK's *Phantasterne* (1857; The Fantasts). But innocuous comedies and feeble late romantic dramas were still performed on the stage. In poetry there was an attempt to reconcile the threatened idealism with reality. Literary criticism called in vain for an ethical literature. It was an era of imitation.

The fact that the world had changed was not recognized. While the new constitution of 1866 put a brake on the democratic development in Denmark that had begun around 1850, the works of Karl Marx and Friedrich Engels were being read and discussed in the rest of Europe. In the natural sciences Darwinism and Auguste Comte's philosophy of positivism opened up completely new perspectives. John Stuart Mill's works called for parliamentarism and female liberation. Christian doctrine was weakened through David Friedrich Strauss's and Ludwig Feuerbach's radical theology. All these ideas suddenly appeared in Denmark around 1870 primarily because of the literary critic Georg BRANDES, who brought about the so-called modern breakthrough with his university lectures. In his lectures, Brandes intended to follow the ideas of liberty, proclaimed in the French Revolution, through the literatures of the major European countries. He himself did not regard his lectures as literary but rather as political, expounding the rights of "free thought" and "free passion." His attacks were directed against anything in contemporary society that prevented the free development of the individual. Brandes's naturalistic and radical point of view was thus not social but individualistic.

Danish intellectual life in the 1880s was almost exclusively dominated by reactions to the "breakthrough" ideas. Politically, the so-called Brandesianism became a power factor because of its affiliation with the large, liberal Peasant Party, but only to a very small extent did it create a lasting naturalistic literature. Georg Brandes's brother, Edvard Brandes (1847–1931), wrote a series of dramas of social criticism; and Sophus Schandorph (1836–1901) produced a number of atheistic problem novels. However, both writers are more noteworthy for their adherence to Brandes's doctrines than for their literary talent. Yet, for two young authors, Jens Peter JACOBSEN and Holger DRACHMANN, Brandes's ideas meant spiritual liberation. Jacobsen was a natural scientist and seemingly the one to become *the* author of Danish naturalism because of his short story "Mogens" (1872), in which human beings are regarded as part of nature and the soul is portrayed only in its relation to physical instincts and reactions. His later works, however, disclosed Jacobsen to be a lyrical dreamer, an atheist with religious longings. Although Jacobsen joined Brandes because of his naturalistic view of life, Drachmann was attracted by Brandes's social criticism. Jacobsen and Drachmann were by nature polar opposites, the former ironical and introverted, the latter passionate and pathetic with a marked affinity for exterior effects. The social, revolutionary attitude of Drachmann's youth was eventually transformed into bourgeois respectability and nationalism, which, in turn, gave way to a bohemian, heroic worship of beauty. The major literary figure outside the circle of "breakthrough" writers was Vilhelm Topsøe (1840–81), a newspaper editor and liberal politician who successfully opposed radical Brandesianism. As an author, Topsøe was a transitional figure. He continued H. E. Schack's criticism of romanticism in his satirical novel *Nutidsbilleder* (1878; Portraits of the Present) and anticipated the nontendentious writers of the following decade through his empathetic realism and excellent psychological characterizations.

The 1880s gradually became marked by large-scale renunciations of the naturalistic movement. Although Drachmann later swung back, the young radical Karl GJELLERUP remained in opposition, and the two major writers of the period, Herman BANG and Henrik PONTOPPIDAN, were completely unaffected by Brandes's ideas. Even the cooperation between the literary Left and the Peasant Party broke down owing to religious and national disagreements. The Peasant Party remained the largest Danish political party. It, therefore, strove to take over the government and to initiate parliamentarism, a fact that did not occur until 1901. The ruling Right, under Prime Minister Jakob Estrup, resisted these demands and from 1885 governed the country autocratically with the help of provisional financial laws. The nation became split over the issue of parliamentarism. Parallel economic and social progress (the cooperative movement began in 1882; trade unions were established from 1879 to 1885) could not prevent political bitterness and passivity among the population, and personal motifs became preponderant among the authors of this period.

The naturalistic moral was most extensively criticized in Pontoppidan's exposure of the exaggerated belief in the nobility of the liberated human being. The main characters of his three large novel cycles all end up in resigned isolation following vain and tragic battles against the burden of prejudice and environment. The foremost epic writer in Danish literature, Pontoppidan "deromanticized" the language as a reaction to both Jacobsen and Drachmann. The other critical realist, Herman Bang, stressed the fact that realism is an art form, not tendentious writing. Only when problems had become expressions of human life did they interest him. Bang's frame of reference was the role of the neglected "quiet existences" in the "so-called life," with its hopelessness, degeneration, and decline. These motifs are all found in his extensive impressionistic writing which followed his first artistic victory, "Ved Vejen" (1886; By the Wayside).

A new generation of writers appearing around 1890 had a revitalizing effect upon the literature. The soul was again recognized as a reality, and a lyrical reaction to the dominating prose and the materialistic philosophy of naturalism took place. The four principal writers of this generation, Johannes JØRGENSEN, Sophus CLAUSSEN, Viggo STUCKENBERG, and Helge RODE had, united in bonds of friendship, begun as righteous disciples of Brandes but later, influenced by Drachmann, Friedrich NIETZSCHE, and modern French literature, rejected scientific observation in favor of mystical and suggestive elements, thereby creating their own language, filled with music and beauty. This symbolic and neoromantic school neither wished to change the social structure nor imitate outer reality. No longer was the author regarded as a radical revolutionary but rather as a visionary. Johannes Jørgensen was the leading transmitter and theoretician of these ideas. As early as 1891 he launched the slogan "The

New Denmark" and, in the following years, violently attacked the present gray realism and the sterile debates about current issues in a series of articles about Stéphane MALLARMÉ, Charles BAUDELAIRE, Joris-Karl HUYSMANS, and Paul VERLAINE. The monthly magazine *Taarnet* (1893–94; The Tower), established by Jørgensen, was widely read and discussed, receiving much praise; but *Taarnet* was also criticized when it became obvious that its key concepts—symbolism, metaphysics, and mysticism—evidenced traits of dogmatic belief.

Two authors, Ludvig HOLSTEIN and Sophus Michaëlis (1865–1932) were also affiliated with neoromanticism. The former, nevertheless, broke with the more intimate style of the 1890s in later pantheistic hymns, and the latter expressed brilliantly and meticulously a refined view of life in a number of poetry collections with Oriental motifs published around 1900. Michaëlis won world fame with one single play, *Revolutionsbryllup* (1906; Revolutionary Wedding), a tragedy of love set at the time of the French Revolution.

Niels Møller (1859–1941) stands completely by himself, a speculative poet with a highly developed metaphoric language. Influenced by Robert Browning, he introduced the monologue poem into Danish literature. His poetry is marked not only by a fine feeling for nature but also by resignation before the merciless coincidence of existence. A selection, *Annabella,* was published in 1931.

Following the lyrical, introspective writing of the 1890s, the turn of the century brought a new realistic and rationalistic wave, the so-called material breakthrough, distinct from the earlier naturalism through a markedly materialistic and partly socialistic attitude. Although Jørgensen's poetry expresses the soulful human being's longing for eternity, Johannes V. JENSEN, the crucial figure of the new literature, represented the active human being in his worship of the technical era and the Industrial Revolution. It is possible to discern two directions within the "material breakthrough": (1) regional literature, which is primarily represented by authors from Jutland, notably Johan Skjoldborg (1861–1936), author of the novel *En Stridsmand* (1896; A Fighter), and Jeppe AAKJÆR; and (2) social agitational writing, combined with regionalism in the works of Skjoldborg and Aakjær and otherwise represented mainly by the proletarian author Martin Andersen NEXØ. Nexø produced numerous collections of short stories, from *Skygger* (1898; Shadows) to *De sorte Fugle* (1930; The Black Birds), containing both social, proletarian motifs and lyrical nature descriptions. However, two monumental novels about the working-class boy and girl, Pelle and Ditte, constitute the central point of his writing. They are the first Danish proletarian novels and Nexø's masterpieces.

Regional literature also provided a frame of reference for the two basically opposite authors Jakob KNUDSEN and Johannes V. Jensen; but whereas Jensen's *Himmerlandshistorier* (1898–1910; Himmerland Stories) simply forms the point of departure for a poetic expansion in time and space, Knudsen opens, on the basis of Christianity, perspectives on the peasant's still pagan view of life. Knudsen sets his characters against society, confronting the individual with God in a relationship that implies absolute obedience but also complete inner freedom. In Knudsen's writing, the individualism of Danish neoromanticism is overcome through religion; in Nexø's, through international communism; and in J. V. Jensen's, through Darwinism. Employing Charles Darwin's evolutionary theory in his works, Jensen brought about the powerful expansion of the present and reality, which lies behind his myths. Some of these myths were published as short prose tales; others, as novels. To Jensen, the myth, which contains both the elementary and the universal elements of life, grows out of reality. Thus the 20th century made its entrance into Danish literature with Jensen, who utilized the motifs of the big city and modern technology, especially in his early works. Like Jensen, Thøger Larsen (1875–1928) was influenced by natural science. His poetry, as in the mature collections *Jord* (1904; Earth) and *Dagene* (1905; Days), has a regional and peasant background; but, through his study of astronomy, Larsen's sense of nature became elevated to a cosmic sense of eternity and of the interrelationship among all things.

The third generation of realists, after the 1870s and 1880s, made their debut ca. 1900. Their most consistent representative, Karl Larsen (1860–1931), created his own domain with portraits of Copenhagen characters and milieus, often colored by dialect. Although Gustav WIED, in his descriptions of provincial life, intermingling idyll and bitter humor, is related to Herman Bang, his later cynical and satirical plays and novels are dominated by the main motifs of naturalism: decadence and love seen as pure instinct. The psychological novel of neoromanticism was also continued in the 20th century. In *Aage og Else* (1902–03; Aage and Else), Harald Kidde (1878–1918) juxtaposes two opposite characters, a young man burdened by guilt and thoughts of death and a vigorous and vital woman who chooses to abandon the man when she realizes that death is stronger than life in him. The principal character in Kidde's masterpiece, *Helten* (1912; The Hero), is an evangelical hero whose attempt to find happiness in humiliation and renunciation, that is, to follow the example of Christ, is portrayed with stirring perception. The major novels of Knud Hjortø (1869–1931), *Støv og Stjerner* (1964; Dust and Stars), *To Verdener* (1905; Two Worlds), and *Hans Raaskov* (1906), form a psychological and philosophical trilogy with one common theme, the inability of fantasts to cope with life. By his use of dream and the subconscious, Hjortø enlarged his human portraits through psychological analyses reminiscent of Sigmund Freud.

The outbreak of World War I brought about a major change in Danish literature. Denmark's neutrality led to an economic boom, a period of stockjobbing and easy wealth for some but also of inflation and bankruptcy for others. In the shadow of a threatening war, zest for life increased. A new generation of poets stepped spontaneously forward, filled with an ecstatic acceptance of the wonders of life. The two distinctive personalities of the group, Emil Bønnelycke (1893–1953) and Tom KRISTENSEN, published a series of sensational collections distinguished by individualistic materialism and sparkling expressionism. Their program, "to get the picture to burst, the lines to explode against each other, the colors to grate from sheer power and splendour," became realized in Bønnelycke's best-known collection, *Asfaltens Sange* (1918; Songs of the Asphalt), untraditional prose poems, influenced by J. V. Jensen's early poetry and by Walt Whitman's universal and positive affirmation of life. They illustrate Bønnelycke's glowing worship of modern cities, technology, and the chaotic contemporary times. But this exalted mood lasted only five years. A serious setback, a condemnation to silence or disillusion, took place ca. 1921 among many of the expressionists. The period had, indeed, begun with great promises on the internal political scene with the eight-hour day in 1919 and the reunion with northern Schleswig in 1920, only to be followed by demonstrations and strikes. The general skeptical atmosphere of the end of the war created an aura of uncertainty concerning the social and moral position among artists. They regarded the European ideals—

Western culture, the peace movement, and humanism—as being bankrupt, and if these values could not be found anew and redefined, pure nihilism seemed the only alternative. Against this confusion, the poet Otto GELSTED posited a rational and critical point of view, determined by a scientific recognition of the interrelationship of all things. Gelsted was the first to react artistically against the materialism of the war years and the subsequent ideological breakdown.

As the creator of a new poetic mentality, Emil Bønnelycke was undoubtedly the central figure of the 1920s, but Tom Kristensen became more important as a poet and intellectual personality. In his first collection of poems, he transforms outer reality into a marvelous orgy of clashing colors. Later he broke with this expressionistic style and achieved a restrained, color-filled form of writing closer to impressionism but unable to hide the feeling of desperation so typical of Kristensen's whole production, culminating in his last novel, *Hærværk* (1930; Eng. tr., *Havoc*, 1968). Besides Kristensen, Jacob PALUDAN must be regarded as the foremost representative of this postwar generation. But whereas Kristensen experienced the chaos within himself, Paludan was a spectator who investigated the misery from a satirical, conservative point of view. From the beginning he was highly skeptical regarding the period, and he was the first to see that the 1930s were not years of peace but interwar years.

Around 1925 the ideological chaos culminated in an impassioned debate. Following the great success of the expressionistic poets, a new generation of writers made their appearance. In various ways they attempted to find their standpoint in a changed world. The new generation's foremost artistic talents were the poets Per Lange (1901–), Paul LA COUR, and Jens August SCHADE and the prose writer Knud SØNDERBY. The poetry in Lange's collections, *Kaos og Stjernen* (1926; Chaos and the Star), *Forvandlinger* (1929; Metamorphoses), and *Orfeus* (1932; Orpheus) contains erotic, mystical, and nature motifs informed by a tragic idealism. Lange attempted to overcome the period's artistic and human dissolution through clarity of thought and a stylistically clear, classical tradition, whereas la Cour tried to penetrate the inner being of nature and matter and his own self in order to perceive the secret of existence. Schade, in his turn, caught the tension between the infinite and the finite in respectless and erotic surrealistic poetry. Artistically, Nis PETERSEN's works are the most convincing expressions of the period's anxiety and nihilism. Petersen was never able to gain a foothold either ideologically or materially, and he succumbed in anxiety and doubt. For him only the untouched world of childhood, death, and finally the hope for divine grace could provide an escape from the existential darkness, three possibilities put forth in his colorful but deeply tragic historical novel *Sandalmagernes Gade* (1931; Eng. tr., *The Street of the Sandalmakers*, 1933). The other major prose work of the 1930s, Hans KIRK's *Fiskerne* (1928; Eng. tr., *The Fishermen*, 1951), is marked by the author's sociological and Marxist point of view. In *Fiskerne*, Kirk describes the development of a society but succeeds in raising the narration above pure propaganda through convincing and realistic portrayals. Despite the fact that a large segment of his production is critical and polemical, Kirk's human outlook was quite positive. This was not the case with another important novelist of the 1930s, Jørgen NIELSEN, whose view of life was marked by pessimism and resignation. The speciality of Aage Dons (1907–) was pure psychological analysis. His novels, for example, *Soldaterbrønden* (1936; Eng. tr., *The Soldier's Well*, 1940), portray the attempts of rootless, lonely human beings to overcome their isolation. A bla-

tant political tendency is obvious in the works of Hans SCHERFIG, next to Kirk the most markedly Marxist writer of the period. For him the apparent absurdity of life becomes a sign of the corruption of capitalism, depicted in a series of satirical and humorous novels with suspense effects. Some social critics like Harald Herdal (1900–78) described the misery of the big city proletariat. Others, like Knuth BECKER in his extensive, autobiographical cycle of novels, directed their criticism at public institutions and the educational system. However, the period was not dominated by this predominantly socialistic or Communist literature, partly because of the Moscow trials of 1936–38, which had quite a deterrent effect upon even the most idealistic sympathizer.

The drama, on the other hand, experienced a time of hectic activity. The plays of Carl Erik Martin SOYA are characterized by brutal realism, merciless satire, and psychological experiments. Kjeld ABELL was, in the beginning, more strongly related to the old naturalism. His successful dramas attacked bourgeois pettiness, as in *Melodien, der blev væk* (1935; Eng. tr., *The Melody That Got Lost*, 1939), but they also proclaim an aggresive humanism aimed at the threatening war. The most interesting figure of the interwar era was, however, Kaj MUNK, a playwright and a clergyman. In the course of a few years, he developed into the foremost preacher, the most controversial spiritual personality, and, without doubt, the major modern dramatist in Danish literature. Munk desired to create a drama full of effects, placing passion and man's relationship with God in the foreground. In his first heroic drama, *En Idealist* (1928; Eng. tr., *Herod the King*, in *Five Plays by Kaj Munk*, 1953), the battle between the man of action and God ends with the defeat of the former. But the hero can also be chosen to defend the cause of truth in a political situation. In a number of dramas from the war years, brutal force (Nazism) is confronted with a Christian humanistic ideal.

Far removed from this current, active engagement was Karen BLIXEN. Her first world success, *Seven Gothic Tales* (1934; Danish tr., *Syv fantastiske Fortællinger*, 1935), deals with the dilemma of destiny, with the necessity to realize oneself and to accept both the good and evil elements in life. Neither realistic nor psychological motifs dominate Blixen's writing. Her work also indicates a sharp break with the dominating naturalistic prose of the 1930s. On the other hand, Hans Christian BRANNER's first novel, *Legetøj* (1936; Toys), is in its composition typical of the 1930s: a collective novel—that is, a novel in which there is no single, major character—about office workers in a commercial firm, a tiny society that with its problems symbolizes society at large. Branner's later, more experimental works are, however, connected with postwar existentialism and deal with the situation of the individual in the present and the fundamental problems of life and death. Martin Alfred HANSEN also began as a realistic social critic, but he later became the chief exponent of the postwar religious and antinaturalistic currents. The events of World War II led to his belief that modern civilization is distinguished by inhumanity and moral dissolution.

The German occupation of 1940 to 1945 initiated a critical period in Danish literature. The majority of writers were decidedly opponents of Nazism. Most of them, socialists, conservatives, and nihilists, joined in the defense of the national culture. But the remaining vestige of the belief in cultural progress was now gone; all the ideals of mankind seemed suspect. The war years and the postwar era gave rise to endless literary motifs, which, however, only several years later were given their artistic form. The larger part of prose writing was simply a continuation of the trends of the 1930s, whereas poetry dominated the 1940s. Most of the poets, notably Ole SARVIG, Ole WIVEL, Thorkild BJØRNVIG and Frank JÆGER, belonged to the circle around the literary journal *Heretica* (1948–53), which displayed a "heretic" attitude toward the dominating rationalism and materialism. *Heretica* thus personified a reaction against the 1930s in a way similar to that in which symbolists of the 1890s reacted against Brandesianism with Rode and Blixen as connecting links and M. A. Hansen as the leading personality. The bond unifying Danish writers proved to be their recognition of the so-called cultural crisis. A common spiritual culture no longer existed. Its place had been taken by a far less universal economic and political unity. The poets were filled with a deep longing for a change of the human mind and a cultural rebirth. Yet fear and desperation prevailed rather than this hope. In connection with the destruction of the common cultural pattern, there was a stylistic and structural crisis that is regarded as an integral part of poetry. The poem is often seen as possessing wisdom that goes beyond intellectual comprehension. In the 1920s, Sophus Claussen adhered to this view as did Gustaf MUNCH-PETERSEN in the 1930s. However, many of the later poets, for example, Tove DITLEVSEN, followed the tradition of rhymed, simple, and melancholic stanzas, or else they strove for clarity and austerity and for a telling use of words, as did Piet HEIN. The most typical poets of the war years were Halfdan RASMUSSEN and Morten Nielsen (1922–44). The Resistance became for them the central event that activated them as artists. Nielsen's two collections, *Krigere uden Vaaben* (1943; Warriors without Weapons) and *Efterladte Digte* (1945; Posthumous Poems), show him as a representative of the young, devoid of illusions but still with the will to risk life for freedom.

The cultural criticism of M. A. Hansen was continued by the principal poet of the era, Ole Sarvig. The experience of the crisis of modern, rational man, isolated from any metaphysical dimensions, is a theme found in several collections of Sarvig's poems published between 1943 and 1948. But the isolation can be overcome through an experience of love, which is felt as grace and salvation in the evangelical sense, also described in a number of later novels. Whereas the mystery of love and grace is regarded by Sarvig as a means of deliverance from chaos and uncertainty, the belief in poetry itself is of decisive importance for the poet Thorkild Bjørnvig. He too regards love as a central motif but views it only as a stage in life that inexorably ends with death. The idea of metamorphosis is also prevalent in the poetry of Ole Wivel, but in connection with the belief in the rebirth of man and culture, a progression from catastrophe to messianic hope. Erik KNUDSEN belonged to the circle around *Heretica* for a short time, but he broke with the journal to join the new, Marxist, rationalistic magazine *Dialog* (1950–61; Dialogue). The feeling of anxiety and powerlessness so typical of his generation does not drive Knudsen to renunciation or religious quest. For him, social criticism and satire (a political commitment) take the place of introspective poetry, which is also true of Wivel in his later collections. By contrast, Frank Jæger, the youngest among the "Heretica" poets, turned demonstratively against the ideological trends, concentrating upon humorous and naive descriptions of the concrete, elementary life in nature. Yet, in Jæger's collections from the 1960s, a number of love poems evidence an increasing feeling of desperation over man's isolation in life, a theme that brings him close to lyrical modernism despite the otherwise classic structure of his poetry.

Jæger's prose is dominated by imaginative elements, and this is typical of many of the Danish prose writers of the 1950s. A characteristic trait of this period was a deep interest in Karen Blixen, very noticeable in the works of Willy-August LINNEMANN, Niels Albert DAM, and Leif Christensen (1924–). They all share the spiritual conviction that man exists to realize himself in his relation to fate. The realistic and psychological human portrayals of the 1930s were continued in a masterly way by the prose writers Hans Lyngby Jepsen (1920–), Poul Ørum (1919–), Erik Aalbæk Jensen (1923–), and Tage Skou-Hansen (1925–), but simultaneously a more experimental tone is also prevalent.

If the "Heretica" poets still belonged to a symbolistic tradition, one can now speak of consistent modernism, which, from a philosophical point of view, continued the existential line, but attempted to break down the barrier between reality and the experience of reality with far greater emphasis. A conscious effort was now made to bring Danish literature into step with European modernism, the organ of which became the journal *Vindrosen* (1954–74; The Compass). In prose, modernism was first represented in the first works of Villy SØRENSEN and Peter SEEBERG published in the 1950s. Sørensen's narrations may be considered the imaginative thoughts of a philosopher, whereas Seeberg's short stories and novels spring from penetrating observations that break with both traditional and more symbolic realism.

Leif PANDURO is less exclusive but far more productive. His novels deal almost entirely with a certain type of human being, the individual who is split because of his dependence on his past. But Panduro attacks not only the traditional concept of the unity of the personality but also basic ideas of what constitutes normality and abnormality and also, in general, the moral hypocrisy of the bourgeoisie. Panduro's dramatic writing is a typical and successful indication of the interest in the theater and the dramatic genre prevalent in the 1960s. A result of this interest is the many stage productions and various experimental theater groups that in the 1970s become more and more political. The greatest success on the stage was enjoyed by Ernst Bruun Olsen (1923–). Aiming at current trends, his plays combine realism with imagination: *Teenagerlove* (1962), satirizing the cult of pop music, and *Bal i den Borgerlige* (1966; Middle-Class Ball), which is a political criticism of halfhearted socialism. Of greater artistic importance is the dramatic production for stage, radio, and television, which Leif Petersen (1934–) began in the 1960s, with its roots in the works of Harold Pinter and William Saroyan.

The real artistic innovation on the threshold of the 1960s, however, was lyrical modernism. The political climate of the 1940s had encouraged the poetry of fear and pessimism, and the reaction to that climate was expressed in a search for cosmic or metaphysical meaning. Around 1960 writers to a much larger extent accepted the welfare state, commercialism, and the atom bomb. Whereas the previous decade had been dominated by primarily literary, nostalgic trends, the new poetry of the 1960s was directed provokingly against the outer and current forms of society, confronting the incompatible elements of reality and sensory impressions with each other. To Klaus RIFBJERG goes much of the credit for the lyrical renewal of Danish literature in the 1960s. His collection *Konfrontation* (1960; Confrontation), which breaks new ground, consists of poems that express the confrontation between consciousness and reality and the sheer experience of matters formulated through the associative power of the language.

Simultaneously with Rifbjerg's prose works, which are quite traditional in form, an experimental prose modernism broke through around 1960, anticipated by Villy

Sørensen and Peter Seeberg in the 1950s. Whereas many novels of the preceding generation had been based on experiences of the war and the occupation, the writers in the 1960s turned their attention to current existential problems, which led to a transformation of the structure of the novel. Influences were felt from the "nouveau roman" of, for example, Alain ROBBE-GRILLET and Samuel BECKETT, causing the elimination of both traditional action and the distance between narrator and narration.

Svend Åge MADSEN has been strongly influenced by the modern French novel. He experiments with various viewpoints on the author and narrative levels in an attempt to reduce human identity and thereby also reduces the structure of the novel. Political and social criticism occupies an increasingly larger role in Madsen's novels of the 1970s. A similar tendency is noticeable in the prose works of Sven HOLM, although he never abandons his imaginative style, characteristic of his analyses of the psychological conflicts within people, conflicts often determined by time and culture. Psychological interest is also typical of two women writers, Cecil Bødker (1927-) and Ulla RYUM. Bødker's novels, *Tilstanden Harley* (1965; The Condition of Harley) and *Pap* (1967; Cardboard), are distinguished by a precise, concentrated, modernistic form, whereas Ryum, like Sven Holm, is a representative of the more fantastic tradition in newer Danish literature characterized by the works of Karen Blixen and Villy Sørensen. Thorkild HANSEN's objective and nonideological writing is in sharp contrast to Madsen's relativistic point of view. Hansen does not attempt to interpret reality, he rather describes actual events. Hansen's documentary production runs parallel to the neorealistic currents that appeared about 1965 and are lyrically expressed in Rifbjerg's *Amagerdigte* (1965; Poems from Amager) and Benny ANDERSEN's humorous and structurally simple poetry. In prose, this neorealism is primarily represented by Anders BODELSEN, Christian KAMPMANN, Henrik Stangerup (1937-), and Ole Hyltoft (1940-). Contemporary types and milieus are described with penetrating satire by Bodelsen and with added polemic precision by Stangerup and Hyltoft, whereas Kampmann's artistic strength lies in his perceptive analysis of bourgeois life and values, revealed with acute irony.

Whereas the modernistic prose of the 1960s had very few forerunners, poetry had a broader background in the experimental lyrical writing of the preceding decade. In 1960, the same year that Rifbjerg's collection *Konfrontation* (Confrontation) was published, Jess ØRNSBO made his debut with *Digte* (Poems). The social commitment found in this volume provides new motifs in modernism, while the principle of composition is the confrontation technique, given its classic expression in Rifbjerg's poetry. Ivan MALINOVSKI also adheres to this aesthetic principle, which is a formal expression of his own experience of life's absurdity, found in *Galgenfrist* (1958; Short Respite), the period's first consistently modernistic collection of poetry. A more intellectual tendency, related to T. S. Eliot, SAINT JOHN PERSE, Gunnar EKELÖF, and Ezra Pound, is cultivated by Jørgen SONNE; and, in the manner of poets, he is familiar with an extensive tradition, alluding to the past and to foreign cultures. Like Sonne, Jørgen Gustava BRANDT is quite skeptically inclined toward all ideologies and political commitments. His attitude is similar to that of a religious mystic whose duty it is to establish contact between the self and its environment through poetry.

Around 1965 and parallel with the development of neorealism there was in Denmark, as in Sweden, a tendency toward concretism, although it was more philosophical and methodically conscious. Words were given their own lives as independent signs. In prose this trend is found in Svend Åge Madsen's tightly structured novels; in poetry it is found in Ivan Malinovski's *Romerske bassinger* (1963; Roman Basins) and, to an even larger degree, in Per HØJHOLT's rather esoteric writing. The inclination of this concretism toward the pedagogical and mechanical, qualities that characterize the work of Vagn Steen (1928-), is replaced by greater illusionary power in the later collections of poetry of Hans-Jørgen Nielsen (1941-). Within this movement, Inger CHRISTENSEN reaches supreme artistic height with *Det* (1969; It), a daring epic, combining poetry, poetics, and philosophy.

If both neorealism and concretism were reactions against the hermetic character of modernism in the 1960s, a similar neoromantic reaction took place in prose and poetry around 1970, mostly rooted in a revolutionary, romantic dream of a new society similar to that which is portrayed in Vagn Lundbye's (1933-) talented, lyrical novel *Smukke tabere* (1970; Beautiful Losers), the beat generation's dream of solidarity, depicted in rich, melodious language, which also characterizes another significant representative of this trend, Rolf Gjedsted (1947-).

Besides the established authors, traditionalists and modernists, a number of young innovative writers have appeared, supporting the impression that current Danish literature is nondogmatic, vital, and richly faceted. Steen Kaalø (1945-) and Henrik Nordbrandt (1945-) adhere to a dreamlike, poetic surrealism, which, in Henrik Bjelke's (1937-) novels, is combined with burlesque and realistic traits. Psychedelic experiences, mixed with science fiction elements, are described by Knud Holten (1945-) and Anders Westenholz (1936-), whereas a more extensive social awareness is evident both in the more traditional, realistic authors Ole Henrik Laub (1937-) and Thomas Brandt (1943-) and the more linguistically oriented writers Dan Turell (1946-), Jens Smærup Sørensen (1946-), Henning Mortensen (1939-), and Kristen Bjørnkjær (1943-). Social commitment again becomes evident in the very talented works of Marianne Larsen (1951-), which includes themes such as class struggle, the battle between the sexes, and political imperialism, all presented in a concise style. A proletarian childhood forms the basis of Lean Nielsen's (1935-) demand for a permanent revolution, whereas Vita Andersen (1944-) unites these motifs in her very successful poetry collection *Tryghedsnarkomaner* (1977; Security Addicts).

These writers hold out the promise that recent Danish literature will continue to develop the versatility, quality, and talent that characterized the 1970s.

See: P. M. Mitchell, *A Bibliographical Guide to Danish Literature* (1951); J. Claudi, *Contemporary Danish Authors* (1952); P. M. Mitchell, *A History of Danish Literature* (1957); S. H. Rossel, *Skandinavische Literatur 1870-1970* (1973), *Scandinavian Literature since 1870* (1980), and *A History of Scandinavian Literature, 1870-1980* (1980).   S.H.R.

D'Annunzio, Gabriele (1863-1938), Italian poet, novelist, short-story writer, and dramatist, was born on the Adriatic coast in Pescara, the principal city of the Abruzzi. He returned periodically to this primitive region, and it remained a fixed point in the elaboration of an aesthetic myth in which an extraordinarily sharp sense of the physicality of natural phenomena mingled with an equally sensitive perception of art objects, finding expression in vivid images and verses of unmatched musicality. He was the leading literary personality of the first two decades of the 20th century in Italy, a cross between Ariel and a latter-day Lord Byron. He attracted attention as much by the unconventionality and flamboyance of his personal life and his military activity during World War I as by the ostentatious splendor and unrestrained sensuality of his work, which drew upon almost all contemporary artistic currents and was itself widely imitated.

A brilliant, precocious student at the Liceo Cicognini in Prato (one of the best schools in Italy at the time), to which he was sent to master Tuscan Italian, D'Annunzio made his debut as a poet at the age of 16 with the publication of *Primo vere* (1879; Early Spring). The poems that compose this work were inspired by Giosuè Carducci's *Odi barbare* (1877; Eng. tr., *The Barbarian Odes*, 1939), in which the dean of Italian poets had experimented with the rhythmic structure of Greek and Latin verse forms, forms fundamentally alien to normal Italian syllabic verse. Because of the enthusiastic reception of *Primo vere*, D'Annunzio was already well known when in 1881 he moved to Rome to attend the university. He quickly became part of the intellectual and cultural life of the new capital of Italy, contributing to such prestigious journals as *La cronaca bizantina*, *Il capitan Fracassa*, and *La tribuna*. His second collection of poetry, *Canto novo* (1882; New Song), was followed two years later by *Intermezzo di rime* (An Interlude of Verses), which sparked a heated controversy about decorum in art because of its overt expression of sensuality. Between 1882 and 1886, D'Annunzio also published three volumes of prose works, *Terra vergine* (1882; Virgin Land), *Libro delle vergini* (1884; The Book of the Virgins), and *San Pantaleone* (1886; Saint Pantaleone), naturalistic sketches and stories that show the influence of Giovanni VERGA and Guy de Maupassant and were later reissued as *Novelle della Pescara* (1902; Eng. tr., *Tales of My Native Town*, 1920). In 1891, D'Annunzio published a Dostoyevskian novel (*see* Fyodor DOSTOYEVSKY), *Giovanni Episcopo* (Eng. tr., *Episcopo and Company*, 1896), a sordid story of degradation and crime set in a petit bourgeois environment unusual for him. His most famous novel, *Il piacere* (Eng. tr., *The Child of Pleasure*, 1898), appeared in the same year. Like *A rebours* (1884; Eng. tr., *Against Nature*, 1959) by Joris-Karl HUYSMANS, a work with which it has points of contact, *Il piacere* is a veritable breviary of decadence in *fin de siècle* Rome.

What has been called D'Annunzio's Roman period came to an end in 1891 when the poet, now separated definitively from Maria Hardouin di Gallese, whom he had married in 1883 and by whom he had three sons, moved to Naples, where his next novel, *L'innocente* (1892; Eng. tr., *The Intruder*, 1898), was serialized in *Il corriere di Napoli*. It is at this time that D'Annunzio's works began to be known outside of Italy, thanks in large part to his French translator, Georges Hérelle (1848–1935). His next two novels, *Il trionfo della morte* (1894; Eng. tr., *The Triumph of Death*, 1896) and *Le vergini delle rocce* (1895; Eng. tr., *The Maidens of the Rocks*, 1898), reflect an overwhelming enthusiasm for Friedrich NIETZSCHE and Richard WAGNER. With his espousal of the myth of the superman, D'Annunzio became the leader for the youngest generation of Italians, disappointed with the results of the Risorgimento, chafing at Italy's position as a second-rate power, and yearning for war and the glory of combat. D'Annunzio's 1895 cruise to the Aegean islands was another result of his encounter with Nietzsche, in particular with the latter's *The Birth of Tragedy*. On the return from that trip, D'Annunzio met the great tragic actress Eleonora Duse once again, a meeting that initiated yet another clamorous love affair and also ushered in one of D'Annunzio's most productive periods. D'Annunzio's direct involvement in the political life of the nation dates from 1897, when he was elected to the Italian parliament for a three-year term.

D'Annunzio became a playwright in the wake of his Greek trip and when Duse decided to limit her future repertoire to his works. His plays range from the lyrical effusions of *Sogno di un mattino di primavera* (1897; Eng. tr., *The Dream of a Spring Morning*, 1903) and *Sogno di un tramonto d'autunno* (1898; Eng. tr., *The Dream of an Autumn Sunset*, 1904) to the glorification of the exceptional personalities of supermen living the "inimitable life" in *La città morta* (1898; Eng. tr., *The Dead City*, 1900), *La Gioconda* (1899; Eng. tr., *Gioconda*, 1902), and *La gloria* (1899; Glory) to the verse tragedies *Francesca da Rimini* (1902; Eng. tr., *Francesca da Rimini*, 1902), his recognized masterpiece, *La figlia di Jorio* (1904; Eng. tr., *The Daughter of Jorio*, 1907), *La fiaccola sotto il moggio* (1905; The Torch under the Bushel), *Più che l'amore* (1906; More than Love—which created a scandal when it was first performed in Rome), *La nave* (1908; The Ship), and *Fedra* (1909; Phaedra). He also wrote three plays in French: *Le martyre de Saint Sébastien* (1911; The Martyrdom of Saint Sebastian—performed with music by Claude Debussy and dances by Ida Rubenstein), *La Pisanelle ou la mort parfumée* (1913; Pisanella or Perfumed Death—with music by Ildebrando Pizzetti and later by Pietro Mascagni), and *Le Chèvrefeuille* (1913; Eng. tr., *The Honeysuckle*, 1916). He also wrote the script for the film spectacle *Cabiria* (1914).

During his liaison with Duse and while his main residence was in the fabulous Tuscan villa of La Capponcina, D'Annunzio published the novel *Il fuoco* (1900; Eng. tr., *The Flame of Life*, 1900), which has been described as the Venetian pendant to *Il piacere* and which caused yet another scandal because of its transparent allusions to his ongoing love affair. To the same period belongs his greatest collection of poetry, *Alcyone* (1903; Alcyone—one of the Pleiades), the third book of a cycle of seven, *Laudi del Cielo del Mare della Terra e degli Eroi* (1903–18), hymns of praise by means of which D'Annunzio planned to celebrate the Heavens, the Sea, the Earth, and Heroes. Only five of the books were actually completed: *Maia* (1903; also known as *Laus vitae*, Hymn to Life), *Elettra* (1903; Electra), *Alcyone*, *Merope* (1912; also known as *Canzoni d'oltremare*, Songs from Beyond the Sea, with reference to Italy's participation in the war against Turkey), and *Canti della guerra latina* (1914–18; Songs of the Latin War, with reference to World War I, originally to have been entitled after another of the Pleaides, Asterope). The poems of *Alcyone* celebrate the days of high summer along the Tuscan coast near the mouth of the Arno—days of "immortal metamorphoses," D'Annunzio calls them, when the objects of nature become transfigured before the poet's eyes to the point of creating new personifications, living figures, and embodiments of the poet's desire, rivaling those of ancient myth.

In addition to the works already cited, while in France (1909–15) D'Annunzio also wrote the prose pieces of *Contemplazione della morte* (1912; Contemplation of Death). These meditations on death were occasioned by the death of the poet Giovanni PASCOLI and the almost simultaneous death of D'Annunzio's aged landlord. They were followed later by similar poetic reminiscences in *La Leda senza cigno* (1916; Leda without the Swan), which draw their subject matter from the French years both in peace and war, culminating with the famous description of Rheims Cathedral in flames during the German advance. Even more striking are the extraordinary prose pieces of *Notturno* (1921; Nocturne), written in utter darkness and immobility while D'Annunzio was recovering from the loss of his right eye in a wartime flying accident in 1916.

An ardent patriot, D'Annunzio not only volunteered for active duty, distinguishing himself by acts of valor, but he continued the irredentist fight for the annexation of Italian-speaking provinces even after the armistice with the occupation of the formerly Austrian city of Fiume on the Yugoslav coast. When he was obliged to relinquish Fiume in 1921, he retired (or voluntarily exiled himself) to a villa on Lake Garda, a residence that he filled with art works and mementos of his life and left to the Italian government, which turned it into a national monument. His later years were devoted to the publication of prose fragments, reminiscences, and the public addresses he had made, as well as his *Opera omnia,* for which a National Institute had been established in 1926.

After his death and especially after World War II, D'Annunzio's reputation suffered a precipitous decline. In the early years of the century, Benedetto CROCE had already reduced his art to dilettantism, a search for sensation for its own sake. Yet the pervasiveness of D'Annunzio's influence, most noticeable in his own day in the desire to imitate his style of life and his mannerisms as well as his works, has been revealed in retrospect to have left its mark on virtually all poets that followed him, even those most hostile to him or to all appearances most distant from him. While he continues to be a favorite subject for titillating and popular biographies, he has also come into his own, together with his contemporary Giovanni Pascoli, as a major subject of study for a better understanding of modern Italian poetry. For a one-volume anthology of his work, with an excellent introduction by Mario PRAZ, see G. D'Annunzio, *Poesie. Teatro. Prose,* M. Praz and F. Gerra, eds. (1966), which also contains extensive bibliographies.

See: P. Jullian, *D'Annunzio* (1973).   O.R.

Däubler, Theodor (1876–1934), German poet, was born in Trieste of German parents and grew up as a bilingual child, equally at home in German and Italian. After his schooling he became a vagrant intellectual. In Naples he conceived the plan of his epic poem *Das Nordlicht* (pub. Florence, 1910; a rev. ed. pub. Geneva in 1922; The Northern Lights).

His years in Paris were Däubler's really formative period. Although essentially a lonely soul, he there became the lifelong friend of Moeller van den Bruck, who in most respects was his spiritual opposite. In Germany during nearly the entire period of World War I he tried repeatedly and unsuccessfully to become a soldier. After the war his homelessness continued; he traveled to Greece and the Near East and visited Egypt and the Scandinavian countries. He died in a sanatorium in the Black Forest.

Under the influence of superstitious servants, Däubler early developed a very personal religion. *Das Nordlicht* is conceived as an original cosmic myth. Only in rare poems did he achieve a perfect expression of his own self, as in *Das Sternenkind* (1917; The Child of the Stars), and *Die Treppe zum Nordlicht* (1920; The Stairway to the Northern Lights).

See: Akademie der Künste, Berlin, *Theodor Däubler* (1968), catalogue on the opening of the Däubler archives.
E.R. rev. A.L.W.

Daudet, Léon (1867–1942), French journalist, memorialist, literary critic, and novelist, was born in Paris. The son of the novelist Alphonse Daudet, he was raised by a loving family and grew up in intellectual and artistic surroundings. While such favorable circumstances do not explain his character or the nature of his political activities, they undoubtedly account for some of his accomplishments as a writer. Young Léon attended the best schools in Paris,

studied medicine for several years, and then gave it up to become a writer. His first book (1891) contained three short stories, but it was the next one, his first novel, *Haeres* (1893), that attracted some attention. *Les Morticoles* (1894), which dealt with the medical world, created a sensation. He asserted himself with his *Voyage de Shakespeare* in 1896. The course of Daudet's life was determined in 1908, when he joined Charles MAURRAS as coeditor of the ultraroyalist *L'Action française.* By 1914 he had published a dozen novels, various essays, and many political articles. Over 50 important books are now listed in his bibliography. Today, Léon Daudet is especially known for the novels *Suzanne* (1897) and *L'Entremetteuse* (1921; The Go-between); the essay *Le Stupide XIXe Siècle* (1922; Eng. tr., *The Stupid 19th Century,* 1928), which should not be taken too seriously; and his six volumes of *Souvenirs des milieux littéraires, politiques, artistiques et médicaux* (6 vols., 1914–21; Eng. tr., *Memoirs of Léon Daudet,* 1925), whose value is certainly more literary than documentary.

During an eventful life, Daudet was in contact with the most prominent men of his own and his father's generation. He married and later divorced the granddaughter of Victor Hugo, fought 14 duels, was elected deputy for Paris, was jailed for accusing the Parisian police of killing his son, and escaped to Belgium, where he lived in exile for two and a half years. He died in Saint-Rémy-de-Provence.

Daudet's writings and political activities entertained, intensified prejudices, and excited hatred. Yet his Rabelaisian verve, humor, and imagination, his picturesque language and truculent style were such that even the readers whom he offended most were at times more amused than irked by his invectives, caricatures, or abuses. While his critical judgment was sometimes suspended, he often revealed himself as an acute observer with a sense of humor, quite capable of judging people, appreciating talent, and perceiving genius. He imposed Marcel PROUST on the Goncourt Prize jury and pleaded in favor of Jean GIRAUDOUX, Guillaume APOLLINAIRE, Louis-Ferdinand CÉLINE, and others, irrespective of their political beliefs or affiliations. He repeatedly acclaimed Pablo Picasso as the greatest living artist and loudly defended Claude Debussy's music. At his best, Daudet was an excellent literary critic.

See: R. Guillou, *Léon Daudet: son caractère, ses romans, sa politique* (1918); E. Mas, *Léon Daudet: son œuvre* (1928).   A.V.R.

Daumal, René (1908–44), French poet, short-story writer, and essayist, was born at Boulzicourt in the Ardennes. He was educated in the lycées of Charleville and Reims. Although his life was brief, he left an extensive body of works of remarkable intellectual quality, the majority of which were published after his death, earning him the rare distinction of being the first 20th-century French author to win posthumous fame. He and Roger Gilbert-Lecomte, surrealists (*see* FRENCH LITERATURE) with mystical tendencies, were founding editors of the avant-garde literary review *Le Grand Jeu* (1928–30). During his lifetime, Daumal published only two complete works: *Le Contre-ciel* (1936; Against Heaven), a collection of poems, and *La Grande Beuverie* (1938; The Great Carousal), a satirical account of Parisian intellectual life in the 1930s. His posthumously published works are the unfinished *Le Mont Analogue* (1952; Eng. tr., *Mount Analogue: An Authentic Narrative,* 1968) and *Poésie noire, poésie blanche* (1954; Black Poetry, White Poetry). Published collections of his essays, stories, translations from Sanskrit, and letters include *Chaque fois que l'aube paraît*

(1953; Each Time Dawn Appears), *Lettres à ses amis* (1958; Letters to His Friends), *Tu t'es toujours trompé* (1970; You Were Always Wrong), *Bharata* (1970); *L'Evidence absurde* (1972; The Absurd Evidence), and *Les Pouvoirs de la parole* (1972; The Powers of the Word).

It is impossible to separate the work of Daumal, the student of the occult, science, mathematics, Oriental religions, and Indian philosophy and literature, from that of the essayist or the poet. All Daumal's voices contribute to a single discourse of which the theme is summed up in a note found among his papers: "Art . . . is knowledge realized in action." Daumal, the spiritual heir of Gérard de Nerval (1808–55) and Arthur RIMBAUD, sought an authentic spiritual experience, not a philosophical or metaphysical system. *Le Mont Analogue,* which he was writing at the time of his death, is a symbolic account of his own spiritual experiments in the search for truth, a search he never abandoned, believing firmly that "the door to the invisible must be visible." In this work, as well as in his poetry and such characteristic articles as "La Révolte et l'ironie" (1924; Revolt and Irony), and essays like "Une Expérience fondamentale" (1943; A Fundamental Experience), one encounters Daumal's belief in an absolute truth, an impersonal, ageless knowledge found in all great traditions, both Eastern and Western.

See: R. Shattuck, preface to *Mount Analogue: An Authentic Narrative* (1968); special no. of *Hermès* 5 (1968).

T.H.G.

Davičo, Oskar (1909–), Serbian poet, novelist, and essayist, was born into a merchant family in Šabac, western Serbia. He became a high-school teacher and was arrested several times as a Communist, spending five years (1932–37) in a penitentiary. During World War II he joined the Partisans after escaping from a prisoner-of-war camp. After the war, he worked as a journalist, and for the last several years he has been a professional writer.

Davičo published his first collections of poems, *Tragovi* (1928; Traces) and *Anatomija* (1930; Anatomy), while he was a member of the surrealist circle of Serbian writers, a small but powerful group who emulated their French counterparts but who tried to give surrealism stronger social overtones. After the Serbian surrealist group broke up, Davičo joined those writers with predominantly socialist tendencies (*see* SERBIAN LITERATURE). His subsequent collections of poetry—*Pesme* (1938; Poems), *Višnja za zidom* (1950; A Sour-Cherry Tree behind the Wall), and *Hana* (1951; Hannah)—established him as a poet of clear orientation and powerful poetic means. His other important collections of poetry are *Nastanjene oči* (1954; Occupied Eyes), *Flora* (1955; Flora), *Kairos* (1959; Cairos), *Tropi* (1959; Tropes), and *Trg M* (1968; The Square M). He has also written long poems, *Zrenjanin* (1947; Zrenjanin) and *Čovekov čovek* (1953; A Man's Man); volumes of essays, *Poezija i otpori* (1949; Poetry and Resistance) and *Pre podne* (1960; Before Noon); and a travelogue, *Medju Markosovim partizanima* (1947; With Markos's Partisans).

Davičo's first novel, *Pesma* (1952; Eng. tr., *Poem,* 1960), a poetic evocation of the maturing of a high-school student into an underground fighter, helped to establish him as an important contemporary Serbian novelist. Other novels—*Beton i svici* (1956; Concrete and Fireflies), *Radni naslov beskraja* (1958; A Limitless Working Title), and *Generalbas* (1962; Thorough Bass)—also deal with ideological and political subjects. Davičo's ambitious tetralogy *Robije* (Hard Labor), consisting of *Ćutnje* (1963; Silence), *Gladi* (1963; Hunger), *Tajne* (1964; Secrets), and *Bekstva* (1966; Escapes), concerns the illegal activity of

prewar revolutionaries and their experiences in prison. It is one of his finest works.

A prolific writer, Davičo has nevertheless displayed some consistent characteristics throughout his literary career. Above all, he uses literature to expound his ideological views, although always in a highly artistic form. He has always been a modernist, bent on experimenting, sometimes to excess, with both ideas and language.

See: M. I. Bandić, "Pesnik kao romanopisac," *Vreme romana* (1958), pp. 156–94; A. Petrov, "Ličnosti i problemi Davičove proze," *Savremenik* 5 (1964): 496–510; J. Melvinger, "Tipovi metafore u poeziji Oskara Daviča," *Godišnjak Filozofskog fakulteta u Novom Sadu* 10 (1967): 263–81.

V.D.M.

De Filippo, Eduardo (1900–), Italian playwright, actor, and director, known as Eduardo, is Italy's foremost Neapolitan dialect dramatist. He began his career as an actor in Neapolitan troupes and did not turn to playwriting until the late 1920s. In 1932, together with his sister Titina and his brother Peppino, he formed the "Compagnia del Teatro Umoristico i De Filippo," which, during the next decade, performed his plays and those of leading Italian authors. In 1944 he reorganized the company without Peppino under the name of "Il Teatro di Eduardo."

Although many are written exclusively in Neapolitan, Eduardo's plays have been performed with notable success throughout Italy. Beneath their spirited fun, his early farces reveal the suffering side of humanity and anticipate the paradoxical, painful humor of his later, more ambitious works. *Sik-Sik, l'artefice magico* (1929; Sik-Sik the Prestidigitator) presents one of Eduardo's prototypical characters: a down-and-out middle-aged man who struggles to maintain his dignity and self-respect. *Natale in casa Cupiello* (1931, rewritten in 1942; Christmas at the Cupiello's) presents a recurrent situation: the misunderstood efforts of a pathetic paterfamilias to preserve tradition and family solidarity in the face of changing values and corrupting influences.

After 1945, Eduardo moved away from pure comedy and toward more serious treatments of universal concerns. At the same time, he began to rely less exclusively on the Neapolitan dialect. *Napoli milionaria!* (1945; Naples's Millionaires) marks this new phase of his career. Set in wartime Naples, this play mingles comedy with the sober reality of human suffering as, once again, Eduardo turns to familiar motifs: the disillusioned father, the breakdown of the family, and moral disorder. During this period, Eduardo also adopted philosophical themes that recall the works of Luigi PIRANDELLO. Man's need for illusion is stressed in both *Questi fantasmi* (1946; Eng. tr., *Oh, These Ghosts,* 1964) and *La grande magia* (1948; Eng. tr., *Grand Magic* in *Three Plays,* 1976). The protagonists of both plays are cuckolds who accept improbable fictions in order to mask an ugly reality. An exception to the serious plays of this period is *Filumena Marturano* (1946; Eng. tr., *The Best House in Naples* in *Three Plays,* 1976), the story of a resourceful ex-prostitute who induces her common-law husband to marry her.

Eduardo's concern for social problems is also evident in *De Pretore Vincenzo* (1957) and in *Il sindaco del Rione Sanità* (1960; Eng. tr., *The Local Authority* in *Three Plays,* 1976), in which he considers the injustice of institutions that compel men to live beyond the law. In *Mia famiglia* (1955; My Family), Eduardo again takes up the themes of moral deterioration and the importance of the family in the face of such threats as war and poverty.

Eduardo's maturity as a playwright is evident in *Il figlio di Pulcinella* (1958; The Son of Pulcinella). The play is both an evocation of the commedia dell'arte mask of

Pulcinella (with whom Eduardo has often been identified) and a rejection of Pulcinella's traditional role as the pliable servant of corrupt masters. The son's discarding of the father's mask and denunciation of his servile antics may well be viewed as Eduardo's own refusal to perpetuate a comic convention devoid of ethical intent.

Eduardo's virtuosity as interpreter of every major role he has created is legendary. He has also directed and acted in numerous films, including several based on his plays (*Napoli milionaria!*, *Questi fantasmi*, and *Filumena Marturano*).

Eduardo's plays written before 1945 are published in *Cantata dei giorni pari* (1959; Song of Even Days). The three volumes of *Cantata dei giorni dispari* (1971; Song of Uneven Days) contain his later plays. His collected verse is available as *Il paese di Pulcinella* (1951; The Land of Pulcinella).

See: E. Bentley, in *In Search of Theatre* (1953); L. Codignola, "Reading De Filippo," *TDR* (Spring 1964); S. Torresani, in *Il teatro italiano negli ultimi vent'anni (1945-65)* (1965), pp. 239-68.   M.R.C.

Dehmel, Richard (1863-1920), German poet, the most distinguished representative of the transition from extreme naturalism to classic restraint, was born the son of a forester in Wendisch-Hermsdorf. The landscape of his poetry is that of Brandenburg, a wide, open plain with huge forests of spruce and pine. In that plain rose the city of Berlin with its factories, forges, and smokestacks. The poet's own landscape has two divergent aspects: giant spruce trees battling with the elements and buzzing telegraph wires and blast furnaces belching smoke and flame. The same dualism is evident in the man: Dehmel was both a realistic naturalist and a visionary seer. On the one hand he exemplifies a daring disregard of conventional forms, while on the other hand his verse displays a painstaking mathematical exactness.

While a pupil in a Berlin gymnasium, Dehmel came into conflict with his orthodox teachers, was ousted, and finished his preparatory schooling at Danzig. At the university there he studied philosophy and literature as well as the natural sciences. He wrote his dissertation in the field of economics and accepted a secretarial position with a fire insurance company. Not until he published two volumes of poetry did he feel he had the right to resign from his position and devote himself to literature. In 1889 Dehmel married Paula Oppenheimer, with whom he collaborated on a volume of verse for children. Their marriage ended in divorce (1899) and Ida Auerbach became Dehmel's second wife. Dehmel preached—and practiced—rigorous self-discipline and was among the first to follow the gospel of Friedrich NIETZSCHE.

As a young man, Dehmel had been rejected for military service, but at the age of 51 the pacifist Dehmel forced the army to accept him for service in the trenches. When World War I ended in defeat, he urged the formation of an "iron guard" in which only volunteers would be allowed to serve. He did not live to realize this last dream of social service.

Dehmel's development in his poems is clearly visible from volume to volume, and even the titles are significant: *Erlösungen* (1891; Releases), *Aber die Liebe* (1893; But Love), *Weib und Welt* (1896; Woman and World); and *Schöne wilde Welt* (1913; Beautiful, Wild World). The first three volumes were carefully revised and radically changed in subsequent editions, and the last volume was greatly enlarged.

Dehmel enriched German poetry with a new and significant note. His lyrics show man in his threefold life as an individual, a member of society, and a bit of cosmic life. His novel in verse, *Zwei Menschen* (1903; Two People), is the work of a great lyric poet. Of his dramas his last seems the most significant. It sums up his war experiences: *Die Götterfamilie* (1921; The Family of Gods), the fantastic vision of an insane world. In 1919, a year before his death, Dehmel's *Kriegstagebuch* (War Diary) was published, with the meaningful subtitle of *Zwischen Volk und Menschheit* (Between the People and Humanity).

See: J. Bab, *Richard Dehmel* (1926); H. Slochower, *Richard Dehmel, der Mensch und der Denker* (1928); H. Fritz, *Literarischer Jugendstil und Expressionismus: zur Kunsttheorie, Dichtung und Wirkung Richard Dehmels* (1969).   F.Br., rev. A.L.W.

Delblanc, Sven (1931-), Swedish novelist and playwright, since 1965 docent in comparative literature at the University of Uppsala, was born at Swan River, Manitoba, Canada, but grew up at Vagnhärad in the province of Södermanland, Sweden. His allegorical first novel, *Eremitkräftan* (1962; The Hermit Crab), concerns a student named Axel, who lives in a society in which citizens are supervised as closely as if they were prisoners. He escapes to The White City, where freedom reigns supreme. ("We do what we ourselves want. We work when we feel like it, and rest when we want to. We are free.") Unable to accept unlimited freedom—irresponsibility and debauchery—he is compelled to return to "Jail" (society), where he can function better within the given limits. ("Only through the lack of freedom can we become humans.") Like a hermit crab that is on the lookout for a larger shell to live in, he returns to what he has had in the first instance.

Delblanc further explored the theme of freedom versus submission of the individual in *Prästkappan* (1963; The Minister's Frock) about Hermann, the vagrant curate who in Prussia in 1784 attempts to realize his ecstatic dreams of power, honor, and happiness attendant upon love. His dreams end in defeat when Frederick the Great himself imparts his total cynicism to Hermann, who reaches his Olympus (his summit, his heavenly palace) thoroughly disillusioned with the possibility of reaching freedom. *Homunculus* (1965; Eng. tr., 1969), subtitled "A Magic Tale," deals with Sebastian, an unemployed chemistry teacher, who in his Stockholm apartment finally succeeds in creating a homunculus, a little man. Around this central line of plot revolve two subplots that are entirely dependent upon each other: an effort on the part of the American Central Intelligence Agency and another on the part of the Russian intelligence staff to obtain Sebastian's formula for the homunculus, potentially a strategic weapon in the balance of terror between the superpowers. Sebastian fails in his quest when, terror-stricken by human cruelty and the lust for destruction, his homunculus is unable to remain among people, and tragedy becomes inevitable. Sebastian is scientist and artist in one person, a Paracelsus and desperado with an apocalyptic vision of nuclear holocaust. Basically, the novel deals with the right of creative persons to control their own creation and make it subservient to the good individuals in a world full of exploiters and evildoers. In a setting fit for *Dr. Strangelove* or *Catch-22*, Delblanc mixes magical elements of alchemy with learned allusions to classic and modern creators, basically individualists.

The novel *Nattresa* (1967; Night Journey) tells of Axel Weber, who with his upper-class socialist girfriend, has returned to his childhood home in an attempt to regain innocence and freedom from responsibility, but it is in vain, for he cannot escape what he knows of misery. "Our world is hell-bent, that is clear enough, but why should I, of all people, set it right again?'' Weber argues, wishing to withdraw into pessimism and passivity, tempted by the San Francisco-based Brotherhood, who rule and exploit the world. He is offered two alternatives: "To be victim or executioner. But I have already been an executioner for a long time. My weakness and hesitation have already designated a choice." In the end he realizes that, through his indecision, he is actually serving those already in power. His activist partner offers an alternative: "Come to us; we have a task for you." In revealing the causes of his problems, Weber finds a way to commitment and involvement in change. A similar view is expressed in Delblanc's novel *Åsnebrygga* (1969; Asses' Bridge), a diary novel. In the novels *Kastrater* (1975; Eng. tr., *The Castrati*, 1979), an 18th-century pastiche from Florence, *Grottmannen* (1976; The Caveman) about Sebastian Delfine, a cultural politician at the Stockholm Film Institute, and *Gunnar Emmanuel* (1978), subtitled "a timeless story," about a man who takes Delblanc's course in creative Swedish at Uppsala University, a main theme is the difficulties to be faced by art and the artist in a corrupt and commercialized society. For these and other works Delblanc has received numerous prizes and wide popular acclaim. Like most of his generation of Swedish authors, he has gradually adopted a more pronounced political stand. In his novels he is the great fabulator, viewing life from a rational and/or mystic angle. Despite excesses and despair, he remains essentially a humanist in his work. Among his plays are *Ariadne och påfågeln* (1964; Ariadne and the Peacock) and *Göm dig i livets träd* (1965; Hide Yourself in the Tree of Life). An excerpt from *Prästkappan* (The Minister's Frock) is included in *Modern Swedish Prose in Translation,* ed. by K. E. Lagerlöf (1979), pp. 181–98.

See: K. E. Lagerlöf, *Samtal med 60-talister* (1965), pp. 127–35; R. B. Vowles, "Myth in Sweden: Sven Delblanc's *Homunculus,*" *BA* 48, no. 1 (1974): 20–25; L. Sjöberg, "Delblanc's *Homunculus:* Some Magic Elements," *GR* 49, no. 1 (1974): 105–24.   L.S.

Deledda, Grazia (1871–1936), Italian novelist and short-story writer, was born in Nuoro, Sardinia, of middle-class stock. Her father served for a time as mayor of Nuoro. Deledda's early reading was wide but unsystematic, and her schooling did not go beyond the secondary level. At the age of 17, she published her first novel, significantly entitled *Sangue sardo* (1888; Sardinian Blood). In 1900 she married Palmiro Modesani, a civil servant from the region of Mantua, and they had two sons. From 1900 until her death Deledda resided in Rome. Sardinia remained, however, a constant inspiration and provided the setting for most of her novels and tales. Neither World War I nor the Fascist Revolution seems to have affected her very deeply. They left no impression on her works, which, in spite of their realistic detail, convey a certain sense of remoteness.

Deledda's production was copious; she made it a rule to write two hours every day and led a rather restricted social life. Between 1900 and 1936 she brought out annually either a novel or a collection of short stories, all characterized by a simple, vigorous style, which became increasingly sober with the passing years, and an absorbing if predictable story line. In 1926 she was awarded the Nobel Prize for literature. It is difficult to single out any one of her 33 novels as the masterpiece or indeed as the most representative. Among the best known, however, are *Il vecchio della montagna* (1900; The Old Man of the Mountain), *Elias Portolu* (1903), *Cenere* (1904; Eng. tr., *Ashes,* 1908), *L'incendio nell'oliveto* (1918; The Fire in

the Olive Grove), and *La madre* (1920; Eng. tr., *The Mother,* 1923).

Deledda's stories possess action and movement, and they are filled with colorful detail. She was to some extent a regionalist, and her interest in the lives of simple folk and their customs gave her something in common with Giovanni VERGA, who probably influenced her. She was not, however, a committed naturalist, and her figures do not attain the almost archetypal dimensions of Verga's padron 'Ntoni or a Mastro-don Gesualdo. Her interest was rather in the portrayal of the conflicts that take place in the hearts of primitive (or at least nonintellectual) men and women. She wrote with intuitive authority about their passions, obsessions, and haunting guilts. Usually, Deledda's protagonists are victims—either of their own passions, of others' lusts or ambitions, of the operations of an unjust society, or of blind fate. But whatever the source of the anguish, its resolution—when there is one—lies in spiritual rather than social adjustment: through expiation, renunciation, or illumination. Deledda's frame of reference is not secular. She is a probing analyst of sin and remorse, and has inevitably been compared to Fyodor DOSTOYEVSKY. One may also see a connection with Antonio FOGAZZARO, whom she admired. Deledda was particularly successful in her depiction of women who, if not the dominant, are often the determinant personalities in her novels. Her art is characterized by simplicity, in which quality lie both her weakness and her strength, for if her tales tend to be simple and her characters though often confused never complex, the honesty of her report and the sharp outlines of her dramatis personae create a powerful impact.

The tone of Deledda's earlier novels is deeply pessimistic. Some of the later works, however, beginning perhaps with *Il Dio dei viventi,* (1922; The God of the Living), indicate a more serene acceptance of the ways of Providence and have caused some critics to see a shift in Deledda's religious stance from the "transcendent" to the "immanent" concept of the deity. One may have some reservations about this thesis. What is certainly clear, however, is that throughout her career Deledda remained remarkably true to her own genius, resistant to passing changes of fashion and never losing either her sense of compassion or her Christian acceptance of the existence of evil. In recent years her prestige has declined somewhat. But if her world now seems archaic and her approach a little dated, the human situations she presents are still moving, and her unpretentious manner still carries conviction.

See: Y. E. Di Silvestro, *La vita e i romanzi di Grazia Deledda* (1945); G. Buzzi, *Grazia Deledda* (1952); L. Russo, in *I narratori* (1958), pp. 192–95; S. Pacifici, in *The Modern Italian Novel from Capuana to Tozzi* (1973), pp. 86–97.   T.G.B.

Delibes, Miguel (1920–), Spanish novelist, short-story writer, essayist, and journalist, was born in Valladolid, where he taught mercantile law after completing his studies in that subject. He has been much involved there with the newspaper *El Norte de Castilla* and was made a member of the Royal Spanish Academy of the Language in 1975.

Delibes began his career with two undistinguished novels, the first of which, *La sombra del ciprés es alargada* (1948; The Long Shadow of the Cypress), nevertheless won the Nadal Prize. The novelist found his authentic voice with *El camino* (1950; Eng. tr., *The Path,* 1961), a Bildungsroman that gives a small boy's account of his childhood on the eve of his unwilling departure on the road that will take him to school in the city. The power of the work (it will undoubtedly remain a minor classic) is a product of its two voices, on the one hand the boy, who sees only the present and the past, and on the other the narrator, who nostalgically shares his protagonist's emotions but knows that there are no options: the road, being time itself, must always be taken. After a fourth and less successful work, *Mi idolatrado hijo Sisí* (1953; My Adored Son, Sisí), there were two diary novels: *Diario de un cazador* (1955; Diary of a Hunter) and *Diario de un emigrante* (1958). Both have the same unconsciously humorous narrator, the simple beadle Lorenzo, whose passion for hunting is shared by the author. One of Delibes's distinctive gifts is his ability to create characters through the use of colloquial language, a talent that first calls attention to itself in the diaries and enhances all of his subsequent works.

The short-story collection *Siestas con viento sur* (1957; Afternoons with the South Wind) is made up of four stories. One of the three long ones, "La mortaja" (The Shroud), is among the finest in the Spanish language. It is an existential portrayal of the lot of man in the world, represented by a small boy who must spend the night alone with his father's naked corpse and take on the role of an adult in an uncaring world, with inner resolve as his only weapon. The theme of natural continuity, one of the constants of Delibes's work, usually manifests itself, as it does here, in the father-son relationship, considered from varying generational perspectives and tonalities ranging from the tragic to the hopeful. His humble characters live in close contact with the natural world. Their portrayal through colloquial language and popular modes of thought produces a striking sense of authenticity.

The protagonist of *La hoja roja* (1959; The Red Leaf) is an old man who, after retirement ("the waiting room of death"), finds himself abandoned by friends, family, and society. The work takes its place with Muriel Spark's *Memento Mori* among the successful fictional treatments of the difficult subject of old age. *Las ratas* (1962; Eng. tr., *Smoke on the Ground*, 1972) returns to the rural world of *El camino*. There is a chill to this story of elemental but contemporary cave dwellers who make their living by killing water rats and selling them to be eaten in the local tavern. The principal character, a small boy from whose perspective the world of the novel is seen, is compared to the child Jesus. He is the village oracle, but his remarkable knowledge is based entirely on observation of the natural world, a simple method foreign both to the villagers and to the government. *Las ratas* is a brilliant study of man's tripartite relation to nature: as animal identified with it, as society out of touch with it, and as understanding collaborator with its forces.

Delibes's 1966 novel, *Cinco horas con Mario* (Five Hours with Mario), incorrectly signaled for many critics his finally joining the ranks of the social novelists. What is new in *Cinco horas*, one of Delibes's most admired books, is its adventurous ironic technique and its mastery of the interior monologue. The novel consists of the thoughts, expressed in colloquial conversational form, of a reactionary widow sitting up with the corpse of her intellectual, liberal husband the night before his funeral. The mismatched pair represent the two Spains, whose opposition has resulted in the endless social conflicts of the country's modern history. Delibes's next novel, *Parábola del náufrago* (1969; Parable of the Shipwrecked Man), exemplifies the increasing experimentation of the recent Spanish novel. While belonging to the tradition of such anti-Utopian novels as Aldous Huxley's *Brave New World* and George Orwell's *1984*, *Parábola* is a much

more difficult work than these. It records the author's nightmare about the destruction of human will and reason. Dream logic (a form of stream of consciousness) governs the style, structure, and happenings of the work, while the literalization of metaphor that is typical of dreams permits the creation of new realities. As a result, the protagonist can literally become a sheep, and all of the author's experiences (his reading of Utopian novels, for example, or of Franz KAFKA's *Metamorphosis*) can enter the play of psychological association.

In two of Delibes's more recent novels, *El príncipe destronado* (1973; The Dethroned Prince) and *Las guerras de nuestros antepasados* (1975; The Wars of Our Ancestors), he draws back from the complexities of *Parábola* without abandoning his essential preoccupations. They are, however, works of lesser artistic stature.

Delibes has been a very productive writer—many of his travel and hunting books, personal diaries, and stories have not been mentioned here—and his career has been one of continuous growth. If he has been felt to be on the fringes of literary trends, it has been because of the uniqueness of his voice. Several of his works are likely to be among the most lasting of the post-Civil War period.

See: J. W. Díaz, *Miguel Delibes* (1971); A. Rey, *La originalidad novelística de Delibes* (1975).   H.L.B.

Derème, Tristan, pseud. of Philippe Huc (1889–1941), French poet, was born in Marmande. He traced his lineage back to the Archbishop of Toulouse Pierre de Marca (1595–1662). A brilliant and precocious student, Derème founded the periodical *L'Oliphant* in Agen in 1905. Later, while employed as a tax assessor, he wrote prolifically under his own name and various pseudonyms. He finally selected that of Derème, yet he also retained the name Decalandre as an alter ego.

Derème is reputed to have known by heart more French poetry than anyone else, and it amused him to write verse in the form of prose or to insert verses by others into his texts. With a computerlike mind—and by close study—he associated poetic practices and their variations across the centuries. He promulgated "counterassonance," that is, retention in rhyme of the same consonants but variation of the vowel. Derème was also a fine Latinist, but he wore his erudition lightly, preferring to treat serious subjects with humor. He entitled an early volume of verse *Les Ironies sentimentales* (1909; Sentimental Ironies), and he called many of his works merely "petits poèmes." His best-known collection of verse is *La Verdure dorée* (1922; The Gilded Verdure), but he continued to write poetry, especially elegies, throughout his career. Spokesman for the "poètes fantaisistes" (*see* FRENCH LITERATURE) before World War I, he was deeply interested in versification and allied subjects. He was also fascinated by the "poetic in the quotidian." These matters are treated somewhat haphazardly in his "arc-en-ciel" (a series of bestiaries in prose): *Le Violon des muses* (1935; The Violin of the Muses), *Le Poisson rouge* (1934; The Red Fish), *L'Escargot bleu* (1936; The Blue Snail), *L'Onagre orange* (1939; The Orange-Colored Onager), and the posthumous *Libellule violette* (1942; Violet Dragonfly). These were all composed at the same time that he was serving as head of the politician Achille Fould's personal secretariat. A witty lecturer, he collaborated with Mme Dussane of the Comédie-Française on debates and impromptus, and—a master craftsman—he "manufactured" articles on any assigned subject. He also wrote a newspaper column on events of interest to him. Derème died of heart failure in his native Béarn.

See: H. Martineau, *Tristan Derème* (1927); S. S. Weiner, "Around Derème," in *PCP* 4 (April 1969): 65–69.

S.W.

De Roberto, Federico (1861–1927), Italian novelist and
critic, was born in Naples. He lived nearly all his life in
Catania and set most of his fiction in Sicily. De Roberto
was a prolific writer, with over 30 volumes of published
works, but his fame rests on two or three novels, including his masterpiece, *I Vicerè* (1894; Eng. tr., *The Viceroys*, 1962), a few short stories, and a one-act play, *Il
rosario* (1912; The Rosary). De Roberto divided his energies between creative and critical pursuits. His first two
publications were a collection of liberary studies, *Ara-
beschi* (1883; Arabesques), and a collection of regionalist
tales, *La sorte* (1884; Fate). During the 1890s there followed short stories, novels, and criticism. From 1900 until
his death, he was a recluse, during which period he turned
increasingly from fiction to critical writing.

With Giovanni VERGA and Luigi Capuana (1839–1915),
De Roberto forms the triad whose writings constitute the
best achievements of Italian literary naturalism. His approach to naturalism, or *verismo* (*see* ITALIAN LITERA-
TURE), was markedly modified by the influence of Paul
BOURGET, contemporary psychological and philosophical
literary currents, and the French realist tradition from
Stendhal to Gustave Flaubert. In his works, De Roberto
attacks traditional romantic conceptions of love, offering
instead purely physiological and environmental explanations for its effects. This view informs the novels *Ermanno Raeli* (1889), *L'illusione* (1891; The Illusion),
whose heroine is an aristocratic, Italian Emma Bovary,
Spasimo (1897; Spasm), and the short-story collections
Documenti umani (1888; Human Documents) and
L'albero della scienza (1890; The Tree of Knowledge), as
well as nearly all his other behavioral studies. De Roberto's vision of life is fatalistic: characters are destined to
unhappy, disillusioned lives by the very nature of the
human condition; man is viciously self-seeking; and there
is no ameliorating progress in the movement of history.
This view is most forcefully presented in the lengthy
historical novel *I Vicerè*. Against the background of the
Risorgimento and the first two decades of Italian nation-
hood, De Roberto traces the vicissitudes of the Uzeda
family, pointing up the consuming greed of human nature,
the manipulative will to power of the few, and the gross
servility of the many. The Risorgimento is seen as having
had no positive effect on the socioeconomic structure of
the Italian south. The Uzedas, descended from the Spanish viceroys of Sicily, retain powers and privileges as the
new masters in a "democratic" state, for the novel ends
with the election to parliament, by popular vote, of the
reactionary Prince Consalvo. In an unfinished sequel,
L'imperio (1929; The Empire), De Roberto traces the
prince-deputy's fortunes in Rome, focusing on the corruption of contemporary political life. De Roberto has
influenced several 20th-century southern Italian writers,
including Luigi PIRANDELLO.

See: G. Mariani, *Federico De Roberto narratore* (1950);
V. Spinazzola, *Federico De Roberto e il verismo* (1961).

J.C.

Derrida, Jacques (1930–), French philosopher and essayist, was born in El Biar, Algeria. He teaches at the Ecole
Normale Supérieure. Two essays on Husserl, *Introduction à l'origine de la géometrie* (1962; Eng. tr., *Edmund
Husserl's "Origin of Geometry": An Introduction,* 1978)
and *La Voix et le phénomène* (1967; The Voice and the
Phenomenon), contain the kernel of what is developed in
better-known works, but *L'Ecriture et la différence* (1967;

Eng. tr., *Writing and Difference*, 1978) and *De la grammatologie* (1967; Eng. tr., *On Grammatology*, 1976) had
immediate, wider repercussion. These volumes reveal a
mind conversant with the full range of Western philosophy and a broad spectrum of literature. The first part of
De la grammatologie (*grammatologie* is the science of
écriture, that is, "scription") harbors some of its most
seminal pages.

Derrida is concerned with breaking out of the ethno-
centrism of Western thought, with stripping the logos of
the superior attributes with which it had been endowed
from Aristotle to Ferdinand de Saussure (1857–1913). He
sees his role as that of a "deconstructor"; along with but
independently from Jacques LACAN he has made it possible to recognize in texts a complex, nonindividual subject rather than a unitary one. He has helped in undermining the Saussurian concept of sign, and he has paved
the way for the study of texts in their materiality and their
ability to produce rather than convey meaning. *La
Dissémination* (1972) brought together three major essays
on texts by Plato, Stéphane MALLARMÉ, and Philippe
Sollers. In *Marges de la philosophie* (1972; Margins of
Philosophy), Derrida pursued his deconstructive work in
essays dealing with linguistic and literary as well as philosophical problems. This has been followed by *Glas*
(1974; Knell), in which he involves himself with an unlikely pair: G. W. F. Hegel and Jean GENET. *Eperons*
(1976; Spurs), a quadrilingual text, finds its point of departure in Friedrich NIETZSCHE. An introduction to Derrida's thought and a clarification of some of his essays
may be found in a series of interviews in *Positions* (1972).
One of these appeared in translation in *Diacritics* 2, no.
4 (1972) and 3, no. 1 (1973). Several recent essays have
been collected in *La Vérité en peinture* (1978; The Truth
in Painting).

See: special issues of *L'Arc* 54 (1973) and *Sub-stance*
7 (1973).

L.S.R.

Déry, Tibor (1894–1977), Hungarian novelist and playwright, was born in Budapest to an upper-middle-class
family. He had a lonely childhood, in part due to an illness
for which he took long cures abroad. As a young man, he
organized a strike while employed at his uncle's firm. He
joined the Communist Party in 1919 and emigrated to
Czechoslovakia in 1920. Déry spent the next 15 years
traveling and living in Vienna, Paris, Perugia, Berlin, Prague, Dubrovnik, and Majorca. Having returned to Hungary in 1936, Dery spent two months in jail (1938) for
translating André Gide's *Retour de l'U.R.S.S.* In 1944,
Déry, who was a Jew, narrowly escaped the Nazi terror.
He joined the newly formed Communist Party in 1945 and
was awarded the Kossuth Prize for his literary work in
1948. Sentenced to nine years imprisonment for his role
in the Hungarian uprising of 1956, he was granted amnesty
in 1960.

In the 1920s, Déry wrote dadaist and expressionist poetry and surrealist prose for the Berlin *Sturm* and other
periodicals. Of the early works, *Országúton* (1930; On the
Road), a novel that purports to demonstrate the bankruptcy of anarchistic flight from society, is the most significant. The road was to become a recurring symbol of
escape in Déry's prose. From 1933 onwards, unable to
publish his original works, he was a detached figure,
somewhat out of tune with his time. Intent upon combining pure art with his own social dictates, he was both an
outsider among Communist workers and an aristocratic
exile in the intimate café society of Budapest. The attempt
to break out of one's own class is in fact the main theme
of the trilogy *A Befejezetlen mondat* (1947; The Unfinished Sentence), which Déry wrote in the years 1933–37.

This novel provides a social and psychological cross section of Hungarian society. Déry was the first writer in Hungary to utilize consciously the modern European writing techniques of such writers as Franz KAFKA, Thoman MANN, and Marcel PROUST. With regard to *A Befejezetlen mondat*, György LUKÁCS, Déry's close friend, called him "the only prose writer in Hungary" between the two world wars.

A long overdue recognition of Déry's work came in 1945. *Alvilági játékok* (1946; Eng. tr., "Games of the Underworld" in *The Portuguese Princess and Other Stories*, 1967) is an autobiographical cycle of short stories. This dramatic tale of the author's survival during the Nazi period and the siege of Budapest heralds a new era. The two-volume *Felelet* (1950–52; The Answer) got its author into trouble again for allegedly underestimating the Communist Party's influence on the working class in the 1930s. Déry then published some new stories, among them *Szerelem* (1955; Love), and a short novel *Niki* (1956; Eng. tr., *Niki: The Story of a Dog*, 1958). These moving, powerful statements about oppression and the abuse of power gained their author worldwide fame. In his later writings, Déry, Hungary's most experimental prose writer, turned away from realism in favor of irony and the parable. By so doing he returned to his early interest in mankind and history in general. The Kafkaesque, anti-Utopian novel *G. A. Úr X-ben* (1964; Mr. G. A. in X), which Déry started in prison, argues the incompatibility of freedom and order. *Kiközösítő* (1966; The Excommunicator) is a pseudohistorical work that parodies the forged trials of the 1950s. Déry's memoirs, entitled *Itélet nincs* (1969; No Verdict) explain and justify his career and political attitudes. History's extremes fill him with pessimism. *Képzelt riport egy amerikai popfesztiválról* (1971; Imaginary Report about an American Pop Festival) denounces the false Utopias of the young. In this book, as in his diary, *A napok hordaléka* (1972; The Debris of My Days), Déry contends that civilization has brought more discontent than gain and extols personal work as the sole redeeming activity left to man. He writes of the erotic fantasies and limitations of old age in the charming *Kedves bópeer . . . !* (1973; Dear Beau-Père). The aged writer's sexual fantasies also figure prominently in *A félfülü* (1975; The Man with One Ear), which is based on the Getty kidnapping in Italy.

See: Gy. Illyés, "Déry Tibor regénye," *Nyugat* 31 (1938): 139–40; G. Lukács, Introduction to T. Déry, *A ló meg az öregasszony* (1955): pp. 5–8; I. Mészáros, "Déry Tibor munkássága," Introduction to T. Déry, *Vidám temetés* (1960), pp. 167–177. F. Fehér, "There Is a Verdict," *NHQ* 10 (1969): 126–36; T. Ungvári, *Déry Tibor* (1973); B. Pomogáts, *Déry Tibor* (1974); I. Sanders, "Tibor Déry at Eighty," *BA* 49 (1975): 12–18.   P.V.

Descaves, Lucien (1861–1949), French novelist and journalist, was born in Montrouge, a working-class quarter of Paris. The atmosphere of Montrouge shaped his career and outlook; its humble inhabitants provided the raw material for his novels and plays, and its spirit of protest against social injustice informed his every public act. Although he never attained greatness, Descaves won prominence early. He was elected to the Académie Goncourt at its inception in 1900 and served for many years first as its secretary and then as its president, positions that always kept him in the public eye. Yet he never settled into a comfortable official role, remaining instead the outspoken rebel, known for more than 40 years as the enfant terrible of the Académie.

A spirit of protest and sympathy for the outsider are indeed the animating perspectives of Descaves's writing,

but careful craftsmanship, scrupulous observation, accuracy of detail, and a clear and unpretentious style were the qualities that impressed his contemporaries. His first three novels, written between 1882 and 1885, when he was in his early twenties, scarcely attracted any notice, however, because they were so patently imitative of the naturalist manner of Joris-Karl HUYSMANS, Edmond de Goncourt (1822–96), and Emile ZOLA, whom he admired. Descaves's uninspired tales of laundresses, shop girls, and artisans nevertheless laid the groundwork for his career.

In 1887, Descaves publicly proclaimed his artistic independence of naturalism by signing, with four young fellow-writers, a manifesto protesting the excesses of Zola's latest novel, *La Terre* (1887; Eng. tr., *The Soil*, 1888). The manifesto caused a sensation and became the occasion of Descaves's first public notoriety. An even more ringing act of protest quickly followed the manifesto and made Descaves one of the most controversial authors of the day: in 1889 he published a novel about the morally damaging effects on sensitive young men of compulsory military service in the peacetime army. This well-written, powerful novel, entitled *Sous-offs* (The Noncoms), caused Descaves and his publisher to be brought to public trial for offense against the army and against public morality. Although he was acquitted, Descaves found himself viewed with suspicion in the literary world for the next several years, thus reinforcing his strong sense of always being an outsider. By 1892, however, he was able to obtain a journalistic position and resume his career, acting as regular book and drama critic while continuing to write novels and plays. His work depicted sympathetically, yet with minute accuracy, the troubled lives of the simple folk in his Paris neighborhood. His novel *Les Emmurés* (1894; The Walled-in Prisoners) is still regarded as one of the most sensitive attempts ever made to articulate the experience of being blind.

In 1901, Descaves tried his hand at historical fiction, producing in *La Colonne* a portrait of the impact of the Commune of 1871 on working-class lives. This effort was so successful that he later produced several other novels on the theme of the Commune, evoking different character types each time. It was Descaves himself who pointed out that his basic literary talent, perhaps inherited from his father, who had been an engraver, was that of an *imagier*, a creator of portraits in print. His notable biographical studies of the poet Marceline Desbordes-Valmore (1786–1859) and of the novelist Huysmans offer additional evidence that portraiture was indeed his forte.

Descaves is not much read anymore, for his talent, however genuine, was a small one. Yet he was not an insignificant part of the literary history of his time, and his works of fiction, his biographies, and his own memoirs, *Souvenirs d'un ours* (1946; Memoirs of a Boor), have left us a valuable portrait of that era.   M.S.

Desjardins, Paul (1859–1940), French educator and critic, was born in Paris, the son of an eminent professor. He himself was a brilliant student at the Ecole Normale Supérieure, obtaining a teaching post and beginning his career as writer and lecturer at the age of 22. For 25 years he taught in various lycées and at the Ecole Normale de Sèvres. His published articles were well received, notably the *Esquisses et impressions* (1888; Sketches and Impressions), a volume that brought together about 30 pieces that had first appeared in *La Revue bleue*, and *La Méthode des classiques* (1904; The Method of the Classics), studies on Pierre Corneille, Nicolas Poussin, and Blaise Pascal.

Desjardins's teaching and writing, however, are less

important aspects of his life than his work as organizer for the advancement of culture and civilization. By 1891 he had already decided to found a society to promote truth and justice over individual interests. Named the "Union pour l'Action Morale," it soon launched a full program of activities; in 1905 the society became the "Union pour la Vérité." A year later, the purchase of an old abbey at Pontigny made it possible for Desjardins to expand his project into one of the greatest intellectual institutions of the 20th century—the "Décades de Pontigny." Every summer from 1910 to 1939, except for the years of World War I, prominent intellectuals of France and elsewhere met there to discuss a given topic. Here men like André GIDE, Paul VALÉRY, André MALRAUX, and Antoine de SAINT-EXUPÉRY exchanged views while others, like Marcel PROUST, eagerly awaited news of what had been said. Today the colloquies of Cerisy carry on the tradition established by this dedicated man.

See: *In memoriam Paul Desjardins* (1949); A. Heurgon-Desjardins, *Paul Desjardins et les Décades de Pontigny* (1964).   L.LeS.

Desnos, Robert (1900–45), French poet, was born in Paris, close to the Halles market where his father was a broker for poultry and game. He was 14 when World War I began, and he soon emancipated himself from school and family, embarking on a succession of jobs. In 1916 he began writing down his dreams. Shortly thereafter, he met former members of the criminal "Bande à Bonnot," an anarchist group that may be the origin of the legendary character Fantômas who appears in his (and others') work. Desnos's long poems, "Le Fard des Argonautes" (The Makeup of the Argonauts) and "L'Ode à Coco" (Ode to Coco), written in 1919, mix echoes of Charles BAUDELAIRE, Arthur RIMBAUD, and Guillaume APÓLLINAIRE with self-mockery, treating the themes of the voyage and of an intoxication due not to drugs but to dreams.

During his military service in 1919, Desnos met André BRETON and soon contributed to the new journal *Littérature*, in which he (literally) published his dreams in 1922. An early star of surrealism (*see* FRENCH LITERATURE), a literary movement that made a point of hypnosis, Desnos was the poet who most brilliantly practiced automatic writing. Breton wrote in *Nadja* (1928; Eng. tr., 1960) of his "astonishing poetic equations," such as the punning aphorisms of *Rrose Sélavy* (1922), for whose title Desnos had appropriated the name (from "arrose, c'est la vie"—"pour on, it's life") with which Marcel Duchamp, then in the United States, was signing his creations and statements. Desnos's other poetic games, *Langage cuit* (Cooked Language) and *L'Aumonyme*—an ambiguous title that contains the word *aumône* (alms) while it suggests the word "anonymous"—appeared in 1923, and are astonishing in their combination of satire, mockery, and poignancy. Some consist of letters to be read aloud, others of notes of music. In his lyrical and powerful poetry, Desnos embraced Breton's aesthetic of the marvelous (Breton had written in the first *Surrealist Manifesto* [1924], "The marvelous is always beautiful"). The short, vehement poems of *C'est les bottes de sept lieues cette phrase "Je me vois"* (1926; It's the Seven League Boots, the Sentence "I See Myself") are written in a somber and quasi-prophetic language. His two works of churning, often obscene yet lyrical prose, *Deuil pour deuil* (1924; Mourning for Mourning's Sake) and *La Liberté ou l'amour!* (1927; Liberty or Love!)—which one is tempted to translate as the ultimatum "Give me liberty or give me love!"—contain cantos reminiscent of LAUTRÉAMONT. The Seine Department's tribunal correc-

tionnel saw fit to have the latter work condemned and mutilated.

In the poems of *A la mystérieuse* (1926; To the Mysterious One), Desnos's love is expressed with a quasi-religious faith. Like Gérard de Nerval (1808–55), whom Desnos admired, he seems to seek a love that he wishes would remain inaccessible. His *Les Sans Cou* (1934; The Neckless Ones), whose title is homophonous with the words "les cent coups" of the expressions "etre aux cent coups" (to be worried) and "faire les quatre cent coups" (to paint the town red), concern decapitated figures that remain intensely human. Desnos's exaltation stems from a spiritualizing of the senses, from a conviction that sensuality seeks to grasp that which is immaterial.

In his poems, death, solitude, and abandonment are accompanied by a conviction that he is living outside the limits of time. The themes of sight, night, darkness, blindness, and absence combine in his poetry with the affirmation of an assertive, often joyous love for a woman or for his fellow men. One group of his poems is entitled "Les Ténèbres" (Darkness), and indeed the theme of the fecundity of night is a particularly frequent one in his writings.

For several years, Desnos wrote for newspapers and created successful ditties for publicity on the wireless, work that Breton condemned in the *Second Manifeste du surréalisme* (1930) as an "activité journalistique" (journalistic activity), in which Desnos "thought he could engage with impunity." Desnos left the surrealist group, while remaining a surrealist in most of his subsequent writings and while sharing Breton's conviction that poetry is the "true working of the mind." There is great variety in Desnos's output, in content as well as form. His work exhibits ebullient lyricism, wit, despair, fraternity, love, patriotism, and, at times, a deliberate commonness; his techniques vary from traditional rhyme and regular verse to elliptical, compact, and free forms or to short and melodious songlike texts written for children.

On February 22, 1944, Desnos, who had been active in the underground group "Agir" (to act), was arrested by the Gestapo and deported to a succession of concentration camps, in the last of which, Terezin (Theresienstadt), he died of typhus after the liberation of the camp by Russian forces and Czech Partisans. He had written much during his captivity, but nothing of this remains. Those of his companions who survived remembered his joyousness and the hope and encouragement he gave to other prisoners.

Desnos's earlier poetry was collected in *Corps et biens* (1930, new ed., 1968; With All Hands). The volume *Fortunes* (1942) contains "Siramour," a long *chantefable* of alternating prose and verse sections whose title combines the words "siren" and "love," as well as other poems from the 1930s. Desnos's posthumous publications include *Domaine public* (1953; Public Knowledge), which includes *Corps et biens, Fortunes*, and a 75-page selection of previously unpublished texts; *Chantefables et chantefleurs* (1955), diaphanous poems written for his friends' children; *La Liberté ou l'amour!* and *Deuil pour deuil*, published in one volume (1975); *Calixto suivi de contrée* (1962; Calixto Followed by Country), a volume of tragic poems, mostly in classical form; and *Cinéma* (1966), a volume of scenarios, synopses of texts for films, and 105 pages of Desnos's inspired articles and reviews on film. The volume *Destinée arbitraire* (1975) includes unpublished as well as inaccessible published texts. Desnos also wrote one novel, *Le Vin est tiré . . .* (1943; The Wine Is Ready), and the long essay *De l'érotisme considéré dans ses manifestations écrites et du point de vue de l'esprit moderne* (1953; Concerning Eroticism Considered in Its Written Manifestations and from the Point of View of the Modern Mind). One of his poems inspired Man Ray's short film *L'Etoile de mer* (1928; The Starfish), in which Desnos appears briefly. Desnos is one of the major French poets of the 20th century and certainly one of the most brilliant ones of the epic period of surrealism.

See: P. Berger, *Robert Desnos* (1949); R. Buchole, *L'Evolution poétique de Robert Desnos* (1956); M. A. Caws, *The Poetry of Dada and Surrealism: Aragon, Breton, Tzara, Eluard and Desnos* (1970); special issue of *Europe*, nos. 517–18 (May–June 1972).   T.W.G.

Desnoues, Lucienne (1921–), Belgian poet, was born in Saint-Gratien, France. She learned at an early age, as the daughter and granddaughter of artisans, the worth of objects. Her poetry does not attempt to magnify objects, but rather tends to accord them a greater viability, a second truth accessible only to those who love them. An epicureanism colored with melancholy permeates her collections: *Jardin délivré* (1947; Liberated Garden), *La Fraîche* (1958; Freshly Gathered), *Les Ors* (1966; The Golds), and *La Plume d'oie* (1971; A Quill Pen). The simplicity of vocabulary, combined with purity and precision, confers an accent of sincerity rarely attained in poetry on Desnoues's work; despite her faithfulness to classical rules, her expressiveness maintains an extreme naturalness; and the gravity of her subject matter, often veiled with irony, in no way lessens the lightness of the rhythm.

See: R. Burniaux and R. Frickx, *La Littérature belge d'expression française* (1973).   R.F.

Destrée, Jules (1863–1936), Belgian writer and essayist, was born in Marcinelle, in the province of Hainaut, a region that constituted a constant source of pride and inspiration. A dedicated Socialist and a fervent supporter of workers' rights, he also defended the rights of the Walloons within the Belgian nation. During his days as a law student at the University of Brussels, Destrée was active in literary and artistic circles. He was the Brussels correspondent for *Le Journal de Charleroi* and *La Flandre libérale*, a member of the literary group "Chapitre," and a peer of Camille LEMONNIER and Emile VERHAEREN. At first influenced by the aestheticism of the group around the review *La Jeune Belgique*, he gradually became disillusioned with purely literary aims. His return to Marcinelle and the realities of *Le Pays Noir*, coupled with the need to impose his political and moral beliefs through his writing, led him to use a rather flamboyant style. In works such as *Bon-Dieu-des-Gaulx, étude d'âmes et paysages au Pays-Noir* (1898; Bon-Dieu-des-Gaulx, a Study of Souls and Landscapes in the Black Land) and *Quelques Histoires de miséricorde* (1902; Several Stories of Mercy), Destrée's descriptions of human misery constitute the means of conveying an understanding of misfortune, a spirit of clemency, and a disinterested dedication to the exoneration of the falsely accused. His studies of Italian art led him to a reevaluation of Walloon art. His two most important works of art criticism, on Roger van der Weyden (1926) and on the Master of Flemalle (1930), emphasize the Walloon heritage of these two artists. His views on the situation of the two Belgian peoples appeared more explicitly in *Le Principe des nationalités et la Belgique* (1916; Eng. tr., *The Principle of the Nationalities and Belgium*, 1916). His dedication to the cause of the Walloons was superseded during World War I by his national commitment to the defense of Belgium. Sent at the outbreak of hostilities to Italy along with Maurice MAETERLINCK and the artist Pierre Paulus, Destrée lobbied valiantly as an orator and writer to persuade the Italians to intervene. He also encouraged British participation in the Belgian defense. He wrote a marionette play to help raise funds for Belgian soldiers' uniforms: *Dramatique mariage de la Princesse Belgia et du Chevalier Honneur* (1916; Eng. tr., *Dramatic Marriage of Princess Belgia and Prince Honour*, 1916). Sent to Petrograd after the Russian Revolution (1917), he produced one of his most moving works, *Les Fondeurs de Neige: Notes sur la Revolution bolchevique* (1920; The Melters of Snow: Notes on the Bolshevik Revolution). Further suffrage reform in Belgium led to a Socialist majority in the Parliament and to Destrée's appointment as minister of sciences and arts. In his new capacity, he continued to press for the interests of the working class. He made modifications in the school curriculum, legislated for artists' pensions, and, in 1921, played a major role in the creation of the Belgian Academy of French Language and Literature. His last years were marked by his writings in favor of a united federation of European nations and by several volumes on art history.

See: P.-J. Schaeffer, *Jules Destrée* (1962), J.-P. Paulus, *Edmond Picard et Jules Destrée* (1971).   A.Rus.

Deyssel, Lodewijk van, pseud. of Karel Joan Lodewijk Alberdingk Thijm (1864–1952), Dutch novelist, critic, and journalist, was born in Amsterdam. He began his literary career by writing critical articles for newspapers and magazines, combining a polemical style with his critical ability. After 1887, his criticism appeared mainly in *De Nieuwe Gids* (The New Guide), where he expressed his admiration for Emile ZOLA and the Goncourts. His attraction to naturalism led him to write his novels *Een liefde* (1887; A Love) and *De kleine republiek* (1889; The Little Republic), in which he combined two of the artistic objectives of the "Movement of the Eighties" (*see* DUTCH LITERATURE), realistic observation and impressionism. The heroine experiences very subjective perceptions, and these form the "sensitivistic" element in the work. From 1882 to 1844, he became interested in what he called "heroic individualism," which manifested itself in dandyism. The literary result was "Het Ik, heroisch-individualistische dagboekbladen" (1890–91; The Ego: Heroically Individualistic Pages of a Diary), an unpublished verse drama, *Napoleon* (1895), and *Caesar* (1898). His disillusionment with Zola had, in the meantime, appeared in *De dood van het naturalisme* (The Death of Naturalism), which was published in *De Nieuwe Gids* in 1891. Then he drew a line from Zola to Maurice MAETERLINCK and Ruusbroec, the medieval mystic, "from observation to impression, sensation, and ecstasy," which he described in *Van Zola tot Maeterlinck* (1895; From Zola to Maeterlinck). His new art emerged as "prose poems," such as, *In de zwemschool* (In the Swimming School), *Menschen en bergen* (1891; People and Mountains), and *Jeugd* (1892; Youth). In these, the writer reproduced the "sensation" that arose through exact "observation" of things. In *Apocalyps* (1893), the "sensation" becomes "ecstasy," and a high point is reached. When, in the same period, he wrote biographical studies of *Multatuli* (1891) and his father, the writer and professor *J. A. Alberdingk Thijm* (1893), his self-controlled, reflective style, enlivened by humor, was quite different from his impressionism. In 1894, he set up the *Tweemaandelijks Tijdschrift* (Bimonthly Magazine) with Albert VERWEY. He later became editor of *De Twintigste Eeuw* (The Twentieth Century), and from 1909 on, he was editor of *De Nieuwe Gids*. Ecstasy and experiences of beauty, happiness, and eternity appear in *Uit het leven van Frank Rozelaar* (1911; From the Life of Frank Rozelaar). He described the many emotions and influences in his life, and revealed himself, the essential van Deyssel, in *Gedenkschriften* (1924; Memoirs).

All his critical and reflective work, including the excellent essays on *Rembrandt* (1906), has been collected in the eleven volumes of *Verzamelde opstellen* (1922-23; Collected Essays). Van Deyssel may be seen as the most important critic in Dutch literature since the "Movement of the Eighties."

See: H. G. M. Prick, *Lodewijk van Deyssel: dertien close-ups* (1964); F. Jansonius, *Lodewijk van Deyssel* ([1954]).   S.L.F.

D'haen, Christine (fully Beelaert-D'haen) (1923-), Belgian (Flemish) poet, was born in Sint-Amands-berg Gent, studied Germanic languages at the University of Ghent and became a teacher at the Bruges state teacher training college. From 1946 on she published poetry in literary reviews, mainly in *Dietse Warande en Belfort* and *Nieuw Vlaams Tijdschrift*, and by her neoclassicism soon became a controversial figure in the critical debates of the period. She was fiercely attacked by the modernist avant garde (notably by Hugo CLAUS), yet consistently defended by the more traditionalist writers and poets of the older generation, such as Raymond Herreman. In 1951 after the publication of her first work, *Gedichten* (Poems), she was awarded the "Arkprijs" (Free Speech Prize) offered by *Nieuw Vlaams Tijdschrift*. A later volume, *Gedichten 1946-1958* (1958; Poems 1946-1958) comprises part of the first collection, yet added later poems. Christine D'haen draws her images and even analogies from mythology, Christianity, and from the history of Middle Ages and Renaissance; she revels in rhetorical figures, uses traditional forms (sonnet, strophical form) and sometimes writes in English. She mainly expresses her love of the rich texture of language and her sensuous sense of (past) life. In 1961 *Gedichten 1946-1958* was awarded the Van der Hoogt Prize.

In the heavily annotated *Vanwaar zal ik u toezingen?* (1966; How Will I Praise Thee?; the title is a Vondel quotation) formal intricacy and mannerism reach a peak yet never combine with either irony or parody. The poems of *Ick sluit van daegh een ring* (1975; Closing A Cycle Today; again the title is a Vondel quotation) are more condensed and hermetic, yet show a marked increase of feeling.

Christine D'haen produced an excellent translation into English of Gezelle's poems (1971).

See P. de Wispelaere, "De poëzie van Christine D'haen", in *Nieuw Vlaams Tijdschrift*, vol. 12 (1958), pp. 969-74; A. Westerlinck, "Nieuwe poëzie van Christine D'haen", in *Dietse Warande en Belfort*, vol. 111 (1966), pp. 370-75.   D. van B.

Dhôtel, André (1900-), French novelist and essayist, was born in Attigny. He was educated in Autun and Paris. A philosophy teacher by profession, he first taught in Athens, then in private schools in France until 1961. Since 1943 his considerable output has amounted to more than 30 novels, among them *L'Homme de la scierie* (1950; The Saw-Mill Man), *Le Pays où l'on n'arrive jamais* (1955; Far Away), *La Chronique fabuleuse* (1955; The Fabulous Chronicle), and *L'Honorable Monsieur Jacques* (1972). The magical realism characteristic of his vision and style is akin to that of Charles Nodier and ALAIN-FOURNIER. The natural settings in which his heroes find themselves resemble his native Ardennes and are perceived as through the wondering eyes of a child, yet described with

great accuracy. His young heroes, optimists all, are untroubled by doubts, social concerns, abstract thoughts, or ingrained habits. Their keen awareness is not introspective, so that they achieve a nearly total identification with the objects or creatures around them.

Dhôtel's plots usually concern quests stemming from remembered or awaited love and involve kidnappings, chance encounters, disappearances, and discoveries. Yet these events tend to be subordinated to the depiction of rural life and to a psychology of anticipation. An unknown order beyond logical causality underlies the manifestations of reality; in the rare moments when time is transcended, his characters are illuminated by grace.

See: B. Jourdan, "Dhôtel et la foi du charbonnier," *Crit* 144 (May 1959): 413-26; K. Obrist, *L'Absence de continuité logique dans l'œuvre d'André Dhôtel* (1974).
                                                    J.-P.Ca

Dias, João Pedro Grabato, pseud. of António Quadros (1933-), Portuguese poet and painter, was born near Viseu. He studied fine arts in Oporto and has been living in Mozambique since 1968, identifying himself with the cultural life of that African country. While there, he founded with others the highly selective literary review *Caliban* (1971-72). As a poet, Dias stands as one of the most brilliant personalities in contemporary Portuguese letters, a position he has held ever since the publication of his first book, *40 e tal sonetos de amor e circunstância e uma canção desesperada* (1970; Some 40 Occasional Love Sonnets and 1 Despairing Song). This was followed a year later by *Uma meditação* (A Meditation) and two long "didactic odes" in free verse, *O morto* (The Dead Man) and *A arca* (The Ark). In 1972, Dias published the *Quybyrycas*, a gigantic spoof (in the classical ottava rima of Renaissance epics), on both the disaster of Kasr el Kebir, Morocco, in which King Sebastian lost his life in 1578, and on the Portuguese in Africa in general. *A pressaga* (1974; The Foreboding One) is an immense collage of original verse and quotations mainly from Mozambican writers, which celebrates the independence of Mozambique that was to come. Dias has a tremendous breath to sustain long poems, a fascinating and imaginative power over words, and an impressive command both of meditation and invective. Above the plainly surrealistic torrent of words, of his violent diction or down-to-earth humor, he usually achieves a superior poetical transfiguration, which fuses all the trends that have appeared in modern poetry during the last decades, and this in a most personal manner.

See: M. de Lourdes Cortez, Introduction to J. Grabato Dias, *Uma meditação . . .* (1971), and "Grabato Dias e as transgressões de linguagem," in her *Craveirinha, Grabato Dias, Rui Knopfli* (1973).   J. de S.

Dicenta, Joaquín (1863-1917), Spanish dramatist, was born in Calatayud, in the province of Zaragoza. His education in a religious school near Madrid produced a rebel against religion and the established social order. Although he began his literary career as a poet and journalist and later published short stories and novels that are now forgotten, he is commonly thought of as the dramatist of the proletariat because of one play, *Juan José* (1895; Eng. tr., 1919), which created a public sensation. He began his career as a playwright with the romantic verse drama *El suicidio de Werther* (1888), and even his later social plays in prose betray the heavy influence of the postromantic school of José ECHEGARAY. Dicenta also inherited many of his themes from the theater of the Spanish Golden Age. *Juan José*, one of the most popular plays of its time, was translated into seven languages. It is considered an important and innovative work because it put working-class characters on stage in serious roles for the first time in Spain and granted them the same dignity as was previously reserved for the upper classes. Juan José is an honest mason who lives with the reformed prostitute Rosa. He is driven to robbery in order to compete with his boss, Paco, who is using his money and position to seduce Rosa. While in jail, Juan José learns that Rosa is living with Paco. He escapes and kills them both. Clearly, in this work the classical Spanish honor play and the postromantic melodrama of jealousy have been overlaid with the more modern problem of class conflict and social injustice. Nevertheless, the play was novel, and it has a certain brute strength. So also does *El señor feudal* (1897; The Feudal Lord), which places the class problem in rural Andalusia, the most common setting of later Spanish plays that treat the class theme. Its basic dramatic situation is also very similar to that of Lope de Vega's 17th-century tragicomedy *Fuenteovejuna*. The themes in both works are honor, jealousy, and vengeance, and in both the people right a social wrong through direct action.

Dicenta's *Daniel* (1906) is a violent play about sindicalist activities in a mine, while his *El lobo* (1914; The Wolf) portrays a hardened criminal transformed by love into a hero. In all of these plays, Dicenta remains fundamentally romantic in spirit. His protest against social abuses, although timely, is mainly sentimental.

See: F. García Pavón, *El teatro social en España* (1962), pp. 31–62.   N.B.A. rev. H.L.B.

Diego, Gerardo (1896–), Spanish poet, was born in Santander. He studied with the Jesuits in Bilbao and at the universities of Salamanca and Madrid, graduating in Romance philology in 1916. In 1920 he was awarded a teaching post in literature at the secondary level. He taught at the *institutos* in Soria, Gijón, Santander, and Madrid. Prior to the Spanish Civil War, he traveled and lectured extensively in Europe, Asia, and South America. Some of his lectures were lecture-recitals on Spanish music, as Diego also became an accomplished pianist.

Diego began his poetic career in the ultraist movement (1919–23), which fused the tendencies of futurism, poetic cubism, and creationism, and in general integrated Spain into the imagist experiments that were then revolutionizing European poetry. Diego's *Imagen* (1922; Image) has been called the most typical and lasting product of this pioneering group. Like the English and American imagists, the ultraists strove for shock effect by creating daring metaphors based on far-fetched comparisons. They also experimented with typography, as Guillaume APOLLINAIRE had done in his *Calligrammes*. Diego himself was particularly influenced by Vicente Huidobro's creationist belief that metaphors should not compare existing objects but create a new visionary reality independent of nature. He continued his avant-garde experiments in *Manual de espumas* (1924; A Seafoam Manual), but he also wrote in traditional forms and in a more sober and direct style, as in *Soria* (1923) and *Versos humanos* (1925; Human Poems), his best known book.

With Dámaso ALONSO, Diego was the most enthusiastic promoter of the Luis de Góngora revival, on the occasion of the baroque poet's tricentennial in 1927. He participated in all of the collective activities and testimonials of the group later to be known as the Generation of 1927, of which Federico GARCÍA LORCA, Pedro SALINAS, Rafael ALBERTI, Vicente ALEIXANDRE, and others were notable members and friends of Diego. Most of these poets published first versions of texts that later became famous, in Diego's little magazine *Carmen* (1927–28). Its iconoclastic supplement, *Lola*, took up literary battles and sometimes

made fun of consecrated poets, including Juan Ramón JIMÉNEZ. *Fábula de Equis y Ceda* (1932; Fable of x and z) was Diego's ironic attempt to revitalize Góngora's style in a modern context. He also edited the Góngora anthology offered as a tribute by members of his group. In 1932, Diego published the still authoritative anthology *Poesía española contemporánea,* which included most contemporary poets since the beginning of the century but for the first time featured the members of the Generation of 1927.

Diego has written some 40 books of poetry. Several volumes contain love poetry, including *Sonetos a Violante* (1962). Other collections contain visions of the Spanish landscape and of the sea. Diego is a master of the sonnet, and his "El ciprés de Silos," in *Versos humanos,* is included in nearly all anthologies of modern Spanish poetry. Along with Jorge GUILLÉN, Diego has reestablished the baroque *décima* as a valid modern form, as in his book of religious poetry entitled *Viacrucis* (1931). Like Guillén, he also translated Paul VALÉRY's *Cimetière Marin* as a rigorous exercise in the classic hendecasyllable.

See: A. G. Morell, *Vida y poesía de Gerardo Diego* (1956); D. Alonso, *Poetas españoles contemporáneos* (1958), pp. 244–70.   J.Cr.

Díez-Canedo, Enrique (1879–1944), Spanish essayist and poet, was born in Badajoz and studied law at the University of Madrid. He began his literary work as a poet in the first year of the 20th century, winning a prize in a contest sponsored by the newspaper *Liberal*. Three books, *Versos de las horas* (1906), *La visita del sol* (1907; Visit from the Sun), and *Del cercado ajeno* (1907; From Another's Garden)—a collection of translations from foreign poets—established his reputation as a poet, translator, and connoisseur of contemporary European poetry. In his own poetry, he first followed the modernist school, imitating Rubén Darío (*see* SPANISH LITERATURE). In *La sombra del ensueño* (1910; The Shadow of the Fantasy) and *Imágenes* (1910; Images), Díez-Canedo appears more intimate, but it is not until *Epigramas americanos* (1928) that he found his innermost personal form.

From 1909 to 1911, Díez-Canedo studied in Paris, where he became acquainted with many Spanish-American writers who were living in or visiting the French capital and whom he introduced to the Spanish public. By this time he began to distinguish himself as an essayist, the most constant literary activity of his life. He contributed to the most important reviews and papers of the Hispanic world and taught French and the history of art. He was also a dramatic critic for *Voz* and *Sol* and for many years was one of the most active and amiable persons in the literary world of Madrid. He lectured in several countries and spent 1931 as a visiting professor at Columbia University. As a result of his close friendship with Manuel AZAÑA, he was appointed ambassador to Uruguay and Argentina from the Spanish Republic. When he entered the Royal Spanish Academy of the Language in 1935, he read an address on a subject he knew particularly well, the literary relations between Spain and Spanish America (*Unidad y diversidad de las letras hispánicas*). Like many other Spanish writers, he lived in exile in Mexico after the fall of the Republic. Well equipped for literary criticism by virtue of his learning, curiosity, and taste, Díez-Canedo's work in this area, although fragmentary and occasional, is broad in scope and in several respects authoritative. Most of his essays have been brought together in the following books: *La poesía francesa* (1913), *El teatro y sus enemigos* (1939), *Juan Ramón Jiménez en su obra* (1944), *Letras de América*

(1944), *Conversaciones literarias* (3 vols., 1964), *Estudios de poesía española contemporánea* (1965), and *El teatro español de 1914 a 1936* (4 vols., 1968). This last collection of essays is a valuable document of the history of the Spanish theater before the Civil War.

See: A. Iduarte, "Adios a don Enrique Díez-Canedo," *CA* 17 (1944): 59–65; J. L. Abellán, ed., *El exilio español de 1939*, vol. 4, *Cultura y literatura* (1976), pp. 43–45, 253–55.   A. del R. rev. J.L.G.-M.

Di Giacomo, Salvatore (1860–1934), Italian poet, short-story writer, playwright, essayist, and chronicler, was born, lived, and died in Naples. He is best known for his poetry in Neapolitan dialect. The son of a physician, he was destined for his father's profession, but in his third year of medical school, he recognized his lack of interest in medicine and his natural disposition for poetry. In the famous "Pagina autobiografica" (autobiographical page) that opens the first volume of his *Opere* (1946; Works), Di Giacomo gives a vivid account of the moment when he finally made the choice between science and art. This masterfully written piece may easily be taken as a paradigm of his entire literary production, reflecting as it does his two constant resources: the world of reality and the world of reverie.

Aside from a few early experiments in school journals such as *Il liceo,* Di Giacomo's literary activity began in 1879, the year he turned from medicine to journalism. He contributed some German-style stories to *Corriere del mattino,* works largely imitative of E. T. A. Hoffmann and Erckmann-Chatrian. During this period, he seems also to have been steeped in Edgar Allan Poe's *Tales of Mystery and Imagination.* He published his collected stories under the ironic title *Pipa e boccale* (1893; Pipe and Mug), dedicated to a hypothetical Professor Otto Zimmermann. Di Giacomo wrote to "Zimmermann" that this volume offered an alternative to Italian narrative of the period, which was "drenched with husbands' honor and dripping lovers' blood and tears."

Shortly afterward, Di Giacomo was attracted to verismo (*see* ITALIAN LITERATURE), a movement characterized by a thirst for truth in art, taking its themes and its sense of reality from actual life. He began to write about the life of the poor and the disinherited in the slums of Naples. This is the focus of *'O funneco verde* (1886; The Green Alley), a volume of sonnets; *Malavita* (1889; Low Life), a collection of theater sketches; and *Novelle napolitane* (1914; Neapolitan Novellas), a volume of short stories. Di Giacomo also proved himself capable of a tragic intensity with plays that dealt with the wretched world of violent, elemental emotions, notably *A San Francisco* (1896) and *Assunta Spina* (1910), in which the theme of jealousy and vengeance has an epic quality that rivals Giovanni VERGA's *Cavalleria rusticana.* Contrary to the tenets of verismo, however, Di Giacomo always sought to render not the actuality of things, but the essence of the impression perceived by his imagination, which preferred the gently vague to the definite. Similarly, his propensity toward realism never checked the sense of *humana pietas* that prevails in all his works.

There is also a peculiar vein of melancholy in Di Giacomo's writing. Its tinge may be found in his early songs for the Piedigrotta festival (Naples's most popular folk festival), in his first, unsurpassed sonnet "Nannina" (1881), and in some poems of *Ariette e sunette* (1898; Ariettas and Sonnets), despite their color and brio. This melancholy reached its highest moments of intensity in the long poem " 'O mese mariano" (1900; The Month of Mary), and especially in the last collection of *Canzone e ariette nove* (1916; New Canzones and Ariettas), which,

with its insistence on advancing age and death, suggests a cosmic sorrow and symbolizes human frailty. Di Giacomo has been hailed by many critics, first among them Benedetto CROCE, not only as the prince of poets in the Neapolitan dialect, but also as one of Italy's finest lyric poets and as an erudite historian of his native city. He was admitted to the Italian Academy in 1929.

See: F. D. Maurino, *Salvatore Di Giacomo and Neapolitan Dialectal Literature* (1951); F. Schlitzer, *Salvatore Di Giacomo* (1966); S. Rossi, *Salvatore Di Giacomo* (1968).   C.A.Me.

Diktonius, Elmer (1896–1961), Finland-Swedish poet, fiction writer, and critic, was born in Helsinki. He came from a working-class background and, by attendance at Finnish-language schools, acquired the complete bilingualism that would one day enable him to write Finnish verse and translate his own novel, *Janne Kubik,* into Finnish. A voracious reader, he came under the influence of such disparate figures as Friedrich NIETZSCHE, August STRINDBERG, Fyodor DOSTOYEVSKY, Walt Whitman, MULTATULI, Knut HAMSUN, and, later on, Pär LAGERKVIST, Edgar Lee Masters, the German expressionist poet Alfred MOMBERT, and the German critic Alfred KERR. His plans to become a composer led him to Gustav Mahler and Arnold Schoenberg, but he early realized that his genius was literary.

Diktonius's literary debut, *Min dikt* (1921; My Poem), was made up mostly of aphorisms but contained one of the most exciting of his early poems, "The Jaguar," in which he stated his intention to "kill the cry of those without feeling, the sympathy of the heartless." "The Jaguar" was then transferred to his first lyric collection, *Hårda sånger* (1922: Hard Songs), serving to introduce verses about his days of revolt ("dynamite symphonies in my hip-pocket") and semistarvation, his erotic sensations ("Eros whoregod godgod stinkpuddle pure spring"), and his brotherhood with the storm and its "laughter-logic," formulations that might have given him a rank had he written in Russian, with Vladimir MAYAKOVSKY, but that were met by lack of comprehension in Finland. The rule's exception was the critic Hagar Olsson, who then introduced him to Edith SÖDERGRAN. *Taggiga lågor* (1924: Barbed Flames) contained themes and forms that, although presented by Diktonius with characteristic explosiveness, were able to appeal to a more conservative public (sentimental poems on children, "portrait poems" of Diktonius's cultural heroes). *Stenkol* (1927; Coke), for all its revolutionary tones (calling attention to the "heroes' graves" of Reds fallen in the Finnish Civil War, predicting a "great moving day" in society), won Diktonius the grudging praise of academic critics and the adulation of young leftist poets in Sweden proper. These events took place when Diktonius's personal fortunes were at their lowest ebb, after a second disastrous trip to Paris (1925–27). *Stark men mörk* (1930: Strong but Dark) marks the end of this Promethean phase. Its famous narrative about "Red Emil" is faintly ambiguous in attitude; the hunger poems are fewer and shorter; music ("To a Bechstein") and Finland's seascape ("Åland Symphony") have become leading objects of praise in his writing.

In the 1930s the strident, "international" Diktonius gave way to a gentler, "national" one. Of the three lyric books published in that decade only the last, *Jordisk ömhet* (1938: Earthly Tenderness), is made up wholly of new verse; *Mull och moln* (1934: Clod and Cloud) combines poems with prose sketches and *Gräs och granit* (1936: Grass and Granite) has "poems new and old." But all three speak of the poet's absorption by Finland's nature, of Finland's heritage (the tribute to J. J. Wecksell), of the threat from the east (the "cannons of Kronstadt" in "Villa Golicke"), and of national unity on the 20th anniversary of the Civil War ("Heart of the World, 1938"). This strain becomes unabashedly patriotic in *Varsel* (1942: Portent), with its tributes to Jean Sibelius, the novelist Frans Emil SILLANPÄÄ, the poet Eino LEINO, and President Kyösti Kallio, who had guided Finland through the Winter War. As the poet declined, though, the prose writer flourished. From a somewhat wordy aphorist, as in *Brödet och elden* (1923: The Bread and the Flame), and likable provider of anecdotes and sketches, as in *Onnela* (1925), Diktonius emerged as a masterful novella writer in some parts of *Ingenting* (1928: Nothing). His complete mastery of prose was evident in the two volumes on *Medborgare i republiken Finland* (1935-40; Citizens in the Republic of Finland), the citizens including Fascists, farmers, orphans, Jews, madmen, devoted mothers. But Diktonius had other prose talents as well. In 1932 he published the experimental novel *Janne Kubik*, with its "woodcut" text and quasi-scholarly commentary, about a sometime member of the Red Guard who becomes rumrunner, Fascist gangster, and dockworker. The next year, *Opus 12*, his volume of music criticisms, appeared— erratic, entertaining, and linguistically inventive. Symptoms of a debilitating illness appeared during the early 1940s. *Hôstlig bastu* (1943: Autumnal Sauna) contains a sad return to the "happy land" of *Onnela* and *Ingenting,* and his last verse collections, *Annorlunda* (1948: Otherwise) and *Novembervår* (1952: November Spring), are— with the exception of a handful of splendid poems, the tribute to Diktonius's dead mother and the portrait of the alcoholized Leino—cranky and tired. Much of Diktonius's energy in these final productive years was given to a rendering into Swedish of Alexis Kivi's Finnish classic, *Seitsemän veljestä*, an eccentric translation, which nonetheless shows Diktonius again to be the creator of a language entirely his own, vulgar, funny, forceful, and sometimes sublime.

See: O. Enckell, *Den unge Diktonius* (1946); T. Henrikson, *Romantik och Marxism: estetik och politik hos Otto Ville Kuusinen och Diktonius till och med 1921* (1971); G. C. Schoolfield, *Elmer Diktonius* (1980).

G.C.S.

Dilmen, Güngör, who also uses the name *Kalyoncu* as a second surname (1930-), Turkish playwright, was born in Tekirdag. He obtained a degree in classical philology at the University of Istanbul. Later he did theater research in Athens and Tel Aviv and studied drama and playwriting at Yale University Drama School and at the University of Washington. Intermittently he has worked for the City Theater of Istanbul as a director and drama consultant. In 1976 he became the theater's research director and editor of its quarterly journal, *Türk Tiyatrosu*. He is also a translator of plays and musicals.

Dilmen's first play, *Midas'ın Kulakları* (1959; Eng. tr., *The Ears of Midas*, in *Modern Turkish Drama,* 1976), launched a verse trilogy based on legends relating to the Phrygian king. The two other plays in the trilogy are *Midas'ın Altınları* (1970; Gold of Midas) and *Midas'ın Kördüğümü* (1975; Midas's Tangled Knot). His *Kurban* (1967; Sacrificial Victim) is an adaptation of the legend of Medea to a Turkish village setting. Dilmen is fascinated by ancient and modern history. Among his best plays are *Akad'ın Yayı* (1967; Akkadia's Bow), based on the Mesopotamian theme; *İttihad ve Terakki* (1969; Union and Progress), a dramatization of the Young Turk Revolution and its aftermath; and *Ak Tanrılar* (1976; White Gods), about the conquest of Mexico. *Canlı Mymun Lokantası*

(1964; Live Monkey Restaurant), a striking play about neocolonialist exploitation, and numerous other plays by Dilmen have won Turkey's top awards. He received the Drama Prize of the Turkish Language Society in 1976.

T.S.H.

Dinesin, Isak: *see* BLIXEN, KAREN.

Diop, Birago (1906-), Senegalese poet and story-teller, was born in Dakar and received his higher education in France. After a long career as a veterinarian, he served as ambassador of Senegal to Tunisia (1961-65). Diop began to write poetry in 1925 while still a student. His collected poems have appeared under the title *Leurres et lueurs* (1960; Lures and Flashes). In the 1930s he became involved in the Paris-based *négritude* movement and contributed to Léopold Sédar SENGHOR's newspaper *L'Etudiant noir* (The Black Student).

Diop has become widely known as one of the most gifted and prominent African francophone writers, chiefly for his work as a story-teller. Without losing the flavor of the original, he has successfully used modern French to express his people's oral tradition and to describe the landscape and rural life of West Africa. In the 1930s, in Senegal, he met a 60-year-old *griot* (African minstrel) whose tales he incorporated in his masterpieces *Les Contes d'Amadou Koumba* (1947; Eng. tr., *The Tales of Amadou Koumba,* 1966) and *Les Nouveaux Contes d'Amadou Koumba*. Diop has also written other stories, published as *Contes et lavannes* (1963; Tales and Riddles), and plays, such as *Sarzan* (1955). He remains one of the most widely read African francophone writers.

B.C.

Dıranas, Ahmet Muhip, whose last name was spelled *Dranas* prior to the 1970s (1909-), Turkish poet, was born in Sinop. He studied law and philosophy and has held various positions, including those of librarian at Istanbul's Academy of Fine Arts, publications director for People's Houses, president of the Association for the Protection of Children, board member of İş-Bank, and member of the literary committee of the Turkish state theaters. Dıranas wrote two plays: *Gölgeler* (1947; Shadows) and *O Böyle İstemezdi* (He Wouldn't Have Wanted It This Way), produced in Istanbul in 1946 and 1948 respectively. His collected poems came out in 1974 under the title *Şiirler* (Poems).

Using the syllabic meters of autochthonous folk poetry reenforced by ingenious rhymes, Ahmet Muhip brought a new lucid diction to Turkish poetry. His poems are distilled evocations of love and suffering. Some of his major poems depict the lives of ordinary people, the disintegration of Istanbul's cultural identity, and scenes of Utopian beauty.

T.S.H.

Ditlevsen, Tove (1918-76), Danish novelist and poet, was born in Copenhagen. She grew up in the Copenhagen slums and made this experience the focal point of her writing. Social description is especially emphasized in her sensitive short stories and novels about the problems of growing up in a poor, working-class milieu, most characteristically portrayed in *Man gjorde et Barn Fortræd* (1941; A Child Was Hurt) and *For Barnets Skyld* (1946; For the Sake of a Child). Man's isolation in the big city is a major theme in Ditlevsen's formally traditional poetry, from *Pigesind* (1939; A Girl's Mind) to *Den hemmelige rude* (1961; The Secret Window). A second theme is the inconstancy of the joy of love experienced in a woman's life, from her immature longings on through love affairs, marriage, motherhood, and catastrophe, to the mature woman's confrontation with her own youthful dreams. Ditlevsen's childhood memories provide the background for the novel *Barndommens Gade* (1943; The Street of Childhood), for the poetry collection *Det runde værelse* (1973; The Round Room), and for her fascinating and ruthlessly honest series of memoirs (1967–71).

See: *Om Tove Ditlevsen*, ed. H. Mogensen (1976).

S.H.R.

Döblin, Alfred, pseud. Linke Poot, (1878–1957), German novelist, playwright, and essayist, had the greatest narrative talent of any German expressionist. A writer of tremendous vitality, fertile imagery, and vision, he was thoroughly grounded in science and philosophy. He was born in Stettin in a Jewish merchant family, but his parents moved to Berlin when he was 10. He studied in Berlin and Freiburg, receiving his M.D. in 1905. He turned to journalism, however, and it was not until 1911 that he practiced as a psychiatrist in the workers' district around the Alexanderplatz in Berlin. He married and had four sons. During the first phase of his life his publications were confined to his professional field and to essays on philosophical and aesthetic questions.

Writing was a passion with Döblin, although most of his early writings remained unpublished. His first public appearance as a writer was made in *Der Sturm*, the spectacular expressionist periodical. The stories published there were collected in *Die Ermordung einer Butterblume* (1913; The Murder of a Buttercup), where vision merges with reality, perspective with romantic distortion, and reflection with symbolism, characteristics revealed also in most of the author's later work. His first great success was the "Chinese" novel, *Die drei Sprünge des Wanglun* (1915; The Three Leaps of Wang-lun), which earned him the Fontane Prize. It is not a story of adventures or curiosities, but rather it is a literary attempt to transplant the soul of the Far East to Europe. Wang-lun, the roving revolutionary and reformer, succumbs to the crude power of the state; but even in his defeat he demonstrates the victory of the nonviolent spirit over brute force.

In World War I, Döblin served for three years at the front as a physician, but even there he continued writing. *Wadzeks Kampf mit der Dampfmaschine* (1918; Wadzek's Battle with the Steam Engine) poses grotesquely and ironically the problem of human beings versus machines. The novel *Der schwarze Vorhang* (1919; The Black Curtain) was followed by the two-volume historical novel *Wallenstein* (1920), written in part at the front during the war. The novel strips history of idealizing embellishments and demonstrates the collapse of mere power, obviously containing Döblin's interpretation of World War I. *Berge, Meere und Giganten* (1924; Mountains, Oceans, and Giants) is a satirical yet powerfully horrible vision of the future of the human race, a nightmare of expressionist conjuration, where heartless modern science leads to a fantastic apocalyptic doom.

Döblin's best-known novel is *Berlin Alexanderplatz* (1920; Eng. tr., *Alexanderplatz, Berlin*, 1931), performed as a radio play in 1976. The best elements of expressionism are fused in this stupendous work, which although it is not an imitation of James Joyce nevertheless strongly suggests him. The story of the fate of a simple, if rude, proletarian, written with consummate skill and with an intimate knowledge of people and locale, contains a variety of prose techniques, including interior monologue, simultaneity, and cameralike panoramas, reminiscent also of John Dos Passos.

When the anti-Semitic tide rose and the Nazis came to power in 1933, Döblin fled to Paris via Zürich; in France he became a naturalized citizen and at the outbreak of the war was a member of the French Ministry of Information. His flight into exile continued in 1940, when he went to New York (and later to Los Angeles), taking the well-known route through southern France, Spain, and Portugal. While in Germany his books were burned, Döblin continued to write in exile. Some of his works from that time are *Babylonische Wanderung* (1934; Babylonian Migration), a novel; *Pardon wird nicht gegeben* (1935; Eng. tr., *Men without Mercy*, 1937), a novel; two exotic historical novels dealing with the Spanish conquistadores, Indians, and Jesuits, *Die Fahrt ins Land ohne Tod* (1937; Journey into the Land without Death) and *Der blaue Tiger* (1938; The Blue Tiger). In 1939 he began his multi-volume *November 1918*, a mixture of reportage and epic that he completed in 1950. His autobiography, *Schicksalsreise* (Fateful Journey), appeared in 1949.

After World War II, Döblin returned to Europe as the cultural attaché with the French military government in Baden-Baden in 1945. He had converted to Catholicism during his flight in 1940, and the novel *Hamlet oder Die lange Nacht nimmt kein Ende* (Hamlet or The Long Night Never Ends) was long in finding a publisher, appearing finally in 1956 in East Germany.

Between 1946 and 1951, Döblin edited the literary magazine *Das goldene Tor*, and in 1949 he was a cofounder of the prestigious Academy of Sciences and of Literature in Mainz. But essentially isolated and forgotten, and disappointed in the political development of West Germany, he went back to Paris in 1951, returning to Germany again only shortly before his death.

See: H. von Hofe, "German Literature in Exile: Alfred Döblin," *GQ* 17 (1944): 28–31; M. Prangel, *Alfred Döblin* (1973); W. Kort, *Alfred Döblin* (1974); K. Schröter, *Alfred Döblin in Selbstzeugnissen und Bilddokumenten* (1978).

W.K.P. rev. A.L.W.

Dobraczyński, Jan (1910–), Polish novelist and journalist, was born in Warsaw and educated there in the School of Business. During World War II he took part in the 1939 September campaign, later fought in the Home Army, was coeditor of the clandestine journal *Walka*, and took part in the 1944 Warsaw uprising. He belongs to the circle of Catholic writers connected with Catholic journals *Dziś i Jutro* and *Tygodnik Powszechny*. In his more than 40 volumes, Dobraczyński deals with a wide range of topics. He has written essays: *Bernanos—powieściopisarz* (1937; Bernanos—Novelist), *Lawa gorejąca* (1939; Fiery Lava) about Giovanni Papini, *Książki, idee i czlowiek* (1955; Books, Ideas and Man), *Wielkość i świętość* (1958; Greatness and Sainthood), *Głosy czasu* (1966; Voices of the Time), and novels about the Nazi occupation of Poland: *W rozwalonym domu* (1946; In a Demolished Home), *Najeźdźcy* (1946–47; Invaders), *A znak nie będzie mu dany* (1957; And He Will Not Be Given a Sign), *Tak biały jak czerwona jest krew* (1972; Just as White as Blood is Red). He also wrote historical novels, often with biblical plots, such as *Dwa stosy* (1947; Two Piles); *Wybrańcy gwiazd* (1948; Chosen of the Stars); *Święty miecz* (1949; Eng. tr., *The Sacred Sword*, 1959), a portrait of the world of early Christianity with Saint Paul as a central character; and *Listy Nikodema* (1952; Eng. tr., *The Letters of Nicodemus*, 1958), a fictionalized story of the influence of the life and ministry of Jesus Christ upon Nicodemus, one of the New Testament characters. He also wrote memoirs, *Gra w wybijanego* (1962; Playing "Knock One Out") and *Tylko w jednym życiu* (1970; Only in One Life). His novel *Wyczerpać morze* (1961; Eng. tr., *To Drain the Sea*, 1964) is a vision of the world partially destroyed by a nuclear explosion. Dobraczyński's writing is inspired by Christian ideas and is permeated with his humanistic belief in man's ability to improve.

See: Z. Lichniak, *Szkic do portretu Jana Dobraczyńskiego* (1962); A. Rogalski, *Dobraczyński* (1969).

A.Z.

Doderer, Heimito von (1896–1966), Austrian writer, was born near Vienna, where he spent most of his life. He held a Ph.D. in medieval history and studied psychology as well. He was a member of the Austrian Nazi party until 1938, and he served as an officer in both world wars. As a writer, Doderer matured slowly. He isolated himself from the literary movements of his time; publication of his works was sometimes delayed for decades, and his fame is still mostly confined to Central Europe. His published oeuvre comprises 10 novels, 5 volumes each of stories and essays, 2 collections of poetry, and selections from his diaries.

Doderer's early, rather insignificant works include the poems in *Gassen und Landschaft* (1923; Alleys and Scenery) and the novels *Die Bresche* (1924; The Breach) and *Das Geheimnis des Reichs* (1930; The Mystery of the Empire). The essay *Der Fall Gütersloh* (1930; The Case of Gütersloh) indicates that his acquaintance with this painter and writer marked Doderer's second birth as a writer—his "conversion to language." He now found the central thematic concern of his work: *Menschwerdung*, or the slow and tortuous process of "becoming human" by traveling a path confused by false perceptions, mistaken directions, impasses, fateful jolts, reversals, and belated insights. Obsessions and *Deperzeption*, the failure or refusal to see things as they really are, prevent the *Menschwerdung* of all but a handful of Doderer's characters.

Doderer's novels of the 1930s explore the theme of *Menschwerdung* in the lives of individual protagonists. In *Ein Mord, den jeder begeht* (1938; Eng. tr., *Every Man a Murderer*, 1964), a self-conscious young man catches up with his own past; at the end of a laboriously systematic but misdirected attempt to solve a "murder" he discovers that he himself unwittingly brought about the death. The realization and acceptance of this guilt finally free him. In 1939, Doderer wrote *Die erleuchteten Fenster* (1951; The Lighted Windows); the *Menschwerdung* of the subtitle is achieved when the protagonist frees himself from a voyeuristic obsession.

As Doderer matured, the scope and design of his novels grew increasingly complex. *Die Strudlhofstiege* (1951; The Strudlhof Steps) and *Die Dämonen* (1956; Eng. tr., *The Demons*, 1961) are intricate fabrics presenting several generations and different social classes from multiple points of view. Written over 24 years, the two novels have overlapping plots and sets of characters. The narratives are anchored in Vienna before and after World War I, but Doderer's search for the hidden roots of characters and events leads to deeper layers of time and personality. External and internal "demons" come dimly into view as intricate emotional, social, and financial relationships are developed, sustained, disrupted, and reformed. Combining precise observation of minute psychological fluctuations and calculated stage managing, Doderer moves about 30 major characters through locales ranging from sewers to palaces and through incidents from precarious idylls to mass riots. The farcical novel *Die Merowinger* (1962; The Merovingians) traces the rise and fall of a latter-day tyrant who terrorizes his "total family" until the victims dispose of him. Doderer, forever distrustful of modern achievements, relentlessly mocked scientists, psychiatrists, and academic scholars.

In *Die Wasserfälle von Slunj* (1963; Eng. tr., *The Waterfalls of Slunj*, 1966), the only completed part of a planned tetralogy, Doderer achieved classic objectivity in telling a tragic story from that artistic distance where serene detachment and a compassionate perception of human entanglements go hand in hand. *Tangenten* (1964; Tangents), his 1940–50 diaries, reveal a writer devoted to his craft and painfully aware of contemporary paradoxes: a Thomist shrinking away from all ideologies, an eclectic elitist longing to be an ordinary man, an individualist pursuing humanist values in an era bent on abrogating them.

See: D. Weber, *Heimito von Doderer: Studien zu seinem Romanwerk* (1963); H. J. Schröder, *Apperzeption und Vorurteil: Untersuchung zur Reflexion Heimito von Doderers* (1976).   W.H.

Dombrovsky, Yury Osipovich (1909–78), Russian novelist, was born in Moscow, where he studied literature and theater. In 1932 he was arrested and sentenced to forced residence in Kazakhstan, where he taught school, wrote for local newspapers, and worked in the National Museum of Alma-Ata. He was arrested again during the terror of 1937 and spent 20 years in labor camps. Finally set free from a Siberian prison in 1957, he returned to and settled in Moscow.

His novels include *Obezyana prikhodit za svoim cherepom* (1959; The Monkey Is Coming to Get His Skull) and *Khranitel drevnostey* (1964; Eng. tr., *The Keeper of Antiquities*, 1969). The second is presented in the form of an allusive essay on despotism, a novel about the 1937 deportations as they were viewed in Alma-Ata. It established Dombrovsky as a writer of first rank. His novel *Fakultet nenuzhnykh veshchey* (Paris, 1978; The Faculty of Useless Things) is an account of his own prison and labor-camp experience, at the same time a panorama of the world of prisons and concentration camps; an inside picture of the NKVD; a study of a schizophrenic society; and a meditation, apropos of the Passion of Christ, about the power of humanism during eras of tyranny. After working on this book for 10 years, Dombrovsky saw no hope of ever seeing it published in the Soviet Union and therefore sent the manuscript secretly to Paris for publication.

As a novelist, Dombrovsky was unclassifiable. He possessed a powerful realistic talent but was notable for his perfection in the techniques of the symbol, the oneiric echo, and the allusion awaiting interpretation. The possessor of a Greco-Latin culture that is very rare in the Soviet Union, Dombrovsky was probably the most profound analyst of Stalinism from the standpoint of universal history.   J.Ca.

Domenchina, Juan José (1898–1959), Spanish poet and critic, was born in Madrid. His first volumes of poetry, *Del poema eterno* (1917) and *Las interrogaciones del silencio* (1918), were taken to represent a transition from modernism to the "new poetry." From the beginning his poetry had an intellectual bent mixed with a Castilian sense of reality and a baroque form of expression. One of his most characteristic early works is *La corporeidad de lo abstracto* (1929; The Bodily Form of Abstraction). The *Poesías completas* of 1936 also include *Dédalo* (1932; Labyrinth) and *Margen* (1933). He wrote two novels, but aside from his poetry he was best known for his *Crónicas de Gerardo Diego* (1935), a collection of newspaper articles in which he incisively judged many contemporary writers.

Domenchina went into exile in Mexico in 1939 and remained there until his death. Exile and nostalgia for

Spain provided the subject matter of the poetry of his last 20 years. Late collections include *Destierro* (1942; Exile), *Pasión de sombra* (1944; A Passion for Shadow), *Exul umbra* (1948), and *La sombra desterrada* (1950; The Exiled Shadow). The "shadow" of these titles represents Spain and the poet's lost past as well as his present shadowy, uprooted existence. *Poesía, 1942–1958* appeared posthumously in 1975.

See: C. Zardoya, *Poesía española contemporánea* (1961), pp. 397–410.   A. del R. rev. H.L.B.

Domin, Hilde (1912–), German poet and critic, was born in Cologne, the only daughter of a wealthy Jewish lawyer. She first studied law, then turned to sociology, economics, and philosophy at the universities of Cologne, Berlin, Heidelberg, and Florence, where she finished her studies with a dissertation on Pontanus, a political theorist of the Renaissance. Becoming aware of impending political troubles, Domin left Germany in 1932 for Italy. There she married the art historian E. W. Palm, with whom she fled to England in 1939 and on to the Dominican Republic a year later. She worked as teacher and translator, turning to poetry only in 1951. In 1954 she and her husband finally returned to Germany, where she now lives in Heidelberg, a free-lance writer.

All of Domin's work (five collections of poetry, short prose, a novel, and essays) was published after 1959 and reflects the writer's life against a kaleidoscopic background of experience abroad and at home. The poetry collection *Nur eine Rose als Stütze* (1959; Only a Rose for Support) conveys the plight of a refugee wandering through alien countries, in a style devoid of artifice or sentimentality, using forceful images of crystalline beauty and simple language, limpid and musical. These are songs of fear, despair, about the search for security, love, and farewell, in quickly passing time. Thematically, *Rückkehr der Schiffe* (1962; Return of the Ships) and *Hier* (1964; Here) are similar, but in them exile is seen as the general fate of man, alienated from a hostile or, at best, indifferent world.

The novel *Das zweite Paradies* (1968; The Second Paradise) deals with crisis in marriage and a weltanschauung of a woman whose life is almost identical with the author's. Returning to Germany in the 1950s, after years of exile, she finds her native country both familiar and changed, and she also experiences a crisis of love. The shock forces her to reexamine all of her relationships. In loosely connected monologues, fragments of dreams, daydreams, and memories, the author recaptures the past and tries to adjust to the present. Only through sacrifice and self-denial does she regain hope for a "second paradise."

The love poetry contained in *Höhlenbilder* (1968; Cave Drawings), written in 1951 and 1952, exudes strong exaltation, whereas the poems of *Ich will dich* (1970; I Want You) demonstrate self-restraint, empathy for human frailty, and understanding of the evanescence of emotion.

According to Hilde Domin's critical work, *Wozu Lyrik heute* (1968; Why Lyric Poetry Today), it is the poet's privilege and duty to show people their right to be free, human, and humane, in spite of social pressure to automatize them within conformist society. She has applied this credo to her own life and work. She is also the author of autobiographical varia in *Von der Natur nicht vorgesehen* (1974; Not Foreseen by Nature) and a best-selling anthology, *Doppelinterpretationen* (1966; Double Interpretations).

See: O. Seidlin, "Bemerkungen zu einer neu-deutschen. Poetik," *GQ* 41 (1968): 505–11.   A.P.O.

Donnay, Maurice (1859–1945), French playwright, was born in Paris. He studied to be an engineer and graduated from the Ecole Centrale in 1885. In 1890 he was a member of the famous Montmartre cabaret, Le Chat Noir, where he presented certain *pièces d'ombres*, including *Phryné* (1891), and *Ailleurs* (1891; Elsewhere). In 1892 he began his real dramatic subjects.

Donnay is one of the most important authors of light comedies. At times he indulged in dramas typical of the boulevard theater—*Education de Prince* (1900; Education of a Prince), *La Patronne* (1908; The Boss), *La Belle Angevine* (1922, with André Rivoire; The Beautiful Girl from Anjou), *Le Geste* (1924, with Henri Duvernois; The Gesture)—and even wrote librettos for musical comedies, such as *Le Mariage de Télémaque* (1910, with Jules LEMAÎTRE; Telemachus's Marriage) and *Le Roi Candaule* (1920; King Candaules). He also contributed plays of deep psychological significance—*Amants* (1895; Eng. tr., *Lovers*, 1915), *La Douloureuse* (1897), *L'Autre Danger* (1902; Eng. tr., *The Other Danger*, 1914), *Paraître* (1906; To Appear)—as well as studies of social problems. Among the latter are *La Clairière* (1900, with Lucien DESCAVES; The Clearing), an amusing satire of a phalanstery; *Le Retour de Jérusalem* (1903; Eng. tr., *The Return from Jerusalem*, 1912), on the Jewish question; *Oiseaux de passage* (1904, with Lucien Descaves; Birds of Passage), on the difficulty people of different races and backgrounds find in understanding each other; *Les Eclaireuses* (1913; The Girl Scouts), on feminism. A skepticism without bitterness and a keen sense of humor prevented Donnay from giving his social dramas the dull character of problem plays.

Although primarily a playwright, he wrote the *Vie amoureuse d'Alfred de Musset* (1926; The Love Life of Alfred de Musset) and volumes of an autobiographical nature, *Pendant qu'ils sont à Noyon* (1917; While They Are at Noyons), *Autour du Chat Noir* (1926; Around the Chat Noir), and *Mes Débuts à Paris* (1937; My Beginnings in Paris). Donnay was elected to the Académie Française in 1907.

See: R. Le Brun, *Maurice Donnay* (1903); P. Flat, "Maurice Donnay," in *RBl* 52 (1914): 359–62; H. Bidou, "Les Epoques du théâtre contemporain en France: IV, La Période Donnay-Capus," in *RH* 30 (1921), vol. 1: 195–210; P. Bathille, *Maurice Donnay: son œuvre* (1933).   M.E.C. rev. D.W.A.

Dorgelès, Roland, pseud. of Roland Lecavelé (1886–1973), French novelist, travel writer, and critic, was born in Amiens. As a youth, he went to Paris to study architecture at the Ecole des Beaux-Arts. He soon left the school, becoming a humorist and journalist and a member of the Montmartre group that included Guillaume APOLLINAIRE, ALAIN-FOURNIER, Francis CARCO, and Pierre MAC ORLAN.

Volunteering for military service in 1914, Dorgelès served at the front for the next four years, was seriously wounded, and was cited for bravery in action. His first novel, *Les Croix de bois* (1919; Eng. tr., *Wooden Crosses*, 1921), received the Femina Prize and nearly won the Goncourt Prize, which went that year instead to Marcel PROUST for *A l'ombre des jeunes filles en fleurs*. Dorgelès's novel, which expressed, in the language used by the poilus at the front, their sufferings and disappointments, became an overwhelming best-seller and continued to be widely read throughout the interwar period. Elected to the Académie Goncourt in 1929 as successor to Georges COURTELINE, he subsequently served as president of that body from 1954, when he replaced COLETTE, until his death. For more than 40 years, Dorgelès wielded immense power as a member of the Goncourt jury.

Although he was the author of more than 30 books, Dorgelès's later work never attained the critical success and public attention that his first novel had won for him. Among his more interesting books are *Saint Magloire* (1922; Eng. tr., *Saint Magloire*, 1923), *Montmartre, mon pays* (1925; **Montmartre, My Hometown**), and *Au beau temps de la butte* (1952; In the Heyday of the Hillock). Dorgelès is also credited with inventing the term *drôle de guerre* (phony war) in 1940 while serving as a war correspondent in Lorraine.

See: G. Senart, "Roland Dorgelès," *Livres et lectures,* vol. 1 (1956), pp. 565–69.   D.O'C.

Dorosh, Yefim Yakovlevich, pseud. of Yefim Yakovlevich Golberg (1908–72), Russian prose writer, was born in Yelizavetgrad. Initially a student of art history, he started publishing stories, mainly on revolutionary themes, in the 1930s. He joined the Communist Party in 1945. As a journalist on the *Literaturnaya gazeta,* he became interested in collective farms, and around 1954–56 he conceived the plan for his *Derevenskiy dnevnik* (Village Diary), a series of sketches comprising a monumental inquiry into the condition of peasants in the Rostov-Yaroslavskiy district of central Russia. *Derevenskiy dnevnik* was regularly published in the periodical *Novy mir* over a period of 12 years: "Dva dnya v Raygorode" (1958; Two Days in Raygorod), "Sukhoye leto" (1961; Dry Summer), "Raygorod v fevrale" (1962; Raygorod in February), "Dozhd popolam s solntsem" (1964; Half and Half Between Sun and Rain), "Ivan Fedoseyevich ukhodit na pensiyu" (1969; Ivan Fedoseyevich Is Pensioned Off), and "Pyatnadtsat let spustya" (1970; Fifteen Years Later). Death prevented Dorosh from completing a series of historical essays, *Proshloye sredi nas* (The Past in Our Midst), which he began in 1967 with *Razmyshleniye v Zagorske* (A Meditation in Zagorsk).

Dorosh's works are an indictment, free of passion but filled with facts, of the economic and cultural decline brought on by an antidemocratic agricultural policy that never took account of either the wishes or the experience of those who cultivated the land. They abound in penetrating reflections about the civilizing role of social forces nowadays held in disdain: the peasantry, the intelligentsia, and the church, with its monasteries. Through his refusal to separate the history of Russia from the history of Europe, Dorosh opposed the neo-Slavophile currents in contemporary Soviet literature. He is linked to both the 19th-century tradition of Gleb Uspensky and the ideas of Ivan Turgenev.   J.Ca.

D'Ors y Rovira, Eugenio (1882–1954), Spanish art critic, essayist, and philosopher of exceptional artistic sensibility, was born in Barcelona. His works and his cultural activities have had an importance of which there is insufficient awareness. In D'Ors, the Generation of 1898's desire for the Europeanization of Spain became a reality. He was the founder of the Catalan movement called *novecentismo,* and he led the cultural activities of the Institute of Catalan Studies. Later he lived in Paris as Spain's cultural representative to the League of Nations. Having earlier organized important art exhibitions throughout Europe, he was put in charge of recovering for Spain art works removed from the country during the Civil War. Finally, he founded the Instituto de España, now the Consejo Superior de Investigaciones Científicas.

D'Ors wrote more than 30 books in Catalan, Spanish, and French. He influenced other philosophers, such as José Luis ARANGUREN, and his view of the baroque has found acceptance. He began his *Glosari* (1906–20; Glossary) in Catalan, but his *Nuevo glosario* (1920–43; New Glossary) and *Novísimo glosario* (1944–45; Latest Glossary) were written in Spanish. These works represent a synthesis of D'Ors's thought. The gloss is a commentary intended to provide the reader with an understanding of a specific cultural phenomenon. So understood, it is original with D'Ors. The gloss differs from the conventional essay in the precision it achieves. D'Ors's "harmonious" thought moves between the extremes of spontaneity and definition. This dualism pervades his philosophy and his view of art and culture. D'Ors defines the baroque, for example, as a historical constant, a permanent and universal cultural style, which is opposed to the other constant—the classical—in the same way as spontaneity and the dynamic are opposed to the principle of ordering, hierarchy, and unity. The baroque is illuminatingly seen as "the eternal feminine." Guided by the concept of opposites, which can also be seen as the contrast between spatial or architectonic values and expressive or musical values in art, D'Ors characterizes all of the paintings in the Prado Museum in his delightful *Tres horas en el Museo del Prado* (1922; Three Hours in the Prado). On the one side are Poussin and Mantegna, on the other side, El Greco and Goya.

D'Ors's theory of the "eones" is the basis of his view of art and culture. To understand it one can begin with his beautiful definition of rhythm: "Rhythm is the insertion of fixed elements in the development of a continuous, variable series." History itself is such a series, which D'Ors places somewhere between amorphism and determinism. He sees history as a variable, indeterminate series within which it is nevertheless possible to detect the presence of fixed elements or constants that repeat themselves. All causal explanations are denied to history because D'Ors replaces the principle of causality with that of required function, in which function is dominant over structure. The cosmos is not a whole held together by causal links but rather by "syntactic relations." These fixed elements are the "eones." One of them is the baroque, as explained in *Lo barroco* (1935) and *Las ideas y las formas: Estudios sobre la morfología de la cultura* (1928).

In many ways D'Ors's philosophy is born of a polemical dialogue with the dominant currents of thought of his time. His principle of required function, for example, represents an obvious intent to move beyond positivism. In his masterwork, *El secreto de la filosofía* (1947), he does not offer a metaphysics but rather an illuminating philosophy of the world based on the decline of classical physics. The cosmos is not an atemporal reality or system in which energy merely changes and is transformed but is neither reduced nor destroyed. Rather, it is a system that loses energy and therefore gradually decays. It has, as a result, a history. *La filosofía del hombre que trabaja y que juega* (1921; The Philosophy of the Man Who Works and Plays) to a certain extent corrects the principle of vital pragmatism, because although it recognizes the universal value of life, action, and practical ends, it also points out that not all activity is useful or end-directed. Alongside *homo sapiens* and *homo faber* stands *homo ludens,* the man who plays. D'Ors's philosophy links artistic activity with cognitive activity and pragmatism without sacrificing or subordinating any of these elements.

See: J. L. Aranguren, *La filosofía de Eugenio D'Ors* (1945); E. Rojo Pérez, *La ciencia de la cultura. Teoría historiológica de Eugenio D'Ors* (1964); V. Aguilera Cerni, *Ortega y D'Ors en la cultura artística española* (1966).   F.F.-T.

Dossi, Carlo, pseud. of Alberto Pisani Dossi (1849–1910), Italian journalist, writer, and diplomat, was born into an aristocratic family in Pavia. He was a precocious writer, and in 1867 he backed the founding of *Palestra letteraria e artistica*, a literary magazine that put him in contact with the *scapigliati* (*see* ITALIAN LITERATURE), a group of late romantics who derived their aesthetics from the French symbolists. In this milieu, he met the novelist Giuseppe Rovani, whom he was to idolize for the rest of his life. In 1868, Dossi published *L'altrieri* (Yesterday), a book of boyhood reminiscences written in what was to become his typical literary manner: a mixture of sketches and impressions drawn from memory and influenced by other artistic media, such as music and painting.

In 1870, Dossi published *Vita di Alberto Pisani* (Life of Alberto Pisani), a continuation of *L'altrieri,* but with more ambitious artistic goals. Patterned on Dante's *Vita nuova*, the book is a mixture of trite romantic themes (such as the suicide of the protagonist for love) and continual literary quotations ranging from Laurence Sterne and Charles Dickens to Jean Paul Richter, with a gusto for the macabre surely drawn from Dossi's avid reading of E. T. A. Hoffman. Dossi's *Vita* is distinguished by a sense of failure. He confesses that at the age of 20 he finds himself at a terminal point in his life, devoid of "virtue, goodness and knowledge." Yet the work is marked by the perfection of his personal style. Ellipses, unorthodox punctuation, word associations with colors and sounds, and sudden digressions create a style very different from the rational, polished manner of Alessandro Manzoni (1785–1873) and his school. But as he had feared, Dossi seemed to lose his inspiration once he exhausted the themes of childhood and infancy. Some of his subsequent works, such as *La colonia felice* (1874; The Happy Colony), betray an attempt to create art forcibly through systematic ideological planning. In other works, Dossi pushes the possibilities of linguistic expression and verbal innovation to extremes. *Note azzurre* (1912; Blue Notes), for example, is a collection of reminiscences, thoughts, suggestions from Latin and Italian classics, plans for future works, and extremely personal and eccentric judgments. He condemns Giacomo Leopardi (1798–1837), for example, as a mediocre poet while he places Rovani in the same class as Dante.

Dossi's linguistic syncretism was accompanied by an extremely stern moral attitude toward contemporary society. Typically, he did not express this attitude in an organized structure or in one work, but in various writings. In *Note azzurre* he underscores the hypocrisy of turn-of-the-century society, while in *Dal calamaio di un medico* (1873; From the Inkwell of a Doctor) he reveals his strong pessimism about human nature. *La desinenza in A* (1878; Ending in A) contains a vitriolic attack on women.

In 1879, Dossi was appointed general consul to Bolivia. There he had time to indulge his passion for archaeology, a pursuit he continued when he moved to Athens as chief of the diplomatic corps. After 1905 he went into retirement and spent the rest of his life working on a book on Rovani, which he never finished.

See: G. Mariani, in *Storia della scapigliatura* (1967); R. Bigazzi, in *I colori del vero* (1969).   D.M.

Dostoyevsky, Fyodor Mikhaylovich (1821–1881), Russian novelist and short-story writer, was born in Moscow. In 1849 he was arrested as a member of the conspiratorial Petrashevsky circle; and, as a consequence, his creative career was interrupted for almost 10 years. After a period of transition from 1859 to 1863, in which his work was not markedly different from the works he had published in the 1840s, his literary career took a leap into greatness with the publication of *Zapiski iz podpolya* (1864; Eng. tr., *Notes from the Underground*, 1913, 1918). His literary career, then, can be divided fairly exactly among the works that he wrote between 1843 and 1849, those that he wrote in the transitional years from 1859 to 1863, and those that he published in the years of literary greatness from 1864 to his death in 1881. A profound change is evident in the quality and philosophical maturity of the works after 1864, and the causes for this change are to be sought in the 10 years of imprisonment and exile. Before he was arrested in 1849, Dostoyevsky shared some of the vague liberal ideals and compassion for the masses of the young men of his generation; and it was these sentiments, as well as considerable restlessness, that probably led him to attend the meetings of the Petrashevsky circle between 1847 and his arrest on April 23, 1849.

Five years before, his literary career began dramatically in 1844 when his first novel, *Bednye lyudi* (Eng. tr., *Poor Folk*, 1894), was greatly praised by Vissarion Belinsky, the most important personage on the Russian critical scene at the time. Belinsky's praise and influence were sufficient to catapult Dostoyevsky into the literary limelight with his first serious literary effort. What Belinsky saw in *Poor Folk* was a continuation of the Nikolay Gogol tradition of seeing and championing the common humanity in insignificant and oppressed people. But Belinsky had serious reservations about Dostoyevsky's second work, *Dvoynik* (1846; Eng. tr., "The Double," 1917), an amazing anticipation of some of Dostoevsky's mature work, and he criticized sharply *Gospodin Prokharchin* (1846; Eng. tr., "Mr. Prokharchin," 1918) and *Khozyayka* (1847; Eng. tr., "The Landlady," 1917). Dostoyevsky was always to react meekly to adverse criticism, and the reservations of Belinsky were to dissolve not only his public acclaim but also his inner confidence. During the rest of the 1840s Dostoyevsky's writings were characterized by a lack of direction and considerable experimentation. He experimented with farcical works such as *Roman v devyati pismakh* (1847; Eng. tr., "A Novel in Nine Letters," 1919) and *Chuzhaya zhena i muzh pod krovatyu* (1848; Eng. tr., "Another Man's Wife," 1919), fantasies such as *Malenkiy geroy* (1849; Eng. tr., "A Little Hero," 1918) and *Belye nochi* (1848; Eng. tr., "White Nights," 1918); social commentary in *Yolka i svadba* (1848; Eng. tr., "A Christmas Tree and a Wedding," 1917), and the sentimental epistolary tale *Netochka Nezvanova* (1849; Eng. tr., "Netochka Nezvanov," 1920). Some of the traits of his mature style and outlook are already present in these tales. His perception in *The Double* that men will choose self-destruction rather than give up their sense of dignity and self-worth is an early example of an important later theme. The suffering buffoon in *Polzunkov* (1848) was to appear repeatedly in his later works, and the tendency of his later characters to protect some dream of their inner excellence by creating conditions that prevent that excellence from being manifested is already present in Yefimov in *Netochka Nezvanova*. But the hints and impulses of the mature style and outlook are scattered and uncertain, and some catalyst is needed to bring them to that tragic view that characterizes the mature works after 1864.

The catalyst was to be the transformation in his views of man that he underwent in prison. Dostoyevsky changed from an adherent of the abstract liberalism of the Utopian socialists to a profoundly tragic conservatism. He came out of prison believing in God and individual responsibility and holding the conviction that man was tragically condemned to destroy himself and others. These changed views do not manifest themselves in the first years after returning from prison and exile. His first publications are comic works: *Dyadyushkin son* (1859; Eng. tr., *Uncle's Dream*, 1888) and *Selo Stepanchikovo i ego obitateli* (1859; Eng. tr., *The Friend of the Family*, 1887); these are followed by *Zapiski iz myortvogo doma* (1861–62; Eng. tr., *Buried Alive*, 1881, *Prison Life in Siberia*, 1887, *The House of the Dead*, 1915), an autobiographical account of his life in prison, and *Unizhonnye i oskorblyonnye* (1861; Eng. trs., *Injury and Insult*, 1886, *The Insulted and Injured*, 1915), a sentimental tale of mediocre quality. The change is pronounced in *Notes from the Underground*, which has been called the philosophical prelude to the great novels that followed. The basic view that is unfolded by the sardonic and self-contradictory narrator is that man by his nature will never permit himself to be subjected to organized happiness because he values his unfettered free will more than anything else. The great novels that follow may be looked on as a series of experiments in which Dostoyevsky takes up again and again the question of the limits of man's nature and the limits of freedom. *Prestupleniye i nakazaniye* (1866; Eng. tr., *Crime and Punishment*, 1886) is such an experiment, in which Raskolnikov tests the limits of his will and right to kill a useless old woman. The novel shows Dostoyevsky's extraordinary ability to use a variety of forms and devices, such as the sentimental tale, the gothic novel, and the novel of adventure, for serious philosophical ends.

In February 1867, Dostoyevsky married Anna Grigoryevna Snitkina, an 18-year-old girl whom he had hired in October 1866 to take his dictation of the text of *Igrok* (1866; Eng. tr., *The Gambler*, 1887). His first marriage to Marya Dmitriyevna Isayeva on Feb. 6, 1857, in Siberia ended with her death in 1874. Dostoyevsky's first marriage and his love affair with Polina Suslova from 1862 to 1865 were turbulent and punishing, but his marriage to Anna Snitkina was to be happy and harmonious. In April 1867 he left with his new bride for Europe, where they remained for more than four years. These were years of ceaseless moving, and of financial and emotional distress because of Dostoyevsky's compulsive gambling. They were also years in which he completed two of his major novels, *Idiot* (1869; Eng. tr., 1887) and *Besy* (1871–72; The Devils; Eng. tr., *The Possessed*, 1914). *The Idiot* was difficult for Dostoyevsky, and the notebooks to the novel show us that he went through a number of plans and changes in the Idiot's character before he was to see him as a modern-day Christ. The novel shows less control of form than does *Crime and Punishment*, but it is rich in imagination and creative energy. Nastasya Filippovna is probably his greatest female creation, and Prince Myshkin is almost unique in world literature. *The Possessed* was provoked by the political murder by Nechayev, a Russian nihilist, of one of his followers, and it quickly became a scorching indictment of Russian radicalism. But before Dostoyevsky was through, portions of an unfinished novel entitled *Zhitiye velikogo greshnika* (The Life a Great Sinner) were incorporated into the work and the political pamphlet had become a masterful interweaving of political and philosophical motifs.

After his return to Russia in July 1871, Dostoyevsky edited the conservative newspaper *Grazhdanin* during 1873 and the first part of 1874 and published as a supplement to this newspaper his *Dnevnik pisatelya* (Eng. tr., *The Diary of a Writer*, 1949), a miscellaneous commentary on various aspects of Russian life. He was to take up *The Diary of a Writer* in 1876 and 1877 and briefly in 1881 as a separate publication; it was in this newspaper that two of his best short stories were published: "Krotkaya" (1876; Eng. tr., "The Gentle Maiden, 1913;" "A Gentle Spirit," 1917; also tr. as "A Meek Young Girl," "The

Meek One") and "Son smeshnogo cheloveka" (1877; Eng. tr., "The Dream of a Ridiculous Man," 1917). Dostoyevsky made an attempt to understand the liberal and radical elements of the time in his writing of *Podrostok* (1875; Eng. tr., *A Raw Youth*, 1916), a novel not up to the quality of his other great novels. *Bratya Karamazovy* (1880; Eng. tr., *The Brothers Karamazov*, 1911) was written between 1878 and 1880, and it must be considered his greatest novel. Sigmund Freud ranked it, along with Sophocles' *Oedipus Rex* and Shakespeare's *Hamlet*, as one of the three greatest literary creations of all time. The novel is the culmination of Dostoyevsky's extraordinary creative vision. The four brothers represent the range of impulses in mankind, and the meeting between Christ and the Grand Inquisitor is a confrontation between the dark and light forces of mankind. In this scene Dostoyevsky presents his readers with a choice between the difficult and perhaps impossible freedom of Christ and the certain security of spiritual and material comfort in the lack of freedom in the organized world of the Grand Inquisitor. Dostoyevsky died on Jan. 28, 1881, about three months after completing *The Brothers Karamazov*.

Dostoyevsky's works are available in numerous translations. For critical interpretation see: K. Mochulsky, *Dostoyevsky: zhizn i tvorchestvo* (1947; Engl. tr., *Dostoevsky: His Life and Work*, 1967); E. Simmons, *Dostoyevsky, The Making of a Novelist* (1950); E. Wasiolek, *Dostoyevsky, The Major Fiction* (1964); D. Fanger, *Dostoyevsky and Romantic Realism* (1965).   E.W.

Drach, Ivan (1936–), Ukrainian poet, was born of peasant stock in the village of Telizhentsi, Kiev province and studied in Kiev and Moscow. A member of the Communist Party, Drach belonged to an unofficial group known as the *shestydesyatnyky* (the Generation of the 1960s), young poets in search of new values during Nikita Khrushchov's "thaw." In 1961, Drach published a controversial philosophical poem, "Nizh u sontsi" (Knife in the Sun). His collections of poetry, marked by striking imagery, include *Sonyashnyk* (1962; Sunflower), *Protuberantsi sertsya* (1965; Protuberances of the Heart), *Balada budniv* (1967; The Ballad of Everyday), and *Do dzherel* (1972; To the Sources). He has also written film scenarios. A selection of his poetry has appeared in English under the title *Orchard Lamps* (1978).   G.S.N.L.

Drachmann, Holger (1846–1908), Danish poet, novelist, playwright, and painter, was born in Copenhagen. His first poetic attempt was directly inspired by Georg BRANDES's provocative ideas (*see* DANISH LITERATURE). Drachmann's debut work, *Digte* (1872; Poems), contains political and social poems that often contain elements of revolutionary pathos. His collection *Dæmpede Melodier* (1875; Muted Melodies), indicates that he was likewise occupied by the struggle between the reactionary old and the victorious new. Besides poems of agitation, one also finds bohemian songs and ravishing poems about the bright nights and the sea as symbols of freedom extending beyond naturalism. This development is particularly noticeable in the novel *En Overkomplet* (1876; A Supernumerary), which, alternating between realism and fantasy, employs the Turgenev-influenced main motif of Drachmann's writing: the strong woman versus the weak man. Simultaneous with his growing spiritual intimacy, Drachmann departed from the Brandesian influence. His travel book, *Derovre fra Grænsen* (1877; Over There from the Border), glorifies Danish nationalism, and his antinaturalistic poem *Prindsessen og det halve Kongerige* (1878; The Princess and Half the Kingdom) rejects gray, ideological literature for the poetry of the fairy tale. This new orientation is most clearly expressed in the three large collections *Sange ved Havet* (1877; Songs by the Sea), *Ranker og Roser* (1879; Vines and Roses) and *Ungdom i Digt og Sang* (1879; Youth in Poetry and Song), through which Drachmann renewed Danish poetry. Adam Oehlenschlager, Henrik IBSEN, and Bjørnstjerne BJØRNSON were the Scandinavian writers who chiefly inspired Drachmann, whereas among the foreign writers, Goethe and Heinrich Heine contributed to his "lieder"-like tone. His broad metrical forms are reminiscent of Algernon Charles Swinburne, his egotism and the heroic attitude, of Lord Byron.

Drachmann's poetry became distinguished by classical tranquillity. Family life is idealized in *Gamle Guder og Nye* (1881; Old and New Gods). The popular and the nationalistic form the main elements in a series of sailor's stories, as well as in the fairy-tale play *Der var engag* (1885; Once upon a Time), Drachmann's most successful dramatic work. Toward the end of the 1880s his poetic vitality diminished, but the meeting with a young cabaret singer, called Edith by Drachmann, brought renewed inspiration. *Sangenes Bog* (1889; The Book of Songs) is dedicated to this new love, but its tone is mixed with grief: behind the hectic feeling of happiness lies the fear of approaching age. The novel *Forskrevet* (1890; Signed Away), in addition to being a critical confession, glorifies Edith as the embodiment of purity and beauty in a hypocritical time. As a stylistic piece of art, the book proves to be a culmination of impressionistic prose.

In the 1890s, Drachmann renewed his dramatic writing with a series of melodramas characterized by compact action and strongly lyrical qualities. The major work of this period is *Vølund Smed* (1894; Wayland the Smith); in the figure of the famous smith from the *Edda*—influenced by Shakespeare and Richard WAGNER—Drachmann created a gigantic symbol of his creative self. Drachmann regarded beauty and freedom as the main motifs of his production. As an extravagant Renaissance figure, he stood above his own down-to-earth times, but his poetry's infinite richness of rhythms and moods significantly influenced later Danish poetry.

See: P. V. Rubow, *Holger Drachmann's Ungdom* (1940), *Holger Drachmann 1878–97* (1945), and *Holger Drachmann Sidste Aar* (1950).   S.H.R.

Drieu la Rochelle, Pierre (1893–1945), French novelist, essayist, critic, and poet, was born in Paris into a middle-class family of Norman extraction. Such ancestry may explain his taste for both adventure and tradition, as well as his later revolutionary and reactionary tendencies. Drieu attended the Ecole des Sciences Politiques with a view to entering the diplomatic service, but he failed his last examination, and in August 1914 he found himself at the Battle of Charleroi. For Drieu, the bayonet charge was a profound experience, second only to the struggles of lovemaking in peacetime, as he makes clear in *La Comédie de Charleroi* (1934; Eng. tr., *The Comedy of Charleroi, and Other Stories*, 1973). All of Drieu's life and work was to be spread between those two poles; married twice, he also had many affairs, which made him a "man overlaid with women"—*L'Homme couvert de femmes* (1925) was, indeed, the title of his first novel—before he tended towards a mysticism he never really achieved. His political preferences passed from communism through a Pan-European socialism to fascism. On the literary scene, he flirted for a while with the surrealists (*see* FRENCH LITERATURE), but at bottom he remained an independent, Baudelairean dandy (*see* Charles BAUDELAIRE).

During World War II, Drieu became the editor of the *Nouvelle Revue française* and, from 1943 to 1944, he wrote for Lucien Combelle's review, *Révolution nationale*. Although in 1942 he again joined Jacques Doriot's Parti Populaire Français, he no longer believed in collaboration with the Nazis, and even less in the victory of the Axis Powers. This did not prevent him, however, from remaining faithful—at least on the surface—to these lost causes. In some ways like his friend André MALRAUX (to whom he stayed close throughout the war, in spite of their political differences), Drieu required contingent commitments, rather than being merely on the proper side. What in the last analysis counted most for him was the testimony of his own intimate yet contradictory demands. He committed suicide in 1945 as much from a metaphysical inclination (already manifest in his childhood) as from disillusionment with himself and with the world. Although his life was in many respects exemplary, Drieu was a "youth of his time" who knowingly explored all his inner contradictions and exposed them in a leisurely manner in his works.

In spite of their lack of constraint (or precisely because of it), Drieu's writings are now recognized as bearing, to a high degree, the modern stamp of authenticity. For instance, *Le Feu follet* (1931; Eng. trs., *The Fire Within*, 1965, *Will o' the Wisp*, 1966) is not only the fashionable story of a young Parisian addict who suffers the multiple effects of drug abuse in a capitalist milieu, it is also an exercise in style that is one or even two literary generations ahead of its time. In *Gilles* (1939), Drieu's most ambitious if not his most significant novel, he paints a fresco of the period between the world wars, where themes both social (culture, politics, religion) and private (aspiration, pleasure, lucidity) affect a protagonist who is very much like the author. In *Mémoires de Dirk Raspe* (1966), a posthumous work left unfinished so that death might complete it after *Récit secret* (1961; Eng. tr., *Secret Journal and Other Writings*, 1973), Drieu at last bridged the dialectic of things sacred and profane. If the plot borrows from Vincent Van Gogh's biography, another man "suicided by society" (as Antonin ARTAUD put it), the motif implies the transcendence of struggle and sex by means of love and art.

Since his first poems of *Interrogation* (1917), which celebrated in Claudelian odes (see Paul CLAUDEL) the "blood wedding" of the human being and the cosmic world, Drieu fundamentally thought that "decadence," whose current signs he identified almost everywhere in the West, could never be overcome in the individual unless he or she withdrew from society. It is indeed significant that the last works of this former "appraiser" of France and of Europe deal essentially with painting, literature, and religion. Of course, as some critics have pointed out, in so doing Drieu may have sought a way to sublimate his political error and failure before taking the ultimate step of suicide. But as a matter of fact he always considered the warrior equivalent to the monk, where both could not coincide as they do in the figure of the Knight Templar. In a decaying age that has surrendered to materialism, it is the function of the artist or the writer to replace the former guardians of the spirit. Hence the change from the first Drieu to the last one, who serenely resolves his contradiction through creativity.

Drieu's books are also noteworthy for their numerous insights into the character of women, especially that of rich women who are pitted against not so rich men, in a social class where love is subordinate to money. For Drieu himself this was a lifelong problem, and he wrote about it quite bluntly. From this point of view alone, his works are unique in contemporary French literature.

See: P. Andreu, *Drieu: témoin et visionnaire* (1952); F.

Grover, *Drieu la Rochelle* (1952); R. B. Leal, *Drieu la Rochelle: Decadence in Love* (1973); D. Desanti, *Drieu la Rochelle ou le séducteur mystifié* (1978); J. Hervier, *Deux individus contre l'histoire: Pierre Drieu la Rochelle, Ernst Jünger* (1978); P. Andreu and F. Grover, *Drieu la Rochelle* (1979).   M.H.

Dubillard, Roland (1923–), French playwright and short-story writer, was born in Paris. He is the author of such plays as *Si Camille me voyait* (1962; If Camille Saw Me), *Naïves Hirondelles* (1962; Naïve Swallows), *La Maison d'os* (1964; The House of Bones), *Le Jardin au betteraves* (1969; The Beet Garden), *Les Crabbes* (1971; The Crabs), and *Où boivent les vaches* (1973; Where Do the Cows Drink); of the essay *Méditation sur la difficulté d'être en bronze* (1972; Meditation on the Difficulty of Being in Bronze); and of short stories, collected in such volumes as *Olga ma vache* (Olga My Cow) and *Confession d'un fuemru de tabac* (1974; Confession of a Tobacco Smoker).

Dubillard's theater is first and foremost a poetic realm, but poetry for Dubillard is a language devoid of content. His dreams do not enact situations, and his characters are not imbued with great passions. Indeed, his protagonists differ from those we are accustomed to seeing in the conventional theater: they are essences living in a kind of anguished solitude, expressing their turmoil in the eternal present, speaking with one another in a language impregnated with dreams, silences, and variegated musical sonorities.

Dubillard's clusters of banalities mask feelings of frustration and solitude. His humor is never cruel or acidulous, but rather tender, restrained, and naive—admirably suited to his childlike characters, who are both present and absent, onstage physically but mentally existing in a world beyond. In *Méditation sur la difficulté d'être en bronze,* he synthesizes the pain of the creative individual (thus his own), who is forever seeking to fix his feelings, thoughts, and inspiration in some concrete object or entity, but who realizes at the same time the impossibility of stabilizing what is ephemeral.

See: G. Serreau, *Histoire du nouveau théâtre* (1966).
                                                                    B.K.

Du Bos, Charles (1882–1939), French critic, was born to a French father highly placed in fashionable racing circles and in the entourage of King Edward VII and to the daughter of an English banker, herself descended from the American Eustis family that supplied an ambassador to France. Du Bos's familiarity with Ralph Waldo Emerson and the English poets whom he read at Oxford (1900–01), as well as his successive sojourns (1902–07) in the Florence of Gabriele D'ANNUNZIO, the Berlin of Stefan GEORGE and Georg Simmel, and the England of Henry James, equipped him for the interpretation of foreign literatures. With the *Nouvelle Revue française* group, he labored, through the interpenetration of cultures, to develop the concept of the "European," synonymous with the fullest humanity.

For Du Bos, the enemy was Cartesian and Voltarian rationalism as well as the (to him) false classical unity that trisects the oneness of creative personality into man, writer, and Christian. This oneness was restored, he felt, by Paul CLAUDEL via Rousseau. Looking first to Henri BERGSON but also and increasingly to neo-Platonism, Du Bos combined moralism (without being moralistic), intuition, and ecstasy. Thus, outside of the France of Blaise Pascal and Charles BAUDELAIRE, he felt particularly at home in English, German, and Russian literatures. His Trinity was Shakespeare, Dante, and John Keats, while

Novalis and Water Pater provided sources of influential revelation. Friedrich NIETZSCHE figured as the noblest of adversaries, challenging him to a systematic distrust of inspired moments, particularly in the years 1918–27. But Du Bos "passed beyond" to Catholicism.

As a translator and as the editor of a series of works by foreign writers, Du Bos, who possessed unusual powers of conversation and extensive friendships, sowed germs of thought and influence freely, like a *grand seigneur* of ideas. His view of literature won him a lodging (not without protest on his part) in Albert THIBAUDET's *Quartier des philosophes*. For Du Bos, literature is "life becoming conscious of itself when, in the soul of a man of genius, it joins its plenitude of expression." By life he meant the experience of a Bergsonian *durée* (*see* Henri BERGSON), the continuity of consciousness in its creative dynamism. The soul, known intuitively—and this was the major conviction of this French introspective—is so related to life in this sense that, in the "act" of writing, it achieves expression of both.

Seven volumes of his *Approximations* (1922–37), gathered into one large volume in 1965, and the *Extraits d'un journal* (1928, enlarged ed., 1931; Extracts of a Journal), followed by nine posthumous volumes of journals (1946–61), bear reciprocal relationships. But the *Journal* is a sketchbook for almost everything Du Bos wrote, including a volume on *Byron et le besoin de la fatalité* (1929; Eng. tr., *Byron and the Need of Fatality,* 1932), one on Benjamin Constant, a figure embodying some of Du Bos's main preoccupations; and one on Goethe. Three articles of extreme subtlety, "Du spirituel dans l'ordre littéraire" (Concerning the Spiritual in the Literary Order, in *Virgile,* 1930), can be read in relation to a *Dialogue avec André Gide* (1929), where the "spiritual interpreter," despite an exceptionally capacious "house of thought," draws the line at what he considers the exploitation of a spiritual gift in the interest of art alone. Du Bos's slight volume *Comtesse de Noailles* (1949; *see* Anna de NOAILLES) is important for the development of an idea of genius taken from Lev Tolstoy: the inability not to do what one does. Appropriately, Du Bos's final essay, *What Is Literature* (1940), was written in English and delivered in 1938 as three lectures before the faculty of Saint Mary's College, Notre Dame, Indiana.

With the advent of the "new criticism," particularly by those termed the "critics of consciousness," Du Bos has been singled out, with Jacques RIVIÈRE, as the founder of a criticism that aims at the transposition of mental worlds, that of the critic into that of the creator. Georges Poulet, himself the champion of a "criticism of identification," has shown how, in the case of Du Bos, thought suddenly comes to life out of an original inertia by the "grace" of a literary or artistic encounter. The critic's mind becomes the willing receptacle for a spiritual life not its own and is rewarded by becoming a second voice, developing and enriching the original creation. In this sense, criticism becomes "literature about literature." To Du Bos, Poulet acknowledges his debt for a point of departure that he himself developed more systematically.

The second of perhaps the two best essays on Du Bos, written by Jean-Pierre RICHARD, emphasizes the special concerns of the author of *Littérature et sensation*. Having characterized Du Bos's *approximation* "sur le milieu intérieur chez Flaubert" (interior landscape in Flaubert) as the source of all "modern" criticism of Flaubert, he studies the critic's language, especially his criticism-metaphors. Yet we must not lose sight of Du Bos's insistence that when he is most "subjective," he finds himself most "objective." This is the philosophical issue at the heart of his "spiritual interpretation."

See: C. Dédéyan, *Le Cosmopolitisme littéraire de Charles Du Bos*, 2 vols. (1967); J.-P. Richard, "La Méthode critique de Charles Du Bos," *MLR* 62 (1967), no. 3; J. Bossière, *Perception, critique, et sentiment de vivre chez Charles Du Bos* (1969); G. Poulet, *La Conscience critique* (1971); A. P. Bertocci, "Charles Du Bos and the Critique of Genius," in *Modern French Criticism*, ed. by J. K. Simon (1972). A.P.B.

Dučić, Jovan (1874–1943), Serbian poet and prose writer, was born in Trebinje, Herzegovina. He was the leading representative of the "Moderna" movement in Serbian literature in the first decades of the 20th century (*see* SERBIAN LITERATURE). After studying to become a teacher, Dučić taught for a while in Mostar. He continued his education in Geneva and then in Paris, where he fell under the influence of the French symbolists. While continuing to write poetry, he entered the diplomatic service in 1907, holding positions in various European capitals until 1941, when he emigrated to the United States. He died in Gary, Ind.

Dučić's first book of poetry, *Pjesme* (1901; Poems), appeared at the time when Serbian literature was drawing closer to the modern European mainstream. Indeed, he actively encouraged this trend. Other collections of poems followed: *Jadranski soneti* (1906; Adriatic Sonnets), *Pesme* (1908; Poems), the prose poems *Plave legende* (1930; Blue Legends), *Carski soneti* (1930; Imperial Sonnets), and others. Dučić also wrote a sophisticated book of travel impressions, *Gradovi i himere* (1932; Cities and Chimeras), which is the best of its genre in Serbian literature; a book of essays in popular philosophy, *Blago cara Radovana* (1932; The Treasure of Tsar Radovan); and essays on various writers and their works. The first edition of his *Sabrana dela* (Collected Works) was published in 1929–32, and the second in 1969.

Dučić was an esthete, with a refined taste and an aristocratic spirit. He strove in his poetry for formal excellence expressed through clarity, precision, elegance, musical quality, and picturesque images. His subject matter and unique style, reflecting the manner of the French decadent poets, brought a new spirit to Serbian verse. Unlike previous Serbian poets, who were either romantically or realistically oriented, Dučić was attracted to such themes as a mournful sunset, a disconsolate weeping willow, a tower clock striking in the silent night. His poems to and about women show the sentiments of a man yearning for satisfaction and yet convinced beforehand of his failure. In fact, Dučić's poetry generally reveals a highly sensitive artist with a basically pessimistic outlook. He has sometimes been criticized for this, as well as for his inclination toward art for art's sake. Nevertheless, he is considered one of the finest craftsmen in Serbian poetry.

See: J. Skerlić, "Jovan Dučić," *LMS* 210 (1901): 77–86; A. G. Matoš, *Eseji i feljtoni o srpskim piscima* (1952), pp. 222–53; B. Popović, "Jedna književna analiza," *Srpski književni glasnik* 32 (1914): 33–40, 126–37, 200–17; P. Slijepčević, "Jovan Dučić," in *Sabrani ogledi*, vol. 1 (1956): pp. 93–147. V.D.M.

Dudintsev, Vladimir Dmitrievich (1918–), Russian prose writer, was born in Kupyansk, in the province of Kharkov, and educated at the Moscow Juridical Institute. He owes his place in Soviet Russian literary history to the great controversy provoked by the publication in 1956 of his novel *Ne khlebom yedinym* (Eng. tr., *Not By Bread Alone*, 1957), which deals with the struggles of an honest, generous, and talented but unknown inventor, Lopatkin, against the stultifying effects of an industrial establishment that is in the control of crude, ruthless, self-indul-

gent careerists, typified by Drozdov. Although the novel is undistinguished as a work of art, its theme obviously struck a responsive chord in the Soviet public, and it was widely read and discussed. Despite the fact that its criticism of the Soviet Drozdovs in no way conflicts with any enlightened interpretation of the official Soviet doctrine of socialist realism, the novel and its author were subjected to a barrage of attacks organized by the Soviet literary establishment.

See: K. Paustovsky, "The Drozdovs," and L. Sobolev, "Millions are Listening," in *The Year of Protest, 1956*, ed. by H. McLean and W. N. Vickery (1961), pp. 156–63. W.B.E.

Duhamel, Georges, pseud. of Denis Thévenin (1884–1966), French novelist, essayist, poet, dramatist, and critic, was born in Paris. The son of a physician, he too earned an M.D. degree. With a group of friends, he founded in 1906 the Abbaye de Créteil, a short-lived colony of young poets and artists seeking self-fulfillment in community living, while earning a livelihood by operating a printing press. It is here that his first book of verse, *Des légendes, des batailles* (Legends, Battles), was printed in 1907. Four more collections of mostly vers-librist poems were to follow between 1909 and 1920, after which Duhamel—who had been appointed poetry critic of the *Mercure de France* in 1911—decided henceforth "to quench his poetic fervor in prose."

Turning to the stage, he had his first two plays, *La Lumière* (1911; Eng. tr., *The Light*, 1914) and *Dans l'ombre des statues* (1912; Eng. tr., *In the Shadow of Statues*, 1914), produced by André ANTOINE at the Odéon. In 1913, Jacques Rouché staged *Le Combat* (Eng. tr., 1915) at the Théâtre des Arts, and in 1920 *L'œuvre des athlètes* (The Work of the Athletes) was presented at Jacques COPEAU's Vieux-Colombier. In 1923, the Pitoëff Company (*see* Georges PITOËFF) performed Duhamel's last play, *La Journée des aveux* (The Day of Avowals), at the Comédie des Champs-Elysées. His failure to achieve notable success eventually discouraged him from further theatrical efforts.

At the outbreak of World War I, Duhamel volunteered as an army surgeon and was put in charge of a front-line mobile surgical unit. The human tragedies that he witnessed supplied the material for two of his highly successful books of short stories, *Vie des martyrs: 1914–1916* (1917; Eng. tr., *The New Book of Martyrs*, 1918) and *Civilisation: 1914–1917* (1918; Eng. tr., 1919), which won the Goncourt Prize. Both war books expose, in compassionate vignettes, the senseless sufferings of the innocent and the inhumanity of a technocratic civilization responsible for a catastrophe of such magnitude. Duhamel's indictment of the excesses of quantitative thinking, his advocacy of peace, individualism, and a humanistic civilization, became the cornerstone of his philosophy.

It was in the interwar period that Duhamel, who from then on devoted all his time to literature, reached the peak of his career as one of France's foremost novelists and thinkers. His five-volume cyclic novel *Vie et aventures de Salavin* (1920–32; Eng. tr., *Salavin*, 1936) relates the adventures of a hapless introvert in desperate search of perfection. Salavin hopes to redeem himself successively through friendship, sainthood, political involvement, and self-sacrifice, until he meets his death, aware of his failure, but convinced that given a chance to relive his quest, he would gain salvation. Duhamel then undertook the monumental task of writing what he believed to be his magnum opus, the 10-volume *Chronique des Pasquier* (1933–44; Eng. tr., *The Pasquier Chronicles* [vols. 1–5], 1937; *Cécile Pasquier* [vols. 6–8], 1940; *Suzanne and Joseph Pasquier* [vols. 9–10], 1946). This work is the saga of a French lower middle-class family's rise to prominence under the Third Republic. Laurent Pasquier, the central figure and the author's fictional counterpart, is a young biologist with high ideals. He achieves fame as a distinguished scholar, but in the face of his family's tribulations and his own quandaries, he ends up in deep disillusionment.

Between the wars, Duhamel wrote many essays. In *La Possession du monde* (1919; Eng. tr., *The Heart's Domain*, 1919), *Querelles de famille* (1932; Family Quarrels), and *L'Humaniste et l'automate* (1933; The Humanist and the Automat), he restated in philosophical terms the criticism voiced in his fictional writings. A tireless voyager, he wrote as many as nine travel diaries. Whereas in *Le Voyage de Moscou* (1927) his distrust of communism did not prevent him from paying tribute to the achievements of the Russian people, no such forgiveness is found in the controversial *Scènes de la vie future* (1930; Eng. tr., *America: The Menace*, 1931) where, following a six-week tour of the United States, he castigated with bitterness and wit American industrial civilization, predicting that Europe would fall victim to its cancerous growth.

During the German invasion of France in 1940, Duhamel again took up medicine and cared for civilian casualties in the Rennes area. Under the occupation, he led a secluded life in Paris, harassed by the Germans and participating in clandestine literary activities. After the liberation of France, Duhamel, then 61, resumed his travels and published more essays and works of fiction, including *Le Voyage de Patrice Périot* (1950; Eng. tr., *Patrice Periot*, 1952), a partly autobiographical novel on postwar polarization within the family and in public life. This also proved to be a time for taking stock, during which Duhamel published his five-volume memoirs under the general title *Lumières sur ma vie* (1944–53; Eng. tr., *Light on My Days*, 1948 [vols. 1–2 only]).

Duhamel was an elegant stylist whose polished if sometimes studied prose abounds in delicately lyrical overtones, flashes of caustic humor, and outbursts of prophetic indignation. While in the 1950s he was eclipsed by the younger literary generation, it was precisely the appeal of the new trends that eventually brought him back into the limelight. Although *The Pasquier Chronicles* continues to be regarded by younger critics as an obsolescent work of largely historic interest, Salavin's spiritual odyssey is now being hailed as an early example of the alienated hero's bewilderment in an absurdly indifferent world. Likewise, Duhamel's attitude toward the mechanical age and its effects on man and his environment speaks with renewed persuasiveness to the critics of wars, pollution, and a conflict-ridden consumer society. Duhamel was elected to the Académie Française in 1935.

See: C. Santelli, *Georges Duhamel* (1947); P.-H. Simon, *Georges Duhamel* (1947); L. C. Keating, *Critic of Civilization: Georges Duhamel and His Writing* (1965); B. L. Knapp, *Georges Duhamel* (1972).   K.H.

Dujardin, Edouard (1861–1949), French novelist, poet, dramatist, critic, historian, and editor, was born in Saint-Gervais. He is best remembered for his novel *Les Lauriers sont coupés* (1888; Eng. tr., *We'll to the Woods No More*, 1938), which was ignored for 35 years and then brought back to life by James Joyce, who acknowledged it as his source for the technique of interior monologue in *Ulysses* (1922). *Les Lauriers*, which appeared serially in 1887 and was published in book form in 1888, 1897, and finally in 1924 with a preface by Valery LARBAUD, is a simple, lyrical love story, composed in short sentences

and told through the images in the inner life (or the unconscious) of a young man.

Dujardin claimed as inspirations the poetry of Stéphane MALLARMÉ, the musical motifs of Richard WAGNER, and the dramatic monologues of Racine. Except for Mallarmé, Joris-Karl HUYSMANS and George Moore, writers and critics did not notice the importance of *Les Lauriers* when it first appeared, and Dujardin continued other literary pursuits. He was among the first of the symbolist poets to write in vers libre, publishing his work in journals between 1885 and 1912 and in a collection, *Poésies* (Poems), in 1913. As a playwright, he used legends and poetry in such creations as *La Fin d'Antonia* (The End of Antonia), whose production in 1895 sparked one of the battles of symbolism. His other plays include *Les Argonautes, Le Mystère du Dieu mort et réssuscite* (The Mystery of the Dead and Resuscitated God), and *Le Retour éternel* (The Eternal Return).

Dujardin also produced several works on religious history. He taught a religion course at the Sorbonne for many years. In *La Source du fleuve chrétien* (1906; Eng. tr., *The Source of the Christian Tradition*, 1911), *Le Dieu Jésus* (1927; God Jesus), and *Demain ici ainsi la révolution* (1928; Tomorrow Here Thus the Revolution), he portrays the origin of Christianity as a necessary expression of the social realities of its time as well as of human spiritual evolution.

As a critic, he describes, in his *Le Monologue intérieur* (1931; The Interior Monologue), the forces that influenced him to write *Les Lauriers,* including his belief in the poetry and music of language and the importance of an inner reality. He shows that Fyodor DOSTOYEVSKY, Robert Browning, and Marcel PROUST do not really use the *monologue intérieur.* Another critical essay is *Les Premiers poètes du vers libre* (1922; The First Poets of the Free Verse). Dujardin also founded important journals, including *La Revue indépendante, La Revue wagnérienne, La Revue des idées, Pages libres,* and *Les Cahiers idéalistes.*

See: J. Cassou, "Edouard Dujardin et l'évolution du symbolisme," *Revue européenne,* vol. 3 (1924); P. Handler, "The Case for Edouard Dujardin," *RR* 56 (1965); R. Bordaz, "Edouard Dujardin et le monologue intérieur," *La Revue des deux mondes* (October-December 1970); F. Weissman, "Edouard Dujardin, le monologue intérieur et Racine," *La Revue d'histoire littéraire de la France* 74 (1974).   C.E.F.S.

Dullin, Charles (1865–1949), French stage director and actor, was born in Yenne, the youngest of 19 children. In 1905 he went to Paris to become an actor, learning his craft first by working in 19th-century melodramas. He then acted successively with André ANTOINE, Jacques COPEAU (with whom he shared ideals and artistic views), and Firmin GÉMIER, before establishing his own theater in Paris, l'Atelier (1921–41). In this "laboratory for dramatic experiment" that was also a rigorous workshop for actors, Dullin, a demanding teacher and an outstanding actor himself, stressed mime and improvisation in an atmosphere of artistic purity and integrity. Aiming at educating his audiences away from the vulgarity of commercial theater, he made known to the French, in free adaptations, the great plays of Aristophanes (*Peace, The Birds*), Calderón, and Shakespeare (*Richard III*) and other Elizabethans (Ben Jonson's *Volpone*). He was the first to stage Luigi PIRANDELLO in Paris, and he also presented the first plays of Marcel ACHARD, Armand SALACROU, Jean ANOUILH, Jean COCTEAU, and Jean-Paul SARTRE. He was later named director of the Théâtre Sarah-Bernhardt (1941–47).

The most influential of the Cartel of Four (which included Georges PITOËFF, Gaston BATY, and Louis JOUVET), Dullin had utmost respect for the text, shunning both naturalism and realism, and instead enhancing the play by use of color, pantomime, ballet, and music. His views on the development of popular theater and the creation of "artistic centers" throughout France were prophetic. Jean VILAR and Jean-Louis BARRAULT, among others, were greatly influenced by him.

See: D. Knowles, *French Drama of the Inter-War Years* (1967), pp. 23–28. A.R.

Duras, Marguerite (1914–), French novelist, dramatist, and filmmaker, was born in Cochinchine (now in Vietnam). In 1932 she moved to Paris, where she studied law, mathematics, and political science. Duras published her first novel in 1943. Her major novels include *Un Barrage contre le Pacifique* (1950; Eng. tr., *The Sea Wall*, 1959), *Moderato cantabile* (1958; Eng. tr., 1960), *Le Ravissement de Lol V. Stein* (1964; Eng. tr., *The Ravishing of Lol Stein*, 1967), *Le Vice-Consul* (1968; Eng. tr., *The Vice-Consul*, 1968), *Détruire, dit-elle* (1969; Eng. tr., *Destroy, She Said*, 1970), *Abahn, Sabana, David* (1970), and *L'Amour* (1972; Love). A two-volume collection of her plays was published in 1965 as *Théâtre* (Eng. tr., 1967). In 1960, Duras wrote the screenplay for Alain Resnais's *Hiroshima mon amour*. She has directed stage productions of some of her own plays, e.g., *Le Shaga* and *Yes, peut-être* (pub. in *Théâtre*, vol. 2, 1968). Duras has also directed film versions of her works, including *La Musica* (1966; Eng. tr., in *Suzanne Andler; La Musica & L'Amante Anglaise*, 1975), *Détruire, dit-elle* (1969), *Jaune le soleil* (1972; The Sun Is Yellow), *Nathalie Granger* (1973), *India Song* (1973; Eng. tr., 1976), and *La Femme du Gange* (1974; The Woman of the Ganges).

The protagonists of Duras's works have broken away from conventions and bourgeois values and live in a state of anguished availability and expectancy. In her earlier books, love is the only escape from bordeom and the aimlessness of life. In later works, however, love is seen as a limited, individualistic solution and becomes subservient to a commitment to total revolution. Always a liberal, and for a time a militant in the French Communist Party, Duras has, in recent years, dissociated herself from both communism and the intellectual Left to advocate the rejection of all forms of social order and the crippling heritage of culture and knowledge. This ideology is reflected in her works. Her characters tend to lose their very identity because of their efforts, whether deliberate or unconscious, to sever themselves from their background, their past, and their memories, and they exhibit signs of schizophrenia and insanity—a condition Duras considers a desirable form of the individual's revolt.

Yet Duras's radicalism is aesthetic as well as ideological. While her early novels were fairly conventional in form and content, her later works increasingly eschewed plot, traditional motivations, and psychology as they dissolved the boundaries between narrative fiction, drama, and poetry. Language is divested of its utilitarian function; through a process of grammatical and syntactic simplification and logical deconstruction, it becomes both the instrument and the result of the "destruction" that Duras sees as the prerequisite to the individual's liberation.

See: A. Cismaru, *Marguerite Duras* (1971); A. Vircondelet, *Marguerite Duras* (1972). M.B.-C.

Durkheim, Emile (1858–1917), French sociologist and philosopher, was born in Epinal. He taught at the University of Bordeaux from 1887 to 1902 and at the Sorbonne for the rest of his life. Some 50 years after sociology had received its letters patent from Auguste Comte, Durkheim found it—in France at least—still inorganic and undeveloped. At the time of his death he had made it, with the semiindependent help of Lucien Lévy-Bruhl (1857–1939), a thoroughly autonomous science, complete with a charter, a program of studies, a review (*Année sociologique*, 1898–1913, continued by others after 1923 and superseded in 1934 by the *Annales sociologiques*), and, last but not least, an impressive team of workers eager to follow in the master's footsteps (including Célestin Bouglé, Henri Hubert, Marcel Mauss, François Simiand, Paul Fauconnet, Maurice Halbwachs, Charles Lalo, and Georges Davy.

Durkheim's four main works are: *De la division du travail social*, his doctoral dissertation (1893: Eng. tr., *Emile Durkheim on the Division of Labor in Society*, 1933); *Les Règles de la méthode sociologique* (1895; Eng. tr., *The Rules of Sociological Method*, 1938); *Le Suicide* (1897; Eng. tr., *Suicide: A Study in Sociology*, 1952); and *Les Formes élémentaires de la vie religieuse: le système totémique en Australie* (1912; Eng. tr., *The Elementary Forms of the Religious Life*, 1915). Two of these are deserving of special mention. *Les Règles de la méthode sociologique*, somewhat reminiscent in title and purpose of the *Discours de la méthode* of Descartes, effects an abrupt separation between sociology and individual psychology and insists that social facts be considered as "things," that is to say, as entirely original syntheses with no relation to their personal constituents. In *Les Formes élémentaires de la vie religieuse*, Durkheim, a deeply religious spirit who counted rabbis among his relatives, asserts that religion is the social fact par excellence, not only because it is social in its essence and origins, but because all collective representations—laws, customs, traditions, fashions, tastes, revolutions—are religious in character, having the same aura of coercion and supra-individual power that surrounds the mystical gatherings of primitive tribes.

See: M. Halbwachs, "La Doctrine d'Emile Durkheim," in *RevPh* 85 (1918): 353–411; G. Davy, *Emile Durkheim* (1927); G. Gurvitch, *Essais de sociologie* (1938), pp. 68–90, 113–69, 189–93, 277–306; H. Alpert, *Emile Durkheim and His Sociology* (1939); D. LaCapra, *Emile Durkheim: Sociologist and Philosopher* (1972); S. Lukes, *Emile Durkheim: His Life and Work, a Historical and Critical Study* (1972); E. Wallwork, *Durkheim: Morality and Milieu* (1972); R. A. Nisbet, *The Sociology of Emile Durkheim* (1974); P. Q. Hirst, *Durkheim, Bernard and Epistemology* (1975). J.-A.B. rev. D.W.A.

Dürrenmatt, Friedrich (1921–), Swiss playwright, novelist, and essayist, was born in Konolfingen, canton Bern. He is Switzerland's most important playwright and one of the most accomplished dramatists in the succession of Bertolt BRECHT. A student of philosophy and theology, Dürrenmatt experimented with short stories reminiscent of Franz KAFKA. In 1947 he created his first theater scandal with the chaotic drama *Es steht geschrieben* (It Is Written), a combination of street ballad and religious comic strip. After the failure of *Der Blinde* (1948; The Blind Man), an allegorical drama in which the struggle between nihilism and faith ends with the victory of the latter, Dürrenmatt experienced his first international success with the "a-historical historical comedy" *Romulus der Groß* (1949; Eng. tr., *Romulus the Great*, 1964). In *Romulus*, the last Roman emperor is portrayed as a timid poultry farmer who allows his empire to perish in order to save humanity.

Dürrenmatt's next important play, *Die Ehe des Herrn Mississippi* (1952; Eng. tr., *The Marriage of Mr. Missis-*

sippi, 1964) reveals his indebtedness to the morality theater of Frank WEDEKIND as well as to the tradition of the baroque "world theater" and its satirization by Johann Nepomuk NESTROY. Dürrenmatt's play concerns three world reformers who fail in their missionary zeal because "everything can be changed, except man." This thesis represents a challenge to Brecht's statement that "the world can be shown on stage if it is shown as a changeable world." Dürrenmatt's religious morality play *Ein Engel kommt nach Babylon* (1953; Eng. tr., *An Angel Comes to Babylon*, 1964) shows the incompatibility of power and grace. A young girl, Korrubi, is given by the grace of God to the most miserable man in Babylon. He is not, as everybody assumes, the beggar Akki but King Nebuchadnezzar, who crushes God's gift and builds the Tower of Babel "aiming at the heart of his enemy."

Dürrenmatt's most successful play—the one that made him a modern classic—is the "tragic comedy" *Der Besuch der alten Dame* (1956; Eng. tr., *The Visit*, 1958). The "richest woman on earth" returns to her native town of Güllen (Swiss-German for "manure") in order to demand the life of a former lover who wronged her. By promising wealth for everyone, she succeeds in inducing the impoverished community to assassinate their fellow citizen, thus demonstrating the corruptibility of human nature. In Dürrenmatt's *Die Physiker* (1962; Eng. tr., *The Physicists*, 1963), three famous physicists seeking a deadly formula hide as patients in an asylum only to witness the formula being stolen by a mad doctor who wants to achieve world domination.

In his essay "21 Points about *The Physicists*" as well as in the elaborate *Theater-probleme* (1955; Eng. tr., *Problems of the Theatre*, 1958) Dürrenmatt tries to explain his theory of the "tragic comedy," which he uses "to correct man's concept of reality." He insists that Friedrich Schiller's idea of the tragic has become unworkable because it presupposes a clear concept of the world that has been lost in the nuclear age. Therefore "we can be reached only by comedy" behind which the tragic becomes visible. Dürrenmatt thus creates grotesque counterrealities (the influence of such writers as Jonathan Swift and Mark Twain is evident) in his plays *Der Meteor* (1966; Eng. tr., *The Meteor*, 1973), *Porträt eines Planeten* (1971; Portrait of a Planet), and *Der Mitmacher* (1973; The Accessory). As a director, Dürrenmatt tried his ideas on the stages of Basel and Zürich with adaptations of plays by Shakespeare, Goethe, Johan August STRINDBERG, and Gotthold Lessing. In addition to his stage works, he has written numerous radio plays, short stories, several detective novels—among them *Der Richter und sein Henker* (1952; Eng. tr., *The Judge and His Hangman*, 1954), and *Das Versprechen* (1957; Eng. tr., *The Pledge*, 1959)—and many essays and speeches conveniently collected in *Theater, Schriften und Reden* (1966; Theater, Essays and Speeches).

See: H. Bänziger, *Friedrich Dürrenmatt* (1960); E. Brock-Sulzer, *Friedrich Dürrenmatt: Stationen seines Werkes* (1973); U. Profitlich, *Friedrich Dürrenmatt, Komödienbegriff, Komödienstruktur* (1973); P. Spycher, *Friedrich Dürrenmatt, Das erzählerische Werk* (1972).

R.K.

Durtain, Luc, pseud. of André Nepveu (1881–1959), French novelist, poet, dramatist, essayist, and critic, was born in Paris. He studied medicine, practicing otolaryngology all his life. Durtain made his literary debut with *L'Etape nécessaire* (1906; The Necessary Stage), a book of brief narratives and impressionistic notes viewed by later critics as foreshadowing dadaism (*see* FRENCH LITERATURE). Introduced by Jules ROMAINS to the writers of the *Abbaye*—so named for their short-lived experiment in community living in a literary and artistic "monastery"—he became a friend and travel companion of Georges DUHAMEL and Charles VILDRAC. After seeing active service as an army doctor in World War I, he traveled extensively in Europe, the Americas, and the Orient. Durtain's voyages supplied the material for his travel books on the USSR, Scandinavia, Indochina, and South America. His 11-volume fictional cycle *Conquêtes du monde* (1906–37; Conquests of the World) has been seen as a cosmopolitan's attempt at self-discovery through the scrutiny of man's fate in a shrinking world. It includes four novels dealing with life in the United States: *Quarantième étage* (1927; 40th Floor), *Hollywood dépassé* (1928; Hollywood Surpassed), *Captain O.K.* (1931), and *Frank et Marjorie* (1934). While deploring the excesses of American industrial civilization, Durtain praised its vitality and progressive outlook. He also devoted a four-volume cyclic novel, *Mémoires de votre vie* (1947–50; Memories of Your Life), to the European scene between 1896 and 1945.

Durtain's prose, forceful, nervous, and abrupt, is marked by unconventional imagery and an occasional touch of hermetic obscurity. His principal books of verse, *Kong Harald* (1914), *Le Retour des hommes* (1920; The Return of Men), and *Perspectives* (1924), were largely inspired by the aesthetic canons of the *Abbaye*. Durtain's plays, *Le Donneur de sang* (1927; The Blood Donor) and *Le Mari singulier* (1937; The Strange Husband), achieved but momentary success. Selections of his critical essays appeared under the title *D'homme à homme* (1932; From Man to Man).

See: C. Sénéchal, *Luc Durtain et les Conquêtes du monde* (1930); Y. Chatelain, *Luc Durtain et son œuvre* (1932).

K.H.

Durych, Jaroslav (1886–1962), Czech novelist and poet, was the outstanding representative of the Catholic movement in modern Czech literature. He was born in Hradec Králové, studied medicine at the University of Prague, and served as an army doctor during World War I. He rose to the rank of colonel in the medical corps of the Czechoslovak army. After World War II the government imposed a ban of silence on Durych because of his conservative political tendencies; the post-1948 Communist regime broadened this ban to complete suppression, although a partial rehabilitation of his work had just begun at the time of his death, in Prague, in 1962.

Durych's short stories and novels have a great variety of settings, but all are variations on one theme: man's desire for divine grace. This grace can be found in mystical union with God, in the love of a pure, simple woman, in the humility of the poorest beggar, and in moments preceding death. Durych, a convinced Catholic of the neo-Thomist persuasion, wanted to create a Catholic art that aspired to the Absolute, while reviving the Catholic glories of Czech history. But these spiritual aspirations were always offset by Durych's strong instincts: his sensuality, which struggled with his cult of innocence and purity; his rebelliousness against social oppression, which seems difficult to reconcile with his glorification of the Counter-Reformation; and his predilection for the horrible and cruel, the grotesque and even brutal, which frequently debased his urge toward mystical ecstasy.

Durych's small legends and fairy tales, graceful or horrible, comprise some of his best work, whereas his full-length novels suffer from disjointed plots, repetitions, and monotony. His novels include *Na horách* (1919; On the Mountains), a poetic love story with a dim medieval setting; *Sedmikráska* (1925; The Daisy); *Paní Anežka Ber-*

ková (1931; Mrs. Agnes Berk); and *Píseň o růži* (1934; The Song of the Rose), the last three set in small towns. Durych's most important novel, *Bloudění* (3 vols., 1929; Eng. tr., *The Descent of the Idol,* 1935), is a large-scale historical novel. It is set during the Thirty Years War, and the figures of the great general Albrecht von Wallenstein and of the Holy Roman emperor, Ferdinand II are part of the background. In the foreground are a Czech Protestant emigrant and a Catholic girl of Spanish origin whose love finds fulfillment only at the hour of death. Although Durych treated the civilization of the Jesuit baroque with sympathy and understanding, his strained and ornate style, fantastic landscapes, feverish visions, superhuman passions, and grandiose battle scenes are "expressionist" in a highly modernistic manner rather than imitations of 17th-century style. At the least, *Bloudění* is a welcome reaction to the antiquarian type of historical writing produced by such authors as Alois Jirásek and Zikmund Winter. A particularly successful example of Durych's mastery of the short story can be found in his next work, a collection of three stories, *Rekviem* (1930; Requiem); a translation of one of them, "Wallenstein's Tomb," appeared in the *Slavonic Review* 11, no. 32 (1932–33): 269–85. Durych's novel *Masopust* (1938; The Carnival), set in the 16th century, contains his usual motifs of random wandering and searching for the one predestined woman, but they are varied with less effect than in *Bloudění*. His final novel, *Služebníci neužiteční* (1940; The Unprofitable Servants), is the first volume of an uncompleted trilogy treating the work of the Society of Jesus, *Země* (The Land).

Durych also wrote distinguished songs and verse, mostly in the simple popular style of ballads, which were collected in *Básně* (1930; Poems), and some dramas on themes of martyrdom, notably *Svatý Václav* (1925; Saint Wenceslaus), which try to revive the form of the 17th-century Spanish *autos*. His miscellaneous prose includes travel impressions from Germany, Italy and Spain, reminiscences, and some criticism expounding neo-Thomist dogmas or attacking different contemporary ways of thinking, for example, *Ejhle, člověk* (1928; Behold a Man), and *Váhy života a umění* (1933; The Scales of Life and Art). Durych admired Otokar BŘEZINA, to whom he devoted an early pamphlet (1918) in which he declared his allegiance to a symbolist art permeated with the Catholic spirit. Of all the many Czech Catholic writers who flourished before 1948, Durych came nearest to achieving such an art.

See: J. Bartoš, *Kdo jest Jaroslav Durych?* (1930); J. Otradovicová, *Básnický profil Jaroslava Durycha* (1943).

R.W.

Dutch literature. Dutch literature of the modern period begins with the literary revolution of the 1880s, or "De Beweging van Tachtig" (The Movement of the Eighties), as it is usually called. A group of young writers in Amsterdam rose up to throw off the dead weight of the past, to get rid of the clichés and meaningless rhetoric of the older literary generation. Powerful currents, generated by two important literary sources, England and France, aided them in their work of renewal. The English romantics, especially Percy Bysshe Shelley and John Keats, inspired the new Dutch poets to express genuine emotions in their verse, and the lyric and the sonnet became their favorite forms. Image, melody, and rhythm—indeed, the word itself—received new attention, as these young writers sought to create an individualistic poetic language. From France came the stimulus of Gustave Flaubert, Emile ZOLA, and the naturalists, which revealed itself most clearly in the development of the Dutch novel.

It would be an oversimplification to pretend that Dutch literature was completely lost in darkness when the leaders of "The Movement of the Eighties" came to rescue it. Everhardus Johannes Potgieter had established *De Gids* (The Guide) in 1837, and with the aid of his fellow editor, Conrad Busken Huet, he attempted to raise the literary standards in the Netherlands and to introduce his readers to the great achievements in other European literatures. In 1865, Huet offended influential sections of the public with two articles he had written, and resigned his editorial position. Potgieter stuck by his friend, and also left *De Gids*. Huet did not publish *Het Land van Rembrand* until almost 20 years later, and although some of the factual material is now out of date, it still remains a highly interesting and perceptive study of Dutch culture in the 17th century. Another forerunner of the literary change that was to sweep Holland was Eduard Douwes Dekker, who, writing under the pseudonym of Multatuli ("I have borne much"), quickly achieved a national and international reputation with his autobiographical novel *Max Havelaar* (1860). A master of satire and sarcasm, he exposed not only the weaknesses and injustices of Dutch colonialism in what was then the East Indies, but the follies and limitations of the bourgeoisie in Holland. Neither Potgieter nor Huet recognized his talent, but his book, which remains the greatest Dutch novel of the 19th century, led to political reform, and earned him the respect of the young leaders of the "Eighties." The seven volumes of his *Ideën* (1862–77; Ideas) contain not only aphorisms and stories, but a five-act play and a long novel.

In poetry, Jacques Perk's sonnet cycle *Mathilde,* which was published only posthumously in 1882, introduced a poetic form that was to become very important in the new literary movement. Hélène Swarth, whose poetry began appearing at the same time, served as a link between Flemish and Dutch literatures. Willem KLOOS admired her verse, and called her "the singing heart in our literature." It was he, too, who published *Mathilde,* and his introductory essay on Perk and poetry is generally considered the manifesto of the "Eighties." In 1885, Kloos, Albert VERWEY, Frederik van EEDEN, Willem Paap, and Frank van der Goes established a magazine, *De Nieuwe Gids* (The New Guide), whose very name proclaimed its opposition to the tradition-bound *Gids*. Although it was a general magazine, and welcomed articles in such fields as politics and science, its primary impetus was literary. Kloos described art as "the most individual expression of the most individual emotion," and "De Nieuwe Gidsers," as the "Eighties" were often called, emphasized the self, beauty, and "art for art's sake." If they adopted Shelley's individualism, they did not share his concern for society, but gave a high place to poetry and to the poet himself. They invented new words, experimented with syntax, and revitalized the language.

De Nieuwe Gids published the first canto of Herman GORTER's "Mei" (May), a long lyrical poem, which recalls Keats's "Endymion." Van Eeden's autobiographical novel *De kleine Johannes* (1887; Eng. tr., *Little Johannes*, 1895) appeared in its first issue. It was also receptive to naturalism, and Lodewijk van DEYSSEL, pseud. of Karel Alberdingk Thijm, who published his praise of Zola in it, also attempted to combine this style with impressionism. A political force, the rising socialist movement, also exerted an influence on the magazine, dividing the editors. Personal differences complicated this division, and by 1894, *De Nieuwe Gids* had lost its influence as a literary and cultural force.

Not all of the leading literary figures of the last two decades of the 19th century, of course, belonged to the group that gathered around *De Nieuwe Gids*. Marcellus EMANTS, for example, was an earlier admirer of Zola and naturalism than van Deyssel. His most important work of fiction is *Een nagelaten bekentenis* (1894; Eng. tr., *A Posthumous Confession*, 1975), in which he proves himself a master of the psychological novel. Such plays as *Domheidsmacht* (The Power of Stupidity) are also in the naturalistic tradition. In his novel, he anticipated van Eeden's *Van de koele meren des doods* (1900; Eng. trs., *The Deeps of Deliverance* 1902, 1974), which portrays the psychological destruction of its heroine. Although he published his first *novellen* in *De Nieuwe Gids,* Jacobus van LOOY, who began as a painter, wove some of his own experiences as a child in an orphanage into the novels *Jaapje* (1917), *Jaap* (1923), and *Jacob* (1930).

A much greater and more prolific novelist, who remained completely outside the "Movement of the Eighties," was Louis COUPERUS. Born in The Hague, he wrote a remarkable novel of upper-middle-class and aristocratic society in his native city, *Eline Vere* (1889; Eng. tr., 1892). The heroine is a victim of her own heredity, and ends by taking her own life. Here Couperus is pursuing the novel as it developed under Emants and the naturalists, rather than van Eeden. In *De stille kracht* (The Silent Force), the hero is destroyed by the mysterious forces of Fate, which fit easily into the East Indies setting. *De boeken der kleine zielen* (1901-03; The Books of The Small Souls), a tetralogy, returns to the atmosphere of The Hague, and offers admirable examples not only of Couperus's narrative skill, but also of his ability to portray character. His last novel about the upper strata of society in The Hague revolves about a couple in their 90s, who were accomplices in the murder of the woman's husband 60 years before. The tension of this secret runs through *Van oude menschen, de dingen die voorbijgaan* (1906; Eng. trs., *Old People and the Things That Pass* 1918, 1963). There is an atmosphere of decadence in this book, as well as in many other novels by Couperus, that is evident in other European writers at the end of the 19th century, but then Couperus was a European, as well as a Dutch writer.

Of the "Eighters," only van Eeden had a serious interest in the drama, and no one else since Multatuli had made a significant contribution to this genre. At the turn of the century, however, Herman HEIJERMANS, the author of a number of works of prose fiction in the naturalistic style, began to reveal himself as a born dramatist, and the only one in modern Holland to win both national fame and a world reputation. He achieved his first success in the theater with *Ahasverus* (1912; Eng. tr., 1929) in 1893, a one-act play about Jewish refugees from the pogroms of Russia. Heijermans followed this up with another drama of Jewish life, *Ghetto* (1899; Eng tr., 1899), which was set in Amsterdam. There followed a series of plays, most of them in a realistic style, which brought Dutch national life to the stage. The most famous of these is *Op Hoop van Zegen* (1900; Eng. tr., *The Good Hope*, 1912), a drama of the life of the Dutch fishermen, but such other plays as *Schakels* (1903; Eng. tr., *Links*, 1927) and *Uitkomst* (1907; The Way Out) are part of his achievement.

Heijermans was interested in socialism, and showed his sympathy for the Dutch working classes in many of his plays. Gorter, who had been an "Eightier," published Socialist poetry in his second volume of *Verzen* (1903; Verses), and played an active role in the affairs of the Socialist Party. In his *Kritiek op de litteraire beweging van 1880 in Holland* (1898-99; Critique of the Literary Movement of 1880 in Holland), he attacked the individualism of the "Movement of the Eighties," and criticized

Kloos, Verwey, and van Deyssel for favoring bourgeois literature. His friend Henriëtte ROLAND HOLST, née van der Schalk, made her literary debut in 1893, with some sonnets in *De Nieuwe Gids*. Although she was an individualist herself, she moved away from the strict sonnet form of the "Nieuwe Gidsers" toward freer rhythms and enjambement. Partly out of humanitarian motives, she turned to socialism, as is evident from *De nieuwe geboort* (1903; The New Birth) and *Opwaartse wegen* (1907; Upward Roads). Like Gorter, she later turned her back on Russia and the Communist Party, and her socialism became religious socialism. Verwey, who had introduced Gorter and Roland Holst to each other, was an influential figure in modern Dutch literature. He came to reject the principles of the writers who had gathered around *De Nieuwe Gids*. In 1894, with van Deyssel as coeditor, he established the *Tweemaandelijksch Tijdschrift* (Bimonthly Magazine), which later became a monthly under the new title of *De Twintigste Eeuw* (The Twentieth Century). Verwey formed a friendship with the German poet Stefan GEORGE, and also met members of his circle. He and George translated each other's work, and in 1896, George published translations of the poetry of Kloos, Verwey, and Gorter in *Blatter für die Kunst*, strengthening the ties between Dutch and German literature. In 1905, after differences with van Deyssel, Verwey founded *De Beweging* (The Movement), and he himself was editor. He had become a Neoplatonist, and regarded the Idea as the most important thing in poetry. Much of his poetry, including three poetic dramas, was published in the three volumes of *Verzamelde gedichten* (1911-12; Collected Poems). Verwey was significant as a poet, but he was even more important as a literary critic and historian. The same issue of *De Nieuwe Gids* that presented the first poems of Roland Holst also included the first verses of Jan Hendrik Leopold. Like Roland Holst, he was also influenced by Baruch Spinoza. Both Leopold and Pieter Cornelis BOUTENS had been students of the classics before they began their careers as secondary school teachers, and their work reflects this interest. Their love for the classics probably explains their adherence to the individualism of the "Movement of the Eighties" and their admiration of beauty. Leopold who was shy and cut himself off from society, partly because of his deafness, was not very well known until Boutens published a volume of his *Verzen* (1912; Verses). This melancholy poet's awareness of his own isolation as an individual was revealed in his epic poem *Cheops,* as well as in his Dutch version of the *Rubaiyat of Omar Khayyam*. Boutens was not only a translator of the *Rubaiyat,* too, but of Homer, Aeschylus, Sophocles, and Goethe. He displayed remarkable skill in his use of the language and in poetic form. His *Verzameld werken* (1943-54; Collected Works) was published in seven volumes. Among the prose writers, who, like van Deyssel, were attracted to both naturalism and impressionism, were Arij Prins, pseud. of A. Cooplandt, and Adriaan van Oordt. They were interested in portraying medieval themes, and are thus often characterized as Neoromantics. Prins's *Uit het leven* (1885; From Life) is a volume of naturalistic sketches, but in his novel *De heilige tocht* (1913; The Holy Expedition), the story of a knight who joins a crusade, he experimented with the syntax of the language, in an attempt to achieve, in prose, the same effect that the impressionists created in painting. In *Irmenlo* (1896) and *Warhold* (1906), van Oordt also presented themes from the Middle Ages, seen from a naturalistic point of view, but described in an impressionistic style.

The outstanding novelist of the late 19th century was Arthur van SCHENDEL, whose first novel, *Drogon* (1896), describes the adventures of a young nobleman of the Middle Ages in a neoromantic style. The novels *Een zwerver verliefd* (1904; A Wanderer in Love) and *Een zwerver verdwaald* (1907; A Wanderer Lost) were in the same style, and again Fate determines the course of events. With *Het fregatschip Johanna Maria* (1930; Eng. tr., *The Johanna Maria*, 1935), *De Waterman* (1933; Eng. tr., *The Waterman*, 1963), and *Een Hollandsch drama* (1935; Eng. tr., *The House in Haarlem*, 1940), however, van Schendel achieved a realistic style. Fate, usually based on heredity and circumstances, plays a decisive role in these novels. Yet, some of his main characters are filled with a feeling of self-sacrifice and duty. The novels of this period border on naturalism, and van Schendel captured the life and the character of the Dutch middle class against the atmosphere of the national landscape. He displayed the same talent for style and character in his shorter fiction and remained the most significant novelist for the period that ended with World War II.

The tradition of the Dutch novel based on life in the East Indies, now Indonesia, had not been forgotten. Augusta de Wit, who had been born there, began her career with a book in English, *Facts and Fancies about Java*. Of more immediate literary importance, however, was her novel *Orpheus in de dessa* (1903; Orpheus in the Dessa), in which, in a poetic, philosophical style that went beyond realism, she took up the relationship between Western and Eastern civilizations. *Gods goochelaartjes* (1932; God's Conjurers) depicts the inner mysteries of life in the same Eastern setting. Van Deyssel had high praise for the work of another writer in this genre, whose naturalistic novels, *Uit de suiker in de tabak* (1884; Out of Sugar into Tobacco) and *Goena-Goena* (1889) appeared under the name of Maurits, pseud. of P. A. Daum.

Israël Querido, another novelist who was influenced by van Deyssel and naturalism, focused his sharp eye on his native Amsterdam in *Levensgang* (1901; The Course of Life), a view of the world of the diamond-cutters, and the tetralogy *De Jordaan, Van Nes en Zeedijk, Manus Peet,* and *Mooie Karel* (Handsome Karel) (1912–25), a view of life in a well-known working-class section of Amsterdam. Herman Robbers wrote novels in a realistic style, portraying middle-class family life. The best examples of his work are *De roman van Bernard Bandt* (1897; The Novel of Bernard Bandt), *De bruidstijd van Annie de Boogh* (1901; The Bridal Days of Annie de Boogh), and the series of novels that form the family chronicle *De roman van een gezin* (1909–33; The Novel of a Family). J. van Oudshoorn, pseud. of J. K. Feylbrief, wrote in a starkly naturalistic style, often reminiscent of Emants. He probed the depths of his psychopathological heroes, whose sexual frustration often led to insanity. In his first novel, *Willem Mertens' levensspiegel* (1914; Mirror of William Mertens' Life), the hero suffers from loneliness and sexual guilt feelings. Similar sexual problems appear in *Louteringen* (1916; Purifications), and *Tobias en de dood* (1925; Tobias and Death) involves a struggle against death, but there is an element of humor in both of them. Van Oudshoorn's reputation has grown in recent years, and he is considered to have links to the writers of the generation that followed him.

Margo Antink is one of a group of gifted women novelists. Her first novel, *Catherine* (1899), reveals the influence of the "Movement of the Eighties" and the combination of naturalism and impressionism. *Sprotje* (1905–09), a group of three *novellen* about a servant girl, betrays no weakening of her powers of observation, but marks the development of a realistic style. There is further development of her psychological realism in the novel *Angelina's huwelijk* (1918; Angelina's Wedding). In 1924,

she married the writer Carel Scharten, and they wrote a number of books together. Another member of this group is Ina Boudier-Bakker who is an excellent storyteller, sets her stories in a comfortable middle-class milieu. Her novel *Armoede* (1909; Poverty), however, written in a realistic style, is a pessimistic book. She achieved considerable success with her novel *De straat* (1924; The Street), and continued her literary career until long after World War II. Top Naeff, née van Rhijn, won early fame with books for girls and also wrote several plays. Her literary reputation, however, rests on her middle-class novels, such as *De stille getuige* (1907; The Silent Witness) and *Voor de poort* (1912; In front of the Doorway). Carry van Bruggen, the sister of the poet Jacob Israël de Haan, described her own youth with sensitivity, intellect, and humor in *Het huisje aan de sloot* (1921; The Little House on the Canal), *Avontuurtjes* (1922; Adventures), and *Vier jaargetijden* (1924; Four Seasons). A woman writer who stands somewhat apart from this group is Nine van der Schaaf, who was born in Friesland, and started out as a servant girl in The Hague. She used fantasy in her early poetry and prose, but after 1920, she became more realistic, and turned to rural Friesland and simple people for her books *Friesch dorpsleven* (1922; Frisian Village Life, repub. in 1936 as *Heerk Walling*), *De uitvinder* (1932; The Inventor), and *De liefde van een dwaas* (1937; The Love of a Fool). P. H. van Moerkerken was a member of *De Beweging* Group, and in keeping with Verwey's theories, he attempted to put ideas into his novels. After writing the satirical novel *De ondergang van het dorp* (1913; The Decline of the Village), he published *De bevrijders* (1914; The Liberators), an ironic account of the liberation of the Netherlands from Napoleon, and an attempt to restore the tradition of the 19th-century historical novel. *De gedachte der tijden* (1919–24; The Thought of the Times) is a series of historical novels, based on the idea of the collective striving of humanity for freedom and happiness.

Both Verwey and van Eeden influenced Nico van Suchtelen. His *Quia Absurdum* (1906) reflects his stay at van Eeden's Walden colony, and it first appeared in *De Beweging*. His philosophical reflection and humanitarianism are evident in *De stille lach* (1916; The Silent Laughter), which takes up the effect of World War I on the sensitive intellectuals of the period.

In poetry, Gorter and Roland Holst, who had both been actively interested in socialism and communism at the time, influenced Abraham Eliazer van Collem, who contributed poetry to their monthly magazine *De Nieuwe Tijd* (New Times). His volumes of verse, *Liederen van huisvlijt* (1917; Songs of Domestic Skills) and *Opstandige liederen* (1919; Rebellious Songs), show social consciousness combined with irony. Van Collem's confidence in the rise of humanity is clear in *Liederen der gemeenschap* (Songs of Community). Carel Steven ADAMA VAN SCHELTEMA became the poet of the workers but his socialism has been questioned. His poetry had a simple style, and he enjoyed great popularity. Among his volumes of poetry are *Zwervers Verzen* (1904; A Wanderer's Verses) and *De keerende kudde* (1920; The Turning Herd).

Geerten Gossaert, pseud. of F. C. Gerretson, was a contributor to *De Beweging,* who wanted to go back to inspired rhetoric in poetry, and he preferred the alexandrine to the sonnet. His reputation as a poet is based on his one volume of verse, *Experimenten* (1911). Jakobus Cornelis BLOEM published his first poetry in *De Beweging*. The feeling of longing in his poetry, a longing for happiness and love, is expressed in the title of his first volume of verse, *Het verlangen* (1921; Longing). There is disillusionment in Media Vita (1931), and in this and

De nederlaag (1937; The Defeat), he turns away from neoclassicism and "inspired rhetoric." Love has lost its meaning, as he contemplates loneliness and death. With Bloem, meanwhile, poetic language had become more colloquial. Pieter Nicolaas van EYCK was opposed to "inspired rhetoric." Like Verwey in his later years, van Eyck sought truth in philosophical speculation and ideas. He began publishing poetry with *De getooide doolhof* (1909; The Decorated Labyrinth), which revealed his passion for sensual beauty, but the soul is not satisfied with this transitory beauty. *Herwaarts* (1939; Hither) represents a later stage of his poetic development, when he is filled with a longing to experience God. His mysticism and philosophical views appear most clearly in the long mythological poem *Medousa* (1947). Van Eyck also remains a significant literary critic.

Like van Eyck, Aart van der Leeuw, another member of the group around *De Beweging*, also opposed "inspired rhetoric," nor was he interested in philosophical speculation. He found happiness in the beauty of life on earth, and his poetry often contains visions of a neoclassical, Arcadian world. He wrote a great deal of poetry, and *Het aardsche paradijs* (1927; Earthly Paradise) is a good example of his verse, but with this book he stopped. Van der Leeuw is also important as a writer of *novellen* and novels, however, and he made his reputation as a writer of fiction with *Ik en mijn speelman* (1927; I and My Minstrel) and *De kleine Rudolf* (1930; Little Rudolf), which, with fine humor, present a view of life as seen through the eyes of an artist. Although he was a contemporary of Verwey, and his first verses appeared in *De Beweging*, Johan Andreas dèr Mouw did not begin to write poetry until he was in his 50s. A classicist and a philosopher, he was an anti-Hegelian, and immersed himself in pre-Indian philosophy. He preferred the sonnet form, and published many mystical and philosophical poems, which he lightened with an excellent sense of humor. Dèr Mouw sought the unity of Cosmos and Self, and his *Brahman I* (1919) and *Brahman II* (1920) were published under the Sanskrit pseudonym of Adwaïta ("he who has risen above duality"). He was not much appreciated in his own day, but he was rediscovered in the 1930s, and there has been renewed interest in him recently. Another poet who was on the fringes of the group around *De Beweging* was Jacob Israël de Haan. His early prose shows his connections with the naturalists—*Pathologieën* (1908). After years as a freethinker and socialist, he returned to the Orthodox Judaism whence he came. The two volumes of *Het Joodsche lied* (1915, 1921; The Jewish Song) form a moving revelation of his feelings for religious traditions, Zionism, and the memories of his youth, along with inner conflicts. Even more of himself appears in *Kwatrijnen* (1924; Quatrains). Jan Prins, pseud. of C. L. Schepp, was also loosely tied to the group around *De Beweging*. A naval officer, he speaks in his poetry of the beauty of the Dutch landscape and its characteristic features in such volumes as *Tochten* (1911; Journeys), *Getijden* (1917; Tides), and *Verschijningen* (1925; Phenomena). *Indische gedichten* (1932; East Indian Poems) contain his observations of scenes in the Indies.

With Adriaan Roland Holst the neoromantic period in Dutch literature came to an end. He was the last upholder of traditional Dutch poetry, which goes back to the last two decades of the 19th century. He had been a student at Oxford, and also came under the influence of William Butler Yeats. The theme of loneliness, which is important in his work, appears in his first volume of poetry, *Verzen* (1911; Verses). In *Voorbij de wegen* (1920; Beyond the Roads) and *De wilde kim* (1925; The Wild Horizon), he longs for the passionate life of a mythical and mystical

past. His fascination with Celtic myths and legends is clear in *Een winter aan zee* (1937; A Winter by the Sea), as well as in the adaptation of such material in *Deirdre en de zonen van Usnach* (1920; Deirdre and the Sons of Usnach), one of his prose works.

Martinus NIJHOFF published his first poems in *De Beweging*, but although he forms a link with the traditionalists who grouped themselves around the magazine, *De wandelaar* (1916; The Walker) already indicates his connections with the modernist poets who gathered around *Het Getij* (The Tide). The traditional, almost classical style of *Vormen* (1924; Forms) offers a contrast to the modernist motifs. *Nieuwe gedichten* (1934; New Poems) includes the long poem *Awater*, in which Awater is an ordinary man, a member of the multitude. Nijhoff made effective use of the vocabulary of everyday life and of colloquial speech, a road that had been begun by Gorter, Bloem, and dèr Mouw. One of the leading figures at *Het Getij* was Herman van den BERGH, whose first volume of poetry, *De Boog* (1917; The Bow) marked the appearance of Dutch expressionism. In his essays, which were published as *Nieuwe tucht* (1928; New Discipline), he called for a new style in life and poetry. After a silence of 30 years, he demonstrated, in such volumes of poetry as *Het litteken van Odysseus* (1956; The Scar of Odysseus) and *Verstandhouding met de vijand* (1958; In Collusion with the Enemy), that his talent had deepened, and that he had a new expressionistic style to present it in. Expressionism became much more of a force in Belgium, under the Flemish poet Paul van Ostaijen, and the only important young Dutch poet who came under the influence of van den Bergh was Hendrik MARSMAN. His first volume of poetry, *Verzen* (1923; Verses), showed enthusiasm and passion, and the imagery is that of expressionism. With *Porta Nigra* (1934), his style and tone changed. There is a contrast between life and death, and the fear of death is present. *Tempel en Kruis* (1940; The Temple and The Cross) appeared just before his death. Written at a time when the Nazis and the fascists were threatening to destroy the civilization of Western Europe, Marsman saw it as based on two components, the tradition of ancient Greece, or The Temple, and Christianity, or The Cross.

Menno ter Braak left *De Vrije Bladen* (The Free Pages), and with Charles Edgar du PERRON and the Flemish novelist Maurice Roelants, founded *Forum*, which became a very influential magazine. Ter Braak was the leading essayist and critic of his day. He was an individualist, who was very learned and polemical in his criticism. An admirer of Multatuli, he lost no opportunity to expose false values. He was also author of two novels. *Hampton Court* (1931) and *Dr. Dumay verliest* (1933; Dr. Dumay Loses). A critic of collective movements, and a fierce opponent of German national socialism, he took his own life when the Nazis invaded the Netherlands. Du Perron, ter Braak's friend and comrade-in-arms at *Forum*, was born in Java, and did not come to Europe until he was 22, when he settled first in Paris, where he made friends with a number of artists and writers, including André MALRAUX. He, too, was an individualist, but his criticism was even more subjective than that of ter Braak. The most important of his works of fiction is *Het land van herkomst* (1935; Country of Origin), an autobiographical novel that is set in both Java and Paris. It does not have the traditional form and structure of the novel, and there is no plot; instead he attempts to define himself, his past and present. Du Perron also wrote a fine and well-documented biography of Multatuli, toward whom he felt a close affinity, in *De man van Lebak* (1937; The Man from Lebak). Jan Jacob Slauerhoff was one of the writers who gathered around *Het Getij* and *De Vrije Bladen*, and he also published in *Forum*. The romantic themes in his work, however, set him off from the other writers of his period. They are evident even in his first volume of poetry, *Archipel* (1923; Archipelago), as well as in such other poetic works as *Oost-Azië* (1928; East Asia) and *Een eerlijk zeemansgraf* (1936; An Honorable Sailor's Grave). He was a ship's doctor, and made long voyages to the Far East. Many of his stories are based on Chinese themes. He was also a talented novelist. Among his novels are *Het verboden rijk* (1932; The Forbidden Realm), which gives an unusual view of the Portuguese poet Camoëns, and *Het leven op aarde* (1934; Life on Earth), which describes the pleasures of opium.

Two other important novelists of this period are Ferdinand BORDEWIJK and Anna BLAMAN, both of whom knew how to make effective use of psychology in their work. Two works, *Blokken* (1931; Blocks), a satire on collective society, and *Knorrende beesten* (1933; Growling Beasts), a satire on automobiles, show the development of Bordewijk's style. Together with *Bint* (1934), the story of a schoolmaster who maintains iron discipline by terrorizing his students, they established his reputation when he was 50. The concise, objective style of *Bint* suits the milieu and the hero perfectly. In *Karakter* (1938; Eng. tr., *Character*, 1966), he skillfully depicts the psychological conflicts between a father and his son. Anna Blaman, pseud. of Johanna Petronella Vrugt, began by publishing poetry in *Criterium* and *Helikon*, but with *Vrouw en vriend*, a story of love's disillusionment, she established her talent for the psychological novel. *Eenzaam avontuur* (1948; Lonely Adventure) is about a novelist whose marriage fails and who writes a novel about it. Her best novel, *Op leven en dood* (1954; Eng. tr., *A Matter of Life and Death*, 1974), is partly autobiographical.

The most versatile and prolific writer of this period is Simon VESTDIJK. He has written poetry, novellas, novels, essays, and criticism. Vestdijk first achieved success as a novelist with *Terug tot Ina Damman* (1934; Back to Ina Damman), a tender recollection of unrequited love drawn from his own experience. It is one of the eight novels in the Anton Wachter series. His mastery of depth psychology is clearly evident in *Else Böhler, Duitsch dienstmeisje* (1935; Else Böhler, German Main), in which the hero destroys himself through his love for the heroine of the title. His best novel, *De koperen tuin* (1950; Eng. tr., *The Garden Where the Brass Band Played*, 1965) reflects, in both background and structure, Vestdijk's love of music. He has also written a number of historical novels. Among the novelists who came to fame after World War II, the most important is Willem Frederik HERMANS, whose first significant novel, *De tranen der acacia's* (1949; The Tears of the Acacias) is set against the background of the war, as is *Ik heb altijd gelijk* (1951; I Am Always Right). His best novel is *De donkere kamer van Damokles* (1958; The Dark Chamber of Damocles), which provides a view of the chaotic world of The Netherlands during the Nazi Occupation. Gerard Kornelis van het REVE's first novel, *De avonden* (1947; The Evenings), presents the gloomy and realistic view of life as it is seen by the generation after World War II. In a different category are the collections of travel letters *Op weg naar het einde* (1963; On the Way to the End) and *Nader tot U* (1966; Nearer to You), which are filled with thoughts of approaching death. Jan WOLKERS's first novel, *Kort Amerikaans* (1962; Crew Cut) contains most of the themes, the father-son conflict, death, sex, loneliness, and alienation, which were to return in his later work. *Een roos van vlees* (1963; Eng. tr., *A Rose of Flesh*) and *Turks Fruit* (1969; Eng. tr., *Turkish Delight*) are autobiographical. Harry Mulisch has not confined himself to the novel, but his best-known novel, *Het*

stenen bruiosbed (1959; Eng. tr., *The Stone Bridal Bed*, 1962), takes place in Dresden, a bombed-out city, after World War II.

Of the poets, Gerrit ACHTERBERG is a metaphysical poet, who hopes to bring the dead beloved back to life through the power of poetry. His imagery is unusual, and he creates new words of his own. This is evident in the well-known volume *Ballade van de gasfitter* (1953). Leo VROMAN lives in New York, where he is a physiologist. In poetry, he is an innovator, who invents new words, and plays with old ones. He often uses a conversational style. He has written some poetry in English. LUCEBERT, pseud. of L. J. Swaanswijk, the painter, is an experimental poet, who creates new words and new forms of the language. His poetry is related to abstract art, and he wants to create a nonsubjective language.

See: T. Weevers, *Poetry of the Netherlands in its European Context, 1170–1930* (1960); R. P. Meijer, *Literature of the Low Countries* (1971); G. P. M. Knuvelder, *Handboek tot de geschiedenis der Nederlandse letterkunde* (1977). S.L.F.

Duun, Olav (1876–1939), Norwegian novelist, was born in northern Trøndelag, a region dominated by fjords, forests, and mountains. The son of a farmer, Duun spent the first few years of his adult life working at home. After attending a teachers college, he became a teacher in a small town on the Oslo Fjord. In 1927 he received an author's stipend from the Norwegian state.

Duun published his first book in 1907, and within only a decade he had won fame and recognition as one of the most important authors in Norway. He wrote in *nynorsk* (*see* NORWEGIAN LITERATURE), a natural choice since it conformed closely to the dialect of Duun's native region. Indeed, Duun felt the need of writing only about what he intimately knew, and Trøndelag is the setting of all his works. His masterful novels are also profound psychological studies, a fact that makes them human documents of the broadest interest.

The fundamental theme of Duun's novels is the battle of man with the forces that attempt to dominate his thoughts and acts. His first novels picture man combatting the forces of nature. In Duun's later works, however, we see man struggling against the forces within himself, forces created by his social surroundings and moral traditions. The monumental work in Duun's oeuvre is a series of six relatively short novels collected under the title *Juvikfolke* (1918–23; Eng. tr., *The People of Juvik*, 1930–35). Constructed much like one of the great Icelandic family sagas, *Juvikfolke* covers a period of a century and a half, relating the determined struggle of successive generations. It culminates in the story of the last man of the family, his mental growth, his maturing, and his final victory over a primitive heritage. Wild self-assertion yields to the nobility of self-sacrifice; the strength of resignation, however, is really won by virtue of inherited will power. Here, through a series of colorful vignettes, Duun presents the education of mankind from barbarism to the highest level of morality.

Duun's next major achievement was a trilogy of novels—*Medmenneske* (1929; Fellow Beings), *Ragnhild* (1931), *Siste Leveåre* (1933; The Last Year of Life)—centered around a good woman who is driven to murder. Finally, through her sufferings, she is able to give an example of purity to the world.

Duun's novels present a galaxy of varied, sharply delineated characters. In his later works, society and surroundings are less and less important, even through their influences are always distinctly felt. Duun never abandoned his interest in the struggle of the individual against the hidden forces of his own soul. Duun himself defined the idea of his entire oeuvre in the title of his last book, *Menneske og maktene* (1938; Man and the Powers, Eng. tr., *Floodtide of Fate*, 1960). His novels recall Henrik IBSEN's dramas in their severe, firm construction, and the Icelandic sagas in that the characters reveal the secrets of their nature through their own acts and words. Duun's style is often surprising for its striking, unaffected paradoxes, and for its subtle irony. He was an exquisite artist, whose every word served the aim of his work and helped illuminate the eternal psychology of struggling manhood.

See: R. Thesen, *Menneske og maktene* (1942); A. Sæteren, *Mennesket og samfunnet* (1956); O. Dalgard, *Olav Duun* (1976); Å. Svensen, *Mellom Juvika og Øyvase* (1978); L. Fetveit, *Juvikfolke og tradisjonen* (1979).

H.K.

Dygasiński, Adolf (1839–1902), Polish novelist, short-story writer, and publisher, was born in Niegosławice, near Pińczów, and died in Grodzisk Mazowiecki. He studied natural sciences at the University of Warsaw, and as a student he took part in the 1863 Uprising. He worked as a teacher, a tutor, and as a publisher of popular scientific works and also served as co-editor of several magazines including *Przegląd Tygodniowy* and later *Wędrowiec, Głos,* and *Wisła.* He started his career as a writer late, in his forties, and wrote about 50 volumes of short stories and novels. These were, however, of very uneven quality. In 1890–91, Dygasiński made a trip to Brazil, later using the observations from this journey in his novel *Na złamanie karku* (1893; Back-breaking Work). He was a positivist and an admirer of science and Charles Darwin, and his prose reflected the influence of naturalism. Darwin's theory of natural selection and of the survival of the fittest played a certain role in the development of Dygasiński's pessimistic view of history and human fate, a view that replaced the positivistic optimism of his first journalistic works.

In the stories of *As* (1896; The Ace) and *Zając* (1900; The Hare), Dygasiński emphasized the dependence of man on nature and found similarities between man and the animal world. *Gody życia* (1902; The Feast of Life) is a kind of lyric poem in prose contemplating nature's beauty and vitality. In such novels and short-story collections as *Nowele* (1884; Short Stories), *Beldonek* (1888), and *Margiela i Margielka* (1901), Dygasiński described in realistic detail the life of the Polish countryside, villages, and manors. *Beldonek,* the story of a poor country boy with artistic talent, is considered one of Dygasiński's greatest literary achievements. The prose of Dygasiński the naturalist combines in an original way elements of the *gawęda* (a Polish spoken tale), folk tales and beliefs, and lyricism.

See: J. Z. Jakubowski, *Zapomniane ogniwo: studium o Adolfie Dygasińskim* (1967); B. Dyduchowa, *Narracja w utworach nowelistycznych Adolfa Dygasińskiego* (1974).   A.Z.

Dygat, Stanisław (1914–78), Polish novelist, satirist, and short-story writer, was born and died in Warsaw. The son of a well-known architect, he studied architecture and philosophy in Warsaw. His first novel, *Jezioro Bodeńskie* (1946; Bodensee), is based on his experiences in the German internment camp at Constance, where, as a French citizen, he spent a year. Unlike other Polish novels dealing with World War II, it treats textbook patriotism with melancholy irony, but still the hero's inner man has a hidden attachment to the Polish romantic tradition of heroic deeds. Other works of fiction followed: a novel, *Pożegnania* (1948; Farewells), a gentle satire in which

Dygat ridicules the social conventions, and *Pola Elizejskie* (1949; Elysian Fields), a collection of skeptical short stories, in which he reevaluates contemporary thought patterns, complexes, and customs. The novel *Podróż* (1958; Journey) is a half-humorous fairy tale about long-cherished but lost illusions and dreams. *Disneyland* (1965; Eng. tr., *Cloak of Illusion,* 1969) is a novel written with bitter humor about contemporary youth; about the basic problems in human life: love, faithfulness, and a need for trust in others and oneself; about disillusionments and the search for honesty in life. *Rozmyślania przy goleniu* (1959; Meditation While Shaving) consists of philosophical feuilletons that Dygat had previously published in Polish cultural weeklies. In his story "Karnawał" (1968; Carnival), Dygat returned to the conflicts and problems presented in his first novel, with a new attitude enriched by his life experience. In 1973, Dygat published the novel, *Dworzec w Monachium* (The Munich Railway Station) and a collection of short stories, *W cieniu Brooklynu* (In the Shadow of Brooklyn).

See: Z. Skwarczyński, *Stanisław Dygat* (1976).

E.M.T. and S.F.

Dyk, Viktor (1877–1931), Czech poet, dramatist, and novelist, wrote the most important political poetry in Czech literature. He was born at Psovka, near Mělník, the son of a steward on an estate. After becoming a journalist, he took a prominent part in editing several periodicals of the sharply anti-Austrian Radical Progressive Party. In 1917 he was imprisoned by the Austrian authorities. After the formation of Czechoslovaki in 1918, he became a member of Parliament and later a senator for the National Democratic Party.

Skepticism and even nihilism dominated Dyk's early poetry, but his despair was always tempered by irony and satire. He used stanzaic forms and loved witticism, paradoxes, and grotesque rhymes. After the publication of his best collection, *Marnosti* (Vanities) in 1900, he slowly turned away from individual problems of futility, and concentrated on political satire and exhortations to his countrymen. The pieces in *Satiry a sarkasmy* (1905; Satires and Sarcasms) and *Pohádky z naší vesnice* (1910; Fairy Tales from Our Village) upbraid the nation for abandoning its old traditions and recommend an uncompromising, conservative nationalism. Dyk's political verse culminates in four collections, *Lehké a těžké kroky* (1915; Light and Heavy Steps), *Anebo* (1918; Or), *Okno* (1920; The Window), and *Poslední rok* (1922; The Last Year), which comment on World War I and postwar developments as well as on the author's experiences in an Austrian prison. Among Dyk's later, less important books, *Devátá vina* (1930; The Ninth Wave) is particularly interesting for its personal tone—the feeling of approaching death unifies a miscellany of intimate lyrics. Besides lyrical poetry, where he is at his best, Dyk also attempted small-scale epics: a cycle of ballads or romances like that on *Giuseppe Moro* (1911), or a short verse story like *Zápas Jiřího Macků* (1918; The Struggle of George Macků), which deals with a peasant's defiance of death.

As a dramatist, Dyk used an effective dialogue technique, with sharp dialectics, which makes each of his plays almost a series of epigrams. *Posel* (1907; The Messenger) is a historical drama that attempts to indict the spirit of Christian pacifism for the loss of Czech independence in the Battle of the White Mountain (1620). *Zmoudření Dona Quijota* (1913; Don Quixote Recovers His Reason) is an ironic dramatization of the conflict between romantic dreams and sober reality, while *Revoluční trilogie* (1921; The Trilogy of the Revolution) consists of three short plays about the French Revolution, all of which reveal the playwright's sarcastic attitude towards idealism.

Least successful of all Dyk's works is his voluminous prose. He did write some good short stories, like "Krysař" (1915; The Pied Piper), which vary the theme of romantic illusionism. But his satirical and political novels are artistic failures, in spite of the interest of their material, which is based on the author's memories of events and personalities. In all his novels, the composition is loose, and debate and discussion crowd out imagination. *Konec Hackenschmidův* (1904; Hackenschmid's End) depicts the students' part in the "Progressive" movement; *Soykovy děti* (1929; Soyka's Children) is a chronicle of the war; and *Děs z prázdna* (1933; Horror Vacui) attempts to reconstruct Czech political life during the early 19th century. Dyk also wrote polemical prose, some criticism, and reminiscences.

Dyk overcame his early nihilism by a fervent nationalism that recommended the most radical measures against Austrian dominion and that, after the establishment of the Republic, turned against socialism and the humanitarian democracy represented by President Tomáš Garrigue MASARYK. Dyk thought of the nation in terms of its historical tradition, conceiving of it as a moral absolute. Artistically, Dyk is important as a lyrical poet, because in a time of rhetoric he cultivated concise, hard, and sharp forms. But his imagination was too frequently sacrificed to sheer intellect. His dramas seem contrived, and his novels suffer from too much topical discussion. Although Dyk has been compared to Maurice BARRÈS, he is far drier, more subdued, and narrower.

See: K. H. Hilar, *Viktor Dyk; essay o jeho ironii* (1910); M. Rutte, *Viktor Dyk; portrét básníka* (1931); H. Jelínek, *Viktor Dyk* (1932); A. Novák, *Viktor Dyk* (1936, in Czech); V. Jirát, *O smyslu formy* (1946), pp. 145–64; J. Hora, *Poezie a život* (1959), pp. 288–304. R.W.

Dzyuba, Ivan (1931–), Ukrainian literary critic, was born in the village of Mykolayioka, Donetsk province. The leading critic of the post-Stalin period, Dzyuba was one of the dissidents (together with Vyacheslav Chornovil, Valentyn Moroz, and many others) who opposed Soviet policies of russification and pleaded for national and civil rights (*see* UKRAINIAN LITERATURE). Author of the clandestine *Internatsyonalizm chy rusyfikatsiya* (Eng. tr., *Internationalism or Russification,* 1968), Dzyuba was arrested, along with other dissenters, in 1972 and released in 1973 after making a public confession of his "political errors." A master of incisive prose, he is the author of essays on Hryhoriy Skovoroda, Taras Shevchenko, and other Ukrainian writers. G.S.N.L.

E

Echegaray, José (1832–1916), Spanish dramatist, was born and died in Madrid. He devoted himself with brilliant success to diverse activities, coming to occupy an outstanding position in the scientific, political, and literary life of Spain. He taught at the School of Civil Engineering until the Revolution of 1868 brought him into the political arena. He was elected to the Cortes Constituyentes, was appointed director of public works and minister of the interior, and was considered an authority on economic questions. Beginning in 1874, however, when his first two plays were presented on the stage, he devoted himself almost exclusively to the theater. The following year the romantic drama *En el puño de la espada,* (At the Hilt of the Sword) established his popularity. For 30 years, Echegaray contributed to the Spanish stage a steady stream of dramas and comedies in prose and verse, and he may well be considered the most genuine representative of the Spanish theater during this period.

His works can be divided into two groups: the romantic dramas, which are in the nature of historical legends, and the dramas that deal with contemporary moral and social problems. The best fall into the latter category, but the difference between the two is more apparent than real. The nature of the dramatic conflict in all Echegaray's work is that of the typical romantic drama. Certain of his later plays, such as *El loco Dios* (1900; Eng. tr., *The Madman Divine,* 1908) and *El hijo de don Juan* (1892; Eng. tr., *The Son of Don Juan,* 1895), are exceptions. In these, inspired by Henrik IBSEN, Echegaray attempted to infuse new life into his work. In general, however, his theater stems directly from romanticism and from classical Spanish drama, especially Pedro Calderón de la Barca. His belated romanticism appeared when the romantic movement had been eclipsed and the powerful reaction of the middle of the century had set in against it. This explains the popularity and resounding success of his plays, which revived the subject matter and procedures of the romantic and, to a certain extent, the classical theater, so deeply rooted in the Spanish people. The conflicts assume stark, violent forms, in which man and human will are playthings of the more powerful fatalities of chance. Clashes between individual characters are calculated, electric, and almost physical. Such is the formula of most of Echegaray's dramas. They revive in modern guise, coldly and with an eye to effect, the old theme of chivalry and honor based on conjugal fidelity. Clouded by the shadow of doubt, marital life becomes full of unbearable anguish. These ideals in their most extreme and unreal forms are the very essence of dramatic tension in several of his best-known plays, such as *O locura o santidad* (1896; Eng. tr., *Madman or Saint,* 1912), the drama of a conscience scrupulous to the point of madness, and *El gran Galeoto* (1881; Eng. tr., *The World and His Wife,* 1908), an account of the tragic power of public opinion. Echegaray's art juxtaposes oversimplified and exaggerated themes to intense theatrical effect. There is a deliberate withdrawal from reality. The characters are types or simply generic human beings, the passions are abstractions and logical principles, and the words are mere rhetoric.

The literary generation that followed Echegaray reacted violently against him when he was at the height of his national popularity and had been internationally recognized as a recipient of the Nobel Prize for Literature, which he shared with Frédéric MISTRAL in 1904. This negative reappraisal now seems likely to be permanent.

See: A. Lázaro Ros, "Prólogo" to J. Echegaray, *Teatro escogido* (1955); F. Ruiz Ramón, *Historia del teatro español,* vol. 1 (1967), pp. 414–22.

F. de O. rev. H.L.B.

Edfelt, Bo Johannes (1904–), Swedish poet, translator, and critic, was born in Kyrkefalla, in the province of Skaraborg. He had his first collections of poems published in the 1920s. His reputation as a poet became established somewhat later with the publication of *Aftonunderhållning* (1932; Evening Entertainment) and above all with *Högmässa* (1934; High Mass). His style, which shows the influence of Birger SJÖBERG's bold and unconventional imagery and of the *neue Sachlichkeit* (new objectivity) of the German poets Erich KÄSTNER and Bertolt BRECHT, is in the latter collection fully formed with restraint and firmness as hallmarks. In these two books, especially *Högmässa,* as in his poetical works from the late 1930s and early 1940s, Edfelt stands out as a poet deeply affected by contemporary events. His poems voice the anguish and fear that many people felt, confronted with the horror and violence of the period. Against everything that degrades man he set off his idealistic belief in certain indomitable qualities of the human genius. The pessimistic key is from time to time relieved by the gentle and warm note that is struck in his love poems. The sexual act becomes a sacramental experience and a final revelation. Edfelt's poems from these years usually have a very simple form. The guiding principles are often antithesis and parallelism, which give each stanza a symmetrical construction. If this pattern is the result of a largely conventional technique, the opposite can be said about his striking and closely knit imagery, which in many respects anticipates Swedish modernist poetry of the 1940s. Edfelt often utilizes symbols and images drawn from the Bible and from the myths of classical antiquity. The past and the present are thus combined to form a harmony rich in associations. *Elden och klyftan* (1943; The Fire and the Chasm) indicates a personal and artistic reorientation, confirmed in the poet's later work. In this collection we find few traces of the contemporary background. The mood is still somber, but the many poems about death or premonitions of death have a more personal ring now. Edfelt looks back on his childhood and youth and tries to recreate the past in lines rich in sensuous impressions of nature and simple household things. This theme recurs, for example, in *Bråddjupt eko* (1947; Precipitous Echo), *Under Saturnus* (1956), and *Ådernät* (1968; Vascular Net), and *Brev från en ateljé* (1976; Letters from a Studio) and is brought out in relief by Edfelt's increasing awareness of old age and estrangement. His later poetry is also characterized by a wider formal range and a suppler diction. Last but not least should be stressed the important part Edfelt has played as an introducer and translator of foreign poetry. Edfelt's *Dikter* (Selections, 1932–76) appeared in 1979.

See: U. B. Lagerroth and G. Löwendahl, eds., *Perspektiv på Johannes Edfelt* (1969).   P.-A.H.

Edschmid, Kasimir, pseud. of Eduard Schmid (1890–1966), German novelist, was born in Darmstadt. He studied Romance philology and became an early representative of expressionism. Three collections of shorter fiction, *Die sechs Mündungen* (1915; The Six Estuaries), *Das rasende Leben* (1916; Delirious Life), and *Timur* (1916) established his reputation. Spurning realism and psychological analysis, he celebrated rapture, brutality, eroticism, and subjectivity in hectic staccato sentences. Heroes like François Villon and Tamerlane live explosively against exotic backdrops ranging from medieval France to the South Seas. In *Über den Expressionismus in der Literatur* (1919) and the periodical *Tribüne der Kunst und Literatur* (1919–20), he expounded his elitist, vitalist, and antiexperimental views. The novel *Die achatnen Kugeln* (1920; The Agate Balls) depicts an heiress's attainment of insight and intensity from living among beggars and prostitutes, while also illustrating the inadequacy of ecstatic prose as a medium for longer fiction. Later works include *Sport um Gagaly* (1927), the first German novel to view sports seriously, and *Lord Byron* (1929; Eng. tr., *Lord Byron;* Am. tr., *The Passionate Rebel,* both 1930), in which the poet's incestuous cravings offer the key to his character. Extensive travel led to the more realistic presentations *Afrika nackt und angezogen* (1929; Africa Nude and Clothed) and *Glanz und Elend Südamerikas* (1930; Eng. tr., *South America: Lights and Shadows,* 1932) and to numerous volumes on Italy and the Mediterranean. With the coming of the Nazis to power in 1933, Edschmid was forbidden to speak publicly; in 1941, to publish. After 1945 he produced accounts of the lives of Georg Büchner (1950) and Simón Bolivar (1954), as well as collections of expressionist documents and manifestos.

See: U. Brammer, *Kasimir Edschmid—Bibliographie* (1970).   G.W.R.

Eeden, Frederik Willem van (1860–1932), Dutch novelist, dramatist, poet, and essayist, was born in Haarlem. He studied medicine in Amsterdam, receiving his degree in 1886, and set up his practice in Bussum. He had become interested in psychiatry and hypnotism in Paris and established a clinic for psychotherapy in Amsterdam. Even in his youth, however, van Eeden displayed literary talent, and his first work, the poetic comedy *Het rijk der wijzen* (1882; The Realm of the Sages), was published anonymously in *Nederland.* Among the other plays he wrote during his student years are *Het sonnet* (1883), *Frans Hals* (1884), *Het poortje of de Duivel te Kruimelberg* (The Little Gate or the Devil at Kruimelberg), *De student thuis* (1885; The Student at Home), and *Don Torribio* (1887). He became one of the founders and first editors of the influential literary periodical *De Nieuwe Gids,* which was to be the voice of a new generation. In its first issue, he began publication of his first novel, *De kleine Johannes* (1887; Eng. tr., *Little Johannes,* 1895; *The Quest,* 1907). With this partly autobiographical novel, cast in the form of a fairy tale, van Eeden achieved great popularity. The novel reflects his lifelong interest in parapsychology and contains a Christ-figure, as do several other works. Parts 2 and 3 did not appear until 1905–06, but in the meantime he continued this book's success with *Johannes Viator: Het boek van de liefde* (1890–1902; Johannes Viator: The Book of Love). His dramas *De Broeders, Tragedie van het recht* (1894; The Brothers, A Tragedy of Justice) and *Lioba, Drama van trouw* (1896; Lioba, Drama of Fidelity) both have heroines who are "virtuous sinners." With *Van de koele meren des doods* (1900; Eng. tr., *The Deeps of Deliverance,* 1902, 1974), however, van Eeden explored the destructive conflicts created in a young woman by the urgings of sex and the restrictions of society, proving himself a master of the psychological novel. For van Eeden, the kind of literary narcissism that characterized the men of *De Nieuwe Gids* was not enough. He shared the feelings of idealistic humanitarianism that were developing in Europe at the time and, indeed, often regarded himself as a potential savior of mankind. Inspired by his reading of Henry David Thoreau's *Walden*—he later wrote a preface to the first translation into Dutch—van Eeden bought property for a Utopian cooperative society, which he named Walden and which was to achieve Christian socialism, in contrast to the Marxist socialism that had attracted some of the other members of "De Nieuwe Gids" movement. The whole project ended in financial disaster, however, and in 1908 he went to the United States for a time to write articles and give public lectures. These experiences are reflected in the dramas *De Zendeling* (The Missionary)—published together with *De Stamhouder* (The Son and Heir) in *In kenterend getij* (1913; In the Changing of the Tide)—*Minnestral, De idealisten of Het beloofde land* (1909; The Idealists, or The Promised Land), and *Het paleis van Circe* (Circe's Palace). *De Nachtbruid* (1909; Eng. tr., *The Bride of Dreams,* 1913), an autobiographical novel, also belongs to this period. Van Eeden's vision of himself as a prophet and even a second Christ, who would save humanity, appears again in *Sirius en Siderius,* a fictional trilogy consisting of *De Ouders* (1912; The Parents), *Het Kind* (1914; The Child), and *Geroepen of verkooren?* (1924; Called or Chosen?). One of his most successful plays is *De Heks van Haarlem* (1915; The Witch of Haarlem), which is based on conflicting views of duty. His poetry, which he began writing at an early age, has lost much of its appeal. Among his poetic works are *Ellen, een lied van de smart* (1891; Ellen: A Song of Pain), *Van de passielooze lelie* (1901; Of the Passionless Lily), *Het lied van schijn en wezen* (1895–1922; The Song of Appearance and Substance), *Dante en Beatrice en andere verzen* (1904), *Pauls ontwaken* (1913; Paul's Awakening)—inspired by the death of his son—and *Aan mijn engelbewaarder en andere gedichten* (1922; To My Guardian Angel and Other Poems). He also admired and translated Rabindranath Tagore. His essays were collected in six volumes of *Studies* (1890–1917) and in *Langs den weg* (1925; Along the Way). He was also coeditor of *De Amsterdammer,* a weekly (1915–22). In 1922 he converted to Catholicism.

Van Eeden was a gifted and versatile man and remains the most interesting writer of his group for the modern reader.

See: H. W. van Tricht, *Frederik van Eeden, denker en strijder* (1934); *Mededelingen van het Frederik van Eedengenootschap* (1935–); A. Verwey, *Frederik van Eeden* (1939); S. L. Flaxman, "Thoreau and van Eeden," in E. Fromm, K. R. Grossmann, and H. Herzfeld, *Der Friede: Idee und Verwirklichung* (1961).   S.L.F.

Egge, Peter (1869–1959), Norwegian novelist, was born in Trondheim. Egge's entire literary production reflects the poverty he knew as a child and as a young man. In the 1890s he wrote short stories about the Trøndelag district that demonstrate a firm grip on realistic portrayal. This artistic command, combined with his psychological insight, made his novel *Hjertet* (1907; The Heart) his first success with both the public and the critics. In later novels, notably *Inde i Fjordene* (1920; In the Fjords) and *Hansine Solstad* (1925; Eng. tr., *Hansine Solstad: The History of an Honest Woman,* 1929), Egge continued to write in a vein of naked realism, yet his compassionate portraits of exploited but strong, proud, and independent women lend warmth and optimism to his accounts. Of his later books, *Minner I–IV* (1948–1955; Memories) are noteworthy for their personal, vivid sketches of Norwegian literary life.

See: B. S. Jystad, *Peter Egge og hans trønderromaner* (1949).   K.A.F.

Eich, Günter (1907–72), German radio play writer and poet, was a pioneer (1929–31) of the radio play. His post-World War II works, such as *Sabeth* (1951), *Träume* (1951; Dreams), *Die Andere und ich* (1951; The Other Woman and I), and *Der Tiger Jussuf* (1952), effectively exploit radio's unique acoustic qualities. They display a desire for individual integration with an atemporal and transcausal natural sphere and yet also stress human interrelatedness and responsibility. This thematic juxtaposition is increasingly uneasy in later radio plays such as *Die Brandung vor Setubal* (1957; Eng. tr., *The Rolling Sea at Setubal,* 1968), *Festianus, Märtyrer* (1958; Festianus, A Martyr), and *Man bittet zu läuten* (1964; Please Ring the Bell).

Eich's poetry developed similarly. His collection *Abgelegene Gehöfte* (1948; Remote Farmsteads), a ruthless stocktaking, influenced a generation of postwar poets. *Botschaften des Regens* (1955; Messages of the Rain)

stresses the themes of mystic integration and human responsibility, but the later collection *Zu den Akten* (1964; For the Record) clearly doubts any ordering principle in man's universe. Eich's last works, such as *Maulwürfe* (1968; Moles), create a linguistic universe only roughly paralleling "reality."

Eich was the husband of the writer Ilse AICHINGER. A selection of his poems is available in English, *Günter Eich,* tr. by T. Savory (1971).

See: E. Krispyn, *Günter Eich* (1971).   W.K.C.

Ekelöf, Gunnar (1907–68), Swedish poet and essayist, was born in Stockholm. He is widely considered his country's most important lyric modernist. His general outlook was that of a nonconformist mystic, and his art can be said to have its roots in a romantic and symbolist tradition. Yet he called himself an outsider and there is hardly a single term that will describe his complex but profoundly consistent poetry.

Ekelöf was all his life haunted by his childhood in an environment that appeared to him far beyond the normal. His father, a stockbroker, grew mentally ill and died before the boy was nine. Ekelöf's relation to his mother, Valborg von Hedenberg, was on the other hand to be one of frustrated love and rebellious disillusion.

The recurring dominant features in Ekelöf's art, revolt and vision, obviously originated in childhood experiences. His revolt found expression in a personally conceived titanism, his need of warmth and affection in a sublimating dream of an unattainable divinity or cosmic mother. He has himself declared that "want" is the only ground on which art can grow.

In his youth loneliness and emotional need could torment Ekelöf almost to the edge of suicide but also direct him towards aesthetic views and a secular mystic outlook on life that in the main became permanent. Oriental speculation combined with Baruch Spinoza's philosophy in particular came to color Ekelöf's efforts to find, beyond dualism, an intellectually viable formula for the oneness of the universe, of which man's inmost essence was at once an integral part and a clear reflection. During the period 1926–27 he became particularly engrossed in the Sufi Muhyi'd Din Ibn al-Árabí. The latter's 12th-century collection of mystical odes, *Tarjúmán al-Ashwáq* (Interpreter of Desire), came to be of lifelong importance to him.

Ekelöf had at that time only sporadic university studies to his credit, including a couple of months of Hindustani at the London School of Oriental Studies. After a long illness he went to Paris to study music (1929–30), but these studies, too, were not completed. Nevertheless they left him with a lasting dependence on music. He soon acquired very considerable learning, however, not least in the field of antiquity. He was made an honorary Ph.D. at Uppsala University in 1958, the same year as he was elected to the Swedish Academy.

During his stay in Paris in the year 1929–30 Ekelöf became acquainted with surrealism and presurrealism, abstract and concrete art. He praised particularly the active artistic integrity of the symbolist Stéphane MALLARMÉ and expressed a certain affinity with Robert DESNOS, whose surrealism seemed to him not very dogmatic. Ekelöf's mainly French orientation in about 1930 resulted in two volumes of translations, *fransk surrealism* (1933) and *100 år modern fransk dikt* (1934).

Ekelöf's very first volume of poetry, *sent på jorden* (1932; late on earth), struck a radically new note in Swedish literature. He called it "a suicidal book" and with its explosive language it was not only beyond the surrealist clichés, it suggested nightmare scenes of a purely emotional logic. His imagery, in fact, owed more to surrealist painting than to French literary experiments, steeped as it was in the same hallucinatory, subconscious, ghostly magic. A Freudian influence is obvious in *sent på jorden*, and the musical inspiration behind the work was above all Igor Stravinsky's *Sacre du Printemps*.

Ekelöf's sensational literary debut coincided with the emergence of the modernist currents in Sweden. He joined the editorial staff of the two avant-garde periodicals *Spektrum* and *Karavan*. But at the same time the situation in Europe had begun to darken. A long visit to Berlin in 1933 convinced Ekelöf that "Hell is drawing near to Earth," a message that he proclaimed in various forms. His feeling, familiar since early youth, that he had a call became stronger. After a disasterous first marriage new disappointments in love intensified his aggressiveness and his pessimism. A violent revulsion against society and the prevailing political mood seized him. His essay "Bcneath the Dog Star" (*Karavan* I, 1934) and the atmosphere of his second book of poems, *Dedikation* (1934), clearly express his revolt and anguish.

Ekelöf was later to characterize the period of the early 1930s as one of neurotic overcompensation. His efforts to understand the "oracle" Arthur RIMBAUD by writing articles and translations brought to the fore his own lengthy struggle against dualism, contributing to a reorientation after the middle of the 1930s. He was always critical of the next two, more traditionally romantic, collections: *Sorgen och Stjärnan* (1936; The Sorrow and the Star) and *Köp den blindes sång* (1938; Buy the Blind Man's Song).

To the very end, Ekelöf regarded *Färjesång* (1941; Ferry Song), his real breakthrough, as a milestone in his development. When it appeared, war and death, alluded to in the title and opening song (that is, Charon's boat), were all around. Ekelöf's realization of the intellectual's moral dilemma in the political struggle accounts for the disenchanted attitude of "Tag och skriv" (Write), the main poem written while he was translating André MALRAUX's novel *L'Espoir* about the Spanish Civil War and later T. S. Eliot's *East Coker*. In the poem, good and evil, The Knight and the Dragon, carry on their infinite struggle while the Princess (the Virgin) is standing by, at once the decoy and the prize of the struggle, the symbol of the innermost heart of existence beyond all categories.

An even stronger indication of Ekelöf's outsider's stance was given in *Non serviam* (1945). If *Färjesång* was a document of intellectual endeavour, its successor was chiefly marked by feeling and temperament. In the words of the fallen angel Lucifer, "I will not serve," Ekelöf hurled forth his refusal to submit to anybody or anything, like Joyce's Stephen Dedalus. He felt a stranger in his own land, "the people's home," welfare Sweden, which he said he had left "for good" three times. In a polyphonically composed group of poems "Havstema" (Sea Theme), elegiac and sensual parts mingle in a fantastic underwater symphony. The great ode "Samothrake" is a vision of humanity's voyage over the ocean of time and death. The winged Virgin indomitably advancing in front of the ship of death is humanity's dream of an ever-eluding victory. In one poem, "Gymnosofisten," he tries like the Indian philosopher to seize the essence of reality through deep meditation, in another, "Absentia animi," to touch the mystical insight in a moment of fortunate half-consciousness, to attain "something beyond-nearby in what is this side faroff."

With its emancipated diction and indications of Ekelöf's "intellectual emotional life," *Om hösten* (1951; In the Autumn) is largely preoccupied with dream and retrospect and introduces the Swedenborgian conception, dear to

Ekelöf, of the cosmos as "the great man." The main poem "Röster under jorden" (Voices under the Ground) is an impressive nightmare recollection of loneliness and paralysis.

With the beginning of the 1950s, the imagist poetry of anguish that had distinguished Swedish literature during the 1940s began to be replaced by a more optimistic current and a simpler style. Once again Ekelöf broke away from the prevailing trend. In *Strountes* (1955; Nonsense) he introduced an antiaesthetic, absurdist conception of art. This also pervades *Opus incertum* (1959) and *En natt i Otočac* (1961; A night in Otočac).

Through long visits to Italy and Greece,—after his marriage in 1951—Ekelöf had greatly increased his knowledge of their cultures. The recurrent antique motifs, often chthonian in character, thus bind together the antiaesthetic poems, just as the mixture of reflection and drastic parody, of nature lyrics and obscene and grotesque material, is common to all his poems.

It was not only by his fidelity to the idea that dreams and the subconscious can attain a reality beyond reality that Ekelöf maintained his continuity. His cosmic Virgin-Mother began to take on the shape of the syncretically conceived Mediterranian goddess and Madonna of the icons that he invoked in his last years.

Between *Opus incertum* and *Otočac* came the publication of the long poem *En Mölna-elegi* (1960; Eng. tr., *A Mölna Elegy*, 1979), which Ekelöf had been working on for more than 20 years, and of which parts had already been published. It is a great composition about time. Ekelöf shared with Joyce, Marcel PROUST and Eliot the Bergsonian conception of time. In *A Mölna Elegy* the action represents a cross section of time, apprehended in a half-conscious moment of the ego as "auditive focus" of a flood of memories, associations and moods, one day during the Indian summer of 1940. The individual's path through the metamorphoses is, like that of human culture, determined by causes and influences stretching back to the fossilized bird, the archaeopteryx, which is in Ekelöf's poetry also an image of the petrification of living emotion. Melodious refrains and symbolic correspondances bind the composition together.

In 1962, Ekelöf published a revised edition with a commentary of *Sent på jorden* with an "appendix" (early Sufic fragments) and a long prose and lyric suite in sonata or symphonic form, "En natt vid horisonten" (A Night at the Horizon), which is of mixed chronology but of great interest. The volume of translations *Valfrändskaper* (1960; Elective Affinities) was a stage in the same attempt to find the thread of scarlet through the work.

Ekelöf was now heading for climax. In apparent defiance of the current intellectual climate he presented an ecstatic and highly personal creed disguised in a setting of the Byzantine Middle Ages and Near-Eastern culture history. *Dīwān över Fursten av Emgión* (1965; Dīwān) was similar to Goethe's *West-Eastern Divan* in that it described a synthesis of East and West, yet it also showed the conditions of modern man reflected in the grim past. When the *Dīwān* was followed by *Sagan om Fatumeh* (1966; Eng. tr., *Selected Poems*, 1971) and *Vägvisare till underjorden* (1967; Guide to the Underworld), surprising and partly contrasting expressions of Ekelöf's mysticism again appeared. The Orient of the *Arabian Nights* and at the same time a looking-glass land and a land of shadows gave the *Saga* its magical atmosphere of fate. The underworld of the *Vägvisare* contained both Antiquity's and Hellenism's worlds of myth. The memories, associations and reactions that the three collections re-created were common not only to them; the whole of Ekelöf's writing had revolved about personal experience, widened into collective human perspectives. The triology, or rather triptych, was an attempt at a summary, what the author called his testament.

It is under the title "Devil's Sermon" that Ekelöf finally presents his secular belief in the Virgin, his artistic creed and his message of love. He has once more become a seer. Ekelöf's personal encounter with the culture of Asia Minor released his artistry in a tremendous inspiration. His philosophy of life is in the end simple: everything comes together in the bosom of the Magna Mater. Life is a narrow chink between darknesses. Ekelöf's own ashes were scattered in the river at Sardis, near the cult of Artemis.

A cross section of Ekelöf's writings may give the impression that his complicated and profound poetry is thoroughly inaccessible and obscure. This is by no means true. He is always close to the reader and speaks directly in his passionate voice and verbal artistry. Not seldom does a joking and puzzling tone break through.

An increasing number of translations into a score or so of languages has brought Ekelöf's poetry over Sweden's frontiers.

See: R. Ekner, *I den havandes liv* (1967) and *Gunnar Ekelöf: en bibliografi* (1970); B. Landgren, *Ensamheten, döden ech drömmarna* (1971); L. Sjöberg, *A Reader's Guide to Gunnar Ekelöf's A Mölna Elegy* (1973); R. Shideler, *Voices under the Ground* (1973); P. Hellström, *Livskänsla och självutplåning* (1976); L. Koch Ausili Cefaro, *L'alto, il basso, la seppia e la spirale: studio sulle varianti a due liriche di Gunnar Ekelöf* (1977).   B.W.

Ekelund, Vilhelm (1880–1949), Swedish poet and aphorist, was born at Stehag in the southern province of Skåne and educated at the University of Lund. The first phase of his career comprises the years 1900 to 1906, during which he published seven collections of poetry, some of it among the very best in the Swedish language. In *Vårbris* (1900; Spring Breeze), *Syner* (1901; Visions), and *Melodier i skymning* (1902; Twilight Melodies), the melodious strains of French symbolism a la Paul VERLAINE are mingled with melancholy imagery derived from the poet's native landscape of beech woods, fertile land, and lakes. *Elegier* (1903; Elegies) and *In Candidum* (1905) are more disciplined in form and reveal the author's growing commitment to the art and ideals of classical antiquity. Classical is the noble resignation that inspires many of the pieces in *Havets stjärna* (1906; Stella Maris), and classical are the light, drunken hymns of *Dithyramber i aftonglans* (1906; Dithyrambs in Evening's Splendor), perhaps Ekelund's finest collection. Ekelund the poet was in many respects a true follower of the romantic idealists and of the symbolists, above all in his extolling of art and absolute beauty as a realm of eternal freedom and escape from the frustrations and sufferings of human life.

In 1908, Ekelund left Sweden in order to evade the legal consequences of a minor offense—participation in a public house brawl—and at the same time he took leave of poetry. He spent the following four years in Berlin in utter poverty, sustaining himself on a diet of Plato, stoicism, and Friedrich NIETZSCHE, learning the hard virtues of self-denial and spiritual discipline. A period of severe illness in Denmark marked his way back to Sweden, where he hoped to become a spiritual leader of the young, but to his bitter disappointment he found himself isolated without a public except for a small circle of devoted followers who made it their concern to print his work. Ekelund's new medium of expression in exile and henceforth was the essay and aphorism, in which he showed himself a master of Swedish prose. *Antikt ideal* (1909; Classical Ideal) is the first of several books of aphoristic

meditation. Others are *Båge och lyra* (1912; Bow and Lyre), *Veri similia* (1915–16), *Metron* (1918), and *På havsstranden* (1922; On the Beach). In spite of disappointment and public rejection, Ekelund gained moral strength and lust for living as he grew older, and the essence of his later work, always exquisite and sometimes a little bookish, is an affirmation of life.

Vilhelm Ekelund is not the only early 20th-century poet to choose silence as a means of powerful poetic expression. Rainer Maria RILKE and Paul VALÉRY afford parallel examples. But, unlike these, Ekelund made a final renunciation of poetry, and on the strength of that renunciation and the noble teaching of his prose books, he became a poet for the poets, perhaps the most influential of contemporary Swedish writers on young poets from the early 1920s to the late 1940s. *Agenda*, a selection of aphorisms, appeared in 1976 (Eng. tr., L. Bruce).

See: A. Werin, *Vilhelm Ekelund*, 3 vols. (1960–61); *Ekelund studier 1912–1976* (1976); L. Gustafsson, *Forays into Swedish Poetry* (1978), pp. 65–72.   S.B.

Elskamp, Max (1862–1931), Belgian poet, was born in Antwerp. He seldom left his native city, where his father was a shipowner and banker. Elskamp studied law but practiced for only one year. His wealth permitted him to indulge in many hobbies, among which were the carving of woodcuts, the collecting of old nautical instruments, and the study of Flemish folklore. He was 30 when he published his first book of poems, *Dominical* (1892; Sunday). This and three succeeding volumes were later collected under the title *La Louange de la vie* (1898; Praise of Life). Meanwhile, Elskamp had aroused hostility among conservative Belgian critics for the liberties he took with syntax, diction, and poetry. His quatrains and couplets, often in lines of five, eight, or nine syllables, resembled folk songs. Defended by Emile VERHAEREN in Belgium and in France by the symbolists, his ingenuous style was compared to that of Paul VERLAINE. Between 1898 and 1921, Elskamp published no poetry, but in the latter year appeared his *Sous les tentes de l'Exode* (Under the Tents of Exodus), the poetic record of four years of exile in Holland during the World War I. There followed years of abundant publication: eight volumes of poetry in three years as well as typescripts of five additional volumes, which did not appear until 1967 in the *Œuvres complètes* (Complete Works). This collection, one thousand pages in length, despite repetition and monotony of themes, reveals new breadth of subject matter: many poems on loved women, on exotic imaginary voyages, on Oriental religion, and on mental suffering. Although many of the lyrics are happy songs, there are more and more of anguished tone. This is not strange, for Elskamp, never in robust health, became seriously neurotic as he grew older and spent his last years in a mental state in which dream and reality, punctuated by imaginary fears, were utterly blended. The echoes of this distressed condition can be found in a collection of poems entitled *Aegri Somnia* (1924: A Sick Man's Dreams). Throughout his poetry runs a constant yearning for religious calm, which he sometimes sought in prayers to the Virgin Mary and again in verses addressed to the Buddha. He deserves mention for his rich variety of verse forms and for his curious patterns of speech, where banal terms are subtly changed into something original. He may have influenced Guillaume APOLLINAIRE, and he is sometimes cited among poets of the Catholic literary revival.

See: R. Guiette, *Max Elskamp* (1956); L. Lebois, *Admirable XIXᵉ Siècle* (1958); B. Delvaille, "Avant-propos" in Elskamp's *Œuvres complètes* (1967); C. Berg, "Max Elskamp et l'esthétique fin de siècle," *BARLLF* 47, no.

2 (1969): 132–55; *Max Elskamp et le bouddhisme* (1969); H. Spencer, ed., *The Penrose Graphic Arts International Annual* 65 (1972); A. Art, R. Fayt, and D. de Papi, *Inventaire de la bibliothèque de Max Elskamp* (1973).

K.Co.

Elsner, Gisela (1937–), German novelist and short-story writer, was born in Nuremberg, the daughter of a director of Siemens, the giant German electrical company. Elsner studied philosophy, German literature, and theater arts in Vienna and lived long in London and Paris. After her initial success in 1956 with the collection of stories, *Triboll*, she was invited to read to "Gruppe 47." *Die Riesenzwerge* (1964; Eng. tr., *The Giant Dwarfs*, 1965), her first and best-known novel, translated into 12 languages, is directed against the postwar German petite bourgeoisie, depicted with great exactness as monstrous, gross, and misshapen. Elsner's next novel, *Der Nachwuchs* (1968; The Descendants), is again critical of society, portraying the bestial and evil aspects of suburbia. *Der Berührungsverbot* (1970; Do Not Touch), a novel of provocation, has as its theme repressed sexual conduct and its relationship to group sex. Elsner caricatures the nouveau riche and their incongruent mores in grotesque fashion. A later novel, *Der Punktsieg* (1977; Winning on Points), is about another affluent industrial family, the Mechtels. A second collection of short stories, *Herr Leiselheimer* (1973), bears the significant subtitle: "Further Attempts to Master Reality."

See: W. Widmer, "Die Züchtung von Riesenzwergen. Von der kalten Wut der Gisela Elsner," in H. L. Arnold, ed., *Geschichte der deutschen Literatur aus Methoden,* vol. 3 (1973), pp. 33–36; E. R. Herrmann and E. H. Spitz, eds., *German Women Writers of the Twentieth Century* (1978), pp. 116–24.

E.H.S.

Eluard, Paul, pseud. of Eugène-Emile Paul Grindel (1895–1952), French poet, was born in Saint-Denis. Eluard first began to write when he was confined at the age of 19 to a Swiss sanitorium for inceptive tuberculosis. There he met his future wife, Gala; on his return to Paris he became part of the *Nouvelle Revue française* group and associated with the young poets and artists who were to embrace the dadaist movement (*see* FRENCH LITERATURE) in Paris. In the 1920s he joined André BRETON and Louis ARAGON in launching the surrealist movement and participated in many of the experimental activities of the group, demonstrating automatic writing, the transcription of dreams, and the simulation of insanity. Eluard collaborated with Breton in exploring the idiom of mental aberration in a work called *L'Immaculée Conception* (1930; The Immaculate Conception). Eluard was also closely associated with the artists Max Ernst and Pablo Picasso. Indeed, the coordination of painting with poetry was one of the fundamental objectives of surrealism. *Les Malheurs des immortels* (1922; The Misfortunes of the Immortals) is an early collaboration with Max Ernst. *Donner à voir* (1940; To Give to See) juxtaposes Picasso drawings with some Eluard poems that provoke the power of extended vision through verbal imagery, demonstrating the theory that in surrealism the objective is not so much the creation of unusual images as the cultivation of the power to provoke sight, of making the invisible visible in what Eluard liked to call "le miroir sans tain" (the mirror without silvering).

Eluard's most famous collections of surrealist verse are *Les Dessous d'une vie ou la pyramide humaine* (1926; The Underside of Life or the Human Pyramid) and *Capitale de la douleur* (1926; Capital of Sorrow); the first gives a plethora of examples both of automatic surrealist texts and of more structured poetry, exploring the bound-aries of dream and death, of the subconscious verging on the unconscious. In *Capitale de la douleur* as well as in *L'Amour, la poésie* (1932; Love, Poetry), Eluard conveys the cloudless, transparent regions attained through the purification of the senses, through unexpected metaphoric associations sometimes verging on the abnegation of physical laws, such as in his famous statement "La terre est bleue comme une orange" (The earth is blue like an orange). Eluard writes of the night, the piercing of blackness, wings, birds, the solitude and the virtually concrete reality of absence, the perceptions of the blind and the deaf, auroras and metamorphoses of natural phenomena, and the serenity of the Beautiful mingled with anguish; from these elements he created a poetry that is limpid yet throbbing, pure and sensual at the same time. Above all, he writes about love, the cult of woman, and the engulfing power of the eternal feminine.

Eluard also successfully wrote prose poems, coupling the abstract with the concrete in the manner of the symbolists. If he is, poetically speaking, a comrade of Breton, he is also a descendant of Racine, Charles BAUDELAIRE, and Paul VERLAINE in the translucence he can achieve and in the richness of meaning he obtains through lexical simplicity. *La Vie immédiate* (1936; Immediate Life) and *Les Yeux fertiles* (1936; Fertile Eyes) suggest the immanence of reality, the abundance of vision, and the catalyzing power of love. In his most famous war poem, "Liberté" (Liberty), he also wrote about the prevailing frenzy for freedom, searching for it in school notebooks, in jungles and deserts, in his daily bread, writing the word "liberty" in the rising sun and in the sea and the mountaintops.

During World War II, Eluard joined the Resistance movement and identified himself with the Communist Party. At the same time he turned from the cryptic, largely analogical poetry of the subconscious to a more direct idiom, moralistic in tenor, more open in meaning, humanistic in objective, patriotic in effect, yet also more hypnotically lyrical and emotionally captivating. Love poetry continued to be Eluard's richest vein. After he had lost Gala to Salvador Dali, he married Nusch who, in turn, became the focus of his love poems, even after her sudden, tragic death. In his post–World War II writings, the theme of love gravitates from the particular to the universal, and personal ecstasy is transformed into love of humanity and a concerted effort toward moral fulfillment.

See: special issues of *Europe* 91–92 (1953), 403-4 (1962), 525 (1973), and of *CduS* 364 (1962); L. Perche, *Paul Eluard* (1964); A. Kittang, *D'amour de poésie: essai sur l'univers des métamorphoses dans l'œuvre surréaliste de Paul Eluard* (1969); R. Vernier, *Poésie ininterrompue et la poétique de Paul Eluard* (1971); P. Nugent, *Paul Eluard* (1974); L. Parrot and J. Marcenac, *Paul Eluard* (rev. 1975).

A.B.

Elytis, Odysseas, pseud. of Odysseas Alepoudelis, (1911–), Greek poet, was born in Herakleion, Crete. He helped revive Greek letters in the mid-1930s. Whereas George SEFERIS expressed the tragic awareness of a long cultural-historical past, Elytis has been predominantly the euphoric voice of youth and rebirth in a sun-drenched Aegean. His brightly sensual, yet thoughtful, imagery derives from his native Herakleion, his ancestral Lesbos, and summers spent on various other islands. Elytis was influenced at first by French surrealism, but he developed his own sense of form and clarity. His first two collections of poems, *Prosanatolismi* (1940; Orientations) and *Ilios o protos* (1943; Sun the First), convey his joyful vision of the Aegean. The long *Iroïko ke penthimo asma yia ton* hameno anthipolohagho tis Alvanias (1945; Heroic and Elegiac Song for the Lost Lieutenant of the Albanian Campaign), inspired by his war experience in 1940, introduces a tragic element into his lyricism.

The volumes Exi ke mia tipsis yia ton ourano (1960; Six and One Remorses for the Sky) and Axion esti (1960; Eng. tr., The Axion Esti, 1974) lifted Elytis's art to the level of a major accomplishment. Axion esti is a complex epico-lyrical work inspired by the Byzantine liturgy. Its first major section, "Genesis," identifies the creator-poet with the Greek people and their history as well as with the entire Aegean world. The second section, "The Passion," leads him through the horrendous events of the 1940s, while the final section hymns the glory of all those elements of Greece—the Aegean, the sun, trees, mountains, stars—that are "worthy" (Àxion) of the poet's devotion and that justify his sacrifices. After Axion Esti, Elytis published, among other things: Asma iroiko kai penthimo via ton hameno anthypolohago tis Alvanias (1962; Heroic and Elegiac Song for the Lost Second Lieutenant of the Albanian Campaign), Thanatos kai anastasis tou Konstandinou Palaiologou (1971; Death and Resurrection of Constantine Palaiologos), O ilios o iliatoras (1971; The Sovereign Sun), and Villa Natacha (1973). In Elytis's more recent collections, his sun-and-love lyricism has reached new heights. He is influential and popular in his own country, and his work has been translated into several foreign languages. He was awarded the 1979 Nobel Prize for Literature. A selection of his poetry is available in English under the title The Sovereign Sun: Selected Poems, tr. by K. Friar (1974).

See: BA (Autumn 1975) (special Elytis issue).   A.D.

Emants, Marcellus (1848–1923), Dutch novelist, poet, and dramatist, was born in Voorburg, a suburb of The Hague. He studied law at Leiden, but because he had an independent income, he was soon able to devote himself completely to literature. Emants did not share the aesthetic views of the men in the "Movement of the Eighties," for he felt that not beauty, but truth, was the essence of art. His first published play, the comedy Jonge Harten (1872; Young Hearts), appeared in Spar en Hulst, a journal that he founded. Juliaan de Afvallige (1874; Julian the Apostate), an historical drama, was his first work to appear in book form and revealed his rejection of both romantic unreality and middle-class narrow-mindedness. In 1875, in De Banier, a magazine he had established with two other men of letters, he published almost all of Op reis door Zweden (1877; Traveling through Sweden); Monaco (1878), a group of stories; and Een drietal novellen (1879; A Trio of Novellas). Although he defended Émile ZoLa's point of view in the preface to the novellas, Emants was no mere follower of naturalism. He rejected his Dutch contemporaries' view of the word as art, however, and wrote in an easy narrative style, without literary pretensions. With Lilith (1879), he scandalized his readers, as he had already done with his earlier work. Just as the casino in Monaco symbolizes an overwhelming evil power, so Lilith, the heroine of Emants's epic, symbolizes sexual desire, which human beings are unable to resist. Hence, human problems are attributable to God, who is responsible for the urge to procreation. Emants sees life as meaningless, and his pessimism appears again in his later epic Godenschemering (1883; Twilight of the Gods), which is based on material from the Edda. Just as Emants viewed Lilith as a contemporary figure, so he interpreted Loki, his hero from the world of Germanic mythology, as a representative of reason, which was not always appreciated in the modern world. Emants's first novel, Jong Holland (1881; Young Holland) was not very

important, but with Juffrouw Lina, een portret (1888; Miss Lina: A Portrait), he developed his own manner. Emants's disillusioned view that love leads to more suffering than pleasure in life reappears in his novel Dood (1892; Death), which is included in the volume Afgestorven/Huwelijksgeluk/Een kind (1967; Dead/Matrimonial Bliss/A Child). Emants won a permanent place for himself in the history of Dutch literature with a grim and convincing psychological novel, Een nagelaten bekentenis (1894; Eng. tr., A Posthumous Confession, 1975). Influenced by a deterministic view of heredity, Emants portrays an antihero in an unfortunate marriage. In the taut and perceptive novel Inwijding (1901; Initiation), the heroine dies of the effects of an abortion. The theme of love as an illusion appears again in Waan (1905; Illusion), a novel of the love of a man for a woman much younger than himself, and in Liefdeleven (1916; Love Life), a novel in which the woman makes life a torment for her husband. Emants's skill in writing dialogue is evident even in his novels. His Adolf van Gelrè (1888) is a verse drama in the romantic tradition, but his later plays, Domheidsmacht (1904; The Power of Stupidity) and Om de mensen (1916; Because of People), reflect his naturalistic point of view.

See: F. Coenen, "Bij de dood van Marcellus Emants," in Verzameld Werk (1956); P. H. Dubois, Marcellus Emants: een schrijversleven (1964).   S.L.F.

Emmanuel, Pierre, pseud. of Noël Mathieu (1916–), French poet, was born in Gan. He has lived in Paris since 1944, but he has also resided abroad, particularly in the United States, where he spent several years of his childhood. In 1938 he began publishing in such leading literary periodicals as Mesures, Cahiers du Sud, Nouvelles Lettres, and the Nouvelle Revue française. His first volume of poetry, Elégies, appeared in 1940, but it was the following year that, with Le Tombeau d'Orphée, (The Tomb of Orpheus), Emmanuel attracted critical attention, reached a wide public, and became a famous poet overnight. Today, 40 years later, his published work exceeds 40 titles comprising collections of poems, essays, autobiographies, lectures, and one novel. These works, among which it is hard to make a choice, deal with the human condition in its multiple forms: political, philosophical, and religious.

From Le Poëte et son Christ (1947; The Poet and His Christ) to Evangiliaire (1961; Evangiliary), from Jacob (1970) to Tu (1978; Thou) and Duel (1979), the main thread of this immense work, baptized "profound rhetoric" by the author himself, is the Christian faith, a poetic and mystical testimony whose high point is Babel (1952). One might also call this thread Judeo-Christian mythology. In fact, Emmanuel has never ceased being inspired by the great Biblical and evangelical texts while, at the same time, projecting into them his most personal problems, his greatest and most painful contradictions, his obsessions, and his fantasies. If the conception of poetry elaborated by Emmanuel remains essentially traditional (an impression and opinion confirmed by the more recent Duel and Una), the originality of the poet consists in associating the Christic revelation with the quest for self. From this attempt at a lyrical synthesis—romantic, supremely eloquent, an undertaking of genius in its epic proportions—there results a private religion that animates book after book with the most diverse sentiments and interpretations. The overriding quality of this all-encompassing, insistent, and totalitarian work contrasts with the effect produced by most contemporary works, and it is not by accident that Emmanuel is compared to Agrippa d'Aubigné, Victor Hugo, or Alfred de Vigny—even to Dante.

Influenced neither by surrealism nor by more recent schools (*see* FRENCH LITERATURE), Emmanuel seems to be, despite his audience and his election to the Académie Française in 1968, a marginal writer, simultaneously concerned with his times (from the Resistance to the present moment, from the communistic fellow-traveling of the 1940s to the post-1958 Gaullism) and violently opposed to them. The basis of this opposition corresponds to the poet's manifestations against atheism and agnosticism, against the domination of Marxist throught or of the neo-paganism of the Right. Rejected, moreover, by Louis ARAGON after 1950 and by the "progressives" linked to the Stalin cult, Emmanuel did not reconvert to liberalism and democratic socialism, being prevented from so doing by his theology, which, although it does not appear to be completely reactionary, has its source in a period much earlier than the Age of Enlightenment, before the scientism and positivism of the 19th century and before the ideologies of the 20th.

To explain Emmanuel more fully, one must go back to the dualism of Pauline Christianity. On the one hand, there is flesh, which is evil; on the other, the spirit, which is the only road to perfection and salvation. This dualism, later taken into consideration by the Reform and by Jansenism, tortures the believer. He wishes to incarnate himself, but then he exposes himself to sin (particularly to the sin of sex); he wishes to purify his mind, but then he runs the fearful risk of angelism. In the extreme form he goes back—and of this Emmanuel is very conscious—to the religion of the Cathars, the consequences of which are well known: spiritual pride, strict morality, and unbridled mysticism. Emmanuel reacted to this by admitting his personal temptations, his obsession with the flesh, and by founding an eroticism capable of unshackling the soul. In other words, by the poetic act, Emmanuel sanctions a kind of liberating behavior linked to the liberation that, according to the gospels, is favored by faith. By a system of complex modalities, faith transcends the body-spirit dualism delivered over to its torments. This implies a search for a new theology and a new ethics. Thus from *Sophia* to *Una ou la mort, la vie* (Una or Death, Life), Emmanuel aims increasingly at giving a privileged position to woman, the feminine half of the human being, a notion already present in his masterpiece, *Babel*. In triumphing over his dualism, however, Emmanuel does not always master abstraction. He creates a Christian philosophy in which some see—as in the case of his "master" Pierre Jean JOUVE—a cohabitation of Sigmund Freud and Jesus, not without conflict or confusion.

Emmanuel's work also presents formal difficulties. As Gaëtan Picon has so clearly suggested: "The words themselves, in their excess, their rhetorical lengthening, carry less weight; this poetry quickly becomes abstract and colorless; the accumulation of epithets and images tends to devaluate the expression." Such works as *Jacob, Sophie* (1973), and *Tu*, imposing, didactic, and heavy, have jeopardized Emmanuel's prestige, whereas there are still admirers of the brief *Cantos* (1942) of the Resistance period or of the 160 "douzains" (12-line poems) of *Una*.

See: A. Bosquet, *Pierre Emmanuel* (1959); S. E. Siegrist, *Pour ou contre Dieu: Pierre Emmanuel ou la poésie de l'approche* (1971); A. Marissel, *Pierre Emmanuel* (1974).   A.M.

Enckell, Rabbe (1903–74), Finland-Swedish poet, playwright, and essayist, was born in Tammela. He was the Sunday child among the Finland-Swedish modernists. Because of the clarity of his verse (and its quite unpolitical nature), he won early acclaim. In his brother Olof, critic, novelist, and literary scholar, he possessed a sympathetic ally. Under no economic pressure, he could develop his talents as he wished. He also achieved substantial success in a second artistic line, as a painter. Throughout a career of 50 years, he was able to maintain a consistently high level of craftsmanship and taste.

Even his debut was sure-handed. The elegant intensity of the love lyrics in *Dikter* (1923: Poems) led to the bridegroom's songs of *Flöjtblåsarlycka* (1925: Flutist's Happiness), rejoicing at the world around him. Young Enckell was a close student of the Finland-Swedish baroque poet, Jakob Frese (ca. 1690–1729), and had learned Frese's natural piety, if not yet his melancholy. *Vårens cistern* (1931: Spring's Cistern) contains more compressed work, "matchstick poems," a capturing of specifically Finnish pastorals in a form not unlike the haiku. Simultaneously, Enckell cultivated a cool but somehow impassioned prose, in which he analyzed himself—*Tillblivelse* (1929: Becoming); and *Ljusdunkel* (1930: Chiaroscuro)—and his first wife, Heidi Runeberg—*Ett Porträtt* (1931: A Portrait). The narrative line of *Landskapet med den dubbla skuggan* (1933: Landscape with the Double Shadow) and *Herrar till natt och dag* (1937: Lords of Night and Day) was less convincing, although the first contains Enckell's masterly sketch of playground cruelty, "The Japanese Children." His collections of poems, *Tonbrädet* (1935; The Sounding Board) and *Valvet* (1937: The Vault) speak of personal crisis, but through classical allusion and odic form; the ensuing tension makes *Valvet,* in particular, a major collection. Enckell's classical studies also resulted in verse plays, first on familiar themes—*Orfeus och Eurydike* (1938), *Iokasta* (1939), *Agamemnon* (1947), *Hekuba* (1952), and *Mordet på Kiron* (1954: The Murder of Chiron)—then, more freely and almost jokingly, on a poet, *Alkman* (1959). With the years, the plays became vehicles for broadcasting. In *Dikt* (1966: Poem), Enckell reprinted the Jokasta play, together with two new plays, written in what Enckell called a more everyday language, on Laius, Oedipus' father, and Latona, the mother of Artemis and Apollo. Enckell's "classical" work has never been academic (unlike that of his predecessor in Finland-Swedish verse, Emil Zilliacus). The loss behind *Valvet,* for example, also informs the drama on Orpheus.

Lutad över brunnen (1942; Bent over the Well), deals, again in Greek (or Biblical) figures, with personal problems and Finland's perils. *Andedräkt av koppar* (1946; Breath of Copper) praises "poets of the hard school" and poetry itself; the long programmatic elegy, "O spång av mellanord" (O Bridge of Words between), shows how the bucolic singer of the 1920s, recently a somber odist, has become the great apologist for his guild and his art. Aware of a watershed in his production, Enckell marked it with the selection from his lyrics *Nike flyr i vindens klädnad* (1947: Nike Flees in the Wind's Raiment), with an introduction by Erik LINDEGREN.

The remainder of Enckell's work can be listed under three rubrics, apart from the completion of the dramatic edifice: (1) lyric, from *Sett och återbördat* (1950; Seen and Regained), past five subsequent collections to the posthumous *Flyende spegel* (1974; Fleeing Mirrors), which sometimes offers a diarylike travel impression, sometimes the quick union of painter's eye and poet's hand, sometimes a resigned epigram; (2) the reflective and aphoristic prose of *Traktat* (1953: Tractate), *och sanning?* (1966; and truth?), *Tapetdörren* (1968: The Tapestried Door), and *Resonören med fågelfoten* (1972: The Reasoner with the Bird's foot), where wisdom and insight are occasionally marred by a snobbish querulousness; and (3) the collected essays *Relation i det personliga* (1950:

Personal Report), a display of his utterly well-founded opinions on letters and painting, and *Essay om livets framfart* (1961: Essay on Life's Sweep), which contains Enckell's portrait of his father, the agriculturist Karl Enckell, and one of his lengthiest efforts to explore—in an objective report, not a confession—his own emotional constitution.

In his precision of language and his magisterial inclinations, Enckell resembles T. S. Eliot but shares neither the latter's religiosity nor his excessive learnedness; from start to finish, Enckell pursued an ideal of reasoned lucidity that makes him a representative of the best in the Finland-Swedish humanistic tradition, albeit a humanist never unaware of the fragility of his emotional and aesthetic world.

See: L. Ekelund, *Rabbe Enckell: modernism och klassicism under tjugotal och trettital* (1974).　　　G.C.S.

Enquist, Per Olov (1934-), Swedish novelist, was born in Bureå, Västerbotten. He lost his father at an early age and was brought up by his mother, a schoolteacher. He has a Fil. Lic. (Ph.D.) from Uppsala University. Enquist's approach to the novel is scholarly, his concern being how the novelist filters his material. After his first two novels, *Kristallögat* (1961; The Crystal Eye) and *Färdvägen* (1963; The Road), exercises into the art, communicating how closely related the real is to the illusionary and how intertwined the genuine is with the false, Enquist's first major work is *Magnetisörens femte vinter* (1964; The Magnetician's Fifth Winter). It is about Anton Mesmer, a figure who once intrigued the romantic poets, for example, E. T. A. Hoffmann, and also inspired Ingmar BERGMAN to create the film *Ansiktet* (1958; Eng. tr., *The Magician*, 1960) who is chosen as model. The conflict stands between the physician and rationalist, Selinger, and the magnetician, who heals people but also manifestly manipulates them.

Enquist's experimentation with the documentary novel began with *Hess* (1966). The title refers to Rudolf Hess, who fled from Hitler's Germany during World War II, but the main character is a scholar writing his dissertation on Hess and running into difficulties. Can Hess be understood? Enquist lays out a kaleidoscope of quotations. The intention is to demonstrate that objective information always is interpreted and turned in the pattern of action and reaction that dominates each era. Change the time and the picture looks different. This idea is behind Enquist's best-known novel, *Legionärerna* (1968; Eng. tr., *The Legionnaires* 1973), which deals with an event that caused great upheaval in Sweden right after the war. The Soviet Union had asked for the return of Baltic military personnel who had worked for the Nazis and then fled from the Russians over to Sweden, where they were interned. The government agreed to the delivery, but among the Swedish people the conviction took hold that these refugees were in a cowardly way being sent to certain torture and death, an impression strengthened by suicide and self-mutilation among the interns. Twenty years later, when the political situation had radically changed, Enquist investigated the event anew and what happened afterward to those people whom most Swedes had forgotten. Enquist traveled to interview them, and his story is a new story, an "undramatization" of the event itself but an intensification of the political drama. Enquist says he tries to "paint with documents." Therefore, he states where he stands, knowing that his political view has been crucial for his choices and his presentation of what happened. In *Sekonden* (1971), Enquist has left the problematics of the author versus his product, but this novel is,

nevertheless, a sophisticated contribution to that discussion. The main character is the son of a pietistic mother and a socialist father who also is a champion in hammer-throwing. In the choice between his parents, the son opts for the uncomplicated and enthusiastic father, becoming his second, following him from contest to contest. The father is a winner until it is discovered that he has cheated and he is suspended for life. The father never understands how it happened. The son, however, becomes scrupulous about obtaining sufficient information, which, in turn, makes him incapable of acting decisively. Enquist is a socialist and interested in sports. How he views the contest between capitalism and socialism over sports is also documented in *Katedralen i München* (1972), a report from the Olympic Games in Munich. *Berättelser från de inställda upprorens tid* (1974; Tales from the Days of Canceled Revolts) is a collection of short stories, most of which are about the United States, which Enquist has visited several times. His play, *Tribadernas natt* (1975; The Night of the Tribades), about August STRINDBERG's view on women, became an international success and even had a short run on Broadway. *Musikanternas uttåg* (1978; The Departure of the Musicians) is a historical novel—about the period 1903-11 in the author's home district—with documentary elements. In the novel, Enquist argues persuasively for a humane socialism. *The Second* (*Sekonden*) appears in *Modern Swedish Prose in Translation*, ed. by K. E. Lagerlöf (1979), pp. 259-77.

See: S. Linnér, *Den moderne roman og romanforskning i Norden* (1971); T. Brostrøm, *Moderne svensk litteratur 1940-1972* (1973; Swedish tr., 1974); J. Stenkvist, *Svensk litteratur 1870-1970*, vol. 3 (1975), pp. 141-48; E. H. Henningsen, *Per Olov Enquist* (1975).　　　B.K.S.

Enzensberger, Hans Magnus (1929-), West German poet, essayist, editor, and cultural and social critic, was the eldest of four sons born to middle-class parents in the Bavarian village of Kaufbeuren. He grew up in Nuremberg, surviving the postwar years by interpreting and bartending for the British and dealing on the black market. He studied languages, literature, and philosophy at Freiburg, Erlangen, Hamburg, and Paris, doing a lot of student theater work and writing his dissertation on Clemens Brentano. After two years of radio work (under Alfred ANDERSCH), he spent the years 1957 to 1960 in the United States, Mexico, Norway, and—on a German government stipend—in Rome. After a stay in Frankfurt as editor at Suhrkamp Verlag, he moved to Norway in 1961, then to Berlin in 1965, where he lived until the end of 1978 (except for his many travels, notably to the United States, where he gave up a fellowship at Wesleyan University on political grounds, and to Cuba for a prolonged stay in 1968 and 1969). He now resides in Munich. Long a member of "Gruppe 47" (*see* GERMAN LITERATURE), Enzensberger has received the literature prize of the German Critics Guild (1962) and the Büchner Prize (1963).

Certainly the most cosmopolitan poet of his generation, Enzensberger is fluent in a number of European languages and has translated from five of them. His first three volumes of poetry, *verteidigung der wölfe* (1957; in defense of wolves), *landessprache* (1960; native speech), and *blindenschrift* (1964; braille), firmly established him as an angry young poet who had clearly learned from Bertolt BRECHT and knew, used, and belonged to the modern poetic tradition from Charles BEAUDELAIRE, Guillaume APOLLINAIRE, Gottfried BENN, T. S. Eliot, W. H. Auden, and on to the present. In 1965, Enzensberger founded the magazine *Kursbuch*, a key forum for the literary and political debates of the late 1960s; he remained its editor until 1975. His early essay focus on specific aspects of mass culture as it is, but from the mid-1960s on, his focus shifted to revolutionary change. Each of his five books between 1968 and 1975 centers around the figure of the revolutionary, at first only in a political sense: *Das Verhör von Habana* (1970; Eng. tr., *The Havana Inquiry,* 1973); *Freisprüche. Revolutionäre vor Gericht* (1970; Verdict: Not Guilty. Revolutionaries at the Tribunal), a documentary "novel"; *Der kurze Sommer der Anarchie* (1972; The Short Summer of Anarchy), about the Spanish anarchist Buenaventura Durruti. Then Enzensberger presented individuals who have effected radical changes in their lives in *Der Weg ins Freie* (1975; The Way Out into the Open), and, in his first poetic work in years, *Mausoleum: 37 Balladen aus der Geschichte des Fortschritts* (1975; Eng. tr., *Mausoleum,* 1976), he presented those who have effected radical changes in Western consciousness. This last is a pessimistic book; the changes bring their authors no happiness, no peace of mind. The young Enzensberger has been compared with the young Heinrich Heine, but Heine could point to liberal France and hope. Enzensberger thought he had found such a model for change in Cuba and in the revolutionary movement of the late 1960s, but he lost that hope; and a later book, *Der Untergang der Titanic* (1978; The Sinking of the Titanic), 49 verse texts woven into a poetic whole, ends with him, a survivor, alone, crying and swimming in a sea empty but for bits of wet, useless baggage and debris, doing the only things he can: going on crying and swimming. Three selections from Enzensberger's early poems are in English: *Poems* (1966), *Selected Poems* (1968), and *poems for people who don't read poems* (1968). Books of selected Enzensberger essays in English translation include *The Consciousness Industry* (1973), *Politics and Crime* (1974), and *Raids and Reconstructions* (1976).

See: J. Schickel, ed., *Über Hans Magnus Enzensberger* (1970); P. Demetz, *Postwar German Literatur* (1970), pp. 92–97; "Hans Magnus Enzensberger," *Text & Kritik* 49 (January 1976).   D.J.W.

Erdman, Nikolay Robertovich (1902–70), Russian playwright and film-script writer, was born in Moscow. In 1924 he collaborated with his brother Boris, an artist and poet, on a Vakhtangov Theater workshop production of the 19th-century farce *Lev Gurych Sinichkin,* for which Nikolay wrote comic interludes. Erdman's first successful play, the comedy *Mandat* (1925; Eng. tr., *The Mandate,* 1975), was staged by Vsevolod Meyerhold. In his portrayal of the Gulyachkin family, he satirized the reactionary hopes aroused by the New Economic Policy: the match for his sister arranged by the Gulyachkin son links him with monarchist malcontents who need the Communist Party card or "mandate" that Gulyachkin pretends to possess. Full of comic surprise and farcical intrigue, *Mandat* satirizes White and Red Russians alike, and its petit bourgeois heroes are left empty-handed as major victims in the end. Erdman's second comedy, *Samoubiytsa* (1928; Eng. tr., *The Suicide,* 1975), was ready through dress rehearsal for presentation at the Meyerhold Theater, but was not allowed to open. A satire in defense of "the little man," it was aimed finally at the Soviet system and at the dictator himself. No wonder Erdman suffered partial repression under Iosif Stalin, after which he no longer wrote original plays but rather adaptations and film scenarios, among them the successful film *Volga, Volga* with M. Volpin and Grigory Alexandrov (1938). For a selection of Erdman's work in English, see N.

Erdman, *The Mandate and The Suicide,* tr. by M. Hoover, G. Genereux, Jr., and J. Volkov (1975).   M.L.H.

Erenburg, Ilya Grigoryevich (1891–1967), Russian novelist and journalist, had a career that represents a curious blend of patriotism, cosmopolitanism, and instinct for survival. Political acumen, cinematic plots, and Western settings lend his fiction the topical appeal of his rousing anti-Nazi war reportage.

Erenburg was born in Kiev and grew up in Moscow, where his father operated a brewery. He fled Russia to avoid trial for revolutionary agitation, and spent much of 1909 to 1917 in Left Bank Paris cafés. Enchanted by Catholic mysticism and medievalism, he almost joined the Benedictines. He returned to Russia after the Revolution of February 1917, the year in which he wrote the anti-Communist poem "Prayer for Russia." He later wrote conciliatory poems, *Razdumiya* (1921; Meditations), but nevertheless returned to Paris in 1921. After being deported to Belgium, Erenburg wrote his first, and best, novel, *Neobychaynye pokhozhdeniya Khulio Khurenito* (1922; Eng. tr., *The Extraordinary Adventures of Julio Jurentio,* 1930), a brutal satire on Russia, the West, and civilization itself (he portrays himself as the picaresque hero's persecuted Jewish disciple). He spurned repatriation but began reporting for *Izvestiya* in 1923. He also wrote numerous pessimistic novels: *Zhizn i gibel Nikolaya Kurbova* (1923; The Life and Death of Nikolay Kurbov) on the downfall of a stereotypical Soviet secret policeman; *Trest D.E.* (1923; Trust D. E.) on American capitalism conquering Europe; *Lyubov Zhanny Ney* (1924; Eng. tr., *The Love of Jeanne Ney,* 1929) on a bourgeois French woman's love for a Russian Communist; *Rvach* (1925; The Grabber), *Leto 1925 goda* (1926; Summer 1925), and *V Protochnom Pereulke* (1927; Eng. tr., *A Street in Moscow,* 1932), all on the disillusionment of Soviet idealists during the period of the New Economic Policy; *Burnaya zhizn Lazika Roytshvanetsa* (1928; Eng. tr., *The Stormy Life of Lazik Roitschwantz,* 1960), attacking all societies that allow a Jewish tailor to escape from Russian anti-Semitism only to be jailed in Western Europe and starve in Palestine; *Zagovor ravnykh* (1929; A Conspiracy of Equals) on the isolation of the French Revolutionary hero François Babeuf; and *Den vtoroy* (1933; Eng. tr., *Out of Chaos,* 1934), on an intellectual crushed by the Five-Year Plan.

Erenburg returned to the Soviet Union shortly before the German invasion in 1941 and thereafter published his most ambitious novel, *Padeniye Parizha* (1941–42; Eng. tr., *The Fall of Paris,* 1942), on the decline of capitalist France. Two Cold War novels, *Burya* (1947; Eng. tr., *The Storm,* 1949) and *Devyaty val* (1951–52; Eng. tr., *The Ninth Wave,* 1955), attack the United States.

A one-time apologist for Iosif Stalin, Erenburg became a leading liberal spokesman after Stalin's death with his novel *Ottepel* (1954; Eng. tr., *The Thaw,* 1955), which gave its name to the relatively less rigid decade to follow. His essays (Eng. tr., *Chekhov, Stendhal and Other Essays,* 1963) deal with artistic freedom; and his memoirs, *Lyudy, gody, zhizn* (1960–65; Eng. tr., *People and Life; First Years of Revolution; Truce; Eve of War; Post-War Years;* 1961–66), casually reintroduce hitherto proscribed Western and Russian cultural figures into Soviet publications.

See: V. Alexandrova, *History of Soviet Literature* (1963).   H.A.G.

Erlingsson, Þorsteinn (1858–1914), Icelandic poet and short-story writer, was born of well-to-do parents at

Stóramörk, Rangárvallasýsla, Iceland. After a happy youth Erlingsson went to school in Reykjavík and then in Copenhagen, where he began by studying law at the university but ended by devoting his time to Icelandic studies and poetry. Here he contracted the tuberculosis of the lungs that finally was to prove fatal. On his return to Iceland, he eked out a meager living by journalism and private teaching.

In Copenhagen, Erlingsson was influenced not only by the realism of Georg BRANDES, but also by the growing socialist movement. He became an ardent socialist, an antimonarchist, and an intrepid attacker of church and clergy. His satire was as sharp as it was brilliantly executed; it proved very effective in demolishing the fundamentalism of the 19th-century Lutheran Church in Iceland. But Erlingsson was far more than a satirist. Fervent love and nature lyrics also came from his pen. He loved nature, and he expressed his sympathy with birds and beasts not only in poems, but also in exquisite short stories cast in the form of Oriental tales. Erlingsson was deeply interested in Icelandic folk poetry; he polished its chief vehicle, the quatrain (*ferskeytla*), to a degree of perfection attained only by the few masters of this form. A high degree of workmanship is characteristic of everything he wrote.

Erlingsson's volume of poems, *þyrnar* (Thorns), was printed in three editions (1897, 1905, and posthumously, with many additions, in 1918). The poem *Eiðurinn* (1913; The Oath), on the same subject as *The Virgin of Skalholt* by Kamban, and the animal tales, *Málleysingjar* (1928; The Dumb Ones), complete the list of his productions.

See: Erlingsson, *þyrnar* (1918), ed. by S. Nordal, with an introduction by several authors.   S.E.

Ernst, Paul (1866–1933), German poet, essayist, and prose writer of fiction and drama, composed many hundreds of essays, several hundred short stories, 6 novels, and 23 works for the theater (comedies, tragedies, historical dramas, and what he conceived of as a new form called "redemption drama" or "meta-tragedy"). Ernst also produced *Erdachte Gespräche* (1921; Imaginary Conversations), two slender volumes of short poems, two epics—the more important of which is *Das Kaiserbuch* (6 vols., 1923–28; The Book of the Emperor)—and two volumes of autobiography, *Jugenderinnerungen* (1930; Youthful Memoirs) and *Jünglingsjahre* (1932; Years as a Young Man), which are actually a comprehensive account of the economic, social, and political conditions and the literary trends in the last three decades of the 19th century. He edited, with critical prefaces, some 50 works from German and other European literatures, in some cases supplying translations.

The author of this enormous output of prose and verse, fiction, drama, and criticism was born in Elbingerode and grew up at Clausthal in the Harz Mountains, the son of a mine foreman. The boy was an omnivorous reader. Destined for the ministry, he felt himself repelled by modern theology and by the indifference of its propounders to social problems and needs. He gave up theology for practical social action, writing both literary criticism and essays on economics, politics, and sociology, later editing the Social Democratic (that is, Marxian) *Berliner Volkstribüne* and making political speeches.

The first of Ernst's published works was his essay *Leo Tolstoy und der slawische Roman* (1889; Leo Tolstoy and the Slavic Novel). Subscribing to Marxian economics, he wrote his doctoral dissertation on *Die gesellschaftliche Reproduktion des Capitals bei gesteigerter Produktivität der Arbeit* (Bern, 1892; Social Increase of Capital through Increased Productivity of Labor). Shortly after, he freed himself from his Marxian connections and at the end of the decade turned to creative literature, writing four naturalistic one act plays.

On a trip to Italy in 1900 he found in the classic forms—both literary and pictorial—the intention of poets and artists, and the means they employed, more congenial to his innate conservatism. Thereafter Ernst was to combat naturalism in art as well as Marxism in all its manifestations, notably in *Der Weg zur Form* (1906; The Way to Form), *Der Zusammenbruch des Marxismus* (1919; The Collapse of Marxism), and *Grundlagen der neuen Gesellschaft* (1930; The Foundations of a New Society).

His political and artistic principles thus clarified, Ernst began his important work at the age of 35 with a strong predilection for drama (which to him was synonymous with tragedy) and a low regard for the novel. Yet some of his novels, such as *Der schmale Weg zum Glück* (1904; The Narrow Path to Happiness) and *Grün aus Trümmern* (1933; Green out of Ruins), found their way to the hearts of a public that remained cold to his dramas. *Der schmale Weg zum Glück* passed through 10 editions. No comparable success greeted Ernst's *Brunhild* (1909), the perfect exemplification of his theory of tragedy, or his *Ariadne* (1912), written after he had received the "grace of faith in Jesus Christ" and had decided that tragedy and its essential pessimism must give way to a form "beyond tragedy," to "redemption drama." The same disappointing reception awaited *Das Kaiserbuch*, which Ernst undertook after World War I, hoping by this panorama of the glorious medieval past to give courage to a defeated and despoiled nation. But the 100,000 verses precluded its becoming the familiar companion of his people. With his novellas, classic in construction and brevity, he became the supreme master of that genre.

The function of the poet—as Ernst conceived it—is that of prophet and high priest of the people. Even with his limitations, Ernst remains a significant writer. More than any other contemporary German thinker outside the church, he pointed the way to the restoration of orthodox Christianity among the intelligentsia.

See: K. A. Kutzbach, *Paul Ernst—Gedenkbuch* (1933); R. Fuerst, *Ideologie und Literatur: zum Dialog zwischen Paul Ernst und Georg Lukács* (1976).

J.F.G. rev. A.L.W.

Ersoy, Mehmet Akif, more commonly known as Mehmet Akif (1873–1936), Turkish poet, was born in Istanbul. He had a thorough religious education and learned Arabic and Persian early in life, later also studying French. He graduated first in his class at the Halkalı School of Veterinary Sciences in 1894 and worked in Rumelia, Albania, and Arabia for four years. Mehmet Akif published his major poems and articles after 1908. He was in Germany during World War I. In 1920 he supported the Turkish national independence struggle and became a member (from the province of Burdur) of the first Parliament. In 1921 he wrote the words for the national anthem. After the Turkish Republic started to initiate religious reforms, he left Turkey in protest and spent more than 10 years in Cairo, where he taught courses in Turkish literature. He returned to Istanbul shortly before his death in 1936.

Employing neoclassical formal structures and conventional prosody with impeccable craftsmanship, Mehmet Akif wrote a large corpus of lyric and didactic poetry dealing with patriotic and religious themes. Some of his best-known poems delineate social problems and the life of the lower classes in Istanbul. He preached the focal importance of the Islamic summum bonum and the ideals of nationalism. His poems were collected in *Safahat* (1911; Phases), *Süleymaniye Kürsüsünde* (1912; At the

Süleymaniye Pulpit), *Hakkın Sesleri* (1913; Voices of God), *Fatih Kürsüsünde* (1914; At the Fatih Pulpit), *Hatıralar* (1917; Recollections), *Asım* (1919), and *Gölgeler* (1933; Shadows). His complete poems have been published many times under the title *Safahat*.

T.S.H.

Ertel, Aleksandr Ivanovich (1855–1908), Russian novelist, was born near Voronezh, son of the manager of an estate. Unable to complete his schooling as a boy, he owed his education largely to his first wife, who also awakened his interest in literature. He is remembered chiefly for his novel *Gardeniny, ikh dvornya, priverzhentsy i vragi* (1888; The Gardenins, Their House, Adherents, and Enemies), a work written when Ertel was under the influence of Lev TOLSTOY, who spoke highly of it. In spirit and methods of treatment Ertel was very close to the Russian Populists, but he believed instinctively, and also because of his knowledge of estate administration, in a more truthful and realistic approach to the peasant problems. In his later years there was also a growing interest in the essence of religion that separated him from many of the Populists. Ertel was a keen observer of the reality of Russian peasant life, looking at it as one who had been reared in a rural environment; he treated less well the decaying gentry and had no reason for feeling that sense of personal guilt and obligation which marked many of his literary associates. Definitely a minor writer, he nevertheless composed in *The Gardenins* one of the best works of the period.

See: F. D. Batyushkov, "A. I. Ertēl, po neizdannym dokumentam," *Sobraniye sochineniy,* vol. 1 (1909), pp. 1–48; A. Kostin, *A. I. Ertel: zhizn i tvorchestvo* (1955), and "Ertel," in *Istoriya russkoy literatury,* vol. 9, part 2, pp. 157–67.   C.A.Ma. rev. W.B.E.

Espanca, Florbela (1894–1930), Portuguese poet and short-story writer, was born out of wedlock and married at 16 in the provincial milieu of Vila Viçosa in the Alto Alentejo province. She soon rebelled against the traditionally inferior status of Portuguese women. At the age of 18 and already divorced, she was busily composing lyric verse and short stories patterned on the symbolist-decadent models of the day. These early products were published posthumously in 1931. By 1917 Espanca was a law student in Lisbon, where she soon remarried. During this period she published her first collection of poems, *Livro das mágoas* (1919; Book of Woes). Following still another divorce, more verse appeared in 1923: *Livro de Soror Saudade* (Book of Sister Saudade), the title of which is an allusion to a sobriquet given her by a friend and fellow poet, Américo Durão. Both books were ignored by the critics of the day, who were perplexed by the poet's unconventional candor. When death came after a lengthy illness, probably by her own hand, on her birthday in 1930, Espanca had married for a third time and was preparing another collection of verse, *Charneca em flor* (Flowering Heath), several editions of which appeared in 1931.

Except for her short stories, dated examples of erotic art nouveau, Espanca's works remain extraordinarily popular—especially her sonnets, which fuse an almost Parnassian discipline with a romantic's reliance on subjective inspiration. Variously characterized as "female Don Juanism" and "erotic egomania," her vision covers a wide spectrum of emotions in a ceaseless search for love, where euphoria alternates with melancholy and a Whitmanlike exultation often gives way to humiliating subjugation. By now this writer is generally regarded as her country's foremost woman poet.

See: J. de Sena, "Florbela Espanca," in his *Da poesia portuguesa* (1959), pp. 115–44; J. Régio, "Florbela," in his *Ensaios de interpretação crítica* (1964), pp. 167–96; A. Bessa-Luís, *Florbela Espanca, a vida e a obra* (1979).

R.A.P.-R.

Espina, Antonio (1894–), Spanish poet, novelist, and essayist, was born and has lived most of his life in Madrid, although he made his home abroad from 1946 to 1955. He edited a number of Madrid dailies and the Republican weekly *Nueva España* (1929–31). He was also much involved with such literary journals as *La Pluma* and *Revista de Occidente*. His two novels, *Pájaro pinto* (1927; Painted Bird) and *Luna de copas* (1929; Moon of Hearts), are metaphorical, dehumanized works principally concerned with playing intellectual games with the reader. Although Espina has often been compared with Benjamín JARNÉS, his novels also have characteristics in common with those of Ramón GÓMEZ DE LA SERNA. Some critics have felt that Espina's narrative talents are more effective in his biographies of the bandit Luis Candelas, the actor Julián Romea, the statesman Cánovas del Castillo, and the Golden Age writers Quevedo and Cervantes. Several collections of his numerous newspaper articles have also appeared, among them *Lo cómico contemporáneo* (1928; Contemporary Humor) and *Audaces y extravagantes* (1959; Rebels and Eccentrics).

His volumes of poetry include *Umbrales* (1918; Thresholds) and *Signario* (1923; Markings). The latter is perhaps his most characteristic work. Like his prose, his poetry is fresh, irreverent, occasionally bitter in the manner of Ramón del VALLE-INCLÁN's late verse of these same years, whimsical, and highly imaginative. In short, Espina's poetry is representative of the isms of the 1920s and 1930s, but it lacks the transcendence of the works of the great Spanish poets of the period.

See: F. Sainz de Robles, *Historia y antología de la poesía española,* vol. 2 (1967), pp. 1804–08; E. G. de Nora, *La novela española contemporánea,* vol. 2 (1968), pp. 197–200.   H.L.B.

Espina de Serna, Concha (1877–1955), Spanish novelist, was born in Santander and encouraged in her youthful literary interests by her affluent family. Married at an early age, she spent three unhappy years with her husband in Chile, where she began work as a journalist. She wrote some 50 books in all genres, but she is best known for her novels and short stories, many of which portray the countryside and customs of the region in which she lived.

Espina de Serna was especially interested in feminine psychology. Many of her women characters share the same traits: they are forbearing, long-suffering, and tragically doomed to unhappiness. Her first novel, *La niña de Luzmela* (1909; The Girl from Luzmela) characteristically uses the Montaña region as a backdrop for the story of a young woman. The most famous of the regional novels, however, is *La esfinge maragata* (1914; Eng. tr., *Mariflor*, 1924), set in the province of León. The heroine of this novel was "born to love and suffer." *Ruecas de marfil* (1917; Ivory Distaffs) treats the same themes in short-story form.

Compassion takes on social significance in *El metal de los muertos* (1920; The Metal of the Dead), a description of mining life and a passionate plea for reforms in this area, as well as an attack on foreign exploitation.

The novelist's travels through Spain, South America, Europe, and the United States produced material for fiction as well as essays and reminiscences, as in *Singladuras* (1932; A Day's Run). Her traditional and Catholic views led her to sympathize with the Nationalists during the Spanish Civil War, but the opposition occupied the region in which she lived during this time. The title of her diary of those experiences explains her attitude: *Esclavitud y libertad: diario de una prisionera* (1938; Slavery and Liberty: Diary of a Prisoner).

Although she went blind in 1937, she continued to write. Her last novel is a fictionalized account of the love of Marcelino MENÉNDEZ PELAYO for his cousin, entitled *Una novela de amor* (1953; A Love Story).

Her self-avowed literary influences include the Bible, classical Spanish writers, and English and French novelists. She has been praised for her brilliant descriptive and lyrical style and her realistic portrayals of life in her region. Excesses of lyricism, romanticism, sentimentalism, and rhetorical passages have been singled out for criticism.

See: M. Fria Lagoni, *Concha Espina y sus críticos* (1929); E. G. de Nora, *La novela española contemporánea*, vol. 1 (1963), pp. 328–41.   M.E.W.J.

Espriu, Salvador (1913-), Catalan poet, novelist, and dramatist, was born in Santa Coloma de Farners and received a joint degree in law and ancient history from the University of Barcelona. Espriu's university formation is reflected in his "encyclopedic" cultural vision, to quote Josip Maria CASTELLET. Before the Spanish Civil War, Espriu wrote mainly prose. He published his first book, *Israel,* biblical sketches, in Castilian in 1929 and *El doctor Rip* in Catalan in 1931, followed by *Laia* (1932), *Aspectes* (1934), *Miratge a Citerea* (1935), *Ariadna al laberint grotesc* (1935), *Letizia* (1938), *Fedra* (1938), and *Petites proses blanques* (1938; Little White Proses). The Civil War greatly influenced Espriu's later work, in which he adopts a moral tone. Representative of this are his play *Antígona,* which he wrote in 1939 but did not publish until 1955, and *Primera història d'Esther (Improvisació per a Titelles)* (Esther's First Story [Improvisation for Puppets]; 1948). He also began to publish his poetic work after the Civil War, beginning with *Cementiri de Sinera* (1946; The Cemetery of Sinera), a mythification of Arenys de Mar, the town where he spent his childhood. Subsequent books of poetry are *Les cançons d'Ariadna* (1949), *Les hores* (1952; The Hours), *Mrs. Death* (1952), *El caminant i el mur* (1954; The Wanderer and the Wall), *Final del laberint* (1955; The End of the Labyrinth), *La pell de brau* (1960; The Bull's Skin), *El llibre de Sinera* (1963; The Book of Sinera), and *Setmana Santa* (1971; Holy Week), for which he won "el Premio de la Crítica." A later theatrical success is *Una altra Fedra, si us plau* (1977; Please, Another Phaedra).

Espriu is one of the first writers to leave the orbit of the "Noucentista" generation, as Josep PLA has perspicaciously made us aware. He is the most prominent member of the Catalan Generation of 1936 and the writer who reacted most vehemently to the Civil War. He lashed out against the war in his theater of puppets and marionettes, and he attempted to counteract the violence by preaching togetherness in his poetry, for example, in *La pell de brau,* where Catalonia is symbolized by the mythical city of Sinera and Castille by "Sepharad," the Hebrew word for Spain. The figure that dominates this poetic universe from beginning to end is death. Espriu himself has said that his work is a "constant and obsessive" meditation on that subject. Nevertheless, Castellet and Moals have emphasized the civic character of his poetry. This quality in particular has made Espriu the mentor of new generations of writers, who have discovered in him the lucid but disconsolate voice that has won him respect not only in Catalonia but also in the rest of Spain and the world. He has been nominated for the Nobel Prize on several different occasions and received the Montaigne Prize in 1971 and the "Ignasi Iglesias" in 1978.

See: A. Vilanova, "La obra de Salvador Espriu," *Revista Destino,* no. 686 (Sept. 30, 1950); J. Molas, Prologue to S. Espriu, *Primera historia d'Esther* (1966); J. Marco, Prologue to S. Espriu *Llibre de Sinera* (1966); J. M. Castellet, *Iniciació a la poesia de Salvador Espriu* (1971); E. T. Lawrence, "Salvador Espriu entre Sinera i el seu cementiri," *Serra d'Or* (June 1978).   J.F.C.

Estaunié, Edouard (1862–1942), French novelist, was born in Dijon. He was educated in Jesuit schools and graduated from the Ecole Polytechnique, becoming a versatile and active high civil servant. Nevertheless, he found time to write 15 books of fiction. The diffident Estaunié was never a widely acclaimed literary figure, and today he is unknown to most French intellectuals, despite his membership in the Académie Française and his term as president of the Société des Gens de Lettres. He considered himself forgotten at least 10 years before he died, and in his old age he thanked F. Lehner, his German translator, for helping to break the critical silence that, he wrote, had always surrounded his work. Although in recent decades there has been little critical interest in Estaunié outside scholarly circles, his self-assessment was unduly severe. Most of his novels were reviewed by influential critics in widely read periodicals and were translated into many languages. Although unpublished, the number of master's and Ph.D. theses on his work, in France and abroad, is considerable. Few unbiased histories of French literature fail to note that he is one of the better minor novelists of his country, and historians such as Henri Peyre have called for a reevaluation of his work.

Estaunié's first novels were inspired by Gustave Flaubert, Emile ZOLA, and Guy de Maupassant, and his scientific training (he was an electrical engineer) made a positivist of him. His later novels, those better known today, were imbued with spirituality. Although he had renounced his naturalist models, he remained a proud Balzacian throughout his career. "The perplexed positivist," as Ruth Holz called him, is an apt expression and one adopted by other scholars, but one can also say that while Estaunié was increasingly drawn back to his childhood faith during the second phase of his writing career, he was no less a perplexed spiritualist. His third novel, *L'Empreinte* (1895; The Imprint), a severe indictment of his Jesuit educators, gained him a measure of fame and the disdain of ultraconservative Catholics. Yet his later work was neo-Christian, leading some historians to classify him, incorrectly, as a "Catholic writer," although it would be idle to deny his rapprochement with the Church at the end of his life.

Such works as *La Vie secrète* (1908; The Secret Life), *Les Choses voient* (1913; Things See), *L'Ascension de M. Baslevre* (1919), and *L'Appel de la route* (1922; The Call of the Road) led Albert THIBAUDET to dub Estaunié "the novelist of sorrow." Despite experiments in narrative technique in *Les Choses voient* and *L'Appel de la route,* Estaunié's essentially traditional approach, his fidelity to Honoré de Balzac, his deliberately sober and methodical style, his self-sacrificing heroes, his refusal to pander to the reader, and his later defense of bourgeois values (which he had attacked bitterly in his first novels) lend his work an air of remoteness today. In many respects, however, he is a worthy elder to Julien GREEN and François MAURIAC.

See: A. Bellessort, *Nouvelles Etudes* (1923), pp. 236–64; J. Charpentier, *Estaunié* (1932); C. Cé, *Regards sur l'œuvre d'Edouard Estaunié* (1935); M. H. Isley, "Edouard Estaunié's Message," *FR* 16 (1942): 46–71; R.

C. Holz, *Edouard Estaunié: The Perplexed Positivist* (1949); G. Cesbron, *Edouard Estaunié: romancier de l'être, suivi de "Récits spirites"* (1977).   E.Har.

Estonian literature. The history of modern Estonian literature may be divided into four distinct periods, the first beginning in 1857. Following the example of Elias Lönnrot's Finnish national epic, *Kalevala* (1835-49), Friedrich Reinhold Kreutzwald (1803-82) compiled *Kalevipoeg* (1857-61; Eng. tr., *The Hero of Estonia*, 1895). This work laid the foundation for a national literature. Three authors, however, brought Estonian literature into the 20th century: Juhan Liiv (1864-1913), who wrote impressionistic nature poetry and verse of prophetic symbolism; Eduard Vilde (1865-1933), the author of naturalistic and historical novels; and August Kitzberg (1855-1927), who wrote plays about country life, occasionally utilizing folklore material.

The second period began in 1905, with the emergence of "Young Estonia," the first important school of native writers. "Young Estonia" successfully championed greater international literary awareness, linguistic reform, stylistic sophistication, and formal perfection. One member of the group, Gustav Suits (1883-1956), later became the first professor of Estonian and world literature at Tartu University. Suits was the author of *Tuulemaa* (1913; The Land of Winds), the first artistically structured collection of Estonian verse. The intricate texture and nationalist symbolism of his poetry has been compared to that of William Butler Yeats. Friedebert Tuglas, pseud. of Friedebert Mihkelson (1886-1971), perfected the short story and introduced the essay and aphorism into Estonian literature as serious literary genres. A radical renewal of language, accomplished through borrowings from the sister-tongue of Finnish, the use of native dialects, and the creation of neologisms, was the work of Johannes Aavik (1880-1973). Other "Young Estonians" were Villem Ridala, pseud. of Villem Grünthal, (1885-1942), the elegiac bard of the Estonian islands; Ernst Enno (1875-1934), a poet of mystical moods; and Jaan Oks (1884-1918), whose expressionistic intensity was championed by the next literary school, "Siuru" (named after a bird of Estonian mythology).

The third period of Estonian literature may be dated from 1917, the year in which the "Siuru" group burst upon the literary scene. On the eve of Estonian independence, the "Siuru" group opened the richest chapter in the literature of this Finno-Ugric language. A many-faceted development in all genres (except drama) was spearheaded by such "Siuru" poets as Marie UNDER and Henrik Visnapuu (1890-1951), the poet-critic Johannes Semper (1892-1970), and the popular, flamboyant novelist August Gailit (1891-1960). These writers were first influenced by expressionism and futurism. Under was the poet who dominated the period of independence. Her peer in fiction was Anton Hansen TAMMSAARE, hailed as the most impressive Estonian novelist to date. August Mälk (1900-), whose works depict the islanders' dramatic life, was among the best-loved novelists of this period. The novellas of Peet Vallak, pseud. of Peeter Pedajas, (1893-1959) offer a gallery of memorable country and city types and exhibit a Chekhovian finesse (*see* Anton CHEKHOV). In spite of a flourishing theater life, drama was the weakest genre during this period. Hugo Raudsepp (1883-1952), a popular author of witty comedies, was surpassed by the novelists Eduard Vilde and Tammsaare in their occasional plays. These feverishly productive years, on the other hand, were rich in poetry. The last school of poets to emerge in independent Estonia was also the first generation of writers to have been entirely educated in their native language. Their work was gathered by the influential critic and translator Ants Oras (1900-) in his anthology, *Arbujad* (1938; Magicians of the Word). The neosymbolist poems of Betti Alver, pseud. of Elisabet Lepik (1906-), have a classical finality that rivals Suits. Her husband, Heiti Talvik (1904-47), was the leading "Arbuja" with his uncompromisingly ethical stance and artistic integrity. The theologican-linguist Uku Masing (1909-) startled his readers with mystically inspired visions that used associative techniques akin to surrealism.

The years 1940-44 cannot be characterized as a separate period in Estonian literature. During the cataclysmic era of Soviet annexation (1940) and Nazi occupation (1941), the literary harvest in Estonia was meager. The fourth period of modern Estonian literature began toward the end of World War II. From 1944 to 1974, there was a bifurcation in literary production. It is no mean achievement for the young literature of one million people to sustain two parallel branches of development through three decades. On the one hand, there was the sovietized literature in Estonia that was revived only in the 1960s, a decade after Iosif Stalin's death. On the other hand, there was a literature in exile, produced and supported by some 70,000 émigrés scattered throughout the West, and particularly in Stockholm, New York, and Toronto. Poetry was the leading genre in Estonia itself. Alver embodied there the same kind of moral leadership that Under did in exile. In this effort, Alver was seconded by another "Arbuja," August Sand (1914-69), a poet and eminent translator. But it was Jean Kross (1920-) who in 1958 first broke the monotony of socialist realism with an experimental verve. Subsequently, he became perhaps the most interesting prose writer in Soviet Estonia, producing a series of historical novels and novellas that employ the interior monologue. Artur Alliksaar (1923-66) cultivated verbal fireworks that were almost surrealist in temperament and founded the Estonian theater of the absurd. Another poet, and a translator of Dylan Thomas, was Paul-Eerik Rummo (1942-), who wrote the most famous Estonian absurdist play, *Tuhkatriinumäng* (1969; Cinderella Game). A mystical prophet of ecology is Jaan Kaplinski (1941-), while Jüri Üdi, pseud. of Juhan Viiding (1948-), continues the main tradition of Estonian verse in his ironic, virtuosic poetry. The impact of Franz KAFKA on Estonian literature has been absorbed in varying ways in the stories of Arvo Valton (1935-), Enn Vetemaa (1936-), and Mati Unit (1943-).

Literary production in exile from 1944 into the 1960s, however, has surpassed that in Estonia both qualitatively and quantitatively. Most established writers of the older and middle generation, such as Aavik, Suits, Under, Karl Rumor (1886-1971), Visnapuu, Artur Adson (1889-1977), Gailit, Mälk, Albert Kivikas (1898-1978), Karl Ristikivi (1912-77), and Bernard Kangro (1910-), chose emigration over life under Soviet occupation. They have continued to write in the West, and émigré fiction has exhibited a particularly high level of accomplishment. Ristikivi's *Hingede öö* (1953; All Souls' Night) explores the refugee's troubled psyche in Kafkaesque ways. His subsequent novels have chosen themes from European history to illuminate present conflicts. Kangro, the only "Arbuja" poet to escape to the West, has occupied a central position in exile letters due to his manifold editorial activities and prolific work in all genres. He employs various narrative perspectives in his six-volume novel about the university town of Tartu in the 1930s and 1940s. Valev Uibopuu (1913-) is a psychologically penetrating novelist who experiments discreetly with new techniques. Among the most promising younger prose writers abroad are Ilmar Jaks (1923-) and Helga Nõu (1934-). Postwar émigré poetry has exhibited great artistic range. It includes Arno Vihalemm's (1911-) mordant irony, Aleksis Rannit's (1914-) worship of art, Kalju Lepik's (1920-) modern adaptation of folk song techniques, Ilmar Laaban's (1921-) surrealist poems, and Ivar Grünthal's (1924-) traditional forms packed with explosive personal and national experiences.

See: W. K. Matthews, Introduction to *Modern Estonian Poetry* (1953); A. Oras and B. Kangro, *Estonian Literature in Exile* (1967); A. Mägi, *Estonian Literature* (1968); E. Nirk, *Estonian Literature* (1970); G. Kurman, *Literatures in Contact: Finland and Estonia* (1979); I. Ivask, ed., "A Look at Baltic Letters Today," *BA* 47 (1973): 623-63; A. Ziedonis, J. Puhvel et al, eds., *Baltic Literature and Linguistics* (1973); T. Parming, E. Järvesoo, eds., *A Case Study of A Soviet Republic: The Estonian SSR* (1978); V. B. Leitch, ed., *The Poetry of Estonia* (1980). I.I.

Etiemble, René (1909-), French literary critic and novelist, was born in Mayenne. Etiemble is very different from the timorous academic, often depicted as concerned only with the past and reluctant to take risks. During his early days at the Ecole Normale Supérieure and then at the University of Chicago where he taught until 1944, Etiemble proved to be a blunt, aggressive judge of literary works and an opponent of all prejudices and conventions. Early in his career, he published *L'Enfant de chœur* (1937; new ed., 1947; The Choir Boy), a courageous, bitter novel, cynical in appearance but tinged with affection and warmth, on the theme of incest between a mother and her son. A subsequent and longer novel, *Peaux de couleuvre* (1948; Snakeskins), attempted to portray a group of students in Paris bidding farewell to their turbulent adolescence, but this work was less successful.

Etiemble has been a prolific critic, impeccably informed, well read in several languages (including Chinese), enjoying savage iconoclasm and fighting against any contamination of pure French by "franglais." His bulky three-volume *Mythe de Rimbaud* (1952-61), a study of Arthur RIMBAUD's posthumous reputation, wields sarcasm and erudition with equal mastery. He relentlessly champions sanity, clarity, and restraint. Jean PAULHAN and Jules SUPERVIELLE are those whom he has praised most warmly among his elders. A bellicose critic and a heretic among Sorbonne professors (and a better writer than most of them), he appears at his truest in his trench-

ant essays collected in five volumes as *Hygiène des lettres* (1952-67; Literary Hygiene). H.P.

Eyck, Pieter Nicolaas van (1887-1954), Dutch poet, critic, and journalist, was born in Breukelen. He studied law at the University of Leiden, but became the London correspondent for the *Nieuwe Rotterdamse Courant*, the Rotterdam daily and one of the leading newspapers in the Netherlands. In 1935 he became a professor of literature at Leiden, succeeding his friend Albert VERWEY. He became the leading critic among the younger group that gathered around the journal *De Beweging* about 1910. He published his first poetry in the volume *De getooide doolhof* (1909; The Decorated Labyrinth), which reveals an urge to the passionate enjoyment of and the surrender to sensual beauty. For the poet there was no psychological satisfaction in the fulfillment of this urge, however, and this led to melancholy. *Getijden* (1910; Tides) combines love and melancholy, but love now has a cosmic scope. With *Uitzichten* (1912; Views) the poet has regained his faith in the life of this earth and the joy of the soul. Van Eyck came under the influence of Baruch Spinoza, and with *Inkeer* (1922; Introspection), he viewed the world as the manifestation of God. *Voorbereiding* (1926; Preparation) is in a somewhat lighter vein and puts more emphasis on the senses. *Herwaarts* (1939; Hither) reveals a longing for the highest happiness, for the direct experience of God. This volume, along with *Verzen* (1940) and *Meesters* (1946; Masters), demonstrates a striking maturity. *Medousa* (1947), a long mythological poem in iambic pentameter, the verse form Willem KLOOS had used for his *Okeanos* and Verwey for his *Persephone*, was a masterful accomplishment. It presents van Eyck's psychological development and is the most comprehensive embodiment of his mystical and philosophical view of life. He gave poetry a religious dimension, and sought to establish direct connection between poetry and the personality of the poet. Van Eyck was editor of the magazine *Leiding* from 1920 to 1931, and in it he published a number of essays on criticism and literary history. He also brought out editions of the work of two of his contemporaries, Leopold's *Verzamelde Verzen* (1935; Collected Verse) and Verwey's *Oorspronkelijk Dichtwerk* (1939; Original Poetry). His own writing has appeared as *Verzameld Werk* (1958; Collected Works), in seven volumes.

See: C. Bittremieux, *Pieter Nicolaas van Eyck* (1947). S.L.F.

F

Fabbri, Diego (1911-), Italian playwright and journalist, was born in Forlì. Since World War II, he has been the leading Italian dramatist of Catholic themes. Fabbri began his playwriting career at the age of 17 with pieces privately staged in provincial circles, but his first artistically significant works, as well as public recognition, date from the early 1940s. He has written over 30 works for the theater, including one-act and radio plays. His reputation abroad is greatest in France, where most of his works have been staged in translation. Fabbri's dramas treat the human condition in terms of Christian pessimism and entail belief in the Christian scheme of God, the soul, and salvation. In Fabbri's view, a psychological malaise, itself the effect of original sin, renders man constitutionally unhappy and prone to despair; this pain of living, which can end only with union with God in the afterlife, can nevertheless be mitigated and made spiritually redemptive

by means of a suprarational faith, embodied in humility and love for one's fellowman. Fabbri's protagonists emerge from tormenting conflicts as Christ figures, "converted" to selfless love and respect for others—an experience the author posits as the ultimate and only possible "good" within reach of vitiated human nature. This theme is prominent in *Orbite* (1941; Orbits), *Paludi* (1942; Swamps), *La libreria del sole* (1943; The Bookshop of the Sun), *Processo di famiglia* (1953; Families on Trial), *Processo a Gesù* (1955; Eng. tr., *Between Two Thieves*, 1959), and *L'avvenimento* (1967; The Event). Fabbri was an active anti-Fascist during the 1940s, and his works of the 1950s and 1960s demonstrate a concern for social reform.

While Fabbri's themes are similar to those of 20th-century French Catholic writers, notably the Christian existentialists, he has also been influenced by the Italian dramatists Ugo BETTI and Luigi PIRANDELLO. Like Betti,

Fabbri proposes an inescapably corrupt human nature, and like both Betti and Pirandello, he probes the self-contradictions of his characters. These two playwrights also influenced the structure of Fabbri's theater, especially such later pieces as *Inquisizione* (1950; Eng. tr., *The Inquisition*, 1963), *Processo di famiglia, Processo a Gesù, Lo scoiattolo* (1963; The Squirrel), and *L'avvenimento*. In these plays, the dramatic conflict incorporates aspects of a legal inquest or the act of confession; choral characters figure as emblems of mankind, and the action involves the audience through "improvised" exchanges between actors and public.

Fabbri has also been active in the Italian cinema, collaborating on over a dozen films as writer, producer, or artistic consultant. He has been a contributor and editor of the literary journal *La fiera letteraria*. His more significant critical and moral essays have been collected and published in two volumes, *Cristo tradito* (1940; Christ Betrayed) and *Ambiguità cristiana* (1954; Christian Ambiguity).

See: G. Pullini, in *Teatro italiano fra due secoli: 1850-1950* (1958), pp. 430-36; S. Torresani, in *Il teatro italiano negli ultimi vent'anni (1945-65)* (1965), pp. 185-215; G. Cappello, *Invito alla lettura di Diego Fabbri* (1979).

J.Ch.

Fabra i Poc, Pompeu (1868-1948), Catalan grammarian, lexicographer, and philologist, was born in Barcelona, where his father was mayor, and died in Prada de Conflent, France. He studied industrial engineering and became a professor of chemistry in Bilbao. He held this position until Enric PRAT DE LA RIBA invited him to join the Institute of Catalan Studies.

HIS literary talent soon became evident in the pages of the journal *L'avenc*, where Casas-Carbó had initiated a campaign to purify the Catalan language. Fabra lent his enthusiastic support to this project. His *Ensayo de gramática del catalán moderno* (A First Grammar of Modern Catalan) was published in *L'avenc* in 1891 and from then on Fabra dedicated himself completely to the task of standardizing and systematizing Catalan on the basis of the Catalan spoken in Barcelona. He wrote *Contribució a la Llengua catalana* (1898; Contribution to the Catalan Language), *Sil labari català* (1904), *Tractat d'Ortografia catalana* (1904; Treatise on Catalan Orthography), *Qüestions de Gramática catalana* (1911; Issues of Catalan Grammar), and *Gramática de la Llengua catalana* (1912; Grammar of the Catalan Language). In 1913 his *Normes ortogràficues* (Rules of Orthography) were officially adopted by the Institute of Catalan Studies. In 1915 linguistic reform triumphed in Valencia and, a short while later, in Majorca, despite continuing vehement opposition, which also existed in Catalonia. Fabra's *Diccionari Ortografic* (1917; Orthographic Dictionary) and *Diccionari general de la Llengua catalana* (1932; General Dictionary of the Catalan Language) contributed decisively to the systematization and standardization of Catalan, as did his continuous efforts as director of the lexicographical service in the philological section of the Institute of Catalan Studies and as professor of the Catalan language in the Senate (Diputació) of Barcelona.

Other books are a new *Gramática catalana* (1918; Catalan Grammar), a *Gramática francesa* (1919; French Grammar), and a *Gramática inglesa* (1924; English Grammar). In the same year he assumed the presidency of the Ateneu and began to contribute to the newspaper *La Publicitat*, to which he submitted his famous *Converses filologiques* (Philological Chats), where he explains his linguistic concerns to the layman. The same ideas continued to preoccupy him in *L'obra de depuració del català*

(1924; Purifying Catalan), *Ortografia catalana* (1925; Catalan Orthography), *Les principals faltes de gramàtica* (1925; Catalan Grammatical Errors), *La conjugació dels verbs en Català* (1926; Verb Conjugation in Catalan), *De la depuració de la Llengua Catalana* (1927; On Purifying Catalan), *Abrede Grammaire catalane* (1928; Short Catalan Grammar), and *Compendio de Gramática Catalana* (1930; Compendium of Catalan Grammar).

In 1931 he became editor of *Butlletí di Dialectologia*, and in 1932 he acceded to a chair at the Autonomous University of Barcelona and to the directorship of cultural affairs of Catalonia. He published *El Català literari* (1932; Literary Catalan) and *L'obra de l'Universitat Autónoma* (1935; The Task of the Autonomous University), collections of speeches and articles, and *Grammaire catalane* (1946; Catalan Grammar). He spent his years of exile in France and died in Prada de Conflent on Dec. 25, 1948, where the annual Pompeu Fabra Popular Festival of Culture is held in his honor.

See: R. Aramon i Serra, ed., *Estudis romanics*, vol. 7 (1963-68); "Estudis de lingüistica i de filologiu catalana dedicats a la memòria de Pompeu Fabra en el centenari de la seva naixenca I (1970)," *BIEC* 8, no. 2 (1970); J. Coromines, "Pompeu Fabra (1868-1948)" in *Lleures i converses d'un filòleg* (1971).

J.F.C.

Fadeyev, Aleksandr Aleksandrovich (1901-56), Russian novelist, was born in the province of Tver to revolutionary parents. A Communist Party member at the age of 17, he was a brigade commissar during the Civil War. Later he was a leader of the Russian Association of Proletarian Writers from 1928 to 1932 and the head of the Soviet Writers Union from 1946 to 1954. As a Marxist literary theorist, he was in the forefront of Soviet literature for 30 years. His first stories, written in 1923, deal with the Russian Revolution and the Civil War in the Far East, as does his widely acclaimed novel *Razgrom* (1927; Eng. tr., *The Nineteen*, 1929; *The Rout*, 1956), which depicts the struggle and defeat of a Red guerrilla detachment whose 19 survivors never lose their fighting spirit. Presenting social psychology through individuals, Fadeyev successfully created real, full-blooded characters. Emulating Lev TOLSTOY, he followed the train of his characters' thoughts and exposed their hidden feelings and motivations by frequent use of the "not because . . . but because" type of sentence. *The Rout* is well organized; its language is dircct and, unlike many of its contemporary Soviet counterparts, almost devoid of ornamental imagery. *Posledniy iz Udege* (1930-40; The Last of the Udege) is lengthy and disjointed. Originally conceived as an epic about the transition to socialism of the Udege, a primitive Far Eastern tribe, it has a multitude of characters from various social strata. *Leningrad v dni blokady* (1944; Eng. tr., *Leningrad in the Days of the Blockade*, 1946) is a collection of sketches inspired by World War II.

With *Molodaya gvardiya* (1945; Eng. tr., *The Young Guard*, 1958,) Fadeyev began to have difficulties with Stalin's censors. This novel describes the activities of the Young Guard, an underground organization that actually existed in a Ukrainian town during the German occupation. Fadeyev's stern realism is mitigated here by lyricism and a romantic idealization of the young Communists. This novel met with Stalin-inspired criticism and has, since 1951, been published in a revised version marred by politically motivated additions. Fadeyev's last novel, *Chornaya metallurgiya* (1954; Black Metallurgy), also underwent a thorough revision when its political and technological orientation became unacceptable after Stalin's death. Relieved of the chairmanship of the Writers Union at the beginning of destalinization and haunted by thoughts of the decimation of the literary profession during Stalin's purges, Fadeyev shot himself in 1956.

See: E. Brown, *Russian Literature since the Revolution* (rev. ed., 1969), pp. 172–79; G. Struve, *Russian Literature under Lenin and Stalin 1917–53* (1971), pp. 134–36, 319–20.   H.E.

Faeroese literature. On the Faeroe Islands, situated in the North Atlantic, Danish was the official language until 1948, when the islands became a self-governing region of Denmark. A major barrier to the development of the Faeroese language was the absence of spelling rules, which were first developed in 1854 by Ventzel Ulricus Hammershaimb (1819–1909). Until then, literary tradition was primarily oral, consisting of riddles, tales, and ballads, which were transmitted from one generation to another.

Modern Faeroese literature begins with national and religious songs composed since the 1870s both by Faeroese students in Copenhagen and on the islands themselves. The three major writers of this period were Fríðrikur Petersen (1853–1917), Jóannes Patursson (1866–1946), and Rasmus Effersøe (1857–1916). Effersøe also wrote plays with motifs from history and daily life, and he edited the first newspaper in the Faeroese language (from 1890). Only in the period after 1900 does a richer and more intimate form of poetry emerge, the foremost representative of which is Jens H. O. Djurhuus (1881–1948)—on the whole the major poet in Faeroese literature. The keynote of his *Yrkingar* (1914; Poems), the first individual collection of poems in Faeroese, is marked by doubt and pessimism, an expression of the author's split personality.

Faeroese prose has its beginnings in Hammershaimb's edition of ballads and folktales, *Færøsk Anthologi* (1884–91; Faeroese Anthology). Regin í Líð (1871–1962), author of short stories and nature descriptions from ca. 1900 on, published the first Faeroese novel in 1909, *Bábelstornið* (The Tower of Babel), a family novel dealing with the social conflicts on the islands between 1850 and 1900. The 20th century is dominated by a number of major prose writers. Heðin Brú's (1901–) novel *Feðgar á ferð* (1940; Eng. tr., *The Old Man and His Sons,* 1970) is a humorous portrayal of the reactions of an old Faeroese to modern times. Brú has written numerous other novels, for example, *Lognbrá* (1930; Mirage), *Fastatøkur* (1935; Firm Grip), and *Men lívið lær* (1970; But Life Laughs), a historical novel, as well as short stories and poetry. In his writing Brú embraces both detailed realism in his descriptions of Faeroese everyday life and a more symbolic narrative technique. He is undoubtedly the foremost stylistically talented author among contemporary writers of the Faeroese language. He not only preserves the ancient dialects but also broadens their viability, as, for example, in translations of Shakespeare.

Two of the most outstanding Scandinavian authors of this century are Faeroese but write in Danish. One is Jørgen-Frantz Jacobsen (1900–38), whose sole literary work was published posthumously, the historical novel *Barbara* (1939; Eng. tr., 1948), which builds on a local tradition from the 18th century. The book paints a fascinating portrait of a woman who completely follows her natural instincts—a Faeroese Madame Bovary. She is the widow of two ministers and married to a third, whom she abandons. But even though Barbara represents the tragic aspects in human relationships, she is the tubercular author's glorification of the precious qualities of life. The writing of William HEINESEN, the second of these two, is more faceted, being partly lyrical, partly epic.

Among the younger representatives of Faeroese literature, Regin Dahl (1918–), Karsten Hoydal (1912–), and especially Jens Pauli Heinesen (1932–) should be mentioned. In contrast to Jens Pauli Heinesen, whose production includes five collections of short stories, three novels, and one play, the most recent authors are primarily devotees of poetry. This is particularly true about the very talented Steinbjørn Jacobsen (1937–) and Guðrið Helmsdal (1941–), the latter of whom writes both Danish and Faeroese.

See: E. Krenn, *Die Entwicklung der föroyischen Literatur* (1940); H. Brønner, *Three Faroese Novelists* (1974); W. Glyn Jones, *William Heinesen, TWAS* 282 (1974).   S.H.R.

Fagus, pseud. of Georges Eugène Faillet (1872–1933), French poet, was born in Brussels, the son of a Frenchman who had been exiled after the Commune in 1871. The family returned to Paris after the amnesty of 1880. As a youth, Fagus was, like his father, a radical, but he was later reconciled to the republic and for some time earned his living as an official at the Prefecture of the Seine; he finally turned into a decided reactionary, a fanatic royalist, and an ardent Catholic. Indifferent to recognition by the general public, he remained, until his death in an accident, *un isolé*. He belongs to the generation of the symbolists, who not infrequently could be called bohemians in their writings and gentlemen in their tastes and their way of living. Hostile to all that savored of vulgarity, Fagus insisted on decency in behavior and manners, and his language was that of a purist. As an artist he belongs to the family of the Villons, with such writers as Mathurin Régnier, Gérard de Nerval, and Paul VERLAINE. Gautier would no doubt have added his name to the list of his *Grotesques*.

The titles of Fagus's collections of poetry, together with the dates of publication, are in themselves somewhat revelatory of his evolution towards an ever more orthodox philosophy and creed: *Colloque sentimental entre Emile Zola et Fagus; poèmes* (1898; Sentimental Colloquium between Emile ZOLA and Fagus; Poems); *Fagus: Testament de sa vie, recueilli et expurgé* (1898; Fagus: Testament of His Life, Gathered and Expurgated); *Ixion; poème* (1903); *Jeunes Fleurs; exercices poétiques* (1906; Young Flowers; Poetic Exercises); *Frère Tranquille; dialogue entre la raison et le spectre de la mort* (1918; Brother Tranquil: Dialogue between Reason and the Specter of Death); *La Danse macabre* (1920; The Dance of Death); *La Prière de 40 heures, ou les 14 Stations sous l'horloge du destin* (1920; The 40-Hour Prayer, or the 14 Stations beneath the Clock of Fate), republished in *La Guirlande à l'épousée* (1921; The Bride's Garland); *Les Ephémères* (1925; The Mayflies); *Le Sacre des Innocents; poèmes* (1927; The Crowning of the Innocents: Poems); *Ballade de Saint Côme offerte à M. Aug. Fournier pour tout l'Hôtel-Dieu et les autres hospitaliers* (1927; Ballad of Saint Como Offered to Mr. Aug. Fournier for All the City Hospital and the Other Hospital Employees). In 1908 was published a small volume, *Aphorismes,* and in 1926 *Clavecin* (Harpsichord), comments on the art of writing. As a scholar he translated Vergil's *Eclogues* (1929) and the *Chanson de Roland* (1929; Song of Roland). He was a contributor to numerous periodicals and for a time, after 1925, wrote "Chroniques" for the *Evénement.*

See: H. Martineau, "Fagus," *Divan* 17, no. 100 (May 1925): 195–312; A. van Bever and P. Léautaud, *Poètes d'aujourd'hui* (1929).   A.Sc. rev. D.W.A.

Falkberget, Johan (1879–1967), Norwegian novelist, was born near the small mining town of Røros. Both his parents were descended from Swedish and Norwegian peasant miners, and Johan, too, began to work in the mines when he was only eight years old. The difficult labor in brutal surroundings was redeemed only by the austere beauty of nature on the treeless mountain plateau. At age 27 he finally left the mines and worked one year as an editor of a Labor Party paper in western Norway before finally settling down in Christiania (now Oslo) as a writer. Falkberget began publishing his first stories at 16 and published his first book at 22, but it was not until *Svarte fjelde* (1907; Black Mountains) that he received critical acclaim. Its subject matter, mining life, was quite new to Norwegian literature, and he revealed in this novel a remarkable narrative gift that has made him one of the most popular authors in his homeland. Outstanding among his earlier books is *Lisbet på Jarnfjeld* (1915; Eng. tr., *Lisabeth of Jarnfjeld*, 1930), the story of a spirited woman from the high mountains, who through a tragic marriage succumbs to the irrational forces of her mind, and *Brændoffer* (1917; Burnt Offering), a novel about the destructiveness of modern industrialism. *Brændoffer*, Falkberget's only novel to describe a contemporary social problem, is not without bitterness, a quality otherwise rarely found in his writings.

In 1922, Falkberget returned to his hometown to take over his father's small farm on the edge of Rugelsjøen. There he lived, studying the background of his family and of the region and identifying himself closely with the people of the community. With *Den fjerde nattevagt* (1923; Eng. tr., *The Fourth Night Watch*, 1968), Falkberget began writing historical novels, a genre in which he was to excel. The central figure of this work is an early 19th-century clergyman who comes to a mining community intending to dominate it, but who learns charity and humility instead. The great trilogy *Christianus Sextus* (1927–35), set in the 18th century, is the story of the mine of that name. It is also a monument to the lives of simple, hard-working people. In 1940, Falkberget fled before the invading Germans, crossing the plateau to Sweden on foot. He carried with him the manuscript of *An-Magritt* (1940), the first volume in the tetralogy *Nattens brød* (1940–59; The Bread of Night), possibly Falkberget's greatest work. In the raw, brutal Røros of the 17th century the author has placed his heroine, An-Magritt; strong, wild, and stubborn, but also sensitive and loving, she is both an unforgettable character and a symbol of Falkberget's belief in the beauty and resiliency of the human spirit.

Falkberget's work shows a deep, genuine understanding of the life of the poor and of their toil and hardships down through the centuries. His struggle on behalf of the working class was inspired by the Utopian socialists, and he believed that change would have to come through work and love based on Christian faith.

See: K. M. Kommandantvold, *Johan Falkbergets bergmannsverden* (1971), T. B. Pettersen, ed., *Falkberget nå* (1980). H.A.L.

Fallada, Hans, pseud. of Rudolf Ditzen (1893–1947), German novelist, was born in Berlin, the son of a judge. He studied agriculture, was for a time a fiscal inspector, and became a journalist before settling in as a free-lance writer, mostly of novels that depict the environmental and sociological predicaments of ordinary people. Concerned mostly with the moral, economic, and social problems that confronted society in the wake of two world wars, although mainly World War I, Fallada's optimistic viewpoint and faith in the life-force of his people made his novels popular, particularly since he wrote in an uncomplicated, often banal, anecdotal style.

Fallada's early novels are *Der junge Goedeschall* (1920; Young Goedeschall), *Anton und Gerda* (1923), and *Bauern, Bonzen und Bomben* (1931; Farmers, Big-Shots, and Bombs), but his greatest success was *Kleiner Mann— was nun?* (1933; Eng. tr., *Little Man, What Now?*, 1933), a novel about the effects of the depression of the 1930s on the lower classes in Germany. Other novels are *Wer einmal aus dem Blechnapf frißt* (1935; Eng. tr., *The World Outside*, 1934), *Wir hatten mal ein Kind* (1934; Once We Had a Child), *Altes Herz geht auf die Reise* (1936; Eng. tr., *An Old Heart Goes A-Journeying*, 1936), *Wolf unter Wölfen* (1937; A Wolf among Wolves), *Das Märchen vom Stadtschreiber, der aufs Land flog* (1938; Eng. tr., *Sparrow Farm*, 1938), and *Der ungeliebte Mann* (1940; The Unloved Man). He wrote two autobiographical works, *Damals bei uns daheim* (1941; Back Then at Home) and *Heute bei uns zu Hause* (1943; The Way It is at Home Today). An autobiographical strain also marks the posthumous novel *Der Alpdruck* (1947; The Nightmare), a work concerned with the postcatastrophic feeling of guilt among survivors in the aftermath of war.

After serving in World War II, Fallada returned to East Berlin, where he worked on the East German journal *Aufbau*. After his death from an overdose of narcotics in the wake of a severe illness, other works appeared: the novels *Jeder stirbt für sich allein* (1949; Everyone Dies by Himself), the story of the resistance and demise of a worker in Berlin after World War II, *Der Trinker* (1950; Eng. tr., *The Drinker*, 1952), and *Ein Mann will hinauf* (1953; A Man on the Way Up). The novel *Kleiner Mann— was nun?* was adapted for the stage by the West German playwright Tankred Dorst.

See: L. Frank, *Hans Fallada* (1962); H. J. Schueler, *Hans Fallada: Humanist and Social Critic* (1970); J. Manthey, *Hans Fallada in Selbstzeugnissen und Bilddokumenten* (1973). A.L.W.

Fargue, Léon-Paul (1876–1947), French poet and journalist, was born in Paris. Fargue began to publish poems in 1893 in the journal *L'Art littéraire*, but the work that in later years he acknowledged to be his first was *Tancrède* (1895). This group of poems in prose and verse presents the sensuous and sentimental confessions of a young artist. The work is in the symbolist manner inspired by Arthur RIMBAUD. Fargue's reluctance to give *Tancrède* a final form is characteristic of his entire life's work; it took 16 years before he allowed his friend Valery LARBAUD to publish these poems in a limited edition (1911). Ten other prose poems, privately printed (1907), became the nucleus of *Poëmes,* a collection published in 1912 and revised several times, a fact that reflects Fargue's constant search for perfection. These musical prose poems, rich in imagery, vocabulary, and emotion, are autobiographical. Some originate in Fargue's despair over the death of his father (1909), who died believing his son to be a total failure, having published no major work. Recurrent themes of *Poëmes* include absence, separation, old homes, unrequited love, and the turbulence of children; favorite words also recur: long ago, dreams, mystery, memories, trains, railroad stations, abyss, loss, bridge.

Much of Fargue's poetry was expressed orally, at the expense of his writing. His conversation was so dazzlingly effervescent, rich in imagery and word-invention, that his company was sought after in spite of his inveterate lateness and absent-mindedness. André Beucler recorded his anecdotes and conversation in his *Vingt ans avec Léon-Paul Fargue* (1952; Eng. tr., *The Last of the Bohemians: Twenty Years with Léon-Paul Fargue,* 1954), as did T. Alajouanine in his *Correspondance Larbaud-Fargue* (1971). Fargue's brilliant talk made him the literary lion of such elegant salons as those of the Duchesse de la Rochefoucauld, who wrote a monograph on him (1950), and of the Princesse de Bassiano, who sponsored the literary review *Commerce* (1924-30) with Larbaud, Paul VALÉRY, and Fargue as coeditors and Adrienne Monnier as secretary. He was among the most faithful visitors at the Maison des Amis des Livres, Monnier's renowned literary bookstore. The circle of his intimates included many leading French and foreign writers, painters, and musicians. Erik Satie, Maurice Ravel, and Ricardo Vinès set some of his poems to their melodies. Yet in spite of Fargue's many friends, one of the constantly recurring moods of his work is loneliness, perhaps caused by the melancholy memories of having been an illegitimate child living with his devoted seamstress mother, beyond the pale of the "respectable" bourgeois of his father's family—until his parents' marriage when he was 31.

A major subject of Fargue's later works is Paris, which he knew well enough to be called "Le Piéton de Paris" (Pedestrian of Paris) from the title of a collection of his prose poems published in 1939. Most of his work appearing in *Commerce, Mesures, Mercure de France, Nouvelle Revue française,* and *Transition* (including English translations, 1927) was collected in 1928-29 in four books with revelatory titles: *Banalité* (basis for his inspiration), *Vulturne* (with its fantastic visions often compared to those of Hieronymus Bosch and Odilon Redon), *Epaisseurs* (density through which his images rise to the surface), and *Suite familière* (his ars poetica). In two later collections, *Haute Solitude* (1941; High Solitude) and *Refuges* (1942), his sensitivity to people and objects was again well served by striking metaphors and inventive Rabelaisian vocabulary. The results of the stroke he suffered in 1943 are reflected in the volume *Méandres* (1946); no longer "Piéton de Paris," he received "le tout-Paris" in his bedroom.

Chronically impoverished, Fargue turned to journalism in the 1930s and wrote several hundred articles, mainly in *Le Figaro* (1934-47), *Les Nouvelles littéraires* (1931-47), and *Aujourd'hui* (1940-43). In these souvenirs of his contacts with people and his endless ramblings in every quarter of Paris, he recreated a whole epoch and a milieu, but these articles, journalistic in nature, lack the quality that distinguishes his poetry. Nevertheless, Fargue had most of these pieces, along with the prefaces he wrote for other authors, published in a dozen books such as *Déjeuners de soleil* (1942; Lunches of Sunlight) and *Lanterne magique* (1944; Eng. tr., *Magic Lantern*, 1946). Hard-pressed financially, he frequently revised his feature articles, using them in various publications—in deference to his readers' limited memory—as if they were new.

See: special Fargue double issue of *LFL libres* 45-46 (June 1927); C. Chonez, *Léon-Paul Fargue* (1950); L. R. Schub, *Léon-Paul Fargue* (1973); J.-C. Walter, *Léon-Paul Fargue ou l'homme en proie à la ville* (1973).   L.R.S.

Faure, Elie (1873-1937), French essayist and art historian, was born in Sainte-Foy-la-Grande, in Gascony. In one of his books, *Les Trois Gouttes de sang* (1929; The Three Drops of Blood), he attempted to characterize the ethnic originality of that French province. His mother came from a well-known Protestant family, the Reclus, and several of his maternal uncles were doctors or geographers. Faure soon revolted against his constricting provincial and religious environment, yet he retained from it an obstinate independence of character. He studied medicine in Paris and practiced it all his life, but his passion was for art and the philosophy of history.

Faure saw the great artists as mirrors of their own ages and molders of the ages to follow. As an art historian, his range was immense, extending to all continents and all periods of history. In his studies, he felt obstinately drawn to the perilous and yet stimulating field of national psychology. He cared little for historical objectivity and for the academic refusal to feel intensely and to venture value judgments. He spurned moderation and that restraint that ends by desiccating the sources of feeling. Several of his volumes of essays exalt energy, war, the genius of Napoleon, and the lyrical rhetoric of Jules Michelet: *La Danse sur le feu et l'eau* (1920; Eng. tr., *The Dance over Fire and Water*, 1926), *Napoléon* (1921; Eng. tr., *Napoleon*, 1924), *Les Constructeurs* (1914; The Builders). But his great work, which has had a profound impact upon a limited but outstanding group of writers, artists, and psychoanalysts, is his *Histoire de l'art* in four volumes (1909; rev. ed., 1920; Eng. tr., *History of Art*, 1921-30), to which he added in 1926 a thought-provoking theoretical volume, *L'Esprit des formes* (Eng. tr., *The Spirit of the Forms,* 1930). Scholars primarily attached to factual objectivity and clinging to noncommittal prudence have balked at the author's imperious generalizations, dazzling intuitions, and hyperbolic tone. Faure's Nietzschean fervor (see Friedrich NIETZSCHE) and the profundity of many of his remarks, his worship of all that is dynamic and intense, weary some readers. Others do not hesitate to hail him as one of the greatest, most generous personalities of the 20th century and a source of illumination on the arcana of artistic creation.

See: special numbers of *Europe* (December 1937) and *CduS* 381 (1965); P. Desanges, *E. Faure* (1963).   H.P.

Faye, Jean Pierre (1925-), French novelist, poet, and essayist, was born in Paris. In addition to poetry—*Fleuve renversé* (1960; River Reversed), *Couleurs pliées* (1965; Folded Colors), and *Verres* (1977; Glasses)—he has written seven novels: *Entre les rues* (1958; Between the Streets), *La Cassure* (1961; The Break), *Battement* (1962; Beating), *Analogues* (1964), *L'Ecluse* (1964; The Lock), *Les Troyens* (1970; The Trojans), and *Les Portes des villes du monde* (1977; The Gates of the Cities of the World). Similarities among the titles of the first three and the fifth (interval, break, pulsation, sluice) point to a unity of purpose in Faye's work. *Analogues* brings together strands of the earlier novels, *Les Troyens* interweaves all six, and the seventh winds its way through "openings" of previous texts; an eighth is to be called *Hexagramme* (which is the subtitle of the sixth). In exploring the nature and effect of the narrative process, Faye relies less and less on realistic underpinnings, stressing instead the gap that separates all narratives from so-called reality and the role narrative plays in shaping and changing one's view of that reality. Such ideas inform *Le Récit hunique* (1967) and *Théorie du récit* (1972). The title of the first is a pun referring to the unified narrative of history and to a hypothetical narrative told by a Hun that would have induced his fellow-tribesmen to cross the Rhine (and thus change history). Two statements from *Théorie* will serve to indicate the direction of Faye's thought: "The history of a Western nation commonly designated by the word 'France' is first of all a tangle of narratives"; "man is the animal who states what he does, who knows what he narrates." What concerns Faye most is how history (as narrative) can affect history (as event or ideology). This has led him to his most ambitious undertaking, *Langages totalitaires* (1972; Totalitarian Languages), which is an endeavor to explain how the language used, first by Fascists, later by Nazis, made possible Adolf Hitler's rise to power and his hold on the people.

Among those impressed by Faye's novels was Philippe Sollers, who invited him to join the editorial board of *Tel*

Quel, on which he remained from 1963 to 1967. He broke with Sollers to establish what he called not a review but a collective, naming it *Change* in clear opposition to the group he was leaving. Although both place their activities within the purview of linguistics, psychoanalysis, and Marxism, and although both have rejected structuralism, *Tel Quel* and *Change* have proceeded along divergent paths. The nucleus of the collective was constituted by Faye, the poet and mathematician Jacques Roubaud, and the novelist Maurice Roche. Roche soon defected, while others were attracted to the group. By the time the eighth "cahier" appeared in March 1971 (32 were published through 1977), a stable group of eight members had been brought together, including novelist-critic Philippe Boyer, novelist Jean-Claude Montel, linguist Mitsou Ronat, and translator Léon Robel. In 1973, assessing what had been accomplished up to then, Faye referred to "the royal way that leads from Roman Jakobson to Noam Chomsky," that is, from the Linguistic Circle of Prague to the theory of generative grammar. Working under the assumption that the concepts that ground the latter are transferable, the collective's aim has been to establish a practice of "generative criticism" (see *Change* 16–17) based on the Chomskian model.

See: P. Boyer, *L'Ecarté(e)* (1973); "The Language-Field of Nazism," *TLS* (Apr. 5, 1974).   L.S.R.

Fayko, Aleksey Mikhaylovich (1893–), Russian dramatist, was born in Moscow. He graduated from the Faculty of History and Philology at Moscow University in 1917, and from 1921 to 1924 worked as coach and actor in the Studio of Improvisations, also writing cabaret sketches. Of his first successful plays, *Ozero Lyul* (1923; Lake Lyul) and *Uchitel Bubus* (1925; Bubus the Teacher) the critic Boris Alpers said: "Melodrama is his element." The "banal cinematographic 'Americanism' of Fayko's first plays" is not altogether overcome in *Chelovek s portfelem* (1928; Man with a Portfolio), his exposure of self-seeking ambition in a socialist society, although another critic considers this play a turning toward realism. Still, the recent republication of Fayko's work points to its continued validity. In 1971 a collection of his works was published under the title *Teatr. Pyesy. Vospominaniya*.   M.L.H.

Federspiel, Jürg (1931–), Swiss novelist, poet, and short-story writer, was born in Winterthur, Zürich canton. His first book is a collection of short stories entitled *Orangen und Tode* (1961; Oranges and Deaths). This title signals the author's obsession with the principles of life and death, which, in his work, frequently takes the form of an ardent, often violent dialogue between them. "I am a sensuous man," he maintains. "If there are no oranges anymore, I am for death. Mine."

Federspiel's language has the power and imagination of Günter GRASS's, although it lacks the latter's ironic distance. His novel *Massaker im Mond* (1963; Massacre on the Moon) is a very critical description of Switzerland in the 1950s that caused considerable annoyance in his homeland. In 1967 he published a volume of poems, *Marco Polos Koffer* (Marco Polo's Suitcase), the result of a unique collaboration with the poet Rainer Brambach. A scholarship enabled Federspiel to spend the year 1967–68 in New York. The result of this experience is the literary "collage" *Museum des Hasses, Tage in Manhattan* (1969; Museum of Hatred, Days in Manhattan), which clearly reveals the influence of Max FRISCH's literary diaries. *Museum* consists of diaristic and autobiographical pieces, pure fiction, reports, and critical essays. Federspiel subsequently has produced more short-story collections, *Die Märchentante* (1971; The Fairy-Tale Teller) and

Paratuga kehrt zurück (1973; Paratuga Returns); in these stories his powerful stream of narration is tamed somewhat by the conciseness of the form. In *Träume aus Plastic* (1972; Dreams of Plastic), Federspiel reveals his talent as a critic of contemporary culture.

See: W. Bucher and G. Ammann, eds. *Schweizer Schriftsteller im Gespräch*, vol. 2 (1971), pp. 85–120.
R.K.

Fedin, Konstantin Aleksandrovich (1892–1977), Russian prose writer, was at the time of his death an influential conservative voice in the Soviet political and literary establishment. Serving as both first secretary and president of the executive board of the Soviet Writers Union and as a deputy to the Supreme Soviet, he was active in censuring disloyal writers.

Educated in his native Saratov and in Moscow, Fedin went to Germany in 1914, where he was interned when World War I broke out. He had published inconsequential pieces as early as 1913–14, but upon returning home soon after the October Revolution, he took up the literary profession in earnest. He was introduced by Maksim GORKY into the Serapion Brotherhood in 1921 (*see* RUSSIAN LITERATURE); and conservative as he was in his literary inclinations, he was not unaffected by the lively and innovative atmosphere of that group.

Although his later works have come to be regarded as models of critical and socialist realism, Fedin began his career with interesting experiments in fictional style and form. The stories comprising *Pustyr* (1923; Wasteland) and *Transvaal* (1926) reveal at times the stylistic influence of Aleksey REMIZOV and a Dostoyevskian psychological concern with people in desperate circumstances. Fedin's major achievement of the 1920s was *Goroda i gody* (1924; Eng. tr., *Cities and Years*, 1962), as the first large-scale Soviet novel. This novel is about a Russian intellectual's formation, his irresolute attitude toward the Russian Revolution, and his eventual liquidation by his former closest friend, a German who has opted for the new order in post-Revolutionary Petrograd. The vivid, kaleidoscopic views of Germany before and during the war and of Russia in the grip of revolution and civil war are enhanced by the use of deliberately confused and confusing chronology, unusual vocabulary and syntax, and shifting narrative planes in the manner of Andrey BELY. The novel set an important theme for Soviet literature: the problems faced by an intellectual in adjusting to a revolutionary society. In his next novel, *Bratya* (1928; Brothers), Fedin returned to this theme, here in the figure of a gifted composer who fails in both music and love.

His two novels of the 1930s, both set in Western Europe, where Fedin was a frequent visitor, are considered less successful. *Pokhishchenye Yevropy* (1933, 1935; The Rape of Europe) attempts to contrast the decadence of Western bourgeois society to the vitality of the USSR at the time of the first Five-Year Plan, but the result is both schematic and static. *Sanatoriy Arktur* (1940; Eng. tr., 1957) is a love story set in a Swiss tuberculosis sanatorium.

Fedin spent over 20 years on what he intended to be his crowning work, the trilogy that includes *Pervye radosti* (1945; Eng. tr., *Early Joys*, 1948), *Neobyknovennoye leto* (1948; Eng. tr., *No Ordinary Summer*, 1950), and *Kostyor* (1962; Eng. tr., *The Conflagration*, 1968). If his earlier work seemed Dostoyevskian, his stylistic models here are Lev TOLSTOY and Maksim Gorky. Spanning the period from 1910 to World War II, these novels attempt to depict in a large cast of diversified characters the vast historical, social, and psychological changes taking place in Russia. Fedin's protagonist, the obligatory positive hero, is well drawn; and the two members of the intelligentsia, in contrast to the author's earlier figures of this type, come eventually to accept the Revolution and to work within the new order. The trilogy is one of the best expressions of the conservatism in Soviet literature that has developed since the end of the 1920s, and it earned Fedin several state prizes.

Fedin's reminiscences are valuable for the information they provide about the history of Soviet literature, particularly his two-volume memoir about his mentor, *Gorky sredi nas* (1943, 1944; Gorky in Our Midst). Although the first volume was highly praised, the second volume, about "vanishing Petersburg," was attacked as anti-Soviet. A revised and expanded version appeared in 1967. Fedin's wide-ranging *Pisatel, iskusstvo, vremya* (1957; Writer, Art, Time; rev., 1961, 1973) is a set of literary portraits, critical sketches, and reflections on the art of literature.

See: E. Simmons, *Russian Fiction and Soviet Ideology* (1958), pp. 9–87; I. Zilbershteyn, ed., *Tvorchestvo Konstantina Fedina* (1966); J. Blum, *Konstantin Fedin* (1967).

R.P.H.

Felipe, León, pseud. of León Felipe Camino Galicia (1884–1968), Spanish poet was born in Tábara. His work shows deep concern with his country's cultural values and contemporary political history and represents one of the best examples of committed poetry in Spain. A tireless wanderer, in his youth Felipe traveled all over Spain and lived in several countries, including the United States, where after receiving a degree from Columbia University he taught for two years at Cornell University (1928–29).

Although his first books, *Versos y oraciones de caminante* (2 vols., 1920, 1929; Songs and Prayers of a Pilgrim) were published in the 1920s, his extremely original style, which recognized no literary school or fashion, was not very well known until the onset of the Spanish Civil War (1936–39), when the poet, after criticizing the injustice of the war in an explosive poem, left his diplomatic post in Panama and returned to Spain to write violently critical poems inspired by the politics of the war. Like many other Republican intellectuals he soon had to leave for Mexico, where he died 30 years later, never having returned to his homeland. Spain always remained his main concern. In exile he published his poems about Civil War in two books: *El payaso de las bofetadas y el pescador de caña* (1938; The Clown Who Gets Slapped and the Man with the Fishing Rod) and *El hacha* (1939; The Axe). A third collection deals with the painful reality of defeat: *Español del éxodo y del llanto* (1939; Spaniard of the Exodus and Tears). These set the tone that is characteristic of most of Felipe's later publications, including, among many others, the very passionate *Ganarás la luz. Biografía, poesía y destino* (1953; You Will Earn the Light. Biography, Poetry and Destiny). The publication in Buenos Aires of his *Obras completas* (1963) gave him full recognition as a major contemporary poet.

Felipe's earlier interest in theater (he had been an actor in his youth) accounts for the dramatic quality of his poetic language. Convinced that poetry has a superior function, he thought of himself as a prophet whose voice had the high pitch of righteousness and the convincing ring of truth. In his Promethean view of the poet as a defender of human freedom he is reminiscent of Walt Whitman, whose poetry he translated into Spanish. Unlike the American bard, however, Felipe makes use of stronger language and is sometimes too blunt in his directness. His lengthy poems are made up of cumulative series of repeated fixed expressions, symbols, metaphors and parabolic images that strikingly communicate a set of basic situations and concepts. The use of free verse

stresses a rhythmical pattern akin to the predicatory repetitiveness of a Biblical prophet whose emotional manifestations of sadness and ire, despair and hope, are born out of an ethical sense of human justice.

During his long period of life in Mexico, Felipe maintained relations with other exiled Spanish writers and even collaborated with Juan LARREA in the founding and publication of *Cuadernos Americanos*, where most of his work appeared for the first time.

See: B. D. Wolfe, "León Felipe: Poet of Spain's Exodus and Tears," *TriQ* 16 (1970): 21–29.   S.D.-T.

Fénéon, Félix (1861–1944), French art and literary critic, was born in Turin, Italy. Educated in France, he excelled in geography and history. Between 1881 and 1894 he was employed at the War Ministry, but when implicated in an anarchist plot (but not prosecuted), he left that post. Little is known of his private life—he was nicknamed "the silent one"—but he did maintain an attachment to anarchism. Interested in art and literature, Fénéon contributed to some 40 little magazines of the decadent-symbolist movement. He founded *La Libre Revue* (1883–84) and *La Revue indépendante* (1884–85), played a major role in *La Revue moderniste* (1886) and *La Vogue* (1886), and directed *La Revue blanche* from 1895 to 1903. He was the first editor of Arthur RIMBAUD's *Illuminations* and of texts by Jules Laforgue. As director of *La Sirène* (1920–24), Fénéon promoted such authors as James Joyce and John Millington Synge. An outstanding art critic—for some, like Jean PAULHAN, he was *the* critic—Fénéon supported such new artists as Georges Seurat, Henri Matisse, Edouard Vuillard, and Pierre Bonnard. In 1912 he organized the first futurist exhibition (*see* ITALIAN LITERATURE) in Paris. He had an extraordinary ability to appreciate contemporaries, writers such as Stéphane MALLARMÉ and Alfred JARRY. Although Fénéon signed most of his early art criticism, his other writings (he wrote sparingly) were pseudonymous or anonymous. He perfected the surprising, three-line anecdote, perhaps an extension of the precise, "lapidary" style (for some neologistic, for others technical and precise) that attempts to state the important and to conclude nothing. Recognized as the gray eminence of symbolism and impressionism, he spent his last years in the house built for François René Chateaubriand at Vallée-aux-Loups.

An edition of Fénéon's works was published, with an introduction by Paulhan, in 1948. Joan Halperin edited a meticulous, augmented edition (2 vols., 1970) with a chronology, introduction, and explanatory notes, entitled *Œuvres plus que complètes* (More Than Complete Works).   S.W.

Fenoglio, Beppe (1922–63), Italian novelist and short-story writer, was born in Alba to working-class parents. He spent all his life in the Langhe region of Piedmont, cut off from the Italian literary scene. Fenoglio's fiction deals with the anti-Fascist Resistance. Most of his work was still unpublished at the time of his death, and this material has since proved difficult to edit. It now seems clear that he intended to produce a massive panorama of the Italian civil war (September 1943–April 1945).

Scholars have recently discovered that many of Fenoglio's major writings are drawn from a much longer chronicle, written after his 18-month experience with the partisans. The language of the chronicle is bold and analogical, often mixing English and Italian quite arbitrarily, as in this passage: "flashing in morbosa fulmineità. . . . poi si arrestò crashingly." The chronicle is the source of Fenoglio's first book, *I ventitré giorni della città di Alba* (1952; The 23 Days of the City of Alba). This volume, published in Einaudi's "Gettoni" series (directed by Elio VITTORINI), is a collection of short stories dealing with partisan warfare and rural life in the Langhe. The first story, which gives the collection its title, is an ironic view of the brief occupation of Fenoglio's native town by the Italian partisans. The novel *La malora* (1945; The Ruin) again deals with rural life, depicting the hardship and extreme poverty of farms in the Langhe. In *Primavera di bellezza* (1959; Spring of Beauty), Fenoglio recounts the adventures of his autobiographical hero, Johnny, his experiences as an officer cadet in Rome, his escape to the Langhe after the Allied armistice, and his encounter with a band of Communist partisans. The novel's compact, forcefully written scenes reflect Fenoglio's considerable mastery of the short-story form. Fenoglio's best-known works are the short-story collection *Una questione privata* (1963; A Private Question) and the novel *Il partigiano Johnny* (1968; Johnny the Partisan). Johnny's further adventures are recounted in *La paga del sabato* (1969; Saturday's Wages), which deals with the ex-partisan's rehabilitation into civilian life.

Fenoglio's unpublished archives show that he read, annotated, and translated much English literature. The influences of Shakespeare, John Bunyan, Thomas Hardy, T. E. Lawrence, Edgar Lee Masters, and Ernest Hemingway can all be felt in his writing. He was particularly fascinated by Firth's life of Oliver Cromwell. Yet the influence of Cesare PAVESE, who would have been the obvious model for his stories about the Langhe, is curiously missing.

See: G. P. Biasin, "An Epic Defeat," *IQ* (Fall 1968): 129–32; M. Corti, in *Metodi e fantasmi* (1969); B. Merry, "More on Fenoglio," *Italica* 49 (1972): 3–17.   B.M.

Fernández Almagro, Melchor (1893–1966), Spanish critic, essayist, and historian, was born in Granada and studied law at the universities of Granada and Madrid. At a very early age he began to write for the Granadan newspapers. After his arrival in Madrid, in 1921, he collaborated on the conservative paper *La Epoca* and wrote essays for *El Sol* and *La Voz*, mainly as a drama critic. In 1934 he became a member of the editorial staff of the newly founded paper *Ya*. During the Spanish Civil War (1936–39) he lived in Salamanca and Burgos, where he served with the Department of Press and Propaganda. In 1939 he returned to Madrid and started writing for *ABC* and soon after for *La Vanguardia*. As an historian, Fernández Almagro is best known for his works on 19th- and 20th-century Spain: *Orígenes del régimen constitucional en España* (1928); *Catalanismo y república española* (1932); *Historia del reinado de don Alfonso XIII* (1933); *Historia de la república espanõla, 1931–1936* (1940); *La emancipación de América y su reflejo en la conciencia española* (1944); *Cánovas: su vida y su política* (1951); *Historia política de la España contemporánea* (1956); and *Viaje al siglo XX* (1962; A Trip to the 20th Century). In recognition of his merits as a writer and historian, he was granted membership in the Royal Spanish Academy of History in 1944. He has also been in charge of the history section of the Institute for Political Studies. In 1951 he was elected to the Royal Spanish Academy of the Language. Although Fernández Almagro was best known among his contemporaries for the essays he published periodically in the most prestigious Spanish newspapers and journals, for the most part they have not yet been collected in book form. He initiated a reevaluation of the Generation of 1898 very early in his career through numerous essays on Joaquín COSTA, Angel GANIVET, Ramón del VALLE-INCLÁN, Federico GARCÍA LORCA, and Gabriel MIRÓ: *Vida y obra de Angel Ganivet* (1925); *Vida y literatura de*

Valle-Inclán (1943); and *En torno al 98: política y literatura* (1948; About the Generation of 1898: Politics and Literature). All of his critical works are distinguished by a sense of objectivity, a wealth of significant details, and a keen perception of cultural and literary values.

See: P. Laín Entralgo, "Melchor Fernández Almagro," *Insula* 233 (1966): 1 and 12.   A. del R. rev. J.L.G.-M.

Fernández de la Reguera, Ricardo (1916–), Spanish novelist, was born in Santander, lived in Chile as a child, but returned to Spain for his education. He is considered a member of the group of postwar realists of the 1950s, although he did not concern himself as much with the social issues so popular in the literature of that period as with the more universal themes of man confronted with a situation often beyond his control. His approach has existential, moral, and ethical implications that transcend the limits of plot. His novels *Un hombre a la deriva* (1947; A Man Adrift) and *Cuando voy a morir* (1951; Eng. tr., *In the Darkness of My Fury*, 1959) present the protagonist in the grip of an overwhelming passion. His best-known work, *Cuerpo a tierra* (1954; Eng. tr., *Reach for the Ground*, 1964), is one of the many war novels of the period. Instead of a partisan approach to the war, however, Fernández de la Reguera presents it from the perspective of an ordinary soldier portrayed as a victim of circumstances beyond his control. *Perdimos el paraíso* (1955; Lost Paradise) describes the world of childhood. *Bienaventurados los que aman* (1957; Blessed Are They Who Love) treats the problem of adultery. The principal characters of *Vagabundos provisionales* (1959; Provisional Vagabonds) are three men whose different points of view together form a composite picture of Spanish and human nature.

Beginning in the 1960s, the writer concentrated his efforts, in collaboration with his wife Susana March, on a series of historical novels collectively entitled *Episodios nacionales históricos* (Episodes of National History), the first volume of which is *Héroes de Cuba* (1962). Designed to extend from 1898 to the post-Civil War period, the series follows the tradition of Benito Peréz GALDÓS's historical novels, interweaving history and fiction. In this case, the novels are heavily documented.   M.E.W.J.

Fernández Flórez, Wenceslao (1885–1964), Spanish novelist and essayist, was born in La Coruña. He distinguished himself at an early age as an ironically humorous writer in essays first published in his native region, in *La Maraña, Diario de Galicia*, and *Tierra Gallega*, and, after 1910, in Madrid. There he was editor of *El Parlamento* but soon after began to write for *El Imparcial, La Ilustración Española e Hispanoamericana*, and, finally, for *ABC*, where he became famous for his witty *Acotaciones de un oyente* (1914–16; A Listener's Notes), chronicles of the parliamentary debates in the Spanish Cortes. In 1917 he was awarded the Fine Arts Circle Prize for his novel *Volvoreta*, still considered one of his best. In 1922 he received the Mariano Cavia Prize. In 1934 he became a member of the Royal Spanish Academy of the Language, although he did not read his inaugural address, "El humor en la literatura española," until 1945.

Fernández Flórez is above all a humorist who in his best works offers a desolate and bitter vision of life and of the world that is both personal and universal. A realistic technique prevails in his first novels: *Luz de luna* (1915; Moonlight), where it is colored by a candid sentimentalism; *Volvoreta* (1917), the most classic and balanced of his novels; and *Ha entrado un ladrón* (1920; A Thief Has Come in). With *El secreto de Barba Azul* (1923; Bluebeard's Secret) Fernández Flórez achieved his most characteristic and personal novel. In 1934 he published a collection of novellas, which includes his three best: "Unos pasos de mujer" (1924; A Woman's Footsteps), "La casa de la lluvia" (1925; The House of Rain), and "Huella de luz" (1925; Trace of Light). In 1926 he published his most famous and highly praised novel, *Las siete columnas* (1926; Eng. tr., *The Seven Pillars*, 1934). Among his other novels the following stand out: *El malvado Carabel* (1931; The Wicked Carabel), *La novela número 13* (1941); and *El bosque animado* (1943; The Lively Forest). The novels of Fernández Flórez cannot be completely separated from his essays, just as his best essays lie halfway between novel and essay. Thus the narrative form along with the exposition of ideas becomes an integral part of his essays in a perfect equilibrium that constitutes one of the peculiar distinctions of Fernández Flórez's style. His most important collections of essays are: *Acotaciones de un oyente e impresiones políticas de un hombre de buena fe* (1914–36; A Listener's Notes and Political Impressions of a Man of Good Faith), collected in volumes 8 and 9 of his *Obras completas* (9 vols., 1945–50); *Las gafas del diablo* (1918; The Devil's Glasses); *Visiones de neurastenia* (1924); *El país de papel* (1929; The Country of Paper); and *El toro, el torero y el gato* (1946; The Bull, the Bullfighter, and the Cat).

See: A. P. Mature, *Wenceslao Fernández Flórez y su novela* (1968); R. Zaetta, "Wenceslao Fernández Flórez: The Evolution of His Technique in His Novels," *KRQ* 17 (1970): 127–37.   J.L.G.-M.

Fernández Santos, Jesús (1926–), Spanish novelist, short-story writer, and journalist, was born in Madrid and studied philosophy and letters at the University of Madrid. As a movie director he has produced a number of documentaries, most notably *España 1808* (Spain 1808), a portrait of Goya. Fernández Santos directed the first university experimental theater in Madrid, Teatro de ensayo universitario, and has performed in the Teatro Nacional de Cámara and on Radio Madrid.

The novel *Los bravos* (1954; The Untamed), one of Fernández Santos's best works, focuses on the poverty, apathy, and misery of a rural community in the province of León. It is characterized by expressive prose, poetic condensation, preponderance of dialogue, and cinematographic presentation. With its realistic and descriptive prose, cinematic style, and absence of judgmental characterizations, *Los bravos* is one of the most representative examples of the "objective realism" cultivated in Spain in the 1950s and 1960s. His subsequent novels, *En la hoguera* (1956; At the Stake), *Laberintos* (1964; Labyrinths), and *El hombre de los santos* (1969; The Man Who Paints Statues), utilize stylistic elements found in *Los bravos*. A later and more ambitious novel, *La que no tiene nombre* (1977; She Who Has No Name), is also a history of Spain from the Middle Ages to the present. Social realism and the problems of the human condition are the main traits of Fernández Santos's fictional world.

See: R. Schwartz, *Spain's New Wave Novelists 1950–1974* (1976), pp 74–86.   J.O.

Ferrater Mora, José (1912–), Spanish philosopher and essayist. Born in Barcelona, he went into exile in 1939. After teaching in Havana and Santiago (Chile), he moved to the United States in 1947. Since 1949 he has been a professor of philosophy at Bryn Mawr College. Ferrater's works can be divided into three thematic groups, which roughly correspond to different periods in his own intellectual development. Immediately after the Spanish Civil War, his books center around Spanish identity and the meaning of Spanish history: *España y Europa* (1942);

Cuestiones españolas (1945); *Unamuno, bosquejo de una filosofía* (1944; Eng. tr., *Unamuno; A Philosophy of Tragedy*, 1962), and essays on literary criticism collected in *Variaciones sobre el espíritu* (1945; Variations on the Spirit). During these years he also wrote *Cuatro visones de la historia universal* (1945; Four Views of Universal History) and the monumental *Diccionario de filosofía* (1941), reissued and revised several times, most recently in 1979. Theoretical rigor and constructive originality characterize these works of a young exile in a world tainted by bloody passions.

In his second period, Ferrater elaborated an original philosophy. Called "Integrationism," it is defined as the attempt to bridge the gulf between philosophies that take human existence and those that take nature as their respective points of departure and frames of reference. Both extremes, says Ferrater, operate on the tacit assumption that the "subject" or its opposite "nature" are absolute entities and, as a result, absolutely opposed to each other. Integrationism rejects that assumption and tries to reconcile the two extremes of the polarity. The main works of this period are *El hombre en la encrucijada* (1952; Eng. tr., *Man at the Crossroads*, 1957); *El ser y la muerte*. *Bosquejo de filosofía integracionista* (1962; Eng. tr., *Being and Death: An Outline of Integrationist Philosophy*, 1965), and *El ser y el sentido* (1967; Being and Meaning).

An important aspect of integrationism is the dialogue between analytical philosophy and phenomenology. In 1955 Ferrater had published *Lógica matemática* in collaboration with Hughes Leblanc, and after *El ser y el sentido* and *Obras selectas* (2 vols., 1967), his writings reflect a "shift of gears." As defined in *Cambio de marcha en filosofía* (1974; Shifting Gears in Philosophy), the change appears to be a humble retreat from the ideal of integrationism to a more analytical viewpoint and increased attention to science. Representative works of this, his third, period are: *Indagaciones sobre el lenguaje* (1970; Inquiries on Language); *Els mots i els omes* (In Catalan, 1970; Words and Men); *El hombre y su medio y otros ensayos* (1971; Man and his Environment and other Essays), *Las crisis humanas* (1972; Mankind's Crises), and *De la naturaleza al espíritu* (1979; From Nature to Spirit).

The theoretical results of Ferrater's experiments in cinema were published in *Cine sin filosofías* (1974; Cinema without Philosophy). An excellent teacher, he has published the most influential book to date on José ORTEGA Y GASSET, *Ortega y Gasset: An Outline of His Philosophy* (1956, 1963), in addition to his *Diccionario de filosofía*. Four features are outstanding in his writings: perfectionism, encyclopedism, clarity of style, and irony. Ferrater's irony results from his practice of qualifying and reversing his own statements, thereby unmasking the absolutist character inherent in language. His influence is visible in the new reconciliation of the "two Spains," in the integration of scientific and existential philosophy, and in the search for accuracy in philosophical writing.

See: A. López Quintás, *Filosofía española contemporánea* (1970); R. Guy, "La théorie du sens chez Ferrater Mora," in *Philosophes ibériques et ibéro-américains en exil* (1977), pp. 115–34.   C.M.A.

Ferreira, José Gomes (1900–), Portuguese poet, short-story writer, and essayist, was born in Oporto but went with his parents to Lisbon at the age of four. As an adolescent, he studied and composed music but eventually took a degree in law at the University of Lisbon in 1924. While there he joined the Academic Batallion, an antimonarchist organization. After spending five years in Norway as a consul (1925–30), he returned to Portugal and became a journalist. Although he published his first volume of verse, *Lírios do monte* (Wild Lilies) in 1918, it was not until 1931, when his poem "Viver sempre também cansa" (To Live without Stop is Such a Bore) came out in *Presença*, the leading literary magazine of the time, that he felt he had found the verse idiom he wanted. His *Marchas, danças e canções* (1946; Marches, Dances and Songs) was followed at regular intervals by other collections of verse, including the prize-winning *Poesia III* (1961) and *Poesia V* (1973). Ferreira's prose includes such fiction as *O mundo dos outros* (1961; The World of Other People), a collection of short stories, two allegorical novels, *As aventuras maravilhasas de João Sem Mêdo* (1963; Fearless John's Marvelous Adventures) and *O sabor das trevas* (1976; The Taste of Darkness), and several books of memoirs, beginning with *A memória das palavras* (1965; Words Remembered) and *Imitação dos dias* (1966; Imitation of Days Past). He has been considered, perhaps incorrectly, to be a neorealist because of the dominant note of social awareness in his poetry and because of his belief that he, as a writer, must document injustice and accuse society of perpetuating it. Fiercely ironic at times, his writing tends to be colloquial. His work is marked by sharp observation and appreciation of what is odd in the commonplace happenings of everyday life. Having begun to write as early as 1918, he has been associated with many literary coteries, including those of *Presença*, Vitorino NEMÉSIO's *Revista de Portugal,* and especially the *Novo Cancioneiro,* although always maintaining an independent position.

See: J. Gaspar Simões, *Crítica II,* vol. 1 (1961); A. Pinheiro Torres, "A poesia de Gomes Ferreira," Preface to J. Gomes Ferreira, *Poesia I* (2d ed., 1962), pp. 160–68.

R.S.S.

Ferreira, Vergílio (1916–), Portuguese novelist and essayist, born in Melo at the foot of the Estréla Mountains, now lives in Lisbon. After several years in a seminary studying for the priesthood, he left and acquired instead a master's degree in classics. He has taught in secondary schools since 1944, the year of the publication of his second novel—a first and youthful one *O caminho fica longe* (It's a Long Way from the Road) had appeared the previous year. These novels and the next one, *Vagão "J"* (1946; Box Car), were written according to the realistic tradition upheld by the social realism school since the late 1930s. *Mudança* (1949; Change) marks a turning point in the novelist's career: not only is it a major work, but it also shows the influence of Sartrian existentialism (*see* Jean-Paul SARTRE) and a technical departure from straightforward realism. Since *Mudança,* an increasingly personal approach to existentialism and a daring experimentalism have shaped Ferreira's novels, which count among the best in contemporary European literature. They voice, through the use of transposed personal experiences or imaginative treatment of reality, a profound moral concern for life in general and in particular for life under the social and political conditions of the protracted dictatorial regime that came to an end in Portugal in 1974. *Aparição* (1954; Apparition), *Estrela Polar* (1962; North Star), *Alegria breve* (1965; Brief Joy), as well as the highly experimental *Nítido nulo* (1971; Neat Null), are some of the landmarks in the novelist's output. The most striking characteristic of Ferreira's fiction is the author's capacity to give life to his philosophical conceptions and at the same time to stress—as he has said—"the unreal quality of reality." Through description, inner monologue, absurd situations, and strange dialogue, he creates a world in which human beings feel alienated from an overwhelm-ing reality that eludes them. Ferreira has also written impressive literary and philosophical essays, the most outstanding of which is the one presenting the Portuguese translation (1962) of Sartre's *L'Existentialisme est un humanisme.*

See: J. Palma-Ferreira, *Vergilio Ferreira* (1972).

J. de S.

Ferreira de Castro, José Maria: *see* CASTRO, JOSÉ MARIA FERREIRA DE.

Ferres, Antonio (1925–), Spanish novelist and short-story writer, was born in Madrid. He worked as an assistant engineer until 1956 and taught literature between 1967 and 1977 at several institutions in the United States and at the Universidad Veracruzana in Mexico. Ferres won the Sésamo Prize in 1956 for his short story "Cine de barrio" (Neighborhood Theater). *La piqueta* (1959; The Pickaxe), the best example of this author's social realism, is the dramatic story of a Spanish migrant family whose shanty is demolished to make way for urban renewal. In *Caminando por las Hurdes* (1960; Walking through the Hurdes), written in collaboration with Armando LÓPEZ SALINAS, the travelogue technique is used to expose the misery of the Hurdes area in the province of Cáceres while the socioeconomic conditions of southern Spain are the theme of *Tierra de olivos* (1964; Land of Olive Trees).

His trilogy *Las Semillas* (Seeds) includes *Los vencidos* (1965; The Defeated), *Al regreso del Boiras* (1975; On Boiras's Return), and *Los años triunfales* (1978; Years of Triumph). These novels describe the social and pychological effects of the Spanish Civil War and contain an underlying criticism of Francisco Franco's regime. This first stage of Ferres's social criticism is characterized by a direct, sober, and colloquial style. Some of his other works, such as *En el segundo hemisferio* (1970; In the Second Hemisphere) and *Ocho, siete, seis* (1972; Eight, Seven, Six), are rooted in the writer's American experience and feature characters who suffer from alienation, neurosis, and a lack of identity. His recent novels utilize more sophisticated technical devices as well as more imaginative themes, but they lack the emotion and vigor that characterize his social realist novels of the 1950s and 1960s.

See: J. Schraibman, "Antonio Ferres y el nuevo realistmo crítico en la novela española," *Homenaje a Sherman H. Eoff* (1971), pp. 247–59; J. Ortega, *Antonio Ferres y Martínez Menchén, novelistas de la soledad* (1973).

J.O.

Feuchtwanger, Lion (1884–1958), German novelist and dramatist, was born in Munich. He became famous for his historical novels, the intellectual basis of which he expostulated in his last, unfinished work, *Das Haus der Desdemona* (1961; Eng. tr., *The House of Desdemona,* 1963). Rather than emphasize the personalities of great historical figures, he studied the external forces of culture, religion, and politics acting upon them.

Reflecting his heritage, Feuchtwanger's work, from his doctoral dissertation on Heinrich Heine's *Rabbi von Bacherach* to his last novels, examines Jewish themes. Two early novels distinguished him internationally: *Die häbliche Herzogin* (1923: Eng. tr., *The Ugly Duchess,* 1928), and *Jud Süss* (1925; Eng. tr., *Jew Süss,* 1926, and *Power.* 1928). *Süss* remains Feuchtwanger's most popular work, having sold over three million copies. The novel tells of a court Jew's rise to power in a gentile world that ultimately destroys him. A corrupted film version of the novel was shown by the Nazis throughout occupied Europe.

The *Wartesaal* (Waiting Room) trilogy—*Erfolg* (1930; Eng. tr., *Success*, 1930), *Die Geschwister Oppenheim* (1933; Eng. tr., *The Oppermanns*, 1934), and *Exil* (1939; Eng. tr., *Paris Gazette*, 1940)—describes vividly the rise of Nazism and its effect on Jewish families. *Erfolg*, (Success), a roman à clef, was the first German novel to portray Adolf Hitler.

Feuchtwanger dealt with contemporary politics from the vantage point of distance in such historical novels as *Der falsche Nero* (1936; Eng. tr., *The Pretender*, 1937) and the Josephus trilogy: *Der jüdische Krieg* (1932–36), consisting of *Josephus* (1932; Eng. tr., 1932), *Die Söhne* (1935; Eng. tr., *The Jew of Rome*, 1936), and *Der Tag wird kommen* (1936; Eng. tr., *Josephus and the Emperor*, 1942). Here, Feuchtwanger presents the historian Josephus as a cosmopolitan, a mediator between East and West who "sought the world too soon."

After 1932, Feuchtwanger lived in France. With his wife, he escaped from Vichy France into Spain in 1940 and in 1941 emigrated to Los Angeles. During his last years he wrote *Goya, oder der arge Weg der Erkenntnis* (1951; Eng. tr., *This is the Hour*, 1951), in which he examines the 50-year-old Goya's intellectual awakening, and *Narrenweisheit, oder Tod und Verklärung des Jean Jacques Rousseau* (1952; Eng. tr., *'Tis Folly to Be Wise*, 1953), a work departing from the actual events in Jean Jacques Rousseau's life and dealing with the philosopher's influence on a young man's social consciousness. *Die Jüdin von Toledo* (1954; Eng. tr., *Raquel, The Jewess of Toledo*, 1956), which is set in the time of Alphonso X of Castile, is partially inspired by the biblical story of Esther. In this novel, Judaism with its espousal of peace and the intellect is juxtaposed with the medieval glorification of warfare. *Jefta und seine Tochter* (1957; Eng. tr., *Jephta and his Daughter*, 1958), deals with the story in Judges 11 and 12 of a leader's rise to power and the sacrifice of his daughter. Feuchtwanger's best-known work for the stage is his adaptation of Christopher Marlowe's *Edward II* (1924), written in collaboration with Bertolt BRECHT. Feuchtwanger will be chiefly remembered for raising the historical novel to new heights. He saw the mission of the poet-historian as interpreting the present by illuminating the past.

See: J. M. Spalek, ed., *Lion Feuchtwanger: The Man, His Ideas, His Work* (1973); L. Kahn, *Insight and Action: The Life and Work of Lion Feuchtwanger* (1975).

K.S.M.

Feydeau, Georges (1862–1921), French writer of vaudeville (light comedy), was born in Paris, the son of Ernest Feydeau, whose novel *Fanny* (1858) was once rated on a par with Gustave Flaubert's *Madame Bovary*. Georges married the daughter of the society painter Carolus Duran, thus increasing his already considerable social stature. A habitué of Maxim's and the Boulevard cafés, Feydeau first wrote monologues that were performed in salons. He earned recognition in 1892 with two comedies (given in England in 1972, but still unpublished): "Monsieur chasse" and "Champignol malgré lui." In his subsequent career as a vaudeville writer, Feydeau became internationally known as an author of bedroom farces and as a brilliant dramatic technician. Some of his best-known works are *L'Hôtel du Libre-Echange* (1894; Eng. tr., *Hotel Paradiso*, 1957), *Un Fil à la patte* (1894; Eng. tr., *Not by Bed Alone*, 1970), *Le Dindon* (1896; Eng. tr., *Paying the Piper*, 1972), and *La Puce à l'oreille* (1907; Eng. tr., *A Flea in Her Ear*, 1968).

Feydeau contrived wild, uproarious, yet logical situations, manipulated at a torrential pace. He also employed sidesplitting comic devices, such as the chair that induces

ecstatic sleep in *La Dame de chez Maxim* (1899; Eg. tr., *The Lady from Maxim's*, 1971), his acknowledged masterpiece. But Feydeau's so-called farces, including *Occupe-toi d'Amélie* (1908; Eng. tr., *Keep an Eye on Amélie*, 1958), also present a cynical picture of the frivolous *grands bourgeois* and nobles of the *belle époque* and of Maxim's clientele of eccentrics and notorious courtesans. Still more vitriolic are Feydeau's views on marriage, as depicted in his one-act plays *Feu la Mère de Madame* (1908; Madam's Late Mother), and *On purge bébé!* (1910; Eng. tr., *Going to Pot*, 1970).

In the 1940s, his popularity was revived by the actor-director Jean-Louis BARRAULT and by the Comédie-Française. Today, Feydeau's plays are frequently televised, filmed, and translated. Critics now explain Feydeau's modern appeal as much by his perceptiveness and sense of the absurdity of life as by his bewildering comic world and famous technique. He raised the vaudeville to the status of a literary genre.

See: A. Shenkan, *Georges Feydeau* (1972). A.S.

Fichte, Hubert (1935–), German novelist, interviewer, essayist, and radio author was born in Perleberg, now East Germany, and grew up in Hamburg. After a decade at various jobs he settled in Hamburg in 1963 as a free-lance writer. Fichte's first book, *Der Aufbruch nach Turku* (1963; Setting Out for Turku), is a collection of short stories. *Das Waisenhaus* (1965; The Orphanage), his first and partly autobiographical novel, deals with a German-Jewish boy in the Nazi years. It reveals Fichte's obsession with outsiders; his subsequent novels treat outcasts and the oppressed. *Die Palette* (1968; The Palette) centers on a homosexual bar in Hamburg. *Detlevs Imitationen 'Grünspan'* (1971; Detlev's Imitations 'Verdigris') depicts the precarious existence of youth as and after the Third Reich ends. The novel *Versuch über die Pubertät* (1974; Treatise on Puberty) juxtaposes Fichte's own youth, Afro-American rituals, and self-portraits of a murderer and an older homosexual. *Xango* (1976), published with the photographer Leonore Mau's volume of the same name, presents research into the rites of the syncretistic Afro-American religions. Fichte's novels analyze puberty as "confrontation with the concept of self" and "describe an experiment: living in order to attain a form of depiction." Three collections of interviews with pimps, prostitutes, and murderers have also appeared: *Interviews aus dem Palais d'Amour etc.* (1972); *Der Ledermann spricht mit Hubert Fichte* (1977; The Leather Man Talks with Hubert Fichte); and *Wolli Indienfahrer* (1978; Wolli India Voyager).

The prizes Fichte has won include the Hermann Hesse Prize (1965), Villa Massimo Grant (1967–68), and Theodor Fontane Prize (1975).

See: R. Mills, "The Leather Man," *Gay Sunshine*, nos. 33–34 (1977): 12–13; G. Ullrich, *Identität und Rolle: Probleme des Erzählens bei Johnson, Walser, Frisch und Fichte* (1977), pp. 64–78. R.M.

Figueiredo, Fidelino de Sousa (1888–1967), Portuguese literary critic and historian, was born in Lisbon and went to Coimbra to study law and literature. Dissatisfied with the Portuguese Republic of 1910, he gathered a group of social-minded traditionalists around his *Revista de história* (1912–28). In 1918–19 he entered the cabinet of the dictator-general Sidónio Pais. When Pais was assassinated, Figueiredo went into exile. He taught in Rio de Janeiro (1920), spent three years in Madrid (1927–30), became a visiting professor at Berkeley, Calif. (1931, 1937), and returned to Brazil, where he taught Portuguese literature at the University of São Paulo (1938–51), training future Brazilian scholars. Finally, with his health broken, he returned to his homeland. But in spite of almost total physical incapacitation during the many years preceding his death, he remained intellectually alert and active as an essayist to the very end.

Guided by ideas received from Benedetto CROCE, Paul BOURGET, and Charles-Augustin Sainte-Beuve, Figueiredo injected a sound critical spirit into the study of Portuguese literature. He applied a psychological method that focused on the personality of each author as the primary factor in his works. The practical outgrowth of his theories was A história literária como ciência (1912; Literary History as a Science) and História da literatura portuguesa (1913-24; History of Portuguese Literature). His sincere friendship for neighboring Spain speaks through his translations of Miguel de UNAMUNO and Marcelino MENÉNDEZ Y PELAYO, as well as through several original studies, especially as As duas Espanhas (1932; The Two Spains) and Pirene (1935; Pyrene). He also wrote fiction in his youth, including the autobiographical novel Sob a cinza do tédio (1925; Under the Ashes of Tedium). His last works are collections of essays in the liberal, humanistic tradition cultivated more commonly in Spain. Among them are Música e pensamento (1954; Music and Thought), Diálogo ao espelho (1957; Dialogue before the Mirror), Símbolos e mitos (1964; Symbols and Myths), and Paixão e ressurreição do homem (1967; Man's Agony and Resurrection).

Figueiredo raised the standards of Portuguese criticism on the basis of individualistic and quasi-scientific principles. Furthermore, he introduced the study of comparative literature into Portugal. A key to his ideas on politics and literature may be found in earlier essays, Notas para um idearium português (1929; Notes for a Portuguese System of Ideas) and Problemas de ética do pensamento: o dever dos intelectuais (1936; Problems of Ethics for Thinkers: The Duty of the Intellectuals).

See: C. de Assis Pereira, Ideário crítico de Fidelino de Figueiredo (1962); J. García Morejón, "Dos coleccionadores de angustias: Unamuno y Figueiredo," Unamuno y Portugal (2d ed., 1971), pp. 462-504; H. Hoeppner Ferreira, "Trajetória espiritual de uma correspondência," Convivium 10 (1971): 79-86.   G.M.M., rev. E.M.D.

Figueiredo, Tomaz de (1920-), Portuguese novelist, was born in Braga but raised in Arcos de Valdevez where he was steeped in the old rural ways of the north. After studying law in Coimbra and Lisbon, he became a notary. His psychological curiosity, craftsmanship, and satiric vein are remarkable. His gift for mockery, as well as his interest in regional subjects and vernacular, link him with Camilo Castelo Branco, the late 19th-century romantic, more than with the contemporary Presença group. Only the musicality of his paragraphs has a modern ring. Figueiredo's fiction portrays kind or wicked individuals in earthy terms that carry the reader back to a rural and feudal past. His works include A toca do lobo (1947; The Wolf's Lair), in one critic's words "a very Portuguese experiment of a novel without action"; Nó cego (1950; Tangled Knot); Fôlego (1950; Vitality); Uma noite na toca do lobo (1952; A Night in the Wolf's Lair); Procissão dos defuntos (1954; Procession of the Dead), three loosely connected tales of wickedness, A Gata Borralheira (1961; Cinderella); D. Tanas de Barbatanas (2 vols., 1962, 1964); Vida de cão (1964; Dog's Life), sories; Monólogo em Elsenor (2 vols., 1972; Monologue in Elsinore); and Tiros de espingarda (1972; Gunshots), tales. Conversa com o silêncio (1960; Conversation with Silence) is a book of memoirs. Figueiredo has also published poetry, such as

Guitarra (1956; Guitar), and plays, for example, Teatro I (1965).

See: D. Mourão-Ferreira, "Tomaz de Figueiredo, prosador-poeta," in his Hospital das letras (1966), pp. 263-69.   G.M.M.

Finland-Swedish literature. The literature written by members of Finland's Swedish-speaking community, known as Finland-Swedish literature, emerged as a distinct entity only at the end of the 19th century, in response to the growing cultural awareness of the Finnish-speaking majority. Earlier, most writers had been educated in Swedish-language schools, and Finnish poets such as Gustav Philip Creutz, Mikael Chorœus, and Frans Michael Franzén considered themselves part of Swedish letters. But the mid-19th-century poets who wrote in Swedish regarded themselves as Finns: Johan Ludvig Runeberg (1804-77) wrote a set of narrative poems celebrating Finnish heroism in the futile 1808-09 war with Russia, Fänrik Ståls sägner (1848-60; Eng. tr., The Tales of Ensign Stål, 1925; 1938), and Zacharias Topelius (1818-98) wrote a series of novellas, Fältskärns berättelser (6 vols., 1853-67; Eng. tr., The Surgeon's Stories, 1872-74), about a Finnish family's deeds in wars of the 17th and 18th centuries. Yet the demands of the Hegelian, Johan Vilhelm Snellman (1806-81) for "one tongue, one spirit" in Finland made Swedish speakers feel threatened.

Other writers held different views of the language problem. Joseph Julius Wecksell (1838-1907) foresaw a fruitful rivalry between Swedish with its rich heritage and Finnish with its youthful vitality. Karl August Tavaststjerna (1860-98) was less optimistic, and the despondency of some of his lyrics and such novels as Barndomsvänner (1886; Childhood Friends) became a hallmark of Finnish-Swedish letters. Jac. Ahrenberg (1847-1914) feared that cultivated Finnish-Swedes would marry Russians, and the "establishment" would be bastardized. This melodramatic stance appealed to Baron Bertel Gripenberg (1878-1947) and Arvid Mörne (1876-1946), poets who often wrote on the problems of Finland's Swedish population, in addition to writing poems on political themes and on nature. It also appealed to the novelists Gustav Alm (pseud. of Richard Malmberg) (1877-1944) and Ture Janson (1886-1954). Lighter works were produced by Carl Gustaf Estlander (1834-1910), Hjalmar Neiglick (1860-89), and Gustaf Mattsson (1873-1914).

In the early 20th centruy, a group known as the "Dagdrivarna" (Loafers) appeared, whose members wrote skeptical, analytical prose pieces. The group's outstanding figure was Runar Schildt (1888-1925), the author of novels and plays distinguished by their psychological insight. Schildt discovered the Swedish-speaking people of east Nyland, doing more artistically what Jonatan Reuter (1859-1947) had done for west Nyland, and what Gustav Alm would do for the Ostrobothnian coast in Fångstmän (1924; Hunters). In Den stora rollen (1923; The Great Role), the best of his plays, Schildt treated Finland's Civil War (1918).

Schildt's closest rival for a large conservative readership was Jarl Hemmer (1893-1944), another member of the "Dagdrivarna," popular for his mellifluous verse and generous personality. But Hemmer also wrote En man och hans samvete (1931; Eng. tr., A Fool of Faith, 1936), which probes important moral questions. Hemmer's humanitarianism is echoed in the essays and critical writings of Hans Ruin (1891-), Erik Kihlman (1895-1931), Yrjö Hirn (1870-1952), and Rolf Lagerborg (1874-1959).

To posterity, the main glory of the 1920s undoubtedly derives from the "modernists," a group whose poetry is characterized by styles and attitudes reminiscent of

Anglo-American imagism, Russian futurism, and German expressionism. The group's pioneer and high priestess was Edith SÖDERGRAN; its revolutionary singer, Elmer DIKTONIUS; its syntactical radical, Gunnar BJÖRLING; its theorist and classicist, Rabbe Enckell (1903–74); its polemicist Hagar Olsson (1893–1978), its golden boy Henry Parland (1908–30); and its provincial the Ostrobothnian R. R. Eklund (1894–1946). The modernists' reforms—their rejection of regular rhymes, rhythms, and easily comprehended images—influenced all Scandinavian poetry.

After the enthusiasm bred by Finland's independence in the 1920s, new waves of anti-Finnish-Swedish feeling at home and the Soviet threat made the minority lose heart in the 1930s. The resultant literary drift toward veiled expression, introspection, and exotic milieus can be found the verse of Kerstin Söderholm (1897–1943), the novellas of Mirjam Tuominen (1913–67), the novels of Tito Colliander (1904–), Göran Stenius (1909–), and Olof Enckell (1900–), and in Hagar Olsson's long fairy tale *Träsnidaren och döden* (1940; Eng. tr., *The Woodcarver and Death*, 1965). The decade's great international success was Sally Salminen's (1906–76) novel *Katrina* (1936; Eng. tr., 1937), while the more valuable work of Anna Bondestam (1907–) and Atos Wirtanen (1906–76) attracted too little attention.

After the wars of 1939–40 and 1941–44, the literary world seemed about to dissolve: the promising lyricist Christer Lind (1912–42) was dead; the prose artist Lorenz von Numers (1913–) was living in France; and writers such as Ralf Parland (1914–), Willy Kyrklund (1921–), Bengt Holmqvist (1924–), and Harry Järv (1921–) had migrated to Sweden. Of the new talents emerging in Finland, Walentin Chorell (1912–) and V. V. Järner (1910–) proved themselves to be gifted playwrights, while the poet Bo Carpelan (1926–) forged his own elegaic style, and Solveig von Schoultz (1907–) wrote lyrics and novellas noted for their solidity, clarity, and subtlty.

New and innovative writers appeared toward the end of the 1950s. Anders Cleve (1937–) published a collection of stories, *Gatstenar* (1959; Paving Stones), which upset some readers by the excessive "Finland-Swedishness" of its language. Also disturbing was Christer Kihlman's (1930–) *Se upp, Salige!* (1960; Pay Heed, O Blest!), a tormented, and tormenting, dissection of the author's linguistic group and himself. Kihlman's attacks on the establishment and his insistence on sexual detail are less upsetting than they once were, for he influenced such writers as the novelist and cabaret writer Johan Bargum (1940–), the leftist Ralf Nordgren (1936–), the determinedly liberated Märta Tikkanen (1935–), and the psychologist-author Claes Andersson (1937–). Lately Swedish Finland had produced two superb essayists, Sven Wilner (1918–) and Johannes Salminen (1925–). Provincial literature, fostered by the novelist Sven-Olaf Högnäs (1910–61), the peasant poet Evert Huldén (1895–1958), and the Ålander Joel Petterson (1892–1937), is continuing to be published by Lars Huldén (1926–), Wava Stürmer (1929–), Hans Fors (1937–), Gösta Ågren (1936–), and the Ålanders Valdemar Nyman (1904–) and Anni Blomqvist (1908–).

If Finland's Swedish culture begins to demise, as has often been predicted, the loss would be great, for no northern body of authors has shown such a fruitful awareness of its heritage and such a gift for useful experimentation.

See B. Holmqvist, *Modern finlandssvensk literatur* (1951); K. Laitinen, *Finlands moderna litteratur* (1968); J. Ahokas, *A History of Finnish Literature* (1973), pp. 35–62, and 385–433; G. C. Schoolfield, *Swedo-Finnish Short Stories* (1974). G.C.S. and K.L.

Finnish literature. The generation of 1880 gave a new direction to Finnish literature. Until approximately that date, most Finnish authors had been educated in Swedish-language schools. Now they began to employ their mother tongue enthusiastically, creating a modern press in Finnish. Yet many important writers still continued to use Swedish, and until this day literature in Finland is bilingual (*see* FINLAND-SWEDISH LITERATURE).

The dominant literary style of the 1880s was realism. Writers of this period were especially influenced by French, Scandinavian, and Russian literature. In the 1890s a change took place, and a new style, called "national neoromanticism," emerged. This was a Finnish version of contemporary European symbolism, incorporating impulses from central European art nouveau as well as national topics and ideas. This style was still prevailing at the beginning of the 20th century. One of its most distinguished representatives was Eino LEINO, a versatile poet, critic, playwright, journalist, and translator. Some former realists joined the new movement, among them the important prose writer Juhani Aho (1861–1921), author of impressionistic short nature stories and of novels like *Juha* (1911), a tragic love story. The beginning of open Russian pressure (the notorious February Manifesto issued by Tsar Nicholas II in 1899) made political themes topical, but they were often discussed in allegorical form. In poetry, contacts with European symbolism proved most fertile for Veikko Antero Koskenniemi (1885–1962) and Otto Manninen (1872–1950). The former was also an influential critic; the latter a splendid translator of Greek plays, Homer Molière, and Henrik IBSEN. Other central figures in early 20th-century poetry were L. Onerva, pseud. of Hilja Onerva Madetoja (1882–1972), and Larin-Kyösti, pseud. of Kyösti Larson (1873–1948). Two poets who wrote in Swedish must also be mentioned, Baron Bertel Gripenberg and Arvid Mörne.

During the first decade of the 20th century, symbolism was opposed by several writers who reintroduced a realistic, in part naturalistic, narrative technique. These writers described backwoods people: poor cottagers, small farmers, people living in primitive conditions far away from the urban world. Their point of view was frequently critical of the bureaucracy and the upper classes, but at the same time their texts were spiced with humor. One of these writers was Ilmari Kianto (1874–1970), who wrote two classic novels, *Punainen viiva* (1909; The Red Line) and *Ryysyrannan Jooseppi* (1924; Ryysyranna's Joseph). Maria Jotuni (1880–1943), a fine short-story writer, also composed a village novel, *Arkielämää* (1909; Everyday Life). Maiju Lassila was the best known of the several pen names of Algoth Untola (1868–1918); under this pseudonym he published his humorous novel, *Tulitikkuja lainaamassa* (1910; Borrowing Matches). Johannes Linnankoski, pseud. of Vihtori Peltonen (1869–1913), was the author of the erotic best-seller *Laulu tulipunaisesta kukasta* (1905; Eng. tr., *The Song of the Blood-Red Flower*, 1920) and a short novel in classical style, *Pakolaiset* (1908; Runaways). Maila Talvio (1871–1951) was a productive woman writer who treated topical themes and later wrote historical novels.

The 1918 Finnish Civil War also left its imprint on the production of other writers. Joel Lehtonen (1881–1934) began as a neoromanticist but turned—influenced in part by French and Italian Renaissance literature—to a more colorful, burlesque style. His magnum opus is *Putkinotko* (1919–20; the name of an estate), a broad description of one single summer day in the life of a poor sharecropper's family. Besides its obvious humor, the work displays a sharp national self-criticism and becomes, in part, a study of the social causes of the Civil War. Similar themes are treated by Frans Emil SILLANPÄÄ in his novel *Hurskas kurjuus* (1919; Eng. tr., *Meek heritage*, 1938).

Many writers of the generation of the early 20th century published their best books in the 1920s and 1930s. Aino Kallas (1878–1956), who spent several years in London as the wife of a diplomat, wrote historical novels on Estonian themes in the archaic style of ancient chronicles. These include her *Reigin pappi* (1926; Eng. tr., *Eros the Slayer*, 1927) and *Sudenmorsian* (1928; Eng. tr., *The Wolf's Bride*, 1930). Volter Kilpi (1874–1939), who began as a typical neoromanticist, later evoked the sea-faring peasants of southwest Finland in a trilogy that opens with the novel *Alastalon salissa* (1933; In the Living Room of Alastalo) and ends with *Kirkolle* (1937; On the Road to the Church). Because of his narrative technique, involving slow tempo, long sentences, minute descriptions, neologisms, and an individual syntax, Kilpi has been compared to both James Joyce and Marcel PROUST.

In the 1920s a modernist group called "Tulenkantajat" (Torchbearers) emerged. Its favorite preoccupations were modern technology, urban life, and picturesque exoticism. Its leader was Olavi Paavolainen (1903–64), a brilliant representative of the contemporary cosmopolitan style who championed new currents of European literature and wrote critical travel books (about Hitler's Germany). His diary of the World War II years, *Synkkä yksinpuhelu* (1946; Gloomy Monologue), sparked heated discussions. The "Tulenkantajat" group was mostly made up of poets, of whom the principal figures were Katri Vala (1901–44), Elina Vaara (1903–), Lauri Viljanen (1900–), Yrjö Jylhä (1903–56), Arvi Kivimaa (1904–), and above all Uuno Kailas (1901–33), the poet of "dreams and death," who early became a classic of his generation. The best-known prose writers were Unto Seppänen (1904–55) and Mika Waltari (1908–79). Waltari, a versatile novelist and short-story writer, became internationally known after World War II for historical novels such as *Sinuhe, egyptiläinen* (1945; Eng. tr., *The Egyptian*, 1949), the story of an innocent hero facing the cruelty of the world. Two other important prose writers, Toivo Pekkanen (1902–57) and Pentti Haanpää (1905–55), had contact with the "Tulenkantajat" group without being members. Both were self-made men with only an elementary school education, but each was successful at describing the economic conditions and crises of contemporary society. Pekkanen's most typical work is *Tehtaan varjossa* (1932; In the Shadow of a Factory). He later published an impressive autobiography, *Lapsuuteni* (1953; Eng. tr., *My Childhood*, 1966). Haanpää's world, on the other hand, is rural, and his heroes are small farmers, lumberjacks, and vagabonds. A witty and scarcastic short-story writer, he was an incisive critic of bourgeois society. He also wrote important novels, most notably *Yhdeksän miehen saappaat* (1945; The Boots of Nine Men) and *Jauhot* (1949; Flour).

The Finnish literary climate again changed. In the 1930s, most poets chose the traditional style, especially the melodic, postsymbolist Kaarlo Sarkia (1902–45) and the young woman poet Saima Harmaja (1913–37). In prose, new psychological aspects and ideas were being explored in the novels of Iris Uurto (1905–), Helvi Hämäläinen (1907–), and Tatu Vaaskivi (1912–42), who was also an acute critic. "Kiila" (The Wedge), a new left-wing literary group, was founded in 1936. Its principal authors were the poets Jarno Pennanen (1906–69), Arvo Turtiainen (1904–), Viljo Kajava (1909–), and Elvi Sinervo (1912–). Sinervo also wrote novels, such as *Viljami Vaihdokas* (1946). Among the relatively few serious playwrights, the Estonian-born Hella Wuolijoki (1886–1954) was probably the most original. She is best known for her

plays about the old farm of Niskavuori. The first of them, *Niskavuoren naiset* (1936; The Women of Niskavuori), was performed in London under the title *Women of Property* (1937).

World War II brought still another transformation—this time a radical one—in the Finnish literary scene. This partly political, partly cultural change was caused as much by the war and its aftermath as by the emergence of a young generation of writers. Their forerunners were such older poets as Aaro Hellaakoski (1893–1952), a master of meditative nature poetry and energetic self-analysis; P. Mustapää, pseud. of Martti Haavio (1899–1973), a folklorist who encouraged new trends with his metrical innovations and fresh imagery; and Aale Tynni (1913–). The young generation was influenced by T. S. Eliot and contemporary Swedish poetry. It preferred unrhymed free verse to traditional forms, favored rich visual imagery, wit, and irony, and was characterized by ideological skepticism and a general distrust of politics. Its foremost representative was Paavo Haavikko (1931–), a poet, playwright, and novelist. In his poetry, Haavikko fuses themes drawn from history with contemporary topics and gives critical attention to the problems of political power (Eng. tr., *Selected Poems*, 1968, 1974). Other figures in this versatile and far from homogeneous "modernist" generation are Helvi Juvonen (1919–59), Eeva-Liisa Manner (1921–), Eila Kivikkaho (1921–), Aila Meriluoto (1924–), Lasse Heikkilä (1925–61), Pentti Holappa (1927–), Lassi Nummi (1928–), and Tuomas Anhava (1927–). Some of Anhava's poems have appeared in English translation as *In the Dark, Move Slowly* (1969).

The post-World War II change in prose was less abrupt than that in poetry. Writers searched for different modes of expression. A few, such as Oiva Paloheimo (1910–73), wrote in a fantastic vein; some probed human nature, both philosophically and psychologically, notably Jorma Korpela (1910–64) and Juha Mannerkorpi (1915–); still others, like Lauri Viita (1916–65), found a solution in vigorous realism. The traditional line of realism and humor was continued by Veikko Huovinen in his best-selling novel *Havukka-ahon ajattelija* (1952; The Thinker of Havukka-Aho). The most celebrated manifestations of traditional fiction, however, are the novels of Väinö Linna (1920–). In *Tuntematon sotilas* (1954; Eng. tr., *The Unknown Soldier*, 1957), Linna describes the war years of 1941–44 critically, yet with humor, from the point of view of the common soldier. His trilogy *Täällä Pohjantähden alla* (1959–62; Here under the Polar Star), gives a cross-section of the social history of Finland from the end of the 19th century to the years after World War II. Veijo Meri (1928–) also evokes the war, but his point of view and technique are quite different. Seldom commenting on the thoughts or reactions of his heroes, Meri builds his narration on grotesque situations and whimsical anecdotes, as in his most remarkable novel *Manillaköysi* (1958; Eng. tr., *The Manila Rope*, 1967). Many of Meri's novels and short stories have been translated into several languages, and he is also an excellent essayist. A similar descriptive style is used by Antti Hyry (1931–) and to some extent by Marja-Liisa Vartio (1924–66), who is at her best in the novel *Hänen olivat linnut* (1966; The Birds Belonged to Her). Topical social and historical themes are treated by many writers who emerged after World War II, especially Eila Pennanen (1916–), Eeva Joenpelto (1921–), Iris Kähäri (1914–), Paavo Rintala (1929–), and Leo Kalervo (1924–).

The generation of the 1960s has been more political than its predecessor and has dealt with more topical social themes. These writers have produced documentary literature and politically committed plays and songs. Political subjects were introduced into poetry again by Pentti Saarikoski (1937–) in his collection *Mitä tapahtuu todella?* (1962; Eng. tr., *Selected Poems*, 1967). Other poets of importance are Pertti Nieminen (1929–), Väinö Kirstinä (1936–), Mirkka Rekola (1931–), Matti Rossi (1934–), and Pentti Saaritsa (1941–). In prose, Hannu Salama (1936–) occupies a central place with his powerful novels *Juhannutanssit* (1964; The Midsummer Dance) and *Siinä näkijä, missä tekijä* (1972; No Deed Remains Unseen). Other prose writers worth mentioning are Eeva Kilpi (1928–), Anu Kaipainen (1933–), Kerttu-Kaarina Suosalmi (1921–), Lassi Sinkkonen (1937–), Alpo Ruuth (1943–), Hannu Mäkelä (1943–), and Juhani Peltonen (1941–).

See: V. Tarkiainen, *Suomalaisen kirjallisuuden historia* (1934, 3d ed., V. Tarkiainen-E. Kauppinen, 1962; R.Koskimies, *Elävä kunsulliskirjallisuus,* 3 vols. (1944–49); M. Kuusi, ed., *Suomen kirjallisuus,* vols. 1–8 (1963–70); K. Laitinen, *Suomen kirjallisuus 1917–1967,* 8 vols. (1967); J. Ahokas, *A History of Finnish Literature* (1973); T. R. Dauenhauer, P. Binham, eds., *Snow in May: An Anthology of Finnish Writing 1945–72* (1978).   K.L.

Fischer, Otokar (1883–1938), Czech poet and critic, was born in Kolín. He studied German literature in Prague and Berlin, and became professor of German literature at the Czech University of Prague. From 1935 to 1938 he was dramatic director of the Prague National Theater. He died of a heart attack on March 12, 1938, while reading the news of Germany's invasion of Austria.

Fischer's poetry—collected under such titles as *Hořící keř* (1912; The Burning Bush), *Léto* (1920; Summer), *Kruhy* (1923; Circles), *Hlasy* (1926; Voices), and *Host* (1930; The Guest), and *Poslední básně* (1938; Last Poems)—expresses the struggle of a sensitive soul with fate and with his own divided mind. His dependence on postromantic poetry such as that of Otakar THEER gave way to a simpler and finer expression in later years, and the early subjective problems of mental isolation were replaced by the tortuous special problems of the Czech Jew and the wider problems of life and death.

Fischer was possibly the best poetic translator in the whole of Czech literature. He combined remarkable scholarship and ingenuity with a real sense of style. His greatest achievement is a 15-volume edition of Johann Wolfgang von Goethe that contains his masterly translation of both parts of *Faust*. He translated dramas by Ewald von Kleist, *Also sprach Zarathustra* by Friedrich NIETZSCHE, the poems of Heinrich Heine, William Shakespeare's *Macbeth,* Christopher Marlowe's *Edward II,* Percy Bysshe Shelley's *The Cenci,* Pierre Corneille's *Polyeucte,* Lope de Vega's *Fuenteovejuna,* as well as selections from François Villon, Emile VERHAEREN, Aleksandr Pushkin, and Rudyard Kipling. Fischer was likewise an ambitious dramatist, and his *Spartakus* (1925) is a successful attempt at poetic drama.

Fischer also achieved great distinction as a literary critic and historian. He began with highly specialized work in German and afterwards wrote monographs on Kleist (1912), Nietzsche (1913), and Heine (2 vols., 1924), all of which show his mastery of facts and ability to analyze difficult personalities. His booklet, *Otázky literární psychologie* (1917; Problems of Literary Psychology), introduced modern psychological trends, including psychoanalysis, into Czech literary criticism. His criticisms and studies, collected in the volumes *Duch a slovo* (1927; Spirit and Word) and *Slovo a svět* (1938; Word and World), are among the most distinguished productions in Czech literary scholarship. *K dramatu* (1919; Toward the Drama) is a collection of his dramatic criticism.

See: V. Jirat and others, *Dílo Otokara Fischera* (1933); R. Wellek, "Otokar Fischer," *SEER* (1938–39): 215-18.
R.W.

Fishta, Gjergj (1871–1940), Albanian poet, was born of peasant parents in a village near Scutari. A Franciscan friar heralded by his admirers as the national poet, he is the outstanding figure among the younger representatives of the Albanian romantic movement (*see* ALBANIAN LITERATURE). Fishta studied theology in Bosnia, where he read such Croatian poets as Kačić and Ivan Mažuranić (*see* CROATIAN LITERATURE), who largely took their themes and models from oral poetry. Inspired by these writers and by North Albanian oral poetry, Fishta wrote *Te ura e Rzhanicës* (1905; At the Rzhanica Bridge), an epic celebrating the battles of the Albanians against the Montenegrins in 1878. Two years later, he published another epic, *Vranina,* concerning an 1858 border clash between Montenegrins and Albanians led by Oso Kuka, a Scutarene folk song hero. These works, together with *Anzat e Parnasit* (1907; The Wasps of Parnassus), a collection of satirical poems, established Fishta as the leading literary figure of his time. In 1913, Fishta founded *Hylli i dritës,* an influential Albanian journal in which he published other epic poems, various lyrics, and polemical articles. Later volumes of Fishta's poetry include *Mrizi i zanavet* (1924; Noontide of the Muses), a collection of political and didactic poems, and *Vallja e parrizit* (1925; The Dance of Paradise), a group of religious hymns in the fashion of Alessandro Manzoni's *Inni sacri.* Fishta also wrote several melodramas and a satirical burlesque, *Gomari i Babatasit* (1923; Babatasi's Donkey), in which he ridicules his political opponents.

Although he was a prolific writer who cultivated almost all poetic genres, it is for his lifelong work *Lahuta e Malciś* (1937; The Highland Lute) that Fishta is chiefly celebrated. This epic poem is a sequence of 30 cantos in rhymed octosyllables—the national verse form—praising the heroism and virtues of the Gheg (northern) highlanders in their battles against the Montenegrins and the Serbs. Begun as a series of random episodes, the poem was later cast into a larger framework, encompassing both episodes of the national struggle for independence as well as other incidents conveying Fishta's personal beliefs concerning "fatherland and religion." In the earlier and by far the best cantos, Fishta is able to capture the heroic spirit of his model, the folk rhapsodies, proving himself to be a superior folksinger. Polemic and ideology mar later cantos, however, which become overwrought and redundant, and in which Fishta's political satire often turns into parody and caricature. Nevertheless the epic is usually considered to be the most representative work of Albanian literature, and it has been translated into Italian and German.

Fishta's passion for politics was inseparable from his religious and literary vocations. He edited a newspaper *Posta e Shqypnís,* a mouthpiece for the Austro-Hungarian authorities of occupation during World War I. He was vice-president of the first Albanian parliament in 1921 and later headed several governmental delegations abroad. Having acquiesced to the Italian occupation of the country, he was made a member of the Fascist Accademia d'Italia in 1939. Fishta's political activity, aggravated by his slavophobia, made him the bête noire of Albanian communism, and his works were banned. Literary criticism has not yet come to grips with Fishta's tremendous verbal power and versatility. He remains the most controversial author in Albanian literature, the object of hyperbolic praises and virulent detractions. A German translation of *Lahuta e Malciś*, tr. by M. Lambertz, appeared in 1958.

See: A. Pipa, *Albanian Literature: Social Perspectives* (1978), pp. 111–19.   A.P.

Flake, Otto, pseud. Leo F. Kotta (1880–1963), German novelist, was born in Metz in Alsace and studied German literature, art history, and philosophy in Strasbourg. In World War I he served in Belgium, going to Zürich in 1918 and in 1920 to Berlin. After travels through Russia, England, and France he settled in Baden-Baden in 1928. A worldly and cultivated narrator, critic, and essayist, Flake supported the idea of a pan-European civilization under the aegis of a renewal of the ideals of antiquity. He began writing with impressionistic fervor in the novel *Schritt für Schritt* (1912; Step by Step) and through the novels *Freitagskind* (1913; Friday's Child), republished in 1928 under the title *Eine Kindheit* (A Childhood), and *Die Stadt des Hirns* (1919; The City of the Brain), but he approached expressionistic fervor with *Nein und Ja* (1920).

During the 1920s, Flake was considered to be one of the better writers of fiction in German. During this time appeared *Sommerroman* (1927; Summer Novel) and *Es ist Zeit* (1929; It Is Time). His essentially conservative viewpoint is clear in works that focused on the past, such as *Badische Chronik* (Baden Chronicle), a two-volume work consisting of *Die junge Monthiver* (1934; The Monthiver Girl) and *Anselm und Verena* (1935), published together as *Die Monthivermädchen* (The Monthiver Girls) in 1952. Flake called for sensibility and pleaded for clarity, sensuality, and energy. Because some of his works published during the Nazi years were little noticed—since he was persecuted for his contributions to the cultural-political magazine *Die Weltbühne* and because his second wife was of Jewish descent—they were republished after World War II. This was the case with *Die Töchter Noras* (1934; Nora's Daughters), republished in 1948 under the title *Kamilla*. During World War II, Flake was forbidden to publish, but he continued writing, later issuing the developmental novel *Fortunat* (1946) in two volumes, from manuscripts written earlier; it was continued with the two-volume *Ein Mann von Welt* (1947; A Man of the World). A two-volume edition of stories appeared in 1947. The novel *Old Man* (1947, in German) was followed by a study of Kaspar Hauser in 1950 and the novel *Die Sanduhr* (The Sand Clock) in the same year. *Lichtenhaler Allee* (1965) contains three short novels, "Hortense," "Scherzo," and "Das Quintet." Flake's autobiography, *Es wird Abend* (Evening Approaches) appeared in 1960, as did the novel *Der Pianist*. Flake never later achieved the prominence he had enjoyed in the 1920s, and he withdrew into a life of poverty in his last years.   A.L.W.

Flers, Robert Pellevé de La Motte-Ango, marquis de (1872–1927), French dramatist, was born in Pont-l'Evêque, of a family prominent in Norman annals since the Middle Ages. He spurned the more austere occupations of his forebears and devoted his life to the theater. In 1901 he married the daughter of the well-known dramatist Victorien Sardou (1831–1908) and began his highly successful collaboration with Gaston Arman de CAILLAVET. The latter died during World War I (1915), and Robert de Flers, having volunteered his services, fulfilled important military and diplomatic missions to Russia and Romania. Too modestly recorded in his volumes *Sur les chemins de la guerre* (1919; On the Roads to War) and *La Petite Table* (1920; The Little Table), they were formally eulogized in the Romanian Parliament. With Francis de Croisset as a new associate, he produced another series of plays, at least one of which, the operetta *Ciboulette* (1926, music by Reynaldo Hahn; Chives), enjoyed the popularity of his former works. By then he held several influential positions, including that of literary director and dramatic critic of *Figaro*. His election in 1920 to the Académie Française, which he had satirized in one of his best-known comedies, *L'Habit vert* (1912; The Green Uniform), served notice upon his bewildered ancestors, two of whom had been members of the Institut, that all roads lead to the Coupole.

See: E. Chaumié, *La Belle Aventure de Robert de Flers: Russie-Roumanie* (1929); F. de Croisset, *Le Souvenir de Robert de Flers* (1929).   J.-A.B. rev. D.W.A.

Focillon, Henri (1881–1943), French historian and philosopher of art, was born in Dijon. In the studio of his father, an engraver, he acquired early a passion for the arts. During his brilliant academic career, Focillon taught at the Ecole Normale Supérieure, the Ecole de Rome, the Collège de France, and Yale University, where he died in 1943, grieved by the condition of his humiliated country. He taught and wrote on many periods and aspects of war, from Romanesque sculpture and mural painting to modern art. His rigorous method as a historian, the boldness of his aesthetic speculations, and the passionate fervor of his devotion to beauty have profoundly impressed his many disciples, French and American. With Elie FAURE and André MALRAUX, he ranks among the greatest French writers on 20th-century art.

Focillon's first significant work was a profound analysis of *Giovanni-Battista Piranesi* (1918), the last of the artistic creators of Italy, a Renaissance visionary born, out of his time, in the 18th century. Focillon's fascination with the visionaries of all ages in art (Hieronymus Bosch, Albrecht Dürer, Rembrandt, Francisco Goya) lasted to the end of his career and found expression in a host of monographs and articles. His outstanding works on medieval art are *L'Art des sculpteurs romans* (1932; The Art of the Romanesque Sculptors) and especially the impressive synthesis *Art d'Occident* (1938; Eng. tr., *The Art of the West in the Middle Ages*, 1963). Focillon often returned to his first love, Italian art, and one of his most sensitive descriptive analyses, posthumously published, was that of *Piero della Francesca* (1952). In the modern field, his two volumes on *La Peinture française aux XIXe et XXe siècles* (1928; French Painting in the 19th and 20th Centuries) have inevitably aged faster, but they constitute an impassioned homage to the artistic and social dynamism of romanticism.

Focillon's philosophical position, underlying his judgments and his method, was opposed to both iconography and to pure history. According to his view, pregnantly embodied in *La Vie des formes* (1934; Eng. tr., *The Life of Forms in Art*, 1942), art is both content and form. While it resides somewhere in time and space, it transcends both, yet in order to exist, it must assume a form. "All is form and life itself is form," Honoré de Balzac had declared. Students of art endeavor to teach the uniqueness of genius or talent, but they must also insert that singular personality within a network of relations, while eschewing all determinism.

See: L. Grodecki, *Bibliographie Focillon* (1963).
                                                         H.P.

Fogazzaro, Antonio (1842–1911), Italian novelist, was born in Vicenza. He learned several languages at an early age, and read widely in English, French, and German literature, a taste fostered by his tutor, Giacomo Zanella, who was himself a poet. Fogazzaro's love of music is apparent throughout his work. His education was interrupted by the revolutions of 1859, but encouraged by his father, he went on to study law in Padua, Turin, and Milan. In 1868 he married Margherita di Valmarana, the daughter of a noble family. Fogazzaro spent the rest of his life in Vicenza and at Oria in Valsolda on Lake Lugano, the inspiration for some of his most lyrical descriptions.

Although Fogazzaro began to write poetry at an early age, he did not publish his first work, *Miranda,* a romantic tale in blank verse, until 1874. *Valsolda,* a volume of shorter poems, followed in 1876. In a lecture in 1872 on the future of the novel, he urged Italian writers to look to England rather than to France for their models. *Malombra* (1881; Eng. tr., *The Woman,* 1907), his own first novel, is indebted both to Wilkie Collins and to Victor Cherbuliez, yet it reveals an unmistakably original talent. His next novel, *Daniele Cortis* (1885; Eng. tr., 1887), is set in Rome and Vicenza, and includes a well-known description of the Villa Valmarana, an estate, belonging to his wife's family, famous for its Tiepolos. Daniele and his beloved Elena won all hearts, and the novel's skillful mingling of ideal politics and ideal love brought Fogazzaro immediate fame. His next, rather slight work, *Il mistero del poeta* (1888; The Mystery of the Poet), was not as successful. In 1896, Fogazzaro was appointed senator. The same year, he published his masterpiece, *Piccolo mondo antico* (Eng. tr., *The Patriot,* 1906), whose hero and heroine, Franco and Luisa Maironi, are idealized versions of his own father and mother. As in *Daniele Cortis* and the later novels, Fogazzaro is here concerned with a man whose Christian faith is more profound than that of the woman he loves. The story ends in 1859 with Franco's death in the battle for Venetian freedom. The fortunes of his son, Piero, form the subject of the somewhat autobiographical *Piccolo mondo moderno* (1900; Eng. tr., *The Man of the World,* 1906), a novel whose minor characters and scenes of provincial life owe much to George Eliot.

In his later years, Fogazzaro's youthful religious doubts were replaced by a devout Catholic faith. *Il Santo* (1905; Eng. tr., *The Saint,* 1906) depicts Piero's attempts to establish a lay mission, his eloquent plea for church reform in a midnight interview with the Pope (based on a similar scene in Emile ZOLA's *Rome*), and his death. The reforms Fogazzaro was advocating were being widely discussed in France and Germany under the name of modernism, and he was shocked when *Il Santo* was placed on the Papal Index, as was its sequel *Leila* (1910; Eng. tr., 1911). It was not until 50 years later that the ideas officially condemned in his novels were sanctioned by the Second Vatican Council.

The influences on Fogazzaro's works, as well as his own interests, make him the most European of Italian novelists. He is unique among Italian writers for his unusually wide range of intellectual concerns, for his psychological perceptions, and for his portraits of elegant, intelligent, and independent women. While his books show the influence of English models, his stories of ambiguous, frustrated love are also tinged with Swedenborgian mysticism. Fogazzaro's studies of crises of conscience owe something to Paul BOURGET and anticipate the French Catholic novelists of the next generation.

See: T. Gallarati-Scotti, *The Life of Antonio Fogazzaro* (1922); P. Nardi, *Fogazzaro* (1938); D. and L. Piccioni, *Antonio Fogazzaro* (1970). B.Co.

Foix, Josep Vicenc (1894–), Catalan poet, was born in Sarriá, Barcelona, where he studied law. He soon abandoned his studies to supervise a local family business. His literary vocation blossomed at an early age, when he gravitated toward the study of poetry. His own works, published in such journals as *L'amic de les arts, Quaderns de poesia,* and *Helix* under the signature J. V. Voix, exhibit surrealistic tendencies. The year 1918 marks the beginning of his diary, fragments of which he published in *Gertrudis* (1927), *KRTU* (1927), *Del "Diari 1918"* (1956), and *L'estrella d'en Perris* (1963). From 1913 to 1936 he composed his book of sonnets *Sol, i de dol* (1936; Alone, and In Mourning). Other works are *Les irreals omegues* (1948; The Unreal Omegas), *On he deixat les claus* (1953; Where I Left the Keys), *Còpia d'una lletra tramesa a na Madrona Puignau de Palau Saverdera* (1951; Copy of a Letter Sent to . . .), *Onze Nadals i un Cap d'Any* (1960; Eleven Christmases and a New Year), *Quatre nus* (1963; Four Nudes), and *Desa aquest llibre al calaix de baix* (1964; Put this Book in the Lower Drawer). In the same year he received the National Prize for Catalan Literature for his collected works, *Obres poètiques.* Subsequently he published *Escenificació de cinc poemes* (1965; Scenario of Five Poems), *Els lloms transparents* (1969; The Transparent Backs), *Allò que no diu "La Vanguardia"* (1970; What "La Vanguardia" Doesn't Say), *Darrer comunicat* (1970; Final Dispatch), and *Mots i maons o A cadascú el seu* (1971; Words and Bricks, or To Each His Own). *Revolució catalanista* (1934; Catalonian Revolution) was written in collaboration with Josep Carbonell.

Foix's perceptiveness enables him to analyze his own poetry and to recognize, as in *L'estrella d'en Perris,* that by following a bold experimental path toward the future one becomes linked with the most authentic past, or what Eugenio D'ORS would have called the genuine tradition. His lucidity shines forth in each of his poems and has captivated the admiration of new generations of poets, who see in the "Master of Sarriá" one of their most important predecessors.

See: J. Romeu, "Aproximacions a l'obra de J. V. Foix" in *Del "Diari 1918"* (1956); J. Marco, "M'exalta el nou u m'enamora el vell (Rellegint J. V. Foix) in *Sobre literatura catalana i altres assaigs* (1968); G. Ferrater, Prologue to J. V. Foix, *Els lloms transparents* (1969); P. Gimferrer, "Sol, u de dol . . . de J. V. Foix" in *Guia de literatura catalana comtemporània,* ed. by J. Castellanos (1973); P. Gimferrer, *La poesia de J. V. Foix* (1974). J.F.C.

Follain, Jean (1903–71), French poet, was born in Canisy. His ancestors were lawyers and teachers. He became a lawyer in Paris in 1928, was appointed judge in Charleville in 1951, and retired in 1961. Follain traveled a great deal and visited the United States in 1960. He was the recipient of many prizes, including the Mallarmé Prize (1939), the Blumenthal Prize (1941), and the great Poetry Prize of the Académie Française (1970). Follain was killed by a car on the Place de la Concorde on March 10, 1971, the same day his last book, *Espaces d'instants* (Spaces of Moments), was published.

In touch with poets of the group "Sagesse," Follain had started to publish in the early 1930s. *La Main chaude* (The Warm Hand) appeared in 1933 with a preface by André SALMON. *L'Epicerie d'enfance* (1937; The Childhood Grocery) described the poet's youth. *Canisy* (1942), *Exister* (1947; To Live), and *Territoires* (1953; Territories) are considered his most important works. He also wrote on religious topics. In still another vein, Follain's *Célébration de la pomme de terre* (1955; In Praise of the Potato) enchanted the gourmets.

The main theme of Follain's work is an endless search to recapture the instant. He wrote of the daily activities of his youth, a realm in which any object can be pregnant with an immense lyricism. Follain's best poems are short and concrete, but in them we find a universe.

See: special no. of *NRF* (June 1971); A. Dhôtel, *Jean Follain* (1972).   J.-C.M.

Fonseca, António José Branquinho da (1905–), Portuguese short-story writer, novelist, dramatist, and poet, a son of the writer Tomaz da Fonseca, was born in Mortágua. He earned his degree in law at the University of Coimbra. While a student there, he was one of the founders (1927) of the review *Presença*, the organ of writers concerned with the aesthetic aspect of literature. His works include poetry: *Poemas* (1926) and *Mar coalhado* (1932; Curdled Sea); plays: *Posição de guerra* (1928; War Post) and *Teatro I* (1939); short stories and novellas: *Zonas* (1932), *Caminhos magnéticos* (1938; Magnetic Paths), *Rio turvo* (1945; Turbid River), and *Bandeira preta* (1956; Black Banner); and two novels: *Porta de Minerva* (1947; Minerva's Gate) and *Mar santo* (1952; Holy Sea). The novella *O barão* (1942; The Baron), first included in *Rioturvo*, has been especially well received.

Fonseca dwells on strangeness amid the everyday routine of life: the penetrating chill of a dead man's hands touched by the heroine of "As mãos frias" (The Cold Hands) or the feeling of being directed by an unseen presence in "O anjo" (The Angel). *O barão*, praised for its construction, takes its unremarkable narrator, a school inspector, to a remote village in the Portuguese uplands and throws him unexpectedly upon the hospitality of the baron, one of the memorable personages in modern Portuguese literature. The character of the baron provides a larger-than-life portrait of decadent rural aristocracy. By turns dictatorial and sympathetic, depraved and idealistic, he leads the narrator on an eerie midnight search through the baronial manor and its grounds. Fonseca combines the real and the plausible with the strange and the mysterious, allowing glimpses of a world of symbols and mythic types.

See: M. Moisés, *A literatura portuguesa* (6th ed., 1968), pp. 306–09; D. Mourão-Ferreira, *Tópicos de crítica e de história literária* (1969), pp. 200–24.   T.Br.

Fonseca, Manuel da (1911–), Portuguese poet, short-story writer, and novelist, was born in Santiago do Cacém, Baixo Alentejo, a province that provides the background for much of his early fiction. He has worked as traveling salesman, a writer for a medical journal, and an advertising agent. True to neorealist tenets—more so than most members of the group—he writes poetry in a simple, direct language that can be easily understood and felt. His first collections of poems, *Rosa dos ventos* (1940; Compass Rose) and *Planície* (1941; Flatlands), were joined in *Poemas completos* (1958; Collected Poems). An enlarged edition appeared in 1963. Fonseca's preoccupation with the hard, almost violent conditions in rural areas and the mediocrity of everyday life in the small towns of Alentejo is prominent in his prose works from the beginning. His first book of short stories, *Aldeia Nova* (1941; New Village), presents harsh reality through the eyes of children. His two novels, *Cerromaior* (1943) and *Seara de vento* (1958; Crop of Wind), may occasionally disclose the neorealists' intent to use literature as a means of social change, but here again Fonseca is usually much more balanced than many fellow writers of the same period, who divide the world between insensitive, rapacious employers and noble, suffering workers. His portrait of a large landowner in "O último senhor de Albarrã" (The Last Lord of Albarrã), a story included in *O fogo e as cinzas* (1951; Fire and Ashes), artistically reveals the nobility and generosity of a member of the rural ruling class.

After a 10-year silence, Fonseca published two more volumes of short stories, *Um anjo no trapézio* (1968; An Angel on the Trapeze) and *Tempo de solidão* (1969; Time of Solitude), which focus mainly on the cold atmosphere of a cynical, corrupt society with an incisive irony that heightens the inequities of today's world.

See: M. Sacramento, *Ensaios de domingo* (1959), pp. 229–36; J. Gaspar Simões, *Crítica II*, vol. 1 (1961), pp. 329–34; M. Dionísio, "Introduction," to M. da Fonseca, *Poemas completos* (2d ed., 1963), pp. xi–xxxix.

E.M.D.

Fontane, Theodor (1819–98), German novelist, was born in Neuruppin, Brandenburg, to a family descended from French Huguenot refugees. Like his father, he became a pharmacist and, after doing his apprenticeship in Berlin, worked in this profession in Leipzig, Dresden, and Berlin from 1841 to 1849. In Leipzig he was associated with the radical Herwegh Club; in Berlin he joined a conservative literary group known as "Tunnel über der Spree." He gave up pharmacy in 1849 to become a free-lance writer, but because of financial difficulties he was forced to accept employment with the Prussian governmental press bureau. He visited England in 1852 as a reporter for the official *Preußische Zeitung*; from 1855 to 1859 he lived in London as a correspondent and semiofficial press agent for Berlin newspapers. Upon his return to Germany, he left governmental service to become the editor in charge of British affairs at the conservative *Kreuzzeitung* (1860–70). Later he worked as a theater critic for the liberal *Vossische Zeitung* (1870–89). From 1859 until his death he lived mainly in Berlin, except for occasional vacations and professional trips as a war historian to the battlefields of 1864, 1866, and 1870–71.

Fontane began his literary career as a poet. Some of his early poetry, written in Leipzig during the *Vormärz* years, was political and expressed a democratic radicalism like that of the contemporary revolutionary poets such as Georg Herwegh and Ferdinand Freiligrath. He established his literary reputation, however, as a writer of ballads dealing with events and personalities in English and Scottish as well as in Prussian history. Inspired by Thomas Percy's *Reliques of Ancient English Poetry* and Walter Scott's *Minstrelsy of the Scottish Border*, he created a distinctive blend of poetic devices taken from both the German and Anglo-Scottish ballad traditions. As a journalist and feuilletonist, he gained invaluable experience for developing his craft as a prose writer. His travel accounts *Ein Sommer in London* (1854), *Aus England* (1860), and *Jenseits des Tweed* (1860; Eng. tr., *Across the Tweed*, 1965) convey vivid impressions of British society and culture during the 1850s. In his *Wanderungen durch die Mark Brandenburg* (4 vols., 1862–82), he paid tribute to the land of his birth by exploring its history, social fabric, art, and natural beauty. In writing these travel books, Fontane sharpened significantly his powers of observation and sense of history; above all, he developed the urbane, detached, and humorous narrative style and attitude that were to become characteristic features of his fiction.

Fontane was almost 60 years old when his first novel was published. In a remarkably sustained flow of creative energy, he produced 17 novels and novellas during the last two decades of his life and became Germany's foremost 19th-century social novelist. Through his choice of subject matter and narrative technique, he aligned himself with the mainstream of European realism and the novel of manners rather than with the German tradition of the Bildungsroman with its narrative introversion and predominant theme of individual self-cultivation. Some of

Fontane's early novels have historical settings, yet the narrative focus is more on human attitudes and social contexts than on the historical events themselves. Thus *Vor dem Sturm* (1878; Before the Storm) provides a panoramic view of various segments of Prussian society on the eve of the war of liberation against Napoleon; *Schach von Wuthenow* (1883; Eng. tr., *A Man of Honor,* 1975) is a compelling case study of human weakness and vanity reflecting the general demoralization of Prussian military and aristocratic circles before the battle of Jena. With *L'Adultera* (1882; Eng. tr., *The Woman Taken in Adultery,* 1979), a tale of marital estrangement, divorce, and remarriage, Fontane turned to the type of novel in which he was to excel, the realistic novel of contemporary society in Berlin and its surrounding countryside. Realism as his avowed literary principle was for him the "portrayal of a life, a society, a group of people as the undistorted reflection of the life we lead"; it excluded the idealistic or romantic interpretation of human affairs as much as the naturalistic preoccupation with the ugly, the sordid, and the problems of the working classes. Fontane drew his fictional characters from the social groups he knew best, especially the landed gentry and the military aristocracy, to a lesser extent from the nouveau-riche middle class and the petite bourgeoisie. In his critical portrayal of the conservative and class-conscious Wilhelmian society, the members of the nobility are cast in a profoundly ambivalent light; their conversational wit and their refined manners and tastes make them aesthetically attractive and interesting individuals, but as a class they appear doomed, owing to their loss of economic power and their lack of moral energy and social adaptability.

Fontane's narrative interest focuses on the subtle portrayal of character and social milieu, not on dramatic action. The external events in his works consist mainly in social gatherings of the leisure classes and their urbane conversations. Beneath the narrative surface of carefree social interaction, Fontane deals with the intense personal conflicts of his protagonists. The dominant theme is that of the precarious relationship between the sexes in a traditional society. Problems of love and marriage become paradigmatic focal points for social analysis. Without moralizing, Fontane recorded how people in a rigidly stratified society become captives of class and convention. In his masterpiece, *Effi Briest* (1895; Eng. tr., 1967), a middle-aged aristocratic civil servant repudiates his young wife and kills her former lover in a duel when he finds out about her one marital infidelity; he does so against his own feelings and despite his awareness that he merely obeys the petrified code of his class. In *Cécile* (1887) and *Unwiederbringlich* (1891; Eng. tr., *Beyond Recall,* 1964), the self-deceptions and pseudovalues of the male protagonists cause marital crises that precipitate the suicide of the principal female character in each novel. Fontane's most artful treatment of the theme of misalliance is *Irrungen, Wirrungen* (1888; Eng. tr., *Trials and Tribulations,* 1917), in which a young nobleman and a working-class woman bow to class barriers by renouncing their love for one another. Middle-class environment and mentality are presented in *Frau Jenny Treibel* (1892; Eng. tr., 1976) and *Mathilde Möhring* (1906); the former deals in a largely comical vein with the poses and pretensions of the newly rich bourgeoisie; the latter shows the futile attempt of a shrewd and energetic young woman to overcome her petit-bourgeois origins by marrying into the educated upper middle class. Fontane's last two works of fiction, *Die Poggenpuhls* (1896; Eng. tr., *The Poggenpuhl Family,* 1979) and *Der Stechlin* (1899), are virtually plotless and portray, mainly through discourse, the economic and political decline of the lower nobility against the background of newly emerging social forces, especially the moneyed bourgeoisie.

The well-tempered realism of Fontane's *Zeitromane* is a late offspring of European realism. Although his novels represent incisive critical analyses of contemporary social conventions and conflicts, they contain relatively little hard-core satire or explicit attacks on the prevailing system, nor do they expound programmatic ideas. In his letters, however, Fontane revealed himself as an outspoken and radical critic of the social and political order. As a theater critic, he lent his support to progressive dramatists such as Henrick IBSEN and Gerhart HAUPTMANN. His craftsmanship as a prose writer had a profound influence on Thomas MANN.

See: P. Demetz, *Formen des Realismus: Theodor Fontane* (1964); H.-H. Reuter, *Fontane* (1968); W. Müller-Seidel, *Theodor Fontane: Soziale Romankunst in Deutschland* (1975); A. R. Robinson, *Theodor Fontane: An Introduction to the Man and his Work* (1976); C. Jolles, *Theodor Fontane,* 2d ed. (1976).   W.Ho.

Forsh, Olga Dmitriyevna (1873–1961), Russian novelist, was born in Gunib, in Dagestan. She first published in 1907 under the pseudonym A. Terek. A major representative of the philosophical or intellectual school of historical novelists, she was one of the founders of the Soviet historical novel. Her first major historical novel, *Odety kamnem* (1924–25; Eng. tr., *Palace & Prison,* 1958), depicting the fate of the young revolutionary, Mikhail Beydeman (1840–87), who was imprisoned in the Petropavlovsk Fortress and eventually went insane, is now a classic. Forsh's special interest in the liberal and revolutionary movements of the late 18th and early 19th centuries is reflected in three novels: *Radishchev* (1932–39), which gives a broad panorama of life under Catherine I; *Mikhaylovsky zamok* (Mikhaylovsky Fortress, 1945–46), dealing with the period of Paul I; and *Perventsy svobody* (1950–53; Eng. tr., *Pioneers of Freedom,* 1958), which treats the Decembrist uprising of 1825.

See: A. V. Tamarchenko, *Olga Forsh: zhizn, lichnost, tvorchestvo* (1966).   L.T.

Forssell, Lars (1928–), Swedish poet, playwright, novelist, and essayist, was born in Stockholm and received his B.A. from Augustana College in Rock Island, Ill., in 1948 and his Fil. kand. degree from Uppsala University in 1952. Erik LINDEGREN met the precocious poet in 1944 and for a decade served as his father figure. Forssell also had an international orientation at an early age through his contacts with the artist Adja Yunkers and with the poet and educator Martin S. Allwood, among others. His first collection of poetry, *Ryttaren* (1949; The Rider), as well as *Narren* (1952; The Buffoon [referring to the poet as a buffoon]), reveals a great talent, which was duly noted by the critics; but these thin books also reveal an appreciable influence from the Anglo-American tradition, especially T. S. Eliot and Ezra Pound, the latter of whom Forssell translated into Swedish in two volumes, *25 dikter* (1953; 25 Poems) and *Cantos I–XVII* (1959). In *F. C. Titjens* (1954), a collection of verse satirizing certain tendencies in contemporary Swedish aesthetic life, one of the most frequent themes in Forssell's writings, the human relation to fear and courage, is expressed. *Telegram* (1957) shows great variety and range, formally as well as intellectually. The book contains references to Horace, Shakespeare, Samuel Taylor Coleridge, Robert Burns, Pound, Eliot, and assorted Swedish poets such as Lasse Lucidor, Gustav FRÖDING, and Birger SJÖBERG; there is even a prose piece, "A. A. Milne in memoriam."

En kärleksdikt (1960; A Love Poem) is impressive in its directness and immediacy, especially when seen as a totality; but there are also individual poems that successfully compete with Forssell's best love poems, for example, "Odysseus på Ithaca" (Odysseus on Ithaca), "Vinter" (Winter), "Som kartan" (Like the Map), and "Jag sover i dig" (I Sleep in You). A selection of Forssell's love poetry, *Det enda vi har är varandra* (All We Have Is Each Other), appeared in 1964. *Röster* (1964; Voices) is simplified and refined with respect to form; the poet engages in writing ballads and ditties. Noteworthy are poems on Hokusai, Don Quixote (referring to Palle Pernevi's sculpture), Kasimir Malevich, and Gustav Fröding, but, above all, the long suite on Vaslav Nijinsky (1963) monumentalizing anxiety, for which the poet makes no claim to biographic authenticity; however, episodes have been taken from Romola Nijinsky's biography of her husband and also from Colin Wilson's *The Outsider*.

A development toward greater personal integration and more clearly defined views and commitments is discernible in *Ändå* (1968; Nevertheless), especially in some travel poems, "Samtal vid Ganges" (Conversation on the Ganges) and its postscript. Forssell's interest in the other popular arts, such as film, cartoons, ballads, ditties, the French chanson, and the cabaret, have found expression in *Snurra, min jord och nya visor* (1958 and 1966; Spin, My Earth, and New Ballads) and in the more aggressive *Jack Uppskäraren och andra visor tryckta i år* (1966; Jack the Ripper and Other Ballads Printed This Year), which have been inspired by such diverse books as Peter Wyden's *The Hired Killers*, Eric Ambler's *The Ability to Kill*, *Dossier Napoléon* (Université Marabout), not to mention matricles from Amnesty International, and Per WÄSTBERG's book *Afrika berättar* (Africa Recounts).

Oktoberdikter (1971; October Poems) consists of seven sections including "Uljanov" and "Lenin talar till arbetarna" (Lenin Speaks to the Workers)—and the contours of Vladimir I. Lenin's portrait are found on the cover. These poems should be read in the light of history, the poet has said. Lenin's dreams of the dictatorship of the people has been turned into the worst nightmares: "practically nothing of Lenin's intentions has been realized in the Soviet Union of today." *Försök* (1972; Attempts) is a somewhat uneven suite, written "actually during a single night" as the poet's frustrated reaction to the resumed bombing of North Vietnam. *Det möjliga* (1974; The Possible) contains deeply pessimistic poems, an attack on politicians, and no fewer than three requiems—to Gunnar EKELÖF, Ezra Pound, and Erik Lindegren—and songs written to a performance of Carlo Goldoni's *Le Baruffe chiozzotte*, *Gruffet*. Several of Forssell's plays, among them *Söndagspromenaden* (1963; Eng. tr., *The Sunday Promenade*), *Galenpannan* (1964; Eng. tr., *The Madcap*, 1973), *Flickan från Montreal* (1968; The Girl from Montreal), *Borgaren och Marx* (1970; The Burgher and Marx), *Show* (unpublished Eng. tr., 1972), have been performed at the Royal Dramatic Theater in Stockholm. In addition, the play *Haren och vråken* (1978; The Hare and the Buzzard) was successfully performed at Göteborg's City Theater in December 1978, and it was published that same year. Forssell's collected dramatic works, *Teater* I-II (1977; Theater) appeared with an introduction "Lyrikern som dramatiker" (The Poet as Dramatist) by Harry Carlson.

The short poetic plays *Kröningen* (1956; Eng. tr., *The Coronation*, 1963), on the theme of the unloved child, Alcestis, and *Charlie McDeath* (1962; Eng. tr., 1963), about a double, have enjoyed many performances in many

countries. Forssell's debut as a novelist came with *De rika* (1976; The Rich Ones), written in Paris in 1973 and Stockholm in 1975. The main characters, Mikael and Aunt Jenny, are seen against a backdrop of the stiflingly "harmonious" family relations of a successful upper-class family. A selection of Forssell's essays were published as *Nedslag* (1969; Downbeats or Impact) and *En bok för alla människor* (1975; A Book for All People). His selected poetry appeared as *Don Quixotes drömmar* (1960; The Dreams of Don Quixote, Poetry from 1949-1959), and *Dikter* (1975; Poems). A large collection of Forssell's many songs appeared under the title *Jag står här på ett torg* (1979; I Stand Here in the Square). Forssell became a member of the Swedish Academy in 1971. A selection of Forssell's poems in English appears in *Modern Swedish Poetry in Translation*, ed. by G. Harding and A. Hollo (1979), pp. 57-70.

See: G. Printz-Påhlson, "Bristens ironi," *Solen i spegeln* (1958), pp. 272-83; H. Carlson, "Lars Forssell— Poet in the Theater," *SS* 1 (1965); 31-57; L. O. Franzén, "I tomhetens bur" in *Omskrivningar* (1968), pp. 60-65; G. Syréhn, *Osäkerhetens teater: studier i Lars Forssells dramatik* (1979). L.S.

Fort, Paul (1872-1960), French poet, was born in Reims. At the age of 18 he became one of the animating forces of French symbolism. Reacting against the naturalistic Théâtre Libre, he founded in 1890 the Théâtre d'Art (later, de l'Œuvre) as a showcase for the idealistic lyric dramas of the symbolists. Fort also founded the important symbolist reviews *Le Livre d'art* (1892) and *Vers et prose* (1905), the second of which he edited until 1914. Both friend and champion of two generations of symbolists, Fort was elected "prince of poets" in 1912, an honor that consecrated his dual role as poet and respected leader.

All of Fort's abundant poetry and verse dramas reflect his close association with symbolism, especially in their use of vers libre. Employing rhythmic prose patterns to mirror the lyric effusions of popular poetic modes, Fort created an original form of the ballad. His *Ballades françaises et chroniques de France* (1897-1953) fills 49 volumes. Yet the new prosody that Fort adopted here is more innovative in appearance than in fact. Despite proselike stanzas arranged in paragraphs, the long periods often reveal fluid alexandrines with caesura and rhyme or assonance. The unusual typography also disguises traditional shorter meters repeating the rhymes and refrains of popular poetry. Fort is a poet of love and life, of French history and of France; he is in the tradition of the folk singer, singing songs that are playful, picturesque, sentimental, and always exuberant. Several charming pieces have been set to music by leading *chansonniers*. But Fort's virtue—facility—is also his downfall: lacking the introspection, depth, and sense of mystery of his symbolist associates, he remains on the surface of French poetry in spite of his enormous production. His literary fame may depend more on his historical role as a catalyst of the symbolist movement than on his achievement as a poet of popular songs.

See: G. A. Masson, *Paul Fort: son œuvre* (1923); P. Béarn, *Paul Fort* (1960). J.Me. rev. M.G.C.

Fortini, Franco, pseud. of Franco Lattes (1917-), Italian poet and critic, was born in Florence. He graduated in 1940 from the University of Florence. Fortini served as a soldier during World War II, but joined the Partisans in 1944. These experiences are recalled in *Sere in Valdossola* (1963; Evenings in Valdossola).

Fortini's early verse, published in *Foglio di via* (1946; Expulsion Order), emancipated itself from Hermetic influence (*see* ITALIAN LITERATURE) and proclaimed his commitment to revolutionary social realities. He espoused the antidogmatic program of Elio VITTORINI's journal *Il politecnico* (1945-47), to which he contributed Marxist analyses of Giacomo Leopardi (1798-1837), Franz KAFKA, Paul ELUARD, and other writers. In his writings, Fortini defended the need for intellectual autonomy against the party-line authoritarianism of the Cold War era. Since 1947 he has published his pungent literary-political criticism in numerous journals. The volume *Dieci inverni* (1957; 10 Winters) is a collection of these articles. The essays in *Verifica dei poteri* (1969; Investigation of the Authorities) are a continuation of Fortini's efforts at demystifying the relationship between culture and power.

In his poetry, Fortini enjoys grim, prophetic allegories in order to create a dialectical relationship between personal experience and the historical process. He harnesses all elements of his formation to an ideal of an integrated culture that he feels poetry is socially mandated to pursue but cannot exhaust. His chief poetical works are *Poesia ed errore* (1959; Poetry and Error), *La poesia delle rose* (1963; The Poetry of the Roses), *Una volta per sempre* (1963; Once and for All), and *Questo muro* (1973; This Wall). His hard-edged imagery acknowledges the influence of Eugenio MONTALE. Fortini has also published two semiautobiographical prose works, *Asia Maggiore* (1956; Asia Major) and *I cani del Sinai* (1967; The Dogs of Sinai). A critical study, *Il movimento surrealista* (The Surrealist Movement) appeared in 1959. He has also translated widely from French and German literature.

See: A. Berardinelli, *Fortini* (1973). M.M.G.

Forzano, Giovacchino (1884-1970), Italian dramatist, librettist, and screenwriter, was born in Borgo San Lorenzo. He studied music and law, sang in opera, and became a journalist. In 1904 he produced operas in Alessandria and Pesaro and so began a distinguished career in the theater arts. Forzano was the official producer at La Scala in 1922-23 and was guest producer at Covent Garden and in Rome for several seasons. He wrote over 30 librettos for Ruggiero Leoncavallo, Ermanno Wolf-Ferrari, Pietro Mascagni, and other composers; his best-known are *Suor Angelica* (1918; Eng. tr., *Sister Angelica*, 1918) and *Gianni Schicchi* (1918; Eng. tr., 1918) for Giacomo Puccini.

In addition to his librettos, Forzano wrote some 20 plays, all of which he produced himself. His skill in light comedy and dramatic effects delighted actors and audiences. Two available in English are *Un colpo di vento* (1930; Eng. tr., *A Gust of Wind*, 1966) and *Don Buonaparte* (1934; Eng. tr., *To Live in Peace*, 1966). Forzano liked elaborate scenery and costumes, and many of his plays have exotic or historical settings: *Tien-Hoa* (1924) is set in China, *Pietro il Grande* (1929; Peter the Great) in Russia, and *Madonna Oretta* (1918) and *Lorenzino* (1922) in Renaissance Florence. *Lorenzino* treats a theme used in *La maschera di Bruto* (1908; The Mask of Brutus) by Sem BENELLI. Forzano also borrowed Benelli's facile verse form for his plays *Sly* (1920) and *Ginevra degli Almieri* (1926). Forzano's debt to Victorien Sardou is evident in several plays dealing with the French Revolution and with Napoleon: *Il Conte di Bréchard* (1923), *Madame Roland* (1926), and *Napoleone e le donne* (1930; Napoleon and the Ladies).

Forzano publicly declared his sympathy with fascism in *Le campane di San Lucio* (1924; The Bells of Saint Lucio) and enjoyed government patronage. Benito Mussolini himself suggested the subjects for *Campo di Maggio* (1931), *Villafranca* (1931), and *Giulio Cesare* (1939; Julius Caesar), all historical parables of Il Duce's mission. In 1933, Forzano formed a motion picture company and filmed several of his own plays, including *Villafranca*. *Camicie nere* (1933; Black Shirts) was a Fascist propaganda film, as was *Tredici uomini e un cannone* (1936; Eng. version, *Thirteen Men and a Gun*, 1938). He also founded the Carri di Tespi, a troupe of mobile theaters, and directed their inaugural plays and their opera seasons from 1930 to 1934. His last published works were *Mussolini autore drammatico* (1954; Mussolini as Dramatist), which includes the three commissioned plays, and *Come li ho conosciuti* (1957; As I Knew Them).

See: M. Ferrigni, *Cronache teatrali* (1931), pp. 270-81; S. D'Amico, *Il teatro italiano* (1932), pp. 201-05; R. Simoni, *Trent'anni di cronaca drammatica*, vol. 3 (1955), pp. 456-60, vol. 4 (1958), pp. 453-56. B.Co.

Foucault, Michel (1926-), French philosopher, was born in Poitiers. He entered the literary arena with *Raymond Roussel* (1963), which deals with the enigma inherent in ROUSSEL's writings. After this work appeared, the importance of Foucault's earlier *Histoire de la folie à l'âge classique* (1961, rev. ed., 1972; Eng. tr., *Madness and Civilization: A History of Insanity in the Age of Reason*, 1965) became apparent. This is a study of society's handling of those elements not integrated into its ideology, of the means by which the Other is kept apart from the Same, and of the neoclassical age's attempt to drive out the irrational. Together with his earlier analysis of linguistic difference and repetition, slippage between language and reality, *Madness and Civilization* points to the central concern of *Les Mots et les choses* (1966; Eng. tr., *The Order of Things*, 1971), in which Foucault defines the epistemic structure of an age through its use of language, its perception and ordering of reality, and its modes of exchange. He identifies two breaks within Western culture: the first when neoclassicism introduced an ideology of representation that replaced the earlier complex world of harmonies and correspondences; the second when romanticism introduced historicity, isolating objects of knowledge into diachronic series, while a literary current emerged whose proponents (such as Friedrich Hölderlin) refused representation. The romantic age also saw Man emerge as an object of knowledge together with a "great eschatological myth"—the illusion that Man, free of alienation and determinations, could become his own master. Foucault then predicted the end of Man, not as object of knowledge but as subject of his own consciousness and freedom. He next published *L'Archéologie du savoir* (1969; Eng. tr., *Archeology of Knowledge*, 1972), in which he explores the grounds of his own methodology, and then a shorter, more accessible work, *L'Ordre du discours* (1971; Eng. tr. included in *Archeology*), describing the many constraints and taboos that preside over the issuance and reception of discourse—whether it be literary, scientific, or philosophical. *Surveiller et punir* (1975; Eng. tr., *Discipline and Punish: The Birth of the Prison*, 1978) follows up concerns of his first work while introducing a new conception of political power. In 1976, Foucault published *La Volonté de savoir* (Eng. tr., *The History of Sexuality, Vol. 1: An Introduction*, 1978), the first installment of a planned six-volume study of the subject.

See: A. Guédez, *Foucault* (1972); special issue of *Crit* 343 (December 1975). L.S.R.

Foulon, Roger (1923-), Belgian poet, was born in Thuin. He is the president of the Association of Belgian Writers. Fascinated by nature, Foulon is appeased and reassured in his writing by the perpetual evolution of the sky, trees, and fountains; but he draws inspiration as well from the distressing consciousness of nature's own precariousness.

He expresses his experience of the world in a poetry composed of incantations, cautious screams, and discreet boldness in its choice of rhythms and images. Variety of style tends to break the monotony of an exacting prosody, characterized by respect for meter, but also by the rejection of gratuitous or forced rhyme. Foulon's work is abundant: *Prières pour un vivant* (1950; Prayers for the Living), *Eve et le songe* (1952; Eve and the Dream), *Rites pour conjurer la mort* (1969; Rites to Conjure Up Death), and *Laudes pour elle et le monde* (1970; Lauds for Her and the World) illustrate the principal phases of an evolution in which *Le Dénombrement des choses* (1973; To Enumerate Things) and *Jardins* (1976; Gardens) constitute the temporary result. Without marking any perceptible increase in themes, these last two collections reveal a deepening of thought and underscore with extraordinary brilliance the formal mastery of the author.   R.F.

France, Anatole, pseud. of Anatole François Thibault (1844–1924), French novelist, short-story writer, poet, and critic, was born in Paris. The only son of a book-dealer, he was educated at a religious institution, the Collège Stanislas, where he was a mediocre student. He married, had a daughter, and was divorced before he met Mme Arman de Caillavet, who was the great love of his life. She was responsible for making him a name in French letters, despite his unaggressive, unambitious nature. Except for a few trips to Italy and a lecture tour in Latin America, France spent most of his time reading, talking, and writing. When this shy man reached 50, he displayed a sharp interest in politics. He participated increasingly in public affairs, and as he aged, he grew more radical. France's literary career had a slow start, but he became one of the most famous writers of his time. He belonged to the Académie Française, was awarded the Nobel Prize for Literature in 1921, and, at his death, was given a state funeral comparable only to the one Victor Hugo had received in 1885. France's reputation never recovered from this excess of honor. The surrealists (*see* FRENCH LITERATURE) attacked him as the symbol of all that they hated, distributing during the funeral a pamphlet entitled "Un Cadavre."

At first, France was a Parnassian poet. His *Poèmes dorés* (1873; Gilded Poems) and his verse drama *Les Noces corinthiennes* (1876; Corinthian Nuptials) were well received, if not met with enthusiasm. France then turned to prose. With *Le Crime de Sylvestre Bonnard* (1881; Eng. tr., *The Crime of Sylvestre Bonnard,* 1890) and *Le Livre de mon ami* (1885; Eng. tr., *My Friend's Book,* 1913), France had found his style: a slow-moving plot, in which reflections and comments are more important than events, and a sentimental story, treated with irony and self-irony. In 1888 he began a journalistic career and was appointed literary critic of the important newspaper *Le Temps.* The champion of subjective criticism, France wrote articles in which he spoke of himself when discussing great men's works. Many of these pieces are collected in *La Vie littéraire* (5 vols., Literary Life). Notable among his other writings of this period are the novels *Thaïs* (1890; Eng. tr., 1891) and *La Rôtisserie de la Reine Pédauque* (1894; Eng. trs., *At the Sign of the Reine Pédauque,* 1912, *The Queen Pédauque,* 1923, *At the Sign of the Queen Pédauque,* 1930, *The Romance of Queen Pédauque,* 1950). In these ironic or parodic reconstitutions of the past, France displays his mature erudition— not for historical purposes but to achieve an aesthetic goal. Yet, at the same time, these books show his strong anticlerical sentiments.

The Dreyfus Affair was the turning point of France's career, as it was for many writers of the 1890s. With Emile ZOLA, France was one of Dreyfus's most outspoken defenders. His four-volume *L'Histoire contemporaine* (Contemporary History)—*L'Orme du mail* (1897; Eng. tr., *The Elm-Tree on the Mall,* 1910), *Le Mannequin d'osier* (1877; Eng. tr., *The Wicker Work Woman,* 1910), *L'Anneau d'améthyste* (1899; Eng. tr., *The Amethyst Ring,* 1919), *Monsieur Bergeret à Paris* (1901; Eng. tr., *Monsieur Bergeret in Paris,* 1922)—certainly his best work, is a fictionalized chronicle of the events, which explains to some extent the loose construction of the story. Here France modified his epicurean attitude so that despite its aloofness, this work made full use of his talents for irony and satire. His protagonist, Professor Bergeret remains the best-sketched character in France's books.

The violence and the bitterness surrounding the Dreyfus case was followed by much disappointment. Dreyfus had been rehabilitated, but the scars remained; victory had been only partial and had not led to any major change in society. Although France became a socialist and participated in many reform campaigns, his writings during this period show his disillusionment. *L'Affaire Crainquebille* (1901; Eng. tr., *Crainquebille,* 1915) is a parody of justice. *L'Ile des pingouins* (1908; Eng. tr., *Penguin Island,* 1914), is a harsh, at times extremely funny satire in which France retells in his way the history of his country. *Les Dieux ont soif* (1905; Eng. tr., *The Gods Are Athirst,* 1913) is a powerful, intelligent novel, set during the French Revolution. But here France is not interested in historical events; what he describes is the endurance of daily life during the most agitated of times. Critics had difficulty reconciling France's socialist writings with this gloomy view of the Revolution. A more serene and detached atmosphere marks two very good but minor books: *L'Histoire comique* (1903; Eng. tr., *A Mummer's Tale,* 1921) and *La Révolte des anges* (1914; Eng. tr., *The Revolt of the Angels,* 1914). The latter is France's last interesting work. Deeply affected by World War I, he remained, during the years preceding his death, the patriarch of letters, a highly respected figure despite his political stands and his cynical lucidity.

For years, critics have been saying with little effect that France, once too highly praised, does not now occupy the place he deserves. Nevertheless, he remains a widely read author, and important scholarly studies have been devoted to his works. On the other hand, France has had no influence on contemporary writers and is seldom mentioned by contemporary critics. His interests are in complete opposition to our present conception of the world as metaphysical and tragic. France realizes how difficult and precarious existence is, but he refuses to dramatize it. Irony and pity are his motto. Even when he is at his most sarcastic, he gives the reader the feeling that life is a game in which France's comments, sad as they may be, deflect the tragedy of situations. Such an attitude is the heritage of both Voltaire and Ernest Renan, who likewise are not among today's favorites. France's much-admired style is today an obstacle; it is too ornate and too self-conscious, especially in the sentimental works that made him famous. These works still appear in anthologies as inoffensive excerpts, but France has not yet been restored to the esteem in which he was once held.

See: J. Sareil, *Anatole France et Voltaire* (1961); M.-C. Barquart, *Anatole France polémiste* (1962); J. Levaillont, *Essai sur l'évolution intellectuelle d'Anatole France* (1965); D. Bresky, *The Art of Anatole France* (1969).

J.S.

Frank, Bruno (1886–1945), German novelist, dramatist, and poet was born in Stuttgart and studied at several universities in southern Germany, taking his Ph.D. at Heidelberg. He lived near Munich until he left Germany after 1933. The United States was his home for some years before his death.

Frank began his literary career in 1905 as a poet *Aus der goldenen Schale* (3d ed. 1907; From the Golden Goblet) contains graceful but not very original lyrics. Selected poems of the next years were published in *Die Kelter* (1920; The Wine Press). Only a few among his many earlier novels, stories, and dramas were successful, notably the novel *Die Fürstin* (1915; The Princess) and the drama *Die Schwestern und der Fremde* (1918; Sisters and the Stranger).

It was not until after 1920 that Frank found the artistic formula that made him internationally known. He once wrote, "The masses detest being bored, they need strong stimuli." Adhering to this formula, Frank built plots full of action around psychologically modernized historical figures or events, as in *Tage des Königs: drei Erzählungen* (1924; Eng. tr., *The Days of the King*, 1927), *Trenck: Roman eines Günstlings* (1926; Eng. tr., *Trenck: The Love Story of a Favorite*, 1928), the drama *Zwölftausend* (1926; Eng. tr., *Twelve Thousand*, 1928); and the novel *Ein Mann namens Cervantes* (1934; Eng. tr., *A Man Called Cervantes*, 1934). He also piqued the reader's curiosity by using well-known, if thinly veiled, contemporary personalities as subjects for more or less fantastic stories, as in *Der Magier* (1925; The Magician) and *Politische Novella* (1928; Political Novella). The novel *Der Reisepass* (1927; Eng. tr., *Lost Heritage*, 1937), a story of love among émigrés, makes use of popular anti-Nazi feelings to hold the interest of the reader. A novel, *Die Tochter* (1943; Eng. tr., *One Fair Daughter*, 1943), was published in Mexico City. A collection in English, *The Magician and Other Stories*, appeared in 1946 after Frank's death.

W.R.G.

Frank, Leonhard (1882–1961), German novelist and dramatist, was born at Würzburg, the son of a cabinetmaker. At the age of 13 he was apprenticed to a bicycle mechanic. For some time he tried to make a living as a factory hand, a chauffeur, a house painter, and a hospital attendant. At 30 he wrote his first novel, *Die Räuberbande* (1914; Eng. tr., *The Robber Band*, 1928), the story of several Würzburg boys named after some characters from Karl MAY's books, who took part as disguised "brigands" in a series of romantic adventures and pranks. In a sequel, *Das Ochsenfurter Männerquartett* (1927; Eng. tr., *The Singers*, 1932), the revolutionary tunes of *Räuberbande* are softened into a bittersweet scherzo on the theme of boys turning bourgeois: the old "brigands," middle-aged men, have abandoned their adventurous spirit after the World War I. Frank's second novel, *Die Ursache* (1920; Eng. tr., *The Cause of the Crime*, 1928), joined the ranks of those that exploited revolt against the old order as a literary theme; it is full of belligerent compassion for the guilty, who are innocent victims of a coercive educational system.

When World War I broke out, Frank left Germany and went to Switzerland as a refugee, where he became a member of a Zurich group of antiwar writers. Here his *Der Mensch ist gut* (1917; Man Is Good) was written, a powerful humanitarian denunciation of the war spirit, the first of its kind in German literature. The book was enough to make Frank again depart from Germany after 1933.

In 1924, still impressed by the revolution of 1918, Frank produced the novel *Der Bürger* (Eng. tr., *A Middle-Class Man*, 1930), less remarkable for its plot than for its style, similar to the technique employed in a movie script with

its rapidly changing scenes. In his short story *Karl und Anna* (1917; Eng. tr., 1929), he succeeded in presenting one of the most original variants of the Enoch Arden motif of the husband's return, but the story is centered primarily around sexual and not patriotic problems. Two years afterward Frank recast this novel into a successful play of the same title (1929; Eng. tr., 1929).

Of his many short stories *Im letzten Wagen* (1925; Eng. tr., *In the Last Coach and Other Stories*, 1935) seems especially typical of his art, which skillfully combines sensationalism and psychological cruelty. More and more Frank disengaged himself from any allegiance to his native land, and the ground of his narratives became the wide world of international affairs.

See: M. Glaubrecht, *Studien zum Frühwerk Leonhard Franks* (1965). H.Sc. rev. A.L.W.

Franko, Ivan (1856–1916), Ukrainian writer and scholar, was born in the village of Nahuyevychi, in the western Ukraine, into the family of a blacksmith. He studied at the universities of Lviv (Lvov) and Chernivtsi (Chernovtsy). A radical socialist in his youth, he remained dedicated to the cause of social and national revolution. In Galicia, Franko's role as national poet-prophet was comparable to that which Taras Shevchenko had played earlier in the eastern Ukraine (see UKRAINIAN LITERATURE). Franko's prodigious literary talent showed itself in poetry, prose, and journalism. He was also a prominent scholar in the areas of folklore and literary history. Some of his stories, such as "Boa constrictor," (1878) and "Boryslav smiyetsya" (1882; Boryslav Is Laughing), deal with the life of the working class, while other works, such as the novel *Zakhar Berkut* (1883; Eng. tr., 1944), are historical. He was also a successful playwright, his most notable stage work being *Ukradene shchastya* (1893; Stolen Happiness).

Franko's greatest achievement, however, was in poetry, in which he departed from the realistic conventions that prevailed in his prose. His best collections of lyric verse are *Zivyale lystya* (1896; Withered Leaves), *Miy izmaragd* (1898; My Emerald), and *Iz dniv zhurby* (1900; From the Days of Sorrow). Different but not less accomplished are his philosophical poems "Ivan Vyshensky" (1900) and "Moysey" (1905; Eng. tr., "Moses," 1938). A remarkable satirical poem is *Lys mykyta* (1890; Mykyta the Fox). Franko was hostile to the Ukrainian modernists, yet like them he himself often transcended realism. Selections of his work in English translation have appeared under the titles *Selected Poems* (1948), *Poems and Stories* (1956), and *Boa constrictor* (n.d.). G.S.N.L.

Fratti, Mario (1927–), Italian playwright, was born in L'Aquila, but is now residing in the United States. Fratti's work is better known to audiences abroad than in his native Italy. He has written more than 40 dramas, in both Italian and English, and has received numerous drama awards in the United States and in Italy. Fratti's work reflects the influences of Luigi PIRANDELLO, the Italian theater of the grotesque, and Bertolt BRECHT. The dominant theme of Fratti's works is the dissonance between reality and appearance, a subject he approaches as a moralist and as an ironic social critic.

Most of Fratti's works date from 1964, when he moved to New York. The focus of his work is frequently on standards of morality and social behavior in the United States. Racial antipathies characterize the six short pieces collected in *Races* (1972), while the "generation gap" and the idealism of American youth in the 1960s animate *L'ospite romano* (1969; Eng. tr., *The Roman Guest*, 1968). Fratti stresses the contradictory American impulses of materialistic self-centeredness as opposed to a traditional concern for others and belief in social progress. In his view, this contradiction motivates characters to commit acts of aggression and gratuitous violence, as happens in *The Bridge* (1969), or reduces emotional relationships to mutual exploitation, as in *Tre letti* (1970; Three Beds), *La vittima* (1972; Eng. tr., *The Victim,* 1972), *Sorelle* (1972; Sisters), and *I frigoriferi* (1964; Eng. tr., *The Refrigerators,* 1968). Fratti's familiarity with two cultures allows him to contrast their mores. In *The Roman Guest,* for example, he examines American and European attitudes towards authority and personal responsibility, while in *The Academy* (1964; rev. title, *The Seducers,* 1972) he compares views on male chauvinism and sexual freedom. Besides theatrical pieces, Fratti has written several radio and television dramas, two volumes of poetry, and a novel. He currently teaches Italian literature at Hunter College in New York.

See: *Crowell's Handbook of Contemporary Drama* (1971), pp. 159–60.   J.Ch.

Frénaud, André (1907–), French poet, was born at Montceau-les-Mines in Burgundy. His father was a pharmacist. At the age of seven, Frénaud discovered Edgar Allan Poe's *Adventures of Gordon Pym.* He studied law and philosophy at the University of Paris and in 1930 was a lecturer at the University of Lwów (then in Poland). He became a civil servant at the Finance Ministry in 1937, and retired in 1967. Frénaud started to write rather late, between 1940 and 1942 when he was a prisoner of war in Germany. *Les Rois Mages* (1943; The Three Magi), a mythical and mystical book published by Seghers, was followed by *Malamour* (1945), *La Noce noire* (1946; The Black Wedding), and *Poèmes de dessous le plancher* (1949; Poems from under the Floor). Frénaud's collected poems were published under the titles of *La Sainte Face* (1948; The Holy Face), and *Il n'y a pas de paradis* (1962; There Is No Paradise). Many of his poems have been translated into more than 20 languages. Frénaud received the great poetry prize of the Académie Française in 1973.

At first glance, Frénaud may seem pessimistic and negative. Everything worries him, he is full of anguish, and he is fascinated by evil and destruction. Yet there is in him a mystical yearning, a quest for a divine meaning. According to Frénaud, the poet must transform despair into hope: he must be a magus. Frénaud is a stoic poet, a traveler who longs for eternity.

See: Gaëtan Picon, *Panorama de la nouvelle littérature française* (1949); G.-E. Clancier, *André Frénaud* (1963); M. Wiedmer, *André Frénaud* (1969).   J.-C.M.

French literature. The closing years of the 19th century had been a period of weariness in France, probably and subconsciously made more acute by the generalized phrase "fin de siècle" and the conviction on the part of many people that they were living in a decadent age, at the end of a vitally creative era in painting, music, and literature. Impressionism and what is now conveniently termed postimpressionism in painting had become exhausted in the last years of the moribund century. No other movement (the "Synthesis," symbolist art, pointillism) appeared to possess enough vitality to renovate the pictorial arts. In 1900, two years after the outcry aroused by Auguste Rodin's *The Kiss* and *Balzac,* the city of Paris at last consecrated that sculptor's genius at the Universal Exhibition. The Dreyfus Affair was on its way to being concluded and Emile ZOLA was to die when the new century was two years old. But by that time not even he and his friends of Médan would have protested through a telegram "Naturalism not dead" against the journalists' haste to bury the movement. Naturalism had spent its force both in fiction and on the stage. Its impact was to be felt much more powerfully outside France—in Germany, Spain, Britain, and the United States. Only by fits and starts, and under very different guises, was something akin to naturalism revived in the 20th century; it reemerged in realistic novels about World War I; in the short-lived "Populism" movement; in proletarian fiction; and in the writings of Louis-Ferdinand Céline, Henri Barbusse, Jean-Paul Sartre (after a fashion), and the pornographic, exalted, and monotonous sex-novels of Raymond Guérin and Pierre Guyotat. The outcry against Zola soon subsided and today, almost 80 years after his death, his greatness as a visionary poet and as the last (or, with Victor Hugo, the only) novelist to have been popular with the masses as well as with the elite is universally proclaimed. He stands second to none among French fiction writers as the hero, or the victim, of rapidly accumulating academic studies.

The early years of the 20th century likewise witnessed a decline—in poetry, drama, and in aesthetic and critical speculation—of what had, in the previous decades, gone by the name of symbolism. This had amounted to nothing less than a gradual invasion of the several branches of literature (fiction, drama, even philosophical and historical writing) by poetry. It had, in opposition to naturalism, insisted on treating the material world as merely a storehouse of signs pointing to a higher and ulterior meaning in another world. The poet was the decipherer of these hieroglyphics. There was no philosophical doctrine and no coherent aesthetics behind the diverse, at times contradictory, expressions of each poet's individual temperament. Yet most of them, reacting against determinism and positivism, concurred in proclaiming the ideal character of the world, the superiority of nonrational and intuitive perception over intellectual and scientific modes of cognition. Harking back to Charles BAUDELAIRE's sonnet "Correspondances," a work hitherto almost unnoticed, they hailed all arts as parallel translations of one fundamental mystery. In poetry, the symbolists had wanted to discard the oratorical and discursive forms of poetical development dear to many romantics and to cultivate esoteric rarity, vagueness, elusive and ethereal imagery and, in Walter Pater's formula, to "aspire to the condition of music."

The prestige and the impact of that vanguard French poetical movement were enormous in other countries: England, Ireland, Germany, and, most of all, Russia. In France, they had encountered much scoffing and hostility. A few vanguard magazines devoted to poetry, *Vers et prose* (1905–14) and *La Phalange* (1906–14), attempted to expand or to prolong the sway of symbolism in France. They reached only a thin cluster of young people until, around 1910 and even more after 1919, Stéphane Mallarmé (first thanks to the critic Albert Thibaudet), then Arthur Rimbaud (worshiped by Paul Claudel), last and least of all LAUTRÉAMONT (hailed by the surrealists), posthumously engineered a return to some of the revolutionary values that lay behind the symbolists' appearance of eccentricity and effeminacy. In retrospect, the spirit of experimentation in symbolism, the fondness for an atmosphere of dream and for melodious prose and verse, appears to us to have been preserved most felicitously by a few great authors, all born around 1870: Claudel, André Gide, Marcel Proust, and Paul Valéry.

There had been no generally acclaimed or influential theorist or critic guiding the poets and dramatists of the symbolist group, although Rémy de GOURMONT seemed for a time to be capable of fulfilling that role. He lacked, however, discriminating taste, and his approach was too intellectual and arid. The philosopher who, in the first two decades of the 20th century, towered above all others in France was Henri BERGSON. Yet although he wrote an artistic prose himself, eschewing all pedantry and technical language, he was only moderately interested in literature. His notions of creative evolution, of the supremacy of intuition over intellectual deduction, of duration as opposed to time, and of the perpetual mobility of a world in which free will was restored and spiritual energy vindicated, corresponded to the aspirations of the generation that, even before most of Bergson's works had actually appeared, had won the battle for symbolism. Georges Sorel, Charles Péguy, and Thibaudet were, outside the professional philosophers, the authors who did most to spread Bergsonism. Bergson's most talented opponents were Julien BENDA, a staunch supporter of pure intellectualism, and Jacques MARITAIN, who took issue with a mode of thought that seemed to distrust intelligence and to ignore Thomistic rationalism.

The other influential thinkers of the years 1900–19 were the sociologists Gabriel de Tarde and Emile DURKHEIM. The latter has grown in stature ever since. His books on suicide, on the division of labor, on elementary forms of religious life, and on the history of education are still highly regarded. His proposed methodology for the consideration of sociological data as objects possessed a rigor that won for that discipline a respected status among the "human sciences." Political thought, meanwhile, had few outstanding representatives and very few, in particular, who attempted to provide liberal or socialistic democracy with a powerfully reasoned doctrine. That lack was fraught with grave consequences in a country in which ideological doctrines hold much fascination for political parties. Georges SOREL blended Bergsonism and Marxism in an original system advocating action and violence as more fruitful than theoretical meditation. Paradoxically, his socialism turned out to be most influential on totalitarian doctrines. Jean JAURÈS, an eloquent orator and a prophetic historian, and Léon BLUM, a subtle literary critic who became a socialist leader, failed to evolve an original body of thought to bolster their generous policies.

The first two decades of the 20th century were marked, in France as in other countries, by a revival of nationalist ideas—witness Rudyard Kipling, the successors of Friedrich NIETZSCHE and of Heinrich von Treitschke, and Gabriele D'ANNUNZIO. Maurice BARRÈS strenuously expounded his romantic religion of the soil, the race, and the dead; after 1900, he resorted to essays, diaries, and travel sketches as a substitute for his failing imaginative powers. Something of his rich, vibrant prose and of his feverish temperament will be found later in writers who, without subscribing to his views, had a somewhat similar sensibility (Charles de Gaulle, André Malraux, Albert Camus). Charles MAURRAS upheld a more coherent nationalist and royalist doctrine, violently reviling democracy under all its forms. His slight literary merits have been overestimated by his fanatical partisans. Léon DAUDET had more warmth and was a biased, grossly partial, but effective polemical journalist. Many of those champions of traditionalism and of what they fancied to be classical values—Lasserre, Henri MASSIS, Jacques Bainville—blindly opposed what was promising and vital in the literature of their time. ALAIN was an extraordinary professor, known for his independent thinking and terse, exact style, but his essays (called by him "propos")—ingenious, often acute, casual, and brief—were never woven into a doctrine. In the realms of aesthetics and philosophy, of practical ethics and politics, they are likely to remain urbane minor pieces, hard to appreciate by anyone not steeped in the tradition of the French moralists. The greatest essayist of the early 20th century was probably Charles PÉGUY, a thinker more illogical than most, but closer to the soul of the people of France and always animated by the élan vital dear to Bergson. Péguy was both a socialist and a Christian, at times a mystic, but a tirelessly reasoning one, and seldom charitable toward those who disagreed with him. He wrote too much and too hastily, indulging in repetitions and mannerisms of style that do, however, impart a racy flavor to this prose. His poetry stood at the opposite end from the symbolist ideal of purity, musicality, and evocative imagery, yet it is nevertheless admired by those few "antimoderns" who claim, contrary to Edgar Allan Poe's theories, that a long poem with epic ambitions is not necessarily a contradiction in terms. Half a century after Péguy's death, a group of critics, most of them Catholic and intent on liberalizing the appeal of the Church to modern democracies, has been active in interpreting and renovating his message.

In the early years of the 20th century, the novel seemed oppressed by the achievement of those great predecessors who, like Honoré de Balzac and Zola, had been capable of embracing a whole society and a whole age within their massive accumulation of works. The symbolist era was hardly favorable to a genre that seldom thrives on abstraction and allegory and that traditionally needs structure, density, and depth in order to create characters. The reputations of few novelists have fallen so abruptly as those of the writers who, until approximately 1920, enjoyed universal fame. It is unlikely that Anatole FRANCE, Pierre LOTI, Paul BOURGET, or Maurice Barrès will ever climb back to the pinnacle of fame to which the middle-class audience had then raised them. Ever since the end of World War I, those gentle and genteel authors and upholders of a philosophical or social message have appeared as second-rate, repetitious tellers of tales, too timid to run risks. Romain ROLLAND, who had remained more independent from the establishment and was more open to the foreign influences (Italian Renaissance art, German music, Indian wisdom) suffered less from the passing of intellectual fashions. His saga-novel, *Jean-Christophe* (1904–12), for which he won the Nobel Prize, has remained popular with readers outside France, although the French balked at the author's inelegant style and at the shallowness of his psychological revelation.

In those same years preceding World War I, the drama failed to match the innovating ardor that had, between 1885 and 1900, enabled the genre to reinvigorate itself through courageous realism (such as that of André Antoine's Théâtre Libre) and through the infusion of strangeness, poetry, and stark, tragic struggles adopted from Henrik IBSEN, August STRINDBERG, and other Nordic authors. These influences are evident, for example, in the works of Aurélien LUGNÉ-POE. The mundane and frothy "theater of the Boulevards" then enjoyed its golden age, hardly challenged as yet by the vanguard stage. Such a theater entertained for the public, as Eugène Scribe (1791–1861) had done for a good part of the 19th century, but it hardly expected to survive as literature. Since 1920 or so, this theater has, to a large extent, been replaced by the cinema. Against the background of the Boulevard playwrights, three dramatists endeavored to treat the conflict of ideas (François de CUREL, Paul HERVIEU) or psychological struggles of sensuous, relentlessly self-analytical couples (Georges de PORTO-RICHE). But they failed to dramatize these tensions with enough force and enough beauty of diction to transmit them to posterity. Ironically, far less serious or pretentious plays, which first broke intentionally with the conventions prevailing among middle-class audiences, have more successfully withstood the wear and tear of the years: *Ubu Roi* (staged in 1896) by Alfred JARRY, *Les Mamelles de Tirésias* (staged in 1917) by the poet Guillaume Apollinaire, and, soon after World War I, *Le Cocu magnifique* (1921) by Fernand CROMMELYNCK.

After the excitement aroused by the symbolists and the decadents in 1885–95, French poetry was marking time. It would be 30 or 40 years before the full import of Stéphane MALLARMÉ, Arthur RIMBAUD, and Jules Laforgue (1860–87) could be weighed and their poetical revolution assimilated. Paul VERLAINE's great, tragic pieces and his bold metrical innovations at first failed to impress his immediate successors; only since 1935 or so has he come into his own, in the estimation of most critics, as a great poet. The symbolists who applied the lessons of those bold innovators proved to be timid followers, decorative talents toying with vague symbols elegantly draped in elaborate folds. Most of them appear to us today to have been but minor talents. Some of them retained only the superficial charm of symbolism: Gustave KAHN, one of the earliest users of vers libre, Henri de RÉGNIER, Albert Samain. Others clamored for publicity in the manner typical of the French: through founding a group of their own, stressing their differences from the symbolist masters to whom they knew themselves to be woefully unequal. The "naturist" school that Saint-Georges de Bouhélier tried to launch lacked the ingredients necessary for survival: genuine talent and a timely message. Another failure was the short-lived "Ecole romane," founded by Jean MORÉAS. The unblushing expression of a bulging ego and gifts of versified eloquence and of facility were the mark of such neoromantics as Edmond ROSTAND (in his much acclaimed plays and in ambitious odes) and Anna de NOAILLES. Others tried to come down to earth and to restore to poetry what the symbolists had almost eliminated from it: humor and playfulness. They are sometimes called the "fantaisist" group and included Paul Jean TOULET and FAGUS. Around the middle of the century, Fombeure, Jacques Prévert, and, with far more originality, Francis Ponge would stand in that same tradition. About 1905 the unanimist group undertook to break away from the proverbial isolation of the self-centered poet, singing instead of the beautiful Utopia of fraternal love binding together individuals and even nations. Inspired by Walt Whitman and the robust talent of Emile VERHAEREN, they advocated the cult of life, of teeming fertile nature, and of the modern city. Jules ROMAINS and, to a lesser extent, Georges DUHAMEL provided the philosophical and sociological substratum of the movement, but their poetical achievement hardly matched the strength of their theoretical conviction. They soon transferred their efforts to plays, novels, and essays. The ambition to bring back poetry to the simplicity of everyday life and to obliterate all difference between the prosaic and the poetical—the goal first of the 18th century, then of Charles Sainte-Beuve (1804–69), Alphonse Lamartine (1790–1869), Baudelaire, and the almost forgotten François Coppée (1842–1908)—had once again been frustrated.

The years preceding World War I appear to us today (although few contemporaries were then aware of it) to have been dominated by two great poetic figures: Paul CLAUDEL and Guillaume APOLLINAIRE. At that time, Claudel composed *Partage de midi* (1905; Eng. tr., *Break of Noon*, 1960) and *L'Annonce faite à Marie* (1910; Eng. tr., *The Tidings Brought to Marie*, 1916), two of the finest lyrical dramas ever written in French, far earthier and less monotonously stilted than most plays written in English or in French under the inspiration of the symbolist movement. Claudel was no less original as a lyrical poet inspired by Catholicism. As a creator of grandiose images, as a cosmic evocator of a universe infused with God's presence, as an eloquent successor to Rimbaud and, little as he would admit it, to Hugo, he restored the lyrical ode, the hymn, and the prayer to the forefront of poetry. His ambitious *Cinq Grandes Odes* (Five Great Odes) appeared in 1910 and his more restrained long poem *Cette heure qui est entre le printemps et l'été* (This Hour That Is between Spring and Summer; reprinted as *La Cantate à trois voix* [The Cantata with Three Voices], 1931) in 1931. Earlier still, Claudel had, in *Connaissance de l'est* (1901, new ed., 1907; Knowing the East) offered the finest examples in the French language of prose poems that eschewed facility and formlessness and blended, according to Mallarmé's dictum, the urge to understand (and to interpret) objects and their poetical transfiguration. Apollinaire, more independent and iconoclastic, thirsting for modernity, shunned eloquence and pomp in his lyrical pieces. His playful humor, his blend of tenderness and of irony, and his amused self-pity recalled and matched the best achievement of Heinrich Heine. He ventured fearlessly into erotic literature, often to mock his own yearnings for female sympathy, and he experimented with language, style, and metrics. He was an obstinate devotee of the literary vanguard. When he died in 1918 at the age of 38, very few suspected that the eternal playboy he had seemed to be would go down to posterity as the pioneer of modern movements in art and literature. Both cubism and surrealism stand in his debt. Half a century after his death, Apollinaire remains one of the best loved and most probingly studied of modern poets. His friend Max JACOB, a tragic figure no less richly gifted and in appearance no less of a perpetual playboy, perished in 1944 as one of the victims of the holocaust. But Jacob's most felicitous works had appeared as prose poems or as hermetic or burlesque dramas before his 40th year (1916). Critical opinion has not yet granted to him, or to the Swiss Blaise CENDRARS, the full recognition that their erratic but genuine talent deserved.

Suddenly, around 1909–13, a number of significant works appeared heralding a new literary age, as if the 20th century, after a few years' hesitation, had discovered its originality. Parallel, synchronic innovations were taking place in several sciences and social disciplines. The new physics, breaking away from rigid determinism, seemed to leave room for indeterminacy. Synthetic chemistry and biology were discovered to be far more flexible in their implications. After a 15-year lag, the theories of Sigmund Freud, and then of Carl Jung, were beginning to enter the consciousness of Western Europe. So were the new ideas in anthropology and in the sociological study of religions. In Vienna and Paris, the philosophy of language, linguistics, painting, and music were suddenly undergoing a renewal. World War I was merely to hasten, in arts as in sciences, the maturing of the innovations that had been attempted in the few years preceding 1914. Russia herself had sent to Berlin and Paris the ferments of a profound cultural renewal: the full appreciation of Fyodor Dostoyevsky, Wassily Kandinsky, Marc Chagall, the constructivists, the Russian ballet, and Igor Stravinsky, whose *Rite of Spring* seized the Parisian public with mad enthusiasm.

In French literature, the writers who heralded that literary flowering were in part men in their early forties who had had to wait 10 or 15 years before finding, or molding, their audiences and publishing their masterpieces. Such was the fate of Claudel's dramas, Péguy's longer works in prose (*L'Argent*, 1901) and in verse (*Eve*, 1914), André Gide's *La Porte étroite* (1909; Eng. tr., *Strait is the Gate*, 1924) and *Les Caves du Vatican* (1914; Eng. trs., *The*

Vatican Swindle, 1925, *Lafcadio's Adventures,* 1927), and Marcel Proust's *Du côté de chez Swann* (1913; Eng. tr., *Swann's Way,* 1922). Several of the authors who voiced the new aspirations grouped themselves in 1913, and then again after an interruption in 1919, around the *Nouvelle Revue française* and the Théâtre du Vieux-Colombier. There soon followed a galaxy of younger talents who all won their first laurels, if with a limited public, just prior to the outbreak of the 1914 war. Some of them were to die on the battlefield: ALAIN-FOURNIER, Ernest PSICHARI, Emile Clermont. Others were to be shaken to their spiritual foundations by it: the critic Jacques Rivière, Henri BARBUSSE, Duhamel, Roger Martin du Gard. Roland DORGELÈS and André MAUROIS also wrote war books, tragic or humorous, that first made them aware of their potentialities. Others among the gifted young men who started publishing before 1914 and who were to become the leaders of the first postwar literary generation were: Francis Carco, Jean Cocteau, Jean Giraudoux, Marcel Jouhandeau, Pierre-Jean Jouve, Valery Larbaud, François Mauriac, Pierre Reverdy, Romains, André SUARÈS, Jules Supervielle, and Charles Vildrac. The war years themselves added a sense of tragic urgency to their writings, accelerating the maturity of their talents, and even more so the maturity of their public.

A number of works of propaganda, political speculation, and history, attempting to explain the most gruesome war yet fought by Europeans, appeared between 1914 and 1918. But the monstrousness of the cataclysm seemed to defy intellectual lucidity and to prevent impartiality. As had been the case during the Napoleonic era, those who might have composed essays and elaborate fictional works of lasting interest had either disappeared in the slaughter or been engrossed by their tasks as soldiers, industrialists, and administrators. The war literature consisted chiefly of diaries and records of the hellish, or simple unendurably boring, experience of the trenches; in a few cases, some authors confessed that they had not altogether disliked the thrill of danger or the revelation of social fraternity between intellectuals serving in the army and the simpler men "from the masses." Some—Apollinaire, Giraudoux, Elie FAURE, Pierre Teilhard de Chardin, Pierre DRIEU LA ROCHELLE—had even welcomed the patriotic exaltation and whatever element of sport persisted amid the barbarity of modern warfare. Still others stressed the sheer absurdity of the massacre and dreamt of a drastic revolution from the Left that would put an end to it once and for all. On the whole, however, few of the fictional works composed during World War I by those who waged it have retained their grip upon our imagination.

The generation that had fought, or lived through, World War I threw itself into the enjoyment of life in the gleeful realization that at least some of them had survived the mass slaughter. This generation felt itself estranged from its elders, who had not known how to prevent the senseless destruction of European youth. It cherished speed, intense living, and professed the cult of the instant. All faith in absolutes had been shattered. That age group resumed the advocacy of modernity and the ambition to express simultaneity through fiction, which had already been the professed aim of the Italian futurists (*see* ITALIAN LITERATURE). These authors prided themselves on exploiting techniques such as interior monologue, the probing into the subconscious, even automatic writing. It became the fashion to compare oneself implicitly to Hamlet, to condone the display of one's hesitations and to describe one's new "mal du siècle" with some complacency. For several years the adolescent became the character favored by such novelists and playwrights as Gide,

Mauriac, Martin du Gard, and Julien GREEN. The adolescent hero was of an uncertain age, nostalgic for the imaginary purity of childhood, yet eager to appear brutal and cynical, sacrificed by his callous elders and hunted by a selfish society that blocked his way to success.

Literary criticism and the multifaceted essay discussing literature, art, ethics, and politics occupied much room in the many lively monthlies and weeklies of the years 1919–30, but few of the reviewers and only five or six of the more reflective critics have continued to be significant for those who read them after 50 years. Through the sheer force of their personality and their vibrant prose, a few essayists—Faure, Suarès, Henri FOCILLON—count among the finest writers of their age, even when they wrote so much as to be uneven and often repetitious. In the field of letters, those who may be singled out as preeminent for their keenness of intellect, their perceptiveness of the new, and their power of synthesis were Jacques RIVIÈRE, who steered the new directions of the *Nouvelle Revue française* between 1919 and his premature death in 1925; Charles DU BOS, generously open to literatures other than French, but often more concerned with moral and spiritual values than with literary ones; Benjamin CRÉMIEUX, a keen and eclectic mind, attentive to the new; Léon Pierre-Quint, one of the very first rightly to appraise Gide, Proust, and Lautréamont; and Albert THIBAUDET, a ubiquitous, garrulous writer who at times was also refreshingly earthy and sane. The criticism written by the creators themselves, on the other hand, that which ultimately outlives a merely ephemeral success, was in those years that of Gide and Valéry, more rarely that of Proust and Claudel.

Never had the literary journals been so numerous and so brilliant. Everywhere, even in the old, staid bimonthlies like the *Revue des deux mondes* and the *Revue de Paris,* editors were competing for new talent, anxious to discover the intentions of the younger generation. The novel, in its variegated forms, proliferated: the personal introspective novel, the *roman fleuve,* and the saga novel aiming at portraying a whole society; the adventure novel, whose rebirth Rivière had announced in a 1913 essay; and the exotic novel, as writers once again delighted in exploring the countries of Asia and of the New World. The novel boldly stepped in where tragedy and the epic had once reigned, claiming rightfully to succeed them, thanks to a technique made richer and more supple by the example of the Russians.

The verdict of half a century has confirmed the towering position that was assigned, hesitatingly at first, to Marcel PROUST by Rivière, Du Bos, Crémieux, and several non-French critics. He is today most admired for what was at first received with doubts and suspicions: his prose style, his comic spirit, the scope and the structure of his work, his ability to impart life to exceptional and unheroic characters. The other two novelists of his generation, André GIDE and COLETTE, fell far short of his supreme eminence. Gide was a superb master of prose, a man of letters of catholic tastes, the trusted counselor of many a young talent and an expert at coquettishly confessional literature. His truly Goethean curiosity and sympathy and the purity of his art were, however, ill suited to the novel. His short novels, which he called *récits,* remain more moving than his overly ambitious and excessively self-conscious *Faux-Monnayeurs* (1926). Gide's creative gifts seemed to have deserted him in the last 20 years of his life. He died in 1951, four years before Claudel and three years before Colette, the other survivors of the great generation born around 1870. Colette, often singled out as the one woman writer of the 20th century to have won universal fame, gave exquisite expression to the world of form, color, and keen sensations. She was, however, more deft at recreating the delicacy of cats and dogs, or the loveliness of plants and fruits, than at rendering the complexity of human beings. Even her eroticism lacked variety and depth. She is likely to be granted only a modest niche in the ruthless ranking that posterity eventually establishes.

It is probable that, exactly as in every other age, only four or five novelists (if that many) and hardly any more poets of the 1920s will continue to be read by any but the specialists. François MAURIAC is likely to remain among those chosen few. He would not experiment with fictional form, vary his own technique, or extend the scope of his observation, but he imparted an original atmosphere to his tales of sin and remorse; he conveyed to his readers the full intensity of their tragic conflicts and, like Proust, he retained the saving grace of poetry throughout his exploration of greed and vice. Roger MARTIN DU GARD, the other Nobel Prize winner (along with Mauriac) among these French novelists, completed only in 1940 his long chronicle of French families begun in 1922, Les Thibault. He appears to us today as the reviver of a deeply modest, compassionate realism, made gripping by the restrained anguish of the author and by his melancholy concern for the modern Europeans, carried away by their urge to self-destruction. Other French authors then tried to emulate the long, meandering, or comprehensive novel that they admired in their Russian or British predecessors: they hoped to go down to posterity more securely if they rode upon the heavy train of 5, 10, or even 25 volumes, loosely linked and embracing either simultaneously all the layers of society or diachronically the continuous evolution of one family. Duhamel scored an undeniable, if not a brilliant and perdurable success with his Salavin series (1920–32; Eng. tr., Salavin, 1936), but he failed to repeat it with a similar but much weaker 10-volume chronicle of the Pasquier family. In a trilogy entitled Psyché (1922–29; Eng. tr., The Body's Rapture, 1933), Romains blended in a heavy-handed manner a cold eroticism and even more frigid psychological developments. This was a prelude to the more ambitious Les Hommes de bonne volonté (see below). René Béhaine (1880–1966), who had been among the first moderns to attempt a saga of contemporary France, was not equal to his vast ambition. As traditional ethics resting upon the family continued their steady decline, novelists seemed to be intent upon fondly conjuring up provincial ancestors, fighting to preserve the integrity of some family estate in a bygone era.

Not a few novelists were in truth storytellers, better qualified to compose artfully written, intelligent vignettes than full-length novels. One of those genteel essayists— urbane, pleasantly ironical, ever anxious not to jolt his public too vigorously—was André Maurois: his best novelistic attempts, Climats (1928; Eng. tr., Atmosphere of Love, 1929) and Le Cercle de famille (1932; Eng. tr., The Family Circle, 1932) are sensitive and expertly told, but they pale beside the greater charm of the biographies that he was to compose later. Valery LARBAUD was, like Maurois, a man of the world, a cosmopolitan amateur, and the introducer of several foreign authors into France. The three nouvelles that make up his best known book, Amants, heureux amants (1923; Lovers, Happy Lovers) are discreet, evocative pieces, among the most felicitous volumes for "the second shelf" of a fastidious amateur's library, as he himself put it. In these works, the device of the interior monologue is subtly put to use by the admirer and translator of James Joyce's Ulysses.

A thundering literary debut, in 1922–23, was that of Paul MORAND, a dashing young diplomat with a brilliant style, a cosmopolitan background, and a gift of incisive satire. Morand never recovered the striking success of those insolent collections of short stories entitled Ouvert la nuit (1922; Eng. tr., Open All Night, 1923) and Fermé la nuit (1923; Eng. tr., Closed All Night, 1924). He may have been prevented from the concentration and the solitude required, as Proust liked to repeat, for a creator's maturation, by his fondness for speed, for clever effect, and for roaming around the planet. Morand's colleague in the foreign service, Jean Giraudoux, indulged with more nonchalance his taste for preciosity and for ornamental and playful surprise. Giraudoux's novels seem to take place in an unreal world from which the brutality of the flesh, the contingencies of real life, sin, remorse, and even anxiety are banished. The first two, Suzanne et le Pacifique (1921; Eng. tr., Suzanne and the Pacific, 1923) and Siegfried et le Limousin (1922), have not totally lost their frail, ironic gracefulness. Later, the charm wore off and the mannerism yielded to facility. A younger man, Marcel ARLAND, who had been among the first to speak in the name of postwar youth, wrote critical essays and tender sketches of simple, rustic people, but his long novel, L'Ordre (1929), lacked imaginative force and intensity. More hope had been set on Raymond RADIGUET, a precocious young man with a singular knack for the thin, sharp psychological novel in a dry vein, reminiscent of Mme de la Fayette (1634–93) and of Benjamin Constant (1767–1830); his premature death at the age of 20, in 1923, did not allow his success with Le Diable au corps (1923) to be repeated.

Only a very few French authors summon up the courage to resist the lure of the capital, its honors, its salons, and its journalists, and resign themselves to residing in the provinces or abroad. Henri Pourrat (1887–), however, remained faithful to his native Auvergne, whose ancient tales he collected; sedulously avoiding stressing the picturesque and what the French derisively call "le folklore," he clung to racy humor and to a sane and robust truth. Joseph Malègue (1875–1940), who also hailed from Auvergne, told with stark simplicity the story of an austere childhood in Pierres noires (1958; Black Stones), after having presented, in Augustin ou le maître est là (1933; Augustine or the Master Is There), one of the most dramatic spiritual conflicts treated in a modern French novel. Maurois's brother-in-law, Jean-Richard BLOCH, enjoyed a striking success with a novel, . . . Et compagnie (1918; Eng. tr., ". . . & Co.," 1930), and several plays, but he later became too committed to the struggle against fascism inside and outside France to continue devoting his energies to literature. To the end, he spurned any compromise with bourgeois and academic values and spent much time in the USSR. The great Swiss novelist Charles-Ferdinand RAMUZ also refused, unlike some of his compatriots, to be fascinated by Paris and by the academic polish of the language written in the capital. His best novels appeared in the mid-1920s: Joie dans le ciel (1925) and La Grande Peur dans la montagne (1926; Eng. tr., Terror on the Mountain, 1967). They have few, if any, equals in the modern Swiss literature written in French.

The 10 years that followed World War I count among the most active in the history of the French stage. Much credit should go to the impulse given in 1913, and again in 1920, by the Théâtre du Vieux-Colombier of Jacques COPEAU. The earlier courageous attempts of André ANTOINE, Aurélien Lugné-Poe, and Firmin GÉMIER were resumed by him and pursued with more ardent faith and a keener artistic touch. Innovations borrowed from talented foreign producers (Konstantin Stanislavsky, Gordon Craig, Vsevolod Meyerhold, Max Reinhardt) were introduced. To technical improvements in the staging, interpreting, and acting of plays, Copeau added an austere insistence upon sincerity, scrupulously patient workmanship, disinterested cooperation of all participants, and art. He avoided the two common pitfalls of vanguard theaters: intellectual snobbery and excessive strangeness. Suggestion, rather than realistic illusion, became the motto of his dramatic performances. They aimed at enhancing the poetical value of the text. The pioneering Vieux-Colombier had to close its doors after five years, harassed by costs, by the loss of successful actors, and by the dearth of new plays of serious quality. Yet for the next 20 years, serious French theaters were to bear the mark of Copeau's teaching. France could then boast of a number of first-rate producer-actors—Charles DULLIN, Louis JOUVET, Georges PITOËFF—who challenged the once all-powerful "theater of the Boulevards." The most substantial result of that dramatic revival was a reconciliation between the stage and literature, something that would have been unthinkable throughout most of the 19th century. But it proved difficult to draw to the stage, and to maintain there, playwrights who might fulfill the requirements of the theater: entertainment and action, as well as dramatic force clad in a literary style likely to survive. Claudel, Romains (*Dr. Knock* was first acted in 1923), and Giraudoux, whose *Siegfried* and *Amphitryon 38* scored a triumph in 1928 and 1929, are outstanding exceptions. Vieux-Colombier audiences were not gripped by plays like Gide's *Saül* or those of Martin du Gard and of Gide's one-time friend, Henri GHÉON, or even by Copeau's own play, *La Maison natale* (1923; The Birthplace), and his adaptations of Lev TOLSTOY and of Fyodor DOSTOYEVSKY.

In other theaters, those directed by Gaston BATY, Dullin, Jouvet, and Pitoëff, playwrights were encouraged to compete with other literary forms in deriving inspiration from the new psychology and from recent poetical moods. Henri-René LENORMAND utilized with obstinacy the revelations of a still primitive psychoanalysis, but also with humorless and often heavy-handed didacticism. Paul Raynal, while addicted to declamatory displays of virtuosity, was the author of *Le Maître de son cœur* (1920), a restrained and forceful drama enacted between love and honor, or sexual attraction and the loyalty to male friendship. Stève PASSEUR and, even more, Simon Gantillon (in *Maya* [1924; Eng. tr., 1930]) united a skillful dramatic structure and a sense of mystery, imparting fleshy concreteness to their symbols without indulging in excessive artificiality. Jean-Victor PELLERIN toyed more dangerously with symbols in his pageant-play *Têtes de rechange* (1926; Spare Heads). The most original note in the drama of that decade was struck by those who, weary with verbosity and equally tired of coarseness and insipid risqué allusions, attempted to blend humor and poetry, tempering sentiment with discreet mockery. A "school" of dramatists came to advocate, along with Jean-Jacques BERNARD, the "theater of silence," almost going back to some of the effects once aimed at by Maurice MAETERLINCK, but in a much simpler, more modern setting. In 1920, Charles VILDRAC held the stage longer than anyone until then with *Le Paquebot Tenacity* (Eng. tr., The Steamship Tenacity, 1921), a play in which nothing happens and very little is said. The greatest success, due in part to the superb acting of a newcomer from Switzerland, Michel Simon, was *Jean de la lune* (John of the Moon) by Marcel ACHARD, produced in 1929 at the Comédie des Champs-Elysées. This playwright subsequently won honors and popular acclaim, but he also forsook his early artistic ambitions and became a mere entertainer.

Poetry, meanwhile, had begun to assimilate the best of the heritage of symbolism while eschewing its mannerism. Claudel was turning away from poetry proper and composing more and more essays in prose (on such topics as Richard Wagner, Japan, religious themes, and art). The brightest star in the poetic firmament, although he had gone almost unnoticed with *La Jeune Parque* (1917; The Young Parca), was Paul VALÉRY, whose slender but invaluable volume *Charmes* appeared in 1922. His profound, often obscure essays had already established him as an illuminating dialectician and an unequalled master of prose. In his concise, melodious, often rarefied verse, he seemed to rival Racine and La Fontaine in pure and fluid music, and Mallarmé in deliberate and elliptic condensation and even in some of his mannerisms. Those poems united with miraculous felicitousness the pangs of the intellect and the sensuous thrills of the flesh; only the heart at times remained unmoved or was silenced by the too lucid consciousness of the self. The images were fused into the stanza or in the poetical speeches of Narcissus, of the Parque, of the serpent tempting Eve, or of the poet craving for meticulously calculated art. Valéry's poetry did not lend itself to being imitated. The poet's theories, which claimed to banish inspiration and all promptings of the subconscious from artistic creation, misled imitators who actually lacked his hidden passion, sensuousness, and depth. Although Valéry himself ceaselessly claimed to be the foe of literature and of critical and philosophical speculation, and to despise "sincere" and indiscreet revelations, he sedulously preserved for posterity his epigrams and aphorisms. SAINT-JOHN PERSE was, among Valéry's slightly younger contemporaries, the only one who might be set up as his equal. His *Anabase* (1924; Eng. tr., *Anabasis,* 1930) first brought him renown beyond a small circle. After he came to live in America in 1940, Perse devoted himself entirely to poetry. His haughty, sumptuous poems unroll with stateliness; occasionally, their elaborate strangeness and their wealth of precious ornaments keep the reader at a distance, dazzled by such hieratic majesty. The Lithuanian Oscar-Vladislas MILOSZ, a lonely mystic and an aristocrat ever aware of his mission as a magus, never pierced through the wall that kept all but a few admirers from meeting him half way. His best poetry appeared under the appropriately forbidding titles of *Ars magna* (1924) and *Les Arcanes* (1926). Léon-Paul FARGUE is a more intimate poet, closer to the daily life of Paris and to the music of popular songs. Jean Cocteau gathered collections of his verse between 1924 and 1927, before he scored his stage and screen triumphs. Had he cared, his gift for effects of surprise and for the coining of fanciful images, for experimenting with words and ideas somewhat as the cubists had treated painting, might have placed him among the outstanding poets of his generation. Readers, however, were more easily drawn to Jules SUPERVIELLE, his elder by a few years, a poet less revolutionary, less paradoxical, more deeply human. Friendship, simple love, family affections, childhood memories, and cosmic visions of oceans and of planets gravitating through the poet's dream are among Supervielle's themes. Jouve, after being inspired by the horror of war and by human passion, found new strains in psychoanalytic explorations and in religious mysticism; he and his slightly younger contemporary Pierre REVERDY count among the very few modern French poets in whom one hears echoes of William Blake, Friedrich Hölderlin, or Baudelaire. Reverdy, who died in 1960, is likely to be appreciated more as years go by.

The group that, after World War I, experimented with the wildest iconoclastic fury, questioning not only its elders but the very legitimacy of literature, was that of the surrealists. Arguments will long persist over the question of the debt that surrealism owed, and seldom openly acknowledged, to its predecessor, dadaism. The members of the two groups, one born in 1916, the other between 1919 and 1924, underlined their points of difference (on the whole minor) in order to assert their originality. Surrealism never rallied more than a handful of men, and few of them remained orthodox surrealists very long. Yet they can lay claim to having constituted the marching wing of French literature between 1924 and 1930, and even later. That very vocal group resorted lavishly to publicity stunts and to exhibitionism, to dogmatic assertions that often nonchalantly contradicted each other, and to untenable psychophysiological or pseudomystical theories. It was fiercely logical even in its madness or in its challenge to reason, scornful of traditional moral and aesthetic conventions while endeavoring to formulate a new morality resting upon the unfettering of desire. Dada had been more international: in sculpture, collages, even in poetry, some of its most admired members had come from Alsace, Germany, or even Romania, the country of its founder, Tristan TZARA, who is today acknowledged as an important innovator in poetry. Georges RIBEMONT-DESSAIGNES was once a bold pioneer, remaining aloof from all coteries. Jacques Vaché (1895–1919) impressed his friend André BRETON with his eccentric personality, but he remains an almost mythical figure since he did not condescend to write anything. His nihilism and his rejection of modern culture were apparently total. For Vaché, suicide was the logical solution, as it was for other surrealists: Jacques Rigaut, René CREVEL, Raymond ROUSSEL. Surrealism took shape officially in 1924 under the guidance and stern rule of Breton, assisted in his early pronouncements by Philippe SOUPAULT, Louis ARAGON, Paul ELUARD and, for a brief while, Robert DESNOS. The most faithful ally of Breton remained Benjamin PÉRET, an authentic and at times a great writer. René CHAR, like many other poets of talent and not a few painters, also began his career under the aegis of the surrealist group. The essentials of the surrealist doctrine as formulated by Breton, the leader of the movement, are largely contained in the two manifestos of 1924 and 1930 and a third profession of faith delivered in 1942 as a lecture at Yale University. But the vicissitudes of politics, the acceptance of communism by a few members of the group, the revulsion against Stalinism in others, the restlessness of erstwhile surrealist artists (Salvador Dali, Joan Miró, Max Ernst, André Masson, and others) under the curbs imposed upon their independence, made the evolution of surrealism between 1924 and 1950 a checkered and confused story. The movement soon became international in character, spreading especially to Spain, Germany, New York, and to London, where it encountered much more resistance. Everywhere it served to stimulate the imagination of the young.

In its negative aspect, surrealism was an all-embracing revolt against the whole legacy of the past—aesthetic, moral, psychological, even political and social. Hence its tone of provoking audacity, assisted somewhat by Freud's theories, in doing away with the moral ban on subconscious and erotic promptings; hence also its subsequent and often stormy association with Marxist and Trotskyite doctrines. Soon, however, it became clear that surrealism had gone beyond its negative stage and had grown into a constructive attempt to annex new provinces to psychology and literature. The main achievements of the surrealists, occasionally disfigured by childish stunts, may be summarized as opening up the vast oneiric domain to literature; breaking the shackles of logic and releasing the forces of imagination and of desire, however irrational and humorously absurd the results might be; recovering the purity of a child's vision of the world and the illogical freshness of a spontaneous flow of images; reaching the "superreal" state in which the subjective and the objective, the ego and the universe, are merged into a higher synthesis. In spite of an excess of obstinate reasoning in its very madness and of questionable claims to scientific validity, surrealism appears, after half a century, as a romantic aspiration toward greater authenticity in literature and toward the liberation of the imagination. The manifestos and the doctrines have attracted much attention from scholars, who are fond of relating literary and artistic achievements to an underlying abstract philosophy. But the often contradictory, at times uneven, poetical work of the dadists and the surrealists is what is ultimately likely to survive. Breton is a genuine poet and, even more often perhaps, a clear and brilliant master of French prose, as in his strange novel *Nadja* (1928; Eng. tr., 1960) and in the original speculations and the artistic style of *L'Amour fou* (1937; Mad Love) and *Les Vases communicants* (1932; Communicating Vases). Eluard counts among the great poets of love in French: love to him is a pathetic struggle against solitude, an aspiration toward purity, the cosmic center of the universe. His delicate music and his fresh and graceful gift for coining images have quickly turned him into a classic. He is dangerously easy to imitate. Aragon, although apparently a more combative temperament and having become in his old days a hallowed fixture of the Communist establishment, was, in fact, more pliable than either Breton or Eluard. His successive works in verse and in prose bore witness to his perilous facility. Aragon's novel *Le Paysan de Paris* (1926; Eng. trs., *Nightwalker,* 1970, *Paris Peasant,* 1971), while it has few or none of the ingredients of the traditional novel, is an imaginative and poetical transfiguration of the city of Paris. It is as a poet that this Communist met his chief success, reaching a surprisingly wide audience when, after the defeat of France in 1940, he untiringly composed patriotic pieces accessible to common men and women, as well as sentimental love poetry lauding his wife and muse, Elsa Triolet. Robert Desnos appeared to be more brutal in *La Liberté ou l'amour!* (1927; Liberty or Love), but in *Corps et biens* (1930; With All Hands), his early verse tinged with combative humor, he demonstrated more fantasy than Aragon, more suppleness than Breton in his exploration of the marvelous. Desnos died tragically after having been sent by the Germans to a prison camp. Péret remained to the last the least histrionic of all the surrealists.

It would seem that by 1930 or 1931 the full élan of the postwar era had begun to subside. Proust's *A la recherche du temps perdu* had by then appeared in its entirety. The creative impulses of Gide, Claudel, Colette, and even Válery had been spent. The complacency with which the young men who had elected the career of literature after 1918 had analyzed their anguish seemed now too egocentric; the short era of prosperity, of faith in a permanent peace and in a security system guaranteed by the League of Nations had come to an end. The problem of misery confronted even the most aesthetically minded authors, since economic imbalance, unemployment, and bank failures had found American and European politicians powerless to act. Violent political feuds in Germany, grave self-doubts among the Austrians, and the failure of nerve among the men at the helm in France and Britain heralded a period of turmoil and anguish in which new structures would have to be established on firmer philosophical foundations. A few exceptionally clear-sighted young men first seemed to be aware of the changes needed in the world around them—André Malraux and three alumni of the Ecole Normale Supérieure: Jean PRÉVOST, bidding farewell to his youth in *Dix-huitième Année* (1929; 18th Year); Robert BRASILLACH, writing bellicose journalistic essays in which he claimed the right to speak in the name of patriotic and nationalist youth; and Jean-Paul Sartre, prophetically opposing the latter (in an interview given in 1929 to *Les Nouvelles littéraires* while he was still a philosophy student). Works that produced the impression of being startlingly new began to appear soon after 1930: Jean Giono's *Regain* (1920; Eng. tr., *Harvest,* 1939), Antoine de Saint-Exupéry's *Vol de nuit* (1931; Eng. tr., *Night Flight,* 1932), Drieu la Rochelle's *Feu follet* (1931; Eng. trs., *The Fire Within,* 1965, *Will o' the Wisp,* 1966), Louis-Ferdinand Céline's *Voyage au bout de la nuit* (1932; Eng. tr., *Journey to the End of Night,* 1934). While, in the political sphere, faith in Franco-German understanding as the foundation for a new Europe had collapsed, in literature France was the first to repudiate the literary fashions of the postwar "mad years" and to grope for new paths. As usual, the newcomers started by turning against the more superficial features of the preceding literary works: the literary inflation that had led to brief, repetitive volumes devoid of solid content; the excessive cerebrality of many postwar novels; the vogue for adolescent characters deficient in willpower and addicted to the selfish analysis of their feelings or of their inability to feel; the escapism that had inspired a plethora of travel books, of nonchalant reveries; and the subtle antics of a revived preciosity. The new period is marked by the eager interest taken by men of letters in political and social problems. Gide led the way when he became, for a brief time only, an enthusiast of the Soviet Union. Malraux, André Chamson, Louis Guilloux, even Jules Romains welcomed the 1936 Popular Front and spoke at the leftist "Maison de la Culture." A few of them traveled to the USSR without losing their faith in the Stalinist regime. Others chose to find their moorings on the Right, belonging to one or another of the para-Fascist leagues that then proliferated; they imitated the Fascists of Italy and dreamt of a friendly understanding with Hitler's Germany. Some of them were not averse to anti-Semitism. They were historians and essayists such as Pierre Gaxotte, Thierry MAULNIER, Maurice BARDÈCHE; novelists with more dialectical skill than imagination (Brasillach and, for a time Claude Roy, who subsequently shifted to a position at the far Left); or simple veterans of World War I like Céline and Drieu la Rochelle, whom the aftermath of victory had bitterly disappointed.

Not all the important books then published were political in character, but few authors could abstract themselves from the pressure of events. Those who might have cultivated philosophical speculation per se (Sartre, Beauvoir, Merleau-Ponty) or polished their poems in isolation (Char, Guillevic, Pierre SEGHERS) were brutally jolted by Munich in September 1938 and then by the French collapse of 1940. Once again, the war that had seemed inevitable for some time did not give rise to a new literature. Eluard, Malraux, Georges BERNANOS, and others, not to mention the surrealists, had been in the public eye before 1939; Sartre and even Albert Camus had by then already written their first books and mastered their technique and their style. The experience of the defeat and of the Resistance gave depth to their writings, enhancing their sense of tragic urgency, but they continued to pursue the path that they had already trodden. The least ambiguous result of World War II was to bring the public into unison with a serious literature, which it might otherwise have resisted for another decade.

In the novel, the outstanding representatives of that generation that held the field from 1930 on included men already in their mid-forties who either had been slow in displaying their full powers (such as Bernanos) or had decided that middle age should be the time for them to undertake a magnum opus reflecting and interpreting all walks of life. In the latter group stood Jules Romains, notable for the sheer weight of his works, their intellectual lucidity, and their skillful although artificial composition. He had been the most determined architect of an ambitious saga-structure. The early volumes of his *Hommes de bonne volonté,* begun in 1933 and appearing at the rate of two or four a year after that date, were received with enthusiasm. Soon, however, the public's excitement flagged as the author's inspiration appeared to run dry. He pursued his self-appointed task laboriously, synthetically combining doses of realism, mystery, sex, political reflection, and visits to England or the USSR by his characters; no inner compulsion was felt on the part of the writer, and the style lacked vividness. Those 20-odd volumes may in the long run be read chiefly as historical documents and for the portrait of French society that they offer. Marcel JOUHANDEAU entertained a few Parisian circles with his acid humor and his exhibitionism in *Chaminadour* (1934) and *Chroniques maritales* (1938), but he hardly won any readers outside his native land. Bernanos was, on the contrary, an intensely passionate novelist and the visionary creator of a world. He broke into the Paris literary circles in 1926 with *Sous le soleil de Satan* (Eng. tr., *Under the Star of Satan,* 1940), a gloomy story of satanism and mysticism that was at once hailed as a masterpiece. His *Journal d'un curé de campagne* (1936; Eng. tr., *Diary of a Country Priest,* 1937), however, had greater concentration and more potent human emotion. From then on, Bernanos was aligned by able critics with the three or four Western European novelists of this age who were not unworthy of Dostoyevsky. *Monsieur Ouine* (1943; Eng. tr., *The Open Mind,* 1945) is a more contradictory work, mixing melodrama, satire (directed notably at Gide), polemics, and intense religious ardor in a complex but masterly fashion. After 1936, Bernanos's self-consuming energy was spent on works of political indignation and moral vituperation as well as some works of fiction.

Among the other significant novelists of that era, Louis-Ferdinand CÉLINE stands out as the most controversial but also, in his brutality, the most powerful. He is at the opposite pole from such introspective, mundane predecessors as Proust and Gide. The truculent force of Céline's writing irrupted into the literature of France, often viewed as the most orderly and the most classical in Europe. His power over language and his use of an artificial style, which he presented as that of the popular classes, were haunting, despite all their mannerisms. The *Voyage au bout de la nuit* (1932) and *Mort à crédit* (1936; Eng. tr., *Death on the Installment Plan,* 1938) are likely to outlast his later novels, in which he harped upon the same themes of universal hatred (thinly covering up a sentimental eagerness to be loved) and wearily used the same gross devices. André MALRAUX's career as a novelist did not extend beyond World War II: its milestones were *La Condition humaine* (1933; Eng. trs., *Man's Fate, Storm in Shanghai,* 1934) and *L'Espoir* (1937; Eng. tr., *Man's Hope,* 1938). Composed in a bold, disconnected technique reminiscent of the cinema, scornful of the traditional reader's demands for clarity, for continuity of interest, and for a few representative characters, his complex plots, taken from lived recent history, reach epic greatness. His heroes, obsessed by their tragic solitude and the constricting conditions meted out to man's fate, desparately yearn for a cause for which to live and die. A few scenes, laden with restrained emotion, vibrating with fraternity and a sense of spiritual communion with one's fellow-beings, count among the most unforgettable in modern fiction. All the while, Malraux also lived the life of a man of action and, after earning a hero's record during World War II, he began a new career as politician, autobiographer, and above all, as a writer on art.

Those who, in the 1930s, were placed on the same level as those two giants now fail to be read with the same admiration. Jean GIONO, self-educated, born and raised in poverty in Upper Provence, early recaptured the spirit and the imaginative style of the Greek classics. He revealed his full stature in his shorter *récits, Un de Baumugnes* (1929; Eng. tr., *Lovers are Never Losers,* 1931), and in a sensuous evocation of his childhood, *Jean le bleu* (1932; Eng. tr., *Blue Boy,* 1946, 1949). He then attempted to scale epic heights, devising more ambitious plots, instilling symbolic meanings and ethical and social teachings into his fictions. His best novels are *Le Chant du monde* (1934) and *Que ma joie demeure* (1935; Eng. tr., *Joy of Man's Discovering,* 1940)—sprawling, diffuse works, showing simple people on Provençal farms living in communion with the earth and the seasons. The descriptions count among the richest and the most sensuously haunting in literature. In subsequent works, Giono, intoxicated by the admiration of those who had hailed him as a prophet and not simply as an artist, marred his tales through his eagerness to deliver ideological sermons. After 1945, he altered his manner altogether, forsook messages, and contented himself with his exceptional gifts as a teller of tales. Henry de MONTHERLANT, slightly younger than Giono, began his literary career earlier, dazzling his age group with his magnificent style and a cynical male insolence that alternated with sincere yearning for heroism and even for a sort of pagan mysticism. He, too, was anxious to impart to his readers his nihilistic outlook on life, his scorn for average human beings, his ethics of self-denial and of stoic pessimism. Several of his volumes of essays, *Service inutile* (1935; Useless Service) in particular, are the work of a superb and haughty moralist. He cannot be called primarily a novelist: his most condensed fictional attempt, *Les Célibataires* (1934; Eng. tr., *The Bachelors,* 1935, 1936, 1960), failed to do justice to his talent, and there are only occasional moments of brilliant satire and of tenderness in the series of sketches entitled *Les Jeunes Filles* (1935–39; Eng. tr., 1937–40). After World War II, the dramatic form served him better. Antoine de SAINT-EXUPÉRY was likewise more gifted as a moralist and as a fastidious craftsman than as a novelist. Like Malraux, he was primarily a man of action; his most pregnant reflections occurred, as they often do in active natures, not when he meditated at a desk in silence but when he was piloting a plane, facing perils. During his lifetime, he was overrated as a thinker, which he hardly was, and as an epic moralist. Yet Saint-Exupéry provided aviation with its letters of nobility in literature, and he succeeded where most French writers have failed: in composing a children's book that delighted children and adults, *Le Petit Prince* (1943; Eng. tr., *The Little Prince,* 1943).

At least some of the secondary writers of the period must also be mentioned. André CHAMSON, who stood close to Malraux in the liberal fights against the threat of fascism in the 1930s and then served with him in the Resistance, promised for a time to be one of the significant novelists of his generation. Chamson's arresting, well-knit works include *Le Crime des justes* (1928; The Crime of the Just, 1930), a portrait of the stern Huguenots of the Cévennes among whom the author lived as a child; *L'Année des vaincus* (1934; Eng. tr., *Barren Harvest,* 1935) and *La Galère* (1939; The Galley), novels with a melancholy political background, reflecting the wreckage of hopes for peace; and *Le Puits des miracles* (1945; Miracle Well), a vivid picture of life in a southern town during the German occupation. But these novels lack the intensity, the technical originality, and the brilliant style that might have assured them a truly eminent place. In that same decade preceding World War II, several novelists, impatient with the bourgeois or effete character of much literature and eager not to exclude the working classes from the benefits of culture, attempted to write about industrial workers, the poor, and the common soldiers who had been the martyrs of trench warfare. Two or three of them—Léon Lemonnier (1890-), André Thérive, and Henri Poulaille—resorted to the familiar device of founding a "school," calling their movement populism. These writers are half-forgotten, and indeed, beside the power of Céline, their well-documented proletarian stories look pale. Eugène DABIT scored some success with *Hôtel du Nord* (1929; Eng. tr., 1931), a picture of a dreary group of humble people huddled together in a hotel in the quarter of Paris where Zola had set *L'Assommoir* (1877). A much stronger work, with a talent for caricature and the boldness of bitter exaggeration that fiction seems to require if it is to strike us as true, is Louis GUILLOUX's *Sang noir* (1935; Eng. tr., *Bitter Victory,* 1936). The author did not duplicate that happy stroke when he followed it with a cumbersome and dreary volume, *Jeu de patience* (Jigsaw Puzzle) in 1949.

Despite the attempts of Van der Meersch, Pierre HAMP, Paul Nizan, Aragon, and Andre Stil to draw the so-called working classes to books and to depictions of their daily struggles, proletarian literature remains an underprivileged province of fiction, in France as elsewhere. The more facile and gentler themes of escape into a world of sentimental adventure and of idealization of reality apparently offer a more vivid appeal to the reading public, still drawn mostly from the middle classes. Hence the moderate success of André DHÔTEL, a novelist of limited talent but gifted with a poetic vision of life. Dhôtel was a secondary-school teacher, as was a man of vaster gifts and greater emotional force, Paul Gadenne (1907-56), who began attracting interest with *Siloé* in 1941. Jean Prévost attempted populist fiction, and, like many academics, rebelled against the teaching profession and against the establishment, but his education had developed in him the critical and evaluative skills. He turned into a vigorous critic and essayist. Prévost wrote a valuable but rather dry novel on a group or generation, in a sharp Stendhalian style, *La Chasse du matin* (1937; The Morning Hunt). Two other graduates of the Ecole Normale also attempted collective novels depicting groups of smart young intellectuals in the Latin Quarter. The protagonists of Paul NIZAN's *La Conspiration* (1938; The Conspiracy) and René ETIEMBLE's *Peaux de couleuvre* (1948; Snake Skins) are philanderers, playing at appearing cynics and scornful of their teachers, while waiting to replace them and to become, in turn, the watchdogs of a newer official philosophy and a refurbished classicism. Nizan, who, like Prévost, was killed in World War II, had satirized his Sorbonne professors in his first novel, *Les Chiens de garde* (1932; Eng. tr., *Watchdogs,* 1972). The one among their elders whom Prévost and Etiemble revered was Jean PAULHAN. Many others were fascinated by his personality, his dilettantist kindliness, and his sharp insight, but posterity is not likely to offer him the same deference. As in the case of Alain, those who have not known Paulhan apparently cannot do him full justice from his published works alone. Such may also be the case with a younger writer, Michel LEIRIS. He is the master of a terse, stripped prose, an ingenious essayist and a tortured mind; he may survive chiefly as the author of one of the most incisive and least mendacious of autobiographies, a masterpiece of the genre, *L'Age d'homme* (1939; Eng. tr., *Manhood*, 1963).

In the years 1930–45 and since, the most widely read novelists were men (some of whom eventually won a seat in the august Académie Française) who should perhaps not be eliminated altogether from literature just because readers have flocked to them in large numbers. Claude Farrère was one of those men with a wide audience. Although he never rose above mediocrity, he was even preferred to Claudel by the Academicians. Farrère later discredited himself, however, by his attitude during World War II. Russian-born Henri TROYAT is a more gifted storyteller and a fertile inventor of plots and characters. His several saga-novels on Russian or French life have brought pleasure to many without requiring undue mental strain. So have the vivid historical novels of Zoé Oldenbourg (1916–), also Russian born. Joseph KESSEL, of Russian-Jewish extraction, was a pioneer of the literature of aviation and a novelist who reached a wide public without ever debasing his pen or yielding to facility. Maurice Druon (1918–), more prolific and more conventional, is also a portrayer of the shallow lives of the upper classes; he lays no claim to literary immortality. Francis CARCO was an even more gifted writer, with a delicate poetical gift; he raised stories of pimps, venal loves, and the underworld to an honorable level. The most gifted and prolific of those novelists, the one whom Gide and other highbrow authors have unashamedly envied while finding him deficient in ideas and in art, is Georges SIMENON. He is uneven, yet a few of his novels evince such a skillful gift for the suggestion of atmosphere and offer such a vivid picture of the lower middle classes in France and elsewhere that they cannot be dismissed altogether as commercial literature. A few of his stories may well outlive the more pretentious and too self-conscious novels of 1965–75 that are accessible only to the unhappy, and gloomy, few.

The remarkable feature of the French theater in the 15 years between the 1929–30 world depression and France's emergence from humiliation in 1945 is that the renewal of directing, staging, and performing due to Jacques Copeau's fervent followers (Jouvet, Baty, Dullin, Jean-Louis BARRAULT) drew to the stage novelists and thinkers who, in earlier times, would probably have kept away from the theater altogether. A few of those who had brought a fresh note of fantasy and poetry into the theater in the 1920s did not resist the temptation of popular success. One of these, Marcel Achard, scored his most lasting hit with *Patate* (1957), a mediocre comedy in which any claim to remain within the literary fold was relinquished by this Academician. Marcel PAGNOL, whose inspiration was more authentic and whose understanding of comedy as keen as any Frenchman's since Pierre-Augustin Beaumarchais (1732–99), triumphed with the general public in *Topaze* (1928; Eng. tr., 1930), then with *Marius* (1929; Eng. tr., 1957) and *Fanny* (1932). He ranks among the few modern playwrights who have been fortunate, or unfortunate, enough to create a type. Armand SALACROU, who made a fortune in pharmaceutical publicity but remained sentimentally attached to those who fail in life (as, he hints, God has failed and most great men also), satirized the complacency of the middle class and sided with the victims of injustice in serious comedies set in a realistic context, such as *L'Inconnue d'Arras* (1935; The Unknown Woman of Arras) and *La Terre est ronde* (1938). He may continue to be considered among the best dramatists of the prewar decade, ingeniously uniting,

through his great technical skill, literary ambitions and an appeal to the curiosity of average audiences. Jean ANOUILH will find it harder, as years go on, to withstand the lure of success and the temptation to repeat himself, stressing the cruder features of his onslaught against organized society and human selfishness and hypocrisy. Overproduction has become his privilege, or his sin, as it had for Eugène Scribe (1791–1861) before him. Indeed, Anouilh became overweeningly confident in his extremely skillful theatrical craft. His most touching pleas for the purity of the young and for the beauty of dreamy, disinterested love were best dramatized in his earlier plays: *Le Voyageur sans bagage* (1937; Eng. tr., *Traveller without Luggage*, 1959), *Le Bal des voleurs* (1938; Eng. tr., *Thieves' Carnival*, 1952), *Eurydice* (1942; Eng. tr., 1948), and *Antigone* (1942; Eng. tr., 1946), his controversial hit of the war years, which has survived as a minor classic.

That same era of ominous expectation and of France's sorrow and tragic pity, 1930–45, was also signaled by a renaissance of tragedy. Jean COCTEAU had been the insolent, extraordinarily intelligent playboy of the stage as early as the period of the Russian ballets, and he long enjoyed acting the part that Sergey Diaghilev and Pablo Picasso expected him to play: a fertile and occasionally profound master of surprise. His early *Orphée* (1926; Eng. tr., 1933) was less hauntingly poetic and disturbing than the film that he later directed on the same theme—a favorite one with him—the obsession of death. His ironical and incisive variation on the Oedipus theme, *La Machine infernale* (1934; Eng. tr., *The Infernal Machine*, 1936) and his tragicomedy in a modern setting, *Les Parents terribles* (1938), are likely to outlive perhaps even his films, certainly most of his novels.

The adjective "tragic" is bound to recur often in any account of the theater in those years during which authors, with even more sensitivity to the portents of the future than powerless politicians, intuited that an implacable fatality was crushing them and that men of heroic stature were urgently needed if the direst catastrophes were to be averted. Jean GIRAUDOUX recaptured tragic emotion, blending it in his plays with irony, wit, and dazzling sophistry. His works are uneven, some probably too far-fetched and too easily enraptured with the brilliance of their own language. The word—"Sire le Mot"—is enthroned in his theater, as it was (with more genius and less preciosity) in Shakespeare and in Racine. Giraudoux's characters are highly intelligent people who delight in delivering tirades and sowing subtle allusions. Such a typically French, or "Latin," theater does not translate to advantage into other languages. Yet Giraudoux's best achievements—*Judith* (1931; Eng. tr., 1963), *La Guerre de Troie n'aura pas lieu* (1935; Eng. tr., *Tiger at the Gates*, 1955), and *Electre* (1937; Eng. tr., *Electra*, 1957)—stand a chance of surviving as literature. The posthumous *Folle de Chaillot* (1945; Eng. tr., *The Madwoman of Chaillot*, 1949), most successful with the foreign audiences, was far from being the best. Henry de Montherlant was an even more "literary" playwright, stern and haughtily geometric in the ethical debates in which his characters fondly indulge. *La Reine morte* (1942; Eng. tr., *Queen after Death*, 1951) is probably the least inhuman of his dramas. The author's quest for a personal ethics, founded upon refusal to compromise with what is vulgar and base, as well as his monumental pride and inflexible individualism could not well win over a wide public in modern democracies. During the war years, Jean-Paul SARTRE, with a much greater dramatic talent, far less egocentricity, more human compassion, and a consistent philosophy of his own, had two or three tragedies staged, works that remain milestones in the modern French theater. *Les Mouches* (1943; Eng. tr., *The Flies*, 1948) is marred by too insistent and didactic a message, pinned upon the ancient theme of Electra and Orestes, the latter intent upon saving men through instilling into them a will to revolt against the gods in the name of freedom. *Huis clos* (1944; Eng. tr., *No Exit*, 1948), more condensed, more profound and subtle in its existentialist implications, is one of the masterpieces of the modern stage, as is, in spite of too violent a string of events emphasizing an abstract theoretical situation, *Morts sans sépulture* (1946; The Unburied Dead). The Belgian Michel de GHELDERODE won an audience in France, and subsequently outside the French-speaking world, only in the 1950s and 1960s. His best plays, strange, dark, almost medieval in their obsession with the themes of Faust and the Devil, were, however, composed in the years preceding World War II. These include *Pantagleize* (1929, pub. 1934; Eng. tr., 1957), *Fastes d'enfer* (1929, pub. 1943; Eng. tr., *Chronicles of Hell*, 1960), and *Mlle Jaire* (1934, pub. 1942; Eng. tr., *Miss Jairus*, 1964). Their merit as important literature is likely to be more generally acknowledged in the years to come.

Surrealism won a number of new adepts in the years 1931–39, but it lost more, and more original ones, than it gained. For a time, it seemed that both poets and painters deserted the movement and its stern constraints as soon as they grew aware of their own originality. Yet it is to Breton's credit that he helped a number of talents develop faster and with greater independence than might have been the case if surrealism, that pole of attraction, had not revealed their vocation to a number of poets. More disappointing was the twofold failure of the surrealists to leave their mark upon the novel and to spread their influence across the English Channel and across the Atlantic. Surrealist painting, which is very far from constituting the best of their achievement, was more easily exported than surrealist literature. The only novelist of note whom surrealism claimed (Aragon's fiction, after 1935 or so, was hardly touched by surrealism) was Julien GRACQ, whose fiction, surrounded with mystery and vaguely suggestive of a misty Celtic atmosphere, is flawed by artifice. Since Dylan Thomas can hardly be linked with the rigorous poetics of surrealism, the only recruit abroad of significance was made during World War II in Martinique: Aimé CÉSAIRE was the most original of the black poets writing in French. American, Belgian, German, Catalan, and Spanish painting, on the other hand, took over and often perfected the best qualities of the original French movement. Jacques AUDIBERTI and the Belgian Henri MICHAUX, two poets exhibiting an uncommon power over language, a flow of imagery and of sonorous words that might have stemmed from the practice of automatic writing, would seem to have been influenced by surrealism, but their originality was in fact independent from the theories and the attitudes of Breton and his friends. Audiberti's verbal facility and vividness of imagery at times recall Victor Hugo or Edmond Rostand. Michaux is a major poet on many counts and a fiercely independent one; he stands among the very few 20th-century poets whose imagination conjures up a visionary world of its own and whose language compels the reader to share its magic.

During World War II, France witnessed a new communion between authors and an enlarged public through poetry. Poets felt that they had rediscovered powerful, collective emotions and had emerged from the solitude that their romantic, Parnassian, and symbolist predecessors had lamented even while cultivating it. The oldest and the greatest of the poets who thus won an enlarged audience, Saint-John Perse, was living in America. His poem *Exil* (1942; Eng. tr., *Exile and Other Poems*, 1949), followed by *Pluies* (1944; Eng. tr., *Rains*, 1944), *Neiges* (1944; Eng. tr., *Snows*, 1945), and *Vents* (1946; Eng. tr., *Winds*, 1953), were proud epic undertakings, rashly defying monotony and frigidity. Jules Supervielle, at the opposite pole of the world of poetry, composed pieces of unassuming, tender, almost prosaic simplicity, directly echoing his sorrow at France's plight. Francis PONGE published in 1942 one of the most strikingly fresh and intelligent volumes of verse of the century, *Le Parti-pris des choses* (Eng. tr., *The Voice of Things*, 1972). He has exploited the same vein of high seriousness ever since, although with less playful humor. Patrice de LA TOUR DU PIN won early applause in 1933 with *La Quéte de joie* (The Quest of Joy). For once, it seemed that a poet had arisen who could sing of innocence and Christian faith, evoking almost Pre-Raphaelite visions. Then La Tour du Pin's inspiration yielded to repetitious facility and vanished. Another Catholic, Pierre EMMANUEL, could compose both elegiac poetry, as in *Le Poète et son Christ* (1942), and wrathful verse inspired by patriotism, as in *Jours de colère* (1942) and *Combats avec tes défenseurs* (1943). He then developed into an official poet and a zealous prose writer. Emmanuel's inspiration often recalls that of an elder poet, Pierre-Jean JOUVE, who published tortured fictional studies of psychological cases as well as ardent, death-haunted verse. *Le Paradis perdu* (1929), *Noces* (1930), and *Sueur de sang* (1934), works at times embarrassingly reminiscent of Friedrich Hölderlin, contain Jouve's starkest, most feverish poetry. Another notable work of the war years was *Les Rois-Mages* (1943), a powerful volume of eloquent, dolorous poetry by André FRÉNAUD, then just freed from a prisoner-of-war camp. Frénaud does not seem to have won the place that is rightfully his in the critical estimate of his compatriots. Among the serious writers of the 1940s, Jacques PRÉVERT pursued the vein of light, fanciful, and humorous verse, bringing poetry within the reach of the common man. Prévert had the audacity to entertain, without any pose or any claim to greatness, and he succeeded brilliantly with *Paroles* (1946; Words). But sentimentality and commonplace facility are the stumbling blocks for popular poets, as they were for the prose-writer Boris VIAN. Like Prévert, Vian was also immensely successful for a time but in danger of being chastised by critics and professors for having entertained them too well. Modern times, nurturing their anguish, have not favored laughter.

For a dozen years after the defeat of Germany, the literature of Western Europe was conditioned by the brutal and far-reaching shocks of the war. The return to normalcy that had served as a motto in the 1920s was out of the question, for it had proved too preposterous an illusion and too cowardly an attitude. The reconstruction to be undertaken was even more formidable than that after the Peace of Versailles, since it entailed a thorough philosophical and spiritual rebuilding from the roots. The parties of the political Right and the forces of conservatism at first seemed to have been totally discredited by the collaboration with Nazi Germany, to which some of their members had subscribed. The Communists claimed to have been the backbone of the Resistance, and they intended to cash in on their prestige. With a few weeklies and monthlies at their disposal, they did not underestimate the power of literature in a country like France. Everywhere the wind appeared to be blowing favorably for new movements and for audacious experiments. Yet victory, the common goal of the war years, was now reached; whatever momentary or superficial unity had existed was soon replaced by feuds and acrid controversies. The two simultaneous but often antagonistic poles of fascination for liberated France were the United States and the USSR. Both had gained immense prestige through their share in the victory. Russian literature, however, seemed to have little to offer that might provide a source of renovation. American literature, on the other hand, became widely popular. It did not present a picture of prosperous, optimistic America but, on the contrary, one of discontent, brutality, and decay. Yet it offered to the French models of vitality and of uncouth youthfulness, turning them away from the finicky excesses of subtle psychological disquisition that their tradition favored. It also opened them up to another technique, less self-conscious, less elaborately Flaubertian, but more effective in its apparent disregard of rules and recipes. At the same time, French literature became fascinated by philosophical speculations and problems. A good proportion of the novelists, poets, critics, and even of the dramatists had, as it happens, studied philosophy. They naturally favored abstract developments and lofty ethical messages, supposedly resting on some epistemological concept or upon the "contestation of Being." Existentialism utilized that trend and strengthened it. In part, the French then found in rarefied speculation and in abstract dialectics an alibi for their blatant inferiority on the technological plane, which had contributed to their defeat. Through a curious process, after having strained every nerve in order not to fall under the intellectual influence of their victors while they were being occupied, they found in G. W. F. Hegel, Edmund Husserl, and Martin HEIDEGGER, not to mention Freud and Marx, their new intellectual guides. They triumphantly mastered all the arcana of German philosophy, but they also allowed themselves to ape the turgidly pedantic style of much Germanic speculation.

Those who survived World War II were, naturally, strongly affected by their attitudes during the crucial era and by the accelerated change of taste that the ordeal brought about. Maurois, Duhamel, Morand, Romains, and Gide himself were suddenly found to have aged and to have lost much of their relevance. Some authors who had committed themselves to the cause of Franco-German cooperation or had consented willy-nilly to the prospect of the paternalistic regime advocated by Vichy would not resign themselves easily to the turn of events. Drieu la Rochelle had gone too far on the road to literary collaboration with Germany and had for several years been obsessed by his own vacillations and his lack of genuine conviction. Courageously, he chose to commit suicide. Henri Massis (among the older reactionary critics), Maurice Bardèche (the most gifted of the younger ones), and half a dozen others who wrote in *Rivarol* or *Ecrits de la France*, stood stubbornly on their positions. Bardèche has since, on the purely literary plane, written the most solid and lucid studies of Stendhal, Balzac, and Proust. Lucien REBATET, who had been a fanatical collaborator with the extreme rightists in France and with the Germans, was later sentenced to death and eventually pardoned. In 1951 he published a long novel, *Les Deux Etendards* (The Two Standards), which counts among the richest portrayals of a youth attracted to Catholicism, music, literature, and political action. His contemporary Marcél AYMÉ, a more prolific and more varied talent, did not conceal his sympathies for the little people who, during the years of German occupation, had not been particularly heroic, but who were roughly treated, in the hour of liberation, by former "Résistants" who themselves had been heroic—or imagined they had been. Aymé's novels are thin, and their realistic, comic picture of peasants and the petty bourgeois, when extended over 200 pages or so into a would-be novel, grows monotonous and flat. But he is a master of the short story, satirical, biting, yet wholesome and written with a conciseness and a vividness that Guy de Maupassant and Ernest Hemingway might have envied.

The events of 1939–45 were probably too close in time and too enormous in scope for imaginative literature to attempt to depict or to interpret them. Only the existentialist authors, bent upon drawing philosophical lessons from recent history, had the audacity to offer narratives of the war, allegorical in the case of Albert Camus, realistic with an ideological orientation in the case of Sartre and Simone de Beauvoir. Montherlant, aloof, self-righteous, and unconcerned with the sordid details of day-to-day history, rarely attempted fiction after the liberation of France, and he failed in it when he did. He found a more congenial medium in the dramatic genre and an even more fitting one in maxims and brief, peremptory essays. Giono discarded his Rousseauistic and Tolstoyan ideology of the prewar years and, disabused of his naive creeds, satisfied himself with his role as a fluent and inventive storyteller, at times Stendhalian almost to a fault, as in *Le Hussard sur le toit* (1951; Eng. tr., *The Hussar on the Roof*, 1954). Among those who had elected a courageous course during the years of occupation, Malraux exhibited the impassioned eloquence of a thinker flagellating human mediocrity and exalting the fight of his compatriots against the demons ever preying upon them in order to debase them. He brought back to life historical characters, artists in particular, as if they were heroes of his own fiction. Younger readers (after 1965 or 1970), having grown weary of his brilliant formulas and of his overpowering personality, were secretly resentful of their inability to live up to what Malraux or de Gaulle expected of them. By 1975, he was still, in his better moments, the greatest writer of the age. Aragon, even older than Malraux (he was born in 1897) and just as indefatigable, at times just as much in love with eloquence and flamboyance, but much less acute as a thinker, continued, in the period 1945–70, to pour out facile, torrential poetry and novels. The best of them, *La Semaine sainte* (1958; Eng. tr., *Holy Week*, 1961) and *La Mise à mort* (1965; The Kill), are not likely to survive as great fiction. They did not attempt to strike new paths in technique and style, but in them, a writer who had maintained all his life an allegiance to the parties of the Left proved that he could appeal to a wide middle-class public just as effectively as Barrès, Loti, or Maurois had once done.

The exhilaration of France after the end of the German occupation was reflected in a number of insolent, carefree novels that served as an antidote to the more severe works being produced by the existentialists groping for a new ethics. Roger VAILLAND provided a spirited, disrespectful picture of the youth engaged in the Resistance in *Drôle de jeu* (1945; Strange Game). He followed it up with one or two dashing stories, *La Loi* (1957; The Law), laid in a remote Italian town, and *La Fête* (1960), on the pursuit of physical love. Vailland's tone sometimes resembles that of Stendhal, although with much more dryness, now that of Pierre Laclos (1741–1803), but with less sharpness of intellect. Vailland probably would not have risen to the stature of a significant novelist even if he had lived longer. Nor could one feel certain that Roger NIMIER, another impetuous and cynical writer (who also died prematurely), would have gained the maturity and depth that might have supplemented the flashy recklessness of his one good book, *Le Hussard bleu* (1950; The Blue Hussar). A third novelist in love with action and with the hazards of wartime existence, Jacques Perret (1901–), failed to follow up the success of *Le Caporal épinglé* (1947; The Pinned-Up Corporal), a first novel replete with entertaining, comic experiences. There was more emotional power and less egocentricity in the early books of Romain GARY, a Russian-born Frenchman who, after serving in the Free French air force, depicted the martyrdom of children in Eastern Europe in a restrained and moving book, *Education européenne* (1945; Eng. tr., *A European Education,* 1960). He then became a prolific storyteller and a strong advocate of the picaresque in fiction. His many works are uneven, some decidedly on the hasty, superficial side. Gary's best book is *La Promesse de l'aube* (1960; The Promise of Dawn), a spirited fictional autobiography.

There is more depth, more range, and more staying power in the novels of Emmanuel ROBLÈS. Like Camus, the North African Roblès is a writer concerned with moral issues and with spiritual debates of conscience. He is often close to Camus in talent and forcefulness and excels him in the depiction of women. Roblès's *Cela s'appelle l'aurore* (1952; Eng. tr., *Dawn on Our Darkness,* 1953) and *Le Vésuve* (1961; Eng. tr., *Vesuvius,* 1970), both set in Italy, the latter during the war years, are among the finest works of fiction in the period that preceded the vogue of the "new novel." Albert MEMMI, a Tunisian Jew, is, along with Camus, Roblès, and Jules Roy (1907–), one of the original talents among the non-Arabs to have emerged from the former French colonies. Memmi's *La Statue de sel* (1953) and a few subsequent novels offer, with quiet anguish, a picture of the isolation and alienation of a writer torn between his origins and the culture of France, in whose language he writes and into which he has been assimilated. Robert Merle (1908–) also comes from Algeria; his novels, however, are set either in France, where he teaches English literature, in some exotic locale, or in an allegorical Utopia. His *Weekend à Zuydcote* (1949) is a vivid record of his experience as a soldier at the Dunkirk evacuation in June 1940. *L'Ile* (1962) and his subsequent novels are marred by too obvious an allegorical intention.

There are other successful, pleasantly readable practitioners of fiction in the years 1945–60, writers whose ultimate ranking with posterity is, in our opinion, in doubt, but who, for a time, voiced the concerns of their own age. Henri BOSCO, like Merle and Memmi a professor, came to the writing of fiction late in his career: *Le Mas Théotime* (1945; Eng. tr., *Farm in Provence,* 1947) and *Malicroix* (1948) were his most striking evocations of the poetry of Provence and of the Camargue. Bosco merged the re-creation of atmosphere with complex but frail and artificial plots that smacked of the detective story. His visionary imagination did not often succeed in making his strained and farfetched inventions acceptable. Hervé BAZIN, a much younger man than Bosco, irrupted into literature and instant success with *Vipère au poing* (1948; Eng. tr., *Viper in the Fist,* 1951), a novel of hatred (of his social class, of bourgeois conventions, of his mother). Bazin then produced a dozen other novels, some comic or satirical, others restrainedly compassionate, that placed him among the most imaginative and the most fertile in his age group, close to Troyat. There is much facility as well as an alert style in the fiction and short stories of the Belgian author Albert Carette, who became French and adopted the name Félicien MARCEAU. His gift of irony, of storytelling, and his acute critical judgment make him a successor, with more acid verve, to Anatole France or to Jules RENARD. Roger PEYREFITTE struck a felicitous theme and treated it with sensitivity and brilliance in *Les Amitiés particulières* (1945), a none too flattering picture of dangerously close male friendships in a Catholic college. He has since chosen to exploit his facility and his genuine gift as a stylist through hasty, provocative books that have discredited him as a serious

author. Raymond QUENEAU, no less keen or less dry an intellect, is an immensely learned man, a master of technique with a remarkable gift of self-control. He is much admired by some, while his excessive artifice and almost scientific calculation leave other readers unconvinced. In the French literary world, he holds a position similar to that of Paulhan in an earlier generation as a trenchant, ironical, yet benevolent critic and adviser of talents less perversely intellectual than his. Jean CAYROL, more sentimental and melancholy, unashamedly lyrical and touchingly compassionate, stands in contrast to the three novelists just mentioned. He is among the few in modern France who have, after Bernanos and Mauriac, attempted a form of fiction inspired by religion, although in a very different key and with much less parading of a sense of tragedy.

Among women writers of the period 1945–60, Françoise SAGAN was, for a brief while, the most popular. Her novel *Bonjour, Tristesse* (1954; Eng. tr., 1955), as well as subsequent clever, dry, and shallow *récits,* depicted a monotonous world of bored pleasure-seekers. Sagan never aimed at depth or forcefulness and, 10 years after her adolescent success, she was already half-forgotten. Françoise Mallet-Joris (1930–) showed far more psychological insight and far more mastery of fictional form at the age of 21 in *Le Rempart des Béguines* (1951), set in her native Belgium. She has since experimented with realistic novels, historical reconstructions, and stories of characters yearning for faith, but she has never matched the extraordinary skill of her first novel. Christiane ROCHEFORT likewise does not appear to have been able to strike a fresh note after her first provoking work, *Le Repos du guerrier* (1958; The Warrior's Rest). She transferred her interest to analyses of children's games, delusions, and Utopias, first in *Les Petits Enfants du siècle* (1961; The Grandchildren of the Century) and then again in a mediocre and flimsy volume, *Encore heureux qu'on va vers l'été* (1975). Violette LEDUC, torn by personal problems and ready to throw all feminine *pudeur* to the winds, gave forceful expression in several novels to her torments, her fierce lesbian loves, and her complexes about her ugliness. Leduc's *La Bâtarde* (1965; The Bastard Girl) is worthy of survival. There is, however, more subtlety and restraint, more technical awareness and stylistic talent in Marguerite DURAS. Duras has written too much not to be often uneven, and she has divided her interest between the cinema and fiction. None of her novels evinces the sustained power of Simone de Beauvoir or of Nathalie Sarraute. Yet Duras has kept within modest, self-imposed limits, and two or three of her evocative, poetical *récits,* revolving around the difficulty of human communication, may remain as original minor productions of the postwar years. Several of her screenplays deserve to hold a place in that new, semiliterary genre.

If any 15-year period could ever be summed up in one representative movement and be said to have acknowledged one leader, the years following the liberation of France in 1945 would be designated as those in which Sartrean existentialism was preeminent. A number of forces then converged to foster the spread of existentialist ideas. Some were superficial and may be ascribed to snobbery and publicity, for the leaders of the new philosophy were not above encouraging and utilizing the public's curiosity, just as the surrealists and, much earlier, the naturalists had done. Other elements that helped make them conspicuous were political: Sartre, his friend and exegete Jeanson, Simone de Beauvoir, and Jean Genet himself, insofar as he can be grouped with the existentialists, loudly proclaimed their opposition to colonial wars and to American imperialism and their outright rejection of bourgeois society (while living as bourgeois). For a time, they appropriated the labels "revolutionary," "ethics of violence," "literature as a form of revolt," expressions that hold a potent appeal for the French. The attitude of the upper Catholic hierarchy and of the self-styled intellectual elite had disappointed many during the gloomy years of German occupation, and traditional philosophy appeared effete and cowardly. Phenomenology and Marxism, at times individually, at times in conjunction, appealed to the young. Phenomenology, illustrated by Maurice MERLEAU-PONTY, indicted intellectualism and stressed behavioral description rather than conceptualization; its key words were "the lived" and the deep-seated "ambiguity" of the human situation. Merleau-Ponty himself, although primarily a philosopher, occasionally included literature and painting (that of Paul Cézanne in particular) among his fields of interest. Sartre also proposed successive, even contradictory philosophical systems through the years; the shifts in his political attitude (toward Marxism, Russian communism, French socialism) have been even more baffling. He may well have given his best in his polemical essays on such subjects as the bourgeois theater, the significance and purpose of literature, black poetry, and various novelists, poets, painters. In his novel La Nausée (1938; Eng. tr., Nausea, 1949), as well as in his short stories, which are perhaps unequalled in 20th-century literature, and in the three volumes of Les Chemins de la liberté (3 vols., 1945–47; Eng. tr., The Roads to Freedom, 1947–50), Sartre boldly attempted a renovation of novelistic technique and composed a fictional summa of a philosophical but also cosmic and worldly character nowhere matched in the achievement of the 20th century since Proust.

The sprawling, often prattling autobiographical works of Simone de BEAUVOIR and even her courageous, but tiresome and often flabby developments in Le Deuxième Sexe (1949; Eng. tr., The Second Sex, 1953) have tended to outshine her meritorious, and even original, novels, L'Invitée (1943; Eng. tr., She Came to Stay, 1949) and Le Sang des autres (1945; Eng. tr., The Blood of Others, 1948). She failed conspicuously in other fictional attempts. Feminists are grieved to watch all her women characters end up as meek, sentimental followers of the males whom they unweariedly pursue and before whom they stand in awe. But if, as we believe and as the examples of Balzac and Tolstoy and Proust seem to indicate, some didacticism has its rightful place in fiction, the intellectual character and the ethical message of Beauvoir's early novels in no way detract from their lasting value. Whether or not Albert CAMUS subscribed to the main existentialist theses and whether his ulterior break with Sartre, Jeanson, and Beauvoir was inevitable or not, posterity will probably link him to those writers with whom he started his literary career. The uncritical acclaim that hailed him, in the 1950s and after his accidental death, as a saint and a prophet inevitably brought about an adverse reaction in those who feel irked if they admire what the common herd lauds. The ultimate verdict will probably be that, while Camus was neither a profound and consistent thinker nor an expert dramatist, he will occupy a permanent place as a moralist and as the author of two masterpieces of minor fiction, L'Etranger (1942; rev. 1953; Eng. tr., The Stranger, 1946) and La Chute (1956; Eng. tr., The Fall, 1957). Jean GENET may be linked with existentialism only artificially, and because Sartre composed a big, indigestible volume on him (and, indirectly, on Sartre's own ideas). A legend has developed around Genet's homosexuality and his career as a professional thief. He himself has strained every nerve to play the part of the revolutionary outlaw that he was supposed to be.

When the aura of superficial scandal surrounding him has been dissipated, he will stand out as a great theatrical craftsman and as a superb master of prose, autobiographical and at times semifictional. In the same age group as these writers, but if anything closer to surrealism than to the positive thinking and underlying optimism of the existentialists is Georges BATAILLE. Between 1945 and 1960, this novelist and essayist, fascinated by the force of evil and of damnation, took on the appearance of a prophet and magician unleasing infernal demons. His volumes of essays on L'Expérience intérieure (1943; Interior Experience) and La Littérature et le mal (1957; Literature and Evil) lack depth, rigor, and even originality; his attempts at some sort of fiction, Dirty (1945) and L'Abbé C . . . (1950), have something childish about them. The Marquis de Sade, Baudelaire, and Proust had explored with far more acuteness "the perilous regions from where destructive forces surge up."

Philosophical speculations in the years 1945–60 were uppermost not only in the minds of the novelists but in those of critics and essayists. Simone WEIL exercised a wide influence through her posthumously published books: La Pesanteur et la grâce (1947; Eng. tr., Gravity and Grace, 1952), La Connaissance surnaturelle (1950; Supernatural Knowledge), and other essays. Even more than Sartre, Weil yearned for the role of a martyr, and she lived her unorthodox ideas with utmost seriousness unto the last. Her doctrine was not a systematic one, and her most illuminating flashes of intuition are found in aperçus (often perversely paradoxical, always heretical). She may well stand out, in the eyes of posterity, as the freest and the deepest thinker among the French women writers of the 20th century. Claude-Emonde Magny née Vinel (1912–66) was another "Normalienne." Her early volumes of literary criticism (on Giraudoux, American fiction, and French novelists) proved her to be, for a score of years after 1940, the most consistently influential critic of her generation, although she is now forgotten. Maurice BLANCHOT lived up to Bataille's requirement that "criticism is nothing if it is not the expression of a philosophy." Blanchot is an expert stylist who, even when attempting the most abstruse fiction, retains an appearance of clarity, as in Thomas l'obscur (1941; Thomas the Obscure) and Aminadab (1942). In his best volumes of critical essays, which also happen to be his earliest ones, Faux-pas (1943; Mistakes) and La Part du feu (1949; Sacrifice to Save the Rest), Blanchot focused insistently on a handful of writers, all of whom call the very existence of literature into question: Hölderlin, Nietzsche, Mallarmé, and Heidegger. Much of the probing exploration of language that was to be attempted after 1960 in France stems from Blanchot's challenging of the act of writing and from his meditations on silence as the ultimate, although often disregarded, goal of the art of writing. He stands out as the first, and the most searching, among the moderns who ceaselessly wonder how literature, that "right to die," can be at all possible. Gaston BACHELARD, on the other hand, can hardly be called a critic of literature in the usual manner. The poetry he was fond of quoting to support his aesthetic and psychological assertions was selected with scant discrimination and with a nonchalant disregard of literary values. But his volumes of psychoanalysis and psychology, his poetical meditations on dreams and daydreaming, and his dissection of imaginative processes have had an impact second to none on the interpretation of literary creation between 1945 and 1960. His phenomenological studies were not those of a cool, detached thinker but of a passionate dreamer, humorously picturing himself as "creating a cosmos every morning." Another romantic and, after a fashion, an explorer of material imagination, was the Jesuit scientist and amateur theologian Pierre TEILHARD DE CHARDIN, a mystic attached to the world of matter. His fame and influence, like those of Simone Weil, were posthumous, in his case on account of the fear that his unorthodox views aroused in the Catholic hierarchy. He was, with no little exaggeration, compared to Galileo, celebrated as a new Saint Thomas Aquinas fired with the prophetic glow of Saint John of Patmos. Teilhard attempted to turn religious thought away from its traditions, from its fixation on revelation and redemption, from its anathematizing of matter and the flesh and, instead, toward the construction of the future. There are many flaws in his enraptured developments on ''the heart of matter,'' on marrying the Christian God and ''the Marxist God of ever forward.'' Scientists and theologians have taken issue with several of Teilhard's impetuous assertions, but some men of letters, including the Senegalese French poet Léopold SENGHOR, have gratefully acknowleged the fertilizing impact of Teilhard's vision upon their thinking. In several ways, that influence supplemented and reinforced that of Claudel.

France's recovery—demographic, economic, political, and spiritual—from the ordeal and the losses of World War II proved to be prompter than that after the severer losses of World War I. By the end of the decade 1950–60, France felt ready for industrial modernization and gave herself a strong government able to settle the long rankling colonial problems and to steer its own course in foreign policy. President Charles de Gaulle who, after 1958, ruled the country like an enlightened monarch, also happened to be a gifted writer; he appointed as his minister of culture a great man of letters and a fiery orator, André Malraux. Yet literature and the arts did not thrive conspicuously during the Gaullist era. Contemporaries have always complained that they were living in an age devoid of greatness and poor in geniuses. It did appear to many of them that the 15 years from 1960 to 1975, even though the country had first an intellectual general and then a professor and lover of poetry at the helm, suffered sadly when its literary output was contrasted with far richer and more innovative period of 1919–30 or even with the reign of Napoleon III.

The contrast was sharpest in poetry. During the war years and the Resistance, poetry enjoyed wide popularity; even after 1945, acclaim was bestowed on Claudel, Perse, and several former surrealists. But readers of poetry soon became few and far between once again. The space granted to verse in literary magazines was stingily meted out, and official or academic recognition did not go to poets as it did to playwrights, novelists, and especially critics. Scholarly and literary journals teemed with exegeses of Rimbaud, Mallarmé, and even earlier poets, but they failed to interpret the poets of their own age. In order to survive as men of letters, poets turned to writing aphorisms, abstruse poetics, and art criticism. The inspiration of the outstanding poets dried up as they reached the middle of their lives: René Char remained the greatest of them, as Camus had proclaimed him to be, but wrote little after 1960; Francis Ponge was tempted to repeat himself and, as he was taken seriously by his admirers and by himself, to lose his fresh humor; Pierre Emmanuel, Jean GROSJEAN, Claude Vigée (1921–), Malcolm de Chazal (1902–) in his native Mauritius, and Léopold Senghor yielded more and more to the temptation of eloquence. Political vituperation did not help Aimé Césaire, the leading black poet of the 20th century, to grow as a poetical figure. Nor did another poet from Martinique, Edouard Glissant (1928–), long continue to dwell on the epic heights to which he had ascended in his ambitious poem

Les Indes, concerning the conquerors and explorers of the New World and their red- and black-skinned victims. Eugène GUILLEVIC lacks magic in his imagery and style. The two outstanding French poets of the 1960s, both expert and lucid critics of poetry as well, are Yves BONNEFOY and the Swiss Philippe Jaccottet (1925–), both haunted by images of nothingness and death. Close to them in age and talent are three other poets, André du Bouchet (1924–), Jacques Dupin (1927–), and Michel Deguy (1930–), equally shy of eloquence and of color, and fond of the sparsest, driest poetrical style, in the tradition of Reverdy and Char.

Much has been written since 1960 on the death of the avant-garde, and the concept has indeed lapsed into disuse except, strangely enough, in the realm of the theater, the one art that normally must wait for the public taste to be ready for its innovations. Nowhere in recent times, not even in the musical and choreographic arts, has the divorce between run-of-the-mill plays aimed at entertaining and the experimenters who frontally scorned or opposed the public taste been so acutely marked. The revolutionary, or at least innovating force on the French stage since 1945–60 came not from playwrights primarily, but from alert and bold directors or, as the French word more aptly puts it, the *metteurs en scène.* Their names have been mentioned earlier in this article. In the post-World War II era, their successors, no less courageous and no less imaginative, were Barrault, Jean VILAR, Roger PLANCHON, and a number of directors of provincial stages or of festivals throughout France. The Parisian stage ceased to be the prime mover in the development of the modern theater. Indeed, the most fruitful models were offered by foreign dramatists: Anton CHEKHOV, Luigi PIRANDELLO, Bertolt BRECHT, and Jerzy Grotowski. The number of French playwrights of foreign origin has been extraordinarily large: Arthur Adamov (Russian), Fernando ARRABAL (Spanish), Samuel Beckett (Irish), Armand Gatti (Italo-Russian), Michel de Ghelderode (Belgian), Eugène Ionesco (Romanian), René de Obaldia (Panamanian), Robert Pinget (Swiss), Medjid Khan Rezvani (Iranian and Russian), George Schehadé (Lebanese), Jean VAUTHIER (Belgian), Romain WEINGARTEN (part Polish). The native predecessors invoked by the most radical of the French theatrical innovators were Jarry, Apollinaire, a few dadaist and surrealist experimenters, and—more modestly—Roger VITRAC, whose *Les Mystères de l'amour* (1924; The Mysteries of Love) and *Victor, ou les enfants au pouvoir* (1928; Victor, or the Children in Power) were sponsored by Antonin ARTAUD. Artaud himself, while hardly significant as an actual author of plays, has, long after the end of his wretched life, become an influential force on the dramatic ideas of France and other countries. His slogan, ''the theater of cruelty,'' is as ambiguous as it is striking. ''Every thing that acts is cruelty,'' he wrote; the chief cruelty is outside man, that of an absurd and violent universe. According to Artaud, a direct contact with the public was to be reinstated through the disappearance of the stage. Speech would become secondary to gesture, motion, and pantomime. Psychology, realism, and understanding would be sacrificed to magic, myth, and dream. Artaud's ideas opened the road to the ready acceptance, after 1955–60, of Beckett, Ionesco, and their successors.

The test of time has already been applied to the older dramatists of the last 20 years, and some of them have stood it victoriously. Ghelderode, who has been diversely characterized as romantic, baroque, devilish, and metaphysical, only came into his own with French audiences after 1960. Eugène IONESCO is more vulnerable; there are facile tricks, mechanical repetitions, and moments of marked unevenness in his plays. As he entered his own second half-century, he was, like Anouilh, Salacrou, Aymé, and others among his predecessors, passing—some would say, sinking—from the advance theater for a few into the more facile group of playwrights who were once called "boulevardiers." Samuel BECKETT is assuredly greater as well as deeper and no less significant as a novelist than as a dramatist. He appears more sternly anguished than his Romanian contemporary, whose anxiety about death is expressed through derisiveness and absurdity. Arthur ADAMOV, George SCHEHADÉ, René de OBALDIA, and Armand GATTI seemed, at age 50 or older, to have lost the power of self-renewal. Robert PINGET, if he does not abandon the stage for the art of fiction, in which he has proved more adept at winning a group of devotees, might enjoy the most lasting success of those experimenters with the drama.

After 1960, structuralism succeeded existentialism as the dominant "ism" in both literature and philosophy. The word itself, with all the ambiguities to which it was susceptible (for it was variously applied, at times, in highly contrasting ways, to linguistics, ethnology, sociology, epistemology, and other disciplines) became fashionable and indispensable by the year 1970. The intellectual attitude to which it pointed was widespread among thinkers and critics. It affected imaginative literature very little, in spite of much confusion between the theories upheld by some "new novelists" and structuralist theses. (A form of positivism, or of phenomenology, might just as legitimately be detected in the early novels of Alain ROBBE-GRILLET or of Claude OLLIER.) If the technicality of linguistic and ethnological structuralism is left out of an article dealing primarily with literature, the general features of structuralism, which served as a substratum for the ideas on literature that gained ascendancy after 1960, might be summed up as follows:

A revulsion occurred against the "romantic" and emotional mood that lay under and behind both surrealism and existentialism. In both groups, the stress had been placed on the creative self; immense, almost unlimited claims had been put forward for man's freedom; the individual was urged to create his own values and to become "like unto the gods," decreeing what is good and what is evil. The march forward (or "progress" in Comtist terminology) was preferred to static order. Existentialism had boasted of being a kind of humanism and had won renewed prestige for that time-honored word. In the realm of ideas and even of literature, the *fond* (that which is signified), had been stressed. The existentialist thinkers had, insofar as one may generalize concerning them, evinced scant interest in science. As a reaction against all this, the new trend moved toward a distrust of excessive subjectivity, attempting instead (as Hippolyte Taine and earlier theorists had once tried) to render the aesthetic judgment objective and "scientific." The new movement denounced and derided humanism, since, after all, many of the crimes and much of the social injustice of our time had been accepted, or accomplished, by so-called elites trained in humanism or in some bourgeois mockery of it. It analyzed "the signifying," the techniques and models (in the scientific use of the word) of the *récit* and the *discours*. With the naive enthusiasm of neophytes, it rediscovered old-fashioned rhetoric. Most vehemently of all, it indicted history, the "diachronic," the contingent, nonnecessary, unpredictable accident, which mocks all strict order. In societies, in non-Western cultures, and in language, the structuralists no longer strove to discover the "meaning," which is but a surface feature, but a more basic network of relations in mutual dependency upon each other. Various elements, each of which if isolated offers little significance, take on their full value only when combined with each other into a whole that, as in Jules Romain's unanimism, is altogether more than the sum of its components.

Claude LÉVI-STRAUSS was championed against Sartre by those who saw in the former the intellectual leader of structuralism. He himself has repudiated all connection with the literary popularizers of structuralism, and he has only seldom been concerned with literature. Several of his books, however, most notably *Tristes tropiques* (1955; Eng. tr., 1974) and even *La Pensée sauvage* (1962; Eng. tr., *The Savage Mind,* 1966), are written with elegance and even with emotion. One of his truest ancestors is Jean-Jacques Rousseau, in his nostalgia for the childhood of man and his dissatisfaction with Western civilization. Michel FOUCAULT, the paradoxical, dogmatic Nietzsche of the movement, has occasionally stood even closer to literature and to art and has retold the history of the modern age in an imperiously arbitrary fashion. Jacques DERRIDA, Gérard GENETTE, and the neo-Marxist Louis ALTHUSSER, like Foucault, all former students of the Ecole Normale, and perhaps even Lucien GOLDMANN might, not without some artifice, be grouped together as the structuralists in criticism. Roland BARTHES has been less abstruse and more influential with literary figures. His subtle and brilliant paradoxes on Racine, Balzac, Jules Michelet, and others have dazzled the intellectual smart set. Still, in contrast to the structuralists, whose criticism almost never concerned itself with discovering new talents and in elucidating contemporary literature for the general reader, the finest critics of those years may well have been the independents who, at times with the help of psychoanalysis or thematic criticism, or simply through being sensitive, acute, and free from the shackles of any system at all, renewed the interpretation of whole eras of the past. Relatively few came from the traditional French academic world: Jean-Pierre RICHARD, Picon, and Doubrovsky. Several were Swiss, including Marcel Raymond, Albert BÉGUIN, Rousset, and Jean STAROBINSKI; one, Georges POULET, was of Belgian origin but close to the so-called Geneva School of critics.

In the past 20 years, the novel form has been practiced by a variety of talents who have addressed themselves either to a vast general public or to a limited group of sophisticated readers, mostly drawn from the academic profession in and outside France. Seldom if ever has the cleavage between the two kinds of literature been so sharp. No writer of very high stature appears to have emerged from that group of novelists who won public recognition through prize-winning novels and struck a new note without posing as the theorists of a new technique. This group includes Marguerite YOURCENAR, whose *Mémoires d'Hadrien* (1951; Eng. tr., *Memoirs of Hadrian,* 1954) was not subsequently followed by works of unchallenged quality; Roger Ikor (1912–), winner of the 1955 Goncourt Prize, André PIEYRE DE MANDIARGUES, a skillful and often arresting author of *récits* and discreetly erotic short stories that are tinged with surrealist weirdness but lack the sustaining force needed for a full novel; José CABANIS, whose *L'Age ingrat* (1952; The Ungrateful Age), a traditional novel, was followed by historical essays of merit; Pierre GASCAR, who won the Goncourt Prize for *Les Bêtes* (1953; The Beasts) and who was perhaps the most gifted of the Prize winners until Michel Tournier (1924–) received the same coveted award for *Le Roi des aulnes* (1970; Eng. tr., *The Erlking,* 1972). Tournier had earlier written the curious, disturbing *Vendredi* (1973; Eng. tr., *Friday & Robinson: Life in the Esperanza Island,* 1972), an original redoing of Defoe's *Robinson Crusoe,* as well as a less exotic volume, *Les*

Météores (1975) on the now banal theme of male love. Jean-Marie LE CLÉZIO, who as he reached the age of 30 did his best to drown his talent in deluges of words, facile collages, and repetitious mannerisms, deserves for his earlier volumes to count among the most promising hopes of the 1960s. A startling debut was later that of Pierre GUYOTAT; his youthful imagination and his verbal, and verbose, abundance have conjured up dreams of mass murders, rapes, and sexual perversions. The novel and the cinema of the 1970s have inured audiences to all the dreary excesses of pornography. Some like to present it as a form of revolution. But nothing ages faster and Guyotat, the successor of Céline as a writer intoxicated with hatred, but also as a naive and frustrated idealist, seems to be sinking into the quicksands of language set free.

Guyotat's work was blessed, or cursed, by an official guarantee from Barthes, Philippe SOLLERS, and other advocates of the "new novel." A strange feature of the 1960s and 1970s was indeed the fact that, decolonization having been achieved (not by the Left but by no other than de Gaulle) and the revolt of 1968 having been followed by an acknowledgment of failure and the rallying of the youth to an ethics of work and to the benefits of a consumer society, a few authors have fancied that they would serve the cause of revolution by turning against the novel and discarding from it plot, character, emotion, psychology, and style. The social significance of the "new novelists" of 1960-75 is indeed scant, and their impact upon French life at large has been almost nil. They have counted relatively few readers. Indeed it often appears that much of the "new novel" was purposely composed so that academic critics might disassemble their elaborate mechanics while ingenious graduate students abroad might rearrange the pieces of their puzzles.

If one refuses to be impressed by the preposterous claims put forward by the "new novelists," who like to contend that a new era has dawned in literature with them, the originality of some of them is undeniable. Inevitably, writers of no consequence such as Marc SAPORTA and Claude MAURIAC jumped on the bandwagon and were for a brief while mistaken for authentic novelists. Others, like Claude Ollier and Jean RICARDOU have proven more adept at evolving dogmatic theories and fighting off those whom they suspect of enmity to the new Gospel than at writing anything gripping, or merely readable. Among the authors of genuine talent who have been lumped together under the all too convenient label, there exist deep differences: Nathalie SARRAUTE has very little in common with Michel BUTOR, and Claude SIMON has even fewer affinities with Robbe-Grillet, whom he amiably parodied in one of his dullest books, *La Bataille de Pharsale* (1969; Eng. tr., *The Battle of Pharsalus*, 1971). Beckett, the most original of them as a novelist, is a solitary writer, fiercely alien to any group. The only great one among the "new novelists" (great only in four or five of his dozen books) may be Claude Simon. Two of Butor's novels, *L'Emploi du temps* (1956; Eng. tr., *Passing Time*, 1960) and *La Modification* (1957; Eng. tr., *A Change of Heart*, 1959), may perhaps still continue to be read by the year 1990. The theories cleverly put together by Robbe-Grillet as well as the stripping of the novel to its lean, desiccated skeleton in Nathalie Sarraute's self-conscious stories were salutary for a time, and it may have been necessary to attempt a geometrization of the novel and to stress space at the expense of time and duration. These exercises have served a useful purpose by putting the novelist on guard against the Bergsonian philosophy of mobility and against anthorpomorphism. Banishing color, emotional heat, poetical style, and moral implications from the art of fiction was probably a healthy undertaking in an era in which science clearly held the primacy in human concerns, and literature meekly endeavored to become objective, coolly descriptive, and unconcerned with human passions, with social protest, with the woes of the poor and of the underprivileged. But it seems doubtful that an art form as flexible and variegated as fiction, ever ready to rise up again from the moribund couch to which doctors have often assigned it in the past, will not be reborn after its abdication of the 1960s and 1970s. In earlier ages, there had occurred periods in French literature that were impoverished through the stronger attraction offered by science, social studies, public administration, and the lures of engineering and of business expansion to the ambitious young. The competition of the cinema, of other mass media, and even that of the detective story and science fiction, has further weakened the appeal of literature. The formidable and forbidding expansion of criticism and the near monopoly of literary interpretation by teachers of philosophy have tilted the balance away from fresh creativity. Imagination, however, will in time recover its rights and its role. The Napoleonic era, the years 1890-1910 when fiction and poetry seemed to have sunk into silence and sterility, were followed by a glorious rebirth. A similar renaissance, freed from the obsession with linguistics, with scientific objectivity, with the hypercritical and myopic exegeses of texts, may well be in store for the last two decades of the 20th century.

See: D. W. Alden, ed., *French XX Bibliography: Critical and Biographical References for the Study of Contemporary French Literature*, nos. 1–31 (1949–79); C.-E. Magny, *Histoire du roman français depuis 1918* (1950); D. Grossvogel, *The Self-conscious Stage in Modern French Drama* (1958); V. Brombert, *The Intellectual Hero: Studies in the French Novel 1880–1955* (1961); M. Esslin, *The Theatre of the Absurd* (1961); J. Guicharnaud, *Modern French Theater from Giraudoux to Genet* (1967); H. Peyre, *French Novelists of Today* (1967); J. Sturrock, *The French New Novel* (1969); L. Roudiez, *French Fiction Today* (1972); J. Bersani et al., *La Littérature en France depuis 1945* (1974); J. Cruickshank, "French Literature since 1870," in *French Literature from 1660 to the Present* (1974); P.-O. Walzer, *Littérature française: le XXᵉ siècle I: 1896–1920* (1975); G. Brée, *Littérature française: le XXᵉ siècle II: 1920–1970* (1978); D. W. Alden and R. A. Brooks, eds., *A Critical Bibliography of French Literature: Vol. VI, The Twentieth Century*, in three parts (1980).   H.P.

Frère, Maud (1923–), Belgian novelist, was born in Brussels. She introduces us to the intimacy of both nature and childhood in her first stories, *Vacances secrètes* (1956; Eng. tr., *Secret Holiday,* 1957) and *L'Herbe à moi* (1957; My Own Grass). Later, other themes appear: the war and the long wait of the Nazi occupation of Belgium (*Les Jumeaux millénaires,* 1962; The Millenarian Twins); the difficulty a woman has when faced with loving and being herself despite temptations of self-denial (*Guido,* 1965). Everywhere in Frère's work this truth inscribes itself in filigree: the important thing is to become what one is while remaining faithful to the somewhat wild frugalities of youth. A knowingly elliptic writing contributes to giving her novels, purposely constructed around an absence or a silence, the "charm of things which one is alone in knowing." She has won two important literary prizes, the Villon Prize in 1960 and the Rossel Prize in 1962.

See: M. Pierson-Piérard, *Maud Frère* (1960).   R.Bu.

Fridegård, Jan (1897-1968) Swedish novelist and short-story writer,, was born in Enköpings Näs. He came from the most deprived group of society, the *statare* (share-cropper) class, and tried first to improve his life by enlisting in the dragoon corps. While confined to the guardhouse, he found a work by Anton CHEKHOV and discovered the joy of reading. He studied much during his frequent periods of unemployment and early became interested in yoga and Ralph Walds Emerson. His first novel, *En natt i juli* (1933; A Night in July), earned him an award. Then came a series of autobiographical novels about Lars Hård. The first, *Jag Lars Hård* (1935; I, Lars Hård), shocked the audience with its cynical attitude to love and its satirical sneer at society's attempts to impose conventional values upon an individual spirit. His experiences of brutality in military life are described in *Äran och hjältarna* (1938; The Glory and the Heroes).

Fridegård, also a renowned discoverer of runic stones, then wrote a trilogy set in Viking times. As opposed to the sagas, he describes the lives of the slaves rather than the masters. In the novels *Trägudars land* (1940; The Land of the Wooden Gods), *Gryningsfolket* (1944; The People of the Dawn), and *Offerrök* (1949; Sacrificial Smoke), he drew implicit parallels between the slaves of the past and the *statare* of the present. Turning back to autobiographical material, he wrote *Lyktgubbarna* (1955; The Lantern Men) and *Flyttfåglarna* (1956; The Migrant Birds) about the *statare* generation of his parents, followed by his memoirs *På Oxens horn* (1964; On the Horn of the Ox) and *Det kortaste strået* (1966; The Shortest Straw).

Among Fridegård's other novels, *Torntuppen* (1941; The Tower Rooster) reflects his interest in spiritualism. The spirit of a dead farmhand flies over the world listening to people's thoughts. The novel ultimately deals with man's relation to death, crime, and punishment. Fridegård's interest in history and spiritualism is fused in *Hallonflickan* (1968; The Raspberry Girl), in which a man dies in a car accident and wakes up in the Bronze Age and then he meets a girl whose remains he was mysteriously drawn to at a visit to a museum.

See: A. Gustafson, *A History of Swedish Literature* (1961), pp. 519–22; L. Furuland, *Statarna i litteraturen* (1962); *SLT* 4 (1970).   T.L.

Fried, Erich (1921–), Austrian poet, translator, novelist, and librettist, was born in Vienna. He emigrated to England in 1938. Primarily a poet, Fried was optimistic about Germany (despite the holocaust in which his parents were killed), writing, until the mid-1960s, brief, intellectual, politically "unengaged" lyrics in which he used myth and experimented with language and form. An example is "Die Flut" ("The Tide") in *Anfechtungen* (1967; Arguments), a typographical representation of the tide's ebb and flow. This poetry, although technically polished, lacked purpose. Fried's optimism eventually waned, and he became convinced that only profound political upheaval would improve the quality of life in Germany (he does not, he asserts, hate Germany). Politically "engaged," technically competent poetry of substantially higher quality followed the political awakening. An example is "Verdammungsurteil" ("Death Sentence") in *Die bunten Getüme* (1977; The Bright Little Monsters), a provocative poem about the suicide of the revolutionary Ulrike Meinhof. Fried has also earned a considerable reputation as a translator (Shakespeare, T. S. Eliot, and Dylan Thomas). His other works include *Deutschland* (1944); *Ein Soldat und ein Mädchen* (1960; A Soldier and a Girl), a novel; and *und Vietnam und* (1966; and Vietnam and).

See: W. Hinderer, "Sprache und Methode," *Revolte und Experiment*, ed. by W. Paulsen (1972), pp. 132–43.
                                                          R.Z.

Frisch, Max (1911–), Swiss novelist, playwright, diarist, and essayist, was born in Zürich. Frisch studied architecture and was a successful architect for several years before he decided in 1954 to devote all his time to writing.

Frisch's first two novels, *Jürg Reinhart* (1934) and *Antwort aus der Stille* (1937; Answer from Silence), reveal the influence of Albin ZOLLINGER's lyrical prose style. At the outbreak of World War II, he published his first literary diary, *Blätter aus dem Brotsack* (1940; Sheets from the Knapsack), about his life as a soldier in the Swiss army. Immediately after the war, Frisch, together with his compatriot Friedrich DÜRRENMATT, created the German postwar drama. His first successful play was *Nun singen die wieder* (1945; Now They Are Singing Again), an impressive indictment of war. The "romance" *Santa Cruz* (1947), is a short play about love, marriage, longing, a dream-world, and "real" life. *Die Chinesische Mauer* (1947; Eng. tr., *The Chinese Wall*, 1961) is a historical farce about the incompatibility of power and humanity. The protagonist, a modern intellectual, tries to demonstrate the madness of the continual power struggle in human history, from the beginnings to the atomic bomb. He is not understood by the people, but the emperor of China, who understands him very well, makes him honorary court jester.

Frisch's next play, *Als der Krieg zu Ende war* (1949; When the War Was Over) deals with the love of a German woman for a Russian officer. In *Als der Krieg*, Frisch's sensitivity toward the image-creating nature of language becomes evident: the love of the couple is based on the fact that they cannot understand each other's language. *Graf Öderland* (1951; Eng. tr., *Count Oederland*, 1962), perhaps Frisch's most difficult play, psychologically probes the anarchic longings of a middle-class man who yearns to grab an axe and break out of his daily routine. *Don Juan oder die Liebe zur Geometrie* (1953; Eng. tr., *Don Juan or the Love of Geometry*, 1969) shows the protagonist as a "Columbus of the soul" searching for a "virgin continent" and ironically ending up married to a former prostitute. *Biedermann und die Brandstifter* (1958; Eng. tr., *Biedermann and the Firebugs*, 1962) deals critically with Bertolt BRECHT's concept of the parable by showing the vagueness of a parabolic lesson; it is also Frisch's first attempt toward a non-Aristotelian concept of dramatic "perpetuity." *Andorra* (1962; Eng. tr., 1962) again discusses the image-creating hence love-destroying power of language by using the word "anti-Semitism" as a model for an analysis of prejudice.

In addition, Frisch developed new trends in the German novel. In *Stiller* (1954; Eng. tr., *I'm not Stiller*, 1958) he treats the problem of self-acceptance and identity; *Homo faber* (1957; Eng. tr., *Homo Faber: A Report*, 1959) concerns the ironic confrontation of a modern technologist with the ideas of fate and predestination. With *Mein Name sei Gantenbein* (1964; Eng. tr., *A Wilderness of Mirrors*, 1965), Frisch joined the avant-garde of modern narrators by telling a story in several possible varieties, thus demonstrating the distance between art and life. Similar in nature, except that it is fashioned for the stage, is his play *Biografie* (1967; Eng. tr., *Biography*, 1969). Frisch can be said to have invented a new type of "consciousness literature" in his famous literary diaries, *Tagebuch 1946–1949* (1950) and *Tagebuch 1966–1971* (1972; Eng. tr., *Sketchbook*, 1974). *Montauk* (1975) continues the series of autobiographical literary works that have become one of the hallmarks of Max Frisch's oeuvre.

See: H. Bänziger, *Frisch und Dürrenmatt* (1960); E. Stäuble, *Max Frisch: Gesamtdarstellung seines werkes* (1967); M. Jurgensen, *Max Frisch: die Dramen* (1968); T. Beckermann, *Über Max Frisch* (1971); R. Kaiser, *Max Frisch: das literarische Tagebuch* (1975).   R.K.

Fröding, Gustaf (1860–1911), Swedish poet, was born near Karlstad in the county of Värmland. In view of his poor health and emotional problems, much of Fröding's poetic oeuvre can be understood as part of his struggle for health and vigor and as prompted by a wish to communicate with a world from which in many ways he was excluded.

Fröding published three major collections of verse in the short span of five years, *Gitarr och dragharmonika* (1891; Eng. tr., *Guitar and Concertina*, 1925), *Nya dikter* (1894; New Poems), and *Stänk och flikar* (1896; Drops and Fragments). Together they form an impressive canon of recorded life, and their popular success in Sweden, and indeed in Scandinavia, has been tremendous. They also give evidence of personal development and growing maturity. Fröding's popularity was founded, above all, upon his familiarity with peasant and small-town life, his sparing but evocative descriptions of the Värmland scenery, and his humor. A rough hunter, a girl of the streets, an incorrigible small boy, a nasal prayer leader, a gay lieutenant, a drunken recruit, even an old mountain troll may emerge as his central figures. Into all he can project himself with humorous detachment and objective imagination. With a few notable exceptions—such as "Den gamla goda tiden," (1892; The Good Old Days)—his verse remains politically neutral, but his journalistic prose and his private letters bespeak a general radicalism in political, social, moral, and religious quesitons.

Technically, Fröding was a traditionalist. Among his models were Robert Burns, to whom he devoted a sympathetic study, Heinrich Heine, Lord Byron, and Goethe, apart from Swedish influences such as Viktor RYDBERG and Verner von HEIDENSTAM. Later Friedrich NIETZSCHE was to make a stimulating and disturbing impact on him. The chains of rhyme and meter have seldom been worn with such grace as by Fröding. As for rhythm, his verse appeared as an advance toward the naturalness of genuine speech; and, as for rhymes, it appeared to thrive upon them, even intellectually.

Stänk och flikar, his most important collection, was written partly under the impact of psychotic, hallucinatory experiences. It perfects a poetic method already employed in the earlier collections, that of imaginative identification either with great figures of the past, biblical or historical, or else with figures of symbolic value, social misfits and outcasts, such as tramps and prostitutes. The humility and tenderness typical of Fröding are particularly noticeable in poems addressed to women, whether they be members of his own class (like his mother and his elder sister and lifelong supporter) or the lower-class girls among whom he found love and acceptance. To this group belong such miracles of poetic diction as "Det borde varit stjärnor" (There should have been Stars), or, in his native dialect, "Nypenrosa" (Brier Rose).

The element of brooding in Fröding's poetry focuses around the perennial feelings of guilt that weighed on his mind. Although there may have been a real foundation for them in the social failure of his Uppsala years, his drinking habits, and his sexual irregularities, they were still largely expressions of a morbid scrupulosity. Be that as it may, they inspired some of his most profound poetry. To this group belong "Flickan i "ögat" (The Girl in the Eyes), "Drömmar i Hades" (Dreams in Hades), and "Sagan om Gral" (The Story of the Grail), in which "the grail" can be seen as a symbol of wholeness, the synthesis of good and evil impulses only to be attained by some superman or dreamed-of redeemer. The poetic cycle "En morgondröm" (A Morning Dream) is a Nietzschean or Aryan fantasy of purehearted and open-eyed love-making. It so outraged the bigoted moralists of the time, who took the poetic dream of pristine innocence for lewdness and depravity, that Fröding was prosecuted in the fall of 1896 for instigating immoral behavior. Defending himself with noble dignity, he was acquitted by the jury. It is generally held, however, that the trial was detrimental to his delicate health and may have hastened his certification and admittance to a mental hospital in 1898.

In the hospital, Fröding presented certain symptoms of schizophrenia, but periodically he continued his reading, especially of the Bible and of intellectually demanding works. He annotated a copy of his collected poems in 1903 with lucid but often self-berating comments. Shortly before his death, while living in quiet surroundings in the care of a devoted private nurse, he even experienced a spell of returning poetic inspiration. The result, remarkable by any standards, can be studied in *Reconvalescentia*, a posthumous collection (1913). The standard edition of Fröding's collected works is *Samlade skrifter*, ed. by R. G. Berg (16 vols, 1917–22). Selected translations are found in C. W. Stork, *Selected Poems* (1916) and *Anthology of Swedish Lyrics* (1930), pp. 183–214, and in A. Gustafson, *A History of Swedish Literature* (1961), pp. 316–24.

See: H. Olsson, *Fröding* (1950) and *Vinlövsranka och hagtornskrans* (1970).   S.A.B.

Fucini, Renato (1843–1921), Italian poet, short-story writer, and educator, was born in Monterotondo, Tuscany. As a writer, he is noted for the purity of his style and for his social concern. Fucini's early reputation was as a comic poet. His *Cento sonetti in vernacolo pisano* (1872; 100 Sonnets in the Pisan Vernacular), is a graphic, witty commentary on the life of the common people of Pisa. Because of the sonnets' popularity, Fucini was readily admitted to the literary and artistic circles of Florence, where he associated especially with the *macchiaioli* (impressionist) painters, but also met journalists and government officials who had come to Florence when it became the capital of Italy.

In 1877 Pasquale Villari, the Neapolitan historian and statesman, sent Fucini to Naples to study its slums and report on them to the rest of the nation. *Napoli a occhio nudo* (1878; Naples: A Close-Up View) consists of nine letters contrasting the vibrant beauty of Naples's countryside with the abysmal conditions in which four-fifths of its population lived. Although ignored for many years, this social document is now recognized as Fucini's best work as well as an outstanding example of verismo (*see* ITALIAN LITERATURE).

In 1878 Fucini became a teacher of Italian in Pistoia and served as inspector of its rural school district until 1900. During this period he published two collections of short stories, *Le veglie di Neri* (1882; Neri's Evening Gatherings) and *All'aria aperta* (1897; In the Open Air), the result of his observations of the people and customs of Tuscany. Fucini's impressionistic technique, influenced by the *macchiaioli*, draws upon realism, humor, and pathos without blending them. His characters are motivated by self-interest, yet are not without traces of generosity and altruism. Unlike Giovanni VERGA's characters, they generally accept their lot, finding relief from their misery in hunting or fishing. These two collections were widely used as school texts as late as 1949.

Between 1901 and 1909, Fucini wrote *Mondo nuovo* (New World) a textbook series for grades 1–6. *Il Ciuco di Melesecche* (1922; Driedapples's Donkey), a volume of children's stories in prose and in verse, appeared posthumously. Fucini also wrote two autobiographical collections of anecdotes, *Acqua passata* (1921; Water Gone By) and *Foglie al vento* (1922; Leaves in the Wind).

See: R. S. Phelps, *Italian Silhouettes* (1924), pp. 142–59; L. G. Sbrocchi, *Renato Fucini: l'uomo e l'opera* (1977).   L.G.S.

Fuks, Ladislav (1923–), Czech novelist and short-story writer, was born in Prague. After studying philosophy and psychology, he took his doctorate at Prague University. Fuks is a writer of the grotesque and bizarre, whose almost exclusive subject is death. He has been much influenced by Franz KAFKA, although not to the point of losing his own identity as a writer. His novel, *Pan Theodor Mundstock* (1963; Eng. tr., *Mr. Theodore Mundstock,* 1968) established his reputation both in Czechoslovakia and abroad. It is a portrait of a Jew doomed to enter a concentration camp who systematically prepares himself to undergo its rigors so that he may survive. Ironically, he is killed by one of the trucks come to take him and other prisoners to the camp. *Spalovač mrtvol* (1967; The Burner of Corpses) depicts the career of an undertaker who puts to death his partly Jewish wife and children, and ends up serving as an operator in the Nazi gas chambers. Fuks's finest work is probably the long novel *Variace pro temnou strunu* (1966; Variations for a Dark Spring), in which, against the background of events leading to the fall of Czechoslovakia, he tells a family horror story that mingles elements of vampirism and lycanthropy. Fuks's later work, such as the novel *Myši Natalie Mooshabrové* (1970; Natalia Mooshaber's Mice) seems increasingly divorced from reality. Some of his stories, collected in *Smrt morčete* (1969; The Death of a Guinea Pig), show a lively humor that contrasts sharply with his more typical obsession with death.

See: T. G. Winner, "Some Remarks on the Art of Ladislav Fuks," *Ricerche slavistiche,* vols. 17–19 (1970–72), pp. 587–99.   W.E.H.

Fulda, Ludwig (1862–1932), German dramatist and translator, was born in Frankfurt am Main. He studied in Heidelberg, Munich, and Berlin and visited the United States in 1906, subsequently writing *Amerikanische Eindrücke* (1906; American Impressions). He became president of the literary section of the Prussian Academy of Fine Arts in 1926. His editing of German poets of the 16th century suggested to him the theme of his first drama. The failure of this dramatization of the tragic fate of *Christian Günther* (1882) is almost symbolic of Fulda's own work, since his keen intelligence sensed ideals that his amiable, versatile, and facile talent was unable to attain.

In spite of his early espousal of Henrik IBSEN, Fulda deviated little in his own productions from the more ordinary French social drama. His award of the Schiller Prize was vetoed by William II, but Fulda received the Viennese Bauernfeld Prize for his comedy *Die Kameraden* (1894; The Comrades). His three-score plays show little or no development except in theatrical skill. Of lasting value, however, is Fulda's achievement as a translator. In this field his empathic and linguistic talents and his gift of versification master the most divergent problems of form.

See: A. Klaar, *Ludwig Fulda* (1922).

E.F. rev. A.L.W.

Furmanov, Dmitriy Andreyevich (1891–1926), Russian "proletarian" novelist and short-story writer, was born into a peasant family but spent his formative years in the major industrial city of Ivanovo-Voznesensk. After serving in World War I, he joined the Bolsheviks in 1918, and began writing for newspapers. Among the posts he occupied during the Civil War was that of political commissar in the famous division commanded by General Vasily Chapayev. This provided material for a work that has become a classic of Soviet literature: *Chapayev* (1923; Eng. tr., 1935). The novel is structured on a contrast that was also honored by many later Soviet writers—between the ideologue and the activist, in this case the political commissar Klychkov (a fictionalized Furmanov), a worker by origin, with little feel for the realities of military leadership and with much apprehension about combat, and the brilliant commander Chapayev, a peasant by origin and an instinctive but untutored revolutionary. As the novel develops, each moves toward the other, Klychkov growing in experience and courage, Chapayev in ideological awareness. A related theme is the nature of heroism—whether embodied in a single individual or in the masses. Based on Furmanov's own diaries, *Chapayev* is documentary in form, and won much acclaim in an age thirsty for literature about "real" life. Furmanov's last novel, *Myatezh* (1925; Revolt), is a semidocumentary account of the suppression of a peasant uprising in Central Asia; it was made into a play.

See: K. Kasper, *Dmitry Furmanov* (Halle, 1962); A. A. Isbakh, *Dmitrii Furmanov* (Moscow, 1967).   R.A.M.

Füst, Milán (1888–1967), Hungarian poet, novelist, and aesthetician, was born Milán Fürst in Budapest. His first work appeared in the literary review *Nyugat* (*see* HUNGARIAN LITERATURE) in 1908, and he remained a contributor to that publication throughout its existence. Füst studied law in Budapest and, after graduation, taught economics in a commercial school, but because of his involvement with the Hungarian Soviet Republic of 1919 he was forced into early retirement. Between the two world wars he traveled extensively abroad and published a volume of his poems in 1934. During World War II, most of his diary, the work of 40 years, was lost. After the war he published the text of his lectures on aesthetics. *Látomás és indulat a művészetben* (1948; Vision and Impulse in Art) still a fascinating testimony to Füst's perception and interpretation of art. From 1951 to 1960 he lectured at Eötvös Loránd University, where his idiosyncratic, passionately expressed views exerted a great influence on generations of students. The publication of his collected works began in 1955. With the French translation (1958) of his best novel, *A feleségem története* (1942; The Story of My Wife), Füst became known in the West as one of Hungary's ablest writers of fiction.

Although the volume of Fust's poetry is small, his poetic achievement is considerable. In his poems, the lyrical ego usually appears masked, speaking through personae. This device enables Füst to express what is eternally human, yet grounded in a particular historical reality. Füst's main preoccupation is with the tragic character of human fate. Although he sometimes breaks into grotesque or even ribald song, Füst's poetry, with its Pindaric meter and biblical overtones, is basically solemn, full of "heroic sadness," expressing a sense of isolation and a nostalgia for "real life." His poetic diction and his use of Pindaric meter and biblical overtones made a great impact upon the poets of the third *Nyugat* generation, such as Sandor WEÖRES. Indeed, his influence is still felt in Hungarian poetry today.

Significant among his novels is *Advent* (1923; Advent), a story of religious persecution in 17th-century England, that was, in fact, a protest against Hungary's counterrevolutionary White Terror of 1920. *A feleségem története* is a compelling, almost hypnotic tale about the growth of pathological jealousy. Füst's models were Shakespeare and Lev TOLSTOY; and his somewhat bizarre but imaginative essays on these two writers were included in *Emlékezések és tanulmányok* (1956; Reminiscences and Studies). As a playwright, Füst was much underrated in his lifetime, but *IV. Henrik király* (1940; King Henry IV) is an impressive historical drama with modern insights and Shakespearean undertones. Füst also translated *King Lear* into Hungarian. His diaries (*Napló*) were published in 1976.

See: L. Kassák, "Füst Milán," *Nyugat* 20 (1927): 279–84; E. Vajda, "Füst Milán Világa," *Ujhold* 2 (1947): 189–96; T. Ungvári, "Arcképvázlat Füst Milánról," *Csillag* 10 (1956): 1006–13; Gy. Somlyó, *Füst Milán* (1969).

G.G.

G

Gabriel y Galán, José María (1870–1905), Spanish poet, was born and grew up in Frades de la Sierra in the province of Salamanca. After a brief period as a rural teacher, he married and became a farmer in an isolated village of Extremadura. His fame came suddenly when he won a poetry reading contest in Salamanca in 1901 with his poem "El ama" (The Housewife). At about the same time, "El Cristu benditu" (The Blessed Christ), a poem to a village shrine written in rural dialect, also became popular. These two poems are representative of all of his work, and their publication brought him immediate fame. Enthusiasm for his noninnovative poetry was sometimes couched in terms of disapproval of the current innovations of modernism (*see* SPANISH LITERATURE). In its small way, Galán's popular traditionalist poetry is also related to the literary revolution of the Generation of 1898 and its glorification of Castile. His is a sentimental poetry of commonplace and insufficiently individualized ideas on such subjects as work, motherhood, patriotism, and faith. His work is deeply felt but in both theme and technique it has little to offer the sophisticated reader. His *Castellanas* (1902; Poems of Castile), the dialect verses of *Extremeñas* (1902; Poems of Extremadura), and *Campesinas* (1904; Country Rhymes) are still popular as recital pieces, somewhat in the manner of the poems of James Whitcomb Riley in the United States.

See: L. Jiménez Martos, "Introducción," to J. M. Gabriel y Galán, *Poesía y prosa* (1970), pp. 9–49.

H.L.B.

Gadda, Carlo Emilio (1893–1973), Italian novelist and essayist, was born in Milan. He fought in World War I and was a prisoner of war. After occasional work as a civil engineer, Gadda turned to writing, contributing numerous topical articles to *L'Ambrosiano* and *La gazzetta del popolo,* later collected in *Le meraviglie d'Italia* (1939; The Marvels of Italy) and *Gli anni* (1943; The Years). He also wrote essays, book reviews, and other short pieces for the journals *Solaria* and *Letteratura,* later included in *La Madonna dei filosofi* (1931; Our Lady of the Philosophers) and *Il castello di Udine* (1934; The Castle of Udine). His first important novel, *La cognizione del dolore* (1963; Eng. tr., *Acquainted with Grief,* 1969), first appeared in serial form in *Letteratura* in 1938.

Gadda's best and most representative work belongs to the postwar period and includes the Milanese tales of *L'Adalgisa* (1944), the novel *Quer pasticciaccio brutto de via Merulana* (1957; Eng. tr., *That Awful Mess on Via Merulana,* 1965), regarded as his masterpiece, and *Eros e Priapo* (1967), a psychosexual harangue against fascism. Gadda's other publications span several genres. *Il primo libro delle favole* (1952; The First Book of Fables), a collection of parodistic aphorisms, was followed by the collection *Novelle dal Ducato in fiamme* (1953; Tales from the Duchy in Flames) and his masterful translation of Joseph Conrad's *The Secret Agent.* In 1955, Gadda published *Giornale di guerra e prigionia* (War and Prison Journals), and the volume *I sogni e la fòlgore* (Dreams and Lightning Bolts), containing *La Madonna dei filosofi, Il castello di Udine,* and *L'Adalgisa.* A book of major

essays, *I viaggi la morte* (Travels Death), appeared in 1958, and a collection of sketches, *Verso la Certosa* (Towards the Charterhouse), in 1961. He won the French International Prize for Literature in 1963 for *La cognizione del dolore.* Gadda's last publications include a new edition of his short stories, *Accoppiamenti giudiziosi* (1963; Judicious Couplings); the historical satire *I Luigi di Francia* (1964; The Kings Louis of France); a satirical play, *Il guerriero, l'ammazzone, lo spirito della poesia nel verso immortale del Foscolo* (1967; The Warrior, the Amazon, and the Poetical Spirit of Foscolo's Immortal Verse); *La meccanica* (1970, Mechanics); and *Novella seconda* (1971; The Second Short Story).

Gadda's prime impulse as a writer is to verify the existence of a rationally governed order, but his perception of chaos weakens his belief in the attainability of such an end. From his early stories to the mature prose of *Quer pasticciaccio,* Gadda's writing is conspicuously fragmentary. In its perennial disorder and lack of symmetry, his work transmits an awareness of an incoherent, unstable, and ambiguous universe. All that is left for Gadda is the contemplation of the "grotesque"—this irrational, disordered complex of phenomena that he seeks to understand—by means of macaronic prose, baroque description, and pastiche. Gadda uses pastiche (the imitation of various prose styles) in order to negate the certainty of traditional literary expression, but this technique is also a means of concealing his own anxiety in the face of a disintegrated world that nevertheless continues to express itself through conventional language.

Gadda's art is best defined, within the context of European expressionism, as that of a writer in crisis. Yet it is the very extremity of his experience that animates his quest for a new realism, qualifying him as an important forerunner of the "new novel" (*see* FRENCH LITERATURE).

See: O. Ragusa, "Gadda, Pasolini, and Experimentalism: Form or Ideology?" in *From Verism to Experimentalism,* ed. by S. Pacifici (1969), pp. 239–69; R. S. Dombroski, "Moral Commitment and Invention in Gadda's Poetics," *RLMC* 25, no. 3 (1972), and *Introduzione allo studio di Carlo Emilio Gadda* (1973).   R.S.D.

Gaiser, Gerd (1908–76), German novelist, essayist, and art historian, was born in Oberriexingen, Wür Hemberg, the son of a Swabian clergyman. He studied art and art history at the art academies of Stuttgart, Königsberg, and the University of Tübingen and traveled extensively throughout southern Europe. During World War II he was an officer in the Luftwaffe. After the war, he taught art and art history in his native Württemberg. Gaiser owes his popularity during the 1950s and 1960s to his retrospective, richly descriptive narratives of World War II. His war narratives are populated by an elite with youth movement ideals, who stoically endure the German defeat. They are protected from feeling the impact of their failure and the failure of their cause by hauntingly beautiful, dreamlike fever trances and a fatalistic incomprehension of their responsibility. The narratives set in a postwar milieu constrast that elite with materialistic, plebian contemporaries of the Federal Republic. Gaiser began to write during World War II in a late-expressionist manner inspired by a Nazified Friedrich Hölderlin and Friedrich NIETZSCHE, as in *Reiter am Himmel* (1941; Riders in the Sky). He continued after the war with short stories whose Fascist spirit is hidden behind lyrical evocations of art, southern European landscape, culture, and modern alienation, as in *Zwischenland* (1949; Land In-Between; and *Am Pass Nascondo*, 1960).

In his novels, Gaiser masked his conservative ideology by adopting modern forms. In *Schlußball* (1958; Eng. tr., *The Final Ball, 1960),* for instance, he related the same events from the perspectives of different characters. In *Die sterbende Jagd* (1953; The Dying Chase), he mixed dream vision, description, and reportage in a style that has been called "magic realism." The subjects of his novels are topical; his first, *Eine Stimme hebt an* (1950; A Voice Sets In), for which he won the Fontane Prize, deals with a soldier's return from war, and his second, *Jagd,* with the Luftwaffe's defeat in the air war. He gives a romanticized view of man and technology in the manner of Antoine de SAINT-EXUPÉRY. His most popular novel, *Schlußball* (translated into nine languages) exposes the corruption and lack of sustaining values of the society of the "economic miracle." Critical opinion on the quality of his work is sharply divided.

See: C. Hohoff, *Gerd Gaiser: Werk und Gestalt* (1962). M. Reich-Ranicki, *Deutsche Literatur in West und Ost: Prosa seit 1945* (1963), pp. 40–56. U.M.

Gala, Antonio (1936–), Spanish playwright, poet, short story writer, and essayist, was born in Córdoba. Although Gala has been active in the theater since the early 1960s, the fact that his plays remained unpublished for some years delayed general awareness of his work. His first play, *Los verdes campos del Edén* (1963; The Green Fields of Eden), winner of the Calderón de la Barca and City of Barcelona prizes, is perhaps his best known. Three of his fundamental preoccupations appear in this poetic but somewhat inexperienced work: man's inability to obtain peace and love, man's solitude, and the playwright's critical perception of contemporary Spanish society. Also present is Gala's tendency to use ambiguous symbols. In doing this, as he writes in his "autocriticism" of *Los verdes campos del Edén,* he attempts to evoke the similarities between seemingly unrelated individuals and events, implicitly affirming that ultimately each shares many of the characteristics of its counterpart. The spectator is asked to perceive universal problems by focusing on individual situations.

See: A. Gala, *El caracol en el espejo. El sol en el hormiguero. Noviembre y un poco de yerba* (1970), with studies by J. Monleón (pp. 9–40), J. M. Rodríguez Méndez (pp. 44–47) and P. Laín Entralgo (pp. 113–18); F. Ruiz Ramón, *Historia del teatro español, siglo XX* (1977), pp. 516–24. L.G.-del-V.

Galaction, Gala, pseud. of Grigore Pişculescu (1879–1961), Romanian novelist and short-story writer, was born in Dideşti-Teleorman. He contributed stories to the journals *Ligă ortodoxă* and *Adevărul.* In 1899 he enrolled at the University of Bucharest to study literature, but he switched to theology, receiving a doctorate in 1909 and, in his 40s, became an Orthodox priest. The story "Moara lui Califar" (1902; Califar's Mill) was noteworthy for its lyrical, transcendent quality. Others appeared in *Linia dreaptă,* then edited by Todor ARGHEZI, and in other leading journals. His short stories appeared in the volumes *Bisericuţa din răzoare* (1914; The Chapel in the Fields), *Clopoţele de la monastirea Neamţu* (1916; The Bells of Neamţu Monastery), *Raboz pe bradul verde* (1920; The Notch on the Green Tree), and *Toamna de odinioară* (1924; Autumn in the Old Days).

Galaction's most important novels are *Roxana* (1930), *Papucii lui Mahmud* (1932; Mahmud's Slippers), and *Doctorul Taifun* (1933; Doctor Taifun). His fiction is imbued with a deep humanitarianism and his characters are often faced with profound moral decisions. In *Papucii lui Mahmud,* Savu Pantofaro kills an innocent Turkish prisoner of war in a drunken rage and is thereafter tortured by visions of his victim in tattered slippers. To amend for his crime, Savu spends the rest of his life making slippers for the poor. Pursued by his visions, he hunts for the bones of his victim and reburies them in Mahmud's family tomb. Savu's expiation becomes complete when he dies in Constantinople and is himself buried in a Muslim cemetery.

See: T. Vârgolici, *Gala Galaction* (1967). V.A.

Gałczyński, Konstanty Ildefons (1905–53), Polish poet and dramatist, was born and died in Warsaw. His rich imagination manifested itself even in his selection of strange pseudonyms: Il de Fons, Kig, Karakuliambro, King Herod, Mandarin Li Coer, and so on. His poetry is a unique blend of the wildest fantasies, plebeian theater imagery, pure nonsense, wit, and sharp satire, combined with the most delicate lyricism. Among his literary ancestors are street minstrels, popular song writers, and medieval jugglers. His general concept of poetry is similar to that of Vachel Lindsay, and, like Lindsay, he recited his own poems movingly and beautifully.

After his literary debut in 1923, Gałczyński became associated with the satirical magazine *Cyrulik Warszawski* (1926–33). In 1929 he published a grotesque and satirical novel, *Porfirion Osiełek czyli Klub świętokradców* (Porphyrion the Donkey, or the Blasphemers' Club), and in 1930 a bizarre semiautobiographical poem, *Koniec świata: Wizje Świętego Ildefonsa czyli Satyra na wszechświat* (The End of the World: Visions of Saint Ildefons, or a Satire on the Universe).

His best poems, however, appeared after World War II: *Zaczarowana dorożka* (1948; The Enchanted Coach), *Ślubne obrączki* (1949; Wedding Rings), *Niobe* (1951), and *Wit Stwosz* (1952). Gałczyński also wrote for the theater: *Będziemy biedni* (perf. on radio in 1938; We'll Be Poor, in collaboration with Jerzy Zagórski), *Babcia i wnuczek, czyli Noc cudów* (1955; Grandma and Grandson, or A Night of Wonders), and *Noc mistrza Andrzeja* (1956; The Night of Master Andrew; in collaboration with Adam Mauersberger). Gałczyński also published numerous film scripts and radio plays. From 1946 to 1950 he was a regular contributor of satirical sketches and poems to the weekly *Przekrój.* The most popular of his series were the grotesque, absurd miniature plays *Zielona Gęś* (The Green Goose) and humourous feuilletons *Listy z fiołkiem* (Letters with Violet).

See: *Słownik współczesnych pisarzy polskich,* vol. 1 (1963), pp. 531–36; M. Wyka-Hussakowska, *Gałczyński a wzory literackie* (1970); W. P. Szymańksi, *Konstanty Ildefons Gałczyński* (1972); A. Drawicz, *Konstanty Ildefons Gałczyński* (1974). E.J.C.

Galich, Aleksandr Arkadyevich, pseud. of Aleksandr Ginzburg (1919–77), Russian poet and dramatist, was born in Yekaterinoslav and died in Paris. He studied at the Moscow Literary Institute and at theater studios directed by the producers Konstantin Stanislavsky and Valentin Pluchek and by the dramatist Aleksey ARBUZOV. During World War II, Galich worked in a theater at the front. In the years following the war he was the author or coauthor of nearly a dozen films, and his plays were produced in various Soviet theaters.

In the 1960s, Galich achieved extraordinary popularity in the Soviet Union and abroad as the composer and singer of songs that were circulated widely in tape recordings and typewritten copies. In 1971 he was expelled from the Union of Soviet Writers and the Union of Cinematographers; in June 1974 he emigrated from the USSR, living first in Norway and then in France, where he met an accidental death a short time later.

Artistically, the most important part of Galich's work consists of his songs and poems, in which he provides a satirical representation of the Soviet way of life. The characters in his songs are typically Soviet bureaucrats, Communist Party members, former prisoners, and petty officials. A few poems—"Poema o Staline" (A Poem about Stalin), for example—gravitate towards meditations of a philosophical and ethical nature. Galich makes abundant use of street slang and prison jargon, as well as colloquial words and phrases that are rarely if ever encountered in the officially approved literature. This peculiarity of his poetry, along with the satirical sharpness of his images, has distinguished him as a dissident poet who shatters the generally accepted aesthetic norms of Soviet literature.

See: E. Etkind, "'Chelovecheskaya komediya' Aleksandra Galicha," *Kontinent* 5 (1975): 405–26; L. Kopelev, "Pamyati Aleksandra Galicha," *Kontinent* 16 (1978): 334–43; V. Betaki, "Galich i russkiye bardy," *Kontinent* 16 (1978): 349–53.   D.K.

Ganivet, Angel (1865–98), Spanish essayist and novelist, was born in Granada into a modest industrial family. He showed remarkable intelligence from childhood through his university studies. In 1892 he obtained a position in the Spanish State Department (Consular Section), a rather inadequate choice for a young man who held a law degree and a Ph.D. in philosophy, and who moreover was totally incapable of any other social attitude than a blunt openness and frankness. In 1891, Ganivet met Amelia Roldán, his lifelong mistress and mother of his two children. From 1892 to 1895 he held a consular position in Antwerp, where, partly as a result of close contact with European ideas, he experienced an intense intellectual and spiritual crisis. In 1895 he was promoted to consul in Helsinki. Soon afterward he wrote for *El Defensor*, a Granada periodical, a series of articles that were later collected under the title *Granada la Bella* (1896). In 1897 he published the *Idearium español* and *La conquista del reino de Maya* (The Conquest of Maya's Kingdom), and, again in *El Defensor*, the *Cartas Finlandesas* (Letters from Finland). Ganivet's most influential book, *Los trabajos del infatigable creador Pío Cid* (The Labors of the Indefatigable Creator Pío Cid), appeared in 1898. This was a critical and fatal year in his life. In August he was nominated Spanish consul in Riga. Amelia, from whom he had been alienated, came to Riga against his wishes. Ganivet had been contemplating suicide for several years, and on the day of Amelia's arrival he threw himself into the river Dvina. Rescued, he jumped again, and this time drowned. Progessive syphilitic paralysis and the arrival of Amelia were influential only in that they precipitated the act.

Ganivet's correspondence shows him to have been, paradoxically, both a divided and a coherent personality. A man of powerful intellect, deeply religious inclinations, and unbending ethical character, he was also a skeptic who could indulge in bouts of unbridled sensuality. This inner conflict came to a crisis in Antwerp where, through a period of "darkness of the soul," Ganivet experienced an illumination that transformed him into an extreme spiritualist. His books and the outlook they reflect are born from this crisis, which took place between 1892 and 1895. It is no exaggeration to say that his work and his life are the coherent expression of a complex but solidly unified system of thought into which his spiritual experience has been absorbed and integrated. In his doctoral dissertation, *España filosófica contemporánea* (1889), Ganivet had already described modern Spain as a divided country where ideas are not instruments of social construction but dangerous weapons used by Spanish political groups for their mutual destruction. In the *Idearium español*, Ganivet expresses his belief in the possibility of changing such a situation: *ideas picudas* ("pointed ideas") can and must be changed into *ideas redondas* ("round ideas"). "Round ideas" are like millstones: from their interaction we obtain our flour. Dialogue, then, must replace conflict. The character of Spain is the result of two components: her geographical territory, which inclines her towards independence, and her racial heritage of Arab, Jewish, and Castilian blood. These elements ideally predispose her for the creation of a contemplative culture that would combine sensual and mystical elements of Semitic origin with Castilian strength and determination. From them modern Spain could derive the spiritual energies which would enable her to become a Christian Athens. Spain failed in the past because she betrayed her identity by becoming a great imperial power.

Mother to so many countries, Spain is like a virgin who has remained faithful to her contemplative vocation throughout an active life but who, although so externally effective, must realize now, at last, her true mission in giving birth to a great society and culture. *Los trabajos del infatigable creador Pío Cid* presents the individual capable of personally endeavoring to put into practice this spiritual vocation. As "Cid" (Conqueror), Ganivet's hero is a man of action, but as "Pío" (Pious Man), his deeds are not of war, but of persuasion and conversion. The "virginity" of his soul is expressed in the detached way in which he influences his world: he teaches a serving maid how to read and write, makes a good mother of a frivolous aristocrat, preaches political honesty but refuses to be involved in practical politics, and is a model family man who refuses to marry. Only by this crucifixion of the flesh, of individual drives and ambitions, can the true soul, both of Pío Cid and of Spain, be born.

Although Ganivet died in 1898 and has often been called a precursor of the Generation of 1898, it is legitimate to consider him actually a member of that movement. In his obsession with individual and national *abulia* (paralysis of the will), this preoccupation with the spiritual regeneration of Spain, which he sees poetically expressed in the moral transformation of his literary characters, his personal commitment, and his history of personal crisis, he is very much an intellectual and moral colleague of Miquel de UNAMUNO, AZORÍN, PIO BAROJA, and Antonio MACHADO. He died when they began to blossom, but his powerful personality left its imprint in works which can legitimately be considered among the most influential of this period.

See: L. Seco de Lucena Paredes, *Juicio de Angel Ganivet sobre su obra literaria* (1962); J. Herrero, *Angel Ganivet, un lluminado* (1966); H. Ramsden, *Angel Ganivet's Idearium Español: A Critical Study* (1967).   J.H.

Gaos, Vicente (1919–), Spanish poet and critic, was born in Valencia. From 1948 to 1956 and in subsequent years he has taught Spanish literature in American universities. His published work as critic and anthologist is abundant and includes *La poética de Campoamor* (1955), *Temas y problemas de literatura española* (1959), *Antología del* *grupo poético de 1927* (1965), and *Diez siglos de poésia española* (1975; Ten Centuries of Spanish Poetry).

Gaos's first book of poetry was *Arcángel de mi noche* (1944; Archangel of My Night), first winner of the Adonais Prize. It was followed by *Sobre la tierra* (1945; On Earth), *Luz desde el sueño* (1947; Light from the Dream), *Profecía del recuerdo* (1956; Prophecy of Remembrance), and *Concierto en mí y en vosotros* (1965; Concerto in Me and in You), among others. His *Poesías completas* have been published in two volumes (1959 and 1974). Gaos's poetry has been given a number of labels, some of them contradictory. He has been considered a neoromantic, a Neoplatonist, a classicist, and a poet who has broken with the neoclassicism of the Generation of 1936. Although he is a bit too young to be a member of this generation, he nevertheless has much in common with them, notably his return to classic forms (much of his work consists of sonnets) and a thematics rooted in human and divine love. Faith, occasionally doubt, and the Christian deity are at the center of his work, while the poetics of social action, common to many of his contemporaries, is absent from it, despite the human solidarity expressed in the long opening poem of *Concierto en mí* and elsewhere. His poetry perhaps lacks a strong individual profile because of the marked tendency to use other writers, poems, and lines as points of departure. Intertextual echoes of such classic poets as Fray Luis de León, Saint John of the Cross, and Garcilaso are mixed with those of Antonio MACHADO, Miguel de UNAMUNO, and poets of the Generation of 1927 such as Vicente ALEIXANDRE, Jorge GUILLÉN, and Pedro SALINAS.

See: V. G. de la Concha, *La poesía española de posguerra* (1973), pp. 423-30.   H.L.B.

Garaudy, Roger (1913-), French philosopher, was born in Marseille to working-class parents. At 14 he converted to Protestantism. In 1933, Garaudy joined the Communist Party and remained a member for 36 years. For 28 years he occupied leading positions as a member of the Executive Central Committee, but after the revelations made by Khrushchev at the 20th Congress, his faith in communism was shaken. He was expelled from the Party in 1970. Along with his political commitments, Garaudy pursued a university career. In 1953 he passed the state doctorate in philosophy with a dissertation on the materialistic theory of knowledge. For several years he has taught philosophy at the universities of Clermont and Poitiers.

Garaudy's publications are numerous and varied, and he has even written novels and plays. His most important writings, however, are works in the general history of ideas, Marxist studies at all levels (specialized or popular analysis, participation in polemics with existentialist and Christian thinkers), research on moral philosophy, and more recently, essays on contemporary art and aesthetics. Among his most important books are *Théorie matérialiste de la connaissance* (1953; Materialistic Theory of Knowledge), *Perspectives de l'homme* (1961; Perspectives of Man), *Le Grand Tournant du socialisme* (1969; Eng. tr., *The Crisis in Communism: The Turning-Point of Socialism,* 1969), *Peut-on être communiste aujourd'hui?* (1968; Can One Be a Communist Today?), *Toute la vérité* (1970; Eng. tr., *The Whole Truth,* 1971), *L'Itinéraire d'Aragon: du surréalisme au monde réel* (1961; The Itinerary of Aragon from Surrealism to the Real World), *Esthétique et invention du futur* (1971; (Aesthetics and Invention of the Future), and *Danser sa vie* (1973; To Dance One's Life), with a preface by Maurice Béjart.

In keeping with Marxist epistemology, Garaudy's major research is on the foundations of revolutionary politics. Following the spirit of Marx, rather than his outdated formulas, Garaudy foresees a solution for contemporary problems in the reconciliation of the double scientific and socialist revolutions. Today man risks alienation of two sorts: technical as well as political. Thus the goal of socialism should not simply be economic and social justice; it should also give each individual his or her personal chances for creativity. This reasoning explains Garaudy's increasing interest in the artistic tradition and the modern arts, for aesthetic creation is one of the few reasons for hope in the modern world.   E.M.-S.

Garborg, Arne (1851-1924), Norwegian poet, novelist, and essayist, was born in Jæren, in southwestern Norway, to a family of poor but independent peasant farmers. When Garborg was about eight years old, his father went through a religious crisis that made the man gloomy and tyrannical, and he forbade the children to attend a "worldly" school or even to read books. Yet Arne managed to read by stealth, resolving to leave the farm, to which as eldest son he had hereditary rights, and to go to the city. Nevertheless, Garborg valued family continuity more and more as he grew older, and he never ceased to regret his own break with his parents.

In Christiania (now Oslo), Garborg studied at the university, supporting himself by writing trenchant, irreverent articles on contemporary issues. He learned to write *riksmål* with great skill, but in his first important book, *Bondestudentar* (1883; Peasant Students), he returned to *landsmål* (*see* NORWEGIAN LITERATURE). (*Bondestudentar* describes a phenomenon new in Garborg's day, the peasant boy uprooted from his environment and unable to fit into the life of the university. *Mannfolk* (1886; Menfolk) is a naturalistic novel describing young men adrift in the city; *Hjaa ho Mor* (1890; At Mother's) is its counterpart, concerning the life of a young girl who tries to maintain her respectability.

Garborg rejected the pietism of his parents, siding with the modernists on the two burning questions of the day: free love and atheism. Yet he opposed ideological fervor and dogmatic attitudes. In *Trætte mænd* (1891; Tired Men), a novel written in diary form, he recorded his doubts about absolute values. This brilliantly written book is filled with a sense of neoromantic resignation. After *Trætte mænd,* Garborg returned to the scenes and subjects of his childhood in Jæren. The tragic novel *Fred* (1892; Eng. tr., *Peace,* 1929), based on the life of Garborg's own father, is a powerful study of Enok Hove, a sincere but unlearned peasant caught in the grip of a fire-and-brimstone religion. The chronicles of the Hove family are continued in a later dramatic trilogy, of which the first play, *Læraren* (1896; The Teacher), has enjoyed the greatest success of any dramatic work written in *landsmål*.

In addition to his fiction and dramatic writing, Garborg wrote and translated philosophical-religious books, published volumes of letters and diaries, and, in 1895, produced the most popular of all his works, the poetic cycle *Haugtussa* (The Hill Innocent). *Haugtussa* tells the story of a young mystic who has the power to see the souls of the dead as well as the invisible trolls and sprites that surround human beings. Her struggle to conquer the powers of darkness is described with a spiritual exaltation that, along with the lyric beauty of the separate poems, the pictures of Jæren landscapes, and the homely, intimate details of peasant life, makes *Haugtussa* one of the most important poetic works ever published in *landsmål*.

See: H. A. Larsen, "Arne Garborg," *ASR* 12 (1924): 275-83; R; Thesen, *Arne Garborg I-III* (1935-39).
H.A.L.

García Hortelano, Juan (1928–), Spanish novelist and short-story writer, was born in Madrid, where he studied law and subsequently worked as a civil servant. His first novel, *Nuevas amistades* (1959; New Friendships), won the Biblioteca Breve Prize. It recounts the empty existence of a group of young people belonging to the Madrid bourgeoisie. The effectiveness of the resulting social indictment is due largely to the dialogues that reveal to the reader the amoral life of this sector of Spanish society. This novel is perhaps the best example of García Hortelano's "critical realism," where the illusion of objectivity is achieved by combining documentarily accurate dialogue with interior monologue. In his second novel, *Tormenta de verano* (1962; Eng. tr., *Summer Storm,* 1962) the novelist reiterates his criticism of moral corruption by focusing on the oligarchy born of the Civil War. *El gran momento de Mary Tribune* (1972; Mary Tribune's Great Moment) is a social and moral indictment of the narrator-protagonist's meaningless existence. Structurally, this work is highly experimental. Stylistically, it exhibits excellent craftsmanship in the use of dialogue, irony, and language appropriate to a variety of social levels. García Hortelano belongs to the social realist Generation of 1950 whose members adhere to the principle of literary objectivity in order to portray the moral chaos produced by the Civil War.

See: P. Gil Casado, *La novela social española* (1968), pp. 41–59; R. Schwartz, *Spain's New Wave Novelists 1950–1974* (1976), pp. 43–52.   J.O.

García Lorca, Federico (1898–1936), Spanish poet and playwright born in Granada, is probably the most widely known Spanish writer since Cervantes. His native Andalusia had a profound impact on his character and his works. He lived his childhood with intense sensitivity, immersed in the popular tradition of Granada, its songs, its poetry, and its folklore. Two phases of his formative years had an equally lasting effect on him: the study of music, which led to active participation in musical activity throughout his career, notably in his collaboration with his fellow Granadan Manuel de Falla, and his affiliation with the Residencia de Estudiantes in Madrid, where he became the close friend of countless writers and artists, among them Luis Buñuel, Pablo Neruda, and Salvador Dalí. He took his law degree in 1923 but never led any professional life other than poet and playwright, along with his artistic avocations of music and painting. Lorca was one of an extraordinary group of poets, the so-called Generation of 1927, whose personal relationships were intimate and who shared in the post-World War I currents of avant-gardism while creating, each in his own way, a complex new poetic style based on image and metaphor. They found precedents and inspiration in Spain's rich lyrical tradition, particularly in the esoteric art of the metaphorical baroque poet Luis de Góngora (*see* SPANISH LITERATURE). The works that brought Lorca the greatest recogniton during his lifetime are those that integrate tradition and modernity in especially dramatic fashion: *Romancero gitano* (1928; Eng. tr., *The Gypsy Ballads of García Lorca,* 1953), and the tragedies of the 1930s. Ironically, his greatest measure of fame stems from his premature death at the hands of Fascist partisans in the early days of the Spanish Civil War. His name has become one of the great antitotalitarian symbols of the 20th century.

Lorca's earliest poetry, *Libro de poemas* (1921), and his first play, the fantasy *El maleficio de la mariposa* (1920; Eng. tr., *The Butterfly's Evil Spell,* 1963), are characterized by the passion of a reflective young poet who experiences the anguishing transition from child to adult. Despite the relative immaturity of these works, certain Lorcan hallmarks are already in evidence, among them the inseparability of poetry and drama, the somber juxtaposition of life and death alongside playful irony, and a profound probing into the chthonic spirit of children, the land, and creatures of nature. His maturation as a poet came quickly. Although he published no other collections until 1927, the six intervening years were a period of great creative activity. Publishing for Lorca meant in large measure reading his works aloud in bardlike fashion, a practice that, given his remarkable vocal ability and personal attractiveness, earned him many admirers and contributed much to his growing reputation as a writer. By 1922 he had completed many of the series of poems entitled *Poema del cante jondo* (Poem of the Deep Song) in which he evokes the rhythms and emotional power of the ancient Andalusian *cante jondo* with its anguished vocal sonorities accompanied by the dramatic chords of the guitar. Several of these poems were read at a festival of the *cante jondo* in that year, but the collection itself was not published until 1931. Throughout his career, Lorca was simultaneously poet and playwright. In the mid-1920s he wrote two puppet farces, the experimental sketch *El paseo de Buster Keaton* (1925; Buster Keaton's Promenade), and his first major play, the delicately poetic *Mariana Pineda,* which was staged in 1927 with the distinguished actress Margarita Xirgu as the heroine. The latter is an historical figure of early 19th-century Granada who had become a legend in the popular poetic tradition of song and ballad. In 1927, Lorca also published his second collection of poetry, *Canciones* (Songs), which he had completed three years earlier. Along with the *Poema del cante jondo,* the *Canciones* may be his purest lyric. They express short, fleeting moments of poetic experience. Many are dedicated to children and best understood, as is *Mariana Pineda,* from the point of view of a child's perception of the world. Although less overtly Andalusian than the *Cante jondo* or *Romancero gitano,* *Canciones* is well marked by the presence of the popular traditions of the region and its three great cities, Córdoba, Seville, and Granada.

The 18 poems which make up *Romancero gitano* were written between 1924 and 1927 and take their form from the medieval Spanish ballads of oral tradition. Like their ancient counterparts, Lorca's poems are both narrative and dramatic. They are so deeply rooted in known reality that despite the complexities of their metaphorical imagery they remain intelligible even to the unlettered Spaniard. The central theme is the gypsy in vital contact with a sensual and violent world of moons, winds, sex, blood, and death, and the ominous presence of the Spanish Civil Guard bent on his destruction. While the gypsy subculture of Andalusia was an integral part of Lorca's personal experience, the world of the American blacks that he discovered in New York in 1929–30, although it inevitably attracted him, was alien to him and defied any traditional mode of expression. To translate into poetry his vision of the alien city and its black subculture, he invented a tumultuous labyrinth of seemingly incoherent and nightmarish images and a dissonant system of free verse forms. His vision of the city shows decay, desolation, and both spiritual and physical corruption. His vision of the blacks is deeply compassionate and points to an ultimate triumph of primitive innocence and elemental forces. The definitive collection of these poems, *Poeta en Nueva York,* was published posthumously in 1940 in Mexico City (Eng. tr., 1940, 1955).

Lorca's triumph as a playwright coincided with the years of the Spanish Republic, under whose aegis he directed a highly successful traveling theater company, "La Barraca." From 1930 to 1936 six of his plays were staged for the first time, with the collaboration of some of the leading actresses of both Spain and Spanish America. Among them are the farce *La zapatera prodigiosa* (1930; Eng. tr., *The Shoemaker's Prodigious Wife*, 1963), the tragedies *Bodas de sangre* (1933; Eng. tr., *Blood Wedding*, 1945) and *Yerma* (1934; Eng. tr., 1945), and the drama *Doña Rosita la soltera* (1935; Eng. tr., *Doña Rosita the Spinster*, 1963). With the exception of his farces, Lorca's theatre is essentially tragic and thematically skeletal. His protagonists are caught in a web of preexisting circumstances from which there is no escape. The dramatic substance is not in the contrivance of events but in the progressive intensification of those circumstances, an intensification that is communicated through systematized poetic language reinforced by song, stylized movement, and any and all resources the stage can offer. For Lorca the theater was a spectacle and a celebration of the poetic imagination. Like his poetry, his plays have deep Spanish roots, but in all but two cases he consciously rejected what is historically recognizable in favor of a generic view of the human condition in its elemental circumstances. The depiction, however, is so vitalized that the universalization or archetype becomes secondary to the spectacle of individual action. The two theatrical genres he most cultivated are those traditional forms which are generic and ahistorical: farce and tragedy. The basic theme of his theater is not unrelated to his vision of the gypsy and the American black as an individual with the right to personal integrity and freedom. The protagonists of his tragedies—*Bodas de sangre*, *Yerma*, and *La casa de Bernarda Alba* (written in 1936)—are denied that fundamental right.

The last major work of Lorca to be published during his lifetime is also a masterpiece of the European elegiac tradition, *Llanto por Ignacio Sánchez Mejías* (1935; Eng. tr., *Lament for the Death of a Bullfighter and Other Poems*, 1937). Some of the verses with which he eulogized his good friend are often considered to be applicable to the poet himself. It is as if he had written the epitaph the world would have written for him.

See: C. Ramos-Gil, *Claves líricas de García Lorca* (1967); J. Guillén, "Federico en persona," in *Obras completas de Federico García Lorca* (1973); S. M. Greenfield, "Lorca's Theatre: A Synthetic Reexamination," *JSSTC* 5, no. 1 (1977): 31–46.   S.M.G.

García Nieto, José (1914–), Spanish poet and critic, was born in Oviedo and has spent most of his life in Madrid. Although he is unlikely to be considered a major poet, his historical importance is assured by his having founded in 1943 and later become director of the journal *Garcilaso*, an important organ of the new "humanized" poetry opposed to the "pure" or "dehumanized" aesthetics of the avant-garde poets. García Nieto was at the center of the group called "Juventud creadora" (Creative Youth), an antecedent of the journal. In his "Poética" he speaks of a belief in everyday poetry and in an everyday man, whose life is made up of everyday time.

García Nieto's abundant production includes *Poesía (1940–1943)* (1944), *Tú y yo sobre la tierra* (1944; You and I on Earth), and *Tregua* (1951; Respite). His complete poems to date were also published in 1951. Later volumes are *La red* (1956; The Net), which won the Fastenrath Prize of the Royal Spanish Academy of the Lanuage, *El parque pequeño y Elegía en Covaleda* (1959; The Little Park and Elegy in Covaleda), *Geografía es amor* (1961), *La hora undécima* (1963; The Eleventh Hour), *Sonetos y revelaciones de Madrid* (1976), and many more. He has also published a number of works of literary criticism and in later years has edited the journal *Poesía española*.

García Nieto's poetry, a good portion of it in sonnet form (one of the classical traditions his group favored), is simple, direct, and graceful, his favorite themes being love and friendship, Spain and its geography, death and time, and above all, thankful dialogue with God.

See: M. Mantero, ed., *Poesía española contemporánea* (1966), pp. 97–100, 255–70; V. G. de la Concha, *La poesía española de posguerra* (1973), pp. 247–66.   H.L.B.

García Pavón, Francisco (1919–), Spanish scholar, drama critic, and fiction writer, is best known for his short stories and novels, many of which are set in his native Tomelloso in the region of La Mancha. His first work, *Cerca de Oviedo* (1946; Near Oviedo), sets the pattern for later works with its humor, description of local events, people, and psychology, and observations on life and human behavior, strung together by a plot full of human interest. Tomelloso is the setting for many of his short stories, some of which evoke periods of the author's life, as in *Cuentos de mamá* (1952; Mama's Stories) and *Cuentos republicanos* (1961; Republican Stories). *Los liberales* (1965; The Liberals) continues the evocation of the past in a hybrid form combining characteristics of both short and long fiction.

One of his recurrent and popular characters is the police chief Plinio, a detective who, accompanied by his Watson-like companion, solves mysteries with his common sense, homespun philosophy, and keen perceptions. Also from Tomelloso, he typifies the qualities of that region and is an ardent spokesman for and representative of the joys of country life. First appearing in various short stories, Plinio is featured in several novels, including *El reino de Witiza* (1968; The Kingdom of Witiza), *El rapto de las sabinas* (1969; The Rape of the Sabine Women), *Las hermanas coloradas* (1970; The Redheaded Sisters), which won the coveted Nadal Prize, and in the collection of short stories entitled *El último sábado* (1974; The Last Saturday). The Plinio series is touted as one of the few examples of Spanish detective fiction to date.

Vivid characters, regional details, folksy humor, and local color bolster the complex, suspense-filled plots of García Pavón's essentially realistic fiction. His detailed descriptions of people, places, and activities associated with an identifiable region are characteristics of the Spanish genre of regional realism, or *costumbrismo* (*see* SPANISH LITERATURE). His style is direct, his straightforward descriptions laced with vigorous, earthy dialogue.

García Pavón is also known for his scholarly work, including several literary anthologies and contributions to drama criticism, among them his *Teatro social en España* (1962; Social Theater in Spain).

See: P. W. O'Connor, "A Spanish Sleuth at Last: Francisco García Pavón's Plinio," *Hispano* 48 (1973): 47–68.   M.E.W.J.

García Serrano, Rafael (1917–), Spanish novelist, essayist, journalist, and founder of the Falangist S.E.U. (Sindicato Español Universitario), was born in Pamplona. A student of philosophy and letters at the outbreak of the Spanish Civil War, he volunteered for the forces of Francisco Franco and spent five years in hospitals following the battle of Teruel. His first literary efforts appeared in *Haz*, a political weekly. He later served as a correspondent in Rome and as director of the newspapers *Arriba*, *Primer Plano*, and the weekly *7 Fechas*. His first novel, *Eugenio o la proclamación de la primavera* (1938; Eugene or the Proclamation of Springtime), is a lyric exaltation of the Falangist ideals of heroism and the warlike spirit, with abstract, idealized characters and a strong dose of demagogy. *La fiel infantería* (1943; The Loyal Infantry) offers a crude and dramatic view of life in the Nationalist trenches. It is of greater value as a testimony of moral and psychological attitudes than as a historical document. *Plaza del Castillo* (1951; The Castle Square), set in Pamplona immediately before the war's inception, is less impassioned and probably his best literary achievement, while *La paz dura quince días* (1960; Peace Lasts Two Weeks) presents the 7th Navarre Brigade during a brief respite following their successful conclusion of the northern campaign in October 1937. In *Los ojos perdidos* (1958; Lost Eyes), the combative tensions of war constitute the background for a sentimental interlude. A collection of short stories, *El domingo por la tarde* (1962; On Sunday Afternoon) ironically portrays the "man in the street" on his day off.

García Serrano has written thousands of newspaper articles and reports, a sampling of which is collected in *El pino volador* (1964; The Flying Pine). Like his fiction, these reflect a decidedly political bent characterized by the same impassioned, arrogant, and aggressive apologia of war and violence. In over a dozen movie scripts and at least 15 books, García Serrano seeks not so much to create characters or well-constructed narrative as to infuse a personal vision of art and literature into his confessional testimony of historical events he has personally experienced.

See: F. C. Sainz de Robles, *La novela española en el siglo XX* (1957), p. 255; E. G. de Nora, *La novela española contemporánea,* vol. 3 (1967), pp. 89–94; F. Lázaro and E. Correa, *Literatura española contemporánea* (1969), p. 289.   J.W.D.

Gárdonyi, Géza (1863–1922), Hungarian novelist and playwright, was born in Agárd. After graduating from a teachers college in Eger, he taught school and later worked as a journalist in various provincial towns. During these years he wrote the cheap crime novels and light sketches of village life that first brought him popularity. In 1897 he moved to Eger and lived there until his death.

Gárdonyi was a prolific but uneven writer. His first work of promise was a book of short stories, *Az én falum* (1898; My Village), an attempt at a realistic depiction of the Hungarian peasant. Because of Gárdonyi's lack of interest in social conflicts, however, the work remained an idyllic representation of peasant life. Gárdonyi scored his greatest success with historical novels and, in fact, owes his lasting reputation to three of them. The first and most popular, *Egri csillagok* (1901; The Stars of Eger), is a realistic, colorful canvas of 16th-century Hungary during the period of Turkish occupation. This novel became a favorite of the young. *A láthatatlan ember* (1902; Eng. tr., *Slave of the Huns,* 1969), although ostensibly a historical novel, is also a statement of Gárdonyi's belief that man is capable of great sacrifices in serving an ideal, in this case selfless love. *Isten rabjai* (1908; Prisoners of God) is an imaginative account of medieval religiosity and its penchant towards a mystical annihilation of the self. The social novel *Az a hatalmas harmadik* (1903; That Powerful Third) reveals Gárdonyi's growing interest in spiritual life as well as his unorthodox views on marriage, to which he preferred the spontaneity of love. Gárdonyi's prose style is characterized by conciseness, plasticity, and simplicity. As a poet, he was a traditionalist. Among his plays, *A bor* (1901; Wine), a good-humored portrait of village life, is considered the best.

See: A. Schöpflin, "Géza Gárdonyi," *Nyugat* 15 (1922): 1245–48; J. Mezei, "Gárdonyi pszichologizmusa," *Itk* 68 (1964): 449–50; J. Reményi, *Hungarian Writers and Literature* (1964), pp. 146–53.   G.G.

Gary, Romain, pseud. of Romain Kasself (1914–), French novelist, was born in Moscow but went to France as a child. He studied for a law degree. During World War II, Gary fought brilliantly as a pilot in the French army. After the war, he entered the diplomatic service and became a writer. He won the Critics Prize with his first book, *Education européenne* (1945; Eng. tr., *A European Education,* 1960), a novel about the Resistance in Poland under German occupation. His next books, *Tulipe* (1946), *Le Grand Vestiaire* (1949), and *Les couleurs du jour* (1952; The Colors of the Day), illustrated the malaise of our postwar civilization.

In 1956, Gary won the Goncourt Prize with *Les Racines du ciel* (The Roots of Heaven), a fable about the killing of elephants in Africa and the inhuman aspects of progress and technocracy. His recent production, such as *Lady L* (1963), is more in the vein of satire or adventure stories. An unusual book, *Chien blanc* (1970; White Dog), is difficult to classify. At once biography and fable, it is a pungent commentary on racism and politics. Gary's best novels, written in a realistic style, are notable for their vigorous defense of humanistic values.   P.Br.

Gascar, Pierre, pseud. of Pierre Fournier (1916–), French novelist, short-story and novella writer, dramatist, and journalist-essayist, was born in Paris. He is the author of over 30 works, a number of which have been awarded major literary prizes. "Les Meubles" (1949; Furniture) and "Le Visage clos" (1951; Closed Face), Gascar's first published short stories, reflect a quasi-documentary realism reminiscent of Guy de Maupassant (1850–93). Later works reveal an undercurrent of hope in the guise of a somber pessimism, perhaps strongest in essays such as *La Chine ouverte* (1955; Open China) and *Voyage chez les vivants* (1958; Journey among the Living). Often likened to Maupassant for his formal techniques, Gascar is also compared to Franz KAFKA for his admixture of fantasy and horror in a world of reverie and nightmare.

Gascar links his writings closely to specific historical contexts, especially to war and his own concentration-camp internment, evident notably in the short stories colleced in *Les Bêtes* (1953; The Beasts), which won the Goncourt Prize, and the novella "Le Temps des morts" (1953; The Time of the Dead). His visionary prose is informed with a violent satire on man's propensity to baseness and bestiality in human relationships. Yet his symbolic fables and bestiaries are ultimately parables of pity and compassion for the inevitable "journey among the living." The first volume of Gascar's memoirs appeared as *Quartier latin* (1973; Latin Quarter). The most elucidating introduction to, and statement on, the author's writings is arguably his own *L'Expression des sentiments chez les animaux* (1964; The Expression of Feelings among Animals) and *L'Homme et l'animal* (1974; Man and Animal).   M.C.

Gatti, Armand (1924), French dramatist, journalist, screenwriter, film director, and poet, was born in Monaco. During World War II he fought in the underground, was arrested and sentenced to death, then pardoned and deported to a German camp. He escaped and resumed fighting as a paratrooper.

Gatti's political and social commitment is evident throughout his works, including *L'Enclos* (1960; The Enclosure), a fiction film on concentration camps; "Le Bombardement de Berlin," a poem; and such plays as *La Vie imaginaire de l'éboueur Auguste Jais* (1962; The Imaginary Life of the Road-Sweeper Auguste Jais), *La Deuxième Existence du camp de Tatenberg* (1962; The Second Existence of the Camp of Tatenberg), *Chant pub-*

lic devant deux chaises électriques (1964; Public Song before Two Electric Chairs), about the Sacco-Vanzetti case, *V. comme Vietnam* (1967; V. as in Vietnam), and *Petit Manuel de guérilla urbaine* (1968; Little Manual of Urban Guerillas), suggested by the events of May 1968. In his depiction of poverty, political oppression, and class struggles (strikes, revolutions, trials), he focuses on, and sides with, the victims—workers, prisoners, American Indians, immigrants—and presents the revolutionary as hero. Thus his concern for contemporary events in Europe, China, the USSR, and Latin America aims at stirring the spectator into political awareness or even militancy.

According to Gatti, the theater should not be mere entertainment, but a "means of liberation," and as such must be made into a popular art, like that of Bertolt BRECHT. With this purpose in mind, he endeavors to create a new theater, mingling fantasy and reality, dialogue and lyrics, and relying upon music, slide projections, filmed sequences, and complex lighting effects. Gatti has worked to make his plays available to audiences everywhere in France through dramatic centers as well as through performances in factories. He also organizes public readings and discussions.

See: G. Gozlan and J.-L. Pays, *Gatti aujourd'hui* (1970). M.B.-C.

Gatto, Alfonso (1909–76), Italian poet, essayist, art critic, and journalist, was born in Salerno. He moved to Milan in 1934 and to Florence in 1938 and became associated with nonconformist intellectual milieus. For a time he contributed articles to architectural journals. In 1938–39 he and Vasco PRATOLINI coedited *Campo di Marte*, a literary and cultural review. *Isola* (1932; Island), his first collection of verse and prose pieces, is devoted to graceful, incantatory visions of the south of his childhood. The poems in this volume are written in traditional meters, particularly the canzonet and ballad, yet they also explore the revolutionary poetic developments of Corrado Govoni (1884–1965), Giuseppe UNGARETTI, and Eugenio MONTALE. The visual and linguistic inventiveness of the poems in *Morto ai paesi* (1937; Dead in the Villages) placed Gatto among the masters of Italian hermeticism (*see* ITALIAN LITERATURE)

During the 1940s, Gatto's poetry combined syntactical complexity, linear and musical purity, and a strong moral sense. *Amore della vita* (1944; Love of Life) shows his concern for humanity, intensified by an anxious sense of man's perennial vulnerability. The poems of *Il capo sulla neve* (1947; The Head on the Snow) are inspired by the Italian Resistance and reflect Gatto's own political imprisonment in 1936. In this work, he simplifies his characteristic eloquence in order to produce a passionate condemnation of the destruction of the human community. After the war, Gatto turned again to the evocation of familiar images, balancing the pleasures of memory with a constant awareness of pain and death. The tension and pathos of this dual comtemplation culminate in the poems of *La madre e la morte* (1960; Mother and Death).

Among Gatto's other works is *Carlomagno nella grotta* (1962; Charlemagne in the Grotto), a collection of essays reflecting his continuing interest in the arcane laws and rituals of southern Italy. His poetic output continued with *La forza degli occhi* (1954; The Force of the Eyes), *Osteria flegrea* (1962; Phlegrean Tavern), *La storia delle vittime* (1966; The Story of the Victims), *Poesie* (1967; Poems), *Rime di viaggio per la terra depinta* (1969; Rhymes of Travel for the Painted Land), and *Poesie d'amore* (1973; Love Poems). Gatto was awarded the Savini Prize in 1939, the Saint Vincent Prize in 1948, the

Bagutta Prize in 1954, and the Viareggio Prize in 1966. He was also a vigilant and experienced critic of the visual arts, having written on the Tuscan painter Ottone Rosai (1939, 1941).

See: E. Mazzali, in *Letteratura italiana: i contemporanei*, vol. 2 (1975), pp. 1575–86; G. Ferrata, Preface to *Poesie*. M.M.G.

Gedeão, António, pseud. of Rómulo de Carvalho (1906–), Portuguese poet and physicist, was born in Lisbon but studied at the University of Oporto. He has been a teacher of physics and chemistry at the Liceu Normal of Lisbon and has written widely on scientific subjects. Under his pen name he has published several volumes of poetry beginning with *Movimento perpétuo* (1956; Perpetual Motion) and including *Poema para Galileo* (1964; A Poem for Galileo) and *Linhas de força* (1967; Lines of Force). His *Poesias completes* (Complete Poems) appeared in 1964 and was enlarged in 1968. Gedeão is also the author of a two-act play, *RTX 78/24* (1963), and of *A poltrona e outras novelas* (1973; The Armchair and Other Tales). Unknown when he published his first poetry at the age of 50, he won immediate critical approval for his originality of style and forcefulness of statement. It was evident that he was an avid reader of Fernando PESSOA, whose fondness he shared for paradoxes and certain kinds of wordplay that are frequent in early and classical Portuguese poetry. Also in the manner of Pessoa, he is interested in speculation as to the human ability to perceive the nature of reality. However, unlike Pessoa, he deeply responds to the problems of human suffering, and among his many poems of social commitment there are powerful antiwar poems. His style is marked by a highly original vocabulary with a large stratum of scientific terms; he draws upon his scientific background, too, for many of his metaphors and symbols. He would like to write verse that would be accessible to the masses, and some of his work is in a clear, almost popular style, but often it remains closer to that of the other epigones of the *Modernista* movement. Gedeão's usual ironic attitude finds expression in parodies, in surprise endings like those of the Brazilian Manuel Bandeira's *piada* (wisecrack) poems, and in the contrast between an apparently laconic, impersonal style and the author's social conscience.

See: J. Gaspar Simões, *Crítica II*, vol. 2 (1961); J. Sena, Preface and Epilogue to António Gedeão, *Poesias completas* (2d ed., 1968). R.S.S.

Gelsted, Otto (1888–1968), Danish poet, was born on the island of Fyn. After matriculating in 1907, he became a journalist and a critic. Gelsted introduced modern literature, painting, and theories (for example, Sigmund Freud's ideas in 1920) to Denmark. In *Jomfru Gloriant* (1923; Maiden Gloriant), Gelsted posited his neorationalism (developed via Greek poetry and Immanuel Kant's philosophy) and Marxism against the interwar worship of the machine age with its nihilistic and ideological chaos. His later collections all express his striving for clarity and harmony, which is flawlessly expressed in *Rejsen til Astrid* (1927; The Journey to Astrid), *Under Uvejret* (1934; During the Storm), *Emigrantdigte* (1945; Emigrant Poems), and *Digte fra en solkyst* (1961; Poems from a Sunny Coast). These collections contain concentrated and form-bound poetry, simultaneously indicating that the desparate feelings of isolation and loneliness expressed in his debut work, *De evige Ting* (1920; The Eternal Things), have given way to a stoic devotion to fate. S.H.R.

Gémier, Firmin, pseud. of Firmin Tonnerre (1869–1933), French actor, theater director, and producer, began his career in 1892 at the Théâtre Libre and soon became one of its leading figures. Occasionally, he also created new parts in other avant-garde theaters, such as Alfred JARRY's outrageous Père Ubu at the Théâtre de l'Oeuvre. For many years, Gémier followed in André ANTOINE's footsteps, succeeding him as director of the Théâtre Antoine (1904–14) and of the Odéon (1921–30). Yet in spite of this close association, Gémier developed dramatic ideals of his own. Like Romain ROLLAND, he envisioned a theater for the people. His goal was to create a spiritual communion between the actors and the masses and to bring about an active participation of a large public. To that end he looked for staging effects that would help bring audience and actors close together. His Théâtre Ambulant, created in 1911 to broaded the theater public, anticipated today's decentralization of French theater. In 1920 he launched the Théâtre National Populaire, which was to become famous under Jean VILAR. Gémier was intensely interested in pageants, and he staged some notable productions in open-air theaters and produced spectacular plays in the huge Cirque d'Hiver. Although Gémier tended to dissipate his boundless energy in multifarious projects, contemporary French theater owes much to his bold experiments.

See: P. Gsell, *Firmin Gémier* (1921); P. Blanchart, *Firmin Gémier* (1954). M.Sa.

Genet, Jean (1910–), French poet, novelist, and playwright, was born in Paris of an unknown father. His mother abandoned him in a maternity ward on the rue d'Assas, and it was not until he reached his 21st birthday that he obtained a birth certificate and found that she had been using the first name of Gabrielle. Genet was brought up by a country couple who acted as his legal guardians. Thus, at a very early stage, Genet began to think that there was no clear-cut distinction between parent, master, and judge, a basic confusion that was to become the cornerstone of his philosophy. At the age of 16, he was charged with theft and sent to a reformatory for young delinquents at Mettray, near Tours. At the age of 20, he escaped from the reformatory and enrolled in the Foreign Legion, but deserted after a few days. For a time he wrote songs with the help of a well-known songwriter, but he revolted against society and became a vagabond seeking his livelihood by begging, prostitution, and dope-smuggling. Crime was for him a ritual with religious overtones. Ten times he was sentenced to prison and, while there, he wrote poems, novels, and plays.

While imprisoned in Fresnes (south of Paris), Genet managed to publish *Le Condamné à mort* (1942; Eng. tr., *The Man Condemned to Death,* 1965), a beautiful, provocative poem of 65 stanzas in memory of his friend, Maurice Pilorge, who had been sentenced to death and executed on March 19, 1939. Thanks to the encouragement and financial support of some other friends, Genet produced the novels that were to make him famous, among which the best known are *Notre-Dame des fleurs* (1944; Eng. tr., *Our Lady of the Flowers,* 1963) and *Miracle de la rose* (1946; Eng. tr., *Miracle of the Rose,* 1966). In 1948, when he was about to be sentenced to prison for life, he obtained a pardon from President Vincent Auriol through the intercession of reputable friends, among whom were Jean-Paul SARTRE and Jean COCTEAU. Once set free, Genet concentrated on his literary work and soon became a writer of international reputation, but still without a fixed domicile, now living in luxury and now in squalor.

Besides *Le Journal du voleur* (1949; Eng. tr., *The Thief's Journal,* 1959), a somewhat autobiographical work, Genet has written and produced several plays:

Haute Surveillance (probably written in 1944, produced in 1949; Eng. tr. in *The Maids and Deathwatch,* 1954), *Les Bonnes* (1948; Eng. tr. in *The Maids and Deathwatch,* 1954), *Le Balcon* (1956; Eng. tr., *The Balcony,* 1957), *Les Nègres* (1958; Eng. tr., *The Blacks,* 1960), and *Les Paravents* (1961; Eng. tr., *The Screens,* 1962). Although Genet has announced other works as being in progress, nothing more has appeared.

In Genet's novels, one is struck by the contrast between the perfect clarity and purity of his style and the crudeness of his message. Speaking from experience, Genet depicts what he knows best, that is, jails and brothels. These places are waiting rooms for violent death, whether through assassinations or through legal executions, and they foster almost unbearable scenes of desperate hatred or love—often homosexual—among the inmates. Genet fancies a microcosm governed by ruthless laws of interchange, where everything must be bought at a high price, now with money, now with loss of ideals, or liberty, or life. These laws, enforced upon characters who are just about as guilty as Sophocles' Oedipus, are obeyed religiously, as if a ritual were being performed. Thus, the tedious daily routine of jail activities becomes a ceremony through which the inmates secretly convey their feelings towards one another, the penitentiary being assimilated to a cathedral where astonishing miracles do occur. The inmates deliberately ignore the rules of a society that has condemned them, and within the walls of their jail they create a new hierarchy, similar to that of a convent (the comparison between a penitentiary and a nunnery being implicit in the title *Our Lady of the Flowers*). For instance, in *Miracle of the Rose,* the heart of the jail is divine Harcamone, a prisoner sentenced to death for the murder of a warden. While waiting for his execution, he is the object of such a cult from all the other inmates that his fetters miraculously intertwine with roses. In this manner, the reader is made aware that any concept can be systematically replaced by its opposite. Vice is not virtue, but it may equal virtue.

This device of the inversion of roles and substitution of partners is most clearly exemplified in Genet's plays. There, maids play the part of their mistress (*The Maids*); the Queen's messenger fights a riot from the balcony of the city brothel, which is a substitute for the Queen's palace, suggesting that the Queen could be mistaken for a prostitute (*The Balcony*); blacks become whites (*The Blacks*); traitors become heroes (*The Screens*). The subversive aspect of this theater is brought about not by language alone, but through plot-substitution patterns. Genet constantly implies that the system would work just as well if bishops were treated as scapegoats; if judges were thrown in prison instead of criminals; if generals were killed at war instead of soldiers; if the whites were discriminated against, and not the blacks; if hoodlums were ruling the country instead of the Queen. Basically, those shifts in values would bring very little change in our so-called advanced society, in which the ruling class only assumes a superficial function of arbitration—as if it were only acting—but is never truly concerned with justice or mercy. In his fight, Genet resembles some of the most famous writers of our time: Fernando ARRABAL, Samuel BECKETT, Louis-Ferdinand CÉLINE. These writers all question the logic and moral value of so-called normal human behavior, and they assert their right to feel and think in a different way. In Genet's case, this rebellion is all the more remarkable since he uses the orthodox language of submissiveness, with which mystics have always expressed their submission to an indefinable divinity, a submission of the most absolute and tyrannical nature.

See: J. H. MacMahon, *The Imagination of Jean Genet*

(1963); J.-P. Sartre, *Saint Genet: Actor and Martyr* (1963); R. N. Coe, *The Vision of Jean Genet* (1968); B. L. Knapp, *Jean Genet* (1968); M. Esslin, *The Theatre of the Absurd* (rev. ed., 1973). A.Ch.

Genette, Gérard (1930-), French critic, was born in Paris. He entered the literary scene in 1959 shortly after the advent of structuralism (*see* FRENCH LITERATURE) in France. Genette immediately viewed literary criticism as necessarily structuralist because, he felt, its practice is analogous to the *bricolage* activity that Claude LÉVI-STRAUSS ascribes to mythical thought. Genette has also acknowledged, with some reservations, the contribution of Russian formalists and linguistics to a structuralist theory of literature. For Genette, the virtues of this approach are manifold: it enables one to examine a work in its specific "literarity" (excluding such matters as biography or sources), to maintain its unity and coherence, to establish a distance between it and the critic, and more broadly, through the concept of "function," to transform the notion of literary history—no longer seen as a sequence of authors, works, or genres, but as a history of the "literary system" in which forms have different functions in different ages.

The structures with which Genette is most concerned are those built on figures of speech ("figures de rhétorique"), although he expands the meaning of the phrase to include narrative forms. His practice has led him both to analyze the works of individual writers (such as Marcel PROUST) and to elaborate a literary theory. On occasion, the two will merge, as in "Discours du récit" (in *Figures III*), a long essay on narrative theory based on PROUST's *A la recherche du temps perdu*. Genette's essays are collected in a series of volumes called *Figures*, of which three have appeared (1966, 1969, and 1972). More recently, he has published what might be called a structural history of rhetorics, starting from Plato's *Cratylus*, entitled *Mimologiques* (1976). L.S.R.

Genevoix, Maurice (1890-), French novelist and essayist, was born in Decize. He was elected to the Académie Française in 1946 and has served as its Secretary General since 1958. Genevoix draws his major inspiration from the region of Orléans. Nature and concern for its preservation are themes of his essays. The protagonists of his novels may be either human—as in *Remi des Rauches* (1922) or *Raboliot* (1925), which won the Goncourt Prize—or animals, as in *Rroû* (1931; Eng. tr., 1932), *La Dernière Harde* (1938; Eng. tr., *The Last Hunt*, 1940), or *Le Roman de Renard* (1958; Eng. tr., *The Story of Reynard*, 1959).

In the traditions of the rustic novel and the naturalist essay, Genevoix's works portray, with profound understanding, the encroachment of modern civilization upon simple, instinctive creatures who value their freedom and are inseparable from their environment. He is a skillful stylist whose precise descriptions of nature are conveyed in a language that is an impressionistic mixture of technical and regional terms with literary prose. His forms of discourse, too, are artfully varied, and his works are written with a fine sense of balance.

See: P. Vernois, *Le Style rustique dans les romans champêtres après George Sand* (1963), pp. 257-63; J. J. Walling, "L'Œuvre de Maurice Genevoix," *BJR* 16 (1969): 45-56. M.I.M.

Gentile, Giovanni (1875-1944), Italian philosopher, educator, literary critic, and editor, was born in Castelvetrano, Sicily. He began his university studies in literature in Pisa in 1893, but he soon turned to philosophy and wrote his doctoral thesis, *Rosmini e Gioberti* (1898), under Donata Jaja. Gentile wrote a series of essays on recent Italian philosophy for Benedetto CROCE's journal, *La critica*. In 1912 he began his most innovative work, a reform of the Hegelian dialectic. His neo-Hegelian theory, called actualism, was first fully expounded in *Sommario di pedagogia come scienza filosofica* (1913-14; Summary Of Pedagogy as Philosophical Science). The most systematic statement of his philosophy is provided by *Teoria generale dello spirito come atto puro* (1916; Eng. tr., *The Theory of Mind as Pure Act*, 1922), his best-known book outside Italy, and *Sistema di logica come teoria del conoscere* (1917, 1923; System of Logic as Theory of Knowing). His most important philosophical works after 1923 are *Filosofia dell'arte* (1931; Eng. tr., *The Philosophy of Art*, 1972) and *Genesi e struttura della società* (1946; Eng. tr., *Genesis and Structure of Society*, 1960). The most important of his works of literary criticism are collected in *Studi su Dante* (1965; Dante Studies) and *Manzoni e Leopardi* (1928). He also edited several journals, founded *Giornale critico della filosofia italiana*, and was the directing editor of the *Enciclopedia italiana*. Gentile was active in education most of his life and taught at the universities of Palermo, Pisa, and Rome. In 1922 he became minister of education under Benito Mussolini, and eventually brought about a major reform of the Italian school system. From 1922 until his assassination in April 1944, Gentile was a loyal defender of the Fascist regime.

Gentile's philosophy is both a science of knowledge, in the tradition of Immanuel Kant, and an ethics of wholeness. He believed that there is no knowledge without action, no action without knowledge, and that neither the active nor the contemplative life is sufficient by itself. The whole of man should be engaged in whatever he does, because what gives reality and value to human activity is the immediately present act of thinking, the examining awareness of the person as he acts. In this sense, every man is a philosopher to the extent that he is attentive to what he is doing. Yet although he sought to unify action and thought, Gentile proposed that it is the thinking subject alone that gives reality and value to the object it contemplates. This emphasis on the power of thought to dominate—even tyrannize—its object made Gentile's philosophy receptive to the rise of fascism.

By 1931, however, Gentile had drastically modified his position. In *The Philosophy of Art* and his two essays on Giacomo Leopardi (1798-1837), Gentile denied that the goal of thought is to possess and master its object. Instead, he now felt that thought should seek to understand its object as free and beyond subjugation. Prior to the rise of fascism, Gentile was ripe for it; five years after its inception, he was, in his finest thought, deeply opposed to its essentially coercive nature. At the end of his life, Gentile was caught in a tragic conflict between thought and action that violated his own philosophical principles.

See: R. Holmes, *The Idealism of Giovanni Gentile* (1937); H. S. Harris, *The Social Philosophy of Giovanni Gentile* (1960); M. E. Brown, *Neo-Idealistic Aesthetics: Croce, Gentile, Collingwood* (1966). M.E.B.

George, Stefan (1868-1933), German poet, was born in the village of Büdesheim near Bingen on the Rhine. He spent his childhood in Bingen and at the Greek and Latin school in Darmstadt, where he completed his schooling in 1888. Subsequently, he devoted himself to the study of modern languages, first in French Switzerland and Paris, later at the University of Berlin. During his frequent long stays in Paris, he had personal contacts with Stéphane MALLARMÉ, Paul VERLAINE, Henri François Joseph de RÉGNIER, and Auguste Rodin. In London he met Ernest

Dowson, and in Belgium and the Netherlands he formed friendships with Charles VAN LERBERGHE, Emile VERHAEREN, Albert VERWEY, and the painters James Ensor, and Toorop. His journeys took him north as far as Copenhagen, east to Vienna, west and south to central Spain, and to Paestum in Italy. After 1914 he left Germany only for vacations in the Swiss Alps, which he preferred to the windy seashore. He refused honors and funds offered him by the Nazi government and died a voluntary exile in Locarno, Switzerland, on Dec. 4, 1933. He is buried in Locarno.

George's work may be divided into five periods. The first period includes poems written up to 1889. At this time George intended to become a painter. The poems show that blend of emotion and philosophy dear to youth and are full of tormenting questions about the meaning of life. Some were written in a language he himself had invented and later transcribed into German. Only selections are extant, published by George himself in the *Fibel* (1901; Primer) and in the last volume of his works.

The second period comprises the *Hymnen* (1890), *Pilgerfahrten* (1891; Pilgrimages), *Algabal* (1892), and *Die Bücher der Hirten-und Preisgedichte der Sagen und Sänge und der hängenden Gärten* (1895; The Books of Shepherds: Poems and Poems of Praise of Sagas and Songs and of the Hanging Gardens). The poetry of this period is symbolistic and impressionistic, in strong oppostion to the naturalistic trend of that time. Not only did George incorporate the elements of French symbolist poets and impressionist painters, but he also set his stamp on the language of his country. He made it sterner and more sparing and utilized vowel sounds in new and richer combinations. Emotions were not described or analyzed but conveyed by ear-and-eye impressions. The composition of *Hymnen* covers the period of a year, the eternal cycle that nature and the human soul, in tune with the changing seasons, require for their renewal. In *Pilgerfahrten* George is no longer satisfied with the creatures of his imagination but searched among his contemporaries for a gesture of deeper understanding. It was at this juncture that, together with the young Austrian poet Hugo von HOFMANNSTHAL and the Belgian Paul Gérardy, he founded the journal *Blätter für die Kunst* (1892–1919), which was published at irregular intervals and only for subscribers. In *Algabal* he dramatized the life of the young Roman emperor Heliogabalus, but he deviated from historical data: his Algabal feels himself close to the passions of the people and is imbued with a sense of remoteness from his environment. *Hirten-und Preisgedichte* represents the poet's recovery from this feverish and futile search for companionship. He takes refuge in the world surrounding him in the unpolluted woods and valleys of his native land and in the simple life of fishermen and shepherds, untouched by the changing centuries.

The next sequence, the monochrome and linear period, embraces *Das Jahr der Seele* (1897; The Year of the Soul) and the volume *Der Teppich des Lebens und die Lieder von Traum und Tod, mit einem Vorspiel* (1899; The Tapestry of Life and the Songs of Dream and Death, with a Prologue). In *Das Jahr der Seele* George is almost reconciled to not finding a companion. An undercurrent of gentle and steadfast melancholy combines even the most contrasting colors into a delicately tinted, homogeneous whole. The poems speak of an "I" and a "you," but more often these terms do not represent two persons but the poet in discussion with himself. From the heights of his solitude he beholds people and objects spread before him like a tapestry of life, and he draws the figures as one sees them on the wall hangings of the Middle Ages, where the most characteristic gesture is arrested at the peak of motion. In the dramatic rise of the "Vorspiel" to *Der Teppich*, the poet expresses his philosophy in a dialogue with an angel, who is none other than his own soul. *Die Lieder von Traum und Tod* supplies a mystical and transcendent close to this period of despair.

The fourth or classical period of George's work comprises *Der siebente Ring* (1907; The Seventh Ring) and *Der Stern des Bundes* (1914; The Star of the League). The poet found the companion for whom he had been searching in a boy who died at the age of 15, after George had known him for about a year. In the poet's life this companion, called Maximin, played a role similar to that of Dante's Beatrice. In *Tage und Taten* (1903; Days and Deeds), George's only volume of prose, he describes his first encounter with Maximin. *Der siebente Ring* reveals the realms thrown open by this friendship. The laws of the new world and the new life are given in *Der Stern des Bundes*. The language of these poems is terse and forceful, and its beauty does not depend on poetic devices or sustaining power of rhyme.

In his last period George is the judge and seer of his time. *Das neue Reich* (1928; The New Realm) treats of the actual problems of his age. The subject matter is wide in scope, ranging from poems on the basic significance of World War I to lyrics akin to folk songs in their poignant simplicity of symbols and meaning.

George published his translations of Shakespeare's *Sonnets* in 1912, of selected cantos from Dante's *The Divine Comedy* in 1909, and of the major part of Charles BAUDELAIRE's *Les Fleurs du mal* in 1901. His *Poems*, Eng. tr. by C. N. Valhope and E. Morwitz, were published in 1943.

See: F. Gundolf, *George* (1930); F. Wolters, *Stefan George und die Blätter für die Kunst* (1930); E. K. Bennett, *Stefan George* (1954); U. K. Goldsmith, *Stefan George: A Study of His Early Work* (1959); M. Gerhard, *Stefan George: Dichtung und Kündung* (1962); M. Winkler, *Stefan George* (1970); M. M. Metzger, *Stefan George* (1972).

E.Mo.

German literature. The spirit and character of literature in Germany in the 20th century has been marked by the creative artists and philosophers of the 19th century. The demonic genius and singularity of mind of Richard WAGNER produced redemptive mythical libretti and heroic music that scored German culture indelibly. The philosophical formulations of Friedrich NIETZSCHE sought a higher form of humankind, breaking with traditional religion, and setting up a tragic optimism in a cycle of "eternal return." The values of the 19th century began to be questioned and overturned by new social awareness and by advances in science, such as Charles Darwin's theory of evolution and Albert Einstein's theory of relativity. The dualistic base of literature in the last quarter of the century, a time of pragmatic thought, produced the black and white imaginary heroics of Karl MAY, a popular author of tales of the Wild West, full of ingenuous native cunning that outwits evil, adventures that appealed strongly to readers in Germany after World War II.

The realistic prose of Theodor FONTANE, a notable regional journalist and surveyor of social crises in the metropolis, as in *Effi Briest* (1895; Eng. tr., 1967); the socially aware novels and stories of Max KRETZER, as in his history of a fictional middle-class family in Berlin in *Meister Timpe* (1888); and the increasingly naturalistic style of the outstanding woman novelist of the time, Clara VIEBIG, were increasingly deplored by the narrative theoretician and storywriter Paul HEYSE, Germany's first recipient of the Nobel Prize for Literature (1910). Ricarda HUCH, who extolled beauty and love even in the most sordid milieu in *Aus der Triumphgasse* (1902; Out of Triumph Alley), turned to criticism, reviving romanticism in *Die Blütezeit der Romantik* (1899; The Time of Blossoming in Romanticism) and *Die Ausbreitung und Verfall der Romantik* (1902; The Expansion and Decline of Romanticism). But the strong tides that rose with naturalism, receding then into impressionism and neoromanticism, only to dash ashore again with the seething angers of expressionism, are met in the work of the poet Richard DEHMEL, "a realistic naturalist and visionary seer," a man caught and tossed by traditions in transition. Hermann SUDERMANN, a realistic dramatist and novelist, himself from the proletariat, found great resonance with his contemporary bourgeois tragedy *Heimat* (1893; Eng. tr., *Magda*, 1896) and with the novel *Frau Sorge* (1887; Eng. tr., *Dame Care*, 1891), but he was eclipsed by the boisterous and original naturalistic dramatist Gerhart HAUPTMANN, whose *Vor Sonnenaufgang* (1889; Eng. tr., *Before Dawn*, 1909) electrified and scandalized the audience in Berlin at its premiere.

Naturalistic plots emphasized the influences of environment, heredity, and social rank in a style that sought to reproduce natural speech, with all its dialectical overtones, its slurred words, pauses, and incomplete phrases. The tragedy of the weavers in Silesia in the uprising of 1844 is found in Hauptmann's *Die Weber* (1892; Eng. tr., *The Weavers*, 1899), a drama that has a whole people as its hero. The fervent resistance to the excesses of naturalism, at first gently in a renewed interest in romanticism, were reflected even by Hauptmann himself in his fairy-tale drama *Die versunkene Glocke* (1897; Eng. tr., *The Sunken Bell*, 1898), a play that struck a chord often heard in the century ahead: the artist who is unable to blend into the fabric of society and who ultimately fails. Carl HAUPTMANN, the elder brother of Gerhart and in many ways his imitator, although he did not share the naturalistic reluctance to elaborate on "the force of the idea," wrote dramas whose characters are influenced by milieu without the undertone of social significance. In his novel *Einhart der Lächler* (1907; The Smiling Einhart) he also describes the life of a misunderstood artist.

A prosaic, minutely detailed, and repulsive naturalistic world is exemplified in the works of Arno HOLZ and Johannes SCHLAF, who collaborated under the pseudonym of Bjarne P. Holmsen in the prose sketch *Papa Hamlet* (1889), which set the model for naturalistic style and content. Holz, who tried to formulate an aesthetic theory that would justify and elucidate naturalism, later wrote "natural" verse, avoiding rhyme and strophes. Schlaf's works stressed the psychological attributes of his characters, an emphasis employed also by Max HALBE, particularly in his successful *Jugend* (1893; Eng. tr., *When Love Is Young*, 1904), a drama that presents the psychology of adolescence. Their contemporary, Ludwig FULDA, never became an outright naturalistic dramatist, remaining closer to ordinary social drama, not written in the crass naturalistic style.

As early as 1891, in the very beginning of the short-lived naturalistic movement, the Austrian Hermann BAHR anticipated the strong reaction against the exaggerations and excesses of naturalism with his critical volume *Die Überwindung des Naturalismus* (1891; Overcoming Naturalism). A member of the "Jungwien" (Young Vienna) group that espoused the emerging neoromanticists and included Arthur Schnitzler and Hugo von Hofmannsthal in its membership, Bahr later helped define the traits of the trend that superseded the decadent symbolic focus of neoromanticism: expressionism. The group of "Jungwien" writers epitomized the sensitivity and morbidity of a society on the verge of obsolescence. The characters in

the works of such authors caper toward self-destruction, as do those of Arthur SCHNITZLER in his psychosexual playlet *Reigen* (1900; Eng. tr., *Dance of Love*, 1965) and in the novella *Leutnant Gustl* (1901; Eng. tr., *None But the Brave*, 1931). A juxtaposition of semblance and reality is presented brilliantly in his short play *Der grüne Kakadu* (1899; Eng. tr., *The Green Cockatoo*, 1943). The early genius of Hugo von HOFMANNSTHAL became evident with his one-act play *Der Tor und der Tod* (1893; Eng. tr., *Death and the Fool*, 1961), which depicts an unfulfilled life. Soon, however, Hofmannsthal underwent a wrenching crisis that he describes in *Ein Brief* (1902; Eng. tr., *The Letter of Lord Chandos*, 1952). Written by a fictional Lord Chandos, the "letter" investigates a demoralizing skepticism about the ability of language to represent reality truly. When his creative impulse threatened to dry up, Hofmannsthal turned to ancient myth to revive his flagging abilities with *Elektra* (1904; Eng. tr., 1963), a play set to music by Richard Strauss in 1909; the collaboration of the two led to *Der Rosenkavalier* (1911) and other operas. The age of baroque literature also served as a source for Hofmannsthal in his morality and spectacle play *Jedermann* (1911; Everyman) as well as in *Das große Salzburger Welttheater* (1922; Eng. tr., *The Salzburg Great Theater of the World*, 1963), a parable of mankind derived from Calderón, whose *La vida es sueño* furnished the source for Hofmannsthal's comment on the decline of contemporary civilization in *Der Turm* (1924; Eng. tr., *The Tower*, 1963), written first with an optimistic ending and in 1927 with a pessimistic one. The encounter with the limits of language, a theme in German literature after World War II, was recorded by Hofmannsthal in *Der Schwierige* (1921; Eng. tr., *The Difficult Man*, 1963), whose hero cannot communicate with those around him for fear he will be misunderstood. Anton WILDGANS, although for a short time director of the Burgtheater in Vienna, will best be remembered for his verse, collected in *Späte Ernte* (1933; Late Harvest), rather than for plays such as *Dies irae* (1919). Josef WEINHEBER received critical attention comparatively late with his volume *Adel und Untergang* (1932; Nobility and Defeat).

The riotous extremes of naturalism were countered effectively in poetry by Stefan GEORGE, an aesthete and perspicacious master of the German language who refined it and imbued it with sensuality of sound and richness of color through his original idiom. From a place of isolation, as in the sequence *Das Jahr der Seele* (1897; The Year of the Soul), George gathered devoted followers and in *Der siebente Ring* (1907; The Seventh Ring) celebrated friendship. With the advent of World War I, which shattered the continuity of intellectual development in Germany, George became the seer of foreboding. He felt the mission of the poet—to warn and to clarify and to celebrate—very deeply; he sought beauty amid ugliness, keeping himself distant and aloof. A member of the circle of poets who admired George was Max KOMMERELL, who believed literature was the vehicle that could establish human morality. The renewed search for mystery amidst the revolt against the cheapening of life is exemplified by an admirer of George, Albrecht SCHAEFFER, and his concern with the meaning of art through the ages.

A combination of spirituality and whimsy is found in the work of Christian MORGENSTERN whose *Galgenlieder* (1905; Eng. trs., *The Gallows Song: A Selection*, 1967; *Gallowsongs*, 1970) established his popularity with grotesque humor that probes the essence of language itself. Doomed by illness to a short life, Morgenstern sought and found solace for his spiritual self in *Einkehr* (1910; Introspection). Like Morgenstern in that he was not involved with a group or a movement, Alfred MOMBERT made mysticism more communicative to a real world in such works as *Tag und Nacht* (1894; Day and Night), the dramatic trilogy of the future *Aeon* (1907-1911), and *Sfaira der Alte* (1936; Sfaira the Elder), verses that present the poet as listener to the worlds of mankind and nature alike. The work of Richard von SCHAUKAL emphasizes the importance of tradition, of the aristocratic, aloof artist, and the central position of art in human affairs.

A strong sense of form and an enduring search for profound religious understanding in eloquent symbol helped make Rainer Maria RILKE the most distinguished lyric poet in German in the 20th century. His sense of spatial form oriented him in a sensitive concern for the visual arts and for the spiritual place of humankind. Rilke was a wanderer—restless, probing, contemplative. *Das Stundenbuch, Das Buch vom mönchischen Leben* (1905; The Book of Hours, The Book of the Monastic Life) heralds the kinship of all human beings, linked to God through the vatic voice of the lyric poet. The *Neue Gedichte* (1907; Eng. tr., New Poems, 1964) focuses objectively, but with penetration on things, often the work of human hands. His autobiographical prose fiction *Die Aufzeichnungen des Malte Laurids Brigge* (1910; Eng. tr., The Journal of My Other Self, 1930) depicts his own psychological development, the fears of childhood, the innate death in every human being, and the stultifying isolation of the individual in a metropolis. His most memorable achievements were the *Duineser Elegien* (1923; Eng. tr., Duinese Elegies, 1930), a mystic investigation of mankind's place in the world, and the *Sonnette an Orpheus* (1923; Eng. tr., Sonnets to Orpheus, 1936), which emphasizes the role of the poet as the mediator who transforms humankind. Both works were finished in fervent haste after years of hesitation and personal crisis. Rilke's private symbols and personal idiom, combined with the clarity of his language, make him a unique phenomenon among poets of the early 20th century, a time when an intense revival of the lyric mode occurred.

Börries von MÜNCHHAUSEN, for example, revived the German ballad, a form that had been ignored for decades. Agnes MIEGEL also contributed to the ballad form with treatments of historical events and supernatural forces, as did Lulu von STRAUSS UND TORNEY, whose ballads deal with heroic figures. Transitional writers in the early years of the century, still lodged securely in tradition yet cognizant of the impending revolution in expressive language, were Eduard, Graf von KEYSERLING, whose style in restraint and realistic language is reminiscent of Fontane; Rudolf BORCHARDT, principally a translator and essayist with a strong nationalistic tendency; and Wilhelm von SCHOLZ, who in both poetry and prose concentrated on the irrational underlayer of demonic dream and hallucination contained within reality. The moorland home of Hermann LÖNS is evoked in *Aus Flur und Forst* (1907; From Field and Forest); the patriotic treatment of old peasant stock in *Der Wehrwolf* (1910; Eng. tr., Harm Wulf, 1931) contributed to his popularity among Nazi readers years later.

The titanic age of German expressionism lay on the horizon in the early years of the 20th century. An increasingly restless urge to break with the past, disgust at tendencies in the development of society, revolt against technology, militarism, the evils of urban inhumanity, all these marked the turn toward an appeal to the spiritual aspects of humankind and the individual human being, toward a spirit of reform, a sense of the perils in political arenas, and a search for essences. Transitional still were the works of Max MELL, who revived the religious folk play for laymen. A forerunner of the expressionist poets was Else LASKER-SCHÜLER, whose poems and plays reflect her Jewish background. The expression of a personal cosmology is found in *Das Nordlicht* (1910; The Northern Lights) by Theodor DÄUBLER. A notable expressionist was August STRAMM, whose curt, compressed language (in his plays as well as in his poems) often consisted of monosyllabic ejaculations and shouts of protest and emphasis. But Georg HEYM slashed decorum to proclaim a vision of horror in war and death in vivid, densely packed lyric verse. In his poems he mocks German classicism and analyzes the madness of his own time unsparingly, sensing the cataclysm about to happen. Although not the follower of any expressionist group, KLABUND embodies a range of imaginative transformations and contrasts in a restless and sometimes grotesque spirit. Ernst STADLER wrote poems that contain a sense of unity and mystic dedication to the future. The morbid awareness of cataclysmic change felt by so many expressionists is clearly present also in the poems of Georg TRAKL, who was a visionary of apocalyptic evil, although he kept his somber language free of expressionistic excesses. Paul ZECH also was more eclectic in his poetic utterances, mixing reminiscences of his early life as a worker with memories of World War I and cosmic visions. The physician Gottfried BENN shocked readers delightedly with the putrefaction of death and decay in his *Morgue* (1912). In later collections of poetry he mourned the schism between mind and body. Benn saw history as essentially irrational, and he became infatuated with the overblown rhetoric of Nazism for a time, but by 1936 he had been publicly reprimanded, reestablishing his reputation with the pithy postmortem statements on modernity in *Statische Gedichte* (1948; Static Poems).

Although the poets were often angry and almost always pessimistic in their forebodings, the essential genre of the German expressionists was the drama, which enlarged the anger and sense of doom. Considered to be a forerunner of expressionism is Frank WEDEKIND, who pioneered in the presentation of eroticism on the stage, convinced as he was of the primary power of the elementary sexual passions. He chastized the adult world for its ignorance and moral hypocrisy in *Frühlings Erwachen* (1891; Eng. tr., The Awakening of Spring, 1909), but the creation of the demonic female Lulu in *Der Erdgeist* (1895; Eng. tr., Earth Spirit, 1914) and *Die Büchse der Pandora* (1903; Eng. tr., Pandora's Box, 1903) remains the strongest statement of Wedekind's perception of the supremacy of primitive emotions over those imposed by a lunatic society. In contrast, Paul ERNST combatted naturalism and conceived of redemption drama, which meant metatragedy, tragedy beyond tragedy, based on a return to orthodoxy in religion.

An important stage critic and champion of Hauptmann and Sudermann, Alfred KERR endorsed the strident voice of expressionism and helped gain its acceptance. The revolutionary and sensational thrust of expressionist drama is exemplified by Walter HASENCLEVER, whose *Der Sohn* (1914; The Son) is paradigmatic for the conflicts felt by members of the younger generation, despising their fathers while feeling themselves to be prophets of peace. The antimilitarism of expressionism is found in Hasenclever's *Antigone* (1917), where popular rage punishes the brutality of a tyrant and pacifism reigns in the end. Arnold BRONNEN, an Austrian in Berlin, pitted son against father in his *Vatermord* (1920; Parricide) and in subsequent plays investigated the opposites of liberation and oppression in emotional and social conflicts, finally attacking tyrannical power in *Gloriana* (1941). Carl STERNHEIM satirized the German bourgeoisie in a series of plays with the typically expressionistic antihero, a shallow and grotesque cynic. Sternheim's language is extreme in its staccato style. The Viennese Karl KRAUSS battled intellectual corruption with scathing wit and in his panoramic drama *Die letzten Tage der Menschheit* (1918–22; The Last Days of Mankind) condemned the desecration of humanity by enslavement to technology, hypocrisy, and fraudulent ideals. The condemnation of war common to expressionist dramatists is found in the work of Georg KAISER, whose *Die Bürger von Calais* (1914; The Citizens of Calais) stresses the search for a "new man," a chief theme of the period. *Von morgens bis mitternachts* (1916; Eng. tr., *From Morn to Midnight*, 1922) is representative in its expressionistic anonymity—most expressionist heroes are nameless and typical—in a man's search for spiritual security. Kaiser's trilogy of antiwar sentiment, in the plays *Die Korale* (1917; Eng. tr., *The Coral*, 1963), *Gas I* (1918; Eng. tr., 1957), and *Gas II* (1920; Eng. tr., 1963), takes mankind from the excesses of wealth and the tyranny of machines of war to the inevitable holocaust. His language is terse, impulsive, full of emotion, and he mixes musical interlude and commentary with broad mime to achieve a pre-Brechtian alienation.

Ernst BARLACH is called an expressionist, although he himself did not view his characters as typical and, in fact, he had a deep sense of spiritual self-identification and was a God-seeker, as were several expressionist dramatists in their own ways. Alfred KUBIN was vehement in his expressionistic art and prose, frequently demonic and dreamlike, as in his novel *Die andere Seite* (1909; Eng. tr., *The Other Side*, 1967). He is the antipode of the writer-sculptor Barlach.

The strong urge for liberation from the political and social fetters of past decades and the search for new modes for the expression of social, artistic, political, and spiritual aspirations are found in the vigorous plays of Ernst TOLLER, who presented a portrait of idealistic leadership among proletarian workers in *Masse Mensch* (1922; Eng. tr., *Masses and Man*, 1923) and a nameless hero who sacrifices himself in the mutinous uprising of machine-enslaved workers in *Die Maschinenstürmer* (1922). Hugo BALL, whose early works were clearly expressionistic, as in *Die Nase des Michelangelo* (1911; Michelangelo's Nose), turned away from activism in content and style when he converted to Catholicism. The radical dogmatism and strong antimilitarism of Fritz von UNRUH are reflected in *Ein Geschlecht* (1916; A Family) and *Platz* (1920; Room), laments that the revolution in Germany following World War I did not bring out the longed for "new man." Reinhard GOERING wrote one of the most compelling and soul-searching pacifist plays with his *Die Seeschlacht* (1917; Eng. tr., *Seafight*, 1940).

While the expressionists railed and protested, transfixing audiences with raw incident and riveting language, other writers emphasized different aspects of the age. Helen VOIGT-DIEDERICHS wrote somber novels whose themes include rural life and the trials of marriage. Josef PONTEN gained distinction for an ambitious series of novels with the collective title *Volk auf dem Wege* (1930–40; A People under Way), in which the migrations of various peoples contribute to the development of the historical processes that engulfed Germany. In Austria Franz WERFEL began with expressionist poetry, wrote dramas that revealed the psychological depths of human beings, as in *Spiegelmensch* (1920; Eng. tr., *Mirror Man*, n.d.) and *Bocksgesang* (1921; Eng. tr., *Goat Song*, 1926), and furnished monuments to the human spirit in the play *Jakobowsky und der Oberst* (1944; Eng. tr., *Jakobowsky and the Colonel*, 1944) and the novel *Das Lied von Bernadette* (1941; Eng. tr., *The Song of Bernadette*, 1942). Like many of his contemporaries, Werfel fled the Nazi tyranny to

the United States and became one of numerous writers who continued their careers in exile.

Another such writer was Alfred DÖBLIN, probably the greatest narrative artist of expressionism, gifted with a vibrant and kinetic imagination, capable of revealing and instructive distortion, ever on the side of the nonviolent spirit and opposed to mindless brute force. His *Berge, Meere und Giganten* (1924; Mountains, Oceans, and Giants) is a novel that posits a future for human beings that is made into a nightmare by science. But Döblin's best-known work is the monumental novel *Berlin Alexanderplatz* (1920; Eng. tr., *Alexanderplatz, Berlin*, 1931), a work that contains the best of his satirical, kaleidoscopic style of expressionist prose, mixed with experimental techniques reminiscent of James Joyce and John Dos Passos. However, one of the most popular authors of the Weimar era was Heinrich MANN, the brother of Thomas, whose *Professor Unrat* (1905; Eng. tr., *Small Town Tyrant*, 1944), well known as the source for the film *The Blue Angel*, made him famous. Concerned for the wellbeing of humanity, Heinrich Mann saw in the author the one artist who could restore the waning power of democracy. Kasimir EDSCHMID, a leading proponent of expressionism, who from the beginning threw himself wholly into the demonic style, later adapted the more repressed but strongly realistic style of the new realism of the 1920s. Leonhard FRANK also took up the theme of revolt against the old order, principally denouncing war, as in *Der Mensch ist gut* (1917; Man Is Good).

The strengths of expressionism lay principally not in prose but in the lyric and in drama, and it was the latter that launched the career of the most influential 20th century dramatist, a revolutionary of art and the spirit and of all that had to do with theater, Bertolt BRECHT. With his first play *Baal* (1918; Eng. tr., 1964) Brecht took up the cause of the outsider, the artist outcast from society, with a work that in its epic style, its inserted songs, and its socially critical outlook is programmatic for his subsequent dramatic output. His political involvement and compassion for the victims of war are found in *Trommeln in der Nacht* (1922; Eng. tr., *Drums in the Night*, 1966), and his recognition of the debilitating and destructive influence of the metropolis in *Im Dickicht der Städte* (1924; Eng. tr., *In the Jungle of Cities*, 1961). The radical political and social satire *Die Dreigroschenoper* (1928; Eng. tr., *The Threepenny Opera*, 1955), set to music by Kurt Weill, brought international fame to Brecht. He became increasingly concerned with the social relevancy of dramatic statements and with the darker side of the irrationality of human beings, anxieties often sanctioned by social and religious forces. He advocated the qualities of epic theater and the abandonment of the Aristotelian unities, and he described what he called "alienation," that is, the involvement of the audience in the realization that it is witnessing a performance, denying it a cathartic experience. Lighting, set decoration, the use of signs and placards, inserted songs, all were designed to interrupt the stage illusion and to shock the audience into reflective awareness. Having fled the Nazi regime, Brecht made his way to Hollywood via a long and tortuous route. There he wrote *Leben des Galilei* (1938; Eng. tr., *The Life of Galileo*, 1947), a drama concerned with the scientist's responsibility to society. It was followed by *Mutter Courage und ihre Kinder* (1939; Eng. tr., *Mother Courage and Her Children*, 1941); a denunciation of war and its dehumanization, *Der gute Mensch von Sezuan* (1940; Eng. tr., *The Good Woman of Setzuan*, 1961), which depicts the dilemma of "being good" in a world corrupted by evil; and *Der kaukasische Kreidekreis* (1945; Eng. tr., *The*

Caucasian Chalk Circle, 1948), which argues that "ownership" is the right of those who make use of the things owned in the best way, here concentrated in a surrogate mother. Brecht never realized the Utopian dream of an instructive theater—his art overwhelmed his pedagogical intentions even in East Berlin after World War II, where he had a theater at his own disposal—but the influence of his revolution in theater extends to the present day in the works of such dramatists as Peter WEISS, Peter HANDKE, and Franz Xavier KROETZ.

An outsider who wrestled with the anxiety that engulfed the 20th century was Franz KAFKA, a singular and unique prose writer whose works also have been unceasingly influential on the idiom of the narrative authors who succeeded him. The spiritual suffering, the social estrangement, and the deep personal anxiety of Kafka are reflected in anecdotes, short prose works such as *Die Verwandlung* (1912; Eng. tr., *The Metamorphosis,* 1948) whose protagonist has turned overnight into a gigantic insect, and in novels not ever really finished. *Der Prozeß* (1914; Eng. tr., *The Trial,* 1937) depicts with agonizing reality and grotesquerie Kafka's world, in which space and time cease to function logically, where cause produces ungainly and inexplicable effect. *Das Schloß* (1922; Eng. tr., *The Castle,* 1930) continues the theme of a man lost in a world that refuses to react in a way that can be rationally grasped. The style of Kafka—terse, dreamlike, explicit but amazingly deceptive—found numerous imitators in the decades following his death. His works have defied the incessant efforts of three generations of interpreters.

The great narrative authors of the century were still to come with Thomas Mann and Hermann Hesse, who were contemporaries of a number of notable prose writers. Ernst JÜNGER the brother of the minor poet Friedrich Georg Jünger, deplored the irrationality and even barbaric technologically captive forces of the century, particularly in his Utopian parable *Auf den Marmorklippen* (1939; Eng. tr., *On the Marble Cliffs,* 1947). Otto FLAKE championed a pan-European society and a sensibility of spirit in such works as *Die Monthivermädchen* (1952; The Monthiver Girls). Rudolf Alexander SCHRÖDER clung to enduring values in his reflective *Der Wanderer und die Heimat* (1931; The Wanderer and the Homeland), and he revived the long-neglected art of hymn writing. Rudolf BINDING stood apart from the mainstream, concentrating on clarity of spirit and the special functions of nature in his legends and autobiographical works. Jakob WASSERMANN emphasized the social injustice suffered by the Jews and the need for feelings of brotherhood that cross racial, religious, and social barriers. Hermann STEHR, immediately called a naturalist on the publication of his early works, quickly turned to mysticism, tracing the divinity of man in *Der Heiligenhof* (1918; The Court of Saints). The novel *Die Biene Maja* (1912; Eng. tr., *The Adventures of Maya, the Bee,* 1922) was the most memorable of the works of Waldemar BONSELS, who turned to examples in nature for qualities lacking in human beings. Ernst WIECHERT also found more positive examples of humanity in nature than in his contemporary world, despising war and searching for meaning in Christian ethic, as in his *Hirtennovelle* (1935). Hans CAROSSA also sought self-discipline and inner peace in meditation on the positive contributions of Christianity to the human condition in *Der Artz Gion* (1931; Eng. tr., *Doctor Gion,* 1933).

A whole generation of German writers had been scarred by World War I. Ina SEIDEL turned to the past to capture the psychic motivations that moved such a man as the

translator of Kalidasa, Georg Forster, in the novel *Das Labyrinth* (1921; Eng. tr., *The Labyrinth,* 1932), as did Alfred NEUMANN in his novel *Der Teufel* (1926; Eng. tr., *The Devil,* 1928) concerning the depredations of power in the person of Louis XI. Stefan ZWEIG, an Austrian Jew, brought a message of peace with *Jeremias* (1917; Eng. tr., *Jeremiah,* 1922) and pointed to critical moments in the history of mankind with his *Sternstunden der Menschheit* (1927; Eng. tr., *Tide of Fortune,* 1955) and a series of major biographies of Marie Antionette, Erasmus, and Mary Stuart. Hermann KASACK concentrated on a surreal world especially in his novel of a city of the dead, *Die Stadt hinter dem Strom* (1947; Eng. tr., *The City beyond the River,* 1953), while the work of Erwin Guido KOLBENHEYER was mainly historical. In his *Die Bauhütte* (1925; The Construction Cottage) he foresaw the ideas of the approaching Nazi era, and in other works he presented the German at bay in a hostile world, a theme he developed in the three-volume historical novel set in the time of Jakob Böhme, *Paracelsus* (1917-23).

Most German writers of the first half of the 20th century were concerned principally with contemporary affairs, even though they occasionally disguised them in historical costume. The pacifist Hans Henny JAHNN envisioned blind creative forces at work on human destinies, particularly those of demonic sensuality struggling for release, as in his immense *Fluß ohne Ufer* (1949-50; River without End). Hermann BROCH explored the stagnation of society in *Die Schlafwandler* (1930; Eng. tr., *The Sleepwalkers,* 1932) and the value of art and life's meaning in the stream-of-consciousness novel *Der Tod des Vergil* (1945; Eng. tr., *The Death of Vergil,* 1945). Robert MUSIL wrote a monument to confused adolescent brutality and sexuality with his *Die Verwirrungen des Zöglings Törless* (1906; Eng. tr., *Young Törless,* 1955) and the incomplete testimony to a man's increasingly vain search for moral sensibility in the immense novel *Der Mann ohne Eigenschaften* (1930-42; Eng. tr., *The Man without Qualities,* 3 vols., 1953, 1954, 1960), which intuits a final void.

The world of Karl Heinrich WAGGERL is one of adults and children and their relationships with one another, exemplified by his *Mütter* (1936). A work called truly surrealistic is the novel by Elisabeth LANGGÄSSER, *Das unauslöschliche Siegel* (1947; The Indelible Seal), which presents the struggle between God and Satan for the soul of a Jew. Werner BERGENGRUEN combined romantic fantasy and psychological realism in such works as *Das Feuerzeichen* (1949), while Gertrud von LE FORT portrayed Christian values in *Das Schweißtuch der Veronika* (1928; Eng. tr., *The Veil of Veronica,* 1932). It was Hans GRIMM who provided a new designation for a people who felt hemmed in by historical forces in his lengthy, relentlessly tortuous novel *Volk ohne Raum* (1926; A People without Space).

The true masterworks of German fiction in the first half of the 20th century were created by two authors, Hermann HESSE and Thomas MANN. Hesse began as a neo-romanticist who was ever cognizant of the dual nature of man, his passionate flesh and inspirited mind. The title character in *Peter Camenzind* (1904; Eng. tr., 1969) seeks refuge in nature from an incomprehensible society. *Demian* (1919; Eng. tr., 1965) emphasizes the dual aspects of art and life, facets of human endeavor in constant strife. The Buddhistic novella *Siddharta* (1922; Eng. tr., 1951) furnishes the solution to the opposing forces that govern human lives. But *Der Steppenwolf* (1927; Eng. tr., *Steppenwolf,* 1963) posits darker sides in the nature of mankind that make strife in civilization inevitable. The psychological portraits of two friends of opposite natures, one a child of the senses and the other a child of the intellect, are brilliantly drawn in *Narziß und Goldmund* (1930; Eng. tr., *Narcissus and Goldmund,* 1968). In *Das Glasperlenspiel* (1943; Eng. tr., *The Glass Bead Game. Magister Ludi,* 1970), Hesse's last major work, he delineates a society of the future that is dominated by the earnestly playful intellect but still finds no solution to the inadequate synthesis of mind and the natural instincts.

The work of Thomas Mann is a panorama of the dilemmas confronting the individual man and society in the first half of the century, beginning with the decline of a family of high social status in *Buddenbrooks* (1901; Eng. tr., 1924) and ending with the parody of an outsider in *Felix Krull* (1955; *Confessions of Felix Krull, Confidence Man, Memoirs, Part I,* 1955). In between Mann, who very early developed a reflective, penetrating, explicit prose style, concerned himself with the role of the artist in a society from which he is instinctively but unhappily alienated. That theme suffuses most of Mann's work, from the satirical *Königliche Hoheit* (1909; Eng. tr., *Royal Highness,* 1916) through the myth-permeated parody of an artist in decline in the novella *Der Tod in Venedig* (1913; Eng. tr., *Death in Venice,* 1925) to the great novel of a civilization on the brink of disaster, *Der Zauberberg* (1924; Eng. tr., *The Magic Mountain,* 1927), in which the processes of death and decay in a representative group isolated from the mainstream of society are depicted. The timelessness of mankind and the necessary subjugation to the powers of social, religious, mythical, intellectual, and artistic strictures are found in the tetralogy *Josef und seine Brüder* (1933–45; Eng. tr., *Joseph and His Brothers,* 1934–45), an immense work interrupted in its composition by the writing of *Lotte in Weimar* (1939; Eng. tr., *The Beloved Returns,* 1940), a carefully detailed snapshot of the old Goethe, where again the artist has set himself a style that makes social acceptance possible. *Doktor Faustus* (1947; Eng. tr., 1948), a profound intellectual exercise combining the philosophy of Nietzsche and the music of Arnold Schönberg in a character who makes a Faustian pact with the devil—all a complex and penetrating paradigm for the Nazi domination and destruction of the German nation—is an apocalyptic portrait of a doomed people. Mann did not again surpass that work either in his wry version of the medieval Pope Gregory in *Der Erwählte* (1951; Eng. tr., *The Holy Sinner,* 1951) or in the tasteless and bitterly anti-American *Die Betrogene* (1953; Eng. tr., *The Black Swan,* 1954), in which the renewed sexual appetite of an aging woman has as its source a wasting and fatal disease. The exaltation of intellect and spirit in Mann's works are constantly in conflict with the subversive and tempting pleasures of the body, and Mann seeks always to find a synthesis, a conciliatory point, to unite the two natures of the human animal.

The advent of the Nazi domination of Germany in 1933 began a 12-year rupture in the development of German literature far worse than the shocks of World War I. The persecution of Jewish writers and the harrowing censorship of any author who wrote in contradiction to official Nazi policy resulted in mass flight on the one hand and in the submergence of writers into public silence on the other. The German language itself became a victim of Nazi oppression and distortion, to the point that phrases and specific words took on connotations that later recalled the horrors of midnight Gestapo raids, often leading to concentration camp annihilation. Gertrud KOLMAR, a Jewish poet whose traditional lyrics were hymns to childlike innocence and the guileless rose, disappeared into a concentration camp in 1943. Albrecht HAUSHOFER, executed in an aborted plot to overthrow Adolf Hitler, criticized Nazi figures in the guise of novels on Roman tyrants and, while in prison, wrote a collection of sonnets, *Moabiter Sonette* (Eng. tr., *Moabite Sonnets,* 1978), that survived him. The propagandistic jargon up to and during World War II furthered the maltreatment of the language. Those authors whose writing was worthwhile were either in exile—all over the world—or they were writing silently, for themselves, for their desk drawers, forbidden to publish in their homeland.

Karl WOLFSKEHL, an admirer of Stefan George, lived in exile in New Zealand. His mystic poems had a hymnlike quality, mournful and reflective, about the fate of the exiled artist. Richard BEER-HOFMANN, an Austrian visionary poet who sought eternal links amid the dislocations of human existence in poems and plays, emigrated to New York. The forces of politics and religion acting upon historical characters were the themes of the novels of Lion FEUCHTWANGER, best known for the novel *Jud Süss* (1925; Eng. tr., 1926); he fled Nazi Germany to Los Angeles, via France and Spain. René SCHICKELE, himself the son of a German father and a French mother, yearned for a supranational unity but took refuge in France after 1933. Even before 1933, Bruno FRANK wrote psychological suspense novels that popularized anti-Nazi opinions, so that he fled to the United States after 1933. An early proponent of surrealism and dada, Iwan GOLL, was blacklisted after 1933 by the Nazis, who were always unfriendly to experimental literature. Goll wrote melancholy poems, compact with cabbalistic images, in French as well as in German, collaborating with his wife Claire Studer (1891–1977) occasionally. Goll fled to New York in 1939, returning to Paris in 1947. The Austrian Joseph ROTH, who depicted the collapse of the Austro-Hungarian monarchy in his masterpiece *Radetzkymarsch* (1932; Eng. tr., *Radetzky March,* 1933), pled for religious tolerance in *Juden auf Wanderschaft* (1927; Jews in the Diaspora) and fled to Paris in 1936. Johannes URZIDIL a friend of Werfel and Kafka in Prague, went to England in 1939 and to the United States in 1941. His works reflect the poet's role as that of a craftsman who serves all humankind in preserving things worth saving.

Nelly SACHS, one of the most remarkable poets of the century, whose agonized suffering found expression in mystical poems that celebrate the exile on earth—the human being—fled with her mother to Sweden in 1940. Paul CELAN, whose poem "Todesfuge" became the symbol for the holocaust that entrapped European Jews under Hitler, went to Paris, where he continued to produce esoteric, haunting lyrics until his suicide. Robert NEUMANN, whose works were burned and banned by the Nazis in 1933, emigrated to England, where he wrote books in English. It was not unusual for exiled German-language authors to be published in English before their works appeared in German. Hermann KESTEN, a man of small stature and enormous courage, provoked Hitler with his novel *Der Scharlatan* (1932; The Charlatan) and had to flee Germany to Holland, from which he went in 1940 to the United States, returning to Rome in 1952. His novels and plays center on the downtrodden, emphasizing the author's liberal viewpoints and defending freedom of expression. Stefan Andres (1906–70), whose novella *Wir sind Utopia* (1942) is a scarcely disguised indictment of Nazi ideology, where the world of intellect and brute force collide, moved to Italy in 1937, where until 1948 he lived in quiet seclusion in Positano. Hilde DOMIN went to Italy in 1932 and fled to England in 1939, traveling on to the Dominican Republic in 1940, where she lived until 1954 before returning to Germany. All of her works were published after 1959 and reflect the life of the wandering émigré, the exile in a hostile world; unsentimental and precise in her poetry and prose, Domin resists the technological automation of humankind. Jakov LIND is typical of the peripatetic exile who paradoxically loses his identity in a fight for survival. He fled Austria in 1938 and, after traveling through several European countries, settled finally in England, where for a time he abandoned his native German to write in English. The grotesque characters in Lind's stories reflect the horror that swept across Europe in World War II.

The aftermath of World War II brought a lasting dichotomy in the political and literary structure of what was once one land with the establishment of two Germanies, East and West. East Germany, a socialist republic, demanded adherence to an official party line by its writers, who were forbidden to emphasize censorship, suicide, and—after it was erected—the Berlin Wall and flight across it into the West. Before the building of the Berlin Wall, Uwe JOHNSON moved from East to West Germany, where he published the first novel that dealt with the problem of the two Germanies, *Mutmaßungen über Jakob* (1959; Eng. tr., *Speculations about Jacob*, 1963). That confrontation was continued in subsequent works, historical chronicles focusing on memorable characters. Johnson's prose style brought immediate comment because of unorthodox punctuation, occasional dialect, and parataxis, all techniques that involve the reader consciously in the construction of the story. His *Jahrestage* (1970–), a projected tetralogy that recapitulates events surrounding the life of Gesine Cresspahl, contains numerous quotations from *The New York Times* from August 1967 to 1968. Another writer from the East, Christa REINIG, left East Germany in 1964. She is a laconic poet, representative of the increasing consciousness of women writers, as scathingly depicted in her novel *Die Entmannung* (1976; Emasculation). Manfred BIELER left East Germany for Czechoslovakia in 1966, moving to the West in 1968 after the Soviet invasion of Prague. Bieler is a chronicler of contemporary life, critical of socialistic repression in *Maria Morzeck* (1965) and upper-class arrogance in *Der Mädchenkrieg* (1975; The Girl's "War"). The poet Peter HUCHEL, editor of the influential East German journal *Sinn und Form* for many years, left East Germany in 1971 for Italy and then went on to West Germany.

While many authors were finding it impossible to remain in the restricted environment of East Germany, others continued to live and write there. The author of one of the most important novels revolving around World War I, Arnold ZWEIG, achieved instant success in his *Der Streit um den Sergeanten Grischa* (1927), the first of four works that emphasize the central position of the individual in the process of history. He lived in Palestine during the Nazi years, returning to East Berlin in 1948, where he was an active Zionist. Ludwig RENN indicted war in his novel *Krieg* (1928; Eng. tr., *War*, 1929), a terse and dispassionate account of the military life. He escaped from a Nazi jail and fled to Switzerland in 1936, played a role in the Spanish Civil War, and returned to East Germany in 1947. The poet Johannes R. BECHER, who lived in the Soviet Union from 1935 to 1945, became one of the most influential East German arbiters of literature, serving as minister of culture for a time, seeking a new voice for a new state dominated by the Communist ideology. The greatest success of Hans FALLADA was *Kleiner Mann—was nun?* (1933; Eng. tr., *Little Man, What Now?*, 1933), a novel about the effect of the depression of the 1930s on the little man. After World War II, Fallada worked in East Germany on the journal *Aufbau*, commenting in his novel *Der Alpdruck* (1947; The Nightmare) on the widespread feeling of guilt that enveloped survivors of the war. Anna SEGHERS, whose novel *Das siebte*

Kreuz (1942; Eng. tr., *The Seventh Cross*, 1942) relates the flight of a group of concentration camp internees, fled to Paris and to Mexico after the Nazi takeover in Germany, returning to live in East Germany in 1947, serving the socialist cause in her novels, for example, *Überfahrt* (1971; Crossing).

The first writer of consequence in East Germany after 1945 was Johannes BOBROWSKI, who was championed by admirers in the West before his untimely death. He is a poet of the landscape of his homeland in *Sarmatische Zeit* (1961; Sarmatian Time), seeking to preserve particular redemptive natural scenes in a time that afflicted human beings with social guilt. His narrative prose, as represented in *Litauische Klaviere* (1966; Lithuanian Pianos), is a lucid presentation of common desperation. Drama in East Germany is represented by Peter HACKS, also a lesser theoretician of theater in the wake of Brecht. The works of Hacks range from a sociological examination of history in *Die Eröffnung des indischen Zeitalters* (1954; The Opening of the Indian Era) to an exploration of contemporary bureaucracy in *Die Sorgen und die Macht* (1958–62; Problems and Power), to adaptation of examples of world theater and a comedy on the theme of the emancipation of women, in *Adam and Eva* (1973). Heiner MÜLLER adapted plays from antiquity and from Shakespeare after he fell from favor in the early 1960s but reestablished himself with *Mauser*, combining verse and prose in an original idiom, dramatizing the brutality of revolution and the doomed destiny of the revolutionary. Christa WOLF was acclaimed an outstanding East German writer upon publication of her first work, a narrative entitled *Moskauer Novelle* (1961; Tale of Moscow) and with her novel *Der geteilte Himmel* (1963; Eng. tr., *Divided Heaven*, 1976), which deals with the conflict of the individual and the communal group in a socialistic nation. Her quest for personal identity is exemplified in the novel *Nachdenken über Christa T* (1968; Eng. tr., *The Quest for Christa T.*, 1970). Ulrich PLENZDORF became the controversial angry young man of East German letters with his *Die neuen Leiden des jungen W.* (1973; The New Sorrows of Young W.), the story of a young representative of the counterculture in the East, a novel that found success in East and West Germany alike. Rolf SCHNEIDER dramatized the conflict between the socialist East and the capitalist West and became one of the foremost practitioners of the documentary drama with his play *Prozeß in Nürnberg* (1967; Trial at Nuremberg). He achieved notoriety with the novel *November* (1979), a daring indictment of the expatriation of cabaret singer Wolf Biermann by East Germany in November 1976.

The years of the ebb and the flow of a hot and cold, restrictive and comparatively tolerant policy by East German authorities in regard to literary expression reached its climax in the expulsion of a number of writers in late 1976 and early 1977, the result of protests that erupted after the refusal of East Germany to permit Wolf BIERMANN to return to East Berlin after a Cologne concert in November 1976. Biermann, a caustic critic of socialist practices while still a devoted adherent to the socialist cause, had been prohibited from performing his critical songs of protest and lament in the East for a number of years. After his expatriation other writers either were expelled or were permitted to leave voluntarily—Thomas Brasch, Volker Braun, Bernd Jentzsch, Sarah Kirsch, Reiner Kunze—and they were followed several years later by Jürek Becker and Günter Kunert, both of whom received permission for extended residency abroad without severing their ties to East Germany entirely. Jürek BECKER is the author of novels that explore the dilemma of the Jew in wartime, as in *Jakob der Lügner* (1968; Eng.

tr., *Jacob the Liar,* 1975); the bureaucratic maze, as in *Irreführung der Behörden* (1973; Confounding the Authorities); and the repressed individual seeking self-expression in a prohibitive society, as in *Schlaflose Tage* (1977; Sleepless Days), a work denied publication in East Germany. A commitment to the human being over the social and political ideologue marks the poetry and prose of Günter KUNERT, who moved to the West in the fall of 1979. Kunert, whose wit and wry humor conceal a deep concern for art and a pessimistic attitude toward the destiny of humankind, very early found a West German publisher for works that could not meet the standards of socialist realism in the East, as with the novel of fantasy and vengeance *Im Namen der Hüte* (1967; In the Name of Hats). Kunert's predilection for justifying his treatment of contemporary East German taboo subjects by dramatizing historical personalities (such as Albrecht Dürer, Heinrich von Kleist, and Heinrich Heine in three radio plays) made him a difficult author for East German literary arbiters and endeared him to the West. His *Der andere Planet* (1974 in the East, 1975 in the West; The Other Planet), written after a sojourn in the United States, is an ambivalent examination of Western political and sociological mores. Contemporary writers in East Germany still struggle with their roles as representatives of a socialist ideology and their innate desire to express their human persuasions freely, as do Günter de Bruyn, Fritz Rudolf Fries, Stefan Hermlin, Stefan Heym, and Eberhard Hilscher, although a writer such as Hermann Kant conforms to socialist literary directives. Now a new generation of young writers, which includes Lutz Rathenow, faces the same dilemma that has prevailed in East Germany since 1945.

An Austrian of multiple talents, Oskar KOKOSCHKA, witnessed the coming and going of styles in literature and art from early in the century to its last decades. Always active as an illustrator as well as a writer, Kokoschka was first known as a representative of *Jugendstil,* although his language was boisterously expressionistic even then. After his irrepressible antics in art and drama early in the century, Kokoschka remained relatively isolated in his ecstatic visions on canvas and more and more infrequently on paper. A fellow countryman, Heimito von DODERER, found his literary voice slowly but steadily, achieving prominence in his thematic search for the understanding of what makes human beings what they are with his novel *Ein Mord, den jeder begeht* (1938; Eng. tr., *Every Man a Murderer,* 1964), in which the protagonist discovers that he is himself responsible for a mysterious death and must himself accept the blame. Doderer followed with a series of complex novels that explored Austrian society and the disruptions of the 20th century, mocking technological, scientific, and intellectual advance. In Germany during World War I and then during World War II in exile, the popular novelist Erich Maria REMARQUE wrote *Im Westen nichts Neues* (1929; Eng. tr., *All Quiet on the Western Front,* 1929) about the first war, and about the second war then with a versatile, dramatic style in works such as *Arc de triomphe* (1946; Eng. tr., *Arch of Triumph,* 1946) and *Der schwarze Obelisk* (1956; Eng. tr., *The Black Obelisk,* 1957). Remarque lived in exile after 1932, saw his books burned in Germany in 1933, was stripped of his German citizenship in 1938, and in 1939 went to the United States, where he became an American citizen. Flight and peril were constant themes in his novels. Gerd GAISER, on the other hand, served with the German air force in World War II and remained in Germany, masking his ideology with a romantic realism, and becoming something of an opportunist with works that record the Nazi defeat in the air, *Die*

sterbende Jagd (1953; The Dying Chase), and criticize the economic policy of the Federal Republic, *Schlußball* (1958).

More typical of the fate of the German writer who remained in Germany and found himself out of favor with the Nazi overlords was Hans Erich NOSSACK, who turned to literature after a career in business, but not in sympathy with the Nazis, did not dare try to publish. All that he had written and secreted away was destroyed in the bombing of Hamburg in 1943. After the war he published a large body of narrative work that probed superficial events to reach the fundamental causes of human actions, evocative in style and theme of the alogical, bizarre world of Kafka. Elias CANETTI published the novel *Die Blendung* (1936; Eng. tr., *Auto-da-Fé,* 1946) in Germany before his emigration to England, but the novel was ignored until after the war, when it was republished twice, first achieving notice only with a small but devoted circle of readers and then reaching public acclaim. Canetti's anecdotes and reminiscences, as well as the sociological treatise *Masse und Macht* (1960; Eng. tr., *Crowds and Power,* 1962), assured his fame. Erich KÄSTNER, whose novel *Emil und die Detektive* (1930; Eng. tr., *Emil and the Detectives,* 1930) brought him international recognition, was another witness of book-burning in Germany. Although he was prohibited from publishing there after 1933, he continued to publish in Switzerland, until 1943 when he was forbidden to write at all. After the war Kästner continued his laconic and satirical inquisition of contemporary society and intellectual pretention. Wolfgang KOEPPEN was unpopular with Nazi authorities but persisted in his writing in Germany, although from 1938 until 1951 he published nothing, reappearing on the literary scene with *Tauben im Gras* (1951; Pigeons in the Grass), a novel critical of the postwar economic "miracle" in Germany. Koeppen favors interior monologue and the collage style of John Dos Passos and James Joyce rather than subscribing to the postwar popularity of Ernest Hemingway and Kafka imitators.

The first writer in Germany to make a debut after the war was Wolfgang BORCHERT, a solitary phenomenon, a man whose health was destroyed in the Third Reich. In a few years he wrote masterful pieces of short prose marked by an individual style of intensity and laconic brevity. His *Draußen vor der Tür* (1947; Eng. tr., *The Man Outside,* 1952) is a drama that was the first and is still the ultimate statement on the misery and misunderstanding that ruined the returning veteran. The year 1947, however, was remarkable for the establishment of a literary practice that exerted a steady and lasting influence on postwar German writing over a period of 20 years. Thwarted by the military government from publishing *Die Skorpion,* a magazine of politically critical but independent new writing, Hans Werner Richter and Alfred Andersch were instrumental with other young writers in founding what came to be known as the "Gruppe 47." Like other returning soldiers, betrayed by a destructive ideology and defeated in war, Richter and Andersch realized the necessity of a new beginning, a critical confrontation, tied to no ideology, free of conformity to any creed. Although the year zero, the year of a completely new start, was an idea that was not valid—writers did have the example of German literature before 1933— Wolfgang Weyrauch did call for a sweeping reform in literature that was meant to revitalize and cleanse the Nazi-dirtied German language. Denied their magazine, Richter and Andersch met informally with concerned writers who read to one another and critized one another's unpublished work. That informal meeting in 1947 resulted in annual and semiannual conferences that set the tone and encouraged writing, eventually catapulting authors such as Günter Grass into fame. Never a formal organization, always a group of friends, the "Gruppe 47" even became a media event, attended by publishers and critics on the lookout for new voices. It came to an abrupt end in 1968, when Russian troops intervened in Czechoslovakia just prior to a meeting scheduled in Prague that was, of course, never held. The influence and endorsement of the group was of importance for a period of two decades, a period that witnessed the reemergence of literature in Germany to one of international importance.

Like others of his generation who had undergone similar experiences, Hans Werner RICHTER wrote about the war in novels such as *Du sollst nicht töten* (1955; Thou Shalt Not Kill) and chronicled the destinies of the doomed generation of the 1920s in *Rose weiß, Rose rot* (1971; Rose White, Rose Red). Alfred ANDERSCH supported the search for freedom in his autobiographical *Die Kirschen der Freiheit* (1952; Cherries of Freedom) and in a series of radio plays, the form easiest to present to the public after the war at a time when there were neither presses nor publishers. Wolfgang WEYRAUCH began publishing in the 1930s but became known only in 1949, with the pioneer presentation of young German writers in an anthology *Tausend Gramm*. He has consistently furthered German writing with other anthologies, by explorative and experimental prose and poetry of his own, and with the establishment of an annual prize for lyric poetry. His contributions to the postwar German radio play established him in that genre. He has continued to question and provoke with spirited and skeptical language in a remarkable miscellany of stories and poems, consistently defiant and unpersuaded.

While the "Gruppe 47" was promoting literature in Germany, it reached into Austria as well to encourage the writers of a new age. One of the first was Ingeborg BACH-MANN, a morose and reclusive poet and writer of prose who found public favor with her volume of poems *Die gestundete Zeit* (1953; Time Suspended) and a collection of stories *Das dreißigste Jahr* (1961; Eng. tr., *The Thirtieth Year*, 1964). Ilse AICHINGER (1921–), another Austrian, married to the German lyric poet Günter EICH, is also representative of the assortment of writers associated with the "Gruppe 47." In her novel *Die größere Hoffnung* (1948; Eng. tr., *Herod's Children*, 1963), as well as in the collection of stories *Der Gefesselte* (1953; Eng. tr., *The Bound Man*, 1956), Aichinger relates the individual's search for a meaningful life, accenting renunciation to achieve symbolic victory over repressive circumstances, often in a surprising flight of fancy and imagery reminiscent of Kafka.

Although there had not been a close association of like-minded writers since the early expressionists—despite the claims of literary critics and scholars that schools such as new realism in the 1920s did exist—an association of this kind did take place in Vienna after World War II, when iconoclastic, critical, experimental writers gathered in what became known as the "Wiener Gruppe." Foremost among them was Ernst JANDL, a prolific and daring linguistic experimentalist, who in poetry and radio play has revealed his scornful skepticism toward human pretensions and amused readers while instructing them in new idioms. His close friend and sometimes his collaborator, Friederike MAYRÖCKER, also brought new realizations of the capabilities of language with laconic puns and the deconstruction of reality, which she reassembles into collage depictions of new realities. Her vulnerability has been a calming factor for Jandl's occasional irascibility. Gerhard RÜHM—also a member of the "Wiener Gruppe," which included Friedrich Achleitner, Konrad Bayer, and

Oswald Wiener—like H. C. Artmann reintroduced the Viennese dialect as a vehicle of social comment, exploring the structural aspects of language and the visual character of words that reflect their content in irrepressible exuberation and open delight. Hans Carl ARTMANN has disassociated himself with the stance of the "Wiener Gruppe" and is now one of the most successful avant-garde experimental poets, an incandescent eccentric who springs with protean alacrity from book to book, from genre to genre, choreographing each according to its fundamental nature. The Austrian Thomas BERNHARD, however, did not associate with the "Wiener Gruppe" but pursued an independent way through bizarre novels and dramas, sometimes frenetic in their denunciation of political parties and intellectual bores, as in *Das Kalkwerk* (1970; Eng. tr., *The Lime Works,* 1973) and *Die Berühmten* (1976; The Famous Ones). But the writer who had the greatest impact outside of Austria is Peter HANDKE, a profligate author of plays, novels, and poetry who from the start used language as a tool to dissect literary styles, genres, and social attitudes and conventions. His *Publikumsbeschimpfung* (1966; Eng. tr., *Offending the Audience,* 1969) became an overnight theatrical sensation. The psychological study of a murderer, *Die Angst des Tormanns beim Elfmeter* (1970; Eng. tr., *The Goalie's Anxiety at the Penalty Kick,* 1972), is typical of Handke's masterful use of linguistic structure and verbal nuance to construct a world beyond reason. He continues his examination of social sensibilities and literary labels, often with wrathful, even merciless precision in an amazing variety of literary styles and vehicles.

The year 1954 is memorable in German letters of the 20th century because of the founding of the most prominent literary magazine, *Akzente,* by Hans Bender and Walter Höllerer. The magazine, published from the beginning by the Hanser Verlag in Munich, celebrated its 25th anniversary in March 1979, still under the editorship of Bender. Höllerer had left as coeditor in 1967 to found a linguistically oriented journal in Berlin, *Sprache im technischen Zeitalter.* Since 1977, Michael Krüger, a poet and editor at Hanser, has assisted Bender with the magazine. Through two-and-a-half decades *Akzente* has been the sounding board for new authors, thanks to the critical judgment of the editors, particularly of Bender, who became the acknowledged discoverer of a progression of authors in Germany and in neighboring German-speaking lands. In a reprint edition in 1977, *Akzente* astonished German publishers with sales of almost 100,000 of a 5-volume, 20-year reprint. With the support of *Akzente,* in which many an author found the first opportunity to appear in print, German literature emerged in the second half of the 20th century as the most consistently productive (and overall the most consistently ignored in the English-speaking world) of European letters. Hans BENDER is a master of the short story in German, recognized as such since the publication of the collection *Wölfe und Tauben* (Wolves and Doves) in 1957. Because of his consistent close contact with German writers and because of his fastidious refusal to become identified with any partisan tendency or literary group, he has also been a foremost editor of anthologies of German-language lyric poetry. Walter HÖLLERER helped Bender shape postwar literature and, as the founder of the Literarisches Colloquium/Berlin, furthered the careers of a number of experimental authors, including Nicolas Born. Höllerer himself introduced semiotics as a literary signpost in his novel *Die Elephantenuhr* (1973).

An author who fits into no scheme in postwar literature in Germany is Arno SCHMIDT, a multilingual radical whose novels have fascinated a generation of readers, from the programmatic *Berechnungen* (1955; Calculations) to his *Die Schule der Atheisten* (1973; The School of Atheists). Always innovative, both in style and in format, Schmidt attained and held tightly to a reclusive existence, constantly challenging his readers with puns, allusions, and encyclopedic parodies.

German prose flourished in the new age of German letters. Paul SCHALLÜCK, although he wrote for radio and television, first became widely known because of his novel *Engelbert Reineke* (1959), which took up a theme that consistently was repeated in the works of a succession of novelists: the difficult task of coming to terms with a historical past that casts a pall of guilt on a whole people. However, the career of Schallück was always overshadowed by that of his fellow resident of Cologne, Heinrich BÖLL, a leading prose writer. Böll began to make a name for himself quite early with stories and novels in which the German experience of war was paramount, as in *Wanderer, kommst du nach Spa . . .* (1950; Eng. tr., *Traveller, If You Come to Spa,* 1956) and *Wo warst du, Adam?* (1951; Eng. tr., *Adam, Where Art Thou,* 1955). Böll continued to criticize the religious and social hypocrisy of postwar Germany in works that found international acclaim, such as *Billard um halb zehn* (1959; Eng. tr., *Billiards at Half-Past Nine,* 1961), *Ansichten eines Clowns* (1963; Eng. tr., *The Clown,* 1965), and *Gruppenbild mit Dame* (1971; Eng. tr., *Group Portrait with Lady,* 1973). In the 1970s he became a controversial figure because of his attacks on an irresponsible press during a time of terroristic attacks on the German establishment.

Another giant of postwar fiction, Siegfried LENZ, in his stories and novels investigates the often questionable ethics of human beings caught up in the storms of war. Questions of moral decisions occur in *Stadtgespräch* (1963; Eng. tr., *The Survivor,* 1965) and in the immense *Deutschstunde* (1968; Eng. tr., *The German Lesson,* 1972), which deals as well with the suppression of art in the Third Reich. The political manipulation of postwar German youth is the theme of the probing *Das Vorbild* (1973; Eng. tr., *An Exemplary Life,* 1976), and the theme of sacrifice for the sake of a greater cause in the service of humanity is depicted in *Heimatmuseum* (1978; Masurian Museum).

Günter GRASS, however, is an incarnation of talent in all literary genres and in art. He burst on the literary scene with his scandalous and scurrilous novel of German guilt and perseverence, *Die Blechtrommel* (1959; Eng. tr., *The Tin Drum,* 1962). A further examination in concise depth of the German conscience was exploited in the novella *Katz und Maus* (1961; Eng. tr., *Cat and Mouse,* 1963) and in the novel of retribution *Hundejahre* (1963; Eng. tr., *Dog Years,* 1965). Grass was an instantaneous success not only because of the iconoclastic thematics of his novels but also because of a style that reshaped and reinvigorated the German language, an indefatigable array of puns, allusions combined with a profound historical awareness and a scourging indictment of the German intelligentsia, unsparing, sometimes vicious, always mercilessly on target. His essentially middle-of-the-road persuasion in political campaigns in support of Willy Brandt brought him enmity from the extremes of left and right. Untouched by criticism and always ready with an appropriate retort, Grass continued his one-man reform of language with *örtlich betäubt* (1969; Eng. tr., *Local Anaesthetic,* 1970), the feminist novel fantasy *Der Butt* (1977; Eng. tr., *The Flounder,* 1978), and the compliment to Hans Werner Richter and the "Gruppe 47," *Das Treffen in Telgte* (1979; The Meeting in Telgte). All along Grass furnished his poems and plays with illustrative graphic comments that elaborate the literary themes.

Rienhard LETTAU is in the realm of anecdote and curt prose sketches on a smaller scale what Grass is in the larger epic, also a scurrilous observer of language and social incident, as in *Schwierigkeiten beim Häuserbauen* (1962; Difficulties in House Construction) and *Feinde* (1968; Eng. tr., *Enemies,* 1973). An author who became a critic of the German economic regeneration and the effect it had on the social and political environment of the nation is Martin WALSER, who in a series of dramas and novels took German society to task for past and present failures. The affluent society of postwar Germany approaches a moribund state in the trilogy comprised of *Halbzeit* (1960; Half-Time), *Das Einhorn* (1966; Eng. tr., *The Unicorn,* 1971), and *Der Sturz* (1973; The Fall). Ultimately Walser's novels and plays amount to a self-searching analysis of the individual role in most memorable interpersonal and intersocial relationships. The disaffection of the individual with German postwar society is exemplified in the critical fiction of the disenchanted Günter HERBURGER, an adherent originally to the new contemporary realism initiated by Dieter Wellershoff. The world of realism meets the realm of the grotesque in such works as *Jesus in Osaka* (1970) and in the multivolume *Flug ins Herz* (1977; Flight into the Heart), in which Herburger demands political and social reforms at every level. Peter HÄRTLING, on the other hand, is concerned with a reconstruction of the fabled past, particularly the role of fathers in such novels as *Das Familienfest* (1969; The Family Feast) and *Neimbsch* (1964), a concern that progresses to the denial of true individuality in *Hubert oder die Rückkehr nach Casablanca* (1978; Hubert or the Return to Casablanca). Heinz PIONTEK, known both as a poet of existential despair and a novelist imbued with an acute awareness of history, has written of the midlife crisis in *Mittlere Jahre* (1967; The Middle Years) and the problems confronting contemporary authors in *Dichterleben* (1976; A Poet's Life), always with clarity and occasional illuminating surreality. A short-lived but influential loose association of writing workers, known as "Gruppe 61," was initiated in 1961 by Max von der GRÜN, whose matter-of-fact prose concentrates on a critical evaluation of contemporary life-styles, particularly focused on workers in *Männer in zweifacher Nacht* (1962; Men in a Twofold Night) and a novel of commitment, *Flächenbrand* (1979; Conflagration). A similar devotion to a new brand of realism is seen in the novels of Dieter WELLERSHOFF, such as *Ein schöner Tag* (1966; Eng. tr., *A Beautiful Day,* 1966) and *Die Schattengrenze* (1969; The Edge of Shadow). Horst BIENEK, a refugee from the East who moved to West Germany in 1955 after a short prison term at Vorkuta in Siberia for political agitation, is a sensitive and trenchantly observant poet, author also of a prison novel *Die Zelle* (1968; Eng. tr., *The Cell,* 1972), and of a tetralogy that narrates events on the eve of the first day of World War II on the Polish border in *Die erste Polka* (1976; Eng. tr., *The First Polka,* 1978), *Septemberlicht* (1977; September Light), *Zeit ohne Glocken* (1979), and a volume yet to appear.

Women writers have also found a voice in contemporary German writing, although not in the numbers expected in today's society and not with the resonance abroad that male authors have enjoyed in small numbers. Barbara KÖNIG focuses on the theme of the multifaceted personality in her *Die Personenperson* (1965) and takes a realistic, unvarnished look at a modern marriage in *Schöner Tag, dieser 13.* (1974; Beautiful Day This 13th). Gisela ELSNER portrays the gross and misshapen social possibilities of the postwar German family in *Die Riesenzwerge* (1964; Eng. tr., *The Giant Dwarfs,* 1965) and in *Der Berührungsverbot* (1970; Do Not Touch) examines the subject of changing sexual mores. Helga NOVAK, who moved from East Germany to West Germany in 1965, has consistently been a spokesman for protest in a mechanistic world unfriendly to its human inhabitants, as can be seen in *Aufenthalt in einem irren Haus* (1972; Stay in a Mad House), and she has served as a partisan in the increasingly militant feminist movement, apparent in *Eines Tages hat sich die Sprechpuppe nicht mehr ausziehen lassen* (1972; One Day the Talking Doll Refused to be Undressed). A critic and satirist of contemporary German society, particularly in relation to the emancipation of women and in interfamilial relationships, is Angelika MECHTEL, whose precision of style and evocation of the past and the potential future have brought a wide readership for her novels, notably *Das gläserne Paradies* (1973; The Glass Paradise) and *Die Blindgängerin* (1974; The Blind Girl). The most productive woman writer is Gabriele WOHMANN, who in exact, analytical strokes lays bare the various levels of German society with irony and sometimes with satirical horror. The isolation of the individual in *Die Bütows* (1967) and *Ländliches Fest* (1971; Country Party) is contrasted with repeated failures to communicate in *Abschied für länger* (1965; A Farewell for a Long Time) and the isolation and struggle of the artist in *Frühherbst in Badenweiler* (1978; Early Fall in Badenweiler).

An irrepressible author of the grotesque and the fantastic, who also has created a graphic world that reflects his inexhaustible imagination, is Christoph MECKEL, an inventor of fabulous worlds that are counterparts to the Earth, as in *Im Land der Umbramauten* (1961; In the Country of the Umbramauts). Meckel's poetry is rhapsodic and melancholy in turn.

German drama had a mixed reception after 1945, centered on but a few authors. A foremost creator of stage plays was Carl ZUCKMAYER, who became a success on the German stage in the Weimar Republic with the comedy *Der fröhliche Weinberg* (1925; The Merry Vineyard) and was celebrated for the satire of pre-Hitler militarism, *Der Hauptmann von Köpenik* (1931; Eng. tr., *The Captain of Köpenick*, 1932), but who had to flee Germany and Austria in 1938 to the United States, where he continued to write plays critical of the new regime, with *Des Teufels General* (1946; The Devil's General), and an indictment of atomic scientists in *Das kalte Licht* (1955; The Cold Light). A short-lived but venturesome and controversial subgenre of drama was the documentary play, initiated by Rolf HOCHHUCH in 1963 with his study of the role of Pope Pius XII in the fate of wartime Jews in the play *Der Stellvertreter* (Eng. tr., *The Deputy*, 1964). Hochhuch followed that extravaganza of historical investigation with a stunning accusation against Winston Churchill for complicity in the death of Władysław Sikorski in *Soldaten* (1967; Eng. tr., *Soldiers*, 1968). His subsequent plays have either concerned themselves with a future political tyranny or with more contemporary themes, and he has written aesthetic inquiries about the theater. Heinar KIPPHARDT also became an international sensation with his documentary play *In der Sache J. Robert Oppenheimer* (1964; Eng. tr., *In the Matter of J. Robert Oppenheimer*, 1967), but he subsequently turned to other genres with less successful effect, such as the novel *März* (1976; March), a psychological study of insanity. The most widely performed dramatist of the documentary play is Peter WEISS, a refugee from Nazi tyranny who fled to Sweden and first wrote the autobiographical, confessional novels *Abschied von den Eltern* (1961; Eng. tr., *Leavetaking*, 1966) and *Fluchtpunkt* (1962; Eng. tr., *Vanishing Point*, 1966), preceded by the exaggeratedly precise and detailed *Der Schatten des Körpers des Kutschers* (1960;

Eng. tr., *The Shadow of the Coachman's Body*, 1969). The first success of Peter Weiss was his pseudodocumentary *Die Verfolgung und Ermordung Jean Paul Marats, dargestellt durch die Schauspieltruppe des Hospizes zu Charenton unter Anleitung des Herrn de Sade* (1964; Eng. tr., 1965), known for short as *Marat/Sade,* and the notorious documentary of the Auschwitz war criminal trials in Frankfurt am Main, *Die Ermittlung* (1965; Eng. tr., *The Investigation,* 1966). Subsequent attempts by Weiss to involve theatergoers in protest against materialist aggression, the Portuguese in *Gesang vom Lusitanischen Popanz* (1967; Eng. tr., *Song of the Lusitanian Bogey,* 1971) and the Americans in *Viet Nam Diskurs* (1967; Eng. tr., 1970), met no public favor. The uncompromising realism of Franz Xaver KROETZ brought him success with short plays that show inarticulate people in *Wildwechsel* (1968; Deer Crossing) and the play without dialogue *Wunschkonzert* (1972; Request Program).

Most authors of postwar German literature have written poems from time to time, often with notable success, as was the case with Wolfgang Weyrauch, Helga Novak, Günter Grass, Heinz Piontek, Christoph Meckel, and others, but there are those whose work has been predominantly lyric. One such author was Maria Luise KASCHNITZ, whose poetry was a sort of self-liberation from the strictures of political and social traumas. Although her preference was for traditional lyric form, the content of her work circles about the alienated condition of humankind and seeks ways to transcend despair. Günter EICH, a pioneer author of memorable radio plays after 1945, also found his main genre to be lyric poetry. His idiom was plainfaced, forthright, and ruthless in *Abgelegene Gehöfte* (1948; Remote Farmsteads), although he turned to mystic worlds that parallel reality in *Botschaften des Regens* (1955; Messages of the Rain) and in the short prose sketches of *Maulwürfe* (1968; Moles). The work of Karl KROLOW shows him to have a profound affinity with nature while not being unaware of the immediate concern for contemporary affairs, often with a laconic tone as in *Nichts weiter als Leben* (1970; Nothing More than Living). The liberating quality of poetry is demonstrated in his *Landschaften für mich* (1966; Landscapes for Me). Ernst MEISTER was always a deeply committed and reflective lyric poet, sensual in his poems but reticent in his personal contacts. His poetry challenged and bewitched readers and critics alike, some of whom remained bewildered by his vision.

The experimental poet in German letters since 1945 has been Helmut HEISSENBÜTTEL, a stylist who has consistently challenged the traditional understanding of what makes a poem, particularly in such works as *Kombinationen* (1954), *Topographien* (1956), and his *Textbuch* series (6 vols., 1960–67). He mixes collage, concrete poetry, and kaleidoscope fragmentation in poems as well as in his novel *Projekt Nr. 1 D'Alemberts Ende* (1970; Project No. 1, The End of D'Alembert) in his persistent effort to reorganize language to reflect experience. Franz MON also has produced lyric poems that have turned poetry inside out, stressing phonetic and syntactic features, providing permutations of reality, mixing stereotype and children's song, always seeking to reorganize the reader's perception of what poetry is. On the other hand Wolfdietrich SCHNURRE has been provocative in more perceptive ways in poetry and prose, in caricatures and fables for children and adults, ever concerned with everyday problems. The slashing political satire of Peter RÜHMKORF in *Irdisches Vergnügen in g* (1959; Earthly Delights in g) and *Kunststücke* (1962; Clever Tricks) is mixed with vulgar children's lyrics collected on the streets of Hamburg and volumes of critical essays and poems, such as

Strömungslehre I (1978; Theory of Currents, I). Hans Magnus ENZENSBERGER has published aggressive attacks on contemporary linguistic practices in the affluent society, all in lyrics that remain objectively cool and effectively restrained. His *Verhör in Habana* (1970; Eng. tr., *The Havana Inquiry,* 1973) put an end to the documentary theater in a chorale defense of Fidel Castro. Rolf Dieter BRINKMANN was an incorrigible and defiant critic of contemporary society, antagonistic, compelled to show his world its dirty side in volumes such as *Was fraglich ist wofür?!* (1967; Questionable What For). He was a merciless realist in *Westwärts 1 & 2* (1975) and had been the principal voice in Germany for American poetry of the 1960s and 1970s. Dieter HOFFMAN has built lyrical monuments to places, art works, and in miniature portraits has erected anecdotal busts of artists from all the realms of art of the past. Nicolas BORN chronicled the doomed student protest movements of the 1960s in his novel *Die erdabgewandte Seite der Geschichte* (1976; The Side of History Turned Away from the Earth) and detailed the horrors of terrorist civil conflict in the Middle East in *Die Fälschung* (1979; The Counterfeit). His poems were always concerned with the role of language and literature in society, a concern that seems to have been common to many authors in Germany in the 20th century.

It must be evident that the literary panorama of German letters in the 20th century is incredibly vast, varied, and consistently lively. Despite the interruption of World War I, a conflict that put an end to the career of several outstanding talents and that produced a spate of pacifist works condemning war, and despite the horrendous and more destructive and crippling rupture of World War II, which brought forth memorable works by exiled authors but produced nothing of consequence by authors allied to the Nazi cause, the end result has been a progressively developing canon in literature that is remarkable for its sustained experimental liveliness, its severe indictments of socially destructive and humanly degrading politics, and ultimately its positive evaluation of the contribution of literary efforts to sustain and elaborate the human condition. The number of authors writing in German has been immense, considering the relative size of the German-speaking population. Authors have consistently been supported by fellowships on national and local levels. From 1968, the year of its founding, to 1979 the literary magazine *Dimension,* published in the United States but devoted to contemporary German writing with facing-page translations, published almost 300 contemporary German-language authors. For a time German publishers became cautious and even reticent about enlarging the stable of known authors, so that late in the 1960s some practitioners and critics of literature declared that German letters were moribund. Recent developments have proved, however, that the new writer is accepted and even on occasion meets with instant acclaim. The lack of an enthusiastic reception through translation in the English-speaking world is regrettable. Perhaps it is in part due to the scorn and revulsion still felt by some for a language whose speakers propelled the world into two wars. But the coming decades will undeniably give German literature the attention it deserves because of its inexhaustible spirit, its linguistic fervor (even in moments of debate about what language is and can be), and its fundamental role as a mediator between the destructive forces of history and the indomitable human individual. German literature today is vibrant, often angry, sometimes desultory and confused, but never saccharine or lachrymose.

See: P. Demetz, *Postwar German Literature* (1970); D. Lattmann, ed., *Die Literatur der Bundesrepublik Deutschland* (1973); K. Franke, ed., *Die Literatur der Deutschen Demokratischen Republik* (1974); H. Spiel, ed., *Die zeitgenössische Litetatur Österreichs* (1976); H. L. Arnold, ed., *Kritisches Lexikon zur deutschsprachigen Gegenwartsliteratur* (1978 ff.).   A.L.W.

Gevers, Marie (1883–1975), Belgian novelist, was born at her family's estate, Missembourg, near Antwerp, where she spent her entire life. Such an uncomplicated existence recalls that of Selma LAGERLÖF at Morbacka or that of Emily Dickinson in Amherst, Mass. But, even though Gevers remained at Missembourg for so many years, she was neither a solitary nor a recluse. When she married in 1908, her husband, Frans Willems, joined her there and many of her relatives lived nearby. Missembourg thus constituted an estate, a family, and a community, as well as a privileged meeting place where generations of writers, artists, and friends gathered. Gevers did not have a formal education: her mother taught her to read and write and to appreciate authors like Jean de la Fontaine and François Fénelon. Her family was typical of many Flemish families in which a French-speaking tradition was maintained. This tradition has contributed to the enrichment of Belgian literature of French expression: Maurice MAETERLINCK, Emile VERHAEREN, Charles van LERBERGHE, Franz HELLENS, Suzanne LILAR, and Françoise MALLET-JORIS, among others. For Gevers, the linguistic situation was neither a problem nor a division. She was as close to Emile Verhaeren (to whom she was related) as to the Flemish writers whom she enjoyed translating.

Her initial literary efforts were in poetry, *Missembourg, Les Arbres et le vent* (The Trees and the Wind). Her first novel, *La Comtesse des digues* (The Countess of the Docks) was published in 1931 and again, in Paris, in 1932, with a translation of Charles VILDRAC. Then followed *Madame Orpha ou la sérénade de mai* (1933; Mrs. Orpha or the May Serenade), *La Ligne de vie* (1937; The Line of Life), *Paix sur les champs* (1941; Peace on the Fields), *La grande Marée* (1945; The Big Tide), and *Château de l'Ouest* (1948; Castle of the West).

Gevers was attracted not only to the novel. In *Guldentop* (1935), she told the story of the ghost of Missembourg. Her exaltation of nature appeared in *Bruyère blanche* (1931; White Bramble), *Plaisir des météores* (1938; Pleasure of the Meteors), *L'amitié des fleurs* (1941; The Friendship of the Flowers), and *L'herbier légendaire* (1949; The Legendary Herbarium). Two trips to Africa and the Congo inspired *Des mille collines aux neuf volcans* (1953; From the Thousand Hills to the Nine Volcanos) and *Plaisir des parallèles* (1958; Pleasure of the Parallels). Finally, reaching into a well of memories of love and of love of life, she published her masterpiece in 1961, *Vie et mort d'un étang* (Life and Death of a Pond).

Marie Gever's life remained calm in spite of incertitudes, happy in spite of much grief. Elected to the Royal Academy of French Language and Literature of Belgium in 1938, she attracted public esteem and admiration as a major literary figure.   G.Si.

Ghelderode, Michel de, pseud. and (after 1930) legal name of Adhemar Martens (1898–1962), Belgian writer of plays and short stories, was born in Ixelles, a suburb of Brussels. Although his parents were of Flemish origin, they decided to raise their children to speak French. Yet Ghelderode was never able to forget the legends and myths of "Mother Flanders" that his mother recounted in Flemish to her children. Forced by illness to abandon his studies with the priests at the Institut Saint-Louis in 1915, Ghelderode ceased to be a practicing Roman Catholic without ever freeing himself from the religious tradition that, along with Flanders, constituted a rich source of artistic inspiration. He continued his education at the

Royal Conservatory of Music and then in museums and in cafés frequented by artists and writers. In 1918 was staged his "La Mort regarde à la fenêtre" (unpublished; Death Looks Out the Window), a one-act play inspired by Edgar Allan Poe; and, in 1919, his "Le Repas des Fauves" (text lost; The Beasts' Meal), a play in three acts based on his own recollections of World War I. In spite of the success of these two plays, Ghelderode's next four years were devoted to narrative prose. The manuscript of "Heiligen Antonius" (1919–21; Saint Anthony), a lively evocation of the temptations of a Flemish Saint Anthony, reveals the efforts of the young story writer to create his own tone and style. His love for the life of the people provided material for his first published book, *L'Histoire comique de Keiser Karel* (1922, 1923; The Comic Story of the Emperor Charles), a collection of droll anecdotes of the life of Charles V, and inspired five plays for puppets, including *Le Mystère de la Passion* (1925; The Mystery of the Passion). The fascination that folklore held for Ghelderode coincided with a renewed interest in the theater and with his contacts with the theater critic Camille Poupeye, whose writings revealed to Ghelderode the work of Luigi PIRANDELLO and of the German expressionists. The influence of these writers appears in *La Mort du Docteur Faust* (1926; Eng. tr., *The Death of Doctor Faust*, 1964) and in *Don Juan* (1928), in which Ghelderode utilized techniques freely borrowed from the music hall, the cinema, the circus, and pantomime. Such a daring reaction to the theatrical practices of the period drew the attention of Johan de Meester, the brilliant director of the Vlaams Volkstooneel (Flemish People's Theater). This itinerant Catholic troupe, whose productions were influenced by Russian constructivism and German expressionism, as well as rooted in the religious and political aspirations of Flanders, attracted a large public among the French-speaking elite, as well as among Flemings. The production, early in 1927, of Ghelderode's *Beeldekens uit het leven van Sint Franciskus van Assisië* (Scenes from the Life of Saint Francis of Assisi)—the original French version was never published—was widely acclaimed; it was followed in 1929 by *Barabbas* (1932; Eng. tr., 1960) and in 1930 by *Pantagleize* (1934; Eng. tr., 1957). Ghelderode's experience with the Volkstooneel led to the creation of the poetic *Christophe Colomb* (1928; Christopher Columbus) and of the intensely dramatic *Escurial* (1928; Eng. tr., 1957), which, although not accepted by the Volkstooneel, became Ghelderode's most often staged play. After the disbanding of the Volkstooneel in 1932, Ghelderode continued to write for the theater: *Magie Rouge* (1935; Eng. tr., *Red Magic*, 1964), *Sire Halewyn* (1943; Eng. tr., *Lord Halewyn*, 1960), *La Ballade du Grand Macabre* (1935), *Mademoiselle Jaire* (1942; Eng. tr., *Miss Jairus*, 1964), *Hop Signore!* (1938; Eng. tr., 1964), and *Fastes d'Enfer* (1943; Eng. tr., *Chronicles of Hell*, 1960). Discouraged by the unenthusiastic reception given to these plays, Ghelderode turned to the writing of short stories; in 1942 he published *Sortilèges* (Sorceries). Subsequently, he composed several plays whose subject had long preoccupied him, notably *L'Ecole des Bouffons* (1942; Eng. tr., *School for Buffoons*, 1964). He had withdrawn from literary activities in 1947, when two young French producers, André Reybaz and Catherine Toth, brought forth *Hop Signor!* Their enthusiasm was soon shared by others who were excited to discover this theater of flesh and blood after the postwar philosophical dramas of Albert CAMUS, Jean-Paul SARTRE, and Gabriel MARCEL. At the Concours des Jeunes Companies in 1949, the first prize was awarded to *Fastes d'Enfer* and the third prize to *Mademoiselle Jaire*. Three years later, at the Théâtre Marigny, the winning play produced one of the most publicized scandals

in contemporary theater. This event represented the beginning of Ghelderode's worldwide reputation. Feeling abandoned, Ghelderode died on April 1, 1962. He did not know that the Swedish Academy, encouraged by Eric Bentley, among others, was seriously considering his candidature for the Nobel Prize for Literature in 1962.

Ghelderode's works have been produced with a growing frequency. His popularity has been greatest, especially in France and the United States, among young theatrical companies and among university students and amateurs, and their enthusiasm suggests a bright future for Ghelderode's theater. In 1978 was founded in Gênes a "Société Internationale des Etudes sur Michel de Ghelderode."

The Belgian dramatist has increasingly been viewed as one of the principal precursors of the "new theater" of the 1950s. It is uncertain whether he influenced writers like Eugène IONESCO, Samuel BECKETT, Jean GENET, and Fernando ARRABAL; but it is unquestionable that many of their "innovations" were already present in his work and that this work contributed to the acceptance of these innovations. Critics often classify Ghelderode with Antonin ARTAUD, yet a great gap stands between the visions and intentions of these two men. Unlike Artaud, Ghelderode did not question the essence of "representative" theater based upon the supremacy of author and text. Rather than seeking to change man, Ghelderode held up a distorted mirror that reflects man's ambiguity and the ridiculous aspects of his condition. But, like Artaud, Ghelderode utilized stage techniques that Artaud called "specifically theatrical."

Ghelderode's theater appeals primarily to the senses through its rich pictorial imagery. He was inspired by Bruegel, Hieronymus Bosch, and, in particular, James Ensor, who was the source of the pantomime *Masques Ostendais* (1935; Masks of Ostend) and of an unpublished antimilitarist satire, "Le Siege d'Ostende" (1933; The Siege of Ostend).

The greater part of Ghelderode's theater has been assembled in five volumes (1950–57); English translations appeared as *Seven Plays* (2 vols.; 1960, 1964).

See: J. Francis, *L'Eternel aujourd'hui de M. de Ghelderode* (1968); R. Beyen, *M. de Ghelderode ou la hantise du masque* (1971); J. Stevo, *Office des ténèbres pour M. de Ghelderode* (1972); R. Beyen, *Ghelderode* (1974).

R.By.

Ghéon, Henri, pseud. of Henri Vangeon (1875–1944), French playwright, critic, poet, novelist, and theatrical producer, was born in Bray-sur-Seine. He showed a precocious talent for drama, writing his first play, "Un mari trompé" (A Deceived Husband), at the age of eight. Ghéon began his literary career while still a medical student, contributing to various reviews, especially the *Mercure de France* and *Ermitage,* for a time all but directing the latter. In 1909 he participated in founding the *Nouvelle Revue française,* and until 1914 he was not only its most prolific but one of its most respected critics. His essays, collected in *Nos Directions* (1911; Our Directions), asserted the *Nouvelle Revue's* position against neoromanticism and naturalism and advocated a truly dramatic, poetic theater, thus heralding the work of the Théâtre du Vieux-Colombier, in which he took part. Coining the expression "nouvelle critique" (new criticism) as he had coined "nouveau roman" (new novel) in 1901, phrases that were to enjoy such a vogue half a century later, he advocated an objective criticism free of all aesthetic, political, or religious bias. Ghéon also wrote in 1914 one of the first interesting articles on Marcel PROUST.

Although he was André GIDE's closest friend and exuberant companion for about 15 years—his motto then was "de tout, beaucoup, deux fois"—Ghéon seems to have been indelibly influenced by Francis VIELÉ-GRIFFIN, as evidenced by his contribution to the theory of vers libre, which he also exemplified in his early poetry, especially *Algérie* (1906). Similarly, although he had attacked naturism, Ghéon's early "popular tragedies," *Le Pain* (1911; Bread) and *Eau-de-vie* (1914; Brandy), bear the mark of naturism and vers-librism. The influence of naturism is also suggested by the titles of Ghéon's most interesting novels, *La Vieille Dame des rues* (The Old Woman of the Streets), serialized long before its publication as a volume in 1930, and *Les Jeux de l'enfer et du ciel* (1929; Games of Heaven and Hell).

In 1915, Ghéon converted to Catholicism, an event recalled in *Témoignage d'un converti* (1919; Testimony of a Convert). His conversion had a profound and lasting effect on his life and work. Gide, for whom Ghéon had been "a soul of crystal and gold full of marvelous sonorities," lamented this conversion, saying, "God has confiscated him from me." But Ghéon was now a militant Christian and patriot. In about 100 plays and several novels, he was inspired by fervent faith, hagiography, and the religious theater of the Middle Ages, as well as by such writers as Hans Christian Andersen, Calderón, and Shakespeare and by European and oriental folklore. Ghéon wrote in all dramatic genres, and his production for the theater, although uneven, is one of the largest in French literature. His best plays, written in a language that is rich, warm, and poetic with a deliberate naiveté, reflect a true sense of the theater and an ability to infuse life into all-but-forgotten figures, mostly saints. Only some can be enumerated here: *La Farce du pendu dépendu* (1920; The Farce of the Unhanged Hanged Man), *Le Pauvre sous l'escalier* (1921; The Pauper under the Stair), *Les Trois Miracles de Sainte Cécile* (1921; The Three Miracles of Saint Cecilia), *Le Triomphe de Saint Thomas d'Aquin* (1924; The Triumph of Saint Thomas Aquinas), *Le Comédien et la grâce* (1925; The Actor and Grace), *Le Mystère de la messe* (1934; The Mystery of the Mass), *Le Noël sur la place* (1935; Christmas on the Square), *Les Aventures de Gilles* (1936; The Adventures of Gilles), *Judith* (1948; pub. 1952), and *Oedipe* (1952).

In spite of his considerable success with the Catholic masses ("le peuple fidelé") everywhere, Ghéon's place in French literature remains difficult to assess as he perilously attempted after his conversion to clericalize, as René ETIEMBLE would say, a long-since secularized genre. Some of his criticism, however, is of unquestionable importance, especially that on the theater, *L'Art du théâtre* (1944; The Art of the Theater), and on Mozart, *Promenades avec Mozart* (1932; Promenades with Mozart).

See: M. Raymond, *Henri Ghéon: sa vie, son œuvre* (1939) and *Le jeu retrouvé* (1943); H. Brochet, *Henri Ghéon* (1946); M. Deléglise, *Le Théâtre d'Henri Ghéon* (1947); A. Gide, *Journal 1899–1939* (1948) and *Feuillets d'automne* (1949).   J.-P.C.

Ghil, René (1862–1925), French poet, was born in Tourcoing, French Flanders. He studied in Paris at the Lycée Condorcet, where he shared the friendship of Ephraïm Mikhaël, Pierre Quillard, Stuart MERRILL, and André Fontainas, all of whom were soon to play a part in the symbolist movement. His first book of poems, *Légendes d'âmes et de sang* (1885; Legends of Souls and Blood), written under the influence of Stéphane MALLARMÉ, was an attempt at applying his scientific conception of poetry. The following year, in the *Traité du verbe* (Treatise on the Word), Ghil defined and expanded his theories. His main purpose was to submit the art of verse to a scientific method by applying to the sounds of speech the principles of instrumental music, creating thereby what he calls *instrumentation verbale*. Taking Arthur RIMBAUD's "Sonnet des voyelles" as a starting point, Ghil claimed that vowels, and even consonants, not only possess color suggestions, but also a particular timbre corresponding to such and such a musical instrument and capable of evoking by sound alone a variety of emotions. He then began to apply this musical technique to the exposition of his philosophical and scientific concepts, and to that effect he published several books of poems. As if to leave no doubt concerning their unity of design, these works bear a unique title, *Oeuvre* (1889–1909), divided into three parts, *Dire du mieux* (Saying of the Best), *Dire des sangs* (Saying of the Bloods), and *Dire de la loi* (Saying of the Law). Although verbal orchestration was his main intent, Ghil dreamed of fusing together all the forms of art—literary, pictorial, plastic, as well as musical. By such means, Ghil aimed at achieving a complete synthesis of man since his remotest origins. In spite of the elaborate treatises in which he explained his intentions—*De la poésie scientifique* (1909; Concerning Scientific Poetry), *La Tradition de la poésie scientifique* (1920; The Tradition of Scientific Poetry), and *Les Dates et les œuvres* (1923; The Dates and the Works)—he had no disciple, but his work remains a curious example of experimentation in the domain of poetic technique.

See: A. Barre, *Le Symbolisme* (1912); C. A. Fusil, *La Poésie scientifique* (1918); A. van Bever and P. Léautaud, *Poètes d'aujourd'hui* (1929); M. Robert, *René Ghil: du symbolisme à la poésie cosmique* (1962); W. Theile, *René Ghil: eine Analyse seiner Dichtungen und theoretischen Schriften* (1965); T. Goruppi, "Simbolismo e positivismo nel *Traité du verbe*," in *Saggi* 16 (1976): 363–409.

M.D. rev. D.W.A.

Gide, André (1869–1951), French novelist, critic, essayist, and dramatist, was born in Paris. He was among the most disturbing and controversial of great contemporaries, for hesitations and contradictions mark all his thought. He insisted that he wrote to be reread; and if he admirably fulfilled his function, which was to disturb and provoke the reader, it is also true that each of his books contains the precise antidote for the poison that it apparently distills.

André Gide was descended, on his father's side, from Cévennes Huguenots and, on his mother's, from Norman Catholics recently converted to Protestantism. In these divergent influences he saw the source of his intellectual contradictions and the reason for his writing, since only in art could he harmonize his opposing tendencies. His father's death in 1880 left André in the care of three austere women whose rigid principles did not prevent their pampering the boy—his mother, his Aunt Claire, and the English spinster Anna Shackleton. An indifferent pupil afflicted with nervous disorders, he studied at the Ecole Alsacienne and under private tutors. The conflict between his intense religious fervor and his awakening to manhood found expression in *Les Cahiers d'André Walter* (1891), begun at 18 and published anonymously as the posthumous diary of an unhappy youth. Although telling in romanticized form the story of his own pure love for his cousin Emmanuèle, this little volume of lyrical prose, soon to be followed by Walter's *Poésies* (1892), also reduced to its essence the philosophico-literary idealism of the epoch and hence opened to its author the door of the *cénacles*. For two or three seasons, Gide circulated among the symbolists, a stiff and artificial figure whose uncompromising intellectualism and devout faith embarrassed his friends. Meanwhile his subtle *Traité du Nar-*

cisse (1892), *Tentative amoureuse* (1893), and *Voyage d'Urien* (1893) further identified him with French symbolism. But in the fall of 1893 he undertook a trip to North Africa that, as he had foreseen when he left his beloved Bible at home, marked the great turning point in his life. Falling ill at Biskra, he narrowly escaped death, and his convalescence taught him the value of life, of the present moment, and of that ardent fervor that gives life its zest. He also learned the secret of his tormented nature and resolved not to stifle his inclinations. Deliberately he renounced his past, seeking the primitive man under the veneer of education. After a year in the desert he recanted his former life in an ironic epitaph, *Paludes* (1895); in 1897 his break with symbolism was confirmed by *Les Nourritures terrestres,* a breviary of revolt that preaches the joy of living by the senses, restlessly eager for every eventuality. On his return to Paris in 1895 he had witnessed his mother's death and married his cousin. Henceforth, with Paris and his two Norman estates as headquarters, he was to travel frequently to Africa, Italy, Germany, England, and eventually Russia.

"To free oneself is nothing; it's being free that is hard"—this is the problem that Gide examined from all sides during the next 20 years. The too receptive Saul and the overgenerous Candaulus, heroes of his beautiful verse dramas *Saül* (1903) and *Le Roi Candaule* (1901), together with the Michel of *L'Immoraliste* (1902), end tragically because of breaking with conventional morality in their search for self-fulfillment. The Alissa of *La Porte étroite* (1909), counterpart of *L'Immoraliste,* illustrates the dangers of the other extreme, renunciation. In *Le Retour de l'enfant prodigue* (1907) Gide's prodigal, while admitting his errors, helps his younger brother to escape. Finally, the seductive Lafcadio of *Les Caves du Vatican* (1914) finds himself the prisoner of a free unmotivated act he has committed to prove his own liberty. Indeed, even during his period of maturity between the two wars, Gide consistently returns to the problem of personal freedom: in his dialogues on the subject of homosexuality, *Corydon* (1924), in his outspoken memoirs, *Si le grain ne meurt* (1926), and in *Les Faux-Monnayeurs* (1926)—the only novel he wrote, for he classified the frankly ironic works as *soties* (*Paludes; Le Prométhée mal enchaîné,* 1899; *Les Caves du Vatican*) and the soberly classical works recounted by one of the protagonists as *récits* (*L'Immoraliste; La Porte étroite; La Symphonie pastorale,* 1919; and a few others). In treating the three themes of his novel—the adolescent revolt, the decaying of bourgeois families, and the creation of a work of art—Gide reveals many of the antinomies upon which his dynamic equilibrium rests: the soul and the flesh, life and art, expression and restraint, the individual and society, classicism and romanticism, Christ and Christianity, God and the Devil. Here, moreover, his predilection for the complex form of a book within a book, which he had originally indulged in his first work, yields its happiest results.

It is natural that his lifelong preoccupation with freedom and his keenly sympathetic nature should have made André Gide a champion of the oppressed. As mayor of a commune in Normandy (1896), later as a juror in Rouen (1912), and finally as a special envoy of the Colonial Ministry (1925–26), he had ample opportunity to observe social injustice. His *Voyage au Congo* (1927) and *Retour du Tchad* (1928), in fact, led to legal reform and eventually to curbing of the industrial concessions in the colonies. When, in the early 1930s, he declared his admiration for Soviet Russia and his sympathy toward communism, Gide shocked the men of his generation, as he had so often done before, and raised another barrier between himself and official honors. After a trip to the Soviet Union, his

Retour de l'U.R.S.S. (1936), which told of his disappointment and criticized the Soviets for abandoning their original principles, momentarily alienated even his young admirers. But Gide was always an independent.

Gide's critical writings, found chiefly in *Prétextes* (1903), *Nouveaux Prétextes* (1911), *Dostoïevsky* (1923), and *Incidences* (1924), have won him a place as one of the most perspicacious literary critics of his time. His double nature permitted him to admire the classical (Johann von Goethe, Jean Racine, Johann Sebastian Bach) while nourishing a predilection for tormented and complicated souls (Friedrich NIETZSCHE, Fyodor DOSTOYEVSKY, William Blake, Walt Whitman, Charles BAUDELAIRE). These and a few others (Michel de Montaigne, Robert Browning, Frédéric Chopin) are the spiritual brothers having most intimate influence on the man who, in a lecture in 1900, made a most eloquent apology for all influences. The same broad sympathies are shown in his clairvoyant criticism of contemporaries, for he was often the first to discern and encourage authentic talent. In 1909 he was a prime mover in founding the *Nouvelle Revue française,* a focal point in modern French literature. His own influence was as wide as that of any writer of his generation; suffice it to mention two Academicians and a Nobel Prize winner who have felt that influence, François MAURIAC, Jacques de LACRETELLE, and Roger MARTIN DU GARD, and certain leaders of the group born around 1900, Jean GIONO, Julien GREEN, André MALRAUX, and Antoine de SAINT-EXUPÉRY.

A skeptic, questioning all values, like Montaigne vaunting his uncertainty and his inconsistencies, Gide early dedicated himself to the study of man. In a style that varies from the colored, ejaculatory prose of his early works to the voluntarily bare understatement of his mature works, he explored the most complex and most disturbing characters, emotions, and ideas. Although "le gidisme" has frequently exerted an unfortunate influence upon those who failed to read to the end his maxim, "It is good to follow your penchant provided you go upward," nevertheless Gide's position as a moral philosopher has only grown with time.

See: C. Du Bos, *Le Dialogue avec André Gide* (1929); R. Fernandez, *André Gide* (1931); L. Pierre-Quint, *André Gide; sa vie, son œuvre* (1932); J. Hytier, *André Gide* (1938).　　　　　　　　　　　　　　　　　　　　J.O'B.

By the time of his death in Paris in 1951 the "inquiéteur" whose beliefs and conduct had so often provoked the shocked condemnation of his contemporaries during the 1920s and 1930s was a doctor *honoris causa* of Oxford and a Nobel Prize laureate (1947). "Seductive Lafcadio" had trod the respectable boards of the Comédie Française in a 1950 adaptation of *Les Caves du Vatican,* while his creator, an old and famous man, was discussing his life and art in a 1949–50 series of radio interviews with Jean Amrouche and showing a partriarchal face on film in *Avec André Gide* (1950).

The moral and aesthetic censure that had followed Gide in life did not abandon him in death—the Catholic Church placed his works on the Index in 1952, and his role as literary innovator went largely unacknowledged by the structuralists (*see* FRENCH LITERATURE)—but "le gidisme," with its influence for good or bad, has long since ceased to be at issue. Gide today is widely translated and republished, and works once decried as morally corrupt occupy places of honor in literature classes around the world.

Gide's repeated insistence that it was from the point of view of art and not of morality that he ought to be judged bore fruit in the years following his death. A steady stream of critical studies devoted to his literary works has revealed the extraordinary scope of his artistic inventiveness; his innovative exploration of self-critical fiction has established Gide, with Marcel PROUST, as the first "modern" writer of the 20th century. Gide can thus say, with the serene hero of his fictional testament, *Thésée* (1946; Eng. tr., *Theseus*, 1948), that he has left his monument behind him.

As an artist, Gide was also the last of the great classical stylists. His measured prose appeared dated in the wake of the new novel (*see* FRENCH LITERATURE) and caused Gide's fiction to lose some of its appeal for a younger generation of critics, who have turned instead to his writings in nonfictional genres, especially autobiography, and to exercises in literary history and publication. Editions of Gide's literary and personal correspondence (with Proust, Paul CLAUDEL, Rainer Maria RILKE, Paul VALÉRY, Rouveyre, Henri GHÉON, Mauriac, Martin du Gard) have appeared regularly since 1948 and, by their quantity, interest, and quality, show Gide, like Voltaire, to have been the foremost letter-writer of his day. The *Journal* (*Journal, 1889–1930* [1939]; *Journal, 1939–1942* [1946]; *Journal, 1939–1949* [1954; Eng. tr., *The Journals of André Gide*, 1947–51]), translated by Justin O'Brien, spans 60 years of lively, restless, and brilliantly lucid inquiry into the nature of life and art. It has come to be recognized as one of the major human and literary documents of its time, and together with *Si le grain ne meurt*, it may indeed prove more enduring that Gide's fiction.

Gide's personal writings, however, frequently hid more than they revealed. The mystery surrounding his private life—and contributing to his public reputation—has been largely cleared away with the posthumous publication of numerous memoirs, diaries, and letters, some of them from Gide's own pen, many from the pen of others. It was Gide himself who first broke the silence protecting his wife, Madeleine (1879–1938). *Et nunc manet in te* (1951; Eng. tr., *The Secret Drama of My Life*, 1951, *Madeleine*, 1952) unveiled the drama—indeed, the tragedy—of their unconsummated "marriage of Heaven and Hell," and the rupture provoked by Gide's affair with young Marc Allégret—an affair that eroded the Gidean myth of the incompatibility of spiritual and physical love. Other equally demythifying evidence subsequently helped both to elucidate the relationship of Gide's life to his works and, together with the passage of time, to disarm much of the debate occasioned by his moral and intellectual stances. The *Cahiers de la Petite Dame 1918–1945* (1973–77), written by Gide's confidante and neighbor Maria Van Rysselberghe (whose daughter, Elisabeth, in 1923 bore Gide's only child, Catherine), is a rich source of information about Gide's domestic life, his literary and personal friendships and activities. Areas that discretion, ignorance, the morality of the day, or the distortions of polemic had obscured during Gide's lifetime—his religious crisis of 1915–16 (otherwise analyzed in his 1922 *Numquid et tu?*), his continual travels and countless homosexual encounters—are discussed by Gide throughout his correspondence and in the reminiscences and reflections of *Ainsi soit-il* (1952). With the appearance of these and other documents, the legend of André Gide has begun to yield to a more balanced understanding of the man and his works, and the earlier interpretation of him as a great moral philosopher, put forth against a historical backdrop of *ad hominem* attacks and hagiographic defenses of Gide's moral, political, and social views, has begun to recede. The wealth of posthumous documentation, together with reinterpretations based on evolving critical and moral perspectives, have lifted Gide's works out of that context, and it is rather his position as one of the

major *literary* figures of the century that has grown with time.

See: G. Brée, *André Gide: l'insaisissable Protée* (1953); J. Delay, *La Jeunesse d'André Gide*, 2 vols. (1956–57); *Bulletin des Amis d'André Gide* (1967–); V. Rossi, *André Gide: The Evolution of an Aesthetic* (1967); W. W. Holdheim, *Theory and Practice of the Novel: A Study on André Gide* (1968); D. Moutote, *Le Journal de Gide et les problèmes du moi* (1968); *Cahiers André Gide* (1969–); G. W. Ireland, *André Gide: A Study of His Creative Writings* (1970); C. Martin, *La Maturité d'André Gide* (1977)   A.L.M.

Gijsen, Marnix, pseud. of Jan-Albert Goris (1899–), Belgian novelist, poet, and critic of Flemish extraction, was born in Antwerp. He studied economic history at Louvain and later taught it, but he also became a government official. From 1941 to 1964, he was director of the Belgian Government Information Service in New York, then a delegate to the United Nations, and still later he became an ambassador and commissioner general. His literary career began with a volume of expressionistic poetry, *Het huis* (1925; The House), but it was not until after World War II that the first of his many novels appeared. In *Het boek van Joachim van Babylon* (1946; Eng. tr., *The Book of Joachim of Babylon*, 1951), he has given a modern interpretation to ancient myth and has presented the Biblical Susanna as a modern wife. Gifted with a supreme sense of irony, Gijsen is also a social novelist and satirist. *Telemachus in het dorp* (1948; Telemachus in the Village) offers an ironic view of the little provincial town where Gijsen grew up. *Klaaglied om Agnes* (1951; Eng. tr., *Lament for Agnes*, 1975), which, like so many of his novels, is also autobiographical, is a poignant story of the lost love of youth. Many of his books, like *De vleespotten van Egypte* (1952; The Fleshpots of Egypt) have an American background; and Gijsen, who has spent more than half his adult life in the United States, has called himself "the Euro-American Homunculus." Although the relationship between the sexes plays an important role in his novels, he does not describe the physical aspects of that relationship in explicit detail. Because his novels are usually fragments of his life recounted by a first-person narrator and his plots are simple, some critics have accused him of lacking inventiveness. But Gijsen is a moralist, and his reflective, intellectual heroes are governed by restraint and control. Nature is of no importance in his fiction, for he is an urban man, a detached observer of human life. His skepticism is essentially modern, but there is something classical, even stoic, in his attitude. In addition to *The House by the Leaning Tree* (1967), a volume of verse in a more traditional style, Gijsen has written several books of stories and a large number of novels, including *De man van overmorgen* (1949; The Man of the Day after Tomorrow), *Goed en kwaad* (1950; Good and Evil), *De kat in den boom* (1953; The Cat in the Tree), *Er gebeurt nooit iets* (1956; Nothing Ever Happens), *Terwille van Leentje* (1957; For the Sake of Leentje), *Jacqueline en ik* (1970; Jacqueline and I), and *De afvallige* (1971; The Apostate). In 1974, Gijsen received the Prijs der Nederlandse Letteren.

See: M. Roelants, *Marnix Gijsen* (1958); "Marnix Gysen 75," *De Vlaamse Gids* 58, no. 11 (1974).

S.L.F.

Gil, Ildefonso Manuel (1912–), Spanish poet, novelist, and critic, was born in Paniza, in the province of Zaragoza, and has long been a professor of Spanish literature at various universities in the United States. In 1934, with

Ricardo Gullón, he founded the journal *Literatura*. Gil is a member of the poetic Generation of 1936, which succeeded the "pure" or dehumanized poets of the Spanish avant-garde and replaced the latter's aestheticism with a return to traditional forms and the everyday concerns of life, love, time, and faith. The generation has not until recently been well studied, perhaps because the Spanish Civil War (1936-39) disrupted its natural development, alienated its members from each other because of their differing political views, and sent many into exile. Gil was one of these.

Two of his early collections are *Borradores* (1931; First Drafts) and *La voz cálida* (1934; The Warm Voice). His maturity was reached in *Poemas de dolor antiguo* (1945; Poems of Long Felt Grief) and such later volumes as *El tiempo recobrado* (1950; Time Recovered), *El incurable* (1957), *Los días del hombre* (1968; The Days of Man), and *Luz sonreída, Goya, amarga luz* (1972; Smiling Light, Goya, Bitter Light). As some of the titles suggest, Gil's poetry primarily expresses his grief for the loss of his past, his family, youth, and Spain. Gil's poetry is sometimes sentimental but always deeply felt and in firm control of the resources of poetic language.

In addition to a number of works of literary criticism, Gil is also the author of several novels: *La moneda en el suelo* (1951; The Coin on the Floor), which won the International Prize; *Juan Pedro el dallador* (1953; Juan Pedro, the Mower); and *Pueblonuevo* (1958). The recurring theme of these works—lives destroyed by unforeseen events—is clearly not unrelated to that of their author's poetry.

See: E. G. de Nora, *La novela española contemporánea*, vol. 3 (1968), pp. 217-19; J. Ferrán and D. Testa, eds., *Spanish Writers of 1936* (1973); F. Pérez Gutiérrez, *La generación de 1936: antología poética* (1976), pp. 57-74.
                                                                H.L.B.

Gil-Albert, Juan (1906-), Spanish poet and prose writer, was born in Alcoy, in the province of Alicante. A member of the Generation of 1936, Gil-Albert had a short but active literary career before the end of the Spanish Civil War (1936-39), only to be forgotten until the late 1960s, when he was rediscovered by young Spanish writers who saw in him a model for their own artistic endeavors. Cofounder of the Republican publication *Hora de España*, he left Spain in 1938. In 1947 he returned from his exile in Latin America to live in the isolation of an "interior exile" in his native Valencia.

His poetry evolved from the formal preoccupations of the sonnets of *Misteriosa presencia* (1936), through the political commitment of *Candente horror* (1936; Burning Horror) to the poems of *Las ilusiones* (1944) and several later books characterized by well-balanced composition using traditional meter, images, and concepts. The attempt to embody a set of ideas in artistically pleasing images defines his style in poetry as well as in prose. More than autobiographies or essays, his many prose works are inquiries into human nature, meditations that combine memories of his personal past with learned comments about historical events, literature, and the meaning of art. Even in his fictional narrative, *Valentín* (1974), he is more concerned with the analysis of specific human motivation than with action. His style is richly complex and somewhat evocative in its tone. A true humanist, Gil-Albert conceives of literature as a method of knowledge different from any other then.

See: L. A. de Villena, "Sobre Gil-Albert y su *Retrato oval*; entre la reflexión y el atrevimiento," preliminary study to J. Gil-Albert, *El retrato oval* (1977).   S.D.-T.

Gil de Biedma, Jaime (1929-), Spanish poet and literary critic of Catalan descent, was born in Barcelona. Along with such other poets as José Angel VALENTE, Angel GONZÁLEZ, and Claudio RODRÍGUEZ, he belongs to the literary Generation of 1950. His three principle books are *Compañeros de viaje* (1959; Traveling Companions), *Moralidades (1959-1966)* (1966), and *Poemas póstumos* (1969).

According to a survey done in 1969 by the journal *Cuadernos para el diálogo*, Gil de Biedma was judged—because of *Moralidades*—one of the most admired Spanish authors writing between 1939 and 1969. He is particularly admired by younger poets like Pere GIMFERRER and Manuel Vázquez Montalbán, who have criticized most of the socially committed literature of that period for sacrificing form to content.

In Gil de Biedma's works one finds social protest, especially against the Catalan bourgeoisie (the milieu in which he was brought up), and identification with the proletariat. This social content coexists, however, with universal themes such as time and poetry itself. The social fervor that dominates his early works does not interfere with the artistic integrity of his later ones. This is especially evident in *Moralidades*. In this book, as Pere Gimferrer notes, Gil de Biedma combines in a unique manner a refined poetic diction with conversational language in order to make of the poem an ambiguous product that means more than it says. The obvious social or political criticism is never the sole motive of the poem but only a point of departure for the poet's penetration into the more universal preoccupations that evolve from the original social theme.

This poetic ambivalence, introduced in *Moralidades*, continues with more emphasis in his *Poemas póstumos*, where the conflict between the present and the past, between the mature poet's despair and the young alter ego's revival of frightening and impossible dreams, becomes one of the defining elements of the book. Gil de Biedma has moved from an objective and social poetry to more subjective and intimate poetic creation, and from the ironic mood of *Compañeros de viaje* to the more ambiguous tone of *Moralidades*, which as its title suggests is a combination of art and ethics.

Gil de Biedma's most important work of literary criticism is *Cántico. El mundo y la poesía de Jorge Guillén* (1960; Canticle: The World and Poetry of Jorge Guillén), a very perceptive analysis of Jorge GUILLÉN's first book of poetry. It is also a key document for understanding many of Gil de Biedma's ideas on poetry, which he developed in his last two volumes of poetry.

See: J. González Muela, *La nueva poesía española* (1973), pp. 81-103; J. Olivio Jiménez, *Diez años de poesía española* (1972), pp. 205-21.   V.C.

Gilkin, Iwan (1858-1924), Belgian poet, was born in Brussels. He is linked to the development of *La Jeune Belgique*, the review that from 1881 to 1897, marked the renaissance of Belgian letters. He was precociously attracted to science and philosophy, nourished by vast readings (the Spanish and Elizabethan theaters, Dante, John Milton, Aeschylus), and impassioned by music. During his youth, he went through a long crisis, in which the discovery of urban pauperism combined with religious doubt. A deep pessimism, reinforced by Charles Pierre BAUDELAIRE and Arthur Schopenhauer, led him to a very tragic kind of poetry. *La Damnation de l'artiste* (1890; The Damnation of the Artist), *Ténèbres* (1892; Darkness), and *Satan* constitute the group entitled *La Nuit* (1897; The Night). The work reflects the obsession with universal evil and the religious, moral, social drama lived by the poet, who was haunted by the contradiction of philosophical systems and who attempted to free himself by a return to self-knowledge. The odelets of *Cerisier fleuri* (1899; Cherry Tree in Bloom) reflect a more peaceful and pantheistic outlook. However, Gilkin remained concerned with the great problems of the end of the 19th century, whether in *Prométhée* (1899; Prometheus), a long poem in which he extols a strange Christian pantheism that reconciles all antagonisms, or in *Le Sphinx* (1923), a representation of the destructive doubt of faith, which Gilkin hopes to vanquish by ending the opposition between science and God. The theater of ideas also interested him: *Les Etudiants russes* (1906; The Russian Students) is a depiction of the Petersburg revolt of 1902, in which Gilkin sides, against the revolution, with eternal and Christian Russia; *Savonarole* (1906) shows Florence torn between asceticism and fundamental powers. A powerful poet, at times overwhelmed by philosophical preoccupations, Gilkin remained a man of the 19th century, animated above all by his struggle against scientism and positivism.

See: H. Liebrecht, *Iwan Gilkin* (1941).   R.T.

Gillès, Daniel (1917–), Belgian novelist, was born in Bruges. He is a lawyer and a businessman. After the short stories of *Mort la douce* (1952; Death, Sweet Death), he oriented himself toward the novel of social observation and manners. Attentive to revealing human reactions beyond conventional attitudes, he attached himself, not without cruelty sometimes, to the bourgeoisie and business milieus in *Jetons de présence* (1954; Tokens of Presence) and *Coupon 44* (1956; Ticket 44). *Les Brouillards de Bruges* (1962; The Fogs of Bruges) indicts provincial mentalities, turpitudes dissimulated under social respectability, whereas *La Termitière* (1960; The Termitary) denounces the failure of the colonization of the Congo. *La Rouille* (1971; The Rust) exposes with irony the false problems of modern psychology while treating the Pirandellian dilemma of truth and the unity of personality. Finally, Gillès published *Le Festival de Salzbourg* (1974; The Festival of Salzburg) and *Nés pour mourir* (1976; Born to Die), the first volumes of a broad fresco in the manner of Lev TOLSTOY, whose characters, borrowed especially from the Belgian and Austrian aristocracy, are confronted with the birth of Nazism. This is a historical, but also realistic and human, novel, which evokes with power and tragedy a world's agony. Equally a biographer (of Tolstoy, D. H. Lawrence, Anton CHEKHOV) and an essayist of talent, Gillès is a classic and sober writer.

See: J. Burniaux and R. Frickx, *La Littérature belge d'expression française* (1973), pp. 82–83; A. Jans, *Lettres vivantes 1945–1975* (1975), p. 87   R.T.

Gilson, Etienne (1884–1978), French philosopher, was associated with the revival of medieval studies in the 20th century. Gilson's numerous works are brilliant, clear, and erudite presentations of the most important theologians and philosophers from the beginning of the Christian era to the Renaissance. His objective and historical interpretations, based on a deep knowledge of Greek philosophy as well as modern intellectual currents, treat medieval thought not only in its historical background and perspective, but in reference to our present culture, which it can help to illuminate.

Gilson's books and articles can be classified into three categories. First, Gilson produced his two doctoral dissertations devoted to the Scholastic sources of Descartes's philosophy. *La Liberté chez Descartes et la théologie* (1913; Liberty in Descartes and Theology) and *Index scolastico-cartésien* (1913; Scholastico-Cartesian

Index). Then there are his historical monographs or syntheses, such as *Le Thomisme* (1922; Eng. trs., *The Philosophy of St. Thomas Aquinas*, 1924, *The Christian Philosophy of St. Thomas Aquinas*, 1956), *La Philosophie de Saint Bonaventure* (1924; Eng. tr., *The Philosophy of St. Bonaventure*, 1924), *La Philosophie au Moyen-Age* (1925; Eng. tr., *History of Christian Philosophy in the Middle Ages*, 1955), *Saint Thomas d'Aquin* (1925; Eng. tr., *Moral Values and the Moral Life: The System of St. Thomas Aquinas*, 1931), *Introduction à l'étude de Saint Augustin* (1929; Eng. tr., *The Christian Philosophy of St. Augustine*, 1960), and *Dante et la philosophie* (1939; Eng. trs., *Dante the Philosopher*, 1948, *Dante and Philosophy*, 1968). Finally, there are the works of historical and critical interpretation, dealing mainly with the problem of Christianity and its meaning in the 20th century, such as *Les Idées et les lettres* (1932; Ideas and Literature), *Christianisme et philosophie* (1936; Eng. tr., *Christianism and Philosophy*, 1939), *La Philosophie et la théologie* (1960; Eng. tr., *The Philosopher and Theology*, 1962), and *Introduction aux arts du Beau* (1963; Eng. tr., *The Arts of the Beautiful*, 1965). Gilson was the cofounder of *Archives d'histoire doctrinale et littéraire du Moyen-Age* and served as its codirector from 1925. He was a professor at the Collège de France, taught in American and Canadian universities, and was elected to the Académie Française.
                                                  E.M.-S.

Gimferrer, Pere (1945–), Spanish poet and literary critic of Catalan descent, was born in Barcelona. He has published poetry in both Spanish and Catalan. In Spanish: *Arde el mar* (1966; Burning Sea), for which he was awarded the National Prize for Poetry; *La muerte en Beverly Hills* (1968; Death in Beverly Hills); and *Poemas 1963–1969* (1969). In Catalan: *Els miralls* (1970; The Mirrors), *Hora foscant* (1972; Darkened Hour), and *Foc cec* (1973; Blind Fire). These last three books and other poems written between 1973 and 1977 have been collected in a bilingual book (Spanish-Catalan) entitled *Poesía* (1977).

Gimferrer's poetry differs profoundly from the religious, existential, and socially oriented poetry of the two previous generations of Spanish poets and is closer to the early poetry of Jorge GUILLÉN, Pedro SALINAS, Vicente ALEIXANDRE, and Luis CERNUDA, members of the Generation of 1927. Gimferrer admires these poets as well as Octavio Paz, Lezama Lima, T. S. Eliot, and Ezra Pound, because he sees that for them the poem, in addition to being the refined product of an artistic process, is also an autonomous world. Gimferrer's art is a complex synthesis of elements from music, painting, sculpture, literature, and the mass media. His approach to composition is not a logical sequence of ideas but rather an irrational juxtaposition of images and symbols embodying a variety of emotions and concepts with which the author has decided to play.

The reader has a mixed reaction to this poetry based on free and seemingly frivolous associations. On the one hand, he feels alienated from its apparently nonsensical form, and on the other, he experiences an exciting confrontation with the exotic and fabulous world of poems that do not mean what they say but only what they elliptically suggest.

Gimferrer's persistent and playful use of cultural elements from the mass media (popular heroes, songs, music, and movie stars) has induced critics to include him in the so-called camp generation along with Guillermo Carnero and Leopoldo María Panero. Whatever labels may be used to identify his poetry, however, it is a radical departure from earlier post-Civil War verse. In all his books, the poet reveals a consistent dislike of the Catholic moral values that shaped his childhood. This leads him to view his childhood as a dead part of his self which must now look for a substitute in order to achieve an identity. This substitute is poetry, which for Gimferrer means a constant and laborious pursuit of form as the only means to acquire personal and artistic freedom.

Gimferrer has a growing reputation as a literary critic. His approach is imaginative in its perceptions and sophisticated in its scope. He views Spanish and Catalan literature in the light of artistic and linguistic developments in other countries. He has also become one of the most active modern researchers on Catalan literature, a field which unfortunately has been neglected in Spain because of the Catalan and Basque separatist movements.

See: J. M. Castellet, *Nueve novísimos poetas españoles* (1970), pp. 153–80; J. González Muela, *La nueva poesía española* (1973), pp. 119–27.   V.C.

Giner de los Ríos, Francisco (1839–1915), Spanish educator, philosopher, essayist, and disciple of Julián Sanz del Río, was the guiding spirit of the educational and intellectual renaissance of modern Spain. Born in Ronda, he studied law and philosophy at the universities of Barcelona and Granada, but it was not until he went to Madrid in 1863 and heard the lectures of Sanz del Río that he found the philosophy of the German thinker Karl Krause, which was to direct all his thinking and action for the rest of his life. In 1868 he won an appointment to the chair of philosophy of law at the University of Madrid, a position he held for over 30 years, with several interruptions. One of these came in 1875 when Giner protested against the unconstitutional infringements made on academic freedom by the restoration government. As a result he was arrested and imprisoned in Cádiz. On his release in 1876, together with some kindred spirits, he founded the Institución Libre de Enseñanza, a private corporation free from any religious, philosophical, or political affiliation, "for the purpose of cooperating in the general progress of education." Its innovations were revolutionary: education was to be not only intellectual but physical and moral as well; students were encouraged to develop a spirit of free inquiry and to form independent judgments; students and teachers went on weekend walking trips into the Sierra de Guadarrama and on short journeys to discover the art treasures of old Spanish towns. It was Giner's profound conviction that the regeneration of Spain could be brought about only by the slow process of education. The Institución was Giner's greatest work. Its greatness was due not so much to the new educational ideas and methods that came from England and Germany as to Giner's own vibrant personality and glowing spirit, which left a deep imprint on the minds of some of the greatest poets, thinkers, and teachers of modern Spain, among them Joaquín COSTA, Leopoldo ALAS, Juan Ramón JIMÉNEZ, Américo CASTRO, and Gregorio MARAÑÓN.

Giner's writings, from his first published volumes—*Estudios jurídicos y políticos* (1875); *Estudios de literatura y arte* (1876); *Estudios filosóficos y religiosos* (1876)—reveal a multiplicity of interests and inexhaustible curiosity. Although they deal with the most varied themes of literature, aesthetics, law, and religion, all have in common a philosophical spirit and a deep social consciousness. On the philosophy of law he wrote a number of works that were widely used: *Principios de derecho natural* (1873) and *Resumen de filosofía del derecho* (1898), both of these in collaboration with his student Alfredo Calderón, and *La persona social* (1899). On educational topics he wrote innumerable works, including *Estudios sobre educación* (1886); *Educación y enseñanza* (1889); *Pedagogía universitaria* (1905); and *Ensayos menores sobre educación y enseñanza* (1913). All of his essays and longer works were gathered together by his friends and disciples in the edition of his *Obras completas* (20 vols., 1916–36).

See: J. B. Trend, *Origins of Modern Spain* (1934), pp. 50–132; *CA* 139 (1965) 61–160, issue devoted to Giner de los Ríos; J. Villalobos, *El pensamiento filosófico de Giner* (1969).   E.F.H. rev. J.L.G.-M.

Ginzburg, Natalia Levi (1916–), Italian novelist, essayist, translator, and playwright, was born in Palermo into a bourgeois family of Jewish intellectuals. In 1919 her father accepted a professorship at the University of Turin, and in that city Natalia was raised and educated. As opposition to Benito Mussolini's dictatorship intensified, the Levi household became a meeting place for many prominent anti-Fascist intellectuals. In 1938, Natalia married Leone Ginzburg, a brilliant Slavist and one of the leaders of the clandestine group "Giustizia e libertà." In 1940, Leone was sent to political confinement, and four years later he died as a result of his imprisonment. In 1950, Natalia settled in Rome and married Gabriele Baldini, a specialist in English and American literature, who died in 1969.

Natalia Ginzburg's literary career began with the publication of short stories in the distinguished Florentine little magazine *Solaria*. Her first short novel, *La strada che va in città* (1942; Eng. tr., *The Road to the City*, 1949), appeared under the pseudonym Alessandra Tornimparte. Five years later, she published a second work, *È stato così* (Eng. tr., *The Dry Heart*, 1949), a story about a young woman's unhappy marriage, which ends with her murder of her husband. *Tutti i nostri ieri* (1952; Eng. tr., *A Light for Fools*, 1957) is an engrossing story about a family's involvement with the Italian Resistance. Another short novel, *Le voci della sera* (1961; Eng. tr., *Voices in the Evening*, 1963), is set in Piedmont around the time of World War II. The humorous, autobiographical *Lessico famigliare* (1963; Eng. tr., *Family Sayings*, 1967) was followed by numerous essays and plays, the short epistolary novel *Caro Michele* (1973; Eng. tr., *No Way*, 1974) and the novel *Famiglia* (1977; Family).

Ginzburg's work is characterized by structural simplicity as well as by a plain style that, despite its homeyness and modesty, manages to achieve highly lyrical effects. Her recurring characters—frustrated intellectuals, sad women unable to find meaning outside the home—are invariably afflicted by two contemporary malaises: tedium and incommunicability. They lead static lives, resigned to pain and loneliness. Ginzburg's milieux are never minutely described, and what happens there could happen anywhere. At times, her heroine's name is revealed only at the end of the story in a strategy aimed at stressing her universality. Ginzburg's pessimistic, but not bitter, vision of the world is relieved by occasional flashes of humor, particularly in her plays and essays.

See: S. Pacifici, in *Le voci della sera* (1971) and in *A Guide to Contemporary Italian Literature* (1972); E. Clementelli, *Invito alla lettura di Natalia Ginzburg* (1972).
                                                                                     S.P.

Giono, Jean (1895–1970), French novelist, was born and died in Manosque. Although Giono's parents, a Protestant shoemaker and a laundress, were uneducated (see *Jean le bleu*, 1932; Eng. tr., *Blue Boy*, 1946, 1949), they early recognized that their only child was gifted and they endeavored to enrich his childhood with classical music and with tutors. Giono's first novel, *Colline* (1928; Eng. tr.,

Hill of Destiny, 1929), introduced by his mentor André GIDE, was a success. Heavily loaded with Provençalisms and poetic place names, this work launched its native author as an original novelist—a pastoralist in the tradition of George Sand, Knut HAMSUN, and D. H. Lawrence. Giono has also been compared to William Faulkner, whom the French novelist much admired.

Giono celebrated his native Alps in more than 26 major works of fiction, 10 essays or collections, 4 plays, 3 volumes of poetry, syndicated columns, and varia. Throughout this voluminous production, he maintained a central philosophical-political position: to offer his readers and disciples, as an alternative to a modern urban and industrial civilization, a Utopian and pastoral universe in the classical manner of Greek mythology. His edition of Virgil, *Les Pages immortelles de Virgile* (1960; The Immortal Pages of Virgil), reintroduced that poet to the general public.

Wounded in World War I, an experience recounted in *Le Grand Troupeau* (1931; Eng. tr., *To the Slaughterhouse,* 1969), Giono increasingly became a pacifist. By 1936 he was openly urging passive resistance, for which he suffered threats of assassination and of an embargo against his work as a writer. He chose imprisonment over military service in World War II. When, however, Giono led his young disciples to an Alpine village, his Utopianism proved less socialist than anarchic (see Lucien Jacques's *Carnets,* 1939). Giono's radical political ideas are set forth in his various treatises: *Refus d'obéissance* (1937; Refusal to Obey), *Les Vraies Richesses* (1936; True Riches), *Le Poids du ciel* (1938; The Weight of Heaven), and *Lettre aux paysans sur la pauvreté et la paix* (1938; Letter to the Peasants on Poverty and Peace). In this last polemic, he addressed women in particular, urging them to outlaw war by refusing to bear children.

When the sanctions imposed as a result of World War II were lifted, academic critics such as Henri Peyre and Maxwell A. Smith hailed Giono's postwar productions in experimental fiction as continuously original and perhaps the most distinguished in modern France. Giono was rewarded by the Prix Monégasque and the Goncourt Prize, both in 1954.

In his scathing, brilliant fiction, Giono indicted modern civilization through a masterful use of the macabre, irony, satire, exuberant rhetoric, and a profusion of metaphor reminiscent of Rabelais. For him, heroes were still as splendid as they had been in medieval epics, modern men as tragic as in Greek and Renaissance times, and family relationships as dark as the Oedipal depths explored by Sigmund Freud. As an admirer of Walt Whitman, Herman Melville, and Faulkner, Giono celebrated women and praised the loving heart of man. The pastoral trilogy *Colline, Un de Baumugnes* (1929; Eng. tr., *Lovers Are Never Losers,* 1931), and *Regain* (1930; Eng. tr., *Harvest,* 1939) remains Giono's most popular work of fiction. Giono was also well known for the film *La Femme du boulanger* (1938; The Baker's Wife), with a screenplay by Marcel PAGNOL.

Deeply attached to his family, Giono suddenly rejected life in Paris for his residences in Manosque and Majorca, supporting himself and his family (mother, wife, and two daughters) entirely from the proceeds of his writings. He thus found leisure to collect books and study Italian history; to write apocalypse and history, such as *Le Désastre de Pavie* (1963; Eng. tr., *The Battle of Pavia,* 1965); to defend a farmer indicted for murder, as he recalls in *Notes sur l'affaire Dominici* (1955; Notes on the Dominici Affair); and to collaborate on translations of such works as *Moby-Dick* (1941).

Giono is very difficult to translate because of his extensive vocabulary and poetic prose. He is, however, much admired for his last polemic, *Provence perdue* (1968; Provence Lost), and especially for his last novels, including *Un Roi sans divertissement* (1947; A King without Distractions), *Noé* (1947; Noah), *Le Hussard sur le toit* (1951; Eng. tr., *The Hussar on the Roof,* 1954), *Le Moulin de Pologne* (1952; Eng. tr., *The Malediction,* 1955), and *Le Bonheur fou* (1957; Eng. tr., *The Straw Man,* 1959).

See: M. A. Smith, *Jean Giono* (1966); W. D. Redfern, *The Private World of Jean Giono* (1967); N. L. Goodrich, *Giono, Master of Fictional Modes* (1973); M. M. Girard, *Jean Giono, Méditerranéen* (1974).   N.L.G.

Gippius, Zinaida Nikolayevna (1869–1945), Russian poet, essayist, literary critic, and writer of prose fiction and drama, was born in the province of Tula. Together with her husband Dmitry MEREZHKOVSKY she played a leading role in the turn-of-the-century Russian religious renaissance and aesthetic revival. The Merezhkovsky salon in Petersburg was a prominent gathering place for the writers and thinkers of the Silver Age (*see* RUSSIAN LITERATURE). Gippius gave the impetus to the organization of the "Religious-Philosophical Assemblies" (1901–03), whose purpose it was to bring together the cultured elements of the clergy and the religious segments of the intelligentsia. She also inspired the creation of the literary journal *Novy put* (1903–04), which was a mouthpiece for the Merezhkovskys' metaphysical preoccupations with religious community. In 1905 they became involved with certain members of the revolutionary populist movement, whom they attempted to convert to their own mystical conception of revolution. While welcoming the February Revolution (1917), Gippius was violently opposed to the Bolshevik Revolution of the following October, and she remained a stauch anti-Communist throughout her life. In 1919, Merezhkovsky and Gippius emigrated from Russia to Poland, finally settling in Paris, where they became influential figures in Russian émigré cultural life.

Gippius wrote in a variety of literary genres. Her short stories, collected in such volumes as *Zerkala* (1898; Mirrors) and *Aly mech* (1906; The Crimson Sword), reflect both the decadent and visionary zeitgeist as do her politically inspired novels *Chortova kukla* (1911; The Devil's Doll) and *Roman-Tsarevich* (1913). Affected by the Nietzschean world view (*see* Friedrich NIETZSCHE), her fictional characters isolate themselves from society in their lonely, difficult quest for a new religious consciousness. Gippius's prose fiction is generally marred by an artificial tone and by ideological schematicism. Her play *Zelyonoye koltso* (1916; Eng. tr., *The Green Ring,* 1920), about the youthful aspirations of the new generation and their desire to establish honest and meaningful relationships, is not very effective. Writing under the male pseudonyms Anton Krayny (Anton the Extreme) and Tovarishch German (Comrade Herman), Gippius wrote sharp, witty literary criticism and brilliant philosophical essays, some of which are collected in *Literaturny dnevnik* (1908; A Literary Diary). Her criticism is frequently very partisan, especially when dealing with an opponent or an alien literary faction. This subjectivity is also apparent in her fascinating memoirs, *Zhivye litsa* (1925; Living Faces). Gippius's outspoken political views are revealed in her diaries, notably *Sinyaya kniga* (1929; The Blue Book), and in *Le Tsar et la révolution* (1907) and *Tsarstvo Antikhrista* (1921; The Kingdom of Antichrist).

Gippius's major contribution to Russian literature is her philosophical poetry about God, love, and death, collected in *Sobraniye stikhov* (vol. 1 1904, vol. 2 1910; A Collection of Poems); and *Siyaniya* (1938; Radiances).

Her unadorned, terse poems are very intense and expressive, reflecting a Dostoyevskian passion for metaphysical ideas. It is a poetry of the swinging pendulum whose movement is caused by the endless search for an indefinable and never attainable faith in God. Despair, expressed by symbols of physical decay, evil, and spiritual loneliness, sets in when the persona is incapable or fearful of moving toward the higher reality. While hoping for the divine revelation, the poet is also afraid that the revelation will take place and bring an end to temporal movement. In her poetry, Gippius finds an answer to man's duality in her androgynous metaphysics of love: the consecration of the flesh or the merging of the spiritual and sensual sides of man will be achieved with the transcendence of the sexual dichotomy.

See: T. Pachmuss, *Zinaida Gippius: An Intellectual Profile* (1971); O. Matich, *Paradox in the Religious Poetry of Zinaida Gippius* (1972).   O.M.

Giraud, Albert (1860–1929), Belgian poet, was born in Louvain. He was one of the first and most faithful collaborators on the review *La Jeune Belgique*. Despite his rigor, his work shows a profound sensitivity and an original temperament. It was in the baroque decor of commedia dell'arte that he first transposed his nostalgia. The atmosphere of *Pierrot lunaire* (1884; Lunar Pierrot) recalls that of Paul VERLAINE's *Fêtes galantes*. With *Hors du siècle* (1888; Out of the Century), Giraud looks, in history and legend, for a remedy to his *mal de vivre* and the opportunity to stigmatize his time; but, just as in *Les Dernières Fêtes* (1891; The Last Holidays) and *Le Sang des roses* (1910; The Blood of the Roses), the dominant theme of the collection is a nostalgia for childhood and a regret for lost purity. Both *La Guirlande des dieux* (1910; The Garland of the Gods) and *La Frise empourprée* (1912; Crimson Borders) renew relations with Leconte de Lisle's pagan dream, whereas *Le Laurier* (1919; The Laurel) ties together poems inspired by World War I. If Giraud's style is occasionally convoluted, his varied inspiration and constant care for formal perfection cannot be denied. An artist with unerring taste, of haughty and melancholy thought, Giraud, along with Waller, Iwan GILKIN, and Valère-Gille, best illustrates the *l'art pour l'art* current in Belgium.

See: G. Charlier and J. Hanse, *Histoire illustrée des lettres françaises de Belgique* (1958); R. Burniaux and R. Frickx, *La Littérature belge d'expression française* (1973); R. Frickx and M. Joiret, *La Poésie française de 1880 à nos jours* (1976).   R.F.

Giraudoux, Jean (1882–1944), French novelist and dramatist, was born in Bellac, the son of a civil servant. A gifted, brilliant student, young Giraudoux was the star pupil of the provincial lycée of Châteauroux before entering the prestigious Ecole Normale Supérieure in Paris. Specializing in German, he spent a year in Germany as a French *lecteur* before entering the French consular service. His career as a diplomat was interrupted by World War I, in which he served for four years and in which he was wounded. After World War I, Giraudoux rose to the important assignment of inspector of diplomatic posts. In 1939–40, he served briefly in the French government as a high commissioner for information. He died in Paris one year before the end of World War II, despondent over the German occupation of France.

Giraudoux's first published writings were the short-story collection *Provinciales* (1909; Sketches from Provincial Life) and the novels *Simon le pathétique* (1918), *Adorable Clio* (1920), *Suzanne et le Pacifique* (1921; Eng. tr., *Suzanne and the Pacific*, 1923), *Siegfried et le Lim-*

ousin (1922), *Juliette au pays des hommes* (1924; Juliet in the Country of Men), *Bella* (1926; Eng. tr., 1927), *Eglantine* (1927), *Les Aventures de Jérôme Bardini* (1930), and *Combat avec l'ange* (1934; Struggle with the Angel). These light, impressionistic, poetic, essentially plotless works frequently centered on the character of a young ethereal woman. *Choix des élues* (1938; Choice of the Elect), a longer, more elaborate "novel," was still a "poetic divagation" and a study in feminine psychology with stylized, idealized characters.

Critics found Giraudoux's early works artificial, precious, and insignificant, and some of them thought of him as an *amuseur*. Indeed, these works were precious and ornate, rich in original images and finely chiseled metaphors, but they did not dispense words only. Giraudoux's preciosity was given substance by his authentic and vast erudition. He knew Plato, Vergil, Tacitus, Rudyard Kipling, Japanese painting, and the symbolists, as well as the German romantics (Jean-Paul Richter, Novalis), who may have influenced him to some degree. Having studied and mastered foreign grammars and literatures, history, and geography, he was able to make subtle use of these varied disciplines in his creative work. Although Giraudoux was a virtuoso of fantasy, he was also—even in his very early works—a poet, a man preoccupied with ethics and philosophy, and a Platonist at heart.

In 1928, Giraudoux entered the world of the theater with the play *Siegfried* (Eng. tr., 1964). With the assistance of an exceptional actor and director, Louis JOUVET, he immediately became France's most successful dramatist of the decade. *Siegfried* was followed by many great plays: *Amphitryon 38* (1929; Eng. tr., *Amphitryon*, 1937), *Judith* (1931; Eng. tr., 1963), *Intermezzo* (1933; Eng. tr., *The Enchanted*, 1950), *La Guerre de Troie n'aura pas lieu* (1935; Eng. tr., *Tiger at the Gates*, 1955), *Ondine* (1939; Eng. tr., 1954), *Electre* (1937; Eng. tr., *Electra*, 1957), *Sodome & Gomorrhe* (1943; Sodom and Gomorrah). Two other plays, *La Folle de Chaillot* (1945; Eng. tr., *The Madwoman of Chaillot*, 1949) and *Pour Lucrèce* (1934; Eng. tr., *Duel of Angels*, 1958), became international favorites and were particularly well received in New York in the adaptations of Maurice Valency and Christopher Fry.

Giraudoux's plays are extremely well written and, like his novels, light and poetic. But he did not think of his stage works as mere exercises in style. For Giraudoux, it was the theater's purpose to purify the souls of the spectators, to erase the coarseness and banality of everyday life. He knew he could accomplish this by respecting "its nobility, which is the Word (*le Verbe*), and its honor, which is Truth (*la Vérité*)." Like Paul CLAUDEL, Giraudoux knew that there is in the universe a mystery to be grasped. His characters, however, are not "aliens" in this world, but rather are constantly tempted by the thought of escape, which they finally reject. They speak for the author, linking his dreams with reality, his ethics with life.

Giraudoux's humor conceals some very serious themes: the spiritual relationships between two countries (France and Germany in *Siegfried*), the inevitability of war (in *Tiger at the Gates*) and of revolution (in *Electra*), the relationships between a mortal and a god (in *Amphitryon 38*) and between the sexes (in *Sodom & Gomorrhe*), and the corruption of modern society (in *The Madwoman of Chaillot*). Some of those plays (especially *Sodome & Gomorrhe*, written during the darkest hours of World War II) are deeply pessimistic.

Yet in Giraudoux's plays, there is always the promise of dawn, even after the desolation of war and murder. "Cela s'appelle l'Aurore" ("Its name is Dawn") is the final line of *Electre*. *Intermezzo* is Giraudoux's most optimistic play. This charming fantasy concerns Isabelle, a young teacher who dreams, like many other Giraudoux heroines, of coming into contact with the supernatural. One day she meets le Spectre, a handsome ghost who haunts the woods around the sleeply little bourgeois city where Isabelle teaches. A school inspector, who is able to feel the poetry as well as the realities of life, will overcome the ghost and cure Isabelle through his love. Graceful and subtle, *Intermezzo* is an intelligent, satisfying play and certainly Giraudoux's comic masterpiece.

In 1941, Giraudoux published *Littérature* (1941), a book of essays that sums up some of his main concerns. It reveals the author as a man of culture whose only "sin" was perhaps, in his own view, to have been isolated from the people by that very culture he loved. In this, he continued the line of the great symbolist generation and of the German romantics. Giraudoux's other publications include a charming essay on La Fontaine, *Les Cinq Tentations de Jean de La Fontaine* (1938; The Five Temptations of Jean de La Fontaine), and some political essays collected in *De pleins pouvoirs à sans pouvoirs* (1935; From Full Authority to No Authority).

See: C.-E. Magny, *Précieux Giraudoux* (1945); H. Sørensen, *Le Théâtre de Jean Giraudoux: technique et style* (1950); M. Mercier-Campiche, *Jean Giraudoux et la condition humaine* (1954); V. H. Debidour, *Jean Giraudoux* (1955); M. L. Bidal, *Giraudoux: tel qu'en lui-même* (1956); R. M. Albérès, *Esthétique et morale chez Jean Giraudoux* (1957); R. Cohen, *Giraudoux: Three Faces of Destiny* (1968). P.Br.

Gironella, José María (1917–), Spanish novelist and essayist, was born in Darníus in the province of Gerona. He entered a seminary but left to engage in a series of minor jobs. Gironella began his literary career as a poet with *Ha llegado el invierno y tú no estás aquí* (1946; Winter Has Come and You Are Not Here). In 1946 he also received the Nadal Prize for his novel *Un hombre* (Eng. tr., *Where the Soil Was Shallow*, 1957).

Gironella's most celebrated work is the tetralogy *Los cipreses creen en Dios* (1953; Eng. tr., *The Cypresses Believe in God*, 1955), *Un millón de muertos* (1961; Eng. tr., *One Million Dead*, 1963), *Ha estallado la paz* (1966; Eng. tr., *Peace After War*, 1969), and *Condenados a vivir* (1971; Condemned to Live). An ambitious literary undertaking in the tradition of Benito PÉREZ GALDÓS's *Episodios Nacionales*, this series fictionalizes the crucial historical period from 1930 to 1950. *Los cipreses*, a bestseller, recreates the social and political climate of Gerona, a microcosm of Spain, during the years that preceded the Civil War. *Un millón* is a documentary of the war years, while the other two volumes deal with the postwar period.

The question of the objectivity and literary merit of this tetralogy has given rise to heated controversy. Many critics find in Gironella a lack of documentation and partiality toward the Francisco Franco regime. The work is difficult to categorize, as it belongs to both fiction and history without always being either one or the other. Gironella is a gifted novelist who employs stylistic devices typical of traditional 19th-century realism, such as lack of autonomy in his characters, accumulation of detail, and excessive digressions.

See: R. Schwartz, *José María Gironella* (1972). J.O.

Giudici, Giovanni (1924–), Italian poet, was born in La Spezia. He attended secondary school and the university in Rome, where he took his degree in French literature. Instead of following an academic career, Giudici worked as a copywriter for the Olivetti company in Turin and Ivrea while freelancing for magazines like *Communità, Aut Aut, Paragone, Rinascita,* and *Quaderni piacentini.* Since 1958 he has lived in Milan. Giudici's collections of verse include *Fiori d'improvviso* (1953; Sudden Blooming), *La stazione di Pisa* (1955; The Pisa Railroad Station), *L'intelligenza col nemico* (1957; Intelligence with the Enemy), *L'educazione cattolica* (1963; A Catholic Education), *La vita in versi* (1965; Life in Verse), *Autobiologia* (1969) and *O Beatrice* (1972). He has also published translations of Hart Crane, Ezra Pound, John Crowe Ransom, and Aleksandr Pushkin. In 1969 he won the prestigious Viareggio Prize.

Giudici's early poetry is characterized by a demure tone of elegy with ironic admixtures and is chiefly indebted to Eugenio MONTALE. The style of his most recent volumes, however, has sharpened into black humor on the one hand, and into soaring hymns (*O Beatrice*) on the other. In both phases of this style, Giudici uses traditional versification and cannily exploited rhyme effects. In recent works, narrative often yields to litanylike repetition. Nevertheless, the thematic center of Giudici's poetry remains the precarious condition of mankind in industrialized society.

See: F. Fortini in *Il menabò* 2 (1960); S. Antonielli in *Aut Aut* 41 (1966); O. Cecchi in *Rinascita* (Dec. 27, 1968 and May 9, 1959); M. Forti, in *Le proposte della poesia* (1971); G. Cambon, in *FI* 7 (March 1973); O. Cecchi, in *Letteratura italiana: i contemporanei*, vol. 6 (1974), pp. 1645–59. G.C.

Gjellerup, Karl (1857–1919), Danish novelist and dramatist, was born in southern Zealand. The son of a minister, he studied theology, but the influence of Georg BRANDES and his reading of Charles Darwin and Herbert Spencer made him an atheist before he had taken his degree in 1878. His major work from this period (1878–83), the novel *Germanernes Lærling* (1882; The Teutons' Apprentice), deals with a young theologian's revolt against religion. But its acceptance of Germanic culture indicates the break with French naturalism, which took place after Gjellerup's travels to Germany, Greece, and Russia in 1883 and 1884. Gjellerup attempted to combine the scientific demand for truth with an idealism colored by Goethe's and Friedrich von Schiller's Greek humanism. This idealism is expressed not only in a series of dramas, but also in several novels dealing with ethical problems, which were influenced by Ivan Turgenev and Fyodor DOSTOYEVSKY. *Minna* (1889; Eng. tr., 1913), considered Gjellerup's finest work, is a melancholy love story whose title character is contrasted with the frivolous artistic circles of the times, whereas *Møllen* (1896; The Mill) is a suspenseful psychological study of a crime of passion, in its detailed symbolism inspired by Emile ZOLA. The final period of Gjellerup's writing (after about 1900) is influenced partly by the Buddhist teaching of self-denial as illustrated by the abstract portrayal of a soul's wandering towards Nirvana in *Verdensvandrerne* (1912; The World Wanderers) and partly by Christianity in a Danish milieu in *Den gyldne Gren* (1917; The Golden Bough). In 1917, Gjellerup shared the Nobel Prize for Literature with Henrik PONTOPPIDAN; today he is undeservedly a forgotten name. S.H.R.

Gladilin, Anatoly Tikhonovich (1935–), Russian prose writer, was born in Moscow. In his youth he worked as a mechanic and in construction, and became acquainted with the life of gold miners and fishermen in the Soviet Far East. Gladilin first called attention to himself with *Khronika vremyon Viktora Podgurskogo* (1956; The

Chronicle of the Times of Victor Podgursky), published in the magazine *Yunost* (Youth). Among his outstanding works are the novellas *Pervy den novogo goda* (1963; The First Day of the New Year) and *Prognoz na zavtra* (1972; Forecast for Tomorrow), published in West Germany.

His characters are mostly members of his own generation, searching for their occupational and intellectual vocations. His style is often slangy, his heroes usually urban, educated, and ironic in their attitudes, repudiating moral and social clichés. Some of his stories deal with simple workers in remote parts of the country.

Gladilin has also written other, longer tales, after the manner of *Prognoz na zavtra*, works that have not yet been published in the USSR. In addition, he is the author of a historical novel-biography about the French Revolution, *Yevangeliye ot Robespyera* (1970; The Gospel according to Robespierre) in the Flaming Revolutionaries series of the Political Publishing House, and a life of the 19th-century revolutionary Myshkin, as well as a screenplay about Feliks Dzerzhinsky, the head of the Cheka (1974).

Along with Vasily P. AKSYONOV, Gladilin was one of the leaders of Soviet urban, psychological prose—clever, witty, irreverent, in some respects reminiscent of J. D. Salinger, although not indebted to him directly. Gladilin achieves complex effects through shifts of narrative point of view and interweaving of chronology. In 1976, Gladilin emigrated to Paris, where he has continued to publish articles and stories, including *Repetitsiya v piatnitsu* (1978; Rehearsal on Friday).   G.Gi.

Gladkov, Fyodor Vasilyevich (1883–1958), Russian novelist, "self-taught" in the tradition of Maksim GORKY, was born in Chernavka, a village near Saratov. He is best known for his proletarian novel *Tsement* (1925; Eng. tr., *Cement*, 1929), which portrays the dramatic national effort of reconstruction in the Soviet Union following the October Revolution of 1917 and the attendant Civil War. His earlier novels include *Izgoi* (1908–09, pub. 1922; Outcasts), about political prisoners in Siberia, and *Ognenny kon* (1923; Fiery Steed), about civil war in the Kuban. Among his numerous later works in the style of socialist realism are *Energiya* (1932–38; Energy), a novel about the construction of Dneprostroy, the huge hydroelectric power plant on the Dnieper River. More successful stylistically are his novelized reminiscences, *Povest o detstve* (1949; Story of My Childhood), *Volnitsa* (1950; Freeman), *Likhaya godina* (1954; Hard Times), and the unfinished *Myatezhnaya yunost* (1958; Eng. tr., *Restless Youth*, 1959.

See: L. N. Ulrikh, *Tvorchestvo Fyodora Gladkova* (1968).   D.Fi.

Gobetti, Piero (1901–26), Italian essayist, critic, and publisher, was born in Turin, where he studied law. In 1918 he founded *Energie nuove*, a biweekly strongly influenced by the idealism of Benedetto CROCE. By 1921, Gobetti was dissatisfied with Croce's intellectual position, which he felt could not lead to practical action. Fascinated by the vitality of Turin's working class, he became drama critic for Antonio GRAMSCI's socialist daily, *L'ordine nuovo*. This contact with the real world inspired Gobetti in 1922 to found *La rivoluzione liberale*, a weekly in which he intended to combine the scholarly study of Italian intellectual history since the unification with a program of concrete cultural action. Gobetti's repeated attacks on the class nature of fascism led to his arrest and brought his political activities to a temporary halt. Forced to concentrate on cultural problems, in 1924 Gobetti founded *Il Baretti*, a periodical that attracted renowned intellectuals

such as Croce, as well as young people destined to literary fame: the poets Umberto SABA, Eugenio MONTALE, and Sergio Solmi; the critic Natalino Sapegno; and the historians Aldo Garosci and Leone Ginzburg. Increasing Fascist control in Italy made it almost impossible for Gobetti to work. At the beginning of 1926, he chose exile in Paris, where soon after he died.

As in the case of many Italian intellectuals of his generation, Gobetti's ideas on art and literature were at first heavily influenced by Croce. His often expressed "need to act," however, led him away from his early master. Under the influence of Gramsci and the classics of Marxism, Gobetti accepted the notion that the meaning and value of a work of art has to be sought within the historical process of the country that produced it. This notion is best expressed in his *La filosofia di Vittorio Alfieri* (1923; The Philosophy of Vittorio Alfieri). Alfieri's originality, Gobetti wrote, lay in proposing a philosophy that was conceived as a basis for action and in his understanding that individuals partake in the elaboration of truth even without elaborating theoretical problems.

The relationship between the intellectuals and the masses was clearly Gobetti's main concern. He wrote about it in *Risorgimento senza eroi* (1926; Risorgimento without Heroes), in which he denounced the lack of participation of the lower classes in the liberal monarchic solution that brought about the unification of Italy, and in *Paradosso dello spirito russo* (1926; Paradox of the Russian Spirit), in which he again stressed that a moral renewal of Italy could take place only through a political struggle spearheaded by the masses. Gobetti also wrote extensively on the theater. In his famous essay on *Hamlet* (published in *Opera critica*, 1927), he saw in that play a dialectic of tragedy and irony, dominated by the minor characters. His reviews of the plays of Luigi PIRANDELLO have a well-established place in Pirandello criticism.

See: G. Carocci, "Piero Gobetti nella storia del pensiero politico italiano," *Belfagor* (1951).   D.M.

Goering, Reinhard (1887–1936), German novelist, dramatist, and poet, was born near Fulda. He interrupted his study of medicine to compose the largely autobiographical novel *Jung Schuk* (1913). In the novel, Schuk's scorn for bourgeois values leads to isolation, and his suicide prefigures the death of his creator. The many parallels to Goethe's *Werther* reveal an affinity between storm and stress and early expressionism. While recuperating from tuberculosis contracted in the army, Goering began writing dramas. His best play, *Seeschlacht* (1917; Eng. tr., *Seafight*, 1940), depicts the perplexity of sailors in a warship's turret before the battle of Jutland. At its premiere it seemed a sensational pacifistic protest. The play *Scapa Flow* (1919) registers the traumatic impact of defeat upon the Germans. In the tragedy *Die Retter* (1919; The Deliverers), Samuel BECKETT's absurdist theater is anticipated. *Die Südpolexpedition des Kapitän Scott* (1930; Captain Scott's South Pole Expedition) lauds the British explorer's courageous fatalism. Its operatic version, *Das Opfer* (1937; The Sacrifice), appeared posthumously with dodecaphonic music by Winfried Zillig and a chorus clad as penguins. Written in the last decade of his life to be read aloud, Goering's short stories celebrate in telegrammatic prose the individualistic rebel's defiant turning to nature.

See: G. Capell, *Die Stellung des Menschen im Werk Reinhard Goerings* (1968).   G.W.R.

Goetel, Ferdynand (1890–1960), Polish novelist and playwright, was born in Sucha and died in London. He studied architecture in Vienna. Goetel was interned in Russia during World War I, witnessed the Russian Revolution (1917), and served for some time in a technical detachment in the Red Army until he managed to return to Poland in 1921. He started publishing in 1911, and his first full-length novel was *Kar Chat* (1922; Eng. tr., *Messenger of Snow*, 1930). Even greater success greeted his next, experimental novel, *Z dnia na dzień* (1926; Eng. tr., *From Day to Day*, 1931). In his introduction to the English translation, John Galsworthy termed the novel an important contribution to the novelistic form, and critics generally considered its intricate pattern of two-level narrative structure a pioneering effort. Goetel also published, among others, the novel *Serce lodów* (1930; Eng. tr., *The Heart of the Ice*, 1931) and a historical play, *Samuel Zborowski* (1929). In 1939, Goetel published a treatise, *Pod znakiem faszyzmu* (Under the Sign of Fascism), in which he came out as a supporter of fascism and Nazism. A controversial figure under the German occupation because of his political stand, Goetel lived in London after World War II. Here he published, among others, a novel entitled *Nie warto być małym* (1959; No Use Being Small) and memoirs, *Czasy wojny* (1955; The War Times).

See: *Słownik współczesnych pisarzy polskich*, vol. 1 (1963), pp. 553–60.   Z.F.

Goffin, Robert (1898–), Belgian poet, novelist, and literary and jazz critic, was born in Ohain. He studied law at the University of Brussels and became a famous barrister. While a student, associated with students' literary movements, he published *Rosaire des soirs* (1918; Evening Rosary) and *Jazzband* (1922), thus moving from the musical symbolism to a half-unanimist, half-surrealist style. After the first years at the bar, he returned to literary spheres and published essays on various subjects, including Arthur RIMBAUD, jazz, and gastronomy, as well as historical biographies, novels, and books of verse molded on the Claudelian (*see* Paul CLAUDEL) versicle, such as *La Proie pour l'ombre* (1935; The Prey for a Shadow) and *Sang bleu* (1939; Blue Blood). At the onset of World War II (May 1940), Goffin left Belgium for the United States. There he supported himself with lectures, articles, and books: several novels, especially *Passeports pour l'Audelà* (1944; Eng. tr., *White Brigade*, 1944), and essays like *Jazz from the Congo to the Metropolitan* (in Eng., 1943, 1976). During the same period, Goffin taught the history of jazz at the New School for Social Research in New York and was proclaimed an honorary citizen of New Orleans and an honorary lawyer of Pittsburgh. After the liberation of Belgium from the Nazis he resumed his seat at the Brussels Court of Appeal and published a new series of poetry books: *Le Voleur de feu* (1950; The Fire Thief), *Foudre natale* (1955; Native Bolt), *Le Temps sans rives* (1958; Time without Edges), *Archipels de la sève* (1959; Lymph Archipelagoes), *Sources du ciel* (1962; Heavenly Springs), *Corps combustible* (1964; Combustible Matter), *Sablier pour une cosmogonie* (1965; Hourglass for a Cosmogony), *Le Versant noir* (1967; The Black Slope), *Faits divers* (1969; Press News), *Phosphores chanteurs* (1970; Singing Phosphorus), *L'Envers du feu* (1971; The Reverse of the Fire), and *Chroniques d'outrechair* (1975; Chronicles beyond the Flesh). In all these works, Goffin has espoused neoclassicism in the manner of Stéphane MALLARMÉ and Paul VALÉRY, even if that most labored technique alternates, from 1958 on, with some long poems written in "spoken style" and dedicated to the popular mythology of the 20th century. Critical essays of this period are *Louis Armstrong, le roi du jazz* (1947; Eng. tr., *Horn of Plenty*, 1947), *Entrer en poésie* (1948; To Take Up Poetry), *Rimbaud et Verlaine vivants* (1948; Living Rimbaud and Verlaine), *Mallarmé vivant* (1956; Living Mallarmé), and *Fil d'Ariane pour la poésie* (1964; Ariadne's Thread for Poetry). Another novel is *Le Roi du Colorado* (1958; The King of Colorado). Goffin is a member of the Royal Academy of French Language and Literature of Belgium, national president and international vice-president of the PEN Club.

See: J.-P. de Nola, *Robert Goffin, poète* (1973); J.-M. Horemans, *Robert Goffin: le poète au sang qui chante* (1976).   J.-P. de N.

Goga, Octavian (1881–1938), Romanian poet and statesman, was born in Rășinari, Transylvania, then a Hungarian province. During his school years, Goga was already a prolific poet whose themes reflected a nationalistic spirit. Before World War I, he was imprisoned by the Hungarian authorities. After Transylvania was ceded to Romania in 1920, Goga began a controversial political career that culminated in his appointment and quick dismissal as prime minister (Dec. 28, 1937–Feb. 10, 1938). He was elected to the Romanian Academy and received the National Prize for poetry.

Although he wrote verse with a decidedly popular appeal, Goga was a serious poet. He introduced new lyrical moods into Romanian poetry, never abandoning the idea of national tradition as the unique source of true literary inspiration. Following *Poezii* (1905; Poems), Goga produced several collections whose titles reflect the main themes of his literary activity: *Ne cheamă pământul* (1909; The Land Beckons Us), *Din umbra zidurilor* (1915; From the Shadows of the Walls), *Strigăte în pustiu* (1915; Cries in the Desert), and *Cantece fără țară* (1916; Songs without a Country). Goga also published a drama, *Domnul Notar* (1914; Mr. Notary) and a translation from the Hungarian of Imre Madách's *The Tragedy of Man* (1934).

See: L. Gáldi, *Esquisse d'une histoire de la versification roumaine* (1964); I. D. Balan, *Octavian Goga* (1971).   P.G.T.

Gojawiczyńska, Pola, pseud. of Apolonia Gojawiczyńska (1896–1963), Polish novelist, was born and died in Warsaw. Through her talent for writing, discovered by a teacher, and her great capacity for work, she won the interest and support of Ignacy Matuszewski, then secretary of the treasury. Her semiautobiographical story "Maryjka" was published in the official *Gazeta polska* (1932) through his help. Thus auspiciously launched, she continued to write, and when a brief residence in Silesia removed her from the center of the literary world, she took advantage of the temporary exile to produce a fine portrait of the mining district, especially of its women, in *Ziemia Elżbiety* (1934; The Land of Elizabeth). On her return to Warsaw, Gojawiczyńska proceeded to recreate in the two novels *Dziewczęta z Nowolipek* (1935; The Girls from Nowolipki) and *Rajska jabłoń* (1937; The Apple Tree of Paradise) the hard, drab world from which she herself had sprung, thereby turning Warsaw's "lower depths" into literary material. Interested primarily in exploring not society as a whole but woman, Gojawiczyńska next pursued, in *Słupy ogniste* (1938; Pillars of Fire), her favorite theme, the tribulations of woman in a man's world. Although this work was distinctly inferior to those that preceded it, Gojawiczyńska was regarded, on the eve of Poland's collapse, as one of the most promising and serious of the younger writers. After World War II she wrote five more volumes of prose: *Krata* (1945; Prison Bars), *Stolica* (1946; Capital City), *Dom na skarpie* (1947; The House on the Slope), *Miłość Gertrudy* (1956; Gertrude's Love), and *Opowiadania* (1956; Short Stories). Gojawiczyńska's novels and short stories are mostly linked with Warsaw. Possessing a genuine ability to depict the atmosphere of the everyday life of the poor and the middle-class, she portrayed her heroes with deep psychological knowledge and understanding.

See: A. P. Coleman, "The Literary Scene in Poland," *NYTBR* (Apr. 9, 1939), pp. 8, 24; D. Knysz-Rudzka, *Pola Gojawiczyńska* (1977).   A.P.C. rev. S.F.

Goldmann, Lucien (1913–70), French sociologist and critic, was born in Bucharest, Romania. He was a Marxist who placed his work under the aegis of G. W. F. Hegel, Sigmund Freud, György LUKÁCS, Antonio GRAMSCI, and Jean Piaget. Goldmann gave new impetus to sociological studies of literature, of which his own dealt mainly with "great" writers whose "creations" he examined as works of art, not documents (his literary terminology was conservative). Goldmann called his method "genetic structuralism" and opposed it to most other structuralist practices (*see* FRENCH LITERATURE). In his view, mental structures change as those of society change: interaction between mental and societal structures constitutes the "genetic" element of the method. As he saw it, the individual is the locus of many structures operating at unconscious, nonconscious, and conscious levels—libidinal ones (on all three) having an individual subject, social ones (on the latter two), a transindividual subject. Domination by the former structures leads to alienation, by the latter to great accomplishments in politics or in the arts. Goldmann argued that in a great writer's work there is a nonconscious generation of mental structures homologous to those in society; they do not reflect the latter but have been engendered by them. The critic's task is to explain the work as a unified whole in terms that account for it in its entirety. Goldmann attempted that in two major works, *La Communauté humaine et l'univers chez Kant* (1948; The Human Community and the Universe in Kant) and *Le Dieu caché: étude sur la vision tragique dans les pensées de Pascal et dans le théâtre de Racine* (1955; Eng. tr., *The Hidden God,* 1964). He also wrote *Pour une sociologie du roman* (1964; For a Sociology of the Novel), where he examines the novels of André MALRAUX. Goldmann's studies of contemporary figures have been collected, along with his theoretical essays, in *Structures mentales et création culturelle* (1970; Mental Structures and Cultural Creation), *Marxisme et sciences humaines* (1970; Marxism and Human Sciences), and *Epistémologie et philosophie politique* (1978; Epistemology and Political Philosophy). His independent, combative stance is displayed in a posthumous text, *Lukács et Heidegger* (1973), in which he tries to reconcile those two very different thinkers (*see* Martin HEIDEGGER).

See: P. V. Zima, *Goldmann* (1973).   L.S.R.

Goll, Iwan, pseuds. Iwan Lassang, Tristan Torsi (1891–1950), German lyric poet and dramatist, was born of Alsace-Lorraine parents in Paris and studied in Strasbourg and in Paris, where he received a Ph.D. in 1912. From 1914 to 1918 he lived in Switzerland, where he befriended James Joyce, Stefan ZWEIG, and Hans Arp, among others. He was married to the lyric poet Claire Studer (1891–1977), with whom he frequently collaborated. In 1919, Goll went to Paris and promoted dada with André BRETON and with Paul ELUARD championed surrealism. After Goll was blacklisted by the Nazis in 1933 he wrote mostly in French. He fled to New York in 1939, returning to Paris in 1947. The last two years of his life he suffered from leukemia.

Goll began as an expressionist lyric poet but turned to surrealism and then to a new realism with compact poetic images. His poems are colored by melancholic, dreamlike visions that draw on mythology, magic, and cabbalistic metaphors. His poetic works include *Lothringische Volkslieder* (1912; Folk Songs from Lorraine), *Der Panamakanal* (1912), *Der Torso* (1918), *Die Unterwelt* (1919; The Underworld), and *Das Herz des Feindes* (1920; The Heart of the Foe); many of his poems were collected in 1924 under the title *Der Eifelturm* (The Eifel Tower).

Goll's grotesque and absurd drama of the eternal bourgeois, *Methusalem,* appeared in 1922, exerting later influence on the early dramas of Martin WALSER and Peter WEISS. The drama *Der Stall des Augias* appeared in 1924 and was followed by three volumes of poetry written with Claire Goll: *Poèmes d'amour* (1925; Eng. tr., *Love Poems,* 1947), *Poèmes de jalousie* (1926), and *Poèmes de la vie et de la mort* (1926). A novel in French, *Le Microbe de l'or* (1927) was followed by three in German, *Die Eurokokke* (1928), *Der Mitropäer* (1928), and *Agnus Dei* (1929). Poems in French were published in three volumes in the years 1936 to 1939 under the title *La Chanson de Jean sans terre.* Other books of poetry are *Atom Elegy* (1946), *Traumgras* (1948; Dream-Grass), and the posthumous volumes *Traumkraut* (1951; Dream-Herbs) and *Abendgesang* (1954; Evening Song). A posthumous play is *Melusine* (1956). Selected works by Goll have appeared in translation: *Songs of a Malay Girl* (1942; from a French text), *Fruit from Saturn* (1946), *Selected Poems* (1968), and *Lackawanna Elegy* (1970).

See: F. J. Carmody, *The Poetry of Ivan Goll* (1956); V. Perkins, *Yvan Goll: An Iconographical Study of His Poetry* (1970); V. P. Profit, *Interpretations of Iwan Goll's Late Poetry* (1977).   A.L.W.

Gołubiew, Antoni (1907–79), Polish prose writer and publicist, was born in Wilno, where he studied history at the university, and died in Kraków. He was one of the founders of the periodical *Żagary* and later editor of the Catholic periodical *Pax.* After World War II he was connected with the Catholic journals *Tygodnik Powszechny* and *Znak.* In 1935, Golubiew published the novel *Mędrcy na arenie* (Sages on the Arena), but he is mainly known as the author of the seven-volume historical novel *Bolesław Chrobry* (1947–74; Bolesław the Brave): vol. 1, *Puszcza* (1947; The Forest); vol. 2, *Szło nowe* (1947; New Times Were Coming); vols. 3 and 4, *Złe dni* (1950; Bad Days); vols. 5 and 6, *Rozdroża* (1954–55; Crossroads) and vol. 7, *Wnuk* (1974; The Grandson). Written in an archaic Polish, this novel presents a vast panorama of life in Poland after the acceptance of Christianity and analyzes the process of historical and social transformation during the establishment of Poland as an independent state. Gołubiew also published collections of short stories and essays dealing with contemporary problems: *Listy do przyjaciela* (1955; Letters to a Friend), *Poszukiwania* (1960; The Search), *Na drodze* (1966; On the Road), *Unoszeni historią* (1971; Carried Off by History), and *Spotkanie na Świętokrzyskiej* (1975; Meeting on Świętokrzyska Street).   A.Z.

Gombrowicz, Witold (1904–69), Polish novelist and playwright, was born in Małoszyce into a landowner's family and died in Vence, France. After graduating in law from Warsaw University he studied philosophy and economics in Paris. Shortly before World War II he left Poland for Argentina, where he stayed until 1963. He spent the last years of his life in France. His first book, *Pamiętnik z okresu dojrzewania* (1933; Memoir from Adolescence), contains seven short stories whose themes and techniques foretell his later development. Gombrowicz is the author of novels that are all first-person narratives, and among them the most popular is *Ferdydurke* (1937; Eng. tr.,

1961). It is not a continuous narrative but a sequence of three important episodes in the life of the narrator, which are combined with two philosophical tales. *Ferdydurke* is a multilevel parody of official values. Its plot is devoted to the phenomenon of human immaturity and centers around a 30-year-old individual brought back to the state of puerility by domineering friends and relatives. The two philosophical tales illustrate the principle that men are not masters of the "Form" they create, but, on the contrary, are its slaves. The conclusion of the novel is that there is no escape from the process of being created by others. *Trans-Atlantyk* (1953; Trans-Atlantic) is an account of Gombrowicz's first years of émigré life in Argentina. Written in a language that parodies Polish baroque memoirs, the novel is devoted first of all to a theme that is present in many of his writings: a revision of the common attitude toward the Polish national myth and to stereotypes of patriotism. *Pornografia* (1960; Eng. tr., 1966) deals, in Gombrowicz's words, with the ideals of a man who "aspires to perfection but is afraid of it because he knows that it is death. He rejects imperfection, but it attracts him because it is life and beauty." *Kosmos* (1965; Eng. tr., *Cosmos*, 1966) is a novel about the nature of the universe and man's position in it, his tragic and unresolved attempt to find out the laws and order of the world. Gombrowicz also published under a pseudonym a sensational novel, *Opętani* (1939; The Possessed). *Iwona księżniczka Burgunda* (1938; Eng. tr., *Princess Ivona*, 1969) is the first of four grotesque plays Gombrowicz wrote, the last of which, *Historia* (1975; History), was left unfinished. A mixture of tragedy and farce, taking place in an absurd fairy-tale kingdom, *Princess Ivona* presents a world of people who play games with one another and become disturbed when suddenly the title character stops playing and there is a danger that the whole system will collapse. About *Ślub* (1947; Eng. tr., *The Marriage*, 1969) Gombrowicz himself wrote: "Here human beings are bound together in certain forms of pain, fear, ridicule, or mystery . . . in absurd relations and situations, and submitting to these forms they are created by what they themselves have created." *Operetka* (1966; Eng. tr., *Operetta*, 1971) parodies the genre to which it purports to belong and at the same time parodies the absurd events of modern history. The plot, consisting of opposing social groups and political ideas in confrontation, is a continuation of Gombrowicz's main problem, a conflict between the desire for maturity and desire for immaturity, between the individual and the form he generates. Gombrowicz's longest work, and chronologically his most extensive, is his *Dziennik 1953-1966* (4 vols, 1957-66; Journal). It is an autobiography and at the same time an autobiographical novel, a discussion of philosophical and literary problems, and a commentary on cultural and social life, his own works, points of view, doubts, and obsessions. Gombrowicz's writing is an original and different manifestation of European existentialism and structuralism. In Polish literature it is an innovative continuation of the trend presented by J. I. Witkiewicz and Bruno Schultz. Gombrowicz's provocative writing was a rebellion against all values in literature, against the accepted rules in social life, and the conventional attitudes toward national tradition. But under the mask of grotesque and sarcastic humor Gombrowicz poses the most important questions about the freedom of man. He provides no positive solution but neither does he reject the search for it. Looking back upon his own output, he remarks in his *Journal:* "The world is an absurdity and a horror for our unrealizable need for sense, justice, and love. As long as I live, and even on my death bed, I will always be on the side of human order (and even on the side of God, although I am not a believer)."

See: W. Gombrowicz, *Dzieła zebrane*, vols. 1–11 (1969–77); C. Jeleński and D. de Roux, eds., *Gombrowicz* (1971); E. M. Thompson, *Witold Gombrowicz* (1979).

E.M.T. and S.F.

Gómez de la Serna, Ramón (1883–1963), Spanish novelist, dramatist, critic, and prose poet, was born in Madrid. Although he studied law, his devotion to writing was unmistakable. His first book, *Entrando en fuego* (1904; Engaging in Battle), was published when he was only 16 years old. His father indulged his vocation and founded a review, *Prometeo* (1908–12), which served him as an outlet for his writing as well as an instrument to educate himself and his contemporaries about the various avant-garde movements that were emerging throughout Europe. On the eve of the Spanish Civil War, Ramón moved to Buenos Aires, where he lived the rest of his life. But before then he carried on flirtations with various cities other than Madrid, to which he devoted some of his most inspired pages. He wrote his novel *La quinta de Palmyra* (1923; Palmyra's Villa) in Estoril, Portugal. Some of the most memorable scenes of *La viuda blanca y negra* (1918; The Checkered Widow) take place in Paris, and *La mujer de ámbar* (1927; The Ambar Lady) is set in Naples. Of course, *La Nardo* (1930) is subtitled "The Novel of Madrid." He wrote *Cinelandia* (1923; Eng. tr., *Movieland*, 1930), his only novel to be translated into English, without having ever been to Hollywood. He was undoubtedly the most picturesque writer Spain has produced since Antonio de Guevara, author of the 1529 European best seller *Reloj de príncipes*. In 1915, Ramón founded a literary *tertulia* at the Café Pombo which lasted, off and on, until he left Spain in 1936. The account of the colorful sessions that transpired there and the list of the famous writers from all nations who passed through its salon can be found in his two-volume chronicle: *Pombo* (1918) and *La sagrada cripta de Pombo* (1924; The Inner Sanctum at Pombo). He was the only Spaniard of the period before the Civil War who tried to create in Madrid a truly avant-garde atmosphere. His amusing antics, his radio talks, and his literally iconoclastic "suitcase lectures" earned him fame as a humorist. Ramón, Charlie Chaplin, and the Italians Massimo BONTEMPELLI and Dino Pitigrilli are the only foreigners ever invited to become members of the French Academy of Humor. When his fame was at its peak, in the 1920s and 1930s, Gómez de la Serna was known as "Ramón" all over Europe and Latin America.

It is a mistake, however, to consider Ramón a mere humorist and enfant terrible of the avant-garde. His writings go beyond humorous and imaginative verbal pyrotechnics and touch on fundamental problems of philosophical importance that transcend comedy and purely superficial verbal invention, however brilliant. His preoccupation with death (in this respect it is important to consider the title of his autobiography, *Automoribundia*, 1948, that is, Studies in Self-Death), with the world of things, and, in turn, with the very nature of reality, led him to write a series of remarkable books. *El Rastro* (1915; The Flea Market), his multifaceted literary re-creation of Madrid's flea market, epitomized his deep concern with things. One of his masterpieces is *El circo* (1922; The Circus), in which he systematically tackles a theme that fascinated many of his contemporaries, including Pablo Picasso, Gertrude Stein, and Max Jacob. Ramón was also one of the first Spaniards of his generation to elevate eroticism to a high literary plane. Novels like *La viuda blanca y negra*, *La mujer de ámbar*, and *La Nardo*, as well as his book *Senos* (1918; Breasts), stand out today as precursors of what has become in our generation the literature of erotic obsessions. He also made important advances in the writing of what today we call "profiles." More than biographies, Ramón's *retratos* are intuitive insights into the figures that he chose as targets of his uniquely personal interpretive method. His collection *Retratos contemporáneos* (1942; Contemporary Profiles) is a priceless gallery of these portraits. Ramón expanded some of his *retratos* into masterful book-length biographies: *Oscar Wilde* (1921), *El Greco* (1935), and *Velázquez* (1943).

Ramón is perhaps best known, however, for his *greguerías,* incongruous juxtapositions or daring metaphors that unite disparate and far removed elements, most often with humorous intent. "The swan sticks his head underwater to see whether there is a robber under his bed," is a *greguería.* It is difficult to ascertain whether the associations are conceptual, as in 17th-century wit, or whether they emerge from the author's subconscious. At times, Ramón impresses one as the direct heir of Francisco Quevedo and Baltasar Gracián. Other times, he writes like a full-fledged surrealist, as in, "If pearls cried, snow would reach the price of gold."

See: R. Cardona, *Ramón: A Study of Gómez de la Serna and his Works* (1957); G. Gómez de la Serna, *Ramón: obra y vida* (1963); L. Granjel, *Retrato de Ramón* (1963); R. Mazzatti Gardiol, *Ramón Gómez de la Serna* (1974).   R.C.

Gonçalves, António Aurélio (1901–), Portuguese writer of short fiction and essayist, was born on the South Atlantic island of São Vicente in the Cape Verde Archipelago. After graduating from Gil Eanes, perhaps the oldest and certainly one of the most prestigious high schools in Portugal's African colonies, Gonçalves went to Lisbon, where he completed his education at the university. His many years in Portugal afforded him a firsthand knowledge of the major literary currents of Europe. Gonçalves's return to São Vicente coincided with the regionalist fervor that swept the tiny island; although he shared in the enthusiasm, he did so with a sober and disciplined perspective on Cape Verdean cultural nationalism. While only occasionally taking part in the controversy that centered around the use of Creole versus standard Portuguese as a literary language or the question of Cape Verde as a case of African versus European regionalism, Gonçalves calmly accepted the islands' black heritage and cultural autonomy. "Bases para uma cultura de Cabo Verde" (1956; Bases for a Cape Verdean Culture), his low-key essay on Cape Verdeanness, contrasts with the romantic and often defensive treatises written by several of his contemporaries.

Gonçalves did not begin to publish fictional works until he was well into his forties, and he expresses his artistic talent with the same circumspection that characterizes his essays. Thus far he has published four of his novellas or "novelettes," as he somewhat modestly terms them: *Pródiga* (1956; Prodigal Girl), *O enterro de Nha Candinha Sena* (1957; Mrs. Candinha Sena's Funeral), *Noite de vento* (1970; Windy Night), and *Virgens loucas* (1971; Foolish Virgins). The two latest works qualify as small masterpieces. All four stories revolve around strong-minded women, whose restlessness reflects the instability of Cape Verdean society, in which male unemployment and emigration have traditionally given rise to precarious common-law marriages. By defying their confining environment, Gonçalves's heroines represent the poor Cape Verdean's will to survive in a harsh climate under impossible economic conditions. By playing down local color and only implicitly suggesting Cape Verdeanness,

Gonçalves has created a sense of the islands' ethos while creating works of haunting beauty and universal appeal.

See: M. Ferreira, *Aventura crioula* (1973), pp. 120, 148–50, 291, 308–9; R. G. Hamilton, *Voices from an Empire* (1975), pp. 325–33.   R.G.H.

González, Angel (1925–), Spanish poet, was born in Oviedo. He belongs to the second generation of post-Civil War poets, or the Generation of 1950. For them the Civil War (1936–39) was a childhood experience that left in their spirits an indelible mark of suffering and despair, later made still more discouraging by the difficult times of the Franco dictatorship. A few years younger than the more conspicuous social poets of the period, he followed some of their basic tenets in his work but introduced a wider variety of subjects and a more careful poetic treatment of his social and political views. He accepted the interpretation of poetry as a means of communication and also believed that the poet has a specific social duty. Like several other Spanish poets of his same age, he has a grim view of his country and feels strongly that as an intellectual he has the responsibility to express his hopes for a better, more humane society. This cannot be done by merely expressing a desire for it but by creating a poetic message made not only of political dissent but of a philosophical view of man in society. The man in society is the poet himself, who in his own human experience summarizes everyone's experience as a simple link in the social chain of historical change. It follows that poetry, which has to be understood by the majority of readers, must be clear of concept and directly communicative, without losing its artistic excellence or its richness of meaning and deeply felt emotion. Consequently, González resorts to a prosaic and concise use of free verse with rhythmical patterns based on the syntactical unities of the poetic discourse. His poems are brief, well-structured, and emotionally controlled. The prevailing tone of his work is one of restrained and subdued expression of a meditative and melancholy spirit alien to any form of excess. This is particularly true of his first book, *Áspero mundo* (1956; Harsh World). In later collections the poet allows certain ironic overtones to enter his work, a reflection of his critical view of the world in general and of Spain in particular. In 1972 his collected poems appeared under the title of a previous book: *Palabra sobre palabra* (Word upon Word). A strongly emotional and critical book, *Muestra, corregida y aumentada, de algunos procedimientos narrativos y de las actitudes sentimentales que habitualmente comportan* (1977; Sample, Corrected and Enlarged, of Some Narrative Procedures and of the Sentimental Attitudes That They Generally Comport), presents the renewed despair of a generation that has reached maturity without having seen its hopes come true.

At present the poet teaches literature at the University of New Mexico, but he keeps in close contact with the main centers of intellectual life in Spain by spending long periods of time there. *"Harsh World" and Other Poems* is available in English translation by Donald D. Walsh (1977).

See: E. Alarcos Llorach, *Angel González, poeta* (1969); G. L. Brower, "Breves acotaciones para una bio-bibliografía de la 'vidorra' de Angel González," *Mester* 5, no. 1 (1974): 10–12.   S.D.-T.

Gorbanevskaya, Natalya Yevgenevna (1936–), Russian poet, born in Moscow, is one of the most lyrically expressive of the post-Stalinist *samizdat* writers. She studied philology at Moscow and Leningrad universities, working afterwards as an editor of technical information, a bibliographer, and a translator. Criticized as a "decadent and pessimist," she has appeared on only three occasions in "official" Soviet publications. A number of *samizdat* collections of her poetry, however, have been distributed since 1964, and in 1968 Gorbanevskaya helped to found the *samizdat* journal *Khronika tekushchikh sobytiy*, which was republished abroad and reported cases of state persecution and abuse of civil rights. She continued to edit the journal, when at liberty, until she was compelled to leave the Soviet Union in 1975. One of the seven Red Square demonstrators against the Soviet Union's invasion of Czechoslovakia in August 1968, she produced a documentary report of their trial: *Polden* (1970; Eng. tr., *Red Square at Noon*, 1970), and she was herself arrested in 1969 and was placed in a psychiatric prison hospital the following year. A selection of poems in English translation with a transcript of her trial and other documents was published in 1972 in England and the United States and in the same year she was released from prison. In 1973, *Poberezhye* (The Littoral), an authorized collection of her poems, was published in the United States. Allowed to leave the Soviet Union with her two children in 1975, Gorbanevskaya settled in Paris and became managing editor of the Russian language magazine *Kontinent*. The bulk of Gorbanevskaya's poetic work is intensely personal, transcending politics. Hers is a poetry of pain and separation, of isolation and despair. Her verse is formally often quite traditional but its tense rhythms and hallucinatory range of sounds bear witness to the poet's determination to remain vulnerable under all circumstances.   D.T.W.

Gorky, Maksim, pseud. of Aleksey Peshkov (1868–1936), Russian novelist, playwright, and essayist, had the unique distinction among Russian authors of playing an equally important role in his country before and after the Revolution of 1917. He could also claim a practically equal significance as man and as writer. So interwoven were the events of his life with those of Russian history and with his literary expression that both in his life and in his work one loses sight of the borderline between *Dichtung* and *Wahrheit*. Born in Nizhni-Novgorod (now renamed Gorky) on the Volga, the restless wanderer learned to know this great river and all his vast native land by tramping over it as he plied the widest variety of trades. This intimate contact with men and life gave Gorky his sense of reality, which coexisted in him with a perpetual dream of a different world and a better life. Realism coupled with romanticism—such was the outlook of Gorky the man and the author.

In his earliest short stories, which he began publishing in 1892, Gorky broadened the thematic range of Russian fiction by introducing his own peculiar form of romantic exoticism, portraying the outcasts of Russian society in the midst of all their squalor and degradation even while showing their kinship as human beings with the reader and occasionally glorifying the rebels among them. Two of his best stories of this period are "Chelkash" (1895; Eng. tr., 1902) and "Dvadtsat shest i odna" (1899; Eng. tr., "Twenty-Six Men and a Girl," 1902).

At the urging of Anton CHEKHOV and the producer Vladimir Nemirovich-Danchenko, Gorky tried his hand at a play, using the same materials that had so captivated the public in his short stories. The result was *Na dne* (perf. 1901; Eng. trs., *Night's Lodging*, 1905; *The Lower Depths*, 1912; *At the Bottom*, 1930), which enjoyed overwhelming success in performance at the Moscow Art Theater under the direction of Konstantin Stanislavsky and soon afterward in Western Europe and the United States. The revolutionary and, at that time, scandalous

overtones of the play, together with its exotic setting, a Moscow flophouse, captivated thousands of spectators.

In general, Gorky was not at his best either in the drama or in the novel, which he first attempted in 1899 with *Foma Gordeyev* (two Eng. trs., 1901), a work portraying the new merchant class in Russia, which is probably Gorky's best achievement in this genre. Far better known but considerably inferior in quality is his novel *Mat* (1907; Eng. tr., *Mother*, 1907), which he wrote in the Adirondack Mountains of New York after escaping from Russia the year before and coming to the United States on an ill-fated mission to raise money for the Russian revolutionaries. He had thrown in his lot with the Russian Social Democrats at the end of the 1890s, although without ever joining their party, and had been arrested briefly during the 1905 Revolution for publicly attacking the tsarist government's excesses in putting it down. His novel *Mother* shows the transformation of a simple, illiterate old woman through her associations with her Marxist revolutionary son and his comrades during a long strike of factory workers. Although beneath criticism as art, *Mother* has proved effective among unsophisticated readers as propaganda, and in the Soviet Union it is considered a classic of revolutionary literature.

In 1913, Gorky started on his best work, a series of autobiographical sketches and literary memoirs. First published serially in the newspaper *Russkoye slovo*, the sketches then appeared in book form as the first two parts of Gorky's autobiography, *Detstvo* (1913; Eng. tr., *My Childhood*, 1915) and *V lyudyakh* (1916; Eng. tr., *In the World*, 1917). Later, in 1921–22, he added a third part, written in a different style, *Moi universitety* (Eng. trs., *My University Days*, 1923; *My Universities*, 1949). Skillfully moving between the persona of the mature and famous Maksim Gorky and the impudent and observant child Alyosha Peshkov, he creates a rare amalgam of deeply painful family reminiscences, petty merchant life in an important Volga River town, and an unforgettably musical reconstruction of everyday Russian language, combined with recollections of his grandmother's colorful folk poetry and his grandfather's almost unbreakable soaked wooden beating rods. Gorky's memoirs of Lev TOLSTOY (1919) are perhaps the most perceptive, and in some ways the most merciless, sketch we have of Tolstoy the man, as opposed to Tolstoy the writer. They have been published in English, along with equally moving memoirs of Chekhov (1905) and Leonid ANDREYEV (1922), as *Reminiscences of Tolstoy, Chekhov and Andreev* (1934).

In 1917–18 the ruthlessness of the new Soviet regime led Gorky to criticize it severely in a series of articles published in his newspaper *Novaya zhizn*, which have since been republished only abroad: *Nesvoyevremennye mysli* (Paris, 1971; Eng. tr., *Untimely Thoughts*, 1968). Gorky's long-standing friendship with Vladimir Lenin and his international prestige as a writer assured him of great influence in post-Revolutionary Russia, which Gorky energetically exploited in an effort to salvage Russian culture and save Russian writers and intellectuals during the destructive turmoil of revolution and civil war (*see* RUSSIAN LITERATURE). This will probably go down in history as his greatest contribution to his native land. Finally, in 1921, exhausted by his efforts, discouraged over the results, and plagued by illness, he left Russia and lived for several years as a voluntary expatriate in the West, during which he produced two more big novels, *Delo Artamonovykh* (1925; Eng. trs., *Decadence*, 1927; *The Artamonov Business*, 1948), in which he returned to the theme of the merchant class; and the first parts of the unfinished tetralogy *Zhizn Klima Samgina* (1925–36; Eng. tr. of part

1, *Bystander*, 1930; part 2, *The Magnet;* part 3, *Other Fires*, 1933; part 4, *The Specter*, 1938), which added little to Gorky's reputation. On the other hand, he produced another volume of memoirs, *Zametki iz dnevnika* (1924; Eng. tr., *Fragments from My Diary*, 1924), which ranks among the best things he ever wrote.

After two triumphal visits to the Soviet Union in 1928 and 1929, Gorky was persuaded to settle there permanently in 1931. In return for his at least outward acceptance and public support of the whole Stalinist system he lived out the last five years of his life cradled in luxury and showered with honors as the most eminent literary personality in the Soviet Union. The record of Gorky's statements and actions during those last five years remains as puzzling and controversial as the circumstances of his death in 1936. During the purge trials two years later, the former head of the Soviet secret police, Genrikh Yagoda, was officially accused of having organized the murder of Gorky as part of an international right-wing Trotskyite plot against Iosif Stalin. According to another theory, Gorky was killed on the order of Stalin himself. According to a third, he may have died a natural death.

See: A. Kaun, *Maxim Gorky and His Russia* (1931); H. Muchnic, *From Gorky to Pasternak* (1961), pp. 29–104; R. Hare, *Maxim Gorky: Romantic Realist and Conservative Revolutionary* (1962); D. Levin, *Stormy Petrel: The Life and Work of Maxim Gorky* (1965); I. Weil, *Gorky: His Literary Development and Influence on Soviet Intellectual Life* (1966).   A.Ka.; I.W.; W.B.E.

Gorodetsky, Sergey Mitrofanovich (1884–1967), Russian poet, was born in Petersburg. He achieved notoriety with his first book of poems, *Yar* (1907; Frenzy), in which he managed to create a stylization of folk motifs and a stylized mythology that impressed Aleksandr Blok and Valery Bryusov, among many others. Today, aside from one or two snatches of song, Gorodetsky's poetry is forgotten. He is remembered mainly as one of the founders of acmeism, and he did write one of the group's manifestoes, in which he called for the joyful, manly acceptance of the world's beauties (its roses) on their own terms and not as symbols of otherworld realities (*see* Russian Literature). From the point of view of literary production, Gorodetsky was a success. Editions of his collected work appeared in 1916, 1936, and 1964. In addition, he published undistinguished prose works, and translated and produced librettos for operas, including a new text for M. I. Glinka's *Ivan Susanin*.

See: Introduction by S. Mashinsky to S. Gorodetsky, *Stikhi* (1964).   H.W.T.

Gorter, Herman (1864–1927), Dutch poet, was born in Wormerveer. He studied classics at Amsterdam, where he wrote his doctoral dissertation on Aeschylus' imagery, and was a high-school teacher in Amersfoort for a time. His study of the classics influenced his poetry. At the age of 25, he suddenly created his literary reputation with *Mei* (1889; May). A long poem, reminiscent of John Keats's *Endymion*, it was the greatest poetic achievement of the Movement of the Eighties. *Mei*, which is partly a reflection of Gorter's own psychological development, tells the story of a young girl, who stands for love and the natural beauty of the month of May. She is hopelessly in love with the blind god Balder. Since she also represents what is human, transitory, and of this world, Balder, who is immortal, and stands for the philosophical and religious world-soul, rejects her. There are some elements of Germanic mythology in the poem, but it is really not an epic, for its predominant mood is lyrical. With brilliant imagery and great musicality, Gorter sings of the beauties of Holland and the Dutch landscape. After the impressionistic sensualism of *Mei*, Gorter became very individualistic. He broke with tradition and attempted to create his own poetic language. In *Verzen* (1890; Verses), he revealed the imaginative power of language and the ability to create mood and atmosphere that showed him to be a poet of the Movement of the Eighties. It was what Verwey called "sensitivistic" poetry. After this he turned to philosophy again, and translated Baruch Spinoza's *Ethica* in 1895. *De school der poëzie* (1897; The School of Poetry) contains both sensitivistic poems and philosophical ones.

In the meantime, Gorter had become interested in socialism, which played an important role in his life. In 1897, he joined the Dutch Socialist Party, which had been formed only three years before. He became an editor of *De Nieuwe Tijd*, where he published his *Kritiek op de litteraire beweging van 1880 in Holland* (Critique of the Literary Movement of 1880 in Holland) in 1898–99, which was revised in 1908–09. Accusing his former literary allies of being proponents of bourgeois art, Gorter denounced decadent middle-class individualism. In the second volume of *Verzen* (1903), he presented socialist poetry. The language is not as innovative as that of the first volume, but the work is still that of a highly individualistic poet, albeit a socialist. In an effort to give more concrete form to the new socialist art, he turned to the epic. *Een klein heldendicht* (1906; A Short Epic) shows a young man hesitating to take part in the railroad strike of 1903. In contrast to the poetic theories of the "Men of the Eighties," it takes up Marxist theories. Gorter belonged to the radical group of socialists, and in 1909, after a conflict with the labor leader Troelstra, he resigned from the party. In the same year, he wrote the epic *Pan* (1912), which he expanded to 12,000 lines in the 1916 edition. It is based on the idea of the liberation of humanity through socialism. Although it contains some excellent lyrics, it is often uninspired, and sometimes grandiose. In 1918, the Social Democratic Party, of which Gorter was a founding member, became the Communist Party. He wrote political essays, and attracted the attention of Vladimir Lenin, but a sharp conflict led to a break with him at the Party Congress in Moscow in 1920. Disillusioned after his trip to Moscow, he resigned from the Party in 1921. Around 1920, he wrote Marxist literary studies of Aeschylus, Virgil, Dante, Chaucer, Shakespeare, John Milton, Vondel, Goethe, and Percy Bysshe Shelley, which were published posthumously as *De groote dichters* (1935; The Great Poets).

Gorter's was the greatest poetic voice of the Movement of the Eighties, and his influence extended to Leopold and Pieter Boutens. An experimentalist, he electrified his contemporaries, and gave them the poetry they had been seeking.

See: H. Roland Holst, *Herman Gorter* (1933); J. de Kadt, *Herman Gorter* (1947); G. Borgers et al., *Herman Gorter* (1966).   S.L.F.

Goul, Roman Borisovich, his transliteration of Gul (1896–), Russian historical novelist, critic, and editor, was born in Penza and educated at Moscow University. After interrupting his university studies to fight in World War I, and then on the White side in the Civil War following the October Revolution, Goul emigrated to the West, living until 1933 in Berlin, then in Paris, and since 1950 in New York. In his historical novels Goul has focused his attention on revolutionary and terrorist personalities. *General Bo* (Berlin, 1929; rev. text, *Azef*, 1959; Eng. trs., *General Bo*, and *Provocateur: A Historical Novel of the Russian Terror*, both 1930; Eng. tr. of rev. text, *Azef*, 1962) has as its chief characters the colorful Socialist Revolutionary conspirator Boris Savinkov (1879-1925) and the sinister double agent Yevno Azef (1869-1918). The work was an immediate success and has since been republished three times in Russian and translated into many languages. Goul is also the author of a historical novel about the revolutionary anarchist Mikhail Bakunin, *Skif* (Berlin, 1931; The Scythian; rev. ed., *Skif v Yevrope,* New York, 1958; The Scythian in Europe; 3d ed., *Bakunin,* New York, 1974); as well as *Dzerzhinsky* (Paris, 1935; 2d ed., New York, 1974), a highly critical biography of the first head of the Soviet secret police, Feliks Dzierzynski; Goul's own autobiography, *Kon ryzhy* (New York, 1952; The Horse That Was Red); and a collection of literary essays, *Odvukon* (New York, 1973; On Two Horses), the title of which reflects the author's view of the dialectical nature of Soviet and émigré Russian literature. In 1959, Goul joined the editorial staff of the well-known New York émigré publication *Novy zhurnal* (The New Review), serving first as coeditor and since 1966 as editor.

W.B.E.

Gourmont, Rémy de (1858-1915), French critic, essayist, and writer of fiction, was born in Normandy, of an old aristocratic family. After studying at the Lycée of Coutances and the University of Caen, he went to Paris and became an assistant librarian at the Bibliothèque Nationale, a position that he was forced to resign after the publication of an "unpatriotic" article in 1891. He was very active in the literary circles of the capital and soon enjoyed considerable prestige, especially among the poets of the symbolist school. His *Le Livre des masques* (1896; The Book of the Masks) is an interesting portrait gallery of the leading writers of that time. In 1889 he joined the group that was founding the *Mercure de France,* to which he contributed regularly until his death in 1915. When Gourmont was in his 30's, a mysterious disease disfigured him almost completely, and thereafter he withdrew more and more among his books to live the semirecluse life of a lay Benedictine.

Gourmont's numerous writings all bear the mark of a brilliant mind endowed with a wide and eclectic curiosity and often attracted by very esoteric studies. His first book of criticism, *Le Latin mystique* (1892; Mystical Latin), an essay on medieval hymnology, shows his interest in little-known subjects and at the same time provides a key to his own poetry (see *Divertissements* [1912]). "Litanies de la rose," "Les Saintes du Paradis," and "Oraisons mauvaises" are all characterized by a Baudelaire-like (*see* Charles BAUDELAIRE) mixture of mysticism and sensuality and reveal an artist enamored of rare and melodious words rather than a really inspired poet. In his short stories also, in *Le Pèlerin du silence* (1896; The Pilgrim of Silence) and *Couleurs* (1908), Gourmont appears more concerned with the artistic arrangement of musical words than with the telling of his sensuous tales. His first novel, *Sixtine* (1890), he himself described as a "novel of the cerebral life," and his later ones, *Les Chevaux de Diomède* (1897; The Horses of Diomedes), *Une Nuit au Luxembourg* (1906; Eng. tr., *A Night in the Luxembourg,* 1912), and *Un Cœur virginal* (1907; Eng. tr., *A Virgin Heart,* 1921), if they may be called novels at all, are likewise largely cerebral. These strange books evince their author's constant preoccupation with sex: both passionate and cold, ardent and ironical, they leave the reader with a sense of unreality. The heroines especially, fleshy and yet ethereal, have the unsubstantial quality of Pre-Raphaelite virgins. Curiously enough, it is Eve, in *Lilith* (1892), a dramatic treatment of *Paradise Lost,* that one remembers as a real woman.

Gourmont's love for words led him to a study of their derivations. This new interest engendered some of his most original works, *L'Esthétique de la langue française* (1899; Aesthetic of the French Language), *La Culture des idées* (1900; The Cultivation of Ideas), and *Le Problème du style* (1902; The Problem of Style). To him words were not chilly and abstract symbols, but living organisms that should be kept alive in all their savor and freshness. From this conception also sprang his theory of the "dissociation of ideas," his desire to break up associations of ideas that have become encysted in stereotyped phrases and threaten to harden a language into deadly woodenness. New fields of study were constantly attracting him—history, philosophy, theology, sociology, biology. His *Physique de l'amour: essai sur l'instinct sexuel* (Eng. tr., *The Natural Philosophy of Love,* 1926) appeared in 1904 when he thought he had discovered a scientific basis for his theory that man's love is only animal instinct. In 1902 was published *Le Chemin de velours,* a reevaluation of the old quarrel between the Jansenists and the Jesuits, favorable in its conclusions to the less inhuman ethics of the latter. He was the most influential of the *Mercure*'s collaborators. His articles cover an ever wider range of subjects, further revealing his insatiable curiosity and his truly encyclopedic knowledge; no matter what their subject, they open new vistas illuminated with flashes of insight. They appeared later in volume form as *Promenades littéraires* (7 vols., 1904-28; Literary Promenades) and *Promenades philosophiques* (3 vols, 1905-09; Philosophical Promenades). The articles on literature reveal a critic of catholic taste, partial perhaps to the very modern writers or to the lesser known of the distant past ("I feel at home before Boileau and after Baudelaire"), a comprehending judge with no set code or doctrine, whose viewpoint is always novel, whose conclusions are always challenging. In his commentaries on current events, on contemporary life and manners (*Epilogues* [1903-07]), he often displays an elegant cynicism, the detached irony of a modern La Rochefoucauld.

The last years of his life were brightened by the visits of a beloved American woman, "l'Amazone," recorded in *Lettres à l'Amazone* (1914; Eng. tr., *Letters to the Amazon,* 1931) and *Lettres intimes à l'Amazone* (1928; Intimate Letters to the Amazon). But the outbreak of World War I gave a new and sadder tone to the commentaries of *Pendant l'orage* (1915; During the Storm), *Dans la tourmente* (1916; In the Tempest), and *Pendant la guerre* (1917; During the War). This lover of beauty, this hater of the coarse and vulgar, died on September 29, 1915, as he was working on an indignant article protesting the German shelling of Reims Cathedral. Many of Gourmont's works have been translated into English.

See: Legrand-Chabrier, *Rémy de Gourmont: son œuvre* (1925); P. E. Jacob, *Rémy de Gourmont* (1931); G. Rees, *Rémy de Gourmont: essai da biographie intellectuelle* (1940); J. B. Barrière, *L'Idée de goût de Pascal à Valéry* (1972), pp. 205-22.

V.G. rev. D.W.A.

Goytisolo, Juan (1931-), Spanish novelist and essayist, was born in Barcelona. During the Spanish Civil War his father was imprisoned and his mother was killed in an air raid. Goytisolo studied law at the universities of Madrid and Barcelona, but writing was his real interest. His maternal great-uncle and his brother José Agustín were poets. Another brother, Luis GOYTISOLO is a novelist. In 1951, with the novelist Ana María MATUTE and others, he founded the "Turia," a Barcelona literary group. In 1957 he moved to Paris in self-imposed exile and worked for the Gallimard Publishing Company. During recent years he has taught literature courses in several universities in the United States. Some of Goytisolo's literary criticism has been collected in *Problemas de la novela* (1959; Problems of the Novel), *El furgón de cola* (1967; The Caboose), and *Disidencias* (1977; Dissident Remarks).

His first novel, *Juegos de manos* (1954; Eng. tr., *The Young Assassins*, 1959), concerns young delinquents who live through the Civil War as children. *Duelo en el Paraíso* (1955; Eng. tr., *Children of Chaos*, 1958), frequently compared to William Golding's *Lord of the Flies*, deals with a gang of refugee children who act out the atrocities lived by adults during the war.

In the second phase of his career, represented by *La resaca* (1958; The Undertow), *La Isla* (1961; The Island), and *Fin de Fiesta* (1962; Eng. tr., *The Party's Over*, 1966), he shifts to an objective and photographic style to capture the moral decay of an affluent society. Dissatisfied with objective realism, Goytisolo evolved new techniques in his famous trilogy: *Señas de identidad* (1966; Eng. tr., *Marks of Identity*, 1969), *Reivindicación del conde Don Julián* (1970; Eng. tr., *Count Julian*, 1974), and *Juan sin tierra* (1976; Eng. tr., *John the Landless*, 1977). *Señas*, perhaps the most ambitious part of the trilogy, is a brilliant attempt to destroy the historical, psychological, religious, and literary myths of Spain through the author's inner investigation of his life during the "25 years of peace" (1939-64). This dissection of reality is achieved by means of multiple stylistic recourses and an elaborate narrative technique. The author's social commitment is shifted to a purely linguistic level in *Reivindicación* and *Juan sin tierra*, two works that represent an exploration into the unlimited possibilities of literary language as well as narrative syntax. Goytisolo is one of the few authors belonging to the social-realist trend of the 1950s who have overcome the limitations of that current by the constant and intelligent renovation of their literary tools.

See: J. Ortega, *Juan Goytisolo: Alienación y agresión en Señas de identidad y Reivindicación del conde Don Julián* (1972); G. Sobejano et al., *Juan Goytisolo* (1975); L. G. Levine, *Juan Goytisolo: la destrucción creadora* (1976).   J.O.

Goytisolo, Luis (1937-), Spanish novelist and short-story writer, the brother of Juan GOYTISOLO, was born in Barcelona, where he studied law and later worked in several publishing houses. In 1956 he won the Sésamo Prize for his short story "Niño mal" (Sick Child) and in 1958 the Biblioteca Breve Prize for his novel *Las afueras* (1959; The Outskirts), an example of social realism. A fluid yet tense style characterizes *Las mismas palabras* (1963; The Same Words), a narrative dealing with the Catalonian oligarchy. *Ojos, círculos, búhos* (1970; Eyes, Circles, Owls) and *Devoraciones* (1976; Devourings) are interesting experimental works.

The novels *Recuento* (1973; Inventory) and *Los verdes de mayo hasta el mar* (1976; The Green of May to the Sea) are the first two parts of a tetralogy entitled *Antagonía*. Stylistically, they are Goytisolo's most ambitious novels. *Recuento* is narrated by a character whose story is identifiable with the novelist's middle-class Catalan youth. The complexity of this text stems from the narrative technique, which is based on the concept of writing as an autonomous generator of new realities. *Los verdes* is a literary reflection on the creative process. *Antagonía*, begun in 1973, represents the maturity of a novelist whose early social and experimental tendencies have evolved into a more skilled literary craftsmanship.

See: J. Ortega, "Asedio a *Recuento* de Luis Goytisolo," *CHA* 317 (1976): 488-94; A. Riccio, "De las ruinas al taller en la obra de Luis Goytisolo," *ANP* 2 (1977): 31-43.   J.O.

Gozzano, Guido (1883-1916), Italian poet, was born in Agliè (Turin). He spent his early years in his family's villa in the Canavese, the region that would become the setting for some of his best poetry, and in Turin, where he studied law and literature without earning a degree in either. He began publishing poetry in 1904 at about the same time that he first became ill with tuberculosis.

Gozzano is the most important and influential of the *poeti crepuscolari* (*see* ITALIAN LITERATURE) active in northern Italy just after the turn of the century. But while he too seeks respite from the hurly-burly of contemporary life, he is not as lachrymose as some of his fellow "crepuscolari." The poems in *La via del rifugio* (1907; Way of Refuge) and *I colloqui* (1911; Conversations) suggest that the poet is a world-weary, rather cynical provincial aesthete, out of tune with his times and incapable of love or belief in the great ideals, which have been rendered "nauseating" for him by previous "rhetoricians." Gozzano uses a sentimental irony to keep at a distance from a world for which he feels no rancor but where he senses he could not survive. Thus the many typical Victorian household objects that figure in his verses, the famous "buone cose di pessimo gusto" ("good things in the worst taste") are precious to him because the demands they make on his sympathies are so minimal and so arbitrary. So, too, the intellectual lawyer of "La Signorina Felicita ovvero la felicità" (Miss Felicity, or Happiness) rather heartlessly makes love to a hopelessly plain but touchingly responsive provincial spinster more at home with *camicie* ("shirts") than with Nietzsche (*see* Friedrich NIETZSCHE), and incapable of understanding his angst. In the poem "Totò Merùmeni," Totò prefers sleeping with his cook to more emotionally engaging amorous adventures. Gozzano also deals with gentle, melancholoy erotic themes in such other well-known poems as "Le due strade" (The Two Roads) and "Cocotte." The form Gozzano finds most congenial for the expression of these themes is the brief narrative, invariably in traditional meters, in which he attempts to halt the flux of time through the vivid evocation of objects or events from the past. This is especially evident in "L'amica di nonna Speranza" (Grandma Hope's Girlfriend), where the cheap bric-a-brac of a mid-19th-century middle-class salon are meant to function as magical talismans against the passage of time.

Gozzano's long years of illness may account not only for the melancholy in his poetry, but also for a resigned, distanced tone that places life's great passions on the same level with commonplace objects. The resulting juxtaposition of the serious and the banal is part of Gozzano's defensive irony and the result of his habitual stance of bemused alienation from the world around him. This attitude, in turn, shows how much he already possessed the modern poetic sensibility typified by such later poets as Eugenio MONTALE (who has written an important essay on him) and T. S. Eliot.

Gozzano's complete works, including several poems not collected during his lifetime as well as the less important prose, are available in A. De Marchi's edition of the *Poesie e prose* (1961; Poems and Prose Works), which also contains the travel journal *Verso la cuna del mondo* (Toward the World's Cradle), an account of Gozzano's trip to India. The love letters he exchanged with the novelist and poet Amalia GUGLIELMINETTI have also been published.

See: G. Getto, "Gozzano," in *Poeti, critici e cose varie del novecento* (1953); E. Sanguineti, "Guido Gozzano," in *Letteratura italiana: i contemporanei,* vol. 1 (1975), pp. 515-29.   C.K.

Grabato Dias, João Pedro, *see* DIAS, JOÃO PEDRO GRABATO

Gracq, Julien, pseud. of Louis Poirier (1910–), French novelist, was born in Saint-Florent-le-Vieil. He studied with the famous philosopher ALAIN at the Lycée Henri IV, was admitted to the Ecole Normale Supérieure in Paris, passed the *agrégation* in 1934, and taught history and geography in various lycées. A discreet, secretive young man, Gracq wrote for a little-known publisher and brought forth singularly mature works. His literary production is not abundant, but each of his books has been admired for its high quality. His four novels are *Au château d'Argol* (1938; Eng. tr., *The Castle of Argol,* 1951); *Un Beau ténébreux* (1945; Eng. tr., *A Dark Stranger,* 1950); *Le Rivage des Syrtes* (1951; By the Shores of Syrtes), winner of the Goncourt Prize, an award that the author refused; and *Un Balcon en forêt* (1958; Eng. tr., *Balcony in the Forest,* 1959).

Gracq's concerns are somber: in the first two novels he deals with the attraction of death, while in the third and fourth with the interlude before an inevitable tragedy. The story line does not constitute the main interest of his works; it is rather only a libretto for magnificent music. Indeed, Gracq's novels are beautifully written, and the magic of his words creates a climate of bewilderment, surprise, and sometimes terror that gradually bewitches his readers, leading them into an entirely new universe of dreams, phantasmagoria, and poetry.

Gracq knows and admires the literature of the Middle Ages (especially the Arthurian legend), Victor Hugo, Gothic novels, Arthur RIMBAUD, LAUTRÉAMONT, Edgar Allan Poe, Richard WAGNER and, last but not least, surrealism (Gracq wrote a book on André BRETON in 1947). In many ways, Gracq's work is the antithesis of Jean-Paul SARTRE's. While Sartre accepts as literature only what is realistic and engagé, Gracq vigorously refuses realism and naturalism and praises, above all, disinvolvement with politics and other practical aims.

Besides his four novels, Gracq has published a triptych of stories entitled *La Presqu'île* (1970; The Peninsula); an important literary essay, *La Littérature à l'estomac* (1950); Literature at the Stomach Level); a collection of prose poetry, *Liberté Grande* (1946; Freedom the Great); and a four-act drama, *Le Roi Pêcheur* (1948; The Fisherman King), inspired by the Grail legend.

See: J.-L. Leutrat, *Julien Gracq* (1967); A.-C. Dobbs, *Dramaturgie et liturgie dans l'œuvre de Julien Gracq* (1972).   P.Br.

Gradnik, Alojz (1882-1967), Slovenian poet, was born in Medana, where he attended primary school. He went to a German gymnasium in Gorica, and studied law at the University of Vienna. After an active legal and governmental career, he retired in 1945 and devoted the remainder of his life principally to translating works from Russian, Italian, English, German, Spanish, and Serbo-Croatian literatures.

Gradnik began to compose poetry while he was still at the gymnasium, where he steeped himself in the German classics. His philosophy of life was strongly influenced by Arthur Schopenhauer's pessimistic view of the world. Along with France Prešeren (*see* SLOVENIAN LITERATURE) and Oton Župančič, Gradnik is considered one of the greatest poets in Slovenian literature. Since he aimed at purity of thought and classical clarity of expression, his poetic devices are simple and sparse. Yet although his

bare, intellectual verse is devoid of emotionalism, it is not without symbolic elements. His poetic creation grew out of his own inner turbulence and pain and his desire to attain the final, definitive truth at all costs. His favorite form was the sonnet, into whose brief span he compressed the fruits of his contemplation about himself, mankind, life, love, and death.

Between 1916 and 1953, Gradnik published 10 collections of poetry, the most important of which are *Padajoče zvezde* (1916; Falling Stars), *Pot bolesti* (1922; The Path of Pain), *De profundis* (1926), *Večni studenci* (1938; Eternal Wellsprings), and *Primorski soneti* (1952; Seashore Sonnets).

See: M. Boršnik, *Pogovori s pesnikom Gradnikom* (1954); B. Meriggi, *Storia della letteratura slovena* (1961); M. Brecelj, *Gradnikova bibliografija* (1964).
                                                   J.P. with W.B.E.

Graf, Oskar Maria (1894-1967), German prose writer and poet, was born in Berg on Lake Starnberg, Bavaria. He was the son of a village baker. Graf learned his father's trade but left home at the age of 16 to escape his brother's tyranny and decided to pursue a career as a writer in Munich. Unsuccessful as a dramatist, he was forced to earn a living doing odd jobs. During World War I, Graf was drafted but forced his release by successfully pretending insanity. Returning to Munich, he took part in the revolution of 1918-19. During the early 1920s he achieved success with several books, especially with the first part of his autobiography, later published in two parts as *Wir sind Gefangene* (1927; Eng. tr., *Prisoners All,* 1928). With the exception of this, all his works were put on the list of recommended literature after Adolf Hitler had assumed power in Germany. Graf protested in his open letter "Verbrennt mich!" ("Burn Me, Too") and did not return from a lecture tour in Vienna. In 1934 he sided with Austrian workers in their revolt against Chancellor Engelbert Dollfuss's government and was forced to flee to Czechoslovakia. In the same year Graf participated in the First International Congress of Socialist Writers in Moscow. From 1934 until 1938 he lived in Brunn, fleeing then to New York. He was chosen president of the German-American Writers Association, but had to wait for American citizenship until 1958 on account of his (successful) refusal to sign the defense clause in the naturalization process.

Two major concerns dominate all of Graf's works: the everyday life of simple farm and village people on the one hand and the adverse circumstances contributing to the rise of totalitarian government on the other. Although his strong sense of realism protected the author from falling in line with the bards of "blood and soil" literature, his social skepticism prevented him from becoming the advocate of any party politics. The plots and characters of his short stories and novels are based upon his personal experiences in his Bavarian homeland, notably in *Kalendergeschichten* (1929; Calendar Tales); *Bolwieser* (1931; Eng. tr., *The Station Master,* 1933), a satirical novel about a married couple; *Einer gegen alle* (1932; Eng. tr., *The Wolf,* 1934), an antiwar novel; *Das Leben meiner Mutter* (1946, preceded by Eng. tr., *The Life of My Mother,* 1940); and *Unruhe um einen Friedfertigen* (1947; Agitations around a Peaceful Man), a novel about belligerent chauvinism and racial hatred. Graf's poetry reflects concerns similar to those of his fiction, for example, *Altmodische Gedichte eines Dutzendmenschen* (1962; partial Eng. tr., *Old-fashioned Poems of an Ordinary Man,* 1962).

See: A. von der Heydt, "Oskar Maria Graf," *GQ* 41, no. 3 (May 1968): 401-12; R. Recknagel, *Ein Bayer in*

Amerika: Oskar Maria Graf—Leben und Werk (1974); H. F. Pfanner, *Oskar Maria Graf: eine kritische Bibliographie* (1976).   H.E.P.

Gramsci, Antonio (1891–1937), Italian politician and essayist, was born in Ales, Sardinia, and studied literature in Turin. In 1913 he joined the Socialist Party, and in 1924 he began to write for the newspaper *Il grido del popolo*. In 1916 he became the editor-in-chief of the Socialist Party paper *Avanti!*, where he was also theater critic. His early articles are collected in *Scritti giovanili* (1958; Early Writings). In 1919 he cofounded, with Palmiro Togliatti, *L'ordine nuovo*, a weekly whose great stress on culture made it a focal point for a whole generation of young socialists. In 1921, Gramsci became a member of the central committee of the newly founded Communist Party, and in 1924 he cofounded the official Party newspaper, *L'unità*. The same year, he was elected to the Italian parliament. Arrested in 1926 on trumped-up charges by the Fascist government, Gramsci was condemned in 1928 to 20 years of imprisonment. During this period, he started work on a series of essays on "the history of the formation and of the development of Italian intellectual groups." The essays, which never took a definitive form, were scattered throughout 32 notebooks and were edited and published only after his death. The material was divided according to subject into six volumes: philosophy, *Il materialismo e la filosofia di Benedetto Croce* (1948; Historical Materialism and the Philosophy of Benedetto Croce); intellectual history, *Gli intellettuali e l'organizzazione della cultura* (1949; Intellectuals and the Organization of Culture); political theory, *Note sul Machiavelli, sulla politica e sullo stato moderno* (1949; Notes on Machiavelli, Politics, and the Modern State); history, *Passato e presente* (1951; Past and Present) and *Il Risorgimento* (1949); and literature, *Letteratura e vita nazionale* (1950; Literature and National Life). A partial English translation, *Selections from the Prison Notebooks*, was published in 1971. Prison conditions aggravated Gramsci's already poor health. Released conditionally in 1934, he died in a Roman clinic three years later.

Gramsci was neither a theoretician nor a literary critic in the technical sense. His importance in the literary world derived mainly from his ability to satisfy post–World II—and specifically Italian—cultural needs. Gramsci provided a conceptual framework significantly different from that of Benedetto CROCE on the one hand and from that of vulgar Marxism on the other. By criticizing the Crocean revision of historical materialism, Gramsci reinstated into Marxism the subjective superstructural element, which freed Marxism from the traditional accusation that it was deterministic and conditioning when dealing with art. Thus, Gramsci made Marxism acceptable to the Italian literary establishment and at the same time provided the tools by means of which a score of Italian intellectuals could free themselves from Crocean cultural hegemony.

Gramsci's interest in popular art forms, such as Grand Guignol and the detective novel, led him to examine these genres for patterns of character behavior and reasons for audience identification. These inquiries, coupled with Gramsci's notion of Italian intellectuals as a "cosmopolitan" class detached from national reality, provided the necessary impetus for many studies of the central problem of Italian culture: the split between literature and national life. In the last years of his life, the great 19th-century critic Francesco De Sanctis (1817–83) had warned against just such a split; 20th-century thinkers felt that the split was aggravated by fascism. Gramsci proposed an ideological basis for a literature of social commitment, na-

tionalist in its scope, populist in its themes, and direct in its style. This program, known as *gramscianesimo*, was in contrast to the elitist aesthetics of poetic hermeticism (*see* ITALIAN LITERATURE) that had flourished in Italy in the late 1930s and early 1940s. Moreover, Gramsci started a trend new to the Italian critical tradition: literary history seen as intellectual history, a concept that revitalized studies of the Italian Renaissance, the Enlightenment, and 19th-century Italian literature.

Gramsci has been credited with having laid the foundations of a Marxist aesthetics. But his interpretations of Dante, Luigi PIRANDELLO, Alessandro Manzoni (1785–1873), and others show a strong debt to Croce in matters of aesthetic judgment. His ideas about the theater, which were overlooked for a long time as a secondary aspect of his thought, stand today as his most original contribution. Gramsci saw the theater not as literature, as in the traditional Crocean view, but as an organization of practical elements that acquires semantic value and becomes a means of artistic expression only in the totality of its parts.

A posthumous selection of Gramsci's letters, mainly to his relatives, *Lettere dal carcere* (1947; Eng. tr., *Letters from Prison*, 1973), was awarded the Viareggio Prize in 1947. This record of Gramsci's life from early imprisonment to his death reveals a writer capable of vivid descriptions of natural events, a storyteller who could recapture the world of his childhood in Sardinia and retell or invent children's stories, and especially an intellectual who was able to look at the Italian south with a compassion and a directness of style that had a parallel only in the masterworks of Elio VITTORINI and Carlo LEVI. The collection owed much of its success to a structure that gave the book the quality of fiction while retaining the immediacy of a diary and the impact of a historical document. The letters were molded into a pattern that followed Gramsci's prison life: at the beginning, a passionate and hopeful Gramsci is reflected in long letters that have the freshness of a journalistic account, but as life, hope, and affection slip away from him, the letters themselves become shorter and shorter until they all but disappear, leaving the reader with the impression of unspoken sentiments, punctuated by the emptiness of the almost white last page. More complete collections of the letters were published in later years, but none enjoyed the success of the first.

See: J. M. Cammett, *Antonio Gramsci and the Origins of Italian Communism* (1967); G. Fiori, *Antonio Gramsci: Life of a Revolutionary* (1970).   D.M.

Grande, Félix (1937–), Spanish poet, fiction writer, and essayist, was born in Mérida in the province of Badajoz and lived in Tomelloso in the province of Ciudad Real until he was 20. Before joining the staff of the Madrid literary journal *Cuadernos Hispanoamericanos* (of which he is now associate editor) he worked as a shepherd, cattle raiser, vintner, office worker, and salesman. He is one of the most important voices of the so-called critical generation rooted in the decade of the 1960s and characterized by its reaction against the dominant rhetoric of the social poets (*see* SPANISH LITERATURE). His first book, *Taranto* (Flamenco), not published until 1971, was written under the influence of the Peruvian poet César Vallejo, while *Las piedras* (1964; Stones), which won the Adonais Prize, could be considered a homage to Antonio MACHADO. In its deep awareness of the loneliness and dissatisfaction of modern man, *Música amenazada* (1965; Threatened Music), winner of the Guipúzcoa Prize, represents a maturation of Grande's earlier promise. *Blanco espiritual* (1967; White Spiritual), first published in Cuba, where it was awarded the Casa de las Américas Prize, is one of his best books of poetry. In it the most everyday aspects of reality are demythified. Dreams and disillusionment, tenderness and grief, love and hate, poverty and injustice all confront each other in a language that represents the search for personal reality. The style is somewhere between stream of consciousness and social testimony, but free of all rhetoric. Grande's fifth book, *Puedo escribir los versos más tristes esta noche* (1971; I Can Write the Saddest Verses Tonight), is an introspective analysis of individual and collective conscience under the insistent press of time.

Grande's is a narrative poetry tied to the phenomena of daily life. Its strength lies in the cumulative whole and in an inspiration that comes not from literature but from life observed in all its multiformity and complexity. This accounts for the poetry's meditative, deeply felt, critical approach to human experience. In other words, Grande sees poetry as a search for authenticity through the creation of a personalized language open to new expressive forms. These in turn open the way to the rehumanization of art. Grande's last book of poems, *Las rubáiyatas de Horacio Martín* (1978), was awarded the National Literary Prize. Using the device of the heteronym, as did Fernando PESSOA and Antonio Machado, the poet brings together the various essentials of his previous work and moves into a new period in which love and language become the substantive elements of creativity.

Grande has also published prize-winning fiction and several volumes of literary criticism.

See: G. Brotherston, "The Speaking Voice in Félix Grande's Poetry," in *Studies in Modern Spanish Literature and Art*, ed. by N. Glendenning (1972), pp. 1–12.

R. de C.S.

Granin, Daniil Aleksandrovich, pseud. of Daniil German (1918–), Russian novelist and short-story writer, was born in Volyn. He was first recognized for his story "Sobstvennoye mneniye" (1956; An Opinion of One's Own), which was published in the journal *Novy mir*. The story describes the moral dilemma of a middle-aged Soviet scientist who recognizes that his plan to follow a courageous path in his work was only a delusion. As a young man, Granin was an electrical engineer, and he wrote several novels and stories about scientific and industrial problems, including *Iskateli* (1954; Eng. tr., *Those Who Seek,* 1957) and *Idu na grozu* (1962; Eng. tr., *Into the Storm,* 1965). He has also written stories of personal emotion, including "Posle svadby" (1958; After the Wedding) and "Dozhd v chuzhom gorode" (1973; Rain in a Strange Town); a cycle of love stories, and several biographical studies of scientists, including *Eta strannaya zhizn* (1974; This Strange Life), about the biologist Lyubishchev, and a screenplay about J. Robert Oppenheimer and other inventors of the atomic bomb. *Sad kamney* (1972; Stone Garden) is an account of a visit he made to Japan. In 1975 he published the screenplay *Vybor tseli* (Choice of Goal) and two long stories *Eta Strannaya zhizn* (This Strange Life) and *Odnofamiliets* (Namesake), and in 1976 the tale *Obratny bilet* (Return Ticket). In these works, he continued to explore the problems of time, science, and links with past generations. A complex and original writer, Granin has served as secretary of the Leningrad Writers Union.

See: K. Armes, "Daniil Granin and the World of Soviet Science," *Survey* 20, no. 1 (Winter 1974): 47–59.

G.Gi.

Gras, Félix (1844–1901), Provençal poet and novelist, was born in Malemort, a small town in the Comtat Venaissin.

He spent most of his life in Avignon as a justice of the peace. Gras sprang from an old family of prosperous farmers and received his education at the Collège of Béziers. While still a student, he became interested in the "Félibrige" (*see* PROVENÇAL LITERATURE). The founders of the movement ranked him as the greatest in the so-called second generation of Félibres. In contrast with them, however, he was to remain all his life an outspoken "Red of the South," that is, a liberal in politics and religion, a firm believer in the ideals of the French Revolution. He was to enjoy also the distinction of being the Provençal writer most read in the United States, not excepting Frédéric MISTRAL.

His important works in verse consist of two somber epic poems in 12 cantos each: *Li Carbounié* (1876; The Charcoal Burners), dramatizing the life of rustic Alpine mountaineers, and *Toloza* (1880), dealing with the Albigensian Crusade, together with *Lou Roumancero prouvençau* (1887; The Provençal Romancers), a series of lyrics evoking the history and legend of medieval Provence. Some of these had appeared previously in *L'Armana prouvençau*, the organ of the Félibrige. Having thus established a solid reputation as an epic and lyrical poet, Gràs turned to prose. He published *Li Papalino* (1891; Stories of Papal Avignon) and *Li Rouge dóu Miejour* (1 vol., with French tr. on opposite pages, 1896; 3 parts, in French, *Les Rouges du Midi,* 1898–1900; Eng. tr., *The Reds of the Midi,* 1896, *The Terror,* 1898, and *The White Terror,* 1899, the last two being the second and third volumes of the series). Gras also published a little pamphlet, *Lou Catechisme dóu bon felibre* (1892), which defines the ideals of the Félibrige.

Li Papalino comprises picturesque and colorful stories permeated with good humor and gaiety, told in an energetic, yet light and harmonious language. It was *Li Rouge dóu Miejour,* however, that won its author a prominent and even original place among the authors of historical fiction. This is the story of the famous battalion of patriots from Marseilles to whose enthusiasm the French owe the name of their national anthem. It is extraordinarily alive, rich in color, swift in action, epic-like in its rhythm. It was published simultaneously in Provençal, French, and English. The English translation has had several American editions. A new edition of the Provençal-French text appeared in 1951.

See: C. P. Julian and P. Fontan, *Anthologie du Félibrige provençal* (1924); M. Jouveau, "Félix Gras," *Le Feu* 20 (1926), 321–30; F. Bertrand, *Félix Gras et son œuvre* (1935).

A.V.R.

Grass, Günter, pseud. Artur Knoff (1927–), German novelist, poet, dramatist, graphic artist, and essayist, was born of German-Kashubian parentage in Danzig-Langfuhr. After attendance at schools in Danzig, Grass entered the German air force in 1944, was wounded, hospitalized, and taken captive by American forces in 1945. After his release from captivity he made his way down the Rhine River, working as he went, finally in a chalk mine. After apprenticing himself in Düsseldorf as a stonecutter and sculptor, he studied at the art academy there with Sepp Mages and Otto Pankok, and in the early 1950s he began to write poetry. After a journey to Italy in 1951 he studied with Karl Hartung at the Berlin Academy of Art, then lived for a time in Paris, where he met his translator, Ralph Manheim. In 1955 he became associated with the "Gruppe 47" (*see* GERMAN LITERATURE) and that same year won third prize in a competition for lyric poems sponsored by South German Radio.

Grass's first volume of poetry, *Die Vorzüge der Windhühner* (1956; The Advantages of Weatherhens), contains the topical themes (political and social), the irrepressible linguistic creativity, the imaginative metaphorical inventiveness, and the accompanying graphic depictions that characterize his entire work. Little noticed at the time of its publication, the volume was issued in a second edition in 1966 (with the same lyric contents but with a variation in graphic art) when Grass had achieved world renown as an author who had given German literature and the German language new vitality. In 1957 the ballet *Stoffreste* (Scraps), for which Grass had written the book, was performed in Essen.

Günter Grass burst upon the literary scene in Germany and around the world with the publication in 1959 of his long novel *Die Blechtrommel* (Eng. tr., *The Tin Drum*, 1962), the story of the dwarf Oskar Matzerath, who entered the pantheon of unforgettable characters in world literature. The novel, spanning more than 30 years of European history from the 1920s into the 1950s, ranging from Danzig through Germany to Paris, centers on the travails of Matzerath, who incorporates the conscience of Germany and its encounter with the Nazi experience. The novel established Grass's reputation for bold incident, irridescent language, and wildly improbable event; it was denounced as blasphemous and obscene but also praised as the most original fictional work in German letters. Grass was awarded the Bremen Book Prize in 1960, but the prize was withdrawn by the Senate of the city of Bremen because of the novel's controversial public reception. It was filmed successfully in 1979.

Grass's second book of poetry, *Gleisdreieck* (1960; Rail Interchange), further established his lyric reputation and brought his artistic development a step further. It was followed in 1961 by a narrative spin-off from *Die Blechtrommel*, the novella *Katz und Maus* (Eng. tr., *Cat and Mouse*, 1963)—filmed in 1966 and a public sensation because of a masturbatory scene—the story of the cryptic fate of a young Danzig German, Mahlke, whose grossly overdeveloped Adam's apple becomes a symbol of his quest for peer acclaim and for an Iron Cross to hide the protuberance from public view. The story is narrated by Mahlke's friend, Pilenz, who writes the tale as penance for his own role in Mahlke's mysterious end. The satanic, pubescent girl Tulla Pokriefka from *Katz und Maus* emerges as a leading figure in the second long novel by Grass, *Hundejahre* (1963; Eng. tr., *Dog Years*, 1965). The novel is concerned with German destiny and the individual flight from reality and centers on three friends, Eddi Amsel (who is also Goldmäulchen and Brauxel—spelled three ways), Walter Matern, and Harry Liebenau. The figure of Brauxel haunts the novel, pursuing the bad conscience of Matern, who himself goes on a vengeful journey of retribution for transgressions in which he played a part. The conscience of Germany is the subject of the book. The language of the narrative further reiterates Grass's peerless reputation as a narrative author who handles puns and parodies (for example, of Martin HEIDEGGER) with equal facility. The three books form what has become known as "The Danzig Trilogy." The year 1963 was also the time when an aesthetic essay by Grass, *Die Ballerina* (The Ballet Dancer), was published in a small edition. His two-act play *Hochwasser* (Eng. tr., *Flood*, 1967) was also published in 1963, although it had first been performed in 1957.

Since 1961, Grass had taken part in German election campaigns, supporting the Social Democratic Party (SPD) and its candidate Willy Brandt with political speeches, which were collected in 1965 under the title *Dich singe ich, Demokratie* (To Thee I Sing, Democracy), five political speeches that had previously been published as pamphlets, with sales proceeds going to purchase books for libraries for the German armed forces, the titles chosen by Grass's author friend Uwe JOHNSON. A collection of miscellaneous essays, political and social commentary, open letters, and aesthetic criticism, *Über das Selbstverständliche* (1968; Eng. tr., selections, in *Speak Out*, 1969), kept the controversially engagé Grass before the public eye.

In 1965 the play *Onkel, Onkel* (Eng. tr., *Mister, Mister*, 1967) was published. It presents the antics of two redoubtable children, who cause the death of a man who has lost contact with the real world. Also in that year Grass received the Georg Büchner Prize and was awarded an honorary doctorate by Kenyon College in Ohio. In 1966 the play *Die Plebejer proben den Aufstand* (Eng. tr., *The Plebians Rehearse the Uprising*, 1966) caused an uproar at its premiere in Berlin, where supporters of Bertolt BRECHT loudly decried the work, which they considered an attack on the East German playwright. Despite Grass's denial that the director in the play is a depiction of Brecht and his inactivity at the time of the uprising of students and workers in East Berlin, some aspects of the famous dramatist can be discerned. Also in 1966, Grass was one of the group of German authors who traveled to the United States for the Princeton meeting of "Gruppe 47" in April.

Between 1966 and 1970, Grass was one of three authors who edited *Luchterhands Loseblatt Lyrik* (Luchterhand's Loose-Leaf Lyrics), broadside sheets of single poems that sold for one mark apiece. His third book of poetry, *Ausgefragt* (1967; Tired of Questions), contains the poetic threnody that has found its way into most of his fictional and dramatic works as well. As with his previous collections of lyrics, Grass furnished trenchant, sometimes shocking illustrations (his favorite themes: cooks, nurses, nuns, fish, eels, snails, phallic mushrooms). The year 1967 also witnessed the boycott of the German newspaper and news magazine publisher Axel Springer by German authors, an event marked by Grass with the publication of *Der Fall Axel C. Springer am Beispiel Arnold Zweig* (1967; The Case of Axel C. Springer on the Example of Arnold Zweig).

For the Literarisches Colloquium in Berlin, Grass contributed stories in *Geschichten* (1968; Stories), under the pseudonym of Artur Knoff. In the same year he published *Briefe über die Grenze* (Letters across the Border), correspondence with Pavel Kohout that was an effort to start an East-West dialogue, and *Über meinen Lehrer Döblin* (On My Teacher Döblin), a small collection of lectures, the title piece of which extols Alfred DÖBLIN, whom Grass holds up as a great forerunner and an influence on his own work.

Grass's third novel, *örtlich betäubt* (1969; Eng. tr., *Local Anaesthetic*, 1970), is not written in the style of his previous novels, nor is it as long. Although the author considered it his best work at the time, it met with less critical acclaim. An associated work was the play *Davor* (premiered 1969, pub. 1970; Eng. tr., *Max*, 1972; also produced in the United States under the title *Uptight*, premiered at the University of Texas at Austin in 1970, produced at the Arena Theater in Washington, D.C., 1971), which recapitulates some events of the novel. The novel and the play portray the insecurity, indecision, and guilt-ridden consciences of German schoolteacher intellectuals and their students in the early years of the 1960s, reflecting the distaste felt generally for the United States's involvement in Vietnam, the whole scene being commented upon by a philosopher-dentist.

The dramatic work of Grass was collected in the volume *Theaterspiele* (Pieces for the Theater) in 1970. In addition to the plays mentioned already, it also includes

Die bösen Köche (Eng. tr., *The Wicked Cooks,* 1967) and *Noch zehn Minuten bis Buffalo* (Eng. tr., *Only Ten Minutes to Buffalo,* 1967). *Four Plays—Mister, Mister, Cooks, Buffalo, Flood*—appeared in 1967. None of Grass's plays has enjoyed critical success in German productions, for which Grass blames uninspired directors and flawed staging. The single critical success was the American productions of *Uptight.* After the collection of plays came the collection of poetry by Grass in 1971, *Gesammelte Gedichte.* Three volumes of selected poems have appeared in English translation: *Selected Poems* (1966), *New Poems* (1967), and *In the Egg and Other Poems* (1977).

Aus dem Tagebuch einer Schnecke (1972; Eng. tr., *From the Diary of a Snail,* 1973) is a work that combines semifictional political campaign reportage with fictional events in Danzig just prior to World War II. The strong autobiographical allusions in the works of Grass, particularly in regard to place, to reading experiences, and to historical reflections, are particularly apparent in *Der Butt* (1977; Eng. tr., *The Flounder,* 1978), another long novel, this time a story of humankind's intersexual struggle, based loosely on the fairy tale of the flounder fished from the sea, "The Fisherman and His Wife," in which the magically endowed, speaking flounder promises three wishes and is thrown back into the sea. The novel, which ranges from prehistoric times to the present day, concentrates on the social and sexual relationships between men and women, with a tribunal of women judging the talkative, perennial, male-chauvinistic flounder for his support of the principle of male domination.

Grass's graphic art, and its close connection in theme and execution to his literary production, are summarized in a sense in the work *Mariazuehren* (1973; Eng. tr., *Inmarypraise,* 1973), a bilingual publication with illustrations. *Liebe geprüft* (1974; Love Tested) is a volume with seven stories and seven etchings by Grass. The long story *Das Treffen in Telgte* (1979; The Meeting in Telgte) is dedicated to Hans Werner Richter, the venerated cofounder of "Gruppe 47," and relates a fictional meeting of baroque poets in Telgte in 1647. Some critics believe the work to be Grass's finest.

Günter Grass continues his active participation in the criticism of social inequities, although he has become less involved with political events. He remains the undisputed leader in German letters since World War II. Because of his unexampled literary virtuosity and his authentic graphic artistry, Grass has an assured place in the history of German literature. In 1979 he established the Döblin Prize, to be given in recognition of the excellence of an unpublished work by a German-language author. The first recipient was the Swiss novelist Gerold Späth.

See: W. J. Schwarz, *Der Erzähler Günter Grass* (1969); T. J. Di Napoli, "The Rhetoric of Religion in the Works of Günter Grass," Ph.D. Dissertation, University of Texas (1971); H. L. Arnold, *Günter Grass—Dokumente zur politischen Wirkung,* (1971); E. Diller, *A Mythic Journey: Günter Grass's Tin Drum* (1974); J. Leonard, *Günter Grass* (1974); K. Miles, *Günter Grass* (1975); J. Reddick, *The 'Danzig Trilogy' of Günter Grass* (1975); P. O.'Neill, *Günter Grass: A Bibliography* (1976).   A.L.W.

Grau, Jacinto (1877–1958), Spanish dramatist, was born in Barcelona and died in Buenos Aires, where he had lived since 1939. His dramatic works, which he began writing in the early years of the 20th century, may be described by the term "disconformity." From the beginning he adopted a critical attitude toward the Spanish theater of his time, accusing it of lacking originality, creativity, and imagination. He was critical of directors, ac-

tors, and critics as well. His plays achieved little success in Spain and are generally little-known.

Grau began his work with the express purpose of going beyond the realistic bourgeois theater dedicated to describing the life and manners of the time. He aspired to the restoration of tragedy, "with the dream," as he confessed, "of reestablishing, as in ancient Athens, the ideal relationship between the theater and public life." In his first tragedy, *Entre llamas* (1905; Amid Flames), he unsuccessfully attempts to combine the psychological analysis of naturalistic drama with elements plucked from classical and romantic tragedy. *El conde Alarcos* (1907; Count Alarcos) follows, and later, *El hijo pródigo* (1917; The Prodigal Son). Although beautiful literary creations, his tragedies are in a certain sense mere substitutes for tragedy, that is, literary pieces that lack an authentic tragic vision. Realizing the fruitlessness of his experiments, Grau abandoned tragedy and wrote plays in a variety of genres. Two of them return to the Spanish myth of Don Juan: *Don Juan de Carillana* (1913) and *El burlador que no se burla* (1930; The Seducer Who Does Not Seduce). *En Ildaria* (1917), criticizes contemporary Spanish society. With *El señor de Pigmalión* (1921; Mr. Pygmalion), Grau made his debut in the farce. This is without doubt his best and most original work. Rejected by Spanish producers, it was translated into French shortly after it appeared in book form in Spain, and was presented in Paris by Charles DULLIN at the opening of the Théâtre de l'Atelier. In 1925, Karel ČAPEK presented it in the National Theater of Prague. Only in 1928, on the heels of its European success, was it presented in Spain.

From 1929 to 1945, Grau wrote a series of plays in which he repeated a single dramatic scheme built around the same characters, ideas, and meanings combined in a number of different plots. Each of them features a man and a woman, strong and superior to all mortals, whose secret consists in the cult of the self and whose strength springs from their absolute egoism, which they consider the source of their power. Around them hover, visible or invisible, destiny, illusion, and death. These works are constructed by means of a succession of vignettes. They attempt to portray contemporary society as driven by the pursuit of success but fundamentally controlled by the three great lords of this world: the devil, illusion, and death. If in concept they reflect Nietzsche's idea of the superman (*see* Friedrich NIETZSCHE), in dramatic form they show the influence of German expressionist theater. Representing this phase are *El caballero Varona* (1929; Varona, the Gentleman), *Los tres locos del mundo* (1930; The Three Madmen of the World) and *La casa del diablo* (1942; The Devil's Home).

Grau's last phase is represented by three farces written between 1949 and 1958: *Las gafas de don Telesforo* (1949; Don Telesforo's Glasses), *Bibí Carabé* (1954) and *En el infierno se están mudando* (1958; Moving Day in Hell). In these plays, Grau abandons superman and destiny and returns to the style of his less conventional works, modeled after *El señor de Pigmalión.* By their cold irony, their function as dramatic parables, their fondness for sarcastic denunciations, and their portrayal of the growth of a dehumanized society, these three plays can be compared to the theater of Friedrich DÜRRENMATT, although they lack the rigor and intellectual complexity of the Swiss author's work. Grau's last play is richer in content than his earlier ones. Here his nonconformity successfully leads him away from theatrical convention toward a drama of commitment and social intimacy. In Spain there has recently begun a movement toward a critical revision of the theater of Grau.

See: L. García Lorenzo, Introduction to J. Grau,

Teatro selecto (1971); M. Navascués, *El teatro de Jacinto Grau* (1975).   F.R.-R.

Greek literature. Modern Greek literature inherits the longest and most continuous tradition of any literature in the Western world, but it also inherits Greece's traditional divisiveness. Until the beginning of the 20th century, there existed three separate literary modes: the "erudite," written in the vocabulary and forms of the archaic Greek language; the "demotic," using the spoken idiom of the people as the basis for literary expression; and the "mixed" mode, attempting to fuse the two. The erudite branch extended a written tradition that had existed without break since Hellenistic times (ca. 325-150 B.C.). Demotic literature has its source in the oral traditions of the common people, i.e., in the folk songs (*dimotika tragoudia*) whose earliest known examples appeared in the 9th century. The mixed mode commenced with the epic *Digenis Akritas,* which probably dates from the 11th century and is normally considered the first written monument of modern Greek literature.

In the areas of the Greek world that came under Turkish control after the fall of Constantinople (1453), the erudite dominated, producing a lifeless literature separated from everyday reality. In the islands under Venetian rule, however, there was a mixed tradition, tending toward the demotic, that flowered into a renaissance in Crete at the end of the 16th century. Works such as Vitsentzos Kornaros's *Erotokritos* (ca. 1650) approached the popular spirit of the folk songs and influenced future Greek poets from Dionysios Solomos to George SEFERIS. But the fall of Crete to the Turks in 1669 aborted this first renaissance, and only the folk songs continued as a truly creative genre.

During the revolutionary period (ca. 1810-30), a new renaissance took place. This second renaissance occurred in the Ionian Islands, the area that produced two great poets, Andreas Kalvos and Solomos, who were the true forerunners of contemporary Greek poetry. Kalvos (1792-1869) belongs to the mixed tradition. His fervent odes hymn the heroic actions of revolutionary Greece. Because his work remained unknown in Greece until 1889, his influence was delayed. Solomos (1798-1857), a champion of demotic, also had to wait for his influence to be felt. This delay is attributable chiefly to two factors: linguistic purism, and Phanariot conservatism. Purism, a well-meaning attempt to bridge Greece's linguistic divisions, was largely the work of Adamantios Korais (1748-1833), who invented a "puristic" language (the *katharevousa*) by adapting the vocabulary of demotic to erudite grammar and syntax. This artificial instrument became the official language of the Greek state.

The learned Phanariots who settled in Athens after the Greek Revolution espoused the puristic idiom. The poets among these conservative aristocrats, descendants of the privileged Greeks who had occupied the Phanar region of Istanbul under the sultan, constituted the Old Athenian School, which deadened Greek intellectual life for 50 years with its archaizing language, pomposity, and extreme romanticism. Nevertheless, the growth of Greek literature was encouraged by such factors as the demotic orientation of the Ionian poets who came to Athens after the islands were joined to Greece (1863), the folkloristic researches of Nikolaos Politis, and the strengthening of the middle class. At the turn of the century, the works of Kostis PALAMAS made Solomos's hopes for demotic a reality. Yannis Psycharis's satirical *To taxidi mou* (1888; My Journey) stimulated the decisive turn toward the demotic, as did Alexandros Pallis's translation of Homer's *Iliad* in 1904.

Constantine CAVAFY was also writing at this time, but in Alexandria, not Greece. The antipode of both Palamas and Solomos in both sensibility and linguistic idiom, Cavafy brought to an end the mixed tradition to which he belonged, while opening new paths of expression for later poets who, like him, had experienced the decline of cherished values.

Palamas and his circle formed the New Athenian School. These poets, besides winning the battle for the use of demotic in poetry, enabled modern Greek letters to assimilate European fashions such as symbolism and Parnassianism while remaining clearly Greek in character. Those poets who reached maturity in the decade 1900-10, and who therefore began to write demotic poetry with the aid of linguistic precedents, were able to advance further in both the aesthetic and ideological spheres. After 1900 the dominant ideological trends were romantic adulation of Greece, Nietzschean worship of power (*see* Friedrich NIETZSCHE), and (after 1917) Marxian socialism. The great jolt to national life caused by the unsuccessful war against Turkey in 1897 and the impasse of the still weak bourgeoisie encouraged these concerns.

The most significant poets of the generation that reached maturity at the beginning of the 20th century are Angelos SIKELIANOS, Nikos KAZANTZAKIS, and Kostas VARNALIS. A secondary figure is Apostolos Melachrinos (1883-1950), a symbolist who attempted to fuse the traditions of Byzantium with the pantheistic mysticism of ancient Greece, and who introduced to Greek letters the theories of Stéphane MALLARMÉ, Henri BREMOND, and Paul VALÉRY. Other poets of note are Myrtiotissa, pseud. of Theoni Drakopoulou (1885-1968); Thrasyvoulos Stavrou (1886-), also a distinguished translator; Fotos Yiofyllis (1887-); and Romos Filyras (1889-1942).

The poets of the period 1910-30 offer a great variety of artistic orientations and intellectual concerns, but they lack the strong faith of their predecessors. The ideals of demoticism and Greekness grew less intense after the Balkan victories of 1912-13. World War I, the schism between Premier Eleutherios Venizelos and King Constantine I, and finally the Asia Minor Disaster of 1922—which brought Greece's irredentist foreign policy in Asia Minor to an abrupt and catastrophic end involving the loss of Anatolia and of any hope to reoccupy Constantinople, as well as burdening an already struggling Greece with over one million refugees—caused disintegration, a spirit of cosmopolitan decadence, and an inclination toward subjectivism and despair. Kostas KARIOTAKIS expressed his despondency in elegaic verse filled with sarcasm. His paradigmatic suicide in 1928 helped create a fashionable but superficial cult of "kariotakism"; not until after World War II was his influence felt more deeply, among poets who had seen all their dreams destroyed. A more lyrical poet of the 1920s was Tellos Agras (1899-1944). Agras was also a distinguished critic, the first to note his contemporaries' turn to Cavafy who, alone among the older poets, spoke to their despondent condition. Others affected by this climate of decadence were Kostas Ouranis (1890-1953), Nikos Hager Boufidis (1899-1950), Mitsos Papanikolaou (1900-43), Napoleon Lapathiotis (1889-1944), and Maria Polydouri (1902-30). An exception was Takis Papatsonis (1895-1976), who escaped pessimism through a mysticism that identified God with nature.

The all-important "Generation of 1930" renewed Greek verse by means of modern poetic technique. It was inevitable that the dismemberment of traditional literary forms in Western Europe ca. 1900-20 should have deeply affected those Greek poets who reached maturity after the Asia Minor Disaster of 1922. Greece's prostration had already been mirrored in the poetry of Kariotakis, but the following generation, distanced from the immediacy of the events, was able to view both tradition and current reality with a critical eye. Two ideological groups must be distinguished here. Writers devoted to socialism tended to be optimistic, nourished by historical reality rather than metaphysical concerns, and influenced by foreign poets such as Paul ELUARD, Vladimir MAYAKOVSKY, Pablo Neruda, and Louis ARAGON. Yannis RITSOS is the outstanding example, but Nikiforos Vrettakos (1911–), Nikos Pappas (1906–), and his wife, Rita Boumi-Pappa (1907–), are also noteworthy members of this group that considers poetry not just an aesthetic contribution but a moral one. Greek poets with a bourgeois orientation were more subjective and pessimistic; their foreign influences were figures like T. S. Eliot, Ezra Pound, and Jules Laforgue. The best of both groups, however, had this in common: while they renewed Greek poetry, they did not cut themselves off from tradition. Ritsos, Seferis, and Odysseas ELYTIS, winner of the 1979 Nobel Prize for Literature, are the most significant figures in this renewal, but credit also belongs to a striking experimentalist, Andreas Embirikos (1901–75), who introduced André BRETON's surrealistic mode of automatic writing to Greek poetry with his *Ypsikaminos* (Blast Furnace) in 1935. Another pioneering surrealist, Nikos Engonopoulos (1910–), is best known for his *Boliver,* inspired by Greece's struggle against the Axis Powers. Nikos Gatsos (1915–) is part of this group even though his sole work, *Amorgos,* appeared in the 1940s. In this work, Gatsos attempted to renew surrealism by inoculating it with Greek folk song, an experiment that underscores surrealism's inability to uproot Greek poetry from its traditions, and that brings us back to the road first opened by Seferis and later extended by Elytis and Ritsos: renewal based not on the denial of tradition but on its creative assimilation. Other poets, like Dimitrios I. Antoniou (1906–), Alexandros Baras (1906–), and Alexandros Matsas (1911–69) followed the same road, each in his own way. Yet some, like Ioannis M. Panagiotopoulos (1901–), remained basically melancholy, while others—Giorgos Sarandaris (1908–41), for example—retained an idealistic faith in mankind.

Only a very few poets of this generation have remained isolated. These seek their deliverance in contemporary psychology or existentialism. Melissanthi, pseud. of Hebe Skanthalaki (1910–), dwells on sin, guilt, love, and the relationship between life and death. An obsession with death is also present in the poetry of Giorgos Vafopoulos (1903–) and Aris Diktaios (1919–).

These same existentialist quests are intensified in the works of various poets who began publishing in the 1940s and 1950s. The wars, social upheavals, and passionate ideological clashes that these poets experienced in their formative years enter their work sometimes as faith, sometimes as disillusion and doubt. Most of them live in Salonika, where a school was developed under the leadership of Giorgos Themelis (1900–76), who considered poetry a "method of self-knowledge." For Zoi Karelli (1901–), poetry represents a struggle between silence and expression. Like Themelis and Karelli, Nikos Pendzikis (1908–) and Eleni Vakalo (1921–) articulate the chagrin of their isolated selves in the belief that they speak for isolated man. Yet they remain essentially subjective even when they are filled with love for "the other."

This isolation is not characteristic of poets who dwell on the political consequences of World War II and the ensuing Civil War. Their work is optimistic and polemical, vibrant with the heroic spirit of the Resistance. Representative figures are Tasos Leivaditis (1922–), Mitsos Lygizos (1912–), Christos Koulouris (1924–), and Giorgos

Gavalas (1922–). This same spirit continues in the robust verse of Dimitris Christodoulou (1924–), which also foreshadows later struggles for peace. But the chief emotions flooding Resistance poetry, especially that of the 1950s, are nostalgia for the 1940s, the heroic decade of occupation followed by the Civil War, bitterness at the defeat of Greek radicalism, wrath against conformist tendencies within its ranks, and fierce pride in its battles for freedom. These emotions are evident in the poetry of Aris Alexandrou (1922–78), Giorgos Sarandis (1920–), Thanasis Kostavaras (1932–), Kleitos Kyrou (1921–), Dimitris Doukaris (1925–), Titos Patrikios (1928–), and Michalis Katsaros (1921–). The most significant poet of this period is Manolis Anagnostakis (1925–), in whom the pain of defeat and disappointment has nurtured an existentialist anguish characterized by fear, not of death itself, but of an improper death concluding a wasted life.

Still another group of poets writes a kind of social poetry devoid of specific political nuance. Kriton Athanasoulis (1917–79) and Takis Sinopoulos (1917–79) are examples of this group, the latter employing a neosurrealistic mode to convey his vision of our fragmented world. Nikos Karouzos (1926–) is entirely individualistic. A writer of religious verse filled with popular color, he projects a humanistic Christianity dwelling not on an abstract God but on Christ and Saint Paul. This generation also has its share of exiles. Andonis Decavalles (1920–) evokes isolation and nostalgia; Nikos Spanias (1924–) reacts with bitter anger to the inhumanity of contemporary life; Petros Andaios (1920–), a political refugee in Moscow, writes revolutionary verse filled with the yearning for return.

For those poets who began to publish in the 1960s, the Resistance and Civil War were not personal experiences. But the struggle for democracy during the colonels' dictatorship (1967–74) constituted a new resistance that showed these poets their kinship with earlier writers such as Ritsos. At the same time, their aesthetic sophistication helped them to assimilate the teachings of Seferis and Elytis. Greece's increased involvement with the outside enabled this generation to feel a close kinship with world poetry, yet the search for a foundation amid modern confusion also brought it back to the folk songs and other traditional roots of Greek verse.

Modern Greek prose must take second place to poetry. Although many novelists have been as talented as the poets, the need after 1900 to apply to prose a literary demotic that had been developed for poetry led certain writers into a rhetorical lyricism often inappropriate for the novel. The 19th-century treatment of peasant mores (the Greek "ethographic" novel or short story) survived into the 20th century in the work of Giorgios Drosinis, Ioannis Kondylakis, Yannis Vlachoyannis, Andreas Karkavitsas, Alexandros Papadiamandis, Kostas Hatzopoulos, and Kostas Theotokis. But migration to the cities had begun to fashion a new way of life in Greece, and this literary form could not longer flourish. As early as the 1890s a new kind of fiction appeared, the city-novel, a subgenre reflecting the egocentricity and domesticity of the bourgeoisie, the socialistic leanings of the workers, and the coming of industrial civilization. Yet the city-novel absorbed these influences only superficially, since Greek prose writers were unable to comprehend the complexity of this transitional period, perhaps because they still looked with nostalgia to the villages where they had been raised. An example of the city-novelists is Grigorios Xenopoulos (1867–1951), whose early works are ethographic and idyllic, but who subsequently attempted, under the influence of Honoré de Balzac, Charles Dickens, and Emile ZOLA, to paint great canvases of urban life. Pavlos Nirvanas (1866–1937) treated the plight of the peasants who had moved to Athens; Dionysios Kokkinos (1884–1967) described fashionable society; and Kostas Paroritis (1878–1931) depicted the poor struggling for survival. The numerous realistic vignettes of Demosthenes Voutyras (1871–1958) capture the despair of the unemployed as they sit in neighborhood taverns. The city-novelists of this period, however, are important chiefly as precursors of the more polished artists of the 1930s who pointed Greek prose in the direction that it still follows today.

Many of these new novelists were not raised in idyllic villages. Typically, they grew up in the decade of uninterrupted warfare (1912–22) and in the ideological vacuum of subsequent years. Renouncing ethography entirely, they aspired to capture the complexities of Greek life in large novels of synthetic understanding. To be sure, one group still took its impetus from the "outdoor Greece" of the ethographic tradition and considered urban life antithetical to the Greek spirit. The most significant figures in this group are Stratis MYRIVILIS and, to some extent, Kazantzakis. Others, such as Fotis Kondoglou (1895–1965), Stratis Doukas (1895–), Tatiana Stavrou (1899–), and especially Ilias Venezis (1901–73), all Anatolians deprived of their ancestral soil, brought new perspectives to Greek fiction. Venezis's *To noumero 31328* (1931; Number 31328) describes the horrible life of prisoners of war. His *Galini* (1939; Serenity) depicts the attempts of Anatolian refugees to reestablish themselves in Greece, while his *Aioliki yi* (1943; Eng. tr., *Aeolia*, 1949; *Beyond the Aegean*, 1956) returns with nostalgia to the author's childhood in a land forever lost. Similarly nostalgic is Pandelis Prevelakis (1909–), whose *Chroniko mias politeias* (1933; Chronicle of a City) recreates the author's birthplace in Crete as it existed ca. 1910–20. Prevelakis followed this work with a series of historical novels dealing with the crucial political eras of modern Crete, and later with works focusing on the individual and his existential angst, an example being *Ilios tou thanatou* (1959; Eng. tr., *The Sun of Death*, 1965).

A second group of the new generation continued the city-novel, making sure, however, that it ceased to be merely ethographic romance in urban disguise. This group divided along ideological lines. Petros Pikros (1900–57), Nikos Katiforis (1903–68), Galateia Kazantzaki (1886–1962), Vasos Daskalakis (1899–1944), and Menelaos Loudemis (1912–76) observed Greek society through the prism of socialism. Of those writers who espoused bourgeois liberalism, Pavlos Floros (1897–), Angelos Terzakis (1907–79), Michalis Karagatsis (1908–60), Thrasos Kastanakis (1901–67), Lilika Nakou (1905–), and Thanasis Petsalis (1904–) are noteworthy, while Giorgos Theotokas (1905–66) is the most representative. His essay *Elefthero pnevma* (1929; Free Spirit) provided a manifesto for liberals disgusted with Greek backwardness, and his huge didactic novel *Argo* (1933–36; Eng. tr., 1951) attempted to create a panorama of Greek social and political life after World War I. Theotokas's greatest gift to Greek culture, however, was his scorn of fanaticism. He remained continually open to all ideas, thus exemplifying the intellectual's responsibility. But the most significant city-novelist of the "Generation of 1930" is Kosmas Politis (1888–1974), whose diverse works treat such subjects as the agonies of adolescence, in *Eroica* (1938), communism versus bourgeois sophistication, in *Treis ylnaikes* (1943; Three Women); life under the German occupation, in *I koromilia* (1959; The Plum Tree); and, in his masterpiece, *Stou Hadzifrangou* (1963; At Hadzifrangos's), Smyrna before and during the Asia Minor Disaster.

In the 1940s—the black years of the occupation and two civil wars—many established writers (and even some young ones) retreated nostalgically to themes of village life or maritime adventures, or focused on the family. After 1950, however, a fiercely ideological naturalism developed, as well as a literature of rage, alienation, and despair. Although the career of Kazantzakis began in 1906, as a novelist he bridges the 1940s and 1950s, his appeal deriving precisely from rage tempered by nostalgic evocation of peasant simplicity. Sea adventures occupied both Yannis Manglis (1909–), who drew on his own experiences as a sponge merchant, and Eva Vlami (1914–74), the daughter of a sea captain. The novel of family life was cultivated by Galatia Sarandi (1920–) and Margarita Liberaki (1912–). Liberaki's *O allos Alexandros* (1950; Eng. tr., *The Other Alexander*, 1959) shows this "private" genre modulating into an examination of war's alienating effect upon the individual.

Of the openly ideological writers, Stratis Tsirkas (1911–) has emerged as the most gifted of the leftists; his ambitious trilogy *Akyvernites politeies* (1960–65; Eng. tr., *Drifting Cities*, 1974) traces the machinations of the Greek government in exile (ca. 1940–45) with an artistry rare in the Greek novel. Others extolling the Resistance are Zisis Skaros (1917–), Dimitris Hatzis (1913–), Sotiris Patatzis (1917–), and Yannis Goudelis (1921–). Prose works biased against the Resistance are rarer. In *Poliorkia* (1953; Siege) by Alexandros Kotzias (1926–), for example, the hero is a nationalist killed by Communist foes. Similar events viewed from a comparable vantage point occupy the early work of Rodis Roufos (1924–72), who emerged in the mid-1960s as a liberal rationalist in the style of Giorgos Theotokas. In the well-known *Ta dontia tis mylopetras* (1955; The Teeth of the Millstone) by Nikos Kasdaglis (1928–), the adherents of both factions are shown to be simultaneously the teeth and the victims of a directionless millstone of fear and hatred that reduces men to the status of hunted animals. Kasdaglis's subsequent work reinforces this extreme cynicism, an attitude completely at odds with the idealism of the Resistance.

The two legacies of the 1950s, rage and cynicism, come together in Vasilis Vassilikos (1934–), whose Kafkaesque (*see* Franz KAFKA) trilogy *To fyllo, to pigadi, t'angeliasma* (1961; Eng. tr., *The Plant, the Well, the Angel*, 1964) begins with idealistic aspirations, descends (in *The Well*) into a denial of them, and ascends again to "heaven" in order to view bourgeois society with bitter sarcasm. In *Z* (1966; Eng. tr., 1968), Vassilikos uses "objective" reportage to bridle his furor against the rightist faction. An exception to the dominant mode of cynicism and rage is Andonis Samarakis (1919–), whose "detective story" *To lathos* (1965; Eng. tr., *The Flaw*, 1969) condemns a totalitarian regime whose mistake it is to undervalue the human heart.

Greek drama, revived in Crete ca. 1580–1660, began to flourish again in Athens 300 years later. In between, if we exempt the "shadow theater" (Karaghiozis) that developed during the Turkish occupation, there were only a few scattered texts. But from roughly 1890 onward, demoticism's energizing effect produced in Greece, if not another renaissance, at least a great amount of theatrical activity. Pandelis Horn (1881–1941) and Dimitris Bogris (1890–1964) transferred the ethographic mode to the stage; Palamas wrote his only play, *Trisevgeni* (1903; Eng. tr., *Royal Blossom or Trisevyene*, 1923), for the "New Stage" founded by Konstantinos Christomanos (1867–1911) in 1901; Spyros Melas (1883–1966), who was influenced by Henrik IBSEN and Nietzsche, composed sociological, historical, and symbolist dramas; Grigorios Xenopoulos captured the psychological traits of Athens's developing bourgeoisie; Kazantzakis and, later, Sikelianos cultivated the symbolical/mythological mode of verse drama. The National Theater was established in 1930 and Karolos Koun's all-important Art Theater in 1942. In the 1930s, although Xenopoulos, Horn, Bogris, and Melas dominated at first, Vasilis Rotas (1889–1977), Angelos Terzakis, Nikos Katiforis, and Alekos Lidorikis (1907–) attempted to escape not only ethography but also the mimickry of European models. The polite comedies of Dimitris Psathas (1907–) provided relief during the occupation and civil wars. In the 1950s, Iakovos Kambanellis (1922–) and other young playwrights brought realism back to the stage, while the novelists Prevelakis, Theotokas, and Kosmas Politis enriched the theater with historical dramas.

Most recently, Greek playwrights have tended to renounce traditional subjects and forms in an attempt to become completely modern and "European." Dimitris Kehaidis, Vasilis Ziogas, and Kostas Mourselas (1930–) are representative figures. Seen as a whole over the past 80 years, drama in Greece has displayed continuous vitality, although it has fallen short of the novel and especially of poetry, the one genre that enjoyed a true rebirth in the 20th century.

See: D. C. Hesseling, *Histoire de la littérature grecque moderne* (1924); A. Mirambel, *La Littérature grecque moderne* (1953); P. Sherrard, *The Marble Threshing Floor* (1956); B. Knös, *L'Histoire de la littérature neo-grecque: la période jusqu'en 1821* (1962); G. Sideris, "The Playwrights of the Modern Greek Theatre," *Thespis* 2–3 (1965): 10–43; M. Gianos, ed., *Introduction to Modern Greek Literature: An Anthology of Fiction, Drama and Poetry* (1969); B. Lavagnini, *La letteratura neoellenica* (3d ed., 1969); R. Dalven, tr., *Modern Greek Poetry* (1971); M. Vitti, *Storia della letteratura neogreca* (1971); C. T. Dimaras, *A History of Modern Greek Literature*, tr. by M. P. Gianos (1972); E. Keeley and P. Bien, eds., *Modern Greek Writers* (1972); K. Friar, ed., *Modern Greek Poetry: From Cavafis to Elytis* (1973); L. Politis, *A History of Modern Greek Literature*, tr. R. Liddell (1973); *Byzantine and Modern Greek Studies* (1975–).

C.A.

Green, Julien (1900–), French novelist, was born in Paris to American parents residing there. His father was from Virginia and his mother from Georgia. Obsessed by the mysteries of remote ancestral influences and by the possibility of reincarnation, Green thought he discovered in his sensibility traces of Irish blood (visionary mysticism), of Scottish ancestry ("the thorn of Puritanism" and the haunting of predestination), and his American legacy. Indeed, he shared with Edgar Allan Poe, Herman Melville, Nathaniel Hawthorne, and William Faulkner an obsession with evil, violence, and "the power of blackness." Green preferred French to English as the language in which he would write, in part because he sought through it a balancing force to reconcile his conflicting tendencies. He was the last of seven children, five of them girls, all brought up in the nostalgic cult of the American South. After his schooling in a Paris lycée, and then two years at the University of Virginia (1919–21), he followed his vocation as a novelist in the French tradition inherited from Honoré de Balzac (1799–1850). His first novel, *Mont-Cinère* (1926; Eng. tr., *Avarice House*, 1927), was laid in an unreal, melodramatic American setting. He returned to Virginia for the scene and the characters of at least two others of his best novels: *Moïra* (1950; Eng. tr., 1951), set in Charlottesville and probably his masterpiece, "a long scream of hatred of the flesh" as Green described it, and again in *Chaque homme dans sa nuit* (1960; Eng. tr., *Each in His Darkness*, 1962), a weird

story of a young Catholic athirst for purity, yet torn by homosexual urges. The most revealing among his several volumes of personal reminiscences—*Partir* (1963; Leaving) and *Terre lointaine* (1966; Distant Land)—are also those in which he conjures up the handsome young men of Charlottesville, to whom he was kept from declaring his feelings through a morbid shyness and scruples of remorse. The seven volumes of his *Journal* (1928–58) offer a picture of the wild dreams, self-doubts, and harrying fears of the tormented diarist, but they also teem with insightful remarks on writers and painters of the past.

Green is an authentic novelist in the 19th-century French tradition. He never indulges in fantasy, levity, or humor, nor does he play with ideas or experiment with form, as other novelists from Anatole FRANCE to André GIDE have done. Green is desparately serious, like a man who had to invent in fiction anguished sinners and victims of morbid fear in order not to be stifled by his own obsessions. He is fascinated both by the force of the sexual instinct and by male beauty, and full of detestation for those uncontrollable forces. He is closer to Anglo-Saxon novelists than to the French when he repeatedly echoes the cry of D. H. Lawrence: "We are crucified by sex." The most haunting among his novels of violence laid in France are *Adrienne Mesurat* (1927; Eng. tr., *The Closed Garden*, 1928), *Léviathan* (1929; Eng. tr., *The Dark Journey*, 1929), *Minuit* (1936; Eng. tr., *Midnight*, 1936), and *L'Autre* (1971; Eng. tr., *The Other One*, 1973). Green's "other" is the person loved, devoured by the avid would-be ravisher, and also the supernatural force (the Devil or God) acting through the tragic tormentors. Unconcerned with the philosophical or ethical fiction of the existentialists or with the experiments and contrived ambiguities of the "new novelists" of 1960–75 (*see* FRENCH LITERATURE), Green has remained faithful to a well-knit plot, and to characters who are the victims of their sensual greed, of panicky fear, and of their own urges for self-destruction. His style is neither poetical nor colorful, but the author succeeds in forcing upon his readers a half-willing suspension of disbelief. He is closest to Georges BERNANOS and François MAURIAC among his French contemporaries, to Graham Greene and, with less trickery, to Iris Murdoch among the British novelists. In 1971, after a decree that allowed him to retain his American nationality and yet to be considered as a French citizen, he became the first non-French writer to be elected (unanimously) to the Académie Française.

See: M. Eigeldinger, *Julien Green ou la tentation de l'irréel* (1947); S. Stokes, *Green and the Thorn of Puritanism* (1955); J. Semolué, *Green ou l'obsession du mal* (1964); R. de Saint Jean, *Green par lui-même* (1967); J. Petit, *Julien Green* (1969).

H.P.

Grieg, Nordahl (1902–43), Norwegian poet, dramatist, and novelist, was born in Bergen to a prominent family. By the age of 22 he had worked as a seaman and journalist, studied at Oxford, completed his degree in Norway with a thesis on Ruyard Kipling, and published both a collection of poetry, *Rundt Kap det Gode Haab* (1922; Around the Cape of Good Hope), and a realistic novel of life at sea, *Skibet gaar videre* (1924; Eng. tr., *The Ship Sails On*, 1927). All of Grieg's works from the 1920s evince a deep empathy for human suffering, a growing social and political awareness, and a strong love of country. In addition to the works mentioned above, these include an account of the Chinese civil war, *Kinesiske dager* (1927; Chinese Days); two plays, *En ung mans kjærlighet* (1927; A Young Man's Love) and *Barrabas* (1927); and two collections of poetry, *Stene i strømmen* (1925; Stones in the Stream) and *Norge i våre hjerter* (1929; Norway in Our Hearts).

The political ferment of the 1930s forced Grieg to confront the conflict between his pacifist leanings and the necessity of force. The play *Barrabas* and *De unge døde* (1932; The Young Dead), an eloquent collection of essays on John Keats, Percy Bysshe Shelley, Lord Byron, and three British poets killed in World War I, provide insights into his struggle. It was, however, Grieg's opposition to Nazism and, more particularly, his espousal of Marxism during a visit to the USSR (1933–35) that provided the external focus and ideological thrust of his major works in the 1930s. During this decade he wrote the plays *Vår ære og vår makt* (1935; Our Honor and Our Might) and *Nederlaget* (1937; Eng. tr., *The Defeat*, 1944), and *Ung må verden ennu være* (1938; But the World Must Yet Be Young), a sweeping novel that encompasses the major political and ideological events of the period while displaying Grieg's faith in the Soviet experiment.

Grieg took an active part in World War II as a soldier and correspondent. Two posthumous collections, *Flagget* (1945; The Flag) and *Friheten* (1943; Eng. tr., *All That is Mine Demand*, 1944), reflect the intensity of his feelings for Norway and for peace. Grieg's wartime activities and his death in an air attack on Germany imparted an aura of importance to his work that subsequent criticism has not sustained. Nevertheless, he remains an important writer of his generation.

See: J. Mjöberg, *Nordahl Grieg* (1947); K. Egeland, *Nordahl Grieg* (1953); F. Haslund, *Nordahl Grieg* (1962).

A.G.A.

Grimm, Hans (1875–1959), German novelist, short-story writer, and essayist, was born in Wiesbaden. He is known not so much for his creative writing—the longer short story—as for his novel *Volk ohne Raum* (1926; A People without Space). The title became a new designation for the German action and a Nazi slogan offering the long-sought "political synthesis." Despite its 1,352 pages and the measured tempo of its style, which seems to echo the plodding feet of the German peasant and emigrant Cornelius Friebott, despite the epic retardation and the repetition of both narrative and conversational formulas, the novel gripped the imagination of German readers, and more than 1 million copies were sold between its appearance in 1926 and the outbreak of World War II in 1939. Set in Africa, *Volk ohne Raum* is one of the most harrowingly painful fictionalized records ever penned. It depicts the senseless suffering of protagonists who are mere struggling victims of a relentless fate, patiently enduring a passion without any scheme of redemption. The same theme is treated, in fact with greater objectivity, conciseness, and artistry, in an earlier work that was perhaps Grimm's best, *Die Olewagen Saga* (1918; The Olewagen Saga).

Prior to the success of his novel, Grimm from 1895 to 1910 had been a merchant apprentice in England and a clerk and independent merchant in Cape Colony. In 1910 he returned to Germany to become a writer. He studied political economy in Munich, fought in World War I, and then settled at Lippoldsberg on the Weser.

His works fall into two distinct groups, the creative writing of the artist and the political writing of the patriot. To the latter category belong, besides the political novel *Volk ohne Raum*, documentary volumes dealing with the sufferings and injustices inflicted on the South African Germans during and after World War I.

His purely creative writing consists of the 30-odd stories that make up the volumes *Südafrikanische Novellen* (1913; South African Novellas), *Der Gang durch den Sand* (1916; The Walk through the Sand), *Der Richter in der Karu* (1930; The Judge in the Caru), and *Lüderitzland* (1934).

See: G. K. Brand, "Hans Grimm," *DnL* 27 (1926): 529–37; G. H. Danton, "Hans Grimm's *Volk ohne Raum*," *Monatshefte* 27 (1935): 33–43; R. T. House, "The South African Stories of Hans Grimm," *AGR* 6 (1939): 16–17, 34; H. Grimm, *Suchen und Hoffen: aus Meinem Leben 1928–1934* (1960). J.F.G. rev. A.L.W.

Grin, Aleksandr, pseud. of Aleksandr Stepanovich Grinevsky (1880–1932), Russian novelist and short-story writer, wrote numerous adventure stories that now enjoy great popularity within the Soviet Union. Grin left his home in Vyatka (now Kirov) before his 16th birthday to seek his fortune in Odessa. He dreamed of becoming a sailor and visiting foreign lands, but his only trip abroad was to Alexandria. After working at a number of jobs throughout Russia and after deserting the army, he joined the Socialist Revolutionaries and was arrested and exiled several times. His literary career began in 1906 when he moved to Petersburg, where he lived for many years. In 1924, he settled for good in his beloved Crimea. Through such works as *Alye parusa* (1923; Eng. tr., *Scarlet Sails*, 1967), *Blistayushchiy mir* (1923; The Radiant World), and *Begushchaya po volnam* (1928; She Who Runs on the Waves), Grin achieved some recognition in the 1920s but his current reputation dates only from 1956, when his works were once again widely published.

Adhering to none of the literary movements of his time, Grin is something of an anomaly in Russian literature. While there is little to distinguish his first writings from the typical realistic prose of the period, he established a manner very much his own as early as the publication of "Ostrov Reno" (1909; Reno Island) and continued to refine it in subsequent years. Grin's work shows the influence of Rudyard Kipling and Robert Louis Stevenson, in addition to that of his childhood reading, which included Thomas Mayne Reid, James Fenimore Cooper, Edgar Allan Poe, and Arthur Conan Doyle, among others. Yet Grin is not quite like any of these writers. His stories take place in a setting of his own invention, called "Grinlandiya" by the critic Kornely Zelinsky, and the same cities—Liss, Zurbagan, Gel-Gyu—reappear in different works. The heroes of these exotic tales are strong individuals, firm in the knowledge of their own righteousness, and in general they lead lives of the kind that Grin apparently wanted for himself. The clear-cut dichotomy between good and evil invokes the world of the fairy tale, as do occasional elements of the fantastic (such as the flying man in *Blistayushchiy mir*). Grin lacked the sophistication of a truly first-rate writer, but the same qualities that have endeared him to children in the Soviet Union have made him a favorite of many adults as well.

See: V. Kovsky, *Romanticheskiy mir Aleksandra Grina* (1969); L. Mikhaylova, *Aleksandr Grin* (1972); N. Luker, *Alexander Grin* (1973); B. Scherr, "The Literary Development of Aleksandr Grin," Ph.D. Dissertation, University of Chicago (1973). B.P.S.

Grochowiak, Stanisław (1934–76), Polish poet, novelist, short-story writer, and playwright, was born in Leszno Wielkopolskie and died in Warsaw. While studying Polish philology at the universities in Poznań and Wrocław, he made his poetic debut in literary periodicals. In 1956 his first books appeared: *Plebania z magnoliami* (The Presbytery with Magnolias), a novel, and *Ballada rycerska* (A Chivalrous Ballad), a collection of poems. He belonged to a circle influenced by Catholic thinking. The roots of Grochowiak's poetry can be found in baroque literature,

Charles BAUDELAIRE, the surrealists, and Cyprian NOR-WID. Because of his fascination with ugliness, the critics gave Grochowiak's poetry the label "turpism" for the Latin word for ugly. However, his sharp irony, parodistic tone, and brutal images are not intended for shocking effects but rather for a profound humanistic protest against all the sadness and suffering in human life. The volumes of poetry that followed are *Menuet z pogrzeba-czem* (1958; Minuet with a Poker), *Rozbieranie do snu* (1959; Undressing for Sleep), *Agresty* (1963; Gooseber-ries), *Kanon* (1965; Canon), *Nie było lata* (1969; There was No Summer), and *Polowanie na cietrzewie* (1972; Hunting the Black Grouse). Grochowiak also wrote two novels: *Trismus* (1963) and *Karabiny* (1965; Rifles), as well as a volume of short stories, *Lamentnice* (1958; The Lamenting Women). As a playwright, Grochowiak is a representative of the most recent development in dra-maturgy: radio and television drama. His *Partita na in-strument drewniany* (Partita for a Woodwind Instrument) won a prize in Italy. Most of his plays are collected in the volume *Dialogi* (1975; Dialogues). His plays are a continuation of the Polish antinaturalistic trend in theater.

See: *Słownik współczesnych pisarzy polskich*, series II, vol. 1 (1977), pp. 301–11.   A.Z.

Grosjean, Jean (1912–), French poet and translator, was born in Paris and spent his youth in eastern France. Gros-jean studied theology, worked in a factory and, while traveling extensively in the Middle East in 1936–37, learned Arabic, Aramaic, and Hebrew. He became a priest in 1939 and spent two years in a stalag in Germany during World War II. Thanks to André MALRAUX, Gros-jean's *Terre du temps* (Earth of Our Time) was published in 1946. In 1950, Grosjean left the Church. In 1967, he became, with Jean PAULHAN and Marcel ARLAND, one of the leading forces of the *Nouvelle Revue française*.

Grosjean has published many volumes of poetry and several outstanding translations, including *Hypostases* (1950); *Le Livre du juste* (1952; The Book of the Just); *Les Prophètes* (1955), translated from the Hebrew; *Aus-trasie* (1960), a volume of short prose poems about birds, plants, and places, reminiscent of Jean FOLLAIN; *Apoc-alypse* (1962); *Elégies* (1967); and *La Gloire* (1969; The Glory). His recent works include *La Nuit de Saül* (1971; Saul's Night) and *Le Messie* (1974; The Messiah). Gros-jean has also translated the New Testament and the Koran into French.

Grosjean belongs to no school. He believes in God and is deeply in touch with Judaism and Islam, as well as Christianity. In certain respects, he can be compared to Paul CLAUDEL. Grojean's poetry—sacred, mystic, and prophetic—possesses a grandeur and a lyricism that re-calls the Song of Solomon.   J.-C.M.

Grossman, Vasily Semyonovich (1905–64), Russian nov-elist, was born in Berdichev and educated at the Institute of Physics and Mathematics in Moscow. He worked as a chemical engineer in the Donbas region and started writing at the beginning of the 1930s. Up to World War II the proletarian theme predominated in his works, no-tably in *Stepan Kolchugin* (1937–40), a novel in four vol-umes that describes the advance of a young worker to-ward Bolshevism.

Between 1941 and 1945 Grossman frequently visited the front as a correspondent for the Red Army newspaper *Krasnaya zvezda*. His newspaper reports served as the foundation for *Narod bessmerten* (1942; Eng. trs., *The People Immortal*, 1943, *No Beautiful Nights*, 1944), the first Soviet novel about World War II, which brought him great fame.

Grossman's difficulties began in 1946. In the issue of *Znamya* for July, the month before the Central Committee of the Community Party passed the resolution launching what has since come to be known as the period of Zhda-nov reaction, Grossman published *Yesli verit pifagore-ytsam* (If We Are to Believe the Pythagoreans), a play he had written before the war on the theme of the eternal return. The play was immediately attacked for "ideolog-ical errors," and it has never been republished or staged in the Soviet Union. In his novel *Za pravoye delo* (1952; For A Just Cause), in which he strove to keep as close as possible to the truth about the war, Grossman stirred up a storm of protest because he deviated from the usual chauvinistic stereotypes. (In addition, Grossman was a Jew, and his book came out at the worst period of Stalinist anit-Semitism.)

Grossman's situation did not improve with the ascent to power of Nikita Khrushchov. In 1961 the KGB confis-cated the manuscript of his "Zhizn i sudba" (Life and Fate), a sequel to *Za pravoye delo* in which he touched on the theme of concentration camps. This was the first case in the post-Stalinist USSR of a police raid with "literary" objectives—a procedure that was to be widely used in the future. Grossman's manuscript was long con-sidered lost, but a copy turned up years later, and ex-cerpts have appeared in the émigré journal *Kontinent*.

Samizdat was to save another novel on the same theme: *Vsyo techot* (1970; Eng. tr., *Forever Flowing*, 1972), which has circulated widely abroad. Presented as the memoirs of a survivor of the prison camps and written in a poignant spirit of humanity, this novel portrays various aspects of the world of the labor camps and reveals Gross-man as in many respects the forerunner of the Aleksandr SOLZHENITSYN who wrote *The Gulag Archipelago*. For Grossman too Stalinism existed before Iosif Stalin him-self, and his subtle and perceptive analysis of Vladimir Lenin appears even more convincing than Solzhenitsyn's indictment.   J.Ca.

Grosso, Alfonso (1928–), Spanish novelist, was born in Seville. In his first novel, *La Zanja* (1961; The Trench), Grosso conceives of literature as an instrument of social change. He clearly misreads the objectivism of Rafael SÁNCHEZ FERLOSIO's influential novel *El Jarama* (1956), turning it into deliberate tendentiousness. In his novel *Un cielo difícilmente azul* (1961; A Stubbornly Blue Sky), Grosso bears witness to rural poverty, and in a travel book written with Armando LÓPEZ SALINAS, *Por el río abajo* (1966; Down the River), he denounces the large landholders of Andalusia. In *Testa de copo* (1963; Cot-tonhead) and *El capirote* (1964; The Hood), Grosso con-demns the exploitation of the Andalusian proletariat. In 1962 he published *Germinal y otros relatos* (Germinal and Other Stories), a collection of his early narratives.

Two factors compelled Grosso to abandon this kind of realism, however, and to manifest his creative genius: the publication of Luis MARTÍN-SANTOS's novel *Tiempo de silencio* (1962) and the new narratives coming out of Latin America. *Inés Just Coming* (1968), a novel about the Cuban revolution, *Guarnición de silla* (1970; Cavalry Troop), and *Florido Mayo* (1973; Flowery May), a col-lection of baroque Andalusian narratives with epic and mythical overtones reminiscent of William Faulkner and James Joyce, are transitional works. At present, Grosso is more attracted by stylistic concerns than by politics. Having concluded that literature cannot alter reality, he has opted for an openly aestheticist stance. In keeping with this, *La buena muerte* (1976; The Good Death) is an ironic thriller that flaunts its own brilliance and reveals on every page the technical artifice, both structural and verbal, that makes a novel what it is.

See: G. Sobejano, *Novela española de nuestro tiempo* (1975), pp. 417–25; D. Villanueva, *Estructura y tiempo reducido en la novela* (1977), pp. 212–21, 299–307.

D.V.

Grubiński, Wacław (1883–1973), Polish short-story writer, novelist, playwright, and theater critic, was born in Warsaw and died in London. Grubiński's narrative prose, variously arranged in almost 10 volumes—for example, *Pocałunek* (1906; The Kiss), *Człowiek z klarnetem* (1927; Man with a Clarinet)—betrays a liking for the paradoxical incidents of human existence and displays a masterly precision of style. Almost the only longer work in this field, *Listy pogańskie* (1938; Pagan Letters), is an epistolary novel projecting Christ's time and story through the eyes of a sophisticated Roman aristocrat.

As a playwright, Grubiński belonged to the "Warsaw School," akin to the French Théâtre du Boulevard. Within this group, he represented the highest level not only thanks to his daring choice of topics and his technical skill, but also to his penetrating psychological insight and mastery of a lively, witty, paradoxical, dramatic dialogue. Characteristic examples among 10 produced and published one-act and full-length plays are *Kochankowie* (1915; Lovers) and *Niewinna grzesznica* (1926; The Innocent Sinner). Grubiński also published his memoirs *Między młotem i sierpem* (1947; Between Hammer and Sickle), about his deportation to the Soviet Union during World War II and his condemnation to death (later commuted to 10 years of imprisonment) for publishing a comedy about Lenin in 1921. They are the work of a true humanist, detached, free from self-pity, and full of quiet courage, which perhaps represents the summit of his literary achievement.

See: *Słownik współczesnych pisarzy polskich*, vol. 1 (1963), pp. 617–20.

T.T.

Grün, Max von der (1926–), West German prose writer and playwright, is the best-established and most important among West Germany's authors who deal with working-class problems. Born in Bayreuth, von der Grün worked in construction after World War II and from 1951 to 1963 as a coal miner in the Ruhr area. In 1953 he started to write about his experiences in the mines, and in 1961 he initiated the "Gruppe 61," a group of writers whose concern was the working class (*see* GERMAN LITERATURE). From the start, von der Grün did not accept literature as *l'art pour l'art* but demanded that it be a realistic, entertaining, and critical reflection of life and its environment—in his case, the life and exploitation of physical laborers.

Von der Grün's first two novels, *Männer in zweifacher Nacht* (1962; Men in a Twofold Night) and *Irrlicht und Feuer* (1963; Fantasm and Fire), describe the hard life in the darkness of the mines, and, when they became best sellers, they provoked extended controversial discussions.

Since 1964, von der Grün has lived as a free-lance writer near the coal pits in Dortmund, where most of his stories and novels take place. In *Zwei Briefe an Pospischiel* (1968; Two Letters to Pospischiel) he tied together several major topics of post-World War II German concern: the fading memories of Nazi terror, the subordination of workers in capitalism, the dependence of freedom on money. *Stellenweise Glatteis* (1973; Icy in Spots) calls for solidarity among workers. But von der Grün's characters are not puppets a la socialist realism; they are real people who seek room for more individual development

and who fight for a more humane life. Everything von der Grün writes is ammunition for this fight—his collections of short stories as well as his fascinating Middle East travelogue *Wenn der tote Rabe vom Baum fällt* (1975; When the Dead Raven Falls from the Tree), his books of literary portraits, *Menschen in Deutschland* (1973; People in Germany) and *Leben im gelobten Land* (1975; Life in the Promised Land), and his widely acclaimed television scripts.

A children's book, *Vorstadtkrokodile* (1976; Crocodiles in the Suburbs), was made into an extraordinarily successful television film. Von der Grün's autobiographicl documentary account of the Nazi years, *Wie war daas eigentlich, Kindheit und Jugend im Dritten Reich* (1979; How Was it Anyway, Childhood and Youth in the Third Reich), was followed by a novel of topical commitment, *Flächenbrand* (1979; Conflagration).

See: H. L. Arnold, ed., *Text & Kritik,* no. 45 (1975).

F.Vi.

Guareschi, Giovanni (1908–68), Italian journalist and comic novelist, was born in Fontanelle di Roccabianca near Parma. He worked as a boarding school teacher and a proofreader on a local newspaper. In 1936 he joined the staff of the humorous Milan periodical *Bertoldo* and became its editor-in-chief in 1937. During World War II Guareschi spent two years in a German prison camp. From 1945 until 1957, he was editor of the humorous Milan weekly *Candido*. During this period, Guareschi was in the forefront of the Italian political scene as a monarchist and an anti-Communist. His bitter political satire and cartoons contributed to the defeat of the Communist bloc in 1948. Nevertheless, he did not spare the new Italian republic. In *Diario clandestino* (1949; Eng. tr., *My Secret Diary, 1943–1945,* 1958), he categorized the new government as "this mock democracy of mock gentlemen." In the early 1950s, he published apocryphal letters in *Candido* that he attributed to Alcide de Gasperi, leader of the Christian Democratic Party. As a result, Guareschi was imprisoned for libel.

Guareschi's writings as a political and social satirist, his cartoons (the famous sketches in *Candido* of Communist hardliners as *trinariciuti* [endowed with three nostrils]), and his humorous novels (complete with his own illustrations) all express a rudely vigorous anti-Left world view. Indeed, from Guareschi's features in *Candido* stem the two series of novels for which he is famous, the political or Don Camillo series, and the sociodomestic or Guareschi family series. In his feature "Mondo piccolo," Guareschi portrayed the parish priest Don Camillo and the Communist mayor Peppone who, in spite of endless violent confrontations, manage to coexist handsomely in their village by the Po. His ability to reduce the complex social-political struggles of the postwar period to human dimensions won Guareschi great popularity both in Italy and abroad. The Don Camillo novels include *Mondo piccolo: Don Camillo* (1948; partial Eng. tr., *The Little World of Don Camillo,* 1950), *Don Camillo e il suo gregge* (1953; partial Eng. tr., *Don Camillo and His Flock,* 1952), *Il compagno don Camillo* (1963; Eng. tr., *Comrade Don Camillo,* 1964), and *Don Camillo e i giovani d'oggi* (1969; Eng. tr., *Don Camillo Meets the Flower Children,* 1969). In the *Candido* feature "Corrierino delle famiglie," Guareschi portrayed a topsy-turvy modern world, as seen through the antics of Giovannino, his wife Margherita, and their children Albertino and La Passionaria. He collected these features into the family novels *Zibaldino* (1948; A Medley), *Corrierino delle famiglie* (1954; Eng. tr., *My Home, Sweet Home,* 1966), and *Vita in famiglia* (1968; Eng. tr., *The Family Guareschi,* 1970). Among

Guareschi's other books are several fantasies, including *Il destino si chiama Clotilde* (1942; Eng. tr., *Duncan and Clotilda*, 1968) and *Il marito in collegio* (1943; Eng. tr., *A Husband in Boarding School*, 1967).

See: G. Casolari, "Guareschi giullare dell'oggi e di Cristo," *Letture* 25 (1970). A.M.G.

Guðmundsson, Kristmann (1902-), Icelandic novelist, was born at Þverfell in the district of Borgarfjörður. His mother's family was deeply rooted in the soil; his father was a temperamental rover. The youth of Guðmundsson was marred by lack of parental care and by sickness, yet he grew up to be a healthy boy whose optimism and enterprising nature nothing could curb. Having been a jack-of-all trades, he finally (1924) decided to go to Norway and become a writer. Two years later his first book of short stories, *Islandsk kjærlighet* (1926; Icelandic Loves), was an immediate success. Many novels and a host of short stories have appeared in Norwegian. Since 1939, Guðmundsson has lived in Iceland and written in Icelandic.

Guðmundsson is a master of the modern romance. Like no other Icelandic novelist he understands the psychology of love, especially young love, and describes it with a realism that nevertheless seems ethereally romantic. With him the spiritual and the physical aspects of love unite in harmony without the bad conscience that troubles some of the prewar writers, such as Guðmundur KAMBAN who, during the 1920s, fought a struggle of emancipation from the older ideology of love. Next to love, character interests Guðmundsson. This is especially evident in his family sagas: *Brudekjolen* (1927; Icelandic tr., *Brúðarkjóllinn*, 1933; Eng. tr., *The Bridal Gown*, 1931), *Livets morgen* (1929; Icelandic tr., *Morgunn lífsins*, 1932; Eng. tr., *Morning of Life*, 1936), *Det hellige fjell* (1932; The Holy Fell), *Jordens barn* (1934; Children of Earth), and *Gyðjan og uxinn* (1937; Eng. tr., *Winged Citadel*, 1940). The last is a historical romance from the Crete of Minoan times, but it is full of allusions to modern psychoanalysis and modern world politics. Perhaps finest of Guðmundsson's characters is the hero of *Morning of Life;* in him the heroic ideal of the sagas is once more incarnated. Not the least source of Guðmundsson's charm is his facile narrative talent, his obvious joy in telling a story. His books have been translated into many languages.

See: G. G. Hagalín, "Kristmann Guðmundsson," *Iðunn* 14 (1930): 55-70. S.E.

Guðmundsson, Tómas (1901-), Icelandic essayist and poet, was born and grew up in Grímsnes in southern Iceland, near the river Sog—an idyllic countryside that early instilled in him a sensitivity to beauty. The river and the surrounding region were later to become important symbols in his poems—not least so in his last collection of verse, *Fljótið helga* (1950; The Sacred River).

Even as a college student in Reykjavik, Guðmundsson attracted notice for poems he had composed. He matriculated in 1921, earned a degree in law from the University of Iceland in 1926, and later operated a law office in Reykjavik and worked for the Bureau of Statistics, but dedicated himself wholly to writing after 1943. He edited the literary magazine *Helgafell* (1942-55) and later another such periodical, *Nýtt Helgafell* (1956-59). He has translated several books into Icelandic, including works by Johan BORGEN, Giuseppe TOMASI DI LAMPEDUSA, and Erich Maria REMARQUE; he has also written a number of books on historical (Icelandic) and biographical subjects, among them a life of the painter Ásgrímur Jónsson.

Guðmundsson's first volume of verse, *Við sundin blá* (1925; Beside the Blue Channels), has the markings of the

new romantic life worship introduced into Icelandic poetry around 1920 through the works of Stefán frá Hvítadal and Davíð STEFÁNSSON. Most of the poems in this book concern the pleasures of youthful love, although there is often an undercurrent of nostalgia for the past—a tone of sadness that grew in intensity in Guðmundsson's later verse. On the whole, these early poems have a thoughtful and intellectual quality, and the romantic sentiment tends to be somewhat detached. The intellectual humor that was later on to play such a prominent role in his later poetry can hardly be detected in this first volume.

With *Fagra veröld* (1933; Beautiful World), Guðmundsson established himself as a mature poet. In addition, the book was a tour de force that gained him immense popularity—among other reasons because many of the poems were about Reykjavik, Iceland's still-young capital, and life there—a subject largely ignored by poets up to that time. Guðmundsson literally opened the eyes of Reykjavik residents to the beauty of their own town. *Fagra veröld* is, at the same time, a make-believe world far from the reality of economic depression and class conflicts that dominated the headlines when the book appeared. As a reward for singing its praises, the city of Reykjavik gave the poet a stipend that enabled him to travel in southern Europe; and some of the poems in his next volume, *Stjörnur vorsins* (1940; The Stars of Springtime), are developed from the experiences of that trip. Although this book has more pure lyricism in it than any other of Guðmundsson's works, it also contains poems on social concerns, such as racial bigotry and the rise of Nazism in the 1930s. The terrors of World War II, however, affected him more profoundly than any other political events, as is clearly seen in *Flótið helga,* his most pessimistic, philosophical, and religious book of verse.

Guðmundsson's poetry has in many respects a classical quality, yet it is shot through with romantic worship of beauty and nostalgic longing. His poetic forms are varied, but long lines of colloquial diction are typical for much of his work. He was fond of paradoxes, and this gives his humor an intellectual cast, but his greatest achievement is perhaps that he was the first mature poetic spokesman for Icelandic city dwellers. He adapted the traditional diction of verse to suit emerging life-styles by using an idiom close to the rhythms of colloquial speech.

See: K. Karlsson, Introduction to T. Guðmundsson, *Ljóðasafn* (1961), pp. vii–xlv. S.S.H.

Guéhenno, Jean (1890-1978), French essayist and critic, was born Marcel Guéhenno in Fougères. In *Changer la vie: mon enfance et ma jeunesse* (1961; To Change Life: My Childhood and My Youth), one of his best books, he tells the story of his childhood and adolescence spent in poverty. He had begun making a livelihood while still quite young and readied himself alone for university studies, which he completed brilliantly. He then had a distinguished university career, while attaining renown through his writings as critic and essayist.

As a scholar, Guéhenno is chiefly known for his works on the historian Jules Michelet, *L'Evangile éternel* (1927; The Eternal Gospel), and especially on Rousseau (3 vols., 1948–52; Eng. tr., *Jean-Jacques Rousseau*, 1966). Guéhenno's most profound essays are found in *Caliban parle* (1928; Caliban Speaks), where he opposes to Marxism his concept of humanism. He became deeply committed to the reformist activities of the Popular Front in the 1930s, about which he wrote in the *Journal d'un homme de quarante ans* (1934; Diary of a 40-year-old Man). During World War II he joined the Resistance. He later wrote several works about this experience, including *Dans la prison* (1944; In Jail), *Journal d'une "révolution"*

(1939; Journal of a "Revolution"), *L'Université dans la Résistance et dans la France nouvelle* (1945; The University in the Resistance and in the New France), and *Journal des années noires* (1946; Diary of the Dark Years).   J.-P.C.

Guelbenzu, José María (1944–), Spanish novelist, poet, and essayist, was born in Madrid. He has studied law and been associated with the publishing industry. His book of poetry, *Espectros, la casa antigua* (Phantoms, the Ancient House), appeared in Barcelona in 1967. Guelbenzu belongs to a new generation of Spanish writers who have rebelled against the realistic fictional interpretation of society that dominated the 1950s and 1960s. In his narrative *El Mercurio* (1968; The Mercury), the novelist skillfully manipulates language and structure to portray the intellectuals and artists of contemporary Madrid, although his main theme is the creative process. *Antifaz* (1970; Veil), based on the mystery of a love relationship, is an experiment in novelistic creation, with the complexity typical of any work written as a literary search. *El pasajero de Ultramar* (1976; The Overseas Traveler) is an elaborate analytical novel based on the love affair of a traveler in search of his identity. In this narrative, Guelbenzu achieves a cohesion of theme and style that was lacking in his previous works. *La noche en casa* (1977; The Night at Home) fictionalizes the frustration and skepticism of two characters belonging to a generation that is incapable of love.

See: J. Rodríguez Padrón, "*Antifaz,* una novela polémica," *CHA* 255 (1972): 609–17.   J.O.

Guglielminetti, Amalia (1885–1941), Italian poet, novelist, short-story writer, and playwright, was born in Turin. She rebelled against the rigid upbringing of her wealthy upper-class family and sought to develop her independence through writing. Guglielminetti was strongly influenced by the early writings of Gabriele D'ANNUNZIO and shares his tendency to blur the border between autobiographical confession and literary creation. Guglielminetti's life, reflected in her portraits of intensely passionate, intelligent women, impatient with convention and avid for strong sensations, made her a controversial figure in her own time. Today, however, she is probably best known for the love letters she exchanged with the poet Guido GOZZANO, now available in the volume *Lettere d'amore di Guido Gozzano e di Amalia Guglielminetti* (1951; Love Letters of Gozzano and Guglielminetti). Her more than 20 published works include the volumes of poetry *Le vergini folli* (1907; The Foolish Virgins) and *Le seduzioni* (1909; Seductions) and the fiction of *I volti d'amore* (1913; The Faces of Love), *Gli occhi cerchiati d'azzurro* (1920; Blue-ringed Eyes), and *Tipi bizzarri* (1931; Strange Types).   C.K.

Guillén, Jorge (1893–), Spanish poet, was born in Valladolid. A member of the so-called Generation of 1927, Guillén was active as a professor of Spanish literature at various European and American universities between 1917 and 1957. He sided with the Republicans in the Civil War and went into exile in 1938. Since 1940 he has resided in the United States. He has been awarded numerous international prizes for poetry.

Until 1957, Guillén was known as the author of a single book of verse, *Cántico,* which was augmented in four successive editions. The first edition dates from 1928 and the definitive edition from 1950. Between 1957 and 1963 his trilogy *Clamor* appeared. In 1967 a third essential work, *Homenaje,* was added. The three titles make up

Aire Nuestro (1968). This volume was followed by *Y otros poemas* (And Other Poems) in 1973. The best-known of his prose works is *Language and Poetry* (1961; Spanish ed., 1962).

Cántico reflects many of the poetic ideals of the 1920s: perfection of form, the cultivation of imagery that coincided with the revival of Gongorism in Spain, objectification, and the rejection of sentimentality. Some critics have called Guillén's verse intellectual poetry, likening it to the works of Paul VALÉRY or Stéphane MALLARMÉ. Although these poets may be similar in their use of condensation, symmetrical structure, and utmost exactness of expression, these aspects do not preclude passion and enthusiasm in Guillén's work. While the French poets raise art above life without being able to escape the cold realm of nihilism, *Cántico's* subtitle reads, "Fe de vida," that is, testimony of and faith in life. The phrase synthesizes Guillén's outlook on human existence: to be born is equal to starting a song of praise. The world is greeted as "well made," and "concrete marvels" everywhere meet the eye. Each poem bursts with life and the endless tension of "becoming." To exist means to strive for perfection, in content and in form. And yet *Cántico* is not an egocentric work: the poetic "I" never ceases to communicate with the surrounding world and to gather strength from each contact. Hence the importance of awakening and dawn, which open each section of the book. The author's stance can be judged by the frequency of such expressions as "thank you," "a gift to me," and "offers itself." He sees his task as that of an interpreter, not a demiurge. It is a loving relationship. The poet feels love of a flower, a lizard, a distant river, but also for the perfect companion, because only through shared love can total plenitude be reached. As this poetry deals with essentials and universals, *Cántico* has often been defined as an ahistorical and apolitical book, although from the very beginning, Guillén emphasizes the importance of experienced events. The language of *Cántico* is often elliptical. The reader must exert himself mentally to grasp the implications. Great density is achieved through connotation, synesthesia, and multitiered metaphors. Many poems have a circular structure, negating linear time and a single interpretation, and affirming the perfection of a form that knows no beginning or end. Nouns predominate, as they stress essence, and verbs are used almost exclusively in the present tense. The tone is terse. The compact verses are interrupted by exclamations, interjections, and interrogations, all manifestations of vital force, enthusiasm, and the desire for a perfect rendering. It is not easy reading. Even the shortest poem condenses a whole world.

The trilogy entitled *Clamor* revolves around the theme of "time in history." It is more negative than *Cántico.* Even the lines abandon their symmetry. Spain's fate becomes an important theme, and the necessity of communication and community between men is accentuated. This development is similar to that experienced by most poets of Guillén's generation and is also found among the younger poets of postwar Spain. New forms are introduced, such as the epigrammatic *trébol* and rhythmic prose paragraphs. Time is recognized as an unavoidable factor. Themes of old age and death appear, as well as nostalgic evocations of the past. Irony and satire irrupt more frequently, but affirmation never cedes to skepticism or despair. Significantly, the entire trilogy is encompassed by a poem entitled "Acorde," which stresses the order and harmony that subdue temporary chaos. A line from "Viviendo" (Living) recapitulates the poet's stance: "I accept my human condition." In *Clamor* not all is light, air, and transparency, as it was in *Cántico,* but the joy that emerges is more mature and has been achieved by unrelenting will power.

Homenaje reaffirms Guillén's determination to consider life and what it brings as a gift. Here again he shows that art transcends time. A number of poems present variations on his reading, ranging from *Genesis* to contemporary literature. When authors are evoked, they appear as human beings, not only artists. The central section, full of youthful vitality, is an homage to love. After *Clamor*'s accent on the passing of things, *Homenaje* stands for regeneration and the continuity of essential human values. The prevailing tone here is that of mature serenity. Having withstood all trials and temptations, the poet rejoices in extolling man's fundamental virtues of sharing, understanding, and perseverance in the pursuit of ideals.

Y otros poemas presents a fusion of actual history and universal, eternal themes. Guillén's poetics are here defined as "Ars vivendi, ars amandi." The impossibility of excluding life from art had been stressed in the first line of *Cántico*. Now, in "The Sybil," the last poem of the volume, Guillén gives a review of his encounters with art, just as the section called "Reviviscencias" offers a retrospective autobiographical synthesis. Both end with an accent on continuity. As in the preceding volumes, the astounding variety of form and expression testifies to the poet's open stance, undiminished intellectual curiosity, and the persistence of the "amorous attention" proclaimed in *Cántico*.

Guillén's poetry is dense and highly affirmative, the result of rigorous discipline and faith in art. Penetrating into the very core of phenomena, it never becomes completely abstract, as the "here and now" is an essential condition of Guillén's creative process. Other outstanding characteristics are the dynamism caused by outbursts of joy, the incessant search for the "exact word," grateful astonishment in the face of a never exhausted universe, and an unceasing determination to achieve fulfillment. Guillén's poetry is available in English translation in the following collections: *Cántico: A Selection*, ed. by N. T. Giovanni (1965) and *Affirmation: A Bilingual Anthology, 1919-1966*, ed. by J. Palley (1968).

See: I. Ivask and J. Marichal, eds., *Luminous Reality: The Poetry of Jorge Guillén* (1969).   B.Ci.

Guillevic, Eugène (1907–), French poet, was born in Carnac, a small village in Brittany famous for its prehistoric alignments of rocks. Guillevic lived in Brittany until 1919, then moved to Ferrette in Alsace. Brittany and Alsace are very much present in his works. Guillevic worked as a civil servant and, in 1935, was appointed to the Finance Ministry in Paris. During World War II he worked in the Resistance, joined the Communist Party, and published his first poems, in the journal *L'Honneur des poètes*, under the pseudonym Serpières.

Guillevic's first major work was *Terraqué*, published in 1942. In this book, he tried to discover an "objective poetry." Man is afraid of being excluded or rejected, yet he must fight back with words, since words are knowledge. *Trente et un sonnets* (1954; 31 Sonnets) is a volume of political poems. *Carnac* (1961) is a long meditation on the immensity of the ocean. *Euclidiennes* (1967) contains poems on various geometrical forms (the ellipse, the lozenge, the circle), while *Ville* (1969; City) describes the city as if it were a human body. In his last work, *Du domaine* (1977; Of the Domain), Guillevic studies the relationship of man to the mystery of the universe. According to Guillevic, the poet responds to everything—both outer and inner—that makes up the world. Although

his poetry is definitely materialistic, it teaches the great lesson of fraternity.

Guillevic has been the recipient of many prizes, including the great Poetry Prize of the Académie Française in 1976 as well as the Yugoslavian Struga Prize that same year.

See: J. Tortel, *Guillevic* (1971); *Littérature de notre temps*, vol. 2 (1971).   J.-C.M.

Guilloux, Louis (1899–), French novelist, was born in Saint-Brieuc, Brittany, to poor working-class parents. Although he has lived in Paris from time to time, he has never strayed far from his birthplace, and it is here that the action of most of his novels is set. After beginning his writing career by working for various Parisian dailies, he published five early novels in rapid succession: *La Maison du peuple* (1927; House of the People), *Dossier confidentiel* (1930), *Compagnons* (1931), *Hyménée* (1932), and *Angélina* (1934). In these books, Guilloux used a deliberately simple style as he drew on vivid early memories of working-class life in order to present the evolution of the political consciousness of proletarians and small businessmen in provincial Brittany.

Guilloux's most important novel, *Sang noir* (1935; Eng. tr., *Bitter Victory*, 1936), describes the last day in the life of Cripure, a lycée professor in an obscure provincial town in 1917. A man whose personality is riddled with contradictions and who is convinced of the rottenness of the world, Cripure still does nothing to change either himself or his surroundings. At the end of the novel, he commits suicide, yet the young Lucien, one of his former students, does act, deciding to set out for Russia to take part in the revolution. Lucien is not optimistic, but in a reversal of the Pascalian wager, he seems to feel he has everything to lose by refusing to believe in the possibility of social change and everything to gain by an act of faith in humanity. The conflict in *Sang noir* is largely between generations, while in the earlier novels Guilloux examined the tension between the wealthy and the deprived.

Guilloux's later novels include *Le Pain des rêves* (1942; Bread of Dreams), *Le Jeu de patience* (1949; Jigsaw Puzzle), *Parpagnacco* (1954), *Batailles perdues* (1960; Lost Battles), and *La Confrontation* (1967), but none of these is as powerful as *Sang noir*. Guilloux's only play, based on *Sang noir* and entitled *Cripure* (1962), met with little success. Autobiographical elements are found in *Absent de Paris* (1952) and *La Bretagne que j'aime* (1973; The Brittany That I Love), two volumes of travel and reminiscence.

See: G. R. Strickland, "The Novels of Louis Guilloux: A Recommendation," *CQ* 5 (1972): 159-80.   D.O'C.

Guimerà, Àngel (1849–1924), Catalan playwright, orator, and poet, was born in Santa Cruz de Tenerife, Canary Islands, of a Catalan father. At the age of seven he went with his parents to Catalonia and received his first impressions of the landscape of the Bajo Penedés. He studied in Barcelona and returned to his father's village to aid his family in the wine business. But he was really interested in literature, and after 1872 he lived in Barcelona, as he considered this the most suitable place in which to make himself known as a writer. He was an assiduous competitor in the poetic contests Jocs Florals. In 1877 he was named *mestre en gai saber* (master troubadour) upon winning the three prizes necessary to obtain this title. He was a frequent collaborator on the newspaper *Renaixença*, which he helped convert into a magazine. From 1872 he was the editor of the publication. In 1874 he identified himself with the patriotic organization Jove Catalunya and in 1895, in a memorable presidential speech in the Ateneo, he enthroned this language. Never playing party politics, he dedicated his efforts to preaching the good news of the renaissance of Catalan culture with the breadth of vision shared by all those identified with the *Renaixença* movement. His patriotic speeches are collected in *Cants a la pàtria* (1906; Songs to the Fatherland). Some of his verse had been gathered in *Poesies* (1887), where he shows himself to be an exalted patriot and employs an energetic language replete with brusque images and outlines. *Segon llibre de poesies* (Second Book of Poems), which appeared in 1920, is very inferior to the first volume of poems.

For the theater Guimerà wrote *Gala Placidia* (1879), *Judith de Welp* (1883), and *El fill del mar* (1886; The Son of the Sea). These plays reveal a tragic dramatist of full stature. *Mar i cel* (1888; Sea and Sky) has the energy of the great German romantic dramas, but the psychological verisimilitude of the characters and the humanness and naturalness of the situations transcend the tenets of any school. Other plays of this period are *Rei i monjo* (1890; King and Monk); *L'ànima morta* (1892; The Dead Soul); and *Les monges de Sant Aymant* (1895; The Monks of Sant Aymant), based on the legend of Count Arnau, a sort of Don Juan, Faust, and Satan rolled into one, whose memory is alive in all Catalonia. *La boja* (1890; The Insane Woman) inaugurates his modern dramas, which include: *En pòlvora* (1893; In Gunpowder); *Maria Rosa* (1894); *La festa del blat* (1896; The Wheat Festival); and *Terra baixa* (1896; Eng. tr., *Marta of the Lowlands*, 1914), a very original play based on the contrast between the purity of the people of the high mountain region and the abject passions that animate those who live in the flatlands. *La farsa* (1899; The Farce), *La filla del mar* (1899; The Daughter of the Sea), *La pecadora* (1902; The Sinner), and others follow. In his final period Guimerà wrote plays based on very abstract ideas and of relatively slight literary value.

See: J. Prepatx, *La Renaissance des lettres catalanes* (1883); J. Yxart, Prologue, to À. Guimerà, *Poesies* (1887); J. L. Pagano, *Attraverso la Spagna literaria* (1902); M. de Montoliu, *Estudis de literatura catalana* (1912); A. Rovita i Virgili, "Àngel Guimerà," *RdC* (August 1924).

F. de P.

Guitry, Sacha (1885-1957), French dramatist, actor, and producer, was born in Petersburg. The son of the great actor Lucien Guitry, he was raised in the theater and lived only for it. He was greatly influenced by "the musketeers": his father and the Boulevard playwrights Alfred Capus, Tristan Bernard, and Jules RENARD. Sacha achieved success with *Nono* (1905), which was soon followed by other light, sentimental comedies: *Chez les Zoaques* (1906); *Le Scandale de Monte Carlo* (1908); *Un Beau Mariage* (1911; A Fine Marriage); *Le Veilleur de nuit*, one of his best plays (1911; The Night Watchman); and *La Prise de Berg-op-Zoom* (1912; Eng. tr., *Fall of Berg-op-Zoom*, 1930). During World War I, his short, three-character comedies—involving Him, Her and the Deceived Husband—raised the morale of the troops. Sacha wrote more serious roles for his father in *Deburau* (1918; Eng. tr., 1921), *Mon Père avait raison* (1919; My Father Was Right), *Pasteur* (1919; Eng. tr., 1921), and *Béranger* (1920), although he treated history lightly.

Guitry's output was enormous: 130 plays and 33 films, in addition to essays, books of maxims, and memoirs. He usually produced and acted in his plays and films with his five successive wives, all of whom he trained (the most famous being Yvonne Printemps). He was made commander of the Legion of Honor in 1936 and was elected to the Académie Goncourt in 1939. A cynical moralist,

Guitry charmed his public with his sprightliness, grace, wit, and fantasy, although he was sometimes criticized for having become shamelessly commercial.

See: A. Madis, *Sacha* (1950); J. Lorcey, *Sacha Guitry* (1971).   A.S.

Gullberg, Hjalmar (1898-1961), Swedish poet, was born in Malmö of well-to-do parents but was brought up as a foster child in a working-class home. At Lund University he read Latin and Greek and later made excellent translations of Sophocles, Euripides, and Aristophanes. Gullberg's academic education determined his poetic career. At a time when the modernists were beginning to introduce free verse in Sweden, Gullberg adhered to traditional patterns of meter and rhyme with perfect ease and skill but not without an ironic twist. Irony is also a prominent device in his handling of the religious subject matter in much of his work. The Christian element in his early poetry is reflected in the titles of some of the collections: *I en främmande stad* (1927; In a Strange City), *Andliga övningar* (1932; Spiritual Exercises), *Att övervinna världen* (1937; Overcoming the World), and *Fem kornbröd och två fiskar* (1942; Five Barley Loaves and Two Fishes). A recurrent theme is Christ's nativity, offering as it did a half-ironic point of identification for the poet who had been brought up as a foster child. He often expresses a feeling of divine vocation, portraying himself as a Saul converted into a Paul. Some of his poems echo Blaise Pascal, Søren KIERKEGAARD, and Saint John of the Cross, whose verses in *The Dark Night of the Soul* he translated. More secular concerns occupied him in *Kärlek i tjugonde seklet* (1933; Love in the Twentieth Century), which, prompted by an experience of deep personal commitment, makes ironic use of the Freudian gospel of sexual liberation then in vogue.

Gullberg remained in Lund until 1934, when he moved to Stockholm, where he became literary adviser to the Royal Dramatic Theater. From 1936 to 1950 he was head of the theatrical department of the Swedish Broadcasting Company. In 1940, when he was elected to the Swedish Academy, his popularity among educated readers was at its peak. His position as a kind of poet laureate of the nation was confirmed by his 1942 collection, which includes declarations of patriotic loyalty in times of war.

When, after a full decade of poetic silence, Gullberg brought out *Dödsmask och lustgård* (1952; Death Mask and Paradise), he revealed a new visage. The mocking irony is largely replaced by a solemn probing of the position of people in a world in which God is dead. The only "helpers" that remain are the half-gods, the heroes, Orpheus, Dionysus, Heracles, and Christ, all of them sprung from the immortal seed of gods but subject to the conditions of human misery and mortality, suffering cruel deaths. In "Sjungande huvud" (Singing Head) the severed head of Orpheus is a symbol of the new role Gullberg wished to assume as a poet: a mouthpiece for suffering humanity seeking to overcome its fate by rising above it and transforming it into art. In these poems based on Greek mythology, Gullberg employs classical Greek meters with unsurpassed mastery. His last years were marked by the painful progress of a paralytic disease, relieved only by the love and care of a distinguished lady friend and by the resurgence from time to time of his creative powers. In *Terziner i okonstens tid* (1958; Terze Rime in the Artless Age) and *Ögon, läppar* (1959; Eyes, Lips), he often reverted to his former manner of rhyming and ironic allusion. Although making use of the new poetic freedom introduced by the school of the 1940s, Gullberg asserted his belief in the timelessness of artistic form by making virtuoso performances in Dante's meter. Challenging but not antagonizing traditional values in literature, Gullberg was one of the last among Swedish poets to attract a wide audience. His *Samlade dikter* (Collected Poems) appeared in six volumes between 1948 and 1963. A volume of *Selected Poems* in English tr. by J. Moffett, was published in 1979.

See: C. Fehrman, *Hjalmar Gullberg* (3d ed., 1968); O. Holmberg, *Hjalmar Gullberg* (2d ed., 1969); I. Algulin, *Tradition och förnyelse* (on Hjalmar Gullberg and Bertil Malmberg; 1969); G. Brandell, *Svensk litteratur 1870–1970*, vol. 2 (1975), pp. 152–62. S.B.

Gumilyov, Nikolay Stepanovich (1886–1921), Russian poet, short-story writer, literary critic, and translator, was born in Kronstadt, the son of a navy doctor. His first book of poems, *Put konkvistadorov* (1905; The Path of the Conquistadors), was published before his graduation from the school of Tsarskoye Selo where the poet Innokenty ANNENSKY was his headmaster and teacher. Gumilyov never republished those derivative, juvenile poems, but the images of the conquistador and later of the poet-warrior were closely associated with him. In 1907 he attended lectures on French literature at the Sorbonne, in Paris, and there published his second volume of verse, *Romanticheskiye tsvety* (1908; Romantic Flowers). At that time he was editing a little magazine, *Sirius,* in which his first stories were published. He also made the first of three trips to Africa, which left an indelible impression on him and came to play a great part in his life and poetry. The poems in *Shatyor* (1918; The Tent) are on African themes, and his charming long poem for children *Mik* (1918) tells of a black African boy and the son of a French consul who run away together and join a tribe of apes. Gumilyov also wrote an account of one of his hunting expeditions in Africa, "Afrikanskaya okhota" (1916; African Hunt).

After returning to Russia from Paris, Gumilyov enrolled at the University of Petersburg, but he never graduated. In 1910 he married Anna Gorenko, who later, under the name of Anna AKHMATOVA, became an even better known poet than he (they were divorced in 1918). His third volume of verse, *Zhemchuga* (1910; Pearls), brought him popularity and fame and was favorably reviewed by Valery BRYUSOV and Vyacheslav IVANOV, two leaders of the symbolist movement (*see* RUSSIAN LITERATURE). Bryusov's influence, along with that of the French Parnassians, was strongly reflected in Gumilyov's poetry. In those years, Gumilyov also published, mainly in the symbolist magazine *Vesy,* a number of stories, most of which were collected posthumously in *Ten ot palmy* (1922; The Shade from a Palm Tree).

Between 1910 and 1914 he was a leading figure on the Petersburg literary scene, not only as a poet but also as one of the principal literary critics of *Apollon* (1909–17), an influential modernist review of arts and letters. The publication in 1912 of *Chuzhoye nebo* (Foreign Skies) marked an important new departure in Gumilyov's poetic development, coming as it did between the founding, on his initiative, of the "Tsekh poetov" (Guild of Poets) and his launching, jointly with Sergey GORODETSKY, of the poetic movement to which they gave the name "acmeism." Its tenets were formulated in two articles by Gumilyov and Gorodetsky, published as literary manifestoes in the first 1913 issue of *Apollon* (a third article, by Osip MANDELSHTAM, remained unpublished at the time). The acmeists were a small group, but they were important for the reaction they led against certain aspects of symbolism. They championed poetry as craftsmanship, in contrast to metaphysics and mysticism, and a balanced use of poetic

means, as against predominant musicality. Although their program was vague, their impact on the Russian poetry of the time was quite significant. Of all of Gumilyov's own volumes of poetry, *Chuzhoye nebo* was perhaps the most truly acmeist. Among its characteristic pieces is a long poem, "Otkrytiye Ameriki" (The Discovery of America).

During World War I, Gumilyov served in the army at the front with distinction until 1917. Much of his war poetry was published in his next book, *Kolchan* (1916; The Quiver), in which war was reflected as a spiritual experience; Gumilyov seemed to be overcoming and outgrowing his acmeism. At about the same time he wrote one of his best verse plays, "Gondla" (1917), which concerns the conversion of Iceland to Christianity by the Irish. In the summer of 1917, Gumilyov was sent to join the Russian expeditionary force in France. While in Paris he feel in love with a young girl of mixed Russian-French parentage and wrote a book of poems to her: *K siney zvezde* (To the Blue Star), published posthumously in Berlin in 1923. After the Russian Revolution (1917) he tried in vain to join the British army in Mesopotamia. In April 1918 he returned to Petersburg and resumed his literary activities. He worked as a translator on Maksim GORKY's "World Literature" project, organized seminars and lectures for budding poets, published another volume of poetry, *Kostyor* (1918; Bonfire), and prepared still another, *Ognenny stolp* (1921; The Pillar of Fire), for publication. Even those critics who are inclined to regard Gumilyov's poetic reputation as overblown admit that by 1918 he had become a first-rank poet (as, for example, Vladimir Markov, in his introduction to *Modern Russian Poetry* [1966]). *Ognenny stolp* contains the remarkable visionary poem "Zabludivshiysya tramvay" (A Streetcar Gone Astray) and the wonderful poetic autobiography "Pamyat" (Memory). Almost on the eve of the book's publication, in August 1921, Gumilyov was arrested by the Cheka on a charge of complicity in an antiregime conspiracy (the so-called Tagantsev plot), which was alleged to involve over 60 people; they were all shot without trial before the end of the month.

In 1922–23 some of Gumilyov's work was still published in Russia but after that his name became virtually taboo. Outside of Russia there were several reprints of his earlier volumes and a separate edition of *Gondla* (1936). Two manuscripts he had left behind in the West did not come to light until much later: a play, "Otravlennaya tunika" (The Poisoned Tunic), and an unfinished novella, "Vesyolye bratya" (The Joyful Brotherhood), both published by Gleb Struve in New York in *Neizdanny Gumilyov* (1952; Unpublished Gumilyov).

See: N. Gumilyov, *Sobraniye sochineniy,* 4 vols., ed. by G. Struve and B. Filippov (Washington, 1962–68); M. Maline, *Nicolas Gumilev, poète et critique acméiste* (Brussels, 1964). G.St.

Gunnarsson, Gunnar (1889–1975), Icelandic poet, dramatist, essayist, and novelist, was born in Fljótsdalur parish in eastern Iceland, where his father was a farmer. Gunnarsson was brought up in Vopnafjörður (also in eastern Iceland) because his father moved there while the boy was still a child. The early death of his mother left deep psychological scars on Gunnarsson, as many passages in his writings clearly suggest. His father was poor, so the boy received little formal education as a youth.

Gunnarsson made his literary debut in Iceland with two collections of verse: *Vorljóð* (1906; Spring Poems) and *Móður-minning* (1906; Remembering Mother). In order to get some education and to establish himself as a writer, he went to Denmark in 1907, enrolling there at the folk high school of Askov, where he was to study until 1909. Later, he stayed in Århus, Denmark, for a year but after that in Copenhagen; he lived there as well as at the country estates of Grantofte and Fredsholm in Zealand until 1939, when he returned to Iceland. Once back in his native country, he was a farmer until 1948 in the parish of his birth at an ancient chieftain estate named Skri-ðuklaustur. From then on, he lived in Reykjavik.

As a writer in Danish, Gunnarsson first published a volume of poems entitled *Digte* (1911; Poems), but his breakthrough work was the tetralogy *Borgslægtens Historie* (The History of the Family at Borg, consisting of *Ormarr Ørlygsson* (1912), *Den danske Frue paa Hof* (1913), *Gæst den enøjede* (1913), and *Den unge Ørn* (1914; abridged Eng. tr., *Guest the One-Eyed*, 1920). This novel sequence is a neoromantic family chronicle set in Iceland and written in a style akin to Norwegian and Swedish *Heimat Dichtung,* a work showing the unmistakable influence of Selma LAGERLÖF. In *Borgslægtens Historie,* Gunnarsson had created a special character type that was to recur frequently in his subsequent fiction: the solid and dependable Icelandic farmer. In this first case, however, the farmer's two sons belong to different worlds; one is a dreamer and a noble-minded artist, torn between the call of his art and that of the soil, where he has his roots, whereas by contrast, his brother is a demonic evildoer whose misdeeds stem from blind instinct. The conflicts in the story grow out of the tension between these two polarities, a dualism that was to become one of the prime characteristics of Gunnarsson's fiction.

World War I was a severe blow for Gunnarsson, demolishing, as he saw it, his ideological world view; and the next phase of his literary career evinces deep pessimism as well as a struggle with psychological and ethical problems. Among his novels having such direction is *Livets Strand* (1915; The Shore of Life). It focuses on the tragic life of a clergyman caught in a conflict between the principle of human reason and his faith in divine providence; the latter fails him, and he is at the same time victimized by an unscrupulous conservative, his worldly competitor. *Varg i Veum* (1916; Wolf in Sacred Places) concerns the ruin of a young man who has rebelled against bourgeois decency. *Salige er de enfoldige* (1920; Blessed Are the Simpleminded; Eng. tr., *Seven Days' Darkness,* 1930) takes place in Reykjavik during seven days in which the Spanish flu is raging—against a backdrop of a volcanic eruption. In this novel, a medical doctor, who believes in the goodness and nobility of mankind, suffers defeat at the hands of a character representing pure evil and treachery; the work ends on a note of liberal resignation with the words "Love one another." Few, if any, Icelandic authors have delved so deeply into the problem of evil as has Gunnarsson or probed so fearlessly the psychological depths that give rise to crimes people commit. A number of plays by Gunnarsson date from this period, too: *Smaa Skuespil* (1917; Small Drama) and *Dyret med Glorien* (1922; The Animal with the Halo); *Rævepelsene* (1930; The Fox Pelts) is of a later composition.

Departing after 1920 from the pessimistic psychological tack, Gunnarsson returned to material from his youth and place of origin with his five-volume fictionalized autobiography *Kirken paa Bjerget* (1923–28; The Church on the Mountain; Eng. tr. of the first three vols., *Ships in the Sky* and *The Night and the Dream,* 1938). *Kirken paa Bjerget* is at once the story of the maturing of a young writer (Bildungsroman) and a significant contribution to cultural history—an account of rural life in Iceland at the turn of the century. The last two volumes describe the author's trials in Denmark until the time when he had established himself as a literary figure and found, through his wife, happiness and a foothold in life, a condition he felt he had been deprived of with the death of his mother.

Between 1920 and 1940, Gunnarsson was a very productive essayist. He lectured extensively in the Nordic countries and also in Germany, where he won acceptance and became a significant influence as an author. The unification of the Nordic countries is a central concept in his essays, which deal, broadly speaking, with Icelandic culture and Icelandic problems. A selection was published as *Det nordiske Rige* (1927; The Nordic State).

Gunnarsson followed up the thoroughgoing self-examination of *Kirken paa Bjerget* by charting in a similar way the nature and fate of the Icelandic nation, a work he envisioned as a 12-volume series of historical novels, although he never completed the sequence. First came *Edbrødre* (1918; Eng. tr., *The Sworn Brothers,* 1920), which is about the first two settlers in Iceland. In *Jord* (1933; Earth), Gunnarsson moved on to the establishment of an organized state in the early history of the nation. This is a book containing a strong element of religious mysticism, with ancient Nordic paganism shown as reverence for life, simple worship, and belief in fate. A similar mystical feeling also runs deeps in *Hvide-Krist* (1934; White Christ), focusing on events leading to Iceland's conversion to Christianity around the year 1000. *Graamand* (1936; The Man in Gray) treats of the incipient dissolution of the Icelandic Commonwealth, and *Jón Arason* (1930) is both the story of the last Catholic bishop in Iceland and a survey of the nation's transition to a new religious order in the Reformation period (the first half of the 16th century).

Somewhat removed from these last works, which draw upon the history proper of Iceland, are a number of others. One of them, *Svartfugl* (1929; Black Gull; Eng. tr., *The Black Cliffs,* 1967), derives its action from a murder case in 1800 or so; it is a novel shot through with religious mysticism, although it is also a psychological probe of the evil in human nature, and the theme of cooperation receives stronger emphasis here than in the remainder of Gunnarsson's writings. Another novel, *Vikivaki* (1932; Folk Dance), Gunnarsson's most enigmatic work of fiction, is an absurd fantasy about the responsibility of an author toward his art and toward humanity.

After his return to Iceland, Gunnarsson wrote and published his books in his native language. He had projected a five-volume series of novels on life and social developments in Iceland during the first half of the 20th century, but he completed only two of the installments: *Heiðaharmur* (1940; Grief in the Mountains) and *Sálumessa* (1952; Requiem). His last work was *Brimhenda* (1954; The Sonata of the Sea), a short novel. Gunnarsson had earlier written some of his best fiction in that very genre, such as *De blindes Hus* (1933; The House of the Blind) and *Adventa* (1937; Eng. tr., *Advent,* 1939, republished as *The Good Shepherd,* 1940).

The hallmarks of Gunnarsson's fiction are strong individualism, psychological insight, and religious mysticism, as well as character creation of an unusual range. Although the bulk of his literary output is the work of an expatriate, Gunnarsson derives his subject matter exclusively from his native soil, and his descriptions of life in Iceland have great immediacy, although he at the same time views what is characteristically Icelandic from an artistic distance.

See: S. Arvidson, *Gunnar Gunnarsson islänningen* (1960); S. Björnsson, *Leiðin til skáldskapar* (1964); K. E. Andrésson, "Kjarninn i verkum Gunnars Gunnarssonar,"

Samvinnan (1973); S. S. Höskuldsson, "Draumur í sýn," *Skírnir* (1974): 114–40.   S.S.H.

Guro, Yelena Genrikhovna (1877–1913), Russian poet, playwright, and artist, born in Petersburg, made an important contribution to the early, impressionistic stage of Russian futurism (*see* RUSSIAN LITERATURE). After publishing a collection of prose, poetry, and drama entitled *Sharmanka* (1909; The Hurdy-Gurdy) and illustrated largely by herself, she joined the group led by David BURLYUK, participating in its first joint miscellany *Sadok sudey* (1910; A Trap for Judges) but occupying an independent position and resisting her fellow futurists' shift to primitivism in 1912. Her best collection, *Nebesnye verblyuzhata* (1914; Little Camels of the Sky), appeared only after her death. Typically, Guro's works are lyrical miniatures, prose poems. Some approach surrealism, but most remain impressionist pictures of Petersburg city life or anthropomorphic nature in the Finnish vacation area. There are also sympathetic portrayals of children, youth, and struggling, unrecognized artists. In her work, more than anyone else's, symbolism and futurism come together.

See: V. Markov, *Russian Futurism* (1968), pp. 14–23 and passim; K. B. Jensen, *Russian Futurism, Urbanism and Elena Guro* (1977).   V.M.

Gustafsson, Lars (1936–), Swedish novelist, dramatist, and critic, was born in Vasteracs. He studied philosophy at Uppsala University where he received his *filosofie licenciat* degree in 1961 and his Fil. dr. (Ph.D.) in 1978. Gustafsson worked as editor of the literary periodical *Bonniers Litterära Magasin* (1961–72); during this period, Gustafsson wrote a number of important reviews, articles, and editorials, contributions to the "cultural debate" in Sweden. His interest in social issues is evidenced in such nonfiction works as *The Public Dialogue* in *Sweden* (1964), in *Den onödiga samtiden* (1974; The Unnecessary Present, with Jan Myrdal), and in much of his fiction.

Gustafsson is best known as a novelist and poet. His first book, *Vägvila* (1957; Road Rest), a novel, is characterized by an interest in metaphysical and philosophical issues. This interest is also evident in the early novels *Poeten Brumbergs sista dagar och död* (1959; The Last Days and Death of the Poet Brumberg) and *Bröderna* (1960; The Brothers).

These novels show the influence of Alain ROBBE-GRIL-LET's theories of the "new novel" and of Ludwig Wittgenstein's philosophical theories. Gustafsson's later fiction is a "system," as he calls it, of five novels that shows the different protagonists' progression from Inferno in *Herr Gustafsson själv* (1971; Mr. Gustafsson Himself) through Purgatory in *Yllet* (1973; Wool), *Familjefesten* (1975; The Family Party), and *Sigismund* (1976) to Paradise in the last novel, *En biodlares död* (1978; The Death of a Beekeeper). In these latest novels, Gustafsson uses a more realistic style and framework without, however, abandoning his inquiry into the problems of being and existence. These receive highly individual treatment; in the last novel, Gustafsson finds the paradisiacal state to equate absence of pain.

Gustafsson is an excellent stylist, with a penchant for the telling, well-turned phrase. His language is clear and precise, his imagery, sensual and original. These qualities have made him a ranking lyric poet. The poems from Gustafsson's first three volumes of poetry (the first was published in 1962) are collected in *En privatmans dikter* (1967; Poems of a Private Man). In his poetry as in his prose, Gustafsson deals with metaphysical problems and delights in esoteric lore. In the long poem *Kärleksförklaring*

till en sefardisk dam (1970; Declaration of Love to a Sephardic Lady), an important section centers on a disued ore hoist. Selections from this poem and from the earlier poetry have been translated by Robin Fulton and published as *Lars Gustafsson: Selected Poems* (1972). Other selections, mainly from *Varma rum och kalla* (1972), translated by Yvonne L. Sandstroem, have been published as *Warm Rooms and Cold* (1975). Gustafsson's latest volume of poetry, *Sonetter* (1977; Sonnets), is an experiment with fixed forms, sonnets and some sestinas, which demonstrates Gustafsson's technical expertise. Gustafsson's *Forays into Swedish Poetry*, tr. by R. T. Rovinsky, was published in 1978. A selection from his short-story collection *Förberedeiser till flykt* is included in *Modern Swedish Prose in Translation*, ed. by K. E. Lagerlöf (1979), pp. 247–58; a selection of his poetry is included in *Modern Swedish Poetry in Translation*, ed. by G. Harding and A. Hollo (1979), pp. 87–107.

Gustafsson has also written three plays, all of which contain social criticism. The strongest of these, *Den nattliga hyllningen* (1970; Homage at Night) describes a confrontation between conservative institutions and anarchical individualism.

See: W. Höllerer, "Der Mensch eine Maschine," *Die Zeit* 49 (1967); L. Sjögren, "Ett egendomligt landskap" *Kritik* 15 (1970), pp. 67–89; Y. L. Sandstroem, "The Machine Theme in Some Poems by Lars Gustafsson," *SS* 44, no. 2 (1972): 210–23; *Bonniers Litterära Magasin* (1978), pp. 67–92, which contains essays on Gustafsson by Erik Hjalmar Linder, Lennart Sjögren, and Per Quale.   Y.L.S.

Guyotat, Pierre (1940–), French novelist, was born in Bourg-Argental. At the age of 18 he fled his liberal Catholic bourgeois background, moving to Paris in order to become a writer. Conscripted into the French army, he spent 20 months in Algeria before publishing his first book, *Ashby* (1964), a Gothic-like romance presenting the conflicts of flesh and spirit, debauchery and purity. *Tombeau pour cinq cent mille soldats* (1967; Tomb for 500,000 Soldiers), a modern epic in seven prose *chants*, depicts a series of killings, rapes, and tortures reducing colonial exploiters and exploited to a state of bestiality. The events of May 1968 led Guyotat to join the Communist Party and put him in contact with the *Tel Quel* group, whose mark can be seen on *Eden, Eden, Eden* (1970), a 270-page, one-sentence novel. The censorship of this work by the French government provoked a vociferous campaign of protest; reactions to this act as well as several interviews with Guyotat himself are collected in *Littérature interdite* (1972; Forbidden Literature).

Guyotat's repeated descriptions of sexual acts of all kinds in *Tombeau* and *Eden* provoke the paradoxical reactions of shock and boredom. Unreadable in a traditional sense, Guyotat's works belong to that contemporary textual activity that—rejecting psychology, rhetoric, and representation—affirms a materialistic notion of language and insists upon the close link between politics and sexuality in writing.

See: P. Sollers, "La matière et sa phrase," *Crit* 290 (July 1971): 607–25; F. C. St-Aubyn, "Pierre Guyotat: Sex and Revolution or Alienation and Censorship," *IFR* 2 (January 1975).   D.B.R.

Gyllensten, Lars (1921–), Swedish novelist, essayist, and short-story writer, was born in Stockholm. He is noted particularly for his treatment of philosophical problems in literary terms and for his stylistic virtuosity. For many years he pursued a medical career, and he has drawn parallels between his scientific and literary work: his books are "experiments" designed to test the validity and consequences of different life-styles. To this end he adopts different roles in his books—like Søren KIERKE-GAARD, whose influence he has repeatedly acknowledged. *Moderna myter* (1949; Modern Myths) is a collection of aphorisms, poems, and short stories that illustrate "the bankruptcy of naiveté": people can no longer believe naively in any absolute truth and must, therefore, create their own meaning in life, living as though they believed in the validity of their own creation. Through a dialectical progression that is an essential feature of his work, Gyllensten puts the opposite point of view in the novel *Det blå skeppet* (1950; The Blue Ship), whose hero is encouraged to stake all on the possibility of a miracle, a force outside humanity and beyond reason. Thesis and antithesis are both present in *Barnabok* (1952; Children's Book), where the conflict is presented in the hero's vacillation between two women, one offering a prosaic, self-disciplined existence and the other offering the possibility of a passion strong enough to sweep away skepticism and reservation. *Barnabok* is written in an expressionistic, syntactically chaotic style that is most effective in conveying the extremes of clinical detachment and violent emotion. Gyllensten reveals deep revulsion and at the same time anger at the human condition in the misanthropic collection of sketches called *Carnivora* (1953). He explores one method of defense against life's shocks in the deliberately narrated *Senilia* (1956), where the hero represents a life-style that regards all change and novelty as the repetition of long-familiar events. Two opposing life-styles are presented in *Senatorn* (1958; The Senator), in which a dedicated Communist, whose rigid ideology is his armor, even—he argues—his essential self, entangles with a woman who is in a constant state of change, "faithless" to her past experiences and personalities. The implications of such "faithlessness" are pursued in *Sokrates död* (1960; The Death of Socrates) through the attitudes of the characters to Socrates' fanatical determination to be executed. *Kains memoarer* (1963; Eng. tr., *The Testament of Cain*, 1967) is a witty illustration of the relativity of truth in the form of an account of the Cainites, a sect who believe truth is only to be glimpsed through the destruction of petrified creeds. This theme of "iconoclasm" is repeated in *Juvenilia* (1965), a fine study of a man's attempt to rejuvenate himself by destroying his old self. An important theme in this book and in much of Gyllensten's more recent work is that of our sympathy for the sufferings of others and of our inability to relieve them. *Lotus i Hades* (1966; Lotus in Hades) is a collection of prose poems about characters who have lost their individual identities. *Diarium spirituale* (1968) is the journal of a writer who descends into linguistic and spiritual impoverishment in order to re-create himself. The problem of human suffering occurs again in *Palatset i parken* (1970; The Palace in the Park), the portrait of a man made up of the memories he awakens, Orpheuslike, from the dead. The impressive triptych *Grottan i öknen* (1973; The Cave in the Desert) reemphasizes that the path to spiritual freedom and renewal leads through isolation and impoverishment like the anchorite's retreat into the desert. In Gyllensten's novel *I skuggan av Don Juan* (1975; In the Shadow of Don Juan), the "hero" is Don Juan's servant, Juanito. *Baklängesminnen* (1978; Memories in Reverse) is a novel about stages of a man's life, beginning with his funeral and ending with his birth. Gyllensten has also published numerous essays and articles—in collected form in *Nihilistiskt credo* (1964; Nihilistic Creed) and *Ur min offentliga sektor* (1971; From My Public Sector), and *Klipp i 70-talet* (1979; Cuttings in the 1970s). In *Mänskan djuren all naturen* (1971; Man, Beast, All of Nature), he expounds in essays and sketches his scientific and literary philosophy of "elective affinities"—that we see in the world what we are predisposed to see, that we find what we seek. In 1977, Gyllensten became the permanent secretary of the Swedish Academy. A selection from *Lotus i Hades* is included in *Modern Swedish Prose in Translation*, ed. by K. E. Lagerlöf (1979), pp. 13–23.

See: L. Sjöberg, "Lars Gyllensten: Master of Arts and Science," *ASR* 55 (1967: 158–62; H. E. Johannesson, *Studier i Lars Gyllenstens estetik* (1973); H. Isaksson, *Hängivenhet och distans: en studie i Lars Gyllenstens romankonst* (1974) and *Lars Gyllensten TWAS* (1978); K. Munck, *Gyllenstens roller: en studie över tematik och gestaltning i Lars Gyllensten's författarskap* (1974).

H.I.

H

Hacks, Peter (1928–), East German dramatist, poet, and theoretician of the theater, was born in Breslau, the son of a Social Democrat lawyer. He lived in Dachau after 1946 and studied philosophy, sociology, literature, and theater in Munich, receiving a Ph.D. in 1951 with a dissertation on Biedermeier drama. Influenced by the dramatic theories and the works of Bertolt BRECHT, and leaning politically toward Marxism, Hacks moved to East Germany in 1955, where he worked as a dramaturgist with the Deutsches Theater in Berlin until his forced removal from that post.

A leading dramatist of East Germany, Hacks wrote early plays that have a historical-sociological focus. His first play, *Die Eröffnung des indischen Zeitalters* (1954; The Opening of the Indian Era), is about the beginnings of capitalism, seen through the enterprise of Christopher Columbus's voyage West, and depicts a vision of the coming exploitation of Indians in the New World. The play won the author a young dramatist's award in Munich. The influence of Brecht, apparent in the first play, is less so in the second, *Das Volksbuch von Herzog Ernst* (premiered 1953, pub. 1956; The Chapbook of Duke Ernst), in which heroism decreases in direct proportion to the increase of power. Hacks's third play, *Die Schlacht bei Lobowitz* (premiered 1956, pub. 1956; The Battle of Lobowitz), is a comedy that pleads for the abolition of war through military desertion. The fourth play, *Der Müller von Sans Souci* (1958; The Miller of Sans Souci), is also a historical drama, in which Frederick the Great calls upon an ordinary miller to battle for his mill and thereby attest to the monarch's power.

Hacks's first play concerned with contemporary themes, *Die Sorgen und die Macht* (first version 1958, second version premiered in 1960, third version 1962; Problems and Power), caused considerable discussion among East German bureaucrats and resulted in Hacks's loss of his position with the Deutsches Theater because of the play's criticism of an emphasis on quantity of industrial production as against quality and because of a statement critical of communism. The comedy *Moritz Tassow* (1965) depicts the anarchistic resistance of a revolutionary opposed to land reform. It was followed in 1967 by another historical drama, *Margarete in Aix* (Margaret in Anjou), which was premiered in Basle in 1969.

Hacks occasionally turned to the adaptation and translation of plays from the repertoire of world theater, as in John Millington Synge's *The Playboy of the Western World—Der Held der westlichen Welt* (1956); H. L. Wagner's play on infanticide—*Die Kindermörderin* (1957); Aristophanes' *Peace—Der Frieden* (1962); John Gay's *Polly* (1965); *Amphitryon* (1968); and a play on the theme of Hercules' transvestite caper, *Omphale* (1970; Eng. tr., 1973 in *Dimension*). His *Adam und Eva* (1973) is a comedy on the theme of the emancipation of women.

The energy and imagination of Hacks has also produced a number of books for children, such as *Das Windloch* (1956; The Wind Hole), *Der Flohmarkt* (1965; The Flea Market), *Der Bär auf dem Försterball* (1972; with Walter Schmögner; The Bear at the Foresters' Ball), *Die Katze wäscht den Omnibus* (1973, with Gertrud Zucker; The Cat Washes the Bus), and *Kathrinchen ging spazieren* (1973; Katy Went Walking). In addition to a few poems and a number of radio plays, Hacks is also the author of several volumes of theoretical writings, more anecdotal than substantively reflective in character, on the theater, in which his early tendency toward didactic plays gives way to an emphasis on formal aspects; they are collected in *Die Massgaben der Kunst* (1977; Measures of Art).

See: H. Laube, *Peter Hacks* (1972).   A.L.W.

Hagalín, Guðmundur G. (1898–), Icelandic novelist, poet, and playwright, was born at Lokinhamrar in Vestfirðir, of robust farmer-fisherman stock. He soon determined to become a writer and after a brief attendance at school acted as editor of several ephemeral newspapers, thus having an opportunity to indulge in his desire to write. He visited Norway in 1925–27. In 1930 he became a librarian in Ísafjörður in his home district and has remained there ever since.

Hagalín made his start in the lyric and national romantic period of the early 1920s. Soon he found his field, however, in short stories and novels describing with humor and gusto the life of the fishermen of Vestfirðir. Sometimes he contrasted the old generation with the new, to the latter's detriment. After 1930 Hagalín, like Halldór LAXNESS, gave up the classical style of his early works for one more redolent of the earth and sea. In rough and robust dialect, assumed in order to depict the primitive characters close to the soil, he has written several short stories and the novels *Kristrún í Hamravík* (1933) and *Sturla í Vogum* (2 vols, 1938). The first pictures an old woman in an isolated cottage facing the Arctic, a widow poor yet perfectly content and self-contained, fearing neither God nor man, a master of her small world. The second describes a rugged, individualistic farmer in his development towards a social consciousness that finds outlet in practical cooperation with his fellow men. Hagalín has also written two adventure biographies of a shark fisherman and a skipper.

See: S. Einarsson, "Guðmundur Gíslason Hagalín," *Iðunn* 18 (1934): 65–88.   S.E.

Halas, František (1901–49), Czech poet, was born in Brno. He is perhaps the greatest Czech poet of the 20th century, and has been an important influence on every succeeding generation of Czech poets. His first book of verse, *Sepie* (1927; The Squid), is derivative, presenting a curious mixture of the two reigning styles of the day, "proletarian" verse and "pure" poetry. The collection reveals the writer's obsession with death, a theme that became dominant in his next volume, *Kohout plaší smrt* (1930; The Rooster Scares Off Death). In this work, decay and degeneration, along with death, emerge as favored themes, and life seems only an illusion. With the collection *Tvář*

(1931; The Face) the theme of love, invariably linked with death and decay, enters Halas's work. *Staré ženy* (1935; Eng. tr., *Old Woman,* 1948) is similar in vein, while *Dokořán* (1936; Wide Open) expresses the inner spiritual anxiety of the poet, who anticipates the coming world holocaust. Halas's few postwar works, including the long poem *Potopa* (The Deluge), first published, only in 1956 in the United States, express his fear of imminent apocalypse. Halas's verse is generally free, both metrically and syntactically; much of it lacks punctuation. His choice of words and images is striking and powerful. A dedicated member of the Communist Party, Halas apparently became estranged from the regime almost as soon as it took power in Czechoslovakia in 1948, and for a time remained under a cloud, although his literary influence was again felt in the 1960s.

See: B. Václavek, in *Tvorbou k realitě* (1937), pp. 35–52; A. French, *The Poets of Prague* (1969).   W.E.H.

Halbe, Max (1865–1945), German dramatist and novelist, was born in northeastern Germany near Danzig, in a district where German and Polish racial elements have intermingled for centuries. Growing estrangement between his parents and social ostracism, which their Protestant neighbors imposed upon them for being Catholics, cast early shadows upon his youth. From 1883 to 1888 he studied first law, then language and history at the universities of Heidelberg, Berlin, and Munich. In Berlin he became acquainted with Gerhart HAUPTMANN and other naturalistic writers.

In his play *Eisgang* (1892; Ice Drift), Halbe pictured a social and psychological problem against the background of a great natural panorama in his homeland. Encouraged by the success of this play, he wrote the drama that was to become his only lasting contribution to German letters, *Jugend* (1893; Eng. tr., *When Love is Young,* 1904). The new element in this play was the psychology of adolescence: two young people, carried away by their love to a fateful end, express their feelings in highly poetic language. From then on, Halbe's dramatic output was a series of failures alternating with mild successes. *Mutter Erde* (1897; Eng. tr., *Mother Earth,* 1913–15), *Haus Rosenhagen* (1901; Eng. tr., The Rosenhagens, 1901), and *Der Strom* (1906; The Stream) are perhaps the only plays that deserve to be saved from oblivion. In 1895, after a short stay in Switzerland, Halbe went to Munich, which was to become his second home. There he joined the groups of writers who made the Bavarian capital a center of literary activity at about the turn of the century. His theatrical ventures, such as an "Intimate Theatre for Dramatic Experiments" and, in 1899, a "People's Theatre," were rather short-lived. He turned to writing fiction, which—with the rural novella *Frau Meseck* (1897)—had brought him some success earlier in his career. His two novels, *Die Tat des Dietrich Stobäus* (1910; The Deed of Dietrich Stobäus) and *Jo* (1917), display a surprising mastery of style and form strangely absent from the historical dramas he wrote during the same period. Alfred Kerr's benevolent judgment of him still stands: "What characterizes Halbe is the fact that he never quite succeeded."

See: A. Kerr, *Die Welt im Drama,* vol. 1 (1917), 163–79; H. von Hülsen, "Max Halbe," *DT* 28 (1925): 56–61.
     W.N. rev. A.L.W.

Halévy, Daniel (1872–1962), French essayist, biographer, and historian, was born in Paris into a prominent family of Jewish-Protestant extraction. Although perhaps not an original thinker in his own right, he acted as a foil to such contemporaries as Georges SOREL and Charles PÉGUY, clarifying at one remove their seminal ideas concerning myth and *mystique*, the role of an elite, and violence in politics. In his day, Halévy stood out as a guide and interpreter, serving as a prism to his times and epitomizing in his life and work the hopes and illusions of the generation that reached adulthood with the Dreyfus Affair. Seen as a whole, his œuvre marks him out as the chronicler of more than half a century of French national experience, a period corresponding almost exactly to the lifespan of a Republican regime whose obscure origins he recounted in his major historical work, *La Fin des notables* (1930; The End of the Notables), and its sequel, *La République des ducs* (1937; The Republic of the Dukes).

The essentially derivative quality of Halévy's thought and the wide range of his interests can be traced to a youth and upbringing almost too generously endowed with varied stimulation. The son of the librettist Ludovic and the younger brother of Elie (the historian of 19th-century England), Daniel was brought up in an ambience dominated by such intellectuals as Ernest Renan and Hippolyte Taine, his father's colleagues at the Académie Française. He fell under the spell of the painter Edgar Degas, whom he later commemorated in *Degas parle* (1960; Degas Speaks). Together with Marcel PROUST and other schoolmates at the Lycée Condorcet, Halévy at first exhibited a literary bent by launching a review called *Le Banquet*, having many affinities with the symbolism of his English teacher Stéphane MALLARMÉ. But the Dreyfus Affair broadened Halévy's interests, and he became a moralist seeking to explain and to judge the springs of human conduct in public affairs. This is the task he set for himself in what will undoubtedly remain his most enduring work, *Charles Péguy et les Cahiers de la quinzaine* (Charles Péguy and the Fortnightly Review), first published in 1918 and reissued in its third version in 1941—an important commentary on his times, recording the transition from the 19th century to the 20th and containing the clue to some of the more elusive trends underlying French political and social thought. Halévy and Péguy did not always agree; as a repentant Dreyfusard, Halévy's *Apologie pour notre passé* (1910; Apology for Our Past) provoked Péguy to reply with a vindication of Republican principles in *Notre Jeunesse* (1910; Our Youth). Yet it was his intimacy with Péguy that led him to explore the rise of syndicalism and the unknown world of the rural masses in such pioneering studies as *Essais sur le mouvement ouvrier en France* (1901; Essays on the Worker Movement in France) and the successive installments of the *Visites aux paysans du Centre* (4th ed., 1935; Visits to the Peasants of the Center). The latter work drew him closer to the provocative ideas of Sorel, whose *Réflexions sur la violence* (1908; Eng. tr., *Reflections on Violence*, 1912) he helped to edit in 1911.

Always inclined to avoid well-trodden paths, Halévy was the first Frenchman to introduce Friedrich NIETZSCHE to his countrymen. He was also instrumental in adapting the ideas of the anarchist Pierre Joseph Proudhon to the quasi-fascist ideology of the corporate state, which theories became an integral part of the intellectual climate of Vichy France. Much of what Halévy published in the decades preceding the fall of France revealed his reaction to the breakdown of parliamentary democracy at the hands of the Radical Party, but such diatribes as *Décadence de la liberté* (1930; Decadence of Liberty) and *La République des comités* (1934; The Republic of the Committees) in no way detracted from his abiding interest in literary criticism, illustrated by his enterprising role as editor of Grasset's *Cahiers verts* series, and from his own solid efforts, through such undertakings as scholarly editions of the papers of Adolphe Thiers (1920) and Léon Gambetta (1938), to make the study of contemporary his-

tory a respectable academic field. His real interest, however, lay in exploring the affinities linking Renan's moral pessimism to Maurice BARRÈS's *culte du moi*, or Nietzsche's heroic vitalism to Henri BERGSON's *élan vital*. With a biographer's flair for translating ideas into the form of character and personality, Halévy also succeeded in shedding light on his country's tradition of socialist dissent by bringing out the connections that bound Péguy's *mystique* and Sorel's syndicalist myth to the libertarian ideas of Proudhon, their common ancestor.

See: A. Silvera, *Daniel Halévy and His Times* (1966).

A.Si.

Halide Edib (Adıvar) (1884–1964), Turkish novelist, was born in Istanbul. She graduated from the American College for Girls in Istanbul in 1901 and published her first novel, *Raik'in Annesi* (Raik's Mother), in 1909. She led a colorful political, academic, and literary life. After teaching at lycées and serving as inspector of schools, she became an instructor of European literature at Istanbul University. In 1919, with her husband Dr. A. Adnan (Adıvar), a leading intellectual and scholar, she joined the national liberation struggle under Kemal Atatürk. After the Turkish Republic was inaugurated, she and her husband were forced to live abroad, because of their opposition to Atatürk's policies. From 1923 to 1938 she lectured in France, India, England, and the United States. She also published several books in English: *Memoirs* (1926) and *The Turkish Ordeal* (1928), both of which chronicle the war of independence and the transition from the Ottoman Empire to the Turkish Republic; *Turkey Faces West* (1930); *Conflict of East and West in Turkey* (1935); and others. The year 1924 saw the publication of the English version of her 1922 novel, *Ateşten Gömlek*, under the title of *The Shirt of Flame*, which was followed by her *Daughter of Smyrna: A Story of the Rise of Modern Turkey on the Ashes of the Ottoman Empire* in 1928. In 1935 she published *The Clown and His Daughter*, a novel in English, about the life of an Istanbul neighborhood and the clash of cultures as reflected by several colorful characters. The Turkish version of this novel, *Sinekli Bakkal*, came out in 1936, received a major award in 1942, and had more than 30 printings by the late 1970s, becoming one of Turkey's all-time best sellers.

Halide Edib returned to Turkey in 1939 and served as professor of English literature at Istanbul University from 1940 to 1950, during which period she wrote a three-volume history of English literature. From 1950 to 1954, she was a member of Parliament from Smyrna.

Her early fiction concentrated on themes of romantic love; deprivations of the Turkish woman, for whose liberation the author campaigned vigorously; and the cause of Turkish nationalism as the ideology of all Turks in the Ottoman lands and abroad. Later she wrote numerous books of patriotic fiction about the war of independence. Her best work from the late 1930s until her death in 1964 depicts in a realistic vein the sociopsychological panorama of Turkey in the first half of the 20th century. Her only play, *Maske ve Ruh* (1945; Eng. tr., *Masks or Souls*, 1953), is a dramatic and philosophical exploration of the cultural heritage of Europe and the Orient. In 1963 she published her memoirs under the title *Mor Salkımlı Ev* (House with Violet Bunches). T.S.H.

Halikarnas Balıkçısı (meaning "The Fisherman of Halicarnassus"), pseud. of Cevat Şakir, whose last name, Kabaağaçlı, never appeared in his publications (1886–1973), Turkish novelist, was born in Istanbul. He received a degree from Robert College, in Istanbul, and from Oxford University (1908). After a 15-year stint as journalist, he was convicted for sedition and imprisoned in Bodrum (ancient Halicarnassus), where he remained after his release in a year and a half. Until his death, he worked on Turkey's Aegean coast as a journalist, tourist guide, and writer. A polyglot, he occasionally wrote in English.

His novels include *Aganta Burina Burinata* (1946), *Ötelerin Çocuğu* (1956; A Child from Beyond), and *Deniz Gurbetçileri* (1969; Exiles of the Sea). He also wrote two historical novels about two Ottoman admirals: *Uluç Reis* (1962) and *Turgur Reis* (1966). Collections of his short stories are *Ege Kıyılarından* (1939; From the Aegean Coast), *Merhaba Akdeniz* (1947; Hello Mediterranean), *Egenin Dibi* (1952; Bottom of the Aegean), *Yaşasın Deniz* (1954; Long Live the Sea), *Gülen Ada* (1957; Island of Smiles), and *Gençlik Denizlerinde* (1973; In the Seas of Youth). He translated about 100 books into Turkish and wrote four major books about Anatolian mythology. In 1961 he published his memoirs, *Mavi Sürgün* (Blue Exile). Halikarnas Balıkçısı specialized in fiction based on his keen observations of sailors, fishermen, and divers, and on the life of coastal villages, often enriching his plots and narration with myths and legends. T.S.H.

Hamp, Pierre, pseud. of Pierre Bourillon (1876–1962), French novelist and sociologist, was born in Nice. The son of a master cook, he always considered manual labor equal in importance to that of any profession. After early wanderings as a cook in England and Spain, Hamp returned to Paris where he attended the then flourishing Université Populaire, later obtaining work with a railroad company in northern France. At this time, he began to write those books on which his reputation is based. This series, entitled *La Peine des hommes* (The Ordeal of Men), includes the novels *Marée fraîche* (1908; Fresh Seafood), on the fishing industry; *Vin de Champagne* (1909; Wine of Champagne); *Le Rail* (1912); *Le Cantique des Cantiques* (1922; The Song of Songs), on the women's clothing industry; *Mineurs et métiers de fer* (1932; Miners and Iron Trades); and *Kilowatt* (1957). These works express Hamp's personal political convictions as a socialist who saw private property and orthodox religion as barriers to the eventual happiness of the working man. In each of these novels, the plot is developed so that the product in question is followed from the stage of raw material to the point of retail sale. Today these books are, if nothing else, valuable and quite readable documents on industrial production at the time.

Among Hamp's many other books, *Gens* (1920; Eng. tr., *People*, 1921) comments on personalities of the day, while his three volumes of essays on work—*Le Travail invincible* (1918; Invincible Work), *Les Métiers blessés* (1919; The Wounded Trades), and *La Victoire mécanicienne* (1920; The Mechanical Victory)—deal with the economic question of the minimum wage, shorter working hours, and what he took to be the need for more American-style energy in one's work. Hamp also wrote a number of plays that are of no consequence, but his autobiographical volume *Mes métiers* (1931; Eng. tr., *Kitchen Prelude*, 1932) illuminates the early life of this original writer.

See: T. W. Bussom, "Pierre Hamp: Prophet of the French Proletariat," *SAQ* 27 (1928): 376–90; D. Saurat, "Pierre Hamp," *NRF* 37 (1931): 539–56. D.O'C.

Hamsun, Knut (1859–1952), Norwegian novelist, dramatist and poet, was born in Lom, Gudbrandsdalen. He is the major prose writer of Norwegian literature and after Henrik IBSEN, its most widely known literature figure. Hamsun grew up in Nordland county, and its landscape and social structure are mirrored in most of his work. As a young man he spent several years in the United States, working at odd jobs, as a streetcar conductor in Chicago, farmhand in North Dakota, and secretary and public lecturer in Minneapolis. The stay had a profound influence on his political views and literary style. Its immediate result was *Fra det moderne Amerikas Aandsliv* (1889; Eng. tr., *The Spiritual Life of Modern America*, 1969), a sarcastic depiction of what he considered America's spiritual poverty. He later, in an article in 1928, modified his views and expressed his indebtedness to American optimism and work ethic. After years of bohemian existence, Hamsun married for the second time in 1909 and settled down as a farmer-writer, first in Nordland, and later (1917) at Nørholm near Grimstad, where he lived until his death. Around the turn of the century, Hamsun published an important volume of poetry *Det vilde Kor* (1904; The Chorus) and several plays that enjoyed considerable popularity, particularly in Russia. He is now chiefly remembered, however, as the author of a dozen significant novels that fall into three major categories: the romantic works of the 1890s, the social novels from the World War I period, and the Vagabond trilogy from the years 1927–33.

Hamsun's early romantic works include his greatest novels: *Sult* (1890; Eng. tr., *Hunger*, 1899), *Mysterier* (1892; Eng. tr., *Mysteries*, 1927), *Pan* (1894; Eng. tr., 1920), and *Victoria* (1898; Eng. tr., 1929). *Hunger*—partly based on Hamsun's own experiences during several unhappy stays in Norway's capital city—describes a few fall and winter months in the life of an impoverished young writer trying to survive in Christiania (now Oslo). Forced and prolonged neglect of his body gradually affects his mind to a point where he can no longer collect his thoughts, and he seeks his escape, not in death—the Hamsun hero's usual way out—but as a deckhand on a small ship bound for England. Throughout the novel, hunger affects the hero's temperament like a mind-expanding drug: against starkly realistic surroundings, *Hunger* juxtaposes colorful fantasies and humorous scenes that are unparalleled in Hamsun's production. Some critics consider this first novel his most powerful work.

The hero of *Hunger* sometimes experiences a splitting of his personality, a motif that Hamsun developed further in other works. In *Mysteries,* the protagonist appears as two separate characters: the charlatan hero Nagel, and the Midget, his alter ego in whom he sees his own exhibitionism mercilessly caricatured. The two watch each other suspiciously, like the antagonists of a detective story. In *Pan,* written during three restless years in Paris, Hamsun expressed his yearning for the peace and natural beauty of Nordland, his childhood county. This short novel, written in the form of a hunter's diary, contains the most exquisite descriptions of nature in Norwegian literature. *Victoria* is Hamsun's sweetest love story. It includes charming pictures of the lovers, Victoria and Johannes, as innocent children, as well as a sentimental ending involving Victoria's fatal tuberculosis and her final confession of undying love.

In spite of their individual differences, however, *Hunger, Mysteries, Pan,* and *Victoria* all feature a Byronic hero, a tragic love story, and an emphasis on what Hamsun, in an important early essay "Fra det ubevidste sjæleliv" (1890; "From the Unconscious Life of the Mind"), referred to as "the whisper of the blood." Rather than employing the typical characters and utilitarian philosophy of novels from the naturalistic period (*see* NORWEGIAN LITERATURE), he wished to illustrate the strange psychology of exceptional people. During this stage of his career, Hamsun's work recalls the art and outlook of Fyodor DOSTOYEVSKY and Friedrich NIETZSCHE. The influence of the former is reflected in his heroes' fluctuations between towering arrogance and deep humility, the latter in Nagel's view of woman and supermen, as well as in the Apollonian-Dionysian conflict of a character such as Lieutenant Glahn in *Pan*. At the same time, however, one can see, particularly in a more realistic early novel like *Ny Jord* (1893; Eng. tr., *Shallow Soil*, 1914), a certain impatience with the youthful Byronic hero.

After a transitional stage in which he wrote poetry, plays, and a couple of lyrical first-person novels, *Under høststjernen* (1906) and *En vandrer spiller med sordin* (1908; both novels published together in Eng. tr., as *Wanderers*, 1922), Hamsun turned to large-scale social novels in which the old artist-hero is reduced to a secondary character, whose comments often reflect Hamsun's opinions. These novels include *Børn av tiden* (1913; Eng. tr., *Children of the Age*, 1924) and *Segelfoss by* (1915; Eng. tr., *Segelfoss Town*, 1925), humorously ironic descriptions of the decline and fall of a small Norwegian community, and Hamsun's poetic eulogy of the practical farmer, *Markens grøde* (1917; Eng. tr., *Growth of the Soil*, 1921). For *Markens grøde,* Hamsun's most monumental, best-known work, he was awarded the Nobel Prize for Literature in 1920. Yet critics who welcomed the optimistic note in this novel were soon disappointed. Hamsun's next two novels are misanthropic, reflecting the author's disillusionment with the outcome of World War I. Then, after a severe crisis followed by psychoanalytic treatment (the first of its kind in Norway), Hamsun produced the three lively novels *Landstrykere* (1927; Eng. tr., *Vagabond*, 1930), *August* (1930; Eng. tr., 1931), and *Men livet lever* (1933; Eng. tr., *The Road Leads On*, 1934), in whom the old artist-protagonist reemerges on a deromanticized level as August, a slightly ridiculous, but very human, charlatan.

In later years, Hamsun's romanticism led him astray politically. His apprentice years in the United States (1882–84, 1886–88) had robbed him of his belief in democracy as a power for advancing the cultural and moral ennoblement of man. Furthermore, his early heroes all reject scientific progress and industrialization and recommend a return to nature and to the values of the old aristocratic society. Hamsun, however, seeing the preservation of a feudal system as anachronistic, slowly came to accept the rugged individualist farmer as his new hero. This trend, coupled with an old admiration of Germany (and an equally old dislike of the English), finally led Hamsun into the camp of the Norwegian Nazis, whom he supported during the German occupation of Norway in 1940–45. During the post-World War II period, that mistake cost him his considerable fortune and, for a number of years, his popularity as a writer. In the two decades following his death in 1952, however, the reissue of his collected works, the publication of his moving memoirs of political imprisonment, *På gjengrodde stier* (1949; Eng. tr., *On Overgrown Paths,* 1967), and the appearance of biographies by his wife and son gradually regained for Hamsun his old position as Norway's most widely read novelist.

See: H. A. Larsen, *Knut Hamsun* (1922); J. W. McFarlane, "The Whisper of the Blood," *PMLA* 71 (1956): 563–94; R. Popperwell, "Critical Attitudes to Knut Hamsun 1890–1969," *Scan* 9 (1970): 1–23; A. Østby, *Knut Hamsun: en bibliografi* (1972); H. S. Naess, *Knut Hamsun og Amerika* (1969). H.S.N.

Handke, Peter (1942–), Austrian writer, born in Griffen, is the most versatile and controversial German-speaking author of his generation. He grew up in Berlin and Aus-

tria, studied law in Graz, and has lived in several European countries. By 1979 he had published 10 prose works, 2 film scripts and a diary, as well as 9 plays, 4 radio plays, and many poems and essays. Handke shows how visual perception, verbal expression, and memory can distort reality. He describes oppressive individual and supraindividual relationships and the attempts at self-realization of human beings caught up in a perplexing interplay of external and internal worlds. He uses language as a precision tool; it might even be the secret hero of his explorations.

Handke launched his career by assailing the "Gruppe 47" (*see* GERMAN LITERATURE) and by assaulting theatrical convention in *Publikumsbeschimpfung* (1966; Eng. tr., "Tongue-Lashing," 1968 in *Dimension*, and *Offending the Audience*, 1969). Like much of his early work, this "speak-in," investigates the nexus between psychological and social structures and aesthetic and linguistic conventions. In Handke's best-known play, *Kaspar* (1968; Eng. tr. in *Kaspar and Other Plays*, 1969), a mute foundling is successfully subjected to "speech torture"; but his mastery of words does not guarantee lasting control over the objects they signify, and in the end chaos destroys the verbal clichés. Later plays include the enigmatic *Der Ritt über den Bodensee* (1971; Eng. tr., *The Ride Across Lake Constance*, 1973) and *Die Unvernünftigen sterben aus* (1973; Eng. tr., *They Are Dying Out*, 1977), in which a successful entrepreneur laments the loss of his ability to experience emotions, comes to see himself as a depersonalized object, and commits suicide.

Handke's early prose, tentative and sometimes derivative (Franz KAFKA, *nouveau roman*), was followed by a small masterpiece, *Die Angst des Tormanns beim Elfmeter* (1970; Eng. tr., *The Goalie's Anxiety at the Penalty Kick*, 1972), which creates a paranoid reality with stunning verbal precision. *Wunschloses Unglück* (1972; Eng. tr., *A Sorrow Beyond Dreams*, 1974) is a brief fictionalized account of the bleak life and suicide of Handke's mother. Later narratives with minimal plots (Handke calls them *Erzählungen*) read like sections of an *Entwicklungsroman*. In *Der kurze Brief zum langen Abschied* (1972; Eng. tr., *Short Letter, Long Farewell*, 1974) and *Die Stunde der wahren Empfindung* (1975; Eng. tr., *A Moment of True Feeling*, 1977), Handke allows some hope for individual change; he portrays protagonists who overcome certain sinister aspects of their former selves. In *Die linkshändige Frau* (1976; Eng. tr., *The Left-Handed Woman*, 1978), a woman throws out her husband but continues in her uneventful suburban existence. With his sparsest prose yet, Handke uses external detail to suggest the woman's pain and her incipient creativity. Handke based his second film on this story (1977). In *Das Gewicht der Welt* (1977; The Weight of the World) he recorded in diary form thousands of "verbal reflexes" triggered by visual perceptions and "events of consciousness." In *Langsame Heimkehr* (1979; The Long Way Home), a geologist, in his contemplation of landscapes and faces in America, experiences the destructive and healing powers of a disjointed universe aspiring toward harmony.

Not yet 40, Handke has created an amazing ouevre and may be expected to deliver further surprises; one indication is the announcement of a long study on *Die Frau über dreißig in ihrer beruflichen, sozialen und sexuellen Selbstverwirklichung* (1980; The Woman Over Thirty: Her Professional, Social and Sexual Self-Realization).

W.H.

Hansen, Martin Alfred (1909–55), Danish novelist and short-story writer, was born in the Zealand village of

Strøby. The son of a farmer, he was a farm worker for a short period. From 1931 to 1945 he taught in Copenhagen. His first novel, *Nu opgiver han* (1935; He Gives Up), treats the conflict between old and new social structures in a peasant society. Its sequel, *Kolonien* (1937; The Colony), deals with the failure of a collective farm experiment. The burlesque novel *Jonatans Rejse* (1941; Jonatan's Journey) shows significant artistic development. Its title figure embodies the harmonious medieval world view. As a contrast to Jonatan, his companion, Askelad, symbolizes critical and analytical rationalism, the victory of which appears in a vision of destruction toward the end of the book. A similar theme is found in *Lykkelige Kristoffer* (1945; Eng. tr., *Lucky Kristoffer*, 1974), this time within a historical frame set in the Renaissance, the period of the rise of modern individualism and materialism. Although Hansen had in *Jonatans Rejse* recognized God and Satan as realities, he now—like Fyodor Dostoyevsky—places their mutual struggle within the human heart. In the short-story collection *Tornebusken* (1946; The Thornbush), this struggle takes place in the present. The theme common to all the stories is the spiritual change in human beings caused by shocking experiences. For Hansen, the major experience is war—the sin—symbolized by the title. In the 12 short stories of *Agerhønen* (1947; The Partridge), Hansen, often in a complicated, modernistic form, also attempts to create symbolic expressions of his knowledge of the power of evil over people. In addition, the book is a sharp attack on the emptiness and barrenness of a nihilistic period. The same ethical and religious dilemma distinguishes Hansen's best-known and last fictional work, the novel *Løgneren* (1950; Eng. tr., *The Liar*, 1954, 1969). Here he has chosen a doubter as a mouthpiece for his Christian view of life. The main character, the parish clerk and teacher Johannes, is a dilettante of the faith, striving to reach a religious standpoint that also entails human responsibilities. The action takes place on a small Danish island during a few spring days when the ice breaks up, creating connection with the mainland—a symbol of resurrection. Like Hansen's other significant books, *Løgneren* is a carefully composed symbolic work mingling precise descriptions of nature with religious and philosophical meditations in a most subtle manner. Hansen was no sharp dialectician but was bound to a tradition expressed in his view of life. One of the greatest Scandinavian writers of the 20th century, he belonged to the same school of thought as Søren KIERKEGAARD, Henri BERGSON, and Dostoyevsky, all of whom strove to substitute a metaphysical outlook for the Utopian belief in progress and the rational creed.

See: T. Bjørnvig, *Kains alter* (1964); O. Wivel, *Martin Alfred Hansen*, vols. 1, 2 (1967–69); F. and N. Ingwersen, *Martin Alfred Hansen* (1976).   S.H.R.

Hansen, Thorkild (1927–), Danish author, was born in Copenhagen. He worked as a journalist and critic for various newspapers and also participated in several archaeological expeditions. Hansen first made his mark with *Det lykkelige Arabien* (1962; Eng. tr., *Arabia Felix*, 1964), a thrilling story of a Danish expedition that was sent to Arabia in the 18th century and from which only one scientist returned. The book thus deals with human beings uprooted from their own cultural milieu and placed in a completely alien surrounding, as does the novel *Jens Munk* (1965; Eng. tr., *The Way to Hudson Bay*, 1970), which describes an unsuccessful attempt to find the Northwest Passage to India and China. The theme of Hansen's trilogy, consisting of *Slavernes kyst* (1967; The Coast of the Slaves), *Slavernes skibe* (1968; The Ships of the Slaves), and *Slavernes øer* (1970; The Islands of the

Slaves), is the Danish slave trade between Africa and the Virgin Islands; the slave trade is strongly criticized by Hansen, who, in effect, abandons the objective reportorial genre for a very subjective style and the frequent use of inner monologue and literary "leitmotivs." As a writer, Hansen combines outstanding artistic creativity with a skillful historical method that makes him one of the forerunners of documentary literature in Scandinavia. His significant position in recent literature was emphasized by the publication of a three-volume work, *Processen mod Knut Hamsun* (1978; The Trial of Knut Hamsun), a deeply committed and critical account of the treason trial of the famous Norwegian author after World War II (*see* HAMSUN, KNUT).   S.H.R.

Harasymowicz, Jerzy (1933–), Polish poet, was born in Puławy. His first book of poetry, *Cuda* (1956; Wonders), was soon followed by others, of which *Powrót do kraju łagodności* (1957; Return to the Country of Gentleness) and *Wieża melancholii* (1958; Tower of Melancholy) made the greatest impact. Harasymowicz was the founder of the poetic group "Muszyna" (1957–63) and co-founder of the group "Barbarus." *Wybór wierszy* (1967; Selected Poems), so far the best selection of Harasymowicz's work, includes some of his longer poems, such as the one on Cracow, in which the town's rich past is the poet's main source of inspiration.

Harasymowicz is in some ways a "primitive" poet. His poetry grows out of a myth of nature and of natural man. He sees reality in terms of a fairy tale. Although his themes are traditional, if not anachronistic, Harasymowicz's technique is modern. In his poems impressionism mingles with a popular version of surrealism, and his dominant verse form is irregular free verse laced with metaphors. His individual imagery and the gentle humor that informs most of his work make it accessible and quite popular with the average reader of contemporary verse.

See: J. Kwiatkowski, *Klucze do wyobraźni* (1964), pp. 118–57; *Słownik współczesnych pisarzy polskich*, series 11, vol. 1 (1977), pp. 325–30.   G.G.

Harding, Gunnar (1940–), Swedish poet, editor, reviewer, and translator, was born in Sundsvall. He has published six volumes of poetry, the most important being *Blommor till James Dean* (1969; Flowers for James Dean), *Örnen har landat* (1970; The Eagle Has Landed), *Skallgång* (1972; Hue and Cry), and *Ballader* (1975; Ballads). His American interests (he spent a year in Iowa) are evident in his poetry, especially his more playful verse of the 1960s, and he has translated American, French, and Russian poetry into Swedish. From 1971 to 1974 he edited the poetry magazine *Lyrikvännen* and the associated list of books. His wide range of sympathies has been shown to good effect in his editorial work, both in the promotion of new native writers and in the introduction of foreign poetry. A short selection from his 1969 and 1970 books, in Robin Fulton's translation, was published in London Magazine Editions in 1973. With A. Hollo he edited *Modern Swedish Poetry in Translation* (1979), which includes a selection of his own poetry on pp. 109–21.

See: L. Frick, *New Swedish Books* (1975–78), pp. 34–35.   R.Fu.

Härtling, Peter (1933–), German novelist, essayist, and poet, was born in the East German city of Chemnitz, now Karl Marx Stadt, part of the German Democratic Republic. Like many writers of his generation, he suffered the loss of his childhood country. This experience lends particular urgency to the theme of memory that dominates his writing. Free-lancing since 1974, Härtling also produced creative publications that date back to the early 1950s. The verse collection *Yamins Stationen* (1955, repr. 1965; Yamin's Stations) established his reputation as a poet, and later lyric publications, including *Spielgeist-Spiegelgeist* (1962; Playspirit-Mirrorspirit) and *Anreden* (1977; Addresses), confirmed it. In keeping with a contemporary trend, Härtling has also written essays on literary topics, among which *In Zeilen zuhaus* (1957; At Home in Verses) deals with "the adventure of the poem, of writing poems, and of reading poems." But in spite of these and other works, such as a children's book and the dramatic excursion into the French Revolution, *Gilles* (1970), Härtling is above all a novelist.

In the two decades since his overly wordy *Im Schein des Kometen* (1959; By the Light of the Comet), some nine prose works have appeared. Several, like *Das Familienfest oder Das Ende der Geschichte* (1969; The Family Feast or the End of History), *Niembsch oder Der Stillstand* (1964; Niembsch or the Standstill), and *Hölderlin* (1976) deal with historical outsider figures. Others are set in modern Germany, especially the Third Reich, and focus on fictional characters, although with frequent autobiographical overtones, such as *Janek. Portrait einer Erinnerung* (1966; Janek: Portrait of a Memory), *Zwettl. Nachprüfung einer Erinnerung* (1973; Zwettl: Verification of a Memory) and *Eine Frau* (1974; A Woman). All these texts show a fascination with history as the possibility of reconstructing the past through both memory and documents. But whereas in the biographical works the evocation of the past is a generic element, reinforced by occasional authorial comments, the novels incorporate the mnemonic process thematically, as the protagonists try to recall earlier figures and events from their lives. Repeatedly an obsession with the memory of the father serves as the focal point for this search after origins.

The ontological implications of the preoccupation with memory are underlined in the correlated topic of "standstill" and "the end of history," personified in the ultimate mental disintegration of Lenau (Niembsch) and Hölderlin. With *Hubert oder die Rückkehr nach Casablanca* (1978; Hubert or the Return to Casablanca), the concept of nonhistorical existence becomes dominant. The title figure has no consistent personality but consists essentially of shifting reflections of reproducible, public clichés like those provided by popular film characters. In this work, Härtling's long-standing concern with the elusiveness of historical truth appears to reach its logical conclusion in the denial of man's very individuality.

See: M. F. Lacy, *Afflicted by Memory: The Work of Peter Härtling 53–69* (1970); F. Gallard, *Zeit und Geschichte in Peter Härtlings Romantrilogie* (1976).

E.Kr.

Hašek, Jaroslav (1883–1923), Czech novelist and short-story writer, was born in Prague, the son of a high-school teacher. He led a bohemian existence, sometimes working as a journalist, sometimes at less regular professions: at one juncture, like his hero Schweik, he forged pedigrees for mongrel dogs. During World War I, Hašek served in the Austrian army, but went over to the Russians. In the Soviet Union, he joined the Communist Party and for two years served in Siberia as a Soviet commissar. He returned to Prague in 1920 to publish his masterpiece, *Osudy dobrého vojáka Švejka za světové války* (4 vols., 1921–23; Eng. tr., *The Good Soldier Schweik*, 1930, unabridged version, 1974). Soon afterward his health, undermined by alcohol, gave way, and he died in Lipnice in 1923. His unfinished *Schweik* was completed, rather ineptly, by the humorist Karel Vaněk.

Hasek wrote a large number of antibourgeois satirical stories and sketches, of a rather crude and vulgar character. But his fame rests on *The Good Soldier Schweik*. This long, anecdotal comic novel presents a good-natured simpleton whose apparent idiocy protects and sustains him through the trials of war. Schweik overfulfills any order given him to the point of rendering it ludicrous and sabotaging its intent. It remains unclear (and deliberately so on the part of the author) whether Schweik is a real idiot or only counterfeiting, but it may be significant that Schweik, like his creator, does surrender to the Russians as soon as the opportunity presents itself. Schweik has been compared to Don Quixote, but the Czech writer Jaroslav DURYCH pointed out that in fact he is Sancho Panza without Quixote; as such he may be an original figure in world literature. He stands for popular, earthy integrity as opposed to tyranny, absolutism, and pompous ideology and rhetoric. It must be mentioned, however, that in spite of its ideological significance and the brilliance of its leading comic idea, *Schweik* is often crude and extremely repetitive. Indeed, shocked by the novel's vulgarity and its antiestablishment ideology, the postwar Masaryk republic was slow to acknowledge *Schweik's* worldwide fame, and Czech readers only slowly came to realize that the work had something genuine to say about the character of the Czech common man as well as about the plight of all little men caught up in the horror of war. The novel has been influential both abroad—on Bertolt BRECHT's drama *Schweyk im zweiten Weltkrieg* (1959) and Joseph Heller's novel *Catch-22* (1961)—and in Czechoslovakia itself, on the stories of Bohumil HRABAL and on Josef ŠKVORECKÝ's novel *Tankový prapor* (1971).

See: J. Durych, *Ejhle, člověk* (1928); E. A. Longen, *Jaroslav Hašek* (1928,); Z. Ančík, *O životě Jaroslava Haška* (1953); B. Frinta, *Hašek, the Creator of Schweik* (1965); J. B. Stern, "On the Integrity of the Good Soldier Schweik," *FMLS* 11, no. 1 (January 1966); 14–24.

W.E.H.

Hasenclever, Walter (1890–1940), German dramatist and poet, was born in Aachen. He saw something of the world in his student years, attending not only the University of Leipzig but the universities of Oxford and Lausanne as well. He was wounded in World War I and spent a year in a hospital.

Hasenclever was nothing if not sensational. His first poems, in *Der Jüngling* (1913; The Youth), were, to be sure, not exciting except for their subject matter: they were the warnings of a confessed libertine. With the play *Der Sohn* (1914; The Son), however, the theme of revolt breaks out. A boy of 20, who refuses to be intimidated any longer by his tyrant father, escapes from home; becomes a revolutionary both socially and politically; and, when the bailiffs haul him again before his outraged parent, threatens his father with a pistol, with the result that the latter dies of a stroke. This play, produced for the first time in 1916, was one of the early shots fired in the battle of expressionism; it also introduced the motif of father-son hatred, which ran like a lurid thread through the literature of the period. As he was drawn into World War I in 1915, Hasenclever became more politically conscious. In that year he wrote a dramatic poem, *Der Retter* (The Rescuer), in which a poet, a prophet of peace and of the brotherhood of man, goes down before the firing squad of a field marshal. Spiritual and political leadership is also attributed to a poet in *Der politische Dichter* (1919; The Political Poet), which contains poetry of a highly revolutionary sort. The most violent of all Hasenclever's works is his drama *Antigone* (1917), in which the Greek story is used as a framework for antimilitary arguments. Creon, a mask for William II, becomes the most brutal of tyrants, who is brought to justice by the rage of the people; the proud Antigone turns democrat and pacifist.

Eventually, Hasenclever found revolution unprofitable. Two experiments with dramatic technique followed, *Die Menschen* (1918; The People), which approaches pantomime because the text consists mostly of interjections, and *Jenseits* (1920; Beyond), a ghostly tragedy with two characters and an implied spook. Later Hasenclever took the path of comedy with *Ein besserer Herr* (1927; A Better Gentleman), *Ehen werden im Himmel geschlossen* (1929; Marriages are Made in Heaven), and *Napoleon greift ein* (1930; Napoleon Attacks). In 1917 he was awarded the Kleist Prize.

See: M. Raggam, *Walter Hasenclever, Leben und Werk* (1973). H.W.P. rev. A.T.W.

Hauge, Alfred (1915–), Norwegian novelist, was born and raised in the Rogaland region of southwestern Norway. Hauge's works express a strong Christian ethical view of life. His early novels, such as *Ropet* (1946; The Call) and *Ingen kjenner dagen* (1955; No One Knows the Day), are psychological studies of the conflicts that arise when pietism confronts the secular world; guilt and repentance are their central motifs. Hauge's principal work to date is a trilogy about the adventurer Cleng Peerson, the leader of the first organized Norwegian emigration to the United States. The trilogy, *Hundevakt* (1961; Midwatch), *Landkjenning* (1964; Sight of Land), and *Ankerfeste* (1965; Anchored)—available in abridged Eng. tr., as *Cleng Peerson* (2 vols., 1975)—is built on thoroughly researched material and has considerable epic power.

Hauge's more recent books, particularly his "Utstein Monastery Cycle"—a series of novels and one collection of poetry whose setting is geographically linked to a medieval monastery in western Norway—treat Christian religious themes. Most of these are also characterized by the author's search for a new fictional form. In *Mysterium* (1967; Mystery), *Legenden om Svein og Maria* (1968; The Legend of Svein and Maria), *Det evige sekund* (1970, The Eternal Second), *Perelmorstrand* (1974; Mother of Pearl Beach), and *Leviathan* (1979), he works with complex structures and untraditional points of view, consciously trying to involve the reader in the problem of creative writing. The two latter works are, besides being part of the "Utstein Monastery Cycle," the first two novels in a series about the character of life in 20th-century Norway. Hauge has published two autobiographical works, *Barndom* (1974; Childhood) and *Ungdom* (1977; Youth), which give fascinating insight into the source material of his production. K.A.F.

Hauge, Olav H. (1905–), Norwegian poet, was born in the Hardanger region of western Norway. Hauge published his first volume of poetry, *Glør i aska* (Glowing Embers), in 1946, but it has only been during the last decade that he has been recognized, not least by the younger generation, as one of the most remarkable new voices among Norwegian poets.

In both language and subject matter, Hauge is rooted in his native region. He writes a conservative version of *nynorsk* (*see* NORWEGIAN LITERATURE) with an admixture of Hardanger dialect, and his favorite motifs are the often harsh environment of fjords and mountains and the ordinary activities of the farmer. Yet Hauge's verse is considered European rather than provincial. Although he is largely self-taught, his poetry reveals a wide-ranging familiarity with literary history and theory. The influences on his writing include Percy Bysshe Shelley, William Blake, Friedrich Hölderlin, Paul VERLAINE, Arthur RIMBAUD, William Butler Yeats, Ezra Pound, Georg TRAKL,

Georg HEYM, Bertolt BRECHT, as well as Japanese haiku. Some of Hauge's highly acclaimed translations of English, French, and German poetry are collected in *Utanlandske dikt* (1967; Foreign Poetry).

Hauge's early work belongs largely to the romantic, visionary tradition exemplified by Olav AUKRUST and Olav NYGARD. His poetry tends toward subjective introspection, a nostalgic longing for transcendence, and a symbolic expression that at times approaches myth. As to form, he favors complicated meters and stanza patterns such as ottava rima. But as early as his second collection of poetry, *Under bergfallet* (1951; Below the Avalanche), Hauge was breaking away to find his own voice. His imagery and his language became sparer, more concentrated, less introspective. This development was carried further in the next two volumes, *Seint rodnar skog i djuvet* (1956; Slowly Turn the Leaves in the Canyon) and *På ørnetuva* (1961; On the Eagle's Hill). With his sixth volume, *Dropar i austavind* (1966; Drops in the Eastern Wind), there was a decisive transformation both in Hauge's general attitude and in subject matter, marking a second phase of his style. In *Dropar i austavind*, as well as in his most recent work, *Spør vinden* (1972; Ask the Wind), Hauge's poetic medium is the plain language of ordinary people. In these volumes he writes of everyday life, often with a touch of humor and irony, and he emulates the unadorned verse forms of Brecht, the proverbial style of the skalds, and the compact realism of haiku.

On the surface, Hauge's technique has become almost myopic. He leads the reader to notice minute details of life, enclosing him, so to speak, within the security of tangible, ordinary reality, its sights, smells, touch, and sounds. But he also causes the reader to remember, to relive his childhood, his dreams, and the experience of earlier generations, and thus guides him into renewed reflection, internal movement, and insight.

See: E. Bjørvand and K. Johansen, eds., *Olav H. Hauge* (1968); I. Stegane, *Olav H. Hauges dikting* (1974); K. Johansen, ed., *Tankar om dikting: til Olav H. Hauge* (1978). H.S.

Hauptmann, Carl (1858–1921), German dramatist and novelist, was born in Obersalzbrunn, Silesia, the elder brother of Gerhart HAUPTMANN. Silesian mysticism, especially the works of Jakob Böhme and Meister Eckhart, early attracted his attention. Interested in the metaphysical approach to natural science, he took his doctorate at Jena under Ernst Haeckel in zoology and Ferdinand Avenarius in natural philosophy. Although he gave great promise as a scientist, his brother Gerhart's literary success started Carl on a new career. When the dramas *Marianne* (1894), *Waldleute* (1895; People of the Forest), and *Ephraims Breite* (1898; Eng. tr., 1900) appeared, the critics proclaimed him a late naturalist, an imitator of his brother, and a talented, forceful writer who, however, might more profitably have confined his endeavors to natural sciences. But the collection of aphorisms and lyrics entitled *Aus meinem Tagebuch* (1900; From My Diary) helped create a better understanding of the man and the poet. He did not share the naturalist's reticence about the "idea"; in fact, the "force of the idea" is a predominant theme.

Carl Hauptmann's dramatic efforts cover an extensive field: tragedy in *Die Austreibung* (1905; The Expulsion), realism in the dramatic poem *Moses* (1906), symbolism in *Die Bergschmiede* (1902; The Mountain Forge), Hauptmann's best-known drama. In *Napoleon Bonaparte* (1911), his crowning achievement in drama, he reconstructed the career of the French emperor within the framework and spirit of Napoleon's own time. Supernatural and realistic elements are interwoven in *Die lange Jule* (1912; Tall Julie) and *Die armseligen Besenbinder* (1913; The Impoverished Broom Makers). Hauptmann turned to comedy in *Die Rebhühner* (1916; The Partridges) and to tragicomedy in *Tobias Buntschuh* (1916), the first play in the trilogy *Die goldenen Straßen* (Golden Streets), of which the second and third parts are *Gaukler, Tod und Juwelier* (Trickster, Death, and Jeweler) and *Musik* (both 1919). *Der abtrünnige Zar* (The Renegade Czar) and *Krieg, ein Tedeum* (Eng. tr., *War, A Tedeum*, in *Drama*, 6 [1916]: 597–653), both published in 1914, predict the coming catastrophe; words are subordinated to plot for a more vivid picture of the nature of things to come.

Two prose works appeared in 1902, the short stories collected under the title *Aus Hütten am Hange* (From Cottages on the Slope) and the novel *Mathilde*—descriptions of milieu and characterizations without the naturalistic undertone of social significance. Hauptmann's striving for perfection in the moral sense reached a climax in the novel *Einhart der Lächler* (1907; The Smiling Einhart), in which he portrayed the life of a misunderstood artist; here again he combined dream with reality. The prose works *Ismael Friedmann* (1913), *Nächte, Schicksale* (1915; Nights, Destinies), and *Das Rübezahlbuch* (1915; The Turnip Paybook), have their setting in Silesia. Hauptmann also commanded the lyric form, as in *Der Sonnenwanderer* (1896; The Sun Wanderer).

See: H. H. Borcherdt, ed., *Carl Hauptmann, er und über ihn* (1911); H. Razinger, *Carl Hauptmann: Gestalt und Werk* (1928); W. Goldstein, *Carl Hauptmann: eine Werkdeutung* (1931); A. Stroka, *Carl Hauptmanns Werdegang als Denker und Dichter* (1965); and H. Minden, *Carl Hauptmann und das Theater* (1976).

L.K. rev. A.L.W.

Hauptmann, Gerhart (1862–1946), German dramatist and novelist, was born in Obersalzbrunn, Silesia. Reared in Protestant orthodoxy, but early exposed to the more emotional teachings of Moravian pietism, he was as a young man subjected to the impact of an almost religious belief in scientific causality and materialistic determinism, tempered by a vague kind of socialistic meliorism, which at that time attracted the young intellectuals of Germany. A failure as a pupil, he turned to farming, sculpture in Breslau and Rome, desultory academic study in Jena and Berlin, and finally to literature. His marriage to a beautiful young heiress, who supported him throughout the four years of their engagement, freed him from the necessity of literary hack work. Marital incompatibilities and a passionate attachment to a young violinist led to more than 10 years of self-torturing inner conflicts, terminating in divorce and a new marriage in 1904. He received the Nobel Prize for Literature in 1912 and honorary degrees from Oxford (1905), Leipzig (1909), Prague (1921), and Columbia (1932). The Weimar Republic bestowed on him the order Pour le Mérite (1922). The Third Reich ignored him, but he remained one of the most popular dramatists on the German stage.

Hauptmann was essentially a product of a time of transition and of uncertain groping, wherein his distinction, as well as his limitations, lies. In a manner unparalleled in German literature, he demonstrated a receptivity to the varied intellectual currents of the age and a sensitivity to new literary movements without persistently following any of them. Few other writers have delved so deeply into the contradictions and irrationalities of human behavior; few have looked at the facts of life and of nature with the same honesty and candor.

After dabbling with epigonic dramas, epics, and social ballads, Hauptmann began to experiment with realistic sketches, some unpublished fragments containing painstaking and minute reproductions of various dialects. When he met Arno HOLZ, he was already well along the road to the naturalistic style of which Holz claimed to be the originator. What he most owed to Holz was encouragment to apply the new technique to the drama. *Vor Sonnenaufgang* (1889; Eng. tr., *Before Dawn*, 1909) marks the birth of the naturalistic drama. This and the other early plays, except for a greater illusion of realism in speech and in situations, were still reminiscent of Henrik IBSEN with his emphasis on milieu, heredity, or education. An entirely new dramatic form was evolved in *Die Weber* (1892; Eng. tr., *The Weavers*, 1899). Five seemingly independent tableaux are organically bound together in a climactic action of overpowering force. From the more than 70 characters, no individual hero stands out. The hero is, in fact, the whole proletarian group. A similar structural principle is observed in *Der Biberpelz* (1893; Eng. tr., *The Beaver Coat*, 1912), one of the few great comedies in German literature. The success of *Die Weber* prompted Hauptmann to apply the same technique to a theme from the Peasants War of the 16th century in *Florian Geyer* (1895; Eng. tr., 1929). The dramatist succeeded here in combining the speech forms, psychology, and cultural and social background of a forgotten age in a stupendous historic pageant. Both plays are typical naturalistic tragedies. There is no clash of ideas—only the collision of great natural forces. No divine order of eternal justice and righteousness is vindicated as in the Hegelian type of tragedy. As in *Oedipus Rex* and *King Lear*, the reader is left with the depressing feeling of the senselessness of human events, the brutality of life, and the dominating role played by error and chance. The neoromantic movement is reflected in Hauptmann's touching dream play *Hanneles Himmelfahrt* (1893; Eng. tr., *Hannele*, 1894), the first play in world literature in which the heroine is a child. The romantic supernaturalism of this play could still be explained on purely psychological grounds as figments of a feverish mind. A complete surrender to romanticism was made in *Die versunkene Glocke* (1897; Eng. tr., *The Sunken Bell*, 1898), the most personal as well as the most popular of Hauptmann's dramas. In most of the plays up to *Die versunkene Glocke*, the tragic outcome is generally the result of man-made causes and could be avoided by man-made reforms. When Hauptmann became more engrossed in his own personal problems, he envisaged tragedy as inherent in human nature itself. Sex reveals itself in its highest sublimation as self-sacrificing love in Hauptmann's most beautiful verse drama, *Der arme Heinrich* (1902; Eng. tr., *Henry of Auë*, 1914), as well as in one of its most pathological expressions, that of nymphomania, in *Kaiser Karls Geisel* (1908; Eng. tr., *Charlemagne's Hostage*, 1915).

Hauptmann's emphasis on nature and character found its most adequate expression in *Fuhrmann Henschel* (1899; Eng. tr., *Drayman Henschel*, 1913) and *Rose Bernd* (1903; Eng. tr., 1913). In these, as in the other naturalistic plays, dialect predominates, but their structure is more closely knit. Also, the characters are no longer examples of static and plastic analysis; they are human beings undergoing an evolutionary change. As if to escape from the brutality of everyday life, Hauptmann turned more and more to legendary, romantic, and balladesque subjects, even though he often gave them a realistic background. The most fascinating and beautiful of these, symbolizing the varied reactions of men to beauty, is found in *Und Pippa tanzt* (1906; Eng. tr., *And Pippa Dances*, 1907), which the poet loved best of all his plays.

As a sort of summing up of a lifelong preoccupation with the figure of Christ, Hauptmann wrote the most profound religious novel of his time, *Der Narr in Christo, Emanuel Quint* (1910; Eng. tr., *The Fool in Christ, Emanuel Quint*, 1911). With sympathetic insight, Quint is portrayed as a modern mystic who tries to carry out literally the simple social precepts of Jesus and meets with a somewhat similar fate. A journey to Greece produced in Hauptmann's travel diary *Griechischer Frühling* (1908; Grecian Spring) a unique appreciation of a pastoral, pre-Socratic, essentially Dionysiac Greece with its serenity and joyous acceptance of life even in its most tragic implications. This new outlook was reflected in the forceful drama *Der Bogen des Odysseus* (1914; Eng. tr., *The Bow of Odysseus*, 1917), in which the hero appears at first almost as a dreamy German who has actually lost the sense of his own identity until he regains his former prowess by contact with his native soil. *Der Ketzer von Soana* (1918; Eng. tr., *The Heretic of Soana*, 1923), a dithyrambic praise of pagan assertion of life and of the senses, is stylistically and structurally the most finished of Hauptmann's narrative works. World War I caused him to withdraw within himself and to continue work on the exotic themes selected earlier. *Der weiße Heiland* (1920; Eng. tr., *The White Savior*, 1924) is an exquisite tragedy in melodious trochaic tetrameters, holding up to scorn Christian fanatic zeal as opposed to the guilelessness of the Christlike Montezuma. *Indipohdi* (1921; Eng. tr., 1925) is steeped in Buddhistic longing for nonexistence.

The epic *Till Eulenspiegel* (1928) is the work that Hauptmann considered his greatest. It contains grandiose and realistic pictures of the depressing and chaotic conditions in postwar Germany and finally takes the hero to Greece, where he lives for a thousand years a characteristically bucolic existence with Baubo, the handmaiden of the gods. After the centaur Chiron has shown him the realm of Platonic ideas, he returns to the phenomenal world and finally seeks death in the Swiss glacier ice. Later works were two dramas, *Iphigenie in Delphi* (1941) and *Iphigenie in Aulis* (1944).

Hauptmann wrote more than 60 books. *Das Abenteuer meiner Jugend* (1937; The Adventure of My Youth) is a detailed and illuminating autobiography of his first 26 years, but he published practically nothing about his later life or about his works. Aphorisms and fragments were brought together in *Ausblicke* (1922; Prospects); and collected speeches, in *Um Volk und Geist* (1932; On the People and Spirit). So-called conversations, *Gespräche* (1932), were written down from memory and arranged by Josef Chapiro.

See: P. Schlenther, *Gerhart Hauptmann* (1897; rev. by A. Eloesser, 1922); H. F. Garten, *Gerhart Hauptmann* (1954;); C. F. W. Behl, *Gerhart Hauptmann, His Life and Work* (1956); L. R. Shaw, *Witness of Deceit: Gerhart Hauptmann as a Critic of Society* (1958); R. Michaelis, *Der schwarze Zeus, Gerhart Hauptmanns zweiter Weg* (1962); J. Améry, *Gerhart Hauptmann, der ewige Deutsche* (1963); E. Hilscher, *Gerhart Hauptmann* (1969); H. Daiber, *Gerhart Hauptmann oder der letzte Klassiker* (1971). F.W.J.H. rev. A.L.W.

Haushofer, Albrecht (1903–45), German poet and dramatist, was born in Berlin-Moabit, the son of a geopolitician. He studied at the University of Munich and after receiving his Ph.D. traveled widely. He became a professor of geopolitics in Berlin in 1940, worked in the Foreign Office in 1941, was dismissed from office and forbidden to speak in public, and then, as a member of the group that plotted to overthrow Adolf Hitler in 1944, was executed by the Gestapo.

Haushofer criticized contemporary affairs in Nazi Germany with dramas about ancient Rome, disguising his reference to Nazi figures, as in *Scipio* (1934), *Sulla* (1938), and *Augustus* (1939). A book of prison sonnets, *Moabiter Sonette* (Eng. tr., *Moabit Sonnets*, 1978), appeared posthumously in 1946, as did his drama *Chinesische Legende* in 1949.

See: U. Laack-Michel, *Albrecht Haushofer und der Nationalsozialismus* (1974). A.L.W.

Havel, Václav (1936–), Czech dramatist, was born in Prague. Havel has been the principal Czech exponent of the theater of the absurd. He studied chemistry but in 1960 joined the staff of the Theater Na zábradlí, the leading avant-garde theater in Prague. Like Eugène IONESCO, Havel is preoccupied with the disease of language and its failure to communicate; like Sławomir MROŻEK, he uses the forms of absurd theater to dramatize the absurd situation of an individual in a satellite socialist state. His first play, *Zahradní slavnost* (1963; Eng. tr., *The Garden Party,* 1969), pokes fun at empty sloganeering; its hero is a philistine who rapidly advances his career by parroting official slogans. The underlying subject of the play is the failure of institutions and their rhetoric to relate to individuals and their needs. The theme is continued in a second drama, *Vryozumění* (1965; Eng. tr., *The Memorandum,* 1967). In this play, a huge enterprise introduces an artificial language called "Ptydepe," to promote precision of thought and communication, but abandons the language when it proves too difficult to learn; nevertheless, a new artificial language, equally difficult, is at once substituted. A somewhat different theme is introduced in *Ztížená možnost soustředění* (1968; Eng. tr., *The Increased Difficulty of Concentration,* 1972), which concerns modern man's inability to cope with complex human relations in his mechanized society. *Protokoly* (1966; Protocols) contains some lively essays as well as a series of amusing graphic poems, called "typograms," composed on the typewriter. Since 1969 Havel has not been published in Czechoslovakia, but several new plays have appeared outside that country, in Czech and in translation.

See: A. J. Liehm, *The Politics of Culture* (1970); pp. 371–94; P. I. Trensky, *Czech Drama since World War II* (1978), pp. 104–24, 182–90. W.E.H.

Háy, Gyula (1900–75), Hungarian playwright, was born in Abony. His political commitment dates from his adolescence when he was involved in the socialist youth movement. Between 1919 and 1923, and again after 1929, Háy lived in Germany. It was there that his first important play, *Isten, császár, paraszt* (1932; God, Emperor, Peasant), was staged, gaining him immediate recognition among intellectuals. After a short stay in Austria and Switzerland, Háy, who had been a card-carrying Communist since 1932, emigrated to the Soviet Union. He returned to Hungary in 1945 and became a professor at the Academy of Theatrical Art in Budapest. Many of his plays were staged at that time, including *Tiszazug* (written 1936; To Have and To Hold), a drama depicting the desperate social situation of the Hungarian peasantry, and *Az élet hídja* (perf. 1946; The Bridge of Life), a "socialist-realist" account of the reconstruction of Budapest's first postwar bridge. During the "thaw" of 1953–56, Háy became an outspoken critic of the Stalinist system, and in 1957 he was sentenced to six years in jail for "counterrevolutionary activities." Released in 1960, he settled in Switzerland.

Háy was a master of stagecraft, but his best plays have historical rather than social themes. These were collected in the volume *Királydrámák* (1964; Royal Dramas). What really interested him was the clash of human passions and ambitions behind the great movements of history. This is the theme of *Isten, császár, paraszt,* which takes place at the Synod of Konstanz; *Mohács* (1964), an exposé of the internal strife and corruption that led to the conquest of Hungary by the Turks in the 16th century; and *Attila éjszakái* (1964; Attila's Nights), the action of which opens on the eve of the Battle of Catalaneum. Another play, *A ló* (1960; Eng. tr., *The Horse,* 1965), is a straightforward farce about the emperor Caligula's "personality cult" centered on his horse. Háy's colorful memoirs, *Geboren 1900* (1971; Born 1900), were first published in German but have lately been translated into English.

See: I. Hermann, *Szent Iván éjjelén* (1969), pp. 213–36; M. Anderson et al., *Crowell's Handbook of Contemporary Drama* (1971), pp. 226–27; G. Gömöri, "Playwright's Progress," *IOC* 5, no. 3 (1976): 91–92.   G.G.

Hazard, Paul (1878–1944), French scholar and critic, was born in the village of Nordpeene, Nord, the son of a schoolmaster. He himself became one of the most eminent teachers and investigators of his generation, joining high professional competence and scrupulousness with qualities of imagination and grace that endeared him to students in two hemispheres. Trained at the Ecole Normale Supérieure, which he entered in 1900, Hazard was appointed to the chair of comparative literature at the University of Lyon in 1910; he was called to Paris to the Sorbonne in 1919 and became a member of the faculty of the Collège de France in 1925. He lectured extensively abroad and received honorary degrees from the universities of Turin, Santiago (Chile), Mexico, Sofia, Harvard, and Columbia. He was visiting professor at Columbia University in alternate years from 1932 to 1940. Near the end of 1939 he was elected a member of the Académie Française.

Hazard's doctoral thesis, *La Révolution française et les lettres italiennes* (1910; The French Revolution and Italian Literature), has been called a model. Here, as constantly in his subsequent writing, he is substantial, documented, but with no suggestion of the ponderous; he is hospitable to general ideas, never irresponsibly affirmative. The multiplicity of his interests is indicated by such titles as *Leopardi* (1913), *Lamartine* (1926), *Stendhal* (1927), and *Don Quichotte* (1931). In 1932 appeared *Les Livres, les enfants et les hommes* (Eng. tr., *Books, Children & Men,* 1944), a sensitive appraisal of works written for very young readers, or taken over by them, throughout Europe and through the centuries. The comprehensive *Histoire de la littérature française* (2 vols., 1923–24; History of French Literature), compiled with Joseph Bédier, ranks with the *Histoire* of Gustave Lanson. Hazard was long an editor of the highly reputed *Revue de littérature comparée* founded by him and Fernand Baldensperger.

Hazard's La Crise de la conscience européenne (3 vols., 1935; The European Identity Crisis) is a study of the mind and the heart of Europe in the decades from 1680 to 1715. One reviewer said that the title of the first chapter, "De la stabilité au mouvement," might have served the entire work, but Hazard while he had the boldness of his lucidity—and he had to endure the not overly devastating reproach of being "un esprit trop clair"—was capable of both seeking and distrusting simplicity. This book is indispensable for any student of the period and of the genesis of a relativistic attitude in modern Europe.

Hazard came to New York for another semester at Columbia University in 1940; he returned to France in January 1941 to remain with his own people in their tragic ordeal. The enemy refused to accept him for the post to which he was then nominated, the rectorship of the University of Paris. He continued to teach, at Lyon and at Paris, and to study. Before his death in April 1944, he had completed, in cruel circumstances and with a true humanist's steadiness, a continuation of his report on the European "conscience," a large new work to be entitled *La Pensée européenne au XVIIIème siècle, de Montesquieu à Lessing* (1946; Eng. tr., *European Thought in the Eighteenth Century from Montesquieu to Lessing,* 1954). Early in 1944 a clandestine review, *France de demain,* published Hazard's characteristically moving exhortation to his countrymen, "Pour que vive l'âme de la France" (So that the Soul of France May Live; republished in the *Romantic Review,* December 1944).

See: J. M. Carré, "Paul Hazard," *RLC* 20 (1940): 5–12; H. Peyre, "Paul Hazard," *FR* 17 (1944): 309–19.
H.Sm. rev. D.W.A.

Hebrew literature. Hebrew literature, extending from biblical times to the present, may be divided into religious and secular writing. Religious writing is that used for sacred ritual. In ancient times, it was that of the Temple; later, the synagogue. Secular literature is that intended for the edification of the individual. Modern Hebrew literature began at that point where the ritual function of literary production vanished, leaving only the secular. This transition took place in the second half of the 18th century in Italy, a country where Jews enjoyed freer contact with their non-Jewish environment than they did elsewhere. With the spread through Central and Western Europe of more tolerant attitudes toward Jews, Hebrew literature began to adopt the forms of the various European literatures. By the end of the 18th century, modern Hebrew literature was flourishing. But the more Jews gained acceptance among the peoples with whom they lived, the less motivation they had to write in the Hebrew language. This being so, by the beginning of the 19th century the center of Hebrew literary activity shifted to areas such as Russia and some parts of the Austro-Hungarian Empire. Here the assimilation of Jews into local Gentile society had remained only partial, and consequently the motivation of writers to express themselves in Hebrew remained strong. The rise of the Zionist movement in the second half of the 19th century aroused an even more powerful urge to write the language of the Old Testament. That movement declared as its aim the regathering and rejuvenation of the Jews in their ancient land. At the end of the 19th century and the beginning of the 20th centuries, Jewish settlement in Palestine was reestablishing the natural territorial base for Hebrew letters. This settlement was accompanied by the revival and transformation of Hebrew from a written tongue into an everyday, spoken language. Even before World War II, Palestine stood out as the creative center of Hebrew literature. After the holocaust, in which the great Jewish communities were exterminated, Palestine—soon to become Israel—remained virtually alone as the center of Hebrew belles-lettres. At the present time, only the United States continues to house a group of Hebrew-language writers, and there are also individual Hebrew poets and novelists in the Soviet Union (the latter are forbidden to publish their works in their own country). Although isolated Hebrew writers can also be found in other countries, contemporary Hebrew literature today means, in effect, Israeli literature.

The close link between modern Hebrew literature and concrete developments in Jewish history provides the key to the subdivision of the literature into periods: the Enlightenment, the Renaissance, the literature of Mandatory Palestine (or prestatehood Israeli literature), the literature of the holocaust and the struggle for independence, and contemporary Israeli literature.

Hebrew Enlightenment literature began with the Italian-born Hayyim Moshe Luzzatto (1707–46), whose dramas combine cabalistic concepts with the influence of Ludovico Ariosto, Torquato Tasso, and Giambattista Guarini. Another Enlightenment figure, Naphtali Herz Wessely (1726–1805), wrote the poetry in *Shirei Tif'eret* (1709–1802; Songs of Praise) under the influence of the German poet Friedrich Klopstock's *Messiade*. Wessely's work gave powerful momentum to the assimilation by Hebrew writers of the forms of European literature. The philosopher Moses Mendelssohn (1729–86), who in 1750 brought out the first Hebrew-language periodical in Berlin, is also one of the important figures of this period and of modern Hebrew literature.

Hebrew Enlightenment literature developed in three main directions: romanticism, allegory, and satire. The appeal of romanticism led poets and prose writers to create fresh depictions of biblical times. Allegory is evident in the didactic dramas. These depicted biblical figures representing moral values, such as Joseph ha-Efrati's (1770–1804) play *Melnchat Saul* (1794; Saul's Kingdom). Satirical works deal with the intra-Jewish struggle between Hassidim (emotionalists) and Mitnagdim (rationalists) as well as with the struggle against the rigid adherence to the prohibitions of Judaism insisted upon by the stricter rabbis. In this last regard, the Russian writer Judah Leib Gordon (1830–92) is a significant figure. Considered the foremost Enlightenment poet, he aroused considerable controversy because his works fought for the liberation of women and against the overzealous application of traditional Jewish laws (*Halakhah*).

The outstanding satirical writer of Enlightenment literature is MENDELE MOCHER SFORIM (Mendele the Bookseller), the literary nom de plume of Sholem Yacob Abramowitz. The period of Mendele's literary activity, which also includes Yiddish writing, excludes him chronologically from the enlightenment period, but the satirical bent of his works, pervaded by a desire to improve the quality of Jewish life, makes him an important spokesman for Enlightenment ideas. Mendele was a novelist of supreme expressive power who succeeded in creating a many-layered language made up of all the linguistic strata of Hebrew sacred writing—biblical, Mishnaic, and Talmudic. Mendele is the first Hebrew novelist of stature whose importance reaches beyond his own period.

In its Renaissance period, European Hebrew literature began to grasp more thoroughly the complex reality of Jewish existence. The biblical novel *Ahavat Tziyyon* (Love of Zion), written in Lithuania in 1850 by Abraham Mapu (1808–67), may be considered the harbinger of Hebrew Renaissance literature, but the period may be properly dated from 1886. In that year, the great anti-Jewish pogroms that took place all over Russia drove Jewish thought away from the notion of assimilation and toward the idea of a national reawakening. This new movement reached its peak in the 1920s with the immigration of a group of Hebrew writers from Odessa to Palestine. This group included the nation's poet laureate Hayyim Nahman Bialik (1873–1933). Bialik is the foremost poet of the Renaissance period, and he is probably the best exponent of Hebrew literature in its move from the diaspora back to its ancient homeland. His poetry demonstrates both a keen awareness of death and annihilation and an enthusiastic desire to achieve total control over the description of reality. Bialik was also a poet of rebuke whose reproofs emerge from his deep identification with the fate of Jewry.

An important contemporary of Bialik was the poet Shaul Tschernichowsky (1875–1943). If Bialik is considered the poet of the sublime, then Tschernichowsky is the poet of beauty. His poetry is influenced by the spirit of ancient Greece, and his message is universal. He translated an enormous variety of texts from all Western literatures into Hebrew and deliberately fitted his own poetry into formal patterns that emphasize his worldwide cultural affinities. A master of the sonnet and the sonnet cycle, he also wrote many ballads, longer poems, and idylls. His sonnet cycles *La-Shemesh* (1921; To the Sun) and *Al ha-Dam* (1923; On Blood) present his faith in a constructive cosmic force, as well as his faith in the potential of art to redeem the world.

The Renaissance period also produced important prose writers. Micha Joseph Berdichevsky (1865–1921) wrote stories based on folklore and fairy tales that exalt the Nietzschean rebel (*see* Friedrich NIETZSCHE). Joseph Hayyim Brenner (1881–1921) was a "prophet of wrath" who foresaw a dire future for his people. Uri Nissan Gnessin (1879–1913) was a master of introspection whose stories are remarkable for their descriptions of the struggles and doubts of their alienated protagonists.

The prestatehood period began around 1930 with the immigration of talented writers and poets to Palestine. Bialik, as already mentioned, arrived in 1920; Tschernichowsky first came in 1907 and finally settled there in 1931. Shmuel Yosef AGNON came in 1913, returned to Germany, and finally settled in Palestine in 1924. Hayyim Hazaz (1898–1972) and others also made Palestine their permanent home. What these writers share is an ability to face the totality of the Jewish experience past and present. Their works do display some tendentiousness in desiring to alter the character of Jewish life, but the epic dimension enjoyed for its own sake grows and becomes dominant in them.

The fever and pathos that had characterised Renaissance writing gave way in this period to a relatively relaxed poetics in which full-length novels took the place of short stories or novels written in fragmented, diary form. The works of Agnon and Hazaz are, in effect, comprehensive histories, written in literary language, of the Jewish people throughout their existence, with special emphasis on more recent times. Indeed Hazaz and Agnon are the great epic writers of renewed Hebrew literature. Hazaz also included in his works the life of Yemenite Jewry, as in his full-scale novel *Ya'ish* (1940–51), which unfolds over four volumes the life story of a Yemenite Jewish mystic.

Poetry, too, underwent an important development during the prestatehood period. Avraham Shlonsky (1900–73) and Nathan Alterman (1910–70) rebelled against the styles of Bialik and Tschernichowsky. Their writing became more symbolistic and more colorful and their Hebrew is more flexible, as befitting a living, spoken language and not solely a literary medium. Neologisms adorn their writing. Alterman's poetry in particular devotes attention to contemporary issues. In poems he himself called "period and periodical poetry," Alterman vents his reactions to current events affecting the Jewish populace of Palestine. While Alterman and Shlonsky were creating new poetic styles in the 1930s and 1940s, other successful poets were continuing in the tradition of Bialik. *Massada* (1924), by Yitzhak Lamdan, is a symbolic, expressionist poem about a Jewish pioneer who comes to reclaim his homeland. The poetry of Shin Shalom (1904–) formulates a contemporary mysticism. Rachel Bluwstein (1890–1931) and Leah Goldberg (1911–70) delicately interwove their personal experiences into the story of nation-building.

The holocaust, the greatest catastrophe ever to befall Jewry, finds its litearary expression in the poetry of Uri Zvi Greenberg (1890-), perhaps the greatest Hebrew poet of all times. As he writes of the holocaust, this wrathful poet-prophet uses a language that seems both ecstatic and carefully polished in preparation for its historic task. His *Rehovot ha-Narhar—Sefer ha-Illiyyut ve-ha-Koah* (1951; Streets of the River—The Book of Eulogy and Strength) is a series of dirges written during the holocaust (1939-44) and immediately afterward. Greenberg employs expansive metaphors and what he himself calls "the rhythm of the sea," eschewing such poetic structures as the sonnet and symmetrical cycles of poems. Instead of restrictive forms, Greenberg is concerned with teleological goals. His vision of the resurrection of the Jewish people gives his poems the firm conclusions of a definite eschatological outlook. Along with Greenberg, poets from outside Israel also describe the holocaust. Aharon Zeitlin (1898-1973), who lived for many years in the United States, wrote *Bien Ha-Esh ve-ha-Ye'sha* (1957; Between Fire and Salvation), a poetic drama utilizing mystical and parapsychological dimensions to depict the tragedy of European Jewry. The poems of Yitzhak Katzenelson (1885-1944) bear living witness to the furnaces, ghettoes, and concentration camps of the Nazis.

At the opposite pole from Greenberg is the poet Yonathan Ratosh, pseud. of Uriel Shelah (1908-), who elaborated in his poetry the so-called Canaanite ideology. This ideology compares the immigration of Jews to Palestine/Israel to the arrival of immigrants in countries of immigration such as the United States. Ratosh's poetry revives ancient, mythical forms of expression, and devotes itself to the development of ritual and ecstatic rhythms.

The literature of the holocaust chiefly directs itself toward Europe, while the literature of the struggle for independence concentrates on Palestine. Independence literature is, for the most part, realistic. Its emphasis is on the individual's self-realization within some collective framework such as the kibbutz or an underground independence movement. Its poetry is impassioned in tone. For example, Hayyim Guri's (1922-) poems on the War of Independence (1948-49) are entitled *Pirhei Esh* (1949; Flowers of Fire). The prose writing of this period abounds with warrior figures. Moshe Shamir's (1921-) *Hu Halakh ba-Sadot* (1948; He Walked in the Fields) tells the life of a "Palmah" (Crush Squads) fighter, and his *Be-Mo Yadav* (1951; By His Own Hands) is a prose eulogy for his brother, killed in the war. In *Melekh Basar va-Dam* (1954; King of Flesh and Blood), a historical novel set in Hasmonean times (140-63 B.C.), Shamir throws light on the modern struggle between those who were demanding political power for Israel and those who preferred to aim at moral and religious superiority. The novelist S. Yizhar (1916-) uses internal monologue in his novel about the War of Independence. Hebrew drama, which had hitherto been almost entirely poetic and not really suited to theatrical production, now became a vehicle for the discussion of current problems.

Since the War of Independence, Hebrew literature has undergone a shift away from realism. One important new style has been metarealism, a depiction of reality, using metaphysical language loaded with symbols and allegories, that shows the influence of Agnon, Franz KAFKA, and Albert CAMUS. The metarealists include David Shahar (1926-), Binyamin Tammuz (1919-), Aharon Appelfeld (1932-), Avraham B. Yeshoshua (1936-), Yitzhak Orpaz (1923-), and Israel Eliraz (1936-). Varied other new prose styles have been adopted by Aharon Megged (1920-), Hanoch Bartov (1926-), and Amos Oz (1940-). Poetry, too, follows new paths. Yehuda Amihai (1924-) leans toward the daring simile, Nathan Zach (1930-) toward style modeled on T. S. Eliot, and David Avidan (1934-) to an atmosphere of intensive irony. Even the finest poets of the previous generation such as Abba Kovner (1918-) and Amir Gilboa (1917-), have now abandoned closed, symmetrical forms for more open ones. Innovative and experimental approaches are also in evidence in modern drama, particularly the plays of Nissim Alloni (1926-).

Among the historians of modern Hebrew literature are Joseph Klausner (1874-1958) and Fishel Lachover (1883-1947), writers who emphasized a biographical point of departure; Hayyim Nachman Shapira (1894-1943) and Baruch Kurzweil (1907-72), whose point of view is ideological; Avraham Shaanan (1919-) who is a comparatist; Shimon Halkin (1898-), who writes from sociological observation; and Dov Sadan (1902-), who draws links between Hebrew and Yiddish literature, and between Hebrew writers and other Jewish writers.

See: S. Halkin, *Modern Hebrew Literature* (1950); Y. Goell, *Bibliography of Modern Hebrew Literature in English Translation* (1968) and *Bibliography of Modern Hebrew Literature in Translation* (1975).   H.B.

Heiberg, Gunnar Edvard Rode (1857-1929), Norwegian critic, dramatist, and essayist, was born in Christiania (now Oslo). The son of a cultivated, conservative family, he early became conversant with Norwegian as well as European cultural traditions. He visited Rome, where he met Henrik IBSEN, and he spent much time in Copenhagen and Paris. These foreign contacts strongly influenced him, and he developed ideas far different from those of his parents. Even as a university student, he had repudiated his family's conservatism, having accepted the more liberal views of Georg BRANDES and others. Heiberg began his literary career in 1878, publishing two poems, but his first important work was a drama, *Tante Ulrikke* (1883; Aunt Ulrikke), which espoused a radical, socialistic doctrine. From 1884 to 1888, Heiberg was artistic director of the National Theater in Bergen, but he was forced out because of his penchant for presenting plays by contemporary authors.

While he lived, Heiberg was considered an important writer. His cosmopolitan orientation, his aristocratic intellectualism, his disdain for philistinism, which he castigated in the drama *Jeg vil verge mit land* (1912; I Shall Defend My Land) and *Paradesengen* (1913; Bed of State), contributed greatly to an emerging sophistication in Norwegian intellectual and critical endeavor. He does not, however, cast a long shadow. His comments on Ibsen, for example, are dated. Indeed, although Heiberg was a disciple of Ibsen, his two most important dramas, *Balkonen* (1894; Eng. tr., *The Balcony*, 1922) and *Kjærlighetens tragedie* (1904; Eng. tr., *The Tragedy of Love*, 1921) show a closer affinity to certain plays by August STRINDBERG. In spite of his diminished reputation, Norwegians still value Heiberg for his maliciously witty essays, published in several collections, notably *Salt og Sukker* (1924; Salt and Sugar).

See: E. Skavlan, *Gunnar Heiberg* (1950).   S.A.

Heidegger, Martin (1889-1976), German philosopher, was born in Meßkirch, Baden. He is best known for his uncompleted book, *Sein und Zeit* (Eng. tr., *Being and Time*, 1962). Published in 1927 while Heidegger was teaching at Marburg, this work is dedicated to the phenomenologist Edmund Husserl, whom Heidegger succeeded as professor at Freiburg in 1928. Heidegger's understanding of phenomenology differed from Husserl's, however, in that it did not shirk ontology and at the same time admitted being a "hermeneutics"—a historically conditioned interpretation—of existence. Instead of bracketing questions about the reality of the natural, ordinary world in order to produce a presuppositionless investigation of pure consciousness, Heidegger maintained that people are beings already in a world that cannot be bracketed. As traditional distinctions like subject and object, self and world, are only abstractions, Heidegger invented a new vocabulary to avoid Cartesian antinomies. People are not spoken of as thinking things or self-conscious egos, but simply as *Dasein* (human existence, or being-there). *Dasein* is not in its world as one thing merely present (*vorhanden*) along with others, like matches in a box. The world is itself neither another present object, like the matchbox, nor a collection of Cartesian *res extensae* existing independently of a theorizing, contemplative spectator. *Dasein*'s world is a perspectival horizon in which things are first encountered functionally in contexts of use—for instance, like a hammer lying ready-to-hand (*zuhanden*) on a workbench. An essentially temporal and historical being, *Dasein* finds itself thrown (*geworfen*) into a world not of its own making. In fact, for *Dasein* genuinely to find itself at all, it must reflectively recover its own individuality from within an inauthentic dispersion in anonymous, average everydayness. Although no one is ever fully authentic all the time, inauthenticity can and should be combated through the freedom revealed principally in the experience of dread. A genuine recognition of finitude and death dispels self-forgetfulness and first makes it possible for *Dasein* to become a unique self. Not everybody has a self in this sense, however, and whether *Dasein* will succeed in its resolution to follow its silent conscience and give a unity to its life depends on the world *Dasein* is in and on the historical destiny of *Dasein*'s community.

Although the analyses of being-in-the-world, inauthenticity, dread, and finitude became cornerstones for later existentialism, Heidegger did not intend *Being and Time* to be a work of philosophical anthropology and subsequently took a different direction. The analysis of *Dasein* was to be only a provisional way of getting to the deeper question of the meaning of Being (*Sein*), a question sometimes expressed in the form: Why is there something rather than nothing? In the *Brief über den "Humanismus"* (1949; Eng. tr., *Letter on 'Humanism'*, 1962) Heidegger dissociated himself from existentialism, which Jean-Paul SARTRE in his discussion with the Marxist humanists had claimed to be true humanism. Humanism makes the mistake, Heidegger believed, of not questioning the metaphysical positing of the human being as subject and as the measure of all things. The central philosophical concern is not simply with the truth about the nature of people but with the very possibility of truth as such, which Heidegger thinks of as *aletheia*, a meaningful lack of concealment or disclosure. Heidegger's favored metaphor for disclosure is that of a forest clearing (*Lichtung*), the open space required for the illumination of otherwise obscure things. If *Being and Time* implies that *Dasein* is the essential place of disclosure, later writings like *Unterwegs zur Sprache* (1959; Eng. tr., *On the Way to Language*, 1971) shift the center of investigation from man to language. Language is most fundamentally not the idle speech of the average person but the horizon of intelligibility in which the truth of Being first discloses itself, however partially. People alone cannot will such disclosure, and their measure could only be revealed as if it were historically sent to them as a gift from beyond themselves (*Seinsgeschick*). Such sendings are recorded in the history of ontology (*Seinsgeschichte*), but only negatively, for Heidegger reads it as a series of ways of forgetting the fundamental question of the meaning of Being. That the history of Western metaphysics eventuates in the nihilism of the modern, technological world view is thus no accident. Technology's manipulation of people and world is the consequence of the metaphysical reductions of men to free-floating subjects, things to quantifiable objects, and knowledge to clear and distinct propositions. A sign of this emergent nihilism is the actual failure of modern philosophy to question these reductions and to overcome metaphysics. The clue to the recall from nihilism is to be found not in further metaphysical ratiocination, but in more thoughtful attention to language itself, and specifically to poetry: *Erläuterungen zu Hölderlins Dichtung* (1951; Eng. tr., *Elucidations of Hölderlin's Poetry*, 1978). Poetry is understood not merely aesthetically, as decorative, figurative-speaking, but ontologically, as the power to call forth and ground a new historical era. A variety of monumental cultural artifacts can be poetic in this sense, and Heidegger's examples include Greek temples, Vincent Van Gogh's paintings, and presumably the Bible, although most significant are the works of poets like Rainer Maria RILKE, Georg TRAKL, Stefan GEORGE and, preeminently, Friedrich Hölderlin.

Less important for the theory of literature than the correctness of Heidegger's readings of these poets is the claim that poetry is most essentially not an aesthetic or formalist concern for words alone but rather an ontological and constitutive response to the world. This response can be historically effective and culturally productive, generating a tradition of reception and influence. Literary historians and critics must question this evolving tradition continually if the force of a poetic creation is to be preserved. Already in *Being and Time* Heidegger stresses that all understanding is conditioned by a prior concern for the subject matter and that any understanding is the result of an inevitably circular process of interpretation. This analysis of the hermeneutic circle gave new life to the tradition of hermeneutics, which was subsequently revived in H.-G. Gadamer's *Wahrheit und Methode* (Eng. tr., *Truth and Method*, 1975).

See: M. Murray, ed., *Heidegger and Modern Philosophy: Critical Essays* (1978); W. Spanos, ed., *Heidegger and Literature* (1979). D.C.H.

Heidenstam, Verner von (1859–1940), Swedish poet and novelist, was born at Olshammar, on Lake Vätter. He spent several years abroad (in Italy, Greece, Syria, Egypt, France, and Switzerland) and returned to live close to Lake Vätter at Övralid in 1925. In 1916 he received the Nobel Prize in Literature. The poems in his first book, *Vallfart och vandringsår* (1888; Pilgrimage and Wanderyears), reflect his travels in the Mediterranean countries with their vivid exoticism. Brilliant in color, indolent, and antiutilitarian in morals, the poems formed a sharp contrast to the prevailing literary mood of the 1880s. Heidenstam became the leading author among the so-called *90-talister* (The 1890s). In the essay "Renaissance" (1889) and other pamphlets, he argued for a union of imagination, of the sense of the beautiful, and of bold realism in literature, and also for what he considered to be "the peculiarities of our national temperament." *Dikter* (1895; Poems) has a rich variety of motifs and themes, but a more restrained moralism and a decided patriotism are obvious. Indeed a vein of patriotism is characteristic of Heidenstam's writings at the turn of the century, manifest in his choice of national themes for his novels and prose writing: *Karolinerna* (1897–98; Eng. tr., *The Charles Men*, 1920), *Heliga Birgittas pilgrimsfärd* (1901; Saint Birgitta's Pilgrimage) and *Folkungaträdet* (2 vols., 1905–

07; Eng. tr., *The Tree of the Folkungs*, 1925). The poetic cycle *Ett folk* (1902; One People) includes "Sverige," sometimes considered as a Swedish national anthem. Heidenstam's last book was *Nya dikter* (1915; New Poems). In this volume the mood of *livsglädje* (joy of living) of his first poems and the mood of patriotism of his middle have yielded to a serene maturity and resignation. The clear, simple form recalls Goethe's lyrics. A book of memoirs from his childhood, *När kastanjerna blommade* (1941; When the Chestnut Trees Were in Bloom), was published posthumously.

See: A. Gustafson, *Six Scandinavian Novelists* (1940), pp. 123–76; F. Böök, *Verner von Heidenstam* (1945, 1946; rev. ed., 1959); S. Björck, *Heidenstam och sekelskiftets Sverige* (1946) and *Verner von Heidenstam* (1947); G. Axberger, *Diktaren och elden* (1959); A. Gustafson, *A History of Swedish Literature* (1961), pp. 295–305.

N.Å.S.

Heijermans, Herman (1864–1924), Dutch dramatist, novelist, short-story writer, and journalist, was born in Rotterdam. At first, business seemed to promise a successful career, but financial failure brought disgrace and the threat of bankruptcy. His early desire to write received new encouragement when *De Gids,* the leading literary magazine, published a story by him. He seized the opportunity to move to the metropolitan and cultural center of Amsterdam, where he found a livelihood writing for *De Telegraaf.* It was his column in this newspaper that gave rise to his famous series of sketches of Dutch life, later known as *Falklandjes.*

The reception of his first play, *Dora Kremer* (1893), was a great disappointment to him. His next play was the one-act *Ahasverus* (1912; Eng. tr., 1929), which he produced that same year under a pseudonym, pretending that it was a translation from the Russian of a certain Ivan Jelakovich. The play proved a huge success, and Heijermans revenged himself upon the critics by revealing that the supposedly talented young Russian was none other than himself and by printing the enthusiastic reviews of the critics alongside their harsh words about *Dora Kremer.* The success of his next play, *Ghetto* (1889; Eng. tr., 1889), established Heijermans upon the Dutch stage. *Het zevende gebod* (1900; The Seventh Commandment) offered another critical view of the middle class and its morality. His most famous play, *Op Hoop van zegen* (1901; Eng. tr., *The Good Hope*, 1912), won him an international reputation. It is a masterful and realistic genre painting of Dutch fishermen at the turn of the century, caught in an unequal struggle against the sea and the shipowners who exploit them. The enormous popularity of the play contributed to the Ships Act of 1909, which provided for better government regulation of seagoing vessels and more protection for the men who sailed them. In a similar manner, Heijermans brought the tillers of the soil to the stage in *Ora et labora* (1903; Pray and Work) and the miners in *Glück auf!* (1911; Good Luck!). His skill and craftsmanship in the creation of middle-class drama are evident in two very different plays about businessmen, *Schakels* (1904–05; Eng. tr., *Links,* 1927) and *De opgaande zon* (1911; Eng. tr., *The Rising Sun,* 1926). Heijerman's love of the world of imagination emerges in *Uitkomst* (1909–11; The Way Out), a tender fantasy growing out of the delirium of a dying child, as well as in *Dageraad* (1920; Dawn) and *De wijze kater* (1919; The Wise Tomcat). His imagination is one of the traits setting him off from the naturalistic school. Among his other important dramas are *Allerzielen* (1905; All Souls) and *Eva Bonheur* (1919), an affectionate and humorous portrait of a crabbed, lonely old woman. Heijermans was

also a talented writer of one-act plays and wrote half a dozen of them in the two years between 1898 and 1900. *In de Jonge Jan* (1903; At the Jonge Jan) and *De Meid* (1911; The Maid) are both one-act dramas that gained fame on stages outside the Netherlands. Heijermans added a new word to the Dutch language with the *Falklandje,* the popular sketch of Dutch life he published every weekend under the pseudonym of Samuel Falkland. The *Falklandjes* appeared weekly for over 20 years, first in *De Telegraaf* and then in the *Algemeen Handelsblad,* two of the largest daily newspapers in Amsterdam. Some of Heijerman's one-act plays first appeared as *Falklandjes.* Among his best-known novels are *Kamertjeszonde* (1898; Sin in a Furnished Room), *Diamantstad* (1904; Diamond City), *Droomkoninkje* (1924; The Little Dream King), and *Duczika* (1926). He also achieved fame in Germany, and his plays have been performed over the world.

Heijermans began his career as a dramatist in the years when the "free-theater movement" was revitalizing the European stage. In the Nederlandsche Tooneelvereeniging (The Netherlands Stage Society), established in 1893, he found an acting company that was to bring to Holland the ensemble system so necessary for the new drama and for the plays he was going to create. Henrik IBSEN, Emile ZOLA, Gerhart HAUPTMANN, naturalism, symbolism, and the "Movement of the Eighties" had filled the air with new ideas. Each made a strong impression on him, and although he eventually rejected all of them, each left some mark upon his work. Yet he maintained his artistic integrity and followed an independent path of development. He never belonged to any school or coterie. In spite of the fact that he was a keen critic of society, he portrayed the middle class with the same skill and warmth he demonstrated in his proletarian dramas. He captured the life and language of the Dutch people on the stage. Heijermans became the greatest Dutch playwright of the modern period, and no one has yet taken his place.

See: B. Hunningher, *Toneel en werkelijkheid* (1947); L. Flaxman, *Herman Heijermans and his Dramas* (1954); E. de Jong, *Herman Heijermans en de vernieuwing van het Europese drama* (1967).

S.L.F.

Hein, Piet, pseud. Kumbel (1905–), Danish poet, designer, and scientist, was born in Copenhagen. The creator of numerous technical inventions, he became an honorary doctor at Yale University in 1972. Hein is internationally known for his *Gruk* (vols. 1–20, 1940–63; Eng. tr., *Grooks,* vols. 1–6, 1966–78), short, often four-lined epigramlike poems containing philosophical and contemporary thoughts. They show exceptional stylistic humor and precision. Apart from *Grooks,* Hein has published more traditional collections with speculative pathetic contents. One selection is published as *Digte fra alle årene* (1972; Poems from All the Years), in which, as in his essays, Hein deals with the modern duality, the split between science and the humanities.

S.H.R.

Heinesen, William (1900–), Faeroese poet, novelist, and short-story writer was born in Thórshavn, where he has lived since 1932. His earliest collections of poetry (1921–30) express an extreme individualism when the self—confronted with Faeroese nature—faces loneliness and death in isolation, whereas the volume *Stjernerne vaagner* (1930; The Stars Awaken) denotes a turning away from mysticism toward social awareness. This tendency is continued in *Panorama med regnbue* (1972; Panorama with Rainbow), but here it is again combined with Heinesen's predilection for cosmic nature. In his prose his social commitment is first noticeable in *Blsende Gry* (1934;

Stormy Daybreak) and the collective novel *Noatun* (1938; Eng. tr., *Niels Peter,* 1940), which describes the individual's battle with harsh Faeroese nature. Heinesen's imaginative narrative talent develops freely first in the three masterful novels *De fortabte Spillemñd* (1950; Eng. tr., *The Lost Musicians,* 1971), *Det gode Håb* (1964; The Good Hope), and *Tårnet ved verdens ende* (1976; The Tower at the End of the World), in which the comic and tragic elements in man's existence are ingeniously mingled in both dramatic and lyrical descriptions of Faeroese life and characters. Heinesen is one of those rare authors who succeeds, both as a poet with a cosmic vision and as a narrator of fabulous tales, in creating his own universe. Behind the outer social and historical period pieces, like those found in *Forīllinger fra Thorshavn* (1973; Stories from Thorshavn), a selection of Heinesen's best short stories, he seeks the poetic experience that is the only thing of lasting value in a changing world.

See: W. Glyn Jones, *William Heinesen, TWAS* 282 (1974). S.H.R.

Heißenbüttel, Helmut (1921–), German poet, novelist, essayist, critic, and radio playwright, was born in Rüstringen near Wilhelmshaven, was drafted into the army during World War II, and served until he was wounded. At the universities of Dresden, Leipzig, and Hamburg he studied architecture, literature, and art history. For two years he worked for a publishing house in Hamburg. Since 1958 he has lived in Stuttgart, where he is the director of the radio essay program of the Süddeutscher Rundfunk.

Stylistic experiments link Heißenbüttel, who rejects traditional modes of writing, to "concrete poetry" and the "new novel." Although a tenuous story line can often be recognized in his work, there is no omniscient observer or well-developed plot. Instead, Heißenbüttel argues, the "word" and clichés must be freed from conventional syntactic units, verse, meter, rhyme, and transcendental meaning and be considered as materials for "new combinations." He produces collages: cut-outs, "combined and glued together" to project a broken reality and the fragmented consciousness of modern industrial society. Attempting to pinpoint the ever-changing aspect of mobile language, he uses key words or sentences in varying contexts and the structural devices of repetition, combination, association, analysis, and synthesis. Often clichés are atomized into particles and restructured at random; sometimes he phrases syllables and letters like tonal patterns in music; occasionally he changes longer syntactic units into elemental predications by reducing transformations. Clearly, Heißenbüttel's prosodic experiments are influenced by transformational linguistics, cybernetics, and communication theory.

The titles of his first two collections of poetry are significantly indicative: *Kombinationen* (1954) and *Topographien* (1956) point in the direction that all his subsequent works would take. In them and in *Textbuch 1* to *Textbuch 6* (1960, 1961, 1962, 1964, 1965, and 1967), Heißenbüttel reveals himself as a member of the avant-garde, using techniques similar to those of "concrete poetry" but not those of the graphic arts. His building blocks are key words and ideas, literary clichés, visual images, random information, and philosophical, psychological, religious, economic, sociological, and political observations. Within collage units, style matches content; adjacent units contrast. Formal essayistic elements are followed by unrestrained colloquial chatter, objective analysis by subjective tirade, history by hearsay. Language is woven into a closely knit fictional fabric to achieve certain effects that may be ironic, playful, or provocative. Heißenbüttel's

collage projects the changing kaleidoscopic experience in the mind of the modern intellectual. His five radio plays also skilfully demonstrate his compositional talent with flashbacks, cuts, repetition, fragmentation, and stereo effects.

However, the best example of his technique, *Projekt Nr. 1. D'Alemberts Ende* (1970; Project No. 1. The End of D'Alembert), his first novel, is a gigantic collage of commentary, clichés, information, interior monologues, and fragments of a story about nine characters and their relationships, all set against the background of modern Germany. Although d'Alembert and his intellectual friends have strong autobiographical traits, the book is not an autobiography because Heißenbüttel denies the very idea of personal identity. Rather, the work is a projection of his concept of writing. Since he believes that "the individual is extinct," and "everything is questionable," all that remains for him is language as a combination of quotations and clichés retrieved from the storehouse of a common cultural and linguistic heritage. The author uses notes, statistics, quotations, personal reminiscences, and observations as raw materials to be cut, arrayed, combined, and restructured. The result is "synthetic authenticity," Heißenbüttel's "new organization of language."

See: R. A. Burns, *Commitment, Language and Reality* (1975); R. Rumold, *Sprachliche Experiment und literarische Tradition* (1975). A.P.O.

Helder (de Oliveira), Herberto (1930–), Portuguese poet and writer of short prose fiction, was born in Funchal, Madeira. While attending the University of Coimbra, he had his first small collection of poems, *O amor em visita* (1958; Love's Visit) published by the surrealist "underground". He gave up his studies to live in Lisbon and work for a publishing house. His subsequent books were mostly poetry. They include *A colher na boca* (1961; Spoon in Mouth); *Poemacte* (1961; Poem-act); *Lugar* (1962; Place); *Os passes em volta* (1963, enlarged 1970; The Footsteps around Us), short stories; *Apresentação do rosto* (19..; Introduction of the Face), short stories; *Electronicolírica* (1964; Electronicalyric); *Húmus* (1967; Humus), a poetic tribute to the writer Raul BRANDÃO; *Ofície cantante* (1967; Singing Profession); *Retrate em movimento* (1967; Portrait in Motion), poetic essays with personal impressions and reactions; and *Vocação animal* (1971; Animal Vocation), poems. *Poesia toda I* (1973; Complete Poetical Works I) contains Helder's poetry to date.

Life, love, loneliness, and death are recurring themes in his writing. After an apprenticeship in surrealism, Helder probes the magic of language, becoming the foremost literary experimenter in Portugal with the visual effects of "concrete poetry" and with combinatory exercises. In his prose fiction, he prefers first-person narrative (as in *Os passes em volta*) to create episodes, generally brief, in which present, past, memory, dream, delirium, or nightmare enter in varying proportions. Strange visions of death intrude in a well-ordered sequence of events, as with the man who is building a house in which to die ("O quarte" (The Room). Yearnings for purity, innocence, and exaltation contend with a miserable human reality. "Teorema" (Theorem) retells with disturbingly effective timelessness the story of King Pedro the Cruel, "mad, innocent and brutal," executing before a "barbarous, pure" people the assassin of his beautiful mistress, Inês de Castro, as if the narrator were the assassin himself.

See: R. Bele, "Poesia e arte poética em Herberto Helder," *O Tempe* 1 (1963). T.Br.

Hellens, Franz, pseud. of Frédéric van Ermengem (1881–1972), Belgian prose writer, poet, playwright, and essayist, was born in Brussels, but he spent his childhood in Wetteren (eastern Flanders) and in Ghent, capital of the same province, where he studied law at the French University. After the World War I and a long stay on the Côte d'Azur, he founded in 1921, with the French poet André SALMON, an important review, successively titled *Signaux de France et de Belgique, Le Disque vert, Ecrits du Nord,* then again *Ecrits du Nord* and *Le Disque vert.* Between 1936 and 1939 Hellens animated the "Groupe du lundi," which proclaimed that the French writers of Belgium were an integrated part of French literature, thus denying the existence of a Belgian national school. Meanwhile, the author had been appointed librarian of the Belgian Parliament. After the superannuation he settled down in La Celle-Saint-Cloud (near Paris). He died in Brussels.

Hellens wrote 122 volumes. His novels and short stories, amply suffused with poetry, move between the two poles of onéirism—with *Les Clartés latentes* (1912; Fading Lights) and mainly *Mélusine* (1920)—and realism—with *La Femme partagée* (1929; The Shared Woman) and *Moreldieu* (1946)—and convey what the author names *Réalités fantastiques* (title of a volume of short stories, 1923; Fantastic Realities) or "Le Fantastique réel" (title of an essay, 1967; The Fantastic Becomes Real). We find another approach to this question in *La Vie seconde ou les Songes sans la clé* (1945; The Second Life or Dreams without a Key). The various expressions of the interaction between life and dream may descend to the gloomy underworld of Ghent—*Les Hors-le-vent* (1909; Out of the Wind)—or wear the tinsel of African magic in *Bass-Bassina-Boulou* (1922). They return to Flanders with *Fraîcheur de la mer* (1933; Freshness of the Sea), reach the supernatural in *Mémoires d'Elseneur* (1954), and resume the thematic of fantastic reality in *Les Yeux du rêve* (1964; The Eyes of the Dream). The autobiographical background of many books, from *Le Naïf* (1926; The Naive One) to *Cet âge qu'on dit grand* (1970; What They Call Ripe Old Age), is evident. Perhaps the work of Hellens is more respected than admired. Often his "invention" is laborious, and, unfortunately, his language is sometimes misused. When he leaves the Flemish inspiration for cosmopolitan or exotic subjects, his style loses originality and vigor. But he has ruled over French literature in Belgium, and his influence is undeniable. He has had his portrait painted by Amedeo Modigliani; he was the discoverer of Henri MICHAUX and Michel de GHELDERODE; he was a friend of Maksim GORKY and Ilya ERENBURG, of Giuseppe UNGARETTI and Vicente ALEIXANDRE, of Jules ROMAINS and Jean PAULHAN. Famous critics like René ETIEMBLE, Jean CASSOU, Léopold Ségar SENGHOR, and Carlo Bo were interested in his work.

As a lyric poet, Hellens observed both the regular prosody and the classical sense of composure and rigor, in spite of a quite symbolist or surrealist complaisance to the "noble putrescence" (see *Pourriture noble,* 1951). In a second phase he inclined to a certain liberation of the verse. His principal lyrics are included in *Poésie complète, 1905–1959* (1959), *L'Age dur, 1957–1960* (1961; The Hard Age), and *Arrière-saisons, 1960–1967* (1967; The Close of the Seasons). For the stage Hellens wrote the farces and tragedies of *Petit Théâtre aux chandelles* (1960; Little Theater by Candlelight).

See: M. Manoll and G. Le Clec'h, *Franz Hellens* (1956); A. Lebois, *Franz Hellens* (1963); A. Vialatte, *Franz Hellens et ses mythes* (1967); R. De Smedt, *Franz Hellens: recueil d'études, de souvenirs et de témoignages* (1971).

J.-P. de N.

Hémon, Louis (1880–1913), French novelist, was born in Brest. He grew up with the spirit of restless independence so often characteristic of seafaring communities. Although he studied law and completed training for a career in colonial administration, he found the thought of a functionary's life unacceptable, turning instead to literature. He first contributed stories and articles to periodicals that dealt with sports and physical fitness, of which he was an enthusiast. When in his mid-20s, Hémon moved to England, where he married and continued to write for French periodicals, expanding his range to include stories of social commentary. The death of his wife in 1911, when he was 31 years old, plunged him into despair, and in another bout of restlessness he sailed for Canada.

Preferring the rural wilderness to the cities, Hémon found employment as a farmhand in the remote Lac Saint Jean region north of Montreal. He was impressed with the patient devotion that the inhabitants displayed towards their austere, joyless life in that thinly populated area. Hémon's admiration for the quiet courage with which these settlers were conquering the wilderness inspired him to write a novel evoking the daily monotony and suffering of that rude existence. He moved back to Montreal to do the writing during the winter and spring of 1912–13, and in early July of 1913 he dispatched his manuscript to the Parisian newspaper *Le Temps.* A few days later, having restlessly taken to the road once again, Hémon was accidentally killed by a train in northern Ontario. Meanwhile, his novel was accepted for publication by *Le Temps;* it appeared in installments during the spring of 1914 under the title *Maria Chapdelaine.*

The serial publication of *Maria Chapdelaine* in Paris attracted little notice, but book publication in Montreal in 1916, arranged by Hémon's father, won the novel rapid recognition among its natural audience, both as a work of art and as an impressive celebration of the pioneering spirit of the French-Canadian farmer. The book quickly took its place as a major landmark in the literature about French Canada, its reputation growing through large sales and successive Canadian editions after 1916. A book edition was also published in Paris in 1921 and won a considerable posthumous reputation for the author in his native land, as well. During the 1920s, several of the novels and stories he had published in installments in periodicals at the start of his career were republished in book form to feed the growing public interest in his work. A diary found among his papers was also published, but nothing appeared to equal the interest and the artistry of *Maria Chapdelaine,* which remains his claim to fame. This remarkably sensitive, poetic novel has earned for Hémon a unique place in the history of French-Canadian letters. He remains the only non-Canadian to have contributed a great classic to the literature of French Canada.

See: A. McAndrew, *Louis Hémon: sa vie et son œuvre* (1936)

M.S.

Herbert, Zbigniew (1924–), Polish poet, essayist, and playwright, was born in Lvov and studied law in Toruń, commerce in Cracow, and philosphy in Warsaw. Although his poems were printed in *Tygodnik Powszechny* as early as the late 1940s, his first book of poetry, *Struna światła* (1956; A Chord of Light), could be published only during the post-Stalin "thaw." His poetry and plays have been translated into most Western languages.

Herbert's poetry is firmly rooted in the historical experience of his generation, which was decimated in the Warsaw uprising of 1944 and demoralized during the years of Stalinist oppression. It also reflects his deep concern about the survival of certain cultural and individual human values. Whereas his historicism, philosophical preoccupations, and references to Greek mythology point to classicist leanings, the impermanence of both tradition and reality are constantly stressed in Herbert's sly parables and ironic "assessments" of situations. *Hermes, pies i gwiazda* (1957; Hermes, Dog and Star) and *Studium przedmiotu* (1961; A Study of the Object) established Herbert as a mature poet, a compassionate observer of the human condition. His book of poetry *Pan Cogito* (1974; Mr. Cogito) marks his return to the everyday problems of existence and a more critical attitude toward certain manifestations of contemporary Western civilization. Herbert's essays discussing Italian and French culture and history, collected in the volume *Barbarzyńca w ogrodzie* (1962; A Barbarian in tne Garden), are impressive in their erudite lucidity. Iis plays, published in book form as *Dramaty* (1970; Dramas), are written more for the radio than for the stage.

See: J. Kwiatkowski, *Klucze do wyobraźni* (1964), pp. 360–74; A. Alvarez, Introduction to Z. Herbert, *Selected Poems,* pp. 265–79; (1968); G. Gömöri, "Herbert and Yevtushenko: On Whose Side Is History?" *Mosaic* 3, no. 1 (1969): 50–61.   G.G.

Herburger, Günter (1932–), German novelist and poet, was born in Isny in Bavaria and studied literature, sociology, philosophy, and Sanskrit in Munich and Paris. He worked at various occupations during travels in France, Spain, North Africa, and Italy, and on his return to Germany was a television editor with the South German television network. An adherent of the new contemporary realism initiated by Dieter WELLERSHOFF in Cologne, Herburger has written film scripts for television and is the author of stories for children, as well as of novels, poems, and short stories.

His first publication, a volume of short stories, *Eine gleichmäßige Landschaft* (Eng. tr., *A Monotonous Landscape,* 1968), appeared in 1964. *Die Messe* (1969; The Fair), his first novel, brings the realistic narrator into contact with the grotesque in the world about him, encounters for which he is in no way prepared. *Jesus in Osaka* (1970) is subtitled a novel of the future and takes place in an unnamed but obviously Japanese landscape in 1984. In a mass society a hippylike Jesus figure comes forward as an anarchistic world messiah who preaches love and brotherhood. At the conclusion of the novel he marches with a group of children through a tropical landscape. In 1972, Herburger declared his allegiance to communism, a persuasion first apparent in the title story of a collection, *Die Eroberung der Zitadelle* (The Conquest of the Citadel) and continued in the multivolume novel *Flug ins Herz* (1977; Flight into the Heart), which he has called his "wish biography" and in which he calls for social and political reform.

Herburger is also the author of volumes of poetry, such as *Ventile* (1966; Valves), *Training* (1969), *Operette* (1973), and *Ziele* (1977; Targets). Most of his poems resemble prose rather than lyric utterances, and most take up the themes of his narrative fiction reflecting his deep concern with contemporary political and sociological problems, as in the poem "Vietnam." *Die amerikanische Tochter* (1973; The American Daughter) contains poems, essays, a radio play, and a story.

Herburger's concern for the future of humankind is evident in his books for children. *Birne kann alles* (1971; Birne Can Do Anything) and *Birne kann noch mehr* (1971; Birne Can Do Even More) were written for his son, who also drew the illustrations. *Helmut in der Stadt* (1972; Helmut in Town) and the third Birne book, *Birne brennt durch* (1975; Birne Breaks Loose) contain Herburger's hope that the children of today can be the emancipators

and creators of new forms of society tomorrow. Herburger is also the author of radio plays, such as *Exhibition oder Ein Kampf um Rom* (1971; Eng. tr., "Exhibition or A Battle for Rome," 1972, in *Dimension*), a piece that provides a panorama of the possibilities of the form in wild parody. He has written a number of television film scenarios, as well as the screenplay adaptation of his story "Eroberung" (1977).   A.L.W.

Herczeg, Ferenc (1863–1954), Hungarian playwright, novelist, and short-story writer, was born in Versec (now in Yugoslavia). He studied law in Budapest, where he lived most of his life. For a brief time, Herczeg hesitated between writing in German or Hungarian, finally choosing the latter as his medium of expression. His family belonged to the middle class, but his taste—and perhaps his vanity—induced him to seek the company of the ruling "historical classes"; he was accepted by them and, in fact, he acted and even thought exactly as members of that particular social stratum were expected to. His devotion to these people made him an observant and forgiving recorder of their idiosyncrasies. Herczeg was editor of *Uj idők,* a popular middle-class magazine, for 50 years. As a writer, he possessed the sort of entertaining imagination and observation that stimulates but does not profoundly stir. His ideology rarely went a step farther than was permissible for a Hungarian gentleman.

Herczeg made use of almost every literary genre, but it is difficult to say how much of his work promises permanent value. Of his gay but superficial tales (several of them dramatized), the best known are *Gyurkovics lányok* (1893; The Gyurkovics Girls) and *Gyurkovics fiúk* (1895; The Gyurkovics Boys). His later fiction is more serious. In his historical novels, such as *Pogányok* (1902; Pagans) and *Az élet kapuja* (1919; Life's Gate), Herczeg delved into Hungarian history to unravel the secret of the East-West duality of the Hungarian soul. His comedies are romantic and pleasant, yet somehow second-rate. His finest psychological play is *Kék róka* (1917; Blue Fox), while his best tragedy is *Bizánc* (1904; Byzantium), a work often staged in Hungary before 1945. Some of his hostorical dramas, such as *A híd* (1925; The Bridge), are paraphrased presentations of modern Hungarian problems.

See: J. Horváth, *Herczeg Ferenc* (1925); J. Barta, "Herczeg Ferenc mai szemmel," *Alföld* 6 (1955): 59–69; J. Reményi, *Hungarian Writers and Literature* (1964), pp. 220–28.   J.R. rev. G.G.

Heredia, José Maria de (1842–1905), French poet, was born in Cuba but went to France in 1851 and spent the rest of his life there. Influenced by the poetry of Charles-Marie-René Leconte de Lisle (1818–94), Heredia became involved in the Parnassian movement, choosing for his own the rigorous and precise form of the Petrarchan sonnet. From 1862 on, Heredia's sonnets appeared in various literary reviews and in *Parnasse contemporain* (1866, 1871, 1876). After 30 years of revision, he selected 118 of his sonnets to be published in one volume, *Les Trophées* (1893; Eng. tr., *The Trophies,* 1910) which was enthusiastically received by the French public. A more inclusive edition of his works, *Poésies complètes avec notes et varantes* (Complete Poems with Notes and Variants), appeared in 1924. *Les Trophées* is composed of five cycles: "Greece and Sicily," "Rome and the Barbarians," "The Middle Ages and the Renaissance," "The Orient and the Tropics," and "Nature and Dream." This collection, often compared to Victor Hugo's *Légende des sièecles* (1859; Legend of the Centuries), is primarily made up of scattered episodes taken from the history of human civilization. Heredia's remarkable erudition, his sure knowledge of art and history, is revealed in every sonnet. *Les Trophées* received the Poetry Prize of the Académie Française. Exemplifying the Parnassian ideals of objectivity, precision, and transposition of the plastic arts into a poetic framework, these sonnets are masterpieces of technical perfection, thoroughly documented and strikingly synthesized.

Shortly after the publication of *Les Trophées,* Heredia was elected to the Académie Française and became literary director of *Le Journal.* He also published several French translations of Spanish literature. In 1901, he was appointed administrator of the Arsenal Library.

See: M. Ibrovac, *José-Maria de Heredia* (1923).

D.C. and A.C.

Herling-Grudziński, Gustaw (1919–), Polish short-story writer, essayist, and literary critic, was born in Kielce. He studied Polish literature and published his first essays in Warsaw. Following the 1939 September campaign at the beginning of World War II, he organized an anti-Nazi underground group. In 1940 he was deported to a Soviet labor camp. Upon his release he joined the Polish army and participated in the Italian campaign of the Allies, including the battle of Monte Cassino. After the war he lived and published in Rome and in London. In 1955 he settled in Naples, Italy, and became a steady contributor to the Italian monthly *Tempo Presente* and to the Polish monthly *Kultura,* published in Paris. He gained wide recognition with his book *Inny świat* (1953; Eng. tr., *A World Apart,* 1951), which is based on his experiences and observations in the Soviet labor camp and which was first published in English with an introduction by Bertrand Russell. The book is quite unique for both its humanitarian and literary values. Herling-Grudziński also excels in the genre of the short story, which he handles in a very original way, in *Skrzydła ołtarza* (1960; The Wings of the Altar) and *Drugie przyjście* (1963; The Second Coming), which appeared in English under the title *The Island* (1967). His critical essays *Żywi i umarli* (1945; The Living and the Dead), *Upiory rewolucji* (1969; The Ghosts of the Revolution), and *Dziennik pisany nocą* (1973; A Diary Written at Night) are remarkable for their brilliance.

See: T. Terlecki, ed., *Literatura na obczyźnie 1940–1960,* 2 vols. (1964); M. Danilewicz Zielińska, *Szkice o literaturze emigracyjnej* (1978), pp. 226–30.   Z.Y.

Hermans, Willem Frederik (1921–), Dutch novelist, critic, dramatist, and poet, was born in Amsterdam. He studied physical geography, receiving his degree in 1955, and became a member of the faculty at the University of Groningen. In 1973 he resigned his academic position and moved to Paris. He won first prize in an essay contest, which led to publication in the *Algemeen Handelsblad* in 1940. Hermans published several volumes of poetry, *Kussen door een rag van woorden* (1944; Kisses through a Cobweb of Words), *Horror coeli* (1946; Horror of the Heavens), and *Hypnodrome* (1948). World War II often forms the background of Hermans's work, as it did for his first important novel, *De tranen der acacia's* (1949; The Tears of the Acacias), and for *Ik heb altijd gelijk* (1951; I Am Always Right), *Herinneringen van een engelbewaarder* (1971; Memories of a Guardian Angel), and *De donkere kamer van Damokles* (1958; The Dark Chamber of Damocles). Hermans has a rather bleak view of the universe, and he does not believe that it is possible to improve people, who live in a chaotic world, as is evident in his first-person-singular novel *Nooit meer slapen* (1966; No more Sleeping). Among his other novels are *De god Denkbaar Denkbaar de god* (1956; The God Is Conceiv-

able, Conceivable Is the God); a sequel, *Het evangelie van O. Dapper Dapper* (1973; The Gospel according to O. Dapper Dapper); and *Onder professoren* (1975; Among Professors). Hermans has also written several volumes of short stories, *Moedwil en misverstand* (1948; Willfulness and Misunderstanding), *Paranoia* (1953), *Een landingspoging op Newfoundland* (1957; A Landing Attempt on Newfoundland), and *Een wonderkind of een total loss* (1967; A Child Prodigy, or A Total Loss) and three plays, *Drie drama's* (1962), consisting of *Het omgekeerde pension* (The Topsy-turvy Boarding House), *Dutch comfort,* and *De psychologische test* (The Psychological Test), as well as two television plays, *King Kong* (1972) and *Periander* (1974). In addition to some interesting volumes of essays—such as the amusing and critical *Mandarijnen op zwavelzuur* (1964; Mandarins in Sulfuric Acid) and *Het sadistische universum* (1964; The Sadistic Universe)— Hermans has also published *Fotobiografie* (1969; Photobiography). He was an editor of both *Criterium* (1946–48) and *Podium* (1950, 1963–64). He feels that his achievements as a scientist have brought him much more recognition than his work as a writer. Having earlier rejected two prizes, the Vijverberg Prize and the P. C. Hoof Prize, Hermans traveled to Brussels to receive the Prijs der Nederlandse Letteren in 1977.

See: J. G. M. Weck and N. S. Huisman, *In contact met het werk van moderne schrijvers, Deel 3: W. F. Hermans* (1972).   S.L.F.

Hermant, Abel (1862–1950), French novelist, playwright, critic, and essayist, was born and raised in Paris. Throughout his career he exhibited the urbane skepticism and satiric wit that are often considered the essence of the Parisian intellectual. In his early twenties, Hermant wrote novels in the then fashionable naturalistic manner, works more bitterly ironic than witty. His first novel, obviously autobiographical, *Monsieur Rabosson* (1884), harshly satirized those intellectual misfits produced by the French university system, while his next novel, *Le Cavalier Miserey* (1887), depicted the gradual moral disintegration of a young cavalry recruit under the relentless pressure of the military system. This second novel, perhaps because of its controversial subject matter, became a succès de scandale and made Hermant well known at a young age. It must be said that the novel was better than the fashionable sensation it seemed to be at the time, for it developed genuine emotional power in recounting not a conventional antimilitaristic narrative but a painful tale of an idealistic young man whose reverence for the military calling is undermined by the inhumanly rigid treatment he encounters.

Fame did not confirm Hermant's naturalistic manner, but instead permitted him to find a more authentic voice in his fiction, a voice that was lighter in tone and expressive of an amused interest, not in social misfits, but in the foibles of the aristocratic and cosmopolitan society of Paris. This somewhat more frivolous subject matter offered the ideal outlet for Hermant's Parisian inclination to be the satirical analyst of social and sentimental behavior. Before long, he embarked on a series of 20 novels of this type, reminiscent of Emile ZOLA's Rougon-Macquart series, but pointedly ranged under the modestly unambitious general title "Mémoires pour servir à l'histoire de la société" (Memoirs to Serve for a History of Society). In these novels, published between 1901 and 1937, as well as the plays he wrote during this period, Hermant was scrupulously careful not to moralize or to urge social reform, confining himself instead to a kind of amused but detached observation. Oddly enough, during the 1920s and 1930s, his impulse to take partisan stands found expression in a series of articles he wrote, under a pseudonym, on questions of language, regarding this journalistic work as part of a campaign to preserve the integrity of the French tongue. Hermant won enough success with his efforts to consent to the publication, in book form, of several collections of his articles under his own name, attesting to the considerable reputation he had earned as an arbiter of good French usage.

Hermant had a long and active career in French letters, although he never again attained with any single work the attention and fame that his youthful novel *Le Cavalier Miserey* had brought him in the 1880s. His steady achievements as a writer eventually won him election to the Académie Française in 1927, but he lived to see himself expelled from that body in 1945, as a consequence of his allegiance to the Pétain regime. He died in 1950, embittered by the political cloud that had fallen over his life's work. Hermant is a relatively minor figure in French literature, but while he lacks artistic stature, he is of more than passing interest as a perceptive historian of the social mores of his time.

See: R. Peltier, *Abel Hermant: son œuvre* (1924); A. Thérive, *Essai sur Abel Hermant* (1926).   M.S.

Hernández, Miguel (1910–42), Spanish poet, playwright, occasional critic, and journalist, was born and raised in Orihuela in the province of Alicante, the "Oleza" of Gabriel MIRÓ, a writer whose influence Hernández acknowledged. Beginning at age 11, he attended the Jesuit Colegio de Santo Domingo for 3 years. Without further formal education, he went to work as a goatherd in his father's family business, but he devoted all his free time to reading and talking with local poets and intellectuals. The classical Spanish poets, the Golden Age drama, the poetry of Juan Ramón JIMÉNEZ, Antonio MACHADO, and the poets of the Generation of 1927—then at the height of their prestige—found fertile ground in Hernández. His friendship with Ramón Sijé, a precocious local thinker who died at 21 and to whom he dedicated a perfect elegy, developed his vocation for poetry. "Life as a shepherd is not appropriate for poetry writing. . . ," he wrote in a letter to Juan Ramón Jiménez. He wanted to join the poets in Madrid, where he established residence in 1934, having paid a short visit to the capital in 1931. While still in Orihuela he had founded with Ramón Sijé a literary magazine, *El Gallo Crisis,* which appeared only during 1935. The group of poets in Orihuela was more or less an offspring of the liberal neo-Christian tendency represented by *Cruz y Raya* (Madrid) and the spiritual Catholicism of Jacques MARITAIN, in France. Once in Madrid, Hernández met José BERGAMÍN, Pablo Neruda, Vicente ALEIXANDRE, and José María de Cossío. These and many other poets and writers became his friends. Some months before the outbreak of the Civil War, he had already detached himself from his Christian ideals, influenced especially by Neruda and the "impure" poetry of the two volumes of Neruda's *Residencia en la Tierra.* Hernández then began to inject into his writings a radical accent and sociopolitical concern. During the Civil War he married Josefina Manresa and lived as a committed poet dedicated to the struggle for the Republic against the Francisco Franco forces. He participated in the anti-Fascist writers' conference in Valencia and visited the Soviet Union as a poet. In 1938 he was awarded the National Prize for Literature, sharing it with Germán BLEIBERG. After the war, he was jailed in Madrid, was discharged for a few days and then imprisoned elsewhere in Madrid. He was transferred to Toledo, then later to Palencia, and finally to Alicante. His health weakened during the long imprisonment. His condition degenerated into tuberculosis, and

he died in the infirmary of the Provincial Prison of Alicante on March 28, 1942.

Hernández's first publications were short poems in local newspapers. They were first collected by Claude Couffon in *Orihuela y Miguel Hernández* (1967), and later by Juan Cano Ballesta (the foremost scholar on Hernández) and Robert Marrast, the latter in *Poesía y Prosa de Guerra y otros textos olvidados* (1977). His first book of poetry, *Perito en lunas* (1933; Expert on Moons), reflects the influence of Gongorism. As expressed by Timothy Baland, "Into the close-knit stanzas used in Spain's Golden Age three hundred years before, Hernández poured the energy of his own twentieth-century childhood, and formed a book anchored in the quiet strength Lorca spoke of in his letter to Hernández." In 1935 he published an *auto sacramental* in *Cruz y Raya,* while still under the baroque spell: *Quién te ha visto y quién te ve y Sombra de lo que eras* (How Changed You Look—A Shadow of What You Were). In 1936 his second book of poetry appeared: *El rayo que no cesa* (The Lightning That Never Stops). This book is mainly a collection of sonnets with a few longer poems, among them the earlier elegy to Ramón Sijé. Its date of publication may explain why critics include Hernández in the Generation of 1936, when he should perhaps be considered the last and youngest voice of the generation of '27. In 1937, during the Civil War, Hernández published *Viento del Pueblo* (Wind from the People), his first collection of war poems. Shortly before the end of the war, he published his second book, *El hombre Acecha* (Man Lies in Wait). As Baland remarks, "two centuries after Goya, Miguel Hernández etched once again the disasters of war in poems bordered with the dark color of blood and silenced longings." In prison he wrote poems collected in the posthumous *Cancionero y romancero de ausencias* (1939–41; Songs and Ballads of Absence). The most famous of these poems is the "Lullaby of the Onion," the subtitle of which reads: "Lines for his son, after receiving a letter from his wife in which she said that all she had to eat was bread and onions." In addition to the *auto sacramental* mentioned before, Hernández published two longer plays: *Los hijos de la piedra* (1935; Sons of Stone) and *El labrador de más aire* (1936; The Most Vital Villager). During the war he wrote several one-act propaganda plays, adopting the term coined by Rafael ALBERTI: "teatro de urgencia" (theater of urgency). Of the plays written during the war, the most significant is *Pastor de la muerte* (1938; Shepherd of Death).

See: J. Cano Ballesta, *La poesía de Miguel Hernández* (1971); V. Ramos, *Miguel Hernández* (1973); J. Cano Ballesta, ed., *En torno a Miguel Hernández* (1978).
                                                              G.Bl.

Hernández, Ramón (1935-), Spanish novelist and short-story writer, was born in Madrid. Since 1966 he has written seven novels and a few short stories. Hernández views man as an entity attempting to justify and understand his existence but who fails to achieve this objective because of the disorientation brought about by the absurd reality surrounding him. Among his best novels are *Palabras en el muro* (1969; Words on the Wall), *La ira de la noche* (1970; The Anger of Night), and *Eterna memoria* (1975). The latter, winner of the coveted Villa de Madrid Prize, is Hernández's finest work to date. It is the story of a man who refuses to join the military establishment and as a result is ostracized by everyone. The work does not attack a given war or society. Its generic view of the horrors of warfare condemns all wars and those societies that bring them about. This is accomplished by presenting the rambling mind of a madman who represents all soldiers. Throughout his career, Hernández has demonstrated his mastery of interior monologue and stream of consciousness. Undoubtedly among the most impressive Spanish contemporary writers of fiction, Hernández has already made tangible contributions to the novel in Spain.

See: V. Cabrera and L. González-del-Valle, *Novela española contemporanea* (1978), pp. 135–218.

L.G.-del-V.

Hertz, Henri (1875–1966), French poet, novelist, journalist, and critic, was born in Nogent-sur-Seine, of Jewish parents from Alsace-Lorraine. He grew up in the turbulent climate of the Dreyfus Affair and, at an early age, began a lifelong campaign against social and racial injustice. Poetry, however, was to remain a profound necessity for him. In Paris, at the turn of the century, he mingled with the literary avant-garde, including Guillaume APOLLINAIRE and Max JACOB.

Hertz's writings are but the reflection of his inner struggles. His early poems, later collected in volume form as *Quelques vers* (1906; A Few Verses), *Les Apartés* (1912; Asides), and *Lieux communs* (1921; Commonplaces), betray the influence of Tristan Corbière and Jules Laforgue and evince a preoccupation with the themes of departure and evasion. The same dreamy quality informs *Passavant* (1938; Pass), in many respects his poetic testament; but the work also has historical dimensions and is replete with dire forebodings. Like his verse, his stories and novels of the period—*Sorties* (1921), *Vers un monde volage* (1924; Towards a Fickle World), *Le Jeu du Paradis* (1927; Game of Paradise), and *Enlèvement sans amant* (1929; Abduction without a Lover)—are all poetic in form and substance, yet are designed to denounce the brutalities and inequities of modern times.

Up to 1938, when he received the Mallarmé Prize, Hertz's career had been a prolific one, extending to the fields of literary and art criticism. World War II muted his voice, although not his spirit, and, despite his advancing years, he played an active part in the French Resistance.

See: A. Spire, "Un Précurseur: Henri Hertz," *Europe* 23 (1955): 192–98, and *Souvenirs à bâtons rompus* (1962), pp. 239–47; articles by S. D. Braun, H. Henry, et al., in *Europe* 48 (1970): 41–86.

S.D.B.

Hervieu, Paul (1857–1915), French novelist and playwright, was born in Neuilly-sur-Seine. He had a career as lawyer and diplomat. His first literary contributions were signed Eliacin. Hervieu became known first as a short-story writer and a novelist with *Diogène le chien* (1882; Diogenes the Dog), *L'Alpe homicide* (1886; The Homicidal Alp), *L'Inconnu* (1887; The Unknown), and *Flirt* (1890). These early works already showed remarkable qualities of analysis.

In 1890, Hervieu wrote his first play, *Point de lendemain* (No Tomorrow), and two years later *Les Paroles restent* (The Words Remain). Then came his two best novels, *Peints par eux-mêmes* (1893; Painted by Themselves)), a bitter satire of French society, and *L'Armature* (1895; The Framework), a study of the importance of money in the modern world. After 1895 he used the theater as a constant vehicle to expose social evils and suggest their possible cure—*Les Tenailles* (1893; The Pincers), *La Loi de l'homme* (1897; The Law of Man), *L'Enigme* (1901; The Enigma), *La Course du flambeau* (1901; The Torch Race), *Le Dédale* (1903; The Labyrinth), *Le Réveil* (1905; The Awakening), *Modestie* (1909; Modesty), *Connais-toi* (1909; Know Thyself), *Bagatelle* (1912; Trifle), *Le Destin est maître* (1914; Fate Is Master). A historical drama, *Théroigne de Méricourt* (1902), was the only interruption to this series of problem plays.

Hervieu's plays treat the eternal themes of divorce, family honor, and the relationship between parents and children. He wrote with an extreme concision and a strict adherence to rules. He continued the tradition of the classic playwright, but his dramas, impeccably put together, suffer from a sort of mathematical logic, from an oversimplification that results in artificiality. His style has often been criticized for its lack of spontaneity and its unnatural pomposity.

See: C. Malherbe, *Paul Hervieu* (1912); T. D. Barker, "Reading List on Paul Hervieu," in *Bulletin of Bibliography* 8 (1914): 40; E. Estève, *Paul Hervieu: conteur, moraliste et dramaturge* (1917); C. Ferval, *Paul Hervieu* (1917); H. A. Smith, *Main Currents of Modern French Drama* (1925, 1968), pp. 246–60.

M.E.C. rev. D.W.A.

Hesse, Hermann (1877–1962), German novelist, essayist, and poet was born in the Black Forest town of Calw, Swabia, into a milieu of Christian pietism, Swabian mysticism, and Oriental influence. His maternal grandfather had won renown as a scholar of Indian dialects, and his parents served as missionaries in India. As a youth, Hesse dropped out of school twice, worked as a mechanic and bookseller, and, determined to become a writer, educated himself by reading voluminously. After a first undistinguished collection of romantic verse and prose, he attained immediate recognition with his first novel, *Peter Camenzind* (1904; Eng. tr., 1969), the story of a provincial dreamer who, after experiencing life in the big city, returns to his mountainous origins to live in the spirit of Saint Francis of Assisi. This was followed by the novels *Unterm Rad* (1906; Eng. tr., *Beneath the Wheel*, 1968), about the pressures of school and society to which a young, sensitive boy succumbs; *Gertrud* (1910; Eng. tr., 1969), about a love triangle in which two artists love the same woman; *Rosshalde* (1914; Eng. tr., 1970), a projection of Hesse's own marital difficulties into a painter's family; and the story of *Knulp* (1915; Eng. tr., 1971), about a childlike vagabond's life-style, which ends with his reconciliation to God's ways. From his early works, Hesse emerges as an amiable romanticist, a melancholy aesthete, and a loving observer of nature. With gentle sadness he reminisced about childhood as a state of blissful innocence. After a trip to India in 1911, which was a disappointment, several personal crises, including the dissolution of his marriage and his traumatic reaction to World War I, Hesse underwent Jungian psychoanalysis in 1916 and 1917. From this time on his provincialism changed to a deep concern with the *malaise humaine*. When he publicly denounced Germany's militarism and the ensuing bloodshed, his countrymen called him a traitor. These personal traumas and his anguish about his own responsibility for the European disaster were reflected in his next novel, *Demian* (1917–19; Eng. tr., 1965), the story of a young sensitive outsider's identity search and development. The dark and the light worlds confront each other to be merged in the all-embracing symbolic figure of Frau Eva. The novel shows influences of psychoanalysis, Friedrich NIETZSCHE, the Bible, and Christianity. In 1919, Hesse settled in Switzerland, where he remarried twice and remained as a Swiss citizen until his death.

Beginning with *Demian,* Hesse's novels all stress the problem of spiritual loneliness and the quest for self-knowledge, for the meaning of life, for the totality of existence, for ultimate reality, and for mystical awareness, usually gained after a deep personal crisis. They tend to be autobiographical, for Hesse believed that his own moral and spiritual dilemmas were representative of those of modern man. *Siddhartha* (1922; Eng. tr., 1951) is the masterfully simple story of the Brahman son who rebels against his father's teachings and tradition and whose road takes him from asceticism to hedonism to the experience of unity and ultimate enlightenment. Formal teaching is repudiated, and a river is regarded as the great teacher. With his next novel, *Der Steppenwolf* (1927; Eng. tr., *Steppenwolf,* 1963), Hesse struck the nerve of the times. It depicts in psychoanalytical and introspective terms the despair of Harry Haller split into man and beast and living in a transitional period. In this work Hesse uncompromisingly indicted middle-class materialism, hypocrisy, and conformity, as well as the manifestations of modern industrial society. Nature and spirit, wolfish instincts and cultured intellect compete. Haller must learn to transcend the lies of the unity and duality of man and accept his multiplicity as part of an all-encompassing totality. *Narziß und Goldmund* (1930; Eng. tr., *Narcissus and Goldmund,* 1968) tells the pseudomedieval tale about an abbot and his worldly pupil, about the thinker and the creative artist, both in search of the Great Mother, of the All. The allegorical *Die Morgenlandfahrt* (1932; Eng. tr., *The Journey to the East,* 1961) is an exploration of the mystical way, of the search for expanded consciousness. *Das Glasperlenspiel* (1943; Eng. tr., *The Glass Bead Game. Magister Ludi,* 1970) is Hesse's last Bildungsroman and the summa of his thought and cultural critique, in which Josef Knecht, after experiencing several "awakenings," resolves to leave his *vita contemplativa* in Castalia, the rarefied world of the intellect, to devote himself to a *vita activa* in the real world. He dies in this undertaking but not without having left a legacy of integrity and commitment to a young pupil. Hesse's poetry, *Die Gedichte* (1953; Eng. tr. of 31 poems, *Poems,* 1970), ranges from highly melodious, idyllic, and romantic verse to very modern, symbolic, confessional lyrics. His essays, collected in *Betrachtungen* (1928) and in *Krieg und Frieden* (1946; Eng. tr., *If the War Goes on . . . ,* 1970), express his pacifism, his opposition to mass movements, and his astute perceptions of a dehumanized world. Hesse received the Nobel Prize for Literature in 1946. As a stubborn nonconformist, he stressed throughout his life self-reliance, a responsible individualism, and the importance of the suprapersonal. With uncanny accuracy he expressed in his writings the moods, fears, frustrations, and visions of two generations within his own lifetime and, posthumously, those of America's youth of the 1960s.

See: T. Ziolkowsky, *The Novels of Herman Hesse: A Study in Theme and Structure* (1965); M. Boulby, *Hermann Hesse: His Mind and Art* (1967); G. W. Field, *Hermann Hesse* (1970); J. Mileck, *Hermann Hesse: Biography and Bibliography* (1977) and *Hermann Hesse: Life and Art* (1978).   I.H.

Heym, Georg (1887–1912), German expressionist poet and prose writer, was born at Hirschberg in Silesia. He first studied law at Würzburg and Berlin, with little relish. Just as he was beginning to establish himself as a writer he was drowned in a skating accident.

In his two books of poems, *Der ewige Tag* (1911; The Everlasting Day) and *Umbra Vitae* (1912); Heym rejected all conventions of decorum and "good taste" to write some of the most savage verse in the German language. His themes extend from the grim realities of life in industrial Berlin to gigantic and complex visions of war, sickness, suffering, and death: a world and an underworld where demons are abroad. His language is vivid, extreme, difficult; the texture of his poems is dense, packed with

simile and metaphor whose aim is not to clarify but to intensify. Heym evolved a private apocalyptic mythology, a vocabulary full of towers and gates, torches, blood, death and decay, red suns and baleful moons—and dreams. A pattern of nightmare runs through his work, as through that of his contemporary, Franz KAFKA. Heym contemplated his visions with a sense of horror combined with intoxication; the influence of Friedrich NIETZSCHE—especially of *Zarathustra*—is clear. Classical allusions are paradoxically frequent, and on occasion, Heym follows his greatest idol, Friedrich Hölderlin, in evoking and reanimating ancient gods. But, like Hölderlin, Heym knew (and Nietzsche had reminded him) that these gods are dead in the modern world. Their place has been taken by other, demonic beings like "Der Gott der Stadt" (The God of the City) and "Der Krieg" (War). So the classical world is often invoked to mock the grotesque reality of a life far removed from the sweetness and light of Greek stereotype; at the end of one poem, "Aurore," appears "in the gateway of the East" to illuminate the carnage of a Napoleonic battlefield. Like Georg Büchner, another of his heroes (who died even younger), Heym despised Germany's literary classicism, calling Goethe a "swine."

Most of Heym's prose appeared in the collection *Der Dieb* (1913; The Thief). The themes of the seven short pieces are familiar from a reading of his poems: madness, disease, mental and physical pain, murder, and—above all—horror. In his diary, Heym noted that it gives him gruesome satisfaction to "dissect and analyze my sufferings with a scalpel," and this is precisely what he practices in his fiction, where the sufferings become his own through an unsparing imaginative identification. The times were such, Heym felt, that "nice" literature was no longer possible. He sensed the approach of a cataclysm; the boredom that is so often mentioned in his later diary entries was the ominous calm before the storm. "Why doesn't something happen?" he asked in 1910. "Why doesn't somebody cut the balloon-seller's string?" He did not live to see the string cut, but in his work he had already foreseen all that would ensue when it was.

See: H. Greulich, *Georg Heym (1887–1912): Leben und Werk* (1931); A. Blunden, "Beside the Seaside with Georg Heym and Dylan Thomas," *GL&L* 29 (1975): 4–14.   A.G.B.

Heyse, Paul (1830–1914), German novelist and dramatist, was born in Berlin, where both his father and his grandfather, the compiler of a standard dictionary, had been well-known linguists. Paul's mother came from the family of a well-to-do Jewish court jeweler related to the Mendelssohns. He studied the classics at the University of Berlin for two years, chose Romance languages for his speciality, and took a doctor's degree, with a dissertation on the poetry of the troubadours. In 1852 he made his first journey to Italy, the land of his deepest and most lasting sympathies, in order to do research on Provençal manuscripts and in preparation for his career as university lecturer. At the age of 24, he was called to Munich to the court of the Bavarian king, Maximilian II. Although he had at this time published only a few romantic stories and verses, one tragedy, and one novella (his renowned *L'Arrabiata,* which, from a technical point of view, he never surpassed), Heyse abandoned Romance philology and settled in the Bavarian capital. After his arrival in Munich, Heyse married, but his wife died in 1862. Although he found happiness in a second marriage in 1867, he went through many personal sorrows. When Maximilian II died in 1864, his successor, Ludwig II, known for his enthusiastic patronage of Richard WAGNER, generously continued the stipend. In the last years of the century, Heyse became one of the most bitter enemies of the naturalistic and impressionistic schools of writers. He disliked what he considered the naturalistic reveling in the baser aspects of life. In 1910 the Nobel Prize for Literature was awarded to him—the first German writer so honored—in recognition of his being one of the finest craftsman of the German 19th-century novel.

Heyse produced about 120 novellas, 6 large novels, numerous narrative and lyric poems, some 60 plays, and many translations from Italian, Spanish, and English literature. Many of the translations are masterly, above all, the versions of modern Italian poets such as Giuseppi Giusti and Giacomo Leopardi. Among Heyse's novellas, the best are *L'Arrabbiata* (1855; Eng. tr., 1855), *Das Mädchen von Treppi* (1858; Eng. trs., *The Maiden of Treppi, Love's Victory*, both 1874), *Andrea Delfin* (1859; Eng. tr., 1864), and *Der Weinhüter von Meran* (1864; The Wine Custodian from Meran). Among his long novels is *Kinder der Welt* (1872; Eng. tr., *Children of the World*, 1882). None of the 60 plays was a stage success. Heyse also published the autobiographical *Jugenderinnerungen und Bekenntnisse* (2 vols., 5th ed., 1912; Youthful Memories and Confessions).

See: A. Farinelli, *Paul Heyse* (1913); W. Martin, *Paul Heyse: eine Bibliographie seiner Werke* (1978).

H.Sc. rev. A.L.W.

Hidalgo, José Luis (1919–47), Spanish poet and painter, was born in Torres, in the province of Santander. He died of tuberculosis in a Madrid sanatorium before his promising talent could produce the work of which it was capable. He was also a teacher of drawing and painting in Valencia and on two occasions had one-man exhibitions of his work in Santander.

He published only three books of poetry. The first, *Raíz* (1944; Root), is quite uneven and reveals the strong influence of other poets, in particular Vicente ALEIXANDRE and the surrealists. In the second work, *Los animales* (1945), each poem concerns a different animal and one of that animal's prime characteristics in relation to emotions or abstractions like time. Although the reader senses a growing concern with things eternal in this collection, just as *Raíz* already established a feeling for telluric values, these themes come together and achieve transcendence only in Hidalgo's last book, *Los muertos* (1947; The Dead), the work on which his fame rests. This moving volume, only put into final form by the poet's friends as his death drew near, appears to have been written in the emotional knowledge of the approaching end of life. It is the poet's bitter, rebellious dialogue with a silent, unjust God who may be only the poet's life itself and who may die with him in a kind of interdependence earlier envisioned by Miguel de UNAMUNO. The theme of divine injustice in Hidalgo has much in common, both in tone and content, with that of his contemporary Blas de OTERO but without the social concerns of the latter.

Like the poetry of the Generation of 1936 or of the early post-Civil War social poets, Hidalgo's work is not formally innovative. He also shares with both of these groups a concern for the Christian deity, a theme absent from the work of the prior Generation of 1927.

See: A. García Cantalapiedra, *Verso y prosa en torno a José Luis Hidalgo* (1971).   H.L.B.

Hierro, José (1922–), Spanish poet, was born in Madrid. He spent five years in prison for political reasons at the end of the Spanish Civil War. He has won the most important Spanish literary prizes and is now one of Spain's most active art critics.

Hierro's first books, *Tierra sin nosotros* (Earth without Us) and *Alegría* (Joy), both published in 1947, appeared when the climate of realism and majoritarian social commitment that was to characterize the first poetic generation of the post-Civil War period was defining itself. This conditioning is apparent in the literary ideas embodied in Hierro's *Antología consultada de la joven poesía española* (1952; Considered Anthology of the Emerging Spanish Poetry). The poet there believes in "speaking clearly" and sees obscurity as an "expressive defect." He defends everyday language and the documentary value of the poem, confesses his opposition to the ivory tower, and claims that the signs of his time are collective and social—even that "the poetry of today should be epic." Although many of his poems of that period reflect these ideas, the bulk of his work nevertheless is lyric and personal, born of an obsession with time. Perhaps for biographical reasons, Hierro feels time to be a great emptiness where something was to have been written but was not and can therefore only be filled with his words. He illustrates his own circumstances and those of his period and also attempts to achieve a personal identity through poetry. The root of the many contrasts in his work is the life/death dialectic and his consequent sense of temporality. These provide the center of his vision of the world.

His later collections include *Con las piedras, con el viento* (1950; With the Stones, With the Wind), *Quinta del 42* (1953; Drafted in '42), *Cuanto sé de mí* (1957; All I Know about Me), and *Libro de las alucinaciones* (1964; Book of Hallucinations). His voice becomes progressively richer and more complex as his verse incorporates vaguely irrational and dreamlike forms and blends daring temporal and spatial concepts. In the prologue to his *Poesías completas* (1962), he defines the two poetic paths he has followed as "reporting" and "hallucinations." In the former he treats themes directly in a narrative manner, avoiding the prosaic by means of "a sustained, hidden rhythm that adds emotion to coldly objective words." In the hallucinations, on the other hand, "everything is cloaked in mist." Emotion is preeminent but scarcely distinguishable from the elements that produce it. It must be said, however, that this theoretically useful distinction is not so neatly made in the poems themselves.

Hierro includes himself among the "testimonial" poets molded by the historical experience of the postwar period, one of "those who give witness to their time from within their 'I' or their 'We'." His poetic voice speaks always of strong emotion and a sense of flowing time, and is strengthened by his extraordinary control of rhythmic values. He is considered one of the major figures of Spanish postwar poetry.

See: J. Olivio Jiménez, *Cinco poetas del tiempo* (1972), pp. 177–326; A. de Albornoz, "Aproximación a la poética de José Hierro," *RP* 5-6 (1974–75): 47–85; P. J. de la Peña, *Individuo y colectividad: el caso de José Hierro* (1978).   J.O.J.

Hikmet, Nazım, Turkish poet, playwright, and essayist, seldom used his surname, Ran (1902–63), was born in Salonika (then part of Ottoman Turkey, now in Greece) and died in Moscow. Turkey's most famous poet at home and abroad, Hikmet revolutionized Turkish poetry in the 1920s and 1930s by introducing free verse, a brave new style, and Marxist-Leninist themes.

On the verge of graduating from the Naval Officers School in Istanbul in 1921, he was given his discharge for medical reasons. After a short stay in Anatolia during the Turkish War of Independence, he went to the Soviet Union, where he studied at the Eastern Workers University in Moscow. There he acquired his lifelong commitment to the Communist ideology and came under the influence of Vladimir MAYAKOVSKY, Sergey YESENIN, and others.

On his return to Turkey he worked for various newspapers and wrote, in addition to a large body of innovative poetry, several avant-garde plays, a substantial number of newspaper articles, numerous novels, and other works. Because of his political ideas, he was jailed several times. In 1938 he was sentenced to a 25-year term for sedition in the armed forces. In 1950 an amnesty resulted in his release, but in 1951, faced with the possibility of draft into the army, he fled Turkey and spent the rest of his life in Bulgaria, Poland, and the Soviet Union. In 1950 he shared the Lenin Peace Prize with Pablo Neruda.

Hikmet's early poems, the first of which came out in 1918, were formal lyrics that expressed romantic sentiments, patriotic attitudes, and an occasional interest in mysticism. In the 1920s he launched his new poetic aesthetics, whose hallmarks included free verse utilizing the heightened rhythms of natural speech, a functional relationship between form and substance, broken or jagged lines, use of rhymes only for special effect, and fresh metaphorical structure. Hikmet's poems, formulated with a dramatic flair and a powerful lyric flow, challenged the establishment values, denounced the exploitation of the masses, rebeled against imperialism and colonialism, attacked religious faith and its entrenched institutions, and evoked the Utopia of a classless society and a unifed world. His influence on 20th-century Turkish poetry has been profound.

His major collections include *835 Satır* (1929; 835 Lines), *Jokond ile Si-Ya-U* (1929; La Gioconda and Si-Ya-U), *Gece Gelen Telgraf* (1932; The Telegram Received at Night), *Benerci Kendini Niçin Öldürdü* (1932; Why Did Benerjee Kill Himself?), *Taranta Babu'ya Mektuplar* (1935; Letters to Taranta Babu), and *Şeyh Bedreddin Destanı* (1936; Eng. tr., *The Epic of Sheikh Bedreddin*, 1977), a verse epic—regarded as one of Hikmet's masterpieces—about the uprising and downfall of a 15th-century universalist and quasi-communistic sect in Anatolia. Some of his major poetic works were published in Turkey posthumously: *Kurtuluş Savaşı Destanı* (1965; The Epic of the War of Liberation), *Saat 21-22 Şiirleri* (1965; Poems of 9-10 P.M.), and his huge five-volume saga, *Memleketimden İnsan Manzaraları* (1966-1967; Human Scapes from My Land). His plays enjoyed success in Turkey in the 1930s and again from the 1960s on. Some of his later plays were produced in the Soviet Union and France to critical acclaim. His novels, essays and articles, tales, and letters have been published posthumously (mostly in the late 1960s).

Hikmet's poetry has been translated into all major and many minor languages. Hikmet collections in English include *Poems by Nazım Hikmet* (1954), *Selected Poems* (1967), *The Moscow Symphony* (1970), *The Day Before Tomorrow* (1972), and *Things I Didn't Know I Loved* (1975). T.S.H.

Hildesheimer, Wolfgang (1916-), German author, was born in Hamburg. He attended school in Mannheim and in England, where he studied painting and stage design in London until 1939. During World War II, he worked for the British in Palestine, and later was a simultaneous translator at the Nuremberg trials. He started writing in 1950. In 1957 he moved from Munich to Poschiavo, Switzerland, where he lives today. Long a member of the "Gruppe 47" (*see* GERMAN LITERATURE), he received the Radio Play Prize of the German War-Blind in 1955, and the Büchner Prize in 1966. Hildesheimer's first collection of satirical short stories, *Lieblose Legenden* (1952; Loveless Legends), and his first novel, *Paradies der falschen*

Vögel (1953; Paradise of Fake Birds), establish his characteristic tone (urbane, ironic, witty, inviting comparison with Lewis Carroll and Thomas MANN) and absurdist focus (rearranging rather than imitating reality). These qualities are also found in his 8 stage and over 20 radio plays. His two later novels, *Tynset* (1965), and *Masante* (1970), record a struggle for clarity and humanity in the face of pervasive angst. He has translated from the English, notably works by George Bernard Shaw, James Joyce, and Djuna Barnes and has written a biography of Wolfgang Amadeus Mozart (1977).

See: D. Rodewald, ed., *Über Wolfgang Hildescheimer* (1971). D.J.W.

Hjartarson, Snorri (1906-), Icelandic novelist and poet, was born at Hvanneyri in the district of Borgarfjörður, in southwestern Iceland, where his father was a school principal. Hjartarson grew up in a prosperous and cultured home, enrolled at the gymnasium in Reykjavik, but contracted tuberculosis and never completed the course of study. He spent some time in Danish sanatoriums while recuperating and then studied to be a painter in Copenhagen and later in Oslo (1931-32).

Hjartarson's first published work was a novel in Norwegian, which dealt with a young Icelandic artist's struggle to choose between life and art. Although this novel won favorable notices, Hjartarson was to write no other work of fiction. He returned to Iceland and became a librarian in Reykjavik, a position he held from 1939 to 1966.

Despite his limited output of verse—only three books: *Kvaeði* (1944; Poems), *Á Gnitaheiði* (1952; On Gnita Heath), and *Lauf og Stjörnur* (1966; Leaves and Stars)—Hjartarson has been a leading voice in Icelandic poetry since World War II. When the modernist school burst upon the scene in Iceland in the 1940s with free forms and complex symbolism, he struck a compromise between old tradition and new style. Thus, he uses conventional rhyme schemes but varies them at times, as by substituting half rhymes. His imagery is modernistic and shows the influence of his background in painting. By reconciling Icelandic tradition in poetry and modernism, he set an example that was followed by many other contemporary poets in Iceland, of whom Hannes PÉTURSSON is the best known. Hjartarson's own development, however, has been such that his last poems show the greatest concentration of images and the highest degree of freedom in form.

Icelandic history and the nature of the country are central motifs in many of Hjartarson's poems, especially those contained in the first two collections. His descriptions of nature are rich in color and of exalted tone; the landscapes often serve to communicate a state of mind. Such pictures, however, are less pronounced in his latest book, where they function more like a backdrop or as a means of underscoring thoughts or sentiments. Longing and the search for happiness are recurring themes in Hjartarson's poetry, but, as he sees it, happiness can only be achieved by undergoing severe trials—and as a result he often shifts from the somber mood associated with ordeal to optimism. *Á Gnitaheiði*, the least introspective of Hjartarson's books of verse, is a good example of the worry and uncertainty that prevailed during the Cold War period. In the face of the concerns that confront him, the poet places his trust in Icelandic nationality and cultural values, constantly celebrating both. *Lauf og stjörnur*, on the other hand, is the most private of his verse collections, characterized by pessimism and disillusionment. Still, art and other achievements of the human spirit are seen here as affording a measure of relief. Many of the poems in this book deal with time and the transitory nature of life, but the poet can accept the prospect of approaching death as long as he can savor the pleasures that art and nature's beauty can afford him.

See: H. Pétursson, "Um skáldskap Snorra Hjartarsonar," *Félagsbréf AB*, 17 (1960): 13–25; I. Orgland, "Snorri Hjartarson," in S. Hjartarson, *Lyng og krater* (1968), pp. 5–42.　　　　　　　　　　　　　　S.S.H.

Hłasko, Marek (1934–69), Polish prose writer, was born in Warsaw and died in Wiesbaden. His remains were brought to Warsaw in 1975. His first volume of short stories, *Pierwszy krok w chmurach* (1956; The First Step in the Clouds), gained wide recognition among the young generation, for whom he became an idol. He went abroad in 1958 and decided to stay there, living first in West Germany, then Israel, then the United States, and finally back in West Germany. Both his next story, "Ósmy dzień tygodnia" (1956; Eng. tr., *The Eighth Day of the Week*, 1958) as well as "Pętla" (The Noose) from the first volume were filmed. Abroad Hłasko published two novels in one volume: *Cmentarze* (Eng. tr., *The Graveyard*, 1959) and *Następny do raju* (Eng. tr., *Next Stop—Paradise*, 1960), the second of which was also filmed. *Cmentarze* depicts the author's bitter experiences during the Stalin years in Poland and the decline of all ideologies. Other works by Hłasko include *Opowiadania* (1963; Short Stories), *Wszyscy byli odwróceni, Brudne czyny* (1964; All Were Turned Away. Dirty Deeds), *Nawrócony w Jaffie. Opowiem wam o Ester* (1966; Converted in Jaffa. I Will Tell You about Esther), *Piękni dwudziestoletni* (1966; The Good-Looking Twenty-Year-Olds), *Sowa, córka piekarza* (1968; The Baker's Daughter). Hłasko's stories reveal him as a portrayer of moral conflicts and social evils. He rebelled against the banality and vulgarity of human existence. His earlier short stories still bear marks of socialist realism, but his later prose turns more into a kind of romantic naturalism. Traces of Ernest Hemingway's style are visible in his writing.

See: *Słownik współczesnych pisarzy polskich*, series 2, vol. 1 (1977), pp. 349–61; M. J. Kryński, "Marek Hłasko—Lyrical Naturalist," *PolR* no. 4 (1961), pp. 12–21.　　　　　　　　　　　　　　　　　　A.Z.

Hochhuth, Rolf (1931–), German dramatist and essayist, was born in Eschwege on the Werra, West Germany. He has lived in Basel, Switzerland, since 1963. Hochhuth left school before graduation and worked as a bookseller and editor while trying to come to terms with his boyhood wartime experiences. Because of the historical theses propounded in his first two plays, he is often called a "documentary dramatist," but he argues that a writer must subordinate historical accuracy to poetic purpose. In contrast to the absurdists, for him tragedy is still possible, given individual freedom within the historical process. He believes theater can still be a "moral institution." His early plays also follow the Schillerian model in their adherence to a traditional form. His first play, *Der Stellvertreter* (1963; Eng. tr., *The Deputy*, 1964), with its controversial portrayal of Pope Pius XII as failing to protest Nazi treatment of the Jews, gave Hochhuth immediate international acclaim. The reaction to *Soldaten* (1967; Eng. tr., *Soldiers*, 1968) was equally stormy, for although treating the problem of Allied civilian bombing in World War II, it implied Winston Churchill's culpability in General Władystaw Sikorski's death. After a third, unsuccessful "tragedy," *Guerrillas* (1970), Hochhuth turned to comedy: *Die Hebamme* (1971; The Midwife), and *Lysistrate und die Nato* (1973), both with political themes. A more recent play, a monodrama, *Tod eines Jägers* (1976;

Death of a Hunter) depicts Ernest Hemingway's suicide and generally reflects on the role of writers in society. For Hochhuth this role is clearly a political one, as revealed by the essays in *Krieg und Klassenkrieg* (1971; War and Class War). Other essays, two novellas—*Die Berliner Antigone* (The Berlin Antigone) and *Zwischenspiel in Baden-Baden* (Intermezzo in Baden-Baden)—as well as poems appeared in the *Hebamme* volume. But the novel *Eine Liebe in Deutschland* (1978; A Love in Germany) is Hochhuth's first major prose work. Through the use of a montage technique, an account of the author's historical research accompanies the story line. Hochhuth thus continues to sift through the *Dokumentenschutt* (rubble heap of documents) in search of the truth in history, in order to create works that have symbolic force.

See: E. Bentley, ed., *The Storm over the Deputy* (1964); R. Taëni, *Rolf Hochhuth* (1977); M. E. Ward, *Rolf Hochhuth* (1977).　　　　　　　　　　　　　　　M.E.W.

Hoel, Sigurd (1890–1960), Norwegian novelist and literary critic, was born in the rural district of Nord-Odal. After his university training in science, he taught for a time in Christiania (now Oslo) and remained in the capital for the rest of his life. Although he achieved distinction as a novelist, he is better known as an essayist and literary critic. Hoel was a man of impressive appearance, with a keen, receptive, inquiring mind. He acquired a phenomenal knowledge of his native literature and of foreign literatures, particularly American, English, and French. He translated works by Erskine Caldwell, Joseph Conrad, and William Faulkner into Norwegian, and from 1929 on edited a lengthy series of translations. His introductions to these, published as *50 gule* (1939; 50 Yellow-Jacketed Books), are excellent critiques. Hoel early hailed Ernest Hemingway as a coming author, and he was one of the first to recognize Albert CAMUS's potentialities as a writer. He published several important critical articles in *Samtiden* (1924, 1925, 1929). Hoel also wrote a number of superb essays, in which he revealed his subtlety of mind, his irony, and his sense of humor.

Hoel's novels and short stories show a marked similarity to Hemingway's. His principal concern—more intellectual than emotional and with a liberal political and Freudian cast—is with the rootless character (familiarized by Knut HAMSUN) who searches for a meaning to the human condition in a world devastated by World War I. The short stories collected in *Veien vi gaar* (1922; The Road We Travel) and the novels *Syvstjernen* (1924; The Pleiades) and *Syndere i sommersol* (1927; Eng. tr., *Sinners in Summertime*, 1930) deal lightly and cynically with the theme of love and are early precursors of a later treatment of that subject. The novels *En dag i oktober* (1931; Eng. tr., *One Day in October*, 1932) and *Fjorten dager før frostnettene* (1935; Fourteen Days before the Frost Nights) show how bourgeois society stifles happiness with fear. *Sesam sesam* (1938; Open Sesame) is an ironic account of literary life in Oslo. Hoel also wrote two memorable books for children, based on Norwegian tales: *Veien til verdens ende* (1933; Road to World's End), and *Prinssessen på glassberget* (1939; The Princess on the Glass Mountain).

The novels Hoel published after World War II are of uneven quality, but two represent the height of his literary achievement. *Møte ved milepelen* (1947; Eng. tr., *Meeting at the Milestone*, 1951) probes the causes of fascism by depicting a group of Norwegian collaborators with the Nazis during the war. The novel reveals Hoel's ability to convey subtle psychological insights as well as his technical mastery of the novel as a literary form. Two years before his death, Hoel published *Trollringen* (1958; The

Magic Circle), a continuation of a much earlier and weaker novel, *Arvestålet* (1941; Ancestral Steel). *Trollringen* is set in Norway in the years after 1814 and gives strong evidence of Hoel's abilities as a sparkling epic narrator. Hoel continued as a central cultural force throughout the postwar years, publishing several collections of essays and articles. His best articles on Norwegian literature are collected in *Tanker om norsk diktning* (1955; Thoughts about Norwegian Literature).

See: J. E. de Mylius, *Sigurd Hoel—befrieren i Jugleham* (1972); A. Tvinnereim, *Risens hjesto* (1975).   S.A.

Hoffmann, Dieter (1934–), German poet, was born in Dresden, where he lived until he left the German Democratic Republic (GDR) in 1957. His first volume of poems, *Aufzücke deine Sternenhände* (1953; May Your Star-Hands Wince), evokes the rural atmosphere of the environs of Dresden, including famous baroque castles such as Pillnitz and Moritzburg. This volume was followed by *Mohnwahn* (1956; Poppy Craze) and *Eros im Steinlaub* (1961; Eros in the Stone Foliage), which contain numerous motifs from Saxony and Baden-Würtenberg. Later collections of poetry include *Stierstädter Gartenbuch* (1964; Stierstadt Garden Book), *Ziselierte Blutbahn* (1964; Enchased Blood Course), *Veduten* (1969; Views), and *Lebende Bilder* (1971; Living Images). *Gedichte aus der augustäischen GDR* (1977; Poems from the Augustan GDR), an ironically titled collection, contains poems inspired by five visits to Dresden between 1974 and 1976 and emphasizes the disparity between the "Golden Age" of Saxony under August the Strong (1670–1733) and the exploitation of this cultural heritage in the GDR.

Many of Hoffmann's poems reveal nostalgia for the Saxony of his youth as well as for the baroque Dresden of August the Strong. "Ein Haus in Sachsen" (A House in Saxony), from *Blutbahn*, evokes a childhood memory of Hoffmann's parents' house in Dresden, while "Lausa," from *Veduten*, refers to the place where he lived after the fire bombing of Dresden in 1945. His poems may be likened to portraits or miniatures of people (such as August the Strong, Immanuel Kant, Ludwig van Beethoven, Georg Friedrich Händel, and Johann Wolfgang von Goethe) and sketches of cities and countries (such as Dresden, Munich, Frankfurt, Rome, Paris, Austria, and Egypt) and castles and parks (Pillnitz, Moritzburg, Schönbrunn, Homburg, and Bayreuth). Other poems are strongly biographical or anecdotal.

Hoffmann has received numerous literary awards, including the Villa Massimo Fellowship (1963) and the Andreas Gryphius Prize (1969). He served a term as vice president of the Literary Class of the Mainz Academy of the Sciences and Literature.   D.H.C.

Hofmannsthal, Hugo von (1874–1929), Austrian poet, dramatist, and librettist, was born in Vienna. He burst upon the Viennese literary scene at the age of 16 in 1890 with precocious brilliance. He stunned older contemporaries with poetry of a richness, luminescence, and intuitive sophistication unequaled in German since Goethe. More significantly, Hofmannsthal's development transcended both early precocity and an intermediate crisis of creativity. He consciously affirmed his role as a legatee and rejuvenator of the multifaceted and multinational Austrian cultural heritage. His passionate (but by no means blind or chauvinistic) moral commitment to this idea was in turn representative of a broad European humanistic tradition and goal. Ironically, events during his lifetime destroyed the political reality of his ideal (causing Hofmannsthal great agony), but in no way does this negate the import and factual successes of his lifelong endeavor.

Hofmannsthal's long-lived reputation as an ultrarefined representative of hermetic impressionism rested largely upon his poetry of the years 1890–99. Indeed, such poems as *Terzinen über die Vergänglichkeit* (1894; Eng. tr., *Stanzas in Terza Rima*, 1961), *Ballade des äusseren Lebens* (1895; Eng. tr., *Ballad of the Outer Life*, 1961), and the verse playlet *Gestern* (1891; Yesterday) are permeated with a dual awareness of ineluctably fleeting temporality juxtaposed with an absolute timeless continuity. The theme of evanescence appealed to the impressionists, and the writer's conviction that he could penetrate surface phenomena to experience an essential unchanging reality was seen by many as the triumphal expression of a poet-prophet. Hofmannsthal's paradoxical aesthetic awareness never led him, however, to ethical indifference or elitism. He quietly declined to join the elite circle of the self-proclaimed poet-prophet Stefan GEORGE.

Hofmannsthal parted company with impressionists, decadents, and advocates of *l'art pour l'art* in the question of involvement. This parting of the ways was implicit in the early parabolic playlet *Gestern*, which depicts the vulnerability and sterility of the impressionistic life-style of the play's late-Renaissance hero, Andrea. The recognition of his lover's infidelity shatters Andrea's conviction that reality is a mere function of his ego and that continuity is only the random flux of consciousness.

Hofmannsthal portrayed full moral implications of impressionistic self-deification in the superb verse playlet *Der Tor und der Tod* (1893; Eng. tr., *Death and the Fool*, 1961), a work inspired by the baroque allegorical tradition. In the play the egocentric aesthete Claudio destroys a former friend, a previous lover, and his mother in the presence of death (an allegorically Dionysian figure) by his sterile manipulative treatment of them. The destructive manipulation has also robbed his own life of meaning. Claudio's determination to read such meaning into his death functions as an ultimate sterile irony.

Hofmannsthal described his early period as one of "Präexistence" (preexistence), in which he felt himself to be a privileged participant in an interconnected world. Toward the turn of the century, the contradiction inherent in temporal discontinuity and mystic interconnection (that of "becoming" versus "being") became a creative crisis for Hofmannsthal, often interpreted as having paradigmatic cultural implications. Expressed most eloquently in his fictional *Ein Brief* (1902; Eng. tr., *The Letter of Lord Chandos*, 1952), the crisis was characterized by corrosive doubt in the efficacy of language itself. Hofmannsthal no longer could trust the rich imagery of his earlier writing. The change, however, was preeminently one of authorial outlook. Works like the fine story *Reitergeschichte* (1899; Eng. tr., *A Tale of the Cavalry*, 1952) demonstrate his unbroken productivity. There was, however, a redirection of effort. Hofmannsthal began to perceive social communion and interconnection as the positive task and goal of art.

An immediate response to the crisis was Hofmannsthal's attempt to deal with the irrational, demonic, and bloody side of human life through a reworking of antique tragedies. Two of the resulting plays, *Elektra* (1904; Eng. tr., 1963) and *Ödipus und die Sphinx* (1906; Oedipus and the Sphinx) develop the theme of fatal predetermination transcended by the protagonists' self-sacrifice and self-overcoming. These works have been misunderstood and rejected by many critics, who see in them only a perverse enjoyment of blood and irrationality.

Hofmannsthal's engaged attitude also led to the writing

of opera libretti. His remarkable collaboration with Richard Strauss began in 1906 and lasted until his death. In opera, Hofmannsthal hoped to create a *Gesamtkunstwerk* (unified work of art) and also occasion a communal cultural experience. The first production was *Elektra* (performed in 1909). Most successful was *Der Rosenkavalier* (performed 1912; Eng. tr., *The Cavalier of the Rose,* 1963). Underlying the gaiety of life in the times of Maria Therese is the serious awareness of passing time that plagues the heroine. Her morally motivated sacrifice in giving up her young lover lends her figure enhanced stature. *Die Frau ohne Schatten* (performed 1919; The Woman without a Shadow) is a deeply symbolic work in a fairy-tale setting. It also portrays heightened humanity gained through self-abnegation.

Yet another contribution to the rejuvenation of culture was Hofmannsthal's involvement in the Salzburg Festival Plays. His reworked morality play *Jedermann* (1911; Everyman) was intended to communicate basic truths about transcience and salvation directly to an audience of the people. Hofmannsthal's later contribution, his *Das große Salzburger Welttheater* (1922; Eng. tr., *The Salzburg Great Theater of the World*, 1963), was inspired by a play by Calderón. It responds to the yawning social divisions imperiling post-World War I Austria. In the Marxistic beggar, who ultimately eschews the violence of the axe (which would surely produce chaos), Hofmannsthal stressed the active moral beneficence of enlightened self-abnegation.

The disruption of World War I also led Hofmannsthal to comedy. *Der Schwierige* (1923; Eng. tr., *The Difficult Man,* 1963) is set against the background of Austrian aristocratic society, whose passing Hofmannsthal deeply rued. It deals lightheartedly with the theme of marriage, which stands symbolically for the continuity and connectedness the author constantly sought. The difficult man, Hans Karl Bühl, is able to achieve an understanding with the ideally suitable Helene Altenwyl only after a near-failure born of reticence.

Hofmannsthal's narrative works are few. Most important of them is the uncompleted developmental novel *Andreas oder die Vereinigten* (1914; Eng. tr., *Andreas,* 1952). The novel's hero must develop to manhood in order to regain a lost union with his beloved, Morgana. Andreas's growth, a complex and variegated process, enables him to penetrate surface phenomena (symbolized by the city of Venice) in order to perceive unifying realities.

The constant search for practical means to unity is dramatically restricted in the author's last work, *Der Turm* (1924, rev. ed. 1927; Eng. tr., *The Tower,* 1963). Both versions of the play are set against an archaic background of mob chaos and corruption of power, which highlights the nobility of the protagonist Sigismund. In the early version, however, his suppression of anarchy is unavoidably violent and peace remains only a promise. The later version ends with Sigismund's heroic nonaction countered by assassination. His glory is without effective resonance in the reality of clashing epochs. Thus, although Hofmannsthal's passionate devotion to the concept of community and reconciliation remained in his later years, his doggedly active optimism was drastically curbed.

Hofmannsthal's works in English translation include H. Broch, ed., *Selected Prose* (1952) and M. Hamburger, ed., *Poems and Verse Plays* (1961) and *Selected Plays and Libretti* (1963); the introductions to these three Bollingen Series volumes are very useful for a general understanding of Hofmannsthal's work.

See: H. Hammelmann, *Hugo von Hoffmannsthal* (1957); B. Coghlin, *Hofmannsthal's Festival Dramas* (1964).

W.K.C.

Hofmo, Gunvor (1921–), Norwegian poet, published her first collection of poetry, *Jeg vil hjem til menneskene* (1946; I Long for Mankind), just as the wave of new verse, inspired by the work of T. S. Eliot and Ezra Pound, hit Norway. Yet although her poetry was inspired by the new form, she never adhered to any program.

Visionary, at times ecstatic, but also penetrated by chilling loneliness and despair, Hofmo's verse grapples with the existential questions of life in complex images that sometimes border on the obscure. Her ethical framework is Christian, but it is never orthodox. Her themes—alienation, separation, departure, death—are always treated in the context of an ultimate order. After her fifth collection of verse, *Testamente til en evighet* (1955; A Will for Eternity), there was a pause of 16 years before she again published. Since 1971, however, Hofmo has produced six more collections. The anguish of human existence is still a main theme in her work, but a new, reconciled view of life is also apparent. Now lifelessness, not death, is the threat. There is a strain of mysticism throughout Hofmo's poetry. Her verse gives evidence of a religious quest, beyond all orthodoxy, seeking to come to terms with life's ultimate questions. Although strangely isolated, she remains a central poet in modern Norwegian literature.

K.A.F.

Højholt, Per (1928–), Danish author, was born in the western Jutland city of Esbjerg. From 1951 to 1965 he was a librarian. Højholt had his breakthrough with the collections of poetry *Min hånd 66* (1966; My Hand 66) and *Turbo* (1968) and the novel *6512* (1969), all published toward the end of the 1960s at a time when modernism was being replaced by concrete poetry. Højholt experiments with all levels of the language: quotations, technical or self-invented words, and slogans. Paper and the typography are used as artistic materials, a cultivation of pure form elements, which, in *Punkter* (1971; Points), transforms the texts into mere signs and closed symbols. *Volume* (1974) is more open, a picture book with clusters of words, masterfully arranged as a collage meant to stimulate the imagination of the reader. Højholt's philosophical and metaphysical point of view as well as his artistic radicalism makes him one of the least accesible authors in Danish literature.

See: N. Egebak, *Højholts metode* (1974).   S.H.R.

Holan, Vladimír (1905–), Czech poet, was born in Prague. He is a complicated artist whose verse lacks obvious external appeal or flair; its strength lies chiefly in its purity of structure and its tight although often enigmatic development of ideas. Holan's principal models are Rainer Maria RILKE and František HALAS. In his early collection, *Triumf smrti* (1930; The Triumph of Death), he sounded the note of tragic individualism that has remained with him throughout his poetic career. The volumes *Vanutí* (1932; Breezes) and *Oblouk* (1934; The Arch) mark the high point of his early poetry. They exhibit a rich use of metaphor, neologism, and linguistic deformation, which represent the poet's attempt to define the limits of being and nonbeing, of the concrete and the abstract. The political events of the late 1930s and World War II tore Holan away from his preoccupation with metaphysical questions, and his verse became more consciously political; the collection *Dík Sovětskému svazu* (1945; Thanks to the Soviet Union) is perhaps the most obvious manifestation of this new consciousness. But Holan found the post-1948 Stalinist regime repressive, and, having fallen into official disfavor, he turned to translating and to writing children's books. With the liberalization of the 1960s Holan, then in his late 50s, underwent a revival and published some of his most inspired poetry in collections such as *Na postupu* (1964; On the Advance) and *Bolest* (1965; Pain). The long poem, *Noc s Hamletem* (1964; A Night with Hamlet), is a meditative dialogue in which the figure of Hamlet is employed as the poet's alter ego. Holan's later poetry is freer in form and stylistically simpler than his earlier rhymed verse; it is individualistic and tragic, with religious overtones. His verse served as a stimulus and a rallying point for the generation of younger poets and readers of the 1960s. In 1965 he was given the title of "national artist." For a selection of Holan's poetry in English, see *Vladimir Holan: Selected Poems*, tr. by J. and I. Milner (1971).

See: A. French, *The Poets of Prague* (1969).

W.E.H.

Holeček, Josef (1853–1929), Czech novelist and poet, was born in Stožice near Vodňany, in southern Bohemia. After becoming a journalist, he served as a war correspondent. He traveled frequently in the Balkans and also visited Russia. In his early years as a novelist and poet, Holeček wrote much about Yugoslavia, especially Montenegro, an interest that led to his translation of Yugoslav heroic folk poetry, *Srbská národní epika* (4 vols., 1909–26; Serbian National Epics), and to imitation of its style in his own poetry about Yugoslav heroes, notably *Sokolovič* (1922). Holeček also translated the Finnish national epic, *Kalevala* (5 vols., 1894–96). But his most important work is the cycle of novels, *Naši* (10 vols., 1898–1930; Our People), which attempts to present a complete study of Czech peasants in southern Bohemia as they were before the advent of industrialization. The action covers the years 1840–66 and centers around an ideal peasant, a "strong Christian," named Kojan. The novel's plot is poorly organized; its interest derives from Holeček's penetrating analysis of the Czech peasant, and the wonderfully vivid and detailed picture he presents of peasant customs, superstitions, and beliefs. Permeating the work is a conservative agrarian ideology with a strong Christian coloring. Holeček was influenced by the Russian Slavophiles, although his religious thought reflects primitive general Christianity rather than the tenets of any particular denomination. He preached love of the soil, family, community, and nation, with a strong emphasis on Pan-Slavism. He depicted the struggle of the peasant with the landlord and the usurer, and succeeded in creating sharply individualized types. The novel—especially the first three volumes—can be compared to Władysław REYMONT's *The Peasants*, not merely as a documentary novel with folkloristic information, but also as a searching analysis of the peasant soul, which to Holeček was identical with the soul of the nation.

See: J. Voborník, *Josef Holecek* (1913); E. Chalupný, *Dílo Josefa Holečka* (1929). R.W.

Höllerer, Walter (1922–), German poet, novelist, dramatist, and critic, was born at Sulzbach-Rosenberg in Bavaria, since 1977 site of the Archives for Contemporary German Literature, founded by Höllerer. After studies at Erlangen, Göttingen, and Heidelberg, he wrote his Ph.D. dissertation on Gottfried Keller in 1949. Since 1959 he has been professor of German and comparative literature at the Technical University of Berlin and since 1973 also at the University of Illinois-Urbana.

Höllerer has been influential in shaping directions for postwar German literature as a prominent critic in "Gruppe 47," as co-editor, wiith Hans Bender, of *Akzente*, and as editor, since 1961, of *Sprache im technischen Zeitalter*. In his critical-theoretical reflections and in his literary texts Höllerer has elaborated and practiced a coherent poetics of the open form, whose central tenets include the critical confrontation of given forms and systems, the transcendence of their boundaries with mixed sign systems, and the elucidation of interrelations and processes of change. He sees literature as a process of communication ranging along a continuum of art, science, and everyday experience. His novel *Die Elephantenuhr* (1973; rev. ed. 1975; The Elephant Clock), combining art and science, poetry and theory, has been described as both a long poem and a novel whose "hero" is theory. Höllerer's conception of semiology, a key metaphor in the novel, referring to the unifying theories and methods of semiotics, has found expression in several astistic expositions directed by Höllerer and in his multimedial composition *Alle Vögel Alle* (1978; All the Birds). The expositions and the literary texts both urge and present redefinitions of language, of literature, and of methods of artistic communication that repair the fractured links between art and other modes of human communication.

J.K.H

Holm, Sven (1940–), Danish novelist and writer of short stories was born in Copenhagen. He matriculated in 1958, was a tutor from 1958 to 1960, after which he held various jobs. Behind the fabulous fairy-tale style of Holm's first collection of symbolic short stories, *Den store fjende* (1961; The Great Enemy), lies a modern theme: the duality and persecution of one's own self. During the following years this perspective is enlarged to encompass the struggle for power among people, as in the political novel *Fra den nederste himmel* (1965; From the Lowest Heaven) and the allegorical short stories in *Rex* (1969). Between these books, which constitute an attempt to unite existentialism and a type of socialism, Holm wrote the gloomy science fiction novel *Termush* (1967; Eng. tr., 1969), which consists of diary entries about a group of people seeking refuge in an isolated hotel after World War III. A completely different tone is found in the satirical and humorous spy novel *Min elskede* (1968; My Beloved). In the partly psychological, partly satirical novels *Syg og munter* (1972; Sick and Merry), *Det private liv* (1974; Private Life), and *Langt borte taler byen med min stemme* (1976; Far Away the City Speaks with My Voice), the main theme is the relationship between the personal and social traits in people, ending in that melancholy realization of impotence and isolation, which even characterizes sexual relationships, as is satirically demonstrated in Holm's novel, *Ægteskabsleg* (1977; Marriage Game.).

S.H.R.

Holstein, Ludvig (1864–1943), Danish poet, was born in Kallhave, in Zealand. He matriculated in 1883 in Copenhagen. Although Holstein lived primarily in Copenhagen, his writing is tied to the experience of nature in Zealand during the four seasons. His first published collection, *Digte* (1895; Poems), expresses the spontaneous joy of nature combined with the dreamlike wistfulness of neoromanticism. Holstein's melancholy drama with a ballad theme, *Tove* (1898)—inspired by Maurice MAETERLINCK's symbolism—was followed by a series of poetry collections, *Mos og Muld* (1917; Moss and Mold), *Æbletid* (1920; Apple Time), and *Jehi* (1919). Holstein viewed the human life cycle as part of nature's eternal renewal. In his poetry one can find some of the most beautiful and serene expressions of religious pantheism in Danish literature. This pantheism is theoretically formulated in the philosophical prose work, *Den grønne Mark* (1925; The Green Field), directed against confessional religion and the egotism of the symbolist movement.

See: E. Frandsen, *Ludvig Holstein* (1931). S.H.R.

Holt, Kåre (1917–), Norwegian novelist, was born in the region of Vestfold on the Oslo Fjord where he has lived most of his life. The son of a railroad worker in a rural community, Holt became aware at an early age of the antagonism between farmers and workers and of the class structure of the Norwegian society of the 1930s. This background has profoundly influenced his writing. He worked in the Resistance movement during World War II, but in his discussions after the war with Nazi collaborators he gained a new insight into the psychological complexity of people's behavior during the war period, and the question of choice became a central problem both in his life and his books.

Holt's first important novel, *Det store veiskillet* (1950; At the Crossroads), treats the choice theme by presenting three different versions of the life of a single person, each version being the result of a different choice. This motif also appears in Holt's later novels. His subsequent major works are a group of novels based on the history of the Norwegian labor movement, *Det stolte nederlag* (1956; The Proud Defeat), *Storm under morgenstjernen* (1958; Storm under the Morning Star), and *Opprørere ved havet* (1960; Rebels by the Sea), and a trilogy about the medieval Norwegian king, Sverre, *Kongen I-III* (1965–69; The King). Among his recent works are *Folket ved Svansjøen* (1972; The People on Svan Lake), a novel based on documentary materials, about a nearly extinct Lapp tribe, *Kappløpet* (1974; The Race), a book about Roald Amundsen that emphasizes the less heroic side of the polar explorer and *Sønn av himmel og jord* (1978; Son of Heaven and Earth) about Hans Egede, 18th-century Norwegian missionary to Greenland. Holt is also the author of several children's books.

See: P. Larsen, *Holt* (1975). K.A.F.

Holz, Arno (1863–1929), German poet, literary theorist, and dramatist, was born in the East Prussian city of Rastenburg. In 1875 his family moved to Berlin, and the boy was brought into contact with the modern urban life that he was to make the subject of his first important volume of verse, *Das Buch der Zeit* (1886; The Book of Time).

Holz's real career, typical of the radical and experimental nature of German literature in the last decades of the 19th century, started with the naturalistic revolution, of which *Das Buch der Zeit* is an important document with its interest in social problems and the modern city and its enthusiasm for Emile ZOLA and Henrik IBSEN. In 1885, Holz was one of the contributors to the naturalistic anthology *Moderne Dichter-Charactere* (Modern Poet Characters). His major contribution to German naturalistic theory was *Die Kunst, ihr Wesen und ihre Gesetze* (1891; Art, Its Nature and Its Laws), an exposition of the theory of so-called *konsequenter Naturalismus* (consistent naturalism). In this essay Holz attempted to formulate an aesthetic theory that excluded the subjective element from artistic creation and gave naturalism a logical, objective theoretic basis. In reality, its extreme ideas undermined the naturalistic position. More important than his theory was his collaboration with Johannes SCHLAF in writing, under the joint pseudonym Bjarne P. Holmsen, *Papa Hamlet* (1889), a phonetic and photographic reproduction of reality. This, with the drama *Die Familie Selicke* (1890; The Selicke Family), produced by the Freie Bühne (Free Stage—a Berlin theater enterprise) in the same year, and *Neue Gleise* (1892; New Tracks), was of great influence in the development of Gerhart HAUPTMANN and naturalistic drama in general. With the decline of German naturalism, Holz turned back to the lyric with a volume of modernistic poetry, *Phantasus* (1898–99). In 1899 was published *Die Revolution der Lyrik*, a theoretical defense of his new poetic technique, in which he championed a poetic form that was a direct expression of subject matter, avoiding rhyme and strophe, a form that is not "free" but "natural" verse. Typographically the lines are centered on the page and not aligned with the left-hand margin, the so-called *Mittelachse* verse. Holz's later career produced additional volumes of lyrics, such as *Dafnis: lyrisches Porträt aus dem 17. Jahrhundert* (1904; Daphnis: Lyrical Portrait from the 17th Century), and several dramas, among them *Traumulus* (1904), written with Otto Jerschke, and *Sonnenfinsternis* (1908; Eclipse of the Sun), a tragedy.

See: O. E. Lessing, *Die neue Form* (1910); R. Ress, *Arno Holz und seine künstlerische Bedeutung* (1913); H. Motekat, *Arno Holz, Persönlichkeit und Werk* (1953); G. Schulz, *Arno Holz: Dilemma eines bürgerlichen Dichterlebens* (1974). W.H.Ro. rev. A.L.W.

Honchar, Oles (1918–), Ukrainian novelist, was born of peasant stock in the Poltava region. He studied journalism in Kharkiv, fought in the Red Army during World War II, and later completed his studies in Dnipropetrovsk (Dnepropetrovsk). During the so-called thaw period in the 1950s, Honchar was president of the Ukrainian branch of the Soviet Writers Union. He is currently a member of the Central Committee of the Communist Party in the Ukraine.

Honchar became popular with a war trilogy, *Praporonostsi* (1947–48; Eng. tr., *Standard-Bearers*, 1948). A prolific writer, he is the author of many novels and long short stories, such as "Shchob svityvsya vohnyk" (1955; So That the Light May Burn). Although a pillar of the Soviet literary establishment, Honchar has sometimes expressed dissenting and nationalistic views, especially in his novel *Sobor* (1968; The Cathedral), which evoked favorable comment from Ukrainian dissidents, notably Yevhen Sverstyuk. Honchar has been awarded the Lenin Prize for Literature. Although his prose attempts to break away from poetic traditions, he remains a "socialist romantic."

G.S.N.L.

Hora, Josef (1891–1945), Czech poet, was born in Dobřín near Roudnice. He was a journalist, first with the Communist and then with the socialist press. Next to Jiří WOLKER, Hora was the most outstanding member of the group that composed "proletarian" verse, and he later wrote metaphysical reflections of considerable power. He began as a follower of Stanislav Neumann. Two collections, *Strom v květu* (1920; The Tree in Bloom) and *Pracující den* (1920; The Working Day), established him in the proletarian group. But his enthusiasm for the revolution was even then tempered by a desire for individual integrity and by a frankly contradictory longing for escape from cities and the masses. Hora's break with the rhetoric of the proletarians occurred with *Srdce a vřava světa* (1922; The Heart and the Tumult of the World), in which he returned to the forms of folk poetry as well as to themes of nature, home, quiet, and even an unproletarian loneliness. The change is complete in *Italie* (1925; Italy), which is ostensibly a travel diary. In this book the poet achieved a style of almost classical serenity and severity. Hora's later collections, among which *Struny ve větru* (1927; Strings in the Wind) is perhaps the best, possess a new metaphysical quality, the result of reading William

James, Henri BERGSON, and modern physics. Often, they are meditations on time and the universe, acute realizations of the dreamlike character of existence that testify to a degree of spiritualization rarely found in recent Czech verse. *Máchovské variace* (1936; Variations on a Theme by Mácha) celebrates the great Czech romantic poet, Karel Hynek Mácha, on the 100th anniversary of his death and demonstrates the author's own affinity with romantic themes and forms. This affinity is obvious in a later volume, *Jan houslista* (1940; John the Violinist), a slight, sentimental story, with an early 19th-century flavor, about the return of a great violinist from the United States to his downtrodden native country. The romantic convention disguises the author's profound and very personal despair over life and the fate of his nation. Hora also wrote a book of ballads, *Tonoucí stiny* (1933; Drowning Shadows), some verse satires, and some less impressive novelistic prose. In his later years he was an extremely successful translator of verse; his paraphrase (1937) of Aleksandr Pushkin's *Yevgeny Onegin* is a masterpiece comparable to the finest achievements of Otokar FISCHER. Apparently an out-and-out modernist and prophet of the coming revolution, Hora found his way back to the sources of poetry in Slavic romanticism, in Mácha and Pushkin and their melancholy. Upon his death in 1945, he was honored by a state funeral and the newly created title of "national poet."

See: F. X. Šalda, *O nejmladší poesii české* (1928); A. M. Píša, *Proletářská poesie* (1936), pp. 16–19; A. French, *The Poets of Prague* (1969).   R.W.

Horváth, Ödön von (1901–38), German dramatist, novelist, and story-teller, was born in Fiume and lived as a free-lance writer in Murnau on the Staffelsee until 1934, when he emigrated to Vienna. He then lived in Henndorf in the vicinity of Salzburg, and in 1938, when the Nazi government integrated Austria into the Third Reich, he went to Paris. There he was killed by a falling tree limb on the Champs Elysées. His dramas and stories, written in a realistic style and concentrating on social and moral criticism of his age, are spiced with humor, moralistic seriousness, and biting satire. He is best known for his dramas, which are topical in theme and present everyday people with their everyday problems. His novels concern the nature of dictatorship.

Horváth's plays, which have in recent years received revived attention, include *Revolte auf Côte 3018* (1927; Revolts on Coast 3018), reissued in 1928 with the title *Die Bergbahn* (The Mountain Railway); *Sladek, der schwarze Reichswehrmann* (1930; Sladek, The Black Reich Soldier); the popular comedies *Geschichten aus dem Wienerwald* (1931; Eng. tr., *Tales from the Vienna Woods,* 1977) and *Italienische Nacht* (1931; Italian Night); *Glaube, Liebe, Hoffnung* (1932; Faith, Hope, and Charity); the comedies *Eine Unbekannte aus der Seine* (1933; An Unknown Woman from the Seine) and *Figaro läßt sich scheiden* (prod. 1934, first pub 1959; The Divorce of Figaro); and *Der jüngste Tag* (1938, published in 1955; Judgment Day). A novel, *Der ewige Spießer* (The Eternal Philistine) appeared in 1930. Two others, *Jugend ohne Gott* (1938; Godless Youth) and *Ein Kind unserer Zeit* (1938; A Child of Our Time) were issued in a single volume in 1953 with the title *Zeitalter der Fische* (Eng. tr., *The Age of the Fish,* 1939). His plays were collected in one edition in 1961.

See: J. Strelka, *Brecht, Horváth, Dürrenmatt* (1962); A. Fritz, *Ödön von Horváth als Kritiker seiner Zeit* (1973); D. Hildebrandt, *Ödön von Horváth in Selbstzeugnissen und Bilddokumenten* (1975); K. Winston, *Horváth Studies: Close Readings of Six Plays* (1977).   A.L.W.

Hostovský, Egon (1908–73), Czech novelist and short-story writer, was born at Hronov in northeastern Bohemia. He studied in Prague and Vienna and entered the diplomatic corps, serving in France and the United States, where he spent the years of World War II. In 1948, when Czechoslovakia went Communist, he was stationed at a diplomatic post in Norway and decided to emigrate. He returned to the United States, where he worked as an active opponent of communism until his death.

Hostovský's novels and stories are psychological melodramas, strongly influenced by Fyodor DOSTOYEVSKY. Their heroes are displaced, rootless beings, consumed by fear and feelings of persecution. Like Hostovský himself, these men are frequently Jewish intellectuals. Their problems stem in part from their hypersensitivity, inferiority feelings, and lack of sure national and social identification. His early novel, *Případ profesora Körnera* (1932; Professor Körner's Case), concerns such a hero. Hostovský's subsequent works are less psychological and more melodramatic, and are set against the background of the wartime world of espionage, exile, and the Nazi and Communist terrors; they frequently suffer from a hectic tone and excessive sensationalism. Such is true of the stories collected in *Listy z vyhnanství* (1941; Eng. tr., *Letters from Exile,* 1942), and the novel *Sedmkrát v hlavní úloze* (1942; Eng. tr., *Seven Times the Leading Man,* 1945). A better work is *Úkryt* (1943; Eng. tr., *The Hideout,* 1945), a short novel that gives a vivid but restrained picture of the feelings of a refugee who hides from the Nazis. Hostovský's latter novels are weaker, although they have been rather popular in English translations; they include *Půlnoční pacient* (1959; Eng. tr., *The Midnight Patient,* 1955) and *Dobročinný večírek* (1958; Eng. tr., *The Charity Ball,* 1957).

See: *Padesát let Egonu Hostovskému* (1958).

W.E.H.

Hrabal, Bohumil (1914–), Czech novelist and short-story writer, was born near Brno and studied law at Prague University, receiving his doctorate in 1946. He worked at various manual and clerical jobs, coming to literature rather late. His first stories appeared in 1956, under the title *Hovory lidí* (People's Conversations); these were followed by the collections *Perlička na dně* (1963; A Pearl on the Bottom) and *Pábitelé* (1964), the latter title a term the author invented for his weird characters and his grotesque narrations. Hrabal was influenced by the humor of Jaroslav HAŠEK and his *Good Soldier Schweik,* as well as by dada and surrealism. His characters are crude commoners and petit bourgeois whose actions are wildly eccentric and whose speech is exaggerated, vulgar and frequently hilarious. Hrabal's short novel, *Ostře sledované vlaky* (1964; Eng. tr., *A Close Watch on the Trains,* 1968), was adapted for the screen as *Closely Watched Trains* and earned an international reputation as one of the most popular Czech films of the 1960s. The story is a Chaplinesque blend of black humor and pathos, about a nondescript youth who overcomes sexual impotence to become a hero of the underground resistance to the Nazis. His long story *Taneční hodiny pro starší a pokročilé* (1965; Dance Lessons for Older and Advanced Pupils), a comic-erotic interior monologue cast as a single sentence, is a kind of parody of the last chapter of James Joyce's *Ulysses.* Hrabal was active in the "Prague Spring" movement of 1968; following that year he fell into official disfavor.

See: W. E. Harkins and P. I. Trensky, eds., *Czech Literature since 1956: A Symposium* (1980).   W.E.H.

Huch, Ricarda (1864–1947), German novelist and historian, who wrote occasionally under the pseudonym of

Richard Hugo, was born in Braunschweig, the sister of the novelist Rudolf Huch and a cousin of Friedrich Huch. Inherited literary talents, the background of a highly cultured home, the opportunity for a university education—a rare privilege then for a woman—together with a zest for work enabled Ricarda Huch to become a leading woman writer in Germany. Her creative work shows none of the paralyzing influences that learning and scholarly inclinations quite often have. Her style, although refined and deliberate in choice of words and structures, remained vigorous and natural; not even the abundance of accurate historical detail displayed in her later novels obstructed the epic flow in her tales. Moreover, although Ricarda Huch was conversant with all current European ideas, emotions and strong instincts nevertheless govern the lives of her characters. The best known among her earlier works, *Erinnerungen von Ludolf Ursleu dem Jüngeren* (1893; Eng. tr., *Recollections of Ludolf Ursleu the Younger*, 1913–15), evokes reminiscences of that long series of European novels portraying the disintegration of a well-to-do family, brought about by an overdose of introspection and intellectual refinement, with an accompanying loss of vitality. With Huch, however, disaster results much less from intellectualism than from the onrush of irrational passion.

Huch combined epic style with the ability to discern, in a welter of conflicts and opposites, the lasting values of beauty and love. No matter to what aspects of life she turned, she always transcended ephemeral phenomena and reconciled conflicts in a vision of final harmony and beatitude, even when she delved into such a sordid milieu of broken lives as in *Aus der Triumphgasse* (1902; Out of Triumph Alley). It was only natural that her predestined epic understanding tended to radiate through ever wider spheres of reality and to turn to vast historic panoramas, as in *Die Geschichten von Garibaldi* (1906–07; Eng. tr., *Defeat*, 1928; *Victory*, 1929), *Das Leben des Grafen Federigo Confalonieri* (1910; The Life of Count Federigo Confalonieri), and the monumental account of the Thirty Years War, *Der große Krieg in Deutschland* (1912–14; The Great War in Germany). Thereafter she devoted all her energies to historical, critical, and philosophical studies, a field in which she was already well accredited by virtue of her two volumes on the romantic movement, *Die Blütezeit der Romantik* (1899; The Time of Blossoming in Romanticism) and *Ausbreitung und Verfall der Romantik* (1902; The Expansion and Decline of Romanticism). The crisis affecting this change was fundamentally intellectual. It is as if once more Huch had wanted to cast off her womanly, harmonizing role and to fling herself into the man-made world of ideas and polemical issues. But it was in vain; whether she sided with Christianity against neopaganism, as in *Der Sinn der Heiligen Schrift* (1919; The Meaning of the Holy Scriptures), or with Mikhail Bakunin's socialism against the bourgeois mentality, as in *Michael Bakunin und die Anarchie* (1923), the balance was soon restored as she revealed deep appreciation of personality, as in *Entpersönlichung* (1921; Depersonalization), or extolled the sturdiness of the German bourgeoisie, as in *Das Zeitalter der Glaubensspaltung* (1937; The Age of the Schism of Faith), dealing with the age of Reformation and its gigantic inner tensions, which showed her power at its best. The same maternal instinct with which other woman writers of her time, notably Agnes Sapper (1852–1929) and Helena Christaller (1872–1953), sanctified life within the precincts of the family or the small community, in the work of Ricarda Huch extended its beneficial function into far wider spheres of time and place.

See: E. Gottlieb, *Ricarda Huch: ein Beitrag zur Geschichte der deutschen Epik* (1914); O. Walzel, *Ricarda Huch* (1916); M. Baum, *Leuchtende Spur, das Leben Ricarda Huchs* (1950); H.-H. Kappel, *Epische Gestaltung bei Ricarda Huch* (1976); J. Bernstein, *Bewußtwerdung im Romanwerk der Ricarda Huch* (1977).

H.Bo. rev. A.L.W.

Huchel, Peter (1903–), German poet, was born in Berlin and spent his childhood in rural Mark Brandenburg. He studied literature and philosophy briefly in Berlin, Freiburg, and Vienna, then worked as a translator and farmhand in France, the Balkans, and Turkey. After serving in the army during World War II, he became artistic director of the East Berlin Radio. Between 1949 and 1962, Huchel was chief editor of the influential East German literary journal *Sinn und Form*. His refusal to adapt his liberal editorial policies to narrow Communist Party guidelines led to his dismissal and to eight years of imposed isolation in Wilhelmshorst near Potsdam. In 1971 he was permitted to emigrate to the west and now lives in Staufen near Freiburg, West Germany.

Long known primarily as an inspired, courageous editor, Huchel only gradually won recognition as a poet of major importance. Although he began to publish poems as early as 1924, his reputation is based entirely on three slim collections of poetry published after the war: *Gedichte* (1948; Poems, republished in somewhat altered form as *Die Sternenreuse*, 1967; The Star Trap), and *Chausseen Chausseen* (1963; Highways Highways) and *Gezählte Tage* (1972; Counted Days), published only in the west. A new volume, *Die neunte Stunde* (The Ninth Hour), appeared in 1977.

Huchel is neither a mere nature poet, as some critics have argued, nor specifically political, as others insist. He should be viewed within the symbolist, hermetic tradition of Friedrich Hölderlin, Charles BAUDELAIRE, Georg TRAKL, and Paul CELAN. Employing nature motifs, particularly from the landscape of his childhood, but also drawing on classical, biblical, and mystical sources, he creates poetic textures of great density and complexity. In recurrent images of evocative richness Huchel expresses his major concerns: the search for meaning in a meaningless and threatening universe; the problematic interrelationships among humanity, nature, time, and death; and a profound skepticism about the efficacy of language as a means of overcoming human isolation.

See: J. Flores, *Poetry in East Germany* (1971), pp. 119–204; H. Mayer, ed., *Über Peter Huchel* (1973); A. Vieregg, *Die Lyrik Peter Huchels: Zeichensprache und Privatmythologie* (1976).

H.S.

Hungarian literature. The beginnings of modern Hungarian literature may be traced to the last decade of the 19th century. The Compromise of 1867 established the dual (Austro-Hungarian) monarchy and created favorable conditions for rapid industrialization. Between 1867 and the end of the 19th century, Hungary was transformed from a semidormant agrarian land into a rapidly developing country with a strong industrial base, on extensive railway network, and sprawling urban centers. The distribution of wealth favored only certain social groups, however, and the growth of the population resulted in agrarian unemployment and stimulated large-scale emigration to the United States. Industrialization created an indigenous working class, the numbers of which grew dramatically between 1890 and 1900, and with the formation of the Hungarian Social-Democratic Party in 1890, the organized struggle for workers' rights began. The main beneficiary of the economic development of the post-1867 period was the bourgeoisie, largely of German and of Jewish origin, the assimilation of which proceeded quickly under successive liberal governments. While the bourgeoisie was gaining in economic strength, it nevertheless left politics to the so-called historical classes, the aristocracy and the gentry (the lesser nobility). The administration of the Hungarian half of the monarchy was almost entirely in the hands of the gentry, which was torn between its political and economic interests: although it resented the increasing impoverishment of the small landowner, the gentry—at least until 1904—supported the administration for fear of losing its social status. The question of national minorities proved to be the most intractable of all the problems left unsolved by the Compromise of 1867, and while it could be dealt with administratively, in the cultural sphere it induced Hungarian escapism into illusions of national grandeur.

This egocentric trend reached a point of culmination in 1896 when Hungary celebrated the millenium, the thousandth year of its national existence. The fiction of unity and social peace could not entirely hide the deep division between nationalities or the antagonism between classes; yet the literature of the period—with some exceptions— was less the reflection or critical analysis of reality than an expression of moral ideals and grand illusions. A "popular national" school set the tone in literature; its leading critic, Pál Gyulai (1826–1909), generally regarded the popular romanticism of Sándor Petőfi (1823–49) and the epic realism of János Arany (1817–82) as binding ideals. Although Gyulai was a distinguished critic in his own right, by the 1890s his criteria of good literature had become largely anachronistic. The "popular national" school was patriotic in its outlook, mediocre and often banal in its style. Together with the popular romantic writer Mór Jókai (1825–1904), sometimes called "the great storyteller," this school became the mainstay of stagnation. Both Gyulai and Jókai represented venerable ideals of a period long bygone, but their disciples were often poor imitations indulging in empty bombast.

The decade 1896–1906 was the gestation period of the modern movement. Its precursors included urban Jewish poets such as József Kiss (1843–1921) and Jenő Heltai; naturalist and critical realist writers such as Sándor Bródy and Zoltán Thury; the lonely aesthete, Jenő Péterfy; and accomplished stylists and critics with a French orientation, such as Dezső Szomory and Zoltán Ambrus. Of the conservative writers Géza Gárdonyi added a new psychological touch in his historical novels whereas Ferenc Herczeg introduced a cautious critical dimension into Hungarian writing. Recognition of the talented newcomers was retarded by the absence of a journal open to literary innovations. From 1900 onwards, however, there were a number of attempts to establish a truly authoritative forum for modern ideas. This period saw the growth of "modernism" in the arts, exemplified by the music of Béla Bartók and Zoltán Kodály and the painting of József Rippl-Rónai and the impressionists of Nagybánya. At the same time, a movement emerged in the social sciences with the aim of fostering free thought and sociological inquiry into the problems of Hungarian society. Its forum, established in 1900, was Huszadik Század (20th Century), the journal of the Social Sciences Association. Despite its low circulation, this periodical played a significant part in the history of Hungarian radicalism, influencing, among others, the young Endre Ady. Ady's important volume of poetry Uj versek (1906; New Poems) coincided with the first offensive of the Hungarian Left against the semifeudal establishment.

Uj versek was the bugle call of new Hungarian literature. Ady provided a symbolic link between "historical" Hungary (represented for centuries by the nobility) and the modern movement rooted in urban conditions. Ady belonged to the gentry, and both his personality and language were imbued with Hungarian tradition. Yet, at the same time, he was steeped in French symbolism and was a determined advocate of a radical restructuring of Hungarian society. Ady was the most prominent figure in the anthology Holnap (Tomorrow) published in 1908 and 1909 at Nagyvárad by a group of young poets, and when Nyugat (West), edited by Paul Ignotus, pseud. of Hugo Veigelsber (1869–1949), Ernő Osvát, and Miksa Fenyő, at last got off the ground in 1908, he soon joined forces with its politically less radical modern writers. The first Nyugat generation was a loose coalition of numerous talented writers who shared an openness to the new philosophical and artistic trends in Western Europe—Friedrich Nietzsche, Henri Bergson, naturalism, symbolism, and impressionism. They wished to modernize the means of literary expression in order to make Hungarian literature "European" in every respect. Yet according to the literary historian Antal Szerb, the result of Nyugat's long and impressive struggle against provincialism and bad literature was "not that Hungarian literature became more Western but it became more deeply and freely Hungarian." Ady became a prophet of the democratic revolution, expressing his views in striking metaphors and powerful symbols. Ady's ideals, however, were not fully shared by other Nyugat writers, with the possible exception of Zsigmond Móricz, some of whose novels sharply condemn the backwardness and smug class prejudice of contemporary Hungarian society.

The first Nyugat generation included many excellent poets and translators. The central figure of the group was Mihály Babits, a learned poet and thoughtful critic in whom Catholicism and the classical tradition, idealism and the passions of a sensitive soul, aesthetic ideals and social reality clashed in an immensely creative struggle. Babits's importance as literary arbiter was greatly enhanced between the two world wars when he became curator of the prestigious Baumgarten Prize and, after Osvát's death, editor of Nyugat. Dezső Kosztolányi, Árpád Tóth, and Gyula Juhász were all poets of genuine talent and remarkable craftmanship, as well as excellent translators of English and French poetry. Kosztolányi later branched out into prose with considerable success, while Tóth and Juhász, both influenced by Ady, remained above all poets. All four poets professed an enlightened "bourgeois" humanism, Kosztolányi fundamentally rejecting politics in the name of "pure art," whereas Tóth and Juhász also voiced socialist sympathies with quasi-religious undertones. A fifth poet of the same generation, Milán Füst, was fated to remain something of an outsider. His poems, although few in number, are impressive in their sonorous, almost classically controlled expressionism. After World War I, Füst's stature grew thanks to his fiction and writings on aesthetics as well; he is now regarded as an important influence on the post-Nyugat modernists.

Although the new literary movement did not have a coherent program, it did have its gifted critics and polemicists, such as Ignotus, Aladár, Schöpflin, and Lajos Hatvany, Ernő Osvát, the almost legendary editor of Nyugat, wrote little himself, but he enjoyed a special reputation for discovering new talent. Schöpflin won admiration for the impartial soundness of his critical judgment. Nyugat prose writers, apart from Móricz, included such masters of the Hungarian language as Gyula Krúdy, Margit Kaffka, and Dezső Szomory, but even the lesser writers connected with Nyugat—Gyula Török, Géza Csáth, Viktor Cholnoky, Ernő Szép—would on occasion produce works impressive for their psychological realism or their evocative impressionism. The success of Frigyes KARINTHY and Jenő J. Tersánszky was mainly due to their imaginative wit. Tersánszky's *Kakuk Marci* (1923–42, Martin Cuckoo) cycle is an interesting example of the modern picaresque novel. Karinthy is best known as a humorous writer and the author of a superb collection of literary pastiches, *Igy írtok ti* (1912; That's How *You* Write), which greatly contributed to the popular acceptance of the modern movement, yet he was also fascinated by scientific progress (he admired H. G. Wells) and wrote an account of a Swiftian misogynist Utopia as well.

Outside the *Nyugat* circle but equally influenced by new artistic trends was Ferenc MOLNÁR, a thoroughly urban writer who came to literature from journalism and soon became the star entertainer of Budapest's "new bourgeoisie." He was enormously versatile, writing ironical novels that dissected the tinsel world of the nouveau riche, such as *Az éhes város* (1900; The Hungry City), sentimental stories that later became youth classics, and cleverly constructed, highly theatrical plays, some of which, like *Liliom* (1909; Eng. tr., 1921), were successes on Broadway. The same period saw the first successes of young playwrights, such as Menyhért Lengyel and Lajos Bíró, who later left Hungary and settled abroad, becoming skillful scriptwriters in Hollywood and Great Britain.

The conservative element in Hungarian literature was too drained of talent to challenge the *Nyugat* writers on purely literary grounds. Attacks on the modernists were, on the whole, based on political innuendo. It was only during World War I that *Nyugat* faced serious competition, and it came not from the conservatives but from the Left, from Lajos KASSÁK's small but vociferous group of avant-garde literati. The jingoistic sloganeering and nationalist intoxication that had characterized the first months of the war gave way in later years to anxiety, despair, and eventually to pacifistic utterances by certain *Nyugat* writers, including Babits, Karinthy, and Tóth. Ady, however, opposed the war from the beginning. Lajos Kassák's program, outlined in his magazine *Tett* (Action), and after its suppression in *Ma* (Today), was directed both against bourgeois convention, championing instead the "new man" shaped by technological progress (a distinctly futurist concept), and against the social system whose manfunctioning led to the senseless holocaust of the war. Kassák's journals accommodated a wide variety of antiwar rebels, some of whom—Aladár Komját, József Lengyel, and József Révai—turned Communist in 1918, while others followed their intransigent leader's "independent revolutionary" line.

The collapse of the Austro-Hungarian monarchy and its turbulent revolutionary and counterrevolutionary aftermath constitute a watershed in the development of modern Hungarian literature. Ady's death in January 1919 symbolized the end of a period rich in both conflict and hope. The revolutionary regime of Count Michael Károlyi and the Socialist-Communist coalition of the Soviet Republic were controversial in their policies, yet they were nevertheless last-ditch attempts to defend Hungarian national interests in a period of chaos and rapacious self-assertion by new national states. In the Trianon Peace Treaty (1920), Hungary lost two-thirds of its prewar territory and had to yield sizable Hungarian minorities to Czechoslovakia, Romania, and Yugoslavia. The counterrevolutionary regime established in 1920 under the leadership of Admiral Horthy had to live with the heritage of the war. For all its nationalist posturing, this government was a narrow-minded continuation of prewar Hungary: a titular kingdom without a king, in which individual aristocrats and the church still owned vast estates and shared economic power with the barons of industry. Unemploy-

ment and the influx of refugees into the small territory that was now Hungary further aggravated the economic situation, while the chauvinistic, antisocialist, and anti-Semitic atmosphere of the first years of counterrevolutionary rule forced many gifted intellectuals to emigrate.

Under such circumstances, it is amazing how resilient literature proved to be. With few exceptions, writers refused to recant their support of the revolution or to make tactical adjustments to the spirit of hysterical nationalism and crusading Catholicism. Counterrevolutionary conservative nationalism did find a learned exponent in the person of Gyula Szekfű, whose *Három nemzedék* (1920; Three Generations) tried to trace the reasons for the disintegration of historical Hungary. But the right-wing radicalism of the impoverished gentry and economically ruined urban middle classes inspired Dezső SZABÓ to write his large expressionist novel, *Az elsodort falu* (1919; The Village That Was Swept Away), which, with its rejection of metropolitan "decadence" and romantic cult of the peasantry, later became a point of departure for some of the populist writers. The "official" literature of the Horthy regime was, of course, conservative and nationalistic. Most conservative authors, such as Ferenc Herczeg and Miklós Surányi, wrote panoramic historical novels or romantic biographies of outstanding artists and composers. By the early 1930s, however, some Transylvanian writers, such as József Nyirő, and Áron Tamási, were taking their themes from the life of the sturdy and resourceful Hungarian peasants. These writers also became popular among the more traditional readership in Hungary. An attractive blend of romanticism and realism characterized the work of Ferenc Móra (1879–1934), whose most successful novel, *Ének a búzamezőkről* (1927; Eng. tr., Song of the Wheat Fields, 1930), depicts the tragic conflicts created by the way in the life of a simple peasant family. Among Catholic writers of the period, two names stand out: Sándor Sík (1889–1963), a Piarist monk who was an influential religious poet and an open-minded teacher of aesthetics, and László Mécs (1895–1978). A Catholic priest from northern Hungary, which after the war became part of Slovakia, Mécs enjoyed unprecedented popularity for some years, although his poetry, preaching a "revolution of love" in a sentimentally affected style, represents a regression to the poetic standards of *Nyugat*.

Between 1920 and 1926 there emerged in Vienna an important new Hungarian literary center created by émigré writers of the Left whose political views ranged from liberal to Communist. It was in Vienna that György (Georg) LUKÁCS wrote his important theoretical essays later published as *Geschichte und Klassenbewusstsein* (1923; Eng. tr., History and Class Consciousness, 1971). Here also some of Ady's former friends and collaborators—Ignotus, Hatvany, Béla Révész—now lived. The most forceful expenent of Hungarian modernism, Lajos Kassák, continued to publish his constructivist review *Ma* in Vienna. Although some of *Ma*'s contributors soon quarreled with him and established their own short-lived periodicals, Kassák's journal published translations of German and French avant-garde poets and provided a forum for younger critics and poets such as Andor Németh, Tibor DÉRY, and Gyula ILLYÉS. Vienna was important both as a clearinghouse for ideas and a focal point from which leftist writers could move on to Hungarian communities outside Hungary: Gábor Gaál and Zoltán Franyó settled in Romania, Ervin Sinkó (1898–1967) in Yugoslavia. Some Communist writers, such as Béla Balázs, left Vienna in the mid-1920s, and in the early 1930s a new exodus took place from there to the Soviet Union. The Moscow group of Hungarian émigré writers did not include a single important poet, although they did produce one good playwright, Gyula HÁY, and—after his many years of suffering—an outstanding prose writer, József Lengyel. Needless to say, this group's theoretical and critical contribution to modern Hungarian literature, exemplified by Lukács and Révai, has a strong Marxist bias.

In Hungary, *Nyugat* remained the leading literary review throughout the period between the two world wars, yet it had lost much of its political militancy and had become a defender of universal humanist values. Babits's program of "pure art" can be interpreted both as a withdrawal from the political arena and as a stand against the advance of totalitarian ideologies. The elitist implications of this program were not lost on his contemporaries, but the Left, fragmented and shattered after 1919, could not challenge *Nyugat*'s position. The best magazine of the non-Communist Left, *Szép szó* (Fine Word), edited by Paul Ignotus, Ferenc Fejtő, and Attila JÓZSEF, could only complement rather than supplant Babits's review. Even Gyula Illyés, generally regarded as a leading populist post, kept very close ties with Babits, after whose death he launched *Magyar csillag* (Hungarian Star), the successor of *Nyugat*.

There was less affinity among the members of the second *Nyugat* generation than had been the case with the first. Its poets—Lőrinc SZABÓ, József Fodor, and György Sárközi—were urban writers with postexpressionist or postsymbolist tendencies and populist sympathies. Yet its leading prose writer, the elegant and erudite Sándor MÁRAI, represented certain "patrician" middle-class values not unlike those of Thomas MANN. A skillful chronicler of family sagas and a dispassionate observer (although not necessarily supporter) of social change, Márai created something of a school. He left Hungary after 1945 and has lived in the United States and, more recently, in Italy. Of his numerous novels, *Egy polgár vallomásai* (1934; Confessions of a Bourgeois) is considered the most successful. Another representative writer of the period, and Márai's fellow émigré from 1948 onwards, was Lajos Zilahy (1891–1974). Zilahy had been first known as a conservative raconteur, but in the 1930s he became a reformist mediator between the government and the young populists; his intimate knowledge of the aristocracy's way of life enabled him to write *Ararát* (1947; Eng. tr., *The Dukays,* 1949), a perceptive account of the disintegration of that class.

The third generation of *Nyugat* writers, sometimes called "the essayists' generation," made its appearance in Hungarian literature in the early 1930s. The essayists—Antal SZERB, Gábor Halász, László Szabó—were contemporaries of the poets of the second *Nyugat* generation, and the apparent delay in the impact on the literary scene of the essayists can be explained by the differences inherent in the two genres. In Hungary the essay was the genre of the intellectual elite. An excellent essayist like Szerb did not achieve wide recognition before the publication of his *Magyar irodalomtörténet* (1934; The History of Hungarian Literature), a book that set standards for literary historians for many years. The English and French orientation of the essayists provided a welcome counterweight to the massive Germanic learning of older literary historians, some of whom, such as László Négyesy and János Horváth, had already applied Wilhelm Dilthey's more modern methods of inquiry into cultural history. Whereas Szerb was particularly interested in modern English fiction, another critic, Albert Gyergyai (1893–), wrote perceptive essays on French literature and translated Gustave Flaubert and Marcel PROUST into Hungarian. Of the younger generation of writers and essayists who made their debuts before World War II, several deserve mention: the Catholic poet and essayist György Rónay, the Catholic novelists Gábor Thurzó and Béla Just, and the "urban rationalists," such as István Sőtér, András Hevessi, and Emil Kolozsvári. All followed, more or less consciously, French models. Perhaps the most ambitious member of this group was Miklós Szentkuthy (1908–), whose long-winded experiments with a kind of "antinovel" have so far produced only questionable results.

The poets of the third *Nyugat* generation were fighting against great odds when they stood up to the challenge of their poetic predecessors. Ady, Babits, Kosztolányi, Füst, Lőrinc Szabó, and Attila József were poets of real stature who exerted considerable influence on their younger colleagues. Hence the slow maturing of the third generation, with the exceptions of the short-lived Transylvanian poet Jenő Dsida (1907–38) and of Miklós RADNÓTI, whose poetry suddenly blossomed into greatness in the shadow of death. Others, such as Sándor WEÖRES, István VAS, György Rónay, and Zoltán Jékely, came of age later, some during World War II and some afterwards. László Kálnoky is at least one case of a very late developer. An important step in the development of this generation was their rejection of avant-garde aesthetics in the name of a rationalist, classical tradition. This was the position of Vas and Radnóti. Yet as the example of Weöres demonstrated, it was also possible to oppose the irrational mythology of fascism in the spirit of an anthropological universalism. Another trait of the third generation is its adventurousness, its interest in the bizarre, the mysterious, and the extraordinary. Although few of these writers are religious in a strict sense of the word, their work has a "metaphysical" aspect.

The populist movement in Hungarian literature began in the early 1930s and produced a large, heterogeneous body of literature, with a special emphasis on rural themes and the need for social reform. In 1932 the talented novelist and essayist László NÉMETH started his one-man magazine *Tanu* (The Witness), which together with *Válasz* (The Answer) launched in 1934, was instrumental in formulating many "populist" ideas. The movement reached its highest point of influence in 1937 with the formation of the "March Front," an anti-Fascist group striving for internal reforms. After 1938, however, the populist movement split into Left, Right, and Center, and while some of its slogans became incorporated into government programs, its hard core around the Center concentrated on preparing Hungary for the changes that were expected to occur after the war. While the political views of individual populists diverged, Németh's ideas about the desirable "revolution of quality" (a moral revolution) and Hungary's right to choose a third road between capitalism and Soviet socialism undoubtedly influenced most of them. Another spokesman of the Center (with a radical leftist past) was Gyula Illyés whose *Puszták népe* (1936; Eng. tr., *People of the Puszta,* 1967) can be singled out as the most influential book of the movement. The Hungarian village was "rediscovered" thanks to the work of Illyés and other populist writers such as Zoltán Szabó, Imre Kovács, Ferenc Erdei, József Darvas, and Géza Féja, whose sociological monographs deepened the awareness of Hungary's anachronistic social structure. From a literary point of view, the movement dated back to Dezső Szabó and József Erdélyi (1896–1978), a lyricist whose simple poems foreshadowed the possibility of a more "popular" type of poetry. It accomodated "documentary realists," such as Péter Veres and József Darvas; neoromantics leaning towards folkloristic or tribal-mythological stylization, such as Pál Szabó, Áron Tamási, István Sinka, Károly Pap, and János Kodolányi; and psychological realists such as László Németh. Illyés, one of the most versatile Hungarian writers of the 20th century, stands apart in that prior to World War II he was best known as a socially committed poet and the author of strongly analytical essays, whereas after the war he developed a reputation as a playwright who dealt with national and universal human problems. Yet, there is a parallel between the work of Illyés and that of Németh: a perceptive essayist and novelist, Németh is also the author of historical plays usually investigating the conflict of outstanding personalities and their social environment. One many conclude that the best populist writers were not only concerned with social reform but also with historical continuity and national cohesiveness.

Alongside the polished, urbane prose of successive *Nyugat* generations and the romantically colored realism of Zsigmond Móricz, the period between the two world wars gave rise to a critical realist approach in literature. Most, if not all, writers of this trend were socialists, although the practical application of their principles often led them to clash with Marxist doctrines or (after World War II) with Communist ideology. Apart from the work of Lajos NAGY and Gyula Illyés, the visionary proletarian tales of Andor Endre Gelléri (1907–45) deserve attention, as do the dark, grim novels of Zsigmond Remenyik (1900–62), which passionately condemn social injustice and human baseness. Remenyik lived abroad for long periods of time, as did Tibor Déry whose socialist convictions could never quite suppress the ironic detachment with which he viewed society. Déry's long novel, *A befejezetlen mondat* (1947; The Unfinished Sentence), was one of the most important works of Hungarian realist fiction written before World War II.

No socialist prose writer, however, surpassed the achievement of Attila József, the greatest revolutionary poet of the period in or outside Hungary. József learned from Ady and the *Nyugat* writers as well as from Kassák and the French surrealists. There are also populist tendencies in his poetry, but his basic tone is unmistakably urban and modern. József was an anarchist rebel in his youth and a Communist organizer around 1930. In the last period of his short life, József described his own alienated experience in gripping poems and explored his subconscious with the aid of Freudian psychoanalysis. József transcends the limitations of "proletarian poetry" by turning his antifascism into an appeal to defend universally cherished values. Although he introduced few formal innovations, his posthumous influence has been enormous. His socialist ideals were so totally Western that he became an inspiration not only to those who wanted to destroy capitalism, but also to successive generations trying to "humanize" socialism.

During World War II, many promising Hungarian writers and poets of Jewish origin perished. Radnóti, Szerb, Halász, Sarközi, and László Fenyő were killed in Hungary; György Bálint, the courageous left-wing critic, and the poet Béla Pásztor disappeared in the Ukraine; Károly Pap, and Gelléri died in German concentration camps. The influx of Communist writers returning from the USSR—Béla Illés, Sándor Gergely, Háy, Balázs, and others—could not make up for these losses. In fact, 1945 did not bring an immediate change in the character of Hungarian literature. While fascist sympathizers amongst the writers, such as Erdélyi, were silenced or jailed and some populists, such as László Németh were victimized, the period between 1945 and 1948 was characterized by the conditions of the "democratic coalition." *Válasz* resumed publication, and several new periodicals sprang up—*Magyarok, Ujhold* (New Moon), *Forum*—each with a different political orientation. *Ujhold* pledged itself to the continuation of Babits's "uncommitted" humanism. Its poets, especially János PILINSZKY and Ágnes Nemes Nagy used sparse, controlled verse to express the feelings of guilt of the Hungarian intelligentsia and the existential anxiety of modern man. The poetic model of *Ujhold,* to which other poets, such as György Rába, László Kálnoky, and Sándor Rákos, also contributed, gained new attractiveness in the intellectually more demanding climate of the 1960s. The same is true for the prose writers connected with *Ujhold*—Iván Mándy, Géza Ottlik, Magda Szabó—whose techniques all differed from realism in one way or another.

A new phase in Hungarian cultural policy was ushered in by the so-called Lukács controversy in which Lukács was castigated by Communist Party spokesmen for preferring "Western" critical realism to (Soviet) socialist realism. Although the era of enforced socialist realism was relatively short (1948–53), its adverse effects could be felt for years afterwards, and only since the early 1960s can one speak of a genuine pluralism in the cultural policy of the government. Nevertheless it was in the early 1950s that a new constellation of poetic talents emerged. These were poets of peasant origin—Ferenc JUHÁSZ, László NAGY, István Simon, Imre Takács, and Sándor Czóri—who soon left behind their primitive realism or initial naive romanticism. These writers, especially Juhász and Nagy, created a syncretic imaginative style that grappled first with problems of the small community and later with those of a chaotic yet interdependent world. Of the urban socialist poets of the period László Benjámin (1915–) is the most important; after a period of uncritical enthusiasm for the new regime, in 1955–56 he became one of the strongest challengers of the Stalinist double standards that were corrupting public morality. In prose, Déry's novel *Feleltt* (2 vols., 1950–52; The Answer) and probing short stories were the best achievements of a period singularly lacking in good fiction, although the talents of some younger writers—István Örkény, Ferenc Karinthy, and Imre Sarkadi—did shine through their pretenses. Their ranks were reinforced during the post-Stalin "thaw" by a new wave of prose writers, sometimes referred to as the "1955 Generation." This group, including László Kamondy, György Moldova, István Csurka, Ferenc Sánta, and István Szabó, introduced a measure of psychological realism and humor into Hungarian prose.

The 1956 Hungarian uprising, which erupted as a consequence of Stalinist abuses and dogmatic resistance to radical reforms, created a new and paradoxical situation. Although the Hungarian Writers Association was suspended and some ex-Communist writers, including Déry, Háy, Tibor Tardos, and Zoltán Zelc were jailed, many formerly suppressed non-Marxist authors reappeared in print. Among these were János Kodolányi, with his popular novels on biblical themes, Magda Szabó, with her acclaimed analytical social novels; László Németh, once again a major novelist; and Sándor Weöres, whose collection *A hallgatás tornya* (1956; The Tower of Silence) was a literary event, demonstrating his stature as a poet. Nevertheless, we cannot speak of a full return to normality in literary life before 1963, when the post-1956 regime felt at last strong enough to relax some of its most objectionable controls.

Hungarian prose flourished throughout the 1960s. Important short novels by Ferenc Sánta and Tibor Cseres probed Hungary's recent past and the individual's responsibility in difficult situations. Endre Fejes, Lajos Galambos, and Gyula Csák wrote perceptive social reportage. A new, existentialist model of reality appeared in the work of Gyula Hernádi. The simultaneous success of Iván Mándy's blurred snapshots, Miklós Mészöly's detached narratives, and István Örkény's grotesque minia- tures indicated that the new diversity in prose was wel- come. If József Lengyel's dramatic report of life in Soviet labor camps was the literary sensation of the 1960s, the best single novel of the post-1968 period has been György Konrád's *A látogató* (1969; Eng. tr., *The Case Worker,* 1974), the visionary narrative of a social worker dealing with the human rejects of society.

In the early 1970s there was little change in the com- plexion of Hungarian poetry. Illyés, Weöres, and Vas have all produced important new work; the influence of the "Ujhold" group has grown, to the detriment of the politically more conformist poets such as Mihály Váci and Gábor Garai; and some of the younger poets—Dezső Tandori, László Marsall, and György Petri—confronted the uncontrolled verbalism of Ferenc Juhász's recent work with an intellectual and axiomatic austerity of their own. In the late 1960s Hungarian drama began to catch up with European development. Some well-known play- wrights, such as Endre Illés and István Örkény, as well as younger ones such as Ferenc Karinthy, István Csurka, and Géja Páskándi, explored the possibilities of the thea- ter of the absurd and the grotesque.

Hungarian literature outside Hungary has been flour- ishing ever since 1919. Romania, with its large Hungarian ethnic minority, provided a vast reservoir of talents be- tween the two wars. During this period, the liberal *Erdélyi Helikon* (Transylvanian Helicon) and the leftist *Korunk* (Our Age) published good literature and provocative crit- icism. Hungarian literature from Romania includes the historical novels of Károly Kós, Sándor Makkai, József Nyírő; Aladár Kuncz's (1886–1931) striking memoirs about his interment in France during World War I; and much realistic and semidocumentary fiction by György Kovács, István Asztalos, and István Nagy, the tradition of which was later revived by the talented novelist and playwright András Sütő. The best Transylvanian writer, Áron Tamási, moved to Hungary in the 1940s. Apart from Lajos Áprily and Sándor Reményik, among the pre-World War II poets only Jenő Dsida (1907–38) deserves separate notice for the perfection of his playful, nostalgic, and musical poetry. While Ernő Salamon (1912–43) enjoys a high reputation for his socialist lyrics, most poets of his generation who survived the war—László Szabédi, Fer- enc Szemlér, Imre Horváth, and Jenő Kiss—were ham- pered by the dogmatic cultural policy of the Communist regime. Only the poets of the 1950s—János Székely, Sándor Kányádi, and Géza Páskándi—and the 1960s— Aladár Lászlóffy and Domokos Szilágyi—managed to in- fuse new blood into Hungarian poetry in Romania. As for Hungarian literature in Slovakia and Yugoslavia, its scope prior to World War II was smaller than in Romania and literary life more parochially localized, although the work of the anti-Fascist essayist Zoltán Fábry (1897–1970) ex- erted influence beyond the borders of the First Republic. In Yugoslavia there were several Hungarian literary mag- azines before the war. Of these, *Híd* (Bridge) became an important forum of modern Hungarian writing in and out- side Yugoslavia in the 1960s. While the outstanding figure of Hungarian literature in Yugoslavia was Ervin Sinkó, author of two autobiographical novels and many interest- ing essays, the Vojvodina region produced such prose writers as János Herceg, Károly Szirmai, and Mihály Majtényi, the essayists Imre Bori, Nándor Major, and János Bányai, and the poets Ferenc Fehér, Károly Ács, József Pap, István Domonkos, and Otto Tolnai.

Among the writers of the Hungarian diaspora (mainly Western Europe and the United States), one can find polished prose writers of prewar fame (Sándor MÁRAI, Lajos Zilahy) as well as brilliant modernists whose work

has attracted attention only in the last two decades (Győző Határ, and the much younger György Ferdi- nandy), cultivated essayists, such as László Cs. Szabó, Zoltán Szabó, and the practically bilingual Paul Ignotus (1901–78). Some Hungarian-born authors such as Ar- thur Koestler and George Mikes are now widely regarded as English writers by virtue of their long-term adherence to English as the language of literary expression. The best émigré playwright was Gyula HÁY although he spent only the last decade of his life on foreign soil. The most rep- resentative poets of the older generation are Győző Határ, György Faludy and Tamás Tűz; as to the "1956 Genera- tion," members of which left Hungary in 1956 and after, it made a collective appearance in the anthology *Uj égtájak* (1969; New Climes). This anthology includes both traditionalists and experimentalists and the main interest of the latter group lies in exploring the mechanism of language. Since 1977 poets of this generation have begun appearing in print in literary journals published in Hun- gary. The most important literary magazines of Hungar- ians abroad are *Uj Látóhatár* (Munich), *Irodalmi Ujság,* and *Magyar Műhely* (both Paris). Among publishing houses, *Aurora* (Munich), *Occidental Press* (Washington, D.C.) and *Szepsi Csombor Kör* (London) have the most distinguished lists of authors.

See: M. Benedek, ed. *Magyar irodalmi lexikon*, 3 vols. (1963–65); T. Klaniczay, J. Szauder, M. Szabolcsi, *His- tory of Hungarian Literature* (1964); J. Reményi, *Hun- garian Writers and Literature* (1964); A. Tezla, *Hungar- ian Authors: A Bibliographical Handbook* (1970).

G.G.

Huysmans, Joris-Karl, pseud. of Charles Marie Georges Huysmans (1848–1907), French novelist and art critic, was born and died in Paris. He was of Dutch descent on his father's side. Huysmans's childhood was a tormented one, exacerbated, like that of his idol Charles BAUDE- LAIRE, by his widowed mother's remarriage when he was nine. Within a month after receiving his *baccalauréat*, he was appointed to a minor post at the Ministry of the Interior, where he remained for 32 years.

Huysmans's service in the war of 1870 provided ma- terial for his first work, "Le Chant du départ" (Farewell Song), which he later reworked into *Sac au dos* (1880; Backpack). His first published work, *Le Drageoir à épices* (1874; Eng. tr., *A Dish of Spices,* 1927), rejected by several publishers, appeared at his own expense under the pseudonym he now adopted. That work brought him the sympathetic attention of major writers, including Emile ZOLA and Edmond de Goncourt (1822–96), whom he cultivated assiduously. In the 1870s, Huysmans began his career as art critic in perceptive articles. Later, in *L'Art moderne* (1883; Modern Art) and *Certains* (1889), he championed new or neglected artists—Gustave Mo- reau, Odilon Redon, Edgar Degas, and Paul Cézanne.

Huysmans established himself as a major follower of Zola with *Marthe, histoire d'une fille* (1876; Eng. tr., *Martha, Story of a Prostitute,* 1948) and reinforced it with *Les Soeurs Vatard* (1879; The Vatard Sisters), which he dedicated to the master. Zola welcomed him to the circle of young disciples that appeared with him in the volume of petulantly antimilitarist short stories, *Les Soirées de Médan* (1880; Médan Evenings). Huysmans's *A vau-l'eau* (1882; Eng. tr., *Down Stream,* 1927) introduced the char- acter of Folantin, whom Guy de Maupassant character- ized as the "Ulysses of the cook-shops."

With *A rebours* (1884; Eng. tr., *Against Nature,* 1959), however, Huysmans created a furor because the novel seemed to repudiate his affiliations with the naturalists. Its protagonist, Jean des Esseintes, incarnates all the morbid, perverse eccentricities associated with "decadent" mentality, preferring the artificial to the real, seeking escape from the banalities of normal existence through refinements so extreme that he is on the point of losing his mind. Prostrate emotionally and physically, his life barely saved by doctors, he wonders whether the only salvation might not be in a return to faith. The novel had a tremendous impact in literary and artistic circles, becoming the breviary of decadence, the bible of Dorian Gray in Oscar Wilde's novel. The implications of the paradoxical conclusion of *A rebours* were immediately recognized by the Catholic novelist Barbey d'Aurevilly, who proclaimed in a famous article that the author of such a work had but two alternatives: the muzzle of a pistol or the foot of the Cross. Huysmans did indeed arrive at the Cross through a tortuous 10-year route, with soul-searing incursions into occultism, sorcery, and demonology, culminating in the satanism of *Là-Bas* (1891; Eng. tr., *Down There*, 1924) before finally fulfilling d'Aurevilly's prophecy in *En route* (1895; Eng. tr., 1920). The author's own dramatic return to Catholicism is depicted in the agonized gropings of the protagonist Durtal, who had been introduced in *Là-Bas*, and who was to reappear as the central character of *La Cathédrale* (1898) and *L'Oblat* (1903; The Lay Brother).

Huysmans continued his studies of the Catholic faith in the hagiographic *Sainte Lydwyne de Schiedam* (1901) and in *Les Foules de Lourdes* (1906; Eng. tr., *The Crowds of Lourdes*, 1925), a direct rebuttal of the thesis Zola had defined in *Lourdes* (1894; Eng. tr., 1894). All of Huysmans's writings employ a distinctive vocabulary. Rare, colorful terms abound in sentences of intricate syntax, producing vivid images that are not incompatible with the robust naturalism he maintained to the end.

Although he had been a hypochondriac most of his life, Huysmans died after real and intense physical suffering due to cancer of the mouth, enduring his long agony with Christian resignation. In contrast to the fate of most novelists of the period, his work, far from undergoing even a temporary eclipse, has increasingly enjoyed popular as well as scholarly attention. *A rebours* remains a classic in its very special area. The Catholic world regards him as one of its distinguished apologists. Art historians turn to his studies for some of the most perspicacious discussions of aesthetics formulated by a 19th-century critic.

See: H. Trudjian, *L'Esthétique de Joris-Karl Huysmans* (1934); H. M. Gallot, *Explication de Joris-Karl Huysmans* (1954); R. Baldick, *The Life of Joris-Karl Huysmans* (1955). A.Ar.

I

Ibrăileanu, Garabet (1871–1936), Romanian critic and literary historian, was born in Tîrgu-Frumos. While still in high school, he founded the society "Orientul," which provided a forum for the discussion of new literary ideas. In 1889 he helped found the journal *Scoala noua*. At the University of Iasi, Ibrăileanu's early commitment to the Marxist interpretation of life and literature was intensified. He taught school and was named professor at Iasi where, for the next several decades, he influenced his many students. Ibraileanu also had an important influence on the public in general through such journals as *Viaţa romănească*, which he founded in 1906, and the daily *Momentul* and the weekly *Însemnări ieşene*, both of which he published between 1916 and 1920. He also published a novel, *Adela*, in 1933.

Ibrăileanu's most important critical works are *Spiritual critic in cultura romînească* (1909; The Critical Spirit in Romanian Culture); a monograph on Alexander Vlahută (1912); *Note şi impresii* (1920; Notes and Impressions); *Scrotori romîni şi straini* (1926; Romanian and Foreign Writers); and *Studii literare* (1930; Literary Studies). A modest, unassuming man, Ibrăileanu was one of the first Romanian critics to recognize the necessity for absolute objectivity in critical judgment. A consistent thread in his critical thinking is a belief in "energism." According to this theory, the artist's temperament has a great role in literary creation, but he is limited by the sociological and psychological implications of his environment. While the writer creates in total freedom, he is limited by a cosmic fatalism.

See: A. Piru, *Garabet Ibrăileanu: viaţa şi opera* (1967); M. Dragan, *Ibrăileanu* (1971). V.A.

Ibsen, Henrik Johan (1828–1906), Norwegian dramatist and poet, was born in the small town of Skien in southern Norway, of well-to-do parents. In 1834 his father's business began to fail, and the next year the family was forced to leave its patrician home. At the age of 15, Ibsen was apprenticed to a pharmacist in Grimstad, an even smaller southern town. When he was 18, he fathered a child. He wrote his first play, *Catilina* (1850), under the influence

of the revolutions of 1848. The publication of the play attracted little notice, but it is significant that its theme, the failure of the main character, Catiline, to keep faith with himself, represents the first appearance of a major theme in Ibsen's mature drama.

A few weeks after the appearance of *Catalina*, Ibsen himself arrived in Christiania (now Oslo) to enter the university, but he never completed his qualifying examinations. (In 1877 the University of Uppsala awarded him an honorary doctor's degree, and Ibsen afterwards used that title.) During his first year in Christiania he contributed to a radical weekly and wrote literary essays and theater reviews for a student publication. From 1851 to 1857 he was assistant stage manager and house dramatist at the Norwegian theater in Bergen, a theater started in an effort to promote Norwegian drama and the Norwegian language, as opposed to Danish (*see* NORWEGIAN LITERATURE). In the spring of 1852, this theater sent him on a study tour of Danish and German theaters. In 1857 he moved back to Christiania as director-manager of the Norwegian theater there, another self-consciously "national" enterprise. Ibsen married Suzannah Thoresen in 1858. The next year their only child, Sigurd, was born. The early 1860s were difficult years for Ibsen. He was a public failure both as a dramatist and as a manager and was miserably poor.

In the plays he wrote in Bergen, Ibsen tried to meet the popular demand for works that would revive national traditions, finding his subjects in saga, history, folklore, and medieval ballads. *Kjærlighedens komedie* (1862; Eng. tr., *Love's Comedy*, 1900), on the other hand, was Ibsen's first "modern" play, a witty verse satire on the conventions of engagement and marriage. *Kongsemnerne* (1863; Eng. tr., *The Pretenders*, 1905) a penetrating history play that owes much to Shakespeare, points forward to Ibsen's later dramas about divided personalities.

As to his political views, Ibsen was a devoted pan-Scandinavianist, deeply disillusioned by the failure of Norway and Sweden to come to the aid of Denmark during that country's war with the German states in 1863–64. The experience of these years strengthened Ibsen's feeling that he could not write in full freedom as long as he remained in Norway, and in the spring of 1864 he traveled to Rome on a small grant. His self-imposed exile lasted for 27 years, interrupted only by brief visits home in the summers of 1874 and 1885. Ibsen took no part in the cultural life of his host countries (first Italy and then, after 1868, mainly Germany), since he felt the need to keep away from whatever might threaten his spiritual and intellectual independence. The plays he sent home from abroad were provocations to his people "to think great thoughts." With remarkable singlemindedness he devoted the rest of his life to drama.

Ibsen's disillusionment with his countrymen is evident in the first two plays he wrote in exile, the verse dramas *Brand* (1866; Eng. tr., 1891) and *Peer Gynt* (1867; Eng. tr., 1892). *Brand* brought Ibsen instant fame throughout Scandinavia. Its uncompromising demand for wholeness of personality and faithfulness to a God-given mission provoked intense debate and created in the public mind the image of Ibsen as a moral prophet. The success of *Brand* earned Ibsen an annual stipend from the state, like the one already given Bjørnstjerne BJØRNSON. After *Brand*, Ibsen said, "*Peer Gynt* followed by itself." Having taken the Peer figure from Norwegian folklore, Ibsen developed him into the antitype of Brand: a charming egoist who dissipates himself in a lifetime of lying and compromise. *Peer Gynt* is Ibsen's wittiest and most imaginative work, mixing national romanticism, topical satire, and metaphysics in a playful allegorical fantasy about a hero who is both the prototypical Norwegian and a modern Everyman in quest of his own identity. But both the critical and popular reception of the play was divided. As a result, Ibsen angrily threatened to turn from poetry to photography—and, in a sense, he did. *De unges forbund* (1869; Eng. tr., *The League of Youth*, 1890) is a light comedy of intrigue, in prose, but its satire on provincial politics and sham liberalism offended many. Four years passed before Ibsen published another play. Meanwhile, he traveled as one of Norway's official delegates to the opening of the Suez Canal in 1869, and he published *Digte* (1871; Poems), a volume of poems.

Ibsen's next play, *Kejser og galilæer* (1873; Eng. tr., *The Emperor and the Galilean*, 1876), is the one that he himself always considered his most important. But although it is pregnant with ideas, the play is heavy with historicity, and the dramatic movement is sometimes slack, particularly in the second of its two five-act parts. In this "world-historical" play of Hegelian dialectics, Ibsen tried to clarify his ideas about cultural evolution. Its hero, Emperor Julian the Apostate (A.D. 361–63), fails to reconcile the joy and beauty of paganism with the moral seriousness of Christianity. Similar conflicts between irreconcilable values arise in many of Ibsen's later plays.

Beginning in 1877 there appeared—almost exactly at two-year intervals—the 12 works of modern realism that established Ibsen's worldwide fame. The first of these were the "social problem plays." These plays are characterized by debates on contemporary issues and plots about the power of bigoted social conventions to inhibit and corrupt the individual. In *Samfundets støtter* (1877; Eng. tr., *Pillars of Society*, 1888), a businessman compromises his integrity for the sake of wealth and power. In *Et dukkehjem* (1879; Eng. tr., *Nora, or a Doll's House*, 1880), a wife walks out on an apparently perfect marriage when she realizes the irreconcilable conflict inherent in the sexual roles imposed by society upon her husband and herself. In *Gengangere* (1881; Eng. tr., *Ghosts*, 1889), on the other hand, the wife does *not* leave, only to find her escape from the ugly past of a loveless marriage

overtaken by tragic retribution. In this drama, the role of the ancient tragic nemesis is taken by the realities of psychological and physical heredity, making *Ghosts* at the same time both the most classical and the most ruthlessly naturalistic of Ibsen's plays. *En folkefiende* (1882; Eng. tr., *An Enemy of the People*, 1890) is a spirited attack on the conservative establishment and "the compact liberal majority" alike. These plays marked the breakthrough of serious literary realism on the stage.

Ibsen's disillusionment with the problem play is signaled in the new note of skepticism and tolerance evident in *Vildanden* (1884; Eng. tr., *The Wild Duck*, 1891), where an officious truth-teller drives a child to pointless suicide. In the plays that followed *Vildanden*, Ibsen dealt increasingly with individual psychology rather than with social issues. Petty politics combine with sexual guilt to cause the death of the two protagonists in *Rosmersholm* (1886; Eng. tr., 1889), yet the core of the play is their failure to reconcile new intellectual convictions with traditional moral feeling. Both *Fruen fra havet* (1888; Eng. tr., *The Lady from the Sea*, 1890) and *Hedda Gabler* (1890; Eng. tr., 1891), are intimate studies of neurotically obsessed women; these two plays are only incidentally concerned with the social conditions that have stunted the growth of these characters into free, happy personalities.

In 1891, Ibsen, wealthy and famous, returned to Norway and settled in Christiania. He had a joyless marriage and his life remained lonely and austere, graced only by a few episodes of friendship with young women. There may be autobiographical significance in the fact that the four plays he wrote after his return all deal with the conflict between art and life. The main characters of *Bygmester Solness* (1892; Eng. tr., *The Master Builder*, 1893), *Lille Eyolf* (1894; Eng. tr., *Little Eyolf*, 1894), *John Gabriel Borkman* (1896; Eng. tr., 1897), and *Naar vi døde vaagner* (1899; Eng. tr., *When We Dead Awaken*, 1900) are forced to recognize that their vocational commitment has led them to betray their human responsibility. The external action in these plays is minimal, and their settings and language are symbolic and metaphorical. *When We Dead Awaken* in particular (a play that Ibsen subtitled "a dramatic epilogue") is an almost wholly introspective work.

In 1898, Ibsen received the world's homage on the occasion of his 70th birthday. Two years later he suffered the first in a series of disabling strokes. On his death in May 1906, the country he had never really left gave him a state funeral.

Ibsen's plays belong to world drama because of their formal beauty and technical skill and because of the scope and depth of their moral vision. The retrospective structure he took over from classical Greek tragedy charges the present with the guilty past and accounts for the compacted intensity of the best of his later plays; a long train of events comes to swift catastrophe on stage, as if impelled by the momentum of its own logic. Mythic patterns of cultural and psychological archetypes lie beneath the surface of Ibsen's social realism, and the trivial objects, actions, and words in his middle-class homes assume larger resonance by being invested with symbolic and allusive power. The controversies that originally attended his plays are largely dead, but that is because Ibsen himself was one of the shapers of the modern consciousness. One reason why drama in recent decades has moved away from the Ibsen tradition in dramaturgy is that both his success and his example incited other playwrights to new ventures. If his plays still hold the world's stages and attract great actors and actresses, it is because the liberal polemicist and realist was also a poet of the theater. "To be a poet is to see," said Ibsen once, and he referred to his plays as "self-anatomies" and "doomsday sessions" on his own soul. What he "saw," in his society and in himself, his imagination turned into stage actions charged with dramatic energy and moral fervor. In an age of collective movements and disintegrating values, his plays challenged the self to take on true selfhood.

See: B. Shaw, *The Quintessence of Ibsenism* (1891, 1913); H. Weigand, *The Modern Ibsen* (1925); B. W. Downs, *Ibsen: The Intellectual Background* (1946) and *A Study of Six Plays by Ibsen* (1950); P. F. D. Tennant, *Ibsen's Dramatic Technique* (1948); J. Northam, *Ibsen's Dramatic Method* (1953); R. Fjelde, ed., *Ibsen: A Collection of Critical Essays* (1965); D. Haakonsen, ed., *Contemporary Approaches to Ibsen,* 2 vols. (1966, 1971); M. C. Bradbrook, *Ibsen the Norwegian* (rev. ed., 1966); J. W. McFarlane, ed., *Henrik Ibsen: A Critical Anthology* (1970); M. Meyer, *Ibsen: A Biography* (1971); M. Egan, ed., *Ibsen: The Critical Heritage* (1972).

H.K. and O.Re.

Icelandic literature. Icelandic literature represents a long, unbroken tradition hailing back to the Middle Ages (13th and 14th centuries), when the Icelandic classics were written. Ever since, Icelandic authors have built on that great cultural heritage, which consists of Eddic and skaldic poetry as well as the sagas—a body of literature that is the actual beginning of the epic-realistic convention characterizing Icelandic fiction. This medieval literary heritage, it is agreed, played a large role in preserving the Icelandic language: the native of today can still read the classics in the original. Icelandic verse is notable for its retention of features from the earliest Germanic poetry known, such as the use of alliteration as a structural device—a technique that has been obligatory in Icelandic poetry until contemporary times.

Even when the Icelandic economy sank to its lowest ebb, in the 17th and 18th centuries, and despite the removal of most of the original manuscripts to Denmark, literary life went on with occasional works of classical quality emerging, both religious and secular, so that continuity was ensured. Although the Enlightenment period, which began by the end of the 18th century, heralded better days to come after a long time of absolute rule and Danish trade monopoly, Icelandic letters made no immediate comeback. It is true, however, that a foundation was then laid for a number of literary developments that were to come into their own in the first half of the 19th century with the advent of romanticism.

When considering trends in Icelandic literature it should be kept in mind that ideological and artistic schools of thought—like enlightenment, romanticism, realism, and so on—have never made themselves felt in Iceland in as unadulterated and dogmatic form as in the European countries of their origin—and this for a number of reasons. There is, for one thing, the inevitable time lag: owing to slow communications, new doctrines had always lost their keenest edge by the time they were introduced in Iceland. Still more important, socioeconomic realities in Iceland, namely, subsistence farming that had seen negligible change since the Middle Ages, had few things in common with the urban cultural settings of Western Europe, where the respective movements had come into being in response to specific conditions.

An important precursor of romanticism in Iceland, the poet and scholar Sveinbjörn Egilsson (1791–1852) researched poetic diction, compiling a reference work entitled *Lexicon poeticum* (1860). He also acquainted his countrymen with the Greek classics through his translations of *The Odyssey* (1829–40) and *The Iliad* (1855). Egilsson prepared the ground for the linguistic renewal of the romantic period, in part by his analysis of the Icelandic classics, but also by paying attention to the purest idiom that he could find among the common people of his own day.

Modern Icelandic literature began with romanticism, a movement that had such a profound and long-lasting effect on Icelandic letters that traces of it can be observed even today. It strengthened and deepened the Icelanders' self-respect by placing emphasis on folk values, nationalism, and Nordic antiquity, including the Icelandic classics—a cue deriving from the Heidelberg school of romanticism. As a result, folktales were collected with great vigor in Iceland, for instance, whereas the aesthetic and philosophical concerns associated with the Jena branch of romanticism found fewer adherent.

The first strong representation of romanticism in Iceland came with *Fjölnir* (1835–47), a magazine published by four Icelandic students in Copenhagen. One of them, Jónas Hallgrímsson (1807–45), ranks indubitably among the greatest poetic geniuses of all time in Iceland. His techniques were evolved from the lyrical aspect of Eddic versification, classical European meters, and contemporary models like Heinrich Heine, out of all of which he created his own unique synthesis. Jónas Hallgrímsson holds a pivotal position in the development of Icelandic verse, so much so that poets antedating him appear to belong to the distant past, whereas his poems still have such freshness that they might as well have been written yesterday. But Hallgrímsson was not only a romantic aesthete, for his work is in many respects of a classical cast, perhaps reminiscent of Goethe, and shows a good deal of social awareness, which is, in fact, typical for romantic poets in Iceland. They were on the whole more realistic and more concerned with social issues than were their European counterparts, who were drawn to philosophical and religious problems, even to the point of at times retreating from worldly matters into a shell of conservative resignation.

Hallgrímsson was followed by a large number of late romantic figures in Iceland: Grímur Thomsen (1820–96), Benedikt S. Gröndal (1826–1907), Steingrímur Thorsteinsson (1831–1913) and Matthías Jochumsson (1835–1920), to name a few. Although none of them equaled the near-perfection that Hallgrímsson had reached in his poetry, they collectively strengthened the nationalistic-romantic mood and thus gave added momentum to the stress on national values and Icelandic self-respect—a trend that was of crucial importance during the struggle for political independence in the 19th century. Romanticism and the quest for political autonomy are inseparable strands in Icelandic history, jointly leading to the reestablishment of the Althing (Parliament) as a consulting body in 1845 and an Icelandic constitution as well as a legislative function for the Althing in 1874.

If Icelandic poetry took a leap across several centuries with the romantic verse of Jónas Hallgrímsson, romanticism, in its late phase, also signaled the return of fiction, a genre that had been in eclipse for several hundred years. Jón Thoroddsen (1818–68) laid the groundwork with his two novels, *Piltur og stúlka* (1850; Eng. tr., *Lad and Lass,* 1890) and *Maður og kona* (1876; Man and Wife), both of them romantic works, yet giving realistic pictures of everyday life among plain country people in Iceland. As a writer of fiction, Thoroddsen was indebted to both the native saga tradition and foreign models—in the latter case especially to Walter Scott.

Realism came to the fore on the Scandinavian literary scene after 1870, not least because of the inspired writings and lecturing of Danish critic Georg BRANDES. Four Icelandic disciples of his, who had been studying in Copenhagen, introduced realism to Icelandic readers with the publication of *Verðandi*, a magazine they launched in 1882. Three of the original four became notable literary figures in Iceland. Hannes Hafstein (1861–1922), influenced by the verse of Holger DRACHMANN, is best known for his masculine poems about love and other worldly pleasures, although he later grew increasingly romantic and nationalistic; he turned to politics and was appointed the first Icelandic minister when home rule came in 1904.

Two of Hafstein's companions left a much deeper imprint on Icelandic literature. Gestur Pálsson (1852–91) was the truest Icelandic representative of realism. Sympathy for the underprivileged runs deep in his stories, which, as the formula expounded by Brandes demanded, take their subject matter from the everyday lives of common people in Iceland and are bitter satirical attacks on the social evils and the power structure of the author's day.

The fourth member of the group, Einar H. KVARAN, however, was to exert an even greater and more enduring influence. He began his literary career by writing fiction of social criticism in the spirit of Georg Brandes, but after the turn of the century his outlook evolved toward bourgeois liberalism. In many of his works, Kvaran chose Reykjavík's emerging middle class as his subject matter, and he may be regarded as the foremost chronicler of that social stratum in his day. This emphasis aside, Kvaran sympathized with society's outcasts and the oppressed, and his short stories, which are his best works, often reveal profound psychological insights. An intellectual of a philosophical and religious bent, he embraced spiritualism after 1900, becoming quite influential as a leading proponent of that movement.

Although not included in the *Verð andi* group, Jón TRAUSTI was the most creative and most influential of all Icelandic writers of fiction taking their artistic orientation from realism. Broad in scope and somewhat diffuse at times, his works often deal with contemporary life in Iceland, whether on farms or in small fishing villages, but he also wrote historical fiction. As for writers of verse, realism was intrinsically less appealing than for those working in fiction, but two major Icelandic poets, nevertheless, owe an ideological debt to Georg Brandes as well as to socialism: Þorsteinn ERLINGSSON and Stephan G. STEPHANSSON.

Shortly after 1890, Icelandic literature had passed another watershed with the advent of the so-called neoromantic poets, who were primarily influenced by French symbolism and the philosophy of Friedrich NIETZSCHE. The foremost of these was Einar BENEDIKTSSON, a towering figure who practically dominated Icelandic verse-making in the first three decades of the 20th century. A world citizen, he lived for extended periods in England and elsewhere in Western Europe, and although he wrote long descriptive poems about foreign scenes and cultural phenomena, he was a deeply religious mystic, forever struggling with philosophical problems. Many other Icelandic poets were influenced by French symbolism, among whom were Guðmundur Guðmundsson (1874–1919), Hulda, pseud. of Unnur Benediktsdóttir Bjarklind (1881–1946), Sigurjón Friðjónsson (1867–1950), Sigurður Sigurðsson (1879–1939), and Jónas Guðlaugsson (1887–1916), although this is most pronounced in the case of Jóhann SIGURJÓNSSON, a lyrical genius, who is, however, best known as a dramatist writing in Danish.

Icelandic drama is, incidentally, the least developed genre of the national literature. There is no reliable evidence that plays were staged in Iceland until the 18th century, and then at the Latin school (Cathedral School) of Skálholt in southern Iceland. "Leikfélag Reykjavíkur"

(Reykjavik Theater Company) was founded in 1897, and Icelandic drama, both playwriting and performances, made a leap forward after the turn of the century, with realism the dominant influence. The leading dramatists in Iceland at the time were Kvaran and Indriði Einarsson (1851–1939); the latter wrote historical plays and family dramas modeled on Henrik IBSEN's. Like Sigurjónsson, Guðmundur KAMBAN wrote plays in Danish; Kamban's best drama works constitute attacks on what the author claims are pathological aspects of Western culture.

A National Theater was opened in Reykjavík in 1950, and the dramatic arts are immensely popular in Iceland today. In the last few decades, various new playwrights have appeared. Drama is, for example, a separate chapter in the literary career of Halldór LAXNESS and Jökull JAKOBSSON is unsurpassed in Iceland to date in technical mastery of effects for the stage. Still another noteworthy recent author of plays is Oddur Björnsson, whose work contains a strong element derived from the theater of the absurd, a drama movement for which he is Iceland's leading champion.

A socioeconomic transformation got under way in Iceland after 1900: towns and villages started to grow, attracting people from the countryside. The ancient agricultural economy gradually gave way to a new order that had its base in urban centers, a development giving rise to polarities that had never been experienced in Iceland: an emerging class of domestic merchants and fishery entrepreneurs on the one hand and a working class on the other, although the latter was at first impoverished and without political leverage. World War I saw the origin of the three-party lineup that has since characterized political life in Iceland: (1) a strong Conservative Party backed by people with interests in commerce, fisheries, and manufacturing; (2) a Socialist Labor Party (which split in the 1930s into Social-Democrats and Radical Socialists); and (3) a moderate, left-of-center party supported by farmer and middle-class city dwellers as well as by the cooperative movement. In 1918 at the end of World War I, Iceland became an independent state, a constitutional monarchy recognizing the Danish king as its sovereign and with foreign affairs entrusted to Denmark.

At this point in Icelandic history, three men of letters were of paramount importance: (1) Stephan G. Stephansson, a poet living in Canada, a socialist, and a pacifist, but also influenced by atheism and naturalism; (2) Einar H. Kvaran, originally a realist, but subsequently a bourgeois humanist with an overriding interest in spiritualism; and (3) Einar Benediktsson, a symbolist with strong overtones from Nietzschean hero worship and admiration for human willpower, as well as a religious mystic and philosopher. Regardless of their vast differences, all three had one thing in common: an intellectual outlook on the problems of human existence. Meanwhile, Gunnar GUNNARSSON resided in Denmark and was rapidly gaining European recognition for his fiction on Icelandic subjects, written in Danish; he was chiefly concerned with probing religious, philosophical, and ethical questions.

As World War I ended, four authors made their debuts, all young men whose works initiated a new epoch in Icelandic literature. Stefán frá Hvítadal (1887–1933) published in 1918 a book of verse: *Söngvar förumannsins* (The Songs of the Vagabond); he had lived in Norway and was influenced by Norwegian poetry. Davíð STEFÁNSSON published *Svartar Fjaðrir* (1919: Black Feathers). Both of these poets used lighter, more lyrical forms than their predecessors. And, departing from the intellectual outlook of their elders, they celebrated instead untrammeled emotional response and, above all, worship of life and its pleasures. As for fiction, Sigurður NORDAL attracted attention for his *Fornar ástir* (1919; Old Loves), a collection of short stories written in neoromantic and expressionistic style, including one bordering on a prose poem. And in 1919, too, the first novel of Halldór Laxness appeared: *Barn náttúrunnar* (Child of Nature), a romantic tale of country life imbued with sentimentality and religious feeling.

New Icelandic literature in the 1920s developed along similar lines. Poetry was dominated by light lyrical forms, and traditional Icelandic features of versification, such as alliteration and rhyme, were retained. Romantic life worship, sentimentality, and self-expression were the order of the day, qualities well represented by, for instance, Tómas GUÐMUNDSSON and JÓHANNES ÚR KÖTLUM as well as by Jóhann Jónsson (1896–1932); the latter was considered a poetic genius by his generation, but he died young from tuberculosis.

The novels written immediately after 1920 deal in the main with psychological, ethical, theological, and philosophical problems. Some of the authors wrote in an epic-realistic style and based their works on liberal bourgeois ideology, for example, Einar H. Kvaran and Guðmundur Kamban. The fiction of others as best described as *Heimat Dichtung*, as in the case of Guðmundur G. HAGALÍN, who took his subjects from the lives of the farmers and fishermen in his home region in the western fjords. The most mature novel within the category of bourgeois realism, however, is *Vefarinn mikli frá Kasmír* (1927; The Great Weaver from Kashmir) by Halldór Laxness, a book also notable for the author's experimentation with surrealist effects as a narrative technique.

A radical change in the attitude of fiction writers was heralded by the epoch-making *Bréf til Láru* (1924; A Letter to Laura) by Þorbergur ÞÓRÐARSON. In its wake came a wave of fiction of social criticism, often colored by socialist ideology, that was to dominate Icelandic fiction of the 1930s. Shortly after 1930, Laxness, an author dwarfing all others in Iceland since then, joined the new trend, and younger prose writers with socialist convictions, like Ólafur Jóhann SIGURÐSSON, came along to swell the ranks. Many poets, too, were caught up by the same development, and the first book of verse strongly suggesting this was *Hamar og sigð* (1930; Hammer and Sickle) by Sigurður Einarsson (1898–1967). Other poets of a socialist stripe soon followed: Jóhannes úr Kötlum, Guðmundur BÖÐVARSSON, Steinn STEINARR, and Jón ÚR VÖR. This literary preoccupation with social issues grew in part out of domestic circumstances—economic depression, stronger labor organizations, and more pronounced class conflicts—but also from alarms over foreign events such as the rise of Nazism and fascism in Europe and the drift toward war. The master ideologue of the radical writers was Kristinn E. Andrésson (1901–74), a brilliant literary critic and book publisher; in 1937 he organized the book club *Mál og menning* (Word and Culture); its magazine, *Tímarit Máls og menningar* (*tímarit* means "periodical"), was for a long time the chief organ of leftist-leaning authors in Iceland.

The isolation of Iceland was suddenly terminated in the spring of 1940 with British occupation of the country, and American troops replaced British forces a year later. Since that time, the United States has maintained a presence of some sort in Iceland, whether as service facilities for military aircraft or military installations. With Allied forces in Iceland and the German's occupying Denmark, all political contact between the two countries was severed; in 1940, Iceland took charge of its own foreign affairs, which up to that time had been controlled by the Danish government. What is more important, however, the occupation of Iceland led to a socioeconomic revo-

lution: the final demise of the old agricultural society. Unemployment was wiped out overnight, and people flocked to urban centers, with the result that more than half of Iceland's inhabitants today live in an urban environment, which, if not fully formed, resembles the city-based societies of Western Europe.

This transformation brought about a corollary development in Icelandic literature: with the eradication of unemployment and growing general prosperity, social criticism entered a decline. Authors like Laxness and Steinarr, among others, abandoned protest for concerns of a more philosophical and individualistic kind. At the same time, a foreign military presence acted to strengthen nationalistic sentiment; especially on the part of leftist writers, who saw that presence and Icelandic involvement in a foreign military alliance as evidence of moral degradation and political corruption.

In addition to the general ideological shift from social issues to psychological, religious, and philosophical concerns, Icelandic poetry entered a new phase, called the *form revolution,* in the 1940s. This drastic change meant, broadly speaking, that the Icelandic verse tradition, with its obligatory rhyme and alliteration, was replaced by much freer forms. The poetical language itself underwent a metamorphosis: there was a large-scale increase in the use of imagery as well as the introduction of fresh, often nonlogical associations. Outward-looking narrative poetry gave way to nondiscursive and concise verse focusing on inner reality, whether the author's own or the universal personal problems of human life. The undisputed pioneer of this new style was Steinn Steinarr, especially in his *Ljóð* (1937; Poems) and in *Tíminn og vatnið* (1948; Eng. tr., *Time and Water,* 1972). His lead was followed by many established poets who had previously written in traditional form, for instance, Jóhannes úr Kötlum, Guðmundur Böðvarsson, and Jón úr Vör, as well as by the great majority of younger poets who appeared after World War II, such as Hannes SIGFÚSSON and Einar Bragi (1921–), the author of refined lyrical verse and the founder and editor of *Birtingur* (1953–68), the chief organ of the modernists.

Icelandic poetry from the period after World War II falls into three main categories: works by authors like Davíð Stefánsson and Tómas Guðmundsson, who more or less adhere to the old Icelandic convention; modernists; and poets seeking a compromise between tradition and free form, such as Snorri HJARTARSON, Hannes PÉTURSSON and ÞORSTEINN FRÁ HAMRI. After 1960 outward-looking poetry of social concern began to reassert itself, and the main direction of Icelandic verse in the last few years appears to be toward even greater openness and more social involvement.

In the sphere of fiction, innovative techniques caught on more slowly than had been the case with poetry. One conceivable reason for this is that the epic-realistic tradition, the hallmark of Icelandic prose from saga times, may have been inherently more powerful than even the original Germanic features of Icelandic verse. It is, however, no doubt of significance that Halldór Laxness, a towering literary figure in Iceland in the year following World War II, had written most of his works in that style, as had a number of other established authors, like Guðmundur G. HAGALÍN and Ólafur Jóhann SIGURÐSSON. For whatever reason, it was not until after 1950, with the prose works of Thor VILHJÁLMSSON, that a totally new way of writing fiction emerged in Iceland, a technique dispensing with all the conventional props, including a definite time, setting, and methods of characterization. In the wake of Vilhjálmsson came such writers as Guðbergur Bergsson (1932–), whose absurd-realistic novel *Tómas*

Jónsson—metsölubók (1966; Tómas Jónsson, Best-Seller) was a tour de force, and Svava Jakobsdóttir (1930–). The latter is best known for her novel entitled *Leigjandinn* (1969; The Renter), an absurd-symbolic work about the fate of an individual or a nation involved with an alien financial power; the book has been interpreted as a comment on Iceland-United States relations.

Like poetry, Icelandic fiction has in recent years moved toward a higher degree of realism and increasing concern with social issues. Notable authors representing this trend are Þorgeir Þorgeirsson (1933–), a radical essayist who has published historical fiction, and Vésteinn Lúðvígsson (1944–), who sees himself as a disciple of the Russian 19th-century novelists and who has written fiction that is a broad mapping of middle-class society in Reykjavik since World War II.

The publishing of books and newspapers has flourished in Iceland during the last few decades, so, despite the competition from new media like movies and television, it is safe to say that the printed word, the lifeblood of Icelandic culture for centuries, is still holding its own as the principal cultural feature in Iceland of today.

See: S. Einarsson, *History of Icelandic Prose Writers 1800–1940* (1948); K. E. Andrésson, *Íslenzkar nutímabókmenntir 1918–48* (1949); R. Beck, *History of Icelandic Poets 1800–1940* (1950); S. Einarsson, *A History of Icelandic Literature* (1957); S. S. Höskuldsson, *Að yrkja á atómöld* (1970).   S.S.H.

Iglesies, Ignasi (1871–1928), Catalan dramatist, introduced individualistic materialism to the Catalan theater. Born in San Andrés de Palomar of a laboring family, he knew from childhood the sufferings of this social class. He glorified the working class in his work and came to be known as the "poeta dels humils." Iglesies began his education in Lérida but soon abandoned his studies in order to dedicate himself to literature. Still very young, he produced *Fructidor* (1897), and *L'escorço* (1902; The Scorpion), in which one can discern the influence of Henrik IBSEN. The struggles of the workingmen and their economic plight were present in numerous works. *Els vells* (1903; The Old Ones) enjoyed an extraordinary success in Barcelona and, translated into French, in Paris. It is perhaps his finest play. *Lari* and *La mare eterna* (1902; The Eternal Mother) were translated into Italian. Another successful work, also social in nature, is the drama *Les Garces* (1905; The Herons). Other works are: *La Resclosa* (The Canal Lock), in which commonplace concepts of morality are criticized; *El cor del poble* (1897; The Heart of the Humble); *Foc nou* (New Fire); and the comedy of manners *Girasol* Sunflower). His last productions include *L'encis de la gloria* (The Charm of Glory) and *La llar apagada* (The Cold Hearth). The theater of Iglesies, while it represented a novelty in the Catalonia of the beginning of the 20th century, seems antiquated today.

See: R. Darío, "Films de Paris," *Nación* (May 2, 1912); J. Bernat i Duran, *Historia del teatro en Cataluña y Valencia* (1924); R. Tasis i Marca, *La literatura catalana moderna* (1937).   J.M.M.iV.

Ilf, Ilya, pseud. of Ilya Arnoldovich Faynzilberg (1897–1937), and **Yevgeny Petrov,** pseud. of Yevgeny Petrovich Katayev (1903–42), Russian humorists, met in 1925 and the next year began collaboration on a series of short stories and novels. Before 1925, Ilf, born in Odessa, had held a variety of jobs, but from 1923 on he worked in Moscow editing the satirical newspaper *Gudok* and writing reviews, sketches, stories, and feuilletons. Petrov, also from Odessa, had an exotic work career too, at one

time serving as a police inspector; but after moving to Moscow in 1923 he wrote feuilletons and stories for the humorous journal *Krasny perets*. In 1927, Petrov's brother, Valentin Katayev, suggested to the two that they write a novel about a search for a set of chairs in one of which diamonds are hidden, and thus one of their best-known works, *Dvenadtsat stulyev* (1928; Eng. trs., *Diamonds to Sit On*, 1930; *The Twelve Chairs*, 1961) was conceived. The novel was an immediate success and is now an established Soviet classic. Its hero, Ostap Bender, is utterly amoral, brazenly imaginative, and one of the major con artists in world literature. His picaresque and ultimately fruitless pursuit of the diamonds leads him all over central Russia in a series of adventures that satirize virtually every aspect of Soviet life in the 1920s. In the last analysis, the novel's world view is bleak, and Bender's murder at the hands of his long-suffering accomplice comes as ambiguously poetic justice.

Bender proved so popular a figure, however, that like Sherlock Holmes, he was resurrected (with a tell-tale scar across his throat) in the novel *Zolotoy telyonok* (1931; Eng. trs., *Little Golden Calf*, 1932, *The Golden Calf*, 1962) in which he tracks down a Soviet underground millionaire. Here the denouement is clearly didactic (wealth is powerless in the New Russia), and Bender's unscrupulousness is less than ingenuous. It is not surprising that Soviet critics have always felt more comfortable with *Zolotoy* than *Dvenadtsat*.

In 1935 the two writers made a tour of the United States. The result was *Odnoetazhnaya Amerika* (1936; Eng. tr., *Little Golden America*, 1937), a satirical but not hostile account of their travels.

Besides their longer works Ilf and Petrov produced a large number of humorous feuilletons, stories, and cycles of stories.

In 1937, Ilf succumbed to tuberculosis. His *Zapisnye knizhki* (1937–38; Notebooks) were published posthumously. After Ilf's death Petrov wrote several film scenarios. He served as a correspondent for *Pravda* during World War II and in 1942 became another of the countless casualties of that war.

See: A. Vulis, *Ilya Ilf i Yevgeny Petrov* (Moscow, 1960).   D.A.L.

Iłłakowiczówna, Kazimiera (1892–), Polish poet, was born in Vilnius. She studied at the Jagiellonian University in Cracow, and at Oxford. Her first volume of poetry, *Ikarowe loty* (1911; Icarus Flights), brought her early recognition, and a steady stream of poetry followed: about 20 separate volumes of lyrics, with such titles as *Śmierć Feniksa* (1922; Death of the Phoenix), *Połów* (1926; Fishing), *Płaczacy ptak* (1927; Weeping Bird), *Zwierciadło nocy* (1928; Mirror of the Night), *Popiół i perły* (1930; Ashes and Pearls), *Ballady bohaterskie* (1934; Heroic Ballads), *Słowik litewski* (1936; Lithuanian Nightingale), and others. After World War II a number of new volumes appeared, notably *Wiersze religijne* (1955; Religious Poems, *Portrety imion* (1957; Portraits of Names), *Szeptem* (1966; In a Whisper), *Liście i posągi* (1968; Leaves and Statues), and others. Iłłakowiczówna's poetry is characterized by sensitivity, refinement, and clarity of tone; by skill in concrete psychological observations; by the connections with folk fantasy; by freshness of lyrical expression; and by a great variety of verse meters. She developed the form of the ballad motifs from folk songs and legends in an original and modern way. Iłłakowiczówna also published a volume of poetical prose, *Z rozbitego fotoplastikonu* (1957; From the Broken Peepshow); a volume of reminiscences, *Ścieżka obok drogi* (1939; Path beside the Road), mainly devoted to Marshal Józef Piłsudski, whose secretary and collaborator she was for many years during her service in the Ministry of War; volumes of sketches and reminiscences, *Niewczesne wynurzenia* (1958; Untimely Confessions) and *Trazymeński zając* (1968; The Trasimeno Hare), and plays, as well as translations from German, Russian, English, and Hungarian literature.

See: *Słownik współczesnych pisarzy polskich,* vol. 1 (1963), pp. 696–701. Z.F. with S.F.

Illyés, Gyula (1902–), Hungarian poet, novelist, playwright, and essayist, was born into a poor family in the Tolna district. He spent his childhood in the isolated world of a *puszta,* a manorial estate, where his father worked as a mechanic. In 1916, Illyés was sent to school in Budapest. As an active supporter of the Hungarian Soviet Republic of 1919 he had to leave Hungary soon after its collapse. After a short stay in Vienna and Berlin, he proceeded to Paris where he attended lectures at the Sorbonne and began writing in earnest. This period of his life was later vividly depicted in his novel *Hunok Párizsban* (1946; Huns in Paris). Illyés returned to Hungary in 1926 and soon afterwards settled in Budapest. He was a contributor to *Nyugat* from 1928 on, and in 1937 he became joint editor with Mihály BABITS. Upon Babits's death in 1941, Illyés took over the editorship, and between 1941 and 1944 he edited *Magyar csillag,* the successor of *Nyugat.* Illyés was a leading figure of the populist movement of the 1930s. His study of village society, *Puszták népe* (1936; Eng. tr., *People from the Puszta,* 1967), was among the first to focus attention on the appalling living conditions of the agrarian proletariat. During the German occupation of Hungary, Illyés went into hiding, and in 1945 he became a parliamentary representative of the National Peasant Party and editor of the literary review *Válasz* (1946–48). A winner of the Kossuth Prize in 1948 and 1953, he was regarded as a distinguished fellow traveler of the Communist regime. Nevertheless, the Hungarian uprising of 1956 prompted him to publish his famous poem "Egy mondat a zsarnokságról" (1956; Eng. tr., *One Sentence on Tyranny,* 1957), a passionate condemnation of Stalinist autocracy. Illyés published nothing between 1957 and 1960 as a token of solidarity with the writers imprisoned after the uprising. In 1965 he won the International Grand Prix for Poetry.

Illyés has made significant contributions to nearly all branches of literature. As a poet he was influenced by French surrealism and Lajos KASSÁK's constructivism before finding his own distinctive voice—a blend of Hungarian "popular realism" and modernist tendencies. Although his poetic language is based on everyday speech, it is not exempt from rhetoric figures. He usually writes in rhyming stanzas, but he has also experimented with a loosely spun blank verse. In the early 1930s, Illyés wrote mainly long narrative poems about the plight of the peasantry and about his own youthful experiences. Of these, *Hősökről beszélek* (1933; I Speak of Heroes), published anonymously, is the best. Illyés's deep sympathy with the poor and the exploited motivated such memorable poems as "Nem menekülhetsz" (1936; Eng. tr., *You Cannot Escape,* 1968), while his conviction that the old world is doomed and will soon collapse makes the message of "A kacsalábon forgó vár" (1936; Eng. tr., *The Wonder Castle,* 1970) almost prophetic. The intense patriotism of the collection *Rend a romokban* (1937; Order upon Ruins) reappears in the restrained fury of "Nem volt elég" (1945; It Was Not Enough), a poetic indictment of conservative Hungary. Illyés's best volumes of poetry since World War II are probably *Kézfogások* (1956; Handclasps) and

Dőlt vitorla (1965; With Tilted Sail). Although he has written both attractive love poems and impressionistic landscape poems, Illyés's real talent is essentially reflective and didactic. His most effective medium is the parable, either natural or historical, which gives expression to his commitment to the underprivileged.

Illyés has also written several plays, the majority of which are on national themes. For example, *Ozorai példa* (1952; The Example of Ozora) and *Fáklyaláng* (1953; Torchflame) exalt the Hungarian War of Independence of 1848–49, while *Dózsa György* (1954) and *Testvérek* (1972; Brothers) concern the leader of the great peasant rebellion of 1514. The tragic hero of *Különc* (1963; The Eccentric) is László Teleki, Lajos Kossuth's envoy to Paris in 1848 and the only Hungarian politician of his time with a truly European vision. The dramatic parable *Kegyenc* (1963; The Minion), a modern version of Teleki's play of the same title, is the tragedy of Maximus, a Roman patrician, dehumanized by his loyalty to a tyrannical emperor. Illyés has also written comedies, but these have had much less impact than his tragedies. In both genres he has remained within the convention of psychological realism. One of Illyés's most successful prose works is his biography of Sándor Petőfi (1936; Eng. tr., 1974), the revolutionary poet whom Illyés regards as his spiritual ancestor. Among his more recent prose works are *Ebéd a kastélyban* (1962; Lunch in the Castle), notable for its acute sociological and psychological observations, and *Hajszálgyökerek* (1971; Capillary Roots), a collection of incisive essays mapping out Hungary's place in contemporary Europe.

See: A. Schöpflin, "Illyés Gyula a költő," *Nyugat* 33 (1940): 276–79; L. Gara, *Az ismeretlen Illyés* (1965); G. Gömöri, *Polish and Hungarian Poetry: 1945 to 1956* (1966), pp. 70–75, 113–15; L. Cs. Szabó, *Hunok Nyugaton* (1967); T. Kabdebo and P. Tabori, eds., *A Tribute to Gyula Illyés* (1960); I. Kenyeres, *Gondolkodó irodalom* (1974), pp. 87–123. G.G.

Inber, Vera Mikhaylovna (1890–1972), Russian poet and prose writer, imitated Anna AKHMATOVA's intimate lyrics before the Russian Revolution (1917) and experimented with constructivist technological imagery after it (*see* RUSSIAN LITERATURE). She was born in Odessa; her father was a publisher and her mother taught Russian. A regular visitor to Western Europe, Inber published her first collection of poems in Paris. Her acceptance of Soviet reality is reflected in her stories; in her travel notes on American utilitarianism in France, *Amerika v Parizhe* (1928; America in Paris), and on Soviet Georgia, *Putevoy dnevnik* (1939; Travel Diary); and in her narrative verse, including the fine *Synu, kotorogo net* (1927; To the Non-Existent Son).

In the 1920s and 1930s, Inber wrote stories, sketches, and narrative verse on Vladimir Lenin, the Revolution, and Moscow, where she lived from 1922 to 1941. She joined the Communist Party during World War II and devoted herself to the patriotic writing that made her famous. Her long poem, "Pulkovsky meridian" (1941; Pulkovo Meridian), which received a Stalin Prize in 1946, describes daily life in besieged Leningrad, as does her Leningrad diary, *Pochti tri goda* (1946; Almost Three Years), which documents her reading and lecturing to workers and soldiers during the war. Despite lapses into egoism or weak generalization, these works exhibit Inber's gentle humor and mastery of realistic detail. After the war she lived in Leningrad, which is the subject of her verse collection *Aprel* (1960; April).

See: I. Grinberg, *Vera Inber: kritiko-biografichesky ocherk* (1961). H.A.G.

Inglin, Meinrad (1893–1971), Swiss novelist and short-story writer, was born in Schwyz. An account of his youth is contained in the autobiographical novel *Werner Amberg* (1949). His father, a goldsmith whose love of nature and hunting he shared, perished in the mountains when Inglin was only 12. His mother died three years later. After attending various schools and working as a watchmaker's apprentice and waiter, Inglin took up the study of philosophy, psychology, and literature. He also became an officer in the Swiss army and was frequently called upon to serve his country. He worked on the editorial staffs of two daily newspapers, spent a year in Berlin, and in 1921 returned to Schwyz, where he spent the rest of his life as a writer.

Inglin's first novel, *Welt in Ingoldau* (1922; World in Ingoldau), concerns Ingoldau, a typical Swiss town of the early 20th century. The young people of Ingoldau, although from different backgrounds, resent the conventionalities of their elders and struggle to prove themselves. The five short stories in *Jugend eines Volkes* (1933; Youth of a People) present Switzerland's historic past as a source of strength for the nation. Inglin's monumental novel *Schweizerspiegel* (1938; Mirror of Switzerland) is a gripping literary account of the numerous problems the country faced during World War I. The children of the bourgeois national councilor and high ranking officer Ammann are drawn apart by the events of their time. Long stretches of military duty and the outbreak of a deadly influenza epidemic scar the people; divided loyalties to warring nations and drastic social changes set individuals and groups against each other.

Inglin's short story-collections *Güldramont* (1943) and *Die Lawine* (1947; The Avalanche) contain psychological sketches of ordinary people in difficult situations, often when they are being challenged by forces of nature. His novel *Urwang* (1954) shows the destructive effects of modern technology on the environment. Indeed, man's relationship to nature is a recurring theme in Inglin's work. He pleads that men be one with nature, rooted in their native soil, which he considers the foundation of a strong human community. Inglin's other works include the novels *Die graue March* (1935; The Gray March), *Erlenbüel* (1965), and the short-story collections *Ehrenhafter Untergang* (1952; Honorable End), *Besuch aus dem Jenseits* (1961; Visit from Yonder), *Erzählungen I* (1968; Stories I), and *Erzählungen II* (1970; Stories II). *Chlaus Lymbacher* is the only play by Inglin. Apparently written during the early 1940s, in dialect, it was discovered only after his death and performed for the first time in 1976 under the title *Der Robbenkönig* (King Walrus).

See: E. Eilhelm, *Meinrad Inglin: Weite und Begrenzung* (1957); A. Hauser, "Begrenzung und Erfüllung: Meinrad Inglin zu seinem 75. Geburtstag," *SchM* 48 (1968): 495–504; B. von Matt, *Meinrad Inglin* (1976).

R.A.Me.

Ionesco, Eugène (1912–), French dramatist, novelist, short-story writer, and essayist, was born in Slatina, Romania. When he was a year old his French mother, Thérèse Icard, brought him to Paris. At the age of nine, he and his younger sister spent some time in the care of a kind peasant family in the small village of La Chapelle-Anthenaise in Mayenne. To this day, Ionesco sees that hamlet, with its public square, village church, and the *école communale* that he attended, as a paradise. With the passing of years, the Edenic image acquired archetypal dimensions in the writer's psyche and in a number of his plays. Upon his return to Paris he wrote his first play, "a patriotic drama."

When Ionesco turned 13, the family returned to Romania to join his father, a lawyer, but shortly afterward, Ionesco's parents were divorced. The boy sided with his mother. The presumption of his father's guilt can perhaps account, to some extent, for the feeling of sinfulness, the mysterious, haunting disquiet that pervades most of Ionesco's plays, as well as the pages of his intimate journals. In Romania, Ionesco learned to speak his father's language and, completing his secondary school training, entered the University of Bucharest. He was 18 when he started teaching French at one of the Bucharest gymnasiums. At the same time, he embarked on a brilliant literary career, publishing poetry and essays in the reviews *Azi, Floarea de Foc, Viaţa literară, România literară,* and *Facla.* His first book, *Nu* (meaning "No"), a collection of essays, was published in 1934.

In 1936, Ionesco married Rodica Burileano, a student of law and philosophy. The couple left Romania in 1938, when Ionesco received a government scholarship to study at the Sorbonne, where he planned to write a thesis on the theme of death in modern poetry. During World War II and the years of German occupation, Ionesco and his wife first sought refuge in the countryside and then lived in Marseille. Their daughter was born in 1944 at the time of the liberation and was named Marie-France.

Returning to Paris in 1945, Ionesco worked as a proofreader. This happy period of his life was also one of great hardship. It was in 1948 that he attempted to learn English by using the Assimil conversation method. The dialogue in the textbook seemed particularly simple-minded as the characters explained to one another that the floor was under their feet, the ceiling above their heads, that the days of the week were Monday, Tuesday, Wednesday, and so on, that they were the Smiths, living near London. As Ionesco, the would-be student of the English language, began to transcribe the sentences into his notebook, the dialogue and the characters took on a life of their own and a play emerged, *La Cantatrice chauve* (1953; Eng. tr., *The Bald Soprano,* 1958). Ionesco still likes to say: "I became a dramatist by accident." Staged by Nicolas Bataille, this "antiplay" was presented on May 11, 1950 at the Théâtre des Noctambules. It went unnoticed and unattended until some established writers, such as the dramatist Jean ANOUILH and the avant-garde novelist Raymond QUENEAU, supported it and embarked on a campaign to attract an audience. This first play was quickly followed by *La Leçon* (1953; Eng. tr., *The Lesson,* 1958), *Jacques ou la soumission* (1953; Eng. tr., *Jack, or the Submission,* 1958), and *L'Avenir est dans les œufs* (1958; Eng. tr., *The Future Is in Eggs,* 1960), a sequel to *Jack.* Ionesco's masterpiece of this first period is *Les Chaises* (1954; Eng. tr., *The Chairs,* 1958). With *Les Chaises,* the theater of the absurd (as Martin Esslin calls the new drama) became the deeper, more philosophical metaphysical farce. Later, when Ionesco began to publish essays on his dramaturgy, he explained that his theater is essentially metaphysical. For a long time, however, he preferred to leave this discovery to those of his critics who detected in his work the ontological intentions of a theater of the mind, thinly disguised under the delightful surface of anarchic humor.

There are indeed two Ionescos: Ionesco the prankster—the neodadaist and heir of Tristan TZARA, the enfant terrible who claims that he belongs to "the cabaret school of literature" and that his true ancestors are not writers but Charlie Chaplin, the Marx Brothers, Buster Keaton, and the comic strips; and Ionesco the Philosopher King—a thinker who reads and rereads Plato, Plotinus, and the Tibetan Book of the Dead. This second Ionesco has written some of the greatest tragic plays of the 20th century, plays about the process of dying, about the gradual disintegration of our planet and our solar system. By exploring our collective subconscious, Ionesco undertakes a voyage into the hidden, atavistic self; his oneiric theater, an architecture of images, presents upon the stage crystallizations of our inner world. Like the tragicomedies of Samuel BECKETT, another practitioner of the metaphysical farce, Ionesco's "comic dramas" question man's existence, conveying a sense of his existential solitude and of his fear of dissolution. His use of clichés as a stylistic device reveals that the banality of the quotidian is permeated by disquieting grotesqueries. His dramaturgy is not unrelated to the aesthetic of French symbolist theater; indeed, Ionesco's protagonists walk through what Charles BAUDELAIRE described in the sonnet "Correspondances" as "forests of symbols." In *Amédée ou comment s'en débarrasser* (1954; Eng. tr., *Amédée or How to Get Rid of It*, 1958), a corpse is afflicted with growth, forcing from their small apartment Amédée, an unsuccessful playwright, and his wife Madeleine, a telephone operator. We are never told how the corpse got there in the first place, or whose corpse it is—it is simply presented as phenomenological evidence. The presence of the corpse causes mushrooms to proliferate through the apartment, and "the geometric progression" of its growth—the cancer of the dead—threatens to split the womblike space. Madeleine urges her weak, passive husband to "get rid of it"; he lowers the body out the window and runs out into the street to drag it to the Seine, but the corpse, grown light and filled with air, floats up, carrying away with it the delighted Amédée, all his cares now gone. Never has the euphoria of freedom been so eloquently depicted. As Amédée flies up into the space of poetry and imagination, he waves farewell to his wife, who must suffer the punishment of being "terre à terre."

The apprehension of weightiness and of sinking informs *Victimes du devoir* (1954; Eng. tr., *Victims of Duty*, 1958), Ionesco's favorite among his plays. A neobaroque drama, it stages by means of a play within the play the protagonist's imaginary voyage into his past. A strong Oedipal motif underlies the action as Madeleine (wife/mother) and the Detective (father/analyst/judge) force the protagonist, Choubert, to plumb his inner world. The gaps in Choubert's memory—his symphony will definitely remain unfinished—are to be filled by the crusts of stale bread he is forced to chew by the Detective (now turned jailor and tormentor). An unexpected guest arrives, the ectoplasmic projection of the wicked parents, Nicolas d'Eu, whose name suggests a kingly title (Nicolas II). The elated Madeleine turns into a frantic hostess, balancing a proliferating number of coffee cups. The rhythm of her entrances and exits and of her juggling act evokes, in its wild progression, the image of the sorcerer's apprentice. One of Ionesco's obsessive images is that of the proliferation of matter (chairs, mushrooms, growing legs, coffee cups). As a bit of stage business, it lends a comic touch to the enactment, as though we were being made to watch the speeded up reel of one of the silent films Ionesco likes so much. Yet this "anarchy of humor"—to use the term coined by Antonin ARTAUD in his *Le Théâtre et son double*—borders on the demonic.

Ionesco's most joyous play is *Le Piéton de l'air* (1963; Eng. tr., *A Stroller in the Air*, 1968). The protagonist is an astronaut who has no need of spaceships: he levitates out of pure joy. A slight bicycle movement is all he needs to climb up, first as high as the treetops, then, as his bicycle is whisked off, higher and higher into space. In this realm, worlds and antiworlds interpenetrate, and in fact, the inhabitants of these antiworlds at times lose their way, wandering into ours. They even look much like us, except for the slightly disquieting fact that their pipes point downward. *Le Piéton de l'air* is a paean to man's imagination, to his ability to rise above the earth and to tread the clouds, if he so wishes. Yet, airy and exultant as it is, *Le Piéton* is tinged with angst. The stroller in space suddenly realizes that the little planet he has left is the only verdant place in the universe, that it is surrounded by "deserts of fire, deserts of ice." This bit of hospitable earth is all we have, Ionesco suggests. Like the French philosopher Blaise Pascal (1623–62), whose Jansenist vision is not too remote from Ionesco's brand of pessimism, the dramatist conveys his sense of terror at the thought of "the silence of these infinite spaces."

The satanic glow that infuses many of Ionesco's plays pervades *La Soif et la faim* (1966; Eng. tr., *Hunger and Thirst*, 1968), which he wrote for the Comédie-Française. With this production, Ionesco was transformed from an avant-gardist into "un classique moderne" (he was, in fact, admitted to the Académie Française in 1971). In this allegorical drama, Jean deserts his wife to go in quest of the ideal, perhaps even the ideal woman. His punishment for this act will be to wait on tables in the monastery where he mistakenly thought he had found refuge. It is a nightmarish vision of imprisonment, both political and metaphysical, suggesting the dictatorships of Eastern Europe, the Gestapo, and the NKVD. But this is also an inferno devised to fit the crime of a particular sinner. The final act of this grandiose and somber play is a Black Mass that could have been painted by Francisco Goya.

The creator of the metaphysical farce is also one of the most politically conscious writers of our time. He has consistently attacked all forms of tyranny and repression, steering clear at the same time of party politics. Ionesco is a libertarian, perhaps even an anarchist, but a quiet, nonviolent one. Two plays serve to reveal this aspect of Ionesco's philosophy: *Tueur sans gages* (1958; Eng. tr., *The Killer*, 1960) and *Rhinocéros* (1959; Eng. tr., *Rhinocéros*, 1960). The first of these shows Bérenger, Ionesco's "hero in spite of himself"—this is the dramatist's own definition of his antihero—in search of an elusive murderer who haunts the ersatz paradise of a perfectly planned neighborhood, "the radiant city." An architectural marvel, one that transcends the wildest imaginings of a Le Corbusier or a Frank Lloyd Wright, it can nevertheless offer its dwellers no protection against mortality, a universal human condition, nor against the murderous will of a "tueur sans gages"—Ionesco invented this term—who, unlike a "tueur à gages" (a hired assassin), kills for no reason of gain, in fact for no reason at all. Bérenger is aghast when the existence of the Killer is revealed to him by the Architect, a cool, efficient technocrat who is able to take the scandal of mortality in his stride. In fact, everyone except for Bérenger seems to know about the Killer—even Edouard, Bérenger's sickly friend, carries in his voluminous briefcase the murderer's list of future victims, his maps and the photos with which he entices his victims to the edge of the fountain, where they fall and drown. Could Edouard be the Killer? Certainly not, but his conspiratorial silence reveals that he is a fellow-traveler. Like the readers of *Mein Kampf* who deluded themselves into thinking that Adolf Hitler's projects were nothing but idle reveries, Edouard does not take these plans seriously. Thus, Bérenger remains alone in his determination to track down the criminal. Caught in the goose-stepping mob of the followers of a female demagogue, La Mère Oie (Mother Goose), Ionesco's antihero is unable to make his way to the police station. He walks on, however, along a deserted road. There he finds himself facing a puny creature; it is the Killer. A dialogue-monologue makes up the final scene. The Killer never answers, he just snickers. As Bérenger talks on, trying to understand the mentality of one who destroys for the sake of destroying, the protagonist finds arguments for his own annihilation. To argue with the Absurd is to enter the void. Although Bérenger is armed—he has old-fashioned guns—the Killer's short knife and long-lasting determination will triumph.

The Bérenger of *Rhinocéros* is another avatar of the protagonist of *Tueur*. Here again the antihero will have courage enough to retain his humanity in the face of universal metamorphosis. Rhinoceritis is the disease of conformity. Bérenger is strangely immune, and yet, sadly, he will remain alone at the end of the play, the last human among beasts. Ionesco's third profoundly political play is *Macbett* (1972; Eng. tr., 1973), his cartoon version of Shakespeare's *Macbeth*. This play examines how absolute power corrupts absolutely.

Although starting with *Amédée*, Ionesco became a writer of full-length plays, he never gave up the one-act form with which he made his fame. His other one-act plays include *Le Salon de l'automobile* (1953; Eng. tr., *The Motor Show*, 1963); *L'Impromptu de l'Alma* (1958; Eng. tr., *The Shepherd's Chameleon*, 1960), a spoof on the dramatist and his critics; *Le Nouveau Locataire* (1958; Eng. tr., *The New Tenant*, 1958); *Le Maître* (1958; Eng. tr., *The Leader*, 1960); *Délire à deux* (1963; Eng. tr., *Frenzy for Two*, 1965); *Le Tableau* (1963; Eng. tr., *The Picture*, 1968); *La Colère* (1963; Eng. tr., *Anger*, 1968); *Scène à quatre* (1963; Eng. tr., *Foursome*, 1963); and *La Lacune* (1966; Eng. tr., *The Gap*, 1969). These short works are mostly entertainments, but at times they touch upon some of the philosophical concerns central to the major plays. *Le Nouveau Locataire*, for example, begins on a realistic note showing a man moving into a new apartment. He talks with his future concierge who is full of good cheer and platitudes, while he obviously cherishes solitude and silence. As his furniture is being brought up, filling his tiny room, enclosing and burying him, we glimpse an Egyptian ruler within his pyramid. Although the proliferation of pieces of furniture suggests our gadget-conscious, materialistic civilization, the image created on the stage transcends time. The new tenant is both the comic victim of mass production and the proud, last representative of a dying culture, one that will disappear with him. Mummified, surrounded, he is a 20th-century pharaoh.

The image of death and of the process of dying finds its most eloquent expression in *Le Roi se meurt* (1963; Eng. tr., *Exit the King*, 1965). Bérenger the First, the sovereign of a decaying country, is informed by Queen Marguerite (his number one wife) and by the court physician that he is to die "at the end of the play." At first he refuses to believe this, but the signs of his end become unmistakable. *Le Roi se meurt* is Ionesco's masterpiece, the most moving tone poem on the process of dying in the dramatic literature of the 20th century. It echoes the lamentations of Job and Shakespeare's Richard II and it reminds one of Fyodor DOSTOYEVSKY's descriptions of the last moments of a condemned man in *The Idiot*. The last monologue of Queen Marguerite, who has become the great divinity of the Beyond, is based on the Tibetan Book of the Dead. Death and murderous rage also pervade *Jeux de massacre* (1970; Eng. tr., *Killing Game*, 1974), *Ce Formidable Bordel* (1973; Eng. tr., *What a Bloody Circus*, 1975), the novel *Le Solitaire* (1973; Eng. tr., *The Hermit*, 1974), and *L'Homme aux valises* (1975; Eng. tr., *Man with Bags*, 1977). This last work is a magnificent dream play, one in which the voyage becomes an allegory of man's search for his identity. The nameless protagonist, L'Homme, is Everyman as Wandering Jew. Although he is best known as a playwright, Ionesco is also a fine essayist. *Notes et contre notes* (1962; Eng. tr., *Notes and Counter Notes*, 1964) is a lucid collection of essays on modern dramaturgy. His other volumes of essays include *Journal en miettes* (1967; Eng. tr., *Fragments of a Journal*, 1968), *Présent passé passé présent* (1968; Eng. tr., *Present Past Past Present*, 1971), and *Antidotes* (1977), a collection of essays on politics and philosophy. He has also written four fairy tales "for children under three," and *Découvertes* (1970), an illustrated volume of childhood reminiscences for which he composed drawings. His "Thèmes et variations ou voyages chez les morts" was published in the *Nouvelle Review française* in 1980.

See: J. H. Donnard, *Ionesco dramaturge ou l'artisan et le démon* (1966); C. Bonnefoy, *Conversations with Eugene Ionesco* (1970); R. C. Lamont, ed., *Ionesco: A Collection of Essays* (1973); R. C. Lamont and M. J. Friedman, eds., *The Two Faces of Ionesco* (1978).

R.C.L.

Iorga, Nicolae (1871–1940), Romanian poet, historian, biographer, and statesman, was born in Botoşani, the son of a lawyer. He graduated from the University of Iaşi and studied history in Paris, Berlin, and Leipzig, where he received his doctorate. In 1894, at the age of 23, he became a professor at the University of Bucharest. An incredibly prolific scholar, Iorga produced some 800 volumes and pamphlets, as well as thousands of articles and reviews. His historical works include *The Byzantine Empire* (Eng. tr., 1907), *Istoria poporului francez* (1919; History of the French People), and *Istoria românilor* (11 vols., 1936–39; History of the Romanians). His broad-ranging works on literature include *Istoria literaturii româneşti* (3 vols, 1907–09, History of Romanian Literature in the 19th Century; 2 vols., 1934, History of Contemporary Romanian Literature; 1901; 2 vol. ed. in 1969; History of Romanian Literature in the 18th Century.

As early as 1903, when he became associated with the journal *Sămănătorul* (*see* ROMANIAN LITERATURE), Iorga viewed literature as a moral force whose function was to give cultural direction to the national ideals of the Romanian people. Because he subordinated aesthetic factors, he did not appreciate the work of such writers as Liviu REBREANU, George BACOVIA, Tudor ARGHEZI, and Gala GALACTION.

Iorga's interest in history permeates his poetry as well as such theatrical works as *Mihai Viteazul* (1911), *Învierea lui Stefan cel Mare* (1912; Resurrection of Stefan the Great), and *Constantin Brâncoveanu* (1920). History is, of course, also the subject of his memorabilia: *Orizonturile mele* (1934; My Horizons) and *Oameni cari au fost* (2 vols., 1967; Men [Remembered] as They Were).

Iorga was a public man who devoted three decades of his life to the political welfare of the Romanian nation. He was elected deputy in 1907, founded the National-Democratic Party in 1908, and served as prime minister in 1931 and 1932. In 1940, Iorga was assassinated because of his antifascist views.

See: I. Rotaru, *O istorie a literaturii române* (1972), vol. 2, pp. 13–22 and passim; D. M. Pippidi, ed., *Nicolas Iorga: l'homme et l'œuvre à l'occasion du centième anniversaire de sa naissance* (1972); M. Bucur, *Istoriografia literară românească* (1973).

V.A.

Irzykowski, Karol (1873–1944), Polish critic of literature and theater, novelist, playwright, short-story writer, and theoretician of cinema, was born in Błażkowa, near Jasło, and died in Żyrardów from wounds received during the Warsaw uprising in World War II.

Before World War I, Irzykowski's greatest achievement was the huge work *Pałuba* (1903; The Hag). It was an experimental novel, opposing all reigning literary conventions, an analytical novel, provocatively introducing a discursive element into the fabric of narration. *Pałuba* anticipated the budding psychological trends (Sigmund Freud, Alfred Adler), as well as many later attempts and discoveries in fiction (Marcel PROUST, James Joyce, André GIDE, and William Faulkner). A premature work, it was never duly appreciated, either in Poland or abroad.

Between the two world wars, Irzykowski assumed the role of a critic—a perpetual contestant, penetratingly probing every cultural phenomenon, every creative personality and trend. He was a fierce dialectician, passionately pursuing rational truth, absolutely independent and incorruptible. This activity is represented by the big book *Walka o treść. Studia z literackiej teorii poznania* (1929; The Struggle for Substance: Studies in Literary Epistemology), most of which consists of polemics with Stanislaw I. WITKIEWICZ's theory of "pure form," and by a collection of always challenging, often revealing essays called, autoironically, *Słoń wśród porcelany* (1924; The Elephant in a China Shop). He also published *Prolegomena do charakterologii* (1924; Prolegomena to Characterology), *Beniaminek* (1933), and *Lżejszy kaliber* (1938; A Smaller Caliber). His other important accomplishment of this period was the precursory work *Dziesiąta Muza. Zagadnienia estetyczne kina* (1924; The Tenth Muse. Aesthetic Problems of the Cinema), a first attempt at a philosophy of the new art of film, in which he sought to define its specificity and its inherent potentialities. His diaries, *Notatki z życia, obserwacje i motywy* (Observations, Motifs, and Notes from Life) were published in 1964).

See: T. Terlecki, "Niełatwy żywot," *Pion* 24, no. 5 (1938) (the whole issue devoted to Irzykowski); *Słownik współczesnych pisarzy polskich*, vol. 1 (1963), pp. 704–11; W. Głowala, *Sentymentalizm i pedanteria. O systemie estetycznym Karola Irzykowskiego* (1972); C. Taylor Sen, "Karol Irzykowski's Pałuba: A Guide to the Future," *SEEJ* 17 (1973): 288–300.   T.T.

Isaksson, Ulla (1916–), Swedish novelist and short-story writer, was born in Stockholm. Her 11 novels feature keenly observed social environments, always with surprising and convincing portraits of women. Her characters often appear to be powerless, "locked into" their feelings and circumstances, but they experience inexplicable moments of freedom, of "grace." These moments may be said to represent the underlying motif of Isaksson's works. Although she made her literary debut in 1940 with the novel *Trädet* (The Tree), which depicts a group of religious adherents, she considers her fourth book, *Ytterst i havet* (1950; At the End of the Archipelago), as her actual debut. In the novel a preacher in a fishing community on a small island discovers—partially through a love affair—that his God has received "a new face" and as a consequence he breaks with his parish. Its narrow framework, the island, makes the novel especially forceful.

With *Kvinnohuset* (1952; The House of Women), about a group of self-supporting, contemporary women, Isaksson achieved public recognition. All the women in *Kvinnohuset* have been obliged to sacrifice the "great dream" of love for trivial, everyday reality. By way of contrast, *Dit du icke vill* (1956; Where You Don't Want to Go) is set in the midst of 17th-century witch trials, and Isaksson reproduces, in a language colored by the official court records, the paranoiac mood of the day in a rural village. After *Klänningen* (1959; The Dress), featuring a modern generation-gap conflict, appeared *De två saliga* (1962;

Eng. tr., *The Blessed Ones*, 1971), a study of love as a folie à deux phenomenon. Thus, a troubled marriage is described partly from the wife's and partly from the psychiatrist-husband's point of view. The novel *Klockan* (1965; The Bell), a portrait of a small town, depicts Isaksson's experiences of the secularization of religion in Sweden, whereas in *Amanda eller Den blå spårvagnen* (1969; Amanda or the Blue Trolley) she tackled the problem of a developing country. As a result of "culture shock," a Swedish civil servant on a mission to Guatemala suffers a breakdown, and part of the novel is comprised of his nightmares. For that book the author systematically made use of her own dreams, recorded during a period of more than a year. In 1973, *Paradistorg* (Paradise Square), a family novel, appeared. In *Paradistorg* the author expresses her deep apprehension about the cold, new type of human being that is being created from the mechanized commercialization of big-city life. As egotism and a need for isolation and indifference steal into the home and—supposed retreat to life-warmth—the family, the tragedy unfolds in the midst of a melancholy-ecstatic description of the pleasures of life during summer. The novel received an important prize from the Swedish Academy.

Isaksson's play *Våra torsdagar* (1964; Our Thursdays) has been performed on several Scandinavian stages. Some of her writings have been filmed. Two dramas, *Nära livet* (Eng. tr., *Brink of Life*, 1958) and *Jungfrukällan* (Eng. tr., *The Virgin Spring*, 1960), were filmed by Ingmar BERGMAN and received a great deal of attention.

See: Å. Kussak, "Insikt och försoning," *BLM* (1959); E. H. Linder, *Böckernas värld* (1970), p. 2; G. Brandell, *Svensk litteratur, 1870–1970*, vol. 2 (1975), p. 269.

L.S.

Iskander, Fazil Abdulovich (1929–), Soviet author of mixed Persian-Abkhazian descent who writes in Russian, was born in Sukhumi and began his career as a poet (1957–64), but his reputation rests above all on the short stories and novels he has written since abandoning poetry. Most of his stories, collected under such titles as *Zapretny plod* (1966; Forbidden Fruit) and *Derevo detstva* (1970; Tree of Childhood) are humorous accounts of the author's early years in Abkhazia. The narrator gently mocks his own quirks and those of the people and society around him. Abounding in exotic local color and zany characters, many of the tales deal with moral crises in the life of the young narrator.

Iskander's novels differ from his stories in length and topicality, but not in composition, digressive as ever. *Sozvezdiye kozlotura* (1966; Eng. tr., *The Goatibex Constellation*, 1975), a satire on Soviet genetics, agriculture, and journalism in the Nikita Khrushchov era, is Iskander's most topical work.

Though usually considered a sunny humorist, Iskander is also the author of poignant tales of love and betrayal such as "Dom v pereulke" (1966; House on the Lane) and "Morskoy skorpion" (1976; Sea Scorpion).

See: H. Burlingame, "The Prose of Fazil Iskander," *RLT* no. 14 (Winter, 1976): 123–65.   D.A.L.

Istrati, Panait (1881–1938), Romanian and French prose writer, was born in Brăila of a Greek father and a Romanian mother. After finishing primary school, he lived the life of a vagabond and traveled widely. He became active in the socialist movement and sent articles from France to the journal *România muncitoare*. An extended bout with tuberculosis confined him to a sanatorium in Lausanne. A correspondence established with Romain

ROLLAND gave Istrati the encouragement he needed to publish, in French this time, his best stories and novels. Thus, a Romanian vagabond emerged as a contemporary French prose writer. In 1928, Istrati went to the Soviet Union for a long visit during which he became a bitter critic of the regime. In his trilogy *Vers l'autre flamme* (1934; Toward the Other Flame), he exposed and condemned the crimes and deportations of Iosif Stalin's reign of terror at a time when almost nobody dared to speak out on the subject. His last articles show a return to Christian ideals.

From 1921, when he committed himself to writing, Istrati's literary production grew tremendously: novels, short stories, and works of nonfiction appeared in both Romanian and French. Some of the best known are *Kyra Kyralina* (1924), *Oncle Angel* (1925; Uncle Angel); *Michaïl* (1927), *Codin* (1926), *Nerrantsoula* (1927), *Les Chardons du Baragan* (1933; Thistle of the Baragan Plain), *La Maison Thüringer* (1933; The Thüringer House), and *Coucher du soleil* (1935; Sunset).

See: A. Oprea, *Panait Istrati: un chevalier errant moderne* (1973).   P.G.T.

Italian literature. Italian literature, as distinct from the literature written in the Italian language since the 13th century, begins in the decade that followed the proclamation of the Kingdom of Italy (1861) when the capital of the new country was transferred from Turin, first to Florence (1864) and then to Rome (1871). Although works of literature continued to be written and, to some extent, published in all parts of the new nation, centripetal forces began to operate to change the character of the traditional Italian centers of culture and to blur if not obliterate distinctive regional differences. Where Florence had been the lodestar that attracted writers from other parts of Italy by the prestige of its Renaissance past and the purity of its tongue, Milan and Rome now took its place. The former became the book-publishing capital of the nation; the latter, center of its political life, the Mecca to which flocked journalists and men of letters who found an outlet for their work in a rich flowering of literary periodicals: *Cronaca bizantina* (1881–85), for instance, for which the young and already flamboyant Gabriele D'ANNUNZIO wrote a fashion column under the pseudonym of "Il duca Minimo," and *Nuova antologia* (founded in Florence in 1866 but moved to Rome in 1878) in which the novels of Giovanni VERGA, Antonio FOGAZZARO, Grazia DELEDDA, Matilde SERAO, and Luigi PIRANDELLO first appeared in serial form.

In the interest of clarity, Italian literature since the unification might be divided into five 20-year periods: the first extending to the turn of the century, the second to the end of World War I, the third corresponding to the Fascist regime, the fourth covering the post–World War II period, and the fifth from the late 1950s to the present. It is obvious that these loose chronological limits clash with the historical (factual) reality of individual literary careers and the progressive evolution of aesthetic doctrines, and—more importantly—with the achieved, "organic unity" of each single work. These are factors that neither the critic nor the historian can ignore. As a matter of fact, it is precisely the awareness of these tensions (variously formulated) that in the 20th century brought about a radical change in the conception itself of literary history and undermined the confidence with which at one time an individual historian—Francesco De Sanctis (1817–83), for instance, in *Storia della letteratura italiana* (1870–71; Eng. tr., *The History of Italian Literature*, 1931)—embarked upon the project of single-handedly writing the history of a whole literature or, as in the case

of Natalino Sapegno's *Storia del Trecento* (1934; History of the 14th Century), of a whole epoch.

The methodological difficulties inherent in trying to fix a large body of heterogeneous material in systematic form have been compounded by the current high degree of specialization in literary studies, which tends to a fragmented view of the whole. Such a systematization has also been hampered by Benedetto CROCE's critical attack on histories of literature organized by periods, schools, genres, themes, and other extrinsic and generalized concepts, as well as later on by the almost complete dominance of the historical approaches to literature by Marxist-oriented critics. Yet there is, by and large, agreement on the characteristics of the successive literary movements to which writers active in this period can be said to have at one time or another belonged or from which they differentiated themselves.

Secondo Ottocento ("the late 19th century," roughly equivalent to the Victorian period in English literature) is the most comprehensive of the terms applied to Italian postromantic literature before decadentism. The nine-volume *Storia della letteratura italiana* (1965–69) edited by Emilio CECCHI and Natalino Sapegno, at present the standard reference work on Italian literature, devotes a whole volume to this period. Its first two chapters deal respectively with (1) narrative literature from the historical novel through the autobiographical writings of participants in the struggle for unity and independence (Risorgimento), and with (2) De Sanctis, thus establishing the novel and criticism as the two areas in which later developments were most closely linked to their immediate predecessors. This is in contrast to the situation in poetry, since no major modern Italian poet has broken completely with a tradition that has kept the language (if not the subject matter and verse forms) of Dante and Petrarch alive. (Giacomo Leopardi [1798–1837], Italy's great romantic poet, is a link with the past, not a separation.) As far as the theater is concerned, postromantic drama in Italy up to the time of Pirandello is derived from French naturalism and Henrik IBSEN, its two indigenous developments, opera and the dialect theater, being only indirectly related to the body of writings that concerns us here.

The dominant intellectual current in Italy, as elsewhere in Europe from the 1860s to the turn of the century, was positivism, so named by Auguste Comte (1798–1857). Positivism can be defined as a philosophical system of thought maintaining that the goal of knowledge is simply to describe perceived phenomena, not to explain them speculatively or metaphysically. Charles Darwin (1809–82), Herbert Spencer (1820–1903), and Hippolyte Taine (1828–93) were its chief exponents in biology, sociology, and criticism, respectively. Positivism's parallel movement in art was the later form of realism known as naturalism in France and *verismo* in Italy. *Gli 'ismi' contemporanei* (1898; Contemporary "isms"), a lively, journalistic survey of the state of Italian literature, was written by Luigi Capuana (1839–1915), Italy's champion of naturalism and *verismo* after 1864 (the year he had his native Sicily for literary life in Florence). This work reflects the waning of positivism and its attendant movements in the arts, and the emergence of idealism in its place.

In addition to its philosophical grounding in positivism and its affinities with French naturalism, *verismo* had its roots in the "new" art that came out of the 1855 Paris Exposition and was propagated in Italy by the Florentine open-air painters known as the *macchiaioli*, and in the decadent romanticism of feuilleton literature as reflected in the work of a group of artists and writers who, regarding themselves as the Italian equivalent of the French *bohème* of the preceding generation, went under the name of *scapigliati* ("the dishevelled ones," i.e., the army of the irregulars). Although the *Scapigliatura* can be considered a forerunner of later avant-garde movements because of its programmatic anticonformism and its search for the novel and the culturally shocking (its repertoire of subjects runs from the macabre through terror, satanism, and necrophilia to the grotesque), its link with 20th-century Italian literature is only indirect. Its major influence was on the development of Verga, probably the single most important writer of this period because of the magnitude of his artistic achievement and because he was "rediscovered" in the second postwar period as a precursor of neorealism.

As a *verista*, Verga is one of a group of writers whose work is characterized on one level by its regionalism and on another by the canon of impersonality, that is, by the author's desire to eliminate his own presence—his own bias, directly expressed—from the text through the adoption of certain narrative and stylistic techniques such as the emphasis on theatrical "scene" rather than narrative "summary" and the widespread use of free indirect discourse in place of the author's direct expression of opinion. But it is the regionalism of *verismo* (the attachment to the survival of the regionally distinct ethnic cultures within the newly formed nation) that is most striking from a comparative point of view and that has led to the prevalent but erroneous notion that *verismo* was an "exclusively southern" phenomenon, "devoted to exposing the wretched conditions of the peasantry" (Carsaniga). It is true that the Sicilian triad Verga-Capuana-Federico DE ROBERTO (to whom could be added the early Pirandello) stands out in relief, but the Sardinian Grazia Deledda, the Neapolitan Matilde Serao, not to speak of the Tuscans Mario Pratesi (1842–1921), Renato FUCINI, and Ildefonso Nieri (1853–1920), the Milanese Emilio De Marchi (1851–1901), the Genoese Remigio Zena (1850–1917), and the Venetian Antonio Fogazzaro, all contributed in varying degrees to the record of the different social realities that comprised Italy in the last decades of the 19th century. And if rural life occupies an important place in the sociohistorical canvas of their collective "étude littéraire" (literary study) and "enquête sociale" (social inquest) (to recall the definition of the novel as an instrument of knowledge that the Goncourt brothers proposed in the preface to *Germinie Lacerteux*, 1864), they do not overlook either urban life—see Verga's *Per le vie* (1883; On the Streets), De Marchi's *Demetrio Pianelli* (1890), and Serao's *Il paese di cuccagna* (1891; Eng. tr., *The Land of Cockayne*, 1901)—or small-town life, where the quintessence of the region can be perceived and the social crossection most economically recreated, as in Capuana's *Il marchese di Roccaverdina* (1901; The Marquis of Roccaverdina) or in Verga's *Mastro-don Gesualdo* (1888–89; Eng. tr., 1893, 1923). As a matter of fact, had the "proletariast fallacy" (i.e., the Christian-romantic belief in the moral superiority of the poor translated into the terms of the Marxist class struggle), projected backward to include the peasant class, not been as dominant both in the initial journalistic criticism of the works of *verismo* and in their later academic collocation in literary history, a more balanced view might have gained general currency instead of remaining strictly the province of specialized scholarship. As it is, the tendency has been to identify those aspects of *verista* writing that are not consistent with the stereotyped view either with what preceded it or with what followed it, with what is sometimes referred to as *secondo* and *terzo romanticismo* (in our usage, *Scapigliatura* and decadentism), the "tired," defeatist weltanschauung that followed the Risorgimento and that

tended to separate and often alienate the artist from the community of men active in government, industry, and commerce.

Because the theater is not considered an integral part of Italian literature, the contribution to *verismo* of plays in dialect and in standard Italian has often been overlooked. Yet it is perhaps in the theater more than anywhere else that the coexistence of different linguistic traditions—a constant in Italian literature that has often been perceived as a cultural problem—can most fruitfully be studied. A misapprehension almost as common as that *verismo* was an exclusively southern phenomenon is that the *veristi* wrote in dialect. To be sure, there is in their work an occasional use (as in Verga) of dialect terms for which there is no ready equivalent in standard Italian, or (as in Fogazzaro) of conversational exchanges in dialect that are not only more "true to life" than their translation into Italian would be but that also document the social environment being represented. Yet none of the narrative writers of this period wrote whole works or even extensive parts of works in anything else than the standard language; the audience itself for which they wrote—mostly urban readers of newspapers, periodicals, and novels—precluded such a practice. The situation is different for poetry (especially for those dialects—Roman, Milanese, Neapolitan, Sicilian—with a strong literary tradition of their own) and, as mentioned above, in the theater, where local companies of itinerant players kept the spirit and techniques of commedia dell'arte alive well into the 20th century. The dialects that produced the best plays were Venetian (Giacinto Gallina [1852–97]), Piedmontese (Vittorio Bersezio [1828–1900]), and Milanese (Carlo Bertolazzi [1870–1916]) in the north; and Neapolitan (Salvatore DI GIACOMO) and Sicilian (see the anthology *Teatro verista siciliano* [1970]) in the south. In the dialect plays, which are usually set in a peasant or working-class environment, local color predominates; psychological introspection is virtually absent. In contemporary theater production in Italian, on the other hand, as well as in *verista* narrative writing dealing with the middle class or aristocracy, psychological introspection is an important feature.

In contrast to the buoyancy of much romantic writing, naturalistic writing is pervaded by a characteristic sense of grayness and hopelessness; for a good example, see Italo SVEVO's early novel *Una vita* (1893; Eng. tr., *A Life*, 1963). This feeling was perhaps engendered as much by an obscure premonition that the region as an independent entity within the nation and as a formative experience for the artist was fated to disappear, as by positivism's accentuation on measurable social phenomena and socialism's aspiration to place art in the service of progress understood as material betterment. The underlying conviction of most Italian naturalists was that progress was at best a two-edged sword and that Utopia could hardly be achieved in the face of the inveterate, ineradicable moral shortcomings of man.

If, chronologically speaking, romanticism and realism can be considered as two sides of the same coin, then the same can be said of *verismo* and decadentism: 1881, the date of Verga's *I Malavoglia* (Eng. tr., *The House by the Medlar Tree*, 1890, 1953, and 1964), is also the year of Fogazzaro's *Malombra* (Eng. tr., *The Woman*, 1907), a novel in which the different manifestations of the "supernatural" cannot be explained away by "science" as they are in De Marchi's *Il cappello del prete* (1888; The Priest's Hat) or Capuana's *Il marchese di Roccaverdina*. The term "decadentism" is more firmly established in Italian literary history than it is elsewhere. In France, where it first came into prominence with the 1886 review

Le Décadent, it was almost immediately and definitively replaced by symbolism. As a term, "symbolism" has the advantage of emphasizing the distinctive feature of the new aesthetics—art must suggest, not state, for the universe consists of harmonies, not of measurable facts—but decadentism embraces more. In its original use, the term celebrated the beauty of the overripe, the languishing, the fevered and ill (the best repertoire of these themes is still Mario PRAZ's *La carne, la morte e il diavolo nella letteratura romantica,* 1930 and subsequent eds., less expressively retitled in the Eng. tr., *The Romantic Agony,* 1933). Yet it soon turned into the disparaging epithet with which post-Risorgimento Italy could be branded for its falling-off in political vigor and civic enthusiasm (not to speak of the financial scandals that rocked the government), and with which its writers were humiliated as the puny offspring of giants. It is in this sense that term and concept appear in Croce's series of critical essays, *La letteratura della nuova Italia* (The Literature of the New Italy, begun in 1903), where Italy's major decadent writers—D'Annunzio, Giovanni PASCOLI, and Fogazzaro, for none of whom, however, the limiting label actually proves adequate—are subjected to quasi-official censure as promoters of a self-indulgent, socially withdrawn art that is the very antithesis of classical equilibrium and of wholesome morality. In a later extension of its meaning—especially popular with post-World War II Marxist literary critics—decadentism came to cover all the "sins" of Italian bourgeois society, from the industrialization that made Italy into a modern nation, to colonialism, interventionism in World War I, and support of fascism. Most inclusively, the term refers to that cult of the individual (not of man, as in Marxism's version of "humanism") that persisted beyond the Nietzschean significance (*see* Friedrich NIETZSCHE) it had for D'Annunzio and remained one of the hallmarks of the civilization of the West until the radical leveling of present-day mass society replaced it with the politics of the interest group.

Because of its negative connotation of decline and deterioration, decadentism never had exponents and programs as such. It never became a movement, that is, in the sense that *verismo* and symbolism were movements. Moreover, the term is imperialistic, capable of annexing meanings to itself, often so contradictory as to make it ultimately unserviceable as an organizing historical principle. It is not without significance that the "ism" against which Capuana battled (see above) was not decadentism but cosmopolitanism. Such was the term chosen by the young Ugo Ojetti (1871–1946) in his series of interviews *Alla ricerca dei letterati* (1895; In Search of the Men of Letters), to name the movement that he felt was—and should be—displacing *verismo.* Cosmopolitanism, of course, sets itself up in direct opposition to regionalism and thus maintains a peculiarly Italian context. In also underlines not only the "international" setting of the novels of D'Annunzio and Fogazzaro (in terms of the social class and the cultural background of their characters), but that desire to bring Italy back into the mainstream of European intellectual and artistic life that has been periodically renewed since the days of the Milanese journal *Il caffè* (1764–66). In the 20th century, this desire is manifest successively, in various guises, in turn-of-the-century aestheticism (one facet of decadentism), with its roots in the art-for-art's sake movement of the Parnasse and in the stylizations of the Pre-Raphaelites; in the iconoclasm and antirationalism of the futurists, with their rage to liquidate the past (classical and romantic) in order to make room for the new civilization of the machine (object of beauty for them, not source of dehumanization and pollution); in the program of deprovincialization of Giu-

seppe PREZZOLINI's review *La voce* (1908–13) with its championing of Hegelian dialectics, Bergsonian vitalism (*see* Henri BERGSON), and the revolutionary syndicalism of Georges SOREL; in the attack by Ardengo Soffici (1879–1964) on Italian academic painting and his promotion of impressionism and cubism; in the attention paid to foreign literatures in the periodicals of the 1920s and 1930s, perhaps best epitomized in *Solaria*'s (1926–34) search for an "Italian Proust" and its discovery of the outsider, the marginal Austrian-Italian-Italo Svevo; in Pirandello's efforts to establish a state theater on the model of other permanent, subsidized theaters; in the attraction felt, especially in the 1940s, for the mythic strength and innocence of an unsullied, barbaric America; down to the radical structural and linguistic experimentalism of Gruppo '63, stimulated by the example of a similar company of programmatic innovators, the German "Gruppe 47." A history of 20th-century Italian literature written from the point of view of the presence in it of foreign stimuli would not only capture one of its continuous cultural realities (present even in the Fascist years of autarchy) but would touch in one way or another upon every single major writer and major movement, pointing to that transnational cultural consolidation and uniformization that is probably the most striking characteristic of the second half of the 20th century and that is on the way to obliterating the sense of distinct national literatures to establish a new canon of writers belonging instead to world literature.

In the age of the triumphant printing press and of what might be called the foreign correspondent for cultural affairs, periodicals offer the best gauge for this stepped-up activity. Literary and cultural periodicals, like the cafés and salons of earlier periods, played an important role in shaping and directing the course of literature in 20th-century Italy. It is customary to group them chronologically and to distinguish their programs by contrast to one another. Indeed, this establishes their different identities in spite of the fact that the same writers often wrote for more than one, either simultaneously or successively. In considering their various objectives, however, it is well to bear in mind that all modern cultural movements—what in European terms may be termed collectively "modernism" (1890–1930)—had in common a perception of themselves as "new," "modern," as breaking—often violently and completely, but always "significantly"—with the past. From this perspective, the 19th century appeared more often than not an undifferentiated monolith ("le bête dix-neuvième siècle" [the idiotic 19th-century], as a Frenchman called it), all of whose achievements, from the political institutions of parliamentary government to historicist scholarship and representational art, must be destroyed.

The most important militant reviews of the pre–World War I period in Italy were *Leonardo* (1903–07), *La voce,* and *Lacerba* (1913–15), all three published in Florence, marking the energetic comeback of that cultural center as a locus of avant-gardism. If *Leonardo* (with Giovanni PAPINI and Giuseppe Prezzolini as its directors) was more concerned with philosophical problems, *La voce* (under Prezzolini's leadership) with the status of Italian intellectual life in a broad, all-encompassing perspective, and *Lacerba* (with Papini and Soffici at the helm) with the possibilities of total subversion inherent in futurism, they were united, as Prezzolini put it in his article on Italian literature in the 1947 edition of the *Columbia Dictionary of Modern European Literature,* in "the task of renewing culture," a task understood by him with characteristic aggressiveness as the battle against positivism in favor of reestablishing the primacy of ideas. Other reviews of the period were *Il convito* (1895–1900), like *Cronaca bizantina* distinguished by its D'Annunzean aestheticism and sumptuous production; *Poesia* (1905–09), F. T. MARINETTI's international review for the diffusion of French poetry in Italy and the defense of vers libre, a first step in setting poetry on the road to *parole in libertà* (words in liberty, freed of their syntactic relationship); *Hermes* (1904–06), directed by Giuseppe Antonio BORGESE, more specifically concerned with problems of literary criticism; and *Il regno* (1903–06), in whose pages the attack on democracy already foreshadows fascism's radical "corrective" of totalitarianism. Unwavering in their proselytizing and tumultuous in their short-lived existences, these reviews for all their differences shared a view of the close relationship between literature (and art) and culture. What is meant by culture in this context is perhaps best illustrated by the Prezzolini article cited above. His understanding of what constitutes literature is surprisingly broad, "impure" by the standards of later New Criticism. He is more interested in "extrinsic" considerations— schools, libraries, museums, the mode of their organization, the policies guiding them—in the social structures, that is, within which (or in spite of which) art occurs, than in the works themselves. The fact that this first group of literary and cultural reviews had objectives that went beyond art explains why they all came to an end with Italy's switching of sides in the political alignment of European powers and its entry into World War I in support of the Allies.

World War I, with its strong demarcation between life at the front and life at home and the participation of virtually the totality of draft-age male populations in battle, created a bigger hiatus in the continuity of European life than did World War II, whose actual destruction was on so much larger a scale. Europe emerged from the first conflict with its map redrawn and its social structure shaken by revolutions, the most important of which, in Russia, left its mark on all subsequent developments. As indices of the tenor of intellectual life, the periodicals that appeared in Italy after the war reflect the magnitude of the change that had taken place. The first group, consisting of Antonio GRAMSCI's *L'ordine nuovo* (1919–21) and Piero GOBETTI's various political reviews, especially his *Il Baretti* (1924–28)—forum of the Turinese anti-Fascists, whose influence was to reemerge, after the fall of fascism, in the group of intellectuals gathered together by the publisher Einaudi—continued the ideological engagement of the reviews of the prewar years but on the opposite political side. More immediately significant and effective was *La ronda* (1919–23), published in Rome under the editorship of Vincenzo CARDARELLI and with Riccardo BACCHELLI and Emilio Cecchi among its chief contributors. *La ronda* took a stand against all pre–World War I orientations and contributed a new "ism"—*rondismo*—to Italian literature. Successful in keeping literature and politics strictly separated in the years that saw fascism's rise to power, *La ronda* called for a "return to order," that is, to the tradition of a controlled and sober prose exemplified in Alessandro Manzoni (1785–1873) and especially in Leopardi. "Art prose" (as opposed to narrative prose, specifically the prose made current by naturalism) is akin to the better known genre of the prose poem. The preferred length is the journalistic essay, the *terza pagina* article of the Italian daily (so called from the page number on which it appeared), the newspaper reader's ration of literature. *Capitoli* (chapters), *elzeviri* (from the type face in which the page was set), *frammenti* (fragments), or *pesci rossi* (golfish, from Cecchi's title for the most famous collection of such pieces) are some of the designations used to describe the personal, refined, often lyrical,

always highly polished, always in some way topical pieces which resulted from this new attention to form. Although the movement was criticized from the perspective of post–World War II political engagement for turning its back on social and political problems, *rondismo* has been praised for the influence it had in improving the general level of prose writing and for having provided many of the writers who came after it with a workshop for linguistic and stylistic training.

We come now to the periodicals of the Fascist period proper. Critics and historians with a strong, unexamined, emotionally determined anti-Fascist bias have created the impression that an undifferentiated pall was spread over Italian artistic and intellectual life during those 20 years— the *ventennio nero,* with the intentional ambiguity of the adjective "black" pointing both literally to the emblematic color of fascism and figuratively to a horrified rejection of the phenomenon. An examination of the evidence (and being time- and place-bound, periodicals make exceptionally good documents) shows that this was not the case. Of course, there was the exile, enforced or voluntary, of leading anti-Fascists; there was the institution of *confino* (banishment for a period of confinement, not actual imprisonment, in some remote hamlet of Italy—Carlo LEVI's *Cristo si è fermato a Eboli* is the record of one such experience); there was censorship; and there was the coercion of the fear of censorship. But in its 20 years of existence, fascism passed through different phases, and human adaptability is such that there are many intermediate steps between complete acquiescence and open rupture. The periodicals of the Fascist period ranged from those that continued the literary emphasis of *La ronda,* through those that joined battle in the polemic of *strapaese* and *stracittà* (Italian cultural life seen as centered around the region and municipality and therefore national and traditional, as against Italian cultural life located in the city and therefore European and modern), to those that represented the official Fascist position on cultural matters and the attempts within it to make room for less conservative directions.

Of these three, the last group has for obvious reasons been the most neglected. The second group, especially Massimo BONTEMPELLI's *'900* (1926–29), with its intention of showing how much the Italy of fascism was part of the 20th century and with its militant anti-"past-ism" reminiscent of futurism, has in recent years received considerable attention as part of a more positive evaluation of Italian avant-garde movements than had been the case in the "classical" part of the century, dominated by Croce. But it is the first group, the literary periodicals, that played the dominant role in their own time and have ever since occupied a place of prestige in presentations of modern Italian literature. *Il frontespizio* (1929–40), *Solaria* (1926–34), *Letteratura* (1937–47), and *Campo di Marte* (1938–39) were all published in Florence, the last two financed by the publisher Vallecchi, one of the last private patrons of the arts in Italy. To their later embarrassment, some of the most representative writers of the anti-Fascist post–World War II period were connected with them: Elio VITTORINI's *Conversazione in Sicilia* (1941; Eng. tr., *In Sicily,* 1947) first appeared in serial form in *Letteratura;* Vasco PRATOLINI was one of the editors of *Campo di Marte.* By virtue of the impact it had on its not numerous but selected readership, *Solaria* was the most important of these periodicals, and the roster of its contributors runs the gamut from Eugenio MONTALE, Carlo Emilio GADDA, Salvatore QUASIMODO, and Cesare PAVESE to Giovanni Comisso (1895–1969), Gianna MANZINI, Sergio Solmi (1899–), Giuseppe Raimondi (1898–), and Vittorini, and includes the critics Gianfranco Contini

(1902–) and Giacomo Debenedetti (1901–67) as well. Like *La ronda, Solaria* succeeded in adding a word to the Italian language: the adjective *solariano* (also used as a noun), which refers to the characteristics common to the writers associated with it. Its day-to-day existence, at a time when the Fascist regime had become fully established and its positions on cultural conformity had hardened, was more difficult than *La ronda*'s had been, and its pages were often mutilated by censorship. Attentive to form and cultivating a poetic, introverted kind of prose in which the "real" world is filtered through memory, *Solaria* yet succeeded in giving Italy a wider literary horizon through its presentation of writers such as Marcel PROUST, James Joyce, and Katherine Mansfield and its "discovery" of three new Italian writers—Umberto SABA, Svevo, and Federico TOZZI—to each of whom it devoted an homage issue. *Solaria* probably played a more decisive role in the development of the modern novel in Italy than is generally recognized; the principal document for this facet of its influence, Debenedetti's *Il romanzo del Novecento* (1971; The 20th-Century Novel), did not appear until many years later.

We have so far left out the most important periodical in the intellectual life of Italy during the first half of the century. Croce's *La critica* (1903–44), "a review of literature, history and philosophy," as the subtitle identifies it, was founded neither as a forum for contemporary creative writing nor as a corrective to Italy's presumed cultural backwardness and inferiority. Its longevity, its ability to survive more than 40 years of radical changes, attests not only to the intellectual forcefulness and the personal energy of its founder (probably the last unaffiliated scholar in Italy), but also to the persistence of intellectual problems and their capacity to generate renewed interest in successive generations. (Croce was consistently anti-Fascist after the instauration of the dictatorship in 1925, but his antifascism was "nonconspiratorial," as Contini has so effectively defined it.) The new periodical, its 1903 Introduction stated, was to deal with interdisciplinary questions and with general problems of scholarship overlooked by the specialized journals. Rather than being eclectic, or worse still, dilettantish, it would adhere to certain basic stated principles, for, as Croce wrote in one of those common-sense formulations so typical of his style, "freedom . . . is better served by offering a clear target to opponents than mixing with them in an insincere fraternization that benefits nobody." The method of inquiry was to be the historical method, carried out, however, not in the spirit of positivism, but of "antimetaphysical" or "realistic" idealism (i.e., art is *not* related to the material existence of the artist, but is a distinct, spiritual activity that cannot be reduced to other activities; it is "lyrical intuition," the perfect synthesis of sentiment and image). In a departure from the basic attitude of scholarship, which looks with suspicion on the treatment of contemporary subject matter, *La critica* from its inception undertook the systematic examination of Italian philosophy and literature since the Unification. For example, Giovanni GENTILE's series of articles on philosophy became the basis for his three-volume *Le origini della filosofia contemporanea in Italia* (1917–23; The Origins of Contemporary Philosophy in Italy), and we have already had occasion to refer to Croce's *La letteratura della nuova Italia*. With these articles, *La critica* entered the arena of "militant criticism," an expression used in first half of the 20th century to refer to journalistic criticism of contemporary literary production, with its frequent but not necessarily exclusive promotion of the new and timely. The opposite of "militant criticism" is "academic criticism," which does not deal

with works of literature as they are being produced and which aims at "scientific" objectivity, adhering to critical principles derived from a definite aesthetic and to a method that is not simply personal preference or accidental reminiscence. If, through his essays on D'Annunzio, Verga, Pirandello, and others, Croce played an important role in the assessment of modern Italian literature, he played an even more important one in academic criticism, both through his direction of the "Scrittori d'Italia" (Writers of Italy) series for the publisher Laterza and by setting the model for the monographic type of criticism that became standard in the middle years of the century. The principal academic critics who followed in Croce's footsteps, although each one was also engaged in his own personal discourse within the shared common direction, were Luigi Russo (1892–1961), Attilio Momigliano (1883–1952), and Francesco Flora (1891–1962). Nor did the immediately following generation—Mario Fubini (1900–78), Natalino Sapegno (1901–), and Walter Binni (1913–)—reject the "lesson" of the man who in the very name of his review had singled out criticism, the need to analyze and judge, to theorize and define, as the dominant intellectual activity of the 20th century. Finally, outside of the professional context of the study and teaching of literature, Croce's influence fostered the appreciation of the unity and uniqueness of the work of art.

Twentieth-century Italian poetry took a more overtly antagonistic stand towards the past than did prose. This was due in part to the fact that the battle in narrative had already been fought with *verismo* and in part to the fact that symbolism was first and foremost a movement in poetry. Although the first comprehensive work to introduce French symbolism to Italy, Vittorio Pica's (1864–1930) *Letteratura d'eccezione* (1899; Literature of Exception), deals with both prose and poetry, it was in the poets, Paul VERLAINE and Stéphane MALLARMÉ specifically, that the new aesthetics, with its rejection of rhetoric (Verlaine's *l'éloquence*) and its privileging of indirect modes of communication (Mallarmé's *suggérer*), was most strongly in evidence. In the dichotomy of Verlaine/Mallarmé (Verlaine, the musical, accessible poet who speaks to the sentiments; Mallarmé, the aloof alchemist seeking unsullied words with recondite meanings who speaks to the intellect), it was to take Italy many years to draw abreast of Mallarmé and, by that time, Paul VALÉRY as well. Indeed, it was not until Francesco Flora's ground-breaking study *La poesia ermetica* (1936; Hermetic Poetry) won currency for the term "hermeticism" (which in Flora's intention had a denigrating sense, however) that Italy's "new" poets, who had been active since the beginning of the century, found a well-defined place in the history of Italian literature with what eventually became a positive label in place of the negative and undifferentiated term "decadentism."

The *crepuscolari* were the first group of poets to distance themselves from the late-19th-century triad, Giosuè Carducci (1835–1907), Pascoli, and D'Annunzio, "le tre corone" (three crowns) as they were dubbed in recognition of their achievement and status. *Crepuscolo* is the Italian word for "twilight" and refers to the lingering light of day at nightfall and, figuratively, to the end period or death of an age. The cult of the individual, which had a heroic dimension in D'Annunzio's will to self-assertion and in his panic (from Pan, not Apollo, as god of poetry) exaltation of nature, has a minor-key pendant in the poetry of Marino MORETTI, Fausto Maria Martini (1886–1931), and Carlo Chiaves (1883–1919)—to whom the designation was first applied—and of Guido GOZZANO and Sergio Corazzini (1887–1907), with whom the term remained more closely identified. These poets wrote about the prosaic aspects of daily life—the ordinary objects that filled their living rooms and their attics—with subdued affection not untouched by irony, and in an unpretentious, conversational tone. In recent years, a more limited view of the *crepuscolari* as innovators has resulted from a closer reading of the work of their predecessors. In each case, a private voice was revealed alongside the public one that the 20th century rejected: in Carducci, a poet of fleeting and evanescent aspects of nature was discovered next to the historical poet of Italy's past; in D'Annunzio, a poet of family affections and languid convalescence appeared next to the poet of the savage joy of sensual pleasure and of violence and war; and in Pascoli, a linguistic experimenter was shown to exist next to the humanitarian prophet, a voice to the disinherited.

The break with the past represented by futurism was infinitely more radical than that of the *crepuscolari*. Here not only tone, subject matter, and lexicon were involved, but even the very appearance of the page on which the poem was printed changed. The visual distinction between prose and poetry disappeared; onomatopoeia was pushed to extremes with different type faces used to enhance its expressivity (Marinetti's "Bombardamento di Adrianopoli" (1914) contains typical passages); numbers and mathematical symbols took the place of words, especially of the "imprecise and ineffectual" adjective. As manifesto upon manifesto called for, "the ridiculous stupidity of the old grammar inherited from Homer" was abandoned in favor of the simple juxtaposition of significant words (nouns and verbs in the infinitive) and of the second terms of analogies standing alone, all tumbling out together as if under the impact of strong, traumatic emotion, to express "the analogical synthesis of the world embraced at one glance" (simultaneity) and to show how "the poetry of the human is to be supplanted by the poetry of cosmic forces" and "the old romantic, sentimental and Christian proportions of the story abolished." Yet in spite of Marinetti's untiring energy, in spite of the meetings at which he officiated with booming voice and unfailing talent for sparking controversy and tumult, in spite of the "sister-arts" that futurism embraced—especially music and painting, but also architecture and theater—no major poet emerged from the movement. Although the futurist voice is unmistakable in Italian poetry of the early 20th century—Marinetti himself singled out Aldo PALAZZESCHI's "La fontana malata" (The Sick Fountain, in *Poesie 1904–1909*) for special praise—it remained marginal and won little prestige outside the circle of the movement's adherents. It has been suggested, however, that in the "manifesto," futurism contributed a new genre to literature, akin to the place won by the poster in art. And certainly the "group work" that Marinetti extolled (in his preface to the 1925 anthology *I nuovi futuristi* [The New Futurists], for instance) has been followed in later collective efforts in which the responsibilities and privileges of authorship are democratically shared.

Italy's major 20th-century poets have almost all in one sense or another been connected to hermeticism, especially if we take the term (from Hermes Trismegistus, reputed third-century author of works on magic and the occult) in its most generalized meaning, that of "difficult" or "closed" poetry. Unlike futurism and like decadentism, hermeticism was not a movement with an explicit program and an easily identifiable following. This explains why there is much fluctuation in defining it and in singling out the specific poets to whom the term should be applied. According to Silvio Ramat (1939–), it should be reserved in its precise, historical significance for poets and critics active in Florence from the time Giuseppe De Robertis (1888–1963) took over the direction of *La voce* in 1914 to

the early 1940s, in particular for Carlo Bo (1911–), Mario LUZI, Alfonso GATTO, Piero BIGONGIARI, Alessandro PARRONCHI, and Oreste Macrì (1913–). Ramat cites Bo's 1938 essay "Letteratura come vita" (Literature as a Way of Life, the opposite of D'Annunzio's Wilde-like slogan "Life Lived as Art") as the manifesto of a new critical language making use of metaphor in place of technical description or commonsense persuasion. He claims as distinctive for Florentine hermeticism a conception of the poetic symbol not as a defense against nothingness, against nonbeing, but as an active, illuminating force consonant with the Catholicism of *Il frontespizio,* the leading periodical of the group. If we accept this definition, a number of poets commonly associated with hermeticism are left out, the most important being Giuseppe UNGARETTI, Montale, and Quasimodo. And indeed Ungaretti and Montale are often considered, like Dino CAMPANA and Arturo Onofri (1885–1928), precursors of hermeticism, or, together with Saba and Cardarelli, are designated *lirici nuovi* (new lyricists), innovators in their adoption of an unrhetorical poetic language but not as impenetrable in their symbolism as the later hermetics.

A frequently repeated explanation for hermeticism's obscurity sees in it a resistance to fascism, a lowering of the tone of the enunciation as a tacit condemnation of public policy and of the grandiloquent style of the regime—an attitude expressed in a different context by Pirandello when, in his 1931 speech on Verga, he separated Italian writers into those of the "style of words" and those of the "style of things," privileging the latter. But a more flexible and nuanced view of literary developments in the first half of the 20th century, one in which the totalitarian ventures of the period between the two wars do not play an apocalyptically determinant role, has shifted the emphasis to "inner" motivations, "inner" both as a continuation and expansion of symbolist poetics explored along the whole gamut of European symbolism as well as in the reactivation of Italian poets such as Petrarch and Leopardi, and as the less literary, more psychological impulse to protect the individual world of consciousness, conscience, and memory against the various forces—political, economic, sociological, and ideological—that were bent on "exposing" it, quantifying it, and commercializing it.

A step back at this point will permit us to trace developments in Italian drama after the period of *verismo,* to which we have already referred. The first major trend in 20th-century drama was introduced by Gabriele D'Annunzio who, together with the actress Eleonora Duse (1858–1924), launched a project in 1898 for an open-air theater in which the production of classical works and of modern tragedies imitative of the Greeks would mark a radical departure from the often trivial realism of the bourgeois theater with its ambition to reproduce the surrounding world on stage within the formal boundaries of the well-made play. D'Annunzio's plays demanded a poetic style of recitation far removed from ordinary spoken language, extravagant and spectacular stage sets, and audience sympathy for psychologically tortured and sensually overexcited characters who find themselves in extreme and morbid situations. His principal followers were Sem BENELLI, Ercole Silvio Morselli (1882–1921), and Gioacchino FORZANO.

Contemporary with poetic drama were a number of quite different works that were later seen as constituting the beginnings of the current of *intimismo,* the theatrical pendant to *crepuscolarismo.* Reminiscent of the more famous works of Anton CHEKHOV and Maurice MAETERLINCK, these plays aimed at suggesting feelings rather than stating them, hence the denomination of *teatro del silenzio* (theater of silence) or *dell'inespresso* (of the unexpressed). In *Tristi amori* (1887; Eng. tr., *Unhappy Love*, 1916) and *Come le foglie* (1900; Eng. tr., *As the Leaves*, 1911) by Giuseppe Giacosa and in *Il piccolo santo* (1909; The Humble Saint) by Roberto BRACCO (see especially the preface, which contains a kind of poetics of *intimismo*), one encounters understated nostalgic depictions of decent people who are engaged in a doomed effort to evade a commonplace existence and who must accept a gray, unheroic routine. These works foreshadow the plays of Fausto Maria Martini (1886–1931) and Cesare Vico Lodovici (1885–1968) and even find echoes in Pirandello and Ugo BETTI.

The early theatrical experiments of futurism also belong to the pre–World War I period. We speak of performances here rather than plays, for what is distinctive about futurist theater is not the interpretation of a dramatic text but the orchestration of a spectacle in which all forms of entertainment mingle: words, songs, music, dance, lighting effects. Futurist "evenings," a kind of extension of the variety show but with the additional intention of shocking the spectator, consisted of the reading of manifestos, the declamation of poetry, the production of familiar and unfamiliar sounds and noises, the staging of brief, "synthetic," largely improvised pieces (comparable to the "two quips," of Achille CAMPANILE), and the inciting of audience participation, sometimes by means of outrageous and puerile devices such as the spreading of itching and sneezing powders in the hall. Futurist "evenings" often ended in brawls and general confusion; they had news value but were considered marginal cultural expressions. Yet there are links between them and other avant-garde groups, such as the "teatro degli indipendenti" (theater of the independents) founded by Anton Giulio Bragaglia (1890–1960). Techniques of the futurist theater also found their way into the work of serious playwrights, such as Pier Maria ROSSO DI SAN SECONDO and Pirandello.

"Teatro nuovo" (new theater) or, more strikingly expressed, "teatro del grottesco" (theater of the grotesque) is the name by which the most significant innovations in 20th-century Italian drama are known. The designation "grottesco" derives from the genre label attached to Luigi CHIARELLI's play *La maschera e il volto* (Eng. tr., *The Mask and the Face*, 1927), written in 1913 but not produced until 1916, by which time it had already become widely known in theatrical circles. The word "grotesque" in this connection is not to be understood in its ordinary meaning of "ludicrous" or "odd" in the sense of "ridiculous," but should be related to the decorative painting particularly popular in the Renaissance that made use of fanciful combinations of human and vegetal shapes. The discordant, contrasting effect of such figures recalls the two-faced statue (one face of which is laughing at the tears of the other) that Pirandello speaks of in a famous metaphor for the intentions of his art. Although Pirandello preferred the more inclusive *teatro nuovo* as descriptive of his plays beginning with *Così è (se vi pare)* (1917; Eng. tr., *Right you Are, if you Think So*, 1923), he is often considered, at least in the first phase of his plays in Italian, as belonging to the current of *grottesco*. In addition to Chiarelli and Pirandello, the principal writers of *grotteschi* were Luigi Antonelli (1882–1942), Enrico Cavacchioli (1885–1954), and Rosso di San Secondo, whose *Marionette, che passione!* (1918; Marionettes, What Passion!) points in its very title to a view of characters as puppets moved by a blind and unfathomable fate, a view emblematic of the human condition in a directionless universe.

Between the two world wars, the Italian theater was dominated by Pirandello. What he calls the "pangs of his spirit" in the 1925 preface to *Sei personaggi*—the anguish engendered by "the deception of mutual understanding founded on the empty abstraction of words, man's multiple personality corresponding to the possibilities of being to be found in each of us, the inherent tragic conflict between life, which is continually moving and changing, and form, which fixes it, immutable"—are themes found in the works of his contemporaries and successors. Italian writers who have been influenced by Pirandello range from Chiarelli to Bontempelli, to Betti, Diego FABBRI, and Eduardo DE FILIPPO. Outside Italy, Thornton Wilder, Eugene O'Neill, Jean ANOUILH, Jean-Paul SARTRE, and Jean GENET are among the writers most often cited as having been influenced by him.

Depending on the point of view, neorealism is the "ism" that either followed or ran parallel to hermeticism: "followed," if its impact in the immediate post–World War II years, contributed to by the success of Roberto Rossellini's film *Roma città aperta* (1945) and other films, is taken as a turning point; "ran parallel," if we consider that the term was first used in 1930 by the "militant" critic Arnaldo Boccelli (1900–76) to describe the literary production of the previous year, among which was Alberto MORAVIA's novel *Gli indifferenti* (Eng. trs., *The Indifferent Ones*, 1932, *Time of Indifference*, 1953). Other works that are usually assigned to the beginnings of neorealism include Carlo BERNARI's *Tre operai* (1934; Three Factory Workers), written and rewritten between 1928 and 1934; Pavese's collection of poetry *Lavorare stanca* (1936; Eng. trs., *A Mania for Solitude: Selected Poems, 1930–1950*, 1969, *Hard Labor*, 1976); Mario SOLDATI's *America, primo amore* (1935; America, First Love); Corrado ALVARO's *L'uomo nel labirinto* (1926; Man in the Labyrinth); and, even further back, Tozzi's *Tre croci* (1920; Eng. tr., *Three Crosses*, 1921) and *Il podere* (1921; The Farm), Borgese's *Rubè* (1921; Eng. tr., 1923), and (retrospectively, after it was published in Italy in 1947) Ignazio SILONE's *Fontamara* (1933; rev. 1958; Eng. trs., 1934, 1960). These works were essentially "antiliterary," rejecting the traditional emphasis on style—*bello scrivere* (beautiful writing)—and holding "content" to be more important than "form." Inasmuch as they did not derive from a common program, they are quite different among themselves. But taken as a group, they stand apart not only from the contemporary works of the hermetic poets but also of prose writers such as Riccardo Bacchelli, Antonio BALDINI, Anna BANTI, Emilio Cecchi, Gianna Manzini, Giuseppe Raimondi (1898–), Bonaventura Tecchi (1896–1968), and Giovanni Battista Angioletti (1896–1961); and from popular novelists appealing to whatever mass market there was at the time, such as Alba de CÉSPEDES, Virgilio Brocchi (1876–1961), Bruno CICOGNANI, Salvator Gotta (1887–), Marino Moretti, and, at quite some distance from the others, Pitigrilli (pseud. of Dino Segre [1893–]) and Liala (pseud. of Liana Negretti [1902–]).

Neorealist works *avant la lettre* reflected the anguished, squalid loneliness of modern life, the problematic relationship between man and reality, his avulsion from historical understanding, and his search for meaning amid the disorder of the first postwar period. Pirandello's 1921 postscript to *Il fu Mattia Pascal* (1904; Eng. tr., *The Late Mattia Pascal*, 1923) is a good indicator of these concerns. Already manifest in these works are characteristics that would remain identified with neorealism proper: certain preferences in subject matter and treatment (the underprivileged classes, the Italian south, provincial life; the analysis of social environment as determinant of the human condition), as well as a new view of America's

primitiveness as an antidote to European hyperciviliza-
tion, and a strong ethical and at times political commitment against injustice, inequality, and oppression.

In a narrower sense, neorealism is a post–World War
II phenomenon, an outgrowth of the Resistance movement and of the literature to which it and antifascism in
its various forms gave rise. Much of this literature was
autobiographical, such as Gramsci's *Lettere dal carcere*
(1947; Eng. tr., *Letters from Prison*, 1973) or Alcide De
Gasperi's (1881–1954) *Lettere dalla prigione* (1955; Letters from Prison), and documentary, such as Carlo Levi's
Cristo si è fermato a Eboli (1945; Eng. tr., *Christ Stopped
at Eboli*, 1947) or Primo LEVI's *Se questo è un uomo*
(1947; Eng. tr., *If This Is a Man*, 1959). It bequeathed to
fictional narrative a sense of urgency, of unmediated directness, of recently shared experience, and lent a haunting first-person quality even to works written in the third
person. This is apparent in writers as different as Pavese
and the early Italo CALVINO, Pratolini, Carlo CASSOLA,
or Giorgio BASSANI. The main objective of this literature
was to bear testimony; its subject matter included partisan
warfare, as in Beppe FENOGLIO; disrupted civilian life, as
in Giuseppe BERTO's *Il cielo è rosso* (1947; Eng. tr., *The
Sky Is Red*, 1948); the dramas of German occupation and
deportation, as in Bassani's stories of Ferrara; and the
eking out of a livelihood in an urban wasteland, as in Pier
Paolo PASOLINI's *Ragazzi di vita* (1955; Eng. tr., *The
Ragazzi*, 1968). Thus neorealism succeeded in placing a
new literary landscape next to those of the late 19th and
early 20th centuries: the Italy of poverty and deprivation,
of makeshift ''Hoovervilles'' and petty crime, of the unemployed and the illiterate, of the homeless and the socially alienated—this next to the Sicilian peasant Italy of
Verga, the cosmopolitan upper-class Italy of D'Annunzio,
and the minor bureaucrats' Italy of Pirandello. By the
early 1950s, however, this reliving of recent Italian history
under fascism, as in Pratolini's *Il quartiere* (1944; Eng.
tr., *The Naked Streets*, 1952), of war experiences, as in
Mario Rigoni Stern's (1921–) *Il sergente nelle neve* (1953;
The Sergeant in the Snow) or Giose RIMANELLI's *Tiro al
piccione* (1953; Eng. tr., *The Day of the Lion*, 1954), and
of the disorientation preceding reconstruction (again Pasolini's *Ragazzi di vita* comes to mind) had run its course.
Neorealism, not to mention the novel, was felt to be in
crisis.

The crisis was first of all ideological. In the initial flush
of the defeat of fascism there had appeared to be a consensus about the solution of social problems, yet that
solution was soon shown to be illusory. The future of
Italy began to be considered with less optimism and specifically, as in the pages of Vittorini's periodical *Il politecnico* (1945–47), the political commitment of intellectuals was discovered to be fraught with greater difficulties
than a theoretical analysis of their role in Italian culture,
such as Gramsci's, had led one to expect. Moreover, the
reconstruction of Italy and stepped-up industrialization,
not only in Italy but in the rest of Europe (with the exodus
of large masses of Italian workers to northern countries),
eventually brought about widespread economic well-
being, the famous ''miracle'' or ''boom,'' unparalleled in
the history of the country. The changed situation was, of
course, accompanied by its own problems, and in the late
1950s and early 1960s, partly as a result of the work of
Vittorini and Calvino's new periodical *Il menabò*
(founded in 1959), numerous books, novels, and surveys
(*inchieste*) dealt with industry and technology, the new
reality of the working lives of the average Italian. Luciano
BIANCIARDI and Lucio MASTRONARDI, Giovanni TES-
TORI, and Ottiero Ottieri (1924–; author of *Donnarumma
all'assalto* [1959; Eng. tr., *The Man at the Gates*, 1962]),

Goffredo PARISE, and Paolo VOLPONI can be cited in this
connection. In several of their works, the anonimity, rep-
etitiousness, and enslavement inherent in the relationship
of man to machine result in full-fledged alienation, either
the social alienation that expresses itself in acts of violence against the factory or the psychological alienation of
paranoia, neurosis, and schizophrenia.

Experimentalism is the last ''ism'' that will concern us
here. The term was first used by Gianfranco Contini in
his studies of the linguistically hybrid Italian literature of
the 13th century, and was chosen by Pier Paolo Pasolini
in his articles for *Officina* (1955–59) to name the expressionistic, rather than mimetic, subversive use of language
in the poetic production of the 1950s. It was also the term
adopted by the new avant-garde, the group of writers that
came together in 1963, called themselves ''Gruppo 63,''
and were dubbed a ''new literary generation'' by their
mentor, Luciano Anceschi (1911–). Anceschi, professor
of aesthetics at the University of Bologna, had written a
dissertation, *Autonomia ed eteronomia dell'arte* (1936;
The Autonomy and Heteronomy of Art), which, although
essentially a historical and theoretical defense of the concept of pure poetry, at the same time reintroduced the
complementary concept of the interdependence of art and
society. Anceschi was a phenomenologist while the philosophical idealism of Croce still dominated Italy. In 1956,
the year of the Hungarian uprising against Soviet control,
Anceschi founded the journal *Il Verri*, which became a
continuing force for cultural and artistic innovation in
Italy. Among the many special publications it sponsored
were a number devoted to the French *nouveau roman*
(''new novel''; *see* FRENCH LITERATURE), one to the
avant-garde and *engagement*, one to the psychopathology
of expression, one to psychoanalysis and poetry, one to
futurism, and so on. An anthology devoted to *I novissimi*
(1961; The Newest Poets) and the anthology-manifesto
that grew out of the meeting of the 1963 group (*Gruppo
'63* [1964]) identified the new writers, stated their position, and illustrated their work. Among the poets were
Elio Pagliarini (1927–), Nanni Balestrini (1935–), Alfredo
Giuliani (1924–), Antonio Porta (1935–), and Edoardo
SANGUINETI; among the prose writers, Alberto ARBA-
SINO, Furio Colombo (1931–), Oreste del Buono (1923–),
Raffaele La Capria (1922–), Luigi MALERBA, Giorgio
Manganelli (1922–), and Piero A. Buttitta (1931–); among
the critics and theorists, Renato Barilli (1935–), Umberto
Eco (1932–), and Anceschi himself. All these writers re-
jected those works of literature whose basic assumption
was that art in some ways mirrors or imitates reality.
Turning their back on the realistic tradition and opting for
experimentalism (variously understood), they ridiculed
the most successful contemporary realists—Moravia,
Bassani, and Cassola—and sought their models in the
radical innovators of the early 20th century—James
Joyce, Marcel Proust, Robert Musil, Svevo, Pirandello,
Franz KAFKA—and in their successors—Alain ROBBE-
GRILLET, Michel BUTOR, and Günter GRASS, and (in
Italy) Carlo Emilio Gadda. As Barilli put it, the new
avant-garde writer was concerned with ''the perceptual
level, with the way in which time and space are conceived, how objects are seen, how feelings are recognized
and designated, how syntax is articulated.'' His project
was cognitional as much as literary.

See: G. Contini, *Letteratura dell'Italia unita 1861–1968*
(1968); E. Cecchi and N. Sapegno, eds., *Storia della
letteratura italiana*, vols. 8 and 9 (1969); F. Sanguineti,
Poesia italiana del Novecento, 2 vols. (1972); E. H. Wilkins, *A History of Italian Literature*, rev. ed. by T. G.
Bergin (1974); F. Jones, *La poesia italiana contemporanea: Da Gozzano a Quasimodo* (1975); S. Ramat, *Storia*

della poesia italiana del Novecento (1976); G. Manacorda, *Storia della letteratura italiana contemporanea: 1940-1975* (1977). O.R.

Ivanov, Georgy Vladimirovich (1894-1958), Russian poet and prose writer, was born at Kovno into the Russian gentry. As a very young man he met Nikolay GUMILYOV and became associated with the latter's acmeist group. His early verse is only a very skilled stylization of the extremely popular and quite original poetry of the older acmeists and of Mikhail Kuzmin, who is assumed (probably rightly) to have been a strong early influence upon him. Along with Georgy ADAMOVICH, Ivanov emigrated to France in the early 1920s. There he became a major Russian poet—bitter, perceptive, difficult as a person, and chilling in his ability to give voice to the despair, the utter negativity of his vision. At the same time there is implicit in his verse an abiding faith in poetry, particularly in the senseless, insane music of verbal art. In this, Ivanov's magic is akin to that of Aleksandr BLOK. In several poems he adopted the bleak outlook and directness of expression advocated by Adamovich, who admired Ivanov's verse even though he never really approved—publicly at least—of his expressiveness. Ivanov's later poetry, written abroad, ranges from simple, bemused observation to capricious surrealism. Always underlying his vision is an irony that has been described as romantic but might just as well be called existential.

Ivanov also wrote several prose works. In 1928 he published his highly imaginative, at least partly fabricated, memoirs of the literary scene in Petersburg from 1913 to the early 1920s called *Peterburgskiye zimy* (Petersburg Winters). His other prose works include fragments of a novel, *Tretiy Rim* (1929; The Third Rome) and the novel *Raspad atoma* (1938; The Disintegration of the Atom), about the disintegration and despair of modern man. *Stikhi* (1958; Poems) contains most of Ivanov's best verse.

See: N. Gumilyov, "Statyi i zametki o russkoy poezii," *Sobraniye sochineniy,* vol. 4 (Washington, D.C., 1968); V. Markov, "O poezii Georgiya Ivanova," *Opyty* 8 (1957): 83-92; G. Ivask, "Russkiye poety: Georgy Ivanov," *NovZ,* no. 98 (1970): 135-43. H.W.T.

Ivanov, Vsevolod Vyacheslavovich (1895-1963), Russian novelist and short-story writer, was born near Semipalatinsk, in Siberia, into a schoolteacher's family. He left home at the age of 15, knocked about in various jobs, and fought in the Russian Civil War, first for the Whites, then for the Reds. In 1916 he broke into print, soon attracting the attention of Maksim GORKY, and in 1920 he joined the Serapion Brothers, a group of writers in Petrograd (*see* RUSSIAN LITERATURE). Ivanov published four novels in close succession, and they established him as a major literary presence: *Partizany* (1921; The Guerrillas), *Bronepoezd 14-69* (1922; Eng. tr., *Armored Train 14-69,* 1933), *Tsvetnye vetra* (1922; Particolored Winds), and *Golubye peski* (1922; Azure Sands). All four are large-scale treatments of the Russian Revolution (1917) and Civil War in either Siberia or Mongolia, and are related in a seemingly discontinuous manner that mixes various styles and lexicons, offers exotic settings and striking turns of plot, and features uncomplicated characters seeking identity through war. The novels impressed most contemporary critics as being "realistic," "joyous," and "life-celebrating," and for a time Ivanov was the most popular writer in the Soviet Union next to Boris PILNYAK. But the critics had misread him. His characters are mostly will-less, instinct-driven creatures who can neither understand nor influence the world; nature is beautiful but

indifferent to their questings, which end in deaths that are at worst humiliating, at best pointless. Unlike Pilnyak, Ivanov had no theory of history or of the Revolution and mocked those of his characters who try to devise one.

Ivanov made one attempt at a "proletarian" novel, *Severostal* (1924; Northsteel); but as the 1920s wore on, his preferred setting was the Russian village, as in *Taynoye taynykh* (1927; Mystery of Mysteries), a short-story collection. He softened his palette and tried to concentrate more on individuals than on panoramas, but his basic outlook remained the same. Finally the critics discerned his pessimism and cynicism and deemed them inappropriate in a Soviet writer. In many later works, Ivanov duly tried to cultivate more positive themes and attitudes. In the stage version of *Armored Train 14-69* (1927), for example, the formerly passive hero is transformed into a vigorous exponent of proletarian ideals. *Pokhozhdeniya fakira* (1934-35; abridged Eng. tr., *The Adventures of a Fakir,* 1935) draws on Ivanov's own experiences as a circus performer; *Parkhomenko* (1939) deals with the famous Civil War commander; a number of novels and stories, none really memorable, were inspired by World War II. Toward the end of his life, Ivanov published interesting memoirs.

See: L. A. Gladkovskaya, *Vsevolod Ivanov: ocherk zhizni i tvorchestva* (1972); R. A. Maguire, "The Pioneers: Pil'nyak and Ivanov," in *Major Soviet Writers,* ed. by E. J. Brown (1973). R.A.M.

Ivanov, Vyacheslav Ivanovich (1866-1949), Russian poet, critic, classical scholar, and philosopher, was born and educated in Moscow. After obtaining his Ph.D. in Berlin as a student of Theodor Mommsen, he traveled widely in Europe and the Middle East. In 1903, shortly after his return to Russia, his first volume of poems, *Kormchiye zvyozdy* (Lodestars) was published. It immediately established him as one of the prominent exponents of the new poetry of "decadentism" or symbolism. He soon also became the leading theoretician of the religiously and philosophically inspired group within the symbolist movement that was led by Aleksandr BLOK and Andrey BELY, as well as by Ivanov himself. Ivanov's home in Petersburg served as a center of literary life in the years between 1904 and 1912. During the October Revolution (1917) he lived first in Moscow and then accepted the chair of classical philology at the University of Baku. In 1924 he emigrated to Italy, never to return to his homeland.

Both his poetry—ornate, studded with archaisms of Old Slavonic and Byzantine provenience, and difficult because it is fraught with allusions to classical thought and mythology—and his theoretical writings show the impact of Fyodor DOSTOYEVSKY, Vladimir SOLOVYOV, Dante, Goethe and, above all, Friedrich NIETZSCHE, whose ideas, however, he developed and interpreted in his own independent way, seeing in the Hellenic religion of Dionysus, the suffering God, a premonition of Christianity. His famous theoretical work *Perepiska iz dvukh uglov* (1920; Correspondence between Two Corners) is important because it expounds his philosophy of creativity in civilization. In *Perepiska* he interpreted his own conception of the significance of the arts and culture in terms of the continuing effect of inborn memory, the Platonic *Mnemosyne*. Memory affirms being, while nonbeing is manifested in terms of forgetting and oblivion. The poet awakens, fructifies, and stimulates memory, thereby revealing glimpses of the meaning of existence. Culture itself is comprehended by the concept of the "thesaurus," the accumulated wisdom and spiritual achievement of fathers and ancestors, which, however, is progressively enriched by the continuing creative labor of the generations. Also essential to Ivanov's philosophic and religious view of man are his two volumes of poetry *Mladenchestvo* (1914; Infancy) and *Chelovek* (1939; Man), in which a realistic, not to say pessimistic, conception of human nature is overcome by the affirmation of a positively Christian humanism.

In 1926, Ivanov was received into the Roman Catholic Church, an act that he did not regard as a "conversion" but as a personal fulfillment of true ecumenicity. At his death he left a volume of poetry, greatly simplified in style as compared to his earlier verse, but profound and enriched by hard-won wisdom and deep insight; and an unfinished, long novel, a metaphysical and historiosophic allegory of the destinies of Russia, which he considered his chief work. The most recent Russian edition of Ivanov's work, ed. by O. Deschartes, is V. I. Ivanov, *Sobraniye sochineniy*, which the Foyer Oriental Chrétien began publishing in Brussels in 1971.

See: F. Stepun, *Mystische Weltschau* (1964); J. West, *Russian Symbolism: A Study of Vyacheslav Ivanov and the Russian Symbolist Aesthetic* (1970). H.A.S.

Ivask, Yury Pavlovich (1910–), Russian poet and critic, was born in Moscow. After the Russian Revolution (1917) his family emigrated to Estonia, where he studied law at the University of Tartu. Having fled to Germany during World War II, he immigrated to the United States in 1949 and embarked upon an academic career. He received a Ph.D. from Harvard in 1954 and was named professor of Russian literature at the University of Massachusetts in 1969. Ivask has published essays on Andrey BELY, Fyodor DOSTOYEVSKY, Osip MANDELSHTAM, Aleksandr Pushkin, and Marina TSVETAYEVA, among others. His monograph on Konstantin LEONTYEV appeared in *Vozrozhdeniye* in 1961–64. He also provided the introduction and notes to two volumes of Leontyev's works in English (1969) and has edited selections from the writings of G. P. Fedotov (1952) and Vasily ROZANOV (1956) and an anthology of Russian émigré poetry (1953).

Ivask's poetry is close to acmeism, featuring colorful images from a mythical landscape of Byzantine-Muscovite and Occidental culture, and echoes of world literature. His later poetry has displayed freer rhythms, surrealist imagery, and a Khlebnikov-like surrender to the mythmaking power of language. Ivask's verses are rich in inner rhymes and modulated sound patterns. His autobiographical poem "Homo ludens" (1973) is an odyssey of a poetic spirit. It is surely one of the most remarkable products of recent Russian poetry. Collections of his poems are *Severny bereg* (1938; Northern Shore), *Tsarskaya osen* (1953; Imperial Autumn), *Khvala* (1967; Praise), and *Zolushka* (1970; Cinderella). V.T.

Iwaszkiewicz, Jarosław, pseud. Eleuter (1894–1980), Polish poet, novelist, short-story writer, and playwright, was born in Kalnik near Kiev, studied law and music in Kiev,

and began writing and publishing poetry in 1915. In 1918 he moved to Warsaw, where he was one of the founders of the "Skamander" group of poets, in which he represents the most consistent line of development from buoyant spontaneous lyrics, free in form, nurtured by profound impressions of nature and strong, almost violent, passions and eroticism, up to more controlled reflective poems with philosophical motifs and formal refinement. His first important volumes were *Oktostychy* (1919; Octostichs) and especially *Dionizje* (1922; Dionysiacs), which was acclaimed as one of the most successful examples of expressionist poetry in Poland. In his later poems he described impressions from his frequent trips to Western Europe and pondered the opulence of nature, the meaning of art, and the inevitable transcience of life; these volumes include *Księga dnia i księga nocy* (1929; The Book of Day and the Book of Night), *Powrót do Europy* (1931; Return to Europe), *Lato* (1933; Summer), and *Inne życie* (1938; Another Life). Simultaneously with his poetry, he wrote short stories, novels, and plays (this simultaneity is a distinct feature of his writing). After his first attempts at writing poetic prose, Iwaszkiewicz wrote his first novels of an autobiographical nature, *Hilary, syn buchaltera* (1923; Hilary, The Bookkeeper's Son), and *Księżyc wschodzi* (1924; The Moon Rises). His short stories written in the 1930s—collected in *Panny z Wilka* (1933; Maidens from Wilko), and *Młyn nad Utrata* (1936; The Mill on the Utrata)—occupy a very significant place in the history of Polish prose. They deal with the passing of time, the awe of death, the tragedy of love, and the restless pursuit of the meaning of life. At the same time, he published a historical novel about the early Middle Ages, *Czerwone tarcze* (1934; Red Shields), which was innovative in the way it reconstructed the past and dealt with the modern problem of people versus history. The novel *Pasje błędomierskie* (1938; The Błędomierskie Passions) deals with the crisis of culture on the eve of World War II. After the war, Iwaszkiewicz published his next collections of short stories, *Stara cegielnia* (1946; The Old Brickyard); *Nowa miłość* (1946; The New Love), which included his famous short stories "Bitwa na równinie Sedgemoor" (Battle on the Plain of Sedgemoor) and "Matka Joanna od Aniołów" (Mother Joan of the Angels) and *Nowele włoskie* (1947; Italian Short Stories) as well as his extensive epic trilogy on the life of Polish society starting with World War I, *Sława i chwała* (1956–62; Fame and Glory), and new volumes of poetry. Iwaszkiewicz also published the plays *Kochankowie z Werony* (1927; Lovers from Verona) and *Lato w Nohant* (1936; Eng. tr., *Summer at Nohant*, 1942), essays about literature, music, travel, impressions and memoirs.

See: R. Przybylski, *Eros i Tanatos: proza Jarosława Iwaszkiewicza 1916–1938* (1970); A. Gronczewski, *Jarosław Iwaszkiewicz* (1972); J. Kwiatkowski, *Poezja Jarosława Iwaszkiewicza na tle dwudziestolecia międzywojennego* (1975); M. Jędrychowska, *Wczesna proza Jarosława Iwaszkiewicza* (1977). Z.F. and S.F.

J

Jacob, Max (1876–1944), French poet, novelist, and artist, was born of Jewish parents in Quimper and died in the Drancy concentration camp. After a brief stay at the Ecole Coloniale, he earned his living as a law clerk, a shop sweeper, a journalist, an art critic, and a piano teacher. Early in his career, his keen interest in art put him in contact with the struggling Pablo Picasso, with whom he later shared a room in the Bateau Lavoir on the

rue Ravignan in Paris. His neighbors and close friends then included such future celebrities as Juan Gris, Pierre MAC ORLAN, Guillaume APOLLINAIRE, André SALMON, and Pierre REVERDY who at the time (1902–06) were formulating the basis for cubism and Art Nouveau, two of the movements that undoubtedly would have the greatest influence on the aesthetics of the 20th century. Jacob's friendships and the publication of his now famous collection of poems, *Le Cornet à dés* (1917; The Dice-box), earned him, for lack of a better classification, the label of cubist poet. In his preface to *Le Cornet,* considered the manifesto of the prose poem, Jacob argued for a new idea of poetry, consciously breaking with the symbolist and postsymbolist tradition and stating that a poem must have "situation and style." The short prose pieces of the collection differed from earlier writings in the variety of the subjects they treated (nightmares and hallucinations mingled with everyday life), in their formal character (riddles, parodies and mystifications), and in their decisive, studied expression. Whether or not cubist poetry indeed existed, or whether Jacob's work deserved that title, there is no doubt that its new form, the disconcerting relationships it established, and its "delightful whimsy" played a fundamental role in the development of modern French poetry. The younger poets continually cited it, and until his death, Jacob avidly corresponded with these writers.

The event that marked Jacob's life most decisively and that probably contributed to his reputation as a clown was his conversion to a devout, yet burlesque, Catholicism. This act followed his visions of Christ, first in his room (1909) and later in a movie house (1914). Finally, in 1915, with Picasso as his godfather, he was baptized into a church that looked upon his conversion with suspicion. In 1921, withdrawing for the first time from his debauched Parisian life, he settled in the Abbey of Saint-Benoît-sur-Loire. He returned to Paris in 1928 only to recommit himself once again in 1936 to a life of seclusion, then supporting himself by the sale of his gouaches and drawings.

From his first publication, the children's story *Histoire du roi Kaboul Ier et du marmiton Gauwain* (1903; The Story of King Kaboul the First and his Kitchen-Helper Gauwain), to his *Méditations religieuses* (1947), Jacob's work is best characterized by its liberation from reality, its mystifying intentions, and its linguistic inventions. Moreover, Jacob repeatedly varied the form of his expression: he wrote prose poems, collections of which were posthumously published as *Le Cornet à dés II* (1955) and *Derniers poèmes en vers et en prose* (1945; Last Poems in Verse and Prose); verse poems, published in *Le Laboratoire central* (1921; The Central Laboratory), *Les Pénitents en maillots roses* (1925; The Penitents in Pink Jerseys), *Fond de l'eau* (1927; Bottom of the Water), *Rivage* (1931; Coast), *Ballades* (1938), and *Poèmes de Morven le Gaëlique* (1953; a pseudonym he took when he "thought in Breton"); the short stories of *Saint-Matorel* (1911), *Cinématoma* (1920), *Le Roi de Béotie* (1921; The King of Beotia), *Le Cabinet noir* (1922; The Black Cabinet), and *La Couronne de Vulcain* (1923; Vulcan's Crown); and the novels *Le Phanérogame* (1918), *Filibuth ou la montre en or* (1922; Filibuth or the Golden Watch), *Le Terrain Bouchaballe* (1923; The Bouchaballe Field), and *L'Homme de chair et l'homme reflet* (1924; The Man of Skin and the Man of Reflection). He also wrote religious texts, such as *La Défense de Tartufe* (1919), which relates his conversion through verse and prose poems, meditations, and quasi-philosophical texts, *Visions infernales* (1924), and *Sacrifice impérial* (1929) as well as what he called "fantaisies," dialogues intended to be read and not performed such as *Dos d'Arlequin* (1922; Arlequin's Back). Finally, Jacob's miscellaneous writings include the critical works *Art poétique* (1922) and *Conseils à un jeune poète suivi de Conseils à un étudiant* (1945; Advice to a Young Poet Followed by Advice to a Student), as well as a *Tableau de la bourgeoisie* (1930) and *Miroir d'astrologie* (1949), an astrological treatise written with Claude Valence (Conrad Moricand).

Although the variety of Jacob's literary production and his multi-faceted personality have often relegated his work to a marginal position in the literary trends of the 20th century, his writing is now considered to hold a pivotal, experimental place in the modern conception of the text.

See: G. Kamber, *Max Jacob and the Poetics of Cubism* (1971); R. Plantier, *L'Univers poétique de Max Jacob* (1976); A. Thau, *Poetry and Antipoetry: A Study of Selected Aspects of Max Jacob's Style* (1976); J. M. Schneider, *Clown at the Altar: The Religious Poetry of Max Jacob* (1978). S.Lé.

Jacobsen, Jens Peter (1847–85), Danish author, was born in the Jutland town of Thisted. After studying natural science, he translated Charles Darwin's theories of evolution, which definitely influenced his writing—in all of Jacobsen's works man is scientifically analyzed as a creature of instincts. Having studied the German critics of the Bible, David Friedrich Strauss and Ludwig Feuerbach, he turned to atheism. Jacobsen was by nature a dreamer, and the increasing struggle between dream and reality became a principal motif as early as in his first immature poems. These were not published until 1886, together with his remaining poetry, as *Digte og Udkast* (Poems and Sketches). Jacobsen's poetry reached its culmination in the cycle "Gurresange" (The Songs of Gurre) and in his arabesques, a series of free images of a penetrating spiritual content shrouded in ornamental language and illuminated by sense impressions and colors. He joined the coterie around Georg BRANDES with the first naturalistic work in Danish literature, "Mogens" (1872), the story of a young fantast's maturing to a final acceptance of reality by way of doubts and misfortunes (*see* DANISH LITERATURE).

During a journey to Italy in 1873, Jacobsen was discovered to be suffering from incurable tuberculosis, which placed the perspective of death upon his later writing. This is not the case, however, in the naturalistic novel *Fru Marie Grubbe* (1876; Eng. tr., *Marie Grubbe,* 1917) in which the dominating motif is eroticism. Marie's fate is determined by her instincts, childhood, and environment, portrayed with a delicacy obviously influenced by Gustave Flaubert's novel *Madame Bovary.* The book is also a historical novel with minutely depicted "scenes from the 17th century" (its subtitle) described in splendidly evocative and colorful language. *Niels Lyhne* (1880; Eng. tr., 1919), on the other hand, is a contemporary novel. It is both a Bildungsroman about dreamers unable to cope with life and a problem novel about emotional atheists unable to accept rational atheism. Lastly, it is a book about death. In both *Marie Grubbe* and *Niels Lyhne,* a lyrical atmosphere gradually takes the place of cold analysis, a method not suitable for detailed naturalism. Jacobsen's personal farewell to life is expressed in the splendid short story "Fru Fønss" (Mrs. Fønss), published with three other stories as part of *Mogens og andre Noveller* (1882; Eng. tr., *Mogens and Other Stories,* 1921, 1972), reiterating the same themes as the novels.

His psychological portraits are evidence that Jacobsen had learned much from French literature (Stendhal and Flaubert), where his discreet understanding of the human being is related to the Russian novelist Ivan Turgenev. To his refined psychology corresponds his exquisite style, occasionally artificial and overloaded, influenced by the prose of Søren KIERKEGAARD and Hans Christian Andersen.

See: A. Gustafson, *Six Scandinavian Novelists* (1940); F. Nielsen, *Jens Peter Jacobsen* (1953); N. L. Jensen, *Jens Peter Jacobsen, TWAS* (1978). S.H.R.

Jacobsen, Rolf (1907–), Norwegian poet, was born in Oslo where he lived until the age of six. He has lived most of his adult life in the island city of Hamar, working as editor and journalist on the local newspaper. Even in his first two collections, Jacobsen distinguished himself from his colleagues in Norwegian poetry. The individualism, nationalism, social criticism, and regular verse meter of other poets had little influence on Jacobsen's unrhymed poems about life in the machine age. Although the conflict of nature versus human civilization was already a central theme in the work of Knut HAMSUN and other writers of the 1890s, Jacobsen is more ambivalent than they, being at once frightened and curiously fascinated by the products of man's technical ingenuity.

After World War II, Jacobsen's poetry developed along two lines, one polemical, with poems ridiculing and warning against the excesses of modern technocracy, and one in which he praises old-fashioned virtues—humility, the blessings of little joys. In this second group of poems, Jacobsen had developed a technique that recalls Hans Christian Andersen's mixture of irony and sentimentality. Of all Norwegian poets, Ivar Aasen (*see* NORWEGIAN LITERATURE) is perhaps closest to Jacobsen's heart, and between the other Scandinavian literatures he has more in common with the light-hearted Danes than with the more heavily symbolic Swedes, but of all poets the American Carl Sandburg has been the single strongest influence in his writing. His verse is characterized by a low-keyed charm that blends humor and humility. Sometimes a religious note appears, giving his poems a hymnlike simplicity that often masks the fastidious craftsman. Although almost entirely outside the general Norwegian tradition of nationalistic and socially engagé poetry, Jacobsen is a poet committed to warning his countrymen that Norway—Europe's last wilderness area—should be kept the way it is. Since this message cuts across party lines, Jacobsen is today one of the most respected Norwegian poets, while at the same time he is finally achieving recognition as the first poet in 20th-century Norwegian literature to adopt the principles of modern verse. His books include *Jord og jern* (1933; Earth and Iron), *Vrimmel* (1935; Myriads), *Fjerntog* (1951; Long-Distance Trains), *Hemmelig liv* (1954; Secret Life), *Sommeren i gresset* (1956; Summer in the Grass), *Brev til lyset* (1960; A Letter to Light), *Stillheten efterpå* (1965; The Silence Afterwards), *Headlines* (1969), *Pass for dørene lukkes* (1972; Beware of the Closing Doors), *Pusteøvelser* (1975; Breathing Exercises), and *Tenk på noe annet* (1979; Think of Something Else).   H.S.N.

Jæger, Frank (1926–77), Danish poet, short-story writer, and essayist, was born in Frederiksberg, near Copenhagen. After obtaining a library degree in 1950, he became a free-lance writer and translator. His first poetry collections, *Dydige Digte* (1948; Virtuous Poems) and *Morgenens Trompet* (1949; The Morning's Trumpet), reveal him as a naive hedonist who has turned his back on bourgeois life and all ideological controversies. Poems that demonstrate Jæger's isolation and impotence as an artist are found in these and all later collections—joy of life is transformed into angst and renunciation. The poet's early easy-flowing, improvised form is abandoned in the more tightly structured volumes *Havkarlens Sange* (1956; Songs of the Merman) and *Cinna* (1959). A growing desperation becomes conspicuous, particularly in the increasingly predominant erotic poetry about love that never is realized, a pessimistic development that culminates in a volume with the ironic title *Idylia* (1967). The poet's crisis in his relationship with love and art and in the tension between idyl and the demonic recurs in the

short stories of *Den unge Jægers Lidelser* (1953; The Sufferings of the Young Jæger) and *Danskere* (1960; Danes). The imaginative element grows to unbridled visionary delusions in *Hverdagshistorier* (1951; Everyday Stories), whereas in *Kapellanen og andre Fortællinger* (1957; The Chaplain and Other Stories) and the historical novella *S.* (1973) Jæger emerges as an outstanding realistic and psychological narrator. More philosophical are the seven stories in *Provinser* (1972; Provinces), the title of which indicates not only a geographical location but also loneliness and isolation. In addition, the collection is a defense of the independent, spontaneous artist, rebelling against the political demands that are placed upon today's author—a problem that Jæger also deals with in his final work, the essay and short-story collection *Udsigt til Kronborg* (1976; View toward Kronborg).

See: F. Hugus, "The Dilemma of the Artist," *SS* 47 (1975): 52–65; B. Brovst Nielsen, *Frank Jæger's forfatterskab* (1977).   S.H.R.

Jahnn, Hans Henny (1894–1959), German novelist, playwright, essayist, and organ builder, was born in Stellingen, near Hamburg, the youngest son of a ship's carpenter. In 1919, Jahnn published his drama *Pastor Ephraim Magnus,* and a year later Oscar Loerke awarded it the coveted Kleist Prize. The storm of controversy that followed has continued unabated, for while Jahnn was undeniably one of Germany's most gifted writers, he was also one of its most bizarre. His almost obsessive preoccupation with sexuality and death, which he mythified and mystified in his major works, calls to mind the worlds of the Marquis De Sade, Joris Karl HUYSMANS, Edgar Allan Poe, H. P. Lovecraft, Hieronymus Bosch, Franz KAFKA, and Isak DINESEN. Jahnn's first published novel, *Perrudja* (1929), was greatly influenced by Joyce's *Ulysses;* nevertheless, his writings are unique, and his style is unmistakably his own.

During World War I, Jahnn, who was a pacifist, went into exile in Norway, accompanied by his friend Gottlieb Harms. The rugged Scandinavian landscape served as the setting for a number of his later works. While in exile, Jahnn wrote dramas and novel fragments. In these the religious fervor of his childhood was replaced by an intense, indignant resentment against what he called the *Schöpfungsprinzip,* the force that, in his view, controlled human destiny—a blind, cold, mechanically creative force, heedless of individual suffering, that produced a never-ending cycle of birth and death, creation and dissolution. In the 1930s, Jahnn was to see his Weltanschauung paralleled in the cosmological-harmonic theories of Hans Kayser.

In 1920, one year after his return to Germany, Jahnn formally left the Lutheran Church and founded the "Glaubensgemeinde Ugrino." This was not a religious sect but rather a cultural organization devoted to furthering Jahnn's own projects: the publication of baroque music, the study of ancient Egyptian and Babylonian—as well as Romanesque—architecture, and the restoration of baroque organs.

In 1923, under the auspices of Ugrino, Jahnn and Harms began to restore the Arp-Schitgar organ in Hamburg's Saint Jakobi Church and thus launched organ reform in Germany. In all Jahnn constructed and restored over 100 organs throughout Europe.

Jahnn married Ellinor Philips in 1926, and three years later their daughter Signe was born. Harms married Ellinor's half-sister Sibylle, and the couples formed a single household. For Jahnn the 1920s was a period of literary creativity and critical recognition. Several of his dramas were produced: *Die Krönung Richards III* (The Coronation of Richard the Third) in 1922; *Pastor Ephraim Magnus,* directed by Brecht and Bronnen, in 1923; and *Medea,* perhaps his greatest drama, in 1926. In 1929 *Perrudja* was published, and Jahnn was elected president of the newly formed "Kartell Hamburger Künstlerverbände." He also headed the experimental division of the German Organ Council and was the organ consultant for the city of Hamburg. When the Nazis came to power, he was removed from these posts and went to Switzerland, where he was supported by the Germanist Walter Muschg. In 1933 Jahnn completed the first draft of his important drama, *Armut, Reichtum, Mensch und Tier* (Poverty, Riches, Man, and Animal), which was not published and performed until 1948.

In 1933, Harms died. Jahnn never entirely overcame his grief, and the colossal, unfinished 2,000-page novel trilogy, *Fluß ohne Ufer* (1949–50, 1962; River without End), is his tribute to their friendship. In 1934 Jahnn exiled himself to the Danish island of Bornholm. There he lived on a farm with his mistress, the young Hungarian Jewish refugee Jüdit Müller-Touraine, his wife and daughter, and Harms' widow and son. Besides managing the farm and writing *Fluß ohne Ufer,* he worked for the Copenhagen organ-building firm Frobenius and began hormone experiments using animals. At the end of World War II the farm was confiscated by Denmark, which considered Jahnn a German citizen. In 1950, after making extended visits to Germany, Jahnn settled again in Hamburg. There he devoted himself to cultivating the musical talents of his godson Yngve Jan Trede, whom he had taken into his family after the child's father died.

Jahnn was elected to the Academy of Sciences and Literature in Mainz in 1954 and became increasingly involved in its activities. He was also the cofounder of the Hamburg Free Academy of Arts in 1950 and served as its first president until his death. In 1955 he became a corresponding member of the German Academy of Arts in East Berlin and even visited Russia. The Literary Prize of Lower Saxony was awarded him in 1954, and in 1955 he received the Lessing Prize from the city of Hamburg. A year later Gustav-Gründgens directed his drama *Thomas Chatterton,* which is perhaps the best-suited for performance of all his plays. Despite critical recognition, his works did not win popular acclaim, and he spent his last years disillusioned, misunderstood, and ignored, occupying himself with writing polemics denouncing atomic war.

See: W. Muschg, "Hans Henny Jahnn," in *Von Trakl zu Brecht: Dichter des Expressionismus* (1961); J. Meyer, *Verzeichnis der Schriften von und über Hans Henny Jahnn* (1967); H. Mayer, "Versuch über Hans Henny Jahnn," in T. Freeman and T. Scheuffelen, eds., *Hans Henny Jahnn: Werke und Tagebücher* (1974), pp. 5–49.

T.P.F.

Jakobsson, Jökull (1933–), Icelandic novelist, essayist, dramatist, and poet, was born in Nordfjörður, in eastern central Iceland, where his father was a clergyman. As a young boy he accompanied his parents to Canada, but the family returned to Iceland in 1940, and Jakobsson has since then lived in or around the capital. He matriculated in Reykjavik in 1953, then attended universities in Vienna, London, and Reykjavik. While a young man, he worked at a variety of jobs, for the longest time as a newspaperman.

His first novel was *Tæmdur bikar* (1951; Emptied Cup), and he has since written four others, besides a collection of short stories. An important theme in his fiction concerns the growing up of young people who are in rebellion against their families or the community at large. The au-

thor's treatment is generally a romantic one, evincing a longing for the pure and uncorrupt—qualities he normally represents in the guise of country folk. Jakobsson has also published a number of travelogues, notably on Greece and the Westman Islands. It is, however, as a playwright that he is best known, and he is without doubt Iceland's foremost living dramatist.

His first play, *Pókók,* was staged by the Reykjavik Theater Company in 1961, and he has since then been a prolific writer of dramas, for the stage as well as for radio and television. In form, his plays are realistic, almost of the type *pièce bien fait;* and such literary influences have been suggested as Anton CHEKHOV and Harold Pinter. In his dramas, Jakobsson typically portrays ordinary people in everyday situations. Instead of using spectacular theatrical effects, he makes his point emphatically through a low-key comical tone. Indeed, a sense of humor is among his key traits as a writer.

In the plays *Hart í bak* (1962; Hard to Portside) and *Sjóleiðin til Bagdad* (1965; Eng. tr., *The Seaway to Baghdad,* 1973), he deals with the lives of common Reykjavik residents of today, and in both plays he places his hope in characters living outside the hurry and competition of the modern world. These two plays, as well as most of Jakobsson's subsequent dramas, focus on persons in search of a dream world—a pursuit always doomed to failure—so that the characters must sadly reconcile themselves to the depressing reality of the actual world. In *Dómínó* (1972), the portrayal of a bourgeois family at times approaches the absurd. In *Kertalog* (1974; Candle Flame), the protagonists are two young people bent on creating for themselves a world free from the status symbols of the acquisitive society, but they fail in this.

All of Jakobsson's longer plays describe opposite states of being, often in conjunction with arrivals and departures. Old friends meet, or people are about to establish relationships; others reminisce about their past or dream about the future while still living in the present as they must. By and large, such dramatic characters are recurring types: rebellious youths, oldsters thinking about the past, men dissatisfied with their role in life and hoping for a new chance, innocent girls with vague dreams about the future, society ladies unhappy in their vanity, the visitor who comes or goes. In all of his major works, Jakobsson creates tension between two poles: past and present, dream and reality, living in the actual world while longing for something that a romantic dream has conjured up.

See: S. A. Magnússon, Introduction to *Modern Nordic Plays,* Scandia Books no. 14 (1973), pp. 7–20.   S.S.H.

Jaloux, Edmond (1878–1949), French literary critic, novelist, short-story writer, essayist, and poet, was born in Marseille. He launched his literary career with a collection of poems in the postsymbolist style entitled *Une Ame d'automne* (1896; An Autumn Soul). His poetry instantly won warm praise from the young André GIDE and from the renowned poet Stéphane MALLARMÉ. Jaloux's fame as a gifted writer spread throughout the Marseille–Aix-en-Provence region until he soon found himself the leader of a small provincial literary school. This circle was occasionally frequented by persons who would later become well-known writers, such as Francis de Miomandre, Jean-Louis Vaudoyer, Stuart MERRILL, and Henri de RÉGNIER, as well as by literary aspirants from the immediate community.

It was not as a poet, however, but rather as a literary critic and as a writer of prose fiction that Jaloux excelled. His first article of pure literary criticism, devoted to Gide's *Les Nourritures terrestres,* appeared in the Marseille newspaper *L'Indépendance républicaine* in 1897.

This was the first major essay to praise the literary genius of Gide and to predict for this future Nobel Prize winner the world acclaim he later received. Out of this article there developed a lifelong literary and personal friendship between the two writers.

Jaloux served as the rallying point for literary life in Marseille from 1893 until 1903. But it soon became evident to him that to succeed as a man of letters in France, he needed to move to Paris, where all of the principal publishers were centered. Upon his arrival in the capital in 1903, Jaloux spent several months as a guest in Gide's home. The poet Stuart Merrill arranged for him to collaborate with the symbolist review *L'Ermitage*. As Jaloux's literary reputation grew, he was invited to contribute articles on a regular basis to the newspaper *Le Gaulois* (1912–22) and to *L'Opinion* (1912–22). The Parisian literary public began to take him seriously when his early novel, *Le Reste est silence* (1909; The Rest Is Silence) won him the coveted Prix Fémina–Vie Heureuse. Despite the fact that he subsequently wrote more than 40 novels and 5 volumes of short fiction, Jaloux never surpassed his first novel from the standpoint of narrative excellence and of penetrating psychological analysis of characters.

Committed to the novel as a literary genre, Jaloux published approximately one novel every year or two during his productive life. In addition to *Le Reste est silence,* other especially noteworthy novels include *L'Incertaine* (1918; The Uncertain Woman), *Fumées dans la campagne* (1918; Smoke in the Countryside), *La Fin d'un beau jour* (1921; The End of a Fine Day), and *Le Pouvoir des choses* (1941; The Power of Things). The American scholar Marthe Rosenfeld divides Jaloux's novels into three distinctive categories: his realistic and regional novels, his novels of poetic imagination and psychological experimentation, and his novels of mystical and symbolic experience.

Jaloux's most fertile period coincided with his tenure, from 1922 until 1940, as the principal literary critic of the prestigious and powerful weekly newspaper *Les Nouvelles littéraires*. His column, "L'Esprit des livres" (The Spirit of Books), which was read avidly by tens of thousands of readers, may well have made of him the most powerful literary critic in France for almost two decades. The author of literally thousands of articles and prefaces, he published frequently in such highly regarded daily newspapers as *Le Temps* (1930–40), *L'Eclair* (1919–23), and *Le Jour* (on and off during the 1930s). Dozens of his more substantial articles appeared in volume form. Noteworthy are *L'Esprit des livres: série I* (1923), *De Pascal à Barrès: L'Esprit des livres: série II* (1927), and *Perspectives et personnages: L'Esprit des livres: série III* (1931). His criticism dealing with foreign writers is collected in *Au pays du roman* (1931; In the Land of the Novel), which deals mainly with English fiction; *Du Rêve à la réalité* (1932; From Dream to Reality), concerning German literature; and *Figures étrangères* (1925; Foreign Faces). Jaloux's most significant critical monographs on individual writers are: *Avec Marcel Proust* (1953; With Marcel Proust), *Edgar Poe et les femmes* (1943; Edgar Poe and Women), *Goethe* (1949), *Souvenirs sur Henri de Régnier* (1941; Memories of Henri de Régnier), and two volumes dealing with the German poet Rainer Maria RILKE: *Rainer Maria Rilke* (1927) and *La Dernière Amitié de Rainer Maria Rilke* (1939; The Last Friendship of Rainer Maria Rilke).

In 1936, Jaloux was elected to the Académie Française, occupying the seat left vacant by the recent death of his close friend Paul BOURGET. Jaloux fled the German invasion of France in 1940 and spent the entire period of the Nazi occupation in exile in or near Lausanne, Switzerland. It is there that he wrote some of his finest, most mature pages of criticism and literary history. His two-volume *Introduction à l'histoire de la littérature française* (1946, 1948; Introduction to the History of French Literature) covers the Medieval and Renaissance periods from the point of view of a critic thoroughly schooled in the most contemporary and boldly innovative literary currents of the first half of the 20th century. In *Les Saisons littéraires* (vol. 1, 1942; vol. 2, 1950; Literary Seasons), Jaloux masterfully recounts both his earliest years of apprenticeship in southern France and the exploits of the writers who shared his own generation of experiences with him. *Essences* (1952), a posthumous anthology of maxims and aphorisms, must be regarded as his fullest and finest statement of personal philosophy.

Jaloux died of a massive coronary attack in Lausanne on Aug. 22, 1949, and is buried in the municipal cemetery there. His widow, Germaine, who had worked closely with him during the greatest part of his professional life, published posthumously what may possibly be his finest anthology of literary criticism, *Visages français* (1954; French Faces).

Jaloux should be regarded as a transitional novelist, one who spanned the gap between the postsymbolist novels of the turn of the century and the experimental novels of the 1930s and 1940s. As a critic, he produced work that assumed three directions. First, he played a decisive role in the discovery of such new talent as Gide, Proust, Paul VALÉRY, Julien GREEN, André BRETON, the surrealists (*see* FRENCH LITERATURE), François MAURIAC, and Jean-Paul SARTRE. Secondly, he was probably the most courageous defender of non-French writers in France and is credited with winning wide acceptance among his generally nationalistic compatriots for such German authors as his close friend Rilke, Thomas MANN, and Hugo von HOFMANNSTHAL, and for such English-language authors as James Joyce, Virginia Woolf, Katherine Mansfield, Maurice Baring, and Aldous Huxley. Thirdly, Jaloux helped restore French interest in the romantic movement and in all other literary movements that served as an antidote for what he regarded as the excessive propensity of the French people for rational, realistic, and unimaginative literature. He passionately maintained that literary criticism was as creative a genre as the novel or the poem.

See: Y. Deletang-Tardif, *Edmond Jaloux* (1947); J.-L. Vaudoyer, *Discours prononcés dans la séance publique tenue par l'Académie française* (1950); J. Kolbert, *Edmond Jaloux: critique littéraire* (1962); M. Rosenfeld, *Edmond Jaloux: The Evolution of a Novelist* (1972).   J.K.

Jammes, Francis (1868–1938), French poet and novelist, was born in Tournay (Hautes-Pyrénées). He was educated at the lycées of Pau and Bordeaux, where he developed an interest in botany and entomology. His formal education completed, Jammes moved to Orthez where he was to spend most of his life. His first collections of verse, *Six Sonnets* (1891) and *Vers* (1892–94), revealed an engaging manner and simple feelings, winning for him the approbation of Stéphane MALLARMÉ and André GIDE, the latter of whom befriended him for almost 20 years. But the work that won Jammes public attention in Paris was *De l'Angélus de l'aube à l'angélus du soir* (1898; From the Morning Angelus-Bell to the Evening Angelus-Bell), a collection of descriptive and nostalgic poems. The work's prefatory manifesto denounced the defective naturism (a virtual adoration of the forces of nature) of Saint-Georges de Bouhélier. "Jammisme," the return to God and to nature that he advocated, is, ironically, perhaps best expressed in his verse up to 1898, prior to his conversion to Catholicism.

The poems collected in *Clairières dans le ciel* (1906; Clearings in the Heavens), the *Géorgiques chrétiennes* (1911–12; Christian Georgics), and the four *Livres des quatrains* (1923–25; Books of Quatrains) reveal a marked evolution in Jammes's manner from the almost paganly sensual atmosphere of his earlier verse to a virtually unrelieved, religiously inspired fervor. All of his writing dating from his return to the Catholic faith in 1905 (under the influence of Paul CLAUDEL) displays a conscious attempt to fuse rustic decor with an unmistakable Christian inspiration. The *Géorgiques chrétiennes* suggests a sprawling epic in which the French countryside provides the backdrop for the dialogue that takes place between the poet and nature in the presence of a personal and paternalistic God. Yet despite the essentially Christian character of his verse collections, Jammes emerges, by and large, as a regionalist poet, ostensibly divorced from all significant literary influence, who celebrates the peasant simplicity of his native Béarn in direct, unassuming language. His simple verse forms (the alexandrine flexibly used, sometimes unevenly with 11, 13, or even 14 syllables) and his almost childlike tone, separated him, finally, from all preceding schools of poetry.

Notable among his prose works are *Clara d'Ellébeuse* (1899) and *Almaïde d'Etremont* (1901), delicately woven tales of exquisite young country ladies. *Le Roman du lièvre* (1903; The Novel of the Hare), which enjoyed wide popularity, relates the story of a rabbit languishing in the boredom of heaven and recalling his more adventurous terrestrial experiences. *Monsieur le curé d'Ozéron* (1918) is an undistinguished novel of provincial clerical life. Jammes's *Mémoires* (1922–23) recall in considerable detail his personal ideas on poetry and his very pronounced concern with religion. He considered himself the inspired poet par excellence, and he once confided to Gide that he felt he had no right to tamper with a verse after it had been written. Such a method of composition naturally begets blemishes; naiveté becomes coquetry and simplicity turns to artifice. Completely enveloped in his self-imposed pastoral world, he often becomes monotonous, and his irony, devoid of humor, is heavy-handed. His *Antigyde* (1932), for example, an attempted satire on Gide's so-called immoral influence, is a case in point.

See: R. M. Dyson, *Les Sensations et la sensibilité chez Francis Jammes* (1954); M. Parent, *Francis Jammes: étude de langue et de style* (1957) and *Rythme et versification dans la poésie de Francis Jammes*, 2 vols. (1957); R. Mallet, *Francis Jammes: sa vie et son œuvre* (1961).

J.Me. rev. R.T.D.

Jandl, Ernst (1925–), Austrian poet and playwright, was born in Vienna. After military service in World War II he studied German and English literature at the University of Vienna, taking a doctorate and then becoming a secondary school teacher for many years. A prolific and inventive writer, member of the group of experimental poets in Vienna and later of the group in Graz, Jandl is a proponent not only of concrete poetry but also of poems that he describes as visual, linguistic, and oral. His experimental writing has had a profound effect on modern German poetry, not only in Austria but throughout the German-speaking countries. A superb performer, Jandl has recorded selections of his own writings in a montage radio play entitled "Das Röcheln der Mona Lisa" (1970; The Death Rattle of Mona Lisa).

With his long-time friend Friederike Mayröcker Jandl wrote the radio play "Fünf Mann Menschen" (1971; A Crew of Five), which won the prize of the German War Blind in 1968. He has translated English poetry into German, such as Robert Creeley's *The Island* (1965), John

Cage's *Silence* (1969), and Gertrude Stein's *Narration* (1971).

Jandl is the author of over 20 books of poetry, some illustrated by his own scurrilous, scrawny drawings. Basically a misanthropic man, Jandl fills his work with scornful skepticism mixed with effervescent linguistic invention, even in his earliest book of poems *Andere Augen* (1956; Other Eyes). Other volumes of poetry include *lange gedichte* (1964; long poems), *klare gerührt* (1964; beaten eggwhites), selected poems in *Laut und Luise* (1966; Sound and Luise), *Sprechblasen* (1968; Speech Bubbles), *Der künstliche Baum* (1970; The Artificial Tree), *Dingfest* (1973; Confirmed by Law), *für alle* (1974; for everyone), *der versteckte hirte* (1975; the hidden shepherd), and *Die Bearbeitung der Mütze* (1978; Hat Manipulation). What he calls "theoretical forays" are collected in the volume of essays, *Die schöne Kunst des Schreibens* (1976; The Fine Art of Writing). Jandl's perceptive ear for language and his playfulness mask a deep concern for meaning and for the potential that lies in language. He combines scorn and delight to produce linguistic concoctions that startle, scathe, titillate, and amuse readers and listeners. Selected works are in English translation in *No Music, Please* (1967).

A.L.W.

Janevski, Slavko (1920–), Macedonian poet and novelist, was born in Skopje. He was a political commissar during World War II and an editor of the Macedonian literary review *Nov Don*. He is a member of the Macedonian Academy of Arts and Sciences.

Janevski made an important contribution to the so-called *poésie engagée* in his early collections of poetry published immediately after World War II, notably *Krvava niza* (1945; Bloody Row), *Pruga na mladosta* (1946; The Tract of Youth), *Pesni* (1948; Poems), *Egejska barutna bajka* (1950; Aegean Gunpowder Tale), *Lirika* (1950), as well as in *Evangelie po Itar Pejo* (1966; Gospel Told by Witty Pejo). His sensitivity to the vicissitudes of man's inner life is revealed in such lyrical works as *Leb i kamen* (1957; Bread and Stone) and *Kainavelija* (1968). Janevski is also a prolific writer of fiction and the author of the first Macedonian novel, *Selo zad sedumte jaseni* (1952; The Village beyond the Seven Ash Trees).

The main theme of Janevski's work is the life of contemporary Macedonia, including the World War II years. He depicts Partisan fighters, the people and atmosphere of the occupied city, the postwar collectivization of villages, and the successes and dilemmas of modern urban life. But he also turns to the more distant past, revealing the perseverance and courage with which the people of this part of the world have managed to survive through the centuries. Janevski is much inclined in his novels to explore psychological problems. In so doing, he constantly makes use of modern narrative techniques. Both his poetry and prose are distinguished by a metaphorical expressiveness and power.

Janevski is also an essayist, a writer of travelogues and screenplays, and a painter. In addition, he has translated the works of several Yugoslav and Russian poets into Macedonian.

See: B. Koneski, *Makedonska književnost* (Belgrade, 1961) and *The Macedonian Novel* (Skopje, 1971).

A.Sp.

Jans, Adrien (1905–73), Belgian poet and essayist, was born in Edeghem. After studies in law and Thomistic philosophy at the University of Louvain, he decided to devote himself to writing. Three of his volumes of poems are particularly noteworthy: *La Colonne ardente* (1954; The Blazing Column), *D'Arrache-cœur* (1960; Fullheartedly), and *La Tunique de Dieu* (1964; The Cloak of God). Written in free verse as well as in more formal frameworks, these poems reflect both a keen aesthetic sense and a deep longing for harmony. Above all, Jans expresses in his poetry the spiritual values that render him akin to a Charles PÉGUY or a Paul CLAUDEL. In *Le Manant* (1953; The Peasant), Jans's religious inspiration gave way to a celebration of the hills of Ardennes. As an essayist, he produced forceful critical essays on such diverse figures as Erasmus, Louise Labé, Jacques RIVIÈRE, Paul Claudel, and Michel de GHELDERODE. A member of the Royal Academy of French Language and Literature of Belgium, he played an active role in the literary and cultural life of his compatriots. His regular contribution to the weekly literary page of the Brussels daily, *Le Soir*, provided an accurate and sophisticated overview of Belgian literature in French during the second half of the 20th century.   G.Si.

Jardiel Poncela, Enrique (1901–52), Spanish playwright, novelist, and script writer, was born in Madrid. Although he had intended to revolutionize the literary world with his unconventional approach to humor, his career suffered so greatly from the gap between his own artistic intentions and the negative judgments of his detractors that most of the sweeping changes he had determined to introduce miscarried. Straining hard on the side of extravagance, Jardiel enriched the theater with his absurdist experimentations, although he failed to exercise a similar influence on the humorous novel of his time.

Jardiel repudiated most of his early work, including 5 novels and 64 plays. His merit as an innovative humorist lies in the 4 major works of fiction, 30 short novels, and 26 full-length plays that escaped the wrath of his self-excoriation. Such comedies as *Eloísa está debajo de un almendro* (1940; Heloise Lies under an Almond Tree) and *Blanca por fuera y Rosa por dentro* (1943; Blanca on the Outside and Rosa Within) consecrated his reputation as a master of sophisticated technical construction, hilarious repartee, and bizarre humor. Many of his inferior works nevertheless abound with too much frivolous nonsense and mawkish slapstick to be taken seriously.

Jardiel's creative genius was all too frequently arrested by his predilection for superficiality. His inventiveness was crippled by unrestraint and his peace of mind ravaged by despair and paranoia. Nevertheless, his energy and idealism injected vigor into the Spanish theater of the 1930s and 1940s, inspiring an entire generation of dramatists to write with a newfound freedom of ideas and expression.

Among Jardiel's published works of fiction, his best novel is *La 'tournée' de Dios* (1932; The Tour of God), a bittersweet burlesque on human folly. He also wrote film scripts for more than 15 movies, which he helped direct in Spain, Argentina, and the United States.

See: D. R. McKay, *Enrique Jardiel Poncela* (1974).
D.R.McK.

Jarnés Millán, Benjamín (1888–1949), Spanish novelist, essayist, and translator, was born in Codo, attended the Pontifical University and studied for the priesthood, leaving the seminary in 1908 before being ordained. Between 1910 and 1919 he married and served in the army. By 1923 he had begun publishing short stories in literary magazines. He joined the editorial board of José ORTEGA Y GASSET's *Revista de Occidente*, which in 1925 published his first novel, *El profesor inútil* (The Useless Professor), launching his literary career. In the ensuing ten years, Jarnés published seven novels, five biographies— among them studies of Thomás de Zumalacárregui (1931),

Emilio Castelar (1935), and Gustavo A. BÉCQUER (1936)— seven collections of essays—two of which, *Ejercicios* (1927; Exercises) and *Rúbricas* (1931; Flourishes), deal with problems of literary style—and eight translations, including the *Song of Roland* (1926), Ben Jonson's *Volpone* (1929), and Erich Maria Remarque's *All Quiet on the Western Front* (1929). In the upheaval of the Spanish Civil War (1936–39), Jarnés served the Republic in the army medical corps until 1939, when he fled first to France and then to Mexico. In addition to teaching occasionally at the National University in Mexico City, he wrote frequently for *Romance* and *España peregrina*, magazines founded by fellow Spanish exiles in Mexico, and edited two anthologies of works by Miguel de UNAMUNO as well as an *Enciclopedia de la literatura* (1947). In the 10 years before his death, Jarnés published two novels, biographies of Manuel Acuña, Stefan ZWEIG (both in 1942), Cervantes (1944), and two more collections of essays: *Cartas al Ebro* (1940; Letters to the Ebro), concerning the art and literature of the Generation of 1927, and *Ariel disperso* (1946; Ariel in Flight), studies of Spanish-American authors. In 1948, his health failing, he returned to Spain, where he died the following year.

Because of their emphasis on poetic style, their lack of attention to plot, and their seeming disinterest in realist techniques, Jarnés's novels exemplify some of Ortega's thinking in *La deshumanización del arte* (1925). Like other members of the Generation of 1927, Jarnés placed the highest value on innovation, creativity, and stylistic grace in his attempt to renovate prose style. The politicization of literature in the 1930s and 1940s cast a shadow over Jarnés's achievement, causing some to criticize him for his presumed insensitivity to social issues. In the decade preceding the Civil War, however, Jarnés succeeded in showing the way for a heightened poetic element in prose. He also performed an extremely important service as a book reviewer for the *Revista de Occidente*, introducing some of the best contemporary writers of Europe to a Spanish audience.

See: P. Ilie, "Benjamín Jarnés: Aspects of the Dehumanized Novel," *PMLA*, 76 (1961): 247–53; J. S. Bernstein, *Benjamín Jarnés* (1972); E. de Zuleta, *Arte y vida en la obra de Benjamín Jarnés* (1977).   J.S.B.

Jarry, Alfred (1873–1907), French dramatist, novelist, and humorist, was born in Laval. To his paternal ancestors— artisans and petty tradesmen—he owed a robust constitution that served for a time to counterbalance a legacy of eccentricity and brilliance from his mother, in whose family there existed a pronounced strain of insanity. He received his early education in the schools of Saint-Brieuc and Rennes before going to Paris in 1891 to pursue his studies at the Lycée Henri IV. After a term of military service, he returned to the capital to devote himself to literature. Jarry's earliest productions in prose and verse appeared in periodicals of the literary vanguard and were collected in 1894 in a small volume entitled *Les Minutes de sable mémorial*, remarkable for its imaginative intensity and verbal resourcefulness. LAUTRÉAMONT's influence can be discerned in this work, and many passages have the nightmare quality of surrealist texts (*see* FRENCH LITERATURE). In this same year, Jarry's portrait was painted by Henri Rousseau and hung in the Salon of the Independents. Jarry undertook to spread the fame of this childlike fellow townsman; the writer nicknamed him "Douanier" and commissioned a lithograph—Rousseau's only known print—which appeared in the second issue (January 1895) of *Ymagier*, a deluxe quarterly founded by Jarry in conjunction with Rémy de GOURMONT.

Sudden and shattering celebrity befell Jarry with the production, on Dec. 10, 1896, of his satirical drama *Ubu Roi* (Eng. tr., 1951) at the experimental Théâtre de l'Oeuvre. Jarry had originally written the play at the age of 15 in collaboration with a classmate at the Lycée of Rennes, with the purpose of ridiculing a pompous mathematics teacher. He later recast and expanded the play, while retaining its original Punch-and-Judy character. Jarry sought to heighten this effect by providing masks for the players, by assigning special voices to each, and by insisting on stylized performances. These innovations, together with the coarseness of the language and the anarchistic implications of the action, outraged the traditionalists in the audience, and the ensuing tumult was later described as "la bataille d'*Hernani* des décadents," alluding to the furor over Victor Hugo's play. In the figure of the ignoble Père Ubu, Jarry created a literary type. Ubu has become the symbol, even in the popular imagination, of bourgeois stupidity grown complacent and irresponsible through abuse of authority. But as if in revenge, this monstrous creation took possession of the personality of its creator; for the rest of his life, Jarry adopted the gestures and intonation of his supermarionette, speaking in clipped, nasal accents and always employing the royal "we."

Until his modest inheritance was exhausted, Jarry continued to write in an involved, strongly personal style characterized by the subtle interplay of humor and lyricism. This manner culminated in *L'Amour absolu* (1899; Absolute Love), a novel of almost impenetrable obscurity. Faced finally by the necessity of supporting himself by his writings, he published *Ubu enchaîné* in 1900 (Eng. tr., *Enslaved*, 1953). Although inferior in verve to the earlier play, the quality of its humor is more cerebral, less gross. It was acted for the first time, with considerable success, at the Paris Exposition of 1937. Like *Ubu Roi*, it is in essence a parody of tragedy; together these plays constitute the entire contribution of the symbolist movement to the field of comedy. More rewarding financially was Jarry's novel of ancient Rome, *Messaline*, which appeared in the pages of the *Revue blanche* in the course of the same year (1900). A feat of impeccable and effortless erudition, its sumptuous, richly figured language matched the splendor of its setting and caused it to be regarded by Jarry's contemporaries as his masterpiece. It now seems inferior to its modern counterpart, *Le Surmâle* (1902; Eng. tr., *The Supermale*, 1968), the last and best constructed of his novels. Here the style is sober, lucid, and balanced—perfectly adapted to supporting the lurid fantasy of a machine that falls in love with its creator. *Le Surmâle* has been called the only strictly surrealist novel.

With his health undermined by poverty and the systematic overuse of alcohol, Jarry was at length able to contribute only an occasional essay to the reviews. His humor, like that of Jonathan Swift and Edgar Allan Poe, is metaphysical and mathematical, involving the logical demonstration of an absurd proposition. It is displayed to best advantage in *Spéculations* (1911), a volume of essays collected and published after his death, together with an earlier "neoscientific" novel in the vein of Rabelais, *Les Gestes et opinions du docteur Faustroll* (1911; The Deeds and Opinions of Dr. Faustroll).

The importance of Jarry's literary contribution was for a while obscured by the persistence of the personal legend he had so deliberately cultivated. Interest in his work was revived by the writers of the 1920s, who discovered in him a precursor. His books were reissued and reappraised, and his position now seems secure as a writer of remarkable gifts of imagination and verbal facility and as a humorist of the highest order.

See: A. Breton, *Les Pas perdus* (1924), pp. 47–65; G. Apollinaire, *Il y a* (1925), pp. 223–34; R. Shattuck, *The Banquet Years* (1958); G. Wellwarth, *The Theatre of Protest and Paradox* (1971), pp. 1–14; M. Arrivé, *Les Langages de Jarry* (1972) and *Lire Jarry* (1976); N. Arnaud, *Alfred Jarry: d'Ubu Roi au Docteur Faustroll* (1976).

A.McV. rev. G.E.W.

Jastrun, Mieczysław (1903–), Polish poet, prose writer, essayist, and translator, was born in Korołówka, near Tarnopol. He studied Polish and German literatures and philosophy at the Jagiellonian University in Cracow. In 1929 he received his Ph.D. degree and from then until World War II he was employed as a high school teacher of Polish. From 1925 on he published poems in *Skamander* and other periodicals, but he did not belong to any literary group. Before the war he published four volumes of poetry: *Spotkanie w czasie* (1929; Meeting in Time), *Inna młodość* (1933; Another Youth), *Dzieje nieostygłe* (1935; Smoldering History), and *Strumień i milczenie* (1937; A Stream and Silence). These volumes revealed Jastrun's connections with the philosophical ideas of Cyprian NORWID, with the tradition of French symbolism, and with the contemplative poetry of Rainer Maria RILKE. In his poetry the theme of transient time became most pronounced, a theme that was to remain one of the most important in his works. During World War II, Jastrun taught clandestine courses and contributed to the underground press. The war found an expression in his volumes *Godzina strzeżona* (1944; The Guarded Hour) and *Rzecz ludzka* (1946; Human Matter), and he returned to these years of horror in his later volumes *Sezon w Alpach* (1948; A Season in the Alps), *Rok urodzaju* (1950; Year of Fertility), and others, showing the ability of human affairs to transcend inhuman times. The wartime holocaust compelled him to pay more attention to current problems, but he retained the attitude of a humanist viewing the events in a historical perspective and fascinated with major cultural trends. A new period in the development of Jastrun's philosophical and existential ideas started in the volumes *Poezja i prawda* (1955; Poetry and Truth) and *Gorący popiół* (1956; Hot Ashes), and especially in such volumes as *Genezy* (1959; Genesis), *Większe od życia* (1960; Bigger than Life), *Intonacje* (1962; Intonations), *Strefa owoców* (1964; Zone of Fruits), and *W biały dzień* (1967; In Daylight), in which he turns to the most universal problems of life and death, and meditates upon the power of art to overcome the age-old human anxiety arising from the Heraclitean stream of time and from the impossibility of knowing the world. In Jastrun's poems the reflective element prevails; he carefully treads the narrow boundary between art and life. He shuns formal controversies, considering poetry to be a cognitive process than emanates from the depths of consciousness. Jastrun has also published an autobiographical psychological novel, *Piękna choroba* (1961; The Beautiful Sickness); biographical studies on Adam Mickiewicz (1949); Juliusz Słowacki, *Spotkanie z Salomea* (1951; A Meeting With Salomeą); and Jan Kochanowski, *Poeta i dworzanin* (1954; The Poet and the Courtier); and volumes of essays, including *Mit śródziemnomorski* (1962; The Mediterranean Myth), in which he points to various aspects of Western culture and weighs its chances for survival. Jastrun is also a translator of French, German, and Russian poetry.

See: J. Trznadel, *O poezji Mieczysława Jastruna*

(1954); J. Błoński, "Mieczysław Jastrun," in *Poeci i inni* (1962), pp. 163–218.   M.G.

Jaurès, Jean (1859–1914), French socialist leader and writer, was born in Castres into a bourgeois family. The branch to which Jaurès belonged was in decline, partly through the fault of his father, an unsuccessful merchant. Devotion to his mother inspired Jean to compensate for his father's failure. Thanks to a scholarship, procured by a relative who was an admiral, Jean and his younger brother Louis were able to study at the lycée of Castres. Singled out by an inspector general of education, Jean went on to Paris to prepare for the Ecole Normale Supérieure; he was first in the examination for admission, and in 1881, Jaurès placed third for the *agrégation de philosophie,* just behind Henri BERGSON. A brilliant university career seemed to open before him. He was appointed professor at the lycée of Albi (1881–87), began work on his doctoral theses, *La Réalité du monde sensible* (The Reality of the World of the Senses) and *Les Origines du socialisme allemand* (1927; The Origins of German Socialism), and was then appointed lecturer at the Faculty of Letters at the University of Toulouse.

It was probably at the suggestion of a cousin already in parliament that Jaurès became a candidate for the legislative elections of 1885. At the age of 26, he became one of the body's youngest deputies. Politically left of center, he was interested in social problems, particularly the matter of retirement benefits for miners, but because some socialists favored violence, he was not attracted to socialism. Defeated in the elections of 1889, he returned to his teaching position at Toulouse and resumed work on his theses. From 1886 on, Jaurès wrote political articles for the daily *Dépêche de Toulouse,* and from 1893 to 1898 he contributed a literary column to that newspaper. In 1890 he entered the municipal council and became deputy mayor.

About this time, Jaurès turned to socialism. Some believe that this shift was due to his contact with the miners of Carmaux, but others (including Charles Andler, Léon BLUM, and Marcel Mauss) attribute it to Jaurès's conversations with Lucien Herr, the librarian at the Ecole Normale who had such a great influence on the generation of Normaliens from 1888 to 1925. In a "partial election" in 1893, Jaurès was chosen to represent Carmaux in parliament. During the period 1892–98, Jaurès was very optimistic about the future of socialism, which he envisioned as being gradually accepted by sincere republicans and wholeheartedly embraced by young intellectuals. He attempted to define his non-Marxist socialism in two bills before parliament (one on the importation of wheat, one on the nationalization of the mines) and in a series of articles in the *Revue socialiste* (March 1895–May 1896). About this time, he helped set up a worker-owned glass factory in Toulouse. Intent on defending every humane cause, he threw himself into the campaign (1894) for the revision of the Dreyfus trial. When, at the suggestion of Herr, he founded his newspaper, he called it *L'Humanité.*

The decade 1898–1908 was a difficult period for Jaurès. Having failed to gain reelection in 1898, he became the editor of the *Histoire socialiste: 1789–1900* (12 vols., 1900–08). His own contribution to this work was republished as *Histoire socialiste de la révolution française* (8 vols., 1922–24; Socialist History of the French Revolution). Jaurès had even considered producing a socialist encyclopedia, but the project fell through. The socialist unity that he had so ardently desired was slow in coming, and when it did materialize it was—to Jaurès's dismay—according to the positions of Karl Marx and Jules Guesde.

Jaurès's concerted involvement in French political life on the eve of World War I was brought to an end by an assassin's bullet on July 31, 1914. Roger MARTIN DU GARD provided a moving account of these events in his cyclical novel *Les Thibault.*

See: *Bulletin de la société d'études jaurésiennes* (1960–); H. Goldberg, *The Life of Jean Jaurès* (1962); G. Lefranc, *Jaurès et le socialisme des intellectuels* (1968).
                                                                    G.L.

Jensen, Johannes Vilhelm (1873–1950), Danish novelist, poet, and essayist, was born in the northern Jutland area of Himmerland. His first experience of Copenhagen as a medical student is told in his first two novels, *Danskere* (1896; Danes) and *Einar Elkær* (1898) both literary incarnations of the decadent fin de siècle mood and both inspired by Johannes JØRGENSEN and Knut HAMSUN. In these novels, Jensen describes two narcissistic provincial students. He broke away from this attitude, however, in *Himmerlandshistorier* (1898–1910; Himmerland Stories), the title denoting a return to his childhood environment. With humor and realism he tells—mingling sympathy and criticism—about ordinary human beings, as well as heroic characters. During his first visit to the United States in 1896, Jensen experienced technology, the modern lifestyle, and the rapid pace, all of which made a lasting impression upon him. In 1898 he began his journalistic career, which took him around the world. All of this experience comes together in *Den gotiske Renaissance* (1901; The Gothic Renaissance) in which he formulates his love of great deeds, a life of action, and modern technology. The historical novel *Kongens Fald* (1900–01; Eng. tr., *The Fall of the King,* 1933) became an attack on the doubting, dreaming Danish nation, personified by King Christian II in his vain battle for power. It also reveals all the dreams and longings behind Jensen's worship of reality. Scenes of brute realism mingled with lyrical passages of overwhelming beauty make the book a work of artistic genius. A second visit to America in 1903 resulted in the novels *Madame d'Ora* (1904) and *Hjulet* (1905; The Wheel), which are, despite excellent descriptions of Chicago and New York, weakened by trite criminal effects and violent polemics against the belief in immortality. Besides *Kongens Fald,* Jensen's finest narrative skills are found in all 11 volumes of his *Myter* (1907–44; Myths). These short prose pieces reproduce primarily intense sense experiences and their perspectives in time and space. In essays and in nature, animal, and travel descriptions, the author presents symbolically his basic ideas: a deep love of reality and a belief in eternity found in a revitalizing nature. Several of the myths laid the foundation for the great novel series, *Den lange Rejse* (1908–22; Eng. tr., *The Long Journey,* 1922–24), for which Jensen was awarded the Nobel Prize for Literature in 1944. In this series he describes the development of man from a half-animal existence in the primeval forests of Jutland to the discovery of America. This evolutionary writing depicts the mighty individual as the creator and the battle against the cold as the main force in cultural progress.

Jensen's poetry is collected in five volumes, of which the first, *Digte* (1906; Poems), introduces a new era in Danish poetry. Landmarks are the prose poems inspired by Walt Whitman and Heinrich Heine and centered around the self, in which Jensen expresses his firm belief in the ecstasy of the moment as well as his unbounded longing for eternity, for example, "Interferens" (Interference). This duality decreases after 1920, when a more classical style dominates in his praise of woman, child, and Danish nature. Jensen was one of the greatest path-finders of the 20th century in Denmark, having had the most crucial influence upon the development of Danish literature. Nevertheless, he also did belong to the generation of the neoromanticists. Jensen's production, one of the most important in European literature, combines the present with eternity in a mythical vision.

See: Aa. Marcus, "Johannes V. Jensen," *ASR*, 20 (1932): 339–47; L. Nedergaard, *Johannes V. Jensen* (1968); O. Friis, *Den unge Johannes V. Jensen*, vols. 1–2 (1974).   S.H.R.

Jersild, Per Christian (1935–), Swedish novelist and physician, was born in Katrineholm. As a physician, Jersild, together with Gunnar and Maj-Britt Inghe, wrote *Recovery in Schizophrenia, a Sociopsychiatric Study* (1970). Jersild's whole authorship is centered in this sphere of interest, the individual against an environment that, with the slightest shift in perspective, seems mad. In all Jersild's early books, *Räknelära* (1960; Basic Mathematics), *Till varmare länder* (1961; To Warmer Countries), and *Ledig lördag* (1963; Free Saturday), the approach is the same. A soft beginning with casual everyday events that suddenly turn fantastic and ghostlike. Jersild makes heavy use of burlesque to put the absurdity of everyday life into relief.

In the picaresque novel *Calvinols resa genom världen* (1965; Calvinol's Journey through the World), Jersild let his movie-inspired hero, Calvinol, fly high through time and space, participating in historic events like El Alamein or Lützen through distorted perspective to disintegration through his manic brain. The book was Jersild's first major success. His next novel, *Prins Valiant och Konsum* (1966; Prince Valiant and the Co-op), plays the same game but from the other side of the table. The very young heroine believes fully in her Prince Valiant, but eventually his image is killed for her by the drab commercial fantasy world. He is replaced by the co-op store. A movie was made from the novel *Grisjakten* (1968; The Pig Hunt) in 1970 by Jonas Cornell. In this novel, Jersild masterfully illustrates how people compartmentalize their lives. The hero, a pedantic bureaucrat, is put in charge of the extinction of pigs on the island of Gotland, and he effectuates this assignment in a thorough manner. He separates completely his life at work from his life at home until one day he is caught himself in the pig hunt.

Jersild's most restrained and perhaps most serious novel, *Vi ses i Song My* (1970; See You at My Lai), criticizes the indoctrination of a society. It is not about the American, but about the Swedish, military establishment. The haphazard hero is Dr. Nylander, a company psychologist, who sets up a small troubleshooting group. Although it seems like a sensible and democratic enterprise, as events follow, the group falls apart. Nylander cannot rescue his project, and it becomes more and more evident that the project means more to him than do the people involved. He is a manipulator of the most insidious kind. He fails in all respects and has to admit that he fails. Nevertheless, in the last chapter he is involved in a similar attempt to organize a new group.

Uppror bland marsvinen (1972; Revolt among the Guinea Pigs) and *Den elektriska kaninen* (1974; The Electric Rabbit) are so-called animal stories. Partly they are about animals and how people treat animals, but partly they, too, illustrate Jersild's favorite themes: the fear that people have of each other and of the unknown and the extent they are willing to manipulate in order to get their favorite fantasy or project to square with reality. Jersild's novel *Djurdoktorn* (1973) appeared in an English translation as *The Animal Doctor* (1975). The novel *Barnens*

Ö (1976; The Children's Island) makes caustic comments on contemporary Swedish society and makes an attempt to explain what has gone wrong. *Babels hus* (1978; The House of Babel) is a novel about a modern metropolitan hospital in Stockholm. The protagonist is a 76-year-old retired man.

See: J. Stenkvist, *Svensk litteratur 1870–1970*, vol. 3, pp. 125–28, and "From Calvinol's Way through the World," in *Modern Swedish Prose in Translation* (1979), pp. 155–65.   B.K.S.

Jesenský, Janko (1874–1945), Slovak novelist, short-story writer, and poet, was born in Turčiansky Svätý in central Slovakia. A lawyer, he served as an officer in the Czechoslovak legions in Russia during World War I. After the war and the formation of Czechoslovakia, he was chosen regional vice-president for Slovakia. Jesenský's first poetry collection, *Verše* (1905; Verses), shows nascent traits of symbolism, but he soon abandoned subjective and intimate poetry for prose with greater social and national consciousness. As a writer of fiction Jesenský was a critical realist; the collection *Malomestské rozprávky* (1913; Small-Town Tales) savagely satirizes the conservative citizenry of provincial towns, and the novel *Demokrati* (2 vols., 1934–37; Eng. tr., *The Democrats*, 1961) ridicules the emerging bourgeoisie, with its career ambition and frequently crude political maneuvering.

Jesenský was an able translator of the Russian classics, above all of Aleksandr Pushkin and Mikhail Lermontov, and at the end of his life he became a poet of resistance to Nazism and local Slovak fascism. His poems from the period of World War II circulated illegally, appearing after the liberation in two collections, *Na zlobu dňa* (1945; For Days of Evil) and *Čierne dni* (1948; Black Days).

See: Various authors, *Jesenský v kritike a spomienkach: sborník* (1955).   F.M.B.

Jilemnický, Peter (1901–49), Slovak novelist, was born in Kyšperk in Bohemia but spent most of his life in Slovakia, where he was a teacher. Imprisoned in a concentration camp during World War II, he served after 1945 as a journalist in Belgrade and as cultural attaché in Moscow. From his youth, Jilemnický had a leftist political orientation, and his writing was influenced by Maksim GORKY. His first novel, *Víťazný pád* (1929; The Victorious Fall), is a lyric picture of the poverty of the Slovak people, but his later *Zuniaci krok* (1930; The Resounding Step), drawn from personal experience, depicts the class struggle in a Soviet village during the 1920s. Without question, Jilemnický's masterpiece is *Pole neorané* (1932; Unplowed Fields), which traces the dramatic evolution of a peasant into a Communist activist. *Kus cukru* (1934; A Piece of Sugar), set in the years of the worldwide economic depression, documents the struggles of the politically evolving Slovak proletariat. His last novel, *Kronika* (1947; Chronicle), faithfully reconstructs the life of a Slovak village during the Nazi occupation and the Slovak national uprising (1944). Although Jilemnický may be considered the founder of Slovak socialist fiction, he largely succeeded in avoiding the rigid and schematic tendencies of socialist realism as practiced in the 1950s.

See: B. Truhlář, *Slovenská próza v Povstaní* (1954); J. Špitzer, *Peter Jilemnický* (1955).   F.M.B.

Jiménez, Juan Ramón (1881–1958), Spanish poet, was born in Moguer, a small Andalusian town. In 1956 he received the Nobel Prize for Literature while in Puerto Rico, where he died. His influence was great among Spanish-speaking poets, especially during the 1920s. Jiménez's work can be divided into two periods: the first, modernist, lasted until 1915; the second begins with the publication of *Diario de un poeta recién casado* (1917; The Diary of a Newly Married Poet). With this book he initiates his "naked" poetry, frequently deep and beautiful, whose attraction seems to lie in its precision. The poetry of his second period, especially in the last years, is nevertheless at times complex and hermetic.

Juan Ramón was always a poet for "the few." He lived in isolation, dedicated to "reliving" his previous poetry, always in search of perfection. The ecstatic contemplation of beauty in nature is one of his distinguishing features, particularly in the second period. In 1900 he went to Madrid for a short period and published his first two books of poetry, characterized by a very romantic and sentimental style. That same year he witnessed his father's death and as a result began to suffer from an acute neurasthenia marked by a pathological fear of death. This fear stayed with him all his life. In 1901 he was admitted to a sanatorium in the south of France and later to one in Madrid, where he remained until 1905. During those years he published *Rimas* (1902), *Arias tristes* (1903; Sad Arias), and *Jardines lejanos* (1904; Distant Gardens). There is in these poems a successful amalgamation of French symbolism and the influence of Gustavo BÉCQUER, as well as the popular Spanish ballad. Nevertheless, many of these poems are overly sentimental, filled with tears, sighs, and dreams of love. From 1905 to 1907, after his return to Moguer, he wrote *Baladas de Primavera* (1910; Ballads of Spring) and *Pastorales* (1911).

From 1908 to 1911, Juan Ramón wrote six more books of poetry. Their style is in general overly ornate, with many "garments," as he said later. The verse is more modernist (*see* SPANISH LITERATURE) and decadent than before and includes exuberant alexandrines.

He moved permanently to Madrid in 1912. There he wrote *Platero y yo* (1914; Eng. tr., *Platero and I*, 1956), a book of lyric prose in which he recalls his walks in Moguer, evoking its landscape and human types. In 1914–15 he wrote *Sonetos espirituales* (1917), in which his love for Zenobia, his future wife, is already evident alongside his obsession with nothingness. This book ended his first period. The next, written in 1915, is *Estío* (1916; Summer). The verse is composed of short stanzas, and the tone is lighter and more cheerful, the product of a new state of mind due to his impending marriage. It is a transitional book that announces the "naked poetry" of the following year.

Juan Ramón left Madrid in January 1916 and went to New York, where he married Zenobia in June. In July they returned to Madrid. During the voyage and while in the United States he wrote much of the verse and prose of *Diario*. Many verses, written without fixed meter or rhyme and little imagery, sound almost like prose. This was the kind of "natural and everyday poetry" he wanted to write. The best poems are perhaps those related to the sea, for they reveal deep and complex emotions. The sea—grandiose, cold, and menacing—is identified with nothingness, and Juan Ramón is seen struggling against falling into dark pessimism.

In 1917 his first anthology, *Poesías escojidas* (Selected Poems), was published in New York. While he was living serenely in Madrid with his young wife and his new "naked poetry," he wrote, from 1916 to 1918, *Eternidades* (1918) and *Piedra y cielo* (1919; Stone and Sky). Later he prepared his *Segunda antolojía poética, 1898–1918* (1922), which included a large selection of revised poems from the first period and from the beginning of the second. In *Poesía* and *Belleza* (Beauty), which appeared in 1923, Jiménez dwells on the meaning of his work and on the role of poetry as a means of overcoming death and oblivion. He also begins to concentrate on what will later become his central theme: the experience of the "eternal instant."

From 1923 to 1936 he did not publish any book of poetry. Some new poems, probably written between 1932 and 1936, appeared in *Canción* (1936; Song) and were republished, together with others written during the same years, in *La estación total* (1946; Total Season). This book, published in Buenos Aires, was practically ignored in Spain. It is nevertheless one of his best. Evident here, expressed with forcefulness and color, is the motif of salvation through the contemplation of beauty. The poet strives to attain an ecstatic identification with all that is beautiful, although he rarely succeeds.

Juan Ramón left Spain with his wife in September 1936. They went first to Puerto Rico and Cuba. In 1939 they moved to Florida and in 1942 to Washington. From there, sick and depressed, Juan Ramón returned to Puerto Rico in 1951. Somewhat recovered, in 1952–53 he prepared *Tercera antolojía poética, 1898–1953* and wrote his last prose works and poems.

His poetic work written in exile is not extensive. Part of it did not appear until 1957, in his *Tercera antolojía*. From 1939 to 1942 he wrote the beautiful *Romances de Coral Gables* (1948; Ballads of Coral Gables). *Españoles de tres mundos* (Spaniards of Three Worlds), a series of penetrating portraits of both living and dead personalities, written in very original prose, appeared in 1944. Also published in 1943 and 1944 were the first two stanzas of "Espacio" (Space), part of a long, obscure, and hallucinatory poem that he had written in 1941 in Miami after being released from the hospital in a state of "rhapsodical intoxication." It is a good example in Spanish of stream of consciousness.

In 1948, Juan Ramón went to Argentina, where he gave lectures. While returning to the United States by ship he had an extraordinary mystical experience that he speaks of in *Animal de fondo* (1949; Animal of Depth). This is a book full of joy and enthusiasm. While contemplating the sea he felt that finally, after many years of search, he had achieved his goal: the union of the inner "god desired" (that is, himself) with the outer "desiring god," the "god of beauty" who had been searching for him. Now everything became one: beauty, the world, and god were in him, and he, as though transported out of himself, was "god." Although at times this book is very beautiful, it is indeed obscure. Juan Ramón speaks only to himself, or to his "god," to the plenitude he has reached, and to beauty.

With the publication of *Tercera antolojía poética* (1957) it was possible for the first time to have a comprehensive view of Jiménez's poetic activity. This anthology included almost everything he had written since he came to America. When it was published in Spain, a year before his death, there was for a while a renewed interest in him and his work. Many of his books went through several editions in the following years and much was written about him. But this interest soon faded. His moment had passed; poetry was now on a different course. He was criticized with some justification then, as well as now, for his egocentrism and eccentricity. This criticism, however, ignores his merits. His place among the great figures of modern Spanish literature seems assured.

See: H. R. Hays, *The Selected Writings of Juan Ramón Jiménez* (1957); A. Sánchez-Barbudo, *La segunda época de Juan Ramón Jiménez* (1962); H. T. Young, *The Victorious Expression* (1964), pp. 77–135.   A.S.-B.

Jóhannes úr Kötlum, pseud. of Jóhannes Bjarni Jónasson (1899–1972), Icelandic essayist, novelist, and poet, was born in Dalasýsla, in western central Iceland. The son of poor parents who lived on an isolated farm, Jóhannes úr Kötlum received little formal education as a youth. He attended a school for young people in his home district but lacked the means to continue his education. Later, however, he enrolled at a teachers college in Reykjavik and became a schoolteacher in 1921; as such, he was first employed in the region of his origin but after that in Reykjavik. From 1933 on, he supported himself exclusively by writing, residing in Reykjavik and Hveragerði. He was, for a time, active in politics and in professional associations of writers, serving, for instance, as a member of the Althing (Parliament) for the Socialist Party in 1941 and the head of an organization of radical writers from 1935 to 1938.

Jóhannes úr Kötlum's first poems appeared in a magazine in 1921, but it was not until 1926 that his first book of verse, Bí, bí og blaka (Lullaby), came out. His last original collection of poems, Ný og nið (Waxing and Waning Moon) was published in 1970. He was a prolific writer for half a century, writing, in all, 15 books of verse, 6 children's books (5 of them poetry), 5 novels, and a volume of essays. In addition to this, he was an active translator, rendering both verse and fiction into Icelandic.

His earliest poems are romantic and characterized by optimism and nationalistic sentiment, many of them expressing a childlike feeling for nature, as well as a degree of religious faith. In both form and substance, his poems from this period resemble the verse of life worship by Davíð STEFÁNSSON and Stefán frá Hvítadal (1887–1933), although echoes from Einar BENEDIKTSSON are also noticeable. In his first few books of poetry, Jóhannes úr Kötlum emerges as more of an Icelandic traditionalist than most of his contemporaries on the literary scene. A key source of inspiration for him was Icelandic folk poetry, a genre influencing his work throughout his entire career.

The volume of poems entitled Ég læt sem ég sofi (1932; I Pretend to Be Asleep) introduced a new dimension into his work: emphasis on social criticism, strongly colored by the author's socialist views. A socialist call to arms is a salient feature in all books of verse by Jóhannes úr Kötlum that appeared in the 1930s. Many of his poems dating from this period deal with international events, such as the rise of Nazism and the intensifying class struggle. Typical of his stance in these years is Hrímhvíta móðir (1937; Snowcapped Motherland), a collection of epic poems dealing not with the romanticized saga heroes of the author's early verse, but instead with nameless protagonists from everyday life, the slaves of the Commonwealth period as well as the fishermen and laborers of his own day. Hart er í heimi (1939; World Is in Chaos) and Sól tér sortna (1945; The Sun Turns Black) testify, respectively, to the poet's fear as he saw World War II approach and his horror when he witnessed the carnage itself. A unique work from this time, however, is Eilífðar smáblóm (1940; The Small Flower of Eternity), a collection of brief lyrical poems on nature. Thus, Iceland and its nature became a refuge for the poet when he found it necessary to avert his gaze from the terrors of war in the larger world. In Sóleyjarkvæði (1952; A Poem on the Sunny Island), Jóhannes úr Kötlum combines nationalism and his socialist outlook in a bitter attack against interests of the United States and the American military presence in Iceland, also denouncing Icelandic politicians who he felt had betrayed their country through submission to a foreign power.

Sjödægra (1955; Seven Days' Journey) marks the beginning of still another phase in the literary career of Jóhannes úr Kötlum. Although many of the poems in this collection had already appeared anonymously in Tímarít Máls og menningar even as far back as 1945, Sjödægra announced him to the public as one of the most significant Icelandic poets of the modernist school. These poems are careful designs in free form, their imagery being fresh and inviting the reader to make sudden, often nonlogical jumps—a poetic style that also characterized the author's subsequent books of verse. In content, Jóhannes úr Kötlum's poetry from this last period tends to be more private and philosophical, whereas political protest occupies a less prominent place, although fear and disillusionment can be noticed in some of the poems.

Although Jóhannes úr Kötlum did not herald new epochs in Icelandic poetry (those beginning in 1918, the 1930s, and the 1940s), he retained the main features associated with these periods longer than others; and no other Icelandic poet reflects more faithfully the artistic currents that made themselves felt during his long career as a poet.

See: I. Orgland, "Jóhannes úr Kötlum," in Jóhannes úr Kötlum, Sjudøgra (1967): 5–42; H. Pálsson, "Myth and Symbol in Jóhannes úr Kötlum's Sjödægra," Skandinvische Lyrik der Gegenwart (1973), pp. 175–81; N. P. Njarðvík, "Vort er ríkið," þjóðviljinn, Nov. 5, 1974; Ó. Halldórsson, " . . . hvernig skal þa ljóð kveða?" Tímarit Máls og menningar (1975), pp. 124–37.   S.S.H.

Johnson, Eyvind (1900–76), Swedish novelist, was born into a working-class family in Svartbjörnsbyn in the province of Norrbotten in the far north of Sweden. Leaving school at the age of 13, he tried a variety of unskilled jobs before escaping to Germany and France, where he spent a great part of the 1920s. During this period he tried to establish himself as a writer. Of his earliest works, the most successful is Stad i mörker (1926; Town in Darkness), about personal and political rivalry in a subarctic town. His increasing rejection of traditional novel forms culminated in Kommentar till ett stjärnfall (1929; Commentary on a Falling Star), with its echoes of Marcel PROUST, André GIDE, James Joyce, and Sigmund Freud. In this novel, Johnson attacked the sterility and rootlessness of capitalist society, and in following novels, like Bobinack (1932) and Regn i gryningen (1933; Rain at Dawn), he toyed with the attractions of a primitivist, less convention-ridden way of life. His celebrated tetralogy, Romanen om Olof (1934–37; The Novel about Olof; Eng. tr. of the first part, 1914, 1970), is a story of adolescence, based largely on his own. The young hero, Olof, develops from being a tongue-tied observer of events to a lively, if wayward, participant, involved with women and politics. Through all his trials, Olof is strengthened by a morality that places responsibility for his fate firmly on himself, and he is consoled by his delight in literature. The Olof novels are distinguished by their blend of fairy tale and realism, in which fantasy both conceals and illuminates a grim reality.

Increasingly disturbed by the dictatorships of the 1930s, Johnson emphasized the nature of totalitarianism and the urgent need to fight it in Nattövning (1938; Night Maneuvers)—an account of Nazi sympathizers in Sweden—and Soldatens återkomst (1940; The Soldier's Return), about a Swedish volunteer who has fought dictatorship in Spain, Finland, and Norway, only to be murdered in a Swedish village. The Krilon trilogy (1941–43), Johnson's "military service," is a rich but diffuse work. On one level it is a moving tale of a group of friends and their struggle to survive personal tragedies. At the same time their adventures are an allegory of the events of World War II. In addition, the novel comments directly on the war and attacks the appeasement policies of the Swedish government. In *Strändernas svall* (1946; Eng. tr., *Return to Ithaca*, 1952), Johnson retells Homer's *Odyssey* in realistic terms and uses it to illustrate the moral dilemma of World War II: that humanist values have to be defended by evil methods. *Krilon* and *Strändernas svall* reveal Johnson's exuberant imagination at its best, although it is balanced by an irony and circuitousness reminiscent of Thomas MANN.

After the war, Johnson continued to present current problems in oblique, usually historical terms. *Drömmar om rosor och eld* (1949; Dreams of Roses and Fire) describes a "witch-hunt" in Cardinal Richelieu's France. The novel is a deep psychological analysis of the evil in man that springs from envy and frustration. *Molnen över Metapontion* (1957; The Clouds over Metapontion) blends a retelling of Xenophon's *Anabasis* with a modern journey; in both works a hard-won victory is followed by an uneasy peace under threatening clouds. *Hans nådes tid* (1960; Eng. tr., *The Days of His Grace*, 1968) describes the fate of a satellite state in Charlemagne's empire. Personal dreams of love and national dreams of freedom are brutally destroyed by a Stalinlike dictator, yet in the end love and freedom are not totally crushed. In the lyrical *Livsdagen lång* (1964; Life's Long Day), the same themes of love and freedom are presented in several different historical guises, flowing into one another. *Några steg mot tystnaden* (1973; Steps into Silence) is a study of a typical Johnson hero, a battered but resilient humanist whose character is presented through his re-creations of two of his ancestors' lives. Johnson's historical sense, his feeling that our time is "a river where many ages flow abreast," is also evident in two novels in contemporary settings—*Lägg undan solen* (1951; Put Away the Sun) and *Favel ensam* (1968; Favel Alone)—and in two novels based on his experiences of the 1920s—*Romantisk berättelse* (1953; Romantic Tale) and *Tidens gång* (1955; The Course of Time). Johnson also wrote many fine short stories—a full collection is *Sju liv* (1944; Seven Lives)—and various travel books and essays, a selection of which is *Stunder vågor* (1965; Moments, Waves). He shared the 1974 Nobel Prize for Literature with Harry MARTINSON.

See: G. Orton, *Eyvind Johnson*, *TWAS* 150 (1972); S. Bäckman, *Den tidlösa historien: en studie i tre romaner av Eyvind Johnson* (1975); L. Sjöberg, "The 1974 Nobel Prize in Literature," *BA* 49, no. 3 (1975): 407–21; O. Meyer, *Eyvind Johnson's historiska romaner* (1977); *SLT* (entire double issue), nos. 3–4 (1977); T. Stenström, *Romantikern Eyvind Johnson* (1978).   G.O.

Johnson, Uwe (1934–), German novelist, was born in Kammin, Pomerania (now part of Poland); in 1945 his family fled to Mecklenburg in East Germany. Johnson studied German literature under Hans Mayer at Rostock and Leipzig, doing free-lance editing and translating (Herman Melville's *Israel Potter* among other works) after completing his studies. He moved to West Berlin in 1959, where he lived, except for three interruptions, until he moved to England, where he lives now. In 1961, Johnson was in the United States at Wayne State and Harvard; in 1962 he spent nine months in Rome on a West German government stipend; and he spent the years 1966 to 1968 in New York, the first as a textbook editor for Harcourt, Brace & World.

Johnson's first two published novels (a previous novel, "Ingrid Babendererde," never saw print), *Mutmaßungen über Jakob* (1959; Eng. tr., *Speculations about Jacob*, 1963) and *Das dritte Buch über Achim* (1961; Eng. tr., *The Third Book about Achim*, 1967), brought Johnson instant acclaim in the West as the "Poet of both Germanies," because in them he confronted the reality of two

distinct German states—a theme conspicuously ignored until then. His intentions are broader, in fact, than the label allows. He chronicles several decades' worth of social and political history as his characters experience it. *Jakob*, published in 1959, takes place in 1956; *Achim* (1961) in 1960; and *Jahrestage* (1970, 1971, 1973, with the fourth and last volume scheduled for 1980; Eng. tr., *Anniversaries* [vols. 1 and part of 2 condensed into one], 1975) records one year starting on Aug. 21, 1967. Although each successive novel dips further back into the characters' past, the center remains in postwar Mecklenburg. Johnson treats his characters—many of whom recur in his writing—with discretion and respect. They frequently speak for themselves; the narrator knows only what they tell him. This he describes in a serious, even tone, set off in recent writing by occasional notes of wry humor or biting irony.

In Johnson's unusual style, most pronounced in *Jakob*, abrupt shifts of narrative technique (internal monologue, dialogue, narration), leaps between present and past, scrupulous attention to accuracy of detail (particularly in technical descriptions), an abundance of adjectives, occasional dialect phrases, unorthodox punctuation, and much parataxis—contrary to modern German practice—all combine to interrupt the narrative flow and make the reader actively construct the story as he reads. Other books by Johnson include *Zwei Ansichten* (1965; Eng. tr., *Two Views*, 1966), a story about the Berlin Wall, seen from both sides; *Eine Reise nach Klagenfurt* (1974), documentation; and *Berliner Sachen* (1975), essays.

Johnson has received the Fontane Prize of the City of West Berlin (1960), the International Publishers Prize (1962), and the Büchner Prize (1971). In 1979 he delivered the Frankfurt Lectures on Poetics.

See: M. Boulby, *Uwe Johnson* (1974); P. Demetz, *Postwar German Literature* (1972), pp. 206–13; W. Schwarz, *Der Erzähler Uwe Johnson* (1970); R. Baumgart, ed., *Über Uwe Johnson* (1970).   D.J.W.

Jonckheere, Karel (1906–), Belgian (Flemish) poet, essayist, and prose writer, was born in Ostend, the "queen of the Belgian sea resorts," which was to play a central role in Jonckheere's work. Although extremely active in various literary domains, he owes his fame primarily to his poetry. A first collection of poems, *Proefvlucht* (Testflight), appeared in 1933. In this volume, the essential features of his entire work are already present: the influence of the well-known Flemish symbolist poet, Karel van de Woestijne, the loss of religious faith accompanied by a questioning of his relationship to his mother, and the childless marriage. As Jonckheere himself noted in the first part of his memoirs, *De Vogels hebben het gezien* (1968; The Birds Are My Witnesses), these various themes unfold before the immutable background of the sea. *Klein Testament* (1938; Last Will) contains his best-known poem of the period, "Bij de Indiaanse in het Maïsveld," which not only recounts a hasty trip to Central America but also sets forth a central problematic: the onset of an earthly joy, a sensuality void of torment, and an awareness of the relativity of things. The childless marriage, one of the recurrent themes of Jonckheere's poetic work, is explicitly dealt with in *Conchita* (1939). The volume is named after a young Spanish fugitive whom Jonckheere adopted and upon whom he projected his longing for a child. *Spiegel der zee* (1946; Mirror of the Sea) sums up his youth and constitutes a kind of spiritual testament, an inventory of everything that still appeared worthwhile to him after 40 years of life.

De hondenwacht (1931; Midnight Watch) can be viewed as the closing piece of the first period. With *Van zee tot schelp* (1955; From Sea to Shell), Jonckheere renewed his style in the light of the stimulating influence of experimental poetry, which swept over Flanders and the Netherlands in the 1950s. He has become increasingly aware of the resources of a poetry that would be less enslaved to rhyme and meter and that would render ideas and feelings in a more concrete and direct way. Indeed, in *Van zee tot schelp,* a number of poems are presented like fables or ballads. Their form is more narrative than that of conventional lyric. Yet, elegiac in essence, Jonckheere's poetry exudes serenity and quiet. It is never tormented with metaphysical speculations but rather put in perspective by a proverbial irony.

Critics have pointed out that much of Jonckheere's work is based on everyday events. Indeed, many of his poems are autobiographical and take a concrete occurrence as a point of departure. The collection of poems entitled *Poëtische inventaris* (1972; Poetical Inventory), for instance, could be read as a reconstruction of the course of life.

Next to the dominant themes touched on so far, one must take into consideration the dynamic life of the author. Personal reasons as well as his work as a civil servant have led Jonckheere to travel a good deal. His activities to promote translations of Flemish literature have earned him the title of ambassador of Flemish letters. Jonckheere's numerous trips gave birth to a number of travel accounts. The best-known of these are *Cargo* (1940), *Tierra Caliente* (1941), *De zevende haven* (1942; The Seventh Harbor), and *Kongo met het blote oog* (1958; Congo with the Naked Eye). His travels were also to have an impact on his poetry. *Van Zee tot schelp* begins with the long "Ballade van de slapeloosheid" (The Ballad of Insomnia), in which Jonckheere enumerates his so-called roadhouses. Romania constitutes a symbol in the travel poems, for Jonckheere considered that country as his second homeland (*Roemeense suite,* 1965; Romanian Suite).

Jonckheere is appreciated not only as a poet, but also as a storyteller and an editor of anthologies. Moreover, he has written critical essays, among which one must mention *Poëzie en experiment* (1956; Poetry and Experience) and *De poezie muur dorrbreken* (1958; To Break through the Wall of Poetry) as well as an overview of Flemish literature (1958). Jonckheere has earned a reputation in public life and in literary circles as an eloquent and witty speaker. In 1967 he published a collection of aphorisms, *Nacht? Zei de zon, nooit van gehoord!* (Night? The Sun Said, "Never Heard of It!"). In the same way, his memoirs are written in a familiar tone. Five volumes of the memoirs have already appeared: *De Vogels hebben het gezien* (1968), *Waar plant ik mijn ezel?* (1974; Where Shall I Put My Easel?), *Mijn dochter wordt sirene* (1975; My Daughter Becomes a Siren), *De man met de ruiker* (1977; The Man with the Bouquet), and *Verbannen in het vaderland* (1977; Exiled in the Home Country).

See: C. Haesaert et al., *7 over Karel Jonckheere* (1967); R. Roemans and H. van Assche, *Bibliografie van Karel Jonckheere* (1967); E. Decorte, *Karel Jonckherre* (1974); Profiel, *Karel Jonckheere* (1976).   P. van A.

Jones, Philippe, pseud. of Philippe Roberts-Jones (1924–), Belgian poet, essayist, and art critic, was born in Brussels. His father, a noted attorney of English descent, was tortured and killed by the Germans during World War II. Jones distinguished himself first as a member of the Resistance and subsequently as a liaison officer in the English army. After the war, he resumed his studies at Harvard University and at the University of Brussels, where he wrote a doctoral disseration on satirical illustrations between 1860 and 1890. This work was to become the cornerstone of a major critical work entitled *De Daumier à Lautrec: essai sur l'histoire de la caricature scandaleuse entre 1860 et 1890* (1960; From Daumier to Lautrec: Essay on the History of Satirical Caricature between 1860 and 1890). Jones gained an international reputation with a series of essays on contemporary art: *Du Réalisme au surréalisme: la Peinture en Belgique de J. Stevens à Paul Delvaux* (1969; From Realism to Surrealism: Belgian Painting from J. Stevens to Paul Delvaux), *L'Art majeur: pamphlet pour un art permanent* (1974; Major Art: Pamphlet for a Permanent Art), and *Magritte, Poète du visible* (1972; Magritte: Poet of the Visible). In these works, Jones not only exhibited his talents as an incisive art critic and philosopher, but also his gifts as a poet to articulate a language to talk about avant-garde manifestations such as pop art. *Racine ouverte* (1976; Bared Root), a collection of poetry, prolongs the questioning of visual representation: "By itself, a tree, be it present or absent, defines a landscape. Erect, it proclaims a domain. By being it becomes a locus of exchange, ranging from the root to the bird." This volume, which opens with a dialogue with the French surrealist poet René CHAR, constitutes a kind of summa of elements of poetry that appeared in previous volumes such as *Graver au vif* (1971; Engrave to the Quick), *Jaillir saisir* (1971; Shooting Forth Grasping), and *Etre Selon* (1973; To Be As May Be), as well as in previously unpublished poetry. Since the publication of his first volume of poetry, *Le Voyageur de la nuit* (1947; The Night Traveler), Jones has developed a voice of his own that transcends diverse tendencies of contemporary poetry. "Word of a dawn which returns each day," the poetry of Jones explores the realm of human destiny in which a "common presence" is the real. A universe of form, colors, language, and, above all, love constitutes the support of long free verses. Jones has continued to pursue this poetic quest while assuming the responsibilities as curator in chief of the Royal Museums of Fine Arts in Belgium.   F.Ve.

Jónsson, Stefán (1905–66), Icelandic poet, short-story writer, and novelist, was born in Hvítársíða in the Borgarfjörður district of southwestern Iceland. His parents lacked the means to establish their own home, so the boy was brought up on various farms where his mother—and sometimes his father also—worked as hired hands. The hardship Jónsson experienced as a youth undoubtedly contributed strongly to the profound sympathy he displays toward all who are weak or oppressed—an attitude permeating all of his writings. Jónsson attended a folk high school and later graduated from a teachers college in Reykjavik in 1933, after which he worked as a schoolteacher for the rest of his life, doing his writing on the side.

His first publication was a book of short stories, *Konan á klettinum* (1936; The Woman on the Cliff), and in its wake came several other collections of short stories. Jónsson also wrote children's poetry, the best-known collection of which is *Sagan of Gutta og sjö önnur ljóð* (1939; The Story of Gutti and Seven Other Poems).

It is in stories for children and young people, however, that Jónsson reaches his greatest artistic heights: he ranks among the very best writers in this genre that have ever lived in Iceland. The most popular of his children's tales is the sequel of stories about a boy named Hjalti, beginning with *Sagan hans Hjalta litla* (1948; The Story of Little Hjalti), a work based in part on his own childhood in Borgarfjörður.

Jónsson selected the Icelandic countryside at the beginning of the 20th century as the setting for most of his stories for children and young people. All such works of his reveal deep psychological insight, humor, and a sound overview of society. The author's understanding of human nature and this sympathy for the weak and unfortunate make these books especially engaging, and they are, moreover, of value as cultural history.

Jónsson's largest work is a novel entitled *Vegurinn að brúnni* (1962; The Road to the Bridge), an account of the maturing of a young man (Bildungsroman) living in the first half of the 20th century. At the same time, it charts the development of Icelandic society up to World War II. This novel is Jónsson's most ambitious attempt to deal with human life on a larger scale than in his books for the young, but its strength lies in the same qualities—psychological insight and deep understanding of human power and weakness.

See: S. Hilmarsdóttir, "Um Hjaltabækurnar eftir Stefan Jónsson," *Mímir* (October 1970): 17–32; E. Bragi, "Af hvaða rót eru þessar sögur runnar" in S. Jónsson, *Ritsafn*, vol. 1 (1972), pp. v–xxxii.   S.S.H.

Jonsson, Thorsten Georg (1910–50), Swedish short-story writer, critic, translator, and journalist, was born in Nordmaling. He began his literary career as a poet but received little recognition. As a prose writer he had much better success. With the two collections *Som det brukar vara* (1939; As It Usually Is) and *Fly till vatten och morgon* (1941; Flee to Water and Morning), he made a name for himself as a master of the short story. He revitalized the genre largely by adopting a concise, unadorned style that points to Ernest Hemingway as his master. But he also learned a great deal from William Faulkner and James Joyce. The latter's stream-of-consciousness technique can thus be detected in some of the stories. For people and background in the first collection, he drew on his knowledge of his native Norrland in a way reminiscent of Eyvind JOHNSON. *Fly till vatten och morgon* is a portrait gallery of society's losers and castaways who try to solve their problems by committing criminal acts. The stories are based, in the true naturalistic tradition, on authentic cases. The narrative objectivity in these stories cannot hide that Jonsson feels pity for at least some of the unhappy offenders. From 1945 to 1946 Jonsson worked in the United States as a correspondent for a big Swedish newspaper. Many of his experiences from this period served as material for his only novel, *Konvoj* (1947), and the four short stories that made up the posthumously published, unfinished *Dimman från havet* (1950; Fog from the Sea), in which Jonsson presents glimpses of some rather sordid aspects of the United States. Jonsson was responsive to the literary development in the United States and wrote penetratingly on Hemingway, Faulkner, James Farrell, and others in, for example, *Sex amerikaner* (1942; Six Americans). His many translations of American writers are brilliant.

See: L. Landen, "Om Thorsten Jonssons författarskan," in *40-talsförfattare*, ed. by L. O. Franzén (1965); G. Brandell, *Svensk litteratur 1870–1970*, vol. 2 (1975), pp. 252–54.   P.-A.H.

Jonsson, Tor (1916–51), Norwegian poet and essayist, was born into a peasant family in Lom. From early childhood, he felt the social and economic injustices of the Norwegian rural community, and those impressions were never erased. His prose writings, for the most part journalistic essays, were published in two collections in 1950 and 1952 under the title *Nesler* (Nettles). These pieces burn with Jonsson's acid hatred of the old social and religious structures, which, in his eyes, destroy the finest human

qualities through their implicit acceptance of poverty and injustice.

Like his prose, Jonsson's poetry conveys irony and sarcasm in terse, epigrammatic phrases. Writing in *nynorsk* (see NORWEGIAN LITERATURE), a language rich in possibilities of poetic expression, Jonsson chose a simple, unembellished style. Yet like Arnulf ØVERLAND, whom he admired, Jonsson sought to give his verse a rhetorical effectiveness; anaphora and alliteration were the poetic figures he preferred. Beneath the social criticism of his first collections, such as *Berg ved blått vatn* (1946; Rock by Blue Water) and *Jernnetter* (1948; Iron Nights), there are currents of despair and loneliness. This side of his personality dominates his final collection, *En dagbok for mitt hjarte* (1951; A Diary for My Heart). In the last reflective poems of this volume, Jonsson's verse rises to a monumental stature as he looks back on his life and forward to death—the solution to his problems—chosen, through suicide, before the book appeared in print.

See: A. Aarseth, "Tor Jonssons diktning," *Edda* (1965), pp. 129–43; L. Mahle, *Frå bygda til verda* (1967), pp. 221–34.   K.A.F.

Jón úr Vör, pseud. of Jón Jónsson (1917–), Icelandic poet, was born in Patreksfjörður in northwestern Iceland and grew up there in dire poverty. The son of the village shoemaker who had 13 other children, Jón was brought up from the age of two by a radical laborer, receiving little education as a youth except for two years at a folk high school, although he later attended evening classes in Reykjavik after moving there. Following the publication of his first book of verse, *Ég ber að dyrum* (1937; I Knock at the Door), Jón úr Vör went to Sweden and was enrolled in 1938 and 1939 at a folk high school run by the Swedish labor movement, spending the next summer at a Nordic folk high school in Geneva, and he had then a chance to travel considerably in Switzerland, France, and Germany. During a second stay in Sweden (1945–47), he became well acquainted with Swedish literature—an important influence on him, especially so in the case of the Swedish proletarian poets, although the Swedish modernist school as a whole left some imprint on him.

A volume of prose poems entitled *Þorpið* (1946; The Village; enlarged edition, 1956) marked a new phase in the poetry of Jón úr Vör. In this most influential of his works, he discards all traditional poetic conventions, his diction is simple and clear, and his message is always unambiguous. The poems focus on everyday life in a desperately poor village—a microcosm obviously modeled on his own birthplace, Patreksfjörður. *Þorpið* has been referred to as the Icelandic example par excellence of social realism, but, despite his objectivity, the author evinces a degree of nostalgia for the past. The poor people depicted in these poems speak for basic values that the poet celebrates and adopts as his own, proclaiming that simple moral code as the best solace in a world of change.

Although Jón úr Vör embraced radical socialism as his creed at the outset of his literary career, his views were characterized by caution and skepticism from the very first, and his doubts have loomed progressively larger in his later books of poetry. With the years, his images have grown more complex, too, and more personal, and his philosophical outlook has become increasingly pessimistic. He especially voices three basic conerns: his fear for the future of humanity in an atomic age, his disappointment with the actual implementation of socialism in the world, and his disillusionment over Iceland's foreign policy.

Confronting a harsh world ready for war, as well as political deceit wherever he looks, Jón úr Vör places all his trust in the honesty of ordinary people, for irrespective of his profound skepticism, he believes in the essential goodness of the little man who cultivates a small plot of ground around his home. As Jón úr Vör sees it, this lowly individual contains in his veins the eternal spirit of the revolution that will be transmitted from generation to generation.

See: E. Bragi, Introduction to J. úr Vör, *loo kvæði* (1967), pp. 7–46.   S.S.H.

Jørgensen, Johannes (1866–1956), Danish poet, was born in Svendborg on the island of Fyn. As a student in Copenhagen in 1884, he came under the influence of Georg BRANDES's naturalism and studied zoology, following Darwinistic theories. Jørgensen soon gave up his studies however, in favor of writing and journalism. A momentary enthusiasm for Friedrich NIETZSCHE and Percy Bysshe Shelley waned under the influence of Catholic philosophy, and Jørgensen's writing progressed toward spiritual, introspective, and metaphysical poetry. In 1896 he converted to Catholicism. Between 1913 and 1953 he lived in Assisi and thereafter in Denmark.

Jørgensen's first work, *Vers* (1887; Verses), influenced by Algernon Charles Swinburne and notable for a style overloaded with adjectives, is an expression of a homeless soul. This feeling of melancholy and longing increases in five novellas published from 1888 to 1894, all about rootless students from the provinces, among which *Livets Træ* (1893; The Tree of Life) expresses Jørgensen's despair over a materialistically limited existence. His spiritual struggle leads to a religious breakthrough in the poetry collection *Bekendelse* (1894; Confession). The first poems indicate a pantheistic belief, but in the final poem, "Confiteor" (I Confess), the Christian faith becomes victorious. Owing to the influence of Charles BAUDELAIRE, Jørgensen changed his early minutely analytical language into a plain, imageless style in later collections, a style that reaches its perfection in *Der er en Brønd, som rinder* (1920; The Well That Flows). His later production becomes a part of international Catholicism. It consists of travel books from Germany and Italy and scholarly and psychologically penetrating biographies of saints: *Den hellige Frans of Assisi* (1907; Eng. tr., *Saint Francis of Assisi*, 1912) and *Den hellige Katarina af Siena* (1915; Eng. tr., *Saint Catherine of Siena*, 1938). Jørgensen's chief prose work, however, is *Mit Livs Legende* (1916–28; Eng. tr., *Jørgensen, An Autobiography*, 1928–29), a candid confession, which, as a psychological document, is comparable to the confessions of Saint Augustine and Jean Jacques Rousseau. Inspired by Goethe and Paul VERLAINE, Jørgensen developed a unique lyrical and transparent style, preferring uncomplicated metrical forms in which the contents are relayed through the intensity of the feelings.

See: E. Frederiksen, *Johannes Jørgensen's Ungdom* (1946); W. Glyn Jones, *Johannes Jørgensen, TWAS* (1969).   S.H.R.

Jouhandeau, Marcel (1888–1979), French novelist and short-story writer, was born in La Clayette (Saône-et-Loire) and grew up in Guéret (Creuse) in a strict Catholic atmosphere. At age 12 he was influenced by a former Carmelite named Jeanne and her sister Emilie, under whose guidance he read extensively in mystical literature. Later he was steeped in religiosity by a certain Mme Caron (she appears in his works as Mme Alban or "the Perfection"). After the end of this relationship, Jouhandeau brilliantly finished his studies in Guéret (see *Chaminadour*, vols. 1–3 [1934–41, definitive ed., 1968]), and in 1908 he went to Paris where he studied literature at the

Lycée Henri IV and the Sorbonne. Three years later, his father learned of his desire to become a writer and stopped supporting him. From 1912 to 1949, Jouhandeau taught at the Collège Libre de Passy, usually the sixth form (see *Ma classe de 6e* [1949]). In 1914, the year of his first passionate homosexual relationship, he burned most of his manuscripts. Drafted in 1915, he served as an army clerk stationed in Guéret until the end of World War I. At this point in his life he almost married.

Upon his return to Paris, Jouhandeau began to submit manuscripts to editors. *Les Pincengrain* (1920), a collection of short stories originally published in the *Nouvelle Revue française*, was soon followed by *La Jeunesse de Théophile* (1921; Théophile's Youth), an ironic, mystical, and autobiographical work. During the following years, Jouhandeau encountered most of the prominent writers of his time, becoming the friend of several of them, including Jacques RIVIÈRE, André GIDE, Jean PAULHAN, Jean COCTEAU, and Henry de MONTHERLANT. Jouhandeau traveled abroad, dabbled in occultism, and had a violent homosexual affair, recounted in *L'Amateur d'imprudence* (1932; The Lover of Imprudence). He turned the people of his hometown against him because of his depiction of them in *Les Térébinthe* (1926) and *Prudence Hautechaume* (1927).

On the advice of his close friend Marie Laurencin, Jouhandeau married Elisabeth-Claire Toulemon, a dancer well known under the name Caryathis. He immortalized her under the name Elise in numerous works: *Monsieur Godeau marié* (1933; partial Eng. tr., *Marcel and Elise*, 1953), *Chroniques maritales* (1938; Marital Chronicles), *Nouvelles chroniques maritales* (1943; New Marital Chronicles), and in the nine volumes of *Scènes de la vie conjugale* (1948–59; Scenes of Conjugal Life). Elise also wrote her own memoirs, published as *Joies et douleurs d'une belle excentrique* (1952–60; Joys and Sorrows of a Beautiful Eccentric).

In the 1930s, Jouhandeau experienced marital and financial problems and underwent a deep psychological crisis (see *De l'abjection* [1939; Concerning Abjection]). He became anti-Semitic and wrote *Le Péril juif* (1937; The Jewish Peril). After World War II, Jouhandeau was accused of having been a collaborationist, and for a time he had to go into hiding. In 1946, with his *Essai sur moi-même* (1947; Essay on Myself), he began to dedicate himself to memoirs and his diary. *Mémorial* appeared in seven volumes between 1950 and 1972; 26 volumes of his *Journaliers* (Dailies) appeared between 1961 and 1978, covering the period 1957–72. In the 1940s, Jouhandeau also began to embrace homosexuality openly, glorifying it in *Chroniques d'une passion* (1944; Chronicles of a Passion), *Carnets de Don Juan* (1947; Don Juan's Notebook), *Eloge de la volupté* (1951; In Praise of Voluptuousness), *Du pur amour* (1955; Concerning Pure Love), and in *Journaliers*. A most prolific writer up until his death, Jouhandeau's œuvre consists of more than 50 published volumes as well as numerous contributions to periodicals and some as yet unpublished works.

A master of introspection, psychological analysis, and spontaneous writing, Jouhandeau exploited his memoirs, especially those concerning his youth and adolescence and his hometown. In a document without equivalent in literature, he described and analyzed his own marital life. In many of his later works he drew on his experiences as a homosexual. Although Jouhandeau's work is generally autobiographical, he stated that "in order for one's own story to be bearable, one must add a little legend to it." Thus his alter ego Godeau and his wife Elise are not merely portraits, but imposing literary creations.

Despite the fact that he was acclaimed as their peer by

many of his great contemporaries, Jouhandeau's following remained quite small until the 1950s. This may be due to the themes he treated and to his disregard for literary structures. Among major 20th-century French authors, he is probably the least known abroad, especially in the United States. In addition to those works mentioned above, Jouhandeau's most important writings include *Monsieur Godeau intime* (1926; Intimate Picture of Mr. Godeau), *Astaroth* (1929), *Le Journal du coiffeur* (1931; The Hairdresser's Diary), *Images de Paris* (1934; Scenes of Paris), *Algèbre des valeurs morales* (1935; Algebra of Moral Values), *L'Oncle Henri* (1943; Uncle Henry), *Petit Bestiare* (1944; Little Bestiary), *La Faute plutôt que le scandale* (1949; Sin Rather than Scandal), *Notes sur la magie et le vol* (1952; Notes on Magic and Theft), *Carnet du professeur* (1953; The Professor's Notebook), *Contes d'enfer* (1955; Tales of Hell), *Carnets de l'écrivain* (1957; The Writer's Notebook), *Saint Philippe Neri* (1957; Eng. tr., St. Philip Neri, 1960), *Théâtre sans spectacle* (1957; Theater without a Play), *Réflexions sur la vie et le bonheur* (1958; Reflections on Life and Happiness), *Descente aux enfers* (1961; Descent to Hell), *Trois crimes rituels* (1962; Three Ritual Crimes), and *Léonora ou les dangers de la vertu* (1969; Leonora or the Dangers of Virtue). Under the name Marcel Provence he published *Les Allemands en Provence* (1919), *Bauxite et aluminium* (*L'Allemagne et l'après-guerre*, 1920), and *Amour*, an anthology of poems.

See: C. Mauriac, *Introduction à une mystique de l'enfer* (1938); J. Cabanis, *Jouhandeau* (1959); J. Gaumier, *L'Univers de Marcel Jouhandeau* (1959).   J.-P.C.

Jouve, Pierre-Jean (1887–1976), French poet, novelist, essayist, and translator, was born in Arras. In his youth he was deeply affected by three things: precarious health; his reading of Charles BAUDELAIRE, Stéphane MALLARMÉ, and Arthur RIMBAUD; and the beginnings of a lifelong love for music. After three years of publishing his own review, *Les Bandeaux d'or*, and some limited contact with the members of the "Abbaye" group of writers (*see* Charles VILDRAC), Jouve published his first collections of verse: *Les Muses romaines et florentines* (1910; Roman and Florentine Muses), *Présences* (1912; Presences), and *Parler* (1913; Talk).

After the outbreak of World War I, in which Jouve saw limited action as a volunteer hospital orderly, those earlier works were followed by the pacifist poems of *Vous êtes des hommes* (1915; You Are Men), *Poème contre le grand crime* (1916; Poem against the Great Crime), and *Danse des morts* (1917; Dance of the Dead). His repeated bouts of poor health and the time he spent with war wounded led to his abstraction of the notion of limit, based on that of death. Acquaintance with Freudian psychology and psychoanalysis, moreover, convinced him of the all-encompassing primacy of human sexuality and eroticism. His consequent perception of man, trapped between the demands of instinctual forces and the limitation of human mortality, led him in turn to conclude that Roman Catholicism afforded the best satisfaction for his spiritual needs.

In 1925, Jouve published the first of two volumes—*Les Mystérieuses Noces* (1925; Mysterious Nuptials), *Les Nouvelles Noces* (1926; New Nuptials)—that were to be reissued in 1928 simply under the title *Les Noces* and which represented for Jouve a break with his poetic past, a rejection of his works already published, and an inauguration for his work yet to come. In *Les Noces*, as in *Le Paradis perdu* (1929; Paradise Lost), *La Symphonie à Dieu* (1930; Symphony to God), and *Sueur de sang* (1933; Bloodsweat), Jouve works constantly to attain a poetry,

justifiable as chant, that will incarnate his spiritual concerns.

At this time, he also turned to novels and short stories. The heroine of *Paulina 1880* (1925), tortured by eroticism and mysticism, echoes the themes and ideas seen in his poetry of the period. This work sets the stage for his succeeding fiction: *Le Monde désert* (1927; Deserted World), *Hécate* (1928; Hecate), *Vagadu* (1931; Vagadu), *Histoires sanglantes* (1932; Bloody Tales), and *La Scène capitale* (1935; Capital Scene). During World War II, instead of repeating the pacifist cries of his poetry of the years 1915–17, Jouve published works that appear as reaffirmations of faith in man's spiritual value: *Vers majeurs* (1942; Major Verse), *La Vierge de Paris* (1944; The Virgin of Paris), and *Gloire 1940* (1944; Glory 1940). Following the war, Jouve returned to his characteristic quest for resolution of man's physical-spiritual dilemma through the medium of poetic language. This was the concern of such works as *Hymne* (1947; Hymn), *Diadème* (1949; Diadem), *Langue* (1952; Tongue), *Mélodrame* (1957; Melodrama), *Inventions* (1958; Inventions), and *Ténèbre* (1965; Shadow).

Throughout his career, Jouve also functioned as an adept translator (of Friedrich Hölderlin and Shakespeare, in particular) and as a brilliant critic. His *Le Don Juan de Mozart* (1942; Eng. tr., *Mozart's Don Juan*, 1957) is a keen, accessible analysis of Mozart's genius as seen in a work that, through its concentration on the themes of love and death, mirrors Jouve's own principal preoccupations.

See: M. Callander, *The Poetry of Pierre-Jean Jouve* (1964); R. Micha, *Pierre-Jean Jouve* (1971); special Jouve no. of *L'Herne* 19 (1972).   J.F.E.

Jouvet, Louis (1887–1951), French actor and director, was born in Crozon. While studying pharmacy in Paris, he met Jacques COPEAU, the founder of the Théâtre du Vieux-Colombier, under whose guidance he acquired a solid artistic and technical preparation. After 1922 he became stage director of the Comédie des Champs-Elysées and, in 1927, the director of that theater. With Gaston BATY, Charles DULLIN, and Georges PITOËFF, he founded "Le Cartel," an association for professional and moral support. The four worked together in this association until 1940. In 1934, Jouvet took over the Athénée, which he ran until his death, except during an extended tour of South America during World War II.

An original actor endowed with a strong personality and a curiously inflected voice, Jouvet left his imprint on numerous roles in plays by Molière, Jules ROMAINS, and Jean GIRAUDOUX, as well as on the screen in such films as *Topaze*, *Carnet de bal*, *Drôle de drame*, and *Hôtel du nord*. As a stage director, he liked only theater having stature as literature. He served as an advisor for several contemporary writers, especially Giraudoux, whose most important plays Jouvet produced; and he gave a new interpretation, both respectful and subtle, to the great works of Molière. Yet his attention to the text did not prevent him from giving prominence to ingenious stage machinery and from seeking the assistance of painters, such as Christian Bérard and Georges Braque. In his later years, Jouvet taught a remarkable course on theater that has been recorded in two posthumous works, *Le Comédien désincarné* (1954; The Actor Disincarnated) and *Tragédie classique et théâtre du XIXe siècle* (1968; Classical Tragedy and Theater of the 19th Century). He also wrote several luminous works on the art of acting.

See: C. Cézan, *Louis Jouvet et le théâtre d'aujourd'hui* (1938, 1948); B. L. Knapp, *Louis Jouvet: Man of the Theatre* (1957).   R.A.

Jovine, Francesco (1902–50), Italian novelist, short-story writer, and critic, was born in Guardialfiera (Molise), the small town that served as inspiration and setting for much of his work. Jovine was the eldest son of a large family of modest means. He attended local elementary schools and graduated from the normal school in Velletri at the age of 16. A year later he began his teaching career as tutor in private boarding schools in Maddaloni and Vasto. In 1925 he was appointed to the elementary schools in Rome and subsequently became school supervisor within the Ministry of Education, a post he held for most of his life.

Jovine's serious literary activity began in Rome with the publication of a few short stories, a children's book, *Berlué* (1929), and numerous critical articles in which he engaged in the ongoing literary polemics with hermeticists, surrealists, and the supporters of Gabriele D'ANNUNZIO and Luigi PIRANDELLO. Jovine's outspoken views and his profound aversion to fascism isolated him from the official literary and intellectual world of the 1930s and early 1940s. He took an active part in the Italian Resistance, and in 1948 he joined the Italian Communist Party.

Jovine's first novel, *Un uomo provvisorio* (1934; A Temporary Man), is the story of a small-town intellectual who finds himself both caught up in and frustrated by the superficiality of city life. Although this work contains all the flaws of a first novel, one can already see in it the elements and themes that will be developed in the writer's later works: the realities and stark poetry of the peasant world, the harshness of the land, and the quiet desperation of the men who inhabit it. Jovine's second novel, *Signora Ava* (1942), was largely ignored when it appeared, but it established him as one of the major writers of the postwar period. Although it is set in Guardialfiera during the last years of the Bourbon rule, the book is much more than a mere historical or regionalistic novel. Its outstanding quality is the perfect balance that Jovine strikes between the nostalgic, fablelike memory of a remote past and the presentation of ironic crude reality. His last novel, *Le terre del Sacramento* (1950; Eng. tr., *The Estate in Abruzzi*, 1952), published shortly after his death, won the Viareggio Prize and represents the fulfillment of his potential as a writer as well as the peak of his ideological development. The characters in the novel are divided into two groups: the landed gentry, with their pride, tawdry ambitions, and timid dreams, and the peasants, strong in spirit and determination but ineluctably doomed to exploitation, failure, and death. The true protagonist of the novel, however, is the land itself, which Jovine views not as wealth to be possessed, but as an instrument for creating the well-being of those who must live on it or perish.

Among Jovine's other works are several collections of short stories, *Ladro di galline* (1940; Chicken Thief), *Il pastore sepolto* (1943; The Buried Shepherd), *L'impero in provincia* (1945; The Empire in the Provinces), and *Tutti i miei peccati* (1948; All My Sins), all of which have been reprinted in *Racconti* (1960; Short Stories). Jovine also wrote two plays, which are as yet unpublished, "Il burattinaio metafisico" (1933; The Metaphysical Puppeteer) and "Giorni che rinasceranno" (1945; Days That Will Be Reborn).

See: G. Giardini, *Francesco Jovine* (1967); M. Grillandi, *Francesco Jovine* (1971).   Z.T.

József, Attila (1905–37), Hungarian poet, was born in Budapest. He is the finest Hungarian socialist poet of the 20th century. József's father left the family when Attila was three years old, after which he and his sisters were supported by their mother, a washerwoman. In 1910 he was sent to the small village of Öcsöd and spent two depressing years there with foster parents. After his mother's death in 1919, his brother-in-law was appointed his legal guardian. József published his first book of poetry, *A szépség koldusa* (1922; Beggar of Beauty), when he was still attending secondary school. In 1924 he entered the University of Szeged to study Hungarian and French literature, but after a year he was advised to leave by a professor Hungarian philology who had decided, on the basis of József's anarchist-minded poem "Tiszta szívvel" (1924; With a Pure Heart), that he was not be be a schoolteacher. The following year, József left for Vienna, where he made a living by selling newspapers and cleaning dormitories. A few months later he moved to Paris, where he first read G. W. F. Hegel and Karl Marx and where his instinctive revolt against society hardened into an attitude of conscious revolutionary negation.

József returned to Hungary in 1927 and, after an unfortunate love affair with a middle-class girl (ending in József's first nervous breakdown), became actively engaged in the socialist movement. He joined the illegal Communist Party in 1930. Unable to support himself from his writing alone, he took all sorts of odd jobs. His aggressive, unjust attack on Mihály BABITS in the review *A Toll* cut him off from an important potential source of financial assistance, the Baumgarten Foundation, of which Babits was curator. József's third volume of poetry, *Nincsen apám, se anyám* (1929; Fatherless and Motherless), shows that he had successfully assimilated the influences of Endre ADY, Gyula JUHÁSZ, and Lajos KASSÁK as well as the new techniques of French surrealism. His defiance and challenge to the established order recall Arthur RIMBAUD. During the period of his closest identification with Communist ideals (1930–32), József's poetry often imitates that of the medieval poet François Villon, whose typical genre, the ballad, became in József's hands a modern verse form capable of expressing the sufferings of the working class and its determination to break its shackles. József's next book of poetry, *Döntsd a tőkét!* (1931; Chop at the Roots! [or] Topple the Rule of Capital!), was confiscated by the public prosecutor who well understood the pun hidden in the title and who took exception to such poems as the dramatic "Szocialisták" (Socialists).

In 1931, József began undergoing psychoanalytic treatment. In that same year, in spite of his active participation in the educational work of the Communist movement, he began to be regarded with suspicion by some of its leaders. This finally led to a break between the poet and the Communist Party. József's "sins" included his rejection of the narrow concept of "proletarian culture" and his insistence on the necessity of a synthesis between Marxism and Sigmund Freud's teachings. Despite the fact that József made proletarian existence the subject of such great descriptive poems and tableaux as "Külvárosi éj" (Night in the Slums), "Elégia," and "Téli éjszaka" (Winter Night), all written in the early 1930s, his poetry was rejected in Communist Party circles and he was not invited to the Soviet Writers Congress in Moscow in 1934. To József this was an act of betrayal.

József's last two books of poetry, *Medvetánc* (1934; Bear Dance) and *Nagyon fáj* (1936; It Hurts Deeply), were received warmly in the literary press, and in 1936 he was at last given a job as editor of the independent left-wing review *Szép szó*. Yet his nervous condition deteriorated rapidly, and in the last two years of his life József suffered severe attacks of schizophrenia. In his lucid intervals, however, he produced scores of beautiful, moving, often "existentialist" poems that remain gems of modern European poetry. Political disappointments could not undermine his belief in such ideals as freedom and a humane socialism. József's most famous love poem is the musical "Oda" (1933; Ode), which takes the reader for a journey around and inside the body of the beloved woman. Another significant poem, addressed to his mother, is an expression of a love-hate complex released by psychoanalytical treatment. Although he was basically a nonreligious man, at the end of his life József turned to God in his desperate search for a figure of love and authority. In December 1937, Attila József committed suicide at Balatonszárszó.

József once defined poetry as "word-magic acting within the soul of a nation." His own poetic achievement cannot be fully appreciated unless one knows Hungarian, yet in his work the combination of dialectical thought, supply and imaginative language, and original patterns of rhythm and rhyme produced a poetry that is firm both in form and substance. Furthermore, his best work, although rooted in the Hungarian poetic tradition, is universal; while his background and themes are often proletarian, his compassion transcends class barriers. József's influence on post-World War II Hungarian poetry has been considerable. He is admired for the clarity, conciseness, and outspoken character of much of his verse as well as for his opposition to the politics and social philosophy of the regime during the 1930s. József's philosophical and aesthetic writings are characterized by a convoluted Hegelianism. His political essays, which advocated, among other things, alliance with all democratic forces even before this platform became official Comintern policy, were included in vol. 3 of his *Összes művei* (1958; Collected Works).

See: A. Németh, *József Attila* (1944); A. Koestler, *The Invisible Writing* (1954), pp. 214-21; A. Sándor, "Attila József," *New Writing of East Europe* (1968); G. Gömöri, Introduction to *Attila József: Selected Poems and Texts* (1973); M. Vágó, *József Attila* (1975).   G.G.

Juhász, Ferenc (1928-), Hungarian poet, was born in Bia, the son of a poor bricklayer. In 1947 he moved to Budapest, where he studied Hungarian philology for a while, later earning his living as a writer and an editor. Juhász's first works, *Szárnyas csikó* (1949; Winged Foal), *A Sántha család* (1950; The Sántha Family), and *Apám* (1950; Father), were heavily influenced by such classic Hungarian writers as Sándor Petőfi and János Arany (*see* HUNGARIAN LITERATURE), yet these volumes give evidence of Juhász's poetic gifts, especially his daring use of imagery. After a period of naive revolutionary optimism, Juhász became disenchanted with the political status quo. The volume *Óda a repüléshez* (1953; Ode to Flight) broke through the rigid canons of socialist realism, and his next work, *A tékozló ország* (1954; The Prodigal Country), a very long epic poem on the peasant revolt of 1514 led by György Dózsa, ends with a passionate hymn to freedom. From an aesthetic point of view, this work, in spite of its heterogeneous character, is an important landmark: it marks the liberation of the Hungarian poetic imagination from the tutelage of old-fashioned realism, and it is also a bold experiment in verse form, demonstrating Juhász's "extended syllabic line."

Juhász's next collection, *A virágok hatalma* (1956; The Power of Flowers), contains some of his most mature and moving work, but it poses the threat that his visionary panbiologism—the proliferation of natural and cosmic imagery in his work—will devour the message and destroy the "traditional" structure of the poem. In the long poem "A szarvassá változott királyfi . . ." (1955; The Boy Changed into a Stag"), Juhász adapted folk motifs used by Béla Bartók in *Cantana Profana*, creating in his poem

a Bartókean synthesis of sound and image. Some years later, in *József Attila sírja* (1963; Eng. tr., *The Grave of Attila József*, 1968), Juhász appeared to have lost the balance between form and content, his theme being overgrown by functionally irrelevant clusters of metaphors. This tendency has continued in *A szent tűzözön regéi* (1969; Tales of the Sacred Fire-Flood), which consists of endless variations on the theme of universal castastrophe and the ultimate devastation of nature and mankind, as well as in *A halottak királya* (1971; The King of Dead), where the poet returns to a more traditional verse form, but remains obsessed with death, corruption, and decay, his images and metaphors gushing forth in a monotonous, exasperating torrent of verse. His poetry has found more than one English translator, including Kenneth McRobbie (1970) and David Wevill (1970).

See: P. Nagy, "A tékozló költő," *Csillag* 8 (1954): 2400-15; B. Abody, *Indulatos utazás* (1956); K. McRobbie, Introduction to F. Juhász, *The Boy Changed into a Stag: Selected Poems* (1970); Z. Kenyeres, *Gondolkodó irodalom* (1974), pp. 306-19.   G.G.

Juhász, Gyula (1883-1937), Hungarian poet and journalist, was born in Szeged. His poetry retained strong connections with this southern city and the countryside around it. In 1899, Juhász entered the Piarist novitiate in Vác but decided to leave only a few months later. He then studied Hungarian and Latin at Budapest University, where he met and befriended Mihály BABITS and Dezső KOSZTOLÁNYI. Between 1906 and 1916, Juhász taught in various cities all over Hungary, including Nagyvárad (now Oradea, Romania), where he participated in the famous *Holnap* anthology, along with the great Hungarian symbolist poet Endre ADY. Juhász's teaching career was repeatedly interupted by fits of depression; in 1914 he attempted suicide. An enthusiastic supporter of the 1918 Hungarian democratic revolution and a literary advisor to the Szeged Theater during the Hungarian Soviet Republic (1919), he was unable to resume teaching in the counterrevolutionary atmosphere of the regime of Miklós Horthy and could barely support himself on his earnings as a journalist. He never recovered his mental health and finally took his life with an overdose of Veronal.

Juhász is in some ways the most "Hungarian" poet of the first *Nyugat* generation (*see* HUNGARIAN LITERATURE). Influenced by Lev TOLSTOY, Friedrich NIETZSCHE, Paul VERLAINE, and the French Parnassians, his is a reflective, sad, gentle symbolism, full of local color and patriotic concern. Juhász called himself "the poet of Hungarian sorrow and human compassion," the latter trait evident in his sympathetic treatment of the life of the poor. While some of his poems proclaim socialist ideals, his most famous pieces lament unrequited love in quasireligious tones or paint the Hungarian countryside in soft pastel colors. With regard to form, Juhász was fairly traditional; apart from the sonnet his favorite structure was the rhyming couplet. Juhász's poetry is uneven and seldom original, yet it created an important link between Ady and Attila JÓZSEF, whom Juhász helped to launch as a poet. Juhász was awarded the prestigious Baumgarten Prize three times.

See: Gy. Illyés, "Juhász Gyula versei," *Nyugat*, 22 (1929): 176-78; L. Bóka, "Juhász Gyula," *Irodalomtörténet* 1 (1951), pp. 80-94; A. Kispéter, *Juhász Gyula* (1956); A. Karátson, *Le Symbolisme en Hongrie*, (1969), pp. 320-39.   G.G.

Jünger, Ernst (1895-), German novelist and essayist, brother of the poet and essayist Friedrich Georg Jünger, was born in Heidelberg, the son of a pharmacist. He volunteered at the outbreak of World War I and, in the course of his military service, he was awarded the highest German military order. During the years between the wars he devoted himself to writing and was a contributor to a number of conservative reviews and newspapers. In 1940 he took part in the French campaign.

The technological and social changes of the 19th century did not, it seemed to Jünger, decrease the perennial threat with which irrational forces confront the unstable life of humankind. Only the constant and total exercise of all human virtues, physical as well as moral and intellectual, will establish the vital harmony that can sustain a culture. The sense of the fearful, elemental fascination of the world is one of the most striking qualities of Jünger's work. His first book, *In Stahlgewittern* (1920; Eng. tr., *The Storm of Steel*, 1929), struck the characteristic theme of extreme action coupled with insight and soldierly pathos. Several volumes followed, essentially observational and reflective rather than narrative in nature. A semiautobiographical account of experiences in southern France and North Africa is *Afrikanische Spiele* (1936; Eng. tr., *African Diversions*, 1954). Jünger's best form, however, is not the novel but the contemplative essay, as in *Das abenteuerliche Herz* (1929; The Adventurous Heart) and *Blätter und Steine* (1934; Leaves and Stones), in which his "stereoscopic" perception is rendered through imagery of extraordinary "perspective" power.

The political implications of his attitude, in some respects reminiscent of T. E. Lawrence, had considerable influence. On one occasion he examined in detail the social and emotional structure of the contemporary worker, in *Der Arbeiter* (1932; The Worker); but it is in the soldier and his reflective counterpart, the poet, that Jünger recognized the human type in which the qualities of alertness, discipline, intelligence, and sensitiveness appear most strikingly. Jünger is an individualist, although much of his work is drawn from his experiences of the wars, as in *Der Kampf als inneres Erlebnis* (1922; Battle

as Inner Experience), essays; *Feuer und Blut* (1925; Fire and Blood); essays, and in the report *Das Wäldchen 125* (1925; Eng. tr., *Copse 125*, 1930). In the mythological parable, *Auf den Marmorklippen* (1939; On the Marble Cliffs), and in the diary of his months in 1940 as an officer in France, *Gärten und Straßen* (1942; Gardens and Roads), Jünger wrote urgently and with concern of the threat to deep-rooted cultural values offered by the forces of undisciplined inhumanity and barbarian dissolution. His thought is always conveyed with the precision of one to whom the distinction between the observable fact and the irrational perspective is only one of degree and intensity. Dream imagery is, therefore, one of his most frequent devices, and his vision of nature has at times the puzzling coherence of a surrealist landscape. By his devotion to the civilized and civilizing qualities of language, as in *Geheimnisse der Sprache* (1934, rev. ed., 1939; Mysteries of Language), he produced some of the finest prose written in Germany; it is lithe, resolute, unsentimental, and radiant.

Jünger became a controversial figure immediately after World War II because of his participation in campaigns in France; for a short time in 1945 he was forbidden to publish. Some held him to be at best a sympathizer of Nazi doctrine, while others defended him as an elite intellectual who kept his ethical and moral prnciples intact. In 1949 he published his war diaries *Strahlungen* (Radiations) and in the same year the somber Utopian novel *Heliopolis*. In 1957 the novel *Gläserne Bienen* (Glass Bees) appeared, and in 1959 he became a coeditor of the journal *Antaios*. His collected works appear in ten volumes between 1960 and 1963.

See: W. K. Pfeiler, *War and the German Mind* (1941), pp. 109–16; E. Brock, *Das Weltbild Ernst Jüngers* (1945); H.-P. Schwarz, *Der konservative Anarchist* (1962); H. L. Arnold, *Wandlung und Wiederkehr* (1965); F. Baumer, *Ernst Jünger* (1967); G. Loose, *Ernst Jünger* (1974); H. P. des Coudres, *Bibliographie der Werke Ernst Jüngers* (1970).

V.La. rev. ALW

K

Kaden-Bandrowski, Juliusz (1885–1944), Polish novelist, short-story writer, and essayist, was born in Rzeszów. He was killed in Warsaw during the Warsaw uprising. Kaden-Bandrowski studied music in Leipzig and Brussels. He occupied a major place in Polish literature between World War I and World War II. Associated with the patriotic movement for his country's independence, he fought actively in Józef Piłsudski's legions (1914–18) and eventually became a literary spokesman for Piłsudski's ideology. Between the two world wars he occupied several major positions in Poland's literary life as president of Writers Union and secretary of Polish Academy of Literature. Kaden-Bandrowski's early novels and short stories published between 1911 and 1914 show his dependence on, and his departure from, the impressionistic lyrical style of "Young Poland." His mature works, such as the political novel *Generał Barcz* (1923), containing an analysis of the problem of power and its moral rights, represent his own highly expressionistic style. A novel in two parts, *Czarne skrzydła* (1928–29; Black Wings), deals with social problems and workers' movements in Silesia; and still another political novel, a sequel to the previous one, *Mateusz Bigda* (1933), criticizes the Polish parliamentary system of that period, bordering on satire of major political leaders. Kaden-Bandrowski also wrote several successful collections of short stories, political

journalism, essays, reminiscences, and short, mostly autobiographical novels, for example, *Miasto mojej matki* (1925; My Mother's Town) and *W cieniu zapomnianej olszyny* (1926; Eng. tr., *Call to the Cuckoo*, 1948), which won him wide recognition and popularity.

See: *Słownik współczesnych pisarzy polskich*, vol. 2 (1964), pp. 62–73; M. Sprusiński, *Juliusz Kaden-Bandrowski* (1971).

J.R.K.

Kaffka, Margit (1880–1918), Hungarian novelist and poet, was born in Nagykároly (now Carei, Romania), into the gentry. She was one of the pioneers of modern Hungarian prose. Kaffka lost her father at the age of six and was educated in an orphanage run by nuns. She became a teacher and taught at Miskolc and Budapest until 1915. After that date, she devoted herself entirely to writing. Kaffka was married twice. She died in the influenza epidemic that swept through Europe at the end of World War I.

Kaffka's first poems were published in the reviews *Magyar Geniusz* and *Hét*, but once *Nyugat* (see HUNGARIAN LITERATURE) was launched, she became a regular contributor and a member of its inner circle. In her social and aesthetic views, Kaffka was influenced first by József Kiss and later by Endre ADY, the greatest Hungarian poet of the period. Although she published five books of poetry, Kaffka never became a really significant poet, yet what she could not achieve in poetry, she did accomplish in prose. Her novels, especially *Szinek és évek* (1912; Colors and Years), represent a new departure in Hungarian fiction. *Szinek és évek* depicts the decline of a gentry family as seen through the eyes of Magda Pórtelky, a woman who is unable to break out of the restrictions imposed upon her by provincial society. Magda, whose daughters received vocational training and are emancipated women, feels a nostalgia for the glittering world of her youth with its balls and feasts, but not without realizing that her own tribulations in life are closely connected to the traditional status of women in small-town and rural Hungary. The book's first-person narrative unfolds through a stream of reminiscences and an impressionistic sequence of episodes. It is full of minute psychological observations related in a highly poetic style.

While the protagonist of *Szinek és évek* is basically nonsensual, the heroine of *Mária évei* (1913; Mary's Years) is a prey to her own feverish imagination and longing for "real" life; She experiences the inner conflicts of a woman who has renounced her traditional role but has not yet found a new one. *Állomások* (1914; final version 1917; Stations), is a broad canvas of the literary life of Kaffka's times and possesses all the inherent shortcomings of a roman à clef. Apart from Kaffka's three major novels, two short ones are noteworthy: *Hangyaboly* (1917; Anthill) and *Két nyár* (1916; Two Summers). In *Két nyár*, she gave voice to her strong pacifist sentiments. Her deep concern for the unequal status of women and the acuteness of her social and psychological observations have made Kaffka a much-read author in present-day Hungary.

See: M. Radnóti, *Kaffka Margit müvészi fejlődése* (1934); A. Schöpflin, *A magyar irodalom története a XX. században* (1937): pp. 216–41; J. Reményi, *Hungarian Writers and Literature* (1964), pp. 284–91.   G.G.

Kafka, Franz (1883–1924), Austrian novelist and short-story writer, was born in Prague, the only son of a successful Jewish merchant. He was educated exclusively in German-speaking schools and, after receiving a degree in law from the German University in Prague in 1906, became an official in a workers' accident insurance company. In order to seek treatment for a tubercular infection that had first been diagnosed in 1917, he resigned the post in 1922. Kafka welcomed his illness as a miracle that released him forever and in a socially acceptable fashion from the duties and responsibilities of bourgeois life. His various attempts to marry failed, and he remained a bachelor all his life. Kafka died of tuberculosis in a sanatorium near Vienna.

Kafka's language and narrative technique place him outside such literary movements of his day as were represented by the neoromantics of Vienna and Prague and the decadent writers of Paris. His prose style reflects the legalistic language of his profession and also shows affinities with the rarefied and bloodless German dialect spoken in Prague and employed in its ruling bureaucratic circles. No matter how emotionally charged Kafka's nightmarish visions of guilt, torture, or endless frustration may be, his language remains sober, crystal clear, and detached. There is never a trace of rhetoric, sentimentality, or surprise.

Kafka regarded his narrative technique as primarily that of a storyteller: "I don't describe people. I tell a story. Pictures . . . only pictures." Since he himself never intruded as an omniscient narrator with philosophical reflections, psychological illuminations, or overt moral judgments, the narrative point of view is limited to the conscious thoughts and perceptions of the protagonist. Kafka's fiction therefore bears certain similarities to a newspaper report, which presents a stark succession of events as well as the comments of those involved but does not attempt to interpret causes or draw conclusions. The result is a highly dramatic style in which all actions are experienced as occurring in the present rather than as being retold. The reader feels trapped within a stream of events from which there is no escape: the Kafkian protagonist's insight into his own behavior as well as his comprehension of the enigmatic world in which he finds himself is not only insufficient for his own coming to terms with experience, it is often misleading and patently false.

Kafka's literary technique moved between two extremes. He described the works written between 1912 and 1916, which embody the theme of guilt and punishment, as an attempt to present his own "dreamlike inner life." If the dream symbol dominates the first part of his work, it is the so-called intentional symbol that dominates the second part. In the works written after 1917, the protagonist himself subjects certain central symbols—such as the Great Wall of China, the Castle, and the burrow—to endless interpretations. Intellectual possibilities are pursued in all directions, but in such a way that the numerous conditions and contradictions expressed seem finally to cancel each other out. The result is that, however compulsive and elaborate the various exegeses may become, they do not serve to interpret the work for the reader. The interpretations of the protagonist are themselves open to further endless interpretation. It is from the very torrent of possibilities, which never culminates in a point of certainty, that the later group of works arises. While the style and mood of the first period is dreamlike, ominous, and tragic, that of the second period is intellectual and ironic, at once playful and morally earnest.

Although Kafka had written some impressionistic sketches before *Das Urteil* (1912; Eng. tr., *The Judgment*, 1948), this story, set down on the eve of Yom Kippur, represents both a breakthrough to what would become his characteristic thematic obsession (the struggle between father and son, which generates feelings of guilt and is eventually resolved through suffering and atonement) and a refinement of his artistic technique (in a narrative point of view limited to the hypocritical and lying perspective of the protagonist). In *Das Urteil*, the struggle for power erupts with Georg Bendemann's announcement to his father of his impending marriage; it is given immediate expression in Georg's attempt to put his father to bed, a symbolic act of wishing to bury him forever. Herr Bendemann thereupon condemns his son to death for being both "a devilish human being" and "an innocent child"; devilish, because of Georg's aggressive wish to remove and destroy his father as head of the household, and innocent, because of his conscious feelings of filial solicitude, which are designed to conceal his unconscious and hostile motives from himself and from his father. It is therefore not Georg but Georg's absent friend in Russia whom Herr Bendemann declares to be "a son after my own heart," for this is a son who chooses not to challenge the father's independence and power but instead retreats into a life of exile, loneliness, illness, and (most important) bachelorhood. From his father's point of view, Georg's wish to marry not only represents an attempt to murder his father; it also means that Georg must deny his friend, that is, repress all those innermost tendencies that lead away from marriage and the world of business. In reality, however, Georg has only been masquerading as a successful bourgeois businessman, for beneath this façade lies a sensitive and rather freakish other self. Herr Bendemann becomes the means by which the truth is revealed to Georg. On behalf of himself and the friend in Russia, Herr Bendemann acts as both prosecutor and judge, thereby meeting Georg's need for punishment. Georg, having recognized and accepted his guilt, is able to die with love for his father in his heart.

Die Verwandlung (1912; Eng. tr., *The Metamorphosis*, 1948) explores the theme of the divided self: Gregor Samsa awakens one morning to find himself transformed into a gigantic insect. Just as Georg Bendemann initially refuses to recognize the existence of the aggressive impulses he directed toward his father, Gregor strives to ignore his metamorphosis. The visible symbol of Gregor's guilt, however, analogous to the manifestation of a neurotic symptom, provides him with two secondary gains while crippling his life. Without incurring any feelings of guilt, Gregor is now able to give up his very unpleasant job and thus all responsibility for supporting his parents. Gregor's metamorphosis also satisfies a need to express his aggression against the family that has been exploiting him. Gregor's deepest impulse was not to be a successful bourgeois businessman and a helpful son but, rather, to retreat ever further into isolation and loneliness. Such an impulse must engender feelings of guilt. On the most fundamental level, therefore, the metamorphosis also satisfies Gregor's need for punishment and self-destruction for what he has felt toward and done to his family.

Kafka's first novel, *Amerika* (1912; Eng. tr., 1940), is a comedy in which the protagonist, Karl Rossmann, continually experiences the typical Kafkian father-son conflict while managing to avoid the tragic consequences suffered by Georg Bendemann and Gregor Samsa. Karl's real father has been left far behind in Central Europe. Instead of his presence, the essential characteristics of the Kafkian father reappear in various figures of authority throughout the novel. The work thus provides the initial point of departure for the gradual depersonalization of the father image that reaches its culmination in *Das Schloß*. In a series of picaresque adventures across America, the adolescent Karl suffers defeat and punishment by various authority figures. But because Karl does not have guilt feelings, the punishment does not satisfy an inner need for atonement that leads to a final feeling of love and a transfiguring moment of joy. The authority figures remain merely sadistic and tyrannical. The novel concludes with Karl's acceptance into the Nature Theater of Oklahoma, a benign paternal organization that presents a Utopian solution directly opposed to the subterranean current of Kafka's work, which presupposes the son's guilt and leads him to an affirmation of the father, though only by means of punishment and the destruction of the self.

In Kafka's second novel, *Der Prozeß* (1914; Eng. tr., *The Trial*, 1937), and in *In der Strafkolonie* (1914; Eng. tr., *In the Penal Colony*, 1948), the dynamics of the family configuration are projected into the outer world. The struggle still revolves about the protagonist's guilt and punishment, but the father now dons the robes of figures of power in a social context—a remote judge and a prison commandant. Crime and punishment have been objectified and depersonalized, the wrath of the bourgeois father having been replaced by a community's legal code. Although Kafka utilizes a legalistic configuration upon which to construct the works, the defendant's right to receive a fair trial by pleading his case before an impartial judge is nonexistent. The emphasis is not upon the revelation of innocence but upon the admission of guilt (*Prozeß*) and the procedure of punishment (*Strafkolonie*).

Joseph K., the protagonist of *Der Proceß*, is arrested one morning without being informed of the nature of his crime. While fervently denying his guilt, he nevertheless pursues endless investigations into the nature of the court system that is accusing him. He discovers that this court is located only in the slum tenements of the city. In the shadow of the court, life exists on the most primitive level, without the sophisticated veneers and prohibitions of bourgeois society. In direct opposition to the cleanliness, order, and isolation of Joseph K.'s life, existence in the court precincts is spontaneous, communal, and sensual. The court presents and represents the valid definitions of the justified life. Joseph K.'s sterile middle-class bachelorhood is, by comparison, an offense against the law. Joseph K. fights conscious recognition of any feelings of guilt until the very end, for he is unable to surrender himself to a court that serves only to degrade its victims while remaining totally inscrutable. Since he does not admit his guilt, he dies "like a dog" without that final moment of joy and love that Georg and Gregor experienced. In Kafka's world, guilt must be consciously accepted for it to have a beneficial psychological effect; its mere presence is not sufficient. Whether one's claim to innocence is real (like Karl Rossmann's) or fraudulent (like Joseph K.'s), it is the very claim itself that prevents inner transfiguration. Joseph K dies wearily in darkness. No truth has been revealed to him.

The accusatory authority in *Der Prozeß*, symbolized by the court bureaucracy as a whole, undergoes a further process of abstraction in Kafka's next major work *In der Strafkolonie*, appearing here as a unique instrument of torture. The apparatus was created by the Old Commandant, who is now deceased. In the world of the New Commandant, it exists merely as a somewhat neglected curiosity at the periphery of society, maintained only by the love of an officer from the Old Commandant's time. The latter had designed the instrument to precipitate in a guilty prisoner a final ecstatic moment of truth. This moment occurs when the prisoner is able to discover the nature of his crime by reading it from the script that the machine has written with needles upon his body. The present prisoner's crime of disobedience—specifically, failing to salute a doorpost—is so obviously ludicrous that an explorer who has come to the Penal Colony to observe feels forced to object to the whole procedure. Because of the explorer's objections, the officer who tends the machine releases the prisoner before subjecting him to its torture. In order to demonstrate his own devotion to the machine, however, he places himself upon the instrument. But he is killed like a dog; "no sign was visible of the promised redemption." The machine then destroys itself. Thus, neither Joseph K. nor the officer benefit psychologically or spiritually from the suffering inflicted by authority. Accusatory authority is revealed as being merely powerful: No feeling of guilt is assuaged and no truth revealed. Because in the modern world of the New Commandant suffering can only brutalize, the two extremes of physical suffering and spiritual ecstasy inherent in the Old Commandant's world are legislated out of existence. But the suspicion remains that someday the Old Commandant will rise again, and in place of the spiritual superficiality of the modern liberal and humanitarian world he will reinstitute suffering and spiritual transfiguration at the center of life, in the form of a machine of torture.

In *Brief an den Vater* (1919; Eng. tr., *Letter to His Father*, 1954), Kafka presents a defense against his father such as he was never able to embody in his fiction (although his father never read the letter). Kafka investigates one central question: Where does the blame lie for his own crippled existence? He declares that the world was for him divided into three parts: the world of his father, infinitely remote, from which orders were issued and anger expressed when the orders were disobeyed; Kafka's own world, in which he was forever unable to obey his father's laws; and finally a third world, in which everyone else lived happily, free of laws and guilt. For Kafka, life had become reduced to a courtroom in which his own father was both judge and prosecutor and in which he constantly argued both for and against himself. Hermann Kafka—self-confident, insensitive, and gross but productive—appeared to be the measure of life. Hence to be unlike his father for Kafka was to be in some degree inadequate to life itself. Kafka accuses himself of leading a sterile and parasitic existence, while at the same time he blames his father for having filled him with a profound sense of inadequacy during his childhood. Thus Kafka admits: "My writing was all about you; all I did there, after all, was to bemoan what I could not bemoan upon your breast. It was an intentionally long-drawn-out leave-taking from you." But fear and guilt kept him chained to his father. It was only with the outbreak of tuberculosis in 1917 that Kafka was able to liberate himself from his own trial. He was able to retire from the daily struggles of life and from the standards imposed by Hermann Kafka. Moreover, Kafka's increasing maturity (he was 36 years old when he wrote the letter) allowed him at last to perceive that his father was as weak and deluded as Kafka himself and that his vision of his father as a superhuman embodiment of truth and vengeance was the distorted creation of his own terrified, childlike mind.

On the first evening that K., the protagonist of *Das Schloß* (1922; Eng. tr., *The Castle,* 1930), arrives in the Village, he fraudulently asserts that he has been called by the Castle to function as a land surveyor. The rest of the novel describes his unsuccessful attempts to make contact with the Castle in order to have his false claim verified. K. assumes an aggressive posture toward the disdainfully remote, labyrinthine, and hierarchical authority of the Castle, an attitude that quickly develops into a monomaniacal quest for personal recognition from above. Because the state functions for him as the sole ground of meaning and existence, he is prepared to sacrifice the security and comforts of everyday existence in the village in order to break through a forbidding maze of intermediaries. Although he writes letters, uses the influence of women, and pleads with countless officials, his every effort is frustrated. One's immediate impression of the Castle is of a paternal organization that is hopelessly corrupt, laughably inefficient, and infuriatingly condescending. But since the narrative point of view is limited to that of K., who never penetrates into the Castle, the Castle cannot be condemned; its ultimate nature and function can never be embraced or comprehended by reason or experience. Everything concerning the Castle remains ambiguous. Even when K. appears to have made contact with the Castle, his success is immediately overshadowed by the problem of how to evaluate the response from "above." K.'s continuing failure—the novel remains a fragment—implies a negative critique of the individual's fanatical quest for an absolute that serves only to degrade him.

In his last years, Kafka wrote a number of short stories, all of them brilliantly realized. Most of these are constructed around the endless and obsessive reflections and ruminations of their animal narrators: *Forschungen eines Hundes* (1922; Eng. tr., *Investigations of a Dog,* 1946), *Der Bau* (1923; Eng. tr., *The Burrow,* 1946), and *Josefine, die Sängerin, oder das Volk der Mäuse* (1924; Eng. tr., *Josephine, The Singer, or the Mouse Folk,* 1948).

Kafka's works have given rise to a number of quite different interpretations. He has been claimed by the existentialists as describing a world of despair and meaninglessness, by social critics as dealing with the inhumanity of totalitarian regimes, by psychoanalytic writers as metaphorically elaborating his pathological relationship with his father; and by his editor, Max Brod, as having written allegories of divine grace. But since Kafka's works are symbolic, the imaginative universe of his fiction—coherent though it may be—will always escape total explanation by any system of abstract thought. Kafka's concerns are much more fundamental than can be expressed solely in language provided by philosophy, psychoanalysis, or political theory. For Kafka himself, his works represented the biography of his inner life in various symbolic disguises. Like his life, his fiction—centered upon the quest for recognition and the desire for self-definition—was forever marked by despair, frustration, and a sense of constant failure.

See: R. Gray, ed., *Kafka: A Collection of Critical Essays* (1962); H. Politzer, *Franz Kafka: Parable and Paradox* (rev. ed. 1966); W. H. Sokel, *Franz Kafka—Tragik und Ironie* (1964) and *Franz Kafka* (1966); W. Emrich, *Franz Kafka: A Critical Study of His Writings* (1968).

F.G.P.

Kahn, Gustave (1859–1936), French poet, essayist, and novelist, was born in Metz. He was an adamant practitioner and theoretician of vers libre. Kahn's first collection of poetry, *Les Palais nomades* (1886; Nomadic Palaces), is a noted example of the symbolist use of free verse. In 1897 he published some earlier poems in one volume, *Premiers Poèmes* (First Poems), incorporating a prefatory essay in defense of a versification liberated from the traditional rules of rhyme and meter. Indeed, his poetry, marked by the imagery of fantasy and myth, is dominated by a preoccupation with form. Other collections of verse worthy of mention are his *Domaine de fée* (1895; Fairyland), *Images bibliques* (1929; Biblical Images), and *Poèmes 1921–1935* (1939).

Kahn was a cofounder of various literary journals, including *La Vogue* and *Le Symboliste.* He also wrote a serialized column, "La Vie mentale," as well as many novels that are rarely read today. *Symbolistes et décadents* (1902; Symbolists and Decadents) and *Origines du symbolisme* (1936; Origins of Symbolism) deal with the literary movement in which he had participated. Kahn also published numerous critical studies of such artists and poets as François Boucher, Auguste Rodin, Jean Honoré Fragonard, Charles BAUDELAIRE, and Jules Laforgue, the latter contained among those portraits presented in *Silhouettes littéraires* (1925; Literary Silhouettes).

See: J. C. Ireson, *L'Œuvre poétique de Gustave Kahn* (1962).

D.C. and A.C.

Kaiser, Georg (1878–1945), German playwright, was born in Magdeburg. He was one of the outstanding exponents of expressionist drama. His vast oeuvre comprises about 70 plays, as well as sketches, poems, essays, and 3 novels. Between 1895 and 1911 he wrote 29 second-rate plays, mostly comedies, in both the naturalist and the neoromantic modes. None of these was performed or published at the time, but the expressionist plays that followed established his success and fame. Joining and sometimes leading the chorus of expressionist voices around World War I, Kaiser wrote plays that describe dehumanized men in industrial society and depict the often-frustrated search for the expressionists' "new man." Ironically, the emergence or apotheosis of this elusive superhuman being is often accompanied by catastrophic destruction. Typified characters and diction reduced to stark essentials are used to enact the interplay of highly antithetical ideas.

In *Von morgens bis mitternachts* (1916; Eng. tr., *From Morn to Midnight,* 1922), Kaiser uses the *Stationendrama* technique popular with the expressionists and takes his protagonist, a petit bourgeois bank teller who tries to break out of a deadly monotonous existence, through a series of "stations" that contrast the shabbiness of domestic and public life with an ecstatically inspired imaginary existence. While the bank teller's self-centered attempt at regeneration fails, *Die Bürger von Calais* (1914; The Citizens of Calais) presents the notion that one man's heroic humanism and exemplary self-sacrifice not only can save a beleaguered community but also can inspire others to become "new men."

The fates of three generations are traced in a trilogy of plays in which the gap between escalating aspirations and failure in reality widens from play to play. In *Die Koralle* (1917; Eng. tr., *The Coral,* 1963) a tycoon mercilessly rules the industrial empire he has built in a futile attempt to overcome his deep-seated existential insecurity, disguised as fear of poverty. In *Gas* (1918; Eng. tr., 1957) the tycoon's son socializes his factories only to watch the workers who cannot share his vision become more and more enslaved to the machines that provide material gain. In *Gas II* (1920; Eng. tr., 1963) the great-grandson, a worker himself, preaches pacifism and nonworldly sufferance in a setting of total war. When his fellow workers side with his antagonist, who tells them they will rule mankind once they have annihilated half of it, the protagonist himself sets off the explosion that destroys the human race. Thus both the social experimentation advocated in *Gas* and the spiritual solution proposed in the sequel are rejected by the unregenerate masses, who follow the technocrats into dehumanization and destruction. Kaiser's most optimistic but unconvincing treatment of the "new man" theme, *Hölle Weg Erde* (1919; Hell Path Earth), expresses the hope that humanity, once awakened, will choose universal brotherhood over selfishness.

During a spectacular trial for embezzlement in 1921, Kaiser based his unsuccessful defense on the claim that the writer was an invaluable asset to society. In the early 1920s he turned away from expressionism and made a success with a series of insignificant and disparate works that included thrillers, cabaret-style reviews, and musicals. In the most interesting play of this period, *Oktobertag* (1928; Eng. tr., *The Phantom Lovers,* 1928), a Utopian dream world of pure love is constructed and presented as victorious.

In 1933 the Nazis burned Kaiser's books and banned the production of his plays. Relegated to obscurity after 15 years of success and fame, Kaiser lived near Berlin until 1938, when he went to Switzerland. The best of several antitotalitarian plays he wrote after 1933 is the pacifist parable *Der Soldat Tanaka* (1940; The Soldier Tanaka). Its protagonist rebels against previously sacrosanct imperial authority when he comes to realize that human degradation and misery are required to maintain the army.

In his last three plays, written during World War II and published posthumously as *Griechische Dramen* (1948; Greek Plays), Kaiser used traditional form (employing five acts, blank verse, and a small cast) and elevated language to present the pitiful fate of lofty ideals (art, love, and innocence) among men. In *Pygmalion,* art is seen as the highest value, but Pygmalion's supreme creation can live for a short time only before she reverts to stone, because not even her artist-creator can unite dream and reality. In *Zweimal Amphitryon* (Twice Amphitryon), the belligerent hero is bested by Zeus, who in turn is vanquished by Alcmene's pure love. In *Bellerophon,* life is depicted as a maze of evil machinations and extreme dangers. The imperturbably innocent young hero triumphs and, united with his beloved, is placed among the stars.

Kaiser's rational inclinations, strikingly evident in his skillful construction of intricate plots, are strangely at odds with his basically irrational view of man and the world. Even after the demise of expressionism, Kaiser pursued the vision of the "new man," a vision he was able to sustain only by resorting to an elitist and despairing denunciation of ordinary men.

See: E. Schürer, *Georg Kaiser* (1971).   W.H.

Kamban, Guðmundur (1888–1945) Icelandic dramatist and novelist, born on Álftanes near Reykjavik, of poor but enterprising parents, was one of a large family. While working his way through school, Kamban came in contact with the cosmopolitan and humanitarian Einar KVARAN, but he went to Copenhagen to study literature and dramatics, and there he joined the group of Jóhann SIGURJÓNSSON with enthusiasm and wrote his first play, *Hadda-Padda* (1914; Eng. tr., 1917), under that influence. Hadda-Padda is a woman whose love is her moral guide, a recurrent figure in Kamban's work. The play was a success at the Royal Theater, but another play in the same national romantic vein was not so successful. After a visit to New York (1915–17), Kamban turned social critic. In *Marmor* (1918; Marble), a play, and *Ragnar Finnsson* (1922), a novel, he criticized the treatment of convicts in prisons in the United States. During the 1920s, Kamban revolted—as was the fashion of the times—against the conventional morals of love and marriage in a series of plays. *Vi Mordere* (1920; We Murderers) was the most successful of the group. *Sendiherrann frá Júpíter* (1927; The Ambassador from Jupiter) closes this period in Kamban's work with a general challenge to the corruption in Western civilization.

After a decade of cosmopolitan subjects, Kamban returned to native themes and wrote the historical novel *Skálholt* (4 vols., 1930–1935; Eng. tr. of vols 1 and 2, *The Virgin of Skalholt,* 1935), about the unhappy love of the proud daughter of Bishop Brynjólfur Sveinsson (1605–75) and about his *mala domestica.* In monumentality of design this work is reminiscent of Sigrid UNDSET's novels, but the philosophy is totally different: again, as in Kamban's first work, the woman's love is her only conscience. The affinity of this proud type with the women of the sagas is obvious, and in *Jeg ser et stort skønt Land* (1936; Eng. tr., *I See a Wondrous Land,* 1938), Kamban had an opportunity to portray the saga women themselves in his retelling of the stories of the discovery of Greenland and Vinland (America).

Kamban was connected with theaters in Scandinavia and Germany. His stay in Iceland (1927–30) resulted in the novel *30. Generation* (1933; The 30th Generation), a description of the modern emancipated and cosmopolitan bourgeoisie of Reykjavik, with whom Kamban obviously was in sympathy.

During World War II, Kamban was in Denmark and Germany, writing several plays. He was killed by mistake by Danish patriots on May 5, 1945.

See: Ø. Ree, "En islandsk dramatiker," in *Nordisk tidskrift för vetenskap, konst och industri utgiven av Letterstedtska Föreningen* (1921), pp. 39–42; S. Einarsson, "Guðmundur Kamban," *Tímarit þjóðrœknisfélags Íslendinga,* vol. 14 (1932), pp. 7–32.   S.E.

Kamensky, Vasily Vasilyevich (1884–1961), Russian poet, novelist, and playwright, was one of the pioneers of Russian futurism. Born in Moscow, he had a colorful, eventful life, which he later described in several autobiographies. After joining the group headed by David BURLYUK (*see* RUSSIAN LITERATURE), he contributed to the collection *Sadok sudey* (1910; A Trap for Judges). Thereafter he briefly abandoned literature for aviation, but after a plane crash rejoined his fellow futurists. He added extreme verbal experiment to the impressionism of his earlier poetry, especially in the "ferro-concrete" poems of *Tango s korovami* (1914; Tango with Cows). Kamensky's central work is the novel *Stenka Razin* (1915), which extolls anarchy in exuberant language that is sprinkled with shouts, Oriental words, and neologisms. After the October Revolution Kamensky belonged to the LEF group, and prolifically wrote poems thereafter about nature and officially desirable subjects. Kamensky's uneven poetry and prose are marked by emotionalism, cheerfulness, folklorism, and loud verbal color.

See: V. Markov, *Russian Futurism* (1968).   V.M.

Kampmann, Christian (1939–), Danish novelist and short-story writer, was born in Copenhagen. He took his degree in journalism. Kampmann made his literary debut with the collection of short stories, *Blandt venner* (1962; Among Friends), but not until the novel *Sammen* (1967; Together) did he find his true field—the penetratingly critical and psychologically analytical study of the bourgeoisie and its life-style. In *Sammen,* Kampmann's style imitates that of the weekly tabloids, and in the novel *Uden navn* (1969; Without a Name) a similar, conscious, clichélike tone marks the descriptions of anonymous everyday people trapped in a trite and unsuccessful marriage. Kampmann considers existential problems in *Nærved og næsten* (1969; Near and Nearly), one of the major Danish prose works of the 1960s. The focal point of this novel is the attitude of six couples toward love, isolation, happiness, and death, with special stress on their attempts to establish contact with others. Kampmann's moral and social viewpoint becomes clearer in *Vi elsker mere* (1970; We Love More), short stories about people unable to reconcile their private moral concepts with the official, more liberal ones. His most significant artistic achievement is the cycle of novels about the greatness and decline of the Copenhagen bourgeoisie after World War II: *Visse hensyn* (1973; Certain Considerations), *Faste forhold* (1974; Firm Relationships), *Rene linier* (1975; Clean Lines), and *Andre måder* (1975; Other Ways), reflecting the Cold War era of the 1950s, the prosperity of the 1960s, and finally the economic crisis of the 1970s. *Fornemmelser* (1977; Feelings) is an autobiographical novel describing the social mechanisms that place the homosexual in a suppressed position. The skillful structure and superior character delineation of this documentary work confirm Kampmann's position as one of Scandinavia's leading realistic authors.   S.H.R.

Kane, Sheikh (or Cheikh) Hamidou (1928–), Senegalese novelist (writing in French) and government official, was born in the Fouta Djallon, Senegal. As a child, Kane spoke only Peul and attended Koranic school. He then went to a French school, receiving his diploma in 1941 and his B.A. in Dakar in 1948. Kane later studied at the University of Paris, received his *licence* in philosophy from the Ecole Nationale de la France d'Outre-mer in 1959, and then returned to Africa as an official of the French colonial regime in Senegal. After the independence of Senegal, Kane became chef de cabinet to the minister of development and planning. He was governor of the district of Thiès from 1960 to 1963. He is presently an official of the United Nations Emergency Fund (UNEF) in Lagos, Nigeria.

Kane's only novel to date, *L'Aventure ambiguë* (1962; Eng. tr., *Ambiguous Adventure,* 1963), is one of the most important works to be produced by French-speaking West Africa. To label this book a novel is not truly correct; in fact, the author called this ambiguous story a *récit,* which is itself an ambiguous French genre. *L'Aventure ambiguë* is a series of tormented dialogues on truth. The ancient human quest for truth is posed anew by the particular set of historical events created by colonialism. In Kane's work, the search for truth goes beyond the anguish of the individual man, involving instead an entire world looking for a new direction. The question that the book is unable to resolve is: Where does the spiritual future of Africa lie? The protagonist of the novel, Samba Diallo, heir of the Diallobé, rulers of the country for generations, is a man helplessly torn between the atheistic West and God-centered Islam. Although he has been raised in the strictest Muslim tradition by the Master, a respected mystic, Samba complies with the times by going to Western schools and eventually to Europe. When he returns to Africa, he is confused, troubled, and no longer able to believe the Master's teaching. After the death of the Master, his disciple, who is called the Fool because he lost his mind as a soldier in the white man's world, kills Samba when he refuses to become the new Master.

The book exposes the dilemma of contemporary Africa in an unprecedented manner. Kane uses different characters to represent not different kinds of individuals but different ideas. The Master teaches the word of God as it has been taught since the beginning of Islam. He proposes only continuation and has no interest in finding a solution to the political and social upheaval besieging the country; solutions mean compromises and one cannot compromise with God. Yet the Master's view is only one pole of the paradox. The opposite view is passionately symbolized by the Most Royal Lady, cousin of Samba Diallo. Since African fiction does not offer many important female characters, it is indeed remarkable that Kane chooses a woman to exemplify the new order. From the point of view of the Most Royal Lady, the Master is teaching Samba Diallo how to die while she wants to teach him how to live, to survive in this new world where only might is right. Hers is a world where God is dead and technical progress is the hope of mankind, even though in such a world the sunset is no more than an easily explained phenomenon. Samba Diallo, unable to find any peace in life, represents a lost generation of Africans caught between two irreconcilable visions of man and his destiny. Kane's beautifully simple and classical style creates an atmosphere of dignity and melancholy for this parable of Africa's dilemma.

See: D. E. Herdeck, *African Authors: A Companion to Black African Writing,* vol. 1, 1300–1973 (1973).

S.M.L.

Kanık, Orhan Veli (1914–50), Turkish poet and translator, who seldom used his last name in his publications, was born in Istanbul. He graduated from the Gazi Lycée in Ankara in 1932 and attended the Faculty of Literature at the University of Istanbul, which he left in 1935 without getting a degree. After working for the Postal, Telephone, and Telegraph Administration for six years, he became a member of the translation bureau of the Ministry of Public Education in 1945. Resigning from the bureau in 1947, he devoted his remaining years to writing. From January 1949 until June 1950 he edited a single-sheet literary magazine called *Yaprak.*

Kanık's entry into the literary world came through formal lyrics published under the pseudonym Mehmet Ali Sel. These early poems show his mastery of conventional stanzaic forms and syllabic meters. Many of them reveal a lively interest in Greek or European literary and mythological themes and also some influences of French symbolists and surrealists. By 1941 he had introduced drastic innovations, which had the effect of revolutionizing Turkish poetry. With the appearance of *Garip* (Strange), a 1941 volume featuring the work of Kanık, Melih Cevdet ANDAY, and Oktay Rifat, a new type of poetry was initiated. The hallmarks of the "Garip" movement were free verse without rhyme or meter, the vernacular full of colloquialisms and slang expressions, the average person as the hero, and a utilitarian function. In their joint manifesto published in *Garip*, Kanık and his two friends stressed the need for "attuning poetry to the tastes of the masses" and for rescuing themselves from "the stifling effects of the literatures that have dictated and shaped our tastes and judgments for too many years." They called for "dumping overboard" everything that traditional literatures taught them, including "language itself."

Kanık's later collections—*Vazgeçemediğim* (1945; What I Can't Give Up), *Destan Gibi* (1946; Like an Epic), *Yenisi* (1947; The New One), and *Karşı* (1949; Across)—furnished further examples of his modernist aesthetics. *Bütün Şiirleri*, his complete poems, first published in 1951, went through at least 13 printings by the late 1970s, making Kanık one of the most popular Turkish poets ever. His colleague Oktay Rifat observed in 1950 that Kanık "lived within his all too brief lifetime the creative adventures of several generations of French poets . . . Thanks to his output Turkish poetry caught up with contemporary European poetry."

Kanık was a prolific translator of poetry and drama (Molière, Nikolay Gogol, Jean-Paul SARTRE, Jean ANOUILH, Arthur RIMBAUD, Paul VALÉRY, Stéphane MALLARMÉ, Louis ARAGON, Guillaume APOLLINAIRE, and others). He also published many essays and his own versions of Jean de La Fontaine's *Fables* and of the anecdotes of Nasreddin Hoca, a 13th-century Turkish humorist. *I am Listening to Istanbul* (1971) is the only collection of Kanık's poems in English translation.   T.S.H.

Karaosmanoğlu, Yakup Kadri (1889–1974), Turkish novelist, was born in Cairo and died in Ankara. After publishing articles and short stories in the Istanbul press in the 1910s, he joined Mustafa Kemal Pasha's (later Kemal Atatürk) national liberation struggle. He served as a member of Parliament in the early years of the Republic and later as Turkey's ambassador in Albania, Czechoslovakia, Holland, and Switzerland. After returning to Turkey, he wrote lead editorials for the Ankara daily *Ulus* and served again as a member of Parliament from 1961 to 1965.

Karaosmanoğlu's literary career, which spanned 65 years, started with short plays, prose poems, and romantic or realistic short stories. He was catapulted to fame by some of his major novels published in the 1920s: *Kiralık Konak* (1922; Mansion for Rent), the story of the fall of the Ottoman Empire as symbolized by an upperclass family caught in disintegration; *Nur Baba* (1922; Father Divine), a depiction of corrupt religious brotherhoods; *Hüküm Gecesi* (1927; Night of the Verdict), about the conspiratorial policies of the Young Turks and the shadowy goings-on around them as the Ottoman state was nearing its end; and *Sodom ve Gomore* (1928; Sodom and Gomorrah), which delineates Istanbul under Allied occupation after World War I and the moral bankruptcy of the Ottoman intellectuals. Karaosmanoğlu's fiction culminated in *Yaban* (1932; Stranger), a poignant study of

an idealistic young urban intellectual who goes to an Anatolian village as a reserve officer and becomes aware of the harsh realities of rural life, of the plight of the peasants ignored by the government, of despair and ignorance and superstition. *Yaban* became the first major literary work to expose the terrifying conditions in Turkish villages. In 1953 and 1954, Karaosmanoğlu published his two-volume *Panorama*, a wide vista of Turkish society presented in scores of vivid episodes. In addition to several volumes of short stories and prose poems, Karaosmanoğlu published monographs about the poet Ahmet Haşim and modern Turkey's founder, Kemal Atatürk. His memoirs have appeared in five volumes. Karaosmanoğlu ranks among the major figures of Turkish fiction.   T.S.H.

Karinthy, Frigyes (1887–1938), Hungarian humorist, playwright, short-story writer, and poet, was born in Budapest and died in Siófok. He achieved his first major literary success with a volume of literary parodies, *Így írtok ti* (1912; That's How *You* Write). In these delightful, trenchant caricatures, Karinthy satirizes the pet themes and characteristic mannerisms of the popular and influential writers of his time, both Hungarian and foreign. But Karinthy was always more than just a humorist; with its speculative undercurrents, his humor went beyond the conventions of his day and often veered toward the grotesque and the tragic.

Karinthy's stories and sketches contain a stunning mixture of adolescent idealism and jeering pessimism. His evocation, in some of his darkest tales, of a disjointed, nightmarish world is strongly reminiscent of Franz KAFKA, although there is no evidence to suggest that he was directly influenced by the German writer. His world view was, however, affected by Freudian psychoanalyis and by August STRINDBERG's paradoxical view of human relationships. These influences are apparent in Karinthy's misogynist *Utopia Capillaria* (1921; Eng. tr., *Capillaria*, 1965), although Karinthy was basically a rationalist with a deep-seated belief in the eventual triumph of scientific progress. One of his most popular works, the semiautobiographical *Tanár úr kérem* (1916; Eng. tr., *Please Sir*, 1968), presents a gallery of portraits of boys growing up in the Victorian society of turn-of-the-century Budapest. Their timidity and repressed grandiosity are revealed in a series of bittersweet vignettes that deal with such things as the rigors of school life, the dreadful prospect of failure, and the mystery of awakening sex. His celebrated *Utazás a koponyám körül* (1937; Eng. tr., *A Journey round My Skull*, 1939), also autobiographical, is an engrossing account of the author's struggles with a developing brain tumor and of his journey to Stockholm to be operated on by a famous Swedish surgeon.

Karinthy was a colorful member of Budapest literary society before World War I. His undisciplined life-style, as well as the grimly exploitative world in which he lived, prevented him from fully realizing his creative potentials—or so he thought. Actually, Karinthy's masterpieces are to be found among the brief sketches and essays that he considered mere trivia. Both his collected short stories, *A lélek arca* (The Countenance of the Soul), and his complete plays, *Hököm-Szinház* (Theater), were published in 1957. A four-volume edition of his humorous writings, *Az egész város beszéli* (The Talk of the Town) appeared in 1958.

See: L. Kardos, *Karinthy Frigyes* (1947); E. K. Grandpierre, "Karinthy," in *Irodalomtörténet* (1956), 397–423; K. Szalay, *Karinthy Frigyes* (1962); J. Reményi, *Hungarian Writers and Literature* (1964), pp. 298–305.

I.S.

Kariotakis, Kostas (1896–1928), Greek poet, was born in Tripolis, Arcadia. He is the most representative Greek poet of the 1920s, expressing in terms of anguish and futility a Greece whose ideals and aspirations had been destroyed in the Asia Minor Disaster of 1922 (*see* GREEK LITERATURE). As an employee of government ministries, Kariotakis hoped to remain in Athens, but he was posted to provincial towns whose dullness aggravated his inherent melancholy and led to his suicide. "I am paying," he wrote, "for all those who, like me, can never find an ideal in their lives." This suicide marked the end of a despondent period in Greek letters, clearing the air for the poetic revival of the 1930s.

In his first volume, *O ponos tou anthropou kai ton pragmaton* (1919; The Suffering of Man and Things), Kariotakis expresses sorrow at the same time that he idealistically contemplates furtive beauty. In *Nepenthe* (1921), his romanticism finds a more realistic expression in the remembrance of lost affections. His last and best volume, *Elegheia kai satires* (1927; Elegies and Satires), passes from a tragic sense of defeat to the futility of escape, and thence to sarcasm about a reality that finally appears wholly negative. Kariotakis's collected works are available as *Poiimata kai peza* (1972; Poetry and Prose), ed. by G. P. Savides.

See: K. Friar, ed., *Modern Greek Poetry: From Cavafiy to Elytis* (1973).   A.D.

Karlfeldt, Erik Axel (1864–1931), Swedish lyric poet, was born at Folkarna in the province of Dalarna and studied at Uppsala University. After some years as a teacher and librarian, he became permanent secretary of the Swedish Academy in 1912. The Nobel Prize for Literature was awarded to him posthumously in 1931. With Verner von HEIDENSTAM and Gustaf FRÖDING, Karlfeldt was the most outstanding lyrical poet of the 1890s. His first book, *Vildmarks-och kärleksvisor* (1895; Songs of the Wilderness and of Love), is opened by the poem "Fäderna" (My Fathers), in which he does homage to the rural traditions in which he was rooted and which he was forced to abandon. This gives the clue to most of his poems. In his following books, *Fridolins visor* (1898; Fridolin's Songs) and *Fridolins lustgård* (1901; Fridolin's Pleasure Garden), he created the figure of fiction Fridolin, who is both an alter ego and, above all, a personal ideal. Fridolin has abandoned his rural home and returned to it again (which Karlfeldt himself never did); he is a poet and a countryman at the same time. He represents the ideal of rootedness and firmness, of spontaneous joy of living and mature consideration. The other side of Karlfeldt's fundamental experiences was incarnated in the figure of "Löskerkarlen" (The Vagrant), uprooted, without a stable form of living, and with a longing for peace and faith. The rootedness in the soil of Dalarna is especially prominent in a suite of poems, "Dalmålningar, utlagda på rim" (Dalarna Wall Paintings in Rhyme), which is included in *Fridolen lustgård*.

Nature and love are two consistently dominating themes in Karlfeldt's poetry. In *Flora och Pomona* (1906) however, Karlfeldt's love poetry became more profound and complex. The love themes and the nature motifs are often deeply interwoven, as in "Nattyxne" (Dame's Violet). *Flora och Pomona* contains perhaps Karlfeldt's finest poetry, although it never won the same popularity as the preceding collections. Karlfeldt was a great artist; he mastered rhyme and meter perfectly. As a lyric poet he had an unexpected shyness about expressing his inner feelings; Fridolin and "the vagrant" are disguises of his own feelings. And he even uses the "wall paintings in rhyme" to give a sort of objectivity to his inner life. His

adherence to old rural customs and to old Swedish poetry from the baroque period and, at the same time, his modern sense of nature and his hidden treatment of his own personal problems give many dimensions to this poetry. His interest in Swedish baroque poetry is a parallel to T. S. Eliot's interest in the metaphysical poets of the 1600s. In his last two collections, *Flora och Bellona* (1918), the title of which hints at the fact that it was published during World War I, and *Hösthorn* (1927; The Horn of Autumn), he was somewhat less restricted in expressing his inner feelings. He made a rather undogmatic confession of his religious belief in the poem "Sjukdom" (Sickness) in *Flora och Bellona* and in the poem "Höstpsalm" (Autumn Psalm) in *Hösthorn*. The final poem in *Hösthorn* is "Vinterorgel" (Winter Organ), a masterpiece of instrumentation, an intricately orchestrated poetic fugue. *Arcadia Borealis*, a selection of Karlfeldt's poems, translated and with an introduction by C. W. Stork, appeared in 1938.

See: T. Fogelqvist, *Erik Axel Karlfeldt* (1931); O. Lagercrantz, *Jungfrun och demonerna* (1938); J. Mjöberg, *Det folkliga och det förgångna i Karlfeldts lyrik* (1945); K.-I. Hildeman, "The Evolution of 'Längtan är min arvedel,'" *SS* 31 (1959): 47–64, and *En löskekarl, en Karlfeldbok* (1977); A. Bergstrand, *Dikter till och om Karlfeldt* (1978).   N.Å.S.

Karpowicz, Tymoteusz (1921–), Polish poet, short-story writer, playwright, and literary critic, was born in Ziełona near Vilnius. He studied Polish philology at Wrocław University, where he received his Ph.D. and later joined the faculty. In 1974 he became professor of Polish literature at the University of Illinois at Chicago Circle. Karpowicz began his writing career with a volume of short stories, *Legendy pomorskie* (1948; Pomeranian Legends), and made his debut as a poet with his volume *Żywe wymiary* (1948; Living Dimensions), which was followed by the volumes *Kamienna muzyka* (1958; Stone Music), *Znak równania* (1960; Equation Sign), *W imię znaczenia* (1962; In the Name of Meaning), *Trudny las* (1964; Difficult Forest), and *Odwrócone światło* (1972; Reversed Light). His poetry, a creative continuation of Polish Vanguard trends, has evolved from the univocal character of the word in his early poems, through the use of allegories in the following volumes, to the equivocal, symbolic nature of the meaning of words in the most recent volumes. His work has been labeled "linguistic poetry" and his expression compared to "a palimpsest in which all semantic layers do not hide one under another, but all try to appear on the surface of the text" (J. Sławiński). Karpowicz uses ambiguity added to words, to their associations, and to syntactical patterns; he attempts to go back to the source of words and their symbols, as a means of conveying intellectual and moral content. He expresses his opposition to the explicitness of words, to associations imposed by linguistic stereotypes and, often parabolically, to stereotypes in life in order to indicate the complexity and the multidimensional character of the world. Such content is decidedly contemporary, treating as it does the fate of man in general, and both postwar and current Polish reality in particular.

Karpowicz began his work in drama with radio and television plays. In 1975, he published his *Dramaty zebrane* (Collected Dramas), consisting of plays that had appeared in *Kiedy ktoś zapuka* (1967; When Someone Knocks), as well as later works first published in the journal *Dialog*. Karpowicz's dramas recall the tradition of both symbolism and the theater of the avant-garde, the theater of the grotesque and of the absurd. The fundamental feature of these plays is their ambiguity, multifariousness, and metaphoric quality. A strangeness and a fantastic element characterize both the psychology of the heroes and the action of the plays. In fact, Karpowicz's plays really contain no action at all. According to him, the action of his dramas takes place in the minds of his characters. The often nightmarish world of these plays, extraordinarily full of insinuation and incomprehensible fears, employ many concrete details drawn in particular from Polish contemporary life. Karpowicz is also the author of a book on Bolesław LEŚMIAN, *Poezja niemożliwa: modele Leśmianowskiej wyobraźni* (1975; Impossible Poetry: Patterns of Leśmian's Imagination).

See: J. Trznadel, "Kształt wyobraźni zorganizowanej," in *Róże trzecie* (1966), pp. 108–31; M. Piwińska, "Zaczarowanc koło Tymoteusza Karpowicza," *Dialog* 8 (1969): 120–25; S. Barańczak, "Tymoteusz Karpowicz albo polifonia," in *Nieufni i zadufani* (1971), pp. 48–68; E. Balcerzan, "Składnia świata Tymoteusza Karpowicza: Mózg człowieka na scenie," in *Oprócz głosu* (1971), pp. 101–17; A. Falkiewicz, "Świat Tymoteusza Karpowicza," in T. Karpowicz, *Dramaty zebrane* (1975), pp. v–xxxv.   S.F.

Kasack, Hermann (1896–1966), German novelist, essayist, and poet, was born in Potsdam, near Berlin, the son of a physician. Exempt from military service during World War I because of a heart condition, he studied German literature and philosophy at the universities in Berlin and Munich. In 1920 he joined the publishing house of Kiepenheuer as a reader, eventually becoming one of its directors. From 1925 to 1927 he was an editor of the publishing house of S. Fischer. After 1927, Kasack became a free-lance writer and was among the first in Germany to employ the broadcast media for literary purposes, notably radio drama and poetry readings.

When the Nazi Party came to power in 1933, Kasack was denied access to public broadcasting but was able to continue his work in publishing. His cultural conservatism placed him in opposition to Nazi ideology, but his opposition never grew into political resistance. Nor did the Nazi Reich Chamber of Literature raise any objections to Kasack's later employment by Suhrkamp publishers (1941–45). Living in Potsdam at the end of World War II, Kasack continued his work for Suhrkamp until 1949, when he moved to West Germany. He founded the German PEN Club, and in 1953 he was elected president of the German Academy of Language and Literature at Darmstadt.

Although Kasack made his debut as a lyric poet and dramatist, he is best remembered for his post-World War II novel *Die Stadt hinter dem Strom* (1947; Eng. tr., *The City beyond the River,* 1953), which reflects the German mentality after 1945. The novel deals with the visit of a scholar to the habitations of the dead, which resemble the burned-out cities of Germany. It was critically acclaimed until the early sixties, when its limitations became apparent: the novel's metaphysical message relies on 19th-century values that are no longer adequate. Kasack's other allegorical narratives, *Der Webstuhl* (1949; The Weaver's Loom) and *Das große Netz* (1952; The Great Net), show the same deficiencies.

Although he started as an expressionist in the 1920s, Kasack finally emerged as traditionalist who combined realism and allegory in the style of Hermann HESSE and Franz KAFKA.

See: W. Kasack, ed., *Leben und Werk von Hermann Kasack* (1966); W. F. Mainland, *Essays on Contemporary German Literature, German Men of Letters,* 4, ed. by B. Keith-Smith (1966), pp. 39–59.   E.B.

Kaschnitz, Marie Luise (1901–74), German poet, short-story writer, novelist, essayist, and radio playwright, was born in Karlsruhe into the old, aristocratic family of von Holzing-Berstett, learned the book trade, and married the Viennese archaeologist Guido von Kaschnitz-Weinberg in 1925. The couple lived in Königsberg, Marburg, Frankfurt, and, for seven years, in Rome, where Kaschnitz-Weinberg died in 1958. Kaschnitz then resided in Frankfurt am Main and in Rome until her death in 1974.

For Kaschnitz, writing was a form of liberating self-scrutiny. Even as a girl she kept a diary, and her working method as a writer was to note events and thoughts as they occurred day by day, then to sort them out and transform them into art. Thus her life and her art were inextricably linked. Her guiding principle was to search for truth, self-knowledge, and insight into the complex world surrounding her. Very widely read, she was influenced by writers of classical antiquity as well as by Georg TRAKL and Friedrich Hölderlin. As can be seen in *Tage, Tage, Jahre* (1968; Days, Days, Years), Kaschnitz was an admirer of Franz KAFKA, Hermann HESSE, and Samuel BECKETT. Her own writing was at first traditional in content and form, but it evolved toward broader concepts and freer form.

Her first two prose works, *Liebe beginnt* (1933; Love Begins) and *Elissa* (1937), are novels that deal with young lovers who face misunderstanding and sorrow. In both, a sensitive girl comes to know herself and her lover; the first ends happily, while the second, a recreation of the myth of Dido and Aeneas, closes with separation.

After two further prose works, *Griechische Mythen* (1943), a clear, succinct retelling of various Greek myths, and *Menschen und Dinge* (1945; Men and Things), essays depicting post-World War II misery in Germany, Kaschnitz turned to poetry. *Gedichte* (1947; Poems), still traditional in form, was followed by *Totentanz und Gedichte zur Zeit* (1947; Danse macabre and Poems for the Times), *Zukunftsmusik* (1950; Music of the Future), *Ewige Stadt* (1952; Eternal City), *Neue Gedichte* (1957; New Poems), and *Dein Schweigen—meine Stimme* (1962; Your Silence—My Voice), which reveal a widening horizon and a freer, particularly cyclic, form. Kaschnitz brought into focus a growing awareness of modern man's alienated existence and a humanitarian commitment to a troubled age. Man has to transcend his despair, the poet urged in *Ein Wort weiter* (1965; One More Word), to master life, and to reach out for hope.

Two short-story collections, *Das dicke Kind und andere Erzählungen* (1951; The Fat Kid and Other Tales) and *Lange Schatten* (1960; Long Shadows), contain similar feelings. Characteristic of the stories as well as of the poetry are acute observations of the most subtle psychic moves, a detached attitude, and emotional control. Particularly sensitive to the difficulty that children experience in growing up—their loss of innocence and protection, their "search, errors, and sufferings"—Kaschnitz observed each individual's path to self-realization.

Many of her protagonists are children or young adults who try to come to grips with life's problems. Kaschnitz treated myth, vision, dream, fear, and death as psychic realities and integral parts of life. In the novel *Das Haus der Kindheit* (1956; The House of Childhood), of which she was particularly fond, dreams and visions are decisive in the self-analysis of an aging journalist. Unable to cope with unresolved childhood complexes, the journalist withdraws from the world—does without a clock, refuses to open letters, and loses all touch with people outside. Only after she has "found herself" through regression in memory can she resume normal life. In *Wohin denn ich?* (1963;

Where Am I To Go?), the idea of suicidal submersion into "the inhuman element, the sea" attracts a desperate woman bereaved of her husband and in deep despair. And in the radio play *Gespräche im All* (1971; Conversations in Space), two spirits, husband and wife in life, speak of death as the ultimate forgetting of everything, including individual thought, and finally becoming part of an all-embracing divine love.

Kaschnitz's other works include: *Gustave Courbet, Roman eines Malerlebens* (1949; Gustave Courbet, Novel of a Artist's Life); *Engelsbrücke: Römische Betrachtungen* (1955; Bridge of Angels: Roman Views); *Hörspiele* (1962; Radio Plays); *Ferngespräche: Erzählungen* (1966; Long-Distance Calls: Stories); *Überallnie: ausgewählte Gedichte 1928-1965* (1965; Not Anywhere: Selected Poems 1928-1965); *Steht noch dahin: neue Prosa* (1970; Still Undecided: New Prose); and *Zwischen Immer und Nie: Gestalten und Themen der Dichtung* (1971; Between Always and Never: Figures and Themes of Literature).
See: A. Baus, *Standortbestimmung als Prozeß* (1974).
A.P.O.

Kasprowicz, Jan (1860-1926), Polish poet, dramatist, and translator, one of the most outstanding representatives of the "Młoda Polska" (Young Poland) period, was born into a peasant family in the village of Szymborze in Kujawy and died in Poronin. He studied philosophy and literature in Leipzig and Wrocław, and he received his doctor's degree in Lvov, where he became professor of comparative literature. Kasprowicz's earliest works are on themes of village life: *Poezje* (1889; Poems), the poem *Chrystus* (1890), and *Z chłopskiego zagonu* (1891; From a Peasant Field). Transitional works reflecting the growing influence of symbolism and impressionism typical of "Young Poland" are the collection *Anima Lachrimas* (1894) and the poem *Miłość* (1895; Love). The collection *Krzak dzikiej rózy* (1898; The Brier Rose Bush), devoted to the Tatra Mountain region as the embodiment of beauty and the eternal harmony of the world, marks the culmination of this trend. Kasprowicz's most representative work consists of two cycles of reflective, philosophical hymns; *Ginącemu światu* (1901; To the Perishing World) and *Salve Regina* (1902), consisting of eight poems and reprinted in 1921 as *Hymny*. The poems in the first cycle range from images of apocalyptic terror showing the division of the world between good and evil, as in "Święty Boże, święty mocny" (O Holy God) to a search for a solution to despair and doubt in "Moja pieśń wieczorna" (My Evening Song). The road from doubt to hope culminates in the second cycle of hymns, in which the principle of life is seen as forgiving, purifying love, and suffering leading to salvation. These hymns draw upon the tradition of the Bible, medieval hymns, Polish peasant church songs, and church iconography. The composition of the hymns resembles that of symphonic musical forms. Besides naturalism and impressionism, the predominant element in their style is a tendency toward expressionism. The hymns are written in irregular free verse, sometimes with rhyme. In 1906, Kasprowicz published a volume of poetic prose, *O bohaterskim koniu i walącym się domu* (On a Heroic Horse and a Crumbling House), a potpourri of genres and themes in which the new element is satire directed against bourgeois ethics and mentality. Subsequent volumes of lyrics, *Ballada o słoneczniku* (1908; Ballad of a Sunflower) and *Chwile* (1911; Moment) continue Kasprowicz's evolution toward religious humility and simplification of poetic expression, begun in *Hymny*. This evolution is completed in *Księga ubogich* (1916; The Book of the Poor), the title alluding to the medieval *Biblia*

pauperum (Books of the Poor). The work expresses a Franciscan love of nature and an affirmation of divine order in the world. Tranquility and consolation permeate this cycle of 43 lyrics, with its free narration, refined simplicity, economy of expression, and intentionally uniform rhythm. *Księga ubogich* is the first instance in Polish poetry of extensive use of tonic verse. A small posthumous collection, *Mój świat* (1926; My World), goes even further toward primitivism, utilizing folk stylizations reminiscent of highland folklore. Kasprowicz also wrote dramas: *Bunt Napierskiego* (1899; Napierski's Revolt), *Uczta Herodiady* (1905; Herodia's Banquet), *Sita* (1917), and *Marchołt* (1920). Kasprowicz's translations include works from the ancient classics (Aeschylus and Euripides) and English literature (Shakespeare and Shelley), as well as others published in five volumes entitled *Obraz poezji* (1931; The Image of Poetry).
See: S. Kołaczkowski, *Twórczość Jana Kasprowicza* (1924); W. Borowy, *Jan Kasprowicz* (1926); J. Lipski, *Twórczość Jana Kasprowicza w latach 1878-91* (1967); A. Hutnikiewicz, *Hymny Jana Kasprowicza* (1973); J. J. Lipski, *Twórczość Jana Kasprowicza w latach 1891-1906* (1975).
S.F.

Kassák, Lajos (1887-1967), Hungarian poet and novelist, was born in Érsekujvár (now Nove Zamky, Czechoslovakia), the son of working-class parents. Kassák was the central figure of the Hungarian avant-garde. As a young man, he worked as a locksmith, first in Győr and later in Budapest. Even before World War I, Kassák's unrhymed, free-flowing poems, which recall Walt Whitman and some of the German expressionists, were making an impact on the reading public. His first book of poetry, *Éposz Wagner maszkjában* (1915; Epic Poem Wearing Wagner's Mask), established him as the undisputed leader of the small but aggressive group of Hungarian modernists. In the same year, he launched his avant-garde review *Tett*, which, besides attacking "bourgeois culture" and challenging the supremacy of *Nyugat* (see HUNGARIAN LITERATURE), also printed antiwar protests. *Tett* was banned in 1916, but Kassák revived it soon afterwards under the title *Ma*.

A Social Democrat and trade unionist of long standing, he greeted the Russian Revolution of 1917 with enthusiasm. Kassák also played an active part in the establishment of the Hungarian Soviet Republic, although he publicly crossed swords with its leader, Béla Kun, over questions of cultural policy. After the collapse of the Kun regime, Kassák was jailed for a short time, but he managed to escape to Vienna. During his stay there (1920-26), he continued publishing *Ma*, but the politically committed futurism that still informed the poems in *Világanyám* (1921; World, My Mother) gave way to a more abstract, "geometric" style. In 1926, Kassák returned to Budapest and began publishing his memoirs, first in the review *Nyugat* and then in book form. The eight volumes of *Egy ember élete* (1928-39; A Man's Life) are considered Kassák's best prose work. They constitute a realistic account of the epoch leading up to historical Hungary's collapse and of a man's relentless struggle for self-advancement. The best parts of this work stand comparison with Maksim GORKY's autobiography. Between the two world wars, Kassák wrote much fiction, including the novel *Angyalföld* (1929; "Angels' Land," a working-class district of Budapest), which is probably his most successful effort in the genre. It depicts the drab life of industrial workers with sympathy and understanding. From 1928 to 1939, Kassák edited the cultural review *Munka*. His political views, usually described as "anarcho-syndicalist," coupled with intolerance of the non-Kassákean trends in poetry, isolated him from both the Right and the Left. After World War II, he played a role in the reorganization of Hungarian literary life and edited the periodicals *Alkotás* and *Kortárs,* but he withdrew into silence during the Communist-sponsored supremacy of socialist realism. Kassák reemerged with the publication of *Válogatott versei* (1956; Selected Poems) and, finally, in 1965, was awarded the Kossuth Prize.

Kassák made his greatest impact on Hungarian literature between 1912 and 1920. During these years, he tried to create an aesthetic and idiological alternative to the impressionistic and postsymbolistic poetry of *Nyugat*. In this he was only partly successful: although he influenced many young poets, the public at large did not really appreciate his work, nor did it value the purity of his lonely struggle. After 1920, Kassák's poetry lost its political message and its futuristic pretensions. The manifestos turned into elegies, and the poet, disenchanted with society, found peace and harmony in nature. The loss of social and experimental momentum resulted in a respectable but rather unremarkable stream of poetry.

See: E. Gáspár, *Kassák Lajos, az ember és munkája* (1924); A. Komlós, "A költő Kassák," *Nyugat* 20 (1927): 338–46; M. Radnóti, "Kassák Lajos költészete," *Nyugat* 32 (1939): 49–52; Gy. Rónay, "Kassák és az izmusok," *Irodalomtörténet* (1959): 43–53; I. Vas, *Nehéz szerelem* (1964, 1967).   G.G.

Kaštelan, Jure (1919–), Croatian poet, was born in the village of Zadučac, in the Polijica region. After studying in Split and Zagreb, he took part in the Partisan movement. After the war, he edited the works of several Croatian authors. Kaštelan lectured at the Sorbonne in the 1950s and later taught literary theory at Zagreb University.

Kaštelan began to write poems as a student. His first volume, *Crveni konj* (1940; The Red Horse), was destroyed by the police. His most important collection, *Pjetao na krovu* (1950; The Cock on the Roof), contains his writing from 1940 to 1949. Kaštelan has written some new poems in his later collections: *Biti ili ne* (1955; To Be or Not to Be), *Malo kamena i puno snova* (1957; A Bit of Stone and a Lot of Dreams), and *Izbor pjesama* (1964; Selected Poems). Although he is best known as a poet, Kaštelan has also written a play, several short stories, and many critical studies, among which the best is his doctoral dissertation on Antun Gustav MATOŠ.

Some critics have seen in Kaštelan's work the influence of folk poetry and surrealism, as well as that of such writers as Dragutin TADIJANOVIČ, Miroslav KRLEŽA, Federico GARCÍA LORCA, and Walt Whitman. Nevertheless, Kaštelan's poetry has its own individual thematic and formal features, and in it many supposedly contrary elements are happily intertwined. Kaštelan's intonation is original, his rhythm is varied, and his lexicon is so well adapted to his content that the two form a harmonious unit.

Kaštelan's experiences during World War II found expression in two major themes that run through his postwar poetry. On the one hand, out of the senseless cruelty of foreign occupation and internecine strife there came such negative existential statements as the powerful and famous poem "Jadikovka kamena" (1951; Lament of a Stone). On the other hand, even in the midst of wartime ferocity, Kaštelan found within the Partisan Resistance movement a spirit of comradeship that brought a glimmer of light into the darkness of his despair and that has inspired many of his best poems.

See: A. Kadić, "Postwar Croatian Lyric Poetry,"

ASEER 17 (December 1958): 521–28; N. Milićević, "Poezija Jure Kaštelana," *ForumZ* 1–2 (1966): 187–91.
                                                          A.K.

Kästner, Erich, pseud. Robert Neuner (1899–1974), German poet, novelist, and author of children's books, was born in Dresden, the son of a saddler. World War I interrupted his preparation to become a schoolteacher, and after the war he was a bank clerk. He then studied German literature in Leipzig, Rostock, and Berlin, receiving his Ph.D. in 1925. After some years as a journalist he found the income from his books of verse, such as *Herz auf Taille* (1928; Heart on Your Sleeve), *Lärm im Spiegel* (1929; Noise in the Mirror), and *Ein Mann gibt Auskunft* (1930; A Man Furnishes Information), sufficient to allow him to be a free-lance writer. The most popular of his books, which also was a successful play and an entertaining film (both in 1930), was *Emil und die Detektive* (1929; Eng. tr., *Emil and the Detectives,* 1930), which was followed by the novel *Fabian, die Geschichte eines Moralisten* (1931; Eng. tr., *Fabian,* 1932), *Drei Männer im Schnee* (1934; Eng. tr., *Three Men in the Snow,* 1935), also filmed, and *Die verschwundene Miniatur* (1936; Eng. tr., *The Missing Miniature,* 1936).

The bitterness of the years after World War I surfaces in his more satiric writings and in his poems. His books were burned in Germany in 1933, and he was refused permission to publish in his homeland, publishing thereafter in Switzerland. He was arrested by the Gestapo in 1934 and again in 1937, when he crossed the border daily to consult with his Swiss publisher, preparing for the publication of his novel *Georg und die Zwischenfälle* (1938; George and Incidents). In 1943 he was forbidden to write at all.

After World War II, in Munich, Kästner founded a cabaret and was an editor for the newly established *Neue Zeitung.* In 1946 he founded the young people's magazine *Pinguin.* After the publication of *Kurz und bündig* (1948; Short and Snappy) he published the novel for children *Das doppelte Lottchen* (1949; Lottie Doubled), which received a prize as a film. *Pünktchen und Anton* (Dottie and Anton), a play for children, appeared in 1952. A volume of poems, *Die dreizehn Monate* (The Thirteen Months) was published in 1955, followed in 1956 by a drama, *Die Schule der Diktatoren* (The School for Dictators). In 1957, the year of the publication of *Als ich ein kleiner Junge war* (When I was a Little Boy) and *Der kleine Grenzverkehr* (Eng. tr., *A Salzburg Comedy,* 1957), he received the Georg Büchner Prize. In the years that followed, Kästner published anthologies of world humor and in 1966 received an international prize for humor for his story "Ist Existentialismus heilbar?" (Can Existentialism be Cured?). In his last years he was honored with numerous prizes and decorations. After his death the Bavarian Academy of Arts established a literary prize in his honor, the first recipient of which was Peter Rühmkorf in 1959.

See: J. Winkelmann, *The Poetic Style of Erich Kästner* (1957); H. Wagener, *Erich Kästner* (1973).
                                                   B.Q.M. rev. A.L.W.

Katayev, Valentin Petrovich (1897–), Russian novelist, poet, playwright, and short-story writer, was born in Odessa and began his literary career in 1910 as a poet, publishing his first stories two years later. He was gassed and wounded while serving in World War I, and in 1919 he was inducted into the Red Army. During the post-Civil War years, Katayev wrote several stories, plays, and novels, the most famous of which is the novel *Rastratchiki* (1926; Eng. tr., *The Embezzlers,* 1929), a satire about a cashier and a bookkeeper who embezzle a large amount of official money and procede to indulge their bourgeois fantasies through adventurous travels about the country. Satire also dominates his play *Kvadratura kruga* (1928; Eng. tr., *Squaring the Circle*, 1936). Katayev's novel *Vremya, vperyod!* (1932; Eng. tr., *Time, Forward!*, 1933), perhaps the best of all Five-Year Plan novels, abandons satire in favor of a fast-paced realistic chronicle of an attempt to beat a concrete production record. Katayev employed extremely short sentences to convey the impression of speed.

In 1936 the first volume of Katayev's tetralogy *Volny chernogo morya* (Black Sea Waves) appeared under the title *Beleyet parus odinokiy* (Eng. tr., *Lonely White Sail*, or *Peace is Where the Tempests Blow*, 1937); it recounts boyhood adventures in the Odessa of 1905. The other volumes in the tetralogy are *Khutorok v stepi* (1956; Eng. tr., *Small Farm in the Steppe*, 1958), covering the years 1910–12; *Zimniy veter* (1960; Winter Wind), set in the Civil War period; and *Za vlast Sovetov* (1947–61; For the Power of the Soviets), set primarily during the World War II defense of Odessa. *Za vlast Sovetov* has appeared in five different versions, partly as a result of political criticism, and is also known under the title *Katakomby* (Catacombs).

Katayev is one of the few Soviet authors to have made continuous and significant artistic contributions during the 1920s, the years of Iosif Stalin's rule and the 1960s, the best of his works appearing in the 1920s and 1960s. While editor of *Yunost* from 1955 to 1962, he helped promote the careers of many young artists, and himself broadened the perspectives of post-Stalin literature with two excellent experimental novels, *Svyatoy kolodets* (1966; Eng. tr., *The Holy Well*, 1967) and *Trava zabveniya* (1967; Eng. tr., *The Grass of Oblivion*, 1969). *Svyatoy kolodets* employs the device of drug-induced dreams to explore the past, and in one sequence introduces a talking cat that represents writers who must mouth official jargon. Another section describes the assassination of John F. Kennedy, president of the United States. *Trava zabveniya* also delves into the past to discuss the two writers Ivan BUNIN and Vladimir MAYAKOVSKY and their contributions to Russian literature. In these works, Katayev proposes a new school of literature, "mauvisme," in which people can write as they choose. His later works include *Kubik* (1971) and *Razbitaya zhizn ili volshebny rog Oberona* (1972; Broken Life, or the Magic Horn of Oberon). Katayev is considered especially good at descriptions of the material world, with a greater appreciation for life and the beauties of nature than for political philosophy. Because of his recent contributions, his present position as a Soviet writer of the second rank may be due for reassessment.

See: V. Braynina, *Valentin Katayev: ocherk tvorchestva* (1960).   S.Sc.

Kaverin, Veniamin Aleksandrovich, pseud. of Veniamin Aleksandrovich Zilber (1902–), Russian novelist, short-story writer, playwright, literary critic and scholar, journalist and memoirist, has been active in Soviet literature since the early 1920s. Born in Pskov, he followed briefly an inherited musical bent as a child. After finishing secondary school in Moscow and one year at the University of Moscow, he transferred in 1920 to Petrograd and simultaneously attended the Institute of Oriental Languages and the University of Petrograd, where he studied literary history. A friend and student of Yury TYNYANOV, he made a speciality of Russian literature. In 1928 he defended his dissertation on the career of the Polish-born Russian writer Osip Senkovsky (J. J. Sękowski), whose

pseudonym became the title of Kaverin's valuable monograph, *Baron Brambeus* (1929; rev. ed., 1966).

During the 1920s, Kaverin was a member of the Serapion Brotherhood (*see* RUSSIAN LITERATURE), belonging to the radical "Western wing." Influenced by Edgar Allan Poe and E. T. A. Hoffmann, he wrote cleverly plotted stories of fantastic adventures. Several of these early experiments form his first volume, *Mastera i podmasterya* (1923; Craftsmen and Apprentices). His love of complicated and adventurous plots is evident as well in *Konets khazy* (1926; End of a Gang), an entertaining short detective novel about the Leningrad underworld. The grotesque and the romantic also dominate in *Bubnovaya mast* (1927; Diamond Suit) and numerous other short stories of the 1920s. A new interest appears in *Devyat desyatykh sudby* (1925; Nine-Tenths of Fate), Kaverin's first novel, in which he explores the psychological problems of the old intelligentsia in revolutionary Russia. The academic and literary world of Leningrad, which he knew at first hand, provides the background for his roman à clef, *Skandalist, ili vechera na Vasilyevskom ostrove* (1928; Troublemaker, or Evenings on Vasily Island).

A work of deep significance, *Khudozhnik neizvesten* (1931; Eng. tr., *The Unknown Artist*, 1947), written in the late 1920s, depicts the clash between an artist of quixotic idealism (modeled on the poet Viktor KHLEBNIKOV) and a pragmatic realist of the Five-Year-Plan period. The book was not well-received in the Soviet Union and was evidently not republished until it was included, somewhat revised, in Kaverin's collected works in 1964.

Kaverin's response to the "social command" was *Prolog* (1930–31), a set of documentary sketches about state collective farms, which represented an important departure for him. Thereafter he published a novel of socialist realism, *Ispolneniye zhelaniy* (1934–36; Fulfillment of Desires; Eng. tr., *The Larger View*, 1938), which is set in an academic milieu and effectively contrasts a young student of literature and his earnest friend, a young man of worker background. Kaverin's next work, *Dva kapitana* (1938–44; Eng. tr., *Two Captains*, 1942), guaranteed him continuing popularity with the reading public. A novel for juveniles, *Dva kapitana* is an exciting adventure tale involving Arctic explorations and a boy's romantic dreams of distant journeys and scientific discovery. In the trilogy *Otkrytaya kniga* (1949–56; incomplete Eng. tr., *An Open Book*, 1955), his last major undertaking in the novel form, Kaverin again deals with the world of science (bacteriology) and with the life of university students. He was one of the first Soviet writers, in the final volume, to broach the taboo subjects of political denunciation and the labor camps.

Also a dramatist of note, Kaverin began writing plays in the early 1930s. The best-known of them are *Ukroshcheniye mistera Robinzona* (1933; The Taming of Mr. Robinson) and a fairy-tale play for children *V gostyakh u Kashcheya* (1941; Visiting Kashchey). The dramatization of *Two Captains* (1948; also filmed, 1955) was successful as well.

During World War II, Kaverin served as a war correspondent, and he published several collections of sketches and documentary short stories between 1941 and 1946. Outstanding amongst a set of short novels of the post-Stalin period are the autobiographical *Neizvestny drug* (1959–60; Unknown Friend), the anti-Stalinist *Kusok stekla* (1960; A Piece of Glass), *Sem par nechistykh* (1962; Seven Pairs of the Unclean), *Kosoy dozhd* (1962; Rain Aslant), and another "scientific" novel *Dvoynoy portret* (1966; Double Portrait) treating denunciation and using a double narrative perspective. In 1972, Kaverin published an interesting epistolary novel, with authorial commentary, *Pered zerkalom* (Before the Mirror), about the life of an émigré Russian woman artist. In later years he increasingly devoted himself to literary memoirs and autobiography.

See: D. G. B. Piper, *V. A. Kaverin: A Soviet Writer's Response to the Problem of Commitment* (1970).

R.P.H.

Kawalec, Julian (1916–), Polish novelist and short-story writer, was born in Wrzawy, near Tarnobrzeg. He studied Polish philology at the Jagiellonian University. Kawalec spent the years of World War II in his native village, where he was connected with the Resistance movement. Since 1945 he has lived in Cracow. In 1957 he began his literary career with the collection of short stories *Ścieżki wśród ulic* (Paths among Streets). This volume was followed by the novels *Ziemi przypisany* (1962; Assigned to the Land), *W słońcu* (1963; In the Sun), *Tańczący jastrząb* (1964; Dancing Hawk), *Wezwanie* (1968; The Call), and *Przepłyniesz rzekę* (1973; You'll Cross the River), as well as by several collections of short stories, including *Blizny* (1960; Scars), *Zwalony wiąz* (1962; Fallen Elm), *Czarne światło* (1965; Black Light), and *Marsz weselny* (1966; Wedding March). Kawalec, who preserved emotional ties with his rural beginnings, is a representative of the peasant theme in literature and a spokesman for the large segment of the population that moved from villages to towns. His work depicts the psychological and moral experiences, including the costs, of this migratory movement.

See: *Słownik współczesnych pisarzy polskich,* series 2, vol. 1 (1977), pp. 435–40. A.Z.

Kazakevich, Emmanuil Genrikhovich (1913–62), Russian novelist and short-story writer, was born in Kremenchug, in the Ukraine, but he lived from 1931 to 1938 in the Jewish autonymous province of Birobidzhan and published his first stories in Yiddish.

After serving as a front-line officer during World War II, he published two war stories that attracted much attention. *Zvezda* (1947; Eng. tr., *Star,* 1950) concerns reports by reconnaissance troops behind enemy lines about the deployment of an SS division. "Dvoe v stepi" (1948; Two Men in the Steppe) is set during the critical war year, 1942. Because of its theme—ruthless death sentences for cowardice under fire—and its clearly artistic point of view, this is one of the most remarkable, although psychologically equivocal, stories in the first wave of Soviet literature about the war (1945–49).

In 1949, as a sequel to "Zvezda," Kazakevich published the war novel *Vesna na Odere* (Eng. tr., *Spring on the Oder,* 1953). Reconnaissance troops play the main role here too, and the story culminates in the occupation of Berlin, in which the author himself participated. Although Kazakevich made an effort to create an exciting plot in *Vesna na Oder,* the scenes on the German side are not very convincing artistically. In addition, the novel's distorted anti-American and anti-British bias reflects the early phases of the Cold War. This is likewise true of its sequel, *Dom na ploshchadi* (1956; Eng. tr., *The House on the Square,* 1957[?]), which describes the 1945 transfer of a city in the Harz Mountains from the Western Allies to the Soviet occupation troops.

Despite the extent to which political considerations influenced Kazakevich, he rendered a relatively unvarnished account of the everyday problems of Russian front-line soldiers, whom he presented without any false monumentalism. And despite its literary cultivation, his language remains authentic and sociologically typical for the wartime situation. Kazakevich's later stories "Pri

svete dnya" (1961; In the Light of Day) and "Priezd ottsa v gosti k synu" (1962; The Father Comes to Visit His Son) belong to the new wave of sober literature growing out of the thaw. In these, characterizations marked by skepticism rather than lyrical romanticism and a restrained, even though benevolent, irony reveal the maturity of the writer, who had freed himself from reliance upon a simple one-dimensional view of reality and had learned to make good use of contrasts in perspective.

See: A. Bocharov, *Slovo o pobeditelyakh: voennaya proza Emmanuil Kazakevicha* (1970). J.Ho.

Kazakov, Yury Pavlovich (1927–), Russian short-story writer, born in Moscow, is one of the best lyrical, personal writers of the 1960s and 1970s. His favorite themes include hunting; the countryside of central Russia and the White Sea; downtrodden, seemingly unimportant people in rural areas and small towns; and trivial but poignant emotional events in the daily lives of ordinary people.

Many collections of his works have appeared in the Soviet Union. The earliest volume was published in 1958, under the heading *Na polustanke* (Whistle Stop). His best known stories are "Na polustanke" (Whistle Stop); "Manka" (Eng. tr., "Marie," 1964); "Zapakh khleba" (Eng. tr., "The Smell of Bread," 1964); "Arktur" (Eng. tr., "Arktur—Hunting Dog," 1965); "Adam i Eva" (Eng. tr., "Adam and Eve," 1964); and "Nestor i Kir" (Nestor and Cyrus). Kazakov became less productive in the 1970s, but what little he wrote continued to be received with acclaim.

Never drawn to public or political themes, Kazakov writes rather in the tradition of Anton CHEKHOV and of the rural stories of Ivan Turgenev and Ivan BUNIN. He loves the sea, the forest, and Old Russia. His works are delicate and rich in mood rather than events. He also has written travel accounts and sketches, including those in the volume *Severny dnevnik* (1961; Northern Diary).

Kazakov relies on natural imagery, and his prose is strongly poetic. In theme he is particularly drawn to misfortune, grief, and disappointment. Typical of his best work is the story "Trali-Vali" (1959; Eng. tr., "Silly-Billy," 1964), also published as "Otshchepenets" (The Derelict), which describes the life of a broken-down ex-navy man who makes his living by taking care of beacons on a river; although he drinks, the man occasionally rises to great emotional heights during trysts with a local peasant woman, particularly when singing folk songs. Although some find Kazakov's range narrow, he must be counted among the very best Soviet prose writers of the 1960s and 1970s.

See: G. Gibian, Introduction to Y. Kazakov, *Selected Short Stories* (1963), pp. ix–xxv. G.Gi.

Kazakova, Rimma Fyodorovna (1932–), Russian poet, was born in Sevastopol. She studied history at Leningrad University and later worked in Khabarovsk as a film editor. In 1955 she began publishing, and even her early collections, *Vstretimsya na vostoke* (1958; We'll Meet in the East) and *Tam, gde ty* (1960; Where You Are) evidence their strong interest in exotic lands. Such later works as *Stikhi* :1962; Poems), *V tayge ne plachut* (1965; They Don't Cry in the Taiga), and *Pyatnitsy* (1965; Fridays) are romantic and personal in their treatment of nature, the Far East, and the heroine's emotions. These poems often tell of the joys and difficulties of life in Siberia and the taiga. *Snezhnaya baba* (1972; The Snow Woman) consists primarily of lyrical love poems many of which, such as the cycle *Sredneaziatskiye strannitsy* (Central Asian Pages), are set in the Far East. Kazakova tends towards traditional poetic forms and extensive use of word play. Her lyric heroine is primarily the voice of Kazakova herself: "Eto ya takaya, ya sama—snezhnaya, zaputannaya baba" (It is I who am such, I myself am a snowy, confused woman).

See: V. A. Zaytsev, *Sovremennaya sovetskaya poeziya* (Moscow, 1969).   L.V.

Kazantzakis, Nikos (1883–1956), Greek poet, novelist, and playwright was born in Herakleion, Crete. He studied philosophy in Paris, where he was influenced by his teacher Henri BERGSON and by Nietzscheanism (*see* Friedrich NIETZSCHE). Kazantzakis fought persistently for social justice, peace, and intellectual freedom, driven by a messianic concern not for established religions but for the primordial anguish of men facing life, death, and the mystery beyond. Although his works abound in harsh realism, they are also preoccupied with metaphysical problems, particularly the relationship between man and God. A "tragic optimist," he believed that life is a crusade in the service of God, and that man's principal duty is to transubstantiate matter continually into spirit. Emphasis on eternal becoming is the main characteristic of his philosophy.

Kazantzakis wrote prolifically in many genres. *Salvatores Dei: Askitiki* (1927; Eng. tr., *The Saviors of God, Spiritual Exercises*, 1960), an essay written in lyrical, biblical form, expounds a philosophical and political credo that is constantly reflected in his other writings. His most impressive achievement is the *Odysseia* (1938; Eng. tr., *The Odyssey: A Modern Sequel*, 1958), a philosophical epic weighty both in size (33,333 lines) and in the questions it explores. It was his novels, however, that made Kazantzakis internationally famous. Although these works are not devoid of preconceived ideas and stock characters, they possess an energy, sincerity, and linguistic richness that give them great appeal. There is an earthy realism, sometimes tender and humorous, as well as a serious philosophical purpose in such novels as *Vios kai politeia tou Alexi Zorba* (1946; Eng. tr., *Zorba the Greek*, 1953), *O Christos Xanastavronetai* (1948; Eng. tr., *The Greek Passion*, 1953), *O Kapetan Michalis* (1958; Eng. tr., *Freedom or Death*, 1956), *O teleftaios peirasmos* (1955; Eng. tr., *The Last Temptation of Christ*, 1960), *O ftochoulis tou Theou* (1956; Eng. tr., *Saint Francis*, 1962), and *Aderfofades* (1963; Eng. tr., *The Fratricides*, 1964). Two novels written in French, *Toda Raba* (1934; Eng. tr., 1964) and *Le Jardin des rochers* (1930; Eng. tr., *The Rock Garden*, 1963), are fictionalized discussions of politics and metaphysics. *Anafora ston Greco* (1961; Eng. tr., *Report to Greco*, 1965) is a revealing spiritual autobiography. Kazantzakis's many plays are more interesting for their poetry and philosophical debates than for purely dramatic qualities. They include *Melissa* (1939), *Kouros* (1955), and *Christophoros Kolomvos* (1956; Eng. tr. of all three, *Three Plays: Melissa, Kouros, Christopher Columbus*, 1969), *Voudas* (1956; Buddha), *Kapodistrias* (1946), and *Konstantinos Palaiologos* (1956). Kazantzakis has been especially appreciated in Greece for his travel books; *Spain* (1937; Eng. tr., 1963), *Japan-China* (1938; Eng. tr., 1963), *England* (1941; Eng. tr., 1965), *Journey to the Morea* (1937; Eng. tr., 1965), and *Journeying* (1927; Eng. tr., 1975) are available in English. He also enriched modern Greek culture with his many translations, the most important of which are his modern Greek versions of Dante's *Divine Comedy* (1934), Goethe's *Faust* (1937), and, in collaboration with Ioannis Kakridis, Homer's *Iliad* (1955) and *Odyssey* (1965).

See: P. Prevelakis, *Nikos Kazantzakis and His Odyssey* (1961); H. Kazantzakis, *Nikos Kazantzakis: A Biography Based on His Letters* (1968); P. Bien, *Nikos Kazantzakis* (1972); P. Bien, *Kazantzakis and the Linguistic Revolution in Greek Literature* (1972).   C.M.P.

Kegels, Anne-Marie (1912–), Belgian poet, was born in Dunes (Tarn-et-Garonne) in France and evinces her rural origin in her work. The earth and the seasons form the habitual decor of a poetry whose dominant themes are love and the zest for life, as well as the keen awareness of the passage of time. This empassioned communion with nature is more than an act of faith; in taking her inspiration from the very sources of life, Kegels appeases or foils the perpetual uneasiness that tortures her. The permanent play of images and the great freshness of verbal associations provide her poetry with its principal power of seduction more subtly than the themes entered upon do. Author of *Rien que vivre* (1951; Nothing But Life) and *Doigts verts* (1967; Green Fingers), Kegels scarcely veers from the proved paths of classical prosody; even if, in *Lumière adverse* (1970; Adverse Light) and *Les Chemins sont en feu* (1973; The Roads Are on Fire), rhyme perchance gives way to assonance and, less frequently, regular verse gives way to free verse, something of the old music remains, guaranteeing the poem its equilibrium and exquisite fluidity.

See: R. Burniaux and R. Frickx, *La Littérature belge d'expression français* (1973); A. Jans, *Lettres vivantes, 1945–1975* (1975); R. Frickx and M. Joiret, *La Poésie française de Belgique de 1880 à nos jours* (1976).   R.F.

Kemal, Yashar (1922–), Turkey's most famous novelist, was born in southern Turkey, where he spent his early years. (The Turkish spelling of his first name is Yaşar, and he never uses his surname, Gökçeli.) He quit secondary school and made a living in his teens and twenties in such occupations as farmhand, cobbler's apprentice, construction worker, clerk, and petition writer. In the 1940s he published poems in a local magazine in Adana in southern Turkey and in small magazines elsewhere. In 1943 he published a collection of folk elegies, which he collected in his region.

In 1951, Kemal settled in Istanbul and became a roving reporter for the leading daily, *Cumhuriyet*. The year 1952 saw the publication of his collection of short stories *Sarı Sıcak* (Yellow Heat). His newspaper interviews and reportorial pieces, which set a new tone and established an innovative literary style in Turkish journalism, were collected in three volumes: *Yanan Ormanlarda Elli Gün* (1955; Fifty Days in Burning Forests), *Çukurova Yana Yana* (1955; Chukurova Up in Flames), and *Peri Bacaları* (1957; Fairy Chimneys).

İnce Memed (1955; Eng. tr., *Memed, My Hawk*, 1961) secured immediate nationwide fame for Kamal. A powerful and poignant saga of the spirit of defiance against oppression and exploitation, this novel has been Turkey's all-time best seller. Kemal's second major novel, *Orta Direk* (1960; Eng. tr., *The Wind from the Plain*, 1962), is a masterful account of a poverty-stricken family that is in search of work and struggling to survive. A prolific writer, Kemal left *Cumhuriyet* in 1963, served on the Central Committe of the Turkish Labor Party, and published *Ant*, an influential Marxist weekly in the 1960s. His fame grew in Turkey and abroad with the publication of many major novels: *Yer Demir Gök Bakır* (1963; Eng. tr., *Iron Earth, Copper Sky*, 1974); *İnce Memed II* (1969; Eng. tr., *They Burn the Thistles*, 1973); *Ölmez Otu* (1969; Eng. tr., *The Undying Grass*, 1977); *Akçasazın Ağaları*, *The Lords of Akchasaz*, consisting of two volumes, *Demirciler Çarsısı Cinayeti* (1974), translated into English as *Murder in the Ironsmiths Market* (1979), and *Yusufcuk Yusuf* (1975). In all these novels, Yashar Kemal unfurls a panorama of deprivation, injustice, struggle, and unhappiness in the countryside, mainly around the Chukurova region; yet he stresses the dauntless spirit of the villagers to endure against all odds. His style is crisp, colloquial, and compelling, with an impressive lyric flow. The characters are often vivid, and his narrative technique ranges from a starkness like that of Ignazio SILONE to William Faulkner's brand of stream of consciousness.

Kemal has consciously created a modern mythology from the legends and folktales of southern Turkey. His profound interest in folklore has yielded several works based on major Turkish legends: *Üç Anadolu Efsanesi* (1967; Three Anatolian Legends), *Ağrıdağı Efsanesi* (1970; Eng. tr., *The Legend of Ararat*, 1975), *Binboğalar Efsanesi* (1971; Eng. tr., *The Legend of the Thousand Bulls*, 1976), and other works.

His fiction in the late 1970s has moved from the countryside to the big city and coastal towns: *Al Gözüm Seyreyle Salih* (1976; Take My Eyes and Watch, Salih), *Kuslar da Gitti* (1978; The Birds Too are Gone), *Deniz Küstü* (1979; The Sea Is Cross), and other novels.

In addition, Kemal has published several collections of novellas, short stories, essays, and articles. Seven of his short stories are available in English translation in *Anatolian Tales* (1968). His work has been translated into nearly 30 languages. He has won numerous awards in Turkey and abroad. He was also mentioned in the European and American press in the late 1970s as a strong candidate for the Nobel Prize in Literature.   T.S.H.

Kemal Tahir (1910–73), Turkish novelist, was born in Istanbul. He left the Galatasaray Lycée when he was a sophomore and worked as an attorney's secretary and reporter from 1928 to 1938. Because of his Marxist ideology, he was sentenced to 15 years of imprisonment. In 1950 he was released and supported himself through his fiction.

During the 1930s his literary output consisted of poems and short stories. His novels came out in quick succession between the mid-1950s and mid-1970s. Of the 16, the following are the most significant: *Esir Şehrin İnsanları* (1956; The People of the Captive City), *Köyün Kanburu* (1959; Hunchback of the Village), and *Bozkırdaki Çekirdek* (1967; The Seed in the Steppe). In addition to these, which deal mainly with the harsh realities of Turkey's rural areas, where feudal exploitation, social injustice, and religious fanaticism oppress the poor people, Kemal Tahir wrote several major novels about Turkish history. *Yorgun Savaşçı* (1965; The Weary Warrior), which was awarded the Yunus Nadi Prize of the important daily *Cumhuriyet*, is an account of the Turkish War of Independence in the early 1920s. *Devlet Ana* (Mother State) of 1967, winner of the coveted Fiction Prize of the Turkish Language Society, is a sprawling episodic saga of the emergence of the Ottoman state seven centuries ago. The author's *Kurt Kanunu* (1969; The Law of the Wolves) depicts the evil plots of the politicians during the period of the transition from the Ottoman Empire to the Turkish Republic. *Göl İnsanları* (1955; Lake People) is Kemal Tahir's only collection of short stories. He also translated many works into Turkish under many different pseudonyms.   T.S.H.

Kerr, Alfred, pseud. of Alfred Kempner (1867–1948), German critic, essayist, and poet, was born in Breslau. Through his articles in *Der Tag* and the *Berliner Tageblatt* he became one of the most influential critics of the German stage at the beginning of the 20th century. He was an early champion of Henrik IBSEN, Gerhart HAUPT-

MANN, and Hermann SUDERMANN, as evidenced in *Davidsbündler! Das neue Drama* (1904), *Schauspielkunst* (1904; The Art of Drama) and *Herr Sudermann* (1903), and was instrumental in bringing about the acceptance of the expressionists. Kerr saw criticism as an art form in itself, and he wrote in what was called an "impressionistic" and "subjective" style, which, although ironical and barbed, never interfered with his objectivity and scholarship. Kerr's polished language also criticized the cultural and political situation in Germany until 1933, when he had to flee the Nazis, who saw him as the prototype of the "ultrarefined Jewish intellectual." In exile he wrote essays, pamphlets, and poetry and broadcast speeches with the main purpose of ridding his beloved Germany of the Nazis.

Between 1923 and 1933 there appeared a series of travel books and during the Nazi period the political works *Die Diktatur des Hausknechts* (1934; The Dictatorship of the House Servant), *Das dritte Reich* (1935), and *Walther Rathenau* (1935).

See: M. Heimann, "Alfred Kerr" (1918) in his *Die Wahrheit liegt nicht in der Mitte* (1966), pp. 214–24; W. Huder, "Alfred Kerr, ein deutscher Kritiker im Exil" *SuF* 18 (1966): 1262–79.   W.T.

Kessel, Joseph (1898–), French novelist and journalist, was born in Clara, Argentina, where his father, a Russian refugee who had completed his medical studies in France, practiced medicine. Kessel himself was educated in France, in Nice and Paris. World War I broke out while he was still studying at the Sorbonne. He enlisted and saw active service as an aviator, receiving the Croix de Guerre. He was then sent to the United States, leaving France the day the armistice was signed. From New York he went to Los Angeles and then on to Siberia, where he joined the French general staff. There he became acquainted with the hetman Semyonov and his Cossacks. Upon his return to France, Kessel published *La Steppe rouge* (1923; The Red Steppe), a group of short stories dealing with the Terror that accompanied the October Revolution of 1917, and *L'Equipage* (1923; The Crew), a war and aviation story that is probably his best novel. As a reporter he attempted to reenter the USSR and narrowly escaped being shot by the Bolsheviks in Riga. His novel *Les Captifs* (1926; The Captives), a somber study of the victims of tuberculosis, was awarded the Grand Prix du Roman by the Académie Française in 1927. *L'Armée des ombres* (Eng. tr., *Army of Shadows*, 1944), a vivid novel concerning World War II, was published in 1944. Kessel's more recent works, such as *Le Lion* (1958) and *Les Cavaliers* (1971), have been for the most part inspired by his numerous travels.   P.Br.

Kesten, Hermann (1900–), German novelist, playwright, translator, and anthologist, was born in Nuremberg of Jewish parents and was educated at Erlangen and Frankfurt am Main. An attack upon Hitlerism in his novel *Der Scharlatan* (1932; The Charlatan) made it necessary for him to leave Germany. In Amsterdam, where he fled, he was from 1933 until 1940 a literary editor for the publisher Albert de Lange. In 1940 the German invasion forced him to emigrate to the United States, where he lived until after the war in New York, becoming an American citizen. Since 1952 he has lived in Rome, traveling frequently both to West Germany and to New York.

Kesten's talent was early recognized; his first novel, *Joseph sucht die Freiheit* (1927; Eng. tr., *Joseph Breaks Free*, 1930), won for him a citation by Hans Henny Jahn at the Kleist Prize awards. Its theme—a youth's painful realization that the supposed virtues of his family existed only in his affectionate imagination and his consequent desire to escape from actuality—is, in Kesten's following novel, *Ein ausschweifender Mensch* (1929; A Dissolute Man), enlarged to a man's attempt to break away from his fatherland. His next book, *Glückliche Menschen* (1931; Eng. tr., *Happy Man!,* 1935), sentimentally melodramatic at the beginning and fantastic and arbitrary in its sequence of events, is nevertheless characteristic of its author, a moralist disguised as a grim joker. Kesten's fictionalized biographies, *Ferdinand und Isabella* (1936; Eng. tr., *Spanish Fire*, 1937, American tr., *Ferdinand and Isabella*, 1946), *König Philipp der Zweite* (1938; Eng. tr., *I, the King*, 1939), are marked by his attention to historical detail and correctness. The confusion and stupidity of the Spanish Civil War are vividly portrayed in *Die Kinder von Gernika* (1939; Eng. tr., *Children of Guernica,* 1939).

Several of Kesten's plays were produced before he left Germany. *Maud liebt beide* (1928; Maud Loves Both), *Admet* (1929), *Die heilige Familie* (1930; The Holy Family), *Babel* (1930), *Einer sagt die Wahrheit* (1931; One Man Tells the Truth), and, in collaboration with Ernst TOLLER, *Wunder in Amerika* (1931; Eng. tr., "Mary Baker Eddy," in Toller's *Seven Plays*, 1935). In Germany, and after his exile in the Netherlands and the United States, Kesten published several anthologies of European literature, his preference often being for the grim and melancholy, even gruesome aspects of life. Both in German and in English he edited the poems of Heinrich Heine, the work of Joseph Roth and G. E. Lessing, and he translated Julien GREEN, Jules ROMAINS, Jean GIRAUDOUX, John Gunther, Stephen Vincent Benét, and E. W. White.

A bantam of a man, and a fierce foe, Kesten has repeatedly stood up for the little fellow, particularly for the one trodden down by political persecution and tyranny. His novel of Germany between the wars, *Die Zwillinge von Nürnberg* (1947; appeared in 1946 in Eng. tr. as *The Twins of Nuremberg*), was followed by *Die fremden Götter* (1949; The Foreign Gods), a novel in which a Jew rediscovers his heritage because of Hitler's persecution. Important for Kesten's liberal viewpoint, which defends freedom of thought, are his biographies, *Copernicus und seine Welt* (1948; Copernicus and His World) and *Casanova* (1952), as well as his depiction of contemporary writer-colleagues in *Meine Freunde die Poeten* (1953; My Friends the Poets), *Dichter im Café* (1959; Poets in the Coffeeshop), and *Lauter Literaten* (1963; Nothing but Writers). Further novels and stories found little acclaim in West Germany, although Kesten has been repeatedly honored with prizes (Georg Büchner Prize, 1974), awards (Nelly Sachs, 1977), and honors (president of PEN in West Germany, 1972; chairman of the Erich Kästner Society in Munich, 1975). The delight he himself finds in his newly discovered talent for verse, as in *Ich bin der ich bin* (1974; I Am Who I Am), is infectious to his readers.   V.La. rev. A.L.W.

Keyserling, Eduard, Graf von (1855-1918), German novelist and dramatist, was born at Paddern, the ancestral estate in the Baltic province of Courland; his distinguished family traced its descent from the Teutonic Knights who had brought Christianity and Western culture to this region in the 13th century. His early education was in Hasenpoth, and he attended the university at Dorpat before going to Vienna to live. After some years at Paddern administering the family estate and further travel in Italy, he settled in Munich in 1899, where he lived with two sisters. An invalid after 1897, he was blind the last 10 years of his life.

Keyserling's literary career began late. His first works, the novels *Rosa Herz* (1883) and *Die dritte Stiege* (1890; The Third Stairs), as well as his dramas *Frühlingsopfer* (1899; Spring Sacrifices), *Der dumme Hans* (1901; Foolish Hans), *Peter Hawel* (1903), and *Benignens Erlebnis* (1906; Benignen's Experience), influenced by early naturalism, are almost forgotten. His later stories show Keyserling at his best. His style is reminiscent of Theodor FONTANE and Ivan Turgenev. The somber landscape and the melancholy isolation of the baronial estates reflect the passive mood and aristocratic restraint so fundamental to an understanding of his characters. His delineations are concise and accurate; his narratives, realistic and objective. His own social and cultural heritage determined his work. The German nobility in the Baltic provinces had enjoyed a unique position of influence for centuries and controlled internal affairs completely, despite the nominal political dependence upon Russia. Even in the late 19th century, after serfdom had been abolished and basic human rights granted to the Lett peasantry, the landed aristocracy dominated. The wide gulf between the masses of people and this small group of cultivated leaders remained unbridged. Keyserling portrayed the life of this select circle.

Among Keyserling's best works are the novels *Beate und Marile* (1903; Eng. tr., *The Curse of the Tarniffs,* 1928), *Dumala* (1907; Eng. tr., *Man of God,* 1930), *Wellen* (1911; Eng. tr., *Tides,* 1929), *Abendliche Häuser* (1913; Houses at Evening), *Am Südhang* (1916; On the South Slope), *Fürstinnen* (1917; Princesses), and *Feiertagskinder* (1919; Holiday Children) and the collections of stories *Schwüle Tage* (1906; Humid Days), *Bunte Herzen* (1908; Bright Hearts), and *Im stillen Winkel* (1918; In a Quiet Corner). His stories are documents of the gradual crumbling of a society that had once been the bulwark of European civilization but was now an anachronism. He ignored the problems of his time and seemed unaware of the significance of the revolt among the Letts (1905–06) that was really a prelude to the final collapse of German supremacy in the Baltic. For Keyserling, human relationships were significant only within the accepted pattern. His characters feel their position, their privileges, and their duties. Love is the motivating factor in his narratives, but it is not an elemental passion. He pictured love as an irrational desire that dislocates the ordinary relationships of life. Every story deals with the destructive influence of illicit love in conventional aristocratic circles, yet Keyserling never becomes tiresome in handling such limited materials.

See: K. Knoop, *Die Erzählungen Eduard von Keyserlings* (1929); R. Steinhilber, *Eduard von Keyserling, lings* (1929); R. Steinhilber, *Eduard von Keyserling:*
W.A.R. rev. A.L.W.

Kharms, Daniil Ivanovich, pseud. of Daniil Yuvachov (1905-42), Russian poet, prose writer, and dramatist, was born in Petersburg. During his lifetime, Kharms was known for his children's stories and verses, as well as for his editorial work on a children's magazine, but he also wrote many poems, sketches, stories, and philosophical and comic prose pieces which have gradually been published, although only in the West. Kharms was associated in Leningrad with the painter Kazimir Malevich and a group of avant-garde writers, painters, musicians, and theater people. His works are grotesque and range from black humor to speculative philosophical reflections. The play *Yelizaveta Bam* (1927) is a precursor of Eugène IoNESCO's theater of the absurd. Kharms belonged to an informal group of writers and artists called the OBERIU, their Russian acronym for "Association for Real Art" (*see* RUSSIAN LITERATURE). The group included Nikolay

ZABOLOTSKY, Aleksandr Vvedensky, and others. In the early 1930s this late flowering of futuristic art came into conflict with the official Soviet line and was silenced. Kharms died in prison. Kharm's *Izbrannoye* (Selections), ed. by G. Gibian, was published in Würzburg, Germany, in 1974.

See: G. Gibian, Introduction to D. Kharms, *Russia's Lost Literature of the Absurd* (1974), pp. 1–35.   G.Gi.

Khlebnikov, Velimir, pseud. of Viktor Vladimirovich Khlebnikov (1885–1922), Russian poet and playwright, was born in Astrakhan province in the Kalmuck steppes. He made his literary debut with a neologistic prose piece which appeared in a Petersburg newspaper. Although encouraged by Vyacheslav IVANOV and M. A. KUZMIN, Khlebnikov was dissatisfied with the reception given his poetry, broke with the Academy of Verse (where he had received the name Velimir) in 1909, and joined a group of unknowns headed by David BURLYUK, eventually called futurists (*see* RUSSIAN LITERATURE), whose first collection was *Sadok sudey* (1910; A Trap for Judges). They proclaimed Khlebnikov a genius and regularly printed his poetry, prose, dramas, and essays in their miscellanies. He acquired a fame of sorts for his short "Zaklyatiye smekhom" (1910; Incantation by Laughter), built on derivations from a single root. Among his works written up to 1914, all of which are characterized by neologisms, metrical and semantical dislocations, fragmentary composition, folkloric tendencies, and lexical mixing, the most outstanding are the Whitmanesque "Zverinets" (Zoo) and two fantasies, the grim "Zhuravl" (The Crane) and the satirical play "Markiza Dezes." When the futurist group, which was calling itself "Hylaea" in 1911, began to stress primitivism, Khlebnikov contributed a series of Slavic idylls, among them "I i E" (1912) and "Shaman i Venera" (1912; A Shaman and Venus). Pagan Russia always attracted him, as is evidenced in "Vnuchka Malushi" (1913; Malusha's Granddaughter), as did Asia, with which the anti-Westernist Khlebnikov more readily identified Russia than with Europe. Among his "Asian" works are "Khadzhi-Tarkhan" (1913), a poem about his home city of Astrakhan; the post-Revolutionary "Persian" poem "Truba Gul-mully" (1928; Gul-mullah's Trumpet); and the prose piece "Esir" (1924).

In 1913, Khlebnikov signed the futurist manifesto "Poshchochina obshchestvennomu vkusu" (A Slap in the Face of Public Taste), which was largely an attack on Russian literature in general, but which also contained the slogan *samovitoye slovo* (self-oriented word) coined by him. This futurist emphasis on language, which resulted in incessant verbal experiment and word-creation, had in Khlebnikov one of its best theoreticians. His talent was evidenced at first in a joint essay with Aleksey KRUCHONYKH, *Slovo kak takovoye* (1913; The Word as Such), and later in "Nasha osnova" (1920; Our Foundation) which sums up his own ideas. Perhaps the most extreme consequence of such emphasis on the "word as such" was the so-called *zaum* (transrational language), a completely new poetical idiom; for Kruchonykh it was the creation of meaningless but expressive pieces of sound, while for Khlebnikov it meant a distillation of the lost primary meaning. As a literary fighter, Khlebnikov was of little help to his fellow futurists. An introvert and eccentric, he lacked both the voice and the temperament to participate in their scandalous public appearances. He was a restless traveler who seldom washed and often forgot to eat, being preoccupied with his calculations of the laws of time. Khlebnikov's linguistics and mathematics of history are inseparable from his poetry, especially

in the post-Revolutionary period. In the year 1914 three collections of Khlebnikov's poetry were in print: *Ryav* (Roar), *Izbornik stikhov* (Selected Poems), and *Tvoreniya* (Creations). It was also, however, the year that F. T. MARINETTI came to Russia, a sojourn that eventually led to a split within Russian futurism and its eventual disintegration. During the October Revolution and Civil War, the hungry and "underdressed" Khlebnikov continued to travel. Although he gave the pagan idyll more depth in "Poet" (1919), his main post-1917 achievements were poems presenting revolution as tragic retribution, notably "Nochnoy obysk" (Night Search); the Utopian poem *Ladomir* (1921); and "Siniye okovy" (Blue Chains), written in free verse. His preoccupation with time and numbers in history is summed up in *Doski sudby* (1922; Tablets of Destiny), and also resulted in the ambitious play *Zangezi* (1922), which crowned his efforts to create the new genre called "trans-tale" (*zapovest*), earlier tried in the imposing *Deti vydry* (1913; Otter's Children). Khlebnikov died in the Novgorod district from malnutrition.

Though habitually identified with futurism—and neologism—Khlebnikov was larger than his movement and an outsider within it. His handling of the poetical medium revealed fascinating vistas. His efforts to open up new thematic areas and to transcend literature proper still await evaluation. Original in both poetry and prose (see especially "Ka," written in 1915), Khlebnikov's ties with the Russian literary tradition were both deeper than those of his fellow futurists and more unexpected (Nikolay Gogol, A. K. Tolstoy, A. Ostrovsky, Griboyedov). It is as an artist, however, that Khlebnikov excelled; some of his poems on revolution, although sympathetic, are the least biased or simplified, as well as the most profound, in Soviet poetry, where his influence was wide and strong. Current volumes of his works include *Sobraniye sochineniy* (Collected Works), vols. 1–4 (Munich: 1968–72) and *Snake Train: Poetry and Prose,* ed. and tr. G. Kern (1976).

See: V. Markov, *The Longer Poems of Velimir Khlebnikov* (1962) and *Russian Futurism* (1968); translations from and articles about Khlebnikov in *RLT* 12 (Spring 1975) and 13 (Fall 1975).   V.M.

Khodasevich, Vladislav Felitsianovich (1886–1939), Russian poet, critic, essayist, memoirist, and translator, was born in Moscow and died in exile in Paris. Vladimir NABOKOV acclaimed him the "greatest Russian poet of our time"; he exaggerated, but understandably so, given the neglect of this important writer. Although Khodasevich excluded his first two books of verse—*Molodost* (1908; Youth) and *Schastlivy domik* (1914; The Happy Little House)—from his *Sobraniye stikhov* (1927; Collection of Poems), they are by no means negligible. His fame, however, rests on the poetry in *Putyom zerna* (1920; The Way of the Grain) and *Tyazholaya lira* (1922; The Heavy Lyre), written for the most part before his emigration from Russia in 1922, and on the small number of poems written in the West and published as the final section of *Sobraniye stikhov* under the title "Yevropeyskaya noch" (European Night).

After 1927, Khodasevich wrote little verse, turning instead to studies of Aleksandr Pushkin and to literary criticism. Some of his critical pieces were collected in *Stati o russkoy poezii* (1922; Essays on Russian Poetry) and *Stati i vospominaniya* (1954; Literary Essays and Memoirs). He also wrote a series of acerbic memoirs, a selection of which appeared as *Nekropol* (1939; Necropolis), and a magnificent biography of Gavril Romanovich Derzhavin (1931). He translated poetry from many languages but most significantly from Polish, Armenian, and especially Hebrew. There is no edition of his collected works.

Khodasevich owes a certain debt to Russian symbolism, but he joined no literary groups, and his finest verse belongs to the postsymbolist era both in chronology and in spirit. Although he deliberately based his mature poetics on those of an earlier age, no reader is likely to confuse his deceptively simple yet astringent "neoclassical" verse with that of Pushkin or Yevgeny Baratynsky. He mastered traditional techniques and language in order to express his personal and corrosively modern vision: a profound awareness of the void of human existence and the tragic split in his own dislocated being, which hopelessly struggles to escape the limitations of the flesh as the world of European civilization disintegrates around him.

In his criticism—and by the example of his verse—Khodasevich passionately defended the essential role of tradition as a living and liberating force in art, thereby placing himself squarely in one of the mainstreams of modernism, along with men as diverse as T. S. Eliot, Igor Stravinsky, and George Balanchine. Translations of his verse are available in *Modern Russian Poetry,* ed. by V. Markov and M. Sparks (1967).

See: R. P. Hughes, "Khodasevich," and V. Nabokov, translations and essay "On Khodasevich" in *The Bitter Air of Exile: Russian Writers and the West 1922-1972,* ed. by S. Karlinsky and A. Appel, Jr., (1977), pp. 52-70, 83-87.　　　　　　　　　　　　　　　　　　　　　　J.E.M.

Khvylovy, Mykola, pseud. of Mykola Fitilov (1893-1933), Ukrainian short-story writer, poet, and essayist, was born in the village of Trostyanets, Kharkiv (Kharkov) province. One of the most prominent literary personalities of the 1920s, Khvylovy was a Communist who ardently believed in the regeneration of Ukrainian culture under Soviet rule. With this aim he organized the group of "proletarian" writers called VAPLITE (1925-28) and stirred up the so-called literary discussion defending the high aesthetic goals of literature and pleading for orientation toward the West (*see* UKRAINIAN LITERATURE). Chided by Iosif Stalin for advocating a policy of turning "away from Moscow," Khvylovy recanted and later tried to regroup the opposition forces. Bitterly disenchanted with ever increasing russification and with Communist Party controls, Khvylovy committed suicide in May 1933.

Khvylovy's first collections of poetry, *Molodist* (1921; Youth) and *Dosvitni symfoniyi* (1922; Morning Symphonies), were full of revolutionary romanticism. Of much greater merit were his short stories in such collections as *Syni etyudy* (1923; Blue Etudes) and *Osin* (1924; Autumn), which employed intricate narration, deep irony, and poetic imagery. His later stories, notably "Ivan Ivanovych," "Revizor" (The Inspector General), were satirical. A novel, *Valdshnepy* (1927; The Woodsnipes), remained unfinished at his death. Khvylovy expressed his views on politics and aesthetics (including his theory of "romantic vitaism") in the brilliant pamphlets *Kamo hryadeshy?* (1925; Whither Are You Going?) and *Dumky proty techniyi* (1926; Thoughts against the Current). After his journal *Vaplite* was closed down in 1928, his followers published *Literaturny yarmarok* (1929; The Literary Fair) and *Prolitfront.* Khvylovy was influenced by Oswald Spengler and, indirectly, by Friedrich NIETZSCHE. His impact was felt not only by his own generation but also by later dissident writers. Some of his short stories have appeared in English translation in *Stories from the Ukraine* (1960).　　　　　　　　　　　　　　　　　　　　　　G.S.N.L.

Kielland, Alexander Lange (1849-1906), Norwegian novelist, short-story writer, and dramatist, was born in Stavanger, to a wealthy family. He received a law degree in 1871 and embarked on a tangled career as a factory owner, journalist, mayor, and, finally, district governor. Bursting upon the literary scene in 1879, he worked feverishly for a decade and then stopped writing as suddenly as he began. Along with Henrik IBSEN, Bjørnstjerne BJØRNSON, and Jonas LIE, Kielland is reckoned as one of the "Big Four" classic Norwegian writers.

Like his contemporaries, Kielland attacked the abuses of social life, but he stood apart from the writers of his generation by virtue of his great personal charm, his brilliant wit, and his unfailing clarity of form. Bjørnson and Georg BRANDES hailed him enthusiastically as an ally in the battle for social and intellectual freedom in Scandinavia. Kielland's attacks on social prejudice stemmed from his sincerity of ethnical purpose, a logical, rationalistic view of the world, and an absolute conviction of the importance of the cause for which he fought. His basic tastes were developed in a precapitalistic, patriarchal economy, an atmosphere of small-town merchant princeliness. This world was reflected in his courtly manners, his proud, reticent character, the deep veneration he nourished for the cultural tradition of his family, and the touch of foppery and dolce far niente that he often regretted but never denied. His loving delineation of the ancestral house stands among the high points of his authorship. But Kielland broke decisively with the political and religious tradition of this background. His years as a factory owner opened his eyes to the position of the laboring man, and his reading after 1870 gave him direction by awakening his anger over the exploitation and inequalities of modern life. The satirical spirit that had been nourished in his student days by the works of Heinrich Heine and Søren KIERKEGAARD was now captivated by the ideas of Georg Brandes and John Stuart Mill and inspired by the narrative art of Charles Dickens, Léon DAUDET, Hans Christian Andersen, and Honoré de Balzac. The theme of Kielland's infinitely varied writing became the glaring discrepancies between wealth and poverty, between the respectable and the outcast. He felt a deep aversion to the anticultural effects of industrial capitalism, which was now approaching, and parted company with his own class by sympathizing with its victims instead of its beneficiaries, by seeking to strengthen those who lacked power, and by encouraging their dissatisfactions.

Kielland poured his satiric vitriol, above all, on the representatives of conservative, institutionalized life: the clergy, the bureaucracy, and the schoolmen. Although his satire began with rapier thrusts, it ended with good, hefty blows of the broadsword. Kielland's first published work was a collection of short stories, *Novelletter* (1879; Eng. tr., *Tales of Two Countries,* 1891; *Norse Tales and Sketches,* 1897). His fame rests chiefly on these and the novels *Garman og Worse* (1880; Eng. tr., *Garman and Worse,* 1885) and *Skipper Worse* (1882; Eng. tr., 1885). The most distinguished of his contemporary satires were the novels *Arbeidsfolk* (1881; Laborers), *Else* (1881; Eng. tr., *Elsie,* 1894), and *Gift* (1883; Poison). His best plays were the satirical comedies *Tre Par* (1886; Three Couples) and *Professoren* (1883; The Professor).

In his writings, Kielland exhibited a cultivation of language; a deft, discreet handling of detail that is often loving in its maliciousness; and a lyric vein that grew out of a passionate fondness for the gray, low-lying shores of southwestern Norway and the sea that incessantly pounds them. At the same time, his works offer a remarkable blending of the Norwegian milieu with the European outlook.

See: G. Gran, *Alexander L. Kielland og hans samtid* (1922); O. Storstein, *Kielland på ny* (1949); N. E. Bæhrendtz, *Alexander Kiellands litteräara genombrott* (1952); O. L. Apeland, *Alexander L. Kiellands romaner* (1971).   E.H.

Kierkegaard, Søren Aabye (1813–55), Danish philosopher, was born in Copenhagen. His father, Michael Pedersen Kierkegaard, a wealthy merchant, was highly gifted and not only trained his son in the art of logic but also encouraged his imagination as well. Kierkegaard withdrew from his theological studies in the 1830s and lived a bohemian life until he experienced a religious crisis in 1838, which led to a firm conviction regarding Christian salvation. In 1840, Kierkegaard passed his theological examinations. Following another crisis of unknown origin, he broke off his yearlong engagement to Regine Olsen in 1841. This caused a scandal in Copenhagen, and it also proved to be of paramount importance to Kierkegaard's writing, the major part of which occurred during the productive years of 1843 to 1846. Kierkegaard's work during those years was inspired by his opposition to Georg Wilhelm Friedrich Hegel's systematic philosophy, which, in its search for the speculative truth, completely ignores the existence of the individual. Beginning in 1846, satirical attacks in the weekly magazine *Corsaren* gave the sensitive Kierkegaard new inspiration for a number of religious treatises, the second phase of his literary career. Eventually the attacks led to his self-chosen martyrdom, which, beginning in 1854, resulted in violent polemics against the official state church, and constituted the third and last, journalistic, phase of Kierkegaard's career.

Kierkegaard's philosophy is permeated with absolute demands, mistrust of human nature, and the belief that truth is something to be gained only through personal suffering. As early as his first major work, *Enten-Eller* (1843; Eng. tr., *Either-Or;* English translations and editions of Kierkegaard's works have been so numerous that no attempt will be made to enumerate them here), Kierkegaard posits the existential choice in the form of different ways of life—the aesthetic and the ethical stages—against the compromise-prone spirit of the times. The first, or aesthetic, stage is characterized by a disharmonious, hedonistic attitude toward life represented by Don Juan and Johannes the Seducer. The second, ethical, stage can be reached only by fulfilling everyday duties and responsibilities. For Kierkegaard, neither is the true stage. Indeed, *Enten-Eller* is simply a preparation for *Stadier paa Livets Vei* (1845; Eng. tr., *Stages on Life's Way*), which again analyzes the aesthetic (in "In Vino Veritas") and the ethical standpoints, illuminated in relation to love and marriage. The third part of the book, ("Guilty–Not Guilty") regards suffering as a prerequisite of the third or religious stage, the only form of existence capable of bestowing value and eternity upon human life. The third stage is described as a paradox wherein the individual can receive no assistance from other human beings but has to face his or her responsibility toward God alone. In *Frygt og Bæven* (1843; Eng. tr., *Fear and Trembling*), Kierkegaard used the biblical tale of Abraham's sacrifice of Isaac in order to illustrate this paradox of faith. Abraham is placed in a situation of choice where he must choose between general ethical duty toward his fellow man and absolute obedience to God. In *Gjentagelsen* (1843; Eng. tr., *Repetition*) the aesthetic viewpoint is placed before the tribunal of faith. The purpose is to illuminate the religious concept, which Kierkegaard called "repetition," that is, the possibility inherent in faith to

win back in spiritual freedom that which was lost in the finite. Job of the Old Testament succeeded in this, but Constantius, the main character of *Gjentagelsen*, fails when he vainly attempts to repeat an aesthetic experience. The paradox of Christian faith is further illustrated in *Philosophiske Smuler* (1844; Eng. tr., *Philosophical Fragments*) by juxtaposing it with Greek Platonic philosophy. To be a Christian requires the acceptance through faith of the paradox that God has become man, that the infinite has become the finite. In contrast to the Socratic philosophy, which holds truth to be inherent in man, the Christian is given truth through an act of grace. The dogmatic condition for this redemption is the awareness of sin, an idea elucidated in *Begrebet Angest* (1844; Eng. tr., *The Concept of Dread*). Dread is the first stage on the way to faith. It makes possible the "leap" that brings the individual in contact with religion, where the spirit becomes aware of itself and the human being recognizes the synthesis of soul and matter. In *Afsluttende uvidenskabelig Efterskrift* (1846; Eng. tr., *Concluding Unscientific Postscript*), Kierkegaard once again explained the individual's road to Christianity, that is, the acceptance of the paradox of faith through the recognition of sin, thereby changing the objective point of view into a subjective, committed relationship with Christ. Thus, subjectivity becomes truth. In this philosophical treatise, Kierkegaard also disclosed that one and the same person was responsible for his hitherto pseudonymous writings. Simultaneously with these, he published, under his own name, a series of *Opbyggelige Taler* (1843–47; Eng. tr., *Edifying Discourses*), in which he directly expressed his fervent, almost pietistic, relationship with God. According to Kierkegaard, this parallel form of publication served to prove that his standpoint from the very outset was Christian. With increasing passion, he expounded the Christian ethic in *Kjerlighedens Gjerninger* (1847; Eng. tr., *Works of Love*) and wrote of despair and its result, sin, in *Sygdommen til Døden* (1849; Eng. tr., *The Sickness unto Death*). The attack on the state church is initiated in *Indøvelse i Christendom* (1850; Eng. tr., *Training in Christianity*), in which Kierkegaard demanded that the Christian shall make himself contemporary with Christ, that is, choose martyrdom. From the standpoint of this absolute demand, Kierkegaard aimed, in the pamphlets *Øieblikket* (1–9, 1855; Eng. tr., *The Moment*), a series of satirical and scathing attacks on the ministers of the church for having made a living out of what should have been a martyrdom. During the bitter polemics Kierkegaard overreached himself and died soon afterward. It was to be his last external disappointment that not even *Øieblikket* succeeded in arousing a reaction from the state church. He was ignored to death. But through his description of the fundamental contrasts between existence, which only can be experienced through life and action and the cognitive thought, which transforms life into general and objective concepts, Kierkegaard's philosophy has become the foundation of modern existentialism, represented by, for example, Karl Jaspers, Martin HEIDEGGER, Albert CAMUS, and Jean-Paul SARTRE. In addition, his influence is noted in such authors as Henrik IBSEN and Franz KAFKA.

See: W. Lowrie, *Kierkegaard* (1938); J. Hohlenberg, *Søren Kierkegaard* (1940), and *Den ensommes vej* (1948; F. Brandt, *Søren Kierkegaard: His Life—His Works* (1963); B. K. Stendahl, *Søren Kierkegaard, TWAS 392* (1976).   S.H.R.

Kijowski, Andrzej (1928–), Polish essayist, critic, and fiction writer, was born in Cracow. His works have appeared in the leading Polish literary periodicals since

1950. Among his works are *Diabeł, anioł i chłop* (1955; The Devil, the Angel, and the Peasant), short stories; *Miniatury krytyczne* (1961; Critical Miniatures) and *Arcydzieło nieznane* (1964; The Unknown Masterpiece), short essays on literary and social subjects; *Dziecko przez ptaka przyniesione* (1968; The Child Brought by the Stork), a novel; and *Listopadowy Wieczór* (1972; A November Night), essays on historical and philosophical subjects related to Polish romanticism. Kijowski specializes in short philosophical tales; some of them are fictionalized, and others take the form of a monologue delivered to a friend. He uses the word "feuilleton" to define the genre he practices, and he believes it to be the successor to the novel. His topic is 20th-century people coping with the inevitable baggage of history and trying to find their place in, and response to, technology and new social mores. Kijowski's style is intensely personal; his philosophical reflections, nontrivial, ironic at times, but seldom bitter.   E.M.T.

Kinck, Hans Ernst (1865–1926), Norwegian short-story writer, novelist, dramatist, and essayist, was born in Øksfjord in Loppa, the son of a physician. After growing up among the "medieval" country folk of Setesdal (from age 7 to 11) and the "salty rationalists" of Hardanger (from age 11 to 17), Kinck received classical schooling. He took a university degree in 1892, winning honorable mention for a thesis on the relation between medieval ballad poetry and the mythical-heroic poetry of northern antiquity. This was the first of his many attempts to reach, by means of a magnificent scholarly intuition (although too often without adequate factual support), a conception of the Norse "folk psyche" in both modern and medieval times.

Kinck is one of the most original, temperamental, and startling writers in Norwegian letters. On the one hand, he was in step with other writers and thinkers of the neoromantic era, yet he also turned his attention to the Middle Ages, seeking there the roots of the nation, "the mystery of a people." Like Henri BERGSON, Kinck praised human vitality, the impulse, the unreflective, the flame of heart and temper. Like Friedrich NIETZSCHE, he saw in history "a series of vast undertakings resulting from the self-willed craving for action of individual personalities." Kinck's entire work was founded in mysticism, but he approached it by way of an ironic, almost corrosive wit and a fantastically imaginative intellect. His earliest novels, *Huldren* (1892; The Half-Wit) and *Ungt folk* (1893; Eng. tr., *A Young People*, 1929), were outwardly naturalistic, but their purpose was to reveal the unconscious urges of the soul. A sojourn in Paris (1893–94) led to his first genuinely original creation, the short-story collection *Flaggermusvinger* (1895; Bats' Wings), and two novels, *Sus* (1896; Soughing) and *Hugormen* (1898; The Adder). Kinck's writings left the public cold, bewildered, and antagonistic, but among writers and connoiseurs he won faithful, even frenzied support.

In 1896, Kinck visited Italy for the first time and was so captivated by its charm that he made it his second homeland. From then on, he varied the settings of his writings between a Norwegian peasant or medieval background and the Italian Renaissance. Those of his masterpieces set in rural Norway include the novel *Emigranter* (1904; Emigrants), the unrhymed dramatic poem *Driftekaren* (1908; The Drover), numerous volumes of short stories and essays, and the monumental *Sneskavlen brast* (3 vols., 1918–19; The Avalanche Broke); their basic themes are class conflicts, and the relation of heritage and environment, or race and individual. Kinck's Italian studies led him to conceive of two polar types in the racial

mixture of Italy: the satirist Pietro Aretino, in the drama *Den sidste gjest* (1910; The Last Guest), and the mystic nationalist Niccolò Machiavelli, in the drama *Mot karneval* (1915; Toward Carnival). Although Kinck was close to Vilfredo Pareto in his views on emotion and was affected by the writings of the German racialists, he did not follow them into fascism, remaining instead sharply opposed to all mechanistic philosophies and mass movements.

Kinck's style is alternately lyric and grotesque, with an overpowering, baroque fantasy that can flare up into burlesque or sadism without warning. His literary medium was a form of Dano-Norwegian such as no one had written before him, shot through with the riches of his childhood dialects, concentrated, impulsive, and difficult to access. Kinck's work contains flashes of authentic genius, even though it reveals an incapacity for sustained narrative or dramatic characterization. The best of his extraordinarily prolific work is found in the short stories; he was less apt to use these as vehicles for philosophical statements and was free to be, as Gunnar HEIBERG once noted, the "pure artist."

See: E. Beyer, *Hans E. Kinck: livsangst og livstro*, 2 vols. (1956, 1965).   E.H.

Kipphardt, Heinar (1922–), German dramatist, novelist, and poet, was born in Heidersdorf, Silesia. He was a practicing psychiatrist until 1951. From 1951 to 1959 he worked with the Deutsches Theater in Berlin. In 1959 he moved to West Germany, where he became internationally famous with his play *In der Sache J. Robert Oppenheimer* (1964; Eng. tr., *In the Matter of J. Robert Oppenheimer*, 1967), a compelling dramatic documentary drawn from transcripts of the American Atomic Energy Commission hearings but shaped by Kipphardt, a la Bertolt BRECHT, to provoke political awareness (Kipphardt considers the work to be drama first, documentary second). Another epic theater documentary, *Joel Brand: Die Geschichte eines Geschäfts* (1965; Joel Brand: The History of a Deal), concerns the Nazi attempt to barter one million Jewish lives for 10,000 trucks. Kipphardt also writes stinging satire such as *Shakespeare dringend gesucht* (1954; Shakespeare Urgently Sought), a humorous play critical of the East German theatrical world and government censorship. He has lately turned to other genres and has indicated less overt concern with political issues (Brechtian influence is still evident, however). *März* (1976; March) is a novel about a psychiatric patient. *Angelsbruckner Notizen* (1977; Angelsbruck Notes), containing poems dating back to the 1940s, includes recent, nonpolitical lyric poems. Kipphardt often writes about topics involving science. He is the author of nine other books, including a film script. In 1964 he received the Gerhard Hauptmann Prize.

See: A. Blume, *Das dokumentarische Theater* (1977).
                                                                R.Z.

Kirk, Hans (1898–1962), Danish novelist and journalist, was born in Hadsund in northwestern Jutland. He received a law degree in 1922. Kirk's first novel, *Fiskerne* (1928; Eng. tr., *The Fishermen*, 1951), is written from a Marxist, sociological viewpoint. It has no main character and tells of a collective community of fishermen moving from the rough west coast of Jutland to a milder area. Their gradual absorption into new surroundings and the ensuing conflicts, particularly between ascetic religion and sexuality, is the theme of the book. Although his psychology contains more artificiality than depth, Kirk's human portraits in *Fiskerne* are believable and realistic. This is not the case in the next two related novels, *Dag-*

lejerne (1936; Day Laborers) and *De nye Tider* (1939; New Times), both describing the industrialization of an old village community and the resulting severe human and economic problems. Kirk departed from contemporary motifs in *Slaven* (1948; The Slave), a philosophical novel about the repression of a slave insurrection on a 17th-century Spanish ship, which is a symbol of the capitalistic society. *Vredens Søn* (1950; The Son of Wrath) also has a historical frame, depicting Jesus as a social rebel and revolutionary and drawing parallels to 20th-century events, especially the German occupation of Denmark from 1940 to 1945. Kirk's later writing thus developed into a more narrow, polemical, and tendentious direction, yet his first novel, *Fiskerne,* places him in the epic and naturalistic tradition alongside such masters as Henrik PONTOPPIDAN and Martin Andersen NEXØ.

See: J. K. Andersen and L. Emerek, *Hans Kirk's forfatterskab* (1972).   S.H.R.

Kirsanov, Semyon Isaakovich (1906–72), Russian poet, was born in Odessa, the son of a tailor. He took a degree in philology at the University of Odessa in 1925 and soon began to publish. In 1925 he also moved to Moscow, where he was close to Vladimir MAYAKOVSKY, whose style had already influenced him. Like Mayakovsky, Kirsanov produced a great deal of versified journalism, such as the narrative poem "Pyatiletka" (1932; Five-Year Plan). His style is marked by whimsical imagery, ingenious metaphors, conceits, and puns, and by a symbolic use of syntactic and sound patterns. Like Mayakovsky, Kirsanov often focussed on the poet's own persona, as in "Moya imeninnaya" (1927; My Nameday Poem). He also wrote versified science, such as "Osada atoma" (1933; Atom under Siege) and "Poema o robote" (1934; Poem about a Robot), which occasionally produces intriguing insights.

Among Kirsanov's poems written during the 1930s are some like "Tvoya poema" (1937; A Poem for You), in which personal suffering is eloquently expressed in haunting images. During World War II he produced his share of patriotic verse, and he played a significant role in the "thaw" after Iosif Stalin's death. His narrative poem "Sem dney nedeli" (1956; Seven Days of the Week) skillfully combines science fiction with moral allegory, describing the implantation of new hearts in the chests of the Soviet citizenry. In later years he turned toward versified *Naturphilosophie* (often in free verse). While much of his poetry is modern and even "Western," he also cultivated the style of Russian folk poetry, as in "Skanzaniye pro tsarya Maksa–Yemelyana" (1962–64). Recent collections of his poetry are *Iskaniya: stikhotvoreniya i poemy, 1923–1965* (1967), *Zerkala: Stikhi* (1972), and *Sobraniye sochineniy,* 4 vols. (1974–75).   V.T.

Kirshon, Vladimir Mikhaylovich (1902–38), Russian playwright, was born in Nalchik. Although a loyal Communist Party activist throughout his adult life, he was executed as an alleged Trotskyite and only posthumously rehabilitated. Kirshon achieved short-lived success as a dramatist by centering his plots around burning issues of the day. Thus, *Relsy gudyat* (1928; The Rails Are Humming) examines the advancement of unskilled workers to managerial positions, and *Khleb* (1930; Eng. tr., *Bread,* 1934), studies the class struggle in the countryside during Iosif Stalin's collectivization campaign. As a member of the "On-Guardists," Kirshon led a vigorous campaign for the psychological portrayal of the individual hero, as opposed to the oversimplified collective hero demanded by the

"Literary Frontists." Unfortunately, his own characters often are little more than mouthpieces of Party ideas.
                                                S.E.R.

Klabund, pseud. of Alfred Henschke (1890–1928), German novelist, dramatist, and poet, was born in Crossen on the Oder, the son of an apothecary. At the age of 24, he was forced by an attack of tuberculosis to abandon his studies. From then on until his death, his time was spent, with ever shorter intervals, in the sanitariums of Davos and other health resorts. He married twice. After the early death of his first wife, the "Irene" (Peace) of his poems, he wrote the exquisite *Totenklage* (1918–19; Death Lament).

The critic Alfred KERR discovered the young Klabund, whose poetry he printed in his periodical *Pan* and whom he staunchly upheld against a scandalized public. Primarily a lyricist, Klabund was at the same time an expressionist, although he never belonged to any of the expressionist groups. He commanded a great variety of types of expression, from the vulgar to the mystic. Most of his "Chinese" poems are not translations but works of his own imagination. His style, diverse in form, is always restless and impatient. His poetry expresses itself preponderantly in contrasts (*Klabund* means "transformation"), which often led to the grotesque and to satire. He was attracted by the genuine and the elemental, an inclination evident in the subject matter of his novellas, of which he wrote some 10. The best known are *Brache* (1918; Eng. tr., *Brackie the Fool,* 1927), *Pjotr* (1923; Eng. tr., *Peter the Czar,* 1925), and *Borgia* (1928; Eng. tr., *The Incredible Borgias,* 1929). Klabund was also a successful dramatist, particularly with his version of the Chinese *Kreidekreis* (1924; Eng. tr., *Circle of Chalk,* 1929) and the social comedy *X Y Z* (1926).

See: H. Grothe, *Klabund: Leben und Werk eines Poeten* (1933); W. Paulsen, "Klabund," *GL&L* 3 (1938–39): 222–30; S. L. Gilman, *Form und Funktion, eine strukturelle Untersuchung der Romane Klabunds* (1971); G. von Kaulla, *Brennendes Herz. Klabund, Legende und Wirklichkeit* (1971).   W.P. rev. A.L.W.

Kloos, Willem Johannes Theodorus (1859–1938), Dutch poet and critic, was born in Amsterdam. He was married to the writer Jeanne Reyneke van Stuwe. Kloos had studied classics at the university, and in 1880 he began his literary career with the publication of the dramatic fragment "Rhodopis" in the magazine *Nederland*. His passionate poetry reached full expression in *De Nieuwe Gids,* the magazine of the "Movement of the Eighties" (see DUTCH LITERATURE), which he helped to found and of which he was editor. He was a friend of Jacques Perk and of Albert VERWEY. Kloos preferred the sonnet, and he had published Perk's sonnet cycle *Mathilde*. His introduction to the book, an essay on Perk's poetry and poetry in general, is considered the manifesto of the "Movement of the Eighties." Kloos's own sonnet cycle, *Het Boek van Kind en God* (1888; The Book of the Child and of God), is a moving work. *Sappho* (1882) remained a fragment. The epic fragment *Okeanos* (1884; Ocean) reveals the influence of John Keat's "Hyperion," but Kloos had already forged a poetic language of his own, in which sound, rhythm, and imagery were paramount. His poetry centered around Beauty and the Self, and his subjective, introverted point of view influenced the poetry of Albert Verwey and Herman GORTER. The emotional element is dominant in his work.

Kloos did not fulfill the promise of his early poetry. His personality and his talent declined sharply after 1891, and *Verzen* (1894), for example, is marred by personal attacks, and the volumes *Nieuwe verzen* (1895; New Verses), *Verzen II* (1902), or *Verzen III* (1913) do not add anything to his reputation. Kloos published several literary studies, such as *Een daad van eenvoudige rechtvaardigheid* (1909; An Act of Simple Justice), a book on Dutch poets of the 18th century. *Veertien jaar literatuurgeschiedenis* (1896: Fourteen Years of Literary History), containing the influential reviews of the first period of *De Nieuwe Gids,* was republished as *Nieuwere litteratuurgeschiedenis* vols. 1-2 (1904-14; Recent Literary History). Volumes 3-5 include the reviews from 1895 to 1915; volumes 6-27, for the years 1916-1937, were published as *Letterkundige inzichten en vergezichten* (1928-38; Literary Insights and Perspectives). Kloos translated Euripedes' *Alcestis*, Sophocles' *Antigone*, and Thomas à Kempis's *Imitation of Christ*. With Kloos, the poetic line became a thing of feeling, originality, and beauty, and he put an end to the traditional and hackneyed verse of the 19th century.

See: K. H. de Raaf, *Willem Kloos, de mensch, de dichter, de criticus* (1934). S.L.F.

Klossowski, Pierre (1903-), French novelist and essayist, was born of Polish parents living in Paris. Brother of the painter Balthus, he started writing in the 1930s, at the same time as Georges BATAILLE, Roger Caillois, and Michel LEIRIS. Of strong Catholic background, Klossowski decided during World War II to enter the religious life, an experience that led to his first novel, *La Vocation suspendue* (1950; The Suspended Vocation). His major work, *Les Lois de l'hospitalité* (1965; The Laws of Hospitality), regroups three earliers novels—*Roberte ce soir* (1953), *La Révocation de l'édit de Nantes* (1959; Eng. tr., *Roberte ce soir* and *The Revocation of the Edict of Nantes,* 1969), and *Le Souffleur* (1960); The Prompter)—to form a triptych in which theology and pornography coexist amidst a dizzying series of debates, dialogues, and *tableaux vivants. Le Baphomet* (1965) uses the persecution of the Knights Templars in 1307 as a pretext for presenting the opposition/nonopposition between God and the Antichrist, the Unique and the Multiple. To these novels one should add Klossowski's essays—*Le Bain de Diane* (1959; Diana's Bath), *Nietzsche ou le cercle vicieux* (1969; NIETZSCHE or the Vicious Circle), and *La Monnaie vivante* (1970; Living Currency).

Klossowski's archaic language and scholasticlike arguments may appear anachronistic. Yet his anti-Cartesianism, his taste for paradox and irony, and his notion of the relation between language and the body all place him squarely in the contemporary "tradition" of dialogism and écriture.

See: M. Foucault, "La Prose d'Actéon," *NRF* 135 (March 1964): 444-59; G. Deleuze, "Klossowski ou les corps-langage," in *Logique du sens* (1969); special Klossowski issue of *L'Arc* 43 (1970). D.B.R.

Kluge, Alexander (1932-), German short-story writer, filmmaker, and media theorist, was born in Halberstadt, now part of East Germany. After studies in law, history, and religous music in Freiburg, Frankfurt, and Marburg, Kluge received a doctorate in jurisprudence in 1956. Although his creative activities have long since overshadowed his legal practice, Kluge's professional training has exerted a strong influence on the content and style of his work. His first collection of short stories, *Lebensläufe* (1962; Eng. tr., *Attendance List for a Funeral,* 1966), won the Berlin Young Artists Award and introduced the detached, ironic tone that has characterized his subsequent literary and cinematic productions.

Kluge's texts are sketchy blends of fact and fiction, often couched in the alienating jargons of the institutions his critical lance loves to score: the courts; the industrial, military, and political bureaucracies; National Socialism; the performance principle. His characters face a common dilemma in the struggle for order and security against the chaotic reality of nature and the bogus reality (*Scheinöffentlichkeit*) imposed by an economic structure beyond their control. In *Schlachtbeschreibung* (1964; Eng. tr., *The Battle,* 1967), a dark satire of the defeat of Hitler's 6th Army at Stalingrad, Kluge began to adapt Brechtian dramaturgy to literature (*see* Bertolt BRECHT). He creates a critical perspective (*Verfremdung*) through a laconic reportage laced with illustrations from field manuals, unacknowledged quotes, ironic footnotes, and news bulletins, all reflecting different—and contradictory—aspects of reality. In *Lernprozesse mit tödlichem Ausgang* (1973; Learning Processes with Fatal Results) and *Neue Geschichten. Hefte 1-18 "Unheimlichkeit der Zeit"* (1977; New Stories. Vol. 1-18 "Disquietude of Time"), Kluge continues to develop this radical technique into a "blizzard of narrative particles" that reflects the experience of random material nature.

Kluge has enjoyed a critical reception in Germany comparable to the international interest in his films, which are often based on his literary texts. In 1979 he won the prestigious Fontane Prize for *Neue Geschichten,* from which the author/director drew material for his award-winning film *Die Patriotin* (1979; The Patriot).

See: U. Gregor and W. Schütte, in *Herzog/Kluge/Straub,* Reihe Film 9 (1976): 17-25, 52-61, 131-78, 229-40. S.Ac.

Klyuyev, Nikolay Alekseyevich (1887-1937), Russian poet, was born to a peasant family in the Olonetsk region and was raised as a deeply religious Old Believer. After two years in a village school, he spent some time in the Solovetsk monastery and fell strongly under the influence of the "Khlysty" sect. Little is known of his early years except that he traveled extensively throughout Russia. His first poems were published in 1904 in the Petersburg almanac *Novye poety,* edited by Nikolay Ivanov. In 1907, Klyuyev began a long correspondance with Aleksandr BLOK, to whom he dedicated his first volume of poetry, *Sosen perezvon* (1912; Chimes of Pines). In 1911, Klyuyev lived in both Petersburg and Moscow, and his deliberate use of peasant speech, village clothing, and exaggeratedly religious mannerisms shocked many who met him. He became known as the leader of a group of so-called peasant poets, which included Sergey Klychkov and Pyotr Oreshin. Klyuyev's sentimentality, sensuality, and religious fervor, which was often viewed as hypocrisy, repelled many of his contemporaries. His relation with the peasant poet Sergey YESENIN were particularly stormy. He identified himself several times with Rasputin, as is evidenced by his 1918 poem "Menya Rasputinym nazvali" (They Called Me Rasputin). The poet Sergey Gorodetsky commented that all of Klyuyev's friends hated him at various times.

Klyuyev's poetry is filled with highly stylized folklore motifs, legends, and proper names. He makes heavy use of dialect, Slavonicisms, and words from the liturgy of the Russian Orthodox Church. His ornate language frequently describes peasant customs and religious rituals. Klyuyev's early poems were immensely popular, and he was viewed as a prophet incarnating the religious consciousness of the Russian peasantry. Yet he soon was disappointed in his own religious populism and in his belief that the 1917 Revolution would bring about an earthly paradise for the Russian peasantry. By the second half of the 1920s Klyuyev was under heavy attack as a mystical reactionary and as a kulak. He was arrested in 1933, probably in connection with his poem *Pogorel'shchina* (Scorched Earth), a lament for rural Russia that was published only in 1954. He was deported and died in unknown circumstances in 1937. He has not been republished in the USSR. A two-volume edition of his works, *Sochineniya*, edited by G. P. Struve and Boris Filipoff, was published in Munich in 1969.

See: R. Poggioli, *The Poets of Russia 1890-1930* (1960); N. Khomchuk, "Yesenin i Klyuyev," *BL*, 2 (1958): 154-168.　　　　　　　　　　　　　　　　　　　　L.V.

Knopfli, Rui (1932-), Portuguese poet from Inhambane in the former East African colony of Mozambique, lived in Lourenço Marques until the country won its independence. Knopfli's poem "Auto-retrato" (Self-Portrait) describes his Portuguese ancestry in romantic and sensual terms; his distant Swiss heritage, on the other hand, consists "of an ancient pocket watch and a strange, obscure name" left to him by a great-grandfather. Despite this acknowledgment of European origins, Knopfli, like other white poets born and raised in Portuguese Africa, occasionally reveals an ambivalence about his cultural identity in the tightly knit free verse of his collections: *O país dos outros* (1959; The Land of Others), *Reino submarino* (1962; Underwater Kingdom), *Máquina de aréia* (1964; Sand Machine), *Mangas verdes com sal* (1969; Green Mangoes with Salt), and *A Ilha de Próspero* (1972; Prospero's Island), the last being a descriptive poetic text with photographs by the author of the city of Ilha de Moçambique. Knopfli affirms his Africanness specifically in "Naturalidade" (Birthright), whereas his poems are generally indistinguishable in attitude and form from those of other European writers.

Knopfli has contended that poetry is an end in itself regardless of the regional and social context that it may reflect. This attitude conflicts with the ideology of those who insist on an African poetry's being valid only when it captures the ethos of black people. Knopfli and those who share his thinking do not deny the validity of such a poetry; they do, however, defend their place in the multifaceted panorama of Mozambican literature.

One critic has called Knopfli's poetry subjective and, as such, removed from social realities. Actually, his individualistic art presents an aesthetic tension between personal lyricism and social concern. In the midst of the polemic, he excels as a poet who cultivates the essence of the word, and his preoccupation with technique and individual style aids him in presenting Mozambique's variegated cultural situation artistically. The tension still pervades the poems of *O escriba acocorado* (1978; The Squatting Scribe), in which the "ex-African poet," deeply hurt, registers the loss of his homeland. He lives in London now.

See: E. Lisboa, "A voz ciciada (Ensaio de leitura da poesia de Rui Knopfli)" *Poesia de Moçambique: Craveirinha, Grabato Dias, Rui Knopfli* (1972), pp. 45-68.　　　　　　　　　　　　　　　　　　　　R.G.H.

Knudsen, Erik (1922-), Danish poet, was born in the Zealand town of Slagelse. Since 1944 he has been a teacher. In his first collections of poems, *Dobbelte Dage* (1945; Double Days) and *Til en ukendt Gud* (1947; To an Unknown God), Knudsen, as a typical representative of the World War II years, expressed his generation's feelings of duality, fear, and powerlessness in a "world full of sick Gods." The struggle between despair and hope, as well as the poet's belief in love as a world-altering

force, is given its fullest artistic expression in Blomsten og Sværdet (1949; The Flower and the Sword). However, Knudsen's naturalistic view of life, most convincingly manifested in the collection *Minotaurus* (1955; Minotaur), is too strong to allow mysticism or aestheticism. The crisis of modern man is regarded as created by society, and Knudsen proves to be an engaged socialistic critic of society and culture in the later collections *Sensation og stilhed* (1958; Sensation and Silence) and *Journal* (1963), as well as in his satirical musical *Frihed—det bedste guld* (1961; Freedom—The Best Gold). Knudsen uses language as a means of agitation, as in the "socialist debate book," *Babylon marcherer* (1970; Babylon on March), in *Vietnam. Artikler, taler og digte* (1973; Vietnam, a collection of articles, speeches, and poems), directed against both the American engagement in Vietnam and capitalism in general and in the poetry collection *Forsøg på ut gå* (1978; Attempts to Walk).　　　　　　　　　　　　　　　　S.H.R.

Knudsen, Jakob (1858-1917), Danish novelist, was born in the south Jutland village of Rødding. Through his father he received a spiritually free but physically authoritarian upbringing, which strongly influenced his view of life. He took a degree in theology in 1881, Later he was a folk high school teacher, minister, and lecturer. Through his realistic portraits of peasant life, Knudsen belongs to Danish regional literature, although his horizon is much wider, marked by an original, religious and ethical complex of problems. His first major work, the novella *Et Gjensyn* (1898; A Reunion), about a childhood and the meeting with that childhood many years later, contains one of the principal elements of Knudsen's philosophy: man's relations with God is as a relationship between father and son. The idea that man's religious outlook is determined without exterior dogmatic and legal rules is also prevalent in Knudsen's breakthrough novel, *Den gamle Præst* (1899; The Old Pastor). It depicts the dilemma of a murderer who is exhorted by a pastor not to surrender to the punishment of the law but instead to accept his responsibility before God through suicide. Knudsen's semiautobiographical double novel, *Gjæring-Afklaring* (1902; Fermentation-Clarification), satirizes his own generation and thus reflects his critical reaction against radical naturalism. This critical attitude is expressed in the plot, which illustrates how faith, inspired by romantic illusions, is destroyed through the confrontation with reality, only to be won back in a more intense manner. In *Sind* (1903; Temper), Knudsen's artistically most significant novel, nature and the peasant population are the focal point of attention. Here also does obedience to divine laws cause a break with society's modern and lenient legal view. The peasant culture is confronted with industrialization in *Fremskridt* (1907; Progress). According to Knudsen, the guilt of modern times lies in the destruction of the human spirit through leveling and mechanization. Whereas social and personal development must rely on firm outer rules to protect the positive, freedom should reign within the spiritual sphere.

Knudsen's novels thus discuss existential dilemmas within social and religious areas. His writing often seems repellent because of the ruthless, uncompromising attitude by which he destroys his opponents. On the other hand, it is captivating not only because of the poetry weaving through even the most dramatic scenes but also because of the intensity and subjectivity of the narration.

See: C. Roos, *Jakob Knudsen* (1954); R. Andersen, *Jakob Knudsen* (1958).　　　　　　　　　　　　　　S.H.R.

Kocbek, Edvard (1904-), Slovenian poet, short-story writer, and essayist, was born near Ščavnica. He studied

Romance languages and literature in Paris, where he was
strongly influenced by the personalist movement of Emmanuel MOUNIER. Between the two world wars, Kocbek
taught at Varaždin and Ljubljana, and during and immediately after World War II he held important political
positions.

With his first collection of poems, *Zemlja* (1934; The
Earth), Kocbek reconciled the opposition in Slovenian
literature between excessive spiritualism and descriptive
realism, producing a kind of metaphysical realism dealing
with the moral problems of contemporary life as well as
with questions about the ultimate nature of reality. During
the Spanish Civil War, Kocbek provoked a crisis in the
Slovenian Catholic intelligentsia with his article
"Premišlevanje o Španiji" (1937; Considerations about
Spain), in which he came out against the Spanish Fascists
and for the secularization of church property. Upon the
outbreak of World War II, Kocbek and his left-wing Catholic associates joined the Partisan movement. He described his wartime experiences in several revealing
works, including two books based on his diaries, *Tovarišija* (1949; Comradeship) and *Listina* (1967; A Document). His collection of short stories *Strah in pogum*
(1951; Fear and Courage) aroused the indignation of Communist Party critics, who called him a representative of
literary nihilism and an advocate of personalism and existentialism. Nevertheless, contemporary Slovenian prose
is rooted to a considerable extent in Kocbek's courageous
writings of the early 1950s. If Slovenian prose has subsequently dealt with the question of who man is, rather
than what man is, Edvard Kocbek is responsible for this
new orientation.

See: A. Kadić, "Some Specific Themes of Contemporary Slovenian Poetry," *JCS* 14–15 (1973–74): 151–54; B.
Pahor and A. Rebula, *Edvard Kocbek: pričevalec našega
časa* (1975).   J.P. with W.B.E.

Koeppen, Wolfgang (1906–), German novelist, was born
in Greifswald, Pomerania, and was raised by a bachelor
uncle in Ortelsburg, Masuria, in a lonely atmosphere that
set the pattern for Koeppen's lifelong penchant for seclusion. His early education was irregular and aimless, as
were his later university studies in Greifswald, Hamburg,
Berlin, and Würzburg. Eager for knowledge and stimulated by his uncle's extensive library, Koeppen devoted
his hated school years to the world of books. His first
publication, an essay on expressionism, appeared while
he was still in school. During a longer voluntary stay
away from school, in Hamburg, Koeppen discovered Caspar David Friedrich, whose paintings of loneliness, melancholy—even nearness of death—left an indelible
impression that seems to have influenced Koeppen's novella *Jugend* (1976; Youth). As a young man, Koeppen
held various jobs as journalist, dramaturgist, assistant
producer, actor, and, from 1931 to 1934, editor on the
Berliner Börsen-Courier, which was banned in 1934.

When his journalistic career ended, Koeppen went to
Italy, wrote his first novel, *Eine unglückliche Liebe* (1934;
An Unhappy Love); and—after his publisher Bruno Cassirer, one of the most respected German publishing
houses, was ostracized—received the first Nazi press defamation for daring to continue the "un-German tradition"
of Thomas MANN and Heinrich MANN, of Alfred DÖBLIN,
and of Lion FEUCHTWANGER. In 1935 Cassirer published
Koeppen's second novel, *Die Mauer schwankt* (The Wall
Is Swaying), a disguised political novel. After Cassirer's
liquidation in 1938 the novel reappeared under the title
Die Pflicht (Duty).

Koeppen withdrew completely from the literary scene
and, except for a short stay in Holland, survived the

Hitler nightmare in Berlin, where his third novel manuscript, entitled *Die Jawanengesellschaft,* burned. When
the World War II ended, Koeppen settled permanently in
Munich. After 15 years of silence he published the first
volume of a postwar trilogy, *Tauben im Gras* (1951; Pigeons in the Grass), in which—for the first time in German
literature—the flaws of the West German postwar economic miracle were mercilessly exposed. *Das Treibhaus*
(The Greenhouse) was published in 1952 and *Der Tod in
Rom* in 1954 (Eng. tr., *Death in Rome,* 1956).

Criticism of *Tauben* was divided. Koeppen's condemnation of postwar Germany was rejected as too negative;
his style was applauded. At a time when most German
writers were following Ernest Hemingway or Franz
KAFKA, Koeppen continued in the tradition of William
Faulkner, John Dos Passos, and James Joyce. *Treibhaus*
and *Tod in Rom,* about rearmament and neofascism, were
either underestimated or completely misjudged. Koeppen's antiheroes all suffer from an existential disease:
anxiety. The themes of loneliness and thwarted attempts
at interpersonal relationships are reflected in the radicalism of Koeppen's narrative art, in his use of collage, in
the Joycean inner monologues, and in the montage of
factual newspaper material, as in the work of Dos Passos.

After four years of renewed silence—"I am a spectator,
a quiet watcher, a silent man, an observer" (from "Not
a Memo," 1971)—Koeppen published *Nach Rußland und
anderswohin* (1958; To Russia and Elsewhere), *Amerikafahrt* (1959; American Journey), and *Reisen nach
Frankreich* (1961; Travels to France). About these impressionistic travel books, Walter Jens wrote, "Next to
Max Frisch, Koeppen is presently the most brilliant stylist
of the German language." Koeppen's reason for writing
such books was "a fondness for traveling and the pleasure
of feeling nowhere at home." After still another silence,
Koeppen published a collection of short prose texts, *Romanisches Café* (1971; Romanesque Café), and *Jugend*
(1976), a fictional autobiographical novel in which the
transformation of reality into the fictional realm of memory constitutes the structural principle.

See: H. L. Arnold, *Gespräche mit Schriftstellern*
(1975); U. Greiner, ed., *Über Wolfgang Koeppen* (1976).
                                                      C.S.

Kokoschka, Oskar (1886–1980), Austrian dramatist,
novelist, essayist, painter, and illustrator, was born in
Pöchlarn on the Danube. He enrolled in 1904 in the Vienna Arts and Crafts School, then still a bastion of academicism and historicism. Kokoschka also worked at the
Wiener Werkstätte (Vienna Workshops), painting postcards, fans, and the like. From 1906 on he also painted
in oils. An admirer of William Morris, Kokoschka wrote,
illustrated, printed, and bound the poem "Die träumenden
Knaben" (1907; Dreaming Youths) and also designed the
typeface. The lithographs are of the *Jugendstil* period,
but the language is expressionistic: a series of disjointed,
emotional pictures. The critics conceded that this "fairytale book" was not for philistine children, but they refused to accept it as literature. The work is an analysis of
youth's breaking out of a protective covering into sexual
maturity, seen both idealistically and as a banality. In
1908 Kokoschka was forced to leave the Arts and Crafts
School because of a poster he drew, a grotesque pietà
with a bloody man in her lap.

Many critics viewed Kokoschka as degenerate, a description he in turn applied to Rainer Maria RILKE, Franz
WERFEL, and Hugo von HOFMANNSTHAL. At the 1909
art show, Kokoschka performed his *Mörder, Hoffnung
der Frauen* (1907; Murderers, The Hope of Women), one
of the earliest expressionistic plays. The short play has

no real plot, only dream associations in elliptical and ecstatic language suggesting drives, feelings, and irrational concepts. The main characters are the "new" man, in conflict with his basic animalistic drives, and the "new" woman, who asserts herself.

From 1907 to 1918, Kokoschka wrote several plays with the theme of the battle of the sexes and sexual isolation. *Sphinx und Strohmann* (1907; Sphinx and Straw Man), a study in ecstatic theater, had a great influence on expressionism and Dada. *Hiob* (1917; Job) and *Der brennende Dornbusch* (1911; The Burning Thorn) are Kokoschka's major plays of the period. Between 1917 and 1973, Kokoschka wrote several short stories, none of which has attained the stature of his early plays.

See: E. Hoffmann, *Kokoschka: Life and Work* (1947); J. P. Hodin, *Oskar Kokoschka, The Artist and His Time: A Biographical Study* (1966).   W.T.

Kolbenheyer, Edwin Guido (1878–1962), German novelist and dramatist, was born in Budapest. His father was for a time employed by the Hungarian government as an architect. After his father's early death, his mother went with the two-year-old boy back to her hometown, Karlsbad. Here Kolbenheyer spent the most impressionable years of his life. Later he moved to Vienna to study philosophy and natural sciences at the university.

Kolbenheyer's one-sided overemphasis on Teutonism, which was in tune with the trend of Hitlerism in Germany, was largely the result of his early years in the atmosphere of a German minority group. Not only in his historical novels but also in his theoretical studies, above all *Die Bauhütte* (1925; The Construction Cottage), he anticipated many ideas of national socialism.

His work is mainly historical. The heroes of his novels and dramas are what he considers "typical Germans," maintaining themselves against a hostile world. This "typical German" is always a mystic revolting against some form of scholasticism, an exponent of the Reformation rebelling against the fetters of an international church. All of Kolbenheyer's historical heroes are in some way or other proclaimers of the spirit of the Reformation, as in his two most important historical dramas, *Giordano Bruno* (1893; later reissued as *Heroische Leidenschaften*, 1921; Heroic Passions) and *Gregor und Heinrich* (1934); the Spinoza novel, *Amor Dei* (1902; Eng. tr., *God-intoxicated Man*, 1933); the novel *Meister Joachim Pausewang* (1910; Eng. tr., *A Winter Chronicle*, 1938), evoking the time of Jakob Böhme; and the three-volume *Paracelsus* (1917–23).

His novels are historical and philosophical works, permeated with a Germanomania. In *Pausewang* and *Paracelsus*, Kolbenheyer tried to reproduce the spirit of the times by creating a semiarchaic language. He also experimented in his dreams and evolved the theory of a "third stage," a dramatic conception of the stage that would extend over the entire theater and make the spectator in the audience an integral part of the play.

See: C. Wandrey, *Kolbenheyer, der Dichter und der Philosph* (1933); E. Frank, *Jahre des Glücks, Jahre des Leids: eine Kolbenheyer Biographie* (1969).
W.P. rev. A.L.W.

Kolmar, Gertrud, pseud. of Gertrud Chodziesner (1894–1943?), German lyric poet and author of plays and prose, was born in Berlin of a middle-class Jewish family. She became a teacher of Spanish and Russian, with positions in Dijon and Berlin, where she worked occasionally with deaf and dumb children. In March 1943 she was arrested and shipped to a concentration camp. No one ever heard of her again.

The small production of Kolmar is marked by strong spiritual feelings and a large, almost cosmological, feeling for nature. Her lyrics were traditional in form, leaning toward rhyme and cycle sequence, often approaching folk song and ballad. Among her main themes were the unborn child and animals, creatures innocent of guile. Her first poems were published in 1917, *Gedichte* (Poems). Further works followed, as in *Preußische Wappen* (1935; The Prussian Coat-of-Arms), *Die Frau und die Tiere* (1938; Women and Animals), and *Welten* (1947; Worlds). Her collected works appeared in one volume in 1955. *Dark Soliloquy* (1975) is a selection of her work in English translation. Her posthumous work was edited by Hermann KASACK. Her mythical, balladlike poems present panoramic visions of human beings and animals. A favorite symbol and bearer of metaphor for her was the rose, an organic center for pure nature.   A.L.W.

Kommerell, Max (1902–44), German poet, essayist, and critic, was an intimate member of the circle of disciples surrounding Stefan GEORGE in the 1920s. His *Der Dichter als Führer in der deutschen Klassik* (1928; The Poet as a Leader in German Classicism) is a monument to the ethics and aesthetics of George, but its penetrating analyses of Goethe, Friedrich Schiller, Friedrich Hölderlin, F. G. Klopstock, and Jean-Paul F. Richter are still forceful today. Even after breaking with George in 1930, his work showed a fascination with literature as the quintessentially moral, norm-founding human activity. His broad erudition produced unorthodox but convincing characterizations of major figures in German literature, as well as seminal essays on Aristotle and on Spanish and French theater. He published several volumes of poetry, of which *Leichte Lieder* (1930; Easy Songs) and *Mein Anteil* (1938; My Share) stand out. The novel *Der Lampenschirm aus den drei Taschentüchern* (The Lampshade Made of Three Handkerchiefs) appeared in 1940, and the play *Die Gefangenen* (The Prisoners), written in 1941–42, appeared posthumously in 1948. The collection of lyrics *Kasperle* (1939; Puppets) and the novel *Kasperlespiele für grosse Leute* (1949; Puppet Plays for Grown-ups) express his interest in commedia dell'arte and folk literature. He was appointed professor at Marburg in 1941, where he worked until his untimely death.

See: I. Jens, ed., *Max Kommerell: Briefe und Aufzeichnungen, 1919–1944* (1967).   L.G.S.

Koneski, Blaže (1921–), Macedonian poet and scholar, was born in Nebregovo, near Prilep. He studied literature in Belgrade and Sofia. Since 1950 he has been editor-in-chief of the scholarly journal *Makedonski jazik*. A major figure in Macedonian cultural life, he is a professor at Skopje University and a past president of the Macedonian Academy of Arts and Sciences. In his first two volumes of verse, *Mostot* (1945; The Bridge) and *Zemjata i ljubovta* (1948; Land and Love), Koneski produced patriotic poetry of high quality. The more recent volumes *Pesni* (1953; Poems), *Vezilka* (1955, 1961; The Embroiderer), and the poetry collection *Zapisi* (1974; Marginalia) reveal the intimate side of the poet. The nature lyric is one of the forms that Koneski commonly uses to express his emotional and intellectual experiences and to reveal his attitudes toward the basic questions of mankind: the meaning of life, happiness, love, triumph and defeat, and the transience of human existence. His inclination toward meditative lyricism has also found expression in a series of short poems or poetic sketches, in which he uses characters from legends and folk tales. These short works are characterized by depth of thought, precision of ideas, and conciseness of expression. Koneski's poetry attempts to develop an increasingly harmonious relationship between emotional and intellectual inspiration so that the two may enrich one another. Although his poetry excels by virtue of its simple form, it is exceptionally cultivated.

Koneski's only book of narrative prose is *Lozje* (1955; The Vineyard), a collection of realistic short stories that depict everyday life and a variety of ordinary individuals and their fates. The author's tone is often humorous, even ironic, but it is never without feeling. In addition to his creative writing, Koneski is the author of a grammar and a history of the Macedonian language, as well as several other works of linguistics and literary history. He is also a translator.

See: H. G. Lunt, "A Survey of Macedonian Literature," *HSS* 1 (1953): 363–96; V. Ognev, ed., *Iz sovremennoj poezii narodov Jugoslavii* (Moscow, 1972).

A.Sp.

Konetsky, Viktor Viktorovich (1929–), Russian fiction writer, was born in Leningrad. A lieutenant in the merchant marine, he began publishing in 1956 while continuing his work as a seaman. Among his work are: the collections of stories *Kamni pod vodoy* (1959; Stones below Water Level), *Nad belym perekryostkom* (1962; Above a White Crossroads), *Luna dnyom* (1963; The Moon in Broad Daylight), and *Ogni na myorzlykh skalakh* (1964; Fires on Frozen Cliffs); the novels *Zavtrashniye zaboty* (1961; Tomorrow's Cares) and *Kto smotrit na oblaka* (1967; He Who Looks at the Clouds); and the travel accounts *Solyony lyod* (1969; Salty Ice) and *210 sutok na okeanskom orbite* (1972; 210 Days on the Ocean).

Although the sea is the setting for most of his stories and travel accounts, Konetsky is much more than a mere writer of sea stories. Through his perpetual inquiry into the incommunicability of human beings, their wasted lives, useless sacrifices, and—above all—their absurd deaths, he has succeeded in rising above the problems of a frustrated generation to become a writer about the human condition.   J.Ca.

König, Barbara (1925–), German novelist and short-story writer and author of radio and television plays, was born in Reichenberg and interned by the Gestapo during her last year in the gymnasium. From 1947 to 1953 she was a journalist and interpreter. König visited the United States in 1950, in 1973, and in 1975 as writer-in-residence at the University of Texas at Austin. She lives as a freelance writer in Diessen am Ammersnee.

In 1958, König published her first short story, "Das Kind und sein Schatten" (The Child and His Shadow), and in 1961 her first novel, *Kies* (Gravel), a haunting tale about woman's fate. König has written several other novels about women: *Die Personenperson* (1965), in which the main character, Nadine, is seen as a group of different persons who interact with her, question her, try out different situations, and argue with each other; and *Schöner Tag, dieser 13.* (1974; Beautiful Day, This 13th), an autobiographical love story in diary form about an upper-middle-class woman and her relationship to her husband, her ex-husband, and a male friend. König combines a realistic and at times cheerful style with a witty-absurd rendition of a many-layered nature. Her dominant themes are the emancipation and the self-realization of woman. König has also written short stories, such as those in the collection *Spielerei bei Tage* (1969; Play in the Daytime), and various radio plays.

See: E. R. Herrmann and E. H. Spitz, eds., *German Women Writers of the Twentieth Century* (1978), pp. 72–76.   E.H.S.

Konopnicka, Maria (1842–1910), Polish poet, short-story writer, critic, and translator was born in Wasiłowska in Suwałki and died in Lvov. After Adam ASNYK, Konopnicka is the most outstanding poet of the period of positivism. While at boarding school in Warsaw, she met Eliza Pawłowska (later the well-known writer Eliza Orzeszkowa); that friendship was to be long-lasting and important for Konopnicka. After separating from her husband, she settled in Warsaw, where she worked for a while as editor of *Świt,* a journal for women. She was one of the first advocates of women's emancipation and sensitive to the suffering of the poor. Some 20 years of her life were spent abroad (in Germany, Switzerland, Italy, and France), and observations from these trips are reflected in her writing. In 1902 she received a small manor in Żarnowiec as a gift from the nation on the 25th anniversary of her literary debut, and there she spent the last years of her life.

Konopnicka began publishing poetry in periodicals in 1875. Her first volume, *Poezje* (Poetry), appeared in 1881, followed by two more volumes with the same title in 1883 and 1886. She then published *Linie i dźwięki* (1897; Lines and Sounds), *Italia* (1901), *Śpiewnik historyczny 1767–1883* (1904; Historical Songbook 1767–1883), *Ludziom i chwiłom* (1905; To People and Moments), and *Głosy ciszy* (1906; The Voices of Silence). In 1908 Konopnicka wrote the patriotic poem "Rota" (The Oath), a work that won great popularity throughout Poland; "Rota" was also set to music. Konopnicka's ardent patriotism was expressed not only in many poems but also in the active role she played in defense of Polish national interests.

Konopnicka was influenced by the great romantic poets Adam Mickiewicz, Juliusz Słowacki, and Victor Hugo. Yet her writing represents new, positivistic ideas: humanism and a democratic, even radical attitude toward social injustice. She became a true bard of the Polish peasants, expressing the sufferings and injustices of their hard life. Indeed, her poetry, which was very popular during her lifetime, is at its best in those lyrics inspired by folk songs. (These poems are especially evident in her first three volumes of poetry.) In some of her poems, Konopnicka introduced a folk-narrator, allowing him to present the story through his own eyes. In 1910 appeared her large poem *Pan Balcer w Brazylii* (Mr. Balcer in Brazil), written in octave rhyme and planned as a folk epic, depicting the Polish emigrants' dramatic struggle for survival in Brazil.

In addition to her poetry, Konopnicka wrote short stories and novellas describing the lives of peasants and workers. Raised in the realistic prose tradition of Henryk Sienkiewicz, Bolesław PRUS, Eliza Orzeszkowa, and Guy de Maupassant, Konopnicka wrote short stories of a high artistic level containing keen, convincing psychological analyses of its protagonists. Her volumes of fiction include *Cztery nowele* (1888; Four Short Stories), *Moi znajomi* (1890; My Friends), *Na drodze* (1893; On the Road), *Ludzie i rzeczy* (1898; People and Objects), and *Na normandzkim brzegu* (1904; On the Norman Seashore); Konopnicka also published books for children, the best known being the novel *O krasnoludkach i sierotce Marysi* (1896; About the Little People and the Orphan Mary), which combines folk and fairy-tale motives with vivid descriptions of the Polish village and nature. Her essays of literary criticism include *Mickiewicz, jego życie i duch* (1899; Mickiewicz, His Life and Spirit) and *O Beniowskim* (1911; About Beniowski). She also translated works by Heinrich Heine, Gerhart HAUPTMANN, Edmond de Amicis, Gabriele d'ANNUNZIO, and Edmond ROSTAND.

See: W. Leopold, *Maria Konopnicka* (1954); A. Brodzka, *Maria Konopnicka* (1961); M. Szypowska, *Kon-*

opnicka jakiej nie znamy (1963); *Konopnicka wśród jej współczesnych* (1976). A.Z. and S.F.

Konwicki, Tadeusz (1926–), Polish novelist, was born in Nowa Wilejka, near Vilnius. During World War II he fought in eastern Poland in the Resistance movement of the home army. Although his first published novel, *Władza* (1954; Power), was written in the clichés of socialist realism, his autobiographical novel *Rojsty* (written 1948; publ. 1956; The Marshes) initiated a series of novels in which his reflections on war experiences are related to no less dramatic contemporary ethical and moral problems. He pursued that motif in *Sennik współczesny* (1963; Eng. tr., *A Dreambook for Our Time*, 1969), *Wniebowstąpienie* (1967; Ascension), and *Nic albo nic* (1971; Nothing or Nothing). In some of his other novels, notably *Dziura w niebie* (1959; A Hole in the Sky), *Zwierzoczłekoupiór* (1969; Eng. tr., *The Anthropos-Specter-Beast*, 1977), and *Kronika wypadków miłosnych* (1974; The Chronicle of Love Events), Konwicki turned to psychological and philosophical problems connected with growing up and the dreams of youth, returning to the land of his childhood in Lithuania in a lyrical manner, expressing his sadness for the loss of this unique world destroyed in the catastrophe of World War II. A semiautobiographical novel, *Kalendarz i klepsydra* (1976; A Calendar and a Water Clock), was followed by the highly anti-Communist *Kompleks polski* (1977; A Polish Complex), a novel published in an uncensored Polish journal, *Zapis*, and reprinted in London in the series Index on Censorship.

See: J. R. Krzyżanowski, "The Haunted World of Tadeusz Konwicki," *BA* 48 (1974: 3. J.R.K.

Korniychuk, Oleksandr (1905–72), Soviet Ukrainian playwright, was born in the village of Khrystynioka, Cherkassy province. He was an exponent of socialist realism (see UKRAINIAN LITERATURE). Some of his plays, such as *Zahybel eskadry* (1934; Death of a Squadron), depict the heroism of the revolutionaries. Others, such as *V stepakh Ukrayiny* (1941: In the Steppes of the Ukraine) and *Front* (1942), deal with Soviet patriotism. After Iosif Stalin's death, Korniychuk wrote a mildly controversial play, *Kryla* (1954; Eng. tr., *The Wings*, n.d.). A very prolific writer, Korniychuk was a representative of the literary officialdom of the Stalin era. He was a member of the Central Committee of the Communist Party.
G.S.N.L.

Korolenko, Vladimir Galaktionovich (1853–1921), Russian fiction writer, was born in Zhitomir of a Polish mother and Russian father. While studying in Petersburg and Moscow he came under suspicion for his association with the Populists and in 1879 was condemned on false charges to several years' exile. Part of his exile was spent in Siberia among the Yakuts, a primitive people who inspired several of his stories, including his most famous, "Son Makara" (1885; Eng. tr., "Makar's Dream," 1892), published shortly after his return from exile. Although Korolenko had been writing stories since 1879, among them "Yashka" (1880; Eng. tr., "Yashka," 1954) and "Ubivets" (1882; Eng. tr., "Killer," 1954), none was so well done as the story of the poor Russian Makar who manages to persuade Toyon, or God, that his hard life should make up for his sins. As the dead Makar eloquently recounts his life, the scales of justice, so heavily weighted with his sins, finally tilt in his favor.

Korolenko's fiction is often too sentimental for modern tastes, but it is usually redeemed by its warm and obviously sincere humanitarianism. A novella with just these qualities is *Slepoy muzikant* (1886; Eng. tr., *The Blind Musician*, 1890). The blind young hero is coddled by his mother and encouraged to develop his faculties by his uncle. He craves light, yet is sensitive to sound and manages to find happiness as a pianist.

Korolenko often based his fiction on a single character, usually suffering from some misfortune. In "Bez yazyka" (1895; Eng. tr., *In a Strange Land*, 1925), for example, Matvey, a Russian immigrant to the United States, cannot fathom the customs or the language of his new country, and for a time is mistakenly considered a wild man who bites people. Matvey finally comes to terms with his new land, but like Korolenko, whose visit to the Chicago Exposition in 1893 prompted this story, he comes to appreciate the fine qualities of his own Russian people more deeply than before.

Korolenko was loved and respected not only as a fiction writer but also as a commentator on issues of the day. He began working on the Populist journal *Russkoye bogatstvo* in 1896 and took over as editor in 1904. He became known for his liberal views, in particular his attack on the death penalty and his defense of persecuted Jews and peasants. He opposed violence, and during the bitter revolutionary period he courageously tried to help victims on both sides (*see* RUSSIAN LITERATURE).

During his late period (1905–21), Korolenko wrote the four-volume autobiographical *Istoriya moyego sovremennika* (1922; abridged Eng. tr., *The History of My Contemporary*, 1972), which renders invaluable glimpses of early influences on Korolenko's career and of life in Russia during the second half of the 19th century.

Aside from the excellent "Makar's Dream," Korolenko's work is less esteemed now than in his own day, perhaps because, like Maksim GORKY, he owed his early fame more to an appreciation of himself as a person than to his writing. Today he has a firm place among the second rank of Russian writers.

See: L. Leighton, "Korolenko's Stories of Siberia," *SEEJ* 49 (1971): 200–13; G. A. Byaly, *V. G. Korolenko* (Moscow-Leningrad, 1949). S.Sc.

Korzhavin, Naum Moiseyevich, pseud. of Naum M. Mandel (1925–), Russian poet, dramatist, essayist, and critic, was born in Kiev. In 1945 he entered the Gorky Literary Institute in Moscow but was arrested two years later, imprisoned for eight months, and banished to forced residence in Siberia as a result of openly writing poems critical of Iosif Stalin. Amnestied after Stalin's death, he returned to Moscow in 1954 and was officially "rehabilitated" in 1956. He was graduated from the Gorky Literary Institute in 1959. His first major publication was 16 poems in the much discussed miscellany *Tarusskiye stranitsy* (1961; partial Eng. tr., including seven of Korzhavin's poems, *Pages from Tarusa*, n.d.). His only book of poems published in the Soviet Union was *Gody* (1963; Years), a selection of 54 poems written from 1941 to 1961 and edited by the poet Yevgeny VINOKUROV, which was praised by the critics and sold out at once. His play *Odnazhdy v dvadtsatom* (Once in 1920), was performed with great success in 1967 at the Stanislavsky Dramatic Theater in Moscow, but was never published in the Soviet Union. At the end of 1973, Korzhavin emigrated and has lived since 1974 in the United States. His second collection of poems, *Vremena* (1976; The Times), was published in Frankfurt am Main in West Germany. Underlying Korzhavin's poetry is an unmistakable religious-philosophical world view; it is a poetry of passionate convictions.

See: N. Korzhavin, "Opyt poeticheskoy biografii," *Kontinent* 2 (1975): 199–279; W. Kasack, "Naum Korzhavin," *Lexikon der russischen Literatur ab 1917* (1976), pp. 187-89; D. Brown, *Soviet Russian Literature since Stalin* (1978), pp. 93-96. V.L.

Kosovel, Srečko (1904-26), Slovenian poet, was born in the barren region of the Karst plateau. He was the outstanding Slovenian lyric poet of the 1920s. After receiving his early education in Ljubljana, he enrolled at Ljubljana University in 1922, but he died of meningitis before completing his university work. He contributed to all the leading Slovenian literary journals of his day and was himself the founder of *Lepa Vida*, a magazine for youth. From the fall of 1925 until his death, Kosovel edited the journal *Mladina*. He also wrote for newspapers and made public appearances, giving lectures and recitations of his poetry in Ljubljana and elsewhere in Slovenia. He prepared a collection of his poetry entitled *Zlati čoln* (1949; The Golden Boat) but did not live to see it in print. A year after his death, a selection of his best poems was published by his friend Alfonz Gspan. In 1931, Anton Ocvirk, in the introduction to a volume of Kosovel's selected poems, wrote the first mature criticism about him and placed him within the framework of Slovenian literature. The same editor brought out three collections of Kosovel's poetry after World War II.

Kosovel's poetry is based on a tragic perception of cosmic alienation and grew out of a feeling of spiritual loneliness. For Kosovel, life was not a condition but a struggle, and in his poetry he tried, through words and images, to influence human beings and to bring about changes in society. The primary thematic concerns of his lyrics are love, loneliness, eternity, dreams and apparitions, revolution, motherhood, and—most important of all—nature and death. For Kosovel contact with nature was the source of spiritual awakening, and through his nature poetry he achieved the fullest expression of his poetic vision. In his poetry, death does not appear as a sudden termination of physical existence but rather as an existential phenomenon in which everything living is reduced to equality and peace.

See: J. A. Vidmar, "Srecko Kosovel Pjesme," *Zapisi i kritike* (1954), pp. 154-63; M. Alyn, "Srecko Kosovel," in *Kosovel* (1965), pp. 8-96. J.P. with W.B.E.

Kossak-Szczucka-Szatkowska, Zofia (1890-1968), Polish novelist, was born in Kośmin and died in Cieszyn. During World War II, she participated in the Resistance. In 1943 and 1944 she was imprisoned in the concentration camp at Auschwitz, and in 1944 she was active in the Warsaw uprising. Between 1945 and 1956 she lived in England. She made her literary debut with an autobiographical account of World War I, *Pożoga* (1922; Eng. tr., *The Blaze*, 1923). A major representative of Polish Catholic literature, she wrote a cycle of historical novels about the Crusades, *Krzyżowcy* (1935; Eng. tr., *Angels in the Dust*, 1947), *Król Trędowaty* (1937; Eng. tr., *The Leper King*, 1945), and *Bez oręża* (1937; Eng. tr., *Blessed Are the Meek*, 1944). Another cycle of novels on Polish history includes *Beatum scelus* (1924; Blessed Sin), *Złota wolność* (1928; The Golden Freedom), *Legnickie pole* (1930; Legnica Field), and *Suknia Dejaniry* (1948; Eng. tr., *The Meek Shall Inherit*, 1948). Among her numerous writings are novels on biblical themes, for example, *Przymierze* (1952; Eng. tr., *The Convenant*, 1951); a collection of lives of saints, *Szaleńcy Boży* (1929; The Holy Fools); and reminiscences of the concentration camp, *Z otchłani* (1946; From the Abyss), as well as short stories for children and memoirs. Her vivid imaginative novels, written with an epic sweep in which she managed to present historical changes in various epochs and their

influence on human psychology, received worldwide recognition and have been translated into many languages.

See: *Słownik współczesnych pisarzy polskich*, vol. 2 (1964), pp. 184-95. J.R.K. and S.F.

Kosztolányi, Dezső (1885-1936), Hungarian poet, novelist, translator, and essayist, was born and educated in Szabadka (now Subotica, Yugoslavia), where his father was head of the local secondary school. Kosztolányi was an outstanding representative of the first *Nyugat* generation (*see* HUNGARIAN LITERATURE). In 1903 he enrolled at the University of Budapest, where he studied philology. It was there that he befriended Mihály BABITS and Gyula JUHÁSZ and began contributing to *Nyugat*. Kosztolányi opposed World War I and hailed the democratic revolution in Hungary in 1918, but he came to disagree with Béla Kun's regime. After the collapse of the Hungarian Soviet Republic in 1919, he wrote articles for a right-wing journal, an act that antagonized many of his former friends and colleagues. Later on he was ashamed of this episode and in his contribution to the debate on Endre ADY's poetry in 1929 he labeled himself *homo aestheticus*, as opposed to the politically committed *homo moralis*. From 1921 to 1936, Kosztolányi worked on the staff of the newspaper *Pesti Hirlap*. In 1931 he was elected president of the Hungarian PEN Club. His foreign connections and travels not withstanding, he was a passionate linguistic purist who wrote numerous articles against the contamination of the Hungarian tongue by unnecessary foreign phrases.

Kosztolányi created works of importance in several genres. As a poet, his first period was characterized by a somewhat theatrical display of changing moods and emotions. The best single volume of this volatile, "decadent" period is *A szegény kisgyermek panaszai* (1910; Laments of a Poor Child), a cycle of poems that probe with an almost neurotic sensitivity, the dreams, anxieties, and delusions of childhood. These poems, which show the influence of Rainier Maria RILKE, blend impressionism and a gloomy symbolism. Kosztolányi's first postwar volumes, *Kenyér és bor* (1920; Bread and Wine) and *A bús férfi panaszai* (1924; Laments of a Sad Grown-up), indicate a new maturity in his richly textured, basically sensual poetry. Now, he says wistfully, he is "at home in this world/ and no longer at home in the sky." The poetry collection *Meztelenül* (1928; Nakedly) is Kosztolányi's answer to expressionism: for the first time he abandons rhyme and adapts free verse to his modern, often ironic themes. The prevalent mood is one of "brotherhood," full of compassion for the poor, the helpless, and the weak, but at the same time contemptuous toward the masses of the modern metropolis. Kosztolányi's last book of poetry, *Számadás* (1935; Account), is a grand summation of his attitudes and delights, stating once again his "aestheticism" and rejection of the new epoch of machines and dictatorships. This volume contains some of his greatest poems, such as "Hajnali részegség" (Drunkenness at Dawn), his confession of awe before the miracle of existence. When Kosztolányi's virtuosity serves his message, as in this poem, instead of outshining it, he is capable of extraordinary poetic effects. He was also a gifted translator of English, French, and German poetry, although with a tendency to paraphrase the original texts.

Kosztolányi's achievement in prose is equally remarkable. His fiction is never verbose; its clarity, conciseness, and psychological insights rivet the reader's attention. His first important novel, *Néró, a véres költő* (1922; Eng. tr., *The Bloody Poet*, 1927, 1947) examines the psychological make-up of the Roman emperor and would-be artist, and his exercise of power. In this novel,

Kosztolányi condemns irrationalism as the nursemaid of all dictatorships. *Édes Anna* (1926; Eng. tr., *Wonder Maid*, 1947), can be read as a powerful protest against social injustice. Society heaps humiliations upon Anna, the patient and attractive serving maid who finally commits a seemingly incomprehensible murder. The construction of the plot simulates a folk ballad: tension grows imperceptibly and Anna's determination ripens under the heavy cloak of her silence. Kosztolányi's superb craftmanship can also be admired in the novel *Pacsirta* (1924; Skylark), the grim naturalism of which is only partly alleviated by a kind of muted lyricism. The setting of *Pacsirta*, a sleepy provincial town in Hungary is also that of *Aranysárkány* (1925; The Golden Kite). A more substantial novel than *Pacsirta*, *Aranyádrkány* depicts the adult's nostalgia for the savage, merrily tragic world of youth. Using the school as a microcosm of human passion, *Aranysárkány* reaches a deeply pessimistic conclusion about the meaning of life. Kosztolányi was also a prolific writer of short stories, among which the collection *Esti Kornél* (1933; Cornelius Nightly), concerning Kosztolanyi's bohemian alter ego, occupies a special place. Kosztolányi's stories are not exempt from Freudian simplifications and from an overapplication of the "surprise" element (somewhat in the manner of André GIDE), yet they amply illustrate his cardinal virtues—wit, clarity, and compassion. His numerous sketches and newspaper articles stamp him as a rare master of the shorter literary forms. Kosztolányi's collected works were published in 11 volumes between 1940 and 1948.

See: F. Karinthy, "Az ötvenéves Kosztolányi," *Nyugat* 28 (1935): 265–72; J. Reményi, *Hungarian Writers and Literature* (1964), pp. 252–65; I. Sőtér, "Kosztolányi Deszo," *Kritika* 3 (1965): 26–34; A. Karátson, *Le Symbolisme en Hongrie* (1969), pp. 144–224. G.G.

Kotsyubynsky, Mykhaylo (1864–1913), Ukrainian short-story writer and novelist, was born in Vinnytsya (Vinnitsa) and educated in a seminary. In his youth he was dedicated to populist causes and dissident activities, but he later devoted himself to literature. His early short stories, such as "Andriy Soloveyko" (1884) and "Dlya zahalnoho dobra" (1895; For the Common Good), reflect a preoccupation with themes of social injustice and the intelligentsia's duty to enlighten the peasants. In his later, mature works these themes remain in the background. A somewhat neurotic man of delicate health, Kotsyubynsky found his work as a government official very depressing. His travels took him to the Crimea, Greece, Italy, and other countries and gave stimulus to some of his stories, such as "Na kameni" (1902; Eng. tr., "On the Rock," 1973). His best short story, "Intermezzo" (1909), has been hailed for its effective juxtaposition of psychological meditation and brute reality and for its fine impressionistic technique. Other stories include "Tsvit yabluni" (1904; Apple Blossom), "Son" (1911; The Dream), and "Persona grata" (1908). Influenced by the events of the Russian Revolution of 1905, Kotsyubynsky wrote the novel *Fata Morgana* (1910). His masterpiece is the novel *Tini zabutykh predkiv* (1911; Eng. tr., *Shadows of Forgotten Ancestors, 1979*), based on the legends of the Hutsul region. Kotsyubnsky acknowledged the strong influence of August STRINDBERG, Knut HAMSUN, and Maurice MAETERLINCK. He is the best representative of Ukrainian modernism, although his earlier work was in the realist tradition (*see* UKRAINIAN LITERATURE). A collection of Kotsyubynsky's short stories has appeared in English translation as *Chrysalis and Other Stories* (1958).

See: E. Wiśniewska, *O sztuce pisarskiej M. Kociubynskiego* (1973); B. Rubchak, "The Music of Satan and the Bedeviled World," in M. Kotsiubynsky, *Shadows of Forgotten Ancestors* (1979). G.S.N.L.

Koziol, Urszula (1931–), Polish poet and novelist, was born in Rakówka, a village in central Poland. She studied Polish literature at the University of Wrocław and worked as a teacher. She gained recognition for her second volume of poems, *W rytmie korzeni* (1963; In the Rhythm of the Roots), and has since published two other volumes, *Smuga i promień* (1965; The Shadow and the Ray), and *Lista obecności* (1967; Attendance List). Highly skillful in her use of contemporary poetic idiom, she succeeds in her best poems in giving individual expression to traditional themes of lyrical poetry. Her *Postoje pamięci* (1964; Stages of Memory) is the story of a village girl's maturation in the 1940s. Her second novel, *Ptaki dla myśli* (1971; Birds for Thought), is a study of an artist's confrontation with the pressures of modern commercialism. B.Cz.

Krains, Hubert (1862–1934), Belgian novelist, short-story writer, and critic, was born in Les Waleffes. He was very attached to his native territory, La Hesbaye, and is one of the most characteristic representatives of Walloon regionalism. His first novel, *Le Pain noir* (1904; The Black Bread), evokes in a rustic context the classic drama of a mother scoffed at by her unworthy son. The scrupulous writing, of a somewhat dry rigidness, perfectly conveys the pessimism of this observer disenchanted with human nature. At the same time that his style became supple, the author of *Figures du pays* (1908; Shapes of Our Land) evolved towards a less bitter conception of life. His "pantheistic hedonism" sparkles in *Mes Amis* (1921; My Friends), about 15 short stories marked by humor and emotion, which rank as first-rate among those of his relatively small literary output. Some of Krains's *Portraits d'écrivains belges* (1930; Portraits of Belgian Writers), devoted notably to Demolder, Charles VAN LERBERGHE, Eekhoud, and Emile VERHAEREN, bear witness to "a penetrating critic and fascinating memorialist" (D. Denuit). He became a member of the Royal Academy of French Language and Literature of Belgium in 1920 and received the Prix triennal du roman in 1921.

See: G. Charlier and J. Hanse, eds., *Histoire illustrée des lettres françaises de Belgique* (1958); D. Denuit, *Hubert Krains* (1959); R. Gustin, *Hubert Krains, conteur et romancier* (1968); *Bibliographie des écrivains français de Belgique*, vol. 3 (1968). R.Bu.

Kranjčević, Silvije Strahimir (1865–1908), the greatest Croatian poet of the second half of the 19th century, was born in Senj. Destined in his youth for the priesthood, he was sent to Rome to study theology, but he showed no vocation for clerical life and remained there for only six months. On his return home, Kranjčević went to Zagreb, where he obtained teaching credentials and was sent to Bosnia-Herzegovina, where he taught in one provincial town after another. In 1893 he was transferred to Sarajevo. He remained there until his death, devoting his time to teaching, to writing, and for several years to editing the literary journal *Nada*.

In his first collection of poems, *Bugarkinje* (1885; Plaintive Songs), Kranjčević showed a certain similarity to such predecessors as both August Šenoa (*see* CROATIAN LITERATURE) and August Harambašić. Yet he gradually distinguished himself from them through his powerful images, the novelty of his daring themes, and his insistence that man must work and fight for a better future. As he demonstrates in his poem "Radniku" (1885; To the Laborer), he appreciated the hard lot of the working man, but Kranjčević also had an almost missionary vision of the duty of the intellectual, whom he regarded, as in the poem "Mojsije" (1893; Moses), as called upon to lead the masses into the promised land of social justice and freedom.

Kranjčević's stay in classical and papal Rome made a deep impact upon him. At times he thundered like an Old Testament prophet, as in "In tyrannos" (1884; Against the Tyrants); at other times he speaks in the voice of a merciful and compassionate evangelist. Even when he had doubts about the existence or the goodness of the Creator, when he indignantly rejected the established church, or when he suggested that a child should go out of the huge cathedral and into nature, Kranjčević always admired Jesus and was deeply moved by his sufferings and his humanitarian ideas. In some of Kranjčević's most radical songs, such as "Resurrectio" (1897), the poet even saw Jesus on the barricades with French revolutionaries.

Kranjčević wrote his best poems before he was 35 years old. These were collected in *Izabrane pjesme* (1898; Selected Poems). His later volumes *Trzaji* (1902; Spasms) and *Pjesme* (1908; Poems), were often darkened by his strong penchant toward pessimism. However, even during his last years, Kranjčević wrote verses that, although not "completely harmonious" (Barac), are intimately linked with "our times and worries" (Krleža).

See: A. G. Matoš, "U sjeni velikog imena," *Savremenik* 12 (1908): 705–14; M. Krleža, "O Kranjčevićevoj lirici," *Hrvatska revija* 3 (1931): 137–58; I. Frangeš, "Rani Kranjčević," *LMS* 6 (1958): 443–65.   A.K.

Krasko, Ivan, pseud of Ján Botto (1876–1958), Slovak poet, was born in Lukovištia in southern Slovakia. He worked as a chemical engineer and after the formation of Czechoslovakia (1918) became a high government official in Bratislava. He served as a delegate to the Czechoslovak Parliament and later as a senator. After 1938 he lived in retirement.

Krasko is considered the outstanding representative of the Slovak symbolist movement known as the "Moderna" (*see* SLOVAK LITERATURE). He replaced the long narrative poetry of his predecessor Pavol Országh Hviezdoslav with poetry in which symbols and intensity of experience are central. His first collection, *Nox et solitudo* (1909; Night and Solitude), reveals his individuality, yet expresses the pessimism of Krasko's comtemporaries of the Moderna movement both in their concern for their own fates and that of their people, and in the banality of their existence and the prevalence of apathy. His imtimate poems are infused with a melancholy lyric quality, but those addressed to the nation anathematize his people until the day they awake from their apathy.

Brighter tones sound in Krasko's second and final collection, *Verše* (1912; Verses), and the two poems "Baníci" (The Miners) and "Otrok" (The Slave) are among the finest Slovak poems of the 20th century.

Krasko was the first poet in Slovak literature to make systematic use of dactylic and dactylo-trochaic verse. His poetic language is distinguished by its high level, its simplicity, and its rich sound, and he is one of the most frequently recited of Slovak poets. Krasko brought Slovak poetry to the level of contemporary Western European poetry. Although he was not a prolific writer, he is considered the father of modern Slovak poetry.

See: J. Brezina, *Ivan Krasko* (1945).   F.M.B.

Kraus, Karl (1874–1936), Austrian essayist, aphorist, and poet, was born in Jičin, Czechoslovakia, but lived mostly in Vienna. After a short career as a journalist and pamphleteer, he was offered an important position with a leading Austrian daily, but inner scruples led him to refuse it. He saw his own intellectual and spiritual integrity as well as the public mind threatened by the corrupt, pseudoliberal press. He, therefore, founded his own periodical, *Die Fackel* (1899–1936), devoted to social and literary criticism; it was written at first largely, then entirely, by himself. This journal, in which most of his works first appeared, became as much admired by the younger generation as it was hated by the established representatives of the bourgeioisie. Kraus's fight against intellectual and economic corruption, carried through with devastating wit, soon took on the wider meaning of cultural criticism and grew to a confrontation of the ideal and the reality of human beings. The human perversion of the machine from a human instrument to a god, the enslavement of nature by commerce, the hypocritical treatment of the sexual instincts, the falsification of literary values—these are Kraus's central themes. Throughout the years he scathingly attacked "journalese" as the most conspicuous expression of that hypocrisy and perversion.

The emotional impact of World War I on Kraus was tremendous. Remaining in Vienna, he gave running commentaries, polemic and satirical, directed against those in power who desecrated human dignity, against the unholy mixture of business and "idealism," militarism and religion. His gigantic drama *Die letzten Tage der Menschheit* (1918–22; The Last Days of Mankind), a documentary and a visionary panorama at the same time, is the supreme monument of the horror of those years. *Worte in Versen, I–IX* (1916–30; Eng. tr., of selections, *Poems,* 1930), the embodiment of Kraus's personal experience and philosophy in lyrical, didactic, satirical verses, also began to appear during the war. Before the war Kraus's fame had already been established by two volumes of prose essays, *Sittlichkeit und Kriminalität* (1908; Morality and Criminality) and *Die chinesische Mauer* (1910; The Great Wall of China); to the same literary genre belong *Weltgericht* (1919; Last Judgment), *Untergang der Welt durch schwarze Magie* (1922; The Decline of the World through Black Magic), and *Literatur und Lüge* (1929; Literature and the Lie). Masterpieces of penetrating wit and precision are his books of aphorisms *Sprüche und Widersprüche* (1909; Sayings and Countersayings), *Pro Domo et Mundo* (1912), and *Nachts* (1919; At Night) and his *Epigramme* (1927). Among his minor works in dramatic form are the parody, *Literatur* (1921), of Franz WERFEL's *Spiegelmensch* (Mirror Man); the satirical version *Wolkenkuckucksheim* (1923; Never-Never Land) of Aristophanes' *Birds*; and the satirical and philosophical *Traumstück* (1923; A Dream Piece) and *Traumtheater* (1924; Dream Theater). In his last book, *Die Sprache* (1937; Language), Kraus discussed with his extraordinary linguistic sensitiveness problems of grammar, style, and poetics.

Through all of Kraus's work runs the conviction of the fundamental moral and aesthetic importance of the way in which words are used; in his own style words and thoughts are inextricably interlocked. Although despising the cheap pun, he made an art of the meaningful play on words, which he sometimes does in a serious vein. Literary art to Kraus resided in the perfect union and mutual enrichment of form and content. This approach to literature he furthered by masterly public readings of William Shakespeare, of unorthodox selections from later writers, and of his own works. These readings became not only occasions of literary enjoyment but also satirical tribunals, just as his written work was equally a moral and aesthetic undertaking, a revision of values in every respect. German polemic prose and the esssay as a literary genre won rare power and beauty through Kraus. The superabundance of verbally and factually interdependent allusions, certain mannerisms in his later writings, the revengeful suppression of his name in the press (which he so persistently fought)—only these have delayed his recognition as one of the greatest German satirists.

See: L. Liegler, *Karl Kraus* (1921; rpt., 1933); K. Kraus, *Introduction to Poems*, tr. by A. Bloch (1930), pp. 9–21; R. von Schaukal, *Karl Kraus* (1933); P. Schick, *Karl Kraus in Selbstzeugnissen und Bilddokumenten* (1965); W. A. Iggers, *Karl Kraus* (1967); H. Zohn, *Karl Kraus* (1971); T. S. Szasz, *Karl Kraus and the Soul Doctors* (1976). F.H.M. rev. A.L.W.

Kretzer, Max (1854–1941), German novelist and short-story writer, was born in Posen, East Prussia, the son of a prosperous restaurateur. The family moved to Berlin, where it merged with the capital's industrial proletariat. Max, then 13, became a factory worker, later a sign painter. An accident he sustained at the age of 25 changed the course of his life, and at that time he took up writing.

Equipped with a keen sense of observation, a facile pen, and an urge to preach on social problems, Kretzer's works display an intimate knowledge of Berlin's proletarian life in the 1880s and 1890s. His first novel, *Die beiden Genossen* (1880; The Two Colleagues), is set against the background of the activities of the Social Democratic Party; *Die Betrogenen* (1882; The Betrayed) dwells on the evils of prostitution; *Die Verkommenen* (1883; The Depraved) describes the fate of the industrial proletariat. In contrast, *Drei Weiber* (1886; Three Females) pictures the rottenness of high Berlin society. *Meister Timpe* (1888), Kretzer's most characteristic novel, traces the history of a family of artisans from economic security to destruction. A strong religious note is struck in *Die Bergpredigt* (1890; The Sermon on the Mount) and *Das Gesicht Christi* (1896; The Face of Christ). The other novels of Kretzer deal mostly with the life of the middle class.

See: G. Keil, *Max Kretzer: A Study in German Naturalism* (1928); H. May, *Max Kretzers Romanschaffen* (1931). G.Ke. rev. A.L.W.

Krėvė, Vincas, pseud. of Vincas Mickevičius (1882–1954), Lithuanian short-story writer and playwright, was born in the hamlet of Subartonys, in Lithuania, and died in Marple Township near Philadelphia, Pa., in the United States. He was one of the initiators of modern Lithuanian literature and became its major figure. Krėvė attended the theological seminary in Vilnius (1898–1900), but later devoted himself to the study of comparative Indo-European philology at the universities of Kiev (1904–05) and Lvov (1905–08). He was professor of Slavic literatures at the University of Kaunas (1922–40), the University of Vilnius (1940–44), and finally at the University of Pennsylvania (1947–53).

Krėvė was a prolific and versatile writer, whose work exhibits great diversity of theme, style, and source of artistic conception. The rich folklore of the southeastern region of Lithuania in which he grew up served as a continual inspiration during his literary career. He began as a romantic with the tale *Gilšė* (1909; Eng. tr., *Gilshe*, 1947). This was followed by a legendary play, *Šarūnas, Dainavos kunigaikštis* (1912; Šarūnas, Prince of Dainava), and a collection of tales, *Dainavos šalies senų žmonių padavimai* (1912; Legends of the Old People of Dainava), the themes of which were taken from Lithuanian legends and folklore. In his own inimitable style, approaching that of the folk ballad, he portrayed the beauty of nature and the vitality of human passion. His play *Šarūnas*, in which

the strong-willed Prince Šarūnas attempts to fuse many tribes into a unified Lithuanian nation, is exemplary of his style and themes. His historical drama *Skirgaila* (1925) presents Prince Skirgaila caught in the turmoil of changing times as Christianity replaces paganism. Krėvė portrayed village and city life in his realistic works: short stories collected in *Šiaudinėj pastogėj* (1922; Eng. tr., The Herdsman and the Linden Tree) and the novella *Raganius* (1939; The Sorcerer). In other prose works, such as *Rytų pasakos* (1930; Tales of the Orient) and *Dangaus ir žemės sūnūs* (1907–54; The Sons of Heaven and Earth) Krėvė probes the spiritual life of Oriental and biblical man. His satirical story *Pagunda* (1950; Eng. tr., The Temptation, 1965) depicts the behind-the-scene aspects of Communist propaganda.

See: V. Maciūnas, "From Native Lithuania to the Distant Orient: A Survey of the Literary Heritage of Vincas Krėvė," *Lituanus* 11 (1965): 18–68; B. Vaškelis, "Vincas Krėvė, the Lithuanian Classic," *Lituanus* 11 (1965): 5–17. B.V.

Kristensen, Tom (1893–1974), Danish poet, novelist, and essayist, was born in London but grew up in Copenhagen. After receiving his university degree in 1919, he taught English between 1919 and 1921, later becoming a journalist. An outstanding and influential literary critic, Kristensen was one of the central figures of the post-World War I generation. His first collection of poems, *Fribytterdrømme* (1920; Pirate Dreams), is reminiscent of contemporary expressionistic painting with its daring color and sound effects. Kristensen's revolutionary tendency—partly political but mainly artistic—was based on an all-embracing feeling of fear, which also is present in *Mirakler* (1922; Miracles) and *Paafuglefjeren* (1922; The Peacock's Feather), the latter collection inspired by a journey to China and Japan in 1922. In these, Kristensen breaks with his expressionistic style, but the formal harmony used only increases the tension in the homeless soul of the poet. In powerful, philosophical poems, he struggles with existential problems concerning art and reality, life and death. Despair is constantly lurking behind the meditative and resigned poems in the later collections, from *Verdslige Sange* (1927; Worldly Songs) to *Den sidste Lygte* (1954; The Last Lantern).

Kristensen's first prose works were two expressionistic novels. In the first, *Livets Arabesk* (1921; The Arabesque of Life), a revolutionary fantasy, both the upper and the lower classes are depicted as equally corrupt. The political aspect of the novel is soon, however, transformed into a religious one, an expression of the author's longing for "divine peace." Kristensen's second novel, *En Anden* (1923; Another), is exceptional for its time because of its exceedingly pliable and precise description of the upbringing of a proletarian boy in Copenhagen. The factual and objective narration, however, is only a pretense. Both novels concern the same problem: the search for the self, the formation of individual personality. In *Hærværk* (1930; Eng. tr., *Havoc*, 1968), which marks the culmination of Kristensen's prose works and is the strongest expression in Danish literature of "the lost generation" of the interwar years, anxiety and despair are openly expressed. The novel's main motif is the fear of the main character, Ole Jastrau, of becoming lost in the world, of not finding himself. Deliverance is achieved neither through communism nor Catholicism, which frighten Jastrau because of their logic, but through self-destruction, which creates the feeling of eternity that his soul is longing for. *Hærværk* is a Danish parallel to Aldous Huxley's *Point Counter Point* and Ernest Hemingway's *The Sun Also Rises*, in addition to being related to James Joyce's *Ulysses* in both style and composition. The novel is unequaled in world literature with respect to its candor and its descriptions of postwar people. After the 1930s, Kristensen seldom published any lengthy works. Besides a series of travel books, his main effort was devoted to the writing of critical essays.

See: N. Egebak, *Tom Kristensen* (1971); M. S. Byram, "The Reality of Tom Kristensen's *Hærværk*," *Scan* 15, no. 1 (1976): 29–37; J. Breitenstein, *Tom Kristensen's udvikling* (1978).   S.H.R.

Kristeva, Julia (1941–), French literary theorist, was born in Bulgaria. She has drawn on a wide international array of critics, philosophers, psychoanalysts, and linguists to elaborate an original and far-reaching theory of textual analysis. It has taken shape in a series of essays published in *Tel Quel, Semiotica,* and elsewhere—a number of which were collected in *Semeiotikè: recherches pour une sémanalyse* (1969; Researches for a Semanalysis) and *Polylogue* (1977)—as well as in comprehensive studies such as *Le Texte du roman* (1970; The Text of the Novel) and especially *La Révolution du langage poétique* (1974; The Revolution of Poetic Language). A brief presentation in English of Kristeva's theory can be found in her "The System and the Speaking Subject" (*TLS,* Oct. 12, 1973).

In Kristeva's view, the text is not a finished, static object that an outside observer can analyze at leisure. It is a signifying process, and "semanalysis," the science that accounts for it, is a typology of signifying practices. A number of concepts she devised have found their way into critical vocabulary: the "dialogic" status of words, which are loci of two lines of significance—the denotive-connotive complex and a reaching out to other texts; "intertextuality," derived from the former, which posits a text (a concept that replaces and displaces the notion of genre) as absorption and transformation of other texts (not the same as source or influence); the "pheno-text" as surface and system of signs and the "genotext" as operation that produces meaning within the apparatus of signifying practices of a given language; the text is seen as "productivity" and the textual signifier thought of as "numberer," which neither "represents nor "signifies" and is materialized in a graphic element called the "signifying differential." Broadly speaking, the signifying process embodies a dialectic between two modes, the symbolic (found in its purest form in artificial languages) and the semiotic (the basis of nonverbal systems such as music). Poetic language, which includes but is not restricted to conventional poetry, partakes of the nature of both modes; it is the main object of Kristeva's investigation, along with its link to the language-learning process in children. In another vein, the essay *Des chinoises* (1975; Eng. tr., *About Chinese Women,* 1977) is a manifestation of Kristeva's concern with the role and status of women.

See: P. E. Lewis, "Revolutionary Semiotics," *Diacritics* 4, no. 3 (1974).   L.S.R.

Krleža, Miroslav (1893–), Croatian writer, was born in Zagreb. After studying at the military academy in Budapest, Krleža volunteered in 1912 for the Serbian army, but he was suspected of being an Austrian spy, expelled from Serbian territory, arrested by the Austrians, and deprived of his officer's rank. During World War I, however, he was sent as a private to the front in Galicia; he became ill there and returned to Zagreb in 1917. His war experiences led Krleža to become an antimilitarist and, after 1918, a Communist. Alone or with others he founded several leftist periodicals: *Plamen* (1919), *Književna republika* (1923–27), *Danas* (1934), and *Pečat* (1939–40). In

the 1920s he was in constant conflict with royalists, freemasons, nationalists, and clerics—experiences he related in *Moj obračun s njima* (1932; My Squaring of Accounts with Them). In *Dijalektički antibarbarus* (1939; A Dialectical Antibarbarian), he scathingly ridiculed the orthodox Stalinists (among whom then was Milovan Djilas) and was expelled from the Communist Party. Consequently, he did not join the Partisans during World War II, but remained in Zagreb until 1945. For a while, Krleža was in disgrace, but he was soon rehabilitated by his friend Marshal Tito and from 1952 on was a driving force in liberalizing Yugoslav culture. He played an important role also as the director of the Lexicographic Institute in Zagreb and the editor-in-chief of the *Enciklopedija Jugoslavije.* Although he supported Croatian national and cultural claims in 1967, Krleža is skeptical of democratic progress, particularly in the Balkans. His views on these issues have been recorded in *Razgovori s Miroslavom Krležom* (1969; Conversations with Miroslav Krleža).

Krleža's significant poetic output may be divided into several cycles. His first poetry is collected in *Pan* (1917) and *Tri simfonije* (1917; Three Symphonies). His poetry soon turned however to war, wounded soldiers, hospitals, and incessant funerals, the subjects of *Knjiga Lirike* (1932; A Book of Lyrics). In *Pjesme u tmini* (1937; Songs in Darkness), he predicted the downfall of the capitalist system, believing that the exploited class would find an exit from the "darkness" of the social structure. In his most important collection, *Balade Petrice Kerempuha* (1936; Ballads of Petrica Kerempuh), composed in the Kajkavian dialect, which had been neglected since the Illyrian movement (*see* CROATIAN LITERATURE), Krleža presents an apocalyptic vision of Croatian history as a series of tragic events leading toward a promise of rebirth.

From the time of World War I, when he wrote his symbolic "legends" about Jesus Christ, Michelangelo, and Columbus, until 1959, when he published *Aretheus,* his "fantasy" about a Roman physician, Krleža also wrote many plays. His stage works reflect several literary trends and treat a variety of themes. At first, under the impact of expressionism, he described tumultuous and bloody scenes, but later he benefited enormously from the influence of Henrik IBSEN, especially in his best dramas, *Glembajevi* (1928; The Glembays) and *U agoniji* (1928; In Agony). In these two plays, Krleža displays a new economy as he minutely analyzes a few members of the decadent Austro-Hungarian nobility.

Krleža denounced the atrocities of war in his poetry and plays, but he sounded this theme most effectively in his collection of short stories, *Hrvatski bog Mars* (1922; The Croatian God Mars), which depicts the miserable condition of the Croatian soldier in the Austro-Hungarian army. In the 1920s and 1930s, he published novellas portraying the conflict between subservient fathers and revolutionary children.

Krleža's first and best novel, *Povratak Filipa Latinovicza* (1932; The Return of Philip Latinovicz) concerns a painter who, having achieved a certain amount of fame in Paris, returns home hoping to discover the identity of his father. Philip's childhood memories are skillfully interwoven with a depiction of the pettiness and corruption of bourgeois society. The novel *Na rubu pameti* (1938; On the Brink of Reason) portrays an individual who, although aware that the effort will be in vain, decides to unmask his employer and reveal man's stupidity, in general. In *Zastave* (1967– ; Banners), of which five volumes have appeared so far, the novelist gives a broad panorama, mixed with biographical reminiscences, of the events between 1912 and 1922.

Krleža's other publications include six volumes of

learned, stimulating, often impressionistic essays on a variety of subjects and an account of his journey to Russia (1926; *Izlet u Rusiju*).

See: M. Matković, "Marginalije uz Krležino dramsko stvaranje," *Hrvatsko Kolo* 2-3 (1949): 410–47; A. Kadic, "Miroslav Krleža," *BA* 4 (1963): 396–400, and "Krleža's Tormented Visionaries," *SEER* 104 (1967): 46–64; I. Frangeš, "Miroslav Krleza," *ForumZ* 1-2 (1973): 114–133. A.K.

Kroetz, Franz Xaver (1946–) West German playwright, was born in Munich. He began studying acting at 15, first in Munich, then in Vienna. He returned to Munich, acted in cellar theaters, worked at odd jobs, and began at 20 to write plays. He quickly found his own set of themes, a distinctive style, and success. The critical "folk plays" of Marieluise Fleisser and Ödön von HORVÁTH provided models: Horváth focused on the discrepancy between what is said and what is meant, a lack of language; from Fleisser's plays come a sympathy for the oppressed, the use of dialect speech, and an honest representation of people powerless to help themselves. Revivals of works by these two in the late 1960s had formative influence on a generation of young dramatists: Wolfgang BAUER, Martin Speer, and Kroetz in particular. But Kroetz's consistent use of an almost genuine Bavarian stage dialect, his uncompromising realism based on close observation, and, above all, his extremely laconic scenes give even his early plays a distinctive stamp. By 1972, nine of his plays had been produced; since then, he has been one of the most performed writers on the German stage.

Again and again, Kroetz's plays show the victims at the bottom of the social pecking order, unable to escape their plight, unable even to articulate what that plight is. Among these early works are *Wildwechsel* (1968; Deer Crossing), *Stallerhof* (1972; Staller's Farm), and the one-person play with no dialog at all, *Wunschkonzert* (1972; Request Program). A growing involvement with Bertolt BRECHT's plays and with the Communist Party (DKP) caused Kroetz to try writing longer plays based on social ideas—including two adaptations of Friedrich Hebbel plays—but he remains most successful with his characteristic compact, minutely observed, realistic plays, although with a less pessimistic outcome. In the recent ones, *Oberösterreich* (1972; Upper Austria), *Das Next* (1974; The Next), and *Mensch Meier* (1977; Man Meier), the character does begin to understand his predicament and to make his way out of it. A selection of his dramatic work is in English translation in *Farmyard and Other Plays* (1976).

See: E. Panzner, *Franz Xavier Kroetz und seine Rezeption* (1976). D.J.W.

Krog, Helge (1889–1962), Norwegian dramatist and literary critic, was born in Christiania (now Oslo), into a liberal, academic family. This heritage always marked him, even though his political views were influenced early by Marxist philosophy and communism. From his first contact with the Marxist-oriented "Mot Dag" movement in 1920, Krog became a sharp, witty critic of capitalism and the established middle-class order, and his social criticism only grew more vitriolic with the years. As a literary critic, he became known for his piercing logic and independent personal engagement, qualities that often led him to produce important correctives in critical thinking. His criticism has been collected in several volumes, including *Meninger om bøker og forfattere* (1929; Opinions on Books and Authors) and *Meninger. Litteratur. Kristendom. Politikk.* (1947; Opinions, Literature. Christianity. Politics).

As a dramatist, Krog was an exponent of the bourgeois realism of Henrik IBSEN and Gunnar HEIBERG. He had the same desire to arouse debate on social issues—the problems of the working class, the oppression of women, the hypocrisy of the established order—but in his dramas his views on these subjects became almost understated; only in his treatment of erotic love did he raise the storm he had hoped for. Krog worshipped woman both as an erotic being and as a symbol of moral integrity. This view of a dual female superiority is the central theme of his three best plays, *Konkylien* (1929; Eng. tr., *Happily Ever After?*, 1934), *Underveis* (1931; Eng. tr., *On the Way*, 1939), and *Opbrudd* (1936; Eng. tr., *Break-up*, 1939), all of which concern strong-willed, independent women who oppose the rules that guide society. A number of Krog's lesser plays, mostly comedies, have also enjoyed great popularity in Scandinavia.

See: S. Arestad, "Helge Krog and the Problem Play," *SS* 37, (1965): 332–51; F. Havrevold, *Helgi Krog* (1959). K.A.F.

Krokann, Inge (1893–1962), Norwegian novelist, was born of old farming stock in the mountain valley of Opdal, where he lived most of his life. Intensely interested in the history of Norway and, in particular, the history of Opdal, Krokann studied extensively and became a knowledgeable, sensitive historian. The result of his research was two significant treatises on changes in the old Norwegian rural society, *Då bøndene reiste seg* (1937; When the Farmers Rebelled) and "Det store hamskiftet i bondesamfunnet" (The Great Transformation of the Rural Society, pub. in *Norsk kulturhistorie*, vol. 5 (1942), pp. 100–95).

Krokann's studies also resulted in several historical novels. His tetralogy about medieval Norway demonstrates that, with the possible exception of Hans E. KINCK and Sigrid UNDSET, no modern Norwegian writer has had a more intimate knowledge of Norway's past coupled with the ability to put that past into a convincing fictional form. The story of the Lo family, told in *I Dovresno* (1929; In the Winds from Dovre), *Gjennom fonna* (1931; Through the Snowdrift), *På linfeksing* (1934; On the Flax-Maned Horse), and *Under himmelteiknet* (1941; Under the Omen in the Sky), is a prose epic of Opdal in the 15th and 16th centuries. Written in the Opdal dialect, these novels are rich, fascinating documents of medieval Norwegian culture. Although Krokann's strength did not lie in the probing analysis of the individual, his psychological representation of the late medieval community as a whole has hardly a parallel in Norwegian literature. A later continuation of the tetralogy, *Gravlagt av lynet* (1952; Buried by Lightning), does not have the epic power of the preceding novels.

See: O. Dalgard, *Inge Krokann* (1970). K.A.F.

Krolow, Karl (1915–), German poet and prose writer, essayist, critic, feuilletonist, and translator of French and Spanish poetry, was born in Hanover. From 1935 to 1941 he attended the universities of Göttingen and Breslau, where his main areas of study were Germanic and Romance languages, philosophy, and art history. He began to write professionally in 1942; since then he has also held guest lectureships at several German universities. A member of several literary societies, Krolow has also been awarded a number of literary prizes, including the Georg Büchner Award (1956) and the Rilke Prize (1975).

Krolow's work holds a central position in postwar German poetry. The earlier poems exhibit a close affinity with nature, in the romantic tradition. Yet he aligns this tradition with surrealism and German expressionism, and with a concern for the immediacy of current affairs (e.g., the threat of atomic war). At times, these poems echo the elegiac tone of Georg TRAKL; at other points, the influence of Oskar Loerke and Wilhelm Lehmann is evident, as well as that of Charles BAUDELAIRE, Federico GARCÍA LORCA, and Arthur RIMBAUD.

The lyrical world that Krolow has since created is uniquely his own. His poems might be viewed as attempts to keep life alive through poetry. Amidst the imagery of agility and transparency characteristic of much of his work, however, an underlying melancholy cannot be overlooked. Krolow's metaphors attest to his power of imagination, yet equally important is his experience of human frailty, articulated in some works, such as *Nichts weiter als Leben* (1970; Nothing More Than Living), as a running thread of laconism.

These newer poems also marked a new direction for Krolow: the growing proximity of poetic and "mathematical" vision, as both combine to produce models with which it may be possible to locate reality. In such works as *Landschaften für mich* (1966; Landscapes for Me), it seems that poetry is in a position to thaw out human torpidity and grant man freedom. Krolow feels his way around the picture we create of the world, transposing it in an effort to go behind the accepted order of things.

As in the long story *Das andere Leben* (1979; The Other Life), Krolow's poetry and prose incorporate a close observation of the literary "scene," an ongoing investigation of the possibilities of contemporary poetry. The record of such thought can be found in his regular contributions to newspapers, magazines, and radio, as well as in his essays in *Schattengefecht* (1964; Shadow-Boxing) and *Ein Gedicht entsteht* (1975; The Origin of a Poem).

See: *Über Karl Krolow* (1972).   C.J.

Kruchonykh, Aleksey Yeliseyevich (1886–1968), Russian poet and critic, born in Olevka in Kherson province, is often considered the most extreme and consistent of the futurists (*see* RUSSIAN LITERATURE). He joined the group headed by David BURLYUK at the time the futurists switched to neoprimitivism. Between 1912 and ca. 1934 nearly 250 booklets appeared containing his poetry, prose, drama, manifestos, criticism, and literary theory; sometimes they were illustrated by the best avant-garde artists; many of them merged poetry and visual art, often whimsically. Kruchonykh's early poetry stressed parody, disorder, coarseness, inconsistency, and just plain silliness; his early volumes include *Pustynniki* (Hermits), *Pomada* (Pomade), *Mirskontsa* (Worldbackwards), and *Vozropshchem,* (Let's Grumble). As a critic, Kruchonykh tirelessly attacked Aleksander Pushkin as well as contemporary symbolists with their ideals of beauty. A well-known theoretician and practitioner of *zaum* (transrational language), Kruchonykh freely invented words expressing emotions intuitively, irrationally, spontaneously, and individually. After the Russian Revolution (1917) he headed *zaum* groups in the Caucasus and in Moscow and briefly belonged to the LEF group. He stopped participating in Russian literary life in the 1930s. An English translation of his opera libretto *Pobeda nad solntsem* (Victory over the Sun) appeared in 1971. A volume of selected works, *Izbrannoye*, was published in 1973.

See: V. Markov, *Russian Futurism* (1968); G. McVay, "Alexi Kruchenykh: The Bogeyman of Russian Literature," *RLT* 13 (Fall 1975): 571–90; C. Douglas, "Views from the New World: A. Kruchenykh and K. Malevich. Theory and Painting," *RLT* 12 (Spring 1975): 323–70.
                                                                                        V.M.

Kruczkowski, Leon (1900–62), Polish novelist, playwright,

essayist, and publicist, was born in Cracow and died in Warsaw. After studying chemistry in Cracow, he worked in the chemical industry and taught in technical schools. He was active from his youth in the socialist movement. He fought in the Polish army in 1939, was taken prisoner, and spent the war years in a prisoner of war camp in Germany. After World War II he was deputy minister of culture (1945–48) and then chairman of the Polish Writers Union (1949–56). Kruczkowski's writing was greatly influenced by Stefan Żeromski, his literary master, and by Marxist ideology. In the historical novel *Kordian i cham* (1932; Kordian and the Boor), based on an authentic diary of a plebeian participant in the 1830 Polish uprising against Russia, he undertook a reevaluation of the romantic legend of the uprising from a new social aspect, introducing a peasant hero. Authentic diaries also provide the basis for his next work, the sociological historical novel *Pawie pióra* (1935; Peacock Feathers), which deals with the class structure of the Polish peasantry at the beginning of the 19th century. A new psychological approach is evident in Kruczkowski's next novel, *Sidła* (1937; A Trap), about white-collar workers. After 1945, Kruczkowski turned mainly to the drama, in which he touched political and moral problems. In his play *Niemcy* (1950; The Germans), he focuses on the problem of the individual's moral responsibility for the Nazi war crimes. His other plays include *Juliusz i Ethel* (1954), about Julius and Ethel Rosenberg's trial, and *Pierwszy dzień wolności* (1960; The First Day of Freedom). In his last play, *Śmierć gubernatora* (1961; The Death of the Governor), he moved away from the realistic idiom of his theater toward a parabolic presentation of the mechanism of power and the moral responsibility for its use.

See: *Słownik współczesnych pisarzy polskich,* vol. 2 (1964), pp. 246–53.   A.W.

Krúdy, Gyula (1878–1933), Hungarian novelist, was born in Nyíregyháza. Memories of his childhood and early youth served as a vast reservoir for the mature writer, whose creative method could be characterized as recollections from a sensuous dream world. Krúdy moved to Budapest in 1896 and lived there for the rest of his life, a journalist and writer much beloved in bohemian circles. He was immensely prolific; his literary output has been estimated at 60 novels and 3,000 short stories, not to mention numerous articles and feuilletons.

Krúdy's early writings show the influence of Mór Jókai (*see* HUNGARIAN LITERATURE), Kálmán Mikszáth, Charles Dickens, and Ivan Turgenev, but later, after a short "critical realist" interlude in which he wrote the novel *Az aranybánya* (1901; The Gold Mine), Krúdy began to evolve a style unmistakably his own. He first evoked his youth in a series of short stories and then embarked upon his first important creative venture, the Sindbad cycle. The novel *Szinbád ifjúsága* (1911; The Youth of Sindbad) was followed by numerous short novels and stories, all revolving around the writer's alter ego, a nostalgic adventurer who roams the country in search of women and memories. The milieu of these works is provided by the manor houses and inns where the gentry lead their unambitious, dissipated lives, but Krúdy goes beyond social reality to create a timeless world where only impressions, passions, and memories matter. A similar mood pervades *A vörös postakocsi* (1913; Eng. tr., The Crimson Coach, 1967) and its continuation, *Őszi utazások a vörös postakocsin* (1917; Autumn Journeys on the Scarlet Stagecoach). Here, however, the setting is metropolitan rather than manorial, and Krúdy fills the two novels with lyrical, often humorous recollections of a bohemian Budapest at the turn of the century. Love, mild intrigues, and the sensuous joys of life dominate the charming novel *Hét bagoly* (1922; Seven Owls), the hero of which, a middle-aged lawyer, visits the capital to relive his youth. There is a noticeable shift toward realism in the prose of the older Krúdy, although it is more a realism of details than one of social movement. His last important novel, *Boldogult úrfikoromban* (1930; When I Was a Young Gentleman), was called by one critic "the most intimate expression of the poetry of urban life." Some of Krúdy's earlier stories and short novels, such as *Az útitárs* (1919; The Fellow Passenger) or *N.N.* (1922), evinced fairy-tale lyricism not unlike that of Virginia Woolf's *Orlando*. In his later short stories, however, collected in *Az élet álom* (1931; Life Is a Dream), the narrator's attention turns from reckless love affairs to the delights of good food.

Krúdy's work is sometimes compared to that of Marcel PROUST, but despite similarities in their narrative technique, their social milieus are quite different, Krúdy's world being held together less by social convention than by poetic imagination. His enthusiasm for life often turns sour when confronted with illness, old age, or loneliness—and these are plentiful on the fringes of society, where his heroes happen to move. His real strength lies not so much in the creation of plot as in the use of language: the texture of his prose is rich and the movement of his sentences suggests musical rhythms. The uniqueness of Krúdy's art resides in this rambling, picturesque style, full of metaphors and seemingly irrelevant reminiscences. He is now acknowledged as one of the great figures of modern Hungarian literature.

See: A. Komlós, "Az élet álom," *Nyugat* 25 (1932): 660–62; J. Szauder, *Szinbád születése* (1960); J. Reményi, *Hungarian Writers and Literature* (1964), pp. 229–38; L. Baránszky-Jób, "Krúdy és Proust," *Híd* 2 (1965): 1423–32; *A magyar irodalom története, 1905–töl-napjainkig*, vol. 3 (1965), pp. 186–99.   G.G.

Kubin, Alfred (1877–1959), Austrian writer and expressionist painter, was born in Leitmeritz, Bohemia. He attended school in the town of his birth and became an apprentice photographer. In 1898 he studied at the school for applied art in Salzburg and then at the academy of art in Munich. In 1905 he traveled in Western Europe and the Balkan countries and after 1906 lived in a castle on the Inn River, working as a painter, graphic artist, illustrator, and free-lance writer. His novels, as well as his works of art, reflect a stubborn willfulness and expressionistic vehemence, often in trancelike visions and demonic dreams as well as in sinister apparitions. His novel *Die andere Seite* (1909; Eng. tr., *The Other Side*, 1967) is a fantasy about a realm of dream. A collection of stories, *Der Guckkasten* (The Peep Show) appeared in 1925. Essays are found in his *Vom Schreibtisch eines Zeichners* (1939; From the Writing Desk of a Graphic Artist), and a collection of drawings is in the volume *Abenteuer einer Zeichenfeder* (1941; Adventures of a Drawing Pen). His *Nüchterne Balladen* (Sober Ballads) were published in 1949, and selected writings in 1950 in *Abendrot* (Red at Evening). The *Phantasien in Böhmerwald* (Fantasies in a Bohemian Wood) of 1951 was followed in 1959 by his autobiography, *Dämonen und Nachtgesichte* (Dreams and Night Visions). His works show the influence of the romantic graphic artist and author of fantasy E. T. A. Hoffmann. Graphic works are available with English commentary in *Dance of Death and Other Drawings* (1973).

See: H. Bisanz, *Alfred Kubin: Zeichner, Schriftsteller, und Philosoph* (1977).   A.L.W.

Kukučín, Martin, pseud. of Matej Bencúr (1860–1928), Slovak novelist and short-story writer, was the outstanding figure in the Slovak realist movement. As a teacher in his native village of Jasenova, he refused to enforce the prescribed policy of magyarization and in 1885 went to Prague, where he studied medicine. He later worked as a physician along the Dalmatian coast of Croatia and in Argentina and Chile. In 1922 he visited Slovakia but returned to Croatia, where he died.

Kukučín enriched Slovak fiction with tales of the Slovak village. He eliminated sentimental lyricizing and romantic pathos, emphasizing instead the character of the Slovak peasant with his inborn sense of humor, original manners, and rich folk speech. His stories open with a briefly sketched situation and precisely conceived characters and then develop through the use of dialogue in which the folk wisdom of the peasant and his commonsense view of life were revealed.

While in Croatia, Kukučín wrote the novel *Dom v stráni* (1903–4; The House on the Hillside), a penetrating analysis of the relations between two opposed classes, the gentry and peasants, which sadly admits that class distinctions are more powerful than love. His last three novels are more expansive: *Mat' volá* (1926–27; Mother Calls) treats the life of Yugoslav emigrants in South America, while *Lukáš Blahosej Krasoň* (1929) and *Bohumil Valizlost' Zábor* (1930) are fictionalized biographies of two Slovak romantic poets. These works lack the vividness of the stories or of *Dom v stráni,* which is perhaps the masterpiece of Slovak realism.

See: C. J. Potoček, "Martin Kukučín," *SEER* 22, no. 2 (1944): 49–60; A. Mráz, *O slovenskych realistickych prozaikoch* (1950), pp. 391–435; various authors, *Martin Kukučín v kritike a spomienkach: sbornik* (1957); J. Noge, *Martin Kukučín, tradicionalista a novator* (1962).
                    F.M.B.

Kulish, Mykola (1892–1937), Ukrainian dramatist, was born in Kherson province of peasant stock. He fought as a Partisan during the Revolution (1917) and later sided with the Bolsheviks. His first play, *97* (1924), was the first part of a trilogy about a Ukrainian village during and after the Revolution. The other parts were *Komuna v stepakh* (perf. 1924, pub. only in rev. version, 1931; A Commune in the Steppes) and *Proshchay selo* (1933; Farewell, Village!). Kulish reached the height of his dramatic power while collaborating with the producer Les Kurbas of the Berezil Theater in Kharkiv. During that period he wrote his masterpiece *Narodny Malakhiy* (1929; The People's Malakhiy), about the "immediate reform of mankind," and *Patetychna sonata* (perf. 1931, pub. 1943; Eng. tr., *Sonata Pathétique,* 1975), a play about the destructive impact of the revolution on personal lives. Although *Patetychna sonata* was staged with great success in Moscow and Leningrad, it was later banned. Kulish also wrote the finest modern Ukrainian comedy, *Myna Mazaylo* (1929). His last major play was *Maklena Grasa* (1932). Kulish was a close associate of Mykola KHVYLOVY and was the president of the literary group VAPLITE (*see* UKRAINIAN LITERATURE). Accused of Ukrainian nationalism, he was arrested in 1934 and died in a Soviet concentration camp. He was partially rehabilitated in 1958.

See: N. Kuzyakina, *Pyesy Mykoly Kulisha* (1970).
                    G.S.N.L.

Kuncewiczowa, Maria (1899–),Polish novelist, short-story writer, and playwright, was born Maria Szczepańska in Samara, Russia. She studied Polish and French literature and music in Poland and France. Kuncewiczowa began publishing fiction in 1918. In her first collection of short stories, *Przymierze z dzieckiem* (1927; Alliance with a Child), and in her first novel, *Twarz mężczyzny* (1928; Face of the Male), she presented herself as a keen observer of feminine psychology, which she described with extraordinary frankness. Her second collection of short stories, *Dwa księżyce* (1933; Two Moons), was followed by *Cudzoziemka* (1936; Eng. tr., *The Stranger,* 1944), one of the most outstanding psychological novels in Polish literature of the period between the world wars, in which in a single day, the last day of the heroine's life, she reexperiences her whole past, with all the strangeness of her individuality and behavior. Before the outbreak of World War II, Kuncewiczowa also published a play, *Miłość panieńska* (1932; Maiden's Love), and literary sketches, *Dyliżans warszawski* (1935; Warsaw Stagecoach) and *Miasto Heroda* (1939; Herod's Town). She also pioneered in radio drama in Poland with a highly successful serial, *Dni powszednie państwa Kowalskich* (1938; The Kowalskis's Everyday Life), the first experiment of its kind in Europe. Kuncewiczowa lived in England from 1940 to 1955, then taught Polish literature at the University of Chicago, and later returned to Poland. Her later works include a diary from the war period, *Klucze* (1943; Eng. tr., *The Keys,* 1946); novels, *Zmowa nieobecnych* (1946; Eng. tr., *The Conspiracy of the Absent,* 1950), *Leśnik* (1952; Eng. tr., *The Forester,* 1954), *Gaj oliwny* (1961; Eng. tr., *The Olive Grove,* 1963), and *Tristan 46* (1967); a play, *Thank You for the Rose* (1950; *Dziękuję za róże,* 1963); and literary sketches.

See: *Słownik współczesnych pisarzy polskich,* vol. 2 (1964), pp. 300–04; S. Żak, *Maria Kuncewiczowa* (1971).

D.W.

Kundera, Milan (1929–), Czech novelist, playwright, short-story writer, and poet, was born in Brno, the son of a well-known musicologist. After studying literature, music, and film, he lectured for a time on world literature for students of film. He began to write lyric poetry, but subsequently turned to drama and then to fiction. An early play, *Majitelé klíčů* (1963; Keepers of the Keys), introduces Kundera's favorite subjects, love and sex, while confronting young people with the choice they must make—either an active social and political role in life or one of passive neutrality. The three volumes of tales that constitute the series *Směšné lásky* (1963–68; Eng. tr., *Laughable Loves,* 1974) embody Kundera's typically ironic, almost cynical view of love and sex, both of which are conceived as giving happiness, but only if a lover can sustain self-deception. Kundera's novel *Žert* (1967; Eng. tr., *The Joke,* 1969) attracted wide attention outside Czechoslovakia. It concerns a student who is sentenced to hard labor because of a joking reference to Leon Trotsky; after his release he seeks to take revenge on the man responsible for his punishment, but discovers that his revenge is not supported by any stable ethical principle, for political morality has shifted so radically that individuals cannot be held accountable for their changing attitudes. Since 1969, Kundera has not been published in Czechoslovakia, and he soon emigrated. He now resides in France, where his novels have gained great popularity. There he has published three more novels, two of which have so far appeared in English versions: *Life Is Elsewhere* (1974), the story of a young poet who destroys himself, spiritually and physically, by collaborating with the Stalinist regime; and *The Farewell Party* (1976), the theme of which is paternity, which avoids, in Kundera's typically ironic manner, any serious conclusion or moral. Kundera is also the author of *Umění románu* (1960; The

Art of the Novel), an important study of the writer Vladislav VANČURA.

See: A. J. Liehm, *The Politics of Culture* (1970), pp. 129–50; P. I. Trensky, *Czech Drama since World War II* (1978), pp. 73–84; W. E. Harkins and P. I. Trensky, *Czech Literature since 1956: A Symposium* (1980).

W.E.H.

Kunert, Günter (1929–), German poet, novelist, essayist, graphic artist, and film and television playwright, was born in Berlin and remained a resident of East Berlin until the autumn of 1979. He studied graphic arts at the Academy at Berlin-Weissensee from 1946 until 1949, when he joined the SED (the State Party) publication *Ulenspiegel.* In 1950 he participated in the first writer's apprenticeship of the East German *Deutscher Schriftstellerverband* (German Writers' Association). Later that same year his first volume of poetry, *Wegschilder und Mauerinschriften* (Road Signs and Wall Inscriptions), was published by Aufbau, an official publishing house of the German Democratic Republic.

In the diary published in 1951, Johannes R. BECHER, noted expressionist writer and then Secretary for Cultural Affairs in East Germany, saw in Kunert's work the advent of a new generation of East German writers "celebrating the deeds and aspirations [of the new socialist republic]." By the mid-1950s criticism was directed at the "coldness" and "intellectualization" of both the satirical prose collection *Der ewige Detektiv und andere Geschichten* (1954; The Eternal Detective and Other Stories) and the poems in *Unter diesem Himmel* (1955; Under This Sky). The television drama *Fratzers Flucht* (1962; Fratzer's Flight), followed a year later by the prepublication, in the *Weimarer Beiträge,* of three poems that later appeared in *Der ungebetene Gast* (1965; The Uninvited Guest), resulted in the first vehement criticism of Kunert's ideological position (cf. the protocols of the Sixth Party Congress [1963], reflecting the "Lyrik Debatte" or poetry controversy of the early 1960s in which Kunert's work played a central role).

Subsequently, an increasing proportion of Kunert's books appeared in West Germany. During the politically sensitive period of the mid-1960s the Carl Hanser publishing house in Munich printed Kunert's first poetry volume to appear in the Federal Republic of Germany, *Erinnerung an einen Planeten* (1963; Memory of a Planet), and continued to publish his work in the ensuing years. Many of Kunert's published works are available only in West Germany, including the poetry volume *Verkündigung des Wetters* (1966; Weather Forecast), the prose volume *Die Beerdigung findet in aller Stille statt* (1968; Private Services Will Be Held), poems in *Warnung vor Spiegeln* (1970; Beware of Mirrors), the short prose volume *Tagträume in Berlin und andernorts* (1972; Daydreams in Berlin and Elsewhere), poems in *Im weiteren Fortgang* (1974; In the Course of Further Events), and the novel *Gast aus England* (1973; Guest from England). Some pieces of short prose and poetry from these volumes have appeared in East Germany, and several of Kunert's books have been printed simultaneously in West and East Germany: *Der andere Planet: Ansichten von Amerika* (1975; The Other Planet: Views about America), *Warum schreiben? Notizen zur Literatur* (1976; Why Write: Notes on Literature), and *Ein anderer K: Hörspiele* (1977; A Different K: Radio Plays). The author's first novel, *Im Namen der Hüte* (1967; In the Name of Hats), the story of a youth capable of transcribing thoughts from the hatbands of hats of previous owners, appeared in Dutch, Italian, French, and Swedish before its publication almost a decade later (1976) in East Germany. On the other hand, since the early 1960s, an equivalent number of volumes have appeared only in East Germany, notably *Kramen in Fächern* (1969; Rummaging through Pigeonholes), whose texts have appeared individually or in anthologies in the West. One short narrative, "Zentralbahnhof" (Central Station), was the basis for a television film for West German TV in 1971. Several of the volumes Kunert has edited are revealing tributes to acknowledged models, notably Bertolt BRECHT's *Kriegsfibel* (1955; War Primer) and a later selection of Brechtian poetry (1970), a collection of poems by Nikolaus Lenau (1969), and Edgar Allan Poe's tales (1974).

Both in the breadth of his publications and in his reading audience, Kunert has been an East German author whose sphere of influence has extended beyond his homeland. He has enjoyed relative freedom of movement to the West. As a guest lecturer at the University of Texas at Austin in the fall of 1972 he edited and wrote the introduction for a special East German issue of the literary magazine *Dimension*. He was a writer-in-residence at the University of Warwick in England in 1975. Like many other East German writers, Kunert's literary fortunes have mirrored cultural policies. Loyalty per se is not at issue, but rather the meshing of loyalty to the state with his own artistic convictions. Early in his career, official criticism was directed only at his aesthetic execution. By the mid-1960s, however, political considerations began to infringe more rigorously on his artistic expression. After Wolf BIERMANN's expulsion from East Germany in 1976, Kunert signed a petition on Biermann's behalf. Related events led to Kunert's expulsion from the Party in 1977 and to his decision in 1979 to live in self-imposed "exile," with a travel visa valid for 1050 days, in Itzehoe, in West Germany.

See: E. Hofacker, "Günter Kunert and the East German Image of Man," *Monatshefte*, 66 (1974): 366–80; D. Jonnson, *Widersprüche—Hoffnungen: Literatur und Kulturpolitik der DDR/Die Prosa Günter Kunerts* (1978); M. Krüger, ed., *Kunert Lesen* (1979). J.Sw.

Kuprin, Aleksandr Ivanovich (1870–1938), Russian fiction writer, was born into the family of a minor civil servant in Penza. He was educated in military schools, served four years in the provinces as an infantry officer, then held a variety of odd jobs, such as actor, surveyor, fisherman, and teacher, all of which nourished the writing he began in the 1890s. In 1901 he moved to Petersburg, where for a time he was associated with the "Znaniye" (Knowledge) group of writers, which was headed by Maksim GORKY and specialized in exposé-type depictions of various aspects of society.

Kuprin first attracted real attention with the novella *Molokh* (1896; Eng. tr., *Moloch*, 1917), an indictment of the brutalities of industrialization. It was *Poyedinok* (1905; Eng. tr., *The Duel*, 1916), however, that made him famous and remains his best-known work. Appearing shortly after Russia's defeat in its war with Japan (1905) and amidst revolutionary turmoil, this novel was widely read as a condemnation of the military system and, by extension, of society as a whole. It is strongly autobiographical, being set among the officer corps of an infantry regiment posted in a dismal provincial town in 1894. Such virtues as honor, valor, and forthrightness are preached by the military establishment but can find no outlet here except in debauchery and cruelty. The reader is shown a variety of character types exemplifying sundry morbidities (sadism, alcoholism, lechery), which Kuprin explored in other works as well. *Poyedinok's* main hero,

Romashov, represents the fullest development of a type that fascinated Kuprin throughout his career: sensitive and idealistic, yet utterly lacking in willpower, he loathes yet cannot escape a milieu legitimized in this case by a system that plays on his basic decency and finally maneuvers him into a duel in which he is killed.

The most sensational instance of the exposé genre in Kuprin's work is the novel *Yama* (1909–15; Eng. tr., *Yama: The Pit*, 1929), which is set in a brothel in Odessa. Kuprin was also renowned as a skillful maker of adventure plots, the best example being *Shtabs-kapitan Rybnikov* (1906; Eng. tr., *Captain Ribnikov*, 1916), which features a Japanese spy in Russian disguise. Much of his work, however, deals with the reactions of ordinary people to such basic realities as love, friendship, and death. Poignancy and even sentimentalism are often the dominant modes here, as for instance in the story "Granatovy braslet" (1911; Eng. tr., "The Garnet Bracelet," 1917), which tells of a simple clerk's grand passion for an elegant and unattainable upper-class woman. Kuprin also had a strong feeling for nature, and in his works men who live close to it have a special radiance, as in *Listragony* (1907–11; Eng. tr., *The Laestrygonians*, 1917, as do the animals who are the protagonists of many of his stories.

Kuprin emigrated from Russia in 1919 and lived the next 17 years mainly in Paris. French scenes and memories of the Russian past dominate his work from this period, notably in the autobiographical novel *Yunkera* (1928–33; The Cadets). In 1937, already gravely ill, he returned to his native land, where he died the following year.

See: V. N. Afanasyev, *Aleksandr Ivanovich Kuprin: kritiko-biograficheskiy ocherk*, (2d ed., Moscow, 1972).
R.A.M.

Kurek, Jalu (1904–), Polish poet and prose writer, was born in Cracow, and studied French at the Jagiellonian University in Cracow and also in Naples. His literary debut, both in prose, with the novel *Kim był Andrzej Panik?* (1926; Who Was Andrzej Panik?), and in poetry, with the volume of poems *Upały* (1925; Heat-Wave), reflects the tendencies that dominated the Cracow avant-garde writers between the two world wars, among whom he was very active (from 1931 to 1933 he edited the avant-garde review *Linia*). Along with his many volumes of poetry, Kurek continued to write prose, and the novel *Grypa szaleje w Naprawie* (1934; Flu Rages in Naprawa) brought him the greatest recognition. In this novel, using innovative technique and structure, Kurek depicts the conflicts and adversities that torment a small village in the Tatra foothills, presenting a somber image of the misery of life in that region. His following novels are devoted to the same problem: *Woda wyżej* (1935; Rising Water) and *Młodości śpiewaj* (1938; Sing, O Youth). After World War II, Kurek's poetry became more personal, dominated by rather lyrical reflections. His postwar poetry includes *Strumień goryczy* (1957; The Stream of Bitterness), *Eksplodują ogrody* (1964; Gardens Explode), and *Śmierć krajobrazu* (1973; Death of a Landscape). In Kurek's prose (which predominates) the theme of the Tatra highland prevails. In addition to the novels *Janosik* (1945–48), *Dzień dobry Toporna* (1954; Good Day, Toporna), *Księga Tatr* (1955; The Tatra Ledger), Kurek also wrote novels about contemporary problems, such as *Ocean Nie-spokojny* (1951; The Un-Pacific Ocean) and *Bestia* (1973; The Beast), as well as a book of memoirs, *Mój Kraków* (1963; My Cracow), short stories, and reportage.

See: *Słownik współczesnych pisarzy polskich*, vol. 2

(1964), pp. 311–16; S. Jaworski, "Pisarz społecznej pasji—Jalu Kurek," in *Prozaicy dwudziestolecia międzywojennego*, ed. B. Faron (1972), pp. 413–31.   A.Z.

Kushner, Aleksandr Semyonovich (1936–), Russian poet, born in Leningrad, is a writer whose work is characterized by reserve and a sense of balance and harmony. A graduate of the Herzen Pedagogical Institute in Leningrad, he has worked as a teacher of Russian literature. His first book, unassumingly entitled *Pervoye vpechatleniye* (1962; First Impression) was apolitical, sensitive, and exhibited a control of the classic metres of Russian verse. Kushner has continued to develop his contemplative, often ironical art. Subsequent volumes of poetry, *Nochnoy dozor* (1966: The Night Watch), *Primety* (1969; Signs), *Zavetnoye zhelaniye* (1973; Secret Wish), *Pismo* (1974; Letter), and *Pryamaya rech* (1975; Direct Speech), demonstrate an ability to confront and assimilate the violence and pressures of the 20th century in disciplined verse. Scenes from life are described as objectively as though they were paintings, and effective use is made of such historical events as the massacre of the Huguenots on Saint Bartholomew's night. His concern with precise, unemphatic language is notable in a literature that has often leaned heavily on rhetoric.   D.T.W.

Kuśniewicz, Andrzej (1904–), Polish novelist and poet, was born in Kowenice, near Lvov. Having studied law at Jagiellonian University and at the School of Political Science, he worked as a diplomat before and after World War II. At the outbreak of the war he was in France, where he joined the Resistance; in 1943 he was arrested and sent to a concentration camp. Since his return to Poland in 1950 he has worked as a journalist and editor. In 1956 he published his first volume of poetry, *Słowa o nienawiści* (Words on Hatred), then *Diabłu ogarek* (1959; The Devil's Stub) and *Czas prywatny* (1962; Private Time). He later turned to prose. In 1961 appeared a novel *Korupcja* (Corruption), followed by *Eroica* (1963), *W drodze do Koryntu* (1964; On the Road to Corinth), *Król obojga Sycylii* (1970; The King of Both Sicilies), *Strefy* (1971; Zones), and *Lekcja martwego języka* (1977; The Lesson of Dead Language).

Kuśniewicz's prose is rich, sophisticated, and philosophical. His works combine keen psychological analysis with broad epic descriptions. *Eroica* is a penetrating psychological analysis of a Nazi officer who gradually suffers complete degeneration. In the novel *Strefy*, Kuśniewicz paints a rich and vivid panorama of eastern Galicia, the land of his childhood, where the cultures and customs of several nationalities were blended.

See: *Słownik współczesnych pisarzy polskich*, series 2, vol. 1 (1977), pp. 570–72.   A.Z.

Kuzmin, Mikhail Alekseyevich (1872–1936), Russian poet, fiction writer, and playwright, was born in Yaroslavl but grew up in Petersburg. He is among the most paradoxical figures in Russian literature. The early works of this "northern Wilde," who was famous for introducing the previously taboo theme of homosexuality into Russian letters, have much in common with the European art nouveau. Yet his "modern" aestheticism coexisted organically with a profound feeling for Russia's ancient past, a fascination with classical antiquity, and a deep interest in Christianity and mysticism (although he was no mystic), drawn from a wide range of sources, among them Plotinus, the Gnostics, Saint Francis of Assisi, Johann Georg Hamann, and Goethe.

A connoisseur of style, Kuzmin was in love with the styles of the past, but everything he wrote was marked by a love for the world of simple things and a joyous, tender affirmation of *this* world, in which man may through love move to perfection. With his vision of beauty as inherent in the world, Kuzmin had nothing in common with the symbolists, with whom he is sometimes erroneously associated: indeed, he can be said to have initiated a revolt against symbolism (*see* RUSSIAN LITERATURE). His works are consistently written in a major key and stamped by an absence of tragic conflict, which makes them unique in the Russian tradition except for the Aleksandr Pushkin period, to which Kuzmin consciously aligned his poetics of "harmonious precision." There is nothing in all of Russian literature, however, like the "seraphic aestheticism" of this master of great art in small forms.

Kuzmin wrote many plays and a mass of fiction. On the one hand, his narrative prose continues the so-called minor line of Russian fiction (Nikolay LESKOV and P. I. Melnikov-Pechersky) with its emphasis on plot and *skaz* narrative; on the other, it attempts to recreate European styles and genres in a highly stylized manner. While his prose works are by no means negligible, his place in Russian literature rests primarily on his achievement as a poet.

The evolution of Kuzmin's poetic style was marked by a drift from an aesthetic of clarity and measure, with a relatively rare use of metaphor—in the collections *Seti* (1908; Nets), *Osenniye ozyora* (1912; Autumn Lakes), and *Glinyanye golubki* (1914; Clay Doves)—to an ever more dense metaphorical style, full of complex, often arcane cultural and personal allusions, best evidenced in *Nezdeshniye vechera* (1921; Otherworldly Evenings) and *Paraboly* (1923; Parabolas). These are best described by the term "hermeticism" as is the poet's final verse collection, *Forel razbivayet lyod* (1929; The Trout Breaks through the Ice), in which some have seen elements of surrealism. His early "poetry of objects" exercised a profound influence on the young acmeists, although he himself denied any identification with them. Kuzmin also published translations and critical works, and was a composer of some talent.

See: J. E. Malmstad, "Mixail Kuzmin: A Chronicle of His Life and Times," in M. A. Kuzmin, *Sobraniye stikhov*, vol. 3 (Munich, 1976), pp. 7–319; V. Markov, "Poeziya Mikhaila Kuzmina," *Sobraniye stikhov*, vol. 3 (1976), pp. 321–426.   J.E.M. and G.Sh.

Kuznetsov, Anatoly Vasilyevich, pseud. since 1969, A. Anatoli (1929–), Russian novelist and short-story writer, was born in Kiev. He first published some short stories in 1946, but achieved recognition with the short novel *Prodolzheniye legendy. Zapiski molodogo cheloveka* (1957; The Continuation of a Legend. Notes of a Young Man), which incorporated his own experience of performing various jobs on building sites, and was one of the first attempts to portray the problems of Soviet youth in a more realistic manner. His most notable work is *Babiy Yar* (1966; Eng. tr. of rev. version, with Soviet-censored passages restored, 1970), a documentary novel based on his childhood memories of Kiev during the German occupation of World War II, and describing the round-up and massacre of the city's Jewish population. His narrative skill is also demonstrated, in a different vein, in the story *Artist mimansa* (1968, in the journal *Novy mir;* the Mime Artist). In 1969, on a visit to London ostensibly to gather material for a book on Vladimir Lenin, he asked for and was given political asylum in England, where he has lived ever since. He brought with him an uncensored copy of *Babiy Yar*, which was published in its full form both in English and in Russian in 1970. An uncensored version of *Artist mimansa*, with comments by the author, was also published (in the New York Russian-language *Novy zhurnal*, 1970). A comparison between the full and censored versions of these two texts offers important insights into the way in which works of literature may be modified by editors and censors before they reach the Soviet public. M.Ha.

Kvaran, Einar Hjörleifsson (1859–1938) Icelandic novelist, dramatist, and poet, was born at Vallanes in east Iceland, the son of a pastor. He went to study political economy in Copenhagen, but instead he joined the Georg BRANDES realists among his compatriots and edited (1882) the periodical *Verðandi*, to which he contributed a rebellious short story. In 1885, Kvaran went to Winnipeg, Canada, where he became an editor of an Icelandic weekly and, in general, a leader of his compatriots. In 1895 he returned to Iceland, there to work as a journalist and political leader until 1906, when he was awarded a governmental grant to devote himself to literature.

The years in Winnipeg mellowed Kvaran's realistic outlook to such an extent that on his return to Iceland he was ready to preach a liberal Christian humanitarianism and to experiment with spiritualism, an apostle of which he soon became. Strongly opposed at first, he and his followers gradually won the day; they still have a considerable following, in spite of attacks from the neo-romanticists (Siqurður NORDAL, 1925) and the Communists (Halldór LAXNESS 1936).

Vonir (1888; Hopes) is the first of a long series of short stories, in which Kvaran is at his best. He is especially fine when he writes about individuals least favored in life, a preferred subject with him. These stories are published in the collections *Vestan hafs og austan* (1901; West and East of the Ocean), *Smælingjar* (1908; The Insignificant), and *Frá ýmsum hliðum* (1913; From Various Viewpoints). In the novels *Ofurefli* (1908; The Unconquerable) and *Gull* (1911; Gold), Kvaran describes the impact of new ideas (the "new" theology) on society in Reykjavik. His later novels, *Sálin vaknar* (1916; The Soul Awakens), *Sambýli* (1918; House-mates), *Sögur Rannveigar* (2 vols., 1919–22; Rannveig's Stories), and *Gæfumaður* (1933; The Fortunate Man), speak eloquently of his humane understanding and breathe the optimism of the convinced spiritualist. Two plays, *Lénharður fógeti* (1913; Eng. tr., "Governor Lenhard," *Poet Lore*, XLIII, 3–55) and *Syndir annara* (1915; The Sins of Others), are partly inspired by the Icelandic struggle for independence, but in *Hallsteinn og Dóra* (1931; Hallsteinn and Dora) the background is spiritualistic. Kvaran has also left a slim volume of poems, thoughtful, melancholy, composed early in life.

As no one else Kvaran represents the optimistic bourgeoisie before World War I. His style is classical—pure, smooth, often argumentative and tinged with humor or irony. But it is somewhat lacking in vigor, color, and manliness. S.E.

Kyrklund, Paul Wilhelm "Willy" (1921–), Swedish short-story writer, novelist, and playwright, was born and educated in Helsinki, Finland, but settled later in Sweden. In 1948 he published *Ångvälten* (The Steamroller), a collection of short stories that shows man's defenselessness in the many cruel situations that fill life. His next book is a kind of philosophical conte that he called *Tvåsam* (1949; Twosome), with a play upon the word. It is a story about a janitor and a chief janitor reminiscent of Franz KAFKA. The men can be seen as two opposed individuals or as conflicting attitudes within one and the same person. The former is browbeaten and unable to adapt himself to life; the latter conforms because he espouses everything that is rule, regulation, or precept—thus he does not have to choose. The influence of existentialist thinking is rather evident here as elsewhere in Kyrklund's work. He feels pity for those who are humiliated and suffer an unjust fate, but compassion is held in check and often concealed by his irony, wit, and cool stylistic perfection. These traits are apparent in the little novel *Solange* (1951), in which a man and a woman, Hugo and Solange, can be interpreted as the chief janitor and the janitor in new disguises. The pattern is repeated in Kyrklund's drama *Medea från Mbongo* (1967; Medea from Mbongo), an original re-creation of a classic marital conflict.

That Kyrklund is a widely traveled man, geographically and culturally, is evidenced also by *Mästaren Ma* (1952; Ma the Master) and by *Polyfem förvandlad* (1964; The Metamorphosis of Polyphemus). The former is a kind of pastiche, the collected words of wisdom of a fictitious Chinese philosopher, Ma. Tension and irony are created by the fact that his words are commented upon by his faithful but unphilosophical wife and by a rather smug scholar of a later period. Kyrklund's later works include *Den rätta känslan* (1974; The Right Feeling).

See: R. Ekner, "*Sagoberättaren Kyrklund*," in K. E. Lagerlöf, *Femtitalet i backspegeln* (1968). J. Stenkvist, *Svensk litteratur 1870–1970*, vol. 3 (1975), pp. 27–29. P.-A.H.

L

Lacan, Jacques (1901–), French psychoanalyst and essayist, was born in Paris. He has been urging a "return to Freud" in opposition to those he terms neo-Freudians—followers of Carl Jung or practitioners of American ego psychology. This means, in part, stressing the role of the unconscious and sexuality. Lacan's fame spread at a time when critics had become disillusioned with the application of psychoanalysis to literature; they welcomed his concern with linguistic phenomena, that is, his linking of Freud's displacement and condensation with metonymy and metaphor. One of Lacan's better-known sayings is that "the unconscious is structured like language." A seminal essay for students of literature is "L'Instance de la lettre dans l'inconscient" (in *Ecrits*, 1966; Eng. tr., *Ecrits/A Selection*, 1977).

Like Jacques DERRIDA (but from a different angle), Lacan attacks the Saussurian concept of sign and the notion of unitary subject. For Lacan, a word is not a sign, but an active nexus of meanings. The implication is that words in a text "work"—as in Freud's dream*work*. Meaning in a text is not determined by the "author," since language can be shown to signify "something quite different from what it says." For Lacan, language serves "to indicate the position of a subject in search of truth." A new truth then requires that the subject find his place within it, but while "one becomes used to reality, one represses truth." Hence a new approach to literary analysis.

Lacan realizes that his theory has applications beyond psychoanalytic practice. By affecting, even slightly, relations between man and his language, he believes that the course of history might be changed "through a modification in the moorings of his being." Lacan's lectures are being published in a 21-volume series called *Le Séminaire* (1973–). The 1973 volume has been translated as *The Four Fundamental Concepts of Psychoanalysis* (1978).

See: special issues of *YFS* 48 (1972) and *L'Arc* 58 (1974); S. Schneiderman, "Afloat with Lacan," *Diacritics* 1, no. 2 (1971); P. Lacoue-Labarthe and J. L. Nancy, *Le Titre de la lettre* (1973); C. Clément, *Le Pouvoir des mots* (1974).   L.S.R.

la Cour, Paul (1902–56), Danish poet, was born in southern Zealand. His unstable childhood—caused by the family's unsettled economy, variable political conditions, and the early death of his father in 1917—forms the basis of the main theme of his writing: uncertainty as an element of his life. This rootlessness, which la Cour tried to replace by experiencing the inner unity of things, first in the meeting with nature and with people and later in poetry, distinguishes *Den galliske Sommer* (1927; Gallic Summer) and *Den tredie Dag* (1928; The Third Day), two early poetry collections written in France. Back in Denmark in 1930, la Cour colored his poetry with his experience of the countryside—his pantheistic attitude made him one of the most outstanding Danish nature poets—and with the threat of a new war. His two main collections of the 1930s, *Dette er vort Liv* (1936; This Is Our Life) and *Alt kræver jeg* (1938; I Demand All), are dominated by feelings of guilt about the fate of Europe as the poet discerns the power of ruthless instinct within himself. Simultaneously, there is in la Cour's work at this time a growing belief in the necessity of change, which in *De hundrede Somre* (1940; The Hundred Summers) reaches messianic perspectives. The result of la Cour's search beyond the intellect is present in his major work, *Fragmenter af en Dagbog* (1948; Fragments of a Diary), a unique mixture of philosophical teaching, poetics, and poetry, which has influenced most of the younger Danish poets. In a series of aphorisms in *Fragmenter,* the unity of existence is expressed in the meeting between rational and irrational forces in art. La Cour's poetry collections of the post-World War II period, *Levende Vande* (1946; Living Waters) and *Mellem Bark og Ved* (1950; Between Bark and Wood), correspond to the world of ideas expressed in the fragments. In these collections, the poet concentrates on the pure image, often an experience of nature with which he is able to identify in his new harmony.

See: O. Kampp Larsen, *På vej med Paul la Cour* (1962); P. Schmidt, *Paul la Cour* (1971).   S.H.R.

Lacretelle, Jacques de (1888–), French novelist, was born in the Burgundian château of Cormatin belonging to his grandfather Henri de Lacretelle, a liberal of the late romantic period and a friend of Alphonse Lamartine. The death of his father, a minor diplomat, and his failure at the bachelor's degree combined to make Jacques de Lacretelle a shiftless young man until, during World War I, he read Marcel PROUST's *Du côté de chez Swann* (1913; Eng. tr., *Swann's Way*, 1922) and eventually went to visit the recluse novelist. Under Proust's influence, Lacretelle produced a somewhat autobiographical novel, *La Vie inquiète de Jean Hermelin* (1920; The Restless Life of Jean Hermelin), which, appearing at a time when the novel of adolescence was in vogue, was an immediate success. He then undertook a longer but never-finished novel, a book he later referred to as "le roman protestant," inspired by his mother's Protestant background. Lacretelle interrupted his writing of this work to publish in the *Revue hebdomadaire* a short story, "La Mort

d'Hippolyte" (1922; The Death of Hippolytus), which, in subject and form, set the style for his classical work. He next expanded an episode of his "roman protestant" into the carefully constructed psychological novel *Silbermann* (1922; Eng. tr., 1923), the story of a Jewish boy who is persecuted by his lycée companions (presumably during the Dreyfus Affair, although Dreyfus is never mentioned) and who dominates the young Protestant narrator until the latter's parents intervene. André GIDE enthusiastically accepted this novel for the *Nouvelle Revue française;* doubtless he was pleased by what he called the *récit* form (first-person narrative) so typical of his own work, by the Protestant background, and by the typically Gidian manner in which the author raised moral issues while avoiding dogmatism.

At a period when Benjamin CRÉMIEUX was imagining a rebirth of classicism, Lacretelle returned to tradition by writing a novel in the manner of the 19th-century realists, *La Bonifas* (1925; Eng. tr., *Marie Bonifas,* 1927), relating the entire life of a homely child who grows into an old maid rejected and persecuted by her provincial town. When this work met only with a succès d'estime, Lacretelle returned to the Silbermann theme with a text that he eventually fragmented (after publishing it as a whole in the weekly *Candide*) to make *Le Retour de Silbermann* (1929; The Return of Silbermann) and *Amour nuptial* (1929; Eng. tr., *A Man's Life,* 1931). *Amour nuptial,* again picking up the story of the Protestant narrator, was highly acclaimed and pronounced Gidian by the critics, its marriage relationship being likened to that in *L'Immoraliste.* Under the urging of Roger MARTIN DU GARD, Lacretelle next undertook a cyclical novel, *Les Haut Ponts* (1932–35; High Bridges), whose four volumes tell the long story of a provincial family that loses its castle but gets it back through the indiscretion of the daughter, only to lose it again because of the grandson's profligacy. Although the setting is Vendée, rather than Burgundy, certain analogies with the history of the Lacretelles at Cormatin can be detected. This admirable novel of provincial mores, with its nostalgic 19th-century atmosphere, was completely out of touch with the 1930s, but it appealed to the reigning critics and won Lacretelle a seat in the Académie Française (1938), of which he became the youngest member and the third person to represent the Lacretelle family. He was highly regarded at this time as a master of French prose and was frequently seen in print. His major collections of short stories are *L'Ame cachée* (1928; The Hidden Soul) and *Histoire de Paola Ferrani* (1929; Story of Paola Ferrani); his principal essays are gathered in *Aparté* (1927; Aside), *Le Demi-dieu ou le voyage en Grèce* (1930; The Demigod or the Trip to Greece), *Les Aveux étudiés* (1934; Carefully Considered Admissions), and *L'Ecrivain public* (1936; The Public Secretary).

Lacretelle has been a director of the newspaper *Le Figaro* since World War II. Immediately after the war, amidst paper shortages, he published in Geneva *Le Pour et le contre* (1946; For and Against), a two-volume novel whose central figure, Olivier Le Maistre, is a writer in whom many autobiographical elements may easily be identified. The themes are frequently Proustian, but the form is more reminiscent of Aldous Huxley's *Point Counter Point* and Gide's *Les Faux-Monnayeurs.* Due to ill-timed publication, however, *Le Pour et le contre* had few readers and has never been reissued in France. Since then, Lacretelle has been satisfied to play the role of a public literary figure. His creative works have been limited to a short Flaubertian novel, *Deux Cœurs simples* (1947; Two Simple Hearts); a published but unproduced play, *Une Visite en été* (1963; A Visit in Summer); and a curious collection of imaginative texts on the frontier between autobiography and the "new novel" (*see* FRENCH LITERATURE), *Les Vivants et leur ombre* (1977; The Living and Their Shadows). Lacretelle also published a brief autobiographical volume, *Le Tiroir secret* (1959; The Secret Drawer), and several collections of articles: *L'Heure qui change* (1941; The Changing Hour), *Idées dans un chapeau* (1946; Ideas in a Hat), *Les Maîtres et les amis* (1959; Masters and Friends), *Portraits d'autrefois et figures d'aujourd'hui* (1973; Portraits of Yesterday and Figures of Today), and *Journal de bord* (1974; Sea Journal).

See: D. Alden, *Jacques de Lacretelle: An Intellectual Itinerary* (1958).   D.W.A.

Laforet, Carmen (1921-), Spanish novelist and short-story writer, was born in Barcelona. She lived in Las Palmas, in the Canary Islands, before moving back to Barcelona, where she studied law and philosophy and letters. Laforet received the Nadal Prize for her first and best novel, *Nada* (1944; Nothing), which initiated the existentialist trend in post-Civil War Spanish narrative. *Nada* reflects the disintegration and bitterness of post-Civil War society by depicting the anguished search of characters who seek to find a meaning for their existence. One of the first literary documents of the moral decay in post-Civil War Spain, *Nada* incorporates neorealistic technique, rapid action, and comprehensive character studies. Laforet's second novel, *La isla y los demonios* (1952; The Island and the Demons), depicts the frustrations experienced by a woman who fails to establish a personal relationship with the world. A woman is also the protagonist of *La mujer nueva* (1955; The New Woman), a novel based on Laforet's conversion to Catholicism. Although this work is technically more innovative than her previous novels, the religious problem is artificially treated. *La insolación* (1963; Sunstroke), the first part of a projected trilogy to be entitled "Tres pasos fuera del tiempo" (Three Steps Outside of Time), presents the conflict of an adolescent with a world alien to any kind of human understanding. Four of her short novels have been collected in *La Llamada* (1954; The Call). *Nada* still remains Laforet's main contribution, as it initiated a renaissance of the novel in Spain.

See: D. W. Foster, "*Nada,* de Carmen Laforet: ejemplo de neo-romance en la novela contemporánea," *RHM* 32 (1966): 43-55; G. Sobejano, *Novela española de nuestro tiempo* (1975), pp. 143-60.   J.O.

Lagerkvist, Pär (1891-1974), Swedish poet, essayist, dramatist, novelist, and short-story writer, was born in Växjö. He carried the religious orthodoxies and provincial conventionalities of this childhood into the aesthetic avant-garde modernism of his maturity. Despite the influences of French painting—naivism, cubism, and fauvism—and the dramatic expressionism of August STRINDBERG on his work, Lagerkvist retained throughout his life an intense interest in the metaphysical questions aroused by the conflict between his inheritance of his grandparents' traditional faith and his own 20th-century skepticism (*see* SWEDISH LITERATURE). Whatever the genre in which he worked and however much his moods and emphases shifted under the stresses of two world wars and the emotional changes from an unhappy first to a satisfactory second marriage, his writing remained committed to an examination of the mysteries of existence, a probing of the nature of good and evil, and an attempt to reconcile or balance the ambiguities of life. His interests and values show a remarkable unity throughout his 40 volumes of work.

Lagerkvist made his initial impact on a Swedish audience as a poet. Although *Motiv* (1914; Motifs)—his first volume of poems and sketches—failed, *Ångest* (1916; Anguish), his second, following the same cubistic principles outlined in his essay "Ordkonst och bildkonst" (1913; Word Art and Picture Art), made a successful assault on the traditional strongholds of 19th-century Swedish romantic poetry. *Ångest* was harsh and strident, and its meters and diction spoke directly to the emotions of a war-torn generation. Throughout Lagerkvist's nine volumes of poetry, cubistic theories shape the structure; his quest for a balance and order to give meaning to existence provides the content. He moved through an angry period in *Kaos* (1919; Chaos) and *Den lyckliges väg* (1921; The Way of the Happy One), probed love in *Hjärtats sånger* (1926; Songs of the Heart), sank to wartime gloominess in *Vid lägereld* (1932; By the Campfire) and *Genius* (1937), and broke into patriotism in *Sång och strid* (1940; Song and Battle) and *Hemmet och stjärnan* (1942; The Home and the Stars). Still his general methods and governing concerns remained the same: an overall dialectic in which poem balances poem, volume responds to volume, in a valiant effort to reach ultimate truth. Even *Aftonland* (1953; Eng. tr., *Evening Land,* 1975), Lagerkvist's final and major achievement in modern Swedish lyric poetry, follows the same pattern and stands at no great distance in these respects from *Ångest.*

Lagerkvist's dramas show a similar unity, whose principles were set form in his *Modern teater* (1919; Eng. tr., *Modern Theater,* 1966). Dissatisfied with Henrik IBSEN's influence on the Scandinavian stage and championing Strindberg's expressionistic opposition to the prevailing naturalism in the theater, Lagerkvist laid out a program for more imaginative drama. He studied a vast array of ancient and modern sources, read intensely the work of Strindberg and the German expressionists, and sought a form that, like his poetry, would permit him full treatment of his metaphysical and ethical interests.

In all, Lagerkvist wrote 13 plays—one a trilogy—which, for all their variety, demonstrate a remarkable unity. Despite their artistic development and response to political and social changes and their reflection of Lagerkvist's changes in emotional states, his dramas cohere around his search into the mysteries of existence, the dualities in life and man's nature: from *Sista mänskan* (1917; The Last Man) to *Låt människan leva* (1949; Eng. tr., *Let Man Live,* 1951). In *Låt människan leva,* Lagerkvist uses a barren stage to set forth the experiences of historical characters through a series of speeches that reveal the continual human struggle to endure against the adversities confronting people in all ages. Love balances hate, good counters evil, and somehow the human spirit manages to survive through the very act of struggling.

The incredible variety of forms that Lagerkvist employed to convey a limited range of themes in his poetry and plays is matched in his fiction. For Lagerkvist, however, prose fiction was the most important of all art forms; he revered it as though it were scripture itself. Although some of his short fiction appeared early in his career, his first important work, *Det eviga leendet* (1920; Eng. tr., *The Eternal Smile,* 1954), was not published until he had already demonstrated his ability in poetry and drama, and his major fiction—the novels—was the work of a mature and accomplished writer. It shares the themes and general interests of his poems and plays, but in craftsmanship it far outdistances the rest of his writing.

Even his shorter novels work through varied forms to give breadth to Lagerkvist's limited scope of fundamental interests. In *Det eviga leendet,* souls in limbo join in a search for God. Their individual voices, distinct in themselves, combine to present humanity's urgent demand for answers to the mysteries of existence. Although dissimilar in technique, *Gäst hos verkligheten* (1925; Eng. tr., *Guest of Reality*, 1936, 1954), raises the same questions. Through a series of tableaux, Lagerkvist's most autobiographical work deals with the gradual unfolding of a youth's discovery of the conflicts between illusion and reality, faith and skepticism. Lagerkvist recreates his own experience of the clash between his grandparents' faith and the modern world's doubts. *Själarnas maskerad* (1930; Eng. tr., *Masquerade of Souls*, 1954) uses yet another means to present a confrontation between man's illusions and the grim reality that he must learn to adapt in order to survive. Duality also marks Lagerkvist's *Bödeln* (1933; Eng. tr., *The Hangman*, 1936, 1954), a novella later adapted for the stage. In *Bödeln*, Lagerkvist explores the relationship of good and evil in the human experience, and, as in all his work, concludes with an acceptance of the fact that people are neither one nor the other, but rather a combination of the two, and that life depends on the proper balance of opposing forces.

Lagerkvist's long novels, written with greater assuredness and considerably more deftness, explore essentially the same ground and arrive at the same destination. As novelist Lagerkvist reached his artistic height, and his first genuine attempt at the genre produced his masterpiece, *Dvärgen* (1944; Eng. tr., *The Dwarf*, 1945). His persona, a dwarf, as twisted in mind as he is deformed in body, presents a view of Renaissance court life whose complexities and ambiguities he interprets simply and absolutely as human baseness, falsity, and hypocrisy. For him human beings are the embodiment of evil. The dwarf regards human bestiality as the totality of human nature, but Lagerkvist makes evident that the dwarf's perspective is a distortion wrought of his own perversity. In contrast, Lagerkvist offers Bernardo, a character resembling Leonardo da Vinci. Capable of cruelty and insensitivity, Bernardo, nevertheless, symbolizes the creative energy of the artistic nature of human beings.

In his later years, Lagerkvist devoted himself primarily to novel writing. From *Barabbas* (1950; Eng. tr., 1951) through *Mariamne* (1967; Eng. tr., *Herod and Mariamne*, 1968), the interest remains the same. Having rejected his forefathers' religion, Lagerkvist sought to replace their God with one that could serve the needs of people today. His last six novels, like a five-act play with an epilogue, dramatize man's quest against the background of the messianic expectations in the centuries around the birth of Christ.

In *Barabbas*, Lagerkvist casts the anguished figure of the convict released from the cross as his protagonist. Barabbas cannot believe, but neither can he escape Christ's shadow. Confused and searching, Barabbas the criminal displays more charity than those who profess Christianity. Along the way, the novel confirms man's need for faith in something, and at the conclusion Barabbas, again on the cross, reaches forth into the darkness to which he delivers up his spirit. Lagerkvist continues what amounts to a dialogue of the soul in *Sibyllan* (1956; Eng. tr., *The Sibyl*, 1958). Whereas in Barabbas skepticism and faith vie with each other within the character, in *Sibyllan* a Christian outcast (Lagerkvist's Wandering Jew) and a profanced Delphic priestess raise their voices in testimony to the desperate need of human beings for faith.

Lagerkvist's quest cycle culminates in the trilogy of *Ahasverus död* (1960; Eng. tr., *The Death of Ahasuerus*, 1960), *Pilgrim på havet* (1962; Eng. tr., *Pilgrim at Sea*, 1964), *Det heliga landet* (1964; Eng. tr., *The Holy Land*, 1966), all collected in *Pilgrimen* (1966; The Pilgrim). The trilogy concerns the passionate quest for the Holy Land

by the unbelieving, yet virtually possessed ruffian soldier Tobias. His narrative brings together the myths of pagan antiquity and primitive Christianity—indicating through their parallelism the similarities in people's needs to affirm their faith in something. Yet when Tobias reaches the Holy Land and dies, it is in the aura of mist and uncertainty, suggesting that for Lagerkvist the arrival is less important than the journey and that if life has significance, it is in living itself.

With *Mariamne*, a kind of coda to these works, Lagerkvist constructs from his biblical material a story that once more demonstrates the intertwining of good and evil in the human experience. Appropriate as a conclusion to his cycle of Crucifixion stories, it also, going back as it does to his earliest theme, recalls the fundamental unity of all Lagerkvist's work, regardless of the genre. With translations into at least 34 languages, his fictional works have gained international recognition. Elected to the Swedish Academy in 1940 and awarded the Nobel Prize for Literature in 1951, he clearly ranks as the foremost Swedish writer of the 20th century. His diaries and notes, edited by his daughter Elin Lagerkvist, were published under the title *Antecknat* (Noted) in 1977.

See: J. Mjöberg, *Livsproblemet hos Lagerkvist* (1954); S. Linnér, *Pär Lagerkvists livstro* (1961); R. D. Spector, *Pär Lagerkvist, TWAS* (1973). L. Sjöberg, *Pär Lagerkvist* (1976); E. M. Ellestad, "Lagerkvist and Cubism: A Study of Theory and Practice," *SS* 45, no. 1 (1973): 38–53.

R.D.S.

Lagerlöf, Selma (1858–1940), Swedish novelist, was born at Mårbacka, the little family estate in Värmland, where she spent her early years and to which she returned in 1907 as a famous author; two years later she was awarded the Nobel Prize for Literature. Her first book was the masterpiece *Gösta Berlings Saga* (1891; Eng. tr., *The Story of Gösta Berling*, 1898). In the folk tales that Lagerlöf listened to while she grew up, she found plenty of exciting adventures and old, fascinating characters in the novel, directly derived from the oral tradition of the countryside, but she had to work hard to make all the pieces fit into an elaborate composition and to find an appropriate style—in a period when the only permissable way of telling a story was the realistic and naturalistic method of Emile ZOLA. Thomas Carlyle's *The French Revolution* helped her to find her form, as well as to legitimate her attitude to her heroes. When the book appeared at the beginning of the 1890s, it happened to be in accordance with the new literary signals from Verner von HEIDENSTAM and Oscar Levertin, and Lagerlöf took her place as the only great novelist in the poetic renaissance of the 1890s. Her next novel, *Antikrists mirakler* (1897; The Miracles of Antichrist), deals with the problems of modern socialism and has its setting in Sicily. At the turn of the century she wrote *Jerusalem I* and *Jerusalem II* (1901, 1902; Eng. tr., 1901-03), a novel of a quite different kind from *Gösta Berlings Saga*. *Jerusalem* is a monumental study of ancient rural traditionalism, confronted with a modern religious revival. The language is simple and powerful, reminding one of the Icelandic sagas, and her attitude to the peasants she admires so much is that of Björnstjerne BJÖRNSTJERNE in his tales of Norwegian peasants.

Lagerlöf published several books of varying character during her long career: short stories, historical tales, legends, for example, *Kristuslegender* (1904; Eng. tr. *Christ Legends*, 1908); a "geography book" for the school, *Nils Holgerssons underbara resa* (1906-07; Eng. tr., *The Wonderful Adventures of Nils*, 1907); and above all—novels. *Körkarlen* (1912; Eng. tr., *The Soul Shall Bear Witness*) is a novel that discusses social problems in the framework of a supernatural folktale. In *Bannlyst* (1918; Eng. tr., *The Outcast*) Lagerlof considered the evils caused by World War I. In the 1920s she wrote a trilogy of novels, *Löwensköldska ringen* (1925), *Charlotte Löwensköld* (1925) and *Anna Svärd* (1928; Eng. tr., of the whole trilogy, *The Ring of the Löwenskölds*, 1931). She also wrote three volumes of autobiography: *Mårbacka* (1922; Eng. tr., 1924), *Ett barns memoarer* (1930; Eng. tr., *Memories of My Childhood*, 1934), and *Dagbok* (1932; Eng. tr., *The Diary of Selma Lagerlöf*, 1936).

See: A. Larsen, *Selma Lagerlöf* (1936); E. Wägner, *Selma Lagerlof*, vols. 1-2 (1942-43); V. Edstrom, *Livets stigar* (1960); A. Gustafson, *A History of Swedish Literature* (1961), pp. 305-16; U.-B. Lagerroth, *Körkarlen och Bannlyst* (1963); G. Brandell, *Svensk litteratur 1870-1970*, vol. 1 (1974), pp. 258-83, extensive bibliography in vol. 2 (1975), pp. 225-26; a series of publications of Lagerlöf is published by the Selma Lagerlöf Sällskapef (society) since 1957.   N.Å.S.

Laín Entralgo, Pedro (1908-), Spanish essayist, was born in Urrea de Gaén, in the province of Teruel, but studied at the University of Madrid. A physician, he holds the chair of the history of medicine at Madrid and has published numerous books in his field, especially on medicine during antiquity. He is also a member of the Royal Spanish Academy of the Language.

Laín Entralgo's primary importance is as a Catholic thinker and essayist on modern Spanish culture. As a Falangist, he was one of the chief contributors to the review *Escorial*, and his writings immediately after the Civil War are characterized by attempt to make the values of traditional Catholic culture viable in Spain. *España como problema* (1949; Spain as a Problem), which includes his controversial essays on *La generación del noventa y ocho* (1945; The Generation of '98), consists of reflections on Spanish culture since the last half of the 19th century. Although in this work he affirms Catholic and Nationalist principles, he also recognizes and attempts to integrate the contributions made by liberal thinkers. Laín Entralgo's later essays, influenced by José ORTEGA Y GASSET and Xavier Zubiri, are often philosophical in nature. Probably his most profound book is *La espera y la esperanza* (1957; Waiting and Hoping), a dialogue between reformed Christianity and existentialism, in which he studies hope as a determinant of human existence. In this regard his *Teoría y realidad del otro* (1961; Theory and Reality of the Other) also deserves mention.

During the 1950s, as Francisco Franco's policies increasingly displeased him, Laín Entralgo became a more liberal thinker. While rector of the University of Madrid, he improved the environment for free intellectual inquiry, and his book *El problema de la Universidad* (1967) is a significant outgrowth of this experience.

See: E. Díaz, *Pensamiento español, 1936-1973* (1974), pp. 27-30, 69-80, 132-41.   E.I.F.

Lalić, Mihailo (1914-), Serbian novelist and short-story writer, was born in Trepča, Montenegro. While a law student at the University of Belgrade, he was often imprisoned for Communist activities. He fought as a Partisan in World War II and spent time in a prisoner-of-war camp. After the war he occupied many positions as an editor and a journalist. In later years he was a professional writer.

Lalić's first book of short stories, *Izvidnica* (1948; Reconnaissance Patrol), attracted the attention of the critics, but he received universal recognition only after publishing

a series of novels—*Svadba* (1950; The Wedding), *Zlo proljeće* (1953; The Evil Spring), *Raskid* (1955; The Break), *Hajka* (1960; The Chase), and *Lelejska gora* (1957, 1962; Eng. tr., *The Wailing Mountain*, 1965). Some of his other works are the short-story collections *Prvi snijeg* (1951; The First Snow), *Gosti* (1967; Guests), and *Posljednje brdo* (1967; The Last Hill), and the novel *Pramen tame* (1970; A Patch of Darkness). His novel *Ratna sreća* (1973; War Luck), is the first in a planned series of novels about the life of the Montenegrins during the last 50 years.

When he writes about World War II, Lalić is not concerned so much with a realistic depiction of fighting as he is with man's behavior toward his fellow man. In *Lelejska gora*, he follows the odyssey of a Partisan leader left behind enemy lines and hunted like a wild animal; freed from the restraints and concerns of civilization, he is faced at last with the naked problem of existence. Although Lalić was long preoccupied with the war and the fratricidal struggle between the Partisans and their opponents in Montenegro, he later indicated a broader interest. In *Ratna sreća*, considered his best work to date, he depicts with epic sweep the Montenegrins' aspirations throughout all of their recent history, both in peace and at war. Here, too, he is very much interested in moral issues and in man's efforts to preserve his humanity.

Through his concern for the universal meanings of existence, his search for moral values, and his understanding of the individual, Lalić has been able to give his voluminous work the dimensions of true greatness, thus emerging as one of the best living Serbian writers.

See: R. Zorić, *Kritički eseji* (1962), pp. 91-108; M. I. Bandić, *Mihailo Lalić: Povest o ljudskoj hrabrosti* (1965); B. Popović, *Romansijerska umetnost Mihaila Lalića* (1972); R. V. Ivanović, *Romani Mihaila Lalicá* (1974).   V.D.M.

Lampo, Hubert (1920-), Belgian (Flemish) novelist, was born in Antwerp. In a long interview with the Flemish writer, Robin Hannelore, *Er is méér, Horatio* (1970; There Is More, Horatio), Lampo suggested that his work could be classified in the following manner: psychological-realistic novels such as *Hélène Defraye* (1945) and *De ruiter op de wolken* (1948; The Horseman in the Clouds); historical novels such as *Don Juan en de laatste nimf* (1943; Don Juan and the Last Nymph) and *De Duivel en de maagd* (1955; The Devil and the Maiden); historical fantasy tales like *Idomeneia en de Kentaur* (1951; Idomeneus and the Centaur) and *De belofte aan Rachel* (1952; The Promise to Rachel); and magical-realistic works such as *Terugkeer naar Atlantis* (1953; Return to Atlantis), *De komst van Joachim Stiller* (1960; The Coming of Joachim Stiller), and *De Goden moeten hun getal* (1969; The Gods Must Have Their Due). To these genres, a fifth one must be added: nonfiction and essays such as *De roman van een roman* (1951; The Novel of a Novel) about the French writer ALAIN-FOURNIER; *De Zwanen van Stonehenge* (1971; The Swans of Stonehenge) about mythological and occult phenomena, as well as De *Kroniek van Madoc* (1975; The Chronicle of Madoc), a search for the author of the medieval tale, "Reinhart and the Fox."

Lampo's birthplace, Antwerp, plays an important role in his epic works. In his autobiography, *De draad van Ariadne* (1967; The Ariadne Thread), which he later reworked under the title *Joachim Stiller en ik* (1978; Joachim Stiller and I), Lampo acknowledged that Antwerp was always present in his dreams. In fact, by subtly combining the world of reality with the world of dreams, Lampo manages to reveal some of the uncanny aspects of reality. Lampo's interest in the writing process comes forth not only in his autobiography but also in the collection of essays entitled *De ring van Möbius* (1966; The Moebius Strip).

Terugkeer naar Atlantis undoubtedly constitutes one of Lampo's soundest achievements. The chief character of the novel is the 40-year-old physician, Christiaan Dewandelaer, who one day comes to the bewildering conclusion that his father did not die 30 years earlier as he had always assumed. Christiaan Dewandelaer starts looking for his father. Yet, neither the old witnesses nor his own guesses help him to reconstruct the truth. Finally, Dewandelaer convinces himself under the pressure of mysterious incidents that life and the world are full of unforeseeable and uncanny elements that give us a glimpse of "another" world longed for by men everywhere. *De komst van Joachim Stiller* and *De vingerafdrukken van Brahma* (1972; The Fingerprints of Brahma) are written in the same vein. The theme of the eternal feminine and of the sister soul also plays a role in some of Lampo's novels such as *Hermione betrapt* (1962; Hermione Grabs) and *De goden moeten hun getal hebben*.

Lampo's early psychological novels (*Hélène Defraye* and *De Ruiter op de wolken*) are most appealing because of their poetic language.

Lampo's pseudohistorical novel, *De Belofte aan Rachel* has often been compared with Marnix GIJSEN's *Joachim van Babylone*. Yet, Lampo focuses on individual cases which he places in a context broader than that of Gijsen. The novel could be termed "pseudohistorical" in so far as Lampo transposes 20th century events into the world of ancient Egypt.   P. van A.

Landolfi, Tommaso (1908–79), Italian novelist, short-story writer, critic, and translator, was born in Pico. A graduate of the University of Florence, where he studied Slavic languages, Landolfi was a distinguished translator of Russian, German, and French literature. His earliest stories were published in the journals *Letteratura* and *Campo di Marte* in the 1930s, when he was regularly linked with the experimentalism of the Hermetics (*see* ITALIAN LITERATURE). As with Carlo GADDA and Eugenio MONTALE, Landolfi's style was often a smokescreen masking his contempt for Fascist society and culture. Although he was by no means a political writer, Landolfi was jailed on the eve of World War II for anti-Fascist beliefs.

Along with Gadda, Landolfi was one of the most important stylists in modern Italian fiction. While charting an independent course, his work reflects a wide range of European influences, including Franz KAFKA, Luigi PIRANDELLO, Marcel PROUST (in the exploration of time recalled) and James Joyce (in the gamut of linguistic reference). The major native influence on Landolfi is Giacomo Leopardi (1798–1837), particularly his *Operette* and the diaristic jottings of the *Zibaldone*. For all his modern sense of the absurd, Landolfi shared with Leopardi an aristocratic respect for language and a taste for inner withdrawal, reflected in the common use of the diary form in his fiction. His talent was suited to the concentrated form of the novella rather than the larger rhythms of the novel, yet the full-length *La pietra lunare* (1939; The Moon Stone), is considered by some to be his masterpiece. This work illustrates Landolfi's characteristic feeling for arcane natural forces, and his partially idolatrous fascination with woman, represented here by the remarkable figure of Gurù, part female, part goat.

Landolfi's central theme is the idea of insufficiency. He deals with man's search for faith, his inability to achieve spiritual grace, and the romantic impulse to sublime love that founders on imperfect social codes. Above all, insufficiency represents for Landolfi the frustration of the artist who cannot find the words to fit his vision. This doctrine is expressed in *La muta* (1964; Eng. tr., *The Mute,* 1971), in which the protagonist murders a dumb girl in order to protect her silent beauty from the defilement of speech. In *Cancroregina* (1950; Eng. tr., *Cancerqueen,* 1971), the lone pilot of a spaceship adrift in the void writes a diary of his fears and feelings, knowing that no one will ever read it. The early *Dialogo dei massimi sistemi* (1937; Eng. tr., *Dialogue on the Greater Harmonies,* 1961) tells of a man's tragic mastery of an apparently nonexistent language. Landolfi is also a critic of intolerance, as in *Le due zitelle* (1946; Eng. tr., *The Two Old Maids,* 1961). This story of a monkey who celebrates mass is more than a surrealistic fantasy, for in it, Landolfi molds his tender reverence for the suffering animal world into a diatribe on religious bigotry, exposing the inability of the established to accept the extraordinary. Because of the difficulties of translation, Landolfi's name has been overshadowed by the more familiar ones of Kafka, Joyce, Pirandello, and Samuel BECKETT. But he is recommended reading for students of the avant-garde as well as for readers curious about the condition of 20th-century man.

See: G. Pampaloni, in *Storia della letteratura italiana,* vol. 9 (1969); E. Sanguineti, in *Letteratura italiana: i contemporanei,* vol. 2 (1975) pp. 1527–39.   H.L.

Lange, Antoni (1861–1929) Polish man of letters, practicing all literary genres from various kinds of poetry to drama, fiction, and science fiction, was born and died in Warsaw. He played an important role in Poland as a gobetween and informant on Western intellectual life, especially poetry. He was the first in Poland to write about the symbolist movement, publishing an essay on it as early as 1887 (reprinted in *Studia z literatury francuskiej,* 1897; Studies in French Literature). Along with popularizing the new trends in French poetry, he also translated the later romanticists, Parnassians, and symbolists, Charles BAUDELAIRE, Theophile Gautier, Stéphane MALLARMÉ, and many others. Subsequently, he extended this activity to other literatures: English and American (Shakespeare, Percy Bysshe Shelley, Edgar Allan Poe), Italian, Spanish, Hungarian, Czech, Russian, and modern Greek. In his untiring drive he also reached for the literatures of the Near and Far East.

Lange the literary activist somehow overshadowed the original, but by no means negligible poet represented by *Poezje* (1895 and 1898; Poems) and many other volumes. He introduced certain motifs (for example, nirvana) for the first time in Polish poetry. The range of his poetry was wide. Besides motifs characteristic of the "moderns," it moves from his early social poems, radical and revolutionary, through poetic orientalism and interest in various religions systems to personal, reflective lyricism of great purity in *Rozmyślania* (1906; Reflections). Lange was also fascinated by the technical aspects of poetry. His famous poem "Rym" (1898; Rhyme) is a virtuoso display of rare rhymes and a treatise on poetry; he experimented with many difficult, elaborate stanzaic and metrical patterns (for example, the Alcaic stanza and the only choridactylic poem in Polish). Lange was one of the first science-fiction writers in Poland, publishing *W czwartym wymiarze* (In the Fourth Dimension) in 1912.

See: W. Borowy, "Antoni Lange jako poeta," in *Dziś i wczoraj* (1934), pp. 196–215; F. Machalski, *Orientalizm Antoniego Langego* (1937); M. Podraza Kwiatkowska, "Ideał jedności doskonałej. O Antonim Langem jako krytyku," *Młodopolskie harmonie i dysharmonie* (1969), pp. 42–95.   T.T.

Langer, František (1888–1965), Czech playwright and novelist, was, next to Karel ČAPEK, the most successful Czech dramatist of the period following World War II. He was born in Prague, to Jewish parents and became a doctor. In 1916 he was taken prisoner by the Russians, but joined the Czechoslovak legions as a member of the medical corps, and took part in their crossing of Siberia. After the war, he continued serving in the medical corps of the Czechoslovak army, eventually becoming a colonel. In 1939 he escaped the Nazi takeover of his homeland by traveling to England. He returned to Czechoslovakia after the war, and in 1947 was awarded the official title of "national artist."

Before World War I, Langer published a collection of short stories, Zlatá Venuše (1910; The Golden Venus), which attracted some attention because of its unusual combination of an exquisite sense of form with a rather crude sensualism. The plays he wrote at that time, Svatý Václav (1912; Saint Wenceslaus) and Miliony (1921; Millions), although skillfully constructed, were unsuccessful.

The war changed Langer's outlook completely: he forgot his early aestheticism and neoclassicism and discovered ordinary man and his moral problems. Velbloud uchem jehly (1923; Eng. tr., The Camel through the Needle's Eye, 1929), his greatest success on the stage, was received with acclaim at home and also in Austria, Germany, and New York. It is clever comedy praising victorious robust health and ordinary common sense. Periferie (1925; Eng. tr., The Outskirts, n.d.), which followed, is drama on the verge of tragedy; in a technique imitating that of moving pictures, Langer tells the story of a murderer who vainly tries to get convicted by the court. Langer subsequently wrote farces and sentimental dramas of little value: Grand Hotel Nevada (1927, original Czech title) is a satire on the absurdities of rich people; Obrácení Ferdy Pištory (1929; The Conversion of Ferda Pištora) concerns a rogue from the slums who is converted against his will; and Andělé mezi námi (1931; Angels in Our Midst) is a sentimental discussion of euthanasia. Only Jízdní hlídka (1935; The Cavalry Watch) represents a new advance. A fairly successful tragedy of collective heroism, the play is drawn from Langer's experiences as a legionnaire in Siberia. Dvaasedmdesátka (1937; No. 72), like Periferie, is an interesting reconstruction of a crime, with the technique of a play within a play used to good effect.

Langer's prose written after World War I is not important. A collection of short stories from Siberia, Železný vlk (1920; The Iron Wolf), reveals his usual constructive skill, but his attempts at humorous sketches and his novel Zázrak v rodině (1929; The Miracle in the Family), are failures. In late life Langer wrote puppet plays. The only important work from this period is a volume of memoirs, Byli a bylo (1963; People and Events), which includes reminiscences about Jaroslav HAŠEK, Josef ČAPEK, and Karel Čapek.

See: P. Buzkova, "F. Langer," in České drama (1932), pp. 196–228; E. Konrad, František Langer (1949).

R.W.

Langgässer, Elisabeth (1899–1950), German poet and writer of fiction, was born in Alzey, Hesse, the daughter of a municipal architect. In Darmstadt she studied to be a teacher, and she taught for 10 years in schools in Hesse, moving to Berlin in 1929, where she was an instructor at the School of Social Work for Women and was a contributor to the literary journal Die Kolonne. In 1935 she married Wilhelm Hoffmann, a philosopher, and in 1936, because of Jewish blood in her family, she was forbidden to publish or work in her profession by Nazi decree.

Although she became a victim of multiple sclerosis, she was forced to work in a clothing factory during World War II, an experience she relates in the story "Die Nähmaschine" (The Sewing Machine). After the war she left Berlin with her family and lived until her death in the village of Rheinzabern.

A devout Catholic, Langgässer was the author of several volumes of religious poetry, including Der Wendekreis des Lammes (1924; The Zodiac Sign of the Lamb). Her novel Proserpina (1932) combines elements from Greek mythology with Christian mystical experience. Her best-known work is the novel Das unauslöschliche Siegel (1947; The Indelible Seal), which relates the conversion of a Jew and the struggle between God and Satan for his soul; the work has been called one of the truly surrealistic novels. The novel Die märkische Argonautenfahrt (1950; Eng. tr., The Quest, 1953) follows the travels of seven people who cross the corpse-ridden countryside after World War II on a pilgrimage search for salvation and a new start for their shattered lives.

Eighteen short stories about the everyday life of the oppressed in Hitler's Germany are found in Der Torso (1947; The Torso). Other works of poetry are Die Tierkreisgedichte (1935; Zodiac Poems), Der Laubmann und die Rose (1947; The Pruner and the Rose), Kölnische Elegie (1948; Cologne Elegy), and Metamorphosen (1949; Metamorphoses). Her poems emphasize human longing for salvation in the midst of a demonic world. Triptychon des Teufels (1932; A Triptych of the Devil) is a collection of stories, as is Das Labyrinth (1949). Her other novel is Der Gang durch das Ried (1936; The Path through the Reeds). Langgässer received the Georg Büchner Prize in the year of her death.

See: J. P. J. Maassen, Die Schrecken der Tiefe: Untersuchungen zu Elisabeth Langgässers Erzählungen (1973).

E.H.S.

Larbaud, Valery (1881–1957), French poet, novelist, essayist, and translator, was born in Vichy the only child of wealthy parents. He was a uniquely self-effacing man of letters who took as much pride in restoring lost literary reputations as in composing his own work. His health was always precarious and he was largely incapacitated, due to aphasia, during his last 22 years. Until then, his life was virtually a "grand tour," as he traveled extensively on the European continent and became fluent in a variety of languages, including English, Spanish, Italian, and Portuguese. Like James Joyce and William Faulkner, whom he admired a great deal, Larbaud began as a poet and later turned to fiction. His career proper was launched with the publication of Poèmes par un riche amateur (1908; Eng. tr., Poems of a Multimillionaire, 1955), a collection of verse indebted to Walt Whitman and to the French symbolists.

Some of the lyricism of Larbaud's early poetry is present in the short novel Fermina Márquez (1911), which concerns a boarding school in France whose international clientele is dominated by South Americans. Adolescent love and pride are the consuming passions of the schoolboys. The Journal de A. O. Barnabooth (1913; Eng. tr., A. O. Barnabooth, His Diary, 1924), a considerably more mature work, is the diary of a South American millionaire. This novel offers a lush itinerary of places seen, of loves experienced, of interior changes undergone. Barnabooth clearly has much in common with Larbaud himself: his considerable fortune, his polyglot talents, and his refined sensibility. The stories collected in Enfantines (1918) concentrate on the intimacies and anxieties of childhood. The final piece in the collection, "Portrait d'Eliane à quatorze ans" (Portrait of Eliane at 14), offers an unusually convincing portrait of a girl at the outer limits of childhood about to negotiate the uncertainties and insecurities of adolescence. The metaphor for Eliane's growing sexual frustration is the drawing of the nude male figure in the *Petit Larousse illustré.*

Larbaud's concern with the erotic carries into what is probably his finest work of fiction, *Amants, heureux amants . . .* (1923; Lovers, Happy Lovers). The three novellas in this collection all have as their heroes young men who pride themselves on their amorous successes. The first of these stories, "Beauté, mon beau souci . . . " (Beauty, My Beautiful Concern), is told in a traditional manner, while the other two, "Amants, heureux amants . . ." and "Mon plus secret conseil . . . " (My Most Secret Counsel), use variations on stream of consciousness. "Amants, heureux amants . . .," dedicated to James Joyce, measures the inward turnings of its hero's mind; his impressions, mainly about the two women in his life, are given to us in sensuous images and occasionally in analogies borrowed from music. "Mon plus secret conseil . . .," dedicated to Edouard DUJARDIN, uses first-, second-, and third-person discourse. The thoughts of the monologist are recorded during a train ride that takes him away from his mistress.

Joyce was central to Larbaud's career not only as an inspiration for certain fictional techniques but also as a subject for critical speculation and translation. Larbaud was the first to offer a "skeleton key" for Joyce's *Ulysses* in a lecture he gave at the Maison des Amis des Livres on Dec. 7, 1921 (published in the April 1922 *Nouvelle Revue française*), and he was involved in the French translation of that book (1929). At Joyce's suggestion, he helped to revive the literary fortunes of neglected writers such as Dujardin and Italo SVEVO. He advanced Faulkner's reputation in France—at a time when he was scarcely known in the United States—by contributing a preface to the French translation of *As I Lay Dying* (*Tandis que j'agonise*, 1934).

Larbaud will probably be remembered longer in France for his translations than for his poetry, fiction, or criticism. A partial list of writers he translated into French includes Samuel Butler, Walter Savage Landor, Francis Thompson, Arnold Bennett, Walt Whitman, Ramón GÓMEZ DE LA SERNA, Gabriel MIRÓ, and Alfonso Reyes. His *Sous l'invocation de Saint Jérome* (1946; Under the Invocation of Saint Jerome) is as fine a book as we have in any language on the role and responsibilities of the translator. Larbaud was accorded many honors during his lifetime, but the finest tribute of all was perhaps the posthumous appearance of his works as *Œuvres de Valery Larbaud* in the prestigious Pléiade edition (1961).

See: J. O'Brien, "Valery Larbaud," *Symposium* 3 (1932): 315–34; G. May, "Valery Larbaud: Translator and Scholar," *YFS* 6 (1950): 83–90; M. J. Friedman, "The Creative Writer as Polyglot: Valery Larbaud and Samuel Beckett," *TWA* 49 (1960): 229–36; F. Weissman, *L'exoticisme de Valery Larbaud* (1966); T. Alajouanine, *Valery Larbaud sous divers visages* (1973).   M.J.F.

Larrea, Juan (1895–), Spanish poet, essayist, art critic, and visionary philosopher, was born in Bilbao. He attended Catholic schools and prepared for a career as a librarian and archeologist. He exercised his profession at the National Historical Archives in Madrid and at the same time began publishing verse in literary magazines such as *Grecia* and *Cervantes.* In 1926 he gave up his career and settled in Paris. He became a friend of Vicente Huidobro and, especially, of César Vallejo, as well as of many of the French surrealists and artists such as Jacques Lipchitz, Juan Gris, and Pablo Picasso. His poetic pro-

duction, written mostly in French and translated into Spanish, appeared in little magazines (*Carmen, Litoral*) and in Gerardo DIEGO's famous anthology, *Poesía española contemporanea* (1932). Larrea wrote all of his verse, as well as some surrealist prose, before 1932.

After the Spanish Civil War, Larrea settled in Mexico, where he was associated with the important Spanish exile publications *España peregrina* and *Cuadernos americanos.* In these and other magazines he published some 100 articles and reviews on history, art, archeology, and literature, with his literary criticism centering on Vallejo. His most important teleological essays date from this period (1939–50). They include *Rendición del espíritu* (1943; The Spirit's Surrender) and *El surrealismo entre viejo y nuevo mundo* (1944; Surrealism between the Old World and the New). His monograph *The Vision of Guernica* (1947) was commissioned by the Museum of Modern Art in New York and is considered one of the best interpretations of Picasso's masterpiece, which Larrea had seen at various stages of its execution.

Larrea lived in New York from 1949 to 1956 as a recipient of several Guggenheim and Bollingen grants for research on the Saint James myth and on the language of the Apocalypse. This research tied in with his earlier interest in pre-Colombian cultures. In fact, Larrea's entire output, including his poetry, is part of an attempt to come into contact with, and decipher, the archetypes of the collective unconscious as they are manifested in all forms of culture, as well as in individual dreams and experiences. He came to believe in a forthcoming mutation in the cultural cycle in which the traditional religious and social institutions of the West, as well as the Western emphasis on individual consciousness, would disappear. A higher form of collective consciousness would emerge, perhaps rooted in the rediscovered primitive cultures of America.

Larrea's collected poems were about to be published in Madrid when the Civil War broke out. His poetry remained mostly unknown until 1963, when Vittorio Bodini, in *I surrealisti spagnoli*, hailed him as "the unknown father of Spanish surrealism." Bodini published the first edition of the collected poems under the title *Versión celeste* (1969), in parallel Italian-French or Italian-Spanish versions. The following year a Spanish edition appeared in Barcelona. Today, Larrea is increasingly recognized as the most genuinely surrealistic Spanish poet, in form as well as in spirit. Since 1956 he has lived and taught literature in Argentina. In 1977 he returned to Spain to lecture on *Guernica.* The same year, he published his *César Vallejo y el surrealismo,* and in 1978 his critical edition of Vallejo's *Obra poética* appeared.

See: D. Bary, *Larrea, poesía y transfiguración* (1976).   J.Cr.

Larson, Alf (1885–1967) Norwegian lyric poet, was born and spent most of his life in Tjøme on the Oslo Fjord, but he also spent several formative years in Denmark and France. He loved the coastal landscape and extolled it in his poetry. Influenced by French symbolism, Larsen's verse has a musical, dreamlike quality. His early collections, the first of which was *Vinterlandet* (1912; The Winter Land), are moody and melancholy. Larsen's later poetry, strongly influenced by Rudolf Steiner's anthroposophy, expresses a religious conception of life. This attitude is represented in such collections as *I vindens sus* (1927; In the Whisper of the Wind), *Jordens drøm* (1930; The Dream of the Earth), *Høsthay* (1958; Autumn Sea), and *Tangkrans* (1959; Wreath of Sea Weed), where nature—the ocean, trees, and animals—takes on a metaphysical dimension, becoming evidence of a reality beyond the one that meets the eye. Lucid and melodious, Larsen's poetry reflects his inquisitive attitude toward life, as well as his profound sense of ultimate harmony.

K.A.F.

Lasker-Schüler, Else (1876–1945), German poet, novelist, and essayist, was born in Elberfeld in the Rhineland, of the famous Schüler family. The Rhineland is one of the sources of her inspiration; others are her deep devotion to Judaism and her ecstatic vision of the Orient. After the dissolution of her first marriage with the physician Lasker, she went to Berlin; became the companion of the prophetlike vagabond poet Peter Hille; and, after his death, married Herwarth Walden, one of the leaders of the expressionist movement and the editor of the periodical *Der Sturm*. She lived, in her writings as well as in her personal life, in a world of wonders, colorful images, and fairy-tale adventure suggestive of the *Arabian Nights* (1912).

The young expressionist generation from 1910 to 1920 recognized in Else Lasker-Schüler a forerunner and a kind of fairy godmother. She, on her part, saw in her many literary admirers some of the strange and fantastic figures of her own wonder world. In some of her books, for example, *Gesichte* (1911; Faces) and *Das Konzert* (1932), is found a variety of literary genres—poems, essays, grotesques, biographies, fairy tales, and autobiographical novellas. At times, as in *Tino von Bagdad* (1907) and *Prinz von Theben* (1914), she transforms herself into this or that figure of the Orient. Her first book of poems, *Styx*, appeared in 1902; her best poems were collected in *Gedichte* (1914; Poems). A later book of poetry is entitled *Die Kuppel* (1925; The Cupola). The Hebraic element became most clearly visible in *Die hebräischen Balladen* (1913) and in the novel *Der Wunderrabiner von Barcelona* (1926; The Miraculous Rabbi of Barcelona). Lasker-Schüler's Rhenish temperament found its strongest expression in an early social play, *Die Wupper* (1908), produced in the expressionistic style in Berlin in 1919, and in the autobiographical story *Arthur Aronymous: Die Geschichte meines Vaters* (1932; Arthur Aronymous: The Story of My Father). There was no room for her in Adolf Hitler's world; she found her second home in Palestine, where she wrote *Hebräerland* (1937; The Land of the Hebrews). After her death appeared a collection of letters to Karl Kraus in 1959, verse and prose from her posthumous papers in 1961, and letters with the title *Lieber gestreifter Tiger* (1969; Dear Striped Tiger).

See: M. Wiener, "Else Lasker-Schüler," in *Juden in der Literatur* (1922); D. Baensch, *Else Lasker-Schüler* (1971); H. W. Cohn, *Else Lasker-Schüler: The Broken World* (1974).

K.Pi. rev. A.L.W.

La Tour du Pin, Patrice de (1911–75), French poet, was born in Paris to a prestigious family of the Sologne region. He felt close ties with his ancestral background and his country. From childhood, the poet sought comfort and inspiration in solitude and in communion with nature. The union of these sentiments with a mystical temperament and poetic talents produced a collection of poetry that is intensely personal and, at the same time, universal. While studying at the Sorbonne and the Institut d'Etudes Politiques, La Tour du Pin was preparing to become a poet. Jules SUPERVIELLE encouraged the young writer to submit *Enfants de septembre* (Children of September) to the *Nouvelle Revue française*; his first collection, *La Quête de joie* (1933, The Quest of Joy), was enthusiastically received by the public.

Like his medieval predecessors, La Tour du Pin seeks grace, the divine love of God, and redemption in his quest for holiness. The spiritual symbolism of *La Quête* animates all of La Tour du Pin's work and like Dante's *Divine Comedy*, the work can be interpreted on several levels. *La Quête* is a search for the essential reality of the self, a discovery of terrestrial joy, an investigation into the sources of poetic creation, and an expression of the poet's yearning for union with the Absolute. In later collections, such as *La Vie recluse en poésie* (1938; The Sequestered Life in Poetry), *La Genèse* (1945; Genesis), *Le Jeu du seul* (1946; The Game of the Solitary Man), *Une Somme de poésie* (1946; A Summa of Poetry), *Le Second Jeu* (1959; The Second Game), and *Lettres aux confidants* (1960; Letters to Confidants), La Tour du Pin traced his spiritual journey toward a personal knowledge of God. *La Genèse* examines the symbiosis of poetic genius and the joy of life. *Le Jeu du seul* and *Le Royaume de l'homme* (The Kingdom of Man) are attempts to discover the goodness and salubrity that exist in the human condition beneath the forces of sin and evil. La Tour du Pin's work as a whole is an affirmation of hope and love and a denial that man is irrevocably doomed to despair because of sin. His participation in World War II and his experiences as a prisoner of war influenced his philosophy of life and his poetry. His attitudes and work were also affected by the writings of Heraclitus, Aeschylus, Plotinus, Charles d'Orléans, John Donne, Novalis, Gérard de Nerval, Giacomo Leopardi, John Keats, Charles BAUDELAIRE.

See: E. Kushner. *Patrice de La Tour du Pin* (1961).

S.H.

Latvian literature or **Lettish literature.** The emergence of modern Latvian literature in the second half of the 19th century coincided with the self-assertion of the Latvian people as a nation after centuries of serfdom. This literary effort was characterized by attempts to develop a modern written idiom and to synthesize the native oral tradition and Western written tradition. By the 1890s the first process was largely completed; the other is still going on in much of Latvian literature.

National romanticism attempted to advance national aspirations by romanticizing the past; western socialist and naturalist ideas, propagated in the 1890s by Jānis Jansons Brauns (1872–1917) and others, opposed these tendencies and found many sympathizers among the younger writers, particularly Eduards Veidenbaums (1867–92), who wrote protest poetry, and Aspazija, pseud. of Elza Rozenberga (1865–1943), who wrote some feminist dramas. Nevertheless, even most of these writers continued to use the ethnic idiom. Thus Aspazija's first important play, *Vaidelote* (1894; The Priestess), is set in the Latvian mythological past, and her husband, Jānis RAINIS wrote folk-song-inspired verse and symbolic dramas. Indeed, Latvian symbolism (which was one way of circumventing tsarist Russia's censorship) derived most of its material from folklore.

A number of diversified literary talents flourished at the turn of the century. Rūdolfs Balumanis (1863–1908), who wrote dramas and carefully constructed novellas, remains unsurpassed as an exponent of psychological realism. Jānis Poruks (1871–1911) revealed his pietist upbringing as well as the influence of Friedrich NIETZSCHE and neoromanticism in his stylistically uneven but emotionally powerful poems and stories. Also at this time, Anna Brigadere (1861–1933) introduced the fairy-tale drama with her play *Sprīdītis* (1903), and Vilis Plūdons (1874–1940) began his career as a master of narrative poetry. Jānis Jaunsudrabiņš (1877–1962) wrote some of his most enduring impressionistic prose early in the century; his collection of childhood reminiscences, *Baltā grāmata* (1914; The White Book), is among the best in this popular genre.

The 1905 Revolution had in Latvia both national and socialist characteristics. It was widely supported in literary circles, and revolutionary poetry thrived. Rainis, the author of *Vētras sēja* (1905; The Sowing of the Storm), and his wife, Aspazija, were forced into exile during the political repression that followed the 1905 Revolution and did not return until 1920. Others, such as Jānis Akurāters (1876–1937), poet, prose writer, and dramatist, and Kārlis Skalbe (1879–1945), poet and master of the literary fairy tale, spent shorter periods abroad. After the 1905 Revolution, debates arose in Latvia proper between the "decadent" advocates of pure literature, led by Viktors Eglītis (1877–1945), and the Marxists, most prominently represented by the novelist Andrejs Upīts (1877–1970).

In the wake of World War I, the emergence of the USSR and an independent Latvia caused a number of splits. A group of Communist writers in exile was formed in the USSR, but its most prominent member, Roberts Eidemanis (1895–1937), and many others perished in Iosif Stalin's purges. So did Linards Laicēns (1883–1938), who had joined the exiles in 1932. Sympathizers who stayed in Latvia fared better. Such recognized Soviet writers as Andrejs Upīts and Jānis Sudrabkalns (1894–1975) continued publishing; the novelist Vilis Lācis (1904–66) and the poet Mirdza Ķempe (1907–74) began their careers during independence. Indeed, that was the time when literary activity reached a high level in Latvia; the ratio of published titles to the population was among the highest in the world.

Although expressionistic tendencies appeared briefly after World War I, particularly in the poetry of Sudrabkalns and Pēteris Ērmanis (1893–1969), style consciousness predominated, especially in the Maupassant-like stories of Jānis Ezeriņš (1891–1924), in the classic, elegant verse of Edvards Virza, pseud. of Edvards Lieknis (1883–1940) and, later, in the poetry and prose of Ēriks Ādamsons (1907–46). Formalism with an ethnic twist is displayed in Jānis Medenis's (1903–61) attempts at neoclassic Latvian meters. The ethnic-national component remained strong and was encouraged, particularly during the authoritarian Ulmanis regime of the late 1930s. The novels of Aleksandrs Grīns (1895–) and Jēkabs Janševskis (1865–1933) romanticized the recent and distant Latvian past, while Jānis Veselis (1896–1962) resurrected mythology in his *Latvju teiksmas* (1943; Latvian Legends). Veselis and Virza also glorified farm life, the latter in his enduring prose epic *Straumēni* (1933; The Straumēni Farmstead). Such "positivistic" tendencies were opposed by postexpressionists and Marxist social critics, among them Sudrabkalns and Laicēns, but most prominently by Aleksandrs Čaks, whose poetry celebrates the city with its underprivileged people. The formal characteristics of his verse—its rhyme, rhythm, and imagery—have influenced succeeding generations of poets.

World War II, the Soviet occupations of 1940–41 and 1945 with their political reprisals and deportations, and the intervening German occupation disrupted many writers' lives and work and opened a chasm between the literature produced in Soviet Latvia and that produced in Western exile. Those leaving Latvia at the war's end included not only established writers like Jānis Jaunsudrabiņš, Kārles Skalbe, and Jānis Veselis, but also many whose activity had just started, such as the lyricists Zinaīda Lazda, pseud. of Šreibere (1902–57), Andrejs Eglītis (1912–), Veronika Strēlerte (1912–), and Velta Toma (1912–). The works of Lazda and Toma are steeped in the folk idiom; Eglītis is best known for his forceful patriotism; and Strēlerte's forte is her fine lyric balance.

Among the novelists who left Latvia were Anšlāvs Eglītis (1906–), Aīda Niedra (1899–1968), Alfrēds Dziļums (1907–), Jānis Klīdzējs (1914–), and the late-starting Jānis Sarma, pseud. of Jānis Kalniņš (1884–). Eglītis, with his penchant for grotesque humor, has become one of the most popular 20th-century Latvian writers. He is also a playwright—he and Mārtiņš Zīverts (1903–), are the most prominent dramatists in exile. Whereas these authors continued writing in Latvian, thus having to face a dwindling audience, Zenta Mauriņa (1897–) turned successfully to the German-speaking public in her humanistic and autobiographical essays and novels. The younger generation of Latvian writers in exile is, for the most part, poetry-minded. In the 1950s such poets as Velta Sniķere (1920–), Dzintars Sodums (1922–), Gunars Saliņš (1924–), Linards Tauns, pseud. of Arnolds Bērzs (1922–63), and Olafs Stumbrs (1931–) started to display literary characteristics steeped in Latvian and foreign traditions. Although the 1960s produced such new poets as Baiba Bičole (1931–), Aina Kraujiete (1923–), and Astrīde Ivaska (1926–), it was primarily a decade of prose. If Gunars Janovskis (1916–) became popular with his realistic novels, Jānis Turbads, pseud. of Valdis Zeps (1932–) created a political stir with an iconoclastic "fairy tale"; Guntis Zariņš (1922–65) was schooled in existentialism; Ilze Šķipsna (1928–) explored man's inner space in her novels and stories, and Aivars Ruņgis (1925–) devoted himself to the problem of the individualist-patriot living among the destructive forces of ideological thinking, exile existence, and mass society. The early 1970s witnessed a new shift to the lyric when the generation of writers born in the 1950s began to publish.

For more than a decade after World War II, literature in Soviet Latvia adhered to the officially prescribed tenets of socialist realism by reliving the battles against the Nazis, being vigilant against saboteurs, eradicating remnants of bourgeois thinking, glorifying the new Soviet regime, and propagandizing Soviet ideology. Liberalization after the post-Stalin "thaw" resulted in new critical attitudes and some formal experimentation. The lyric genre showed the greatest vitality here as well, particularly in the work of Ojārs Vācietis (1933–), Māris Čaklais (1940–), Vizma Belševica (1931–), Imants Auziņš (1937–), Jānis Peters (1939–), and Imants Ziedonis (1933–), the latter poet being the most versatile of them all. The basic tendency among the lyric poets is to develop fully the expressive range of the poetic language itself, absorbing, specifically, colloquial and idiomatic elements to create verse that is simultaneously contemporary and steeped in tradition. Albert Bels's (1938–) prose fiction shows innovative tendencies, but original drama in Soviet Latvia has not flourished; the most promising young playwright is Gunārs Priede (1928–). Despite relaxations, literary activities are monitored by Communist Party ideologues, and writers are reprimanded for deviations from official ideology and signs of national sentiment. Although visits by exiled writers to Soviet Latvia are encouraged, exile literature, with few exceptions, is not permitted to circulate freely, and strict separation is the rule.

See: J. Andrups and V. Kalve, *Latvian Literature* (1954); R. Ekmanis, *Latvian Literature under the Soviets: 1940–1975* (1978).   V.N.

Laurent, Jacques, pseud. of Jacques Laurent-Cély (1919–), French novelist and critic, was born in Paris. He has published a large number of works under at least three well-known pseudonyms. Laurent began his prolific writing career after World War II. Reacting against those who remained traumatized and preoccupied by their war experiences, he and a group of young writers wrote numerous pamphlets that were as brilliant as they were virulent. The targets of his attacks were committed writers, existentialists, and ideological writers in general. For almost 20 years, Laurent edited newspapers and wrote reviews for *Arts, La Table ronde*, and *La Parisienne*, which he founded. At the same time, he was able to write a series of extremely popular novels: *Caroline chérie* (1950; Eng. tr., *Caroline Chérie*, 1952) and its sequels, as well as *Passagers pour Alger* (1960; Passengers for Algiers) and *Hortense* (4 vols., 1963–67), which he published under the pseudonym Cécil Saint-Laurent.

Under the name of Jacques Laurent he published his more serious works, novels in which one detects the influence of Jean GIRAUDOUX and especially Stendhal: *Les Corps tranquilles* (1948, 1949; The Peaceful Bodies); *Le Petit Canard* (1954; The Little Duck); *Les Bêtises* (1971; Foolish Things), for which he received the Goncourt Prize; *Histoire égoïste* (1976; Selfish Story); and *La Fin de Lamiel* (1966), a completion of Stendhal's *Lamiel*. Under another pseudonym, Albéric Varenne, he published such historical studies as *Quand la France occupait l'Europe* (1948; When France Occupied Europe).

Laurent not only wrote under several names; he skillfully imitated the style of other writers. In *Neuf perles de culture* (1952; Nine Pearls of Culture), he superbly parodied Albert CAMUS, Simone de BEAUVOIR, André MALRAUX, François MAURIAC, and especially Jean-Paul SARTRE. In *Paul et Jean-Paul* (1951), Sartre is also ironically shown to be a disciple of Paul BOURGET. Laurent's penchant for parody and polemics has no doubt been responsible for his not having received the critical attention he deserves. Nonetheless, he is one of the most gifted of contemporary writers. Laurent's most recent critical essay, *Le Roman du roman* (1978; The Story of the Novel), synthesizes his concept of the traditional novel as truly creative and unencumbered by partisan ideology.

J.-P.C.

Lautréamont, pseud. of Isidore Ducasse (1846–70), poetic prose writer, was born of French parents in Montevideo, Uruguay. At the age of 10 he was sent to Tarbes and later to Paris to acquire a French education and training in engineering. Little else is known about Lautréamont's life except what can be gleaned from the textual analysis of his two writings, *Les Chants de Maldoror* (1868) and *Les Poésies* (1870).

His more celebrated work, *Les Chants*, is comprised of six cantos in which the narrator and Maldoror, an imaginery bestial creature, are sometimes alter egos and sometimes a single subjectivity set on doing evil to mankind and its creator, "who should not have created such a vermin." In a moving, long-winded, accentuated prose, the self-styled count takes the reader through nocturnal visions of murder, rape, and copulations that violate the barriers of the species. The *Chants* depicts the confrontation of man with an existing but frightful deity whose omnipotence is accepted but decried. This rebellion at a critical moment in human civilization marks the cracking of the anthropocentric universe, foreshadowing the notion of the absurd. The weapons that Lautréamont uses to gird himself against the vulnerability of the human condition are those of masochism, sarcasm, and sadism. He manifests a sublime anguish that pierces through the rhinoceros skin he has alledgedly acquired. In Lautréamont's web of ruthless analogies, man is reduced on the Darwinian scale to the level of "brother to the toad." The concept of beauty is subjected to the same vilification. One analogy affecting the notion of the beautiful—"beautiful as the fortuitous meeting of a sewing machine and an umbrella on a dissection table"—was to be taken out of

context by the surrealists (*see* FRENCH LITERATURE) and repeatedly quoted as the paradigm of their analogical system, based on the juxtaposition of distant realities. With ideas such as this, Lautréamont introduced a gauge of beauty compatible with an insensitive world: beauty of the grotesque, the sanguinary, the monstrously incongruous. His writing was self-destructive as he probed mercilessly the fibers of the human psyche.

Immediately after publication, *Les Chants de Maldoror* was withdrawn by its shocked publisher. In what was presumably a last-minute reversal of his subversive writing, Lautréamont wrote a series of aphorisms, entitled *Les Poésies,* in which he extolled the good and the traditionally beautiful. The authenticity of this stance, however, remains highly contestable. The dictums may well have been written in blood, belying their overt significations as a final demonstration of black humor.

Lautréamont has often been classified as a latter-day romanticist, his nocturnal visions compared to those of Edward Young (1683–1765) and his apostrophes to the sea to those of James Macpherson's (1736–96) Ossian poems. The surrealists, however, have considered him their major precursor because of his sense of the unconscious forces in man and beast and because of his power to convey the irrational through logical language. They have also identified with his spirit of rebellion, which extended beyond the social to the metaphysical. A number of surrealist artists, including Salvador Dali, have illustrated his work.

See: L. Pierre-Quint, *Le Comte de Lautréamont et Dieu* (1928, 1967); M. Jean and A. Mezei, *Lautréamont* (1947); G. Bachelard, *Lautréamont* (1956); P. Zweig, *Lautréamont: The Violent Narcissus* (1972).   A.B.

Lavelle, Louis (1883–1951), French philosopher, was born in Saint-Martin-de-Ville-réal (Périgord). He devoted his life to the teaching of philosophy and the writing of books, the latter ranging from specialized research to popular essays that have been read by a very wide public. He taught in provincial French high schools, at the Sorbonne, and, after 1941, at the Collège de France, where he held the famous chair of philosophy, and as such was Henri BERGSON's successor. In 1934 he founded, with René LE SENNE, the movement "Philosophie de l'Esprit" and directed the series connected with it, in which for more than 20 years most of the French philosophers of that period were published. The movement was a definite effort to react against scientific imperialism and positivistic philosophy, which then dominated the Sorbonne and the French universities. It invited a revival of metaphysical meditation following the great tradition of French spiritualism represented in the last three centuries by Nicolas de Malebranche, Marie-François-Pierre Maine de Biran, Jean Ravaisson-Mollien, Octave Hamelin, and Bergson.

Lavelle's own philosophy was a metaphysical optimism for which the human act and personal expression constitute participation in the universal being and the eternal value of God. Such a philosophy is not a form of dogmatism, but a spiritualistic experience that reunites knowledge and prayer, while human consciousness participates in the total and infinite presence of the spirit. Among Lavelle's most specialized books are *De l'être* (1928; Eng. tr., *Introduction to Ontology*, 1966), *La Présence totale* (1934; The Total Presence), *De l'acte* (1937; Concerning the Act), *Du temps et de l'éternité* (1945; Concerning Time and Eternity), and *Traité des valeurs* (1951; Treatise on Values). Among his popular essays, written in a style that recalls François Fénelon's elegance and suppleness, are *La Conscience de soi* (1933; Consciousness of Self), *Le Moi et son destin* (1936; The

Ego and Its Destiny), *L'Erreur de Narcisse* (1959; Eng. tr., *The Dilemma of Narcissus*, 1973), *Le Mal et la souffrance* (1940; Eng. tr., *Evil and Suffering*, 1963), and *Les Puissances du moi* (1948; The Powers of the Ego).

E.M.-S.

Lavrenyov, Boris Andreyevich (1891–1959), Russian short-story writer and dramatist, was born in Kherson, graduated from Moscow University, and fought in both World War I and the Russian Civil War.

Lavrenyov is at his best in his early stories such as "Veter" (1924; Wind); "Sorok pervy" (1924; The Forty-First); and "Rasskaz o prostoy veshchi" (1924; Eng. tr., "Such a Simple Thing," Moscow n.d.), which are all set against a background of the Russian Revolution or Civil War. These stories are filled with action, their plots are complex, and their characters are portrayed romantically. A recurrent theme in most of his stories of the 1920s, as well as in his popular play *Razlom* (1928; The Breakup), is the role of the intelligentsia in the Revolution and under the new regime. Lavrenyov's talent declined in later years, reaching its nadir in plays such as *Golos Ameriki* (1949; The Voice of America) and *Lermontov* (1953).

See: I. Vishnevskaya, *Boris Lavrenyov* (1962).

S.E.R.

Laxness, Halldór (1902–), Icelandic poet, dramatist, essayist, and novelist, was born in Reykjavik. When he was three years old, his parents moved to Laxnes, a farm in nearby Mosfellssveit parish; in addition to his farming, the father worked as a road construction foreman. By his own account, in his autobiographical *Í túninu heima* (1975; In the Hayfields of Home), Laxness began to try his hand at writing as a child. He first left home to study music, then attended a special secondary school (gymnasium) in Reykjavik but did not graduate. Instead, he dedicated himself to writing, publishing his first novel, *Barn Náttúrunnar* (1919; Child of Nature), at the age of 17.

Following this, he stayed for a time at the Benedictine monastery of Saint Maurice de Clervaux in Luxembourg, where he studied and led a life of religious devotion; he was received into the Catholic Church in 1923. Laxness spent the next year at a Jesuit-run school in England—Champion House in Osterley, Middlesex—and then alternately in Iceland and on the continent of Europe, including Sicily, where he worked on *Vefarinn mikli frá Kasmír* (1927; The Great Weaver from Kashmir). A tour de force, this broadly based novel tells of the struggle of a young man torn between his religious faith and the pleasures of the world; although he rejects the latter for his calling, he pays a high price. The book is clearly influenced by most of the artistic and cultural currents that placed their mark on Western Europe in the years after World War I, although Laxness's writings from this period specifically bear the imprint of surrealism and Catholic mysticism and, as for individual figures, the influence of August STRINDBERG and Otto Weininger (1880–1903). The style and narrative technique of *Verfarinn mikli frá Kasmír* made a clean break with the epic-realistic tradition of Icelandic fiction—a tradition that Laxness, however, was to readopt in the next phase of his literary career in which he wrote his broad novels of social criticism. Because Laxness abandoned the Catholic faith during the writing of this first major effort of his, *Vefarinn* signals the end of the first stage in his development, which might be described as bourgeois psychological fiction.

In 1927, the year when *Vefarinn* appeared, Laxness, went to the United States, where he stayed until 1929.

This experience caused a profound change in his ideological outlook. He observed glaring social inequities and turned to socialism, as he claims in the autobiographical *Skáldatími* (1963; Poets' Time)—more because he saw the unemployed poor in parks than from reading socialist writings. While in the United States, he, nevertheless, became acquainted with the novel of social concern through the works of authors like Upton Sinclair and Theodore Dreiser. Laxness's newly adopted socialist views soon found strong expression in a collection of essays entitled *Alþýðubókin* (1929; The Book of the Plain People). In the next year he published of his only volume of verse: *Kvæðakver* (1930; A Sheaf of Poems), which evinced more pronounced surrealist effects than any other book of Icelandic poetry from this period.

Although Laxness has lived in Iceland since 1930, he has also traveled extensively, and some of his many stays in Europe have been of long duration, so that his works have been written in foreign parts as well as at home. His permanent residence is at Gljúfrasteinn in Mosfellssveit, the parish of his youth.

Laxness's fiction dealing with social issues began with *Þú vínviður hreini* (1931; You Pure Vine) and its sequel, *Fuglinn í fjörunni* (1932; The Bird in the Shore; Eng. tr. of both, *Salka Valka*, 1936). The scene is a small Icelandic fishing village early in this century, where an awakening labor movement is pitted against merchants and fishing entrepreneurs. In *Sjálfstætt fólk I–II* (1934–35; Eng. tr. *Independent People*, 1945), Laxness turned to the life and condition of Icelandic farmers; the central character is the peasant Bjartur, who, although forever doomed to be the slave of prosperous farmers and their commercial interests, stubbornly views himself as the most independent person on earth. The author takes a still another tack in a subsequent tetralogy comprised of *Ljós heimsins* (1937; The Light of the World), *Höll summarlandsins* (1938; The Palace of Summer Land), *Hús skáldsins* (1939; The Poet's House), and *Fegurð himinsins* (1940; The Beauty of the Sky; Eng. tr. of all four vols., *World Light*, 1969). Here, the protagonist is Ólafur Kárason, a hapless folk poet in Iceland, whose obvious faults do not prevent him from winning the reader's sympathy.

By 1940, and especially later, Iceland's independence and its place in the world became a central theme in Laxness's essays, a theme that also gave rise to a trilogy of historical novels with a focus on a peasant living around 1700: an archetypal Icelander locked in a dubious contest with oppressive authorities and foreign power. On one level, the work—consisting of *Íslandsklukkan* (1943; Iceland's Bell), *Hið ljósa man* (1944; The Bright Maiden), and *Eldur í Kaupinhafn* (1946; Fire in Copenhagen)—symbolizes the eternal struggle of the Icelandic nation for its existence in the past. But it also points to the present and the future, implying a warning concerning the fate of Iceland in a world of conflict between large powers, particularly in the context of foreign military bases. The facilities made available to the United States became an overriding issue in Icelandic politics soon afterwards, and Laxness's *Atómstöðin* (1948; Eng. tr. *The Atom Station*, 1961) assails bourgeois politicians for having sold out to American interests.

Laxness wrote one more novel that belongs to the social-issue phase of his career, *Gerpla* (1952; Eng. tr., *The Happy Warriors*, 1958), a satirical work with a setting in the Middle Ages and deriving from *Fóstbræðra Saga* and Snorri Sturluson's *Heimskringla*, among other sources. Still the author addresses himself to contemporary realities: the Cold War and the worship of dictators like Adolf Hitler and Iosif Stalin. The novel is specifically an attack on blind political loyalties and on warfare and its atrocities. Imbued with a pacifist spirit, *Gerpla* describes the tragic fate of a poet victimized by his belief in the power and glory of a worldly ruler.

Although all the major works of fiction written by Laxness from 1930 to 1952 have a pervasive element of sharp and alert social criticism, they also contain various strands that foreshadow his later emphases, such as folk wisdom molded by Icelandic tradition and Oriental philosophy akin to the Taoism of Lao-tze, a school of thought of crucial importance for him.

Laxness was awarded the Nobel Prize for Literature in 1955, an honor that led to a world tour in 1957 and 1958, at the invitation of the United States, China, India, and others. In Laxness's writings since that time, social criticism has yielded to philosophical concerns and closer focusing on individual problems. The first such work, *Brekkukotsannáll* (1957; Eng. tr., *The Fish Can Sing*, 1966), has as its themes the destructive effect of faked renown and the danger threatening the artist who serves any interest outside his creation. On the other hand, the Taoist ideal—to avoid aggression and to help all—is held up as a means of salvation.

Paradisarheimt (1960; Eng. tr., *Paradise Reclaimed*, 1962) traces the experiences of a convert to a new religion, who moves to another part of the world to seek the paradise that has been promised him. Unable to find it there, he returns to his abandoned farm in Iceland, realizing that the most important human task is to cultivate the place of one's own origin, a conclusion recalling Voltaire's *Candide,* a work Laxness translated into Icelandic. He has also translated fiction by Ernest Hemingway and Gunnar GUNNARSSON.

In his writings from the last two decades, Laxness has persistently voiced his skepticism of all systematized ideologies, glorifying instead undogmatic protagonists—his own mouthpieces, it seems; as a rule, they are people who have separated themselves from the world by refusing to participate in the mundane affairs of ordinary human beings.

Laxness wrote little fiction during the 1960s but turned to drama instead—a genre he had actually worked in much earlier, although on a minor scale: *Straumrof* (1934; Short Circuit) and *Silfurtúnglið* (1954; The Silver Moon). But now the several plays appeared in a rapid succession: *Strompleikurinn* (1961; The Chimney Play), *Prjónastofan Sólin* (1962; The Sun Knitting Shop), and *Dúfnaveislan* (1966; Eng. tr., *The Pigeon Banquet,* 1973). His plays are typically humorous and of satirical intent, showing obvious influences from Bertolt BRECHT and the theater of the absurd. They have, however, not matched his fiction in popular appeal.

Collections of essays by Laxness have appeared at a steady rate throughout his entire career, and he has been an enthusiastic proponent of intellectual debate in Iceland. In his later years, he has published numerous essays within the general sphere of medieval studies and early Icelandic history. By the late 1960s, he had resumed his writing of fiction. His recent novel *Kristnihald undir Jökli* (1968; Eng. tr., *Christianity at Glacier,* 1972) is heavily influenced by Taoism, as is the documentary novel *Innansveitarkronika* (1970; A Parish Chronicle). *Guðsgjafarþula* (1972; A Rhyme of God's Gift) has a setting strongly resembling that of *Salka Valka*; the action is, however, seen from a diametrically opposed vantage point, and the author's attitude has changed from radical social criticism to liberalism of a mildly conservative cast.

Halldór Laxness is by far the most famous Icelandic writer of the 20th century. His creative powers are unequaled: no other author has dealt so imaginatively with practically all aspects of human life in Iceland, and he has at the same time, more than anyone else, given direction to the self-understanding and the general outlook of his countrymen of today. He is an absolute master of style. His adaptability has few parallels anywhere. Time and again he has shifted his ideological position in drastic ways, and his entire career as an author has been a restless search for whatever it takes to create the ultimate text. But despite the many facets of his art, all works by Laxness carry one unchanging signature, namely, the bantering wit of the true humanist.

See: P. Hallberg, *Den store vävaren* (1954), and *Skaldens hus* (1956); *Scan* (special issue devoted to the work of Halldór Laxness: supplement [May 1972]; *Sjö erindi um Halldór Laxness* (1973); P. Hallberg, *Halldór Laxness* (1971), and *Halldór Laxness* (1975). S.S.H.

Léautaud, Paul (1872–1956), French essayist and memorialist, was born in Paris, the son of an unwed actress who abandoned him to the care of his father, a prompter at the Comédie-Française. The early deprivation of affection left an indelible mark on young Paul, who grew up in Paris as a keen and suspicious observer of human frailty. He developed an appreciation of 18th-century skepticism and direct expression in the manner of Stendhal. He wrote poetry for a while (1893–95), and then produced his *Essais de sentimentalisme* (1897–98; Essays toward Sentimentalism). Together with his friend Adolphe van Bever, Léautaud edited the highly successful—and influential—*Poètes d'aujourd'hui* (1900, 1908, 1929; Contemporary Poets), although he later disclaimed any reliance on the values of poetry. He became known for the frankness of his autobiographical novel *Le Petit Ami* (1903; The Paramour), which related his upbringing and his meeting with and incestuous attraction towards his mother, who was by then married. A candidate (unsuccessfully) for the Goncourt Prize, *Le Petit Ami* is a small masterpiece of observation, suggestion, and interpretation.

Léautaud's search for "authenticity" led him to prefer the spontaneously written essay or chronicle. Secretary of the *Mercure de France* (1908–41), he also reviewed plays under the pseudonym Maurice Boissard; when the play failed to interest him, he wrote about himself or about cats—he was undoubtedly one of the chief feline fanatics of the 20th century. But the bulk of his observations, experiences, and opinions—aside from occasional *plaquettes* (small, thin books)—went into his *Journal littéraire* (18 vols., 1954–56; index, 1966; Literary Journal). Some of his sexual experiences and feelings, however, were reserved for the *Journal particulier* (2 vols., 1956; Private Diary). These jottings, sometimes inconsistent in opinion, sometimes boring in their repetitions and details, are his attempt to be himself without artifice. In this work, Léautaud's independent and frank judgment won him a succès de scandale. His public fame, however, was based mainly on the series of radio interviews (1950–51) with Robert Mallet. These *Entretiens* were published in unexpurgated form in 1951. A complex character to some, yet simple to others, Léautaud was himself the chief preoccupation of his writings.

See: R. Mahieu, *Paul Léautraud: la recherche de l'identité, 1872–1914* (1975); S. S. Weiner, "Sincerity and Variants: Paul Léautaud's *Petit Ami,*" *Symposium* 14, no. 3 (1960): 165–87. S.W.

Lec, Stanisław Jerzy (1909–66), Polish poet, satirist, and translator, was born in Warsaw into a rich Viennese-Galician Jewish family. He studied law and Polish literature in Lvov, and his poems first appeared in 1929. From 1941 to 1943 he was in a German concentration camp, from which he escaped to join the Aymia Ludowa, the Communist underground army. In 1945 he was editor of the satirical paper *Szpilki* in Łódź, and from 1946 to 1950 he worked in the Polish diplomatic service in Vienna. He emigrated to Israel in 1950 but two years later returned to Poland, where he was blacklisted by the authorities; the ban on him was lifted only during the "thaw" in 1956. Although he published several collections of short lyrical and satirical verse before as well as after World War II, the best of which is collected in *Wybór wierszy* (1968; Selected Poems), Lec became internationally known only thanks to his witty, mordant, "philosophical" aphorisms printed in 1956 and later in a number of Warsaw literary journals. These aphorisms, published in book form as *Myśli nieuczesane* (1957; Eng. tr., *Unkempt Thoughts,* 1962) and *Myśli nieuczesane nowe* (1964; New Unkempt Thoughts), were expressions of the "collective wisdom" of the Polish intelligentsia, which, from 1939 onwards, had found that traditional modes of thinking and reasoning became inadequate when confronted with naked terror or the peculiar dialectics of totalitarianism. Lec was a master of paradox; he used wry humor and irony to deflate the demands of those who manipulate life in order to justify "historical necessity." G.G.

Lechoń, Jan, pseud. of Leszek Serafinowicz (1899–1956), Polish poet, satirist, and literary critic, the youngest member of the "Skamander" group (see POLISH LITERATURE), was born in Warsaw and died in New York. He wrote altogether four small volumes of poetry. Two appeared after World War I, *Karmazynowy poemat* (1920; A Crimson Poem) and *Srebrne i czarne* (1924; Silver and Black). Two more were published after a gap of almost 20 years, *Lutnia po Bekwarku* (1942; Bakfark's Lute) and *Aria z kurantem* (1945; Aria with Chimes). Lechoń's *Poezje zebrane* (1954; Collected Poems) comprise 118 items in slightly over 160 pages, but they represent poetry of rare intensity, utmost condensation, and impeccable formal perfection.

Lechoń's first collection of only eight longer poems voiced simultaneously a rebellion against the subservience of poetry to the national cause and the deepest attachment to the romantic tradition. At the same time Lechoń was active as a venomous satirist, inspired by staunch, uncompromising patriotism as, for example in *Rzeczypospolita babińska* (1920; The Republic of Babin). His second prewar volume of poems, *Srebrne i czarne,* is an extreme expression of philosophical pessimism, hopelessness, and the absurdity of existence, but this vision is presented with surprising restraint and a rigorous precision of poetic diction.

Lechoń's second creative phase seems, on the surface at least, more uniform. It betrays a passionate commitment to the fate of the poet's fatherland and an obsessive preoccupation with personal sorrows. These feelings are expressed in an idiom crowded with cultural, historical, and literary allusions, characterized by crystalline transparency and a complete control over verse rhythm.

Lechoń was active as a critic of literature. In the first months of World War II, he delivered in Paris a series of lectures that were published in book form as *O literaturze polskiej* (1942; About Polish Literature). He likewise tried to tackle political and ideological problems in a large essay about the role of the United States in the postwar world, *Aut Caesar aut nihil* (1955; Eng. tr., *American Transformations,* 1959).

After Lechoń's suicide in New York, three volumes of his diary was published, embracing the years 1949 to 1951.

See: M. Grydzewski, ed., *Pamięci Jana Lechonia* (1956); Z. Folejewski, "Jan Lechoń's Poetic Work," *PolR* 9, no. 4 (1956): 3–8; *Słownik współczesnych pisarzy polskich,* vol. 2 (1964), pp. 329–33. T.T.

Le Clézio, Jean-Marie G. (1940–), French novelist and occasional critic, was born in Nice, where he teaches and still lives. He shuns Parisian literary life. The son of a British father, Le Clézio has close connections with England, and he has traveled in Nigeria, Thailand, Mexico, Japan, and the United States. His first novel, *Le Procès-Verbal* (1963; Eng. tr., *The Interrogation,* 1964), published when he was 23, was awarded the Renaudot Prize. *La Fièvre* (1965; Eng. tr., *Fever,* 1966) followed, a brilliantly original collection of 10 short pieces. Le Clézio has since published several novels in rapid succession: *Le Déluge* (1966; Eng. tr., *The Flood,* 1968), *Terra amata* (1967; Eng. tr., *Terra Amata,* 1969), *Le Livre des fuites* (1969; Eng. tr., *Book of Flights,* 1971), *La Guerre* (1970; Eng. tr., *War,* 1973), *Les Géants* (1973; Eng. tr., *The Giants,* 1975), and *Voyages de l'autre côté* (1975; Trips on the Other Side). He has also written two essays, *L'Extase matérielle* (1967; Material Ecstasy) and *Haï* (1971), which describes his encounter with the Panamanian Indians, and *Les Prophéties du chilam Balam* (1976).

Le Clézio is, passionately, a man of his time. Aware of the technical experiments introduced by the novelists of the 1950s, he makes free use of verbal collages from the world of reality, meticulous enumerations and descriptions of everyday objects, and shifting registers in narrative tone (epic, lyric, visionary, satiric, familiar) and mode (inserted dialogue, letters, notes, diary). His indeterminate characters are loners who venture forth in wonder, pain, doubt, or terror on unspecified quests in a stupefying world of supermarkets, airstrips, traffic lanes, sirens, television, plastics—in other words, our world. Le Clézio has single-mindedly pursued one adventure: to express what it means to be alive, to hear, touch, feel, see, apprehend a life, the strangeness of which he tries to grasp, convey, and elucidate. A richly dynamic flow of language sustains the enterprise of a writer who wants his works to convey "the joy and pain of mortal things."

See: P. Lhoste, *Conversations avec J.-M. G. Le Clézio* (1971). G.Br.

Leduc, Violette (1913–72), French novelist, was born in Paris. Her works, including *L'Asphyxie* (1946; Eng. tr., *In the Prison of Her Skin,* 1970), *Ravages* (1955), *La Vieille Fille et le mort* (1958; The Old Maid and Death), and *L'Affamée* (1948; The Starved Woman), are highly personal accounts of a woman's life in a vicious society dominated by men, a cry of rage wrung from the desperate loneliness of a lesbian imprisoned in her sexuality. Leduc is best known for her autobiographical *La Bâtarde* (1964; Eng. tr., *La Bâtarde: An Autobiography,* 1965), a realistic, sometimes shocking self-portrait reminiscent of Jean-Jacques Rousseau's *Confessions*. The work is also a fascinating depiction of an era and of the author's friends, especially Maurice Sachs. Leduc's other works include *The Golden Buttons* (1961), *La Femme au petit renard* (1965; Eng. tr., *The Lady and the Little Fox Fur,* 1967), *Thérèse et Isabelle* (1967; Eng. tr., *Thérèse and Isabelle,* 1968), and *La Folie en tête* (1970; Eng. tr., *Mad Pursuit,* 1971). D.Br.

Le Fort, Gertrud, Freiin von (1876–1971), German poet and novelist, was born in Minden of an aristocratic Huguenot family that had found refuge in Germany. She enjoyed a thorough university training in history and philosophy. After editing the theological writings of her teacher, the Protestant philosopher Ernst Troeltsch of Heidelberg, in 1925, she entered the Catholic Church. Her magnificent *Hymnen an die Kirche* (1924; Eng. tr., *Hymns to the Church,* 1937) had already been published. In the novel *Das Schweißtuch der Veronika* (1928; Eng. tr., *The Veil of Veronica,* 1932), she portrayed within a single German household living in modern Rome four typical attitudes toward the church, the "good pagan," the devout daughter of the church, and two types of conversions. Her two historical novels, *Der Papst aus dem Ghetto* (1930; Eng. tr., *The Pope from the Ghetto,* 1934) and *Die magdeburgische Hochzeit* (1939; Wedding in Magdeburg), and one historical novella, *Die Letzte am Schaffott* (1931; Eng. tr., *The Song at the Scaffold,* 1933), combine the fruits of extensive research with deep poetic insight and great literary gifts. Her *Hymnen an Deutschland* (1932; Hymns to Germany) contains a Christian appeal to the nation. She was also the author of essays, such as *Die ewige Frau* (1934; The Eternal Woman) and *Das Reich des Kindes* (1934; The Kingdom of the Child). Her other works include notebooks and reminiscences in 1951, *Die Krone der Frau* (1952; The Crown of Womanhood), *Gelöschte Kerzen* (1953; Snuffed Candles), *Am Tor des Himmels* (1954; At the Gate of Heaven), a Christmas book (1954), *Die Brautgabe* (1955; The Dowry), a volume of poems in 1958, *Die letzte Begegnung* (1959; The Last Encounter), hymns to the church in 1961, memoirs in 1965, and *Der Dom* (1968; The Cathedral). Four novellas appeared in translation in *The Judgment of the Sea* (1962).

See: T. Kampmann, *Gertrud von Le Fort* (1935); I. O'Boyle, *Gertrud von Le Fort: Introduction to Her Prose Work* (1964); G. Kranz, ed., *Gertrud von Le Fort: Leben und Werk* (1976). C.E.F. rev. A.L.W.

Leino, Eino, pseud. of Armas Eino Leopold Lönnbohm (1878–1926), Finnish poet, novelist, playwright, essayist, journalist, and translator, was born in Paltamo. While still in school he began writing poems, publishing his first book, *Maaliskuun lauluja* (1896; Songs of March), at the age of 18. With his brother, the poet Kasimir Leino, he edited a cultural review, *Nykyaika,* and joined the editorial staff of the liberal newspaper *Päivälehti* (later *Helsingin Sanomat*).

Eino Leino was a highly versatile poet and the most eminent representative of the generation that introduced "national neoromanticism" into Finnish literature in the 1890s (*see* FINNISH LITERATURE). He was influenced by Finnish folk songs and the *Kalevala,* the Finnish folk epic compiled by Elias Lönnrot (1935–49), but also by Heinrich Heine and contemporary European symbolist poetry. Leino's early work is characterized by a melodic, musical diction. He wrote with ease and liked to improvise poems for various occasions. In his following phase, Leino's youthful optimism turned into Nietzschean "tragic optimism" (*see* Friedrich NIETZSCHE); the poet knows that the time of his personal happiness is over, and this realization finds expression even in the titles of his books, such as *Talviyö* (1905; Winter Night) and *Halla* (1908; Frost). From the beginning of the 20th century on, nature symbols are powerfully used in Leino's patriotic poems. His finest achievement was *Helkavirsiä* (1903–16; Holy Songs), a cycle, or rather cycles, of mythical poems, written in the style and employing the meter of folk poetry. Yet, although Leino did borrow certain poetical devices from folk poetry, these poems are in essence profoundly personal philosophical visions that reflect the problems of the author's time and reveal his own inner world. In addition to poetry, Leino wrote novels, plays, and excellent essays. Among the authors he translated are Dante, Corneille, Racine, Goethe, and Schiller.

See: L. Onerva, *Eino Leino,* 2 vols. (1932; 2d ed. 1979); O. Nuorto, *Eino Leino* (1938); V. Tarkiainen, *Eino Leinon runoudesta* (1954); M.-L. Kunnas, *Mielikuvien taistelu* (1972). K.L.

Leiris, Michel (1901–), French poet, was born in Paris. He took his place among the surrealists (*see* FRENCH LITERATURE) with *Simulacre* (1925; Semblance), before giving new impetus to autobiographical confession as a genre. For Leiris, wordplays and the search for truth constitute the same quest for "the sacred in daily life." Several books of his poetry, collected chiefly in *Haut-Mal* (1943, 1969; Falling Sickness), reveal the restrained tension of a metaphysical drama through ambivalent images of mineral coldness and liquidity. An oneiric, revolted imagination also lies behind his surrealist "gothic novel" *Aurora* (1946; written 1927). The Ariadne's thread leading the reader through this work is a play on words similar to those in *Glossaire, j'y serre mes gloses* (1925–40; Glossary, I Shut My Glosses [also malevolent gossip] in It) and *Mots sans mémoire* (1969; Words without Memory). Each of these works is a kind of antidictionary (questioning word meanings by multiplying puns and verbal associations) as well as an essential game, whereby language becomes a poetic oracle, a revelation of our reasons for living. In addition to these investigations into language, Leiris wrote *L'Afrique fantôme* (1934; Phantom Africa), the logbook of a field trip turned into a diary of the explorer's disillusions and inhibitions. With this work, be began a career in anthropology, writing a half-dozen important studies.

Leiris's best known autobiographical work is *L'Age d'homme* (1939; Eng. tr., *Manhood,* 1963), which he defended in his essay "De la littérature considérée comme une tauromachie" (1946; Literature Considered as Bullfighting). An account of the "progressive degeneration" of his life in the Paris of the surrealists, *L'Age d'homme* audaciously avows his intimate moral and physiological deficiencies. Nevertheless, it calls for a deeper tragic communication. Symbolical figures largely contribute to the disclosure and mythical magnification of the personal drama. The sense of Leiris's endeavor is confirmed with *La Règle du jeu* (1948; The Rules of the Game), which includes three (probably greater) autobiographical volumes: *Biffures* (1948; Deletions), *Fourbis* (1955; Odds and Ends), and *Fibrilles* (1966; Fibrils). The rules to be discovered should be at the same time a poetic art and a *savoir-vivre.* These are first based on a revival of the magical language of childhood, but the quest widens from the combination of words to those events: their conjunctions or shiftings become the "bifurs" (crossroads), the very material of the writer's "biffures" or deletions groping for life's truth. Multiple relations also intertwine past and present, giving the recollection a quasi-Proustian density (*see* Marcel PROUST). Moreover, the biographical reality opens to contemporary history, thereby assuming other mythical dimensions. Leiris however, always trapped in a quest both revelatory and deceptive, relates in *Fibrilles* his abortive attempt at suicide followed by a reassertion of his poetic vocation.

See: M. Nadeau, *Michel Leiris et la quadrature du cercle* (1963); P. Chappuis, *Michel Leiris* (1973). D.Ba.

Lem, Stanisław (1921–), Polish science-fiction writer, was born in Lvov into a physician's family, studied medicine in Lvov and Cracow, and began to publish in 1946. His first two science-fiction novels, *Astronauci* (1951; The Astronauts) and *Obłok Magellana* (1955; Magellan's Cloud), which optimistically describe two social Utopias based on interplanetary journeys, were followed by a great variety of novels, short stories, and essays in which Lem discusses the cultural impact and moral implications of modern science and technology. Lem's growing fears for the future of civilization, his questions about the changes in the behavior and psychology of man under the influence of technological developments and contacts with interplanetary space, and his concern about the moral responsibility of scientists for the consequences of their inventions are reflected in such works as *Powrót z gwiazd* (1961; Return from the Stars), *Solaris* (1961; Eng. tr., 1970), *Niezwyciężony i inne opowiadania* (1964; Eng. tr., *The Invincible*, 1973), *Opowieści o pilocie Pirxie* (1968; Stories about Pilot Pirx), and *Głos Pana* (1968; The Voice of the Master). Perhaps the most notable of these is *Solaris*, a horrifying story about human explorations of a planet entirely covered by an ocean that has the power to turn the subconscious thoughts and feelings of human beings into living creatures.

Lem's most distinctive contribution to the genre of science fiction lies in his use of a brilliant comical style, shot through with tongue-in-cheek irony, word play, paradox, and parody, as a means of discussing a broad array of serious human problems, ranging from historiosophy and sociology to cybernetics and philosophy. This fusion of the serious and the comic is nowhere better illustrated than in *Dzienniki gwiazdowe* (1957; Eng. tr., *The Star Diaries*, 1976) and *Ze wspomnień Ijona Tichego. Kongres futurologiczny* (1971; Eng. tr., *The Futurological Congress*, 1974), two cycles of stories linked together through a character reminiscent of Münchhausen and Gulliver who travels about among the galaxies; the amusingly grotesque *Pamiętnik znaleziony w wannie* (1961; Eng. tr., *Memoirs Found in a Bathtub*, 1973); *Bajki robotów* (1964; Robot Fables); and *Cyberiada* (1965; Eng. tr., *The Cyberiad*, 1974), a cycle of hilarious tales with profoundly serious implications about two inventive robots who exercise their creative talents on a scale ranging from the invention of a poetry-writing machine to tinkering with the structure of the universe.

Lem is also the author of philosophical essays, *Dialogi* (1957; Dialogues), *Summa technologiae* (1964), *Filozofia przypadku* (1968; The Philosophy of Chance), and *Fantastyka i futurologia* (1971; Science Fiction and Futurology), as well as a three-volume non-science-fiction novel about his experiences during World War II, *Czas nieutracony* (1955; Time Not Wasted).

See: E. Balcerzak, *Stanisław Lem* (1973); D. Suvin, Afterword to S. Lem, *Solaris* (1970), pp. 205–16; M. Kandel, Introduction to S. Lem, *Mortal Engines* (1977), pp. vii–xxiv.   E.M.T. with S.F. and W.B.E.

Lemaître, Jules (1853–1914), French critic, essayist, and playwright, was born in Vennecy near Orléans. A brilliant student, he received his doctorate from the Ecole Normale Supérieure in 1882. Trained as a scholar, he taught at the universities of Besançon and Grenoble, but teaching proved a disappointment and he gave it up in 1884 for a career in literature, beginning as a critic for Paris journals. He achieved almost instant success, notably with an irreverent piece on Ernest Renan in the *Revue bleue*. In 1885 he became drama critic for the *Journal des Débats*, by which time he had already written two slim books of Parnassian poetry (1880, 1883). There followed a pair of indifferent novels (1886, 1893); 8 volumes of excellent short stories (1889–1914); more than 15 graceful, witty, and psychologically sound plays (1889–1912), beginning

with *Révoltée* (1889; The Rebel); and some polemical tracts, such as *Discours royalistes: 1908–1911*). Today, however, Lemaître is best remembered for his criticism, collected in *Les Contemporains* (7 vols., 1885–99; vol. 8, 1918; Contemporaries) and *Impressions de théâtre* (10 vols., 1888–98; vol. 11, 1920; partial Eng. tr., *Theatrical Impressions*, 1924). Late in life he published *Jean-Jacques Rousseau* (1907; Eng. tr., 1907), *Jean Racine* (1908), *Fénelon* (1910), and *Chateaubriand* (1912).

Lemaître produced impressionistic criticism. The critic, he wrote in 1887, should record, sincerely and carefully, impressions just of the moment, since appreciation for an author often changes dramatically, as from love to indifference, or from scorn to adoration. Criticism, he decided, should be basically sympathetic; finding faults is all too easy and likely to prove sterile (this from the man who began his career by attacking Renan and by utterly destroying the once respected dramatist Georges Ohnet). Although Lemaître's tastes were catholic, he preferred contemporary literature. Even so, he faulted naturalism for lacking truth, and symbolism for lacking clarity, only to brush aside his censure as mere fleeting impressions. He objected to systematic, general criticism and masses of scholarly impedimenta, which he said prevented any real literary enjoyment. He was called a dilettante (Ferdinand BRUNETIÈRE accused him of affecting literary dandyism), and at times he seems to embrace the charge gladly. Yet he observed that completely individualistic criticism is nonexistent. Any reader measures what he reads against all other similar works and then judges; thus the subjective approach reaches the same goal as the objective, if more humbly. Actually, Lemaître is probably less subjectively impressionistic than he would have us believe. Solidly trained in Greco-Latin humanism during his university days, he possessed a tough core of classic balance, evident as early as the 1890s in the moralizing tendency of his dramas. In his pose of subjectivity and capriciousness he may well be at least partly humoring his magazine audience.

The Dreyfus Affair (1894–1906) politicized Lemaître's outlook, as it did that of so many of his contemporaries. He soured on liberalism and the Third Republic, and began to laud conservatism, patriotism, and morality. He even abandoned literature to found and head the Ligue de la Patrie Française, organized to combat radicalism, and he eventually joined the Royalist cause. Fortunately, he returned to literary preoccupations with four series of lectures on Rousseau, Chateaubriand, Fénelon, and Racine. Chateaubriand he condemned for pacifism, Rousseau for being a foreigner and responsible for the French Revolution (although politics aside, Lemaître could praise him). The portrait of Racine is overly worshipped but charming and acutely limned. All his faults considered, Lemaître remains one of the finest French critics, and not quite fairly treated in the well-known phrase that counts him among "Sainte-Beuve's small change."

See: H. Morice, *Jules Lemaître* (1924); G. Durriére, *Jules Lemaître et le théâtre* (1934).   A.E.S.

Lemonnier, Camille (1844–1913), Belgian art critic and novelist, was born in a suburb of Brussels. He led an uneventful life devoted solely to writing. His first work, *Salon de Bruxelles*, inaugurated his career as an art critic and was followed by studies of Gustave Courbet, Alfred Stevens, Félicien Rops, and others. The influence of plastic artists is clearly discernible in all his work, and it is often easier to trace the inspiration of his novels to a painter than to any purely literary model. Lemonnier prided himself on being a Proteus and always gave full vent to his lyric genius: "I have been only a creature of instinct, intoxicated by the beauty of life," he declared. His adoration of nature in all its aspects constitutes the unifying principle of his work. Yet while this outlook at times led him to commune with the French naturalistic school, his Dionysiac temperament prohibited any suggestion of pessimism.

The novel *Le Mâle* (1881; The Stud), belongs to the early period of Lemonnier's work, that designated by Léon Bazalgette as the period of unconscious pantheism, and remains his masterpiece in fiction. It is realistic in the sense that it was conceived and written among the actual scenes and characters portrayed, but the old Flemish masters, such as Peter Paul Rubens, Jacob Jordaens, and David Teniers, were still guiding his eye. The theme of the work is the free, exuberant life of forest and countryside, instinctively enjoyed without the intrusion of debatable social theories. *La Mort* (1882; Death) recalls Emile Zola's *Thérèse Raquin*. In sharp contrast to *Le Mâle*, *Le Mort* stigmatizes the physical and moral depravity of two peasants. In 1883 appeared *L'Hystérique,* a work that began a belligerent defense of the claims of nature. Based on pathological data, it was perhaps influenced by *La Sorcière* (The Witch) of Michelet, for whom Lemonnier expressed warm admiration. The subject is the misery stemming from the ascetic education of a priest. This novel marks the transition to what Bazalgette calls Lemonnier's second period, one of uncertain psychological groping.

Lemonnier's sympathies lay with the unfortunate and the oppressed. In the company of the Belgian painter Constantin Meunier, he observed the wretched life of toilers in the rolling mills. At times, Lemonnier felt that he was himself the victim of oppression. Prosecuted at Paris in 1888 for a short story, he replied vigorously in *Le Possédé* (1890; The Possessed), in which he exposed the degradation of a magistrate, a lecherous Torquemada persecuting uncompromising art. Another trial, which resulted in acquittal, inspired *Les Deux Consciences* (1902; The Two Consciences), in which Lemonnier analyzed his own development. In other novels he defended the right of women to develop fully their own personalities. *L'Arche* (1894; The Arch) is the journal of a mother who rebuilds the family fortunes; in *Le Bon Amour* (1900; The Proper Love), an estranged couple reunite in philanthropic activity; and *Madame Lupar* (1888) analyzes the mercenary vice of the heroine. Both naturalistic and psychological trends were combined in *La Fin des bourgeois* (1893; The End of the Bourgeois). In this work, Lemonnier observes that since society is itself an agent of corruption, it must be changed through a return to a state of nature.

In the last period of his life, Lemonnier celebrated the naive virtues of peasants and championed a conscious pantheism. Novels like *L'Ile vierge* (1897; The Virgin Island), *Adam et Eve* (1899), and *Au cœur frais de la forêt* (1900; In the Cool Heart of the Forest) suggest the freshness of a Theocritean idyll combined with the majesty of biblical poetry. His immediate inspiration for these books may have been the scenes of nature painters like Velvet Brueghel, Emile Claus, and Jean Baptiste Camille Corot. With *Le Vent dans les moulins* (1903; The Wind in the Mills), Lemonnier returned to a more marked realism. His last book, *La Chanson du carillon* (1911; The Song of the Carillon), inspired by Georges Rodenbach's *Bruges-la-morte* and by the paintings of Hans Memling, crowns the work of the writer whom Rodenbach had named "the Marshal of Belgian Letters." In addition to his novels, Lemonnier wrote numerous short stories, mysteries, and children's stories. Particularly noteworthy are the *Contes flamands et wallons* (1875; Flemish and Walloon Tales), in which Belgian national life appears in a sympathetic and even idyllic light. Lemonnier's vocabulary is as extensive as his subject matter, but, rather than borrowing from dialect, he sought picturesque expressions and nuances.

In its scope and variety, Lemonnier's work defies facile categorization. His writings do not fall neatly into either "romantic" or "realist" schools. As an author of Flemish background writing in French and celebrating the beauties of both Flemish and Walloon areas of Belgium, Lemonnier transcends the differences between the two cultures and takes a place as a truly national figure. Several of Lemonnier's short stories have been collected and translated as *Birds and Beasts* (1944).

See: G. Rency, *Camille Lemonnier (1844–1944): son role, sa vie, son œuvre* (rev. 1944).   B.M.W. rev. M. R.L.

Lengyel, József (1896–1975), Hungarian novelist, was born in Marcali into a middle-class family. He began his literary apprenticeship with Kassák by writing expressionist, avant-garde, and socialist revolutionary poetry during World War I. A founding member of the Hungarian Communist Party, Lengyel was an active participant in the 1918 revolution and in the formation of the short-lived Hungarian Soviet Republic of 1919. After the collapse of the republic, Lengyel moved to Vienna, Berlin, and, in 1930, to Moscow. During these years, he worked as a writer and editor for film journals and Communist Party publications. Lengyel dedicated two works to the Hungarian Soviet Republic. The first were semidocumentary memoirs entitled *Visegrádi utca* (1957; Visegrad Street), whose earlier 1932 Russian edition included an introduction by Béla Kun. The second work is *Prenn Ferenc hányatott élete* (1958; Eng. tr., *Prenn Drifting,* 1966), a picaresque novel about a roughneck who becomes a revolutionary. Lengyel maintained a lifelong interest in the possibilities of combining facts with story elements, and he characterized his own writing as "reports," "mirrors," and "documentations."

Arrested in 1938; Lengyel spent the next 17 years in Siberian concentration camps and in compulsory residence in the USSR. He returned to Hungary in 1955. With the publication of *Elévült tartozás* (1964; Expired Debt), a major author, virtually unknown, appeared on the literary scene at the age of 68. This collection of short stories, based on personal experience, describes life in the Soviet camps and in Siberia. Here man's grim predicament is redeemed only by nature's beauty, the kindness of a few people, and the inner strength of the individual. The restrained, poetic narrative demonstrates Lengyel's firm belief in human integrity. The finest pieces in the collection, "Igéző" (The Spell), first published in 1958, and "Kicsi mérges öregúr" (Little Angry Old Man), are impressive tributes to man's dignity.

A committed writer, Lengyel was always passionately for or against something. His uncompromising stand against the abuse of power resulted in a filmscript, *Isten ostora* (1972; God's Scourge), about Attila the Hun. His novel *Szembesítés* (*Confrontation,* 1973), published only in English, reaffirmed the importance of disclosing the crimes of Stalinism. Although Lengyel never lost his total dedication to the cause of communism, he was a relentless critic of its practices.

See: A. Diószegi, "Lengyel József útja," *ÚÍ* 5 (1965): 236–43; P. Ignotus, "The Return of József Lengyel," *Encounter* (May 1965): 88–91; J. Szabó, *Lengyel József: alkotásai és vallomásai tükrében* (1966); M. Almási, *Ellipszis* (1967); G. Gömöri, "Jósef Lengyel: Chronicler of Cruel Years," *BA* 49, no.3 (Summer 1975): 471–474.

P.V.

Lenormand, Henri-René (1882–1951), French playwright, critic, poet, and novelist, was born in Paris, the son of a noted musician. He was France's leading dramatist from 1915 to 1935 and one of the most important observers of the French theatrical scene until his death. Eventful as his life was, it was intimately allied with the theater of his epoch and often became the subject of his drama. His intellectual interests as a young man were in Elizabethan drama, the works of Edgar Allan Poe, and the Russian novelists, and each influenced his burgeoning career as a playwright. His fascination with terror, the grotesque, and the uncharted depths of the human psyche can be traced to his early readings. His lifelong interest in exotic countries gave rise to his concept of the influence of climate on human actions.

Lenormand's first published work was a volume of prose poems, *Les Paysages d'âme* (1905; Landscapes of the Soul). Immediately following were his first play, *La Folie blanche* (1905; The White Madness), presented at the Grand Guignol, and a novel, *Le Jardin sur la glace* (1906; The Garden on Ice). His remarkable growth as a dramatist may be seen by comparing his second play, *Le Réveil de l'instinct* (1908; The Awakening of Instinct), with its later incarnation, *Le Simoun* (1920; The Simoom). Incest, superficially treated in the former, becomes a harrowing and tragic obsession in the latter, one of Lenormand's finest plays and one of the first in which the climate becomes an unseen but crucial character (here the essential antagonist of the main character, Laurency). The first play to demonstrate his mastery of theatrical techniques as well as his originality is *Terres chaudes* (1913; Tropic Lands), later slightly revised and presented as *A l'ombre du mal* (1924; In the Shadow of Evil). The study of evil as a cosmic force and man's inability to avoid it places Lenormand in the line of such philosophers as the Marquis de Sade and LAUTRÉAMONT. In this work, Lenormand innovatively creates almost unbearable theatrical tension through his use of tom-toms to punctuate the action. (The American playwright Eugene O'Neill later also made effective use of tom-toms in *The Emperor Jones* [1921].) A series of major works, most of them performed and/or directed by the Pitoëffs, were produced from 1919 to 1924. These plays include *Le Temps est un songe* (1919; Eng. tr., *Time Is a Dream*, 1923), *Les Ratés* (1920; Eng. tr., *Failures*, 1923), *Le Simoun, Le Mangeur de rêves* (1922; Eng. tr., *The Dream Doctor*, 1928), and *L'Homme et ses fantômes* (1924; Eng. tr., *Man and his Phantom*, 1928).

Lenormand had read Sigmund Freud in 1917, but the influence of the Viennese psychoanalyst can be seen principally in the plays produced after 1920. An analyst named Luc de Brontë is a major character in several of them. Lenormand's mastery in presenting characters with troubled, often psychotic personalities can be seen in *Le Temps*, which deals with a neurasthenic man torn between Eastern mysticism and Western metaphysical anguish. As in the other plays of this period, the climate (here the oppressive climate of Holland) becomes a major character. The characters of *Le Mangeur de rêves* include an emotionally disturbed woman, Jeannine, whose disintegration at the hands of her psychoanalyst lover is powerfully portrayed. Lenormand demonstrates here the danger of playing with the psyches of others, a concern found in several later plays as well. *L'Homme* is a study of a modern Don Juan the basis of whose amatory actions is an unconscious attraction to and fear of homosexuality. Although Lenormand's psychological insights into the Don Juan legend are profound and stimulating, the play is weakened by the sensationalism of the final scenes. *Une Vie secrète* (1924; A Secret Life) is one of several studies by Lenormand of the process of artistic creation. This process is nourished by the antisocial instincts of the artist who destroys in order to create but who, at the same time, is tormented by his conscience. *Le Lâche* (1925; Eng. tr., *The Coward*, 1928) and *L'Amour magicien* (1926; Love the Magician) lack both the dramatic conciseness and artistic conviction found in the earlier plays, and the second deals luridly but unconvincingly with spiritualism. *Mixture* (1927) contains one of Lenormand's finest theatrical creations, Fearon, a woman of doubtful virtues and remarkable insights into the problems of existence. She serves as raisonneuse both in this play and in *Le Mangeur de rêves*. But *Mixture,* as well as *L'Innocente* (1928) and *Les Trois Chambres* (1931; The Three Rooms), repeat themes presented more forcefully in the earlier plays. *Asie* (1931) is a weak retelling of the Medea legend. In 1934, however, *Crépuscule du théâtre* (Eng. tr., *In Theatre Street*, 1937) was produced. Although this play is a dramatic failure, it is significant for its vitriolic attack on and insights into the modern theater—its directors, actors, technicians, and audience. Lenormand decries the decadence of the theater, which, he feels, has made the public turn to the cinema for entertainment. The poet is no longer the center of theatrical work; he is subservient to the whims of outrageous directors, egocentric actresses, and avaricious financiers. His last plays, *La Folle du ciel* (1937; The Madwoman of the Sky), a poetic fairy tale about a bird-woman, and *La Maison des remparts* (1942), are further examples of Lenormand's declining dramatic powers. Only in the novels *Une fille est une fille* (1949; Eng. tr., *Renée*, 1951) and *Troubles* (1950; Eng. tr., *The Rising*, 1952) are there characters as well portrayed as those in Lenormand's finest plays.

Aside from the plays written before 1925, Lenormand's posthumous fame depends strongly on his theatrical essays and the *Confessions d'un auteur dramatique* (2 vols., 1949, 1953; Confessions of a Dramatic Author). The *Confessions* is an important autobiographical work, dealing as it does with the processes of artistic creation, but more significantly it is a brilliant commentary on and analysis of the French theater of the first half of the 20th century. A wealth of information about the period's directors—especially those of the Cartel (*see* Gaston BATY, Charles DULLIN, Louis JOUVET, Georges PITOËFF)—as well as stage designers, authors, and actors is found in this work, as is Lenormand's philosophy of the theater and its relation to the other arts and society. Notable is his treatment of the censorship policies of the French government. The *Confessions* is one of the great works of theatrical criticism and analysis written in the 20th century.

At his best, Lenormand was an experimental dramatist who enlarged the scope of the theater through his portrayals of clinical personalities confronting an alien world, and many of his characters are the prototypes of the 20th-century alienated hero. Although he does not deal in the great emotions found in the classical or romantic theater, Lenormand does portray the anxieties, fears, desires, and impulses that lurk beneath the conscious mind and ultimately determine man's fate. His characters, whom he sees as representative of contemporary men and women, are unable to distinguish between illusion and reality or between desire and death, and thus destruction, whether of themselves or of others, becomes a way of life. Lenormand's theater is ultimately pessimistic, but it does contain some of the most memorable characters in contemporary drama.

See: P. Blanchart, *Le Théâtre de H.-R. Lenormand: apocalypse d'une société* (1947).　　　　R.E.J.

Lenz, Hermann (1913–), German novelist and poet, was born in Stuttgart, the son of a teacher. He studied theology in Tübingen and archaeology, art history, and German literature in Heidelberg and Munich. He was a soldier in World War II and spent some time in American captivity. From 1951 to 1972 he was the secretary of the South-German Writers Association, during which time he became a free-lance writer. He has called himself a maker of mirrors and has characterized his works as mirrors in which readers can glimpse themselves. In many ways a traditionalist, Lenz has named Eduard Mörike, Adalbert Stifter, and Thomas MANN as writers who influenced him. He himself has translated Washington Irving and Anthony Trollope. His novels take place not in a historically fixed world but inwardly, in the consciousness of the narrator.

The first small book of poetry by Lenz appeared in 1936, *Gedichte* (Poems). *Das stille Haus* (1947; the Quiet House), a long story, was followed by three stories in *Das doppelte Gesicht* (1949; The Double Face). Reading them, Thomas Mann called Lenz "an original, dreamily bold, and remarkable talent." The novel *Der russische Regenbogen* (1959; The Russian Rainbow) was the first of a series of novels that attracted little public notice but found a steady, small readership. Among them are *Die Augen eines Dieners* (1964; The Eyes of a Servant), *Verlassene Zimmer* (1966; Abandoned Rooms), *Andere Tage* (1968; Other Days), *Im inneren Bezirk* (1970; In the Inner Precinct), *Der Kutscher und der Wappenmaler* (1972; The Coachman and the Coat-of-Arms Artist), and *Neue Zeit* (1975; New Time). Lenz attracted the attention of Peter HANDKE, whose support in public statements brought Lenz a wider public. In 1978 he received the prestigious Georg Bǔchner Prize. A.L.W.

Lenz, Siegfried (1926–), German fiction writer, dramatist, and essayist, was born in the Masurian town of Lyck, East Prussia. After World War II he studied philosophy and German and English literature at the University of Hamburg and then turned from journalism (1948–51) to creative writing. While his first two novels, *Es waren Habichte in der Luft* (1951; Hawks Were in the Sky) and *Duell mit dem Schatten* (1953; Duel with a Shadow) tend toward symbolical representation, the novel *Der Mann im Strom* (1957; The Man in the River), the story of an aging diver, and *Brot und Spiele* (1959; Bread and Games), a sports novel, are more firmly rooted in contemporary reality. The novel *Stadtgespräch* (1963; Eng. tr. *The Survivor*, 1965) probes the ethical dilemma that confronted a member of the Resistance when he fought the German occupation troops in Norway and had to choose between self-sacrifice and sacrificing the lives of innocent hostages.

Lenz's masterpiece *Deutschstunde* (1968; Eng. tr. *The German Lesson*, 1972) deals with the suppression of artistic freedom during the Third Reich. Required to write an essay on the "Joys of Duty," the youthful narrator recounts the obsessive, inhumane dedication to duty of his father, a policeman, who is charged with the supervision of the painter Nansen (that is, Emil Nolde). Lenz sees the persistence of perverted concepts of duty in postwar society as an indication that the vestiges of the Nazi past have not yet vanished. *Das Vorbild* (1973; Eng. tr. *An Exemplary Life*, 1976), another substantial novel, draws attention to the potential manipulation of youthful enthusiasm by the propagating of false models. In the partly autobiographical novel *Heimatmuseum* (1978; Masurian Museum), the narrator delves deeply into his own past and the history of his native Masuria to justify his having set fire to the museum that he had reestablished

in the Federal Republic but that was in danger of being propagandistically exploited by a group of refugees from former East Prussia.

Lenz's mastery of the short story is primarily evident in four collections: *Jäger des Spotts* (1958; The Ridiculed Hunter), *Das Feuerschiff* (1960; Eng. tr., *The Lightship*, 1962), *Der Spielverderber* (1965; The Spoilsport), and *Einstein überquert die Elbe bei Hamburg* (1975; Einstein Crosses the Elbe near Hamburg). Ernest Hemingway's influence is evident in the hunter's stoic dignity in the face of defeat in such early stories as *Jäger*. Later stories tend to exhibit a more pronounced social awareness, albeit in an often ironic, satiric, or Kafkaesque guise. The versatile storyteller Lenz also penned several collections of humorous tales, notably the tribute to Masuria, *So zärtlich war Suleyken* (1955; So Tender Was Suleyken). Although Lenz's forte is the radio play rather than the drama, his play *Zeit der Schuldlosen* (1962; Time of Guiltless) attracted attention. His personal and critical essays were published under the title *Beziehungen* (1970; Relationships).

See: C. A. H. Russ, "The Short Stories of Siegfried Lenz," *GL&L* 19 (1966): 241–51; H. Wagener, *Siegfried Lenz*, (1976); Peter Russell, "The 'Lesson' in Siegfried Lenz's *Deutschstunde*," *Seminar* 13 (1977): 42–54; B. Murdoch and M. Read, *Siegfried Lenz* (1978). S.M.

Leonov, Leonid Maksimovich (1899–), Russian novelist, short-story writer, dramatist, and journalist, was born in Moscow. He is one of the most individual of Soviet writers, even though his work long seemed to reflect the fever chart of literary politics in the Soviet Union. His often tragic or ambiguous views of moral and ethical problems in post-1917 society have frequently drawn the unfriendly attention of orthodox critics.

Before establishing himself as a writer of realistic prose and drama, Leonov tried his hand at verse and several poetic, "ornamental" stories of romantic fantasy, all published before 1924. In two novellas published in 1924, *Zapisi Andreya Petrovicha Kovyakina* (Notebooks of Andrey Petrovich Kovyakin) and the forceful *Konets melkogo cheloveka* (End of a Petty Man), Leonov experimented respectively with a *skaz* technique (stylistically individualized first-person narration) that owed much to Nikolay Gogol, Nikolay LESKOV, and Aleksey REMIZOV and with the character types, situations, and style developed by Fyodor DOSTOYEVSKY, aspects that became central to his work. *Konets* is perhaps a key document in Leonov's evolution, and in it he depicted the purposeless career of a gifted scientist who gradually comes to an awareness of the revolutionary upheaval around him; in the end, however, he is inveigled by his Dostoyevskian double into destroying the results of his important research.

For all its stylization and use of symbolism, Leonov's next work, *Barsuki* (1924; Eng. tr., *The Badgers*, 1947), is a further step toward realism. The counterrevolutionary representative of the "rural," to whom greater sympathy is attracted, eventually capitulates to his "urban" brother, who has become a Soviet commissar. One of the *skaz* tales introduced into the narrative, about the "furious Calaphat," is a satirical fantasy concerning a kind of hypertrophied totalitarianism. Several cuts were made in it in later editions. The hero of Leonov's ambitious second novel, *Vor* (1927; Eng. tr., *The Thief*, 1931), is a tortured figure who cannot accept the revolutionary new order, or rather the social and economic retrenchment signalized by the New Economic Policy (NEP). A disillusioned former commissar with murder on his conscience, he becomes the leader of a powerful band of criminals. Like Raskolnikov, the "thief" seems ultimately to undergo a reformation. This already complex work is further complicated by the presence as a character of a limited and not-always-reliable novelist who is writing a book about the other characters. *Vor* was not republished in its original form after 1936, and the author subjected it to radical revision in 1959.

Leonov maintained his prolific output during the 1930s. The novella *Sarancha* (1930; Locusts) was the result of a trip to Turkmenia as a member of a writers' brigade. His contributions to Five-Year Plan literature include the novels *Sot* (1930; Eng. tr., *Soviet River*, 1931) and *Skutarevsky* (1932; Eng. tr., 1936). The first deals with the building of a paper mill in backwoods Russia, ultimately successful despite the opposition of reactionary peasants, superstitious monks, and saboteurs. The theme of sabotage is also important in the second novel, which is concerned with the activities of a famous scientist in the Soviet electrical industry. With *Doroga na Okean* (1935; Eng. tr., *Road to the Ocean*, 1944), Leonov paid an idiosyncratic tribute to socialist realism: the author himself participates in the novel's action, his psychologically complex, incurably ill hero is a committed Communist, and his plot line, in the "present," runs parallel to two others, one in the pre-Revolutionary past and another (principally in the footnotes) in a Utopian future. The multifarious characters and narrative planes are not always well integrated, but the novel is nonetheless an interesting experiment.

During the World War II, Leonov's energies were devoted primarily to drama and journalism, but his novella *Vzyatiye Velikoshumska* (1944; Eng. tr., *Chariot of Wrath*, 1946), which culminates in an exciting episode involving an attack by a single Soviet tank on a German corps operating in the Ukraine, is a considerable achievement. The large-scale *Russkiy les* (1953; Eng. tr., *The Russian Forest*, 1966) is permeated by a deeply felt ecological concern for Russian natural resources, which extends symbolically to the human waste of Iosif Stalin's purges and the labor camps. Leonov has produced nothing of comparable scope or value since the publication of *Russkiy les*. The novella *Yevgeniya Ivanovna* (1963; Eng. tr., 1964), about the life of a Russian émigré woman, is a revision of an unpublished work written in 1938.

The plays Leonov wrote during the 1920s, including a dramatization of *Barsuki*, are psychological and ethical investigations—usually embodied in quirky characters in strange situations—of old ways in the new Soviet society. *Skutarevsky* was dramatized in 1932. *Polovchanskiye sady* (1938; Eng. tr., *The Orchards of Polovchansk*, 1946) and *Volk* (1938; Wolf) are suspenseful dramas culminating in the exposure of an enemy agent. *Metel* (1940; Snowstorm) and *Zolotaya kareta* (1946; Golden Coach; rewritten 1955) were both suppressed, but a revised version of the first was a success in 1963. Particularly well received were Leonov's war plays *Nashestviye* (1942; Eng. tr., *Invasion*, 1944) and *Lyonushka* (1943). Leonov's only original new work of recent years is the film script *Begstvo mistera Mak-Kinli* (1961; Mr. McKinley's Flight), a disappointing lampoon of Western warmongers.

See: E. J. Simmons, "Leonid Leonov," in *Russian Fiction and Soviet Ideology* (1959), pp. 89–161; H. Muchnic, *From Gorky to Pasternak* (1961), pp. 276–303; B. Thomson, *The Premature Revolution* (1972), 277–95; and "Bibliography of the Works of Leonid Leonov," *OSP*, vol. 11 (1964): 137–50.   R.P.H.

Leontyev, Konstantin Nikolayevich (1831–91), Russian novelist and conservative thinker, was born in Kudinovo. After studying medicine in Moscow, he served as an army doctor during the Crimean War. Later he was a diplomat, journalist, and censor in the Balkans. He was consecrated as an Orthodox monk shortly before his death.

For Leontyev, writing was often a psychotherapeutic means of resolving mental conflicts arising from his bisexuality, the homosexual side of which had to be suppressed. He himself appears in disguise in some of his works, usually as a Narcissus, preaching that all is good if it is beautiful and strong. His early novels *Podlipki* (1861; Under the Lindens) and *V svoyom krayu* (1864; Back Home) portray idyllic gentry life on a manorial estate and introduce features that would become Leontyev's hallmark: impressionistic style, manipulation of time, de-emphasis of plot, heightened eroticism, and rejection of everything coarse and unrefined. The novella *Ispoved muzha* (1867; A Husband's Confession) is striking for its modern theme: a middle-aged, impotent husband encourages his young wife to have an affair with a young Greek, during which the girl falls in love with the boy, while the husband becomes passionately attached to both the boy and girl. Of Leontyev's novels based on his life in the Balkans, *Yegipetskiy golub* (1881; Eng. tr., *The Egyptian Dove*, 1969) is the best. Its aura of refined decadence, its expression of a pagan joy in life and beauty, and its musical composition were in advance of their time in Russian literature. In his ideological writings, such as *Vizantizm i slavyanstvo* (1875; Byzantinism and Slavdom), Leontyev expounded his "triune" theory of history, according to which all states, like all organisms, pass through stages of primeval simplicity, complex flowering, and resimplification and death. He maintained that by rigorously fighting the leveling processes of democracy, some states still in the second stage could preserve the complex beauty of their civilization and postpone final decay.

Leontycv also wrote about literature. His *Analiz, stil i veyaniye o romanakh gr. L. N. Tolstogo* (1890; Eng. tr., *The Novels of Court L. N. Tolstoy: Analysis, Style, and Atmosphere*, 1968), while written in a somewhat awkward and disjointed style, is a clever and deeply perceptive examination of Lev TOLSTOY's works from the standpoint of formal, analytical, and aesthetic criticism. Many consider it the finest piece of 19th-century Russian criticism.

See: Yu. Ivask, *Konstantin Leontyev* (1961–64); S. Lukashevich, *Konstantin Leontyev* (New York, 1967).
                                                                            S.E.R.

León y Román, Ricardo (1877–1943), Spanish novelist, was born in Barcelona. The son of an army officer, he was raised in Málaga. Later he was employed by the Bank of Spain, first in its Málaga branch, later in Santander and in Madrid, where he died. His first and best-known novel, the story of a nobly born youth who neglects his ancient heritage for the frivolous gratification of his restless desires, was completed in 1905. Only after repeated rejections by Madrid publishers did it finally appear in Málaga as *Casta de hidalgos* (1908; Eng. tr., *A Son of the Hidalgos*, 1921). It had an immediate, overwhelming success. Over the next four years appeared such novels as *Alcalá de los Zegríes* (1909), the story of a conflict between a man's political ambitions and his domestic responsibilities; *El amor de los amores* (1910; The Love of Loves), a demonstration of the superiority of sacred to profane love; and *Los centauros* (1912), an indictment of the futility and shallowness of modern life.

Brought up in the conservative tradition of reverence for throne and altar, León was never converted to 20th-century liberalism with its belief in scientific progress and political democracy. Unlike most Spanish writers of his generation who, shocked by the national catastrophe of

1898, thought that their country's hope for the future lay in its gradual Europeanization (see SPANISH LITERATURE), León steadfastly maintained that it was Spain's destiny to restore Christian morality to Europe by returning to the virtues which had graced the Spaniards of the Golden Age. From 1912 to 1922 he wrote no novels, but produced two volumes of essays proclaiming this creed as well as three volumes of impressions of World War I. The novels that appeared after 1922 were increasingly propagandistic arguments against the evils he believed to be destroying the world: *Humos de rey* (1923; King's Airs) speaks against the irreligious frivolity of the younger generation, *El hombre nuevo* (1925; The New Man) against the fallacies of "progress," *Los trabajadores de la muerte* (1927; Death Workers) against the international "war makers," *Jauja* (1928; Shangri-la) against the vulgarities of modern life, *Bajo el yugo de los bárbaros* (1932; Under the Barbarians' Yoke) against the revolution of 1931, and *Roja y gualda* (1934; Red and Yellow) against the policies of the Second Republic. His last novel was *Cristo en los infiernos* (1943; Christ in Hell).

Although popular in its day and even critically acclaimed, León's work is now little-read and seems anachronistic, rhetorical, and false.

See: E. G. de Nora, *La novela española contemporánea*, vol. 1 (1963), pp. 309–28.   E.H.H. rev. H.L.B.

Lera, Angel María (1912–), Spanish novelist, was born in Baides in the province of Guadalajara and took courses at the Seminary of Vitoria and at the University of Granada. His first literary success was *Los clarines del miedo* (1958; Eng. tr., *The Horns of Fear,* 1961), a criticism of bullfighting rooted in the tradition of the writers of the Generation of 1898. *La boda* (1959; The Wedding) is a realistic account of the amorality and backwardness of rural Spain, while *Las últimas banderas* (1967; The Last Flags) documents the last days of the Spanish Civil War from the viewpoint of the defeated. Lera's social concerns are again reflected in *Hemos perdido el sol* (1965; We Have Lost the Sun), a novel about the emigration of Spanish workers to Germany. Although this novel is technically superior to his other works, its melodramatic tone betrays a writer more interested in anecdote than in style. His emphasis on current Spanish topics, his social commitment, and the realistic presentation of literary material have made Lera one of the most popular writers of his time.

See: A. R. de las Heras, *Angel María de Lera* (1971).
          J.O.

Lerberghe, Charles van (1861–1907), Belgian poet, was born in Ghent and came from a prosperous family. He attended several schools, among which was the Collège Sainte-Barbe, where two future poets, Maurice MAETERLINCK and Grégoire Le Roy, were his classmates. The three were welcomed to the literary world by Georges RODENBACH in an 1876 essay in *La Jeune Belgique*; the following year all three contributed to *Parnasse de la jeune Belgique*. Soon these young men allied themselves with the French symbolists. Van Lerberghe went to Brussels in 1890, enrolled in graduate study, and obtained a docorate in literature and philosophy in 1894. He made a halfhearted attempt to obtain a teaching position but quickly resumed his writing, living in Brussels or traveling about in Europe and England. He was 38 when he published his first volume of verse, *Entrevisions* (1898; Glimpses), but he was somewhat known in Paris, where his poetic drama, *Les Flaireurs* (The Trackers), had been presented in 1892 and again in 1896. His second volume of poetry, *La Chanson d'Eve* (1904; Song of Eve), was also his last, for he suffered a stroke in 1906. His constant

poetic theme had been the search for the ideal woman.

See: H. Juin, *Charles van Lerberghe* (1969).   K.Co.

Le Senne, René (1882–1954), French philosopher, was born in Elbeuf. His life was that of a professor who based his teaching on his personal research and realized the unique harmony of meditation, pedagogical generosity, and incessant intellectual leadership. In 1934 he and Louis LAVELLE founded the movement "Philosophie de l'Esprit" in reaction to the technological and positivistic philosophy then dominant in the French universities. It was the goal of the movement to transform philosophical analysis into an existential reflection on man and his personal destiny. His concrete philosophy of human liberty explains the choice of the two domains into which Le Senne's publications fall. The first is research on metaphysical and moral experiences, the subject of *Le Devoir* (1931; Duty), *Introduction à la philosophie* (1925, rev. 1970), *Obstacle et valeur* (1934; Eng. tr., *Obstacle and Value*), *La Destinée personnelle* (1951; Personal Destiny), *La Découverte de Dieu* (1955: Discovery of God), and *Traité de morale générale* (1943; Treatise on General Morality). The second is research on the most intimate structures that give to individuals their distinct patterns and that Le Senne, following the French tradition of the moralists, called man's "character"; this is the focus of *Le Mensonge et le caractère* (1930; Lying and Character) and *Traité de caractérologie* (1949; Treatise on Characterology).

In opposition to Freudian psychology, which interprets the dominant trait of an individual by the first experiences of its birth and the parental system, Le Senne believed in the existence of a biopsychological "given" that is permanent and that serves as a continuous substructure for the historical evolutions of the individual within a definite but small margin of freedom. Thus, to act and to create—be it in terms of intellectual, artistic, or religious innovation—is to become conscious of those limits, to transcend them, to convert them into dynamic powers. Le Senne's philosophy can be termed a metaphysical personalism.   E.M.-S.

Leskov, Nikolay Semyonovich (1831–95), Russian novelist and short-story writer, was born at Gorokhovo, near Oryol. His father was a seminarian turned government official; his mother, the daughter of an impoverished gentleman and a merchant-class woman. Leskov thus had direct exposure to many different classes and styles of life and in his work could and did authentically describe Russian society from top to bottom. He attended the Oryol gymnasium, but dropped out before completing the course. He then held several different jobs—in the Oryol criminal court, in an army recruiting office in Kiev, and in the agricultural management firm of a Russified Scotsman who was married to Leskov's aunt. For the latter, his duties involved much travel within Russia, which he later drew on for his stories. In 1860 he became a professional journalist and settled in Petersburg for the rest of his life.

Leskov's earliest writings were economic and social reportage, but in 1862 he tried his hand at fiction and discovered a notable talent. In the same year, although his political views were progressive, he got into a bitter wrangle with the nihilists, retaliating against their attacks on him by writing the polemical romans à clef *Nekuda* (1864; No Way Out) and *Na nozhakh* (1871; At Daggers Drawn). For the first he was virtually excommunicated by the radical high priest, the literary critic Dmitry Pisarev. Despite the political passions that mar those novels, Leskov produced some of his best stories during this period: "Ovtsebyk" (1863; Eng. tr., "The Musk-Ox," 1944), "Ledi Makbet Mtsenskogo uyezda" (1864; Eng. tr., "Lady Macbeth of the Mtsensk District," 1922), and "Voitelnitsa" (1866; Eng. tr., "The Amazon," 1949). It was in this period also that he wrote his most famous novel, or "chronicle," *Soboryane* (1872; Eng. tr., *The Cathedral Folk*, 1924), and two of his most popular stories, "Zapechatlenny angel" (1873; Eng. tr., "The Sealed Angel," 1913) and "Ocharovanny strannik" (1873; Eng. tr., "The Enchanted Wanderer," 1924).

Leskov's short-lived alliance with the right-wing publisher Katkov was broken off in 1874; and in 1875, during a trip to Western Europe, he underwent a major reassessment of values that resulted in his total rupture with the Orthodox Church. His religious position was an antimystical, antisacramentalist, ethically centered radical Protestantism, which ultimately, in 1887, led him to join forces with Lev TOLSTOY. In the meantime, with burned bridges on both left and right, he was hard put to find outlets. For some years he held a part-time post in the Ministry of Education, but in 1883 was abruptly dismissed for his satirical representations of the clergy, especially in *Melochi arkhiereyskoy zhizni* (1877–78; The Little Things in a Bishop's Life). After 1886 he gradually became reconciled with the highbrow reviews. The allegiance to Tolstoyanism remained unshaken until Leskov's death, although he had differences with some Tolstoyans and disagreed with Tolstoy himself on certain points (for example, the concept of "simplification").

The writings of Leskov's later years are voluminous and diverse, including problem stories such as "Na krayu sveta" (1876; Eng. tr., "On the Edge of the World," 1922); portraits of contemporary "saints," such as "Nesmertelny Golovan" (1880; Eng. tr., "Deathless Golovan," 1946); adaptations of early Christian legends, such as "Gora" (1890; The Mountain); and mordant satires, such as "Polunoshchniki" (1891; Eng. tr., "Night Owls," 1969), "Zimniy den" (1894; Eng. tr., "A Winter Day," 1969), and "Zayachiy remiz" (written 1891–94; published 1917; Eng. tr., "The March Hare," 1949).

Leskov's works are notable for their diverse character types and broad social range. He is famous for his colorful style, which is full of puns, malapropisms, and other verbal fireworks, and especially for his use of frame stories with narrators speaking highly marked language—for instance, the celebrated "Levsha" (1881; Eng. tr., "The Steel Flea," 1916).

See: V. Setschkareff, *N. S. Leskov: Sein Leben und sein Werk* (Wiesbaden, 1959); for bibliography of English articles, see W. Edgerton, ed., *Satirical Stories of Nikolai Leskov* (1969), p. 411; H. McLean, *Nikolai Leskov: The Man and His Art* (1977).   H.McL.

Leśmian, Bołesław, pseud. of Bołesław Lesman (1878–1937), Polish poet, prose writer, and essayist of Jewish extraction, was born and died in Warsaw. He studied law in Kiev, spent several years in Paris before World War I, and then lived the rest of his life in Poland, mostly in Warsaw. In 1933 he was elected a member of the Polish Academy of Literature.

In his youth, Leśmian published two cycles of poems in Russian in the journals *Zolotoye runo* (1906) and *Vesy* (1907) and wrote a Russian drama, now lost. *Sad rozstajny* (1912; The Orchard at the Crossroads) was his first volume of Polish poetry. Then followed his finest collections, *Łąka* (1920; The Meadow) and *Napój cienisty* (1936; A Shadowy Potion), and a posthumous volume, *Dziejba leśna* (1938; Forest Happenings).

Leśmian wrote a highly original variety of symbolist poetry. His imagery comes from Polish country life and folklore, and occasionally from Oriental folklore and mythology. His haunting, fantastic world has built-in components of arbitrariness and nonexistence—hence a profusion of negative particles and linguistic signals of indefiniteness. In *Łąka* one finds some of the most powerful poems in the Polish language celebrating sensuous love, but most of his poems are a sort of elegiac protest against the limitations of human life. The poet escapes into a fantastic world of his own making, always bitterly conscious of its arbitrary and illusory character. In his vitalism and antiintellectualism he was influenced by Henri BERGSON. His favorite genres were short lyrics and ballads, and his verse forms are traditional and very regular and have an incantatory character. He took great liberties with the language and introduced into his poetry a profusion of bold neologisms, "Leśmianisms." Owing to them, his poetry is barely translatable.

During his lifetime he had a small group of ardent admirers, but at large he was considered to be an eccentric, a marginal figure, eclipsed by the members of the "Skamander" group. After World War II came the recognition of his stature as one of the greatest Polish poets. He also published two volumes of Oriental fairy tales in poetic prose, *Klechdy sezamowe* (1913; Sezam Fairy Tales) and *Przygody Sindbada Żeglarza* (1913; The Adventures of Sinbad the Sailor). His finest poetic prose, *Klechdy polskie* (1956; Polish Fairy Tales), based on freely treated folklore motifs and akin in subject matter to his ballads, was published posthumously. He translated the *Tales* (1845) of Edgar Allan Poe: *Niesamowite opowieści* (1914).

See: J. Trznadel, *Twórczość Leśmiana* (1964); M. Pankowski, *Leśmian: la révolte d'un poète contre les limites* (1967); *Studia o Leśmianie,* ed. by M. Głowiński and J. Sławiński (1971); T. Karpowicz, *Poezja niemożliwa. Modele Leśmianowskiej wyobraźni* (1975); R. Heller Stone. *Bołesław Leśmian: The Poet and His Poetry* (1976).   W.W.

Lettau, Reinhard (1929–), West German prose writer, was born in Erfurt and studied German literature at Heidelberg and at Harvard, where he received his Ph.D. in 1960 for a dissertation on the Utopian novel. He taught on the faculty of Smith College, Massachusetts, for a time after 1957, spent semesters occasionally as a free-lance writer in Berlin, and since 1967 has been on the faculty of the University of California at San Diego (La Jolla). He became well known for his scurrilous, surrealistically tinged short prose texts with his first book, *Schwierigkeiten beim Häuserbauen* (1962; Difficulties in House Construction), which was followed in 1963 by *Auftritt Manigs* (Manig Comes on the Scene), in which he reduces narrative to its bare bones, depicting a single scene in the fewest possible words but suggesting a larger, more comprehensive matrix of incident. In 1967 he edited a handbook on "Gruppe 47," a literary circle of friends that met annually (*see* GERMAN LITERATURE), and in 1968 he published a slim volume of poems, *Gedichte*.

Lettau's satirical volume *Feinde* (1968; Eng. tr., *Enemies*, 1973) aims at the absurdities of human existence, particularly at the militaristic preoccupations of mankind. *Täglicher Faschismus, Amerikanische Evidenz aus 6 Monaten* (1971; Daily Fascism, American Evidence from 6 Months) is a selection of news articles from the time of student unrest and Vietnam protest, which shows an ugly side of the United States. The book reveals the bias of Lettau against his adopted country and for a time it created disgust for America in some circles of readers in Germany. *Immer kürzer werdende Geschichten* (1973; Stories that Get Shorter and Shorter) is a reissue of some of the short prose of Lettau plus prose miniatures and aphoristic, unrhymed lyric utterances. Lettau's *Frühstücksgespräche in Miami* (1977; Breakfast Conversations in Miami) depicts a conference of dictators, "servants of reason," in Miami, a witty and disturbing confrontation between Lettau and language that serves the forces of oppression.

See: C. P. Harris, *Reinhard Lettau and the Use of the Grotesque* (1972).   A.L.W.

Lettish literature: *see* LATVIAN LITERATURE or LETTISH LITERATURE.

Levi, Carlo (1902–75), Italian novelist, essayist, and journalist, was born in Turin. In 1923 he received his medical degree from the University of Turin. His mother was the sister of Claudio Treves, one of the leaders of the Italian Socialist Party. Levi frequented Turin's progressive artistic and political circles, and he gained an early reputation as a painter. He was arrested for anti-Fascist activities in 1935 and sent to confinement in Gagliano (Lucania). Levi described this period in *Cristo si è fermato a Eboli* (1945; Eng. tr., *Christ Stopped at Eboli*, 1947). The book is a unique blend of personal and political experience, revealing Levi as an independent social observer and a writer resisting narrow classification. *Cristo* is the nucleus of his work, establishing his major concerns and offering a structural design visible in the books to come. In this work, Levi defines the social classes as he sees them (peasants and social rejects on the one hand, the eternal bureaucrats, who stifle dissent, on the other) and examines the daily struggle, intensified under totalitarianism, between the individual and the state. Like all his books, *Cristo* is a chapter in an intellectual odyssey, a journey into Italy's forgotten past and neglected present. Sent to Gagliano to learn obedience, Levi becomes the counselor for social upheaval. In the south he discovers a primitive society, its people virtually stateless and cut off from civilization. The gentry, bitterly resented by the peasants, rule their fiefdoms in the name of the state. Levi the political prisoner establishes an immediate rapport with the peasants. His final, radical appeal is for a new order in which the south would assume a form of autonomy from Rome. After his release from confinement in Gagliano, Levi lived for a time in France. Here he began to write a meditation on the roots of fascism entitled *Paura della libertà* (1946; Eng. tr., *Of Fear and Freedom*, 1950). *Cristo si è fermato a Eboli* is an extension of this meditation.

After World War II, Levi served as editor of *L'Italia libera*, the mouthpiece of the Action Party, to which he belonged. He described the atmosphere of liberated Italy in *L'orologio* (1950; Eng. tr., *The Watch*, 1951). Levi's continued concern with the problems of the south characterize two other books: *Le parole sono pietre* (1955; Eng. tr., *Words Are Stones*, 1958), set in Sicily, and *Tutto il miele è finito* (1964; All the Honey Is Gone), set in Sardinia. These books deal with such familiar themes as the survival of feudalism and the peasants' retreat into a private culture, but *Le parole sono pietre* also reveals some militancy stirring below its surface. Levi broadened the scope of his concerns in two other works. The journey to the USSR in *Il futuro ha un cuore antico* (1956; The Future Has an Ancient Heart) is an inquiry into the directions of a revolution made in the name of a forgotten peasantry. *La doppia notte dei tigli* (1959; Eng. tr., *The Linden Trees*, 1962) takes the author back to postwar Germany and back to a question posed in *Paura della libertà*: what was it in the nature of man and German society that tolerated the rise of Nazism?

"The individual and the State coincide in theory, they must be made to coincide in practice," wrote Levi in *Cristo si è fermato*. This statement of his humanitarian, moderate socialist beliefs is consistently reiterated throughout Levi's works.

See: H. Rosenberg, in *The Tradition of the New* (1959), pp. 199–206; D. Heiney, in *America in Modern Italian Literature* (1964), pp. 126–31; *Galleria* XVII 3–6 (special Levi issue, May-December 1967); M. Aurigemma, in *Letteratura italiana: i contemporanei*, vol. 3 (1975).   H.L.

Levi, Primo (1919–), Italian short-story writer and novelist, was born in Turin into a Jewish middle-class family. His Jewishness determined the course of his life and his literary career. Levi was arrested in December 1943 by the Fascist militia. Several weeks later, he and 650 other Jews began the long, terrifying trip by train to Auschwitz. When the advancing Russian armies liberated the concentration camp two years later, Levi was still alive. He returned home and shortly afterwards recorded the tragic experiences in the camp for himself and posterity. This short book, *Se questo è un uomo* (1947; Eng. tr., *If This Is a Man*, 1959), scored an almost immediate success in Italy and abroad, where it appeared in various translations. Written with rare simplicity and objectivity, Levi's account of the concentration camp is at once compassionate and penetrating, full of insights not only into the bestiality of man but also into the heroism of the persecuted and their capacity to endure violence both to the body and the spirit. *La tregua* (1963; Eng. tr., *The Reawakening*, 1965) takes up where *If This Is a Man* left off, providing a masterful account of Levi's last, harrowing weeks at Auschwitz and his journey home. The work is especially successful in its presentation of a gallery of unforgettable figures: Hurbinek, "a nobody, a child of death, a child of Auschwitz"; Mordo Nahum, a clever, enterprising Greek whose astuteness injects a note of humor into what is an otherwise somber story; and Cesare, a first-class mime and charlatan whose gifts save him from frequent difficulties. While the focus of the book is on people, Levi courageously broaches difficult philosophical and political questions: What should the world say or think about the concentration camps? Can one take refuge behind a screen of ignorance? What have the horrors of World War II taught mankind?

Levi has also produced two collections of short stories: *Storie naturali* (1966; Nature Stories) and *Vizio di forma* (1971; Flaw of Form). These stories, however, are not about wartime crises, but draw instead on Levi's experiences as the technical director of a paint-and-varnish firm (he holds a degree in chemistry). The stories reveal him as a gifted, at times supremely original artist whose "masters" include Aldous Huxley, Luigi PIRANDELLO, and Italo CALVINO.

See: P. Milano, *Espresso* (Oct. 3, 1966); S. Pacifici, *SatR* (May 15, 1966); G. Manacorda, in *Storia della letteratura italiana contemporanea* (1967).   S.P.

Lévi-Strauss, Claude (1908–), French anthropologist, was born in Brussels. His theoretical originality and personal style were largely responsible for the emergence of structuralism (*see* FRENCH LITERATURE) as a major intellectual movement in the 1960s. Trained as a philosopher at the Sorbonne, he turned his back on what he saw as the aridity and self-satisfaction of French philosophy and went to Brazil as a professor of sociology. He romantically described his field trips to the Brazilian interior, especially among the Bororo and Nambikwara, in the autobiographical travelogue *Tristes Tropiques* (1955; Eng. tr., 1974) (he reported on them more technically in various communications to the Smithsonian Institution). These investigations provided him with a body of first-hand anthropological material that was subsequently generalized at second-hand to something of global proportions.

In his early theoretical work, Lévi-Strauss was devoted to an analysis of kinship as an unconscious structure of society in which women form a medium of exchange between groups (this part of the theory was an extension of Marcel Mauss's theory of the gift). The formalisms of the theory borrowed heavily from linguistics, which Lévi-Strauss had discussed at length with Roman Jakobson when both were in New York towards the end of World War II. In *Les Structures élémentaires de la parenté* (1949; Eng. tr., *The Elementary Structures of Kinship,* 1969) and *Anthropologie structurale* (1958; Eng. tr., *Structural Anthropology,* 1963), Lévi-Strauss brilliantly forged theoretical anthropology and Saussurean linguistics into a powerful combination that, following the leads provided by Lewis H. Morgan and Karl Marx, came to be known as structuralism. In *La Pensée sauvage* (1962; Eng. tr., *The Savage Mind,* 1966), he generalized this theory into an account of all products of the human mind as such, thus bringing art and literature into its domain.

The basic idea of structuralism is that all intelligible complexes are built up from elements entering into sets of relationships (or structures) of a relatively simple and characteristically human kind, operating on diverse contents. Although human culture tends to use as elements complexes inherited from former generations or borrowed from other cultures (a process called by Lévi-Strauss *bricolage,* which roughly means handiness with what is available) the resulting artifacts may nevertheless be of very great complexity. The object of structural analysis is to uncover the various layers of relatively simple relationships that yield this complexity as their end-product and to show the transformations by means of which one apparent structure passes over into another.

The fact that the elements of structure are themselves relational accounts for Lévi-Strauss's stress on binary oppositions and his tolerance for wide variance of content. It may be that the basic structure, of which all manifestations in a given domain are special cases under one transformation or another, appears nowhere at the apparent level and has to be conjectured as their common origin; the concept of the human mind (the invisible or absent guest) is a case in point. On the other hand, for purposes of analysis, a member of a family of apparent structures may be chosen almost arbitrarily as a point of departure. In his later, monumental series *Mythologiques—Le Cru et le cuit* (1964; Eng. tr., *The Raw and the Cooked,* 1969), *Du miel aux cendres* (1966; Eng. tr., *From Honey to Ashes,* 1973), *L'Origine des manières de table* (1968; The Origin of Table Manners), and *L'Homme nu* (1971; Naked Man)—Lévi-Strauss undertook such an analysis for a very large corpus of myths drawn especially from Indian cultures of North America.

Lévi-Strauss's importance for students of literature lies largely in the influence he exerted in Paris during the 1960s on a brilliant generation of writers, influential in their turn, including Roland BARTHES and Michel FOUCAULT, among others. Although no member of this group was, strictly speaking, a disciple of Lévi-Strauss, there can be little doubt that his initiative made possible the convergence and flowering of a number of already existing tendencies that, without him, might have remained minor: Jacques LACAN's neo-Freudian psychoanalysis, Louis ALTHUSSER's Marxism, Georges Dumézil's history of religion. Lévi-Strauss's own cultural interests, however, have tended to concentrate rather on art and music than on literature. In keeping with his Marxist sympathies, he has described his philosophical position as a kind of popular materialism. Lévi-Strauss was elected to the Académie Française in 1973.

See: J. Pouillon, "L'Œuvre de Claude Lévi-Strauss," in Lévi-Strauss, *Race et histoire* (1961); C. Backès-Clément, *Claude Lévi-Strauss on la structure et le malheur* (1970); J. Lyons, *Claude Lévi-Strauss* (1970).

P.Ca.

Libedinsky, Yury Nikolayevich (1898–1959), Russian fiction writer and dramatist, was born in Odessa, the son of a doctor, but he won fame as a representative of "proletarian" literature. He fought in the Civil War on the Bolshevik side, joined the Communist Party in 1920, and played an aggressive role in the savage literary polemics of the first decade following the October Revolution.

Libedinsky's first novel, *Nedelya* (1922; Eng. tr., *A Week,* 1923), was his most influential work. The rudimentary plot deals with the attempts of a group of Party functionaries to establish authority in a recalcitrant provincial town in 1920. All the characters are one-dimensional, yet each represents a type of Bolshevik that became virtually formulaic in proletarian literature thereafter: the all-wise but physically debilitated ideologue; the indecisive intellectual; the opportunist; the inarticulate but perceptive peasant. Libedinsky's later works are more ambitious in conception and scope, and interesting as responses to topical issues. *Zavtra* (1923; Tomorrow) reflects the demoralization felt by many Communists at the partial return to capitalism instituted in the early 1920s; the novel's apparent advocacy of world revolution as the best way of saving the Revolution in Russia brought charges of "Trotskyism." *Komissary* (1925; Commissars), which may have been written in atonement, presents a variety of human types, issues, and states of mind within the Communist Party just after the Civil War. *Rozhdeniye geroya* (1930; Birth of a Hero) stirred great controversy because of its account of the private life of a Communist functionary who develops, then overcomes, deep doubts about the direction being taken by Soviet society. Libedinsky also wrote about the impact of the Revolution on the history and life of the Caucasus, in such novels as *Gory i lyudi* (1947; Mountains and People) and *Zarevo* (1952; Sky Glow), and his service in World War II as a newspaper correspondent inspired various sketches and stories. The best known of his plays is *Vysoty* (1929; Heights), which explores a standard theme of the 1920s: the danger of relying on highly skilled but ideologically unsound technicians for building socialism.

Libedinsky got into deep political trouble during the 1930s. Although reinstated, he is not highly regarded today in the Soviet Union.   R.A.M.

Lidin, Vladimir Germanovich, pseud. of V. G. Gomberg (1894–), Russian author of 17 novels, several hundred short stories, and numerous collections of articles, is probably best known for his novel *Otstupnik* (1927; Eng. tr., *The Apostate,* 1931, and *The Price of Life,* American ed., 1932), about a student who becomes involved in a murder conspiracy and finally, after much soul searching, decides to confess his guilt and return to society. Although it is more valuable as a portrayal of Soviet life during the New Economic Policy (NEP) period than as a psychological study, this novel is typical of Lidin's tendency to focus on the problems of individuals rather than on social or political issues. His generally liberal views are reflected in his reminiscences, among them *Lyudi i vstrechi* (1957, 1961, 1965; People and Meetings).

See: *Russkiye sovetskiye pisateli: prozaiki,* vol. 2 (1964); S. Mashinsky, Foreword to V. Lidin's *Sobraniye sochineniy v tryokh tomakh* (Moscow, 1973).   D.Fi.

Lidman, Sara (1923-), Swedish novelist, playwright, and essayist, was born at Missenträsk, a village in Västerbotten, northern Sweden. She came of a farming family. At age 14, she contracted tuberculosis, and it was during her one-year hospitalization and thereafter that she discovered the literature of the 1930s and eagerly began to write. Living in an isolated rural area, she was obliged to obtain her secondary education by correspondence. She later continued her education at a private school and at the University of Uppsala.

Lidman studied and admired Fyodor DOSTOYEVSKY, Halldór LAXNESS, Albert CAMUS, Stina Aronsson, Harry MARTINSON, and Thorsten Georg JONSSON. In her first novel, Tjärdalen (1953; The Tar Well), about a villain who destroys the "tar valley," she pleads the cause of "the unloved ones," the suppressed and exploited crofters of the Västerbotten of the past. She indignantly attacks those who compromise and create injustice, wherever it occurs, but she does so with a love and compassion that have captivated large audiences.

In Hjortronlandet (1955; Cloudberry Land), a collective novel about four crofter families, Lidman presents excellent individual portraits of several characters, including Frans, his clumsy daughter Claudette, and her opposite, the charismatic and enigmatic Märit. The time is the period between the world wars. If the poverty, hunger, and filth among the crofters are shocking, there is also a wealth of comic, powerful, or tragic situations in the novel, all thoroughly engrossing to the reader.

Regnspiran (1958; Eng. tr., The Rain Bird, 1963) centers on Linda Ståhl, from Ecksträsk, a self-assertive artist by nature, an egotist who stands aloof and becomes indifferent to the sufferings of her neighbors. Yet without participating herself, she manages to arouse compassion, even feelings of guilt, among the social outcasts. Turning increasingly into an outsider in Lidman's next novel, Bära mistel (1960; Wearing the Mistletoe [that is, getting married]), Linda Ståhl tries to atone for her wrongdoing in a hopeless love relationship with a homosexual man, who is unable to respond sexually.

In her deeply religious childhood home, Sara Lidman learned to stand up for the underdog. It is characteristic that, when her literary domains expanded beyond the borders of her home region, to Africa and Asia, she continued to deal with the oppressed—even more grossly abused—and continued to plead their case. Lidman's stay in South Africa (1960–61) resulted in a novel, Jag och min son (1960; I and My Son), about an unsuccessful Swedish technician who, in his eagerness to make money, morally fails the black people with whom he works. In her novel about Kenya, Med fem diamanter (1964; With Five Diamonds), Lidman portrays a black man's moral degradation, caused by his encounter with a degenerate and exploitative white civilization.

Lidman's volume of reportage, entitled Samtal i Hanoi (1966; Conversations in Hanoi), is a leftist's clearly partisan account of travels and talks in North Vietnam at a relatively early point in the Vietnam War as is her volume of articles Fåglarna i Nam Dinh (1972; The Birds of Nan Dinh). In Sweden she has also found discontent and frustration among the miners in the far north in Gruva (1968; Mine). Her provocative essays published in Vänner och u-vänner (1969; Friends and Third World Comrades) received considerable attention. Lidman returned to fiction with her novel Din tjänarehör (1977; Thy Servant Heareth), the first novel in a planned trilogy about how the Sweden of yesterday becomes modern Sweden. "From Cloudberry Land," translated by V. Moberg, is included in Modern Swedish Prose in Translation, ed. by K. E. Lagerlöf (1979), pp. 57–80.

See: L. Bäckström, Under välfärdens yta (1959); H. Borland, "Sara Lidman's Progress: A Critical Survey of Six Novels," SS 39, no. 2 (1967): 97–114, and "Sara Lidman, Novelist and Moralist," SLT 36, no. 1: 27–34; C. Mannheimer, "Från angelägenhet till angelägenhet," in Femtitalet i backpegeln, ed. by K. E. Lagerlöf (1968), pp. 81–86; J. Stenkvist, Svensk litteratur 1870–1970, vol. 3 (1975), pp. 74–78, 117–19.   L.S.

Lie, Jonas (1833–1909), Norwegian novelist, was born in Eiker, near Drammen, in southern Norway. When he was only five years old, the family moved to Tromsø. The future author was inspired by this arctic town, with the glamor of its nightless summers and the terror of its winter storms, its fishermen and seafarers, and the exotic element furnished by Russian traders, Lapps, and Finns. His first book, a short novel entitled Den fremsynte (1870; Eng. tr., The Visionary, 1894), is a delicate love story set against a Nordland background. After some less successful books, he produced three significant novels, Lodsen og hans hustru (1874; Eng. tr., The Pilot and His Wife, 1876), Rutland (1880), and Gaa paa (1882; Go Ahead). Although these novels are about seafaring people and contain magnificent descriptions of storms at sea, their focus is family life, the forces that tear at its fabric and those that protect it.

These motifs also occur in Familjen paa Gilje (1883; Eng. tr., The Family at Gilje, 1920), which is rightfully considered the masterpiece among Lie's social novels. In this work he demonstrates his sensitivity toward society's maltreatment of all women, even those of the educated classes. The mother, isolated from all social contacts, is worn out by the endless tasks of a big household with its servants, dependents, and a well-meaning but tyrannical husband; the daughters are pushed into marriages with elderly suitors because the young men with whom they are in love have no prospect of being able to provide for them. These tragic conflicts, however, emerge in a setting of almost idyllic charm. The masterfully drawn, impressionistic images of the happy moments of the Gilje family are rendered with a warmth that sets the tragic episodes into an even more glaring contrast. Kommandørens døtre (1886; Eng. tr., The Commodore's Daughters, 1892) treats the same social theme, but is more bitter in its arraignment of the social tyranny that ruins the happiness of young girls. Two other novels, Livsslaven (1883; Eng. tr., One of Life's Slaves, 1895), a story of the slums, and Maisa Jons (1888), the tale of a poor seamstress, contain scathing indictments of a ruthless society.

Lie won the affection of his readers with his clear-eyed stories of everyday family life. As he grew older, however, a submerged mystical quality, which earlier had been visible only in Den fremsynte, resurfaced and found expression in a two-volume collection of short stories, Trold (1891–92; Eng. tr. in Weird Tales from Northern Seas, 1893), in which Lapp magic and Norwegian superstition are strangely blended. These stories portray human beings as still partly bound by the mysterious forces of nature. Many of them are classics of their kind, written in a simple epic style that contrasts with the scintillating, impressionistic manner of Lie's novels. In his later novels, he returned to his earlier realism, but with the exception of certain compositional experiments the works are unoriginal, lacking the freshness and poetic expression that mark his earlier works.

Lie was very happily married to his cousin, Thomasine Lie, who collaborated in his work. They lived for many years abroad, in Rome, Paris, and Berchtesgaden, but returned in 1906 to Norway, where she died in 1907 and he in 1909.

See: A. Gustafson, *Six Scandinavian Novelists* (1940), pp. 25–72; I. Hauge, *Jonas Lies diktning* (1970); S. Lyngstad, *Jonas Lie, TWAS* 434 (1977).   H.A.L.

Lilar, Suzanne (1901–), Belgian novelist, playwright, and essayist, was born in Ghent. She first gained fame with *Le Burlador* (Eng. tr., *The Burlador*, 1966), a play performed in Paris in 1946. This was a new version of the Don Juan legend, the first ever written by a woman. Two novels, *Le Divertissement portugais* (The Portuguese Divertissement) and *La Confession anonyme* (The Anonymous Confession), prolong in 1960 this analysis of amorous desire and the disorders of sensual pleasure. Developed with rigor and subtlety in a series of essays, these same themes then came to inscribe themselves in a vast dialectic of opposites that revived the fundamental intuitions of Rainer Maria RILKE, Novalis, and Hugo von HOFMANNSTHAL. The poet's "analogical" vision reveals essential meanings, just as love, if it avoids the impasses of eroticism or idealism, assumes its "sacral" nature as a link between flesh and spirit, as in *Le Couple* (1963; Eng. tr., *Aspects of Love in Western Society*, 1965). In *A propos de Sartre et de l'amour* (1967; About Sartre and about Love) and *Le Malentendu du deuxième sexe* (1969; The Misunderstanding of the Second Sex), Lilar puts the notions of the harmonious bisexuality and complementarity of the sexes in opposition to the theses of Jean-Paul SARTRE and Simone de BEAUVOIR—something that completes the conferral of an original place in present-day feminism on her. In 1950, the author of *Le Burlador* published in New York an essay on the contemporary Belgian theater of both French and Flemish expression, *The Belgian Theater since 1890*. Lilar won the Prix Sainte-Beuve in 1954 and the Prix Quinquennal de la critique et de l'essai in 1972. In 1956 she became a member of the Royal Academy of French Language and Literature of Belgium.

See: R. Burniaux and R. Frickx, *La Littérature belge d'expression française* (1973); A. Jans, *Lettres vivantes 1945–1975* (1975); S. Lilar, *Une enfance gantoise* (1976).
                                                                       R.Bu.

Linares Rivas, Manuel (1867–1938), Spanish playwright, was born of a prominent family in Santiago de Compostela. He studied law but did not continue in that career. As a politician, he served as deputy to the Cortes and later as lifetime senator.

Although he wrote a number of musical comedies and plays in verse, most of Linares Rivas's theatrical works are militant satires of social or political aspects of contemporary Spanish life. Unlike Jacinto BENAVENTE, with whom he was sometimes compared, Linares does not satirize human character but rather attacks social customs or the law. Two of his plays make a plea for the legalization of divorce: his first play, *Aire de fuera* (1903; Fresh Air), in which the problem leads to suicide, and *La garra* (1914; The Claws), his best-known work. Others criticize such social problems as exaggerated pride in one's lineage—*El abolengo* (1904; The Family Tree)—and slander—*La cizaña* (1905; Discord). There are many more plays in this vein, all of them forgotten today.

Linares Rivas's work is no longer viable as drama or literature. He wrote outdated romantic melodrama with poorly integrated social theses. The theme was his only concern, and his characters mere pretexts to serve it. As a result, every aspect of his work, enslaved by the author's will, is arbitrary and false.

See: E. Díez-Canedo, *Artículos de crítica teatral*, vol. 1 (1968), pp. 177–216.   H.L.B.

Lind, Jakov (1927–), Austrian novelist, dramatist, and memoirist, was born in Vienna. He began an 18-year odyssey in 1938 when he fled the Nazis and wandered from Holland to Germany, Israel, and other European countries, working on a barge and in many other jobs before deciding on a literary career. He finally settled in London.

The holocaust and the exile experience have shaped Lind's literature. A Jew himself he indicates in *Selbstporträt* (1969; Eng. tr., *Counting My Steps*, 1969) that in order to survive he had to learn to hate Jews, but, in surviving, he paradoxically denied his own identity. The persecution and his ambivalence about his identity led to nightmarish images of fear, depravity (often cannibalism), insanity, and inhumane action. Lind's ambivalence carries over into his choice of language: he rejected German and in 1968 began publishing in English, but he assists a translator in reworking his books into German. The paradox concerning his survival as a Jew is rendered on a more general level in "Hurrah for Freedom," from *Eine Seele aus Holz* (1962; Eng. tr., *Soul of Wood*, 1964), in which Lithuanian refugees to Sweden commit incest and cannibalize their children to survive, while damning the Soviet Union and praising Sweden for its freedom (without a hint of irony). Lind blends realistic detail and elements of the grotesque in a Kafkaesque fashion, ending many stories with horrifying twists (for example, the suicide of the priest in "The Pious Brother" from *Eine Seele*). Among his nine other works are *Eine bessere Welt* (1966; Eng. tr., *Ergo*, 1967), a novel; *The Silver Foxes Are Dead* (1968, Eng. original; German tr. *Das Sterben der Silberfüchse*, 1965), a collection of plays; and *Numbers* (1972; Eng. original), a continuation of his autobiography.

See: S. P. Rosenfeld, "Jakov Lind: Writer at Crossroads," *MAL* 4, no. 4 (1971): 42–47.   R.Z.

Lindegren, Erik (1910–68), Swedish modernist poet was born in Luleå. In his poetic technique, he was a follower of T. S. Eliot, but he was Eliot's opposite in matters of ideology and personal belief. A metaphysically thwarted atheist in religion and a disappointed radical in politics, he turned to art and love for a purpose in life. In 1931 he settled in Stockholm as critic, translator, and free-lance writer. His first book of poetry, *Posthum ungdom* (1935; Posthumous Youth), is an elegantly ironical exercise in traditional meters. His *mannen utan väg* (1942; Eng. tr., *The Man without a Way*, 1969), gained recognition during the 1940s as a pioneer work in lyrical modernism (*see* SWEDISH LITERATURE). In the form of unrhymed sonnets, the 40 pieces of the book employ an abbreviated syntax and a bold, disjointed imagery that was much copied by lesser poets of the following decade. *Sviter* (1947; Suites) contains poems of a more popular appeal celebrating erotic love, as well as highly obscure compositions full of literary allusions, such as "Hamlets himmelsfärd" (Hamlet's Ascension). Lindegren's fourth and last collection of poetry is named by an oblique allusion to Igor Stravinsky's *Sacre du printemps*, *Vinteroffer* (1954; Winter Sacrifice) and deals with the themes of personal and artistic sterility and rebirth, utilizing the "mythic method" derived from Eliot and subject matter culled from Sir James Frazer's *The Golden Bough*.

As is indicated by the titles of his last two collections, Lindegren deliberately strove to model his poetry on musical patterns of composition. Occasionally, he indulged in an almost musical euphony and line of melody, but more often he drew on the abstract, intellectual elements in music. He also did some excellent work in translating opera librettos for the Royal Opera House in Stockholm and rearranging Harry MARTINSON's space epic *Aniara* (1956; Eng. adaptation, 1963) for the operatic purposes of Karl Birger Blomdahl, the composer. During his last 10 years he contributed texts to a series of mythological ballets. *Tangenter* (Keys/Tangents), a selection of criticism edited by K. B. Lindegren, appeared in 1974.

See: L. Bäckström, *Erik Lindegren* (1962); F. Sandgren, *Erik Lindegren*, a bibliography (1971); G. Bergsten, "Lindegrens 'Arioso' som idédikt," in *Från Snoilsky till Sonnevi* (1976), pp. 173–181; C. Hermelin, *Vinteroffer och Sisyfos* (1976); E. Törnqvist, "Hamlets himmelsfärd," in *Studies in Skandinavistiek* (1977), pp. 175–87; K. Hallind, *Tavlor och deviser: studier i Erik Lindegren dikter till Halmstadgruppens måleri* (1978). S.B.

Linnemann, Willy-August (1914–), Danish novelist, was born in southern Schleswig. This conflict-filled region situated between Denmark and Germany constitutes the geographical basis of Linnemann's entire writing. His novel *Natten før Freden* (1945; The Night before the Peace), for example, is a Bildungsroman depicting the experiences of a young Schleswig man in the Resistance against the German occupation of 1940–45. Linnemann's early works are the forerunners of his five-volume cycle, *Europafortællinger* (1958–66; European Stories), in which he mingles suspenseful narrative art with philosphical reflections. The cycle's framework is the life stories of a group of people hiding in a shelter during an air raid, who attempt to find a pattern in their fate and the hidden face of God (the title of volume 1 is *Bogen om det skjulte Ansigt* [The Book about the Hidden Face]). For Linnemann, as for Karen BLIXEN, God is the organizing principle behind coincidences. His second large (seven-volume) prose cycle (1968–74) is less philosophical and more of a social criticism. In it he portrays the lives of seven members of an old Schleswig family, taking the story up to contemporary times, which are depicted in the last volume, *Protestanten* (1974; The Protestant). Despite his sharp protest against the custodianship and technocracy of the welfare state and his longing for a new, more artistic, era—also expressed in a later novel, *Bølgerne på fjorden* (1977; The Waves on the Sound)—one notices Linnemann's conviction that all is governed and overseen, which bestows a visionary character upon this monumental work.

See: E. Fredericksen, *Willy-August Linnemann* (1969). S.H.R.

Linze, Georges (1900–), Belgian poet, founded the "Groupe Moderne d'Art de Liège" and the journal *Anthologie*. Fascinated by sports, speed, travel, and cinema, this prolific and original poet has championed the technical and material developments of contemporary society, whose concrete, skyscrapers, and supersonic planes give life a new rhythm. Rejecting whatever might stand in the way of the harmony between man and his material environment, Linze has tried to show that happiness and human dignity are not incompatible with technological progress. His futuristic materialism coupled with his humanism emerges in such volumes as *Ici* (1920; Here), *Danger de mort* (1933; Danger of Death), *Orages sur la France* (1935; Storms over France), *Poème de la ville survolée par les rêves* (1948; Poem of the Town Being Flown Over by Dreams), *Poème de la grande invention* (1968; Poem of the Great Invention), and *Poème du bon dialogue universel* (1972; Poem of the Upright Universal Dialogue). Seeking to exalt modern life in a form that reflects this life's rhythm, Linze chose an unrhymed, fragmented verse, a broken delivery, and a succession of illuminating and often disconcerting images. To be sure,

the rapidity of expression is not always accompanied by density or richness: a certain monotony emerges, particularly if the breaking up of the verse does not appear to be dictated by absolute necessity. In general, however, Linze's forceful expression translates remarkably well the speed of a world in evolution. R.F.

Linze, Jacques-Gérard (1925–), Belgian poet and novelist, was born in Liège. He is the nephew of the poet Georges LINZE. A lawyer and poet himself, the author of *Passé midi* (1974; Past Noon), he was a probationary lawyer at the Liége bar and then exercised various professions before entering the advertising profession in Brussels. After having published a traditional, but well-written, adventure story, *Par le sable et par le feu* (1962; Through Sand and through Fire), Linze published four novels better in tune with modern sensibilities and in which the influence of the *nouveau roman* can be seen: *La Conquête de Prague* (1965; The Conquest of Prague), *Le Fruit de cendre* (1966; The Fruit of Ash), *L'Etang-cœur* (1967; The "Etang Coeur"), and *La Fabulation* (1968; Fabulation).

Abundant recourse to modern techniques of composition and writing (confusion of chronology; repetitions; use of pronouns, initials, incidental clauses, and parentheses) contributes to making Linze's novels among the most interesting that have been produced since World War II. In this respect, *La Conquête de Prague* perfectly realizes the equilibrium between the author's sensitivity and his technical virtuosity.

See: R. Brucher, "Double hommage: A Jacques-Gérard Linze," *Dryade* 76 (Winter 1973): 7–18; R. Burniaux and R. Frickx, *La Littérature belge d'expression française* (1973); A. Jans, *Lettres vivantes 1945–1975* (1975). R.F.

Lisboa, Irene (do Céu Vieira) (1892–1958), Portuguese poet, fiction writer, essayist, and educator, who wrote sometimes under the pseud. João Falco, was born in Arruda dos Vinhos, near Lisbon, the illegitimate child of a fairly prosperous landowner. She studied at the normal school in Lisbon and became an elementary schoolteacher. She went to Geneva for two years on a scholarship and spent another year in Belgium and France perfecting her knowledge of elementary education. After teaching for many years, she was forced to retire on a meager pension in 1940 because of her opposition to the Portuguese dictatorship. From then on she devoted herself completely to writing. She published more than 15 books of prose and verse besides contributing regularly to Portuguese magazines, especially *Seara Nova*.

One of the most original of contemporary Portuguese writers, Lisboa developed her own forms, wrote in a prose that is almost indistinguishable from her verse, and crossed the boundaries of genre to produce a kind of short story that approaches nonfiction. Her subject matter in both verse and prose is limited to the facts of her own experience and her reactions in depth to them. Thus her characters appear to be people she has known and thought about for a long time, and her locales are places obviously familiar to her. The characters are almost always the underprivileged. To these charwomen, domestics, underpaid teachers, and half-starved farmhands she extends unlimited sympathy, even when realizing that their plights are often of their own making. She often wrote about Lisbon, for example, in *Esta cidade* (1942; This City) and *Lisboa e quem cá vive* (1940; Lisbon and Those Who Live in It)—three *folhetos* or booklets of stories about Lisbon life. Lisboa also published two other collections of short stories, *Título qualquer serve* (1958; Any Title Will Do), and *Crónicas da serra* (1962; Highland

Sketches), in which she perfected her seeming formlessness. Most of her verse, also confessional and apparently artless, is contained in *Um dia e outro dia* (1936; One Day and Another) and *Outono, havias de vir* (1937; Autumn, You Were Bound to Come). Like her prose, Lisboa's verse exemplifies her theory of banality, being written in a style almost free of traditional techniques. She published two brief volumes of autobiography, *Começa uma vida* (1940; A Life Begins) and *Voltar atrás para quê* (1956; Turning Back—What For?), calling them *novelas* (novellas). *Contarelos* (1926; Tiny Tales) and *Queres ouvir, eu conto* (1958; Would You Like a Story, I'll Tell You One) are volumes of tales for children.

See: J. Alves das Neves, "Irene Lisboa: contador de histórias," *Anhembi* 34 (March 1959): 6–14; R. S. Sayers, Irene Lisboa as a Writer of Fiction," *Hispania* 45 (1962): 224–32.   R.S.S.

Lithuanian literature. Long wars for physical survival kept Lithuania removed from the Christian faith and from Christian letters through most of the Middle Ages, and foreign domination prevented the development of a national literature until the 19th century. Before then, gentle folk songs, deeply rooted in pre-Christian perceptions, were the chief verbal means of artistic expression. The first important Lithuanian writer was Kristijonas Donelaitis (1714–80), a pastor in East Prussia. His *Metai* (1818; The Seasons), a rural epic, remains a major landmark in Lithuanian letters.

The spark of a national revival in Lithuania ignited resistance against russification, and the aroused ethnic consciousness found its voice mainly in the romantic-liberal magazine *Aušra* (The Dawn), founded by Jonas Basanvičius (1851–1927), and in *Varpas* (The Bell), edited by the militant patriot Vincas Kudirka (1858–99). Both journals were printed in East Prussia and smuggled across the border to defy the Russian ban (1865–1904) on Lithuanian publications in the Latin alphabet. Kudirka himself wrote fierce anti-Russian satires and translated dramatic works by Friedrich Schiller and Lord Byron, because he felt in them the bracing wind of freedom. The historian Simanas Daukantas (1799–1848) resurrected an idealized vision of Lithuania's medieval past by using material from the archives of the ancient University of Vilna. Bishop Motiejus Valančius (1801–75) upheld the people's sobriety, morality, and Catholic faith in his realistic, didactic country tales. An outstanding talent among the educated clergy and physicians who nurtured the fledgling Lithuanian literature was Bishop Antanas Baranauskas (1835–1902), author of *Anykščių šilelis* (1858; The Sylvan Glade of Anykščiai), a lovely, melodious, syllabic poem about his native place.

Freedom of the press brought forth many new writers. Žemaitė, pseud. of Julija Žymantienė (1845–1921), wrote strong, pithy, naturalistic stories of Lithuanian village life. Šatrijos Ragana, pseud. of Marija Pečkauskaitė (1878–1930), depicted the patriotic idealism emerging among the country gentry. Jonas Biliūnas (1879–1907) was a suffering, romantic dreamer with Marxist leanings, whose heart was with the peasants and proletarians oppressed by the tsar. His best work is a short story, "Liūdna pasaka" (1907; A Sad Tale), describing the 1863 Lithuanian uprising against the Russians. Vaižgantas, pseud. of Juozas Tumas (1869–1933) was a priest, patriot, and public figure. His popular novel *Pragiedruliai* (1920; Cloud Breaks) is a chatty yarn, full of joie de vivre, which depicts the growth of Lithuanian national consciousness and economic self-reliance. Lithuanian literature found its only theosophical mystic in the person of Vydūnas,

pseud. of Vilius Storasta (1868–1953), who sought truth and love in the ancient Aryan symbols of eternal light.

The best poet writing on the threshold of Lithuanian independence in 1918 was Maironis, pseud. of the Reverend Jonas Mačiulis (1862–1932).. In his intensely patriotic verse, deep private feelings are both confessed and transmuted into noble cadences full of sorrow and love for his land. A master of poetic form, Maironis taught many later poets how to mold the ancient Lithuanian tongue into a weapon and a melody. His best-known verse collection is *Pavasario balsai* (1895; The Voices of Spring).

The foremost Lithuanian prose writer is Vincas KRĖVĖ, who saw Lithuania's freedom won and lost, lived under two foreign occupations, and finally went into exile. He wrote tales about ancient heroes in a stylized, quasi-folkloric idiom, but switched to the realistic mode in such stories as "Skerdžius" (1923; The Shepherd). His historical plays, *Šarūnas* (1912) and *Skirgaila* (1925), probe the hearts of strong men who try to bend the very life-force to their own will. The secret strength of man, the child and challenger of nature, is an underlying theme in all of Krėvė's works. His contemporary, Antanas Vienulis, pseud. of Antanas Žukauskas (1882–1957), remained in Soviet Lithuania. His initial fascination with the exotic is revealed in *Kaukazo legendos* (1907; The Legends of the Caucasus). Later he became a realistic, rather Chekhovian (*see* Anton CHEKHOV), observer of ordinary men caught in the changing patterns of time; he observed with understanding the poignant hidden tragedies of village life, among déclassé aristocrats, and, in the novel *Prieš dieną* (1925; Before Daybreak), described the emergence of small-town Lithuania. His last novel, *Puodžiūnkiemis* (1952; The Puodžiūnas' Homestead), portrays the collectivization of Lithuanian farms from the socialist-realist point of view. Krėvė's contemporary, Ignas Šeinius, pseud. of Ignas Jurkūnas (1889–1959), was an impressionist writer with literary Scandinavian leanings. His best works are the novels *Kuprelis* (1913; The Hunchback), which depicts the struggle, within an intelligent and sensitive man, between a crippled body and beautiful dreams, and *Siegfried Immerselbe atsijaunina* (1934; Siegfried Immerselbe Rejuvenates Himself), which satirizes a Nazi who gains longevity by transfusions of Jewish blood but loses his "ideals" in the process. Another sardonic commentator, Jurgis Savickis (1890–1952), was a diplomat by profession. His elegant, finely tuned short stories show a cool yet sympathetic understanding of the blindness of small men to the enormity of life passing them by. The poetry and prose of Kazys Boruta (1905–65) reveal a passionate love of life, an unyielding, rebellious heart, and, at times, an impish wit. This latter quality is evidenced in the story *Baltaragio malūnas* (1945; Baltaragis's Windmill), where it is combined with symbolic, fairy-tale visions emanating from plain country landscapes.

In poetry, Jurgis Baltrušaitis (1873–1944), a member of the Russian symbolist circle, wrote austere, pensive verse in Lithuanian. A symbolist presence is also apparent in the work of PUTINAS, whose verse is vibrant with tension between the symbols for luminous visions of unearthly love and those for lust for earthly life. Balys Sruoga (1896–1947) also inclined his verse toward symbolism while following his instinct for musical patterns of word and sound recurrences. His verse play *Milžino paunksmė* (1932; The Shadow of the Giant) probes the weary heart of a king. *Dievų miškas* (1960; The Forest of the Gods), which treats the agony and resilience of man's spirit, is a personal memoir about Sruoga's years in a Nazi prison.

During the 1920s, the "Four Winds" movement reflected the futuristic trend. Its guiding spirit was Kazys Binkis (1893–1932), a dashing poet of bold images and sprightly wit. The revolutionary and machine-worship aspects of futurism, however, did not take root in the green Lithuanian countryside. A stronger group, the "Third Front," emerged in the 1930s; it was composed of leftist writers and critics. The group's best poet, Salomėja Neris, pseud. of Salomėja Bačinskaitė (1904–45), wrote gracefully and poignantly of personal sorrows in a verse of musical lift, echoing folkloric images. But Neris later became "a woman of great fury," harshly proclaiming Soviet ideals and extolling Communist leaders. Petras Cvirka (1909–47) expressed his views in the novel *Žemė maitintoja* (1935; Earth the Provider), about a young farmer oppressed by an unjust socioeconomic system. His novel *Frank Kruk* (1934) is a satire involving a Lithuanian immigrant to the United States who makes money by dishonest means only to be swindled out of it back home by the local bourgeoisie. Cvirka's short stories written during and after World War II praise the Russians and the Soviet regime.

The remarkable novel *Aukštųjų Šimonių likimas* (1935; The Fate of the Šimonys of Aukštujai) by Ivea Simonaitytė (1897–) has both pathos and epic sweep in its description of the downfall of an old Lithuanian family through several generations. Her Soviet novel, *Vilius Karalius* (1956; Vilius the King), depicts peasant life in the socialist-realist manner. A subtle master of style, Antanas Vaičiulaitis (1906–), broke new ground with his impressionistic novel *Valentina* (1936), a delicate portrayal of a woman's withdrawal from the challenge of love. His short stories are mostly about country life, where simple people try to meet capricious fate amidst changing times and their own uncertain passions. Vaičiulaitis, now in exile, has also written fairy tales of careful design and graceful wit.

The poetry of Jonas AISTIS is an evocative blend of French modernistic devices, echoes of folklore, and Aistis's personal "metalanguage," in which intense feeling reshapes mundane speech into haunting new patterns of love, longing, and sorrow. He is also known as a pungent, idiosyncratic essayist and critic. A Christian mystic and also a romantic patriot, Bernardos Brazdžionis (1907–) has produced rhetorical, emotional poetry. In his *Ženklai ir stebuklai* (1936; Signs and Wonders) and *Viešpaties žingsniai* (1944; The Steps of the Lord), life is conceived of as a lyrical interlude on the journey to eternity. Later, in *Šiaurės pašvaistė* (1947; Northern Lights) and *Didžioji kryžkelė* (1953; Great Crossroads), this journey becomes the tragic path of exile.

With the return of the Soviets in 1944, many important Lithuanian writers became refugees in the West. Some continued to write of an unchanged, but now imaginary, Lithuania; others sought ways to confront the new literary, cultural, and existential challenges open to them. In his *Kyržiai* (1943; The Crosses), the novelist Vincas Ramonas (1905–) presents bitter pro- and anti-Soviet conflicts, whereas the prolific and sardonic Aloyzas Baronas (1917–) writes paradoxical novels about exile, morality, and death. Marius Katiliškis (1915–), at heart a displaced farmer, possesses a goodly store of rich country speech, a generous imagination, and a sense of total unity with his distant native soil. His best novel is *Miškais ateina ruduo* (1957; Autumn Comes Through the Forests).

The greatest émigré poet, Henrikas RADAUSKAS, writes not of exile, but of art itself, in its relation to life as a screen of death. He seeks perfection of form with intense intellectual passion and achieves thereby great depth of thought and feeling. His verse is polished, controlled, and extraordinarily multifaceted; it can be modernistic or classical, violent or lyrical, humorous or tragic. Radauskas is unique among the older poets in that his best work appeared abroad.

In 1952 a group of writers wishing to raise the standards of both art and criticism joined in the "Earth" collective. Its prime mover was Kazys Bradūnas (1917–), a pastoral poet who in his numerous works strives to unite an elemental love of his native soil and its pagan heritage with his own Christian world view. The verse of Henrikas Nagys (1920–), a poet and critic of the "Earth" group, is essentially romantic, filled with a deep loneliness that is assuaged by visions of a poetic brotherhood of free, creative individuals. *Mėlynas sniegas* (1961; The Blue Snow) is the best of his several books. Nyka-Niliūnas, pseud. of Alfonsas Čipkus (1919–) is the most philosophical poet and astute critic in the "Earth" group. In *Praradimo simfonijos* (1946; The Symphonies of Dispossession) he combines the agony of exile with the sense of cosmic solitude felt by a man who lives among lost illusions. *Orfėjaus medis* (1954; The Tree of Orpheus) and *Balandžio vigilija* (1957; The Vigil of April) expand these perceptions and relate them to ancient myth and modern existentialism.

Close to "Earth" is Algirdas Landsbergis (1924–), author of plays and fiction. His novel *Kelionė* (1954; The Journey) shows the world of a young exile, which he sees as broken fragments of time and space. *Penki stulpai* (1966; Five Posts), a play, describes, often lyrically, the nightmare world of anti-Soviet guerrillas. A fellow writer, Antanas Škėma (1911–61) stood alone in existentialist despair; the novel *Balta drobulė* (1958; The White Shroud) portrays a mind disintegrating in the meaningless postwar world, and the play *Pabudimas* (1966; The Awakening) presents human endurance being tested by tyranny. Death comes onstage in the plays of Kostas Ostrauskas (1926–); sardonic and relentless, death toys with men's hopes in *Pypkė* (1954; The Pipe) and buries them alive in *Duobkasiai* (1967; The Gravediggers). Ostrauskas writes in an absurdist vein—with biting wit and hidden terror—of the uniqueness of human life before commonplace death.

Death brings the theme of exile to grim perfection in the poetry of Algimantas Mackus (1932–1964). In the name of today's lost and murdered children, his verse speaks of hope betrayed and truth forgotten; his language, although harsh and terse, preserves a hidden music but uses the images of life to signify oblivion. Liūnė Sutema, pseud. of Zina Katiliškienė (1927–), writes with a similar bleak honesty, but her poems seem more lyrical, more vulnerable to hope, because of her love for living things. Finally, the filmmaker and poet Jonas Mekas (1922–), seeks a reconciliation with exile by offering his loyalty to all places through which he has passed with an open heart. Within the Soviet Union, the Stalinist grip relaxed around 1956 to permit some freedom of expression, but socialist realism is still the official norm. Eduardas Mieželaitis (1919–), an old Communist and a pupil of the "Third Front" writers, likes to experiment with poetic language and with literary genres allied to poetry. His *Žmogus* (1962; Man) exudes a "cosmic optimism" faintly reminiscent of Walt Whitman. Justinas Marcinkevičius (1930–) can write graceful poetry, but he often speaks of bitter and bloody things—his country's tragic past and present history: *Kraujas ir pelenai* (1960; Blood and Ashes), a narrative poem that depicts the wartime destruction of a Lithuanian village by the Nazis, whereas *Katedra* (1971; The Cathedral), a verse play, confronts the dichotomy between power and art.

An older writer, Juozas Grušas (1901–), still writes in the traditional realistic mode, but his fiction and plays, such as the historical drama *Herkus Mantas* (1967), contain a moral challenge to the accepted notions of reality in the prevailing social order. His young colleague, Kasys Saja (1932–), conceals his biting satire of official myths under a mask of the theater of the absurd. The prose of Mykolas Sluckis (1928–) conforms to traditional standards, but his characters lack the moral force needed to make them stand out as "positive heroes" of socialist art. On the other hand, Icchokas Meras (1934–), now living in Israel, has produced exciting experimental prose in which the world's absurdity and cruelty are juxtaposed in an almost cubist manner against the innate dignity and nobility of man. He speaks in agony of the grotesque sufferings of the Jews but commits himself to all mankind in its search for creative integrity. Jonas Avyžius (1922–), also tends toward the grotesque. He looks at the world through the minds of his heroes, for whom everything seems strange and absurd, since there is nothing in the world to their sense of moral values that alone can give meaning to life.

Some fine Lithuanian poets have emerged since 1950. Janina Degutytė (1928–) writes romantic, patriotic verse, which is closely bound to nature and to folkloric imagery. With the courage of Antigone, she mourns the dead on both sides of the internal strife that still afflicts her country. Sigitas Geda (1943–), an orphic poet, has learned the magic of nature's message. The complex images in *26 rudens ir vasaros giesmés* (1972; 26 Songs of Autumn and Summer) derive from Geda's great love of life. Judita Vaičiūnaitė (1937–) speaks in iridescent lines of the old city of Vilnius, of ancient myth, and of her own consuming passions. Tomas Venclova (1937–) is an intellectual poet, a scholar, and a translator of works from world literature. His verse has a severe texture that does not quite hide deep, symbolic structures and modern poetic images.

If human values prevail, Lithuanian language and literature should have the inner strength to serve the Muses well in the world of the future.

See: J. Mauclaire, *Panorama de la littérature lithuanienne contemporaine* (1938); A. Vaičiulaitis, *Outline History of Lithuanian Literature* (1942); J. Balys, *Lithuanian Narrative Folksongs: A Description of Types and a Bibliography* (1954); A. Senn, *Storia della letteratura lituana* (1957); A. Rubulis, *Baltic Literature* (1970); R. Silbajoris, *Perfection of Exile: Fourteen Contemporary Lithuanian Writers* (1970).   R.Š.

Livshits, Benedikt Konstantinovich (1887–1939), Russian poet and translator, was born in Odessa. His first book of verse, *Fleyta Marsiya* (1911; The Flute of Marsyas), was in the symbolist-decadent tradition. He joined David BURLYUK's group of "cubo-futurists" in 1912 (*see* RUSSIAN LITERATURE), and applied the methods of French postimpressionist art in the poems of *Volchye solntse* (1914; Sun of the Wolves). Livshits took part in the futurist group's notorious public appearances and acted briefly as its chief theoretician, particularly in his essay "Osvobozhdeniye slova" (1913; Liberation of the Word). He was soon alienated by Burlyuk's opportunism, however, and withdrew into his own brand of aesthetical anti-Europeanism, resulting in a joint manifesto "Myi Zapad" (1914; We and the West), with the composer Artur Lurie and the painter Georgy Yakulov, and in the allusive poems about the "Medusa of the Swamps" in his little book of poems *Iz topi blat* (1922; Out of the Swamp). Livshits later wrote an absorbing memoir, *Polutoraglazy strelets* (1933; Eng. tr., *The One-and-a-Half-Eyed Archer*, 1977), about his three years with the futurists. In 1928 he combined all his poetry, including *Patmos* (1926), a book of neo-Pythagorean metapoems, in *Krotonskiy polden*

(Crotonian Noon). He also translated a volume of French poetry, from Victor Hugo to Paul ELUARD, which is the best in Russian. Livshits died in 1939, the victim of a purge.

See: V. Markov, *Russian Futurists* (1968).   V.M.

Lo-Johansson, Ivar (1901–), Swedish author of novels, short stories, and essays, was born in Ösmo. He held many jobs, traveled widely, and published travel books, short stories, and poetry before the appearance of his first novel, *Måna är död* (1932; Måna Is Dead), an autobiographical story about erotic passion and impossible love. Then followed his well-known works about the *statare,* a disadvantaged group of farm laborers or sharecroppers into which he was born. With social pathos resembling that of John Steinbeck in *The Grapes of Wrath,* he describes their oppression and subhuman lives shockingly and with epic magnificence. First came *Godnatt, jord* (1933; Good Night, Earth) and then over a hundred short stories collected in *Statarna I–II* (1936–37; The Sharecroppers I–II) and *Jordproletärerna* (1941; Proletarians of the Earth). Lo-Johansson's writings contributed much to improving the conditions of these people. In *Bara en mor* (1939; Only a Mother), about the individual versus the collective, he creates a fine portrait of a sharecropper woman's destiny: her spontaneous nude bath in a lake, although taken in decent seclusion, is condemned by her peers; and, rejected by a good man, she marries an inferior man. Worn out by childbirth and hard labor, fighting poverty in vain, she dies early after a life of little joy. *Kungsgatan* (1935; The King's Street) describes the encounter between two innocent farm youths and big-city corruption. The portrait of the girl's turning prostitute shocked readers with its frankness and implied social criticism.

Lo-Johansson's series of autobiographical novels starts with *Analfabeten* (1951; The Illiterate), a respectful portrait of the author's father, which is mixed with indignation toward a society that would victimize an honest man for being naively trustful and uneducated. The titles of the other novels indicate their themes, for example, *Gårdfarihandlaren* (1953; The Peddler), *Journalisten* (1956; The Journalist), *Författaren* (1956; The Writer), and *Lyckan* (1962; Eng. tr., *Bodies of Love,* 1973).

After a science fiction novel, *Elektra* (1967), Lo-Johansson wrote an "epic of passions" published in seven volumes, one for each passion, or vice, for example, *Girigbukarna* (1969; The Misers), *Vällustingarna* (1970; The Libertines), and *Lögnhalsarna* (1971; The Liars).

Lo-Johansson's most important nonfiction writing is his protest against the treatment of old people in *Ålderdoms-Sverige* (1952; Sweden for the Aged), which led to reforms of old people's homes. His fame rests, however, first and foremost on his fiction, which blends social consciousness with imagination, historical perspective, and humor into great art. The first volume in Lo-Johansson's memoirs is *Pubertet* (1978; Puberty).

See: R. Oldenberg, *Ivar Lo-Johansson* (1957); L. Furuland and R. Oldenberg, *Ivar Lo-Johansson i trycksvärtans ljus* (1961); A. Gustafson, *A History of Swedish Literature* (1961), pp. 515–19; E. H. Linder, *Ny Illustrerad svensk litteraturhistoria,* vol. 5 (1966), pp. 565–76; G. Brandell, *Svensk litteratur 1870–1970,* vol. 2 (1975), pp. 113–19.   T.L.

Løland, Rasmus (1861–1907), Norwegian novelist, was born in the western coastal district of Ryfylke. Throughout his life he was hampered by neurotic sensitivity and poor health. His early years were spent in shy isolation and poverty. In 1895 he finally broke away from Ryfylke and established himself in Christiana (now Oslo), where he worked as a writer, translator, and editor of a newspaper for children.

During his short period of literary activity (1892–1900), Løland published an astounding number of books, many of them experimental, and in their structure and setting drawing on his experiences, through childhood and youth, as a socially and physically handicapped person. His creation is limited by his somewhat narrow circle of experience; but one finds character and a deep personal honesty in everything he did. Two representative works are Løland's autobiographical novel *Aasmund Aarak* (1902) and the posthumous novel *Hundrad aar* (1910; Hundred Years). Løland's great achievement, however, is his series of children's books describing the life of a group of boys in his home district. These books were collected in a three-volume edition *Barnebøker* (1923–25; Children's Books). In a masterly way, Løland makes the life of these farm children emerge as an autonomous world, distinct from the clumsy, incomprehensible realm of adults. With its own laws and proportions, its own light and shadows, this children's world is filled with drama and passion, tragedy and deep joy. *Barnebøker* has made Løland a classic of Norwegian literature.

See: S. Eskeland, *Rasmus Løland* (1910).   S.Sk.

Löns, Hermann (1866–1914), German novelist and poet, was born in Kulm on the Vistula, far from the Lüneburger Heide that he came to love and on the poetic description of which rests his literary fame. His extensive knowledge of plant and animal life later was the foundation for his scientific investigations. In 1891, Löns gave up his medical studies to become a journalist in Hanover and Bückeburg. Although his novels are written hastily, his descriptive scenes from nature are inimitable. Never before had the thrills of the born hunter of small game been depicted so vividly and accurately as in *Mein grünes Buch* (1901; My Green Book). The scientist and huntsman are merged with the poet in *Mein braunes Buch* (1906; My Brown Book), Löns's first literary success. He was the first to reproduce in literature the infinite variety of colors in the somber moorlands. His stories from animal life are a combination of scientific accuracy and poetic imagination. The former predominates in *Aus Flur und Forst* (1907; From Field and Forest), originally a commentary for photographs from animal life; the latter prevails in *Mümmelmann* (1909), humorous animal tales. In his novels on peasant life, as in *Der letzte Hansbur* (1909; The Last Hansbur), Löns wished to awaken sympathetic understanding for the reticent and proud peasants of the Lüneburger Heide. *Der Wehrwolf* (1910; Eng. tr., *Harm Wulf*, 1931) pictures them in the terse style of an ancient peasant chronicle with many dialect words of old Germanic stock. The autobiographical novel *Das zweite Gesicht* (1911; The Second Face) provides some insight into the conflicting forces in Löns's restless mind. *Der kleine Rosengarten* (1911; Eng. tr., *The Little Garden of Roses*, 1929) so successfully entered into the spirit and style of the old folk song that its tunes and lyrics captured the popular fancy.

Löns was killed before Reims in September 1914. He had become a favorite of the German youth movement. With his emphasis on national literature, race, and soil, he later became an idol of national socialism.

See: W. Deimann, *Hermann Löns* (1939), and *Der andere Löns* (1965).   E.Ho. rev. A.L.W.

Looy, Jacobus van (1855–1930), Dutch short-story writer, poet, and painter, was born in Haarlem, where he grew up in the orphanage. He had already become an artist when he began publishing *novellen* in *De Nieuwe Gids* in 1885. In such stories as "De nachtcactus" (1888; The Night Cactus) and "De dood van mijn poes" (1889; The Death of My Pussy-Cat), his impressionistic perception and description of reality reflect his background as a painter. These stories were later collected in *Proza* (1892). Van Looy's view of life as something meaningless and painful, even when it seems beautiful, often gives a tone of melancholy to his work. Later this tone softened, and his love for daily life and the ordinary man, his interest in the outside world, as seen through the eye of an artist, appeared in the prose pieces published as *Feesten* (1902; Feasts). The *Wonderlijke avonturen van Zebedeus* (1910; The Strange Adventures of Zebedeus), the fantastic and whimsical prose sketches that were first printed in *De Nieuwe Gids* and the *Tweemaandelijksch Tijdschrift*, were later continued in two volumes of *Bijlagen* (1925; Supplements). Autobiographical elements emerged in the moving and penetrating observations of childhood entitled *Jaapje* (1917) and continued as *Jaap* (1923) and *Jacob* (1930). Van Looy wrote two volumes of travel sketches about Morocco, *Gekken* (1892; Fools) and *Reizen* (1913; Travels). *Nieuw Proza* (1929; New Prose) contains his last sketches and travel impressions. His poetry was collected posthumously as *Gedichten* (1932; Poems).

See: M. Augusta Jacobs, *Jacobus van Looy en zijn literair werk* (1945).   S.L.F.

Lopes, Baltasar (1907–), Portuguese novelist, short-story writer, poet, and essayist, who signs his poems with the pseud. Osvaldo Alcânbara, was born on São Nicolau Island, Cape Verde. After graduating in law and Romance languages in Lisbon, he returned to his native islands to become a high school teacher and attorney. In 1936 he was among the writers who founded *Claridade*, a literary review that had a profound impact on the evolution of modern Cape Verdean literature by drawing attention to local topics and problems. In 1947 he published *Chiquinho* (Frankie), a novel depicting social conditions in Cape Verde. The novel's protagonist realizes that his education will not assure him of a suitable position in his arid, underdeveloped islands, and he decides to emigrate to the United States, perhaps to work beside his father in a New Bedford, Mass., cotton mill. The novel had decisive influence in catalyzing Cape Verdeen fiction toward dealing with the pressing local problems of drought, famine, and emigration, as well as with the folkways and speech patterns of the archipelago. Lopes also portrays the people and atmosphere of Cape Verde in several short stories published in the journals *Claridade, Vértice,* and *Cabo Verde*. Some are included in anthologies, such as his own *Antologia da ficção cabo-verdiana contemporânea* (1960; Anthology of Contemporary Cape Verdean Fiction). His poems appeared mainly in *Claridade*. His study *O dialecto crioulo de Cabo Verde* (1957; The Creole Dialect of Cape Verde) represents the first major work in its field.

See: N. Araujo, *A Study of Cape Verdean Literature* (1966), pp. 132–45; M. Ferreira, *Aventura crioula* (2d ed., 1973), pp. 101–11, 213–15.   E.M.D.

Lopes, Manuel (dos Santos) (1907–), Portuguese novelist and poet born on São Vicente Island in the Cape Verde archipelago, is one of Cape Verde's foremost writers and one of the staunchest defenders of the archipelago's Creole culture within the Portuguese sphere of the tropics. In his youth, he was a member of the *Claridade* group. Then he went to live in the Azores, but most of his later years have been spent in Portugal. Like most of the islands' elite, Lopes sees Cape Verde as a society composed of African and European elements—but more European than African. This conviction, coupled with what some younger Cape Verdeans have termed an escapist stance, clashes with their idea of Cape Verde as an extension of Africa. According to Lopes's detractors, evasion means the diminishment of Cape Verde's African substance, the failure to deal with chronic socioeconomic problems, and the escape from the islands to a more comfortable life in Europe. The accusations against him and others of his generation may not be totally warranted when seen in the context of the overwhelmingly Western upbringing of Cape Verdean intellectuals.

The resignation and resilience of the Cape Verdean poor is a major theme in Lopes's prose fiction, including the short-story collection *O galo cantou na baía* (1959; The Rooster Crowed in the Bay); in his novels *Chuva braba* (1956; Heavy Rain) and *Os flagelados do vento leste* (1959; The Victims of the East Wind); and in his poetry, most of it contained in the volumes *Poemas de quem ficou* (1949; Poems of One Who Remained Behind) and *Crioulo e outros poemas* (1964; Creole and Other Poems).

Despite his supposed escapism and self-conscious eschewal of Africanism, Lopes has succeeded in re-creating a Creole world faithfully and thus has helped to further Cape Verde's literary maturity.

See: N. Araujo, *A Study of Cape Verdean Literature* (1966), pp. 111–32; O. Lopes, "Ficção cabo-verdiana," *Modo de Ler: crítica e interpretação literária*, vol. 2 (1969), pp. 135–47.   R.G.H.

López Pacheco, Jesús (1930–), Spanish novelist, short-story writer, poet, and translator, was born in Madrid. He spent his early years near various power plants where his father was employed and later returned to Madrid to study philosophy and letters at the university there. In 1955–56 he founded the University Congress of Young Writers, the first university movement organized against the regime of Francisco Franco. In 1968 he moved to Canada, where he has taught for several years.

In 1952, López Pacheco published a book of poems, *Dejar crecer este silencio* (Let This Silence Grow), and in 1955 he received the first Sésamo Prize for his short story "Maniquí perfecto" (The Perfect Mannikin). Preoccupation with social problems, a recurrent theme in his three volumes of poetry published in 1961, persists in more recent poetry such as *Algunos aspectos del orden público en el momento actual de la histeria de España* (1970; Some Aspects of Public Order at the Present Moment in the Hysteria of Spain).

His novel *Central Eléctrica* (1956; Power Plant), considered the first social novel after the Civil War to present the proletariat as a protagonist, criticizes the injustices suffered by the working class and is also a testimony to the struggle of the common people against technological progress. The social realism of this novel has a mythical and universal dimension. An obsession with exile is reflected in one of his more recent novels, *La hoja de parra* (1973; The Fig Leaf). López Pacheco's work has remained faithful to the aesthetic principles of the social realism of the 1950s.

See: P. Gil Casado, *La novela social española* (1967), pp. 132–51.   J.O.

Lòpez-Picó, Josep Maria (1886–1959), Catalan poet, and an extraordinarily productive writer, was born in Barcelona. The emphasis on witticism in his early work gave way to a more epigrammatic and occasionally hermetic style. Despite his substantial lyrical talent, his verse often seems cold, although it is never mediocre. The outstanding virtue of his poetry, and the element that has exerted

a notable influence on later generations of Catalan writers, is the constant renovation of images—images of material reality (the house, the landscape) as well as images of subjective experience (love, serenity). Despite its wide circulation in Catalonia, Lòpez-Picó's poetry seems unlikely to last. His disciples, mostly "decadent" symbolists, emphasized his enigmatic tone, which is not in keeping with the mainstream of Catalan poetry.

After 1913 he published at least a volume a year, with the exception of 1939, when Francisco Franco's forces invaded Catalonia. Among his most important works are *Intermetzzo galant* (1910; Gallant Intermezzo), *Torment froment* (1910; Trembling Torment), *Poemes de port* (1911; Harbor Poems), *Amor, Senyor* (1913; Love, the Lord), *Espectacles i mitologia* (1914; Spectacles and Mythology), *Epigrammata* (1911); *L'ofrena* (The Offering), *Paraules* (1916; Words), *L'instant, les Noces i el càntic serè* (The Instant, the Betrothal and the Serene Song), *El meu pare i jo* (My Father and I), *Primer recull de poesies* (First Collection of Poems), *Moralitats i pretextos* (Moralizings and Pretexts), *Dietari espiritual* (Spiritual Calendar), *L'oci de la paraula* (1927; The Leisure of Words), and *Epitalami* (Epithalamium). Upon publication of *Epitalami*, his 25th book, Lòpez-Picó was honored by the "Revista" group which prepared an anthology of his poetry. He collaborated on many Catalonian journals, especially *Vell i nou, Empori, Quaderns d'estudi*, and *Quaderns de poesia*. He helped found the so-called *Almanac de la Poesia*, which since 1912 has published a yearly collection of verse from various sources. In 1915, with Joaquim Folguera, he founded the *Revista*, a bimonthly that published poetry and essays and captured the aesthetic ideals of the generation. Many of the poet's compositions have been translated into English, Italian, Spanish, French, and German. The suppression of Catalan culture by the Franco regime inhibited Lòpez-Picó's literary and editorial work in his final years.

See: M. de Montoliu, *Estudi d'història literaria de Catalunya* (1912–14); A. Plana, *Estudi preliminar de l'antologia de poetes catalans* (1915); J. Folguera, *Les noves valors de la poesia catalana* (1919); R. Crossmann, *Katalanische Lyrik der Gegenwart* (1923); C. Giardini, *Antologia dei poeti catalani contemporanei, 1845–1925* (1926).   J.M.M.iV.

López Pinillos, José (1875–1922), Spanish novelist, playwright, and journalist, left his native Seville for Madrid at the age of 20 and soon made a name for himself as a journalist, writing for a number of newspapers under the pseudonym of Pármeno, a name taken from the 15th-century classic *La Celestina* and suggestive of honesty and frankness. His novels tend to be violent. They include *La sangre de Cristo* (1907; The Blood of Christ); *Doña Mesalina* (1910), considered his best work; *Las águilas* (1911; The Eagles), an antibullfight tract in the tradition of Vicente BLASCO IBÁÑEZ's *Sangre y arena* (1908; Blood and Sand) but without the admixture of glory Blasco provides; and *Cintas Rojas* (1916; Red Ribbons), whose unfeeling protagonist kills eight people in succession on a single afternoon so as to be able to buy a bullfight ticket. With hindsight, the contemporary reader can see López Pinillos as a predecessor of Camilo José CELA and the so-called *tremendismo* (sensationalism) of the 1940s. He is also one of Spain's many late naturalists.

López Pinillos supported himself in large part with newspaper work and by writing plays, a number of which were great theatrical successes. Representative of his rural dramas are *El pantano* (1913; The Swamp), *Esclavitud* (1918; Slavery), and *La tierra* (1921; The Land). These are melodramatic family honor plays filled with distorted sexuality, bloody revenge, and often an element of class struggle and social protest. They clearly were produced by the same currents that inspired Jacinto BENAVENTE's rural dramas of these same years as well as the later poetic transcendence of this subject matter in Federico GARCÍA LORCA's rural trilogy.

For the most part, López Pinillo's work suffers from crudity, lack of restraint, and an insistence on violent effects at the expense of all other aesthetic concerns. At present it is little known.

See: E. G. de Nora, *La novela española contemporánea,* vol. 1 (1963), pp. 261–75; J. C. Mainer, *Literatura y pequeña burguesía* (1972), pp. 89–120.   H.L.B.

López Rubio, José (1903–), Spanish dramatist, was born in Motril in the province of Granada. He wrote his first plays *De la noche a la mañana* (1929; From Night to Morning) and *Casa de naipes* (1930; House of Cards), in collaboration with Eduardo Ugarte. In the early 1930s he went to Hollywood with Enrique JARDIEL PONCELA and Edgar Neville to assist Gregorio MARTÍNEZ SIERRA in preparing of films for release in Spanish-speaking countries. He returned to Spain after the Spanish Civil War and began his theatrical career with *Alberto* (1949) and *Celos del aire* (1950; Jealousy in the Air). In these two plays he wrote in a clever way about love, fantasy, and infidelity, establishing a style he would continue to cultivate. His plays, like those of Alejandro CASONA, Víctor RUIZ IRIARTE, and Edgar Neville, have been classified as "teatro de evasión" (evasion theater), that is, works that offer a new perspective on situations that are sometimes comic, sometimes serious. In *La venda en los ojos* (1954; Eng. tr., *The Blindfold,* 1970), winner of the National Theater Prize, he creates one of his most unforgettable characters. Abandoned by her husband, Beatriz appears to reject reality in order to live in a world of fantasy. Her parents, convinced that her insanity protects her from a painful truth, believe, support, and even enjoy her charade. The play suddenly becomes serious when the husband returns. In a scene that proves that Beatriz is far from crazy, she rejects her errant spouse. After his departure, and much to the relief of her parents, Beatriz resumes her antics and the comedy of appearances begins again. *La otra orilla* (1954; The Other Shore), a very successful play reminiscent of Noel Coward's *Blithe Spirit,* uses detective story elements and features some very lively, very witty phantoms. López Rubio, who also writes for television and translates and adapts foreign works for films, is known for his excellent dramatic technique and his ability to create interesting scripts with a minimum of elements. He is particularly adept at amusing repartee and at shifting the dramatic mood from humor to emotional tension and back to humor, as in *La venda en los ojos.* Among his other important plays are: *Una madeja de lana azul celeste* (1951; A Ball of Sky-Blue Yarn) and *Las manos son inocentes* (1958; Innocent Hands).

See: A. M. Pasquariello and J. V. Falconieri, Introduction to *La otra orilla* (1958); M. Holt, *The Contemporary Spanish Theater (1949–1972)* (1975), pp. 34–51; Rodríguez de León, "El humor en el teatro de López Rubio," in *El teatro de humor en España* (1966), pp. 151–68.

P.W.O'C.

López Salinas, Armando (1926–), Spanish novelist and short-story writer, was born in Madrid, attended high school at the Instituto Lope de Vega, and afterwards worked for a while as a manual laborer. A self-taught writer, López Salinas portrays the worker as a fundamental element in the class struggle. *La mina* (1960; The Mine), his best-known book, recounts the exodus of an Andalusian family to the mines in a direct and sometimes lyrical style. He is the coauthor of several travel books: *Caminando por las Hurdes* (1960; Walking through the Hurdes), *Río abajo* (1966; Downstream), and *Viaje al país gallego* (1967; Journey to Galicia), which are also excellent chronicles of working-class life throughout Spain. *Año tras año* (1962; Year After Year) is a vivid testimony to the physical and moral climate of post-Civil War Madrid. López Salinas's works represent an effort to present and condemn the precarious social conditions of the underprivileged Spaniard.

See: R. Bosch, *La novela española del siglo XX,* vol. 2 (1970), pp. 327–32.   J.O.

Loreau, Max (1928–), Belgian poet and prose writer, was born in Brussels and educated at the University of Brussels, where he received a doctorate in philosophy. The complex interrelationship between literary practice and philosophical questioning constitutes a central concern of Loreau's work. *Cri: éclats et phases* (1974; Cry: Bursts and Phases), a long philosophical poem, examines, through the myth of the "cry" as origin, the rebirth of light and appearance. In *Nouvelles des êtres et des pas* (1976; Tales of Beings and Steps), sight functions as a mechanism for the exploration of the self.

The true originality of Loreau's poetic vision resides in his attempt to delineate within writing the locus of a vanishing point, of an abyss that not only pervades the philosophical discourse but also operates within representation and language. Loreau thus emerges as a hyper-Platonic thinker dissatisfied with the scene of the cave proposed by Plato. Implicit is the question of what happens if the prisoners are not chained and if, when looking back and walking toward the light, they only wander forever within a semiobscurity. If the light—the Good— is not a given, where does it come from, how is it fostered, and what is to become of the appearance once it ceases to be an idea endowed with luminosity? Highly sensitive to the "vision" of the visual arts, Loreau has published numerous critical studies on art, including *Jean Dubuffet: stratégie de la création* (1973) and *Dotremont Logogrammes* (1975). For Loreau, literature is, above all, the locus where things and words show themselves forth; the task of literature is to make language alive and hence to bring to life the men who inhabit language. Such an aesthetic impulse questions received ideas, even though its foundations may be rooted in classical traditions. In this, his work is akin to that of Henri MICHAUX, Maurice BLANCHOT, and even Franz KAFKA.   M.R.

Lorenzo, Pedro de (1917–), Spanish novelist, poet, essayist, and journalist, was born in Casas de Don Antonio, in the province of Cáceres. Although he is frequently compared to Gabriel MIRÓ and AZORÍN, his absolute independence of literary fashions has caused many to overlook or underestimate the real excellence of his novels. *La quinta soledad* (1943; Fifth Solitude), whose title alludes to Luis de Góngora's *Soledades,* reveals his baroque tendencies, anticipating by over two decades the present stylistic mode in fiction. A novel about a prisoner in his cell, it is an often existential meditation upon incarceration. *La sal perdida* (1947; Lost Salt) presents reflections on life, love, the writing profession, and problems of the novel. It experiments with narrative viewpoint and rejects literary "sociology." In its clear use of cinematographic techniques—varied narrative planes, flashbacks, "traveling," and fades—*La sal* also anticipates the French *nouveau roman* (*see* FRENCH LITERATURE). *Una conciencia de alquiler* (1953; Conscience For Rent), among the most significant post-Civil War novels, begins the projected seven-novel cycle "Los descontentos." In addition to *Una conciencia, Cuatro de familia* (1956; Four in the Family) and *Los álamos de Alonso Mora* (1970; The Poplars of Alonso Mora) have appeared to date. A saga of the Mora family and of the countryside, peasants, and miners of Extremadura, the cycle continues Lorenzo's use of evocation, fantasy, indeterminate time, and kaleidoscopic vision in exquisitely stylized prose. *Cuatro de familia* utilizes a Grand Guignol technique found in later experimental Latin American narratives, while *Los álamos* is a delicate and lyrically introspective novel of childhood. *Tu dulce cuerpo pensado* (1947; Your Sweet Body in Thought) exemplifies Lorenzo's poetry, while the poetic prose of *Angélica* (1955) presents a defense of cultured, aesthetic writing against the day's neonaturalism. Travel books and landscape portraiture include *Tierras de España* (1953; Spanish Landscapes), *Extremadura, la fantasía heroica* (1961; Extremadura, The Heroic Fantasy), and *Viaje de los ríos de España* (1968; Trip on Spain's Rivers), awarded the National Prize for Literature. Among Lorenzo's volumes of essays are *Fantasía en la plazuela* (1953; Fantasy in the Square), *Fray Luis de Léon* (1964), *Elogio de la Retórica* (1969; In Praise of Rhetoric), and *La medalla de papel* (1970; The Paper Medal).

See: D. Pérez Minik, *Novela española de los siglos XIX y XX* (1957), pp. 325–26; E. G. de Nora, *La novela española contemporánea*, vol. 3 (1967), pp. 266–71; A. Balbuena Prat, *Historia de la literatura española*, vol. 4 (1968), pp. 894–96; F. Martínez Ruiz, "Pedro de Lorenzo: La vuelta de un gran novelista," *LEL* 500 (Sept. 15, 1972): 24–27.   J.W.D.

Loti, Pierre, pseud. of Julien Viaud (1850–1923), French novelist, was born in Rochefort into a distinguished Huguenot family. He won recognition as a master of colorful, nostalgic descriptions of exotic scenes and for his portrayals of the grimness and majesty of death. At the age of 15, Loti decided to become a naval officer, and two years later he entered naval school. In 1910, at the end of a long professional career, he was retired with the rank of captain. The French navy buried him with national pomp in the grove of his ancestral home at Saint-Pierre d'Oleron. He had been elected to the Académie Française in 1891.

From early childhood, Loti kept a diary, published in part as *Journal intime* (1926; Private Journal), that later became the source of his literary production. He wrote more than 40 volumes of touching memoirs and of impressions gleaned in endless voyages and wanderings. Loti's contact with Polynesia provided the background for *Rarahu,* later called *Le Mariage de Loti* (1880; Eng. tr., *Rarahu; or, The Marriage of Loti,* 1892). He recalled Turkey in *Aziyade* (1879), *Les Désenchantées* (1906; Eng. tr., *The Disenchanted,* 1906), and *Suprêmes Visions d'Orient* (1921); West Africa in *Le Roman d'un spahi* (1881; Eng. tr., *The Romance of a Spahi,* 1890); Brittany in *Mon Frère Yves* (1883; Eng. tr., *My Brother Yves,* 1887) and *Pêcheur d'Islande* (1886; Eng. tr., *An Icelandic Fisherman,* 1888); Japan in *Madame Chrysanthème* (1887; Eng. tr., 1889); China in *Matelot* (1893; Sailor); the Middle East in *La Galilée* (1895); the Basque country in *Ramuntcho* (1897); Iran in *Vers Ispahan* (1904; Towards Ispahan); Cambodia in *Un Pèlerin d'Angkor* (1906; A Pilgrim of Angkor); and Egypt, Morocco, and India in various other works. *Pêcheur d'Islande* is probably his masterpiece.

The religious doubts that crept into Loti's mind at a tender age molded his whole life. Bereft of a faith that

had promised everlasting communion with his mother—the only woman he ever truly loved—he lived thereafter in mortal dread of losing her. A haunting presentiment of the utter solitude that must one day befall him, the sense of his own fragility and of the futility of life, affected him profoundly. He sought eagerly and enviously, in later life, the secret of the abiding faith of humble folk, through the Moslem world of the Prophet, in the footsteps of Jesus in Galilee, and at the shrines of the Indian theosophists in holy Benares. On the other hand, his life as a sailor hardened his character in some respects and helped his talent to blossom. Loti found that by simply confiding in his readers, "unknown friends," he could procure some solace for his chagrin and anxiety. His deeply emotional prose has earned him a place among the best of the subjective writers.

Although Loti is usually considered the initiator of modern exotic fiction, the bond between him and the many authors of exotic and regional novels (who more or less consciously derived their inspiration from him) is as slight as his connection with Jacques-Henri Bernardin de Saint-Pierre (1737–1814) and François-René de Chateaubriand (1768–1848), with whom he has been too readily associated. Whether we consider Loti as a writer of works of fiction, in which his characters clearly appear to be projections of his inner self, or as a writer of travel books, in which the very universe seems to revolve around his person, we find him in every sense identical with the Loti of those gems of introspective study, *Le Roman d'un enfant* (1890; The Romance of a Child) and *Prime Jeunesse* (1919; Early Youth). His depth of human understanding would justify placing his whole production under the title of one of his most stirring books, *Le Livre de la pitié et de la mort* (1890; The Book of Pity and Death). Loti was also a talented painter in the manner of the impressionists.

See: N. Serban, *Pierre Loti: sa vie et son œuvre* (1924); P. Brodin, *Loti* (1942).   P.A.C. rev. P.Br.

Louÿs, Pierre, pseud. of Pierre Louis (1870–1925), French poet and novelist, was born in Ghent, Belgium, of French parents. Educated in Paris, he made his entry into the world of letters by founding, with André GIDE, Paul VALÉRY, and Henri de RÉGNIER, *La Conque* (1891), a symbolist review in which were published his first poems, soon afterwards collected under the title *Astarté* (1891). Five years later, the same four writers founded the sumptuous review *Le Centaure.* Louÿs was the disciple of José de HEREDIA, and in 1899 he married the youngest daughter of this leading poet of the Parnassian school.

A man of insatiable intellectual curiosity and passionate devotion to art, at once a sensuous pagan and a refined aesthete, Louÿs celebrated the free life of ancient Greece and proclaimed sensual fulfillment a condition essential to artistic creation and spiritual development. As a Greek scholar, he translated *Poésies de Méléagre de Gadara* (1893) and *Scènes de la vie des courtisanes de Lucien* (1894; Scenes from Lucian's Life of Courtisans), graceful, piquant works that foreshadowed the erotic and Hellenistic tendencies of his later writings. When Louÿs published his own *Les Chansons de Bilitis, traduites du grec par Pierre Louÿs* (1894; Eng. tr., *The Songs of Bilitis, translated from the Greek,* 1904), several scholars mistook the licentious poems in classical style for an authentic work by a contemporary of Sappho. Louÿs's novel of Alexandrian manners, *Aphrodite* (1896; Eng. tr., *Aphrodite, a Novel of Ancient Manners,* 1900), makes an appeal for the rehabilitation of physical love and naked beauty. Although shallow and unreal in its psychology, the work attests to a remarkable historical knowledge and has pages luminously picturesque and exquisitely pure in form. In *La Femme et le pantin* (1898; Eng. tr., *Woman and Puppet*, 1908), Louÿs's interest becomes entirely psychological. Restrained yet vigorous in its expression, this Andalusian novel recounts the pathetic experience of a man to whom sensuality has brought complete servitude and ruin. Among Louÿs's numerous short stories of classical or fictitious inspiration, those collected in *Les Aventures du roi Pausole* (1901; Eng. tr., *The Adventures of King Pausole*, 1926) are especially noteworthy for their graceful and spicy drollery.

Although the success of certain of his works was founded as much on their licentious character as on their literary merit, some of Louÿs's poems, such as those in *Poésies* (1927), may well be remembered for their grace, clear imagery, and pure and flexible harmony. Indeed, few poets have ever had a more fervent worship of beauty and a more profound respect for form.

See: E. Gaubert, *Pierre Louÿs* (1904) and *Le Tombeau de Pierre Louÿs* (1925); A. Gide, *Si le grain ne meurt* (1926), passim; R. Cardinne-Petit, *Pierre Louÿs intime; le solitaire du hameau* (1942); R. Fleury, *Pierre Louÿs et Gilbert de Voisins* (1973).												B.R.L.

Lovinescu, Eugen (1881–1943), Romanian critic and literary historian, was born in Fălticeni. He was educated in classical philology at Iaşi, the University of Bucharest, and the Sorbonne, and he later became a teacher at Ploeşti and Bucharest.

Although Lovinescu was a prolific writer in several genres, he is important as a major critic of Romanian literature between the two world wars. He early declared himself to be a critic in the tradition of Titu MAIORESCU, and joined the editorial staff of the journal *Convorbiri literare*. By temperament a polemicist, he encouraged Romanian ventures into modernism, especially impressionism, and strongly advocated the autonomy of literature. Two collections of his articles, *Paşi pe nisip* (1906; Steps in the Sand) and *Critice* (1909, rev., 1925–29), established his reputation. Shortly thereafter he began to produce his series of monographs: *Grigore Alexandrescu* (1910), *Costache Negruzzi* (1918), and *Gheorghe Asachi* (1921). As editor of the journal *Sburătorul* (1919–21; 1926–27), Lovinescu promoted the reputation of Lucan BLAGA, introduced the poetry of Ion BARBU, and was the first to proclaim the literary merit of Livia REBREANU's *Ion*. Lovinescu's major works are *Istoria civilizaţiei române moderne* (1924–25; History of Modern Romanian Civilization); the authoritative *Istoria literaturii române contemporane* (1926–29, rev., 1937; History of Contemporary Romanian Literature), containing his theory of the mutation of values; *Titu Maiorescu* (1940); *Titu Maiorescu şi posteritatea critica* (1943; Titu Maiorescu and His Critical Posterity); and *Memorii* (1930, 1941; Memoirs).

See: I. Negoiţescu, *Eugen Lovinescu* (1970); E. Simion, *Eugen Lovinescu: scepticul mîntuit* (1971).												T.A.P.

Luca de Tena, Juan Ignacio (1897–), Spanish playwright, was born in Madrid. He rose to political prominence before the Civil War, when he served as deputy from Seville to the Spanish Cortes. For several years he directed the Madrid newspaper *ABC* and the prestigious weekly magazine *Blanco y Negro*. Following a four-year term as Spanish ambassador to Chile, he diverted his strong Loyalist sympathies from the active political arena to the legitimate stage, writing nearly 50 plays in a 40-year span.

While his monarchist stance has elicited an affectionate public response in Spain, the ideological content of several of his historical and sentimental dramas has incensed a few critics who, like Francisco Ruiz-Ramón and Gonzalo TORRENTE BALLESTER, unjustly deprecate the best of his structurally sound plays. Most noteworthy in his repertory are two related works about the Bourbon rule of Alfonso XII and María Cristina, *¿Dónde vas, Alfonso XII?* (1957; Where Now, Alfonso XII?) and *¿Dónde vas, triste de ti?* (1959; Where Now, Sad Friend?). An early Pirandellian (*see* Luigi PIRANDELLO) experiment, *¿Quién soy yo?* (1935; Who Am I?), first staged when Luca de Tena was 38 years of age, enjoyed an unprecedented revival in 1966 and prompted him to write the equally popular sequel, *Yo soy Brandel* (1969; I Am Brandel). The plays deal with the provocative theme of the impersonation of a political leader.

While some critics struggle to identify neo-Pirandellian thought in Luca de Tena's most recent plays, his audiences have been satisfied to be amused and entertained by the uncomplicated and ephemeral comedy of his many nostalgic and romanticized farces. His principal artistic merits reside in the careful construction of well-made plays and the skillful use of the passage of time as a thematic or symbolic motif.

See: W. Newberry, "Luca de Tena, Pirandello, and the Spanish Tradition," *Hispania* 50 (1967): 253–61.
												D.R.McK.

Lucebert, pseud. of Lubertus Jacobus Swaanswijk (1924–), Dutch poet, painter, and photographer, was born in Amsterdam of a working-class family. He is the most important representative of the experimental use of poetic language in the generation after World War II. Lucebert achieves his effects not by rhythm or by the structure of the poetic line, but by the creative use of language. He puts letters together to form words that have no meaning. Other words have several layers of meaning, which the reader must explore for himself. He thus expects great associative powers in his readers, and his poetry can be quite cerebral, especially in such early volumes as *Triangel in de jungle* (1951; Triangle in the Jungle) and *Apocrief* (1952; Apocryphal). On the other hand, as Lucebert himself has said, much of his poetry should be read aloud, in order to achieve its full effect. One of the most versatile poets of his generation, he manipulates the language in an entirely new way. He attempts to restore the unity of man and nature, and he connects the universe with his own existence. More than any other poet of the "Experimentalist" group, he has made image the essence of his poetry. His imagery is more transparent and his diction is simpler in his later poetry, *Van de afgrond en de luchtmens* (1953; Of the Abyss and the Air Man), *Alfabel* (1955), and *Amulet* (1957). The poems are more traditional, but retain their irony, satire, and humor. *Val voor vliegengod* (1959; A Trap for a God of the Flies) contains some prose. Most of his work is collected in *Gedichten 1948–1963* (1965; Poems, 1948–1963); . . . *En morgen de hele wereld* (1972; . . . And Tomorrow the Whole World) includes drawings.

See: R. A. Cornets de Groot, *De open ruimte* (1967), pp. 119–89.												S.L.F.

Lugné-Poe, Aurélien (1869–1940), French actor, director, and producer, was born in Paris. After André ANTOINE's Théâtre Libre ceased to function, Lugné-Poe became France's leading theatrical innovator. He studied at the Conservatoire (1888–92) and served his apprenticeship (1888–90) under Antoine at the Théâtre Libre. Under the stimulus of his friendship with the Nabi painters, Lugné-Poe developed an interest in the symbolist movement, and he joined Paul FORT's Théâtre d'Art (1891), soon assuming its direction. Following his successful production of Maurice MAETERLINCK's *Pelléas et Mélisande,* Lugné-Poe converted the theater into the Théâtre de l'Œuvre (1893), a company that represented a poetic and idealistic reaction to Antoine's stark realism.

L'Œuvre's first season was entirely dedicated to Henrik IBSEN's plays, but to Ibsen's dismay, Lugné-Poe staged his dramas according to the technique used for symbolist works. Ibsen's advice, however, later induced the producer to adopt a mitigated realism. In subsequent seasons, Lugné-Poe continued to champion Ibsen and Scandinavian dramatists as well as other foreign playwrights: Gerhart HAUPTMANN, August STRINDBERG, Oscar Wilde, Nikolay Gogol, Arthur SCHNITZLER, Gabriele D'ANNUNZIO, George Bernard Shaw, as well as the Sanskrit dramas of India. Lugné-Poe thus continued Antoine's work of making the French more receptive to foreign plays. His company's repertory also included new French authors. His stagings of Alfred JARRY's *Ubu roi* (1896) and of Paul CLAUDEL's *L'Annonce faite à Marie* (1912; Eng. tr., *The Tidings Brought to Marie,* 1916) are landmarks in the development of contemporary French drama. Lugné-Poe undoubtedly excelled as a *metteur en scène,* and Konstantin Stanislavsky acknowledged his debt to him. His main strength, however, lay probably in his ability to recognize new talent and in his willingness to produce any work of originality without hoping for a wide appeal. Although he abandoned his theatrical career in 1929, the Théâtre de l'Œuvre has endured to the present, and contemporary French drama is richer for the foreign masterpieces he introduced into France and for the talents he discovered.

See: G. Jasper, *Adventure in the Theatre: Lugné-Poe and the Théâtre de l'Œuvre to 1899* (1947).   M.Sa.

Lukáč, Emil Boleslav (1900–), Slovak poet, was born in Hodruša, central Slovakia. A Protestant pastor, politician, and editor of several literary journals, he was also a translator of French poetry. His own verse, although clearly inspired by native poetic trends, betrays the influence of Paul VERLAINE, Rainer Maria RILKE, Paul CLAUDEL, and Otokar BŘEZINA. Lukáč and Ján SMREK were the outstanding Slovak poets between the two world wars. In contrast to Smrek's optimistic verse, however, the poetry of Lukáč is deeply pessimistic, albeit concerned with metaphysical Christian humanism and pacifism. The ecstatic mysticism of his early collections *Spoved'* (1922; Confession) and *Hymny k sláve Hosudarovej* (1926; Hymns to the Glory of the Lord) yields to skepticism and disillusionment in his next two books, *Križovatky* (1929; Crossroads) and *Spev vlkov* (1929; Song of the Wolves). He senses the imminent catastrophe of war in *Moloch* (1938), a collection using subjects from the Spanish Civil War, while *Babel* (1944) and *Dies irae* (1946) are further expressions of his Christian humanist point of view. Lukáč's language is ornate and baroque, often influenced by the Bible, and his metaphysical imagery is replete with elaborate symbolism.

See: M. Tomčík, *Súčasná slovenská literatúra* (1960).
F.M.B.

Lukács, György (1885–1971), Hungarian philosopher and literary critic, was born in Budapest into a wealthy upper-middle-class Jewish family. He was one of the most influential Marxist thinkers of the 20th century. Lukács was educated in Budapest and Berlin, taking degrees in law and philosophy. His first important study of aesthetics was published in 1909 in the Budapest review *Nyugat* (*see* HUNGARIAN LITERATURE). The following year he published a collection of essays, *A lélek és a formák* (The

Soul and the Forms). In this work, as well as in *A modern dráma fejlődésének története* (2 vols., 1911; The History of the Evolution of the Modern Drama), Lukács still adhered to Wilhelm Dilthey's antipositivistic method of understanding the past through an act of imaginative recovery. Lukács lived in Heidelberg between 1912 and 1918, a crucial period in his development during which he became associated with Max Weber and was influenced by the philosophy of Emil Lask. After 1918, Lukács wrote mainly in German and became known abroad as Georg Lukács. Indeed, his *Die Theorie des Romans* (1920; Eng. tr., *The Theory of the Novel,* 1971), a neo-Hegelian inquiry into the connections between the development of aesthetic forms and history, made a much greater impact in Germany than anywhere else. World War I radicalized Lukács's thinking; although he had not been a Marxist before, he joined the newly formed Hungarian Communist Party in 1918 and became commissar for education during Béla Kun's Soviet Republic.

From 1919 to 1929, Lukács lived in Vienna, where he published his most influential political and philosophical treatise, *Geschichte und Klassenbewusstsein* (1923; Eng. tr., *History and Class Consciousness,* 1971), which he later repudiated. This work addressed itself to Lenin's theory of the role of the Communist Party. Lukács's work stated, to quote George Lichtheim, that "the Party was a classless force which had imposed itself upon an immature labor movement." Such an "elitist" emphasis, coupled with his critique of Engelsian materialism, brought down upon Lukács furious attacks and accusations of "Hegelianism" from Communist Party theoreticians. Between 1929 and 1931 and again between 1933 and 1945, Lukács lived in the USSR where he worked for various Russian, German, and Hungarian cultural publications. From 1931 to 1933 he was in Berlin taking part in the ideological work of the German Communist Party.

In the 1930s he turned his attention to aesthetics, writing extensively on such topics as art and realism. Lukács's theory of realism, expounded in *A realizmus problémái* (1948; Eng. tr., *Studies in European Realism,* 1950), treats the world as an objective category reflected in the artist's consciousness. According to this theory, the central category of realism is "typicality," for it is through human types that the general unites with the particular. Lukács rejected modernism as "subjectivistic," and in *A történelmi regény* (1947; Eng. tr., *The Historical Novel,* 1962) as well as in other essays he held up the "great realism" of Honoré de Balzac and Lev Tolstoy as a model worth following. In *Goethe und seine Zeit* (1947; in Hungarian, 1946; Eng. tr., *Goethe and His Time,* 1967) Lukács judged Goethe's work as the crowning achievement of the German Enlightenment, presenting the author of *Faust* as a complete rationalist. Lukács condemned irrationalism as the source of Hitlerism and blamed German idealist philosophy after Hegel for the holocaust of World War II; but the book that put forward this thesis, *Az ész trónfosztása* (1954; The Destruction of Reason), is regarded by most Western critics as a polemical exercise of little merit. Lukács's work on aesthetics culminated in the two volumes of *Die Eigenart des Aesthetischen* (1963; Characteristics of the Aesthetic), in which he partly revised his earlier theory of "reflection," stressing the cognitive value of art. During the 1950s and 1960s, he wrote many critical essays, of which the most important are those on Thomas MANN and Aleksandr SOLZHENITSYN. Lukács's last major work, an attempt to create a Marxist ontology, remained unfinished.

Lukács's impact upon Hungarian literature has been much slighter than his influence on modern Marxist thought. Between 1946 and 1950, during which time he served as editor of the journal *Forum*, Lukács helped shape Hungarian cultural policy and advocated "socialist humanism" in the arts. In 1949 he was attacked by József Révai, Communist Party spokesman on cultural affairs, for preferring "bourgeois [critical] realism to socialist realism" and was forced to recant. As a former member of Imre Nagy's 1956 revolutionary government, he was repeatedly attacked in the late 1950s for his "mistakes and deviations." In the mid-1960s, however, Lukács regained political favor. A German edition of his collected works was published in 12 volumes in 1968.

See: V. Zitta, *Georg Lukács's Marxism* (1964); F. Benseler, ed., *Festschrift zum 80. Geburtstag* (1965); G. Lichtheim, *Lukács* (1970); G. H. R. Parkinson, et al., *Georg Lukács: The Man, His Work and His Ideas* (1970); T. Hanák, *A filozófus Lukács* (1974).   G.G.

Lunacharsky, Anatoly Vasilyevich (1875–1933), Russian Marxist politician, critic, aesthetician, and dramatist, was born in Poltava. He joined the Social Democrats in 1892 and was arrested several times as a revolutionary. Despite earlier differences with Vladimir Lenin, he was named commissar of enlightenment in 1917, and retained the post until 1929. He died shortly after being appointed Soviet ambassador to Spain.

Lunacharsky's aesthetics exemplify a "biological" version of turn-of-the-century Marxism that was strongly influenced by Charles Darwin, Herbert Spencer, and especially Richard Avenarius. In Lunacharsky's view, art works by "infection" and thereby enables us to experience the healthy and joyful values of life in a concentrated and variegated way. The gratification derived from art is inversely proportional to the amount of energy expended in apprehending it, as, for example, when forms and rhythms most closely resemble natural body movements and structures. Such ideas de-emphasized the shaping role of history in art, and proved offensive to Lenin, Georgy PLEKHANOV, and later Soviet aestheticians.

Lunacharsky advocated a new art embodying proletarian themes and values. By way of example he wrote several plays, most notably *Oliver Cromwell* (1920), whose hero is anachronistically "progressive." At the same time, he believed that much pre-Bolshevik culture should be reinterpreted and made usable by Soviet society. As commissar, he did much to alleviate the hard lot of the old intelligentsia, and encouraged variety and experimentation in the arts. After years of neglect, his importance is again being acknowledged in the Soviet Union.

See: S. Fitzpatrick, *The Commissariat of Enlightenment* (1970); A. A. Lebedev, *Esteticheskiye vzglyady A. V. Lunacharskogo* (2d ed., Moscow, 1970).   R.A.M.

Lundkvist, Artur (1906–), Swedish poet, short-story writer, novelist, essayist, anthologist, and translator, was born in Oderljunga. He started to write poems at an early age. In 1927 he translated poems by Edgar Lee Masters and Carl Sandburg, and the following year he made his literary debut with *Glöd* (1928, new ed., 1966; Fervor, or Embers), a collection of free verse, which was influenced by Elmer DIKTONIUS, Sandburg, Walt Whitman, Emil Bönnelykke, and the early Pär LAGERKVIST. These poems express ecstatic attitudes toward life and boundless faith in human instincts and drives. With this book, Lundkvist became the strongest force in Swedish modernist poetry. It was followed by the important anthology *Fem unga* (1929; Five Young Men), to which he contributed (*see* SWEDISH LITERATURE); *Naket liv* (1929; Naked Life); *Jordisk prosa* (1930; Earthly Prose), including prose poems and sketches; and *Svart stad* (1930; Black City).

All of these proclaim the vitalist (or primitivist) approach to life and revolutionary commitment. In *Vit man* (1932; White Man) the vitalism and the exultation over the possibilities of the machine appear somewhat toned down. In these books an influence from Jungian and Freudian psychology and a modified surrealism are noticeable. Change and movement are the main themes.

Lundkvist translated Paul ELUARD and introduced André BRETON in the magazine *Karavan* (1934–35), in which he wrote on the technique of surrealism. *Nattens broar* (1936; The Bridges of Night) characteristically contains these lines: "At night I love someone I can never find in the daytime," and *Sirensång* (1937; Siren Song) explores the new modes of studying the dream. Human isolation and brooding, rather than joy of life and faith in the future, now become main themes. *Korsväg* (1942; Crossway) is particularly memorable for the two cycles "The Song of the Father" and "The Song of the Woman" and for excellent "portraits" of Erik Johan Stagnelius, Friedrich Hölderlin, Lautréamont, and Sigmund Freud. Lundkvist's main themes from then on are loneliness and communion in a personal as well as collective sense, often with international perspectives. *Dikter mellan djur och Gud* (1944; Poems between Animal and God) has a deepened pessimism. *Skinn över sten* (1947; Skin over Stone) and *Fotspår i vattnet* (1949; Footprints in the Water), which are formally related to the books of the late 1930s, are more hopeful than the poetry of the war years. *Skinn över sten* contains such pieces as "Fresco: Brasilia"; "Pampas: Uruguay"; "Coast Town: Antofagasta"; "The South: Louisiana"; "New York"; and also "portraits" of "Orozco, Mexico"; "Melville, America"; and "Neruda, Chile"; and also a "Biography for the Wind."

Worship of the anonymous riches of nature is expressed in these books as well as in *Liv som gräs* (1954; Lives as Grass) and in *Vindrosor, moteld* (1955; Wind Roses, Counterfire), which, like all of Lundkvist's poetry, contain an abundance of suggestive images, angry indictments of oppression, and an affirmation of revolution. There are also bird poems, for example, one about the magpie, which opens like this:

The bird of my breezy humor
flies whirling like a helicopter
a sphere of wings on the wind.
The magpie, merry widow laughing,
despite her neglected children, Laughing
at thefts she has committed and intends to commit. Black-
    white bird of birches
at home even in trees that stand out black against the snow.
Tr. by W. H. Auden and Leif Sjöberg,
                    New Directions 29, p. 167.

Agadir (1961; Eng. tr., *Agadir*, 1979) is a poetic account of the 1960 earthquake that took thousands of lives and destroyed almost the entire Moroccan city of Agadir. Lundkvist and his wife, who were there, survived. The destruction of the city provided the poet with a reminder of "the greater destruction, / a world in ruins, earth laid waste, only Death trailing smoke / and disappearing into space." Agadir, "white city, life clasped by death" (tr. by William Jay Smith and Leif Sjöberg) Whereas Voltaire, in "Poème sur le désastre de Lisbonne" (1756), made philosophical and antimetaphysical statements, Lundkvist renders his reportage lyrical and extremely moving without turning it into a religious experience. However, in one section a voice says: "No, God was nowhere around; / we plunged into the void, into space ready to become our tomb, / no sign of wings to carry us away." In the following section there is a countervoice: "Just as I plunged into the dark I felt that God existed, / I was seized with terror and joy: God made his presence known, demonstrated his power over the world, showed that there is no relief from God except in God." This touch was new in Lundkvist's writing.

In *Ögonblick och vågor* (1962; Moments and Waves), Lundkvist attacked Western civilization with its "freedom to put God on the company payroll and to build the church on the bank's lot," with "freedom from taxes and freedom of the press for those who can pay, plus freedom of inquisition, freedom of invasion and innumerable other freedoms." But there is also growing alienation on the part of the poet toward the younger generation: Lundkvist even displays resignation and a recognition of the aging process. He reveals his fear of perfection and thereby describes his method of creating, just as nature does, by improvisation ("a poem must be disconnected or it will die in perfection"). However, as human beings are merely a link in nature's creative process in which the H-bomb has no place, it is up to people to defend themselves against the destructive forces ("humans rule and serve simultaneously"). But there are complications for the poet living in this degradation, for each thing includes its own opposite: "humanity must be defended, but by whom". . . how shall I be able to amputate myself? /who is healthy and who is sick /of the two who battle within me?" *Ögonblick och vågor* also contains poems on Albert Einstein, Paul Robeson, Patrice Lumumba, and the Ecuadorian mountain Chimborazo. In spite of the poet's feeling of approaching death (a sense of being made out of sand and gradually dissolving), he proclaims, with refined ambivalence: "I am with the revolutionaries as long as they have not reached their goals."

Lundkvist's collections of poetry include *Texter i snön* (1964; Texts in the Snow) and *Besvärjelser till tröst* (1960; Incantations for Consolation), and in them all there are cascades of images that cogently sum up his experience. It would be impossible to limit someone as creative as Lundkvist to one single genre, and it is characteristic that in most of his fictional prose there are interspersed pages of poetry rich in imagery. To this group belong *Vandrarens träd* (1941; The Tree of the Wanderer); *Malinga* (1952); *Spegel för dag och natt* (1953; Mirror for Day and Night; *Darunga eller Varginnans mjölk* (1954; Darunga or the Milk of the She-Wolf); *Berget och svalorna* (1957; The Mountain and the Swallows); *Ur en befolkad ensamhet* (1958; From a Peopled Loneliness); *Orians upplevelser* (1960; Orian's Experiences); *Det talande trädet* (1960; The Speaking Tree); *Sida vid sida* (1962; Side by Side); *Sällskap för natten* (1965; Company for the Night); *Mörkskogen* (1967; The Dark Forest); *Himlens vilja* (1970; The Will of Heaven), on Genghis Khan; *Lustgårdens demoni* (1973; The Garden of Delights), on Hieronymus Bosch, and *Livsälskare, svartmalåre* (1974; One Who Loves Life and Paints in Black), on Francisco Goya, and several other titles, including *Slavar för Särkland* (1977; Slaves for Särkland).

Lundkvist has also written travelogues of considerable artistic merit, such as *Negerkust* (1933; Negro Coast) and *Negerland* (1949; Negro Land), both about Africa; *Drakblod* (1936; Dragon's Blood), about Spain; *Indiabrand* (1950; India); *Vallmor från Taschkent* (1952; Poppies from Tashkent); *Den förvandlade draken* (1955; The Transformed Dragon), about China; *Vulkanisk kontinent* (1957; Volcanic Continent), about South America; *Hägringar i handen* (1964; Mirages in Hand), about Israel; *Så lever Kuba* (1965; How Cuba Lives); and *Antipodien* (1971; The Antipodes), about Australia.

His books of essays have been eye-openers for Swedes. *Atlantvind* (1932; Ocean Winds) presented Carl Sandburg, Walt Whitman, Eugene O'Neill, Sherwood Anderson, Thomas Wolfe, and John Dos Passos. *Ikarus flykt* (1939; The Flight of Icarus) is about James Joyce, William Faulkner, surrealism (as opposed to naturalism), Henry Miller, and SAINT-JOHN PERSE. *Amerikas nya författare* (1940; America's New Writers); *Diktare och avslöjare i Amerikas moderna litteratur* (1942; Authors and Informers in Modern American Literature); *Poeter i profil* (1958; Poets in Profile); *Utsikter över utländsk prosa* (1959; Views on Foreign Prose); *Från utsiktstornet* (1963; From the Lookout Tower); and *Utflykter med utländska författare* (1969; Excursions with Foreign Authors)—all contains presentations of several (often radical) American writers. Tirelessly, Lundkvist has introduced contemporary authors to Swedish readers. He became a member of the Swedish Academy in 1968.

See: K. Espmark, *Livsydrkaren Artur Lundkvist: studier i hans lyrik t.o.m. Vit Man* (1964); G. Brandell, *Svensk litteratur 1870–1970*, vol. 2 (1975), pp. 197–203; P. Lindblom, *Artur Lundkvist i en föränderlig värld* (1976); L. Sjöberg, "An Interview with Artur Lundkvist," *BA* 50, no. 2 (1976): 329-36.   L.S.

Lunts, Lev Natanovich (1901-24), Russian playwright, short-story writer, and literary theoretician, was born in Petersburg. While still a student at the university in postrevolutionary Petrograd, he began his short-lived literary career as a leading member of the Serapion Brotherhood (*see* RUSSIAN LITERATURE), a highly talented group of 12 young writers who were drawn together by their independent-minded interest in literature as art rather than as propaganda. Yevgeny ZAMYATIN and Maksim GORKY considered him one of the most promising playwrights in postrevolutionary Russia, but a fatal illness struck him down just one week short of his 23rd birthday.

Along with eight short stories published during his lifetime, Lunts wrote four dramas that have been undeservedly neglected at home and abroad. *Vne zakona* (1923; Beyond the Law) is set in a mythical, symbolic "Spain" and deals with the revolutionary overthrow of a tyrannical local duke by the proletarian Alonzo Enríquez, a stonecutter, who then becomes a tyrant himself. The play was staged in Berlin, Vienna, and Prague, but it was forbidden by the censors in Soviet Russia. Lunts's last play, *Gorod pravdy* (1924; The City of Truth), published posthumously in Berlin by Gorky, has been compared to Zamyatin's novel *My* (We) in its anti-Utopian portrayal of the communist state of the future.

In his essays, Lunts criticized current Russian writers for their dullness and their inability to handle plot, and he urged that they learn from the Western masters of plot and the adventure story. His principal essay on this subject is "Na Zapad" (Eng. tr., "Go West!" 1975).

See: W. Edgerton, "The Serapion Brothers: An Early Soviet Controversy," *ASEER* 8, no. 1 (1949): 47–64; G. Kern, Introduction to *The Serapion Brothers: A Critical Anthology*, ed. by G. Kern and C. Collins (1975), pp. ix-xxxviii.   W.B.E.

Luzi, Mario (1914-), Italian poet and critic, was born at Castello, near Florence. He wrote his dissertation on the French Catholic novelist François MAURIAC and has taught French in various institutions, including the University of Florence. Luzi's interest in poetry and literary criticism has gone hand in hand with his interest in the religious philosophy of the West as well as in Oriental philosophy and mysticism. He began his career as a Hermetic poet (*see* ITALIAN LITERATURE) with *La barca* (1935; The Boat) and *Avvento notturno* (1940; Nocturnal Advent), in which style and imagery betray some influence of French symbolism and surrealism (*see* FRENCH LITERATURE). In his later collections, *Un brindisi* (1946; A Toast), *Quaderno gotico* (1947; Gothic Notebook),

Primizie del deserto (1952; Early Fruits of the Desert), and Onore del vero (1957; The Honor of Truth)—all collected in Il giusto della vita (1960; What Is Just in Life)—Luzi achieved greater philosophical depth and his style became more discursive.

Although he began as a self-conscious young aesthete whose writing was especially influenced by Giuseppe UNGARETTI, Luzi emerged in the post-World War II period as a notably individual poet, the verbal and technical efficacy of whose experimentalism was aptly matched with the creative process of his mind and thought. A constant preoccupation in his poetry is the desire to transform what is personal and individual into something universal and to give the edged outline of a personal emotion to what is universal. Like the poetry of Eugenio MONTALE, Luzi's verse attempts to probe the depth of existentialist and metaphysical anguish and uncertainty, but with the difference that it does so from the center of his Catholic faith. In his best poems, Luzi succeeds in expressing the inexpressible by giving a concretely metaphorical form to what is abstract and intangible.

In his most recent collections, Nel magma (1963; In the Mire), Dal fondo delle campagne (1965; From the Depth of the Countryside), and Su fondamenta invisibili (1971; On Invisible Foundations), the central theme is love in its human rather than ideal or philosophical essence, and the woman loved is not so much a spiritual and mystical entity as a person of flesh and blood. Luzi's poetry adds to contemporary Italian poetry the voice of spiritual interiority, rendered in terms of a semimystical, semiromantic passion. Indeed, this passion figures as a key experience in the poet's exploration of reality.

Luzi is also the author of an important book of critical essays, L'inferno e il limbo (1964; Hell and Limbo), dealing with, among other subjects, Vincenzo CARDARELLI, Gabriele D'ANNUNZIO, and Paul ELUARD; of an anthology of the symbolist movement from a comparative point of view, L'idea simbolista (1959; The Symbolist Idea); and, together with Carlo CASSOLA, of a dyptich, Poesia romanzo (1973; Poetry/The Novel), which contains two excellent introductory essays on the two genres.

See: C. Bo, in Nuovi studi (1946); V. Sereni, FLe (Aug. 14, 1955); G. Singh, BA (October 1968); G. Zagarrio, Luzi (1968); C. Scarpati, Mario Luzi (1970); W. Craft, "Mario Luzi," BA (Winter 1975); R. Squires, "The Dark Body of Metamorphosis," MQR (Winter 1975). G.S.

M

Macedonian literature. Literature in Church Slavonic was produced as late as the beginning of the 19th century in Macedonia, which is now the southernmost republic in Yugoslavia. Only then did the first signs of linguistic modernization appear, including the reformation of the literary language on the basis of folk speech. The range of 19th-century Macedonian literature was very limited. The outstanding poets of the period were Konstantin Miladinov (1830–62), Rajko Zinzifov (1839–87), and Grigor Prličev (1830–93). A great deal of work was done in the collection of folk literature, but the question of a unified literary language remained unsettled. At the beginning of the 20th century, significant work in the area of language reform was carried out by Krste Misirkov (1874–1926). Only in 1945, however, after the formation of the Macedonian Republic as a part of Yugoslavia, was a Macedonian standard language finally established. This standardization was very important in the development of Macedonian literature.

In the period between the two world wars, there was an upsurge of literary activity among Macedonians in Yugoslavia and Bulgaria, even though neither Macedonian nationality nor the Macedonian language was officially recognized. Macedonian literature in this period was limited mainly to poetry and drama, both of which had been strongly influenced in their development by the folklore tradition. These works depicted current social conditions and expressed dissatisfaction over the lack of national rights. In Yugoslavia, Vasil Iljoski (1902–), Anton Panov (1906–68), and Risto Krle (1900–) published prose sketches of Macedonian life. Kočo Racin's (1908–43) collection of poems, Beli mugri (1939; White Dawn), is representative of the stage of development of Macedonian literature at that time. The themes of his poems were social in nature. They all sprang from his love for his oppressed countrymen. In the years before World War II, there was also a Macedonian literary circle active in Sofia.

Even after World War II, poetry remained the major genre of Macedonian literature, thanks largely to the work of such poets as Slavko JANEVSKI, Blaže KONESKI, Aco Šopov (1923–), and Gane Todorovski (1929–). In drama, Iljoski successfully continued his work, and later he was joined by Kole Časule (1921–), Tome Arsovski (1928–), and others. The introduction of new genres, especially in prose, was an important feature of Macedonian literature in the period immediately after the war. Pioneering work in this area was carried out by Vlado Maleski (1919–), Janevski, Jovan Boškovski (1920–68), and Ivan Tocko (1914–73). The sudden growth of the young literature was also accompanied by the appearance of criticism and discussions of literary theory by writers such as Dimitar Mitrev (1919–), Aleksandar Spasov (1925–) and Milan Djurčinov (1928–). The first period of postwar Macedonian literature was greatly enriched by the development of its means of expression, which were freed from narrow ties to folklore. Literary activity still suffered, however, from inadequate development and the restrictive model of socialist realism.

During the 1950s, certain basic changes resulted in increasingly close connections with literary events in Western Europe and the rest of the world. Macedonian writers became more and more concerned with fundamental problems of human existence. Literary procedures were broadened to include even the techniques of surrealism. In the 1960s pluralism in expressive approaches was an accepted fact. A new generation of poets was already developing in this changing climate. Among them were Mateja Matevski (1929–), Cane Andreevski (1934–), Jovan Koteski (1936–), and Radovan Pavlovski (1936–). Prose writing also developed, especially in the area of the novel. Stale Popov (1902–67), Gorǵi Abadžiev (1910–63) and Jordan Leov (1920–) concerned themselves with the depiction of the past and of patriarchal life. War themes were developed by Vlasle Maleski. The younger writers Dimitar Solev (1930–), Simon Drakul (1930–), Taĭko Georgievski (1935–), Metodija Fotev (1932–), Zivko ČINGO, and others worked successfully on stories and novels, at times reevaluating earlier interpretations of essential questions facing Macedonia past and present. Čingo's language, style, and imagery have won high critical praise, and his stark portrayal of man's cruelty to his fellow man makes him an innovator in Macedonian literature.

See: H. G. Lunt, "A Survey of Macedonian Literature," *HSS* 1 (1953); B. Koneski, ed., *Makedonska književnost*, (1961); B. Meriggi, *Le letterature della Jugoslavia* (1970); M. Djurčinov, "La poésie macédonienne" in *Anthologie des origines à nos jours* (1972); A. Kadíc, *From Croatian Renaissance to Yugoslav Socialism* (1969); V. D. Mihailovich, and M. Matejić, eds., *Yugoslav Literature in English: A Bibliography* (1976).   B.Ko.

Macedonski, Alexandru (1854–1920), Romanian poet and critic, was born in Craiova. After traveling abroad, he finished his studies at the University of Bucharest. Macedonski's first volume of experimental verses, *Prima verba* (1872; First Words), was published when he was only 18. After serving a brief prison term for writing antimonarchist pamphlets, he challenged the autonomy of Titu MAIORESCU and the "Junimea" literary circle. Claiming descent from writers of the Generation of 1848, Macedonski founded his own literary circle and a journal, *Literatorul*, which promoted both the social and political involvement of literature as well as the new literary modernism imported from France. Dedication to social issues soon turned his attention to the new movement of realism. Macedonski's second book, *Poezii* (1882; Poems), was primarily a protest against the facile conventional lyricism of the day and against all "tyrants." *Poezii* includes some of his best lyrics: "Focul sacru" (Sacred Fire); "Răspuns la cîțiva critici" (Reply to Some Critics), "Poeții," "Homo sum," the love song "Întîiul vînt de toamna" (First Autumn Wind), and the "Nopți" (Nights) poems, with their compassion for the man of genius in his lonely moral world. The volumes *Excelsior* (1895) and *Flori sacre* (1912; Sacred Flowers) reveal a transition from the erotic toward more rustic inspiration. There was little audience for Macedonski's Romanian poetry, however, and so he sought recognition abroad by writing in French. His French works include *Bronzes* (1897; Bronze Figures), a volume of poetry; *Le Calvaire de feu* (1906; The Flaming Calvary), a novel; *Le Cloître—Vers et proses* (1912; The Cloister: Verse and Prose); and *Le Fou* (1921; The Madman), a play. His last years were devoted to the rondel. These verses, among his best, were published posthumously in *Poema rondelurilor* (1927; Poem of the Rondels). A collection of his many articles, edited by Tudor Vianu, was published in 1946.

Macedonski's literary reputation rests upon his having introduced symbolism and other modern concepts of poetry into Romania. He later narrowed that interest to the literary movement called instrumentalism. His lyrics, marked by vigor, optimism, stylistic versatility, and a new, unexpected imagery, and his social verse, with its sharp satire, realism, and pathos, constitute a significant enrichment of the Romanian literary language.

See: T. Vianu, "Alexandru Macedonski," in *Studii de literatură română* (1965); A. Marino, *Viața lui Alexandru Macedonski* (1966); M. Zamfir, *Poezia lui Alexandru Macedonski* (1972); D. Eulert and S. Avadănei, *Modern Romanian Poetry* (1973), pp. 12–15.   T.A.P.

Mach, Wilhelm (1917–65), Polish novelist, essayist, and literary critic, was born in Kamionka, near Dębica, into a peasant family. He committed suicide in Warsaw. Mach studied Polish philology at the Jagiellonian University in Cracow. During World War II he fought in the 1939 September campaign and was active in the clandestine cultural movement. Mach's literary career began in 1950 with the novel *Rdza* (Rust), in which he showed the psychological process of maturing and overcoming one's prejudices during dramatic wartime experiences. In the novel *Jaworowy dom* (1954; Sycamore House), he depicted changes in the life of village inhabitants. *Życie duże i małe* (1959; Life Great and Small) is an analysis of a child's memories as seen through the eyes of the adolescent hero. *Agnieszka, córka Kolumba* (1964; Agnes, the Daughter of Columbus), the story of a devoted schoolteacher, is set against an epic depiction of the countryside. *Góry nad Czarnym Morzem* (1961; Mountains by the Black Sea) represents an interesting example of the Polish "new novel" (*see* FRENCH LITERATURE), with a multilevel plot and essayistic polemical inserts. Mach also wrote two volumes of literary essays and sketches: *Doświadczenia i przypadki* (1954; Experiences and Accidents) and *Szkice literackie* (1971; Literary Sketches).   A.Z.

Machado y Ruiz, Antonio (1875–1939), Spanish poet and essayist, was born in Seville. While still a child he moved with his family to Madrid, where he studied at the Institución Libre de Enseñanza (Institution for Free Learning). In 1899 he worked with his brother Manuel at a publishing house in Paris. He returned to Paris for a short period in 1902, when he met Rubén Darío (*see* SPANISH LITERATURE). At the end of that year, Machado published his first book, *Soledades* (1902; Solitudes). Corrected and enlarged, it appeared later with the title *Soledades, galerías y otros poemas* (1907; Solitudes, Galleries, and Other Poems). The "galleries" are the inner passages of the soul, an enchanted world of dreams, hopes, and memories. *Soledades* is perhaps his best book, the most symbolist, and of great importance in the history of Spanish poetry. There is musicality, color, ambiguity, and great beauty in many of his verses, which seem to be uttered in a quiet, whispered voice. There are also a profound connection and a harmony between the exterior world, real or dreamed, which the poet suggests in the brief description of a garden, a field, or a deserted plaza, and the sentiment of a frequently hesitant traveler who is lost in the world, alone with his wonder and his profound sorrow.

In 1907, Machado was appointed professor of French at the Institute of Secondary Education in Soria. The change from Madrid to Soria had important repercussions for his life and work. For some time, Machado had been dissatisfied with poetry in which the poet only exhibits his emotions. His daily contact with the Castilian people and landscape gave him the opportunity to write more descriptive poetry. Another factor was that shortly after he arrived in Soria, Machado fell in love. Leonor had just turned 15 when he married her in 1909. Freed from his solitude and melancholy, Machado could then look more objectively toward the outside world. Early in 1911, with the help of a scholarship, he and his young wife went to Paris, where he attended Henri BERGSON's classes. Shortly afterward, Leonor fell seriously ill, and in September they returned to Soria. *Campos de Castilla* was published in June of the following year. Most of the poems describe the Sorian landscape vividly and with great richness of color. They also speak of the peasants of that impoverished land. Reflections of a historical nature, criticism of the present Spanish reality, and hope for Spain's future were thus blended in lyrical stanzas and deeply felt descriptions. All of this is typical of the Generation of 1898, but it sometimes gives the book an excessively "sociological" character, detracting from its freshness.

In August 1912, a few days after Leonor died, Machado left Soria. By autumn, he had a new post in Baeza. Alone again, his old melancholy now bordering on desperation, Machado felt like a stranger in his own Andalusion homeland. His heart turned nostalgically to Soria. For the first time he names or clearly alludes to Leonor in his poetry. He even talks to her in short, deeply felt poems, as if she were at his side, strolling with him through the Sorian countryside. In these poems the landscape becomes stylized and more refined. It is painted with light strokes and transformed into a lovingly contemplated "landscape of the soul."

Machado thought that during the years he spent in Baeza he had lost his "voice" or poetic inspiration. The fact is that while in Baeza, as well as later on, he continued to write magnificent poems. It is true, however, that after Leonor's death, Machado's poetry tends to be conceptual and philosophical. In Baeza, Machado read a great deal, above all philosophy, and devoted much time to philosophical reflection.

In 1917 the first edition of his *Poesías completas* was published, including *Soledades* and *Campos*. Added to this last book were the poems written from 1912 to 1917. The poems collected in *Poesías completas* are varied in theme, tone, and rhyme. In general, Machado's is a sad poetry, the work of a man without love and without God. Frequently his poems close with a hopeful outlook and the possibility of love. It is the work of a solitary man who continually yearns and searches for the "other," a man who lifts his heart toward the mystery of an always distant and unreachable deity. This poetry, often of misleading simplicity and deceptive clarity, has always been appreciated by the common reader of Spanish poetry, but it has been even more admired by distinguished poets of various generations and studied by critics of different tendencies, especially since the war.

In 1919, Machado moved to Segovia, and in 1924 he published *Nuevas canciones* (New Songs). This was an uneven and varied book in which what stands out are the *canciones* apparently derived from traditional Castilian lyrical songs and popular Andalusian couplets. It also included "proverbs," in which Machado frequently refers to the ethical need to be aware of the existence of "the other," and some strange and enigmatic sonnets that are among the most beautiful of his poetry. The second edition of *Poesías completas* appeared in 1928 and included *Nuevas canciones* and the poems written later. He also added new poems to the editions of 1933 and 1936. Of note are the "Songs to Guiomar," the great and secret love of his later years. From 1926 to 1932, several of his dramas, written in collaboration with his brother Manuel, were performed.

From 1928 onwards, an "Apocryphal Songbook" in verse and prose appeared as an appendix to editions of the *Poesías completas*. In it Machado speaks through a fictional Andalusian philosopher named Abel Martín and his disciple Juan de Mairena. This device gave him narrative distance and a humorous, skeptical tone. The obscure philosophical and somewhat humorous poems and prose commentaries of the appendix give the impression of a confused and disorganized miscellany. Nevertheless, the attentive reader can discover the basic themes of "temporal poetry," which is contrasted with the cold conceptualization of time; the "heterogeneity of being," that is, the individual's need and desire for "the other," without which he cannot become "one"; and being and nothingness. He repeated and clarified some of these ideas in prose articles written between 1934 and 1936 and collected in *Juan de Mairena* (1936; Eng. tr., 1963). Others were published in 1937 and 1938 in the periodical *Hora de España* and collected in a volume after his death.

Juan de Mairena deals with a variety of themes, but purely philosophical problems predominate. Martin HEIDEGGER is mentioned several times. Surely the poet had read the Spanish translation of *What is Metaphysics?*

(1929), published in 1933. Heidegger's ideas about being and nothingness are essentially the same as those conveyed by Machado in his poem "Al gran cero" ("To the Great Zero"), published in 1926. For that reason, Machado could later say that he was "somewhat Heideggerian without having been aware of it." Although incomplete, Machado's knowledge of Heidegger's early works helped him clarify and confirm his own "poet's metaphysics," which he had outlined before Heidegger.

Because his poetry combines trends deriving from the Spanish or Spanish American tradition, as well as the influence of French symbolism, Machado can in a broad sense be included in the group of Spanish modernists (*see* SPANISH LITERATURE). But the aesthetic vision of the Castilian landscape and the preoccupation with the past, present, and future of Spain—a peculiar mixture of sadness and hope for Spain's destiny—that characterize his *Campos de Castilla* place him quite definitely among the writers of the Generation of 1898 (*see* SPANISH LITERATURE).

At the outbreak of the Civil War, Machado declared himself firmly in favor of the Republican government and against the military rebellion. He departed into exile on Jan. 22, 1939, and died a few days later in Collioure, France.

See: W. Barnstone, *Eighty Poems of Antonio Machado* (1959); R. Gullón and A. W. Phillips, eds., *Antonio Machado* (1973); A. Sánchez Barbudo, *Los poemas de Antonio Machado* (1976).   A.S.-B.

Machado y Ruiz, Manuel (1874–1947), Spanish poet and dramatist, son of the founder of the first folklore society in Spain, was born in Seville. His early education took place in the lay atmosphere of the Institución Libre de Enseñanza in Madrid, but he finished university studies in Seville, where he became enamored of the local color of Andalusia. In Paris at the turn of the century, he worked as a translator, met Oscar Wilde and Jean MORÉAS, and fell under the influence of Paul VERLAINE, whose work he translated. His first book, *Alma* (1902; Soul), reflects a strong *modernista* background (*see* SPANISH LITERATURE), and he helped found two journals associated with the new poetry: *Electra* and *Juventud*. After taking a degree in library science in 1912, he worked briefly in Santiago de Compostela and then assumed a position at the Biblioteca Nacional in Madrid. In 1916 he became a drama critic, first for *El Liberal* and later for *La Libertad*, and in this role exercised a great deal of influence. In collaboration with his brother Antonio MACHADO Y RUIZ, he wrote seven fairly inconsequential but popular plays, the most famous of which, *La Lola se va a los puertos* (1930; Lola Heads for the Ports), idealizes a flamenco singer. At the outbreak of the Spanish Civil War, he was in Burgos, where he chose to remain. He associated himself with the cause of Francisco Franco, and was elected to the Royal Spanish Academy of the Language in 1938. Manuel Machado's fame and influence during his lifetime have been eclipsed in death by the enormous reputation now enjoyed by his brother Antonio.

The best of Machado's poetry displays a clear, honest, and sometimes ironic skepticism. Partially influenced by the ennui prevalent in poetic circles at the turn of the century, but also possessed of a native note of stoicism, he proclaimed often that he expected nothing from life and had no answers. He was content to acknowledge the importance of the physical senses by celebrating women and flamenco. Yet his much-admired "Felipe IV" based on portraits by Velázquez, reveals a fine poetic intelligence. *El mal poema* (1909; The Bad Poem) offers in almost conversational style a glimpse of the seamy side of city life.

See: G. Brotherston, *Manuel Machado: A Revaluation* [*sic*] (1977).   H.T.Y.

Machar, Josef Svatopluk (1864–1942), Czech poet and essayist, was the leader of the realist movement in Czech poetry. He was born in Kolín and in 1891 became a bank clerk in Vienna, where he lived until 1918. In 1916 he had been imprisoned by the Austrian authorities for his anti-Austrian underground activities. Machar was named an inspector general in the Czechoslovak army (largely in charge of the educational program) in 1919, but was compelled to resign in 1924. This affair drove him into bitter opposition to his former friend, President Tomáš Garrigue MASARYK. At the time of his death in 1942, Machar was in complete retirement.

Machar's first literary attempts were lyrics in the tradition of Heinrich Heine and the Czech poet Jan Neruda, later collected in three volumes entitled *Confiteor* (1887–92). In contrast to the decorative diction of poets such as Jaroslav Vrchlický and Svatopluk Čech, Machar wrote in a simple, almost prosaic style, and, lacking their buoyant optimism, he sang only of his heart's disillusionments, which he bore with ironical skepticism. Many of these early poems, which were followed by a brilliant series of sonnets (1891–93), are extremely witty as well as genuinely poetic in their sharp outlines, vivid impressionism, and slightly cynical pessimism. Happier in mood is the collection *Výlet na Krym* (1900; A Trip to the Crimea), a subjective travel diary in verse that reveals an undiminished power of observation and description. But Machar soon broadened his themes to include political and social questions. *Tristium Vindobona* (1893) is a series of satirical and skeptical meditations on the politics and ideology of his own nation. Machar suspected romantic nationalism and disliked the ineffectiveness of the Czech parliamentary opposition in Vienna. Although his original attitude toward woman was satirical, he eventually saw them as victims of circumstance and pleaded for their emancipation in a volume of sketches and portraits of women called *Zde by měly kvést růže* (1894; Here Should Roses Bloom). *Magdalena* (1894; Eng. tr., *Magdelen*, 1916) is a highly amusing novel in verse about a prostitute who marries respectably but is forced back to her "establishment" by the relentless persecution of small-town gossips.

With *Golgotha* (1901) Machar embarked on a series of books that he came to call *Svědomím veků* (The Conscience of the Ages), which covers the history of the world from the florescence of Babylon to World War I. Victor Hugo and Jaroslav Vrchlický were obviously before his eyes. The title poem of *Golgotha* provides a clue to Machar's philosophy of history: Satan upbraids Christ for having founded Christianity, which will bring only weakness, suffering, cruelty, and slaughter to humanity. Another volume of the series is thus appropriately entitled *Jed z Judey* (1906; The Poison from Judaea). Other volumes glorify the virtues Machar admired—the bright intellect of the Greeks and the power of the Romans. The series as a whole is founded on the contrast, derived from Friedrich NIETZSCHE, between classical joy and Christian morbidity. It includes *V záři hellenského slunce* (1906; In the Glow of the Greek Sun), *Barbaři* (1911; Barbarians), *Pohanské plameny* (1911; Pagan Flames), *Apoštolové* (1911; Apostles), *Oni* (1921; They), and *On* (1921; He).

After World War I, Machar resumed his satirical writing with *Tristium Praga* (1926), in addition to many epigrams and satires against political conditions in Czechoslovakia. Machar's prose, like his poetry, is always lucid and readable. He was a brilliant polemicist and satirist as well as storyteller. His many volumes of reminiscences, notably *Konfese literáta* (2 vols., 1901; The Confessions of a Literary Man), *Kriminál*, (1918; Eng. tr., *The Jail*, 1922), *Pět let v kasárnách* (1927; Five Years in the Barracks), and his literary portraits, such as *Vídeňské profily* (1919; Viennese Profiles), rise far above the level of mere good journalism. In a widely read travel book, *Řím* (1907; Rome), Machar again expounded his philosophy of history, but in this work his uncritical glorification of antiquity and superficial anticlericalism sounds even more blatant than it did in his more imaginative verse.

Machar's historical importance is considerable: his return to colloquial diction, his dislike of the 19th-century belief in progress, his hatred of the Hapsburgs and of Catholicism, his pleas for the emancipation of women, all left a permanent impress on wide selections of Czech public opinion. But the Nietzscheanism and bitter political resentments of his later years again isolated him, and his influence has declined steadily. Artistically, his early work is preferable; the volumes of poetry comprising *Svědomím věků* (The Conscience of the Ages) are frequently hasty improvisations, and his late prose works also display many lapses of taste and power.

See: V. Martínek, *Josef Svatopluk Machar* (1912; rev. ed., 1948); Z. Pešat, *Josef Svatopluk Machar básnik* (1959).   R.W.

Mac Orlan, Pierre, pseud. of Pierre Dumarchey (1883–1970), French novelist, essayist, poet, and *chansonnier*, was born in Péronne in northern France, where his heart always belonged, and died at Saint-Cyr-sur-Morin. Much of his life was spent in Paris, but he traveled extensively in France, Europe, and the rest of the world. Mac Orlan's writing is at once exotic, realistic, fantastic, poetic, and musical. A master stylist, he charmed a public of connoisseurs by means of a peculiarly true and enigmatic vision, combining the cosmopolitan and the poetic. Although he early earned recognition, his work has always (unjustly) seemed marginal because undue attention has been paid to certain of his works devoted to the world of gangsters. Mac Orlan's own formula, "chimères sociales," aptly defines many of his works. Thus, the novel *La Cavalière Elsa* (1921) might have appeared to be a work of social anticipation in the early 1920s, yet today it seems tritc in many of the aspects which then seemed fantastic or unreal. The horrors of totalitarian regimes, World War II, and other excesses may have dulled our senses; but Mac Orlan's fantasy finds a secret way to please us. At the other end of the spectrum, the novel *Quai des Brumes* (1927) (not to be confused with the film of the same title) is a charming chronicle of Montmartre.

Among Mac Orlan's other notable works are his accounts of his travels, *Le Chant de l'équipage* (1918; The Song of the Carriage) and *A bord de l'Etoile matutine* (1920; Eng. tr., *On Board the Morning Star*, 1924), and his *Chansons pour accordéon* (1953; Songs for the Accordion). As sung by Juliette Greco and others, Mac Orlan's chansons met with appreciative public reception. He wrote his memoirs more than once, but his best version of them is probably *La Petite Cloche de Sorbonne* (1959; The Little Bell of the Sorbonne), which rings like the immemorial echo of a true *moraliste*. He even produced some children's stories, *Pig, le petit cochon savant* (1956; Pig, the Little Talking Pig) and *Calamity Bob et autres histoires* (1961; Calamity Bob and Other Stories). His complete works, in process of publication, comprise 25 volumes. Posterity might well decide that this poet-novelist, who is so originally an imaginative witness of our time, is a classical author of the 20th century.

See: P. Berger, *Pierre Mac Orlan* (1951); A. Bloch, "Pierre Mac Orlan's Fantastic Vision," *MLQ* 24, no. 2 (1963): 191–96; J. Queval, "Une lecture de Mac Orlan," *NRF* 273 (September 1975): 122–27. J.B.

Madariaga, Salvador de (1886–1978), Spanish essayist, novelist, and poet, was born in La Coruña. Trained as an engineer at the Ecole Polytechnique in Paris, he moved to London in 1916 and devoted himself to journalism. In 1921 he entered the League of Nations Secretariat, becoming director of the disarmament section in the following year. He held this post until 1927. From 1928 to 1931 he held the chair of Spanish studies at Oxford University. He served as ambassador of the Spanish Republic to the United States (1931) and to France (1932–34). After the Spanish Civil War (1936–39) he established himself as an exile in England. He did not return to Spain until 1976, after Francisco Franco's death.

A product of three cultures, speaking and writing Spanish, English, and French with equal perfection (all translations of his books are his own), Madariaga is considered the most cosmopolitan thinker of 20th-century Spain. This spirit of cosmopolitanism, or rather humanism, is reflected in his political philosophy, which is based on the double principle of the liberty of the individual and the solidarity of mankind. Hence his interest in the problems of international relations and world organization as a means to realize this double principle and to attain peace. These subjects are discussed in his political essays: *Disarmament* (1929); *Discursos internacionales* (1934); *Anarquía o jerarquía: idearío para la constitución de la tercera república* (1935; Eng. tr., *Anarchy or Hierarchy*, 1937); *Theory and Practice in International Relations* (1937); *The World's Design* (1938); *Bosquejo de Europa* (1951; Eng. tr., *Portrait of Europe*, 1952); *Europe a Unit of Human Culture* (1952); *The Anatomy of the Cold War* (1955); *De l'angoisse à la liberté: profession de foi d'un libéral révolutionnaire* (1954; From Anxiety to Liberty: a Liberal Revolutionary's Profession of Faith); and *Memorias, 1921–1936; Amanecer sin mediodía* (1974; Eng. tr., *Morning without Noon; Memoirs*, 1974). Hence also his interest in the problems of national psychology as a political factor in the relations between countries, of which his *Englishmen, Frenchmen, Spaniards* (1928) is the best example. His interest in international affairs, however, did not lessen his preoccupation with Spain. As Madariaga lived most of his life abroad, especially in England, his task in this respect consisted mainly in presenting and interpreting Spain—its land and its people, its problems and its values—to the outside world. In this vein are his historical essay *Spain* (1930; a new English edition, 1958, covers the period 1930–57 as well) and several books on different phases of Spanish and Latin American history and literature: *Shelley and Calderón* (1920); *The Genius of Spain and Other Essays on Spanish Contemporary Literature* (1923); *Guía del lector del "Quijote"* (1926; Eng. tr., *Don Quixote*, 1934); *Christopher Columbus* (1939); *Hernán Cortés* (1941; Eng. tr., 1941); *El auge del imperio español en América* (1945; Eng. tr., *The Rise of the Spanish American Empire*, 1947); *El ocaso del imperio español en América* (1945; Eng. tr., *The Fall of the Spanish American Empire*, 1947); *Bolívar* (1951; Eng. tr., 1952); *Mujeres españolas* (1972; Spanish Women); *Españoles de mi tiempo* (1974; Spaniards of My Time); and *Dios y los españoles* (1975; God and the Spaniards).

Madariaga also cultivated other literary genres with varied success, but in them, especially in the novel and in his dramatic writings, the intellectual and the essayist emerge with such strength that they dominate the works

and repress the creative process. Among his works are: poetry, *Romances de ciego* (1922; Blind Man's Ballads and *La fuente serena* (1928; The Tranquil Fountain); theater, *Elysian Fields* (1937); *El Toisón de Oro* (1950; The Golden Fleece); and *Don Juan* (1950); fiction, *La jirafa sagrada* (1924; Eng. tr., *The Sacred Giraffe*, 1925); *Arceval y los ingleses* (1925; Arceval and the English); *El enemigo de Dios* (1936; The Enemy of God); *Ramo de errores* (1952; Eng. tr., *A Bunch of Errors*, 1954); *La camarada Ana* (1954); *El corazón de piedra verde* (1942; Eng. tr., *The Heart of Jade*, 1944); *Guerra en la sangre* (1957; Eng. tr., *War in the Blood*, 1957); *El semental negro* (1961; The Black Stud); and *Sanco Panco* (1964).

See: J. Pemartín, "La obra de Salvador de Madariaga," *Arbor* 26 (1953): 173–217; E. G. de Nora, *La novela española contemporánea*, vol. 2 (1968), pp. 80–93; S. F. Toman, "Don Salvador de Madariaga: A Provocative Interpreter of Spanish America," *SAQ* 71 (1972): 257–67.
C.Ba. rev J.L.G-M.

Madsen, Svend Åge (1939–), Danish novelist, was born in the Jutland city of Århus. A heavily experimental modernist influenced by the French "nouveau roman" (*see* FRENCH LITERATURE), Madsen, in his first novels, *Besøget* (1963; The Visit) and *Lystbilleder* (1964; Lust Pictures), attempts to analyze minutely a chaotic world. The seven stories in *Otte gange orphan* (1965; Eight Times Orphan) describe in the first person seven different abnormal mental conditions, all seven of which function according to extreme but logical principles. To Madsen prose fiction is an existential process: the author does not describe reality; he creates it. This theory is demonstrated in *Tilføjelser* (1967; Additions), consisting of a box with five independent volumes: five ways to look upon the world. In *Liget og lysten* (1968; The Corpse and Desire) and *Tredje gang så ta'r vi ham* (1969; We'll Get Him the Third Time), Madsen unites his existential dilemma with a political criticism of the restrictions in society. The fictional problem is again discussed in *Sæt verden er til* (1971; If the World Exists). In *Dage med Diam* (1972; Days with Diam), a novel with 32 possible solutions, the reader has to combine the selves and the actions according to which story he or she desires to read, that is, which reality he or she wishes to create. The same relative view of the fictional world is also present in *Jakkels vandring* (1974; The Wandering of Jakkel) and brought about a renewal of Madsen's authorship, the result of which is seen in the pseudodocumentary novel *Tugt og utugt i mellemtiden* (1976; Decency and Indecency in the Meanwhile), a political, social, and psychological analysis of everyday life in Denmark in the 1970s. S.H.R.

Maeterlinck, Maurice (1862–1949), Belgian playwright and poet, was born in Ghent. He was reared in an upper middle-class family of francophone and Catholic tradition. After law studies, a sojourn in Paris in 1885 put him in touch with a group of young post-Parnassians who venerated Paul VERLAINE and Philippe de Villiers de l'Isle-Adam. Maeterlinck's first poetry, published in the ephemeral *Pléiade*, started to appear in 1886. He attributed an important part of his formation to his personal meeting with Villiers, the Wagnerian taken with occult sciences and haunted by the hereafter and unknowable. In fact, Maeterlinck already possessed elements of the symbolist aesthetic and a sense of mysticism. As early as 1885 he dreamed of translating John Ruysbroeck l'Admirable's *Ornement des noces spirituelles*, and 1886 was the year that saw Arthur RIMBAUD's *Illuminations*, René GHIL's *Traité du verbe*, and the launching of the Belgian symbolist review *La Wallonie*.

A "decadent" aesthetician, nourished on Shakespeare, Edgar Allan Poe, and the Pre-Raphaelites and linked with Iwan GILKIN, Emile VERHAEREN, and Albert MOCKEL, Maeterlinck published the 33 poems entitled *Serres chaudes* (Warm Hothouses) in 1889. It is fin-de-siècle, mysterious poetry, of a heavy and oppressive nature, dominated by ennui and the refusal of real life; the soul, choked by routine, aspires to another world, as in "Oraison" (Prayer), "Oraison nocturne" (Nocturnal Prayer), and "Offrande obscure" (Obscure Offering). Vegetal and floral images invade an incoherent, absurd universe while the poet suffocates in his "hothouse," in an immobile atmosphere crossed by evanescent dreams. In *Douze Chansons* (1896; Eng. tr., *Twelve Songs*, 1902), which increased to 15 in 1900, the poetry has become more natural and repudiates deliquescence in the search for musicality. The soul is always in pursuit of an unattainable happiness, but the tone—that of a litany of popular songs—already has the harmonics of Maeterlinck's early theater.

For it is indeed as a playwright that Maeterlinck was destined to become famous. *La Princesse Maleine* (Eng. tr., *Princess Maleine*, 1911), with a printing of 30 copies, elicited in the Aug. 24, 1890, *Figaro* a dithyrambic article by Octave MIRBEAU, which rendered the young author from Ghent famous overnight. Circumstances explain, in part, this success. In 1890, if symbolism triumphed in poetry, theater was still at the point of "slice of life" drama or a mediocre theater of ideas. At the other end of this strict realism, Maeterlinck repudiated eloquence, speeches. He placed his characters outside the bounds of real time and space and tried to translate the ineffable. As early as *Maleine*, situated in an unreal Flanders in an undetermined time, the keynotes of his theater began to be affirmed: condemned purity, unavoidable submission to fate, to death. Maleine does not act; she lets herself be carried away by an unjust and capricious destiny. Unknown and hostile powers hover over fragile heroines promised to death, without possibility of action. Maeterlinck himself found in these characters "the appearance of somewhat deaf sleepwalkers constantly pulled towards a painful dream."

This static state is accentuated again in *L'Intruse* (1890; Eng. tr., *The Intruder*, 1918), in which the theme of the fatality of death is treated with all the resources of the symbolist arsenal. The poet is looking for the effect of mystery here, but the characters, more and more deprived of humanity, are scarcely more than uneasy marionettes from a Bruegel painting, just as in *Les Aveugles* (1890; Eng. tr., *The Blind*, 1908).

In 1892, *Pelléas et Mélisande* (Eng. tr., *Pelléas and Mélisande*, 1920), a masterpiece of the symbolist theater, a story of juvenile and tragic lovers, appeared. An admirable song of love in the *Tristan et Yseult* or *Romeo and Juliet* vein, the work lacks vigor. These diaphanous and bloodless characters experience passion or jealousy only as conventional feelings. They do not have the necessary energy for theater dialogue. Maeterlinck's plays are more poetic than scenic. Pretty scenes give the impression of a dream or of life in slow motion. This first style closes with the "three little dramas for marionettes" (1894). *Alladine et Palomides* (Eng. tr., *Alladine and Palomides*, 1899) and *La Mort de Tintagiles* (Eng. tr., *The Death of Tintagiles*, 1899) recall *Pelléas* by their poetic charm and their fairy-tale tonality, but they create a feeling of repetition. Large castles penetrated by endless corridors, idyllic lovers destined for death, blond heroines disarmed in the hand of destiny. To these works of a "terror-stricken and somber harmony," *Intérieur* (Eng. tr., *Interior*, 1914), the last of the "three little dramas,"

carries with it more vigor. Illustrating the unavoidable approach of death, the work is very superior to *L'Intruse* in its controlled and serious dialogue, its sobriety in the expression of the precariousness of the human condition, which is only "immense and useless weakness."

At this time, Maeterlinck decided to be done with certain melodramatic aspects of symbolism; the will of change was accentuated again after his meeting, in 1895, with the singer Georgette Leblanc, with whom he had a liaison for 25 years. *Aglavaine et Sélysette* (1896; Eng. tr., *Aglavaine and Sélysette*, 1911) moves toward serenity, psychological deepening, and interior dramatic movement. Henceforth, his heroines fight, marking the victory of the forces of love over the forces of death: *Soeur Béatrice* (1901; Eng. tr., *Sister Beatrice*, 1901) and *Ariane et Barbe-bleue* (1901; Eng. tr., *Ariane and Barbe Bleue*, 1910). *Monna Vanna* (1902; Eng. tr., *Monna Vanna*, 1905), a historical drama situated in the quattrocento, even presents a Montherlant-style heroine, headstrong and thoughtful, who dominates her destiny. Love will once again be victorious in *Joyzelle* (1903; Eng. tr., *Joyzelle*, 1920), but Maeterlinck's last great triumph was the worldwide success of *L'Oiseau bleu* (1908; Eng. tr., *The Blue Bird*, 1910), an admirable, optimistic fairy scene on the theme of the search for happiness.

The poet obtained the Nobel Prize for Literature in 1911. In 1939, he withdrew into the Orlamonde Palace, near Nice, and he was made a count by King Albert in 1932. His theatrical career, however, was finished, and the plays he was yet to publish added nothing to his glory: *Marie-Magdeleine* (1913; Eng. tr., *Mary Magdalen*, 1910), spoiled by philosophical intentions; *Le Bourgmestre de Stilmonde* (1919; Eng. tr., *The Burgomaster of Stilemonde*, 1918), a patriotic play; *Juda de Kérioth* (1929); *Jeanne d'Arc* (1948; Joan of Arc); and some unedited plays, which appeared in 1959—*L'Abbé Sétubal* (Father Setubal), *Les Trois Justiciers* (The Three Justiciaries), and *Le Jugement dernier* (The Last Judgment).

Finally, Maeterlinck was also an essayist of renown, oriented towards occultism and the hereafter. *Le Trésor des humbles* (1896; Eng. tr., *The Treasure of the Humble*, 1897) refuses positivism and suggests communication by silence; *La Sagesse et Destinée* (1898; Eng. tr., *Wisdom and Destiny*, 1898) proposes a stoic and optimistic moral. Led by theosophy and occultism, Maeterlinck believed in reincarnation and metempsychosis—*La Mort* (1913; Eng. tr., *Death*, 1911); he discussed universal suffrage in *Le Double Jardin* (1904; Eng. tr., *The Double Garden*, 1904). His famous *Vies* of animals—*La Vie des termites* (1927; The Life of the Termite)—and *L'Intelligence des fleurs* (1907; Eng. tr., *The Intelligence of Flowers*, 1907) are still valued for their very beautiful pages, at the same time poetic and penetrating. However, even if he treated death and the absurdity and incoherence of the world, themes that contemporary theater will take up again, Maeterlinck does not work well today. His pseudoscientific theories no longer concern us; a part of his theater is dependent on the symbolist bric-a-brac. To appreciate him fully, situate him in his time and measure his contribution to the theater at the end of the 19th century. Maeterlinck's last work, published the year before his death on May 6, 1949, is a delightful volume of recollections, *Bulles bleues, Souvenirs heureux* (Blue Bubbles, Happy Memories), in which, without affectation or grandiloquence, he painted the serene portrait of a man who made a success of his life.

See: E. Thomas, *Maurice Maeterlinck* (1911, 1974); P. Mahony, *The Magic of Maeterlinck* (1951, 1969); *Annales de la Fondation Maurice Maeterinck*, vol. 1 (1955); W. D. Halls, *Maurice Maeterlinck, A Study of His Life and*

Thought (1960); J. Hanse and R. Vivier, *Maurice Maeterlinck 1862–1962* (1962); A. Pasquier, *Maurice Maeterlinck* (1963); M. Riffaterre, "Decadent Features in Maeterlinck's Poetry," *Lang&S* 7, no. 1 (Winter 1974): 3–19; B. Knapp, *Maurice Maeterlinck* (1975).   R.T.

Maeztu, Ramiro de (1876–1936), Spanish publisher, diplomat, politician, lecturer, critic, dramatist, and above all journalist, was born in the Basque city of Vitoria to a well-to-do Cuban father and an English mother. When financial reverses and the death of his father plunged the family into bankruptcy, Ramiro, having only completed the equivalent of a high-school degree, traveled to Paris seeking a business education with which to support his family. Subsequently he went to Cuba to stave off the loss of an inherited sugar plantation. Having failed at both and armed solely with a minimal formal and practical education, in 1895 he began to write newspaper articles for the local Bilbao daily *El Porvenir Vascongado*. This marked the beginning of a 40-year career in journalism that produced some 15,000 essays. Only a fraction of these have been catalogued or put into book form to date. Maeztu himself published only a few books: *Hacia otra España* (1899; Toward a New Spain), *Inglaterra en armas* (1916; England at War), *Authority, Liberty and Function in the Light of War* (1916), *La crisis del humanismo* (1916), *Don Juan, Don Quijote y la Celestina* (1925), and *Defensa de la Hispanidad* (1934).

Maeztu's essayistic journalism was of a critical and reflective nature. A man of strong convictions, he was a totally humorless writer, passionate, patriotic, and intent on shaking his readers out of their sociopolitical and economic complacency. His work is neither rigorous nor scholarly, and his concern for structural values is almost nil. His one apparent goal is to preach a doctrine and ensure its impact on the mind of the reader. His own mind was more receptive than creative. This is borne out by an examination of the evolution of his ideology. Maeztu's initial residence in Madrid (1891–95) evinced no single heartfelt conviction other than a revolutionary idealism held in common with his literary contemporaries of the famous Generation of 1898. Representative of this first stage is the revisionist prose of *Hacia otra España*, where traditional values and social institutions are excoriated in favor of a new order. The period spent in London (1905–19) as a foreign correspondent proved to be the most significant in the definitive formation of his intellectual convictions. Having seen firsthand the horrors of World War I, and after a bout with liberal socialism, he there came under the influence of T. E. Hulme and became a philosophically convinced Christian. *La crisis del humanismo* expounds on this strange newly found mixture of conservative and paternalistic socialism. The third phase in Maeztu's ideological evolution began upon his return to Spain in 1919, when his latent conservatism turned archreactionary. Political authoritarianism and religious orthodoxy became his only ideals in the last years of his life. Even *Don Quijote, Don Juan y la Celestina*, his only book of any literary value, studies each of the characters in the title from the standpoint of his or her moral, social, and political significance. For Maeztu, Don Quixote represents love, Don Juan, power, and Celestina, wisdom. His last book, *Defensa de la Hispanidad*, the doctrinal treatise for which Maeztu is best remembered, advocates as Spain's only possible salvation from the imminent devastation of the Civil War a return to the old ideals which had carried his nation to her greatest glory in history: the conquest and civilization of the New World. These were the ideals of homeland, faith, language, and culture. Such are the three distinguishable stages of this seemingly radical evolution that began with anarchism, passed through socialism, and ended in a reactionary fascism that foreshadowed Francisco Franco's dictatorial regime.

See: M. Nozick, "An Examination of Ramiro do Maeztu," *PMLA* 69 (September 1954): 719–40; V. Marrero, *Maeztu* (1955); R. Landeira, *Ramiro de Maeztu* (1978).   R.L.

Maiorescu, Titu (1840–1917), Romanian critic, philosopher, and public figure, was born in Craiova. He attended school in Braşov, Vienna, and Berlin, where he received a diploma in philosophy in 1861. He returned to Romania where he soon became professor and then rector at the University of Iaşi. From this time forward, Maiorescu was continually involved in public life either as a teacher or a lawyer. In 1865 he was one of the founders of the "Junimea" society, a group formed to give new direction to Romanian culture under the democratic government of Alexandru Ion Cuza.

Maiorescu gave intellectual direction to an entire generation. He was interested in grammatical theory and suggested the use of phonetical writing. In 1867 he wrote an important study of contemporary Romanian poetry, *O cercetare critică asupra poezi románe de la 1867* (A Critical Study of Romanian Poetry since 1867). In his essay "Despre reforma învătămîntului public," (1870; Concerning Reforms in Public Education), he stressed that it was the lower schools that should first be put on a solid foundation, and then the universities. Maiorescu was the first critic in Romanian literature with a system that was both theoretical and practical, an accomplishment overshadowed during his lifetime by his public career. Only after his death did his critical and philosophic works receive the attention that they deserved.

See: S. Cioculescu, ed., *Istoria literaturii romane,* vol. 3 (1973), pp. 449–506; M. Bucur, *Istoriografia literară românească* (1973), pp. 70–73.   V.A.

Majerová, Marie, pseud. of Marie Bartošová (1882–1967), Czech novelist, was born in Úvaly, near Prague, but grew up in the mining region of Kladno, which is the setting of many of her novels and tales. She became a socialist and subsequently a member of the Communist Party, working as a journalist. In 1947 she was given the honorary title of "national artist."

Majerová's novels and tales possess a special pathos, strongly subjective and rooted in a point of view that allowed the author to identify with her characters—the victims of capitalist oppression. Although sentimental and lacking in objectivity, her works have warmth and life and are infectious. Her early novel, *Náměstí Republiky* (1914; Place de la République), the result of a stay of several years in Paris, portrays the world of Parisian revolutionaries. Her subsequent novels include: *Nejkrásnější svét* (1920; The Most Beautiful World), about a young country girl's movement towards socialism; *Přehrada* (1932; The Dam), a somewhat pretentious attempt at a Utopian novel in which the building of a great dam symbolizes the growth of the socialist movement; *Siréna* (1935) a large-scale chronicle of social development and change over four generations of the Kladno mining country; and *Havířská balada* (1938; Eng. tr., *Ballad of a Miner*, 1960) the moving story of a poor mining family struggling to live decently and honestly during the period of worldwide economic depression.

After Czechoslovakia turned to socialism in 1948, Majerová was hailed as one of the leading Czech writers, but with time it became clear that her talents were insufficiently objective and that the novelistic forms she attempted were too large in scale for her to fill. Before her death, Majerová wrote mostly children's literature.

See: J. Hájek, *Národní umělkyně Marie Majerová* (1952).   W.E.H.

Makal, Mahmut (1930–), Turkish essayist, was born in the village of Demirci, in the province of Niğde. He became the first villager to write a book about the plight of poverty-stricken peasants in Anatolia. In 1947 he graduated from a Village Teachers Institute and served for two years as a teacher in a village not far from his birthplace. He first attracted attention with his village vignettes published in the leading literary journal, *Varlık,* starting May 1948. The collection of these vignettes under the title of *Bizim Köy* (Our Village) in 1950 marked the beginning of a new type of literature committed to exposing the backward conditions and the deprivations in the rural areas. It also caused the ire of the government: Makal was arrested for a brief period. Later he received a higher degree from the Gazi Educational Institute and worked as an inspector of elementary schools and a teacher of literature at a secondary school. Retiring in 1968, after 20 years in the educational system, he started his own publishing firm.

Makal's books include *Köyümden* (1952; From My Village; reissued in 1957 under the title *Hayal ve Gerçek,* Dream and Reality), *Memleketin Sahipleri* (1954; Owners of the Country), *Kuru Sevda* (1957; Dry Love), *17 Nisan* (1959; April 17), *Köye Gidenler* (1959; Bound for the Village), *Kalkınma Masalı* (1960; Myth of Development), *Kamçı Teslimi* (1965; Handing Over the Whip); *Yer Altında bir Anadolu* (1968; Anatolia Underground), *Bu Ne Biçim Ülke* (1968; What Sort of Country Is This), *Kokmuş Bir Düzende* (1970; In a Stinking Social Order), and others, all of which deal with problems of rural and urban poverty, economic injustice, and oppression. English translations of Makal's *Bizim Köy* and *Köyümden* are available in *A Village in Anatolia,* tr. by Sir Wyndham Deedes (1954).   T.S.H.

Maksimov, Vladimir Yemelyanovich (1932–), Russian novelist, born in Leningrad, began publication with a volume of poems (1956), but subsequently became established mainly as a novelist. The distinctive feature of his work is his exploration of the "lower depths" of Soviet society, which he came to know in childhood as an inmate of "juvenile colonies" (for delinquents, waifs and strays), and then as a laborer on construction sites in many parts of the country. His first prose work, a story called "My obzhivayem zemlyu" (We Settle the Earth) appeared in 1961 in the celebrated miscellany *Tarusskiye stranitsy* (Abridged Eng. tr., *Pages from Tarusa,* 1964), edited by Konstantin Paustovsky. His best-known short story published in the Soviet Union is "Zhiv chelovek" (1962, and as a play, 1965; Eng. tr., *A Man Survives,* 1963) a vivid account of life "on the run" in the Soviet criminal underworld. In "Zhiv chelovek," Maksimov showed considerable narrative talent in depicting the seamy side of Soviet existence. Not surprisingly, his choice of subject matter made it increasingly difficult for him to publish in his own country; and his next lengthy novel, a candid exposé of everyday life, could only be circulated in *samizdat,* eventually appearing in print in West Germany under the title *Sem dney tvoreniya* (1971; Eng. tr., *Seven Days of Creation,* 1974). Two other novels, *Karantin* (1973; Quarantine) and *Proshchaniye iz niotkuda* (1973; Farewell from Nowhere) have been published abroad; both embody a good deal of picaresque material, much of it evidently autobiographical, and testify to undiminished story-telling powers—regrettably marred by a tendency

to moralize. In 1973, Maksimov was expelled from the Union of Soviet Writers, and in the following year was allowed to emigrate to the West, where he now lives in Paris and edits the literary journal, *Kontinent.*   M.Ha.

Malanyuk, Yevhen (1897–1968), Ukrainian poet and essayist, was born in Kherson province. An active participant in the 1917 Revolution on the nationalist side, he emigrated to the West in 1920, living in Prague and Warsaw and, after World War II, in the United States. A most influential personality among the émigrés, Malanyuk belonged to the literary group centered around the monthly *Visnyk* published by Dmytro Dontsov in Lviv (Lvov) (*see* UKRAINIAN LITERATURE). Malanyuk was a first-rate poet, influenced in his early career by the Russian acmeists (*see* RUSSIAN LITERATURE). His poetry deals mostly with national and historical themes, which are handled with great originality. His collections of verse include *Zemlya i zalizo* (1930; Earth and Steel), *Zemna madonna* (1934; The Earthly Madonna), *Persten Polikrata* (1939; The Ring of Polycrates), and *Ostannya vesna* (1959; The Last Spring). His essays have been collected in the two-volume *Knyha sposterezhen* (1962; The Book of Observations).   G.S.N.L.

Malaparte, Curzio, pseud. of Kurt Erich Suckert (1898–1957), Italian essayist, novelist, playwright, and poet, was born in Prato of German-Italian parentage. He fought in World War I before the Italian intervention (which he advocated) and was gassed on the French front in 1918. Malaparte soon dissented from the official views of the conflict and put forward, in *La rivolta dei santi maledetti* (1921; The Rebellion of the Accursed Saints), his interpretation of the Italian defeat at Caporetto (now Kobarid, Yugoslavia) as a social, not a military phenomenon. In the immediate postwar years, Malaparte traveled and read widely, continuing to nettle his contemporaries by taking provocative and often contradictory stands. He alternated between cosmopolitan yearnings (witness his collaboration with Massimo BONTEMPELLI on the journal '*900* and his own founding of another international review, *Prospettive*) and violently reactionary outbursts defending the parochial viewpoints of the *strapaese* literary movement (*see* ITALIAN LITERATURE). His collection of burlesque ballads, *L'Arcitaliano* (1928; The Arch-Italian), was influenced both by contemporary nationalism and by a sophisticated literary tradition of Tuscan wit extending from the 13th to the 19th centuries, from Cecco Angiolieri through Grazzini and Doni to Giuseppe Giusti (1809–50) and Renato FUCINI. Respect for tradition seems to have been a necessary basis for Malaparte's dissent, as if he could only reject what he had passionately accepted.

In 1931 he criticized Adolf Hitler and Benito Mussolini in his pamphlet *Technique du coup d'état* (Eng. tr., *Coup d'etat: The Technique of Revolution,* 1932), in which he attempted to show that the conquest and defense of the state were technical, not political problems. He further incurred the enmity of Nazi and Fascist authorities by his brilliant but depressing war correspondence from France in 1940–41, *Il sole è cieco* (1947; The Sun Is Blind), and from the USSR in 1941–42, *Il Volga nasce in Europe* (1943; Eng. tr., *The Volga Rises in Europe,* 1957). While in Finland, Malaparte wrote his best book, *Kaputt* (1945; Eng. tr., 1946), a horrific vision of Europe crumbling under the onslaught of war. His peculiar sensitivity to the contradictoriness and social unbalance of European culture was given dramatic form in the contrast between a few refined cosmopolitan characters, expressing their elegant pessimism through sharp witticisms and scintillating paradoxes, and the holocaust of whole peoples.

During the last months of World War II, Malaparte served as the Italian Army Contingent liaison officer with the Allied Command. The literary result of this experience was *La pelle* (1949; Eng. tr., *The Skin*, 1952), which describes the complete collapse of social life and conventional morality in Naples following the Allied occupation. The novel caused a scandal because, in the new cultural climate, it was mistaken for a realistic work. Yet it was, in fact, the fulfillment of Malaparte's surrealistic tendencies, springing partly from French decadentism filtered through Gabriele D'ANNUNZIO, and partly from the pictorial tradition extending from Hieronymus Bosch and Matthias Grünewald through Francisco Goya to Edvard Munch and Salvador Dali.

After a few theatrical flops and a moderately successful film, *Cristo proibito* (1951; Christ Prohibited), which he wrote and directed, Malaparte again took up his old role of intellectual sniper. His most successful work, *Maledetti toscani* (1956; Eng. tr., *Those Cursed Tuscans*, 1964), belongs to this period. More than ever aware of the limitations of bourgeois culture, of which he was both a creature and a prisoner, he found his ideological targets everywhere in the political spectrum. His contrasting attitudes must therefore be seen as complementary aspects of his effort to break through to freedom. He failed, however, to realize that freedom is not only an intellectual concept, but also a political goal requiring definite political choices. For all his literary skill and cultural insight, Malaparte's political thought seldom raised itself above the level of passionate moralism. Toward the end of his life, he became interested in the Maoist model of communism and accepted an invitation to visit China. His journey, related in the posthumously published journal *Io in Russia e in Cina* (1958; Myself in Russia and in China), was cut short by illness, and he returned to Italy. His deathbed conversion to Catholicism aroused a final flurry of controversy over his ideological allegiance.

See: G. Grana, in *Letteratura italiana: i contemporanei*, vol. 2 (1975), pp. 1227-79.   G.Ca.

Malerba, Luigi, pseud. of Luigi Bonardi (1927-), Italian novelist, short-story writer, and screenwriter, was born in Berceto (Parma). He lives in Rome. Fascinated by language, its paradoxes, insufficiencies, and relation to reality, and by the act of literary invention, Malerba has always made writing itself the subject of his experimental novels. Early signs of this concern appear in the naturalistic stories of *La scoperta dell'alfabeto* (1963; The Discovery of the Alphabet). The extravagant "chronicles" of *Le rose imperiali* (1974; The Imperial Roses), set in an imaginary ancient China, use violence, arbitrariness, and the marvelous to effect, among other things, an incursion into the unnatural power of language. *Il serpente* (1966; Eng. tr., *The Serpent*, 1968), an alarming and very funny novel, is molded by the lies and unreliability of its first-person narrator, a music-loving stamp dealer who loves and murders a woman who may not exist. Underpinning the enigmatic plot are the polarized images of garbage, vermin, serpents, and birds, airplanes, and angels. *Salto mortale* (1968; Eng. tr., *What Is This Buzzing, Do You Hear It Too*, 1969) is a detective story that mockingly calls into question not only the slippery identity of the peripatetic junk-collecting "Giuseppe called Giuseppe" who narrates the murder mystery, but even the identity of language and the book itself. The title of *Il protagonista* (1973) refers to the penis; a comic hallucinatory fantasy written in coarse, ungrammatical language, this novel confronts the mystery of human potency and impotency.

Malerba often parodies literary as well as linguistic conventions to spark a questioning of received notions.

This method is apparent even in his brief children's tale *Pinocchio con gli stivali* (1977; Pinocchio-in-Boots). In addition to a catalogue of regional words, *Le parole abbandonate* (1977; Abandoned Words), his recent works include *Storie dell'anno Mille* (1972; Stories of the Year 1000; coauthored with Tonino Guerra and dramatized for Italian television) and *Il pataffio* (1978; The Hodgepodge). In an inimitable fusion of realism and the comic-macabre, both works are set in a medieval landscape, ravaged by war and nature, in which hunger and self-survival motivate all action. Yet Malerba is able to turn even this subject into an allegory about the power of language.

See: P. Mauri, *Luigi Malerba* (1977); M. Schneider, "To Know Is to Eat: A Reading of *Il serpente*," *YaIS* 2 (1978): 71-84.   M.Sc.

Malewska, Hanna (1911-), Polish novelist, short-story writer, and translator, was born in Grodzisk Mazowiecki. She studied history at the Catholic University in Lublin. Her first novel, *Wiosna grecka* (1933; The Greek Spring), was based on the youth of Plato and the Olympic Games. During World War II she belonged to the Polish underground and took part in the Warsaw uprising, settling after the war in Cracow. In her volume of short stories, *Stanica. Opowieści rzymskie* (1947; The Watchtower. Roman Tales), and in *Sir Tomasz More odmawia* (1956; Sir Thomas More Refuses), she muses upon feats of endurance and spiritual strength, for example, the death of Archimedes, who until the very last did not abandon his geometry; and she intimates that even if a hero becomes a victim of violence, his moral resonance is not wasted. Her major works—*Żelazna korona* (1937; The Iron Crown), linked with the reign of Charles V; *Kamienie wołać będą* (written in 1939; pub. 1946; Stones Will Bear Witness), evoking the medieval builders of the cathedrals; *Przemija postać świata* (1954; Fleeting Is the Shape of the World), based on events of the 7th century A.D.—convey the atmosphere of cultural clashes and the emergence of new order. While relying on thorough documentation, Malewska kept her focus upon the guiding ideas of history but avoided oversimplification. She parted with the traditional techniques of plot development and made her narrative reminiscent of a chronicle. *Panowie Leszczyńscy* (1961; The Leszczyński Gentlemen) is the story of a Polish aristocratic clan during the 17th century; *Apokryf rodzinny* (1965; The Family Apocrypha) is also linked with the native background. Malewska's most recent works include *Labirynt. LLW czyli co się może wydarzyć jutro* (1970; The Labyrinth. LLW, or What May Happen Tomorrow), which proclaims the independence of the historical novelist from current doctrines, and *Żniwo na sierpie* (1947; Harvest On the Sickle), a fictionalized biography of the poet Cyprian NORWID.

See: Z. Starowieyska-Morstinowa, "Epos i historia," in *Kalejdoskop literacki* (1955), pp. 58-98.   M.G.

Malinovski, Ivan (1926-), Danish poet, was born in Copenhagen. He is an excellent translator of German and Russian poetry. The guiding principle of Malinovski's writing is the confrontation technique of modernism, a formal expression of the poet's experience of existence as meaningless and divided into numerous contradictions. His pessimistic and tragic view of life, related to that of the Swedish poet Gunnar EKELÖF, is convincingly expressed in *Galgenfrist* (1958; Short Respite). The enumerative prose poetry in *Romerske bassiner* (1963; Roman Basins) is more hermetically sealed, containing the left-wing author's reflective thoughts on man's chaotic condition, which, to him, illustrates Karl Marx's theory of alienation. Similar ideas are found in the concentrated haikulike aphorisms *Poetomatic* (1965). Malinovski's revolutionary attitude is most noticeable in *Leve som var der en fremtid og et håb* (1968; Living As If There Were a Future and a Hope) and *Kritik af tavshed* (1974; Critique of Silence). The former volume evidences no change in his artistic attitude, whereas the latter is a distorted contribution to the current political debate.   S.H.R.

Mallarmé, Stéphane (1842–98), French poet and aesthetician, was born in Paris. He spent some 30 years teaching English, first in such provincial towns as Tournon and Besançon, and finally in the more congenial environment of a Paris lycée. His eagerness to read Edgar Allan Poe in the original rather than in Charles BAUDELAIRE's remarkable translations had led to his entrapment in a teaching career, which he saw as the only alternative to perpetual employment in a registry office. In keeping with his chosen profession, he composed a textbook, *Petite Philologie à l'usage des classes et du monde: les mots anglais* (1878; Little Philology for Classroom Use and for Society: English Words), of far greater linguistic and literary interest than pedagogical value; he also wrote important studies of Shakespeare's *Hamlet,* William Beckford's *Vathek* (1876), and the poetry of Alfred Lord Tennyson and Charles Algernon Swinburne, and translated the poems of Poe. He also published *Les Dieux antiques* (1880; The Ancient Gods), a book on mythology.

In spite of his tedious teaching assignments, the cares of raising a family on a tight budget, frequent bouts of ill health, and protracted periods of sterility, Mallarmé succeeded, while still exiled to the provinces, in writing some of his finest poems and elaborating a coherent theory of literature. His circle of literary acquaintances already comprised his close friends Henri Cazalis, Emmanuel Des Essarts, and Lefébvre as well as the more influential Théodore de Banville, Catulle Mendès, and François Coppée. At Tournon, he added the Provençal poets Frédéric MISTRAL and Théodore AUBANEL. Back in Paris, Mallarmé led, as far as time would allow, the typical existence of a man of letters. He directed *La Dernière Mode,* a fashion magazine, while writing articles for it (some on gastronomy) under such pseudonyms as Marguerite de Ponty and Miss Satin. At the same time, he was contributing poems, studies, and reviews to various journals, including *L'Artiste, Le Parnasse contemporain,* and *La Revue wagnérienne.* Tactful and modest, but also stimulating and gregarious, Mallarmé frequented an international coterie of intellectuals, including the painters James McNeill Whistler, Edouard Manet, Paul Gauguin, Edvard Munch, Pierre Renoir, and Félix Vallotton, each of whom drew his portrait; Berthe Morisot, about whom he wrote an article; his close friends Edgar Degas and Odilon Redon; and many of the great writers of his day, such as Philippe-Auguste Villiers de l'Isle-Adam, Jules Laforgue, Paul VERLAINE, Arthur RIMBAUD, Oscar Wilde, Swinburne, and Stefan GEORGE. Mallarmé's celebrated Tuesdays, where flocks of admirers came to hear his brilliant improvisations on a variety of subjects, attracted in particular three young men: Paul CLAUDEL, André GIDE, and his spiritual heir, Paul VALÉRY, who became almost as famous as Mallarmé himself. Practically unknown until 1884, Mallarmé suddenly acquired notoriety thanks to Verlaine's *Poètes maudits* and Joris-Karl HUYSMAN's *A rebours* (1884; Eng. tr., *Against Nature,* 1959). Indifferent to the noisy acclaim so eagerly sought by many poets, Mallarmé started the fashion, current to this day, of publishing his poetry in expensive, limited editions; *L'Après-midi d'un faune* (The Afternoon of a Faun) appeared in 1876, adorned with colored woodcuts

by Manet, and *Les Poésies* was printed in 1887, a facsimile of his manuscript with an engraving by Félicien Rops. Interested but impecunious readers had to wait until 1893 for *Vers et prose*, a less expensive selection of his creative writings that nevertheless contained a remarkable lithographic portrait by Whistler.

Mallarmé's passion for poetry started very early. As a schoolboy, he filled page after page with skillful imitations of Pierre-Jean Béranger, Alphonse Lamartine, and Victor Hugo. Finally, he discovered Baudelaire, generally considered the first true modernist in poetry. After approximating in theme no less than in technique some of the more splenetic poems among the *Fleurs du mal* (1857, 1861, 1868; Eng. tr., *Flowers of Evil,* 1909), he soon developed his own unique style and formulated his own aesthetic theories. Mallarmé's admiration for Théophile Gautier and Leconte de Lisle may have encouraged him to seek ever greater rigor, abstraction, and density.

Even more consistently than Baudelaire, Mallarmé chose as his subject matter poetic creation and, going perhaps a step further than his predecessor, the act of writing, with its attendant risks and absurdities. Electing as his sole protagonists the Poet and Poetry personified (as in the sonnet "Ses purs ongles" [1887; Her Pure Nails] and "Hérodiade" [1869–71]), he expressed the wish of transforming the universe into a book, the only act capable of giving a semblance of meaning to an otherwise godless existence. As early as 1866, he endeavored to create his *grand œuvre* (supreme opus), going so far as to regard each one of his finished texts as mere stages on the way toward an unattainable goal, the definitive expression of Totality. A reader of Plato and, in all probability, G. W. F. Hegel, Mallarmé saw in the verbal alchemy of poetry the only means to abolish the object as such, together with chance, so as to reveal the Ideal. For Mallarmé, the function of poetry consisted in restoring, thanks to a demonic search for analogies, the real world obscured by everyday existence. Indeed, he considered the poet the one true mediator of the Absolute.

Although Mallarmé, a dedicated Parnassian, composed many prose poems, including his two masterpieces *Igitur* in 1868, (pub. 1925) and, toward the end of his life, *Un Coup de dés* (A Cast of the Dice), he scrupulously adhered to all the traditional rules of prosody. And it so happens that he attained poetic heights, unapproached before or since, in seven or eight sonnets, including "Ses purs ongles," some of them written quite early, but frequently revised so as to increase their harmony, their luminosity, their concentration and, concomitantly, their hermeticism, as well as the subtlety of their erotic suggestiveness.

Historically, Mallarmé's originality consists to a large extent in the establishment of a novel relationship between the creative artist, willfully dispossessed of personal idiosyncrasies, and the world, as well as in a radically new conception of language, considered sufficient unto itself. Baudelaire before him had all but destroyed the barriers separating the self from the nonself and had substituted a functional poetic persona for the lyrical "I" or personal presence so characteristic of his romantic predecessors. In Mallarmé, destruction gives way to a multiplicity of equations, a veritable algebra of negativity that sets off the poem from external phenomena and from lyrical confession, thus transforming it into an autonomous verbal artifact, irreducible either to experience or to ordinary communication. The poet eschews all anecdotal and descriptive content apart from a few familiar and highly suggestive objects—furniture, a room, stars—which he proceeds to structure and interrelate, usually by means of metaphor, subdued puns, syntactical displacement, and frequent recourse to various forms of negation. As Mallarmé expected from his readers an effort similar to his own, his poetry marks a drastic change in the relationship between author and audience. Instead of passively succumbing to the emotional persuasiveness of the romantics or serving as accomplices in Baudelaire's poetic transgressions, Mallarmé's readers must become manipulators of language in their own right and actively construct for their own enjoyment the recondite drama of the poems.

Mallarmé had a keen sense of the dramatic. He composed his famous *L'Après-midi d'un faune* and "Hérodiade" with every hope of seeing them performed on the stage with elaborate sets, musical accompaniment, and complex choreography. He shared with Richard WAGNER, for whom he professed the greatest admiration, as Baudelaire had before him, the dream of a total spectacle where all art forms would combine so that beauty might triumph over existence in all its aspects.

While contemporary poetry has assimilated the revolutionary innovations of Baudelaire and Rimbaud, if not those of LAUTRÉAMONT, Mallarmé's hermetic texts, particularly *Un Coup de dés*, continue to challenge all those who search for a breakthrough in poetry, including Yves BONNEFOY and other contributors to *L'Ephémère*, and Denis ROCHE and Marcel Playnet of *Tel Quel*.

The first edition of Mallarmé's *Œuvres complètes* (Complete Works), carefully assembled by H. Mondor, appeared in 1945. Mondor and L. J. Austin have edited the *Correspondance*, with C. P. Barbier adding the *Documents Stéphane Mallarmé* (1968–76). J. Schérer's *Le Livre de Mallarmé* (The Book of Mallarmé) and J. P. Richard's *Pour un tombeau d'Anatole* have made available additional fragments pertaining to Mallarmé's *grand œuvre*.

See: A. Thibaudet, *La Poésie de Stéphane Mallarmé* (1912); H. Mondor, *Vie de Mallarmé* (1941–42); C. Mauron, *Introduction à la psychanalyse de Mallarmé* (1950); W. Fowlie, *Mallarmé* (1953; G. Poulet and J. P. Richard, *L'Universe imaginaire de Mallarmé* (1961); R. G. Cohn, *Toward the Poems of Mallarmé* (1965); J. Kristeva, *La Révolution du langage poétique* (1974).   J.D.H.

Mallet-Joris, Françoise (1930–), Belgian novelist, was born in Antwerp. She has studied in Philadelphia and at the Sorbonne. A French citizen by marriage, she lives in Paris. At 17, she published a collection of verse, *Poèmes du dimanche* (1947; Sunday Poems). Her first novel, *Le Rempart des Béguines* (1951; Eng. tr., *The Illusionist*, 1952), tells the story of a 16-year-old girl who is drawn into a homosexual relationship by her father's mistress. In the sequel, *La Chambre rouge* (1955; Eng. tr., *The Red Room*, 1956), the young heroine, proud and self-contained after her lover has married her father, finds herself the disdainful disciple of her former lover, who had promised but not fulfilled the possibility of transcending female contingency. Central themes in both works are human isolation and the impossibility of genuine communication. Self-mastery is the goal of most of Mallet-Joris's fictitious characters. It is achieved through the supremacy of the will and implies assuming a mask to hide one's vulnerability. Her third novel, *Les Mensonges* (1956; Eng. tr., *House of Lies*, 1957), for which she was awarded the Prix des Libraires in 1957, presents the struggle for power within an old bourgeois family. Mallet-Joris's main thematic concerns are mendacity, hypocrisy, will, and truth.

With the publication of *L'Empire céleste* (1958; Eng. tr., *Café Céleste*, 1959), for which she received the Prix Fémina in 1958, Mallet-Joris placed herself in the tradition of the French moralist and social observer. *Les Person-*

nages (1961; Eng. tr., *The Favourite*, 1962) uses a historical setting, the intrigue around Louise de La Fayette at the court of Louis XIII, to describe how a tormented soul after immense suffering becomes reborn in faith. Mallet-Joris herself became converted to Catholicism in mid-life. *Les Signes et les prodiges* (1966; Eng. tr., *Signs and Wonders*, 1966) treats contemporary political and social problems, but the contemporary world is only a setting, as is the historical one. Mallet-Joris deals with the timeless themes of human weakness and clash of passions—hers is a Balzacian world.

Her two autobiographical novels, *Lettre à moi-même* (1963; Eng. tr., *Letter to Myself*, 1964) and *La Maison de papier* (1970; Eng. tr., *The Paper House*, 1971), convey the image of a passionately alive and active woman, mother, and writer. Daily commonplaces fascinate her as much as world events. She likes delving into the mysteries of everyday existence, looking for a guiding thread in the incongruities of the daily life.

Le Jeu du souterrain (1973; Eng. tr., *The Underground Game*, 1975) questions the very foundations of writing: words and their meanings. Mallet-Joris concludes that although stories may serve no purpose, they must be told as long as people function within the universe of language. In her recent novel *Allegra* (1976) the heroine sacrifices her life in the attempt to transform into speech the silence of a mute boy.

Mallet-Joris approaches her subject matter in the traditional way of the French "romancier," with the "old tools" of plot and character. She has consciously avoided both contemporary experiments with unusual ways of expression and play with form.

She has also written a number of historical novels: *Marie Mancini, Le Premier Amour de Louis XIV* (1964; Eng. tr., *The Uncompromising Heart: A Life of Marie Mancini, Louis XIV's First Love*, 1966), *Trois âges de la nuit* (1966; *The Witches' Three Tales of Sorcery*, 1970), and *Jeanne Guyon* (1977).

See: R. D. Reck, "Mallet-Joris and the Anatomy of Will," *YFS* 24 (Winter 1959); G. Delattre, "Mirrors and Masks in the World of Françoise Mallet-Joris," *YFS* 27 (Spring 1961).   E.Ha.

Malmberg, Bertil (1889–1958), Swedish poet, was born in Härnösand. He was the last champion of Platonic idealism in Swedish letters, influenced by Friedrich von Schiller, whose philosophical poetry he translated, and by Stefan GEORGE, whose prophetic pose he sometimes imitated. In *Atlantis* (1916), his first mature book of verse, the glory that was Greece is invoked in magnificent stanzas. In 1917, Malmberg settled in Munich for almost a decade, and his firsthand experience of the political and social collapse of Germany at the end of World War I precipitated a personal crisis. His dissipations, nervous breakdowns, and bitter remorse are candidly confessed in the autobiographical work *Ett stycke väg* (1950; En Route) and give a somber emotional coloring to *Orfika* (1923), containing grandiose, although somewhat rhetorical visions of heaven and hell.

As he grew older and more disillusioned, Malmberg moved away from the cult of absolute beauty toward a concern with the destiny of European civilization and the existential position of man. *Dikter vid gränsen* (1935; Poems at the Limit) reflects the impact of Nazi mythology. In his late collections, for example, *Med cyclopöga* (1950; With a Cyclop's Eye), free verse and a colloquial idiom are employed to reveal bitter moral insights. An altogether different side of the author emerges in the partly autobiographical childhood stories, *Åke och hans värld* (1924; Eng. tr., *Åke and His World*, 1940).

See: A. Ahlberg, *Bertil Malmberg* (1939); E. Bergman, *Diktens värld och politikens: Bertil Malmberg och Tyskland 1980–28* (1967); I. Algulin, *Tradition och modernism: Bertil Malmbergs och Hjalmar Gullbergs lyriska förnyelse efter 1940-talets mitt* (1969); G. Brandell, *Svensk litteratur 1870–1970,* vol. 1 (1974), pp. 335–42; L. Gustafsson, *Forays into Swedish Poetry* (1978), pp. 27–32.   S.B.

Malraux, André (1901–76), French novelist, essayist, and art critic, was born in Paris. The child of separated parents, Malraux grew up in Paris, left the lycée without a *baccalauréat*, and worked briefly for bookdealers such as René-Louis Doyon and publishers such as Daniel Kahnweiler and Simon Kra. He married Clara Goldschmidt (see her autobiographical *Nos Vingt Ans* (1966; Our Twenties), and went with her in 1923 to Indochina, where they hoped to rediscover the Khmer temples along the old Buddhist pilgrimage route through the jungles of Laos and Cambodia.

Malraux was arrested for removing public property in the form of sculptures from the temple at Bantai Srey and was sentenced to three years' confinement. The sentence was subsequently reduced by a colonial appeals court and finally voided entirely by the Cour de Cassation in Paris, but only after the Parisian press had enjoyed no little sport at his expense. For some months he edited an anticolonialist newspaper, *L'Indochine,* in Saigon, an activity that brought him in contact with the local leaders of the Left wing of the Kuomintang.

Malraux's three novels on revolutionary themes, *Les Conquérants* (1928; Eng. tr., *The Conquerors,* 1929), *La Condition humaine* (1933; Eng. trs., *Man's Fate,* 1934; *Storm in Shanghai,* 1934), and *L'Espoir* (1937; Eng. trs., *Man's Hope,* 1938; *Days of Hope,* 1938), earned international acclaim and established him as a leader of the pro-Communist intellectual Left. His other fiction, *La Voie royale* (1930; Eng. tr., *The Royal Way,* 1935), *Le Temps du mépris* (1935; Eng. trs., *Days of Contempt,* 1936; *Days of Wrath,* 1936), and *Les Noyers de l'Altenburg* (1943; Eng. tr., *The Walnut Trees of Altenburg,* 1952), impressed critics as brilliant but technically less successful. Malraux first aroused critical attention with his "semisurrealist" fantasy tales *Lunes en papier* (1921; Paper Moons) and *Le Royaume farfelu* (1922; rev. 1928; The Mad Realm), concerning the significance of which students of his work remain divided: those impressed by the absence of fantasy from his later writing feel that a marked change of manner differentiates it from the earlier, while others point to a similarity of thematic materials in both as evidence of a pervading unity throughout. Another early work, *La Tentation de l'occident* (1926; Eng. tr., *The Temptation of the West,* 1961), is a fictional exchange of letters between a young European and a young Asian intellectual that reveals a serious and grave awareness of the plight of such individuals in an absurd world.

After 1933, when the success of his novels allowed Malraux to indulge his taste for exotic archaeology, his expedition to the oases of Central Asia led to his discovery of Gothico-Buddhist art, and an exploration by airplane of the Arabian hinterland (with the aviator Edouard Corniglion-Molinier) resulted in his finding the lost city that had been the seat of the Queen of Sheba. He abandoned such enterprises abruptly, however, with the outbreak of the Spanish Civil War, in which he served from the outset as a member of the Republican Air Force.

When the Republicans were defeated, he returned to France, joined the French army as a private, and was captured by the Germans during the breakthrough of 1940. He escaped from the prison camp at Sens and remained underground until late in the war, when he undertook the unification of the disparate Resistance groups in southwest France. Following the arrival of the Allies, he became one of the colonels to command the Alsace-Lorraine Brigade, a regrouping of former soldiers from the eastern provinces that spearheaded the liberation of Strasbourg.

After the war, Malraux became Charles de Gaulle's minister of information in the short-lived coalition government of 1945. Malraux's enthusiasm for communism had not survived the Spanish Civil War, so that his apparently dramatic political turnabout was far less radical than it seemed to an unforewarned public. Whereas *Les Conquérants, La Condition humaine,* and *Le Temps du mépris* concerned heroes who found in revolution a sense of human solidarity to relieve their innate feeling of isolation and alienation, those in *L'Espoir* and *Les Noyers de l'Altenburg*—the latter less a novel than a meditation on human nature—had already discovered that solidarity inheres in the nature of man himself. This same idea pervades Malraux's subsequent writing about art.

Malraux had emerged from World War II with the conviction, also held by such writers as Albert CAMUS and Jean-Paul SARTRE, that demoralized France needed to be remoralized. After "the years of shame," of division and collaboration with the enemy, it needed—as he said in his famous "Address to UNESCO" (1946)—"a new idea of man." His books on art, including *La Psychologie de l'art* (3 vols., 1947–50), revised and enlarged as *Les Voix du silence,* (1951; Eng. tr., *The Voices of Silence,* 1953), *Saturne: essai sur Goya* (1950; Eng. tr., *Saturn: Essay on Goya,* 1957), *La Métamorphose des dieux* (1957; Eng. tr., *The Metamorphosis of the Gods,* 1960), and *La Tête d'obsidienne* (1974; Eng. tr., *Picasso's Mask,* 1976), are most intelligible if understood as a persistent and continuing effort to develop and expand this "new idea."

Thanks to photographic reproduction in color, Malraux argued, all art, including painting, sculpture, architecture, and film, can be brought together in a sort of "museum without walls" where it can be studied as a coherent whole. When studied together, prehistoric and primitive art, as well as the art of historical periods, reveals a constant preoccupation with expressing an intuition of what Malraux called "the sacred," a term embracing both the divine and the demonic. Changes from one art style to another correspond, he held, to the changes that have taken place in mankind's response to the super- or extranatural. Except in certain special moments, such as Classical Greece and the Renaissance, these changes manifest mankind's refusal to accept the limitations of the human condition. "Art," according to Malraux's often-quoted sentence, "is an antidestiny."

Professional art experts have strenuously rejected Malraux's approach, either because it is arbitrary (who can say objectively *what* a work of art expresses?) or because putting all art in an imaginary museum infallibly distorts by reducing all the works to a common scale. Other readers, however, have long preferred to read these studies as an eloquent, if sometimes elliptical and inchoate, testimony to man's eternal continuity and identity with himself. Art is man speaking across the ages of himself and to himself. Thus, human solidarity is also eternal.

With de Gaulle's return to power in 1958, Malraux was entrusted with the Ministry of Cultural Affairs, and again his writing was interrupted. His speeches, delivered on solemn occasions on the general's behalf, are collected in *Oraisons funèbres* (1971; Funeral Orations), but his principal activity during these years was an effort to restore the primacy of French culture and its prestige outside France. After de Gaulle's final withdrawal from public life, Malraux turned to writing his *Antimémoires* (1967; Eng. tr., *Anti-memoirs*, 1968), of which only the first of four projected volumes appeared before his death. Under this title, chosen to distinguish the work from memoirs in which the author plays a primary role, he exhibits a gallery of exemplary human types, some being taken from his own fiction and others being historical figures like Jawaharlal Nehru, Mao Tse-tung, Chou En-lai, and de Gaulle. A supplementary volume, *Les Chênes qu'on abat* (1971; Eng. tr., *The Fallen Oaks*, 1972), reports a real or imaginary final conversation with de Gaulle that may have occurred shortly before the latter's death.

In his later years, Malraux tended to think of himself as a "witness" and of his work as "testimony" concerning the varying forms of human nature and human destiny. From a strictly literary point of view, however, his novels must be regarded as his major achievement. To the extent that each is set against the background of a real historical event, such as the insurrection in Shanghai of 1927 and the Spanish Civil War, they are already dated. Yet the events are not of paramount importance, since they serve primarily as temporal backdrops against which eternal human traits are clearly illuminated.

Although Malraux may once have been the most conspicuous revolutionary writer in Europe, his novels reflect less of the influence of Karl Marx than that of Friedrich NIETZSCHE and Fyodor DOSTOYEVSKY. Working-class characters play no major roles in his fiction. His heroes are alienated bourgeois, concerned with alleviating the anxieties and obsessions generated by an existential awareness of the universal human predicament. That predicament is a trap from which they know they can never escape and is in this sense tragic. Especially in the earlier novels, such subjects as the certainty of death, the unacceptable meaninglessness of life, human isolation and communion, and human dignity and humiliation recur in thematic patterns. The characters try to relieve their metaphysical anguish through participating in violent action, or through dominating other individuals, or through breaking contact with reality by various artificial means such as opium and intellectualized sex. Technically, the stories are constructed so as to lead up to intense climactic scenes, such as the celebrated "Descent from the Mountain" sequence in *L'Espoir*, a passage of cinematic brilliance and great emotional impact.

Malraux's briefer incidental writings, such as his introductions to volumes of art reproductions, his studies of literature collected in *Le Triangle noir* (1970; The Black Triangle), his essay on film entitled *Esquisse d'une psychologie du cinéma* (1946; Sketch for a Psychology of the Cinema), and *Lazare* (1974; Eng. tr., *Lazarus*, 1976), a meditation on a nearly fatal illness, reveal the constant adventurousness of a brooding, curious, and immensely perceptive mind whose powers did not diminish with age.

See: W. M. Frohock, *André Malraux and the Tragic Imagination* (1952); C. M. Jenkins, *André Malraux* (1972); W. G. Langlois, *André Malraux: The Indochina Adventure* (1966); A. Vandegans, *La Jeunesse littéraire d'André Malraux* (1966).
W.M.F.

Mammeri, Mouloud (1917-), Algerian novelist writing in French, was born in the tiny mountain village of Taourirt Mimoun in Kabylia, a predominantly Berber region of Algeria. His father was an *amin*, a traditional village leader. At the age of 11, Mammeri left the village for further schooling, first to attend the Lycée Gourand in Rabat, Morocco, then the Lycée Bugeaud in Algiers, and finally the Lycée Louis-le-Grand in Paris. His studies were interrupted by World War II, during which he was drafted into the French army. After the war, Mammeri

finished his studies in Paris and returned to Algeria in 1947 to begin a career as a teacher of French and Latin in Algiers.

Mammeri brings to Algerian literature the perspective of a man imbued with the Berber tradition of his native Kabylia, an area that was the setting for much of the fiercest fighting during the liberation struggle (1954-62). Mammeri's work is an attempt to capture a society in transition, one that is affected first by World War II and then by the Algerian struggle for independence. His three novels form a trilogy. *La Colline oubliée I* (1952; The Forgotten Hill) presents a world firmly rooted in tradition, struggling to remain closed within itself. *Le Sommeil du juste* (1955; Eng. tr., *The Sleep of the Just,* 1956) accentuates the conflict between two opposing worlds, East and West. *L'Opium et le bâton* (1965; Opium and the Stick) presents a realistic account of the struggle against French colonialism. In all three works, the reader discovers a land of impoverished mountain villages where the old order, as exemplified by a rigid honor code and a history of tribal vendettas, is first besieged and finally defeated.

Mammeri's protagonists are men like himself, Algerians born into traditional society and forced by life's circumstances into the modern world. The novels reflect a a gradual acculturation of the hero within the modern sector. Whereas the protagonists of *La Colline oubliée* know of no life beyond the mountains, the hero of *Le Sommeil du juste* rejects ancestral tradition as well as French colonialism. *L'Opium et le bâton* accentuates the distance between protagonist and village; its main character, a doctor, is barely attached to his native Kabylia, and when he chooses to join the liberation struggle, he assumes a national, not a regional, identity.

When Algeria gained its independence, Mammeri became professor of anthropology at the University of Algiers and then director of ethnographic research at the Bardo Museum in Algiers. In this latter position he has furthered the study of oral literature and tradition. In 1969, Mammeri published *Les Isefra*, a bilingual French and Berber anthology of and commentary on the poems of the Berber poet Si Mohand-ou-Mhand. Mammeri has also written several scenarios for the Algerian cinema.

As a chronicler of his nation and his times, Mammeri situates contemporary Algeria within its social and historical context and reveals the attitudes of its people towards their past, present, and future. As a novelist, he expresses the dilemma faced by most writers of the Third World: how best to affirm one's originality, preserve age-old traditions, and yet move with assurance and optimism towards the future.

See: I. Yétiv, *Le Thème de l'aliénation dans le roman maghrébin d'expression française 1952-1956* (1972), pp. 114-33; J. Déjeux, *Littérature maghrébine de langue française* (1973), pp. 180-208; A. Roche, "Tradition et subversion dans l'œuvre de Mouloud Mammeri," *Revue de l'occident musulman* 22 (2e semestre 1976), pp. 99-107.
M.P.M.

Mandelshtam, Osip Emilyevich (1891-1938), Russian poet, was born in Warsaw to a Jewish leather-goods dealer. He grew up in Petersburg, however, and it is with this city that the poet's name is principally associated. His parents were not religious, and the boy grew up with little consciousness of his Jewish heritage; but his father was eccentrically intellectual and his mother, a piano teacher, more conventionally so, with the result that the poet's first home combined petty commercial with liberal bookish interests. He was taught by the usual tutors and governesses and completed his secondary education at the

Tenishev School, an excellent institution of an advanced sort. Most of what is known concerning the foregoing period of his life comes from his autobiographical *Shum vremeni* (1925; Eng. tr., *The Noise of Time*, 1965). From 1907 to 1910, Mandelshtam traveled in Europe and studied briefly at the Sorbonne and at Heidelberg; on returning to Russia, he entered the University of Petersburg but left before receiving a degree. His first poems appeared in 1910 in *Apollon*, a prominent journal of art and literature. His first book, *Kamen* (1913; Stone), brought him a sudden if narrow celebrity as a member of the acmeist group of poets (*see* RUSSIAN LITERATURE). This group was dispersed by World War I, although Mandelshtam himself was not called to serve. While difficult to follow his movements, it is clear that he avoided the worst disorders and deprivations of the Revolution (1917) and Russian Civil War by frequent trips to the south. His second collection of poems, *Tristia* (1922), appeared on his return to the capitals and confirmed his status as a leading poet. To earn a living, however, Mandelshtam was forced to do a good deal of literary hackwork: he worked as a journalist, a writer of children's books, a translator, and as an editor for various state publishing houses. He was still able to find time for his own work and in 1928 published collections of his best writing in three genres, his poems in *Stikhotvoreniya* (Poems), his prose in *Yegipetskaya marka* (Eng. tr., *The Egyptian Stamp*, 1965), and his criticism in *O poezii* (On Poetry). This outward appearance of success is nevertheless deceptive, for Mandelshtam, whose loyalty to the Bolshevik regime had always been rightly suspect, had for several years been falling increasingly from favor. By the end of the decade he was forced to flee his highly placed enemies in the capitals by accepting a journalistic assignment in the distant provinces. The result of this move, *Puteshestiviye v Armeniyu* (1933; Eng. tr., *Journey to Armenia*, 1973), a work of great literary merit and political daring, was violently attacked and proved to be his last publication in the Soviet press for over 30 years. In 1934 he was arrested for an epigram that he had composed on Iosif Stalin and after weeks of interrogation in prison was exiled, first to a small town in the Urals and then to Voronezh, where he remained until 1937. The period of exile was marked by bouts of nervous collapse and failing physical health, but the poetry that he managed to compose is among the greatest of his life and of modern Russian literature. In the months remaining after his release, Mandelshtam and his faithful wife Nadezhda wandered homelessly in search of work and shelter. He was arrested again in 1938, and eventually was sent to a transit camp near Vladivostok. There he is officially reported to have died on Dec. 27, 1938, but that date, like most events surrounding the end of his life, cannot be confirmed (*see* RUSSIAN LITERATURE).

Mandelshtam served his apprenticeship as a poet under the influence of the dominant symbolist school, but by the time of his first collection his allegiance had palpably shifted to the acmeists. The poems of this early period are marked by brevity of form, clarity of image and rhythm, and a certain coldness and solemnity in the treatment of themes severely limited to the world of art itself. As his mastery grew, so did his subject matter, the mere enumeration of which testifies to both the range (the whole span of Western culture) and the narrowness of his interests (almost exclusively the world of high art). His subjects include the catalogue of ships in the *Iliad*; the meter of Homer; the exile of Ovid; the architecture of Hagia Sophia, Notre Dame, the cathedrals of old Moscow, and the classical buildings of Petersburg; the music of Bach; the tragedies of Jean Racine; and the novels of

Charles Dickens. Not only because of this subject matter, but also because of its abstruse and incantatory verbal patterns, Mandelshtam's early verse caused him to be known as a "poet's poet."

Many poems of the 1920s and early 1930s are also thick with reference to art and the ancient world, but both the general mood and the specific references are now different. The mood is one of loss and farewell, the dominant myth that of the underworld. The title poem of *Tristia* begins

> I have studied the science of saying good-bye
> in bareheaded laments at night

and the goddess of Mandelshtam's second book is Persephone. The poems are often dangerously unambiguous in revealing his reaction to what had befallen his country. The following lines, for example, had to be altered before he could republish them in *O poezii*:

> For the blessed meaningless word
> I shall pray in the Soviet night

The poems of exile are often fragmentary and even textually dubious, but among them are masterpieces that open new paths into the possibilities of Russian verse. They manage to be, as Mandelshtam's best work always was, uncompromisingly cerebral and dense with verbal and thematic allusion while conveying human emotions that challenge the adequacy of language itself. Some are predictably bleak but many others celebrate the gift of life with infectious joy. Such poems have contributed to the current evaluation of Mandelshtam as the preeminent Russian poet of the 20th century.

His collected works can be found in *Sobraniye sochineniy*, 3 vols. (New York, 1964–71); *Stikhtvoreniya* (Leningrad, 1973); and *Selected Poems* (Oxford, 1973) and (New York, Atheneum, 1974).

See: C. Brown, *The Prose of Osip Mandelshtam* (2d ed., rev., 1967), and *Mandelstam* (1973).   C.B.

Mann, Heinrich (1871–1950), German novelist, essayist, and dramatist, was born in Lübeck into a prominent merchant family, portrayed by Thomas MANN, Heinrich's younger brother, in the novel *Buddenbrooks*. Heinrich believed he inherited a southern temperament from his mother, a Brazilian of German and Portuguese extraction, and Germanic traits from his father.

From 1893 until World War 1, Heinrich Mann spent most of his time in Italy and France. The new family home in Munich did not appeal to him. The years until 1922 were marked by a personal, artistic, and ideological rivalry between the two literary brothers. Whereas Thomas was influenced greatly by the Russian novelists of the 19th century, Heinrich was well versed in the works of Gabriele D'ANNUNZIO, Friedrich NIETZSCHE, and the French novelists. Heinrich's mission was always to show the responsibility of the artist, in contrast to what he considered to be Thomas's escape into refined language and sensibilities. Heinrich argued his point in more than 900 essays, 21 novels, 10 plays, and many short stories. In all but his very earliest works he was an unrelenting critic of an unjust and narrow-minded society, of militarism, and of the pompous, self-serving bourgeoisie. During the 1920s both he and Thomas Mann were *the* representatives of German letters; Heinrich was chosen president of the literary section of the Prussian Academy of Arts, and Thomas won the Nobel Prize for literature.

Heinrich's politics were decidedly to the Left, and shortly before his death in California he was invited by East Germany to return to Berlin and to the Academy as one of the new nation's most celebrated artists.

It was only during the short life of the Weimar Republic

that Heinrich Mann's works were widely read and appreciated. The novels written before World War I were acclaimed for the beauty of their composition, but it was not until the publication of *Der Untertan* (1912–18; Eng. tr., *The Patrioteer*, 1921) that Heinrich became known and widely read all over Europe. Today he has many admirers in East Germany, in the Soviet Union, and in Poland, as well as, increasingly, in the West.

The early novels (through *Untertan*) show Mann's development from being an apologist of the status quo—as in *In einer Familie* (1894; In One Family)—through being a satirist of Wilhelminian society—*Im Schlaraffenland* (1900; Eng. tr., *In the Land of Cockaigne*, 1925)—to a role as a conscious opponent of the monarchy in *Die kleine Stadt* (1909; Eng. tr., *The Little Town*, 1931), a democratic pastorale. *Zwischen den Rassen* (1907; Between the Races) is, unlike Thomas Mann's novels of the early 20th century, not a melancholic view of an era nearing its end but rather a work in praise of democracy. The trilogy *Die Göttinnen* (1902; Eng. tr., *The Goddess*, 1918; *Diana*, 1929), consisting of *Diana*, *Minerva*, and *Venus*, is an ambiguous work, evoking both the "aestheticism" of turn-of-the-century Europe and the vital self-determinism of a new age.

Die Jagd nach Liebe (1903; The Hunt for Love) was not successful, but *Professor Unrat* (1905; Eng. tr., *Small Town Tyrant*, 1944), later made into the film *Der blaue Engel* (*The Blue Angel*), was to become Heinrich Mann's best-known work. Professor Unrat the tyrannical Wilhelminian schoolmaster, is brought to his downfall by the femme fatale Lola-Lola, a seductive dancehall singer.

Der Untertan, the first volume of the trilogy *Das Kaiserreich* (The Empire), began publication in installments when World War I broke out. It was, of course, then banned, but upon the cessation of hostilities the work struck a chord in the German people and made its author one of the most read of the Weimar era. The novel uncovered the shallowness of the prewar society, and its sequel *Die Armen* (1917; Eng. tr., *The Poor*, 1917) is logical: it is a novel of the working class that also shows Mann's ignorance of socialist theory and practice. The third volume of the trilogy, *Der Kopf* (1925; Eng. tr., *The Chief*, 1925), continues the fight for a civilized humanity.

Heinrich Mann was intensely concerned with the condition of humanity and with the elements that make a human society worthwhile. After World War I he turned all his efforts toward a reconciliation between France and Germany. In his famous essay *Zola* (1915) he formulates the *role* of the writer in society, the relationship between literature and politics, and the *responsibility* of the writer, namely to work for democracy, an interest Heinrich saw decidedly lacking in the German intelligentsia. He held Emile ZOLA to be the activist whom writers of his era should emulate, much to the chagrin of his brother Thomas. It was not until the 1920s that Thomas came to see Heinrich's veiwpoint, but in 1918 his reply was *Betrachtungen eines Unpolitischen* (1918; Reflections of an Unpolitical Man), a nationalistic, chauvinistic tract that attacked Heinrich directly. The falling-out, by that time long brewing, was complete and lasted several years.

While the imperial years saw the creation of most of Heinrich Mann's short stories, the Republic was the era of the essay—commentaries on politics, society, and the arts. Mann did not advocate class struggle to right the ills of society; he believed in the restorative powers of democratic freedom and equality. The Weimar years also saw the publication of *Mutter Marie* (1927; Eng. tr., *Mother Mary*, 1928), *Eugénie oder die Bürgerzeit* (1928; Eng. tr., *The Royal Woman*, 1930), *Die große Sache* (1930; The Important Matter), and *Ein ernstes Leben* (1932; Eng. tr.,

The Hill of Lies, 1935). Heinrich's ideas did not sit well with the Nazis, and from 1933 to 1940 he lived in the south of France and from then on in Los Angeles.

The years of exile in France produced what many consider Heinrich Mann's greatest novels, *Die Jugend des königs Henri Quatre* (1935; Eng. tr., *Young Henry of Navarre*, 1937) and *Die Vollendung des Königs Henri Quatre* (1938; Eng. tr., *Henry, King of France*, 1939). The novels are a complex, often difficult portrayal of Henry IV of France, a study of the problem of human greatness.

Emigration meant obscurity for Heinrich. His wife was mentally ill and died in 1945. He was supported in Los Angeles mostly by his brother Thomas, who had gained greatly in fame, and he spent his last few years lonely, hardly able to speak English, in a strange land. His last undertaking was *Ein Zeitalter wird besichtigt* (1945; Review of an Age), a volume of autobiographical sketches.

See: A. Banuls, *Heinrich Mann, le poète et la politique* (1966, German abridgment, 1970); K. Schröter, *Heinrich Mann in Selbstzeugnissen und Bilddokumenten* (1960); R. N. Linn, *Heinrich Mann* (1967); H. L. Arnold, ed., "Heinrich Mann," *LuK* (1971).   W.T.

Mann, Klaus (1908–49), German novelist, essayist, and playwright, was born in Munich, the son of Thomas MANN and the nephew of Heinrich MANN. By his 20th year he had written a play, *Anja und Esther* (produced in 1925); short stories, *Vor dem Leben* (1925; Life Ahead); and a novel, *Der fromme Tanz* (1926; The Pious Dance). There quickly followed the comedies *Revue zu Vieren* (1926; Four in a Revue); *Gegenüber von China* (1929; Opposite China); and *Geschwister* (1930; Siblings), an adaptation for the stage of Jean COCTEAU's *Les Enfants terribles*; and another volume of short stories, *Abenteuer* (1929; Adventures). The vivid recollection of his own childhood lent understanding and accuracy to his characterizations of Frau Christiné's youngsters in *Kindernovelle* (1927; Eng. tr., *The Fifth Child*) and to the portraits of his family and associates in his "autobiography," *Kind dieser Zeit* (1932; *Child of This Time*). In an *Anthologie jüngster Lyrik* (2 vols., 1927–29; Anthology of Recent Lyric Poetry) and an equally provocative *Anthologie jüngster Prosa* (1928; Anthology of Recent Prose), he published characteristic specimens of his contemporaries. With his sister Erika, he wrote accounts of trips about the world in *Rundherum* (1929; All the Way Around) and *Das Buch der Riviera* (1931; The Riviera Book), and in 1931 appeared a collection of essays on the predicament of the European literati, *Auf der Suche nach einem Weg* (In Search of a Way). His next novel, picturesque and startling in its thesis concerning the success of Alexander the Great, *Alexander: Roman der Utopie* (1929; Eng. tr., *Alexander*, 1930), indicated his interest in semihistorical themes, which he reasserted some years later in his Tchaikovsky novel, *Symphonie pathétique* (1935; Eng. tr., *Pathetic Symphony*, 1938), and in the tale of Ludwig II of Bavaria, *Vergittertes Fenster* (1937; Barred Window).

In 1933, Klaus Mann left Germany. He edited the literary anti-Nazi magazine *Die Sammlung* (1933–35) and *Decision* (1941–42); and time and again he demanded greater political awareness on the part of younger writers (see *Escape to Life* [1939], *The Other Germany* [1940], both in collaboration with Erika Mann, and his autobiographical commentary on his own generation, *The Turning Point* [1942]). At the same time creative writing continued to engage him, with the novels *Mephisto* (1936; Eng. tr., *Mephisto*, 1977) and *Der Vulkan* (1939; The Volcano), as an editor of an anthology, *Heart of Europe*

(1939; with Hermann KESTEN), and as a critic in *André Gide and the Crisis of Modern Thought* (1943). Martin Gregor-Dellis has edited three volumes of his assorted essays and letters in *Prüfungen, Schriften zur Literatur* (1968; Trials, Essays on Literature), *Heute und morgen, Schriften zur Zeit* (1969; Today and Tomorrow, Essays on the Age), and *Briefe und Antworten* (1975; Letters and Replies).

See: W. Dirschauer, *Klaus Mann und das Exil* (1973); P. T. Hoffer, *Klaus Mann* (1978).   V.La. rev A.L.W.

Mann, Thomas (1875–1955), German novelist and essayist, was born in the Hanseatic city of Lübeck, the son of a wealthy grain merchant and his wife, of German-South American extraction. After his father's death, Mann and the family moved to Munich, where he worked first in an insurance office and later on the staff of the magazine *Simplicissimus*, attended the university, and wrote his early short stories, such as "Gefallen" (1894; Fallen) and the Collection *Der kleine Herr Friedemann* (1898; Little Herr Friedemann). During a stay in Rome with his older brother Heinrich, he began his first novel, *Buddenbrooks*, which was published in 1900 (Eng. tr., 1924). Conceived on a small scale as merely "a protracted finger practice with no ulterior advantages," the book developed into a broad account of the history of a Hanseatic family whose strength and prosperity are gradually undermined by the disintegrating fascination that the arts, Richard WAGNER's music, and Schopenhauerian ideas exercise upon its successive generations. The central theme of this brilliant naturalistic novel is the emerging relationship between the bourgeois life of the 19th century and the precarious modern sensibility of the artistic temperament— an issue that occupied Mann throughout his earlier work, especially in his verse drama *Fiorenza* (1906; Florence), and in his three superb short stories "Tonio Kröger (1913; Eng. tr., 1914); "Bekenntnisse des Hochstaplers Felix Krull" (1911; enlarged, 1937), which in 1954 he extended into a work the length of a novel, intending to continue it—*Bekenntnisse des Hochstaplers Felix Krull, der Memoiren I* (Eng. tr., Confessions of Felix Krull, Confidence Man, Memoirs Part I, 1955), later made into a successful film with the actor Horst Bucholz; and *Der Tod in Venedig* (1913; Eng. tr., Death in Venice, 1925); the first tale "dearest to my heart," the second suggested by the memoirs of Manolescu, "the best and happiest thing I have done," and the third one of the most perfect and widely admired *petits romans* written in the 20th century.

The first literary fruit of his marriage in 1905 to the daughter of the mathematician A. Pringheim was *Köngliche Hoheit* (1909; Eng. tr., *Royal Highness*, 1916), "a comedy in the form of a novel," in which the artistically minded aristocratic hero, preoccupied with his private problems, eventually works out his salvation within the social framework of duty and sacrifice instead of becoming a victim of life.

The years during and after World War I drew Mann, whose tastes and cultural traditions, as he himself insists, were "moral and metaphysical, not political and social," into an ever greater concern with the issues of the day. A long essay, "Friedrich und die große Koalition" (1915; Eng. tr., in *Three Essays*, 1929), and the volume *Betrachtungen eines Unpolitischen* (1918; Meditations of an Unpolitical Man) represent his "war service with the weapon of thought" and the substance of his conservative political speculations during the European conflict. Especially in the essay "Von der Tugend" (in *Betrachtungen*) he deplores the political ineptitude of German writers, and in this and subsequent pleas (*Von deutscher Republik*, 1923)

he calls for a genuine mobilization of the German intellectuals in support of the new Weimar state.

In 1924 appeared *Der Zauberberg* (Eng. tr., *The Magic Mountain*, 1927), a spectacular novel of ideas, which was begun in 1912 during a three-week visit to Davos. The minutely detailed canvas of this characteristically German Bildungsroman catches the spiritual pattern of European civilization during the first part of the 20th century and projects it into the rarefied atmosphere of a Swiss sanatorium. There, drawn into many baffling relationships, a youthfully innocent and impressionable German engineer, Hans Castorp, discovers the problematical nature of life and death. In the midst of sickness and decay and surrounded by exponents of every conceivable human attitude, especially the extremes of devitalized reasoning and overrationalized living, he resolves to respect and maintain the profound distinction between life and death: "For the sake of goodness and love," he concludes in the cardinal chapter, "Schnee" (Snow), "man shall let death have no sovereignty over his thoughts." The breadth of its intelligence, the subtlety of its arguments, the precision of observation, and the consummate craftsmanship of its composition have made *Zauberberg* one of the most conspicuous German contributions to the modern European novel.

Work on *Der Zauberberg* was accompanied by the publication of a delightful prose idyl, *Herr und Hund* (1919; Eng. tr., *Bashan and I*, 1923), and the writing of several volumes of critical essays, such as *Rede und Antwort* (1922; Speech and Reply) and *Bemühungen* (1925; Endeavors). Later collections of critical prose, like *Die Forderung des Tages* (1930; The Challenge of the Day), reaffirm the subtlety of Mann's critical perception and testify to the alertness of his response to the cultural challenges of the time. Apart from frequent tribute to those writers to whom he felt himself most closely related—Novalis, Heinrich Heine, Walt Whitman, Theodor FONTANE, Henrik IBSEN, Lev TOLSTOY, Joseph Conrad, André GIDE—he devoted one volume of studies, *Leiden und Größe der Meister* (1935; Eng. tr., *Freud, Goethe, Wagner*, 1937), to influential writers, including August von Platen and Theodor Storm.

During the 1920s, Mann insisted on the spiritual and political obligations that the humanistic heritage of the European tradition imposed upon the liberal European writers, as in *Pariser Rechenschaft* (1926; Accountable in Paris). His intellectual convictions were based on Friedrich NIETZSCHE and the German conservative tradition and sprang from a lively sense of historical continuity and spiritual order. In the story *Unordnung und frühes Leid* (1925; Eng. tr., *Early Sorrow*, 1929), he portrays, against the background of his own family and with melancholy irony, the moral and social confusion that resulted from the chaotic years of the German inflation of values. In 1930, the year after he was awarded the Nobel Prize for Literature, there appeared the novella *Mario und der Zauberer* (Eng. tr., *Mario and the Magician*, 1930), a "tragedy of travel" with "moral and political implications."

In the meantime the plan was being formulated for what became Mann's most profound and elaborate statement of his vision of man's timeless nature—although not, perhaps, his most pleasing work. A portfolio of illustrations depicting the story of Joseph, for which he was asked to write an introduction, suggested to him the subject of the novel tetralogy *Joseph und seine Brüder* (Joseph and His Brothers), the first volume of which was not published until 1933. Not unlike *Der Zauberberg*, this impressive narrative emphasizes the cultural obligations that a purposeful life imposes on a human being. The biblical world is seen through the ever-sharpening eyes of the young Joseph, another Hans Castorp, whose environment, manners, and language are reproduced with meticulous archaeological accuracy, but who is, at the same time, endowed with the knowing perception of a modern observer. The four bulky volumes, *Die Geschichten Jakobs* (1933; Eng. tr., *The Tales of Jacob*, American title, *Joseph and His Brothers*, both 1934), *Der junge Joseph* (1934; Eng. tr., *The Young Joseph*, 1935), *Joseph in Aegypten* (1936; Eng. tr., *Joseph in Egypt*, 1938), and *Joseph, der Ernährer* (1944; Eng. tr., *Joseph the Provider*, 1944), represent Mann's most positive treatment of the social frame outside of which civilized living is impossible. The broader problem of cultural unity has thus absorbed in Mann's later work the issue of the artist's personal relationship to society. In *Lotte in Weimar* (1939; Eng. tr., *The Beloved Returns*, 1940), which relates the historic visit in 1816 of Werther's Lotte to the aged Goethe, the stress is not so much upon the problematical figure of the artist as upon the humanistic achievement of a man whose self-denying and stylized life is, to the bourgeois observer, not without strangeness and tragedy. In that work and in the short novel *Die vertauschten Köpfe* (1940; Eng. tr., *The Transposed Heads*, 1941) the delicacy and refinement of Mann's detachment become disturbing, and his style is often pedantic, pontifical, and mannered, although his talents as storyteller are as apparent as ever.

After 1933, Mann lived in Switzerland, where he edited the literary journal *Maß und Wert*. After his emigration to the United States in 1938 he took an active part in the discussion of current political issues, as in *The Coming Victory of Democracy* in 1938 and *This Peace* in the same year, without achieving in America the effectiveness of argument or speech for which his earlier German essays had made him so distinguished. From 1942 to 1952 he lived in Pacific Palisades, California, having become an American citizen in 1944. But disappointed with the American persecution of Communist sympathizers, he returned to Europe in 1952, living in Switzerland until his death.

Soon after his arrival in the United States he was asked to write a preface to a collection of stories by international authors, based on the Ten Commandments; instead of a preface, however, he wrote the story of Moses, filled as he was still of the world of Joseph; *Das Gesetz* appeared in 1943 and was quickly translated as *The Tables of the Law* in 1945. After a volume of essays on the problem of humanism, *Adel des Geistes* (1945; Nobility of Spirit), Mann published the breathtaking symbolic novel, *Doktor Faustus, das Leben des deutschen Tonsetzers Adrian Leverkühn, erzählt von einem Freund* (1947; Eng. tr., *Doctor Faustus, The Life of the German Composer Adrian Leverkühn, as Told by a Friend*, 1948), a monumental work that combines the life of Friedrich Nietzsche, the legend of the pact with the devil by Faust, and the Nazi evil against the background of the innovative 12-tone music of Arnold Schönberg, also at the time an exile in California. It is an apocalyptic novel, a portrait of a nation at an epochal time in world history. In 1949 came Mann's *Die Entstehung des Doktor Faustus, Roman eines Romans* (Eng. tr., *The Story of a Novel: The Genesis of Doctor Faustus*, 1961), in which he details the origins of the novel. The genial *Der Erwählte* (1951; Eng. tr., *The Holy Sinner*, 1951), for which he used the medieval epic about the legendary pope Gregorius, by Hartmann von Aue, told the story of the trials and temptations of a man torn between the demands of flesh and spirit. *Die Betrogene* (1953; Eng. tr., *The Black Swan*, 1954), in which he takes a bitter inspection of the American character, is a novel that relates the diseased late blooming of a woman

who longs for a lost youth. His last work, the unfinished *Felix Krull,* is surprisingly light-hearted, but still absorbed with the meaning of human existence. Mann remains a monumental figure in German letters of the 20th century, a master of prose style, a man torn himself by the temptations of flesh and the exaltation of spirit.

See: T. Mann, *A Sketch of My Life* (1930); J. Cleugh, *Thomas Mann: A Study* (1933); H. J. Weigand, *Thomas Mann's Novel 'Der Zauberberg'* (1933, repr. 1964); H. C. Hatfield, *Thomas Mann* (1951); H. Eichner, *Thomas Mann, eine Einführung in sein Werk* (1953); R. H. Thomas, *Thomas Mann, The Mediation of Art* (1956); E. Heller, *The Ironic German* (1958); R. Baumgart, *Das Ironische und die Ironie in den Werken Thomas Manns* (1964); K. W. Jonas, *Fifty Years of Thomas Mann Studies* (1955) and *Thomas Mann Studies* (1967); E. Kahler, *The Orbit of Thomas Mann* (1969); A. Bauer, *Thomas Mann* (1960; Eng. 1971); W. A. Berendson, *Thomas Mann, Artist and Partisan in Troubled Times* (German, 1965, Eng. 1973); T. J. Reed, *Thomas Mann, The Uses of Tradition* (1974); H. L. Arnold, "Thomas Mann," *Text & Kritik,* special issue (1976); N. Hamilton, *The Brothers Mann* (1978). V.La. rev. A.L.W.

Manzini, Gianna (1896–), Italian novelist and short-story writer, was born in Pistoia. For several years she lived in Florence, where she wrote for the newspaper *La nazione* and for *Solaria* and *Letteratura* (see ITALIAN LITERATURE). Her fiction was decidedly influenced by the style of these journals and by the lyrical psychologizing of its writers. She later moved to Rome, where she wrote on fashion under the name of Vanessa.

Manzini's first novel, *Tempo innamorato* (1928; A Time of Love), was well received. It was soon followed by several volumes of short stories: *Incontro col falco* (1929; Meeting with a Falcon), *Boscovivo* (1932; Livewood), *Casa di riposo* (1934; Rest Home), *Un filo di brezza* (1936; A Breath of Air), *Rive remote* (1940; Far Shores), *Venti racconti* (1941; 20 Tales), and *Forte come un leone* (1944; Strong as a Lion). Manzini's second novel, *Lettera all'editore* (1945; Letter to the Editor), is a complex work on both psychological and narrative levels. It shows the influence of André GIDE, Marcel PROUST, Virginia Woolf, and Katherine Mansfield, all writers admired by the *Solaria-Letteratura* circle. The book won the Costume Prize.

Manzini's next collection of stories *Il valzer del diavola* (1947; Devil's Waltz) won her the Soroptimist Prize for its combination of lyricism and psychological realism, refracted through subtle, complex, and often self-conscious images. *Ho visto il tuo cuore* (1950; I Saw Your Heart), *Animali sacri e profani* (1953; Sacred and Profane Animals), and *Foglietti* (1954; Notepaper) were followed by the novel *La sparviera* (1956; The Sparrow Hawk), which won the coveted Viareggio Prize. This work, written in faultless *prosa d'arte* (see ITALIAN LITERATURE), is a somewhat autobiographical love story involving Stella, Giovanni, and the ever-present Sparviera, the personified consumptive cough to whose seduction Giovanni finally succumbs. The collection of short stories *Cara prigione* (1958; Beloved Prison) was followed by *Arca di Noè* (1960; Noah's Ark), a volume of fanciful animal stories, and *Ritratti e pretesti* (1960; Portraits and Pretexts), a collection of essays on contemporary writers. Then came *Un'altra cosa* (1961; Something Different), *Il cielo adosso* (1963; The Sky upon Me), *Album di ritratti* (1964; Portrait Album), and *Allegro con disperazione* (1965; Allegro with Despair), which won the Naples Prize. *Allegro con disperazione* concerns the marriage between Marcello, obsessed with living in "truth," and Angela, whose tragic secret is her childhood rape by a family friend. Disaster strikes when their child sees his father dressed for his job as a female impersonator and is attracted to this "corruption." Manzini's recent works include *Ritratto in piedi* (1971; Standing Portrait), an exploration of her feelings of love-hate for her father, and *Sulla soglia* (1973; On the Threshold), a series of stories that explore her feelings for her mother.

See: G. Pampaloni, *NA* 502 (1968); O. Sobrero, in *Letteratura italiana: i contemporanei*, vol. 2 (1975), pp. 1163–84.   J.M.P.

Maragall i Gorina, Joan (1860–1911), Catalan poet and essayist, was born in the city of Barcelona of a very well-to-do middle-class family and received a very careful education. For some time he was a journalist, imparting to his articles a quality that sometimes gave them the value of literary essays. He revealed himself to be a poet of lofty inspiration when he participated in the "Jocs Florals" of Barcelona in the year 1881. His first volume of poetry appeared in 1895 with the title *Poesies*. This was followed by *Visions i cants* (1900; Visions and Songs), *Les disperses* (1904; The Dispersed), *Enlla* (1906), *Seqüències* (1911; Sequences). Elected president of the *Ateneo* of Barcelona in 1903, he read his essay "Elogi de la paraula" (Praise of the Word) which, along with his "L'elogi de la poesia" (The Praise of Poetry) stands as a minor masterpiece in this difficult genre. He translated the *Ifigènia a Taurida* and *Eridon i Amina* (1904) of Goethe, an author who greatly influenced his thought and work, and Novalis's *Enric d'Ofterdinger* (1907), and *Himnes Homèrics*. His complete works were published by his own sons (*Obres completes*, 21 vols., 1929–1935) with eloquent prologues and essays by distinguished critics.

As a literary theorist Maragall advocated an absolute spontaneity and was opposed to rewriting and editing. His theory of the "living word" influenced his disciples considerably, although the danger of approving all that is instinctive and undeveloped was seen when, after his death, less talented followers became the custodians of his doctrines. Living in Barcelona at the beginning of the 20th century, when it was in a state of upheaval and full of hatreds and struggles between the workers and the powerful middle class, Maragall revealed himself to be a very humane poet and writer although he never went beyond the limits of a broad and Christian sympathy for the humble folk. Barcelona indeed makes itself felt in all his work; his language is "characterized by a sweet Barcelonian impurity," as has been said, and his themes, especially the "Oda a Barcelona" (Ode to Barcelona), presents the great Mediterranean city in all its grandeur—and in its defects as he sees them.

Maragall was one of the keenest spiritual guides and critics of the Catalan middle class, although he was not an actual radical. His pretended anarchism was purely intellectual in nature and for the most part no more than a certain rebelliousness directed at his immediate surroundings. Some of his observations and intuitive deductions were brilliantly presented, as in his article "L'església cremada" (The Burned Church), where he declares that he senses God more among the ruins of a church devastated by the fury of the revolutionists than in the churches frequented by the rich and powerful. He exerted an immediate influence on various writers and is still a much-read poet in the Catalan-speaking countries. At times he treated expertly themes of extraordinary breadth, as in his "Comte Arnau." In this traditional figure of Catalan poetry he saw the incarnation of what for Friedrich NIETZSCHE was the prototype of the super-

man. In translation he is much esteemed in Spanish-speaking countries. Miguel de UNAMUNO proclaimed him at his death "the best Peninsular lyric poet."

See: J. Folguera, *Les noves valors de la poesia Catalana* (1919); M. Sants Oliver, Prologue to J. Maragall, *Obres completes* (1929); J. Pijoan, *El meu don Joan Maragall* (n.d.).   F. de P.

Márai, Sándor (1900–) Hungarian novelist and essayist, was born in Kassa, one of the most influential Hungarian writers of the period between the two world wars. Márai studied law in Budapest and between 1919 and 1923 studied law at various German universities. On his return to Hungary, Márai embarked upon a journalistic career and was a staff member of *Az Úsag* and *Pesti Hirlap*. He left Hungary in 1947 and has lived abroad ever since, lately in Italy.

In his two best novels, *Egy polgár vallomásai* (1934; Confessions of a Bourgeois) and *Féltékenyek* (1937; The Jealous Ones), Márai presents an "inside" view of the Hungarian provincial middle class. There is a certain amount of nostalgic idealization in these works, but there is also an irony reminiscent of Thomas MANN's *Buddenbrooks*. Like Mann, Márai has been a staunch defender of the culture-loving European bourgeosie. He remained aloof from politics, for he felt that any kind of political upheaval would hasten the destruction of that class and its values. In addition to the works cited above, Márai has written a number of novels, including *Válás Budán* (1935; Divorce in Buda), *Vendégjáték Bolzánóban* (1940; Guest Performance in Bolzano), and *A nővér* (1946; Sister), and some plays, such as *Kaland* (1941; Adventure) and *Varázs* (1945; Magic). Yet these works have become dated much faster than have his autobiographical writings. Two travel journals, *Napnyugati őrjárat* (1936; Western Patrol) and *Európa elrablása* (1947; The Abduction of Europe), are especially interesting. Márai has been quite receptive to Western literary currents. The influence of a number of European writers can be discerned in his works, particularly that of Jean COCTEAU, in *Zendülők* (1930; The Rebels), a story about adolescents, and Georges DUHAMEL, in the early novel, *Bébi vagy az első szerelem* (1928; Baby, or First Love). His recent works include the novel *Béke Ithakában* (1957; Peace Comes to Ithaca), *Napló: 1945–1957* (1958; Journal), and the incisive memoirs recalling the end of World War II, "*Föld. . .föld*" (1972). Most of Márai's novels have a historical setting but the conflicts that unfold against them are universal human conflicts.

Márai is essentially a solitary intellectual. His style—the famous "Márai-sentence," much-admired by a whole generation of Hungarian writers and readers—fuses erudition with the lyricism and subtle tonalities of an aesthete. His fluid, vibrant, utterly sophisticated prose has become increasingly mannered and precious in his more recent works, but that unique blend of rigorous intellectuality and extreme subjectivity remains his most important literary asset.

See: A. Komlós, "Márai," *Nyugat* 28 (1935): 32–37; I. Örley, "Klasszicizálódás vagy útvesztés," *Magyar Csillag* 4 (1944): 175–79; J. Reményi, *Hungarian Writers and Literature* (1964), pp. 409–13; M. Sükösd, *Küzdelem az epikával* (1972), pp. 241–51.   I.S.

Maramzin, Vladimir Rafailovich (1934–), Russian writer of short fiction, was born in Leningrad. A stylistically innovative satirist of Soviet society, he became known when several long stories and "cycles" of short sketches, most of which had been written years earlier, were published in the West, following his emigration in 1975. Maramzin is at his best when he uses the *skaz* technique, in which stories are told in the words of naive narrators and unskilled writers. One such story is "Blondin obeyego tsveta" (1975; A Blond of Both Colors), an invidious portrait of a ruminative hack artist. In this story, Maramzin's brilliant use of street slang, solecism, bureaucratic pleonasm, elaborate punning, and journalistic cliché is in the tradition of Nikolay LESKOV, Mikhail ZOSHCHENKO, and Andrey PLATONOV. Another long story, "Istoriya zhenitby Ivana Petrovicha" (1975; Eng. tr., "The Story of the Marriage of Ivan Petrovich," 1976), tells the tale of Ivan, who fell in love with Dusya, a young factory worker so desperately short of money that she decided to sell herself to the next passing stranger—who happened to be Ivan. In this story the individual manages to assert himself against the determinism of Soviet city life. Less successful in asserting himself is the narrator of "Ya, s poshchochinoy v ruke" (1965; Eng. tr., "A Slap in the Face," 1975), whose effort to slap the anonymous bureaucrat responsible for his misery only backfires against himself. Maramzim's basic theme of the survival of the personality through all that may befall it is illustrated in his "Chelovek, kotory veril v svoyo osoboye naznacheniye" (1977; The Man Who Believed in His Special Mission).

See: Y. Maltsev, *Volnaya russkaya literatura* (1976); L. Lifshits, *Kontinent* 10 (1976); N. Rubinshteyn, *Grani* 100 (1976). D.F.

Marañón, Gregorio (1887–1960), Spanish biographer, essayist, and literary critic, was born and died in Madrid. He was the most prominent and prolific member of a group of scientists and physicians who shortly after World War I applied their scientific expertise to Spanish art, biography, history, and literary criticism.

An internationally recognized endocrinologist, Marañón initially explored aspects of human sexuality, emotion, and temperament. He wrote prodigious numbers of scientific monographs and more general essays such as *Biología y feminismo* (1920) and *Tres ensayos sobre la vida sexual* (1926; Three Essays on Sexual Life). His subsequent writings attempt to elucidate the useful contributions that biology and psychology can make to the humanities. The most important works in this category are his numerous articles on Don Juan, *Amiel: Un estudio sobre la timidez* (1932; Amiel: A Study of Sexual Timidity), *El Conde-Duque de Olivares (La pasión de mandar)* (1936; The Count-Duke of Olivares: The Will to Rule), *Las ideas biológicas del Padre Feijóo* (1934), and *Antonio Pérez* (1947; Eng. tr., *Antonio Perez, Spanish Traitor*, 1954).

Having discovered Sigmund Freud, through his clinical research, independently of the undifferentiated sexuality of the infant, Marañón was intensely interested in the psychoanalytic movement and was the first prominent Spaniard to apply psychological constructs such as the Oedipus complex, ambivalence, and the inferiority complex to both Spanish literary criticism and biography. With Otto Rank and Otto Fenichel, he believed that the Don Juan persona exemplifies a psychological type, unfortunately rather common in Hispanic culture, incapable of attaining full psychosexual development. His biographies have in common with those of Stefan ZWEIG, André MAUROIS, and Lewis Mumford, among others, the notion that every personality can be understood once the "key to character" (such as "a will to rule," "overriding resentment," or "sexual timidity") is found.

Marañón's career is paradigmatic of the potential as well as the limitations of the Spanish scientist-intellectual during the first half of the 20th century. He was an important activist during the period leading up to and including the Spanish Republic. He proposed university reform, women's suffrage, and equal access to employment and education, along with such startling concepts for that time as sexual education for Spanish children and adults and women's right to artificial insemination. He was also a member, with José ORTEGA Y GASSET and Ramón PÉREZ DE AYALA, of the "Intellectuals at the Service of the Spanish Republic." After the Civil War (1936–39), however, he willingly accepted the role of "official" intellectual in the Franco regime, often contradicting or twisting his most original and valuable ideas.

Marañón's *Obras completas* (1968–77) have been published in 10 volumes.

See: L. S. Granjel, *Gregorio Marañón: Su vida y su obra* (1960); P. Laín Entralgo, *Gregorio Marañón: vida, obra, y persona* (1969); G. D. Keller, *The Significance and Impact of Gregorio Marañón* (1977). G.D.K.

Marcel, Gabriel (1889–1973), French philosopher, playwright, literary critic, and composer, was born in Paris. He was drawn to Christian existentialism because of a need to combine his metaphysical intuitions with a concrete experience. Marcel attached great importance to his plays, 27 in number, of which only a few have been performed. Indeed, these works prompted the insights that led to some 12 philosophical essays, for which Marcel is well known. Lectures given at Harvard University, published as *The Existentialist Background of Human Dignity* (1963), provide a relatively accessible account of the itinerary of his search.

Marcel's drama bears the influence of the postnaturalist well-made play. They are not thesis plays, and no miracles occur as in the works of Paul CLAUDEL or Georges BERNANOS. Crises (illness, divorce, death, or political perils) in a contemporary setting lead the characters (and the spectators or readers) to questions concerning man's existence. Marcel insisted that he left his characters free to seek their own solutions, but, at the very end, they often coincide with the author's. Nonetheless, these conclusions are reached only after a forceful development of opposite attitudes. The strength of Marcel's drama is, indeed, that he never sets up straw men, but allows his characters to present areligious positions at their best. His attempts to "encounter the transcendental" in the very real occurrences on stage are, on the other hand, less convincing. There may be a contradiction inherent in his often stated intention to be "concrete" (which he is), and at the same time to use quasi-musical suggestion, that is, to be poetic, which he often is in the sudden intuitions of the very last scenes of his plays.

In *Le Quatuor en fa dièse* (1925; The Quartet in F-sharp), Claire Mazère is able to go beyond her narrow, egotistical motivations thanks to a revelation that comes to her while listening to a musical composition. "Intersubjectivity," communion with others, leads to knowledge of self and to "being." In Marcel's view, death purifies, since one remembers the deceased's essential being, not his "having" (all the activities and possessions that one can dispense with and that obscure "being"). But in *La Chapelle ardente* (1931; Eng. tr., *The Funeral Pyre* in *Three Plays*, 1958), the parents cling possessively to the memory and the things left by their dead son. His fiancée, however, eventually finds a new direction in what seems at first simply a marriage out of pity. "I exist, now that someone needs me." When is sacrifice overbearing? In a discussion of *Le Chemin de crête* (1936; Eng. tr., *Ariadne* in *Three Plays*, 1958), Marcel himself wonders whether Ariane's selflessness in offering to divorce her husband and assist his new marriage financially is genuine or is a form of manipulation: "How is one to know?" In *Le Dard* (staged in Paris in 1937; The Dart), his strongest play, Marcel opposes political rebellion to practical Christian charity, which in its movement towards "thou," achieves transcendence and "being." Marcel's insistence on freedom appears in *Rome n'est plus dans Rome* (1951; Rome Is No More in Rome), in which a professor, pressured by his wife against his better conscience, flees the Communist menace in France only to be confronted by clerico-military thought-control in Brazil.

Like all existentialists, Marcel is opposed to mere abstraction: "concepts need ceaseless replenishment" by a return to "the sting of the real." Marcel is non-Cartesian, he does not seek to verify, and he is nonsystematic. "Being" is a mystery, hence his "concrete philosophy." One can, however, thanks to a certain "existential security," rely on one's intuition, to which reflection confers some knowledge. (Marcel put some stock in the phenomenon of mental telepathy.) The antimony between "having" and "being" is fundamental in Marcel's philosophical works, such as *Etre et avoir* (1935; Eng. tr., *Being and Having*, 1965). Modern man is especially preoccupied with "having." As Marcel asserts in *Les Hommes contre l'humain* (1951; Eng. tr., *Man against Mass Society*, 1952), Western technocracy and particularly Eastern Communism have exacerbated the possessiveness and the material pursuits of a superficial existence to the detriment of a sense of "being." Citing Claudel, he would want to be a "sower of silence and solitude," creating the condition for the restoration of "ontological weight" to existence, for the fullness that is "being." "Concrete approaches to the mystery of being" are "fidelity" (a transcendence towards the other), "hope" (akin to a prophetic affirmation), and "love" (a communion haunted by the absolute). Marcel avoids as useless any objective proof of God's existence. He insists on the teleological character of man's ontological exigence, the fundamental impulse towards God.

See: J. Chenu, *Le Théâtre de Gabriel Marcel et sa signification métaphysique* (1948); K. T. Gallagher, *The Philosophy of Gabriel Marcel* (1962).   B.Su.

Marías Aguilera, Julián (1914-), Spanish philosopher, critic, professor, and social scientist, was born in Valladolid. The foremost disciple of José ORTEGA Y GASSET, under whom he studied at the University of Madrid from 1931 to 1936, Marías collaborated with his mentor in founding the Instituto de Humanidades (Humanities Institute) in Madrid in 1948. Since 1951, Marías has taught in more than a score of countries and in dozens of universities.

Marías has expanded Ortega's philosophy of life as the radical reality, synthesizing it with the work of such notable Spanish thinkers as Miguel de UNAMUNO and Zubiri. He refers to these and a number of other figures such as Manuel García Morente and José Gaos as "the Madrid School of Philosophy," and sees himself as the heir to an intellectual mood and movement originating with the Generation of 1898 (*see* SPANISH LITERATURE). Nevertheless, his writings reveal a broad knowledge of traditional European philosophy, and his commentaries on German thought (in particular Edmund Husserl, Immanuel Kant, and Martin Heidegger) are worthy of especial note. Among Marías's several original contributions to philosophical thought are his theory of the empirical structure of life, expounded in *Antropología metafísica* (1970), his concept of literary genres in philosophy, in *Ensayos de teoría* (1953; Essays in Theory), and his analysis of social reality, in *La estructura social* (1955). Unlike the existentialist writers with whom the "Madrid School" is often

identified, Marías maintains, as does Ortega, that life is inherently reasonable and structured. Indeed, they argue that in its highest and most proper form reason is both vital and historical. This being the case, Marías is able to restore metaphysics to respectability in philosophy not as an exercise in abstraction, but as a theory of human life. In so doing he reaffirms the bond between philosophy and art, and he willingly accepts the testimony of poets and artists even when dealing with the most rigorous concepts.

An acknowledged master of the essay, Marías writes with exemplary clarity and precision, successfully blending popular themes and metaphors with extraordinary classical erudition. Besides the aforementioned works, Marías's 40-odd books include *Historia de la filosofía* (1942); *Biografía de la filosofía* (1953), and *La España real* (1976; Real Spain). Most of his works written before 1970 are included in his *Obras* (8 vols., 1957-70). In his most recent works—*La Expaña real, La devolución de España* (1977; The Return of Spain), and *España en nuestras manos* (1978; Spain in Our Hands)—Marías emerges as one of the most authoritative voices in Spain and enhances the stature he has enjoyed since 1964 as a member of the Royal Spanish Academy of the Language.   H.R.

Marinetti, Filippo Tommaso (1876-1944), Italian poet, essayist, and dramatist was born to wealthy Milanese parents in Alexandria, Egypt. There he attended French Jesuit schools before being sent to a Paris lycée in 1893 and, two years later, to Pavia and Genoa to study law. He soon established his bohemian credentials in Italy and France by composing modernist verse and plays in both languages, the appearance of which made him a minor international succès de scandale. It was not until the publication of his *First Futurist Manifesto* (1909) in the Paris *Figaro*, however, that Marinetti found his true calling as the creator, propagandist, and high priest of futurism (*see* ITALIAN LITERATURE), one of the most prophetic, influential, and subsequently neglected avant-garde artistic movements of the early 20th century. Marinetti's followers included such writers, composers, and artists as Aldo PALAZZESCHI, Francesco Ballila Pratella, Corrado Govoni, Luigi Russolo, Gino Severini, Carlo Carrà, Paolo Buzzi, and Umberto Boccioni. Until World War I inhibited their activities, Marinetti and his followers wandered throughout Europe, including Great Britain and Russia, trumpeting the futurist gospel. Marinetti was the star and impresario of their riotous lectures and poetry readings, theatrical performances, dance recitals, musical concerts, film showings, and art exhibits—all staged to assault conventional bourgeois taste. These events often ended in pitched battles between audience and actors. As a result of high-spirited promotion, by 1914 the term "futurist" had become universally synonymous with everything new and modern. The *First Manifesto* calls for the demolition of libraries, museums, and academies ("those cemeteries of wasted efforts, those calvaries of crucified dreams") and for the deliverance of Italy from the "canker of professors, archaeologists, cicerones and antiquaries."

Taking cues from past and contemporary iconoclasts (Giambattista Vico, Friedrich NIETZSCHE, Walt Whitman, Arthur RIMBAUD, Gabriele D'ANNUNZIO, Alfred JARRY, Guillaume APOLLINAIRE), Marinetti reflected his generation's disillusionment with the established institutions of the day. His weapons of lunatic buffoonery and vulgar mockery were aimed at the total overthrow of the past in an effort to rejuvenate the present and to revolutionize the future. Thus the futurists' search for novel, more authentic means of expression and artistic subject matter, and their infatuation with the inventions and artifacts of the industrial world: automobiles, locomotives, airplanes, electricity, radio, motion pictures. Thus, too, their celebration of the quickened tempo and spirit of the times: kinetic activity, speed, danger, natural disasters, nationalism, militarism, and warfare, the last unfortunately extolled as the "hygiene of the world." This appallingly innocent aspect of futurism, its naiveté and aggressiveness, was at once a forecast of World War I and one of the main causes of the movement's postwar oblivion. The flirtation of some futurists with fascism, despite Marinetti's defection from the Fascist Party in 1920 and his open condemnation of anti-Semitism in 1938, only hastened its demise.

Nonetheless, the impact of Italian futurism on 20th-century artistic theories and techniques belies the brevity of the movement's history and the ephemeral nature of its own production, particularly in literature. Marinetti's *Technical Manifesto* (1912), also first published in *Figaro*, formulated a number of poetic doctrines that later became the stock-in-trade of more celebrated modernist movements such as dadaism, surrealism, imagism, vorticism, and expressionism, in addition to Russian futurism and Italian hermeticism (*see* ITALIAN LITERATURE). Only some of the similarities among these groups can be explained by reference to their common symbolist sources. Indeed, Marinetti can be credited with organizing and synthesizing symbolist ideas into a cohesive, organic theory of poetry. Symbolist free verse, for example, was behind Marinetti's notion of *parole in libertà* (words in liberty), described as an "uninterrupted sequence of new images" spontaneously emerging from the poet's psyche with complete disregard for the rules of grammar, punctuation, and syntax. Marinetti also insisted upon the centrality of images as the "life-blood of poetry," not as mere ornamentation, and he conceived of images as analogies that "tie up objects that are apparently diverse and hostile," i.e., as the kind of radical imagery and farfetched metaphors that are the hallmark of modern verse. Futurist poetry's international kinship is revealed by its typographic gymnastics, verbal acrobatics, fractured syntax, and disjointed semantics, all of which Marinetti saw as the products of the "wireless imagination." Of all his works, the *Technical Manifesto* alone should secure his place among such figures as Pablo Picasso, Ezra Pound, Igor Stravinsky, and Guillaume Apollinaire as one of the great movers and shapers of modern art. Marinetti's other works include such volumes of poetry as *La Conquête des étoiles* (1902; Conquest of the Stars), *Destruction* (1904), *La Momie sanglante* (1904; The Bleeding Mummy), and *Le Monoplan du Pape* (1912; The Pope's Monoplane), and such plays as *Le Roi Bombance* (1905; Ital. tr., *Il re Baldoria*, 1920) and *Poupées électriques* (1909; Electric Dolls). A selection of his works is available in English as *Marinetti: Selected Writings*, ed. by R. W. Flint and tr. by A. A. Coppotelli (1971).

See: M. Kirby, *Futurist Performance* (1971); A. Frattini, in *Letteratura italiana: i contemporanei*, vol. 1 (1975), pp. 183–210.   W. De S.

Marinković, Ranko (1913–), Croatian short-story writer, dramatist, and novelist, was born on the island of Vis. He studied literature in Zagreb and published his first short stories in Miroslav KRLEŽA's journal *Pečat*. During World War II he was imprisoned by the Italians, and after their capitulation in 1943, spent a year at a Yugoslav refugee camp at El Shatt, Egypt. After the war, he became director of the Zagreb Theater and later a professor at that city's Academy of Drama.

With his postwar volume *Proze* (1948; Prose Pieces)

and even more with his collection of stories, *Ruke* (1953; Hands), Marinković established himself as one of the leading Croatian writers. The protagonists in his stories are representatives of the small-town, prewar bourgeoisie that lived in the shadow of Saint Cyprian's bell tower in Vis: fat canons, silly old virgins, decrepit landowners, corpulent innkeepers, and gendarmes who abused law and order. Their conversations, worries, and malicious gossip are drawn from the author's own experiences with these people, whom he often portrays with more sarcasm than irony or satire. In *Ruke*, however, Marinković's bitterness has diminished and his scope broadened. Certain of his stories—such as "Zagrljaj" (The Embrace), "Ruke" (Hands), and "Andjeo" (The Angel)—are masterpieces, and there is no anthology of modern Yugoslav prose that does not include at least one of them.

Despite his early play *Albatros* (1939), Marinković became known as a playwright only with his *Glorija* (1956; Gloria), which attracted wide attention. This work purports to expose "priestly ruses" designed to keep alive the faith of the simple-minded, but the play fails to do proper justice to those who take their beliefs seriously.

Marinković's generally praised novel *Kiklop* (1965; The Cyclops) is a complex work in which three themes are interwoven: life in Zagreb before World War II, the story of Odysseus and his attempt to escape from the cave whose exit is guarded by the one-eyed monster Polyphemus, and the fate of a crew shipwrecked among Polynesian cannibals. Written in an elaborate style that is filled with allusions to prewar Croatian writers, this difficult but rewarding novel stands at the peak of contemporary Yugoslav prose and is worthy of comparison with the best works of Western authors.

See: M. Vaupotić, "Odiseja intelektualca u Zoopolis," *Kolo* 3 (1967): 232–36; A. Kadić, *From Croatian Renaissance to Yugoslav Socialism* (1969), pp. 237–38, 288–89.
                                                        A.K.

Maritain, Jacques (1882–1973), French theologian and philosopher, one of the foremost exponents of Catholic doctrine in the 20th century, was born in Paris into a Protestant family. His father, who had served as secretary to the statesman Jules Favre, and his mother, née Geneviève Favre, raised him in the liberal tradition of Protestantism. He was educated at the Lycée Henri IV, where he became a friend of Ernest PSICHARI. At the Sorbonne, he met Raïssa Oumansoff, a Jewish Russian student, who became his wife in 1904 and remained his devoted intellectual partner. Maritain graduated as a *agrégé* in philosophy in 1905 and was converted to Roman Catholicism in 1906, largely under the influence of the strange, vociferous mystic Léon BLOY. He pursued studies in biology at Heidelberg in 1906–08 and then attended Henri BERGSON's lectures at the Collège de France. But Maritain grew dissatisfied with the "scientist" attitude then prevalent among secular thinkers, and he likewise criticized Bergsonian views on intuition and on creative evolution as being too lax. Only in the rigorous intellectual system of Saint Thomas Aquinas did he find a haven of certitude. He taught at the Paris Institut Catholique from 1914 to 1939, lectured widely in North and South America, and then taught at Toronto and Princeton. Charles de Gaulle appointed Maritain ambassador to the Vatican for the period 1945–48.

Maritain exerted a profound influence on many 20th-century thinkers and artists, including Jean COCTEAU, Julien GREEN, Marc Chagall, Pierre REVERDY, and Georges Rouault. After 1945, however, as the French turned toward existentialism (atheistic or Christian) and, in the religious realm, to Simone WEIL and TEILHARD DE CHARDIN, Maritain's influence began to wane. In his latter years, Maritain, then a widower, withdrew to a monastery near Toulouse, where he died at the age of 91. His last years were saddened by what he deplored as an excessive liberalization of Catholic doctrine and particularly by the vogue of Teilhard de Chardin, whose poetical thought, ignoring original sin, revelation, and even redemption, at times approaching pantheism, seemed to turn its back on neo-Thomism. Forsaking charity for once, Maritain vituperated against that new modernism in *Le Paysan de la Garonne* (1966; Eng. tr., *The Peasant of the Garonne*, 1968), a clear allusion to La Fontaine's "Paysan du Danube," in which he told the Romans some blunt truths. The subtitle of the volume is explicit: "An Old Layman Questions Himself about the Present Time." In religion as in ethics and politics, an aged liberal is likely to be the most critical of new liberals.

Maritain's temperament was clearly that of a stern redresser of what he judged to be the errors of the modern world. He was harshly unfair to Bergson's alleged "irrationalism" and "pragmatism," and with the wrath of a neophyte, he condemned much in the modern world in *Antimoderne* (1922) and *Trois Réformateurs* (1925; Eng. tr., *Three Reformers*, 1928). The three thinkers he singled out for endangering Christianity (or at least Catholicism) were Martin Luther, René Descartes, and Jean-Jacques Rousseau, Rousseau being especially reprehensible on account of his advocacy of natural goodness and of an all-powerful state to which, through an implicit compact, the individual surrendered all. Maritain also judged Blaise Pascal to be a mediocre theologian, well-nigh ignorant of Thomism. For Maritain, it was the system of the Schoolmen (which he reduced too summarily to an imaginary unity) that alone could preserve intelligence, wisdom, and Christian civilization. It represented an Aristotelianism enriched and fulfilled by Christian thinking; it respected mystery as the nourishment of the intellect; and although it refused to deify man, it showed him as reaching "integral humanism" when he is inhabited by God. The light of Thomism alone could today guide Christians amid their intellectual chaos.

Maritain's many philosophical treatises are abstruse and technical: *Eléments de philosophie* (1923–30; Eng. tr., *An Introduction to Philosophy*, 1930–37); *Distinguer pour unir, ou les degrés du savoir* (1932; Eng. tr., *The Degrees of Knowledge*, 1937); *Humanisme intégral* (1936; Eng. tr., *True Humanism*, 1938). He also wrote widely on poetry and painting, and he attempted, with questionable success, to devise a coherent aesthetics based on the Schoolmen in *Art et Scolastique* (1920; Eng. tr., *Art and Scholasticism*, 1930). His later *Creative Intuition in Art and Poetry* (1955), composed during his stay in America, is more subtle.

From his metaphysics, Maritain derived his ethical and political position: man should first of all know who he is and how he stands in relation to God before he can know how he should act. After having stood perilously close to the ideas of Charles MAURRAS, a vehement foe of Rousseauist concepts of democracy, Maritain parted from him, and in *Primauté du spirituel* (1927; Eng. tr., *The Things That Are Not Caesar's*, 1930), he endorsed the Pope's condemnation of Maurras's doctrines. He became an unrelenting denouncer of the totalitarian regimes, advocating more unselfishness in bourgeois capitalism and more generous concern for the dignity of the working man. He explained how renovated education might hasten the dawn of a more just Christian society in such works as *The Rights of Man and Natural Law* (1943), *Le Philosophe dans la cité* (1960; The Philosopher in the City),

and *Education at the Crossroads* (1943; Fr. tr., *Pour une philosophie de l'éducation*, 1943).

Non-Catholics and Catholics alike have questioned many of Maritain's theses. Yet while his system may not have proved a flawless armor to withstand the onslaught of those who assert the "death of God," the personal warmth of the man and his commitment to his ideas are less easily refuted or denied than his neo-Thomistic system. In the years 1925–50, it was easy to agree with T. S. Eliot, who had proclaimed Maritain's influence "probably the most powerful force in contemporary philosophy."

See: G. Phelan, *Jacques Maritain* (1937); J. Evans, *Maritain: The Man and His Achievement* (1969).   H.P.

Marquina, Eduardo (1879–1946), Spanish dramatist and poet, was born in Barcelona. He is remembered as the reviver of poetic theater and as the principal Spanish exponent of historical verse drama in the early 20th century, despite the fact that recent critics of his work agree that his historical plays are not his best. Examples of these are: *Las hijas del Cid* (1908; The Daughters of the Cid), his first success, and *En Flandes se ha puesto el sol* (1910; The Sun Has Set in Flanders), his best-known play. The last of these early historical dramas was *El gran Capitán* (1916). They are all concerned with the nostalgic idealization of national myths and glories as exemplified in the heroic figures of the past. Written in the wake of the Spanish-American War, these plays represent an evasion of the problematic present, that same present that Marquina's near contemporaries, the Generation of 1898 tried to face up to.

Increasingly aware of what he called the "affectation" of his historical plays, in which quite often the poetry was at odds with the drama, Marquina turned to rural theater in verse, although other historical plays were to be scattered among his remaining works. Although little known, two of these rural plays with realistic settings are among his most effective works: *El pobrecito carpintero* (1924; The Poor Little Carpenter) and *La ermita, la fuente y el río* (1927; The Hermitage, the Fountain, and the River). In the 1930s and 1940s, Marquina produced a number of religious plays that represent the third important classification of his work. Three of these are comparable in quality to his best rural dramas: *El monje Blanco* (1930; The White Monk), *Teresa de Jesús* (1932), and *María la viuda* (1943; Maria the Widow). The last is considered by some to be his finest play. All of the plays in the three mentioned categories are in verse, although Marquina did write a number of pieces with contemporary settings in prose, a genre to which his talent, exceedingly unmodern in spirit and technique, was ill-suited. Marquina's protagonists are usually maternal women. Good and evil, unambiguously portrayed, are often incarnated in feminine opposites. He is not concerned with everyday life in a social environment. His plays tend to be set in distant times and places and to be concerned with traditional Spanish religious and moral values seen from an uncritical, rightist perspective.

See: J. Montero Alonso, *Vida de Eduardo Marquina* (1965); M. de la Nuez, *Eduardo Marquina* (1976).

H.L.B.

Marsé, Juan (1933–), Spanish novelist, was born in Barcelona. He earned his living first in a jewelry shop and later in Paris in the Pasteur Institute. In 1959 he received the Sesamo Prize for his short story "Nada para morir" (Nothing for Death). The novels *Encerrados con un solo juguete* (1960; Locked Up with Just One Toy) and *Esta cara de la luna* (1962; This Side of the Moon) deal with the degraded world encountered by young people growing up after the Spanish Civil War. *Últimas tardes con Teresa* (1966; Last Evenings with Teresa) is also a portrayal of Spanish society, in which Marsé employs a new and more complex prose stye. *La oscura historia de la prima Montse* (1970; The Obscure History of Cousin Montse) is the tragic story of a man who tries to preserve his integrity in an immoral milieu. *Si te dicen que caí* (1973; If They Tell You That I Fell) documents, in allegorical fashion, the violent past of its main character. This novel offers a multiple perspective through the fusion of realistic and mythical levels of narration. All of Marsé's works, including his novel *Confidencias de un chorizo* (1977; Confidences of an Informer), expose the chaotic social and moral conditions of post-Civil War Spain in a bitter, corrosive, and sarcastic language reminiscent of Camilo José CELA and Ramón del VALLE-INCLÁN.

See: M. Vargas Llosa, "Una explosión satírica en la novela española moderna," *Insula* 233 (1966): 1; J. C. Curutchet, *Cuatro ensayos sobre la nueva novela española* (1973), pp. 71–87.   J.O.

Marshak, Samuil Yakovlevich (1887–1964), Russian children's writer and translator, was born in Voronezh. He studied at London University from 1913 to 1914 but was back in Russia during and after World War I. He was active in children's relief work, and he organized and wrote short sketches for one of the earliest theaters for children. Later, as editor of several magazines and as organizer of the juvenile division of the State Publishing House, Marshak played a leading role in establishing the direction that Soviet children's literature was to take. In addition to his writings for children, Marshak produced admirable translations of Shakespeare's sonnets, of many of the English romantics' works, and of English and Scottish folk ballads. He was an adroit and resourceful craftsman, and his translations retain whatever is possible of the literal meaning without going beyond the resources of traditional Russian verse. He has left an account of his life in *V nachale zhizni* (1960; At the Beginning of Life) and of his literary views and reminiscences in *Vospitaniye slovom* (1961; Education by the Word).   C.B.

Marsman, Hendrik (1899–1940), Dutch poet, novelist, and critic, was born in Zeist. He studied law at the University of Utrecht and later lived in France. He drowned in the English Channel, when the ship on which he was hoping to escape to England was torpedoed. He came under the influence of Herman van den BERGH and wrote poetry in the expressionistic style. His form was freer than van de Bergh's, however, for Marsman was a modernist poet. He traveled through Germany in 1921, and this trip led to a group of poems describing German and Dutch cities in an expressionistic style. Beginning in 1919, his poetry was printed in various magazines, and then a volume of it appeared as *Verzen* (1923; Verses). This contained expressionistic poetry, but after its publication, he turned away from the expressionistic style. In 1927, *Paradise Regained* was published, and while there are expressionistic characteristics here, especially in the imagery, there are also stanzas that herald the later Marsman. In 1933, with *De dood van het vitalisme* (The Death of Vitalism), he proclaimed the end of the movement by which the Dutch form of expressionism had become known; he mourned the fact that he had not attracted a younger generation of Dutch followers. *Porta nigra* (1934) reveals a simplification of the poet's language, but there is also fear of the absolute void, and there is the contrast between life and death. Marsman felt both a fear of death and a longing for it. He was a very lonely poet and

attempted to connect himself with the cosmos. His last great poetic work was the cycle *Tempel en Kruis* (1940; The Temple and the Cross), in which he viewed Western civilization at the outbreak of World War II, combining intellectual analysis with lyrical poetry. In this view, the Temple symbolized the civilization of ancient Greece, and the Cross, Christianity. The poet finds himself attracted to the tranquility of antiquity, and he flees Christianity. Only the Dionysian element in modern civilization attracts him. In writing this poetry, he was influenced by Friedrich NIETZSCHE, whose *Also sprach Zarathustra,* he translated into Dutch (with the aid of P. Endt).

Marsman also tried his hand at experiments in prose, which were not as successful as his poetry. He rewrote his first novel, *Vera,* several times, and finally rejected it himself. It was published only posthumously in 1962. *De dood van Angèle Degroux* (1933; The Death of Angèle Degroux) is more effective, although the lyrical passages do not strengthen the structure of the novel. Together with Simon VESTDIJK, he wrote an epistolary novel, *Heden ik, morgen gij* (1937; Today I, Tomorrow You). Marsman was also a literary critic, but he was extremely subjective, and thus, sometimes adopted a very high-handed tone. A year after the magazine *De Vrije Bladen* was founded in 1924, he became editor, and with the disappearance of *Het Getij* at the same time, it became the magazine of that generation. His leadership was not quite successful, however, and conflicts developed among the contributors to *De Vrije Bladen*, with Marsman resigning in 1926, and returning as editor from 1929 to 1931. He published essays on *Herman Gorter* (1937) and *Menno ter Braak* (1939). The publication of his *Verzameld werk* (1938; Collected Work) marked the end of a period of his life that he himself regarded as past.

See: W. L. M. E. van Leeuwen, *Drie vrienden* (1947); A. Lehning, *De vriend van mijn jeugd* (1954).   S.L.F.

Marti, Kurt (1921–), Swiss poet and essayist, was born in Bern. He studied law and theology and became a Protestant minister. In the pugnacious tradition of Martin Luther, Ulrich Zwingli, and Jeremias Gotthelf, Marti uses the power of the word—both of the Gospel and of literature—to change the consciousness of his readers. He discovered that the traditional lyric poetry of his own (Bernese) dialect was bound to passé models. Yet Marti detected Traklean, Rilkean, Georgean, dadaist, and surrealist elements in his dialect, and, under the influence of such "concrete" poets as Eugen Gomringer and Helmut Heißenbüttel he began to modernize the Alemannic dialect poem. Marti's four major volumes of poetry—*republikanische gedichte* (1959; Republican Poems), *rosa loui* (1967), *leichenreden* (1969; Obituaries), and *undereinisch* (1973; Suddenly)—have brought him international recognition. Critics have praised him for overcoming the pastoral sentimentalities of traditional Swiss-German dialect poetry and for linking the Swiss-German poem to world poetry. Characteristically, Marti's poems are not translatable. He consciously writes for the very small circle of his congregation. Helmut HEISSENBÜTTEL maintains that in his poetry Marti has succeeded in suspending the apparent antithesis of formalism and engagement by "unexpectedly pouring polemics and satire into his linguistic style, thus achieving a new kind of naiveté. . . ." Marti has also written a political diary, *Zum Beispiel Bern 1972* (1973; For Instance Bern 1972), and many critical essays on theology and literature.

See: W. Bucher and G. Ammann, eds., *Schweizer Schriftsteller im Gespräch*, vol. 2 (1971), pp. 121–46.   R.K.

Martin du Gard, Roger (1881–1958), French novelist and playwright, was born in Neuilly-sur-Seine of a well-to-do middle-class family. He was trained as an archivist at the Ecole des Chartres, from which he graduated in 1906. His thesis was published in 1909 under the title *L'Abbaye de Jumièges: Etude archéologique des ruines* (The Abbey of Jumièges: Archaeological Study of the Ruins). After studying under several well-known psychiatrists in Paris, he published his first novel, *Devenir!* (Becoming), in 1908. His first major novel, however, was *Jean Barois* (1913; Eng. tr., 1949), written partially under the influence of Marcel Hébert, a modernist priest. The year 1913 marked the beginning of Martin du Gard's lifelong friendship with André GIDE, Jean SCHLUMBERGER, Jacques COPEAU, and other members of the *Nouvelle Revue française* group. Martin du Gard's prewar writings also include a peasant farce, *Le Testament du père Leleu* (1914; Old Leleu's Will), which was performed at the Théâtre du Vieux-Colombier. It was adopted into the repertory of the Théâtre-Français in 1938.

After World War I, in which Martin du Gard served in a motor transport division, he began his major work, *Les Thibault* (Eng. tr., *The World of the Thibaults*, 2 vols., 1939–41), a novel cycle in eight parts, the composition of which covered the period between the two world wars (*Le Cahier gris*, 1922; *Le Pénitencier*, 1922; *La Belle Saison*, 1923; *La Consultation*, 1928; *La Sorellina*, 1928; *La Mort du père*, 1929; *L'Eté 1914*, 1936; *Epilogue*, 1940). This monumental synthesis of the spirit of an epoch (from the turn of the century through 1918) and the troubled meditations of the author takes the form of a family history, that of the Roman Catholic Thibaults. The authoritarian father represents a set of dying bourgeois values, against which the two sons, Antoine and Jacques, must struggle during their formative years. Antoine is so absorbed in his promising medical career that, like many others at that time, he fails to see the signs of the approaching war. When he is caught unprepared by a gas attack at the front, an exposure from which he cannot recover, he decides that he will take his own life rather than endure long suffering. During his illness, he keeps a diary that is a richly human summation of the values of his life. Jacques's egocentric yet idealistic rebellion takes him from confinement in an adolescent "penitentiary," to involvement in the socialist movement. Jacques is attempting to distribute pacifist pamphlets by air when his plane crashes. The counterpoint to the Thibaults is provided by a Protestant family, the Fontanins. The mother's Christian Science beliefs provide a background for the "miraculous" cure of her fatally ill daughter, who will later become the wife of Jacques. The second child, Daniel, leads the life of an undisciplined artist.

In 1928, Martin du Gard published a second peasant farce, *La Gonfle* (The Swelling). The period following 1929 was marked by a series of crises: he was involved in a serious automobile accident, changed his plan for *Les Thibault*, and destroyed a partially completed volume ("L'Appareillage"; The Preparation). During the early 1930s he also wrote several shorter works, including *La Confidence africaine* (1931; African Confession), a technically perfect short story about a "natural" incest; *Un Taciturne* (1932), a play in which the hero discovers his own homosexuality; and *Vieille France* (1933; Eng. tr., *The Postman*, 1954), somber sketches of peasant life. Martin du Gard's other minor published works include "L'Une de nous. . ." (1910; One of Us. . .), a story extracted from an aborted novel, "Marise"; *Témoignage* (1921; Testimony), a tribute to Marcel Hébert; *Noizemont-les-Vierges* (1928); and *Dialogue* (1930).

While writing *Les Thibault*, Martin du Gard was a reg-

ular visitor at the symposia organized by Paul DESJARDINS at Potigny, although he refused to participate actively in the public discussions. He disliked the literary life of Paris and withdrew to Le Tertre, a Norman country estate at Bellême, where he received his friends and served as mentor to many younger writers. Forced to flee before the German invasion in 1940, he spent the war years in Nice. In 1951, after the death of Gide, he published extracts from his journal, under the title *Notes sur André Gide*, in order to counter distorted public statements about his friend.

During his lifetime, Martin du Gard maintained an extensive correspondence, most of which remains unpublished as of 1978. The two published volumes of letters exchanged with Gide (1968) and two others with Copeau (1972) reveal warm literary friendships and the fascinating interplay of quite different personalities reacting to each other, to their works, to their mutual friends, and to the 1913–51 epoch. Martin du Gard's epistolary style is free and easy, full of verve, in contrast to the carefully controlled style of the novels, which aims at a self-effacing banality. The journal he kept from 1919 until 1949 is mostly unpublished, as is also "Souvenirs du Colonel Maumort," a long novel on which he worked from 1941 until his death. Martin du Gard's manuscripts are in the Bibliothèque Nationale in Paris.

As is usual for a first novel, *Devenir!* is flawed, but the work is interesting for the dialogic opposition of its two protagonists. In one of these, Martin du Gard created a character whose life is a failure, in order to exorcise the fears of his own failure as novelist (he had abandoned his first attempt at a novel, "Une Vie de saint" [A Saintly Life]). In *Jean Barois*, the dialogic pattern is repeated. The novel traces the life of its late 19th-century hero from youth to death, through personal conflicts as well as the intellectual and moral crises of the period, chiefly the struggle between science and religion, and the Dreyfus Affair. Progressively freeing himself from religious beliefs and family ties, Jean Barois indulges in a willful affirmation that is philosophical, social, and political. With the coming of old age, however, be abandons his aggressively liberated stance and is happy to accept the comforts of religion. His downfall is accompanied by the rise in importance of his dialogic partner, Luce, who suffers less from human frailties and maintains his liberated stance to the end.

In *Les Thibault* this pattern finds its most profound expression through the opposing temperaments of the brothers Jacques and Antoine. Not only do they represent two sides of Martin du Gard's personality, but their scope is such that they illustrate two dominant modes of the 20th-century mind. Antoine's calm, stable insistence on the satisfactions of the human reason makes him the incarnation of an evolved Cartesianism. He seems to carry with him the aura of a character from Martin du Gard's master Lev TOLSTOY. Jacques's insistence on a conscious life and a conscious death leads directly to the heroes of Albert CAMUS. On the other hand, Jacques's obsessive, troubled rebellions, in the course of pursuing his quest for a personal and social ideal, express the 20th-century rediscovery of the irrational. Antoine is the pragmatist of *Les Thibault* and Jacques is the poet. The dialogic structure of *Les Thibault* embodies the 20th-century struggle between madness and reason. Furthermore, *Les Thibault* expresses, better perhaps than any other modern French novel, the relation of the individual to history, another of the major themes of 20th-century literature.

All of Martin du Gard's novels focus on the exhilarating yet tragic process of an individual's becoming, his *devenir*. He has always been an author with a broad and constant reading public, as evidenced by the production figures for his works. But with the passing of time it has become clear that he is not only a writer to be read, but as Gide said about himself, a writer to be reread. Since 1955, when Camus expressed his admiration for Martin du Gard's writings in a preface to the *Œuvres complètes* (Complete Works), there has been a resurgence of critical interest in his work. Martin du Gard was awarded the Nobel Prize for Literature in 1937.

See: R. Robidoux, *Roger Martin du Gard et la religion* (1964); D. Schalk, *Roger Martin du Gard: The Novelist and History* (1967); C. Savage, *Roger Martin du Gard* (1968); R. Roza, *Roger Martin du Gard et la banalité retrouvée* (1970); R. Garguilo, *La Genèse des "Thibault" de Roger Martin du Gard* (1974); G. Kaiser, "Roger Martin du Gard devant la critique," *SFr* 20, no. 2 (1976): 248–62.   G.E.K.

Martínez Ballesteros, Antonio (1929–), Spanish playwright, was born in Toledo, where he resides and works as a civil servant and shopkeeper while applying his craft as an "underground" playwright. His theater is for the most part a satirical protest, sometimes acerbic, sometimes openly farcical, against the injustices and fetishes of the tyrannical mentality. His target may be a totalitarian regime, a bureaucratic hierarchy, or the victims themselves, who because of their greed, stupidity, or conformism are intimidated by the system. Like other avantgarde playwrights of the Francisco Franco era, Martínez Ballesteros disguises his satires of the dictator by situating them symbolically outside of Spain, as in *En el país de jauja* (1962; Eng. tr., *The Best of All Possible Worlds*, 1966) and *Sultanísimo, por la gracia de Alá* (1973; Super-Sultan, by the Grace of Allah). The veil of abstraction, however, deceived neither the censor nor the impresarios, so that many of his plays remain unpublished and unperformed. A distinctive aspect of his theater is its use of short, abstract allegories, in the form of theatrical fables, designed to satirize modern society. These include *Farsas contemporáneas* (1969), which burlesque violence, consumerism, classism, and conformism; *Retablo en tiempo presente* (1970; Altarpiece in Modern Dress); *Las estampas* (1971; Prints); and *Fábulas zoológicas* (1974; Animal Fables). Most of these works were published soon after they were written. Several have won both national and international prizes, and some segments have been published in English translation.

See: G. E. Wellwarth, *Spanish Underground Drama* (1972).   S.M.G.

Martínez Mediero, Manuel (1939–), Spanish dramatist was born in Badajoz. He was representative of the "underground" (also "censored," "clandestine," "silenced," "avant-garde," "young," or "new wave") playwrights whose aggressive, antiestablishment views in combination with non-naturalistic styles made their works unacceptable to the doctrinaire, conservative government censors of the dictatorship of Francisco Franco (1939–75). Comparable in some ways to the theaters of the absurd and of cruelty, these plays characteristically use allegory, farce, and black humor to portray the evils of excessive power, and their heroes tend to be victims of social or economic oppression. Although theoretically applicable on a universal level, these works show a definite relationship to the experiences of authors living under a repressive regime. While underground plays have rarely been performed by other than amateur groups, several texts have been published in theater journals such as *Primer Acto, Yorik, Pipirijaina,* and *Estreno*. For the most part, however, scripts have circulated in mimeographed form among fellow writers and theater scholars. In addition to Martínez Mediero, the best known of the underground group are: Francisco Nieva, José RUIBAL (*see* SPANISH LITERATURE), Jerónimo López Mozo, Antonio MARTÍNEZ BALLESTEROS, and Juan Antonio Castro. Although Martínez Mediero's work is representative of underground theater in form and content, this author holds the distinction of having had several of his approximately 20 plays performed commercially in Madrid. *Las hermanas de Búfalo Bill* (1974; Buffalo Bill's Sisters), moreover, was a major success of the season. On the surface, this play deals with two sisters who have been put in chains by their despotic brother, Buffalo. When the tyrant finally dies, the sisters throw off their chains and dance joyfully. After a time, however, they begin to miss Buffalo and ultimately resurrect him. The play deals with the responsibility as well as the fear of freedom. Oppression, the author suggests, may be the result of laziness and habit. Other commercial productions by Martínez Mediero are: *Mientras la gallina duerme* (1967; While the Hen Sleeps), *El bebé furioso* (1974; The Furious Infant), and *Las planchadoras* (1978; The Ironing Women). The unperformed *El convidado* (1967; The Guest) is fundamental in the works of Martínez Mediero and has been included in several theater anthologies. The guest, a deaf-mute whose tongue was cut out in the war, symbolizes the losers of the Spanish Civil War and, by extension, individuals oppressed by any system. The ruling class is portrayed by an evil, elegantly dressed father and his spineless son, who diabolically ply their guest with such dishes as salt-mustard soup, cow dung, and needles. Martínez Mediero's first play, *Jacinta se fue a la guerra* (1967; Jacinta Went to War), was written in naturalistic style and published in *Yorik*. This author won the Sitges Theater Prize for the animal allegory *El último gallinero* (1969; The Last Henhouse). After the death of Franco in 1975, he wrote a parody of the political changes in Spain entitled *La banda que j. . . virtuosamente* (1978; The Band That F. . . Like a Virtuoso).

See: G. F. Wellwarth, *Spanish Underground Drama* (1972), pp. 91–96.   P.W.O'C.

Martínez-Menchén, Antonio (1930–), Spanish novelist, short-story writer, and essayist, was born in Linares. He studied law in Madrid, where since 1960 he has worked for the civil service. Some of his literary essays have been collected in *Del desengaño literario* (1970; Of Literary Disillusion). He has also written sociological criticism.

In Martínez Menchén's first novel, *Cinco variaciones* (1963; Five Variations), the anonymous characters are detached from the outside world and search within themselves for a way to overcome their isolation. Their emotional experiences, revealed by interior monologues, are the only resources left to them in questioning an alienated and fragmented world. In *Las tapias* (1969; Walls), the social barriers that separate the characters from the exterior world are so insurmountable that their alienation, as in the fiction of Franz KAFKA, becomes pathological. The impersonal and shadowy characters of *Inquisidores* (1977; Inquisitors) escape the cruelty and solitude of society by exercising their private fantasy and imagination. Childhood memories of the Civil War and the psychological effects of a repressive postwar society characterize the 11 stories that comprise this volume. Linguistic precision and an imaginative and meticulous treatment of the alienated man are the most noteworthy features of his prose.

See: J. Ortega, *Ensayos de la novela española moderna* (1974), pp. 109–35.   J.O.

Martínez Sierra, Gregorio (1881–1947), Spanish dramatist, was born in Madrid. He began his career by writing prose poems and novels. Examples of the former are *El poema del trabajo* (1898; Labor's Poem) and *Flores de escarcha* (1900; Frost Flowers). His novel *Tú eres la paz* (1907) was translated into English as *Ana María* (1921). Martínez Sierra's first dramatic work consists of four Maeterlinckian fantasies (*see* Maurice MAETERLINCK) in dialogue form, published under the title *Teatro de ensueño* (1905; Dream Theater). The first of his plays actually to reach the stage, *Vida y dulzura* (1908; Life and Sweetness), was a collaboration with the Catalonian dramatist Santiageo RUSIÑOL. *La sombra del padre* (1909; Father's Shadow) was far more realistic. More successful was *El ama de la casa* (1910; The Mistress of the House), the story of a stepmother who triumphs over difficulties through good sense and sheer goodness. *Canción de cuna* (1911; Eng. tr., *Cradle Song*, 1917), is the author's most famous play. A charmingly sentimental portrayal of women living in a convent, *Cradle Song* played in New York in 1921, in London in 1926, and again in 1927 in New York with Eva Le Gallienne. *Cradle Song* toured the United States, had several performances in Oxford, Liverpool, and Dublin, and in 1933 was made into a movie. *El reino de Dios* (1915; Eng. tr., *The Kingdom of God*, 1923) traces the career of a nun from youth to old age and offers a fine role for a character actress. It was performed in London in 1927. Ethel Barrymore starred in the 1928 New York production, which inaugurated the theater named for her. *Sueño de una noche de agosto* (1918; Eng. tr., *The Romantic Young Lady*, 1923) is a typically pleasant Martínez Sierra production, with a romantic heroine, a sophisticated novelist-hero, a sprightly thrice-married grandmother, and amusing situations and dialogue. *Triángulo* (1930; Triangle) presents a man whose supposedly drowned first wife returns after he has married a second. He loves them both equally. Because there is no solution to his dilemma, after the curtain falls at the end of the play, the husband escapes into the audience, turning from protagonist into spectator.

These plays are fairly representative of the several score turned out by Martínez Sierra in intervals between managing the Eslava Theater, running the Renacimiento publishing house (later the Biblioteca Estrella), and writing poems, novels, short stories, and essays. His nondramatic works fills more than 40 volumes. Martínez Sierra also translated or adapted five volumes of Maeterlinck's plays, Shakespeare, Carlo Goldoni, Alexandre Dumas fils, Eugène BRIEUX, Bjørnstjerne BJØRNSON, Henrik IBSEN, Charles Dickens, James M. Barrie, and George Bernard Shaw. In his literary work, he had considerable collaboration from his distinguished wife, Doña María de la O. Lejárraga (1874–1974). Many critics have attributed to her influence the definitely feminine and feminist tone of his productions. Like Jacinto BENAVENTE, Martínez Sierra was cosmopolitan in his interests and usually presented the upper strata of Madrid society. His characters are plausible, his dialogue is always sprightly, and his dramatic technique is excellent. His very considerable success on the stage was further assured by the talented first lady of his theater company, Doña Catalina Bárcena.

See: M. Martínez Sierra, *Gregorio y yo* (1953); R. Gullón, *Relaciones amistosas y literarias entre Juan Ramón Jiménez y los Martínez Sierra* (1961); P. W. O'Connor, *Gregorio and María Martínez Sierra* (1977).

N.B.A. rev. P.W.O'C.

Martín Gaite, Carmen (1925–), Spanish novelist, short-story writer, and essayist, was born in Salamanca. A doctor in philosophy and letters, she is married to novelist Rafael SÁNCHEZ FERLOSIO. Martín Gaite's *El balneario* (1954; The Spa), is a collection of short stories in which she treats the obsessions of a spinster with sensibility and precision of expression. The problematic world of a group of unmarried women in a provincial town of Castile is depicted in her first novel, *Entre visillos* (1957; Behind Window Curtains) whereas *Ritmo lento* (1962; Slow Rhythm) deals with society's condemnation of a nonconformist. *Retahílas* (1974; Thread of Discourse) consists of a dialogue between an aunt and her nephew during a single night; the past that prevented them from establishing any kind of communication is counterbalanced by a dialogue that functions as an emotional discourse. *Fragmentos de interior* (1976) is the story of one woman's inability to be integrated into the world of Madrid's upper bourgeoisie. The use of vivid language drawn from different social strata illuminates many degrees of social alienation as well as the novelist's literary skill. In *El cuarto de atrás* (1978; The Back Room), dialogue is again the literary instrument that serves to recreate, through historical and imaginary situations, the traumatic experience of a woman whose life spans the years of the Francisco Franco regime. Martín Gaite's social concern is expressed in this plain but effective use of language combined with her feminine aesthetic sensibility.

See: G. Sobejano, *Novela española de nuestro tiempo* (1975), pp. 493–502.   J.O.

Martín Recuerda, José (1925–), Spanish dramatist, was born in Granada. He is associated with the realistic generation of social dramatists who drew attention to a variety of Spain's problems during the dictatorship of Francisco Franco (1939–75). Martín Recuerda's theater can be divided into two periods, the first of which extends from 1954 to 1959 and includes *La llanura* (1954; The Plain). *El payaso y los pueblos del sur* (1956; The Clown and the Villages of the South), winner of the Lope de Vega Prize, and *El teatrito de Don Ramón* (1959; The Little Theatre of Don Ramón). In these early works, the protagonists, victims of some form of social injustice, agonize and seethe in frustration but fail to rebel. A statement made by Martín Recuerda after the performance of *El teatrito* makes the transition between periods clear: "One must take risks. I promised myself that my characters would always revolt, always listen to their consciences, would scream and never let themselves be defeated; the Spaniard needs strife, passion, action, rebellion, consolation, affection, and especially not to die in his own misery." The second period, which includes the more successful plays, shows cruel oppression as well as open opposition to the established order. The work that begins the cycle, *Los salvajes en Puente San Gil* (1963; The Savages of San Gil Bridge), later made into a movie, portrays a group of puritanical older women who successfully and savagely block the performance in their village of a musical review involving scantily clad chorus girls. The attitude of the women, representative of a tyrannical, repressed Spain, contrasts with and explains the sexual desperation of the village men, who break down the doors of the theater in search of all the actresses. In this play, the author gives the public all he had promised in 1959. This and subsequent plays display a special fury reminiscent of Ramón del VALLE-INCLÁN and not found in other writers of the realistic generation with the possible exception of José María RODRÍGUEZ MÉNDEZ. *Como las secas cañas del camino* (1965: Like the Dry Reeds along the Road) concerns a new teacher in an Andalusian village who loses her position because of a misunderstood gesture of affection to a student and the gossip this occasions. The old women of the village, again symbolic of a cruel, inquisitorial Spain, stone the teacher as she leaves. In *Las arrecogías del Beaterio de Santa María Egipcíaca* (1974; The Prisoners of the Lay Sisters of Saint Mary), written in 1970 but forbidden by censorship at that time, Martín Recuerda recreates the Granadine heroine, Mariana Pineda, who was executed in the 19th century by a repressive Spanish government for embroidering a republican flag. This Mariana, unlike Federico GARCÍA LORCA's *Mariana Pineda* (1927), is a political revolutionary destroyed by a system with parallels in contemporary Spain. With an elaborate staging by a first-rate director, Adolfo Marsillach, *Las arrecogías* made a bid for amnesty for political prisoners—a timely subject in 1976—and enjoyed considerable success in Madrid and on tour.

Martín Recuerda is sometimes compared to García Lorca. They share a common origin (Granada) and a common font of inspiration, and both use Andalusian settings. Both show a preference for female protagonists, attack tyranny and hypocrisy, and portray much frustration. García Lorca tends to be poetic and subtle, while Martín Recuerda is openly critical and violent. Martín Recuerda won his second Lope de Vega Prize in 1976 for *El engañao* (The Deceived). Currently he is a professor of theater arts at the University of Salamanca.

See: F. Ruiz Ramón, *Historia del teatro español: siglo xx* (1975), pp. 502–9.   P.W.O'C.

Martín-Santos, Luis (1924–64), Spanish novelist, was born in Larache, Morocco. He studied medicine in Salamanca, Madrid, and Heidelberg, and practiced psychiatry in San Sebastián, where he was killed in an automobile accident at the age of 40. His first writings are studies in philosophy and psychology.

His only full-length novel, *Tiempo de silencio* (1962; Eng. tr., *Time of Silence*, 1965), represents a radical break with the conventions of the straightforward descriptive narrative then prevalent in Spanish fiction. The author's verbal and stylistic virtuosity is reminiscent of James Joyce's *Ulysses*. His literary method is based on what the writer himself called "dialectical realism," through which the antithesis between subjectivism and objectivism is overcome. *Tiempo de silencio,* based on the novelist's own social and moral vision, deals with the protagonist Pedro's painful search for professional and ethical goals, which is ultimately defeated by the social environment. This novel is also a psychoanalytical and devastatingly satirical dissection of the submissive society of post-Civil War Spain. Because of its stylistic and thematic richness, *Tiempo de silencio* is one of the most innovative and influential works of contemporary Spanish fiction.

Some of Martín-Santos's short stories and unpublished material have been collected in *Apólogos* (1970; Apologues), and an incomplete novel, *Tiempo de destrucción* (1975; Time of Destruction), has been carefully edited by José Carlos Mainer. This second novel, whose protagonist resembles Pedro of *Tiempo de silencio,* is full of literary allusions and provides valuable material for speculation about the creative process.

See: J. C. Curutchet, "Luis Martín Santos, el fundador," *CRI* 17 and 18 (1968): 3–18 and 3–15 respectively; J. Ortega, "La sociedad española contemporánea en *Tiempo de silencio,*" *Symposium* 22 (1968): 256–60; A. Rey, *Construcción y sentido de Tiempo de silencio* (1977).
                                                                J.O.

Martinson, Harry Edmund (1904–78), Swedish poet, novelist, essayist, and dramatist, was born and grew up at Jämshög, in the province of Blekinge. He was the son of a sea captain and a woman who, after her husband's death in 1910, headed for California, leaving her children to public welfare. After spending humiliating years with his guardians, Harry Martinson ran away to sea at the age of 14 and later, from 1920 to 1927, shipped out 14 times, serving as a "deckhand, stoker, coaltrimmer, and all-round kitchen menace." At times he bummed his way "for thousands of miles, especially in India, on the European continent, and in the Americas." Having acquired tuberculosis at sea, he came ashore for good and his disease was arrested. Martinson made use of his experiences in his writings. His literary debut in *Spökskepp* (1929; Spook Ship) was heavily influenced by Rudyard Kipling, Gustaf FRÖDING, and Dan ANDERSSON. In 1929 he married the outstanding proletarian writer Moa MARTINSON. With his next books of poetry, *Nomad* (1931) and *Natur* (1934), Martinson established himself as a poet in his own right, albeit, as Ingvar Holm and Kjell Espmark have shown, he was influenced by such varied writers as Kipling, Walt Whitman, Carl Sandburg, Edgar Lee Masters, and their Swedish heir, Artur LUNDKVIST. (*see* SWEDISH LITERATURE).

Mixing poetry and philosophy with exotic reportage, Martinson received great popular acclaim from his "travelogues," *Resor utan mål* (1932, Travels without Destination) and *Kap Farväl* (1933; Eng. tr., *Cape Farewell,* 1934), in which he elaborated upon his years at sea. Of even greater appeal to the general reading audience was his autobiography, *Nässlorna blomma* (1935; Eng. tr., *Flowering Nettle,* 1936), in which he described his colorful life as a runaway orphan. And finally, the next year, came *Vägen ut* (1936; The Way Out), describing his adolescence.

Thus, the first phase of Martinson's authorship is oriented toward the telling and analysis of firsthand personal experiences. His books of essays, *Svärmare och harkrank* (1937; Sphinx Moth and Daddy Longlegs), *Midsommardalen* (1938; The Midsummer Valley), and *Det enkla och det svåra* (1939; The Simple and the Difficult), indicate a great change in his position. Earlier in the 1930s he had widened his horizon to adopt a broadly defined humanistic pursuit of culture. In accord with his new guidelines, he abandoned private symbolism and experience for the largest theme of all, nature. In these essays he allied himself with a fine Swedish tradition that began even before the time of Linnæus. From a few square feet of nature that Martinson studies, researches, observes, and describes, he finds his way to broad cultural perspectives and to a magnanimous philosophy of life. In his later writings, such as *Utsikt från en grästuva* (1963; View from a Tussock), the author has still managed to retain the larger, even cosmic perspectives.

In Martinson's first proper novel, *Den förlorade jaguaren* (1941; The Lost Jaguar) ("written in too great haste"), he satirized the hyperefficiency of contemporary times. War he saw as a result of the "power-civilization" created by the totalitarian states, which he had opposed in his essays. When the first Finno-Russian War broke out, Martinson volunteered on Finland's side (he had visited the Soviet Union in 1934 and was on the whole unhappy with what he saw there), and in 1940 he published *Verklighet till döds* (Reality unto Death) about his war experiences. His health had understandably deteriorated during his years at sea, and his winter in Finland was followed by a few years of illness and silence.

Martinson returned with a collection of poems, *Passad* (1945; Trade Winds), dedicated to the wife he had married in 1942, Ingrid, née Lindcrantz. Here he had abandoned traveling in an outward sense; instead he traveled inwardly, seeking the ties between the extrovert traveler, the "World Nomad," and the brooding introvert. The former sailor Martinson employed the concept of "trade wind" as a unifying symbol. "There exists something universally compelling which still cannot be materialized. The wind is a good symbol of this, and among the winds the trade wind is the best symbol of human reasonableness and human desire for airing things. It symbolizes a mental set which takes the sea atmosphere for a model, with its openness uniting with the eye's openness for new vistas and new lands." (Harry Martinson, in *Vänkritik*, 1959; Criticism among Friends). The poet Martinson placed his faith for the future in a combination of Western humanism and a personally conceived taoist mysticism.

Martinson's philosophical bent and his imaginative coinage of new words (see his travelogues) were much in evidence in his "novel" *Vägen till Klockrike* (1948; Eng. tr., *The Road*, 1955). The scene of the book is southern Sweden in 1898 and up to the time of the general strike in 1909, that is, a period of enormous social and economic upheaval in the wake of industrialization and the exploitation that went along with it, a time when solutions still might work and it was still possible to reverse the tide of ecological insanity. The main character, Bolle, is a tramp (like his philosophical vagrant companions) and a cigar roller by trade. He is a self-styled individualist, a down-home philosopher who considers work in a noisy, ugly machine shop to be demeaning. Like many of his fellow anarchist-tramps, he "feels hatred for work since it is harnessed to death's work and is furthering the forces of destruction." In *The Road* Martinson created a genre of his own, neither autobiography nor novel proper, for he had "done away with plot and strictly individualized people, as well as home regions and cities." (K. Jaensson, *DN* 12/14, 1948).

In 1949, Martinson became the first autodidact to be elected to the Swedish Academy, and he received an honorary doctorate at the University of Göteborg in 1954. His epic poem *Aniara* (1956; Eng. adaptation, 1963) established Martinson as the first poet of the space age, and later the work was translated into a thrilling space opera by Karl-Birger Blomdahl (Columbia M2S902). The epic poetic cycle *Aniara*, comprising 103 cantos, tells of a giant spaceship hurtling through the universe on an irreversible journey with 8,000 evacuees on board, after technological man has made the earth uninhabitable. *Aniara* deals with a journey into outer space, and it is thought to occur in a very distant future when "the possibilities of imagination" have been neglected and rejected. Launched a few years before the first satellites, *Aniara* "contains essential extracts from modern thought in the natural sciences, but rendered naturally in a supremely personal, or, if you like, subjective fashion" (G. Quarnström). "If, in the poetry of the past, space was endless, it was a beneficient infinity, related to God's eternity. In our time, in the era of cosmonauts, space, with its planets, has come to mean extreme emptiness and hostility to life" (S. Landquist, 1969). This concept of space thus gives the poet the opportunity to expose humanity's historical grounds for consolation and to put them to the test, as it were.

Martinson's other books of poetry appeared under the titles *Cikada* (1953), *Gräsen i Thule* (1958; The Grasses in Thule), and *Vagnen* (1960; referring to "the carriage" and "the car"), all of which reflect to poet's growing alienation from the modern world. As the reception of *Vagnen* was mixed, Martinson vowed to publish no more poetry. However, in 1971 he published the award-winning *Dikter om mörker och ljus* (Poems about Darkness and Light) and *Tuvor* (1973; Tussocks), which apostrophizes trees like pine, birch, sallows, alder trees, but especially the dark spruce tree. *Tuvor* is basically nature observed,

approvingly, without the interference of human greed or exploitation. Martinson here connects with the religion he had endorsed some 30 years earlier. In 1974, Martinson shared the Nobel Prize for Literature with Eyvind JOHNSON. A selection of Martinson's posthumous poetry, *Längs ekots stigar* (Along the Paths of the Echo) appeared in 1978. *Friends, You Drank Some Darkness* (1975), ed. and tr. by R. Bly, includes a selection of Martinson's poems.

See: I. Holm, *Harry Martinson, Myter, målningar, motiv* (1960, 1974); E. O. Johannesson, "Aniara: Poetry and the Poet in the Modern World," *SS* (November 1960): 360–71; J. Wrede, *Sången om Aniara: studier i Harry Martinsons tankevärld* (1965); B. Steene, "The Role of the Mima: A Note on Martinson's Aniara," in *H. G. Leach Festschrift* (1965); K. Espmark, *Harry Martinson erövrar sitt språk* (1970); L. Sjöberg, "Harry Martinson: Writer in Quest of Harmony," *ASR* 60, no. 4 (1972): 360–71, and "Harry Martinson: From Vagabond to Space Explorer," *BA* 48, no. 3 (1974): 476–85; G. Tideström, *Ombord på Aniara: en studie i Harry Martinsons rymdepos* (1975).

L.S.

Martinson, Moa (1890–1964), Swedish novelist and poet, was born in Norrköping. She wrote political articles in the labor press before she turned to fiction. In 1929 she married Harry MARTINSON. Her novels, containing many autobiographical elements, describe, sometimes with brutal realism, the hardship of working-class women, the only stable factor in a world of drinking husbands and too many children to raise on a mere pittance. A sequence of three novels beginning with *Mor gifter sig* (1936; Mother Gets Married) is regarded as her best work. In *Den osynlige älskaren* (1943; The Invisible Lover) she portrayed a young woman who dreams romantically about an ideal man while she is forced to frigidity by a naively brutal husband and the fear of bearing more children than their resources can support. Managing to raise the family from poverty to a sort of material security, she earns the respect of everybody. Martinson also wrote novels with historical settings, the best perhaps being *Drottning Grågyllen* (1937; Queen Grågyllen). She is praised for her portraits of proletarian women, who in their struggle against a paternalistic system both within the family and in society reflect the condition of all women regardless of class.

See: M. Stiernstedt, *Moa Martinson* (1946); A. Gustafson, *A History of Swedish Literature* (1961), pp. 522–23; E. Hj. Linder, *Ny Illustrerad Svensk Litteraturhistoria*, vol. 5 (1966), pp. 576–83; G. Brandell, *Svensk litteratur 1870–1970*, vol. 2 (1975), pp. 122–23.   T.L.

Martynov, Leonid Nikolayevich (1905–), Russian poet, was born in Omsk. He has been greatly influenced by the futurists Vladimir MAYAKOVSKY and Nikolay ASEYEV as well as by Boris PASTERNAK, and has also assimilated the rich tradition of Russian folklore into his semiallegorical poetry. The son of a Siberian railroad worker, Martynov had little opportunity for formal study but started writing and publishing poetry at an early age. At the end of the 1920s and the beginning of the 1930s he traveled widely as a journalist in Siberia and Turkey. His *Gruby korm* (1930; Crude Food) is a collection of reports from this period. A 1939 volume of Martynov's narrative poems caused little stir, but after World War II he was condemned by the increasingly repressive regime as "apolitical" and "timeless"—that is, insufficiently concerned with immediate political objectives. In 1945 he published the long poem *Lukomorye* (Cove) on the traditional theme of the search for a long lost fairy-tale land. This poem represents a kind of culmination of Martynov's early explorations of Siberian remoteness, its history, its myth, and its present-day reality. He was not published again until a new volume of poetry appeared in 1955, after Iosif Stalin's death. Since then this contemplative and staunchly independent poet has been accorded national recognition, winning the Gorky Prize in 1966 for his volume *Pervorodstvo* (1965; Primogeniture) and the State Prize bf the USSR in 1974. A two-volume collection of his poetry was published in 1965. Martynov's writing is rich in image and highly allegorical and yet colloquial and linguistically lucid. D.T.W.

Masaryk, Tomáš Garrigue (1850–1937), Czech statesman, philosopher, and critic, was a national leader and the first president of Czechoslovakia (1918–35). He was born in the Moravian city of Hondonín. Masaryk played a significant part in the evolution of Czech ideas on philosophical and sociological subjects and must be included in any consideration of Czech literature. He was an important and highly influential critic of the history of his country and of its writers, turning the Czechs away from romantic nationalism and giving them a new ideology with roots in their own past. Masaryk assigned his nation a special role in the realization of a high idea of humanity. In books such as *Česká otázka* (1895; Eng. tr., *The Meaning of Czech History*, 1973), *Jan Hus* (1896), and *Karel Havlíček* (1896), he expounded a whole philosophy of Czech history: the Hussite period appears as the summit of Czech history, and the Bohemian Brethren are presented as the finest embodiment of the ideal of humanity. To Masaryk, the Czech national revival seemed a direct continuation of the Czech Reformation, and the modern Czech democracy that he and his followers advocated was merely a fulfillment of the early promises of the Czech tradition. These views also imply a conception of Czech literary history in which the ideological and theological elements are of particular importance.

Masaryk began to discuss literature in his early writings, attacking the authenticity of the so-called Old Czech Manuscripts, which were actually produced in the early 19th century by Václav Hanka and his associates. He expounded his own literary views in a little pamphlet, *O studiu básnických děl* (1884; On the Study of Poetry), and in a wider context in *Moderní člověk a náboženství* (1898; Modern Man and Religion), as well as in his many studies of intellectual history, the most important of which is *Rusko a Evropa* (2 vols., 1913; Eng. tr., *The Spirit of Russia*; the revised English edition in 3 vols. 1961–67, includes his study on Fyodor DOSTOYEVSKY, never published in Czech). Masaryk was first of all a moralist, intensely preoccupied with the ethical and social implications of literature. He sharply criticized romanticism, subjectivism, and titanism wherever he found them: in Goethe's *Faust*, and in works by Friedrich NIETZSCHE and Alfred de Musset, Emile ZOLA and Arne GARBORG. He shocked his contemporaries by his lack of reverence for great names and in particular by his merciless analysis of the intellectual shoddiness of a drama and a poem by his celebrated compatriot, Jaroslav Vrchlický. Although fascinated, he was ultimately repelled by Dostoyevsky, who seemed to him the reductio ad absurdum of romanticism and mysticism. He disliked French romanticism, in which he saw only the symptoms of decadence. But he never wearied of praising the sanity, humanity, and Protestant Christianity of the English tradition. Obviously, Masaryk had little interest in English poetry, and he severely criticized Lord Byron as a specimen of romantic titanism. He was repelled by novelists such as James

Joyce and George Moore, who seemed to him decadent and false. But he loved the main tradition of the English novel from Daniel Defoe to H. G. Wells, and he was particularly appreciative of women writers like Charlotte and Emily Brontë and Elizabeth Barrett Browning. Clearly, Masaryk was above all a general critic largely interested in literature as a mirror of society. His rigid moralism and his lack of interest in problems of form frequently led him astray, but the very bluntness with which he expounded his antiromantic point of view profoundly influenced 20th-century Czech literary criticism. Whatever may be said about certain deficiencies of Masaryk's literary insight, he was in criticism as elsewhere a leader and a liberator.

See: biographies by J. Herben, 3 vols. (1926–27), K. Čapek, 3 vols. (1928–35; Eng. tr., *President Masaryk Tells His Story*, 1934; *Masaryk on Thought and Life*, 1938), Z. Nejedlý, 5 vols. (1930–37), and P. Selver (1940). Also J. L. Hromádka, *Masaryk* (1930); articles in the *Festschrift Th. G. Masaryk zum 80. Geburtstag* (1930); W. P. Warren, *Masaryk's Democracy* (1941); R. Wellek, "Masaryk's Philosophy," in *Essays on Czech Literature* (1963), pp. 62–70; M. Machovec, *Thomas G. Masaryk* (1969); R. Wellek, Introduction to T. G. Masaryk, *The Meaning of Czech History* (1973). R.W.

Massis, Henri (1886–1970), French critic and essayist, was born and educated in Paris. He attended the Lycée Henri IV, where he came under the spell of ALAIN, the free-lance professor of philosophy who exercised a powerful influence upon many students of his generation. Although not exactly a skeptic, Alain delighted in exploding the doctrines and ideas that his students had accepted during their earlier school days; they generally left his courses without any personal philosophical convictions, but ready to let themselves be carried away by new enthusiasms. So it happened that the very young and very intelligent Massis began by airing his views on Emile ZOLA in *Comment Zola composait ses romans* (1906; How Zola Composed His Novels). He then became interested in Anatole FRANCE in *Le Puits de Pyrrhon* (1906; The Well of Pyrrhon) and a little later turned his attention to Maurice BARRÈS in *La Pensée de Barrès* (1908; The Thought of Barrès). These fugitive little books were soon forgotten when he became one of the editors of *Opinion*, which was, for a time after the storm raised by the Dreyfus Affair, the alert organ of young men in search of new ideas. It was in *Opinion* that Massis and Alfred de Tarde, jointly using the pseudonym Agathon, wrote a series of articles that were reissued in book form in 1911 under the title *L'Esprit de la Nouvelle Sorbonne: La Crise de la culture classique, la crise du français* (The Spirit of the New Sorbonne: The Crisis in Classic Culture, The Crisis in French). Those sensational articles were savage attacks upon Gustave Lanson and others who, according to the authors, had replaced the old philosophical appreciation and criticism by an academic, dry-as-dust method imported from Germany. That German method, it may be remarked, went back to Hippolyte Taine and Ernest Renan. In 1913 there were new attacks in *Les Jeunes Gens d'aujourd'hui* (The Young People of Today).

World War I gave the ardent young protagonist of purely French traditions further occasions to combat German methods and ideas, this time from a political angle. His articles and books at this period breathe an ardent patriotism. *Le Sacrifice: Impressions de guerre* (1914–16; The Sacrifice: Impressions of War) was officially praised by the Académie Française, and Massis wrote *La Vie d'Ernest Psichari* (1916; The Life of Ernest PSICHARI), a moving book on his personal friend, the author of *Le*

Centurion and Renan's grandson, who had died in action. Massis also wrote a pamphlet attacking Romain ROLLAND, *Romain Rolland contre la France* (1915; Romain Rolland against France).

Shortly afterwards, Massis allied himself momentarily with the neo-Thomist movement, seeming to find in Jacques MARITAIN the standard by which to judge—more often to condemn—authors who were frequently under discussion at that time: Renan, Rémy de GOURMONT, André GIDE, Georges DUHAMEL, and Julien BENDA. His ever impassioned and dogmatic pronouncements of that period were published in two volumes, *Jugements* (1923–24). In 1920 he founded with Jacques Bainville the *Revue universelle*, the nationalistic, Catholic, and monarchist fortnightly published by Larousse until 1937.

In *La Défense de l'Occident* (1925; Eng. tr., *Defense of the West*, 1928), Massis tried to give a sort of philosophical unity to all his more recent writings. With utter conviction he declared that the French nation alone is capable of giving the world a civilization worthy of the name, that of "the Occident," while under the designation "the Orient" he classes all that is not what he terms the "Latin inheritance." The Orient includes not only Asia and its peoples (who constitute the yellow peril), but also the Turks and the Russians. According to him, it was the Reformation that broke the back of Latin Europe and threw the "white man" into obscurity. What is more, he argued, the Turks and the Eastern powers have found an accomplice in a Germany obsessed by her disaster of 1918. The enemy host is Johann Fichte, Oswald Spengler, Eduard KEYSERLING, Rudolf Steiner, and *tutti quanti*, with whom he associates Mahatma Gandhi, Rabindranath Tagore, Arthur Gobineau, Immanuel Kant, and even Ernest Seillière and a formidable array of others, with whom the reader is supposed to believe that the author himself is familiar. All this was to arouse France from her inertia. The Académie Française awarded him the Grand Prix de Littérature for the total of his publications.

In spite of the enormous output of his own books and articles, Massis found time to publish an important edition of Pascal (1926). In 1937 appeared his *Le Drame de Proust* (The Drama of Marcel PROUST) and *L'Honneur de servir* (The Honor of Serving), wherein he expresses the hope that a revival of 13th-century France will blot out the memory of the France of Renan and of Anatole France. In 1940 he once more expressed his detestation of the Orient, of Germany, and of Gobineau in a series of essays entitled *La Guerre de Trente Ans: destin d'un âge, 1904–1939* (The Thirty Years War: Destiny of an Age). Later in that same year Massis lost no time in turning "collaborationist" (see *Les Idées restent* [1941; The Ideas Remain]). After the war, however, he resumed his career as a writer, publishing *Visage des idées* (1959; The Face of the Ideas) and *De l'homme à Dieu* (1961; From Man to God). In spite of his rightist ideas (or perhaps by that time because of them) he was elected to the Académie Française in 1961. Like so many authors, Massis finished with memoirs, *Au long d'une vie* (1967; In the Course of a Life), as well as studies of the leading rightist figures: *Charles Maurras et notre temps* (1951; Charles MAURRAS and Our Time), *Barrès et nous* (1962; Barrès and Us), and *Le Souvenir de Robert Brasillach* (1963; The Memory of Robert BRASILLACH).

See: P. Moreau, "Henri Massis," in *Le Victorieux XXᵉ Siècle* (1925). A.Sc. rev. D.W.A.

Mastronardi, Lucio (1930–79), Italian novelist, was born in Vigevano, near Milan. Vigevano's thriving shoe industry and enterprising inhabitants form the nucleus of his work. *Il calzolaio di Vigevano* (1962; The Shoemaker of Vigevano), the earliest installment of what might be called a trilogy about provincial life in the industrialized north, was first published in 1959 in Elio VITTORINI's avant-garde review *Il menabò*. A novel with a heavy infusion of Milanese dialect, this work adheres to the type of linguistic experimentation through which Carlo Emilio GADDA and Pier Paolo PASOLINI sought to capture the immediacy and pristine flavor of the spoken language. The story of a small entrepreneur who rises from a job as a worker in a shoe factory to becoming its co-owner serves as a pretext to underline the mimetic function of the dialect. In *Il maestro di Vigevano* (1962; The Schoolteacher of Vigevano), Mastronardi's own experiences as a schoolteacher, filtered through a mordant satire often laced with humor, are used to expose the pettiness, rigid hierarchy, and formalistic pedagogy of elementary education. The dreary atmosphere of a small town, with its monotonous life and puppetlike parade of familiar faces, serves as background for the psychological portrait of the main character, a middle-aged schoolteacher. The substance of the book lies in the revelation of the protagonist's sterile, purposeless existence, sublimated by absurd erotic fixations and surrealistic daydreams. *Il meridionale di Vigevano* (1964; A Southerner in Vigevano) again employs the social milieu and local dialect of *Il calzolaio*, but a discordant mixture of Milanese and Neapolitan dialects is woven into the dialogue. The main character of this work, a southern bureaucrat, is, much like Mastronardi's schoolteacher, an introverted, colorless figure. His quest for social acceptance meets with deep-seated prejudice against southern Italians.

Mastronardi's next work, *A casa tua ridono* (1971; Your Own Family Is Laughing at You), with its fragmented narrative, is more attuned to the trends of new avant-garde prose fiction. Superseding the story is a steady, albeit oblique, effort to delve into the consciousness of the main character and to highlight those incidents that define his distorted psyche.

See: G. Bàrberi-Squarotti, in *Poesia e narrativa del secondo Novecento* (1961); G. Pullini, in *Volti e risvolti del romanzo italiano contemporaneo* (1971). A.Pal.

Matoš, Antun Gustav (1873–1914), Croatian poet, short-story writer, essayist, and critic, was born in Tovarnik. He is considered the central figure in Croatian letters before 1914. Matoš attended secondary school in Zagreb and went to Vienna in 1891 to study veterinary medicine. When he was drafted into the army, Matoš deserted. Escaping to Belgrade in 1894, he remained there for three years before going to Western Europe, where he spent about a year in Geneva and five years in Paris. His stay in the French capital was of great importance for his intellectual development. The works of Charles BAUDELAIRE and Paul VERLAINE aroused his enthusiasm, and under their influence he overemphasized aesthetics and the formal aspects of art. He later adopted, to some degree, the theoretical and political ideas of Stendhal and Maurice BARRÈS. After returning to Belgrade in 1904, Matoš visited Croatia illegally several times before being granted amnesty in 1908 and finally settling in Zagreb. In poor health, he traveled to Italy in 1911 and 1913, seeking the benefits of the sunnier climate. He died in Zagreb from throat cancer.

Matoš's first works are short stories and prose sketches collected in *Iverje* (1899; Chips), *Novo iverje* (1900; New Chips), and *Umorne priče* (1909; Weary Tales). Although he later proved to be a better writer in other genres, Matoš never abandoned the short story. His stories can be divided into two groups: those concerned with patriotic themes and those dealing with the neurotic intellectual.

The macabre tales of the second group, betraying the influence of Edgar Allan Poe, have vivid and interesting descriptions but unconvincing plots. In spite of their shortcomings, however, they were a refreshing novelty in Croatian prose at the turn of the century.

Matoš's decisive influence on the development of Croatian literature is primarily the result of his volumes of essays, reviews, feuilletons, and travelogues. The most important include *Ogledi* (1905; Essays), *Vidici i putovi* (1907; Perspectives and Paths), *Naši ljudi i krajevi* (1910; Our Folk and Regions), and *Pečalba* (1913; Migrant Labor). His sound knowledge of Western and southern Slavic literatures, his deep feeling for musicality in verse, his independent and uncompromising spirit, and his militant support of various worthy causes all made Matoš the leading figure among the Zagreb literati. Some of his weaknesses are by now obvious, yet he nevertheless remains one of the most stimulating Croatian critics. Although his highly original style is sometimes more fascinating than his views, Matoš was a sincere, passionate thinker.

Matoš also wrote travelogues in which he described superbly the uniqueness and charm of renowned European cities (Paris, Geneva, Florence, Rome, and Venice). Certain passages of these books reveal that they are obviously the work of a poet well versed in history and art. Here Matoš demonstrates his sensitivity to the harmony existing between nature and edifices: the aging buildings like their former masters, whisper a lament of bygone glories.

For many years, Matoš earned his living in part as a cellist in various orchestras. After 1906, when his right hand had grown helplessly stiff, he turned to writing poetry. His verse was collected in *Pjesme* (Poems) in 1923 and republished several times. The most accurate edition, with many valuable comments, was prepared by Dragutin TADIJANOVIĆ. In his poetry, Matoš expressed his feelings of disillusionment, unhappy love, loneliness, and melancholy, as well as his patriotic sentiments (he was an ardent disciple of Ante Starčević, the Croatian nationalist leader). In the political songs, he touched upon the glory and misery of the Croatian past, the political tyranny exercised mostly by foreigners, the exploitation of the small farmer who was obliged to emigrate, the beautiful Croatian scenery, and his deep conviction that Croatia would survive in the hearts of its people.

See: A. Barac, "Matoševa lirika," *Savremenik* 10 (1919): 467–75; Š. Vučetić, "Matoš pripovjedač," *Rep* 1 (1951): 86–92; M. Matković, "A. G. Matoš kao kritičar," *Rep* 11–12 (1951): 832–44; A. Kadić, "Današnje značenje A. G. Matoša," *Hrvatska revija* 2 (1973): 191–212.

A.K.

Matute, Ana María (1926–), Spanish novelist and short story writer, was born in Barcelona and obtained her high school diploma after studies there and in Madrid. The Civil War broke out when she was 10 years of age, and the personal trauma this caused is the recurrent theme of her narrative.

Matute's first novel is a family chronicle called *Los Abel* (1948; The Abels). Inspired by the story of Cain and Abel, this work deals with the loss of innocence in childhood and adolescence. Hatred between two stepbrothers is also the leitmotif of *Fiesta al noroeste* (1953; Festivity in the Northwest), while *Los hijos muertos* (1958; Eng. tr., *The Lost Children*, 1965) is a pessimistic view of alienation and discontent brought about by the Civil War and its aftermath.

Matute's several books of short stories, *El tiempo* (1951; Time), *Los niños tontos* (1956; Eng. tr., *The Fool-*ish Children*, 1961), and *Tres y un sueño* (1961); Three and a Dream), depict the lonely and alienated world of childhood and adolescence.

Her trilogy *"The Merchants"*—*Primera memoria* (1959; Eng. tr., *Awakening*, 1963), *La Trampa* (1969; The Pitfall), and *Los soldados lloran de noche* (1964; Soldiers Cry at Night)—is perhaps the best example of this writer's novelistic art. It describes the psychological crises of a young girl from the beginning of the Civil War to the 1960s. *Primera memoria*, the best of the three, is a delicate and lyrical evocation of the solitude experienced by an orphan in a morally disintegrated world.

Some of Matute's later works, such as *La torre vigía* (1971; The Watchtower), show the writer to be in a new experimental phase without having abandoned the themes associated with her previous publications: solitude, alienation, and the futility of life.

What distinguishes Matute's fiction are her sensitive personal, and poetic characterizations, especially of children and women.

See: M. Jones, *The Literary World of Ana María Matute* (1970); J. Díaz, *Ana María Matute* (1971); J. Ortega, "La frustración femenina en *Los Mercaderes* de A. M. Matute," *Hispano* 54 (1975): pp 31–8.   J.O.

Matveyeva, Novella Nikolayevna (1934–), Russian poet, was born in Pushkin. Like Bulat OKUDZHAVA, she is known also for her songs, which she performs to her own guitar accompaniment. Physically handicapped, Matveyeva studied by correspondence at the Gorky Literary Institute and her first collection of poems, *Lirika*, appeared in 1961. Other volumes of poetry followed, including *Korablik* (1963; The Little Boat) and *Dusha veshchey* (1966; The Soul of Things). Matveyeva is unusual among Soviet artists for the element of almost childlike fantasy and the dreamlike atmosphere that often pervade her work. Her language is strongly metaphorical and avoids the familiar and worn; it is sensuous and resonant in a way that is sometimes reminiscent of Marina TSVETAYEVA. Her poetry has a visionary quality and often speaks on an allegorical level. A sharper note does occasionally enter her work, however, such as when she comments on the degradation of women, on the universal human tendency to gossip about or inform upon others, or on the suppression of nonconformity. The sensuousness of Matveyeva's language, together with an ironic tone that reaches beneath the surface, makes hers a distinctive voice in comtemporary Soviet poetry.   D.T.W.

Maulnier, Thierry, pseud. of Jacques Talagrand (1909–), French essayist, literary critic, and playwright, was born in Alès. He was educated in Paris at the Ecole Normale Supérieure, where Robert BRASILLACH and Roger VAILLAND were his classmates and friends. After obtaining the *agrégation* in literature, Maulnier took up journalism and has, since 1930, been a frequent contributor to periodicals and the author of numerous monographs and pamphlets. Prior to World War II, he was associated with the ultraconservative group Action Française, and in a number of brilliantly written essays he has defended a rightist and Catholic ideal.

After the war, he and François MAURIAC, founded the magazine *La Table ronde*. Maulnier's political views do not intrude in his literary essays, however, unless very discreetly in the preference that he shows for works in the classical tradition and his indifference towards many moderns. His study of Racine (1934) is the work best known to students of literature. In emphasizing language rather than psychology, Maulnier presented an image of Racine that has only recently been superseded by the one offered by Roland BARTHES. The theater is Maulnier's particular area of competence. He has written several plays himself and made adaptations and translations, all distinguished for their literary style. He has also had a long career as a drama critic, notably for *Combat* and the *Revue de Paris*. In 1965 he was appointed to the program committee for French television. In whatever capacity, Maulnier conceives of the theater as a tribune or forum where ideas and doctrines can be discussed on a high level of seriousness.

Maulnier was awarded the Grand Prix de Littérature in 1959, and in 1964 he was elected to the Académie Française. He continues to write plays, essays, and articles on a variety of subjects. In recent years he has frequently contributed articles to *Le Figaro*.

See: J. Bersani et al., *La Littérature en France depuis 1945* (1970); *Dictionnaire de la littérature française contemporaine* (1966).   L.LeS.

Mauriac, Claude (1914-), French novelist and critic, was born in Paris. For years he felt so overshadowed by his father, François MAURIAC, that he confined himself to criticism, writing books on Marcel JOUHANDEAU, Honoré de Balzac, André MALRAUX, André BRETON, and Marcel PROUST; vivid personal reminiscences of André GIDE, Jean COCTEAU, and Charles de Gaulle (for whom he served as personal secretary from 1944 to 1949); essays on the cinema; and a weekly column of book reviews of the *Figaro littéraire*. With the publication of a perceptive and highly personalized appreciation of *L'Alittérature contemporaine* (1958; rev. 1969; Contemporary Nonliterature), Mauriac became one of the first to signal new tendencies in fiction.

Mauriac ultimately ventured into fiction with a group of experimental novels, of which *La Marquise sortit à cinq heures* (1961; The Marquise Went Out at Five) and *L'Agrandissement* (1963; The Enlargement) are the most original. He incorporated techniques of the "new novel" (*see* FRENCH LITERATURE): absence of plot, anonymity of character, preoccupation with spoken language, and a detective-story appeal to the reader's collaboration. The main work of his increasingly prolific career is the voluminous *Temps immobile* (1974-; Time Immobilized), an open-ended project based on the journal that he has kept since adolescence. Reflecting a Proustian obsession with time, "the only subject possible," the book that Mauriac calls the "novel" of his life is a cinematographic montage of crisscrossing journal entries, the random juxtaposition. of which appears to eradicate the passage of time by fusing past and present in an illusion of simultaneity. Mauriac's close association with the chief political and intellectual figures of his time makes his work a personal footnote to contemporary French history.

See: S. Johnston, "Structure in the Novels of Claude Mauriac," *FR* 38, no. 4 (February 1965): 451-58; R. Kanters, *L'Air des lettres* (1973), pp. 305-15.   G.R.B.

Mauriac, François (1885-1970), French novelist, was born in Bordeaux, the city in which most of his novels are set. Mauriac was the last of five children; his father died before he was two, and his mother gave him an austere, pious Catholic education. His own shy, anguished adolescence is often portrayed in his fiction. Like many of his characters, Mauriac moved from Bordeaux to Paris. He studied at the Ecole des Chartes, but he soon deserted history for the writing of poetry and fiction. He immersed himself in his favorite authors: Pascal, Racine, Maurice de Guérin (1810-39), Charles BAUDELAIRE, and Maurice BARRÈS (who first praised his young talent), then Paul CLAUDEL, André GIDE, and Marcel PROUST, although

Mauriac had reservations on the moral, or amoral, teachings of the last two. After serving in World War I, he devoted himself to his career as a novelist (he was never to be fully successful either as a poet or as a dramatist). Mauriac achieved early success and was elected to the Académie Française in 1933. He was awarded the Nobel Prize for Literature in 1952. Between Proust and Gide, some 15 years his elders, and André MALRAUX and Jean-Paul SARTRE, 15 or 20 years younger, Mauriac was the outstanding French novelist.

His early novels, while still strained in the depiction of contrasting characters impersonating diverse views of life, already reveal Mauriac's permanent themes: the turbid moods of adolescence, torn between manhood and regret for the child's purity, the insidious lure of the flesh and the delight of sin; the hatreds that tear families apart; the monstrous avidity and destructiveness of sex; and the ludicrous attachment of people to their possessions, especially to the vineyards and pine forests of southwestern France. In some of his novels, Mauriac presented an oversimplified view of human life, a conflict between the treacherous temptations of the flesh and the supreme temptation of God. In these books the characters, having plumbed the depths of misery in a godless world, are awakened to remorse and humility. In his more sophisticated novels such as *Genitrix* (1923; Eng. tr., *The Family*, 1950), *Le Désert de l'amour* (1925; Eng. tr., *The Desert of Love*, 1929), and *Thérèse Desqueyroux* (1927; Eng. tr., *Thérèse*, 1928), however, Mauriac resisted the temptation of converting his heroes and heroines. While his fiction always remains permeated by a Christian view of life, it neither simplifies reality as earlier Catholic novelists (notably Paul BOURGET) had been tempted to do, nor advocates religion as commendable for ethical, social, or political reasons. One of his novels, La Pharisienne (1941); Eng. tr., *A Woman of the Pharisees*, 1946), offers a pitiless delineation of a Catholic woman devoid of charity and, under the cover of her faith, greedy for control of creatures weaker than herself. Even when, as in *Le Nœud de vipères* (1932; Eng. tr., *Viper's Tangle*, 1933), the protagonist finally opens himself up to altruistic love, the total impact upon the reader is that of mutual suspicion, hatred, lust for revenge, and wounded pride in the members of a nominally Christian family all expert at inflicting wounds upon each other and upon themselves.

Mauriac insisted that an imaginative creator's concern should be to keep within his own limits and to depict the sort of universe that he knows best and that haunts him. The setting of Mauriac's fiction seldom varies: it is that of provincial life, in and around Bordeaux, hemmed in with all the constraints and taboos of the small city. The more adventurous characters eventually flee from the city that they simultaneously love and hate to Paris, where they attempt to lose themselves in greed, passion, or vice. The novels are brief and dense; their very feverishness, the burning intensity of the passions they depict, and their linear structure, eschewing both comic relief and episodic diversions, impose upon them a concentration reminiscent of Racinian tragedy. All takes place in a present enriched by the anticipations of a tragic denouement and, even more, by memories of past joys and sorrows crowding upon the present. Mauriac is a master in the expert use of the technique of reminiscence: characters afflicted with nostalgia, remorse, and regret for their lost innocence relive their past and relentlessly analyze themselves. At the same time, Mauriac's probing psychological novels are laid in a setting of nature (conjured up in the majesty of trees, the voluptuous fragrance of flowers, the changes of the seasons) that endows it with a poetic quality similar to that of Proust.

Mauriac remained a novelist ever open to the problems of his age: moral, political, aesthetic. Among the novelists of his age group, he alone was endowed with the gifts of a journalist, polemicist, and political commentator. His articles, written for the daily or the weekly press, were collected in successive volumes of his *Journal* from 1934 on, and then in *Block-Notes* which appeared in *Le Figaro* and *L'Express*. These publications supplemented several volumes of highly personal criticism, notably *Dieu et mammon* (1929; Eng. tr., *God and Mammon*, 1936) and *Le Romancier et ses personnages* (1933; The Novelist and His Characters), in which he expounded his views on the problems and techniques of fiction. Mauriac deplored the preoccupation of the younger French fiction writers with purely technical questions. He regretted the disintegration of personality and the disappearance of characters in the novel, and it was his own aim to retain some consistency and inner logic in his imaginary creations while still preserving the indeterminacy and mystery of life. In the realm of politics, Mauriac upheld an extremely liberal Catholicism, often conflicting with orthodoxy and antagonizing the conservatives. For many years he professed an almost mystical cult for the personality and the ideas of Charles de Gaulle. Throughout his life, he fought with zest and youthfulness for the causes in which he believed.

See: C. E. Magny, *Histoire du roman français depuis 1918* (1950), pp. 128–45; N. Cormeau, *L'Art de Mauriac* (1951); H. Peyre, *French Novelists of Today* (1955).

H.P.

Maurois, André, pseud. of Emile Salomon Wilhelm Herzog (1885–1967), French novelist, biographer, essayist, and historian, was born in Elbeuf, where his family had moved from Alsace after the Franco-Prussian War establishing in that town a prosperous woolen mill. Maurois first studied at the lycée of Elbeuf, then at the lycée of Rouen, where he had as professor of philosophy ALAIN. Alain's influence on Maurois was deep and long-lasting, affecting not only his literary taste but also his social ideas and even the choice of a career. In 1904, following Alain's advice, he went to work in his father's mill and for 10 years was a very successful, imaginative businessman. In 1914, at the beginning of World War I, he was appointed a liaison officer and interpreter to the Ninth Scottish Division fighting in France. Here Maurois gathered the material for his first novel, *Les Silences du Colonel Bramble* (1918; Eng. tr., *The Silence of Colonel Bramble*, 1919), which was an immediate and surprising success. Maurois's vocation as a man of letters was thus decided, but later novels, such as *Les Discours du docteur O'Grady* (1922), *Bernard Quesnay* (1929; Eng. tr., 1927), *Climats* (1928; Eng. trs., *Atmosphere of Love*, 1929; *Whatever Gods May Be*, 1929; *The Climates of Love*, 1957), *Le Cercle de famille* (1932; Eng. tr., *The Family Circle*, 1932), and *Nouveaux Discours du docteur O'Grady* (1950; Eng. tr., *The Return of Dr. O'Grady*, 1951), did not fulfill his expectations. Indeed, Maurois's reputation rests essentially on his achievements as a biographer. His theories on that genre was propounded in the lectures he gave at Cambridge in 1928, published as *Aspects de la biographie* (1928; Eng. tr., *Aspects of Biography*, 1929).

Influenced by the English biographers, notably George Henry Lewes and Lytton Strachey, Maurois explained that biography should be a science, an art, and a means of self-expression. The biographer should therefore apply first the rigorous method of history, consulting all available documents, correspondence, and private papers, and seeking the testimony of competent witnesses. As an art,

biography should read like a novel, sustaining interest with picturesque episodes, anecdotes, and a lively style. Choosing as his subjects literary and political figures in some way akin to his own nature, Maurois applied his theories in numerous, frequently masterful, always highly readable biographies. The first, *Ariel, ou la vie de Shelley* (1923; Eng. trs., *Ariel: A Shelley Romance*, 1924, *Ariel: The Life of Shelley*, 1924) was followed by *La Vie de Disraeli* (1924; Eng. tr., *Disraeli: A Picture of the Victorian Age*, 1928). Responding to criticism that these works lacked solid documentation, Maurois wrote *Byron* (1930; Eng. tr., 1930), marked by painstaking research and an elaborated bibliography. He thus began a new series of biographies that included *Chateaubriand* (1938; Eng. trs., *Chateaubriand*, 1938, *Chateaubriand: Poet, Statesman, Lover*, 1938; repub. as *René: ou la vie de Chateaubriand*, 1966), *Lélia: ou la vie de George Sand* (1952; Eng. tr., *Lelia: The Life of George Sand*, 1953), *Olympio: ou la vie de Victor Hugo* (1954; Eng. trs., *Victor Hugo*, 1956, *Victor Hugo and His World*, 1966), *Les trois Dumas* (1957; Eng. tr., *The Titans: A Three-Generation Biography of the Dumas*, 1957), *Adrienne: ou la vie de Madame de La Fayette* (1960; Eng. tr., *Adrienne: The Life of the Marquise de Lafayette*, 1961), and *Prométhée: ou la vie de Balzac* (1965; Eng. tr., *Prometheus: The Life of Balzac*, 1965).

Maurois made important contributions to the field of literary criticism with both specialized studies, such as *A la recherche de Marcel Proust* (1949; Eng. trs., *Proust: Portrait of a Genius*, 1950, *The Quest for Proust*, 1950), or with more general works such as *De Proust à Camus* (1963; Eng. tr., *From Proust to Camus: Profiles of Modern French Writers*, 1966), *De Gide à Sartre* (1965), and *D'Aragon à Montherlant* (1967). Maurois's rather banal philosophy, based essentially on the respect for traditional values, appears in essays such as *Un Art de vivre* (1939; Eng. tr., *The Art of Living*, 1940), and *Ce que je crois* (1951; What I Believe). Maurois made frequent trips to England and the United States and resided in New York for four years after the fall of France in 1940. His familiarity with both countries led him to write *Edouard VII et son temps* (1933; Eng. trs., *The Edwardian Era*, 1933, *King Edward and His Times*, 1933), *Histoire des Etats-Unis* (1934; History of the United States), *Histoire d'Angleterre* (1937; Eng. tr., *A History of England*, 1937); and *Etats-Unis 39: Journal d'un voyage en Amérique* (1939; United States 39: Journal of a Trip to America). Maurois left abundant autobiographical information in *Mémoires* (1942; Eng. tr., *I Remember, I Remember*, 1942), *Mémoires 1885–1967*, (1970; Eng. tr., *Memoirs: 1885–1967*, 1970), and in *Portrait d'un ami qui s'appelait moi* (1959; Portrait of a Friend Called Me). An extremely prolific writer, Maurois lacked depth, but he was always charming, elegant, and a master of good style.

See: J. Suffel, *André Maurois* (1963); G. E. Lemaître, *Maurois: The Writer and His Work* (1968); L. C. Keating, *André Maurois* (1969). F.V.

Mauron, Charles (1899–1966), French literary critic, was born in Saint-Rémy-de-Provence. At his death he was a professor at the University of Aix-en-Provence. Mauron came to literature late; failing eyesight caused him to give up a career in chemistry and carve a new one out of his hobby. He had always loved poetry, had read Stéphane MALLARMÉ at the age of 14, and knew a considerable amount of verse by heart. He looked at poetry as he would have a science and developed an experimental method to study the psychology of artistic creation. This method, which he called psychocriticism, amounts to a close comparison of an author's texts in order to uncover motifs that originate in the unconscious—in Mallarmé the obsession with a female form, in Charles BAUDELAIRE the feeling of a pull backwards. Psychocriticism resembles psychoanalysis in that it focuses beneath consciousness, yet Mauron's method differs from classical psychoanalysis in that it is interested only in detecting the personal mythology manifest in an artist's work.

The first major application of psychocriticism was the *Introduction à la psychanalyse de Mallarmé* (1950), followed by *L'Inconscient dans l'œuvre et la vie de Racine* (1957; The Subconscious in the Work and Life of Racine), which Mauron presented as a thesis at Aix-en-Provence. These studies were followed by one embracing several other poets and dramatists in which Mauron, with missionary determination, reiterated his claims and fought off his adversaries. This work, *Des Métaphores obsédantes au mythe personnel* (1963; From Obsessive Metaphors to Personal Myth), obtained for Mauron the *doctorat d'etat* from the Sorbonne. With his method thus vindicated and validated, Mauron continued his investigations, although at this point he had been blind for 25 years and had only three years to live. His final stimulating studies of Molière, Baudelaire, and Jean GIRAUDOUX no doubt constitute the lasting contribution of this courageous scholar who helped to develop the "new criticism."

See: L. LeSage, *The French New Criticism* (1967), pp. 99–101.   L.LeS.

Maurras, Charles (1868–1952), French journalist, poet, and literary critic, was born in Martigues. He was the leader and theorist of the neoroyalist movement. Maurras attended the Catholic College of Aix-en-Provence and, in 1885, moved to Paris, where he set out to complete his education by plunging headlong into the study of history, philosophy, and the social sciences. Most of the articles he published at that time (the first in February 1886) were critical reviews of books on these subjects. After having analyzed the doctrine of counterrevolution in an important essay on "L'Evolution des idées sociales" (1891; The Evolution of Social Ideas), Maurras turned most of his attention to art and literature. During the next five or six years, he took an active part in the literary discussions of the day, writing numerous articles of criticism, short stories, and poems, some of these in Provençal. He was one of the founders of the short-lived Ecole Romane (1891) and of the Ecole Parisienne du Félibrige (1892), but he never entirely neglected political and social questions.

With the outbreak of the Dreyfus Affair, Maurras threw himself entirely into political journalism. His main concern then was the elaboration of a system of thought that would solve French social problems. With this in mind, he joined the political group Action Française, whose aim was then limited to the reorganization of Republican France. Under Maurras's influence, Action Française soon became the nucleus of a new royalist movement. It adopted the doctrine of "integral nationalism" (that is, placing the nation's interest above everything else), which for Maurras necessarily entailed the restoration of an absolute monarchy and the power of the Church. Maurras's faith in a set of values based on tradition and what he called reality led him to make systematic and relentless attacks upon most of the public figures of his time. In January 1945, he was brought to trial as an enemy of the Republic and condemned to life imprisonment. He was granted a "grâce médicale" (medical pardon) in April 1952, seven months before his death.

Most of Maurras's writings have been collected and published in book form. His five-volume *Dictionnaire politique et critique* (1932–34; Political and Critical Dictionary) is the most convenient work of reference to the ideas he expressed in practically every field of thought. More strictly limited to political questions are *Enquête sur la monarchie: 1900–1909* (1909; Investigation Concerning the Monarchy: 1900–1909), a compact volume containing the essentials of his teaching. The story of his polemics on the religious question will be found in *La Démocratie religieuse* (1921; Religious Democracy). His articles on French foreign policy between 1895 and 1905 were collected in *Kiel et Tanger* (1910), which caused a sensation at the time of its publication. There are pages of very fine literary criticism in such books as *Trois Idées politiques* (1898; Three Political Ideas), dealing with François-René Chateaubriand, Jules Michelet, and Charles-Augustin Sainte-Beuve; *Les Amants de Venise* (1902; The Lovers of Venice), which concerns the well-known love affair of George Sand and Alfred de Musset and which is Maurras's only important book not made up of selected articles and miscellaneous writings; *L'Avenir de l'intelligence* (1905; The Future of Intelligence), dealing especially with the concept of order, the basic principle of his traditionalism in all domains of human endeavor; and *L'Etang de Berre* (1915), chiefly about Provence and modern Provençal literature. From an artistic and literary point of view, Maurras's finest works are *Le Chemin de Paradis* (1894; The Road to Paradise), a collection of philosophical short stories; *Anthinéa* (1901), letters from Greece, Italy, Corsica, and England; and, above all, *La Musique intérieure* (1925; Interior Music), a selection of poems preceded by a long and interesting biographical essay that contains some of the most beautiful pages Maurras ever wrote.

During the last eight years of his life, Maurras contributed regularly to the weekly *Aspects de la France* and wrote and published some poetry, the semiautobiographical novel *Le Mont de Saturne* (1950), and a large number of sketches that include reminiscences as well as literary and political criticism. *Le Soliloque du prisonnier* (The Prisoner's Soliloquy), a 62-page brochure, was published in 1963. In this work, he explained his attitude during the German occupation, defended the idea of the Utopian Latin union, expressed the belief that the great majority of the French admired Francisco Franco, and belabored his old arguments against the democratic form of government.

In art and literature, Maurras opposed the classicism of the 16th and 17th centuries to the romanticism of the 18th and 19th. He pitilessly analyzed the ills of modern society, invariably putting the blame on democracy, romanticism, or "Rousseauism." He was a powerful polemist, one who aroused much intense hatred among his contemporaries, yet his sincerity of purpose has rarely been questioned, and the best critics recognized him as one of the ablest thinkers and most forceful prose writers of his time. He has exerted a deep influence upon modern French thought, whether positively or negatively. Through his clear and direct style, vigorous logic, and constant appeal to reason, he has performed the feat of holding the admiration, respect, and even the interest of readers who have never been bewitched by the logic of his political philosophy. Maurras was elected to the Académie Française in 1938, at the age of 70.

See: A. Thibaudet, *Les Idées de Charles Maurras* (1920); A. V. Roche, *Les Idées traditionalistes en France de Rivarol à Charles Maurras* (1937); E. Roussel, *Les Nuées maurrassiennes* (1937); L. S. Roudiez, *Maurras jusqu'à l'Action Française* (1957); M. Mourre, *Charles Maurras* (1958); I. O. Barko, *L'Esthétique littéraire de Charles Maurras* (1961).   A.V.R.

May, Karl (1842–1912), German novelist, was born in Hohenstein-Ernstthal, the son of a weaver. He taught school until discharged for misdemeanors and in 1874 turned to writing travel and adventure stories. During the rest of his life his literary output was enormous, and his popularity was national, especially among younger readers, for whom his work supplied enchanting vistas into romantically conceived distant lands. Although May had no direct experience of the United States, in such books as *Helden des Westens* (1890; Heroes of the West), *Winnetou* (3 vols., 1893), *Old Surehand* (1894), *Der Schatz im Silbersee* (1894; The Treasure in Silver Lake), and many others, he conveyed memorable fictional pictures of a colorful wild West frontier land. With amazing literary agility he published in 1892 alone six long tales with a Near Eastern setting in *Durch Wüste und Harem* (Through Desert and Harem), *Durchs wilde Kurdistan* (Through Wild Kurdistan), *Von Bagdad nach Stambul* (From Baghdad to Istanbul), *Durch die Schluchten des Balkan* (Through Balkan Gorges), *Durch das Land der Skipetaren* (Through the Land of the Skipetaren) and *Der Schut*. Other parts of the world, charged with mystery and indescribable dangers, are the background of such best sellers as *Das Vermächtnis der Inka* (1895; The Legacy of the Incas), *Im Lande des Mahdi* (3 vols., 1896; In the Land of the Mahdi), and *Im Reich des silbernen Löwen* (4 vols.; 1898–1902; In the Realm of the Silver Lion). The Karl-May Stiftung, founded in 1913, continued to publish the sources of May's literary remains in the *Karl-May-Jahrbuch*, from 1918 on.

In May's work, memories of the noble savage, aspects of James Fenimore Cooper, and the most striking features of travel and detective literature are effectively intermingled. His tales are fashioned after the black-and-white pattern of a melodramatic chase sustained by treachery and deceit and by the superhuman display of endurance and cunning until Old Surehand or Kara Ben Nemsi fires the redeeming shot. One work, *Captain Cayman*, appeared in English in 1971. He also wrote *Mein Leben und Streben* (1910; My Life and Striving).

See: W. Raddatz, *Das abenteuerliche Leben Karl Mays* (1965); H. Wollschläger, *Karl May in Selbstzeugnissen und Bilddokumenten* (1965). V.La. rev. A.L.W.

Mayakovsky, Vladimir Vladimirovich (1893–1930), Russian poet and playwright, was born in Bagdadi (now Mayakovsky), Georgia, the son of an impoverished Russian nobleman. In his youth Mayakovsky was actively engaged in the Social-Democratic movement, but after receiving an 11-month prison sentence he abandoned political activity for the arts. At first he was more attracted to painting (particularly cubism) than to literature. His first poem, written in 1912, was published in the cubo-futurist manifesto and miscellany *Poshchochina obshchestvennomu vkusu* (1912; A Slap in the Face of Public Taste) (*see* RUSSIAN LITERATURE).

Like most futurists, Mayakovsky considered the existing arts excessively pastoral and reactionary and thought that artists should devise new techniques that would better express the modern ethos. Traditional poetic tropes and themes, therefore, appear in his poetry only as targets of ridicule. Mayakovsky's style is loud and declamatory; indeed, the very appearance of his verse on the page, with each line subdivided into smaller units, contributes to this brashness. His imagery is aggressively down-to-earth. Other stylistic features include a fondness for neologisms, especially deformations of existing words through the use of unusual prefixes and suffixes; a new system of rhyme, based on the accented vowel and the preceding consonants; and an original approach to rhythm, rejecting the established syllabotonic meters for a freer and more declamatory type of line, usually with three or four accents, in which rhythmic tension is created largely by unexpected rhymes and dramatic contrasts in intonation.

In the pre-1917 period, Mayakovsky believed that art should be free of any utilitarian function, and his approach was primarily aesthetic. Several of his shorter lyrics from these years are simply formal exercises; but the longer works are remarkable in their power and intensity. Mayakovsky's characteristic themes are adumbrated in "Vladimir Mayakovsky. Tragediya" (1913; Eng. tr., 1968) and "Oblako v shtanakh" (1914–15; Eng. tr., "A Cloud in Trousers," 1945). Foremost among these themes is the image of the poet as a superman who is frustrated by an unsympathetic and senseless universe. These motifs are developed and expanded in later poems: the torments of love in "Fleyta-pozvonochnik" (1915; Eng. tr., "The Backbone Flute," 1960); the poet as scapegoat and redeemer in "Voyna i mir" (1915–16; War and the World); and finally, the total frustration of the poet's endeavors by an indifferent universe in "Chelovek" (1916–17; Man).

Although social dissatisfaction is present in Mayakovsky's early poetry, it is usually subsumed in a more general theme of cosmic frustration. When the Revolutions of 1917 came, however, Mayakovsky greeted them ecstatically and was one of the few artists to support the Bolsheviks from the start. During the Civil War he contributed hundreds of posters and slogans to the Red cause, and his play *Misteriya-Buff* (1918; Eng. tr., *Mystery-Bouffe*, 1933) and his long poem *150,000,000* (1919–20) are among the classics of Revolutionary literature. Mayakovsky's style in the Revolutionary period, although based on the same principles as his pre-1917 verse, is much simpler and more popular: the elliptical concision is replaced by garrulity, the note of tragedy by broad comedy; it is aimed at the masses, no longer at the artistic avant-garde.

Mayakovsky was convinced that futurist art had played and would continue to play a major part in the destiny of the Revolution. Accordingly, he founded LEF (Left Front of the Arts), a radical artistic movement with roots in futurism that was sympathetic to Marxism. Mayakovsky's activities in the 1920s included public readings in barracks and factories, advertisements for state stores, versified journalism for Soviet newspapers, and written accounts of his travels in the West. He justified these activities both as functional art and as aesthetic education for the culturally illiterate. In criticism, Mayakovsky's judgments were frequently harsh, but they were founded on genuine perception and a coherent aesthetic position. He was particularly interested in photography and cinematography, and he wrote several film scenarios.

With the end of the Civil War and the introduction of the New Economic Policy (NEP) in 1921, Mayakovsky's honeymoon with the Revolution ended. The conservative artistic tastes of the Bolshevik leaders, the rise of a new bureaucracy, the reemergence of bourgeois values among both the population at large and the Communist Party all conflicted with Mayakovsky's hopes and ideals. His greatest work of these years, "Pro eto" (1923; Eng. tr., "About This," 1965), returns to the themes of his pre-Revolutionary poetry. The themes take on added intensity, however, as the Revolution seems to have come and gone without changing anything. From this time satirical elements become prominent in his work, culminating in the two plays *Klop* (1929; Eng. tr., *The Bedbug*, 1960), and *Banya* (1930; Eng. tr., *The Bath-House*, 1963). Both plays are about the betrayal of the Revolution by its self-appointed officials.

Mayakovsky's fame in the Soviet Union rests mainly on three large works. *Vladimir Ilich Lenin* (1924) was inspired by the death and funeral of Lenin. *Khorosho!* (1927; Good!) is a celebration of the tenth anniversary of the October Revolution. The unfinished *"Vo ves golos"* (1929–30; Eng. tr., *At the Top of My Voice*, 1940) appears to have been intended as an introduction to a poem on the first Five-Year Plan. These works are public and rhetorical pieces, and are not without humor and even lyricism. As always, the theme of death inspires some of Mayakovsky's most powerful poetry.

In his later years, Mayakovsky came under increasing attack from more orthodox Soviet writers and critics, both for his unconventional view of art and for his outspoken comments on Communist officialdom. Finally, he was even persuaded to abandon LEF for RAPP (Russian Association of Proletarian Writers), which was the most reactionary of all the literary groups. Despite this "conversion," however, Mayakovsky was still not completely accepted as a Soviet writer and was repeatedly snubbed and humiliated by his new colleagues. This experience, along with various setbacks in his private life, undoubtedly contributed to his suicide on Apr. 14, 1930.

At first his death was greeted with shock and anger in the Soviet press, but in 1935, Iosif Stalin unexpectedly declared that "Mayakovsky was and remains the best and most talented poet of our Soviet epoch," and that "indifference to his memory and works is a crime." Imitation of Mayakovsky thus became incumbent on Soviet poets. They adopted his typographical style and imitated the grand gestures of his verse, usually falling into bombast as a result; the more intimate side of his poetry was left unexplored.

See: L. Stahlberger, *The Symbolic System of Mayakovsky* (1964); E. Brown, *Mayakovsky: A Poet in the Revolution* (1973).   R.D.B.T.

Mayröcker, Friederike (1924–), Austrian poet and author of stories and radio plays, was born in Vienna, where she studied English and after receiving her degree began to teach that language in Viennese schools. After her friendship with Austrian poet Ernst JANDL began in 1954, she collaborated with him in the writing of experimental poetry and radio plays, including *Fünf Mann Menschen* (1971; A Crew of Five), which was awarded the German War Blind Prize in 1968. Mayröcker's first book was the prose volume *Larifari* (1956), which was followed in 1965 by poems in *metaphorisch* (metaphorical) and then by the poetic *texte* (texts) in 1966. Her texts are pieced together like a collage where intuitive association plays a large role; each part leads directly to another, the end result being a new awareness about language and human relationships, with a large measure of skepticism also present. Her "poetic texts" were collected in 1966 in a volume of lyrics entitled *Tod durch Musen* (Death through the Muses). The poems in *Sägespäne für mein Herzbluten* (Sawdust for My Heart's Blood) were published in 1968. *Fantom Fan* (1971) was followed by *Arie auf tönernen Füszen* (Aria to Feet of Clay) in 1972, a volume that bears the subtitle "Metaphysical Theater."

Mayröcker's poems are distinguished by laconic linguistic puns and juxtaposed images that have been compared to the abstract paintings of the cubists. She breaks reality into pieces that she then reassembles into a new kind of reality. *Blaue Erleuchtungen* (1972; Blue Illuminations), with the childlike drawings typical of the author, bearing the subtitle "First Poems," being poems she wrote between 1945 and 1950, was followed by a story, *je ein umwölkter gipfel* (1973; always a beclouded peak). The poems *In langsamen Blitzen* (1974; In Slow Flashes)

were followed by *Das Licht in der Landschaft* (The Light in the Landscape) and then by *schriftungen oder gerüchte aus dem jenseits* (scribbles or rumors from the beyond), both in 1975. The prose volume *Fast ein Frühling für Markus M* (1976; Almost the Springtime of Marcus M) was followed by a volume *heisze hunde* (hot dogs) in 1977, with illustrations by Jandl. A volume of prose, poems, and texts, *rot ist unten* (red is below), appeared in 1977. In 1979 appeared collected poems from 1944 to 1978 in *Ausgewählte Gedichte*.

Other works by Mayröcker include *Heiligenanstalt* (Institute for Saints), being biographical exercises on Frédéric Chopin, Robert Schumann, Anton Bruckner, and Franz Schubert, *Schwarmgesang, Szenen für die politische Bühne* (Swarm Chorale, Scenes for the Political Stage), and *Tochter der Bahn* (Daughter of the Railway), all 1978. Mayröcker is also the author of books for children, as in *Sinclair Sofokles der Babysaurier* (1971; Eng. tr., *Sinclair Sophocles, The Baby Dinosauer*, 1974) and *meine träume ein flügelkleid* (1974; my dreams a wingéd gown). About herself, Mayröcker has written: "At the moment, my platonic life, in the shadow of a bird's wing; or speaking of theory, there is less and less the problem that one has inspiration, rather that one can keep an irreducible vulnerability—that is, one mustn't want to don armor against the world, however much you'd like to at times."

See: *Neue Texte* 20/21 (1978).   A.L.W.

Mechtel, Angelika, pseud. of Angelika Eilers (1943–), German poet, novelist, and playwright, was born in Dresden. She became editor of *Aspekte-Impulse* in 1965 and of *Publikation* in 1972. As a member of "Gruppe 61" (*see* GERMAN LITERATURE), Mechtel developed an interest in workers' literature that produced two documentaries: *Alte Schriftsteller in der Bundesrepublik* (1972; Old Writers in the Federal Republic) and *Ein Plädoyer für uns* (1975; A Plea for Us), interviews with women whose men are in prison. Mechtel has written several volumes of poems, among them *Gegen Eis und Flut* (1963; Against Ice and Flood), and several of stories, such as *Hochhausgeschichten* (1971; High-Rise Stories), about the affluent Germans of today, and *Das Puppengesicht* (1977; The Doll's Face).

In her novels Mechtel is critical of contemporary German society: *Kaputte Spiele* (1970; Ruined Games) concerns the counterculture; *Das gläserne Paradies* (1973; The Glass Paradise) satirizes family life among the upper-middle class; *Die Blindgängerin* (1974; The Blind Girl) portrays a blind woman who regains her sight but still has to grope toward emancipation; *Wir sind arm, wir sind reich* (1977; We Are Poor, We Are Rich) portrays a young girl in war-torn Nazi Germany.

See: "Protokoll eines Interviews mit Angelika Mechtel," in *Basis* 5 (1975): 139–48; E. R. Herrmann and E. H. Spitz, *German Women Writers of the Twentieth Century* (1978), pp. 133–39.   E.H.S.

Meckel, Christoph (1935–), German poet and graphic artist, was born in Berlin and grew up in Freiburg im Breisgau. After one year of formal study at the art academy there he studied for half a semester in Munich, then struck out on his own as a freelance artist. He traveled widely in West Africa, Europe, the southwestern United States, and Mexico, and between the mid-1960s and mid-1970s lived alternately in France and West Berlin.

Meckel's first cycle of etchings, *Moël* (1954), completed when he was 19, is a work of prodigious invention and technical skill, but it received little notice. That cycle led to others, in each case a book of about 50 etchings: *Die*

Stadt (The City), *Der Krieg* (The War), *Welttheater* (The World Theater), all 1960, remodel certain expressionist influences, but *Der Turm* (1961; The Tower) *Das Meer* (1965; The Ocean), and *Der Fluß* (1976, but completed in 1969; The River) are quite independent in their idiom. In these picture books, various recurrent motifs in fantastic configurations do suggest narrative links, but the story aspect is strictly subordinated to graphic principles. Meckel has published in small presses many booklets of writings with graphic designs, for example, *Gedichtbilderbuch* (Poem Picture Book) in 1964, *In der Tinte* (1968; Ink's the Fix You're In), and *Zettelphilipp* (1971). His first books of poems were *Tarnkappe* (1956; Cloak of Invisibility) and *Hotel für Schlafwandler* (1958, rev. 1970; Hotel for Sleepwalkers). With *Nebelhörner* (1959; Foghorns), the volatile oddity and vital fantasy of his poetry began to attract attention. Since then, eight books of poems and seven of prose have appeared. The prose oeuvre began with the singularly concrete fantastic observations of *Im Land der Umbramauten* (1961; In the Country of the Umbramauts). His fabulous (rather than realistic) vein has passed through many modifications since that work, but the later narrative, *Licht* (1978; Light), following the novel *Bockshorn* (1973; Goat's Horn), although combining fabulous with realistic elements, is still metaphoric in its diction and rhapsodic in its rhythms.

New traits in Meckel's prose, with essayistic and documentary accents, appear in his memoir of Johannes Bobrowski (1978). A reflective note in poetry is reflected in the cycle *Säure* (1979; Acids). For a selection of his work, see *Werkauswahl* (1971; Selected Work). Unpublished are six recent cycles (each about 12 sheets) of delicate colored drawings, in which Meckel's flair for zest and mystery command new motifs and tonalities. For translations see *Dimension* 1 (1968): 292–311; 4 (1971): 90–117, and 6 (1973): 80–99.

See: "A New Visual and Poetic Fantasy" *TLS* (April 28, 1961); G. Bracker-Rausch, "Christoph Meckel," in *Schriftsteller der Gegenwart*, ed. by K. Nonnenmann (1963), pp. 221–27; W. Segebrecht, "Christoph Meckels Erfindungen," *Merkur* 214 (1966): 80–85; W. Segebrecht, "Christoph Meckel als Erzähler," in C. Meckel, *Der glückliche Magier* (1967). C.M.

Medina, Vicente (1866–1937), Spanish poet, was born in Murcia. In 1899 he won acclaim with a volume called *Aires murcianos* (Airs from Murcia), which initiated a type of regional poetry that was to become widespread and of great influence among local and regional poets of other sections of Spain and Spanish America. Vicente Medina's achievement consists in creating a new style of rustic poetry. His poetry does not deal with local color, as did the regional literature of the 19th century, nor is he interested in the people because of their unusual or picturesque attributes, as were the romantics, or in the physical and social aspects of their environment, as were the realists. It was the soul of the people he sought to express: their emotions, conflicts, and human qualities as manifested in their ingenuous, unstudied, elemental, and primitive aspects. The "flavor" of Medina's poetry comes from certain outstanding dialectal characteristics which are perfectly intelligible to anyone who knows Spanish. The defect of his poetry is its monotony. Throughout his life, Medina merely repeated himself. He was never able to give new dimensions to his work, not even by changing the regional theme, as he attempted to do in the popular poems he wrote about Argentina, where he lived for over 20 years. *Poesía* (1908) contains much earlier work not previously published in book form, but

Medina's place in Spanish poetry is due almost solely to *Aires murcianos*. Its regional naturalism is not unlike that of José María GABRIEL Y GALÁN in Extremadura.

See: J. M. de Cossío, *Cincuenta años de poesía española, 1850–1900*, vol. 2 (1960), pp. 1248–54.

F. de O. rev. H.L.B.

Medio, Dolores (1914–), Spanish novelist, was born in Oviedo of a modest bourgeois family that was reduced to economic straits on her father's death. She changed from a teaching career to journalism before finally devoting herself full time to writing fiction. Her novels fall into two general categories. In the first, the female protagonists both participate in and comment on the action. *Nosotros los Rivero* (1953; We Riveros), which won the Nadal Prize, describes Lena Rivero's childhood and adolescence. A portion of *La pez sigue flotando* (1959; The Fish Stays Afloat) deals with Lena as a writer, and *Diario de una maestra* (1961; Diary of a Schoolteacher) tells of Irene's personal and professional experiences. The autobiographical implications are clear.

The second group is characteristic of the social novel popular in Spain during the 1950s, in which there is often critical intent and characters are often considered in their dual roles as both individuals and representatives of a group (*see* SPANISH LITERATURE). *Funcionario público* (1956; Public Servant) chronicles Pablo's failure as a social entity and as a husband. *Bibiana* (1963) presents the social and personal relationships of a housewife. Both *La pez* and *Farsa de verano* (1973; Summer's Farce) use the multiple protagonist in intricately interwoven sets of personal and social dramas. The same themes and techniques appear in her novelettes and collections of short stories, including *Andrés* (1967).

Early literary affinities point to the realism and naturalism of Benito PÉREZ GALDÓS and Clarín (*see* Leopold ALAS), while later influences include José ORTEGA Y GASSET and social realism. Her primary interest is in the common man, preferably from the lower or middle class, whom she never separates from his social and historical milieu. On the basis of hypothetical or actually observed situations, Medio fictionalizes questions of social adaptation, reality vs. personal aspirations, and the place of women in 20th-century Spain, among others.

See: J. Winecoff, "Fictionalized Autobiography in the Novels of Dolores Medio," *KFLQ* 13, no. 3 (1966): pp. 170–78; M. E. W. Jones, *Dolores Medio* (1974).

M.E.W.J.

Mehren, Stein (1935–), Norwegian poet and novelist, was born and raised in Oslo. He became a prominent figure among the young poets of the 1960s. From his first collection, *Gjennom stillheten en natt* (1960; Through Silence One Night), through his latest, 13 collections in all, Mehren has shown himself to be a poet of fresh, original verse and profound philosophical commitment. He has engaged in a romantic quest to find congruence between spiritual experiences—of love, nature, beauty—and poetic expression. In his early collections in particular, Mehren struggles with this age-old problem with an intensity and sense of poetic expression that gives it original force. In later collections he has attained new confidence, not the least in *Aurora: det niende mørke* (1969; Aurora: The Ninth Darkness), a cycle of poems about life, love, and loneliness that belongs among the finest Norwegian literary works of the 1960s.

Mehren's growing awareness of the artificiality of 20th-century life is reflected in his later collections, such as *Dikt for enhver som våger* (1973; Poems for All Who Dare), *Det trettende stjernebilde* (1977; The Thirteenth

Constellation), *Vintersolhverv* (1979; Winter Solstice). This perception was treated at length in his two novels, *De utydelige* (1972; The Obscure Ones) and *Titanene* (1974; The Titans). Both works mirror the intellectual climate of Oslo in the early 1970s—bland tolerance, doubt, superficiality—and express a profoundly pessimistic opinion of the quality of modern man.

See: H. Naess, "Stein Mehren: Dialectic Poet of Light and Dream," *BA* 47 (1973): 66–70.   K.A.F.

Meister, Ernst (1911–1979), German poet, was born in Hagen-Haspe in Westphalia. He first studied theology and then philosophy, German literature, and art history. He served in the German army in World War II, and from 1939 to 1960 he was employed in his father's factory. Primarily a poet, he also published stories and wrote radio plays and one drama. His first volume of poetry, *Ausstellung* (Exhibition), appeared in 1932. Almost 20 years passed before he began to publish his hermetic, cryptic poems systematically.

Meister's volumes of lyrics, combining the melodic and the reflective modes, include *Unter schwarzem Schafspelz* (1953; Under a Black Sheepskin), *Dem Spiegelkabinett gegenüber* (1954; Opposite the Mirror Cabinet), *Der Südwind sagte mir zu* (1955; The Southwind Suited Me), *Fermate* (1957; Musical Pause), *und Ararat* (1957; And Ararat), *Pythiusa* (1958), *Zahlen und Figuren* (1958; Numbers and Figures), *Lichtes Labyrinth* (1959; The Labyrinth of Light), *Die Formel und die Stätte* (1960; Formula and Places), *Flut und Stein* (1961; Flood and Stone), *Zeichen um Zeichen* (1968; Signs about Signs), *Es kam die Nachricht* (1970; The News Came), *Sage vom Ganzen den Satz* (1972; Say the Whole of the Sentence), *Im Zeitspult* (1976; In the Fissure of Time), and *Wandloser Raum* (1979; Unalterable Space).

The considerable body of his work was Meister's public appearance, since he was reticent and somewhat reserved personally. His dialectical poems, marked by linguistic concentration and vision, combining abstraction and sensuality, were his trademark. Though critics held him to be imponderable and difficult, his poetry challenged and enchanted them. He was honored with prizes such as the Annette von Droste-Hülshoff Prize (1957), the Petrarch Prize (1976), the Rilke Prize (1978), and—in the first such action of its kind—the distinguished Georg Büchner Prize of the Darmstadt Academy for Language and Literature, awarded posthumously. His collected poems 1932–79 appeared just prior to his death and were reissued immediately with later poems, including the last he wrote, in the summer of 1979. Few readers knew that Meister was an accomplished artist as well as a poet.   A.L.W.

Mell, Max (1882–1971), Austrian poet and dramatist, was born in Styria at Marburg. His father was made director of the state institute for the blind in Vienna, and the family moved there. Mell took his Ph.D. degree at the University of Vienna, majoring in German literature, but he resolved to devote himself to writing and sought no position or office. While still at the university, he published his first book of stories, *Lateinische Erzählungen* (1904; Latin Tales), characterized by polished form and conscious artistry. He continued to improve his style and technical competence by translating and emulating foreign writers, and his prose came to combine Austrian grace and classical purity. His first poems, *Das bekränzte Jahr* (1911; The Wreathed Year), sing of his beloved Styria in all its aspects, seasons, and moods; and a simplicity akin to that of the folk song marks these and his subsequent lyrics.

matic production, which won him recognition throughout the German-speaking lands for his revival of the old-time *Laienspiel*. Modeled on the style of the old folk play, inspired by religious feeling, and rendered more poignant by the destruction and distress of World War I, Mell's three *Legendenspiele* (Legend Plays)—*Das Apostelspiel* (1923; Eng. tr., *Apostle Play*, 1934), *Das Schutzenelspiel* (1923; The Guardian Angel Play), and *Das Nachfolge Christi-Spiel* (1927; The Followers of Christ Play)—were played everywhere.   B.Q.M. rev. A.L.W.

Memmi, Albert (1920–), French-speaking novelist, essayist, short-story writer, and scholar, was born in Tunis, Tunisia, at the crossroads of three cultures: Arab, Jewish, and French. Since childhood, Memmi has known cultural, ethnic, and social alienation. The son of a poor harness-maker, he first spoke Arabo-berber. After studying at the rabbinical school and at the Israeli Alliance, he attended the French lycée in Tunis and then the University of Algiers, where he specialized in philosophy. During World War II, he was sent to various forced labor camps in Tunisia. After the war, he went to Paris, where he prepared his *agrégation* in philosophy at the Sorbonne, married a French woman, and then returned to Tunis to teach philosophy and to direct a psychosociological laboratory. In September 1956, Memmi finally settled in Paris. Currently associated with the National Center of Scientific Research, he lectures at the Ecole des Hautes Etudes. In 1972 he was appointed professor of sociology at the University of Nanterre.

Memmi's work is dominated by two themes: alienation and oppression. In both his novels and his sociological essays, he treats these concerns with great sincerity and perception. Memmi moves with ease from imaginative creation to scientific analysis, from metaphor to the play of concepts. Rooted in individual experience, his work accomplishes the difficult passage from the self to the universal, making this writer one of the essential witnesses to the problems of the postwar period, particularly those dealing with decolonization and the liberation of peoples.

Memmi's *La Statue de sel* (Eng. tr., *The Pillar of Salt*, 1955), an autobiographical and ethnographical novel, was published in 1953, with a preface by Albert CAMUS. This severe indictment of colonial life concerns an adolescent who is "a native in a colonized country, a Jew in an anti-Semitic universe, an African in a world where Europe is triumphant." In *Agar* (1955), Memmi writes about a couple who must deal with the shock of two conflicting cultures (French and Tunisian Jewish); the novel transcends personal experience, however, to reveal its general sociological import. *Portrait du colonisé* (Eng. tr., *The Colonizer and the Colonized*, 1965), published in 1957 with a preface by Jean-Paul SARTRE, is an essay on the drama of colonization and its effects on the two partners of the relationship: the colonizer and the colonized. *Portrait d'un juif* (1962; Eng. tr., *Portrait of a Jew*, 1963) and *La Libération du juif* (1966; Eng. tr., *The Liberation of the Jew*, 1966) resemble the novel in "the sensory richness of experience" and the essay in the effort at synthesis and the ambition to elevate an experience to an exemplary level. In *L'Homme dominé* (1968; Eng. tr., *Dominated Man: Notes toward a Portrait*, 1968), a sociological study of oppression, Memmi treats the oppression of women, colonized peoples, blacks, proletarians, and domestics. His method here is that of the two preceding works: a dialogue of individual experience and an effort at systematization.

In *Le Scorpion; ou la confession imaginaire* (1969; Eng. tr., *The Scorpion, or the Imaginary Confession*, 1971),

Memmi reconsiders the themes of previous works, but he also attempts to pause, to make a second evaluation; this is the work of a mature man who questions himself about all his projects. Metaphysical in tone, its structure inspired not by traditional French forms (as was the case in Memmi's previous works) but by the Talmud, *Le Scorpion* marks a turning point in his thought and aesthetics. Literature, which had previously seemed to Memmi to be the preferred vehicle for information, disclosure, communication, and combat, now appears as only a relative means, one among many others. *La Terre intérieure* (1976; The Interior World) is another summation, this time in the form of an interview with a journalist. *Le Désert* (1977) suggests that Memmi has been completely liberated from Western forms, for here he gives himself up to the pleasure of using the Arabian tale, with its lyricism and voluptuousness, as a means of expressing his philosophy.

Although Memmi writes in French, his thematic and aesthetic preoccupations are profoundly different from those of his French colleagues. Translated into 15 languages, he is read more extensively in the United States than he is in France. *Le Portrait du colonisé* has been especially popular with black American readers. Memmi is also widely popular throughout Africa.

See: A. Khatibi, *Le Roman maghrébin* (1968); I. Yétiv, *Le Thème de l'aliénation dans le roman maghrébin d'expression française: 1952–1956* (1972); J. Déjeux, *Littérature maghrébine de langue française* (1973), pp. 301–31; J. Leiner, "Interview avec Albert Memmi," *PFr* 6 (1973): 71–88.   J.Le.

Mendele mocher sforim, pseud. of Sholem Yakob Abramowitz (1836–1917), Hebrew-Yiddish novelist, poet, and essayist, was born in a shtetl in Belorussia. Here he received the traditional Jewish education, with its emphasis upon the Bible, the Torah, and religious commentaries. At the age of 14, when his father died, he became a wandering scholar. For a while, he attended famous rabbinical schools at Slutsk and Vilna, but when an itinerant mendicant fired the young man's imagination with stories of prosperity in the Ukraine, the two set out for that region. Begging his way from town to town, Mendele acquired a fund of experiences, and an insight into Jewish and Russian folkways that would later be expressed in his writings. Mendele finally broke away from the older vagabond, then found refuge with Abraham Baer Gottlober, a leader of the Enlightenment of "Haskalah," who arranged for his education and published his first literary efforts.

Mendele's first essays and tales were written in Hebrew, and he is still venerated as a pioneer and innovator of modern Hebrew prose. (*see* HEBREW LITERATURE). He soon realized, however, that most readers of secular literature did not have sufficient command of Hebrew to enjoy works written in the sacred tongue. In 1863 he turned to Yiddish as the most suitable vehicle for his popular tales. Unlike his contemporaries, Mendele labored no less diligently over his Yiddish style than over his Hebrew, writing and rewriting his essays and stories until they attained their most perfect form. He is certainly the finest Yiddish prose stylist. Indeed, he is revered as the "grandfather of Yiddish literature," and together with SHOLOM ALEICHEM and Yitzkhok Leibush PERETZ, he forms the triumvirate of classical Yiddish literature.

Mendele's principal subject is life in the Russian Pale of Settlement, the area where Jews were allowed to live. His intellectual roots are in the enlightened humanitarianism of the 18th century, and he aims not merely to entertain but also to reform his readers. In his long, satirical verse-allegory *Die Klatshe* (1873; Eng. tr., *The*

Nag, 1954), he depicts the hapless lot of Russian Jewry in the figure of an old horse, undernourished, overworked, beset on all sides by aristocratic steeds, and beaten by unpitying ragamuffins. In his novel *Fishke der Krume* (1869–88; Eng. tr., *Fishke the Lame,* 1960), Mendele draws upon his youthful experiences as wandering mendicant and rouses sympathy for outcasts, vagabonds, thieves, and the poorest of the poor. His most ambitious work, *Masoës Beyamin Hashlishi* (1878; Eng. tr., *Travels and Adventures of Benjamin the Third,* 1949), is a prose epic of East European Jewry, modeled after Cervantes's *Don Quixote.* Mendele's most mature novel is *Dos Vintshfingerl* (1889; The Wishing Ring), in which he portrays the dreams, longings, experiences, and disillusionment of his entire generation, seduced by the doctrines of the Enlightenment only to be hurled back into the dark reality of Jewish affliction by the pogroms of the 1880s.

See: S. Niger, *Mendele mocher sforim* (1936); D. Miron, *A Traveler Disguised* (1973).   S.L.

Menéndez Pelayo, Marcelino (1856–1912), Spanish critic, historian, and humanist, was born in Santander. He spent two years at the University of Barcelona (1871–73) studying with the philologist Milá i Fontanals and the philosopher Lloréns. In Madrid he had an unpleasant experience with Professor Nicolás Salmerón, an adherent of the German philosopher Karl Krause. As a result, Menéndez Pelayo took an examination at the University of Valladolid. There he met the conservative Gumersindo Laverde, who influenced him deeply. The *krausistas* blamed the Inquisition and Catholicism in general for the lack of freedom in Spain and for the nonexistence of genuinely Spanish philosophy and science. Encouraged by Laverde, Menéndez Pelayo engaged in a polemic that constitutes his first work, published when he was 19: *La ciencia española,* 3 vols., 1876; Spanish Science). Precociousness, incredible erudition, and a synthetic approach, features of Menéndez Pelayo's entire work, are already visible in *La ciencia española.* At the age of 22 he won the chair for General and Spanish Literature at the University of Madrid, a position he held until 1898, when he was named director of the National Library.

The basic subject of Menéndez Pelayo's work is Spanish literature, in a broad sense encompassing even scientific writing. Spain included for him Portugal and Spanish America. The discovery and colonization of America was for him Spain's greatest contribution to world history. Two traits are distinctive in Spanish civilization: Latinism and Catholicism. Anything in the Spanish world that deviates from the path marked by these two lines is a digression or an aberration. The *Historia de los heterodoxos españoles* (1881) tries to prove this point. In his prologue to the second edition of this work, he recants the intemperate style of certain attacks but nothing of their contents. In 1893 he published *Antología de poetas hispanoamericanos.* The prologues to this anthology constitute the first systematic and scholarly approach to Spanish American literature written in Spain. They inaugurate Spain's new view of the Spanish-speaking countries not as ungrateful daughters, but as partners in a common cultural effort. With many additions and revisions, these prologues were later published under the title: *Historia de la poesía hispanoamericana* (1911). Other examples of his massive projects are the *Antología de poetas líricos castellanos* (1890–1908), several editorial projects, and the incomplete and hasty translation of Shakespeare into Spanish.

Menéndez Pelayo's most important work is his *Historia de las ideas estéticas en España* (9 vols., 1883–91). It covers Spain in her European context up to the end of the 18th century. The last three volumes survey the rise of aesthetics as a new discipline in England, France, and Germany, as well as the origins of European romanticism. This work was meant as the background for a study of Spanish romanticism, but the plan was never carried out. The *Historia* was conceived as the introduction to an intended history of Spanish literature. Aesthetics for Menéndez Pelayo includes what today we call critical theory and the study of human response to works of art, as well as the evaluation of the poetic character of literary works. With this comprehensive approach he produced excellent studies of Immanuel Kant, Friedrich von Schelling, George Wilhelm Friedrich Hegel, and other German philosophers whom he had mentioned with disdain in his youth. The main characteristics of Menéndez Pelayo's literary theory are sensitivity to the poetic character of the literary text in contrast to mere erudition or intellectual analysis, and a deep interest in classical and Renaissance humanism in contrast to the philologists of his time, who devoted more attention to the Middle Ages. Spanish literature was for him an expression of the national character, which itself is a fusion of learned and popular elements. By contrast, in Miguel de UNAMUNO's concept of *intrahistoria* (intrahistory) and in Ramón MENÉNDEZ PIDAL's concept of traditional poetry, we find at least a stylistic emphasis on the popular character of Spanish civilization, as if the popular element were more authentic than the learned one.

Menéndez Pelayo's library, rich in manuscripts and rare books, is now open for research in his native city of Santander. The organ of the library is the *Boletín de la Biblioteca Menéndez Pelayo*. Distinguished scholars such as Adolfo Bonilla y San Martín, Ramón Menéndez Pidal, and Agustín González de Amezúa were his disciples.

See: P. Laín Entralgo, *Menéndez Pelayo* (1944); M. Olguín, "Marcelino Menéndez Pelayo's Theory of Art, Aesthetics and Criticism," *UCMP* 28, no. 6, (1950): viii; 333–58; G. Lohmann Villena, *Menéndez Pelayo y la hispanidad* (1957).   C.M.A.

Menéndez Pidal, Ramón (1869–1968), Spanish philologist, literary critic, and historian, was born in La Coruña. He studied at the University of Madrid with Marcelino MENÉNDEZ PELAYO, married the distinguished historian María Goyri, and in 1899 obtained the newly created chair for Comparative Philology of Latin and Castilian (Miguel de UNAMUNO applied for it but later withdrew from the competition). In the meantime, Menéndez Pidal had published his first major work: *La leyenda de los Infantes de Lara* (1896; The Legend of the Noble Brothers of Lara). It was hailed by European scholars as the most important Spanish contribution to date in the field of Romance philology. The characteristics of Menéndez Pidal's method are already visible in this work: rigor and accuracy in establishing and dating textual sources, and the comparison of the poetic text with contemporary historical documents in order to follow the process of mythification of the heroes and to pursue the transformations of the legend through different genres and periods. His early works touch on different aspects of this comprehensive methodology: *Catálogo de la Real Biblioteca. Manuscritos. Crónicas de España* (1898), *Primera Crónica General* (1906; First General Chronical), and *Cantar de Mío Cid. Texto, gramática y vocabulario* (1908–1911). These books brought him international recognition. In 1902 he was admitted to the Royal Spanish Academy of the Language, and in 1909 he delivered the Turnbull Lectures on poetry at the Johns Hopkins University in Baltimore, Md. In those years he also visited several Latin American countries.

Attention to detail never blinded Menéndez Pidal to the need for a comprehensive view of literature within the society from which it emerges. The lectures at Johns Hopkins contain a general study of medieval Spanish epic entitled *L'Épopée castillane à travers la littérature espagnole* (1910). The title *La España del Cid* (1929; Eng. tr., *The Cid and His Spain,* 1934) indicates that he never lost sight of the historical context in the study of individual biography. The same applies to his *El Padre Las Casas. Su doble personalidad* (1963). In *Los españoles en la historia y en la literatura* (1951; Eng. tr., *Spaniards in Their History*, 1966), he attempts to give a synthetic view of the most basic traits of Spanish civilization.

The *Romancero* (corpus of Spanish ballads) attracted his attention from the beginning of his career. He collected ballads in all Spanish-speaking countries and among the Sephardic Jews. In 1899 he published "Notas para el romancero del conde Fernán González" in *Homenaje a Menéndez Pelayo* (vol. 1, pp. 429–507). This study was followed by "Los romances tradicionales en América" *Cultura Espanola* (vol. 1 (1906), pp. 72–111). In 1928 the delightful *Flor nueva de romances viejos* appeared. All this work culminated in the vast project of the *Romancero hispánico. Hispano-portugués, americano y sefardí. Teoría e historia*, (2 vols., 1953). Menéndez Pidal left behind a massive collection of ballads which is being edited by his disciples (see S. Armistead, *El romancero judeo-español en el archivo Menéndez Pidal*, 3 vols., 1978).

The basis of Menéndez Pidal's approach to literature is the concept of "national soul." In 1910 he called his research "psychological archeology." Unlike Menéndez Pelayo, Menéndez Pidal emphasizes the popular aspect of literature as the more authentic expression of the national spirit. Hence the relative neglect of the learned poetry of the Middle Ages in his work. On the basis of the oral character of popular epic and the ballads, he stressed the "traditional" character of Castilian poetry. This poetry lives in its variants, and sometimes in a "latent state," until its age-old themes emerge in a different form or genre. A representative work for the study of these ideas is *Poesía juglaresca y juglares* (1924; The Jongleurs and Their Poetry). Menéndez Pidal's "traditionalist" theory for the study of the medieval epic in Spain and Europe was attacked by positivists like J. Bédier, stylists such as Leo Spitzer, and by E. R. Curtius, who studied the vernacular European literatures in the light of the Latin tradition. Menéndez Pidal answered all criticism and tested his theory in the *Chanson de Roland* itself, where the positivists had seen the best proof of their thesis (see *La Chanson de Roland y el neotradicionalismo*). He fought not only for his literary theories, but for more practical concerns as well. Several pages in *La España del Cid*, for example, are a direct reply to José ORTEGA Y GASSET's diagnosis of invertebrate Spain.

Linguistics is the basis of his literary criticism. Menéndez Pidal's major work in this field is *Orígenes del español* (1926). For him language is both *langue* and *parole*, in Ferdinand de Saussure's terminology. As the literary text is an example of *parole*, today, when Saussure is criticized from the point of view of a linguistics of the text, Menéndez Pidal's concepts merit new attention.

See: D. Catalán, *La escuela lingüística española y su concepción del lenguaje* (1955); C. Morón Arroyo, "La teoría crítica de Menéndez Pidal," *HR* 38 (1970): 22–39.
C.M.A.

Merezhkovsky, Dmitry Sergeyevich (1865–1941), Russian novelist, poet, dramatist, critic, essayist, religious and social thinker, was born in Petersburg. He began his literary career as a civic poet in the populist tradition before initiating the symbolist movement in Russian literature with his collection of verse *Simvoly* (1892; Symbols) and his manifesto *O prichinakh upadka i o novykh techeniyakh sovremennoy russkoy literatury* (1893; On the Reasons for the Decline and on New Trends in Contemporary Russian Literature). Only briefly under the influence of Friedrich NIETZSCHE and the French decadents Paul VERLAINE and Charles BAUDELAIRE, Merezhkovsky advocated mystic content, symbols, and the broadening of artistic impressionability as the basic elements of the new art.

Merezhkovsky's innate religiosity began to dominate his thought and his writings soon after his marriage to the poet Zinaida GIPPIUS in 1889. In his trilogy of novels *Smert bogov: Yulian Otstupnik* (1896; Eng. tr., *The Death of the Gods*, 1901); *Voskresshiye bogi: Leonardo da Vinci* (1901; Eng. tr., *The Forerunner*, 1902); and *Antikhrist: Pyotr i Aleksey* (1905; Eng. tr., *Peter and Alexis*, 1905), as well as in numerous essays and his study *L. Tolstoy i Dostoyevsky* (1901–02; Eng. tr., *Tolstoy as Man and Artist, With an Essay on Dostoievski*, Merezhkovsky sought to reconcile the dichotomy between the earthly and human virtues of Hellenic paganism and the spirituality of Christ that he considered to have been lost in Christianity in its historic manifestations. In his view of history, these two extremes had been and would ever be in conflict. He therefore rejected "historic" Christianity and developed a personal, apocalyptic Christianity of the Third Testament in which these extremes would be synthesized when history had come to an end. Prominent among his religious beliefs is the concept of the Eternal Woman-Mother as the Holy Spirit, the third hypostasis of the Trinity.

An opponent of Russian Orthodoxy and autocracy, Merezhkovsky supported the abortive Revolution of 1905 in the hope that it would become a religious revolution that would overthrow existing state and church forms and then lead to religious sociality and to the establishment of the kingdom of God on earth. Such views fill his essays from 1905 on, particularly in the collection *Le Tsar et la révolution* (1907), which he wrote together with Z. N. Gippius and D. V. Filosofov, in his second trilogy, comprising the drama *Pavel I* (1908), for which he was accused and subsequently acquitted of the crime of lèse-majesté, and the novels *Aleksandr I* (1913) and *Chetyrnadtsatoye dekabrya* (1918; Eng. tr., *December the Fourteenth*, 1923).

Merezhkovsky and his wife fled from Soviet Russia in 1920. At first in Poland and later in Paris, he remained a bitter and vociferous foe of communism and the Soviet state: *Tsarstvo Antikhrista* (1921; The Kingdom of Antichrist), which he wrote along with Z. N. Gippius, D. V. Filosofov, and N. V. Zlobin, reflects these views. As an émigré, Merezhkovsky wrote only two works of fiction, the novels *Rozhdeniye bogov: Tutankamon na Krite* (Prague, 1925; Eng. tr., *The Birth of the Gods*, 1925) and *Messiya* (Paris, 1926–27; Eng. tr., *Akhnaton, King of Egypt*, 1927), abandoning belles lettres in order to devote himself exclusively to the further evolution of his religious thought, in which divine sensuality and the androgyny as the perfect being came to figure prominently. In a series of biographies and in a third trilogy—*Tayna tryokh: Yegipet i Vavilon* (Prague, 1925; The Secret of the Three: Egypt and Babylon); *Tayna zapada: Atlantida-Yevropa* (Belgrade, 1930; Eng. tr., *The Secret of the West*, 1933); and *Iisus neizvestny* (Belgrade, 1931; Eng. tr., *Jesus the Unknown*, 1933; and *Jesus Manifest*, 1935)—Merezhkovsky attempted to reconcile all pre-Christian pagan religions with the teachings of Christ and to unite the whole of humanity in his apocalyptical Christianity.

See: Z. Gippius-Merezhkovskaya, *Dmitry Merezhkovsky* (1951); C. H. Bedford, *The Seeker: D. S. Merezhkovskiy* (1975); B. G. Rosenthal, *Merezhkovsky and the Silver Age* (1975).   C.H.B.

Merleau-Ponty, Maurice (1908–61), French philosopher, was born in Rochefort-sur-Mer. For the last 20 years of his life, Merleau-Ponty was a dominant intellectual figure in France, first through his association with Jean-Paul SARTRE and his collaboration on *Temps modernes*, a periodical founded in 1945 and an active instrument of existentialism. He later separated from Sartre because of their divergent political views and ceased to write for the *Temps modernes*, but his chair at the Collège de France, where he replaced Louis LAVELLE in 1952, gave him a place from which he could address the French intelligentsia and French youth.

His first two books, *La Structure du comportement* (1941; Eng. tr., *The Structure of Behavior*, 1963) and *Phénoménologie de la preception* (1945; Eng. tr., *Phenomenology of Perception*, 1962), which are his doctoral dissertations, dealt with the basic problems of scientific psychology: how does one define and interpret biological and, more specifically, human behavior? and (the classic problem for French philosophers since Descartes) how does human consciousness perceive the external world? In the first study, Merleau-Ponty rejected the analytical method of American behaviorism, intending to prove instead that animal or human behaviors are not isolated units, but more or less complex structures. In *Phénoménologie de la perception*, by which he became famous and part of the new philosophical movement, Merleau-Ponty exposed the respective weaknesses of the two dominant philosophies of perception since Descartes, the intellectualist and empiricist interpretations. To describe and understand perceptive processes as relations between the subject and the object of consciousness, he used Edmund Husserl's methodology of transcendental phenomenology and fundamental theory of consciousness as a priori intentionality. His analyses of the function of the world as horizon and of "meaning" as the relation between signs and objects have had an influence parallel to that of Sartre's interpretation, in *L'Etre et le néant* (1943; Eng. tr., *Being and Nothingness*, 1956), of consciousness as the experience of "néantisation." Merleau-Ponty developed those basic concepts in research on the psychology of language, as can be seen in his last and posthumous book, *Le Visible et l'invisible* (1964; Eng. tr., *The Visible and the Invisible*, 1968).

Merleau-Ponty was also a brilliant essayist. In a nonsystematic way, he applied the phenomenological method to moral, artistic, and political problems of the postwar period, thus participating in the most important discussions of the 1950s. He was interested in the relation between art and literature as, for example in *Sens et non-sens* (1948; Eng. tr., *Sense and Non-Sense*, 1964). In connection with the problem of the Cold War and European communism, he wrote *Humanisme et terreur* (1947; Eng. tr., *Humanism and Terror*, 1969). In 1955, *Les Aventures de la dialectique* (Eng. tr., *Adventures of the Dialectic*, 1973) presented his conflict with Sartre, showing more clearly than before that his philosophical methodology and principles were very different from Sartre's existentialism. The opposition between the two philosophers concerned their psychology of man as well as the moral and political options of the period. In his eulogy of Merleau-Ponty, Sartre himself recognized the irreducible character of their divergent choices, for Merleau-Ponty remained close to Husserl's phenomenological approach and way of thinking, while Sartre was inclining toward G. W. F. Hegel and Karl Marx. Like Sartre, however, Merleau-Ponty was obsessed by the human search for freedom. In his problematics of liberty, he refused to believe in the Hegelian or Marxist principle of synthesis or totalization of History since he felt that human experience is, by nature, ambiguous. The true human problem is to learn how to remain lucid within the complexity and confusion of social experiences.   E.M.-S.

Merrill, Stuart (1863–1915), French poet born in Hempstead, New York, and educated in France, waged the early battles of symbolism with René GHIL and Mikhaël, classmates at the Lycée Condorcet. Influenced by Ghil's theory of "verbal instrumentation," Merrill sought to create a highly musical verse through corresponding sounds and sensations. Using the multiple resources of rhythm and sound, he evoked legendary medieval settings as a sumptuous decor for ideal quests in his first volumes of poetry, *Les Gammes* (1887; The Scales) and *Les Fastes* (1891; The Annals). If the first collection uses more discreet sonorities to convey a melancholic nostalgia for the past, the second flamboyantly mixes strident consonants and vowels in striking alliterations and onomatopoeia to evoke the brilliant coloring and orchestration of Wagnerian mythology. A more discreet tone and style characterize *Petits Poèmes d'automne* (1894; Little Poems of Autumn), in which Merrill moves away from his symbolist manner toward a more direct expression of his sentiments. Finally, *Les Quatre Saisons* (1900; The Four Seasons) and *Une Voix dans la foule* (1909; A Voice in the Crowd) reflect his humanitarian concerns and prove that his socialism, like his aestheticism, derives from a lifelong commitment to an ideal of beauty.

See: M. L. Henry, *Stuart Merrill* (1927).   M.G.C.

Mesa y Rosales, Enrique de (1878–1920), Spanish poet and drama critic, was born and educated in Madrid. As drama critic of *El Imparcial*, he aroused resentment and won respect for his frank appraisals of the work of actors and authors. The best of these criticisms were published under the title *Apostillas a la escena* (1929; Notes on the Theater). Other volumes of his prose are *El retrato de Don Quijote* (1905; The Portrait of Don Quixote) and *Andanzas serranas* (1910; Mountain Wanderings).

It is as a poet, however, that Enrique de Mesa won fame. *Tierra y alma* (1906; Earth and Soul) contains poetry in the traditional manner and meters of the classical Spanish poets. His three most significant volumes of poetry, *Cancionero castellano* (1911; Castilian Songbook), *El silencio de la Cartuja* (1916; The Silence of the Carthusian Monastery) and *La posada y el camino* (1928; The Inn and the Road), form a spiritual whole. His theme is the Castilian countryside, with its mountains and mountain dwellers, its arid plains, and its sense of antiquity and timelessness. While country things and places are called by their popular names, the intense feeling and restrained expression of his lyrics convey a sense of the emotion of the landscape. His evocation of Castile's past reflects the literary mode of his day.

See: F. de Onís, *Antología de la poesía española e hispanoamericana* (1961), pp. 689–702.

K.R.W. rev. H.L.B.

Michaux, Henri (1899–), Belgian painter, poet, narrator, playwright, and essayist, was born at Namur. He lived in Paris when he did not travel to distant countries. Michaux is equally important as a writer and a painter. His writings include verse and prose poems, narratives and voyages, and a play, as well as essays on art and literature. Since the 1920s his texts have appeared in avant-garde reviews such as *Le Disque vert, Cahiers du Sud, Minotaure, L'Arche, Fontaine,* and *Commerce*. His major works include *Un Certain Plume* (1930; A Man Named Plume), *Un Barbare en Asie* (1931; Eng. tr., *A Barbarian in Asia,* 1949), *Voyage en Grande Garabagne* (1935; Journey in Grande Garabagne), *Au pays de la magie* (1941; In whe Land of Magic), *L'Espace du dedans* (1944; Eng. tr., *The*

Space Within, 1951), *Epreuves exorcisme* (1945; Trials, Exorcism). *La Vie dans les plis* (1940; Life in the Folds), *Misérable miracle* (1956; Eng. tr., *Miserable Miracle,* 1964), *Connaissances par les gouffres* (1960; Eng. tr., *Light Through Darkness,* 1964), *Passages* (1963), and *Emergences-Résurgences* (1972), as well as a number of texts illustrated by himself: *Exorcismes-Apparitions* (1946), *Meidosems* (1948), *Peintures et dessins* (1946; Paintings and Drawings), and *Paix dans les brisements* (1957; Peace within Shatters). Most of his writings elude classification by genre—to the extent that any distinction between a prose poem and a narrative, a critical statement and an imaginary account, becomes meaningless. In his very gnomic verse poems, he eschews rhetoric and disrupts syntax as well as prosody. His fragmented, mutilated verse, which sometimes appears to parody the nonsensical ravings of a madman, is in reality perfectly controlled, endowed with highly suggestive verbal power and rarely wanting in humor. Repetitive sound patterns emphasizing dissonance and seemingly mechanical forms of recurrence produce the effect of feverish acceleration that goes beyond the traditional or organic rhythmic patterns associated with poetry. Short narratives and prose poems, structured by description or metaphor, vary in tone from matter-of-fact statements to the most personal pleas. The style, which in some instances emulates the concision of maxims or syllogisms, in others simulates the complex and searching meanderings of philosopical meditations.

The complexity induced by the narrative voice, whether it be through complicity with the reader or identity or distance between author and narrator, manifests itself in Michaux's narratives. The presence of the first-person singular requires of the reader not only awareness of all the strategies of fiction, but also empathy because of the strong confessional element involved. When Michaux records his adventures as a traveler or his experiments with drugs, the autobiographical aspects cannot be overlooked. But as transformation in all instances outweighs recollection, Michaux's works can never be construed as a mimetic attempt to reproduce the high points of experiences instigated, to begin with, as a radical departure from the ordinary self and its relation to the environment.

To what extent each of Michaux's writings pertains to an imaginary, even fantastic realm and to what extent they reflect a distilled or intensified form of reality remain difficult to determine. Evocations of remote or Utopian domains, whether they bear recognizable names or not, tend to be interlaced with satire and social commentary. By thus endowing his strange or remote lands with characteristics pertinent to modern societies, the poet brings dramatic tensions to his visions. More rarely he utters thinly disguised diatribes against political tyranny or absurd bureaucratic structures. He casts suspicions on the actual organizations that govern our lives and on the fantastic structures conceived by a perverted intellect or fostered by a wild imagination. The vitality of alienation produces the greatest shock to his readers, particularly when he forces them to identify with imaginary creatures such as Plume or the Meidosems. Michaux's bewildering creations or "generations" may bring to life new myths or give new meaning to old ones, such as that of Sisyphus. His monsters no longer involve, as do those of Goya, the sleep of reason, but they express the inner vision of the poet and of most of his contemporaries.

Several of Michaux's works show a preoccupation with space by frequently referring to the world within, to its haunting obscurity. Through recurrent nightmares, restlessness, obsessions, the poet gives shape to the struggle of his divided self, at once persecutor and persecuted, henchman and victim. He transforms himself into a battlefield of endless cruelty and torture, where hostility to oneself and aggression toward the outside world become indistinguishable. And the violent conflicts, unexplainable in psychological or social terms, acquire the permanence and absoluteness associated with metaphysics and theology. Questioning and exploring the self lead to the formulations of exorcism rather than to knowledge.

For Michaux, writing can have little to do with an aesthetic because it is an existential necessity that, by conjuring up sufficient strength to neutralize evil spirits, provides one with the only means for a few frustrating moments of liberation. It concretizes with extraordinary immediacy the relentless struggle of an "organism." This explains the persistent presence of the poet as a body that, far from being the counterpart of the soul, is the siege of a hypersensitive, fragmented, mutilated human being. Ultimately reduced to his nervous system, the poet records shocks and other interferences that can never subside and in which we see the most significant and tangible signs of an existence from which there is no escape.

In 1966, Michaux published a dense autobiographical work, *Les Grandes Epreuves de l'esprit et les innombrables petites* (Eng. tr., *The Major Ordeals of the Mind and the Countless Minor Ones*, 1974).

See: R. Bertelé, *Henri Michaux* (1946); R. Brechon, *Michaux* (1959); R. Bellour, *Henri Michaux ou une mesure de l'être* (1966); R. Bellour, ed., *Henri Michaux* (1966); M. Bowie, *Henri Michaux: A Study of his Literary Works* (1973); M. Béguelin, *Henri Michaux, esclave et démiurge* (1974); R. Dadouin, P. Kuentz, J.-C. Mathieu, C. Mouchard, M. Mourier, *Ruptures sur Henri Michaux* (1976).   R.H.

Michiels, Ivo, pseud. of Henri Ceuppens (1923–), Belgian (Flemish) novelist, was born in Mortsel, near Antwerp. His quiet youth in a small family was brought to an abrupt end by the outburst of World War II. By government order he left for the south of France and subsequently (1943) was forced to serve in the hospital corps in Schleswig-Holstein. The war touched Michiels and his work by its complex intertwining of loyalty and disloyalty, of power and weakness, by its deceptive rhetoric, and, above all, by its anguish and death.

In his first writings, *Zo ga dan! Kronijk van een opgang* (1946–47; May It Be So! Chronicle of an Uprising), *Het Vonnis* (1949; The Verdict), *Kruistocht der Jongelingen* (1951; Crusade of the Youth), and *De Oganbank* (1953; The Eyebank), Michiels's traditional style, weighted down with a strict Catholic upbringing, opens on to an existentialism akin to that of Jean-Paul SARTRE and Albert CAMUS. With each book the doubt grows, as Michiels's own life is marked by his divorce, by his turning away from the institution of the Church, and by a great interest in the development of the visual arts and the cinema. In 1955, he collaborated with Roland Verhaevert on a first film, *Meeuwen sterven in de Haven* (Seagulls Die in the Harbor). His interest in the cinema continued in his work as a teacher of "film language and analysis" and as the author of the screenplays for *Albisola Mare, Savona* (1963), *Het Afscheid* (1966; The Parting), which won a prize at the Venice Film Festival, *Met Dieric Bouts* (1975; With Dieric Bouts), and, finally, *Een tuin tussen Hond en Wolf* (1977; A Garden between Dog and Wolf). The last, made in collaboration with André Devaux, is based on a novel by Michiels.

In 1963 appeared *Het boek Alfa* (The Book Alpha), marking a culmination of his earlier works and constituting the first of a series of works that make Michiels

perhaps the most important Flemish writer of his generation. In *Het boek Alfa*, the character disappears as an anecdotal assumption, the use of the flashback diminishes, and a fragmentary structure dominates. The war again serves as a backdrop, notably in passages where a soldier hesitates between the sentimental imperative to desert and go to his wife and the military imperative to stand in place. In other fragments, doubt and compulsion play an important role. *Het boek Alfa* inaugurated a cycle of five works (originally intended to be only four; *Samuel, o Samuel* [1973] was inserted as book number $3\frac{1}{2}$), including *Orchis Militaris* (1969), *Exit* (1972), and *Dixi(t)* (1979).

In *Orchis Militaris*, language is reduced to essentials. The central character has no name. Whereas war is breaking out in *Het Boek Alfa*, *Orchis Militaris* takes place in the midst of the war. The book gives a merciless account of both the violence of war and sexual violence. The dialogue, the litany form, and the confessional style ("yes, general"—"I swear"—"I believe") accurately render the painful humiliation and dehumanizing process. Michiels himself views *Orchis Militaris* as his most important work. In *Exit*, the abstraction and the language reduction become more and more evident. There are still situations like the card game but these situations become linguistic events. For instance, the expression "I pass" leads to a serial effect: "All of you pass." "You are passing too." "I pass because I have bad cards." "I have bad cards too. Somebody must have had good cards and have nevertheless passed." In other terms, Michiels attacks the language of clichés, the means by which one can cheat and fake thinking. *Samuel, o Samuel* was written for radio. The first letters of the title form an S.O.S. that is worked into the dialogue, giving the impression that the voices must learn again to speak according to a ritual of conversation and repartee. *Dixi(t)*, the last book of the *Alfa* cycle, is a book about life even though a good deal of it concerns death. In *Dixi(t)*, Michiels again employs autobiographical detail (the death of the mother) and the short-story format. Yet the style here is more sober, purified, and moving. Between the fragments of the story, the reader finds the typical textual innovations that underline, broaden, and unify the narrative structure. The overall title of the *Alfa* cycle is "In the Beginning Was the Word."   M. van P.

Miciński, Tadeusz (1873–1918), Polish poet, dramatist, novelist, and ideologist, was born in Łódź and killed near Czyryków (Belorussia). A man of great and many-sided erudition, he elaborated an original philosophical system that was never completed and has not yet been thoroughly investigated. It can roughly be defined as a combination of Polish romantic messianism and a particular mystic brand of Pan-Slavism plus Manichaeism.

This specific conception of the world found its relatively clearest expression in lyric poetry, represented by the collection *W mroku gwiazd* (1902; In the Dusk of the Stars). Its greatest value is the fusion of cosmic imagery, conceptual content, and sonorous effects into a balanced whole.

Miciński's vision of historical and metaphysical reality was exposed on a larger scale in two closet dramas and two long quasi novels published in his lifetime. *Kniaź Patiomkin* (1906; Prince Potemkin) was inspired by the abortive rebellion of Russian sailors on board the battleship *Potemkin* in the Black Sea in 1905. The plotless drama combines realistic and fantastic, tragic and grotesque scenes, projecting the struggle of good and evil for the immortal soul of Russia and opposing to the revolution the idea of moral revival. More daring and of larger proportions is Miciński's second dramatic work, *W mrokach złotego pałacu czyli Bazilissa Teofanu* (1909; In the Darkness of the Golden Palace or the Empress of Teophan), based on the stormy history of Byzantium in the 10th century. It is a huge antiquarian drama, overflowing with authentic decorative elements, but conceived by a fiery mystic, a poet of exceptional, sometimes bewildering visionary power. Set against a sumptuous background, the work unfolds the story of the title heroine, an outsize, superhuman demoniac woman, inebriated with lust for power and sex and eventually defeated in her Luciferism.

This leading motif dominates two big prose compositions: one of them is *Nietota. Księga tajemna Tatr* (1910; Nietota: The Secret Book of the Tatra Mountains); the other is *Xiądz Faust* (1913; The Reverend Faust). Both are highly personal and contemporary (the first can even be regarded as a roman à clef), but they deal with the moral and religious problems of an individual, of Poland, and of Slavdom. They display an anti-Roman Catholic edge, hailing Polish-Russian brotherhood and proclaiming a new syncretic religion. Both can be defined as novels of mystical initiation. Structurally, they are experiments, opposing all conventional types of fiction and anticipating expressionism and even surrealism (after World War II the Polish expressionists adopted Miciński as one of their patrons; his influence on "Witkacy"—Stanisław I. WITKIEWICZ—is beyond doubt). What is peculiar to Miciński and can be traced back to Polish romanticism is the apostolic zeal of the ideologist. This urge found expression also in outright propaganda for his cherished ideas.

See: B. Danek Wojnowska, J. Kłosowicz, "Tadeusz Miciński," in *Obraz literatury polskiej XIX i XX wieku. Literatura okresu Młodej Polski* (1967), vol. 3, pp. 269–326; D. Gerould, "Magnus Tadeusz Miciński," *Y/T* 1 (1976), pp. 58–65; E. Rzewuska, *O dramaturgii Tadeusza Micińskiego* (1977); J. Prokop, *Żywioł wyzwolony* (1978).

T.T.

Miegel, Agnes (1879–1964), German poet and short-story writer, was born in Königsberg, East Prussia, the only child of a merchant. In *Kinderland* (1930; Land of Children), she tells of her happy childhood in Königsberg and of her first acquaintance with the sea, which made a lasting impression on her. After completing her elementary education, Miegel attended a girls' finishing school in Weimar and traveled, first to Paris, then to England, where she stayed for two years. A number of her ballads deal with themes taken from the history of England and France. Returning from England, she spent several years in Berlin doing newspaper work, but she never felt at home there and longed for East Prussia. Back in Königsberg, she worked on the staff of the *Königsberger Zeitung* until 1927.

Miegel's talent was essentially lyrical. She expressed her love, suffering, and longing in simple, moving poems, traditional in form. She is best known, however, for her stirring ballads, dealing with historical events as well as with magic and supernatural forces. These ballads are direct and forceful in style; the fusion of lyrical and narrative elements results in poems quite different in form and appeal from the usual narrative ballad, evident in *Gesammelte Gedichte* (1927; Collected Poetry). In her prose tales, the most powerful of which is *Die Fahrt der sieben Ordersbrüder* (1926; The Journey of the Seven Friars), she emphasized detail and description in order to create local color as well as mood and suspense. After the separation of East Prussia from the Reich in 1919, Miegel became more and more the spokesman of her native land. She voiced the hopes and fears of its people, as in *Herbsttage* (1932; Days of Autumn), and she explained her own work in a conversation with ancestors in

Unter hellem Himmel (1936; Under a Clear Sky). A volume of poems, tales, and reminiscences appeared in the year after her death.

See: M. Schochow, *Agnes Miegel: eine Studie* (1929); A. Piorreck, *Agnes Miegel, Ihr Leben und Ihre Dictung* (1967).   O.S.F. rev. A.L.W.

Migjeni, pseud. of Millosh Gjergj Nikolla (1911–38), Albanian poet, was born in Scutari to poor parents of Slavic origin. He studied in Yugoslavia to become an Orthodox priest, but he later became an atheist and worked as a village schoolteacher until his death from tuberculosis in an Italian sanatorium.

Migjeni's poems and sketches brim with sympathy for the poor and the oppressed. His appearance on the Albanian literary scene marked the end of the romantic and postromantic movement that had begun with Girolamo de Rada's *Milosao* in 1836 (*see* ALBANIAN LITERATURE). Migjeni shocked the public by portraying the North Albanian highlanders as starved and sick, cringing before the authorities to obtain a bag of corn, a view in sharp contrast to the idealized depictions of these people by Gjergj FISHTA, the outstanding poet of the time. Migjeni's pictures of city life are equally grim: unemployed workers turning into drunkards, orphans begging in the streets, girls turning to prostitution to earn a living. It is on behalf of these people that Migjeni's poetry rises up against King Zog's semifeudal regime and its servants and allies, the clergy and the intellectuals. His poem "Scandalous Song" is a cry of rebellious apostasy. Yet he lacked the Dantesque anger to persevere in his unorthodox beliefs. As a result of his illness, he often took refuge in melancholy or sank into despair.

Migjeni's poetry, with its mixture of the revolutionary and the decadent, constitutes the most advanced experiment in Albanian poetry of the 1930s. His *Vargjet e lira* (1936; Free Verse) was censured and confiscated, but the book was published in 1944 and has had two editions since, its author being hailed as a forerunner of socialist literature. This is only true in part, however, for the decadent trend in his poetry is hardly less conspicuous. Migjeni is a highly original poet with a rare gift for metaphor. His language cannot be molded into conventional forms, yet he does not reject them completely. Among Albanian poets, Migjeni alone has been widely translated and studied.

See: A. Pipa, "Le mythe de l'Occident dans la poésie de Migjeni," *Südost-Forschungen* (1971), pp. 142–75; G. E. Eintrei, *Tvorchestvo Midjeni* (1973).   A.P.

Miguéis, José Rodrigues (1901–), Portuguese novelist and story writer, was born in Lisbon, where he took his law degree. Since 1935, except for several years spent in Brussels studying for a master's degree in education, occasional visits to Portugal, and a year (1949–50) spent in Brazil, he has lived in New York, whose life he portrayed in short stories and sketches of great beauty. He was known in literary and political circles—having joined the *Seara Nova* group in 1922—when he published *Páscoa feliz* (1932; Happy Easter), a novella that was hailed as a turning point in Portuguese modern fiction, owing to its psychological and social insights. From then on, Miguéis grew to be a major figure and the greatest living fiction writer in Portuguese literature. Judging from the dates of his books, it would seem that his production has been intermittent. Nothing of the sort happened; but because he published many of his works haphazardly or by instalments in magazines, they were consigned to volume form only after many years of painstaking revision.

Thus, the novella *Léah* (1940), a masterpiece of subtle

realism, did not appear in book form until 1958 (*Léah e outras histórias*; Léah and Other Stories). *Onde a noite se acaba* (1946; Where Night Ends), *Gente de terceira classe* (1962; People in Third Class), *Comércio com o inimigo* (1973; Trading with the Enemy), and *As armonias do "Canelão"* (1974; "Canelão's" Harmonies) are also collections of excellent short stories. *Uma aventura inquietante* (1958; A Disquieting Adventure) is a moral parable disguised as a delightful detective story centered in Belgium, whereas *Um homem sorri à morte com meia cara* (1959; A Man Smiles at Death with Only Half a Face) is the impressive and stark account of a serious illness the author endured in New York. *A escola do paraíso* (1960; The School of Paradise) evokes, under the cover of fiction, Miguéis's childhood in Lisbon at about the time when the monarchy came to an end. *Nikalai! Nikalai!* (1971) is a satirical spoof of Russian émigrés in Brussels. It includes the novella *A múmia* (The Mummy), a masterful story, set in Portugal, of frustration in love. A late novel, *O milagre segundo Salomé* (2 vols., 1974; The Miracle according to Salome) combines the sentimental rags-to-riches story of a country girl ravished in the city with a satirically rational explanation of the apparitions of Our Lady of Fátima. Either recalling his life in Portugal or using his cosmpolitan experiences, Miguéis is a realist endowed with imagination, wit, tenderness, and delicacy of touch and tone, who does not lack awareness of any of the technical conquests of modern literature. Novels, short stories, sketches—all of them vibrate with a lucid humanism. An ironic, yet sentimental philosophy of life permeates his writing. His fluent, precise style looks like simplicity itself—and turns out to be a very sophisticated one.

See: O. Lopes, "O pessoal e o social no obra de Miguéis", in his *Cinco personalidades literárias* (1961), pp. 49-84; J. A. Kerr, Jr., "Aspects of Time, Place and Thematic Content in the Prose Fiction of José Rodrigues Miguéis as Indications of the Artist's Weltansicht," Ph.D. Dissertation, University of Wisconsin (1970) and *Migúeis—to the Seventh Decade* (1977). J. de S.

Mihăescu, Gib (1894-1935), Romanian novelist, short-story, writer and dramatist, was born in Drăgăşani. His law studies were interrupted by World War I, during which he probably contracted the tuberculosis that afflicted him later in life. After the war he practiced law in Chişinău. In 1919 his novella "Linia întâi" was printed in *Luceafărul* and the novella "Soldatul Nistor" (Private Nistor) appeared in Eugen LOVINESCU's *Lecture pentru toţi* (Reading for Everyone). In 1921, Mihăescu moved to Cluj where, with Lucian BLAGA and Cezar Petrescu, he founded the review *Gîndrea*, in which he published various novels and short stories. Mihăescu returned to his native village in 1924, married, and again practiced law. He published a volume of novellas, *La Grandiflora* (At Grandiflora), in Craiova in 1928, and in the same year the National Theater produced his drama *Pavionul cu umbre* (Shadowed Ward). Mihăescu's second volume of short novels, *Vedenia* (The Apparition), appeared in 1929. The principal character of the novel *Braţul Andromedei* (1930; Andromeda's Arm) is an amateur astronomer modeled after Mahăescu himself. His best-known novel, *Rusoaica* (The Russian Girl), appeared in 1933 and *Donne Alba*, another of his novels, was published in 1935, shortly after his death.

See: L. Ulici, "Gib Mihăescu, scriitor al obsesiei," in *Viaţa românească*, vol. 2 (1967); A. Piru, *Varia* (1972). P.G.T.

Mihura Santos, Miguel (1905-77), Spanish playwright,

was born and raised in Madrid amidst the miseries and jubilations of the acting profession. His father, a skilled actor and theater manager, exposed young Miguel to the complexities of stagecraft, introducing him to such prominent figures as Pedro MUÑOZ SECA and Enrique Garcia Alvarez, two of the playwrights whose bizarre humor foretokened the absurdist posture Mihura adopted a decade later.

Between 1934 and 1952, Mihura worked as dialoguist on 25 motion pictures. He also founded the wartime humor magazine, *La Ametralladora* (1936-39) and edited the popular weekly periodical, *La Codorniz* (1941-44), known for its abstract satire, colloquial nonsense, and extravagant dialogues. The badinage he cultivated for *La Codorniz* carried over into the writing of three full-length plays in collaboration with Joaquin CALVO-SOTELO, Antonio de Lara, and Alvaro de Laiglesia. This period culminated in the celebrated performance of his first and most notable comedy of single authorship, *Tres sombreros de copa* (1952; Three Top Hats).

Over the next 16 years, Mihura staged 19 plays of varying artistic merit. They range from tantalizing but shallow farces of intrigue, such as *Melocotón en almíbar* (1958; Peaches and Syrup), to works of solid construction in which parody, satire, and caricature are effectively infused with sophisticated dialogue, a profound sense of humanity, and engaging character development. The outstanding plays of this period include *Mi adorado Juan* (1956; My Beloved Juan), *Maribel y la extraña familia* (1959; Maribel and the Strange Family), and *La bella Dorotea* (1963; Lovely Dorotea).

Mihura's plays present a smiling acceptance of reality and an admission that, although human predicaments are not always surmountable, ideals and illusions are worthwhile commodities of the spirit. Above all, his writings affirm that individuals acquire positive values by liberating themselves from constricting habits and social conformity.

See: R. McKay, *Miguel Mihura* (1977). D.R.McK.

Miłosz, Czesław (1911-), Polish poet, essayist, novelist, and translator, was born in Šeteiniai, Lithuania, and studied law at the University of Vilnius, where he belonged to the literary group "Žagary." He spent the years of World War II in occupied Poland. He was connected with the Resistance and edited a clandestine anthology of anti-Nazi poetry, *Pieśń niepodległa* (1942; Invincible Song). He was sympathetic to the social reforms in postwar Poland and served as cultural attaché in Washington and Paris. In 1951, however, he left Poland and settled in France, where he became a leading contributor to the émigré periodical *Kultura*. He became well known in the West as the author of *Zniewolony umysł* (1953; Eng. tr., *The Captive Mind*, 1953), a penetrating study of the predicament of intellectuals in a totalitarian system, and the political novel *Zdobycie władzy* (1955; Eng. tr., *The Seizure of Power*, 1955), which won the Prix Littéraire Européen. In 1960, Miłosz moved to California, where he became professor of Slavic literatures at the University of California, Berkeley.

Miłosz is a writer of great range and power of expression, and his poetry stands apart from the dominant European and American trends. His early poems, *Poemat o czasie zastygłym* (1933; A Poem of Congealed Time) and *Trzy zimy* (1936; Three Winters), are impressive for their intensely personal vision and apocalyptic themes. In contrast, his poetry of the war period and the early postwar years, including the volume *Ocalenie* (1945; Rescue), struck a note of hope and affirmation and was an attempt to overcome the trauma of the "shattered garden" and to seek once more "a world objectively beautiful and true." *Światło dzienne* (1953; Daylight), although containing some of his best lyrical poetry, is also remarkable for its brilliant satirical and discursive verse, and *Traktat poetycki* (1957; A Treatise on Poetry) is perhaps the best example of his classical style. His "Californian" poetry focuses increasingly on the crisis of modern culture, remembrance of things past, and existential themes: *Gucio zaczarowany* (1964; Bobo's Metamorphosis), *Miasto bez imienia* (1969; City without a Name), *Gdzie wschodzi słońce i kędy zapada* (1974; Where the Sun Rises and Where It Sets). Related in these are his prose works, which include *Dolina Issy* (1955; The Valley of Issa), a fictional evocation of a childhood full of metaphysical intimations; *Rodzinna Europa* (1958; Eng. tr., *Native Realm*, 1968), a "search for self-definition"; and *Widzenia nad zatoką San Francisco* (1969; Visions by San Francisco Bay), a book of meditations on European and American civilization, "to exorcise the evil spirits of contemporary times."

Of his other books, *Kontynenty* (1958; Continents), *Prywatne obowiązki* (1972; Private Obligations), *Człowiek wsród skorpionów* (1962; Man among Scorpions), *Ziemiaś Ulro* (1977; The Land of Ulro), *Emperor of the Earth* (1977), and *Ogród nauk* (1979; The Garden of Knowledge) are literary essays. His translations include the first Polish version of T. S. Eliot's *The Waste Land* (1946), poems of Walt Whitman, and Oscar Miłosz, as well as the volume *Postwar Polish Poetry* (1965). His own poetry has been translated into several languages (Eng. tr., *Selected Poems*, 1973) and *Bells in Winter* (1978). Miłosz is also the author of a comprehensive *History of Polish Literature* (1969).

See: M. Danilewicz Zielińska, *Szkice o literaturze emigracyjnej·* (1978), pp. 200–12; WLT (special Miłosz issue) 52, no. 3 (1978).   B.Cz.

Milosz, Oscar-Vladislas de Lubisez (1877–1939), Lithuanian-French poet, novelist, dramatist, and philosopher, was born in Chereya, USSR (but "historic Lithuania," as he himself noted). His father was from an old, noble family, his mother of Jewish Polish extraction. The family moved to Paris in 1889, where he attended the Lycée Janson-de-Sailly, and then studied ancient Semitic languages and civilization. At the same time, he was writing and publishing poetry, *Le Poème des décadences* (1899; The Poem of the Decadences) and *Les Sept Solitudes* (1906; The Seven Solitudes), revealing a sensitivity for verbal music and a mystic temperament, but not sufficient to distinguish him greatly from the contemporary Decadents. Until the outbreak of World War I, he traveled all over Europe and North Africa, living the life of a rich cosmopolitan aristocrat.

Milosz's novel *L'Amoureuse Initiation* (1910; Amorous Initiation) and the three plays *Miguel Mañara* (1912; Eng. tr., 1919), *Mephiboseth* (1913), and *Saul de Tarse* (written 1914, pub. 1970) show that he considered himself an "homme de lettres." The poems he wrote between 1915 and 1922, collected in *Symphonies, Adramandoni*, and *La Confession de Lemuel* (1922), mark a steady increase in preoccupation with spiritual problems and the mystery of the universe. The Russian Revolution (1917) deprived him of his ancestral estates, but he continued to fight for the independence of his little country as minister of Lithuania to France and to the League of Nations. He kept this post until his death, even though in 1931 he had become a French citizen. Near the end of his life, he led an increasingly secluded existence.

In two books of prophetic poetry, *Ars magna* (1924) and *Les Arcanes* (1926), Milosz gave some idea of his system, an exotic blend of Catholicism, Jacob Böhme, Swedenborg, the Cabala, alchemical tradition, and modern physics (like Einstein, he focused his philosophy on the concept of relativity). These "metaphysical" poems are probably his best.

Milosz has been accused of pretentiousness and obscurity by some and hailed as one of the greatest modern French poets by others. He himself said that he wrote with "l'âme des mots" (the soul of the words), and as he grew older this verbal concentration, combined with the esoteric nature of his subject matter, made the texts more difficult to comprehend. But modern readers and contemporary critics find in this writing a pithiness, a depth, and a magic that gradually display their inexhaustible wealth.

See: J. Buge, *Milosz en quête du divin* (1963); *Cahiers de l'Association des Amis de Milosz* (1967–77); J. Bellemin-Noël, *La Poésie-philosophie de Milosz* (1975); A. Silvaire, ed., *Lire Milosz en 1977: colloque de Fontainebleau pour le centenaire de la naissance de Milosz* (1977).   J.B.-N.

Mirbeau, Octave (1850–1917), French playwright, novelist, and essayist, was born in Trévières, the son of a middle-class doctor. An unhappy childhood, complicated by unfortunate experiences in the Jesuit college at Vannes, affected him deeply and may account in part for the bitter tone of much of his mature work. The range of his thought runs from the conservative antirepublicanism of his youth to a highly charged expression of a radicalism that borders, at times, on the anarchistic. He quickly rose to a position of influence in artistic and literary circles and gave real support to the efforts of such innovators as Vincent Van Gogh, Auguste Rodin, Edouard Manet, Claude Monet, Paul Cézanne, Claude Debussy, and Maurice MAETERLINCK. The fiercely independent nature of Mirbeau's temperament is best seen in his journalistic articles for *L'Illustration, L'Ordre*, and *Le Gaulois*. As cofounder with Paul HERVIEU of the intransigent weekly *Grimaces*, Mirbeau in his editorials provoked the indignation of numerous spokesmen for conservatism in art and politics.

A strong note of protest also dominates most of Mirbeau's creative work. His first notable play, *Les Mauvais Bergers* (1897; The Bad Shepherds), directed against those dishonest politicians who exploit the common laborer, paved the way for the memorable drama and popular success *Les Affaires sont les affaires* (1903; Business Is Business), a bitter indictment of business ethics and the financial world. The comedy *Le Foyer* (1908) issued a sharp attack on deceit and mismanagement in charitable institutions. His early novels, *Le Calvaire* (1886; Calvary), *L'Abbé Jules* (1888), and *Sébastien Roch* (1890), are largely autobiographical. Noteworthy among his later novels is *Le Jardin des supplices* (1899; Eng. tr., *Torture Garden*, 1931), a study of oriental sadism prompted to a degree by the development of the Dreyfus Affair. *Le Journal d'une femme de chambre* (1900; Eng. tr., *Celestine, Being the Diary of a Chambermaid*, 1930) stands out as the most truly naturalistic of Mirbeau's works. The vigor of his prose and the fearlessness of his attack made these novels notoriously popular at the time of their publication.

Ideologically, Mirbeau inherited more from Jean-Jacques Rousseau than from Emile ZOLA and his followers at Médan. His novels may be viewed as explicit condemnations of that which ultimately serves to blunt man's instincts and to rob him of his individualism. If Rousseau presented man with the Social Contract in order to extract him from his dilemma, Mirbeau carried his thesis through with a kind of unswerving logic, spelled out unremittingly in the bleak message of *Les Affaires sont les affaires* and in the sadism of *Les Jardin des supplices*.

See: M. Revon, *Octave Mirbeau: son œuvre* (1924); M. Schwarz, *Octave Mirbeau: vie et œuvre* (1966).

R.J.N. rev. R.T.D.

Miró Ferrer, Gabriel (1879–1930), Spanish novelist and short-story writer, was born in the Mediterranean city of Alicante. The second child of a devoutly Catholic family, he was sent to the nearby Jesuit school in Orihuela when we was eight years old. A boarder for nearly five years, the impressionable youth did not fare well and spent long periods in the school's infirmary through whose windows he contemplated his first "aesthetic sadnesses," as he labeled the many sunsets viewed from his sickbed. He later recalled the austere climate of these times in *Libro de Sigüenza* (1917; Book of Sigüenza), one of his best-known works. Miró's subjective art constituted, to a great extent, his life. The only obstacle to the total identification of his inner self and his work was so-called aesthetic distance, that transubstantiation that daily changes reality into universal art.

At the age of 20, Miro wrote *La mujer de Ojeda* (1901; Ojeda's Woman). Along with *Hilván de escenas* (1903; A Threading of Scenes), and *Del huerto provinciano* (1912; From the Country Orchard), he later repudiated this work. In his 20s, Miró built his intellectual and artistic foundations. It was a time of trial and error, of indecision and of constant thinking about what would ultimately constitute his aesthetic. During this period, Miró's enigmatic alter ego, Sigüenza, whose life span parallels Miró's own, made his first appearance, in *Del vivir* (1904; About Life). Most of Miró's early works betray a slight romanticism, and all are brief and written in the style that later crystallized into his "telling by insinuating." *Las cerezas del cementerio* (1910; The Cherries of the Graveyard), a long novel with decadent overtones and motifs, opens the middle stage of Miró's literary production. The knowledge acquired during a year and a half as editor of a failed Catholic encyclopedia was the source of his most controversial and least understood book, but the one that made him known to readers inside and outside Spain. Entitled *Figuras de la Pasión del Señor* (1916–17; Figures of the Lord's Passion), it was received with much skepticism and soon denounced as unorthodox vis-à-vis Catholic hagiography. A two-volume work, it is structured as a series of religious vignettes in which biblical characters are viewed from an intrinsically literary perspective. At about the same time, Miró wrote *El humo dormido* (1919; The Sleeping Smoke), a book of poetic narrative essays, fictional but of autobiographical inspiration. *El abuelo del rey* (1915; The King's Grandfather) and the *Libro de Sigüenza* also date from this period. The latter gathers most of the essays and stories whose protagonist is the same Sigüenza of *Del vivir*. Miró wrote his most aesthetically perfect books in the last decade of his life (1920–30). He worked slowly and devotedly on these works, carefully distilling his narrative resources until he successfully produced a pure and elliptical prose. In his 40s, Miró published only three new novels: *Nuestro Padre San Daniel* (1921; Our Father Saint Daniel), *El Obispo leproso* (1926; The Leprous Bishop), and *Años y leguas* (1927; The Years and the Leagues). Strictly speaking, the first two are really one book, as they share the same literary microcosm. They should be regarded as a bipartite novel. If this last stage of Gabriel Miró's life does not seem prolific, at least it brought him more peace and recognition than previous years. The Mariano de Cavia Prize awarded by the prestigious Madrid daily *ABC* for his story "Huerto de cruces" ("The Cross Orchard")

must have helped ease the repeated slights of the Royal Spanish Academy of the Language, which denied him a chair and twice failed to consider him for the Fastenrath Prize. A resigned and serene tone permeates the major works of this third period of Miró's career, a fitting end to the even-tempered fiction of a sensitive, exquisite, and transcendent writer.

See: E. L. King, "Gabriel Miró y 'el mundo según es'," *PSA* 62 (May 1961): 121–42; V. Ramos, *El mundo de Gabriel Miró* (1964); R. Landeira, *An Annotated Bibliography of Gabriel Miró (1900–1978)* (1978).   R.L.

Mistral, Frédéric (1830–1914), Provençal poet, was born, lived, and died at Maillane near Avignon. His father, a well-to-do farmer, felt honor-bound to give him a good classical education. At the College Royal of Avignon, Frédéric proved to be an excellent student, but reading Homer and Virgil barely consoled him for the loss of actual contact with country life and people who spoke Provençal, his mother tongue. He had his revenge by composing verses in that speech, which was spurned by official education and derided by his schoolmates. One day he was elated to hear one of his teachers, Joseph ROUMANILLE recite some poems in the despised tongue. This marked the beginning of a lifelong friendship and fruitful collaboration. Later Mistral went to study law at the University of Aix-en-Provence. After receiving his diploma (1851), he returned home determined to devote his life to the task of reviving Provençal consciousness among his countrymen. This he hoped to accomplish through the prestige of poetry in the vernacular which, like Roumanille, he was intent upon restoring to literary dignity.

Mistral's first publications were two French poems written in a period of republican and humanitarian enthusiasm (1848), but he attracted considerable attention only when some of his early compositions in Provençal were included in *Li Prouvençalo* (1852), an anthology of living poets edited by Roumanille. From then on his prestige increased rapidly. He was the most brilliant star of the pleiade that founded the "Félibrige" school (*see* PROVENÇAL LITERATURE, MODERN) in 1854. His first important work, *Mirèio* (1859; Eng. trs., *Mireio*, 1867, *Mirelle*, 1868, *Mireio*, 1872), established his reputation outside of Provence. This, a long poem in 12 cantos, a rustic idyl cast in epic form, was a revelation with regard to the richness and poetry of both language and subject matter. It was crowned by the French Academy, later translated into the main European languages, and turned into an opera by Charles Gounod.

Besides *Mirèio*, Mistral's works in verse comprise other poems of the epic type: *Calendau* (1867), symbolizing Provence in its struggle against centralization, and *Lou Pouèmo dóu Rose* (1897; Eng. tr., *Anglore: the Song of the Rhone*, 1937), depicting the life of the Rhône boatmen before the advent of the steamship, as well as two volumes of collected lyrical poems, a versified novella, and a lyrical tragedy. Mistral's prose work includes *Moun espelido; memóri e raconte* (1906; Eng. tr., *Memoirs of Mistral*, 1907); a collection of speeches; and three volumes of *Prose d'almanach* (1926–30), published posthumously with, opposite the Provençal text, a French translation from the pen of the editor. To these must be added a scholarly work, *Lou Tresor dóu Felibrige; dictionnaire provençal-français embrassant les divers dialectes de la langue d'oc* (1876–86), which is indeed a treasure of science and poetry, and a translation of Genesis into Provençal prose. In 1904, Mistral shared the Nobel Prize in Literature, for both his literary works and his contribution to philology. He used the proceeds of the prize to house the Museon Arlaten, a museum of ethnography that he had just founded in Arles and to the enrichment of which he was to devote the last 10 years of his life. When he died, he had been the leading spirit of the Félibrige for nearly 60 years.

Mistral's works are better known to the general public by their French titles, such as, *Mireille, Calendal, Mes Origines.* The French translations accompanying the original are by the author himself. While chiefly considered a Provençal patriot and poet of the soil, Mistral has also been studied as a reviver and defender of classical traditions. Served by a powerful genius and a keen artistic sense he has been able to produce works with a strong and universal appeal, characterized by both perfection of form and the omnipresence of a noble ideal.

See: M. Decremps, *Mistral, Mage de l'Occident* (1954); R. Lafont, *Mistral ou l'Illusion* (1954); R. Aldington, *Introduction to Mistral* (1956); L. Bayle, *Grandeur de Mistral essai de critique littéraire* (1964).   A.V.R.

Mňačko, Ladislav (1919–), Slovak novelist and journalist, was born in Valašské Klobouky in Moravia. From 1945 on, he worked in Slovakia as a journalist, writing political and economic articles on the building of socialism. His articles written abroad (Vietnam, Albania, and Israel, including reports on the trial of Adolf Eichmann) reveal not only a keen journalistic ability, but also a real literary talent. In 1963, Mňačko upset the tranquillity of Slavic literary life by publishing two collections, *Kde končia prašné cesty* (Where the Dusty Roads End) and *Oneskorené reportážo* (Delayed Reports), which depict the tragic fate of innocent victims of Stalinist socialism, and which were inspired by actual cases.

Mňačko's works of fiction often treat moral themes. The partly autobiographical novel, *Smrť sa volá Engelchen* (1959; Eng. tr., *Death Is Called Engelchen*, 1961), depicts the dramatic torment of a man who believes himself guilty of causing the destruction of a Moravian village by Nazi troops. His next novel, *Alo chutí moc* (1967; Eng. tr., *The Taste of Power*, 1967), was first published in Austria in German; it vividly portrays the moral degeneration of a Communist leader who, from a thirst for power, betrays the ideals for which he once fought.

In August 1968, Mňačko left his native country and settled in Austria. Outside Czechoslovakia he has published the satirical novel *Súdruh Münchhausen* (1972; Comrade Munchhausen), which ridicules the paradoxes and absurdities of the Stalinist period (again the work is based on actual cases), and two works of fiction published in German, *Der Vorgang* (1970; Priority) and *Einer muss überleben* (1973; A Man Must Survive), both of which insightfully probe the psychic reactions of people faced by agonizing choices between life and death.   F.M.B.

Moberg, Vilhelm (1898–1973), Swedish novelist and dramatist, was born in rural Småland, the son of a soldier-peasant. After a varied youth, in which periods of unskilled work alternated with periods of study, he took up journalism in 1919. He also began writing tales and plays of peasant life. His literary breakthrough came with the novel *Raskens* (1927; The Rasks), a story of life on a soldier's croft in the late 19th century. The novel is built around the characters of the energetic, if violent, Rask and his long-suffering but faithful wife, Ida; yet the real value of the book lies in its vivid presentation of a particular way of life—its daily routine and its special ceremonies. Folk traditions and customs predominate in *Långt från landsvägen* (1929; Far from the Highway), an account of rural Småland in "the old century"; its sequel, *De knutna händerna* (1930; The Clenched Fists) is a mov-

ing picture of an old peasant who clings convulsively to the past as industrialization changes the traditional way of life. Moberg's journalistic experiences as local correspondent in a small community are reflected in *A. P. Rosell, bankdirektör* (1932; A. P. Rosell, Banker). This disenchanted picture of a small town at the time of the Great Depression shows the local businessmen as embezzlers and the formerly idealistic journalist as cynical and corrupted. *Mans kvinna* (1933; Man's Woman) is a love story set in Småland in the 1790s. The romance is between the dispossessed peasant Håkan and his neighbor's wife, Märit. Their passionate affair and their final elopement as outlaws are a hymn to life outside the bounds of society's conventions—a primitivist vision. As always in Moberg's works, the routine of the farming year and the social background are excellently and knowledgeably described and there is a lyrical quality about the novel that is a minor, but important feature of his works. The *Knut Toring* trilogy (1935–39; Eng. tr., *The Earth is Ours*, 1940) is uneven.

During World War II, Moberg was a fierce opponent of the Swedish government's appeasement of Adolf Hitler. This opposition is expressed in *Rid i natt!* (1941; Eng. tr., *Ride This Night!*, 1943), a novel of 17th-century Småland, in which the German lord of the manor tries to introduce feudal practices among the free Swedish peasantry. The peasants eventually give in to his threats, with the exception of Ragnar Svedje, who takes to the forests as an outlaw rather than become a serf. The novel's message is clear, and the book was an enormous success. The novel *Soldat med brutet gevär* (1944; Eng. tr., *When I was a Child*, 1956) is the story of Valter Sträng from birth to manhood and in outward events is based on Moberg's own life. It is a Bildungsroman about a boy determined to find an ideal to fight for and in this fight to overcome "the short and inadequate life that is the body's." The novel is also a fascinating social history of popular movements in Sweden in the early 20th century, particularly socialist groups. Valter finds his ideal in the struggle for the rights of his underprivileged social class, and he comes to the conclusion that he can best help "my people" by giving them a voice in literature. Whereas the novel is an account of the years leading up to the Social Democrats' breakthrough in Sweden, it is simultaneously a thinly veiled attack on what Moberg saw as the party's betrayal of its early ideals once it was in office. *Brudarnas källa* (1946; The Bridal Spring) is a lyrical intermezzo: four stories from four historical periods that emphasize the repeated cycle of life and death. Moberg's postwar writing is dominated by his tetralogy on Swedish immigration to America: *Utvandrarna* (1949; Eng. tr., *The Emigrants,* 1951), *Invandrarna* (1952; Eng. tr., *Unto a Good Land,* 1954), *Nybyggarna* (1956), and *Sista brevet till Sverige* (1959) (abridged Eng. tr., of *Nybyggarna* and *Sista brevet till Sverige, The Last Letter Home,* 1961). The first volume of this epic work describes a group of peasants from Småland who typify different reasons for emigrating to America in the mid-19th century. The second volume depicts their arrival in the promised land, and as the group splits up, attention is increasingly focused on the energetic but obstinate Karl Oskar and his gentle wife, Kristina. Karl Oskar has left an oppressive Sweden for a land where his initiative brings success, but Kristina never overcomes her homesickness, dies young, and Karl Oskar enters a bitter old age. His brother Robert, seeking absolute freedom and independence through easy riches, sets off on the California Trail in search of gold, but his companion dies in the desert, and his riches turn to ashes; his desire for freedom turns to a longing for death. A modern sequel to the emigrant novels is *Din stund på jorden* (1963; Eng. tr., *A Time on Earth*, 1965), about an old Swedish immigrant who, from the Hotel Eden in California, between the twin dangers of the Pacific and the main highway, reviews his failed life and seeks consolation in his memories of his Småland childhood. It is a quietly lyrical book, with an undertone of fatalism. Moberg's last novel, *Förrädarland* (1967; Traitors' Land), is set in the 16th century and describes the tribulations of a population caught on either side of an arbitrary and disputed frontier. Taken together, Moberg's novels form a great social history of Småland from the 16th century to the present day. Moberg also began a history proper of Sweden, a history that was to be that of the peasants, not the rulers. Only the first two parts appeared before his death: *Min svenska historia* (1970, 1971; Eng. tr., *A History of the Swedish People*, 1972, 1973). Moberg also achieved great popular success as a dramatist. His plays repeat the themes of his novels: peasant life in *Hustrun* (1928; The Wife), social criticism in *Våld* (1933; Violence), and a more private preoccupation with death in *Nattkyparen* (1961; The Night Waiter). He adapted several of his novels for the stage, including *Mans kvinna* (1943; Eng. tr., *Fulfillment*, 1953). Moberg had occasional brushes with what he saw as an obstructive and corrupt establishment; his campaigns find literary expression in the satirical novel *Det gamla riket* (1953; The Old Kingdom) and the play *Domaren* (1957; The Judge). In lighter vein is a collection of autobiographical essays, *Berättelser ur min levnad* (1968; Stories from My Life).

See: G. T. Alexis, "Vilhelm Moberg: You Can Go Home Again," *SS* 40 (1968): 225–32; P. A. Holmes, "Symbol, Theme and Structure in *Utvandrarromanen*," *Perspektiv på Utvandrarromanen* (1971), pp. 239–48; G. Eidevall, *Berättaren Vilhelm Moberg* (1976); P. A. Holmes, *Vilhelm Moberg, TWAS* (1980).   G.O.

Mockel, Albert (1866–1945), Belgian poet, was born in Liège. He was influenced by René GHIL and by Stéphane MALLARMÉ. He founded the review *La Wallonie* in 1886, and, seeking to establish his poetic work on theoretical bases, he published *Propos de littérature* (Topics of Literature) in 1894. But it was his *Chantefable un peu naïve* (A Rather Naive Chantefable), which had appeared in 1891, that first presented his aesthetic: a musical, imprecise, and fluid vision, resting on an abundant use of vague and abstract terms and accompanied by preciosity, affectation, and mannerism. Richard WAGNER's influence is perceptible in the structure of the work; that of Ghil and Mallarmé, in its syntax and vocabulary. Certain dialogues, moreover, evoke the atmosphere of Maurice MAETERLINCK's first plays, whose "magic" nature and power of charm Mockel greatly appreciated. More clarity, more simplicity, and more naturalness characterize subsequent collections, but Mockel's fidelity to his aesthetic principles (architectural proportions, rejection of a personal theme and reality, search for abstraction and suggestion, recourse to dialogue and legendary subjects) confers on his poetry a factitious and antiquated aspect that the use of an obsolete vocabulary reinforces all the more. The reading of Mallarmé strongly imbues the first part of *Clartés* (1901; Lights), in which the poet's "dreaming" becomes enraptured and "lasts forever" in the midst of a universe of reflections, delicate forms, evanescent lines, and abstract contours. *La Flamme immortelle* (1924; The Immortal Flame) is Mockel's most vast and polished work. In it, two important preoccupations are evident: the will to structure matter according to architectonic rules and the desire to break with the personal theme in favor of a less rigid formula. For the traditional "I," Mockel thus substitutes two characters, "She" and

"He," whom he situates in an ideal time and whose voices alternate all along the nine sections of the poem. But Mockel's faithfulness to the symbolist aesthetic gives *La Flamme immortelle* an anachronistic aspect, and its awkwardness and naiveté prevent one from appreciating the scholarly searches for rhythm and harmony at their full value.

See: C. Hanlet, *Les Ecrivains belges contemporains de langue française, 1800–1946*, 2 vols. (1946); G. Charlier and J. Hanse, *Histoire illustrée des lettres françaises de Belgique* (1958); A. Mockel, *Esthétique du symbolisme, Propos de littérature (1894), Stéphane Mallarmé, un héros (1899), Textes divers* (1962); H. Braet, *L'Accueil fait au symbolisme en Belgique, 1885–1900* (1967); R. Burniaux and R. Frickx, *La Littérature belge d'expression française* (1973); R. Frickx and M. Joiret, *La Poésie française de Belgique de 1880 à nos jours* (1976).   R.F.

Moens, Wies (1898–), Belgian (Flemish) poet, essayist, and politician, was a student at the University of Ghent (1916–18) at a time when courses were given in Flemish under the sponsorship of the German occupiers. From 1918 to 1921 he was imprisoned because of his affiliation with the so-called activist wing of the Flemish movement, which had grown weary of awaiting equal rights for the Flemish-speaking community from the Belgian government. His first works, the collection of poems *De Boodschap* (1920; The Message) and the prose work *Celbrieven* (1920; Letters from Prison) were published while he was in prison. *De Boodschap* combined characteristic expressionist traits (extreme yet vague idealism, cosmic imagery, free lyrics) with Christian and Flemish nationalist overtones that were traceable to Moens's own situation. Poetically these works constitute a remarkable achievement because of their idealism (neither bombastic nor moralistic) and their imagery and fluent diction. These qualities turned Moens at once into one of the leading figures of the review *Ruimte* (1920–21), the voice of Flemish humanitarian expressionism and the fierce opponent of the naturalist and impressionistic literature. To the younger generation Moens seemed to labor for a complete formal renewal of Flemish poetry.

By its autobiographical and moral slant, however, *Celbrieven* clearly announced Moens's switch to predominantly Catholic and Flemish-nationalist objectives. Although *De Tocht* (1920; The Journey) still retained an organic unity of form, with *Opgangen* (1922; Progress) and *Landing* (1923) his idealism slowly became programmatic, his optimistic tone strained. The review *Pogen* (1923–25), founded by Moens after the disappearance of *Ruimte*, defended a strictly Catholic view of art and literature. Yet Moens's broadly humanitarian stand still appeared in his serving as secretary (1922–26) to the Flemish Popular Theater, which aimed at the political and social revival of the Flemish-speaking community through theatrical means.

In the later poems of such volumes as *Golfslag* (1935; Undertow) and in the review *Dietbrand* (1933–39), the narrowing of Moens's ever present Flemish nationalism induced a corresponding view on culture. He accepted a leading position with the Brussels broadcasting station during the 1940–44 German occupation of Belgium, pursuing his own ideal of an independent nation comprising Holland and the Flemish community. After World War II, he was sentenced to death in absentia. He settled in Holland continuing his poetic and essay work without response from his home country.

See: F. von Passel, *Het tijdsschrift Ruimte (1920–1921) als Brandpunt van het humanitair expressionisme* (1958); E. Verstraete, *Wies Moens* (1973).   D. van B.

Mogin, Jean (1921–), Belgian poet and playwright, was born in Brussels. He began his career with the poetic collections *Les Vigiles* (1950; The Vigils) and *Les Pâtures du silence* (1956; Pastures of Silence). As a playwright, he wanted to establish a theater of fervor and spoliation, of absolute requirements. *A chacun selon sa faim* (1950; To Each According to His Hunger) is the story of a Portuguese nun who objects to any compromise with a priest whom she deems unworthy: a Montherlantian subject treated with an astonishing psychological density and a great austerity. *Le Rempart de coton* (1952; The Cotton Rampart) is again, within the context of the War of Secession, the story of an intransigent being's refusal. *La Fille à la fontaine* (1955; The Girl at the Fountain), in its proud search for purity, is close to Fernand CROMMELYNCK's *Carine*, whereas *La Reine de neuf jours* (1963; The Nine-Day Queen) traces the brief destiny of Lady Jane Grey, queen of England in spite of herself, who will know how to assume the role to which a convulsion of history bids her. Mogin is fond of whole, infrangible beings and heroic confrontations in which human depth is lost and the character turns to entity—a theater of challenges in which the hero is sometimes called upon to muster all his resources. Mention should also be made of a truculent, less happy farce, *Les Archanges Gabriel* (1966; The Archangels Gabriel), and an excellent assemblage of medieval texts from French and Walloon, *Le Mystère de la Nativité, de la Passion et de la Résurrection de Notre-Seigneur* (1966).

See: J. Burniaux and R. Frickx, *La Littérature belge d'expression française* (1973), p. 102; A. Jans, *Lettres vivantes 1945–1975* (1975), pp. 307–08.   R.T.

Moll i Casanovas, Francesc de Borja (1903–), Menorcan philologist, was born in Ciudadela, where he studied for eight years in the seminary. He studied Romance philology and linguistics and in 1921 began working with Antoni M. Alcovar on the *Diccionari català-valencià-balear* (Catalan-Valencian-Balearic Dictionary). After Alcovar's death in 1932, he continued the work, completing the dictionary in 1962. He also coauthored the *Atlas Lingüístico de la Península Ibérica* (Linguistic Atlas of the Iberian Peninsula). Other books include a *Gramàtica històrica catalana* (1952; Historical Grammar of Catalan), *Els Llinatges catalans (Catalunya, País Valencià, Illes Balears)* (1959; Catalan Names [Catalonia, Valencia, and the Balearic Islands]), and *Un home de combat (Mossén Alcovar)* (1962; Mossén Alcovar, A Fighting Man). In 1962 he set up the cultural foundation Obra Cultural Balear, which widened the scope of his editorial work in the journal *Les Illes d'Or,* founded in 1934, and *Raixa,* which began as a little magazine and by 1954 had grown into a publishing house. In 1963 he founded *Els treballs i els dies* (Works and Days), a series of literary publications.

In 1931, with his *Ortografia Mallorquina segons les normes de l'Institut* (Majorcan Orthografy Following the Rules of the Institute), he had joined the ranks of the movement to renovate and standardize the Catalan language. He later published a *Vocabulario Mallorquí-castellà* (1965; Majorcan-Castilian Word List), *Gramàtica catalana referida especialment a les Illes Balears* (1968; Catalan Grammar, with Special Reference to the Balearic Islands), and *L'home per la paraula* (1974; Man in His Words). Among his prizes are the Philology Prize of the Institute of Catalan Studies, the Prize of Honor for Catalan Studies (1971), and the Ossian Prize (1978), which he received on April 21, 1978. He holds honorary doctorates from the universities of Barcelona and of Basilea (1976) and is an honorary member of the Institute of Catalan Studies, vice-rector of Llulian studies, and a member of the Academy of Bones Lletres of Barcelona.

See: A. M. Badia i Margarit, "Reply to the Acceptance Speech at the solemn investiture of F. de B. M. C. as Doctor 'Honoris Causa' at the University of Barcelona" (1976).   J.F.C.

Molnár, Ferenc (1878–1952), Hungarian playwright, novelist and short-story writer, was born in Budapest and died in New York. As a young man he studied law at Budapest, but he preferred journalism, the stage, and literature. Molnár was first acclaimed as a clever and witty journalist—he had taken up writing in 1896—and soon afterward as a gifted playwright. Molnár spent much of his time away from Hungary, living in Western Europe in the 1920s and, finally, leaving Hungary for the United States, where he lived from 1940 until his death.

As a playwright, Molnár won international fame for his cleverly constructed plays with either sentimental or cynical overtones. His heroes and heroines encounter difficulties caused by a transgression of convention or by an irrational approach to rational problems, but these are rarely those tragic or comic complications that one discerns in the works of the greatest playwrights. Yet Molnár possessed an innate taste that made him avoid the temptation merely to play tricks, and that enabled him at times to assert a real poetic sensitivity (as in *Liliom* 1909; Eng. tr., 1921). He had the urge of the genuine writer, but in most of his plays he mingled romanticism and realism, creating a heterogeneous sort of artistic experience involving unexpected scenes, lively dialogue, manufactured excitement. Many of his plays have been produced in the United States, including *Az ördög* (1907; Eng. tr., *The Devil,* 1908), *A testör* (1910; Eng. tr., *The Guardsman,* 1924), *A hattyú* (1920; Eng. tr., *The Swan,* 1922), *Olympia* (1928; Eng. tr., 1928), *Valaki* (1932; Eng. tr., *Arthur,* 1946). In 1947, *The Guardsman* was adapted for radio by Arthur Miller. The play *Liliom,* which had its successful run on Broadway, reveals aspects of Molnár's talent seldom displayed elsewhere in his works. The play is unpretentious, and its fablelike atmosphere is credible because it is poetically vivid and convincing. Molnár's other plays, despite their skilled technique, their ingeniousness, and in some instances their brilliance, seldom rise to the level of supreme literary art.

Molnár's novels and short stories are entertaining, if not as skillfully constructed as his plays. One of his most successful works of fiction is the much-translated *A Pál utcai fiúk* (1907; Eng. tr., *The Paul Street Boys,* 1927), a novel of young Budapest boys playing "war games." This work has epic attributes; it is simple and tragic, solid and humane. Molnár's first novel, *Az éhes város* (1900; The Hungry City), is perhaps his most realistic piece of fiction. English translations of Molnár's other works of fiction include *Egy gazdátlan csónak története* (1901; Eng. tr., *The Derelict Boat,* 1926), *Éva* (1903; Eng. tr., 1926); *Rabok* (1907; Eng. tr., *Prisoners,* 1925); *Zenélö angyal* (1933; Eng. tr., *Angel Making Music,* 1935) and *Isten veled szivem* (1947; Eng. tr., *Farewell My Heart,* 1945). Molnár's last work, *Utitárs a száműzetésben* (1958; Eng. tr., *Companion in Exile,* 1950), which bears the subtitle "notes for an autobiography," is a tribute to his lost secretary and companion, providing rare glimpses into Molnár's private life.

In the field of nonfiction Molnár's best work is probably *Egy haditudósító emlékei* (1916; Memoirs of a War Correspondent). It observes and records human goodness, decency and solidarity in the gray, monotonous horror of World War I. This warmhearted book shows a passion of the spirit that one often misses in Molnár's other, technically highly competent works.

See: A. Schöpflin, "Molnár Ferenc," *Nyugat* 21 (1928):

497-500; D. Belasco, Foreword to *All the Plays of Molnár* (1937); J. Gassner, *Masters of the Drama* (1940), pp. 479-80; E. Illés, *Krétarajzok* (1957): 316-19; I. Sötér et al., *A magyar irodalom története*, vol. 5 (1965): 476-79.

J.R. rev. G.G.

Mombert, Alfred (1872-1942), German poet and author of modern "myths," was born in Karlsruhe, not far from the Rhine, the river he loved so deeply, which became a kind of homely leitmotiv in his poetry. He was an outstanding literary personality not connected with any school or clique and little known to a wide public. Mombert studied law and philosophy at the universities of Heidelberg, Leipzig, Munich, and Berlin. After six years of law practice, he retired from all public activities and devoted himself to a life of contemplation. He lived in Heidelberg, absorbed in his books and a collection of minerals that he brought home from trips all over Europe and northern Africa. He was an enthusiastic walker, and the greater part of his poetry was written not in his study but while wandering about the country.

Mombert's first volume of verse, *Tag und Nacht* (1894; Day and Night), was influenced by the poets of German romanticism, but at the same time it was inspired by a strange psychological insight, making the interior life transparent and mysticism a realistic affair. His next books, *Der Glühende* (1896; The Glowing Man), *Die Schöpfung* (1897; The Creation), *Der Denker* (1901; The Thinker), and *Die Blüte des Chaos* (1905; The Blossom of Chaos), describe the experiences of the human soul in pictures of emotional grandeur and in words of rhythmic power. Many of these poems have been set to music.

In the years that followed, Mombert made the attempt to create a "myth," based on his personal philosophy. His most important work during this period is the trilogy *Aeon* (1907-11), written in dramatic form. The first part concerns the relations between the world and the human soul; the second, the dilemma of the ego placed between chaos and cosmos. The third part deals with the materialization of the human soul in the history of the nations. These dramatic poems were not for the contemporary stage but were meant to be presented to audiences of the future. Of a proposed second trilogy, *Aigla,* the poet finished only two parts (1928-31). During the same period two of his greatest lyrical works, *Der Held der Erde* (1919; The Hero of Earth) and *Atair* (1925), were published.

In his seventh decade Mombert turned to a new realism. In *Sfaira der Alte* (1936; Sfaira the Elder), the wise old poet who is the central figure of this book of verse does not have "imagination" and does not talk about things; he is simply the most sensitive and understanding of listeners. The trees, the mountains, the lakes, the parks, the old inns—all talk to him. The world is pictured as it looks to them and not from the point of view of a reflective poet.

In the fall of 1940, Mombert was arrested and moved to the concentration camp of Gurs, France, where he fell seriously ill. In 1941 friends succeeded in having him released to reside in Switzerland. He died in Winterthur after celebrating his 70th birthday with his friends. He had finished and revised a second part (1941) of *Sfaira der Alte*.

See: E. Michel, *Der Weg zum Mythos* (1919); F. D. Benndorf, *Mombert: Geist und Werk* (1932); H. Carossa, *Führung und Geleit* (1933); F. J. Petermann, *Symbolik und Problem der Gestalt bei Alfred Mombert* (1960).

M.F. rev. A.L.W.

Mon, Franz, pseud. of Franz Löffelholz (1926-), German experimental poet and theorist, was born in Frankfurt am Main. From his first book, *artikulationen* (1959), he has presented an intense double effort to define, in poetic and theoretical texts, the nature of the poem as a "process" that "must always have begun before." Thus the single poem is not a self-contained structure, but a "shape of articulation" making visible the passage of time and especially (by stressing phonetic and syntactic values over semantic ones) the material character of language.

Mon's poems range from visual, "concrete" constellations, collage and décollage, to systematic permutations, always with appealing variety and playfulness: *sehgänge* (1964; seeways), *5 beliebige fassungen* (1966; 5 optional versions), *Lesebuch* (1967; Reader). His long prose, *herzzero* (1968; heartzero), explores, in two parallel columns, phrases out of phase, studded with puns, allusions, and permutations, with the sequence left to the reader's discretion. Besides his essays on poetic theory, collected in *texte über texte* (1970), Mon has also written and edited books on avant-garde art: *movens* (1960) and *Prinzip Collage* (1968). R.Wa.

Montal, Robert, pseud. of Robert Frickx (1927-), Belgian poet, novelist, and essayist, was born in Brussels. He is a professor at the University of Brussels. The profound unity of his work assumes various aspects. First there is his poetry. *Patience de l'été* (1965; Summer Patience) and *Un royaume en Brabant* (1969; A Kingdom in Brabant) are collections in which, in a very pure language, both love of life and the sharp awareness of its precariousness are expressed. This sensitive acuity of vision recurs in *La Traque* (1970; The Hunt), a novel that retraces a sentimental education marked by a certain inaptitude in living. In the short stories of *La Courte Paille* (1974; Drawing Lots), Montal remains faithful to poetry, which willingly assumes the visage of a curious uncanniness in which it happens that dream meets impertinence and humor. His essays (the last to appear are signed Robert FRICKX) bear witness to his critical lucidity at the same time they reflect the whole of his preoccupations and anxieties: *René Ghil* (1962), *Gérard de Nerval* (1965), *Rimbaud* (1968), *Lautréamont* (1973), *Ionesco* (1974)—so many innovators who have questioned themselves about both the form of their art and the profound meaning of life.

See: *Bibliographie des écrivains français de Belgique,* vol. 4 (1972); A. Jans, *Lettres vivantes 1945-1975* (1975).

R.Bu.

Montale, Eugenio (1896-), Italian poet, essayist, critic, and translator, was born in Genoa. He is largely self-taught; his formal education was interrupted by ill health at the age of 14. Montale spent the first 30 years of his life in his native city and the nearby coastal town of Monterosso, whose rocky shores and sun-drenched hills provided the setting of his first book of poems, *Ossi di seppia* (1925; Cuttlefish Bones). Montale's determination to shun the "eloquence" of Giosuè Carducci (1835-1907), Giovanni Pascoli, Gabriele D'Annunzio, and their imitators gave added impetus to the renovation of Italian poetry that his older contemporary, Giuseppe Ungaretti, had set in motion during the previous decade. From the outset, Montale's style has been sober, yet intense and melodiously compelling. A central theme and abiding concern of his work is the human condition, often viewed with sadness, at times even despair (especially in *Ossi di seppia*), but never totally without hope. Despite the warning, in an early poem, that a poet can only tell what we are *not*, what we do *not* want, Montale never loses his fascination with life's overwhelming, albeit inscrutable power. Thus his darkest lyrics, dwelling on the "evils" of man's existence, are counterbalanced by poems that strike a very different note: not one of unreserved optimism, to be sure, but certainly of faith in life's endurance and persistence, and in the regenerating force of love.

In 1929, after settling in Florence, Montale became the director of the international lending library Gabinetto Vieusseux, a position from which he was summarily dismissed in 1938 because of his refusal to join the Fascist Party. Soon thereafter he published his second collection of poems, *Le occasioni* (1939; Occasions). The work's at times highly compressed, telescoped images and private allusions plunged him into the controversy over obscurity in poetry. Accused of writing hermetic verse (*see* ITALIAN LITERATURE), Montale replied that no poet is hermetic or cryptic on purpose, insisting, however, that no one would write poetry if his overriding aim were merely to be understandable. An outstanding part of *Le occasioni* is the central section, entitled "Mottetti" (Motets), consisting of 20 brief poems addressed to an unnamed lady. This same lady or woman-angel—Montale's personal emblem of salvation in what he now saw as a rapidly decaying world—reappears, under the mythical names of Clytie and Iris, in his third verse collection, *La bufera e altro* (1956; The Storm and Other Poems). The "storm" refers to the grim experiences of World War II in Fascist Italy; "La primavera hitleriana" (The Hitler Spring), for example, concerns Hitler's ominous visit to Florence in early 1938. The "other poems" of the collection are, for the most part, love lyrics, among the most striking to be found in modern Western literature.

By the time *La bufera* was published, Montale had moved to Milan, where in 1948 he became literary editor and special correspondent (later music critic) for the city's major newspaper. Over a period of almost 20 years, he composed a series of transparently autobiographical prose pieces that form a sort of counterpoint to many of his poems. These were collected under the title *Farfalla di Dinard* (1956; Eng. tr., The Butterfly of Dinard, 1971). This volume was followed by *Auto da fè* (1966), a selection of critical essays; *Montale-Svevo. Lettere* (1966), the poet's correspondence with the novelist Italo SVEVO; *Fuori di casa* (1969; Away from Home), a selection of articles written as a roving reporter on various assignments, mostly abroad; and *Sulla poesia* (1976; On Poetry), a collection of Montale's major writings on his own poetic experience, on problems of aesthetics and literary criticism, and on the works of numerous Italian and foreign poets, mainly French and Anglo-American. Three more books of collected poems, *Satura* (1971), *Diario del '71 et del '72* (1973; Diary of 1971–72), and *Quaderno di quattro anni* (1977; Four-Year Notebook), in which his pessimism is mitigated by gentle irony and humor, confirmed Montale's stature as one of the major European poets of the 20th century. General esteem and acclaim in his own country and abroad resulted in his appointment as Italian senator for life (1967), in the conferral the same year of an honorary degree in letters from Cambridge University and, in 1975, in the award of the Nobel Prize for Literature.

Of special interest are Montale's numerous translations, particularly those from English and American authors, including John Steinbeck, Herman Melville, Nathaniel Hawthorne, Mark Twain, William Faulkner, Eugene O'Neill, Shakespeare, and T. S. Eliot. A collection of his versions of works by foreign poets, *Quaderno di traduzioni* (Translation Notebook), was published in 1975. Montale's own poetry has been widely translated into English, beginning with the version of one of his cardinal poems, "Arsenio," in T. S. Eliot's *Criterion* (June 1928). Some of Montale's work is available in English in *Poesie/Poems*, tr. by George Kay (1964); *Selected Poems*, various translators, introduction by Glauco Cambon (1966); and *Provisional Conclusions*, tr. by Edith Farnsworth (1970).

See: J. Cary, *Three Modern Italian Poets: Saba, Ungaretti, Montale* (1969); G. Cambon, *Eugenio Montale* (1973); M. Forti, *Eugenio Montale* (1973); G. Singh, *Eugenio Montale* (1973). L.R.

Monteiro, Adolfo Casais (1908–72), Portuguese poet, essayist, literary critic, and novelist, was born in Oporto and became a high school teacher. Arrested in 1936 for opposing the dictatorship of Oliveria Salazar, he was thereupon forbidden to teach in Portuguese schools. In 1938 he settled in Lisbon, working for a publishing house as a translator. In 1954 he moved to Brazil and from then on lectured at universities. He acquired Brazilian citizenship in 1963 and lived the rest of his days in his adopted country, except for a short period when he taught at the University of Wisconsin.

Monteiro's first book of poems, *Confusão* (1929; Confusion), was published while he was still a student. It was soon followed by *Poemas do tempo incerto* (1934; Poems of an Uncertain Time) and *Sempre e sem fim* (1936; Always and without End). By 1931 Monteiro had become director of the literary review *Presença,* and his poems of that time share the basic attitudes defended by the *presencistas:* introspection, a search for originality, freedom of artistic creation, and a certain aestheticism. Monteiro's first three volumes of poetry were condensed in *Versos* (1944). In his *Poesias completas* (1969; Collected Poems) are also found later poetic works including *Canto da nossa agonia* (1942; Song of Our Agony), *Noite aberta aos quatro ventos* (1943; Night Open to the Four Winds), *Europa* (1946), *Simples canções da terra* (1948; Simple Songs of the Earth), and *Vôo sem pássaro dentro* (1954; Flight without a Bird Within).

"My poems were always born out of a state of dissatisfaction, discontent, and lack of balance. They are, almost all of them, the voice of the shadows, melancholy, despair, anxiety or else of states or moments of positive exaltation, of ecstasy if you prefer," Monteiro wrote in 1944, prefacing *Versos.* Some critics mention that a harsh, almost brutal quality exists in the poems of the early period. This is somewhat tempered in his later work, which shows a deeply humanistic outlook and a reconciliation with reality. The Portuguese critic Jorge de Sena points out a paradox in Monteiro's verses: their intemporality side by side with their revolt against contemporary attacks on human dignity. *Adolescentes* (1945), his only novel, belongs to the psychological trend that *Presença* launched. In it the author analyses the emotional crisis of a young, irresolute college student who finds no meaning in his life.

Monteiro was also one of the most lucid critics and essayists of his time. Having started young with a study of the poet Mário de SÁ-CARNEIRO (1933), he went on to write three major works: *De pés fincados na terra* (1941; With Feet Firmly Planted on the Ground), *Fernando Pessoa, o insincero verídico* (1954; Fernando Pessoa, Truthfully Insincere), and *Romance, teoria e crítica* (1964; The Novel: Theory and Criticism).

See: J. Gaspar Simões, "Breve introdução à poesia de Adolfo Casais Monteiro," in his *O mistério da poesia* (1931), pp. 280–90; J. de Sena, "O poeta Casais Monteiro," in his *Da poesia portuguesa* (1959), pp. 203–13, and Preface to Adolfo Casais Monteiro, *Poesias escolhidas* (1960). E.M.D.

Monteiro, Domingos (1903–), Portuguese story writer and novelist, was born in Barqueiros, in the province of Trás-os-Montes. He studied engineering, switched to law, and became a publisher. In his teens he published his first verse, inspired by the late symbolists. He returned to poetry in *Evasão* (1953; Evasion) to explore modern man's crisis of identity. He became prominent, however, as an author of novellas and short stories. His most popular collections are *O mal e o bem* (1945; Evil and Good), *Contos do dia e da noite* (1952; Tales of Day and Night), and *Histórias castelhanas* (1955; Castilian Stories). In most of his stories and in his two novels—*O caminho para lá* (1947; The Road There) and *Letícia e o lobo Júpiter* (1972; Leticia and the Wolf Jupiter)—Monteiro creates plots whose characters free themselves from some form of bondage. A secular idealist opposed to the limitations of social protocol, common sense, and psychological realism, he effectively shows how everyday events can have transcendence. Setting is secondary in these revelations of human ingenuity, episodes involving poetic whimsy, altruism, and, perhaps most often, deception. The importance given to individual initiative and will-power that asserts itself in unexpected ways explains the author's preference for first-person accounts. The result is a very traditional plot structure. He relies heavily on dialogue with one speaker clearly in the foreground, and he is patently at his best with male protagonists.

See: Á. Ribeiro, *Escritores doutrinados* (1965), pp. 113–239. R.A.P.-R.

Montesquiou-Fezensac, Count Robert de (1855–1921), French poet, essayist, and art critic, was born in Paris. Of an aristocratic family descended from one of the four baronies of Armagnac and claiming among its forebears some famous military and governmental figures of the late 18th and early 19th centuries (as well as d'Artagnan, the hero of Alexandre Dumas's *Three Musketeers*), Montesquiou felt a closer kinship with his ancestors than with the living members of his family. For a young nobleman of the Faubourg Saint-Germain, he was remarkably well educated, first at the hands of private tutors, then at the Lycée Bonaparte (later called Condorcet) and by the Jesuits. Reviewing his first volume of collected verse, *Les Chauves-souris* (1892; The Bats), Anatole FRANCE wrote that "there is something of the musketeer turned into an artist and a poet in M. Robert de Montesquiou, who is, if you like, the d'Artagnan of the rare and the exquisite." By this time, the count was something of a legend in Paris society by reason of his haughty bearing, his caustic wit, his culture, and his eccentric ways. In the same review article, France had felt called upon to deny that the count had been the inspiration for Joris-Karl HUYSMANS's character Des Esseintes.

Montesquiou wrote poetry and prose with great facility, albeit with a certain preciosity. He gave elaborate receptions for each new volume he published, and he was assiduous in obtaining publicity for them in the press. But he was too esoteric to attract the attention of the public, and in his own circle he made more enemies than friends. His collected verse includes *Le Chef des odeurs suaves* (1893; The High Priest of Suave Fragrances), *Le Parcours du rêve au souvenir* (1895; The Route from Dream to Memory), *Les Hortensias bleus* (1896; Blue Hydrangeas), and a volume of 93 sonnets on Versailles entitled *Les Perles rouges* (1899; Red Pearls). His 17 volumes of prose met with no greater success than his verse, yet his wide knowledge and taste gave real merit to some of his criticism. Among the many subjects of such volumes as *Roseaux pensants* (1897; Pensive Reeds) are Jean Auguste Dominique Ingres, Théodore Chassériau, Alfred Stevens, Paul Helleu, Léon Bakst, Emile Gallé, and René Lalique.

It was Montesquiou's fate, however, to attain immor-

tality not through his own efforts but in spite of them. He is remembered because of Marcel PROUST, an aspiring young writer who was presented to him in Mme Madeleine Lemaire's salon on April 13, 1893. Proust was at once intrigued by this eccentric nobleman whose pride of birth was matched by his wit and learning. He soon learned to imitate Montesquiou's voice, style, and mannerisms, and when he came to write his novel *A la recherche du temps perdu* (*Remembrance of Things Past*), he endowed his Baron de Charlus with a parody of Montesquiou's conversation as well as with some of his quirks of character.

See: G. D. Painter, *Proust: The Early Years* (1959) and *Proust: The Later Years* (1965); P. Jullian, *Robert de Montesquiou: un prince 1900* (1965; Eng. tr., *Prince of Aesthetes*, 1968). P.K.

Montherlant, Henry de (1896–1971), French novelist, dramatist, and essayist, was born in Paris. His expulsion from the Sainte-Croix Catholic school in Neuilly deeply affected him and later became the subject of his play *La Ville dont le prince est un enfant* (1951; The City Whose Prince Is a Child). Similarly, his first play, *L'Exil* (1929), was inspired by his resentment of his mother's refusal to allow him to enlist (out of respect for her, he did not publish the play in her lifetime). Montherlant extolled the life of the athlete, fought bulls in Spain, and rose to fame and membership in the Académie Française, but he disdained the world and his public. With characteristic stoicism, he took his own life when threatened with blindness.

Montherlant published widely and brilliantly in various literary forms, but he is best known for his plays (1942–65), nobly poetic "costume tragedies" set in the 16th and 17th centuries, such as *La Reine morte* (1942; Eng. tr., *Queen after Death,* in *The Master of Santiago and Four Other Plays,* 1951), *Malatesta* (1946; Eng. tr., in *The Master of Santiago,* 1951), *Don Juan* (1958), and *Le Cardinal d'Espagne* (1960; Eng. tr., *The Cardinal of Spain,* 1969). He is especially remembered for his "Catholic trilogy": *Le Maître de Santiago* (1947; Eng. tr., *The Master of Santiago,* 1951), *La Ville dont le prince est un enfant,* and *Port Royal* (1954; Eng. tr., 1962). These works, although nominally historical, concern the tragic destiny of man, his absurd paradoxes, and his frailty as he confronts the malevolence of a formless earth under a lightless heaven. Again and again, Montherlant's heroes and heroines face God/nothingness, while their creator belligerently pursues his lifelong campaign on behalf of the individual, defending intellectual, martial, and physical culture over mediocrity and despair, advocating courage, purity, patriotism, and self-sacrifice as opposed to cowardice, hypocrisy, and subservience.

Montherlant's career as author of 13 works of fiction commenced none too promisingly with *Le Songe* (1922; Eng. tr., *The Dream,* 1962), an autobiographical account of World War I that may have inspired Ernest Hemingway. His second novel, *Les Bestiaires* (1926; Eng. trs., *The Bullfighters,* 1927, *The Matador,* 1957), won several prizes. His tetralogy *Les Jeunes Filles* (1936–39; Eng. trs., 1937–40 and *The Girls: A Tetralogy,* 1968), attacked by Simone de BEAUVOIR as antifeminist, has still failed to reach a wide public in the United States. Montherlant's most popular novel to date remains *Les Célibataires* (1934; Eng. trs., 1935, 1936, and as *The Bachelors,* 1960), which tells of two elderly brothers, comic misfits in modern Paris, one of whom kills the other.

Montherlant's psychological penetration deepened over the course of his career, and shortly before his death he published four moving novels that treat his preferred materials with even greater authority. Bullfighting in Spain is the subject of *Le Chaos et la nuit* (1963; Eng. tr., *Chaos and Night,* 1964), and French colonial Morocco is the focus of *La Rose de sable* (1954, 1968; Eng. tr., *Desert Love,* 1957). His two final novels, *Les Garçons* (1929, 1969; The Boys) and *Un Assassin est mon maître* (1971; An Assassin Is My Master), concern parochial school education and the murderous nature of power in our daily lives. These rhetorically admirable novels, classical in style and content, probe beneath the traditional bases of Freudian psychology, exploring modes of consciousness open to the novelist's art.

When controversy raged around political rightism, Montherlant trumpeted unpopular, nationalistic views and espoused an eclectic set of stances ranging from orthodox Christianity to Jansenism, Manichaeanism, stoicism, skepticism, asceticism, and even paganism. Privately he admired Renaissance and classical heroes (see *Le Treizième César* [1970; The 13th Caesar]), and it is said that the example of Cato the Younger enabled him to commit suicide at the onset of blindness.

Montherlant's notebooks, from *Carnets: 1930-44* (Notebooks) to *La Marée du soir* (1972; Evening Tide), cover the period 1930-71; these volumes are represented in *Selected Essays* (1960). Together with prefaces, poetry fiction, polemics, and dramas both historical and modern, they constitute a precious treasury of documents and an extensive monument to this twice-wounded veteran of World Wars I and II. Because of the beauty, elegance, and sobriety of his French, Montherlant has been called a modern classicist. In his own extensive literary criticism, he praised rigor, or what he termed "style naturel."

See: J. W. Batchelor, *Existence and Imagination: The Theatre of Henry de Montherlant* (1967); R. B. Johnson, *Henry de Montherlant* (1968); L. Becker, *Henry de Montherlant: A Critical Biography* (1970); J. Robichez, *Le Théâtre de Montherlant* (1973).   N.L.G.

Morales, Tomás (1884-1921), Spanish poet, was born in Moya, a little seacoast town on the island of Grand Canary. He is often associated with two other Canary Island poets who were contemporaries and friends of his: Alonso Quesada and Saulo Torón. Morales studied medicine in Cádiz and Madrid and spent several years as a country doctor in Agaete, a town on the island of his birth. There he married and began to raise a family. He later moved to the capital, Las Palmas, where he became interested in politics. But his principal and unwavering vocation was his poetry, in which every phase of his brief existence is reflected. His childhood is presented in a series of poems entitled "Vacaciones sentimentales." Subjective in feeling and characterized by a delicate, sentimental prosaicness, these poems are typical of the postmodernist period and of the poetry of the Canary Islands. Then comes the intimate, sentimental poetry of the sea and the waterfront in their most commonplace, everyday aspect. Finally, there is his more ambitious work, represented by the "Oda al Atlántico" and the "Canto a la Ciudad Comercial" (Song to the Commercial City), presenting a mythological version of the sea. They are at once classical and modern, and reveal the great rhetorical gifts Morales inherited from the modernists (*see* SPANISH LITERATURE). This poetic production—varied, intense, personal, and universal in appeal—is contained in two books: *Poemas de la gloria, del amor y del mar* (1908; Poems of Glory, of Love, and of the Sea) and *Las rosas de Hercules* (1922). They have the unmistakable flavor of Morales's native region and have had a strong influence on other poets of the Canary Islands.

See: S. de la Nuez, *Tomás Morales. Su vida, su tiempo y su obra* (1956).   F. de O. rev. H.L.B.

Morand, Paul (1888-1976), French novelist and diplomat, was born in Paris. Having been sent to England for several summers to study English, in 1908 he was permitted by his father to spend a full year at Oxford. Upon his return to France, Morand began a brilliant diplomatic career. After a short stay in the Protocol Section, Morand was sent to England (1913-16), Rome (1917), and then to Madrid (1918). During the years 1919-25, he was engaged at the Ministry of Foreign Affairs in Paris, and it was then that he began to write. His first publications—*Lampes à arc* (1919; Arc Lamps) and *Feuilles de température* (1920; Temperature Records)—were collections of short poems. *Tendres Stocks* (1921; Eng. tr., *Green Shoots,* 1923), with a preface by Marcel PROUST, contained three short stories about three young women adrift in wartime London. The short-story collections *Ouvert la nuit* (1922; Eng. tr., *Open All Night,* 1923) and *Fermé la nuit* (1923; Eng. tr., *Closed All Night,* 1924) brought Morand instantaneous fame. The novel *Lewis et Irène* (1924; Eng. tr., *Lewis and Irene,* 1925), however, was not an unqualified success. The stories and sketches of *L'Europe galante* (1925) presented the same themes as the *Nuits,* but in a more daring key.

In 1923, the Ministry of Foreign Affairs sent Morand to Siam to take charge of the legation in Bangkok. To reach his new post, where he remained only a short time, Morand traveled halfway round the world. For several years thereafter he spent a large part of his time traveling. Some of his books, such as *Rien que la terre* (1926; Eng. tr., *Earth Girdled,* 1928), *Le Voyage* (1927), *Paris-Tombouctou* (1928), and *Hiver caraïbe* (1929; Caribbean Winter), were accounts of his travels. Others were studies of various cultures: the Oriental, in *Bouddha vivant* (1927; Eng. tr., *Living Buddha,* 1927); the African, in *Magie noire* (1928; Eng. tr., *Black Magic,* 1929), the American people, in *Champions du monde* (1930; Eng. tr., *World Champions,* 1931). His later books were mostly of five kinds: travel books, such as *Flèche d'Orient* (1931; Eng. tr., *Orient Express,* 1932) and *Air indien* (1932; Eng. tr., *Indian Air,* 1933); studies of cities, such as *New York* (1929; Eng. tr., 1931), *London* (1931; Eng. tr., *A Frenchman's London,* 1934), and *Bucharest* (1935); political works, such as *1900* (1931; Eng. tr., *1900 A.D.,* 1931), *France-la-Doulce* (1934; Eng. tr., *The Epic Makers,* 1935), and *Rond-Point des Champs-Elysées* (1935); autobiographical works, such as *Papiers d'identité* (1931; Identity Papers) and *Mes Débuts* (1933; My Beginnings); and psychological novels, such as *Le Flagellant de Séville* (1951; Eng. tr., *The Flagellant of Seville,* 1953).

See: G. Guitard-Auriste, *Paul Morand* (1956).   P.Br.

Morante, Elsa (1918-), Italian novelist, short-story writer, and poet, was born in Rome. She married Alberto MORAVIA in 1941. Morante's first book, *Il gioco segreto* (1941; The Secret Game), consisted of short pieces previously contributed to well-known periodicals. She wrote and illustrated a children's book, *La bellissime avventure di Caterì dalla trecciolina* (1942; The Marvelous Adventures of Cathy Pigtail), revised and expanded as *Le straordinarie avventure di Caterina* (The Extraordinary Adventures of Cathy) in 1959. Her first novel, *Menzogna e sortilegio* (1948; Lies and Sorcery), won the Viareggio Prize. This work is a lengthy saga about three generations of a southern Italian petit bourgeois family told by the last descendent, Elisa, who rebelled against impossible social and historical conditions by creating her own fantasy world. Because of the book's unrealistic, poetic language and its emphasis on memory, quite strongly influenced by Katherine Mansfield (some of whose work Morante had translated), critics said that the work harked back to the literature of the 1930s, dominated by the periodical *Solaria* (*see* ITALIAN LITERATURE). Yet the novel was meant as a tragic epic: an ideological expression of the current crisis of the Western bourgeoisie.

Morante's next novel, *L'isola di Arturo* (1957; Eng. tr., *Arthur's Island*, 1959), won her the Strega Prize. Arturo is an adolescent who has lived an isolated life, immersed in dreams of his dead mother and fabulous visions of his father's marvelous voyages. He is rudely initiated into "reality" when he becomes aware of his quasi-incestuous love for his young stepmother and of the fact that his father's journeys are limited to the homosexual circuit near Naples. Arthur is saved from total despair by the reappearance of his (male) childhood nurse, and they leave the island together to enlist. Morante's genius lies in expressing her Freudian themes through intensely poetic imagery and in her highly allusive, musical, lyric language, by means of which she achieves a balance between her extremely bitter vision of reality and Arturo's iridescent fantasy world.

The poetry of *Alibi* (1958) serves, as she put it, as an echo or chorus to her novels. *Lo scialle andaluso* (1963; The Andalusian Shawl), a book of short stories, reaffirms her psychological and lyric gifts. *Il mondo salvato dai ragazzini* (1968; The World Saved by Children) is an ambitious Christian and Marxist mixture of poetry in various styles meant to serve as an epic comment on the unhappy many and the happy few, ending in an expression of hope. Morante's *La Storia* (1974; Eng. tr., *History: A Novel*, 1977) won popular acclaim at the time of its publication as the novel of the century. The work, set in Rome during World War II, was successful partly because of the appeal of its pseudo-Christian and Marxist message, and partly because of the political tensions in Italy. The story concerns Iduzza, a half-Jewish schoolteacher, and her child Useppe, born of her wartime rape by a German soldier. Useppe dies of an epileptic attack at the age of six. His mother goes mad, and his sheep dog Bella, a maternal Christ figure who has told him that the weak of this world are the really beautiful, is killed protecting his body from the authorities. The narration is omniscient with occasional interruptions by a reportorial "I." The language shows some traces of Morante's delicate poetic skill but is on the whole simplistic and sentimental.

See: A. R. Pupino, *Struttura e stile nella narrativa di Elsa Morante* (1968).   J.M.P.

Moravia, Alberto, pseud. of Alberto Pincherle, (1907–), Italian novelist, essayist, playwright, and journalist, was born in Rome into a well-to-do Jewish-Catholic family. During his adolescent years, he was bedridden with tuberculosis of the bone. Although his formal education was scanty, he read widely in world literature and began to write in his early teens. His first novel, *Gli indifferenti* (1929; Eng. trs., *The Indifferent Ones*, 1932, *Time of Indifference*, 1953), was published at his own expense; it was an instant success. Intended primarily as a literary exercise in applying the techniques of the theater to the novel, the work was interpreted by its readers as an indictment of the decadent Italian bourgeoisie. Later critics saw in it the first European existentialist novel, and it remains Moravia's most important work. *Gli indifferenti* contains most of Moravia's later themes: the superficiality of the bourgeoisie and the gap that separates them from the people, the roles that sexuality and money play in the lives of men, and, above all, the relation between man and reality, which Moravia has called the dominating theme of his work. Although some of the author's best

short stories were written during the 1930s, his next novel, *Le ambizioni sbagliate* (1935; Eng. tr., *Wheel of Fortune*, 1937), was undistinguished. His anti-Fascist tendencies were becoming increasingly suspect to Benito Mussolini's government, and in order to baffle the censors he turned to satire, allegory, and other indirect modes of expression. These devices characterize the novel *La mascherata* (1941; Eng. tr., *The Fancy Dress Party*, 1952) and two collections of stories, *I sogni del pigro* (1940; The Lazy Man's Dreams) and *L'epidemia* (1944; The Epidemic). Finally, after the restoration of the Fascist regime in 1943, he was forced to flee Rome with his wife, the novelist Elsa MORANTE. They spent nine months living with peasants in the hills near Fondi, an experience that strengthened Moravia's social conscience and his Marxist leanings. His new sympathy for the people made its first appearance in the short novel *Agostino* (1944; Eng. tr., 1947), in which an adolescent becomes aware of the existence of sexuality and of the lower classes. It is Moravia's most artful work, classic in its sober style, rigorous composition, and psychological penetration.

A second stage in Moravia's evolution was signaled by an essay written in 1946, "L'uomo come fine" (1954; Eng. tr., *Man as an End*, 1965). In it the author analyzes the ills of the world, and the muted optimism of the essay envisions the possibility of establishing an authentic rapport between man and reality, a new humanism in which man would be an end and not a means. Believing that such a rapport already existed among the people, Moravia, like many other Italian writers of the postwar era, decided to follow Marxism and "go to the people," and he began a series of works dealing with the working class and the petite bourgeoisie of Rome. *La romana* (1947; Eng. tr., *The Woman of Rome*, 1949), which reaffirmed in Italy and abroad his position as a major novelist, depicts the difficult but ultimately satisfying life of a Roman prostitute. His best novel, *La ciociara* (1957; Eng. tr., *Two Women*, 1958), narrates the wartime experiences of two refugees, a shopkeeper and her adolescent daughter, who finally succeed in adapting themselves to a radically changed world. During the postwar decade, Moravia also wrote over 130 short stories in which he attempted to capture the flavor of Roman speech by imitating dialectal syntax. These stories were later collected in the volumes *Racconti romani* (1954; Eng. tr., *Roman Tales*, 1956) and *Nuovi racconti romani* (1959; Eng. tr., *More Roman Tales*, 1963). The other novels of this period—*La disubbidienza* (1948; Eng. tr., *Disobedience*, 1950), *Il conformista* (1951; Eng. tr., *The Conformist*, 1951), and *Il disprezzo* (1954; Eng. tr., *A Ghost at Noon*, 1955)—do not represent the best of Moravia.

By the mid-1950s, Moravia's attraction to the myth of the people had begun to wane: whether or not the people enjoyed an authentic rapport with reality in no way resolved the alienation of the bourgeoisie, which required an intellectual, not a Marxist, solution. A new type of novel was also necessary. Abandoning the third-person narrative because it presupposed an objective, knowable reality, Moravia turned to narration exclusively in the first person, one that reflected the subjective nature of his view of the world. Moreover, since the cinema had preempted so much of the novel's narrative function, he proposed the "essay-novel," in which the author's ideology would take precedence over the narration of a story. This third stage in Moravia's evolution was introduced in *La noia* (1960; Eng. tr., *The Empty Canvas*, 1961), whose protagonist is unable to relate to the world around him. Only after he has been near death and then "reborn"—a theme common in Moravia—does he come to terms with life. Heavily influenced by the ideas of

Ludwig Wittgenstein, *La noia* investigates more thoroughly than any of Moravia's previous works the relation of man to reality. Its quasi-mystical conclusion proffers the moral that contemplation, not action, is the only means of overcoming alienation. *L'attenzione* (1965; Eng. tr., *The Lie,* 1966), technically Moravia's most complex novel, purports to be the diary of a novelist writing a work entitled *L'attenzione.* Exploring the relation between his novel and the reality he seeks to depict, the narrator concludes that it is not possible to write an "authentic" realistic novel, because any action—and even reality itself—is inherently inauthentic.

Throughout the 1960s, Moravia continued to write short stories—collected in *L'automa* (1962; Eng. tr., *The Fetish and Other Stories,* 1964), *Una cosa è una cosa* (1967; Eng. tr., *Command and I Will Obey You,* 1969), and *Il paradiso* (1970; Eng. tr., *Paradise,* 1971)—which, treating the general theme of alienation, complement and sometimes clarify his longer fiction. In addition to his historical tragedy *Beatrice Cenci* (1957; Eng. tr., 1965), he also wrote a number of plays during the 1960s, only one of which, *Il dio Kurt* (1968; The God Kurt), was a popular success. The others, *Il mondo è quello che è* (1966; Eng. tr., *The World Is What It Is,* 1967) and *La vita è gioco* (1969; Life Is a Game), are reminiscent of Luigi PIRANDELLO in their philosophical intentions. They proved of little interest, however, to either critics or public.

Moravia's third period closes with *Io e lui* (1971; Eng. tr., *Two: A Phallic Novel,* 1972). In this comic novel, the author portrays a pseudointellectual screenwriter whose ambitions lead him into droll and often humiliating situations. The originality of the work lies in the conversation between the narrator and his penis. Interpreted as the Freudian ego and id, the two interlocutors provide a study of man's relation to himself, a modern debate between the body and the soul. In the novel's self-critical conclusion, Moravia seems to be saying that he has exhausted the intellectual content of his fiction and that it is time to treat topics of wider appeal.

Most recently, Moravia has published a travelogue on Africa, *A quale tribù appartieni?* (1972; Eng. tr., *Which Tribe Do You Belong To?,* 1974), which complements his similar works, *Un mese in U.R.S.S.* (1958; A Month in the USSR), *Un'idea del'India* (1962; An Idea of India), and *La rivoluzione culturale in Cina ovvero il convitato di pietra* (1967; Eng. tr., *The Red Book and the Great Wall: An Impression of Mao's China,* 1968). Two volumes of short stories, *Un'altra vita* (1973; Eng. tr., *Lady Godiva,* 1975) and *Boh* (1976), continue the author's investigation of the female psyche begun with *Il paradiso.*

With Italo SVEVO, Alberto Moravia is one of Italy's leading novelists of the 20th century. Although his critics have reproached him for his failure to advance the technique of the novel and for having too narrow a register of themes, nearly all recognize his merits as a storyteller, his intelligent portrayal of contemporary European civilization, and his dedication to the humanistic aims of literature.

See: E. Sanguineti, *Alberto Moravia* (1962); G. Dego, *Moravia* (1966); J. Cottrell, *Alberto Moravia* (1974).

L.K.

Moréas, Jean, pseud. of Iannis Papadiamantopoulos (1856–1910), French poet, was born in Athens, where his family was prominent in Greek military and judicial affairs. A French governess inspired young Moréas with a love of French literature that was to dominate his life. When he was allowed to make a European tour as preparation for the study of law, Moréas went to Paris (1872) and was straightway captivated by the metropolis. Re-

turning to Athens, he became increasingly obsessed by love of literature, compiled an anthology of modern Greek verse, and made translations from French and German. In 1878 his first volume of poetry appeared. It contained both Greek and French poems and bore the title *Tourterelles et vipères.* Moréas returned to Paris in 1879, ostensibly to study law, but he immediately began frequenting literary cafés and neglecting his studies. First identified with the "Hydropathes" and the "Zutistes," he wrote several poems that were published in the *Nouvelle Rive gauche.* His volume of verse *Les Syrtes* (1884), in which the influence of Charles BAUDELAIRE and Paul VERLAINE is visible, earned him the esteem of the young poetic generation. The year 1886 saw the appearance of his volume *Les Cantilènes* (The Cantilenas), of two novels written in collaboration with Paul Adam, and of a manifesto (in the supplement of *Figaro* on September 18) that defended the symbolists against the accusations of the conservatives. A new manifesto, which appeared as the preface of *Le Pèlerin passionné* (1891; The Passionate Pilgrim), suggests the trend toward classical inspiration that his poetry was to assume. Soon he had founded the Ecole Romane, with Charles MAURRAS, Maurice du Plessys, Raymond de la Tailhède, and Ernest Raynaud as disciples. This school called for the return of classic forms, for the inspiration of the Middle Ages, of Ronsard, and of the 17th century. It sought to discredit the romanticists, the Parnassians, and the symbolists, all of whom it accused of breaking the Gallic tradition. In practice this meant the abundant use of mythological references, of archaic words, and of traditional poetic forms. The vices and virtues of this new poetic manner are best demonstrated in Moréas's *Enone au clair visage* (1893; Oenone of the Fair Face) and *Eriphyle* (1894). By virtue of his personality, of his manifestos, and of these books, Moréas became the recognized leader of a school of poetry. He was encouraged by Léon Deschamps, the director of *Plume,* from whose presses appeared *Les Stances* (The Stanzas; Books 1–2, 1899; Books 3–6, 1901). In 1903, Moréas published *Iphigénie,* a drama in verse that closely followed Euripides in action and content but that showed originality in images and metrics. Moréas also wrote prose works, of which the best is perhaps *Esquisses et souvenirs* (1908; Sketches and Memories). Ten years after the death of Moréas appeared the *Septième Livre des Stances* (Seventh Book of the Stanzas).

Moréas's literary reputation is not yet firmly established. Blind adoration from his disciples is offset by accusation that he was only a pedantic and servile imitator. It is certain that his personality had much to do with his position as *chef de file.* A great part of his existence was spent in Parisian cafés where his commanding presence, his incisive voice, his flashing monocle, and his black mustache usually dominated a group of admiring young poets. He appears to have been exceedingly vain, but neither to his friends nor in his verse did he yield the secrets of his emotional life. Perusal of his successive volumes of poetry give the impression of a man who suffered much and who became increasingly melancholy and disillusioned, but these are the overtones rather than the matter of his verse. His career was an evolution toward clarity, order, and restraint; had he not been so faithful in imitation of Ronsard and Malherbe, so prone to weight his poems with mythological references, he might have gained a surer reputation. Even detractors will admit his fine sense of rhythm and his ability to lift the commonplace to poetic level.

See: E. Raynaud, *Jean Moréas et les Stances* (1929); R. Georgin, *Jean Moréas* (1930); R. Niklaus, *Jean Moréas, poète lyrique* (1936); J. B. Butler, *Jean Moréas:*

A Critique of His Poetry and Philosophy (1967); R. A. Jouanny, *Jean Moréas: écrivain français* (1969) and *Jean Moréas, écrivain grec: la jeunesse de Ioannis Papadiamandopoulos en Grèce (1856–1878)* (1975).

W.K.Co. rev. D.W.A.

Moreau, Marcel (1933–), Belgian novelist, was born in Boussu. He is the author of a number of novels, all of which describe a barbarian festival, at once sacrificial and ceremonial, which unfolds in two steps: that of the extermination of rational and social nonvalues and that of the impassioned celebration of instinctive and nocturnal forces, conjointly running wild in sexuality and artistic creation. Moreau's is a baroque art of display, of immoderation. Frequently tempted by the essay or manifesto, he willingly opposes his visceralism to surrealism, which he finds superannuated and cerebral (*Les Arts viscéraux,* 1975; The Visceral Arts). In short, the author of *Quintes* (1962; Quintes) and *Ecrits du fond de l'amour* (1968; Writings from the Depths of Love) has never ceased straddling what he calls *La Pensée mongole* (1972; Mongol Thoughts), both atheistic and irrational. But, behind these paroxysms, there is the grievously livid experience of the most ordinary prisons: claustral childhood that he retraces in *L'Ivre Livre* (1973; The Drunken Book); a bureaucratic existence whose annihilation he dreams of in *Julie ou la Dissolution* (1971; Julie or the Dissolution). Much admired by Anaïs Nin, Moreau's novels reveal an experience that writing and the very contemporary desire to unite Scream and Style transfigure magnificently.

See: R. Burniaux and R. Frickx, *La Littérature belge d'expression française* (1973); A. Jans, *Lettres vivantes 1945–1975* (1975). R.Bu.

Moreno Villa, José (1887–1955), Spanish poet, was born in Málaga and educated there by the Jesuits. In 1904 he went to Germany to prepare himself for a business career, but he soon found that he was more interested in literature and art. In 1910, after returning to Spain, he began to study archaeology and architecture, which were to have a profound influence on his writing. After five years (1916–21) of editorial work, he became a librarian, first in Gijón, then at the University of Madrid. While practicing his profession, he edited the magazine *Arquitectura,* lectured on architecture and the fine arts, and exhibited his own paintings.

Moreno Villa belongs to the moment of transition from traditional to "pure" poetry, which uses image, metaphor, and allusion, not for the logical expression of ideas, but to dissolve old associations and create new realities stripped of all but purely poetic values. *Garba* (1913; Sheaf), his first book of poetry, is Andalusian in its clarity and grace. It is a poetry of acceptances, of the passing of youth, of the limitation of human effort, and of the triumph of the commonplace. With his second book, *El pasajero* (1914; The Traveler), the poet enters upon a course of exploration. *El pasajero* and *Evoluciones* (1918) reflect his interest in medieval life and art. The evocations of old Castilian towns and human types recall the work of Antonio MACHADO and others of the Generation of 1898 (*see* SPANISH LITERATURE). Additional titles include *Luchas de pena y alegría* (1915; Struggles of Grief and Joy), *Puentes que no acaban* (1933; Bridges without End), and *Salón sin muros* (1936; Room without Walls). *Colección* (1924), *Jacinta la pelirroja* (1929; Jacinta the Redhead) and the three series of *Carambas* (1931; Exclamations) have strong avant-garde tendencies, including touches of surrealism. "Cuadro cubista" (Cubist Painting), for example, might well be a poetic transcription of a Salvador Dalí painting. His later books express an unmistakable disillusion with life and art.

Moreno Villa's poetry is colored by the nostalgia he felt for his native Málaga between 1934 and his death, when he lived in Mexico. His autobiography, *Vida en claro* (A Life Explained), appeared in 1944. In addition to an extensive anthology of his work, several volumes of poems were published during the years of exile. The last of these, *Voz en vuelo a su cuna* (1961; Voice on the Wing to Its Source), appeared posthumously in the city of his birth. His work, light and graceful rather than profound, is not well known.

See: L. Cernuda, *Estudios sobre poesía española contemporanea* (1957), pp. 151–63; J. F. Cirre, *La poesía de José Moreno Villa* (1963). D.K.A. rev. H.L.B.

Moretti, Marino (1885–1979), Italian poet and novelist, was born in Cesenatico of seafaring stock. His mother, a significant figure in his life, was a schoolteacher. Moretti's early ambition was to be an actor. He attended the drama school in Florence in which Aldo PALAZZESCHI, destined to be a lifelong friend, was also enrolled. After his period of training, Moretti served for a while as secretary to the school's director. During World War I, he was a male nurse in an army hospital. For a brief time he collaborated with Federigo TOZZI in managing a publishing house, and for many years he was a regular contributor to *Corriere della sera.* Moretti was one of the signatories of Benedetto CROCE's anti-Fascist manifesto. In 1944 he firmly and unostentatiously declined the prize awarded him by Benito Mussolini's Accademia d'Italia. Most of his life was spent in Cesenatico with frequent visits abroad, especially to France.

Moretti's works are numerous and varied. He was one of the first—and most gifted—of the "Twilight" poets. Indeed, it was his *Poesie scritte col lapis* (1910; Poems Written with My Pencil) that moved Giuseppe BORGESE to create the term *crepuscolare* (*see* ITALIAN LITERATURE). This term came to signify the movement of simple and sentimental reaction against the pretentious rhetoric of Gabriele D'ANNUNZIO that dominated in the early years of the 20th century. Moretti had already written a number of short stories when he turned to the novel with the highly acclaimed *Il sole del sabato* (1916; Saturday's Sunshine). Its protagonist, Barberina, is a humble woman who learns through a series of misfortunes "how to love and pray and suffer." In outline and characterization this novel is typical of much of Moretti's production, which deals with the poor and afflicted members of society. There are, however, other novels in which a kind of acrid realism predominates as, for example, *L'Andreana* (1936), called by Francesco Casnati Moretti's most powerful work. His autobiographical evocations in such works as *Mia madre* (1924; My Mother), *Via Laura* (1931), and *Il libro dei miei amici* (1958; The Book of My Friends) have a charming sincerity. As remarkable as his copious production was Moretti's enduring vitality. In later years he returned to poetry, and his *Tre anni e un giorno* (Three Years and a Day), published in 1971, has all ·the vigor and honesty of the young *crepuscolare.*

See: F. Casnati, *Marino Moretti* (1952); S. Guarnieri, in *Cinquant'anni di narrativa in Italia* (1955); S. Pacifici, in *The Modern Italian Novel from Capuana to Tozzi* (1973); F. Casnati, in *Letteratura italiana: i contemporanei,* vol. 1 (1975), pp. 649–68. T.G.B.

Morgenstern, Christian (1871–1914), German poet-philosopher, admired for his profound spirituality and whimsical humor, was born in Munich, the son and grandson of well-known artists. His philosophical mind was early attracted to Arthur Schopenhauer; but in 1893, when Morgenstern's tubercular condition confined him to his room for months, Friedrich NIETZSCHE first exerted on him the overpowering influence that was to dominate his student years in Berlin. Convinced of the boundless power of the human mind, he expressed his spiritual elation in humorous dithyrambic fantasies in *In Phanta's Schloß* (1895; In Phanta's Palace), in which cosmic, mythological, and modern concepts are playfully combined. Morgenstern's lyric talent, revealed also in two subsequent collections, *Auf vielen Wegen* (1897; On Many Paths) and *Ich und die Welt* (1898; The World and I), was recognized by his naturalistic colleagues in Berlin; and he was asked to translate Henrik IBSEN's poems and dramas in verse. *Ein Sommer* (1899; One Summer), poems written in Norway, shows a family heritage in the artist's growing appreciation of the physical beauty of this earth.

About this time medical examination revealed the certainty of his early death. Beside the impressionistic daintiness of the "silken" verse of Morgenstern, there is in *Melancholie* (1906) the inexorable seriousness of his longing for, and the awareness of participation in, a spiritual realm not yet clearly discerned. The grotesque humor of his *Galgenlieder* (1905; Eng. trs., *The Gallows Songs, A Selection,* 1966; *Gallows Songs,* 1967; *Gallowsongs,* 1970) and *Palmström* (1910), which established the poet's widespread popularity among the sophisticated, is just another way of liberating the mind from the world of matter. Morgenstern's "superior nonsense" assigns human attributes and functions to everything, even mere words and sounds. Grotesque scenes are evolved from a literal interpretation of conventional phrases. New objects are created by analogy of mere words, ridiculing the assumption that name and thing are identical.

In the winter of 1905–06, when Morgenstern studied Buddha, Fyodor DOSTOYEVSKY, and Meister Eckhart, through the Gospel of Saint John he experienced the crowning realization of many years of meditation: that God, immanent in the world and evolving through it, reaches His highest stage of consciousness in the spiritual person (I and the Father are one). When God becomes conscious of Himself in us, all suffering in the world becomes our suffering; time and eternity become one. In the lyrics of his *Einkehr* (1910; Introspection) is found the spirit of harmony and gratitude of one who has found his spiritual self, but also the subdued pain of one who is gradually disengaging himself from this physical plane. Morgenstern had reconciled himself to the idea that he must finish his way in solitude when, in 1908, he found through his love for Margarete Gosebruch, who was to become his wife, companionship and new horizons that transfigured the last years of his life. The sonnets and songs of *Ich und du* (1911; Thou and I) are among the purest and loftiest poems of love in all German literature. The final phase of Morgenstern's religious development is reflected in his last collection of poems, *Wir fanden einen Pfad* (1914; We Found a Path), dedicated to Rudolf Steiner. Two of Morgenstern's posthumous works constitute a priceless record of the poet's inner development and wisdom: a book of aphorisms and notes called *Stufen* (1918; Steps) and *Mensch Wanderer* (1927; Man the Wanderer), a collection of hitherto unpublished poems. In 1973 there appeared two selections of poetry translated into English, *Selected Poems* and *The Daylight Lamp and Other Poems.*

See: M. Bauer, *Christian Morgensterns Leben und Werk* (1933); J. Walter, *Sprache und Spiel in Christian Morgensterns Galgenlieder* (1966); H. Gumtau, *Christian Morgenstern* (1971); M. Beheim-Schwarzbach, *Christian Morgenstern in Selbstzeugnissen und Bilddokumenten* (1973); E. Hofacker, *Christian Morgenstern* (1978; in English). E.Ho. rev. A.L.W.

Móricz, Zsigmond (1879–1942), Hungarian novelist, was born in Tiszacsécse into a large family. His father was a poor farmer who worked his way up to become a house builder, and his mother came from a line of Protestant ministers. Although his ideals were closer to those of his mother, Móricz viewed the peasantry with great sympathy; many of his heroes are strong, ambitious peasants. Having completed his secondary education in various towns of eastern Hungary, Móricz studied theology in Debrecen, but he soon switched to law. In 1900 he moved to Budapest, where he attended university lectures on law, linguistics, and literature but did not take a degree. In 1903 he joined the staff of a Budapest newspaper and worked there until 1909.

During his years in the capital, Móricz's cultural horizons broadened considerably, but he kept his interest in the country and often toured northeastern Hungary on foot, collecting folklore and folk poetry. Sándor BRODY's influence awakened his social consciousness, and the revolutionary poet Endre ADY provided him with a program calling for radical democratization of "half-dormant" Hungarian society. Literary success, however, eluded Móricz until 1908 when the moving short story "Hét krajcár" (Seven Pennies) brought him popular recognition. A collection of stories bearing the same title appeared in 1909 and was soon followed by the novel *Sárarany* (1910; Pure Gold [or] Golden Mud). This uneven, partly romantic, partly naturalistic story of Dani Turi, a peasant hero of great strength and impressive sexual potency, reflected Móricz's preoccupation with the untapped energy of the Hungarian peasant. Frustration, another one of Móricz's favorite themes, sets the tone of *Isten háta mögött* (1911; Behind God's Country), in which the pettiness and inertia of small-town life are shown to stifle the possibility for dramatic action.

During the next seven years, Móricz wrote mainly about the life and declining fortunes of the gentry, a class for which he still had considerable sympathy at the time. These novels are readable but relatively unimportant, and their precise, anecdotal realism is often superseded by the romantic posturing of the characters. During World War I, Móricz wrote "Szegény emberek" (1917; Poor People), a story with a strong antiwar tone, as well as a novel, *A fáklya* (1918; Eng. tr., *The Torch,* 1931), which is justly regarded as Móricz's most radical work up to that time. The title refers to the main character, a Protestant minister whose ambition it is to be a "torch" to his people but who is unable to prevent injustice and the triumph of class interests in his village because he has neither the strength nor a sufficiently clear program to change the order of things.

Móricz's opposition to the class structure of old Hungary made him a natural ally of the Hungarian Soviet Republic (1919). He came out publicly for the contemplated land reform, with the result that after the fall of that republic, he was harassed by the authorities and boycotted by most reviews except *Nyugat.* It was then that he wrote his most subjective and passionate book, *Légy jó mindhalálig* (1920; Eng. tr., *Be Faithful unto Death,* 1962), the story of the unjust treatment suffered by a poor student, Mike Nyilas. This novel, an assertion of the writer's belief in truth and decency, was adapted for the stage and is now considered a classic. The rustic love story *Pillangó* (1925; Butterfly) displays Móricz's poetic vein, while *Boldog ember* (1932–35; A Happy Man) is a tour de force, a painstakingly realistic narrative of a peasant's life as told by the hero himself. Móricz also wrote a series of novels depicting the material and moral decline of the Hungarian gentry. Of these, *Kivilágos kivirradtig* (1926; Till Daybreak) is thought to be the best, although there are many fine pages in *Úri muri* (1928; Gentry Roistering), with its unbridled eating, drinking, carousing, and ultimate tragedy, or in *Rokonok* (1932; The Relatives), a depressing tale of corruption and nepotism.

Lately, an increasing number of critics believe that Móricz's greatest achievement lies in the genre of the historical novel. His trilogy *Erdély* (1922–35; Transylvania), set in the 17th century, concerns the reigns and struggles of two successive Transylvanian princes, the impulsive and reckless Gábor Báthory and the wise and strong Gábor Béthlen. The trilogy, written in an archaic but powerful idiom, is a vast canvas of war, intrigue, and love. Here Móricz displays a gallery of grand characters as well as psychological insights into male-female relationships. If the main theme of *Erdély* is the survival of a small country caught between rapacious empires, the two-volume novel *Rózsa Sándor* (1941–42) is an inquiry into the possibility of social action from "below." Its hero is a famous peasant outlaw granted amnesty by Lajos Kossuth in 1848 so that he might join in the war against Austria.

A master of the short story and of the realistic novel, Móricz proved less successful as a playwright. His writing, however, exerted a great influence on post-World War II Hungarian prose.

See: G. Juhász, *Móricz Zsigmund* (1928); L. Németh, *Móricz Zsigmond* (1943); P. Nagy, *Móricz Zsigmond* (1953; 1962); M. Czine, *Móricz Zsigmond útja a forradalmakig* (1960); J. Reményi, *Hungarian Writers and Literature* (1964), pp. 326–40.   G.G.

Morits, Yunna Pinkhusovna (1937–), Russian poet, was born in Kiev. A word-conscious writer in the tradition of Marina TSVETAYEVA, she studied at the Gorky Literary Institute and published her first volume of poetry, *Razgovor o shchastye* (Talk of Happiness) in 1957. She has a strong attachment to nature, particularly its more rugged aspect, and to the people contending with it. This affection for nature is reflected in *Mys zhelaniya* (1961; Cape of Desire), which contains poems that show Morits's response to her trips to the far north. Other collections of her poetry include *Loza* (1970; The Vine) and *Surovoy nityu* (1974; With a Coarse Thread). In 1964, Morits published a collection of Russian translations of works by the Jewish poet M. Toif. Morits's poetry is powerfully atmospheric, with intimations of loss, separation, and spiritual suffering. Often deeply melancholic, it can also celebrate the color and vivacity of southern scenes and landscapes, and the free imagination of childhood.
          D.T.W.

Morshen, Nikolay, pseud. of Nikolay Nikolayevich Marchenko (1917–), Russian poet, was born in Kiev. He left the USSR in 1943 and began publishing his poetry in émigré periodicals in 1947. His earlier poetry, simple and artless, reflects the shock of *yezhovshchina* and exile. Morshen eventually immigrated to the United States, where he has continued to publish sparingly: only three collections, *Tyulen* (1959; The Seal), *Dvoyetochiye* (1967; Colon), and *Ekho i zerkalo* (1976; Echo and Mirror). Morshen's focal theme, treated in many variations, yet always head-on, concretely, and in modern terms, is that of the poet's quest for the transcendent confrontation with "the second law of thermodynamics." To him poetic pessimism is "a shameful surrender of poetry to the obvious." Hence the title of his second collection, lifted from lines in which he views death as a "colon" not a "full stop." Morshen is a master of conceit, word play, and "literary echo." His versification, while traditional, is never trite. His verses are fresh and vigorous, resembling Boris PASTERNAK's in many ways without being imitative.   V.T.

Morstin, Ludwik Hieronim (1886–1966), Polish dramatist, poet, and novelist, was born in Pławowice, a manor near Cracow, and died in Warsaw. He first came to public attention as the cofounder (with Władysław Kościelski) of the literary journal *Museion* (1911–13). His career as a diplomat spanned the years 1919 to 1925, which he spent mostly in Rome and Paris. Returning to Poland, he again took up writing, first editing the magazine *Pamiętnik Warszawski* (1930–31) and later translating various classics, including Sophocles, Lope de Vega, Pedro Calderón, and Goethe.

After World War II, Morstin continued playwriting. As literary consultant to the Silesian Theater (1946–48) and the Słowacki Theater in Cracow (1949–61), Morstin was able to offer his own plays for production. Always interested in ancient culture and literature, he published several plays on these subjects: *Panteja* (1937; Pantheia), *Obrona Ksantypy* (1939; The Defense of Xanthippe), *Penelopa* (1945), and *Kleopatra* (1950). His other dramas include *Lilie* (1912; The Lilies), *Zakon Krzyżowy* (1948; Knights of the Holy Cross), and *Przygoda florencka* (1957; The Florentine Adventure). His most significant novel, *Kłos Panny* (1929; The Stalk of Virgo), deals with the life of Nicholas Copernicus.

See: *Słownik współczesnych pisarzy polskich,* vol. 2 (1964), pp. 503–10.   E.J.C.

Mounier, Emmanuel (1905–50), French philosopher and journalist, was born in Grenoble and died in Châtenay-Malabry. After having studied in his native city, he went to Paris, where he was strongly influenced by Henri BERGSON's philosophy, Jacques MARITAIN's Thomism, and especially by Charles PÉGUY's militant Christian socialism. His first book was *La Pensée de Charles Péguy* (1931; Charles Péguy's Thought).

Mounier rapidly became a leading Catholic thinker. In 1932 he founded the periodical *Esprit,* which became the leading force in French Catholic thought during the next three decades. Foreseeing the development of a working-class society, Mounier moved to the Left and strove to dissociate spiritual values from the order established and dominated by the middle class. Like earlier Catholic thinkers, he worked to reconcile socialist and Christian ideals, while consistently opposing political systems based on materialism and all forms of totalitarianism. His dominant concern for respect for the human being is evident in even his earliest works: *Révolution personnaliste et communautaire* (1935; Personalist and Communal Revolution), *De la propriété capitaliste à la propriété humaine* (1936; From Capitalist Property to Human Property), and *Manifeste au service du personnalisme* (1936; Manifesto in the Service of Personalism). He took a stand on all crucial issues of his time, especially against the rise of fascism and the specter of war (see *Pacifistes ou bellicistes?* [1939; Pacifists or Bellicists?]).

During World War II, Mounier participated in the Resistance and wrote two of his major works, *L'Affrontement chrétien* (1945; The Christian Challenge) and *Traité du caractère* (1946; Treatise on Character). He was also keenly attuned to major philosophical and political developments. After the war, his influence grew considerably. He was able to discern the relevance of existentialism to Christian idealism, as in *Introduction aux existentialisme* (1946; Eng. tr., *Existentialist Philoso-*

phies: An Introduction, 1948). He also foresaw some of the momentous changes that were to occur on a global scale, such as decolonization, on which he wrote in *L'Eveil de l'Afrique noire* (1948; The Awakening of Black Africa). The essence of his thought can be found in *Personnalisme* (1950; Eng. tr., *Personalism,* 1952). His major works were reprinted under the title *Oeuvres de Mounier* (4 vols., 1961–65).

See: commemorative Mounier issue of *Esprit,* 174 (December 1950); C. Moix, *La Pensée d'Emmanuel Mounier* (1960); L. Guissard, *Emmanuel Mounier* (1962); J. Conilh, *Emmanuel Mounier, sa vie, son œuvre avec un exposé de sa philosophie* (1966); W. Rauch, *Politics and Belief in Modern France: Emmanuel Mounier and the Christian Democratic Movement, 1932–1950* (1972); J. Amato, *Mounier and Maritain: A French Catholic Understanding of the Modern World* (1975).   J.-P.C.

Mourão-Ferreira, David (1927–), Portuguese poet, dramatist, and critic, was born in Lisbon and became a university teacher of literature. He began to write poetry as a student and edited with others the artistically conservative review *Távola Redonda* (1949–54), continued in *Graal* (1956–57), which for a while revived the individualism and spirituality of the *Presença* movement. Mourão-Ferreira's first book of poems was *A secreta viagem* (1950; The Secret Voyage), enacting, like the second, *Tempestade de verão* (1954; Summer Tempest), the drama of loss of childhood innocence through the first experience of love. Associating love and death, the poet uses the Arthurian-Wagnerian myth of Tristan and Isolde but gives it a modern Lisbonese setting. These collections were followed by *Os quatro cantos do tempo* (1958; The Four Temporal Cantos), *In memoriam memoriae* (1962; In Memory of Memory), *Infinito pessoal ou a arte de amar* (1962; Personal Infinite or The Art of Love), *Do tempo ao coração* (1966; From Time to Heart), *Matura idade* (1973; Ripe Age) and *Sonetos do cativo* (1974; The Captive's Sonnets). Mourão-Ferreira's poetry is dominated by a grave and intimate tone that turns with disgust from the vulgarity and impersonality in contemporary civilization. The discipline with which the poet constructs his verse, his striving for technical perfection—"but above all, implacable, the meter . . . unfolding one unchanging verse forever"—are evident in a variety of forms including haiku and sestinas, the demanding arrangement rarely attempted in Portuguese since the 17th century.

Mourão-Ferreira has also written evocative, dreamlike tales, collected in *Gaivotas em terra* (1959; Seagulls on Land) and *Os amantes* (1966; The Lovers) and a few plays, such as the verse play *Isolda* (1948), *Contrabando* (1950), and *O irmão* (1965; The Brother). His principal volume of critical writings, which deal with poets and poetry, is *Motim literário* (1962; Literature in the Fray), a collection of polemical essays. In 1978 he traced the impact of the *Presença* movement in *Presença da "Presença"* (The Presence of *Presença*).

See: J. Gaspar Simões, *Crítica II,* vol. 1 (1961), pp. 195–206; J. Palma-Ferreira and E. Prado Coelho, Introductions to D. Mourão-Ferreira, *A arte de amar* (1973); V. da Graça Moura, *David Mourão-Ferreira ou a mestria de Eros* (1978).   G.M.M.

Mozhayev, Boris Andreyevich (1923–), Russian novelist and social commentator, was born in Pitelino. He has continued the tradition of Valentin OVECHKIN by writing frank sketches of village life, criticizing bureaucratic practices, and by implication recommending more autonomy for the peasants. Unlike Ovechkin, however, Mozhayev

has also written novels, in which he develops an altogether livelier language (using peasant speech for the narration) and depicts thoroughly robust and idiosyncratic characters. His best-known peasant figure is Fyodor Kuzkin, hero of *Iz zhizni Fyodora Kuzkina* (1966; From the Life of Fyodor Kuzkin), whose capacity to defend himself, his family, and his inherited values, in irreverent disregard of overweening and ignorant officials, aroused both admiration and alarm in literary establishment circles. *Iz zhizni* was followed by a long silence, broken by a few articles and short stories, until the publication of *Muzhiki i baby* (1976; Menfolk and Womenfolk), a novel about the early stages of collectivization and the campaign against well-to-do peasants in the mid-Volga basin. The author's narrative viewpoint throughout implies support for many of the forms of village solidarity (the cooperative, the manufacturing and commercial *artel*) that were destroyed by the Communist Party in 1930.

See: G. Brovman, "Talant i napravleniye: o sovremennoy povesti i yeyo kritikakh," *Don,* no. 7 (1967): 159–68.   G.H.

Mrożek, Sławomir (1930–), Polish dramatist and prose writer, was born in Borzęcin near Cracow. He studied architecture in Cracow and there began his career as a journalist, a writer of humorous stories, and a cartoonist. He has lived abroad since 1963 and currently resides in Paris. His early short-story collections were translated into many languages and established his reputation: *Słoń* (1957; Eng. tr., *The Elephant,* 1962), *Wesele w Atomicach* (1959; Eng. tr., *A Wedding in Atomtown*), and *Deszcz* (1962; Eng. tr., *Rain*). A selection of stories from these last two volumes, appearing in English under the title *The Ugupu Bird* (1968), also included the satirical novella *Ucieczka na południe* (1961; Eng. tr., "Escape Southward"). Mrożek's short stories indulge in grotesque parodies of hackneyed verbal expressions and stereotypes of human nature, whether they are relics of the past or the absurdly deformed product of contemporary social pressures. His biting, surrealistic humor strikes at the heart of phenomena and reveals how they operate in social life.

Since the publication and staging of his play *Policja* (1958; Eng. tr., *The Police,* 1967), the major developments in Mrożek's work have been in the field of drama. In *Policja,* the efficiency of an overly powerful police force has led to the disappearance of all signs of resistance or disloyalty to the government; and so, in order to justify their continued existence, the police must manufacture suspects. In *Męczeństwo Piotra Ohey'a* (1959; Eng. tr., *The Martyrdom of Piotr Ohey,* 1967), one of Mrożek's most surrealistic plays, the hero is compelled to sacrifice himself for the higher good of the state. *Indyk* (1960; The Turkey) parodies a situation in which everything is explained by the platitude "a crisis of values." Three one-act plays, *Na pełnym morzu* (1961; Eng. tr., *Out at Sea,* 1967), *Karol* (1961; Eng. tr., *Charlie,* 1967), and *Strip-Tease* (1961; Eng. tr., 1972), considered a triptych, treat the relationship between executioneer and victim. In *Out at Sea,* three shipwrecked men are afloat on a raft without provisions; with the approval of Medium, Fat decides that one of the three survivors must be eaten and it is immediately obvious that it will be Thin. Ultimately, Thin accepts Fat's cynical clichés about the necessity for sacrifice. In *Charlie,* for no apparent reason a half-blind old man and his crude grandson hunt down someone named Charlie. An oculist, whom they consider to be Charlie, circumvents his own murder by turning over his patients as "Charlies" to Grandpa. In *Strip-Tease,* two men with briefcases sit in a room; they are compelled by an unknown voice to remove their clothes, all the while discussing their attitudes toward freedom. In the process of undressing, both reveal their equal readiness to submit to any degradation. At the end of the play, a mysterious gigantic hand appears and pulls the men offstage, presumably to their doom. Mrożek's next plays were *Zabawa* (1962; Eng. tr., *The Party*, 1972), *Kynolog w rozterce* (1962; Dog Lover in a Dilemma), and *Czarowna noc* (1963; Eng. tr., *Enchanted Night*, 1972).

Mrożek's first full-length play, *Tango* (1964; Eng. tr., 1968), is also the one that is best known. Translated into many languages and performed in many countries, *Tango* signals a new direction in the playwright's work. It is a multileveled play, saturated with allusions to concepts and ideas. It is a work grounded in Polish reality, both past and present, but one that nevertheless has universal significance. Seemingly a family drama, *Tango* is actually a parable of European intellectual, social, cultural, and political history from modernism up to contemporary totalitarianism. *Tango* is concerned with the crisis of a culture and the responsibility of its leaders for the success of brute force in political life. Three generations are portrayed in the play: the now middle-aged characters represent the modernists' slogans of freedom from all constraints; the characters from the older generation, raised on traditional principles, are now totally demoralized. Artur, the representative of the younger generation and the protagonist in the play, organizes a domestic coup d'état, hoping to renew the family and rebuild the world through a return to order and harmony. He turns to old forms and reinstitutes an old-fashioned parlor, dress, and manners, but he himself eventually comes to the conclusion that the old forms are only a masquerade, and that external form without an internal idea cannot save the world. Artur looks in vain for such an idea in contemporary life and finally turns to totalitarian power, declaring that "power alone can exist in a vacuum." Artur's totalitarian gesture does not secure power for him, however; Edek, the vulgar, loutish butler, fells Artur with a single, savage blow. In the person of Edek, sheer force takes over. In the finale, Edek, "the new man," and the cynical older Uncle Eugene dance the once popular tango, "La Cumparsita," over Artur's body.

In Mrożek's next plays, thematic and formal exploration is apparent, but horror and pessimism are felt even more strongly. *Testarium* (1968; Eng. tr., *The Prophets*, 1972) treats power and revolution, while *Drugie danie* (1968; Eng. tr., *Repeat Performance*, 1972) deals with differences between generations, the relationship between father and son, and the collapse of the ideals of rebellion, ending in conformity. *Wacław* (1970; Eng. tr., *Vatzlav*, 1970), is a surrealistic political parable about a shipwrecked slave whose noble social and political plans end in fiasco. Mrożek himself describes *Rzeźnia* (1973; The Slaughterhouse) as a play about the disillusionment resulting from a confrontation between culture conceived as an absolute value and suffering, killing, and death. *Emigranci* (1974; The Emigrés) is a shocking drama about emigration, and the Polish emigration in particular. Mrożek's short story "Moniza Clavier" in the collection *Dwa listy* (1970; Two Letters) also treats the problems of emigration.

Mrożek's work is an original continuation of the tradition of the Polish absurdist drama begun by Stanislaw Ignacy WITKIEWICZ and Witold GOMBROWICZ. Certain elements in Mrożek's plays are also connected with the development of the theater of the absurd as seen in the works of Eugène IONESCO and Samuel BECKETT.

See: *Słownik współczesnych pisarzy polskich*, series 2, vol. 2 (1978), pp. 122–39; J. Kelera, "Mrożek—dowcip wyobraźni logicznej" and "Mrożek na etapie syntezy,"
in *Kpiarze i moraliści* (1966), pp. 85–114, 183–93; E. J. Czerwiński, "Sławomir Mrożek: Jester in Search of an Absolute," in *CASS* 3, no. 4 (1969): 629–45; M. Esslin, *The Theatre of the Absurd* (1969); pp. 272–76; M. Piwińska, "Mrożka dialektyka magiczna," in *Legenda romantyczna i szydercy* (1973), pp. 345–60; D. Gerould, Introduction to *Twentieth-Century Polish Avant-Garde Drama* (1977), pp. 77–83. S.F.

Mulisch, Harry (1927–), Dutch novelist, dramatist, and journalist, was born in Haarlem. At first he studied chemistry, but then he turned to literature. His first novel, *Archibald Strohalm* (1952), depicted an artist in conflict with his time and won him the Reina Prinsen Geerligs Prize. *De diamant* (1954; The Diamond) traces the history of a gem through the ages. That Mulisch is very much concerned with the world of his own day, that he is engagé, appears very closely in his best-known novel, *Het stenen bruidsbed* (1959; Eng. tr., *The Stone Bridal Bed*, 1962). He does not see World War II in the perspective of the older generation, and the surrealistic visions of his fiction may be more appropriate to the apocalyptic events of our age. The American ex-bomber pilot of *The Stone Bridal Bed* is, indeed, an anti-hero. Mulisch is an experimental writer, and he soon turned to reportage and the documentary. Thus, he has produced accounts of the Adolf Eichmann trial in *De Zaak 40/61* (1962; The 40/61 Case), the provos and the riots in Amsterdam in *Bericht aan de rattenkoning* (1966; Report to the King of the Rats), and the revolution in Cuba in *Het woord bij de daad* (1968; The Word to the Deed). *De toekomst van gisteren: protokol van een schrijverij* (1972; The Future of Yesterday: The Record of a Piece of Writing) has been called an antinovel, and *Het seksuele bolwerk* (1973; The Sexual Bulwark) is a documentary novel of the life of the psychiatrist Wilhelm Reich. There is autobiographical material in both *Voer voor psychologen* (1961; Fodder for Psychologists) and *Wenken voor de jongste dag* (1967; Hints for Judgment Day). In addition to the plays *Tanchelijn* (1960), *De knop* (1960; The Button), *Oidipous Oidipous* (1972), and two volumes of verse, *De vogels* (1974; The Birds) and *Tegenlicht* (1975; Opposing Light), Mulisch has also written *Chantage op het leven* (1953; Blackmailing Life), *Het mirakel* (1955; The Miracle), and *Het zwarte licht* (1956; The Black Light).

See: N. Gregoor, *In gesprek met Harry Mulisch* (1965); "Harry Mulisch-nummer," *De Vlaamse Gids* 58: 5 (1974). S.L.F.

Müller, Heiner (1929–), German dramatist, was born in Eppendorf, Saxony, one of two sons in a working-class family. His childhood was shaped by the trauma of national socialism, his family's political opposition, and the regime's retaliation, all related in *Die Schlacht* (1951, 1974; Eng. tr., *The Slaughter*, 1977). The difficult attempt to build a new Germany with the German Democratic Republic is reflected in Müller's early writings of the 1950s, especially in the "production pieces," that is, plays set in a contemporary workplace: *Der Lohndrücker* (The Wage Shark), *Die Korrektur* (The Correction), *Die Umsiedlerin/Die Bauern* (The Resettlement/The Peasants), *Traktor*, and *Der Bau* (The Construction).

Barely recognized as a promising young writer, Müller fell into political disfavor in the early 1960s. Forced to abandon contemporary material, in the 1960s and 1970s he translated and adapted works from classical antiquity (with the figures Philoctetus, Heracles, Oedipus, and Prometheus), from Shakespeare (the comedies, *Hamlet*, and

Macbeth), and from Soviet classics (Fyodor GLADKOV's *Cement* and Mikhail SHOLOKOV's *And Quiet Flows the Don*, the latter under the title *Mauser*). *Mauser* brought international recognition and, finally, acclaim in the German Democratic Republic. Müller resides in East Berlin and travels widely.

Endowed with a gift for writing verse interspersed with lyrical prose, a poetic language unique in contemporary German drama, Müller reshapes literary conventions as instruments for dramatizing the interdependence, indifference, and brutality between individuals and society. His depiction of the individual entangled in systems and machines as victim/victimizer—a major concern throughout Müller's work—addresses the permanent crisis and the gnawing angst of 20th-century audiences.

See: T. Girshausen, ed., *Die Hamlet-maschine: Heiner Müllers Endspiel* (1978).   B.N.W.

Münchhausen, Börries, Baron von (1874–1945), German poet and essayist, was born in Hildesheim. He was a doctor of civil and canon law, honorary doctor of philosophy, canon of the Protestant cathedral of Wurzen, captain of the Saxon Guard Cavalry Regiment of the Reserve, and senator of the German Akademie der Dichtung. He was not, however, a lineal descendant of the distinguished soldier and world-renowed fabulist Hieronymus von Münchhausen (1720–97), who left no heirs, although, as the head of the widely ramifying Münchhausen clan that traces its descent from one Rembertus von Münchhausen, he had in his keeping at Schloß Windischleuba all the family treasures, including the souvenirs of the famous *Lügen-Baron* (the Baron of Tall Tales). As interesting as a work of fiction is the 20th-century Münchhausen's *Geschichten aus der Geschichte einer alten Geschlechtshistorie* (1934; Stories from the History of an Old Family History), in which he tells of those members of his family who have made that family important in the annals of Hanover and two of whom have made it known and loved in two hemispheres.

The poet published his first volume of poems, *Gedichte* (Poems), in 1897 and became famous with his sonorous *Juda* (1900) and his first *Balladen* (1901). *Das Balladenbuch* (1924; The Book of Ballads) contains all his ballads, and *Das Liederbuch* (1928; The Book of Songs), all the other poems that had appeared previously in numerous collections. His *Fröhliche Woche mit Freunden* (1922; Merry Week with Friends) and *Die Garbe* (1933; The Sheaf) contain collections of essays filled with information about the poet.

Münchhausen's name is most closely associated with the German ballad. A century and a quarter after Gottfried Bürger and the Hainbund and while Münchhausen was still a student at Göttingen, he and a group of his friends infused new life into the form. Acknowledging Moritz Strachwitz as his starting point, Münchhausen gave to the ballad a new content, an aristocratic tone that helped to resolve the cacophony of naturalism. This he accomplished, as much by his humor as by the "ethical-causal relation between the beginning and the end of the external action," in his *Weltanschauungsballaden*. The astounding range in time and space covered by his ballads is apparent from a glance at the arrangement of them according to subject that precedes the index in *Das Balladenbuch*. The author was a master of the dramatic and onomatopoetic possibilities of the German language. In his *Meisterballaden: ein Führer zur Freude* (1923; Master Ballads: A Guide to Joy), he analyzed 11 great ballads of his precursors and contemporaries.

See: H. Spiero, *Deutsche Köpfe* (1927), pp. 299–308; M. Ritscher, "Börries von Münchhausen," in *Die schöne Literatur* 31 (1930): 6–17; W. Kaiser, *Geschichte der deutschen Ballade* (1936), pp. 275–82, 284–89.

J.F.G. rev. A.L.W.

Munch-Petersen, Gustaf (1912–38), Danish poet, was born in Copenhagen. He was killed during the Spanish Civil War while serving as a volunteer on the Republican side. His first collection, *det nøgne menneske* (1932; Naked Mankind), containing unrhymed rhythmic poems, shows him to be a modern writer, clearly influenced by French surrealism and the Finland-Swedish modernists Elmer DIKTONIUS and Edith SÖDERGRAN, whereas his ideas concerning human solidarity are founded on socialism. The title poem of *det underste land* (1933; The Land Below) sums up his social dream of community and happiness by laying bare the life sources of the subconscious. The relationship between social reality and the subconscious is stressed in *nitten digte* (1937; Nineteen Poems) through pathetic political confessions as well as precise observations of nature and things. Through the acute precision of his senses, Munch-Petersen created a concentrated lyrical style of imagery corresponding to Ezra Pound's imagism, thereby becoming a forerunner of Danish modernistic poetry.

See: P. M. Mitchell, "The English Poetry of Gustaf Munch-Petersen," *OL* 27 (1967): 352–62.   S.H.R.

Muñiz, Carlos (1927–), Spanish playwright, was born in Madrid, where he still lives, dividing his professional time between his career as a civil servant and a private law practice. Muñiz began to write for the stage in the 1950s. The harshly realistic dramas of his first phase depict the socioeconomic bleakness of contemporary Spanish life. The most notable of these is *El grillo* (1957; The Cricket). The sense of desolation and despair carries over into Muñiz's second phase, although he abandons his realistic technique in favor of a stylized expressionism that mixes Kafkaesque nightmarishness with absurdist black comedy (*see* Franz KAFKA). The first of this series, which spans the 1960s, is *El tintero* (1961; The Inkwell). It provides the prototype of the plays that follow and reveals Muñiz at his most creative. The main character is a contemporary Everyman with the very un-Spanish name of Crock. This innocent rebel's simple needs and pleasures are subverted at every turn by the tyranny of a bureaucratized society, and he is left with no way out but the nostalgic recollection of the simple joys of the free spirit, and eventually death. The protagonists of *Las viejas difíciles* (1969; The Intransigent Crones) find themselves similarly destroyed when they challenge institutionalized self-righteousness. Muñiz's theatrical orientation changed once more in the 1970s, when he began to direct his spirit of protest toward Spanish history with the intent to demythify. The first of these efforts, *La tragicomedia del serenísimo príncipe don Carlos* (1972; Tragicomedy of the Most Serene Prince Don Carlos), is a new version of the often dramatized conflict between Philip II and his son, Don Carlos.

See: L. L. Zeller, "La evolución técnica y temática en el teatro de Carlos Muñiz," *Estreno* 2, no. 2 (1976): 41–49.   S.M.G.

Munk, Kaj (1898–1944), Danish dramatist, was born in Maribo on the island of Lolland. He received his degree in theology in 1924. The same year Munk became pastor in Vedersø, western Jutland, where he lived until his murder by the Nazi Gestapo in 1944. His contempt for the weak democracies of his time and his romantic hero worship are expressed in his first play, *En Idealist* (1928; Eng. tr., *Herod the King*, in *Five Plays by Kaj Munk*,

1953). The despot Herod sacrifices everything for the sake of power but is nevertheless destroyed because of his defiance of God. In *Han sidder ved Smeltediglen* (1938; Eng. tr., *He Sits at the Melting-Pot*, in *Five Plays by Kaj Munk*, 1953), Munk again deals with the conflict between the man of power and the message of love. God speaks through a feeble human being—a Jewish scientist—who thereby becomes strong enough to revolt against the masters of this world, in this case, the Nazis. Munk's earlier hero worship is now transformed into a call for resistance to tyranny. This development is evident in the historical drama *Niels Ebbesen* (1942; Eng. tr., in *Scandinavian Plays of the 20th Century*, series 2, 1944), directed against the German occupation of Denmark (1940–45), and in the one-act play *Før Cannae* (1943; Eng. tr., *Before Cannae*, in *Five Plays by Kaj Munk*, 1953), in which Hannibal (Hitler), the tyrant, is confronted with the pure humanistic ideal, Fabius (Churchill). Next to power, love is the other important motif in Munk's writing. Most frequently, both motifs are woven together as in *En Idealist*, where Herod sacrifices his beloved and consequently his happiness for an idea: power. Quite apart are two dramas, both set among western Jutland peasants and dealing with the problem of faith. In *Ordet* (1932; Eng. tr., *The Word*, in *Five Plays by Kaj Munk*, 1953), Munk's greatest success, he boldly creates a miracle on the stage in order to shock the habitual Christians and provoke the nonbelievers. *Kærlighed* (1926; Love) portrays a minister who preaches a faith he does not have himself, but which he is able to get others to accept. For Munk, the theater was meant to entertain as well as to shake the audience. He reached his aim of preaching a Christian humanism and reviving the languishing Danish theater by creating a drama in which violent passions met in life-and-death struggles.

See: A. Henriques, *Kaj Munk* (1945); N. Nøjgaard, *Kaj Munk* (1958). S.H.R.

Muno, Jean (1924–), Belgian novelist, was born in Brussels. The son of the novelist Constant BURNIAUX, he published *Le Baptême de la ligne* (The Crossing of the Line) in 1955 and asserted himself with *L'Hipparion* (1962; Hipparion) as an incisive observer of everyday reality and as a gifted and very fine storyteller. The precise and amused paintings of beings and things is accompanied, however, by a marvelous fancifulness, which is found again in *L'Homme qui s'efface* (1963; The Self-Effacing Man) and in several short stories of *La Brèche* (1973; The Breach). *L'Ile des pas perdus* (1967; The Island of Pacing Steps) is a bitter and sober novel, a disillusioning meditation on existence and the difficult relationships between human beings; but in *Le Joker* (1967), the author resumes the satiric vein in which he excels in order to present a psychological portrait that has an exactness of tone. At the same time cruel and sensitive, Muno's novels bear witness, under modesty of expression and the discretion of means used, to a lucid and formidable intelligence and a great faculty of invention.

See: A. Jans, *Lettres vivantes 1945–1975* (1975).

R.F.

Muñoz Seca, Pedro (1881–1936), Spanish dramatist, was born in Puerto de Santa María, in the province of Cádiz, and died in Madrid. He taught Latin and Greek in academies and private schools and eventually entered government service. He became a very clever writer of one-act farces (*sainetes*) and situation comedies, which were in vogue at the time and were being written in abundance by writers like Carlos ARNICHES and the ALVAREZ QUINTERO brothers. His theater of caricature, jokes, and word

play owed its great popularity to wit, lively dialogue, and clever theatrical devices. He also created the *astracanada* (an untranslatable term), in which nonsensical actions, plays on words, and puns, designed to keep the public in a continual state of hilarity, were exploited to their limit. The *astracanada* is a parody of the traditional theatrical portrayal of reality rather than a parody of reality itself. This concept is probably not unrelated to the much more transcendent *esperpento* of Ramón del VALLE-INCLÁN.

Muñoz Seca wrote some 100 works on his own and another 200 in collaboration with such writers as Fernández Pérez and Enrique García Alvarez. Among his better-known works are *La barba de Carrillo* (1918; Carrillo's Beard), *Pepe Conde* (1920), and *La venganza de don Mendo* (1918; Don Mendo's Revenge). This last is a full-length parody of neoromantic tragedy but follows the general lines of the *astracanada* in its outrageous word plays, unlikely but hilarious rhyme schemes, characters who are killed but come back to life, and a protagonist who assassinates himself and confesses while punning on the slang word for "I myself" (*menda*) and his name, Mendo. This play is the author's most ambitious work. Like Federico GARCÍA LORCA, Muñoz Seca was absurdly assassinated at the beginning of the Spanish Civil War, but by opposite forces.

See: F. Ruiz Ramón, *Historia del teatro español, II, Siglo XX* (1971), pp. 59–62. E.G.-L. rev. H.L.B.

Muschg, Adolf (1934–), Swiss novelist, short-story writer, and playwright, was born in Zollikon near Zürich. In addition to writing, he has pursued an academic career, and has taught at the International Christian University in Tokyo, Göttingen University, Cornell University in the United States, and the University of Geneva. For several years he has been professor of literature at the Swiss Institute of Technology in Zürich.

Muschg is among the most original of the younger Swiss writers of fiction. His first novel, *Im Sommer des Hasen* (1965; Summer of the Hare), is set in Japan. Subsequent novels, *Gegenzauber* (1967; Counterspell), *Mitgespielt* (1969; Gone Along), and *Albissers Grund* (1974; Albisser's Motive), treat the mentality of the Swiss middle class. All of these works have autobiographical elements. Muschg is revealed as a master teller of precise and compact short stories in the collections *Fremdkörper* (1968; Foreign Bodies) and *Liebesgeschichten* (1972; Love Stories). His plays include the "middle-class tragedy" *Rumpelstilz* (1968), the radio play *Das Kerbelgericht* (1969; The Dish of Chervil), and an adaptation of a play by Goethe, *Die Aufgeregten* (1969; The Excited Ones).

See: W. Bucher and G. Ammann, eds., *Schweizer Schriftsteller im Gespräch*, vol. 1 (1970), pp. 143–68.

R.K.

Musil, Robert (1880–1942), Austrian novelist and essayist, was born in Klagenfurt, the only child of an aloof professor of engineering and a highly temperamental mother given to periodic hysterical seizures. While Musil's father dedicated himself totally and successfully to his profession, his mother formed an intimate relationship with a teacher who moved in with the family one year before Musil's birth and remained for the next 40 years. It was as the extraneous element in this perfectly functioning triangle that Musil grew up, a lonely, withdrawn, and melancholy child. In the third grade he had to be sent home for half a year in order to recuperate from a nervous breakdown, and he was sent away from home as soon as it became socially feasible. Thus, at the age of 12 in 1892, Musil was enrolled in a military academy, but he later rejected his father's recommendation for a military career in favor of one in engineering. He received his diploma from the Technical University of Brünn in 1901 but two years later decided against this profession and began the study of philosophy, psychology, and mathematics at the University of Berlin, where he remained for five years, submitting his dissertation on the epistemology of Ernst Mach in 1908.

The publication of Musil's first novel, *Die Verwirrungen des Zöglings Törless* (1906; Eng. tr., *Young Törless*, 1955), brought him some recognition as a writer, and it was at this time that he decided against an academic career. In 1911 he married and also published two short stories, "Die Vollendung der Liebe" (The Perfecting of a Love) and "Die Versuchung der stillen Veronika" (The Temptation of Quiet Veronika), which were collected under the title *Vereinigungen* (1911; Eng. tr., *Unions*, 1965). During World War I, Musil was an officer in the Austrian army, and from 1918 to 1922 he held various semimilitary posts in the government. His two plays, *Die Schwärmer* (1921; The Visionaries) and *Vinzenz und die Freundin bedeutender Männer* (1923; Vincent and the Girl Friend of Important Men), were both commercial failures. From 1922 until his death, Musil lived as a freelance writer of essays, literary criticism, and articles for literary journals and newspapers. In 1924 he published three short stories, "Grigia," "Die Portugiesin" (The Lady from Portugal), and "Tonka," under the collective title *Drei Frauen* (1924; Eng. tr., *Three Women*, 1965). He dedicated the remaining years of his life to his second novel, *Der Mann ohne Eigenschaften* (1930–42; Eng. tr., *The Man without Qualities*, 3 vols.: 1953, 1954, 1960).

Shortly before the entrance of Adolf Hitler's armies into Vienna in 1938, Musil and his Jewish wife left Austria forever and took up residence in Switzerland. His last great novel remained a half-completed fragment. Not only did he die sooner than he anticipated, but also *Der Mann ohne Eigenschaften* presented problems that he finally felt went beyond his powers to resolve. His last years in exile were marked by ever-increasing weariness, poverty, and embitterment, exacerbated by the complete absence of public recognition.

The protagonist of *Der Mann ohne Eigenschaften* once asks: "A man who is after the truth sets out to be a man of learning; a man who wants to give free play to his subjectivity sets out, perhaps, to be a writer. But what is a man to do who is after something that lies between?" Musil himself was perpetually searching after "something that lies between," for he wanted to be like one of those "masters of the hovering life" whose "domain lies between religion and knowledge, between example and doctrine, between *amor intellectualis* and poetry." Since Musil felt himself to be equally a poet and a scientist, a mystic and a rationalist, it is not surprising that his intentions as a writer were extraordinary and far-reaching.

A constant oscillation between the two worlds of reason and mysticism was the fundamental characteristic of Musil's mind as well as of his art. When Musil regarded everyday reality as a rationalist, he approached the perspective of the nihilist: he perceived a world without God, a world that appears to have been shattered into meaningless and unrelated fragments under the onslaught of man's analytical attitude. As a mystic, however, Musil believed that man remains able to recapture in mystical states of self-absorption that feeling of unity, of wholeness and harmony, that vanished with the death of God. His fiction is ultimately directed toward a Utopian synthesis of these opposites. Musil asserted that life in the 20th century would become increasingly decadent and sterile until the ultimate task of synthesis had been achieved. He set himself nothing less than the accomplishment of this task through his fiction. Fiction alone, he believed, was able both to "hover" over all aspects of modern life that appeared fragmented into mutually exclusive opposites under the dialectic of intellect and soul, mind and emotions, reason and mysticism, and to capture and structure through aesthetic means all the possibilities inherent in life to produce a formal synthesis of all opposites in the ideal of the balanced life. Through his fiction, Musil therefore attempted nothing less than the creation of a new morality for Western man, which had to be founded on the synthesis of reason and mysticism. Once noting that there is a type of man who is aesthetically sensitive, Musil placed his allegiance in the opposite camp: "I am morally sensitive," he proudly declared.

Musil's prose reveals a high degree of abstraction from everyday reality, as that reality is experienced in all its concreteness and triviality. This abstraction is manifested in two ways, depending upon whether the protagonist is male or female. In the first, "masculine," instance, Musil's fiction often includes a large amount of intellectual material: the reader of *Törless* and *Der Mann ohne Eigenschaften* is immediately aware that Musil's preoccupations and his manner of considering various problems are generally philosophical. Ideas are often explored at great length by an omniscient narrator who, for the reader's benefit, may offer his own interpretations directly and in an extremely analytical fashion. Such a didactic style results in a generalizing tendency in Musil's fiction, and some readers have objected that his characters often seem to represent nothing more than the embodiments of various philosophical positions.

The second, "feminine" kind of abstraction in Musil's fiction appears in its most extreme form in *Vereinigungen*, where he explores mystical states in the feminine psyche and attempts to render the most subtle and minute shades of feeling by means of a dense web of metaphors. In these stories Musil's style is not analytical, nor does the work progress in the direction dictated by a narrator's logical explanations. Instead, the reader is plunged into a churning sea of feeling without visible horizons and left to swim (or sink) as fleeting sense impressions, half-completed thoughts, and momentary waves of emotion circle about him.

Both kinds of abstraction result in the relative absence in Musil's work of the two most common characteristics of the traditional novel and short story: description of the external world and the unfolding of a plot. The outer world seems to lack a sense of form, solidity, and stability. Thrown either upon his endlessly fertile intellect or upon his complex and formless emotional life, Musil's protagonist possesses an unsettling intuition of a void existing above and below him. Outer reality is not denied, but it enters Musil's fiction only as far as it impinges upon the protagonist's intellectual or emotional life, and the intellectual and emotional life of the Musil protagonist (male or female) is in general as self-sustaining and self-sufficient as it is possible to imagine.

In *Törless*, Musil analyzed an early adolescent's experience of certain mystical (specifically Dionysian) states that one day suddenly and without warning begin to assail him, threatening to destroy not only his previously unquestioned, childish vision of the pristine world of his parents but also his image of himself as a known quantity. Through a series of bizarre experiments, ranging from the systematic torture of a fellow student to the intellectual application of mathematical propositions and Kantian metaphysics, Törless desperately seeks a point of synthesis, of balance in his life between the demands of sexuality and those of rational everyday reality. After the failure of his experiments, he eventually emerges from his confusions with the clear recognition that a darker, richer, and entirely separate mystical dimension resides within the human psyche but cannot be encompassed by the rational mind. He therefore decides not to concentrate his energies upon finding some synthesis but, rather, upon cultivating the growth of his personality in all its varying dimensions.

In the stories of *Vereinigungen,* the two women protagonists undergo a kind of "nervous breakdown," during which their rigid and carefully constructed psychic stability is assaulted and eventually collapses under the onslaught of their long-repressed sexual lives. In *Die Vollendung einer Liebe,* Claudine, leaving the domestic tranquility of a perfect, bourgeois marriage for the first time, takes a short trip away from home and has a brief affair with an animal-like stranger. This affair represents a replay of episodes typical of her earlier life, which was characterized by sexual promiscuity and which she had thought to have overcome once and for all with her marriage. In *Die Versuchung* Veronika struggles against sexual temptation emanating from two different kinds of young men, both cousins, both living with her in the same house. By keeping Johannes and Demeter at arm's length, Veronika desperately strives to prevent her first, long-repressed sexual experience from emerging into consciousness. In contrast to Claudine's, Veronika's past sexuality involved not an animal-like stranger but a real animal, her dog. While Claudine, like Törless, manages to return to the everyday world, Veronika, sublimating her sexual energies into a state of mystical self-absorption, slips away from the everyday world and into irreversible madness.

The protagonists in the collection *Drei Frauen,* respectively an engineer, a soldier, and a young scientist, are subjected to the temptations of an irrational mystical world that confronts them in the form of three rather threatening women who appear in their lives as silent, shadowy, and mysterious creatures existing on the periphery of rational masculine culture. Only the soldier, Ketten, through his marriage, eventually achieves a form of balance between reason and mysticism, between masculine and feminine perspectives ("Portugiesin"). The engineer surrenders all desire to live and dies while his mistress lives on ("Grigia"). The young scientist asserts the powers of his reason and thus survives while his pregnant mistress dies ("Tonka"). Admittedly, the price of his survival is the suppression of his emotional life and the assumption of a future existence based on reason alone.

Musil undertook his most grandiose experiment in the synthesis of reason and mysticism in *Der Mann ohne Eigenschaften.* The hoped-for synthesis is predicated upon two experiments initiated by the protagonist Ulrich. In the first of these, Ulrich bases his life upon standards of behavior consciously derived from the scientific method as practiced in the laboratory and attempts to become an objective recording consciousness. This experiment inevitably leads to a state of paralysis and eventual mental collapse. The second experiment involves an attempt to recover pure feeling in a state of mystical intensity induced by the protagonist's love for his sister Agathe. Such an experiment involves a dialectical reversal: the unalloyed masculine perspective of Ulrich the scientist is replaced by an exclusively feminine attitude toward life in Ulrich the mystic. Unfortunately, the mystical experiment also fails, because Ulrich comes to the conclusion that no form of life that attempts to exist completely outside all social structures can long survive. Thus the synthesis between reason and mysticism remains unachieved in this fragmentary work.

Because of the failure of all Musil's protagonists to achieve the Utopian synthesis, his readers may well experience a sense of never arriving at a conclusion. But the heroic and complex literary spectacle of Musil's ever-continuing, albeit ever-failing, quest for the balanced life carries its own justification as a realistic reflection of modern man's inability to solve ultimate problems. In spite of the fact that the purity of his Utopian vision seemed finally not to bring him any closer to the perfect synthesis but only to exacerbate the intensity of the struggle in the present, Musil remained a dedicated and uncompromising Utopian writer. His integrity never faltered.

See: B. Pike, *Robert Musil: An Introduction to His Work* (1961); E. Kaiser and E. Wilkins, *Robert Musil: eine Einführung in das Werk* (1962); W. Rasch, *Über Robert Musils Roman Der Mann ohne Eigenschaften* (1976); F. G. Peters, *Robert Musil: Master of the Hovering Life* (1978).   F.G.P.

Myrivilis, Stratis, pseud. of Efstratios Stamatopoulos (1892–1969), Greek novelist and short-story writer, was born on the island of Lesbos, the setting for many of his works. In 1918 he served in the trenches on the Macedonian front, an experience that provided material for the powerful novel *I zoi en tafo* (1924, rev. 1930; Eng. tr., *Life in the Tomb,* 1977), the first volume of his "Trilogy of the War." His experiences during the Asia Minor Disaster of 1922 are reflected in the second volume, *I daskala me ta chrysa matia* (1933; Eng. tr., *The Schoolmistress with the Golden Eyes,* 1964), a novel about an embittered veteran's discovery of creativity and love. The third volume, *I panaghia i gorgona* (1949; Eng. tr., *The Mermaid Madonna,* 1959), documents the establishment of a village of Asia Minor refugees on Lesbos.

Myrivilis's greatness may be obscured in the novel form because of his inability to control his love for the Greek language. The short story, however, provided the limitations his genius required. Several collections fully justify his reputation in this genre. The story "O Vasilis o Arvanitis" (Basil Arvanitis), in *To galazio vivlio* (1939; The Blue Book), is particularly outstanding. In both the stories and the novel trilogy, Myrivilis demonstrates that he is a master stylist, a celebrant of the pagan view of Greek nature, and a defender of the individual against the impersonal forces of war, bureaucracy, and custom.

See: A. Mirambel, "Stratis Myrivilis romancier de la Grèce des légendes et de la réalité," *MdeF,* no. 1165 (1960): 90–112; A. Karandonis, *Pezographoi kai pezographimata tis yenias tou '30* (1962), pp. 13–50.   T.D.

N

Nabert, Jean (1881–1960), French philosopher and teacher, had a deep influence on many generations of students at the Lycée Henri IV in Paris. Raised himself in the intellectual tradition of Immanuel Kant's epistemology and ethics, Nabert's writings are examples of the strict, scrupulous analysis that tries to express the complex and reflective movements of human consciousness as an ethical experience of freedom within basic moral sentiments such as the awareness of human finiteness and the desire of justification related to a need for an absolute recourse. With extreme subtlety and fastidiousness, Nabert developed critical moral and metaphysical interpretations based on experiences of human alienation, self-intimacy, guilt and solitude, failure and hope. More than any other French philosopher of the period 1930–50, he showed how the Kantian method of critical exploration permits understanding of the deep, essential movements of human conscience. His publications, such as *L'Expérience intérieure de la liberté* (1923; The Interior Experience of Freedom), *Eléments pour une éthique* (1943; Eng. tr., *Elements for an Ethic*, 1969), *Essai sur le mal* (1955; Essay on Evil), and *Le Désir de Dieu* (1966; The Desire for God), reveal the progressive deepening of a true moral and tragic existentialism.   E.M.-S.

Nabokov, Vladimir Vladimirovich (1899–1977), Russian and American novelist, poet, playwright, and literary scholar, was born in Petersburg, son of a liberal politician. He emigrated after the Revolution in 1919 and was educated at Cambridge. Nabokov published four volumes of poetry in Russia and in Berlin prior to the appearance of his first novel, *Mashenka* (1926; Eng. tr., *Mary,* 1970). Then came the following Russian novels, all written in Berlin and published under the pen name V. Sirin: *Korol, dama, valet* (1928; Eng. tr., *King, Queen, Knave,* 1968); *Zashchita Luzhina* (1930; Eng. tr., *The Defense,* 1964); *Soglyadatay* (1930; Eng. tr., *The Eye,* 1965); *Kamera obskura* (1932; Eng. tr., *Laughter in the Dark,* 1938); *Podvig* (1933; Eng. tr., *Glory,* 1971); and *Otchayaniye* (1936; Eng. tr., *Despair,* 1937; revised tr., 1966). These novels all present Nabokov's central theme that life may be converted into art by turning a given project or course of action into a creative act. His profound involvement with lepidoptery and the theory of chess brought to his literary art a precision of observation and an objectivity that are greatly at variance with the moral and sociological preoccupations of the earlier Russian tradition.

Two novels crown the achievement of Nabokov's European period. *Dar* (serialized in 1937; pub. in book form in 1952; Eng. tr., *The Gift,* 1963) hybridizes fictional narrative devices with those of literary scholarship, the book being both a novel and an intellectual history of 19th-century Russia. *Priglasheniye na kazn* (1938; Eng. tr., *Invitation to a Beheading,* 1959)—like the subsequent novel *Bend Sinister* (1947)—is a political fantasy that depicts in vivid surrealistic images the destruction of individuals by the impersonal machinery of 20th-century totalitarian states.

In 1940, Nabokov moved to the United States and switched to English as his principal literary language. Beginning with *The Real Life of Sebastian Knight* (1941), all his novels were written in English, a case of thorough bilingualism that is without precedent in modern literature. *Lolita* (1955), a sensitive examination of a European intellectual's love for an American teenage girl, was an international best-seller and a landmark in the Western world in promoting new freedom in the literary treatment of sexual themes. *Pnin* (1957), a comical novel about a displaced Russian on an American college campus, continues the Nabokovian themes of exile and of nostalgia for the vanished culture of pre-Revolutionary Russia. These themes reach their imaginative climax in *Ada or Ardor: A Family Chronicle* (1969), a science-fiction-like fantasy that superimposes the reality of 20th-century America upon the background of 19th-century Russian culture and literary allusions. The hybridization of fictional devices with scholarly methodology that was inaugurated in *Dar* is intensified in *Pale Fire* (1962), where the narrative takes the form of annotations to a long poem. Nabokov's most important collections of short stories are *Vozvrashcheniye Chorba* (1930; Eng. tr., *The Return of Chorb,* 1976), *Nine Stories* (1947), *Vesna v Fialte* (1956; Rus. version of a collection including "Spring in Fialta"; 1947), and *A Russian Beauty and Other Stories* (1973). His novel *Transparent Things* (1972) is an expansion of the title story from the first of these collections.

Nabokov's two major plays are *Sobytiye* (1938; The Event) and *Izobreteniye Valsa* (1938; Eng. tr., *The Waltz Invention,* 1966). His memoirs appeared first in English as *Conclusive Evidence* (1951), which Nabokov himself translated into Russian as *Drugiye berega* (1954; Other Shores), and later translated back, with substantial revisions, into English as *Speak, Memory* (1967). The novel *Look at the Harlequins!* (1974) is an anti-autobiography that outlines the life of a writer whose life and writings are the opposite of Nabokov's and yet parallel them and coincide with them in time. He published a Russian translation of Lewis Carroll's *Alice's Adventures in Wonderland* (1923), an idiosyncratic study of Nikolay Gogol (1944), and an annotated four-volume English translation of Aleksandr Pushkin's *Eugene Onegin* (1964). Nabokov's Russian and English novels have now been translated into most of the major languages and have noticeably influenced the development of imaginative fiction in the Western countries.

See: A. Field, *Nabokov: His Life in Art* (1967); L. S. Dembo, ed., *Nabokov: The Man and His Work* (1967); A. Appel, Jr., and C. Newman, eds., *Nabokov* (1970).

S.K.

Nagibin, Yury Markovich (1920–), Russian short-story writer, was born in Moscow into an educated family. His studies at the Moscow Institute of Cinematography were interrupted by World War II. He went to the front as a correspondent, but his reportage soon developed into creative writing distinguished by a light, lucid, and readable style. Although Nagibin started publishing during Iosif Stalin's lifetime, he is a typical representative of the liberal, "middle course" movement in post-Stalin literature. Pro-Soviet in his basic views, he departs from the ideology of socialist realism because he is much more concerned with the private, inner world of the individual than with political and public issues.

Most of Nagibin's stories can be grouped into five thematic categories: war, nature, love, children, and autobiography. The war stories such as "Vaganov" (1946) have a romantic flavor. In the nature stories the environment serves to reveal man's basic moral and psychological makeup. For example, two types of hunters are shown, those who love nature, as in "Poslednyaya okhota" (1957; The Last Hunt), and those who abuse it through aggressiveness and greed, as in "Pogonya" (1962; The Chase). The love stories are sophisticated and subtle, often dealing with unconventional subjects such as relations between middle-aged lovers, "Vecher v Khelsinki," (1956; An Evening in Helsinki). Nagibin's stories about children, notably "Zimniy dub" (1952; Winter Oak) and "Ekho" (1960; The Echo) are among his best. He portrays children as sensitive and vulnerable human beings who suffer from being misunderstood. Of Nagibin's autobiographical accounts *Chistye Prudy* (1961), which describes his childhood, is exceptionally good. His painstakingly honest and often self-critical approach brings to mind Lev Tolstoy's *Childhood*. In Nagibin's output, a place apart is held by a film scenario about the Umberto Nobile expedition to the North Pole, *Ne day yemu pogibnut* (1967; Do Not Let Him Perish).

See: D. J. Richards, Introduction to I. Nagibin, *Selected Short Stories* (1963).   I.H.C.

Naglerowa, Herminia (1890–1957), Polish novelist and short-story writer, was born in Zaliski, near Brody, and died in London. She studied history at the University of Lvov, where she received her doctoral degree. During World War II she was deported to the Soviet Union. She later served in the Polish army in the Near East and Italy. From 1946 on, she was active in the Polish Writers Union in London.

Naglerowa published several novels. *Krauzowie i inni* (1936; Eng. tr., *Loves and Ambitions*, 1954), the first three volumes of an unfinished cycle, brought her recognition. This work is a broad panorama of life in a small town situated in her native region. After the war she wrote another unfinished cycle of novels, *Za zamkniętymi drzwiami* (Behind Closed Doors), the first two parts of which are *Sprawa Józefa Mosta* (1953; Józef Most's Affair) and *Wierność życiu* (1959; Faithfulness to Life). She also wrote a collection of short stories, *Kazachstańskie noce* (1958; Kazakhstan Nights). S.F.

Nagy, Lajos (1883–1954), Hungarian novelist and short-story writer, was born in Apostag-Tabányitelek and died in Budapest. He was the illegitimate son of a peasant servant-girl, and this fact had a significant effect on his life and works. The defiance and bitterness that characterizes his writings can in some ways be related to early childhood stigmatization. From the very beginning of his career, Nagy was an angry radical writer; but he came into conflict with the illegal Hungarian Communist Party of the 1930s, as well as with the post–World War II Communist establishment, for not having the proper Party spirit. Indeed, revolutionary romanticism and fervor were always alien to Nagy; his artistic temperament found its finest expression in a rigorously plain, even abrupt style of writing. His compromisingly critical outlook prompted one of his critics to call Nagy a "born dissenter."

Nagy's early short stories are notable for their eroticism. A disciple of Freudian psychoanalysis, Nagy was one of those radical Hungarian writers—like the poet Attila JÓZSEF—who attempted to reconcile Marxist teachings with psychoanalytic theory. In the 1920s and early 1930s, Nagy was attracted to avant-garde literary trends. In some of the short stories written during this period, such as "Tornázó diákok" (1920; Students in Gym), "Jeremiád" (1927), and "Lecke" (1930; Lesson), Nagy employed a rapid-fire expressionistic narrative. In "Napirend" (1927; Order of the Day) and "Bérház" (1931; Tenement) he used quasi-documentary montage techniques.

Nagy was at his best when he was examining, with dispassionate precision, the social and psychological ills of his country. In "1919 Május" (1932; May 1919), undoubtedly his finest short story, he exposes the unbridgeable gap between rich and poor, oppressor and oppressed. In his documentary novel *Kiskunhalom* (1934), he depicts the dreariness and despair of a Hungarian village. *A lázadó ember* (1956; A Man of Revolt) is a volume of autobiographicl reminiscences.

Nagy is a prolific writer, but the quality of his total literary output is somewhat uneven. Like many a talented Hungarian writer, he was not always able to give his favorite themes adequate artistic form.

See: P. Kardos, *Nagy Lajos élete és művei* (1958); I. Sötér, et al., *A magyar irodalom története*, vol. 6 (1966), pp. 385–407; A. Schöpflin, *Válogatott tanulmányok* (1967), pp. 493–96. I.S.

Nagy, László (1925–78), Hungarian poet and translator, was born at Felsőiszkáz into a peasant family. He studied painting and later Hungarian literature in Budapest. Nagy belonged to that generation of young artists from the countryside for whom post–World War II social changes brought a real possibility of advancement and liberation from the constraints of village life. He published his first poems in the review *Valóság* in 1946, and his early poetry was affirmative and full of revolutionary optimism. But the increasingly repressive character of the Communist regime, affecting both political and creative freedom, filled him with bitterness and despondency. This mood inspired the long poem "Gyöngyszoknya" (1953; Skirt of Pearls) as well as such lines of self-encouragement as "don't be ashamed of illusions that were/ pressed upon you." Nagy's rebellion against the rigid literary canons of socialist realism came to fruition in the slim but significant volume of poetry *A nap jegyese* (1954; The Bride of the Sun). In this collection, love and fascination with nature take precedence over social commitment. The long poem "A vasárnap gyönyöre" (1955; Eng. tr., *Pleasuring Sunday*, 1973) reprinted in the collection *A vasárnap gyönyöre* (1956) is an impressive cantata of life's simple pleasures and a poem that showed Nagy at the apogee of his creative strength.

Nagy's first, "naive" period as a writer came to an end in 1956–57. The aftermath of the 1956 Hungarian Uprising as well as his personal anxieties and suffering introduced new, almost surrealistic accents into his poetry. His next book, *Himnusz minden időben* (1965; Hymn for Anytime), is an important achievement consisting of poetic variations on the anthropocentric myth of the "human community." Most of Nagy's long poems are about archetypal, symbolic situations, described in long, flowing lines, full of striking metaphors and vigorous images. His technique shows certain similarities with that of Dylan Thomas and Federico GARCÍA LORCA, although his interests have a broader range. In the oratorio "Ég és föld" (1969; Eng. tr., *Sky and Earth*, 1973), included in the volume *Versben bujdosó* (1973; Hiding in Verses), he illustrated, by means of a dramatic clash between a father and his sons, the break-up of the traditional agrarian way of life. Nagy translated García Lorca into Hungarian and published two anthologies of Bulgarian folk poetry in Hungarian translation. In 1966 he was awarded the Kossuth Prize, postwar Hungary's highest literary distinction. His collected poems and verse translations were published in three volumes in 1978.

See: T. Déry, *Útkaparó* (1956); I. Bata, *Képek és vonulatok* (1973); G. Gömöri, Foreword to L. Nagy, *Love of the Scorching Wind* (1973); K. McRobbie, "The Scorching Wind Was His Religion; László Nagy," *WLT* 52, no. 4 (Autumn 1978): 538–41. G.G.

Nałkowska, Zofia (1884–1954), Polish novelist and playwright, was born and died in Warsaw, the daughter of Wacław Nałkowski, an eminent geographer and a literary and social critic. In 1906, at the age of 22, she published *Kobiety* (Eng. tr., *Women*, 1920), the first of a series of novels about the women of the Polish intelligentsia in the period before World War I. In these early works, as Czesław MIŁOSZ has put it, "she committed successively all the sins of that era: aestheticism, oversophistication, and psychological sham profundity."

World War I brought about a profound change in Nałkowska's outlook, which was reflected in both the themes and the manner of her writing. In a series of well-constructed novels, written in a style of increasing simplicity, she explored a wide range of social and moral problems confronting Western society in the period between the two world wars. Among her most notable works during these years were *Romans Teresy Hennert* (1924; The Romance of Teresa Hennert), a broad panorama about cynical materialism in bourgeois Polish society in the early postwar period; the autobiographical *Dom nad łąkami* (1925; The House on the Meadows); *Choucas* (1927; The Jackdaw), a novel set in a Swiss sanatorium that invites comparison with *The Magic Mountain* of Thomas MANN; *Ściany świata* (1931; The Walls of the World), an unsparing study of prison life; and *Granica* (1935; The Boundary), which is generally considered to rank among her most mature and finest works.

World War II marked the beginning of Nałkowska's third and final period, during which she was very active in the intellectual life of postwar Poland. Among the most notable works of this period are *Medaliony* (1946; Medallions), a collection of stories about Nazi concentration camp atrocities that are all the more powerful in their impact because of the restraint and simplicity of their style. *Widzenie bliskie i dalekie* (1957; Vision Far and Near), a collection of Nałkowska's essays and critical works, and *Dzienniki czasu wojny* (1970; Wartime Diaries) were published posthumously.

See: W. Wójcik, *Zofia Nałkowska* (1973); E. Frackowiak-Wiegandtowa, *Sztuka powieściopisarska Nałkowskiej. Lata 1935–1954* (1975).   Z.F. with W.B.E.

Namora, Fernando (1919–), Portuguese novelist and poet, was born in Condeixa-a-Nova near Coimbra and received a degree in medicine from the University of Coimbra. As a young doctor, he worked in remote areas among peasants and miners. In 1950 he moved to Lisbon to work at the Cancer Institute until 1965, when he decided to abandon his profession and devote his full time to literature.

When he was still a medical student, Namora published *Terra* (1941; Earth), the first installment of *Novo Cancioneiro* (New Songbook), a poetry collection that favored a social approach. His first significant novel, *Fogo na noite escura* (1943; Fire in the Dark Night) confirmed the trends he had already revealed in his poems and contributed to establishing him among the ranks of the emerging neorealists. His experiences as a doctor among the poor led to his prose works *Casa da malta* (1945; Tramps' House), *Minas de San Francisco* (1946; The Mines of San Francisco), and *Retalhos da vida de um médico* (2 series, 1949—Eng. tr., *Mountain Doctor*, 1956—and 1963; Fragments of a Doctor's Life). Other fiction includes *A noite e a madrugada* (1950; Night and Dawn), *O trigo e o joio* (1954; Eng. tr., *Fields of Fate*, 1970), *Domingo à tarde* (1961; Sunday Afternoon), and *Os clandestinos* (1972; The Underground). In addition to *Terra*, he wrote two other books of poems, *As frias madrugadas* (1959; Chilly Dawns) and *Marketing* (1969), the latter satirizing modern technology. In recent years, Namora has published several volumes of reflections about contemporary society, for example, *Os adoradores do sol* (1971; Sun Worshippers) and *Estamos no vento* (1974; Windswept), addressed to the younger generation.

Three main stages can be perceived in Namora's work. In the first, best illustrated by *Fogo na noite escura*, he combines psychological analysis with a portrayal of social problems. Beginning with *Casa da malta*, he reveals the then prevalent attitude that literature should be an instrument of social struggle. His third phase, including *Domingo à tarde*, reverts to introspection, but with a considerably more subtle approach, which also distinguishes *Os clandestinos*, where Namora contrasts the protagonist's clandestine love affairs with his underground politics. He turned to autobiography in *A nave de pedra* (1975; The Stony Ship).

See: A. Casais Monteiro, "Fernando Namora," in his *O romance e os seus problemas* (1950), pp. 304–6; A. Franco Nogueira, "Fernando Namora," *Jornal de crítica*

literária (1954), pp. 129–44; J. do Prado Coelho, "Dois livros de Fernando Namora," in his *Problemática da história literária* (1961), pp. 287–94.   E.M.D.

Nastasijević, Momčilo (1894–1938), Serbian poet, short-story writer, playwright, was born in Gornji Milanovac. For most of his life he was a high school teacher in Belgrade, where he died in 1938.

Nastasijević began his literary career as a short-story writer and dramatist, but he later turned to poetry. His collection of short stories, *Iz tamnog vilajeta* (1927; From the World of Darkness), drew immediate attention to its author for the novelty of his style. His best play, *Medjuluško blago* (1927; The Treasure of Medjulug), showed similar tendencies. But it was in poetry that Nastasijević achieved his full potential. Between his first collection, *Pet lirskih krugova* (1932; Five Lyric Cycles), and his last, *Pesme* (1938; Poems), lies a brief but intense creative period. There are also two posthumous collections of his verse, *Rane pesme i varijante* (1939; Early Poems and Variants) and *Sedam lirskih krugova* (1962; Seven Lyric Cycles).

Nastasijević is perhaps the most enigmatic of Serbian poets. He developed independently of literary groups and movements, endeavoring to create his own idiom. His style is characterized by extremely concise, archaic, and often cryptic expressions, through which he hoped both to enrich the modern language and to fathom the national and religious character of his nation. He drew heavily from folklore and the distant past, as well as from his deeply religious, even mystical outlook on life. He was often preoccupied with metaphysical and moral questions, which he tried to resolve through his own highly individualistic, hermetic art. As a poet, he remained a loner, understood and admired only by his closest friends. Lately, however, his work has begun to exert a noticeable influence on younger Serbian poets and to be be studied by critics.

See: M. Pavlović, "Momčilo Nastasijević," *Osam pesnika* (1964), pp. 163–203; N. Milošević, "Beleška o strukturi Nastasijevićevog književnog izraza," *Delo* 5 (1969): 509–30.   V.D.M.

Nazor, Vladimir (1876–1949), Croatian poet and short-story writer, was born in Postira, on the island of Brač. He was one of the most prolific of Croatian writers, remaining active for half a century. Nazor attended secondary school in Split and studied natural sciences in Graz, then becoming a teacher, first in Split and Zadar, and later (from 1903 to 1918) in various Istrian schools. Between the two world wars, he was appointed superintendent of the orphanage in Crikvenica and then director of a gymnasium in Zagreb.

Nazor published his first book of poems, *Slavenske legende* (Slavic Legends) in 1900. Its vocabulary and style were influenced by Victor Hugo and Giosuè Carducci. In this book's lengthy compositions, Nazor glorified ancient gods and heroines and tried to instill in his countrymen an admiration for heathen times. In *Hrvatski kraljevi* (1912; Croatian Kings), Nazor avowed his belief that the Croatian people had not lost their pristine courage and the determination to be masters of their own territory, nor their strong desire to rebuild a national state. Among Nazor's significant literary productions during his years in Istria, *Istarske priče* (1913; Istrian Tales) should be singled out. This collection included his famous short story "Veli Jože" (1908; The Great Joe), whose protagonist awaits a propitious moment to lead his brothers against their exploiters. In 1917, Nazor prepared a collection of his selected poems, *Pabirci* (Gleanings), in which he stressed that the salvation of his people would not come from kings or governors, nobles or merchants, but only from below, from the small, insignificant, and oppressed people, the silent and faithful masses. Nazor was a glorifier of various mythologies, a lover of natural sciences, and often labeled a pantheist, yet in the aftermath of World War I, living withdrawn in Crikvenica, he took refuge in Catholicism and produced a famous collection of poems on religious themes, *Pjesme o četiri arhandjela* (1927; Songs about Four Archangels). For a time he was considered one of the leading Catholic poets.

In later years, he also produced two volumes of outstanding autobiographical short stories, *Priče iz djetinjstva* (1924; Stories from Childhood) and *Priče s ostrva, iz grada i sa planine* (1927; Stories from the Island, the City, and the Mountain).

Nazor spoke the Čakavian dialect at home and heard variants of Čakavian while stationed in Istria. Since some of his poetry is in this dialect, he was instrumental in reviving this most ancient vehicle of Croatian literature.

Nazor's departure for Partisan territory at the end of 1942 contributed much to Marshal Tito's prestige. His *Pjesme partizanke* (Partisan Poems) was published in 1944, and his diary, *S partizanima* (With the Partisans), in 1945. At the time of his death, Nazor was president of the Croatian Republic.

See: A. Barac, *Vladimir Nazor* (1918); M. Žežel, *Vladimir Nazor* (1960). A.K.

Necatigil, Behçet (1916–), Turkish poet, was born in Istanbul. He led an uneventful life, teaching literature at various lycées from 1940 to 1972, when he retired. Besides many books of poems, he published his translations of fiction and poetry by Heinrich Heine, Knut HAMSUN, Miguel de UNAMUNO, Heinrich BÖLL, and others. His radio plays, which he collected in four volumes, have been broadcast on Turkish radio; some of them have been produced on West German radio as well. Necatigil has compiled a *Who's Who* in Turkish literature, a dictionary of mythology, and a guide to Turkish fiction and drama. In 1957 he won the Yeditepe Poetry Prize; and in 1964, the coveted Poetry Award of the Turkish Language Society.

Necatigil, whose first poem appeared in the influential journal *Varlık* in 1935, is one of Turkey's foremost intellectual poets, and he has remained staunchly independent, choosing to shun the numerous schools and movements. In his own words, Necatigil has, throughout his poetic career, "concentrated on evoking the life of the average citizen as individual from birth to death, and on capturing the real and the imaginary experiences he has within the triangle of home—family—immediate environment." The summary holds true for his earliest collections, including *Kapalı Çarşı* (1945; Grand Bazaar), *Evler* (1953; Houses), and others. His later volumes, from *Arada* (1958; In Between) to *Kareler Aklar* (1975; Squares and Whites), are virtually cubistic depictions that display bold intellectual complexities and highly innovative structural and stylistic devices. *Sevgilerde* (1976; In Loves), a substantial selection of his best poems, traces Necatigil's evolution from simple lyrics to a synthesis of poetic subtleties.

See: Y. Pazarkaya, *Behçet Necatigil: Gedichte* (1972). T.S.H.

Nedreaas, Torborg (1906–), Norwegian novelist and short-story writer, was born and raised in Bergen. As early as her second short-story collection, *Bak skapet står øksen* (1945; The Axe behind the Closet), she demonstrated her ability to create, within a traditional narrative form, sensitive psychological portraits of women and children. This quality is characteristic of her whole production.

Nedreaas's finest works—*Trylleglasset* (1950; The Magic Glass), a short-story collection, and *Musikk fra en blå brønn* (1960; Music from a Blue Well) and *Ved neste nymåne* (1971; By the Next New Moon), both novels—constitute a loosely tied trilogy. The story of Herdis, a sensitive, dreamy young girl, is told with humor, irony, and compassion. In these works, Nedreaas also reveals exceptional stylistic skill in the creation of mood and atmosphere. Underneath the mood and surface story structure, however, lurk serious social issues, for this socially conscious author has always sought to awaken her reader's conscience to the callousness of society toward its defenseless members. In 1952, Nedreaas published her most controversial book, *De varme hendene* (The Warm Hands), an indignant protest against the rising power of the military establishment and political expediency permeating all levels of Norwegian politics.

See: B. Model, ed., *Festskrift til Torborg Nedreaas* (1976). K.A.F.

Nekrasov, Viktor Platonovich (1911–), Russian writer, was born in Kiev, spent his early years in Paris, but later returned to Kiev, where he subsequently earned a degree in architecture.

Nekrasov served in the Red Army during World War II and participated in the historic battle of Stalingrad, which he later described in his first book, *V okopakh Stalingrada* (1946; Eng. tr., *Front-Line Stalingrad*, 1962). One of the most honest, realistic, and nonheroic portrayals of war in Soviet literature, this work brought him a Stalin Prize. It was followed by *V rodnom gorode* (1954; In the Home Town), a novel about the aftermath of war and the emotional problems of ex-soldiers. In 1961 he published one of his most controversial novels, *Kira Georgievna* (Eng. tr., 1962), a sensitive psychological study of a woman artist and her conflict with her former husband when he returns from a concentration camp. Although it is rather pedestrian in style, *Kira* is free of socialist-realist platitudes.

In 1960, Nekrasov spent two weeks touring the United States and Italy. His description of these trips in *Po obe storony okeana* (1962; Eng. tr., *Both Sides of the Ocean*, 1964) caused a great stir, and he was accused of slandering the Soviet Union and of trying to curry favor with the "bourgeois public." The book is in reality an objective record of personal observations and comparisons, leveling a fair degree of criticism at both sides.

In the late 1960s, Nekrasov wrote a number of essays about literature and art and came to be known as an advocate of the human rights movement in the USSR. He was expelled from the Communist Party in 1972 for supporting Aleksandr SOLZHENITSYN and Andrey Sakharov, and his works have since then been barred from publication. After steadily increasing harassment from the Soviet authorities, he emigrated and settled in Paris in 1975.

See: E. Kulukundis, Translator's Foreword in V. Nekrasov, *Both Sides of the Ocean* (New York, 1964). I.H.C.

Nemésio (Mendes Pinheiro da Silva), Vitorino (1901–78), Portuguese poet, short-story writer, novelist, and scholar, was born on Terceira Island in the Azores. After a youth spent in the Atlantic archipelago, which was to figure prominently in his writings of later years, Nemésio completed his studies in 1931 at the University of Lisbon. In subsequent years he taught literature in France and Belgium and from 1937 to 1940 edited his short-lived but important *Revista de Portugal*. In 1940 he was named to the Chair of Letters at his alma mater, from which he retired in 1972.

Nemésio's fame as a creative writer began with a collection of short stories, *Paço do Milhafre* (1924; Kite's Palace), which was later enlarged and revised as *O mistério do Paço do Milhafre* (1949; The Mystery of Kite's Palace). Critics hailed the author's verbal skill in distilling literary experience from an island boyhood. The islands continued to figure in subsequent narratives, including a novel, *Varanda de Pilatos* (1926; Pilate's Porch), and a collection of novellas, *A casa fechada* (1937; The Closed-Up House). But the greatest acclaim was reserved for *Mau tempo no Canal* (1944; Rough Weather in the Channel), a saga of the Azores during the first quarter of this century and quite possibly the most significant contemporary Portuguese novel. As a poet, Nemésio was one of the first in his country to cultivate the style of the early surrealists. His *O bicho harmonioso* (1938; The Harmonious Animal) marks a milestone in its free association and daring imagery. Other works in verse include his earliest, *Canto matinal* (1916; Morning Song); adaptations of popular ballad forms from the Azores in *Festa redonda* (1950; Round Feast Day); and lyrical complements to his Brazilian travel journals, *Ode ao Rio* (1965; Ode to Rio) and *Violão do môrro* (1968; Guitar from Shantytown Hill). The poet echoes the modern era's spiritual crisis with ironic detachment and verbal austerity, as in *Nem toda a noite a vida* (1952; Life Not All Night Long). Beginning with *O pão e a culpa* (1955; Bread and Guilt), he expresses a unified vision resulting from a recovery of religious faith, without being devotional in any traditional sense. The poems in *Limite de idade* (1972; Age Limit) still judge modern life with humor.

See: D. Mourão-Ferreira, "Sobre a obra de Vitorino Nemésio," in his *Tópicos de crítica e de história literária* (1969), pp. 159–89; E. Prado Coelho, "Vitorino Nemésio—A gramática de Deus ou a ficção reversível," *Colóquio,* 4 (1971): 33–43; M. L. Lepecki, "Sobre *Mau tempo no Canal,*" *Colóquio,* 4 (1971): 44–49.

R.A.P.-R.

Németh, László (1901–75), Hungarian novelist, playwright, essayist, and translator, was born in Nagybánya (now Baia-Mare, Romania). In his many-faceted oeuvre, Németh was often concerned with uniquely Hungarian political, ethnic, and cultural problems. Yet although he could hardly be called a "Westerner," his nationalistic attitudes reveal a profound awareness of the Western tradition.

Németh's literary career began in 1925 with the publication, in the periodical *Nyugat,* of a masterful short story about the death of a peasant woman, "Horváthné meghal" (Mrs. Horváth Dies). By the early 1930s he had also made a name for himself as a critic, on the basis of his highly personal, although erudite and polished, appraisals of some of the great figures of Western literature. Németh was a man of bold vision. Basing his ideological conviction on a curious mixture of Nietzschean elitism (*see* Friedrich NIETZSCHE) and Christian and socialist egalitarianism, he became an advocate of a "revolution of quality," i.e., a moral revolution. The basic tenet of his writing is that life's deep-rooted ills can only be remedied by moral example. In the 1930s Németh rejected both capitalism and communism, believing that the real revolution must take place within the individual consciousness. This ethical impulse informs virtually all of his novels and plays, which deal invariably with the noble and tragic struggle of individual genius against mass stupidity and intolerance. The names alone of the historical personages around whom he built some of his dramas—

Galileo, Jan Hus, Mahatma Gandhi—indicate the nature of his concerns. In subtler ways, his novels exemplify the same outlook. The nonconformist hero of *Emberi színjáték* (1929; Human Comedy) becomes a Nietzschean moral giant and the heroines of *Égető Eszter* (1956) and *Irgalom* (1965; Compassion), although realistically conceived, are symbols of human goodness and endurance. Németh, the father of four daughters, had a predilection for strong female characters. This impulse is evident, for example, in the novel *Gyász* (1936; Mourning), a finely wrought story about a proud peasant widow whose grief over her husband's death turns into an awe-inspiring obsession. Németh's best novel, *Iszony* (1947; Eng. tr., *Revulsion,* 1965), is about a cold, virginal, but highly sensitive woman's tragic marriage to a jovial, sensuous man. *Bűn* (1936; rev. Eng. tr., *Guilt,* 1966) is Németh's most "Russian" novel. The title refers to the guilt felt by sensitive members of the upper class—here represented by a wealthy intellectual—in the face of social inequality.

Németh's career as a fiction writer was not his only one. A physician by profession, he practiced as a school doctor for a number of years. In the 1930s he edited a periodical, *Tanu,* which was one of those curious ventures not entirely unprecedented in Hungarian literature: a journal written by one man. During the late 1940s and early 1950s—until he reached a modus vivendi with the new regime—he earned his living by teaching in a secondary school and translating foreign classics into Hungarian. It was at this time that he completed his brilliant translation of Lev TOLSTOY's *Anna Karenina.*

Németh's intense moral commitment and aesthetic sensitivity earned him the admiration of a whole generation of Hungarian intellectuals. Yet some of his prewar ideas—his controversial distinction between "deep" and "skindeep" Hungarians, for instance, as well as his subtly intellectual anti-Semitism—also turned many of his liberal countrymen against him. He is considered today one of the giants of modern Hungarian literature, despite the fact that Marxist critics dismiss his ethical-ideological convictions as illusionary Utopianism. While Németh did come to accept socialism, in his literary works the redeeming power of solitary moral exemplars remained strong.

See: P. Gulyás, *Németh László* (1932); K. Kerényi, "On László Németh," *HungQ* 3 (1962): 33–38; J. Reményi, *Hungarian Writers and Literature* (1964), pp. 394–401; L. Vekerdi, *Németh László alkotásai és vallomásai tükrében* (1970).

I.S.

Nesin, Aziz (1915–), Turkish novelist, playwright, and short-story writer, and Turkey's best-known satirist, was born in Istanbul. He graduated from the Military Academy in 1937. After about seven years as a career officer, he became a newspaper columnist. In the late 1940s he published a variety of satirical periodicals and was jailed several times because of his leftist views. One of Turkey's most prolific writers, he has published about 70 books since 1945. With income from his many best sellers and from foreign royalties, he established in 1972 the Nesin Foundation, which provides full scholarships for children of poor families.

In addition to more than 30 collections of short stories, he published many novels, several volumes of autobiography, a collection of satirical verse, children's stories, and travel notes. He also wrote 10 plays, many of which were either produced or published or both. His published work includes a critical anthology of Turkish satire, collections of tales, and newspaper essays and articles, and other literary efforts. He won many awards in Turkey, Italy (Gold Palm, 1956 and 1957), Bulgaria (Gold Porcupine, 1966), the Soviet Union (Krokodil, 1969), and the Asian-African Writers Union's Lotus in 1975.

Available in many major and minor languages, his work is represented in English by numerous short stories in journals and anthologies. By 1980 only one Nesin book was published in the English-speaking world, *Istanbul Boy* (1977), which is a major segment of the first volume of Nesin's autobiography.

Nesin's satire presents the trials and tribulations of ordinary people beleaguered by the hostile forces of modern life, lambastes bureaucracy, and exposes the injustices of the capitalist economy. He runs the entire gamut of humor from the subtlest irony to the broadest types of burlesque, and he achieves his most impressive success in poking fun at political institutions and human foibles, particularly hypocrisy. T.S.H.

Neumann, Alfred (1895–1952), German novelist and poet, was born in Lautenberg, West Prussia. After having attended school in Berlin and in Rostock, he became a reader for the Georg Müller publishing house in Munich (1913–18) and in 1917 published his *Lieder vom Lächeln und der Not* (Songs of Smiling and Agony). From 1918 to 1920 he was dramatic adviser for the Munich Little Theater. The most noteworthy of his earlier works is a story entitled *Der Patriot* (1925; Eng. tr., 1928), which deals with the murder of the Emperor Paul of Russia. The dramatic version (1926) was staged in London (1928) under the title *Such Men are Dangerous*. His first literary recognition, however, came with the Kleist Prize for his novel *Der Teufel* (1926; Eng. trs., *The Devil* and also *The Deuce*, both 1928), in which lust for power during the reign of Louis XI is the theme. In the next year he published *Rebellen* (Eng. tr., *The Rebels*, 1929), with the Carbonari revolution as a background. A kind of continuation of *Rebellen* is *Guerra* (1928; Eng. tr., 1930), dealing with the leader of the Italian independence movement. The murder of Walther Rathenau in 1922 suggested *Der Held* (1930; Eng. tr., *The Hero*, 1931), and the *Memoiren des Ritters Hans von Schweinichen* (Memoirs of the Knight, Sir Hans von Schweinichen) led to the composition of *Narrenspiegel* (1932; Eng. tr., *The Mirror of Fools*, 1933). A selection of Neumann's stories appeared in English in 1930 under the title *King Haber and Other Stories*. *Königen Christine von Schweden* (1926; Eng. tr., *The Life of Christina of Sweden*, 1935) represents a historical portrayal of the Swedish queen with some attention to her erotic peculiarities.

Neumann's dramas, *Königsmaske* (1928; The Mask of Kings), *Frauenschuh* (1929; Lady's Shoe), and *Haus Danieli* (1931; The House of Danieli), may be mentioned in passing. He left Germany under the Nazi regime and took refuge in the United States. Among his works written in exile were *Neuer Caesar* (1934; Eng. tr., *Another Caesar*, 1934), *Kaiserreich* (1936; Eng. tr., in America, *The Gaudy Empire*, in England, *Man of December*, 1937), and *Goldquelle* (1938; Gold Source). He is also the author of *Volksfreunde* (1941; republished in 1952 with the title *Das Kind von Paris*; Eng. tr., *The Friends of the People*, 1942), a story that takes place at the time of the Paris Commune; *Es waren ihrer sechs* (1947, with the Eng. tr. appearing first with the title *Six of Them*, 1945), the tale of the tragic anti-Nazi rebellion of the brother and sister Scholl and their compatriots in Munich in the late years of World War II; and a strangely prophetic novel about a 19th-century dictator in Nicaragua, *Der Pakt* (1950; Eng. tr., *Strange Conquest*, 1954).

Neumann contributed to the revival of the historical novel, using the past, however, to symbolize present political situations and problems. His lack of hero worship

and his tendency to pacifism probably rendered his works, from the Nazi viewpoint, suitable for the notorious book burning in 1933.

See: A. Neumann, "Autobiographische Skizze," *Blätter der Bücherstube am Museum Wiesbaden* 3 (1927): 6–7; "Skizze des Lebens," *Bergische Bühnenblätter* 7, no. 28 (1927): 4–5; "Selbstdarstellung," *Die literarische Welt* 6, no. 45 (1930): 1. F.Sp. rev. A.L.W.

Neumann, Robert (1897–), Austrian novelist and parodist, was born in Vienna, the son of an engineer-banker-mathematics professor. He himself studied chemistry, medicine, and German literature in Vienna, where he then worked as a bookkeeper, bank official, broker, and factory director before he experienced financial ruin through the inflation of the 1920s. He served as a sailor on a Dutch tanker and, after his books were burned and banned by the Nazis in 1933, he emigrated to England, where he became an English citizen and wrote in English in Cranbrook, Kent. Later he lived in Locarno.

After early books of poetry, Neumann attracted public notice with parodies in *Mit fremden Federn* (With Foreign Pens) in 1927. Always interested in topical themes, as in the collection of stories *Jagd auf Menschen und Gespenster* (1928; Chase after People and Ghosts) and the novel *Sintflut* (1929; Flood), Neumann wrote entertaining prose that was rational but also psychological. His *Hochstaplernovelle* (1930; The Novella of an Embezzler) appeared in 1952 under the title *Die Insel der Circe* (The Island of Circe). The novel *Sir Basil Zaharoff, der König der Waffen* (Eng. tr., *Zaharoff*, 1935) appeared in 1934. The novel *Struensee* (1935) was reissued in 1953 under the title *Der Favorit der Königin* (The Queen's Favorite). The novel *Eine Frau hat geschrien* (1938; A Woman Screamed) appeared in 1958 under the title *Die Freiheit und der General* (Freedom and the General).

In exile in England, Neumann published several works in English before they appeared in German, a not infrequent experience for German authors in exile. Among others were the novels *An den Wassern von Babylon* (*By the Waters of Babylon*, 1939 in English, German in 1945) and *Tibbs* (1942 in English, German in 1948). The novel *Die Kinder von Wien* (*Children of Vienna*), first in English in 1947 and in German in 1948, tells the story of a Negro priest who seeks to help needy children but is denounced. Controversial themes and political backgrounds mark the work of Neumann, such as the flight before the prevalence of power and persecution in the much-praised novel *Bibiana Santis* (*The Inquest*, 1945 in English, 1950 in German). After other prose works he published parodies, the source of his first fame, in a volume in 1962.
A.L.W.

Neumann, Stanislav Kostka (1875–1947), Czech poet, was one of the most influential and popular Czech writers of free verse. Neumann was born in Prague, took part in the abortive anti-Austrian conspiracy of the 1890s, "Omladina," and for a while cultivated an aristocratic anarchism. He became a journalist and served in the Austrian army during World War I. After the war he was a member of Parliament representing the Czech Socialist Party, but in 1922 he joined the Communist Party and edited its periodicals. He was awarded the title of "national poet" in 1945.

Neumann began his writing career as the poet of fashionable anarchism and Nietzschean individualism (*see* Friedrich NIETZSCHE). The titles of two early verse collections, *Jsem apoštol nového žití* (1896; I Am the Apostle of a New Life) and *Satanova sláva mezi námi* (1897; Satan's Glory among Us), suggest both the crude ideology and the rhetorical style of the young author. But Neumann soon discovered social and national issues: *Sen o zástupu zoufajících* (1903; A Dream of the Despairing Mass) expresses his vision of the horrors of social oppression and his hopes for its removal. Neumann then turned to individual problems. Possibly his best work is included in two collections written before World War I. *Kniha lesů, vod a strání* (1914; The Book of Woods, Waters, and Slopes) contains frankly sensual poems in praise of nature, open air, and sex. The rich, sonorous free verse, the charmingly vivid and colorful metaphors, convey a zest for life and sheer animal enjoyment rare in Czech poetry. *Horký van a jiné básně* (1918; The Hot Breath and Other Poems) includes a naive celebration of the pleasures of the marriage bed. But a completely new ideology and technique appear in Neumann's postwar collections. *Nové zpěvy* (1918; New Songs) represents his sudden discovery of the beauties of machine civilization, and *Třicet zpěvů z rozvratu* (1918; Thirty Songs from the Time of Upheaval) versifies his experiences in Hungary and the Balkans during the war. The technique of these two collections is futurist—a mosaic of colors and impressions, a flow of free-verse rhetoric that frequently violates all standards of taste and good sense but never loses vitality. Several later volumes, notably *Rudé zpěvy* (1923; Red Songs), are only versified propaganda, but one collection, *Láska* (1933; Love), returns to the theme of sexual love in sober, mature tones and even uses old-fashioned, concise song and stanza forms. Neumann's prose is less important than his verse, much of it being either polemics or propaganda; there are also books of reminiscences from World War I and two travel books about postwar Czechoslovakia. Among Neumann's other prose works, a love story, *Zlatý oblak* (1932; The Golden Cloud), is trivial, and his histories of love, of woman, and of the French Revolution are mere potboilers.

Neumann's youthful enthusiasm, which outlasted maturity, his frankly "pagan" sensualism, his glorification of the wonders of modern civilization, the zest and flow of his rhetorical verse, and the color of his metaphors endeared him to the generation of readers immediately following World War I, and he, more than any other older poet, influenced the young "proletarian" movement, as well as the socialist poets who emerged during the late 1940s. Yet his naive ideology and lack of subtle emotions and ideas exclude him from the first rank of Czech poets.

See: B. Polan, *Se Stanislav Kostka Neumannem* (1919); B. Václavek, *Stanislav Kostka Neumann* (1935); J. Lang, *Stanislav Kostka Neumann* (1957); E. Strohsova, *Zrození moderny* (1963), pp. 43–55.   R.W.

Nexø, Martin Andersen (1869–1954), Danish novelist, was born in the slums of Copenhagen, the fourth of 11 children. His boyhood was spent on the island of Bronholm as a shepherd. He attended folk high school between 1891 and 1893, at which time he began writing. A convinced Communist, Nexø stayed in Sweden as a refugee during World War II, thereafter for a while in the USSR, and after 1951 in East Germany. Relentlessly, but without bitterness, Nexø recorded the memories of his proletarian youth in four volumes (1932–39), which have become classics of Danish autobiography and provide the background to his two major novels (*see* DANISH LITERATURE). *Pelle Erobreren* (1906–10; Eng. tr., *Pelle the Conqueror*, 1913–16) follows the progress of the Danish labor movement around 1906 toward its victory, but the description of "the worker's heavy stride across the earth on his endless semiconscious wandering toward the light" becomes a general symbol of human striving forward. The achievement of the light is symbolized by the ideal-

ized main character's development from being the child of poor parents (the novel has autobiographical traits) to becoming an organizer in the workers' struggle for social equality. The novel is a masterpiece owing to the epic force of the narrative, Nexø's social passion, and his belief in the inherent goodness of people. This belief is similarly expressed in *Ditte Menneskebarn* (1917–21; Eng. tr., *Ditte: Girl Alive, Ditte: Daughter of Man, Ditte: Toward the Stars,* 1920–23). This novel is not a political parallel to *Pelle Erobreren* even if Ditte also starts at the bottom of society and possesses the same strong progressive drive and vitality as Pelle. Whereas Pelle is engaged in political activity to build up a new world, Ditte has to fight poverty alone and succumbs as a servant girl and unmarried mother in the city slums. The novel *Midt i en Jærntid* (1929; Eng. tr., *In God's Land,* 1933) is a satirical attack on the economic abuses during World War I by Danish farmers. *Morten hin Røde* (1945; Morten the Red) continues the earlier *Pelle Erobreren*. Here Pelle has become a Social Democratic prime minister, sharply criticized for his middle-class values and mentality. The revolutionary spirit that he previously possessed is now found in the title figure, Nexø's alter ego. Nexø has become the inspiration for many younger Danish and foreign proletarian authors. In contrast to these, however, he believed in human goodness—throughout all social and economic conditions.

See: S. Erichsen, *Martin Andersen Nexø* (1938); H. A. Koefoed, "Martin Andersen Nexø—Some Viewpoints," *Scan* 4, no. 1 (1965): 27–37.   S.H.R.

Nezval, Vítězslav (1900–58), Czech poet, dramatist, and novelist, was born in Biskupky near Třebíč, in western Moravia, the son of a schoolteacher. He went to Prague to study languages and succeeded in earning his living by writing. He made several visits to Paris and the Soviet Union. In 1945, Nezval was named chief of a division in the Ministry of Information. After Czechoslovakia turned Communist in 1948, he became virtually an official "poet laureate" in his support of the Stalinist regime.

Nezval was the founder of a movement he called "poetism." He had begun as an adherent of "proletarian" poetry, but reacted against its preoccupation with rhetoric and propaganda, although he never gave up his sympathies for communism. "Poetism" was a new name for "pure poetry" devoid of thought and of propaganda, for poetry as a play of fancy and association. Nezval carried out his theory in several collections, notably *Menší růžová zahrada* (1927; The Smaller Rose Garden), in which (to borrow the title of one of his poems) he proved himself an "admirable magician," an astonishing virtuoso of poetical fireworks, an inventor of fantastic rhymes, illogical chains of associations, grotesque fancies, whole topsy-turvy little worlds. Nezval's affinities with Italian futurism (*see* Filippo MARINETTI) and Guillaume APOLLINAIRE are frequently obvious, but he had his own peculiar themes and techniques. After about 1928, Nezval's tones began to change and deepen; feverish visions and dreams replace the bright daylight of his early books. His poetry of this later period centers around night, death, time, and inexorable change. His best collection, *Básně noci* (1930; Poems of the Night), is well named, and his masterpiece, "Edison," combines a celebration of technical civilization with the cult of night and sorrow. Nezval's other collections are repetitious and show a decline in inventive power, although a number of individual poems are as fine as ever. *Snídaně v trávě* (1930; The Breakfast in the Grass), *Jan ve smutku* (1930; John in Mourning), *Skleněný havelok* (1932; The Havelock of Glass), *Zpáteční lístek* (1933; The Return Ticket), and

Sbohem a šáteček (1934; Good-bye and a Hankerchief) are some of the fancifully named volumes, all of which indicate an increasing lack of self-criticism.

In about 1934, Nezval embraced the creed of French surrealism and tried to write according to the recipes of André BRETON. As a surrealist, he viewed poetry as a mere overflow of the subconscious, almost automatic writing as practiced by mediums. Nezval's surrealist collections include *Žena v množném čísle* (1936; Woman in the Plural), *Praha s prsty deště* (1936; Prague with the Fingers of Rain), *Absolutní Hrobař* (1937; The Absolute Gravedigger), and *Pět minut za městem* (1939; Five Minutes behind the Town). The last volume represents a return to public themes: one poem, "Historický obraz" (A Historical Picture), is an impressive attempt to express the feeling of the Czech people after the Munich Pact. Nezval's long poems, *Stalin* (1949) and *Zpěv míru* (1950; Eng. tr., *Song of Peace,* 1951), are no more than bad propaganda. Some of the lyrics produced in his final years, however, retain at least a trace of the verve, freshness, and imagist virtuosity of his early work: these are found in collections such as *Křídla* (1952; Wings) and *Nedokončená* (1960; Unfinished).

Nezval did verse translations, very free, from the works of Edgar Allan Poe, Arthur RIMBAUD, and Stéphane MALLARMÉ and wrote verse plays that try to achieve the effect of improvisation in the style of the commedia dell'arte. *Schovávaná na schodech* (1931; Hide and Seek on the Stairs) is based on a comedy by Pedro Calderón de la Barca, and *Milenci z kiosku* (1932; The Lovers from the Newsstand) is an original entertainment that had considerable success on the stage. Nezval's prose is on a lower artistic level than his verse or drama. His novels, which include *Posedlost* (1930; Obsession), *Dolce far niente* (1931), and *Jak vejce vejce* (1933; As Like as Two Peas) are loosely composed long stories that frequently border on pornography or Marxist propaganda. Nezval wrote a number of manifestos, as well as many reviews, critical essays, and aphorisms on literature and art. He also published a few travel sketches. His memoirs, *Z mého života* (1959; From My Life), which recall many literary and artistic personalities of the interwar period, played a role in bringing about a more liberal attitude toward modernist trends in poetry and art at the end of the 1950s.

Nezval was not a man of ideas or even intellect, but his work displays an amazing vitality, a lively play of fancy, and an inexhaustible inventiveness in rhyme and metaphor, all of which outweigh his frequent bad taste and schoolboyish coarseness.

See: F. Soldan, *O Nezvalove a poválečné generaci* (1933); L. Kratochvil, *Wolker a Nezval* (1936); A. Jelínek, *Vítězslav Nezval* (1961); J. Svoboda, *Přítel V. Nezval* (1966); A. French, *The Poets of Prague* (1969).   R.W.

Niccodemi, Dario (1874–1934), Italian playwright, was born in Livorno but spent his early youth in Buenos Aires. He is remembered especially for having directed the premiere of Luigi PIRANDELLO'S *Sei personaggi in cerca d'autore* (1921; Eng. tr., *Six Characters in Search of an Author,* 1922). While still in his twenties, Niccodemi wrote two plays in Spanish. In 1900 he became the secretary of the French actress Réjane and accompanied her to Paris, where he wrote (in French) *L'aigrette* (1912), one of his most successful plays, translated immediately into Italian. During World War I he returned to Italy where he wrote and presented, among other dramas, the highly acclaimed *L'ombra* (1915; The Shadow), *Scampolo* (1916), and *La maestrina* (1918; The Little Teacher). In 1921 he founded a very successful dramatic company.

Niccodemi's plays are written for the entertainment of the bourgeoisie. They are technically excellent and characterized by facile, lively dialogue and well-contrived plots. They combine a certain worldliness with an appealing sentimentalism; the formula is that of the Parisian theater exemplified by Henry BERNSTEIN. Witty, fast-moving, and plausible, Niccodemi's plays are still viable, yet to the present generation they seem conventional in design and superficial in content.

See: R. Bianchi, *Dario Niccodemi* (1924).   T.G.B.

Nicolau d'Olwer, Lluis (1888–1961), Catalan critic and essayist, was an outstanding figure in Catalan letters and was also very active in liberal-nationalistic politics after the Spanish Republic was proclaimed in 1931. He was born in Barcelona, and his father, a lawyer, provided him with an excellent education. Before finishing his studies, including law, he had already published several literary essays which gave evidence of a precocious talent: *Sobre les fonts catalanes de "Tirant lo Blanch"* (1907; On the Catalonian Sources of 'Tirant lo Blanch') and *Notes sobre les regles de trobar, de Jofre de Foixà i sobre les poesies que li han atribuit* (1907; Notes on Jofre de Foixà's 'Regles de Trubar' and the Poems Attributed to Him). He was later elected a member of the Institut d'Estudis Catalans (the most distinguished cultural institution of Catalonia), in which he distinguished himself by his work in the philological section. Among his learned and critical works are: *Sobre la influència italiana en la prosa catalana* (Concerning Italian Influence on Catalonian Prose), *Bernat Metge, Francesc Alegre* (1908); *Del classicisme a Catalunya* (1909; On Classicism in Catalonia); *Jaume I i els trobadors provençals* (1909; James I and the Provençal Troubadors); *Gerbert (Silvestre II) i la cuotura catalana del segle X* (1910; Gerbert [Silvestre II] and the Catalonian Culture of the 10th Century); *Jordi de Sant Jordi* (1915); *Tractat de linguistica* (1917; Treatise on Linguistics); and *Resum de literatura catalana* (1917; Summary of Catalonian Literature).

Nicolau began his political career when he was elected councilman of the municipal government of Barcelona (1918–21). With his friend Bofill i Mates he founded the party Acció Catalana in 1922. From 1923 to 1930 he worked to harmonize nationalistic and republican ideas; and from 1930 to 1939 he held various representative offices. He continued to be deeply interested in literature and history and produced numerous studies: *Del diàleg de la poesia medieval catalana* (1920; The Dialogue in Medieval Catalonian Poetry); *L'escola poètica de Ripoll en els segles X-XIII* (1920; The Poetic School of Ripoll from the 10th to the 13th Centuries); *L'expansió de Catalunya a la Mediterranea oriental* (1926; The Expansion of Catalonia in the Eastern Mediterranean); *L'expedició dels catalans a Orient* (1926; The Expedition of the Catalonians to the Near East); and *Paisatges de la nostra història* (1929; Landscapes of Our History). Of a political nature are *Comentaris* (1920; Commentaries) and *La llicó de la dictadura* (1931; The Lesson of the Dictatorship). *El pont de la mar blava* (1928; Bridge over the Angry Sea), a purely literary work, consists of impressions of a trip through Tunis, Sicily, and Malta. Nicolau's style is notable for precision, clarity, and simplicity.

A refugee in France in 1939, he was obliged to endure incarceration with common offenders. He was eventually set free and after living under surveillance in a small village was able to move to the French capital, where in vain he awaited the liberation of his native country. He died in Mexico.   J.M.M.iV.

Nielsen, Jørgen (1902–45), Danish novelist and short-story writer, was born in central Jutland. He began as a farm-hand, but later he became a journalist in the provinces.

As an author, Nielsen moved to Copenhagen in 1933 but subsequently returned to his home region. His literary production deals primarily with the post-World War I collapse of the value system in a peasant society where the confrontation between a modern relativistic intellectualism and an older moral and religious view of life was felt most acutely. This theme is found in Nielsen's major works, the collections of short stories *Lavt Land* (1929; Low Country), *Vi Umyndige* (1934; We, the Dependents), and *Figurer i et Landskab* (1944; Figures in a Landscape). His first two novels, *Offerbaal* (1929; Sacrificial Bonfire) and *De Hovmodige* (1930; The Haughty), describe man's natural desire for light and happiness, which conflict with the dark, puritanical compulsions in the life of the rural poor, ending in resignation. The same mood also dominates Nielsen's most successful book, the love story *En Kvinde ved Baalet* (1933; A Woman by the Bonfire). All themes are finally present in the novel *Dybet* (1940; The Deep), which describes the hopeless disease of a farmer's wife and the husband's instinctive desire for her death.

See: N. Nilsson, *Jørgen Nielsen: en Digterskæbne* (1951).   S.H.R.

Nietzsche, Friedrich Wilhelm (1844–1900), German philosopher, was born at Röcken in Prussian Saxony, the oldest child of a Lutheran minister. His father died in 1849 of a brain injury caused by a fall, and the following year the family moved to Naumburg. There Nietzsche attended secondary school (1854–58) and the academy (1858–64). The next year he spent at Bonn in the study of theology and philology and then transferred to Leipzig, where he completed his studies in philology. While in Leipzig he came under the influence of Arthur Schopenhauer and made the personal acquaintance of Richard WAGNER, two events of great importance in his life. In 1869 he was called to the chair of classical languages at Basle, and in view of his brilliant record as a student the University of Leipzig conferred the doctor's degree upon him without a formal dissertation.

In the Franco-Prussian War, Nietzsche volunteered for ambulance duty and was in the war zone from August until October 1870. The strenuous work and the sight of suffering proved too much for him, and he returned to his teaching after a severe illness. At Basle his most important association was with Wagner at the latter's home in Triebschen, near Lucerne (1869–72). Both men were interested in the relation of music and tragedy in their bearing on the ethical meaning of life. Wagner regarded Nietzsche as his most brilliant adherent. Coolness developed between the two, however, with Nietzsche's increasing independence. Nietzsche was present at the laying of the cornerstone in Bayreuth (1872), and he attended the opening of the theater in 1876, but by that time he had broken his allegiance to Wagner and was launching out in new ways of his own. For some years his health had been declining because of what was probably syphilis contracted in his youth, and in 1879 he had to resign his professorship. A small private income, supplemented by a pension from the university, enabled him to live independently on a very modest scale. The next 10 years were spent in growing isolation as Nietzsche traveled about in search of a favorable climate. He suffered a mental breakdown at Turin in 1889, his mind was beclouded, and he became progressively worse in his insanity until his death at Weimar in 1900.

Nietzsche's efforts were directed to a single goal: the definition of a higher type of human character and its realization in a new frame of existence. He believed that man had come to the end of a long period of civilization and faced a catastrophic dissolution of all his former ideals. It was now a question of complete nihilism or of creating a new goal. The ethical and moral ideas fostered by religions and metaphysics, especially Schopenhauer's pessimism, encouraged an attitude of resignation and held up nirvana or an imaginary future life as humankind's highest hope. Particularly the Christian religion, with its doctrine of total depravity, broke all that was courageous in mankind. Psychologically this meant that the human being was enslaved by a powerful escape complex that made him unfit for the mastery of life and of himself. In opposition, Nietzsche set up the ideal of tragic optimism, or heroic pessimism, which views life as a tragic process but regards tragedy as the source of new life and power. Ethical rank is determined by the capacity to endure suffering and rise superior to it in a new creative effort. The symbol Nietzsche used for his ideal was the Greek god Dionysus. As a new metaphysical frame, although he ostensibly repudiated metaphysics, he evolved the ideas of the "will to power" and the "external return" as his highest expression of the affirmation of earthly existence—in a sense another concept of an "absolute" and another version of immortality. The hypothesis underlying the "will to power" is that in all existence the urge of each vital unit is to secure at every moment the utmost feeling of power, in whatever disguised ways and according to the "eternal return," life in all its forms will be repeated without change in ever-recurring cycles.

Nietzsche first proclaimed his theory of heroic pessimism in *Die Geburt der Tragödie* (1872; see below for translations of all Nietzsche's works), which connected the rebirth of the tragic spirit with Wagner's music dramas. At the same time he was advancing new educational ideas in certain public lectures at Basle and in his *Unzeitgemäße Betrachtungen* (1873–76, in four parts), all of them centering on the differences between learning and culture. A new series of analytical studies began with *Menschliches Allzumenschliches* (1878–80). Rounding out this group were *Morgenröte* (1881) and *Fröhliche Wissenschaft* (1882). At the outset of this period, pure knowledge is represented as mankind's highest achievement and greatest consolation. Metaphysics, religion, and the aesthetic arts reflecting them, are subjected to dispassionate criticism, not without nostalgic relapses. Saint, poet, and philosopher are superseded by the scientist. Biological determinism relieves the human being of a great burden of responsibility and fear accompanying a "free will." Nietzsche begins his history of moral ideas and shows his hostility to the state as a menace to true culture. As he proceeds he questions the sufficiency of pure knowledge and ends with the idea of "joyful knowledge." This period finds its climax in *Also sprach Zarathustra* (1883–92, in four parts), his greatest bid for the popularization of his ideas. The limitations of man in his highest forms are exposed. In the figure of Zarathustra (Zoroaster) a new type is foreshadowed. He has been through all the "thou shalts" and "thou shalt nots" and, having gained mastery over his baser passions, can now safely entrust himself to a creative morality of "I will."

After *Zarathustra,* Nietzsche again returned to the rational principles of his thinking. In *Jenseits von Gut und Böse* (1886), a fifth part of *Fröhliche Wissenschaft* (1887), and *Zur Genealogie der Moral* (1887), he produced some of his best writing. More and more stress is laid upon the function of the so-called evil forces in the economy of life, and the idea of the "will to power" emerges clearly. What probably would have been Nietzsche's greatest book, in which he intended to develop his ideas in their philosophical and ethical implications, remained unwritten. Materials for it are to be found in *Der Wille zur Macht,* compiled by his sister and Peter Gast on the basis of a brief outline left by Nietzsche (1901). The three works written and published in 1888, *Der Fall Wagner,*

Götzendämmerung, and *Der Antichrist,* and two other composed in that year but published later, the autobiographical *Ecce Homo* (1900) and *Nietzsche contra Wagner* (1901), represent a final effort to gain general recognition. They are somewhat uneven, frequently rising to Nietzsche's accustomed height but occasionally falling into old ruts of thought, imitation, and ranting. Megalomania appears. Nietzsche regards himself as Dionysus, victor over Christ after two thousand years of dominion. The Nazi theoreticians interpreted Nietzsche for their own purposes, and brought him for a time into disrepute, but it is generally believed that their claim to Nietzschean ideas as a basis for Nazism is perverse.

For Nietzsche in German, see the 23-volume Musarion edition (1920-29). For English translations see *The Portable Nietzsche* (1965), which includes *Thus Spoke Zarathustra, Twilight of the Idols, The Antichrist,* and *Nietzsche contra Wagner;* and *Basic Writings of Nietzsche* (1968), which contains *The Birth of Tragedy, Beyond Good and Evil, On the Genealogy of Morals, The Case of Wagner,* and *Ecce Homo.*

See: E. Förster-Nietzsche, *The Young Nietzsche* (1912) and *The Lonely Nietzsche* (1915), tr. from German; G. B. Foster, *Friedrich Nietzsche* (1931); E. Bertram, *Nietzsche* (1933); C. Brinton, *Nietzsche* (1941); G. A. Morgan, Jr., *What Nietzsche Means* (1941); W. A. Kaufman, *Nietzsche: Philosopher, Psychologist, Antichrist* (1950, 4th ed. 1974, the principal translator of Nietzsche); M. Heidegger, *Nietzsche* (1961); A. C. Danto, *Nietzsche as Philosopher* (1965); K. Jaspers, *Nietzsche: An Introduction to the Understanding of His Philosophical Activity* (1965; Eng. tr. of German work of 1936); I. Frenzel, *Friedrich Nietzsche: An Illustrated Biography* (1967); F. C. Copleston, *Friedrich Nietzsche: Philosopher of Culture* (1975); R. J. Hollingdale, *Nietzsche: The Man and His Philosophy* (1975). T.M.C. rev. A.L.W.

Nijhoff, Martinus (1894–1953), Dutch poet, critic, and translator, was born in The Hague. He studied law at the University of Amsterdam, and 20 years later took up the study of Dutch at Utrecht. In 1916 he began publishing sonnets in *De Beweging.* He started out under the influence of the group that had gathered around the magazine, but in his poetry there are more tensions and less control over his feelings. There are expressionistic characteristics in his first volume of poetry, *De wandelaar* (1916; The Walker), but there is also a fear of life. Nijhoff had a few simple motifs to which he returned from time to time: the mother, the child, the soldier, the clown. *Vormen* (1924; Forms) is his most important volume; it reveals a dualistic attitude toward the world, ranging between acceptance and rejection. As a poet he had a strong feeling for reality. With *Nieuwe gedichten* (1934; New Poems), a new period in the poet's life begins, and the fear of life is gone. Occasionally, too, social consciousness appears. The long poem at the end of the volume, "Awater," is in experimental form. Awater is an ordinary man, who represents the multitude and, therefore, modern society. The poet hopes to make contact with that society, for he feels himself to be an ordinary human being. Here Nijhoff dropped the disguises he had used in *De wandelaar* and *Vormen.* There is an affinity between Nijhoff and T. S. Eliot, and both used the language and rhythm of everyday speech, but Nijhoff also had ample precedent for this in the work of Herman GORTER and Jakobus Cornelis BLOEM. *Het uur U* (1937; Zero Hour) is also a long narrative poem, but here the poet does not present himself in the poem. A man passes through a street and is able to return the people who live there to a state of innocence and purity, to the finest hour of their lives, but when he turns the corner, they go back to their old ways. The identity of the man is not made clear. *Het uur U* was rewritten and republished along with *Een idylle* (1942; An Idyll), the last long poem written before his death. The two poems are related, although *Een idylle* is based on a theme from Greek mythology. Nijhoff also had some interest in the drama. He turned the legend of *De Vliegende Hollander* (1930; The Flying Dutchman) into a play performed by the students of the University of Leiden. *Het heilige hout* (1950; The Holy Wood) is a group of three religious plays. Part of his critical work appeared as *Gedachten op dinsdag* (1931; Thoughts on Tuesday). Nijhoff was also editor of *De Gids* from 1926 to 1933. He translated Eliot's *The Cocktail Party,* as well as several of his poems, and the Dutch prize for translation is named in his honor. His poetry, prose, and translations were published as *Verzameld Werk* (1954; Collected Work).

See: T. de Vries, *M. Nijhoff: wandelaar in de werkelijkheid* (1946). S.L.F.

Nikitin, Nikolay Nikolayevich (1895–1963), Russian novelist, short-story writer, and playwright, was born in Petersburg. He was a member of the Serapion Brotherhood (*see* RUSSIAN LITERATURE) and wrote a number of highly experimental works during the early 1920s. Along with his fellow Serapion Vsevelod IVANOV, he wrote in an ornamental manner reminiscent of the works of Yevgeny ZAMYATIN and Boris PILNYAK. His first major work, "Rvotny fort" (1922; Fort Vomit), and all his early stories are centered around the events of the October Revolution and the Civil War. These works are notable for their ideological detachment—politics gives way to blunt and unemotionally depicted scenes of sex, brutality, and violence. The narrative is nearly always fragmented with action shifting rapidly along several loosely related lines or with various digressions, including, for example, the interpolation of supposedly factual or historical material. Plots, if they exist at all, are purposefully obscure and often incomplete. Nikitin's vocabulary and syntax sometimes seem deliberately imitative of folk speech or of speech patterns from different milieus. Unfortunately, this stylization frequently seems strained and artificial. In the late 1920s, Nikitin began to write in a more traditional realistic manner. His novel *Prestupleniye Kirika Rudenko* (1927; Kirik Rudenko's Crime) and his play *Liniya ognya* (1931; The Line of Fire) are both examples of more stylistic and ideological conformity. His novel *Severnaya avrora* (1950; Aurora Borealis) received a Stalin Prize in 1951.

See: L. Plotkin, "Nikolay Nikitin," in N. Nikitin, *Pogovorim o zvyozdakh* (1959); H. Oulanoff, *The Serapion Brothers: Theory and Practice* (1966). B.P.S.

Nilsen, Rudolf (1901–29), Norwegian poet, was born and raised in the poverty of Oslo's East End. Although he received a good education, he continued to identify with the working class, and he spent his brief life working for the political and social revolution that he believed had to come. He died of tuberculosis.

Nilsen published only three collections of poetry, *På stengrunn* (1925; On Stony Ground), *På gjensyn* (1926; We'll Meet Again), and *Hverdagen* (1929; Everyday Life). His lines are simple and lucid, employ traditional rhyme, and possess a musical quality that has tempted many composers. Whether his focus be impassioned calls for rebellion, as in "Revolusjonens røst" (1926; The Voice of Revolution) or, as was mostly the case, images of everyday life from the working quarters of Oslo, his poetry had a general and immediate appeal.

Nilsen's verse became the model for the new generation

of working-class poets in Scandinavia who saw, in his example, a way to bring a new social milieu into literature. Together with Oskar BRAATEN, Nilsen did much to extend the social dimensions of Norwegian literature.

See: J. F. Bjørnsen, *Rudolf Nilsen* (1951).   K.A.F.

Nilsson Piraten, Fritiof (1895–1972), Swedish storyteller, was born in Vollsjö, in the province of Skåne, where his father was the stationmaster. This southern province has lent its dialect and local color to most of the stories. Nilsson Piraten studied law in Lund and became a practicing lawyer, and his experiences in the profession assisted him in acquiring the insight into human behavior that he generously displayed in his stories. These became so popular that they have been printed in many editions, and they are read aloud in homes and in schools and are often heard over the radio.

Nilsson Piraten's first book and greatest success, *Bombi Bitt och jag* (1932; Eng. tr., *Bombi Bitt*, 1932), is a series of adventures of two young boys reminiscent of Mark Twain. Most of Nilsson Piraten's stories take place in some indefinite "sometime-ago," and his characters behave in a wildly original fashion associated with the past. His technique as short-story writer was to tell a big, surprising, and delightful lie, which he propped up with a number of down-to-earth, realistic details. His perfect sense of timing spaced the crazy blows just right enough to catch the reader unawares. Although many of the stories have a sad quality, they are never sentimental. "What our eyes saw and our ears heard has been stored by time and purified by the yeast of fantasy. What remains are images whose contours keep their fresh naiveté and clear colors. The perspective has deepened without letting the shadows obscure the essential. These images we call forth when we seek to return ourselves to the joy of our childhood—and to its fearfulness—these remains are the truth," says Nilsson Piraten in a story, "Mannen som blev ensam" (1940; The Man Who Became Lonely) about a learned minister and botanist who was never understood and became isolated and is a good deal like Fritiof Nilsson Piraten himself.

Other collections of stories are *Bock i Örtagård* (1933; The Goat in the Garden), *Bokhandlaren som slutade bada* (1937; The Book Dealer Who Ceased Bathing), *Historier från Färs* (1940; Tales from Färs), *Bombi Bitt och Nick Carter* (1946), *Småländsk tragedi* (1936; Småland Tragedy), *Skepparhistorier av mig själv och andra* (1952; Tall Stories by Myself and Others), *Vänner emellan* (1955; Between Friends), *Millionären och andra historier* (1965), and finally the collection that was published posthumously, *Historier från Österlen* (1972). Nilsson Piraten also wrote one novel, *Tre Terminer* (1943; Three Semesters).

See: M. von Platen, *Biktare och bedragare* (1958); C. Fehrman, "Konsten att ljuga eller lögnens lekar. En studie i Fritiof Nilsson Piraten's fabulering," *SLT* (1965); *SLT* 25, no. 3 (1972): 1–53, entirely devoted to studies of Nilsson Piraten; J. Stenkvist, *Svensk litteratur 1870–1970*, vol. 3 (1975), pp. 101–03.   B.K.S.

Nimier, Roger, pseud. of Roger Nimier de la Perrière (1925–62), French novelist, was born in Paris. He was the best-known member of that small group of anti-Sartrian writers (*see* Jean-Paul SARTRE) nicknamed "les Hussards," who, after World War II, resolutely refused political commitment and tried to write in the tradition of Cardinal de Retz, Stendhal, Henry de MONTHERLANT, and Jean GIRAUDOUX. Nimier published a few elegant, brilliant, cynical novels and essays that received immediate acclaim. His best works are the essay *Le Grand*

d'Espagne (1949; Spanish Grandee) and three novels, *Le Hussard bleu* (1950; The Blue Hussar)—probably the most successful one, *Les Enfants tristes* (1951; The Sad Children), and *Histoire d'un amour* (1953; Story of a Love). Nimier was killed in 1962 in an automobile accident. *Journées de lecture* (1965; Reading Days) is a posthumous collection of his articles and short essays. P.Br.

Nizan, Paul-Ives (1905–40), French pamphleteer, essayist, journalist, critic, and novelist, was born in Tours. As an adolescent he became involved with various journals. After brilliant studies in Jean-Paul SARTRE's company, Nizan received the *agrégation* in philosophy in 1929. Nizan combined a solid classical training with a thorough knowledge of Dada, the surrealists (*see* FRENCH LITERATURE), and Marxism.

Like his contemporaries André MALRAUX, Pierre DRIEU LA ROCHELLE, Louis ARAGON, and Paul ELUARD, Nizan was obsessed with a vision of a "new man." To this end he joined the Communist Party in January 1926, only to leave and rejoin in the winter of 1927–28. He became France's first Marxist writer, touring Europe untiringly to denounce the capitalist world. At the invitation of the Comintern, he visited the USSR in 1934. With Malraux, Aragon, Jean-Richard BLOCH, and Vladimir Pozner, he attended the first Congress of Soviet Writers that year. After traveling through central Asia, Nizan returned to Paris and participated in the Congrés International pour la Défense de la Culture in 1935.

From 1929 until his death, Nizan espoused Marxism-Leninism in numerous journals: *La Revue marxiste* (1929), *Bifur* (1930), *Le Monde* (1931), *La Revue des vivants* (1932), *La Nouvelle Revue française* (1932), *Europe* (1933), *Commune* (1933), *La Litérature internationale* (1933), *Vendredi* (1935), *Les Cahiers de la jeunesse* (1937), and *Les Cahiers du bolchevisme* (1938). Nor did this militant journalism exhaust his energies as a writer. Nizan produced numerous pamphlets, essays, and novels during the 1930s depicting the problems of the West. His trip to Aden (1926–27), which revealed to him a capitalist society stripped of its disguises, prompted his first such pamphlet, *Aden Arabie* (1932; Eng. tr., 1968). Utilizing a style by turns coarse, lyrical, and even sublime, Nizan denounced the bourgeoisie, their education, culture, and philosophy. In *Les Chiens de garde* (1932; Eng. tr., *Watchdogs*, 1972), a work midway between the essay and the pamphlet, Nizan used a collage of newspaper clippings and quotations from philosophers in order to demonstrate that one must transform the world, not (as the philosophers do) interpret it. His next publication, the novel *Antoine Bloyé* (1933; Eng. tr., 1973), was an attempt at the "socialist realism" advocated by the Kharkov Writers Congress (1932). The work was praised by Eluard, who expressed delight at finding "Nizan the writer and Nizan the militant Communist united toward the same end." Yet it is in *Le Cheval de Troie* (1935; Eng. tr., *The Trojan Horse*, 1975), that Nizan first offered his readers a "positive hero." This novel, a kind of semi-documentary inspired by the journalistic technique of American writers, superbly illustrated the theories of Nikolay Bukharin as expressed at the Moscow Congress of 1934.

In *La Conspiration* (1938; The Conspiracy), a novel influenced by Stendhal, Nizan broke with the literary theories of the Moscow and Kharkov Congresses. That same year, he was awarded the Prix Interallié. Nizan's spectacular rupture with the French Communist Party following the German-Soviet Pact of 1939 proved a setback for his reputation. Although he was killed during the Dunkirk retreat of 1940, his books were withdrawn from the "comptoir des écrivains combattants" (counter of war writers) after the liberation of France. The "affaire Nizan" came to a head in 1946–47, but the republication of *Aden Arabie* in 1960, with an enraptured preface by Sartre, revived interest in this writer's work.

See: J. Leiner, *Le Destin littéraire de Paul Nizan* (1970); W. D. Redfern, *Paul Nizan: Committed Literature in a Conspiratorial World* (1972); A. King, *Paul Nizan écrivain* (1976).   J.Le.

Noailles, Anna Elisabeth de Brancovan, comtesse de (1876–1933), French poet and prose writer, was born in Paris. She spent her life in Paris and at Amphion, a family estate on Lake Geneva. Noailles's earliest poems, composed in 1889, embody many elements characteristic of her adult works: musicality, a sensual awareness of self, and an intense craving for love. *Le Cœur innombrable* (The Innumerable Heart), her first published collection of poems, appeared in 1901, four years after her marriage to Count Mathieu de Noailles and a year after the birth of her only son, Anne-Jules. This publication, enthusiastically received by the French public, is characterized by the juxtaposition of two forces: the vigorous poet herself and her spiritualized, bucolic nature. Subsequent collections, *L'Ombre des jours* (1902; The Shadow of Days) and *Les Eblouissements* (1907; Bedazzlements), written in her liberated version of the traditional rhyming alexandrine, reflect the same sensual exhilaration. In these volumes there are sketches of Asia Minor and Greece and echoes of Noailles's early travels, as well as effusive descriptions of the French countryside.

Beneath the primary themes of love and nature in Noailles's poetry there is an undercurrent of existential fear. This is made explicit in "Les Espaces infinis" from *Les Forces eternelles* (1920; The Eternal Forces). Noailles exhibited a growing preoccupation with death and suffering in *L'Honneur de souffrir* (1927; The Honor of Suffering) and *Derniers Vers* (1934; Last Poems), the pessimistic, resigned, often despairing creations of her maturity.

Noailles's prose works reflect the joyous lyricalness of her earlier poetry. She published three novels—*La Nouvelle Espérance* (1903; The New Hope), the story of a worldly young woman at the turn of the century; *Le Visage émerveillé* (1904; The Amazed Face), the scandalous diary of a nun's love; and *La Domination* (1905)—and *Les Innocentes ou la sagesse des femmes* (1923; The Innocents or the Wisdom of Women). Her published memoirs include *Le Livre de ma vie* (1932; The Book of My Life), a volume of reminiscences up to the year 1896. Noailles received the Grand Prix de Littérature of the Académie Française (1921) and was elected to the Belgian Academy (1922) and the Legion of Honor (1930).

See: E. de la Rochefoucauld, *Anna de Noailles* (1956); L. Perche, *Anna de Noailles* (1964).   D.C. and A.C.

Noel, Eugenio, pseud. of Eugenio Muñoz Díaz (1885–1936), Spanish novelist and journalist, was born in Madrid and died in Barcelona. Son of a servant girl and a blindman's guide, he lived a youth of extreme poverty followed by unfinished seminary studies and enlistment in the army as a last resort. He first attracted attention with his book *Lo que vi en la guerra* (1912; What I Saw in the War), a denunciation of the Moroccan war of 1909. He was popular for his picturesque appearance and his campaigns against certain social ills which had earlier attracted the attention of intellectuals like AZORÍN and Jacinto BENAVENTE. Indeed, Noel was a veritable caricature of the Generation of 1898. Unamuno called him "a man of pas-

sion" thanks to whom "the soul of Don Quixote has not yet disappeared."

His campaigns produced books and pamphlets of documentary interest such as *República y flamenquismo* (1912; Republic and Gypsy Ways), *Las capeas* (Village Bullfights), *Señoritos, chulos, fenómenos, gitanos y flamencos* (Playboys, Bullies, Freaks, Gypsies, and Hooligans), and *Las raíces de la tragedia española* (The Roots of the Spanish Tragedy), all published in 1915. Of greater literary interest are certain of his sketches and travel books such as *Semana Santa en Sevilla* (1916; Holy Week in Seville) and *Aguafuertes ibéricos* (1927; Iberian Etchings).

Noel wrote many short novels and one extravagant and unsuccessful long one called *Las siete cucas: una mancebía en Castilla* (1927; The Seven Cuco Women: A Brothel in Castile). The novels—little read today—demonstrate a vigorous talent but a lack of technical command that results in digressions, gratuitous authorial commentary, and arbitrary development.

See: E. G. de Nora, *La novela española contemporánea,* vol. 1 (1963), pp. 285–98.   H.L.B.

Noël, Marie, pseud. of Marie Mélanie Rouget (1883–1967), French poet and prose writer, was born in Auxerre, where she spent her entire life. This seclusion is reflected in her poetry, which remains untouched by contemporary literary trends. The prime inspiration for her verse is the medieval song, from which she borrowed both meter and imagery. Her *Œuvre poétique* (Poetic Works), published in 1956, contains *Les Chansons et les heures* (1920; Songs and Hours), *Le Rosaire des joies* (1930; Rosary of Joys), *Les Chants de la merci* (1930; Songs of Thanks), and *Chants et psaumes d'automne* (1947; Songs and Psalms of Autumn). Noël's most noted prose publications are her intimate, poignantly written journal, *Notes intimes* (1959; Eng. tr., *Notes for Myself,* 1968), and numerous short stories. *Le Jugement de Don Juan* (1955), a miracle play in verse, displays the religious sentiment that permeates her entire literary creation. Her writings are dominated by the intertwining themes of nature, love, solitude, anguish, death, and God. Noël emphasized the inherent musicality of her verse by setting much of it—such as *Chants sauvages* (1936; Wild Songs)—to music of her own composition.

See: R. Escholier, *La Neige qui brûle* (1957); A. Blanchet, *Marie Noël* (1962); M. Manoll, *Marie Noël* (1962).
D.C. and A.C.

Nordal, Sigurður (1886–1974), Icelandic poet, critic, and scholar, was born at Eyjólfsstaðir in Vatnsdalur, north Iceland. He studied Old Norse-Icelandic philology at the University of Copenhagen, taking his M.A. in 1912 and his Ph.D. in 1914 with a study of the sagas of the Norwegian kings. He studied psychology and philosophy at Oxford in 1917–18 and became professor of the Icelandic-language and literature at the University of Iceland in 1918, holding the post until 1945. He frequently lectured in Scandinavia and in England, and in the United States he held the Charles Eliot Norton professorship of poetry at Harvard University in 1931–32.

Nordal's short stories and prose poems are all contained in one slim volume, *Fornar ástir* (1919; Old Loves). The short stories are of the psychological kind and of no unusual merit. But the prose poem "Hel" is unequaled in Icelandic literature for beauty of style and originality of conception. The influence of French "decadent" masters is obvious. Unfortunately, the work has had no imitators. But as a critic in the tradition of Sainte-Beuve and of Ernest Renan, his favorite, Nordal was extremely influ-

NORWEGIAN LITERATURE

ential in Iceland. In the modern field he wrote brilliant essays on the most prominent figures. He has also attacked the pre-war liberalism, especially as mixed with the spiritualism of Einar KVARAN, demanding more discipline in thought and action. Finally, he emphasized the principle of continuity in Icelandic literature and thought and urged deference for national values, whether they date from the golden age of the saga or are more recent, such as the modern rustic culture of Iceland. In the Old Icelandic (Norse) field his studies and essays on Snorri Sturluson (1920), *Völuspá* (1923), and Egill Skallagrímsson (1924) are of fundamental importance. His plan for a new epoch-making literary edition of the sagas is well begun, with many volumes already published (1933-). But his masterpiece will undoubtedly be *Islenzk menning* (1942-; Icelandic Culture), of which only the first volume has appeared. It is a thoroughly new evaluation of Iceland's contribution to world literature and world civilization, a masterful study of the small nation and a remarkable synthesis of a lifetime of study.

See: S. Einarsson, "Sigurður Nordal," *Timarit þjóðræknisfélags Íslendinga* vol. 13 (1931), pp. 7–18.

S.E.

Norge, Géo, pseud. of Georges Mogin (1898-), Belgian poet was born in Brussels. His poetry is characterized by jubilation, excitement, and, at times, impatience. Although apparently simple, his language reveals many refinements of expression that establish the author of *Râpes* (1949; Rasps) as a veritable craftsman. His work is similar to that of Henri MICHAUX in its lexicological audacity but dissimilar in its vigor and alacrity; it rests on a firm belief in the value of life and on an insatiable appetite for the words that best express this ideal.

Norge's materialism is accompanied by a robust hedonism. These characteristics are apparent in *Famines* (1950; Famines), *Les Oignons* (1953; The Onions), and *Les quatre saisons* (1960; The Four Seasons). The poet displays a taste for verbal games and intellectual traits that do not entirely dissimulate the personality of a moralist fond of people and things. If his irony occasionally reaches angry extremes, it also gives way to humor and to touching emotion. The fervor for life and the need to grasp each moment are rendered in a rapid and clear diction that is void of eloquence and superfluous imagery. A "modern poet" in the full sense of the term, Norge leaves the deceiving past for a very real present. As is the case with every true epicurean, the lust for life is imbued with a certain dose of skepticism. Too perceptive to be tricked. Norge ultimately emerges as a humanist—many of his poems hide the wisdom of a fable within the fleeting charm of a children's rhyme.

See: R. Rovin, *Norge* (1956). R.F.

Norwegian literature. In 1871, when the Danish critic Georg BRANDES delivered his lectures at the University of Copenhagen calling for writers to reject traditional romantic aestheticism and fasten their attention upon the problems of society, he found a particularly attentive audience among young Norwegian authors. These younger writers, who displayed an amazing vitality, came to dominate the Norwegian literature of the last quarter of the 19th century, and their influence was soon felt outside their homeland.

In the early years of the union with Sweden (1814–1905), Norway had struggled through economic hardship and survived a series of political crises before gaining stability and a position of uncontested self-rule within the union. A dominant figure in this struggle was the poet Henrik Wergeland (1808–45). Wergeland stood at the cen-

ter of every national cause, and after his early death, his life and monumental work became a symbol of national pride and self-assertion. The nationalistic sentiments of Wergeland and J. S. C. Welhaven (1807–73), a highly gifted author of refined romantic verse, found further support in the rich treasure of folktales collected and published between 1841 and 1847 by P. C. Asbjørnsen (1812–85) and J. Moe (1813–82), as well as in the medieval ballads published in 1853 by M. B. Landstad (1802–80). Furthermore, Ivar Aasen (1813–96), a brilliant, self-taught linguist and an original poet, created, for national as well as for practical reasons, a new language, based on the rural dialects of southern Norway and Old Norse, called *landsmål* (after 1929 *nynorsk*). The first examples of *landsmål* were published in 1853. Peter Andreas Munch (1810–63) and Rudolf Keyser (1803–64) founded modern Norwegian historical research and expressed as one of their central views the belief that the Norwegian people and its culture were products of a unique and uninterrupted historical process going back to the pre-Viking age. All these efforts strengthened romantic nationalism in Norwegian cultural life, an atmosphere further nurtured by writers who otherwise did not identify with romanticism, such as Aasen and the poet-critic Aamund Olavsson Vinje (1818–70).

This cultural narcissism, resulting from Norway's centuries of political dependence upon other countries, thus lingered on into the 1850s and 1860s, when it inevitably came into conflict with political and social realities. Symptoms of this development included the pioneering work of the sociologist Eilert Sundt (1817–75), which eliminated all romantic notions about life in rural Norway, the rise of a radical labor movement led by Marcus Thrane (1817–90) shortly after the February Revolution of 1848, and the emergence of a united opposition in the Storting (national assembly) against the policies of the government. The political and cultural battles of the 1880s were extensions of these confrontations. Yet the prologue to these struggles had begun much earlier. Camilla Collett (1813–95), the first active feminist in Norwegian letters, had registered the advance of the new age with her depiction of the oppression of women in *Amtmandens døtre* (1854; The Governor's Daughters). A. O. Vinje had given realistic accounts of life in rural Norway in *Ferdaminni fraa sumaren 1860* (1861; Travel Memoirs from the Summer of 1860). But this new development was led, above all, by Bjørnstjerne BJØRNSON, who broke with romanticism both in style and theme in his early peasant stories, treated middle-class marriage in his drama *De Nygifte* (1865; Eng. tr., *A Lesson in Marriage,* 1911), and finally achieved his international breakthrough with his social problem play *En fallit* (1875; Eng. tr., *The Bankrupt,* 1914), which treated hypocrisy and dishonesty in the bourgeois business world. By the 1870s, Henrik IBSEN, the other dominant literary figure of the age, had also turned toward the realistic drama. His first attempt, *De unges forbund* (1869; Eng. tr., *The League of Youth,* 1890), satirizes political corruption and opportunism. In 1877, with *Samfundets siøtter* (Eng. tr., *Pillars of Society,* 1888), he turned all his attention toward the issues of the day and created, over the next decade, the modern drama of social realism. In his zealous quest to uncover the hypocrisy of the social, political, and religious order of his time, Ibsen was by no means alone. On most issues he was joined by Bjørnson, who became increasingly active in social and political affairs. Ibsen received even stronger support from two new major writers, Jonas LIE and Alexander KIELLAND. Lie, the less controversial of the two, was above all a master of realistic portrayals of family life; he often depicted seafaring people, but no domestic milieu seemed foreign to him. A writer more conscientious in his drive for social change, Alexander Kielland used his acerbic wit and glittering style to castigate and ridicule the schools, the church, and the business community for their hypocrisy and exploitation of helpless human beings. Realism also had a typical representative in Kristian Elster (1841–81), a sensitive artist who in novels such as *Solskyer* (1887; Sunny Clouds) and *Tora Trondal* (1879) demonstrated his unusual awareness of the demands that the social and ethical problems of the new age placed upon the individual.

The idealism that was apparent in the early realistic literature gradually gave way, however, to a literature of greater cynicism. This development is clearly discernible in the depiction of woman. In the early Norwegian novels she was a regenerative force, but in the naturalism of the 1880s, writers point to the misery of her lot. This representation of women is characteristic of much of the new literature after Ibsen's *Gengangere* (1881; Eng. tr., *Ghosts,* 1889). Major works on this theme are Lie's *Familjen paa Gilje* (1883; Eng. tr., *The Family at Gilje* (1883; 1920) and *Kommandørens døtre* (1886; Eng. tr., *The Commodore's Daughters,* 1892), and Amalie SKRAM's *Lucie* (1888) and *Forraadt* (1892; Betrayed). Skram was committed to the philosophy of naturalism as was no other Norwegian writer, and she shocked the public and the critics with her outspoken novels on the social and sexual oppression of women. With her psychological insight and blunt honesty, she became a major force in the heated debate on sexual morality that had started with the publication of Hans Jæger's (1854–1910) *Fra Kristiania-Bohêmen* (1885; From the Christiania Bohême). Jæger's novel advocated sexual license and created a furor that left no one untouched, polarizing the literary and cultural forces of Norway. Among the many new and older authors who, through their creative writing as well as through essays and articles, took Jæger's side in the debate, Arne GARBORG had the clearest head and the sharpest wit. In essays and polemical novels, Garborg fought the hypocrisy of the established order. He created a major work of Norwegian naturalism with his *Bondestudentar* (1883; Peasant Students), a novel that shows how unspoiled country students succumb to the forces of opportunism and corruption in their encounter with urban values and practices.

The debate on morality was symptomatic of the cultural and social forces that clashed in the decade of the 1880s. The values of the old social, political, and moral order were pitted against those represented by the changes sweeping in from continental Europe—industrialization, advances in science, the new philosophies. Parliamentarianism was introduced, the franchise was expanded, and emigration, reaching its peak, threatened to upset the old rural equilibrium. Yet to the radical forces that dominated the cultural life of this decade no profound changes were evident. In their view the new order building on these changes was as dogmatic as the old. The result was a certain measure of apathy. Therefore, the seemingly abrupt transformation that now took place in literature had a background in the domestic, social, and political situations as well as in the larger context of European philosophical and literary development. The new wave has been termed neoromanticism. This phenomenon of the 1890s has one of its literary roots in the plays of Ibsen. Starting with *Vildanden* (1884; Eng. tr., *The Wild Duck,* 1891), Ibsen began to employ poetic symbols in his portrayals of human irrationality. Another forerunner of this new literary style was Nils Collett VOGT, who published his first collection of poetry in 1887. Two years later,

Jonas Lie also published a collection, his first in nearly 25 years.

The approaching new age, of which these works are symptoms, received its manifesto in an article by Knut HAMSUN, published in the periodical *Samtiden* in the fall of 1890. In this article, "Fra det ubevidste sjæleliv" (From the Unconscious Life of the Mind), Hamsun called for a new literature that would deal with the mysterious, irrational life of the unconscious forces in man. He himself became the most brilliant exponent of this program through the major novels that he now produced—*Sult* (1890; Eng. tr., *Hunger,* 1899), *Mysterier* (1892; Eng. tr., *Mysteries,* 1927), *Pan* (1894; Eng. tr., 1920), and *Victoria* (1898; Eng. tr., 1929)—all breaking the conventions of the naturalistic novel and marking a watershed in the development of Norwegian prose fiction. Arne Garborg, the brilliant critic and naturalist, also turned his back on social and political problems. *Trætte Mænd* (1891; Tired Men), a pessimistic, resigned novel of decadent city life, marks the change in his concerns. After this work, Garborg spent much of his time in rural Norway, and four years later he published his monumental poetic cycle about a visionary half-wit, *Haugtussa* (1895; The Hill Innocent), a central work of the period. Jonas Lie, who had shown an interest in the irrational forces in man as early as 1870 with his novel *Den fremsynte* (Eng. tr., *The Visionary,* 1894), now wrote wondrous tales of life in northern Norway. Alexander Kielland, the realist, stopped writing altogether. Of the principal novelists of the 1880s, only Amalie Skram persisted with her naturalistic accounts of human, and particularly female, degradation. Ibsen remained the overpowering force in drama, and his plays, which had long contained important elements of neoromanticism, moved after *Hedda Gabler* (1890; Eng. tr., 1891) toward symbolism and allegory. Lyrical poetry flourished. Nils Collett Vogt, a refined poet of lyrical verse, published some of his best love and nature poetry in the 1890s, and Sigbjørn OBSTFELDER, the conscious dreamer, became for later generations the embodiment of that period. Although Obstfelder shows a clear affinity with the French symbolists, he created original poetry that was remarkable for its expressions of beauty, ecstasy, and alienation. He became a forerunner of the richly talented generation of lyrical poets who were to attract attention a few years after his death in 1900.

Norwegian society underwent radical changes during the first two decades of the 20th century. Independence from Sweden (1905) was followed by rapid industrialization and, during World War I, by explosive changes in old social and political patterns. These events paved the way for the social democratic rule of the 1930s. Although the Norwegian workers' movement of the period before 1920 was one of Europe's most militant, its writers were moderates and humanists. Per SIVLE's novel *Streik* (1891; Strike) was the most aggressive attempt to depict the worker's point of view in the brutal process of humiliation and dehumanization of the early industrial period. Oskar BRAATEN, Johan FALKBERGET, and Kristofer UPPDAL, all from working-class backgrounds, wrote their first stories and novels just after the turn of the century. These writers were humanists, committed to the values of Christian ethics and to the cultural traditions of rural Norway. Uppdal and Falkberget created profoundly convincing psychological analyses of the uprooting process that took place when individuals and families moved from a primitive rural society into a capitalistic economy. Uppdal's 10-volume novel *Dansen gjenom skuggeheimen* (1910–24; The Dance through the Shadow Land) and Falkberget's two multivolume works *Christianus Sextus* (1927–35) and

Nattens brød (1940–59; The Bread of Night) are monuments to the Norwegian working class, even though they treat different ages and milieus. Braaten, a writer of more limited talent, brought the daily life of the workers into literature, not least through his immensely popular comedies. Sigrjd UNDSET also took the motifs of her early novels and stories, primarily in the short-story collection *Fattige skjæbner* (1912; Humble Existences), from the harsh realities of urban life in her depictions of poor unmarried or unhappily married women.

The "new realism," of which these works were expressions, had its roots in the naturalism of the 1880s, although its social tendency was less explicit and the depth of its psychological portraits greater than in the naturalistic era. But the new realism of the early 20th century was also partly a result of a distinct current of realist prose that had survived, during the 1890s, in the work of the regional writers. A number of fine, although lesser, authors had appeared in these years. In western and southern Norway, Rasmus LØLAND, Jens TVEDT, Thomas Krag (1868–1913), Vilhelm Krag (1871–1933), and Gabriel Scott (1874–1958) wrote about the material they knew best: life in their local communities. Although these writers belong to the realistic tradition, they also had an open eye for the irrational forces at work in man and nature. Hans AANRUD, and Tryggve ANDERSEN, and Sven Moren (1871–1938) did the same for eastern Norway. Out of this literary regionalism there also sprang the first works of Hans E. KINCK, whose combination of intuitive psychological insight and stark naturalism places him beside Hamsun in creative originality. Although Kinck used his vast knowledge of Italian and Norwegian history in his plays and short stories, he let his poetic instincts and fantastic imagination guide his writing. In most of his short stories and in the verse drama *Driftekaren* (1908; The Drover), Kinck weaves vivid, sometimes bizarre poetic patterns of human behavior in 19th-century rural Norway, while in his main novels he depicts in a more realistic manner his fear of the destructive advance of the forces of capitalism. Johan BOJER and Peter EGGE also emerged from the undercurrents of the 1890s. By 1910 they had established themselves as writers in the realistic tradition, first with short stories about rural Norway and later, while focusing on the psychology of the individual, with broader epics about the clashes between the forces of tradition and change. A writer of greater depth was Olav DUUN. Duun's roots were in the region of Trøndelag, which is also the setting of his celebrated main work, *Juvikfolke* (1918–23; Eng. tr., *The People of Juvik*, 1930–35). Writing in *nynorsk*, the language of Aasen, Vinje and Garborg, Duun is clearly a regionalist, but his incisive probing of the elemental forces of destruction and preservation lifts him above most other writers. A novelist of tremendous power, Duun conveys a message of compassion and humanistic commitment. A common feature of the writers in this group is their deep sense of the value of the cultural traditions of rural Norway.

It is no coincidence that a majority of the regionalist writers used *nynorsk* as their medium or let the characters in their works speak in dialect. After Aasen exhibited his new language in 1853, *nynorsk* rapidly gained recognition in rural Norway. A large part of the population found it to be the natural written and spoken mode of expression, and in 1885 the new form was recognized as the second official Norwegian language. Its wealth of poetic expression and its ties with the old rural culture made it a natural tool for many new writers around the turn of the century. The second and the major language, *bokmål* (before 1929 called *riksmål*), which in the early years after 1814 was nearly indistinguishable from Danish, had given in to specific Norwegian syntactical and orthographical influences during the latter half of the 19th century. This development was greatly accelerated through the first half of the 20th century and has increasingly made *bokmål* the preferred language in Norway, even among writers of rural background.

In the 20th century, not all genres of Norwegian literature developed to the same extent. Drama, which through the efforts of Ibsen and Bjørnson, had become a major genre in the latter half of the 19th century, has received little infusion of original talent in the 20th century. Besides Gunnar HEIBERG's lyric-erotic drama, Helge KROG's social-psychological plays, and Nordahl GRIEG's political drama, only scattered plays of note have been written.

In poetry, however, the situation has been different. Simultaneously with the generation of prose writers who appeared in the post-1905 era, there emerged a group of lyric poets who were to put their mark on the poetry of the next 30 to 50 years. Herman WILDENVEY's billowing lines and charming epicurism won him both critical acclaim and the popularity of the reading public. Arnulf ØVERLAND, whose first verse showed an affinity for the symbolists, moved gradually into political activism and in the 1930s became an ardent champion of the rights of the oppressed. Olaf BULL, a poet of penetrating intellect and unique artistic temperament, treated traditional themes of lyric poetry in the symbolist vein and created some of the most memorable verse of Norwegian literature. Kristofer Uppdal was the most original poet of the early 20th century. Uppdal's poetry breaks with the principal aesthetic tradition of Norwegian poetry as well as with symbolist influence, utilizing a deeply personal poetic language to express the anxiety of the times. In his poetic structures, Uppdal anticipated the later, modernistic forms of expression. Although greatly different in social background and philosophical outlook, these writers were primarily connected to the urban industrialized Norway of the 20th century. Another group of poets, writing in *nynorsk*, had strong common bonds in their deep, lasting commitment to the ethical and cultural traditions of rural Norway. In the work of Olav NYGAARD this bond is perhaps less conscious than in the works of Olav AUKRUST, Tore ØRJASÆTER, and Aslaug VAA. The poetry of these four writers is visionary, reflecting strains of Christian mysticism, and is imbued with an intense experience of Norwegian nature and culture.

World War I, the Russian Revolution of 1917, and the complex social and political situation that followed Norway's rapid industrialization raised profound questions that no writer could avoid. In some cases, as in Hamsun's novels *Segelfoss By* (1915; Eng. tr., *Segelfoss Town*, 1925), *Konerne ved Vandposten* (1920; Eng. tr., *The Women at the Pump*, 1928), and *Markens grøde* (1917; Eng. tr., *Growth of the Soil*, 1921), the weight of these issues fostered a fiction of pessimism or escapism. But the insecurity of the age more often led to probing examinations of fundamental ethical questions. On the whole, there runs through the Norwegian literature of the 1920s and 1930s a strong commitment to the ideals of Christian and humanistic ethics. Part of this current seeks its answers in the old, traditional society of the past with its universe of moral absolutes. To this group belong the *nynorsk* poets Nygaard, Aukrust, Ørjasæter, and Vaa as well as such writers as Duun, Uppdal, Falkberget, Inge KROKANN, and to a degree, Tarjei VESAAS. Sigrid Undset, whose early novels depicted the moral confusion of the modern urban class, underwent the most dramatic changes. She now sought and found new faith and inspiration in Catholicism, the inspiration for her monumental historical novels of life in medieval Norway, *Kristin Lavransdatter* (1920–22; Eng. tr., 1923–27) and *Olav Audunssøn* (1925–27; Eng. tr., *The Master of Hestviken,* 1928–30, 1934). The other branch of the Christian-humanist current is represented by the novels of Sigurd CHRISTIANSEN and Ronald Fangen (1895–1946), who attempted to represent humanistic or, in Fangen's later works, Christian ideals in a contemporary urban setting.

While these writers sought the answer in a reaffirmation of old cultural and ethical values, another, far more vocal group was inspired by the forces of change. These writers sought a more active role in the shaping of the new society and found the Russian Revolution of 1917 a source of inspiration rather than of fear. Consequently, they gravitated in the 1920s toward communism and the Marxist doctrines before turning their backs on Moscow (with the exception of Nordahl Grieg) under the impact of the Soviet political purges of the mid-1930s. These writers were all intellectuals and, with the exception of Rudolf NILSEN, representatives of the urban middle class. Sigurd HOEL, a witty, sarcastic, and glittering stylist, soon became a major force of the cultural Left. Despite this, his portrayal of childhood and domestic crises in the urban middle class reveals more interest in psychoanalysis than in political issues. The dramatist Helge Krog also played down the political dimension of his work, while Arnulf Øverland and Rudolf Nilsen (the only working-class representative of this group) called for social and political revolution. These vocal figures were joined by Nordahl Grieg, who in his political plays and in his journal *Veien frem* (1936–37) fought for the ideals of communism and against the forces of capitalism, of which this group of writers considered fascism to be a manifestation. To this group also belonged one of the most original of the new writers, Aksel SANDEMOSE, who despite radical political views owed much to James Joyce and psychoanalysis. Sandemose's principal novels, *En flyktning krysser sitt spor* (1933; Eng. tr., *A Fugitive Crosses His Tracks,* 1936) and *Det svundne er en drøm* (1946; The Past Is a Dream), are works of deep psychological insight, remarkable poetic force, and great structural complexity. Sandemose was indeed one of the first to seek new forms in prose fiction, breaking with the traditional narrative that, despite Hamsun's early novels, still dominated Norwegian literature. Many of the literary influences reaching the young writers were transmitted by Sigurd Hoel, who as editor of a series of translations published from 1929 on introduced Franz KAFKA, François MAURIAC, William Faulkner, and Ernest Hemingway, among others, to the Norwegian reading public. As an innovator in contemporary prose fiction, Sandemose was joined by Gunnar Larsen (1900–58), the author of *Weekend i evigheten* (1934; Weekend in Eternity), and Emil BOYSON, whose early novels, such as *Yngre herre på besøk* (1936; A Young Gentleman Visiting), show the influences of Joyce and Kafka, employing chaotic structures of time and action and a refined stream-of-consciousness style.

The occupation of Norway by the Germans in 1940 meant that little of literary significance was published in the following five years. Poetry and essays were circulated illegally, but most of the literature of this period was stored away or published by writers in exile, primarily in Sweden. After World War II, the gates were opened and the market was flooded with war literature. Most of this was of little lasting value, but there were also moving accounts of heroism, tragedy, and, as in Sigurd Hoel's *Møte ved milepelen* (1947; Eng. tr., *Meeting at the Milestone,* 1951), profound psychological analyses of the war experience. When the euphoria of peace had passed and the memories of wartime communion had faded, Norwegian writers were left to face a shattered world. The fighting, idealistic humanism of the earlier era was replaced by the world of the atomic bomb and the balance of terror. Literature produced further explorations of the states of isolation, loneliness, and guilt. Such works are characteristic of nearly all collections of poetry published during the first decade after World War II. These themes were given new formal expression in the "modernistic" works of two widely different poets, Paal BREKKE and Gunvor HOFMO, who share the influence of Ezra Pound and T. S. Eliot. The broken rhythm and unrhymed lines of Brekke and Hofmo were not, however, entirely new to Norwegian literature. The poetry of Rolf JACOBSEN, Emil Boyson, and above all Claes Gill (1910–73) had been early precursors of the new poetic forms.

On the whole, the pre-World War II generation of writers provided the inspiration for the next two decades of Norwegian literature. In poetry this came about through the innovative force of the writers mentioned above, although in this genre the conservative, traditional elements remained strong; not until 15 years after the war could one speak of a breakthrough in poetic form. Within the novel, however, the situation was different. The main pillars of the old tradition, Duun, Undset, and Christiansen, had all died by 1949, and other prominent members of the prewar generation showed both the willingness and the ability to add new dimensions to their art. This development gave the older writers a central and even dominant position within this genre for the next two decades. Tarjei VESAAS, who in his early novels of the 1920s and 1930s had adhered to traditional realism, now rapidly became a main exponent of innovation in fiction. A writer with a unique poetic talent, he mixed allegory and symbolism with poetic expressionism in such works as *Kimen* (1940; Eng. tr., *The Seed,* 1964) and *Huset i mørket* (1945; House in Darkness), in which he sought to give fictional representation to the fears of the age. Hoel and Sandemose, with less insight than Vesaas into the irrational forces in man, continued to depict fear and loneliness along more traditional lines. Besides Vesaas, Johan BORGEN was the writer who underwent the most startling development. From a prewar position of relative obscurity he now emerged as an exceptional short-story writer and, from 1955 on, as an important novelist. His novel *Lillelord* (1955; Little Lord), set in the early part of the 20th century, was also an indication of a changing climate: it was now possible to write novels without making reference to the immediate postwar world. The fear of a nuclear holocaust had receded, and writers turned to new, less angst-ridden themes. Agnar Myle's (1915–) erotic novels and Jens BJØRNEBOE's bitter attacks on social institutions are examples of this development.

Despite strong, new developments from Vesaas, Sandemose, Brekke, and Hofmo, the formal approaches in all genres of Norwegian literature remained overwhelmingly traditional throughout the 1950s. Not until the end of that decade did the conservative aesthetics of the Øverland-Hoel generation lose its grip. Stein MEHREN's literary debut in 1960 showed that a new artistic consciousness was emerging in poetry. The year before, Johan Borgen had published *"Jeg"* (1969; "I"), an experimental fictional representation of schizophrenia that breaks all the conventions of the novel structure, and in 1961 Vesaas published his novel *Brannen* (1961; The Fire), a work that functions exclusively on the symbolic level. Both Borgen and Vesaas continued their experimental, symbolic novels and, despite their age, continued to represent the avant-garde of Norwegian prose fiction through most of the 1960s. In the latter half of that decade, however, a distinctly new generation of writers appeared. Most of them clustered around *Profil*, a literary journal published at the University of Oslo, and attacked what they saw as the irrelevancy of most new Norwegian literature, along with its critical reception. These writers sought out foreign influences ranging from the theoreticians of the French "new novel" to poetic concretism and William Burroughs. They soon felt the futility of theoretical experimentation, however, and finding a new basis in political and social engagement, they attempted to represent the realities of Norwegian society through an extreme simplicity of style and expression. Although they sought changes in society based on Marxist doctrines, the most talented of these writers, Espen Haavardsholm (1945-), Paal-Helge Haugen (1945-), Tor Obrestad (1938-), Jan Erik Vold (1939-), Einar Økland (1940-), and Dag Solstad (1943-), have shown an artistic commitment that promises them a central role in Norwegian literary life. Outside this group, Knut Faldbakken (1941-) and Kjartan Fløgstad (1944-) are incisive and undogmatic social critics with great narrative talents. Bjørg Vik (1935-) is the leading artist among a large and increasingly important group of young women writers. Her short-story collections are among the finest in Norwegian literature of the last 15 years.

In 1965 the Norwegian Storting voted to protect the production of literary works by buying 1,000 copies of each book for distribution to state and municipal libraries. During the following decade, there was a dramatic increase in the number of fictional works published each year, a significant rise in literary quality, and a noticeable measure of optimism in Norwegian literary life. K.A.F.

Norwid, Cyprian Kamil (1821-83), Polish poet, playwright, short-story writer, essayist and painter, was born in Laskowo-Głuchy in central Poland, the son of impoverished Lithuanian gentry. He went to school in Warsaw, where afterwards he studied painting. In 1842 he left Poland, never to return. After years of wandering, mostly in Italy, he settled in Paris in 1849. In 1852, driven by poverty, he emigrated to the United States, lived in New York, and then in 1854 returned to Paris, where he spent the last six years of his life in an asylum for paupers.

Norwid wrote a poetry charged with ideas. Belonging to a generation that came after the great romantic poets, he developed in opposition to them a highly individual and difficult idiom, allusive, ironic, compressed, carefully avoiding traditional grandiloquence, resorting to shortcuts, exploring etymological meanings of words, and using idiosyncratic graphic devices. He was also a daring innovator in matters of versification. A Catholic, imbued with a sense of the importance of tradition, he at the same time acutely felt the need for the modernization and democratization of Polish life. Hence his ambiguous attitude toward the United States, a model of a democratic vigorous society, which he bitterly criticized for its materialism and, in two poems provoked by the execution of John Brown, its racism.

Except for his early years, Norwid had great difficulties throughout his life with the printing of his works and managed to publish only one large collection, *Poezje* (1863; Poetry). Undaunted by that failure, although embittered by it, he feverishly worked up to the last months in the paupers' asylum and left behind a vast and varied oeuvre in manuscript. Discovered at the turn of the century by the poet-critic Zenon Przesmycki, he was soon hailed as a great writer. He played an important part in

the development of the 20th-century Polish poetry and is today the favorite poets' poet.

Lyrical poetry occupies the central part in his literary output. His main collection of 100 poems, *Vade-mecum*, composed in 1865 and 1866 and characterized by Norwid as "poetry of history," was not published as a whole until 1947. The best-known poem from that collection, published separately earlier, is "Fortepian Szopena" (written in 1863; Chopin's Piano), in which free verse is used. Outside of the collection is another of his lyrical masterpieces, "Bema pamięci żałobny rapsod" (written 1851; Funeral Rhapsody in Memory of Bem). Among his longer narrative poems are "Quidam" (written 1855-57; Someone) about the Rome of Hadrian; "Assunta" (written 1870-79; The Glance), a lyrical and dramatic love poem; his outstanding late philosophical and satirical composition "A Dorio ad Phrygium" (written 1871; From Doric to Phrygian), a half-nostalgic and half-ironical evocation of Polish country life, left incomplete; and his often quoted "Promethidion" (1851), a dialogue in verse form, dealing with problems of the social function of art. Norwid's plays are highly original and subtle poetic closet dramas, especially a diptych, *Tyrtej—Za kulisami* (written ca. 1865-69; Tyrtaeus—in the Wings), which contains a bold juxtaposition of ancient Athenian and Spartan life with contemporary Polish life, and the historical tragedy *Kleopatra i Cezar* (written ca. 1870-79), both incomplete. Among his other dramatic works mention should be made of the historical mystery plays, *Wanda* (written 1850), and *Krakus* (written 1851; pub. 1863), and the experimental tragedy defined by Norwid as "white tragedy," *Pierścień Wielkiej Damy* (written 1872; The Ring of a Grand Lady). He also wrote several short stories gravitating toward parables, such as "Cywilizacja" (1863; Civilization), the so-called Italian Trilogy (written 1882 and 1883); "Stygmat" (Stigma), "Ad Leones" (For Lions), and "Tajemnica lorda Singelworth" (Lord Singleworth's Secret). Remarkable also for their rich intellectual content, bitter irony, and epigramatic formulations are some of Norwid's essays and letters: *Czarne kwiaty* (1856; Black Flowers), philosophical and aesthetic reflections and reminiscences, about, among others, Frederick Chopan, Juliusz Słowacki, and Adam Mickiewicz; *Białe kwiaty* (1856; White Flowers), philosophical and aesthetic reflections and reminiscences; and *Milczenie* (written 1882; Silence), a treatise on the theory of silence. Norwid wrote also articles and essays about fine art, music, and literature, for example, *O Juliuszu Słowackim* (1861), and he was active as a painter, engraver, and sculptor.

See: K. Wyka, *Cyprian Norwid, poeta i sztukmistrz* (1948); W. Borowy, *O Norwidzie* (1960); Z. Łapiński, *Norwid* (1971); I. Sławinská, *Reżyserska reká Norwida* (1971); *Pisma wsystkie*, ed. J. W. Gomulicki, vols. 1-11 (1971-76); *Cyprian Norwid. W 150-lecie urodzin* (1973); G. Gömöri, *Cyprian Norwid* (1974); J. Trznadel, *Czytanie Norwida* (1978).   W.W.

Nossack, Hans Erich (1901-77), German novelist, essayist, poet, and playwright, was born in Hamburg, the son of a successful coffee merchant. Nossack began to write at the age of 14, when he discovered Friedrich Hebbel's diaries in his father's library. Moved profoundly by them, he decided to keep diaries himself. Three years later he heard a recitation of August STRINDBERG's *Dream Play*, which led him to the works of the expressionist dramatists. His mature style, however, owes most to Stendhal.

Nossack began his university studies at Jena (1919-22) with courses in Old French and Old English philology. Yielding to paternal pressure, he took up the study of law but soon gave it up. As part of his rebellion, he withdrew from the traditional student fraternal organizations and, in his drive for independence, refused further financial support from his parents. The father of a Jewish school-mate found a position for him in a bank. Having left the university, Nossack managed to subsist largely on bread and coffee, spending what little money he had on books, while he wrote his early dramas.

In 1925, Nossack married Gabriele Knierer. In 1929, he visited Brazil for a few months to consider taking over a branch of his father's firm, but he decided against it and returned to Germany. As the Nazis began their rise to power, Nossack became increasingly sympathetic to the Communist Party—primarily because of its opposition to Adolf Hitler. From 1930 to 1933 he was an active Party member. Nossack's decision not to emigrate in 1933 was based partly on his assumption that Hitler's control of Germany would be short-lived and partly on his feeling that he would not be happy living in exile. Taking over the family firm in Hamburg, he acquired a cloak of re-spectability that enabled him to survive the years of World War II despite harassment, interrogations, and searches by the Gestapo.

The turning point in Nossack's career came with the destruction of Hamburg. During the bombing, from July 24 to Aug. 3, 1943, Nossack's apartment and his posses-sions, including nearly all his manuscripts, were de-stroyed. This experience became the basis for much of his later writing. Up to this point he had worked exclu-sively as a dramatist, but he turned now to novels. Having been unable to publish during the Third Reich, he made up for lost time and wrote over a dozen novels after World War II. He gave up the coffee business to devote himself entirely to writing and was soon highly regarded, not only in Germany but also in France, where Jean-Paul SARTRE "discovered" and promoted his work.

Nossack characterized his writing style as "conversa-tional." The main character in his novels is often the narrator, who unfolds the plot in a dramatic monologue. Nossack saw his preference for this perspective as a carry-over from his earlier endeavors as a dramatist. Large portions of his novels read like bureaucratic re-ports—the protocols of court hearings or police interro-gations. Nossack was fond of beginning his works with apparently ordinary people in everyday situations and then following the structure of the detective novel by retracing the past to show that things are not really what they seem. The goal of his writing, as he saw it, was to raise questions and to cast doubt on what is taken for granted. The grotesque, bizarre twists and dry humor of Nossack's novels, miniatures, and parables and the re-portorial style of his prose are reminiscent of the work of Franz KAFKA. Nossack first read Kafka in 1949, before he had written most of his own novels. The "dream logic" of Kafka's prose made a lasting impression on him. Like Kafka, Nossack concentrated on perspectives suggested by a hero's inner consciousness.

The central images of Nossack's works are persistently autobiographical. Very often the narrator is a survivor of some great cataclysm who reflects on life in the old world and on changes that have come in the new. Another recurring theme is the image of the "angel," which is not so much an evocation of the supernatural as it is a sym-bolic reference to the underdeveloped potentialities and possibilities in the lives of human beings.

In 1961, Nossack was sent to the Rabindranath Tagore celebration in New Delhi as a representative of West German writers. He received the Georg Büchner Prize (1961) and the Wilhelm Raabe Prize of the City of Braun-schweig (1963). However, his demanding work did not attain widespread appeal.

Nossack's works include the following novels: *Nekyia, Bericht eines Überlebenden* (1947; Nekyia, A Survivor's Report); *Interview mit dem Tode* (1948; Interview with Death, republished in 1950 as *Dorothea*); *Spätestens in November* (1955; Not Until November); *Der Neugierigie* (1955; The Curious Man); *Spirale: Roman einer schlaf-losen Nacht* (1956; Spiral: Novel of a Sleepless Night); *Der jüngere Bruder* (1958; The Younger Brother); *Nach dem letzten Aufstand: Ein Bericht* (1961; After the Last Revolution: A Report); *Das kennt man* (1964; This Is Known); *Das Testament des Lucius Eurinus* (1965; The Testament of Lucius Eurinus); *Der Fall d'Arthez* (1968; Eng. tr., *The d'Arthez Case,* 1971); *Dem unbekannten Sieger* (1969; Eng. tr., *To the Unknown Victor,* 1974); *Die gestohlene Melodie* (1972; The Stolen Melody); *Bereit-schaftsdienst* (1973; Rescue Squad); and *Ein glücklicher Mensch. Erinnerungen an Aporeé* (1975; A Fortunate Per-son: Memories of Aporeé). Besides these novels, Nos-sack published collections of essays, stories, miniatures, parables, poetry, speeches, and essays.

See: C. Schmid, *Monologische Kunst: Untersuchungen zum Werk von Hans Erich Nossack* (1968), and ed., *Über Hans Erich Nossack* (1970). T.P.F.

Nourissier, François (1927–), French essayist, novelist, and literary critic, was born in Paris. He is one of the most active and versatile men of letters in Paris today. His first book, *L'Homme humilié* (1950; Humiliated Man), dealing with displaced persons, already revealed a talent for social commentary. His essays have dealt with many subjects—with the sexual mores of the middle class; with the literary world; and with France and the French, as in *Les Français* (1968; Eng. tr., *The French,* 1968) and *Vive la France* (1970; Eng. tr., *Cartier-Bresson's France,* 1971). Nourissier's career as a novelist began in the an-tiexistentialist revolt of the early 1950s, when writers favored a return to the novel of personal analysis. From *L'Eau grise* (1951; Gray Water), his first novel, on, Nour-issier has written wistful adventures that focus on indi-viduals and their souls. Yet in his books, the description of a sensibility is never independent of a description of the contemporary society. *Bleu comme la nuit* (1958; Blue as the Night) and *Un Petit Bourgeois* (1963), for example, provide both portraits of characters and broad frescoes of the malaise of the times. *Une Histoire française* (1966; A French Story) shows more muscle than Nourissier's preceding five novels, but its preoccupations are the same.

With Nourissier, essay and novel tend to fuse into a new, hybrid form, something like a diary to which fic-tional devices lend an added dimension. This medium is well suited to his wide range of subjects: life on earth, problems of personality and human relationships, pets and housekeeping. *La Crève* (Done In) won the Femina Prize in 1970. Nourissier has also enjoyed a long and varied career in journalism, working as editor of *La Pa-risienne,* as a book reviewer for the *Nouvelles littéraires,* as a film critic for *Express,* and as a frequent contributor to other periodicals. In his articles, as in all his writing, Nourissier's views are stimulating and his expression graceful.

See: A. Bourin and J. Rousselot, *Dictionnaire de la littérature française contemporaine* (1966). L.LeS.

Nouveau, Germain (1851–1920), French poet, was born in Pourrières (Var). He was almost totally unknown until the day when young Louis ARAGON proclaimed that Nou-veau was "not Rimbaud's epigone but his equal." Nou-veau moved to Paris in 1872 and quickly frittered away his small inheritance in the company of Jean RICHEPIN,

Maurice Bouchor, Léon Valade, and the Parnassians. At the same time, he published strikingly personal verse in Emile Blémont's *La Renaissance*. An acquaintance of Charles Cros and Paul BOURGET, Nouveau also met Arthur RIMBAUD, whom he followed to London (March-June 1874). Certain manuscripts of Rimbaud's *Illuminations* are in Nouveau's hand. In the summer of 1875 he also made the acquaintance of Paul VERLAINE, who was perhaps responsible for his conversion to Roman Catholicism.

Returning to Paris, Nouveau became an intimate of Nina de Villars and her group and collaborated in the *Dixains réalistes*. In 1878, Nouveau entered the Ministry of Public Education, painted, and joined the Hydropathes. In 1879 he began to write the religious poems that were to become the *Doctrine de l'amour* (The Doctrine of Love), finished in August 1881 and signed with the pseudonym Humilis. In 1883, Nouveau gave up his civil service appointment, and the following year he sailed to Beirut, where he taught for a few months and where he wrote his *Sonnets du Liban* (Sonnets from Lebanon). Sent home by the consulate, he returned to Paris, where he fell in love with Valentine Renault. She occupied his attention for nearly two years, inspiring the inventive, frivolous outpouring of the verses of *Valentine*. Having become the drawing master of the lycée Janson-de-Sailly, he was suddenly overcome by an attack of mystical insanity on May 15, 1891. After a five-month internment at the Bicêtre hospital, he followed the route of the great pilgrimages of Italy and Spain, attired in the lice-infested garb of a hermit. Nouveau finally retired, first to Aix where he begged for alms under the porch of the cathedral (Cézanne, it is said, gave him a penny each Sunday), and then in his native village, where he lived from 1898 until 1920 on public charity. He had almost completely given up literature. Entirely against Nouveau's wishes, his friend Léonce de Larmandie published *Savoir aimer* (1904; Know How to Love; later called *Doctrine de l'amour*), which was published a second time in 1910 as *Poésies d'Humilis*. After Nouveau's death, Ernest Delahaye published *Valentines et autres vers* (1922; Valentines and Other Verse) and *Poésies d'Humilis et vers inédits* (1924; Poetry of Humilis and Unpublished Verse), which contain the essential part of his work.

Judged by classical norms, Nouveau's poetry is exceedingly uneven, but the best is worthy of the two major poets, Rimbaud and Verlaine, whose friend he was. "Poison perdu" (Lost Poison) was long thought to be by Rimbaud. Since his inspiration was divided between carnal and spiritual love, one cannot avoid comparisons between *La Doctrine de l'amour* and Verlaine's *Sagesse*, between certain of his prose works and Rimbaud's *Illuminations* or the prose poems of Charles Cros. His musicality and fantasy helped prepare the way for Guillaume APOLLINAIRE and Max JACOB. Indeed, this poet fascinated the surrealists (*see* FRENCH LITERATURE), who greeted him as one of the great innovators in the history of poetry.

See: L. Forestier, *Germain Nouveau* (1971).   P.-O.W.

Novák, Arne (1880–1939), Czech critic and literary historian, was the son of the writer Teréza NOVÁKOVÁ. Born in Litomyšl in Bohemia, he studied in Prague and Berlin and began teaching at the University of Prague in 1906. In 1920 he became professor of Czech literature at the newly founded Masaryk University at Brno, Moravia. He was its rector when the university was dissolved by the Germans in 1939, and he died shortly afterward.

Novák ranks next to František Xaver ŠALDA as the most important critic in Czech literature. Although a master of psychological portraiture, he knew that the critic's most important function is judgment. Novák stressed the national tradition of Czech literature. His political outlook was conservative, and he was cool toward the most modernist literary tendencies. But he never forgot that literature is, first of all, an art. Novák's criticism, written in a somewhat precious style, has been collected in many volumes, including *Mužové a osudy* (1914; Men and Fates), *Myšlenky a spisovatelé* (1914; Thoughts and Writers), *Zvony domova* (1916; Bells of Home), *Krajané a sousedé* (1921; Countrymen and Neighbors), *Duch a národ* (1936; Spirit and Nation), and the small handbook, *Literární kritika* (1916; Literary Criticism). Novák was also a profound student of literary history, writing both monographs, the most important of which are studies of Jan Neruda (1919) and Svatopluk Čech (2 vols., 1921–23) and general histories of Czech literature. His German *Geschichte der čechischen Literatur* (1907; History of Czech Literature), written with Jan Jakubec, attracted attention because of its skillful ordering of materials and sharp judgments on local celebrities. *Přehledné dějiny české literatury* (1909; A Survey of the History of Czech Literature) was repeatedly expanded and rewritten until the fourth edition (1936–39) covered all periods of Czech literature. A more synthetic work, *Die tschechische Literatur*, was written especially for foreign readers, published in 1931 as volume 18 of Oskar Walzel's *Handbuch der Literaturwissenschaft;* the Czech version appeared in 1933 as volume 7 of the *Československá vlastivěda*, and reappeared in 1946, revised and supplemented by Antonín Grund, as *Dějiny českého písemnictví* (Eng. tr., Czech Literature, 1975). Novák's insight into the movement of ideas as well as into the evolution of the art of literature is as remarkable as his powers of characterization and analysis. He was also interested in the plastic arts and published *Praha barokní* (1916; Baroque Prague), a sympathetic interpretation of 17th-century architecture and civilization.

See: J. Heidenreich, *Arne Novák* (1940); J. Horák, A. Pražák, and others, *Strážce tradice: Arnu Novákovi na památku* (1940); I. Liškutín, *Arne Novák* (1940); A. Pražák, *Arne Novák* (1940).   R.W.

Novak, Helga, pseud. of Helga Maria Karlsdottir (1935–), German poet, writer of short prose, radio plays, and reports, was born in Berlin, studied journalism and philosophy at Leipzig, and lived in East Germany until 1961, when she moved to Iceland. She now lives in West Germany. She worked as a laboratory technician, bookseller, and factory worker. Novak began writing in East Germany in 1955 but was unable to publish until 1965, after her move to the West, when her collections of poems, *Ballade von der reisenden Anna* (1965; Ballad of Itinerant Anna) and *Colloquium mit vier Häuten* (1967; Colloquium with Four Skins), appeared. She writes in free verse, a form of protest lyric aimed directly at the social order, critically describing her own environment. Her first book of short prose "texts," *Geselliges Beisammensein* (1969; Social Get-Together), satirically describes a mechanical world without human contact. *Aufenthalt in einem irren Haus* (1972; Stay in a Mad House) is a collection of 11 stories about the helpless and the downtrodden in everyday life. *Eines Tages hat sich die Sprechpuppe nicht mehr ausziehen lassen* (1972; One Day the Talking Doll Refused To Be Undressed), a feminist work, deals with the emancipation of women. *Die Landnahme von Tore Bela* (1972; Taking Over the Land in Tore Bela) portrays a cooperative in Portugal. Novak's social criticism takes issue with anarchism and terrorism, one report being a documentation of the writer and anarchist, Peter-Paul Zahl (1976).

In 1978 she published a volume of poems, *Margarete mit dem Schrank* (Margarete with the Cupboard). Selections of Novak's work in translation have appeared in *Dimension: Poetry*, 2, no. 1 (1969); "Two Stories," tr. L. Willson, 2, no. 1 (1969); "Main Post Office," 2, no. 1 (1969); "Journey of a Woman Nihilist to Verona in Late Autumn," tr. P. Spycher, 6, no. 3 (1973); and in E. Rütschi Herrmann and E. Huttenmaier Spitz, eds., *German Women Writers of the Twentieth Century* (1978), pp. 106–14.

E.H.S.

Nováková, Teréza (1853–1912), Czech novelist, was born Teréza Lanhausová in Prague and died there. But she spent some 20 years in Litomyšl, in eastern Bohemia, where she was married to a teacher at the gymnasium. Her son, Arne NOVÁK, was a noted critic and literary historian. Nováková came to take a deep interest in the common people of the Litomyšl region, which at first found expression in fine folkloristic and topographical studies. Later she depicted the life of these people in novels, evidencing the same faithfulness with which Karolina Světlá and Josef HOLEČEK described the peasants of northern and southern Bohemia. Nováková's own voice sounds in some of her short stories and the romantic pessimism of her personal outlook on life is evident. Her best novels, however, are admirably objective studies of religious and social problems: *Jan Jílek* (1904) concerns an 18th-century Czech who emigrates because of religious scruples; *Jiří Šmatlan* (1906) traces the development of a fervent Protestant sectarian into an enthusiastic socialist; *Děti čistého živého* (1909; The Children of the Pure and Living) describes the decay of a remarkable pantheistic sect; and *Drašar* (1914) attempts to depict an early 19th-century priest and writer who is wrecked by his passions. In tightness of composition and penetration of psychological insight, Nováková's best work surpasses the comparable work of Světlá and Holeček, but as a writer, she lacks their vitality.

See: F. X. Šalda, "Teréza Nováková," in *Duše a dílo* (1913); J. Novotný, *Kraj a dílo T. Novákové* (1924); A. Novák, *O Teréze Novákové* (1930).

R.W.

Noventa, Giacomo, pseud. of Giacomo Ca'Zorzi (1898–1960), Italian poet and journalist, was born of noble stock in Noventa di Piave. After graduating from the University of Turin in 1923, he made the acquaintance of Piero Gobetti, Eugenio MONTALE, and Umberto SABA. Traveling from city to city, in Italy and abroad, Noventa cultivated philosophical and political passions without settling for a precise vocation. During the heyday of hermeticism (*see* ITALIAN LITERATURE), he and Alberto Carocci edited *La riforma letteraria* (1936–38), a Florentine journal distinguished by general anticonformism. Deploring ideological sectarianism and ivory-tower intellectualism, Noventa argued for a traditionalist culture embracing liberal, socialist, and Catholic values. His views found no consistent support, but his moral integrity and caustic wit endeared him to young intellectuals (notably Franco FORTINI) dissatisfied with the culture of the 1930s. Noventa continued to work in the field of political journalism until 1954. His articles are gathered in *Il vescovo di Prato* (1958; The Bishop of Prato), *Nulla di nuovo* (1960; Nothing New), *Il grande amore* (1960; The Great Love), and *I calzoni di Beethoven* (1965; Beethoven's Trousers).

Noventa's poetry, gathered in *Versi e poesie* (1960; Verse and Poems) and *Versi e poesie di Emilio Sarpi* (1963; Verse and Poems of Emilio Sarpi), was composed in total independence of contemporary fashions. Peripheral by choice, he assumed as his medium the Venetian dialect. Romantic in timbre, reactionary, defiant, and vol-

atile, his poems focus on patriotism, love, and the social function of the poet. They are vigorous and metrically versatile, tender and ironic, showing a uniquely aristocratic handling of a popular instrument. In 1956, Noventa was awarded the Viareggio Prize.

See: F. Fortini, in *Il Ponte* (August 1956); G. Pampaloni, in *Letteratura italiana: i contemporanei*, vol. 3 (1975), pp. 281–98.

M.M.G.

Novomeský, Ladislav (Laco) (1904–), Slovak poet, was born in Budapest, Hungary. After World War I he worked as a Communist journalist; after World War II he served as a high government official in Slovakia. Accused of bourgeois nationalist deviationism early in the 1950s, he was sentenced to a long prison term, but in the late 1960s he was rehabilitated and his literary reputation restored. Novomeský is the outstanding writer of Slovak proletarian poetry (*see* SLOVAK LITERATURE). The influence of Czech "poetism" or "pure poetry" (*see* Vítězslav NEZVAL), can be seen in his collections *Nedel'a* (1927; Sunday), *Romboid* (1932; The Rhomboid), and *Otvorené okna* (1935; Open Windows); the verse in these collections, which treat the fates of the poor, introduced new thematic and lexical elements into Slovak poetry, achieving a synthesis between ballad form and modernist content. Another collection, *Svätý za dedinou* (1939; The Saint behind the Village), was inspired by the Spanish Civil War, while the poems published under the title *Pašovanou ceruzkou* (1948; With a Smuggled Pencil) are a vehement protest against fascism.

After his release from prison, Novomeský published the cycle *Vila Tereza* (1963; Villa Tereza), in which he evokes the struggle of the Prague leftist intellectuals in the 1930s for avant-garde art. The apex of his creation is the collection *Stamodtial'* (1964; From Over There), which contains his poems written in prison. In these the poet racks his conscience, unable to explain the absurd events he is experiencing; he comes to the conclusion that the road he has followed is the correct one, and that he cannot recant.

See: V. Reisel, *Poézia Laca Novomeského* (1946); A. J. Liehm, *The Politics of Culture* (1970), pp. 93–113.

F.M.B.

Nowaczyński, Adolf (1876–1944), Polish dramatist, satirist, journalist, and pamphleteer, was born in Podgórze, a suburb of Cracow. Educated in Cracow and Munich, Nowaczyński began his career in a manner prophetic of his later iconoclasm, when he publicly proposed a toast to anarchy in a Cracow café on receipt of the news of the Empress Elizabeth's assassination (1898). A tireless, vitriolic pamphleteer, full of eccentricities, spites, and prejudices—many of the latter grossly unworthy of a man of his ability and standing—Nowaczyński was Free Poland's greatest literary curiosity. He would treat any subject under the sun, including many he knew nothing about, such as the American scene, and he wrote in a style that was often turgid, ostentatious, and overloaded with foreignisms. Yet his readers were legion. He liked nothing better than to deflate the reputations of the great and, as in *Warta nad Wartą* (1937; Watch on the Warta), a rehabilitation of several men of western Poland, to extol the neglected. Among his many plays, in all of which history is ruthlessly distorted, are *Car Samozwaniec* (1908; The Tsar Pretender); *Wielki Fryderyk* (1910; The Great Frederick); *Pułaski w Ameryce* (1917; Pułaski in America); *Wiosna narodów w cichym zakątku* (1929; The Spring of Nations in a Quiet Corner), a satire on the events of 1848 in Cracow; and *Cezar i człowiek* (1937; Caesar and Man), a drama concerning Nicolaus Copernicus and the Borgias. Nowaczyński's historical dramas resemble chronicles written in dialogue, employing picturesque panoramic backgrounds and huge crowds and centered around interesting historical figures. Nowaczyński's final work before the debacle of 1939 was the fascinating *Młodość Chopina* (1939; Chopin's Youth), a semifictional reconstruction of the early life of the great composer with interesting revelations of the Polish sources of Chopin's genius. Nowaczyński has been called the Polish Daudet (*see* Léon DAUDET).

See: Z. Dębicki, *Portrety*, vol. 2 (1928), 213–30; A. Hutnikiewicz, "Adolf Nowaczyński," in *Obraz literatury polskiej XIX i XX wieku. Literatura Młodej Polski*, vol. 2 (1967), pp. 359–91. A.P.C. rev. S.F.

Nowak, Tadeusz (1930–), Polish poet, short-story writer, and novelist, was born in Sikorzyce, near Dąbrowa Tarnowska into a peasant family. While studying Polish philology at the Jagiellonian University in Cracow he published his first poems. Nowak has written several volumes of poetry: *Uczę się mówić* (1953; I Learn to Speak), *Porównania* (1954; Comparisons), *Prorocy już odchodzą* (1956; The Prophets Are Already Leaving), *Jasełkowe niebiosa* (1957; The Heavens of Nativity Plays), *Psalmy na użytek domowy* (1959; Psalms for Home Use), *Ziarenko trawy* (1964; A Grain of Grass), and *W jutrzni* (1966; At Dawn). Nowak's poetry is based on folk traditions, but it has found its own tone, sophisticated yet resembling the fresh observations of the peasant child. He is considered a "peasant surrealist."

About 1962, Nowak gave up poetry and began to write novels and short stories, such as *Przebudzenia* (1962; Awakenings), *Obcoplemienna ballada* (1963; Ballad of a Foreign Tribe), *Takie większe wesele* (1966; A Bigger Wedding), *A jak królem, a jak katem będziesz* (1968; When You'll Be a King, When You'll Be an Executioner), *Diabły* (1971; Devils), and *Dwunastu* (1974; The Twelve). Elements of folk tradition are also present and alive in his prose, but they are seen through the perspective of revaluating confrontation with the contemporary world.

See: *Słownik współczesnych pisarzy polskich*, series 2, vol. 2 (1978), pp. 176–81. A.Z.

Nowakowski, Tadeusz (1918–), Polish novelist, was born in Olsztyn. During World War II he spent five years in German concentration camps and two years after the war in a displaced persons' camp. His first collection of short stories, *Szopa za jaśminami* (1948; A Shed behind the Jasmine Trees), was followed by several novels, all dealing mainly with problems of Polish displaced persons in Germany during and immediately after the war: *Obóz Wszystkich Świętych* (1957; Eng. tr., *The Camp of All Saints*, 1962), *Syn zadżumionych* (1959; The Son of the Plague-Stricken), and others. In his later novels, Nowakowski presents various problems connected with life in contemporary Poland; among them are *Happy End* (1970), and *Byle do wiosny* (1975; Until the Springtime), in which he also returns to the theme of the concentration camps as seen from the perspective of later years. J.R.K.

Nowakowski, Zygmunt (1891–1963), Polish novelist, short-story writer, columnist, dramatist, and actor, was born Zygmunt Tempka in Cracow and died in London. He made a name for himself as an actor and director while simultaneously studying Polish literature at Jagiellonian University in Cracow, from which he received a doctorate. From 1926 to 1929 he was director of the City Theater in Cracow. After his literary debut in 1917, he wrote a score of novels, short stories, and feuilletons. Of his novels, *Przylądek Dobrej Nadziei* (1931; Eng. tr., *The*

Cape of Good Hope, 1940), which was translated into six languages, stands out. As a dramatist he achieved his greatest success with the play *Gałązka rozmarynu* (1938; A Twig of Rosemary). Nowakowski was a prolific writer who did not shun writing for young readers, preparing textbooks. A collection of his feuilletons, *Lajkonik na wygnaniu* (The Hobbyhorse in Exile), appeared in London in 1963.

See: *Słownik współczesnych pisarzy polskich*, vol. 2 (1964), pp. 562–67; T. Terlecki, ed., *Literatura polska na obczyźnie 1940–1960*, 5 vols (1965). Z.Y.

Nušić, Branislav (1864–1938), Serbian dramatist, short-story writer, and novelist, was born and educated in Belgrade, where he studied law. He subsequently held a number of government posts in the Serbian ministries of foreign affairs and education and later served as director of state-subsidized theaters in Belgrade, Novi Sad, Skopje, and Sarajevo.

Nušić was a versatile, prolific author. Aside from his numerous prose writings, his 25 volumes of collected works include practically every kind of dramatic composition, from tragedy to farce. His earlier plays include historical patriotic dramas, *Knez Ivo od Semberije* (1900; Duke Ivo of Semberia) and *Hadži Loja* (1908); several lachrymose romantic pieces; and the tragedy *Nahod* (1923; The Foundling). Although these works initially enjoyed some popularity, they failed to survive the test of time. It was only when Nušić turned to comedy that his dramatic talent achieved its fullest potential. A satirist of the first magnitude, he created a panoramic view of the late-blossoming Serbian bourgeoisie, plagued by the abuses of political, bureaucratic, and police power, the peddling of influence, greed for money, and the craving for advancement and honors. These are the subjects of such memorable plays as *Narodni poslanik* (1883; The Member of Parliament), *Sumnjivo lice* (1887; A Suspicious Character), *Protekcija* (1889; Favoritism), *Običan čovek* (1900; An Ordinary Man), *Svet* (1906; The World), and *Put oko sveta* (1910; A Trip around the World). Nušić's satirical bite became even stronger after World War I, when he completed *Gospodja ministarka* (1929; The Cabinet Member's Wife), *Ožalošćena porodica* (1934; The Bereaved Family), *UJEŽ* (1935; acronym for the Association of Yugoslav Emancipated Women), and *Pokojnik* (1937; The Deceased), in which Nušić amply augmented a picture of the well-known social ills of the new South Slav state, Yugoslavia, with a devastating satirical comment upon the universal foibles of human nature.

Among Nušić's noteworthy nondramatic prose works are his three volumes of short stories and the novel *Opštinsko dete* (1902; The Parish Child), all characterized by a wealth of humorous detail, lively characters, and the rare authenticity of its milieu. Although in both his dramatic and prose compositions Nušić occasionally succumbed to his audience's thirst for easy comic effects and laughter for its own sake, his work still remains a striking exposé of the Serbian bourgeois upstart.

See: M. Djoković, *Branislav Nušić* (1964); *Nušićev zbornik* (1965); V. Gligorić, *Branislav Nušić* (1968). N.M.

Nygard, Olav (1884–1924), Norwegian poet, was born on a small farm in Modalen, north of Bergen. This district's dramatic landscape appears, symbolically veiled, throughout his poetic production. Although Nygard received little education beyond the elementary level and had to struggle with poverty and disease all his life, he managed to teach himself English and publish translations of Shakespeare, Robert Burns, and John Keats. As a poet, Nygard worked incessantly on form, and his struggles were undoubtedly due in part to his encounter with the poetry of Keats. His self-criticism and his agony over the limitations of language caused him to publish only four small volumes: *Flodmål* (1913; The Voice of the River), *Runemål* (1914; The Voice of the Runes), *Kvæde* (1915; Poems), and *Ved vebande* (1923; By the Magic Circle). They contain, however, poems of the highest order.

Like Henrik Wergeland (*see* NORWEGIAN LITERATURE) and Nygard's contemporary Olav AUKRUST, in most respects his closest kin among Norwegian writers, Nygard was a visionary. Yet unlike them, Nygard did not dwell on sentiments of nationalism and patriotism, nor did he have an eye for the common things in life. He writes about transcendence, love, and death, and his unforgettable images of nature are extensions of these themes. In *Ved vebande*, for example, published shortly before he succumbed to tuberculosis, he employs his fabulous visual power to blend the dramatic western Norwegian landscape with cosmic visions of nature and human life. Nygard's poetry, written in traditional verse, is strikingly rich in poetic imagery. He wrote in *nynorsk* (*see* NORWEGIAN LITERATURE), adding freely to it from his own dialect to create a strongly personal poetic language. A demanding craftsman, he sought a stringency of expression that yielded sublime visions of pain and beauty.

See: J. Dale, *Olav Nygard* (1957). K.A.F.

O

Obaldia, René de (1918–), French playwright, novelist, and poet, was born in Hong Kong to a French mother and a Panamanian father. Obaldia studied at the Lycée Condorcet in Paris. During World War II he was a prisoner in Silesia. He published a book of prose poems, *Les Richesses naturelles* (The Natural Wealth), in 1952 and a novel, *Tamerlan des cœurs* (Tamerlan of the Hearts), in 1954. In *Tamerlan*, Obaldia fused the legend of the conqueror with the world of 1939. While working as deputy director of the International Cultural Center at Royaumont near Paris, Obaldia began writing short plays; *Le Défunt* (1967; The Deceased) and *Le Sacrifice du bourreau* (1967; The Executioner's Sacrifice) were produced by Marc Gentilhomme at the Théâtre de Lutèce in 1957. That same year, Obaldia became the literary editor of the Horay Press. In 1959, he received the Combat Prize for his novel *Le Centenaire* (The Centenarian), the subject of which is, in Obaldia's words, "senility considered as one of the fine arts."

Obaldia's first important success was *Genousie* (Eng. tr., 1970), produced in 1960 by Jean VILAR at the Théâtre Récamier in Paris. This play tells the story of Madame de Tubéreuse, an eccentric who entertains distinguished snobs in her castle. In 1965, the famous actor Michel Simon starred in *Du vent dans les branches de sassafras* (Eng. tr., *Wind in the Branches of the Sassafras*, 1969), a "sitting-room western." *Innocentines*, a book of poems "for children and a few adults," was very popular when it was published in 1969.

An heir to the surrealist movement (*see* FRENCH LITERATURE), Obaldia can also be called an exponent of the theater of the absurd, although he himself refuses this label. His language is at the same time poetic and amusing, and his extraordinary humor is most communicative.

J.-C.M.

Obey, André (1892–1975), French dramatist, was born in Douai, where he was educated. He also published essays and novels, among the latter *Le Joueur de triangle* (1928; The Triangle Player), which won the Théophraste Renaudot Prize. Turning to the dramatic form, Obey collaborated with Denys AMIEL on *La Souriante Madame Beudet* (1921; The Smiling Madame Beudet) and *La Carcasse* (1926; The Carcass). He dated his dramatic success, however, from *Noé* (1931; Noah). Obey wrote three other, less successful works for the Compagnie des Quinze: *Le Viol de Lucrèce* (1931; The Rape of Lucretia), *La Bataille de la Marne* (1931; Battle of the Marne), and *Vénus et Adonis* (1932).

Greatly influenced by Paul CLAUDEL, Henri GHÉON, and Jacques COPEAU, Obey was eager to try new theatrical techniques and novel approaches to traditional themes. Some of his successful adaptations include versions of Aeschylus's *Oresteia,* Shakespeare's *Richard III,* and Tennessee Williams's *Cat on a Hot Tin Roof.*

Obey was director of the Comédie-Française (1946–47), which he reorganized. At the same time, the Odéon theater was placed under his supervision for the production of modern plays, and it became, for a time, a "branch" of the Comédie. His later successes include *L'Homme de cendres* (1949; The Phoenix) and *Une Fille pour du vent* (1953; Sacrifice to the Wind). E.D.C. and J.M.L.

Obstfelder, Sigbjørn (1866–1900), Norwegian poet, was born in Stavanger, the son of a baker, and the grandson of a German physician. He typified the fin de siècle in Norwegian poetry. Appreciated by only a narrow circle during his lifetime, he has been repeatedly "rediscovered" since his death. As a young man, Obstfelder demonstrated many talents. He produced his first creative writing when he was 11; he began his university studies in philosophy, but quickly shifted to engineering; he dabbled in painting, played various instruments, and won considerable skill as an improviser on the violin. Divided as he was among these various interests, he was unable to concentrate on any one of them until his return from an eight-month stay in the United States in 1891 and his recovery from a subsequent nervous breakdown. From 1892 until his untimely death, he developed one of the most refined and eccentric literary personalities in Norwegian literature. This personality is exhibited in such volumes as *Digte* (1893; Eng. tr., *Poems,* 1920); *To novelletter* (1895; Two Short Stories); *Korset* (1896; The Cross), a novella; *De røde dråber* (1897; The Red Drops), a play; *En præsts dagbog* (1900; A Pastor's Diary), and *Efterladte arbeider* (1903; Posthumous Writings).

Obstfelder wrote a prose with rhythm and a poetry without rhyme, often seeking to give the effect of music through the sound of words. His themes were the universe, the soul, woman, God, and eternity, all treated in a mystic, brooding spirit reminiscent of Eduard von Hartmann and Arthur Schopenhauer. His overpowering sense of the terror and mystery of life, his own loneliness, and his attempts to express the inexpressible, remind one of the paintings of his countryman and contemporary, Edvard Munch. Obstfelder was a pure neoromantic without a trace of the poseur, and even today his slender production is impressive for its limpid depth and the haunting music of its lines.

See: J. F. Bjørnsen, *Sigbjørn Obstfelder* (1959); A. Hannevik, *Obstfelder og mystikken* (1960); R. Ekner, *En sällsam gemenskap* (1967). E.H.

Odojewski, Włodzimierz (1930–), Polish novelist, short-story writer, and playwright, was born in Poznań. He studied sociology at the University of Poznań and made his debut as a writer with poems and in the field of journalism. He also wrote radio and television plays. His first novels include *Miejsce nawiedzone* (1959; A Stricken Place), *Wyspa ocalenia* (1964; Eng. tr., *No Island of Salvation*, 1965), and *Czas odwrócony* (1965; Time Reversed). He also published collections of short stories, such as *Kwarantanna* (1960; Quarantine) and *Zmierzch świata* (1962; Eng. tr., *The Dying Day*, 1964). Since 1972, Odojewski has lived in West Germany. In 1973 he published a novel, *Zasypie wszystko, zawieje* (All Will Disappear under the Snow), which is considered his major achievement so far. Most of Odojewski's novels and short stories are set in prewar eastern Poland on the Polish-Ukrainian border. They deal with themes of human tragedies, the conflict of nationalities, and the German occupation of this region during World War II.

See: *Słownik współczesnych pisarzy polskich*, series II, vol. 2 (1978), pp. 190–94; J. R. Krzyżanowski, "The Land of No Salvation," *PolR* 23, no. 2 (1978): 17–30.   D.W.

Odoyevtseva, Irina Vladimirovna, pseud. of Iraida Gustavovna Ivanova, née Heinicke (1901–), Russian novelist and poet born in Riga, Latvia, became the youngest member of the Petersburg "Poets Guild" (*see* RUSSIAN LITERATURE). She published her first volume of verse, *Dvor chudes* (1922; Court of Wonders), in Petersburg before emigrating with her husband, the poet Georgy IVANOV, in 1923 and settling in Paris. During the following three decades she published mostly prose. Her novels, *Naslediye* (?; Heritage), *Angel smerti* (1927; Angel of Death), *Izolda* (1931), *Zerkalo* (1939; Mirror), *Ostav nadezhdu navsegda* (1954; Eng. tr., *All Hope Abandon*, 1949), and short stories, successful with the public and translated into several languages, display a fluent style, but are essentially "entertainments." Odoyevtseva's later poetry is remarkable for its formal discipline, which contrasts with the dreamlike vagueness of her images and their capricious, sometimes surrealist, concatenations. Her verses are perhaps the purest example of the "Parisian mood" (*parizhskaya nota*) in Russian émigré poetry, meaning a surrender to aesthetic and emotional hypersensitivity disturbed by a constant, nagging awareness of death. Her collections of poetry include *Kontrapunkt* (1951), *Stikhi napisannye vo vremya bolezni* (1952; Verses Written while Ill), *Stikhi* (1960), *Desyat let* (1961; Ten Years), *Odinochestvo* (1965; Solitude), and *Zlataya tsep* (1975; The Golden Chain). In Odoyevtseva's memoirs, *Na beregakh Nevy* (1967; On the Banks of the Neva), fact and fiction form an intriguing union.   V.T.

Okudzhava, Bulat Shalvovich (1924–), Russian poet and prose writer, was born in Moscow of Armenian and Georgian parentage. He is most widely known for his interpretations, to his own guitar accompaniment, of his topical and sardonic ballads. Okudzhava was directly affected by both the Stalinist purges and World War II. His father perished in the purges of 1937, and his mother was sent to a labor camp. In 1942, while still in high school, Okudzhava volunteered for the army. After the war, he studied philosophy at the University of Tiflis and then worked as a village teacher in Kaluga from 1950 to 1955. With the release of his mother in 1955, Okudzhava returned to Moscow and thenceforth supported himself with his literary earnings.

His first volume of poetry, *Lirika*, was published in 1956. In 1959, Okudzhava began a series of private performances that won him much popularity, especially among Soviet youth. Tape recordings of these performances were widely circulated in the comparatively relaxed post-Stalinist period and were succeeded by public performances in the early 1960s. His first prose publication, "Bud zdorov, shkolyar" (Good Luck, Schoolboy), appeared in Konstantin PAUSTOVSKY's important anthology, *Tarusskiye stranitsy* (1961; Eng. tr., *Pages from Tarusa*, 1964). A truthful, unidealized account of the war, the story was strongly criticized by idealogues for being too pacifistic and for the "infantile psychology" of its hero. Okudzhava has published several other volumes of poetry, including *Ostrova* (1959; Islands) and *Arbat moy Arbat* (1976; Arbat, My Arbat), and a historical novel, *Bedny Avrosimov* (1970; Poor Avrosimov; repub. as *Glotok svobody*, 1971, A Gulp of Freedom) about the Decembrist Pavel Pestel.

Beginning as a poet with a sharp and skeptical eye for the unheroic aspects of war, Okudzhava has developed into an ironic, if sometimes romantic, commentator on city life in post-Stalinist Russia. Although some of his poetry might be described as whimsical, it reflects his determination not to adhere to any rigid or falsifying literary codification.   D.T.W.

Olbracht, Ivan, pseud. of Kamil Zeman (1882–1952), Czech novelist, was perhaps the most gifted of the Czech fiction writers who flourished during the period between the two world wars. He was born in Semily in northeastern Bohemia, the son of a writer, Antonín Zeman, who produced early realist novels under the pseudonym Antal Stašek. Although Olbracht studied law, he became a journalist in the labor movement, writing for socialist and, later, Communist newspapers. He spent several short periods in jail because of revolutionary writings and in 1942 was arrested by the Nazis. In 1945 he was made chief of the broadcasting division of the new Ministry of Information, and in 1947 he was awarded the title of "national artist."

Olbracht's first book was a fine collection of romantic stories about tramps and circus people, *O zlých samotářích* (1913; Of Evil Solitary Men); but his rise as an artist began during World War I, with a strangely powerful novel, *Žalář nejtemnější* (1916; The Darkest Prison), which recounts the jealous pangs of a blind man. Olbracht's next long work, *Podivné přatelství herce Jesenia* (1919; The Strange Friendship of the Actor Jesenius), placed him in the front rank of Czech novelists. Based on the motif of split personality, the novel includes extremely vivid scenes of the war and of green-room life. Its moral indicates a victory of collective belief over narrow egoism and barren introspection. Olbracht apparently took the lesson of this book to heart, with a vengeance. His next novel, *Anna proletářka* (1928; Anne the Proletarian), about the Communist uprising of 1920, is merely heavy-handed propaganda, and the prison stories collected in *Zamřižované zrcadlo* (1930; The Grated Mirror) are also failures. But Olbracht again captivated the reading public with his next novel, *Nikola Šuhaj, loupežník* (1933; Eng. tr., *Nikola Šuhaj—Bandit*, 1954), a brisk story of Subcarpathian Russia told with epic speed, tight composition, and balladlike objectivity. The novel centers around the deeds and misdeeds of a popular revolutionist who took the law into his own hands against the Czech police authorities. *Golet v údolí* (1937; Eng. tr., *The Bitter and the Sweet*, 1967), is an excellent series of stories about the poor Orthodox Jews of Subcarpathian Russia. Olbracht's other work is journalistic in nature and includes *Obrazy ze soudobého Ruska* (1920; Pictures of Present-Day Russia), an enthusiastic travel book about the Soviet Union, and *Hory a staletí* (1935; Mountains and Centuries), a fine descriptive account of Subcarpathian Russia and its social problems.

Olbracht's adherence to strong leftist ideology did not mar his deep humanity and sure artistry. His evolution from an analytical novelist of the subconscious to a writer of epic grandeur is a sign of revolt against the excesses of introspection and heralds the revival of the almost forgotten·art of storytelling. In *Nikola Šuhaj,* perhaps his greatest achievement, Olbracht tells his story interestingly, objectively, with sharp outlines, in fine, clear Czech prose, and succeeds in endowing it with something of the monumentality of a primitive epic.

See: B. Václavek, *Tvorbou k realitě* (1937); A. M. Píša, *Ivan Olbracht* (1949); W. E. Harkins, "Nikola Šuhaj the Bandit," in *Czechoslovakia Past and Present,* ed. by M. Rechcigl, Jr. (1969), vol. 2, pp. 993–1001.   R.W.

Olesha, Yury Karlovich (1899–1960), Russian novelist, short-story writer, and dramatist, was born in Elizavetgrad and grew up in Odessa. His first novel, *Zavist* (1927; Eng. tr., *Envy,* 1936; 1947; *The Wayward Comrade and the Commissar,* 1960), earned him an extremely promising reputation, but with the passage of time he found it more and more difficult to adapt to the political and social demands put on him as a Soviet writer. During the mid-1930s he wrote several film scripts, but after 1936 he virtually disappeared from literature, to be rehabilitated only several years before his death in 1960.

Olesha was concerned with the conflict between life and its needs, on the one hand, and the inhuman and inhumane forms of modern technological and bureaucratic civilization on the other. This conflict is the theme of *Envy,* which pits an individualist, the romantic dreamer Kavalerov, against a soulless order ruled by bureaucratic planners and "sausage makers." Still, Olesha's sympathies were divided: Kavalerov is a rather unsympathetic character, and the author was himself clearly awed by the rude, self-confident technocrats to whom the future apparently belongs. The strongest element of *Envy* is its fresh, sparkling form: the novel is filled with imaginative metaphors and similes; even in its negative and philistine aspects, it bubbles with life. Olesha was clearly aware of and influenced by contemporary expressionist, cubist, and vitalist trends in Western European literature.

His early stories (Eng. tr., *Love and Other Stories,* 1967) are philosophic; strongly influenced by Henri BERGSON, they display the same conflict between vitalism and mechanism that is found in *Envy.* In "Lyubov" (1929; Love) the world appears irrational to a young Marxist in love; as he flies through the air, violating Newton's law of gravitation, a color-blind observer seeks to reduce the world to a cold, schematic, black-and-white order. "Vishnyovaya kostochka" (1930; The Cherry Stone) suggests a resolution of Olesha's usual conflict of vitalism and mechanism in a future Utopian order: a new building of concrete and steel will have a garden in which a cherry stone, symbolizing the narrator's unrequited love, can germinate and grow. "Liompa" (1928) contrasts the world of the infant, nameless but intensely alive, with that of a dying man, for whom only meaningless names are left.

Olesha wrote several plays. *Zagovor chuvstv* (staged in 1929, pub. in 1968; Eng. tr., *The Conspiracy of Feelings,* 1969) is a rather pallid, watered-down version of his novel *Envy,* designed ·to make the theme more acceptable politically. *Spisok blagodeyaniy* (1931; Eng. tr., *A List of Assets,* 1963) shows an attempt, again rather pallid, to fulfill the requirements of the official line: the heroine of the play is a Russian actress who idealizes the West but,

emigrating, falls victim to capitalist intrigues and is finally killed by a Russian émigré.

Olesha also wrote a novel for children, *Tri tolstyaka* (1928; Eng. tr., *The Three Fat Men,* 1964), a fairy tale about the events of the October Revolution. Olesha's essays and his volume of memoirs, *Ni dnya bez strochki* (1965; Not a Day without a Line), although uneven, are instilled with keen imagination and warm humanity.

Perhaps no other Russian writer of fiction since the 1920s possessed stylistic and imagistic gifts equal to Olesha's. Especially noteworthy is his ability to pose the dilemmas of vitalist philosophy in terms of vivid images and lively characters. Even though he was often treated by critics as a writer unsympathetic to the October Revolution who hankered for the return of an older order of "feelings," Olesha was in fact supremely ambivalent: He clearly felt estranged from both the old and new orders. Moreover, the problems of technology and bureaucracy described in his works are as applicable to the West as they are to the Soviet Union. One can only regret the failure of history to permit Olesha a normal artistic development.

See: E. Beaujour, *The Invisible Land* (1970); A. Belinkov, "The Soviet Intelligentsia and the Socialist Revolution: On Yury Olesha's *Envy," RusR* 30 (1971): 356–68 and (1972): 25–37; M. Chudakova, *Masterstvo Yuriya Oleshi* (1972); N. Nilsson, "Through the Wrong End of Binoculars: An Introduction to Jurij Olesha," and W. E. Harkins, "The Theme of Sterility in Olesha's *Envy,"* in *Major Soviet Writers: Essays in Criticism,* ed. by E. J. Brown (1973), pp. 254–94.   W.E.H.

Oliveira, Carlos (Alberto Serra) de (1921–), Portuguese novelist and poet, was born of Portuguese parents in Belém, Brazil, but went to Portugal as a child. He studied at Coimbra, where he became a member of the neorealist group that published the *Novo Cancioneiro* (New Songbook) in 1941. His first volume of verse, *Turismo* (1941), was followed by eight others, including *Entre duas memórias* (1971; Between Two Memories). Carlos de Oliveira brought out an anthology, *Poesias* (1945–1960), in 1962 and collected his poetry in two vols. as *Trabalho poético* (1976?; Poetic Labor), including a new section, *Pastoral.* Of his five brilliant novels, *Casa na duna* (1943; House on the Dune) and *Uma abelha na chuva* (1953; A Bee in the Rain) are the most striking; *Finisterra* (1978; Land's End) is the most recent. His volume of nonfiction, *O aprendiz do feiticeiro* (1971; The Sorcerer's Apprentice), contains personal essays, autobiography, and literary criticism. Like the other early neorealists, this writer was concerned from the beginning of his career with social and economic problems in the countryside and took as his subject matter the relations between the haves and have-nots of small towns and villages. His novels, all of which are short, tell tales of greed, violence, and grinding poverty in the undeveloped region just behind the coast of central Portugal. Sparse in structure and concise in style, they show that the author had read Ernest Hemingway and the novelists of northeastern Brazil, especially Graciliano Ramos. In spite of Oliveira's lifelong social commitment, his verse, which has become increasingly abstract, does not emphasize the social protest that is found in his novels but is personal and constructed of memories and impressions long stored in his subconscious. At first traditional, it has gradually freed itself from fixed meters and rhyme. Often his poems are no more now than brief utterances in short lines and single sentences.

See: A. Franco Nogueira, *Jornal de crítica literária*

(1954), pp. 145–74; J. Gaspar Simões, *Crítica II,* vol. 1 (1961), pp. 335–48, and *Crítica III* (n.d.), pp. 171–96.

R.S.S.

Oller i Moragues, Narcis (1846–1930), Catalan novelist, was born in the city of Valls and he died in Barcelona. He was a notary, and his highly successful participation in Catalan letters only came late in his life through the intervention of his cousin, the critic Josep Ixart, who presented him to a group of writers taking part in the Jocs Florals. These poetic competitions, restored in 1859, were at that time contributing to the rebirth of Catalan literature. His first works were published in *Renaixença,* at the beginning in collaboration with Ixart. His reading of Emile ZOLA's works influenced him greatly in his decision to become a novelist. The literary world of Barcelona was not receptive to naturalism, however, and Narcis Oller adapted what he could from the school in the light of his public's taste. In his first book, *Croquis del natural* (1875; Sketches from Nature), he essayed his powers as a realistic writer. *Sor Sanxa* (Sister Sanxa) was published in 1880, followed by another novel, *Isabel de Galceran. La papallona* (1882; The Butterfly), the portrait of a masculine character, all movement and madness, was one of the author's most popular novels, the one that contributed most to his fame and has been translated into various languages. *L'escanya pobres* (1884; The Exploiter of the Poor), *Vilaniu* (1886), and the *Febre d'or* (1890; Gold Fever) are his first ventures in the thesis novel, a genre dear to naturalism. Rather than literary creations they are like photographs taken in a sordid milieu of repugnant characters. *La borgeria* (1898; The Bourgeoisie) presents the problem of insanity and its social consequences. Some consider *Pilar Prim* (1906), a novel of middle-class urban life, the crowning achievement of Narcis Oller's career. Also to be mentioned among his narrative writings are *Notes de color* (Color Notes), *De tots colors* (1888; In All Colors), *Figura i paisatge* (1897; Figure and Landscape), *Rurals i urbanes* (From the Countryside and the City), and *Al llapis i a la ploma* (1929; With Pen and Pencil). The titles of these works suggest parallels with the plastic arts, in particular painting and drawing.

In following the French naturalistic school, Narcis Oller developed marked talent as an observer, although, as may happen with practitioners of this genre, he frequently presented incarnations of vices and passions rather than men of flesh and blood. Yet his realism is never crude, and he showed rather a keen desire to present great social problems in thesis form, as in his works on the insane asylum, usury, slander, and the desire for wealth. In this sense his work is always moralizing and has an essential didactic purpose.

See: A. Savine, *La Littérature catalane* (1888); C. Fortuny, *La novela catalana* (1912); M. de Montoliu, "Estudi critic" (prologue to the complete works of the author published by Gustau Gili, Barcelona, 1928–30).

F. de P.

Ollier, Claude (1922–), French novelist, was born in Paris. He studied law and then held various positions in the private and public sectors. Ollier's first novel, *La Mise en scène* (1958; Stage Directions), received the Médicis Prize and established him as a promising "new novelist" (*see* FRENCH LITERATURE). *Le Maintien de l'ordre* (1961; Eng. tr., *Law and Order,* 1976), *L'Eté indien* (1963; Indian Summer), and *L'Echec de Nolan* (1967; Nolan's Failure), which completed his first tetralogy, were less successful, despite critical praise. After an interruption of several years, during which he worked as film critic, radio-play

writer, and lecturer, Ollier published in rapid succession the volumes of his second tetralogy: *La Vie sur Epsilon* (1972; Life on Epsilon), *Enigma* (1973), *Our ou vingt ans après* (1974; Our, or 20 Years Later), and *Fuzzy Sets* (1975). This series of novels transposes the main themes of his earlier work into a science-fiction setting. Although readers of the "new novel" have a great respect for his work, Ollier has remained largely unknown by the general public.

All of Ollier's novels are strongly marked by structural devices associated with the "new novel," especially by a multilevel organization that allows for several readings of the text, each one referring to others by means of a strict system of correspondences. Names of characters, geographical locations, temporal segments, stylized and/or ritualized gestures and situations, landscapes and objects thus form networks of meaning associating a legendary past with a fictional present and a prophetic future. South America's jungles are connected with the jungle of Manhattan; Arab deserts with the desert of space; adventures of explorers, filmmakers, detectives, and astronauts, as well as all narrated stories, are linked with the narration of the story of their writing. But each of Ollier's novels has its own style, and in each tetralogy, Ollier moves from powerful realism to increasingly arcane poetry and formal disintegration. Nevertheless, his work always ends on a positive note.

See: J. Ricardou, *Pour une théorie du nouveau roman* (1971); L. Roudiez, *French Fiction Today* (1972), pp. 233–58.

J.V.A.

Olmo, Lauro (1922–), Spanish playwright, novelist, and short-story writer, was born in Barco de Valdeorras, in the province of Orense. Olmo is a self-taught writer who has worked at various minor jobs. The action of his novel *Ayer, 27 de octubre* (1958; Yesterday, October 27) spans one day in the lives of the tenants who inhabit a block of flats in one of Madrid's seedier districts. In this work realism is combined with lyricism through the flexible use of narrative. *Doce cuentos y uno más* (Twelve Tales and One More) won the Leopoldo Alas Prize for short stories in 1955.

Primarily a dramatist, Olmo has published several plays: *La camisa* (1962; The Shirt), *La pechuga de la sardina* (1963; The Breast of the Sardine), *English Spoken* (1964), *El cuerpo* (1966; The Body), *Mare Nostrum* (1966), and *El cuarto poder* (1967; The Fourth Power). *La camisa,* his most acclaimed play, concerns the socioeconomic problems of a shanty town on the outskirts of Madrid and represents a new departure in post-Civil War Spanish theater. Social criticism is conveyed in a realistic style characterized by an economy of words and faithful reproduction of popular and colloquial speech.

See: J. Monleón, "Lauro Olmo, o la denuncia cordial," Introduction to *Lauro Olmo: la camisa, el cuerpo, el cuarto poder* (1970), pp. 9–47; F. Ruiz Ramón, *Historia del teatro español siglo XX* (1975), pp. 494–501.

J.O.

Ömer Seyfettin (1884–1920), Turkey's first major short-story writer, was born in Gönen. He had military training and served as a career officer until 1910. The remaining ten years of his life were devoted to writing, briefly interrupted by further service as an army officer, and to teaching literature (1914–20).

Following the publication of his first major article, "Yeni Lisan" (The New Language), in 1911, which criticized the turgid style of most of his predecessors and contemporaries, he wrote fiction that marked a significant departure: Ömer Seyfettin stressed a simple and clear style, based on the vernacular, streamlined plots filled with gripping action and unexpected twists, colorful dialogue, and explorations into human motivation. Many of his short stories and novellas are among the best specimens of Turkish satire and humor. In addition to vivid depictions of the social and political upheavals he witnessed in the closing years of the Ottoman Empire, he wrote about legends and historical events as well as his recollections of childhood and army life. His so-called social novel *Ashab-ı Kehfimiz* (Our Seven Sleepers) was published in 1918; and his novellas *Harem* and *Efruz Bey,* in 1918 and 1919 respectively. His 140 short stories were compiled and published posthumously in eight volumes: *Efruz Bey, Kahramanlar* (The Heroes), *Bomba* (The Bomb), *Harem, Yüksek Ökçeler* (High Heels), *Kurumuş Ağaçlar* (Withered Trees), *Yalnız Efe* (The Solitary Swashbuckler), and *Falaka* (Bastinado).   T.S.H.

O'Neill, Alexandre (1924–), Portuguese poet, was born in Lisbon, where he still lives. He was one of the founders of the first surrealist group in Portugal (1947), and his activities as a writer were very influential in the group's manifestations. Soon he came to follow a way of his own, becoming one of the important Portuguese poets of the second half of the 20th century. His poetry, however, retained many of its surrealistic traits, which he turned into instruments for a very satirical treatment of contemporary society. With a superior command of language and poetical forms and continuing a tradition of ironic commentary on life that stemmed from 18th-century neoclassicism, he wrote poetry that is at the same time sarcastic and sentimental and that, hiding behind the eccentric virtuosity, possesses a definite moralistic bent that caricatures the biases and prejudices of the Portuguese middle class with accurate precision and imaginative wit. But the poet is not only a satirist: in many poems he has been able to convey a deep poignancy that springs in fact from a dark vision of life. At its best, his poetry is a sharp and moving portrayal of the plight of being a Portuguese in the last decades. Using the title of a previous book of his, he collected his poetry in *No reino da Dinamarca* (1968; In the Kingdom of Denmark). Since then he has published a collection of newspaper columns, *As andorinhas não têm restaurante* (1970; Swallows Have No Res-taurant), and a small volume of new satires in verse, *Entre a cortina e a vidraça* (1972; Between the Curtain and the Pane), accompanied by a recording of his aim: "to strip others, but first of all myself, of the importance we imagine we have."   J. de S.

Orhan Kemal (1914–70), Turkish novelist, short-story writer, and playwright, was born in Ceyhan in southern Turkey. In 1930 he was forced to cut his secondary school education short when he left Turkey with his father, a former member of Parliament, who fled to Syria to escape prosecution because of his opposition to the government. After returning to Adana in 1932, he worked in textile factories and later became a clerk. He moved to Istanbul in 1950 and earned his living through journalistic and literary writing. He died in Sofia, Bulgaria, where he was undergoing treatment for cancer.

After publishing poems in the late 1930s under the pseudonym Raşit Kemal, he started writing short stories in 1940. Between 1949 and 1968 he published 11 collections of short stories, all of which depict the predicament of workers and poor people. Of his 26 novels, the most significant are *Baba Evi* (1949; Father's Home) and *Avare Yıllar* (1950; Idle Years), semiautobiographical evocations that won him early renown; *Murtaza* (1952), a bittersweet

narrative of a colorful lower-class man eking out a measly living in the big city; *Bereketli Topraklar Üzerinde* (1954; On Fertile Soil), a grim depiction of village life; *Gurbet Kuşları* (1962; Birds of Exile), a novel of peasants migrating to the urban areas; and several other works of fiction. He wrote one play, *İspinozlar* (1965; Chattering Birds)ʹ, which had several productions, and adapted four of his works of fiction to the stage. Of these, *72. Koğuş* (1966; Ward 72) was a long-time hit in Ankara and won a major drama award. *Önce Ekmek* (Bread First), a collection of short stories he published in 1968, received both the Sait Faik Prize and the Fiction Award of the Turkish Language Society in 1969. Many of his books have been published posthumously in the 1970s. In 1972 an annual Orhan Kemal Fiction Prize was established in his memory. Orhan Kemal ranks as one of the most effective proponents of social realism in Turkish fiction. His works have been translated into many major and minor languages.   T.S.H.

Ørjasæter, Tore (1886–1968), Norwegian poet, dramatist, and prose writer, was born in the mountain valley of Gudbrandsdal in central Norway and lived there most of his life. From early childhood he felt a deep allegiance to the close-knit farm society and to its venerable, overpowering heritage. But, at the same time, as the son of a schoolteacher he did not really belong to this traditional rural world, and his personal development made him rise in revolt, manifested in his spending the next several years away from his home community. He traveled extensively all over Europe before he again settled down in the Gudbrandsdal valley in 1921. The dualism between tradition and revolt reflected in his lifestyle in these years is also apparent in his poetry, which oscillates between expressions of calm and harmony—dissonance and despair. In his best poems he is one of the finest poets of *nynorsk* literature (*see* NORWEGIAN LITERATURE), expressing a noble sincerity and a lucid depth of feeling and expression.

His literary creations are essentially philosophical works, built on the conflict—sharpened by his own experience—between the free soul and "the powers" that limit that freedom. His first collections of verse express a spontaneous attachment to his milieu and its secure traditions. Like all his poetry, these works are set against a background of sublime mountain landscapes. His following books, however, are monuments to crises. In the great verse-cycle *Gudbrand Langleite* (3 vols., 1913–27), Ørjasæter creates a loose epic narrative on the theme of struggle: the revolt of the individual against surroundings and heritage; man's will against the ensnaring powers of love and home; the artist's dream against everyday life; the soul against its fate; and the painful duality within the protagonist himself, resolved at last in religious understanding. An independent collection of poems, *Skiringsgangen* (1925; Purgatory), concerns the same circle of ideas. Both works are conceived in terms of symbols of original beauty and with an intensity and grandeur of thought and emotion. Three of Ørjasæter's four plays, all inspired by elements of August STRINDBERG's later dramas, employ similar motifs. In his strongly expressionistic play *Den lange bryllupsreise* (1949; The Long Honeymoon), however, written in the aftermath of World War II, his perspective is wider. The frightening realization of man's capacity for self-destruction has shaken him. Yet in his later collections of poetry, strongly reminiscent of the much earlier collection *Elvesong* (1932; Song of the River), *Ettersommar* (1953; Late Summer) and *Klårhaust* (1963; Clear Autumn), Ørjasæter expresses a quiet faith in the ultimate harmony of life.

See: R. Thesen, *Tore Ørjasæter* (1935); L. Mæhle in *Frå bygda til verda* (1967). S.Sk.

Orkan, Władysław, pseud. of Franciszek Smreczyński (1875–1930), Polish novelist, poet, and playwright, was born in a poor settlement, Poręba Wielka, in the Carpathian Mountains and died in Cracow. He managed to get to schools in Cracow, where he began writing in contact with the lively artistic movement known as "Young Poland" (*see* POLISH LITERATURE). From early poems rather imitative of symbolism, Orkan soon developed a style of his own. He wrote short stories and novels of an authentic, realistic character, although not entirely free from naturalistic and modernistic influences. His works were couched in an idiom in which the regional mountain dialect is fused with the literary language in a logical way, suggestive of the social and geographical milieu. In a series of short stories, *Nowele* (1898; Short Stories) and *Nad urwiskiem* (1900; On the Brink of a Precipice), and novels—*Komornicy* (1900; Tenant Farmers), *W roztokach* (1903; In Mountain Valleys), *Pomór* (1910; The Plague), *Drzewiej* (1912; In the Olden Days), and *Kostka Napierski* (1925) as well as the play *Skapany świat* (1903; Guttered World)—Orkan depicted both his contemporary world and the world long past of the Carpathian Mountains and their inhabitants, with all their poverty and deprivations and with all their dreams, ambitions, struggles, and loves.

See: S. Pigoń, *Władysław Orkan* (1958). Z.F.

Ørnsbo, Jess (1932–), Danish poet, was born in Copenhagen. He received his university degree in 1964. His first collection, *Digte* (1960; Poems), a modernistic work, shows an extraordinary social concern focusing upon a Copenhagen working-class milieu. The locale, however, is subordinate to the confrontations with the hopelessness and evil of modern city life. An even greater expansion of Ørnsbo's almost baroque metaphors is found in *Myter* (1964; Myths), an attempt to enlarge his range of motifs to include the subconscious. The crucial themes—alienation, aggression, instincts, and death—are described with glaring stylistic effects. These are also found in the two absurd plays *Dværgen der blev væk* (1962; The Dwarf That Disappeared) and *Hypdangbok* (1966), in which Ørnsbo uses a compact verbal construction and grotesque caricatures, making staging a difficult task. More easily accessible are *Tusdigte* (1966; Twilight Poems) and *Kongen er mulat, men hans søn er neger* (1971; The King Is a Mulatto, but His Son Is a Negro), 24 poems, desperate protests against antihumanity and violence. A similar sentiment is found in the absurdist story *Dullerdage* (1976; Days of Duller), a combination of prose, dramatic monologues, and poetry. In *Digte uden arbejde* (1977; Poems without Work) Ørnsbo returns to the motifs of his first work, whereas in *Mobiliseringer* (1978; Mobilizations) this social criticism is given political overtones in almost anarchistic protests against a society in the process of dissolution. S.H.R.

Ortega y Gasset, José (1883–1955), Spanish philosopher, essayist, and cultural critic, was born in Madrid. He studied at the university there, obtaining his doctorate in 1904, and the following year went to Germany. After some vacillations about his career plans he settled for philosophy. He spent one year (1907–08) at the University of Marburg, a center of neo-Kantianism, under the guidance of Hermann Cohen and Paul Natorp. A fervent neo-Kantian, Ortega engaged in the disputes over the historical role of Spain that became commonplace in the wake of the Spanish-American War of 1898. While the older generation, including Miguel de UNAMUNO, approached the problem of Spain from the point of view of "national spirit" or "national psychology," Ortega considered these concepts romantic and barbaric. He maintained that the salvation of Spain lay in her Europeanization, and that Europe could be identified with science. Against the nebulous sociology of the "national soul," Ortega proposed a sociology based on science, rational ethics, and aesthetics.

In 1910 he was named professor of metaphysics at the University of Madrid, a position he held until 1936. He published *El Espectador* (8 vols., 1916–34), and in 1923 founded the *Revista de Occidente,* a monthly magazine destined to exert a profound influence in the Spanish-speaking world. The dictatorship of Miguel Primo de Rivera (1923–30) convinced Ortega that the monarchy was no longer capable of uniting the Spaniards towards a common goal. He denounced the monarchy and became a Republican. Soon after the advent of the Spanish Republic (1931), however, he warned that its radicalism would prevent it from consolidating its power. He left Spain at the outbreak of the Civil War in 1936 and returned in 1946, although he maintained his official residence in Lisbon. In 1948 he founded in Madrid the Instituto de Humanidades (Humanities Institute), but lack of support and official mistrust forced its closing after two years of operation. In 1949 he was invited to the Center for the Humanities in Aspen, Colo. He died in Madrid in 1955.

Although Ortega intended to produce systematic works of philosophy, he rarely succeeded. His books are for the most part collections of articles and essays. The most famous are: *Meditaçiones del Quijote* (1914; Eng. tr., *Meditations on Quixote,* 1961), *España invertebrada* (1921; Eng. tr., *Invertebrate Spain,* 1937), *El tema de nuestro tiempo* (1923; Eng. tr., *The Modern Theme,* 1961), *La deshumanización del arte* (1925; Eng. tr., *The Dehumanization of Art,* 1948), *La rebelión de las masas* (1930; Eng. tr., *The Revolt of the Masses,* 1932), *History as a System* (1935), *El hombre y la gente* (1957; Eng. tr., *Man and People,* 1957), and *La idea de principio en Leibniz* (1958; Eng. tr., *Leibniz' Idea of Principle,* 1971).

Ortega's intellectual development exhibits four distinctive stages, each with its characteristic influence: from 1908 to 1914, neo-Kantianism; from 1914 to 1920, the synthesis of neo-Kantianism and Max Scheler's philosophy of values; from 1920 to 1927, under the influence of the "philosophy of life," Ortega formulated his theory of "vital reason" and, inspired by Oswald Spengler's *Decline of the West,* turned his attention to history, emphasizing the decadence of European civilization and of Spain in particular. From 1927 onward, Ortega's work shows the profound influence of Martin HEIDEGGER. Through Heidegger he discovered Wilhelm Dilthey, corrected the biologistic tone of his third period and defined man as "project, mission, and authenticity" (see *La rebelión de las masas,* 1930). These undeniable influences do not diminish Ortega's originality. He had an extraordinary capacity for discovering excellence and a talent for applying the philosophical principles he came across to fields that had not attracted the attention of his sources. He also made available to Spanish and Latin American readers the best and the most recent work that was being published in Germany.

The key concepts of Ortega's philosophy are: *vigencia* (prevailing, being in force), generation, perspective, life, vital reason, the dichotomy of the masses and the elite, the dehumanization of art, and level. The concept of level is basic to his theory of knowledge and hermeneutics. For example, at what point can I say, "I know *Hamlet*"? What is the appropriate level of knowledge in the humanities? Criticism purports to reconstruct the internal logic of a given text, while historical research attempts to define the main ideals and contents of a given society and the prevailing values to which that society conforms. The "conforming" elements of a text or a society are their *vigencias*. But *vigencias* change, and as a result the historian must outline a conscious theory of periodization. According to Ortega, the "generation" that brings about a change of collective *vigencias* every 15 years is the basic historical unit. In his elaboration of this concept, Ortega anticipates the basic idea of structuralism: that the interpreter or historian cannot eliminate in the search for the core of a text his own subjective capacity and social situation. This being the case, all interpretations will necessarily be limited, and none will entirely capture the internal logic or conforming values of a remote text or society. This awareness of interpretive limitation pervades Ortega's perspectivism, which is nevertheless far removed from relativism.

For him the subject of philosophy was "human life." While Heidegger eliminated this term in order to avoid the biological overtones, Ortega clung to it and redefined it in accordance with his general thinking. In his neo-Kantian period, Ortega defines human life as culture, reason, and a universally valid restraint against the exercise of spontaneous sensitivity. In *Meditations on Quixote* he defends a synthesis of rationality and spontaneity: he still considers German rationalism to be the exemplary level, but being a Spaniard, he felt bound to accept and explain "Mediterranean superficiality." In this context he wrote the sentence "I am I and my circumstances," which has nothing in common with Heidegger's definition of human existence as "being in the world." In *The Modern Theme*, Ortega introduced the concept of "vital reason" with a rather vague meaning, but certainly biologistic in tone. Reason must recognize that it is an element of human biology and make spontaneous biological energies the main subject of its research. When reason renounces its biological origin it becomes enervating byzantinism. After Heidegger's *Sein und Zeit* (1927; Eng. tr., *Being and Time,* 1962), Ortega redefined human life as "biography," not as "biology." Instead of "vital reason" he now preferred the use of terms like "living reason" and "historical reason."

According to Ortega's best known book, *The Revolt of the Masses,* society is composed of masses and dominant minorities. Typical of the modern epoch is the revolt of the masses, while in other periods of history the masses recognized the superiority of the elite. The elite is defined in relation to the degree of self-demand and readiness for sacrifice one individual or group can muster. The masses, on the contrary, are guilty of irresponsible self-complacence. Ortega's concepts of the masses and the elite are ambiguous in both a quantitative (majority-minority) and a qualitative (self-demand, self-complacence) sense. He corrects this ambiguity in *Man and People,* in which the relationship between individual and society is studied without the moral qualifications of the previous work.

In 1925, Ortega published *The Dehumanization of Art and Ideas on the Novel.* The term "dehumanization" is used in two different senses throughout the book. It is first of all a historical explanation and justification of abstract painting and poetry, which eliminate the human figure and human metaphors. Secondly, it expresses the fact that the quality of the work of art is not based primarily on its content but on its form. "Dehumanization" stands for the tendency of the avant-garde to convert the means of expression into the very substance of the work of art. In this sense it is a new expression for what had been traditionally called "ideal nature," "aesthetic dis-

tance," or, in the formulation of Hermann Cohen, "aesthetics of pure feeling." Ortega's theory and practice of literary criticism are unusually original and far reaching in their implications. His theory of the novel, first expounded in 1914 and later included in *The Dehumanization of Art,* anticipates Lukács's early ideas, which like Ortega's theory derive from neo-Kantian idealism.

See: J. Ferrater Mora, *Ortega y Gasset: An Outline of His Philosophy* (1963); C. Morón Arroyo, *El sistema de Ortega y Gasset* (1968); R. McClintock, *Man and His Circumstances: Ortega as Educator* (1971); P. Silver, ed., *Phenomenology and Art: José Ortega y Gasset* (1975).

C.M.A.

Ory, Carlos Edmundo de (1923–), Spanish poet, essayist, and fiction writer, was born in Cádiz. He has lived outside of Spain since 1955, first in Paris and Lima, and since 1967 in Amiens, France, where he has been librarian of the Maison de Culture and is at present teaching at the University of Picardy. Ory is the creator and principal poet of the avant-garde movement called *postismo,* which arose in Madrid in 1945. He is one of the most original voices in contemporary Spanish literature and an essential key to understanding the "late avant-garde" in Spain. *Postism* was an extreme departure from an anachronistic postwar literary culture that ignored tragic realities. It was a provocative, lucid reaction, a dynamic *conceptismo* and a reinvention of poetic language that proposed the values of imagination and freedom as antidotes to the placid neoclassicism of the first post-Civil War years. It was both a synthesis and the last of the European "isms," including cubism, dadaism, and surrealism, which had had less than direct expression in Spain.

The evolution of Ory's work became clear in 1951 with his manifesto *Introrrealismo.* In this work, Ory calls for the introspective development of a less ludic, more human violence that is free of the strict limits of literature, and the creation of an essential and vital poetry that finds its meaning in a painful, interior reality. The third phase of his aesthetic evolution began with the creation of the "Atelier de Poésie Ouverte" (A.P.O.) in France in 1968. In this period Ory arrived at a synthesis of the poetic process: language finds its freedom and its projection in collective creativity; the social meaning of art is expressed in the concept "l'imagination au pouvoir" (power to the imagination); and art is no longer seen as a concept distinct from life. Poetry, for Ory, is both open and active.

Ory's many poetic works have usually been published late, in incomplete form, and in anthologies. Among these works, the following stand out: *Los sonetos* (1963); *Poemas* (1969); and *Poesía 1945–1969* (1970), the Félix GRANDE edition that led to Ory's definitive recognition in Spanish literature. Since 1970 the following collections have appeared: *Técnica y llanto* (1971; Technique and Tears), one of his most dramatic books; *Los poemas de 1944* (1973); *Poesía abierta* (1974; Open Poetry), an anthology prepared by Jaime Pont; *Lee sin temor* (1976; Read Without Fear), which includes four books; and the anthology *Metanoia* (1978), which covers the period 1944–77 and contains an introduction and study by Rafael de Cózar Sievert. *Energeía* (1978) and *La flauta prohibida* (in press; The Forbidden Flute) are his latest retrospective collections. Ory's prolific talent has also produced a published diary, several books of short stories, and some important critical essays.

R. de C.S.

Orzeszkowa, Eliza (1841–1910), Polish novelist, short-story writer, and journalist, was born Eliza Pawłowska in the manor Milkowszczyzna, near Grodno. In her 16th year she was married to the landowner Piotr Orzeszko, whom she divorced in 1869, moving thereafter to Grodno, where she lived until her death. She was engaged in clandestine political activities before and during the 1863 uprising against Russia, and later was placed under police surveillance for three years for her educational and editorial activity (she organized a Polish publishing house in Vilnius).

Orzeszkowa was one of the most representative prose writers of the period of positivism and one of the outstanding advocates for the emancipation of women. She discussed this problem not only in her novels but also in such essays as *Kilka słów o kobietach* (1888; A Few Words about Women), where she wrote about women's rights in the United States and came to the conclusion that the problem of women's emancipation was already resolved there. Her first books, overloaded by journalistic elements and didacticism, deal with various social matters, such as the inappropriate upbringing of women and their inability to live an independent life. These are the concerns of *Pamiętnik Wacławy* (1871; Wacława's Memoir); *Pan Graba* (1872; Mr. Graba); *Marta* (1873), which was soon translated into German and gained widespread popularity; *Na prowincji* (1870; In the Countryside); and *Rodzina Brochwiczów* (1885; Brochwicz's Family). Orzeszkowa's novels advocate not only women's emancipation but also equal rights for the Jews. In *Eli Makower* (1875) and *Meir Ezofowicz* (1878), she brought this issue to public attention. Young Meir Ezofowicz, who draws his noble ideas from Jewish philosophy and from the tradition of humanism and the Enlightenment, revolts against his conservative milieu.

Discouraged by urban civilization, Orzeszkowa turned her interest toward the life of the village. But even there she found evil, ignorance, exploitation, humiliation, and poverty, themes she treated in *Niziny* (1885; Lowland), *Dziurdziowie* (1888), *Cham* (1889; The Boor), and *Bene nati* (1892; Noble Birth). Orzeszkowa's greatest achievement is her novel *Nad Niemnem* (1888; On the Bank of the Niemen). In this novel, which is a broad panorama of Polish society, Orzeszkowa presented social conflicts and differences between manor and village, gentry and peasantry, but at the same time proclaiming solidarity in the name of the common good of the whole nation. The upper-class heroine of the novel, Justyna, decides to marry a young man from the village—which means giving up her privileges for farm life and manual labor. The novel also introduces the theme of the 1863 uprising, although obliquely (the graves of the Polish insurgents from the uprising are a symbol of the past, ever present in the thoughts of the people living around them). The 1863 Uprising and its martyrs are treated more openly in Orzeszkowa's late collection of short stories, *Gloria victis* (1910; Glory to the Defeated).

See: E. Jankowski, *Eliza Orzeszkowa* (1964); M. Żmigrodzka, *Orzeszkowa. Młodość pozytywizmu* (1965); J. Detko, *Eliza Orzeszkowa* (1971).   A.Z. and S.F.

Osorgin, Mikhail Andreyevich, pseud. of Mikhail Andreyevich Ilyin (1878–1942), Russian novelist and journalist, is the author of *Sivtsev Vrazhek* (1928; Eng. tr., *Quiet Street*, 1930), a novel following the fortunes of a professor's family in Moscow during World War I and the February and October Revolutions of 1917. This work expresses a pacifist, anti-Marxist philosophy, while at the same time advocating acceptance of the October Revolution. Less popular but more innovative stylistically are his novel *Volny kamenshchik* (Paris, 1937; Freemason) and his autobiography *Vremena* (Paris, 1955; Seasons).

Born in Perm and educated as a lawyer in Moscow, Osorgin was imprisoned six months for supporting the Russian Revolution of 1905. He took political refuge in Italy, where he became a well-known foreign correspondent for the liberal Russian press. Returning to Moscow in 1916, he continued to express his nonconformist and even anarchist views until he was expelled from Russia by the Bolsheviks in 1922. Most of his fiction was written during his subsequent exile in Paris, where he contributed to expatriate Russian periodicals. He died in poverty in the French village of Chabris as a refugee from the Germans.

Osorgin belongs to the humanitarian and moral tradition in Russian literature, which includes such figures as Vissarion Belinsky, Lev TOLSTOY, Maksim GORKY, and Aleksandr SOLZHENITSYN. He published over 2,000 articles, and his 20 books include 5 novels and 10 collections of stories or essays. For a selection of his works in English, see *M. A. Osorgin: Selected Stories*, ed. and tr. by D. Fiene (1980).

See: N. Barmache, D. Fiene, and T. Ossorguine, comps., *Bibliographie des œuvres de Michel Ossorguine* (1973).   D.Fi.

Ossendowski, Ferdynand Antoni (1878–1945), Polish novelist and short-story writer, was born in Vitebsk, Russia, and died in Żółwin near Warsaw. He became a writer after a relatively long career in other professions (including scholarship and journalism) and after periods of tempestuous experience. He participated in the Russian Revolution of 1905 and spent two years in prison. Much later, in 1919, he was associated with the anti-Soviet government of Admiral Aleksandr Kolchak, whose defeat forced Ossendowski to escape to the Far East. After visiting the United States, he settled in Poland. He also traveled extensively later in northern and central Africa, European countries, and the Middle East.

The main body of Ossendowski's fiction and documentary writing is based on his personal experience, adventures, and travels. Among more than a dozen translations of his books published in Britain and in the United States is *Przez kraj ludzi, zwierząt i bogów*, published almost at the same time in Polish and in English (1923; Eng. tr., *Beasts, Men and Gods*, 1922) and considered his major work, in which he described his sensational adventures in Russia and Mongolia. Other popular works were *Od szczytu do otchłani* (1925; Eng. tr., *From President to Prison*, 1925) which relates Ossendowski's activities during the Russian Revolution of 1905 and his imprisonment, and the biographical novel *Lenin* (1930; Eng. tr., 1931), translated into more than 10 languages.

See: *Słownik współczesnych pisarzy polskich*, vol. 2 (1964), pp. 583–92.   S.S.

Ostaijen, Paul van (1896–1928), Belgian (Flemish) poet, was born in Antwerp, where he studied and worked as a clerk. After World War I, van Ostaijen was obliged to leave Belgium because of his activist sympathies. He went to Berlin, where he became acquainted with the members of the *Sturm* group and with dada (*see* FRENCH LITERATURE). After having fulfilled his military obligations in Germany, he returned to Belgium in 1923. He lived for a while in Antwerp and, in 1925, he moved to Brussels where he opened an art gallery. He died of tuberculosis in the sanatorium of Miavoye-Anthée. The letters he wrote from Miavoye-Anthée were published in 1932.

Van Ostaijen entertained a close friendship with a number of expressionist artists such as Oscar and Floris Jespers, Paul Joostens, and Heinrich Campendonck, as well as with writers such as Gaston Burssens and Edgar du Perron. Near the end of his life, he directed the magazine *Avontuur* with Burssens and du Perron. The three of them had previously collaborated in two other magazines, *Ruimte* and *Vlaamsche Arbeid*. As a poet and as a critic, van Ostaijen stands as one of the most eminent pioneers of the modernist movement in Flanders. He evolved rapidly from a fin-de-siècle dilettante into a humanitarian expressionist (*Het Sienjaal* [1918; The Signal]) via a short stint as a unanimist (*Music-Hall*, 1916). During his stay in Berlin, van Ostaijen was influenced by nihilist trends. Later on, he turned to a more formal, yet experimental mode of writing. Such works as *De feesten van Angst en Pijn* (1919–21; The Feasts of Anguish and Pain) and *Bezette Stad* (1921; The Occupied City) are characterized by typographical innovations and by a "concentrated" lyrical mode. These works are in many ways akin to those of August STRAMM. In subsequent volumes, van Ostaijen resorted to associative musical principles and created a genre he termed "organic" and "classical" expressionism.

Although nature played a significant role in his poetry, life in the big city constitutes one of van Ostaijen's favorite themes. The choice of this subject matter was in itself innovative in the context of Flemish and Dutch poetry. Ultimately, van Ostaijen rejects lyrical effusion as well as verses with a message, striving instead for an individualistic art in which the poem unfolds as an autonomous piece of work. By the same token, even the most simple word is endowed for van Ostaijen with a revealing power that, through its deep resonances in our unconscious, calls forth the Platonic Idea. Essays such as *Expressionisme in Vlaanderen* (1918; Expressionism in Flanders), which van Ostaijen wrote at the beginning of his career, helped him to elaborate his poetic theory. The influence of Wassily Kandinsky, *Der Sturm*, Guillaume APOLLINAIRE, and the theoreticians of cubism had a considerable effect on him. His posthumous *Gebruiksaanwijzing der Lyriek* (How to Use Lyric) distinguishes him from the surrealists (*see* FRENCH LITERATURE). For van Ostaijen, poetic consciousness is an aesthetic process, one that is always controlled.

Van Ostaijen is also known as a prose writer who deals with grotesque elements, for instance in the social satire *Vogelvrij* (1927; Outlawed). In 1924, he translated into Dutch some short stories of Franz KAFKA.

During his lifetime, van Ostaijen's work received relatively little attention. Gaston Burssens was his only "comrade in arms." But the *Vijftigers* (the poets of the 1950s) who explored experimental poetry looked upon him as one of their major forerunners. On the other hand, his critical essays and his prose in the grotesque mode reveal a strong intellectual personality. His best poems strike the reader by their simplicity, their musicality, and their plasticity. Along with Guido Gezelle and Karel van de Woestijne, van Ostaijen ranks among the greatest of Dutch-language lyric poets to emerge since romanticism.

See: E. Schoonhoven, *Paul van Ostaijen: introduction à sa poétique* (1951); G. Burssens, *Paul van Ostaijen, de dichter* (1957); H. Uytterspot, *Paul van Ostaijen en zijn Proza* (1959); P. Hadermann, *De kringen naar binnen: de dichterlike wereld van Paul van Ostaijen* (1965) and *Het vuur in de verte: Paul van Ostaijen's kunstopvattingen in het licht van de Europese Avant-garde*; G. Borgers, *Paul van Ostaijen: een documentatie* (1970).   P.H.

Ostrovsky, Nikolay Alekseyevich (1904–36), Russian novelist born in the Ukrainian village of Viliya, is venerated in the Soviet Union for his heroic life and his first novel. Born into a worker's family, Ostrovsky left school early and subsequently had many odd jobs. He worked for the Bolshevik underground during the October Revolution (1917) and became a member of the Communist Party in

1924. That same year he began a struggle with an illness that gradually paralyzed and blinded him. Bedridden, he attempted to inspire Communist ideals in young people through *Kak zakalyalas stal* (1932–34; Eng. tr., *The Making of a Hero*, 1937), a largely autobiographical novel that tells the story of Pavel Korchagin, a poor boy who overcomes insurmountable obstacles to become a writer and an ideologist. An immediate success, the novel remains very popular in the Soviet Union. *Rozhdyonnye burey* (1934–36; Eng. tr., *Born of the Storm*, 1939), another political novel, was left unfinished after Ostrovsky's death. Although the characterization is oversimplified, in both works, the narration is skillful.

See: S. A. Tregub, *Zhizn i tvorchestvo Nikolaya Ostrovskogo* (3d ed., 1975).   E.B.N.

Otero, Blas de (1916–79), Spanish poet, was born in Bilbao. He was one of the most representative and well-known writers of post-Civil War Spain. His first compositions appeared in the early 1940s, but it was not until the publication of *Ángel fieramente humano* (1950; Fiercely Human Angel) that his work made an impression on the public. At the beginning his poetry was mainly concerned with the individual's metaphysical inquiries about the self. Existentialist in nature, his religious poems were characterized by a deeply felt anguish that, although constrained to a technically perfect traditional versification, was expressed in a strong emotional tone. His voice had a lyrical force that was missing in other authors who dealt with these themes common to many Spanish poets of the period. He later grew more interested in the rest of mankind and in the external, concrete world of man in society, but he did not abandon his obsessive need to delve painfully into the mysteries of human nature. The profoundly ethical attitude underlying his social beliefs is present in *Redoble de conciencia* (1951; Drumroll of Conscience), his second book. In *Pido la paz y la palabra* (1955; I Ask for Peace and the Right to Speak) his poetry becomes truly social. Focused on the contemporary situation of Spain and on the human suffering caused by social injustice, it expresses in tense and vigorous language the indignation felt by those who are victims of an inhuman political system. This kind of committed poetry should be seen as the natural outgrowth of the poet's spiritual evolution from an individualistic search for a final meaning in his own self to the discovery of his essential similarity to the rest of mankind. A similar inspiration is to be found in his other works, *En castellano* (1960; In Spanish), *Que trata de España* (1964; About Spain), *Mientras* (In the Meantime), and *Escrito para* (1974; Written for).

Like other Spanish social poets he believed that poetry is a form of communication between men and that the writer should try to reach through his work a "vast majority" of readers. Consequently, he wrote in a clear language in which concepts and human emotions are openly and directly expressed. The most outstanding characteristics of his style are the use of idiomatic or common expressions slightly transformed for poetic effect and the reiterative structure of his poems. He wrote with great care, and the small volume of work he produced is the result of a slow creative process in which an intensely emotional life looks for the perfect poetic form to communicate its experience.

See: E. Alarcos Llorach, *La poesía de Blas de Otero* (1973); *Papeles de Son Armadans*, vol. 85 (1977).
                                              S.D.-T.

Otero Pedrayo, Ramón (1888–1975), Spanish essayist, poet, novelist, historian, and geographer, was born and died in the Galician city of Orense. After studying in

Santiago de Compostela and Madrid he returned to his ancient birthplace, where he spent most of his life. Fondly referred to as the modern patriarch of Galician letters on account of his belletrist output, Otero Pedrayo participated actively in the renaissance of his region's language (similar to Portuguese) and culture in this century. Aside from holding a doctorate in philosophy, he was an attorney, a professor of geography at the University of Santiago de Compostela, and a member of the Cortes in the 1930s. He was also one of the founders of the group "Nós" formed in 1920 with the intent of opening up Galicia to modern European currents in order to renew its folkloric and linguistic vigor.

Otero Pedrayo wrote in every literary genre: poetry, novel, theater (one closet drama), and the essay. His poetic production, though not abundant, is significant because it bridges late 19th-century symbolism and the more cultivated imagery of early 20th-century modernism. His best poems are in *Bocarribeira* (1958; Mouth of the River) and *Escolma de poesía galega* (1955; Anthology of Galician Verse). Otero's novels are written in a historical fashion with manor house settings. They mourn the passing of country nobility and archtraditional customs. Between his first novel, the tripartite *Os camiños da vida: Os señores da terra, A maorazga, O estudante* (1928; The Walks of Life: The Lords of the Land, The Heiress, The Student), and *O señorito da Reboraina* (1960; The Lord of Reboraina), his last, Otero wrote four other novels and dozens of short stories. All are steeped in the semilegendary peaceful and feudal Catholic atmosphere of a perfectly ordered and perhaps apocryphal world. In the realm of nonfiction he excelled in the essay. The amorphousness of this genre lent itself well to Otero Pedrayo's boundless enthusiasm and dedication. Of a general nature are his *Guía de Galicia* (1965; Travel Guide to Galicia), *Ensaio sobre a cultura galega* (1933; Essay on Galician Culture), *Síntese xeográfica de Galicia* (1926; Geographical Synthesis of Galicia), and *Pelexinares* (1929; Pilgrimages), in which his fondness for the idealized, extinct Galician countryside and its history are once more patent. Otero mistrusted liberalism and progress, believing that such forces would destroy forever the essential spirit of his beloved region. He collaborated in the journal *Nós* as the foreign literature critic, introducing to fellow Galicians the works of Aldous Huxley, Marcel PROUST, Rainer Maria RILKE, Goethe, Charles PÉGUY, and James Joyce, whose *Ulysses* he translated when few even knew of the novel's existence. The staggering volume of Otero's writings—his essays number in the thousands—precludes a measured and polished style; his is characterized instead by a lyrical and spontaneous fluidity. In Galician letters, Ramón Otero Pedrayo represents the major link between a generation of intellectuals, the "Nós" group, wholly dedicated to the revival of an ancestral regional culture, and today's Galicians who, thanks to their literary forefathers and a favorable political turn, are within reach of their age-old goal of a genuinely autonomous Galician culture.

See: R. Carballo Calero, *Historia da literatura galega contemporánea* (1975); X. R. Barreiro Fernández et al., *Los Gallegos* (1976); V. F. Freixanes, *Unha ducía de galegos* (1976). R.L.

Ovechkin, Valentin Vladimirovich (1904–68), Russian social commentator, was born in Taganrog. He initiated the revival of an old Russian literary genre, the *ocherk* (sketch), with his *Rayonnye budni* (1952; Workaday Life in the District). Practiced in the 19th century by Gleb Uspensky, Mikhail Saltykov-Shchedrin, and Vladimir KOROLENKO, the *ocherk* is a piece of extended reportage,

often embroidered and supplemented as a work of fiction, but always with strict adherence to verisimilitude. It can be an effective political weapon. Ovechkin (and his patron Nikita Khrushchov) wanted to paint a relatively frank picture of the appalling conditions in the post-World War II rural Soviet Union in order to arouse support in the Communist Party and the intelligentsia for a program of reform. What Ovechkin recommended was less centralized control of agriculture and more attention to the needs and expertise of the peasants themselves. Although fiction, his sketches, collected in *Izbrannye proizvedeniya* (2 vols., 1963; Selected Works), are a straightforward apologia for his own point of view. In them he contrasts Brozov, the authoritarian Party secretary who has little practical agricultural knowledge, with Martynov, his eventual replacement, a gentler man who knows and trusts the peasants. Ovechkin's works are devoid of any literary subtlety, but they were undeniably effective in rousing public opinion, and indeed in stimulating later and better works of literature (*see* RUSSIAN LITERATURE).

See: I. Vinogradov, "Derevenskiye ocherki Valentina Ovechkina," *NovM*, no. 6 (1964): 207–29; P. Carden, "Reassessing Ovechkin," in R. Freeborn et al., eds., *Russian and Slavic Literature* (1976), pp. 407–24.
G.H.

Øverland, Arnulf (1889–1968), Norwegian poet, was born in Kristiansund. He was devoted to the ideal of "forging a sword," that is, of making his poetry into a social weapon. Yet there was no sign of this commitment in his earliest verse, which showed the influence of the symbolists and which appeared in such collections as *Den ensomme fest* (1911; The Lonely Feast), *De hundrede violiner* (1912; The Hundred Violins), and *Advent* (1915). These poems are in the tragic mood of Sigbjørn OBSTFELDER, but they have a tense, compressed power that was unknown to the poets of the 1890s. They are lonely, bitter cries against the vanity of all things, expressing devotion to the dream that alone satisfies. Øverland's poems were acclaimed by critics for their fastidious restraint of form, their elimination of all rhetoric, and their truly monumental use of simple, unadorned words. These qualities remained characteristic of his verse.

World War I and the peace of Versailles awoke in Øverland an awareness of social injustice. In *Brød og vin* (1919; Bread and Wine), he admonishes his readers to fight for freedom and justice. Turning from the cultivation of his own soul, he became a rather obstreperous warrior of the extreme Left. His collections of poetry from the late 1920s and the 1930s are not one-sided social commentaries, for there is love and beauty in them, but they display a growing faith in the mystic value of sharing life with one's fellow men. This religious devotion to the ideal of socialism became a substitute for the Christianity against which Øverland turned all his scorn. He repeatedly appropriated religion's own vocabulary and form, even to the extent of creating a socialistic ritual in the volume *Ord i alvor til det norske folk* (1940; Words in Earnest to the Norwegian People). From the very beginning Øverland had been aware of the nature of the new regime in Germany, and in flaming poetic prophecies he tried to awaken his countrymen to the menace of Nazism. In *Den røde front* (1937; The Red Front) he published his famous indictment of and warnings against Nazi Germany—"Guernica" and "Du må ikke sove" (You Must Not Sleep). After the German invasion of Norway in April 1940, he continued to heap scorn on the Nazis, and to exhort his countrymen to continue the fight. These efforts earned him several years in a German concentration camp, a punishment he miraculously survived. During those years he became, together with Nordahl GRIEG, a symbol of Norway's will to resist. His poetry from the war years was collected and published in *Vi overlever alt* (1945; We Will Survive) and *Tilbake til livet* (1946; Back to Life).

After World War II, Øverland married for the second time and became a father. A new mellowness entered his poetic world remaining with him until his death, but even in his later collections he could burn with the old passion against social and political injustice, and against the Creator, whose existence he denied but who nevertheless remained his antagonist. His later collections include *Fiskeren og hans sjel* (1950; The Fisherman and his Soul); *Sverdet bak døren* (1956; The Sword behind the Door), and *På Nebo Bjerg* (1962; On Mount Nebo).

See: O. Gelsted, *Arnulf Øverland* (1946); D. Haakonsen, *Arnulf Øverland og den etiske realisme* (1966).

E.H.

P

Paço d'Arcos, Joaquim, pseud. of Joaquim Belford Correia da Silva (1908–79), Portuguese novelist, dramatist, essayist, and poet, was born in Lisbon, the son of Vice Admiral Carlos Eugénio Correia da Silva, first count of Paço de Arcos. He has traveled widely and held several public offices, including that of chief of press services in the Ministry of Foreign Affairs. His literary production has been copious, and many of his novels have been translated. A number of them reflect his travels: *Herói derradeiro* (1933; Last Hero), his first novel, takes place in Mozambique; *Diário dum emigrante* (1936; Diary of an Emigrant) is set in Brazil. *Amores e viagens de Pedro Manoel* (1935; Pedro Manoel's Amours and Travels), *Neve sobre o mar* (1942; Snow over the Sea), and *O navio dos mortos e outras novelas* (1952; The Ship of the Dead and Other Tales) are collections of novellas and short stories. International settings continue in "Evangeline," in *Neve sobre o mar*, which deals with a refugee from the Spanish Civil War living in the United States. The novelist's most ambitious project has been a series of novels he calls "Crónica da vida lisboeta" (Chronicle of Lisbonese Life), beginning with *Ana Paula* (1938). In the series, the modern political history of Portugal forms the background for individual human dramas. Thus, *Espelho de três faces* (1950; Three-Part Mirror) portrays the country after World War II, with its refugee Germans, political prisoners, monarchists, and Communists. Rightists and leftists pursue their own goals, frustrating the hero in his effort to humanize technology and attenuate the social problems of Portugal. *Memórias duma nota de banco* (1962; Eng. tr., *Memoirs of a Bank Note,* 1968) pulls together the cosmopolitan and Lisbonese themes: like a passive picaresque hero, a banknote describes its various owners and the society in which they move. Unifying this episodic plot is the endeavor to formulate a consistent and compassionate view of man. A more recent novel, *Cela 27* (1965; Cell 27), combines ideological conflict and personal jealousy in a story of two women prisoners condemned to each other's company.

Paço d'Arcos has written about the art of the novel in *O romance e o romancista* (1943; Novel and Novelist) and *Confissão e defesa do romancista* (1946; Confession and Defense of the Novelist). Among his works for the theater are *Paulina vestida de azul* (1948; Pauline Dressed in Blue) and *Antepassados, vendem-se* (1970; Ancestors for Sale). His poetry is collected in *Poemas imperfeitos* (1952; Eng. tr., *Nostalgia,* 1960). He began to publish his memoirs, but death prevented him from completing his account—*Memórias da minha vida e do meu tempo* (3 vols., 1973–79; Memoirs of My Life and Times).

See: R. Hilton, "Joaquim Paço d'Arcos and Contemporary Portuguese Literature," *Hispania* 36 (February 1953): 85–87; A. Álvaro Dória, *Joaquim Paço d'Arcos* (1962). T.Br.

Paemel, Monika van (1945–), Belgian novelist, was born in Poesele. The rural atmosphere in which she grew up permeates her work. Her first novel, *Amazone met het blauwe voorhoofd* (1971; The Blue-Crested Amazonian Parrot), received a literary prize and revealed her persistent themes: the submersion in memory, the paradise (and the inferno) of childhood, the simultaneity of levels of consciousness, and an extremely keen perception of sensations. Her writing is characterized by the absence of lyricism and of description, much like the "neue Sachlichkeit," but it also suggests the terseness of Franz KAFKA. A second book, *De Confrontatie* (1974; The Confrontation), sets forth two faces of femininity (Zoe and Mirjam), complementary yet opposed, in a dialogue that contains elements of a private diary. Here again appear the rejection of an ensnaring world, the memories of childhood, and the descent into the inner self. *Marguerite* (1976) evokes, by means of a painting in the Museum of Arles, the troubled postwar period and a grandmother who is authoritarian as well as sensitive and eccentric. Through this fascinating character, van Paemel explores and seeks to define her own being. This same quest for the self through parental relationships and this same obsession with truth appear in a fourth novel, *De Vermaledijde Vaders* (1978; These Cursed Fathers).

Although van Paemel's style is characterized by a density approaching aphorism and by a rejection of facile quaintness, poetic expression is not excluded. The complex structure of her works is built upon levels of awareness and of memory that combine without ever giving the reader the impression of arbitrariness or of mere playfulness. This uncompromising author is one of the most promising figures in contemporary Flemish literature.

R.Mo.

Pagnol, Marcel (1895–1974), French playwright, film director, and novelist, was born in Aubagne, near Marseille, where his father was a schoolteacher. He studied first at the Lycée of Marseille, then at the University of Montpellier. Having obtained his *licence-és lettres,* he taught English in several secondary schools in the French provinces, and finally at the Lycée Condorcet in Paris. He remained there until 1929, when he resigned in order to devote all his time to the stage and the cinema. His first play, *Jazz* (1926), brought him a measure of success, but real fame came with *Topaze* (1928; Eng. tr., 1930), a sharp yet witty and amusing satire on political corruption. It was, however, in Marseille that Pagnol found the inspiration for his greatest and lasting triumphs with his trilogy *Marius* (1929; Eng. tr., 1957), *Fanny* (1932), and *César* (1936). Set around the old harbor, the three plays present the same characters caught in their everyday occupations, embroiled in a dozen petty intrigues, boasting, talking loudly in their earthy, picturesque language, fiercely proud of their city, yet sentimental and rather likable. From the same vein, Pagnol drew *Cigalon* (1935; Eng. tr., 1948) and *Merlusse* (1935), both written directly for the screen. In collaboration with Jean GIONO, he adapted many of his own and Giono's works to the screen (where some of their interpreters were Raimu and Fernandel), producing such extremely popular films as *César* (1936), *Regain* (1937; Harvest), *La Femme du boulanger* (1938; The Baker's Wife), and *La Fille du puisatier* (1940; The Well-Digger's Daughter).

Pagnol's three-volume autobiography, *Souvenirs d'enfance*—*La Gloire de mon père* (1957, *Le Château de ma mère* (1958; Eng. tr. of both, *The Days Were Too Short*, 1960), and *Le Temps des secrets* (1960; Eng. tr., *The Time of Secrets*, 1962)—offers abundant information on his life, upbringing, and his family, combined with lively descriptions of Provençal scenes and customs. Sharply delineated Provençal types also appear in Pagnol's novel *L'Eau des collines* (1962; The Water of the Hills), the story of a city-bred man who wants to succeed as a farmer, struggling against both the elements and envious and clannish neighbors. Although he fails, he is revenged after his death by his daughter. The novel abounds in delightful evocations, often touching, sometimes humorous, always authentic, of loves and hatreds in a little village near Aubagne. Incensed by the lack of understanding and pretentiousness of professional critics, Pagnol inveighed against them in the pungent satire *Critique des critiques* (1948; Criticism of Critics). Pagnol also wrote on the nature of the comic, in *Notes sur le rire* (1950; Notes on Laughter), and on the technique of the cinema, in *Cahiers du film*.

See: M. Achard, *Marcel Pagnol, mon ami* (1964).

F.V.

Palacio Valdés, Armando (1853–1938), Spanish critic and novelist, was born in Entralgo (Asturias). He was from a well-to-do middle-class family (his father was a lawyer, his mother a landowner) and received his education in Oviedo, the capital of Asturias and land of his ancestors as well as the setting of many of his novels. During his school days there he developed a lasting friendship with Leopoldo ALAS. Their philosophical views were similar, and after leaving Oviedo both studied law at Madrid. They lived through the liberal revolution of 1868, which confirmed them in their liberalism, although Palacio Valdés became a conservative later on. Regardless of their personal similarities, their literary work is quite different. Palacio Valdés was a less biting and more humorous social critic than Alas, and although his fiction outranks Alas's in quantity, the opposite could be said about its quality. The opinion that Armando Palacio Valdés is not one of Spain's greatest novelists was voiced repeatedly during his lifetime in and outside Spain. He is, on the other hand, more than respectable in comparison with lesser writers.

Palacio Valdés began his writing career as a critic. He wrote four volumes of criticism: *Los oradores del Ateneo* (1878; The Atheneum Speakers), *Los novelistas españoles* (1878), *Nuevo viaje al Parnaso* (1879; Parnassus Revisited), and, in collaboration with Leopoldo Alas, *La literatura en 1881* (1882). Rather than a born critic, he was a well-read man whose interest in the world of letters and fine literary sensibility characterize his impressionistic criticism. He mixed his reactions to texts with occasional reflections on the creative process that no doubt derived from his own experience as a fiction writer. This is the most valuable aspect of his criticism, especially when considered in conjunction with the prologues to some of his novels and his 1921 acceptance speech to the Royal Spanish Academy of the Language.

His ideas about the novel reflect a moderate personality. He disliked realism as too crude and was wary of the excesses of idealism, preferring a middle ground. For him, the novel was above all art as an embellishment of reality and should be leavened with humor. During his long career he touched on a variety of themes and often used his native Asturias as a setting. His first novel, *El señorito Octavio* (1881), is weak, but in *Marta y María* (1883; Eng. tr., 1886) he scored his first success. A novel rich in observation and minute character studies, it holds the reader's interest despite its skimpy action. *El idilio de un enfermo* (1883; The Idyll of an Ill Man) also suffers from insufficient action. With *José* (1885; Eng. tr., 1901), however, Palacio Valdés enters his best creative period: the action is intense, and the story, the love between the fisherman José and Elisa, is told very effectively. This time the artistic equilibrium is threatened by an excess of sentimentality, which also runs through *Riverita* (1886) and *Maximina* (1887), although the theme of the latter, the love of a couple, is movingly presented. *El cuarto poder* (1888; Eng. tr., *Fourth Estate*, 1901), an evocation of the world of journalism, is a fine collection of ironic scenes. *La hermana San Sulpicio* (1889; Sister Saint Sulpice), set in Andalusia, is his best-known novel. Its colorful detail shows Palacio Valdés at his peak: witty, lavish, in full control of compositional problems, and able easily to develop the story of the love between Gloria, a would-be nun, and the doctor who finally wins her over to matrimony. *La espuma* (1891; The Foam) introduces the new techniques of naturalism. In this work the wealthy class of Madrid is presented in contrast to the mineworkers. *La fe* (1892; Faith) is an attack on false mysticism. *La alegría del capitán Ribot* (1899; Eng. tr., *Joy of Captain Ribot*, 1900) tells of the platonic love between a sailor and a married woman and again shows Palacio Valdés in good form, balancing his tendency to study manners, here of Valencia, with sound character analysis. Two less important fictional works are worth mentioning: *La aldea perdida* (1903; The Lost Village), a poetic novel, and *Tristán o el pesimismo* (1906), a psychological novel and precursor of the pessimistic subjectivism of 20th century fiction. Four volumes of short stories, his memoirs of his youth—*La novela del novelista* (1921; The Novelist's Novel)—and some historical works round out his production. His value today rests mainly on his natural style, his fine humor, and his ability to create atmosphere. His characters, although somewhat superficial, delighted millions in his own time, as his novels were translated into many languages. The appeal of his novels continues to rest on their relaxing lack of complexity.

See: J. M. Roca Franquesa, *Palacio Valdés: técnica novelística y credo estético* (1951); M. Pascual Rodríguez, *Armando Palacio Valdés* (1976).   G.Gu.

Palamas, Kostis (1859–1943), Greek poet and essayist, was born in Patras and grew up in Missolonghi. He attended the University of Athens and later served as its general secretary (1897–1928). He was the leading figure of the "Generation of 1880," a group of poets and intellectuals dedicated to the popular tradition and to the establishment of the spoken idiom (the demotic) as the language of literature and of national life in general. In this area, Palamas followed and fulfilled the ideals of Dionysios Solomos, whose work was a milestone in the revival of the demotic literary tradition. Palamas was a man of great learning, a wise and venerated cultural leader, and a stalwart polemicist against the Greek literary establishment that adhered to the archaic idiom (the purist) and to other anachronistic or moribund cultural fashions. He devoted his creative energies to the regeneration of Greek life by bringing into his writings the living elements of his tradition as well as the heritage of Western Europe. At the same time, he always fused his personal passions and visions with the external, historical reality that he absorbed. Together with Angelos SIKELIANOS, who succeeded him as spokesman for the spiritual consciousness of the Greek people, Palamas was a supreme singer and celebrator of the Hellenic spirit.

Among Palamas's most important works are: *Tragoudia tis patridos mou* (1886; Songs of My Country), his first collection of poetry in the demotic; *Ta matia tis psychis mou* (1892; The Eyes of My Soul); *Iamvi kai anapaisti* (1897; Iambs and Anapests); *O taphos* (1898; Eng. tr., *The Grave,* 1930), a hauntingly beautiful lament for the death of his beloved little boy; *Thanatos pallikariou* (1891; Eng. tr., *A Man's Death,* 1934), a novella; *Trisevgeni* (1903; Eng. tr., *Royal Blossom or Trisevyene,* 1923), a poetic drama that, like *A Man's Death,* exalts the living forces of the demotic tradition; *Vomi* (1915; Altars); and *Ta dekatetrasticha* (1919; The Sonnets).

Towering above these are three masterpieces. The first is *I asalefti zoi* (1904; Eng. tr. of part 1, *Life Immovable,* 1919; Eng. tr. of part 2, *A Hundred Voices, and Other Poems,* 1921), which contains some of Palamas's most exquisite short lyrics as well as longer poems expressing his chief psychological, social, and metaphysical concerns. The second is *O dodekalogos tou gyftou* (1907; Eng. trs., *The Twelve Words of the Gypsy,* 1964; *The Twelve Lays of the Gypsy,* 1969; *The Twelve Words of the Gypsy,* 1974), a long epico-lyric poem embodying in its hero-symbol, the gypsy, many of the central themes and ideals of Palamas's entire oeuvre, such as freedom, individualism, and artistic creation in relation to Hellenic reality. The third is *I flogera tou vasilia* (1910; Eng. tr., *The King's Flute,* 1967), a historical epic recreating Greece's perennial convulsions and achievements as experienced by the poem's hero, the Byzantine emperor Basil II. In this work, Palamas sings some of his most beautiful hymns to living Greece and to eternal Hellenic values. Palamas's remarkable insights into the Greek world, more than his innovations in poetic form, account for his overwhelming influence on subsequent writers. Although his works often appear rhetorical and longwinded to modern taste, they contain some of the most beautiful verse in the Greek language. Palamas's *Apanta* (Complete Works) are in the process of being published (1960–).

See: A. E. Phoutrides, "A New World-Poet," Introduction to K. Palamas, *Life Immovable* (1919); T. Maskaleris, *Kostis Palamas* (1972).   T.M.

Palazzeschi, Aldo, pseud. of Aldo Giurlani (1885–1974), Italian poet and fiction writer, was born in Florence of Umbrian stock, the only son of a well-to-do merchant and his wife. After completing his training for a career as an accountant, Palazzeschi enrolled in a school for acting also attended by Marino MORETTI, destined to be a lifelong friend. Four years on the stage were sufficient. Palazzeschi left the theater in 1906 and turned to writing. Unlike many Italians of the middle class, he did not welcome World War I. He served as a common soldier when called to arms but saw no combat. Palazzeschi was by nature an apolitical man, taking no part in public affairs. He maintained an undisguised if unaggressive aversion to fascism but had no specific party loyalties. Indeed for Palazzeschi, his art was his life. Except for a brief association with *Lacerba* in the years preceding World War I, he had little to do with journalism; he practiced no profession (his only doctorate is honorary, conferred by the University of Padua in 1962); and he never married. For many years he maintained residences in Venice,

Paris, and in Rome, where he finally made his permanent home.

Palazzeschi's first publications were in verse. *Cavalli bianchi* (White Horses) appeared in 1905 and was followed by four other volumes within the decade. His poems were collected in *Poesie* (1930). Palazzeschi's lyrics have a recognizable affinity with the *crepuscolari* (Moretti and Sergio Corazzini [1887–1907] were good friends of Palazzeschi) and the *futuristi* (*see* ITALIAN LITERATURE); Palazzeschi was for a time openly associated with the latter movement but broke with it in 1914. Critics have found influences of the French symbolists in these poems, yet they have a very distinctive quality in which ethereal fantasy is combined with a certain element of mischievous mockery set to simple, incantatory rhythms. Palazzeschi's first notable work in prose is the brief and somewhat enigmatic *Il codice di Perelà* (1911, Eng. tr., *Perelà, The Man of Smoke*, 1936), of which the protagonist, literally fashioned of smoke, is destined to undergo comic, tragic, and perhaps instructive adventures in this world of coarser fiber. *Perelà* is a kind of *grottesco* (*see* ITALIAN LITERATURE), yet although resemblances between it and the works of Luigi PIRANDELLO are not lacking, in texture and manner it is unique. *Le sorelle Materassi* (1934; Eng. tr., *Materassi Sisters*, 1953) is of a very different nature. Written in a somewhat academic prose, it is a realistic story—with moral overtones—concerning two old maids and their obsession with a youth who exploits them. Palazzeschi's other works of note are *I fratelli Cuccoli* (1948; The Cuccoli Brothers), which presents—again with a touch of surrealistic mischief—the vicissitudes of a bachelor adoptive father; *Roma* (1953; Eng. tr., *Rome*, 1965), the somewhat melodramatic account of an aristocratic Roman family beleaguered by contemporary democracy; and the collection of short stories *Il palio dei buffi* (1936; The Parade of the Odd Fellows), the title of which is self-explanatory. Like Moretti, whose example may have inspired him, Palazzeschi also wrote personal memoirs, such as the evocative *Stampe dell'Ottocento* (1932; 19th-Century Prints), and *Tre imperi . . . mancati* (1945; Three Empires—That Failed), in which he speaks eloquently of his youthful experiences.

Palazzeschi had a long literary career and was active until the end. *Via delle cento stelle* (Street of the Hundred Stars) appeared in 1972. He always wrote to please himself. In a man of less humane nature this attitude could have been disastrous. In Palazzeschi's case it resulted in the production of a number of unique artifacts, recognizably responsive to the fashions of his times yet somehow standing apart. Historians of the narrative will never be able to overlook *Le sorelle Materassi*, and such lyrics as "Rio Bo" and "Palazzo Rari Or" will continue to charm readers for generations to come.

See: L. Russo, in *I narratori* (1958); G. Pullini, *Aldo Palazzeschi* (1965); G. Spagnoletti, *Palazzeschi* (1971); S. Giovanardi, *La critica e Palazzeschi* (1976); F. P. Memmo, *Invito alla lettura di Aldo Palazzeschi* (1976).   T.G.B.

Palm, Göran (1931–), Swedish essayist and poet, was born in Uppsala. He also studied in Uppsala, where his father was a minister. Palm made a name for himself during the 1950s by editing his own literary magazine, *Upptakt*. His impressive knowledge, coupled with an intellectual playfulness presented in an energetic prose, made him a welcome contributor to other journals. He soon realized, however, that the poets and the literary critics wrote for each other, and his aim became to write simply and concretely in order to be a voice for the broader public. Palm began to write poetry that could be easily understood, and his program known as *nyenkel-heten* (the new simplicity) won many followers. During the early 1960s he published two collections, *Hundens besök* (1961; The Dog's Visit) and *Världen ser dig* (1964; The World Sees You). One of his recurring themes is the insufficiency of the worn-out language: "The air is thick of used up words which hinder new ones." "Själens furir," the first poem he ever worked on is included in *Världen ser dig*, and it deals with the conscience that society makes human beings internalize and that then presses so many divergent demands on them. Conscience itself has become secularized. It is the world, not God, that sees us. Consequently, are human beings responsible to the world? That "I" am a part of "them" and "they" are a part of "me" is a complicated reality that Palm has tried to express as concretely as he could without sounding deep and learned. Driven by his social conscience, Palm then wrote *En orättvis betraktelse* (1966; Eng. tr., *As Others See Us*, 1968), which has an explosive effect. In the book he depicts the behavior of the industrialized countries as seen through the eyes of the people in the developing nations. With that book Palm radicalized a whole generation. He continued the same line of examination in *Indoktrineringen i Sverige* (1968; Indoctrination in Sweden) and also in *Vad kan man göra* (1969; What Can Be Done?). As a personal answer, Palm felt he had to do more than to write books. For a year he worked in a factory. The result was two books: one of straight, realistic reportage, *Ett år på LM* (1972; A Year at LM), which states: "If you want to get far away from the revolution then take a job at L. M. Ericsson"; the other, a long prose poem, *Varför ha nätterna inga namn?* (1971; Why Don't We Call the Nights by Name?), in which Palm recapitulates his development ideologically, linguistically, and morally and in which his words have specific weight when he says: "My conviction becomes again my own." Palm has also published *Sweden Writes* (1965; together with Lars Bäckström) and translations of (with introductions to) the works of Amilcar Cabral and Tadeusz Różewicz. *Modern Swedish Poetry in Translation*, ed. by G. Harding and A. Hollo, includes a selection of Palm's poetry on pp. 171–82.

See: P. O. Enquist, ed., *Sextiotalskritik* (1966), pp. 300–42, which includes important essays by G. Palm; K. E. Lagerlöf, *Samtal med 60-talister* (1965), pp. 47–58; T. Broström, *Moderne svensk litteratur 1940–1972* (1973), pp. 181–85; K. E. Lagerlöf, *Strömkantringens år och andra essäer, om den nya litteraturen (1975)*, pp. 143–45; J. Stenkvist, *Svensk litteratur 1870–1970*, vol. 3 (1975), pp. 158–61. B.K.S.

Paludan, Jacob (1896–1975), Danish novelist, was born in Copenhagen. A visit to Ecuador and the United States in 1920 and 1921 led to Paludan's renunciation of American materialism and superficiality. This critical attitude is—in a somewhat abstract form—evident in his literary debut, the emigrant novel *De vestlige Veje* (1922; The Western Roads). In *Søgelys* (1923; Searchlight), the satire on the Danish life-style is not only more effective but also more tied to the period, the "century of mediocrity," or 1922, to be more specific. Paludan attacks not only the materialistic superficiality of the people but also the expressionistic poetry and female emancipation of the 1920s. Not until *Fugle omkring Fyret* (1925; Eng. tr., *Birds Around the Light*, 1928) does Paludan display his great talent by artistically reshaping a current topic. The dramatic action of this social novel—the destruction of nature through technology—symbolizes the love story of the novel itself, as well as the post-World War I period's devastating effect upon humanity. In his next work, *Mar-*

kerne modnes (1927; The Ripening Fields), a tragic novel about an artist, Paludan's ability to create contrasts and sharply defined types is further developed. All his ideas and inspirations are gathered together in *Jørgen Stein* (1932–33; Eng. tr., 1966), the most important Bildungsroman of recent Danish literature. The novel portrays the attitudes of three generations to the cultural breakdown that occurred during World War I: Jørgen's father is lost when his conservative, national world breaks down; Otto, his brother, becomes involved in monetary speculations leading to materialism and suicide; whereas Jørgen himself is able neither to accept these possibilities nor find new ideals. He goes through a process, from the storm-and-stress period of youth via failure to resignation in a life of duty and responsibility, based on a pessimistic insight into everything's relativity. *Jørgen Stein* is Paludan's last novel. Like Tom KRISTENSEN, he concentrated thereafter upon writing critical essays dealing primarily with nature and art, philosophy and religion.

See: E. Frederiksen, *Jacob Paludan* (1966). S.H.R.

Panduro, Leif (1923–77), Danish author, was born in Frederiksberg, near Copenhagen. He became a dentist in 1947 and lived in Sweden between 1949 and 1956. Like Villy SØRENSEN, by whom he was influenced, Panduro described psychological and social abuses both within and outside people. These themes are found in the monologue novel *Øgledage* (1961; Saurian Days), in which the saurians symbolize the suppressed taboos in society as well as in individuals. Puberty, that time in life when youth capitulates to the well-organized adult world, is depicted in Panduro's first major success, *Rend mig i traditionerne* (1958; Eng. tr., *Kick Me in the Traditions*, 1961). Inspired by J. D. Salinger's *The Catcher in the Rye*, Panduro humorously describes a young boy's escape from school, his escapades in the city, and his imprisonment in a mental institution where he refuses to let himself become "normalized." Characters from this novel are also found in *Fern fra Danmark* (1963; Fern from Denmark), initiating the identity question. The novel's main character suffers from amnesia and refuses to accept the role in society that everybody wants to impose upon him. Panduro's next novels, in which he moves from puberty to the schizophrenia of the adult world, are written in traditional prose like all his newer works, with the narrator—the "I" of the books—explaining the extent of his alienation from the self. *Fejltagelsen* (1964; The Mistake) portrays a hypochondriac who has escaped from the present into sickness, an escape into irresponsibility. This neurotic person is portrayed with sympathy, whereas the normal characters are depicted as a deterrent to others. The insanity of normality is also the theme of the exciting, action-packed novel *Daniels anden verden* (1970; The Other World of Daniel), which, like *Amatørerne* (1972; The Amateurs), deals with the contrast between established society, that is, the middle-aged generation, and the revolutionary youth, which stands for necessary changes and a new way of life. *Den ubetænksomme elsker* (1973; The Thoughtless Lover) is both a variation of the theme of normal-abnormal and a captivating psychological thriller about love and responsibility, as in Panduro's last novel, *Høfeber* (1975; Hay Fever). In addition, Panduro wrote revue texts, film scripts, and the short-story collection *Den bedste af alle verdener* (1974; The Best of All Worlds), and a large number of television plays, which reiterate the themes of his novels. *Farvel, Thomas* (1968; Goodbye, Thomas), *I Adams verden* (1973; In Adam's World), and *Louises hus* (1977; Louise's House) are culminations of Scandinavian television drama.

See: J. C. Jørgensen, *Leif Panduro* (1973); J. E. Tiemroth, *Panduro og tredvernes drøm* (1977). S.H.R.

Panero Torbado, Leopoldo (1909–62), Spanish poet, was born and died in Astorga, in the province of León. He completed a degree in law and later in life was book critic for *Blanco y Negro*, editor of *Correo Literario*, and editorial director of the Spanish edition of *Reader's Digest*.

Panero wrote poetry in the late 1920s and throughout the 1930s, although this work did not appear in book form until much later, some of it posthumously in anthologies prepared by the poet's son, Juan Luis. The early poems were written under the sway of the surrealists and the poets of the Generation of 1927, in particular Jorge GUILLÉN, whose *Cántico* Panero had memorized. His *La estancia vacía* (The Empty Room) was published in the journal *Escorial* in 1944, and *Versos del Guadarrama* (1930–39; Verses from the Guadarrama Mountains) first appeared in 1945 in *Fantasía*. He was awarded the Fastenrath Prize of the Royal Spanish Academy of the Language for *Escrito a cada instante* (1949; Written at Each Instant), his best-known work, and the National Prize for Literature for the polemical *Canto personal* (1953), a response to Pablo Neruda's *Canto general*.

Panero belongs to the insufficiently defined Generation of 1936, which includes such poets as Germán BLEIBERG, Miguel HERNÁNDEZ, Luis ROSALES, and Luis Felipe Vivanco, a group that reacted against the pure poetry and the experimentalism that preceded them, only to see their own brief moment followed by the post-Civil War poetry of intense social commitment. The Generation of 1936, not an innovative group, was characterized by moderation and tolerance and a return to classic simplicity after the hermeticism of the 1927 group. As the latter identified with the 17th-century baroque master Luis de Góngora, the new group swung to his Golden Age "opposite," the Petrarchan, bucolic, 16th-century Garcilaso de la Vega. Their journal bore his name.

The fundamental note in Panero's work is a "new humanism," successor to the famous "dehumanization" (Ortega's term) of the great poets who were at the height of their maturity when Panero began to write. With him and such fellow poets as Rosales, the Christian God, whom Juan Ramón JIMÉNEZ, Federico GARCÍA LORCA, Jorge Guillén, and others had replaced with art, returned to poetry. Panero was concerned with a daily, lived reality rooted in a specific time and place. His poetry expresses man's hopeful search for lasting values in the face of the irreparable passage of time. His peaceful but melancholy rural poetry, in which his family is very much present, insistently posits the living man behind it. His major themes are the landscape of León, the search for God, the permanence of personal relations, and the power of love.

See: *CHA* 187–88 (July-August 1965), entire issue; E. Connolly, *Leopoldo Panero: la poesía de la esperanza* (1969); C. Aller, *La poesía personal de Leopoldo Panero* (1976). H.L.B.

Panova, Vera Fyodorovna (1905–73), Soviet Russian writer, was born in Rostov-on-Don, the daughter of a bank clerk. In 1922 she joined the staff of a small local newspaper and pursued a journalistic career until 1946. Her partially autobiographical novel *Sentimentalny roman* (1958; A Sentimental Story) reflects some of her experiences as a young reporter. Her later years were spent in Leningrad.

Panova began to write plays in 1933 but, by her own admission, did not succeed as a playwright. In 1946 she published a short novel, *Sputniki* (Eng. tr., *The Train*, 1948), which describes a group of people working in a military hospital train during World War II. This plotless, "open-ended" story is composed of series of episodes and pen portraits in which Panova explores the nuances of human relationships made poignant by the wartime situation. She merits a comparison with Anton CHEKHOV for her ability to create dramatic tension despite a minimum of action. In 1947, Panova wrote *Kruzhilikha* (Eng. tr., *The Factory*, 1949), a novel of uneven quality about an industrial enterprise. Its artistically strongest element is the portrayal of Listopad, the manager, a domineering, egocentric, yet likeable man. Critics following the Communist Party line were annoyed that Listopad could not be clearly categorized as a negative or positive hero, and they chided Panova for her "ambiguity." In *Yasny bereg* (1949; Bright Shore) Panova depicted everyday life on a collective farm. The sequel to this mediocre work is *Seryozha* (1955; Eng. tr., *Time Walked*, 1957), a first-rate story about a little boy. With extraordinary sensitivity and gentle humor Panova revealed in *Seryozha* the inner world of a child, his happy and painful experiences. Her short stories "Valya" and "Volodya" (1959) are penetrating studies of children and adolescents uprooted by war. Panova wrote several other novels and stories about contemporary life (*see* RUSSIAN LITERATURE) as well as some historical novellas about Russian princes and saints. A number of her works have been filmed.

Panova was not a great writer, but her works are very popular with Soviet readers because she wrote with sympathy and understanding about ordinary people and their personal, social, and professional problems. She was unpretentious and disarmingly sincere, and she courageously retained her integrity throughout the oppressive years of Stalinism.

See: V. Alexandrova, "Vera Panova," in *A History of Soviet Literature* (New York, 1963), pp. 272–83; Z. Boguslavskaya, *Vera Panova: ocherk tvorchestva* (Moscow, 1963). I.H.C.

Panzini, Alfredo (1863–1939), Italian novelist, critic, lexicographer, and teacher, was born in Senigallia. He pursued classical studies at the Marco Foscarini Academy in Venice and literary and philological studies in Bologna, where he was a student of Giosuè Carducci (1835–1907). For many years, Panzini taught in secondary schools in Milan and Rome. A prolific writer, he contributed to numerous publications, notably *Nuova antologia* and *Corriere della sera*. In 1905, he published his *Dizionario moderno delle parole che non si trovano nei dizionari comuni* (A Modern Dictionary of Words Not Found in Ordinary Dictionaries), which is now in its 10th edition. Textbooks, criticism, novels, and short stories followed in profusion. He was a member of the Italian Academy.

Profoundly imbued with classical culture, Panzini endeavored to come to grips with the cynical, mechanically oriented, noisy, and unattractive bourgeois world. Thanks to his unwavering faith in a harmonious world of virtue, beauty, and heroic deeds, he could view the 20th century with a gentle irony and genial humor that only in later years became tinged with acerbity. He was essentially a moralist after the fashion of Jean de la Bruyère, an observer who penned deft, memorable vignettes of all kinds and conditions of men. His stories and novels. are flimsy in plot and development, but he is less a novelist than an essayist or fabulist who discourses with learning, elegance, and often delightful humor upon mankind and its foibles. His characters and plots are, for the most part, either projections of his own states of mind or outrightly autobiographical. His style is characterized by an inherent lyricism coupled with an exquisite sense of order and balance. Yet at the same time it is subtly academic; Panzini's appeal is to the lettered reader rather than to the general public.

Apart from the *Dizionario*, school anthologies, and treatises on rhetoric and stylistics, he produced estimable critical essays on such subjects as macaronic poetry, Matteo Boiardo (1441–94), Carducci, and Giacomo Leopardi (1798–1837). Outstanding among his novels and collections of short stories are *Il libro dei morti e dei vivi* (1893; Book of the Dead and Living), *La lanterna di Diogene* (1907; Diogenes' Lantern), *Santippe* (1914), *Il viaggio di un povero letterato* (1919; Voyage of a Poor Man of Letters), *Il mondo è rotondo* (1921; The World Is Round), *I tre re col Gelsomino, buffone del re* (1927; The Three Kings with Gelsomino, the King's Buffoon), and *Il bacio di Lesbia* (1937; Lesbia's Kiss).

See: A. Borlenghi, in *Narratori dell'Ottocento e del primo Novecento* (1966); G. De Rienzo, *Alfredo Panzini* (1968). G.P.O.

Papini, Giovanni (1881–1956), Italian critic, novelist, and poet, was born in Florence. His avant-garde polemics made him one of the most influential Italian writers of the first quarter of the 20th century. Papini's dramatic shifts from pragmatism to futurism (*see* ITALIAN LITERATURE), from atheism to Roman Catholicism, from severe judgments of contemporary literary life to appreciative historical reappraisals of Italian national and literary values reflect a tortured effort to give expression to the contradictory and often paradoxical impulses in his nature. With Giuseppe PREZZOLINI he was cofounder of the short-lived but important literary periodical *Leonardo* (1903–07), in which he attacked with relentless energy the positivist philosophy then permeating Italian literature and politics. In 1913 he launched the journal *Lacerba*, attracting to it many young writers. His contributions to other important journals such as *Hermes, Il regno,* and *La voce* inspired an entire generation of new authors.

Papini saw in the contemporary scene a fossilization of values, an uncritical veneration for the past, against which he lashed out both as a journalist and as an author. His vitriolic style, always rooted in authoritative and informed judgments, is the keynote of such works as *Il crepuscolo dei filosofi* (1906; The Twilight of the Philosophers), *Il pilota cieco* (1907; The Blind Pilot), and *Chiudamo le scuole* (1919; Let Us Close the Schools). In the autobiographical *Un uomo finito* (1912; Eng. tr., *The Failure,* 1924), his restless spirit found its ideal expression in an honest appraisal of the paradoxes of his own nature—the frenetic search for knowledge, deep dissatisfaction with prevailing notions, and aggressive idealism. This memorable account of his psychological and cultural identity assured Papini's fame.

In denouncing academic traditionalism, Papini spared no one—not even such eminent figures as Benedetto CROCE. Dedicated to demolishing cultural deadwood, Papini went beyond the obvious to the basic philosophical and scientific notions of his time, attacking them with the same forcefulness that he displayed in his judgments of contemporary poetry and prose. His critical essays, vigorously iconoclastic and always intensely personal in their intellectual commitment, are, in spite of a certain boastful self-indulgence, unerring in their insights.

Typical of a more traditional assessment of Italian literature is his ambitious *Storia della letteratura italiana: Duecento e Trecento* (1937; History of Italian Literature: The 13th and 14th Centuries), the only volume of a large-scale project to appear. In this same category stands his sympathetic portrait of the great Italian poet-critic Giosuè Carducci (1835–1907), *L'uomo Carducci* (1918; The Man

Carducci). His mature years are marked by his conversion to Roman Catholicism and a defense of national roots, evident in *Storia di Cristo* (1921; Eng. tr., *Life of Christ,* 1923) and *Italia mia* (1939; My Italy). The Catholic commitment is strong in such later works as *Il diavolo, appunti per una futura diabologia* (1953; Eng. tr., *The Devil,* 1954), but by that time, Papini had lost much of his influence over the younger generation of writers. A man of deep paradoxes, he appeared to many as an untrustworthy guide when he submitted to the authority of the Roman Church. This decline of literary influence has made a true assessment of his merits difficult.

Yet Papini deserves to be remembered for his unceasing efforts to recapture the true spirit of Italian literature, his sound and genial use of philosophical and historical ideas, his keen insights into contemporary affairs, his recognition of originality in new writers, and his enthusiasm for established authors who, in his opinion, reflected the genius of the national character. Always personal and highly emotional, often bitterly polemical, he must nevertheless be credited with a passionate zeal to expose easy myths and intellectual mediocrity. A crusading perfectionist to the end, his pessimism must be interpreted, in the light of his far-reaching ideals, as a forceful assertion of hope in the future of national literary and religious values. He worked relentlessly to shape a literary reality that would give new vigor to Italian literature, a goal that was recognized in official circles in 1939, when he was honored with the title "Accademico d'Italia."

See: G. Prezzolini, *Discorso su Giovanni Papini* (1915); B. Croce, in *Conversazioni critiche,* vol. 4 (1932); L. Russo, in *La critica letteraria contemporanea,* vol. 2 (1943); F. Flora, in *Storia della letteratura italiana,* vol. 5 (1947). A.Pao.

Parandowski, Jan (1895–1978), Polish novelist, short-story writer, essayist, and translator from classical languages, was born in Lvov and died in Warsaw. He studied classical philology and archaeology at Lvov University and began to publish in 1913. From 1933 on, he was president of the Polish PEN Club, and during World War II he was active in the cultural underground movement in Warsaw. In 1945 he became professor of ancient culture and later of comparative literature at the Catholic University in Lublin. His fiction and essays, written in a limpid, classic style, deal mainly with the themes of the ancient Greek and Roman culture and history and with the tradition of European humanism. They include: *Eros na Olimpie* (1924; Eros on Olympus); *Mitologia* (1924; Mythology); *Dwie wiosny* (1927; Two Springs), a collection of short stories, *Dysk olimpijski* (1933; Eng. tr., *The Olympic Discus,* 1939), a slightly fictionalized account of the ancient Greek Olympic Games in 476 B.C., which is a sharp-eyed presentation of Hellenic life written with the humanist's love for that life. Parandowski received a bronze medal for this novel at the Olympic Games in 1936. His collection of short stories *Trzy znaki Zodiaku* (1938; Three Signs of the Zodiac) deals with the tradition of freedom in Poland and the world, starting with ancient times. Parandowski is also the author of a *vie romancée* of Oscar Wilde, *Król życia* (1930; The King of Life), and of a novel, *Niebo w płomieniach* (1936; Heaven in Flames), about a religious crisis experienced by a young boy. After World War II he published a number of new works: a collection of short stories *Godzina śródziemnomorska* (1949; Mediterranean Hour); *Alchemia słowa* (1951; Alchemy of the Word), about the phenomena of literary creation; *Zegar słoneczny* (1953; The Sundial), a book of reminiscences of his childhood; and others. Parandowski was also a translator of Greek,

Roman, and French literature. His translations include a prose rendering of Homer's *Odyssey*.

See: *Słownik współczesnych pisarzy polskich*, vol. 2 (1964), pp. 611–19; G. Harjan, *Jan Parandowski* (1971); W. Studencki, *Alchemik słowa. Rzecz o Janie Parandowskim*, 2 vols. (1972–74). E.M.T. and S.F.

Pardo Bazán, Emilia (1851–1921), Spanish novelist, short-story writer, and critic, was born in La Coruña. The only daughter of a well-to-do family that entered the aristocracy in 1871, when her father was made a count, she inherited the title in 1890. Her education, like that of most Spanish women of the upper classes, was limited to a boarding school. Nevertheless, she continued learning on her own, following a systematic program of readings in contemporary affairs and literature. She belonged to an elite of intellectual women including Cecilia Bohl de Faber (pseud. Fernán Caballero), Concepción Arenal, and Gertrudis Gómez de Avellaneda. These women struggled for proper recognition of their intellectual endeavors in a society totally dominated by men. An intrepid fighter, Pardo Bazán was an irrepressible polemicist. She ardently defended causes like women's rights, the poor, Catholicism, and naturalism, although when her polemics are examined in the broad perspective of her works, some contradictions become apparent. For example, although compassionate towards the disadvantaged, she never failed to defend social stratification. Similarly, when defending naturalism she rejected its cruder aspects, advocating instead the elements that liken it to realism. Her major social accomplishments as a writer were to become the director of the Atheneum of Madrid and to be named professor of Romance literatures at the University of Madrid. Neither position had ever been held by a woman.

Pardo Bazán's literary activities began with the publication of some romantic poems, a series of pseudoscientific articles, and *Pascual López* (1879), a weak novel. Naturalism had appeared in Spain in 1876, but it was not until 1880 that it occupied the limelight of literary discussion. Pardo Bazán soon carried the banner of the new creed. The prologues to *Un viaje de novios* (1881; Eng. tr., *A Wedding Trip*, 1891) and *La Tribuna* (1883; The Woman Orator), together with the collection of articles, *La cuestión palpitante* (1883; The Burning Question), are the essential texts for understanding Pardo Bazán's brand of naturalism. Her defense of the movement earned her great popularity and also created a heated controversy. Some regarded her as a follower of the latest Parisian fad, others as a defender of an atheistic literature that was unacceptable in Spanish society, especially when advocated by a married woman. Today the noisy polemic seems disproportionate to the moderation of Pardo Bazán's ideas, as her espousal of naturalism was full of reservations. First of all, she rejected the ideological core of the movement, believing its deterministic aspects to be responsible for the sordid elements she scorned. She accepted naturalism as a veiled defense of realism and an antidote to the idealism that had dominated Spanish letters during the first half of the century. She understood naturalism as a return to what she considered the traditional modes of Spanish literature, in particular the realism of the picaresque novel. *Un viaje* is a good example of her ambiguous stance. It is a realist novel dotted with naturalistic touches, but naturalistic techniques like the photographic description of objects and emphasis on the characters' physical characteristics are little used and inevitably weakened, in a literary sense, by the romantic plot. In *La Tribuna* she follows Emile ZOLA's formulas more closely, basing her novel on research into the life of women workers in a tobacco factory in La Coruña and

thus presenting a fairly authentic picture of the lowest classes in an urban setting. The narrative technique is loosely impersonal, but the social implications are more poignant. After *El cisne de Vilamorta* (1885; Eng. tr., *The Swan of Vilamorta*, 1891), a great success with the reading public, her talent crystallized in *Los Pazos de Ulloa* (1886; The Manor of Ulloa) and its sequel, *La madre naturaleza* (1887; Mother Nature), undoubtedly her masterpieces. This two-volume work is the story of the declining rural gentry in Galicia. By allowing their lives to be governed by uncontrolled instincts, the characters descend to a level of bestial depravity. This debasement of human life is epitomized by Pedro Moscoso, the young owner of the decaying estate; Primitivo, a shrewd foreman who runs the place with self-serving cleverness; Sabel, the foreman's daughter and lover of the landowner; and Perucho, the couple's illegitimate son. A priest and a young woman, Nucha, enter the life of the manor, the former as a financial and spiritual counselor and the latter as Pedro's wife. Their arrival dramatizes the differences between uncivilized and educated life. The characters are not seen as determined by their own physiology or hereditary traits but as infected by the sensual, cruel manifestations of nature.

Two other short novels fall under the heading of naturalism: *Insolación* (1889; Sunstroke) and *Morriña* (1889; Eng. tr., *Morriña—Homesickness*, 1891). As the author of more than 500 short stories, Pardo Bazán was the most prolific author of her time in this genre, and also the best. In addition to short stories, from 1890 to 1910 she wrote and edited a magazine, *El Nuevo Teatro Crítico* (1891–93) and published *Cuentos de Marineda* (1892; Tales of Marineda) and many novels, including *Una cristiana* (1890; Eng. tr., *A Christian Woman*, 1891), *La prueba* (1890; The Test), *Doña Milagros* (1894), and *Memorias de un solterón* (1896; Memories of a Bachelor). The most distinctive works of this second phase, *La quimera* (1904; The Chimera) and *La sirena negra* (1907; The Black Mermaid), show that she was attuned to the new modernist attitudes and sensibility.

See: D. F. Brown, *The Catholic Naturalism of Pardo Bazán* (1957); C. Bravo Villasante, *Vida y obra de Emilia Pardo Bazán* (1962); W. T. Pattison, *Emilia Pardo Bazán* (1971). G.Gu.

Parise, Goffredo (1929–), Italian novelist, essayist, and journalist, was born in Vicenza, where he spent his childhood and lived through World War II. He traveled widely as a correspondent for leading Italian newspapers. Collections of his reportages include *Cara Cina* (1967; Dear China), *Due, tre cose sul Vietnam* (1967; Two, Three Things about Vietnam), and *Biafra* (1968). Parise has also collaborated on film scripts with Federico Fellini, Mauro Bolognini, and Marco Ferreri.

Parise's first two novels are *Il ragazzo morto e le comete* (1951; Eng. tr., *The Dead Boy and the Comets*, 1952) and *La grande vacanza* (1953; The Great Vacation). His best-known novel is *Il prete bello* (1954; Eng. trs., *Don Gastone and the Ladies* and *The Priest among the Pigeons*, 1955), in whose wake came *Il fidanzamento* (1956; The Betrothal) and *Amore e fervore* (1959; Love and Fervor), reissued as *Atti impuri* (1973; Impure Acts). His trilogy on the theme of the relationship between the ruler and the ruled consists of the novel *Il padrone* (1965; Eng. tr., *The Boss*, 1966), the dialogue (between a man and a woman) entitled *L'assoluto naturale* (1968; The Natural Absolute), and the short-story collection *Il crematorio di Vienna* (1969; Vienna's Crematorium).

The theme of Parise's first two novels is adolescence, rendered with morbid sensuality and an obsession with the death of the flesh. His work combines realism with the macabre and the grotesque; expressionism becomes surrealism. In the 1950s his novels became more realistic, containing mild satire of the religious customs of the region where Parise was born. This satire becomes increasingly bitter until the late 1960s. The latest stories of *Sillabario n. 1* (1972; Primer No. 1) mark a return to the elementary sentiments of man, named in the alphabetically ordered titles of the stories.

See: C. Altarocca, *Parise* (1972). G.-P.B.

Parnicki, Teodor (1908–), Polish novelist, was born in Berlin and spent his childhood in Moscow. During the Russian Revolution (1917) he wandered to Manchuria. In 1928 he arrived in Lvov to study English, Oriental, and Polish literatures. Deported to Soviet Russia during World War II, he moved in 1943 to Teheran, to Palestine, and finally to Mexico, and then in 1967 he returned to Poland. He tried various genres of creative prose, but excelled in the writing of historical novels. For several decades he was fascinated by the fall of the Roman Empire, and *Aecjusz, ostatni Rzymianin* (1937; Aetius, the Last Roman) portrays the declining Empire in the 5th century A.D. Several later works—*Koniec "Zgody Narodów"* (1955; The End of the "Covenant of Nations"), *Słowo i ciało* (1959; The Word and the Flesh), and *Twarz księżyca* (1961; The Face of the Moon)—were devoted to the preceding centuries, but *Śmierć Aecjusza* (1966; Aetius' Death) marked a return to the Roman Empire. *Srebrne orły* (1944–45; The Silver Eagles) describes the reign of the Polish king Bolesłav the Brave in the 11th century. Early Polish history is also the background of *Nowa baśń* (1962–70; The New Fairy Tale), consisting of six bulky volumes. *Tylko Beatrycze* (1962; Only Beatrice) develops an episode from the beginning of the 14th century and *I u możnych dziwny* (1965; Strange Even among the Mighty) and *Inne życie Kleopatry* (1969; The Other Life of Cleopatra) are connected with the 17th century. Some novels are linked with more recent times, for example, *Tożsamość* (1970; Identity) and *Muza dalekich podróży* (1970; The Muse of Distant Travels). At first Parnicki's narratives resembled traditional structural patterns, respected chronology, and maintained a detached point of view; his treatment of characters was influenced by Sigmund Freud. Later he began to write works that owed their basic impulse to history, as historical novels. He argued that in the sphere of novel writing there can be transformations of the author into his characters, and literary characters into the author. He drew radical conclusions about the writer's literary omnipotence, indulging in a mixture of history, autobiography, and fantasy. He combined various kinds of prose: lengthy dialogues, memoirs, letters, documentation, and so on. His technique coincides with the antinovel and other experimental writings of the West.

See: W. Sadkowski, *Parnicki. Wprowadzenie w twórczość powieściową* (1970); M. Czermińska, *Teodor Parnicki* (1974); A. Chojnacki, *Parnicki w labiryncie historii* (1975). M.G.

Parronchi, Alessandro (1914–), Italian poet and art critic, was born and educated in Florence. There, in the late 1930s and early 1940s, he became closely identified with the *ermetici* (*see* ITALIAN LITERATURE), those young poet-critics and scholars, such as Mario LUZI, Piero BIGONGIARI, Carlo Bo (1911–), and Oreste Macri (1913–), who brilliantly dominated poetry and criticism in those years. The several collections of what Parronchi defined as his "youthful verse," gathered together and republished under the title of *Un'attesa* (1962; Expectation),

share a common linguistic audacity with his fellow hermetics, and, initially at least, a wide-ranging, all-inclusive literary syncretism. This quality is understandable in someone who, like Parronchi, has translated a great deal, particularly from the French romantic and symbolist poets. What quickly and clearly emerges as the dominant and most original element in these intensely personal poems, however, is the Petrarchan note, incarnated in the leitmotiv of absence-presence. In this regard, Parronchi is indebted to Gérard de Nerval, Eugenio MONTALE's *Le occasioni,* and Dino CAMPANA's *Canti orfici.*

In the final three sections of *Un'attesa,* there emerges a movement away from an overtly memorial poetry. This tendency continues in the four slim volumes Parronchi wrote in the 1950s, republished under the title *Coraggio di vivere* (1961; Courage to Live). Here Parronchi builds a series of contrasts between an orphic, dreamlike past and a present, finite reality, using a discursive, frequently gnomic, occasionally precious verse to convey the predicament of many of his generation, "crawling," as Boris PASTERNAK said, "between heaven and earth." It is precisely from the awareness of this predicament (of being destined to be a spectator rather than an actor in life) that the poems derive much of their force and anguish. The more occasional poems of *Pietà dell'atmosfera* (1970) exhibit a greater linguistic verve and a new note of irony, yet they remain essentially faithful to the historical pessimism of the 1950s, which Parronchi shared with Luzi. These poems show a strong concern for moral truth that, at least in intention, brings them close to the later poems of Giacomo Leopardi (1798–1837). In addition to his poetry, the prolific, wide-ranging art studies of Parronchi also merit serious consideration.

See: S. Antonielli, *Aspetti e figure del Novecento* (1955); O. Macri, *Caratteri e figure della poesia italiana contemporanea* (1956); P. P. Pasolini, *Passione e ideologia* (1960); G. Bàrberi-Squarotti, *Letteratura italiana: i contemporanei,* vol. 3 (1975), pp. 781–95. T.O'N.

Parun, Vesna (1922–), Croatian poet, was born on the island of Zlarin. After her happy childhood in sunny Dalmatia, the horrors of World War II aroused within Parun an abhorrence of inhumanity in all its forms and a commitment to the building of a "new society." When her first—and perhaps best—collection of poems, *Zore i vihori* (Dawns and Gales), was published in 1947, however, she was attacked from the Left as too individualistic. She was especially criticized for writing in the manner of earlier Croatian poets—a style that had nothing in common with the prescriptions of socialist realism.

Although Parun was silenced for a certain period, she continued to write but did not publish anything. Another important collection of her poetry, *Crna maslina* (The Black Olive Tree), was issued in 1955, and during the following decade several more books appeared. During these years, she became detached from national issues and concentrated instead on her personal experiences and emotions, analyzing in detail her frequent romantic entanglements, with their few blissful moments regularly followed by disillusionment. Her best poems can be found in two selections: *Konjanik* (1962; The Horseman) and *Bila sam dječak* (1963; I Was a Boy).

Parun has written particularly attractive poems for children. She has traveled to Bulgaria and Romania and written about her experiences there. In January and February 1971, Parun created a sensation when she published articles in a Catholic periodical, *Glas koncila,* in which she described and defended her return to Catholicism. On account of these statements, she has been condemned as a reactionary by certain Yugoslav literary critics.

See: Z. Tomičić, "Vita nuova pjesnikinje Parun," *Rep* 9 (1955): 726-33; A. Kadić, "Postwar Croatian Lyric Poetry," *Slav R* 6, no. 3 (December 1958): 514-20; T. Sabljak, "Parun: Bila sam djěčak," *Kolo* 8 (1963): 390-402. A.K.

Pascoaes, Joaquim Teixeira de, pseud. of Joaquim Pereira de Vasconcelos (1877-1952), Portuguese poet, was born at his family's estate, Pascoaes, near Amarante in northern Portugal. That area he used very early as the landscape of his poetry, with the Támega River and the Marão Mountains as its constants, and he continued to use it in this way throughout his life. After studying law at the University of Coimbra, he returned home in 1901 to practice law for 10 years, first in Amarante, then in Oporto. He was to remain in the region of Amarante for the rest of his life, except for brief trips to Spain, France, and England; sojourns in Lisbon, mainly in the 1920s; and frequent excursions to Oporto.

After a false start with two volumes of verse written in adolescence and subject to a strong influence from Guerra Junqueiro (1850-1923), Pascoaes published his first characteristic book of poetry, *Sempre* (Forever) in 1898. Here the poet asserts his independence not only from Junqueiro but also from the other leading poets of the time—António Nobre, Eugénio de Castro, and Cesário Verde. Much later, in his *Livro de memórias* (1928; Memoirs), Pascoaes was to declare: "I was born to live beyond life," an assertion as fundamental to his poetry as to his biography. Three titles of his early collections of poetry are revealing: *Sempre,* already mentioned, for the timelessness of the poet's concerns, and *Vida etérea* (1906; Ethereal Life) and *As sombras* (1907; Shadows), for their indications of the poet's attitude toward physical reality.

Throughout his poetry, Pascoaes is deeply involved with both his native landscape and those who dwell there—be they villagers or ghosts of villagers, trees, clouds or their shadows. The dedicatory poem of *As sombras* is inscribed: "To a tree and to my sister Maria." In a poem in *Elegias* (1912), the poet presents a landscape of moonlight playing over crags and herdsmen piping their rustic melodies; as he suffuses this scene with his deeply felt emotion, the inanimate springs to life: caverns murmur, trees pray in ecstasy, and fantastic crags melting in meditation stand against a sky that is wounded by the first stars. Such a spectrally dynamic landscape is typical of Pascoaes. The poet is not only in communion with all aspects of nature; his is the essence of creation to the extent, as he says in *Sempre,* that the external reality of the world may be nothing more than "the shadow of my verse." As early as 1903, when he published *Jesus e Pan,* Pascoaes was concerned with building a philosophy that would synthesize the Greco-Roman and the Christian systems. But instead of seeking such a synthesis in a particular historical figure, Pascoaes chose to set it in the permanent character of the Portuguese people, typified in his mind by *saudade,* a word that embraces both recollection of the past and longing for the future. In his collections of poetry *Senhora da noite* (1909; Lady of the Night), *Marános* (1911), and *Regresso ao paraíso* (1912; Return to Paradise), this doctrine, known as *Saudosismo,* is affirmed. Not limited to literature, *Saudosismo* looked to a general renaissance of Portugal, culturally, socially, and politically—a Utopia such as had been dreamed of in connection with the messianic figure of King Sebastian.

In 1910, Pascoaes became very active in a group of young writers and intellectuals committed to reforms in the cultural, moral, and political spheres. Appropriately, they called their movement *Renascença Portuguesa* (Portuguese Renascence). Besides Pascoaes, the group included Afonso Duarte, Afonso Lopes Vieira, Jaime CORTESÃO, Leonardo Coimbra, and Veiga Simões, among others. In 1910 they launched as their organ *A Águia,* and two years later Pascoaes assumed the editorship of this journal, whose cover proclaimed it to be a "monthly review of literature, art, science, philosophy and social criticism." Pascoaes made *A Águia* his forum to spread the doctrine of *Saudosismo* and continued to proclaim it as a panacea for all the country's woes in lectures delivered as far afield as Barcelona, but most notably in two new books, *Verbo escuro* (1914; Darksome Word), a most successful sequence of prose poems, and *A arte de ser português* (1915; The Art of Being Portuguese), a less impressive series of essays designed for use in the schools. *Saudosismo* was not long in bringing the poet in conflict with several figures of the *Renascença Portuguesa,* led by the formidable rationalist António SÉRGIO. During the long polemic that ensued, Pascoaes's theory was clearly unable to withstand the dialectics of Sérgio, and in 1916 Pascoaes withdrew from the direction of the journal and from public life in general. Not until 1923 did *A Águia* publish another contribution from the poet. Fidelino de FIGUEIREDO stated the limitation of Pascoaes's theories more succinctly than anyone: "*Saudosismo* is not a political concept or program . . . [but] only a state of mind."

From his estate, Pascoaes continued to write and publish poetry. Among his best works from this period are *Cantos indecisos* (1921; Vague Songs), *Elegia do amor* (1924; Elegy of Love), *Cânticos* (1925; Canticles), *Versos pobres* (1949; Artless Verses), and *Últimos versos* (Last Poems), published posthumously in 1953. As late as 1935, the year that saw the publication of *Painel* (Panel), still another poetic production, Pascoaes had not abandoned faith in the application of *Saudosismo* to public life; but by 1949, the year of *Versos pobres,* he appears to have restored it to the emotional and spiritual realm to which it pertains. He also wrote four biographies: *São Paulo* (1934; Eng. tr., *Saint Paul,* 1937), concerned with the end of the Greek and Semitic civilizations; *São Jerónimo e a trovoada* (1936; Saint Jerome and the Thunderbolt), treating the fall of the Roman Empire; *São Agostinho* (1945; Saint Augustine); and *Napoleão* (1940), which traces the career of Napoleon from Waterloo to Saint Helena. Two important books that elucidate Pascoaes's thought are *O homem universal* (1937; The Universal Man) and *Duplo passeio* (1942; Double Walk).

Many writers and poets came to visit Pascoaes in his hideout, among them Miguel de UNAMUNO, with whom Pascoaes maintained a correspondence for nearly 30 years, and Gabriela Mistral, the Chilean poet. The influence of Pascoaes's poetry is undeniable on that of Jaime Cortesão, Mário Beirão, Domingos MONTEIRO, and António Alves Martins; possibly, too, on the Fernando PESSOA of *Mensagem.* Jorge de SENA gave this evaluation of Pascoaes: "I am attempting . . . to raise him to the level to which he is entitled and which in point of fact is his: that of one of the most prodigious poetic constitutions in our literature, a man who by the intensity and vitality of his inspiration is akin to Camões and Pessoa, just as he resembles Gomes Leal in his visionary qualities, a noble and an extraordinary spirit no matter where, but above all an extremely important figure in whom is summarized almost every experience, *good and bad,* of seven and a half centuries of Portuguese poetry."

See: J. do Prado Coelho, *A poesia de Teixeira de Pascoaes* (1945); J. de Sena, *Da poesia portuguesa* (1959), pp. 95-106; A. Margarido, *Teixeira de Pascoaes* (1961); M. da Glória Teixeira de Vasconcelos, *Olhando para trájvejo Pascoaes* (1971). R.M.-L. and W.H.R.

Pascoli, Giovanni (1855-1912), Italian poet, was born, the fourth of 10 children, in San Mauro, Romagna, where his father managed the Torlonia estate. A sequence of family tragedies (the first of which was his father's unsolved murder in 1867) blighted his childhood and marked him for life. By the time he was 21 he found himself the head of a decimated family, with a deep sense of responsibility toward his two surviving sisters, for whom it became his ambition to restore a family home. Pascoli received an excellent classical education and, after many hardships (including a brief period of detention for taking part in socialist agitations while a student), earned his doctorate in 1882. His first teaching assignment was in southern Italy at the *liceo* of Matera. Posts in Tuscany followed, until in 1896 he had his first university appointment at Bologna. Both at Bologna and Messina, to which he moved next, he was professor of Greek and Latin. In 1905 he succeeded Giosuè Carducci (1835-1907) in the chair of Italian literature at Bologna, where he continued to teach until his death.

Pascoli's first collection of poetry, *Myricae* (1891), was published, like many others of his works, as a wedding gift for a friend. The 22 poems of the original edition subsequently grew to 156. The title, derived from Vergil's Fourth Eclogue—"arbusta iuvant humilesque myricae" (the orchards please and the lowly tamarisks), symbolizes the humble, everyday objects, situations—and feelings that occasion the poems. Dedicated to his father, *Myricae* opens with the commemorative "Il giorno dei morti" (All Souls' Day) in which the traditional graveyard theme is given powerfully haunting expression by the transposition of the familiar domestic scene around the hearth to the cold, wind-blown, and rain-soaked cemetery where the dead members of the family have *not* found their rest. The words that they address to the living in never-ending yearning are echoed in one of the last poems of the collection, "Colloquio," the poet's dialogue with his dead mother. Aside from the framing poems and a few scattered ones, the collection is arranged thematically, including such topics as childhood memories (as in the poem "Ricordi"), scenes of country life—"L'ultima passeggiata" (The Last Walk) and "In campagna" (In the Country), elegies and moments of sadness—"Elegie," "Tristezze"—and trees and flowers—"Alberi e fiori." But if in its tone and subject matter *Myricae* has much in common with contemporary Italian decadentism and precrepuscularism (*see* ITALIAN LITERATURE), in poetic technique (language and versification) it is strikingly original and strongly experimental. Impressions, sensations, vignettes, thumbnail portraits, genre scenes, and fragments of experience and consciousness tap the expressive resources of language at all levels, from inarticulate onomatopoeias and the rhythms of everyday speech to technical terms and dialect words. Pascoli uses assonance and alliteration extensively and operates subtle modifications in the traditional verse forms.

His next collection, *Poemetti* (1897; Short Narrative Poems), later divided into *Primi poemetti* (1904) and *Nuovi poemetti* (1909), adds short narrative poems to the lyric genres of *Myricae*. Georgic in inspiration, terza rima in verse form, *Poemetti* is composed of scenes of rustic life centered around the seasonal activities of a family of farmers in the remote Tuscan region of Garfagnana. The slight plot line follows the story of the courtship and marriage of the oldest daughter, Rosa, and the hunter Rigo. Pascoli's literary models here are Homer and Vergil. Although the poems can be read independently of one another, they are united by plot, literary imitation, and an underlying ideology. Writing in the early years of the modern industrialization of Italy, shortly after the achievement of political unity and independence, Pascoli regressively champions agriculture as the foundation of a stable and healthy society governed by the very rhythms of nature. In his view of Italy's working classes, a special place is occupied by the growing masses of immigrants forced to leave their country in search of work elsewhere. To them is dedicated a sequence of poems, the two *canti* (entitled "Italy") about a family returning from Cincinnati, Ohio. The poems are noteworthy linguistically for the presence of English and Italian-American words and expressions. The disquieting and problematic "Digitale purpurea" (Foxglove) is perhaps the best-known poem of *Primi poemetti*: passionate, dark-haired Rachel and innocent, flaxen-haired Maria, archetypal figures of romanticism, recall their years at convent school and the attraction-repulsion they felt for the poisonous flower, symbol of the union of Eros and Thanatos. The allusion in the last lines of the poem to something mysteriously sweet and at the same time deadly has induced critics to advance the most disparate and contradictory interpretations of the work.

Pascoli's *Canti di Castelvecchio* (1903; Songs of Castelvecchio) returns to the more homogeneous lyricism of *Myricae*. This volume recalls the earlier collection through the use of the same epigraph and its dedication to the memory of the poet's mother. The title refers to Castelvecchio di Barga, the locality in Garfagnana where, in 1895, Pascoli rented the house that he henceforth considered his home and in whose chapel he is buried. The collection opens with "La poesia" (Poetry), an *ars poetica* in which poetry is compared to a burning lamp whose light accompanies man, the pilgrim, on his journey through life. *Canti di Castelvecchio* is distinguished by Pascoli's sharpened sense of every manifestation of life, not only in the universe but in the cosmos, and his impulse to sacrifice his own personality in order to give other beings, animate or inanimate, a voice. From the different and distinctive bird sounds of "The Hammerless Gun" to the shepherd's pipes of "Le ciaramelle," from the cries of chimney sweep and tinker in "I due girovaghi" (The Two Hawkers) to the church bells in "L'ora di Barga" (The Hour of Barga), Pascoli's poetic universe is filled with voices that, he feels, poetry must and can recover. The familiar themes of loss and simple affections lose the realistic anecdotal grounding of the earlier collections in favor of an all-encompassing symbolism. Thus, the mother's voice that is heard in one of the most famous poems, "La voce" (The Voice), becomes the barely perceptible breath that vanishes in the nickname "Zvanî" (from Giovannino), which sounds as a warning and an exhortation to the poet at important turning points in his life. Similarly in "Il bolide" (The Meteor), the poet's experience of seeing a falling star is expanded into a hallucinatory vision of the earth as a planet in the universe.

The volumes *Odi e inni* (1906; Odes and Hymns), *Poemi conviviali* (1911; Convivial Poems), and the posthumous *Poemi italici* (1911; Italic Poems), *Canzoni di Re Enzio* (1908-09; Songs of King Enzio), and *Poemi del Risorgimento* (1913; Poems of the Risorgimento) contain Pascoli's historical and public poetry. Yet his reworkings of Greek, biblical, and medieval material—Ulysses' return to Ithaca in "L'ultimo viaggio" (The Last Voyage), the battle against the forces of evil in "Gog e Magog" (both in *Poemi conviviali*), 13th-century episodes from the history of Bologna (in *Canzoni di Re Enzio*)—and his use of modern and contemporary subjects—"Napoleone" and the sequence on Giuseppe Garibaldi (both in *Poemi del Risorgimento*), episodes from the Italian colonial wars in "La sfogliatura" (The Corn Harvest in *Odi e inni*)—evidence the same characteristics in interpretation and style that one finds in his more personal poetry.

In addition to poetry in Italian, Pascoli also wrote verse in Latin. This won him a sequence of gold medals awarded by the Academy of Sciences in Amsterdam. Much of it is available in the two posthumous volumes entitled *Carmina* (1914; 1930). Pascoli's Latin poetry was not a separate and marginal activity, but was written concurrently with the poetry in Italian and reflects the same themes and same technical achievement. Its setting is ancient Rome, usually the transitional period between paganism and Christianity, a fact that has reminded some critics of Walter Pater's *Marius the Epicurean* (1885). Also related to his classical studies and his academic activity are the school anthologies that he prepared: *Lyra* and *Epos*, devoted respectively to Latin lyric and epic poetry, and *Sul limitare* (On the Threshold) and *Fior da fiore* (Selected Passages), devoted to Italian literature. As Gianfranco Contini has pointed out, the notes in these anthologies are critical essays in miniature. Pascoli's ideal of world literature as belonging equally to all peoples without regard to linguistic or national barriers was expressed further in the collection of translations from Sanskrit and ancient and modern Greek prepared under his direction. His own many translations, mostly from Greek and Latin but also from French and English, were first collected in *Traduzioni e riduzioni* (Translations and Arrangements) in 1913 and subsequently expanded.

Pascoli's essays on Dante—*Minerva oscura* (1898), *Sotto il velame* (1900; Under the Veil), *La mirabile visione* (1902; The Admirable Vision)—occupy an important, although somewhat anomalous, place in Dante studies. *Il fanciullino* (1897; The Child) is Pascoli's essay on poetry. By means of an image derived from Plato's *Phaedrus,* the poetic faculty is compared to the child-like capacity for wonder and spontaneous enthusiasm that persists in man beneath his rationality. Tapping the collective subconscious, the poet does not create (fashion) but discovers (unveils) what all men know without knowing that they do so.

Pascoli's place in the history of Italian literature has been radically reassessed in recent years, first by Pier Paolo PASOLINI, who placed his linguistic experimentalism in the context of popular and dialectal poetry, and then by Contini, who showed that he belongs not in a marginal and provincial literary tradition but in the main line of European symbolism. Some of Pascoli's poetry has been translated into English (1923, 1927, 1938). Italian editions include *Poesie* (4 vols., 1968), with two introductory essays by Contini, and *Poesie,* ed. by G. Nava (1971), an anthology with notes, some excerpts from the prose works, and a selection of critical essays.

See: M. Luzi, in *Storia della letteratura italiana* (1969), ed. by E. Cecchi and N. Sapegno, vol. 8, pp. 731–811.

O.R.

Pasinetti, Pier-Maria (1913–), Italian novelist, is professor at the University of California, Los Angeles. Pasinetti has written for the reviews *Il Ventuno Primato* and *Cinema* and has contributed to film scenarios. His four major novels, published in his own Italian and English versions, are tangentially interrelated and range in subject from contemporary events backward to the protagonists' adolescence and early maturity and forward into the future. Although carefully self-contained, each novel spotlights some region of a vast network of relationships created by the cycle of generations, friendship, chance, travel, war, and personal crises. *Rosso veneziano* (1959; *Venetian Red,* 1960), set in haut-bourgeois Venice, concerns young Elena and Giorgio Partibon, sister and brother, whose mysterious uncle helps them to launch their lives in the dangerous world of World War II Europe. A Partibon cousin is the protagonist of *La confusione* (1964; Eng. tr., *The Smile on the Face of the Lion,* 1965); his return to Italy after 20 years in America as an art expert introduces elements of the postwar intelligentsia of both continents. So far the widest extension of earlier themes is contained in *Il ponte dell'Accademia* (1968; Eng. tr., *From the Academy Bridge,* 1970) whose protagonist, Gilberto Rossi, appeared only briefly in the earlier novels and whose view of Italy and the world is rendered through his work at a mythical Institute for Language and Communication Analysis in California. Pasinetti's next novel, *Domani improvvisamente* (1971; Eng. tr., *Suddenly Tomorrow,* 1972), satirizes the computerized man of international conglomerate life.

In his novels, Pasinetti vividly renders the complexity of character and of human relations. He employs a sinuously intellectual but direct spoken language that is unrivaled in modern Italian literature. Pasinetti's other works include *L'ira di Dio* (1942; The Wrath of God—three novellas, one of which appeared in *Southern Review,* 1939) and scores of articles for such publications as *Corriere della sera, L'Europeo,* and *Italian Quarterly*.

See: R. W. B. Lewis, *SatR* (May 28, 1960); D. Della Terza, *IQ* 8 (Spring 1964); D. N. and A. Curley, eds., *A Library of Literary Criticism: Modern Romance Literatures* (1967); E. Janeway, *NYTBR* (Apr. 5, 1970); G. Contini, *Altri esercizi* (1972). L.N.

Paso, Alfonso (1925–78), Spanish comic dramatist, was born in Madrid. Son of the comic playwright Antonio Paso and actress Juana Gil, Paso was very talented and knowledgeable about every facet of the theater. He directed, produced, and performed in many of his works for theater, movies, and television, and translated, adapted, directed, and produced plays of such diverse national and international figures as Ramón del VALLE-INCLÁN, AZORÍN, Tennessee Williams, and Neil Simon. As a student at the University of Madrid in the 1940s, Paso allied himself with Alfonso SASTRE and others in "Arte Nuevo," an association devoted to experimentation with dramatic form and the use of the theater as a medium for social change. During this period he saw his one act play *Un tic-tac de reloj* (1946; A Tic Toc of the Clock) performed at the Beatriz Theater. After graduation, Paso put aside experimentation to court the acceptance of the conservative, bourgeois audiences who attended theater for amusement and to see their own values reflected. Between 1950 and 1970 he wrote over 200 plays, most of which enjoyed commercial success if not the acclaim of the more discerning critics. In 1952 he married Evangelina Jardiel Poncela, daughter of Enrique JARDIEL PONCELA, a playwright to whom Paso has often been compared. In his second full-length play, *Una bomba llamada Abelardo* (1953; A Bomb Called Abelard) the central character, a trained gorilla, ridicules pseudointellectualism. The play illustrates Paso's outlandish comic style as well as his early interest in social criticism. In the more than 30 plays that he produced in the 1950s, Paso portrayed such serious national problems as unemployment, emigration, and political corruption in a comic (he preferred the term "tragi-comic") manner rather than the serious fashion characteristic of the more respected dramatists of the period, like Antonio BUERO VALLEJO, Alfonso Sastre, and others of the realistic generation. In *Catalina no es formal* (1958; Catalina Is Not Serious), Paso portrays a Russian empress who has no choice but to remain married to her imbecile husband. This play may be the author's defense of his capitulation to the audience, as the empress's situation parallels Paso's bondage to an intellectually sluggish public. Other important plays of the 1950s include *Los pobrecitos* (1957; The Poor Little People), *Juicio contra un sinvergüenza* (1958; Judgment against a Scoundrel), and *No hay novedad, doña Adela* (1959; Nothing's New, Miss Adela). In the 1960s, Paso sustained his incredible productivity as he shifted ideologically to the Right. By the mid-1960s he had completed his metamorphosis from youthful, nonconformist idealist to established, conservative materialist. In program notes to spectators, he bid for approval and lauded in his works the attitudes that he had formerly hoped to chastise. Among characteristic plays of this decade are *Las buenas personas* (1961; The Good People), *Buenísima Sociedad* (1962; High Society), and *La corbata* (1963; The Tie). By the end of the decade, Paso's plays became excessively repetitive and the public tired of him. When he turned to writing works with Freudian, sexual overtones, these also failed to interest. He wrote more and more articles for magazines and newspaper, principally the ultraconservative Madrid daily, *El Alcázar*, while some of his short plays were performed before the even less demanding audiences of cabaret theater. Between 1973 and 1977 no Paso play opened in a Madrid theater. His last play, *La zorra y el escorpión* (1977; The Fox and the Scorpion), features the sadomasochistic relationship of an English lady and her butler. It was unsuccessful. At the time of his death in 1978, two brief works, *En pelota viva* (Stark Naked) and *Los últimos cachondos* (The Last Horny Ones), were running at cabaret theaters, and a revival of *Cosas de papá y mamá* (1963; Mom and Dad's Business) was doing respectable business at a commercial theater. Paso was buried in a monk's habit, a detail that recalled his pleasure at being compared to Lope de Vega, an author with whom he shared certain virtues as well as vices.

See: A. Marqueríe, *Alfonso Paso y su teatro* (1960); F. García Pavón, *El teatro social en España* (1962), pp. 162–72; J. Monleón, "Alfonso Paso y su tragicomedia," in *El teatro de humor en España* (1966), pp. 247–68.

P.W.O'C.

Pasolini, Pier Paolo (1922–75), Italian critic, poet, novelist, film director, and screenwriter, was born and educated in Bologna, although he spent most of his childhood at Casarsa della Delizia, his mother's birthplace in Friuli. His first volume of poems, *Poesie a Casarsa* (1942; Poems at Casarsa—later published with other poems written in the 1940s as *La meglio gioventù* [1954; The Best of Youth])—written in Friulian dialect, is composed of a series of motets, similar to those of Eugenio MONTALE, in which Pasolini nostalgically evokes the world of childhood with verse of lyrical intensity. These poems reveal Pasolini's knowledge not only of the poetry of Giovanni PASCOLI (on whom he later wrote his doctoral thesis) and Montale, but also of a wider European tradition, evidenced in the influence on Pasolini of the Spanish poet Antonio MACHADO.

Pasolini's early Italian poems, later published in *L'usignolo della Chiesa Cattolica* (1958; The Nightingale of the Catholic Church), date from the same period as his Friulian verse. The world of his youth, reflected objectively in the timeless innocence of Friuli and transcribed in the spontaneity of its dialect, here clashes with the world of maturity and of history. The myth of the noble savage clashes with that of progress within history, and the resultant contrast, which is never resolved, is to be observed in all his future works. This contrast, communicated in verse that owes much to the French *poètes maudits*, especially Paul VERLAINE, is poetically pre-

sented through frequent recourse to oxymoron, self-irony and, particularly, *dédoublement*, that is, the splitting of the poet's personality into heart and reason within a continuous, conflicting dialogue. In the best of these poems, this contrast, lived out in all its anguish, is expressed with rare poetic intensity.

Pasolini's precocious poetic activity was accompanied by similar activity in the field of literary criticism with the publication of some review articles, still little known, in the April to December 1942 issues of *Architrave*, the politico-literary monthly of the students of the University of Bologna. This activity, strongly influenced by two of Italy's leading critics, Giuseppe De Robertis and Gianfranco Contini, and their particular attention to close textual analysis, culminated in two essays: one on Pascoli and Montale (1947)—probably a reworking of part of his thesis—published in the Bolognese review *Convivium*, and one on Giuseppe UNGARETTI, written in the years 1948–51, and now included in *Passione e ideologia* (1960), a volume of selected essays.

Pasolini's almost total obscurity during the 1940s was followed by the notoriety of the 1950s, mainly due to the publication of the first two parts of a projected trilogy of novels, *Ragazzi di vita* (1955; Eng. tr., *The Ragazzi*, 1968) and *Una vita violenta* (1959; Eng. tr., *A Violent Life*, 1968). A narrative tendency was noticeable in his poetry of the late 1940s, and in 1949–50 he had already drafted the manuscript of his first novel, *Il sogno di una cosa* (1962; The Dream of Something). The timeless innocence of adolescent life in Friuli still constitutes its subject matter, although the work incorporates a sociopolitical strand, reflecting the neorealistic (*see* ITALIAN LITERATURE) climate of those years. In this the other novels do not differ, except that they are set in the subproletarian shantytowns of Rome. The picaresque life of the undifferentiated mass of youngsters from these areas is reflected in the deliberate formlessness of the first novel. This situation is slightly modified in the second one through the emergence of a Lukácsian (*see* György LUKÁCS), "typical" protagonist, the story of whose unself-conscious existence, told in the first part of the work, is followed by that of his awakening to social awareness in the second. The full development of the social consciousness of the protagonist would have constituted the story of the uncomplicated "Il rio della grana" (The River of Cash).

The notoriety and novelty of these works was exaggerated; they are superficially works of protest, but they reveal in effect a strong thematic continuity with the early poems and *Il sogno*. Their language too, a mixture of Italian and Roman dialect, had a precedent in the early Friulian poems, although here one can see the influence of the 19th-century Roman dialect poet Giuseppe Gioacchino Belli (1791–1863) and the modern novelist Carlo Emilio GADDA, whose *Quer pasticciaccio brutto de via Merulana* (1957; Eng. tr., *That Awful Mess on Via Merulana*, 1965), written in a mixture of Italian, Roman, Venetian, and Neapolitan dialects, had already appeared in five parts in the Florentine review *Letteratura* in 1946. Pasolini's concern with language and dialect is also evident in the criticism of these years, which, although frequently producing flashes of genuine insight, tends to be prescriptive rather than descriptive in nature.

The poetry Pasolini wrote during this period, published as *Le ceneri de Gramsci* (1957; Gramsci's Ashes), continues the narrative, realistic tendency of the poetry of the late 1940s in its long, detailed descriptions of the outskirts of Rome. But against this background there is projected, as always, the person of the poet himself, torn between attraction and revulsion for the world he contemplates, totally incapable of resolving the old antithesis of nature-history that he sees reflected in it.

Although he continued to produce poetry and criticism in the late 1960s and 1970s, it was not the equal of his earlier writing. His attention during these years was increasingly directed to his work as a film director. Among his films are many based on literary sources: *Il Vangelo secondo Matteo* (1964; The Gospel According to Saint Matthew), *Edipo re* (1967; Oedipus Rex), *Medea* (1969), *Il Decameron* (1971; The Decameron), *I racconti di Canterbury* (1972; The Canterbury Tales), *Il fiore del mille e una notte* (1973; The Arabian Nights), and *Salò o le 120 giornate di Sodoma* (1975; Salò or the 120 Days of Sodom). Based on his own subjects are *Accattone* (1961; Beggar), *Uccellacci e uccellini* (1966; Hawks and Sparrows), *Teorema* (1968), and *Porcile* (1969; Pigsty).

See: G. C. Ferretti, *Letteratura e ideologia* (1964); A. A. Rosa, *Scrittori e popolo* (1965); T. Anzoino, *Pasolini* (1971); K. Von Hofer, *Funktionen des Dialekts in der italienischen Gegenwartsliteratur* (1971).   T.O'N.

Passeur, Stève, pseud. of Etienne Morin (1899–1966), French dramatist, was born in Sedan. His early works, which demonstrate psychological insight along with a flair for the light touch, were staged by Aurélien LUGNÉ-POE. The mingling of serious and comic in the same play remained a permanent feature of Passeur's drama.

Although Passeur claimed that all his characters enjoy equal status, women play a dominant role in his works, whereas his men are passive and submissive. Women plead for their lovers' welfare in *Pas encore* (1927; Not Yet) and accept men's vices in *Suzanne* (1929); in *L'Acheteuse* (1930; The Buyer), they force straying husbands back to the marital fold. In Passeur's plays, love is a violent emotion, irrational and perverse. Men enjoy brief liaisons, as in *Les Tricheurs* (1932; The Tricksters), where amusement is substituted for true feeling. Love and hate coexist in *Le Château de cartes* (1937; The House of Cards), and crimes of passion are perpetuated in *La Visiteuse* (1943; The Visitor) and *La Traîtresse* (1946; The Traitress). Less violent although equally excessive behavior is evident in the obsession of *La Bête noire* (1934; The Pet Aversion), the guilt of *Le Témoin* (1935; The Witness), and the regression to childhood of *Le Vin de souvenir* (1946; The Wine of Memory).

Passeur's drama deals with exceptional characters swept up in equally extraordinary circumstances, and his dialogue overflows with bitterness and anger. He wrote more than 40 works, over half of which have been performed. Passeur stands in the tradition of the theater of love of Georges de PORTO-RICHE and Henry BERNSTEIN, but by virtue of his corrosive treatment of the vagaries of passion, he also foreshadows Antonin ARTAUD and the theater of cruelty.

See: B. Ratiu, *L'Œuvre dramatique de Stève Passeur* (1964).   A.J.W.

Pasternak, Boris Leonidovich (1890–1960), Russian poet and prose writer, was born in Moscow to a family where dedication to art was taken for granted: His father Leonid was a well-known portrait painter; his mother Rose, a pianist. Strongly influenced by Aleksandr Skryabin, Pasternak at first envisioned a musical career. He then studied philosophy at the universities of Moscow and Marburg, but finally, in 1913, turned to poetry. His early collections of verse, *Bliznets v tuchakh* (1914; The Twin in the Clouds) and *Poverkh barierov* (1917; Above the Barriers), contain poems of striking originality. But it was for *Sestra moya zhizn* (1922; My Sister, Life) and *Temy i variatsii* (1923; Themes and Variations) that Pasternak

won recognition and acclaim from critics and fellow poets. Throbbing with lyrical excitement and blending emotional intensity with an impetuous boldness of imagery, these two volumes rank among the landmarks of modern Russian poetry.

Although Pasternak composed the nature and love poems of *Sestra moya zhizn* in a kind of trance during the summer of 1917, the theme of the Russian Revolution appears obliquely, and only as a sense of turmoil and renewal. By the mid-1920s, he clearly felt the need to address historical experience more directly in his verse—and thus to transcend the purely lyrical realm. In the longer poems *Devyatsot pyaty god* (1926; The Year Nineteen Five) and *Lyutenant Shmidt* (1926–27), and also in the unfinished novel in verse *Spektorsky* (1931), he attempted to grasp the meaning of the Revolution by describing its immediate antecedents. Except for a number of memorable passages, these experiments with the epic genre are not entirely successful, and in 1932, Pasternak returned to the lyric mode in *Vtoroye rozhdeniye* (The Second Birth). Here the verbal dynamism of the earlier cycles is held in check, although not inhibited, by a deliberate effort at "simplicity," conceived not as artlessness but as a greater intelligibility and directness of statement.

Pasternak's poetic self-expression was effectively inhibited by the intellectual climate of the 1930s. Repeatedly accused of subjectivism, aestheticism, and irrelevance, he turned away from poetry and instead devoted much of his creative energy to translation of the Western classics, notably William Shakespeare, Goethe (*Faust*), Friedrich Schiller (*Maria Stuart*), John Keats, Percy Bysshe Shelley, and Paul VERLAINE. Especially impressive are his translations of eight Shakespeare plays. If they occasionally fall short of the dazzling verbal richness of the originals, they are, on the whole, distinguished dramatic poetry in their own right, underpinned time and again by Pasternak's perceptive reading of Shakespeare.

Pasternak's own voice was heard again in 1943, amid the ordeals of World War II, in *Na rannikh poezdakh* (On Early Trains), a collection of verse that sounds quietly but poignantly the theme of solidarity with the poet's severely tested countrymen. In 1954, the Soviet literary journal *Znamya* published a number of his lyrics under the title "Poems from a Novel." Several years later the novel in question, *Doktor Zhivago,* made Pasternak a celebrity in the West even as it exposed him at home to the most virulent attack of his entire career.

Doktor Zhivago was not Pasternak's first venture into narrative fiction. He had tried his hand at artistic prose in densely textured if somewhat baffling and contrived stories, including "Apellesova Cherta" (1915; Eng. tr., "Il Tratto di Apelle," 1945), "Pisma iz Tuly" (1918; Eng. tr., "Letters from Tula," 1945), and "Vozdushnye puti" (1924; Eng. tr., "Aerial Ways," 1945). His most successful prose pieces are "Detstvo Lyuvers" (1918; Eng. tr., "Childhood of Luvers," 1945), a poetically delicate portrayal of a young girl's discovery of the world around her; "Povest" (1929; Eng. tr., "The Tale," 1941), a partly autobiographical story; and "Okhrannaya gramota" (1930; Eng. tr., "Safe Conduct," 1945), a remarkable if somewhat cryptic autobiography. This memoir was later continued in the equally illuminating if less intricate "Avtobiograficheskiy ocherk" (1956; Eng. tr., "I Remember," 1959).

Sometime in the 1930s, Pasternak embarked on his first full-length novel, *Doktor Zhivago*. He seems to have completed the manuscript in 1954 and, encouraged by the general relaxation in Soviet cultural policy after Stalin's death, was hopeful of publishing it in the Soviet Union. The relatively liberal journal *Novy mir* turned down the novel, however, adjudging it a repudiation of the October Revolution. In the meantime, a publishing house in Milan, previously authorized by Pasternak to bring out the Italian version of *Doktor Zhivago,* proceeded to do so in 1957. The French, German, and English versions promptly followed, and soon the number of translations reached 18.

The ensuing "Pasternak affair" brought to the attention of the Western reading public one of the finest poets of our time. The belated recognition of Pasternak's achievement, coupled with admiration for his courage and sympathy for his ordeal, found expression in the Nobel Prize for Literature in 1958. Faced with a campaign of abuse in the Soviet press and such reprisals as expulsion from the Soviet Writers Union and possible banishment, Pasternak was compelled to turn down the Nobel Prize. He died in Peredelkino in 1960. In 1965, the publishers of the prestigious series "Biblioteka poeta" brought out an extensive and judicious selection of his verse, with an affectionate and perceptive introductory essay by Andrey SINYAVSKY. Five months later the introduction was promptly withdrawn, however, when Sinyavsky was arrested and it became known that the critic Andrey Sinyavsky and the underground writer Abram Tertz were one and the same person.

In the West, the official Soviet ban on *Doktor Zhivago* was deplored, but the critical assessments of the novel differed widely. Edmund Wilson hailed it as "one of the very great books of our time," but others found it diffuse or ill-constructed. It might be argued that some of these strictures rested on a partial misjudgment of the actual thrust and texture of a novel that is essentially brooding and lyrical, designed to be more suggestive than vivid. In spite of its panoramic scope and wide moral relevance, *Doktor Zhivago* is, above all, a poetic biography of a richly endowed individual and the story of his unremitting efforts to maintain creative integrity amid the overwhelming pressures of war and revolution. Criticisms that the author and the hero cannot be wholly identified are valid, but the strong kinship between the two is certainly apparent in Zhivago's religious reverence for life and love, and in his challenge of the Marxist pieties on behalf of a sui generis Christian personalism.

Pasternak's readiness to incur considerable risk in publishing *Doktor Zhivago* is a measure of the importance he attached to his novel. He once called it the most significant thing he had succeeded in doing, and in the same statement dismissed his early works as mere trifles. Critics of neoclassical persuasion were quick to seize upon this pronouncement and to proclaim the "simplicity" of Pasternak's late works and of their spiritual ambience, the ultimate payoff of his ultramodernistic experimentation. Conversely, some Pasternakians miss in such later works as "Kogda razgulyaetsya" (1956–59; When the Weather Clears) the creative vitality of the earlier *Sestra moya zhizn*. These discriminations, however legitimate, should not blind the student of Pasternak to the underlying continuity of his oeuvre. Throughout his long and turbulent career, Pasternak remained his own man—a maverick and a nonjoiner, striving for absolute freshness of perception and utmost directness of statement, rubbing shoulders affectionately with his "sister, life," and stubbornly refusing to subordinate the dictates of his poetic vision to the strident demands of political or literary dogma.

See: D. Davie and A. Livingstone, eds., *Pasternak: Modern Judgments* (1969); H. Gifford, *Pasternak: A Critical Study* (1977).   V.E.

Patrício, António (1878–1930), Portuguese playwright, poet, and story writer, was born in Oporto. He became a medical doctor and, as a diplomat, devoted himself to the cause of the fledgling Portuguese Republic of 1910. Even as a medical student in his native city, Patrício published his first poetry, *Oceano* (1905), replete with the suggestive imagery and aesthetic refinements typical of late symbolism. *Poesias* (1942), published long after his death, reveals the same secular mysticism that unites poet and nature in meters as musical and varied as the language is opulent. In 1910, Patrício published a collection of short stories, *Serão inquieto* (Disquieting Soiree), mood pieces rich in imagery and rhythmical phrases like the poems. A combination of aristocratic stoicism and an obvious human sympathy saves the book from the excesses of morbid sentimentality.

Patrício attempted with fair success to give a dramatic expression to his symbolist-decadent orientation. *O fim* (1909, republished in 1974; The End) is a two-act play that predicted the imminent fall of the monarchy in its portrayal of a senile queen surrounded by the ruins of regal splendor. Other plays, such as *Dom Pedro o Cru* (1918; King Peter the Cruel), transfer to Portugal's past a similar vision of royalty's decline. Patrício's most significant contribution to the symbolist theater is *Dom João e a máscara* (1924; Don Juan and the Masque), in which the insatiable desires of Don Juan lead him to a spiritual quest and ascetic peace with Lady Death, the ultimate mistress.

See: M. Tânger Corrêa, "António Patrício: poeta trágico," *Ocidente* 57–59 (1959–1960), seven articles; U. Tavares Rodrigues, "Uma releitura crítica de *O fim* de António Patrício," *Colóquio* 3 (1971): 63–65.

R.A.P.-R.

Patti, Ercole (1904–76), Italian journalist, short-story writer, and novelist, was born in Catania. In 1921 he moved to Rome, where he lived until his death.

As a reporter for *Gazzetta del popolo,* Patti traveled throughout the Far East. *Ragazze di Tokio* (1934; Girls of Tokyo), a series of impressions of India, China, and Japan based on his experiences as a journalist, foreshadows the narrative quality of his later work. *Quartieri alti* (1940; Elegant Neighborhoods) is a collection of sketches satirizing the frivolity and pretentiousness of life in Rome under the Fascist regime. Catania and Rome often complement each other in Patti's works, as in the short-story collection *Il punto debole* (1952; Achilles' Heel), where Catania is seen in retrospect and Rome is the present reality; at times one city is ancillary to the other, as in Patti's first novel, *Giovannino* (1954). Both cities give expression to the writer's dominant themes: the desire to be young, the search for happiness, the passing of time, and the inevitability of death. The novel *Un amore a Roma* (1956; A Love Affair in Rome), concerns Marcello, a journalist and literary critic who falls in love with a movie actress. The difficulties of the relationship are subsumed under the protagonist's failure to find innocence and truth. Yet the memories of his youth and the intimacy he feels for certain aspects of Rome become a reassuring evidence of stability.

Between 1965 and 1970, Patti wrote three novels set in Sicily: *La cugina* (1965; The Cousin); *Un bellissimo novembre* (1967; Eng. tr., *That Wonderful November,* 1969); and *Graziella* (1970), for which he received the Tremoli Prize. These works treat the passing from adolescence to adulthood against an awareness of death that becomes more acute than it had been in his earlier works. *Roma amara e dolce* (1972; Rome Bitter and Sweet) is an autobiographical account of Patti's experiences between 1921 and 1945. The anguish of the political realities and his search for a personal and artistic maturity provide the matrix for the title itself. *Diario siciliano* (1971; Sicilian Diary) is a collection of stories more than half of which are drawn from some of his earlier works, such as *Le donne* (1959; The Women) and *L'incredibile avventura di Ernesto* (1969; Ernesto's Incredible Adventure). Narrated in the tone of an autobiographical elegy, they are arranged in reverse chronological order. The characters are universal types portrayed in a landscape that itself seems eternal. The conflict between the concern with death and the sensual attachment to things past finds a denouement in *Gli ospiti di quel castelo* (1974; The Guests of That Castle), Patti's last novel and the only one narrated in the first person. In this story of a 23-year-old man who enters a surrealistic world and finds himself 40 years older, the succession of conscious states—the erotic, the political, and the literary—blend into one another, and death itself is taken as one of several but equal facets of existence.

See: U. Bosco, *Introduzione a tutti i romanzi di Ercole Patti* (1972); E. Lauretta, *Invito alla lettura di Patti* (1975).   R.J.T.

Paulhan, Jean (1884–1968), French essayist and critic, was born in Nîmes. He received his *licence-ès-lettres* at the Sorbonne in 1907 and spent the next four years on the island of Madagascar teaching at the lycée of Tananarive, searching for gold, and learning the Malagasy language. In 1912, Paulhan became professor of Malagasy at the Ecole des Langues Orientales in Paris. His earliest published work, *Les Hain-Tenys Mérinas* (1913), a study of Malagasyan poetry based on examples he had collected and translated, reveals Paulhan's passionate interest in the analysis of the uses and possibilities of language and in the relationship between what seems evident in poetry and what is obscure. Wounded at the front in 1914, Paulhan wrote his first major work, *Le Guerrier appliqué* (1917; The Applied Warrior), during his convalescence. This *récit* on the metaphysics of war concerns a soldier's efforts to find the most accurate and adequate linguistic expression for his thoughts and feelings. As editor of the *Nouvelle Revue française* from 1925 to 1940 and again from 1953 until his death, he continued his meditation on language. This meditation began with a condemnation of the old rhetoric in favor of what the dadaists called "terror" (an exploitation rather than an exploration of the irrational); it culminated in a series of attempts at a logical formulation of a new rhetoric that would demystify the domain of letters by adhering exclusively to the order and the laws implicit in language: *Les Fleurs de Tarbes* (1941; The Flowers of Tarbes), *Clef de la poésie* (1944; The Key to Poetry), *Petite Préface à toute critique* (1951; Short Preface to Any Criticism), *La Preuve par l'étymologie* (1953; Proof by Etymology), and *Les Incertitudes du langage* (1970; The Uncertainties of Language).

Paulhan came to be considered an éminence grise by the principal writers of his time, a critic of critics whose advice on literary and artistic questions they sought and generously received in conversations and correspondence. He also encouraged new talents—Marcel JOUHANDEAU, Jean GIONO, Francis PONGE, Henri MICHAUX, Jean-Paul SARTRE, Albert CAMUS, René DAUMAL—and in *F. F. ou le critique* (1945; F[élix] F[énéon] or the Critic) and *Le Marquis de Sade et sa complice* (1951; The Marquis de Sade and His Accomplice) he rediscovered works of literature that had been excluded from the official canon of accepted great texts.

Paulhan's evolution followed the critical debates on the nature of literary language from Stéphane MALLARMÉ and Félix FÉNÉON through Paul VALÉRY, dadaism, and surrealism and was a forerunner of many of the premises of the structuralist and poststructuralist critics (*see* FRENCH LITERATURE). He insisted, but always sotto voce, on the separation of life and art, of thought and language, on the specificity of the literary text and the need for a scientific as opposed to an impressionistic approach. The importance of his writings has been obscured by the paradoxical and elliptical tendencies of his elegant style and by his refusal to adhere to the dogmatic positions, in art and in politics, of most of his contémporaries.

During the occupation of France (1940–45), Paulhan wrote for the underground newspaper *Résistance*, and in 1941 he founded, with Jacques Decour, *Les Lettres françaises*, the clandestine literary review of the C.N.E. (Comité National des Ecrivains). At the end of the war, Paulhan opposed the persecution of collaborationist writers, and in *De la paille et du grain* (1948; Straw and Grain) and *Lettre aux directeurs de la Résistance* (1952; Letter to the Leaders of the Resistance), he engaged in active polemics with the Communist Left. In 1945 he was awarded the Grand Prix de Littérature of the Académie Française, and in 1951 he received the Grand Prix de la Ville de Paris. Paulhan was elected to the Académie Française in 1965.

Paulhan is a curious phenomenon: a man of letters who ruled inconspicuously and discreetly over one of the most influential centers of Parisian literary activity. He wrote hundreds of short pieces, including prefaces, reviews, notes, and some 25 book-length essays. Among these are three essays on art: *Braque le patron* (1945; Braque the Master), *Fautrier l'enragé* (1949; Fautrier the Violent One), and *L'Art informel* (1962; Informal Art), in which Paulhan continued his search for the laws that order and govern the signs of modern painting. His most significant and perhaps his best-known work, *Les Fleurs de Tarbes*, is a model of his endeavor and his achievement. What begins as a plea for the rehabilitation of commonplaces becomes an essay on the functioning of the human mind; an apparently simple subject becomes the pretext for reviewing, with a light touch, the gravest questions that man asks about his language.

See: M. J. Lefèbre, *Jean Paulhan: une philosophie et une pratique de l'expression et de la réflexion* (1949); J. Judrin, *La Vocation transparente de Jean Paulhan* (1961); special Paulhan no. of *NRF* 17, no. 197 (1968).   E.M.

Paustovsky, Konstantin Georgiyevich (1892–1968), Russian memoirist, essayist, publicist, fiction writer, and playwright, was born in Moscow but grew up in Kiev. He is known for his excellent autobiography, the six-part *Povest o zhizni* (1945, 1955, 1957, 1960, 1961, and 1964; American tr. of parts 1, 2, and 3 in *The Story of a Life*, 1964; British trs., *Story of a Life*, 1964; *Slow Approach of Thunder*, 1965; *In That Dawn*, 1967; *Years of Hope*, 1968; *Southern Adventure*, 1969; and *The Restless Years*, 1974). The first four parts cover Paustovsky's boyhood in Kiev through his university days in Moscow; his hospital-train service during World War I; his detached, civilian reactions to the February and October Revolutions of 1917 and the ensuing Civil War; and his life as a journalist in Soviet Odessa in the early 1920s, where typhus, famine, and inflation were rampant. These parts possess a unique combination of childlike charm, sensitivity for beauty, and muted self-criticism, along with vivid descriptions of both people (such as Isaak BABEL) and events (such as senseless killing). The fifth volume declines in quality, perhaps because the times described have neither the freshness of childhood and youth nor the excitement of revolution and war. The final volume, although the weakest of all, contains a noteworthy reminiscence of his boyhood schoolmate Mikhail BULGAKOV. It describes

Bulgakov as an adult in Moscow, telling of how he fantasized writing letters to Iosif Stalin signed "Tarzan."

One of Paustovsky's best essays, "Meshchorskaya storona" (1939; Eng. tr., "Meshchora Country," 1970), concerns the Meshchora countryside not far from Moscow, which he called his "second native land." In beautifully wrought and vividly evocative prose, he conveyed his joyful wonder at the modest glories of the Russian countryside.

Paustovsky's writings on current affairs, done largely in his last decade, helped to solidify his reputation as a man who combined loyalty to the Soviet regime with kindness and personal integrity. Perhaps his best article is "Besspornye i spornye mysli" (*Literaturnaya gazeta*, May 20, 1959, Eng. tr., "Indisputable Thoughts and Controversial Ones," *Current Digest of the Soviet Press*, 1959). It is a sensible and impassioned attack on the contemporary bureaucratization of the Russian language and the "harmful tradition" in Soviet literature of ignoring human sorrow and suffering. He published a book on writing, *Zolotaya roza* (1955; Eng. tr., "The Golden Rose," Moscow, 1957), containing some interesting observations on Russian words and writers. In 1956 he gave a speech on Soviet philistines, "The Drozdovs," which, although available in French and English, has not been published in the Soviet Union.

Paustovsky's fiction is much less successful than his nonfiction and is sometimes escapist. In his longer works, the plots tend to become episodic, whereas his shorter pieces suffer from sentimentality and repetition of devices. Neither are his plays very successful. It must be concluded that he is at his best when describing topics and events from his own experience.

Paustovsky's best work is filled with the romanticism of travel and with closely made observations about nature and people. His finest writing is about his own life or about nature.

See: E. H. Lehrman, "Konstantin Georgievich Paustovsky," in *Soviet Leaders*, ed. by G. Simmonds (New York, 1967), pp. 296–309; W. Kasack, *Der Stil Konstantin Georgievič Paustovskijs* (1971).   E.H.L.

Pavese, Cesare (1908–50), Italian novelist, poet, and critic, was born in Santo Stefano Belbo in the Piedmontese hills. Throughout his life, he considered this village his real home. He studied at the classical *liceo* and at the University of Turin, where he specialized in English and American literature and wrote a dissertation on Walt Whitman. During the next 12 years he wrote poems, a novella, and a novel, and translated Edgar Lee Masters, Sinclair Lewis, Herman Melville, Sherwood Anderson, James Joyce, John Dos Passos, Charles Dickens, Daniel Defoe, Gertrude Stein, and William Faulkner. The results of his studies of American literature were published in *La letteratura americana e altri saggi* (1951; Eng. tr., *American Literature: Essays and Opinions*, 1970).

Pavese's contributions to the publisher Einaudi's anti-Fascist review, *La cultura*, and some politically compromising letters to a woman friend led to his arrest and 10 months' *confino* at Brancaleone Calabro in 1935. This experience left a deep mark on him, as did the marriage of the woman he loved to another man. In 1943, after a period as director of Einaudi's Rome office, he retreated to Serralunga in the foothills of Piedmont, then a battleground for the Partisans and the German army. He returned to Turin as editorial director of Einaudi in 1945, contributed to the Communist newspaper *L'unità*, and was temporarily a member of the Communist Party. During his last five years, he published short stories, novellas,

and five novels. On Aug. 27, 1950, shortly after winning the Strega Prize, he committed suicide.

For many years, Pavese had been torn between a desire for participation in life and a contemplative disposition for creative solitude. This tension is expressed in a number of themes that reveal a creative personality in search of maturity, struggling with remembrances of childhood and adolescence, arriving at myth, and ending with what Gian-Paolo Biasin has called "poetics of destiny." Along the way, he examined the tragic nature of solitude, love, and violence, as well as the quintessential problem of modern man: human incommunicability.

Pavese's first poems in *Lavorare stanca* (1936; Eng. trs., *A Mania for Solitude: Selected Poems, 1930–1950*, 1969, *Hard Labor*, 1976) seem to bridge the separation of self and world, of individual and society, by praising work as an escape from sex and as a way of possessing nature and controlling chaos. But his early stories uncover obstacles. The hopes for participation and communion do not materialize. In fact, the tragic importance of solitude as part of an inescapable human condition becomes more and more apparent. Episodes of solitary wandering become more and more prominent. Developed in a style of quick, idiomatic dialogue, these episodes crop up with various nuances and slight variations throughout Pavese's work.

In their struggle between reality and fantasy, Pavese's early characters shrink from both love and action. In *Il carcere* (1949; Eng. tr., *The Political Prisoner*, 1955), Stefano's desire for human companionship is vitiated by his dread of intimacy and violence. When Berto, in *Paesi tuoi* (1941; Eng. tr., *The Harvesters*, 1961), comes in close contact with the violence unleashed by sexual passion, he discovers that it is impossible for him to belong to a world that is fundamentally bloody and cruel. Stefano and Berto are only two of many characters who exemplify what for Pavese must have been a deep, unresolved, and unconscious ambivalence toward violence, which many of his critics have attributed to a clinical condition of impotence.

The tragic action recurring in all Pavese's works is most profoundly recreated in its various mythological origins and incarnations in *Dialoghi con Leucò* (1947; Eng. tr., *Dialogues with Leuco*, 1965). The dialogues identify violence, even when it is transfigured and admired in nature, as the source of most adult problems, especially those of love. *Il diavolo sulle colline* (1948; Eng. tr., *The Devil in the Hills*, 1954) further shows how this tragic tendency interferes with the attainment of maturity and communication with others. The ending of *Diavolo* seems especially sad because the novel starts on a note of joy, adventure, and the unexpected. Workdays, holidays, and sacred festivals alternate in an ancient rhythm pervaded with the rituals of *homo ludens* and the hope of romance. But the return to country, childhood, and a poetic past serves only to expedite the discovery of sex, sickness, and death.

It is especially sex, which for Pavese is rarely liberating, that reveals the utter fragility of happiness. Hence, the search for reality, self, and one's own metaphysical being in the grain fields, vineyards, and hills does not culminate in the hoped for escape from the temporal dimension into mythical reality. Instead, happiness seems composed mainly of words and, as in *La bella estate* (1949; Eng. tr., *The Beautiful Summer*, 1955), leads only to disillusionment and boredom.

The lack of communication among the bourgeoisie is examined in *Tra donne sole* (1949; Eng. tr., *Among Women Only*, 1959), a novel about the antithesis of the dolce vita and work. Three memorable characters try to deal with this conflict, each in her own way. Momina's intellectual strategy proves utterly sterile, while Rosetta's almost pathological fear of ugliness and relativity leads her to suicide. Only Clelia is temporarily saved through her insistence on work. But even she only rarely breaks through her inability to communicate with others. The dialectic of her situation is not merely a private one; her predicament is clearly part of the macrocosm of history.

In *La casa in collina* (1949; Eng. tr., *The House on the Hill*, 1956), Pavese no longer treats failures in family life and in the field of political responsibility as private fates but as part of a collective human destiny. The mysterious origins and mythic manifestations of this destiny are contemplated by Pavese in what some consider his best novel: *La luna e i falò* (1950; Eng. tr., *The Moon and the Bonfire*, 1953). The protagonist, Anguilla, returns to his place of origin in search of his true self and timelessness, but he discovers that the years and life's violence have destroyed his youth. After this realization, he reluctantly decides to resume his wandering. In *La luna e i falò*, Pavese the writer exhibits, as Biasin has written, a "total comprehension of human life, from birth to death; virile acceptance of the mystery behind life; the maturity that derives from understanding and acceptance." Unfortunately, this was not enough to satisfy the metaphysical yearnings of Pavese the man. As the last poems, *Verrà la morte e avrà i tuoi occhi* (1951; Death Will Come and Its Eyes Will Be Yours), and his diary, *Il mestiere di vivere* (1952; Eng. tr., *The Burning Brand*, 1961), demonstrate, Pavese's deeper need was no longer to write about suffering, but to become himself the exemplary artist-hero who accepts the ultimate suffering of death as the supreme token of his seriousness.

In the end, it was this relentless and intense seriousness that made Pavese the most complex writer of his generation. Lyrical and elegiac by temperament, he nevertheless fashioned a lucid prose in whose clarity and precision the reader can sense the best of classicism, Italian *verismo* (*see* ITALIAN LITERATURE), American realism, and European symbolism. His style combines first-person narrative with rapid, broken dialogue that at first emphasizes and sustains the narrative and then trails off into evocative, if sometimes disquieting and melancholy, impressions. In the mastery of this technique, Pavese has few equals.

See: G. P. Biasin, *The Smile of the Gods: A Thematic Study of Cesare Pavese's Works* (1968); D. W. Heiney, in *Three Italian Novelists: Moravia, Pavese, Vittorini* (1968).   F.S.

Pavlović, Miodrag (1928–), Serbian poet, was born in Novi Sad. In 1950 he abandoned a medical career in order to devote his full time to professional writing. Since then he has published several collections of poems, plays, short stories, and essays, many of which have been translated into several European languages. He became one of the editors of the Prosveta publishing house.

Together with Vasko POPA, Pavlović is recognized as one of the leading figures in postwar Serbian poetry. He is undeniably a poets' poet. The verse collected in such volumes as *87 pesama* (1952; 87 Poems), *Oktave* (1957), *Mleko iskoni* (1963; The Milk of Yore), *Velika skitija* (1969; The Great Scythian), and *Svetli i tamni praznici* (1970; Bright and Dark Holidays) requires a serious intellectual effort on the part of the reader in order to be understood and appeciated. The poetry is neither declarative, narrative, nor confessional, but it is thought-provoking and visionary. While Pavlović's work may appear cold, rational, and almost hermetic, it is in fact deeply spiritual and unmistakably humanistic. Its essence is a

philosophical preoccupation with the metaphysics of life and man, a profound intellectual contemplation of man's destiny, and a compassionate plea for the restoration of human dignity. Pavlović's poetry also seeks the meaning of history and a declaration of human grandeur overshadowed by moral chaos, intellectual depravity, and social degradation. His style is characterized by emotional restraint and the suppression of romantic and sentimental subjectivism. For this reason his poetry, although modern in every sense of that word, is at the same time classical.

See: S. Velmar-Janković "Poezija Miodraga Pavlovića," *Savremenici* (1967), pp. 178–97.   M.M.

Pawlikowska-Jasnorzewska, Maria (1891–1945), Polish poet and playwright, was born in Cracow and died in Manchester, England. She was born Maria Kossak into a family of famous painters. Beginning with her first volumes of poems, *Niebieskie migdały* (1922; Fiddle-Faddle), *Różowa magia* (1924; Pink Magic), and *Pocałunki* (1926; Kisses), she established herself as a sharply defined and very original, if not unique, creative personality. Her poetry was a daring revelation of modern, but not conventional femininity. It was characterized by the utmost emotional and stylistic discretion, restraint, and conciseness. *Pocałunki* comprised over 60 quatrains, which have been compared to Alexandrian and Roman epigrammatic poetry or to the Japanese tanka and haiku. Their main thematic interest is love, expressed in a natural, colloquial language and encompassing a large gamut of tones. In the poetic instrumentation of these miniatures, Pawlikowska-Jasnorzewska revealed an unusual metaphorical inventiveness, a virtuosity of metric form, and a mastery of the surprising pointe.

In the later volumes—*Dancing* (1927), *Cisza leśna* (1928; Forest Stillness), *Paryż* (1928; Paris), *Profil białej damy* (1930; A Profile of the White Lady), *Śpiąca załoga* (1933; A Sleeping Crew), *Krystalizacje* (1937; Crystallizations), and others—the seeming frivolity that misled some critics began to reveal the deeper recesses of the personality, a growing obsession with the biological process of decay and death. It led to new spheres of interest (for example, occultism, spiritism) and became the basis of a poetic philosophy of nature, akin to Hinduism. This phase ended with a catastrophic premonition of the approaching war.

Pawlikowska-Jasnorzewska spent her last years in exile in France and Great Britain. Her poetry voiced one of the most outspoken humanitarian protests against the horrors of war as well as a poignant nostalgia for her homeland and her family. The volumes *Róża i lasy płonące* (1940; The Rose and the Burning Forests), *Gołab ofiarny* (1945; The Sacrificial Dove), and a rich collection published posthumously, *Ostatnie utwory* (1956; Last Works), bring the poetic output of Pawlikowski-Jasnorzewska to a total of 16 volumes.

The plays (more than 10 produced and only a few published) represent the less important part of her work, but they bear the stamp of her keen intelligence, poetic finesse, delicate humor and mastery of the art of witty dialogue. Among the best are *Szofer Archibald* (1924; Archibald the Driver) and *Baba Dziwo* (prod. 1938, pub. 1966; The Wondrous Hag), a metaphorical drama with a sharp antitotalitarian, anti-Nazi satirical edge.

See: *Słownik współczesnych pisarzy polskich*, vol. 2 (1964), pp. 628–35; J. Kwiatkowski, Introduction to M. Pawlikowska-Jasnorzewska, *Wybór wierszy*, (3d ed., 1972).   T.T.

Pedro (da Costa), António (1909–66), Portuguese poet and theater director, a native of the Cape Verde Islands, was the first in his country to come out openly and totally in defense of surrealism. While an announcer for the Portuguese language programs of the British Broadcasting Company in London during World War II, he belonged to a surrealist group there (1944–45), and after his return to Lisbon, he served as a mentor for a similar Portuguese group (1947). As a poet, he published *Diário* (1929; Diary), a book strongly influenced by motifs of his Cape Verde childhood, which contributed to the flowering of regional literature in the archipelago. The *Protopoema da Serra d'Arga* (1948; Protopoem of the Arga Mountains) reflects his interest in surrealism and displays his linguistic skills. Pedro is also the author of a work of fiction, *Apenas uma narrativa* (1942; Only a Tale). As a theater director, he strove to react against the commercialization and decadence of Portuguese drama in the 20th century. In 1948–49 he worked with the experimental group *Pátio das Comédias* (The Play Pit), Lisbon, which did much to revive interest in the stage by updating basic concepts; and in 1953 he became director of the Experimental Theater in Oporto. He was also active in the JUBA movement, which in the period from 1949 to 1955 organized highly popular weekly sessions in a fashionable Lisbon movie theater where classical and avant-garde films were shown and discussed by distinguished critics.

In spite of his relatively early death, Pedro stands out as one of the most enthusiastic and versatile members of the belated and dispersive Portuguese surrealist movement.

See: M. Ferreira, *A aventura crioula* (1973), pp. 280–87.

E.M.D.

Péguy, Charles (1873–1914), French poet and essayist, was born in Orléans. His father a cabinet-maker, died a few months after his birth, and he was brought up by his mother, a chairseat-maker. Thanks to various scholarships and a brilliant record as a student, he was admitted to the Ecole Normale Supérieure in 1894. His family life and subsequent education contributed to those qualities that were to be characteristic of Péguy's life and work: a knowledge of, and a love for, the common man (that is, peasants and artisans) and the poor; feelings of melancholy, tenderness, and timidity in the presence of women; a respect for children, family, work, and knowledge; an admiration for classical culture; patriotism, and exasperation at the defeat of 1870; republicanism, viewed as a triple aspiration toward justice, fraternity, and liberty; and anticlericalism. Péguy's mistrust of an authoritarian Church compromised by association with the rich is demonstrated in *Pierre: commencement d'une vie bourgeoise* (1898; Pierre: The Beginning of a Bourgeois Life), *Par ce demi-clair matin* (1906; On This Half-Clear Morning), and especially *L'Argent* (1901; Money).

Although fully indoctrinated by catechism courses, he abandoned all religious observance for political, philosophical, and theological reasons, and, for 20 years, he declared himself to be an atheist. He originally planned a teaching career, which he considered "the finest of all trades." Throughout his life he was attracted to three disciplines: literature, philosophy, and history. All three inspired his first work, *Jeanne d'Arc* (1897), a play in three acts whose characters include a poet, still the prisoner of traditional forms, and a prose writer, whose language, both learned and familiar, gives evidence of exceptional gifts. Dedicated to "those who have lived . . . and who have died for the coming of the Universal Socialist Republic," *Jeanne d'Arc* bears witness to the spiritual upheaval that he himself was then undergoing. Moved by the poverty and wretchedness of the pro-

letariat, strongly attracted by the personality and thought of Jean JAURÈS, he had become converted to socialism around 1895. Abandoning his teaching career, he sank his personal funds and those of his wife into founding the "Librairie Socialiste" (1898) and into publishing that same year his "Utopia": *Marcel: premier dialogue de la cité harmonieuse* (Marcel: The First Dialogue of the Harmonious City). The Dreyfus Affair only strengthened his determination to engage in political action, as is evident in *Cahiers de l'amitié Charles Péguy* (1957) and *Notes politiques et sociales,* a collection of articles originally published in the *Revue blanche* in 1899.

As a socialist, Péguy is authentic, because he gives absolute priority to the war on poverty, and orthodox, because he preaches an "economic revolution." Péguy's socialism rejects materialistic monism and class struggle while it abhors all dogmatism, all propaganda, and all Party discipline. Without completely excluding violence, he believed revolution to be possible through free education for the common people. From the very start, the "anarchistic communism" to which he always remained faithful made Péguy a "contestataire," a heretic, perpetually outside the pale of those who compromise or betray the socialist "mystique"; Jaurès himself and the five directors of the "Librairie Socialiste" expelled him from "his company" for not being orthodox.

The decisive act of Péguy's career was his founding of the *Cahiers de la quinzaine* (Fortnightly Notebooks) in January 1900. Unique in the history of the French press, this enterpise was to continue for 15 years, despite numerous difficulties and much anxiety, without recourse to advertising and without the smallest subsidy from any political party or from the government. Indeed, the publication existed with only the support of a few generous friends and subscribers, never numbering more than 1,200. The 229 cahiers Peguy issued constituted a monumental collection. Although certain famous writers collaborated on it (Henri BERGSON, Romain ROLLAND, the THARAUD brothers, Georges SOREL, André SUARÈS, Daniel HALÉVY, Julien BENDA), Péguy was the manager, by far the principal author, and sometimes even the typographer. Beginning with the first number, he published extremely varied personal works: dialogues, narratives, book reviews, fantasies, and even songs. The *Cahiers* was also a forum for essays, critical, polemical, comical, or serious, at first rather brief and incisive, then longer and longer. Not one of these essays, generically entitled *De la situation faite à . . .* (Concerning the State of . . .), including those in five volumes still unpublished, is not a work of combat. In them, Péguy battled in the name of truth and liberty; against the abuses of colonialism, French as well as foreign (in Indochina, the Congo, Madagascar); against anti-Semitism; against the temporal and spiritual domination of the "intellectual party" and of the politicians who had come to power after the Dreyfus Affair; against the sectarian anticlericalism (very different from his) of left-wing governments; against literary historians, plain historians, and sociologists whose presumption was equaled only by their incapability of arriving at "sacred reality"; and, finally, for France, threatened in 1905 by a new German invasion and whose defeat would signify, in Péguy's opinion, the end of the socialist dream.

While pursuing his polemical work, Péguy was engaged in a search for truth (metaphysical and religious) that led him to declare that he had "found faith again." A long work, *De la grippe* (Concerning Flu), took shape in 1900 in three notebooks in which, under the influence of Bergson, Blaise Pascal, and the "sacred texts," Péguy discovered that certain realities of another order (and, as such, inaccessible to science) reveal themselves to Christians. His *Clio: dialogue de l'histoire et de l'âme charnelle* (1909; Clio: Dialogue of History and the Carnal Soul), is a major work (rewritten and augmented in 1912 with a slightly different title) containing a long meditation on the human condition and the mystery of Christ. Nevertheless, Péguy did not renounce his implacable accusations against the modern Catholic Church, whose doctors remained for him forever suspect. At no moment did he become a practicing Catholic, but this great faith of "a half-rebellious grown-up son" became purer between 1910 and 1914 under the combined influence of reflection, prayer, and trials of all kinds. Péguy's faith found expression in poetry, which he had also rediscovered. For example, while writing his play *Le Mystère de la charité de Jeanne d'Arc* (1910; Eng. tr., *The Mystery of the Charity of Joan of Arc,* 1950), an expansion of parts of his earlier play on the subject, he substituted supple verse for passages he had first written in prose. Similar to *Le Mystère* in inspiration and style are *Le Porche du mystère de la deuxième vertu* (1911; The Porch of the Mystery of the Second Virtue), *Le Mystère des Saints Innocents* (1912; The Mystery of the Holy Innocents), and the *Ballade du cœur qui a tant battu* (Ballad of the Heart That Has Beaten So Much), a series of unfinished quatrains that remained for a long time unpublished.

Péguy's last poetical works, such as *Sonnets, prières, tapisseries* (Sonnets, Prayers, Tapestries), were written about the time of his pilgrimage to the cathedral of Chartres (1912) and are composed in classical alexandrines. His theologico-poetic monument is *Eve* (1914) in which Jesus speaks to Eve, his "venerable ancestor," in a language of noble simplicity that is also rich in images sensual, rustic, and familiar. In this work, Péguy the poet-prophet unfolds the Christian vision of history from primitive Eden to the resurrection of the dead. Although *Eve* is sometimes tiresomely repetitious, it is, taken as a whole, one of the most astonishing French poems since Victor Hugo.

Péguy's mature prose works are no less profound a record of his spiritual and creative growth. Varied though it is, this work is first of all a way of confiding his process of creation and his spiritual itinerary. Such is the case with *Notre Jeunesse* (1910; Our Youth), in which the former Dreyfusard cuts short any attempt at recuperation by the nationalistic, clerical, and monarchistic Right. Such is also the case for *Victor-Marie, comte Hugo* (1910); the virulent *Un Nouveau Theologien: Monsieur Fernand Laudet* (1911; A New Theologian: Mr. Fernand Laudet), in which Péguy tackles the new adversaries, bourgeois and right-thinking Catholics; *L'Argent: suite* (1913; Money: A Continuation), in which he proclaims the French to be the chosen people bearing the message of liberty; and *Note sur M. Bergson et la philosophie bergsonienne* (1914), in which he defends his "liberator" from the attacks of Jacques MARITAIN.

On Sept. 5, 1914, Lieutenant Péguy was killed in battle at Villeroy. Yet in the last quarter of the 20th century, he remains very much alive, passionately admired and discussed, although his work, still not properly published, is somewhat inaccessible. Collected fragments of his work were published for the first time in English by Ann and Julien GREEN as *Basic Verities* (1943) and *Men and Saints* (1944).

See: D. Halévy, *Charles Péguy et les Cahiers de la quinzaine* (1918, 1944); R. Secretain, *Péguy: soldat de la vérité* (1941; 1973); A. Béguin, *La Prière de Péguy* (1944); R. Rolland, *Péguy* (1944); J. Onimus, *Péguy et le mystère de l'histoire* (1958); B. Guyon, *Péguy: l'homme et l'œuvre* (1960, 1973); J. Viard, *Philosophie de l'art littéraire et*

socialisme selon Péguy (1968); J. Sabiani, *La Ballade du cœur* (1973); B. Guyon, *Péguy devant Dieu* (1974).

B.G.

Pellerin, Jean Victor (1889–1970), French dramatist, after writing a novel, *Insulaire* (1920), made his debut in the theater in 1922 with a one-act play called *Intimité* (Intimacy). In it the author used a scenic effect that served him in good stead for many years: the characters, husband and wife, are engaged in a conversation that is far from transmitting their true thoughts, which are represented at the rear of the stage by other actors and actresses. The effect is highly satiric. *Le Plus Bel Homme de France* (1925; The Handsomest Man in France) was slightly less of a success. A deceived husband and his wife's lover are themselves deceived by "the handsomest man in France." The fault of the play lay in the fact that the author strove to transform his characters into symbols; they became lifeless, illogical, meaningless. *Têtes de rechange* (1926; Spare Heads) was well received by the critics. Pellerin again made use of the effect that had first won him fame. A young man called Ixe is visited in his office by his uncle, Opéku, who has come to ask his nephew for some financial advice. While the elder man is talking, the young man's mind wanders, and the scenes that follow represent his daydreams. This is typical of the author's predilection for "externalizing" his hero's thoughts. The play cannot really be classified as drama, but rather as a pageant; it calls attention to a certain restlessness characteristic of the era.

It was apparently the author's intention, in *Cris des cœurs* (1928; Heart Cries), to present a vast triptych depicting once again this same restless feeling so prevalent among his contemporaries. In the first act, a young man is set upon by his ideas come to life. The setting of the second act represents the facade of a home, which fades away to reveal four apartments and four couples. As they are picked out by the spotlight, each character tells of his or her desires and sorrows. The theme that runs through their dialogue is the dissatisfaction of modern man who, torn by conflicting instincts and intellectually ill, seeks refuge in love, only to find that it too fails to provide the desired peace. In the third act, a philosophical sculptor proposes a double solution—work and religion. Obviously inspired in part by Francis JAMMES and Paul CLAUDEL, the play remains rather naive, arbitrary, and disconcerting.

Pellerin's plays seem to lose with age. Their complement of surprise lost, they appear dated. Something of their satirical value, however, remains.

See: E. Sée, *Le Théâtre français contemporain* (1928), pp. 167–68, and *Le Mouvement dramatique* (1930–1935), vol. 1: 85–86; vol. 3: 186–90; D. Knowles, *French Drama of the Inter-War Years* (1968), pp. 125–28.

P.Br.

Pemán, José María (1897–), Spanish essayist, playwright, novelist, and poet, was born in Cádiz and studied law at the universities of Seville and Madrid. In 1920 he became a member of the Spanish-American Academy of Cádiz. Pemán was first known as a poet, author of *De la vida sencilla* (1923; On the Simple Life), *Nuevas poesías* (1925; New Poems), *A la rueda, rueda . . .* (1928; Round and Round . . .), and *El barrio del Santa Cruz* (1931; The District of Santa Cruz). His poetry is evocative of popular motifs and regional color. Pemán owed his popularity, however, to his work as a playwright. He has written more than 70 plays, beginning with *El Divino impaciente* (1933; Eng. tr., *A Saint in a Hurry,* 1935), a highly successful drama that earned him the Cortina Prize of the Royal Spanish Academy of the Language. With this work, and following the example of Eduardo MARQUINA, he initiated a series of plays in verse: *Cuando las Cortes de Cádiz* (1934; When the Cortes of Cádiz Met), *Cisneros* (1934), *Julieta y Romeo* (1936); *La santa virreina* (1939; The Viceroy's Sainted Wife), and *Metternich* (1942). These are traditional and propagandistic plays, which present a simplistic vision of history. They are at the same time popular theater representative of the bourgeoisie of Francisco Franco's Spain. Perhaps the worst short-coming of Pemán's work is its strong ideological character, for he was induced to become a defender of the conservative political and religious ideals of postwar Spain. Nevertheless, a more liberal ideological orientation becomes apparent in his later comedies of manners, which he calls "popular farce," such as *Los tres etcéteras de Don Simón* (1958; Don Simon's Three Etceteras).

Even though Pemán started as a poet, gained international fame as a dramatist, and is also a novelist, his best and most numerous works are his essays. In 1935 he received the Mariano Cavia Prize, awarded to the best newspaper article of the year, for his essay "Nieve en Cádiz" (Snow in Cádiz), published in *El Debate*. In 1936 he became a member of the Royal Spanish Academy of the Language, and he was its director from 1940 to 1947. His essays appeared regularly in the pages of the best newspapers and journals of Spain and Spanish America, especially in *La Vanguardia, ABC, Mundo Hispánico, Blanco y Negro,* and *Gaceta Ilustrada*. The first volume of his *Obras completas* appeared in 1944, and of the seven volumes already published, three are devoted to his essays. With some exceptions, including *De doce cualidades de la mujer* (1947; On Twelve Qualities of Woman) and *Ocho ensayos religiosos* (1948; Eight Religious Essays), most of Pemán's essays had not been published in book form until they were collected in the *Obras completas*. Among his latest books of essays the following stand out: *Ensayos andaluces* (1972; Andalusian Essays) and *Mis encuentros con Franco* (1976; My Encounters with Franco).

See: A. Barbadillo, ed., *En torno a Pemán* (1974); P. Laín Entralgo, "La Andalucía de Pemán," *Arbor* 354 (1975): 7–24.   J.L.G.-M.

Penna, Sandro (1906–77), Italian poet, was born in Perugia. After 1922 he lived mostly in Rome. Penna's poems are contained in the collections *Poesie* (1939; Poems), *Appunti* (1950; Notes), *Una strana gioia di vivere* (1957; A Strange Joy of Living), *Croce e delizia* (1958; Suffering and Delight), and *Tutte le poesie* (1970; Complete Poems). *Un po' di febbre* (A Degree of Fever), a book of sketches and memoirs, was published in 1972.

Most of Penna's poems deal with the theme of homosexual love, which appears essentially as the revelation of an unattainable object. Dramatizing the tension between the real and imaginative world of erotic experience, Penna depicts the circumstances and effects of his passion with synthetic and epigrammatic clarity. His poetic vocabulary, compared to that of his contemporaries, is notably simple, restricted to the use of only a few images, such as light, dawn, evening, and dream. But his originality consists precisely in his quest for the essential and natural. His most suggestive lyrics are short, although subtly modulated and, at times, strangely ambiguous. His young boys appear in flashes against the background of daily urban life, on buses, in doorways and train stations, or in fields and public gardens. Their real or desired

presence allows for the poet's temporary reconciliation with an oppressive and insensitive world.

Critics have compared Penna's verse with that of his friend and mentor Umberto SABA and, more appropriately, with the monodic lyric of classical Greece, which it resembles in its grace and transparent structure.

See: R. S. Dombroski, "The Undisciplined Eros of Sandro Penna," BA 47, no. 2 (1973); 304–06; G. Mariani, in *Letteratura italiana: i contemporanei,* vol. 3, pp. 479–94.   R.S.D.

Pereda, José María (1833–1906), Spanish novelist and short-story writer, was born in Polanco, a village in the province of Santander. The youngest son of a large family of the local gentry, his education was strict and traditional and left an indelible mark on him. For his entire life he respected the status quo, believed in an inalterable social structure, and remained a devout Catholic. He made relatively few forays outside Santander, but they affected his life greatly, especially his two years in Madrid, where he did his preparatory study before entering the Artillery Academy in Segovia. During this time he observed and participated in the city's cultural life, and developed so profound a distaste for that life that he returned to Santander physically ill and mentally troubled. This antipathy can be seen in his rejection of the ways of the capital in his writings. Later in life, after the liberal revolution of 1868, Pereda plunged into a campaign against the liberals, first with violent newspaper articles and later as a congressman on the traditionalist side. But this view of his personality, based on his public self, may prove distorted if not balanced with what we learn from his personal correspondence and friends, who portray Pereda as a simple man with traditional ideas and a fine sensitivity to art and life which earned him not only the respect but also the friendship of such liberal writers as Benito PÉREZ GALDÓS and Leopoldo ALAS.

Pereda's first book, *Escenas montañesas* (1864; Mountain Scenes) is a collection of articles and sketches that depict the customs, peculiarities, architecture, and speech of the mountainous region of Santander province, near the sea. Two characteristics stand out: Pereda's love for his native land and his dedication to the description of social manners. The people portrayed are types, not characters, for Pereda was interested more in portraiture and the landscape than in the interaction of character and circumstance. Ideologically, the stories reveal a traditionalist author opposed to innovation. As fiction the sketches are interesting as possible settings for plot development. Neither Pereda's ideological stance nor his prose craftsmanship changed substantially during his lifetime. *Tipos y paisajes* (1871; Types and Landscapes), *Bocetos al temple* (1876; Sketches in Distemper), *Tipos trashumantes* (1877; Nomadic Types), and *Esbozos y rasguños* (1881; Outlines and Sketches) are not very different from his first book, although Pereda attempted to inject some fictional narrative into the scenes.

For Pereda the novel was the repository of tradition and, in a way, a form of patriotism: it was an appropriate instrument of defense against the rapid changes of society, whose old values were either being lost or endangered, even in his remote region. This attitude prevailed as a basic tenet of his fiction, giving it a didactic, moralistic tone. His first full-fledged novel, *El buey suelto* (1878; The Bachelor), was a failure because of its biased view. From then on, his observation of reality grew more complex and subtle. *Don Gonzalo González de la Gonzalera* (1879), *De tal palo tal astilla* (1880; A Chip off the Old Block), and *El sabor de la tierruca* (1882; Redolent of the Soil), show a new understanding of liberal idealism. His characters are less flat, his gentleman protagonists more human. Even the narrative techniques are more elaborate, especially in *El sabor*. With *Pedro Sánchez* (1883), Pereda achieves his first novelistic success. A more inspired work and less dependent on a priori conceptions, *Pedro Sánchez* is based on Pereda's recollection of his student days in Madrid. It is narrated in the first person. His imagination is freer, the prose flows with a new ease, and the descriptions of manners in Santander and Madrid are finally integrated into the artistic whole. The four novels that followed this huge success are less important, the most memorable being *La puchera* (1889; The Stew). Next comes the zenith of his career: *Sotileza* (1885), a description of the maritime life of Santander. The scenes are vivid, recalling *Escenas*, but also more ebullient. Among the characters are Father Apolinar, a superb portrait of a truly Christian priest, and Muergo, a naturalistic creature who personifies both the brutality inherent in the poverty-stricken life of the fishermen and the tenderness of a naive man. Above all there is Sotileza, a woman of exemplary humility and simple pride. The elements used previously to vivify the scenes now play a dominant role. The sea, for example, incarnates the awesome power of the unknown, when during a storm it is transformed from a routine place of work into a battlefield where man is forced to become a hero in order to survive. In this work Pereda finally brings together his talent for fictional portrayal, his close knowledge of the life of the region, and his ideology. *Peñas arriba* (1895; Up in the Mountains) is his other most remembered novel. These two masterpieces have a lasting place in 19th-century fiction, although as novels they are clearly surpassed by others. Their aesthetic value resides in the richness of detail and scenic composition. Pereda's imagination copes best with compositional problems on a small scale. In his quest for regional realism, Pereda was able to create a literary replica of the popular language, for which other writers of his time were indebted to him.

See: J. M. de Cossío, *La obra literaria de Pereda, su historia y crítica* (1934); J. F. Montesinos, *Pereda o la novela idilio* (1959); L. H. Klibbe, *José María de Pereda* (1975).   G.Gu.

Pereleshin, Valery, pseud. of Valery Frantsevich Salatko-Petrishche (1913–), Russian émigré poet and translator, was born in Siberia, lived for many years in Harbin, China, and finally settled in Brazil. An acknowledged follower of Nikolay GUMILYOV and the acmeists, Pereleshin did not receive the wide recognition that his poetic gift deserved until late in his life. In the words of Alexis Rannit, Pereleshin's poetry is characterized by "laconicism, spareness in the use of artistic devices, [and a] striving for sculptural clarity of form and for plastic perfection of rhythmic outline." He published four collections of poems in China; his works since then include *Yuzhny dom* (1968; The Southern House), *Kachel* (1971; The Swing), *Zapovednik* (1972; The Preserve), and *S gory Nevo* (1975; Down Mt. Nebo). His translations include an anthology of classical Chinese poetry as well as poems by Samuel Taylor Coleridge, Fernando PESSOA, and many Brazilian poets.

See: A. Rannit, "Valery Pereleshin," *NovZ* no. 107 (1972): 280–82.   H.W.T. and W.B.E

Péret, Benjamin (1899–1959), French poet and essayist, was the closest disciple of André BRETON. Péret never deserted the camp of surrealism or betrayed its early enthusiasm for automatic writing. He was one of the most vivid practitioners not only of the enforced meeting of images beyond the limits of rational choice (and yet within the bounds of "normal" syntax) but also of surrealist theory. This commitment was manifested in his unrelentingly antiestablishment gestures and writings, particularly the volume of poetry *Le Grand Jeu* (1928; The Great Game) and the short stories collected in *Le Gigot, sa vie et son œuvre* (1957; The Leg of Lamb, His Life and Work). His hobby, he said, was spitting at members of the clergy, and photographs provide convincing testimony of the claim. The military received no better treatment, nor did the actively patriotic: thus his attack on Resistance poetry in *Le Déshonneur des poètes* (1945; The Dishonor of Poets), a criticism of Paul ELUARD's famous contributions to the collective volume *L'Honneur des poètes* (1943–44), an anthology of "committed" poetry, which Péret called nationalistic and propagandistic "litanies."

Péret worked with anarchists in Spain in 1936–37, and he always remained loyal to the Trotskyite ideals of surrealism. *Je ne mange pas de ce pain-là* (1936; I'm Not Swallowing Any of It), the title of one of his volumes of poetry, might stand as the motto for all his work. His *Anthologie des mythes, légendes et contes populaires d'Amérique* (1960; Anthology of Myths, Legends, and Popular Stories of America) is an invaluable testimony to the deeply poetic strength of primitive imagery and language, whereas his *Anthologie de l'amour sublime* (1956; Anthology of Sublime Love) bears eloquent witness to his conception of "sublime love," comparable to Breton's "amour fou" or irrational love.

See: C. Courtot, *Introduction à la lecture de Benjamin Péret* (1966); M. A. Caws, "Benjamin Péret's Game and Gesture," in *The Inner Theatre of Recent French Poetry* (1972), pp. 75–105; J. H. Matthews, *Benjamin Péret* (1975).   M.A.C.

Peretz, Yitzkhok Leibush (1852–1915), Yiddish poet and novelist, was born in Zamość, a town in the province of Lublin, Poland. Besides the traditional education in the Bible, the Talmud, and Hebrew, he received private instruction in Russian, German, and other secular subjects. Brooding over problems of life, death, God, and fate, the youth set out to find an answer in books. He obtained access to a rich private library, where he read the German, Polish, and Russian volumes without much discrimination and then taught himself French so that he could devour the French books as well. Physics and fiction, law and philosophy, were pored over with equal zeal, but his longing for a definitive solution of eternal problems remained unsatisfied.

Peretz began to write at the age of 14. After experimenting with Polish and Hebrew, he finally decided upon Yiddish as a literary vehicle, since only in this tongue could he be adequately understood by the Jewish working masses, whom he was interested in enlightening. His first major Yiddish poem, "Monish," appeared in 1888, and his first collection of Yiddish tales was published in 1890 under the title of *Bekannte Bilder* (Familiar Portraits). During the next quarter of a century he forged ahead as the supreme figure in modern Yiddish literature. Peretz's social lyrics were recited and his love lyrics were sung throughout Eastern Europe. His short stories stirred to pity and to action. The best known of these, "Bontsie Shvaig" (Bontsie Silent), is centered about an inarticulate, lowly worker, who finds no reward in this world of illusion, but for whom there is reserved in the kingdom of heaven a seat at the side of the saints and patriarchs of Israel.

Peretz furthered the development of the Yiddish theater with three major mystical dramas, of which the best-known is *Di Goldene Keyt* (1909; The Golden Chain). Peretz pleads the cause of the heart as against the claims of the intellect, the cause of the poor as against the arrogance of the rich, the cause of the Chassidim or mystics as against their deriders, the practical people who lay claim to the goods of this earth. Peretz, MENDELE MOCHER SFORIM, and SHOLEM ALEICHEM form the triad of classical Yiddish literature.

See: A. A. Roback, *Peretz, Psychologist of Literature* (1935); S. Liptzin, *Peretz* (bilingual edition, 1947); M. Samuel, *Prince of the Ghetto* (1948).   S.L.

Pereverzev, Valerian Fydorovich (1882–1968), pioneer Marxist critic and historian of Russian literature, and principal theoretician of the so-called sociological method in literary analysis in the 1920s, was born in Bobrov and studied at the University of Kharkov, where the influence of philologist A. A. Potebnya was strong. He joined the Social Democratic movement in 1902. After the 1917 Revolution he was associated with various literary institutes.

Apart from his two major works, *Tvorchestvo Dostoyevskogo* (1912; The Creative Work of Dostoyvsky) and *Tvorchestvo Gogolya* (1914; The Creative Work of Gogol)—both of them landmarks in scholarship—Pereverzev wrote theoretical works on Marxian literary theory as well as studies on Ivan Goncharov, Maksim GORKY, Dmitry Pisarev, the early 19th-century writers V. I. Narezhny and Aleksandr Veltman, as well as a posthumous published work on old Russian literature. Pereverzev's unpublished works include studies on Aleksandr Pushkin's narrative poems, on Vissarion Belinsky and the theater, and a theoretical work entitled "On the Foundations of Eidological Poetics."

In 1928, at the peak of his influence as a Marxist literary theoretician, Pereverzev edited a collection of essays, *Literaturovedeniya* (The Study of Literature), in which the views of his sociological "school" are expounded. Pereverzev's "sociological method" (he preferred the term "historical-materialistic method") was extensively debated in the Soviet press in the late 1920s. In 1930 it was officially condemned as a "vulgar materialist revision of revolutionary Marxism." At its best, Marxist criticism of Pereverzev sought to transcend the limitations of the "genetic" approach to literature. In the main, however, the criticism of Pereverzev was itself "vulgar," one-sided, and politically charged.

A scholar of extraordinary talents, Pereverzev continued G. V. PLEKHANOV'S quest for the "sociological equivalent" of literary phenomena. Pereverzev, however, insisted on the primacy of textual analysis. He was the first Russian Marxist scholar to put into practice the notion that the real validation of the materialist interpretation of culture must take place first of all in studies analyzing the materials of art—style, structure, imagery, genre. In this sense his prerevolutionary works may be defined as among the earliest examples of Marxist "chamber" scholarship. Pereverzev's writings strongly reflect the 19th century's concern for determinism and "law" in all areas of science and culture (Hippolyte Taine, Karl Marx, Charles Darwin, Claude Bernard, Emile ZOLA, Sigmund Freud). What gives his work its paradoxical character is his effort to fuse a narrow materialism with a valid psychological theory of aesthetic intuition.

Pereverzev's Marxian aesthetics, whatever its strengths or limitations, had nothing in common with the prescriptive "Marxian" criticism of most of his Soviet critics. He was unalterably opposed to the so-called social command in art. His theory of "ideology in image," his idea that the writer cannot escape the "magic circle" of his imagery (that is, cannot create artistically successful works

except out of his own social and psychological experience) earned him the title of "literary fatalist." His ideas were unacceptable to the ruling Party critics and propagandists who sought to bend writers to the utilitarian and "revolutionary" demands of Stalinist social and cultural politics.

Pereverzev's writings remain an important source for the study of Russian literature and for the examination of sociological approaches to literature. His passionate rationalism and confidence in the scientific method mark him in certain respects as a forerunner of 20th-century structuralist critics.

See: H. Ermolaev, *Soviet Literary Theories: 1917–1934* (1963), pp. 93–99; R. L. Jackson, "The Sociological Method of V. F. Pereverzev: A Rage for Structure and Determinism," in *Literature and Society in Imperial Russia, 1800–1914,* ed. by W. M. Todd III (1978), pp. 29–60.
                                                                R.J.

Pérez de Ayala, Ramón (1880–1962), Spanish novelist, poet, and essayist, was born in Oviedo. The son of a Castilian businessman established in Asturias, he belonged, like so many Spanish intellectuals, to the relatively well-off middle class. When he was eight, his parents sent him to a Jesuit academy, where he had a very bad time of it. Years later he wrote an autobiographical novel, *A.M.D.G.* (1910), relating this experience. When he undertook law studies in Oviedo, the university there had a roster of professors of high quality and liberal bent, influenced by the philosophy of Karl Krause that so powerfully informed Spanish intellectual life from the second half of the 19th century on. Leopoldo ALAS, the great novelist, was among his professors.

Pérez de Ayala wrote his first important works around 1910. Although he was somewhat younger than the members of the Generation of 1898, who inaugurated contemporary Spanish literature, some of them, notably AZORÍN and Ramón del VALLE-INCLÁN, were his close friends. He inherited from the Generation of 1898 a critical preoccupation with the problems of the Spanish people as manifested in the progressive national decay that began in the 16th century and reached its nadir with Spain's defeat in the Spanish-American War. Nevertheless, Pérez de Ayala's attitude coincides more with that of the so-called *novecentista* group. José ORTEGA Y GASSET and Gregorio MARAÑÓN, for example, were his colleagues in political activity. This group is characterized by its rigorous intellectual training, a decided attitude of openness to Europe, and a growing social and political consciousness that began at the end of World War I and culminated in public action on behalf of the Second Spanish Republic, proclaimed in 1931.

Pérez de Ayala's novels were not to follow the realistic line of Benito PÉREZ GALDÓS, whom he greatly admired, but rather that of Alas: the intellectual novel, rich in ideas and concerns, and centered on the critical vision, bitter and ironic, of social reality in a Spanish provincial capital. Oviedo was to be as implacably protrayed by Pérez de Ayala, who called it Pilares, as it had been by Alas under the name of Vetusta. Alas and Pérez de Ayala were at one and the same time novelists, thinkers, and critical spirits of great intelligence. They were also great pessimists, but their pessimism was softened by the presence of two apparently typical elements of the Asturian spirit: the lyrical appreciation of nature and a very mellow sense of humor.

Throughout his life, Pérez de Ayala was a great lover of England. He shared with the English his sense of humor and his profound liberalism, which, in the case of the Spanish writer, was not solely a political opinion but a basic belief and general, almost religious attitude toward life. This kind of liberalism has very deep roots in the writer's personality and finds expression in the most varied endeavors of the human spirit. For Pérez de Ayala, in short, the fundamental virtues were tolerance and respect for the ways and thoughts of others.

Pérez de Ayala took part in various political enterprises of an intellectual nature, all of them liberal, Republican, and with lay tendencies. The most important was the Association in Service of the Republic, which he founded with the philosopher Ortega y Gasset and the essayist Marañón. The advent of the Republic represented the triumph of this association and these intellectuals. The Republic came into being with a very marked intellectual character. It sent out as ambassadors figures of recognized prestige, including Pérez de Ayala himself, who was named ambassador to his beloved England. Nevertheless, his position as a moderate liberal (like his friends Ortega y Gasset and Marañón) was undermined by the most extreme elements of the Spanish Republic. With the advent of the Popular Front in 1936 he ceased to be an ambassador.

His dedication to politics, furthermore, was fatal to his work as a novelist. He had early begun a very intense literary life, writing books of poetry, novels, and essays, and he had achieved popular fame primarily because of the scandal created by the publication of *A.M.D.G.* His last novel nevertheless carries the date 1926. At that time he was 46 and fully recognized by the most exacting international criticism. He had won the National Literary Prize and was spoken of now and again as a possible Nobel Prize candidate. He was to live another 36 years. In this long period he wrote many newspaper articles, later collected into books, but not one novel.

The Pérez de Ayala novel belongs to the type usually known as the "intellectual novel" or the "essay novel," similar to what has been done by the Englishman Aldous Huxley, the German Thomas MANN, and the Argentinians Ernesto Sábato and Julio Cortázar. In Spain a distant antecedent is Juan VALERA, and the immediate master is Alas. This type of novel coincides in part with Miguel de UNAMUNO's *nivola* concept and is continued after the war in the works of Francisco AYALA and Luis MARTÍN-SANTOS. Pérez de Ayala inserted in his novels digressions on varied themes, and his characters embody or discuss permanent problems of man in all periods and all countries. This does not mean that he disregarded the here and now, the concrete Spanish reality of his time.

His first four novels are *Tinieblas en las cumbres* (1907; Darkness on the Heights), *A.M.D.G.*, *La pata de la raposa* (1912); Eng. tr., *The Fox's Paw*, 1924), and *Troteras y danzaderas* (1913; Mummers and Dancers). After writing three "poematic" short novels, he began his second period with *Belarmino y Apolonio* (1921) and two novels in two parts each: *Luna de miel, luna de hiel* (Honeymoon, Bitter Moon) and *Los trabajos de Urbano y Simona* (The Labors of Urbano and Simona), both published in 1923, and *Tigre Juan* and *El curandero de su honra* (The Healer of his Honor) (both of 1926; Eng. tr., *Tiger Juan*, 1933).

With the Civil War of 1936-39 there began for Ayala, as for many other Spaniards, intellectuals or not, bitter years of exile. Pérez de Ayala's return to Spain (he died in Madrid) was purely private and did not signify any public stand on the problems of his country.

See: M. C. Rand, *Ramón Pérez de Ayala* (1971); A. Amorós, *La novela intelectual de Ramón Pérez de Ayala* (1972), and *Vida y literatura en "Troteras y danzaderas"* (1973).

A.As.

Pérez Galdós, Benito (1843–1920), Spanish novelist, dramatist, and critic of politics and the arts, was born in Las Palmas on Grand Canary Island. His family decided that he should go to Madrid to study law, and in September 1862 he enrolled at the university there. Galdós felt very much at home in Madrid and gradually developed a great fondness for this city, which was destined to become the background for most of his novels. His interest in writing soon found an outlet when he became the art and drama critic for the newspaper *La Nación*. Drama was his primary interest at this time, but after writing 3 plays, none of which was produced, he gave up the idea of writing for the theater for nearly 30 years. In May 1867, Galdós made his first trip to Paris. It is quite likely that his interest in the novel had been awakened as early as November 1865 by his readings of Honoré de Balzac, since the list he kept of books purchased between 1865 and 1867 includes some 15 novels by the French master. Be that as it may, Galdós devoted the rest of his life to the great genre of the 19th century. He contributed over 100 works that, taken as a whole, present one of the most complete panoramas of Spanish life (from 1804 until the restoration of the Bourbons in the 1870s), in all of its historical, political, and social aspects. In addition, this output reflects the evolution of the European novel during the second half of the 19th century. Galdós's output ranges from the historical novel with romantic leanings, through the realist and naturalist novels that typify the genre of that period, albeit in Spanish guise, on to the spiritualist and semiallegorical works that are not unrelated to the symbolist movement. In 1870–71, Galdós published *La Fontana de Oro* and *El audaz* (The Radical), historical novels that he had conceived with the idea of probing the immediate past in the hope of discovering the cause of the present ills of his country. From 1873 until 1879, with mechanical regularity, he completed his first two series of *Episodios nacionales,* which consist of 20 volumes. In them he gives a very complete and detailed picture of Spain from the Battle of Trafalgar (1805) to the end of the War of Independence, when Spanish forces aided by British troops under the Duke of Wellington defeated Napoleon's army in the battle of Los Arapiles (1812). In this first series, Galdós gives aesthetic expression to the patriotic forces that for a while united the whole nation. The second series deals mostly with the events that followed the defeat of Napoleon in Spain, in particular the period of oppression under Ferdinand VII and the struggle against the absolutism of this despicable monarch. This second series introduces the theme of the two Spains that struggled for political supremacy throughout the greater part of the 19th century. In April 1876, however, before he had completed the first two series of *Episodios,* his first social novel, *Doña Perfecta,* appeared. From this year until 1879 he devoted himself to writing both historical novels and novels of social criticism. The latter he grouped, along with *La Fontana de Oro* and *El audaz,* under the general heading of *Novelas de la primera época;* they include, besides *Doña Perfecta, Gloria* (1877), *La familia de León Roch* (1878), and *Marianela* (1878). Except for the last one, the novels of this period have been categorized as thesis novels in which Galdós exposes the basis of the fundamental division that was plaguing Spain, namely, the religious problem.

In 1881, with the appearance of *La desheredada* (Eng. tr., *The Disinherited Lady,* 1957), Galdós launched a new series of novels in which he sought to portray the society of his own time. To this group, which he called *Novelas contemporáneas,* belong his most important novels: *Fortunata y Jacinta,* (1887–88; Eng. tr., *Fortunata and Ja-*

cinta, 1973), *Miau* (1888; Eng. tr., *Miau,* 1963), *Angel Guerra* (1890–91), *La de Bringas* (1884; Eng. tr., *The Spendthrifts,* 1962), *Nazarín* (1895), *Misericordia* (1897; Eng. trs., *Compassion,* 1962, 1966), etc. In 1898, however, Galdós went back to historical novels. Alternating between the writing of plays and three more *Novelas contemporáneas,* he published three more series of *Episodios nacionales.* The last series, the fifth, consists of six volumes, unlike the other four, which consist of ten each. The last three series of *Episodios* deal primarily with the very complicated political and social events that took place in Spain from 1834 to 1879. The other novels that belong to this period, 24 of them comprising 32 volumes, present a vast panorama of Madrid life into which Galdós weaves the lives of literally hundreds of characters from all levels of society, who appear and reappear, producing the illusion of real life. Even though this technique of reintroducing characters and the attempt to portray the whole fabric of society may have come to Galdós from French novelists like Balzac and Emile ZOLA, Galdós's novels emerge fundamentally as the product of his own vision of life and are immersed in the truly Spanish tradition of Cervantes, and the painters Velázquez and Goya. When Galdós comments upon the novel as a genre and writes of its origins, he refers to Cervantes as its father and points out the influence that this author and the Spanish picaresque novel had on the European novel in general.

It would be difficult to imagine Galdós, an eminently realistic novelist, giving life to such a complete world as he presents to us in his novels, without firsthand observation. Galdós's world is not the type that can be invented. In his address to the Royal Spanish Academy of the Language upon taking his seat in 1897, Galdós was quite explicit about his aesthetic creed:

> The novel is an imitation of life, and the art of writing one consists of being able to reproduce human characters with their passions, their weaknesses, their greatness and their pettiness, their bodies and their souls; everything spiritual and physical that surrounds them; their language, the most characteristic trait of a country; their dwellings, which are the mark of the family; and their clothing, which expresses the final external signs of personality: all of this without forgetting that there must be a perfect balance between accuracy and beauty of reproduction.

It is difficult to imagine anyone trying to fulfill this ideal without devoting much time to direct observation of the life that he is portraying. Around 1889, possibly as a reflection of the spirit of the time, Galdós's novels begin to show an interest in psychological and spiritual problems. He began by questioning the very nature of "reality" in his pair of novels *La incógnita* (1889) and *Realidad* (1889). The latter reintroduces the very same plot presented in the first novel from a single observer's point of view, through a direct dramatization of it. Here Galdós experiments with the dramatic possibility of presenting a character through the use of a direct introspective soliloquy that he contrasts with the social exteriorizing of the same ideas in dialogue form. Eugene O'Neill attempted a similar experience much later in his play *Strange Interlude* (1928). In 1892, Galdós took *Realidad* to the stage. From that date on, he consistently used the theater to express his concerns, whether spiritual or ideological. Some of his most successful plays were translated and produced in the United States.

The post-World War I years brought about a radical change in the aesthetic sensibility of the intellectuals, and for some time it was fashionable to criticize and deride Galdós. With the exception of a few enlightened critics like Joaquín Casalduero, Angel del Rio, H. Chonon Berkowitz, and a few others who began to study Galdós in the 1930s and early 1940s, it took the upsetting experience of the Civil War in Spain (1936–39) to bring about another change in sensibility and a reevaluation of Galdós's work. Today he is considered, almost unanimously, the most important literary figure of 19th-century Spain and the greatest novelist that Spain has produced since Cervantes. Galdós takes his place among the most genuine and most representative novelists of 19th-century Europe, alongside such figures as Charles Dickens, Honoré de Balzac, Fyodor DOSTOYEVSKY, Lev TOLSTOY, and Henry James.

See: J. Casalduero, *Vida y obra de Galdós* (1943); H. Chonon Berkowitz, *Pérez Galdós, Spanish Liberal Crusader* (1948), R. Gullón, *Técnicas de Galdós* (1970); *AGald* (1966); C. P. Snow, *The Realists* (1978), pp. 217–55.   R.C.

Périer, Odilon Jean (1900–28), Belgian poet, dramatist, and novelist, was born in Brussels. His family belonged to the upper bourgeoisie,, and his grandfather, General Thys, had an important share in the colonization of the Congo. Périer's first poems gave signs of an unusual personality. His position in Belgian literature is unique, for the young poet's spiritual attitude was a reaction both against the current tendencies of Belgian writers and against the solemn and puritanical atmosphere of his family life. His best poems are those inspired by his native town, however, and, curiously enough, his criticism, by its moralizing tone, has forced him into an attitude akin to puritanism.

In contrast to the language of all the Belgian writers of the preceding generation, that of Périer is exceedingly pure, without any superfluous ornament; it is sober, concise, always avoiding emphasis and eloquence. In *La Vertu par le chant* (1920; Virtue through Song), as well as in *Notre Mère la ville* (1922; Our Mother the Town), Périer concentrates in a few lines of blank verse the anxieties of his restless soul. Faith would probably have appeased his anguish, but, although far from being an agonist, the poet never found the consolation of religion. Therefore, the ethical problem that constitutes the background of all his poems remains unsolved. In 1924 he wrote *Le Citadin, ou éloge de Bruxelles* (The Townsman, or Praise of Brussels), a poem in classical French alexandrine verse, in which he draws a vivid description of Brussels and life in Brussels in the 1920s, as seen through the eyes of a refined and gentlehearted young man belonging to the ruling class. *Le Citadin,* Périer's masterpiece, is his best chance for attaining immortality.

The young poet had been very well received in Parisian literary circles. The *Nouvelle Revue française* published his last poems, *Le Promeneur* (1927; The Stroller), and also a curious novel, *Le Passage des anges* (1926; The Crossing of the Angels). His play, *Les Indifférents* (1925; The Indifferent Ones), which reflects his moral attitude and his perpetual scruples, was favorably received in Brussels. Périer, who had always been ailing, died of heart disease in Brussels in January 1928. He was buried on the very day of the birth of his only child, a son. His poems are to be found in most anthologies of French contemporary poems.

See: J. Stevo, "Le Poète et sa Ville: Odilon-Jean Périer," *Bulletin officiel de l'Association des Ecrivains belges* vol. 13, no. 11 (1949): 388–96; R. Frickx and M. Joiret, *La Poésie française de Belgique de 1880 à nos jours* (1977).   L.Ko.

Pernath, Hugues C., pseud. of Hugo Wouters (1931–75), Belgian (Flemish) poet, was born in Antwerp. His first three volumes of poetry, *Het uur Marat* (1958; The Hour Marat), *De adem ik* (1959; The Breath I), and *Het masker man* (1960; Man the Mask), were assembled in 1963, together with new poems, in *Instrumentarium voor een winter* (A Winter's Paraphernalia). In the meantime, while he was serving as a regular army officer, he had published his *Soldatenbrieven* (1961; Soldiers' Letters), a correspondence in verse with Paul SNOEK. These early works are predominantly characterized by a tremendous deviation from current syntax. For this pessimistic author, life can never be cleared of an inevitable sense of guilt. Opposites such as love and hate, good and evil, disclosure and obscurity, solitude and craving for sympathy appear to be inseparable pairs and reflect his incurable inner torment. Language provides the materials to erect the *monumentum aere perennium*, but it is also the immediate cause of an increasing confusion of tongues. This self-tormenting poet cannot decide between feminine grief and manly revolt. An honorable, aristocratic acceptance of this limitation forms Pernath's bitter consolation. *Mijn gegeven woord* (1966; My Given Word) elaborates on the same themes but is marked by a relatively less disturbed syntax, so that critics have praised the volume for its perfect balance between explicitness and suggestive power. This evolution toward more accessibility also determines *Mijn tegenstem* (1973; My Counter Voice), a collection including *Index-gedichten* (Index-Poems), which clearly bear the marks of the social commitment of the 1960s. The remaining series of the volume deal with more private feelings in music, highly polished verse. Strictly anecdotal elements, however, are masterfully universalized at every turn. Pernath was awarded the Triennial State Prize for Poetry for his *Nagelaten gedichten* (1976; Posthumous Poems). His unique style had greatly influenced younger generations. By the time of his death he had become the leading figure of Pink Poet, an Antwerp poetry club.

See: M. Bartosik, "Door het drieluik van de tijd heen. De thematiek van Hugues C. Pernath," *NVT* 4, 5 (1973); *NVT* 6, 7 (1976), entirely devoted to Pernath; P. Conrad, *Hugues C. Pernath* (1976). M.B.

Perret, Jacques (1901–), French novelist and essayist, was born in Paris. Instead of pursuing a career, he traveled and lived abroad until his mid-thirties. Perret's first two novels, *Roncon* (1936) and *Ernest le rebelle* (1937), were not especially promising. During World War II he was drafted and taken prisoner to Germany, but he escaped in 1942 and joined the Resistance. This experience inspired his masterpiece, *Le Caporal épinglé* (1947; The Pinned-Up Corporal, one of the best French novels on World War II. Perret's other novels, *Le Vent dans les voiles* (1948; Eng. tr., *The Wind in the Sails*, 1954), *Bande à part* (1951; Their Separate Way), *Les Biffins de Gonesse* (1961; The Troopers from Gonesse), and *Rôle de plaisance* (1957; Pleasure Role), are not nearly as well structured nor were they as successful.

Since 1945, Perret has also written numerous short stories, collected in *Histoires sous le vent* (1944; Stories under the Wind), *L'Oiseau rare* (1947; The Rare Bird), *Objets perdus* (1949; Lost Objects), *La Bête Mahousse* (1951; The Monstrous Beast), and *Le Machin* (1955; The Gizmo). His style and his interest in fantasy are reminiscent of Marcel AYMÉ, whom he admires.

Perret's most recent works are the first two volumes of his memoirs, *Grands cheveaux et dadas* (1975; Great Horses and Fancies) and *Raisons de famille* (1976; Due to Family Reasons). These volumes exhibit his lack of restraint and especially his mastery of the language. Although Perret's conservatism and patriotism are quite present here, the tone of these memoirs does not approach the reactionary, chauvinistic stance of his essays of the 1940s and 1950s. Perret's conservatism has no doubt prevented him from receiving the recognition he deserves for his *Caporal épinglé* and for rendering, with incomparable fidelity, the tone of the French language as spoken by ordinary people at mid-century. J.-P.C.

Perron, Charles Edgar du (1899–1940), Dutch novelist and critic, was born in Java. A cosmopolitan man of the world, he was quite different from his contemporaries. He did not arrive in Europe until he was 22, when he settled in Paris, where he made friends with a number of artists and writers. The result of the first year of his experience there was a novel, *Een voorbereiding* (A Preparation), with which he was never satisfied. He remained an individualist, and his criticism was highly personal. It appeared under the title of *Cahiers van een lezer* (A Reader's Notebooks). As is evident from the title of one of his volumes of criticism, *Vriend of vijand* (Friend or Foe), he seemed mainly interested in finding out whether the writer behind the work was a friend or an enemy. His most important prose work is *Het land van herkomst* (1935; Country of Origin), an autobiographical novel, in which his hero gives an account of his life in Paris in the 1930s and connects it with the memories of his youth in Java. Conversations, diaries, letters, and narrative are combined, and the novel has no plot, which du Perron regarded as an artificiality. Yet the novel forms a unified whole, for the events of the present and past are carefully selected. It is an excellent example of du Perron's belief that the writer should be present in his work. His skill as a craftsman is evident from the way in which he wove all of the episodes together. His poetry was published as *Microchaos* (1932), and some of it had first appeared under the pseudonym Duco Perkens. Du Perron was the most stimulating and influential Dutch critic of the 1930s. His literary criticism appeared as *Voor kleine parochie* (1931; For a Small Parish) and *Blocnote klein formaat* (1936; Small-Sized Writing Pad). His polemical essays were published as *De smalle mens* (1934; The Thin Man). He was very much interested in Multatuli, for whom he felt a great affinity. He wrote an excellent biography of him, *De man van Lebak* (1937; The Man from Lebak), as well as *Multatuli, tweede pleidooi* (Multatuli: Second Plea for the Defense) and *De bewijzen uit het pak van Sjaalman* (The Proofs from Sjalman's Bundle). His writings were published in six volumes as *Verzameld werk* (1954–58); Collected Works). With Menno ter BRAAK, he established the literary magazine *Forum* in 1932.

See: S. Tas, *Een critische periode* (1946); G. Stuiveling, *Steekproeven* (1950). S.L.F.

Perzyński, Włodzimierz (1877–1930), Polish playwright, novelist, and short-story writer, was born in Opoczno and died in Warsaw. After an inconclusive poetic debut, he became a prominent representative of realistic comedy and the novel of manners. His first play, *Lekkomyślna siostra* (1907; The Lighthearted Sister), was a study in the hypocrisy of the middle class, which blames its offspring first for her "immoral" conduct and later for her "stupid" rejection of the material gain ensuing from it. Among his more than 20 plays, 2 others have permanent value: *Aszantka* (1907; Cocotte) and *Szczęście Frania* (1914; Franio's Luck). The latter, called "a comedy about a saint," revealed Perzyński's specific trait: the sadness of the ironist, a discreet and unsentimental compassion in the sharp observer of human psychology and social life. Many collections of serious and humorous stories—the best being *Cudowne dziecko* (1921; The Child Prodigy)—recommended themselves by their conciseness and precision of structure. Perzyński's most masterful novels date from his last period: *Raz w życiu* (1925; Once in a Lifetime), *Nie było nas, był las* (1927; Before Us Was the Forest), *Klejnoty* (1930; The Gems), the latter tending toward the *roman à thèse*. Throughout his life, Perzyński published collections of feuilletons—they were his apprenticeship and later the workshop of a realist writer. In every genre he practiced, Perzyński proved himself a master of the "invisible" style, devoid of tropes, colloquial, deceptively simple, but perfectly functional. It can be compared to that of Stendhal, Guy de Maupassant, and Anton CHEKHOV.

See: J. Lorentowicz, *Współczesny teatr polski* (1935); K. W. Zawodziński, "Perzyński, powieściopisarz na tle swojej epoki," *Powieści o powieści* (1963), pp. 238–45.

T.T.

Pessanha, Camilo (1867–1926), Portuguese poet, was born in Coimbra, the illegitimate son of a law student—who became a judge—and his housekeeper. During his childhood he traveled through continental Portugal and the Azores with his parents. Later on, after he settled in Coimbra, his father acknowledged his paternity. Pessanha took a law degree in 1891, became an assistant public prosecutor for a time, and then practiced law privately. He was sent to Macao in 1894 to teach in the Portuguese lycée, and, except for occasional visits to Portugal, he remained in the colony for the rest of his life. He taught most of that time, though for a period he had a position in the local civil service. During the years he spent in Macao he suffered frequent illnesses, which occasioned visits to the homeland for medical treatment. Yet he succumbed to the spell of the Orient like his colleague at the school Venceslau de Morais, and he is said to have smoked opium habitually. He had one son, born to him by his housekeeper.

During his lifetime Pessanha published only one volume of poetry, *Clepsydra* (1920; Water Clock). It was edited for him by João de Castro Osório (1899–), hardly out of his teens at the time. Osório also prepared the subsequent editions, the last of which came out in 1969, containing new material and further commentary by Osório. Pessanha's only other book that has been published is called *China: Estudos e traduções* (1944; China: Studies and Translations); it contains prose translations from the Chinese with an interesting introduction and essays about Chinese culture. Pessenha's work shows the influence of the great French symbolists—Paul Verlaine, Stéphane MALLARMÉ, Arthur RIMBAUD—and of Rubén Darío, their Spanish-American follower and counterpart, as well as that of Charles BAUDELAIRE. In his early verse, one can detect certain reminiscences of his older Portuguese contemporaries Cesário Verde and Gomes Leal. He developed rapidly through an early stage of sensuality and a brief period of Parnassianism into the most profound and original of the Portuguese symbolists. Mastering the music of Paul Verlaine and the suggestive, ambiguous kind of symbol practised by Mallarmé, he took for his subject matter dreams, fragmented images, and surprising associations from the depths of his subconscious. Thus he produced a startling series of confessional poems that both reveal his inner anguish and conceal, almost always effectively, its sources and bases. There is no doubt, however, that this poetry represents a bitter revolt against his situation in life: his clouded birth, his lifelong ill health, and his separation for so many years from other Portuguese writers, a separation that he could not or

would not end. In China he was a stranger in a very alien land, for in spite of the translations he published, he never learned Chinese well enough to establish verbal contact with a culture that he greatly admired. The extent of his alienation from Chinese inspiration is shown by the fact that only two of his lyrics may be even remotely considered as emerging from his Chinese experience. His influence on later Portuguese poetry and especially on that of the *Presença* group (see PORTUGUESE LITERATURE) is marked, and Fernando PESSOA himself once said that he knew much of Pessanha's work by heart.

See: A. Dias Miguel, *Camilo Pessanha* (1956); B. Vidigal, ed., *Camilo Pessanha: Poesia e prosa* (1965); J. do Prado Coelho, "Camilo Pessanha," *Dicionário das literaturas portuguesa, brasileira e galega* (2d ed., 1969).

R.S.S.

Pessoa, Fernando (1888–1935), Portuguese poet, born in Lisbon, where he lived for the greater part of his life and where he died, spent his childhood in South Africa. His secondary studies in Durban gave him a British upbringing and culture, most uncommon in Portuguese letters. He is the greatest poet in Portuguese in the first half of the 20th century and an outstanding member of the generation of Mário de Sá-CARNEIRO, José de ALMADA-NEGREIROS, and others, who starting with the review *Orpheu* (1915), brought the avant-garde to Portugal. His influence in both Portugal and Brazil upon younger poets has been immense; and through translations into French, English, German, Spanish, and other languages he is increasingly recognized as one of the greatest poets of the century in any literature.

In his early years, Pessoa published poems in English (*English Poems*, 3 vols., 1921; 1. *Antinous*, 2. *35 Sonnets*, 3. *Epithalamium*)—only a small part of his production in that language—that are interesting and revealing. His poetry in Portuguese, aside from the slim, prize-winning volume, *Mensagem* (1934; Message), remained unpublished during his lifetime except for a small portion that appeared in reviews. Of his complete poetical opus, posthumously edited since 1942, 11 volumes have been issued to date, and more are to come. Anthologies in English translation were published by F. E. G. Quintillana, P. Rickard, and E. Honig, all in 1971. Some individual pieces had previously been translated by the poets Roy Campbell (1960) and Thomas Merton (1966).

Against this impressive background, the book *Mensagem* represents only the facet of patriotic and messianic beliefs that links Pessoa's poetry with the old Luso-Brazilian tradition of illusory hopes for King Sebastian's return. The vast bulk of his other poetic production is what is truly significant. Pessoa unfolded his contradictory self by projecting it into four main lyrical personalities—his own and an imaginary trio characterized by district individual qualities: Álvaro de Campos, Alberto Caeiro, and Ricardo Reis. These names are not pseudonyms, but—as the poet called them—"heteronyms," that is, perfectly autonomous entities as regards their natures and modes of expression. Pessoa defined them psychologically and biographically, even to the point of making them write critically about each other. Through them he endeavored to give form to different facets of his being. Caeiro in his colloquial free verse contends that there is nothing beyond what one sees and that it is irrelevant to *think* about things that are supposed to be seen only. Campos, writing also in free verse, develops from futurism a highly imaginative style to express a dramatic anguish that is existentialistic in character. Reis, confining himself to language, meters, and stanzas that recall Horace, states a severe Epicurean philosophy of life. Pessoa himself—or the "orthonym," as he said—keeping most of the time to traditional forms of verse, mirrors the void of a soul that has stripped itself of its options and takes refuge in a Platonic and esoteric view of reality. Pessoa's poetry—his "own" as well as that of the heteronyms—like the poetry of many of his peers in modern literature, represents an intellectualization of internal emotion or, as he expressed it in a famous line, "What in me feels thinks." Yet beyond the intellectual lucidity that expands from analysis to analysis into a critique of knowledge and of the traditionally unified ego, sparing none of the accepted illusions of thought and ordinary life, there are a tremendous lyric power and a capacity for feeling at the very border of despair, which, tragically, assume an ironical tone. Whether in long poems or short ones, Pessoa and his heteronyms, each following his own trends, display an amazing wealth of insights and subtle undertones, molded in styles whose peculiarities have changed poetry in Portuguese forever.

As a literary critic and theorist, Pessoa is also outstanding, and several volumes of his prose have been published.

See: J. Gaspar Simões, *Vida e obra de Fernando Pessoa,* 2 vols. (1950); A. Casais Monteiro, *Estudos sobre Fernando Pessoa* (1958); J. de Sena, *O poeta é um fingidor* (1961); J. do Prado Coelho, *Diversidade e unidade em Fernando Pessoa* (4th ed., 1973); E. Lourenço, *Pessoa revisitado* (1973); J. Griffin, Introduction, to *Fernando Pessoa: Selected Poetry* (1974).　　J. de S.

Petersen, Nis (1897–1943), Danish poet and novelist, was born in southern Jutland. He became an orphan at the age of two and was brought up by his grandmother, whose strict religious attitude both attracted and repelled him, an ambiguity also found in his relations with the bourgeoisie. Throughout his life he was ideologically and materially unable to find an anchorage. He roamed about as a vagabond and bohemian, finally perishing in despair and doubt. Petersen made his debut as a poet with *Nattens Pibere* (1926; The Pipers of the Night), which expresses the duality of his mind in its vacillation between a zest for life, a yearning for death, a longing for faraway places and for home, between defiance and humility. His later collections, *En Drift Vers* (1933; A Drove of Verses), *Til en Dronning* (1935; To A Queen), *Stykgods* (1940; Mixed Cargo) and *Stynede Popler* (1943; Pollarded Poplars), contain the same moods but with an alteration of form, from rhetorical, firm, and rhythmical poems, influenced by Rudyard Kipling and Oscar Wilde, to plain verses of exquisite beauty.

An atmosphere of rootlessness and uncertainty is also present in Petersen's novel *Sandalmagernes Gade* (1931; Eng. tr., *The Street of the Sandalmakers,* 1933), a worldwide success that was translated into more than 20 languages. The book is an artistic panorama of life in ancient Rome, but at the same time a novel of the modern period. The Rome of antiquity corresponds to Copenhagen, and the author illuminates the negative relationship of both epochs with the Gospel's message of love. Petersen's second novel, *Spildt Mælk* (1934; Eng. tr., *Spilt Milk,* 1935), is a story of disillusionment about the Irish Civil War of 1922. From the author's later years stem four collections of short stories (1937–43), like his novels rather weak in composition but all showing his fascinating personality, the most typical expression of the anxiety and nihilism of the Danish interwar period.

See: H. Brix, *Nis Petersen, Liv og Digt* (1947); J. Andersen, *Nis Petersen* (1957).　　S.H.R.

Petrescu, Camil (1894–1957), Romanian novelist, dramatist, philosopher, and poet, was born in Bucharest. He began writing for the journals *Facla* and *Cronica,* the latter then edited by Tudor Arghezi. During World War I he partially lost his hearing. After the war, Petrescu founded several journals in Timişoara and Bucharest, and contributed to most of the other leading periodicals of the day. In his poems, published as *Versuri* (1923; Verse) and *Transcendentalia* (1923), there is a tendency toward abstractionism. His dramas are generally nonscenic and seem to anticipate the existentialism of Jean-Paul Sartre and Albert Camus. They include *Jocul ielelor* (1919; Dance of the Elves), *Act veneţian* (1919; Venetian Interlude), *Danton* (1926), *Mitica Popescu* (1926), *Mioara* (1943), and *Iată femeia pe care o iubesc* (1944; This Is the Woman I Love). Petrescu's important *Modalitatea estetică a teatrului* (Aesthetics of the Theater) appeared in 1937, two years before he was appointed director of the National Theater. He also published *Husserl: o introducere în fenomenologie* (1938; Husserl: Introduction to Phenomenology), as well as a book of travel impressions, *Rapid-Constantinopol-Bairam* (1933; Constantinople-Bairam Express).

Petrescu's fame rests on his prose fiction. His novel *Ultima noapte de dragoste, iniţia noapte de război* (1930; The Last Night of Love, the First Night of War) is felt by some critics to be unsuccessful because of excessive philosophic speculation. *Patul lui Procust* (1933; Procrustian Bed) presents a picture of Bucharest society after World War I. According to Petruscu's own words, the novel is a "dossier of existence." A number of individuals are placed in a temporal situation, and the point at which their lives intersect provides the novelist with possibilities for subtle psychological analysis from different perspectives. With its subtle examination of character, *Patul lui Procust* is one of the first examples of psychological analysis in Romanian literature.

See: A. Oprea, *Prozatori iluştri* (1971); I. Rotaru, *O istorie a literaturii române,* vol. 2 (1972), pp. 609–38 and passim.　　V.A.

Petrović, Rastko (1898–1949), Serbian poet and prose writer, was born in Belgrade. While in Paris, he became acquainted with the modernist trends in French literature. Petrović entered the diplomatic service in 1923. In 1928 he made a trip to Africa, recording his impressions in his excellent travelogue *Africa* (1930) and in *Ljudi govore* (1930; People Speak), a fictionalized dialogue with Spanish fishermen. From 1935 until the end of World War II he was a Yugoslav diplomatic representative in the United States, where he remained as an émigré until his death. His last work, *Dan šesti* (The Sixth Day), published posthumously in 1961, is a novel based on his experiences in 1915 with the retreating Serbian army as it marched through the snowy mountains of Albania.

At the beginning of his career Petrović was inclined toward surrealism, but in the early 1930s he broke with surrealists over their leftist political tendencies (*see* Serbian literature). Petrović's works are characterized by a keen interest in the psychological and the primordial, in dreams and hallucinations. He approaches and depicts life as a blind force, unrestricted by any ethical barriers. Lack of restraint is, in fact, one of the shortcomings of Petrović's poetry, for example, in *Otkrovenje* (1922; Revelation). His lyricism is overly ecstatic; his narration recognizes no rational limitations. Syntactic and logical disorder interferes with the aesthetic quality of his works. Yet in his attempts to capture emotions and thoughts too strong and deep to be expressed in words, Petrović appears to be striving to reach the very roots of life.

See: V. Gligorić, "Rastko Petrović," in *Ogledi i studije* (1959), pp. 167–93; M. Dedinac, "Prevedeno s uspomena," Afterword to R. Petrović, *Dan šeti* (1961), pp. 620–22. M.M. with W.B.E.

Pétursson, Hannes (1931–), Icelandic essayist, novelist, and poet, was born in the village of Sauðárkrókur in Skagafjörður in central northern Iceland, where his father was a postmaster. Pétursson received a classical humanistic education, matriculating in Reykjavik in 1952 and then pursuing Germanistic studies for two years in Cologne and Heidelberg. He earned a degree in Nordic philology and literature from the University of Iceland in 1959.

Among the most prolific writers of his generation in Iceland, Pétursson has published a collection of short stories, *Sögur að norðan* (1961; Tales from the North), the documentary novel *Rauðamyrkur* (1973; Red Darkness), two travelogues, and an ambitious work on Steingrímur Thorsteinsson (1964), a prominent romantic poet in Iceland. He has also translated Rainer Maria RILKE, Franz KAFKA, and Halldis Moren VESAAS into Icelandic and has edited and rewritten introductions to books by many authors, as well as published the reference work *Bókmenntir* (1972; Literature).

It is, however, as a poet that Pétursson ranks among the most outstanding authors in Iceland today. Since his first book of verse, *Kvæðabók* (1955; Book of Poems), he has published six other volumes of poetry. His first collection of verse shows the influence of Snorri HJARTARSON, and Pétursson has followed his example of steering a middle course between Icelandic tradition and modernistic forms. As for foreign influences on him, Rilke and Stefan GEORGE have been cited.

Pétursson combines his keen intellect and power of observation with sentiment, and as a result his poems develop a classical tone. Icelandic history and mythology are the sources of many of his themes, and he has especially strong ties to the district of his youth. On the other hand, his vision is also international in scope, for he is preoccupied with the uncertain future of the human race in a world of turmoil, the powerlessness of people in the face of the terrors of war, the strength and weaknesses of verbal art in a world of technology, and other such problems of global magnitude.

The passage of time is a central theme in much of Pétursson's poetry. Aware of constant changes that demand ceaseless reexamination of all values and seeing Icelandic culture as forever exposed to alien influences, he seeks to define the position of people in the context of their culture. He is bent on establishing values through focusing on the everyday world we live in, and he finds the sublime by exalting the commonplace. Broadly speaking, the nature of human life and human aspirations are the main concerns in all of Pétursson's verse. His point of view was at first hedonistic: The human being is God, and there are no other deities. In his later poetry, however, his outlook has grown somewhat ambivalent; he is still preoccupied with philosophical and theological issues, but he has become more reconciled to the mystery of death; in fact, it appears at times that he conceives of the region of his birth as a nirvana that he is destined to return to.

See: S. S. Höskuldsson, "Det moderna genombrottet i isländsk lyrik," in H. Pétursson, *Tid och rum* (1965), pp. 3–9; I. Orgland, "Hannes Pétursson," in H. Pétursson, *Krystallar* (1965), pp. 5–35. S.S.H.

Peyrefitte, Roger (1907–), French writer, was born in Castres. After attending a Jesuit school, he studied at the Sorbonne and the Ecole des Sciences Politiques. Peyrefitte had a short career as a diplomat, and after 1944 he devoted himself to literature.

Peyrefitte's first book, and perhaps his best, is *Les Amitiés particulières* (1945; Private Friendships), a psychological novel about forbidden passion in a private school. The plot of the work may be less important than its atmosphere; its tone is a mixture of tenderness and irony, innocence and perversity. The book won the Théophraste Renaudot Prize and was highly praised by critics. After 1951, Peyrefitte abandoned the psychological novel to concentrate on the collecting of anecdotes and *faits divers* and satire. His subjects were the diplomatic world, as in *Les Ambassadeurs* (1953; The Ambassadors); the Catholic Church, as in *Les Clés de Saint Pierre*, (1955; The Keys of Saint Peter); and various groups, as in *Les Juifs* (1965; The Jews) and *Les Américains* (1968; The Americans).

Peyrefitte is a cultured, intelligent stylist, the last nonchalant and detached heir of Ernest Renan and Anatole FRANCE. His sometimes licentious themes, however, are not always worthy of his literary talent.

See: C. Garnier, *L'Homme et son personnage* (1955); D. Bourdet, *Pris sur le vif* (1957); P. Brodin, *Présences contemporaines* (1957). P.Br.

Philippe, Charles-Louis (1874–1909), French novelist, was born in Cérilly. He was educated in Moulins and then worked in Paris as a city clerk. His novels and short stories display two tendencies: realism with naturalistic overtones, and poetic idealism mixed with sentimentality. Philippe wrote out of the experience of his own life. He recorded the feelings of people around him, transforming them into characters with whom he fully sympathized. In *La Mère et l'enfant* (1900; Mother and Child), Philippe's poetic account of his own childhood, he described with infinite devotion the affection his mother had showered upon him. In the unfinished *Charles Blanchard* (1913; with several versions and a preface by Léon-Paul FARGUE), whose title character was inspired by his own father, he portrayed the misery of the impoverished peasantry. Indeed, the theme of poverty dominates much of his work, and most of his characters, humble and oppressed, are described with deep compassion. The rare rich persons in Philippe's novels are ridiculed as parasites or ignoramuses.

Another major theme of his work is illness in its many forms. Since the age of seven, Philippe himself had suffered from a maxillary infection that left him with an unsightly scar that his beard could not conceal. Maxillary osteitis, consumption, blindness, and syphilis afflict his characters, as in *Le Père Perdrix* (1903; Eng. tr., *A Simple Story*, 1924). Philippe's medical problems, along with his short stature, made him self-conscious and shy, particularly with women, of whom he knew only two aspects: the idealized, represented by his half-sister, who is portrayed in *La Bonne Madeleine et la pauvre Marie* (1898; Good Madeleine and Poor Marie), and the realistic, which for Philippe was limited to prostitutes, as portrayed in *Marie Donadieu* (1904), *Croquignole* (1906), and *Bubu de Montparnasse* (1901; Eng. tr., 1932). Woman as wife seemed inaccessible to the poor and ugly novelist.

Seeing himself as idealistic but weak, Philippe was very much impressed by Friedrich NIETZSCHE, and in the three realistic novels noted above, a woman is fought over by two men. *Marie Donadieu* is based on an autobiographical episode, except that the ending betrays the author's wishful thinking (the weakling wins the woman); in the other two novels, the Nietzschean strong man brutally triumphs over the Philippe-like character.

Philippe was influenced by the symbolists, such as Paul CLAUDEL, whose cosmic images he imitated, and by André GIDE, an associate at the *Nouvelle Revue française*. From Gide he adopted the idea of the gratuitous act, developed in *Contes du matin* (1916; Tales of the Morning), and of the concept of gratification in seeking rather than finding. Although Philippe made an objective study of prostitution before he wrote *Bubu*, the novel itself, because of its sentimentality, is not naturalistic. His descriptions of vulgar characters are softened by his pity for all human suffering, as well as by the influence of Fyodor DOSTOYEVSKY and Lev TOLSTOY; thus coarseness is mitigated by adjectives: "la pauvre petite putain trotteuse" (the poor little scampering whore).

Philippe's style is always simple, "spoken" rather than "written," with many examples of onomatopoeia, ordinary words, naive expressions, and direct address—all used to get the reader directly involved. Other stylistic devices include frequent rhythmic repetitions; vague, suggestive images and colors; frequent use of the imperfect tense (to lessen the abruptness of actions by making them seem habitual and long-lasting; and enumerations introduced by "il y avait" to lend a sense of fatality (Philippe's characters are usually dominated by events).

After a life of illness, Philippe died of syphilitic meningitis. But he had enjoyed many deep friendships with major writers, for whom he was to remain "le doux Philippe"; on occasions, as in the case of Valery LARBAUD and Marguerite Audoux, he strongly influenced their development.

See: special Philippe no. of *NRF* 2, no. 14 (Feb. 15, 1910); H. Bachelin, *Charles-Louis Philippe* (1929); L. Lanoizelée, *Charles-Louis Philippe: l'homme—l'écrivain* (1953); special Philippe issue of *CVL* 13 (May 1975); *Bulletin de la société des amis de Charles-Louis Philippe*.

L.R.S.

Piccolo, Lucio (1901-69), Italian poet, was born in Palermo and died at Capo d'Orlando, Messina. His published works are *Canti barocchi e altre liriche* (1956; Baroque Songs and Other Lyrics), *Gioco a nascondere: canti barocchi* (1960; Hide and Seek: Baroque Songs), and *Plumelia* (1967; Eng. tr., *Collected Poems of Lucio Piccolo*, 1972). Piccolo was a cousin and close friend of Guiseppe TOMASI DI LAMPEDUSA, who wrote *Il gattopardo* (1958; Eng. tr. *The Leopard*, 1960), encouraged by Piccolo's success at a literary conference at San Pellegrino in 1954, where he was introduced by Eugenio MONTALE).

Piccolo has been called "the last Gattopardo," and his avowed intent in *Canti barocchi*, his best book, was to evoke the Sicilian world of Palermo which is fast disappearing. The theme of the decay of the great house provides a constant ground bass in this work. *Canti barocchi* is a cycle of poems. The influence of Luis de Góngora (1561-1627) can be felt in its ambience and luxuriance, its baroque churches, Easters, and sirocco nights. There hangs over all a sense that the best has been. It is interesting to note that Piccolo was very familiar with the poetry of William Butler Yeats and that he had corresponded with him as a boy. Moreover, both poets were mystics, and they shared common esoteric interests.

Piccolo's last book (although we do not know how many others there may be in his library, sealed off by litigation) is *Plumelia*, perhaps the most mysterious and metaphysical of the works, but they are all remarkably of a piece. Perhaps, as Montale suggested, Piccolo's poetry might have gone on to develop along lines of greater simplification. Piccolo is the poet of contrapuntal melody and thick texture, whose roots in the symbolist movement draw sustenance from the subterranean self in all its complexities.

See: M. Ricciardelli, "A Baroque Life: An Interview with Lucio Piccolo," *BA* 47 (1973): 240-53.   B.Sw.

Picón, Jacinto Octavio (1852-1923), Spanish novelist, short-story writer, and critic, was born in Madrid. He was educated first in France and later at the University of Madrid, where he studied law. Essentially a fiction writer, he began his literary career as an art critic. His biography of Velázquez and his book on the evolution of caricature are readable works of sound scholarship.

Picón's early novels are really elongated short stories, such as *Lázaro* (1882), a genre that he cultivated impressively. As a novelist he lacked creative power, although he often achieved effectiveness by sheer intellectual effort. His plots are slight and in their stereotyped artificiality are reminiscent of the classical Spanish *comedia*.

A naturalist, Picón had two favorite themes: anticlericalism, as exemplified in *El enemigo* (1887; The Enemy), and unconventional love, as in *Juanita Tenorio* (1914) and *Dulce y sabrosa* (1891; Sweet and Tasty). The latter is perhaps his best work. Yet his conception of love is romantic. Were it not for the veil of delicacy that his cultivated style casts over details, Picón's fiction might justly be called erotic. Although sparingly humorous, his work is always ironical and occasionally self-consciously literary. A pure Madridian, Picón builds his scenery out of local vignettes and the capital's argot.

Picón's strength and weakness both derive from the fact that he aimed to reproduce rather than to create, to appeal to sentiment and not to imagination, to please and not to moralize, and to extract from Castilian as much of its inherent beauty as possible.   H.C.B. rev. H.L.B.

Pidmohylny, Valeriyan (1901-41), Ukrainian novelist and short-story writer, was born in Katerynoslav (Yekaterinoslav). A talented prose writer who avoided political and social themes, he was a member of the "Lanka" group (*see* UKRAINIAN LITERATURE). Among his best short stories are "Viyskovy litun" (1924; A Military Pilot) and "Problema khliba" (1927; Eng. tr., "The Problem of Bread," 1973). His most popular novel was *Misto* (1928; The City), about the life and loves of a young Ukrainian writer in Kiev. His last "pre-existential novel" was *Nevelychka drama* (1930; Eng. tr., *A Little Touch of Drama*, 1972). Pidmohylny also translated from French literature, which influenced him a great deal. He died in a Soviet concentration camp.   G.S.N.L.

Pierson-Piérard, Marianne (1907-), Belgian novelist and short-story writer, was born in Frameries. She is the daughter of Louis Piérard. Her first novel, *Millie* (1938), obtained the Prix de Brabant. She next published *Inconstances* (1946; Inconstancies) and *Dora* (1951) and then launched out into the short story with *Les Beaux Etés* (1954; The Beautiful Summers). Of the abundant output that followed, it is worth while to single out *Entre hier et demain* (1967; Between Yesterday and Tomorrow), a novel in the first person about an unsuccessful escape; *Oslo au mois d'août* (1971; Oslo in August); and two collections of short stories, *Les Cloches d'Ostende* (1970; The Bells of Ostend) and *La Dernière Journée* (1974; The Last Day). Faithful to a traditional conception of the psychological novel, Pierson-Piérard excels in translating into delicate notations the states of feeling of her heroines, whether they be little girls, young girls, or women. Love and death are the dominant themes of her engaging work written in a simple and sober style, devoid of affectation as well as pathos.

See: A. Jans, *Lettres vivantes 1945-1975* (1975)

R.F.

Piętak, Stanisław (1909-64), Polish poet, novelist, and essayist, was born in Wielowieś, near Sandomierz, into a peasant family. He committed suicide in Warsaw. Piętak studied Polish philology at the Jagiellonian University in Cracow. In 1935 appeared his first collection of poems, *Alfabet oczu* (Alphabet of Eyes), followed by *Legendy dnia i nocy* (1935; The Legends of Day and Night) and others, but he first won recognition with *Młodość Jasia Kunefała* (1938; The Youth of Jaś Kunefał), a novel with an unconventional structure in which folk tales, dreams, and a diary are inserted into the narrative. He was called a "peasant surrealist." Among Piętak's several volumes of prose are *Białowiejskie noce* (1939; Nights at Biała Wieś) and *Ucieczka z miejsc ukochanych* (1948; Escape from Beloved Places). In both his prose and in his poetry he remained faithful to reminiscences from childhood; they are enveloped in a visionary, fablelike atmosphere. Piętak's writing combines lyric and epic elements.

See: B. Faron, "Ziemi przypisany—Stanisław Piętak," in *Prozaicy dwudziestolecia miedzywojennego*, ed. by B. Faron (1972), pp. 523-52.

A.Z.

Pietrkiewicz, Jerzy, later changed to Peterkiewicz (1916-), Polish poet, novelist, short-story writer, critic, and translator, was born in Fabianki, near Bydgoszcz. Since 1951 he has written in English, even though he preserves some ties with Polish literature. Pietrkiewicz studied journalism and history at the University of Warsaw. At the beginning of World War II he left Poland and settled in England, where he earned a Ph.D. at King's College in London. Since 1950 he has been Professor of Polish language and literature at the University of London. Before the war he published two volumes of poetry: *Wiersze o dzieciństwie* (1935; Poems about Childhood) and *Prowincja* (1936; Countryside). His next books appeared in England. His volumes of poetry include *List otwarty do Emigracji w Zaduszki* (1940; Open Letter to the Emigration on All Soul's Day), *Znaki na niebie* (1940; Signs in the Sky), *Pokarm cierpki* (1943; Acrid Food), *Pogrzeb Europy* (1946; Europe's Funeral), and *Piąty poemat* (1950; Fifth Poem). He has also written two volumes of prose: a novel, *Po chłopsku* (1941; Peasantlike), and a collection of short stories, *Umarli nie są bezbronni* (1943; The Dead Are Not without Weapons), about the Nazi occupation of Poland. His poetic credo is expressed in the essay "Nowoczesność w tradycji" (1946; Modernity in Tradition), in which he advocates following the postulates of the avant-garde and seeking the sources of modern poetry in baroque poetry and in Cyprian NOR-WID. Pietrkiewicz is also active as a translator and was chosen as the editor and translator of the poems of Karol Wojtyła—Pope John Paul II—published under the title *Easter Vigil and Other Poems* (1979).

A.Z.

Pieyre de Mandiargues, André (1909-), French essayist, poet, and novelist, was born in Paris. His grandfather, Paul Bérard, was a collector of impressionist paintings. Pieyre de Mandiargues studied archaeology and has traveled a great deal, particularly in Italy, Spain, and Mexico. His first work, *Dans les années sordides* (1943; The Sordid Years), is a volume of prose poems. *Le Musée noir* (1946; The Dark Museum) contains several short stories, striking for their baroque, erotic atmosphere.

Pieyre de Mandiargues had been influenced by surrealism even before he met André BRETON in 1947. *Le Lis de mer* (1956; Eng. tr., *The Girl beneath the Lion*, 1958), is the story of a girl who chooses her first lover and, after one night with him, disappears forever. *Feu de braise* (1959; Eng. tr., *Blaze of Embers*, 1971) is a collection of short stories. *L'Age de craie* (1961; The Age of Chalk) brings together most of Pieyre de Mandiargues's poetry.

With *La Motocyclette* (1963; Eng. tr., *The Motorcycle*, 1965), Pieyre de Mandiargues reached a wide audience. His reputation was confirmed with *La Marge* (1967; Eng. tr., *The Margin*, 1969), which won the Goncourt Prize. In 1974, Pieyre de Mandiargues wrote a play for Jean-Louis BARRAULT entitled *Isabelle Morra* (1973). He has also written many essays on art and literature, collected in *Le Belvédère* (1958; The Gazebo), *Deuxième Belvédère* (1962; Second Gazebo), and *Troisième Belvédère* (1971; Third Gazebo). Artists such as Leonor Fini, Sugai, and Hans Bellmer have particularly interested him. The marvelous, the fantastic, and the erotic are Pieyre de Mandiargues's favorite themes. He is an expert at creating sensuous theatrical works that are always poetic, even when written in prose.

See: B. Pingaud, *Ecrivains d'aujourd'hui* (1960); *Dictionnaire de littérature contemporaine* (1963); *Littérature de notre temps*, vol. 3 (1971).

J.-C.M.

Pilinszky, János (1921-), Hungarian poet, was born and educated in Budapest. He became a soldier in 1944, was evacuated to Germany and spent several months in Allied prison camps during World War II. From 1946 to 1948, he coedited *Ujhold,* a modernist literary and critical quarterly, supported by the younger generation of Hungarian writers, which followed Western European trends and the literary traditions represented by *Nyugat.* Pilinszky's first volume, *Trapéz és korlát* (1946; Trapeze and Bars), demonstrated that he was an original poet. This abstract, austere book, reflecting his traumatic personal experiences, won him the prestigious Baumgarten Prize in 1947. With the Communist takeover of Hungary, *Ujhold* was banned, and Pilinszky was silenced for over 10 years.

Pilinszky's next book of poetry, *Harmadnapon* (1959; On the Third Day), was an important literary event. In these poems, he reflects on the holocaust of war and the degradation suffered by concentration camp inmates, prisoners of war, and—by implication—the victims of Communist repression. Pilinszky is committed to an understanding of these events because "only the victims have reached the reality of the past tense. Theirs is all the meaning today."

Pilinszky's poetry shows the influence of Catholic mystics such as Saint Francis of Assisi and Saint John of the Cross, and of modern Christian thinkers such as Simone WEIL. His oratorio, *Sötét mennyország* (1964; Dark Heaven), was set to music by Endre Szervánszky. Yet he is not a Catholic poet in the classical sense. His vision of the utter loneliness and helplessness of man borders on agnosticism. His poetic style also reflects a fascination with the theater of the absurd. He even wrote several avant-garde film scripts reminiscent in their structure of Samuel Beckett's *Film.* In the 1970s, however, Pilinszky's poetic language became more austere, "a kind of language without language," as he describes his collection *Nagyvárosi ikonok* (1970; Metropolitan Icons). For this volume he was awarded the Attila József Prize in 1971. Pilinszky's recent publications include *Szálkák* (1973; Splinters), a book of poems, *Végkifejlet* (1974; Final Development), a collection of poems and four plays, and *Beszélgetések Sheryl Suttonnel* (1977; Conversations with Sheryl Sutton), a unique document of the human relationship between the poet and a black American actress.

His poems have been translated into English by Ted Hughes, David Wevill, and Peter Jay.

See: Gy. Rónay, "Trapéz és korlát," *Magyarok* 2 (1946): 402–03; G. Gömöri, "Pilinszky: The Lonely Poet," *HungQ* 5 (1965): 43–47; I. Bata, *Arcok és vonulatok* (1973): 153–65; T. Hughes, Introduction to J. Pilinszky, *Selected Poems* (1976).   I.Si.

Pillecijn, Filip de (1891–1962), Belgian (Flemish) prose writer, studied Germanic philology before becoming a teacher and a journalist. During World War II, he occupied an important post in the Ministry of Education, as a result of which he was sentenced, after the war, to five years in jail. The early work of de Pillecijn won acclaim because of its neoromantic elements (such as a predilec tion for the past) and because of its poetic language and style. In such short stories and novels as *De rit* (1927; The Ride), *Blauwbaard* (1931; Bluebeard), *Monsieur Hawarden* (1934); *Hans van Malmédy* (1935), and *Schaduwen* (1937; Shadows), de Pillecijn wrote of restless wanderers and adventurers without any real homeland. They return from the war to find only solitude and nostalgia. The character of Blauwbaard could be considered as archetypal: de Pillecijn puts more emphasis on the moods and emotions that overcome Blauwbaard than on the actual murders he commits. The main character in *De soldaat Johan* (1939; Johan the Warrior), one of de PIllecijn's best novels, is another outlaw, consumed with restlessness, melancholy, and a vague sense of grief. *De soldaat Johan* recounts the life of a soldier who return to Flanders after the battle of Nancy (1477) and tries to enjoy the harmonious life of a farmer. He reaches this goal only after enduring several conflicts that help him to appreciate the value of freedom and to love his country.

After the war, de Pillecijn's work entered a new phase. His personal fate, a genuine concern for social injustice, and a readiness to forgive and to be compassionate become recurrent themes. Besides such works as *De Veerman en de Jonkvrouw* (1950; The Ferryman and the Lady), *Vaandrig Antoon Serjacobs* (1951; Antoon Serjacobs, the Standard-Bearer), and *Anvaard het leven* (1956; Facing Life As It Is), the novel *Mensen achter de dijk* (1949; The People That Live beyond the Dike) stands out as the best prose work published by de Pillecijn during that period. In *Mensen achter de dijk,* the reader is confronted with the personal recollections of Henri, the son of simple peasants. The tragic events that mark Henri's life stem not only from conflicts between individuals or from differences between social classes but from such external factors as hunger, epidemics, and mechanization.

See: B. Ranke, *Filip de Pillecijn, een proeve van synthese der persoonlijkheid* (1941); A. van Wilderode, *Filip de Pillecijn* (1960); B. F. van Vlierden, *De romankunst van Filip de Pillecijn* (1961).   P. van. A.

Pilnyak, Boris, pseud. of Boris Andreyevich Vogau (1894–1941), Russian novelist, short-story writer, journalist, and essayist, was born in Mozhaysk, the son of a veterinary surgeon. Small towns and ordinary people were always the focus of his writings. His steady output began about 1915 with a series of stories, the best of which were collected in *Bylyo* (1920; Bygone Days). They were mostly built on a conflict that, in various ways, remained his characteristic theme: between instinct and reason, nature and civilization. It was elaborated in *Goly god* (1921; Eng. tr., *The Naked Year,* 1928, 1975), his first novel and the first important work of Soviet literature to attempt a picture of the 1917 October Revolution's shattering impact on society at large. That great upheaval is seen as the latest (but not the last) manifestation of a tension set up by the pull, throughout Russian history, of two opposing elements: "east" (formlessness, instinct, movement) and "west" (symmetry, logic, stasis). As ideologues, the Bolsheviks are "western" and therefore hostile to true revolution, which is marked by a life-affirming violence and is embodied in the peasantry. *Mashiny i volki* (1924; Machines and Wolves) restated the same conflict in its very title and further contributed to the already sizable body of anti-industrial fiction in Russian literature. These ideas owed much to greater writers, such as Andrey BELY and Aleksey REMIZOV, as did the manner of narration: seemingly random juxtapositions of different styles and genres; radical shifts in time and space; elaborate sound effects, rich literary allusions, highly obtrusive narrators; crude naturalism coupled with lofty rhetoric; a greater concern with settings and scenes than with characterization. As vehicles of the new themes of Revolution and Civil War, however, Pilnyak's early works seemed fresh and original, made him enormously popular, and inspired numerous imitators.

At first, many Marxist critics thought that Pilnyak's manner reflected the disorder of the new society, and deemed it "realistic." Soon, however, they began to find him "decadent," "fatalistic," and basically anti-Bolshevik. From the mid-1920s on, he moved toward a greater simplicity and straightforwardness. Much of his best work in the next decade was a kind of lyrical reportage, as in *Korni yaponskogo solntsa* (1926; Roots of the Japanese Sun). Although he generally avoided overtly political themes, two works brought him much trouble. The short story "Povest nepogashennoy luny" (1926; Eng. tr., "The Tale of the Unextinguished Moon," 1967) was a thinly fictionalized account of the suspicious death of Mikhail Frunze, commissar of military and naval affairs. Pilnyak's public apology mollified the authorities. But three years later, the novel *Krasnoye derevo* (1929; Eng. tr., *Mahogany,* 1965) touched off a protracted campaign of vilification. Here Pilnyak saw the interests of the proletariat best served by an ideal communism based on charity, not on industrialization. Worse, the novel was published abroad after being banned at home.

Thereafter Pilnyak trod more cautiously. *Volga vpadaet v Kaspiyskoye more* (1930; Eng. tr., *The Volga Falls to the Caspian Sea,* 1931) borrowed much material from *Mahogany* but, in its account of a gigantic dam-building project, glorified the ideals of socialist construction as promoted by the first Five-Year Plan (1928–33). Pilnyak was allowed in 1931 to accept an invitation by Metro-Goldyn-Mayer to visit Hollywood and work on the script of a picture about Russia. Deeming the material anti-Soviet, he soon resigned, but traveled extensively throughout the United States and recorded his experiences in *O'key* (1933; Okay), which combined admiration for American technology with disapproval of American society. A 1932 trip to Japan yielded a book of impressions, *Kamni i korni* (1934; Stones and Roots). Other major works of the 1930s include *Sozrevaniye plodov* (1936; The Ripening Fruits), based on observations of the famous folk-painters of the village of Palekh; and *Solyanoy ambar* (1937; Salt Barn, pub. only in part), dealing with the revolutionary movement in the Russian provinces during the early 20th century. These later works combined many features of Pilnyak's earlier style and themes with obvious attempts to stress "positive" sides of Soviet life. Pilnyak was arrested in 1937 and charged with being a Trotskyite and a Japanese spy. Death came four years later. For many years his writings were banned and his name all but unmentionable in public. Recently, however, some of his better work—notably *The Naked Year*—has been reissued, and Soviet critics have again begun to discuss him.

See: R. A. Maguire, *Red Virgin Soil: Soviet Literature in the 1920's* (1968), especially Chapter 4; V. Reck, *Boris Pilnyak: A Soviet Writer in Conflict with the State* (1975).

R.A.M.

Pinget, Robert (1919–), French novelist and playwright, was born in Geneva. He studied law there and practiced from 1944 to 1946. After a short stay in England, where he taught drawing and French, Pinget moved to Paris in 1951 and began writing. His first novels, *Mahu ou le matériau* (1952; Mahu or the Material) and *Le Renard et la boussole* (1953; The Fox and the Compass), are ironic, satirical narratives. *Graal flibuste* (1957; Filibustering Grail), on the other hand, recalls the imaginary world of Henri MICHAUX. *Baga* (1958) and *Le Fiston* (1959; Sonny) helped Pinget to sharpen his technique and paved the way for what is probably one of his best novels, *L'Inquisitoire* (1962). This work deals with a policeman who interrogates an old servant about a crime he may have witnessed. By means of the questions and answers, we learn about the servant, about his masters, about life in the castle in the French provinces where they live, and about provincial people and their habits. A world unfolds that is at the same time bizarre and fascinating, weird and familiar, real and imaginary. *Quelqu'un* (1965; Someone), which won the Femina Prize, is also a major novel. It focuses on a solitary figure who sits writing, despising the activity yet continuing to pursue it.

After two other novels, *Libera* (1968) and *Passacaille* (1969), Pinget announced that he had nothing more to say. But then in 1975 he published *Cette Voix* (This Voice). In this work, a voice strives to bring the past back to the surface while at the same time hating this futile enterprise. Like Samuel BECKETT, to whom he is often compared, Pinget is of the opinion that it is impossible to write because there is nothing to write; yet, he feels, one has to continue to do so. Such a declaration of impotence might lead a reader to expect sterility or dryness from Pinget's work but, on the contrary, his many novels contain a Balzacian multiplicity of characters. He excels at reproducing banal conversations and the little concerns of everyday life, and he obviously enjoys coining proper names for people and places, inventing genealogies, and using popular expressions. Pinget boasts of having an unlimited love for the French language, and in fact he has said that what one can say or signify is not in itself interesting, only the way in which it is said is. Pinget has also written plays—*Lettre morte* (1959; Dead Letter), *La Manivelle* (1960; The Handle), and *Ici ou ailleurs Architruc: l'hypothese* (1961; Here or Elsewhere Archthingamagig: The Hypothesis). These works recall the plays of Beckett and Eugène IONESCO, but they are little known and rarely performed.

See: V. Mercier, *The New Novel: From Queneau to Pinget* (1971), pp. 363–415; *Le Nouveau Roman hier et aujourd'hui* (1972); L. Roudiez, *French Fiction Today* (1972), pp. 183–205.

D.S.

Piontek, Heinz (1925–), German poet, short-story writer, novelist, radio playwright, translator, essayist, and critic, was born and raised in Kreuzburg, Upper Silesia, and served in World War II. Afterward he held different jobs, studied German literature, philosophy, and art history, and started his writing career as a nature poet under the influence of Wilhelm Lehmann's *Naturmagie*. Since 1961 he has lived in Munich.

Piontek's first three poetry collections, *Die Furt* (1952; The Ford), *Die Rauchfahne* (1953; The Wisp of Smoke), and *Wassermarken* (1957; Watermarks), consist of series of images in which he sketched landscapes and events with graphic precision in simple language. Man is seen as part of nature, swinging between the joy of living and existential despair. Although the author prefers to dwell in physical nature with its ahistorical cyclic patterns, he remains painfully aware of history and industrial society. In *Mit einer Kranichfeder* (1962; With a Crane Feather) he praised beauty in elaborate language, but in the following collections, *Klartext* (1966; Clear Text) and *Tot oder lebendig* (1971; Dead or Alive), he reverted to simplicity of expression; abandoned rhyme, meter, and verse to write prose poems; and added irony, playful fantasy, and surreal elements. Gradually and with great versatility, Piontek has modified his initial model under the influence of modern writers, but he has remained a lyric poet.

Besides poetry, Piontek has written prose since 1955, when he published the collection of stories *Vor Augen* (Before Our Eyes), followed by *Kastanien aus dem Feuer* (1963; Chestnuts from the Fire). Two novels, *Mittlere Jahre* (1967; The Middle Years) and *Dichterleben* (1976; A Poet's Life), are autobiographical remembrances of youth, war, the cultural past, love and loss, and midlife crisis and contain as well vivid sketches of postwar Germany, scenes of pastoral bliss, and thoughts about writing, other authors, and man's problems in the modern world. Piontek clearly uses the same themes in prose, poetry, radio plays, and essays. Together they form a gigantic mosaic—clusters of miniature sketches. Like a panning camera, Piontek briefly focuses on people or objects; strikes off minute, clear-cut impressions; and sets them off against a dark background. Clear language matches clear perception, the whole representing external nature as well as the inner landscape of the human mind. Further works includes volumes of radio plays and essays, as well as the collected poetry of 1949 to 1974 (published in 1975 as *Gesammelte Gedichte*). Piontek is also the translator of John Keats into German.

See: J. P. Wallmann, *Argumente, Informationen und Meinungen zur deutschen Literatur der Gegenwart* (1968).

A.P.O.

Piovene, Guido (1907–74), Italian journalist, essayist, novelist, and short-story writer, was born in Vicenza into an aristocratic Catholic milieu. He spent his childhood and adolescence in the Veneto mainland, the location of most of his narrative works. After studying philosophy, he embarked on a career as a journalist, and over the years he contributed to periodicals such as *Il convegno, Pegaso, L'Ambrosiano, Solaria, Pan,* and *La lettura,* and to the dailies *Corriere della sera* (1935–52) and *La stampa* (1952–74). In 1974 he cofounded, with Indro Montanelli, the newspaper *Il giornale.*

The subjects of Piovene's writings range from strictly literary, aesthetic, and cultural matters to various topical questions and extensive reporting during travel assignments. These reports constitute the basis for his important essaylike travel books: *De America* (1953; About America), *Viaggio in Italia* (1957; Trip through Italy); *La gente che perdè Ierusalemme* (1967; The People Who Lost Jerusalem), and *L'Europa semilibera* (1973; Eng. tr., *In Search of Europe,* 1975). To the same genre belong his long essays: *Lo scrittore tra la tirannide e la libertà* (1952; The Writer between Tyranny and Liberty) and *Processo dell'Islam alla civiltà occidentale* (1957; Western Civilization on Trial before Islam); his early essay collection *Furti del portalettere* (1928; Thefts by the Letter Carrier); the unique *La coda di paglia* (1962; How to Be a Coward), consisting of an autobiographical essay and diarylike comments; and the fairytale *Il nonno tigre* (1972; Grandfather the Tiger). All these reveal the specific qualities that earned him the title of *il saggista-principe* (the prince of essayists). Piovene's deepest concern, however, was with his fiction, which, in contrast to his travel books, is highly subjective. As a prose writer he has been defined as a moralist in the French tradition, eager to probe into the depths of human nature and behavior and into the force of traditions. Among his recurrent themes are evil, the absence of personal responsibility in modern man, egotism, introversion, passivity, death, and false piety and pity. The many autobiographical elements present in his writings suggest his despair over the distortion and transcience of all traditional values in our "post-Christian" era. This despair expresses itself in the relentless analysis of public and private failures. His first attempts at fiction were short stories, of which only those in *La vedova allegra* (1931; The Merry Widow) have been collected.

During his intensely creative middle period he published four novels: the highly acclaimed epistolary novel *Lettere di una novizia* (1941; Eng. tr., *Confession of a Novice,* 1951; film version, 1960), centering on a Pirandellian investigation into truth and appearance (*see* Luigi PIRANDELLO); *La gazzetta nera* (1943; The Black Gazette), concerned with the concept of evil as a force vital to life and art; *Pietà contro pietà* (1946; Pity against Pity, written in 1943–44); and *I falsi redentori* (1949; The False Saviors, written in 1943). The last two works explore, with Freudian and existentialist overtones, the negative personal relationships of his antiheroes. In *Pietà,* however, Piovene distinguishes a ray of hope in the saving forces of active participation in life; this anticipates the more positive developments in *Le furie* (1963; The Furies). The mature Piovene counterbalances his self-doubting, semiautobiographical, passive heroes with active, courageous figures and considers creative work to be the modern intellectual's only alternative to nothingness and despair. In *Le stelle fredde* (1970; The Cold Stars), Piovene once again takes up the topic of self-evaluation, summing up past goals and future expectations—worldly, personal, and spiritual—and defines the writer's task to be, through his work, "the memory of the world." With *Le furie* and *Le stelle,* he transcends the sphere of private concerns, becoming a witness to and interpreter of our age and a pioneer in redefining the role of the artist. He widens his themes to include general historical, political, cultural, and artistic issues and shows a penchant for the mythical as well.

See: M. L. Caputo-Mayr, "Guido Piovenes Romanwerk," Ph.D. Dissertation, University of Vienna (1966); G. Catalano, *Piovene* (1967); G. Marchetti, *Invito alla lettura di Guido Piovene* (1973).   M.L.C.-M.

Pirandello, Luigi (1867–1936), Italian playwright, novelist, short-story writer, critic, and poet, was born in Agrigento. In 1934 he won the Nobel Prize for Literature for his "bold and brilliant renovation of the drama and the stage." The son of a Sicilian sulphur mine owner, Pirandello earned his doctorate in Romance philology at the University of Bonn with a dissertation on the dialect of his native Agrigento. By 1893, when he settled down to a literary life in Rome, he had two collections of poetry to his credit, had translated Goethe's *Roman Elegies,* and had written his own *Elegie renane* (1895; Rhenish Elegies). His poetry is literary, echoing the major Italian poets of the 19th century from Ugo Foscolo (1778–1827) to Giosuè Carducci (1835–1907). Under the impact of Sicilian *verismo* (*see* ITALIAN LITERATURE), he turned to narrative; his admiration for *verismo*'s major exponent, Giovanni VERGA, is evident in the speech he delivered on the latter's 80th birthday in 1920. Yet Pirandello's manner is more violent than Verga's, and his preference for the

distorted and grotesque is quite distant from Verga's resigned pessimism and Olympian compassion, and closer to his mentor Luigi Capuana's (*see* ITALIAN LITERATURE) mixture of positivism and melodrama. In its radical devaluation of "facts" as the determinants of action and the bases for judgment, Pirandello's first full-length novel, *L'esclusa* (1901, written 1893; Eng. tr., *The Outcast,* 1925), already points the way to his rejection of naturalism. Its theme is adultery, and its ironic twist is that the husband spurns his wife when without justification he suspects her of being unfaithful and takes her back after the adultery has actually occurred. His most famous novel, *Il fu Mattia Pascal* (1904; Eng. tr., *The Late Mattia Pascal,* 1923), written at a time when he had had to turn his talent into a financially profitable activity, presents another ironic twist in the opportunity offered its antihero—the inept, "stranger of life" Mattia—to start life over again elsewhere as a self-constructed someone else. But unable to exist without a social identity, Mattia must return to the place and situation he had hoped to escape, only to be forced to undergo yet another metamorphosis. As his own still living "late" self, he finally turns to the only outlet left him, that of writing the story of his life.

In *Il fu Mattia Pascal,* relativism gives rise to the "philosophy of the little lamp," a blend of belief in occultism and faith in the power of illusion, which, like the "philosophy of remoteness" in the short story "La tragedia di un personaggio" (1911; Eng. tr., "A Character in Distress," 1938), serves as a remedy or palliative for the ills of existence. Related to these two "philosophies" is the aesthetic theory presented in *L'umorismo* (1908; Eng. tr., *On Humor,* 1974). Based on the contrast between the "perception of the incongruous" and the "feeling of the incongruous," that is, on the capacity of seeing the comic and tragic sides of things simultaneously, this theory does much to explain the underlying attitude from which Pirandello viewed his own fictional subject matter. But *L'umorismo* also contains a phenomenology of humor, a review of works in European literature to which the label can be applied. Although often ignored, this second aspect of the essay shows that it properly belongs with general works on the comic or, more specifically, on the ironic.

Pirandello's first short story, "Capannetta" (1884; Eng. tr., "The Little Hut," 1965), is a Sicilian sketch in the manner of Verga. By 1908 he had written just under 100 more short stories: some, like "Scialle nero" (1900; Eng. tr., "The Black Shawl," 1959), "Il 'fumo'" (1901; Eng. tr., "Fumes," 1959), or "Lontano" (1901; Far Away), approaching the novel in length and format; others, like "La paura" (1897; Eng. tr., "Fear," 1965), "Lumie di Sicilia" (1900; Eng. tr., "Sicilian Limes," 1932), or "Amicissimi" (1902; Eng. tr., "The Best of Friends," 1965), little more than anecdotes. After appearing in periodicals, the short stories were regularly collected into volumes, until in 1922 there were enough of them to warrant the comprehensive title of *Novelle per un anno* (A Year's Worth of Stories) for a new edition. This narrative corpus of short prose fiction, the most significant in Italian literature after Boccaccio and comparable in other respects to that of Guy de Maupassant, has only occasionally been considered as a whole. Attention has focused selectively on the stories that contributed the seminal idea or plot for a play, on those in which the preponderance of dialogue already points to the dramatic form, and especially on "La signora Frola e il signor Ponza, suo genero" (1915; Eng. tr., "Signora Frola and Her Son-in-Law, Signor Ponza," 1965) in which the narrating voice prefigures the emergence of a fully rounded character on stage, the typical Pirandellian spokesman such as Laudisi of *Così è (se vi pare)* (1917; Eng. tr., *Right You Are, if You Think So,* 1923). Although Pirandello wrote fewer short stories once he became absorbed in the theater, some of the most powerful and disquieting ones belong to his later years: "Pena di vivere così" (1920; Eng. tr., "Such Is Life," 1959), "La distruzione dell'uomo" (1921; Eng. tr., "Destruction of Man," 1965), and "Cinci" (1932; Eng. tr., 1959).

Of the plays that Pirandello reputedly wrote as early as 1886-96, very little remains. In the years bridging the 19th and 20th centuries he shared the generally disdainful attitude towards the theater of other Italian writers who found the stage a crude, insensitive medium in comparison to the novel. His debut as dramatist occurred in 1910 with two one-act plays. In 1915 his first three-act play, *La ragione degli altri* (The Others' Point of View), was a failure. Pirandello's unconventional conception of the wife instead of the mistress as the principal sympathetic character clashed with the view made popular a half-century earlier by Alexandre Dumas *père*'s defense of the fallen woman in *La Dame aux camélias* (1848). Many of his subsequent plays gave rise to similar misunderstandings as time and again his own views regarding the predicaments of his characters contrasted with established values and the norms of the romantic and naturalist theater against which he reacted. A fundamentally antithetical position, a being at odds with or out of tune—going back perhaps to the separation that Sicilians continued to feel between themselves and other Italians even after the unification of Italy—is at the root of Pirandello's polemical bent, the spring of the creative energy that by 1936 produced the 43 plays of *Maschere nude* (Naked Masks), the collective title he first gave his plays in 1918 and to which he remained faithful.

The idea of the "naked mask" as emblematic of the authentic individual who lives and suffers beneath the social role imposed upon him originated with the play *La maschera e il volto* (1916; Eng. tr., *The Mask and the Face,* 1917), in which Luigi CHIARELLI gave the name of *teatro del grottesco* (theater of the grotesque; *see* ITALIAN LITERATURE) to the "new theater" to which Pirandello too rallied. He had by that time written or translated into Sicilian dialect a number of plays that became successful through the work of the great character actor Angelo Musco (1892-1937). *Così è (se vi pare)* marked the most important turning point in his production. Labeled a "parable" and intent on dramatizing the concept of the relativity of truth and pleading for compassion as the prime social, interpersonal virtue, the play marks the road to that transcending of mimetic realism that was to be the distinguishing feature of Pirandello's later work, especially of the plays of the theater-in-the-theater and of the myths: *Sei personaggi in cerca d'autore* (1921; Eng. tr., *Six Characters in Search of an Author,* 1922), *Ciascuno a suo modo* (1924; Eng. tr., *Each in His Own Way,* 1924), *Questa sera si recita a soggetto* (1930; Eng. tr., *Tonight We Improvise,* 1932); *La nuova colonia* (1928; Eng. tr., *The New Colony,* 1958), *Lazzaro* (1929; Eng. tr., *Lazarus,* 1929), *I giganti della montagna* (left unfinished; Eng. tr., *The Mountain Giants,* 1958).

A different line of development can be traced in those plays both before and after *Così è* that are centered around a protagonist of exceptional psychological complexity, caught in a dilemma for which he can find only an unnatural and often self-damaging solution. Such are the clerk Ciampa in *Il berretto a sonagli* (1917; Eng. tr., *Cap and Bells,* 1974); Chiàrchiaro, the reputed bearer of the evil eye, in *La patente* (1918; Eng. tr., *The License,* 1964); Baldovino, the ex-gambler and now husband-in-name-only, in *Il piacere dell'onestà* (1917; Eng. tr., *The*

Pleasure of Honesty, 1923); Leone Gala, the cool-headed rationalist, all "mask," in *Il giuoco delle parti* (1918; Eng. tr., *The Rules of the Game,* 1959); the nameless protagonist playing the role of a paranoid emperor in *Enrico IV* (1922; Eng. tr., *Henry IV,* 1923); the governess Ersilia Drei in *Vestire gli ignudi* (1922; Eng. tr., *To Clothe the Naked,* 1924); and the Father in the inner story of *Sei personaggi.* Pirandello's principal male figures were created with the actor Ruggero Ruggeri (1871-1953) in mind, the "lyric elocutionist" whom contemporary reviewers described with the same adjectives they used for Pirandello himself: "cerebral" and "made" (as opposed to "spontaneous" or "born").

Pirandello found his ideal female lead in Marta Abba, whom he engaged for his own company, the "Teatro d'Arte di Roma" (1924-28), and for whom he wrote *Diana e la Tuda* (1926; Eng. tr., *Diana and Tuda,* 1950), *L'amica delle mogli* (1927; Eng. tr., *The Wives' Friend,* 1949), *Come tu mi vuoi* (1930; Eng. tr., *As You Desire Me,* 1948), *Trovarsi* (1932; Eng. tr., *To Find Oneself,* 1943), and other plays. In the life/form dichotomy ("the inherent tragic conflict between life which is always moving and changing and form which fixes it, immutable," as Pirandello expressed it in the preface to *Sei personaggi*), woman represents the former, all instinct and passion, except when she is "frozen" in the static role of Mother.

A great theatrical innovator in a period of extraordinary theatrical experimentation, Pirandello is seen more and more frequently to have been a forerunner of German and French existentialism and the theaters of cruelty and of the absurd.

See: G. Giudice, *Luigi Pirandello* (1963; Eng. tr., *Pirandello: A Biography,* 1975); G. Cambon, ed., *Pirandello: A Collection of Critical Essays* (1967); O. Ragusa, *Luigi Pirandello* (1968) and *Pirandello: An Introduction to His Theatre* (1979).   O.R.

Pires, José Cardoso (1925-), Portuguese novelist, dramatist, and essayist, was born in Pêso da Régua, in the province of Trás-os-Montes. He studied mathematics at the University of Lisbon and has worked at many callings: interpreter, pilot in the merchant marine, literary director of a publishing house, and newspaper editor. His works include the stories in *Os caminheiros e outros contes* (1946; The Tramps and Other Stories); *Histórias de amor* (1952; Love Stories), suppressed by the censor because of allusions to the Underground; and *Jogos de azar* (1963; Games of Chance), new versions of earlier stories. He wrote the novella *O ango ancorado* (1958; The Angel Anchored); the essay *Cartilha do marialva* (1960, enlarged 1966; Marialva Reader), attacking the irrationality of the archaic upper class typified in an 18th-century noble (the Marques de Marialva) but aiming at 20th-century Portugal; the play *O render dos heróis* (1960; The Conquering of Heroes), about the peasants' revolt of 1846; and the novels *O hóspede de Job* (1963; Job's Guest) and *O delfim* (1968; The Dolphin), the latter a brilliant application of his ideas on the *marialva.* In a lighter vein he composed the satire *Dinossaure excelentíssime* (1972; His Imperial Highness, Dinosaurus I), about a nobody who made himself the ruler of a fictitious (?) country.

The novella *O anjo ancorado* contrasts the psychology of an affluent couple with the villagers who watch them as the husband goes skin diving for fish and the wife attempts to save a bird that an old man has caught for his dinner. The couple's dialogues and reminiscences alternate with scenes revealing the villagers' struggle for the necessities of life. *O hóspede de Job* presents two poor country people, father and son, trying to cope with forces beyond their control or understanding. Through a triple view of the various characters as individuals, types, and symbols, which is Pires's original contribution to neo-realism, their pressing problems are dramatically shown. The result is a composite portrait of a suffering people.

See: J. Gaspar Simões, *Crítica III* (n.d.), pp. 437–40; J. Palla e Carme, *Do livro à crítica* (1971), pp. 95–118; M. L. Lepecki, *Ideologia e imagináro: Ensaio Sobre José Cardoso Pires* (1977). T.Br.

Pitarra, Serafí, pseud. of Frederic Soler i Huber (1839–95), Catalan playwright, was born in Barcelona, where he was apprenticed to a watchmaker and later ran a shop that made and sold clocks and watches. Frederic Soler was first known as the author of poetry characterized by "humorisme gras" (broad humor). Ruiz i Calonja considers this typical of his early works, named the *Gatades* after *La Gata*, a section of the Odéon Theater. Soler created the *Gatades* with his friend and collaborator, the musician Joan Jariols Sariols, and published them as "singlots poetichs" (poetic hiccups). "El Castell dels tres dragons" (1865) is a particularly amusing example.

Soler's play *La butifarra de la llibertat* (prod. 1865; The Sausage of Liberty) ridicules the war in Africa, and other works parody particular incidents of the war or contemporary literary works. The Palou i Coll's Almudaina's Bell (1863) inspired Soler's *Lésquella de la Torratxa* (prod. 1866; The Cow-Bells of the Tower), while the romantic *Flor de un Dia* is transformed into his *Ous del dìa* (prod. 1866; Eggs of the Day). Soler was one of the best practitioners of the *grimegia* or supermockery that Eugenio D'ORS considers to be a Catalan tradition. The success of *Tal farás tal trobarás* (prod. 1865; What You Shall Do You Shall Find) by Eduard Vidal i Valenciano inspired him to write a new series of plays, which he signed with his real name, Frederic Soler. The series begins with *Les joies de la Roser* (prod. 1866). As it is impossibile to cite all of Soler's numerous works, we shall mention only *Lo Rector de Vallfogona* (prod. 1871); *Les francesilles* (prod. 1868); *Batalla de reines,* whose Castilian version received a prize from the Royal Spanish Academy of the Language in 1888; *Lo Comte Arnau* (prod. 1900); *La dida* (prod. 1872; The Wet Nurse); *Lo ferrer de tall* (prod. 1879; The Ironmonger); *Les eures del mas* (prod. 1869; The Summer House's Orchard); *Lo pubill* (prod. 1886; The Heiress's Husband); *Lo collaret de perles* (prod. 1886; The Pearl Necklace); *Lo veguer de Vich* (prod. 1870; The Magistrate of Vich); and *O rey o res* (prod. 1866; Either King or Nothing).

In all of his plays, first written in verse and later in prose, he used a colloquial language that drew him close to the general public. Soler created a demand for theater in Catalan that later flowered in the work of Angel GUIMERÀ.

See: Anonymous, *Frederich Soler y son teatre* (1873); J. M. Poblet, *Frederic Soler Serafí Pitarra* (1967); M. Fabre Pont, *Pitarra (L'home del Romea)* (1969). J.F.C.

Pitoëff, Georges (1886–1939), French stage director, designer, and actor, was born in Tiflis, Georgia, where his wealthy Armenian father directed a theater. Pitoëff was first trained in engineering and law before studying acting and directing (1912–15). With his wife Ludmilla, an actress of great charm and sensitivity, he created his own company in Geneva, presenting 74 plays by 46 authors between 1915 and 1922. In Paris, from 1927 on, Pitoëff was a member of the famous Cartel of Four, along with Gaston BATY, Charles DULLIN, and Louis JOUVET.

Pitoëff preferred idealistic, poetic plays (it was he who introduced Anton CHEKHOV to the French in his own adaptations) and those expressing the unrest of the post–World War I generation. The most prolific worker of the Cartel, he presented the largest, most international repertory, including Jean ANOUILH, Paul CLAUDEL, Jean COCTEAU, Marcel ACHARD, André GIDE, Henri LENORMAND, Shakespeare, Luigi PIRANDELLO, George Bernard Shaw, August STRINDBERG, Lev TOLSTOY, Henrik IBSEN, and Eugene O'Neill. Of the 210 plays he produced, only a third of them were by French authors. Independent and inventive, Pitoëff detested systems and conventions. He had an almost religious respect for the play itself, searching to express its essence with simplicity, ingenuity, and boldness. Some of his productions—Shakespeare's *Hamlet* and *Macbeth,* Pirandello's *Six Characters in Search of an Author,* Dumas's *Camille (La Dame aux camélias),* Ferenc MOLNÁR's *Liliom*—remain landmarks in the history of modern staging. His son Sacha Pitoëff (1920–), a well-known theater director, possesses similar ideas about the theater.

See: H.-R. Lenormand, *Les Pitoëff: souvenirs* (1943); A. Frank, *Georges Pitoëff* (1958); J. Hort, *La Vie héroïque des Pitoëff* (1966). A.R.

Pla i Casadevall, Josep (1897–), Catalan novelist, was born at Palafrugell into a well-to-do rural family. A journalist and traveler in his youth, Pla later returned to his family home, where he has become, without apparent effort, the most famous Catalan writer of our time. Both the quantity—Albert Manent estimates that Pla has written 30,000 pages of memoirs—and the quality of Pla's work are amazing. He wrote his first work, *El quadern gris* (The Gray Notebook), at the age of 21, although he did not publish it in its entirety until 1966. In 1920 he published a biography of the sculptor Casanovas and following that, *Coses vistes* (1925; Known Quantities) and *Llanterna màgica* (1926; Magic Lantern). The subtitle of the latter, *Cápitols de novel·la, Viatges sense objecte, Retrats* (Chapters from Novels, Haphazard Journeys, Portraits), could serve as a description for his entire literary production. As a novelist he has written works like *El carrer estret* (1952; The Narrow Path), *Nocturn de primavera* (1953; Spring Nocturn), and other narrative works of the most diverse nature. His travel books begin with his second book, *Rússia* (1925), and include *Cartes de Lluny* (1928; Letters from Lluny), *Viatge a Catalunya* (1934; Travels to Catalonia), *Viatge en autobus* (1942; Bus Journey), *Week-end (d'estiu) a New York* (1955; Summer Weekend in New York), and *De l'Empordanet a Barcelona* (1956). These last two books reveal the author's interest in describing faraway lands as well as his immediate surroundings. His biographical writings begin with a series published in *L'Anuari dels catalans,* commissioned by Rovira i Virgili as "Retrats a la ploma" (Pen Portraits). His skill as a biographer reached its zenith in *Vida de Manolo (contada per ell mateix* (1928; Life of Manolo as Told by Himself), *Un senyor de Barcelona* (1952; A Gentleman from Barcelona), *Santiago Rusiñol i el seu temps* (1955; Santiago Rusiñol and His Period), and finally in the various series of *Homenots,* begun in 1960, and in *Retrats de passaport* (1970; Passport Photos).

Pla's autobiographical narratives and his enormously personal memoirs nevertheless constitute the core of his work. Pla himself said: "literature is no more than a struggle against oblivion." Fundamental works like *Girona (Un llibre de records)* (1952; Gerona: A Book of Memoirs) and *Barcelona (Papers d'un estudiant)* (1956; Barcelona. A Student's Papers) may be grouped with others in which the writer meditates on the world around him, such as *Els pagesos* (1952; The Peasants), *Els anys (El pas de la vida)* (1953; The Years: The Rhythm of

Life), and *Les hores (El pas de l'any)* (1953; The Hours. The Rhythm of Life).

Faithful to his name, Pla's work is "pla" or "smooth," as befits the first writer to react against Eugenio D'Ors's "Noucentisme."

See: J. Fuster, "Notes per a una introducció a l'estudi de Josep Pla" in J. Pla, *Obra Completa* (1966); J. Martinell Puig, *Josep Pla, vist de prop* (1972); A. Manent, "Josep Pla: treinta mil páginas de memorias" in *Tres escritores catalanes: Carner, Riba, Pla* (1973); J. M. Castellet, *Josep Pla o la ráo Narrativa* (1978).   J.F.C.

Planchon, Roger (1931–), French stage director, actor, and dramatist, was born in Saint-Chamond into a family of peasant origin. He was brought up in Lyon and was self-educated. In 1952, Planchon founded a permanent theater company, the Théâtre de Comédie, which produced, in a hall with only 100 seats, 26 plays in 5 years. Invited in 1957 to direct the municipal theater at Villeurbanne, a working-class suburb of Lyon, he created the Théâtre de la Cité, which was soon promoted to the rank of national dramatic center.

With the aid of a talented staff, Planchon seeks to create a repertory relevant to the modern world, whether he is illuminating the classics (Marlowe, Shakespeare, Molière, Marivaux) with his rare critical intelligence or is staging contemporary plays by Arthur ADAMOV, Vinaver, or Bertolt BRECHT. Planchon has been decisively influenced by Brecht, not because he accepts the German playwright's didactic purpose, but because he learned from him how to use a new realism, as far from copying reality as it is from trusting to dramatic illusion. Since 1962, Planchon has been alternating the presentation of his own works (*La Remise; Blue, blanc, rouge; L'Infâme; Le Cochon noir*) and of great classical plays, Shakespeare's *Troilus and Cressida*, Racine's *Bérénice*, and especially Molière's *Tartuffe*, for which he proposed new interpretations. In 1973, the Théâtre de la Cité, which had become one of the most famous Theaters in Europe, succeeded the Théâtre National Populaire, inheriting its name and taking up the mission of disseminating its productions throughout France. At Planchon's request, the young stage director Patrice Chéreau (1941–) became codirector of the company.

See: E. Copfermann, *Planchon* (1969).   R.A.

Platonov, Andrey Platonovich, surname officially changed from Klimentov (1899–1951), Russian fiction writer, dramatist, poet, and critic, is gaining posthumous recognition in the Soviet Union and abroad for his highly original work in prose fiction. Born on the outskirts of Voronezh, Platonov left school at 15. He served during the Civil War on the side of the Bolsheviks, and completed his education as an electrical engineer in 1924.

His first writing—short stories, poems, war reporting, and articles—began to appear in the provincial press in 1918. Closely identified with the proletarian cultural movement, he dealt in much of his early work with the conquest of nature by machines in the dithyrambic style of the Smithy and Cosmist writers, but his pastoral writing about village life lent credence to charges of ideological duality.

After leaving the Communist Party in 1921, Platonov worked as a specialist in land reclamation and electrification in the Voronezh region. He resigned from a post in Moscow in 1927 to devote full time to literature. His first prose anthology, *Yepifanskiye shlyuzy* (1927; The Locks of Yepifan), was followed by *Lugovye mastera* (1928; Masters of the Meadowlands), *Sokrovenny chelovek* (1928; The Inner Man), and *Proiskhozhdeniye mastera* (1929; The Origin of a Master); and his stories began to appear in leading journals.

In the late 1920s, Platonov looked back with irony, sometimes with wistful nostalgia, on his earlier romantic hopes for the Revolution. With "Lunnaya bomba" (1926; The Moon Bomb) and "Gorod Gradov" (1927; Eng. tr., "The City of Gradov," 1973), a satire on the excesses of science and bureaucratism begins to dominate. In "Usomnivshiysya Makar" (1929; Doubting Makar), *Kotlovan* (1968; Eng. tr., *The Foundation Pit*, 1973, 1975), and *Chevengur* (incomplete edition, 1972; Eng. tr. of complete text, 1978), he deeply probes the spiritual consequences of total organization from above. Centralized state power is symbolized by an insensate monolith akin to Pushkin's Bronze Horseman ("Makar"), while images of the maelstrom and the pit characterize the fate of simple people drawn into the rush of revolution. Rustic wisdom is opposed to Soviet New Thought as his picaresque and questing heroes often take to the road like Russian "Wanderers" and find briefly near the end the anarchist ideal of brotherhood. In "Ivan Zhokh" (1927) and *Chevengur*, that ideal is a legendary city, a refuge where men manage their own lives free from state controls. Platonov draws from Cervantes's *Don Quixote* for a number of character types. Parallels with Fyodor DosTOYEVSKY are also to be found, particularly in *Kotlovan*, with Platonov's portrayal of alienation, brotherhood, and the myth of the golden age.

Platonov's anarchistic tendency brought him under increasing attack. He was finally barred from publishing after the appearance of "Vprok: bednyatskaya khronika" (1931; For Future Use: A Poor Farmhand's Chronicle). When again permitted to publish, he replaced satire with a lyrically sympathetic treatment of basic human needs. Among the best of his later stories are "Fro" (1936; Eng. tr., 1970), "Tretiy syn" (1936; Eng. tr., "The Third Son," 1970), and "Dzhan" (1964; Eng. tr., 1970).

Platonov won popularity during World War II for his nationalistic war stories, but was attacked for "slandering Soviet society" in his story of postwar readjustment, "Semya Ivanova" (1946; Eng. tr., "Homecoming," 1970), and suffered official disfavor during his remaining years.

He is now highly regarded for the integrity of his artistic vision and the inimitable texture of his language. What has been termed the "Platonov dialect" is an expressive although often difficult-to-digest mixture of Soviet "Newspeak" and rustic philosophizing sprinkled with semantic surprises. His rehabilitation, however, remains incomplete. *Kotlovan* and *Chevengur* have never been published in the Soviet Union, and other important works from the 1920s are missing from recent Soviet editions.

See: L. Shubin, "Andrey Platonov," *Voprosy literatury*, no. 6 (1967); *Tvorchestvo A. Platonova: stati i soobshcheniya* (Voronezh, 1970); M. Jordan, *Andrei Platonov* (1973); J. W. Shepard, "The Origin of a Master: The Early Prose of Andrej Platonov," Ph.D. Dissertation, Indiana University (1973).   J.W.S.

Plekhanov, Georgy Valentinovich (1857–1918), Russian Marxist philosopher and aesthetician, was born in the village of Gudalovka, in the province of Tambov. He was one of the founders of the Emancipation of Labor Party (1883), out of which the Social Democrats developed. For a time he was involved in the Bolshevik-Menshevik struggle, but eventually detached himself from both factions, and even opposed the October Revolution of 1917.

Plekhanov was the first to attempt a systematic Marxist theory of art. Among his most important works are *Pisma bez adresa* (1899–1900; Eng. tr., *Letters without Address,*

1953); *Frantsuzskaya dramaticheskaya literatura i frantsuzskaya zhivopis XVIII veka s tochki zreniya sotsiologii* (1905; Eng. tr., *French Drama and Painting of the Eighteenth Century,* 1936); and *Iskusstvo i obshchestvennaya zhizn* (1912–13; Eng. tr., *Art and Social Life,* 1936). He believed that art develops along with society and serves the purposes of particular classes. In content art is like any other form of ideology, but differs in the means it employs, that is, images (not concepts). On these points most Marxists would agree. What distinguishes Plekhanov is his strong interest in the relevance of anthropology to a study of the development of art; his attempt to blend Marxism and Darwinian evolutionism; and especially his recognition that although the forms art takes are socially conditioned, art ultimately answers a biological instinct for beauty and is a means of disinterested enjoyment. By seeing art as simultaneously inside and outside history, Plekhanov created a dualism that he never resolved and that some of his followers, like Aleksandr VORONSKY, pushed much farther. In practice, he favored works that express general, universal qualities, and he insisted that good artistry counts as much as ideological correctness. He raised, although he did not solve, virtually all the important questions of Marxist aesthetics. Under Iosif Stalin, he was rather neglected for having played down the ideological importance of art; but by the 1970s he had been largely "rehabilitated" in the Soviet Union as a major Marxist figure.

See: S. Baron, *Plekhanov, the Father of Russian Marxism* (1963); P. A. Nikolayev, *Estetika i literaturnye teorii G. V. Plekhanova* (1968). R.A.M.

Plenzdorf, Ulrich (1934–), East German prose writer and playwright, is one of the most influential and popular authors in East Germany. He achieved international recognition in 1973 with his controversial novel *Die neuen Leiden des jungen W.* (The New Sorrows of Young W.), the story of a 17-year-old socialist dropout, and for his screenplay *Die Legende von Paul und Paula* (1974). Born in Berlin of working-class parents, he studied philosophy in Leipzig and then served as a stagehand for the DEFA (state-owned film studio) from 1955 to 1958. In 1963, following military service and four years of training at the Babelsberg film academy, Plenndorf began working as a scenarist and producer for the DEFA.

Although not a prolific writer, Plenzdorf has been able to accomplish something no other German author has done in recent times: to write a play that aroused passionate interest and sympathy in East and West Germany. As a result he has become—in the period following the 1972 publication of *Die neuen Leiden* as a screenplay—the most discussed, reviewed, and performed East German writer since Bertolt BRECHT.

See: I. H. Reis, *Ulrich Plenzdorfs Gegen-Entwurf zu Goethes "Werther"* (1977). R.A.Z.

Plisnier, Charles (1896–1942), Belgian poet, novelist, and short-story writer, was a Communist Party militant who later evolved toward a kind of Christian deism. Although excluded from the Party in 1928 for Trotskyism, he nevertheless drew from this affiliation the admirable short stories in *Faux passeports* (1937; Eng. tr., *Memoirs of a Secret Revolutionary,* 1938), which won the Prix Goncourt in 1937. This work is dominated by the combative exaltation of a militant deceived by the ensuing bureaucratic and efficacious Stalinism. Although materialists, the persons in these stories are mystics who have become won over to the point of abandon and are willing to destroy themselves with the passion of sacrifice. Plisnier's poetry is violent, vehement, penetrated with interrogations and doubts, animated with pity for men, and avid with hope. His volumes of poetry include *Brûler vif* (1923; Burn to the Quick), *Prière aux mains coupées* (1930; Prayers with Severed Hands), *Odes pour retrouver les hommes* (1935; Odes to Meet Again with Men), *Sel de la terre* (1936; Salt of the Earth), and *Ave Genitrix* (1943). As a novelist, he portrayed a bourgeois and provincial society whose pharisaism and lack of ideals he denounced. *Mariages* (1936; Eng. tr., *Nothing to Chance,* 1938) condemns the social conventions of a milieu that prefers security and calculation to love. *Meurtres* (1939–44; Murders) pits a hero eager for purity and an ideal against the bourgeois and hypocritical law of "respectability." With *Mères* (1946–49; Mothers), where the return to Christian ethics is sketched, Plisnier sings a hymn to maternity, to "genetrix" (mother). *Beauté des laides* (1951; The Beauty of Ugly Women) is the psychological analysis of a soul inexorably condemned to destroy itself. Plisnier's narrative work has its tedious passages. It is valued more for its architectural ensemble in the style of Honoré de Balzac and for its use of rich and complex plots than for any subtlety of psychological analysis—with the exception of *Beauté des laides*. But his work is fervent in its quest for the ideal. R.T.

Pogodin, Nikolay Fyodorovich, pseud. of Nikolay Stukalov (1900–62), Soviet Russian playwright, of peasant origin, was born near Rostov-on-Don and worked for nine years as a *Pravda* correspondent before devoting himself entirely to playwriting. His plays are episodic, contain a multitude of characters, and present numerous technical difficulties. While little more than journalistic commentaries in dramatic form on the industrialization of the country, Pogodin's early works, such as *Temp* (1930; Eng. tr., *Tempo,* 1934), have an infectious enthusiasm and a rather charming humor. But their characters are superficially delineated and tend to fade into each other. Better written is *Aristokraty* (1934; Eng. tr., *Aristocrats,* 1937), a "serious comedy" about a ragbag group of criminals sentenced to a forced labor camp building on the White Sea-Baltic Canal. The characters in Aristokraty are vividly drawn, and their down-to-earth dialogue is fast moving and witty. Unfortunately, Pogodin allows them to be rehabilitated without much psychological justification, and from that point on his play moves quickly downhill.

In 1959, Pogodin was awarded a Lenin Prize for his trilogy consisting of *Chelovek s ruzhyom* 1937; The Man with a Gun), *Kremlyovskiye kuranty* (1941; Eng. tr., *The Chimes of the Kremlin,* 1946), and *Tretya pateticheskaya* (1958; The Third Pathetic). In these plays his purpose was to show Vladimir Lenin not only as an awesome leader but also as a sympathetic human being. While they do contain some cleverly written and theatrically effective scenes, their stress on ideology overpowers any dramatic element. A surprisingly different work is *Sonet Petrarki* (1957; Eng. tr., A Petrarchan Sonnet, 1968), a small-scale, quiet love story, which attacks Communist Party officials and others who, under the pretext of guarding "Communist morality," meddle in the personal lives of private citizens. Although Pogodin's 40 plays have a rather broad range and sometimes show flashes of brilliance, they remain of purely local interest.

See: K. Rudnitsky, *Portrety dramaturgov* (1961). S.E.R.

Polish literature. The opening of the modern period in Polish literature is associated with the name Cyprian NORWID, who, from the moment of his rediscovery at the end of the 19th century, became and remains the great patron of contemporary poetry. Unappreciated during his own lifetime and overlooked by his peers of the positivist generation, Norwid's work was discovered only by the "Młoda Polska" writers, who saw in him a precursor of their own poetics and a link between themselves and romanticism. But Norwid has been considered a forerunner not only of "Młoda Polska" but also of many later movements in poetry, up to and including contemporary literature. During the "Młoda Polska" era, Stanisław Brzozowski developed Norwid's philosophy of art as the product of work. Many similarities exist between Bolesław Leśmian and Norwid in subject matter, imagery, and creative word formation. The topics of culture and art in poetry liken the work of Leopold Staff to that of Norwid. Mieczysław Jastrun is greatly indebted to Norwid's thinking on the subject of historical time. All the poetry of different literary groups of the period between the world wars has developed under Norwid's aegis. After World War II, Norwid again inspired new trends. Throughout the whole of his work, Czesław Miłosz recalls Norwid's philosophy, questions treated in his poetry, and his style. The interest in Mediterranean civilization evidenced by Zbigniew Herbert and other poets derives from Norwid. The young Polish émigré poets in London invoke Norwid's name; Norwid's dictum of correspondence between word and object pervades the work of many poets of the current generation. As Norwid himself had foreseen, his poetry, while incomprehensible to his own contemporaries, was accepted by his grandsons.

The year 1864, the year of the defeat of the anti-Russian January uprising (begun in 1863), is customarily considered the date that closes the long period of romanticism in Poland. Subsequently a new phase opens known as positivism, a term that refers both to critical realism in literature and to cultural life as a whole. The catastrophic defeat of the uprising and the wave of severe repression that followed prompted reconsideration of the idea of an armed struggle for independence from the partitioning powers, an idea rooted in romanticism, and marked the beginning of an intensification of the debate with romantic literature. The origins of the new literary features that soon became dominant can be traced back to an earlier period and are connected not only with Polish literature, but also with broad changes in European literature and culture. The views of August Comte, harking back to the tradition of the French Enlightenment in which science was considered the single reliable means of knowing reality, formed the philosophical basis of positivism. The empiricism and utilitarianism that distinguished Polish positivism, however, derived primarily from Comte's English followers, Herbert Spencer and John Stuart Mill. Polish positivism's practical program of social reform, reactivation of both economic and cultural life as expressed in the slogans "organic work" and "work at the foundations," demanded that literature and journalism join in the struggle against ignorance and reaction so as to work for a society based on new principles. Literature and journalism were expected to treat contemporary problems and the concerns of the common man. The short story and the novel replaced drama and poetry, the major romantic genres. Warsaw was the most important center of positivism. The most prominent journalist and theoretician of "Warsaw positivism" was Aleksander Świętochowski (1849–1938), a novelist and dramatist, as well as the author of articles for the positivist platform *Absenteizm* (1872), *Praca u podstaw* (1873; Work at the Foundations). Świętochowski also published the journal *Prawda*, which along with *Przegląd Tygodniowy* was one of the main theoretical organs of positivism. The literary historian Piotr Chmielowski (1848–1904) also took part in the shaping of the ideas of Warsaw positivism, and the novelist Eliza ORZESZKOWA was active in early positivist journalism. Like Świętochowski and Chmielowski, Bolesław PRUS and Henryk SIENKIEWICZ were graduates of the Szkoła Główna, a university founded in Warsaw in 1862, then subsequently closed and turned into a Russian university in 1869. Three of the most outstanding representatives of Polish prose in the second half of the 19th century, Orzeszkowa, Prus, and Sienkiewicz, began writing as positivists. In their early, socially tendentious and didactic short stories, they introduced such topics as the emancipation of women, the oppression of the peasants, and the wretched fate of a talented village child. Nevertheless, in the 1870s and 1880s a crisis occurred in the early optimistic phase of positivism. Due to the growth of social strife and the return of the revolutionary ideals of romanticism (ideals stifled in the early periods of positivism in favor of social and economic change), writers began to drift away from didacticism. Depictions of various segments of society in villages and cities, portrayal of characters, and the personal and social motivations of conflict now appeared as multifaceted and complex. In Orzeszkowa's *Nad Niemnem* (1888; On the Banks of Niemen), for example, positivistic ideals are combined with a depiction of their limitations and with recollections of the armed struggle for independence. A dramatic reinterpretation of romantic and positivistic ideals appears in the parallel narratives in *Lalka* (1890; Eng. tr., *The Doll*, 1972) by Bolesław Prus. In both of these novels elements signaling the subsequent period, "Młoda Polska," can be found. Further, the historical novel, a genre avoided in the early stages of positivism, now came to the fore, primarily in the works of Sienkiewicz, although it was also cultivated by Prus and some minor authors. The leading representatives of the "poetry of these un-poetic times," as Julian Krzyżanowski termed the period, are two poets of rather different personalities, Adam ASNYK and Maria KONOPNICKA. In addition to writing poetry, Konopnicka wrote short stories. Józef Bliziński (1827–93) and Michał Bałucki are the most famous dramatists of the period; Bliziński wrote plays bordering on comedy and farce, such as *Pan Damazy* (1877; Mr. Damazy) and *Rozbitki* (1881; Wrecks).

The influence of naturalism, which reached Poland from France at about this time, was a turning point in the literature of the period. While an outgrowth of positivistic realism, naturalism was at the same time a factor in its deepening crisis. The theory of biological determinism stamping the naturalists' works with elements of fatalism and pessimism undermined positivism's optimistic vision of the world. Naturalism demanded from the writer an objective, almost scientific rendering of a slice of contemporary life, a presentation based upon the author's own observations, a demand that constituted a departure from tendentious literature. Antoni Sygietyński (1850–1923), a novelist, critic, and translator of Hippolyte Taine, was the first writer to foster an interest in the French naturalists; Sygietyński's fascination with Gustave Flaubert, and to a lesser extent, Emile ZOLA, appeared in his articles on the contemporary novel in France. In the years 1884 to 1888, the Warsaw weekly *Wędrowiec*, edited by Artur Gruszecki (1853–1929), was the organ of the naturalists. An active contributor was Stanisław Witkiewicz (1851–1915), a painter, critic, and author of a collection of sketches on Tatra Mountain themes, *Na przełęczy* (1891; On the Pass), which combined ideas of naturalism with impressionism. The most outstanding representatives of naturalism in Polish literature are Adolf DYGASIŃSKI and Gabriela Zapolska, but links with the subsequent period, "Młoda Polska," are evident in both writers. Instances of a symbiotic relationship between these two literary currents can be observed in the works of many writers belonging to the "Młoda Polska" era, such as Stefan ŻEROMSKI, Władysław REYMONT, Wacław SIEROSZEWSKI, and Wacław BERENT. Neither the lives nor the works of the most important writers of the period can be contained within the chronological dates accepted for positivism and naturalism. Eliza Orzeszkowa and Maria Konopnicka both died in 1910; Bolesław Prus in 1912; Henryk Sienkiewicz in 1916; Adolf Dygasiński in 1902; and Gabriela Zapolska in 1921. Prus's *Faraon* appeared in 1896, but Orzeszkowa's *Gloria victis* (Glory to the Defeated) only in 1910. Sienkiewicz published *Quo vadis* (Eng. tr., 1896) in 1896, *Krzyżacy* (Eng. tr., *The Knights of the Cross*, 1900) in 1900, and other novels still later. A series of Konopnicka's novels as well as volumes of her poetry appeared toward the end of her life. Dygasiński's *Gody życia* (The Feast of Life) appeared in 1902. Zapolska's best plays, *Moralność pani Dulskiej* (Mrs. Dulska's Morality) and *Panna Maliczewska* (Miss Maliczewska), appeared in 1907 and 1912, respectively. Numerous interrelationships crop up between declining positivism and the new trend, connections important for the development and continuity of Polish literature.

"Młoda Polska" (Young Poland) is a particularly original variant of a larger European trend that in various countries and at various stages of its development is termed modernism, symbolism, and neoromanticism. To these labels, signifying different tendencies often not appearing in isolation, are added other designations for further diverse directions taken by the movement, such as impressionism and expressionism. In the Polish "Młoda Polska," all these elements appear in varying degrees and in different proportions than in other countries. The name "Młoda Polska" was coined by a writer and literary critic, Artur Górski (1870–1959) by analogy with other new generations of writers and artists, like "Young Scandinavia," "Young Belgium," and "Young Germany." Górski's series of programmatic articles entitled "Młoda Polska," appearing in 1898 in the Cracow journal *Życie* was recognized as the literary manifesto of the new movement; the articles emphasized, among other things, the links between the new trend and romantic and patriotic traditions. In 1899, a second manifesto appeared in the pages of *Życie,* this manifesto entitled "Confiteor," and penned by Stanisław PRZYBYSZEWSKI, the journal's new editor. In his "Confiteor," Przybyszewski coined the phrase, "the naked soul," pronouncing that art is its own absolute. The literary critic Zenon Przesmycki (1861–1944), known under the pseudonym "Miriam," was the first to pave the way for modernism in Poland. Starting in the Warsaw journal *Życie* in 1887, Miriam described the very latest developments in Western European literature. A poet, an admirer of Parnassianism, and a translator of Maurice MAETERLINCK, Miriam also edited the journal *Chimera* (1901–07), in which many excellent works by "Młoda Polska" writers appeared. Miriam is perhaps most important, however, for his discovery and publication of the works of Cyprian Norwid.

As in France and other countries, the extraordinarily heterogenous program of "Młoda Polska" was symptomatic of the cultural crisis experienced throughout all Europe at the close of the 19th century, a crisis in philosophical systems, a crisis of optimism in the area of the theory of knowledge, and a sense of disillusionment caused by the collapse of former values. It was a revolt against the utilitarian aspect of positivism and a peculiar return to the ideals of romanticism, to great national and universal concerns. A sign of the new ideological opposition to positivism was the cult of individualism, a phenomenon traceable to the individualistic philosophical

systems of Arthur Schopenhauer and Friedrich NIETZSCHE. The return to romantic tradition in general, and to Polish romanticism in particular, is especially evident in the cult of Juliusz Słowacki, acclaimed as the precursor of the new movement, for example, in the study *Słowacki i nowa sztuka* (1902; Słowacki and New Art) by the brilliant critic of the period, Ignacy Matuszewski (1858–1919).

The "Młoda Polska" period begins around 1890 with the appearance of the first works of Jan KASPROWICZ, Wacław ROLICZ-LIEDER, Kazimierz TETMAJER, Antoni LANGE, and then just prior to the end of the century, the works of Wacław Sieroszewski, Stefan Żeromski, Władysław Reymont, Władysław ORKAN, and Stanisław WYSPIAŃSKI. The peak of the "Młoda Polska" period occurs between 1900 and 1907, the latter date being the year of Wyspiański's death. During these years, the major works of the period's most distinguished writers appeared: Kasprowicz's *Hymny* (Hymns); Żeromski's *Ludzie bezdomni* (Homeless People) and *Popioły* (Ashes); Wyspiański's *Legion, Wesele* (The Wedding), *Wyzwolenie* (Liberation), *Noc listopadowa* (November Night), and *Akropolis;* Orkan's *W roztokach* (In Mountain Valleys); and the first volumes of Reymont's *Chłopi* (The Peasants). As younger writers entered the literary scene during these years, a second phase opened in "Młoda Polska." The works of writers like Leopold STAFF, Bolesław LEŚMIAN, Wacław BERENT, Tadeusz MICIŃSKI, Stanisław BRZOZOWSKI, Karol IRZYKOWSKI, Adolf NOWACZYŃSKI, Andrzej STRUG, and Tadeusz Żeleński (Boy), while shaped in the artistic atmosphere of "Młoda Polska," nevertheless reflect some fundamental changes. Many of these writers continued to produce through the interwar period, and in the case of Staff also after World War II. At the same time, elements of epigonism and decline started to become evident; criticism, polemics, and evaluations of the whole trend flowed from the pens of Brzozowski, Irzykowski, and Żeleński (Boy). The end of World War I in 1918 is considered the closing date of this period in Polish literature.

The beginning of "Młoda Polska" is connected with the return of poetry. Slighted by the positivists, poetry had heralded the coming of a new trend in literature; poetry's development is related to the various currents within "Młoda Polska," currents sometimes difficult to demarcate. The poetry of Lange and Rolicz-Lieder reflects Parnassianism, but symbolist qualities appear as well, especially in works by the latter writer. After an initial naturalist and impressionist period, Kasprowicz imbued his *Hymny* with elements of symbolism and expressionism. The impressionistic lyrics of Tetmajer typify decadent features like melancholy, catastrophism, and eroticism. The works of Staff, after an early Nietzschean phase, later combined various tendencies, such as neoclassicism, and others. Leśmian's poetry moved from an affinity with symbolism and expressionism to later work containing elements connected with the avant-garde movement.

These heterogeneous affiliations are reflected in the unusually varied subject matter of poetry, ranging from Kasprowicz's discussion concerning the nature of the world and the essence of good and evil, to Tetmajer's apotheosis of art and reflections full of bitterness and pessimism, to the affirmation of life and beauty in Staff, and finally to Leśmian's fantastic and grotesque fairytale-like perception of the world.

The extraordinary role of the Tatra Mountains and the Podhale region as subject matter for poetry during this period constitutes a separate topic. While these themes appear earlier, they are particularly connected with

"Młoda Polska." Discovery of both the primitive beauty of the mountains and of highland folklore resulted from "Młoda Polska's" return to folk culture for inspiration. This interest finds its finest expression in the poetry of Tetmajer and Kasprowicz.

"From the point of view of their own theories, the poets of Młoda Polska had nothing in common with the preceding generation. The situation of prose writers was different" (K. Wyka). National and social issues had lost none of their importance and the vivid imagery and style of naturalism was still a novelty; thus, those prose genres practiced in the preceding period could be continued. This literary inheritance is evidenced by the persistence of subject matter concerned with social issues, and also by the continuation of the harsh vision of naturalism. Simultaneously, however, the introduction of new literary techniques and topics overlapped with these tendencies. Social conflicts in village life and in the city, injustice, poverty, and backwardness (which Żeromski exposed and portrayed with such extraordinary power) also appeared in the novels and short stories of Reymont, Berent, Orkan, and Strug. Further, in the works of these writers the subject of struggle for social justice is combined with the fight for national independence. In the "Młoda Polska" period, a new topic in literature is historicism— interest in the epoch of uprisings and the fight for liberation. Żeromski treated this painful theme the most extensively and with the greatest fervor, but it appears in the works of Reymont and Strug as well. Psychologism, characteristic of the period, influenced the "Młoda Polska" novel; its attainments are evident in the prose of Żeromski and Strug. Żeromski also created uncompromising champions of moral truth and social progress, while revolutionary protagonists appear in the novels of Brzozowski and Strug. In varying degrees, lyricism pervades the prose of different "Młoda Polska" writers. This quality is most pronounced in Żeromski, where it causes a loosening of traditional novelistic structure. Lyric elements are also present in Reymont, Berent, and Orkan. Elements of poetic stylization and rhythmicality are particularly noticeable in the novels of Żeromski and Orkan. Expressionism appears not only in the poetry of "Młoda Polska," but in the prose of Berent and Tadeusz Miciński as well.

The situation of drama during the "Młoda Polska" era was similar to that of poetry. A new theater could not be created based upon the dramaturgy of the preceding period. Innovative efforts in the theater had to seek inspiration in the new types of drama in Western Europe as well as in the great native tradition of romantic drama. The "monumental theater" of Stanisław Wyspiański is an innovative and original fulfilment of symbolic drama. National and social issues form the subject matter of his plays. In a manner typical of "Młoda Polska" historicism, Wyspiański returned to the struggle for national independence in the 19th-century Polish uprisings; at the same time, in his *Wesele* (The Wedding), Wyspiański created a tragic picture of contemporary Polish reality. Elements of expressionism are already present in this play, but later the principles of expressionism are still more evident in *Wyzwolenie* (Liberation).

Wyspiański's unique plays do not exhaust the unusually varied dramaturgy of this period. The most typical examples of expressionism in Polish drama close to surrealism are the plays of Tadeusz Miciński. In very different ways, both Jerzy Żuławski (1875–1915) and Adolf Nowaczyński treated historical subjects. Elements of realism, naturalism, and symbolism are combined in the dramas of Jan August Kisielewski (1876–1918). His plays *W sieci* (1899; In the Net) and *Karykatury* (1899; Carica-

tures) treat a problem often portrayed in the literature of the times: the conflict between the artist and bourgeois society. Karol Hubert Rostworowski's dramatic output prior to World War I also developed within the parameters of symbolist and expressionist aesthetics. In addition to theater inspired by the innovative tendencies of "Młoda Polska," social drama in the realist style continued to evolve. The most important exponents of this trend were two writers of comedies: Włodzimierz PERZYŃSKI and Wacław GRUBIŃSKI. Tadeusz Rittner (1873–1921), who wrote both in Polish and in German, also belongs to this category. Among his best-known plays are: *W małym domku* (1904; In a Little House) and *Głupi Jakub* (1910; Silly Jack).

While, according to accepted chronology, the year 1918 closes "Młoda Polska," the period's significance for the subsequent development of literature does not end here. Poland, which had been erased from the map of Europe and divided among the three partitioning powers at the end of the 18th century, regained her status as an independent nation in 1918. From "Młoda Polska," the new, young nation inherited a literature that had excellent writers to its credit, a literature that for the first time in its history had developed evenly in all genres—in poetry, drama, and prose—as well as in literary criticism. And in each field Polish letters had produced works of the highest value.

In contrast to the two preceding periods, the years of independent Poland, from 1918 to 1939, are not dominated by any single literary trend. The variety of contradictory and changing tendencies that became prominent during this time cannot be encompassed in a single descriptive term. The initial phase of the period between the two world wars remains rooted in "Młoda Polska." These early years are marked by a discussion about the waning "Młoda Polska" era that involved not so much its discreditation as its interpretation, and, not infrequently, the development of its inherent possibilities. Prominent writers of the older generation such as Stefan Żeromski played a significant role in literary life for many years. In 1925, the year of his death, Żeromski published the most outstanding political novel of this period, *Przedwiośnie* (Before the Spring), and his finest play as well: *Uciekła mi przepióreczka* (A Quail Escaped Me). Kasprowicz's last volume of poems, written in a stylized primitivism and entitled *Mój świat* (My World), appeared just after his death in 1926. Strug, Leśmian, and Berent published the bulk of their work in the years following World War I. Staff continued his poetic development and was recognized by the most influential literary group, "Skamander," as its master. Tadeusz Żeleński (Boy) and Karol Irzykowski both played important roles in literary criticism of the period. Literature strongly reflected the change caused in national life by the recovery of independence; but innovative trends in European culture also exerted a marked influence on this period. Nevertheless, ties with the preceding era remained an important factor in interwar literature.

Revitalization of literary life was one of the primary features of the new period as numerous groups with various programs appeared on the scene: expressionists, futurists, the "Skamander" and "Kwadryga" groups, and—somewhat later—avant-garde groups among others. Historically the earliest of these was the expressionist group, which was connected with German expressionism and centered in Poznań around the journal *Zdrój* during the years 1917 to 1920 and in 1922. Jerzy Hulewicz (1886–1941), a painter, dramatist, and novelist, was its editor, but its patron was Przybyszewski. His programmatic introductory statement written in the spirit of his earlier manifesto opens the journal's first issue, in which works by Berent, Orkan, and Kasprowicz appeared. Both Józef WITTLIN and Emil ZEGADŁOWICZ were among the writers connected with *Zdrój*. Zegadłowicz later transmitted certain aspects of the *Zdrój* program, combined with the cult of folk primitivism, to a group of regional poets who took their name from the periodical *Czartak,* of which three issues appeared at Wadowice in the years 1922 to 1928. However, the activities around *Zdrój* neither initiated nor concluded the expressionist movement in Poland. Expressionist elements had manifested themselves in Polish poetry, dramaturgy, and fiction in the very first years of the 20th century in the works of Kasprowicz, Wyspiański, and—later—Miciński. Expressionist tendencies independent of *Zdrój* would continue to appear in the works of Juliusz KADEN-BANDROWSKI, Stanislaw Ignacy WITKIEWICZ, Bruno SCHULZ, and others, and in post-World War II literature as well. The most influential group in poetry during these years was "Skamander," which during the years 1920 to 1928 and 1935 to 1939 published a monthly under that same name; after 1924 their most important publication was the weekly, *Wiadomości Literackie,* the finest literary journal of the interwar period. Mieczysław Grydzewski (1894–1970) edited both journals. Basically, the group consisted of five founding poets of entirely different literary styles: Jan LECHOŃ, Julian TUWIM, Kazimierz WIERZYŃSKI, Antoni SŁONIMSKI, and Jarosław IWASZKIEWICZ. Kazimiera Iłłakowiczówna and Maria PAWLIKOWSKA-JASNORZEWSKA were loosely connected with the group. Among the younger "Skamandrites," Stefan Napierski (1899–1940) and Stanisław BALIŃSKI should be mentioned. The chief critic of "Skamander" was Karol Wiktor Zawodziński (1890–1949), a literary critic as well as a theorist and historian of literature. The group formulated no program of its own, but instead proposed the principles of unhampered development of every kind of creative talent, the relating of poetry to contemporary life, a joyful vitalism, the introduction of urban themes into poetry, the use of everyday language, the combining of irony and humor in the lyric, the maintenance of ties with both native and foreign literatures, and the preservation of traditional forms of expression. Their poetry was a manifestation of the atmosphere of great joy caused by the fact that the country had finally attained freedom. It expressed the conviction that literature, released from the obligation to promote the idea of struggle for independence, would be able to break away from the subject of national martyrdom and relate poetry to contemporary life. Their moderate poetic program was matched by a correspondingly middle-of-the-road democratic social and political program.

Views diametrically opposed to those of the "Skamander" poets were proposed by avant-garde groups. The futurists, organized in Warsaw and Cracow between 1917 and 1920, were the earliest of these. Their program remained under the influence of Filippo MARINETTI and of dadaism and their poetics linked them to the Russian futurists. But most of their social views were connected with Communist ideology. They expounded a radical severing with tradition and a search for new poetic expression through technique, and for some futurists, in folk primitivism. The founders of this group were Bruno Jasieński (1901–39), a writer of poetry, prose, and drama, among whose works are the long poem, *Słowo o Jakubie Szeli* (1926; Song of Jacob Szela), and the novel *Palę Paryż* (1929; I Burn Paris); the poet Stanisław Młodożeniec (1895–1959); the poet and prose writer Anatol Stern (1899–1968), and Aleksander WAT. Tytus Czyżewski (1885–1945), poet, painter, dramatist, and

member of the Cracow formists, was associated with the futurists. In his *Pastorałki* (1925; Pastorals), he transformed folk motifs from carols of the Tatra foothills region through a new verse instrumentation. This return to folk primitivism exemplifies a broader, unusually varied movement having different sources and applications. It encompasses both the poetry of Leśmian and the expressionism of the "Czartak" group, futurists like Czyżewski, and also Jasieński, Młodożeniec, and even a poet close to the "Skamander" group like Iłłakowiczówna.

Futurism was a short-lived phenomenon in Polish poetry, but certain futurist elements, although differently understood, were incorporated by the literary group known as the "Avant-Garde," also termed the "Cracow Avant-Garde," or the "First Avant-Garde." The most important group after "Skamander" and opposed to it, the "Avant-Garde" took from futurism the idea of art as dependent upon changes in modern civilization and a fascination with city and machine. The "Avant-Garde" was centered around the journal *Zwrotnica,* which appeared during the years 1922 to 1923 and 1926 to 1927. The chief representatives of the group were Julian PRZYBOŚ, Jalu KUREK, and Jan BRZĘKOWSKI. The group was conceived by the poet Tadeusz Peiper (1894–1969) who formulated their program in an essay on poetry in *Nowe usta* (1925; New Voices), as well as in articles later collected in the volume, *Tędy* (1930; In this Direction). The principles of the program were: the opposition of culture to nature, the apotheosis of modern civilization as expressed in the slogan, "City-Masses-Machine," and the concept of work as the source of art. Some of the "Avant-Garde's" statements resembled French purism, and also Brzozowski's ideas about culture. Peiper opposed romantic inspiration, impressionism, the spontaneity of futurism, and surrealism; instead, he proposed the ideal of a rigorously disciplined poetry, a cult of poetic craftsmanship, and in his theory of language he emphasized the difference between poetry and prose. Upon the transforming power of technique Peiper not only based a new poetics but a Utopian society as well. Peiper's theory of maximum precision of the word in poetry found its most refined expression in his collections: *A* (1924), *Żywe linie* (1924; Living Lines), and *Raz* (1929; One Time Only). The Cracow "Avant-Garde's" primary theorist and practitioner in his own poetry was Julian Przyboś, who diverged from Peiper by introducing the idea of imagery and imagination. The changing views of the group appeared in their subsequent journal, *Linia* (The Line), published from 1931 to 1933 by Jalu Kurek, Przyboś, and Brzękowski, but without the participation of Peiper.

The opposition between the "Skamander" and the "Avant-Garde" groups dominated the literary life of this period, but other literary groups and other poets appeared that were only loosely connected with the two major groups. For example, the so-called revolutionary or proletarian poetry produced by various writers constitutes not so much a group, as an orientation in their work. Certain writers like Jasieński, as well as Ryszard Stande (1897–1939?) and Witold Wandurski (1891–1937?), exemplify this orientation, but its most famous representative is Władysław BRONIEWSKI. In so far as the style of his poetry continued the tradition of Polish poetry, Broniewski was similar to the "Skamander" poets, but he did not share their total acceptance of contemporary Polish reality.

A rather heterogeneous group of poets that opposed "Skamander" took their name from the journal *Kwadryga,* published in Warsaw from 1927 to 1931, and then after 1937 under the name *Nowa Kwadryga*. While in their poetics the "Kwadryga" poets were not unlike the

"Skamander" group, they objected to the latter's aestheticism. The "Kwadryga" group proposed a socially oriented literature and introduced themes of a technological civilization into their lyrics, but their identification of word with action and the concept of art as inseparable from work harked back to Norwid and Brzozowski. The finest poet of the group was the one most loosely connected with it: Konstanty Ildefons GAŁCZYŃSKI. Zbigniew Uniłowski also belonged to "Kwadryga." The poet, essayist, and playwright Stefan Flukowski (1902–72) was closest to the "Avant-Garde." Among his volumes of poetry are: *Słońce w kieracie* (1929; The Treadmill Sun), *Dębem rosnę* (1936; I Grow Like an Oak Tree), as well as a collection of short stories, *Pada deszcz* (1931; It's Raining). Revolutionary poetry was written by Stanisław Ryszard Dobrowolski (1907–), poet, essayist, and author of volumes of poetry about Warsaw, such as *Powrót na Powiśle* (1935; Return to Powiśle). Lucjan Szenwald (1909–44), author of the long poem *Sceny przy strumieniu* (1936; Scenes by the Stream) and later collections of verse, also used revolutionary themes. Counted among the "Kwadryga" poets was Władysław Sebyła (1902–41), author of poems in the collections *Pieśni szczurołapa* (1930; Songs of a Pied Piper), *Koncert egotyczny* (1934; Egotistic Concert), and *Obrazy myśli* (1938; Images of Thoughts). These last two volumes contained Sebyła's metaphysical reflections, intuitions of impending catastrophe and destruction. Włodzimierz Słobodnik (1900–), Aleksander Maliszewski (1901–78), and Marian Piechal (1905–) were also part of the "Kwadryga" group.

The term "authenticism" refers to some poets' attempt to oppose both the program of "Skamander" and the "Avant-Garde" as well. The trend was launched by Stanisław Czernik (1899–1969), editor of the monthly journal *Okolica poetów*, published between 1935 and 1939. The poet and essayist Jan Bolesław Ożóg (1913–) belonged to this group. The purpose of authenticism was to grasp contemporary problems, in particular those of village life, through personal experience.

A separate phenomenon in the period is the poetry of Adam WAŻYK at this time. Because the sources of his inspiration are associated with cubism and French surrealism, Ważyk's poetry represents these tendencies in the Polish poetry of the period. Likewise, Mieczyslaw JASTRUN was unaffiliated with any group. The poetry of his first volumes, while similar to neoclassicism, possesses a symbolic visionary quality that shows the growing catastrophism in literature at this time.

New literary groups appear around 1930; these groups are known under the collective name of the "Second Avant-Garde." The group includes young Warsaw and Cracow poets, the Vilnius "Żagary" group, and a group of younger poets from the Lublin region who published the journal *Reflektor* during the years 1923 to 1925. The most outstanding poet of this last group is Józef CZECHOWICZ. The program of the Cracow "Avant-Garde" was the point of departure for all these groups, but most often it represented attitudes against which the "Second Avant-Garde" might react. Differences of opinion about poetry, programs, and the principles of poetics intensified. While acknowledging the formal innovations of the "First Avant-Garde," poets in the second movement endeavored to supplement it with a broad philosophical and metaphysical perspective. The "Żagary" group centered around a journal of the same name that appeared in the years 1931 to 1932; they changed their journal's name to *Piony* in 1932, but then between 1933 and 1934 it appeared again as *Żagary*. Czesław MIŁOSZ is the finest representative of this group. Among others who belonged to it were: Jerzy Zagórski (1907–), author of the poetry col-

lection *Przyjście wroga* (1934; The Coming of the Enemy), Aleksander Rymkiewicz (1913–), author of the long poem *Tropiciel* (1936; The Pathfinder), and Jerzy Putrament (1910–), author of many subsequent political novels, such as *Wrzesień* (1951; September). As Czesław Miłosz says of the "Żagary" poets: "Because of their dark visions in which the political was translated into the cosmic by means of a new kind of symbolism, they were soon recognized as the instigators of a 'school of catastrophism.'"

Changes occurred not only within the "Avant-Garde" groups; the "Skamander" poets also went through a significant evolution characterized by a growing neoclassicism. This tendency did not affect "Skamander" alone. It appeared in the work of Leopold Staff and of several poets belonging to "Kwadryga," and even among poets of the "Second Avant-Garde," such as Miłosz. An increasing metaphysical uneasiness, pessimism, and catastrophism marked a change in the writing of the 1930s. This is evident in the work of the chief "Skamander" poets: Słonimski, Wierzyński, Tuwim, Iwaszkiewicz, and Pawlikowska-Jasnorzewska. It appears in the work of younger poets sympathetic to "Skamander." Examples are the dramatic and deeply religious verse of Jerzy Liebert's (1904–31) *Gusła* (1930; Rites) and *Kołysanka jodłowa* (1932; The Fir-Tree Lullaby), and the collections of the religious poems by Wojciech Bąk (1907–1961); *Brzemię niebieskie* (1934; Heavenly Burden), *Monologi anielskie* (1938; Angelic Monologs), and others.

The monumental output of Leśmian evolved independently of these groups and debates. The metaphysical fear that emanates from some of his works was not provoked by external reality, but was born in the highly extraordinary inner world of his poetry. Due recognition of his poetry comes only later, after World War II.

In different ways from poetry, and yet parallel to its exploration in craft and changes in content, the prose of the 20-year interwar period underwent major changes. As in the rest of Europe after World War I, novels appeared that were devoted to the recently experienced tragedy. Józef Wittlin's pacifist novel, *Sól Ziemi* (1936; Eng. tr., *Salt of the Earth*, 1939), best represents this kind of novel. The problems connected with the political and social situation of the first years of independence soon eclipsed the topic of war. A series of political novels by Andrzej Strug and Juliusz Kaden-Bandrowski appeared that contained various evaluations of many facets of the current situation in Poland. Reflection upon the subject of the human personality and upon the psychological drives of the individual became a significant factor in all postwar prose. This current recalled the tradition of the European psychological novel: the philosophical bases upon which it developed and which were reflected in the programs of modernism, and in the postulates of "Młoda Polska" concerning the depth of the individual's experience. Application of the new theory of personality proposed by Freudianism was an essential element in this current. In various forms, these theories are reflected in the fiction of Zofia NAŁKOWSKA, Maria KUNCEWICZOWA, Jarosław IWASZKIEWICZ, and Ewa SZELBURG-ZAREMBINA, as well as the earliest novels of Tadeusz BREZA, Jerzy ANDRZEJEWSKI, and Adolf RUDNICKI. *Zazdrość i medycyna* (1933; Eng. tr., *Jealousy and Medicine*, 1946) by the novelist and short-story writer, Michał Choromański (1904–72), belongs to this current. Choromański is also the author of a collection of tales entitled *Opowiadania dwuznaczne* (1934; Ambiguous Tales), as well as many later novels and short stories published after World War II. The numerous novels of the period dealing with recollections from childhood arise from the desire to explain the sources and nature of human personality. Examples are novels by Maria Dąbrowska, Juliusz Kaden-Bandrowski, Zygmunt Nowakowski, and all the works of Janusz Korczak (1878-1942). Korczak, an educator and theorist of child-raising, was the author of books both for and about children, such as *Król Maciuś Pierwszy* (1923; Eng. tr., *Matthew the Young King*, 1945), *Bankructwo małego Dżeka* (1924; Young Jack Goes Broke), and many others.

Subtle psychological analysis is contained in Maria Dąbrowska's *Noce i dnie* (1932-34; Nights and Days), the finest social epic of the period, which resumes the tradition of realistic prose of the positivist period in the form of a family saga.

The rich diversification that the historical novel underwent at this time testifies to the variety of existing suggestions, areas of interest, and attitudes related to this genre. To this category belong Zofia KOSSAK-SZCZUCKA's cycles of historical novels connected with a Catholic world view, and also Leon KRUCZKOWSKI's novels based upon an attempt at a class interpretation of Polish history. Jarosław Iwaszkiewicz's *Czerwone tarcze* (1934; Red Shields) is an innovative novel about the past. New approaches to the historical novel distinguish the first works of Hanna MALEWSKA and Teodor PARNICKI.

The social and environmental novel forms a separate category in the prose of this period. The founding of the literary group "Przedmieście" in Warsaw in 1933 by Helena Boguszewska (1886-1978) and Jerzy Kornacki (1908-) indicated interest in this type of novel. These writers cooperatively published novels related to the literature of fact, such as *Jadą wozy z cegłą* (1934; The Brick Carts are Running) and *Wisła* (1935; Vistula). During these years, Boguszewska also published a psychological novel, *Całe życie Sabiny* (1934; All Sabina's Life). A trend toward truthfulness of observation, authenticism, and regionalism distinguishes the novels of Zbigniew Uniłowski, Pola Gojawiczyńska, and Jan Wiktor. These same qualities are also seen in the early works of Gustaw Morcinek (1891-1963), such as his epic novel about Silesia, *Wyrąbany chodnik* (1931-32; Mining Tunnel) and in Piotr Choynowski's (1885-1935) novel about Warsaw in the year 1920, *Dom w śródmieściu* (1924; A House Downtown).

The interwar period, particularly its second decade, is distinguished by the development of novels and short stories based upon themes of village life. The achievements of two writers are particularly noteworthy: Jalu Kurek's *Grypa szaleje w Naprawie* (1935; Sickness Sweeps Naprawa) and Stanisław Piętak's *Młodość Jasia Kunefała* (1938; The Youth of Jaś Kunefał). Despite the many differences between these novels, such as the reportage character of the former or the autobiographical elements of the latter, they are joined by their continuation of the tradition initiated by Władysław Orkan, wherein the peasant world is observed from the inside. Furthermore, these novels are similar in their combining of authenticism with "Avant-Garde" experimentation.

Polish literature's rich tradition of interest in the culture of the ancient world had appeared in the "Młoda Polska" period in the works of Stanisław Wyspiański, Jan Kasprowicz, and later Leopold Staff and Wacław Berent. Now, during the interwar period, this subject matter appeared in the works of Ludwik Hieronim Morstin and Jan Parandowski. Among other important types of novels, the category of the fantastic should be noted. Tales of the fantastic were written by Stefan Grabiński (1887-1936), the author of collections of short stories such as *Demon ruchu* (1919; Demon of Movement) and *Księga ognia* (1922; Book of Fire). The writers Melchior WAŃKOWICZ and Ksawery PRUSZYŃSKI developed new forms of reportage during this period.

The works of Stanisław Ignacy Witkiewicz and Bruno Schulz, as well as the early works of Witold GOMBROWICZ, open up a totally new vista in the development of Polish letters. Despite all differences among these creative literary personalities, they were united by their radical break with the traditional "mirror of life" novel, with traditional forms of narration, and their creation of intellectual novels that are philosophical, multifaceted, and multileveled.

The development of the theater in the interwar period took varied directions. The quite different plays of Jerzy Szaniawski, Zofia Nałkowska, Maria Kuncewiczowa, and Karol Hubert Rostworowski nevertheless all represent a theater of realism and psychological problems. The plays of Jarosław Iwaszkiewicz and Ludwik Hieronim Morstin are also part of this line of development. Historical drama is represented by the plays of Adolf Nowaczyński and, although based upon completely different concepts, the plays of Maria Dąbrowska. But it is the plays of Witkiewicz and the unique continuation of his principles by Gombrowicz that constitute the most original phenomenon in the Polish theater at this time. Witkiewicz foreshadowed a new kind of drama, one linked with the experiments in European drama that are termed "surrealist." The works of Witkiewicz and Gombrowicz gave rise to a kind of Polish theater of the grotesque, an unusual and to a certain extent anticipatory expression of the European theater of the absurd.

With the outbreak of World War II in 1939 and the collapse of the Polish state, the prophecies and forebodings of doom expressed by Polish writers came true. There began a time of torment, terror, atrocities, death, and devastation. But Polish culture, a culture that would not yield to destruction, refused to interrupt its development. All public forms of cultural life were forbidden for five years. High schools, universities, libraries, museums, theaters, newspapers, and publishing were all closed down. Nevertheless, cultural life did not die; it simply went underground. A considerable number of writers remaining in Poland participated in the various forms of cultural life that developed alongside the armed Resistance movement. Despite threats of execution for such activity, as many as 1,123 different journals were published. Among these were 40 strictly literary periodicals of various ideological and artistic orientations. One of the most important of the underground periodicals was the mimeographed monthly, *Sztuka i naród*, printed from 1942 to 1944. Of its four editors, all of whom perished during the German occupation of Poland, two were outstanding writers. Andrzej Trzebiński (1922-43), the initiator of the journal's program, wrote *Aby podnieść różę* (1970; Eng., tr., *To Pick Up the Rose*, 1977), an unusual drama about the absurdity of totalitarianism, written in the grotesque style of Witkiewicz and Gombrowicz. Trzebiński was also the author of an unfinished novel, *Kwiaty z drzew zakazanych* (1972; Flowers from Forbidden Trees), as well as a diary and some verse. Tadeusz Gajcy (1922-44) wrote volumes of poetry, published by the underground in mimeographed form, and entitled *Widma* (1943; Phantoms) and *Grom powszedni* (1944; An Everyday Thunderclap). Gajcy is also the author of two grotesque plays, *Misterium niedzielne* (1952; Sunday Mystery Play), *Homer i Orchidea* (1952; Homer and the Orchid), and a book of short stories *Cena* (1975; The Price). Another fine poet among those young writers who made their debuts during the occupation is Krzysztof Kamil BACZYŃSKI, who was associated with another underground literary monthly, *Droga*. These writers' works, influenced by the "Second Avant-Garde," reflected an atmosphere of catastrophism, but at the same time contained an attempt to both evaluate and make an ethical and philosophical statement about the tragic experience of occupation. Tadeusz BOROWSKI was also associated with the monthly journal *Droga*. His two collections of poetry printed in the underground press, full of sarcasm and bitter irony, express an ever more desperate pessimism. Sad reflections upon the subjects of war, man's fate, and the ruins of Warsaw appear in Czesław Miłosz's *Wiersze* (Poems), published by the underground press in 1940. From 1940 to 1944, a series of anthologies of contemporary poetry were printed by the underground press in Warsaw. Among these are *Pieśń niepodległa* (1942; Independent Song), published by Czesław Miłosz; and *Słowo prawdziwe* (1942; The Word That Does not Lie), a collection edited by Jerzy Zagórski and Jan Dobraczyński. *Antologia poetycka* (An Anthology of Poetry) appeared in Cracow in 1944 through the efforts of Julian Przyboś and others. In 1944, a collection of poetry devoted to the Jews fighting in the Warsaw ghetto was printed. Entitled *Z otchłani* (Out of the Abyss), the volume contained poetry of Czesław Miłosz and Mieczysław Jastrun. These anthologies also contained verse by Polish poets then living abroad such as Antoni Słonimski, Julian Tuwim, and Kazimierz Wierzyński. On the other hand, *Antologia poezji współczesnej* (Eng. tr., *A Call from Poland: Anthology of Underground Warsaw Poetry*, 1944), a work printed first in Warsaw in 1941, was reprinted in England with a preface by the literary historian and critic, Tymon Terlecki (1905-). Much prose and drama was also written during the occupation, but found its way into print only after the war. Such was the case with writers like Jerzy Andrzejewski, Kazimierz Brandys, Jan Dobraczyński, Stanisław Ryszard Dobrowolski, Stanisław Dygat, Jarosław Iwaszkiewicz, Hanna Malewska, Ludwik Hieronim Morstin, Zofia Nałkowska, and others.

During World War II, many Polish writers found asylum in Western Europe, the United States, or the Soviet Union; there they continued to write, publishing their own work and periodicals as well. The writers Jan Lechoń, Julian Tuwim, Józef Wittlin, and Kazimierz Wierzyński first emigrated to France and later reached the United States, where they edited the publication *Tygodnik Polski* (1943-44). Witold Gombrowicz landed in Argentina. Living in England were Stanisław Baliński, Maria Pawlikowska-Jasnorzewska, Maria Kuncewiczowa, Zofia Kossak-Szczucka, Ksawery Pruszyński, and Antoni Słonimski. The literary monthly *Nowa Polska* appeared under the editorship of Słonimski from 1942 to 1946. As early as 1940, *Wiadomości Literackie* began to be reissued in Paris, at first called *Wiadomości Polskie,* but still under the editorship of Mieczysław Grydzewski. Later moved to England, the weekly continues to appear under the name *Wiadomości*. A succession of literary works as well as journals appeared wherever the Polish army was located, for example, in Italy or in the Near East, where Władysław Broniewski found himself after serving a term in a Soviet prison. Several writers, such as Jerzy Putrament, Lucjan Szenwald, Adam Ważyk, and others, ended up in the Soviet Union during the war. There they worked with the monthly journal, *Nowe Widnokręgi* (1941-46). Despite the tragic conditions of life at home and the difficult situation of writers in emigration, despite the heavy toll literature took in loss of human lives, and despite the imprisonment of writers in prisoner of war and concentration camps, wartime was not a period of stagnation in Polish literature. In the literary output of many writers, this period is distinguished by first-rate works that constitute an important achievement in their careers. Among the prose genres, reportage made significant strides during this period. Aleksander Kamiński's

(1903-) story about the participation of Polish youth units in the Resistance movement, *Kamienie na szaniec* (1943; Eng. tr., *Stones for the Rampart,* 1945) appeared in Warsaw printed by the underground. Janusz Meisner (1901-78) wrote about the life of Polish pilots in England in *Żądło Genowefy* (1943; Genevieve's Sting) and *"L" jak Lucy* (1945; Eng. tr., *L for Lucy,* 1945). Arkady Fiedler (1894-) described the fighting of Polish pilots in the Battle of Britain in his *Dywizjon 303* (1942; Eng. tr., *Squadron 303,* 1942) and of Polish sailors in *Dziękuję ci kapitanie* (1944; Eng. tr., *Thank You, Captain, Thank You,* 1945). Ksawery Pruszyński and Melchior Wańkowicz wrote stories of reportage about battles involving Polish soldiers on the various European fronts.

A new Polish state was created in 1945, which in 1952 was named the Polish People's Republic. Both its borders and political system were different from before the war. Two literary milieus, one at home and one abroad, were born as well. Their make-up fluctuated, for some writers returned to Poland after a period of time. Others, like Gombrowicz, Lechoń, Wierzyński, and Wittlin—to name only the most famous—remained abroad. Later, Czesław Miłosz joined them and in successive years, other writers emigrated as well: Marek Hłasko, Leopold Tyrmand (1920-), Arnold Słucki (1920-72), Stanisław Wygodzki (1907-), Witold Wirpsza (1918-), Henryk Grynberg (1936-), and Włodzimierz Odojewski.

The chief question that postwar literature addressed is one that had already appeared in some works of the underground writers, namely, the problem of the war and occupation. Literature began to search for new genres and new forms of expression in order to satisfy the need to understand the causes and the meaning of that incomprehensible catastrophe, the tragic overthrow of the foundations of humanism that the barbarity of wartime represented. Although this subject reached an acute intensity in the years immediately following the end of the war, it has not ceased to absorb Polish writers even today. It is one of the important topics continually recurring in postwar Polish literature. Many novels and short stories illustrate the various approaches to the tragedy of the wartime nightmare that were necessitated by lack of appropriate literary models from the past. A matching of literary form to description of human experience in inhuman situations is evident in the psychological prose of Jerzy Andrzejewski's short stories in *Noc* (1945; Night), in the almost passionless factualism of Zofia Nałkowska's *Medialiony* (1946; Medallions), in the terse description of systematic human depravity in Tadeusz Borowski's Auschwitz stories, in the combined description, recollection, and moral commentary of Adolf Rudnicki's stories about the extermination of the Jews, and in the stream-of-consciousness narrative used by Leopold Buczkowski to convey an apocalyptic vision of a collapsing world. The authenticism and psychological study in Gustaw HERLING-GRUDZIŃSKI's *Inny świat* (1953; Eng. tr., *A World Apart,* 1951), describing man's degradation in a camp in the north of Russia, is part of this search for form. The subjects of occupation and camp life appear in various prose treatments in the documentary novel *Dymy nad Birkenau* (1945; Eng. tr., *Smoke over Birkenau,* 1947) by Seweryna Szmaglewska (1916-), in the novel *Czas nieludzki* (1946; Time of Inhumanity) by Stefan Otwinowski (1910-76), in Kornel Filipowicz's (1913-) short stories entitled, *Krajobraz niewzruszony* (1947; Impassive Landscape), and in the works of Gojawiczyńska, Iwaszkiewicz, Zawieyski, Żukrowski, and others. Poetry collections of Julian Przyboś, Mieczysław Jastrun, and Czesław Miłosz published in 1944-45 also dealt with the experiences of war and occupation, historiosophical and ethical reflections upon the tragedy of these experiences, and the need to express both doubt and the overcoming of despair. By means of an existential "antipoetry," void of any stylistic embellishment and confined to the simplest diction, Tadeusz Różewicz initiated a new phase in poetry that was a reaction to the period of values scorned and destroyed. Leon Kruczkowski's play, *Niemcy* (1949; The Germans), attempted a broader examination of the causes and environment engendering Nazism in German society, as well as an objective confrontation between German and Polish mentalities.

War and occupation were not the only subjects in literature, however. The generation of writers that remembered Polish society before the war, its politics and the role of the intelligentsia, recreated prewar reality in their works. Examples are Tadeusz Breza's *Mury Jerycha* (1946; The Walls of Jericho) and Zofia Nałkowska's *Węzły życia* (1948; The Knots of Life). A return to various aspects of life in Poland prior to 1939, often with touches of nostalgia, irony, or criticism, stands out in the first postwar novels of Stanisław Dygat and Kazimierz Brandys, in the novel *Sprzymierzenie* (1947; Blood Brothers) by the Catholic writer and journalist Stefan Kisielewski (1911–), and in the novel *Sedan* (1948) by the poet and essayist Paweł Hertz (1918–). Jerzy Putrament, Wojciech Żukrowski, and Jan Dobraczyński all approached the September military catastrophe from different points of view. Postwar Polish reality constitutes another subject in prose. Jerzy Andrzejewski's *Popiół i diament* (1948; Eng. tr., *Ashes and Diamonds,* 1962), based upon a dramatic political and moral dilemma in the postwar setting, occupies a special place among novels dealing with this period.

New topics in literature, particularly the subjects of war and occupation, influenced changes taking place in prose genres. Kazimierz Wyka (1910–75), a critic and literary historian, has termed this phenomenon the "borderline novel." In this genre, elements of fiction are mixed with documentary material and authorial commentary. In varying degrees, such elements appear in the novels of writers like Adolf Rudnicki, Zofia Nałkowska, Stanisław Dygat, and Kazimierz Brandys. A genre that developed at this time was the biographical novel, for example the fictionalized biographies of Jan Kochanowski, Adam Mickiewicz, Juliusz Słowacki by Mieczysław Jastrun, and the novels about Andrzej Frycz Modrzewski by Anna Kowalska (1903–69): *Wójt Wolborski* (1954; The Bailiff of Wolbor) and *Astrea* (1956).

Beginning in 1949 and continuing for the next five years, the development of literature was markedly retarded by the officially imposed, uniform model of socialist realism. Resistance and unabating sharp criticism from many writers contributed to a revitalization of literature after the relaxation of this dogmatism. Evidence of positive change appeared as early as 1954–55 and openly bloomed in 1956 after the October crisis. With the "thaw" there began a period of new creative exploration and experimentation in all literary genres. Prose reflected these changes by reaching out for fresh subjects and exploring new techniques. These two characteristics did not always go hand in hand, but both thematically and formally, the great diversity of experimentation was pronounced. One feature of this exploration was the swing away from the model of the conventional 19th-century novel, especially promoted in the early postwar years, and a general rejection of any single pattern in favor of creative freedom and experimentation. Links were sought with contemporary innovations in European prose, with French literature and existentialism, with the new American novel, and with the unique native tradition of Stanisław Ignacy Witkiewicz, Witold Gombrowicz, and Bruno Schulz. The moral concern permeating all of Jerzy Andrzejewski's work now found expression in a new parabolic prose and, while in historical garb, a universalizing and questioning of contemporary life through use of the stream-of-consciousness technique. Leopold Buczkowski's novels represent an original kind of antinovel, in their progressive abandonment of all rules of prose fiction: action, narration, composition. The prose achievement of Tadeusz Konwicki is based upon multiple plots, mixing of time, fragmentariness and allusion, and reality portrayed through the convention of nightmare. Wilhelm Mach's *Góry nad Czarnym Morzem* (1961; Mountains by the Black Sea) utilizes autothematic tendencies recalling both Gombrowicz and the French antinovel. A broad application of the absurd, surrealist grotesque is another feature of the prose of this period; first and foremost, this tendency is exemplified by Sławomir Mrożek, but it is also represented by Stanisław Zieliński (1917–), the author of several collections of short, humorous sketches and tales, such as *Statek zezowatych* (1959; A Ship for the Cross-Eyed).

Departure from traditional novelistic forms led to an intensification of intellectual reflection and to a blurring of the distinctions between imaginative fiction and the essay. This rich growth in various parafictional prose genres appears in the works of Adolf Rudnicki, Kazimierz Brandys, and Tadeusz Breza. Further examples are Jacek Bocheński's (1926–) historical parable, *Boski Juliusz* (1961; The Divine Julius); Paweł Jasienica's (1909–70) huge cycle of historical essays, beginning with *Polska Piastów* (1960; Poland Under the Piasts); and Leszek Kołakowski's (1927–) philosophical parables. The aphorisms of Stanisław Jerzy Lec best represent the development of shorter literary forms during this period. The genre of science fiction deserves special attention; the novels and short stories of Stanisław Lem represent innovative achievements in this literary form.

A typical feature of the years following 1956 was a new portrayal of the underground Resistance during the German occupation of Poland. The most representative work in this area is a novel depicting the armed struggle of youth fighting for the home army: Roman Bratny's (1921–) *Kolumbowie. Rocznik dwudziesty* (1957; The Columbuses. Date of Birth: 1920). Another return to the theme of wartime is *Tren* (1961; Lament) by Bohdan Czeszko (1923–). Tadeusz Hołuj (1916–) treated the Resistance movement in Auschwitz in his *Koniec naszego świata* (1958; The End of Our World).

Creative experimentation occurred in the historical novel. Teodor Parnicki's novel cycles present a historical vision of ancient and medieval times; Parnicki portrays a cross section of different epochs, cultures, and religions mirrored in the consciousness of contemporary characters. Hanna Malewska's historical novels center around both moral problems conflicting with the laws of history, and the limitations upon the individual's role in history. Historical novels form the bulk of the work of Andrzej Kuśniewicz, Tadeusz Łopalewski (1900–), and Karol Bunsch (1898–).

Malewska's name is also associated with the concept of a Polish Catholic novel, a form represented by a number of outstanding historical writers, such as Antoni Gołubiew, Jan Dobraczyński, Zofia Kossak-Szczucka, and such writers as Stefan Kisielewski, Jerzy Zawieyski, and Wojciech Bąk.

With the year 1956 came a renewal in novels on rural or peasant themes. Maria Dąbrowska's epic portrayal of contemporary village life in all its complexity and ambiguity, *Na wsi wesele* (1955; Eng. tr., *A Village Wedding,*

1957), played a significant role in this renewal. Among others who took part in this renewal, Wilhelm Mach and his *Dom jaworowy* (1954; A House of Sycamore) should be mentioned. Evidence of the rich development of the rural novel during this period is found in the works of Julian KAWALEC, Tadeusz NOWAK, and Józef Morton (1911-), particularly in his *Mój drugi ożenek* (1961; My Second Marriage). Younger writers involved in this trend are Urszula KOZIOŁ, Marian Pilot (1936-), Edward Redliński (1940-), and Wiesław Myśliwski (1932-), author of the novels *Nagi sad* (1967; The Bare Orchard), and *Pałac* (1970; The Palace). New works on rural subjects were published at this time by peasant writers like Stanisław PIĘTAK; other works by peasant writers are Stanisław Czernik's *Ręka* (1963; The Hand), and Jan Bolesław Ożóg's *Popiół mirtowy* (1962; Myrtle Ash).

The appearance of another new subject, that of the social fringe in the city, is associated with this period. Marek HŁASKO initiated the topic, and most of the works of Marek Nowakowski (1935-), the author of *Ten stary złodziej* (1958; This Old Thief) and *Zapis* (1965; The Record), are devoted to this theme.

Poetry of the immediate postwar years both at home and abroad continued the major trends and groups that had been active during the interwar period. The most distinguished poets of "Skamander" and the "Avant-Garde" continued to write and publish. In the work of many of these writers a renewal in poetic techniques and subject matter occurred due to the influence of their wartime experiences. Soon, however, there appeared a new poetic wave, initially represented by Tadeusz Różewicz. Różewicz's poetic style is reduced in the extreme; it is reminiscent of the catastrophism in Krzysztof Kamil Baczyński's poetry and continues certain elements of the prewar "Avant-Garde" found most notably in the work of Józef Czechowicz. The revitalization of poetry in 1956 was so intense that it might be termed a poetic explosion. In the year 1956 and the years immediately following, numerous poets made their debuts, some of which had been delayed, such as Miron BIAŁOSZEWSKI, Zbigniew HERBERT, and Stanisław Swen Czachorowski (1920-); the reappearance of other writers marks the beginning of their real literary output. In this latter group belong Tadeusz Nowak, Tymoteusz KARPOWICZ, and Wislawa SZYMBORSKA. Moreover, Stanisław GROCHOWIAK, Andrzej Bursa (1932-1957), Jerzy HARASYMOWICZ, Jarosław Marek Rymkiewicz, Urszula Kozioł, and many others began to publish in 1956. This heterogeneous constellation of poetic talents is generally known as the "1956 Generation," or "Współczesność Generation," from the title of a literary journal published between 1956 and 1971 in which some of the poets had made their debuts. The new situation in poetry could not be labeled with any single program, since the poets of this generation represented a variety of approaches toward poetics. What united them all was their common opposition to constricting patterns of creativity. This generation represented a decisive turn toward free utilization of a broadly conceived avant-garde poetic model, toward a restoration of the ambiguity of the word, toward perception of the world in all its complexity and multidimensionality. This crisis stemmed from numerous causes, from both French existentialism and surrealism, from the native literary tradition of the baroque and romanticism, from Norwid, Leśmian, Przyboś, Czechowicz, Miłosz, and Baczyński, as well as from Staff and Gałczyński. The immediate appearance of differences among the poets who comprised this renewal demonstrated the range of Polish poetry during this period. Proof of the wealth of poetic possibilities appears in the following writers: Różewicz's strict moralism and antipoetici-

zation, his language stripped of metaphor and approximating ordinary speech; the various poets characterized as linguistic poets, such as Miron Białoszewski, Tymoteusz Karpowicz, and Zbigniew Bieńkowski (1913-); Stanisław Grochowiak, the chief exponent of "turpism," poetry that highlights ugliness, the ordinariness of human existence, a brutalization of the poetic image, and a return to the contrastive effects of baroque poetry. Marian Grześczak (1934-), the author of *Lumpenezje* (1960), is a poet most similar to Grochowiak. Jarosław Marek Rymkiewicz (1935-), the author of the manifesto *Czym jest klasycyzm?* (1967; What is Classicism?) and many volumes of poetry, such as *Konwencje* (1957; Conventions), and Jerzy Stanisław Sito (1934-), the author of *Wiozę swój czas na ośle* (1958; I Carry My Time on a Donkey's Back), represent a neoclassicism associated with the baroque, T. S. Eliot, Czesław Miłosz, and a concept of the unity and continuity of culture. The new flourishing in poetry is represented by Zbigniew Herbert, a poet of humanitarian culture and perfection of simplicity, by Jerzy Harasymowicz's fairy-tale imagination and folk fantasy, and Stanisław Swen Czachorowski's daring experimentation. The Biblical allegorism and folklore interwoven in the poetry of Tadeusz Nowak, the stoicism reminiscent of Staff in the poetry of Urszula Kozioł, the lyric simplicity of the poetry of Wisława Szymborska, are further examples of poetry's vitality. Even this survey should be supplemented by such names as Artur Międzyrzecki (1922-), Jerzy Ficowski (1924-), Witold Wirpsza (1918-), Wiktor Woroszylski (1927-), Tadeusz Kubiak (1924-79), Anna Kamieńska (1920-), Jan Śpiewak, (1908-1967), and Mieczysława Buczkówna (1924-), and others.

In the 1960s and 1970s, another generation of young poets entered the literary scene, poets who formulated new poetic theories through both their programs and practice of their art. Numerous groups appeared, and they were often very active, publishing their own almanacs and collections of their own first works. The best known of these are: "Hybrydy" in Warsaw; "Próby" in Poznań; "Agora" in Wrocław; "Wymiary" in Toruń; and "Teraz" in Cracow. This latter group represents the so-called naked poetry; a number of original poets belong to "Teraz," such as Julian Kornhauser (1946-) and Adam Zagajewski (1945-). Associated with this group, but differing in their attitude toward language as a continuity of tradition, are Stanisław Barańczak (1946-), author of *Dziennik poranny* (1972; The Morning Daily), Ryszard Krynicki (1943-), and Edward Balcerzan (1937-). Representing a separate variant of "naked poetry" is Rafał Wojaczek (1945-1971). Uncensored publications are a noteworthy example of the activity of these groups in recent years. The Wrocław "Agora" group and the Cracow "Teraz" have printed volumes of uncensored poetry; prose has appeared in uncensored journals as well, such as *Puls; Spotkania,* a journal by young Catholics; and *Zapis.* Many volumes of prose, poetry, and essays banned by the official censorship have been published by the uncensored publishing house Niezależna Oficyna Wydawnicza, including also works of émigré writers.

The postwar stages of development in drama match those of poetry and prose. Theater developed along two lines, one growing out of the realistic tradition and one out of a parabolic theater of the grotesque and the absurd. The former dominated in the years immediately after the war; the latter produced significant achievements after 1956. Ludwik Hieronim Morstin produced his dramas on ancient classical and historical themes during the realistic period. In his popular play, *Dwa teatry* (1946; Two Theaters), Jerzy SZANIAWSKI combined elements of realism with poetic vision and grotesque deformation. The primary exponent of realistic theater was Leon Kruczkowski; however, his dramaturgy also underwent an evolution in which he introduced metaphoric elements and even traces of the grotesque, as can be seen in his last play, *Śmierć gubernatora* (1961; The Death of a Governor). Jarosław Iwaszkiewicz continued to write plays within the realistic and psychological conventions. Maria Dąbrowska published her second historical drama, *Stanisław i Bogumił* (1948). Jerzy Zawieyski produced more plays on both biblical and contemporary themes. Historical and biographical dramas as well as plays on war themes were written by Roman Brandstaetter (1906–). Examples of these are his play about Rembrandt, *Powrót syna marnotrawnego* (1948; The Return of the Prodigal Son); his play about Mickiewicz, *Noce narodowe* (1949; National Nights); and a drama about war time, *Dzień gniewu* (1962; The Day of Wrath). Aleksander Maliszewski (1901–78), Kazimierz Korcelli (1907–), and Halina Auderska (1904) also wrote plays on historical subjects.

Artur Maria Swinarski (1900–1965) continued comedy writing and published his most famous comedy, *Achilles i panny* (1956; Achilles and the Maidens). Another theater trend during the years 1946 to 1950 is represented by Konstanty Ildefons Gałczyński and his cycle of grotesque miniature scenes, entitled *Zielona gęś* (The Green Goose), and based upon nonsense, fantasy, and absurd humor. The revival of theater dates from 1956, when drama picked up the tradition begun by Witkiewicz and continued during the war by Trzebiński and then carried on by Gałczyński. A multifarious, grotesque parody of totalitarian power and the demogoguery of slogans about freedom forms the basis of one of the first plays staged after the 1956 crisis: *Święto Winkelrida* (1946; Winkelried's Feast), by Jerzy Andrzejewski and Jerzy Zagórski. A subsequent play in allegorical form, this time dramatizing post-October 1956 discussions about the abuses of power, was the dramatic triptych, *Imiona władzy* (1957; The Names of Power), by the novelist and dramatist Jerzy Broszkiewicz (1922–). New directions in the development of drama after 1956 were staked out by the stunning work of Sławomir Mrożek, who in an extraordinary and prolific way has continued and transformed the tradition of Polish theater of the absurd. Mrożek's theater is, however, only one branch of this important current. Tadeusz Różewicz represents another approach in his grotesque antidramas, his cruel theater in which every action is suspect, every pose is demasked. The fantasy of Tymoteusz Karpowicz's dramas renders everything strange and recalls the tradition of symbolism as well as the theater of the grotesque and absurd. Also part of this line of development is the work of Stanisław Grochowiak, whose burlesque and degrading tone is most like that of Gombrowicz. In a still different manner, Miron Białoszewski and Zbigniew Herbert continue this trend in their short theater scenes, as does Jaroslaw Marek Rymkiewicz in his farce, written in the spirit of Gombrowicz: *Król Mięsopust* (1970; King Carnival). *Dialog*, a monthly devoted to contemporary drama, began to appear in 1956 under the editorship of Adam Tarn (1902–), and it immediately became the platform of the new wave in Polish theater.

Works by émigré writers constitute an important element in the total picture of contemporary Polish literature. Although scattered throughout many countries, émigré writers have two major centers where their publications appear. The first of these is Paris, where the Instytut Literacki is located. Since 1947, the Instytut Literacki has published the monthly *Kultura*, edited by Jerzy Giedroyć, as well as the series "Biblioteka Kultury," in which more than 300 titles have appeared, including works by Witold Gombrowicz, Czesław Miłosz,

Kazimierz Wierzyński, and Jerzy Andrzejewski. The second center is London, where since 1946 the weekly *Wiadomości* has been published under the successive editorship of Mieczysław Grydzewski, Michał Chmielowiec, and Stefania Kossowska. Also located in London are the offices of the publishing house Oficyna Poetów i Malarzy, directed by Czesław and Krystyna Bednarczyk. Since 1966, they have published a quarterly devoted primarily to poetry, entitled *Oficyna Poetów,* in whose pages have appeared works by both émigré writers and those living in Poland. Most of the numerous books they have published have been in the field of poetry.

The bulk of Witold Gombrowicz's work was written in Argentina, and later in France. A great innovator in prose and avant-garde drama, a classic in Polish literature, and a writer of worldwide reputation and overwhelming influence upon all postwar Polish literature, Gombrowicz's work constitutes one of its most lively and creative currents. Prior to their return to Poland, numerous works were written abroad by such writers as Teodor Parnicki, Maria Kuncewiczowa, Zofia Kossak-Szczucka, and Melchior Wańkowicz. Likewise written abroad were the last works of Aleksander Wat and Marek Hłasko. Stanisław VINCENZ, bard of the foothill country of the Hutzuls, continued his essaylike writings, a form difficult to categorize. The essay genre proper is represented by Jerzy Stempowski (1894–1969), who under the pseudonym Paweł Hostowiec wrote *Dziennik podróży do Austrii i Niemiec* (1946; Diary of a Trip to Austria and Germany), *Eseje dla Kasandry* (1961; Essays for Cassandra), and *Od Berdyczowa do Rzymu* (1971; From Berdyczew to Rome). Aleksander Janta-Połczyński, (1908–74) a prolific writer, produced both poetry and prose. Among his works are the short-story collection *Flet i Apokalipsa* (1964; Flute and Apocalypse), the collection of sketches and essays *Losy ludzkie* (1961; Human Destinies), and *Przyjemnie zapoznać* (1972; Nice to be Acquainted). Writers of the older generation who published their last works while living abroad are Józef Wittlin, Ferdynand Goetel, Wacław Grubiński, Herminia Naglerowa, Zygmunt Nowakowski, and Sergiusz Piasecki (1899–64). Czesław Straszewicz (1904–63), who had begun writing before the war, continued to publish such works as *Turyści z bocianich gniazd* (1953; Tourists from Crow's Nest), a humorous tale about the adventures of Polish seamen in Latin American ports and in postwar Poland. Having begun writing before the war with his *Bunt rojstów* (1938; The Revolt of the Marshes), Józef Mackiewicz (1902–) a prolific novelist and political writer, published a novel cycle abroad: *Droga do nikąd* (1955; Eng. tr., Road to Nowhere, 1963), *Karierowicz* (1956; The Careerist), and *Lewa wolna* (1965; Keep Left), a panorama of life in Lithuania against the background of dramatic political changes in this region during both world wars. Florian Czarnyszewicz (1895–1964) is the author of an epic trilogy, *Nadbereżyńcy* (1942; The Inhabitants of Berezina Country), about the lives of Poles and Belorussians in the western portions of Belorussia during the 1917 Civil War and prior to World War II. The work of Paweł Łysek (1914–78) is associated with another region of Poland. Łysek's Beskid trilogy, of which the first novel is *Przy granicy* (1966; Eng. tr., At the Border, 1977) is an epic story, written in dialect, of the life, customs, and peculiar mentality of the inhabitants of the western Carpathian foothills. Many works written abroad portray wartime and concentration-camp experiences, such as the early novels of Tadeusz Nowakowski. The novels of Zofia Romanowiczowa constantly deal with the psychological deformations caused by the experiences of the war years, concentration camps, and emigration. The experiences of

Polish émigrés in the United States after World War II are the subject of a cycle of novels written by Danuta Mostwin (1921–) of which first is the *Ameryko! Ameryko!* (1961; America! America!). Polish émigrés in Australia are frequently the subject of stories by Andrzej Chciuk (1920–).

A crucial segment of Polish literature, one without which its description would be incomplete, is poetry written in emigration. During and immediately following the war, "Skamander" poets dominated: Maria Pawlikowska-Jasnorzewska, Kazimierz Wierzyński, Jan Lechoń, Stanisław Baliński. Soon, however, poets associated with the avant-garde movements appeared. Jerzy Brzękowski, a cofounder of the Cracow "Avant-Garde" who later resided in Paris, wrote new volumes of poetry. Marian Czuchnowski, associated for many years with the "Avant-Garde," published new collections of verse as well. Another follower of the "Avant-Garde," trend was Stefan Borsukiewicz (1920–42), the author of a volume of poetry, *Kontrasty* (1941; Contrasts). Having begun writing as a part of a circle of Lublin Avant-Garde poets, Józef Łobodowski (1909–), the author of the volumes *Rozmowa z ojczyzną* (1935; Conversation with my Native Land) and *Demonom nocy* (1936; To the Night Demons), continued his poetry with several postwar collections and with autobiographical novels. The prewar period saw the publication of the first volumes of poetry by Bronisław Przyłuski (1905–), the author among other works of *Strofy o malarstwie* (1953; Stanzas About Painting); as well as the first works of Wacław Iwaniuk (1913–), the author of *Ciemny czas* (1968; Dark Times) and many other volumes of poetry. Marian Pankowski's (1919–) poetry and prose is related to modern literary trends. The same should be said about the poetry of Józef Bujnowski (1910–). The work of Tadeusz Sułkowski lies within the "Avant-Garde" poetic tradition of precision and philosophical interest reminiscent of Norwid. Jerzy Pietrkiewicz also acknowledges the influence of Norwid on the new poetry. Pietrkiewicz formulated an "Avant-Garde" poetic program and implemented it in his own work. A group of London poets was formed who continued the ideas of the "First" and "Second Avant-Gardes." This group was known as "Kontynenty," from the journal of the same name which appeared between 1959 and 1964. Members of this group were Bogdan Czaykowski, Adam Czerniawski, Jerzy S. Sito, Zygmunt Ławrynowicz (1925–), Florian Śmieja (1925–), Andrzej Busza (1938–), Jan Darowski (1926–), and Bolesław Taborski (1927–), the author of the poetry collections *Czasy mijania* (1957; Times of Passage), and *Głos milczenia* (1969; Voice of Silence). "Kontynenty" published an anthology of the works of member poets: *Ryby na piasku* (1965; Fish on the Sand). With its preface by Julian Przyboś, *Ryby na piasku* testifies to the community of interests which these émigré poets share with poetic movements in Poland after 1956. One of the most original writers in contemporary Polish literature, Czesław Miłosz, whose poetry, prose, and essays embrace ever broader expanses of human thought, continued his remarkable creative work in emigration.

See: R. Dyboski, *Modern Polish Literature* (1924); K. Czachowski, *Obraz współczesnej literatury polskiej 1884–1935* (1938); M. Kridl, *A Survey of Polish Literature and Culture* (1956); M. M. Coleman, *Polish Literature in English Translation: A Bibliography* (1963); *Słownik współczesnych pisarzy polskich*, ed. by E. Korzeniewska, vols. 1–4 (1963–66), series 2, ed. by J. Czachowska, vols. 1–3 (1977–80); *Literatura polska na obczyźnie 1940–1960*, ed. by T. Terlecki, vols. 1–2 (1964–65); *Obraz literatury polskiej XIX i XX wieku*, series 4, *Literatura polska w okresie realizmu i naturalizmu*, vols. 1–4 (1965–69), series 5, *Literatura okresu Młodej Polski*, vols. 1–4 (1968–77), series 6, *Literatura w okresie międzywojennym*, vols. 1–2 (1979); R. C. Lewanski, *The Literatures of the World in English Translation: A Bibliography*, vol. 2, *The Slavic Literatures* (1967); J. J. Maciuszko, *The Polish Short Story in English: A Guide and Critical Bibliography* (1968); C. Miłosz, *The History of Polish Literature* (1969); *Bibliografia literatury polskiej "Nowy Korbut," Literatura pozytywizmu i Młodej Polski*, vols. 13–15 (1970–77); L. Ryll and J. Wilgat, *Polska literatura w przekładach. Bibliografia 1945–1970* (1972); J. Hoskins, *Polish Books in English* (1974); J. Kleiner, *Zarys dziejów literatury polskiej 1918–1966*, supplement by W. Maciąg (1974); *Prozaicy dwudziestolecia międzywojennego*, ed. by B. Faron (1974); *Literatura polska 1918–1975*, vol. 1, *Literatura polska 1918–1932* (1975); L. S. Bartelski, *Polscy pisarze współcześni. Informator 1944–74* (1977); *Historia literatury polskiej*, ed. by K. Wyka, H. Markiewicz, *Pozytywizm* (1978); J. Krzyżanowski, *History of Polish Literature* (1978); M. Danilewicz Zielinska, *Szkice o literaturze emigracyjnej* (1978).   S.F.

Pondal, Eduardo (1835–1917), Spanish poet, was born at Ponteceso in Galicia. He studied medicine in Santiago de Compostela and took part in liberal student agitation that culminated in a banquet given for the workers of Conjo, a village near Santiago. He was threatened with punishment by the authorities because of the fiery tone of his anarchical verses. He was graduated as a physician in 1860 and spent most of his life in retreat in his native village. His poetry is contained in two books, *Rumores de los pinos* (1877; Murmurs of the Pines), written for the most part in Castilian with a few poems in Galician, and *Queixumes dos pinos* (1886; Complaints of the Pines), entirely in Galician. At his death he left unpublished an extensive poem of epic cast, "Os Eoas" (the title refers to the seafaring people of the east), written in Galician and relating the deeds of the discoverers of America.

In the renaissance of Galician poetry, Pondal represents the romanticism of the Celtic school. The murmuring of the pines of Bergantiños resounds in his ears like the harps of the ancient singers, and the trees from legions of Celtic warriors. Pondal feels himself to be a bard from pre-Christian times.

Pondal possessed great humanist-literary learning (he read Tasso, Camões, Latin and Greek authors, and mythology), an understanding of the Celts and sympathy with the aura of fantasy that surrounds them, and an exquisite sensibility that allowed him to portray the remote past in terms of the present. No one has written Galician poetry with more austere sonority and grandeur.

On rare occasions his poetry expresses the nostalgic melancholy characteristic of other Galician poets of this period. In his most famous composition, "A campana d'Anllons" (The Bell of Anllons), for instance, a captive in Africa evokes his native country under the spell of an hallucination in which he hears the sound of his village bell on a night of full moon. Among Galician poets, Pondal stands worthily next to Rosalía de Castro.

See: R. Carballo Calero, *Historia de literatura galega contemporánea* (1975), pp. 237–333.

R.M.-L. rev. H.L.B.

Ponge, Francis (1899–), French poet, was born in Montpellier. He published *Douze Petits Ecrits* (12 Small Pieces) in 1926, but while this limited edition brought him the sympathetic attention of Jean PAULHAN and other critics, Ponge remained virtually unknown by the literate public until the end of World War II. His second book, *Le Parti-pris des choses* (1942; Eng. tr., *The Voice of Things*, 1972) was singled out for praise by Jean-Paul SARTRE in his essay "L'Homme et les choses" (Man and Things) in *Situations I* (1947). In *Le Parti-pris,* meticulous descriptions of ordinary objects—an oyster, a cigarette, a cut of meat—are presented, usually in brief prose poems. Lyrical effusions are deliberately avoided as signs of anthropocentric bias. It thus appeared that Ponge, alone among poets, could be said to illustrate the phenomenological preoccupations of existentialism. This assumption was paradoxically challenged by Ponge himself in *Proêmes* (1948), whose title can be read as a fusion of the words *prose* and *poème.* In this work as elsewhere, Ponge clearly expresses his desire to abolish the distinction between poetry and prose. His rejection in this volume of the terms "poet" and "poem" applies to himself and his work.

In *Le Grand Recueil* (1961; The Grand Collection), which incorporates under the subtitle *Méthodes* the Pongian equivalent of an *ars poetica,* and in *Pour un Malherbe* (1965; Toward a Malherbe), it became increasingly clear that Ponge's materialism is merely a vehicle for an approach to language and, ultimately, to man. His antilyrical description of things is an exercise toward a restorative critique of language, which will in turn contribute to rectifying man's consciousness of his important, but not unique, place in the universe.

Ponge's work is a multidimensional research into the potential or habitually submerged values of words: every semantic, etymological, visual, and phonetic dimension of a word must be explored in order to perceive its total relationship with the thing it designates. The texts resulting from Ponge's simultaneous interrogation of words and things become rambling, autonomous objects, integrating his research notes (particularly from the Littré dictionary), observations of the object and of the author's reactions to it, and the unrestricted linguistic associations suggested by the word. *Le Soleil lu à la radio* (1950; Reading the Sun on the Radio) is typical of such texts and their unstable equilibrium between wordplay and phenomenological inquiry. Ponge defines this mode of composition as the *"objeu."* The untranslatable *objeu* is a combination of *objet* and *jeu* (game), i.e., a new form of text born of the fusion of the object (or *pre*-text) with the linguistic games it suggests.

In spite of such apparent playfulness, whereby Ponge explicitly accepts the consequence of "the good, the lovable kind of preciocity," his identification with Malherbe and the masters of 17th-century French classicism is justified by his search for definitive formulas and lapidary texts in which literature might realize its potential as an exact science. His rejection of conventional forms and lyricism and his emphasis on language as an object of scientific inquiry have made his work especially relevant to those young writers who, under the structuralist (*see* FRENCH LITERATURE) label, challenged the traditional concepts of literature. Their review *Tel Quel* (founded in 1960) opened its first issue with Ponge's *La Figue* (The Fig).

See: P. Sollers, *Francis Ponge* (1963).   R.V.

Ponten, Josef (1883–1940), German novelist, a native of the countryside near Aachen, was born at Raeren. He combined the geniality of the Rhenish temperament with serious endeavor in the study of geography, philosophy, architecture, and history. Although he spent a large portion of his life traveling extensively in Europe, the Americas, Asia, and Africa, and although he chose Munich as his domicile for the last 20 years of his life, he never relinquished the fundamental emotional and spiritual stimuli of his native scene on the Rhine—the simple life

of the country folk, the impressive natural environment, the lively river traffic, the celebrated Rhenish art and architecture, the eventful history of one of the oldest provinces of Germany, and—last but not least—the historical and legendary figure of Charlemagne.

Ponten's literary significance is primarily based on the extensive series of novels under the collective title *Volk auf dem Wege* (A People under Way), which, composed from 1925 on, began to appear in 1930. Before 1925, however, Ponten gained considerable repute through several short stories and novels such as *Jungfräulichkeit* (1906; new version, 1920; Virginity), *Siebenquellen* (1908; Seven Springs), *Die Insel* (1918; The Tower of Babel), *Die Bockreiter* (1919; The Coachbox Riders), *Der Meister* (1919; The Master), *Der Gletscher* (1923; The Glacier), *Die Uhr von Gold* (1923; The Golden Clock), and *Der Urwald* (1924; The Primeval Forest). In the same group belong *Salz* (1927; Salt) and *Die Studenten von Lyon* (1927; The Students of Lyons). Most of these works, participating in the prophetic tone of expressionism without sharing its frenzy, pose in one form or another the problem of the cultural crisis of people today. They do not voice violent protest or accusation; as long as they can proclaim the continuity of life, they are willing to accept the tragic destruction of the individual.

Although these earlier works often assumed allegorical dimensions, *Volk auf dem Wege* is grounded more on observation, experience, and source studies. Chancing upon the settlements of Volga Germans in 1920, Ponten planned to present the poetic history of German emigration in various cycles, covering several continents. In 1930 and 1931 the first volumes appeared, *Wolga, Wolga* (Volga, Volga) and *Rhein und Wolga* (Rhine and Volga); they were soon withdrawn and rewritten. From 1933 onward were published *Im Wolgaland* (1933; In the Volga Land), *Die Väter zogen aus* (1934; The Fathers Set Out), *Rheinisches Zwischenspiel* (1937; Rhenish Intermezzo), *Die Heiligen der letzen Tage* (1938; The Saints of the Final Days), and *Der Zug nach dem Kaukasus* (1940; The March to the Caucasus). Tracing the various waves of emigration as far back as 1689, Ponten portrayed the most diverse causes and motives of "German unrest" and the aspirations and disillusions that accompanied it. With humanistic restraint he pictured historical events as natural processes, as it were, subject to the polarity of being and becoming, of existence and change. Devotion to objective reality, marked by the absence of sentimental evaluation, pervaded Ponten's essays on nature and art in works from 1910 to 1928.

See: W. Schneider, *Josef Ponten* (1928); L. A. Shears, "The Novellen of Josef Ponten," *GR* 9 (1936): 50–55; H. Rehder, "Josef Ponten, Gestalt und Werk," *Monatshefte* 33 (1941): 124–37.   H.Re. rev. A.L W.

Pontoppidan, Henrik (1857–1943), Danish novelist, was born in the Jutland town of Fredericia, the son of a clergyman. He grew up in the city of Randers. As a protest against the ecclesiastical traditions of the family, Pontoppidan studied engineering but interrupted his studies in 1879 to become a writer. He lived in the Zealand countryside until 1910 and thereafter in Copenhagen. In 1917, Pontoppidan shared the Nobel Prize for Literature with Karl GJELLERUP. His first work, *Stækkede Vinger* (1881; Clipped Wings), describes the inexorable power of environment over human beings and is symptomatic of the pessimism with which Pontoppidan continued the realism of the 1870s (*see* DANISH LITERATURE). He strongly opposed all social evils. The miserable situation of the peasant proletariat is described from a politically radical viewpoint in a series of stories, *Landsbybilleder* (1883;

Pictures from the Countryside) and *Fra Hytterne* (1887; From the Cottages). The short stories in *Skyer* (1890; Clouds), however, evidence a more objective attitude as Pontoppidan also aims his sharp criticism at naturalism. Two major motifs run throughout his extensive literary production: (1) the contrast between nature and culture and (2) the failure of idealism owing to a destiny determined by environment and heredity. These motifs are discernible in a series of short novels, *Sandinge Menighed* (1883; Sandinge Parish); *Isbjørnen* (1887; The Polar Bear), an amusing satire on an eccentric minister's struggle with his colleagues; and *Nattevagt* (1894; Night Watch), which depicts the conflict between a spiritual and a naturalistic point of view. These same motifs are thoroughly analyzed in three major novel cycles all constructed along similar lines of action: the main character proceeds from illusion to disillusion and resignation. The first cycle, *Det forjættede Land* (1891–95; Eng. tr., *The Promised Land*, 1896) is, in addition to being a satirical period picture, a penetrating psychological study of the tragedy of a religious idealist, Emanual Hansted. The title character in Pontoppidan's next cycle, *Lykke-Per* (1898–1904; Lucky Per), is also a fortune seeker. But whereas the clergyman Emanuel was driven by unselfish thoughts, Per Sidenius is simply striving to find his own happiness, reaching it only after having lost everything except himself. Like Emanuel, Per is regarded as a national type; Denmark is a nation of "Sideniuses," lyrically gifted but passionless and inactive. A number of minor novels are forerunners of the final phase of Pontoppidan's literary production. His last novel cycle, *De Dødes Rige* (1912–16; The Realm of the Dead), is dominated by universal despair. The author condemns his own age by describing the humiliation and destruction of ordinary people when confronted with the corrupt morals and political conditions of the times. This novel cycle is permeated with gloomy pessimism. It is exceptional in Scandinavian literature because of its recognition of the nothingness of existence—connected with the moral experience of its worthlessness. In Pontoppidan's final novel, *Mands Himmerig* (1927; Man's Heaven), his despair concerns the destruction of the Danish nation during World War I. The book tells of the tragedy of a ruthless man in a country dominated by a corrupt press, government, and population solely desiring to benefit from the war. No other Danish writer has succeeded in portraying his own age, its main currents, and its people so completely and with such artistic precision as Pontoppidan.

See: K. Ahnlund, *Henrik Pontoppidan* (1956); P. M. Mitchell, *Henrik Pontoppidan*, TWAS 524 (1979).

S.H.R.

Popa, Vasko (1922–), Serbian poet, was born in Grebenac, Banat. He is considered by many critics to be the finest living Serbian poet. During World War II, Popa fought in the ranks of the Partisans. He studied during and after World War II at the universities of Vienna, Bucharest, and Belgrade, receiving his degree in literature at Belgrade in 1949. Since then he has worked as an editor in several publishing houses.

Popa had published four books of poetry as of 1977: *Kora* (1953; Bark), *Nepočin-polje* (1956; The Unrest Field), *Sporedno nebo* (1968; The Secondary Sky), and *Uspravna zemlja* (1972; Earth Erect). His poetry has been translated into many languages. In 1968 he received the National Austrian Prize for European Literature.

Together with Miodrag PAVLOVIĆ, Popa contributed decisively to the victory in the early 1950s of the modernists of Serbian poetry in their struggle against the traditionalists (*see* SERBIAN LITERATURE). Popa's language is often aphoristic and elliptic, bearing resemblances to folk poetry, to the poetry of Momčilo NASTASIJEVIĆ, and to the work of the Serbian surrealists. Yet despite some affinities with other poets Popa's distinctive style makes him a unique poetic figure in modern Serbian literature, influential but difficult to emulate. Even in his early work, Popa showed a predilection for the concrete object rather than for abstractions, for specifics rather than generalities. In his poetry, the inert object often appears as a symbol for the poet's own concepts and attitudes. Popa's poems are often written in cycles, each cycle being a self-sustaining entity, unified by a common subject matter and style. Popa eschews both rhyme and the excesses of free verse, but his terseness of expression lends his verses an unassuming yet strong rhythm.

See: T. Hughes, "Introduction to the Poetry of Vasko Popa," in V. Popa, *Selected Poems*, tr. by A. Pennington (1969), pp. 9–16; V. D. Mihailovich, "Vasko Popa: The Poetry of Things in a Void," *BA*, 43 (1969): 24–29.

V.D.M.

Poplavsky, Boris Yulianovich (1903–35), Russian poet, novelist, and critic, was born in Moscow but emigrated to Paris at the age of 16. His entire literary career, lasting for only six years, developed in emigration in Paris. Apart from Aleksandr BLOK, his formative influences were all non-Russian: Charles BAUDELAIRE, Guillaume APOLLINAIRE, the French surrealists, and James Joyce. His first collection of verse, *Flagi* (1931; Flags), evokes the confusion of post-World War I Europe in colorful surrealistic imagery, at once flamboyant and visionary. In his later verse, published in three posthumous collections, *Snezhny chas* (1936; The Snowy Hour); *V venke iz voska* (1938; In a Wreath of Wax); and *Dirizhabl neizvestnogo napravleniya* (1965; Dirigible of Unknown Destination), the verbal color is toned down and the poet is more concerned with conveying his mystical experience. Poplavsky's novels *Apollon Bezobrazov* and *Domoy s nebes* (both written ca. 1930–35 and published in serialized form only; Eng. tr. of a portion of the latter novel, *Homeward from Heaven*, 1973) depict the lives of Russian émigré dropouts in Paris, prefiguring many of the attitudes and interests of the 1960s hip culture in the West. The same is true of fragments from his journals, *Iz dnevnikov, 1928–1935*, published in 1938. Poplavsky is considered by many, including D. S. Mirsky and Vladimir NABOKOV, to be the most original poet produced by the Russian emigration.

See: A. Olcott, "Poplavsky: The Heir Presumptive of Montparnasse," in *The Bitter Air of Exile: Russian Writers in the West 1922–1972*, ed. by S. Karlinsky and A. Appel, Jr. (1977), pp. 274–88.

S.K.

Porto-Riche, Georges de (1849–1930), French dramatist, was born in Bordeaux. He was a member of the Académie Française. Porto-Riche's early poetic and dramatic efforts went unrecognized by both public and critics until *La Chance de Françoise* (1889; Françoise's Luck) was staged by André ANTOINE in 1888. This work probes into a marriage in which each partner loves the other, but with differing degrees of feeling. *Amoureuse* (1891; Lovey), hailed for the directness and sincerity of its emotion, describes a wife whose ardor repels a husband too weak to break away. Like *L'Amoureuse*, *Le Passé* (1897; The Past) illustrates the power of the sexual drive to enslave; the wife in this play relives the memory of earlier pleasures while her husband is involved with current conquests.

Three minor works followed *Le Passé*: *Les Malfilâtre* (1904), based on Victor Hugo; *Zubiri* (1912); and *Les*

Vrais Dieux (1929; The True Gods). In *Le Vieil Homme* (1911; The Old Man), Porto-Riche focused on the character of an unhappy son, unloved by his parents, who kills himself after an infatuation with an older woman. In *Le Marchand d'estampes* (1917; The Dealer in Engravings), a man consumed by sensuality also resorts to suicide as the only solution to his dilemma. *Les Vrais Dieux,* set in early Christian times, concerns a grieving widow who is encouraged to remarry. Love becomes the "true god" that triumphs over conscience.

In his treatment of love, Porto-Riche broke with romantic tradition by stripping the emotion of its sentimental trappings and viewing its ravaging effects with a clinical eye. His characters are appealing in their vulnerability and—especially his heroines—in their qualities of intelligence and sensitivity. Although his women understand the nature of their subjugation, they prefer the pangs of conscience and unrequited love to separation and loneliness.

See: W. Müller, *Georges de Porto-Riche 1849–1930: l'homme—le poète—le dramaturge* (1934). A.J.W.

Portugal, José Blanc de (1914–), Portuguese poet, was born in Lisbon, where he has lived, except for long sojourns in several overseas colonies and abroad. A graduate in geological science, he has been for years a director of the Meteorological Services. In 1940 he joined some hitherto unknown poets (Jorge de SENA, Sophia de Mello Breyner ANDRESEN, and others) in founding the review *Cadernos de Poesia.* Standing at equal distance from the literary humanism of the *Presença* group (see PORTUGUESE LITERATURE) and from the social realism propounded at the time by the "neorealists," they were trying to recapture the spirit of the avant garde in a new context.

For many years, Portugal's poetry appeared in literary reviews, and only in recent times has he published some collections of verse. That poetry, which springs from a dramatic Catholicism and a vast encyclopedia culture, is characterized by great dignity of diction and severity of expression. Both qualities at once conceal and reveal an anguished humbleness, a somewhat black humor, and a tragic consciousness of the contradictions of the modern world. Abrupt rhythms and elliptical statements make for a highly daring and original language that keeps a precarious balance—to the poet, the very image of human life—between an almost surrealistic inspiration and a sternly demanding lucidity. Portugal is nationally one of the best poets to appear in the second half of the 20th century. He is also one of the country's foremost music critics; and his literary essays, *Anticrítico* (1960; Anticritic), full of paradoxes, are of the highest distinction. The titles of his poetical collections reflect the same mood, for example, *Odes pedestres, precedidas de autopoética* (1965; Pedestrian Odes, Preceded by Autopoetics). J. de S.

Portuguese literature. By the third quarter of the 19th century, after the long crisis occasioned by the implantation of liberalism and its embodiment into the historical structure of the country, Portuguese romanticism, belated, attenuated, and altogether moderate, had produced everything that could be expected of it. This movement has been divided, with some overlapping, into three periods. An "initial romanticism" (1825–51) produced three leaders, Almeida Garrett (1799–1854), Alexandre Herculano (1810–77), and António Feliciano de Castilho (1800–75). Upon Garrett's death, the germ of liberal action inherent in the movement was personified in Herculano—he himself called his work "the first attempt at a critical history of Portugal"—but any militant intervention in

public affairs—politics, education, relations between church and state, censorship—ceased with his withdrawal to the village of Vale de Lobos in 1867. Only Castilho remained; around him had collected the greater part of the writers who were to constitute the "second romanticism" (1851–71). A master of the language, but possessing scant creative imagination, Castilho personified the adaptation of romanticism to the old culture of Portuguese society. He became the obstacle in the path of the new generation that introduced the "third romanticism" (1871–90), which soon evolved into a frank realism, marking the beginning of contemporary questioning. This third movement began with the rebellion of the "Generation of Coimbra." Two very distinct personalities, Antero de Quental (1841–91) and Teófilo Braga (1843–1924), both from the Azores, were the visible heads of the insurrection. Camilo Castelo Branco (1826–90), the great independent novelist, who was to have subsequent encounters with the same younger generation, threw himself into the controversy, attacking the Coimbra group with his pungent sarcasm, whereas José Maria Eça de Queiroz (1845–1900), a member of the group and inventor of Fradique Mendes, its ideal representative, said of "the ardent and fantastic Coimbra" of his day: "Over the railroads that had opened the peninsula, whole waves of new things descended upon us every day from France, and Germany by way of France: ideas, aesthetic systems, forms, sentiments, humanitarian concerns."

The aggressive Generation of Coimbra produced three figures of the highest rank: Quental in poetry, Eça in the novel, and Joaquim Pedro de Oliveira Martins (1845–94) in historical writing. Continuing the criticism but not the medievalism of Herculano, Oliveira Martins also exerted an influence on the Generation of '98 in Spain. Other writers were more popular at the time: Guerra Junqueiro (1850–1923) and Gomes Leal (1849–1921), eloquent poets with civic-social preoccupations, and João de Deus (1830–96), a poet noted for the delicate, unadorned, amorous poems in *Flores do campo* (1869; Field Flowers).

The novel reached its apogee with Eça, whose brilliance observed other talented fiction writers, notably Teixeira de Queiroz (1848–1919), who between 1876 and 1919, published two series of novels that were contemporary character studies, *Comédia do campo* (The Country Comedy) and *Comédia burguesa* (Middle-Class Comedy); Abel Botelho (1854–1917), whose *Patologia social* series of 1891 to 1910 followed the naturalistic method precisely; Júlio Lourenço Pinto (1842–1907), the theoretician of the group; and Fialho de Almeida (1857–1911), whose satirical *Os Gatos* (1884–93; The Cats) sought to continue *As Farpas* (1871–83; The Darts), the monthly started by Eça and Ramalho Ortigão (1837–1915).

The British ultimatum of 1890 to stop Portuguese expansion in southern Africa and a republican revolt in Oporto weakened the monarchy decisively while national literature plunged into pessimism. A Spanish observer, Miguel de UNAMUNO, felt that the wave of suicides among prominent Portuguese, such as Camilo Castelo Branco and Quental, manifested the profound malaise. As had happened a quarter of a century before, writers split along ideological lines, but this was done within an ever more nationalistic framework. On one hand, the subjective critique of modern urban life, foreshadowed in the poetry of Cesário Verde (1855–86), was carried further by Gomes Leal and Guerra Junqueiro in antiplutocratic, antimonarchical, and anticlerical verse, such as the latter's *Finis patriae* (1891; End of Our Country) and *Os Simples* (1892; Simple Folk). On the other hand, there was an escape to exotic themes and places in the poetry of António Feijó (1862–1917) and the prose of Wenceslau de

Morais (1854–1929), both of them describing life in the Far East, where Morais settled and died. Some of those who stayed at home reverted to a sentimental, neoromantic treatment of traditional lore that was termed neo-Garrettism, although their devotion to Garrett's memory stopped short of adopting his liberal creed. Instead, they concentrated on exquisite form, picking up symbolist tendencies in France. A very academic poet, Eugénio de Castro (1869–1944), became the leader of these *nefelibatas* (cloud walkers), named thus in mockery. His *Oarystos* (1890; Discourse) caught the attention of Spanish-American *Modernistas* and brought him more fame abroad than at home. Others renewed the traditions of melancholy effusion and the nostalgia of the bucolic Portugal. The most gifted were two lonely, hypersensitive poets, António Nobre (1867–1900), whose *Só* (1892; Alone) became a modern classic, and the musical Camilo PESSANHA, whose *Clépsidra* (1920; Water Clock) was not appreciated until long after his death. *Só* has been called a "work that marks the return, not only to Garrett, but to all the morbid poetical weaknesses of the national spirit."

Almost symbolically, the 20th century began with the deaths of the poet Nobre and the novelist Eça de Queiroz. Indeed, until the outbreak of World War I, Portuguese literature seemed orphaned, as its finest writers had prematurely died (Verde, Quental, Eça, Nobre) or withdrawn (Pessanha), leaving the field to epigones, such as Eugénio de Castro and Júlio Dantas (1876–1962), who charmed the public with his mundane playlet *A Ceia dos cardeais* (1902; The Cardinals' Supper), the poet Afonso Lopes Vieira (1878–1946), who tried to enrich the national literature with old masterpieces that had originally been written in Spanish, or António Corrêa d'Oliveira (1879–1960), who sentimentalized rural tradition in popular verse.

Political events dispelled the stagnation, although only for a brief moment. The murder of King Charles I in 1908, the end of the seven-centuries-old monarchy through the establishment of the Republic in 1910, the entry into World War I on the Allied side—all encountered much opposition within the country and were followed by military revolts, thus creating an atmosphere of instability that quickly led to the disappointment of great expectations. In 1912 a large, heterogenous movement among the intellectuals founded the *Renascença Portuguesa* (Portuguese Renaissance), a society that pinned on the Republic its hopes for a return to public morality and a renewal of the national traditions and ambitions of the Age of Discoveries when little Portugal sought to establish the first seaborne empire of worldwide proportions. The group was led by impractical idealists arrayed in futile battle against the greedy party politicians. The high intellectual stature of three presidents of the Republic was of no avail: old Teófilo Braga; the skeptical aesthete Manuel Teixeira-Gomes (1860–1941), author of sensuous prose works, such as *Inventário de Junho* (1899; June Inventry) and the comedy *Sabina Freire* (1905); and the anthropologist and educator Bernardino Machado (1851–1944), author of essays written with admirable clarity and high moral standards. The idealists of the *Renascença* were headed by the great poet Joaquim Teixeira de PASCOAES, editor of its review *A Águia* (1910–32; The Eagle), whose national philosophy of *saudade* or *saudosismo* (nostalgia), although positively aimed toward the future, was too hazy to provide guidelines for action. His closest collaborators, the philosophers Leonardo Coimbra (1883–1936) and António SÉRGIO, as well as the historian Jaime CORTESÃO, were dedicated teachers. Even the young Fernando PESSOA, who had just returned from South Africa,

was so inspired by the idea of a national rebirth that he envisioned a great spiritual empire of the Portuguese language, with himself perhaps as its singer. "Because the present political situation is so shabby and pitiful," he wrote in 1912, "we are precisely for that reason led to conclude that a super-Camões is about to appear in our country." The group soon broke apart. Its most active members, guided by António Sérgio, formed a kind of Fabian society, the *Seara Nova* (New Crop) in 1921. Opposed to expediency and authoritarianism of all kinds, it had a lasting effect, although it could not carry out its cooperative and educational programs. With the aid of the socialists, it served as the chief bulwark of democratic resistance to tyranny through the long flourishing review of the same name, faltering only after 1974. It attracted some of the best writers, among them Raúl BRANDÃO, Aquilino RIBEIRO, Ferreira de CASTRO, and José Rodrigues MIGUÉIS. Their tolerant spirit could not prevent the growing polarization in the country, as its economy deteriorated even faster than that of Europe as a whole. Thus, a pre-Fascist, monarchic, and Catholic movement was inaugurated by the poet and essayist António Sardinha (1888–1925); it was modeled after the French *Action Française* and had the name *Integralismo Lusitano* (Lusitanian, that is, Portuguese, Integralism). A few important writers followed Sardinha's lead, among them the essayists Hipólito Raposo (1885–1953) and José Osório de Oliveira (1900–68). Others kept aloof from all political groupings, perhaps out of a feeling of profound disillusionment deepened by over three centuries of national weakness, initiated by the disastrous union with Spain under the Hapsburgs (1580–1640).

This disillusionment is particularly evident in the negative, self-destructive spirit—symbolized by the hopeless hope for a return of past glory known as Sebastianism (from King Sebastian, 1557–78)—that dominates and spoils a large part of the thoughts and writings of Fernando Pessoa, the greatest Portuguese poet of the 20th century. In him it combines with a very modern dissociation and dramatization of the divergent egos within the human breast. Pessoa was the genius behind the shortlived review *Orpheu* (1915; Orpheus), the organ of an intentionally esoteric and provocative artistic movement reflecting French and Italian experimentation with "dynamic" forms of new consciousness, in a "synthesis of all modern literary movements" (Pessoa), sometimes labeled *modernismo*. It associated Portuguese writers, such as the innovative Mário de SÁ-CARNEIRO and the many-sided painter José de ALMADA-NEGREIROS, with the Brazilian poet Ronald de Carvalho. Shortsighted critics saw *Orpheu* as no more than the product of a bunch of "lucid madmen," whereas, in fact, it was a most lively manifestation of disinterested, high-minded art. Nor did this mean that the review dissociated itself from the strivings for national renewal. It aimed to carry on the efforts of the few genuine Portuguese symbolists, and it led to a loose grouping around the review *Presença*, "Folha de Arte e Crítica" (1927–30; 1930–40; Presence, Pages of Art and Criticism). *Orpheu*'s influence finally can be traced to the—belated—appearance of the surrealists after World War II. *Presença* was started in Coimbra by a group of young students who were to dominate Portuguese literature for 20 years afterwards: José RÉGIO as a critic and poet, João Gaspar Simões (1903–) as a critic, António José Branquinho da FONSECA as a story writer, Miguel TORGA as a poet, and, a little later, Adolfo Casais MONTEIRO, also as a critic. All of them typically combined creative writing with literary theory and criticism, in an aura of sophistication from which only Branquinho da Fonseca and Torga escaped. In his editorials, Régio proclaimed the primacy of artistic originality and sincerity, later on expanded to include psychological introspection and the aesthetic autonomy of art, also referred to as individualism and authenticity. Fyodor DOSTOYEVSKY, Marcel PROUST, and André GIDE were the acknowledged models. So much pontification led to splits within the individualistic group, but the review *Presença* continued. Its high literary standards attracted many fine authors, who resisted political pressures to enlist their art. Among them were Pessoa, his friend António BOTTO, Edmundo de Bettencourt (1899–1973), Irene LISBOA, and Vitorino NEMÉSIO. Miguéis should be mentioned also because of his introspective tendency and careful craftsmanship, although he remained committed to the humanistic socialism of *Seara Nova*. An unforeseeable consequence of *Presença* was its contribution to the birth of a literature on the Cape Verde Islands off Africa dedicated to expressing the islanders' psyche "authentically." After founding the review *Claridade* (intermittently since 1936; Brightness), Cape Verdean writers came to national attention for the first time, with the poetry of Jorge BARBOSA and the stories of António Aurélio GONÇALVES, Baltasar LOPES, and Manuel LOPES, as well as those of a mainlander, Manuel Ferreira (1917–). Equally new was a second influence on the writers in this and other parts of Portuguese-speaking Africa, especially Angola; the social protest fiction of a similar region, northeastern Brazil. Young African writers, many of them educated mulattoes, were stimulated by Brazilian fiction (reinforced by "black" writing elsewhere) and decided to band together to produce a decidedly African literature in the Portuguese language. They adopted such slogans as *négritude* and *Vamos descobrir Angola* (Let's Discover Angola). In vain, their mentors among Portuguese officialdom tried to perpetuate colonial dependence through their spokesmen José Osório de Oliveira and Amândio César. The African pioneers of this self-discovery were the poet Francisco José TENREIRO from São Tomé Island and several Angolans—the novelist Castro SOROMENHO, the folklorist Óscar Ribas (1909–), the poet Alda Lara (1930–62), and the poet-sociologist Mário António (1934–). When the Salazar dictatorship tightened the screws, they were supplanted by militants: the essayist Mário Pinto de Andrade (1928–), the story writer Luandino VIEIRA, and the poets Agostinho Neto (1922–) and António Jacinto (1924–), men who were jailed or exiled but could not be silenced permanently. Mozambique, culturally more conservative and less homogeneous than Angola, contributed few voices to the rising chorus, although a poet, José CRAVEIRINHA, and later on a story writer, Luís Bernardo Honwana (1942–), gained an international audience owing to general interest in the struggle for Africa rather than to artistic excellence alone.

In Portugal proper, a literature of social protest marched forward under the banner of "neorealism," with extraliterary functions, such as proletcult, education in economics, and resistance to the rightist government. The term *proletcult* was first used by Joaquim Namorado (1914–) when writing about a Brazilian novelist in 1938. Committed to social change, the neorealists reverted to a purposely plain way of writing, often to the point of sociological reportage, and, like their Brazilian counterparts, were wedded to descriptions of regional life, which was fatally narrow and provincial in Portugal. Reacting to the metaphysical and aesthetic stance of Régio and his *Presença*, the neorealists expressed their views in the journals *Sol Nascente* of Oporto (1937–40; Rising Sun) and *Vértice* of Coimbra (since 1942; Zenith). They gathered strength as the result of two ideological wars: the

disastrous Spanish Civil War, during which their government aided the murderers of Federico GARCÍA LORCA, and World War II against the three totalitarian regimes. The victory of the "democracies" roused false hopes among Portuguese writers. When these hopes were dispelled, the neorealists became intellectually and artistically more mature.

Neorealism had forerunners in two novelists. Ferreira de Castro, whose early Brazilian experience immunized him against the provincialism that made most of the work of the other writer, Aquilino Ribeiro, a closed book for foreign readers. Aquilino, as he was fondly called, had stronger ties to the soil and a better command of the vernacular—a quality always greatly admired in Portugal. Neorealism had its poets—Políbio Gomes dos Santos (1911–39), Manuel da FONSECA, Carlos de OLIVEIRA, and José Gomes FERREIRA—a playwright in the person of Romeu Correia (1917–), and a host of novelists who made the 30 years beginning about 1940 the richest period in prose fiction that Portugal has known, as they vied with excellent craftsmen of various other tendencies—Régio, Miguéis, Tomaz de FIGUEIREDO, Branquinho da Fonseca, Domingos MONTEIRO, Joaquim PAÇO D'ARCOS, and Fernando NAMORA. With his novel *Gaibéus* (1939; Day Laborers), Alves REDOL started a populist literature of books for the people by the people, a program to which the bulk of the semiliterate population failed to respond. Less known neorealists are Joaquim Pereira Gomes (1910–49), Alexandre CABRAL, and Faure da Rosa (1912–). Symptomatic of developing divergences is the case of Vergílio FERREIRA, who turned existentialist under the impact of Jean-Paul SARTRE. Nevertheless, the neorealists' social commitment still seemed valid to a newer generation—a "second wave," to which the poet Manuel Alegre (1937–) and the novelist José Cardoso PIRES belong. Thus they answered the question about the vitality of neorealism which was so hotly debated for many years.

It could not be otherwise as long as the reactionary dictatorship ruled through more or less hidden terror, under the shrewd direction of two former university professors, António de Oliveira Salazar and, for a brief spell, Marcelo Caetano. At first, the dictatorship had benefited from the bankruptcy of the weak parliamentary republic, which it had taken over. It found a smart journalist, António Ferro, friend of many writers, to organize its cultural propaganda office, the *Secretariado Nacional de Informação* or S.N.I. Ferro invited prominent foreign intellectuals to visit Portugal, promoted the fine arts, subsidized folklore groups, attempted to bring theater to the "masses," and created annual prizes for literary and journalistic works, keeping in mind the interests of the *Estado Novo* (New State), organized in 1933 along Fascistic lines. The prizes rarely went to the best writers—most of them refused to compete for them, especially after the dismissal or exclusion of many eminent intellectuals from teaching, among them the literary historian and essayist Fidelino de FIGUEIREDO, the philologist Manuel Rodrigues Lapa (1897–), the prose writer Irene Lisboa, the essayist Agostinho da Silva (1906–), the critic Óscar Lopes (1920–), and many dozens more—a grievous "brain drain" for a small country. A notorious instance of poor judgment was the award of a mere consolation prize to Pessoa for his patriotic cycle *Mensagem* (Message) in 1934. He also wrote satires that circulated clandestinely, as did writings by other unquestionable patriots, such as Pascoaes and Lopes Vieira. The insidious precensorship of the press and the theater further alienated the intellectual world. Notorious scandals broke out when the aged Aquilino was to be tried for "ridiculing the judiciary" in a novel in 1959; again in 1964, when a jury was arrested for awarding a prize to Luandino Vieira, and the too independent Portuguese Writers' Association of which the jury was a part was dissolved. In spite of its long duration—1926–74—the dictatorship was unable to direct culture along safe channels or to break the stubborn resistance of most of the intelligentsia, splintered as it was. A price had to be paid; Mário Cesariny de Vasconcelos points to the "ominously representative suicide of Florbela ESPANCA and "Pessoa's assassination by his own heteronyms."

Nipped in the bud were the hopeful beginnings of experimentation during the short-lived Republic—the futuristic verse of Pessoa, the expressionist drama of Alfredo CORTEZ, the polemic essays of António Sérgio, the frenetic prose and poetry of Sá-Carneiro, the sexual liberation in the poetry of Florbela Espanca, and, later, the wild libertarianism of the surrealists. Pessoa's mastery was realized in Portugal only after his death, when his works were slowly being brought out from 1942 on. A similarly late recognition awaited lesser poets, such as the Cape Verdean Eugénio Tavares (1867–1930) and the Mozambicans Reinaldo Ferreira (1922–59) and Rui de Noronha (1909–43), not to mention the relative obscurity to which great but unpopular writers like Pascoaes and Miguéis were relegated. In vain did some exercise moderation who joined forces in the Cadernos de Poesia (1940–42; 1951–53; Leaflets of Poetry), with the motto "A poesia é só uma" (All Poetry Is One); they included Tomaz Kim (that is, Joaquim Monteiro-Grillo, 1915–67), Jorge de SENA, José Blanc de PORTUGAL, Eugénio de ANDRADE, and Sophia de Mello Breyner ANDRESEN. No wonder, therefore, that the end of the dictatorship found the intellectuals bereft of their most capable leaders, who had either died off (Sérgio, Cortesão, F. de Figueiredo, Pessoa, A. Ribeiro, and, shortly after the liberation, Ferreira de Castro), had remained in exile, or had grown too old. A void exists that recalls the situation at the beginning of the century.

Presently there is no dearth of young writers, but none has achieved prominence yet. In poetry, those who began as surrealists introduced the principle of free association after World War II, while attacking the neorealists for lacking imagination and a radical love of liberty. Early halfhearted attempts by António PEDRO were followed by group expositions and "communiqués" in Lisbon (1949–50). Mário Cesariny de VASCONCELOS remains about the only active surrealist in Portugal today since the early death of António Maria Lisboa (1928–53), the desistance of Alexandre O'NEILL, and the exile of Mário Henrique Leiria (1923–). António GEDEÃO has been unique in relating science and poetry. Herberto HELDER excels in strange metaphors. Linguistic and communication theories have led to visual and morphological experimentation, which two poets, Maria Alberta Menéres (1930–) and her husband, Ernesto Manuel de Melo e Castro (1932–), joined by Ana Hatherly (1929–), learned from the Brazilian "concretist poets." Coming from the rather academic Távola Redonda group (1949–54; Round Table), among whom the poet and critic David MOURÃO-FERREIRA stood out, Menéres began publishing her poems in 1952 (Interval). The couple edited an Antologia da novíssima poesia portuguesa (1959; Anthology of the Most Recent Portuguese Poetry), brought up to date by António Ramos ROSA in Líricas portuguesas, 4.ª série (1969; Portuguese Verse).

Perhaps in poetry, as in other genres, new vitality may stream into Portuguese literature from Africa, with its aspirations towards freedom. At least in Mozambique,

there have appeared Rui KNOPFLI and a brilliant painter-poet who calls himself João Pedro Grabato DIAS and has demonstrated rare powers of inventive magic and ethical pathos in several "didactic odes."

For the first time in Portugal, women excel among prose writers, having gradually conquered for themselves a freedom of expression and life-style that were symbolically conceded with the squashing of the trial of the "Three Marias"—Maria Isabel Barreno, the well-known poet Maria Teresa Horta (1937–), and Maria Velho da Costa—authors of the boldly feminist Novas cartas portuguesas (1972; New "Lettres Portugaises"), written in prose and verse. Agustina BESSA-LUÍS changed the novel with her sombre and cruel analysis of social relations in the north from 1948 on. The stories of Maria Judite de CARVALHO, wife of the journalist, novelist, and critic Urbano Tavares RODRIGUES, have similarly dealt with modern incommunicability and frustration. Neither writer has made feminism her battle cry, as had predecessors, such as Maria Archer (1905–) or Judite Navarro (1910–).

In comparison with earlier generations, there are fewer writers of prose fiction in the late 20th century. The satirical José Cardoso Pires and the philosophically inclined Augusto Abelaira (1926–), both concerned with the plight of man, contrast with more experimental writers such as the storytellers Armando Ventura Ferreira (1920–), Almeida Faria (1943–), and Luiz Pacheco (1934–), the author of the disturbingly cynical Exercícios de estilo (1971; Exercises in Style). Here, too, Africa has something new to contribute in the works of Luandino Vieira, who is reshaping the Portuguese language in the manner of the Brazilian Guimarães Rosa.

There always have been stirrings in the theater. Despite the discouraging condition of the stage, many writers continue to use the dramatic form, affecting the few intrepidly innovating groups of amateurs or university players. From the symbolist plays of António PATRÍCIO and the preexistentialist works of Raul Brandão on, the 20th century is replete with plays that for the most part remain teatro de gaveta, that is, confined to the desk drawer. The vogue of the documentary and epic drama is represented in Portugal by Bernardo SANTARENO.

In short, the Portuguese literature of the 20th century still seems to lack the strong movements of the 19th century. Its best authors, however, are striving to recapture the universal, humanistic spirit that had been its glory in the Renaissance, that golden age when Gil Vicente wrote plays; João de Barros, imperial history; Fernão Mendes Pinto, of adventures in the East; and Camões, lyric and epic poetry. For too long, regionalism, often, as with the neorealists, in combination with social protest, has dominated prose, while poetry continues in the amatory, melancholy, or satiric modes that have been cultivated since the Middle Ages. The domain of Portuguese letters has widened the awakening of Portuguese-speaking Africa. Women are more visible. And for the first time, Brazil is making its weight felt.

See: F. de Figueiredo, Depois de Eça de Queiroz (1933); J. A. França, ed., Tetracórnio: meio século de literatura portuguesa (1955); M. Moisés, ed., Bibliografia da literatura portuguesa (1968); J. do Prado Coelho, ed., Dicionário das literaturas portuguesa, brasileira e galega (2d ed., 1969); J. J. Cochofel, ed., Grande dicionário da literatura portuguesa e de teoria literária (1971–); M. Moisés, ed., Literatura portuguesa moderna (guia biográfico, crítico e bibliográfico) (1973); A. J. Saraiva and O. Lopes, História da literatura portuguesa (5th ed., n.d.); R. G. Hamilton, Voices from an Empire: A History of Afro-Portuguese Literature (1975). G.M.M.

Poulet, Georges (1902–), Belgian literary critic, was born in Chênée. He is generally recognized as the foremost among the critics of consciousness of the Geneva school. He was educated at the University of Liège and has taught at the universities of Edinburgh, Johns Hopkins, Zürich, and Nice. After youthful experiments with fiction, he discovered in literary criticism a form of literature as creative in its own way as poetry or fiction. Poulet defines the critical act as an act of total empathy with an author, in which the critic participates in and recreates, from within the author's own consciousness, as it were, the thematic patterns through which the latter has sought to structure the world and, in so doing, grasp his own subjective truth. First inspired by Charles Du Bos, Jacques Rivière, Marcel Raymond, and Alfred Béguin, Poulet was concerned with the creative role of human consciousness as inseparable from a literary concern with a work's instrinsic structure and movement. In each writer's total oeuvre, he uncovers an initial cognito, the moment in which a mind first awakens to its own ontological reality, distinct from—and independent of—the transience and contingency of existence; and from there he retraces, in the form of a dramatic critical narrative, the successive stages whereby that mind and, in a larger perspective, the age that it reflects, have sought to transmute the fragile, discontinuous moments of existence into a coherent duration. Poulet's profoundly original contribution to criticism can be seen in the four-volume *Etudes sur le temps humain* (vol. 1, 1949; Eng. tr., *Studies in Human Time*, 1956) which also includes *La Distance intérieure* (vol. 2, 1952; Eng. tr., *The Interior Distance*, 1959), *Le Point de départ* (vol. 3, 1964; The Starting Point), and *Mesure de l'instant* (vol. 4, 1968; Measure of the Moment), as well as in *Les Métamorphoses du cercle* (1961; Eng. tr., *The Metamorphoses of the Circle*, 1967), *L'Espace proustien* (1963; Eng. tr., *Proustian Space*, 1977), *Trois Essais de mythologie romantique* (1966; Three Essays on Romantic Mythology), and *La Conscience critique* (1971; The Critical Awareness). This vast body of essays on individual writers, which ranges over four centuries of French literature but has focused increasingly on Poulet's contemporaries, constitutes a unique history of modern man's quest to transcend, through consciousness embodied in literary form, the confines of time and space.

See: P. de Man, "The Literary Self as Origin: The Work of Georges Poulet," in *Blindness and Insight* (1971), pp. 79–101; R. Wellek, "Poulet, Du Bos and Identification," *CLS* 10, no. 2 (June 1973): 173–93; P. Yu, "Georges Poulet and the Symbolist Tradition," *Criticism* 16, no. 1 (Winter 1974): 39–57.   G.R.Bl.

Pourrat, Henri (1887–1959), French novelist and essayist, was born in Ambert and lived in Auvergne. The four novels that compose *Les Vaillances: farces et aventures de Gaspard des Montagnes* (1922–31), tell a tragic story set in the early 19th century. While developing this narrative, drawn from local legend, Pourrat describes the daily life of the Auvergnats and relates numerous regional and national folktales. In keeping with the oral tradition, the action is narrated by a storyteller. The language is rich in imagery and patterned after the speech of local peasants.

Folklore is also the subject of *Le Trésor des contes* (1948; Eng. tr., *A Treasury of French Tales*, 1953), a work that has earned Pourrat the title of "France's Grimm" from at least one critic. Pourrat's essays defend his native province and the rustic way of life, as well as presenting a theory of rustic literature.

See: W. Bal, *La Comparaison: son emploi dans Gaspard des Montagnes d'Henri Pourrat* (1958); M. Bémol,

"Henri Pourrat et *Le Trésor des contes*," *AUS* 10 (1961): 179–82; P. Vernois, *Le Roman rustique de George Sand à Ramuz* (1962), pp. 349–406.   M.I.M.

Prados Such, Emilio (1899–1962), Spanish poet, left his native Málaga to attend the Residencia de Estudiantes in Madrid, where his friendship with Federico García Lorca and the presence of Juan Ramón Jiménez proved to be decisive influences. An early reading of Plato and of Sigmund Freud in French translation also left indelible marks. After a sojourn in Switzerland, he returned to Málaga and with Manuel Altolaguirre founded the poetry review *Litoral* (1926–29). Published with special attention to format, this journal opened its pages to young poets and brought out some of their most important works. At the outbreak of the Civil War, Prados pledged loyalty to the Republic and devoted himself to political activity. His poetry reflects this concern. The defeat of his cause took him into exile in Mexico. He worked for Editorial Séneca and continued to write poetry until his death. His volume *Tiempo* (1925; Time) diligently records transitions of light, sound, and color garnered from the contemplation of nature. *Cuerpo perseguido* (1928; Body Pursued) is an insufficiently appreciated love poem in which the metaphor for love is flight, air, wind, and soaring as recorded by the poet's eyes. The intensity of his love leads Prados to the Neoplatonic paradox of a longing that transcends the desired body. During the Civil War, Prados edited *Romancero general de la guerra de España* (1937; Ballad Book of the Spanish War), an anthology of 302 poems by various hands. Exile in Mexico reconfirmed his longfelt attraction to solitude. *Jardín cerrado* (1946; Closed Garden) restates the importance of the individual in confrontation with nature, and *La piedra escrita* (1961; The Written Stone) develops this relationship in cosmic metaphors.

See: C. Blanco Aguinaga, "Emilio Prados: vida y obra," *RHM*, 26 (1960): 1–107; C. B. Morris, "The Closed Door," in *A Generation of Spanish Poets* (1969), pp. 143–71.   H.T.Y.

Prat de la Riba, Enric (1870–1917), Catalan politician and writer, was born in Castellterçol, where he died on Aug. 1, 1917. He studied law at the University of Barcelona, where he became an outstanding young leader of the student center of Catalonia. His early work, *La nació com a subjecte de Dret Natural* (1890; The Nation as Subject to Natural Law), led many to predict a political future for him. This suspicion was strengthened by the publication of *Compendi de doctrina catalanista* (1894; Survey of Catalonian Doctrine), written in collaboration with Pere Muntanyola, and, more especially, by *La Nacionalitat catalana* (1906; Catalonian Statehood). From that moment on, he was the "Seny ordenador de Catalunya" (The Guiding Wisdom of Catalonia), as Eugenio D'Ors later called him, as well as the creator of "Noucentisme," a movement that brought Catalan culture into the European mainstream. Prat de la Riba's support for this movement was enormously effective, as he became president of the Diputació Provincial de Barcelona in 1907 and president of the Mancomunitat de Catalunya in 1914. He also founded the influential political party La Lliga, which he directed from 1906.

Prat de la Riba's political ideas are reflected in his *Manifestos Als Catalans* (Manifesto to the Catalonians) and *Al Poble Català* (To the Catalonian People). Other important works are *Compendi de la Història de Catalunya* (1898; Survey of Catalonian History) and *Història de la nació catalana* (1917; History of the Catalonian Nation). In the previous year he had published his manifesto, *Per Catalunya i l'Espanya gran*, the best résumé of his political ideas, which were adopted by the parliamentarians of Catalonia.

His work as a journalist is also significant. He was an influential writer for both *La Renaixença* and *La Veu de Catalunya*, a newspaper read by many intellectuals who wanted to contribute something to the future of Catalonia, a purpose to which Prat de la Riba dedicated his whole life.

See: X. Fort i Bufill, *Prat de la Riba* (1967); J. Sole-Tura, *Catalanisme i revolució burgesa: la sintesi de Prat de la Riba* (1967); A. Rovira i Virgili, *Prat de la Riba* (1968); J. M. Ainaud and E. Jardi, *Prat de la Riba, home de govern* (1973). J.F.C.

Pratolini, Vasco (1913–), Italian novelist, was born and raised in Florence. He is the first major proletarian writer of modern Italy. Pratolini's early works are autobiographical; *Il tappeto verde* (1941; The Green Carpet) and *Via de' Magazzini* (1942; Magazzini Street) describe his childhood in Florence. Written in a poetic prose style, both works underline the pathos and loneliness of a child who has lost his mother and thus a close family life. *Le amiche* (1943; The Girl Friends) is a series of character sketches and descriptions of several young Florentine girls all of whom lead unfulfilling lives. In the writings of this first phase, Pratolini relied upon personal reminiscences for his subject matter. The works are a young author's attempt to write what was then in vogue—recollective prose—without the distance that experience and objectivity bring. These early pieces are, however, valuable for the insights they provide into his later, more successful neorealistic (*see* ITALIAN LITERATURE) novels.

The second phase of Pratolini's development began with the publication of *Il quartiere* (1944; Eng. tr., *The Naked Streets*, 1952) and can be traced through *Cronache di poveri amanti* (1947; Eng. tr., *A Tale of Poor Lovers*, 1949) and *Le ragazze di San Frediano* (1949; The Girls of San Frediano). Here the limiting subjectivism of his early novels is replaced by a broader fictional perspective. One observes a more dynamic style, characterized by an urgent concern for social issues. In these works, the wartime Resistance code is transposed into fully developed literary themes: the importance of class solidarity and a sense of fraternity among those who share a common plight. Although Pratolini's protagonists are politically unsophisticated, his novels offer a sense of immediacy and a neorealistic solution to what historians refer to as the social polemic of fascism versus communism. In each of the works, the protagonist is actually a group of individuals who function as one and whose actions, thoughts, and words produce a single thematic statement. Pratolini writes most effectively about the ordinary life of the people of Santa Croce and San Frediano, the poor districts where he grew up. Luigi Russo, praising his eye and ear for the human values in everyday life, has rightly called Pratolini "the poet of his neighborhood." The novels of Pratolini's second phase have been judged artistically his most successful.

In the late 1940s, with the publication of *Un eroe del nostro tempo* (1949; Eng. tr., *A Hero of Our Time: A Novel*, 1951), Pratolini's writing took a new direction. His sociological perspective was broadened to include a more expanded polemic. *Metello* (1955; Eng. tr., *Metello: A Novel*, 1968), the first novel in the trilogy *Una storia italiana* (An Italian History), deals with the early problems of unionization in late 19th-century Italy from the point of view of a worker who becomes actively involved in the struggle against management. The novel effectively draws generalizations concerning the powerful control of the capitalists and their inhumane treatment and misunderstanding of the labor force. Management is forced to come to grips with the growing awareness and concerted action of the workers to protect themselves and their families. The second novel of the trilogy, *Lo scialo* (1960; The Waste), is a lengthy treatment of the Italian middle class in the early 20th century. It ends with the rise of fascism and draws the inevitable conclusion that the lack of moral fiber of the bourgeoisie was responsible for the disastrous political events of that era. The last novel of the three, *Allegoria e derisione* (1966; Allegory and Derision), is a personal description of the life of an intellectual in modern Italy. *La costanza della ragione* (1963; Eng. tr., *Bruno Santini*, 1964) treats the adolescent years of a boy who is trying to find a place in the work force of lower-class Florence. This protagonist stands opposed to the antihero of *Un eroe del nostro tempo*, who represents the complete moral bankruptcy of a typical postwar Fascist youth.

See: A. Asor Rosa, *Vasco Pratolini* (1958); F. Rosengarten, *Vasco Pratolini: The Development of a Social Novelist* (1965); W. Mauro, "Vasco Pratolini," in *Letteratura italiana: i contemporanei*, vol. 2 (1975), pp. 1639–56. J.M.K.

Praz, Mario (1896–), Italian scholar, literary critic, and essayist, was born in Rome. He was professor of Italian at the universities of Liverpool and Manchester (1924–34) and professor of English at the University of Rome (1932–64). Praz is among the most stimulating exponents of comparative literature today and an equally perceptive and original amateur of the visual arts. His works are characterized by a wide-ranging curiosity, profound erudition, and a felicitous style. *Seicentismo e Marinismo in Inghilterra* (1925; Eng. tr. of the essay on Crashaw in *The Flaming Heart*, 1958), a study of the baroque elements in John Donne and Richard Crashaw, was followed by *La carne, la morte e il diavolo nella letteratura romantica* (1930; Eng. version *The Romantic Agony*, 1933; 2d enl. ed., 1951), which analyzes the erotic and morbid aspects of the romantic sensibility from Percy Bysshe Shelley to Gabriele D'ANNUNZIO. This pioneering study is now a classic. Further essays related to this theme are collected in *Il patto col serpente* (1972; The Pact with the Serpent). *Studi sul concettismo* (1934; Eng. tr. by Praz, *Studies in 17th-Century Imagery*, vol. 1, 1939; vol. 2, 1947; 2d enl. ed., 1964) contains the first comprehensive bibliography of emblem books. *Gusto neoclassico* (1940; Eng. tr., *On Neoclassicism*, 1969) preceded by many years the revival of interest in this period. *La crisi dell'eroe nel romanzo vittoriano* (1952; Eng. tr., *The Hero in Eclipse in Victorian Fiction*, 1956) studies the relationship between the Victorian novel and 17th-century Dutch genre painting. *La casa della vita* (1956; Eng. tr., *The House of Life*, 1964), a lyrical catalogue of the contents of Praz's apartment in the Palazzo Ricci, Rome, from the 1930s to the 1960s, is the most complete expression of Praz the man and the passionate, learned collector of Empire and Regency art. *Mnemosyne: The Parallel between Literature and the Visual Arts* (1970), the Andrew W. Mellon Lectures in the Fine Arts delivered by Praz in Washington in 1967, sums up the author's lifelong interest in these correlations. *Mnemosyne* was written in English, as were some of the essays in *The Flaming Heart*.

Praz's detailed and affectionate knowledge of Rome is distilled in *Panopticon romano* (1967), while the four volumes of *Cronache letterarie anglosassoni* (1951, 1966; Anglo-Saxon Literary Chronicles) gather some of his valuable essays on Anglo-American subjects. Praz has also translated works by Charles Lamb, Walter Pater, George

Moore, and T. S. Eliot. He has contributed to the *Enciclopedia italiana* and has served as editor of *English Miscellany* since 1956.

See: V. Gabrieli, ed., *Friendship's Garland: Essays Presented to Mario Praz on His Seventieth Birthday* (1966).   S.Pa.

Preda, Marin (1922–), Romanian novelist, short-story writer, and essayist, was born into a large peasant family in Siliştea-Gumeşti on the Bărăgan plain. He attended secondary school in Bucharest, where he became a journalist after 1941.

Preda joined the literary circle of the journal *Sburătorul* in 1942 and began to write realistic stories about contemporary peasant life. Eight of them were published under the title *Întîlnirea din pămînturi* (1948; Encounter in the Fields). In his candidly realistic other works, as well, Preda creates portrayals of the changing social system, and he is sensitive to the moral dilemmas and the human need for values within this system. The stories "Defăşurarea" (1952; Eng. tr., "In a Village," 1956), "Ferestre întunecate" (1956; Darkened Windows), and the masterful novel *Moromeţii* (part 1, 1955; part 2, 1967; Eng. tr. of part 1, *The Morometes*, 1957), reveal a developing analytical skill and a deepening understanding of peasant psychology. The novels *Ana Roşculeţ* (1949) and *Risipitorii* (1962; rev. 1965, 1970, 1972; The Squanderers) turn to the problems of contemporary urban life. Preda's preoccupation with ethical issues is intensified in *Intrusul* (1968; The Intruder) and *Marele singuratic* (1972; The Great Lonely One). He aroused controversy at home and abroad, however, with *Delirul* (1975; Delirium), an attempt to portray objectively the Antonescu era (1940–44).

Preda has enriched Romanian literature with a body of memorable characters such as the mischievous, generous Paţanghel from "O adunare liniştită" (1948; A Quiet Meeting), Anton Modan in *Îndrăzneala* (1959; excerpted in Eng. tr., "Darling," 1966), and Ilie Moromete. *Imposibila întoarcere* (1971, rev. 1972; There Is No Turning Back) is a collection of philosophically contemplative, sometimes reminiscent essays. Preda is also the author of a play, *Martin Bormann* (1966). A moderate usually removed from politics, he has recently become a spokesman for literary integrity. He has also recently been a vice-president of the Writers Union.

See: J. Steinberg, *Introduction to Rumanian Literature* (1966), pp. 299–313; M. Ungheanu, *Marin Preda: vocaţie şi aspiraţie* (1973); I. Balu, *Marin Preda* (1976).
T.A.P.

Pregelj, Ivan (1883–1960), Slovenian writer, was born into the family of a tailor near Tolmin. He studied Slavic literature in Vienna and later taught in secondary schools. He is considered the leading representative of Slovenian expressionistic prose (*see* SLOVENIAN LITERATURE).

Pregelj's literary career is remarkable for the variety as well as the quality of his work. He made contributions to poetry, drama, essays, criticism, philology, and the theory and history of literature; he was active as an editor and translator; and he was, above all, an original and outstanding writer of prose fiction. He treated contemporary themes in the novels *Mlada Breda* (1913; Young Breda), *Otroci sonca* (1919; Children of the Sun), *Oče, budi tvoja volja!* (1926; Father, Thy Will Be Done!), and *Umreti nočejo* (1930; They Do Not Want to Die). He also wrote historical novels, often set in the period of the Reformation and Counter-Reformation, and these include some of his most outstanding works, notably *Tlačani* (1915–16; The Serfs), *Zadnji upornik* (1918–19; The Last Rebel), *Plebanus Joannes* (1921), *Bogovec Jernej* (1923;

Bartholomew the Theologian), *Zgodbe zdravnika Muznika* (vol. 1, 1923; vol. 2, 1929; The Adventures of the Physician Muznik), and *Magister Anton* (1929–30).

The most frequent theme in Pregelj's work is the dichotomy between the sensual and spiritual elements of man's inner world. But whether he is concerned with this polarity or with social questions, his approach is that of a committed Catholic, viewing the human condition from the standpoint of Catholic morality. Pregelj's themes and ideas as well as the purely formal qualities of his art place his works among the classics of Slovenian literature. The distinctive features of his writing altered the whole course of Slovenian prose. The most complete edition of his works is *Izbrani spisi* (vols. 1–10, Ljubljana, 1928–35), and volume 11, *Moj svet in moj čas*, ed. by T. Debeljak (Buenos Aires, 1954).

See: T. Debeljak, "Opombe z življenjem in delam," in I. Pregelj, *Izbrani spisi,* vol. 11 (Buenos Aires, 1954), pp. 279–339.   J.P. with W.B.E.

Prévert, Jacques (1900–77), French screenwriter and poet, was born in Neuilly-sur-Seine to a Breton father and an Auvergnat mother. He attended Parisian schools where, according to himself, he did badly. By the time he was 15 he was working in a store on the Rue de Rennes. After holding various odd jobs, he entered the army (1920) where he met Yves Tanguy and Marcel Duhamel. Subsequently the three, together with Jacques's brother Pierre, rented a house on the Rue du Château, near Montparnasse. Prévert and his friends took part in surrealist activities and spent much of their time going to the movies. In 1928, André BRETON expelled Prévert from the surrealist group.

Prévert's first published writings, "Souvenirs de famille ou l'ange garde-chiourme" (1930; Family Recollections of the Jail-Keeper Angel) in *Bifur* and "Tentative de description d'un dîner de têtes à Paris-France" (1931) in *Commerce,* reflect surrealist notions. It was also at this time that he began working with films and theater. Prévert wrote his first script, "L'Affaire est dans le sac" (1932; It's in the Bag) for his brother, Pierre. He became involved with the *groupe Octobre* (1932) and its "théâtre social," wrote for the troupe (notably "La Famille Tuyau de Poêle" [The Stovepipe Family] and "Le Tableau des merveilles" [The Picture of Marvels]), acted in its plays, and accompanied it to Moscow (1933), where he directed his own "La Bataille de Fontenoy" (The Battle of Fontenoy). Increasingly, however, Prévert concentrated on the movies. Significant films for which he wrote scripts between 1935 and 1946 include *Le Crime de M. Lange* (1935), directed by Jean Renoir; *Adieu, Léonard* (1943), directed by Pierre Prévert; and the documentary *Aubervilliers* (1945), directed by Eli Lotar. His most successful collaboration was with the director Marcel Carné, starting with *Drôle de drame* (1937; Crazy Drama) and *Le Quai des brumes* (1938; Quay of the Mists) and ending with his own favorite, *Les Enfants du paradis* (1943–44; Children of Paradise), which has become a classic, and *Les Portes de la nuit* (1946; The Gates of Night).

After World War II, Prévert became all the rage in the nightclubs and cafés of Saint-Germain-des Prés. Many of his poems, as well as short plays like "Branle-bas de combat" (1949; Clearing for Action), a satire of war movies, were, according to Raymond QUENEAU, directed toward the same youthful audience that listened to Jean-Paul SARTRE in the café Flore. Among the interpreters of his jazzy, sweet songs, those that come nearest to evoking his unique bridging of the gap between the dramatic and the lyric are probably Juliette Greco and Les Frères Jacques. In 1948, as a result of a bad concussion, Prévert abruptly withdrew from the world of cinema and nightclubs; thereafter he turned increasingly to poetry. As a poet, he had already been discovered, in a sense, by René Bertelé, who undertook the vast job of editing Prévert's first book of poetry, the best-seller *Paroles* (1946; Words), and who remained his editor. A first version of *Histoires,* in collaboration with André Verdet, appeared that same year. There followed, among other works, *Spectacle* (1951), *La Pluie et le beau temps* (1955; Good Weather and Bad), and *Fatras* (1966; Rubbish), which contains reproductions in black and white of Prévert's vivid collages (exhibited in 1957 at the Adrien Maeght Gallery). At the same time, he wrote children's books (a genre that he took seriously), illustrated by artists and the photographers Ylla and Izis. In 1964, *Les Chiens ont soif* (The Dogs Are Athirst) first appeared, as a "livre de peintre" with etchings and lithographs by Max Ernst.

Prévert reflected in his songs and dialogues the various fevers of his age, from flirtations with the unconscious to apprehensions of the absurd. At the same time, he provided a healthy contrast to more pessimistic French artists. His humorous fantasy seems to spring from an ear for word games and an optimistic, if sharp, awareness of flaws in the social order. Satire is his element and puns are his hallmark, in the post-Freudian era that legitimized the pun. Above all, a deceptive simplicity characterizes Prévert's affirmation of love and his undermining of such bourgeois institutions as the Pope, Descartes, and human will. Although a minor figure who never reached the heights of his friend Henri Michaux, Prévert has a recognized place in the history of films, and he remains the writer who in his day was the most read and the most sung, the most "popular" of living poets, in the full sense of the word.

See: "Jacques Prévert," special no. of *PrP* 14 (November 1960); W. E. Baker, *Jacques Prévert* (1967); A. H. Greet, *Jacques Prévert's Word Games* (1968); A. Thirion, "La Rue du Château en 1927," in *Révolution sans révolutionnaires* (1972); J. Sadeler, *A travers Prévert* (1975). A.H.G.

Prévost, Jean (1901–44), French essayist and novelist, attended the Lycée Henri IV in Paris, where he studied under ALAIN, whose disciple he remained. In 1919, Prévost entered the Ecole Normale Supérieure and the Ecole des Langues Orientales Vivantes. Jacques RIVIÈRE welcomed him in 1924 to the *Nouvelle Revue française.* In 1925, Prévost published "Tentative de solitude" (Attempt at Solitude), a short essay in which he attempted to carry isolation and self-analysis to the extreme. The same year, he wrote *Plaisirs de sports* (Pleasures of Sports) which consists of a series of analyses of internal sensations and of the movements of the human body. In his *Essai sur l'introspection* (1927; Essay on Introspection), he described a series of intellectual and emotional states commonly believed to be spiritual, in which respect he seemed to adhere to Baruch Spinoza's doctrine. Besides a rather inadequate *Vie de Montaigne* (1926; Life of Montaigne), which is in the nature of an educational pamphlet, Prévost also published in 1926 *Brûlures de la prière* (Burns of Prayer), the fictional diary of a mystic. As editorial secretary on the *Navire d'argent* from 1925 to 1926, and then on the staff of the magazine *Europe,* he contributed philosophical essays to those reviews. A novel, *Merlin,* was published in 1928. *Polymnie* (1929) described with almost excessive minuteness the facial and nasal movements of movie actors. The same year also saw the appearance of *Dix-huitième Année* (18th Year), a volume of Prévost's boyhood recollections, which reflects the spirit of his generation. His novel *Les Frères*

Bouquinquant (1930; The Bouquinquant Brothers) is considered by many critics as one of the best representations of "populist" literature.

Prévost also wrote essays such as *Les Epicuriens français* (1931; The French Epicureans); works of history, such as *Histoire de France depuis la guerre* (1932; History of France since the War); short stories, such as those collected in *Nous marchons sur la mer* (1931; We Walk on the Sea) and *Lucie-Paulette* (1935); intelligent but hasty novels, such as *Rachel* (1932), *Le Sel sur la plaie* (1935; Salt in the Wound), and *La Chasse du matin* (1937; The Morning Hunt); and a volume about American civilization, *Usonie* (1939).

A member of the fighting forces of the Resistance, Prévost fell in the maquis of Vercors in 1944. P.Br.

Prežihov, Voranc, pseud. of Lovro Kuhar (1893–1950), Slovenian novelist, was born into a poor peasant family in Carinthia. After a haphazard education, Prežihov was caught up in World War I and drafted into the Austrian army, from which he escaped in 1916 to Italy in a vain attempt to enlist against the Austrians. In 1920 he joined the Communist Party and for the rest of his life devoted himself to a dual career as a professional revolutionary and as a writer of politically oriented fiction. In 1930 he escaped arrest by fleeing abroad, where he continued his revolutionary activities. At the outbreak of World War II in 1939, he returned secretly to Slovenia. He was arrested in 1943 and spent the rest of the war years in various German concentration camps. After the war he returned to Yugoslavia, occupying a position of honor in the cultural and political life of the new state until his death in 1950.

Among the literary influences upon Prežihov's work, Yugoslav critics have called particular attention to the great Russian writers, notably Lev TOLSTOY, Fyodor DOSTOYEVSKY, and Maksim GORKY, and to his fellow Slovene Ivan CANKAR. In his narrative technique, his themes, and his ideological commitment, Prežihov stands firmly in the tradition of realism, and indeed is reminiscent of Gorky. He began his career as a writer of short stories, drawing his materials almost entirely from the Slovenian peasant society in which he had grown up. Toward the end of the 1930s, his career took a new turn with the novels *Doberdob* (1940) and *Jamnica* (written 1941, published 1946), in which he examined the political and social dilemmas confronting the Slovenes during the early part of the 20th century. After World War II, Prežihov published two books of memoirs, *Borba na tujih tleh* (1946; The Fight on Foreign Soil), which deals with his experiences in various foreign countries as a Communist activist, and *Naši mejniki* (1946; Our Landmarks), which describes the wartime struggle of the Slovenes to regain their national territory. His last published work, *Solzice* (1949; Lily of the Valley), is a poetic evocation of the Slovenian countryside in the form of lyrical reminiscences.

See: S. Janež, *Istorija slovenačke književnosti* (1959), pp. 413–22; M. Boršnik, "Prežihov Vorance," in *Studije in fragmenti* (1962), pp. 335–58. W.B.E. and A.K.

Prezzolini, Giuseppe (1882–), Italian essayist, critic, and journalist, was born in Perugia. He was self-educated. While in Paris in 1902, he was strongly influenced by Henri BERGSON's philosophy, which, combined with the ideas of Novalis, Giovanni GENTILE, and William James, helped to foster the extreme subjectivism that Prezzolini advocated from the pages of *Leonardo,* a journal that he launched with Giovanni PAPINI in 1903 to combat determinist positivism. In the next few years, Prezzolini also contributed to other reviews and published many eclectic works of philosophical, social, or educational import, notably *Il linguaggio come causa d'errore* (1904; Language as a Cause of Error); *La cultura italiana* (1906; Italian Culture), written with Papini to attack the Italian cultural establishment; *L'arte di persuadere* (1907; The Art of Persuasion), a paradoxical defense of Machiavellian lying; and *Benedetto Croce* (1909), a brilliant essay on the Neapolitan thinker whose ideas, largely nurtured by Giambattista Vico and G. W. F. Hegel, made for a more concretely historical approach to the problems of knowledge and life than Prezzolini had initially envisaged. Together with a later study on Papini (1915) and two essays on the statesmen Giovanni Amendola and Benito Mussolini, the essay on CROCE was reissued as a book under the title *Quattro scoperte* (1964; Four Discoveries). Divergent as they were, Croce and Papini brought out the best in Prezzolini's literary talent: provocativeness, discrimination, empathy, and lucid concision—all of which made him an effective propagandist of culture and a superb editor.

Crocean thought played its part in *La voce*, a new joint venture by Papini and Prezzolini. This Florentine periodical was to leave an indelible mark on the Italian cultural scene. Prezzolini's editorship (from 1908 to 1913) gathered around *La voce* the new forces of the Italian intelligentsia while also attracting important contributions and reactions from abroad. In this journal, social, political, and educational issues were pragmatically debated, while new poets found an outlet for their work. The scope of that pioneering forum can now be judged from Prezzolini's *Il tempo della "Voce"* (1960; The Time of *La voce*), a collection of editorial correspondence from a great variety of sources; *Storia di un'amicizia*, (2 vols., 1966, 1968; History of a Friendship), which documents the planning and editing phase of the journal through the exchange of letters between Papini and Prezzolini; and *La voce 1908-1913: cronaca, antologia e fortuna di una rivista* (1974; *La voce* 1908-1913, Chronicle, Anthology and Fortune of a Magazine) by Prezzolini and Emilio Gentile, which provides invaluable extracts, collateral material, and commentary.

After serving in World War I, Prezzolini revived the name *La voce* as that of a book publishing outfit. He then acted as correspondent for an American press agency and helped to promote international intellectual cooperation in the framework of the League of Nations. From 1930 to 1950 he taught Italian literature at Columbia University; in 1961 he returned to Italy and a few years later moved to Lugano, Switzerland. He has since kept up his prolific activity as a writer with typical polemical zest. His latter-day conservatism has made him a controversial figure, especially in view of his detached but far from negative attitude toward fascism. Among his many books are *Repertorio bibliografico della storia e della critica della letteratura italiana* (1937-39, 1942; Bibliographical Repertory of the History and Criticism of Italian Literature); *The Legacy of Italy* (1948; Ital. tr., 1959); *L'italiano inutile* (1953; The Useless Italian), an autobiographical essay; *Machiavelli anticristo* (1954; Machiavelli Antichrist); *I trapiantati* (1963; The Transplanted), a skeptical view of Italian emigration to the United States; and *Ideario* (1967; Dictionary of Ideas), an anthology of self-quotations in a strikingly Voltairean spirit.

See: W. Binni, in *Critici e poeti dal Cinquecento al Novecento* (1951); *FLe* (July 1955); A. Romanò, in *Antologia della "Voce"* (1960); G. Cambon, "Two Friendships," *Umanesimo* (November 1966); E. Gentile et al., *Prezzolini 70* (1971); A. Mazzotti, in *Letteratura italiana: i contemporanei* vol. 1 (1975), pp. 397-429.   G.C.

Prieto, Antonio (1930-), Spanish novelist and critic, was born in Almería. Although he first took up medicine, he completed his studies in Renaissance literature. He has taught at universities in Spain and Italy and is much involved in the publishing world. He is the author of *Morfología de la novela* (1975) and other essays. He first attracted attention with *Tres pisadas de hombre* (1955; Three Men's Footsteps), which won the Planeta Prize. With the same multiple perspective technique that characterizes his earlier work, he produced a testimonial novel entitled *Buenas noches, Argüelles* (1956). Thereafter he departed from the social realism in vogue in the 1950s and turned to more intellectual and transcendent concerns. The attitudes of man toward universals like love and, especially, death are now expressed in allegorical-symbolic form. To that end he turns repeatedly to mythical or literary correlatives that are, nevertheless, elaborated in a geography identifiable with the author's native land. *Vuelve atrás, Lázaro* (1958; Go Back, Lazarus) blends the Gospel story with the return to Ithaca of Homer's Odysseus; *Encuentro con Ilitia* (1961; Meeting with Ilythia) brings together the myth of the eternal return with that of the Fates; and *Elegía por una esperanza* (1962; Elegy for a Hope) links the Homeric episode of Nausicaä with the abduction of Europa and the *Ninfale fiesolano* of Boccaccio. After *Prólogo a una muerte* (1965; Prologue to a Death) came a work of marked Petrarchan resonance, *Secretum* (1972), and *Carta sin tiempo* (1975; Timeless Letter), written in the form of a critical edition of a treatise on love by an anonymous Spaniard of the Renaissance. All in all, Prieto's fascinating but difficult symbiosis of everyday realities and timeless symbols has not been achieved with complete success.

See: G. Sobejano, *Novela española de nuestro tiempo* (1975), pp. 485-88.   D.V.

Prisco, Michele (1920-), Italian novelist, was born in Torre Annunziata. Shortly after receiving a degree in law, Prisco turned exclusively to literature, publishing his first stories in *La lettura* and *Gazzetta del popolo* when he was 20. Essentially a realist and a regionalist, he conforms, however, to no particular school or trend. His novels remain rather in the 19th-century tradition, carefully structured stories, leisurely recounted in ample detail. In the last decade his work has shifted gradually from a focus on southern Italy to a more general view of man; with this shift he has become increasingly involved in psychological and moral speculation.

Winner of the Strega and Venezia Prizes, Prisco has enjoyed a greater reputation at home than abroad. His better-known works include: *La provincia addormentata* (1949; The Slumbering Province), *Gli eredi del vento* (1950; Eng. tr., *Heirs of the Wind*, 1953), *Figli difficili* (1954; Troublesome Children), *La dama di piazza* (1961; Lady of the Square), *Una spirale di nebbia* (1966; Eng. tr., *A Spiral of Mist*, 1969), *I cieli della sera* (1970; Evening Skies), and *Gli ermellini neri* (1976; The Black Ermines).

See: P. Giannantonio, *Invito alla lettura di Prisco* (1977).   G.P.O.

Prishvin, Mikhail Mikhaylovich (1873-1954), Russian novelist, ethnographer, and naturalist, was born near Yelets into an impoverished merchant family. He was expelled from high school because of impudence to a teacher, the writer Vasily ROZANOV. He later studied at the Riga Polytechnic Institute (1893-97), was imprisoned and exiled for revolutionary activity, and graduated from Leipzig University in agronomy in 1902. While working in this field and writing for Petersburg newspapers, he was encouraged by the ethnographers and folklorists N. E. Onchukov and A. A. Shakhmatov to collect popular epic poetry and folktales. Traveling through northern Russia, Norway, and later Kazakhstan, he artfully cast his observations of nature, customs, habits, speech, and tales into travel sketches, and was elected to the Imperial Geographic Society. His volumes of travel sketches include *V krayu nepuganykh ptits* (1907; In the Land of Unfrightened Birds), *Za volshebnym kolobkom* (1908; Follow the Magical Loaf), *U sten grada nevidimogo* (1909; At the Walls of the Invisible City), and "Chorny arab" (1910; Eng. tr. in *The Black Arab and Other Stories*, 1947). The folkloric tradition, *skaz* narration, attention to provincial Russian *byt*, mixture of dream and reality, and masterful style of his stories "Krutoyarskiy zver" (1911; The Beast of Krutoyarsk), "Ptichye kladbishche" (1911; The Cemetery of Birds), "Nikon Starokolenny" (1912), and "Ivan Oslyanchik" (1912) were inspired by Aleksey REMIZOV.

Prishvin's autobiographical novel *Kashcheyeva tsep* (1923–60; The Chain of Kashchey), on which he worked for more than 30 years, depicts the author's philosophic and moral quest. *Zhuravlinaya rodina* (1929; Crane's Birthplace) focuses on the artist's creative process. Prishvin also wrote hunting and phenological sketches collected in *Rodniki Berendeya* (1925–26; Springs of Berendey), which was later expanded as *Kalendar prirody* (1937; Eng. tr., *The Lake and the Woods*, 1952, and *Nature's Diary*, 1958). His tale, *Zhen-shen* (1933; Eng. tr., *Jen Sheng: The Root of Life*, 1936), best exemplifies his basic principle of "seeing man's soul in nature's images." He perfected miniature prose poems—*Lesnaya kapel* (1940; Forest Drip-Drop)—and unique combinations of folktales with observations of nature—*Kladovaya solntsa* (1945; Eng. tr., *The Treasure Trove of the Sun*, 1952, and *The Sun's Storehouse*, 1956) and *Korabelnaya chashcha* (1954; Eng. tr., *Shiptimber Grove*, 1957). His delightful sense of humor, joy of constant discovery, love of nature, keen observation, and fine style have earned him a unique position in Soviet Russian literature.

See: T. Khmelnitskaya, *Tvorchestvo Mikhaila Prishvina* (1959); M. Slonim, *Soviet Russian Literature: Writers and Problems, 1917–1977* (2d rev. ed. 1977), pp. 109–15.   A.M.S.

Proust, Marcel (1871–1922), French novelist, essayist, and critic, was born in the Paris suburb of Auteuil. On his father's side he was a descendant of a middle-class family established as early as the 16th century in the town of Illiers, near Chartres. His father, Adrien Proust, had a brilliant career in medicine and governmental service as a professor of hygiene, member of the Academy of Medicine, and inspector general of sanitary services. His mother, born Jeanne Weil into a wealthy Jewish family, was a highly educated woman of sterling character and keen intellect. She was a grand-niece of Adolphe Crémieux, a prominent lawyer, cabinet minister, and senator. Marcel Proust, born July 10, was the elder of two sons. When nine years of age, he suffered his first severe attack of asthma, an ailment whose organic and psychological effects were to darken the rest of his life. Marcel was a precocious child, neurotic, hypersensitive, avid of affection and companionship, having a lively sense of humor, fervent for the beauties of nature and the fine arts. While attending the Lycée Condorcet (1882–89), he displayed a marked inclination toward literature, philosophy, history, and botany. Despite frequent absences due to illness, he took his bachelor's degree with honors. A year of military service at Orléans provided him with the benefits of an orderly, disciplined life, and impressions that he later would transcribe in the Doncières episode of

his novel. Vacations spent at Illiers and at his maternal grand-uncle's country estate in Auteuil would be the models for the Combray of his novel.

Proust took degrees in law and philosophy at the Sorbonne and began to move in Paris society, meeting artists, writers, and aristocrats in the salons of Mme Emile Straus (Bizet's widow), Mme Arman de Caillavet, Mme Madeleine Lemaire, and Mme Aubernon. During the same period, he published his first essays in *Le Banquet,* a privately printed monthly that he founded with Fernand Gregh and other friends. Proust collected these sketches, together with poems and short stories, to make his first book, *Les Plaisirs et les jours* (1896; Eng. tr., *Pleasures and Regrets,* 1948). Anatole FRANCE, who took a fatherly interest in him, signed the preface, while Madeleine Lemaire illustrated the volume. Issued only in a deluxe edition, it failed to reach the general public. André GIDE later expressed astonishment that the young author's genius had not immediately been apprehended in this volume. He was unaware that its qualities had at once been recognized by such critics as Charles MAURRAS and Léon BLUM.

In the previous year, Proust had begun writing a sort of autobiographical novel, later published as *Jean Santeuil* (1952, 1971; Eng. tr., 1955), but he had neglected to make adequate plans for its plot and structure. As a result, he accumulated a vast number of episodes recounting his hero's experiences without sequence or unity. When the Dreyfus Affair was at its height, Proust took an active part by gathering signatures for petitions. He also added several chapters to his novel, chronicling some of its events. Finally, after four years' work, he abandoned the project, despairing of imposing order and unity on it. The sacrifice, however, was only temporary: most of the ideas, themes, and even some episodes were to find expression in his great work (later, for instance, he would examine the effects of the Dreyfus Affair on certain of his characters). In 1899 he began his studies and translations of John Ruskin, for whom he had unbounded admiration. Knowing no English, he had to rely on his mother to translate for him, while he reworked the text, writing his own annotations and prefaces. He completed *The Bible of Amiens* in 1904 and *Sesame and Lilies* in 1906. Proust's work on Ruskin impelled him to make two trips to Venice in 1900, enriching his knowledge of art and providing impressions that would serve him later for the splendid evocation of that city in *Albertine disparue.*

The death of his father (1903), and of his mother (1905), whom he worshiped, disrupted his life for some time. But he set to work again in 1907, after a sojourn at Cabourg, on the Channel coast, where he once had stayed with his beloved maternal grandmother, whose portrait—like that of his mother—adorns his novel. There he would return each summer to enrich his experience of nature and of the people he met, all to be transposed later to the Balbec of his novel. Early in 1908, the editor of the newspaper *Le Figaro* asked Proust to write about Lemoine, a swindler arrested for selling a spurious formula for manufacturing synthetic diamonds. Proust wrote a hilarious series of sketches on the affair in the style of such writers as Honoré de Balzac, Gustave Flaubert, Charles-Augustin Sainte-Beuve, the Goncourts, and Louis Saint-Simon. Maurice BARRÈS complimented Proust on having found a new form of literary criticism, but no publisher was willing to accept the series.

After some false starts, Proust set the plan for his novel and began writing in earnest. Within a few months, he had established the work's basic structure by writing its first and its last chapters. The same editor of *Le Figaro* offered to publish the novel serially, but a misunderstanding caused the plan to miscarry. So Proust pursued his "architectural" labors, as he called them, until his first 700 pages were ready in typescript, the remainder in manuscript. After four publishing houses had rejected it, he contracted to have it published, at his own expense, under the general title *A la recherche du temps perdu (Remembrance of Things Past)*. Reluctantly, he allowed it to be divided into several volumes under separate titles. The first, *Du côté de chez Swann* (1913; Eng. tr., *Swann's Way*, 1922), came out shortly before the outbreak of World War I. Once it had appeared in print, its success was modest but certain, for it went through several printings within a few months. Gide, who had been largely responsible for the novel's rejection by the *Nouvelle Revue française*, at once made an offer to publish the remainder of the book. The outbreak of war gave Proust an opportunity to rework some portions of his novel, such as Albertine's death (partly inspired by that of Alfred Agostinelli, whom Proust had met at Cabourg) and some episodes showing the effects of wartime on certain characters and on society in general. After the war, his second volume, *A l'ombre des jeunes filles en fleurs* (1919; Eng. tr., *Within a Budding Grove*, 1924), finally appeared. It won the Goncourt Prize and made Proust famous. This installment was followed by *Le Côté de Guermantes I* (1920; Eng. tr., *The Guermantes' Way*, 1922), then part II together with *Sodome et Gomorrhe I* (1921; Eng. tr., *Cities of the Plain*, 1927). The last volume to appear during Proust's lifetime was *Sodome et Gomorrhe II* (1922). Unable to correct proof for these volumes, he devoted his last efforts to preparing the next part. The posthumous volumes of the works are *La Prisonnière* (1923; Eng. tr., *The Captive*, 1929); *Albertine disparue* (1925; Eng. tr., *The Sweet Cheat Gone*, 1930), also called *La Fugitive*; and *Le Temps retrouvé* (1927; Eng. tr., *Time Regained*, 1931), the only part not translated into English by C. Scott Moncrieff (two other different translations bear the title *The Past Recaptured*).

Proust's *A la recherche du temps perdu* marks the greatest innovation in French novelistic technique of the 20th century. Although he was steeped in the literary art of his predecessors, Proust broke with all traditions of the so-called classic French novel to create a type that is original in form and content. Its structure is based in part on the symmetry of certain sections and on a system of interlocking themes, metaphors, and other unifying elements. For instance, the opening pages, where Proust presents his principal themes, characters, and places, have as a counterpart the final chapter of the entire novel, "Matinée chez la princesse de Guermantes," just as the chapter entitled "Combray" is in parallel with the beginning of *Le Temps retrouvé*. The denouement of the work occurs when the narrator discovers his vocation, the quest for which has motivated his peregrinations; he thereupon states the aesthetic principles that will guide him in writing the novel that the reader is about to finish, and he explains some of its mysteries. So the novel's ending leads to its beginning.

Taking as his principal theme "that invisible substance called time," Proust attempts to give the reader a vivid impression of its passage as it unfolds in the lives of his main characters. He intends to show the transformation he observes in late 19th-century society, disrupted successively by the Dreyfus Affair and by the war of 1914, finally leading to a fusion of the aristocracy and the bourgeoisie. These two social entities are designated by the titles of two volumes: *Swann's Way* and *The Guermantes' Way*. The narrator will evoke his past life through the phenomenon of involuntary memory (memory being an important theme). Proust rejects voluntary memory in favor of recollections born of sensory impressions; thus his past life as a child in Combray is revived through the taste of a madeleine cake dipped in a cup of tea.

Another of the novel's themes is "le moi multiple" (the multiple ego). This theme is demonstrated "in action" by means of a technique that Proust devised for the presentation of some of his principal characters. He calls them his "prepared" characters because the narrator's first impressions of them may be contradicted by later ones. Proust seems to be misleading us by the surprises he had prepared for us, but in fact he is simply imitating life instead of following the simplistic logic of traditional fiction. One example is Vinteuil. Swann and his other neighbors at Combray suppose him to be insignificant, a painfully timid, modest piano teacher. No one suspects that he is a great composer whose music would later reveal his inner nature to have been bold and vigorous. This technique of character presentation lends itself particularly well to Proust's portrayal of homosexuals (who represent one facet of the theme of love), notably Baron de Charlus, a member of the Guermantes clan, who is partly modeled on Count Robert de MONTESQUIOU-FEZENSAC. Some early critics, disconcerted by such characters, called them "illogical," forgetting about Fyodor DOSTOYEVSKY's characters and failing to comprehend an innovation demonstrating the complexity of human nature. This technique was, in fact, a transposition into novelistic terms of objectives embodied in a critical essay Proust had undertaken before he began his novel. His purpose had been to attack the validity of the method originated by Sainte-Beuve, the famous literary critic who had sought to understand writers by investigating their heredity and environment, but who had nevertheless underestimated the greatest poets and novelists of his time. Proust, claiming that "a book is the product of another self than the one which we manifest in our habits, in society, in our vices," accused the critic of having confused the writer with the man. We know from Proust's correspondence, however, that he was as curious as Sainte-Beuve about the private life of creative artists. This discrepancy between Proust's theory and his practice perhaps discloses a desire to hide his own personal foibles. If he abandoned his critical essay, it was doubtless because he had found a way of amalgamating its aims in his novel, chiefly through his presentation of characters. In *A la recherche*, instead of attacking Sainte-Beuve, he widens his angle of vision to apply it to humanity in general. Thus he makes clear, in the case of Vinteuil, Charlus, and others, how easy it is to misjudge people in society, just as Sainte-Beuve had done in literature (*Contre Sainte-Beuve*, 1954; Eng. tr., *On Art and Literature, 1896–1919*, 1958, originally presented by B. de Fallois as the critical essay, although it appears in part to embody an early version of the novel).

Proust is outstanding in his masterful use of dialogue. The language of each individual reflects an intellectual and social level as well as the inner psyche. He is also one of the great stylists of French prose. His versatility is noteworthy especially in the use of syntax and metaphor. His use of linked imagery (for example, the water imagery associated with Guermantes' Way, the "mountains of the sea" associated with Albertine) has a structural value having the effect of a leitmotiv. Much of the charm of his manner is due to the poetic use of metaphor to evoke the beauties of nature, and to the humor that permeates most of the novel.

At first, the action of the novel seems to lag, or to be lacking, because the narrator tells of a world seen through the eyes of a child. Gradually the rhythm accelerates, bringing a sequence of surprises and dramatic incidents.

The novel's unity discloses itself in a myriad of hidden devices that enhance the beauty of the whole. Although the plot consists of the narrator's quest for his true vocation, he recounts only the pivotal events in his life. Yet he tells them with a fully scientific precision. His purpose is to show how apparently insignificant details can have their importance, and how complex life really is. He pretends to no omniscience and draws no conclusions, at least until the end. He prefers to allow his readers to judge for themselves, and, in a sense, to be the readers of themselves. Like an oculist, he simply offers them a lens to help them to read. In telling his life's adventures, he is in fact seeking to fathom the nature of friendship, of love, of happiness, attempting to determine the "laws" that govern human conduct. Nor does he neglect to consider the enigmas of sickness, death, and the afterlife. While he follows no dogma, his reflections are imbued with a deep religious sentiment. Ultimately, he turns toward artistic creativity, deeming it to be the highest order of human endeavor.

Proust's masterpiece has had a profound influence on world literature. Indebtedness to him has been recognized by Virginia Woolf, John Cowper Powys, and Lawrence Durrell in England; by Edith Wharton and Thomas Wolfe in the United States; by Robert MUSIL in Austria; by Azorín in Spain; by the surrealists, Jean-Paul SARTRE, and the "new novelists" in France (see FRENCH LITERATURE); and by writers in many of the countries of Latin America, in Japan, and elsewhere.

See: A. Maurois, *Portrait of a Genius* (1950); J. M. Cocking, *Proust* (1956); D. Painter, *Proust: The Early Years* (1959) and *Proust: The Later Years* (1965); G. Brée, *The World of Marcel Proust* (1966); H. Peyre, *Marcel Proust* (1970); J. Y. Tadié, *Proust et le roman* (1971); P. Kolb, "Proust (Marcel) 1871–1922," in *Encyclopaedia Universalis,* vol. 13, pp. 713–17.   P.K.

Provençal literature, modern. Modern Provençal literature is the literature that has been written and published in the various dialects of southern France during the last 150 years.

Modern Provençal should not be confused with Old Provençal, the literary language of the troubadours of the 12th and 13th centuries, which was known at first as the "Langue d'Oc." This appellation derived from the fact that "Oc" (Latin *Oc*) was the term used in all the romance dialects of the South to express affirmation and assent, as "Oïl" (Latin *hoc ille*) expressed it in the North. Besides "Langue d'Oc," the terms "Limousin," "Gascon," and "Provençal" were also used during different periods when referring to the Oc dialects viewed in the aggregate. Provençal, occasionally utilized by Dante and Petrarch, was to prevail, and it is still the term accepted by scholars in the United States and in most European countries. Attempts are now being made, however, especially in France, to limit its application to the dialects of Provence proper and to replace it by "Occitan" whenever the Oc dialects are considered as a whole—a debatable and widely debated question.

After the disappearance of the troubadours following the Albigensian Crusade (1201–29), the Langue d'Oc (Old Provençal or Occitan) degenerated into an indefinite number of patois, but the significant fact is that the dialects and subdialects themselves survived the disaster, and new generations of poets resorted to them, each generation writing in its own local or regional tongue and using its own system of spelling and orthography, if any. The result was that the greater number of these writers contributed more to the degradation of the vernacular than to its enrichment. But a few of them emerged, their

work to be saved from oblivion and appreciated by posterity. In the 16th century, the Béarnais Pey de Garros, who wrote in Gascon, the Toulousain Godolin (or Goudelin) and the Provençal Bellaud de la Bellaudière each had a lasting audience, and since then their works have been studied and often cited; in the 17th century, the Provençals Nicholas Saboli and Claude Brueys revealed themselves; in the 18th century, the Languedocian writer Abbé Favre may well have been the most popular Provençal poet of his time. In the first half of the 19th century lived the Gascon barber Jacques Boë, who wrote under the pen name Jasmin and who is regarded today as the most eminent precursor of the Provençal renaissance that developed toward the end of the romantic era.

Jasmin was not much concerned, however, with the purification of his mother tongue or the reviving of its literature, the very questions that stirred a group of poets from Avignon and vicinity into action. On May 21, 1854, these seven or eight enthusiasts formed a sort of pleiad and called themselves "Félibre"—a term of doubtful meaning and obscure origin—to distinguish themselves from the Marseilles modern "troubaire" and others who wanted to remain independent. Terms derived from "Félibre," such as "Félibrige," the name of the association, and "félibresso" (Provençal poetess), were later coined.

The three outstanding founders of the Félibrige, often referred to in French as "les primadiers," were Joseph ROUMANILLE, a minor poet but an active and clever organizer, Théodore AUBANEL, a great lyric poet whose fame keeps on increasing a century after his death, and Frédéric MISTRAL, whose first masterpiece insured the initial and lasting success of the movement. More details on their activities and accomplishments are found or suggested in the articles devoted to them in this volume, which contains also short articles on Felix GRAS and Joseph d'ARBAUD with remarks concerning the foundation, development, and evolution of this rather unique literary society that is still progressing after 125 years of existence.

The publication of Mistral's *Mirèio* in 1859 with the author's French translation on the opposite page, made the people of northern France in general, and the intellectuals and literary critics in particular, suddenly aware of a genuine Provençal language. The following year, while Roumanille's popular tales charmed the readers of the *Armana prouvençau*—the Provençal almanac that since 1855 has remained the official organ of the Félibrige, another amazing book, Aubanel's *La Miougrano entreduberte,* came out of the Avignonese press. Other works kept on appearing. When, years later, a new round of recognition for the language was won with Mistral's *Tresor dóu Félibrige* (1878–86), which is a monumental Provençal-French dictionary, the beauty, richness, and vitality of Provençal were never to be questioned again.

At first a purely linguistic and literary movement, the Félibrige, had acquired, as an organized group, a social and even political character because of its insistence on the principle of decentralisation. It was soon to encounter many difficulties, some of them created by its own members: personal frictions between individuals; petty local quarrels; conflicts of interests, ideas, and feelings between social and geographical bodies. Even attempts to revive the old North-South antagonism have occurred and may occur again, but the main issue has never been lost sight of by the leaders of the movement who have consistently insisted on the rehabilitation of the mother tongue through education in the French schools and its illustration in a wholesome and dignified literature.

The Félibrige reached the climax of its development

toward the end of the 19th century. By then, hundreds of works inspired by the group had appeared in the various regions of the Midi. The fact that a few of the authors had never been members of the association and some had left it does not deny nor decrease the importance and value of its influence. Nevertheless, by 1914, the year of Mistral's death, the movement appeared to have reached the end of its course. After World War I—in which the French elite had been decimated in every province—a rather large number of young writers set out to resume Mistral's work.

Every year since the 1920s, many anthologies of modern Provençal poetry, short stories, and selected pieces, as well as novels in the vernacular of the different regions, have been published in France. New Provençal plays are annually performed, and scholarly works on the great Provençal poets of the 19th century continually appear. In 1950 a law was passed allowing the teaching of dialects in elementary schools, and since that time new grammars, dictionaries, and selections of Provençal prose and poetry designed for classroom use have also been published, and the number of lycée and university students interested in Provençal has steadily increased. It may therefore be presumed that the founders of the Félibrige would be satisfied with the progress realized by their followers.

Regarded from a strictly literary point of view, the Provençal movement has developed considerably in the past 60 years. Poetry and the short story have always been the most popular forms of expression. For 50 years after the foundation of the Félibrige in 1854, the work of Provençal poets reflected the influence of French literature, particularly that of the romantic and Parnassian schools. The poetry was mostly descriptive, concerned with local color and picturesqueness. During the 20th century, however, Provençal poets became much more concerned with the great universal human problems. In addition, they evidenced more interest in lyricism, and with form and expression. This shift of emphasis, first evident in d'Arbaud's early poems, became marked in the work of the younger poets writing after World War II. It was encouraged by both the example and the teaching of Sully-André Peyre (1874–1961), who urged his admirers and "companions" (not "disciples") to be themselves and assert their originality. Most of the important Provençal authors—Mistral, Gras, d'Arbaud—have been masters of the short story, a form that has been popular since 1855, when Roumanille began publishing his facetious tales in the *Armana prouvençau* (Provençal Almanac). Twentieth-century practitioners of the form, however, tend to produce more sophisticated stories, which often lack the spontaneity and joy that mark Roumanille's and Mistral's *cascareleto* (facetious tales). The Provençal novel, which developed toward the end of the 19th century, is now a well-established genre. Although about half the novels currently published are of the romantic, sentimental kind, other types—historical, biographical, philosophical, psychological, regional, and social novels—are also available. The drama, especially comedy and farce, has always been a very popular form of entertainment in southern France. Except for the traditional "pastorale," however, serious drama has failed to attract a large audience. The languedocian Emile Barthe (1874–1939), whose comedy *Los Profichaires* (The Profiteers) had a long run during the interwar period, was the most popular Provençal playwright of his day. Another landuedocian of the same generation, François Dezeuze (1871–1949), is considered a master of the farce. It should be noted that a few important studies and critical essays in Provençal can be found in literary reviews such as *Lo Gai Saber* (The Gay Savoir), *Oc*, and *L'Astrado* (The

Bright Star). The most important single critical work by a Provençal writer is undoubtedly Charles Mauron's *Estùdi Mistralen* (1954; Essays on Frédéric Mistral), an original discussion of Mistral's subconscious sources. Mauron, well known throughout France, also applied his "psychocritique" to Stéphene MALLARMÉ, Nerval, and Jean Racine. The continued development of Provençal literature can be assured only if the various Provençal dialects are combined into a single literary language. And there are formidable obstacles to such an eventuality. To begin with, the average Frenchman believes that French should be the only national language, and he is not interested in dialects and subdialects. Also, the provincial dialects have disintegrated to a point beyond recovery, and thus any attempt to unite them would be foredoomed to failure. Finally, history has shown that it is utterly impossible for regional spokesmen to agree, not only on the choice of a dialect as a basis for a unified language, but also on the question of a common orthography for all the dialects involved. Yet, despite these difficulties talented Provençal writers appear with each new generation, eager to explore the beauties of modern Provençal. They may discover and perhaps create new ones, if the vernacular was their mother tongue and has remained their main source of inspiration.

See: G. Jourdanne, *Histoire du Félibrige, 1854–1896* (1897); E. Ripert, *La Renaissance provençale, 1800–1860* (1918); C. Camproux, *Histoire de la littérature occitane* (1953); A. V. Roche, *Provençal Regionalism* (1954); R. Jouveau, *Histoire du Félibrige, 1876–1914*, vol. 1 (1970) vol. 2, *1914–1941* (1977); R. Lafont and C. Anatole, *Nouvelle histoire de la littérature occitane* (1970); H. Marrou (Davenson), "Il n'y a jamais eu d'occitanie," *Esprit* (January 1975); 99–105.   A.V.R.

Prus, Bolesław, pseud. of Aleksander Głowacki (1847–1912), Polish novelist, was born in Hrubieszów and died in Warsaw. As a young man he took an active part in the Polish uprising against the Russians in 1863. Later he entered the University of Warsaw, became a journalist, and eventually became a major author. An ardent advocate of the positivist philosophy, in his journalistic writings and his fiction, he called for the economic betterment of his country, stressing the role of education and social progress as opposed to a narrow-minded conservatism and traditionalism. His first collections of short stories, published in the 1870s, as well as his short fiction, for example, "Kamizelka," (Eng. tr., "The Waistcoat," 1930), blending humor with sentimentalism and great compassion for underprivileged people, often served to illustrate his philosophy of life; soon, however, they also achieved an artistic level unmatched by contemporary fiction. Many of them were based on the exploration of childhood experiences and its psychology. His first novel, *Placówka* (1886; Eng. tr., *The Outpost,* 1921), presented in a realistic manner the problems facing the Polish peasants driven out of their native lands by the Prussian colonists and successfully combined the psychological, social, and political problems of the period. Although Prus's literary reputation was firmly established, it was not until the 1890s that he became a major Polish novelist with the publication of his contemporary novel *Lalka* (1890; Eng. tr., *The Doll,* 1972). Against the rich social background of the Warsaw of the late 1870s, he projected the personal conflict of the protagonist, whose efforts to advance himself socially were met by the prejudice, obscurantism, and intellectual backwardness of society, particularly its upper classes. Blending humor and irony with sharp social criticism in an interesting and well-maintained plot, Prus created the first major realistic novel in Polish literature, raising it to the level of the leading European fiction of that period. The novel has become a classic in Polish literature.

Although his next contemporary novel, *Emancypantki* (1893; The Emancipated Women), was largely a failure owing to its faulty composition—overdrawn characters, moralizing rather than acting, slow pace of the plot, satirical overtones, and so on—nevertheless, it showed Prus's awareness of one of the most acute contemporary problems of the femininist movement. He reestablished his reputation as a skillful novelist with the publication of his historical novel *Faraon* (1897; Eng. tr., *The Pharaoh and the Priest,* 1902), which under the disguise of a story from the ancient Egypt presented another contemporary problem, the power struggle between science and religion, education and obscurantism, thus becoming partly a modern political novel. The conflict between the pharaoh, enthusiastic and socially progressive but without political experience, and the established rulers of Egypt, the priests who possessed practical knowledge of politics and had mastered science, was presented in a colorful action novel, with well-sustained plot and well-developed historical background.

A master short-story teller, Prus often resorted to fiction in order to present some pressing issue, but he never abandoned his journalistic career and contributed his weekly column to the leading Warsaw newspapers. An impressive collected edition of his *Kroniki* (1956-70; Chronicles), comprising 20 volumes, represents an important source for the study of the social, economic, and political problems that Poland faced at the turn of the century. His columns revealed a master of the genre of the journalistic feuilleton and established it firmly in the Polish literary tradition.

Prus, together with his contemporaries Henryk SIEN-KIEWICZ and Eliza ORZESZKOWA, represents the highest achievements of Polish realistic fiction, and he can be regarded as one of the founders of modern Polish literature. Although his work still remains relatively unknown outside of his native country, his short stories and novels occupy a major place in Poland and have enjoyed popular appeal ever since they were published 100 years ago. Twenty-nine volumes of his works, *Pisma,* edited by Z. Szweykowski, have been published.

See: Z. Folejewski, "Turgenev and Prus," *SEER* 29 (1950): 132-38; K. Tokarzówna, S. Fita, *Kalendarz życia i twórczości* (1969); Z. Szweykowski, *Twórczość Bolesława Prusa,* vols. 1-2, (2d ed., 1972); J. R. Krzyżanowski, "Boleslaw Prus' *The Doll:* An Ironic Novel," *Russian and Slavic Literature,* ed. R. Freeborn et al. (1976), pp. 266-82.   J.R.K.

Pruszyński, Ksawery (1907-50), Polish fiction writer, journalist, and essayist, was born in Kierekeszyn in Volhynia into a landowner's family and died in an automobile accident near Hahn, Germany. He studied at the Jagiellonian University in Cracow. During World War I he fought in the Polish army in France and Norway and served as a diplomat in the Polish government in exile. After the war he returned to Poland and resumed his career in the diplomatic service. He started his literary career as a journalist. His first collection of reports, *Sarajewo 1914–Szanghaj 1932–Gdańsk 193?* (1932), the fruits of keen observation, which predicted the danger of war, was followed by his travel reports, *Palestyna po raz trzeci* (1933; Palestine for the Third Time), *Podróż po Polsce* (1937; A Trip around Poland), and *W czerwonej Hiszpanii* (1937; In Red Spain). He included his experiences during World War II in the journalistic reports *Poland Fights Back* (1941) and *Russian Year* (1944), as well as in his novel

Droga wiodła przez Narvik (1941; The Road Led through Narvik), a fictionalized report on the fight of Polish forces on the Norwegian front. In his collections of short stories *Trzynaście opowieści* (1946; Thirteen Tales) and *Karabela z Meschedu* (1948; The Mesched Saber), he presented the fate of Polish wartime exiles, soldiers and civilians, and also included colorful and exotic stories grounded in the life of the Polish gentry, Jews, and peasants, as well as stories about the people, historical events, and legends from different countries. Pruszyński's stories, reflecting the temperament of a true reporter, are written in a memorable style and with vivid narration and high intellectual values. He is also the author of a historical work, *Margrabia Wielopolski* (1944), a reevaluation of the 19th-century Polish statesman, and of a biographical sketch, *Adam Mickiewicz: The Life Story of the Greatest Polish Poet* (1950).

See: Z. Ziątek, *Ksawery Pruszyński* (1972); J. Pacławski, *Ksawery Pruszyński* (1974).   E.M.T.

Przyboś, Julian (1901-70), Polish poet and essayist, was born in Gwoźnica, in the Rzeszów region, and died in Warsaw. He graduated in Polish philology at the Jagiellonian University, and later taught in high schools. During his studies he became a member of the "Cracow Vanguard" literary group, developed and propagated their ideas, and became associated with their periodicals, *Zwrotnica* and *Linia.* The years 1937-39 he spent in Paris. Between 1947 and 1951 he served as the Polish legate to Switzerland. In his first volumes of poetry, *Śruby* (1925; Screws), and *Oburącz* (1926; With Both Hands), the dominating themes are the city and a fascination with the achievements of technical civilization. The main topics of his later volumes—*Zponad* (1930; From Above), *W głąb las* (1932; Into the Heart of the Forest), and *Równanie serca* (1938; Equation of the Heart)—are different; they include the village landscape, Parisian impressions, and reflections upon current social and political problems on the threshold of World War II. In the volume *Póki my żyjemy* (1944; As Long as We Live), Przyboś collected his poems written during the war and German occupation, full of hope despite the years of horror. He published eight volumes of poetry after the war: *Miejsce na ziemi* (1945; A Place on the Earth), *Rzut pionowy* (1952; Vertical Projection), *Najmniej słów* (1955; The Fewest Words Possible); *Narzędize z swiatla* (1958; The Tool of Light), *Próba całości* (1961; The Test of the Whole), *Więcej o manifest* (1969; More on the Manifesto), *Na znak* (1965; As a Sign), and *Kwiat nieznany* (1968; Unknown Flower). In all of these, changes are visible in the strengthening of lyrical and autobiographical elements, in the poet's return to the war seen now from the point of view of human solitude and suffering, and in his attempt, especially in his last volume, to embrace "the world of man in its temporal and spatial dimension" (J. Kwiatkowski). This last volume contains the longer poem "Wierzchołek imperium" (The Top of the Empire State) written after the poet's visit to New York. Przyboś replaced the romantic concept of "melodious lines" and "inspiration" with a demand for maximally condensed, crystal-clear phrase construction, full of dynamic and precise phrases that are a succession of artistic metaphors and images. The purpose of this rhetoric is an objective presentation of reality as it forms and develops. His intellectual and innovative lyrics are characterized by extraordinarily visual sensitivity, which connects them with modern painting, by an attempt to revive the meaning of words as well as the system of language and versification, and by an effort to create a new order of poetic expression. The critical works *Linia i gwar* (1959; Line and Buzz) and *Sens poe-*

tycki (1963; A Poetic Meaning) contain the poet's statements on the subject of the lyric, both his own and those of others (primarily the lyric poetry of the "Vanguard"), information about literary movements and modern painting, and sketches about outstanding Polish writers. Przyboś's valuable treatises on the poetics of Mickiewicz have been collected in the volume *Czytając Mickiewicza*. (1950; Reading Mickiewicz's Works). Przyboś also edited *Jabłoneczka. Antologia polskiej pieśni ludowej* (1953; Anthology of Polish Folk Songs). The influence of Przyboś's poetry and the Vanguard poetic is seen in the works of the younger generation of poets.

See: J. Kwiatkowski, *Świat poetycki Juliana Przybosia* (1972); W. P. Szymański, *Julian Przyboś* (1978).

M.P. and S.F.

Przybyszewski, Stanisław (1868–1927), Polish essayist, playwright, and novelist, was born in Łojew in the Kujawy region of Poland and died in Jaronty. While studying in Berlin, he became especially interested in psychiatry, and this had a strong impact on his later writing.

Przybyszewski gained recognition in the modernist circles of Germany by his initial literary work in German, notably *Chopin und Nietzsche* (1892) and *Totenmesse* (1893; Requiem Mass). He returned to Poland in 1898, preceded by his fame as an eminent writer and eccentric. He took over as editor of the Cracow literary periodical *Życie* and made it the main voice of the new literary and artistic movement called "Young Poland." Later on he became a cofounder of Polish expressionism. Przybyszewski's innovative role in Polish literary life was reinforced by his programmatic pronouncements (*Confiteor*, 1899; Creed), in which he proclaimed, "Art has no aim, it is aim in itself, it is the absolute because it is a reflection of the absolute in the soul." The pronouncements also contained a vehement condemnation of bourgeois mentality and of the artistic taste of the "Philistines."

Przybyszewski's reputation as a rebellious artist owed much to his bohemian habits and life-style, filled with private scandal and even personal tragedy. He ostentatiously made use of this experience in his fiction and plays. Almost everything he wrote was full of affectation and of obtrusive stylistic mannerisms, but his plays and novels were praised both in Poland and abroad, especially in Russia, where his works were frequently translated and performed, and also in Czech literary circles.

More than a decade before Freudian psychoanalysis came to the fore, Przybyszewski was much concerned in his writing with problems of the unconscious, for example, in his novel *Homo sapiens* (1895–98; Eng. tr., 1915) and in the dramas *Dla szczęścia* (1900; Eng. tr., *For Happiness*, 1912), *Złote runo* (1901; The Golden Fleece), and *Śnieg* (1903; Eng. tr., *Snow*, 1920). He also proclaimed the sexual drive as the most powerful force in human personality.

In the last years of his life, in the shadow of his past notoriety, Przybyszewski wrote his memoirs, *Moi współcześni* (1926–30; My Contemporaries). Along with his early writings in German, they are considered his most interesting works, although very typical of his egocentric and exhibitionist attitude.

See: M. Herman, *Un sataniste polonais: Stanisław Przybyszewski* (1939); A. Hutnikiewicz, "Stanisław Przybyszewski 1868–1927," in *Obraz literatury polskiej XIX i XX wieku. Literatura okresu Młodej Polski*, vol. 2 (1967), pp. 107–52; S. Helsztyński, *Przybyszewski* (1973).

S.S.

Psichari, Ernest (1883–1914), French novelist, was born in Paris. He was the grandson of Ernest Renan. As an adult, he turned to nationalistic pride and religious fervor as a means of quelling his personal doubts and anxiety. Educated at the lycées Montaigne, Henri IV, and Condorcet, Psichari received his *licence* in philosophy from the Sorbonne. In 1903 he decided on a career in the army and spent most of the remainder of his life in military service in Africa. The sojourn in Africa and his military service revealed the two great loves of his life that profoundly affect his literary works: his love of France and his devotion to the Catholic faith.

Psichari's first literary work, *Terre de soleil et de sommeil* (1908; Land of Sun and Sleep), reflects the author's spiritual awakening to the full significance of military duty. His novel *L'Appel des armes* (1911; The Call to Arms), more objective than the earlier work, is constructed on the thesis that the military is a safeguard of the faith of the people and imbues a sense of pride and joy in the young people it attracts. After a period of spiritual frustration, Psichari found solace in religion during his stay in Africa in 1911–12; upon his return to France for a visit in 1913, he was formally received in the Catholic Church. *Les Voix qui crient dans le désert* (1920; The Voices Crying in the Desert) is a compilation of fragmentary notes that recount his travels and activities in Africa as well as his soul's pilgrimage in search of God. From these notes, Psichari developed the novel that is considered his masterpiece, *Le Voyage du centurion* (1914; The Centurion's Voyage), written during the last year of his life when he was a practicing Catholic. The theme of the novel is the gradual possession of a soul by God, a possession leading ultimately to mystical union. This work, like all of Psichari's literary productions, is highly autobiographical and reflects the influence of writers whom Psichari admired throughout his life—Blaise Pascal, Maurice BARRÈS, Jacques MARITAIN, and, above all, Charles PÉGUY. Psichari was killed in battle during the first month of World War I at Rossignol, Belgium.

See: W. Fowlie, *Ernest Psichari: A Study in Religious Conversion* (1939); Daniel-Rops, *Psichari* (1942). S.H.

Putinas, pseud. of Vincas Mykolaitis (1893–1967), Lithuanian poet, novelist, and playwright, was born in Kačerginė. He entered the Roman Catholic priesthood in 1915, studied literature in Petersburg and in Switzerland, and became professor of Lithuanian literature at the University of Kaunas in 1923. Caught between the vocation of a priest and that of a poet, between earthly and divine love, Putinas opted for poetry and marriage and was excommunicated in 1936. These inner conflicts are reflected in his novel *Altorių šešėly* (1933; In the Shadow of the Altars), the first major psychological novel in Lithuanian.

Putinas's verse, the main collections of which are *Tarp dviejų aušrų* (1927; Between Two Dawns) and *Keliai ir kryžkeliai* (1936; Roads and Crossroads), expresses similar tensions. The early influence of Russian symbolism led Putinas to construct distant images of unearthly perfection that alternated with his ardent professions of love for the sinful earth. In some of his poems God is a cold ruler, inaccessible to human prayers across the endless cosmic void; in others, he is a roadside Christ, carved by the peasants, His face lined with all their sorrows. Moments of worshipful tenderness alternate with grand gestures of revolt. Putinas's poetry achieves unity not through resolution of these conflicts, but rather through the poet's intensity of feeling, controlled and structured by the power of his language. Similar dichotomies appear in his play *Vladovas* (1930; The Ruler).

After World War II, Putinas had to face another dilemma, a choice between his talent and the demands of socialist realism. His novel *Sukilėliai* (1957; The Rebels), about the 1863 Lithuanian uprising against the Russians, bears the scars of this new battle. Putinas died reconciled with the Catholic Church.

See: J. Grinius, *Vincas Mykolaitis-Putinas als Dichter* (1964); A. Sietynas, "The Condition of Free Prisoner: Poetry and Prose of Vincas Mykolaitis-Putinas," *Lituanus* 11 (1965): 48–63.   R.Š.

Q

Quart, Pere, pseud. of Joan Oliver Sallarés (1899–), Catalan poet, novelist, and dramatist, was born in Sabadell. Among his ancestors are such notable members of the bourgeoisie of the city of western Valles as the economist Joan Sallarés and Pla i Pere Oliver, founder of the Savings Bank Caixa d'Estalvis in Sabadell. He studied law and practiced that profession for some time. In addition he contributed to various newspapers and founded the publishing house La Mirada with his friend Francesc Trabal. As a result of the Spanish Civil War he went into exile in France and later Chile. In Chile he founded the journal *Germanor* and another publishing house.

Sallarés began his existence as Pere Quart in 1934 with the publication of *Les decapitacions* (The Beheadings), having previously published a play, *Gairebé un acte o Joan, Joana, i Joanet* (1929; Almost an Act, or, Joan, Joana, and Joanet). Other works of this period are *Cataclisme* (1935) and *Allò que tal vegada s'esdevingué* (1936; What Might Happen). He received the Joaquim Folguera Prize for *Bestiari* (1937; Bestiary) and soon thereafter wrote *Contraban* (1937; Contraband) with his play *Cambrera nova* (1937; New Waitress).

The shock of the Civil War permeates *Oda a Barcelona* (1936; Ode to Barcelona) and *La fam* (1938; Hunger). From his exile in Chile he wrote *Saló de tardor* (1947; Autumn Room), and on returning to Catalonia he published *Terra de naufragis* (1956; Land of the Shipwrecked), which had won the Ossa Menor Prize in 1955, and *Las tres comedias* (1960; Three Comedies). In 1960 he published *Vacances pagades* (Paid Vacations), for which he received the Ausias March Prize in 1959 and the Lletra d'Or Prize in 1961. Other works are *Los dotze giguaforts de Granyer* (1962; Granyer's Twelve Etchings), *Circumstancies* (1968), and *Tros de paper* (1970: A Piece of Paper). He received the Premi de les Lletres Catalanes in 1970. In 1975 his poetical works were published as the first volume of his *Obra Completa*. In his poetry one can discern the modernity and realism of an exemplary poet writing in the Catalonian tradition.

See: Ferrater Mora et al., *De Joan Oliver a Pere Quart* (1969); J. M. Castellet, "La poesia de Pere Quart y La narrativa de Joan Oliver" in *Questions de Literatura, Politica i Societat* (1975).   J.F.C.

Quasimodo, Salvatore (1901–68), Italian poet, translator, critic, and essayist, was born in Sicily, and his writings reflect nostalgia for that island's life and culture. Quasimodo's work falls into two parts, linked by a gradually evolving Sicilian myth. The first of these, his hermetic period (*see* ITALIAN LITERATURE), began after he gravitated to the mainland in the late 1920s and became, along with Eugenio MONTALE, Umberto SABA, and others, a contributor to the review *Solaria*. His first volume of verse, *Acque e terre* (1930; Waters and Lands), was closely followed by *Oboe sommerso* (1932; Submerged Oboe) and *Erato e Apòllion* (1936; Erato and Apollyon). The poems in these volumes become increasingly complex. The volume *Ed è subito sera* (1942; And It Is Suddenly Evening) gathers together all the poems of this period, and the "Nuove poesie" (New Poems [1936–42])

section of this last volume prepares the way for Quasimodo's later, more discursive verse.

Apart from brief autobiographical lapses in the first collection, Quasimodo's early poetry is characterized by a style described by Oreste Macrì as "la poetica della parola" (the poetics of the word), a combination of harsh, intellectualized sentiment with a genuine feeling for primitive Sicily, often expressed in vegetative imagery of growth or decomposition. Quasimodo's use of ethereal analogies gradually leads him into a solipsistic stance, symbolized by the biblical demiurge, Apollyon. From this crisis, however, a new type of poetry emerges, one which moves away from the metaphysical dream toward a form of integration into real life. Thus, Quasimodo's later poetry is often punctuated by his substitution of the rain-swept landscapes of northern Italy in place of the sun-drenched south.

The real break (if such it can be called) in his poetry, however, took place after the appearance of his Greek translations in 1940, an undertaking that helped him to develop new discursive patterns. His war poetry is more meditative and open, elegiac, and critical of man's cruelty to man. This attitude is illustrated in *Giorno dopo giorno* (1947; Day after Day) and *La vita non è sogno* (1949; Life Is No Dream). By this time Quasimodo's poetic creed had changed completely. Instead of continuing to adhere to the hermetic doctrine of involuted detachment, he became a poet of *engagement,* using the slogan "rifare l'uomo" (remake man) is a means of revaluing society.

In addition to the above-mentioned volumes, *Il falso e vero verde* (1953; The False and True Green), *La terra impareggiabile* (1958; The Incomparable Land), and *Dare e avere* (1966; Giving and Taking) form the basis of Quasimodo's humanistic period. The poems of this period, lacking his earlier hermetic intensity, adopt a classical prosody and fixed melodic patterns. Quasimodo is at his best when he integrates his early hermetic techniques into a new discursive tone, but at times his poetic content becomes too factual, too prosaic, bordering on the documentary. It is his aim, however, to create a new, inner chronicle of events, rather than mere propaganda. He develops a series of modern myths, emphasizing on the one hand the need for solidarity in the face of death, and on the other, individual self-fulfillment. Regrettably, this new period failed to reach final maturity, since Quasimodo died suddenly. Nevertheless, he occupies an important place in contemporary Italian culture, for he presided over the transition between the world of prewar hermeticism and postwar social and cultural innovation. Quasimodo was awarded the Nobel Prize for Literature in 1959.

See: C. M. Bowra, "An Italian Poet: Salvatore Quasimodo," *Horizon* 16 (1947); N. Tedesco, *Quasimodo* (1959); F. J. Jones, "The Poetry of Salvatore Quasimodo," *IS* 16 (1961), and *La poesie italiana contemporanea* (1975); C. M. Bowra, *L'isola impareggiabile* (1977); G. Finzi, ed., *Quasimodo e la critica* (1969).   F.J.J.

Queneau, Raymond (1903–76), French writer, was born in Le Havre. He is best known for his *Exercices de style*

(1947; Eng. tr., *Exercises in Style*, 1958), which treats the same event in 99 different ways, and for the mathematical/musical experiments of *Bâtons, chiffres, et lettres* (1947; Strokes, Figures, and Letters). His passion for the spoken tongue comes near to that of James Joyce, and in the first pages of *Le Chiendent* (1932; Eng. tr., *The Bark-tree*, 1968), he even attempted a "Joycean" translation of Descartes. Much of Queneau's work—for instance, the opening phrases of his *Zazie dans le métro* (1959; Eng. tr., *Zazie*, 1960)—must be read aloud in order to render it comprehensible, since it consists of phonetic transcriptions. Queneau called this language a third or neo-French.

From dada and surrealism (*see* FRENCH LITERATURE), Queneau retained a fascination with shock and with the idea of a self-making literature, that is, one that might approximate in the reader (as in the author) those spontaneous mental reactions or that lyric attitude the surrealists called poetry. Queneau was the most illustrious member of the Collège de Pataphysique, an organization devoted to continuing the stupefyingly complicated, serious humor of Alfred JARRY. He was also associated with OULIPO (OU.LI.PO=Ouvroir de Littérature Potentielle), which sponsors experiments in open-ended storytelling.

Although humor is probably the most salient characteristic of his writing, Queneau also demonstrated a profoundly intellectual curiosity for the workings of the human mind and the human language. Like Blaise CENDRARS, he relied heavily on Joseph Vendryes's *Le Langage* (1921) in this regard. Queneau experimented with pictograms and with many forms of poetry, regular and irregular. Yet he was also the director of the *Encyclopédie de la Pléiade* and the author of many novels that are as

readable as they are "novel": *Loin de Reuil* (1944; Eng. tr., *The Skin of Dreams*, 1948), *Pierrot mon ami* (1942; Eng. tr., *Pierrot: A Novel*, 1950), and *Le Vol d'Icare* (1968; Eng. tr. *The Flight of Icarus*, 1973). The latter treats a Pirandellian theme (*see* Luigi PIRANDELLO), the relation between an author and his characters.

See: J. Bens, *Queneau* (1962); C. Simonnet, *Queneau déchiffré* (1962); A. I. Bergens, *Raymond Queneau* (1963); J. Guicharnaud, *Raymond Queneau* (1965); special Queneau no. of *L'Arc* 28 (1966). M.A.C.

Quiroga, Elena (1919–), Spanish novelist, was born of a noble family in Santander. She has lived in La Coruña and Madrid. Her novel *Viento del norte* (1950, North Wind) is the love story of an old gentleman and his maid in a Galician setting. Naturalism is combined in this novel with a number of conventional formulas. Quiroga's later novels mark a departure from regionalism. In *La sangre* (1952; Blood) the first person is used to narrate the melodramatic story of four generations, while *Algo pasa en la calle* (1954; Something Is Happening in the Street), perhaps her best novel, is a well-written and skillful study of psychological and social problems, with a simple narrative structure. *La careta* (1955; The Mask) offers an in-depth analysis of the bourgeoisie in postwar Spain, and in *La última corrida* (1958; The Last Bullfight) the dialogue efficiently conveys the story of an old and frustrated bullfighter. Quiroga's most recent novels, *Tristura* (1960; Sadness), *Escribo tu nombre* (1965; I Write Your Name), and *Presente profundo* (1973; Deep Present), show some technical progress.

See: G. Sobejano, *Novela española de nuestro tiempo* (1975), pp. 251–58. J.O.

R

Radauskas, Henrikas (1910–70), Lithuanian poet, was born in Cracow, Poland. He studied literature at the University of Kaunas and later worked as a radio announcer and as editor for a commission on book publishing established by the Lithuanian Ministry of Education. After several years of exile in Germany, Radauskas emigrated to the United States in 1949. He did manual labor until 1959, when he joined the staff of the Library of Congress, where he remained until his death.

Radauskas wrote four books of verse: *Fontanas* (1935; The Fountain), *Strėlė danguje* (1950; Arrow in the Sky), *Žiemos daina* (1955; The Song of Winter), and *Žaibai ir vėjai* (1965; Lightnings and Winds). His poems offer balanced contrasting structures in which sharply observed mundane details are imaginatively transformed into fairy-tale vistas, surrealistic flights of fancy, deep evocations of sorrow, or humorous grotesques. Violence is often allied with beauty in a transport of Dionysiac joy, or time and eternity meet in deathless agony—the infinitely extended moment of dying. Ancient myths and symbols become entrapped among the ironies of technological civilization; death and madness mistake each other for beauty. All these worlds float in a heady air of magic and, like magic, they vanish quickly in the clear light of reason that is the knowledge of death.

The complex patterns of images in Radauskas's work do not embody a philosophy, but rather an aesthetic: a faith in art as a transfiguring force answering man's deep-rooted need to make himself equal to his dreams, and perhaps also to his nightmares. The poet achieves this by focusing vague and transient human fantasies into succinct, evocative statements of permanent, classical grace

through the integration of feeling with sound, image, object, and rhythm. In this Radauskas, resembles Osip MANDELSHTAM, who said that, in poetry, form *is* content.

Radauskas stands quite apart from the Lithuanian poetic tradition of patriotic romanticism or religious and philosophical symbolism. To some extent, his work reflects the influences of modern Russian and Western European poetry, but in essence he remains unique and alone.

See: R. Šilbajoris, "Henrikas Radauskas—the Passion of the Intellect," in his *Perfection of Exile: Fourteen Contemporary Lithuanian Writers* (1970), pp. 25–55. R.Š.

Radiguet, Raymond (1903–23), French novelist and poet, was born in Parc-Saint-Mer, the son of a popular but poor cartoonist living just west of Paris. Radiguet has entered Parnassus with perhaps the least baggage any author has ever had. When he was 14 or 15, he showed some of his verses to Guillaume APOLLINAIRE, who was not impressed. "Don't despair, Monsieur," he said; "Arthur Rimbaud didn't write his masterpiece before he was 17."

The disturbingly precocious adolescent had better luck with Jean COCTEAU, whose mother's maid announced the arrival at their door of "a child with a cane." Until Radiguet's death about five years later, the two writers' lives and careers were intimately connected. Radiguet began work as early as 1919 on his best-known work, *Le Diable au corps* (1923; Eng. tr., *The Devil in the Flesh*, 1932). The novel was launched by Grasset with what was denounced as an "American-style" publicity campaign. The first-person narrative, at least partly autobiographical, recounts the story of a 14-year-old who falls in love with the fiancée—subsequently the bride—of a poilu whose wartime duties permit a freely erotic vacation for his pubescent rival. The book enjoyed immediate success in spite, or because, of the virulence of its detractors. From March 1923 on, Radiguet put his new-found opulence to good use, but he also proceeded with work on *Le Bal du comte d'Orgel* (1924; Eng. trs., *The Count's Ball*, 1929; *Count d'Orgel Opens the Ball*, 1952; *Count d'Orgel*, 1953), in part at Arcachon, where he contracted the typhoid fever that resulted in his death just before the year's end.

Radiguet's poetry combines echoes of 17th- and 18-century classicism with frequent traces of the winds of modernity that were blowing through postwar Paris. His novels have surely been overpraised for their resemblance to the author's obvious model, Madame de La Fayette. Their carefully worked-over prose, presenting a striking fusion of a conservative literary aesthetic with a typically modern sense of sophisticated cynicism, constitutes no small achievement for a writer who died at the age of 20.

See: K. Goesch, *Radiguet* (1955); D. Noakes, *Raymond Radiguet* (1968); N. Odouard, *Les Années folles de Raymond Radiguet* (1973).   D.N.

Radnóti, Miklós (1909–44), Hungarian poet and translator, was born in Budapest. Having lost his mother at birth and his father when he was 12, Radnóti was brought up by relatives. He later described the shock of finding himself an orphan in a moving autobiographical sketch, *Ikrek hava* (1939; Eng. tr., *The Month of Gemini*, 1979).

Radnóti's first book of poetry, *Pogány köszöntő* (1930; Pagan Greeting), strongly influenced by European, especially French, expressionism, exults in life and denounces social injustices. A Barbussean socialist at the time (*see* Henri BARBUSSE), he established some ties with the then clandestine Hungarian Communist Party, but his "proletarian" posturing was short-lived and his poems of the 1931–32 period have a hollow ring. As a student of Hungarian and French literature at the University of Szeged, he became friendly with a group of young intellectuals involved in the budding populist movement "Szyedi Fiatalok" (Youth of Szeged) and studied with the Catholic poet-priest Sándor Sík (*see* HUNGARIAN LITERATURE). In 1931, Radnóti's new book of verse, *Ujmódi pásztorok éneke* (The Song of Modern Shepherds), was confiscated by the public prosecutor; Radnóti drew a light jail sentence for his "defamation of religion." Although he completed his degree at the university, he was unable to secure a teaching post, and he supported himself by means of free-lance literary work, mainly translation, and the assistance of a rich uncle. In 1935, Radnóti married and settled in Budapest. By this time his poetry had lost its shrill, provocative edge and occasional mannerisms. Like other members of his generation, he reverted to classical poetic forms, partly in protest against the irrationality and antihumanist bias of the Hitler era. Radnóti was a frequent contributor to the literary review *Nyugat*, edited by Mihály BABITS.

Radnóti won the Baumgarten Prize for his collection *Járkálj csak, halálraitélt* (1936; Man Sentenced to Death, Just Keep Walking). The book spelled out what was to become the obsessive theme of his work: the inevitability of violent death as a result of war or persecution. Following a visit to Paris, where he had contact with left-wing circles, Radnóti became preoccupied with the Spanish Civil War and Federico GARCÍA LORCA's tragic fate. Indeed, these events took on a symbolic meaning for him. He spent his last eight years in a struggle to accept and spiritually overcome the near-certainty of his martyrdom.

Although he was of Jewish extraction, Radnóti inwardly embraced Christianity years before his actual conversion. He found consolation in faith and, to a certain extent, in the hope for peace and a new, just society. At the same time, his poetry sought refuge in Greek and Western classical models. Radnóti's posthumous collection *Tajtékos ég* (1946; Eng. tr., *Clouded Sky*, 1972) contains dramatic ecologues contrasting the horrors of war with an Arcadia of the soul as well as odes to his beloved wife, letters, and poetic fragments written in a rich yet serene idiom. Although his poetry is personal, it is not exempt from a noble brand of rhetoric, emotional yet polished; in it the traditions of the *Nyugat* postsymbolists (*see* HUNGARIAN LITERATURE) blend with the innovations of Guillaume APOLLINAIRE. Radnóti was an outstanding translator of poetry, both old and new: the translations gathered in his *Orpheus nyomában* (1942; In the Footsteps of Orpheus) are models of conscientious craftmanship. In 1944, Radnóti was sent to a labor camp near Bor, in occupied Yugoslavia, from where his unit was led on foot toward Germany. One of his most dramatic poems, "Forced March" (Eng. tr., 1972), describes this event. Near the Hungarian village of Abda, Radnóti was summarily executed and buried in a mass grave. He is now recognized as the finest Hungarian poet of the war years, his tragic death sanctioning his literary achievement in a compelling manner.

See: L. Lator, "Radnóti Miklós költői fejlődése," *Irodalomtörténet* (1954), pp. 259–74; Gy. Ortutay, *Radnóti Miklós: 1909–1944* (1959); I. Bori, *Radnóti Miklós költészete* (1965); B. Pomogáts, *Radnóti Miklós* (1977); C. Wilmer and G. Gömöri, Introduction to M. Radnóti, *Forced March* (1979).   G.G.

Rainis, Jānis, pseud. of Jānis Pliekšāns (1865–1929), Latvian poet, dramatist, and statesman, was born in Rubene parish and educated as a lawyer. In the 1890s he started his literary career as a publicist in the socialist press as a translator of German and Russian. Indeed, his translation of Goethe's *Faust* (1896) crowned the 40-year development of Latvian as a modern literary language and influenced its 20th-century poetic idiom. Because of his association with socialist causes, Rainis and his wife, the poet and dramatist Aspazija, pseud. of Elza Rozenberga (1865–1943), were exiled to Russia. They returned to Latvia in 1903, but after the suppression of the 1905 Revolution in Latvia went to Switzerland and remained their until 1920. In independent Latvia, Rainis directed plays and served as a member of Parliament, minister of education, and theater director.

Rainis's literary production is characterized by strong symbolic and folkloristic tendencies and by philosophic attempts to reconcile individual, social, human and national concerns. In his first collection of poems, *Tālas noskaņas zilā vakarā* (1903; Distant Moods at Twilight), the exile motif predominates; *Vētras sēja* (1905; The Sowing of the Storm) expresses revolutionary sentiments; and *Tie, kas neaizmirst* (1911; Those Who Do Not Forget) combines the poet's moods, in exile with his hope for the future. *Gals un sākums* (1912; The End and the Beginning) marks the culmination of Rainis's philosophic poetry.

In Rainis's first major drama, *Uguns un nakts* (1905; Fire and Night), based on the folk epic *Lāčplēsis* (1888; The Bearslayer) by Andrejs Pumpurs (1841–1902), national and philosophic concerns are expressed symbolically. *Zelta zirgs* (1910; The Golden Steed) is a fairy-tale drama, again with a rich symbolic texture. In *Indulis un Ārija* (1911; Indulis and Arija) historical conflicts assume contemporary political significance. Rainis started a series of "folk song" dramas with *Pūt, vējiņi* (1913; Blow,

Winds). His tragedy *Jāzeps un viņa brāļi* (1919; Joseph and his Brethren) treats the problem of the isolated individual, a recurrent motif in all his work. Attempts by Soviet Latvian critics to depict Rainis as a confirmed Marxist disregard or misinterpret much of his output. Among his suppressed works is the dramatic poem *Daugava* (1919), which celebrates the advent of a Latvian state.   V.N.

Rakić, Milan (1876–1938), Serbian poet, was born in Belgrade. While studying law in Paris from 1898 to 1902, he became well acquainted with French poetry, particularly with the Parnassians and the symbolist poets. Rakić entered the diplomatic service in 1904. From 1908 to 1911 he was the Serbian consul in Priština, and after World War I he served in Copenhagen, Sofia, and Rome. Along with Jovan Dučić, Rakić raised the quality of Serbian poetry to new heights. The volume of Rakić's poetry, however, is very small: 49 of his poems were published during his lifetime and an additional 3 posthumously. Editions keep appearing, however (1956, 1960, 1961, 1963, 1968, 1970), and Rakić's poetry is today an integral part of all Yugoslav anthologies. Thematically, his poems fall into three major categories: love lyrics, meditations, and patriotic verse. Most of them are characterized by stylistic perfection, intellectual maturity, and poetic excellence. Rakić's love lyrics are markedly sensual and erotic. In his patriotic poems, such as the famous Kosovo cycle (1905–11), in which he revived Serbian patriotic poetry, his pessimism takes the form of longing for the past glories of medieval Serbia. His meditative poems contain a note of tragedy and restrained pessimism reflecting Rakić's deep awareness of the transitoriness of man and the world. Nevertheless, the dominant note of his work is not a sentimental self-pity, but rather, like Job, he feels an "anguish of spirit," bitterness, and eventual resignation.

See: Z. Gavrilović, *Od Vojislava do Disa* (1958), pp. 70–116; J. Skerlić, *Pisci i knjige*, vol. 5 (1964), pp. 39–53; I. Sekulić, Introduction to M. Rakić, *Pesme* (1968), pp. 5–36.   M.M. with W.B.E.

Ramuz, Charles-Ferdinand (1878–1947), Swiss poet, novelist, and essayist, was born at Cully, a small town on Lake Geneva in the canton of Vaud. After completing his studies at the University of Lausanne, he went to Paris, where, from 1902 to 1914, he lived in obscurity and wrote four volumes of poetry in addition to eight novels and two collections of short stories, none of which attracted attention outside a small circle of friends and admirers. Longing for an atmosphere truly congenial to his artistic temperament, he decided to go back to his native Cully. This proved to be a momentous step in his life.

The 20-odd volumes of fiction written by Ramuz since 1914 contain a searching analysis of the primitive emotions that give the life of the simple folk in his canton its distinctive tonality. Peasants, winegrowers, small craftsmen, and fishermen live vividly before the eyes of the reader. Ramuz chiseled a language and expressed himself in a style that were new, daring, and deliberately regional, bursting open the narrow boundaries of a literature increasingly dulled by Parisian fashions. He awakened French Swiss writers to a new awareness and pride and urged them to strive for an existence of their own. Although his work is regional, it is by no means merely picturesque. Visual in his approach, he restricted himself only to what he could touch, see, and hear; and yet, out of the antipoetical grew the song. His novels have a power of incantation reminiscent of biblical hymns; they often grow to symbolic dimensions, or, like epic poems, unfold their slow and poignant beauty.

Ramuz's work is a victory over the pessimism and introspection that might easily have dampened his creative impulses. His diary (*Journal* 1895–1920, 1939–1947), his correspondence, and several of his essays show how much he was tormented by self-doubt and what it cost him to overcome it. A tension between depression and exaltation can be found throughout his work.

In several essays, among them *Adieu à beaucoup de personnages* (1914; Farewell to Many Characters), Ramuz drew a conclusion to his first creative period, which ended with his return home from Paris. Among the novels that followed were *La Guérison des maladies* (1917; The Curing of Diseases) and *Les Signes parmi nous* (1919; The Signs in Our Midst), in which the conflict lies not in the hero himself but in his confrontation with others. Ramuz's lasting friendship with the Russian composer Igor Stravinsky began in 1915, when Ramuz had achieved full control of his art. It further stimulated an interest in Russia that had begun in Ramuz's teen years when he read Tolstoy, and led to Ramuz's collaboration with Stravinsky on the libretto of his opera *L'Histoire du soldat* (1920; Eng. tr., *The Soldier's Tale*, 1950). *Salutation paysanne* (1921; Rustic Greeting) and *Passage du poète* (1923; The Poet Comes Along) are good examples celebrating this happy period. Ramuz's expansive mood coincided with an increasing concern for freedom; in *Le Grand Printemps* (1917; The Great Spring) he enthusiastically greeted the first, democratic, Russian Revolution of 1917. His critical interest in the Marxist ideology underlying the October Revolution of 1917 later manifested itself in such essays as *Taille de l'homme* (1933; Stature of Man) and *Besoin de grandeur* (1937; Need for Grandeur), and in the novel *Farinet, ou la fausse monnaie* (1932; Farinet, or Counterfeit Money). *Le Règne de l'esprit malin* (1917; Eng. tr., *The Reign of the Evil One*, 1922), *La Grande Peur dans la montagne* (1926; Eng. tr., *Terror on the Mountain*, 1967), and other works show how limitation in space and spirit can lead to separation, intolerance, and irrational fear. Among still others, *Beauté sur la terre* (1927; Eng. tr., *Beauty on Earth*, 1929) and *Le Garçon savoyard* (1936; The Savoyard Lad) deplore the fact that even in love there is never total communication. Ramuz ends on a pessimistic note: in spite of the triumph of solidarity which, in *Derborence* (1934; Eng. tr., *When the Mountain Fell*, 1949), makes the rescue of the victim possible, nature asserts itself as a dangerous and insensitive protagonist.

See: A. Béguin, *Patience de Ramuz* (1949); A. Guisan, *C. F. Ramuz* (1966).   U.S.

Rasmussen, Halfdan (1915–), Danish poet, was born in Copenhagen. He held various jobs but was also out of work for extended periods of time. The German occupation of Denmark (1940–45) became for Rasmussen the central experience activating him as a poet. The traditional, romantic poetry of his first collections changes in *Digte under Besættelsen* (1945; Poems during the Occupation) to a series of concrete polemical poems founded on the feeling of unity during the Resistance. Rasmussen's postwar collections are dominated by retrospective poems, burdened by the memory of the dead and by the guilt of having survived. After the fighting spirit of the war years there follows a period of doubt, but the gloomy brooding and the dread of a new war in *Aftenland* (1950; Evening Country) are, in *Skoven* (1954; The Forest), changed to a passion for nature seen as the sole way out of fear and loneliness. This leads to more extroverted and realistic poetry in the travel book *Stilheden* (1962; The

Tranquillity). Rasmussen gained very great popularity subsequently through his *Tosserier* (a selection in 1969; Tomfooleries), nonsense verse of great humor and stylistic significance.   S.H.R.

Rasputin, Valentin Grigoryevich (1937–), Russian novelist, is the youngest of the major "village" writers. He is unusual among them in that his language is much more discursive and classical and his analysis of individual psychology much more detailed. These qualities are especially noticeable in *Zhivi i pomni* (1974; Live and Remember), in which Andrey Guskov, a wartime deserter, gradually destroys his wife, Nastyona, by returning to live clandestinely outside their Siberian village. Rasputin's main theme is traditional village communal solidarity and the nature of those forces undermining it. *Posledniy srok* (1970; The Last Stage) views the dissolution of a remote hamlet from the perspective of a dying old woman, and at the same time analyzes what death means to the individual, the family, and the community. Rasputin's major theme is treated even more drastically in *Proshchaniye s Matyoroy* (1976; Farewell to Matyora) about the planned submergence of a village in a hydroelectric power scheme on the Yenisey River. The novel's focus is on the old people, whose message to their descendants is that man will destroy himself if he ignores or represses the ancestral, collective, and inherited layers of his personality in heedless technological "progress." Not surprisingly, this message has stimulated some cool reviews in the Soviet press; what is perhaps more surprising is the positive evaluation his work continues to receive.

See: W. Kasack, "Walentin Rasputin," *Osteuropa*, no. 7 (1975): 489–90; E. Starikova, "Zhit i pomnit," *NovM*, no. 10 (1977): 236–48.   G.H.

Rea, Domenico (1921–), Italian novelist and short-story writer, was born in Nocera, in the province of Naples. His parents were poor, and his youth was full of hardships, climaxed by the trials Naples suffered during World War II. Rea's stories depict the difficult lives of the working class and unemployed of Naples and its region. His avowed purpose is to reveal the grim truth beneath the conventional picture of a city of singers and guitar players.

Rea's first book, *Spaccanapoli* (1947), which takes its name from a region of the city, contains lively sketches, recounted with a brio that sometimes obscures his social intention. *Gesù, fate luce* (1950; Jesus, Give Us Light), which was awarded the Viareggio Prize, and *Quel che vide Cummeo* (1955; What Cummeo Saw) have a similar background and purpose. *Cummeo* is the more effective in its depiction of the misery of the poor. Rea's gifts for swift and vigorous portrayal of characters and description of scenes are best displayed in his short stories. He has, however, written a novel of substance, *Una vampata di rossore* (1959; Eng. tr., *A Blush of Shame*, 1963). *Il re e il lustrascarpe* (1961; The King and the Bootblack) is a collection of essays and tales, full of Neapolitan color. In 1960, Rea became an editor of *Le ragioni narrative*, a review published in Naples and devoted to the study of southern literature. He has also written a play, *Le formicole rosse* (1948; The Little Red Ants).

See: L. Russo, in *I narratori* (1968); G. Manacorda, in *Letteratura italiana: i contemporanei*, vol. 5 (1974), pp. 1287–1304; C. Piancastelli, *Rea* (1975).   T.G.B.

Rebatet, Lucien (1903–72), French novelist, journalist, and pamphleteer, was born in Moras-en-Valloire, a small village in southeastern France (Drôme) where his father

was a notary. By the time he finished his secondary studies in a Catholic boarding school, he had lost his faith. It was soon replaced by the philosophy of Friedrich NIETZSCHE, which spawned in Rebatet his cult of the elite and his hatred of democracy. Rebatet earned his license in philosophy in the early 1920s. Beginning in 1929 he worked for the newspaper *Action française*, and he wrote for the pro-Fascist weekly *Je suis partout* off and on from 1932 until 1944, with time out for military service in 1940.

In 1942, Rebatet published his memoirs, entitled *Les Décombres* (The Ruins). In this successful work, he assigned blame for France's defeat to both the Right and the Left. After the war, he was tried and condemned to death in 1946, although the sentence was commuted the following year. At the time of his imprisonment, Rebatet had begun writing his powerful novel *Les Deux Etendards* (1951; The Two Standards). The thousand-page *Etendards* treats the philosophical struggle between Régis, a young Jesuit, and Michel, a neopagan, for Anne-Marie. At the beginning of the novel, she plans to become a nun and share her love for Régis on a divine plane. By the end of the work she has had an affair with Michel but refuses to marry him, while Régis remains true to his vocation. The novel was responsible, at least in part, for Rebatet's release from prison in 1952.

Rebatet maintained a lifelong interest in music. His second novel, *Les Epis murs* (1954; The Ripened Ears of Corn), artfully portrays the fictional biography of a musical genius who is killed in World War I. Rebatet's *Histoire de la musique* (1969; History of Music) is especially concerned with Richard WAGNER.

See: P. Vandromme, *Rebatet* (1968).   D.O'C.

Rebora, Clemente (1885–1957), Italian poet, translator, and essayist, was born and educated in Milan. He contributed to *La voce* and other avant-garde reviews and also became well known as a translator of Russian literature. He is best known, however, for his poetry, of which he published three major collections: *Frammenti lirici* (1913; Lyrical Fragments), *Canti anonimi* (1922; Anonymous Songs), and *Canti dell'infermità* (1956; Songs of Illness). These works and a number of scattered verses were collected together in 1961 as *Le poesie (1913–1957)*.

Having begun to write poetry just before World War I, Rebora absorbed some of the lyrical traits of crepuscularism and futurism (*see* ITALIAN LITERATURE). Nevertheless, his poetry pulsates with a form of religious anxiety and a sense of redemption that are clearly his own. His lyrical world amounts to a constant dialectical movement between God and reality; his poetry appears to be a titanic orchestration of the life-force as it strives blindly, but not ineffectively, to achieve God's designs. His imagery mirrors his religious message through the turmoil of the senses. During the 1920s when his poetry was becoming more cerebral, Rebora underwent a severe religious crisis, after which he entered the priesthood. Thereafter his lyricism tended to crystallize into doctrinal verse, yet his earlier insights still occasionally reappear in all their lyrical vigor to redeem his heavier theological vein.

The main tension in Rebora's poetry is between nature and man. He uses the real as a stepping-stone in his ascent through personal anguish toward a clearer view of human destiny. Sometimes his insights are gained through the intensity of his sense of participation, and sometimes through a subtle combination of ingenious, "metaphysical" imagery. In "Gira la trottola viva" (The Living Top Spins, pub. in *Canti anonimi*), for example, the earth is represented as a top and the whip driving it as God. As it spins, the colors on its surface merge into one unified hue, intended to symbolize God's hidden harmony.

Rebora's manner is not based on the dulcet word-music of the decadents but is rather a modern version of Dante's "rime petrose" (stony rhymes). Indeed, Rebora's temperament seems to have much in common with Dante's, for example, an affinity for linguistic eclecticism. Rebora introduces many dialectal features into his poetry, straining or actually breaking grammatical rules, and indulging in jarring, dislocated rhythms and grating alliterative sequences. These devices have led critics to conclude that he is a poet with precious little music in his soul, yet his cacophonies are not wholly negative. His expressionistic word-music is also a corrective to the overly mellifluous verse of the *crepuscolari* and a reflection of his own intensely virile lyrical persona. His tortured style, expressive of his struggle to liberate himself from the sins of modern life, allows him to provide a fresh perspective on society within a Christian context.

See: M. Marchione, *L'imagine tesa* (1960); M. Guglielminetti, *Clemente Rebora* (1961); M. del Serra, *Clemente Rebora: lo specchio e il fuoco* (1976).   F.J.J.

Rebreanu, Liviu (1885–1944), Romanian prose writer, was born in Tîrlisiua in Transylvania, then a Hungarian province. He attended the Hungarian lyceum at Năsăud and later an officers' school in Hungary. In 1908 he published his first story, "Codrea," in the journal *Luceafărul*. He was soon encouraged to come to Bucharest, where he contributed to the journal *Convorbiri literare*.

Rebreanu's first volume of short stories, *Frămîntari* (Vicissitudes) appeared in 1912 and was followed by *Golanii* (Vagabonds) and *Mărturisire* (Confession) in 1916. It was the novel *Ion* (1920), however, with its unforgettable characterization, that definitely insured Rebreanu's place in Romanian literature. Ion, a peasant who is capable of performing the most odious deeds, cannot live until he feels he is master of his own land, but all his material greed cannot bring him happiness. In *Pădurea spînzuraţilor* (1922; Eng. tr., *The Forest of the Hanged*, 1922), a war novel, and *Răscoala* (1932; Uprising), a novel inspired by the rebellion of 1907, Rebreanu probes the psychology of the masses. *Adam şi Eva* (1925; Adam and Eve) turned the psychological probing inward. Rebreanu was also interested in the theater. He wrote the comedies *Cadrilul* (1919; The Quadrille) and *Plicul* (1923; The Envelope), and served as codirector of the National Theater in Bucharest from 1928 to 1930.

See: L. Raicu, *Liviu Rebreanu: eseu* (1967); A. Piru, *Liviu Rebreanu* (1968).   V.A.

Redol, (António) Alves (1911–69), Portuguese novelist, was born in Vila Franca de Xira, northeast of Lisbon. At the age of 16, he emigrated to Portuguese Angola, where he lived for three years as a private teacher and office worker. Back in Lisbon, he turned to a literary career. *Glória—uma aldeia do Ribatejo* (1938; Gloria, a Village of the Ribatejo) is an "ethnographic essay" dealing with his native region. *Gaibéus* (1939; Migrant Workers) marked the official beginning of the neorealist school of writing with its social protest and leftist bias. Redol remained a lifelong neorealist. In a foreword to *Gaibéus*, he wrote that this novel made no claim to be a work of art but rather was intended primarily as a human documentary on the Ribatejo region. The story deals with migrant agricultural workers who arrive in the Ribatego rice fields for the harvest season. There is no central character but rather a series of men and women, treated, and visited again, one after another. Redol describes the hardships suffered by the migrants, inflicted both by

human beings (exploitation) and by nature (weather, mosquitoes, malaria). The workers constitute a collective hero made up of individuals—each with different but related problems; all with no real hope, only illusion. The most any of them can do is stave off disaster for another season. Among Redol's many works are *Nasci com passaporte de turista* (1940; I Was Born with a Tourist Passport), short stories, and numerous novels, including the three of his "Port Wine Cycle": *Horizonte cerrado* (1949; Clouded Horizon), *Os homens e as sombras* (1951; Men and Shadows), and *Vindima de sangue* (1953; Blood Vintage). The more recent *A barca dos sete lemes* (1958; Eng. tr., *The Man With Seven Names*, 1964) is one of his best. In this novel Redol concentrates on a single character, a man imprisoned for murder, who tells his story to another Portuguese, a political prisoner in wartime France. Prison scenes alternate with phases of the murderer's life, giving a chilling and yet not unsympathetic account of the progressive dehumanization of a man.

Redol has also produced two books for children and a regional songbook and has collaborated on a collection of ballads.

See: J. de Almeida Pavão, *Alves Redol e o neorealismo* (1959); M. Moisés, *A literatura portuguesa* (6th ed., 1968), pp. 316–21.   T.Br.

Régio, José, pseud. of José Maria dos Reis Pereira (1901–69), Portuguese poet, playwright, literary critic, and novelist, born in Vila do Conde, north of Oporto, acquired a degree in Romance philology from the University of Coimbra and taught French and Portuguese in Portalegre, Portugal. In addition to teaching and writing, he traveled all over Portugal to collect works of religious art, especially sculpture.

Régio's prolific career as a writer began with *Poemas de Deus e do Diabo* (1925; Poems of God and the Devil). In 1927, while still in Coimbra, he joined João Gaspar Simões and António José Branquinho da FONSECA to found *Presença*, the most influential Portuguese literary journal of this century after *Orpheu*. He remained its editor during the 13 years of its existence. His subsequent volumes of poetry were *Biografia* (1929), *As encruzilhadas de Deus* (1936; God's Crossroads), *Fado* (1941; Fate), *Mas Deus é grande* (1945; But God Is Great), *A chaga do lado* (1954; The Wound in the Side), *O filho do homem* (1961; The Son of Man), and *Música ligeira* (1970; Light Music). Except for the predominantly satirical tone of *Fado* and *A chaga do lado*, these works provide variations on the theme of an unresolved conflict between creature and Creator, flesh and spirit, reason and faith, good and evil, Christ and the Devil, time and eternity. As a poet, Régio almost totally ignored the formal innovations of the *Orpheu* generation (see PORTUGUESE LITERATURE). As a lifelong teacher of literature, he preferred tradition to experiment. Whether writing satire or meditations, he usually presented his subjects with fervor, poignant sincerity, sonority, and vivid imagery. Most of Régio's nine plays are similar to his poems in theme and style. The best known, *Jacob e o anjo* (1941; Jacob and the Angel) and *Benilde ou a virgem-mãe* (1947; Benilde or the Virgin Mother), are religious and metaphysical in theme, symbolic, and somewhat expressionistic in tone. Régio believed that his theater was "the most original and therefore least understood part" of his vast production. The novel *O príncipe com orelhas de burro* (1942; The Prince with Donkey Ears) and the delightful collection *Histórias de mulheres* (1946; Stories about Women) probe psychological depths in polished prose. The author also fictionalized his own early experiences in a series of novels, *A velha casa* (5 vols., 1945–66; The Old House).

Régio's thousands of critical articles enhanced appreciation of art and literature in Portugal. His poetry was widely read, and his theater remains the best produced in his generation.

See: O. Lopes, *A obra de José Régio* (1956); E. Lisboa, *José Régio* (1957); Various Authors, *In memoriam de José Régio* (1970); E. Lisboa, *José Régio: a obra e o homen* (1976) and *José Régio: uma citeratura viva* (1978); J. G. Simões, *José Régio e a história do movimento da "Presença"* (1977).   A.A.C.

Régnier, Henri François Joseph de (1864–1936), French poet and novelist, was born in Honfleur. His writings reveal successive tendencies towards the Parnassian, symbolist, and ultimately the neoclassical schools of thought. His earliest collections of poetry—*Lendemains* (1885; Aftermaths), *Apaisemente* (1886; Appeasement), and *Sites* (1887)—are primarily Parnassian, with an emphasis upon precision and plasticity of form. Symbolist leanings, with a characteristic obscurity of image and a haunting musicality, predominate in his next poetic productions: *Poèmes anciens et romanesques* (1890; Ancient and Romanesque Poems), *Tel qu'en songe* (1892; As in a Dream), and *Les Jeux rustiques et divins* (1897; Rustic and Divine Games). In these works, Régnier breaks away from more rigid prosodic forms and turns towards a well-modulated free verse, retaining a strong sense of rhyme and assonance, particularly in the *odelette* (little ode). His images often derive from the mythology of ancient Greece.

Around the turn of the century, Régnier's poetry became more regulated or "classical" in nature, a reversal attributed to the influence of his famous father-in-law, José Maria de HEREDIA. Typical of this period are his *Médailles d'argile* (1900; Clay Medals) and *La Cité des eaux* (1902; The City of Waters), the latter evoking, in descriptive alexandrines, images of the past splendors of Versailles. Representatives of this reversion to traditional versification include *La Sandale ailée* (1906; Eng. tr., *Poems from the Winged Sandal*, 1933) and *Le Miroir des heures* (1910; Mirror of the Hours). These collections exhibit a striking sensitivity to physical beauty, be it in nature or in woman. Yet a strong undercurrent of weariness and nostalgia also flows beneath the surface of these primarily descriptive evocations of the 17th and 18th centuries, stressing the ephemerality of pleasure and of all human endeavor. The elegant, refined poetry of Régnier's old age, such as *Vestigia flammae* (1921) and *Flamma tenax* (1928), reflects the inspiration of a more sober, experienced, and meditative muse.

Like his later prose works, Régnier's early short stories exhibit an essentially precious style. His novels, drawn with indulgent amusement, are set in the 17th or 18th centuries, as in the case of *La Double Maîtresse* (1900; The Double Mistress), *Le Bon Plaisir* (1902; Good Pleasure), and *Les Rencontres de M. de Bréot* (1904; Eng. tr., *The Libertines*, 1929), or in the present, like *Le Mariage de minuit* (1903; Midnight Marriage) and *Les Vacances d'un jeune homme sage* (1903; The Vacation of a Well-Mannered Young Man). These tales, told in a highly decorative, elaborate manner, have shallow characterization and often symbolic settings, such as decaying Venice.

See: R. Honnert, *Henri de Régnier: son œuvre* (1923); E. Jaloux, *Souvenirs sur Henri de Régnier* (1941); M. Maurin, *Henri de Régnier: le labyrinthe et la double* (1972).   D.C. and A.C.

Reinig, Christa (1926–), German poet, novelist, playwright, and short-story writer, was born in Berlin and lived there until 1964. Trained as a florist, she worked as an unskilled laborer during the reconstruction of the city. In 1957, following four years of study in art history and archaeology at Humboldt University, she assumed a curatorial position at the Märkisches Museum, which she held until her move to West Germany in 1964. Devoting herself since then to writing, she has received several distinguished literary prizes.

However much Reinig's experiences as a citizen of four German states in succession may have shaped her ideas and her language, her political history is less evident to the reader than are the singularities of her tastes, preoccupations, and modes of apprehension. Her cool, laconic poems, prized for their ease of diction and clarity of vision, have been collected in several volumes, including *Der Abend—der Morgen* (1951; Evening—Morning), *Die Steine von Finisterre* (1960; The Stones of Finisterre), and *Die Schwalbe von Olevano* (1969; The Swallow from Olevano). Her works for children include a book of verse, *Hantipanti* (1972) and the story *Der Hund mit dem Schlüssel* (1976; The Dog with the Key, 1976). Of her several radio plays, the best known is the prize-winning *Aquarium* (1968). Reinig's autobiographical novel *Die himmlische und die irdische Geometrie* (1975; Heavenly and Earthly Geometry) and the subsequent novel *Die Entmannung* (1976; Emasculation) mark the beginnings of an attempt to define a peculiarly feminine consciousness and a language appropriate to it. In these novels, as well as in a number of scarcely classifiable works—including a "new Zodiac," *Orion trat aus dem Haus* (1969; Orion Left the House); an "eccentric anatomy," *Das große Bechterew-Tantra* (1970); and "exotic products of Old India," *Papantscha-Vielerlei* (1971; Papantsha-Potpourri)—Reinig shows herself a master of satire and grotesquerie in a tradition that encompasses the mordancy of Jonathan Swift and the humor of Mark Twain. Long disabled by Techterew's disease, she maintains in her writings a vigorous voice and an animating intellect.

See: D. Hülsmanns and F. Reske, eds., *Gratuliere: Wort und Bildgeschichte zum 50. Geburtstag von Christa Reinig* (1976).   S.J.

Reiss-Andersen, Gunnar (1896–1964), Norwegian poet, was born in Larvik on the Oslo Fjord and lived most of his life in that area. His first collection, *Indvielsens aar* (1921; The Years of Initiation), showed the influence of Olaf BULL and Herman WILDENVEY, whose poetry was then reaching its artistic peak. Reiss-Andersen's great facility for melodious rhythm and rhyme gave a soothing quality to his early poems on love and nature. During the 1930s, his poetry became increasingly an expression of social and political engagement. This development is evident in *Horisont* (1934; Horizon) and *Vidnesbyrd* (1936; Testimony) and reached its peak in the patriotic poems Reiss-Andersen wrote in exile in Sweden during World War II. The finest of these is the monumental "Norsk freske" (Norwegian Fresco) in *Dikt fra krigstiden* (1945; Wartime Poems).

After the war, Reiss-Andersen became increasingly preoccupied with metaphysical questions and new formal approaches. The broken world of postwar Europe was reflected in his increased use of symbolism and in experimental, fragmented structures. These tendencies were evident in *Usynlige seil* (1956; Invisible Sails) and found their richest expression in his last collection, *År på en strand* (1962; Years on a Beach).   K.A.F.

Remarque, Erich Maria (1898–1970), German novelist, gained world-wide fame with his war novel *Im Westen nichts Neues* (1929; Eng. tr., *All Quiet on the Western Front*, 1929). He was born the son of a bookbinder in

Osnabrück and attended schools there. He served and was wounded in World War I. Later he tried his hand at several professions, finally becoming the editor of a sports journal. In this position he wrote his famous novel, in which he claimed to be a spokesman for "a generation that was destroyed by war, even though it might have escaped its shells." The heroes of Remarque in this novel are not representative of a whole generation but only of a certain type, but the novel is an authentic record, and it has literary merit. Remarque was able to draw characters and situations, engage attention, and arouse sympathy. His language was, and remained always, versatile and concise, rich in contrast and interspersed with pertinent reflections. His composition is based upon excellent stage technique, and his novels were frequently turned into successful films. Lyric and idyllic scenes alternate with the coarsest and most lurid realism. The intricate problems of life and of war are reduced to plain propositions. The first successful novel gave eloquent expression to the cry "No more war," although World War II then came, furnishing Remarque with renewed thematic material for several more novels.

The fate of the surviving heroes in the chaotic time after World War I is told in *Der Weg zurück* (1931; Eng. tr., *The Road Back*, 1931). This novel falls short of its predecessor, although it has narrative interest. In 1932, Remarque moved to Switzerland, and in 1933 his books were burned by the Nazis. He was stripped of his German citizenship in 1938, and in 1939 he emigrated to the United States, where in 1947 he became a citizen. World War II and its epic events supplied Remarque with exciting material for other works of fiction after *Drei Kameraden* (1938 in German, preceded by *Three Comrades* in English in 1937). *Flotsam* (1941, in German and English) depicts the plight of castaways of wartime, fleeing the Gestapo. *Arc de triomphe* (1946; Eng. tr., *Arch of Triumph*, 1946) takes place in wartime Paris, relating the story of a woman doctor in flight from pursuing Gestapo agents. A prisoner in a concentration camp is the central character of *Der Funke Leben* (1952; Eng. tr., *Spark of Life*, 1952). It was followed by *Zeit zu leben und Zeit zu sterben* (1954; Eng. tr., *A Time to Love and a Time to Die*, 1954), *Der schwarze Obelisk* (1956; Eng. tr., *The Black Obelisk*, 1957), *Der Himmel kennt keine Günstlinge* (1961; Eng. tr., *Heaven Has No Favorites*, 1961), *Die Nacht in Lissabon* (1962; Eng. tr., *The Night in Lisbon*, 1964), and *Schatten im Paradies* (1971; Eng. tr., *Shadows in Paradise*, 1972), all more or less concerned with human beings in moments of peril and pursuit. His one play was *Die letzte Station* (Eng. tr., *Full Circle*, 1974).

See: F. Baumer, *Erich Maria Remarque* (1976).

W.K.P. rev. A.L.W.

Remizov, Aleksey Mikhaylovich (1877–1957), Russian novelist and playwright, was born in Moscow, the son of a merchant, and raised in a strict religious atmosphere. He studied natural science at Moscow University until his arrest and expulsion in 1897 for participating in a student demonstration. After eight years of prison and exile he settled in Petersburg, having begun publishing in modernist journals in 1902. He emigrated to Germany in 1921 and lived in Paris from 1923 until his death.

According to D. S. Mirsky, Remizov's work is varied "to such an extent that few of his admirers can embrace the whole of it in their admiration." Much is derivative, encompassing the entire Russian tradition from pagan mythology through Russianized forms of Byzantine Christianity to 19th-century Slavophilism. His derivative work includes: numerous volumes of folktales—*Posolon* (1907; With the Sun), *K moryu-okeanu* (1911; To the

Ocean-Sea), *Ukrepa* (1916; Buttress), *Sredi murya* (1917; Amid the Swarm), and *Russkiye zhenshchiny* (1918; Russian Women); parables, and canonical and apocryphal legends—*Limonar: Lug dukhovny* (1907, expanded 1911; The Spiritual Meadow), *Za svyatuyu Rus* (1915; For Holy Russia), *Nikoliny pritchi* (1917; Legends of Saint Nicholas), *Zvezda nadzvyozdnaya* (1928; Stella Maria Maris), *Povest o dvukh zveryakh: Ikhnelat* (1950; Ikhnelat: A Tale of Two Beasts), *Besnovatye* (1951; The Possessed), *Melyuzina. Bryuntsvik* (1952); and four plays on similar derivative themes. Although his religious parables and apocrypha found no imitators, his folktales did influence Mikhail PRISHVIN and Vyacheslav SHISHKOV.

Characterized by fragmented composition, lyric refrains, the grotesque, and a curious fusion of bookish and colloquial elements, Remizov's original fiction is firmly rooted in Nikolay Gogol, Nikolay LESKOV, and Vladimir Dal, and it stylistically influenced a whole generation of writers, including Yevgeny ZAMYATIN and Boris PILNYAK. His gloomy, ponderous novels *Prud* (1907, rev. ed. 1912; The Pond) and *Chasy* (1908; Eng. tr., *The Clock*, 1924) depict a merciless world ruled by senseless fate, as do his best works, the tales "Krestovye syostry" (1910; Sisters of the Cross), "Neuyemny buben" (1910; Eng. tr. in *The History of the Tinkling Cymbal and Sounding Brass*, 1927), and "Pyataya yazva" (1912; Eng. tr. in *The Fifth Pestilence*, 1927). In sharp contrast is the light tone of *Vesenneye poroshye* (1915; Spring Trifles), a collection of stories based on Remizov's understanding observations of children.

In emigration, Remizov developed an introspective, surrealistic amalgam of memoir, dream, lyric, and fiction evident in the works *Shumy goroda* (1921; The Sounds of the City), *Krashenye ryla* (1922; Painted Mugs), *Akhru* (1922), *Vzvikhrennaya Rus* (1922; Russia in a Whirlwind), *Po karnizam* (1929; Along the Cornices), *Myshkina dudochka* (1953; A Flute for Mice), *Podstrizhennymi glazami* (1953; With Clipped Eyes), and in the fictionalized biography of his wife, *V rozovom bleske* (1952; In a Rosy Light), which includes *V pole blakitnom* (1927; Eng. tr., *On a Field Azure*, 1946). The dream book *Martyn Zadeka* (1953) and the essays in *Ogon veshchey* (1954; The Fire of Things) further testify to the importance of dreams in Remizov's art.

See: D. Mirsky, *Contemporary Russian Literature, 1881–1925* (1926), pp. 281–91; N. Kodryanskaya, *Aleksey Remizov* (Paris, 1959); K. Geib, *Aleksej Michajlovič Remizov: Stilstudien* (Munich, 1970); A. Shane, "A Prisoner of Fate: Remizov's Short Fiction," *RLT* 4 (Fall 1972): 303–18.

A.M.S.

Renard, Jules (1864–1910), French novelist, playwright, and diarist, was born at Châlons-sur-Mayenne but spent most of his life in the Nivernais region of Burgundy and in Paris. His relatively short life was uneventful: a childhood made unhappy by a bigoted and unloving mother, secondary studies in Nevers and Paris, an early interest in writing, desultory white-collar jobs, and then marriage in 1888. From that date on, Renard divided his time between his writing and his family. Always ardently anticlerical, he came to count Léon BLUM and Jean JAURÈS among his personal friends.

Renard's writings fall into three groups: the novels and sketches, such as *L'Ecornifleur* (1892; Eng. tr., *The Sponger*, 1957), *Le Vigneron dans sa vigne* (1894; The Vineyardist in His Vineyard), *Poil de Carotte* (1894; Eng. tr., *Poil de Carotte* [Redhead], 1967), *Histoires naturelles* (1896; Eng. tr., *Natural Histories*, 1966), and *Nos Frères farouches: Ragotte* (1908; Our Rustic Brothers: Ragotte); the plays, of which the most successful are *Le Plaisir de rompre* (1897; Eng. tr., *Good bye!*, 1916), *Le Pain de ménage* (1898; Eng. tr., *Home-made Bread*, 1917), and the dramatized version of *Poil de Carotte* (1900; Eng. tr., *Carrots*, 1946); and finally the correspondence and, above all, the posthumous *Journal: 1887–1910* (1925–27; selected Eng. tr., *Journal*, 1964). The three groups really form a unity, for the novels and sketches are latent in the *Journal*, while the plays are adaptations from the novels and sketches.

Renard was a kind of pointillist Gustave Flaubert. He developed a meticulous and fragmented realism, stemming from a deep distrust of human motives, an equally deep distrust (or lack) of imaginative and intellectual faculties, a cult of the precise word, and an addiction to the condensed and witty image. His most finished novel is *L'Ecornifleur*, an acid and unrelenting transposition of a banal autobiographical episode. The equally autobiographical book, *Poil de Carotte*, is much more moving. This series of vignettes details the war of ruses between a psychotic mother and her hated youngest child. The long one-act play that Renard drew from the book is a modern classic. The overly arch images and mots of the animal pieces in *Histoires naturelles* have aged considerably, but the stark notations on peasants and village life in such collections as *Ragotte* preserve all their immediacy.

It is the *Journal*, however, that is now recognized as Renard's most important work. This diary is a succession of introspective notes, brief accounts of family crises, sardonic maxims, devastating social and literary chit-chat, and occasional poetic flashes. Unfortunately, the manuscript of the *Journal* was destroyed, and we possess only an unavoidably defective text; yet this self flagellating document nevertheless remains a fascinating chronicle of the fin de siècle and the *belle époque*.

See: L. Guichard, *L'Œuvre et l'âme de Jules Renard* (1935). A.J.K.

Renn, Ludwig, pseud. of Arnold Friedrich Vieth von Golssenau (1889–1979), German novelist, was born in Dresden, scion of an old and noble family with Irish and Russian ancestors. Following tradition he became an officer in 1911 and saw combat and staff service in World War I. Changed in his whole outlook by the experiences of war, especially after he had "ceased to drink," Renn began to write, in a factual style especially influenced by the travel books of Sven Hedin. After the war he turned to the political left and became a Communist. He studied at the universities of Göttingen, Munich, and Vienna and undertook extensive trips through the Mediterranean lands and Russia.

His fame rests on his first novel, *Krieg* (1928; Eng. tr., *War*, 1929), one of the few great books that came out of World War I. It presents a simple factual acceptance of the war, with a minimum of reflection, sentiment, and didacticism, and is a more powerful indictment than any elaborate harangue could be. Renn's style is terse, graphic, and clear, revealing a complete mastery of his subject. Pertinent criticism of the conditions of military life is tempered by an insight into general human weakness, and the distribution of light and shadow is done with fairness and objectivity.

In his later works Renn was less successful. *Nachkrieg* (1930; Eng. tr., *After War*, 1931), gives a picture of the hopeless mess of contradictory and aimless political strife in the Weimar Republic. A later volume, *Rußlandfahrten* (1932; Journeys in Russia), tells of his travels and impressions in the Soviet Union. Jailed for several years after Adolf Hitler's ascent to power, Renn escaped to Switzerland in 1936, where he wrote *Vor großen Wandlungen*

(1936; Eng. tr., *Death without Battle*, 1937). He took a prominent part in the Spanish Civil War, after which he lived in France, writing a treatise on warfare and society. He subsequently lived in Mexico, where he published his autobiographic novel *Adel im Untergang* (1944; The Decline of Nobility), but in 1947 he returned to East Germany, where he was professor of anthropology in Dresden before settling in East Berlin. He was the author of two books for children, *Trini* (1954) and *Der Neger Nobi* (1955; The Negro, Nobi). The autobiography *Meine Kindheit und Jugend* (My Childhood and Youth) was published in 1957, the same year as the novel *Krieg ohne Schlacht* (War without Battle). The novel *Auf den Trümmern des Kaiserreichs* (On the Ruins of the Emperor's Realm) appeared in 1961.

See: W. K. Pfeiler, *War and the German Mind* (1941), pp. 150–64. W.K.P. rev. A.L.W.

Rèpaci, Leonida (1898–), Italian novelist and playwright, was born in Palmi. After serving in World War I in a flamethrowers unit, he earned a degree in law at the University of Turin and practiced law in Milan. In 1919 he obtained the acquittal of an anarchist accused of terrorist bombings. Rèpaci started writing in the early 1920s and was involved in journalism for most of his life. In 1922 he became the drama critic of the Roman Communist daily *L'unità*. Arrested in 1925 for anti-Fascist activities, he spent seven months in jail awaiting trial and was finally acquitted. He established a significant reputation in the 1930s and 1940s with his cyclical novel *Storia dei fratelli Rupe*. Rèpaci founded the Viareggio Prize and developed it into an influential—although controversial—literary institution. He is president-for-life of the society that awards it. Rèpaci has traveled extensively throughout the world, writing articles and books on foreign lands and customs. He appeared in Federico Fellini's film *La dolce vita*, giving a short speech on Oriental women in the scene of a party in a writer's home. In 1971, Rèpaci left Rome to live in seclusion in a villa on the sea in his native town in Calabria.

Passion and violence in a primitive setting are recurring motifs in Rèpaci's works, but he is also concerned with social problems. In the novel *L'ultimo Cireneo* (1923; The Last Man of Cyrene), a war invalid plots the murder of his cousin because he unjustly suspects the latter of having a love affair with his wife. He then compares the murder to the savage massacre of World War I. Rèpaci's play *La madre incatenata* (1925; The Mother in Chains) deals with family rivalries. The novel *La carne inquieta* (1930; The Restless Flesh) concerns an unhappy love between a poor peasant and a rich lady. After having been falsely convicted of raping her, the peasant becomes demented and commits suicide; the lady spends a few years in a convent and then becomes a kept woman. The novel *Il deserto del sesso* (1956; The Desert of Sex), concerning the exploits of a pro-Fascist nymphomaniac, was the object of a legal suit for pornography that ended in the author's acquittal. The four-volume *Storia dei fratelli Rupe* (History of the Rupe Family) intersperses the deeds and travels of 10 Calabrian brothers and sisters with the main political events of the 20th century, ranging in setting from Italy to the United States and the USSR. The novel devotes special attention to the political and sexual activities of Leto Rupe, a largely autobiographical character.

Critical attention to Rèpaci's works (amounting to some 30 volumes) has been quite modest, even though they have been popular with Italian readers. None have been translated into English.

See: A. Altomonte, in *Letteratura italiana: i contemporanei,* vol. 3 (1975), pp. 323–47.   A.T.

Reve, Gerard Kornelis van het (1923–), Dutch novelist and translator, was born in Amsterdam of a working-class family. He began his literary career with the publication in the magazine *Criterium* of his novella *De ondergang van de familie Boslowitz* (1946; The Decline of the Boslowitz Family), a chilling account of the beginning of World War II and the coming of the Nazis to the Netherlands. His first novel, *De avonden* (1947; The Evenings), is a gloomy and realistic portrayal of the postwar generation's view of life. It has no plot, but describes the evenings in the life of the hero, a young office worker who drifts along aimlessly in frustration. *Werther Nieland* (1949) is an excellent autobiographical work. Feeling that he was not appreciated in his own country—he lost a travel grant that he had been awarded—he decided to leave the Netherlands, and took up the study of English. In 1956, he published *The Acrobat and Other Stories,* which was later translated into Dutch as *Vier wintervertellingen* (1963; Four Winter Tales). The collections of travel letters published as *Op weg naar het einde* (1963; Approaching the End) and *Nader tot U* (1966; Nearer to You) belong to a different period in his life. Both reveal thoughts of approaching death. Two other volumes of prose fiction are *De taal der liefde* (1972; The Language of Love) and *Lieve jongens* (1973; Dear Boys). He is an admirer of Ivan Turgenev. Van het Reve has been influenced by Harold Pinter, and he has translated *The Caretaker* and *The Collection.* He has also translated Edward Albee's *Who's Afraid of Virginia Woolf?* Van het Reve was an editor of the magazine *Tirade.*

See: K. Beekman and M. Meijer, *Kort Revier: Gerard Reve en het oordeel van zijn medeburgers* (1973).

S.L.F.

Reverdy, Pierre (1889–1960), French poet, was born in Narbonne. The son of an artist father, Reverdy was first attracted to the plastic arts, and on arriving in Paris in 1910 he joined artists such as Juan Gris, Pablo Picasso, and Georges Braque. In 1917, Reverdy helped found the review *Nord-Sud,* which provided a climate of avant-garde aesthetics for such future surrealists as Louis ARAGON, André BRETON, and Philippe SOUPAULT, as well as for the Chilean poet Vicente Huidobro. As an early mentor of the surrealists and a contemporary of the cubists, Reverdy maintained the consistency of his literary signature through changing modes and eras.

Reverdy's first comprehensive collection of poetry, *Les Epaves du ciel* (1924; Chips from Heaven), contains poems written between 1915 and 1918, its title appropriately indicating the intermingling of chips of heaven and the bric-a-brac of earth. *Le Gant de crin* (1927; The Glove of Horsehair) consists of his observations on the creative power of the poet and his dialectics between spirituality and reality. Without overt reference to the role of the subconscious, Reverdy provides a bridge between Arthur RIMBAUD and the surrealists in the recognition of the unpredictable psychic forces that catalyze verbal encounters. A second volume of maxims, written between 1930 and 1936, was entitled *Le Livre de mon bord* (1948; My Logbook). An enlarged edition of *Les Epaves* appeared in 1945 under the title of *La Plupart du temps* (Most of the Time), and the rest of his poems of the period 1913–49, including *Ferraille* (1937; Scrap Iron) as well as those written in Solesmes during the Nazi occupation, were collected in *Main d'œuvre* (1949; Manpower).

Solesmes became Reverdy's permanent residence after his marriage, but he preserved a continuous contact with the Paris artistic milieus and made brief but frequent returns to the capital. Solesmes, with its poplar trees, gray skies, Benedictine monastery, and utter silences became an a posteriori correspondence to the inner landscapes that Reverdy had projected into his poetry. Reality confirmed the visionary structure of his inner world; words, complex in their simplicity, populated the empty canvas with isolated realities of plural significants, blocked sometimes by walls, by darkness, and by death. When Reverdy's world seems to stop turning, he is not overwhelmed by a Sartrian nothingness (*see* Jean-Paul SARTRE) but rapt with the mystery of existence. For Reverdy, the material world, which at all moments made its perishable quality felt, was the funnel for his metaphysical search.

Becoming less Promethean during World War II, he evoked, in "Le Chant des morts" (Song of the Dead), a mutilated world by using to advantage his special technique for creating concrete, disconnected images. Particularly adept with the prose poem, which he used intermittently with free verse, Reverdy discreetly avoided all standard metrical structures. His last prose poems, *Une Aventure méthodique* (A Methodical Adventure) and *La Liberté des mers* (The Liberty of the Seas), written in 1956, were published posthumously with lithographs by Braque.

See: R. Brunner, *Pierre Reverdy: de la solitude au mystère* (1966); M. Guiney, *La Poésie de Pierre Reverdy* (1966); R. Greene, *The Poetic Theory of Pierre Reverdy* (1967); A. Balakian, *Surrealism: The Road to the Absolute* (1970); A. Rizzuto, *Style and Theme in Reverdy's Les Ardoises du Ciel* (1971).   A.B.

Reymont, Władysław Stanisław (1867–1925), Polish novelist, was born in Kobiele Wielkie and died in Warsaw. His road to literature was a long and complicated one. Not having received any formal education, he toiled at many jobs before he became a writer. His youthful experiences with a traveling theatrical company provided him with topics for his first two novels, *Komediantka* (1896; Eng. tr., *The Comedienne,* 1920) and *Fermenty* (1897; Ferment). Although limited in scope to the world of actors, both novels provide an interesting insight into life in Poland in the 1880s and show Reymont's mastery in portraying such problems as the artist versus society, alienation, and psychological desintegration under pressure. His ambitious novel *Ziemia obiecana* (1899; Eng. tr., *The Promised Land,* 1927) depicts the industrial city of Łódź in all the national and social complexity caused by its Polish, German, and Jewish elements, making it not only a major manufacturing center but also a modern urban metropolis with all the problems of a rapidly industrializing society. It merits recognition as one of the first European novels to present those issues.

Reymont attracted worldwide attention with his major novel *Chłopi* (1902–09; Eng. tr., *The Peasants,* 1924–25) a broad panorama of a Polish rural community with all the customs, traditions, and peculiarities against which a complex family tragedy is depicted. The relationship between the events in the Bornya family—a son's rivalry with his father over his stepmother, eventually growing to the major proportions of a classical Greek tragedy—and the community of Lipce makes the novel structurally coherent and gives it a universal meaning that reaches far beyond merely local boundaries. The realism of the novel is heightened by its stylistic perfection, and the descriptions of the countryside blend with the narration and dialogues in a unique combination of poetic lyricism, realistic exactness, and local folkloristic elements. For that novel, translated into every major language, Reymont received the Nobel Prize for Literature in 1924.

His historical trilogy *Rok 1794* (1913–18) recreates the last years of the Polish Republic before its partitions by Russia, Prussia, and Austria. Ambitious in scope, it never became as successful as some historical novels by Reymont's contemporaries, Henryk SIENKIEWICZ and Stefan ŻEROMSKI. Nevertheless, some parts of it are quite impressive, particularly those devoted to the Kosciuszko insurrection against the Russians.

Reymont also wrote numerous short stories and short fiction, gradually evolving from his early naturalistic manner of writing, for example, *Śmierć* (1893; Eng. tr., *The Death,* 1921) toward realism and eventually symbolism in his later works, such as *Wołanie* (1915; Eng. tr., *The Mother,* 1947). Although artistically uneven, they represent an important contribution to the development of Polish fiction at the turn of the century. His collected works, *Pisma,* are being published (vols. 1–8, 1968–75).

See: J. R. Krzyżanowski, *Władysław Stanisław Reymont* (1972).   J.R.K.

Riba, Carles (1893–1959), Catalan poet, was born in Barcelona and studied law and literature at the university there. He was a professor of Greek in the Library School, clerk of the Generalitat and of the university, and director of the Bernat Metge Collection under the auspices of the politician Cambo. He was married to the Catalan poet Clementina Arderiu. He first made a name for himself as a translator of *Las Bucòliques* (1911) of Virgil. The same year an eclogue of his won the Natural Flower of the Floral Games of Gerona. Riba's first book of criticism, *Escolls* (1921), shows him to be a fervent adherent of the "Noucentisme" of Eugenio D'ORS. During the first 35 years of his life, Riba cultivated the art of writing narrative prose, the subject of an informative study by Maurici SERRAHIMA. Riba's prose works include his delightful children's stories, *Les aventures d'en Perot Marrasquí* (1924) and *Sis Joans* (1928), his collection of fantastic tales, *L'ingenu amor* (1924), and other works of criticism, such as *Els marges* (1927), *Per comprendre* (1937), and . . .*més els poemes* (1957). He translated classical works like *L'Odissea* (1919), *Antígona, Electra* (1920) by Sophocles, and *Vidas D'Alexandre i Cesar* (1920) by Plutarch, and modern works like Edgar Allan Poe's *Històries extraordinaries* (1915) and *Els assassinats del carrer Morgue* (1918).

But Riba's true vocation was poetry. He first became known for *Primer Llibre d'estances* (1919), a genuine revelation of poetic talent. He published it together with *Segon Llibre d'estance* in 1930 as *Estances. Tres suites* (1937) confirmed Riba's mastery, and his poetry achieved its maximum expression in *Elegies de Bierville* (1942), written in exile. Here his basic humanism, touched by the winds of war and exile, turned to a politicized poetry committed to the search for liberty. He began writing a day-to-day chronicle, in which his nostalgia for his homeland never defeated his determination to create a poetry of civil character and personal justification, through which he was also able to communicate with his God.

After his return to Catalonia he published *Del joc i del foc* (1946; Of Play and Fire), a book of tankas that further develops the hermeticism already present in the earlier book of sonnets, *Estances, Salvatge Cor* (1946). Riba's *Obra Poética* was published in 1956 by *Insula* in Madrid, with Castilian translations by Alfonso Costafreda, Paulina Crusat, and Rafael Santos Torroella. These translations helped to make him better known in Castile. In *Esbós de tres oratoris* (1957; Sketch of Three Oratories), his last work, he poetically glosses three themes from the New Testament. In this work, Riba seemed to approach a new poetic horizon that he would never reach, as he died unexpectedly on July 12, 1959.

At the end of his life his wisdom and his accomplishments were acknowledged by the younger generations of Catalan poets and by Spanish poets who, led by Dionisio RIDRUEJO, paid him public homage. Riba's conciliatory attitude served as an example both to Catalonia and to the rest of the Iberian Peninsula. He had always favored a continuous dialogue with Castilian intellectuals and attended various meetings of poets, in which his very presence was a guarantee that the best of Catalonia would support any valid attempt at mutual comprehension and understanding.

See: J. Ferrate, *Carles Riba, avui* (1955); M. Serrahima, *Dotze mestres* (1972); A. Manent, *Tres escritores catalanes: Carner, Riba, Pla* (1973).   J.F.C.

Ribeiro, Aquilino (1885–1963), Portuguese novelist and essayist, was born of peasant stock in Carregal da Tabosa, a mountain hamlet of the "rough and ascetic" backlands in the former province of Beira. He won fame as the most accomplished fiction writer in modern Portugal, both through the vigor of his style and the diversity of his subjects, and is at his best when recreating the life of his native province of Beira. When a student, he was jailed for conspiring against the monarchy but was able to escape and continue his studies in Lausanne and at the Sorbonne in Paris. It was perhaps in Paris that he acquired the irreverent irony, reminiscent of Anatole FRANCE, that pervades his stories and cools the ardor of their glorification of nature, life, and love. At the same time, the author never lost the sense of human solidarity that made him join the *Seara Nova* (New Crop) group (see PORTUGUESE LITERATURE) and devote the best of his talent to recounting the humble lives of Portuguese peasants. In 1914 he returned to Portugal to teach high school and administer the ecclesiastical libraries seized by the Republic. Keeping faith with his republican and anticlerical convictions, he actively opposed the dictatorship that came to power in 1926. An exile in France in 1927 and 1928, he returned to join an abortive uprising against the regime, escaped from a military prison, and again went to Paris for two years (1930–31). Upon his definitive return to Portugal (1932), he became practically the only Portuguese man of letters who could subsist as a professional writer. He was briefly jailed and prosecuted for political reasons just before his death.

Ribeiro's style already attained maturity in his first book, *Jardim das tormentas* (1913; Garden of Storms), 11 tales about human frailty, written from 1910 to 1912 in Paris. Four of the tales introduced the Beira peasants, their worldly priests, haughty *fidalgos,* and corruptible magistrates. Other regional works followed, written in a rich vernacular and narrating stories of rural passions, relieved now and then by pantheistic landscapes and the pageantry of folklore. These include *Terras do Demo* (1917; Lands of Satan); *Andam faunos pelos bosques* (1926; Fauns Roam the Woods); and the diffuse *Volfrâmio* (1943; Tungsten), showing how the coveted metal supplied the Devil with a new means of corruption. In *A casa grande de Romarigães* (1957; The Great House of Romarigães) Ribeiro traced the decadence of a landed family, and in *Quando os lobos uivam* (1958; Eng. tr., *When the Wolves Howl,* 1963) he injected a note of political protest into his description of the communal way of life in a mountain village, threatened by the official decision to reforest its pasture lands. Although at his best as a regional writer, for example, in his most popular tale, *O Malhadinhas* (1922; Little Piebald), Ribeiro knew also how to analyze modern city life, as in *O homem que matou o Diabo* (1930; The Man Who Killed the Devil). With the same ease he wrote animal stories for children, such as *Romance da raposa* (2 vols., 1924; Reynard the Fox), or transplanted the theme of *Thaïs* into a Portuguese setting in *S. Banaboião anacoreta e mártir* (1937; Saint Banaboião, Anchorite and Martyr). With a European conscience, he viewed sympathetically French reactions in 1914 and German prostration in 1920. He also wrote a great deal of biography and history, painting earthy, unorthodox portraits of the great in past and modern Iberian literature, among them Cervantes, Camões, Camilo Castelo Branco, and Eça de Queiroz (see PORTUGUESE LITERATURE). His own memoirs appeared only in 1974, with an introduction by J. Gomes Ferreira: *Um escritor confessa-se* (Confessions of a Writer).

See: C. Branco Chaves, *Aquilino Ribeiro* (1935); M. Mendes, *Aquilino Ribeiro* (1960); O. Lopes, "Aquilino Ribeiro: alguns livros e uma panorâmica," in his *Cinco personalidades literárias* (1961), pp. 23–48.

G.M.M. rev. E.M.D.

Ribemont-Dessaignes, Georges (1884–1974), French dramatist and novelist, was born in Montpellier. He was associated with the dada movement and then, briefly, with surrealism (*see* FRENCH LITERATURE). In such writings as his *Manifeste à l'huile* (1920; Manifesto in Oil) and *Manifeste selon Saint-Jean Chrysopompe* (1920; Manifesto According to Saint-John Chrysopompe), Ribemont-Dessaignes made a colorful attack on André BRETON's second surrealist manifesto, accusing him of being a combination policeman and pope, a "tadpole of the font," and a "littérateur."

Ribemont-Dessaignes's major achievements are his plays, works that combine a baroque lyricism with an exalted intensity, violence of action, and apparent illogicality in what may well be the most successful realization of Antonin ARTAUD's theater of cruelty. In *L'Empereur de Chine* (1921; The Emperor of China), a princess is raped by her father in a demonstration of royal "conception to the second power," but she later demonstrates the extent of her own cruelty. She herself is finally beheaded, as the collective force of the system destroys the individual, even the most royal. In "Le Serin muet" (1966; The Mute Canary), a one-act play heavy with irony, a false sovereign fires upon his wife and her lover. At the end of the play, he remains alone with a caged, mute bird and his conviction that he is the supreme realist and the "master of Europe." An interesting and highly peculiar early novel, *Ariane* (1925)—resembling Breton's *Nadja* (1928; Eng. tr., 1960) in its presentation of a woman unlike all others—concerns a naked woman who wanders about, the antithesis of the practical, domestic, and "odious species of girl promised to the patented domesticity of the spouse." Ribemont-Dessaignes's later novels deal with related themes. *Le Temps des catastrophes* (1947; The Age of Catastrophe) examines the obsession of self carried about as baggage, whereas *Smeterling* (1945) portrays a revolt against the "guardians of order" whose watchdog is God.

See: J. P. Begot, *Ribemont-Dessaignes: 1915–1930* (1975).

M.A.C.

Ricardou, Jean (1932–), French critic and novelist, was born in Cannes. He is known as one of the chief exponents of French new criticism (*nouvelle critique*). His articles on the "new novel" (*see* FRENCH LITERATURE), first published in *Tel Quel* and other progressive literary reviews, have been collected in *Problèmes du nouveau roman* (1967; Problems of the New Novel), *Pour une théorie du nouveau roman* (1971; Toward a Theory of the New Novel), and *Le Nouveau Roman* (1973). In his debates on the function of literature he has elicited the opinion of numerous writers, including Simone de BEAUVOIR and Jean-Paul SARTRE.

Ricardou's novels, *L'Observatoire de Cannes* (1961; The Cannes Observer), *La Prise de Constantinople* (1965; The Fall of Constantinople), which won him the Fénéon Prize, and *Les Lieux-dits* (1969; Place Names), as well as a volume of short stories entitled *Révolutions minuscules* (1971; Minute Changes), reflect his concept of fiction and illustrate his theory that description determines the narrative of a fictional work. Ricardou is also known for his studies of the relationship between film and literature.

B.C.

Richard, Jean-Pierre (1922–), French literary critic, studied at the Ecole Normale Supérieure. Richard has taught in London and Madrid. He is now professor of literature at the Vincennes branch of the University of Paris.

Richard first attracted attention with a striking series of four studies (on Stendhal, Gustave Flaubert, Eugène Fromentin, and the Goncourts) entitled *Littérature et sensation* (1954), a volume that may still be his finest work. Inevitably, some monotony crept into Richard's method as he published volume after volume of thematic criticism, reconstructing from a dazzling (and almost confusing) multitude of examples the manner in which a writer perceives and elaborates into images the material world. At least three of his volumes, *Poésie et profondeur* (1955; Poetry and Profundity), *L'Univers imaginaire de Mallarmé* (1961; Mallarmé's Imaginary Universe)—his challenging doctoral thesis, and *Onze études sur la poésie moderne* (1964; Eleven Studies on Modern Poetry), deal with French poets: Gérard de Nerval, Charles BAUDELAIRE, Paul VERLAINE, Arthur RIMBAUD, Stéphane MALLARMÉ, and more recent writers from Pierre REVERDY to Jacques Dupin.

Richard may have displayed his rare sensitivity and insight even more brilliantly in his volumes on prose writers, *Le Paysage de Chateaubriand* (1967; Chateaubriand's Landscapes) and, to a lesser degree, *Proust et le monde sensible* (1974; Proust and the World of the Senses). Deliberately discarding biography, discussion of ideas, and even form and style, Richard delves into the sensations through which the sensibility and imagination of a writer are closely bound up with the material world. For Richard, everything begins in sensation. Georges POULET, Maurice BLANCHOT, and especially Gaston BACHELARD paved the way for this kind of criticism, yet Richard, more thoroughly and perhaps more successfully than they, has remained close to the concrete, a modest and piercingly attentive reader of the texts he illuminates.

H.P.

Richepin, Jean (1849–1930), French poet, novelist, and dramatist, was born in Médéa, Algeria, the son of an army doctor. His early years were spent in the atmosphere of an army garrison; then followed an education in Parisian lycées, a course in medicine at Douai, and, in 1868, the Ecole Normale Supérieure, which he left in 1870 to fight in the Franco-Prussian War. A period of bohemianism ensued, during which Richepin made his headquarters in Montmartre and supported himself by desultory journalism, yielding at intervals to a passion for wandering that took him over much of Europe and during which he worked at a variety of trades, from farm hand to juggler. In these years a group formed around Richepin, including such men as Ponchon, Bouchor, Germain NOUVEAU, and even for a while Arthur RIMBAUD. Calling themselves *les vivants,* they scorned conventions, both social and literary, were interested in popular poetry and folk song, and believed that the proper material for the artist was the life of the common people and that the artist's achievement could best be estimated by the extent to which he appealed to the uneducated masses.

This revolt against convention and interest in the lower classes is evident in all Richepin's early work, which began typically with *Les Etapes d'un réfractaire* (1872; The Stages of an Insubordinate), a study of Jules Vallès, and is particularly marked in *La Chanson des gueux* (1876; The Song of the Beggars), his most famous book. In these poems, Richepin continued the portrayal of the vagabond, the *gueux,* which is at least as old as François Villon, writing of the lives of these wanderers both in Paris and in the provinces with an unabashed realism and a use of argot that shocked his contemporaries. He was imprisoned and fined for *outrage aux mœurs,* but the book's reputation, and his, was made. There can be no doubt that Richepin did a great deal to capitalize on this notoriety. His striking physique, handsome face, and grand manner, plus his attitude of romantic defiance, completely satisfied the public's notion of all that a poet should be. Richepin, a born actor, adapted himself to what was expected of him, allowing romantic speculations to spring up as to his ancestry (actually he was descended from perfectly respectable country folk of the Ardennes) and encouraging the legend of his vagrant nature, familiarity with the seamy side of life, and excessive virility. *Les Caresses* (1877), poems written in frank praise of physical love, as well as *Les Morts bizarres* (1876; The Strange Deaths), a collection of short stories in the style of E. T. A. Hoffmann and Edgar Allan Poe, increased his notoriety. In the following years there was no lack of work from his pen—indeed, all his life he was constantly turning out journalistic work of some sort in addition to his more formal productions—notably *La Glu* (1881; The Slime), a study of a female Don Juan; *Miarka* (1883), the story, rich in local color, of a gypsy girl growing up among townspeople in Richepin's beloved district of Thierache; *Les Blasphèmes* (1884; Blasphemies), a group of strident poems proclaiming Richepin's materialism and atheism; and *La Mer* (1886; The Sea), poetry milder in tone, finding its inspiration in the sea and in the dangerous, humble lives of its followers. At the same time a series of plays were winning him an even wider popularity, especially *Le Flibustier* (1888; The Pirate) and *Le Chemineau* (1897; The Tramp).

Richepin's personal life grew more stable as the years passed (he was received into the Académie Française in 1908), and his work, although still in the main concerned with the grotesque and the abnormal, lost much of its truculent style. He continued to be prolific in prose, poetry, and the drama, but none of the work he did after the turn of the century can be considered as having added to his stature, unless it be the charming dramatization—so unexpected from Richepin—of Charles Perrault's *La Belle au bois dormant* (1907; Sleeping Beauty). He took with grace and humor the honors with which his later days were decked.

In his own day, Richepin's personal charm inevitably influenced his critics; looking back on his work at present and divorcing it from the man, one can judge more soberly. Historically there is no doubt that it is of considerable interest. Richepin's depiction of the lower classes inspired many imitators. *Le Chemineau* can share with Edmond Rostand's *Cyrano* the credit for a temporary revival of the romantic drama in verse, and much of Richepin's prose and poetry can be said to have encouraged the development of naturalism. From a purely aes-

thetic point of view, Richepin's work does not fare so well. A few of the novels, *Braves Gens* (1886; Fine People) and *Le Cadet* (1890; The Younger Brother) in particular, can hold their own, and there is, no doubt, a considerable body of good poetry scattered through Richepin's plays and volumes of verse. But most of his work seems not only dated but essentially superficial. He exploited his flamboyant personality to the utmost in his work. Fond of simple, direct, sensual pleasures, rough, uncomplicated characters, and a wandering, rootless life, he was able to present in a forceful way the surface of things but not their depths. His skillful rhetoric is too often hollow; the devices of technique that he perfected as he grew older, his ability to write a sonorous alexandrine or a theatrically effective scene, fail to hide the essential intellectual poverty of his work.

See: J. Lemaître, *Les Contemporains,* sér. 3 (1894); V. Thompson, *French Portraits* (1900); H. d'Alméras, *Avant la gloire* (1902); F. W. Chandler, *The Contemporary Drama of France* (1920); A. Séché, *Dans la mêlée littéraire* (1935); H. Sutton, *The Life and Works of Jean Richepin* (1961); J. Renaitour, *Erato* (1972), pp. 161–80.

C.W. rev. D.W.A.

Richter, Hans Werner (1908–), German novelist and mentor of post-1945 writers through the famed "Gruppe 47," was born in Bansin on the island of Usedom, the son of a fisherman. He became a bookdealer in Swinemünde and Berlin, then lived in Paris in 1933–34, after which he returned to Berlin and worked as a filling station attendant and chauffeur until he again became a book dealer in 1936. He served in the German armed forces in Poland, France, and Italy in World War II and spent the years 1943 to 1945 in the United States in American captivity. It was during the years as a prisoner of war that he and his friend and fellow author Alfred Andersch conceived a magazine for prisoners of war, *Der Ruf.*

Upon his return to Germany after the war Richter worked to publish an independent, nonaligned periodical, *Die Skorpion,* which was banned by American military government authorities and never distributed. It was at that point that Richter and like-minded author-friends met informally to read to one another and mutually criticize their literary efforts, which was the birth of the "Gruppe 47." The phenomenal influence of the "Gruppe" on postwar literature in Germany, through critics and publishers, can hardly be measured. It prospered until 1968, when a scheduled meeting in Prague was nullified by the Russian occupation of Czechoslovakia.

Like his peers, Richter was concerned about the experiences of the recent war, as in his first novel *Die Geschlagenen* (1949; Eng. tr., *Beyond Defeat,* 1950), which relates the experiences of a German corporal, Gühler, who suffers captivity and the interrogations of conquerors. The central contradiction of the novel, for Gühler hated Hitler and yet fought for his cause, was a problem that plagued many a German soldier. Later novels, such as *Sie fielen aus Gottes Hand* (1951; Eng. tr., *They Fell from God's Hand,* 1956), the autobiographical novel *Spuren im Sand* (1953; *Tracks in the Sand*), and the novel on the business of publishing, *Linus Fleck oder der Verlust der Würde* (1959; Linus Fleck or The Loss of Dignity), were written in a realistic style that critics found banal. The experiences of war, as in the novel *Du sollst nicht töten* (1955; Thou Shalt Not Kill), play a large role in Richter's writing. In 1962 he edited an informative volume about the "Gruppe 47," *Almanach der Gruppe 47,* which included literary contributions by the friends who made up the group. Stories from the place of his birth, *Blinder Alarm, Geschichten aus Bansin* (False

Alarm, Stories from Bansin), appeared in 1970. The novel *Rose weiß, Rose rot* (1971; Rose White, Rose Red) follows the doomed generation of the 1920s in its path to betrayal and defeat. Richter achieved an almost mystical leadership of German authors during the heyday of the "Gruppe 47" and remained afterwards an admired and respected literary connoisseur.   A.L.W.

Ridruejo, Dionisio (1912–75), Spanish poet, journalist, and essayist, was born in the province of Soria and died in Madrid. In 1933, during the Second Republic and in the midst of his law studies, he joined the Falange, the government's rightist opposition. From the beginning of the Civil War in 1936 he was much involved in political matters and in 1937 headed the Falange in Valladolid. A year later he was named chief of the Nationalist Propaganda Service. The war over, in 1940 he and Pedro LAÍN ENTRALGO founded the key literary journal *Escorial*. Shortly thereafter he joined the Spanish Blue Division that fought alongside the Germans on the Russian Front. After his return to Spain in 1942, he resigned all government posts in disillusionment and addressed a critical letter to Francisco Franco. Thereafter he was several times imprisoned and exiled. He later claimed that the Civil War had been "an absolutely unpardonable historical mistake," and from 1951 on his political activities were in the service of democratic ideals. In 1957 he founded the illegal Socialist Party for Democratic Action and in 1974 was one of the founders of the Spanish Union for Socialist Democracy. His integrity and courage in the service of an intensely felt but disinterested political evolution earned him the admiration of friends and enemies alike.

Ridruejo's poetic production, still insufficiently studied, began with *Plural* (1935) and includes among other volumes *Poesía en armas* (1940; Poetry at War), *Sonetos a la piedra* (1943; Sonnets to the Stones), and *Elegías* (1948). *En once años* (1950; In Eleven Years) and *Hasta la fecha* (1960; To Date) are collections of previously published work. Late books are *Cuaderno catalán* (1966; Catalan Notebook) and *Casi en prosa* (1972; Almost in Prose), the latter dealing with the poet's experience of the United States. Among his collections of essays are *Dentro del tiempo* (1959; Inside Time); *Escrito en España* (1962; Written in Spain), which had to be published in Argentina; and the fascinating posthumous collection *Sombras y bultos* (1977; Shadows and Forms), containing insightful studies of both literature and political history.

As a poet, Ridruejo belongs to the Generation of 1936. Like that of his fellow poets of the group, his work represents a return to the classical forms (the sonnet is very frequent) and "rehumanization" after the experimentalism and aestheticism of the prior Generation of 1927. Time, landscape, and the everyday life and death of man, together with human and divine love, are the center of Ridruejo's poetics.

See: L. F. Vivanco, *Introducción a la poesía española contemporánea* (1971), vol. 2, pp. 311–54; C. A. Gómez, ed., *Dionisio Ridruejo: casi unas memorias* (1976).
                                                                H.L.B.

Rifbjerg, Klaus (1931–), Danish author, was born in Copenhagen. He studied at the University of Copenhagen. Rifbjerg was a film director from 1955 to 1957 and a literary critic after 1955. In his third poetry collection, *Konfrontation* (1960; Confrontation)—which contains poems that exclusively relay precise observations—the form and themes of modernistic poetry have their true breakthrough in Denmark. His next collection, *Camouflage* (1961), is a grandiose and ecstatic (but not easily accessible) attempt to overcome outer reality by means

of a journey through the unconscious back to the myths and a personal past. The confrontation technique of classic modernism becomes modified in Rifbjerg's later poetry. *Amagerdigte* (1965; Poems from Amager) is distinguished by a very factual and reportorial style, inspired by the so-called new simplicity in modern Swedish literature. This collection depicts Rifbjerg's childhood milieu, a private motif that also is the essence of *25 desperate digte* (1974; 25 Desperate Poems), a naked portrayal of the author himself. The volume *Ved stranden* (1976; At the Beach) resumes the uninhibited and expansive fantasy flights of the earlier works in a new, original attitude of confrontation with nature. Rifbjerg's more than 60 works include not only poetry and prose but also a number of revue texts, scripts, and less successful dramas, revealing the extent to which his talent is tied to language rather than to the scenic and dramatic.

Rifbjerg's prose writing is mostly traditional. His first novel, *Den kroniske uskyld* (1958; The Chronic Innocence), describes the painful mystery of puberty, the in-between phase that, when confronted with the adult world, leads to catastrophe. The same motif is present in many of the short stories in *Og andre historier* (1964; And Other Stories), *Den syende jomfru* (1972; The Sewing Virgin), *Sommer* (1974; Summer) and *Det korte af det lange* (1976; In Short), the last three of which are less experimental than the 1964 collection. The problems of insecure youth are also the focal points in the novels *Arkivet* (1967; The Archives) and *Lonni og Karl* (1968; Lonni and Karl). The latter is a comic and satirical revolutionary fantasy, dedicated to Fidel Castro.

Rifbjerg directs his psychological exploration at the established adult world in a series of novels. *Operaelskeren* (1966; The Opera Lover) depicts a cold rationalist who discovers that his hitherto secure world is manipulated by forces beyond his control. The full consequence of this is felt by the principal character of *Anna (jeg) Anna* (1969; Anna (I) Anna), one of the major works of recent Danish literature. Anna, a neurotic diplomat's wife, escapes from her luxurious existence by traveling across Europe with a young criminal hippie type. The escape motif is also present in *Brevet til Gerda* (1972; The Letter to Gerda), an anguished outcry against the static and passive, which mask a fear of life that in reality is a fear of death. This theme, which is related to the theme of a journey back to one's human and social origins by means of liberation from any suppression, is repeated in the novel *Vejen ad hvilken* (1975; The Road along Which). In *R.R.* (1972) the criticism is directed at the crippling and leveling effects of rationalism, to which the main character—a Faustuslike type—has sold his soul. A similar complexity characterizes *Kiks* (1976; Miss), a satirical and political novel, employing Rifbjerg's earlier confrontation technique, whereas *Dilettanterne* (1973; The Dilettantes) and the "family chronicle" *De beskedne* (1976; The Modest), which tells of Danish everyday life during the 1950s and 1960s, are more easily accessible. Nevertheless they, together with perhaps Rifbjerg's most significant novels of the 1970s, *Tango* (1978) and *Joker* (1979) confirm his position in Scandinavian literature as an exceptionally sensitive and prolific writer.

See: T. Brostrøm, *Klaus Rifbjerg—en digter i tiden* (1970); C. S. Gray, "Klaus Rifbjerg: A Contemporary Danish Writer," *BA* (January 1975): 25–28; P. Øhrgaard, *Klaus Rifbjerg* (1977).   S.H.R.

Rilke, Rainer Maria (1875–1926), German poet, was born in Prague, Czechoslovakia, of old Bohemian and Alsatian stock. After a few unhappy early years (1886–91) at the military academies of Saint Pölten and Weisskirchen, a year at school in Linz, and four in Prague, he moved to Munich. Untouched by the naturalistic and impressionistic tendencies, he completed in 1894 a collection of indifferent love poems in the conventional style of Heinrich Heine, *Leben und Lieder* (Life and Songs). Even in his second and more distinctive volume of poetry, *Larenopfer* (1896; Sacrifice to the Lares), he revealed little beyond a sentimental attachment to his native city, Prague, and a lively although undisciplined sensitivity to aesthetic impressions. He had not yet brought himself to the intensity of devotion or, above all, to the sharpness of specific observation that became the conspicuous quality of his later poetry. In *Traumgekrönt* (1897; Crowned by Dream), *Advent* (1898), and *Mir zur Feier* (1899; In Celebration of Myself), Rilke moved toward a depersonalized idiom in an attempt to convey, in contemplation and suspense, the emotional unity that thereafter characterized his poetic landscape of things and creatures. The first part of *Das Stundenbuch, Das Buch vom mönchischen Leben* (The Book of Hours, The Book of the Monastic Life), written in 1899 and published in 1905 together with *Von der Pilgerschaft* (1901; On Pilgrimage) and *Von der Armuth und vom Tode* (1903; Eng. tr., *Poems from the Book of Hours*, 1941), intensifies the impression of a fervent although loosely religious imagination.

From 1899 on, Rilke wandered restlessly from one country to another; he traveled in Russia, learned Russian, and, on two occasions, in 1899 and 1900, visited Lev TOLSTOY. Overwhelmed by the immensity of the eastern landscape, he crystalized his discovery of the immeasurable presence of God in his delightful *Geschichten vom lieben Gott* (1900; Eng. trs., *Stories of God*, 1931, 1963). He seemed at home in all parts of Europe; whether in Paris or Munich, Scandinavia, Spain, Italy, or Switzerland, he developed and realized his characteristic sense of space and physical reality. For two years he lived in the painters' colony at Worpswede (*Worpswede*, 1903), where, determined to rid his poetry of all narrative or merely lyrical elements, he wrote most of the poems that were published under the characteristic title *Das Buch der Bilder* (1902, in two parts; 2d ed., enlarged, 1906; Book of Images). Superbly skillful though most of this work has seemed to some, to Rilke it still lacked that firmness of distinct bodies in space in which he felt most palpably the presence of a moving God.

His association with Auguste Rodin in Paris represents perhaps the most significant turn in his poetic career. He had always found himself in sympathy with much of French culture, and he had translated Maurice de Guérin, André GIDE, and Paul VALÉRY; but Rodin (like the equally influential Paul Cézanne) became to him a symbol not so much of the French character in general as rather of a hardworking craftsman grappling with the completely significant world of tangible objects. The artist's work, Rodin insisted, is the only satisfactory mode of religious activity. Much of Rilke's happy recognition of this attitude entered into his account of the master, *August Rodin* (1903; Eng. tr., 1919). But the two volumes of *Neue Gedichte* (1907–08; Eng. tr., *New Poems*, 1964), the second dedicated to Rodin, "mon grand ami," show the turn in Rilke's conception of the artist even more clearly; they contain his first distinctly mature poetry. In these poems he not only developed a peculiarly objective and sculpturesque form, which has, somewhat misleadingly, become known as *Dinggedicht*, but he advanced from his earlier private and impressionistic aestheticism to an integration and transformation of his intense vision into more impersonal symbols. At the same time the poems in *Neue Gedichte* represent, together with the delicate and melancholy prose of his only major narrative work,

Die Aufzeichnungen des Malte Laurids Brigge (1910; Eng. tr., *Journal of My Other Self*, 1930; *The Notebook of Malte Laurids Brigge*, 1958, 1959), the last work in which his impressions, however sublimated and embodied, supplied the material for, and the aim of, his poetry.

His life and his poetry began to change. In spite of his rapidly increasing fame and the astonishing popularity of his earlier, sentimentally melodramatic *Die Weise von Liebe und Tod des Cornets Christoph Rilke* (1906; Eng. tr., *The Tale of the Love and Death of Cornet Christopher Rilke*, 1932) and in spite of a singularly extensive correspondence with a large circle of friends (*Briefe*, from 1929 on; Letters)—many exchanges of letters have been translated into English—there followed years of profound despair, frustration, and helplessness. In August 1914, for once inspired by a feeling of solidarity with his countrymen, he passed through a brief period of exaltation and wrote, in the ecstatic style of Friedrich Hölderlin's last poems, *Fünf Gesänge* (Five Songs). But this elation did not last. As early as the winter of 1911–12 he had begun at the castle of Duino in Istria a series of elegies that he seemed unable to complete until, in an extraordinary burst of inspiration, he finished the last of the ten poems in 1922 at Castle Muzot in the Swiss Valais. The *Duineser Elegien* (1923; Eng. trs., *Duinese Elegies*, 1930; *Elegies from the Castle of Duino*, 1931; *Duino Elegies*, 1939, 1961, 1978; *The Duino Elegies*, 1957, 1972; *Duinesian Elegies*, 1975; with *Sonnets to Orpheus*, 1945, 1977) Rilke regarded as his supreme achievement; the elegies are, at the same time, the most impressive sequence of great poetry in modern European literature. Their theme is the human, and particularly the poet's, struggle for clarity and coherence; with two exceptions, they are written in a rhythmically dithyrambic vers libre, and even though they are naturally charged with elements of philosophical reflection, their appeal is, in the main, to the creative and nervous sensibility such as sustained the poet himself. The poems offer the evidence of an overwhelming religious crisis, but, with their recurrent emphasis upon the succession of struggle, death, and regeneration, they represent only one aspect of Rilke's vision. The other, his sense of joy, affirmation, and praise, is the keynote of *Die Sonette an Orpheus* (1923; Eng. trs., *Sonnets to Orpheus*, 1936, 1942, 1960, 1971), a series of 55 brilliant and exuberantly positive "songs," written in a state of astonishing inspiration while he finished the last of the *Elegien*. A few additional poems, *Späte Gedichte* (1934; Eng. tr., *Late Poems*, 1938), which reiterate the allegorical manner of the later elegies, were published after his death; but with his two incomparable statements of the cosmic experience, progress, and achievement of the poet, Rilke ended a creative career that is as unique in recent times as it is difficult to appreciate.

To contrast him, as is often done, with his great German contemporary, Stefan GEORGE, is merely to stress the peculiarly personal nature of his imagination. Unlike the rigidly stylized and monumental George, Rilke is ultimately a sensitive and, at his best, supremely realistic poet who succeeded in finding the symbols of a modern religious eloquence. It is perhaps not altogether just to dismiss most of his work prior to the *Neue Gedichte* as unoriginal and dangerously subjective. But it is true that many of even the more popular poems in *Das Stundenbuch* and in *Das Buch der Bilder* lack the authoritative gesture. Rilke was, after all, an artist whose perception and intensity of application were throughout most of his life greater than his power of resolute mastery. In his earlier poems it is difficult to escape a feeling of glibness and unmerited ease of mystical intuition. The characteristic poetic figure of the "Angel" (Eng. tr., *Angel Songs*,

1958), in which he frequently focused and through which he realized the strength of his overpowering inspiration, occurs in his early work as well. It is not until after the years of complete despondency, however, that the symbol of the Angel emerges in the *Elegien,* in severe and peremptory images, as the absolute of vision and completeness. Within the allegorical world of a modern paradise in which, innocently close to the animals, Rilke seeks his way, there is no immediate contact with God, but the Angel appears to the poet as does God to the medieval saint. To approach this source of terrible strength is a task almost too great for a man: in children, lovers, and heroes Rilke felt it present, and of them the elegies say much. But the cardinal theme of the *Elegien,* especially of the superb fifth elegy, is the precariousness of human life. And if, as the work draws to a close, the sense of inadequacy gives way to one of trust and affirmation, it is because the poet transmutes what is merely seen or "blindly" lived into the exaltation of a vision (in the seventh elegy) of death as the final transformer. The experience of grief for the dead was probably for Rilke the most moving human experience (Eng. tr., *Requiem and Other Poems,* 1935). In the *Elegien,* therefore, death resolves the discrepancies of human life. But in the subsequent *Sonette an Orpheus,* Rilke presented the complement to this vision. Here the poet's song serves to transform even the mutability of life into the permanence of absolute creation.

A constant and repeated challenge to translators into English, the following works have also found accepters of the challenge: *Das Marien-Leben* (1913; The Life of the Virgin Mary, 1951), poetic cycle; the posthumously published narrative tale *Ewald Tragy* (1944; Eng. tr., 1958); and selections of poetry, *Poems 1906-1926* (1957), *Poems* (1965), *Possibility of Being* (1977), as well as *Selected Works* (from 1960 on). Of particular interest are the little-known plays, collected in English in *Nine Plays* (1979).

See: F. Olivero, *Rainer Maria Rilke: A Study in Poetry and Mysticism* (1931); E. C. Mason, *Rilke's Apotheosis* (1938); E. M. Butler, *Rainer Maria Rilke* (1941); H. E. Holthusen, *Rainer Maria Rilke: A Study of His Later Poetry* (Eng. tr. from the German, 1952); W. L. Graff and N. Fuerst, *Phases of Rilke* (1958); F. H. Wood, *Rainer Maria Rilke: The Ring of Forms* (1958); H. F. Peters, *Rainer Maria Rilke: Masks and the Man* (1960); E. C. Mason, *Rilke, Europe and the English-Speaking World* (1961); S. Mandel, *Rainer Maria Rilke: The Poetic Instinct* (1965); K. A. J. Batterby, *Rilke and France* (1966); J. Rolleston, *Rilke in Transition: An Exploration of His Earliest Poetry* (1970); H. E. Holthusen, *Portrait of Rilke: An Illustrated Biography* (Eng. tr. from the German, 1971); A. Bauer, *Rainer Maria Rilke* (Eng. tr. from the German, 1972).   V.La.

Rimanelli, Giose (1926–), Italian novelist, essayist, and critic, was born in Cascalenda. He received international attention with his first novel, *Tiro al piccione* (1953; Eng. tr., *The Day of the Lion,* 1954). Based on the author's own experiences, the novel offers a sensitive portrayal of a rebellious adolescent's coming of age in wartime. To escape the stifling life of a southern Italian town, Marco falls in with the ragtail Fascist army; matured by the savagery of civil war and by a romantic attachment ending in delusion, he emerges from the chaos around and within him able to accept family, village, and the future. Among the many Italian novels of the 1940s and 1950s based on the events of World War II, *Tiro al piccione* is unusual for its sympathetic presentation of the losing side. A direct, personal testimony to events, the work is linked stylistically to Italian literary neorealism (*see* ITALIAN LITERATURE). A film version of the novel appeared in 1961. Rimanelli's other published novels are *Peccato originale* (1954, Eng. tr., *Original Sin,* 1957), also set in wartime Italy, and *Una posizione sociale* (1959; A Social Position). All three novels have been translated into several languages.

Rimanelli's minor works include short stories and two plays, *Tè in casa Picasso* (1961; Tea at the Picassos) and *Il corno francese* (1961; The French Horn). In the 1950s, he created a stir among Italian literary circles with polemical articles of literary criticism. These appeared in an Italian weekly under the pseudonym "A. G. Solari" and were later collected as *Il mestiere del furbo* (1959; The Sneak's Craft). Rimanelli has lived in Canada and in the United States (where he now resides) and has taught Italian literature at universities in both countries. His Canadian experience underlies *Biglietto di terza* (1958; Third-Class Ticket), while *Tragica America* (1968; Tragic America) contains his reflections on the United States. His published poetry includes *Carmina blabla* (1967), experimental pieces with drawings by the author; *Monaci d'amore* (1967; Monks of Love), English translations of erotic medieval Latin verse; and *Poems Make Pictures Pictures Make Poems* (1972), a volume of poetry for children. He coedited *Modern Canadian Stories* (1966) and a festschrift for Thomas G. Bergin, *Italian Literature: Roots and Branches* (1975).

See: S. Antonelli, in *Belfagor,* no. 5 (1953); F. Virdia, in *La fiera letteraria* (Apr. 12, 1959); G. Titta Rosa, in *Corriere lombardo* (Jan. 8–9, 1960); G. Pullini, in *Il romanzo italiano del dopoguerra* (1965).   J.C.

Rimbaud, Arthur (1854–91), French poet, was born in Charleville of an irresponsible father and an authoritarian mother. He is the prodigy of French poetry, whose career as a poet spans five years (1870–75). Dating his poetic awareness from "Les Poètes de sept ans" (Seven-year-old Poets), Rimbaud was first a social romantic, denigrating the French Revolution as a failure, as in "Le Forgeron" (The Blacksmith), and expressing several aspects of his personal rebellion while still using the standard poetic idiom of the day. Yet he was soon to outstrip his elders in the richness and versatility of his poetic lexicon, particularly in the poem "Le Bateau ivre" (The Drunken Boat). In a second stage of his rapid development, he went through a religious and moral crisis, crystallized in a Dantesque descent into hell in *Une Saison en enfer* (1871; Eng. tr., *A Season in Hell,* 1932). He then expressed his metaphysical yearnings in a more sophisticated and cryptic form of writing, *Les Illuminations* (1873–75; Eng. trs., *Prose Poems from the Illuminatinos,* 1932, *Rimbaud's Illuminations,* 1953) in which he heightened his powers of vision through verbal and artificial stimulants to achieve "Noël sur terre" (Christmas on earth), the intensified reality of a sky purer than blue and of an earth washed to a state of antediluvian innocence. René ETIEMBLE's enlarged edition of *Le Mythe de Rimbaud* (1952-61) is not up to date with the multiplying critical writings on Rimbaud, yet despite the proliferation of criticism on the poet, much may forever remain obscure about his life and the rational significance of his work. A hundred years after the end of his literary career, it has not been possible to determine the chronology of *Une Saison en enfer* and *Les Illuminations.* Nor has there been conclusive evidence of the sincerity of Rimbaud's religious stance, although the frame of reference and language of his analogical system is fundamentally anchored in Catholic doctrine, whether in affirmation or negation of it.

As a child, Rimbaud played the truant, fleeing several times to Paris and assuming the role of ambulant vagabond. In the course of his adolescent vagrancies, he was rescued by Sisters of Charity, established writers like Paul VERLAINE, and most often by his sympathetic teachers. To one of them, Paul Demeny, he wrote a letter at the age of 16 known as "lettre du voyant" (letter of the seer) that was to become not only his own *ars poetica* but the manifesto of future generations of poets. Summarizing his dissatisfaction with the romantics, the young Rimbaud proffered the notion that to be a poet meant to be supremely wise, to cultivate one's faculties to the limit of a "rational disorder of all the senses" until one became truly a visionary, not of another eventual existence as in the Swedenborgian attitude popular with the romantics, but of the self and the human universe. This philosophy of immanence was to be the matrix of a future revolution in poetry and art.

In his vagaries in Paris and in voyages to Belgium and England in the company of Verlaine, the adolescent Rimbaud's behavior gave rise to scandal and legend. In 1873, his intimate relationship with Verlaine ended in a crisis that sent Verlaine to prison for assault. It has been suggested that the incident may have precipitated Rimbaud's decision to abandon literature. After the break with Verlaine, Rimbaud became a trader in Ethiopia. He returned to die of cancer of the leg in Marseilles.

Mysteries surround Rimbaud's life and work. What is the meaning of the famous sonnet "Les Voyelles" (The Vowels), in which he attributes a color to each vowel and associates with each a cryptic, multidimensional analogy? Was it an exercise in linguistic virtuosity meant to suggest the kind of symbolistic synaesthesia popularized by the Swedenborgian cult of the 1850s and 1860s? Or does the poem encode a secret message—erotic, pornographic, or mystical? In the last line of the sonnet, "O l'Oméga rayon violet de Ses Yeux" (O the Omega violet ray of the [his/her] eyes), the ambiguity of the French possessive adjective makes it possible for Rimbaud to equate, linguistically at least, the power of Woman and the power of that mystic force that he sometimes called "Génie."

In Rimbaud's writings, love is more closely identified with the Christian concept of charity than with sexuality. His poetry contains a dialectical representation of both his particular and the universal movement from the love force to the destructive instinct, from the saintly to the perverse. Another perplexing question revolves around the limits of his work: has all that Rimbaud wrote been uncovered? Many of the pieces that comprise *Les Illuminations* were first published in 1886 in the review *La Vogue*, after remaining for more than 10 years in the possession of various friends and colleagues. They were, furthermore, delivered to the editors on bits of paper that seldom indicated their chronology. The sequence is therefore largely arbitrary and determined a posteriori. In view of the casual manner in which Rimbaud copied his poems or had them recopied by friends, such as Germain NOUVEAU, and transmitted them to others, one also wonders if any have been lost. And what of his alleged magnum opus, "La Chasse spirituelle," which he is supposed to have burned before abandoning his literary pursuits? In 1948 a hoax was perpetrated in the *Mercure de France,* claiming the recovery of the apocryphal volume.

Whether one reads *Une Saison en enfer* or *Les Illuminations,* the one written in direct subjective discourse, the other in ellipitic, hermetic structure, the essential Rimbaud emerges: the spirited youth who scorned the stunted *assis* (the seated ones) of established society, the adventurer into perilous sensory experiences whose sense of an animated, ignited physical world created the immediacy of heightened reality. His work expresses nostalgia for a Golden Age, and his telescopic view of vanished civilizations and of their legacy of material encumbrances is accompanied by a will to prevail and to thrust toward light, toward "splendid cities," toward an ideal *génie* in the guise of a superstar, luminous, perfect, pure. Without the descent there is no elevation, and the sense of sin envelops his self-immolating autobiography, *Une Saison en enfer,* as he arises from corruption to retribution through the "alchemy of the Word."

Rimbaud belongs to no literary classification or school. His rhymed poetry has a stark concreteness, and there is rebellious indignation and irony in his realistic portrayal of a young boy in need of decontamination and of love in "Les Chercheuses de poux" (Women Looking for Lice), or of a stolid church congregation in "Les Pauvres à l'église" (The Poor in Church), or of a boy sleeping with a bullet in his side in "Le Dormeur du val" (The Sleeper in the Vale), or of the gun-holding hands of the revolutionary in "Les Mains de Jeanne-Marie" (Jeanne-Marie's Hands). His "illuminations" achieve a suggestive density of meaning through the ambiguous juxtaposition of unreferenced and unrelated concrete images. Although he did not cultivate the vague and the veiled as did Verlaine and the subsequent symbolists, Rimbaud does share with them a certain hypnotic use of language, evoking a nonconnotative mood of mystery, particularly in his ballad poems such as "O Saison, o châteaux" (O Season, O Châteaus) and "Age d'or" (Golden Age). His famous "Bateau ivre," resplendent in exotic images of sea, land, and sky, is in fact an antivoyage into the subconscious and the dream, lived in broad daylight. Indeed, Rimbaud had the power to convey the vision of childhood with the verbal power of the mature artist.

Too many critics have used the works of Rimbaud as a vehicle for their own self-analysis and self-discovery. The best commentaries on Rimbaud's work have appeared in annotations of his texts and in single articles rather than in monographic studies. See commentaries by Jean-Pierre Richard, Bouillaune de Lacoste, Albert Py, Emile Noulet, Suzanne Bernard, Pierre Brunel, and Louis Forestier.

See also: E. Starkie, *Arthur Rimbaud* (1938, 1973); W. Fowlie, *Rimbaud* (1946, 1966); H. Bouillane de Lacoste, *Rimbaud et le problème des Illuminations* (1949); E. Noulet, *Le Premier visage de Rimbaud* (1953); H. Miller, *The Time of the Assassins: A Study of Rimbaud* (1956); W. M. Frohock, *Rimbaud's Poetic Practice* (1963); P. Brunel, *Rimbaud* (1973); M. Frankel, *Le Code dantesque dans l'œuvre de Rimbaud* (1975).   A.B.

Ritsos, Yannis (1909–), Greek poet, was born in Monemvasia. He came to maturity in the 1930s, the decade that saw a revitalization of Greek verse. A tragic childhood, owing to disease and insanity in his family, was made more difficult still by the social problems in Greece following the Asia Minor Disaster of 1922. In the wake of these experiences, he resolved to aid the oppressed by means of poetry that responded to their needs and hopes. While George SEFERIS, Odysseas ELYTIS, and other writers associated with the Athenian periodical *Nea grammata* were oriented toward the bourgeois culture of Western Europe, Ritsos and Kostas VARNALIS embraced socialism and looked toward the Soviet Union. Both fractions, however, drew primarily from Greece's own tradition in their works. Ritsos has never been a narrowly political writer, but rather a poet in the widest sense, producing intensely personal poems of pure lyricism as well as public, engaged verse.

Ritsos first displayed his full poetic force in *Epitaphios* (1936), a dirge lamenting the murder of striking workers by police. This work displays a masterful use of the 15-syllable rhymed couplets of Greek folk poetry. In his subsequent verse, however, Ritsos abandoned stricter forms for unrhymed free verse. His first work in this form was *To traghoudi tis adelphis mou* (1937; The Song of My Sister), which counterbalances his sister's tragic insanity with the redemptive power of poetry. Since then, Ritsos has produced a flood of triumphant lyricism matched in Greek letters only by Angelos SIKELIANOS. At the same time, he has continued his political witness, as in *Romiosini* (1954; Eng. tr., 1969), which celebrates Greek resistance to fascism. He has also experimented with dry, terse poetic statements, such as those in *Martyries* (1963, 1966; Testimonies), which offer pained yet affirmative vignettes of life's perplexities. A form Ritsos has increasingly cultivated is the dramatic monologue, in which he usually voices contemporary concerns through a persona from Greek myth. Examples are *I sonata tou selinophotos* (1956; Eng. tr., "The Moonlight Sonata," 1979), *To nekro spiti* (1962; Eng. tr., "The Dead House," 1974), *Philoktetes* (1965; Eng. tr., 1975), *Orestes* (1966), *Ismene* (1972), and *Phaedra* (1978). His more recent publications include *O toikhos mesa ston kathrefti* (1975; The Wall in the Mirror) and *Hartina* (1975; Of Paper), consisting of epigrammatic, sometimes cryptic poems in which the real and the imaginery alternate within a context of nightmare; *Petrinos chronos* (1975; Year of Stone), written in the Makronisos concentration camp in 1949; and *Epikairika 1945–1969* (1976; Timely 1945–1969), containing long poems expressing the struggles and sufferings of the Greeks during this troubled period. Ritsos has published about 80 collections of poems, some of which have been translated into 36 languages.

Both Ritsos's writings and his personal life have been characterized by a fortitude that retains a vibrant, unsentimental faith in the goodness of man and of nature. He has been immensely popular with the Greek people, partially through settings of his verse by the composer Mikis Theodorakis, and he has also been a strong influence on younger poets. English versions of Ritsos's works are available in *Gestures and Other Poems*, tr. by N. Stangos (1971), *Selected Poems*, tr., by N. Stangos (1974), *The Fourth Dimension: Selected Poems of Yannis Ritsos*, tr. by R. Dalven (1977), *Chronicle of Exile*, tr. by M. Savvas (1977), and *Ritsos in Parentheses* (1979), as well as in K. Friar, ed., *Modern Greek Poetry: From Cavafis to Elytis* (1973).

See: W. V. Spanos, "Yiannis Ritsos' *Romiosini*: Style as Historical Memory," *APR* (Sept.–Oct. 1973): 18–22. *The Falcon* 9, no. 16.   C.A. with P.B.

Rivière, Jacques (1886–1925), French essayist, novelist, and critic, was born in Bordeaux, the son of a physician. He prepared for the Ecole Normale Supérieure at the Lycée Lakanal, where he met his lifelong friend Henri ALAIN-FOURNIER, whose sister Isabelle he married. Taken prisoner in 1914, Rivière spent three years in German prison camps and a year interned in Switzerland. He died of typhoid fever at the age of 38.

Rivière has attained increasing recognition for his fervent espousal of pitiless self-scrutiny, his discriminating literary foresight, and his influence on the artistic currents of his day. Most of his essays on literature, art, music, the ballet, politics, religion, and morals, republished as *Etudes* (1911; Studies) and *Nouvelles études* (1947; New Studies), first appeared in the *Nouvelle Revue française*. Rivière was associated with that publication from its third issue (1909), becoming its secretary in 1911 and editor in 1919. During his years of imprisonment, he worked on an autobiographical novel, *Aimée* (1922); two studies of national character, *L'Allemand* (1922; The German) and *Le Français* (1928; The Frenchman); and his *Carnets* (1974), deeply self-revelatory diaries reflecting personal and religious crises, originally published in part as *A la trace de Dieu* (1925; On the Track of God). Rivière's best lectures were issued as *Quelques progrès dans l'étude du coeur humain (Freud et Proust)* (1926; Some Progress in the Study of the Human Heart [Freud and Proust]) and *Moralisme et littérature* (1932). Noteworthy also are his introduction to Alain-Fournier's *Miracles* (1924), his own *Rimbaud* (1938), and his correspondences with Alain-Fournier, Paul CLAUDEL, Marcel PROUST, and Antonin ARTAUD. *Florence* (1935), a novel, was left unfinished.

An understanding of Rivière's work has been distorted by hasty generalizations. His complex, contradictory personality resists facile analysis, and separate aspects of his work cannot be considered except in relation to the whole. He was not an eternal disciple, but took from each of his successive masters an understanding of a different facet of his personality, after which his detachment from them was complete. His criticism does not divide neatly (as some claim) into lyrical prewar studies with precisely appropriate images and a postwar insistence upon intellectual analysis. On the contrary, he continuously maintained that intuition and "the heart," understood in the Pascalian sense, often reveal reality more truly than can the intellect.

Rivière's criticism is characterized by a rare sensitivity and sensuality that allow both a subtle approach to the core of an author's work and then a dispassionate interpretation of the emotional experience. It is characterized by the absence of a priori moral judgment, by minute psychological analysis based on mistrust of the obvious, by a consideration of the inner world as an object to be explored and defined, by a separation of the author from his creation, and by a belief in intelligibility. Neither dogmatic nor impressionistic, his method was pliable and open; it was in full evolution at the time of his premature death. Most of Rivière's postwar positions were defined in opposition to trends and techniques he deplored. Yet the theorist who was shaping literary tendencies through his major articles should be distinguished from the editor who greeted innovations with interest and published work of unknown authors whose aesthetics differed radically from his own. His essays on Arthur RIMBAUD, Claudel, André GIDE, Proust, Igor Stravinsky, and the Dada movement remain models of the genre.

See: M. Turnell, *Jacques Rivière* (1953); B. Cook, *Jacques Rivière: A Life of the Spirit* (1958); H. Naughton, *Jacques Rivière: The Development of a Man and a Creed* (1966); M. Raymond, *Etudes sur Jacques Rivière* (1972); special Rivière no. of *CahiersVS* 3 (1975).   H.T.N.

Robbe-Grillet, Alain (1922–), French novelist, essayist, and film director, was born in Brest. He completed his secondary and higher education in Paris, graduating from the National Agricultural College. While working at the Citrus Fruit Institute, he began writing fiction. Although his first published novel, *Les Gommes* (1953; Eng. tr., *The Erasers*, 1964), was not a success, it did establish him as a literary figure. In 1955 he became a consultant for the Editions de Minuit and published *Le Voyeur* (Eng. tr., *The Voyeur*, 1958), which received the Critics Prize. A number of theoretical and polemical articles, later reissued as *Pour un nouveau roman* (1963; Eng. tr., *For a New Novel*, 1965), as well as a third novel, *La Jalousie*

(1957; Eng. tr., *Jealousy,* 1959), made him the acknowledged spokesman for the "new novel" group (*see* FRENCH LITERATURE).

Robbe-Grillet's fourth novel, *Dans le labyrinthe* (1959; Eng. tr., *In the Labyrinth,* 1960), was followed by his *ciné-roman* (cinema-novel) *L'Année dernière à Marienbad* (1961; Eng. tr., *Last Year at Marienbad,* 1962), the screenplay for Alain Resnais's film. Robbe-Grillet then turned to filmmaking himself, first with *L'Immortelle,* published as a *ciné-roman* in 1963, then with *Trans-Europ-Express* (1967), *L'Homme qui ment* (1968), and *L'Eden et après* (1970). At the same time, he continued his activity as a novelist, although at a slower pace: *La Maison de rendez-vous* (1965; Eng. tr., 1966), *Projet pour une révolution à New York* (1970; Eng. tr., *Project for a Revolution in New York,* 1972), and *Topologie d'une cité fantôme* (1975; Eng. tr., *Topology of a Phantom City,* 1977). During the 1970s, Robbe-Grillet also wrote a number of shorter fictional texts, reminiscent of his earlier *Instantanés* (1962; Eng. tr., *Snapshots,* 1968). He has lectured frequently in Europe and the United States, remaining one of the most active advocates of what has become the "new new novel."

Like those of other "new novelists," Robbe-Grillet's novels are particularly interesting because of their technical innovations. Influenced by Jean-Paul SARTRE's existentialism, and believing that man's marginal position in the modern world no longer justified an anthropomorphic and anthropocentric vision of the fictional world, Robbe-Grillet stressed in his earlier works the description of *choses* (things) as they are by themselves, that is, geometrical shapes and volumes, and cleansed of any projections of human feelings. Conversely, the background and personality of his characters were progressively reduced to the point of disappearing altogether in *La Jalousie,* where the action is related to the viewpoint of a nonexistent narrator. At the same time, the traditional hero-centered novel was also undermined through a radical dechronology of the plot that made it impossible to reconstitute a logical story line. Yet as early as *Les Gommes,* this dehumanizing orientation was paralleled and compensated by a growing reliance on the subjective representation of the world in the human mind, mixing imaginary and real scenes. In *Dans le labyrinthe,* as well as in the first films, this undifferentiated recording consciousness was then merged with Robbe-Grillet's own imagination in the process of writing or directing his fictions. Circular structures, blurred transitions between multiple levels of narration and reality, complex montages of recurrent descriptions, contradictory statements, variations of names, mirror effects, and intertextuality (*see* Julia KRISTEVA) in terms of earlier works culminated in the virtuosity of *La Maison de rendez-vous.*

Robbe-Grillet's later novels show few new technical developments, despite his claim that, together with the other "new new novelists," he has been moving increasingly toward a "self-generation" of the text, produced by associations of words or images rather than by a concerted organization. It would be more correct to say that the obsessional nature of his imagination, first noticed in *Le Voyeur,* with its stress on eroticism and violence, has clearly emerged as a guiding drive behind the apparent fragmentation of the fictional universe. Things have lost their cold objectivity; translated into frightening clichés of the urban landscape, they have become nightmarish reflections of desires and fears.

See: B. Morrissette, *Les Romans de Robbe-Grillet* (1963); O. Bernal, *Alain Robbe-Grillet: le roman de l'absence* (1964); J. Alter, *La Vision du monde d'Alain Robbe-Grillet* (1966). J.V.A.

Roblès, Emmanuel (1914–), French novelist and playwright, was born in Oran, Algeria, to working-class parents of predominantly Spanish stock. He studied at the Ecole Normale of Algiers and has traveled widely. Since his first novel, *L'Action* (1938), he has published more than 20 works, mostly fiction. Chief among these are *Les Hauteurs de la ville* (1948; City Heights), which won the Femina Prize, *La Mort en face* (1951; In the Face of Death), *Cela s'appelle l'aurore* (1952; Eng. tr., *Dawn on Our Darkness,* 1953), and *Le Vésuve* (1961; Eng. tr., *Vesuvius,* 1970). His most significant play is *Montserrat* (1949). As a translator and as editor of the Seuil publishing firm, he has introduced a number of North African and Spanish authors to the French reading public.

Roblès's works, firmly rooted in reality and the human experience, attest to a tragic sense of life. His characters are aware of their ultimate defeat in death, yet refuse to yield to despair. Man is alone in his all too human condition (God is dead), but by confronting and overcoming the absurd, he asserts his conscience and his dignity in the face of an unjust, often incoherent world. The main tension of Roblès's works stems from the dialectical play between individualism and solidarity, pleasure and selflessness, complacency and revolt, fate and freedom, brutality and tenderness. His protagonists possess an intense lust for life, but also a strong sense of honor and defiance. Their passionate enjoyment of sensory experience and their personal happiness collide with their sense of responsibility towards others. Thus the tragic crises they encounter often lead to violence and death, but also to an exultant pride.

Unlike his contemporaries Albert CAMUS, André MALRAUX, and Jean-Paul SARTRE, whose views on individual responsibility and the absurd he generally shares, Roblès remains apolitical and ideologically uncommitted. His works are unencumbered by intellectual or metaphysical concerns. Rather, it is the passions of men and the drama of life itself that inform his fiction. Structurally and stylistically, his work is traditional, devoid of formalistic experimentation. His short stories—a genre often disparaged in French literary circles—have earned high praise.

See: G.-A. Astre, "Emmanuel Roblès, romancier par exigence," *LiF,* no. 2 (1965); M. A. Rozier, *Emmanuel Roblès ou la rupture du cercle* (1973). J.-P.Ca.

Roche, Denis (1937–), French writer of the extreme avant-garde, was born in Paris. From 1938 to 1946, he and his parents lived in the West Indies, Venezuela, and Brazil. He studied medicine and dentistry in France. Since 1962, Roche has published poems, usually in "series" preceded by theoretical prefaces. His second collected volume, *Récits complets* (1963; Complete Narratives), initiated what he calls an "open" poetics and a practice founded on the ambiguous nature of language itself as a purely human and social act. From 1963 to 1973, he was a member of the editorial committee of *Tel Quel.*

Roche's rejection of conventional poetics and the avatars of the sacred are further evident in *Les Idées centésimales de Miss Elanize* (1964; The Centesimal Ideas of Miss Elanize), becoming more polemical in *Eros énergumène* (1968; Eros the Energumen). These two collections of "poems" are characterized by a kind of "massive fractioning" on the level of "ideas" but also on the level of the "signifiers"; an associative process, but one that is *not* the surrealists' (*see* FRENCH LITERATURE) "automatic writing," replacing traditional composition ("Miss Elanize" is a play on the English word and genre "miscellanies"); and the "dé-figuration" and "dé-sacralisation" of poetry, aimed at the liquidation of what still survived from the symbolist tradition, including the outworn "ideology" that—with rare exceptions—has continued to make French poetry the "written concretization of bourgeois idealism," as Roche insisted in the *Tel Quel* group volume *Théorie d'ensemble* (1968; Basic Theory).

Roche abandoned discussions of poetics and poetic practice—at least under those names—in his provocative presentation in the *Tel Quel* colloquium on Antonin AR-TAUD and Georges BATAILLE at Cerisy-la-Salle (July 1972) and in *Le Mécrit* (November 1972), announced as his "last" collection of poems (really antipoems). A "mécrit" (a neologism composed of the noun *écrit* with the negative/pejorative prefix *mé-*) is a text that magnifies and distorts conventional poetic devices to reduce the degree of "poeticity" to zero, a "bad" writing that demonstrated, once and for all, the inanity and the nullity of "poetry."

Roche did not abandon, however, his efforts to lay bare the world of excrement, sexuality, and death that our institutions try, with our complicity, to hide. We cannot escape them, says Roche, even in pursuing our fantasies and our "desire." Using a tape recorder, a camera, and all the "mechanical" resources of his typewriter, he began producing texts he calls "prose" aimed at provoking what Sigmund Freud called "the return of the repressed," yet not in "sublimated" figures (aesthetic/idealistic "displacements" or "substitutions"), but in all their immediacy. *Louve basse* (1976; Low She-Wolf), grouping 13 such texts, is called a novel, but whatever coherence it has comes from recurrent "themes" and the narrator's "voice." The "low she-wolf" is not the protagonist, but the horizon-figure of the autobiographical narrator's fantasies and obsessions, especially those associated with death as decomposition/putrefaction. The wolf also represents what Roche calls "language-death"—not only conventional and "literary" uses of language but the essential inability of any language to grasp the immediacy of experience. The writer's typewriter here becomes a "bulldozer" (to use Philippe SOLL-ERS's term), violently breaking up the entire "cultural field," preventing any kind of "recuperation," including the symbolists' "salvation through art."

In 1978, Roche published *Notre antéfixe*, an album of 40 photographs, mostly of himself and his companion Françoise Peyrot, in hotel rooms they occupied during their travels. Preceded by a preface this book, too, is characterized as a "novel."   C.L.

Roche, Maurice (1925–), French novelist, was born in Clermont-Ferrand. After the liberation of France, he moved to Paris, where he studied music and science. He began his career as a journalist, and then became a test-driver for racing cars. From 1946 to 1961 he composed music for the stage and for concerts; during the same period he toured Europe as an actor. In 1960 he published a book on Claudio Monteverdi and participated in the issue of the review *Esprit* devoted to new music.

Roche's first novel, *Compact* (1966), was hailed by well-known French, Brazilian, and German critics. It was followed by *Circus* (1972), *Codex* (1974), and *Opera bouffe* (1975). Roche's eclectic life and various interests might explain the peculiarities of his writings. If one had to classify these novels, it could be said that they belong to the "new new novel" (*see* FRENCH LITERATURE), since they do away completely with linear narrative. These texts juxtapose and mesh several languages and various types of writings—even extracts of advertisements, political slogans, business, literary, and medical jargons, and musical notations and allusions. Roche also employs different alphabets and types of printing as well as various symbols, such as Zodiac signs. His novels are thus a

typographical festival, a study in space. Yet this avant-garde experiment in novel writing, fascinating for its inventiveness, is not a purely formal construct; it confronts us with the problems of death, sickness, alienation, and the objectivization of man in a consumer society.

See: "Entretien avec A. Fabre-Luce," *QL* 139 (1972): 3–4; "Spécial Maurice Roche," *EV* 74 (1973).   D.S.

Rochefort, Christiane (1917–), French novelist, was born in Paris. Her first novel, *Le Repos du guerrier* (1958; The Warrior's Rest), established her reputation. Its daring elemental realism and clear character delineation made it an immediate success, although it shocked some readers. *Les Petits Enfants du siècle* (1961; The Grandchildren of the Century), which won the Populist Prize, and *Stances à Sophie* (1963; Stanzas to Sophia) are well-written, very popular books with a strong feminist slant and some social overtones. *Une Rose pour Morrison* (1966; A Rose for Morrison) was more experimental in its style than were her earlier works.   D.Br.

Rode, Helge (1870–1937), Danish author, was born in Copenhagen. His early pessimistic view of life underwent a change owing to a personal mystical experience of the soul behind nature. This became the main background of his first collection of poems, *Hvide Blomster* (1892; White Flowers). In ca. 1894 he joined the neoromantic symbolic movement, becoming its most original thinker and creating the masterpieces of his youth, the drama *Kongesønner* (1896; Sons of the King), influenced by Maurice MAETERLINCK, and the collection *Digte* (1896; Poems). The two sons in *Kongesønner* personify the basic forces—life and death—representing Rode's own dual personality: his practical nature and his speculative spirit. The same duality is found in the tragedy *Grev Bonde og hans Hus* (1912; Count Bonde and His Manor), inspired by Lev TOLSTOY. Another personal experience of the belief that only death gives meaning to life by liberating the spirit is reflected in *Kampene i Stefan Borgs Hjem* (1900; The Battles in the Home of Stefan Borg), a brooding, fatalistic tragedy about the triumph of love over the cynicism of a superman. The last years of Rode's writing were dominated by a series of contemporary and social dramas. Rode's major lyrical works, *Ariel* (1914) and *Den stille Have* (1922; The Quiet Garden), exude a spiritualism derived from Percy Bysshe Shelley. With delightful inspiration, Rode proclaimed his mystical conviction that love and beauty know neither change nor death. His reaction against rationalism and materialism is critically expounded in the historical, philosophical essays collected in *Krig og Aand* (1917; War and Spirit), whereas his religious outlook, which approaches a confessionless Christianity, is presented in *Pladsen med de grønne Træer* (1924; The Square with the Green Trees). Rode reached a larger public through his religious ideas than through his lyrical works. For 40 years he was a major figure in Danish intellectual life.

See: H. Juul Hansen, *Dramatikeren Helge Rode* (1948).   S.H.R.

Rodenbach, Georges (1855–98), Belgian poet and novelist, was born in Tournai but spent most of his early years in Ghent, where he attended school, first at the Collège Sainte-Barbe, then at the University of Ghent, where he received a degree in law. When he was 21, he left for Paris, where he found easy access to literary groups upon publication of his first volume of poems, *Le Foyer et les champs* (1877; Hearth and Fields), shortly followed by two other collections. In 1885 he returned to Belgium and was admitted to the bar in Brussels, but after a few months he left for Paris, where Lemerre had just published his *Jeunesse blanche* (1886; Candid Youth). At this time, abandoning emulation of Victor Hugo and François Coppée, he sought more subtle musical effects; his new idol was Stéphane MALLARMÉ. All of Rodenbach's poetry has a single tonality. It is the verse of muted sounds, of memories, of the convent bells and sleepy canals of Belgium. *Le Règne du silence* (1891; Reign of Silence), *Le Voyage dans les yeux* (1893; Journey in the Eyes), and his last volume, *Le Miroir du ciel natal* (1898; Mirror of the Native Sky), are the principal collections of his verse. As a novelist, he is best known for *Bruges-la-Morte* (1892; Bruges the Dead City) and *Le Carillonneur* (1897; The Bell Ringer). All his fictional settings, like those of his verse, are in Flanders.

See: T. I. A. Bodson, *L'Esthétique de Georges Rodenbach* (1942); P. Maes, *Georges Rodenbach (1855–1898)* (1952); G. Violato, *Bibliographie de Georges Rodenbach et Albert Samain en Italie* (1967); H. Juin, *Ecrivains de l'avant-siècle* (1972) and "Le Mouvement symboliste en littérature," *Revue de l'Université de Bruxelles* 3–4 (1974); M. Luzi, *L'idea simbolista* (1976).   K.Co.

Rodrigues, Urbano Tavares (1923–), Portuguese writer of fiction, essayist, and journalist, was born in Lisbon but grew up in the province of Alentejo. After graduating from the University of Lisbon in 1949, he taught at the universities of Montpellier and the Sorbonne in France; and, on his return to Portugal in 1955, he began to teach at his alma mater. His career has been chiefly that of a journalist.

Rodrigues has published several volumes of travel articles and a large body of criticism that appeared first in the daily press, for example, *Santiago de Compostela* (1949), *De Florença a Nova Iorque* (1963; From Florence to New York), *Noites no teatro* (2 vols., 1961–62; Theater Evenings), and *Realismo, arte de vanguarda e nova cultura* (1966; Realism, Avant-Garde Art, and New Culture). However, it is as a prolific writer of fiction that he is best known; for he has written more than 15 novels and collections of short stories, beginning with *A porta dos limites* (1952; The Gate at the Boundary). The tales gathered in *Uma pedrada no charco* (1958; A Stone Cast into the Swamp) earned him an important literary award. There is much variety in themes and subject matter in this vast fictional production, but two constants emerge: compassion for the victims of social injustice and interest in and sympathy for the maladjusted individual, for example, in *Dissolução* (Dissolution), a 1974 novel about the catharsis of a neurotic, coinciding with the Portuguese April coup d'etat of that year. Because of his use of the Alentejo province as the background for some of his fiction and because of his continuous social criticism, Rodrigues has occasionally been considered a neorealist. But his impressionistic delight in beauty, his concern with language, and his use of foreign locales and characters, as in *Exílio perturbado* (1962; Disturbed Exile) and many other works of fiction, link him also to the tradition of such cosmopolitan novelists as Manuel Teixeira-Gomes, about whom he has written an important study. Recently he published other literary essays, *Ensaios de escreviver* (1970; Essays of Livewriting); stories, *Estrada de morrer* (1972; Death Road); and even a two-act play, *As torres milenárias* (1973; Millenary Towers.)

See; J. Gaspar Simões, "Romancistas contemporâneos," *Crítica III* (N.D.); T. Linhares, ed., *Antologia do moderno conto português* (1968), pp. 223–24; J. Palla e Carmo, *Do livro à leitura* (1971), pp. 168–82, 254–60; P. Companiço, *Urbano Tavares Rodrigues: escritor da fraternidade* (1979).   R.S.S.

Rodríguez, Claudio (1934–), Spanish poet, was born in the provincial capital of Zamora. A semiorphan at age 10, he completed early studies in his home town and went on to study law, although he took a degree at Madrid in Spanish literature. While an undergraduate, he astounded Madrid literary circles by winning the coveted Adonais Prize in 1953. In 1958 he began a teaching career in England (Nottingham and Cambridge) that lasted until 1964, when he returned to Spain to teach in the foreign students' programs and at the University of Madrid. In spite of his long residence in Madrid, Rodríguez's poetry draws its peculiar power from a deep attachment to his native Zamora, with its 12th-century Cistercian cathedral, the River Duero, and the surrounding empty plains. In the tradition of the Generation of 1898 (*see* SPANISH LITERATURE), Rodríguez knows vast reaches of the Spanish heartland firsthand. At the same time he is an extremely literate poet, with a passionate reader's knowledge of Dante, Shakespeare, Racine, Charles BAUDELAIRE, and Arthur RIMBAUD, as well as Saint John of the Cross and Saint Teresa.

His first book, *Don de la ebriedad* (1953; Gift of Drunkenness), contains a Rimbaudian celebration of the poet's vocation and freedom, couched in the concrete, everyday language of Miguel de UNAMUNO, BLAS DE OTERO, and the Spanish mystics. *Conjuros* (1953; Incantations), Rodríguez's second book, is a perfect example of his highly personal, allegorical style, in which worm-eaten rafters exposed to the night sky symbolize human solidarity, and a shirt hung up to dry, his refurbished soul. His third book, *Alianza y condena* (1965), is considered a modern classic. It continues his movement toward themes of a collective nature, such as family, kinship, and national regeneration. Since 1965, Rodríguez has published *El vuelo de la celebración* (1976; Flight of Celebration), which contains poems of earth-centered mystical celebration, together with darker meditations on death and reconciliation with the past.

While his early visionary poems bear some resemblance to Rimbaud's, Rodríguez's poetry is fundamentally original. Although he seems to share the theme of celebration with Vicente ALEIXANDRE, celebration has uniquely tragic overtones in Rodríguez's work. Appearing first in 1953, his work signaled a change in Spanish letters. With him, poets like Francisco BRINES and José A. VALENTE stemmed the tide of social poetry. Younger poets such as Pere GIMFERRER and Guillermo Carnero have merely consolidated this new direction.

See: J. O. Jiménez, *Diez años de poesía española 1960–1970* (1972), pp. 145–74; H. St. Martin, ed. *Roots and Wings: Poetry from Spain 1900–1975* (1976), pp. 452–65.   P.W.S.

Rodríguez Méndez, José María (1926–), Spanish dramatist, was born in Barcelona. Chronologically, thematically, and stylistically, he is associated with the social playwrights of the *generación realista* (realistic generation) composed of Antonio BUERO VALLEJO, Alfonso SASTRE, Lauro OLMO, José MARTÍN RECUERDA, and Carlos MUÑIZ among others. Writing under a highly doctrinaire, puritanical system of government censorship, these opposition writers, whose period of maximum activity and prestige was the 1950s and 1960s, tried to make their voices heard through their art, since a more direct form of criticism was forbidden under the dictatorship of Francisco Franco (1939–75). Unlike the conformists and the light comedy writers, by whom Spain was frequently portrayed as the best of all possible worlds, Rodríguez Méndez and other playwrights of the realistic generation explored a variety of national problems. While other dramatists of the group have tended to employ a theatrical naturalism, Rodríguez Méndez's style frequently runs to farce, caricature, and the grotesque in the tradition of Ramón del VALLE-INCLÁN, with his protagonists ranging from the economically disadvantaged laborer and the unemployed to such social outcasts as prostitutes and homosexuals. Rodríguez Méndez also distinguishes himself from others of the realistic generation by attempting to write not only *about* the disadvantaged but *for* them as spectators. So far, however, he has been unsuccessful in producing this totally popular theater, as public spectacles in Spain are almost exclusively commercial ventures, and the audiences he wants to reach cannot afford the price of admission. Because Rodríguez Méndez has been somewhat ideologically, as well as stylistically, aggressive, many of his works either did not pass censorship or were not contracted by producers, a necessary step in the censorship process during the Franco years. Rodríguez Méndez's theater has been almost exclusively limited to performances by nonprofessional, noncommercial groups in Barcelona and environs. *Los inocentes de la Moncloa* (1960: The Innocents of Moncloa), however, enjoyed a successful engagement in Madrid and is Rodríguez Méndez's best-known work. Dealing with the alienation and selfishness created by a system that forces those who seek the economic security of a government job to undergo *oposiciones* (extremely long and extremely competitive examinations), the action takes place in a cheap boarding house in the Moncloa section of Madrid where several candidates are preparing for this physically and emotionally exhausting ordeal. Absorbed in their studies and conditioned to worry about their own very limited chances to win a position, they fail to notice that a fellow aspirant has become seriously ill. Surrounded but virtually abandoned, he dies before their unseeing eyes. Although the characters show no moral awakening in the course of the play, the author's purpose is to draw attention to the destructive and inhuman resources of the *oposición* system.

Rodríguez Méndez began his writing career with *El milagro del pan y los peces* (1952; The Miracle of the Loaves and Fishes). His published works include *El círculo de tiza de Cartagena* (1964; The Cartagena Chalk Circle); *La batalla de Verdún* (1966; The Battle of Verdun); *Bodas que fueron famosas del Pingajo y la Fandanga* (1965; That Famous Wedding of Pingajo and Fandanga), performed in Madrid in 1978; and *Auto de la donosa tabernera* (1968; The Witty Barmaid's Play). After the death of Franco in 1975, Rodríguez Méndez adapted his 1973 unpublished and unperformed play, *Flor de otoño: una historia del barrio chino* (Autumn Flower: A Tale of Prostitute Row), for the movie *Un hombre llamado flor de otoño* (1978; A Man Called Autumn Flower). This highly successful film stars Spain's most popular actor, José Sacristán, as Lluis, a homosexual transvestite. Lluis dons feminine attire by night to become "Flor de otoño," a cabaret singer in Barcelona's red-light district. By day, Lluis, in conventional male attire, is a labor lawyer as well as an anarchist who plots to assassinate the dictator Miguel Primo de Rivera. When the plot fails, Lluis and others involved in the scheme are summarily executed by the government. Based on an historical character of the 1920s, *Flor de otoño* sympathetically portrays the homosexual community as well as the anarchist cause. Perhaps this brief summary will suffice to explain why much of Rodríguez Méndez's work remained unperformed during the Franco dictatorship.

See: F. Ruiz Ramón, *Historia del teatro español: siglo XX* (1975), pp. 509–16.   P.W.O'C.

Roelants, Maurits (1895–1966), Belgian (Flemish) poet and novelist, was born in Ghent. He began his literary career as a humanist poet of melancholy refinement and engaging charm. In 1930 he published a volume of poetry, *Het verzaken* (Renunciation), in which death, love, and God are the main themes. A few months before his death, Roelants wrote *Vuur en Dauw* (1965; Fire and Dew), a series of poems in which he explores his dual nature.

Roelants is, however, perhaps best known for his novels and short stories. He is a classicist, and the drama in his books is essentially internal. His novels reveal a shrewd but sympathetic analyst of human nature and have none of the traditional Flemish rural and folklore elements. Roelants's style is limpid and intense. In *Komen en gaan* (1927; Come and Go), *Het leven dat wij droomden* (1931; Life as We Dreamed It), *Alles komt terecht* (1935; Everything Settles Itself), and *De jazzspeler* (1928; The Jazz Band Player), as well as in *Gebed om een goed einde* (1944; Prayer on the Occasion of a Good Death), painfully acquired wisdom is meted out without condescension and with great subtlety. An author of wide renown in Holland and in Belgium, Roelants has often been considered one of the fathers of the Flemish psychological novel.

See: J. Eeckhout, *Litteraire profielen*, vol. 8 (1939); F. Closset, *Maurits Roelants* (1946); *Van en over Maurits Roelants* (1956); A van der Veen, Introduction to *Maurits Roelants* (1960).   J.-A.G.

Rof Carballo, Juan (1905–), Spanish medical anthropologist, psychotherapist, psychoanalytic critic, and essayist, was born in Lugo and educated in medicine at the universities of Madrid, Cologne, and Vienna (1928–35). Upon his return to Spain he collaborated with leading medical figures such as Jiménez-Díaz and Gregorio MARAÑÓN. In the late 1940s he became interested in medical anthropology, psychoanalysis (both orthodox and existential), and social psychology. He was influenced by such American theorists as Franz Alexander, Erik Erikson, and René A. Spitz. At the same time he absorbed the ideas of the existential analysis schools headed by Ludwig Binswanger and Victor von Weizaecker, as well as the views of such orthodox Freudians as Michael Bálint and Gustav Bally, and the Jungian Erich Neumann. To these influences should be added the pervasive presence of two philosophers: Martin Heidegger and Xavier Zubiri.

Rof's medical anthropology is expounded in three principal works: *Patología psicosomática* (1949), *Cerebro interno y mundo emocional* (1952; The Inner Brain and the Emotional World), and *Urdimbre afectiva y enfermedad* (1964; Affective Texture and Illness). He is considered a leading theorist on the psychological dimension of interpersonal relations.

In addition to his contributions to psychobiology and neurophysiology, Rof is the first genuine psychoanalytic critic of society and culture in post-Civil War Spain. His essays range from studies of Galician folklore and superstition to character analyses of Philip II and Miguel de UNAMUNO. The best examples of this genre are found in the collection *Entre el silencio y la palabra* (1960; Between the Silence and the Word), a study of the mythical motifs and symbolism in the works of Rainer Maria RILKE, Søren KIERKEGAARD, and Rosalía de Castro. Longer essays, such as *Violencia y ternura* (1967; Violence and Tenderness), contain original interpretations of such literary figures as Oedipus and Segismundo, who become symbolic cultural personifications of contemporary spiritual crisis and dramatize man's blindness to the perils of technology, his rootlessness, and his atheism.

Other significant studies are *Rebelión y futuro* (1970) and *El hombre como encuentro* (1973; Forms of Human Encounter).   T.Me.

Rojas, Carlos (1928–), Spanish novelist was born in Barcelona, studied philosophy and letters, and has been a professor of literature in the United States for some years.

Metaphysical and existential problems have characterized Rojas's narrative since his first novels, *De barro y esperanza* (1957; Of Mud and Hope) and *La ternura del hombre invisible* (1963; The Tenderness of the Invisible Man). Historical figures and periods provide the structure of many of his works. *El asesino del César* (1959; Caesar's Assassin) is a chronicle of the corruption of power, while *Auto de fe*, which won the National Prize for Literature in 1968, is a historical reconstruction of the reign of Carlos II. The author concentrates his baroque vocabulary and flexible style on the physically and mentally deformed denizens of Carlos II's court. *Azaña* (1973) is a fictionalization of critical years in the life of the president of Spain's Second Republic. The inclusion in this novel of extensive texts written by Azaña has produced a heated polemic. The use, and sometimes abuse, of historical material continues in Rojas's works: *El Valle de los Caídos* (1977; The Valley of the Fallen) and *Los dos presidentes* (1977; The Two Presidents).

See: M. García-Viñó, "Carlos Rojas y su por qué," in *Novela española actual* (1967), pp. 203–17.   J.O.

Roland Holst, Adriaan (1888–1976), Dutch poet, prose writer, and editor, was born in Amsterdam, the son of a businessman. He studied at Lausanne and Oxford. In 1908, he published his first poems in *De Twintigste Eeuw* (The Twentieth Century). His first volume of poetry was *Verzen* (1911; Verses), in which loneliness first appeared as an important theme. Loneliness is also a theme in *De belijdenis van de stilte* (1913; Avowal of Silence). In his later work, *Voorbij de wegen* (1920; Beyond the Roads) and *De wilde kim* (1925; The Wild Horizon), he has accepted this loneliness, and longs to return to a lost Elysian world of the past. He shuns the world of his own time. In *Een winter aan zee* (1937; A Winter by the Sea), he goes back to the myths and legends of Homeric Greece and to the beauty of Helen of Troy. The sea and the winter wind are important aspects of nature that express his real world of long ago. He also reveals himself as a gloomy prophet who foresees the end of civilization. This work demonstrates one of his greatest achievements and demonstrates his mastery of language. During his years as a student in England, he became interested in Celtic mythology, and he also came under the influence of the poetry of William Butler Yeats. He gave his interest in the Irish myths and sagas creative form in *Deirdre en de zonen van Usnach* (1920; Deirdre and the Sons of Usnach), *Tusschen vuur en maan* (1933; Between Fire and Moon), and *De dood van Cuchulainn van Murhevna* (1951; The Death of Cuchulainn of Murhevna), all written in his poetic prose. *Uit zelfbehoud* (1938; Out of Self-Preservation), *Onderweg* (1940; On the Way), and *Tegen de wereld* (1947; Against the World) all reflect a greater interest in the world of his own time and the events of World War II. Among his other volumes of poetry are *In gevaar* (1958; In Danger), *Omtrent de grens* (1960; Around the Border), *Uitersten* (1967; Extremes), *Vuur in sneeuw* (1968; Fire in Snow), and *Met losse teugel* (1970; With Loose Reins). Roland Holst revealed something of his poetry in *De afspraak* (1927; The Agreement) and of himself in *Eigen achtergronden* (1945; Own Backgrounds). His poetry and prose were collected in *Verza-*

melde Werken (4 vols., 1948; Collected Works), and a new edition of his poetry appeared as *Verzamelde Gedichten* (1971; Collected Poems). He was awarded the Constantijn Huygens Prize (1948), the P. C. Hooft Prize (1955), and the Prijs der Nederlandse letteren (1959). Roland Holst was the last of the modern romantics.

See: J. van der Vegt, *De brekende spiegel: ontwikkeling, samenhang, achtergronden bij A. Roland Holst* (1974).   S.L.F.

Roland Holst, Henriëtte Goverdine Anna (1869–1952), Dutch poet and prose writer, was born Henriëtte van der Schalk in Noordwijk. She began her literary career in 1893, with the publication of some sonnets in *De Nieuwe Gids*. Her first volume of poetry, *Sonnetten en verzen in terzinen geschreven* (1895; Sonnets and Poems Written in Terza Rima), show her originality in the use of the sonnet form. She turned from the musicality of Willem KLOOS and Herman GORTER to freer rhythms and the effective use of enjambement. *De nieuwe geboort* (1903; The New Birth) reveals the conflict between the ideals of a new socialist world and her own individualism. In *Opwaartsche wegen* (1907; Upward Roads), her socialist convictions became more positive and enthusiastic. The pain and disappointment that followed the break with the Socialist Party appeared in *De vrouw in het woud* (1912; The Woman in the Wood). The title alludes to Dante, who along with Baruch Spinoza was one of the great influences in her life. Here she also became more concerned with the conflict between the dream of the socialist state and the harsh action needed to create it. Her interest also turned to the women's movement, and she portrayed the state of the future in *Het feest der gedachtenis* (1915; The Feast of Commemoration). *Verzonken grenzen* (1918; Sunken Borders), written after the death of her mother, contains mystical thoughts about dying and eternity. It also indicates her loss of faith in the idea of revolution, and in *Tusschen twee werelden* (1923; Between Two Worlds), she rejected the Russian Revolution of October 1917. In her epic *Heldensage* (1927; Heroic Saga), she praised the revolution, but condemned what it had turned into. That same year she left the Communist Party and moved toward religious socialism, emphasizing love and cooperation in *Verworvenheden* (1927; Achievements) and *Vernieuwingen* (1929; Renewals). *Tusschen tijd en eeuwigheid* (1934; Between Time and Eternity) consists of poems on old age, approaching death, and preparations for a realm beyond this earth. *Wordingen* (1949; Origins) portrays her own intellectual development. At the age of 80, she wrote her memoirs, *Het vurr brandde voort* (1949; The Fire Burned On). In addition to her poetry, she published a number of volumes of prose, including biographies of Jean Jacques Rousseau, Lev TOLSTOY, Gezelle, Gorter, Rosa Luxemburg, Romain ROLLAND, Gandhi, and her own husband, the artist R. N. Roland Holst. Her dramatic work included *Thomas More* (1912) and several other plays.

Roland Holst's life infuses her work. Although she enjoyed a significant popular reputation, some critics have found that her imagery and even the structure of her sentences are sometimes faulty. Yet her work marks the trend away from the literary ideals of the "Movement of the Eighties" (*see* DUTCH LITERATURE).

See: R. Antonissen, *Herman Gorter en Henriëtte Roland Holst* (1946); B. Verhoeven, *De zielegang van Henriëtte Roland Holst* (1939).   S.L.F.

Rolicz-Lieder, Wacław (1866–1912), Polish lyric poet and Orientalist, was born and died in Warsaw. He published five numbered collections of poems, *Poezje I, II,* and *Wiersze III* (1889, 1891, 1895; Poetry); a cycle of sonnets, *Moja muza* (1896; My Muse); and *Wiersze V* (1897; Poetry); and a few odd ones. He was intimately linked with the German poet Stefan GEORGE; they translated each other's poems and dedicated some of them to each other; the Polish poet can be regarded as a member of the "George Circle." Rolicz-Lieder also had a strong allegiance to the poetry of his mother country, especially to the Renaissance poet Jan Kochanowski and to the romantic poet Juliusz Słowacki. In his own verse he fused native and Western elements (Parnassian and symbolist) with Oriental influences to create a unique combination.

Rolicz-Lieder started out as a poet with decadent mannerisms and later adopted the symbolist technique of musicalization, but he had an original profile of his own. His poetic idiom was characterized by emotional restraint, condensation, precision, and a daring use of concrete imagery. He practiced the cult of art for art's sake and took a stoical personal stance. His hermeticism, aloofness, and certain whimsicalities of style, spelling, and punctuation resulted in a conflict with critics and the reading public, leading subsequently to underestimation of his value and even to oblivion. But opinion changed before World War II, and he is now the object of considerable interest in his own country and abroad.

See: S. Napierski, *Zapomniany modernista polski* (1936); M. Podraza-Kwiatkowska, *Wacław Rolicz-Lieder* (1966).   T.T.

Rolin, Dominique (1913–), Belgian novelist, was born in Brussels. Her first novel, *Les Marais* (1942; The Swamps), received the praise of Max JACOB and Jean COCTEAU. Having moved to Paris in 1946, she won the Femina Prize in 1952 for *Le Souffle* (The Breath). She was a member of the Femina jury from 1958 to 1964, but quit because of the difficulty of defending a strictly literary point of view. (Indeed, most major French literary prizes are increasingly tied to the needs of the publishing industry; hence, the writers who are called to award such prizes must reckon with circumstances that in fact have little to do with literature per se.) In major works from *Lit* (1960; Bed) to *La Maison, la forêt* (1965; The House, The Forest), *Maintenant* (1967; Now), *Les Eclairs* (1971; The Flashes), *Lettre au vieil homme* (1973; Letter to the Old Man), *Deux* (1975; Two), *Dulle Griet* (1977), and *L'Infini chez soi* (1980; The Infinite at Home), Rolin has moved from a classical technique to experimentation close to that of the French "new novel" (*see* FRENCH LITERATURE) and the *Tel Quel* group. She does not engage in superficial language games; her goal seems rather to write a single great work, at once diary, epic, and lyrical narration, incessantly examining a memory of the family cell's complex intertwining. Characterized by determination and rare exuberance, her highly original project appears to consist in describing, in a thousand different strokes and approaches, the deadlock in the relationship between the sexes, beginning with that between her own parents. As in the work of William Faulkner, the setting of Rolin's fiction is always the same. Flanders becomes as fantastic as the southern United States. The passions of the father, the mother, and the children are taken up again and again, like a repetitive, slowly varied, hallucinatory piece of music. The vision is that of Hieronymus Bosch, of Pieter Bruegel, and even of Jan Vermeer. On the one hand, there is meticulous, lucid order; on the other, baroque folly.

Rolin's art is essentially visionary and pessimistic, as if to suggest, in an elaborate, rhythmic prose, the lure of a concealed void. Thus, the fascination of such an orig-inal work emerges gradually. Essentially metaphysical, Rolin's novels transcend the narrow classification of "feminine writing." They are serenely savage in their portrayal of an accelerated series of births and deaths— mere bubbles of sights and sounds destined to explode in the dark, sensually suffocating, burning atmosphere. The importance of this sincerity in writing is bound to be increasingly recognized in the future.   P.So.

Rolland, Romain (1866–1944), French novelist, playwright, and musicologist, was born in Clamecy. In 1886, after studies in Parisian lycées, he was admitted to the Ecole Normale Supérieure. Trained especially in the discipline of history, and a passionate musician by nature, he filled the first chair of musicology at the Sorbonne and gave courses on art and music in the Ecole des Hautes Etudes Sociales, the Ecole Normale, and the Sorbonne until his resignation in 1912. Rolland was a fellow of the Ecole Française de Rome from 1889 to 1891, and he was also in Italy on an official mission for the Ecole des Beaux Arts in 1892 and 1893. During these years, he conducted research that helped reveal the music of such early masters as Claudio Monteverdi. His marriage to Clotilde Bréal in 1892 was dissolved in 1901, and he remained alone, closely attached to his parents, particularly his mother, until her death. In 1934 he married Mme Marie Koudacheva, the half-French widow of a Russian nobleman. Rolland resided principally in Switzerland from 1914 until 1937–38, when he moved to Vézelay, near his birthplace.

Before the turn of the century, Rolland had begun to perceive in the socialist movement an act of faith and energy that he believed would replace the current social structure. His convictions were put to the test in the years of World War I, when he attempted to judge equally all the warring nations, particularly in *Au-dessus de la melée* (1915; Eng. tr., *Above the Battle,* 1916). He hailed the Russian Revolution of 1917 and the new socialist state as a new hope for humanity, but he did not scruple to criticize its mistakes. He soon acquired a reputation as an ardent Communist, although he never joined the Communist (or any other) Party. From Switzerland, he carried on a long and unremitting struggle for social and political justice, for freedom of the individual conscience, and against all forms of imperialism, nazism, and fascism. In 1935, Rolland visited the USSR under the sponsorship of Maksim GORKY and returned with great expectations.

Rolland's ardent wish to participate actively in the intellectual and spiritual life of society led him to write first for the stage; only later did he turn to fiction. His earliest published works were plays—*Saint-Louis* (1897) and *Aërt* (1898), collected later in *Les Tragédies de la foi* (1913; Tragedies of Faith)—intended to arouse hope, faith, courage, and energy in the France of his day, a nation in which he found apathy, discouragement, and a lack of will and energy. He also wrote a series of plays set in the period of the French Revolution, *Les Loups* (1898; Eng. tr., *The Wolves,* 1918), *Le Triomphe de la raison* (1899; The Triumph of Reason), *Danton* (1899; Eng. tr., 1918), and *Le Quatorze juillet* (1902; Eng. tr., *The Fourteenth of July,* 1918), as well as *Le Temps viendra* (1903; The Time Will Come), concerning the Boer War, and *La Montespan* (1904; Eng. tr., *The Montespan,* 1923). After World War I, he again wrote plays with this setting, including *Le Jeu de l'amour et de la mort* (1925; Eng. tr., *The Game of Love and Death,* 1926), *Pâques fleuries* (1926; Eng. tr., *Palm Sunday,* 1928), *Les Léonides* (1928), and *Robespierre* (1939), the latter written for the screen.

Besides numerous articles on musicians and musical history, Rolland's works of nonfiction include the biographies *Beethoven* (1903; Eng. tr., 1917), *La Vie de Michel-Ange* (1906; Eng. tr., *The Life of Michael Angelo,* 1912), *Haendel* (1910; Eng. tr., *Handel,* 1916), and *Tolstoï* (1911; Eng. tr., *Tolstoy,* 1911). These books were, in part, written as examples of heroic and inspiring lives; they constitute parts of a projected series that was never completed.

During these years, Jean-Christophe Krafft, an imaginary heroic character, lived vividly in Rolland's mind. The 10 volumes of the cyclical novel *Jean-Christophe* (Eng. trs., *Jean-Christophe,* 1913, *John-Christopher,* 1910–13) were published between 1904 and 1912. This work, for which Rolland received the Nobel Prize for Literature in 1915, is the life story of a German musician (elements of the lives of Beethoven, Wagner, Mozart, and others can readily be discerned) whose musical career takes him to Paris, Italy, and Switzerland. He is a pure, simple, and uncompromising soul who sees France first from the outside and then from within, and who also sees Germany from the same perspectives. Through the life of this character, Rolland is able to express criticism, indignation, and praise concerning his own country and its artists, politicians, and simple citizens. In part, Rolland intended Christophe to be an inspiration for his contemporaries. The character is filled with boundless energy and optimism and is stubbornly courageous and candid, if blundering, in his approach to his fellow men and their problems. In the first part of the novel, the young Christophe is nourished on a puritan asceticism, while in the second part, powerful inner forces burst through the restraint of the past. The third part concerns the transformation of Christophe's soul; after transgression, penitence, and resurrection, he achieves the best that is in him. The novel is not strictly linear, and there are various flashbacks as well as episodes not truly related to Christophe's life (one of them—*Antoinette*—is a complete short novel). Despite its forward movement, *Jean-Christophe* is circular; the end of the protagonist's life and of the novel rejoins the beginning in a vision of the River of Life, flowing into the great Ocean of Being. Christophe's romantic qualities—his exclusive devotion to music, his exaggerated simplicity and stubbornness, his deep and stormy feelings (he does not attain peace of mind until very late in his life), his unconsummated love for Grazia— no longer appeal greatly to the older reader. Uneven in quality and interest, the various parts of the work offer a variety of structures and styles. The least interesting now is *La Foire sur la place* (The Market Place), which consists largely of harsh criticism of the literary and artistic scene in Paris during the last years of the 19th century. Among the best parts of the novel are those concerning Christophe's childhood and youth, the enduring friendship of Christophe and Olivier, the testing of Christophe in the fire of passion (the episode of Anna Braun and Christophe), and his suffering after Olivier's death. Antinationalist and antiwar, the novel is a vigorous affirmation of life.

Rolland's next novel, *Colas Breugnon* (Eng. tr., 1919), written in 1913, was not published until 1919. This short tale, a Gallic counterpart to *Jean-Christophe,* consists of episodes in the life of a 16th-century wood carver whose love of life, in spite of its griefs and difficulties, is as great as Christophe's and much gayer. After World War I, Rolland published *Liluli* (1919; Eng. tr., 1920), a satire on war; *Clerambault* (1920), the story of a free conscience during a war; and *Pierre et Luce* (1920; Eng. tr., *Pierre and Luce,* 1922), a short, idyllic prose work that ends in the death of the young lovers in the ruins of the Church of Saint-Gervais.

In 1922, Rolland published the first volume of his sec- ond cyclical novel, *L'Ame enchantée* (1922–33; Eng. tr., *The Soul Enchanted,* 1925–35). The enchantment referred to is the stripping away of illusions, of layers of protective deceptions, and the development of an intelligent young woman. There are three protagonists: Annette, Sylvie (her half-sister), and Annette's son Marc. Annette's overpowering personality is occasionally stifling, both for the reader and for the other characters. Sylvie's mixture of frivolity and seriousness, her Parisian grace and pertness, contrast pleasingly with Annette's character. Marc belongs to a long line of struggling adolescents in more or less open revolt against society. Annette is pitted against society by her decision to remain independent and to rear her child alone. Sylvie, who had always been in such a situation, accepts society as it is and uses it for her own ends. But Annette revolts, and the last two volumes— entitled *L'Annonciatrice* (*La Mort d'un monde, L'Enfantement*) (Annunciation [Death of a World, Birth])—are filled with social comments and criticism, as well as allusions to political and social movements. Although these are stirring pages, future generations will regard them as a fictionalized historical account, neither history nor fiction. The subtitle of *L'Annonciatrice— Anna Nuncia*—suggests by its play on Annette's name the position of the heroine; she is the precursor of a future society and of a new kind of woman. Rolland, however, failed to create a truly sympathetic character here, as he had in Christophe. Annette is admirable in her courage and her sincerity, but she seems to remain nothing more than an alter ego of the author. Marc is an intolerant young man who lacks Christophe's generous and overflowing life and who fails to arouse sympathy, emulation, or admiration. Christophe, in spite of his romantic nature, lives on; Marc and Annette, in spite of their realistic portrayal, do not. Apart from *Jean-Christophe,* Rolland will be remembered as one of the most active and determined defenders of human dignity and freedom and as an eager advocate of a more just and humane social order.

See: M. Doisy, *Romain Rolland* (1945); M. Descotes, *Romain Rolland* (1948); W. T. Starr, *A Critical Bibliography of the Published Writings of Romain Rolland* (1950) and *Romain Rolland* (1971); J. Robichez, *Romain Rolland* (1961).   **W.T.S.**

Rølvaag, Ole Edvart (1876–1931), Norwegian-American novelist, was born on Dønna, an island just below the Arctic Circle. His childhood was dominated by the stark beauty of nature, which he came to love and fear; by the state-sponsored Lutheran Church, against whose dogmatism he rebelled; and by the patriotic movement, with its enthusiasm for Norwegian rather than Danish language and culture. After a meager education, he spent five winters as a fisherman and then in 1896 emigrated to the United States. Arriving in South Dakota, he worked as a farmhand to earn money to continue his education. After three years at Augustana Academy, he enrolled in Saint Olaf College in Northfield, Minn., where he cultivated his interest in Norwegian literature. Graduating in 1905, Rølvaag had found his life's mission: through teaching and writing to foster among Norwegian-Americans the best of the European values that were being lost through Americanization. He returned to Norway for a year of graduate work in Norwegian studies at the University of Christiania and then accepted a position at St. Olaf.

During his teaching years, Rølvaag found time to develop his talent as a writer. Although his seven novels were written in the Nordland dialect, they have a distinctly American flavor. *Amerika-Breve* (1912; Eng. tr., *The Third Life of Per Smevik,* 1971) recounts through letters the experiences of a young Norwegian farmhand in South Dakota. *Paa glemte veie* (1914; On Forgotten Paths) is interesting chiefly because its main characters are prototypes of Beret and Per Hansa in *Giants in the Earth*. *To tullinger* (1920; Eng. tr., *Pure Gold*, 1930) is a powerful, naturalistic account of a rootless Norwegian-American couple who barter their souls for riches. In *Længsælens baat* (1921; Eng. tr., *The Boat of Longing*, 1933), the problem is still the difficulty of immigrant transplantation, but here a fledgling artist remains true to his vision. Rølvaag's most admired work, *I de dage* (1924; Eng. tr., *Giants in the Earth*, 1927), the first volume of a trilogy, is unique in American fiction because of its focus on the psychological conflict inherent in immigrant life on the prairie. The succeeding novels, *Peder seier* (1928; Eng. tr., *Peder Victorious*, 1929) and *Den signede dag* (1931; Eng. tr., *Their Fathers' God*, 1931), although not so finely wrought, are persuasive accounts of the pioneer settlement's struggle to found school, church, and state and to achieve a Norwegian-American identity.

Rølvaag's best novels are distinguished by a skillful use of myth, by simple, lyrical language, and by the presence of elemental characters in communion with nature. In spite of his sensitivity to the tragic possibilities in the immigrant experience, he belongs to the European rather than to the American realistic tradition and is closer in mood and style to Knut HAMSUN than to Willa Cather.

See: T. Jorgenson and N. Solum, *Ole Edvart Rølvaag* (1939); P. Reigstad, *Rølvaag* (1972). P.R.

Romains, Jules, pseud. of Louis Farigoule (1885–1972), French poet, novelist, dramatist, and essayist, was born in Saint-Julien-Chapteuil, but he was raised and educated in Paris where his father, a schoolteacher, had been transferred. In 1906, he was admitted to the Ecole Normale Supérieure. He received the *agrégation* in 1909 and subsequently taught in several lycées until 1919, when he resigned. Romains was the founder of the unanimist school. In 1903, while still a student at the Lycée Condorcet in Paris, he had discovered the fundamental principle of unanimism: the importance of the crowd as a distinct entity, possessing a collective soul and specific qualities. In the crowd, Romains found a new source of inspiration, one that literature, solely preoccupied with the psychology of the individual, had so far ignored.

In 1906, Romains, Georges DUHAMEL, and other writers participated in an experiment in community life known as "L'Abbaye." After an enthusiastic start, "L'Abbaye," torn by internal dissensions, soon ended in failure. Romains's first poems, *La Vie unanime* (1908; Unanimist Life), as well as the later *Un Etre en marche* (1910; A Being on the Move) and *Odes et prières* (1913; Odes and Prayers), are lyrical evocations of the crowd. His first novels also demonstrate aspects of the crowd psychology. *Mort de quelqu'un* (1911; Eng. tr., *Death of a Nobody*, 1944), describes the formation of a unanimous feeling caused by the death of Jacques Godard, a man quite unknown to his neighbors until then. *Les Copains* (1913; Eng. tr., *The Boys in the Back Room*, 1937) recounts, through humorous episodes, a plot to generate a unanimist consciousness in two sleepy towns, Ambert and Issoire. But *Psyché*, in three volumes—*Lucienne* (1922), *Le Dieu des corps* (1928), and *Quand le navire* (1929; Eng. tr. of the three vols., *The Body's Rapture*, 1933)—is more a psychological novel dealing with the unrequited love of the Darbelenet sisters for their cousin Pierre Febvre. These works might all be considered as a kind of preparation for Romains's 27-volume *Les Hommes de bonne volonté* (1932–46; Eng. tr., *Men of Good Will*, 1944–46),

which is the most imposing example of the unanimist theories applied to literature. In its aims, method, and structure, this roman-fleuve differs fundamentally from the traditional novel. Romains sought to present a complete picture of French society between 1908 and 1933, a period of startling innovations and changes caused by the industrial revolution, World War I, and the advent of communism. These and other events had different effects on various social groups—businessmen, politicians, the army, the clergy, the nobility, the bourgeoisie and the working classes, the intellectuals, writers, and teachers. Eleven hundred characters represent these groups, the most important of them being Jallez and Jerphanion, who are Romains's spokesmen. There is no continuity in the narrative from one volume to another, and even sometimes from one chapter to the following one. The story moves from Paris, where it begins on October 6, 1908, to the provinces, to several foreign countries, and then back to Paris, where it ends on October 7, 1933. In later years, Romains wrote less ambitious novels, including *Le Fils de Jerphanion* (1956; The Son of Jerphanion), *Une Femme singulière* (1957; A Strange Woman), and *Un grand honnête homme* (1961; A Great Upright Man).

Romains also used the stage to demonstrate his unanimist theories, and he did so with considerable success. M. le Trouhadec, professor of geography at the Collège de France, is the central character of an extravagant trilogy: *M. le Trouhadec saisi par la débauche* (1923; M. le Trouhadec, a Prey to Debauchery), *Donogoo-Tonka* (1931), and *Le Mariage de M. le Trouhadec* (1935). But his most popular play and probably his masterpiece is *Dr. Knock, ou le triomphe de la médicine* (1923; Eng. tr., *Dr. Knock*, 1925), a hilarious comedy in which a clever scoundrel, having established himself as a doctor in a village in the French Alps, succeeds in persuading the inhabitants that they are all sick and in need of medical attention. Employing highly effective comic devices and an admirable knowledge of peasant psychology and language, Romains depicts a community finally united in the same fears and the same hopes. In collaboration with Stefan ZWEIG, Romains also wrote a much acclaimed adaptation of Ben Jonson's *Volpone* (1928).

Romains published many essays dealing with social, political, literary, and even philosophical questions. *Problèmes européens* (1933; European Problems) and *Sept Mystères du destin de l'Europe* (1941; Eng. tr., *Seven Mysteries of Europe*, 1941) disclose the author's political views and his role in national and international affairs. In *Saints de notre calendrier* (1952; Saints of Our Calendar), he names the authors he admires most and who have influenced him. Romains's *Manuel de déification* (1910) is a kind of art of living, while *Situation de la terre* (1958; Situation of the Earth) and the humorous *Interview avec Dieu* (1952; Interview with God), published under the pseudonym of John H. Hicks, express the anguish of humanity uncertain of its destiny. Romains made several trips to the United States and briefly lived in New York in 1940, after the fall of France. *Visite aux Américains* (1936) and the delightful *Salsette découvre l'Amérique* (1940; Eng. tr., *Salsette Discovers America*, 1942) describe his American experience. The author's final judgment on his works, as well as his views on the nature and purpose of literature, appear in *Ai-je fait ce que j'ai voulu?* (1964; Have I Done What I Wanted?). Romains considered literature not only an art but also a trade that requires training and application as well as innate ability.

See: M. Berry, *Jules Romains: sa vie, son œuvre* (1953); A. Cuisenier, *Jules Romains et l'unanimisme*

(1935) and *L'Art de Jules Romains* (1948); A. Figueras, *Jules Romains* (1952); D. Boak, *Jules Romains* (1974).

F.V.

Romanian literature. Romania had little opportunity to develop a literary tradition before the 1830s and the beginning of romanticism. The work of the chroniclers and religious writers of earlier centuries such as Antim Ivireanul, Grigore Ureche, Dosoftei, and Miron Costin were certainly not without literary merit, but it was not until the mid-19th century that the Moldavian chronicles were published by Mihail Kogălniceanu (1817–91) and thus became part of literary tradition. Another significant event during the early period of Romanian literature was Kogălniceanu's founding of the journal *Daciei literare* (Literary Dacia), which provided a rallying point for the writers of the two principalities, Wallachia and Moldavia. A second important figure in the early modern period was Ion Heliade Rădulescu (1802–72), a great prose writer and cultural innovator who not only established libraries, journals, and printing presses but also encouraged the translation of foreign plays into Romanian and gathered into his circle the men who were to play prominent roles in the revolution in 1848. Other major writers during this period were Costache Negruzzi (1808–68), the first modern Romanian prose writer; Grigore Alexandresou (1810–85), a poet and translator of Lord Byron and Alphonse Lamartine; and Vasile Alecsandri (1821–90). Alecsandri, the greatest Romanian poet before Mihail Eminescu, paid particular attention to literary expression, pioneered the dramatic poem, and influenced the development of Romanian drama. Nicolae Filimon (1819–65) is noteworthy because of his *Ciocoii vechi si noi* (Upstarts, Old and New), one of the few early novels that are still readable.

During the last half of the 19th century, Romanian criticism and art came to maturity. This period was dominated by Titu MAIORESCU, an outstanding figure because of his influence as a teacher and leader of the "Junimea" (Youth) circle and its literary journal, *Convorbiri literare* (Literary Conversations). Unlike his rival critic the Marxist Constantin Dobrogeanu-Gherea (1855–1920), Maiorescu generally avoided politics as a source of inspiration. Instead, he established high critical standards that helped to create a new literary style. *Convorbiri literare* introduced to the public Romania's greatest storyteller, Ion Creangă (1837–89), and its most illustrious poet, Mihail Eminescu (1850–89). A master of language and poetic technique, Eminescu is a symbol of the essential spirituality of the Romanian nation. In his poetic masterpiece *Luceafărul* (Hyperion; or Evening Star), Hyperion gives up his immortality in order to love a girl who returns his love, but when Hyperion discovers that she has another emotional attachment, he delicately assumes his immortality again. Eminescu strove for perfect form in every genre he explored: nature poems, philosophical poems, poems of love or protest. He also captured in his verse the biography of his own troubled life. Romania's greatest playwright, Ion Luca CARAGIALE, also strove for perfect form, but his temperament was different and his predominant mood, unlike Eminescu's romanticism, was ironic.

Toward the end of the 19th century, the "Junimea" became less influential and other literary movements took precedence. The doctrines of *sămănătorism* (*semăna*, "to sow") and *poporanism* (*popor*, "the people") were opposed to both those of the "Junimea," which were viewed as too cosmopolitan, and those of the symbolists, which were seen as too foreign, too decadent. Sămănătorists expressed sympathy for the peasants and believed that literature should be inspired by the past.

Their journal *Sămănătorul* (The Sower), published by Alexandru Vlahuţa (1858–1919) and George COŞBUC, was also supported by Nicolae IORGA. The poporanists and their journal *Viaţa românească* (Romanian Life) also supported the peasantry, but this movement advocated a realistic, unidealized portrayal of peasants in literature. Closely associated with poporanism were such writers as Garabet IBRĂILEANU, Gala GALACTION, Ion AGÂRBICEANU, and George TOPÎRCEANU.

Symbolism, another challenge to the "Junimea," was introduced to Romanian literature by Alexandru MACEDONSKI. This movement fostered new themes, new styles of writing, and new lyrical attitudes that further refined the poetic language. The symbolist movement and its journal *Literatorul* (The Literary Man) proved that it was possible to import French literary symbolism and to give it a characteristic Romanian flavor. The movement's influence was felt by such writers as George BACOVIA, Ion Minulescu (1881–1944), and Dimitrie Anghel (1872–1914). Ovid Densuşianu (1873–1937) founded *Viaţa noua* (New Life), another symbolist journal.

The journal *Sburătorul* (The Goblin) and the critic Eugen LOVINESCU supported the renovation of Romanian literature through increased contact with foreign literatures. Although Lovinescu ridiculed the passive ruralism of the sămănătorists, he was one of the first critics to recognize the genius of Liviu REBREANU's rural novel *Ion*. Lovinescu's modernism encouraged a new type of protagonist—the city dweller, the intellectual—as well as a new emphasis on the introspective, the cerebral, and the psychological. In contrast to *Sburătorul* and Lovinescu, *Gîndirea* (Thought), the most interesting journal of the period between the two world wars, believed that Orthodox Christianity and the village, not the city, should provide the foundation of Romanian literature. Established by Cezar PETRESCU (1892–1961), *Gîndirea* sponsored such writers as Tudor ARGHEZI, Zaharia STANCU, and Lucian BLAGA.

In recent years, the Romanian tradition of excellence in literary criticism has been continued by such critics and literary historians as George CĂLINESCU; Perpessicius, pseud. of Dimitrie S. Panaitescu (1891–1971); Tudor Vianu (1897–1964); Serban Cioculescu (1902–); Alexandre Dima (1905–); Adrian Marino (1921–); and Matei Călinescu (1934–).

Despite some interesting experiments and notable successes, contemporary Romanian dramatists have not yet equaled the achievement of Ion Luca Caragiale. Alex Davila's (1862–1929) *Vlaicu-voda* (Lord Vlaicu) is a romantic drama with Shakespearean overtones. Tudor Muşatescu (1903–70) has been one of the most prolific dramatists, but his work is of uneven quality. Other noteworthy dramatists are Victor Eftimiu (1889–), Victor Ion Popa (1895–1946), George Mihail Zamfirescu (1898–1939), and Mihai Sebastian (1907–45). By 1948, the Romanian theaters had become state-owned. In the last 30 years there have been new audiences and new playwrights: Horia Lovinescu (1917–); Mihail Davidoglu (1910–); and Aurel Baranga (1913–), whose comedies have enjoyed a constant success.

Postwar innovations in Romanian literature are most conspicuous in poetry. Numerous young poets, utilizing various techniques and approaches, have been given encouragement by contemporary journals. Mihai Beniuc (1907–) became the chronicler of the new socialist epoch. Romanian letters have been enriched by the ideological militancy of Maria Banuş (1914–), the brief meteoric career of the adolescent genius Nicolae Labiş (1935–56), the massive imagination and prodigious exuberance of Adrian

Paunescu (1943-), the sensitivity of Nina Cassian (1924-), the poetic directness of Ana Blandiana (1943-), and the daring imagery of Constanţa Buzea (1941-), particularly in her volumes *Agonice* (1970; Agony) and *Coline* (1970; Hills).

The postwar Romanian novel has also achieved remarkable success. There has been a move away from strict socialist realism, so that writers are now exploring reality from many angles. Modern psychology has helped the novelist to better understand his characters and thus better delineate their position in their sociohistorical context. Zaharia Stancu's *Desculţ* (1948; Barefoot) marked a turning point in the Romanian novel and has had great influence in molding the viewpoint and technique of other writers. There has been a new literature inspired by the peasants and rural life, an area in which Marin PREDA has achieved the most significant success. World War II as a subject has tempted some writers, such as Laurentiu Fulga (1916-), the author of *Eroica* (1956; Heroic Years). Fanuş Neagu (1932-), a powerful novelist, is one of the first of his generation to use folkloristic elements, but his purpose is not to produce quaint effects but rather to produce an ambivalent tension and atmosphere. Alexandru Ivasiuc's (1933-77) novel *Vestibul* (1967) recounts the tribulation of a professor of neurology who is loved by one of his students, a love that provides a pretext for an analysis of his entire life.

See: J. Steinberg, *Introduction to Rumanian Literature* (1966); I. Rotaru, *O istorie a literaturii române*, 2 vols. (1971); S. Cioculescu et al., *Istoria literaturii române*, vol. 3 (1973); E. Barbu, *O istoria polemica şi antologica a literaturii române de la origini pînă în prezent* (1976).

V.A.

Romanov, Panteleymon (1884-1936), Russian novelist and short-story writer, was born in a village near Tula, in central Russia, of a noble family, and studied law at the University of Moscow. He was one of the most popular Soviet writers in the 1920s, when his books occupied the first place in lending libraries throughout Russia. A keen observer, with a sense of humor and an extensive knowledge of various strata of Russian society, Romanov gave a broad picture of the innumerable changes in social conditions and in the mentality of his fellow countrymen after the 1917 October Revolution. New bureaucrats, peasants, workmen, party members, young students, old intellectuals—all were represented in his sketches with the directness and accuracy of a literary camera. They were often called "the minutes of our times." Romanov, like a literary thermometer, registered all the ups and downs of social temperature in Soviet Russia between 1922 and 1930. He made a sensation with his collection of short stories on sex and love during the first period of the Revolution, *Bez chereyomukhi* (1926; Eng. tr., *Without Cherry Blossom*, 1930). His novels dedicated to different aspects of moral conflicts in Soviet society—*Novaya skrizhal* (1928; Eng. tr., *The New Commandment*, 1933), *Tri pary sholkovykh chulok (Tovarishch Kislyakov)* (1931); Eng. tr., *Three Pairs of Silk Stockings*, 1931), *Sobstvennost* (1933; Property)—are badly constructed and lack psychological insight, but they nevertheless can serve as literary illustrations of a certain period.

M.Sl. rev. W.B.E.

Romanowiczowa, Zofia (1922-), Polish novelist and short-story writer, was born Zofia Górska in Radom. Active in the underground movement during World War II, she was arrested in 1941 and sent to a concentration camp in Ravensbrück. After the war she lived in Italy, where she then finished high school. In 1946-49 she studied French philology in Paris, where she has since made her home.

Romanowiczowa's first poems, written in the concentration camp, appeared in the anthology *Ravensbrück. Wiersze obozowe* (1961; Ravensbrück: Concentration Camp Poems). In 1956 she published her first novel, *Baśka i Barbara*, which was followed by the novels *Przejście przez Morze Czerwone* (1960; Eng. tr., *Passage through the Red Sea*, 1962), *Słońce dzięsieciu linii* (1964; The Sun of 10 Degrees), *Szklana kula* (1967; The Glass Ball), *Łagodne oko błękitu* (1968; A Blue Compassionate Eye), *Groby Napoleona* (1972; Napoleon's Tombs), *Sono felice* (1977; I Am Happy), and a volume of short stories entitled *Próby i zamiary* (1965; Attempts and Intentions). *Baśka i Barbara* deals with the experiences of motherhood and with problems arising from the exposure of children to bilingualism. In *Groby Napoleona,* Romanowiczowa is concerned with the relationship between a mother and an adolescent daughter. In *Sono felice,* interweaving the narrative with memories and reflections, Romanowiczowa depicts a young woman's desperate struggle to find happiness and meaning in life after the horrors of war. Among the major themes of her novels are the concentration camps, life during the Nazi occupation, and the psychological deformations caused by these experiences, as well as problems of alienation, difficulties in adapting to life in exile, and the inability of human beings to achieve real communication with one another.

Romanowiczowa is a representative of the "new novel" in Polish literature. She makes frequent use of such techniques as internal monologue and the alternation between present and past. Her prose is concise and the structure of her novels is clear and consistent. She has also done translations from the French, a notable example being *Brewiarz miłości. Antologia liryki staroprowansalskiej* (1963; Breviary of Love: Anthology of Old Provençal Lyrics).

See: *Słownik współczesnych pisarzy polskich*, series 2, vol. 2 (1978), pp. 351-55; T. Terlecki, "Zofii Romanowiczowej proza czysta," in *Wiadomości* 13-14 (1978).

A.Z.

Romero, Luis (1916-), Spanish novelist, short-story writer, essayist, and poet, was born in Barcelona, the setting of most of his fictional works. After fighting in the Civil War and with the Spanish Blue Division, Romero became an insurance agent, traveled throughout his homeland, and was exposed to many of the social problems his novels depict. His first book, a poetry collection, *Cuerda tensa* (1950; Tense Cord), reveals Romero's intense love for life in contrast to the pervasive presence of death about him and a concern for social justice, both of which become constants in his later fiction. Romero's best novel, *La noria* (1951; The Treadmill), received the Nadal Prize, encouraging him to become a full-time writer. *La noria* is an account of contemporary urban reality related within strict limitations of time and place. It consists of 37 short chapters, each of which examines a moment in the life of a new and distinct character in a seemingly complete panorama of society. Since the publication of *La noria,* Romero has written eight novels, two collections of short stories, and three historical works employing techniques normally associated with fiction. Romero's contribution to the novel is not extraordinary, but his place to date within post-Civil War narrative is comparable in quality to that of other significant members of his generation.

See: L. and A. González-del-Valle, *Luis Romero* (1976); D. Villanueva, *Estructura y tiempo reducido en la novela* (1977), pp. 131–57; L. González-del-Valle and B. A. Shaw, *Luis Romero* (1979).   L.G.-del-V.

Rosa, António Ramos (1924–), Portuguese poet, translator, and critic, was born in the southern town of Faro, where he lives today. He began writing under the combined aegis of humanistic concern and surrealism. His early poems of 1945–52, *Grito claro* (1958; Clear Cry), republished with later work in *Viagem através duma nebulosa* (1960; Voyage across a Nebula), evoke the plight of contemporary people as victims of impersonal forces and abstract ideologies. Rosa believes that one can find relief only by discovering one's own place in the world. The poet thus rejects the abstract rationalism implicit in discursive thought and strives for verbal creation of a prelogical state of pure perception. Prior to such a state, the poet sees himself as a "faceless shadow" as he puts it in *A construção do corpo* (1969; The Construction of the Body). He achieves freedom by abandoning himself to the world as verbal image: "I do not construct. I merely yield to this vague/ desire that suffuses the air," he writes in *Ocupação do espaço* (1963; Taking up Space). The 10 volumes that comprised Rosa's work by 1972, when he published *A pedra nua* (The Naked Stone), create the illusion of an immediately apprehended universe. Normally static images—a silent house, stones, stucco walls—suggest an extraordinary range of emotional resonances. In recent years, Rosa has checked a tendency to dispersal and lexical paucity by introducing greater metric regularity, richer imagery, and a distinctly erotic tone, especially in *Nos seus olhos de silêncio* (1970; In Your Eyes of Silence) and *Não posso adiar o coração* (1974; My Heart Can't Be Put Off). He has stated his views regarding poetry in the introduction to an anthology of essays edited by him, *Poesia, liberdade livre* (1962; Poetry, Free Freedom).

See: E. M. de Melo e Castro, "Para a poesia de António Ramos Rosa," Introduction to Rosa's *Ocupação do espaço* (1963), pp. xi–li.   R.A.P.-R.

Rosales, Luis (1910–), Spanish poet and critic, was born in Granada and has spent much of his life in Madrid. He was associated with the journals *Cruz y Raya* and *Escorial* and the current *Cuadernos Hispanoamericanos*. He has been a member of the Royal Spanish Academy of the Language since 1964.

Rosales's first book, *Abril* (1935; April), contains religious love poetry and is usually taken to represent the beginning of a new generational poetics in Spain. It followed hard upon Pablo Neruda's "Manifiesto de la poesía impura," published in that same year in the first issue of *Caballo verde para la poesía* in Madrid, where Neruda had just arrived as Chilean consul. The book represented, and the manifesto called for, a new vitalism and humanism after the "pure" poetry of the great poets of the preceding Generation of 1927. The ideal was to capture the pulse of life wherever it might be found. Much of the poetry of the group, including that of Rosales, is concerned with love, family, time, and the deity in existential but Catholic terms. It tends to be a calm poetry of classic forms based on the word rather than image or structural metaphor. The early post-Civil War journal *Garcilaso*, named for the 16th-century bucolic, Petrarchan poet of that name, was one of its organs. The Writers Congress of 1937, in which poets of the generation participated, defined "humanism" as "that which attempts to understand man, all men, in depth."

Among Rosales's later collections are: *La casa encendida* (1949; new version, 1967; The Lighted House), perhaps his finest work; *Rimas* (1951), which won two literary prizes; and *Como el corte hace sangre* (1974; Since the Cut Draws Blood). An anthology of his poetry appeared in 1976.

Rosales is also an excellent researcher and critic whose many prose works include *Cervantes y la libertad* (2 vols., 1960) and *El sentimiento del desengaño en la poesía barroca* (1966; The Sense of Disillusionment in Baroque Poetry).

See: L. F. Vivanco, *Introducción a la poesía española contemporánea,* vol. 2 (1971), pp. 113–49; L. Jiménez Martos, *La generación poética de 1936* (1972), pp. 333–52.   H.L.B.

Rosny, J.-H. aîné, pseud. of Joseph-Henri-Honoré Boëx (1856–1940), French novelist and essayist, was born of French-Belgian parents in Brussels. He and his brother, Séraphim-Justin-François (1859–1948), known as J.-H. Rosny *jeune* after 1909, came to Paris as young men and collaborated on a number of novels, mostly in the naturalist vein, under the collective pseudonym of J.-H. Rosny. Author and signer of the "Manifesto of the Five" against Emile ZOLA's *La Terre,* J.-H. Rosny *aîné* was more allied in fictional style and taste to the manner of the Goncourt brothers than to the directness of Zola. If he recognized the worth of the naturalist aesthetic, he also insisted on the value of a kind of symbolism and fantasy that at times betrayed an actual disregard for reality. Yet such novels as *Vamireh* (1892) and *Eyrimah* (1895), which deal with prehistoric times, attest at once to the scientific and encyclopedic bent of his educational training and to the presence of a highly active imagination. His scholarly interest in prehistory, physiology, and ontology invests both his theory and practice of writing with a fairly sophisticated and plausible scientific substratum. Either explicitly or implicitly, most of his fiction reflects the view that science is man's principal educator and benefactor. Ideally, the rules that direct social and moral behavior should derive from the scientific premise. To a significant extent, the characters that people his novels illustrate these basic theses. His protagonists emerge, more frequently than not, as unnuanced types rather than as embodiments of real-life characters.

J.-H. Rosny *aîné*'s half-hearted adherence to the naturalist code is best illustrated in his novel of London low life, *Nell Horn, de l'armée du salut* (1886; Nell Horn of the Salvation Army). This is ostensibly the story of a young working girl who first seeks and finds solace for her miserable plight in the Salvation Army, abandoning it when she falls in love with a Frenchman. When he leaves her penniless and with child, she ekes out a meager subsistence through a life of prostitution. The first section of the novel, replete with richly documented descriptions of slum neighborhoods, park orators, unruly crowds, and street fights, conforms closely to Zola's prescriptions and constitutes the most successful part of the exposition. But the second half of the novel disintegrates into a series of treatises on the Salvation Army, mysticism, and deplorable hospital conditions, all of which are meant to enlist the sympathy and pity of the reader for the wretched condition of the less fortunate members of society. Both the nature and the tone of these sermons suggest a greater affinity with romantic and symbolist attitudes than with naturalism.

J.-H. Rosny *aîné*'s other so-called humanitarian novels, such as *Le Bilatéral* (1887) and *Marc Fane* (1888), dealing with socialist and anarchist circles in Paris, underscore the thesis of possible social amelioration through nonviolent scientific evolution. *Le Termite* (1890) remains a highly readable fictional portrait of the literary world of the naturalist and symbolist writers. The story of *Daniel*

Valgraive (1891) is hardly more than a veiled plea for the founding of a new scientific morality that would reconcile egotism with altruism. Other novels, such as *La Vague rouge* (1912; The Red Wave), *L'Appel du bonheur* (1919; The Call to Success), and *Les Pécheresses* (1928; The Sinful Women), reveal that J.-H. Rosny *aîné* frequently allowed his fiction to become sidetracked by lengthy digressions, incoherent subplots, and downright indigestible scientific jargon. Among his more readable literary and scientific essays, *La Vie amoureuse de Balzac* (1929; Balzac's Love Life) and *La Pluralité: essai sur la discontinuité et l'hétérogénéité des phénomènes* (1919; Plurality: Essay on the Discontinuity and Heterogeneity of Phenomena)—the latter signed with his real name—shed considerable light on his complex mind.

See: G. Casella, *J.-H. Rosny: biographie critique* (1907). R.T.D.

Rosso di San Secondo, Pier Maria (1887–1956), Italian dramatist and short-story writer, was born of an aristocratic family in Caltanissetta but left his native Sicily for Rome at an early age. He first came in contact with northern Europe during a long stay in Holland when he was barely 20, and the north continued to attract him for the rest of his life. In the dualistic vision of Rosso's works, the south represents ardor, brilliance, and instinctual passion; the north, stable and disciplined rationalism. Among the writers with whom he has been thought to have affinities are Maurice MAETERLINCK, Frank WEDEKIND, Georg KAISER, Franz KAFKA, and Thomas MANN.

Rosso's literary production, beginning in the first decade of the 20th century and lasting into the 1950s (the 1920s being the period of his most intense activity), runs the gamut from naturalistic Sicilian drama to the theater of the grotesque (*see* ITALIAN LITERATURE), symbolism, expressionism, and finally to experimentations in which cinematic techniques were adapted to the stage. In this last category is the one-act play *Da Wertheim—Emporio berlinese* (1928; At Wertheim's Berlin Department Store). Among his early works are two collections of short stories inspired by his first discovery of northern Europe, *Elegie a Marike* (1912; Elegies to Marike) and *La Signora Liesbeth* (1914), and a collection of seven one-act plays or "scenes," described as *Sintesi drammatiche* (1911; Dramatic Syntheses). His third collection of short stories, *Ponentino* (1916; West Wind), contains the story that Rosso rewrote as a play, *Marionette, che passione!* (1918; Marionettes, What Passion!), reportedly on the advice of Luigi PIRANDELLO, who was at the time himself turning from narrative to drama. In *Marionette, che passione!*, the work that made Rosso famous, puppetlike characters move in an allusive, poetic atmosphere that has abandoned the props of realism. Three characters, identified only by an article of clothing each wears, meet in a post office one dreary Sunday afternoon. Their lives become momentarily intertwined as each plumbs the depth of his existential despair and dreams of an impossible escape from his destiny, yet they are as permanently attached to their passions as puppets are to the strings that make them move. Rosso felt that the crisis of his time lay in the realization of "the absolute absence of any freedom, in feeling oneself imprisoned in one's own life first, among the lives of others later."

Rosso's plays are not comedies and tragedies, nor are they dramas. They are referred to by the author himself as "scenes," "syntheses," "grotesques," "moments," "plays in color" whose anguished, restless characters speak a convulsive, lyrical language in which they reveal their sudden private epiphanies. Critics generally agree that *La bella addormentata* (1919; The Sleeping Beauty), "a colored fairy tale," is his best play.

See: W. Starkie, *Pirandello* (1926), pp. 21–28; L. Ferrante, *Rosso di San Secondo* (1959). O.R..

Rostand, Edmond (1868–1918), French poet and dramatist, was born in Marseille, of a well-to-do and cultured family. On marrying the poet Rosemonde Gérard, he presented her with a volume of verse, *Les Musardises* (1890). Soon afterwards, at a time when stark naturalism triumphed on the stage, he undertook to revitalize the old romantic drama in verse, enlisting in the process the friendship and assistance of some of the foremost contemporary actors. Le Bargy interpreted *Les Romanesques* (1894; Eng. tr., *The Fantasticks*, 1900); Sarah Bernhardt at the height of her glory created the title roles of *La Princesse lointaine* (1895; Eng. tr., *The Princess Faraway*, 1899), *La Samaritaine* (1897; The Samaritan Woman), and *L'Aiglon* (1900; Eng. tr., 1900); the inimitable Coquelin headed the cast of *Cyrano de Bergerac* (1897; Eng. tr., 1898), and Lucien Guitry that of *Chantecler* (1910; Eng. tr., 1910). *Cyrano de Bergerac*, by no means a faithful rendering of the true historical figure but a clever and lively reconstruction of the Louis XIII period in which he lived, enjoyed the most enthusiastic popular reception ever granted a poetic drama and has preserved, despite the rationalizations of hardened critics, its ever fresh and youthful appeal. It spread Rostand's fame far and wide, forced for him—at the age of 33—the doors of the venerable Académie Française, and, one must add, made him a slave to his tremendous reputation. Laboring under the glare of unwanted publicity, he produced *Chantecler*, his most uneven, yet his most remarkable work, a bold experiment in dramatic technique that carries to the boards the animal world of La Fontaine. *Chantecler* by any standards but those of *Cyrano* would have been called a success; instead, it was pronounced a failure. Shaken in health and spirit, Rostand ended his days in virtual retirement at his luxurious villa "Arnaga" in Cambo (at the foot of the Pyrenees) and lived long enough to see his two sons, Maurice and Jean (*see* Jean ROSTAND), enter upon literary careers of their own.

There can be no doubt that Rostand set himself up ostentatiously as the successor of Victor Hugo and shared the latter's exalted conception of the poet as a teacher of lofty ideals. His romanticism, however, retains a distinct southern flavor. It basks in the dreamy, unreal sun of his native province. Rooted in the ancient tradition of Italo-Provençal chivalric literature, mixing the old themes of love and war, it revels now in pathos and *préciosité,* now in grandiloquence and bombast, only to end with a flourish—*beau geste, panache*—the very arabesque of which carries a suggestion of wistfulness and futility. Thus Rostand's best-known characters—Cyrano, the would-be poet and lover; the eaglet (Napoleon II) deprived of his wings; Chantecler, the cock who discovers that his crowing does not make the sun rise—all illustrate their creator's diffidence and reveal sadness and frustration beneath their superficial bravura. Paradoxically enough, Rostand's theater, the object of equally extravagant praise and abuse in his lifetime, is being reassessed today in terms of this very sincerity and valued, over and above its emotional thrills, as a lucid and moving dramatization of his own sense of unfulfillment.

See: J. Suberville, *Edmond Rostand: son théâtre, son œuvre posthume* (1921); P. Faure, *Vingt Ans d'intimité avec Edmond Rostand* (1928); M. J. Premsela, *Edmond Rostand* (1933); R. Gérard, *Edmond Rostand* (1935); E. Ripert, *Edmond Rostand: sa vie et son œuvre* (1968); M. Migeo, *Les Rostand* (1973). J.-A.B. rev. D.W.A.

Rostand, Jean (1894–), French biologist and essayist, was born in Paris. He has reached an enormous public with works of what has appriately been called *haute vulgarisation*. The son of Edmond ROSTAND, he did not follow conventional studies but received his main scientific training while working in hospitals during World War I. He subsequently conducted research, mainly on toads and frogs, in his private laboratory. The suggestion that he derived part of his enthusiasm for these creatures from the toads' banquet in the fourth act of his father's *Chantecler* (1910) may not be wholly fanciful. His first published work, *Le Retour des pauvres* (1919; The Return of the Poor), was issued at his own expense under the pseudonym Jean Sokori; dealing with the exploitation of the poor in the Great War, the book provides evidence of a characteristic social—and personal—conscience. *Ignace, ou l'écrivain* (1923; Ignace, or the Writer), a satiric portrait of an intense but hypersensitive writer (drawn no doubt from Rostand's experiences with his father and his brother Maurice), maybe taken as representative of his early works. Fictionalized essays, written for the most part with wit and irony, are excerpted in *Pages d'un moraliste* (1952).

Rostand's major works are manuals and treatises on various aspects of biology, works characterized by a humanistic outlook and a tone of moral sagacity. Many of them have become standard in French schools and universities. Among the most successful is *L'Aventure humaine* (1933; Eng. trs., *Adventures before Birth*, 1936; *Life: The Great Adventure*, 1955), a biologist's view of the seven ages of man. Of more interest from a literary point of view are his excursions into history, including a life of Charles Darwin and an enormously erudite essay on the idea of atomism in biology. He followed this with a series of aphoristic works, including *Carnet d'un biologiste* and *Inquietudes d'un biologiste* (Eng. tr., *A Biologist's View*, 1956), more or less consciously evoking La Rochefoucauld or even Blaise Pascal. In spite of some trenchant moments, however, Rostand's efforts are less incisive than their models.

A synoptic view of Rostand's writings is available in his *Pensée scientifique et œuvre littéraire* (1968; Scientific Thought and Literary Work). Two relatively late works are of special interest: *Ce que je crois* (1953; What I Believe) and *Bestiaire d'amour* (1958; Bestiary of Love), the latter ending with a note of caution about man's ability to intervene wisely in his own biological makeup. Rostand is a liberal nature-philosopher of the old school. A convinced atheist (yet one who can remark that he thinks more about God's absence than the believer about His presence), he is nevertheless resigned to the inescapable limitations of the human: "Having sensed the overwhelming magnitude of the problems posed by the human mind," Rostand has reinforced in himself "the sentiment of an essential incomprehension." Rostand is a member of the Académie Française.

See: A. Juste, *La Vie et l'œuvre de Jean Rostand* (1971). P.Ca.

Rostworowski, Karol Hubert (1877–1938), Polish dramatist, poet, theater critic, and publicist, was born in Rybna, near Cracow, and died in Cracow. He began with poetry, but his true vocation was drama. In over a dozen works he experimented with many types of drama: realistic plays and comedies of manners, historical and contemporary dramas, medieval dramatic forms, and philosophical grotesques. This varied and rather uneven output displays two artistic peaks. The first is marked by three poetic dramas in the earlier part of his life—*Judasz z Kariothu* (1913; Judas Iscariot), *Kajus Cezar Kaligula* (1917), and *Miłosierdzie* (1920; Charity). The first two propose revisionist interpretations of two historical figures. Judas is a poor petty shopkeeper who did not grasp the core of Christ's teaching, and Caligula, a "Roman Hamlet," is desperately fighting the baseness of his subjects and breaks down under this burden. *Miłosierdzie*, a drama-oratorio, was an attempt to deal with the phenomenon of revolution (specifically, the Russian October Revolution of 1917) in the spirit of Christian universalism, Christian pessimistic ethics. All three works hold a special place within symbolist drama, thanks to the daring device of polyphonic orchestration of dialogues and especially of crowd scenes.

Rostworowski's second summit reveals an absolutely different style. It is a realistic, even naturalistic, trilogy, written in prose and using peasant dialect: *Niespodzianka* (1929; Surprise), *Przeprowadzka* (perf. 1931; The Move), and *U mety* (perf. 1932; At the Winning Post). In the first part a desperately poor peasant woman unwittingly murders her elder son, a returning immigrant from America, in order to help her younger son realize his aspiration for an education and social advancement. The following parts disclose the moral ordeal of children suffering for the faults of their parents. The drama, especially its first and artistically most perfect part, has the severe contours and the monumental proportions of antique tragedy.

See: *Słownik współczesnych pisarzy polskich*, vol. 3 (1964), pp. 36–47; J. Goślicki, "Karol Hubert Rostworowski," in *Obraz literatury polskiej XIX i XX wieku. Literatura okresu Młodej Polski*, vol. 2, (1967), pp. 425–62. T.T.

Roth, Joseph (1894–1939), Austrian novelist, was born in Schwabendorf, Volhynia, of an Austrian officer father and a Russian-Jewish mother. Left to the care of his paternal relatives, he grew up alienated from his provincial home and desirous of metropolitan fame. He was about to begin his studies in Vienna when World War I began. Roth volunteered, saw action, and was mustered out in Vienna, where he recovered from his psychic wounds for several years while doing odd jobs. He began his literary career as a correspondent for the *Frankfurter Zeitung* and became independent with the publication of a series of largely autobiographical novellas, now included in his collected stories, *Erzählungen* (1973), and the novel *Hotel Savoy* (1924), which touched a sympathetic chord in his generation.

Roth's apartness and his bitter experiences of society came gradually to the fore as he expanded his range in *Die Flucht ohne Ende* (1927; Eng. tr., *Flight without End*, 1930), the story of the simultaneous breakdowns of the spirit of a returned officer and of the fabric of Austrian society. He then made use of the rampant inflation of the time as a correlative to moral devaluation and cultural confusion in *Zipper und sein Vater* (1928; Zipper and His Father). This led Roth in turn to politics, which he viewed with a sarcastic eye in *Rechts und Links* (1929; Right and Left). This series reached its culmination in his epic *Radetzkymarsch* (1932; Eng. tr., *Radetzky March*, 1933, 1973) and its sequel *Kapuzinergruft* (1938; The Tomb of the Kapuziners). These masterworks trace the decay of the Austro-Hungarian monarchy during Franz Josef's reign by recounting the fortunes of the von Trotta family, and particularly those of its last member, Josef. Roth's mordant wit and his sense of historical forces are nowhere better exemplified.

Roth's dark and mystical side is evident in his works beginning with *Hiob* (1930; Eng. tr., *Job*, 1931), a retelling of the biblical legend. This long work was much acclaimed in its time but is now rather less read than the Nikolay

Gogol-like *Tarabas, ein Gast auf dieser Erde* (1934; Eng. tr., *Tarabas, A Guest on Earth*, 1934), a full-blown mystical work. In *Juden auf Wanderschaft* (1927; Jews in the Diaspora) and *Der Antichrist* (1934; Eng. tr., *The Antichrist*, 1935), Roth pleaded for racial and religious tolerance. In his *Beichte eines Mörders* (1936; Eng. tr., *Confession of a Murderer*, 1937) and his very original presentation of Napoleon as seen through the eyes of an adoring servant in *Die Hundert Tage* (1936; Eng. tr., *Ballad of the Hundred Days*, 1936), Roth presented rather affected but influential literary experiments.

Having been persecuted both in Germany and in Austria, Roth fled to Paris in 1936 and turned to drink. His last work, *Die Legende vom heiligen Trinker* (1939; The Legend of the Holy Drunk), returns to autobiographical material to tell of his poverty, misery, isolation, and dreams. Roth's reputation was eclipsed by World War II and did not revive until the mid-1960s, when other empires began to collapse.

See: H. Linden, ed., *Joseph Roth, Leben und Werk* (1949); W. Sieg, *Zwischen Anarchismus und Fiktion* (1974).   V.La. rev. N.R.

Roumanille, Joseph (1818–91), Provençal poet and raconteur, was born at Saint-Rémy-de-Provence, near Avignon. Like Frédéric MISTRAL he was an educated man of the soil who had spent his childhood among the country people, speaking their language. He attended the College of Tarascon and began his career as study supervisor and teacher in a private school. He later occupied the position of proofreader in a printing house and finally established himself as a publisher and bookseller in Avignon. His shop became famous as a literary center. Roumanille wrote his first Provençal verse for the mere purpose, he said, of satisfying a literary fancy, of showing what could be done with the home speech that had been "dishonored" by low and coarse rhymesters. He also told how, some time later, he resolved to use it as a sole means of literary expression because his mother had been unable to understand a poem he had written in French. The important fact, however, is that he was living at a time when various trends were pointing toward the Provençal renaissance, and that his activities were to lead to the founding of the "Félibrige" (1854). The program of this literary school, whose initial aim was the revival of the language and literature of the ancient troubadours, became more ambitious with the rising fame of Mistral, but Roumanille had been its true and active promoter. Indeed, this is the principal claim to fame of him who was called "le père du Félibrige."

Unlike other Félibres, Roumanille did not publish his works with a face-to-face translation. He was writing for a limited public, the countryfolk of Provence. His first book, *Li Margarideto* (1847; The Daisies), was a collection of short poems of a sincere, delicate, and tender realism, written in a light and easy style. He republished them in a larger volume, *Lis Oubreto en vers* (1859; Minor Works in Verse), which contained Christmas carols, didactic stories, and other types of familiar poetry. In that same year appeared *Lis Oubreto en proso*, a book of selected political articles and pamphlets written during the Second Republic. Roumanille displayed much verve and great talent as a defender of traditional order. He was one of the first to use Provençal prose effectively, making everybody laugh, even his opponents. His real fame as a writer rests principally on the short stories that, from 1855 to his death, he contributed to the *Armana prouvençau*, the annual organ of the Félibrige.

Roumanille was not a great poet, but he was an inimitable storyteller, an acute observer of human nature, a wholesome "Rabelais de famille," as he has been called. He was able to raise the popular tale to a certain literary dignity and turn it into a genre that satisfied both the common people and the well-read man, amusing them while teaching a lesson. Some of his best stories were published in book form, *Li Conte prouvençau e li cascareleto* (1883; The Provençal Book of Tales and Facetiae) and *Contes provençaux par Joseph Roumanille avec le texte provençal et la traduction française* (1911). Many of them had previously appeared in Parisian newspapers and periodicals, translated and commented on by authors such as Alphonse Daudet, Paul Arène, and Armand de Pontmartin. Among the best known are "Lou Curat de Cucugnan," "Lou Mege [physician] de Cucugnan," and "L'Ermitan de san Jaque," presented by Daudet as "Le Réveillon de Saint Jacques."

See: S.-R. Taillandier, "La Nouvelle Poésie provençale," *Revue des Deux Mondes* (Oct. 15, 1859): 807–44; E. Ripert, *La Renaissance provençale, 1800–1860* (1917), pp. 361–403; R. Dumas, *Vint conte de Jousè Roumaniho em'uno prefàci de Reinié Dumas* (1968).

A.V.R.

Roussel, Raymond (1877–1933), French prose writer and playwright, was born in Paris. A wealthy traveler obstinately devoted to his writing, Roussel poses one of the strangest cases of literary genius. His attempt to transcend reality through experimentation with language made him a figure hailed as a forerunner by the surrealists (*see* FRENCH LITERATURE). For him, "the work must contain nothing real . . . nothing but completely imaginary combinations." *Comment j'ai écrit certains de mes livres* (1935; How I Wrote Certain of My Books) partly explained his inventive devices: by pairing approximately or actually homonymous words, he built up the first and last sentences of a work, phonetically analogous but with different meanings. He then discovered more materials by multiplying phonetic and semantic duplication of words or by distorting images or syntactic patterns. This rigorous elaboration, combined with a realistic precision in dealing with the imaginary, produced cryptograms of infinite structural complexity. André BRETON credited Roussel with intents of initiation to esoteric doctrines.

Roussel's first publication, *La Doublure* (1897; Understudy [or Lining]), was a long, versified poem-novel. Repetition, here as elsewhere a theme in his work, seems to be an effort to transcend time, to gain access to a state of childhood or Promethean ecstasy. In *Impressions d'Afrique* (1910), for example, a shipwrecked party of white men detained by a black king participate in strange shows where reproducing machines play an important part. In an episode of *Locus solus* (1914; Only Place), corpses in a glass cage reenact significant moments of their lives. *La Vue* (1904; The View) provides very detailed descriptions of miniature scenes, while *Nouvelles Impressions d'Afrique* (1932; New Impressions of Africa) is constructed by multiplying parentheses encased within each other. Roussel also wrote plays, but such lavishly staged works as *L'Etoile au front* (1924; The Star on the Forehead) and *La Poussière de soleils* (1926; A Dust-Cloud of Suns) were notorious failures.

Although it is possible to find in Roussel's work the anxieties and myths of Western culture, his verbal creation seems to refer essentially to the very space of language itself. His writing skill may perhaps point to no other secret than his own demiurgic functioning.

See: J. H. Matthews, in *Surrealism and the Novel* (1966), pp. 41–55; B. Caburet, *Raymond Roussel* (1968); C. Veschambre, "Sur les" 'Impressions d'Afrique,'" *Poétique* 1 (1970): 64–78.   D.Ba.

Rozanov, Vasily Vasilyevich (1856–1919), Russian philosopher, essayist, critic, and memorist, was born in Vetluga into a humble family. The penury and want of his childhood left a noticeable impression on him, leading to his later glorification of home and family and his "Old Testament religiosity," as expressed especially in the aphoristic, autobiographical books *Uyedinyonnoye* (1911; Eng. tr., *Solitaria, 1927*) and *Opavshiye listya* (1913–15; Eng. tr., *Fallen Leaves, Bundle One*, 1929). After graduating from Moscow University he taught for several years at high schools in small provincial towns. But his essay entitled *Legenda o velikom inkvizitore F. M. Dostoyevskogo* (1894; Eng. tr., *Dostoevsky and the Legend of the Grand Inquisitor*, 1972) found a wide audience in literary and philosophical circles. In the early 1890s, Rozanov moved to Petersburg, where, through the influence of literary friends and well-wishers, he obtained a minor post in the Russian civil service. In 1899, Aleksey S. Suvorin, the proprietor and chief editor of the influential, conservative newspaper *Novoye vremya*, invited him to join the staff. This job gave him financial security so that along with journalistic work he could devote himself to his literary, philosophical, and theological studies. The October Revolution of 1917, which he opposed, deprived him of his livelihood. He died in the monastery at Sergiyevski Posad (now Zagorsk), a victim of poverty and starvation, reconciled to his native Russian Orthodox Church, which he had often attacked vehemently.

Rozanov's most profound and intimate experience was his childhood encounter with Christianity in the guise of the Russian Orthodox Church, with its popular piety, asceticism, and peculiar spiritual and liturgical aesthetics. Religious questions preoccupied him throughout his life. He repeatedly tried to come to grips with the fundamental problem of Christianity, which he saw as the contrast between the vitalistic, patriarchal religion of the Old Testament and the ascetic, negativistic, acosmic doctrines of the New Testament. At times he would reject the church and faith of his forefathers in the name of erotic-vitalistic ideals, and at other times he would defend his native church. Doubtless, Rozanov was one of the most pronounced rebels in the history of Russian religiosity, with a well-nigh Dostoyevskian subtlety and a brilliant talent for polemics and invective. But he remained within the tradition, detesting all positivistic, materialistic, "enlightened" modernism. Only one thing was important to him: the telluric-erotic I and the soul—man between God and the cosmic-vitalistic powers.

Rozanov also enjoyed considerable fame as a stylist. His diction is characterized by informality, nonchalance, and raciness, and his writings bristle with pithy colloquialisms taken from everyday talk, rich imagery, unexpected, paradoxical metaphors, and picturesque idioms. His is the style of a man who spoke to himself rather than to others. Although Rozanov's work is still under a strict taboo in the Soviet Union, there is no doubt that his style influenced Soviet Russian writers, especially during the 1920s. Recent editions of Rozanov's works include *Izbrannoye* (New York, 1956); *Izbrannoe/Ausgewählte Schriften* (Munich, 1970), and *La face sombre du Christ* (Paris, 1964). H.A.S.

Różewicz, Tadeusz (1921–), Polish poet, playwright, and short-story writer, was born in Radomsko. During World War II he fought in the underground home army. He later studied the history of art at Jagiellonian University. His early volumes of lyrics, *Niepokój* (1947; Anxiety) and *Czerwona rękawiczka* (1948; The Red Glove), written in an "antipoetic" style with the use of simple, colloquial, and harsh words, are shadowed by the horror of war and

occupation and the corruption of human values, which remain his constant points of reference in his discussion of contemporary problems. His consternation arising from the cruelty of war and from the conviction that war shattered the basis of European culture found expression not only in the bitterness and irony of his poems but also in his rejection of all literary conventions of genre, meter, rhyme, and metaphor. In his later poems, published in the volumes *Rozmowa z księciem* (1960; Conversation with a Prince), *Głosanonima* (1961; The Anonymous Voice), *Nic w płaszczu Prospera* (1962; Nothing in Prospero's Cloak), *Twarz* (1964; The Face), *Twarz trzecia* (1968; The Third Face), *Regio* (1969), and others, Różewicz's severe moral judgment embraced the whole of contemporary civilization. After 1956, Różewicz moved toward drama written in the idiom of his poetry as "antidramas" and applied in a creative, innovative way the technique of the theater of the absurd. In his first play, *Kartoteka* (1960; Eng. tr., *The Card Index*, 1969), the hero, lying in bed, "witnesses the whole of his phantomlike life" (Czesław MIŁOSZ). Simultaneously, various stages of his life appear through the interrogations of different characters. In *Świadkowie albo Nasza mała stabilizacja* (1962; Eng. tr., *The Witnesses*, 1970), the insensitivity and moral indifference of a contemporary civilized man are penetratingly analyzed. *Wyszedł z domu* (1964; Eng. tr., *Gone Out*, 1969) is a grotesque, absurdist parody of a family drama, with a father escaping from reality into debilitating amnesia. *Akt przerywany* (1964; Eng. tr., *The Interrupted Act*, 1969) is a radical example of antitheater consisting mainly of stage directions, designed to prove the ineffectiveness of existing dramatic conventions. In *Stara kobieta wysiaduje* (1968; Eng. tr., *The Old Woman Broods*, 1970), Różewicz comes close to Samuel BECKETT's pessimistic and tragic vision in his own version of the end of the world as an old woman with a dried-up womb on a heap of rubbish. The author left open the way in which this play could be staged. *Przyrost naturalny* (1968; Eng. tr., *Birth Rate*, 1976), with the subtitle: "The Biography of a Play for the Theater," is a text about a play that the author is not able to write and that a director has to compose on the stage. Różewicz is also the author of several collections of short stories, *Opadły liście z drzew* (1955; The Leaves Have Fallen from the Trees), *Przerwany egzamin* (1960; The Interrupted Examination), and *Wycieczka do muzeum* (1966; An Excursion to a Museum); a short novel, *Śmierć w starych dekoracjach* (1970; Death amidst Old Stage Props), and other literary efforts. He has also published *Poezje zebrane* (1971; Collected Poems) and *Sztuki teatralne* (1972; Plays).

See: H. Vogler, *Tadeusz Różewicz* (1972); M. J. Kryński and R. A. Maguire, Introduction to T. Różewicz, *"The Survivor" and Other Poems* (1976), pp. ix–xix; K. Wyka, *Różewicz parokrotnie* (1977); S. Gębala, *Teatr Różewicza* (1978). A.W. and S.F.

Rozhdestvensky, Robert Ivanovich (1932–), Russian poet, was born in the Altay region. After graduating from the Gorky Literary Institute in Moscow he began to publish in 1950 and gained popular acclaim with "Moya lyubov" (1955; My Love), a polemical poem satirizing the contemporary world. His first published poetry collection was *Flagi vesny* (1955; The Flags of Spring), which was followed by *Ispytaniye* (1956; Trial), *Dreyfuyushchi prospekt* (1959; Dreyfus Avenue), *Rovesniku* (1962; To a Contemporary), *Neobitayemye ostrova* (1962; Uninhabited Islands), *Radiyus deystviya* (1965; The Radius of Action), and *Syn very* (1966; Son of Faith), a pun on his mother's name Vera (faith). Rozhdestvensky's travels to the United States, France, and Italy are often reflected in his verse, which closely follows the oratorical and didactic tradition of Vladimir MAYAKOVSKY. He has also written on World War II—*Rekviem* (1961; Requiem)—and frequently treats such contemporary topics as space exploration, atomic power, and the world of the future. "Pismo v tridtsaty vek" (1963; Letter to the Thirtieth Century) stresses the work and ideals of contemporary Soviet life.

See: V. A. Zaytsev, *Sovremennaya sovetskaya poeziya* (Moscow, 1969).   L.V.

Rozov, Viktor Sergeyevich (1913-), Russian dramatist, born in Yaroslavl, began his theatrical career as an actor and director in the Moscow Theater of the Revolution. During World War II, he was wounded while playing in theaters at the front. He subsequently studied at the Gorky Literary Institute in Moscow and wrote successful plays on the conflict between generations. His *Vechno zhivye* (1956; Eng. tr., *Alive Forever*, 1968), the play with which the Contemporary Theater opened, became known in the West in its screen version entitled *Letyat zhuravli* (1957; The Cranes Are Flying). Rozov has frequently contributed plays to the Soviet repertory on problems of individual life: *V poiskakh radosti* (1957; Eng. tr., *In Search of Happiness*, 1961) dramatizes a boy's rejection of his parents' false idolatry of things; *V den svadby* (1964; On the Wedding Day) concerns a bride who cancels her wedding when she realizes the groom is marrying her out of obligation, not love; *S vechera do poludnya* (1970; From Night till Noon) explores impartially the rights of an American mother and a Soviet father to their son's love.

See: W. Kasack, "Viktor Sergeevič Rozov," *ZSP* 38, no. 1 (1975): 157-77.   M.L.H.

Rubió i Ors, Joaquim (1818-99), Catalan poet and scholar, was born in Barcelona. He is intimately associated with the literary movement known as "Renaixença" (*see* CATALAN LITERATURE). He abandoned a career in the church for one in letters. In 1847 he was appointed to the chair of general and Spanish literature in the University of Valladolid. In 1858 he moved to the University of Barcelona to occupy the chair of universal history of literature. His major efforts were directed toward the revival of the Catalan language and literature. In 1839, under the pseudonym Lo gayter del Llobregat (The Piper of Llobregat), he published his first Catalan composition in the *Diario de Barcelona*. No one, with the exception of the editor of the newspaper, knew the identity of the new troubadour who, with exemplary faithfulness, kept writing Catalan poems for the most important daily papers of Catalonia. His verse was widely and avidly read. In *Lo gayter del Llobregat* (1841; The Piper of Llobregat) he collected previously published poems, adding new ones and an important prologue in which he demanded literary independence for Catalonia and urged love and veneration for the native tongue. The prologue had the value of a political-literary manifesto.

Rubió i Ors was one of the restorers of the poetic festival known as the Jocs Florals (*see* CATALAN LITERATURE) in 1859. He produced works of literary investigation for different Catalan and foreign journals and with his friend Josep Maria Grau began the publication of a collection of old Catalan writers. His work has had a wide influence in the Catalan-speaking countries.

See: F. Tubino, *Historia del renacimiento literario contemporáneo en Cataluña* (1880); M. Menéndez y Pelayo, Prologue, in Rubió i Ors, *Lo gayter del Llobregat* (1889); M. de Montoliu, *Manual d'història crítica de la literatura catalana moderna* (1922).   J.M.M.iV.

Rud, Nils Johan (1908-), Norwegian novelist and short-story writer, was born in Ringsaker, north of Oslo. At the age of 15 he had to assume the support of his family, but he still managed to create a name for himself as a writer at an early age. In 1932, Rud became the editor of *Arbeidermagasinet,* a popular magazine that under his editorship became an important stepping-stone for promising young writers. Rud's early novels treat the psychology of poor white-collar workers, but with *Jakten og kvinnen* (1939; The Hunt and the Woman), he arrived at the central theme of his fiction: man and his relationship to nature. Indeed, Rud often worships woman as earthbound, impulsive, and somehow akin to nature itself. Of Rud's later novels the most important are the trilogy *Fredens sønner* (1947; The Sons of Peace), *Kvinner i advent* (1948; Women in Advent), and *Vi var jordens elskere* (1949; We Were the Lovers of the Earth). In these novels, which concern a farmer's departure for war and his difficult return, Rud continues to express his naive, romantic view of nature and erotic love as well as his awareness of the destructive inauthenticity of modern life. In *Gå hvor du har drømt* (1978; Go Where You Have Dreamed), he portrays an old man's return to his childhood home with a lyrical power and a psychological insight that again demanded critical attention throughout Scandinavia. The same capacity for lyrical-romantic description and for revealing moods and states of mind gives a Chekhovian, dreamlike quality to his short stories, among which are some of the finest in Norwegian literature. Rud's *Novellier i utvalg* (Selected Short Stories) was published in 1972.   K.A.F.

Rudnicki, Adolf (1912-), Polish novelist, short-story writer, and essayist, was born in Warsaw and has spent most of his life in that city. At the outbreak of World War II he fought as a soldier in the Polish September campaign of 1939, and during the Nazi occupation he participated in clandestine publishing activity and took part in the 1944 Warsaw uprising. His first novel, *Szczury* (The Rats), a kind of memoir of a young man, appeared in 1932. He published four more books before the war: *Żołnierze* (1933; Soldiers), *Niekochana* (1936; Unloved), *Lato* (1938; Summer), and *Doświadczenia* (1939; Experiences).

Rudnicki's prose combines various genres: literary fiction, reportage, and memoirs. *Niekochana* is a refined psychological study of passionate love, a theme that was to appear often in Rudnicki's further writing, including *Pałeczka* (1950; "Narzeczony Beaty" (1961; Beata's Fiancé), and "Pył miłosny" (1964; Love Dust). The other issue dominating Rudnicki's postwar short stories is his attempt to give a testimony to the tragic fate of the Jews during World War II. These stories appeared in the collections *Szekspir* (1948), *Ucieczka z Jasnej Polany* (1949; Escape from Yasnaya Polyana), *Żywe i martwe morze* (1952; Eng. tr., *The Dead and the Living Sea and Other Stories*, 1957), *Krowa* (1959; The Cow), *Kupiec łódzki. Niebieskie kartki* (1963; The Merchant from Łódź. Blue Pages), and *Weiss wpada do morza. Niebieskie kartki* (1965; Weiss Falls into the Sea: Blue Pages). After 1956, Rudnicki also began publishing highly personal feuilletons in periodicals. Constituting a kind of diary about people, books, and various contemporary problems, they were later collected in several volumes under the title *Niebieskie kartki* (Blue Pages).

See: *Słownik współczesnych pisarzy polskich*, vol. 3 (1964), pp. 52-59; H. Zaworska, "Proza Adolfa Rudnickiego czyli Hołd każdemu na miarę jego cierpień," in *Prozaicy dwudziestolecia międzywojennego*, ed. by B. Faron (1972), pp. 555-91.   A.Z.

Rueda, Salvador (1857-1933), Spanish poet, novelist, and playwright, was born in Málaga. He is remembered only for his verse, which has undeniable historical importance. Although there is still debate over whether he or Rubén Darío fathered Spanish *modernismo* (*see* SPANISH LITERATURE), it can be claimed that both poets, among others, revolutionized the poetic means and intentions of the Spanish and Spanish American lyric, giving it new subjects, colors, meters, and rhythms. Rueda also introduced Darío to Spanish literary circles in which the great Nicaraguan was to be immensely influential. By 1900, Rueda had already published some 20 volumes, and hardly a prominent writer of the period failed to provide him with a prologue: Gaspar Nuñez de Arce, Leopoldo ALAS, Benito PÉREZ GALDÓS, and Miguel de UNAMUNO. Darío himself wrote the introduction to *En tropel* (1892; In a Rush), one of Rueda's best collections.

Rueda's early work, as in *Cuadros de Andalucía* (1883; Andalusian Scenes) and *Noventa estrofas* (1883; Ninety Stanzas), is naturalist and *costumbrista* in the Andalusian regional manner. The innovations came later, when he began to show signs of dissatisfaction with the lofty romantic poetry of the period. Although it appeared the same year as Darío's *Azul,* the work that is considered to signal the affirmation of modernism in Spanish America, Rueda's *Sinfonía del año* (1888; Symphony of the Year) is already markedly modernist in form, technique, and subject matter. It clearly looks forward to Ramón del VALLE-INCLÁN's four seasonal "sonatas," written in 1902-05. Other representative works are *Himno a la carne* (1890; Hymn to the Flesh) and *Piedras preciosas* (1900; Precious Stones), a collection of 100 sonnets. The titles of these books reveal their literary affiliations.

Rueda's modernist or premodernist verse is a facile, colorful, exuberant, musical poetry of effects and of the senses, not a poetry of transcendence. The influence of the French Parnassians and symbolists is obvious, and although Rueda denied this, it was admitted by Darío. Rueda was a precursor of the great Spanish literary figures to follow. Although he wrote little after 1900, his extraordinary early prominence is exemplified by his reception in Spanish America in 1910, when he was crowned with laurel in Havana and lionized throughout the southern continent. Thereafter he quickly fell into oblivion, and his last years were embittered. Ongoing critical attempts to define his historical importance now invariably recognize its magnitude, but only the same few poems find their way into anthologies.

See: D. Fogelquist, "Salvador Rueda y Rubén Darío," *RHM* 30 (1964): 189-204; R. Morales, *Los 100 poetas mejores de la lírica castellana* (1967), pp. 676-86.

H.L.B.

Rühm, Gerhard (1930-), Austrian poet and prose writer, was born in Vienna. He studied composition before his interest shifted to literature, where he claims German baroque poetry—as well as Dada, surrealism, and constructivism—as his heritage. In the early 1950s he formed the "Wiener Gruppe" (*see* GERMAN LITERATURE) with Friedrich Achleitner, Hans Carl ARTMANN, Karl Bayer, and Oswald Wiener; and he edited a book about the group, *Die Wiener Gruppe* (1967). His first publication was a book of poems in Viennese dialect, *hosn rosn baa* (1959, with Achleitner and Artmann), which uses dialect as an alienation effect, exploiting the tension between spoken immediacy and the outlandish look of the words spelled phonetically. Rühm's subject matter is the structures and mechanisms of language itself, which he explores with a great variety of techniques and inventiveness. The main body of his work is "concrete poetry," which stresses either the sound, as in *Wahnsinn Litaneien* (1973; Madness Litanies), or the visual side of words in nonlinear, spatial constellations, as in *Gesammelte Gedichte und visuelle Texte* (1970) and *Mann und Frau* (1972). Montage dominates in his important prose work, *Fenster* (1968; Windows), and in his dramatic pieces *Ophelia und die Wörter* (1972).

See: R. Waldrop and H. Watts, eds., *Six Poets from Vienna* (1979).

R.Wa.

Rühmkorf, Peter, pseud. Leslie Meier (1929-), German poet and parodist, was born in Dortmund, attended school in Stade, and studied art history, German lierature, and psychology at the University of Hamburg. He worked at various occupations from 1951 to 1958, when he became an editorial reader for the Rowohlt Verlag in Hamburg. In 1963 he served on the staff of the Literarisches Colloquium in Berlin, and he spent the year 1964-65 as a fellow at the Villa Massimo in Rome. Since 1966 he has been a free-lance writer.

Known as a first-rate parodist and lyrical social critic, Rühmkorf founded the magazine *Zwischen den Kriegen* with Werner Riegel in 1951. His first volume of poetry, *Heiße Lyrik* (Fiery Lyrics), was published with Riegel's collaboration in 1956. For a time he was an editor and critic for the journal *Studenten-Kurier* (later *Konkret*), an aggressive magazine of social persiflage. Always politically aware, Rühmkorf gave even his nature poetry a touch of political satire. He is acerbic in the lyric collection *Irdisches Vergnügen in g* (1959; Earthly Delights in g), whose title is reminiscent of the massive collection of topical poems by 18th-century versifier Barthold Hinrich Brockes. The g of the title refers both to God and to the gravity of earth; the poems are modeled on the irrepressible critical commentary on society found in cabaret songs.

Rühmkorf is a master of poetic forms, which he uses to good effect in perverse and topically critical imitations. The collection of poems in *Kunststücke* (1962; Clever Tricks), which he has characterized as "recognitions and discouragements," closes with a critique of lyric poetry. His short biography of *Wolfgang Borchert* appeared in 1961. A collection of often obscene children's songs and rhymes, recorded on the streets and in the alleys of Hamburg, was *Über das Volksvermögen, Exkurse in den literarischen Untergrund* (1967; On the Wealth of the People: Excursions into the Literary Underground), which was preceded in 1962 by a collection of essays in the volume *Bestandsaufnahme* (Inventory). Rühmkorf's attempts at drama, as in *Was heißt hier Volsini, Szenen aus dem klassischen Wirtschaftsleben* (1969; What Do You Mean Volsini: Scenes from a Classical Economic Life), *Lombard gibt den Letzten* (1972; Lombard Gives His All), and *Die Handwerker kommen, ein Familiendrama* (1974; The Handicraftsmen Are Coming, A Family Drama), did not meet with friendly critical receptions. A volume of reportage, *Die Jahre die ihr kennt* (1972; The Years that You Know), was followed in 1978 by a brash critical volume, *Walther von der Vogelweide, Klopstock, und ich* (Walther von der Vogelweide, Klopstock, and Myself), in which Rühmkorf compares his own work with that of the medieval lyric poet and the 18th-century poet of sentiment and political defiance. Rühmkorf's own poems are collected in a volume published in 1976, in *Gesammelte Gedichte*. His book of essays, letters, and poems, *Strömungslehre I* (Theory of Currents, I), was published in 1978. He received the Hugo Jacobi Prize in 1958 and in 1979 the Erich Kästner Prize.

See: T. Verweyen, *Eine Theorie der Parodie: am Beispiel Peter Rühmkorfs* (1973).

A.L.W.

Ruibal, José (1925–), Spanish playwright born in Pontevedra, began writing for the theater while working as a
journalist in South America in the 1950s. Most of his
plays were written in Madrid in the 1960s, when political
repression made him a full-time playwright by stripping
him of the opportunity to continue his career in journalism. His dissident themes and unconventional style severely limited both publication of the plays and the possibility of staging them in his own country, thereby
consigning them to the status of "underground theater."
From its initial application to Ruibal, the term "underground theater" acquired a general applicability to many
inventive playwrights who were forced to undergo isolation and the threat of oblivion during the Franco era.
Ruibal's theater is composed of 18 plays, most of them
short pieces. They present an acidly satirical view of
modern society and the human condition that is communicated through the use of richly creative language, uninhibited and sometimes frenetically kinetic images, and
the allegorical projection of animal figures with roots in
the ancient anthropomorphic animal fables of the fly, the
octopus, the ass, the codfish, and the monkey, among
others. His major plays are *El hombre y la mosca* (written
1968; Eng. tr., *The Man and the Fly*, 1970; first Spanish
ed., 1977) and *La máquina de pedir* (1970; Eng. tr., *The
Begging Machine*, 1975). His *Teatro sobre teatro* was
published in 1975.

See: G. E. Wellwarth, *Spanish Underground Drama*
(1972). S.M.G.

Ruiz Iriarte, Víctor (1912–), Spanish dramatist born in
Madrid, is the author of over 30 plays, most of which can
be classified as light comedy. Adjectives commonly applied to his theater are: witty, well-constructed, delicate,
entertaining, lighthearted, refreshing, optimistic, poetic,
and charming. Dealing frequently with the theme of reality and illusion in the tradition of Luigi PIRANDELLO and
NIKOLAY YVREINOV, his plays usually fall into the category
of "teatro de evasión" (theater of evasion), as do those
of his fellow Spaniards Alejandro CASONA, José LÓPEZ
RUBIO, and Edgar Neville. Ruiz Iriarte frequently selects
a commonplace situation and embellishes it with clever
dialogue and charm. When he selects a more serious
theme, he extracts the pain by offering whimsical scenes
and comforting consequences. His first full-length play,
El puente de los suicidas (1944; Suicide Bridge), featuring
a happiness specialist in the business of preventing suicides, recalls Casona's *Prohibido suicidarse en primavera*, (1937; Suicide in Springtime Is Forbidden) and *Los
árboles mueren de pie* (1949; Trees Die Standing). Ruiz
Iriarte's best known work, *El landó de seis caballos*
(1950; The Six-Horse Carriage), deals with four old people
who reject the harsh realities of life in favor of a world of
fantasy. His treatment of insanity here resembles Pirandello's in *Enrico IV*. Other important works by Ruiz Iriarte are: *Academia de amor* (1946; The Academy of
Love), for which he won the Piquer Prize of the Royal
Spanish Academy of the Language; *Juego de niños* (1952;
Children's Game), winner of the National Theater Prize;
Esta noche es la víspera (1958; Tonight Is the Eve); *El
aprendiz de amante* (1949; The Apprentice Lover), his
first big hit; *El carrusel* (1964; The Carousel); *Un para-
guas bajo la lluvia* (1965; An Umbrella in the Rain); and
La Muchacha del sombrerito rosa (1967; The Girl in the
Little Pink Hat).

See: A. Baquero Goyanes, "El humor en el teatro de
Ruiz Iriarte," in *El teatro de humor en España* (1966),
pp. 183–99; P. Z. Boring, *Víctor Ruiz Iriarte* (1979); M.
P. Holt, *The Contemporary Spanish Theatre (1949–1972)*
(1975). P.W.O'C.

Rusiñol, Santiago (1861–1931), Catalan novelist, dramatist, and essayist, was born in Barcelona. His father was
a businessman, and the son followed this example until
he was 25. This period of his life and the atmosphere of
Barcelona at that time are described in his novel (later
dramatized) *L'auca del senyor Esteve* (Spanish tr., 1908;
Mr. Esteve's Praise). From then on until his death he
devoted himself to painting and to literature. He died at
Aranjuez, the Spanish royal country palace whose gardens
he was fond of painting. His book *Jardins d'Espanya*
(1903; Spanish tr., *Jardines de España*, 1914; Gardens of
Spain) contains 40 reproductions of these paintings with
comments by the author. His literary works, which were
almost always written in Catalan and translated into Spanish, were many and varied and achieved great popularity
throughout Spain. They include collections of articles on
life, travels, and landscape such as *Anant pel mon* (1896;
A Traveler in the World), *Oracions* (1897; Prayers), *Fulls
de la vida* (1898; Pages from My Life), and *L'illa de la
calma* (ca., 1922; Spanish tr., *La isla de la calma*), the
last a description of the island of Majorca. He is the
author of novels as well, the most outstanding being *El
poble gris* (1902; Spanish tr. by G. Martínez Sierra, 1904;
The Gray Town), a satirical description of small town
life. But most famous of all are his dramatic works, among
them the operetta *L'alegria que passa* (1901; Spanish tr.
by Vital Aza, *La alegría que pasa*, 1906; Transient Happiness), *El pati blau* (1903; Spanish tr., *El patio azul*; The
Blue Patio), and *El mistic* (1904; Spanish tr. by J. Dicenta,
El místico, 1904; The Mystic). *El mistic* enjoyed a huge
success in all Spain because of its religious and historical
significance, dealing as it did with the life of the greatest
of Catalan poets, the priest Jacint VERDAGUER. These
many and diverse works are united by Rusiñol's particular
point of view, a blend of humor and sentimentality, of the
joy of living and wry skepticism, of brutal realism and
romantic idealism.

See: G. Desdevises du Dézert, *Le Théâtre catalan de
Santiago Rusiñol* (1906); R. Darío, *Cabezas* (1919), pp.
29–35; J. Ochoa, *Santiago Rusiñol: su vida y su obra*
(1929); J. Passarell and A. S. Escó, *Vida, obra i anecdotes d'en Santiago Rusiñol* (1931). F. de O.

Russian literature. For a variety of reasons Russian literature developed much later than the other major literatures of Europe. Its beginnings date back to the 10th
century, when Grand Prince Vladimir of Kiev accepted
the Byzantine form of Christianity on behalf of himself
and his subjects and married the daughter of the Byzantine emperor. At that time the capital of Byzantium, Constantinople, was a center of European culture. The family
of Vladimir's son, Yaroslav the Wise, married into several
of the major royal families of Europe. For the next 200
years relations between Kievan Russia and the rest of
Europe were far less restricted than in many later periods
of Russian history. The invasion of Russia by the Mongols
in the first decades of the 13th century brought an end to
the Kievan era in Russian history and cut Russia off from
normal contacts with the rest of Europe for nearly 250
years. By the 17th century, however, Western influences
began to grow in Russia, and these Westernizing and
secularizing tendencies were accelerated at the end of the
century by the headlong efforts of Peter I to transform
the Russian state into a modern European nation. By
1799, thanks to a remarkable literary apprenticeship carried out by several generations of energetic and talented
writers, Russia had become a part of the European community of letters. Out of the two languages current in
Russia at the beginning of the century—an untutored spoken Russian and an artificial Church Slavonic—there was

created by the end of the century a flexible and expressive literary language, which like English owed much of its richness to its hybrid origin. By a process of accelerated literary development, 18th-century Russian literature adopted and assimilated in rapid succession the baroque, neoclassical, and sentimental influences that it acquired from the West. By the end of the century, along with a host of worthy talents in poetry and drama and several in prose, it had produced a major poet, Gavriil Derzhavin.

Between 1799 and 1828, the birth dates of Aleksandr Pushkin, the great Russian poet, and Lev Tolstoy, one of the two greatest Russian novelists, Russia produced a generation of literary figures comparable only to those of Elizabethan England, the Spanish Golden Age, and the period of Louis XIV in 17th-century France. That short span of 29 years saw the birth not only of Pushkin and Tolstoy but also of the other three giants of Russian fiction—Nikolay Gogol, Ivan Turgenev, and Fyodor Dostoyevsky—as well as a host of literary figures worthy of comparison with all but the greatest in Western European literature—the poets Mikhail Lermontov, Fyodor Tyutchev, Afanasy Fet, and Nikolay Nekrasov; the novelist Ivan Goncharov; the satirist Mikhail Saltykov-Shchedrin; the dramatist Aleksandr Ostrovsky; the critics Vissarion Belinsky and Apollon Grigoryev; and the gifted, unclassifiable *homme des lettres* Aleksandr Herzen.

Certainly one important force stimulating 19th-century Russian literature was Russia's ambivalent position on the periphery of European culture. The authoritarian Muscovite state that emerged from Mongol bondage in the 17th century resembled its erstwhile Asiatic masters in many more respects than it resembled its Western neighbors. Indeed, the masses of Russian peasants—more than 80 percent of the population—remained largely untouched by the Western influences that penetrated the country after the mid-17th century. The ultimate effect of these influences was to create a gulf between the French-speaking educated class that was largely Western in its outlook and the conservative, illiterate peasant masses. The ensuing creative tension between the "Westernizers" and the "Slavophiles," between those who would bring Russia closer to European culture and those who favored cultivating native Russian traditions, can be traced through Russian history and literature from the end of the 18th century up to the present day.

Another characteristic feature of Russian literature grew out of the fact that neither the tsarist autocrats nor those of the post-1917 period ever allowed public opinion to express itself directly in political matters. Thus, Russian literature—particularly literary criticism—has been almost the only available forum for a discussion of public issues. This tended during much of the 19th century to place undue emphasis upon the social or political message of literature, a situation that led both the public and the government to take writers and their works far more seriously than they were taken in freer societies.

Perhaps the most distinctive feature of the 19th-century giants of Russian literature is their preoccupation with the great moral and philosophical questions of good and evil, the problem of suffering, the nature and destiny of man, and the ultimate meaning of the universe. Indeed, the Russians have always tended to be so religious by temperament that even the atheists among them turn their atheism into a religion. It was the high seriousness of Russian literature that struck readers and critics alike in Western Europe and the United States when they suddenly discovered the Russian novel in the 1880s. The contrast to the soulless amoral naturalism then current in France was so great that the Russian masters took Western readers by storm.

At the very time when enthusiasm for the Russian novelists was at its height in the West, however, Russians at home considered their literature, and indeed their culture in general, to be in the doldrums. The assassination of Alexander II in 1881 had abruptly ended the age of reform associated with his name and ushered in another of those periods of reaction and repression so frequent in Russian history. By 1883 both Dostoyevsky and Turgenev were dead, and Tolstoy had undergone the dramatic inner revolution that led him to place his literary genius henceforth at the service of his new doctrine of Christian anarchism.

Lev Tolstoy remained the dominant figure in Russian literature until his death in 1910. His assumption around 1880 of the role of religious and social prophet by no means involved an abandonment of his role as an artist. His writings during the last three decades of his life can be grouped in three main categories. The first, comprising the works in which he set forth his religious convictions, began with *Ispoved* (1879–80; Eng. tr., *A Confession*, 1887), which in its unsparing honesty, emotional power, and sheer artistry ranks among the greatest confessions in Western literature. The other works that make up Tolstoy's most important statements about his religious philosophy are *V chom moya vera?* (1882–84; Eng. tr., *What I Believe,* 1885), *O zhizni* (1887; Eng. tr., *On Life,* 1888), and *Tsarstvo Bozhye vnutri vas* (1894; Eng. tr., *The Kingdom of God Is Within You*, 1894). Taking nonresistance to evil as the principal doctrine of Jesus' Sermon on the Mount, Tolstoy proceeded to build on it a philosophy of Christian anarchism that rejected, just as completely as any revolutionaries, all the institutions of his own society—government, law courts, prisons, armies, and the established church.

The second group of Tolstoy's postconversion writings comprises literary works based on his new philosophy and addressed to his own educated class. Among these are a number of fine short stories, including the masterpiece, "Smert Ivana Ilyicha" (1886; Eng. tr., "The Death of Ivan Ilyich," 1887); and "Kreytserova sonata" (1890; Eng. tr., *The Kreutzer Sonata,* 1890), and the didactic novel *Voskreseniye* (1889–99; Eng. tr., *Resurrection,* 1899).

The third group of Tolstoy's postconversion writings are the simple stories he wrote for the masses of Russian peasants and city workers. In 1884, Tolstoy and several of his followers established a special publishing house, "Posrednik" (The Intermediary), for the purpose of making good literature available to the masses at prices low enough for them to buy it.

All these categories of writings serve as illustrations of the controversial aesthetic theory Tolstoy set down in 1897 in *Chto takoye iskusstvo* (Eng. tr., *What Is Art?*, 1898). His theory of art as the "infection" of its audience with feelings is in itself broad enough to allow of "infection" through a wide variety of art. Tolstoy's own application of this theory to great works of art, however, makes it clear that he himself arbitrarily limited "good" art to realistic and moralistic art of a very simple kind.

When the novels of Fyodor Dostoyevsky were first translated in the 1880s, Western readers were bewildered, but in the wake of World War I, they more fully appreciated his work. With the old illusions about the rationality of human nature undermined by Freudian psychology, the old religious certainties challenged by the natural sciences, and the very foundations of human society undermined by war and revolution, postwar readers discovered that the basic problems confronting modern man had been anticipated in uncanny fashion nearly half a century earlier in the novels of Dostoyevsky.

From the perspective of the late 20th century it is clear

that the two greatest Russian writers of the 1880s after Tolstoy were Nikolay LESKOV and Anton CHEKHOV. During his lifetime, Leskov was popular with Russian readers but either misunderstood or neglected entirely by Russian critics. In the early 1860s the literary radicals wrongly interpreted him as a reactionary and subjected him to a literary boycott, and later he was subjected to similar harassment by the government and its censors for alleged radicalism. Of the five fictional works of novel length that he wrote in the early years of his career, the only unqualified success was *Soboryane* (1872; Eng. tr., *The Cathedral Folk*, 1924), the first major work in Russian literature to have members of the Russian Orthodox clergy as its principal characters. The rich, colorful language of this work anticipates Leskov's development in the 1880s and 1890s into a stylist noted for his use of dialect, jargon, puns, malapropisms, and a highly personal and peculiar form of satirical word deformation. Leskov is famous for his ironical use of a first-person narrator, often within a frame-story setting, whose account is presented in his own peculiar language and from a point of view that tends to differ markedly from that of the author. His most famous stories are "Levsha (Skaz o tulskom kosom Levshe i o stalnoy blokhe)" (1881; Eng. tr., "The Steel Flea," seven versions, 1916 to 1969) and "Ledi Makbet Mtsenskogo uezda" (1865; Eng. tr., "Lady Macbeth of the Mtsensk District," 1922).

By the time of Leskov's death in 1895, Anton Chekhov had become a master of the short story. Before his own death in 1904 he was a master of the drama as well: he was the first Russian playwright in history to exert an influence on the development of drama throughout Europe. His four great plays, *Chayka* (1896; Eng. tr., *The Seagull*, 1923), *Dyadya Vanya* (1897; Eng. tr., *Uncle Vanya*, 1923), *Tri sestry* (1901; Eng. tr., *Three Sisters*, 1923), and *Vishnyovy sad* (1904; Eng. tr., *The Cherry Orchard*, 1912), reflected Chekhov's interest in the new dramatic techniques in the West, particularly in the drama of Bjørnstjerne BJØRNSON, Gerhart HAUPTMANN, Henrik IBSEN, Maurice MAETERLINCK, and August STRINDBERG. Russian audiences brought up on the straightforward plots and obvious characterizations of Aleksandr Ostrovsky were at first bewildered and then entranced by the breathtaking freshness of Chekhov's innovations—his creation of dramatic tension in situations with almost no external action, his portrayal of characters who cannot fully understand themselves or one another, and his use of dialogue to convey several levels of meaning at once. Chekhov's success as a dramatist was linked with the success of the Moscow Art Theater, which was founded in 1896 by Konstantin Stanislavsky and Vladimir Nemirovich-Danchenko and presented Chekhov's *Seagull* as the first production in its long and distinguished history.

In both the drama and the short story, Chekhov broke with the old Russian tendency to use literature as a pulpit for sermons of social significance, and yet a close examination of his art serves to confirm the evidence provided by his life: he was a writer whose humanity and tolerance neither obscured nor compromised his firm ethical principles. He once said that the duty of the writer was not to provide solutions for problems but to state the problems correctly. This is just what he accomplished in his tightly constructed stories and plays, written in the spare, fresh, evocative style that is the hallmark of his genius. The perspective and critical sophistication of the 20th century have begun to reveal Chekhov's true stature as an artist worthy of being ranked among the giants of Russian literature.

Vladimir KOROLENKO began publishing in the same year as did Chekhov. A writer of the second rank, he is remembered above all for his early short story "Son Makara" (1885; Eng. tr., "Makar's Dream," 1892) and his four-volume autobiography, *Istoriya moyego sovremennika* (1922; abridged Eng. tr., *The History of My Contemporary*, 1972). From the mid-1890s until his death in 1921 Korolenko devoted a large measure of his literary talent to a noble and courageous kind of journalistic statesmanship, largely in the pages of the periodical *Russkoye bogatstvo* (Russian Wealth). He defended Siberian natives against the oppression of the Russian government; he joined Chekhov in resigning honorary membership in the Imperial Academy of Science as a protest against the government's annulment of the election of Maksim Gorky to the Academy; he vigorously campaigned against the still endemic anti-Semitism in Russia; and during the terror that followed the Bolshevik seizure of power in 1917 he protested against the new government's excesses with equal forthrightness and courage. The letters of protest he wrote to Anatoly Lunacharsky, the commissar of education, were published in Paris the year after his death, in the volume *Pisma k Lunacharskomu* (1922), which still remains a courageous and eloquent protest against man's inhumanity to man.

What looked to contemporaries like stagnation in the literature of the 1880s turned out to have been only a transition between the great age of the Russian novel and a new era of brilliance in almost all the arts, especially poetry, painting, and the theater. A paradoxical figure worthy of brief mention in this transitional period is Konstantin LEONTYEV, who began his life as an aesthetic immoralist and ended it as an Orthodox monk, and who wrote highly original literary and cultural criticism.

During the 1890s, Russia was invaded by a host of new ideas from the West that challenged the principal assumptions upon which Russian intellectual life had rested throughout most of the 19th century: realism and utilitarianism in literature, positivism in philosophy, and revolutionary populism in social thought and politics. From France came the poetry of Charles BAUDELAIRE, Stéphane MALLARMÉ, Paul VERLAINE, and Arthur RIMBAUD, with its divorce of aesthetics from morality as well as from utilitarianism; and with its emphasis upon the word both for its purely musical values (as in Verlaine) and as a symbol linking the visible world to a transcendent reality (as in Mallarmé). From Belgium came the poetic symbolist dramas of Maeterlinck; from Scandinavia, the tortured dramas of Strindberg and the protean dramatic genius of Ibsen. The witty writing and flamboyant personality of Oscar Wilde, the satanism of Joris Karl HUYSMANS and Stanisław PRZYBYSZEWSKI, the poetry of Emile VERHAEREN and Walt Whitman, the hedonistic heroics of Gabriele D'ANNUNZIO—these are only samples of the literary influences then sweeping into Russia from the West.

In its first stage, during the 1890s, the Russian response to the new Western influences assumed forms that have commonly been given the label "decadence." Art was proclaimed as a value in itself, often as the supreme value in life; and this emphasis on pure aestheticism tended to be associated with the cult of the ego and the senses, with the alienation of the artist from society and consequently his divorce from all social responsibility, and with a moral nihilism that occasionally led to such extremes as the outright rejection of good in favor of evil.

A lecture in 1892 by D. S. Merezhkovsky, "O prichinakh upadka i o novykh techeniyakh sovremennoy russkoy literatury" (On the Causes of the Decline and on the New Currents in Russian Literature), was greeted at the time as a manifesto of the new decadent movement; but its real pioneers were Konstantin BALMONT and Valery BRYUSOV. Balmont's collection of poems *Pod severnym nebom* (Under the Northern Sky) and Bryusov's three little anthologies *Russkiye simvolisty* (Russian Symbolists) created a *succès de scandale* when they burst upon the Russian reading public in 1894 and 1895. While the two poets were alike in the egocentricity and the flamboyant amoral aestheticism that earned them the label of decadence, they were otherwise vastly different. Balmont looked like the public's image of a daring, dashing, romantically rebellious poet, and he dramatized himself in real life as well as in his books. While his verse lacks real feeling and depth, its musicality and general technical virtuosity are probably unequaled in all of Russian poetry. A large part of Balmont's poetic production consists of translations, including works by Edgar Allan Poe, Percy Bysshe Shelley, Calderón de la Barca, E. T. A. Hoffmann, Gerhart Hauptmann, and Ibsen, and poems from both European and non-European literatures.

In Vladimir Markov's striking image, both Balmont and Bryusov flitted from flower to flower in the garden of literature; but the former was a brilliantly colored butterfly while the latter was a hard-working, purposeful bee. An adequate assessment has yet to be made of Bryusov's important contribution to Russian literature not only as an original poet but also as a writer of prose fiction, a translator, a literary theoretician and critic, and an indefatigable organizer and editor. Unlike Balmont, who emigrated to France after the Russian Revolution (1917) and died there alone and almost forgotten in 1942, Bryusov threw in his lot with the new Soviet government, joined the Communist Party, and organized an institute for creative literature in Moscow.

At the same time that Balmont and Bryusov were leading the modernist revolt in poetry during the 1890s, a similar movement was in preparation in the field of art. It sprang up among a cosmopolitan group of young painters who had studied together in Petersburg at the end of the 1880s and were in rebellion against the didactic art of social significance associated with the older "Peredvizhniki" (Wandering Artists). The new movement culminated in the launching of a lavish new magazine, *Mir iskusstva* (The World of Art) at the end of 1898, edited by Sergey Dyagilev, which proclaimed the autonomy of art and the primacy of artistic craftsmanship. During its six years of publication, *Mir iskusstva* dominated the cultural life of Russia, acquainting Russian readers with the whole range of new art movements in the West; encouraging a reevaluation of the painting and architecture of Old Russia; and supporting such original new figures in Russian art as Valentin Serov, Mikhail Vrubel, and Isaak Levitan. The artistic momentum created by *Mir iskusstva* also influenced the theater, notably theatrical decor and the ballet. One of Dyagilev's most spectacular successes was the organization of the Ballets Russes de Diaghilev, which opened in Paris in 1909 and has influenced all subsequent developments in Western European and American ballet—even though, ironically, it never performed in Russia itself.

Mir iskusstva played a role of very great importance in literature as well. The circle of artists and writers who gathered regularly in the Petersburg apartment of Dyagilev was dominated by Dmitry MEREZHKOVSKY and his brilliant wife, the poet and essayist Zinaida GIPPIUS. Other frequent literary visitors included the poet Nikolay Minsky, who had come to modernism by way of the writings of Friedrich NIETZSCHE; the pessimistic decadent Fyodor SOLOGUB, who is remembered above all

today for his remarkable novel *Melkiy bes* (1907; Eng. tr., *The Little Demon*, 1916); and the paradoxical Vasily RoZANOV, who combined a peculiar moral nihilism with an intense interest in a highly personal form of Christianity.

By the time *Mir iskusstva* was founded in 1898, there appeared a growing emphasis upon the two aspects of what would become an important new movement, symbolism. All the symbolists were in revolt against positivism and utilitarianism; but the "decadent" aesthetic symbolists, led by Balmont and Bryusov, saw art as the revelation of the poet's personality, while the metaphysical symbolists saw art and the artist as instruments for the revelation of a truth that lay above and beyond the phenomenal world. Both groups were preoccupied with nonrational approaches to art, but for the metaphysical symbolists art was a path to religion; for the aesthetic symbolists art itself was religion.

The revolt against positivism had led in the West as well as in Russia to a renewal of interest in religion. The Russian metaphysical symbolists were also strongly influenced, however, by the thought of the brilliant mystical philosopher Vladimir SOLOVYOV. To Solovyov belongs much of the credit for undermining the 19th-century Russian cult of atheistic scientism and making religion a respectable subject for discussion among Russian intellectuals. The influence of Solovyov's apocalyptic ideas about Antichrist and an ultimate conflict between Europe and Asia, which are found in his essay *Tri razgovora o voyne, progresse i kontse vsemirnoy istorii* (1900; Eng. tr., *War, Progress, and the End of History*, 1915), can be traced through the novels of Merezhkovsky, certain poems of Aleksandr Blok, and various writings of Andrey Bely. Vyacheslav Ivanov in particular was the heir to Solovyov's aesthetic philosophy, according to which the artist contributes to the transformation of society by portraying and evaluating reality in the light of his intuitive vision of the divine order.

Dmitry Merezhkovsky's inclination toward mysticism and symbolism in literature and his growing preoccupation with religious questions had been encouraged by his marriage in 1889 to the 20-year-old Zinaida Gippius, a brilliant and forceful young woman who was considerably more talented than her husband and has been called (by Vladimir Markov) possibly the greatest religious poet of Russia. The Merezhkovskys' interest in religion led them in 1901 to organize a series of "Religious-Philosophical Assemblies" in Petersburg. The purpose of the meetings was to open a dialogue between leading members of the Russian intelligentsia and the Russian Orthodox clergy, in the hope of bridging the long-standing gulf in Russia between two cultures, the secular and the religious. The minutes of most of these 22 meetings were published in 1903–04 in the short-lived journal *Novy put* (New Path). The announced purpose of Merezhkovsky and Gippius in founding *Novy put* was "to permit the expression in any literary form . . . of those new trends which appeared in our society with the awakening of religious and philosophical thought." The great weakness of *Novy put* and the weakness of the Religious-Philosophical Assemblies were the same: their premature effort to appeal simultaneously to the culturally isolated Orthodox clergy and the traditionally secular-minded intelligentsia aroused the misgivings of both groups.

Merezhkovsky and Gippius supported both the 1905 Revolution and the democratic February Revolution of 1917, but they were violently opposed to the Bolshevik government that seized power later that year, and at the end of 1919 they escaped over the border into Poland. With the passage of time, Merezhkovsky's reputation has faded as steadily as that of his more gifted wife has grown. Nevertheless, the importance of the role they both played in Russian literary life from the 1890s until 1917 has been seriously undervalued, particularly in the Soviet Union.

Along with the wave of modernism in literature and the arts, a similar wave of new ideas in economics and politics swept into Russia from the West in the 1890s. In the early 1880s Georgy PLEKHANOV had returned home from Western Europe and begun spreading Marxist doctrines in Russia; but it was only in the 1890s that Marxism began to take hold among the workers in the cities and became fashionable among Russian intellectuals. The most notable convert to Marxism in literature was Maksim GORKY, whose early stories so captivated the reading public in the 1890s that in 1902, at the age of only 33, he was elected an honorary member of the Imperial Academy of Science—only to have his election immediately annulled by the government for political reasons. He was to remain a Marxist for the rest of his life, closely associated with the Bolshevik leaders who took power in October 1917 but at times highly critical of their actions.

Gorky's short stories of the 1890s were characterized by what might best be called lyrical realism. He enlarged the thematic range of Russian literature to include the outcasts of society, often portraying them in sordid and depressing settings; but he wove into this material a lyrical affirmation of human beings—of their sensitivity to beauty and goodness and their potential for growth and self-emancipation. This attitude led Gorky to sympathize with the downtrodden victims of an oppressive society, such as the bakers in "Dvadtsat shest i odna" (1899; Eng. tr., "Twenty-six Men and a Girl," 1902), and to romanticize bold, strong-willed rebels against society, whether their rebellion was motivated by mere criminality, as in the thief-hero of his story "Chelkash" (1895; Eng. tr., 1902), or by revolutionary ideology, as in the novel *Mat* (1906; Eng. tr., *Mother,* 1907). This same lyrical realism characterizes Gorky's first play, *Na dne* (1902; Eng. tr., *The Lower Depths,* 1902), which is set in a Moscow flophouse. It was enthusiastically received upon its first performance at the Moscow Art Theater.

In university circles the most prominent converts to Marxism in the 1890s followed a very different course from the one taken by Gorky. Known in history as the "Legal Marxists" because they published in the open rather than the underground press, this brilliant group of scholars included the philosopher Nikolay BERDYAYEV, the economist Sergey Bulgakov, the economist and statesman Pyotr Struve, and the philosopher of Jewish origin S. L. Frank, all four of whom moved on beyond Marxism, became converts to Christianity before the 1917 Revolution, and played important roles in the post-Revolutionary emigration as Russian Orthodox leaders. As early as 1902 three of the four—Berdyayev, Bulgakov, and Frank—gave evidence of their break with Marxism by contributing to a collection of essays entitled *Problemy idealizma* (Problems of Idealism). Three years later, on the eve of the 1905 Revolution, Berdyayev and Bulgakov joined the staff of a new literary journal, *Voprosy zhizni* (Questions of Life), which was in many respects a continuation of the Merezhkovskys' *Novy put.* Like its predecessor, *Voprosy zhizni* was short-lived, but was significant because of the two groups of contributors it brought together: religiously oriented scholars who had passed through Marxism and outgrown it; and writers like Vyacheslav Ivanov, Aleksandr Blok, the Merezhkovskys, Aleksey REMIZOV, Fyodor Sologub, Andrey Bely, and Georgy Chulkov (1879-1939), most of whom were attracted to symbolism as a kind of mystical, quasi-religious approach to reality through art.

The first dozen years of the 20th century were a period of remarkable animation and complexity in Russian literary life. In Moscow in 1900 Bryusov joined forces with S. A. Polyakov, the talented son of a wealthy manufacturer, in founding the "Skorpion" Press, which for the next 15 years played a role of capital importance in disseminating the works of Western European and Russian writers who represented the new spirit in literature. In 1904, largely on Bryusov's initiative and under his de facto editorship, the Skorpion Press began publishing *Vesy* (The Scales), a sophisticated and beautifully printed literary journal. During the six years of its existence *Vesy* served not only as a leading Russian symbolist literary journal but also as the most important source of information in Russia on literary developments throughout Europe. The prestige it enjoyed was directly responsible in 1906 for the launching of a rival modernist review in Moscow, *Zolotoye runo* (The Golden Fleece). Financed by a wealthy but uncultivated Muscovite named Ryabushinsky, *Zolotoye runo* at first attracted the leading figures in Russian symbolism as contributors but ultimately failed because of Ryabushinsky's constant and clumsy interference with the work of his editorial staff. The modernist spirit in literature also led to a proliferation of new publishing ventures, including new presses such as "Grif" 'and "Musaget" in Moscow; and "Shipovnik," "Ory," "Siren," and "Alkonost" in Petersburg.

Further evidence of the new vitality in Russian cultural life could be seen in the wide variety of informal circles and salons that sprang up. In Moscow the most important of these took place in the homes of Judge Pavel Astrov and Margarita Kirillovna Morozova, the daughter and widow of two of Russia's wealthiest industrialists. Morozova's salon gradually evolved into one of several religious-philosophical societies that followed in the wake of the meetings organized in Petersburg by the Merezhkovskys in 1901-03. This led in turn in 1909 to the organization of "Put" (The Way), a publishing house financed by Morozova and devoted largely to books reflecting the 20th-century Russian renaissance in philosophical and religious thought. In Petersburg the most important literary gatherings were the "Wednesdays" of the erudite symbolist poet Vyacheslav IVANOV and his wife.

Vyacheslav Ivanov was without any question the most scholarly poet in the Russian symbolist movement. The three major influences upon his thought were his classical education, Friedrich Nietzsche, and the mystical Russian thinker Vladimir Solovyov, with whom he became personally acquainted just before Solovyov's death in 1900. In his basically philosophical poetry, Ivanov strove to achieve a syncretic fusion of pagan Hellenism with mystical Christianity. Following Solovyov's lead, Vyacheslav Ivanov developed the most consistent aesthetic philosophy to be found among the Russian metaphysical symbolists. Like Solovyov, he saw art as a means of penetrating beyond the visible world to an intuitive perception of a higher, spiritual, reality, which the artist could convey to his audience only through the use of symbols drawn from the world of visible phenomena. In this process the artist not only helped to reveal the higher reality but also helped to transform the visible world; for art contributed, in Solovyov's words, to the "spiritualization of matter."

It was during this period that the two greatest Russian symbolists, Aleksandr BLOK and Andrey BELY, reached their maturity. Both of them came from families of prominent intellectuals; they were born in the same year, 1880; and their lives were destined to become entangled in extraordinary ways. Like many others, both young men were profoundly influenced by the mystical philosophy of

Solovyov. The haunting, ethereal image of the unknown Beautiful Lady, which can be traced throughout Blok's poetic production, has much in common with Sophia, the feminine incarnation of divine wisdom and truth, who was the chief source of inspiration for Solovyov's philosophy, and who according to his own account had appeared to him on three separate occasions in a vision. Bely became acquainted first with Blok's poetry and then with Blok himself through Sergey Solovyov, the philosopher's nephew, who was Bely's closest boyhood friend. Bely, Blok, and young Solovyov were drawn together by their shared enthusiasm over the mystical idealism of Vladimir Solovyov, and this in turn led them to surround Blok's young wife, Lyubov, the daughter of the great Russian scientist Dmitry Mendeleyev, with their own exalted mystical cult of the Eternal Feminine. Bely and Blok remained in close contact until Blok's death in 1921, but their relations were consistently stormy. Perhaps the most profound cause of strain between the two men was their difference in temperament and world outlook. The identity of views based on Solovyov's philosophy that Bely at first thought linked Blok and himself turned out to be largely the product of Bely's wishful, worshipful thinking. Blok was capable of uncanny flashes of intuitive insight, but his approach to Solovyov was essentially that of a poet, and he was left cold by the strained efforts of Bely and his young Moscow friends to build up a quasi-religious cult around the memory of the philosopher.

Blok remained a symbolist poet to the end of his career, but symbolism for Blok was an organic part of his poetic temperament, whereas for Bely symbolism was a set of beliefs, an ideology, to the service of which he devoted his highly original poetic talent. Through Blok's poetry can be traced his various responses to the Eternal Feminine in its various manifestations in his life, his growing disillusionment with the various mystical cults he had known, and his increasing preoccupation toward the beginning of World War I with the theme of his native land. His collection *Stikhi o Rossii* (Poems about Russia), with its complex evocation of sinful, slothful, backward Russia which was, nevertheless, "dearer to me than all other lands," was greeted upon its publication in 1915 with overwhelming approval on all sides.

Bely's growing reputation in Russian literature is due not so much to the artistic perfection of his works as to their remarkable originality. His first prose works were entitled *Simfonii* (1905; Symphonies) and represented an effort to apply the principles of musical structure to narrative fiction. He will probably be best remembered in the future, however, for three extraordinary novels. *Serebryany golub* (1909; Eng. tr., *The Silver Dove*, 1974), portrays the ultimately tragic encounter of a young Western-oriented intellectual with a secret peasant sect whose members call themselves "Doves." *Kotik Letayev* (1917–18; Eng. tr., 1971) is a remarkable first-person account of the hero's experiences and impressions between the ages of three and five. *Peterburg* (1916, rev. 1922; incomplete Eng. tr., *St. Petersburg*, 1959; complete, annotated Eng. tr., *Petersburg*, 1978), is one of the masterpieces of 20th-century Russian literature, the importance of which can only now be recognized in the English-speaking world with the appearance in 1978 of a complete and fully satisfactory translation. All three novels reflect Bely's concern with the fate of Western civilization; and none of the three can be adequately understood without taking into consideration Bely's lifelong interest in suprarational approaches to reality, particularly his adherence, from 1912 on, to the anthroposophical doctrines of Rudolf Steiner.

At the same time that the symbolists were creating a new artistic culture in Russia, during the 1890s and the first decade of the 1900s, another group of younger writers continued along the well-worn path of realism marked out by the great Russian masters of the 19th century. The focal point of their activity was the publishing house "Znaniye" (Knowledge), which Gorky joined and reorganized in 1900, transforming it into a cooperative enterprise designed to foster tendentious, socially critical, realistic literature and to combat the decadent tendencies then spreading in Russia. There were few common denominators among the Znaniye writers. Gorky, the most popular of them, held to the ethical idealism of the older Russian intelligentsia even as he threw in his lot with the new Marxist movement. In the disillusionment that followed 1905, the shrill pessimism of Leonid ANDREYEV temporarily brought him a fame almost rivaling that of Gorky. A writer whose modest reputation has faded less than Andreyev's is Aleksandr KUPRIN, who first attracted attention with *Poyedinok* (1905; Eng. tr., *The Duel*, 1916), and *Yama* (1909–15; Eng. tr., *Yama* [*The Pit*], 1922). The most outstanding literary artist of the Znaniye group was Ivan BUNIN, who wrote in a fashion that might be called lyrical realism. He continued to grow in stature after emigrating in 1920, and in 1933 he became the first Russian writer to win the Nobel Prize for Literature. Among other Znaniye writers worthy of mention are Ivan SHMELYOV and Boris ZAYTSEV, both of whom emigrated after the October Revolution (1917); Mikhail PRISHVIN, who became famous in the Soviet period for his nature stories and sketches; Aleksandr SERAFIMOVICH, whose very modest claim to a place in literary history rests on one novel about the Civil War, *Zhelezny potok* (1924; Eng. tr., *The Iron Flood*, 1935); and Vikenty Veresayev (1867–1945), who wrote a series of fictional works about the fate of the Russian intelligentsia from the 1890s to the 1930s, among which the most remarkable is *V tupike* (1922; Eng. tr., *The Deadlock*, 1928).

The years from 1905 to 1909, when Vyacheslav Ivanov's famous literary "Wednesdays" dominated the literary scene in Petersburg, marked the high point in the history of Russian symbolism. When *Vesy* ceased publication in 1909, Bryusov in a final editorial sanguinely explained its closing with the argument that its goal of establishing symbolism had now been achieved. Before the year was out, Sergey Makovsky founded a new journal in Petersburg, *Apollon*, and gathered around it as contributors many of the leading symbolist figures. Within its first year of existence, however—and within the pages of *Apollon* itself—evidence began to appear of a split in the modernist movement and a challenge to the tenets of symbolism. The first sign of the schism was an article by the young poet Mikhail KUZMIN entitled "O prekrasnoy yasnosti" (On Beautiful Clarity), published in the January 1910 issue of *Apollon*, which pointed the way toward a revolt against the vagueness and obscurity of symbolism, with its emphasis on the hieratic role of the poet as an interpreter of otherworldly truth. A new movement was founded in 1912 as the "Poets Guild" by Sergey GORODETSKY, a minor poet who after the Revolution worked mainly as a translator and opera librettist, and the far more significant poet Nikolay GUMILYOV, the recognized leader of the group. A forerunner of the new movement was the classical scholar Innokenty ANNENSKY, who died in 1909 but whose works continued to influence both the acmeist poets and later the younger generation of poets in the Russian emigration. By late 1912 the new movement had taken the name of acmeism and become an invigorating force in Russian poetry. While sharing with symbolism an essentially aesthetic approach to poetry, the acmeists rejected what they called the "obligatory mysticism" of the Russian symbolists. Stressing the function of the poet as craftsman, they looked upon the poem itself as an artifact. In the often-repeated words of Gorodetsky, "For the acmeists the rose has again become beautiful in itself, because of its petals, fragrance, and color, and not because of its conceivable likeness to mystical love." Among the numerous young poets who came out of the Poets Guild and the acmeist movement, by far the most important were Anna AKHMATOVA and Osip MANDELSHTAM, both among the greatest Russian poets of the 20th century. Beginning her career in the shadow of Gumilyov, to whom she was married until 1918, but rapidly surpassing him, Akhmatova lived out her long and productive life under Soviet conditions that alternated between official neglect and official harassment. Mandelshtam's poetic reputation has continued to grow both at home and abroad ever since his death in 1938 in a Soviet forced-labor camp. Among other gifted acmeists were Georgy IVANOV, who after the Revolution became one of the leading émigré poets in Paris, and Mikhail Lozinsky (1886–1955), who turned to translation in the Soviet period.

The decline of Russian symbolism in 1910 led to challenges not only by the acmeists but also by a second group of poets who later took the name of futurists—thus setting in motion a stream of still unresolved speculation about their possible connections with the futurism bombastically proclaimed in Italy by Filippo MARINETTI in 1909. The Russian futurists did share with Marinetti an addiction to scandalizing the public with juvenile high jinks, and a rejection of traditional aesthetic and cultural values, but Russian futurism proved to be a far more fruitful literary movement than Marinetti's incipient literary fascism. The Russian futurists took much of their inspiration from avant-garde painting, and indeed a number of them were as well known in the graphic arts as in literature—for example, David BURLYUK, Yelena GURO, Aleksey KRUCHONYKH, and Vladimir MAYAKOVSKY. Four separate groups of futurists can be distinguished: the Petersburg ego-futurists, organized in 1911 by the once fashionable Igor SEVERYANIN; the Mezzanine of Poetry, organized in Moscow in 1913 by Vadim Shershenevich (1893–1942), who is remembered rather for his role as the leader of Russian imaginism; Centrifuge, also organized in Moscow in 1913, which was linked in its orientation to both futurism and symbolism, and included among its members the distinguished Boris PASTERNAK and the still remembered Nikolay ASEYEV; and "Hylaea," in Moscow, later known as cubo-futurists, who burst upon the Russian public in December 1912 with a provocative manifesto entitled "A Slap in the Face of Public Taste," signed by Burlyuk, Kruchonykh, Mayakovsky, and Viktor (Velemir) KHLEBNIKOV. Kruchonykh's cult of the word took its own peculiar form, which he called *zaum*, or trans-sense language, and which consisted essentially of the manipulation of sounds and syllables without regard to meaning. Other poets of importance in Hylaea were Yelena GURO, Vasily KAMENSKY, and Benedikt LIVSHITS.

By the outbreak of World War I in 1914, the intellectual ferment of the preceding three decades had thoroughly transformed the cultural life of Russia. From about the 1860s to the end of the 1880s, Russian cultural life had been dominated by an intellectual caste that took as its basic articles of faith a naive and dogmatic worship of materialism and utilitarianism, automatic opposition to everything associated with church and state, and an apocalyptic faith in revolution. In the brilliance and excitement of the "Silver Age" of Russian culture that flourished from the 1890s to World War I, this older type of intelligentsia began to appear almost comically out of date.

World War I interrupted Russia's accelerating economic development, cast a pall over the cultural renaissance that had brought Russia fully into the mainstream of European artistic life, and finally produced the stresses and strains that led to the collapse of the tsarist regime in February 1917 and the overthrow by Lenin and the Bolsheviks in the following October of the provisional government that replaced it. The Bolshevik seizure of power abruptly destroyed the "Silver Age" of Russian culture just when it had reached its apogee, and produced a wave of shock and dismay that swept a large part of the Russian cultural elite over the frontiers into exile. The number of Russians who left their homeland in the first years after the October Revolution has been variously estimated—by Soviet sources at 860,000 and by Russian émigré sources themselves at 1 to 3 million. The resulting dislocation led to extreme physical hardships for the émigrés and serious cultural impoverishment in the homeland; but the émigrés succeeded in creating and maintaining a worldwide diaspora of Russian culture abroad.

Until the end of the 1920s communications between Russian intellectuals at home and in emigration continued with a freedom scarcely imaginable to those who are familiar only with Soviet conditions since that time. The center of this East-West traffic was Berlin, where several important Russian publishing houses were established with a view to serving both the Soviet and émigré markets, and where émigré writers mingled freely with such Soviet visitors as Mayakovsky, Viktor SHKLOVSKY, and Sergey YESENIN, and with other Russian writers such as Andrey Bely, Ilya ERENBURG, and Aleksey TOLSTOY, who at that point had not yet made a decision whether to remain in the West or return home. In addition to Berlin, practically every important city in Europe had its Russian émigré colony, the major émigré center being Paris; an important center of Russian émigré culture outside of Europe was Harbin, in Manchuria.

Among the leading émigré writers of the older generation were Ivan Bunin, Dmitry Merezhkovsky and Zinaida Gippius, Konstantin Balmont, Vyacheslav Ivanov, Ivan Shmelyov, Boris Zaytsev; the philosophers Nikolay Berdyayev and Lev SHESTOV, both of whom made an impact on literary and social thought beyond Russian émigré circles; the poet and critic Vladislav Khodasevich; and the original and profoundly Russian writer Aleksey Remizov. Several writers had begun their careers before the Revolution but achieved real fame only in emigration. Among them were the novelist Mark ALDANOV; the poet Georgy IVANOV; the journalist and fiction writer Mikhail OSORGIN, and TEFFI (N. A. Buchinskaya), whose humorous stories and sketches made her one of the most widely read Russian émigré writers between the two wars. Among the principal émigré humorists—Don Aminado, Sasha CHORNY, Arkady AVERCHENKO—Teffi has the best claim to a lasting place in Russian literature, and selected editions of her works have now begun to appear in the Soviet Union.

A few émigré writers of importance returned to Soviet Russia after spending some time abroad. Aleksey Tolstoy, one of the first writers to emigrate after 1917, published the first part of his novel about the Revolution, *Khozhdeniye po mukam* (Berlin, 1922; Eng. tr., *The Road to Calvary*, 1923), in the leading émigré literary journal, *Sovremennye zapiski* in 1920–21, and then rewrote it in a very different spirit after returning to Soviet Russia in 1923. The gifted poet Marina TSVETAYEVA returned to Russia in 1939 and committed suicide two years later. Ilya Erenburg, who had lived abroad from 1913 to 1917, left Russia again in 1921 and spent much of the next 20 years abroad, finally returning there to play a complicated dual role as a sophisticated Soviet propagandist and crypto-liberal.

In the lively discussions that occupied the pages of émigré periodicals in the 1920s and 1930s the poet-critics Georgy ADAMOVICH and Vladislav Khodasevich were central figures in a long and far-reaching controversy over the existence and nature of an émigré literature and its relation to the literature of the homeland. Each of them also had a considerable following among the younger émigré poets, with Khodasevich insisting on a neoclassical respect for craftsmanship and the cultivation of form and Adamovich emphasizing, in the spirit of Lev Tolstoy, simplicity and humanity in poetry rather than formal experimentation. Among the numerous young poets who came under Adamovich's influence, Anatoly STEIGER and Lidiya CHERVINSKAYA are particularly noteworthy. Khodasevich and Georgy Ivanov are now generally recognized as the greatest Russian émigré poets of the period between the two world wars. Two other poets of importance in the Paris emigration were Irina ODOYEVTSEVA and the highly gifted Boris POPLAVSKY, who died tragically at the age of 32. Next to Paris, the most important center of émigré poetry was Prague, where a group of young writers known as "Skit poetov" (The Poets' Cloister) wrote and published under the leadership of the eminent émigré scholar and critic Alfred Bem (1886–1945), whose influence was also strong among the émigré poets in Warsaw. Other talented émigré poets were Yury IVASK in Estonia, Igor CHINNOV in Latvia, and Valery PERELESHIN, who began publishing his poetry in faraway Harbin, but later moved to Brazil.

Among all Russian émigré writers, Vladimir NABOKOV occupies a unique position. Educated in England at Cambridge University after his family emigrated in 1919, he created two distinguished literary careers for himself in one lifetime, the first in Europe between the two world wars as a Russian émigré writer and the second in the United States as a novelist in English. Toward the end of his life he fused his two literary personalities by freely translating several of his earlier works from Russian into English and his later ones from English into Russian.

The achievements of the Russian émigré writers between the two world wars have still not been given the recognition they merit. In addition to the usual problems of émigré writers, the Russian émigrés faced a special form of discrimination in the naive 1930s at the hands of Western intellectuals who still automatically identified all criticism of the Soviet regime with reaction.

The Bolshevik seizure of power in October 1917 shocked even Lenin's friend Gorky with its ruthlessness and its disregard for elementary human rights. The coup prompted Gorky to write a long series of courageous, critical articles that he published in his journal *Novaya zhizn* (New Life) from April 1917 until Lenin himself closed down the journal in July 1918. They have been reprinted several times in other countries, but have not been reprinted in the Soviet Union since 1918. After depriving Gorky of all opportunities to publish in the homeland, Lenin persuaded him to accept a truce under which, in return for halting his public criticism, Gorky would be given a measure of support in his effort to save Russia's cultural heritage. From the end of 1918 to the middle of 1921, Gorky threw himself into a vast program of organizational work that involved not only saving the treasures of Russia's heritage in art and literature, but also literally saving the lives of countless scholars, writers, and other intellectuals by providing for such elementary needs as food, clothing, and shelter, and in numerous cases interceding with the government when they were arrested. Although Gorky achieved much, the cost to him

was great, and in October 1921 he left Russia at Lenin's urging to get treatment in the West for his chronic tuberculosis. His triumphant return in 1928 to spend the last eight years of his life in service to Iosif Stalin's Soviet state has left many unanswered questions about his motivation as well as his mysterious death in 1936.

The period of War Communism in Russia, from 1918 to 1921, brought about the virtual collapse of cultural life as well as the economy. Poetry survived those strenuous times better than any other genre. At first there were poets of various persuasions—Aleksandr Blok, Sergey Yesenin, Nikolay KLYUYEV, Andrey Bely—who greeted the October Revolution as a cleansing force, or as an assertion of Russia's own national character, or (in terms reminiscent of 19th-century Polish messianism) as Russia's national sacrifice for the redemption of mankind. Early in 1918, Blok wrote a masterful summation of the revolution in his poem "Dvenadtsat" (Eng. tr., "The Twelve," 1920), in which 12 marauding revolutionary soldiers march through the streets of Petrograd, and in the very last line of the poem Jesus Christ is revealed to be marching at their head. Maksimilian VOLOSHIN, who had lived abroad for years, returned to Russia in 1917 and created his greatest poetry in response to the cataclysm of the Revolution and Civil War. The gifted peasant poet Sergey Yesenin at first welcomed the October Revolution in the belief that it would lead to a golden age of peasant culture, but his growing disillusionment led him to commit suicide in 1925. The futurist poets welcomed the Revolution wholeheartedly and tried without much success, to gain a dominant position for themselves in Revolutionary literature. Mayakovsky, the greatest of the futurists, placed his extraordinary talent entirely at the service of the new Soviet state.

As early as the mid-1920s, Russian poets themselves recognized Boris Pasternak as their master, and his innovations influenced a whole generation of poets. The publication of his novel *Doktor Zhivago* (Milan, 1957; Eng. tr., *Doctor Zhivago,* 1958) practically everywhere except in the Soviet Union brought him a worldwide audience and led indirectly to his award in 1958 of the Nobel Prize for Literature.

Until the end of the 1920s the Communist Party leadership maintained a policy of allowing free competition among all literary movements and factions as long as they did not directly attack the new regime and the supremacy of the Party itself. As a result, the 1920s were a period of remarkable initiative and variety in all the arts, particularly after Lenin in 1921 proclaimed his New Economic Policy (NEP), which reopened the country to limited forms of private enterprise, including publishing houses. In that year the authorities revived the 19th-century Russian literary tradition of the "thick journal" by founding *Krasnaya nov* (Red Virgin Soil) under the editorship of the moderate Communist literary critic Aleksandr VORONSKY.

By 1921 it had become clear that most of the literary talent in the new Soviet society was to be found among the members of the old intelligentsia who still remained in Russia. Through these "fellow travelers" of the Revolution, as Leon Trotsky dubbed them, many of the same literary trends that had been dominant in the Silver Age can be traced throughout the literature of the 1920s, and one of the leading figures in the revival of prose fiction was Yevgeny ZAMYATIN, an accomplished stylist who had begun to publish in 1908. A major figure in 20th-century Russian prose literature, Zamyatin is best known for his anti-Utopian novel *My* (written 1920, complete Russian text pub. in New York, 1952; Eng. tr., *We,* 1924), which is a forerunner of Aldous Huxley's *Brave New*

World and George Orwell's *1984* and has not to this day been published in the Soviet Union. Zamyatin also played an influential role as a teacher of writing in the "House of Arts" established in Petrograd by Gorky, where Zamyatin guided the literary development of a gifted group of 12 intellectuals who banded together there in the name of artistic freedom and called themselves the Serapion Brothers. All 12 of them went on to achieve distinction in literature. Viktor Shklovsky made a name for himself as a literary theoretician and critic in the well-known Russian formalist movement. Vsevolod IVANOV and Nikolay NIKITIN are best remembered for their fiction and plays about the Revolution and Civil War. Mikhail SLONIMSKY likewise began with stories about the Revolution and Civil War but then turned to long, old-fashioned, and more colorless chronicles about the tensions and conflicts between the individualistic intellectual and the new collectivist society. This theme is treated with greater artistic success in the works of two other Serapion novelists, notably in Konstantin FEDIN's *Goroda i gody* (1924; Eng. tr., *Cities and Years,* 1962) and *Bratya* (1928; Brothers); and Veniamin KAVERIN's *Khudozhnik neizvesten* (1931; Eng. tr., *The Unknown Artist,* 1947). Other notable Serapions were Mikhail ZOSHCHENKO, who was to become the most popular humorist and satirist in the Soviet Union, the poet Nikolay Tikhonov (1896–), whose poetic technique in the 1920s owed much to Pasternak, and the brilliant young dramatist and unofficial leader of the Serapions, Lev LUNTS.

Along with Zamyatin, the leading figure in the revival of Soviet literature in the 1920s was Boris PILNYAK, whose *Goly God* (1922; Eng. tr., *The Naked Year,* 1928, 1975) was hailed as the first important novel dealing with the revolutionary upheaval. Pilnyak's flawed but compelling talent reveals a kinship with the Russian Eurasian thinkers in his view of the October Revolution as an assertion of the primitive, Asiatic, essentially peasant elements in Russia's culture.

Of all the writers in the 1920s who dealt with the theme of the Russian Civil War, none has achieved a more lasting reputation than Isaak BABEL, who first attracted attention in 1923 with his colorful stories about Jewish life in his native Odessa and then went on to create in *Konarmiya* (1926; Eng. tr., *Red Cavalry,* 1929) a chilling masterpiece.

Perhaps the most important literary event of 1927 was the appearance of *Zavist* (Eng. tr., *Envy,* 1936), a short novel by Yury OLESHA portraying the conflict between the "Babbitts" of the new Soviet society and Olesha's romantic rebels.

In the 1920s, Mikhail BULGAKOV was known above all as the author of a novel and a play about the Whites in the Civil War and several satirical plays and stories. Not until 1965 did the general public learn that just before his death in 1940, Bulgakov had completed a novel that is now recognized as one of the greatest works in 20th-century Russian literature, *Master i Margarita* (censored text, Moscow, 1965–66; complete Russian text, Frankfurt, 1969; Moscow, 1973; complete Eng. tr., *The Master and Margarita,* 1967).

Other fellow travelers who were active in the literature of the 1920s included Boris LAVRENYOV and Marietta SHAGINYAN, who wrote poetry and prose, and the minor novelists Lidiya SEYFULLINA, Panteleymon ROMANOV, and Vladimir LIDIN. Of greater interest and importance are Leonid LEONOV and Valentin KATAYEV. Leonov began writing under the strong influence of Dostoyevsky. Katayev's first work of note was *Rastratchiki* (1926; Eng. tr., *The Embezzlers,* 1929), an amusing satire on bureaucratic corruption in the NEP period. The literary talents of both Leonov and Katayev were mobilized during the first Five-Year Plan, and in the restrictive atmosphere of the period since 1930, their literary development has been hampered but by no means stifled. Two older fellow travelers found their own escape from post-Revolutionary restrictions: Mikhail Prishvin in his nature stories and sketches set in Siberia, and Aleksandr GRIN in his highly popular stories about a fantastic land of his own invention named Grinlandiya.

Although the various Marxist groups in the 1920s were unable to match the literary achievement of the fellow travelers, they tended to make up in militancy for what they lacked in artistry. They constantly discussed how to keep the fellow travelers from dominating the literary scene, how to create a proletarian literature, what the nature of that literature should be, and to what extent all literary production should be subject to Communist Party control.

Even before the Bolsheviks came to power, Marxists headed by Aleksandr Bogdanov had organized the proletcult, a movement designed to create a new proletarian culture. Soon after the October Revolution, the proletcult launched a vigorous campaign to produce a mass proletarian culture by training thousands of young workers in a vast network of studios and literary workshops. The principal result of the proletcult experiment was to prove that genuine culture cannot be mass-produced overnight and that neither proletarian class origin nor ideological purity is an adequate substitute in literature for talent. In 1920 several poets in Moscow broke away from the proletcult and formed their own organization, *Kuznitsa* (The Smithy), proclaiming their opposition to the nonpolitical literature and the formal experimentation of various "bourgeois" groups and declaring their aim to be the creation of a genuinely proletarian literature. Two years later appeared a still more militant group calling itself "October" (whose members were also known as "On-Guardists"), and it immediately launched a campaign to drive the fellow travelers out of literature. The On-Guardists were opposed by LEF (the Left Front of Art), an organization launched at the end of 1922 by a group of futurists led by Mayakovsky, for the purpose of creating an art that would be revolutionary in technique as well as in theme. The dogmatism and intolerance of the On-Guardists and others led to the formation of *Pereval* (The Pass), a group that was closely associated with the moderate Marxist critic Voronsky and that shared his sympathetic views concerning the coexistence of various literary tendencies. This position found support in the moderate Communist Party resolution of June 1925, which set forth the Party policy on literature, and which enabled the relative freedom of literary expression to continue until the launching of the first Five-Year Plan in 1929.

Most of the leading "proletarian writers" in the 1920s were proletarian by ideology rather than class background. Yury LIBEDINSKY, whose short work *Nedelya* (1922; Eng. tr., *A Week,* 1923) is considered the first proletarian novel, was the son of a Moscow physician. Three other leading proletarian writers had served as political commissars with the Red Army during the Civil War: Aleksandr TARASOV-RODIONOV, the author of *Shokolad* (1922; Eng. tr., *Chocolate,* 1932), about the Soviet security police; Dmitry FURMANOV, who is remembered mainly for his novelized account of the peasant and guerrilla leader Chapayev; and Aleksandr FADEYEV, the author of *Razgrom* (1927; Eng. tr., *The Nineteen,* 1929), which deals with a Red guerrilla campaign. Fyodor GLADKOV, a village schoolteacher of peasant origin, was catapulted to official fame in 1925 with *Tsement* (Eng. tr.,

Cement, 1929), about human relations in a worker's family during the period of reconstruction after the Civil War. A place apart among proletarian writers belongs to the Don Cossack Mikhail SHOLOKHOV, whose novel *Tikhiy Don* (1928–40; The Quiet Don; Eng. tr., vols. 1–2, *And Quiet Flows the Don,* 1934; vols. 3–4, *The Don Flows Home to the Sea,* 1940), avoids the stereotyped characterizations then common in proletarian fiction and depicts in colorful style and with epic sweep the story of the Revolution and Civil War through the experiences of a wavering Cossack, Grigory Melekhov. The novel was highly popular, and Sholokhov is the only Soviet author to have been awarded both the Order of Lenin and the Nobel Prize for Literature.

Despite the cultural upheaval brought on by the Revolution and Civil War, it is possible to argue persuasively that the literature of the 1920s has more in common with the literature that preceded it than with the literature that followed. To be sure, the dominant theme among writers of all persuasions in the 1920s was the Revolution and Civil War. Yet the fiction of Fadeyev and Sholokhov shows the unmistakable influence of Tolstoy; Gladkov's early work, including his novel *Cement,* echoes Lermontov and Dostoyevsky; and the convoluted "ornamental prose" of Bely, Sologub, and Pilnyak left its impress for better or worse among numerous young writers of the 1920s.

In poetry the link with the Silver Age was maintained through the continued presence in Soviet Russia of such notable figures as Akhmatova, Mandelshtam, Blok, Bryusov, Sologub, and Gumilyov (until his execution in 1921). In 1919, Mayakovsky and the futurists were outstripped in their attention-getting offenses against public taste by a new group that took the name of imaginists, with the former ego-futurist Vadim Shershenevich as their leader and Yesenin as their most notable member. Among the many short-lived poetic movements that sprang up was constructivism, launched in 1924 under the influence of the Russian constructivist movement in art and architecture; it had as its goal the creation of a socialist art through the fusion of science and technology with poetry. Among the leading constructivist poets were Ilya SELVINSKY, Eduard BAGRITSKY, and Vera INBER. A much less well-known but equally interesting group bore the name OBERIU, a playful Russian acronym for *Obyedineniye realnogo iskusstva* (Association for Real Art). Although the group never had more than seven members, it had much talent and originality. Its best-known member was Nikolay ZABOLOTSKY, and three other members are beginning to be rediscovered: Aleksandr Vvedensky (1904–41), a forerunner of the modern literature of the absurd; Daniil KHARMS, a talented humorist and children's writer; and the poet and novelist Konstantin Vaginov (1889–1934).

The bold experimentalism and vitality in the arts during the 1920s was particularly evident in the theater, which had been brought to a position of international prominence by the innovative directors Konstantin Stanislavsky, Vsevolod Meyerhold, Aleksandr Tairov, and Yevgeny Vakhtangov. The October Revolution gave new impetus to their efforts. Meyerhold in particular carried out striking experiments in staging techniques along constructivist lines. Developments in the drama, however, lagged behind the impressive achievements in the theater, and Russian directors after the Revolution continued to rely heavily on foreign plays for their repertoires. Most of the new Russian plays produced in the early 1920s were by writers who were not primarily dramatists, notably Mayakovsky, Vsevolod Ivanov, Bulgakov, and Konstantin TRENYOV. Among the best of the younger dramatists were Nikolay ERDMAN, whose brilliant satire

on contemporary opportunism, *Mandat* (Eng. tr., *The Mandate,* 1975), made a sensation when it was staged in 1925 by Meyerhold; and Aleksey FAYKO, who had a rare talent for combining fantasy with realism and whose themes ranged from social satire to serious moral issues. A neglected figure in Russian theatrical history just before and just after the Revolution was the dramatist, director, and theorist of the drama Nikolay YEVREINOV.

The Communist Party's moderate 1925 resolution on literature did not put an end to power struggles among the various factions that claimed to represent the correct Marxist position on literature. The result was that by 1929 the Russian Association of Proletarian Writers (known by its Russian initials as RAPP) had emerged with virtually dictatorial powers over Russian writers, journals, and publishing houses. The hegemony of RAPP came soon after the launching of the first Five-Year Plan by the government at the end of 1928, which had as its goal the rapid industrialization of the Soviet Union and the collectivization of agriculture. In this national effort RAPP assumed responsibility for the mobilization of literature, using essentially the same methods of propaganda and coercion upon writers that were applied to the masses of factory workers and peasants. Just as groups of workers were challenged to engage in "socialist competition" with each other in production, writers were similarly challenged to compete with one another in the production of stories, sketches, or poems about coal-mining or the pouring of concrete. Thousands of workers and peasants with literary aspirations were mobilized to increase the production of Five-Year Plan literature. The result of all this was dismay and dissension that led the head of the State Publishing House himself to admit later that 75 percent of all the books published in 1928–31 had been worthless. Among the few Five-Year Plan novels that rose above the level of mediocrity were Valentin Katayev's *Vremya, vperyod!* (1932; Eng. tr., *Time, Forward!,* 1933); Mikhail Sholokhov's *Podnyataya tselina* (1932; Eng. tr., *Virgin Soil Upturned,* 1935); Leonid Leonov's *Sot* (1930, 1931; Eng. tr., *Soviet River,* 1932); and Boris Pilnyak's *Volga vpadayet v Kaspiyskoye more* (1930; Eng. tr., *The Volga Falls to the Caspian Sea,* 1932). Among Five-Year Plan dramas Nikolay POGODIN's *Temp* (1929; Eng. tr., *Tempo,* 1934) about the building of the Stalingrad tractor plant and Vladimir KIRSHON's *Khleb* (1930; Eng. tr., *Bread,* 1934) about the collectivization of agriculture enjoyed an ephemeral success.

RAPP also continued its attacks against all rival literary organizations and against all writers too independent to accept its dictates. Late in 1929 it attacked the still relatively independent All-Russian Union of Writers by mounting a campaign of vilification against its principal leaders, Yevgeny Zamyatin and Boris Pilnyak. Both men, along with the entire executive committee of the organization, were driven from office, and the new leaders issued a policy statement declaring that the aim of Soviet literature was, "while reflecting and explaining the world, to remake it." Soon thereafter, RAPP broke the power of the prominent Marxist literary scholar and critic Valerian PEREVERZEV. A similar campaign by RAPP against Mayakovsky is generally considered to have contributed to his suicide in April 1930. In the course of 1930, RAPP brought to a victorious climax the campaign that had been launched as early as 1924 by militants associated with the On-Guardists against both the independent-minded writers' group *Pereval* and its mentor Voronsky. Among the targets of this campaign was Andrey PLATONOV, who as the son of a Voronezh locomotive mechanic was one of the few writers of talent who could lay claim to a genuine proletarian origin.

The RAPP dictatorship in literature produced such disarray that finally, on April 23, 1932, the Central Committee of the Communist Party issued a decree disbanding all literary organizations, including RAPP, and setting up one Union of Soviet Writers, which was to "unite all writers supporting the platform of the Soviet government and aspiring to take part in the building of socialism." The measure ushered in a period of stability and relative freedom, although the new era was considerably more restrictive than the era from 1921 to 1928. A third requirement for membership in the new Union of Soviet Writers was added in 1934, at its first congress: socialist realism was adopted as the obligatory method to be used in Soviet literature. Socialist realism was officially defined as "the truthful, historically concrete representation of reality in its revolutionary development," and it was to be "linked with the task of ideological transformation and education of the workers in the spirit of socialism."

The adoption of this vaguely formulated requirement marked a watershed in the history of 20th-century Russian literature. Henceforth art was to be subordinated to utilitarianism; literature was to be regimented for service to the state; and writers were to carry out assigned tasks. In return, writers were offered an ever-growing number of material benefits and privileges. Their task, in the phrase attributed to Stalin, was to be "engineers of human souls": they were to contribute to the molding of the new Soviet man and the building of the new collective society. Maksim Gorky's novel *Mat* (Mother) about the political and personal transformation of the illiterate widow of a factory worker through the influence of her revolutionary son, was held up for emulation as the first example of socialist realism in Russian literature.

In general, the literature of the period between 1934 and the Nazi invasion of the Soviet Union in 1941 reflected a reaction against both the dreary mediocrity of the RAPP dictatorship and the bold stylistic and structural experimentation of the NEP period. The most successful works were those that met the demand of readers for interesting literature about believable people and real-life experiences while not straying too far from the requirements of socialist realism. Well-established older writers such as Fedin, Katayev, Kaverin, and Leonov worked out individual compromises with these requirements.

The new era for writers corresponded to a conservative trend in Soviet society. The new society was to be held together by two basic forces: first, an ideology, Marxism Leninism, which is officially defined as a science but is actually treated like a militant, authoritarian religion, with ancient prophets (Marx and Engels), infallible heads of the church (Lenin, and Stalin from about 1930 until 1956), holy scriptures (the writings of Lenin, and of Stalin until 1956), a devil (Trotsky), a priesthood (Communist Party members), and heretics (Tito, Mao Tse-tung); and second, the militarization of civilian society, with a hierarchical structure of authority, a harshly enforced system of discipline, and a tendency to approach all problems in terms of military thinking.

The new conservatism in the 1930s led to a reappraisal of Russia's past as part of an effort to create a new Soviet patriotism. One result of this was the encouragement of new directions in the writing of historical fiction, which had hitherto been confined to the treatment of revolutionary figures of the past in such novels as Aleksey CHAPYGIN's *Razin Stepan* (1926; Eng. tr., *Stepan Razin*, 1946). Notable examples of the new trend are Aleksey Tolstoy's *Pyotr Pervy* (1929–45; Eng. tr., *Peter the First*, 1959) and Sergey SERGEYEV-TSENSKY's *Sevastopolskaya strada* (1937–39; The Ordeal of Sevastopol).

The waves of terror that engulfed the Soviet Union in the latter half of the 1930s and again in 1946–53 can be traced back in part to the tendency of the Bolsheviks, beginning with Lenin, to approach the solution of all problems in a frame of mind that was essentially sectarian and military rather than scientific and humanistic. As a result, Stalin interpreted all differences of opinion as heresy; and whenever difficulties arose, he looked for enemies to be destroyed rather than problems to be solved. The total number of victims of this tendency is variously estimated at from 3 to 15 million, among whom were the poets Gumilyov, Mandelshtam, and Klyuyev; the prose writers Babel, Pilnyak, and Tarasov-Rodionov; the leaders of OBERIU, Kharms and Vvedensky; and the theatrical director Meyerhold.

The labor-camp system became a theme of Soviet literature as early as 1933. Immediately after the completion of the Belomor Canal, which was built in 20 months entirely by forced labor under the direction of the security police, an all-day steamboat excursion on the canal was arranged for 120 writers, after which 36 of them, headed by Maksim Gorky, contributed to a unique commemorative book glorifying the construction project as a means of rehabilitating criminals and enemies of the state, *Belomor-Baltiyskiy kanal imeni Stalina, Istoriya stroitelstva* (1934; The Stalin White Sea-Baltic Canal: The History of Its Construction). Apart from a few similar works, this theme did not reappear in Soviet literature until after Nikita Khrushchov's famous secret speech denouncing Stalin, which he delivered at the 20th Congress of the Communist Party in February 1956. The increasing appearance in fiction of discrete references to the labor camps reached a sudden dramatic climax in 1962 with the publication—authorized by Khrushchov himself—of Aleksandr SOLZHENITSYN's *Odin den Ivana Denisovicha* (Eng. tr., *One Day in the Life of Ivan Denisovich*, 1963), the first legal appearance in the Soviet Union of an honest literary work that had its setting in a forced-labor camp. Since that time the terror and the labor camps have been the theme of numerous works written in the Soviet Union but published so far only abroad. Solzhenitsyn led the way with his two big novels *V kruge pervom* (written 1955–66, Frankfurt and New York, 1968; Eng. tr., *The First Circle*, 1968) and *Rakovy korpus* (written 1963–66, Milan, 1968; Eng. tr., *Cancer Ward*, 1968) and his huge three-volume nonfictional study of the whole labor-camp system, *Arkhipelag Gulag* (Paris, 1973–75; Eng. tr., *The Gulag Archipelago* (1973–78). *Krutoy marshrut* (Milan, 1967; Eng. tr., *Journey Into the Whirlwind*, 1967) by Yevgeniya Ginsburg, the mother of the writer Vasily AKSYONOV, gives an unforgettable account of Ginsburg's personal experience as a devoted Communist Party member in the 1930s who saw the Stalinist terror sweep away one associate after another, including her own husband, and who finally was arrested herself. A parallel treatment of the same theme, can be found in the short novel *Opustely dom* (written 1939–40, accepted for publication in Moscow 1963, rejected 1964, pub. Paris, 1965; Eng. tr., *The Deserted House*, 1967), by Lidiya CHUKOVSKAYA, the prominent dissident daughter of the still more prominent writer Korney CHUKOVSKY. The Stalinist persecution of the poet Osip Mandelshtam, culminating in his death in a labor camp, is described by his widow Nadezhda Mandelshtam in two masterpieces of memoir literature, *Vospominaniya* (New York, 1970; Eng. tr., *Hope Against Hope*, 1970) and *Vtoraya kniga* (Paris, 1972; Eng. tr., *Hope Abandoned*, 1974). A fictional masterpiece is Georgy VLADIMOV's *Verny Ruslan* (written 1963–65, pub. Frankfurt, 1975; Faithful Ruslan), a short novel about a faithful guard dog in a forced-labor camp. Varlam SHALAMOV's *Kolymskiye rasskazy* (Stories from

Kolyma), based on the 17 years he spent in the labor camps, were published in the West only after they had first circulated secretly in the Soviet Union. A remarkable exception is Yury DOMBROVSKY's novel *Khranitel drevnostey* (1964; Eng. tr., *The Keeper of Antiquities*, 1969), a grimly comical account of the terror of the 1930s as reflected in the atmosphere of a provincial archeological museum, which was first published in considerably censored form in the Soviet journal *Novy mir* in 1964 and in book form in 1966.

The crisis provoked by the Nazi invasion of the Soviet Union on June 22, 1941, led to an immediate shift in the Communist Party line from ideology to patriotism. The mobilization for defense against the Nazi invaders was total, and close to 1,000 writers placed their literary talents in the service of the war effort. Predictably, most of what they published during the war itself was journalism rather than art, but there were notable exceptions that had great appeal for the beleaguered Soviet population, among them Konstantin SIMONOV's novel about the battle of Stalingrad, *Dni i nochi* (1943–44; Eng. tr., *Days and Nights*, 1945) and his extraordinarily popular, if sentimental, lyric "Zhdi menya" (1941; Eng. tr., "Wait for Me," 1943); Vasily GROSSMAN's novel *Narod bessmerten* (1942; Eng. trs., *The People Immortal*, 1943, and *No Beautiful Nights*, 1944); Leonov's short novel *Vzyatiye Velikoshumska* (1944; Eng. tr., *Chariot of Wrath*, 1946); and the poetry of Olga BERGGOLTS and Margarita ALIGER. A special place belongs to Aleksandr TVARDOVSKY's humorous and highly popular epic poem about a simple Russian soldier, *Vasily Tyorkin* (1941–45).

The wartime emphasis upon patriotism lent encouragement to writing on themes from Russian history. Aleksey Tolstoy wrote two plays about Ivan the Terrible that defended the tsar's tyranny and cruelty on grounds of the national interest. Sergey Sergeyev-Tsensky published three novels about tsarist Russia's part in World War I.

As might be expected, the tragedy of World War II continued to be a major theme in postwar Soviet literature. Two of the best works on this theme were Viktor NEKRASOV's sober documentary novel *V okopakh Stalingrada* (1946; Eng. tr., *Front-Line Stalingrad*, 1962) and Vera PANOVA's first novel, *Sputniki* (1946; Eng. tr., *The Train*, 1948), based on her experience on a hospital train. Aleksandr Fadeyev's *Molodaya gvardiya* (1945; Eng. tr., *Young Guard*, 1959), a novel based on actual documentation about Young Communists operating in German-occupied territory, won a Stalin Prize for 1945 but then was attacked in 1947 for not showing the alleged leadership of the Communist Party in the exploits of his young heroes, and Fadeyev obediently published a mutilated version of his novel in 1951. Emmanuil KAZAKEVICH wrote a gripping short novel *Zvezda* (1947; Eng. tr., *Star*, 1950) about the tragic end of a reconnaissance unit trapped behind the German lines.

In the midst of their enormous suffering the Russians were sustained by the hope that the wartime relaxation of certain ideological controls would lead to a freer and better life when the war was over. In 1943 and 1944 the government had regularized its relations with the Russian Orthodox Church and the various non-Orthodox religious groups through the establishment of two councils for religious affairs. In literature the relaxation led to the reappearance in print of selected poems by Boris Pasternak and Anna Akhmatova. Then on Feb. 9, 1946, Stalin abruptly wiped out the wartime policy of ideological relaxation in a speech announcing three new Five-Year Plans and leading to a massive effort to seal off the Soviet population from all Western contacts and influences and to impose the tightest possible controls over intellectual

life. The first victims of the new offensive were the writers. On Aug. 14, 1946, the Central Committee of the Communist Party passed a resolution attacking the journals *Leningrad* and *Zvezda* for ideological laxness and kowtowing to the West, particularly by publishing the works of Anna Akhmatova and Mikhail Zoshchenko. This resolution marked the beginning of the grim era in Soviet intellectual history known as "Zhdanovism," from the name of Andrey Zhdanov (1896–1948), the secretary of the Central Committee. In quick succession the journal *Leningrad* was suppressed, the editor of *Zvezda* was dismissed, and Akhmatova and Zoshchenko were expelled from the Union of Soviet Writers. Further Party resolutions soon followed, aimed against "servility to the West" and "rootless cosmopolitanism" in such fields as drama, the film, linguistics, comparative literature, music, art, science, and history. In addition, the effort to isolate the Soviet Union from Western influences was accompanied by an increased emphasis on the cult of Stalin as the greatest genius of mankind and by an inspired campaign designed to claim priority for the Russians in various scientific and technical developments.

In literature as in every other aspect of Soviet life, Stalin's death on March 5, 1953, was a watershed comparable in importance only to the Bolshevik seizure of power in 1917. It left in disarray and confusion the bureaucratic conservatives who had dominated the Soviet literary scene, and this very confusion made it possible at last for Soviet literature to begin to free itself. Within less than a month after Stalin's death an amnesty decree led to the gradual return of surviving inmates from prisons and labor camps, including many writers. Censorship began to be applied in a somewhat less restrictive manner. Several articles appeared in print calling for greater honesty and humanity in Soviet literature, the most notable and widely discussed being Vladimir Pomerantsev's (1907–) essay "Ob iskrennosti v literature" (On Sincerity in Literature). In May 1954 the journal *Znamya* published the first part of Erenberg's *Ottepel* (Eng. tr., *The Thaw*, 1961), a novel whose political importance far outweighs its artistic value, and whose very title was taken as the name for the period following Stalin's death. Toward midsummer a reaction set in, and a process of polarization began in the Soviet literary world between the "Stalinists," who still held most of the positions of power, and the "revisionists," who were determined to bring literature back to life. In December 1954 the Second Congress of the Union of Soviet Writers took place. Control of the Congress remained firmly in the hands of such faithful Party functionaries as Aleksey Surkov (1899–) and Aleksandr Fadeyev; but they faced a groundswell of criticism about the sorry state of Soviet literature. While recognizing that they could not challenge the monopoly position of the Communist Party or the sacred doctrine of socialist realism, the critics attacked the leadership of the Writers Union for their ruthless control of Soviet writers and demanded freedom for each writer to deal honestly and in his own way with the real human problems that concerned Soviet readers. The Congress ended in a standoff in which the Party made certain concessions, notably by restoring Anna Akhmatova to membership in the Writers Union (Zoshchenko had been restored in the previous July); adding liberals to its Presidium; providing for secret voting in Union elections; and modifying the definition of socialist realism in the Union's constitution so as to require only the "truthful, historically concrete representation of reality in its revolutionary development," without any longer requiring that this representation be "linked with the task of ideological transformation and education of the workers in the spirit of socialism." While this omission in itself provides no guarantee of greater freedom for the writer, it has since been privately interpreted as a tacit recognition that the doctrine of socialist realism is bankrupt.

As the "thaw" gathered momentum in 1955, numerous writers who had perished under Stalin were posthumously rehabilitated. Their names were permitted once again to appear in print and new editions of their works began to come out. The range of works allowed to be published was expanded to include living writers such as Akhmatova, Olesha, Zoshchenko, and Zabolotsky, as well as selected émigré writers, such as Bunin, who were safely dead. The first steps were taken toward overcoming the disadvantages of the Soviet Union's long isolation from the West: a new journal, *Inostrannaya literatura* (Foreign Literature), was established for the purpose of filling the gap with translations of important foreign literary works, and Soviet restrictions on travel were cautiously eased. The thaw reached a dramatic climax in February 1956 at the 20th Congress of the Communist Party when Khrushchov made his famous secret speech denouncing Stalin. The startling suicide of Aleksandr Fadeyev the following May is generally attributed to the combined effect of Khrushchov's speech and the steady return from the labor camps of writers who had been arrested during Fadeyev's tenure under Stalin as general secretary of the Writers Union.

There soon appeared more and more works written in what might well be called the new spirit of Soviet critical realism. In *Vremena goda* (1953; The Four Seasons) Vera Panova dealt critically but sympathetically with human relations, human weaknesses, and the corrupting effects of power among the middle levels of educated Soviet society. In *V rodnom gorode* (1954; Home Town) Viktor Nekrasov wrote sensitively about the postwar problems of adjustment that confronted both the returning soldiers and those who had stayed behind and been caught in German-occupied territory. The most sensational examples of this new critical spirit, all of which appeared in 1956, were Vladimir Dudintsev's (1918-) evocatively titled novel *Ne khlebom yedinym* (Eng. tr., *Not By Bread Alone*, 1957), printed in *Novy mir* (New World), which until 1970 was the leading liberal journal in the Soviet Union; and two remarkable miscellanies entitled *Literaturnaya Moskva* (Literary Moscow), which were edited by a distinguished group of writers and to which almost all the leading Soviet Russian writers contributed. The main targets of criticism in these works were the cynical, bureaucratic members of the Soviet ruling class, so corrupted by power and privilege that they had lost their capacity for the essential human virtues. The works aroused great excitement and lively discussion, but the appearance of Dudintsev's novel and the second—and more controversial—volume of *Literaturnaya Moskva* coincided in time with the Hungarian anti-Communist revolution; and the role played by Hungarian writers in preparing the way for it led the Soviet leaders again to tighten their controls.

The rejection of Pasternak's novel *Doktor Zhivago* by the editors of *Novy mir* in 1956 called forth the next great literary crisis during Khrushchov's rule. The publication of an Italian translation of the novel in Italy in 1957 led immediately to its appearance in all the major languages of the world and to the award of the Nobel Prize for Literature to Pasternak in October 1958. After first accepting, the author was subjected to an overwhelming barrage of vicious attacks in the Soviet press and finally, under threat of deportation, was compelled to withdraw his acceptance.

On the defensive after the Pasternak fiasco, Khrush-chov cautiously swung back toward a slightly more liberal position. In 1962 he created a sensation by personally authorizing Tvardovsky, the editor of *Novy mir,* to publish Aleksandr Solzhenitsyn's *Odin den Ivana Denisovicha*. During the months that followed, Khrushchov apparently tried to establish a kind of moderate, stable authoritarianism in which a limited degree of liberty would be allowed as long as it did not threaten Communist Party control. But his colorful career in politics was abruptly brought to an end when he was ousted from power in October 1964 and replaced by Leonid Brezhnev. Since that time there has been a gradual but steady erosion of the ground that had been gained for freedom in literature and the arts since the death of Stalin.

The public revulsion against the evils of the Stalinist period was both reflected and encouraged in the poetry of the late 1950s and 1960s. In September 1955 an annual Day of Poetry was established, which led to a new annual publication of poetry under the same name, *Den poezii*. Subsequently the demand for public readings of poetry was so great that they were frequently held in stadiums, with as many as 15,000 persons attending. Among the most popular poets taking part in these huge gatherings were Yevgeny YEVTUSHENKO, Andrey VOZNESENSKY, and Robert ROZHDESTVENSKY, all of whom recited poetry in keeping with the new liberal spirit. Always a nation of poetry lovers, the Russian people after the Stalinist famine were insatiable in their appetite for the works of good poets, ranging from Anna Akhmatova and Boris Pasternak, the last great survivors of the pre-Revolutionary Silver Age, and such middle-aged poets as Nikolay Zabolotsky. Arseny Tarkovsky (1907-), Pavel ANTOKOL-SKY, Leonid MARTYNOV, Boris SLUTSKY, Vladimir Lugovskoy (1901 57), and Semyon KIRSANOV, to the new generation of young poets that emerged in the post-Stalin period, including Iosif BRODSKY, Yevgeny VINOKUROV, Naum Korzhavin (1925-), and David SAMOYLOV, and the gifted women poets Bella Akhmadulina (1937-), Rimma KAZAKOVA, Yunna MORITS, and Novella MATVEYEVA, as well as Aleksandr KUSHNER, Viktor SOSNORA, and Vladimir Tsybin. All these poets emphasized the individual poetic vision (undistorted by the ideological demands of the Stalinist period), and such simple, old-fashioned virtues as sincerity, honesty, and humanity. Some of those who came to maturity during the Stalinist period sounded notes of self-reproach as they recalled their inescapable involvement in the hypocrisy and moral compromise of the era, whereas those who went through World War II often revealed the scars of their war experience. The post-Stalin generation of poets that rebelled against Stalinism anticipated and partly coincided with the general revolt of youth in Western Europe and America, but the movements had little in common. The young Soviet dissidents were seeking to recover the very values that the romantic young Marxists in the West were undermining, and this led the young Russians in the very act of revolting to rediscover and cultivate the best elements of their older cultural tradition—the great living links with pre-Revolutionary literature, Akhmatova and Pasternak; the martyred writers of the Stalinist period; even the long-submerged Russian religious heritage.

In prose the new winds of change led writers to explore the present and reexamine the past in the spirit of critical realism without directly challenging either the Party's power or its moribund doctrine of socialist realism. Following in the footsteps of Chekhov, and sharing Chekhov's preference for the shorter fictional forms, the most gifted young writers of the Khrushchov period—Andrey Bitov, Daniil GRANIN, Yury KAZAKOV, Yury NAGIBIN, Vladimir TENDRYAKOV—explored a wide range of problems without drawing conclusions or proposing solutions but also—like Chekhov—without leaving any doubt about their moral and social values. Unlike their immediate predecessors, the writers of the post-Stalinist period took the socialized, industrialized Soviet state for granted as the setting for their works, and their dominant themes were Soviet variations on the universal themes of all literature: man's self-discovery; the nature of good and evil, and of justice and truth; and the intricate web of relations that links individuals together in society. In addition, however, a theme unique to Soviet literature since destalinization has been Stalinism itself. Yet post-Stalinist literature is created in a society that is still only partly destalinized. With the whole state still under the control of the Communist Party and the security police, with the censorship system still intact, and with socialist realism, albeit modified, still obligatory, certain literary devices in the work of an independent-minded writer take on the additional function of obscuring his meaning for the authorities while conveying it to perceptive readers. The reaction of younger writers such as Vasily Aksyonov to the hypocritical stereotypes and meaningless clichés of socialist realism has led some of them to seek greater immediacy of effect through the creation of a racy, ironical style combining slang with parodies of Soviet journalese, and through experiments with narrative focus and with both direct and reported dialogue that are far more innovative in the Soviet Union, just emerging from a quarter century of isolation, than they would have appeared to contemporary Western readers.

The new critical spirit also led to a reexamination of World War II in the novels of Grigory BAKLANOV, Yury BONDAREV, the Belorussian writer Vasily BYKOV, Viktor Nekrasov, and Bulat OKUDZHAVA. A similar critical treatment of the Soviet Revolution and Civil War is to be found in such novels as Pavel Nilin's (1908–) *Zhestokost* (1956; Eng. tr., *Comrade Venka,* 1959) and Sergey ZA-LYGIN's *Solyonnaya pad* (1967; Salt Hollow). In Nekra-sov's *Kira Georgiyevna* (1961; Eng. tr., 1962), Tendry-akov's *Svidaniye s Nefertiti* (1964; A Rendezvous with Nefertiti), and Bondarev's *Tishina* (1962; Eng. tr., *Si-lence,* 1965) and *Dvoye* (1964; Two People), human relations in the early postwar period are treated in a way that would not have been conceivable while Stalin was alive.

Since the 1960s the main theme of Yury TRIFONOV's fiction has been the entanglements in the private lives of the urban intelligentsia, while the urban working class provided the setting for Vitaly Syomin's much-discussed novel *Semero v odnom dome* (1965; Seven in One House). Before his death in mid-career, Vasily SHUKSHIN won a prominent place for himself in films, in which he both acted and served as director, as well as in fiction. Seafaring life provided the setting for most of Viktor KONET-SKY's works, but his characters transcend this setting as they struggle with profound moral problems.

One of the most striking developments in post-Stalin literature has been the emergence of what is known as "village prose," dealing with life among the peasants who until recently made up the overwhelming majority of the Russian population. Ever since the Soviet Revolution, doctrinaire Marxist-Leninists had viewed the peasants with hostility as a backward, conservative class that was destined to disappear. By 1952, however, the plight of the peasants and the condition of Soviet agriculture had become so bad that the authorities allowed Valentin OVECH-KIN, himself a Communist Party member and a former collective farm chairman, to begin publishing a series of fictionalized sketches in which he boldly criticized conditions on the collective farms. Ovechkin was essentially a crusading journalist rather than a literary artist, and his

failure through his writings to bring about the necessary reforms led ultimately to an attempt at suicide and his incarceration for a time in a mental hospital. Nevertheless, his sketches opened up new thematic territory that has since been explored by a host of other writers, including Fyodor ABRAMOV, Vasily BELOV, Yefim DO-ROSH, Boris MOZHAYEV, Valentin RASPUTIN, Vladimir SOLOUKHIN, Aleksandr Solzhenitsyn, Aleksandr YASHIN, and Sergey ZALYGIN. Taking the traditional peasant values and way of life as their point of departure, these writers have gone on to discuss moral and philosophical problems, giving many of their works a resonance that has meaning for mankind in general.

An interesting new development in Soviet literature is the appearance of several important writers from the national minorities who have made their reputations with works written in Russian. Among the most notable of the non-Slavs are the bilingual Kirgiz prose writer Chingiz AYTMATOV, whose masterfully written stories of his fellow Kirgiz in confrontation with the new industrialized, collectivized Soviet order provoked wide discussion; and the attractive Abkhazian storyteller Fazil ISKANDER, beneath whose sunny, humorous style there lurks a serious moralist and social critic. A place apart belongs to the extraordinary Chuvash poet Gennady Aygi, whose Russian poems have been translated and published abroad in at least six foreign languages but circulate in the Soviet Union largely in manuscript copies.

In addition to the two streams of Russian literature that have coexisted ever since the Soviet Revolution—censored literature published in the homeland and uncensored literature published by émigrés abroad—two new streams have come into existence since the death of Stalin. One is underground literature, which circulates in the homeland in various kinds of copies—all of which are known as products of *samizdat,* a colloquial Russian word meaning the "Do-It-Yourself Publishing House." The other stream is literature smuggled out of the Soviet Union and published abroad, for which the word *tamizdat,* "publication over there," has been created—an obvious pun on *samizdat.* The distinctions among all four of these streams are complex and shifting. For example, Solzhenitsyn began his career with five short works published in the censored press of the homeland, but then his works began to circulate in *samizdat,* later they were published in Russian and in translation abroad, and finally—after his expulsion in 1974 by the Soviet authorities—they began to be published abroad in the émigré press. From 1956 until their arrest in 1965, Andrey SIN-YAVSKY and Yuly DANIEL maintained dual careers, publishing "innocent" scholarly works and translations in the censored Soviet press while secretly publishing important dissident literary works abroad under the pen names of Abram Tertz and Nikolay Arzhak. A number of suppressed works by other writers, as well as the full texts of censored works published in the Soviet Union, are now available in Western editions. These include works by Andrey Platonov, Andrey Bitov, Fazil Iskander, and Yury Dombrovsky, among many others. The most complete collections of several major writers of the Soviet period, including Pasternak, Mandelshtam, Akhmatova, Gumilyov, and Kuzmin, are available only in scholarly editions published outside of the Soviet Union. A growing number of writers still living in the Soviet Union have been publishing works abroad that could not get through the Soviet censorship. These works include the memoirs of Nadezhda Mandelshtam, Lev Kopelev, and Yevgeniya Ginsburg; short novels by Lidiya Chukovskaya; the most recent works of the highly popular science-fiction writers Arkady and Boris STRUGATSKY;

Georgy Vladimov's *Verny Ruslan*; and all the most recent fiction of Vladimir VOYNOVICH. A highly popular form of poetry that has flourished since the end of the 1950s on the border between legality and underground is the satirical ballad, sung to the accompaniment of a guitar. During the Khrushchov period these ballads were sung at public gatherings; toward the end of the 1960s, when such large meetings began to be suppressed, tape recordings of ballads, especially those of Bulat OKUDZHAVA and Aleksandr GALICH, circulated privately.

Events since the death of Stalin in 1953 make it clear that no future literary historian can discuss 20th-century Russian literature without keeping constantly in mind the dialectical relation between the homeland and the West. The cultural achievement of the "first emigration"—Russians who left immediately after the Soviet Revolution— has yet to be adequately assessed. The "second emigration"—those who left during World War II—included relatively few writers of stature, apart from the poets Ivan YELAGIN and Nikolay MORSHEN and the distinguished poet-scholar Vladimir Markov. But the personal contact of masses of Soviet citizens with life in Central Europe during and immediately after the war produced a cultural shock that evidently played no small part in Stalin's decision in 1946 to seal off the Soviet Union once more from contacts with the West. Within three years of Stalin's death, important literary works written in the Soviet Union began to appear in print in the West, some sent out secretly by their authors, others published without the knowledge or approval of their authors after circulating in the homeland in *samizdat,* and still others published openly abroad by authors still living in the Soviet Union. A major shift of Russian literary talent occurred in the 1970s with the beginning of the "third emigration," which was made up in part of "troublesome" dissidents and in part of persons emigrating legally through the establishment of a claim to some Jewish ancestry. Among the most notable writers in the third emigration were the Nobel Prizewinner Aleksandr Solzhenitsyn, Viktor Nekrasov, Iosif Brodsky, Andrey Sinyavsky, the heroic poet Natalya GORBANEVSKAYA, a founder of the famous underground newspaper *Khronika tekushchikh sobytiy* (Chronicle of Current Events); the poet Naum Korzhavin; the balladeer Aleksandr Galich; and the fiction writers Vladimir MAKSIMOV, Vladimir MARAMZIN, Yevgeny Ternovsky, and Anatoly GLADILIN. An important new periodical founded by third-emigration writers is *Kontinent,* which is published in Western Europe under the editorship of Maksimov, Nekrasov, and Gorbanevskaya. A significant feature that distinguishes *Kontinent* from other leading Russian émigré periodicals such as *Novy zhurnal* is the frank inclusion of religion within its sphere of interests. The prominence of the religious theme in contemporary Russian literature, a striking characteristic of works by Brodsky, Solzhenitsyn, Sinyavsky, Maksimov, and Pasternak, has led to what the Polish scholar-poet Czesław MIŁOSZ calls "a formidable paradox: in the countries where Christian churches thrive there are practically no genuinely Christian novels. Truly Christian writing has had to come from Russia where Christians have been persecuted for several decades."

It would, of course, be hazardous indeed to attempt to predict the course of Russian literature for the rest of the 20th century. A few observations can be made, however, with some confidence. One is that Lenin's theory of the coexistence of two cultures is even more applicable to post-Revolutionary Russia than it is to capitalist countries; but instead of Lenin's opposition between bourgeois and proletarian culture there is in the Soviet Union an opposition between a bureaucratized, dehumanized official culture based on the threadbare myths of Marxism-Leninism, and a schismatic, independent culture of the intelligentsia. The loss of literary talent through emigration since the beginning of the 1970s has been serious, and the obstacles to creativity confronting all émigré writers are well known, but there are still some grounds for refusing to despair about the future. The traditional Russian association of literature with truth, humanity, moral integrity, and the search for eternal values has reasserted itself in the homeland since the death of Stalin and is strong in the third emigration. Thanks in part to technological developments, literary communications between Russians at home and Russians abroad are remarkably effective. Finally, although the long years of cultural isolation under Stalin cut Russian writers off from literary developments in the rest of the world and have given an old-fashioned appearance to much Russian literature, more than 60 years of strenuous post-Revolutionary experience in a Marxist-Leninist ideocracy has given the best Soviet writers a kind of worldly wisdom that is sadly missing today in the common run of Western and Third-World writers.

See: D. S. Mirsky, *A History of Russian Literature* (1949); G. Struve, *Russkaya literatura v izgnanii* (1956); V. Zavalishin, *Early Soviet Writers* (1958); E. J. Brown, *Russian Literature Since the Revolution,* (2d ed., 1969); G. Struve, *Russian Literature under Lenin and Stalin 1971–1953* (1971); M. Dewhirst and R. Farrell, eds., *The Soviet Censorship* (1973); M. Slonim, *Soviet Russian Literature, Writers and Problems 1917–1977,* (2d rev. ed., 1977); D. Brown, *Soviet Russian Literature since Stalin* (1978).

Reference works: S. V. Utechin, *A Concise Encyclopaedia of Russia* (1961); *Literaturnaya entsiklopediya,* vols. 1–9, 11 (1929–39); *Kratkaya literaturnaya entsiklopediya,* vols. 1–9 (1962–78); Wolfgang Kasack, *Lexikon der russischen Literatur ab 1917* (1976).

Bibliographies: K. D. Muratova, ed., *Istoriya russkoy literatury kontsa XIX—nachala XX veka: bibliograficheskiy ukazatel* (1963); *Russkiye sovetskiye pisateli-prozaiki: bibliograficheskiy ukazatel,* vols. 1–7 (1959–72); A. Tarasenkov, *Russkiye poety XX veka, 1900–1955: bibliografiya* (1966); R. Lewanski, comp., *The Slavic Literatures—Beginning to 1960* (1967); S. A. Zenkovsky and D. L. Armbruster, *A Guide to the Bibliographies of Russian Literature* (1970); L. A. Foster, comp. *Bibliography of Russian Émigré Literature 1918–1968,* 2 vols. (1970); *Russkiye sovetskiye pisateli-poety,* vols. 1–3– (1977–79–).

W.B.E.

Ruyra i Oms, Joaquim (1858–1939), Catalan prose writer, was born in Gerona, where he received his secondary education. He studied law at the University of Barcelona but did not take a degree. Instead he retired to his ancestral house in Blanes, where he wrote, unhurriedly and with the patience of an embroiderer, the marvelous pages in which sailors, workmen, and farm boys are observed not only in their external characteristics but also in the most hidden folds of their simple, candid, and frequently contradictory souls. His penchant for mathematics, to which he turned for relaxation from his literary labors, explains in part, perhaps, his style, which is characterized by simplicity and a perfect clarity and order of thought. His entire work embodies a lofty moral purpose without for this reason being didactic. The same combination is found in his poetic production, especially in "El pais del Pler," an allegorical poem.

His literary initiation came late. He was 45 when he produced his first book, *Marines i boscatges* (1903; Seascapes and Coppices). These model prose descriptions, which won prizes in 1895 at the Jocs Florals (the paramount poetic festival of the Catalan-speaking countries, restored, in 1859 through the agency of the *Renaixença*), possess the immutable characteristics of his style. The stories "Mar de llamp" (Sea of Lightning) and "Les senyorestes de mar" (The Young Ladies of the Sea) reveal his great narrative talent. His style was hailed as "trailblazing," and in 1902, when *Jacobé* was awarded a prize at the Jocs Florals, Josep Pijoan enthusiastically exclaimed that that year's festival would forever be identified with this profoundly human short novel, an evocation of "landscapes possessing a soul" and peopled by vibrant, tragic figures.

After *Marines i boscatges,* Ruyra i Oms fell silent. He suffered a grave cardiac illness, and he moved to the Canary Islands in search of rest. His next book, *La Parada* (1919; The Stop), a collection of stories and short novels, appeared 16 years later. During these years there had been notable changes in the literary tendencies of Catalonia. Ruyra, however, true to himself, remained faithful to his initial aesthetic creed. He stood apart from the influence of French naturalism and still farther from romantic and sentimental affectations. He himself confessed that, suspecting a lack of balance in his own imagination, he had read Emile ZOLA, but that the French author soon began to lose prestige for him, and he finally could not read a single page of Zola's novels. Ruyra wrote journalism in addition to fiction. Many short articles of his, which have their own originality, were published in Catalan journals like *Renaixença, Veu de Catalunya, Joventut,* and *Ilustració catalana.* All of these articles, along with the works already mentioned and his later books, *Pinya de Rosa* (1920; Cone of Roses) and *Entre flames* (In the Flames), were to be collected in a complete edition of his works planned by the Institució de les Lletres Catalanes, but the project was interrupted by the invasion of Francisco Franco's forces in 1939. His *En garet a l'enramada,* an adaptation for the stage of one of his short stories, was presented in the Poliorama Theater in Barcelona. He also translated into Catalan poems of Mosco, Horace, Dante, Paul VERLAINE, and Jean Racine, and tales of Erckmann-Chatrian. Some of his own works have appeared in Spanish, Italian, French, and Finnish. He was a member of the Institut d'Estudis Catalans, the most highly esteemed institution in Catalonia. He distinguished himself in the philological branch of that body, to which he contributed countless idioms gathered from among the people and which were to enrich the great projected Catalan language dictionary, patiently prepared by the Institut, a work also interrupted by the events of 1939.

In 1938, at 80 years of age, he was honored by the Catalan writers and by the *Govern de Catalunya* in a ceremony of intimate simplicity that took place in the Conselleria de Cultura. Ruyra's attitude toward the Spanish Civil War was governed by the Christian and patriotic virtues that were a part of his very fiber and soul. He declared that he would feel himself to be less a Christian if, to defend any theologically isolated religious interests, he should resort to the anti-Christian violence of the Falangists and aid in the destruction of the living work of God, his country, his Catalonia. This explains the official silence at the time of his death. A simple family note—in Spanish—announced to the grief-stricken Catalan people the death of their great prose writer. Ruyra's style, although deeply personal, is clearly based on Catalan writing. The unanimously favorable reception that public and critics gave to Ruyra's later work was linked with the success of *Marines i boscatges* and of *Jacobé,* but the fact is that Ruyra's art will be, for all ages, removed from

tendencies and schools. "Amidst my suffering," he wrote when his second book was published, "I have enjoyed a privilege granted to few men: for, having passed a great number of years dead, as one might say, I have had the pleasure of seeing that my work survived."

See: J. M. Capdevila, "La obra de Joaquim Ruyra," *Hora de España* 21 (Sept. 1938): 73–82; C. Riba, "Memoria de Joaquim Ruyra," *Revista de Catalunya,* 4th period, no. 95, pp. 9–16.   J.M.M.iV.

Ruyslinck, Ward, pseud. of Raymond De Belser (1929–), Belgian (Flemish) novelist, was born in Antwerp. Ruyslinck belongs to the generation of writers whose adolescence was marked by World War II, although the war as such did not become a leitmotiv in their work; war, violence, and social injustice were for them aspects of the reality one has to become acquainted with sooner or later. War and anguish do, however, constitute the background of Ruyslinck's early works. The short novel *De ontaarde slapers* (1957; The Deadbeats), the short story "Wierook en tranen" (1958; Incense and Tears), and some of the short stories gathered in *De Madonna met de buil* (1959; The Bruised Madonna) are also characterized by an awareness of social issues and by a romantic sensitivity mixed with irony.

In 1961, Ruyslinck published one of his best novels, *Het dal van Hinnom* (The Valley of Gehenna). The valley of the story symbolizes the hell in which the characters exist. At the center of the novel is the family Roseboom (father, mother, and sick little daughter), pariahs for whom life is nothing but a series of setbacks. They are surrounded by people who, be they rich or poor, are all maimed physically or spiritually. Such characters as Floers, the undertaker, his intolerant, frustrated wife, and the Russian émigré Zapotin illustrate Ruyslinck's pessimistic view of the human condition. Yet his sympathy for these outcasts never sounds pathetic or sentimental. On the contrary, he portrays the pain of these vulnerable people with precision and with a grim, dark sense of humor. A similar atmosphere of pain and misfortune pervades *Het reservaat* (1964; The Reservation).

From 1965 to 1970, Ruyslinck published a series of satirical pieces such as *De paarde vleeseters* (1965; The Horse-Meat Eaters), *Golden Ophelia* (1966), *Het ledikant van Lady Cant* (1968; The Cot of Lady Cant), and *De Karakoliërs* (1969; The People of Karakolia). In 1972, Ruyslinck published *De heksenkring* (The Fairy Circle), one of his masterpieces. This novel deals with the revolt of the poor Argentinian population against the corrupt people in power. Ruyslinck returns here to one of his original themes, the social and humanitarian concern for the persecuted, the oppressed, and the exploited. *Het ganzenboord* (1974; The Game of Goose) is another important novel in which Ruyslinck looks back on his life. In *De sloper in het slakkehuis* (1977; The Breaker in the Cochlea), Ruyslinck tackles the issue of noise in modern society. The novel *Op toernee met Leopold Sondag* (1978; Touring with Leopold Sondag) represents an attempt to summarize the craft of the writer. A gift for introspection and a keen sense of social problems dominate the work of this important Flemish author.

See: T. Schalken, *Ward Ruyslinck* (1966); L. Scheer, *Röntgens van Ruyslinck* (1973); J. G. M. Weck, ed., *In contact met het werk van moderne scrijvers: Ward Ruyslinck* (1974); *Profiel Ward Ruyslinck* (1974); A. de Bruyne et al., *Gewikt en gewogen* (1977).   P. van A.

Rydberg, Viktor (1828–95), Swedish poet and novelist, was born in Jönköping. His studies were seriously hindered by his poverty. In 1855 he began working as a journalist on the liberal newspaper *Göteborgs Handels-och Sjöfartstidning,* and in 1884 he was appointed professor of the history of culture at the University of Stockholm. He had already published several novels, which were to be renowned later on, when in 1862 he published the first book that attracted general attention, *Bibelns lära om Kristus* (The Doctrine of Christ in the Bible). This book revealed a profound theological learning and was an attack on the dogma of the divinity of Christ. Rydberg subsequently became famous as a freethinker (*see* SWEDISH LITERATURE). His scientific work was later focused upon the old Scandinavian and Teutonic mythology, *Undersökningar i germanisk mytologi* (1886; Eng. tr. in part, *Teutonic Mythology,* 1889).

In the 1850s, Rydberg wrote many historical novels in the manner of Sir Walter Scott, which were published as serial stories in newspapers. The novels had the same liberal tendency as the rest of his journalism. He described his novel *Den siste athenaren* (1859; Eng. tr., *The Last Athenian,* 1869) as "a spear which I have thrown against the ranks of the enemy in the warrior's permissible intent to wound and to kill." The setting of the book is from classical antiquity, but the aim of its attack is the contemporary lack of liberty of thought and of faith. In the 1850s, Rydberg also wrote a rather short romantic novel, *Singoalla* (1857; Eng. tr., *Singoalla, A Medieval Legend,* 1903). The principal character is a gypsy girl, and historical romanticism is thus combined with exotic gypsy romanticism. In his last years, Rydberg again took up the writing of novels and published *Vapensmeden* (1891; The Armorer). This book is about the struggle between Lutheran Protestantism and Roman Catholicism in 16th-century Sweden, and in it Rydberg still fought fanaticism and dogmatism, and his ideal was still humanity and liberty.

Even though Rydberg accomplished remarkable achievements as a scholar and as a novelist, his foremost achievement was as a poet. He published two collections of poems (*Dikter*; Poems), the first as late as 1882 and the second in 1891. Rydberg's poetry reveals both his adherence to romantic idealism, as in "Kantat" (Cantata) and romantic dreams, as in "Drömliv" (Dream Life), and also his confrontation with the new scientific and philosophical materialism, especially the Darwinian theory of evolution, as in "Prometeus och Ahasverus." He often used old Scandinavian myths in his poems. His most shocking poem with a social tendency is "Den nya grottesången" (1891; The New Song of Grotti). In this, the myth from the Eddic poem is used for a description of modern industrialism, of child labor, and of the destructive consequences of free competition. Rydberg's humanitarian liberalism never accepted the laissex-faire theory.

See: O. Holmberg, *Viktor Rydbergs lyrik* (1935); Ö. Lindberger, *Prometeustanken hos Viktor Rydberg I–II* (1938); A. Gustafson, *A History of Swedish Literature* (1961), pp. 230–36; H. Granlid, *Vår dröm är frihet: nya greppp i Rydbergs lyrik* (1973).   N.Å.S.

Rylsky, Maksym (1895–1964), Ukrainian poet, was born in Kiev, the son of a prominent Ukrainian intellectual of Polish descent. His first collection of verse was *Na bilykh ostrovakh* (1910; On the White Islands). During the 1920s, Rylsky belonged to the Neoclassicist group (*see* UKRAINIAN LITERATURE), even though his poetry was essentially symbolist in nature. Rylsky's best poems, written in this period, include the collections *Synya dalechin* (1922; The Blue Distance), *Trynadtsyata vesna* (1926; The 13th Spring), and *De skhodyatsya dorohy* (1929; Where the Paths Meet). For a while, Rylsky was out of political favor, but with the onset of Stalinism, he began to turn to social and political themes. The quality of Rylsky's poetry, however, did not suffer as much as that of other poets also writing under political pressure. During World War II, Rylsky wrote two remarkable long poems: *Zhaha* (1943; Thirst) and *Mandrivka v molodist* (1944; Journey into Youth). During the so-called Khrushchov thaw, Rylsky was able to recapture some of his earlier power, as is evident in the volume *Holosiyivska osin* (1959; The Autumn of Holosiyiv). He also supported the young poets in their struggle against Communist Party controls. Rylsky was one of the best translators of other Slavic poets, notably Adam Mickiewicz and Juliusz Słowacki and Aleksandr Pushkin. He received the Order of Lenin three times.   G.S.N.L.

Ryum, Ulla (1937–), Danish novelist and playwright, was born in Copenhagen. She is mainly interested in those tragic characters who search for meaning during a whole lifetime but can find it only in death. Such a person appears in *Natsangersken* (1963; The Night Singer), a fascinating psychological and symbolical portrait of a woman abandoned by life and love. A leading motif in Ryum's writings is the insurmountable distance between human beings. This tragic situation is thoroughly illustrated in *Latterfuglen* (1965; The Laughing Jackass), a variation on the classical Orpheus myth, and in two collections of short stories, *Tusindskove* (1969; Thousand Forests) and *Noter om igår og idag* (1971; Notes about Yesterday and Today), both of which show a strange mingling of miracle and social realism. *Jakelnatten* (1967; The Night of the Puppet) concerns a person who disappears without a trace, a puppeteer whose monologue on his deathbed constitutes the larger part of the novel. As a contrast to Ryum's fantastic and fabulous art in fiction, her dramas attack our dehumanized world, as in *Myterne* (1973; The Myths), and lead to the author's demand for political and social solidarity in *Natten, krigen* (1975; The Night, the War) and the radio play *Denne ene dag* (1976; This Only Day).   S.H.R.

S

Saba, Umberto, pseud. of Umberto Poli (1883–1957), Italian poet, was born in Trieste and lived there most of his life. The only child of a broken family, he was raised in the Jewish quarter by his mother, several aunts, and an especially beloved Slovenian nurse whose surname (Sabaz) is significantly echoed in his nom de plume. Poor, fatherless, his affections disputed by an embittered mother and a possessive nurse, Saba's youth was emotionally a hard one. His precocious passion for the Italian classics from Petrarch to Giacomo Leopardi (1798–1837), as well as his own efforts to emulate them, no doubt began as imaginative compensation for his unhappy lot. A self-made poet, Saba's formal education was minimal. In 1902, at age 19, he committed himself to poetry, quit his clerkship, and lived by his wits for the next five years, roaming through Tuscany while writing occasional journalistic pieces and his own first mature verse. After a year's military service in Salerno he returned to Trieste in 1908, married a local girl, had a child, and settled down to almost half a century of an outwardly uneventful existence.

Saba wrote many poems, published them frequently

and unprofitably (his first book was issued in 1911), kept clear of the various coteries of literary modernism, and earned a modest living for his little family as the proprietor of an antiquarian bookshop.

In 1921 he began the practice of collecting his poems—often revised and rearranged—under the general title of *Il canzoniere* (The Songbook). It is in this massive lyric autobiography, containing in its final form over 400 poems written between 1900 and 1954, that the bulk of his generous, idiosyncratic genius resides. Saba used a variety of traditional closed forms, including sonnets and *canzonette;* only toward the end of his life did he begin to experiment with the freer patterns he associated with his contemporary Giuseppe UNGARETTI. Saba considered his *Canzoniere* to be "the history . . . of a life relatively poor in external events but rich in emotions and inner resonances, in the people whom the poet loved in the course of his long life." This description from his remarkable book-length autocommentary, *Storia e cronistoria del Canzoniere* (1948; History and Chronicle of the Canzoniere), is apt enough, for Saba's material follows his biography like a shadow. In poem after poem, sequence after sequence, his story unfolds: torments and secret joys of childhood and adolescence, the army, courtship and marriage, the servitude and grandeur of domesticity, erotic adventures real and fancied, vignettes of friends and strangers, the bookshop, the liberating experience of his psychoanalysis, old age embittered by Fascist persecution and what he felt to be critical neglect. It is the story of a lifetime lived almost entirely in one place, Trieste, and Saba is the poet of that city as his friend Italo SVEVO is its novelist. Hills and harbor, streets and houses and shops, men and women and children—all are fused in the pages of the *Canzoniere* through Saba's unique sympathy and limpid language.

Despite its title, the *Canzoniere* builds to far more than a collection of individual lyric on the Petrarchan model. In the humanity of his vision and abundance of his inspiration, Saba manages to produce a "horizontal" sense of homely continuity and living process in which the single stunning poem (and there are many) acquires fullest resonance in the context of its place in the story as a whole. By the same token, lesser lyrics borrow peculiar power from the company they keep, from their contribution to the "chapter." It is right, however, to stress the *Canzoniere*'s integrity, its ultimate stature as *poema,* a whole poem, for beneath the weight of particulars and the narrative specificity there is a sense of the characteristically human and communal that deserves to be called epic. As the critic Quarantotti Gambini has said, the *Canzoniere* is "more than a songbook: [it is] a type of odyssey of man in our times."

See: G. Debenedetti, *Saggi critici* (1952); E. Caccia, *Lettura e storia di Saba* (1967); J. Cary, *Three Modern Italian Poets: Saba, Ungaretti, Montale* (1969).   J.C.

Sá-Carneiro, Mário de (1890–1916), Portuguese poet and fiction writer, born in Lisbon, killed himself by taking poison in Paris after earlier attempts at suicide. He, with Fernando PESSOA, José de ALMADA-NEGREIROS, and a few others, was one of the initiators of the Portuguese avant-garde with the founding of the review *Orpheu* (1915) (*see* PORTUGUESE LITERATURE). He had already issued a slim collection of verse, *Dispersão* (1914; Dispersion), and a narrative, *A confissão de Lúcio* (1914; Lucio's Confession). In 1915 he published some short stories, *Céu em fogo* (Sky on Fire). His later poems, *Indícios de oiro* (Gold Tokens), appeared only in 1937 as a book.

Sá-Carneiro is one of the most strikingly original poets in the Portuguese language and certainly one of the most interesting members of the avant-garde anywhere. Unfortunately, his poetry has not caught the attention of translators as much as Pessoa's has done. His fiction, on the other hand, although very arresting, especially for its use of themes that illuminate the poet's soul, nevertheless retains too many fin de siècle mannerisms. It was, however, through a desperate and paroxysmic use of those same mannerisms that Sá-Carneiro achieved the masterly originality of his poetry, whose main theme is the divided self—the contradiction between common human nature and an anxious drive for spiritual completeness. Hardly at any time does the poet depart from traditional forms of verse, with their patterns of meters and rhyme, but his language transforms entirely all the paraphernalia of aestheticist sumptuousness and sensibility into a moving and dazzling vehicle for telling about what is beyond words: the tragic consciousness of a dreamer who does not believe in any transcendence. To suit its ends, that language alters the normal functions of grammar, distorts established meanings in a highly imaginative fashion, and coins composite words through an intense use of synesthesia. Sá-Carneiro's poetry achieves thus an extraordinary shift from exacerbated symbolism to the experimentalism of the avant-garde. This poetry, which is so ambitiously formalistic, conveys an overpowering sense of doom, desperation, and sarcastic self-pity. It attains a piercing poignancy and soaring lyricism, be it in its visionary postures, its debasing statements, or its erotic undertones. The verse itself is extremely musical in a paradoxical way: it is as if the sumptuousness of the imagery and the surprising effects of a highly personal diction were fused together with rhythm to create the tone of a majestic and at the same time childlike lamentation, which never loses elegance or imaginative distinction.

See: D. Wohl, *Wirklichkeit und Idealität in der Lyrik Mário de Sá-Carneiros* (1960; rev. ed. in Portuguese, *Realidade e idealidade na lírica de Mário de Sá-Carneiro,* 1968); M. ALiete Galhoz, *Mário de Sá-Carneiro* (1963); J. Régio, "O fantástico na obra de Mário de Sá-Carneiro," in his *Ensaios de interpretação crítica* (1964).
J. de S.

Sachs, Nelly (1891–1970), German poet and playwright, was born and grew up in Berlin, the only child of a wealthy Jewish manufacturer. Educated by private tutors and at a girls' high school, she never attended a university but studied music, dance, and literature on her own and at one time intended to become a dancer. Later she turned to literature (her father's library was well stocked with the works of Goethe, Friedrich Schiller, the German romantics, and Western and Eastern mystics). In her 20s her enthusiasm for modern writers was limited to the Swedish author Selma LAGERLÖF, whose *Gösta Berling* she had read at the age of 15 and with whom she had corresponded. In 1940, when the danger of deportation to a concentration camp became imminent, Lagerlöf helped Sachs and her mother to emigrate to Sweden. Life in Sweden was difficult, even after Sachs learned Swedish and supported herself and her mother by translating Swedish poetry into German. From a distance she also shared the agony of her people, finding words to express man's inhumanity to man in sorrowful hymns of great beauty.

In her early 20s, Sachs had written neoromantic nature poetry, published under the title *Legenden und Erzählungen* (1921; Legends and Stories), but she has never been a part of the literary or political scene in Berlin. In Sweden everything changed radically. Deeply moved by the tragedy of the Jews and inspired by the empathy and humanitarian vision of modern Swedish poets, Sachs began to write powerful poetry of her own. To her, writing meant "surviving" and uttering a "mute outcry" against Nazi brutality. At the same time she continued to read, particularly Hasidic literature and the Bible. Sachs thought she would not find a publisher for her poetry, but in 1946 her first collection of poems, *In den Wohnungen des Todes* (In the Habitations of Death), was published in East Germany, and the second, *Sternverdunkelung* (1949; Eclipse of a Star), in the Netherlands. Both contain the main themes and form of the works that followed and are lyrical renderings of the tragedy of European Jewry during the Adolf Hitler regime. The only difference between the collections is their mood. Whereas the first conveys primarily the despair of the death camps, the second reflects greater tranquility. Job, the epitome of suffering, is seen in misery but also in the inherent greatness that "shall make all rising suns blanch." Sachs views the victims as part of the eternal cycle of life and death where, out of the "magic substances of pain," planets are born. Youth must again build houses "to face the sun: God." In every death the poet anticipates rebirth; beyond cataclysm and transcience Sachs seeks hope and love.

The imprint of suffering still marks her third collection, *Und niemand weiß weiter* (1957; No One Knows the Way), published in West Germany, but the note of hope is even stronger and the agony of the Jews is linked more clearly to man's fate on earth, perceived according to the laws of nature: eternal metamorphosis, death and rebirth, ebb and flood. Man is but a sign, a little arabesque in the dust; formations are pointed out by fingers; body parts are arranged in "dying delineations." Delineations are also the poet's word, written on the blank page. The poet makes the "alphabet's corpse" rise from the grave and infuses new life into it. Chrysalis becomes butterfly; the poet's creation unfolds for a moment of splendor, soon to return to dust.

Sach's next collection, *Flucht und Verwandlung* (1959; Flight and Metamorphosis), continues a vision of the world in eternal metamorphosis. Man, perceived as an exile on earth, holds "instead of a homeland/the metamorphosis of the world" in his hand. With this collection, and in 1962 with the mystery play *Eli*, a moving tale of a Jewish boy's death in Poland and the search for his murderer, Nelly Sachs became known to a large public in West Germany. Although she subsequently received a number of coveted literary prizes, she was still relatively unknown in Europe when she shared the Nobel Prize for Literature in 1966 with S. Y. AGNON. When public recognition and success did reach her, she was physically exhausted. Tortured by thoughts of persecution, she had relived the agonies of her people, and she died on May 12, 1970, in Stockholm.

Scholars have pointed out that the roots of Sachs's art can be found in the Cabala, the Bible, and Hasidic texts, and in the works of Rainer Maria RILKE and Friedrich Hölderlin. They argue convincingly, to be sure, but they fail to explain the particular impact of Sachs's poetry. Her verse defies explanation because it appeals to universal feelings. She reached back beyond accidental moments in history into a human experience of ancient origins. Intuitively felt, her poems have a mystical, transcendental hue. Her God is, amidst the holocaust, not faith but presence, and her art the weapon to overcome fear and misery.

Other works include *Der magische Tänzer* (1959; The Magic Dancer); *Fahrt ins Staublose: die Gedichte der Nelly Sachs* (1961; Journey into Dustlessness: The Poems of Nelly Sachs); *Zeichen im Sand: Szenische Dichtungen der Nelly Sachs* (1962; Signs in Sand: The Poems of Nelly Sachs); and *Suche nach Lebenden: die Gedichte der Nelly Sachs,* second volume (1971; Search for the Living). Selected English translations include *O the Chimneys* (1967) and *The Seeker and Other Poems* (1970).

See: W. Berendsohn et al., eds., *Nelly Sachs zu Ehren* (1961); S. Spender, "Catastrophe and Redemption," *NYTBR,* (Oct. 8, 1967); J. B. Bauke, "Nelly Sachs, Poet of the Holocaust," *JH* (Spring 1968). A.P.O.

Sadoveanu, Mihail (1880–1961), Romanian novelist, was born in Paşcani, Moldavia, the son of a lawyer. His mother, who was a peasant, remained in his memory as a symbol of his ties with the common people. After graduating from the lyceum at Iaşi, Sadoveanu married and began working as a school inspector, a position he held until 1907. For nine years (1910–19), he was the director of the National Theater at Iaşi. He was elected to the National Academy in 1923.

A prolific author, Sadoveanu's works fill 120 volumes. He was also a masterful teller of tales, the social emphasis of which is strongest in his early works: in the novella *Crîsma lui Moş Precu* (1904; Old Man Precu's Tavern), he is concerned with the fate of the peasantry; in the story "Hoţul" (The Thief), a poor man, tired and sick, steals some wood from a forest but is caught and beaten by the landowner. Sadoveanu wrote much historical fiction, including such novels as *Soimii* (1904; The Soimar Lineage); *Povestiri din razboi* (1906; Eng. tr., *Tales of War,* 1962), which recounts the difficulties involved in freeing Romania from Turkish domination in 1877; and *Viaţa lui Stefan cel Mare* (1934; Life of Stefan the Great). While his major contribution lies in the emphasis he placed on the Romanian national spirit, Sadoveanu also possessed a prose style of an almost perfect lyric realism, as well as having a remarkable feeling for nature, in which he regarded animals, vegetables, and minerals as living in a kind of reciprocal relationship. *Nopţile de Sinzieni* (1934; June Nights) is the story of a forest destroyed through modern economic exploitation.

See: J. Steinberg, *Introduction to Romanian Literature* (1966), pp. 29–76; E. Luca, *Mihail Sadoveanu sau elogiul ratiunii* (1972). V.A.

Sagan, Françoise, pseud. of Françoise Quoirez (1935–), French novelist and playwright, was born in Cajarc. At the age of 19, after an indifferent and hectic school career, Sagan achieved instant international fame with her first novel, *Bonjour tristesse* (1954; Eng. tr., 1955), which she had written the year before. The book won the Critics Prize. Sagan's novels, including *Un Certain Sourire* (1956; Eng. tr., *A Certain Smile,* 1956), *Dans un mois, dans un an* (1957; Eng. tr., *Those without Shadows,* 1957), *Aimez-vous Brahms . . .* (1959; Do You Like Brahms . . .), *Les Merveilleux Nuages* (1961; Eng. tr., *Wonderful Clouds,* 1961), *La Chamade* (1965; Eng. tr., 1966), *Un Peu de soleil dans l'eau froide* (1968; Eng. trs., *A Few Hours of of Sunlight,* 1971, *Sunlight on Cold Water,* 1971), *Des bleus à l'âme* (1971; Eng. tr., *Scars on the Soul,* 1974), *La Garde du cœur* (1968; Eng. tr., *The Heart-Keeper,* 1968), and *Un Profil perdu* (1974; Eng. tr., *Lost Profile,* 1976), as well as her short stories, collected in *Des Yeux de soie* (1976; Eyes of Silk), have nearly all been best-sellers.

In her clear, flowing style, Sagan usually tells of sad little love affairs in an amoral society composed essentially of bored, lonely young women and young or middle-aged men, all of whom drive powerful, shiny cars. She paints a world of seemingly resigned desperation whose inhabitants cling to pleasure as to a life preserver. Sagan has also written plays, among them *Château en Suède* (1960; Château in Sweden), *Les Violons parfois* (1963; Violins Sometimes), *Bonheur, impair et passe* (1964; Happiness, Blunder and Pass), *Le Cheval évanoui* (1966; The Vanished Horse), and *Un Piano dans l'herbe* (1969; Piano in the Grass), in which she often shows a flair for vivid dialogue and a brilliant sense of the theatrical.

See: G. Mourgue, *Françoise Sagan* (1959).   D.Br.

Sagarra i Castellarnau, Josep Maria de (1894–1961), Catalan poet and playwright, was born in Barcelona of an aristocratic family, a descendent of one of the branches of the ancient *Comtes-Reis* (Count-Kings). After an elementary education from the Jesuits of Barcelona, he studied law at the university of that city. He never practiced that profession, devoting himself instead, from an early age and with extraordinary industry, to literature. His first verses were published when he was 12. At the age of 20 he published his *Primer llibre de poemes* (1914; First Book of Poems), followed by *El mal caçador* (1916; The Bad Hunter), *Cançons d'abril de novembre* (1918; April and November Songs), *Cançons de taverna i d'oblit* (1922; Songs of the Tavern and of Forgetfulness), *Cançons de rem i de vela* (1924; Songs of the Oar and the Sail), and *Cançons de totes les hores* (1925; Songs of All the Hours). In all this verse one feels the originality of Sagarra's style and spirit. It is easy to understand how he touched the sensibility of his compatriots. He uses a living language, direct and without pedantry, elevated through its grace to poetic inspiration. From the time of the "Renaixença" the Catalan reader had encountered little but archaisms and artifice whereas Sagarra, like Jacint VERDAGUER and Joan MARAGALL, found his poetic voice in the language of the people. His unique style is clearly discernible in his first novel, *Paulina Buxareu* (1919), and in *All i Salobre* (1929; Garlic and Salt), *Cafè copa i puro* (1929; Coffee, Liqueur and Cigar), and *Vida privada* (1932; Private Life), awarded the Crexells Prize of the Generalitat (1932). He had many imitators.

His first poetic plays, *Rondalla d'esparvers* (1918; Serenade of Blackbirds) and *Dijous Sant* (1919; Holy Thursday), were an indication of the ease with which he was to progress in the dramatic art. The tone of his dramatical poetry encouraged the renovation of the Catalan theater, which had turned away from verse. From *L'estudiant i la pubille* (1921; The Student and the Maid) to *Roserflorit* (1935; Rosebush in Bloom) he was a central and immensely popular figure in Catalan theater. Important theatrical works are: *Les veus de la terra* (1923; The Voices of the Soil); *Marçal Prior* (1926); *L'assassinat de lay senyora Abril* (1927, in prose; The Slaughter of Lady April); and *L'hostal de la glòria* (1931; The Inn of Glory), for which he received the Ignasi Iglesies prize of the Generalitat. These dramatic poems alternated with farces like *La Llucia i la Ramoneta* (Lucy and Little Raimona) and *Amàlia, Emèlia i Emilia* (1929). He also cultivated the tragic poem in *Judit* (1929; Judith) and *La filla del carmesí* (1930; The Crimson Daughter). As a result of his extraordinary facility and the overabundance of his plays, his theater became somewhat affected, with recurring types and analogous situations, although his plays are generally redeemed by the grace and originality of his vocabulary. The same eagerness to portray popular types endowed with the qualities of faith and love as well as the most diverse passions—exemplified already in *El mal caçador*—inspires his longest and most famous poem, *El Comte Arnau* (1928; Count Arnau). In spite of the monotony of some passages, in this work Sagarra attains real genius. His last book of poems, *La rosa de cristall* (The Crystal Rose), which he won the Folguera Prize of

the Generalitat, demonstrates the continuity of his poetic conception.

See: J. Folguera, *Les noves valores de la poesia catalona* (1919); C. Giardini, *Antologia dei poeti catalani contemporanei, 1845–1925* (1926).   J.M.M.iV.

Saint-Exupéry, Antoine de (1900–44), French aviator and writer, was born in Lyon into an old family; one of his ancestors had fought with the Americans at Yorktown. Saint-Exupéry's books show the clear traces of a solid humanistic education as well as the author's eagerness to analyze his inner life and to establish his own scale of ethical values. Drawn to a career of adventure, he flew as an airmail pilot in the early years of transoceanic aviation, narrowly escaping death several times. He served as a pilot in the first year of World War II and again in 1943–44 in North Africa. While on a reconnaissance mission over France in 1944, he was shot down.

Saint-Exupéry's very first volume, *Courrier Sud* (1929; Eng. tr., *Southern Mail,* 1933), revealed him as an acute analyst of the changes brought about in the relationship between man and woman by the abnegation required from an airman, but the plot was weak and the author's personality stifled that of his characters. The author was clearly not a novelist in the traditional sense. He proved more successful in *Vol de nuit* (1931; Eng. tr., *Night Flight,* 1932), reaching a tragic greatness in the depiction of man's unequal struggle against the elements and against the ordinary human affections. *Terre des hommes* (1939; Eng. tr., *Wind, Sand and Stars,* 1939) is a series of finely wrought, elaborately written vignettes interspersed with moral reflections; it vibrates with affection for one's fellow men and with love for the earth, seen from the air as frail and threatened. *Pilote de guerre* (1942; Eng. tr., *Flight to Arras,* 1942) is no less moving as an exploration of the flyer's mind as he accomplished a perilous and vain mission during the French defeat of 1940.

Saint-Exupéry increasingly became a poetical moralist. The reflections collected in the bulky, posthumously published *Citadelle* (1948; Eng. tr., *The Wisdom of the Sands*) are neither lucid nor profound and point to a strangely paternalistic political ideal. Saint-Exupéry was a better imaginative poet in prose than he was an abstract thinker. His most lasting and perennially young work is likely to remain *Le Petit Prince* (1943, Eng. tr., *The Little Prince,* 1943), one of the few classics of children's literature of the 20th century.

See: P. Chevrier, *Saint-Exupéry* (1950); L. Estang, *Saint-Exupéry par lui-même* (1956); C. François, *L'Esthétique de Saint-Exupéry* (1957).   H.P.

Saint-John Perse, pseud. of Alexis Saint-Leger Leger (1887–1975), French poet and diplomat, was born on an islet off Pointe-à-Pitre, Guadeloupe. The first 10 years of Leger's life were spent in and around Guadeloupe, where his family, chiefly of Burgundian ancestry, owned plantations. In this setting of lush vegetation and tropical seas, Alexis learned to swim, sail, and ride when still very young. In 1898 his family was obliged to move to metropolitan France, settling in the resort town of Pau, where Alexis attended the lycée and frequented the town's cosmopolitan society. After studies at the University of Bordeaux, he prepared for the competitive Foreign Service Examination, which he passed in 1914.

Leger began writing poetry very early, but prior to 1914 he published only the slim volume *Eloges* (1910; Eng. tr., *Eloges and Other Poems,* 1944), under the name "Saint-Léger Léger." The poems in *Eloges* celebrate the lost paradise of an Antillean boyhood. In form and idiom they are already wholly characteristic of his later work: devoid of traditional prosody (but strongly rhythmical), abundantly metaphorical, and almost hieratic, in tone. The unusual quality of these poems immediately struck Jacques RIVIÈRE, André GIDE, and Valery LARBAUD.

Throughout his diplomatic career (1914–40), Leger avoided any public participation in literary matters. In the early 1920s he attached the pen name "St.-J. Perse" (later expanded to "Saint-John Perse") to the few poems that did find their way into print. The most important of these was *Anabase* (1924; Eng. tr., *Anabasis*, 1930), which Leger composed during his diplomatic stint in China (1916–21). The poem is a radically compressed epic recited by a nomad leader who tells of an expedition into the fastnesses of Asia and of the human spirit. The narrative condensation, the elliptical imagery, and the poetic exploitation of technical terms combine to give *Anabase* great intensity. It was T. S. Eliot who prevailed upon Leger in 1930 to let him translate it, thus introducing Perse to the English-speaking world. *Amitié du prince* (1924; Eng. tr. in *Eloges and Other Poems*, 1944), although shorter than *Anabase*, is in no way inferior to it and is the only other major poem to survive from the diplomatic years. Manuscripts of at least five other long poems were confiscated and presumably destroyed by the Gestapo in June 1940.

In 1921, when Leger was a delegate at the Washington Conference on the Limitation of Armaments, he was singled out by the head of the French delegation, Aristide Briand. From then until Briand's death in 1932, Leger was one of the "Great Peacemaker"'s closest associates. In 1933, Leger was appointed Secretary General of the Ministry of Foreign Affairs, a post he held until forced out by Paul Reynaud in May 1940, shortly before the fall of France. Leger reached the United States in July 1940, remaining there in voluntary exile until long after the end of World War II. At the instigation of Archibald MacLeish, he accepted a modest, privately funded position as a consultant in the Library of Congress.

Shortly after his arrival in the United States, Leger resumed writing poetry. *Exil* (1942) was soon followed by three other major pieces (Eng. tr., *Exile and Other Poems*, 1949). These poems alternate between invective and elegy, singing of the universal exile that is man's lot and of the human ties that transcend that exile. *Vents* (1946; Eng. tr., *Winds*, 1953), a long, violent poem in which the discovery and exploitation of the New World constitute the culminating episode in the history of Western Man, is the climactic work of the first phase of Perse's "American" period. In *Vents*, Leger mentions an eventual return to France, and he finally did revisit his homeland in 1957, a few years later establishing residence there with his American wife. The poems that follow the crisis of *Vents*, those collected in *Amers* (1957; Eng. tr., *Seamarks*, 1958), *Chronique* (1960; Eng. tr., 1961), and *Oiseaux* (1962; Eng. tr., *Birds*, 1966), are once again *éloges* ("praises"), developing themes of reconciliation and acceptance. *Amers*, an elaborate ode to the sea, is Perse's longest published poem, and the section entitled "Etroits sont les vaisseaux . . ." ("Narrow are the vessels . . .") is one of the great erotic sequences of French literature.

Perse regarded the poetic experience as one of the most ancient and efficacious forms of confronting life's mysteries. The poet's aim is thus not to produce an imperishable artifact but, as he said in his Nobel Prize acceptance speech, "to live better." Perse was uncompromisingly pagan, and his identification with great natural forces makes one think of Walt Whitman, although nothing could be less Whitmanian than Perse's sense of hierarchy or his sustained aristocratic diction. Arthur RIMBAUD and the

early Paul CLAUDEL are often cited as his sources, but Perse's poetic realm is wholly his own.

Perse used to be the poet of a small international elite, but this is no longer true. In 1960 he was awarded the Nobel Prize for Literature. French editions of his works proliferated after that date, and in 1971 a parallel English-French edition of French *Collected Poems* appeared. The Pléiade edition of his *Œuvres complètes* (1972; Complete Works), which includes many prose pieces and hitherto unpublished letters, finally consecrated Saint-John Perse as one of the greatest poets of 20th-century France. His papers and library, along with other Perseana, are now permanently housed at the Fondation Saint-John Perse in the *hôtel de ville* of Aix-en-Provence.

See: A. J. Knodel, *Saint-John Perse: A Study of His Poetry* (1962); "Biographie," pp. ix–xlii, and "Notices et notes," pp. 1087–392, in Saint-John Perse, *Œuvres complètes* (1972). A.J.K.

Saint-Pol-Roux, pseud. of Paul-Pierre Roux (1861–1940), French poet, dramatist, and essayist, was born in Saint-Henry, near Marseille. Saint-Pol-Roux, frequently called "le Magnifique," began his literary career in Paris among the younger symbolists as a frequenter of Stéphane MALLARMÉ's Tuesday evening gatherings. He also participated in founding the review *La Pléiade*, and was one of the seven signers, along with Joséphin Péladan and five others, of the manifesto "la Rose-Croix esthétique" (Aesthetic Rosicrucianism). From 1898 until the end of his life, he resided in Brittany, principally in his manor of Coecilian, an eight-turreted Elsinor-like château he built at Camaret-sur-Mer. He published little, intending rather to entrust his complete works to posterity. Tragically, most of his unpublished manuscripts were destroyed by a marauding German soldier who also mortally wounded the poet.

Of the few works published during his lifetime, Saint-Pol-Roux's principal poetry is contained in *Les Reposoirs de la procession* (1893; The Repositories of the Procession), republished as three separate volumes: *La Rose et les épines du chemin* (1901; The Rose and the Thorns on the Way), *De la colombe au corbeau par le paon* (1904; From the Dove to the Raven through the Peacock), and *Les Féeries intérieures* (1907; Inner Enchantments). These three volumes, along with *Anciennetés* (1903; Antiquities), contain virtually all Saint-Pol-Roux's poetic output from the years 1885–1906. In these works, as in his most important dramatic work, *La Dame à la faulx* (1899; The Lady with the Scythe), Saint-Pol-Roux shows himself to be indeed a precursor of surrealism, as André BRETON called him, as well as one of the primary links with the themes and preoccupations of the symbolist school. His works, teeming with and celebrating life, usually present a profusion of images (some bordering on the preposterous) that are linked unrestrainedly, in a manner foreshadowing later surrealist imagery. Some texts enunciate; others attempt to illustrate his aesthetic system of "ideorealism": the poet must "magnify" reality, reuniting the elements of eternal Beauty dispersed throughout the universe and recreating spiritual reality, thereby renewing archetypical Divine thought.

Some of the manuscripts salvaged by his daughter in 1940 have recently been published. *Le Trésor de l'homme* (1970; Man's Treasure), *La Répoétique* (1971; Res poetica), *Cinéma vivant* (1972; Living Cinema), and *Vitesse* (1973; Speed) reveal Saint-Pol-Roux's deep faith in modern technology and the future, and his profound fascination with the phenomenon of poetic language and its application to all forms of art.

See: J.-L. Steinmetz, "Saint-Pol-Roux ou les dangers

de l'écriture," *AnBret* 73 (1966): 463–82; T. Briant, *Saint-Pol-Roux* (1971).   J.F.E.

Sait Faik (Abasıyanık), (1906–54), Turkish short-story writer, was born in the Anatolian town of Adapazarı. He never completed his graduate studies at universities in Istanbul, Lausanne, and Grenoble. Except for a few brief stints as a secondary school teacher, grain merchant, and court reporter, he never held any jobs. He lived on his inheritance from his father. Ten years after his death, his family house on Burgaz Island near Istanbul became the Sait Faik Museum. In addition to two short novels—*Medar-ı Maişet Motoru* (1944; Fishing Boat of Livelihood) and *Kayıp Aranıyor* (1953; Search for a Missing Person)—and a collection of poems, *Şimdi Sevişme Vakti* (1953; Now is the Time for Love), he published 13 collections of short stories, including *Semaver* (1936; The Samovar), *Lüzumsuz Adam* (1948; Unnecessary Man), *Havada Bulut* (1951; Cloud in the Sky), *Havuz Başı* (1952; By the Pond); *Son Kuşlar* (1952; Last Birds), and *Alemdağında Var bir Yılan* (1954; There's a Snake at Almedağ), among others.

Sait Faik's stories depict the fishermen, workers, clerks, children—in general, the common people—of Istanbul. Many of his principal characters are from the non-Muslim communities. The author often speaks in the first person and figures prominently in some of the stories as a persona. With a subtle style that, despite occasional complexities, was attuned to the simple natural rhythms of colloquial Turkish, Sait Faik portrayed the predicaments, maladjustments, and disillusionments of the average person, frequently himself, living on the fringes of society.

In 1953 the Mark Twain Society (United States) made him an honorary member. In Turkey the Sait Faik Prize, established in 1955, is a major award given each year to the best collection of short stories. French translations of Sait Faik's short stories were published in Leiden, Holland, under the title *Un point sur la carte* (1962) and in the United States as *A Dot on the Map* (1979).   T.S.H.

Salacrou, Armand (1900–), French playwright, was born in Rouen. He first worked as a journalist and became wealthy in pharmaceutical publicity, but he soon turned his talents to the theater. The first 10 years of his career as a dramatist may be represented by the sentiment of the student in Salacrou's *L'Inconnue d'Arras*: "I wish to be compromised with my own generation." Such was Salacrou's own desire. He made his debut with a one-act play, *Le Casseur d'assiettes* (1924; The Breaker of Dishes). *Tour à terre* (1925; Tour on Earth) proved disconcerting to the majority of critics, but was warmly defended by Aurélien LUGNÉ-POE and Henri Bidou; Pierre Brisson insisted on its "absolute originality in literature," thus managing to convey both high praise and severe criticism. *Le Pont de l'Europe* (1927; The Bridge of Europe) was no less heatedly discussed. It consists chiefly, with slight dramatic action, of a poem in which a king, reminiscent of Hamlet, expresses in eloquent monologues his dream of becoming "the world's passer-by." The principal character of *Patchouli* (1930) is another dreamer for whom love is something else than happiness. In this work, Salacrou gave unbounded liberty to his imagination, accepting no literary discipline and yet producing a play impressively lyrical and bitter.

Salacrou's sympathy for failures was again evident in *Atlas-Hôtel* (1931). "God himself has failed; all great enterprises fail"—such is the final speech of Auguste, the Don Quixote of the hotel business. *La Vie en rose* (1931; Life through Rose-Colored Glasses) was, as the author

himself admitted, nothing more than an excuse for songs, costumes, and setting, offered by one born at the beginning of the century who recalled prewar days through the eyes of his childhood. *Les Frénétiques* (1934) was a vigorous satire of the movie world and its conventional characters, although Salacrou himself did not entirely succeed in creating original figures. In *L'Inconnue d'Arras* (1935; The Unknown Woman of Arras) he took for his subject the few seconds granted a dying man to see his life pass before him and to evaluate its true worth. This creation, tender and fantastic, has earned Salacrou high rank among dramatists of his generation. His other successful plays include *Histoire de rire* (1941; Laughing Matter), *Les Fiancés du Havre* (1944), *Les Nuits de la colère* (1947; The Nights of Anger), and *Boulevard Durand* (1960).

See: P.-L. Mignon, *Armand Salacrou* (1960).   P.Br.

Salaverría e Ipinza, José María (1873–1940), Spanish essayist of Basque descent, was born in the Mediterranean coast town of Vinaroz. Although he wrote novels and shorter fiction, he is known almost solely as an essayist. The fundamental concerns of his work are similar to those of his better-known contemporaries, the Generation of 1898, arising from the analysis of the soul of the Spanish nation in the aftermath of the disastrous Spanish-American War, in terms of the dichotomies of will or apathy, isolationism or Europeanization, the glorious past or the uncertain future. Many of the essayists of the period proposed the transformation of Spain along the lines of European development. Salaverría, whose values were not unlike those of Ramiro de MAEZTU, advocated a return to the national traditions manifested in the heroic acts of the past. As a result, many of his books focus on Spain's heroes, the glorious achievers. Typical of these works are *Vieja España* (1907; Old Spain), *Las sombras de Loyola* (1911; Shadows of Loyola), *La afirmación española* (1917), *España: Pueblos y paisajes* (1936; Spain: Peoples and Landscapes), and *Retrato de Santa Teresa* (1939; Portrait of St. Theresa).

Salaverría was a great traveler and knew Spanish America very well. Its literature and heroes provided him with subjects, and some of his articles were published in Argentine newspapers. These studies express the familiar faith in the heritage of Spain, but now in a New World setting. They include *El poema de la Pampa* (1981), *Los conquistadores* (1918), *Bolívar el Libertador* (1930), and *Vida de Martín Fierro* (1934). Salaverría specialized in biographical portraits, dedicating a number of them, from his traditionalist perspective, to contemporary writers.

See: F. Caudet Roca, *Vida y obra de José María Salaverría* (1972).   H.L.B.

Šalda, František Xaver (1867–1937), Czech critic, poet, and novelist, is the most prominent literary critic in Czech literature. The son of a civil servant, he was born in Liberec in northern Bohemia. He studied law at the University of Prague, but became a free-lance writer and the editor of several critical journals. From 1916 on, he taught the history of Western literatures at the University of Prague. In 1928 he founded the journal *Šaldův zápisník* (Šalda's Notebook), which he filled himself, from cover to cover, until his death.

Šalda was a practical critic—a master of portraiture, psychological interpretation, stylistic analysis, and critical judgment—rather than the expounder of a systematic literary theory. During his long career, he frequently shifted his point of view and changed his allegiances, but there is continuity behind the baffling variety of his judgments. Šalda always advocated a vital, contemporary art:

in the 1890s this made him a champion of symbolism against naturalism and after World War I the godfather of "proletarian" poetry. He wanted a highly poetical, metaphorical poetry and disapproved of all purely naturalist or didactic writing. Yet, in spite of his stress on form and expression, Šalda was never an aesthete pure and simple; he always understood the artist's responsibility to society and, especially in his later life, saw literature as closely connected to religion and philosophy. His work increasingly became a general criticism of society and modern civilization, and in his last years his voice was widely listened to as that of a moralist and prophet. Šalda managed to combine a belief in the value of the individual and of individuality with a belief in the necessity for superpersonal values in literature. The scope of his changing interests can be suggested by noting that his critical studies include works on all the major figures of modern Czech literature and range over many other literatures as well. He wrote on Jean-Jacques Rousseau and Arthur RIMBAUD, on Gustave Flaubert and Emile ZOLA, on Dante Alighieri and William Shakespeare. He discussed such subjects as the immortality of a work of poetry and the relation of art and religion. He surveyed modern Czech literature several times and made and unmade the reputation of many Czech writers. In his criticism, Šalda used all types of approach, from careful analyses of style to synthetic and wide surveys of development, from fierce polemics to lyrical meditations. His works are written in a very personal literary style, in which the most diverse elements are combined; learned terminology can be found cheek by jowl with trivial colloquialisms, lyrical metaphors with drastic sarcasms. Collections of his criticism include *Boje o zítřek* (1905; Battles for Tomorrow); *Duše a dílo* (1913; Soul and Work), his best volume; *Juvenilie* (1925; Early Writings); *Mladé zápasy* (1934; Young Struggles); and *Časové a nadčasové* (1936; Matters Ephemeral and Eternal). Much of his best writing, however, is still scattered in pamphlets, buried in the files of short-lived periodicals and newspapers, or mixed with ephemeral polemics in the nine volumes of *Šaldův zápisník* (1928-37). The projected monumental edition of his complete writings, begun in 1947, remains unfinished, although it has succeeded in bringing together most of his early work.

Šalda was not content with being only a literary critic. For a time he was prominent in art criticism, largely as an early champion of French impressionism; his art criticism is collected in *Tajemství zraku* (1940; The Mystery of Sight). Šalda was also a creative writer of great ambitions. His poetry, symbolist in style, is preoccupied with problems of death; it sometimes compares with the best work of Antonín SOVA or Otokar BŘEZINA, the two Czech poets he admired most. His particular poetic quality is well represented in a collection of elegies, *Strom bolesti* (1920; The Tree of Pain), written at the death of the novelist Růžena SVOBODOVÁ, who was his intimate personal friend. Šalda's three attempts at drama were failures, and his long novel, *Loutky i dělníci boží* (1917; Puppets and Laborers of God), seems stilted and cerebral and is overloaded with discussion. The short stories collected in *Život ironický a jiné povídky* (1912; The Ironical Life and Other Stories) and *Dřevoryty staré i nové* (1935; Woodcuts Old and New), however, are fine, as is *Pokušení Pascalovo* (1928; Pascal's Temptation), a philosophical legend, half essay, half visionary story, which is particularly impressive.

See: A. Novák, *Zvony domova* (1916); R. I. Malý and F. Pujman, eds., *František Xaver Šaldovi k padesátinám* (1918); J. Hora, ed., *František Xaver Šaldovi k 22. prosinci 1932* (1932) O. Fischer, *Šaldovo češství* (1936); B. Lifka, ed., *Na pamět František Xaver Šaldy* (1939); J.

Mukařovský in *Kapitoly z české poetiky* (1948), I: 303-36: R. Wellek, "Modern Czech Literary Criticism and Literary Scholarship," in *Essays on Czech Literature* (1963), pp. 179-93; F. Vodička, ed., *František Xaver Šalda: 1867, 1937, 1967* (1968).   R.W.

Salinas, Pedro (1891-1951), Spanish poet of the Generation of 1927, was born and educated in Madrid. Like his lifelong friend Jorge GUILLÉN, he combined creative writing with a distinguished career as a scholar, critic, and teacher of literature. He was lecturer in Spanish at the Sorbonne and at Cambridge University and held the chair of Spanish literature at the University of Seville (1919-28). He founded the Contemporary Literature section of the government-sponsored Centro de Estudios Históricos and edited its journal, *Índice literario* (1932-36). In 1936, invited to teach at Wellesley College, he established residence in the United States, where he remained as an exile from the regime of Francisco Franco. From 1940 until his death, he held a chair at Johns Hopkins University while also lecturing at many other universities in North and South America and in Puerto Rico. For many summers he taught at the Middlebury Language School. He died of cancer in a Boston hospital in December 1951.

As a poet, Salinas followed the spiritual tendency of Juan Ramón JIMÉNEZ. Among the Spanish classics, his sensibility brought him close to the Neoplatonic poets, Garcilaso de la Vega, and the mystics. His relation to Luis de Góngora—to whom his generation rendered a special cult—was limited to a taste for *conceptismo* and word play, but he avoided the sensuous delights of Gongorism's descriptive imagery. His poetry is made of psychological subtleties, and his images are built upon concepts and ideas rather than on sensations. The world is for him a sort of formless life. The poet's task, and his greatest joy, consists of giving it order and sense. In his *Reality and the Poet in Spanish Poetry* (1940), published in English, a lucid critical work, Salinas said that "the poet places himself before reality . . . in order to create something else." All of Salinas's books, when seen in this light, present an extraordinary example of unity in the development of the central poetical idea that poetic intuition is a correlative force that brings a new vision to be shared by all as part of an ever richer collective consciousness and cultural tradition. In his early books—*Presagios* (1923; Presages), *Seguro azar* (1929; Steadfast Chance), and *Fábula y signo* (1931; Fable and Sign)—Salinas reveals a certain metaphysical anguish in the face of the deceitfulness of appearances. His themes, often taken from aspects of modern city life, always express a poetic eagerness to transform the external perception into a superior unchangeable reality from which the emotions of love and happiness are derived.

Salinas's best-known works are *La voz a ti debida* (1933; The Voice Owed to You) and *Razón de amor* (1936; Love's Reason), which contain love poetry judged by many to be among the best of the 20th century. The books can be viewed as collections of poems on the contradictory aspects of love or, taken together, as a cycle that recreates the lovers' private world: a biblical Eden first discovered, then lost, and finally regained when love is understood as an external force or a soul reincarnated in each new generation of lovers. The love theme is still present in *El contemplado* (1946; The Contemplated Sea), written in Puerto Rico. This long poem is a sustained dialogue with the sea as symbol of essential reality, eternal and complete in itself, yet constantly recreated in an endless dynamic cycle. *Confianza* (1954; Confidence) is a posthumous collection of nature poems in which Salinas restates his basic enthusiasm for life.

The most significant book written by Salinas in exile is *Todo más claro* (1949; All Things Made Clearer), in which he denounces the materialistic values of modern society. Its famous "Nocturno de los avisos" (Nocturn of the Signs) is a satirical description of New York's Times Square as symbolic of a dehumanized, valueless world. "Cero" (Zero), the long poem that ends the book, is a protest against war. Written in 1944, it has seemed to many an uncanny prophecy of the atomic destruction that took place a few months later. War protest is also the theme of Salinas's Orwellian novel, *La bomba increíble* (1950; The Incredible Bomb).

Salinas also wrote short stories, plays, critical editions, and seven volumes of essays and criticism. Among his best scholarly works are *Jorge Manrique, o tradición y originalidad* (1947), a penetrating essay on the medieval concept of literary tradition and creation, and *La poesía de Rubén Darío* (1948). *El defensor* (1948; The Defender) is made up of five essays on modern culture, in which Salinas denounces the contemporary fetishes of time, efficiency, and material success that have contributed to the individual's increasing isolation from his contemporaries, as well as to his estrangement from past generations. Salinas particularly criticizes man's growing indifference to the spoken and written word as one of the telling signs of a lessening of the spiritual quality of modern life.

An ample selection of Salinas's poems has been translated into English by Eleanor L. Turnbull, *Lost Angels and Other Poems* (1938), *Truth of Two* (1940), *Zero* (1947), with Spanish and English on opposite pages. Edith Helman and Norma Faber published a bilingual selection of his love poetry entitled *To Live in Pronouns* (1974), and the first volume of the love cycle was translated by Willis Barnstone as *My Voice Because of You* (1976, preface by Jorge Guillén).

See: A. de Zubizarreta, *Pedro Salinas, el diálogo creador* (1969); J. Crispin, *Pedro Salinas* (1974); D. L. Stixrude, *The Early Poetry of Pedro Salinas* (1975).

A. del R. rev. J.Cr.

Salmon, André (1881–1969), French poet, novelist, and art critic, was born in Paris, where he lived most of his life. Early in his career, he associated with such artists and writers as Guillaume APOLLINAIRE, Max JACOB, and Pablo Picasso, figures at the center of various modernist movements (such as cubism and art nouveau). While he never claimed to belong to any of these groups, Salmon's first collections of poetry show similar concerns; *Les Clés ardentes* (1905; The Burning Keys), *Féeries* (1907; Enchantments), and *Le Calumet* (1910) exhibit a tendency toward play and fancy that came to characterize his work.

Salmon apprehended a new relationship between reality and imagination: his poems slip back and forth between everyday life and the fantastic, between the exotic and the modern world. At the same time, he questions the function of poetry and the role of the poet in a technological society. *Prikaz* (1919), written after several trips to the USSR that profoundly changed his political orientation, is an epic poem on the Russian Revolution of 1917. In the same vein is *L'Age de l'humanité* (1922; The Age of Humanity), which depicts the postwar restlessness and shifting standards of his own generation. Both poems, written in a discursive style broken up by short tales, tableaux, and imaginary effusions, are attempts at the "acceptance" of reality "on an imaginary plane." *Le Livre et la bouteille* (1920; The Book and the Bottle) addresses itself to the same epistemological question: "Cabaret ou bibliothèque" (the cabaret or the library) are the choices facing the poet in his endeavor.

Salmon's novels, *Tendres Canailles* (1913; Sweet Scoundrels) and *La Négresse du Sacré-Coeur* (1920; Eng. tr., *The Black Venus*, 1929), fabricate a fantastic picture of bohemia intermingled with the underworld. His other prose works include a number of books on modern art: *L'Art vivant* (1921; Living Art), *Propos d'atelier* (1923; Studio Talk), *Cézanne* (1923), *André Derain* (1923), *Modigliani* (1926), *Henri Rousseau dit le douanier* (1927), and *Chagall* (1929). Later in his life, he produced a two-volume essay on the anarchist movement, *La Terreur noire: chronique du mouvement libertaire* (1959; The Black Terror: Chronicle of the Libertarian Movement). His most important prose work is his autobiography, *Souvenirs sans fin* (3 vols., 1955–56; Endless Memories), an enlightening and fascinating account of the personal, intellectual, political, and artistic aspects of a what has become known as modernism.

See: P. Berger, *André Salmon* (1956).   S.Lé.

Salom, Jaime (1925–), Spanish dramatist born in Barcelona, is the author of dramas of amorous conflict involving cultural and moral issues frequently set in a detective-story framework. The predominance of love and intrigue in his work might seem to place Salom with the light comedy writers, while his interest in social problems suggests an association with the realistic generation. Salom, however, belongs to neither group. His lighter works are too substantive for light comedy, and his serious plays not only lack the social and political commitment of the realistic generation, but his characters typically belong to the upper classes. In addition to love, Salom frequently turns to problems involving duty, God, religion, war, sin, guilt, innocence, hypocrisy, marriage, the generation gap, family conflicts, and the passage of time. Salom began his theatrical career with *El mensaje* (1955: The Message), a love triangle in the old style. *La casa de las chivas* (1969; Goats' House), one of the longest-running Spanish plays of the 20th century, established Salom as an important playwright. Based on an actual event of the Spanish Civil War, the work involves two young women, their father, and three soldiers in a struggle for survival in a house close to the front lines. In this atmosphere of extreme tension, elemental emotions explode. In a lighter vein, *El baúl de los disfraces* (1964; The Costume Trunk) explores the theme of appearance versus reality in dealing with the masks people wear. As in other works, the actors in *El baúl* shift roles within the play. In his highly successful *La piel de limón* (1976; The Skin of the Lemon), Salom uses this same technique to advantage as he makes an eloquent plea for the legalization of divorce in Spain. Other of his better-known plays are: *Los delfines* (1969; The Heirs Apparent), *La noche de los cien pájaros* (1972; The Night of the Hundred Birds), and *Tiempo de espadas* (1972; A Time for Swords). Although Salom has had approximately 25 plays performed in Madrid, the theater capital of Spain, he has not moved there. An eye specialist as well as a dramatist, he lives and practices medicine in Barcelona.

See: A. Marquerie, *Realidad y fantasía en el teatro de Jaime Salom* (1973); P. Z. Boring, *Jaime Salom* (1979).

P.W.O'C.

Samoylov, David Samuilovich, pseud. of David Samuilovich Kaufman (1920–), Russian poet, translator, and literary critic, was born in Moscow. He studied at the Institute of Philosophy, Literature, and History from 1938–1941 and then enlisted in the army. His first poems, about World War II, were published in 1941. One of Samoylov's major concerns is the generation of the 1940s; "Sorokovye, rokovye" (The Fatal Forties) is one of his most famous poems. Utilizing traditional forms and language, his works include both philosophical and love lyrics. The popular historical poem "Stikhi o Tsare Ivane" (A Poem about Tsar Ivan) deals with the death of Ivan the Terrible. His later collections include *Ravnodenstviye* (1972; Equinox) and *Volna i kamen* (1974; Wave and Stone). Samoylov has written a critical study of Russian rhyme, *Kniga o russkoy rifme* (1973; A Book on Russian Rhyme) and has planned a continuation. He is also well known as a translator from Polish, Czech, Hungarian, and the Asian languages of the USSR.

See: E. Sidorov, "Gluboko lichnaya prichastnost," *Znamya* 7 (1964): 243–44.							L.V.

Sánchez Ferlosio, Rafael (1927–), Spanish novelist, short-story writer, and essayist, was born in Rome. He studied philosophy and letters and is married to the novelist Carmen MARTÍN GAITE. Since publishing his widely acclaimed novel *El Jarama* he has devoted himself to the study of linguistics. Some of his essays have appeared in the book *Las semanas del jardín* (1974; The Weeks of the Garden).

His novel *Industrias y andanzas de Alfanhuí* (1951; The Labors and Fortunes of Alfanhuí) is a poetic narrative about the travels and inventions of a roguish young boy. Its rich and sober prose and the plasticity and lyric quality of its sensory imagery make this text a model of literary virtuosity. In contrast to the lyricism of *Alfanhuí, El Jarama* (1956; Eng. tr., *The One Day of the Week*, 1962) is the supreme monument to objectivism in post-Civil War narrative. It recounts the bored way in which a group of youngsters from Madrid spend a Sunday at the Jarama, a nearby river. The excursion ends with the drowning of one member of the group. With linguistic precision the narrator portrays the triviality of the people and the landscape. This faithful and detailed description is nevertheless permeated with poetic overtones. A master of the intricacies of the Spanish language, Sánchez Ferlosio produced an extremely influential work in this novel.

See: E. C. Riley, "Sobre el arte de Sánchez Ferlosio: Aspectos de *El Jarama*," *Filología* 9 (1963): 201–21; J. Ortega, "Tiempo y estructura en *El Jarama*," *CHA* 201 (1966): 801–08; D. Villanueva, *El Jarama de Sánchez Ferlosio, su estructura y significado* (1973).							J.O.

Sandel, Cora, pseud. of Sara Fabricius (1880–1974), Norwegian novelist, was born in Oslo. Between the ages of 12 and 25 she lived in Tromsø in northern Norway, an area that provides the cold, provincial background for much of her writing. As a young woman she studied painting and in 1905 she left Norway to continue her training as an artist in France. During the 15 years she spent there Sandel gave up her intention to become a painter and began her career as a writer, initially out of economic necessity, by contributing stories to Norwegian newspapers. Her marriage to the Swedish sculptor Anders Jönsson ended in divorce in 1926. After 1920, with the exception of a three-year stay in Norway, she lived in Sweden, where she raised her son.

Sandel's development as a writer came relatively late. Her first novel, *Alberte og Jacob* (1926; Eng. tr., *Alberta and Jacob*, 1962), won immediate acclaim. With its companion volumes, *Alberte og friheten* (1931; Eng. tr., *Alberta and Freedom*, 1963) and *Bare Alberte* (1939; Eng. tr., *Alberta Alone*, 1965), Sandel's place in 20th-century Norwegian literature was firmly established. The trilogy concerns Alberta's struggle to develop herself both as an artist and as a human being. The theme of a woman's quest for self-realization is central to Sandel's major

works. It is most succinctly portrayed in *Kranes konditori* (1945; Eng. tr., *Krane's Café,* 1968), a novel that, in its economy of language, unity of composition, and dramatic structure provides the best example of Sandel's stylistic excellence. *Kjøp ikke Dondi* (1958; Eng. tr., *The Leech*, 1960), also shows many of the same stylistic and thematic characteristics. Yet this work is a variation on her principal theme in that it portrays a woman whose efforts to free herself end in failure.

Between her novels, Sandel published a number of excellent short-story collections: *En blå sofa* (1927; A Blue Sofa), *Carmen og Naja* (1932), *Mange takk, doktor* (1935; Many Thanks, Doctor), *Dyr jeg har kjent* (1945; Animals I Have Known), *Figurer på mørk bunn* (1949; Figures on a Dark Background), *Vårt vanskelige liv* (1960; Our Difficult Life), and *Barnet som elsket veier* (1973; The Child Who Loved Roads).

See: O. Solumsmoen, *Cora Sandel* (1957; Å. Hiorth Lervik, *Menneske og miljø i Cora Sandels diktning* (1977).							A.G.A.

Sandemose, Aksel (1899–1965), Norwegian novelist, was born and raised in the small town of Nykøbing Mors, Denmark. He is noted chiefly for his profound analyses of the sources of violent, destructive, and irrational behavior in the individual. His approach was partly inspired by Freudian psychology and partly based on sociological analysis, which emphasizes the disastrous effects of conformity. Memories of his youth and childhood in a small town (which in some books he calls Jante) served as material for his description of the system of reciprocal repression within a social group, codified in what he called *Janteloven* (the Jante law), which has become a household term in Norway.

Sandemose's six books in Danish show little of what was to become his main theme, but are rather conventional action-filled fiction, reflecting the influence of the Danish author Johannes V. JENSEN as well as that of Jack London, among others. By the time he published his first volume of short stories, *Fortællinger fra Labrador* (1923; Stories from Labrador), Sandemose, despite his sparse education, had already acquired experience at jobs of many kinds, notably as a sailor and as a lumberjack in Newfoundland. He again visited China and the United States in 1927–28, this time as a newspaper correspondent. His last novel written in Danish, *Ross Dane* (1928), draws on material he collected in Scandinavian immigrant settlements in western Canada during those years.

Sandemose published his most important books after his emigration to Norway, the country of his mother, in 1930. They are written in brilliant Norwegian prose, almost without a trace of the author's Danish origin. *En sjømann går i land* (1931; A Sailor Disembarks) is the story of Espen Arnakke, a youth who jumps ship in Newfoundland, kills a man in Misery Harbor, and eventually becomes happy and prosperous on the Canadian prairie. The optimistic mood and happy ending of this novel, however, contrast sharply with the next book about Espen, the monumental *En flyktning krysser sitt spor* (1933; Eng. tr., *A Fugitive Crosses His Tracks,* 1936). Here the main character becomes the author's alter ego. The reader's knowledge of the murder in Misery Harbor is taken for granted, and the novel concentrates on the psychological and sociological conditions in Espen's past that made him a murderer, while also establishing the process of self-perception that finally liberates him from his guilt. The book has no chronology and no plot, and Sandemose insisted that it should not be called a novel. Nevertheless, although many details are autobiographical, the murder itself is fictitious—as far as we know. The style of this book was at the time a novelty in Scandinavian literature, its composition reflecting the Freudian principle of free association. A number of Sandemose's other novels from the 1930s also appear in unconventional, experimental forms. In *Vi pynter oss med horn* (1936; Eng. tr., *Horns for Our Adornment*, 1938), for example, the story of the North Atlantic crossing of the schooner *Fulton* and its crew becomes both myth and symbol through a collage of inserted essays, visions, newspaper clippings, and miniature tales. This book is the most eminent in a series of novels about sailors and sailing ships that includes *Mænd fra Atlanten* (1924; Men from the Atlantic); *Klabavtermanden* (1927), and its substantially rewritten Norwegian version, *Klabautermannen* (1932; The Hammer Man); and *Myteriet på barken Zuidersee* (1963; The Mutiny on the Bark *Zuidersee*).

In 1942, Sandemose escaped from the Gestapo to neutral Sweden. During his wartime Swedish exile, he wrote another of his major works, *Det svundne er en drøm* (1946; The Past Is a Dream), the principal character of which is another victim and prisoner of his past. Sexual frustrations and defeat have given the Norwegian-American John Torson a schizoid personality, rendering him capable of doing immense harm to others.

In subsequent years, Sandemose became increasingly preoccupied with the problem of jealousy, and *Varulven* (1958; Eng. tr., *The Werewolf*, 1966), a novel that for the first time brought him a large number of readers and financial success, is his final effort at a comprehensive treatment of this theme in fiction. Works of nonfiction and semifiction are an important part of Sandemose's writing, and his essays and epistles on virtually every aspect of human life number more than 1,000. Some of them appeared in the 13 volumes of his one-man periodical *Årstidene* (1951–55).

See: C. E. Nordberg, *Sandemose* (1967); F. Johansen and J. Væth, *Aksel Sandemose og Skandinavien* (1969); N. B. Wamberg, ed., *Sandemoses ansigter* (1969); J. Væth, ed., *Om Sandemose* (1974).   A.L.

Sanguineti, Edoardo (1930–), Italian critic, poet, novelist, and essayist, was born in Genoa. He earned his doctorate at the University of Turin with a dissertation on Dante. Sanguineti is an outstanding figure among the generation of Italian writers that expressed itself most pugnaciously and polemically through the so-called *neo-avanguardia* and "Gruppo '63" (*see* ITALIAN LITERATURE). By 1963, when Sanguineti became the leader of the literary revolt, he was already well known in and outside Italy, having worked along with painters and musicians and having figured in the anthology *I Novissimi: poesie per gli anni '60* (1961).

Sanguineti has written four books of poetry: *Laborintus* (1956), *Erotopaegnia* (1959), *Purgatorio de l'Inferno* (1963; Purgatory of Hell), and *Wirrwarr* (1972), a book of collected poems and brief theoretical essays entitled *K e altre cose* (1962; K and Other Things); seven books of critical essays on aspects of Italian literature from Dante to Alberto MORAVIA; and two books of narrative fiction, *Capriccio italiano* (1963) and *Il giuoco dell'oca* (1967; The Goose Game). He has also edited an anthology, *Poesia del Novecento* (1969; 20th-Century Poetry). Several of his works have been translated into French, German, Spanish, and other languages.

Sanguineti's essays consistently shed light on his creative works in relation to his central preoccupation with the link between language and ideology and with the basic function of language not as a literary contrivance but as a medium that must be rebuilt upon present historical

exigencies and new standards of value. In his first three volumes of poetry, Sanguineti moves within the realm of a fragmented and hostile reality; if his language is often willfully "obscure," his rational and conceptual meanings are essentially clear, as they are in his numerous essays, especially in *Ideologia e linguaggio* (1965; 1970, 2d ed.; Ideology and Language). In his two works of narrative fiction, Sanguineti breaks away from the tyranny of rational consciousness in yet another attempt to resuscitate the medium of prose through a lucid and calculated subversion of structural and stylistic techniques. Yet in both novels, the overlay of meanings never hides the solid structure or ultimate adherence to a more real reality.

At this point, it may appear that Sanguineti's achievement as a critic is more definitive than his work as a creative writer. On the other hand, his writing, regardless of form, is always a "creative" effort, both structurally and functionally.

See: T. Wlassics, in *Letteratura italiana: i contemporanei*, vol. 6 (1974), pp. 1917–57.   P.Fr.

Santareno, Bernardo, pseud. of António Martinho do Rosário (1924–), Portuguese playwright, was born in Santarém, Portugal, from which he derived his pen name. In 1950 he obtained a medical degree from the University of Coimbra and went to Lisbon to practice. Although he became the best-known dramatist of contemporary Portuguese letters, he, like almost every Portuguese author, began by writing poetry. Since 1957, when he published his first volume of plays—*A promessa* (The Promise), *O bailarino* (The Dancer) and *A excomungada* (The Excommunicated Woman)—he has devoted himself to the theater, with the exception of *Nos mares do fim do mundo* (1959; On Distant Seas), a physician's poetic diary of a journey to Newfoundland and Greenland with the Portuguese fishing fleet. The dominant themes in Santareno's plays are violence, innocence and guilt, human suffering, and tyrannical sex. Sex is a constant in his dramas—incest in *António Marinheiro, ou O Edipo de Alfama* (1960; Sailor António, or the Alfama Oedipus) and homosexuality in *A traição do padre Martinho* (1969; Father Martin's Betrayal). His choice of symbols and situations indicates an influence by Freud.

Santareno's theater is also characterized by local color. His most successful plays present farmers and fishermen as their central characters in an atmosphere of cosmic violence and sinister events. He often introduces a youth whose role it is to foresee the catastrophe and redeem others through self-sacrifice. His women excel in human courage, in demonic powers, or, sometimes, in monstrous malice. Unlike some of his more audacious peers, Santareno usually prefers traditional dramatic devices. Aware that censorship would prevent performance of most of his plays on the stage, he wrote *Os anjos e o sangue* (1961; Angels and Blood) for television. In 1966, *O Judeu* (The Jew) appeared, a long documentary play denouncing the tyranny of his time while seeming to expose the abuses of the Inquisition in 18th-century Portugal. Immediately after the April 1974 coup, Santareno had *Escritor e português, 45 anos de idade* (Writer and Portuguese, Age 45) produced in Lisbon, a frontal attack against those who had oppressed Portugal for 48 years. Four more plays, "Restos" (Remnants), "A confissão" (The Confession), "Monsanto," "Vidabreve em três fotografias" (Life's Brevity in Three Snapshots), were included in *Os marginais e a revolução* (1979; Marginal Lives and Revolution).

See: F. Mendonça, *Para o estudo do teatro em Portugal, 1946–1966* (1971), pp. 54–83.   A.A.C.

Saporta, Marc, pseud. of Marcel Saporta (1923–), French jurist, novelist, and literary critic, was born in Constantinople to a Jewish family originally from Salonika. He had a brief and rapid career as a jurist specializing in international law, in the course of which he published *La Convention universelle de l'Unesco* (1952; UNESCO's Universal Copyright Convention) and, in collaboration with Jacques Lacombe, *Les Lois de l'air* (1953; Aviation Laws). Saporta then devoted himself to American studies with *Le Tour des Etats-Unis en 80 jours* (1958; Tour of the United States in 80 Days), distinguished from other travel books by the precision of his observations and his ability to synthesize. This work was a prelude to his monumental study of American culture, written in collaboration with Georges Soria, entitled *Le Grand Défi U.S.A.-U.R.S.S.* (1967–68: The Great Challenge U.S.A.-USSR). His other essays are more specialized: *Histoire du roman américain* (1970; History of the American Novel), which includes the best study of Edgar Allan Poe and Herman Melville and their contribution to the French *nouveau roman* ("new novel"; *see* FRENCH LITERATURE); *La Vie quotidienne contemporaine aux Etats-Unis* (1952: Contemporary Daily Life in the United States), written in the second person so as to involve the reader in the text; and *Go West* (1976), the account of a trip across the United States, illustrated with photographs by Bernard Plossu.

During a long hiatus in his judicial publications, from 1959 to 1964, Saporta engaged in intensive literary activity, writing novels on the fringe of the experiments of the *nouveau roman* and proposing to literary critics several structural problems that are far from solution at the present time. *Le Furet* (1959; Hunt the Slipper) does not stray far from the so-called *école du regard* (school of the observer), in which objects are treated as characters and influence events, but in *La Quête* (1961; The Search), the novelty consists of the presence of two narrators animating the plot. The molecular motion sketched by the two characters in their peregrinations, one in search of the other, already anticipates Julio Cortázar's experiments in this area. That same year, Saporta published *La Distribution* (1961; The Distribution), which has the distinction of being the first novel written in the future. Although that tense is never used, "futurity" arises from the connections among the author, the characters, and the reader; it becomes an indispensable element in this checker game in which everything is related and comes to life as one advances in the reading of the play "La Pinède" (The Pine Forest), whose outlines form the subject of the novel itself. With *Composition n. I* (1962; Eng. tr., *Composition n. I*, 1963), Saporta introduced into literature, under the inspiration of Alexander Calder, the concept of mobility, an idea of which Stéphane MALLARMÉ had already conceived. This novel, composed of 149 detached sheets, unnumbered and printed only on the front, is made available in a box and is to be shuffled like a game of cards. The combinations for reading are almost infinite. But it is with *Les Invités* (1964; The Guests) that Saporta has given us his most mature and solid work in respect to the dimension and complexity of the characters. Most of the narrative resources already used by him previously, as well as the techniques that he owes to his predecessors (a debt that he readily acknowledges)—Melville, James Joyce, e. e. cummings, Marcel PROUST, John Dos Passos, William Faulkner and Fyodor DOSTOYEVSKY—make this his most dense and most ambitious novel. His metaphysical trajectory is of equal importance to his narrative itinerary and his formalist concerns harmonize extraordinarily well with his existentialist preoccupations. With this novel, Saporta frees himself from the purely experimental progression of the *nouveau roman* and demonstrates that he has not only an original way of telling the story but also something to say.

See: R. Grimm, "Marc Saporta: The Novel as Card Game," in *ConL* 19, no. 3 (Fall 1978): 280–99; S. Spencer, *Space, Time and Structure in the Modern Novel* (1971); L. S. Roudiez, "Marc Saporta," in *French Fiction Today* (1972), pp. 259–77.   P.F.

Sarment, Jean, pseud. of Jean Bellemère (1897–), French actor, poet, novelist, and dramatist, was born in Nantes. A member of Jacques COPEAU's company in America (1917), Sarment was first acclaimed after Aurélien LUGNÉ-POE produced his *La Couronne de carton* (1920; The Cardboard Crown). This play deals with Musset-like romantics who, even though dissatisfied with their lives, are ill-equipped to shape their own destinies.

Influenced by Sigmund Freud, Sarment's earlier plays show touches of real comic technique and sensitivity to human frailty. His later works, however, become more conformist and mark a tendency toward vaudeville and light comedy. One of his best-known plays is *Le Pêcheur d'ombre* (1921; Shade Fisherman), in which a youth bent on suicide over an unrequited love affair is restored to sanity by the woman he loves. Yet he eventually becomes disillusioned and kills himself, convinced that all forms of love are meaningless shadows. *Les plus beaux yeux du monde* (1925; The Most Beautiful Eyes in the World), another well-known play, concerns a triangle in which two young men vie for the love of a blind girl.

Sarment wrote more than 20 plays in prose and in verse and acted in them as well. They were produced at the Comédie-Française and the Odéon as well as in many other European theaters.   E.D.C. and J.M.L.

Sarraute, Nathalie (1905–), French novelist, essayist, and playwright, was born in Ivanovo-Voznesensk, Russia, of Jewish parents with liberal and intellectual propensities. After their divorce, her childhood was spent partly in Russia and Switzerland, but mostly in Paris, where she studied at the Lycée Fénelon and grew up among émigrés of prerevolutionary Russia. After World War I, she studied English at the Sorbonne, history at Oxford, and sociology at the University of Berlin. She then graduated from the Paris Law School and practiced law for about 12 years. By this time, she had married Raymond Sarraute, a lawyer like herself, and had become the mother of three daughters. She had just published *Tropismes* (1938; Eng. tr., *Tropisms*, 1963)—the initial sketches of which dated back to 1932—and begun *Portrait d'un inconnu* (1948; Eng. tr., *Portrait of a Man Unknown*, 1958) when the war forced her into hiding for several years. Her literary career proper started only after World War II when *Portrait* was published with a preface by Jean-Paul SARTRE. Because of her unusual writing style, recognition came slowly to Sarraute. Her literary fame continued to grow, however, both in France and abroad. She has traveled widely throughout the world and has visited the United States several times. Her other published works include the novels *Martereau* (1953; Eng. tr., 1959), *Le Planétarium* (1959; Eng. tr., *The Planetarium*, 1960), *Les Fruits d'or* (1953; Eng. tr., *The Golden Fruits*, 1964), *Entre la vie et la mort* (1968; Between Life and Death), and *Vous les entendez?* (1972; Eng. tr., *Do You Hear Them*, 1973); a volume of literary criticism, *L'Ere du soupçon* (1956; Eng. tr., *The Age of Suspicion*, 1963); and such plays as *Le Silence, le mensonge* (1967; Eng. tr., *Silence and The Lie*, 1969) and *Isma* (1970).

Although Sarraute is a frequent reader of Russian, French, and English psychological novelists—especially

Fyodor DOSTOYEVSKY, Gustave Flaubert, Marcel PROUST, and Virginia Woolf—her own work does not follow this tradition. She is regarded as the initiator of the French "new novel" (*see* FRENCH LITERATURE) because of her consistent rejection of plots, characters, descriptions, and psychological analysis. She draws her subjects from her "sensations" of people and events, as well as from the stylistic adventures entailed in the rendering of these sensations. All realistic or didactic elements are eliminated, since the substance of the novel, according to Sarraute, should not be what things are but what they feel like. This presupposes an observer (as in *Tropismes*) who subsequently becomes a narrator (himself observed by the author); indeed, from *Planétarium* onwards, each character acts in turn as observer and observed in relation to all others or to a multiform anonymous "they." This mosaic of viewpoints opens up new possibilities of "micropsychology."

While focusing on the subliminal, Sarraute discovered "tropisms"—incessant psychic movements as inconspicuous as those of plants. Tropisms differ from motivations, even unconscious ones, in that they do not require the existence of a structure ego, however rudimentary and unreflective, but rather suggest some undifferentiated, sensitive substance at the roots of the psyche in which characters, reader, and, supposedly, the author-narrator are abolished as persons. In such a psychological environment, any kind of objective reality becomes questionable. The only language appropriate to render this new experience is one that substitutes the immediacy of images for the conceptual vocabulary of descriptive psychology. Conceptualizing these matters would betray on insidious will to immobilize tropisms into reassuring social stereotypes, themselves aesthetically and intellectually stultifying. While the image is the spontaneous rendering of elementary psychic motions, images do not simply flash here and there as discrete phenomena; instead, they tend to cluster and, when sustained by a strong emotion, to organize themselves into minute dramas. This wide variety of images and dramatic motions—ranging from spring cleaning to visions of shipwrecks or raging flames—is the most evident characteristics of Sarraute's style.

Another identifying feature of Sarraute's style is the use of "sous-conversations" (subconversations), the incipient transformations of images into words as suggested by interrupted sentences. Here lurks the double danger of losing one's grip on the sensation or seeing it congeal into dead words. The process must be stopped at the precise point where the words, "propelled" by the sensation, are on their way to grammatical structuration while still retaining the ability to disrupt it. In a remarkable chapter of *Entre la vie et la mort*, Sarraute has attempted to render the actual process of creation, pinpointing the moment when the still formless sensation is about to crystallize into images and words.

See: L. Janvier, *Une Parole exigeante* (1964), pp. 65–87; Y. Belaval and M. Cranaki, *Nathalie Sarraute* (1965); H. Peyre, *French Novelists of Today* (1967), pp. 363–68; L. Roudiez, *French Fiction Today* (1972), pp. 28–54. M. Tison-Braun, *Nathalie Sarraute ou la recherche de l'authenticité* (1971).   M.Br.

Sarrazin, Albertine (1937–67), French writer, was born in Algeria. An outlaw, a thief, and a prostitute, Sarrazin was the product of foster homes, reform school, and prison, but she was also a brilliant student and a vivid, sensitive writer. *L'Astragale* (1965; Eng. tr., *Astragal*, 1968) is the story of her escape from jail and of the man who helped her, Julien Sarrazin, whom she later married. *La Cavale*

(1965; Eng. tr., *The Runaway*, 1968) continues the story. Her diaries, notes, and letters were published under the title *Le Passe-peine* (1976; Passing through Punishment).

See: J. Duranteau, *Albertine Sarrazin* (1975).   D.Br.

Sartre, Jean-Paul (1905–80), French novelist, playwright, philosopher, essayist, literary critic, and political activist, was born in Paris. He saw himself primarily as a creative writer, since "logical discourse is only a way to understand one's intuition." Yet one can best elucidate the widening spirals of Sartre's work from the vantage point of his philosophical development, for it is especially here that the originality of his coherent, encyclopedic undertaking is to be found.

As a child in his grandfather's house, Sartre experienced both his contingency (a lack of any reason for being) and the adults' refusal to recognize their own, a hypocrisy he was later to call their "spirit of seriousness." In adolescent writings (a short story and a fragment of a novel), he derided them bitterly: he must have felt that they were free to do otherwise.

Sartre first attempted to define this freedom during his years at the Ecole Normale Supérieure, an inquiry that later led to the publication of four monographs on phenomenological psychology (1936–40). In Edmund Husserl's phenomenology, he had found what he was seeking: a validation of the "lived-world" (the prescientific, preconceptual world of spontaneous experience) that allowed him to turn his back on the traditional epistemological enterprise while giving full weight to the literary one. Literature, in its prereflexive perception and intuition is disclosure, as is praxis in the social arena in the later Sartre. Sartre's point of departure remained Cartesian, the subjectivity of the *cogito*, but he now recognized two levels to consciousness: the level of the prereflexive consciousness, which is the spontaneous perception of the world, and that of the reflexive consciousness, which is at a distance from the world. In the latter, Sartre saw one of the structures of man's freedom; the other is imagination, which can summon up the past or envision a nonexistent future. And in *Nausea*, he found that ontologically man is free since in his contingency he alone can give meaning to his life.

Armed with this phenomenology, Sartre could by 1943 enlarge his scope to develop an ontology in *L'Etre et le néant* (Eng. tr., *Being and Nothingness*, 1956). In Sartre's view, consciousness, a Nothingness without substance, reflects—or reflects on—Being. Amid the infinite variety of the human endeavor, Sartre discerned a common denominator in the "project," an original choice that man in his freedom makes of himself. Man's project may lead him, in "authenticity," to tear himself away from his "situations"—his hereditary, historical, sociological, or psychological conditioning—or, in "bad faith," to accept it as determining him. *Le Mur* (1938; Eng. tr., *The Wall and Other Stories*, 1948) depicts episodes in which most people act in bad faith. In *La Nausée* (1938; Eng. tr., *Nausea*, 1949), which has remained his major novel, Sartre describes the profound crisis of Antoine Roquentin, a man who comes to realize that he ought to change his fundamental project. Roquentin is overwhelmed by the stubborn being of things, their "facticity," while "nothing, absolutely nothing, can justify his existence," certainly not his dissertation on a historical figure nor the desperate, unsuccessful attempt by his friend Anny to make an art of life. At the end of *La Nausée*, Roquentin envisions a possibility: could he not give some meaning to his life by writing a book against the pretentious spirit of seriousness of his small-town middle class? This effort could function much in the same way as a certain recurring jazz melody has expressed the forlornness (contingency) of the downtrodden. The play *Huis clos* (1944; Eng. tr., *No Exit,* 1948) powerfully enacts the importance that one's relationship to "the other" has in determining the opinion each one forms of himself. Others can be "hell" for the person who does not break out of the pattern of bad acts by deciding on a fresh departure.

As a soldier and prisoner of war, Sartre came to see that man was caught up in history, a fact with which he tried to come to terms in his political activity (he joined the Resistance and founded the group "Socialism and Freedom") and in his extensive writing between 1940 and 1960, notably his "theater of situations." *Les Mouches* (1943; Eng. tr., *The Flies,* 1948), played before the eyes of the Nazi occupiers in the deceptive trappings of classical antiquity, depicts an Orestes acting to free Argos, while Electra wavers, a prisoner of her past. *Les Mains sales* (1948; Eng. tr., *Dirty Hands,* 1949) deals with the problem of Communists, ruthless and Moscow-oriented, and of the compromises necessary in politics. Another play, *Le Diable et le bon dieu* (1951; Eng. tr., *The Devil and the Good Lord,* 1960), dramatizes the agony of a military leader who, in the absence of God, must give direction to his own actions. Finally, after a number of other plays, *Les Séquestrés d'Altona* (1960; Eng. tr., *The Condemned of Altona,* 1961) vividly relives Nazi culpability at the time of the French war in Algeria. In an earlier, three-volume novel, *Les Chemins de la liberté* (1945–47; Eng. tr., *The Roads to Freedom,* 1947–50), a Professor Matthieu seeks the way to a meaningful commitment.

"Every novelistic technique reveals a metaphysics," Sartre said. And Sartre's own writings, in their reflection of existential concerns and freedom, are not lacking in originality. The temporality in his fiction is a perpetual present, carrying forward the past but open to an ever-present future. Usually, the author disappears behind the various subjective and autonomous points of view of the characters, yet sometimes a certain irony of situation reveals Sartre's position. His acid prose provokes the reader to an awareness that should lead him to conscious commitment ("to know is to be responsible").

Sartre explained man through history by founding a Marxist anthropology in the *Critique de la raison dialectique* (1960; Eng. tr., *Critique of Dialectical Reason,* 1976). He then turned his efforts to rendering a historical period intelligible through the descent into the "lived world" of one individual. As early as *Baudelaire* (1947; Eng. tr., 1950), Sartre had begun what might be called a new genre, that of existentialist biography. In this work he showed a man who suffered for being too lucid to believe in his self-deception, but who was capable of transferring his profound intuitions into incomparable poetry. A second, far more complex biography, *Saint Genet: comédien et martyr* (1952; Eng. tr., *Saint Genet: Actor and Martyr,* 1963), combined sociological and psychoanalytical analyses and dealt with a criminal outcast working at his own metamorphoses. Through his novels, rites reenacting his "passion," Jean GENET gained the distance necessary for a liberation from his past. It was, however, in *L'Idiot de la famille: Gustave Flaubert de 1821 à 1857* (3 vols., 1971–72; The Family Idiot: Gustave Flaubert from 1821 to 1857), that Sartre most fully developed the genre of existentialist biography and provided a model for existentialist anthropology as well. This work may well come to be known as Sartre's summa, since it integrates the theories that he had developed as psychologist, philosopher, anthropologist, and literary critic within the life of one single individual. It is through Sartre's "empathy" with Flaubert's almost everyday evolution that these cat-

egories become concrete and intelligible in a "true novel." Sartre, still opposed to any determinist psychology, replaced Freud's concept of the subconscious by that of "comprehension," which he defined as "a silent accompaniment of what is lived, a familiarity of the subjective attitude with itself . . . but without explication . . . an obscure awareness . . . [that is] prereflexive." Following the heuristic method of research he developed in the *Critique,* Sartre traces Flaubert's "totalization," that is, his movement towards a unification of his intimate experience and his way of living contemporary history through a series of internalizations, later exteriorized in his attitudes, correspondence, and writing. Sartre makes progressive-synthetic probes, constantly checked in reverse by retrogressive-analytic ones, until a complex but coherent pattern emerges, spanning the achievement of Flaubert's life up to 1857, from his original project to his "totalization" in *Madame Bovary.* The evolution of Flaubert's concept of the artist and his writings up to *Madame Bovary* are explicated in their interrelation with his life and his times, leading to an understanding of a man believed impossible hitherto.

Sartre's ontology of freedom required an ethics of commitment but, being existentialist, it could not be normative. Thus the promised second volume of *L'Etre et le néant* and the fourth of *Les Chemins de la liberté* were never written. Throughout Sartre's vast output—not only in creative writing and philosophy but also in literary criticism, in essays on art, music, and the social scene, and in his outright political interventions such as *Qu'est-ce que la littérature?* (1948; Eng. tr., *What Is Literature?,* 1949), the collection of essays in *Situations I–X* (1947–76), *On a raison de se révolter* (1974; One Has the Right to Revolt), and his own journal *Les Temps modernes* (1945–)—one recognizes what was fundamental to his many-sided undertaking: a minimizing of the utilitarian aspect in human relations.

In a harsh, ironic reminiscence of his childhood, *Les Mots* (1964; Eng. tr., *The Words,* 1964), Sartre broke with his original motivations, a belief in some kind of "mandate" and his hope in "salvation" through literature. But he came to accept that literature gives to any "traveler without a ticket" his own image and a "sense of his life," an awareness that is an appeal to commitment.

In 1964, Sartre refused the Nobel Prize for Literature, resisting "recuperation by the establishment." His last years were marred by near blindness. He stopped writing but continued to express his thoughts in interviews, wherein he wished to complete his work. He now saw ethics as an exigence arising in consciousness as it relates to the other; violence erupts when "fraternity" is breached. *Les Ecrits de Sartre* (1970; Eng. tr., *The Writings of Jean-Paul Sartre,* 2 vols., 1974) provides an annotated bibliography as well as a selection of fragments and interviews.

See: R. D. Cumming, *The Philosophy of Jean-Paul Sartre* (1972); B. Suhl, *Jean-Paul Sartre: The Philosopher as a Literary Critic* (1973); B. T. Rahv, *From Sartre to the New Novel* (1974). B.Su.

Sarvig, Ole (1921–), Danish poet and novelist, was born in Copenhagen. An art critic as well, he traveled in Europe from 1947 to 1950 and lived in Spain from 1954 to 1962. Sarvig's cycle of poems in five volumes, the most important being *Grønne Digte* (1943; Green Poems), *Jeghuset* (1944; The House of Self), and *Menneske* (1948; Man), may be regarded as the major Danish lyrical achievement of the 1940s (*see* DANISH LITERATURE). Using modern, metaphoric language related to abstract art, Sarvig created a carefully composed description of modern man at a cultural and historical turning point. His poems seek an answer to this crisis. The central texts of *Grønne Digte* present a coherent metaphysics of history. The tone is often surprisingly harmonious and contrasts sharply with the atmosphere of crisis in *Jeghuset,* in which the big city is discovered as the scene where the destiny of modern man is completed. The feeling of desperation is overcome in *Menneske,* where the conclusive motifs are the awareness of God and the love between man and woman.

Until his first novel in 1955, Sarvig's writing evolved around the same theme: human beings and their time. His novels are a farewell to something abandoned and destroyed, which must be analyzed in order that humanity may rise above the ruins. *Stenrosen* (1955; The Rose of Stone) is set in Berlin, a city that, as a symptom of demonic modernism, was destroyed but is rebuilt in the old spirit. *De Sovende* (1958; The Sleepers) and *Havet under mit Vindue* (1960; The Sea beneath My Window) are composed as detective novels whose traditional mystery is combined with the identity motif; that is, to solve the crime is equivalent to acknowledging the power of evil and destruction and finding the way to a new life. In *Limbo* (1963) the lyrical element breaks through at the expense of a more traditional novel structure. The book is a description of the waiting human being, of a woman and her dead husband's continued life in her soul. Normal time sequence is broken, thereby transforming the novel, into a vision of eternal love. Criminal elements, although completely devoid of metaphysical aspects, are again found in the novel *Glem ikke* (1972; Do Not Forget), a burlesque satire on Denmark. *Glem ikke,* however, is completely overshadowed by *De Rejsende* (1978; The Travelers), Sarvig's most significant prose work, which on one level relates a middle-aged Danish-American's attempts to settle accounts with his childhood myths but in truth deals with the problem of finding oneself, one's identity in today's world. This is a basic motif in Sarvig's writings, one that he also treats in *Forstadsdigte* (1974; Suburban Poems), a retrospective cycle, denoting a return to his artistic point of departure: the cultural crisis, described in images of city life, which is overcome through a mystical experience of Christ and love.

See: C. M. F. Jørgensen, *Ole Sarvig's lyrik* (1971); S. H. Rossel, "Crisis and Redemption: An Introduction to Danish Writer Ole Sarvig," *WLT* 53, no. 4 (1979).

S.H.R.

Sastre, Alfonso (1926–), Spanish playwright, critic, novelist, poet, and translator, was born in Madrid and received his university education in the capital and in Murcia. In 1945, Sastre and several other aspiring playwrights founded "Arte Nuevo," an experimental theater group designed to revitalize the stagnant national theater. Included in this innovating vein are his dramas *Uranio 235* (1946), *Cargamento de sueños* (1946; Cargo of Dreams), *Ha sonado la muerte* (1946; Death Has Sounded), and *Comedia sonámbula* (1947; Sleepwalking Comedy). The recurrent theme of these plays is man's frustration in the face of social evils. Sastre became the first theater editor of *La Hora* (1948–50), and this activity led to the founding in 1950 of "Teatro de Agitación Social." Censorship doomed this project, however, and, with José María de Quinto, Sastre issued a manifesto proposing the formation of the "Grupo de Teatro Realista."

Sastre's fight for artistic freedom, as well as the social denunciation in his plays, invited opposition from the censor, with the result that very few of his plays were performed. His first success as a playwright was with the production of *Escuadra hacia la muerte* (1953; Eng. tr.,

Condemned Squad, 1964), although the play was closed by military authorities after its third performance. In this work the characters are caught in a conflict between authority and liberty created by a disciplinarian officer who is finally killed by his men.

Some of the most important plays written by Sastre, such as *La mordaza* (1954; The Gag), *Muerte en el barrio* (1955; Death in the Neighborhood), *Guillermo Tell tiene los ojos tristes* (1955; William Tell Has Sad Eyes), *La cornada* (1960; Eng. tr., *Death Thrust,* 1967), *En la red* (1961; In the Net), and *Oficio de tinieblas* (1967; Work of Darkness), have on the existentialist tensions created by men who try to give meaning to their lives through action. Plays by Sastre written after 1965, such as *M.S.A. o La sangre y la ceniza* (1965; M.S.A. or Blood and Ashes), *La taberna fantástica* (1966; The Fantastic Tavern), *Crónicas romanas* (1968), and *El camarada oscuro* (1972; The Gloomy Comrade), fall under what the author terms "complex tragedies," a new tragic form that integrates the theories of Aristotle, Bertolt BRECHT, Ramón del VALLE-INCLÁN, and Samuel BECKETT.

As a theorist of dramatic art, Sastre has written *Drama y sociedad* (1965), *Anatomía del realismo* (1965), *La revolución y la critica literaria* (1970), and *Crítica de la imaginación* (1978). He has written poetry, narrative prose—*Las noches lúgubres* (1964; Dismal Nights), *El Paralelo 38* (1965), *Flores rojas para Miguel Servet* (1967; Red Flowers for Miguel Servet)—and several movie scripts.

See: C. C. DeCoster, "Alfonso Sastre," *TuDR* 5 (Winter 1960): 121–32; F. Anderson, *Alfonso Sastre* (1971).

J.O.

Sawa y Martínez, Alejandro (1862–1909), Spanish novelist and journalist, was born in Seville and died in poverty—ill, blind, and insane—in Madrid. Little is known of this early life, and such literary importance as he has is due to his personal relationships with the great writers of his time, among them Rubén Darío, AZORÍN, Pío BAROJA, and Ramón del VALLE-INCLÁN, the latter two of whom immortalized him in their works. When Sawa died, Valle-Inclán wrote to Darío, "I wept before the body, for him, for me, and for all poor poets." He was the model for Rafael Villasús in Baroja's novel *El árbol de la ciencia* (1911; The Tree of Knowledge) and for the blind poet Max Estrella of Valle-Inclán's play *Luces de Bohemia* (1920; Bohemian Lights).

Four early novels make up the bulk of Sawa's work: *La mujer de todo el mundo* (1885; Everybody's Wife), *Crimen legal* (1886; Legal Crime), *Declaración de un vencido* (1887; Confession of a Defeated Man), and *Noche* (1888; Night). An anarchist and atheist, Sawa expressed in these novels his anticlericalism and his disillusionment with bourgeois values and a corrupt Spanish society. All are naturalistic in the manner of Emile ZOLA and quite unsuccessful. His second period—of outlook, not of productivity—followed six happy years in Paris where he worked as a translator, hosted Rubén Darío, came to know many French writers, and returned to Madrid in 1896 a disciple of the symbolists and Parnassians. As spokesman for French literary currents and the works of such poets as Paul VERLAINE and Stepháne MALLARMÉ, he exercised a noticeable influence on other writers. His posthumously published personal journal *Iluminaciones en la sombre* (1910; Lights in the Darkness), with a prologue by Darío, is of documentary interest.

Not unlike Valle-Inclán himself, Sawa was long a picturesque bohemian figure on the streets and in the literary cafés of Madrid. Hardly a great figure of the time failed to record his felt presence in memoirs, letters, poems, and essays. In the end he came to incarnate for them mortality, with society and art on either side.

See: A. W. Phillips, *Alejandro Sawa: mito y tradición* (1977); I. M. Zavala, "Estudio preliminar" to A. Sawa, *Iluminaciones en la sombre* (1977).					H.L.B.

Sbarbaro, Camillo (1888–1967), Italian poet, was born in Santa Margherita Ligure. He spent almost all his life in Liguria, moving to Genoa at an early age and retiring in 1941 to Spotorno. A solitary figure who prefered personal liberty to financial reward, Sbarbaro devoted his life to his writing, which he considered the sole means of salvaging something from the chaos of existence. He eked out a living from occasional private lessons, translations, and the sales of his collections of rare plants and, more importantly, his lichens, symbols of his love for all neglected forms of existence.

Apart from the juvenile *Resine* (1911; Resins), Sbarbaro's works are largely autobiographical and betray a central paradox: a sense of almost total alienation, not merely from society, but from life itself, and, simultaneously, a bitter, tenacious attachment to life. The discursive, often prosaic poetry of his best-known work, *Pianissimo* (1914), and the prose poems of *Trucioli* (1920; Wood Shavings) into which it logically progresses, show the author's connection with the "Voce" movement (*see* ITALIAN LITERATURE) and its insistence on truth, ruthless self-examination, and confession. Its use of the fragment provided an ideal vehicle for Sbarbaro's lyricism. Both *Pianissimo* and *Trucioli* show the poet trapped in the arid wasteland of the city, a desert that mirrors his own inner drought. Communication with others—who are considered grotesque, mutilated marionettes, cruel reminders of his own state—is impossible, as is escape or revolt. Sbarbaro can only withdraw into his own indifference, attaining a momentary state of petrification, inertia, often termed "absence," whereby he can participate in the nonlife of objects surrounding him, until, as if by a miracle, a more normal self-affirmation returns.

After the publication of *Liquidazione* (1928; Liquidation), in which he seeks refuge in an overly elaborate, involuted prose style, Sbarbaro's existential anguish gave way to the resigned bitterness of the revised *Trucioli* (1948; 2d. ed., 1963), which, incorporating both new and old prose works, shows signs of tiredness and repetition. The republication in 1954 of *Pianissimo*, which had become a collector's item, and its inclusion in *Poesie* (1961, 1971; Poems), gained Sbarbaro long overdue public acclaim, as did *Rimanenze* (1955; Remainders), containing a series of bittersweet love poems and a melodious, if uncharacteristic, hymn to Liguria. Later prose works such as *Fuochi fatui* (1962; Will O' the Wisp), *Gocce* (1963; Droplets), and *Quisquilie* (1967; Trifles), containing fragments, aphorisms, and comments on life and art, display the growing warmth and humanity of one who has suffered, but not in vain.

See: L. Polato, *Sbarbaro* (1969).					I.Sk.

Schack, Hans Egede (1820–59), Danish novelist, was born in the Zealand town of Sengeløse. He received his law degree in 1844. Schack had a political career that was distinguished by his eloquence as a speaker and skill as a debater. His novel *Phantasterne* (1857; The Fantasts) became a forerunner of later Danish naturalism because of its realistic style as well as its condemnation of romantic fantasy. In *Prantasterne*, Schack penetratingly analyzed the development of three young daydreamers, one toward incurable mental illness, the second toward earthbound realism, and the third (the main character, Conrad) toward a well-balanced life-style. The posthumous fragment, *Sandhed med Modification* (1954; Truth with Modification), a contemporary social novel aiming to illuminate the lie, its inner character and meaning, testifies to Schack's masterful talent for psychological penetration.

See: H. Hertel, ed., *Omkring Phantasterne* (1969).

S.H.R.

Schade, Jens August (1903–78), Danish poet and novelist, was born in the Jutland city of Skive and lived all his life as a bohemian in Copenhagen. The major motif of Schade's writing—the coincidental unity between everyday life and cosmic Eros—is fully developed in his first collection *Den levende Violin* (1926; The Living Violin). The lyrical novel, *Sjov i Danmark* (1928; Fun in Denmark; "Sjov" is also the name of the hero) is partly an ironical autobiography, partly a satiric portrait of contemporary Denmark. Later collections, written in a colorful, surrealistic style, from *Hjertebogen* (1930; The Heart Book) to *Overjordisk* (1973; Supernatural), are all characterized by bold, often disrespectful love poems, erotic nature poems and cosmic day-dreams. Schade's models are Sophus CLAUSSEN and D. H. Lawrence. Their theories that the unfolding of life is an intoxication and that poetry is able to penetrate all aspects of human relationship are combined with Schade's all-embracing sexual message, which is strikingly expressed in the titles of his two lyrical novels, *Den himmelske Elskov paa Jorden* (1931; Heavenly Love on Earth) and *Mennesker mødes og sød Musik opstaar i Hjertet* (1944; People Meet and Sweet Music Fills the Heart).

See: F. Stein Larsen, *Jens August Schade* (1973); P. Houe, *Jens August Schades naturlyrik* (1973).					S.H.R.

Schaeffer, Albrecht (1885–1950), German poet, novelist, and essayist, was born in Elbing, West Prussia. His childhood was spent in Hanover. He studied in Munich and in Berlin, tried his hand at journalism, but soon gave it up and settled in the Inn valley of southern Bavaria. He was writing poetry at the age of 14, and all his early compositions were in metrical form—poems, romances, verse epics, plays—with the exception of the novel *Helianth* (1920), which established his reputation as a writer. *Helianth* is a three-volume novel of apprenticeship in the tradition of Goethe's *Wilhelm Meister* and Gottfried Keller's *Der grüne Heinrich*, deeply concerned with the meaning and value of art. The young author's guiding spirit was Stefan GEORGE. With George he revolted against materialism and cheap opportunism, seeking "the radiant mystery of things" and their adequate poetic expression. A searching study of Geroge forms the major essay in his volume *Dichter und Dichtung* (1923; Poets and Poetry). Some of his short stories, for example, "Der Hund" (1918; The Dog), "Der höllische Sebastian" (1928; Satanic Sebastian), and "Das Opfertier" (1936; The Sacrificial Animal), as well as episodes in most of his works, pay tribute to naturalism, although an undercurrent of mysticism seems to suggest subtler, symbolic meanings.

Religion of a mystical and speculative but emphatically Christian kind, the classics, nature, and life close to the soil are the dominating elements in Schaeffer's work. *Der göttliche Dulder* (1920; The Divine Sufferer) retells the adventures of Ulysses; *Parzival* (1922) is a new and imaginative adaptation of the medieval epic; *Alphaia: der Weg der Götter, Völker und Zahlen* (1937; Alphaia: The Way of Gods, Peoples, and Numbers) gives a mystical interpretation of certain numbers and their relations to religion, art, and the evolution of national cultures, based on the proportions of an ancient Greek temple. On the other hand, Schaeffer's novels *Cara* (1936) and *Ruhland: Lebensbild eines Mannes* (1937; Ruhland: The Life of a

Man) grew out of the deep contentment their author had found at least in working the land and sharing the community of country people. Schaeffer left Germany before World War II to live in the United States.

See: W. Muschg, *Der dichterische Charakter* (1929).

E.M.F. rev. A.L.W.

Schaffner, Jakob (1875-1944), Swiss novelist and political essayist, was born in Basel and orphaned at an early age. A distressing picture of his childhood and the years he spent in "Demutt" (Beuggen), a religiously oriented orphanage near Basel, can be found in his most famous novel, *Johannes* (1922). This novel has been praised as the best Swiss educational novel since Gottfried Keller's *Der grüne Heinrich*, and for it Schaffner won the 1930 Swiss Schiller Prize. Schaffner eventually became a shoemaker. He described his experiences as an apprentice in Basel in the novel *Die Jünglingszeit des Johannes Schattenhold* (1930; The Youth of Johannes Schattenhold), and the following years of vagrant life in *Eine deutsche Wanderschaft* (1931; A German Journey). Schaffner held many different jobs, but after his initial literary success was able to devote all his time to writing. From 1911 on he lived in Germany. During World War I he married a German, but did not lose all ties with Switzerland. His novel *Die Glücksfischer* (1923; The Fishers for Luck) deals with the fascinating power a great neighbor and an elegant Lorelei have on two rather naive Swiss citizens. The tension between his small homeland and the Reich, however, could not be called harmless after 1933.

Schaffner's subsequent political behavior resembles that of such literary figures such as Knut HAMSUN, Ezra Pound, and Felix Timmermanns. He embraced national socialism because in the Nazi myth of a revival of the Teutonic spirit he saw the possibility of redemption from (Swiss) pedantry. Schaffner was killed in an air raid on Strassbourg in 1944.

As a writer, Schaffner was not innovative: the Alemannic landscapes and characters in his works are reminiscent of Keller, his romantic craftsmen and wanderers similar to those of Hermann HESSE. He was fond of earth and rivers, of history and music. Longing for his lost mother informs a number of his books. *Die Erlhöferin* (1908) contains memorable portraits of women; the problems of unsteady men are presented in *Konrad Pilater* (1910); politico-historical questions are raised in his history of Switzerland (1915) and in *Das heimliche Alemannien* (1933; The Secret Alemannia); and the novellas in *Die Laterne* (1907; The Lantern), *Die goldene Fratze* (1912; The Golden Grimace), and *Liebe und schicksal* (1932; Love and Fate) are replete with humor and picturesque details. Although Schaffner has been repudiated by his countrymen for his Nazi leanings, his contribution to Alemannic litterature, especially to the history of the realistic novel, was considerable and cannot be denied.

See: P. Fässler, *Jakob Schaffner: Leben und Werk* (1937); H. Bänziger, *Heimat und Fremde* (1958); D. Fringeli, *Dichter im Abseits* (1974).   H.Bä.

Schallück, Paul (1922-76), German novelist and playwright, was born in Warendorf, Westphalia, the son of a German father and a Russian mother. He was seriously wounded in World War II. After his release from a French prisoner-of-war camp in 1946, he studied German literature, history, and philosophy in Münster and theater science in Cologne. Following the broadcast of his radio play *Gericht über Kain* (Judgment of Cain) in 1949 and the publication of theater reviews for several papers, he terminated his studies in 1950, without a degree, to become a freelance writer.

Schallück wrote numerous plays for the stage, for radio, and for television, and also some poetry, but he became well known as a novelist. His first novel, *Wenn man aufhören könnte zu lügen* (1951; If One Could Stop Telling Lies), about young people who look for a new sense in life after the war, did not draw much attention, but his second novel, *Ankunft null Uhr zwölf* (1953; Arrival at 0:12 O'clock), written as a fascinating sequence of 12 short stories, brought immediate fame and made him a member of "Gruppe 47." *Die unsichtbáre Pforte* (1954; The Invisible Gate) was less well received. In 1959 international recognition came to Schallück after the publication of his fourth novel, *Engelbert Reineke*. The novel concerns the conflicts of a German teacher who has to deal with colleagues who once brought his father into a Nazi concentration camp, where he was murdered. Although this novel is one of the strongest accounts of the hypocrisies in post-Fascist Germany to be found in literature, in his fifth and last novel, *Don Quichotte in Köln* (1967; Don Quixote in Cologne), Schallück gives a profound literary analysis of West German life in the 1960s.

It is perhaps tragic that Schallück always lived and published in the shadow of his friend and long-time neighbor, Heinrich BÖLL. Both suffered similar circumstances during and after the war; both started out at the same time in the same small publishing house; both had a similar style, characterized by "Kahlschlag" realism and the bitterly satirical humor and honest sentimentality of Rhinelanders; and, above all, both were obsessed by similar topics.

See: A. F. Keele, *Paul Schallück and the Post-War German Don Quixote* (1976).   F.Vi.

Schaukal, Richard von (1874-1942), Austrian poet, novelist, and essayist, was born in Brünn, Austrian Moravia, the son of an apothecary. He studied law at the University of Vienna, entered the service of the Austrian state in 1897, and achieved distinction as a state official; when the Austrian monarchy collapsed in 1918, Schaukal lived in retirement in a suburb of Vienna. His literary production, although not extensive, is of high quality. While his prose fiction, as in *Eros Thanatos* (1906), a collection of stories, is respectable, his few essays, as in *Giorgione* (1907), noteworthy; and his translations of Charles BAUDELAIRE and Paul VERLAINE in *Nachdichtungen* (1906; Paraphrases), distinguished, he is likely to live longest through his lyric poetry, the first volume of which was published before he was 20, *Gedichte* (1893; Poems). Sloughing off a certain amount of affectation and posing, a blasé weariness and pallor, Schaukal began to come into his own around 1900 and thereafter steadily grew in power and assurance. At the same time he was establishing the principles that were to govern his lyric utterance. These are mainly three: insistence upon the validity and necessity of tradition in life as in art, consistent and conscious advocacy of the "aristocratic" point of view, and the conception of artistic form as central and not peripheral. Constantly filing and polishing his poems, he reissued them as if executing a trust with *Ausgewählte Gedichte* (1909; Selected Poetry) and *Gedichte 1891-1918* (Poems 1891-1918).

See: K. Mayer, *Richard von Schaukals Weltanschauung* (1960).   B.Q.M. rev. A.L.W.

Schehadé, George (1910-), French poet and dramatist, was born in Alexandria into an old Lebanese family of French culture. He returned to Lebanon with his family at age six. After secondary and higher education (including a law degree) in French schools in Lebanon, punctuated by long sojourns in Paris, Schehadé published his first book of poetry, *Etincelles* (Sparks), in 1928. Three volumes of *Poésies* were published in 1938, 1948, and 1949 (in 1952 they were grouped together in one volume). Then followed a novel, *Rodogune Sinne* (1947), "written upon leaving secondary school," *L'Ecolier Sultan* (1950; The School Sultan), and *Poésie zéro* (1951). Like his poetry, *Rodogune Sinne* shows a strong surrealist inspiration (*see* FRENCH LITERATURE).

Despite his poetic output, it is as a dramatist that Schehadé has gained renown. His plays are distinguished for what critics have called their "theatricalized poetry." The arrangement of the plays is governed not by traditional rules or fixed forms but rather depends upon the poetic quality of language and dialogue and upon the author's creative imagination. Schehadé's is a theater of wonder where poet-characters seek a world of innocence, a universe situated far from any contact with the reality of the corrupt and corrupting world of "grown-ups." These "children," naive creatures whose gaze demystifies the false appearance of a world inhabited by "serious" people, play the principal roles. But the dramatic work of this poet is certainly not just a fairy tale for children. Not only do Schehadé's plays draw upon rich dramatic sources—the dream and the journey—they possess a tragic dimension, as well. The inhabitants of this poetic universe are vulnerable, and their flight toward the summits of their dreams collides with hostile elements—material reality, war, old age, death. The journey upward always ends in a descent, a testimony to the fragility of childhood, of dreams, and of the world of pure poetry.

In *Monsieur Bob'le* (1951), for example, a philosopher adored by the inhabitants of Paola Scala decides to leave his village. He leaves his fellows a book containing his meditations, maxims, and proverbs. Later, heeding the pleas of those he left behind, he decides to return, but he falls ill and dies during his return trip. His influence is nevertheless so strong that Paolo Scala will continue to be a place where "happiness is a very ordinary event." With the droll *La Soirée des proverbes* (1954; The Evening of Proverbs), Schehadé provoked a battle between his enthusiastic partisans and his scandalized adversaries, complaining they had understood nothing. *Histoire de Vasco* (written in 1956; Story of Vasco) was another controversial work. First staged in France in 1957, when the Algerian War was at its height, it presents a simple, fearful man involved in the war-machine in spite of himself. His naiveté prevents him from recognizing in time the evil and the traps that await him. *Les Violettes* (1960) is a satirical game in which Schehadé denounces the threat that science and technology pose to mankind. Like *Histoire de Vasco*, *Le Voyage* (1961) and *L'Emigré de Brisbane* (1961) mingle dream and journey motifs with a denunciation of the absurd.

See: R. Abirached, "Schehadé," in *Ecrivains d'aujourd'hui 1940–1960*, ed. by B. Pingaud (1960), pp. 463–70; B. Knapp, "George Schehadé: 'He who dreams diffuses into air . . .'," *YFS* 29 (1962): 108–15; J.-P. Richard, *Onze Etudes sur la poésie moderne* (1964), pp. 141–60; J. Silenieks, "The Transfiguration of a Poetic Theater," *MD* 10 (September 1967): 151–60; S. Khalaf, *Littérature libanaise de langue française* (1974), pp. 70–77, 98–118.   W.L.

Schendel, Arthur van (1874–1946), Dutch novelist and short-story writer, was born in Batavia, Indonesia. He became a high-school teacher of English, and taught in England for a time, before turning to literature. He also lived in Italy for a number of years. In his first story, *Drogon* (1896), the hero of the title is a young nobleman of the Middle Ages.

The romantic longing and sexual passion that are combined in this novel reappear in *Een zwerver verliefd* (1904; A Wanderer in Love) and *Een zwerver verdwaald* (1907; A Wanderer Lost), and again fate determines the outcome. With *De berg van droomen* (1913; The Mountain of Dreams), the romantic longing becomes attached to a more definite, concrete object; it becomes something more practical—a search for happiness in love. This change appears in such novels as *Der liefde bloesems* (1921; The Blossoms of Love), *Rose Angélique* (1922), *Blanke gestalten* (1923; Shining Figures), and *Angiolino en de lente* (1923; Angiolino and Spring).

His approach to reality reached a climax with *Het fregatschip Johanna Maria* (1930; Eng. tr., *The Johanna Maria*, 1935), in which van Schendel turned to Dutch life of the recent past. All his life, Jacob Brouwer has sailed aboard the *Johanna Maria*, and now he is filled with a desire to own her. Just after he realizes his dream, however, fate intervenes and plays a greater and more terrible role. Brouwer dies on his own ship. Van Schendel's new period included views of the Dutch in Indonesia, as in *Een eiland in de Zuidzee* (1931; An Island in the South Seas) and *Jan Compagnie* (1932). The new development reached its height, however, with another group of novels set in the Netherlands: *De waterman* (1933; Eng. tr., *The Waterman*, 1963); *Een Hollandsch drama* (1935; Eng. tr., *The House in Haarlem* ([1940]); *De rijke man* (1936; The Rich man); and *De grauwe vogels* (1937; Eng. tr., *Grey Birds*, 1939). Van Schendel again combines the two themes of the sailor and his ship and of fate in his best novel, *De waterman*. Unlike Jacob Brouwer, however, Maarten Rossaert uses his ship not only for self-fulfillment, but to help his fellowmen. Yet, in the end, death also claims him, as it has his mother and his son. The novel is a powerful portrayal of the Dutch character and of the land itself. The other novels in this group all show heroes whose lives are consumed by self-sacrifice, and the characters are drawn from the Dutch middle class. With their attention to milieu, upbringing, and heredity, they are much closer to naturalism, or "realism," as van Schendel liked to call it. *De wereld, een dansfeest* (1938; The World, a Dance) marks a third period in van Schendel's work. Although it is still a tragedy, it also contains a whimsical humor and a light-hearted tone. Yet there are a vagueness and a shadowy nature to the characters, which may be due to van Schendel's view of them from the distance of an interested spectator, and to his feeling that human beings and their motives are impenetrable, after all. This is evident in such works as *Mijnheer Oberon en Mevrouw* (1940; Mr. and Mrs. Oberon), *De Menschenhater* (1941; The Misanthrope), *Het oude huis* (1946; The Old House), and *Voorbijgaande schaduwen* (1948; Passing Shadows).

Van Schendel was a master of style and character, and he is the greatest novelist of the period up to the end of World War II. He also excelled at the shorter forms of fiction, as is evident from such collections of his stories as *De wedergeboorte van bedelman* (1942; The Rebirth of the Beggar Man), *Nachtgedaanten* (1938; Figures in the Night), and *Anders en eender* (1939; Different and All the Same). He was posthumously awarded the P. C. Hooft Prize in 1947.

See: J. Greshoff, *Arthur van Schendel* (1934); G. H.'s-Gravesande, *Arthur van Schendel* (1949); F. W. van Heerikhuizen, *Het werk van Arthur van Schendel* ([1961]).   S.L.F.

Scherfig, Hans (1905–79), Danish novelist, was born in Copenhagen. He made his debut as a painter in 1928. His literary production is distinguished by sharp social criticism and satire based on a Marxist point of view. Scherfig's novels most frequently start with a murder, which is solved toward the end, used as a symbol of the degeneration of bourgeois society. In between the murder and its solution lies the major message, the satire. In *Den forsvundne Fuldmægtig* (1938; Head Clerk Disappeared), bureaucracy and the mechanized existence of people in bourgeois life is attacked whereas the target of *Det forsømte Foraar* (1940; Neglected Spring) is the traditional, unrealistic system of education, which stifles the imagination and warps the subsequent careers of the students. *Idealister* (1945; Eng. tr., *Idealists,* 1949) is directed against psychoanalysts, spiritists, and other "idealists" who believe they can save the world with one single universal solution. Many of these idealists are also encountered in the semidocumentary *Frydenholm* (1962), which describes the corruption, the men of the Resistance, and the collaborators during the German occupation of Denmark (1940–45), while stressing the positive role of the Communists. Unfortunately, Scherfig's character portrayals are occasionally unfaceted and his tendency artistically unfinished—a shortcoming not found in *Det forsømte Faraar,* his classic masterpiece.

See: S. M. Kristensen, "How to Castigate Your Public—and Write Bestsellers," *DJ* 76 (1973): 26–29; J. Moestrup, *Hans Scherfig* (1977). S.H.R.

Schickele, René (1885–1940), German novelist, poet, and dramatist, was born in Oberehnheim, Alsace, the son of a German father and a French mother. He manifested in his life and works the fate of a citizen in a boundary land between two great cultures. Schickele studied in Strasbourg and then turned to journalism and the publishing of magazines. IIis first volumes of poetry were collected in *Der Ritt ins Leben* (1905; The Ride into Life). Torn between the elemental "natural force" of his paternal ancestry and the greater "historical force" exerted by France, he developed his ideal of the supernational European who is indebted to both "fatherlands." *Der Fremde* (1907; The Foreigner), Schickele's first novel, reveals the contradictory elements in the character of its author, who later alternated between expressionist and impressionist modes of style. Several volumes of poetry were followed by the novel *Benkal, der Frauentröster* (1914; Benkal, the Comforter of Women), an impressive fantastic vision of the coming war and its implicit absurdity. After the outbreak of World War I—Schickele was then living in Berlin—he wrote within a few months the successful drama *Hans im Schnakenloch* (1916; Hans in the Mosquito Hole). The hero, a full-blooded, impetuous farmer, stands between two nations and two women. When the hour strikes, all those about him make clear decisions and know where they stand; only Hans is torn within himself. Death in the French army, which he expects to be defeated, is the last hope of the fugitive from home. Soon banned in Germany and condemned in France, the drama gives evidence of the trend of Schickele's development.

In December 1914, Schickele had become the editor of *Die weißen Blätter.* He transferred the journal from Berlin to Zurich and made it the effective mouthpiece of European antiwar sentiment. Soon disappointed after the war, he retired to the Black Forest and wrote the trilogy *Das Erbe am Rhein* (The Inheritance on the Rhine), an epic of Alsace and the Alsatians, comprising *Maria Capponi* (1925; Eng. tr., 1928), *Blick auf die Vogesen* (1927; Eng. tr., *Heart of Alsace,* 1929), and *Der Wolf in der Hürde* (1929; The Wolf in the Herd).

Driven to France after 1933, Schickele wrote the novel *Die Flaschenpost* (1937; Mail in a Bottle), the tragedy of an individualist who, in the confusion of modern times, finds ultimate peace in an insane asylum. A book on D. H. Lawrence (1934) had shown Schickele to be a lucid and passionate interpreter of creative genius.

See: F. Bentmann, *René Schickele: Leben und Werk* (1974). W.K.P. rev. A.L.W.

Schlaf, Johannes (1862–1941), German dramatist and novelist, was born in Querfurt, Saxony, where he received his early education until his parents moved to Magdeburg in 1874. In childhood he showed literary and artistic inclinations that his parents discouraged and suppressed. After two semesters at Halle, where he switched from theology to philosophy, he completed his training as a philologist in Berlin in 1887. He became a member of the literary group "Durch," in which young enthusiasts like Heinrich and Julius Hart, Bruno Wille, Wilhelm Boelsche, and Leo Berg discussed the requisites of "modern" literature. Already familiar with the new trends and basically in sympathy with them, Schlaf accepted an invitation to collaborate with Arno HOLZ in putting such theories into practice. The winter of 1887–88 yielded a series of sketches, three of which were published as *Papa Hamlet* (1889), under the pseydonym Bjarne P. Holmsen. Their accurate presentation of everyday life in its most prosaic and minute details was carried out with scientific precision and utilized photographic and phonographic techniques. The mannerisms and speech differences of each character were carefully noted and became valuable adjuncts of these milieu studies, which aimed at depicting, not interpreting life. The sketches launched German naturalism, from which emerged Gerhart HAUPTMANN. Earlier and similar sketches, "Die papierne Passion" (The Paper Passion), were finally published in a collection, *Neue Gleise* (1891; New Rails), together with *Papa Hamlet* and the drama *Die Familie Selicke* (1889). The last, a drab and depressing milieu study of an incompatible bourgeois marriage that gradually killed any hope of happiness for a whole family, set the pattern of consistent naturalism *(konsequenter Naturalismus).*

After 1892, Schlaf and Holz wrote independently and indulged for years in disputes regarding their individual shares in their joint efforts. A reasonable and fair estimate must emphasize that Schlaf had the deeper poetic nature whereas Holz was the energetic and aggressive theorist who formulated the principal ideas of German naturalism and gave final form to their cooperative writings. Schlaf published *Meister Oelze* (1892; rev. 2d ed., 1908), technically perhaps the best naturalistic drama, although never successful in the theater. In contrast to the crass naturalism of these works are *In Dingsda* (1892; In That Place) and *Frühling* (1894; Springtime), delicate impressionistic sketches of idyllic contentment far from city turmoil and strife. After a serious nervous collapse (1893–96), Schlaf wrote more dramas and stories, followed by ambitious novels that attempted to combat the decadent spirit of the age and to present the problematic nature of people today in terms of a new positive faith in spiritual values. He stressed the psychological analysis of character in conflict with the world and itself in novels such as *Das Dritte Reich* (1900; The Third Reich), *Die Suchenden* (1901; The Searchers), and *Peter Bojes Freite* (1902), which were followed by three more, *Der Kleine* (1904; The Little Boy), *Der Prinz* (1906), and *Am toten Punkt* (1907; At Dead Center), in which literary artistry seems secondary to philosophical and religious interests. Schlaf wrote essays on Walt Whitman, Emile VERHAEREN, and Maurice MAETERLINCK and translated from their works. W.A.R. rev. A.L.W.

Schlumberger, Jean (1877–1968), French essayist and novelist, was born into a wealthy Protestant family in Guebwiller, Alsace, which he left for Paris at the age of 15 in order to retain his French nationality. After studying the history of religions, he began his literary career as a poet with *Poèmes des temples et des tombeaus* (1903; Poems of Temples and Tombs), Goethean in inspiration and Parnassian in form, and *Epigrammes romaines* (1910; Roman Epigrams). His first novel, *Le Mur de verre* (1903; The Glass Wall), met with respectable success, although he soon disavowed it and regarded *Heureux qui comme Ulysse* (1906; Happy Who Like Ulysses)—later expanded into the triptych *L'Inquiète Paternité* (1911; Restless Paternity)—as his true beginning as a fiction writer.

In 1909, Schlumberger cofounded the *Nouvelle Revue française*, whose guidelines ("Considérations") he wrote and whose director he in effect was until 1912, even though André GIDE, his lifelong friend, was the spiritual leader of the review. The following year, Schlumberger became one of Jacques COPEAU's most essential aides in founding the Théâtre du Vieux-Colombier. Schlumberger wrote the most extensive account of the first years of the *Nouvelle Revue* and the Vieux-Colombier in his memoirs, *Eveils* (1950; Awakenings).

Before World War I, in which he served, Schlumberger had hoped to succeed in the theater. Most of his plays, however, were succès d'estime: *Les Fils Louverné* (1914; The Louverné Sons), *La Mort de Sparte* (1921; The Death of Sparta), and *Césaire* (1921), although the last certainly deserved more attention.

In the 1920s, Schlumberger developed as a novelist and essayist. *Un Homme heureux* (1921; A Happy Man) and *Saint-Saturnin* (1931), his most successful novels, are works of exhaustive psychological analysis set in the complex social milieu of the upper bourgeoisie. Although a sequel to *Saint-Saturnin, Les Quatre Potiers* (1935; The Four Potiers) is a story of the Depression as well as an allegorical account of the *Nouvelle Revue* from 1909 to 1914. Schlumberger's more original fiction includes novels that could best be called *Romans-essais* (novel-essays), such as *Le Camarade infidèle* (1922; The Unfaithful Comrade) and *Stéphane le Glorieux* (1940); a historical novel, *Le Lion devenu vieux* (1924; The Lion Grown Old), whose central character is the Cardinal de Retz; and collections of short stories, *Les Yeux de dix-huit ans* (1928; 18-Year-Old Eyes) and, to a lesser degree, *Passions* (1956). Overshadowed by Gide, Schlumberger's works have not sufficiently been studied to reveal their stylistic quality. Some aspects of his style and his techniques in *L'Inquiète Paternité, L'Enfant qui s'accuse* (1919; The Child Who Accuses Himself), and *Les Yeux de dix-huit ans* anticipate those of the "new novel" (*see* FRENCH LITERATURE).

After World War I, Schlumberger endeavored to foster a Franco-German rapprochement. From the 1930s on, he showed a keen interest in social issues and in the renewal of France in numerous articles published in *Vendredi* and *Le Figaro*.

At the present time, Schlumberger's place in French letters rests mainly on his role in the *Nouvelle Revue* and the Vieux-Colombier; his criticism published in the *Nouvelle Revue* and in such works as *Plaisir à Corneille* (1936; Pleasure in Corneille) and *Madeleine et André Gide* (1956); and his philosophical essays, *Sur les frontières religieuses* (1934; On the Frontiers of Religion), *Essais et dialogues* (1937; Essays and Dialogues), *Jalons* (1941; Landmarks), and *Nouveaux Jalons* (1945; New Landmarks), which reveal rare intellectual and moral qualities. Schlumberger's *Œuvres* (7 vols., Works) were pub-lished between 1958 and 1962. The "Notices" that preface each of his works are of particular interest.

See: M. Delcourt, *Jean Schlumberger* (1956); special issue of *CS* 5 (1956); J.-P. Cap, *Techniques et thèmes dans l'œuvre romanesque de Jean Schlumberger* (1971) and "Jean Schlumberger et la *N.R.F.* 1909–1914," *ECr* 14, no. 2 (Summer 1974): 99–109.   J.-P.C.

Schmidt, Arno (1914–79), German novelist, translator, literary theoretician, historian, and (media) essayist with a radically divergent and experimental style, was born in Hamburg. He spent his adolescence in Silesia, displaying an early inclination toward mathematics and astronomy. The Third Reich rendered the pursuit of his academic and literary plans impossible, forcing him first into the textile trade, then into the military. After World War II, during which he saw duty in Norway, he worked for a time as an English interpreter, settling as a confirmed recluse in 1958 in the heath village of Bargfeld.

Schmidt's characteristic settings reflect this sparse north German Lüneberg landscape, although they assume increasingly "mythicized" features. A semiautobiographical strain is intensified in Schmidt's later work; *Abend mit Goldrand* (1975; Dusk with a Golden Frame) not only introduces the author's quasi-alter egos (Eugen and Egon) but also incorporates the novelist's experiences from birth to young adulthood (1914–32) and passages from an unpublished first novel, "Pharos." His later writings, moreover, tend to focus on aging characters, intellectuals who feel threatened by the flow of time and who echo their creator's idiom as well. Nevertheless, Schmidt shuns mimetic realism, pursuing instead postmodern "perceptional" realism. In his works, plot is secondary, and consciousness, recall, and daydreaming mechanisms are primary, as in the work of Marcel PROUST and James Joyce. Schmidt's unique narrative is brisk, leaping, and disjunctive. His punctuation resembles that of comic-book inserts. Similarly, his printed page is typographically unconventional, varying according to the specific prose medium, with some forms intershifting text blocks and others employing multiple text columns.

A thoroughly original theorist of narrative, Schmidt, in *Berechnungen* (1955; Calculations), issued four programmatic blueprints for model perceptual or prose grids. Actuating these schematics as "Fotoalbum" and "längeres Gedankenspiel" (extended cerebral gamesmanship), he redesigned the fourth type of "dream" during the 1970s in a Joycean and Freudian direction. He remains innovative, however, in his "correction" of Freud's theory of personality by adding a postgenital or impotence phase. This "Theorie der 4. Instanz" forms for Schmidt both an analytical and a creative instrument. For him, an author's imagination, in analogy to Freud's *Traumarbeit* or projection, continuously transforms innermost desires into sexoid images, motifs, and settings, since the preconscious and subconscious "Speaks in etyms." On the one hand, the interpreter Schmidt, especially during the 1960s, attempted to decode this type of Freudian-slip art (*Verschreibkunst*) in the works of Karl MAY, Adalbert Stifter, and James Joyce. *Finnegans Wake*, which Schmidt partially translated during his active endeavors embracing the Anglo-American literary heritage, "is not actually written with words, but rather etyms" (*Der Triton mit dem Sonnenschirm*, 1969, p. 281; The Triton with His Parasol). On the other hand, the later Schmidt lends an additional fictional dimension to his works with the inclusion of similar and intentional misreadings and misspellings. "Word contaminations," associations, and punning "reconstructions" of phonetically transcribed quotes (phallus/palace) produce the multivalence of Schmidt's more psychoanalytical texts after "Caliban über Setebos" (1964, in *Kühe in Halbtrauer*; Cows in Semigrief), culminating in his multilingual magnus opus *Zettel's Traum* (1970; Bottom's [or: Notecards'] Dream). Neoexpressionist *mots justes*, metaphors, and images now become less visible. Here, as earlier, Schmidt appears accurate to the point of "accuratomania," cultivating an encyclopedism whose scope rivals that of Thomas MANN's *Magic Mountain* and infusing his books with quotes, allusions, and parodies of well-known literary works or popular fiction, as in *Die Schule der Atheisten* (1973; The School of Atheists), freely adapting Jules Verne's *School of the Robinsons*.

Like Joyce, the later Schmidt tended to construct his fictions as recurrent myth. Thus, his mature oeuvre blends ahistoric and predominantly collective archetypes with subjective regionalized mythology. Externally, this stylistic change is demonstrated by the shift from prose sketches and Utopian or dysutopian short novels, such as *Schwarze Spiegel* (1951; Black Mirrors), and *Die Gelehrtenrepublik*, (1957, The Republic of Savants), to facsimile texts in oversize folio. In his characterizations this is marked by the absence of the earlier land surveys, mathematicians, and other protechnocrat, reformist members of the intelligentsia. In their place, there now appear presenile authors who dote voyeuristically on young girls while intensifying the sexual frustration of their own mates. Likewise, there is a shift away from both the tradition of the Enlightenment and the commitment to political and cultural criticism, whereby Schmidt sought to come to terms with the present reality of a divided Germany (post and neofascism, reestablishment of a West German Christian bourgeoise, and the bureaucratically entrenched Marxism of the German Democratic Republic). In spite of Schmidt's recent apolitical, literarily egocentric stance, which incorporates an antiyouth bias, his popularity has nonetheless broadened with the publication of numerous paperback editions and generous critical study in the *Bargfelder Bote* (since 1972), a journal dedicated exclusively to Schmidt studies. For English translations of Schmidt's work, see *Die Gelehrtenrepublik,* tr. Michael Horovitz, in *German Writing Today*, ed. by Christopher Middleton, (1967), pp. 94–99; from *Die Schule der Atheisten,* tr. Ralph R. Read/Hans-Bernhard Moeller, in *Dimension*, 6 (1973), 250–51.

See: T. Phelan, *Rationalist Narrative in Some Works of Arno Schmidt* (1972); J. Drews and H.-M. Bock, eds., *Der Solipsist in der Heide* (1974).   H.-B.M.

Schneider, Rolf (1932–), East German playwright, novelist, poet, and author of radio and television scripts was born in Karl-Marx Stadt. From 1951 until 1955 he studied German literature and philology at the university in Halle, after which he worked in Berlin as an editor of the cultural journal *Aufbau*. He first became known as a writer of politically committed radio plays that sought to present the ethical dilemmas brought about by the conflict between socialist values of the German Democratic Republic of the west, considered exploitative and neofascist, they include, *Der dritte Kreuzzug*, (1960; The Third Crusade), *Prozess Richard Waverly* (1961; The Trial of Richard Waverly, and *Der Mann aus England* (1962; The Man from England). His most successful endeavor during the 1960s was the play *Prozeß in Nürnberg* (1967; Trial at Nuremberg), which established him as one of the foremost writers of documentary drama in Germany. His prose works include volumes of stories: *Brücken und Gitter* (1965; Eng. tr., *Bridges and Bars*, 1967) and *Nek-*

rolog (1974; Necrology); and several novels: *Die Tage in W.* (1967; The Days in W.), *Der Tod des Nibelungen* (1970; The Death of the Nibelung), and his most controversial work in this genre to date, *November* (1979), a thinly disguised roman á clef that deals with the political events surrounding the expatriation in November, 1976 of the East German poet Wolf BIERMANN. Schneider has been awarded the prestigious Lessing Prize (1962) and has achieved recognition in the West with the reception in 1966 of the Prize of the German War-Blind for his passionate anti-Nazi radio play *Zwielicht* (Twilight). He is a member of the PEN Club and makes his home in Schöneiche near Berlin.

See: R. Seeliger, "Gespräch mit DDR-Autor Rolf Schneider," *DL* 17 (1975): 152.   T. Di N.

Schnitzler, Arthur (1862–1931), Austrian dramatist and short-story writer, was born in Vienna and stood squarely within that extraordinary burgeoning of Viennese culture at the end of the 19th century. He pursued his literary career contemporaneously with such notable figures as Hugo von HOFMANNSTHAL, Hermann BAHR, Georg BRANDES, Jakob WASSERMANN, Heinrich BEER-HOFMANN, and Karl KRAUS. Each member of this ("Jung Wien") group (*see* GERMAN LITERATURE) reflected in characteristic ways the peculiar dissonance, sensitivity, richness, and morbidity of a society doomed to destruction and utter transformation. In Schnitzler's case, this sensitivity to Austrian society is expressed in both his plays and short stories of the pre-World War I period. Characteristically, these works portray the frivolously self-destructive caperings of worldly upper-class Viennese (figures whose effete egocentric "decadence" has all too often been ascribed to Schnitzler himself), with a detached and subtly ironic awareness. The psychosexual acuity of Schnitzler's works has led many critics to stress (often inaccurately) the striking similarities between them and the theories of his fellow Viennese Sigmund Freud.

Best-known of the early plays that established Schnitzler's fame and notoriety are the *Anatol* playlets (1899–92; Eng. tr., 1956), *Liebelei* (1896; Eng. tr., *Light-O'-Love,* 1941), and *Reigen* (1900; Eng. tr., *Dance of Love,* 1965), the latter a work of majestic thematic impact and considerable abstraction. It is a stunning portrayal of the circular flow of sexuality that binds and equalizes all levels of society. Another play, *Der grüne Kakadu* (1899; Eng. tr., *The Green Cockatoo,* 1943), takes place in Paris on the eve of the French Revolution. Its brilliant interweaving of illusion and reality in a murderous love triangle is literally acted out for representatives of an ethically moribund aristocracy. Its mood of impending chaos lends the play distinct topicality.

Schnitzler's short stories of the prewar period are of interest mostly for their stylistic inventiveness (the author being an early and skilled employer of the interior monologue). By far the best is the novella *Leutnant Gustl* (1901; Eng. tr., *None But the Brave,* 1931). This is an intricately interwoven and devastatingly ironic representation of the bewildered thoughts of a lieutenant in the Imperial army, whose sense of impaired "honor" demands his suicide. The story aroused perfervid indignation upon publication and led to Schnitzler's dismissal as a military surgeon. Two other short works of this period, now widely admired, are *Die Toten schweigen* (1897; Eng. tr., *The Dead Are Silent,* 1947) and *Der blinde Geronimo und sein Bruder* (1900; Eng. tr., *The Blind Geronimo and His Brother,* 1961).

The intervening years up through World War I mark a

span of somewhat diminished production for Schnitzler. Generally, most critical attention has been directed toward the short novel of this period, *Der Weg ins Freie* (1908; Eng. tr., *The Road to the Open,* 1923), largely due to its essentially ancillary discussion of Jews (Schnitzler himself was Jewish) and their ambiguous status in Imperial Austrian society. More successful artistically was the "comedy" *Professor Bernhardi* (1912; Eng. tr., 1936). As is usually the case in Schnitzler's works (despite numerous evaluations of the author as a proponent of amorality), the play is concerned with a question of morality. It deals with the ambiguities resulting from the protagonist's willingness to take a private moral stand without acknowledging the public implications of his action.

In Schnitzler's later years (from 1918 until his death in 1931), the emphasis in his writings was upon the extended short story, several of which are outstanding. In general Schnitzler's stories employ the author's intensely psychological techniques while presenting grand thematic opposites reminiscent of the great Austrian baroque tradition (albeit in secularized form): life versus death; the game or the dream in juxtaposition with reality. *Fräulein Else* (1926; Eng. tr., 1931) returns to a brilliantly executed inner monologue in its depiction of a vital young girl forced by her family's debts into a defiant form of prostitution and eventual suicide. *Traumnovelle* (1926; Eng. tr., *Rhapsody,* 1931) explores the realm of unconscious sexuality in and about the marriage of the couple Fridolin and Albertine. Its dreamlike sequences of wild and subtly perilous erotic adventure lead eventually to an ethical reaffirmation of the marriage itself. Schnitzler's last novella, *Flucht in die Finsternis* (1931; Eng. tr., *Flight into Darkness,* 1931), is a highly realistic portrayal of how a man's descent into madness, born of pathologically introspective suspicion, results in his brother's murder. The symbolic aspects of the story's fraternal love-hate relationship, however, lend it a broader scope. Despite its pessimistic tone, the story affirms Schnitzler's lifelong conviction regarding the ethical necessity of human interconnectedness. Among Schnitzler's works in English are *Viennese Novelettes,* tr. by R. A. Simon, W. A. Drake, O. P. Schinnerer, and A. Jacques (1931), and *Reigen, The Affairs of Anatol and Other Plays,* tr. by M. Mannes and G. B. Colbron (1933).

See: M. Swales, *Arthur Schnitzler: A Critical Study* (1971); R. Urbach, *Arthur Schnitzler* (1971).   W.K.C.

Schnurre, Wolfdietrich (1920–), German poet, editor, critic, and commentator, was born in Frankfurt am Main and attended school in Berlin from 1928 to 1939. As a soldier in Adolf Hitler's army (1939–45) he was repeatedly arrested for "defeatism"; in 1945 he deserted and returned to the eastern sector of Berlin, where he began writing his first short stories, later published as *Man sollte dagegen sein* (1960; People Ought to Be Opposed). From 1946 to 1949 Schnurre worked as a book, theater, and film critic for the *Deutsche Rundschau.* In 1947 he cofounded the "Gruppe 47" and opened the group's first session with a reading of his short narrative *Das Begräbnis* (1946; The Burial). This story, which depicts the burial of God and rejects spiritual consolation as senseless, is thematically similar to early works by Wolfgang BORCHERT and Heinrich BÖLL. The earliest stories in the collection *Eine Rechnung die nicht aufgeht* (1958; A Calculation That Doesn't Work Out) were also written at this time.

In 1948, ordered by the Soviet cultural officer in East Berlin to cease writing for publications licensed by the Americans and the British, Schnurre moved to West Berlin, where he contributed regularly to newspapers and periodicals such as *Neue Zeitung, Die Welt,* and *Neuer Film* and completed his first book, *Die Rohrdommel ruft jeden Tag* (1950; The Bittern Calls Every Day). Schnurre's work of the early post-World War II period shows a deep concern with the tasks of the activist writer in Germany. For him art exists not for itself but for man, and his carefully constructed narratives portray the anxiety, uncertainty, and despair of soldiers, refugees, and children persecuted by the war itself and by memories of it. Schnurre was active politically, and in 1962 he produced a film documentary about the construction of the Berlin Wall.

Schnurre's lighter satirical works are often about animals; *Sternstaub und Sänfte, Aufzeichnungen des Pudels Ali* (1951; Stardust and Sedan-Chairs: Sketches by Ali the Poodle), caricatures the aesthetic "poet" who attempts to escape or to ignore reality. He has published two volumes of poetry—*Kassiber: Gedichte* (1956; Prison Letters: Poems) and *Kassiber: Neue Gedichte* (1964; Prison Letters: New Poems)—numerous radio and television plays, and fables and parables—such as the Kafkaesque tales in *Das Los unserer Stadt* (1959; The Fate of Our City) and *Rapport des Verschonten* (1968; Report of One Who Was Spared).

Throughout his literary career, Schnurre has eschewed longer forms such as the novel in favor of short stories, sketches, anecdotes, fables, dialogues, and verse. Even those works that he labels "novels," for example, *Als Vaters Bart noch rot war* (1958; Back When Father's Beard was Red) and *Richard kehrt zurück* (1970; Richard Returns), are really collections of short, thematically related narratives. Schnurre's multifaceted writing of the past 30 years varies greatly in subject matter and technique and shows an affinity to writers as diverse as Franz KAFKA, August STRINDBERG, Friedrich DÜRRENMATT, and J. D. Salinger. To this day he remains a "committed" writer concerned with the problems of average people in everyday situations.

Ich frag ja bloß (1973; I'm Just Asking) consists of dialectical dialogues for adult readers, in which German children's unabashed questions about sex, religion, war, hunger, work, politics, and family matters humorously reveal parental and societal prejudices and taboos. In "Pappa erinnert sich" (Daddy Remembers), a father's nostalgic memories of comradeship in wartime are "spoiled" by his child's realistic comment about death and destruction, and in "Ersatz" (Substitution), parents replace their child's gruesome war comics with sadistic verses by Wilhelm Busch, which they consider suitable for children. Most of the dialogues in *Ich brauch dich* (1976; I Need You) depict various kinds of male-female encounters or relationships, such as a discussion between ex-husband and ex-wife after the divorce proceedings in "Wendemarke" (Turning Point), an engaged couple's analysis of their previous night's sexual activities in "Im Vorfeld" (In the Perimeter), an amusing portrayal of an immature husband's experience with a prostitute in "Intimität," a murderess persuading a young priest to help her dispose of her husband's corpse in "Zuflucht" (Refuge), and an older man's reluctance to tell his wife he has lost his job in "Die Basis." The narrative *Eine schwierige Reparatur* (1976; Eng. tr., "A Difficult Repair Job," in *Dimension* 9 [1976]) humorously depicts a would-be atheist's relationship to a carving of Jesus.

See: K.-G. Kribben, "Wolfdietrich Schnurre," in *Deutsche Literatur seit 1945 in Einzeldarstellungen* (1968), pp. 279–96; H. Lehnert, "Die Gruppe 47, Ihre

Anfänge und ihre Gründungsmitglieder," in *Die deutsche Literatur der Gegenwart* (2d, ed., 1976), pp. 43–52.

D.H.C.

Scholz, Wilhelm von (1874–1969), German dramatist, novelist, lyric poet, and essayist, was born in Berlin. He was a descendant of the older, conservative bureaucracy (his father was secretary of finance in Otto von Bismarck's cabinet), and he was reared in the traditions of the 19th century. Scholz kept aloof from the changing tendencies of the times, alternating his residence between Berlin and Lake Constance. From 1910 to 1923 he was dramatic director of the stage at Stuttgart. Afterwards he remained an independent writer, except for serving as president of the Deutsche Dichterakademie at Berlin for several years.

After symbolistic beginnings in such dramas as *Der Besiegte* (1899; The Vanquished Man) and *Der Gast* (1900; The Guest), Scholz consistently interpreted the world of poetry as a net of irrational, magic relations superimposed upon the world of reality. Consequently, most of his works dealt with dreams, hallucinations, and related demonological topics, achieving at times a singular transparency, especially in the treatment of historical situations of the Middle Ages. Among his dramas *Der Jude von Konstanz* (1905; The Jew of Constance), *Vertauschte Seelen* (1910; Transposed Souls), *Gefährliche Liebe* (1913; Perilous Love), *Der Wettlauf mit dem Schatten* (1922; The Race with the Shadow), and *Die gläserne Frau* (1924; The Woman of Glass) met with widespread success. His adaptations from Pedro Calderón, as well as his revival of the miracle play and the marionette play, were well received. The author turned to novels rather late. Among them *Perpetua* (1926) and *Der Weg nach Ilok* (1930; The Way to Ilok) express the tragic struggle between the natural and the supernatural in people. Scholz's short stories, the genre in which he was a master, appeared in two collections, *Erzählungen* (1924; Tales) and *Die Gefährten* (1937; The Companions)

Aside from a few collections of lyrics, for example, *Der Spiegel* (1908; The Mirror) and *Neue Gedichte* (1913; New Poems), and from several autobiographical works, especially *Wanderungen* (1934; Wanderings) and *Jahrhundertwende* (1936; Turn of the Century), which abound in remarkable nature descriptions, Scholz's significance rests upon his theoretical writings, for example, *Gedanken zum Drama* (1905, 2d rev. ed. 1915; Thoughts on Drama), *Der Zufall, eine Vorform des Schicksals* (1924; Coincidence, a Preform of Destiny), *Droste-Hülshoff* (1904), and *Hebbel* (1905) and upon his many editions of German classics, such as the *Deutsches Balladenbuch* (1905; Book of German Ballads), *Deutsche Dramaturgie* (1907–12; German Dramatic Art), *Deutsche Mystiker* (1908, German Mystics), *Mörike* (1922), *Novalis* (1922), *Hebbel* (1923), *Eichendorff* (1924), and *Das Buch des Lachens* (1938; The Book of Laughter). Scholz's abiding interest in theater produced *Das Drama, Wesen, Werden und Darstellung der dramatischen Kunst* (1956; The Drama, the Nature, Development, and Depiction of the Dramatic Art) and *Mein Theater* (1964; My Theater). His novel about an investigator, *Theodor Dorn*, was published in 1967.

See: F. Droop, *Wilhelm von Scholz und seine besten Bühnenwerke* (1922); O. Loerke, "Wilhelm von Scholz," *Die neue Rundschau* 46, no. 1 (1935); 206–14.

H.Re. rev. A.L.W.

Schröder, Rudolf Alexander (1878–1962), German poet and essayist, was born in Bremen of a patrician family. In 1898, with his cousin Alfred Walter Heymel, he founded the review *Die Insel* (1898–1902) and the Insel-Verlag, one of the distinguished publishing houses of Germany, now a part of the Suhrkamp Verlag. In 1912, with Hugo von HOFMANNSTHAL and Rudolf BORCHARDT, he helped establish the Bremer Presse, which set a high standard for presswork and literary quality. He was also an architect, decorator, and painter. As a Protestant and a conservative, Schröder kept aloof from neopagan and totalitarian tendencies. About 1934 he left his home city and lived near the Chiemsee in Bavaria.

A writer of witty and elegant verse (*Hama*, 1908), Schröder concentrated more and more upon poetry. He translated *The Rape of the Lock* (1908); the *Odyssey* (1910) and the *Iliad* (1943); Horace (1935); Vergil's *Georgics* (1924), *Eclogues* (1926), and a canto of the *Aeneid* (1931); Jean Racine (1932); many Flemish and Dutch lyrics (for example, Guido Gezelle in 1917 and Geerten Gossaert in 1929); three plays of Shakespeare; and T. S. Eliot's *Murder in the Cathedral* (1946).

Schröder's prose is stately and leisurely, reflective and meandering, as in *Der Wanderer und die Heimat* (1931; The Wanderer and the Homeland) and *Aus Kindheit und Jugend* (1934; From My Childhood and Youth). His greatest achievements were wrung from a profound pessimism, as in the philosophical sonnets *Die Zwillingsbrüder* (The Twin Brothers), in the elegy *In Memoriam*, and in some of his odes and religious poems. He clung to what he thought might last; country, friendship, poetry, faith. With the years his religious heritage asserted itself strongly; he studied the history of Protestant verse and revived the art of hymn writing.

His volumes of early poetry include *Unmut* (1899; Annoyance); *Lieder an eine Geliebte* (Songs to a Beloved), *Empedokles*, and *Sprüche in Reimen* (Proverbs in Rhymes), all 1900; *An Belinde* (1902; To Belinde); *Sonette zum Andenken an eine Verstorbene* (1904; Sonnets in Memory of a Dead Woman); and *Lieder und Elegien* (1911; Songs and Elegies). To the collection of his mature poetry, *Die weltlichen Gedichte* (1940; Worldly Poems), and his religious poems, *Mitte des Lebens* (1930; Midway in Life), have been added *Ein Weihnachtslied* (1935; A Christmas Song), *Ein Lobgesang* (1937; A Hymn of Praise), *Osterspiel* (1938; Easter Play), and *Kreuzgespräch* (1939; Dialogue on the Cross). A volume of letters between Schröder and Siegbert Stehmann, written between 1938 and 1945, was published in 1962 under the title of *Freundeswort* (Words of Friends).

See: *Werke und Tage: Festschrift für Rudolf Alexander Schröder zum 60. Geburtstag* (1938); R. Adolph, *Schröder Bibliographie* (1953); K. Berger, *Die Dichtung Rudolf Alexander Schröders* (1954). H.St. rev. A.L.W.

Schulz, Bruno (1892–1942), Polish writer and graphic artist of Jewish extraction, was born and went to school in Drohobych, a small town in Galicia. He studied architecture in Lvov and fine arts in Vienna; from 1924 to 1939 he was an art teacher in a Drohobych gymnasium. He made his debut as a writer with book reviews in *Wiadomości Literackie*, and in 1938 he was awarded the Golden Laurel of the Polish Academy of Literature. Between 1939 and 1941 he lived in Soviet-occupied territory and was shot dead by a German officer in the ghetto of Drohobych in 1942.

Schulz is one of the most original Polish writers of the period between the world wars. His *Sklepy cynamonowa* (1934; Eng. tr., *The Street of Crocodiles*, 1963) and *Sanatorium pod klepsydra* (1937; Eng. tr., *Sanatorium under the Sign of the Hourglass*, 1978) are collections of stories reflecting Schulz's obsessive world created from his "private mythology." The central character in these stories, reminiscent of Franz KAFKA in their threatening and bizarre atmosphere, is the Father. The narrator's attitude toward him is distinctly ambiguous; he represents traditional power and authority, which is challenged by forces of a new, coarser reality. In spite of the mythological framework, Schulz's stories abound in realistic detail— elements of a grotesque surrealism and descriptive microrealism are welded together in his flowing and elaborate style, which has its roots in neoromantic prose of the fin de siècle. Although Schulz's province has been left behind by the times, life is in constant ferment and flux, and substances take different forms all the time; hence all manifestations of life have to be treated with suspicion and irony. This ironical approach to reality is implicit in most of Schulz's fiction, and even the masochism that is apparent in his writings can be interpreted as a form of self-irony. Schulz translated Kafka's *The Trial* into Polish. The most complete collection of his work is *Proza* (1964; Prose), which, along with his stories, includes all his surviving letters and literary reviews.

See: J. Ficowski, *Regiony wielkiej herezji: szkice o życiu i twórczości Brunona Schulza* (1975).   G.G.

Schwob, Marcel (1867–1905), French short-story writer, novelist, poet, essayist, and critic, was born in Chaville, of Jewish parents. A precocious child and a brilliant student, he quickly mastered German and English, which he spoke fluently. Leaving Nantes, where he spent his childhood, in 1882, he continued his studies at Sainte-Barbe and the Lycée Louis-le-Grand in Paris, where he made friends with Léon DAUDET and Paul CLAUDEL. Armed with a knowledge of the classical languages, he began writing a philosophical drama in verse on Prometheus, composing an original drama on the theme of Faust, and preparing a translation of Catullus done in the style of the 16th-century poet Clément Marot. He became interested in argot and wrote *Etude de l'argot français* (1889; Study of French Slang), influenced in part by a lifelong obsession with François Villon. At the Sorbonne, he studied under the philosopher Emile Boutroux; encouraged, too, by Michel Bréal, he acquired an intimate knowledge of ancient Greece and studied High German, Sanskrit, and Indo-European phonetics. Other influences during this period include Edgar Allan Poe, whom he admired; Robert Louis Stevenson, with whom he corresponded; Daniel Defoe, whose *Moll Flanders* he translated in 1895; Walt Whitman; and Mark Twain.

From all evidence, Schwob's readings and erudition were a means of escape and sublimation. A frail man, he could only enjoy the adventures of others by identifying with them through his imagination. He launched his literary career by contributing to the newspaper *Evénement* and by sending the first of his many stories to the *Echo de Paris*. Several collections of them—*Cœur double* (1891; Double Heart), *Le Roi au masque d'or* (1892; The King with the Golden Mask), *Mimes* (1894)—recreate (somewhat like Hugo's *Légende des siècles),* through their many portraits, the legends of Buddha and the world of Greek antiquity. As he searched for himself, Schwob employed humorous and fantastic disguises, blending his artistic imagination with his erudition. His ethic, an integral part of his aesthetics (which, incidentally, also reflects the Flaubertian importance he gave to perfection of form in his poetic prose), can best be seen in *Le Livre de Monelle* (1894; Eng. tr., *The Book of Monelle,* 1929), inspired by an acquaintance he had made with a prostitute. In this book, Schwob expresses pity and love for all suffering, frightened creatures who face the threat of the outside world.

In 1895, Schwob underwent surgery that left him in ill health for the remainder of his life. Impelled, perhaps, by his condition to escape from himself, he concentrated on biographical tales, in *Vies imaginaires* (1896; Imaginary Lives), a volume inspired by his reading of old texts, and on historical subjects, as in *La Croisade des enfants* (1893; Eng. tr., *The Children's Crusade,* 1898). Viewing biography as a "higher realism" and as a "mode of fiction," he described these lives as a quest for unity. For Schwob, life is chaos. He sympathetically views each individual as unique, driven by the fundamental duality of egoism and charity. For similar reasons, he emphasized his personal identification with such writers as Villon, Poe, Stevenson, and George Meredith, on whom he wrote critical studies in *Spicilège* (1896), and with *Moll Flanders* and *Hamlet* (1896), which represent some of his translations and adaptations.

Schwob's last writings include *Lampe de Psyché* (1903), which contains some of his earlier stories, and his scabrous *Parnasse satirique du XVme siècle* (1905; Satirical Parnassus of the 15th Century). Ironically, although he failed to be admitted to the Ecole Normale Supérieure, he finally became a professor at the Sorbonne in 1904, where he lectured on Villon. The book he was preparing on that poet, *François Villon: rédactions et notes* (1912), did not appear during Schwob's lifetime. As an outstanding antinaturalistic writer of poetic prose, he influenced, among others, Charles-Louis PHILIPPE, Guillaume APOLLINAIRE, and Henry BATAILLE. His genius did not go unnoticed by Alfred JARRY, Paul VALÉRY, Rémy de GOURMONT, and a host of other well-known writers.

See: P. Champion, "Vie de Schwob," in Schwob, *Œuvres complètes* (1927), vol. 1, and *Marcel Schwob et son temps* (1927); G. Trembley, *Marcel Schwob faussaire de la nature* (1969).   S.D.B.

Sciascia, Leonardo (1921–), Italian novelist, critic, and journalist, was born in Recalmuto (Agrigento), where his father worked as a sulphur miner. He has lived all his life in the Sicily that provides a background for his writings. After completing school, he became a functionary in a Fascist agency concerned with the requisitioning of farm produce. In 1949 he began teaching in an elementary shcool in Caltanissetta, where he remained until he moved to Palermo in 1957. In 1968 he relinquished his teaching post to devote his full time to writing.

Sciascia's literary career began in the early 1950s with the appearance of an Aesopean satire on the Fascist regime, *Favole della dittatura* (1950; Fables of the Dictatorship), and a short collection of lyric verse, *La Sicilia, il suo cuore* (1952; Sicily, Its Heart). His first truly successful publication, however, was *Le parrocchie di Regalpetra* (1956; Eng. tr., *Salt in the Wound,* 1969), a collection of stories set in a fictitious parish.

His fascination with what he terms *sicilitudine* (the quality of being Sicilian) is expressed in a series of fictions and "histories." The four stories of *Gli zii di Sicilia* (1958; The Uncles of Sicily) were published by Einaudi under the sponsorship of Elio VITTORINI.

Sciascia's favorite genre, however, is the *giallo* or mystery novel. Three such novels, *Il giorno della civetta* (1961; Eng. tr., *Mafia Vendetta,* 1964), *A ciascuno il suo* (1966; Eng. tr., *A Man's Blessing,* 1968), and *Il contesto* (1971; Eng. tr., *Equal Danger,* 1974), are staged in a realm of silence pervaded by the Mafia, a land where men participate futilely in the "dialogue of the deaf" that characterizes for Sciascia the perennial individualism of Sicilian culture. Sciascia considers these novels not mysteries but "parodies" of mysteries. The atomization he sees as endemic to Sicilian society is reminiscent of

Luigi PIRANDELLO's relativism: the Mafia thus becomes a poor but necessary substitute for social virtue and one of the very few *momenti storicizzabili* (moments where history can be written and thereby be made understandable) helping to define *sicilitudine*.

In his two other novels, *Consiglio d'Egitto* (1963; Eng. tr., *Council of Egypt,* 1966) and *La morte dell'inquisitore* (1964; Eng. tr., *The Death of the Inquisitor,* 1969), as well as in his only historical drama, *Recitazione della controversia liparitana dedicata ad A.D.* (1969, Recital of the Lipari Controversy Dedicated to A.D. [Alexander Dubček]), Sciascia investigates the past with a perspective and rhythm that suggest the confident probing of a detective. The kind of truths recoverable through historiography are examined in *Consiglio*, where a convincingly falsified manuscript suggests the fictitious nature of all past events.

Secondary to Sciascia's favorite mode of "historical" investigation are his dramas, such as *L'onorevole* (1965; The Honorable One), and his shorter fiction, a form to which he returned in 1973 with *Il mare colore del vino* (The Sea the Color of Wine). In his miscellaneous essay collections, *Pirandello e il pirandellismo* (1953), *Pirandello e la Sicilia* (1961), and *La corda pazza* (1970; The Crazy Rope), Sciascia has dealt eloquently with the writers of his Sicilian heritage as well as with contemporary social and political phenomena, particularly the Mafia. As an editor, he has provided prefaces and annotations for a variety of books, including the photographic essay *Le feste religiose in Sicilia* (1965; The Religious Festivals of Sicily) and various poetic texts. His recent publications include *Todo Modo* (1974; Eng. tr., *One Way or Another,* 1977) and *Candido* (1977; Eng. tr., *Candido, or a Dream Dreamed in Sicily,* 1979). Sciascia has been the recipient of several literary awards.

See: W. Mauro, *Sciascia* (1970). J.T.S.W.

Seeberg, Peter (1925-), Danish novelist and short-story writer, was born in the Jutland village of Skrydstrup. He received his university degree in 1950. Seeberg has participated in several archaeological expeditions, and he became curator of the Viborg Museum in Jutland in 1960. His literary production is founded on exceptionally precise and subtle observations related in a stylized language. His novel *Bipersonerne* (1956; The Subordinate Characters) describes a group of foreign slave laborers working in a German movie studio during World War II. They are uninvolved in the war drama itself, thus symbolizing the anonymous human being of the 20th century. In *Fugls Føde* (1957; Bird Pickings), Seeberg deals with conscious escapism. Tom, a writer, attempts to write something *real*, that is, to break out of nihilism, but the result is only a few unacceptable lines: "My eyes are blind; my hands are withered; my mind is dominated by destruction." The short stories in *Eftersøgningen* (1962; The Search) tell of the search for identity, truth, or reality in a universe that is not the outer world but human nature. These major themes indicate Seeberg's indebtedness to the great absurdists, Samuel BECKETT and Eugène IONESCO. His novel *Hyrder* (1970; Shepherds) is a seemingly realistic story about ordinary people. We are all each other's shepherds, and the author opens a perspective toward the dilemma of responsibility and identity. The interrelationship of individuals with society is the theme of the 19 short stories in *Dinosaurusens sene eftermiddag* (1974; The Late Afternoon of the Dinosaur), in which revolutionary attempts to break the imposed social frames are rejected in favor of evolutionary development. In his next work, *Argumenter for benådning* (1976; Arguments for Mercy), Seeberg again points to man's insignificance and

impotence. Through compassion and tolerance, however, it is possible to overcome life's absurdity, a possibility that is less apparent in Seeberg's latest novel, *Ved havet* (1978; At the Sea).

See: I. Bondebjerg, *Peter Seeberg* (1972); V. Thule, *Peter Seeberg* (1972). S.H.R.

Seferis, George, pseud. of Giorgios Seferiadis (1900-71), Greek poet, critic, and diplomat, was born in Smyrna. Although he left his birthplace at the outbreak of World War I, the subsequent displacement of Smyrna's Greek community after the Asia Minor Disaster of 1922 remained for him a personal loss and contributed decisively to the tragic sense of life that dominates his poetry. In 1918, Seferis went to Paris to study at the Sorbonne. After receiving his law degree in 1924, he traveled to London to perfect his English in anticipation of entering the Greek diplomatic service. Thus began his long and fruitful association with England. A tour of London as vice-consul in 1931 introduced him to the poetry of Ezra Pound and T. S. Eliot. This visit also gave him his first sense of nostalgia for the Mediterranean and perhaps the sharpest intimations of the exile theme that was to become so central to his later work.

Seferis's early volumes of poetry, *Strophi* (1931; Turning Point) and *I Sterna* (1932; The Cistern), were the beginning of an oeuvre that revitalized Greek verse. (For translations of these and subsequent volumes, see *Collected Poems, 1924-1955,* translated by Edmund Keeley and Philip Sherrard.) These works reveal Seferis's keen interest in the tonal and stylistic experiments of his French contemporaries, including the "pure poetry" of Paul VALÉRY. This early poetry also demonstrates the poet's awareness of his own tradition by exploiting forms, themes, and diction from folk poetry and demotic (vernacular) literature. It is this literature that Seferis often writes about in *Dokimes* (1962, 1974; partial Eng. tr., *On the Greek Style,* 1966), generally regarded as the best volume of literary criticism in contemporary Greek letters. The influence of Pound, and especially of Eliot, can be felt throughout Seferis's mature verse, including such volumes as *Mythistorima* (1935), *Tetradio gymnasmaton* (1940; Book of Exercises), *Imerologio katastromatos I* (1940; Logbook 1), and *Imerologio katastromatos II* (1944; Logbook 2). In these works, Seferis adopts a poetic voice that combines the language of everyday speech with the poetic forms and rhythms of traditional usage to create the effect of both density and economy.

Seferis served as Greek ambassador to Great Britain from 1957 until his retirement in 1962. This and other diplomatic appointments required him to live outside Greece for many years. His travels are reflected in the personal mythology of his verse, whose recurrent persona is a modern Odysseus, tormented by alienation and a longing to return to a distant "other world." Seferis's direct involvement in the diplomacy of national crises (such as the German invasion of Greece in 1941 and the Cyprus issue of the 1950s) gave his poetry another of its major strengths: an ability to capture the meaning of historical events by means of metaphors universal enough to convey the mood of the poet's own times. *Imerologio katastromatos III* (1965; Logbook 3), a volume of poetry dedicated to the people of Cyprus, transcends mere political commentary to explore the tragic realities of war. During his retirement in Athens, Seferis produced a final volume, entitled *Tria kryfa poiimata* (1966; Eng. tr., *Three Secret Poems,* 1969), with verse as cryptic as its title suggests, but with a linguistic resonance in the manner of Dionysios Solomos.

In 1963, Seferis was awarded the Nobel Prize for Literature, the first such award made to a Greek national. As a result both of this international recognition and of his dramatic condemnation of the Papadopoulos dictatorship in 1969, Seferis's funeral drew thousands to the Athens cemetery to honor him as a national spokesman for those with a faith in freedom. Seferis's *A Poet's Journal: Days of 1945-1951*, tr. by A. Anagnostopoulos, was published in 1974. English translations of Seferis's poems include *Poems*, tr. by Rex Warner (1960), and *Collected Poems, 1924-1955*, tr. by E. Keeley and P. Sherrard (1969).

See: E. Keeley, "Seferis and the 'Mythical Method,'" *CLS* 6 (1969): 109-10.   E.K.

Segalen, Victor (1878-1919), French poet, novelist, dramatist, physician, and amateur sinologist, was born in Brest. He divided his work into what he called four cycles: Maori, heroic, Chinese, and those projects "deposited on account." Segalen's Maori cycle includes a novel, *Les Immémoriaux* (1907; The Immemorial), published under the pseudonym Max Anély, and an article on Maori music (1907). His heroic cycle includes his drama *Siddhartha* (1974). This play led to a collaboration with Claude Debussy on *Orphée roi* (1921; Orpheus the King), which the composer was to have set to music.

Most of Segalen's work belongs to his Chinese cycle. His masterpiece is *Stèles* (1912; partial Eng. tr., *Stelae*, 1964), a collection of prose poems inspired by his travel and residence in China and his studies of Chinese language and culture. Other collections include *Peintures* (1916; Paintings), in which he explores Taoism as well as Chinese art, and *Equipée* (1929; Escapade), based on an actual journey in China, but representing, as does all his work, a "voyage au fond de soi" (journey to the bottom of the self). His novel *René Leys* (1921; Eng. tr., 1974), in which the central figure witnesses the collapse of the Manchu dynasty, revolves around the ambiguous relation of the real and the imaginary. Segalen's contribution to sinology stems from a major archaeological expedition he undertook with Auguste Gilbert de Voisins and Jean Lartigue, the results of which were reported in the *Journal asiatique* (1915-16) and in *L'Art funéraire à l'époque des Han* (1935; Funereal Art in the Period of the Han).

As for Segalen's last cycle, many projects were announced in the *Lettres de Chine: 1909-1910,* published by his widow in 1967. In recent years, his daughter Annie Joly-Segalen has seen to the publications of many incomplete manuscripts, including *Briques et tuiles* (1967; Bricks and Tiles), *Chine: la grande statuaire* (1972; Eng. tr., *The Great Statuary of China,* 1978), *Imaginaires* (1972), and *Le Combat pour le sol* (1974; Battle for the Soil).

See: H. Bouillier, *Victor Segalen* (1961); J.-L. Bédouin, *Victor Segalen* (1963).   G.Bi.

Šegedin, Petar (1909-), Croatian novelist, short-story writer, and essayist, was born in Žrnovo, on the island of Korčula. After obtaining teaching credentials in Dubrovnik, he studied philosophy in Zagreb. He served as secretary to various Croatian cultural organizations and as cultural attaché to the Yugoslav embassy in Paris (1956-60). In 1964 he became a member of the Yugoslav Academy. He was very active in the Croatian political and cultural "mass movement" (1967-71) and thereafter, although not imprisoned, led a precarious existence under police surveillance.

Šegedin began his literary career with an essay, published in Miroslav KRLEŽA's prewar journal *Pečat,* about his journey to the New York World's Fair in 1939. He has continued to travel widely, writing about his journeys

in *Na putu* (1953; On the Road) and *Susreti* (1963; Meetings). Yet we learn little from his travelogues about the countries he saw or the people he met, because in these works Šegedin is concerned above all with his own moods and impressions.

During the period (1945-50), when Yugoslav literature was dominated by the dogma of socialist realism, Šegedin dared to write in his own way and about his own preoccupations. His subjects are often his unhappy childhood in Žrnovo or the figure of the solitary, usually neurotic, intellectual who rarely succeeds in establishing meaningful contact with anyone. When his two novels, *Djeca božja* (1946; God's Children) and *Osamljenici* (1947; The Lonely Ones), appeared, they were hardly noticed; only later, upon their republication in 1961-62, were they greeted as forerunners of a new Yugoslav prose.

Šegedin's numerous short stories, first issued in literary journals and then collected in several volumes, seldom describe happy incidents. With multiple digressions and meditations, the author minutely examines why his characters have failed and who is responsible for their suffering. It is true that they search for a way out of their impasses, but their lives are dominated by darkness and despair. The absurdity of human endeavors is a major theme in Segedin's works, which are slow-moving and difficult to read, and are appreciated mostly by the intellectuals.

In contrast to his fiction, Šegedin writes in a direct, logical style when discussing the economic and cultural grievances of his people. These are the concerns of *Svi smo odgovorni?* (1971; Are We All Responsible?), a clearly written analysis that judiciously draws its arguments from daily life or history. In this work he has proved in critical moments (in the late 1960s) to have the stamina for a leading role in defense of Croatian national interests.

See: P. Džadžić, "Strah i usamljenost u prozi Petra Šegedina," *Nova Misao* 9 (1953): 513-16; T. Ladan, "Omnia mea mecum," *Telegram*, Dec. 14, 1962, p. 5; A. Kadić, *From Croatian Renaissance to Yugoslav Socialism* (1969), pp. 229-30, 285-88; N. Disopra, "Dvije knjige proze Petra Šegedina," *Mogućnosti* 1 (1970): 79-95.
                             A.K.

Seghers, Anna, pseud. of Netty Radványi (1900-), East German novelist, was born Anna Reiling in Mainz, the only daughter of a Jewish dealer in antiques. She studied art history and sinology at the universities of Cologne and Heidelberg. While still a student, Seghers joined a group of left-wing intellectuals, and by the time she married the Hungarian Communist sociologist Laszlo Radványi in 1925, she shared his political views, convictions that grew stronger with each passing year and that dominated her life and work.

In *Aufstand der Fischer von St. Barbara* (1928; Eng. tr., *The Revolt of the Fishermen*, 1930), Segher's first publication, a revolutionary incites fishermen to rebel against a mighty monopoly. Although unsuccessful, the rebellion gives meaning to the uneventful lives of alienated people. Some of the protesters experience freedom and happiness only in the hour of their death. *Auf dem Wege zur amerikanischen Botschaft* (1930; On the Way to the American Embassy), a collection of stories about poverty-stricken workers who vegetate in dingy homes, takes place in the same environment of daily work that is routine and of days that "seem endless and thin like stretched elastic." Only when individuals join in revolutionary action do they regain their human dignity and their place in history. Essentially the same thoughts underlie the novel *Die Gefährten* (1932; The Companions), which describes the life stories of several revolutionaries in Eastern European countries and China against backgrounds of adverse conditions, and *Der Weg durch den Februar* (1934; The Path through February), which deals with the Engelbert Dollfuss uprising in Austria. Revolution is seen as essential to release the energy of the proletariat in an eruption of collective action and as the only way to achieve social change.

After Adolf Hitler came to power, Seghers and her family fled to Paris and then to Mexico. Disillusioned by most German workers' indifference toward and acceptance of the Nazi takeover, Seghers did not glorify revolution; she contended that the proletariat had been lured into the wrong kind of solidarity and advocated the formation of a socialist underground. *Der Kopflohn* (1933; The Bounty) deals with farmers in a village infiltrated by Nazis; *Die Rettung* (1937; The Rescue) focuses on the misery of a group of miners; *Das siebte Kreuz* (1942; Eng. tr., *The Seventh Cross*, 1942) is a moving account of flight from a concentration camp and the resulting solidarity of oppressed people who work for a future socialist revolution. The novel *Transit* (1943; Eng. tr., 1944), dealing with a refugee who seeks a visa and sailing papers amidst an infernal Kafkaesque bureaucracy, reaffirms Seghers's belief in human dignity and future collective action that will bring the end of the fascist regime. It also expresses her belief that the work of the writer can help the cause of the proletariat.

Seghers moved to East Germany in 1947 to serve the socialist cause. *Die Toten bleiben jung* (1949; Eng. tr., *The Dead Stay Young*, 1950), written while she was still in exile, asserts that sons inherit the duty to avenge the injustice done to their fathers by reactionaries; the author sees the world as divided into good revolutionaries and bad reactionaries, without broader human concerns. *Die Entscheidung* (1959; The Decision) and *Das Vertrauen* (1968; Trust) deal with two steel mills. One, in West Germany, oppresses its workers and teaches them to hate East Germany, whereas a new steel mill in East Germany makes great progress in satisfying the workers' needs. Nevertheless, there are sobering observations of East German life, where workers are pressed to achieve production goals and streets look "gray" in contrast to streets inundated by light in West Berlin. Color and shadow also play a role in *Überfahrt* (1971; Crossing), in which a young Brazilian-born physician, Triebl, returns to East Germany—where he had studied and known a girl with "gray" eyes—because he feels that it is the home of men of goodwill.

After her return from exile, Seghers clearly adopted socialist realism as her sole credo and firmly embedded her work in the East German cultural scene. The Communist tendencies of the early works were strengthened, making her a Communist writer.

See: H. Neugebauer, *Anna Seghers, Ihr Leben und Werk* (1970); T. Huebener, "Anna Seghers," in *The Literature of East Germany* (1970). A.P.O.

Seghers, Pierre (1906–), French poet, essayist, and editor, was born in Paris. He studied at the Collège of Carpentras in Vaucluse, where his father's wandering had then taken the family. In 1939, while living in Villeneuve-lès-Avignon, he published on his own press his first collection of poems, *Bonne Espérance* (Good Hope). This was followed by *Pour les quatre saisons* (1942; For the Four Seasons), *Chien de pique* (1943; Pointer), and other volumes. (A selection of his poetry in English translation has been published as *Poèmes* [1956]). In 1939 he also founded a magazine devoted to poetry, *P.C. 39* (selected Eng. tr., *Poésie 39–45*, 1947), and in 1944 he established

the series *Poètes d'aujourd'hui*, wherein each number is devoted to a single poet. Paul ELUARD, Louis ARAGON, and Max JACOB were presented in the first three issues, accounting in part for the remarkable success of the collection. (Issue 164, published in 1967, is on Seghers himself.) In collaboration with Jean Charpier, Seghers produced *Art poétique* (1956; Poetic Art), an anthology of the poetic opinions and judgments formulated by ancient and modern poets on the nature of poetry and its modes of expression. Again with Charpier, he published *L'Art de la peinture* (1957; Eng. tr., *The Art of Painting*, 1964). For Seghers, poetry consists essentially in a docile submission to inspiration, to life in its manifold manifestations. His poetry is thus intensely personal and often obscure, requiring the participation of the reader to reveal its ultimate meaning. F.V.

Seidel, Ina (1885–1974), German poet and novelist, was born in Halle an der Saale. She was steeped in literature throughout her life. The prolific historical novelist Georg Ebers (1837–98) was her mother's stepfather; and her husband, Heinrich Wolfgang Seidel (1876–1945), author of *Erinnerungen* (1912; Memories), *Abend und Morgen* (1934; Evening and Morning), and *Das Seefräulein* (1937; The Ocean Nymph), was the son of Heinrich Seidel (1842–1906), the once popular author of the sentimental story *Leberecht Hühnchen* (1881). Ina Seidel married in 1907, hovered for months between life and death after the birth of her first child, and in this period of solitude and spiritual growth turned to self-expression in poetry. She began her writing with lyric poetry: *Gedichte* (1914; Poems), *Neben der Trommel her* (1915; Next to the Trumpet), and *Weltinnigkeit* (1918; World Inwardness). In 1917 she published her first work of fiction, *Das Haus zum Monde* (The House at the Moon). Five years later she had already gained enough strength and substance to compose a powerful and significant novel, *Das Labyrinth* (1921; Eng. tr., *The Labyrinth*, 1932), the life story of a strange and enigmatic figure, Georg Forster, whose career she traced more on the psychic than on the material plane.

But Seidel was not yet fully equipped for the theme she had first set herself, and definite expression came only in 1930 in *Das Wunschkind* (Eng. tr., *The Wish Child*, 1935). This story of a widowed mother, who has literally wrested her child from the reluctant clasp of fate, only to lose him to a more inexorable destiny in the Prussian wars of liberation, is one of the great books of its generation. Seidel's shorter prose was published in *Der vergrabene Schatz* (1955; The Buried Treasure) and *Die alte Dame und der Schmetterling* (1964; The Old Woman and the Butterfly). A collection of poetry appeared in 1957. Her late novels were *Das unverwesliche Erbe* (1958; The Incorruptible Inheritance) and *Michaela: Aufzeichnungen des Jürgen Brook* (1959; Michaela: Notebooks of Jürgen Brook). A volume of essays, *Frau und Wort* (1965; Woman and Word), was followed by autobiographical works in *Vor Tau und Tag: Geschichte einer Kindheit* (1962; Before Dew and Day: Story of a Childhood) and *Lebensbericht 1885–1923* (1970; Life Story 1885–1923).

See: K. A. Horst, *Ina Seidel: Wesen und Werk* (1956). B.Q.M.

Seifert, Jaroslav (1901–), Czech poet, was born in Prague. As a young man he passed through the then-dominant phase of "proletarian" poetry, as revealed in his first two collections, *Město v slzach* (1921; The City in Tears) and *Samá láska* (1923; Nothing but Love). He also experienced the succeeding "pure poetry" phase, as evidenced by *Na vlnách T.S.F.* (1925; On Radio Waves) and *Slavík* *zpívá špatně* (1926; The Nightingale Sings Badly). Seifert found his true poetic forte in the early 1930s with *Jablko z klína* (1933; An Apple from the Lap). In this collection the clever manner and fireworks of the earlier works have been abandoned for a new style, one notable for its sincerity and directness and for its cultivation of natural, unaffected images rendered in fresh, at times almost colloquial, language. Love, including its sensual aspects, a frequent theme in Seifert's earlier collections, is his dominant subject in *Jablko*, and continues to dominate his next collection, *Ruce Venušiny* (1936; The Arms of Venus). *Zhasněte světla* (1938; Put Out the Lights) betrays the poet's disquiet after the betrayal of Czechoslovakia at Munich. *Světlem oděná* (1940; Dressed in Light), written during the Nazi occupation of Czechoslovakia, is a poetic tribute to Prague, the poet's native city, while *Přilba hlíny* (1945; The Helmet of Clay) celebrates the 1945 Prague uprising against the Germans. During the repressive period following the Communist takeover of Czechoslovakia in 1948, Seifert wrote mostly children's literature. In the 1960s he, along with his fellow poet František Hrubín, played an outstanding role in calling for greater freedom in Czech literature.

See: V. Černý, *Jaroslav Seifert* (1954); A. French, *The Poets of Prague* (1969).   W.E.H.

Sekulić, Isadora (1877–1958), Serbian short-story writer, novelist, and critic, was born in Mošorin, Bačka. She is one of the very few female writers to have won a place of distinction in the pantheon of Serbian literature. Sekulić trained to be a teacher and held a Ph.D. from a German university. Through sojourns in Norway, France, and England, she broadened her cultural horizons and perfected her knowledge of several foreign languages.

Sekulić established herself as a writer with the publication of a highly original, introspective collection entitled *Saputnici* (1913; Fellow Travelers). Its beautiful prose is characterized by lyricism, eloquence, and erudition. Sekulić's next publication, *Pisma iz Norveške* (1914; Letters from Norway), was interpreted by Jovan SKERLIĆ as a sign of indifference to the fate of her native Serbia. Five years later, however, in her novella *Djakon Bogorodičine crkve* (1919; The Deacon of the Church of Our Lad), she gave clear evidence of an identification with her Serbian Orthodox heritage. This identification can be traced throughout her subsequent literary works. A highly cultivated critic, she is nevertheless valued more for her intuitive insights than for factual detail. Her best-known critical works are *Njegošu knjiga duboke odanosti* (1951; A Book of Deep Homage to Njegoš) and *Mir i nemir* (1957; Peace and Unrest). In *Govor i jezik* (1956; Speech and Language), she discusses the difficulty of translating Yugoslav literature into Western European languages.

See: B. Novaković, "Nemiri i napori Isidore Sekulić," *Susreti* (1959), pp. 109–41; Z. Mišić, "Podvig jednog života i pisanja," *Reč i vreme*, vol. 2 (1963), pp. 142–47; J. Skerlić, "Dve ženske knjige," *Pisci i Knjige*, vol. 5 (1964), pp. 278–87.   M.M. with W.B.E.

Selvinsky, Ilya (Karl) Lvovich (1899–1968), Russian poet, playwright, and novelist, was born and grew up in the Crimea. In 1921 he moved to Moscow, where he soon became the central figure in Russian constructivism (1922–30) (*see* RUSSIAN LITERATURE) and the chief rival to Boris PASTERNAK in poetical prestige. As a constructivist, Selvinsky strove for a colorful lexicon, stressed the narrative, and practiced the kind of Russian accentual verse called *taktovik*. He was a virtuoso of verse (as evidenced by his "wreaths of sonnets") and a master of tours de force, which abound in his first and best book,

Rekordy (1926; Records), especially in his imitations of Cossack and gypsy songs. His ambition, however, was to write epics and tragedies. His early narrative poems, *Ulyalayevshchina* (1927), a portrait of a Civil War anarchist leader; *Zapiski poeta* (1928; Notes of a Poet), which features a satirical alter ego; and *Pushtorg* (1929; Fur Trade), a "novel in verse" about the problems of the intelligentsia during the period of the New Economic Policy (NEP), were highly praised, but they were criticized even more by the orthodox critics. Selvinsky's first drama in verse, *Komandarm 2* (1930; Army Commander #2), portraying both true and false revolutionaries, was produced by Vsevolod Meyerhold; and *Pao-Pao* (1933), a philosophical grotesque, has an ape with a human brain for its protagonist. All these major works including *Umkabely medved* (1935; Umka the Polar Bear), a play about the Sovietization of a Siberian minority, were radically rewritten by Selvinsky in later years. More in tune with the prescribed canons of socialist realism, but often of high literary quality, are the play *Rytsar Ioann* (1939; The Knight John), the patriotic trilogy *Rossiya* (1944–57), and the poet's polemics with Goethe, *Chitaya 'Fausta'* (1952; Reading *Faust*). In his late years Selvinsky published a sumiautobiographical novel, *O yunost moya* (1966; O My Youth).

See: A. Kaun, *Soviet Poets and Poetry* (1943); O. Reznik, *Zhizn v poezii* (1967).   V.M.

Sena, Jorge de (1919–78), Portuguese poet, playwright, short-story writer, critic, and essayist, was born in Lisbon and graduated in engineering from the University of Oporto. He worked for the Portuguese Highway Department until 1959, when, although already recognized as an outstanding literary figure, he found the dictatorial atmosphere in Portugal so stifling that he emigrated and took a teaching position at the University of Assis, in Brazil. He lectured at this and other universities in the state of São Paulo for six years before moving on to the United States, teaching first at the University of Wisconsin and then at the University of California at Santa Barbara, while he pursued his career as a creative Portuguese writer.

Sena revealed himself as a surrealist poet even before surrealism took hold in Portugal and also wrote excellent neorealistic verse without actually belonging to the school of that name. With José Augusto França, he resurrected the *Cadernos de Poesia* in 1951 (*see* PORTUGUESE LITERATURE). Under Sena's orientation, the publication declared itself for a type of poetry based on "a commitment established between a human being and his time, between a personality and its own sensitive conscience of the world, which mutually define each other." In his poetry, a vast array of techniques and attitudes is to be found: *Perseguição* (1942; Pursuit), *Coroa da terra* (1946; The Earth's Crown), *Pedra filosofal* (1950; Philosopher's Stone), *Peregrinatio ad loca infecta* (1969; A Journey to the Dark Places), *Exorcismos* (1972; Exorcisms), and the collection of early works entitled *Trinta anos de poesia* (1972; Thirty Years of Poetry). These and others, however, collected in *Poesia* (3 vols., 1961–78), have in common an intellectual, austere search for the meaning of life. There is even a certain aggressive quality in Sena's often sarcastic denunciation of society's evils and in his desire to offer a new truth, based on coexistence of fantasy and reality. He could be very sophisticated in his poetry, being familiar with the best contemporary lyric poets of the Western World, witness his exquisite translations and comments in *Poesia do século XX* (*De Thomas Hardy a C. V. Cattaneo*), published posthumously in 1978.

Within Sena's dramatic production, the four-act tragedy *O indesejado: António, Rei* (1951; King Antonio the Unwanted) has been singled out by some critics as one of the most significant Portuguese plays of the century. His fictional work comprises two remarkable collections of short stories, *Andanças do Demónio* (1960; The Devil's Wanderings), *Novas andanças do Demónio* (1966; The Devil's New Wanderings), and *Os grão-capitães* (1976; enlarged ed. 1979; The Captains-General), in which occasional surrealistic overtones blend into his perceptive humanistic outlook.

As a critic and essayist, Sena wrote more than 60 works on Portuguese, French, and English topics, including a history of English literature (1963) and his *Estudos de história e de cultura*, 2 vols. (1967, 1969; Studies on History and Culture), dealing with Spanish and Portuguese literature of the 16th and 17th centuries. In his later life, Sena became the leading authority on Camões. His Camoniana include *A poesia de Camões* (1951; The Poetry of Camõns), *Uma canção de Camões* (1966, A Canzone by Camõns), and *Os sonetos de Camões e o soneto quinhentista peninsular* (1969; The Sonnets of Camões and the Sixteenth-Century Peninsular Sonnet). Likewise, he has been an early editor and commentator of Fernando PESSOA, beginning with an edition of the latter's *Páginas de doutrina estética* (1947; Pages of Aesthetic Doctrine). He also translated into Portuguese works by André GIDE, André MALRAUX, Ernest Hemingway, Erskine Caldwell, and Graham Greene, as well as a great number of poems from various languages, compiled in *Poesia de 26 séculos* (2 vols., 1971–72; Poetry of 26 Centuries).

See: "Homenagem a Jorge de Sena," homage vol. of *O Tempo* 59 (April 1968); F. G. Williams, "Prodigious Exorcist: An Introduction to the Poetry of Jorge de Sena," *WLT* 53, no. 1 (Winter 1979): 9–15.   E.M.D.

Sender, Ramón José (1902–), Spanish novelist and critic, was born in Chalamera de Cinca, in the region of Aragon. Although he has lived in exile since 1939, mainly in the United States, he has never lost his feeling for his native land. A journalist in his youth, he published his first novel in 1930. Entitled *Imán* (Eng. tr., *Pro Patria*, 1935), it is a devastating criticism of the Spanish army and its war in Morocco in the early 1920s. This work is the first in a series of novels dealing with Spain's past and present history. Sender gave testimony to many events and social movements that took place during the Republic (1931–36). *O.P. (Orden Público)* (1931; Public Order) and *Siete domingos rojos* (1932; Eng. tr., *Seven Red Sundays*, 1936), both deal with the problems of injustice and revolt in a bourgeois society. Sender's sympathy for the anarchist movement in Spain, combined with his clear understanding of its contradictions and limitations, is expressed in these writings. The peasant revolt of Casas Viejas in 1933 and the repression that followed it became the subject of *Viaje a la aldea del crimen* (1933; Trip to the Village of the Crime). More a documentary than a novel, this book exposes the cruelty inflicted upon a group of Andalusian peasants, ironically by the liberal Republican establishment. *Mr. Witt en el Cantón* (1936; Eng. tr., *Mr. Witt among the Rebels*, 1937) focuses on the Cartagena separatist revolt of 1873. By creating a character alien to the historical events, Mr. Witt, an Englishman, Sender affords himself a certain detachment in dealing with the passions and Utopian dreams of the Cartagena rebels. This novel earned Sender the National Prize for Literature in 1936.

The Civil War of 1936–39 was a turning point in the life of Ramón Sender, as it was in the lives of many Spaniards. The front lines separated him from his wife, who was later shot by the Nationalists. His war experiences became the subject of another documentary book, *Contra-ataque* (1938; Eng. tr., *Counter-Attack in Spain*, 1937), published abroad one year prior to the Spanish edition. This book was written to arouse sympathy for the Republican cause, and parts of it reappeared later blended into Sender's main novel of the Spanish Civil War, *Los cinco libros de Ariadna* (1957; The Five Books of Ariadne). This work is a detailed narration in which fact and fantasy, autobiography and poetic imagination, are fused into a web of past, present, and future action. The main character, like the author himself, is strongly individualist and fated to come into conflict with Communist ideology. In *El rey y la reina* (1949; Eng. tr., *The King and the Queen*, 1968) the Civil War is the background for the story of a man and a woman of very different social classes, who face a new reality in which class differences have disappeared. His best novel of the Civil War, however, is rather short. First published in Mexico as *Mosén Millán* (1953), it was published again in New York in a bilingual, English-Spanish edition, as *Requiem por un campesino español* (1960; Eng. tr., *Requiem for a Spanish Peasant*). The tragic aspects of the Civil War are recreated in this novel not on the scale of a wide, all-encompassing mural, but rather within the very limited bounds of the life of a small village and of some of its inhabitants. The main characters are the peasant Paco and the village priest who baptized him and who ends up unwittingly turning him over to his Fascist executioners. The priest feels unable to stop the violence and the killings inflicted on his flock by those who claim to be on the side of religion. Indirectly connected with the Civil War is *El verdugo afable* (1952), which was expanded in its English translation, *The Affable Hangman* (1963). It is the story of a man who decides to become a hangman and thus attract general contempt, in order to expiate the sins of the real killer, society. Hypocrisy is presented as the main characteristic of an established order that despises the man it hires to commit its own legal killings.

Exile, first in Mexico and later in the United States, meant for Sender a new environment from which to extract his literary creations and a chance to look back at his childhood and adolescence in the lost land of Spain. Several novels that had been published separately later appeared together under the title *Crónica del alba* (1963), in which Sender reminisces about his youth, his first love, and the conflicts of growing up in a society of whose shortcomings he was increasingly aware. The first novel of the series appeared in English as *Chronicle of Dawn* (1944). An introduction to the *Crónica* explains that it was written by a Spanish Republican officer who died in one of the refugee camps in southern France after the end of the Civil War. Having lost his native land, he was no longer interested in living.

Far from Spain, Sender found inspiration in America, especially in Spanish-speaking America north and south of the United States-Mexican border. *Epitalamio del prieto Trinidad* (1942; Eng. tr., *Dark Wedding*, 1948) is a story of survival in the cruel environment of a tropical prison island. *Mexicayotl* (1940) and *Novelas ejemplares de Cíbola* (1961; Exemplary Novels of Cíbola) are collections of short stories dealing with pre-Hispanic Mexico and with the North American area colonized by the Spaniards.

His long exile and proclaimed displeasure during the years of the dictatorship of Francisco Franco kept Spanish readers in a state of ignorance about this author. Only in 1965 was *Crónica del alba* published in Spain, and Sender became known again in his own country, in which he had won a national literary prize in 1936. Many of the novels published in exile were printed in Spain for the first time, and those that had given him a literary reputation before 1936 were printed again after a silence of 30 or more years.

Sender has also written for the theater: *Hernán Cortés* (1940), expanded and republished later as *Jubileo en el Zócalo* (1964; Celebration on the Square). *Examen de ingenios: los 98* (1961; Talents Considered: The 98ers) is a collection of literary studies on Miguel de UNAMUNO, Ramón del VALLE-INCLÁN, and Pío BAROJA, among others. Sender has also published a book of poetry, *Las imágenes migratorias* (1960; Migratory Images). He is one of the most prolific of contemporary writers and considered by some critics to be one of Spain's finest living novelists.

See: M. C. Peñuelas, *La obra narrativa de Ramón J. Sender* (1971); C. L. King, *Ramón J. Sender: An Annotated Bibliography, 1928–1974* (1976).   L.S.P. de L.

Senghor, Léopold Sédar (1906–), black French poet, essayist, and statesman, was born in Joal, Senegal, then a French colony. After attending secondary schools in Dakar, he went to Paris where he studied at the Sorbonne, receiving the *agrégation* in 1935. He taught in several French lycées. Drafted into the French army in 1939, he was taken prisoner in 1940 and spent two years in a German stalag. In 1945, Senghor was elected deputy of Senegal to the French Constituent Assembly, and, in 1960, he became the first president of the new Republic of Senegal. In 1929, while still a student in Paris, he and Aimé CÉSAIRE collaborated on founding the journal *L'Etudiant noir*, wherein Senghor coined the term *négritude*. This term, later explained in many essays such as "Ce que l'homme noir apporte" (What the Black Man Brings), is the key to Senghor's political activity and to his poetic inspiration. It denotes the contributions of the black man to modern, and especially European, civilization: sentiment, passion, spontaneity, a sense of mystery, and an intimate communion with nature. Senghor's poetry, distinguished by a mixture of pagan and Christian symbols, exhibits these qualities as well as a pride in his own race and pity for the downtrodden, particularly the victims of the colonial era. His first collection of poems, many of them previously published in the journal *Présence africaine*, appeared in 1945 under the title *Chants d'ombre* (Songs of the Shadows). Senghor's other collections include *Hosties noires* (1948; Black Consecrated Wafers), *Chants pour Naëtt* (1949; Songs for Naëtt), *Ethiopiques* (1956; Ethiopics), and *Nocturnes* (1961). Some of these poems were published in English translation as *Selected Poems* (1964). Senghor's poems can also be found in numerous anthologies, such as *Anthologie de la nouvelle poésie nègre et malgache* (Anthology of the New Negro and Madagascan Poetry), with its preface, *Orphée noir* (Black Orpheus), by Jean-Paul Sartre (1948), and in *Poèmes d'expression française*, by L. G. Damas (1947).

See: A. Guibert, *Léopold Sédar Senghor* (1961).
                                                                    F.V.

Serafimovich, Aleksandr, pseud. of Aleksandr Serafimovich Popov (1863–1949), Russian novelist and short-story writer, was born in the Don River region. He was a political exile from 1887 to 1890, and he joined the Communist Party in 1918. In 1889 he began publishing populist-type stories about the privations of the underprivileged; after the Russian Revolution of 1905, he added the revolutionary theme. Both a collection and a three-volume edition of his stories appeared between 1901 and 1908. His story "Peski" (1908; Eng. tr., "Sand," in *Sand*

and Other Stories, 1957), portraying the self-destructiveness of human greed, drew praise from Lev TOLSTOY. Serafimovich published two novels, *Gorod v stepi* (1912; A Town in the Steppe), which deals with the development of Russian capitalism, and the celebrated *Zhelezny potok* (1924; Eng. tr., *The Iron Flood,* 1935), which shows how the Bolshevik will transforms unruly peasant masses into an iron force during the Russian Civil War in the northern Caucasus. *Zhelezny potok* is noted for its deliberate lack of individual characterization and for its stylistic mixtures of traditionalism and modernism. The author's clear intent was to endow the mass movement with an aura of epic grandeur by employing, like Nikolay Gogol in *Taras Bulba*, the stock attributes of folk poetry, and by creating impressionistic imagery that occasionally borders on surrealism and that contrasts sharply with the earthy Ukrainian spoken by the characters portrayed. *Zhelezny potok* was intended as a part of "Borba" (The Struggle), a projected series of sociopolitical novels that never was written. The stories and sketches Serafimovich published after *Zhelezny potok* add no new dimensions to his writing.

See: E. J. Brown, *Russian Literature since the Revolution* (rev. ed. 1969), pp. 157–61.   H.E.

Serao, Matilde (1856–1927), Italian novelist, was born in Patras, Greece, of a Greek mother and a Neapolitan father. Brought to Italy at the age of four, she studied in Naples with her mother, attended normal school, worked in the telegraph office, and had her first writings accepted by Neapolitan journals. She soon turned her vast energy to journalism and fiction and achieved success and fame in both. In 1882 she moved to Rome where, together with Edoardo Scarfoglio, Giosuè Carducci (1835–1907), and Gabriele D'ANNUNZIO, she helped to make *Il capitan Fracassa* the sprightliest Roman paper of its day. In 1884 she married Scarfoglio, and their combined journalistic ventures enjoyed varied success for two decades. *Il mattino* of Naples, which they founded and edited, was for many years the most substantial newspaper of southern Italy. Upon her separation from her husband in 1904, Serao also left *Il mattino* and founded her own daily, *Il giorno*, which she edited until her death in Naples in 1927.

Serao's vast literary output appeared in some 50 volumes from 1878 to 1926. It embraces, besides her novels and stories of Neapolitan life, many novels of passion among the idle rich, mystery stories, works of religious edification, books of travel, literary essays, diaries, volumes of letters, and a book on etiquette. Her significant fiction on Neapolitan and Roman subjects of the 1880s, which earned her an eminent place in Italian letters, is to be found in some 10 volumes, almost all of the decade 1881–91. *Fantasia* (1883; Eng. tr., *Fantasy*, 1890) is a bold, psychophysiological study of feminine perversity. *La virtù di Checchina* (1884) is the probing yet sympathetic story of a middle-class housewife whose virtue is saved by a doorman's scrutiny. *La conquista di Roma* (1885; Eng. trs., *The Conquest of Rome,* 1902, 1906) recounts the failure of a politician with Roman ambitions. *Il romanzo della fanciulla* (1886; On Girls), is a collection of stories about middle-class girls and their lives of *decente miseria* (respectable poverty). *Vita e avventure di Riccardo Joanna* (1887; Life and Adventures of Riccardo Joanna) tells the story of the turbulent, not too ethical journalism in the Rome of the 1880s. *All'erta, sentinella* (1889; Eng. tr., *On Guard*, 1901), is a collection of Neapolitan stories, including "Terno secco," a tale of a winning lotto draw and its effect on a whole neighborhood, and "O Giovannino o la morte" (Either Giovannino or Death), a girl's tragic idyll. *Il paese di cuccagna* (1891;

Eng. tr., *The Land of Cockayne,* 1901) concerns the Neapolitan mania for lotteries. *La ballerina* (1899; Eng. tr.,
The Ballet Dancer, 1901) tells the story of the sordid life
of a chorus girl. *L'anima semplice: Suor Giovanna della
Croce* (1901; Eng. tr., "Sister Giovanna of the Cross,"
1901) is the tragic tale of a cloistered nun forced back into
the world. *Il ventre di Napoli* (1884; The Bowels of Naples), Serao's only outstanding work of nonfiction, is a
socioeconomic report on the Neapolitan slums of the
1880s.

See: H. James, *Notes on Novelists* (1914), pp. 294–313;
E. Caccia, in *Letteratura italiana: i minori*, vol. 4 (1962);
A. M. Gisolfi, *The Essential Matilde Serao* (1968); M. G.
Martin-Gistucci, *L'Œuvre romanesque de Matilde Serano*
(1973).   A.M.G.

Serbian literature. The first two decades of the 20th century saw the rise of a new trend in Serbian literature
sometimes referred to as the "Moderna" (modernism).
The Moderna was a result of the sharply increased but
still indirect and somewhat vague influence of the leading
literary movements in Europe, notably symbolism. This
influence was more pronounced in Croatian and Slovenian literatures than in the Serbian, where it had a greater
effect on mood and aesthetic attitude than on literary
craftsmanship. The character of the Moderna was manifested most keenly in the works of two poets, Jovan
Dučić and Milan Rakić. Dučić was a man of refined
taste, with a preference for things past. His melancholic,
almost fatalistic disposition reflected the decadent fin de
siècle mood of the French symbolists, whom he admired.
Rakić, although similar to Dučić in basic attitude, was
more contemplative and pessimistic. His outlook was reflected in his small number of analytical poems, permeated with an awareness of unavoidable fate. The third
leading poet of this time was Aleksa Šantić (1868–1924).
His poetry was much simpler, concerned with love, patriotism, and social themes, but what he lacked in sophistication and philosophical approach to problems he
made up for with his sincerity and pathos.

Other poets struck out on independent paths, often with
remarkable results. Vladislav Petković-Dis (1880–1917),
Milutin Bojić (1892–1917), Sima Pandurović (1883–1960),
and Veljko Petrović (1884–1967) all showed a surprising
savoir-faire, sophistication, and maturity in poetic matters. Most of these poets were pessimists, while at the
same time warmly patriotic in supporting their country's
cause on the eve of World War I.

At the beginning of the 20th century, a new generation
of prose writers also made its presence felt. Perhaps the
best of these was Borisav Stanković, a writer of boundless imagination but somewhat limited skill. His best
work, *Nečista krv* (1911; Tainted Blood), is considered
one of the finest Serbian novels despite its technical shortcomings. Stanković's world is the quaint town of Vranje,
near the border between Serbia and Macedonia, a symbol
of a traditional world of merchants and landowners that
was disappearing in the wake of the Turkish retreat. Svetozar Ćorović (1875–1919) similarly depicted his native
Herzegovina, where the changes brought about by the
shift of the Muslim population were most severely felt.
Ivo Ćipiko (1869–1923), like Simo Matavulj (1952–1908)
before him, presented a picture of the South Adriatic that
was not always sunny or blue. There is a sense of alarm
concerning the deterioration of social conditions present
in Ćipiko's best work, the novel *Pauci* (1909; The Spiders). Another regional writer, Petar Kočić (1877–1916),
described in highly lyrical prose the Bosnian Serbs and
their struggle for independence from the Austro-Hungarian Empire and for unification with Serbia. In his most

enduring work, the satire *Jazavac pred sudom* (1904; The
Badger before the Court), Kočić sharply ridiculed the
right of the Austro-Hungarians to rule over the Slavic
people. The Bosnian peasant, by nature sly, suspicious,
and witty, is shown here as morally superior to his foreign
oppressors.

Among other writers who achieved prominence during
this time were the erudite novelist and essayist Isidora
Sekulić, the satirist Radoje Domanović (1873–1908), the
short-story writer Veljko Petrović (1884–) and the novelist
Milutin Uskoković (1884–1915). The finest playwright of
this period was Branislav Nučić, whose fruitful career
spanned half a century. He wrote scores of plays, most
of them highly entertaining comedies into which he managed to inject stinging satire against the causes of social
ills. The notoriously weak Serbian drama was enriched
by Nušić's works. Serbian literature was further enhanced by several capable critics educated in the West,
especially Jovan Skerlić and Bogdan Popović (1863–
1944). Skerlić, with his sweeping historical surveys, and
Popović, with his refined, Western aestheticism, not only
evaluated the achievements of Serbian writers, but also
guided them in the direction of modern world literature.

World War I is a natural watershed in the development
of Serbian literature. Although the majority of prewar
writers reappeared at the end of the conflict, it was mainly
a younger generation that advanced literary developments. Six groups of authors can be distinguished according to the nature of their writing. The first group
showed strong expressionistic tendencies. Miloš Crnjanski, Rastko Petrović, Stanislav Vinaver (1891–1955),
Dušan Vasiljev (1900–24), and Risto Ratković (1903–54)
embodied and exploited the postwar mood in their works.
On the one hand, they were revolutionary in their demands for a new approach to life's problems, but they
also showed signs of revulsion and fatigue after the colossal human slaughter they had just witnessed. The writers of this group sought new forms that would provide for
literary expression. The entire first decade of the postwar
period was enlivened by innovations and heated polemics
between supporters and opponents of modernism as well
as among the modernists themselves. A further issue was
whether literature should primarily concern itself with
social themes.

A counterforce to the modernists was provided by a
number of prewar and new writers who, while enriching
their language with new means of expression, generally
shied away from experimentation and instead followed
traditional realism. During this period, Ivo Andrić grew
into a mature short-story writer; his skill, poise, and ann-
encompassing scope made him one of the most significant
Serbian authors between the two world wars. Other eminent writers in this group were Velimir Živojinović-Mas-
suka (1886–1974), Desanka Maksimović (1898–), Desimir
Blagojević (1904–), and Dragiša Vasić (1885–1945). While
some prewar writers continued their well-trodden paths—
Dučić, Rakić, and Šantić in poetry; Stanković, Ćipiko,
and Veljko Petrović in prose; Nušić in drama—most of
the others stopped writing, realizing that their era had
ended with the war.

A third group may be called, for a lack of a better term,
the folklorists. These writers resemble the so-called traditionalists in that they too were realistic and conservative
in their outlook and their treatment of subject matter. But
the folklorists clung to their own narrow regions and were
untouched by outside literary currents. They limited
themselves to the description of people, customs, and
problems in their home provinces, renewing the tradition
prevalent in Serbian prose during the second half of the
19th century. Like their predecessors, the 20th-century

folkorists also attempted to focus on the universal condition by focusing on the little man, usually a peasant. Some of their stories and novels have withstood the test of time. Among the more prominent folklorists and their concerns are Grigorije Božović—Sandžak and Old Serbia, Dušan Radić (1892–1938)—central Serbia, Isak Samokovlija (1889–1955)—the Jews of Bosnia, Andjelko Krstić (1871–1952)—Macedonia, and Branko Ćopić (1915–)—Bosnia.

Early in this period, a small but vocal group of young writers declared its allegiance to the French surrealist movement and tried to transplant it to Serbian literary soil. The Serbian surrealist episode was very important for the development of the literature. Its leading representatives were Marko Ristić (1902–), Milan Dedinac (1902–66), Dušan Matić (1898–), Aleksandar Vučo (1897–), and Oskar DAVIČO.

Those writers with an exclusively socialist orientation formed another small but highly vocal group. Although few of them achieved notable quality in their literary output, their works were both a symptom of and a self-professed cure for the social ills that beset the country. Most of these writers excelled in criticism: Milan Bogdanović (1892–1964), Djordje Jovanović (1909–43), Jovan Popović (1905–52), and Velibor Gligorić (1899–) are notable examples.

Finally, a few highly individualistic writers wrote in the seclusion of their private worlds. The best example of this group is Momčilo NASTASIJEVIĆ, a darkly strange and powerful creator whose works have yet to be fully fathomed.

The busy period between the two world wars left some lasting works: poems by Nastasijević, Crnjanski, Vinaver, Vasiljev, Maksimović, and Rastko Petrović; stories by Andrić, Veljko Petrović, Vasić, and Ćopić; distinguished novels such as Crnjanski's *Seobe* (1929; Migrations) and Branimir Ćosić's *Pokošeno polje* (1934; The Mowed Field); and plays by Nušić. A large number of lesser works are not to be underestimated, however. For some writers, this was the period of maturation, and after World War II it was these writers—notably Andrić with his novels—who gave Serbian literature a new impetus.

Except for a few poems, the literature of the World War II period was negligible. In the first postwar years, the socialistically oriented prewar writers and the former surrealists clearly attempted to establish the literary doctrine of socialist realism in Yugoslavia. But the course of political developments soon proved this attempt abortive. The whole of Yugoslav literature slowly freed itself from a dictated literary policy, and socialist realism never took root in the country.

In the late 1940s and early 1950s, two literary groups fought for supremacy. These were the so-called realists, who advocated the straightforward, utilitarian use of literature, and the modernists, who demanded greater freedom, especially in matters of form. The struggle ended in the mid-1950s with the victory of the modernists. Since then, Serbian literature has enjoyed a slow but steady progress. In 1961, Andrić received the Nobel Prize for Literature. Even though the cultural atmosphere has not always been propitious, Serbian writers have persevered in their quest of artistic truth and excellence, their ranks periodically strengthened by the advent of a new generation of talented writers.

The tone of post–World War II Serbian poetry was set by such prewar poets as Davičo, Matić, Maksimović and later Crnjanski. By the beginning of the 1950s, however, new poets began to appear, notably Vasko POPA and Miodrag PAVLOVIĆ, who were instrumental in the struggle for modernization. Although quite different, these two writers together raised the quality of Serbian poetry to new levels and began to influence younger poets. Other postwar poets also contributed to the success of Serbian poetry, each adding his own touch. Stevan Raičković (1928–) retreats from city life into nature; Jovan Hristić (1933–) displays contemplation, erudition, and adherence to classical tradition; Ivan V. Lalić (1914–) shows a similar predilection for classical motifs, along with intellectualism and a refined skill. Branko Miljković (1934–61), who died prematurely, was a pessimist and a rebel, much concerned with the role of the poet in society. Borislav Radović (1936–) combines emotionalism with calm thoughtfulness, and romanticism with an inclination toward rationalistic treatment of the subject. Božidar Timotijević (1932–) is a pure lyricist, somewhat romantic but always personal and direct. The younger poets—Ljubomir Simović (1935–), Branislav Petrović (1937–), and Matija Bećković (1939–), and the still younger generation that follows in their footsteps—reveal a thoughtful lyricism, a renewed interest in the distant past, and yet a lively concern with the problems of today. What binds these poets together, despite their diversity, is a sense of method, a striving for high standards, an openness to the currents of world poetry, and an incessant search for poetic truth.

Post-World War II writers again represent a combination of the older and younger generations. Andrić is unanimously considered to be the best Serbian fiction writer of the 20th century. Crnjanski has produced several new novels. Of Davičo's many prose works, perhaps the best are his novels *Pesma* (1952; The Poem) and *Robije* (1963–66; Hard Labor) a tetralogy in which he expounds the theme of revolution. Branko Ćopić, a very prolific and popular writer, also depicts the revolution in his short stories and novels, but he often does so in a humorous vein.

Of the authors who first appeared after World War II, two stand out: Mihailo LALIĆ and Dobrica ĆOSIĆ. Although both are preoccupied with the theme of the revolution (Lalić exclusively so), they are quite different in approach. Lalić penetrates deeply into the problems of the World War II period, while Ćosić has a much wider scope, reaching in his series of novels as far back as the 19th century. A third writer, Erih Koš, is one of the few true satirists in contemporary Serbian literature. His *Veliki Mak* (1956; The Great Mac), an allegorical tale about a stranded whale on the Adriatic coast, has enjoyed international success. A Bosnian, Meša Selimović, (1910–), has published several widely acclaimed novels, the best of which, *Derviš i smrt* (1966; The Dervish and Death), deals with some of the basic dilemmas of existence: life and death, the contemplative versus the active life, and the effects of power upon men.

Among younger writers, by far the most outstanding is Miodrag Bulatović (1930–). In his novels *Crveni petao leti prema nebu* (1959; The Red Cock Flies to Heaven), *Heroj na magarcu* (1964; Hero on a Donkey), and *Rat je bio bolji* (1969; War Was Better), Bulatović exposes an eerie world in which the characters are held captive by their own shortcomings and idiosyncrasies, but also by violence and war, which in Bulatović's human menagerie are seen as sexual aberrations. Next to Andrić, Bulatović is the most widely translated Serbian writer, enjoying greater acclaim abroad than at home. Other promising younger writers are Radomir Konstantinović (1928–), Borislav Pekić (1930–), Radomir Smiljanić (1934–), and Branimir Šćepanović (1937–).

In the 1970s, two playwrights, both satirists and writers of farce, achieved great success with innovative, bold plays. Velimir Lukić (1936–) uses classical myths and problems. Aleksander Popović (1928–) employs street jargon in dealing with contemporary problems. In addition to the traditional genres, radio and television drama has also emerged as a new development in Yugoslav literature.

See: A. Barac, *A History of Yugoslav Literature* (1955; 1973); A. Kadić, *Contemporary Serbian Literature* (1964); S. Lukić, *Contemporary Yugoslav Literature: A Sociopolitical Approach* (1972); V. D. Mihailovich, "Yugoslav Literature," in *World Literature since 1945* (1973), pp. 682–700.   V.D.M.

Sereni, Vittorio (1913–), Italian poet, was born in Luino. He earned his doctorate at the University of Milan with a dissertation on Guido GOZZANO. World War II is the subject of his first two volumes of poetry, *Frontiera* (1941; Frontier) and *Diario d'Algeria* (1947; Algerian Diary), the latter dealing directly with his experience as a soldier and American prisoner of war in Algeria and French Morocco (1943–45). Sereni's early verse is characterized by an attitude of self-searching, a nostalgic but unsentimental evocation of the past, and a feeling of warmth for the woman he loves. His third volume of poetry, *Gli strumenti umani* (1965, 2d ed., 1975; The Human Instruments), marks a decisive development in his work, resulting in a more complex and mature verse. His self-analysis becomes more intense, his musings characterized by disillusionment. The subject of his work is now the imprisonment of modern man, a condition both reflected in and exacerbated by the inexorable monotony of industrial life. In such a world, even writing poetry becomes a routine exercise, a periodic catharsis. Sereni's most recent volumes of poems are *Un posto de vacanza* (1973; A Vacation Place) and *Poesie scelte (1935–65)* (1973; Selected Poems).

Sereni's three prose works are *Gli immediati dintorni* (1962; The Immediate Surroundings), pages from a personal diary; *L'opzione e allegati* (1964; Option and Enclosures), a novel set in the editorial world of the Frankfurt Book Fair; and *Letture preliminari* (1973; Preliminary Readings). He has also translated poems by Ezra Pound, William Carlos Williams, Paul VALÉRY, and René CHAR.

See: C. Bo, "Parlando di Sereni," *Letteratura* (July–October 1966); G. Singh, "*Gli strumenti umani*," *BA* (Summer 1966); M. Grillandi, *Sereni* (1972); F. Fortini, in *Saggi italiani* (1974); P. V. Mengaldo, in *La tradizione del Novecento* (1975); E. Montale, "*Gli strumenti umani*," in *Sulla poesia* (1977).   G.S.

Sergeyev-Tsensky, Sergey Nikolayevich, pseud. of Sergey Nikolayevich Sergeyev (1875–1958), Russian novelist, was born in a small village in the province of Tambov, the son of a veteran of the defense of Sevastopol in 1854–55. He published his first work in 1898. A prolific writer, he began with poetry, short stories, and novellas, and by 1908 he had published his first novel, *Babayev*, which deals with the Revolution of 1905.

Relatively early in his career, Sergeyev-Tsensky displayed a penchant for documentary and historical themes, especially those depicting various aspects of the Russian social fabric. His novel *Preobrazheniye* (1914; Eng. tr., *Transfiguration*, 1926) which portrays the Russian intelligentsia of the early 20th century, brought him wide critical acclaim. It was also the novel that gave the title to his 12-volume cycle, *Preobrazheniye Rossii* (The Transfiguration of Russia), consisting of 12 novels, 3 novelettes, and 2 études, which were written over a period of 44 years (1914–58). All of these works have the same major characters, and all stress the necessity for transforming

both individual and bourgeois society. The subject matter deals with pre-Revolutionary Russian society, the events of World War I, and the February Revolution of 1917. One of the more significant works in this cycle is a novel of World War I, *Brusilovskiy proryv* (1943; Eng. tr., *Brusilov's Breakthrough*, 1945).

Sergeyev-Tsensky's major work is his massive historical novel *Sevastopolskaya strada* (1937–39; The Ordeal of Sevastopol), which recounts the events of the Crimean War and the defense of Sevastopol by the Russians from August 1854 to December 1855.

See: P. I. Pluksh, *Sergey Nikolayevich Sergyev-Tsensky (Zhizn' i tvorchestvo)* (1969).   L.T.

Sérgio (de Sousa), António (1883–1969), Portuguese essayist and historian, primarily a rational philosopher and social reformer, although he has also written in many other fields, was born in Daman, then part of Portuguese India. When his father, the governor, was recalled, nine-year-old Sérgio went to Portugal with his family. A descendant of aristocrats, colonial administrators, and admirals, he began his career as a naval officer, abandoning it in 1910 for politics and literature. Convinced of the urgent need for reforms in Portugal, he tried to impress the young elite with his ideas on culture, education, and political economy. He adhered to the group called *Renascença Portuguesa* (see PORTUGUESE LITERATURE) and its review *A Águia* in Oporto, but he left the group to found his own review, *Pela Grei*, in 1917. In 1921, on his return from publishing work in Brazil (1919–20), he participated in the organization of *Seara Nova* (New Crop), a cooperative group of educators, economists, and writers, in whom he saw an intellectual and moral elite capable of guiding the young republic. Named director of the National Library in Lisbon, he was active in founding writers' organizations and promoting the *União Cívica* (Civic Union), a vast political association. In 1923 he entered the government as secretary of education but soon resigned, unable to carry out any reforms. Because of his leading role in the 1927 revolt against the recently imposed military dictatorship, he had to flee to Paris. Later he returned to Lisbon; and, in spite of repeated arrests for political reasons, he continued to write and act with the courage of his convictions, a staunch defender of democracy, rationalism, and freedom of thought.

Sérgio first became known through his *Notas sobre . . . Antero de Quental* (1909; Notes on . . . Antero de Quental). Besides translations of rationalists such as Benedict Spinoza, Gottfried Wilhelm Leibniz, René Descartes, and Bertrand Russell and countless articles on national problems, he reedited Portuguese 17th- and 18th-century thinkers, in order to "reform Portuguese mentality." The *Ensaios*, 8 vols. (1920–58; Essays) contain most of his didactic studies, including some on literature, for example, on Oliveira Martins. He turned political historian in *O desejado* (1924; The Longed-For King), attacking with documents in hand the romantically vague and indolent messianism of the nationalists, abhorrent to him, the disciplined, critical thinker. He eagerly engaged in many personal polemics, one of them with the poet Joaquim Teixeira De PASCOAES, another with the philosopher Leonardo Coimbra, a third with the critic António José Saraiva. He also rewrote Portuguese history from an economic standpoint—as a struggle of the seaport merchants against the rural landowners. He outlined his findings in *Bosquejo da história de Portugal* (1923; Eng. tr., *A Sketch of the History of Portugal*, 1928) and expanded them to *História de Portugal* (available only in a Spanish tr., 1929). Because of censorship, the still larger Portuguese edition was not allowed to progress beyond its first volume, a geographical introduction (1941). Another version, *Breve interpretação da história de Portugal* (1972; A Brief Interpretation of Portuguese History), was found among his papers at the time of his death.

Sérgio has rightly been called "a universal man," being a poet—his first book was *Rimas* (1908; Rhymes)—a mathematician, philosopher, economist, historian, literary critic, journalist, educator, politician, and, above all, a humanist. He retired from literary activities in 1960.

See: J. Moneva y Puyol, "Prólogo," in Spanish tr. (1929) of A. Sérgio, *História de Portugal*, pp. 7–13; V. de Magalhães-Vilhena, *António Sérgio, o idealismo crítico e a crise da ideologia burguesa* (1964); J. Serrão, ed., "Breve introdução ao ensaísmo sergiano," in *Prosa doutrinal de autores portugueses*, vol. 2: *António Sérgio* (1967), pp. xi–1.   G.M.M. rev. E.M.D.

Serra, Renato (1884–1915), Italian literary critic, was born in Cesena. A precocious scholar, he received a degree in letters in 1904 from the University of Bologna, where he was a student of Giosuè Carducci (1835–1907). After a year of military service, he attended the Institute of Higher Studies in Florence. He returned to Cesena to become director of the Malatestiana Library (1909), a position he held until 1915 when, having been recalled to arms, he died a hero in combat, at the age of 31, on the slopes of Mount Podgora.

Serra considered himself heir to Carducci's "religion of literature," while representing what he himself termed the "moment of criticism": an epoch of transition and renovation in which the critic was to play a preeminent role as *coscienza* ("conscience" and "consciousness") of the entire culture. He was linked, primarily through correspondence, to writers surrounding the innovative Florentine review *La voce* (*see* ITALIAN LITERATURE), to which he contributed articles beginning in 1910. Yet he remained an independent practitioner of what he considered the "art" of criticism, while cultivating the role of "provincial reader" and literary conscience of his generation. He radically defined literary criticism as "pure and simple reading with a few notes in the margin" and the critic as a scrupulously educated humanist who is collaborator, rather than judge or theoretician, of the text. His method, which he preferred to call his manner or technique, was to reduce the intrinsic stylistic features of a textual fragment to their essence and thence to "reconstruct with dialectical force," within a spontaneous essay, the poetic persona or "moral portrait" of the author.

Among Serra's most important essays, collected in his *Scritti* (1938; Writings), are "Giovanni Pascoli" (1909), notable for its linguistic analysis; "Per un catalogo" (1910; For a Catalog), a comparison of Carducci and Benedetto CROCE; "Ringraziamento a una ballata di Paul Fort" (1914; Thanks to a Ballad by Paul Fort), a critical reading that best exemplifies his lyrical style; and "Esame di coscienza di un letterato" (1915; Examination of the Conscience of a Litterateur), a spiritual testament written shortly before his death. The only volume Serra published during his lifetime, *Le lettere* (1914; Literature), considered his masterpiece by his disciple Giuseppe De Robertis, is a "chronicle" of contemporary Italian literature.

Despite his own cordial relationship with Croce, Serra became the standard-bearer of postwar anti-Crocean and antiintellectual sentiment. Less than one month after his death, *La voce* dedicated an entire issue to Serra, proclaiming him the "poet of criticism" and the herald of a new generation of aesthetic readers of literature.

See: G. De Robertis, "Coscienza letteraria di Renato Serra" in R. Serra, *Scritti*, vol. 1 (1938), pp. v–lxv; G.

Contini, "Serra e l'irrazionale," in *Altri esercizi* (1972), and *Scritti in onore di Renato Serra* (1974).   C.As.

Serrahima i Bofill, Maurici (1902–), Catalan writer, was born in Barcelona, where he studied law. He was attracted to political life from an early age. In 1931 he signed the manifesto of the Democratic Catalonian Union, for which he was forced to go into exile after the Spanish Civil War. On his return he fought constantly in favor of democracy, and, after the first free elections in 1977, the king, Juan Carlos, appointed him to be a senator. His literary career began in 1934 with a novel, *El principi de Felip Lafont*, and his *Assaig sobre novela* (Essay on the Novel). He wrote short stories like "El seductor devot" (1937; The Devout Seducer), "Petit mon efebrat" (1947; Little Feverish World), and "Contes d'aquest temps" (1955; Stories from Back Then), and novels like *Després* (1951; Loose) and *Estimat Senyor Fiscal* (1955; Dear Tax Collector). He also wrote literary criticism: *La crisi de la ficció* (1965); *Sobre llegir i escriure* (1966), for which he won the Josep Yxart Prize; and *Dotze mestres* (1972). He turned his attention to the biographical essay, with *Democràcia i sufragi* (1962); *Realitat de Catalunya* (1969), a book that he had published in 1967 in Castilian as a reply to the *Consideración de Cataluña* by Julian Marias; and *Marcel Proust* (1971).

Salvador ESPRIU believes that Serrahima's fiction portrays the upper bourgeoisie of Catalonia. Although this is undoubtedly true of some works, others, like *El fet de creure* (1967; The Fact of Belief) and *De Mitja nit ença (1939–1966)* (1970; From Midnight Onward), reflect a communitarian spirit like Emmanuel Moulnier's. The chronicles that have followed *De Mitja nit ença* give us a better understanding of Serrahima as a fundamental figure in the recovery of democratic normality in Catalonia. The latest volumes are *Del passat quan era present, Volumen I, 1940–1947* (1972) and *Volumen II, 1948–1953* (1974). In addition to writing fiction, he continues to be concerned with the study of the phenomenon of literature.

See: J. Lores, Prologue to M. Serrahima, *El fet de creure* (1967); J. Molas, Prologue to M. Serrahima, *Marcel Proust* (1971).   J.F.C.

Serrano Poncela, Segundo (1912–76), Spanish novelist and essay writer was born in Madrid. He studied law and philosophy and letters at the University of Madrid. Exiled after the Spanish Civil War (1936–39), he taught Spanish literature at several universities, primarily in Puerto Rico, Santo Domingo, and Mexico. He eventually established himself in Caracas.

Serrano Poncela first became known for his essays on Antonio MACHADO and Miguel de UNAMUNO: *Antonio Machado, su vida y su obra* (1958) and *El pensamiento de Unamuno* (1952; The Philosophy of Unamuno). Later, in combination with his teaching career, he dedicated himself to the novel, which from 1954 on he wrote entirely in exile.

Due as much to his date of birth as to the characteristics of his prose, he belongs to the Generation of the Civil War, also known as the Generation of 1940, the Divided Generation, the Generation of 1936, and so on. His adherence to traditional realism nevertheless makes him a nonconformist within this generation.

Serrano Poncela's fiction consists for the most part of stories and short novels. He wrote only two long novels, *Habitación para hombre solo* (1963; Room for a Single Man) and *El hombre de la cruz verde* (1969; The Man with the Green Cross). Combined as a whole, his work can be divided into two stages. The first is characterized by his affinity for the novelistic methods peculiar to realist writers of the 19th century. This affinity manifests itself principally in the creator-reader relationship with the author's intruding in the first person to give his opinions and lead the reader by the hand, in the use of periphrastic style, anticipation, and in the taste for affected language. The year 1963 marks the beginning of his second stage. After the appearance of *Habitación para hombre solo*, Serrano Poncela altered his narrative technique. His phrasing became more concise, his style lighter, and his plots unfolded rapidly. The writer now studies in depth the inner elements of his characters and the motives for their conduct, along with the outer world, and the ramifications of the situations created. Serrano Poncela's corrosive humor, which often turns into sarcasm, is the common denominator of both literary phases. The humor is more crude in the first period, while the second is characterized by its sustained irony. In both periods, however, humor is used to highlight the undesirable aspects of society and to draw attention to the myths of "official" Spanish history.

Serrano Poncela's most successful work is probably *El hombre de la cruz verde*, whose title refers to the lawyer Juan Bracamonte. The story revolves around the inquiry made by this member of the Inquisition immediately following a strange historical occurrence: the accident suffered by Prince Charles, the son of Philip II, in the course of an amorous adventure. The inquiry provides a lucid and lively exposition of the Counter-Reformation, a time in which there existed a peculiar fusion and confusion among the powers of church, state, and king. No one but Serrano Poncela has been able to capture so well the mendacity of the powerful men who prospered in the court of Philip II. The gestures, the words, and the thoughts of the characters, magnificently presented, show how they survive in a devious world where craftiness is a necessity and where the least suspicion can be severely punished.

See: J. R. Marra-López, *Narrativa española fuera de España* (1963), pp. 413–41; E. G. de Nors, *La novela española contemporánea*, vol. 3 (1962), pp. 279–81.

P.G.C.

Severyanin, Igor pseud. of Igor Vasilyevich Lotaryov (1887–1941), Russian poet, was born in Petersburg, the son of an army officer. He began to publish impressionist verse in 1904. By 1909 he had developed his own style, characterized by a—slightly ludicrous–penchant for decadent elegance, philosophical pseudoprofundities, synesthetic effects, neologisms, modern (and foreign) vocabulary, and virtuosic word play. In 1911 he published a brochure, *Prolog Ego-Futurizm*, and an "ego-futurist" group of poets was formed (*see* RUSSIAN LITERATURE). Its manifesto (1912) proclaimed unlimited individualism (against a backdrop of theosophy and cosmic intuitions) and radical modernity of poetic form.

Severyanin broke with the ego-futurists late in 1912 and, briefly, joined the cubo-futurists. In 1913 his volume *Gromoshipyashchiy kubok* (Thunder-Seething Goblet) was extremely successful, and several collections that followed were likewise popular successes. After the October Revolution (1917), he lived in Estonia. His poetry became tamer and more conventional, yet it sometimes states moral and civic points with dignity and expresses personal emotions with grace and simplicity. In his later years, Severyanin translated a great deal of poetry, especially from the Estonian.

See: V. Markov, *Russian Futurism* (1968).   V.T.

Seyfullina, Lidiya Nikolayevna (1889–1954), Russian novelist, was born at Varlamovo in Orenburg province. She was the daughter of an Orthodox priest of Tartar origin and a Russian peasant woman and received her education in the high school of Omsk. After teaching school for some years, she began her literary career in 1922 with the novel *Pravonarushiteli* (Criminals) followed by *Peregnoy* (1923; Manure), comprising four stories, and the short novel *Virineya* (1925). Seyfullina generally gave a psychologically accurate and objective estimate of her characters, who all belong to the Revolutionary period. She made no effort to embellish her pictures and wrote in a direct and simple if undistinguished style. As in the case of her heroine Virineya, she frequently (and perhaps unconsciously) portrayed the emptiness of a soul deprived of faith and moral standards, and not even her loyalty to the prevailing ideology could hide this situation from her.

S.H.C. rev. W.B.E.

Shaginyan, Marietta Sergeyevna (1888–), Russian poet and novelist, of Armenian descent, was born in Moscow. After obtaining a degree in philosophy, she continued her studies in Germany until they were interrupted by the outbreak of World War I. Goethe's thought had a powerful and lasting influence on her.

Shaginyan is the author of several novels, short stories, and dramas and of numerous articles devoted to current events, literary criticism, philosophy, and social problems. Together with her husband, Y. S. Khachatryants, she published studies on Armenian folklore. But it was poetry, which she later abandoned, that first brought her success; her *Orientalia* (1912) was rated among the best productions of the younger symbolists. Her first novel, *Svoya sudba* (1918; One's Own Fate), is largely of philosophical inspiration. Social motives appear in *Peremena* (1922; The Change); they are emphasized in later works, namely in her series *Mess-Mend* (1925–26), which uses the devices of a mystery novel to present a violently grotesque picture of capitalist society collapsing in a world revolution (for the title the author took at random two words from an English-Russian dictionary). To the literature of socialist realism Shaginyan contributed a novel, *Gidrotsentral* (1931; The Hydroelectric Station), describing with a wealth of technical detail the building of a power plant in Armenia. In later life she wrote several novels about Vladimir Lenin and his family, as well as memoirs.

Shaginyan's style is objective and precise. Intricate plots are developed in a manner which is more narrative than directly suggestive of reality. She rightly disclaims any influence of the Russian realistic novel and traces her literary parentage to Voltaire, to Aleksandr Pushkin, and also to Wilkie Collins, whom she translated into Russian.

See: A. Margaryan, *Marietta Shaginyan: tvorcheskiy put* (1956).   L.St. rev. W.B.E.

Shalamov, Varlam Tikhonovich (1907–), Russian poet and prose writer, was born in Vologda. Arrested during the great purge of 1937, he was released and "rehabilitated" only after Iosif Stalin's death. In the Soviet Union he is known mainly for the several volumes of verse published since his release, such as *Moskovskiye oblaka* (1972; Moscow Clouds). His major prose work, *Kolymskiye rasskazy* (Stories from Kolyma), a series of documentary sketches of his life as a prisoner in the concentration camps in the Kolyma region of northern Siberia, have been published only abroad—mostly in the New York Russian-language journal, *Novy zhurnal*, in successive issues between 1969 and 1975. Containing an abundance of sharply observed detail about everyday life in the frozen "ninth circle" of

Gulag, these stories provide a unique literary record of an experience to which there are few surviving witnesses.

M.Ha.

Shestov, Lev, pseud. of Lev Isaakovich Schwarzmann (1866–1938), Russian critic, essayist, and religious thinker, was born in Kiev. He studied law, then lived abroad from 1895 to 1898 and again from 1908 to 1914. From 1920 on he lived in exile in Paris. Shestov called William Shakespeare his "first teacher of philosophy" and saw in Hamlet's "the time is out of joint" the unsettling truth that *every* time is a threat to free individuals. His first book, *Shekspir i yego kritik Brandes* (1898; Shakespeare and his Critic Brandes) sounds the theme of the "unbearable horrors of human existence," which Shestov subsequently developed brilliantly in such works as *Dobro v uchenii gr. Tolstogo i F. Nitshe* (1900; The Good in the Teaching of Tolstoy and Nietzsche) and *Dostoyevsky i Nitshe* (1903; combined in Eng. tr. as *Dostoyevsky, Tolstoy, and Nietzsche*, 1969), and *Apofeoz bespochvennosti* (1905; The Apotheosis of Groundlessness; Eng. tr., *All Things Are Possible*, 1920). Shestov discovered Søren KIERKEGAARD late but found his position highly congenial, as evidenced in *Kirgegard* [sic] *i ekzistentsialnaya filosofiya* (1939; Eng. tr., *Kierkegaard and the Existential Philosophy*, 1969). Shestov's style is elegant, ironic, aphoristic, and questioning. His mature work constitutes a single-minded, impassioned attack on the "tyranny of reason." He rejects theoretical truth in the name of the values of human existence, placing his faith not in impersonal necessity but in a free personal God for whom "all things are possible"—even the revoking of "irrevocable" human loss. His other major works are *Anton Chekhov and Other Essays* (1916, 2d ed. 1966)—drawn from both *Nachala i kontsy* (1908; Beginnings and Endings) and *Velikiye kanuny* (1910–12; Great Vigils); *Na vesakh Iova* (1929, 2d ed. 1975; Eng. tr., *In Job's Balances*, 1932, 2d ed. 1975); *Afiny i Ierusalim* (1951; Eng. tr., *Athens and Jerusalem*, 1966).

See: V. V. Zenkovsky, *A History of Russian Philosophy* (1953), vol. 2, pp. 780–91; G. L. Kline, *Religious and Anti-Religious Thought in Russia* (1968), pp. 73–90; C. Milosz, "Shestov, or the Purity of Despair," *TriQ* 28 (1973): 460–80.

G.K.

Shishkov, Vyacheslav Yakovlevich (1873–1945), Russian novelist, was born in Bezhetsk in the province of Tver, and spent much of his early manhood in Siberia as a civil engineer. He began his literary career in 1908 with neorealist stories about Siberian life. His first novels developed similar themes, culminating in *Ugryum-reka* (1933; Ugryum River), a two-volume work about wealthy Siberian merchants. The Russian Civil War inspired *Vataga* (1924; The Gang) and *Peypus-ozero* (1925; Lake Peipus). Contemporary Soviet reality is reflected in his ingenuous *Shuteynye rasskazy* (1926–29; Humorous Stories), as well as his novel *Stranniki* (1931; Eng. tr., *Children of Darkness*, 1931), about juvenile delinquents. Shishkov is best known for his three-volume historical novel *Yemelyan Pugachov* (1941–47), a colorful panorama of the 18th-century Cossack and peasant uprising, which won a Stalin Prize.

See: V. Bakhmetyev, *Vyacheslav Shishkov* (1947).

A.M.S.

Shklovsky, Viktor Borisovich (1893–), Russian writer and literary critic, was born in Petersburg and studied literary history there at the university. He was one of the founders of the Society for the Study of Poetic Language (*Opoyaz*), the main center of the so-called formalist school of criticism, and its leading spokesman and most pungent phrasemaker. His programmatic essay "Iskusstvo kak priyom" (1917; Eng. tr., "Art as Technique," 1965) launched the influential concept of "defamiliarization" (*ostraneniye*) (presenting the familiar as if it were seen for the first time) as the central literary strategy. He urged other formalist tenets—such as the notion of the conventionality of literary art, a conventionality that is periodically dramatized or "laid bare"—in the provocative essays collected in *Khod konya* (1923; The Knight's Move) and *Literatura i kinematograf* (1923; Literature and the Cinema), in short studies such as *Rozanov* (1921), and, more extensively, in *O teorii prozy* (1925; The Theory of Prose), a seminal if one-sided contribution to the theory of narrative fiction.

In the mid-1920s, Shklovsky sought to modify his initial position by incorporating some elements of the sociological approach to literature. His hastily assembled "socio-formalist" method was tested in *Material i stil v romane L. N. Tolstogo Voyna i mir* (1928; Materials and Style in L. Tolstoy's War and Peace). In 1930, in the face of the mounting pressure for methodological conformity, he offered a hedged apology for his original "scientific error" and for two decades thereafter abandoned literary theorizing. He turned to his other fields of interest, notably film criticism and script writing, popular historical fiction, and memoirs, a particularly notable memoir being *O Mayakovskom* (1941; Eng. tr., *Mayakovsky and His Circle*, 1971). If Shklovsky's 1953 volumes of criticism, *Zametki o proze russkikh klassikov* (Notes on the Prose of Russian Masters) are a timid and uncharacteristic performance, his more recent studies such as *Za i protiv. Zametki o Dostoevskom* (1957; Pro and Contra: Notes on Dostoyevsky) endeavor with varying degrees of success to recapture the liveliness and vigor of the early period.

When still at the peak of his influence as a critic, Shklovsky encouraged hybrid—half-documentary, half-fictional—modes as a solution to the impasse allegedly reached by Russian artistic prose. Some of his own writings are attempts to implement this injunction. *Sentimentalnoye puteshestviye* (1923; Eng. tr., *A Sentimental Journal; Memoirs, 1917–1922*, 1971), a whimsical and candid autobiography, blends scenes of revolutionary turmoil with lyrical effusions and sorties into literary criticism. *Zoo ili pisma ne o lyubvi* (1923; Eng. tr., *Zoo or Letters not about Love*, 1971) is a record of the author's actual romantic involvement cast in the form of an epistolary novel.

See: R. Sheldon, "Shklovsky, Gorky and the Serapion Brothers," *SEEJ* (Spring 1968): 1–13; V. Erlich, *Russian Formalism—History-Doctrine* (3d ed., 1969); R. Sheldon, "The Formalist Poetics of Viktor Shklovsky," *RLT* 2 (Winter 1972): 351–71.

V.E.

Shmelyov, Ivan Sergeyevich (1873–1950), Russian novelist and short-story writer, was born in Moscow into a well-to-do merchant family and died in France, where he had lived as an émigré since 1923. Nine of his 26 volumes of fiction were published in Russia before he emigrated. They include two of his most notable works: *Chelovek iz restorana* (1911; The Waiter), a sympathetic portrayal of the little man in Russian society that combines the humanitarian tradition of Nikolay Gogol and the early Fyodor DOSTOYEVSKY with a stylized first-person narrative manner reminiscent of Nikolay LESKOV; and *Neupivayemaya chasha* (1919; Eng. tr., *Inexhaustible Cup*), the story of a deeply religious and highly talented serf artist in preemancipation Russia that again shows Shmelyov's affinity in a number of respects with Leskov, whose work he greatly admired.

The unifying theme of all Shmelyov's writings in exile is Russia. *Solntse myortvykh* (1923; Eng. tr., *The Sun of the Dead,* 1927) is a documentary account in loose fictional form of the material, cultural, and spiritual devastation of Russia that followed the October Revolution of 1917. *Leto Gospodne* (1933; The Year of Our Lord) and *Bogomolye* (1935; Pilgrimage) are examples both of Shmelyov's autobiographical fiction and of his growing preoccupation after the Russian Revolution with religious themes. Now admired in his homeland as well as in the emigration for his mastery of the Russian *skaz* style (first-person narration in the peculiar language of the persona), Shmelyov has still not received the recognition he merits in the English-speaking world, owing in considerable measure to inadequate translations.

See: G. Struve, *Russkaya literatura v izgnanii* (1956), pp. 94–98, 256–59; O. Sorokin, *Ivan Šmelëv: His Life and Work* (1965).   W.B.E.

Sholokhov, Mikhail Aleksandrovich (1905–), Russian novelist and publicist, was born at Kruzhilino farmstead, in the village of Veshenskaya, Don Military Region, and began to write with little formal preparation. He completed only the fourth form in school and participated intermittently in writers' "seminars" during his two-year residence in Moscow (1922–24). The son of a merchant-class father originally from Ryazan and an illiterate mother, who learned to read and write in order to correspond with her son, he lived in a White-occupied area at the beginning of the October Revolution (1917) but identified with the Reds. He knew Cossack life well without being a Cossack himself. Thus he was in a position to admire the Cossacks for their virtues without blinding himself to their shortcomings or to their place in the Soviet state with its urban working-class orientation. Until the 1930s, nonetheless, doctrinaire Communists repeatedly attacked him for dramatizing rural prejudices, for adopting uncritically a conservative Cossack point of view, and for excessive objectivity. He was also accused of plagiarizing portions of his novel on the Revolution. Although a court exonerated him, the rumor persists. From 1930 onward, Sholokhov became more active politically: he joined the Communist Party, agitated for collectivization, interceded on behalf of purge victims (for example, for the son of Andrey PLATONOV) and was elected to the Supreme Soviet. He served as a correspondent during World War II. Since that time he has published little, although he rewrote the second volume of *Virgin Soil Upturned* after earlier drafts perished during the war. Recipient of Stalin and Lenin prizes, he won the Nobel Prize for Literature in 1964. He is officially regarded as the greatest Soviet prose writer. His works have appeared in 78 Soviet languages and have been translated in 43 nations outside the Soviet Union; total copies exceed 75 million. Sholokhov has written short stories, novels, and journal articles. During his apprenticeship he wrote short fiction about the Civil War and its aftermath in the Don region. In these stories he avoided the tendencies to glamorize Communists and blacken their enemies; hence the stories seem at times gratuitously brutal, comparable to those of Isaak BABEL. They were published in *Donskiye rasskazy* (1924; Don Tales) and in an enlarged collection, *Lazorevaya step* (1926; Eng. tr., *Tales from the Don,* 1961). He returned to the short story during and after World War II, producing a powerful anti-Nazi story, "Nauka nenavisti" (1942; The Science of Hatred), and a moving tale about reconstruction, "Sudba cheloveka" (1956; Eng. tr., *One Man's Destiny,* 1967).

Sholokhov's three large-scale novels, the third unfinished, comprise his major work. The first, *Tikhiy Don*

(1928–40, The Quiet Don; Eng. abridged tr., *And Quiet Flows the Don,* 1934, and *The Don Flows Home to the Sea,* 1940; a more complete tr. in 4 vols., *And Quiet Flows the Don,* Moscow 1960) remains the classic literary rendering of the Soviet Revolution (1917) and the supreme portrayal of Cossack life. Embracing the decade from before World War I to the end of the Revolution and containing approximately 800 characters, the work is epic in scope. One may call Sholokhov the Homer of Soviet literature. His second novel, *Podnyataya tselina* (1932–59; Eng. tr. of part 1, *Virgin Soil Upturned,* 1935 [retitled *Seeds of Tomorrow* in the American ed.], and *Harvest on the Don,* 1960) is the major fictional depiction of collectivization. It became required reading for all collective farm directors and high school students. Not as massive as *Tikhiy Don* because it focuses on a limited setting and fewer characters, it dramatizes the Communist Party's effort to liquidate independent peasants and eradicate private property. The third novel, *Oni srazhalis za rodinu* (1943–59; Eng. tr., "They Fought for their Country," in *Soviet Literature,* July and August, 1959), tells the story of World War II in southern Russia but seems fragmentary.

Throughout his career, Sholokhov has written articles and given speeches on political as well as literary themes. These exhibit his patriotism, loyalty to the Communist Party, concern for the future of Russian literature, and hostility toward dissident intellectuals, especially writers. Much of this material has been collected in *Po veleniyu dushi* (1970; Eng. tr., *At the Bidding of the Heart,* 1973).

Sholokhov once noted with amusement that his fiction was first condemned as anti-Soviet and then canonized as a model of "socialist realism." In technique, he followed the tradition of Lev TOLSTOY, Anton CHEKHOV, and Maksim GORKY. Except for some "ornamental prose" imitating the "Odessa School" in his early work, there is no evidence that the literary experimentation of the 1920s influenced him. His profoundly regional inspiration combined with his faith in Leninist communism provided him with a unique ability to balance the particular and the universal that perhaps explains the power and appeal of his masterpiece, *Tikhiy Don.*

Sholokhov's work serves as a reminder that, of the first 60 years of Soviet history (1917–77), fully 15 were spent in civil strife and war. Sholokhov concentrates on the three periods of acute trauma, which explains why his work emphasizes physical rather than intellectual activity. Moreover, he portrays not Russia as a whole but a single, exceptional Russian subculture. Cossack culture developed in a "frontier" environment that engendered a spirit of independence and an attachment to private property far exceeding that of the Russian peasant. The industrialization of Russia, whether conducted by bourgeois or working-class ideologists, destroyed the conditions for Cossack survival. Thus the events that convulsed Russia after 1917 occurred with heightened intensity in the Cossack areas.

Like many 19th-century Russian writers, Sholokhov dramatized the fate of an entire people with great passion and care. But if he understood and accepted the historical necessity of extinction for Cossack life, he probably did not understand that his own inspiration would expire with it, nor that the new order would be so bleak. *Tikhiy Don* has become a lonely monument marking Russia's passage into the modern world.

Allegations that Sholokhov plagiarized parts of *Tikhiy Don* began in the 1920s and have caused considerable controversy in the 1970s, although Sholokhov himself has not commented publicly about the recent charges. After visiting the Soviet Union, the Canadian C. J. Newman wrote a novel entitled *The Russian Novel* (1973), based in part on Sholokhov's rumored plagiarism. In 1974, Aleksandr SOLZHENITSYN published an anonymous Russian's attribution of major portions of the novel to F. D. Kryukov (1870–1920), a Cossack author well known before World War I: *Stremya "Tikhogo Dona,"* (The Current of *The Quiet Don*). An English translation of R. A. Medvedev's *Problems in the Literary Biography of Mikhail Sholokhov* (first pub. in French tr., *Qui a écri "le Don paisible?",* 1975) appeared in 1977 and lent further credence to this claim. But Herman Ermolaev's reviews of both books disclose their numerous factual errors and flawed stylistic analyses (*Slavic and East European Journal*, 1974, 1976). The Norwegian Slavist Geir Kjetsaa conducted a computer-assisted examination of Kryukov's and Sholokhov's styles and demonstrated more consistency within Sholokhov's work than between it and Kryukov's (*Scando-Slavica*, 1976). Additional information relevant to the controversy may be found in A. Brian Murphy's textual studies of *Tikhiy Don* in the *New Zealand Slavonic Journal* (1975–77) and the *Journal of Russian Studies*, no. 34 (1977).

See: L. Yakimenko, *Tvorchestvo Mikhaila Sholokhova* (1964; Eng. tr., *Sholokhov: A Critical Appreciation*, 1973); D. H. Stewart, *Mikhail Sholokhov: A Critical Introduction* (1967); C. G. Bearne, *Sholokhov* (1969).

D.H.S.

Sholom Aleichem, pseud. of Sholom Rabinowitz (1859–1916), Yiddish novelist, short-story writer, dramatist, and humorist, was born in Pereyaslav, a shtetl in the province of Poltava, in the Ukraine. He received his early education in the neighboring community of Voronkov, which served as the model for Kasrilevke, the locale of many of his short stories. Before the age of 30, he was well known to the Yiddish reading public. As editor of the annual *Die Yiddishe Folksbibliotek* in 1888 and 1889, he attracted the best Yiddish writers, especially since temporary wealth enabled him to play the role of a generous patron. His own longer tales, *Stempenyu* (1889; Eng. tr., 1913) and *Yosele Solovey* (1890), also appeared in this publication. But his wealth was soon exhausted, and the man who had once been a businessman had to devote the last 25 years of his life to a desperate struggle for bread. Yet the more difficult his economic plight became and the poorer the state of his health, the more he sought relief in laughter. In his bitterest years, he wrote the sketches collected in *Tovye der Milkhiger* (1894; Eng. tr., *Tevye's Daughters*, 1949, *Tovye Stories*, 1965). The unheroic hero Tovye is a lighthearted pauper who drives his rickety milkwagon in search of a bare pittance, but his thoughts traverse the entire globe and reach up to God. Despite the severest trials, this simple being wipes away his tears and rejoices that he still lives in God's sunlight on this beautiful earth. With an ironic smile, Tovye reminds us that as bad as things are, they could after all have turned out worse. The epistolary novel *Menakhem Mendl* (1895; Eng. tr., *Adventures of Menachem Mendel*, 1969), presents Tovye's partner as a Jewish schlemiel resembling Don Quixote, chasing after mirages and engaging in speculative ventures that promise wealth but that always end in failure. He is a caricature both of the author's earlier self and of the generation of Jews to which he belonged, those who left the shtetl for the perilous maelstrom of the big cities.

Sholom Aleichem taught a people steeped in tragedy to laugh at its troubles. He loved his men and women for their weaknesses and their follies no less than for their quiet heroism and inarticulated idealism. His deepest love, however, was reserved for children who refused to grow up and to accept the established order of things. The most attractive of these children appear in the serialized sketches in *Motel Peyse dem Khazns* (1907–16; Eng. tr., *Adventures of Motel, the Cantor's Son,* 1953). The orphan Motel cannot adjust to adults' concepts and manages to turn every situation topsy-turvy. He is to the Yiddish reader what Tom Sawyer is to the American. The Motel sketches are tragicomic, didactic, ironic commentaries on the human species. Sholom Aleichem's sketches have often been dramatized for Yiddish audiences, and his satiric monologues enrich Yiddish radio programs. As a dramatist, Sholom Aleichem's most successful plays were *Die Goldgreber* (1907; The Gold Diggers), *Shver Tsu Zein a Yid* (1914; Hard to be a Jew), and *Dos Groise Gevins* (1916; The Jackpot).

After the outbreak of World War I, Sholom Aleichem found refuge in New York. His fame has continued, and even among non-Jews he is the best known of Yiddish writers because of numerous translations of his works and because of *Fiddler on the Roof*, the successful musical based on his Tovye sketches.

See: M. Samuel, *The World of Sholom Aleichem* (1943); S. Gittelman, *Sholom Aleichem* (1974).　　　　S.L.

Shukshin, Vasily Makarovich (1929–74) Russian author of short stories, novels, and film scripts was born in Siberia. His works, which are often set in Siberia, are notable for their frank depiction of Soviet life. His is best known for *Kalina krasnaya* (1973; Eng. tr., *Snowball Berry Red*, 1979), a novel about a repentent thief, and he also directed and played the leading role in the extraordinary popular film based on this novel, which appeared in 1974. His novel *Ya prishol dat vam volyu* (1968; I Have Come to Give you Freedom) is about the 17th-century peasant insurrectionary Stepan Razin. Among Shukshin's other published works are the novel *Lyubaviny* (1965) and six collections of stories: *Selskiye zhiteli* (1963; Countryfolk); *Tam, vdali* (1968; Over Yonder); *Zemlyaki* (1969; Landsmen); *Kharaktery* (1973; Characters); *Besedy pri yasnoy lune* (1974; Conversations under a Clear Moon); and *Brat moy* (1975; Brother Mine). There have been numerous posthumous anthologies of his work, including a collection of film scripts, *Kinopovesti* (1975), and a two-volume collection of both short and long works, *Izbrannye proizvedeniya* (1975).

See: V. Korobov, *Vasily Shukshin: literaturny portret* (1977); V. Shukshin, *Snowball Berry Red and Other Stories*, ed. by D. Fiene (1979), which contains three critical articles and a full bibliography of works by and about Shukshin in Russian and English.　　　　D.Fi.

Shvarts, Yevgeny Lvovich (1896–1958), Russian playwright, was born in Kazan into a family of Jewish intellectuals. After an unsuccessful attempt to study law, he became an actor in a provincial experimental theater that in 1921 moved to Petrograd (Leningrad). When the troupe disbanded, Shvarts remained in the city, which became his permanent home and where he began his literary career in the 1920s.

Shvarts is a rare example of a writer equally gifted in the fields of children's and adults' literature. His zestful and imaginative fairy-tale plays for children, notably *Krasnaya Shapochka* (1937; Little Red Riding Hood), *Snezhnaya koroleva* (1938; The Snow Queen), *Skazka o poteryannom vremeni* (1939; A Tale about Lost Time), and *Dva klena* (1953; Two Maples) are very popular in the USSR. His major plays for adults, *Goly korol* (1934; Eng. tr., *The Naked King*, 1968), *Ten* (1940; The Shadow), *Drakon* (1943; The Dragon), and *Obyknovennoye chudo* (1945; An Ordinary Miracle) have received praise from drama connoisseurs, although, for ideological reasons, the production of these plays in the USSR is restricted.

Goly korol, a free rendering of Hans Christian Andersen's "Emperor's New Clothes," portrays a corrupt ruler, whose public disgrace and subsequent overthrow represent the victory of integrity and courage over hypocrisy and fear. Also adapted from Andersen, *Ten* shows a man's unending crusade against evil. *Drakon* is based on the myths of Perseus and Saint George and reveals the moral degradation of a society governed by a dictator. *Obyknovennoye chudo* is a poetic fairy tale about freedom and love.

The characterizations in Shvarts's plays range from subtle psychological portraits, to grotesque charicatures. The dialogue is precise and witty, and the general tempo is vigorous, marked with swift transitions from lyrical to farcical moods. Shvarts's favorite device was "realization of metaphor," that is, taking figurative expressions literally or developing them into dramatic episodes to achieve irony and freshness of perception.

In stage technique, Shvarts owed much to the Russian avant-garde theater of the 1920s (*see* RUSSIAN LITERATURE). Startling visual effects, acrobatic movements, contrasting moods, and situations calling for improvised humorous dialogue in the style of the commedia dell'arte all reflect the influence of the noted *régisseurs* Vsevolod Meyerhold and Yevgeny Vakhtangov. Most characteristic are Shvarts's attitude of detachment toward the subject and his philosophy that drama is a spectacle, not a "slice of life"—all of which makes him unique among contemporary Soviet playwrights.

Several of Shvarts's plays have been translated and staged in Europe and the United States. He also wrote film scenarios, *Zolushka* (1947; Cinderella), *Don Quixote* (1957); stories, *Pervoklassnits* (1947; The First Grader); essays; and memoirs.

See: S. Tsimbal, *Yevgeny Shvarts: kritikobiograficheskiy ocherk* (Leningrad, 1951) and, ed., *My znali Yevgeniya Shvartsa* (Moscow 1966); I. Corten, "Evgenij Švarc: Man and Artist," Ph. D. Dissertation, University of California at Berkeley (1972).   I.H.C.

Sienkiewicz, Henryk (1846–1916), Polish novelist and short-story writer, was born in Wola Okrzejska, in northeastern Poland and died in Vcvcy, Switzerland. In 1866 he entered Szkoła Główna, the Polish University in Warsaw, initially studying medicine and law and then switching to history and literature. His first novel, *Na marne* (1872; Eng. tr., *In Vain,* 1899) depicts student life. He subsequently turned to journalism, contributing theatrical reviews and feuilletons based on petty daily events. When the actress Helena Modjeska and her friends planned to establish in California a settlement comparable to Brook Farm, Sienkiewicz went to the United States in 1876 as an advance agent. The writer reported his American impressions in *Listy z podróży* (1876–77; Eng. tr., *Portrait of America, Letters,* 1959). The journey inspired several short stories, of which "Latarnik" (1882; Eng. tr., "The Lighthouse Keeper," 1893) is the most popular. In the tales published after his return to Warsaw in 1879, he attacked political and social evils, for example, in *Szkice weglem* (1880; Charcoal Sketches) and "Janko muzykant" (1880; Eng. tr., "Yanko the Musician," 1893).

In 1882, Sienkiewicz began to work on his trilogy of historical novels, *Ogniem i mieczem* (1884; Eng. tr., *With Fire and Sword,* 1890), *Potop* (1886; Eng. tr., *The Deluge,* 1891), and *Pan Wołodyjowski* (1887–88; Eng. tr., *Pan Michael,* 1893). The trilogy made him a celebrity, even though its message aroused controversial opinions. Struc-

turally, its separate parts were an amalgamation of the narrative technique of Walter Scott, the French romance of adventure, and the epic. The text was based on painstaking historical studies. The incidents convincingly reflect the belligerent atmosphere of the 17th century, which abounded in military clashes. The characters, although lacking psychological depth, are colorful and believable. The sinister aspects of warfare are brightened by sparks of humor. Interest is enhanced by deft manipulation of the effects of suspense and surprise, mystery and anticipation. Sienkiewicz's optimistic note, addressed primarily to his countrymen, turned out to have a more universal appeal. In his next book he took up contemporary themes. *Bez dogmatu* (1890; Eng. tr., *Without Dogma,* 1893) portrays a gifted intellectual infected by the apathy of his times. This novel was followed by *Rodzina Połanieckich* (1894; Eng. tr., *Children of the Soil,* 1895), which introduces an unsophisticated businessman, who, although selfish and shortsighted, manages his affairs well and contributes to the welfare of his own family and country. Next, the author sprang another surprise by turning to the ancient past, when the religious dogmas of the Western world were being shaped. *Quo vadis* (1896; Eng. tr., 1896) conveyed the message of faith and hope, not to a single nation, but to all contemporaries breathing the morbid air of the fin de siècle. The decadence of Rome, personified by the immoral ruler with artistic ambitions and the refined patrician scorning the existing order but unwilling to change it, was confronted with the humble, but invincible Christians. The book became a best seller and made Sienkiewicz a figure of international standing. In 1900 he published the large novel *Krzyżacy* (Eng. trs., *The Knights of the Cross,* 1900, *The Teutonic Knights,* 1943), based on the medieval struggle between the Order of the Cross, settled at the Baltic seashore, to convert the local population, and the Polish, Lithuanian, and Ruthenian neighbors. The work clearly referred to the aggressive policy of the modern German state towards the Poles.

In 1905, Sienkiewicz was awarded a Nobel Prize for Literature. The peak of his creative vigor was over, but he still continued writing. The novel *Wiry* (1910; Eng tr., *The Whirlpools,* 1910) reflects his anxiety in view of the revolutionary brooding that was dissipating national energies. *W pustyni i w puszczy* (1911; Eng. tr., *In Desert and Wilderness,* 1912) is a story of adventure addressed to the youth and presenting the ideal resembling the Boy Scout movement; it exploited the author's brief expedition to Africa. When World War I began, Sienkiewicz left for Switzerland, where he joined the Red Cross and the committee for the victims of war in Poland. He died in November 1916. Almost all his works were translated into English, sometimes by several different translators. Published in 50 languages, they were often reprinted, making Sienkiewicz one of the most popular modern authors. His collected works have been published: *Dzieła,* ed. by J. Krzyżanowski, vols. 1–60 (1948–55).

See: M. Gardner, *The Patriot Novelist of Poland, Henryk Sienkiewicz* (1926); J. Krzyżanowski, *Henryk Sienkiewicz. Kalendarz życia i twórczości* (1956); M. Giergielewicz, *Henryk Sienkiewicz* (1968); K. Wyka and A. Piorunowa, eds., *Henryk Sienkiewicz: twórczość i recepcja światowa* (1968); Z. Szweykowski, *Trylogia Sienkiewicza* (1973); J. Krzyżanowski, *Twórczość Henryka Sienkiewicza,* (3d ed., 1976).   M.G.

Sieroszewski, Wacław (1858–1945), Polish novelist and short-story writer, was born in Wólka Kozlowska and died in Piaseczno. He was deported in 1880 to Siberia for participation in underground socialist activites and spent 12 years there living among the Yakuts. This experience, as well as Sieroszewski's later travels to Japan, Korea, and Ceylon, provided him with subject matter and settings for the main body of his fiction, ethnological studies, and travel reporting. Sieroszewski's main monograph *Yakuts* (1896), originally published in Russian and a few years later in the Polish version as *Duanaśeie lat w kraju Jakutów* (1900; Twelve Years in The Yakut Country), brought him much praise and made possible his return home. Precise Siberian settings are characteristic of his best works, such as his most popular novel *Na kresach lasów* (1894; In the Borderlands of the Forest), the collection of short stories *W matni* (1897; In the Snare), the stories *Dno nędzy* (1899; The Depth of Misery), and *Ucieczka* (1904; The Flight). These works, as well as Sieroszewski's Far Eastern short stories and novels, are permeated with insight and compassion for the people of other civilizations.

Both before and especially after his return from Siberia, Sieroszewski was very active in Poland's political life and in the national movement for independence led by Józef Piłsudski. An admirer and staunch supporter of Piłsudski, Sieroszewski became a soldier in spite of his age in Piłsudski's Polish legion fighting against the Russians in World War I.

In 1920, Sieroszewski visited the United States, lecturing before Polish immigrants. As the dean of Polish writers, Sieroszewski became president of the Polish Academy of Literature, established in 1933.

See: A. Lam, "Wacław Sieroszewski," in *Literatura polska w okresie realizmu i naturalizmu,* vol. 4 (1971), pp. 429–72; H. M. Malgowska, *Sieroszewski i Syberia* (1973).   S.S.

Sigfússon, Hannes (1922–), Icelandic novelist and poet, was born in Reykjavík. He reached maturity there in impoverished circumstances during the economic depression after 1930. Sigfússon received a limited formal education, but instead worked at various jobs—as a salesman, farmhand, laborer, fisherman, and lighthouse keeper—gaining from all these a rich store of experience to which he added an educational dimension through independent reading.

He went to Sweden in 1945, staying there and in Norway for a year and a half, during which time he became acquainted with Swedish modernism, a school of writing that was to become one influence on his work. Sigfússon's early books of verse also show influence from surrealism and from T. S. Eliot. Echoes from Eliot's *The Waste Land* are unmistakably present in Sigfússon's first book of poetry, *Dymbilvaka* (1949; Passion Week Vigil), a volume containing a lengthy series of poems derived from the author's experiences as a lighthouse keeper on the rugged southwestern coast of Iceland. From the landscapes so well known to him, Sigfússon has fashioned a picture of a world in chaos, seen from the perspective of the poet's doubts about communism, his fears associated with the Cold War, and the memories of the terrors of a recent world war.

Imbrudagar (1951; Ember Days) is another collection of poetry with the same general theme, although surrealistic effects have by now become more pronounced. The author's stance has shifted, too. He voices greater optimism, concluding the book with an invocation to revolution, asking that it sing a requiem over the defunct capitalist system. In his only novel, *Strandið* (1955; The Shipwrek), Sigfússon draws upon an event he witnessed as a lighthouse keeper. A starkly realistic work, it also symbolizes the collapse of capitalism.

In Sigfússon's two books of poetry published since 1960, *Sprek á eldinn* (1961; Firewood) and *Jarteikn* (1966;

Tokens), the images are more concentrated and the outlook more optimistic than in the problem-centered works of his earlier years. The latter book is his most ambitious attempt at harnessing his poetic energy to further the creation of a decent world by affirming human values that he regards as positive. In general, Sigfússon's poetic idiom is rich and powerful with an enchanting tone that is best described as magical.

Sigfússon has lived in Norway in later years, working as a librarian in Stavanger. While there, he has been a productive translator of Scandinavian verse into Icelandic, and he has published the collection *Norræn ljóð 1939–69* (1972; Nordic Poetry, 1939–69).

See: E. Bragi, "Viðtal vid Hannes Sigfússon," *Birtingur,* 1 (1958): 1–8; I. Orgland, "Hannes Sigfússon" in H. Sigfússon, *Så fløder havet inn* (1974), pp. 5–27.

S.S.H.

Sigurðsson, Ólafur Jóhann (1913–), Icelandic poet, short-story writer, and novelist, was born in Garðahreppur, near Reykjavik, but grew up mostly in Grafningur, in southern Iceland, where his father was a farmer. At only 15, Sigurðsson moved to Reykjavik to become a writer. Although primarily self-educated, he studied in Copenhagen (1936–37) and in New York (1943–44).

His first book was a collection of short stories for children, *Við Álftavatn* (1934; At Swan Lake). Other children's books by him are *Um sumarkvöld* (1935; In the Summer Evenings) and *Spói* (1962; Curlew). Sigurðsson's first novel, *Skuggarnir of bænum* (The Shadows of the Farm), appeared in 1936, and his major works of fiction since then are the sequel *Fjallið og draumurinn/Vorköld jörð* (1944/1951; The Mountain and the Dream/Cold Earth in Spring), *Litbrigði jarðarinnar* (1947; The Colors of the Earth), *Gangvirkið* (1955; The Mechanism), and *Hreiðrið* (1972; The Nest). He has also published a number of collections of short stories and is one of the modern Icelandic masters of that genre. He is the author of three books of verse, the last two of which *Aðlaufferjum* (1972; By the Leaf Ferries) and *Að brunnum* (1974; At the Wellsprings), earned him the Nordic Council Prize in 1976.

Sigurðsson emerged as an author during a time of severe economic depression and fierce labor unrest in Iceland, and he immediately joined ranks with writers who held radical socialist views, a position that was to become a permanent influence on his work. In his formative years, Icelandic society was in a flux, rapidly changing from a primitive but stable farm economy to urban living, which had no precedent in the country. Sigurðsson's work as a whole documents social and cultural changes in Iceland since the turn of the century, constantly focusing on ethical standards and conflicts between values.

Essentially, Sigurðsson praises the simple life of a disappearing rural society, but criticizes what he sees as the moral dissolution of the newly rich generation of city dwellers, who have abandoned the values that sustained the lowly people of days gone by. Consistent with this view, he has been critical of modernistic experimentation on the literary scene.

His own style of writing is characteristically refined and lyrical, and in both his fiction and poetry he seeks to reconcile old literary tradition and modern outlook, forever emphasizing moral honesty and stability, the two most significant themes in his works.

See: H. J. Halldórsson, "Ólafur Jóhann Sigurðsson," *Tímarit Máls og menningar* (1960), pp. 367–76; V. Ólason, "Ein moderne tradisjonalist," *Norsk litterær årsbok* (1976).   S.S.H.

Sigurjónsson, Jóhann (1880–1919) Icelandic dramatist and poet, was born at Laxamýri in Þingeyjarsýsla in the north of Iceland. His parents were well to do, and there was poetic talent in his mother's family (*e.g.*, Jónas Hallgrímsson, pioneer of the romantic movement). The boy was able to follow his inclination to study, and, being attracted to natural science, he chose the study of veterinary medicine in Copenhagen (1899). He had almost finished when he determined to devote his whole time and energy to becoming a writer—a great and famous writer it must be. As a shortcut to literary fame he decided to write plays in Danish. He was thus the first of his compatriots to cut across the narrow confines of his mother tongue (spoken by a population of about 100,000) to gain a wider audience, and more were to follow his example. He was soon one of the most brilliant members of the bohemian art circle in Copenhagen, a group that tasted the excesses of French fin-de-siècle decadence and shared the soaring ambitions of Nietzschean geniuses.

His first two plays, *Dr. Rung* (1905) and *Bóndinn á Hrauni* (1908; Eng. tr., *The Hraun Farm*, 1916), were immature, but the latter treated an Icelandic subject for the first time. With *Bjærg-Ejvind og hans Hustru* (1911; Icelandic, *Fjalla-Eyvindur*, 1912; Eng. tr., *Eyvind of the Hills*, 1916) Sigurjónsson attained meteoric fame. He was acclaimed by the best critics such as Georg BRANDES and wooed by both the Scandinavian and the German stage (*Fjalla-Eyvindur* was first produced in Reykjavík Dec. 25, 1911; in Copenhagen May 20, 1912). The fame of the play spread even to France, England, and the United States; a French critic gave the author a seat of honor beside Scandinavia's big three, Bjørnstjerne BJØRNSON, Henrik IBSEN, and August STRINDBERG. Later Victor Sjöström was to make one of the first artistic films out of the play. *Fjalla-Eyvindur* is based upon an Icelandic folk tale about real 18th-century outlaws (sheep thieves). In the play Fjalla-Eyvindur's wife becomes the true hero, living for her love only and perishing in the end because her love is shattered against the elemental forces of hunger in the wilderness. This great tragedy is projected against the colorful background of Icelandic folkways and magnificent mountains. It is ennobled by the rich lyric expression of the author, who has left other perfect gems of lyric poetry apart from the songs in his plays. His next play, *Ønsket* (1915; Icelandic tr., *Galdra-Loftur*, 1915; Eng. trs., *Loftur*, 1939, "Loft's Wish," *Poet Lore*, XLVI, 99–146), was also based on a folk tale. Loftur is an Icelandic Faust whose towering ambition is to harness the powers of darkness—for higher purposes. He fails utterly because of his selfishness. The same ambition burns in *Løgneren* (1917; The Liar), a play drawn from *Njála*, the most famous of the Icelandic sagas. These two works, though good, did not attain the success of *Fjalla-Eyvindur*.

Sigurjónsson's untimely death cut short a career of unusual brilliance. Those who knew him best all agreed that his life was beautiful poetry even to a greater degree than his written works. He left an unfinished play, *Elsa*, which points to a new, more subdued period in his development. S.E.

Sikelianos, Angelos (1884–1951), Greek poet, was born on the island of Levkas. He entered law school in 1900 but gave up his studies to devote himself exclusively to literature. In 1907 he married Eva Palmer, an American heiress. In 1927 and 1930, they attempted together to revive the ancient Delphic festivals, inspired by the poet's quixotic humanistic hope to bring about the regeneration of modern culture and the spiritual union of all mankind by means of poetry. Although the festivals were artistically successful, they failed in their Utopian purpose.

Sikelianos's first important work was *Alafroiskiotos* (1909; The Visionary), a lyrical masterpiece that established him at once as a major poet. In this work, he reveals what he considered to be the two main creative sources of life: nature and tradition. In the five slim volumes constituting his *Prologos sti zoi* (vols. 1–4, 1915–17; vol. 5, 1947; Prologue to Life), Sikelianos continued to seek a deep, mystical contact with the life-force, articulating his "consciousness" of five vital sources: nature, race, love, religion, and, as the ultimate synthesis, the will to create. It is this will that aims to unite man with God, that is, with the creative power whose most perfect manifestation is man himself. The same themes, treated in a more complex and poetically mature manner, recur in later works.

By means of mythic and symbolic figures, such as Dionysos, Orpheus, Christ, and the Virgin Mary, Sikelianos endeavored to contain eternity within the present and the present within eternity. He viewed poetry as the most authoritative instrument for uniting verse. In *Mitir theou* (1917–19; Mother of God), he employs the figure of Mother Nature, as she existed from prehistoric times to the time of the Virgin Mary, to portray life as a regenerative force in which death is continually destroyed by rebirth. This poem offers the most vivid expression of the poet's pantheistic materialism, which finds in nature's eternal process of rebirth an immortality capable of destroying decay. In *To Pascha ton Ellinon* (1919 [fragments], 1947; The Easter of the Greeks), he is concerned with Christianity not as a dogma but as a universal myth expression the sufferings and aspirations of all mankind.

Quite aside from his mystic search for eternity, however, what truly distinguishes Sikelianos as a great poet is his militant humanism and the powerful beauty of his lyricism. Indeed, his many shorter lyrics are artistically more perfect and ideologically more restrained than his longer works. His dramas, such as *Sivylla* (1944; Sibyl) and *O Daidalos stin Kriti* (1943; Daidalos in Crete), are theatrically ineffective, yet they are outstanding for their lyricism and humanistic zeal. Their central theme is always the conflict between freedom and tyranny. Sikelianos expressed this same theme in many poems that he circulated illegally during the German-Italian Occupation in an effort to sustain the Greek people's spirit of resistance. Sikelianos was a great lyricist and visionary, deeply disturbed by man's alienation from life in our profit-seeking, logic-bound culture. Convinced of the poet's role as initiator and prophet of spiritual renewal, he was frequently but not always successful in giving contemporaneously meaningful expression to his world view. For a selection of his poetry in English, see *Angelos Sikelianos: Selected Poems*, ed. and tr. by E. Keeley and P. Sherrard (1979). Six volumes of Sikelianos's *Apanta* (Collected Works), ed. by G. P. Savidis, have been published (1965–69).

See: E. Keeley and P. Sherrard, eds., *Six Poets of Modern Greece* (1960); P. Sherrard, *The Marble Threshing Floor* (1965); K. Friar, ed., *Modern Greek Poetry: From Cavafis to Elytis* (1973). C.A.

Sillanpää, Frans Emil (1888–1964), Finnish novelist, was born in Hämeenkyrö, central Finland, the son of a small farmer. He studied biology at Helsinki University but did not take a degree. In 1939 he was awarded the Nobel Prize for Literature.

Sillanpää's production can be divided into two main periods. To the first belong his first, lyrical novel, *Elämä ja aurinko* (1916; Life and Sun), and *Hurskas kurjuus* (1919; Eng. tr., *Meek Heritage*, 1938), which describes the Finnish Civil War of 1918. The second period begins with *Nuorena nukkunut* (1931; Eng. trs., *The Maid Silja,* 1933, *Fallen Asleep while Young,* 1939), a novel about the disappearance of a farmer's family. It continues with *Miehen tie* (1932; A Man's Road), in which the plot follows the rhythm of the seasons; the novel *Ihmiset suviyössä* (1934; Eng. tr., *People in the Summer Night,* 1966), in which the narrative is a lyrical mosaic; and *Elokuu* (1941; August), a family drama.

In both periods of his work, Sillanpää sees man as an integral part of nature, intimately connected with its great rhythm. Indeed, his novels usually have rural settings. He often speaks in his essays of "the basic man," by which he means the qualities that are common to all men and form the basis of life itself. It follows from his premises that all forms and expressions of life are valuable; the most humble persons can be real heroes and have a rich inner life. In this respect, Sillanpää writes in the great rural and human tradition of Finnish prose that began with Kivi.

See: T. Vaaskivi, *F. E. Sillanpää* (1937); A. Laurila, *Frans Emil Sillanpää* (1958); A. Ojala, *Kohtalon toteuttaminen* (1959); A. Laurila, *Frans Emil Sillanpää romaanitaide* (1979). K.L.

Silone, Ignazio, pseud. of Secondo Tranquilli (1900–78), Italian novelist and social critic, was born in Pescina. His family, small landholders of the district, provided him with an education in Catholic schools, but his attitudes were chiefly shaped by his close contact with the impoverished peasants of the countryside in which he grew up and by the social injustices he witnessed and rebelled against in early youth. After the death of his mother and five brothers in the 1915 earthquake, he and a surviving brother left the Abruzzi for Rome where for a time he edited the socialist weekly *L'avanguardia*. In 1921 he made the first of several trips to the USSR as a member of the Italian Communist delegation. In Trieste, aided by his brother, he edited the proscribed daily *Il lavoratore*. Sought by the Fascist police, he escaped to his native hills where he was hidden by the peasants for several years. (His brother was captured and eventually died of prison beatings.) In 1930, Silone succeeded in crossing the border into Germany and found eventual refuge in Switzerland. The following year, with an anguish that colored the rest of his life, he broke with the Communist Party. It was thus in separation from all that had been precious and familiar that Silone began his career as a writer. He remained in Switzerland until the events of 1944 permitted his return to Italy.

All of Silone's writings spring from his early indignant sympathy for the oppressed and his ethical conception of socialism. His fiction and essays alike reflect his views on the oppression of power and point to the need for an awareness and correction of the problem through action rather than remote theory. Silone explicitly links the idea of socialism with that of liberty, but he does not assume liberty to be a natural or necessary outcome of socialism. Like Giuseppe Mazzini, of whom he wrote in *The Living Thoughts of Mazzini* (1939; first published in English), he expected his country to be saved, not by outside intervention, but from within. Writing in 1939, he declared himself to be a member of no political party, but "an anti-Fascist partisan" in the civil war raging throughout the world, and he expressed his disappointment with the parties and programs of a Left that had lost all effective contact with reality. He saw World War II as only too likely to result in "the fascistization of the democratic countries," and he was unable to condone those socialists who "with the very best anti-Fascist intentions . . . put

their own theories in mothballs" in order to cooperate with men of opposing ideologies in the struggle against a common enemy. To the convinced socialist (and Silone's life has borne this out), it remained to refuse compromise and to live in strict accord with an ethical ideal. By 1944, Silone had already expressed much of this in the three novels, the drama, and the two works of nonfiction that he published in exile. When he returned to Italy, Silone revised and republished all that he found worth keeping and, at the same time, began a series of new books and essays. He became known in his own country. He reentered political life, but soon withdrew again. From 1956 to 1968 he coedited with Nicola CHIAROMONTE the international cultural review *Tempo presente*.

The cogency of Silone's fiction lies in its humanity, its biting realism, and its irony. Indeed, irony is the overall tempering element, yet it derives not from scorn but from deep and offended love. This certainly applies to *Fontamara* (Ger. ed., 1930, Ital. ed., 1933, rev. 1958; Eng. trs., 1934, 1960), Silone's first novel, written in exile. In its original version, this story of a despoiled, abased peasant village in the Abruzzi during the Fascist period, told with flashing scorn, pride, and wit, was hailed as a masterpiece. Translated into 17 languages during its first year, the novel had the curious distinction of remaining unknown only in Italy. In *Pane e vino* (1937; Eng. tr., *Bread and Wine,* 1936; rev. version, *Vino e pane,* 1955, Eng. tr., *Bread and Wine,* 1962) and in its sequel, *Il seme sotto la neve* (1941, rev. ed., 1953; Eng. trs., *The Seed beneath the Snow,* 1942, 1965), the central character is an intellectual son of gentry, a native of the same Fucino valley hills that yielded Fontamara. Pietro Spina returns from exile to Italy, from the realm of revolutionary theory to the realm of human reality and, after experiencing some of the limitations to which man's love of liberty may be subject, finally finds himself truly at home in the "poor, barren country" that is "the country of his soul." Spina sheds a delusive political partisanship in favor of a concrete, living Christian ethic, sharing his life with the humble company of those with whom he can break bread in poverty and charity.

The first of Silone's three postwar novels, *Una manciata di more* (1952; Eng. tr., *A Handful of Blackberries,* 1953), deals both grimly and farcically with what happens in a rural community when there is an abrupt political shift from extreme right to left. *Il Segreto di Luca* (1956; Eng. tr., *The Secret of Luca,* 1958) and *La volpe e le camelie* (1960; Eng. tr., *The Fox and the Camellias,* 1961) are both essentially minor works.

The earliest of Silone's work of nonfiction is his history of the origins and early years of the Fascist movement in Italy, published only in Switzerland as *Der Fascismus: seine Entstehung und seine Entwicklung* (1934; Fascism: Its Origin and Development). *The School for Dictators* (1938; Italian ed., *La scuola dei dittatori,* 1962) is a satiric treatise on the grooming of modern tyrants, written in the form of a series of dialogues between an aspirant to American dictatorship, a scholarly American windbag, and a European who styles himself Thomas the Cynic. The work acidly views the manners, attitudes, dreams, and myths of dictators past and present. Of paramount interest is *Uscita di sicurezza* (1965; Eng. tr., *Emergency Exit,* 1968). At first glance, this seems to be a random collection of personal and political reminiscences, but as one comes to grasp its ingenious unity, *Uscita di sicurezza* reveals itself as the autobiography of a conscience. Made up of several sketches from the writer's boyhood, a long and moving memoir of his Communist experience, and a number of political essays, it ends with a searching study of the idea of progress in the 20th century. The whole bears witness to the fact that in Silone, the experience of adversity only deepened and purified his convictions.

In addition to these works and a second drama, *L'avventura di un povero cristiano* (1968; The Adventure of a Poor Christian), based on the life of Celestine V, the celebrated abdicator of the papal throne, Silone published numerous articles in European and American books and periodicals.

See: E. Wilson, "Malraux and Silone," *NY* (Sept. 8, 1945); R. W. B. Lewis, *The Picaresque Saint* (1959); I. Howe, *Politics and the Novel* (1961).   I.B.

Simenon, Georges (1903–), Belgian novelist, was born in Liège. The provincial and middle-class environment of this city permeates his writings. Attracted at an early age by literature and journalism, he left Liège before he was 20 in order to pursue a career in Paris. He was able, from 1924 onward, to live from his writings. Between 1923 and 1933 he published, under a number of pseudonyms, many tales and articles, as well as detective stories and romantic and adventure novels. But his readings and his numerous travels, which revealed the mind of a perceptive journalist, produced another kind of writer. His real beginning in the detective novel dates from *Les Treize Mystères* (1929; The Thirteen Mysteries). The first hero named "Maigret" appeared in *Pietr le letton* (1930; Eng. tr., "The Case of Peter the Lett" in *Inspector Maigret Investigates*, 1933); the series experienced an immediate success. Changing to the publisher Gallimard in 1933, Simenon rejected stereotyped themes and turned to first-person accounts and more complex fiction. In *Le Testament Donadieu* (1936; Eng. tr., *The Shadow Falls*, 1945), the plot is only the pretext for the portrayal of individualists (most often marginal) and of provincial settings. In 1938, Simenon published *Le Bourgmestre de Furnes, l'homme qui regardait passer les trains* (Eng. tr., *The Bourgomaster of Furnes*, 1952) and, in 1940, *Les Inconnus dans la maison* (Eng. tr., *Strangers in the House*, 1951). This same period saw the development of the Simenon myth; he became known for his wealth, his pipe, his frequent withdrawals, and his work's "instinctive development." His worldwide success has been phenomenal: only the Bible and the works of Vladimir Ilyich Lenin and Mao Tse-tung have been published in greater numbers. In 1945, Simenon left a weary Europe for North America, where he traveled widely, from Quebec to Arizona and from California to Florida. Several of his most important novels were written in this period: *Trois chambres à Manhattan* (1946; Eng. tr., *Three Beds in Manhattan*, 1964), *Lettre à mon juge* (1947; Eng. tr., *Act of Passion*, 1953), and *La neige était sale* (1948; Eng. tr., *The Stain on the Snow*, 1953). Simenon returned to France in 1955 and moved to Switzerland in 1957. Thereafter he traveled less and less and produced only three or four novels per year, including *Le Fils* (1956; Eng. tr., *The Son*, 1958), *Les Anneaux de Bicêtre* (1962; Eng. tr., *The Bells of Bicêtre*, 1964), and *Le Chat* (1966; Eng. tr., *The Cat*, 1967). From 1960 to 1962 he wrote a diary laced with philosophical reflections and scientific commentaries, *Quand j'étais vieux* (1970; Eng. tr., *When I was Old*, 1971). This work did not provide the first occasion for Simenon to take himself as the object of his writing. In addition to the autobiographical elements, reworked by a rich memory, which appear throughout his works, Simenon had previously produced *Je me souviens* (1945; I Remember), later expanded as a novel in *Pedigree* (1948; Eng. tr. *Pedigree*, 1962). In the early 1970s, Simenon's work began to lessen in quantity and quality. In 1973, the writer decided to set aside his pen. He sold his house in Epalinges in order to settle in a smaller residence, he gave his manuscripts and collections to the University of Liège, and he began to dictate his memoirs. Less a systematic autobiography than a collection of reflections, this new phase of his work began with the rather repetitive *Lettre à ma mère* (1974; Eng. tr., *Letter to My Mother*, 1976).

Georges Simenon has without doubt given a new life to the detective novel by endowing this genre with a human dimension. The same human sensitivity, expressed with remarkable insight, appears as well in his psychological novels, which have gained him the reputation of an Honoé de Balzac of the 20th century.

See: T. Narcejac, *Le Cas Simenon* (1950; Eng. tr., *The Art of Simenon*, 1952); B. de Fallois, *Simenon* (1961); R. Stéphane, *Le Dossier Simenon* (1961); Q. Ritzen, *Simenon, Avocat des Hommes* (1961); L. Raymond, *Simenon in Court* (1969); F. Lacassin and G. Sigaux, *Simenon* (1973); T. Young, *Georges Simenon: A Checklist of His "Maigret" and Other Mystery Novels* (1976).   J.-M.K.

Simon, Claude (1913–), French novelist, was born in Tananarive, Madagascar. He was educated in France and England and studied painting (a lifetime interest) with André Lhote. In the 1930s, he traveled through Europe, especially in Republican Spain at the time of the Civil War. The writing of his first novel, *Le Tricheur* (1945; The Cheat), begun in 1938, was interrupted by World War II. Captured by the Germans in the 1940 debacle, he escaped six months later. A recurrent, obsessive theme in his novels is war, particularly the Spanish Civil War, which furnished the setting for *Le Palace* (1962; Eng. tr., *The Palace*, 1963). Throughout his writing, there are also reminiscences of World War II, an episode of which provided the setting for his most widely read novel, *La Route des Flandres* (1960; Eng. tr., *The Flanders Road*, 1961); of post-Liberation France; of World War I; and of colonialism. Although Simon is not concerned with these events as such, but rather with their fragmentary, confused presence in his characters'—and his own—consciousness, these recollections exist side by side with a host of other memories and perceptions.

Since 1940, Simon has devoted himself to writing, having settled down in the Pyrenees region in 1946, where he cultivates his vineyards. He has published 13 novels from *Le Tricheur* to *Triptyque* (1973), as well as an essay, *Orion aveugle* (1970; Blind Orion), explaining his innovative methods of composition, and a play, *La Séparation* (1963). Simon's early novels, *Le Tricheur*, *La Corde raide* (1947; The Tightrope), *Gulliver* (1952), and *Le Sacre du printemps* (1954; The Anointment of Spring), were written in a traditional mode. He has since developed into one of the most independent of the French experimental novelists. Despite his association with the experimenters, his allegiance to Gustave Flaubert, Marcel PROUST, James Joyce, Franz KAFKA, and William Faulkner is strong, and he is widely acquainted with the novelistic tradition in general.

Simon's later work falls into two main groups. Four novels published in rapid succession brought him recognition: *Le Vent, Tentative de restitution d'un rétable baroque* (1957; Eng. tr., *The Wind, Attempted Restoration of a Baroque Altarpiece*, 1959), *L'Herbe* (1958; Eng. tr., *The Grass*, 1960), *La Route des Flandres*, and *Le Palace*. These novels deal with the themes of time, accumulated memory, history, and private story. The protagonist, in a catalytic moment of stress that releases a confused "magma" of memories and perceptions, attempts and fails to discern a continuity or pattern in his life. In order to suggest the processes of memory, Simon devised a style consisting of long, unwinding paragraphs rich in parentheses, doubling back and forth through recurrent images, projecting a kind of spatial counterpart of the past through a graph of the jumbled paths of memory. A five-year silence preceded his next four works: *Histoire* (1967; Eng. tr., 1968), *La Bataille de Pharsale* (1969; Eng. tr., *The Battle of Pharsalus*, 1971), *Les Corps conducteurs* (1973; Eng. tr., *Conducting Bodies*, 1974), and *Leçon de choses* (1975; Lesson in Things). In these books, Simon experimented with a new form of composition; starting from separate series of images, he works out the purely linguistic processes they trigger. Through ''metaphoric association, superimpositions, contrasts, oppositions,'' they interact and are woven into a single text.

See: *Nouveau Roman: hier, aujourd'hui*, vol. 1: *Problèmes généraux*; vol. 2: *Pratiques* (1972); L. S. Roudiez, ''Claude Simon,'' in *French Fiction Today* (1972), pp. 152–82; C. Du Verlie, ''Interview with Claude Simon,'' *Sub-stance* 8 (Winter 1974): pp. 21–33; J. Fletcher, *Claude Simon* (1975); S. Jimenez, *Claude Simon* (1975); J. A. E. Loubère, *The Novels of Claude Simon* (1975). G.Br.

Simon, Pierre-Henri (1903–75), French novelist and critic, was born in Saint-Fort-sur-Gironde. He had a distinguished career as a professor of literature in France and abroad.

Simon's novels include *Les Valentin* (1931; The Valentins); *L'Affût* (1950; The Watch); *Les Raisins verts* (1950; Green Grapes); *Les Hommes ne veulent pas mourir* (1953; Men Do Not Want to Die); *Elsinfor* (1956); the short novel *Portrait d'un officier* (1958; Eng. tr., *An End to Glory*, 1961); his masterpiece, *Figures à Cordouan: Les Somnambules* (1960; The Sleepwalkers of Cordouan); and *Histoire d'un bonheur* (1965; A Story of Happiness). Masterfully using all the techniques of the novel, as well as his keen understanding of the modern world, Simon analyzed the reactions of individuals to contemporary problems. His fiction as well as his philosophical and literary essays reflect a very high sense of values drawn from a profound Christian humanism.

Among his numerous philosophical essays one might select *La France à la recherche d'une conscience* (1944; France in Search of a Conscience), *Contre la torture* (1957; Against Torture), *Ce que je crois* (1966; What I Believe), *Pour un garçon de vingt ans* (1967; For a Boy of 20), and *Parier pour l'homme* (1973; Bet on Man). In addition to studies of such authors as Georges DUHAMEL, Albert CAMUS, and François MAURIAC, he undertook many cross-sectional studies of 20th-century French literature: *L'Homme en procès: Malraux, Sartre, Camus* (1950; Man on Trial: André MALRAUX, Jean-Paul SARTRE, Camus), *Procès du héros: Montherlant, Drieu la Rochelle, Jean Prévost* (1950; Heroes on Trial: Henry de MONTHERLANT, Pierre DRIEU LA ROCHELLE, Jean PRÉVOST), *Diagnostic des lettres contemporaines* (1966; State of Contemporary Letters), *L'Esprit et l'histoire: essai sur la conscience historique dans la littérature du XXe siècle* (1954; Spirit and History: Essay on the Historical Consciousness in 20th-Century Literature), *La Littérature du péché et de la grâce: essai sur la constitution d'une littérature chrétienne depuis 1880* (1957; The Literature of Sin and Grace: Essay on the Elaboration of a Christian Literature since 1880), *Témoins de l'homme* (1951; Witness of Man), and *Théâtre et destin* (1959; Theater and Destiny). The best synthesis of his literary criticism is his *Histoire de la littérature au XXe siècle* (1957, 1967; History of the Literature of the 20th Century). From 1961 until his death in 1975, Simon was the principal literary critic for *Le Monde*. He was elected to the Académie Française in 1966. J.-P.C.

Simonov, Konstantin (real first name: **Kirill) Mikhaylovich** (1915–79), Russian playwright, novelist, journalist, essayist, and editor, was born in Petersburg and educated in Saratov and at the Gorky Literary Institute in Moscow. He began to publish poetry in 1934. After the invasion of the Soviet Union by Germany during World War II, he became famous as a war correspondent for the newspaper *Krasnaya zvezda*. His war plays, *Paren iz nashego goroda* (1941; A Lad from our Town), *Russkiye lyudi* (1942; Eng. tr., *The Russians,* 1943), and *Tak i budet* (1944; So Be It), are still performed in the USSR. Simonov is best known for his war poems, which are autobiographical, lyrical, and emotional in tone, and in some cases are highly charged politically, as, for example, ''Ubey ego'' (1942; Kill Him), a call to kill the enemy mercilessly (*see* RUSSIAN LITERATURE). Many of his poems have been set to music. Simonov's first long prose work, *Dni i nochi* (1943–44; Eng. tr., *Days and Nights,* 1945), is also highly patriotic, dealing with the battle of Stalingrad. In 1945 he published collections of sketches of his travels with the Russian army to Romania, Bulgaria, Yugoslavia, Poland, and Germany. Simonov's postwar trips to Europe and the United States inspired his play *Russkiy vopros* (1946; The Russian Question), which criticizes the American system, and the book of poems *Druzya i vragi* (1948; Friends and Enemies). His play *Chetvyorty* (1961; The Fourth) deals with the fate of American soldiers after the war. Indeed, for at least a quarter of a century after 1945, a major theme of Simonov's fiction continued to be World War II.

Simonov has also worked extensively as a screen writer and has been very active as an editor and administrator. He has served as secretary of the Union of Soviet Writers and editor in chief of both the literary magazine *Novy mir* (1946–50, 1954–58), and the newspaper *Literaturnaya gazeta* (1938, 1950–54).

See: V. Alexandrova, *A History of Soviet Literature 1917–1962* (1963) pp. 276–79, 287–88; G. Struve, *Russian Literature under Lenin and Stalin 1917–1953* (1971) pp. 312–13, 324–27); I. L. Vishnevskaya, *Konstantin Simonov: o cherk tvorchestva* (1966); S. Fradkina, *Tvorchestvo Konstantina Simonova* (1968). L.V.

Sinyavsky, Andrey Donatovich (1925–), Russian novelist, short-story writer, and critic, is one of the leading figures in the rebirth of Russian literature after the death of Iosif Stalin. Born in Moscow, he received a degree in philological science from Moscow State University in 1952. He then became a senior research fellow and teacher at the Gorky Institute of World Literature, where he worked until his arrest in 1965. In 1956, Sinyavsky began to write under the pen name Abram Tertz; his works circulated in *samizdat* editions and were also published outside the Soviet Union. The works of Abram Tertz may all be seen as stages in a daring and solitary act of self-liberation. They reveal Sinyavsky's struggle from Marxism to a religious position that may be defined as a kind of nonmythological late Christianity in which God the Father is the inspiration and Christ the example. The ethics Sinyavsky developed out of his religious discoveries is akin to that elaborated by Martin Buber in his *I and Thou*.

Sinyavsky is one of the few genuine avant-garde writers of his era. He has created a new literary form that he calls ''fantastic realism,'' which combines the human psyche and external reality into a single image. This equation well describes the situation of contemporary man, whom Sinyavsky sees as a flux between historical cycles. In his works of fiction, the tension between the fantastic and the real produces satire with romantic and metaphysical resonances.

Two of Sinyavsky's most important works, *Chto takoye sotsialisticheskiy realizm* (1960; Eng. tr., *On Socialist Realism*) and *Sud idyot* (written 1956; first published in French, Polish, and Italian translations, 1959; Russian text published in 1967; Eng. tr., *The Trial Begins*, 1961), examine Soviet communism as a tragicomic confusion of ends and means. *Mysli vrasplokh* (New York 1966; Eng. tr., *Thought Unaware*, 1965) is a collection of aphorisms on many subjects (sex, death, original sin), written in an intimate, conversational style. *Fantasticheskiye povesti* (Paris, 1961; Eng. tr., *Fantastic Stories,* 1963) contains experiments in form whose results are put to their fullest use in his novel *Lyubimov* (Eng. tr., *The Makepeace Experiment,* 1965), which is a serene but satiric meditation on the fate and character of the Russian nation. Sinyavsky's criticism published in the Soviet Union under his own name, a long essay on Boris PASTERNAK and *Poeziya pervykh let revolutsii 1917–1920* (1964; The Poetry of the First Years of the Revolution 1917–1920), written in collaboration with A. Menshutin, are of significant critical value.

In 1966, Sinyavsky and Yuly DANIEL were tried and convicted of writing and sending abroad stories slanderous to the Soviet Union. They were convicted and sentenced to seven years in prison. Their trial initiated the crackdown on dissent by the regime of Leonid Brezhnev. In 1973, Sinyavsky emigrated to France and has since been teaching at the Sorbonne. His later works include a new collection of aphorisms, *Golos iz khora* (London 1973; Eng. tr., *A Voice from the Chorus,* 1976), *Progulki s Pushkinym* (London 1975; Walks with Pushkin), and *V teni Gogolya* (London, 1975: In the Shadow of Gogol).

See: M. Mihajlov, *Russian Themes* (1968); R. Lourie, *Letters to the Future: An Approach to Sinyavsky Tertz* (1975).   R.Lo.

Sion, Georges (1913–), Belgian essayist and playwright, was born in Binche and educated at the University of Louvain, where he received his doctorate in law. Sion has been a major force in the development and spread of the French-language culture of Belgium: for many years, he has been director of the *Revue Générale*; his weekly chronicles on literature and the arts in *Le Soir* are well-known; and he teaches the history of the theater at the Conservatoire de Bruxelles. Yet Sion is known above all as a playwright. In plays such as *La Matrone d'Ephise* (1943; The Ephesian Matron), *La Princesse de Chine* (1951; The Princess of China), and *La Malle de Pamela* (1955; Pamela's Trunk), he combines a sharp sense of humor with subtle poetic insights in a style akin to that of Jean GIRAUDOUX. In *Charles Le Téméraire* (1944; Charles the Bold) and *Le Voyageur de Forceloup* (1952; The Traveler from Forceloup), two widely acclaimed plays, he treats difficult subjects with courage and originality. Since 1955, Sion has demonstrated a rare talent in adapting works by Ben Jonson, Robert Bolt, Thomas Wolfe, and Arthur Wing Pinero. His French versions of plays by William Shakespeare, including *Anthony and Cleopatra, Richard II,* and *A Midsummer's Night Dream,* have enjoyed widespread success. A series of journeys in the Orient, Africa, the United States, and Mexico led him to write *Voyage aux quatre coins du Congo* (1953; Journey to the Four Corners of the Congo) and *Puisque chacun a son Amérique* (1956; Since Everyone Has His America). In 1962, he was elected to the Royal Academy of French Language and Literature of Belgium; in 1972, he succeeded Marcel THIRY as perpetual secretary of this academy. A writer and critic whose reputation is international, Sion is the only Belgian member of France's Goncourt Academy.   M.-R.L.

Sivle, Per (1857–1904), Norwegian poet, was born in Voss in western Norway, the son of a farmer. He spent much of his adult life, however, in the Oslo area, working as a journalist. Sivle's first mature work was a collection of short stories, *Sogor* (1887; Stories), containing sensitive portrayals of young boys growing up in a milieu characterized by spiritual and material poverty. The stories are classics of Norwegian literature. A short novel about the working class, *Streik* (1891; Strike), although written in the traditional literary language, has of late received new attention as the first Norwegian novel to present the workers' side in the 19th-century class struggle. Sivle's main, lasting works also include a number of national poems, some written in *riksmål* and some in *landsmål* (*see* NORWEGIAN LITERATURE), many of them taking their subject from national history, and all of them battle songs for Norwegian independence. Because of their epigrammatic form and imaginative power, these poems soon became classics and have been among the most widely read poems in Norway in the 20th century. Sivle's collected works, *Skrifter,* were posthumously published in three volumes in 1909–10.

See: A. Hovden, *Per Sivle* (1905); B. Birkeland, *Per Sivle* (1961).   H.K.

Sjöberg, Birger (1885–1929), Swedish poet, novelist, journalist, and songwriter, was born in Vänersborg and spent most of his working life in Hälsingborg on the south coast of Sweden. He fused the sceneries and social life of those two towns into one in his creative writing. His social perspective was that of the provincial lower middle class, which he pictured with warmhearted irony. One of the few genuinely comical writers in 19th-century Swedish literature, his work has been immensely popular, and some of his lyrics, set to his own music, have become poetic evergreens. His first published work was *Fridas bok* (1922; Frida's Book), a collection of songs put in the mouth of a somewhat priggish, self-educated shop assistant who seeks to improve the mind of his sweetheart, Frida, by explaining the wonders of the universe to her and pointing out the social injustices prevalent in their little town. The satirical and subtly self-ironical attitude sometimes gives way to a simple romantic tone in the hero's naive declarations of courtly love. Touring Sweden, Sjöberg gave numerous highly successful recitals of his songs to his own guitar accompaniment, which exposed him, however, to severe nervous strain. A second series of songs was published posthumously in *Fridas andra bok* (1929; Frida's Second Book). Equally popular was his novel, *Kvartetten som sprängdes* (1924; The Dispersed Quartet), a gay comedy of manners set in a post-World War I provincial town.

Sjöberg's spectacular success as a touring troubadour threw him off his always delicately poised psychic balance and plunged him into a deep emotional crisis, reflected in the collection of poems *Kriser och kransar* (1926; Crises and Laurels). Scorning popular success and bourgeois narrow-mindedness, he undertook in the collection a searching scrutiny both of his own ambitions and of the role of the poet in society. True to his journalistic training, he often took a piece of news as his starting point for a poem, developing it into a composition of far-reaching moral and metaphysical implications. His poetic technique owed something to German expressionism as did his tendency to paint the contemporary scene in apocalyptic colors. Frida's homely lover has turned into a disillusioned exposer of self-deceit and smug hypocrisy, revealing depths of destructive anxiety beneath the thin crust of personal security and social respectability. Many of Sjöberg's poems are devoted to the theme of death and an uncertain hope for immortality. As the author of *Kriser och kransar*, Sjöberg ranks as one of Sweden's first lyrical modernists. Since 1962 the Birger Sjöberg Society has published a series of books on Sjöberg, including a bibliography.

See: A. Peterson, *Birger Sjöberg den okände* (1944); G. A. Axberger, *Lilla Paris' undergång* (1960); L. H. Tunving, ed., *Sypunkter på Birger Sjöberg* (1966); C. J. Lawton, "Birger Sjöberg's Kriser och kransar," Ph. D. Dissertation, University of Hull (1978).　　　　S.B.

Sjöstrand, Östen (1925–), Swedish poet, was born in Göteborg. A modernist of the Paul VALÉRY and T. S. Eliot school, he cut a distinguished poetic profile even in his first two collections of verse, *Unio* (1949) and *Invigelse* (1950; Consecration). The *unio* of the first title is a twofold union: with the elements of water and wind, which permeate all Sjöstrand's poetic writings, and with a nameless spiritual source of being that, at the time, he interpreted in terms of Thomist theology, although the then-current vogue for French existentialism had made a deep impression upon him as well. His first and very successful attempts to write poetry were prompted by visionary experiences that occurred during a personal crisis and by the urge to transform obsessive musical rhythms into words. Some of his early work is modeled on Claude Debussy's piano music.

Although self-educated, Sjöstrand has acquired considerable learning in modern languages and literature, biology and physical science, and musicology, all of which have contributed to the form and subject matter of his poetic work. In *Återvändo* (1953; Return), he abandoned the high-strung lyrical intensity of his earlier work and embarked upon a course of intellectual and spiritual exploration that increasingly alienated him from the Roman Catholic Church and turned him into a passionate defender of the common spiritual heritage of the human race in a world threatening to destroy both inner and outer environment. This course is marked by a number of collections of poetry such as *Främmande mörker, främmande ljus* (1955; Strange Darkness, Strange Light), *Hemlöshet och hem* (1961; Homelessness and Home), and *En vinter i Norden* (1963; A Winter in the North). Some of Sjöstrand's most original achievement is to be found in *I vattumannens tecken* (1967; In the Sign of Aquarius), in which the painful birth of a new historic era is prophesied in startling symbols derived from fields as varied as astrology, post-Einsteinian physics, and Indian philosophy. What might have become too intellectual compositions are turned into compelling poetry by means of the author's unquestioning reliance on the lasting sensuous impressions of the seaside scenery of his childhood and on the deep creative sources that reveal themselves to him in visions and dreams. Candid confessions of hallucinatory states of mind form part of the poems in *Drömmen är ingen fasad* (1971; The Dream Is No Facade), which also contains fruits of the author's collaboration with the composer Sven-Erik Bäck in attempts to combine the resources of poetry and electrophonic music. Together with Bäck, he has also written an opera, *Gästabudet* (1962; The Banquet). His collection of poetry, *Strömöverföring* (1977; Transmission of Power) signals a change in both philosophy and poetic diction. For a selection of Sjöstrand's poetry in English, see *The Hidden Music*, tr. by R. Fulton (1974), and *Modern Swedish Poetry in Translation*, ed. by G. Harding and A. Hollo (1979), pp. 197–211.

See: S. Bergsten, *Östen Sjöstrand, TWAS* (1974).
　　　　S.B.

Skard, Sigmund (1903–), Norwegian poet and literary scholar, grew up in Kristiansand, in southern Norway, in a family active in political and cultural life. After finishing his university degrees, he worked as librarian and research associate before assuming the professorship of American literature at the University of Oslo, a position he held from 1946 to 1973.

Skard's first collections of poetry, *Lang vår* (1946; Long Spring) and *Vestanfor havet* (1946; West of the Ocean), contain poems written in his youth and during his five-year stay in the United States during World War II. These volumes, with their images of love, nature, and patriotism, show Skard to be a *nynorsk* poet (*see* NORWEGIAN LITERATURE) in the tradition of Olav AUKRUST and Olav NYGARD. But in *Vestanfor havet*, and even more in *Sola går mot vest* (1948; The Sun Goes toward the West), Skard turned to the new style of unrhymed verse and to matter-of-fact observation of life around him. This development is clearer still in his later collections, *Haustraun* (1966; Autumn Ash), *Poppel ved flyplass* (1970; Poplar by the Airport), and *Auga og hjarta* (1973; Eye and Heart), which reveal both Skard's awareness of the emotions that cluster about common things and his intellectual cosmopolitanism. Indeed, his poetry demonstrates that everything in the world is the poet's material. In his love poetry, among the finest in Norwegian literature, he demonstrates deep emotional involvement; in other poems, he shows his detached, searching mind. In his two latest collections, *Ord mot mørkret* (1976; Words against the Darkness) and *Skymingssong* (1979; Twilight Song), his main theme is age and approaching death, but as he has done throughout his literary productions, Skard demonstrates that his world is essentially harmonious: man, animal, life, war, and death take their places in the cosmic order.

Besides his wide-ranging scholarly work, Skard has produced a number of translations of American, Latin, and French poetry.　　　　K.A.F.

Skerlić, Jovan (1877–1914), Serbian literary historian and critic, was born in Belgrade into a prominent family. He was educated at the universities of Belgrade and Lausanne where, as a disciple of Georges Renard, he absorbed a number of socialist ideas. Skerlić soon revealed a talent for scholarly, analytical thinking and for literary criticism. Upon the completion of his doctoral work in Lausanne in 1901, he spent some time in Paris, where he broadened his knowledge of Western European thought and literary theory and fell under the influence of the French thinker Jean-Marie Guyau. After his return to Serbia in 1904, Skerlić was offered a chair of national literature at the University of Belgrade, a position that he held throughout the rest of his short but very productive life.

In a single decade of scholarly and critical activity, Skerlić published several hundred essays and critical studies on all the major Serbian authors, collected in nine volumes as *Pisci i knjige* (1907–26; Writers and Books), as well as a cluster of longer monographs, the most notable of which are *Jakov Ignjatović* (1904), *Omladina i njena književnost 1848–71* (1906; Young Serbia and Its Literature 1848–71), *Vojislav Ilić* (1907), *Srpska književnost u XVIII veku* (1909; Serbian Literature in the 18th Century), and *Svetozar Marković* (1910). These monographs provided the foundation for his major critical study, *Istorija nove srpske književnosti* (1914; A History of Modern Serbian Literature), completed only two months before his death. The *Istorija* contains an objective, erudite, and thorough critical analysis of the whole of Serbian cultural and literary life in the 18th, 19th, and 20th centuries.

Skerlić was both the most skillful and the most authoritative Serbian advocate of ethical positivism in literary creation. As such he left a lasting imprint upon the development of modern Serbian letters. Much like the Russian liberal critics of the second half of the 19th century and their Serbian disciple Svetozar Marković, Skerlić regarded literature in the context of the broad social and political developments of its era. As a positivist, he longed for social commitment in all artistic endeavor and expected literature to play a dynamic, progressive role in the service of national aspirations and ideals. For that reason, he detested excessive verbosity, pessimism, and the extravagance of romanticism, championing instead the realistic mode of expression characterized by soundness of subject matter, frankness of tone, and brevity of utterance. Skerlić's spiritual idealism, cosmopolitan literary taste, rare ability for synthesis, and exceptional stylistic polish have made him one of the most prominent literary figures in the entire modern Serbian literary tradition.

See: V. Glušac, *Dr. Jovan Skerlić* (1926); V. Milojević, *Jovan Skerlić* (1937); M. Begić, *Jovan Skerlić et la critique littéraire en Serbie* (1963).   N.M.

Skram, Amalie (1846–1905), Norwegian novelist, was born Amalie Alver into a middle-class family in Bergen. When very young she married a sea captain, whom she divorced after a short, unhappy marriage. She later married the Danish writer Erik Skram and lived in Denmark for the greater part of her life.

Skram's first important work, *Constance Ring* (1885), revealed her to be a disciple of the naturalistic school, which at that time, through the influence of Gustave Flaubert and Emile ZOLA, had begun to dominate the younger generation of Norwegian writers. *Constance Ring* is the story of a tragic marriage, told with all the minute detail that characterizes naturalism. Marital turmoil is again the theme of *Lucie* (1888) and of the intense, original *Forraadt* (1892; Betrayed).

The work that has assured Skram a place among the masters of Norwegian letters is the great four-volume epic novel *Hellemyrsfolket* (The People of Hellemyr), comprising *Sjur Gabriel* (1887), *To venner* (1887; Two Friends), *S. G. Myre* (1890), and *Afkom* (1898; Offspring). The epic is set in Bergen, where the novelist had spent her childhood and youth, and is alive with that town's sights, sounds, and smells. An almost uncanny insight into human nature permits Skram to reveal to her readers the crisscross of motives directing the life of her unsavory hero, S. G. Myre. The son of incurable drunkards, Myre is himself a vain, weak coward who by devious means succeeds in entering the middle class, to which he has always aspired, yet he ends his life in prison. A deep, genuine sense of human destiny, and of the inescapable logic of fate permeates this somber epic in which the author's naturalistic conception of a world dominated by biological factors is transformed and illuminated by a poet's feeling of tragic necessity.

Among Skram's other books, the autobiographical novel *Professor Hieronymus* (1895; Eng. tr., 1899) is noteworthy for the controversy it aroused over its presentation of the treatment of the mentally ill.

See: B. Krane, *Amalie Skram og kvinnens problem* (1951) and *Amalie Skrams diktning* (1961).   O.P.G.

Škvorecký, Josef (1924–), Czech novelist and short-story writer, was born at Náchod, in northeastern Bohemia. He studied English literature at Prague University and worked as a translator and editor of the journal *Světová literatura*. In 1968 he emigrated for political reasons to Canada, where he founded a publishing house for émigré Czech writers.

The publication of Škvorecký's first novel, *Zbabělci* (1958; Eng. tr., *The Cowards*, 1970), afforded early evidence of relaxation in Czechoslovakia after the Stalinist regime of terror with its dogmas of socialist realism. The novel concerns a group of young men who take part in a local uprising against the withdrawing German forces. With their pro-Western tastes and love of jazz they are, from a disciplined Communist Party point of view, nothing but rootless, bourgeois, "cosmopolitans," yet they become heroes in the resistance to the Germans. The novel is characterized by unusually frank, often scatological speech. It created a sensation and was subsequently withdrawn, but was later republished in 1964.

Škvorecký's later novels have largely failed to achieve the success of *The Cowards*, although his *Konec nylonového věku* (1967; The End of the Nylon Age) is a notable, Hemingway-like portrait of the decay of the gilded, anglophile youth of Prague during the first wave of communization that followed 1948. *Lvíče* (1969; The Lion Cub), published in Czechoslovakia but subsequently withdrawn from circulation, is constructed like a detective story, and is an exposé of the Stalinist line as followed in the publishing business. *Tankový prapor* (1971; The Tank Battalion) reveals the ideological excesses and contradictions of the Stalinist doctrines applied to the army; its anecdotal, often hilarious humor suggests the influence of Jaroslav HAŠEK's *Good Soldier Schweik* as well as of the author's own period of Czech military service in the early 1950s. Since leaving Czechoslovakia, Škvorecký has written two novels that mingle in an interesting way the author's reminiscences of political events in Czechoslovakia (World War II, the liberation, the "Prague Spring," and the Soviet occupation of 1968) with satirical portraits and anecdotes of the American and Canadian society in which Škvorecký now lives: these are *Mirákl* (1972; The Miracle) and *Příběh inženýra lidských duší* (2 vols., 1977; The Tale of an Engineer of Human Souls).

Škvorecký has translated works of several American writers, including Ernest Hemingway and William Faulkner. He has written a number of detective novels and stories, as well as a volume of stories concerning the fate of Jews during the Nazi occupation of the Czech lands, *Sedmiramenný svícen* (1965; The Seven-Branched Candlestick). His *All the Bright Young Men and Women* (1971), written in English, is a lively history of the Czech new wave films of the 1960s.

See: A. J. Liehm, *The Politics of Culture* (1970), pp. 151–80.   W.E.H.

Slauerhoff, Jan Jacob (1898–1936), Dutch poet novelist, and translator, was born in Leeuwarden. He studied medicine at the University of Amsterdam and became a ship's doctor, traveling widely. He journeyed to China and South America, for example, and became a wanderer. For a while, he was a physician in Tangiers. Slauerhoff belongs to the generation of poets between the two world wars, which gathered first around the magazines *Het Getij* and *De Vrije Bladen,* and later *Forum*. He was an individualist and a romanticist, who rebelled, even in his student days, against middle-class society. Longing for untouched countries and for grand ages of the past, he searched for a great adventure. In his antisocial behavior, his inability to find happiness in life, he recalls the French *poètes maudits*. He began by publishing poetry in *Het*

Getij, and his first volume of poetry, *Archipel* (1923; Archipelago) revealed his mastery of poetic technique. If his verse was sometimes careless or uneven, he put his own personality into it. Dissatisfied with himself, filled sometimes with a revulsion against life, he was a lonely searcher for exotic lands. Other volumes of his poetry are *Clair-Obscur* (1926), *Oost-Azië* (1928; East Asia), which he published under the pseudonym John Ravenswood, *Eldorado* (1928), *Soleares* (1933), and *Een eerlijk zeemansgraf* (1936; An Honest Seaman's Grave). His *novellen* are often based on Chinese themes, as in the volumes *Het lente-eiland* (1930; Spring Island) and *Schuim en asch* (1930; Scum and Ashes). *Het verboden rijk* (1932; The Forbidden Empire) is a novel that combines the lives of the 16th-century Portuguese poet Camõens and a ship's radio operator, a man of the 20th century, who symbolizes Slauerhoff's own life. The hero of *Het leven op aarde* (1934; Life on Earth) is also a radio operator, who loses himself in the oblivion of opium. The two novels were intended as the parts of a trilogy, but the third part was never written. *De opstand van Guadalajara* (1937; The Revolt of Guadalajara) is about the poor Indians of Mexico. In 1931, Slauerhoff wrote a play, *Jan Pietzersz. Coen.* He also did several translations from works in Spanish and Portuguese.

See: C. J. Kelk, *Leven van Slauerhoff* (1971).

S.L.F.

Sletto, Olav (1886–1963), Norwegian novelist and dramatist, was born and raised in Hallingdal in central Norway, the setting of many of his novels. Like Olav AUKRUST and Inge KROKANN, Sletto was influenced early by Rudolf Steiner's anthroposophy, and, partially inspired by him, he created a number of works that oddly combine paganism, Christianity, and religious nationalism. Sletto's books include a biography of Christ entitled *Tenaren* (1913, rev. 1952; The Servant) and his visionary, four-volume epic based on Old Norse mythology: *Loke* (1913), *Domen* (1916; The Judgment), *Millom Eldar* (1917; Between Fires), and *Skymring* (1918; Dusk).

Sletto's principal work, *Soga om Røgnaldfolket* (5 vols., 1943–50; The Story of the Røgnald People), traces the growth and development of one Hallingdal family from the 17th century to the 20th century, when the old culture clashes with modern technology and new values. The Røgnald novels combine naked realism and roguish humor with rich psychological portraits in a manner strongly reminiscent of Olav DUUN's *Juvikfolke.*

In his dramas about individuals from the local rural community, Sletto again voiced his religious humanism. His best stage work is the expressionistic "mystery play" *Domhuset* (1936; House of Judgment). Sletto also wrote a number of children's books that are among the finest in modern Norwegian literature.

See: J. Dale and L. Reinton, eds., *Ei bok om Olav Sletto* (1966).

K.A.F.

Słonimski, Antoni (1895–1976), Polish poet, essayist, novelist, and playwright, was born and died in Warsaw. After studying painting in Warsaw and Munich, he began his literary career in 1918 with a volume of *Sonety* (Sonnets), which revealed a masterful command of poetic craftsmanship reminiscent of Parnassianism. He was a cofounder of the influential literary monthly *Skamander.* His poetic volume *Parada* (1920; The Parade) struck a few notes of social radicalism, with a reflective mood prevailing over emotional chords. Beginning in 1924, he published weekly feuilletons in *Wiadomości Literackie.* He waged a regular campaign against bigotry, militarism, megalomania, and fascist tendencies, proclaiming humane

universalism and rational democracy. Wit made his sallies popular and effective. His ideas found reflection in his satirical comedies, *Wieża Babel* (1927; The Tower of Babel), *Murzyn warszawski* (1935; The Warsaw Negro); *Lekarz bezdomny* (1930; The Homeless Physician), and *Rodzina* (1934; The Family). Słonimski traveled widely, visiting South America, the Middle East, the Soviet Union and his impressions resulted in the writing of the travel books *Pod zwrotnikami* (1925; Under the Tropics), and *Moja podróż do Rosji* (1932; My trip to Russia). A Wellsian spirit discreetly marked the novels *Teatr w więzieniu* (1922; The Theater in the Prison), *Torpeda czasu* (1924; The Torpedo of Time), and *Dwa końce świata* (1937; Two Ends of the World), which anticipated the holocaust of World War II. After the German invasion of Poland, Słonimski succeeded in escaping to France and settled in London. Although faithful to his pacifist pènchant, he published the poetic volume *Alarm* (1940), whose title poem was a passionate call for relentless struggle; it had tremendous resonance in Poland and abroad. The poem "Popiół i wiatr" (Ashes and Wind), containing his nostalgic memoirs, was published in 1942. After his return to Poland in 1951 he supported liberal trends. He published several volumes of verse and essays and a number of his prewar feuilletons, *Kroniki tygodniowe* (Weekly Chronicles), appeared in 1956 as well as his personal encyclopedia of reminiscencies, *Alfabet wspomnień* (1975; Alphabet of Reminiscences).

See: *Słownik współczesnych pisarzy polskich,* vol. 3 (1964), pp. 159–66; A. Kowalczykowa, *Liryka Słonimskiego 1918–35* (1967).

M.G.

Slonimsky, Mikhail Leonidovich (1897–1972), Russian writer (a cousin of the Polish poet Antoni STONIMSKI), was born in Petersburg, fought in World War I, and began his career working for military newspapers in 1917. He was early encouraged by Maksim GORKY and as a member of the Serapion Brotherhood came under the literary influence of Yevgeny ZAMYATIN. In 1922 he published his first story, "Dikiy" (Wild), as well as his best-known work, the slender short-story collection *Shestoy strelkovy* (Sixth Rifle Regiment), which reveals the cruel absurdities of wartime military life and contains several fine sketches of individual soldiers. His novella *Mashina Emery* (1924; Emery Machine) develops the postwar theme of mechanization, and his novel *Sredniy prospekt* (1927; Middle Avenue) treats another popular theme, the place of the war hero in postwar society during the period of the New Economic Policy. *Lavrovy* (1926; The Lavrovs), perhaps Slonimsky's best-known novel, returns to the theme of war and postwar efforts to adapt to the new society. *Foma Kleshnyov* (1930) is a less successful novel about the new Communist man. Slonimsky's trip abroad in the 1930s produced some sketches and stories with a German motif, among them "Povest o Levine" (1935; Story about Levin), about a German Communist who died in 1919. After World War II, Slonimsky returned to the post-Revolutionary years in the trilogy *Inzhenery* (1950; Engineers), *Druzya* (1954; Friends), and *Rovesniki veka* (1959; Contemporaries of the Century). *Kniga vospominaniy* (1966; A Book of Memories) includes sketches of the Russian writers Aleksandr GRIN, Olga FORSH, Vsevolod IVANOV, Boris PILNYAK, Nikolay NIKITIN, Mikhai ZOSHCHENKO, Yevgeny SHVARTS, and others. Slonimsky's earliest work, which is marked by a terse style and occasionally striking imagery, is generally regarded as his best.

See: A. Gorelov, *Put sovremennika: o tvorchestve Mikh. Slonimskogo* (1933).

S.Sc.

Slovak literature. After the Austro-Hungarian *Ausgleich* of 1867 the Slovaks, faced with pressure to magyarize as well as with social discrimination, had to struggle for their very national existence. The three Slovak lyceums were closed, and in 1875 the Matica Slovenská, the single Slovak scholarly institute, was also shut down. The generation of writers who followed the Slovak romantics and drew inspiration from them, now sought to maintain the morale of the nation through works of a didactic and apologetic character, but they were unable to find new perspectives for the national literature.

Slovak literature was rescued from this stagnation by the realists, who appeared belatedly in comparison with those in Western Europe or Russia, but who advocated a dynamic program: literature must be more than a means of defense; it must also serve as a component in the struggle for national independence. The realists drew their themes from contemporary life, and they introduced elements of colloquial Slovak speech into the literary language.

The poet Pavol Országh-Hviezdoslav (1849–1921) combined the roles of several generations in his work. He developed a new type of reflective lyric, which was both a modern poetic narrative form and a verse play. In addition he translated world classics into Slovak (among them the works of Shakespeare, Goethe, and Adam Mickiewzic). His contemporary, the realist poet Svetozar Hurban Vajanský (1847–1916), worked unstintingly to organize Slovak national life, editing the journal *Slovenské Poh' lady* from 1881 to 1890. He also wrote poetry and fiction. In his novels, Vajanský attempted to define the roles of the intelligentsia and the gentry in Slovak life. The outstanding representative writer of Slovak realist fiction is Martin KUKUČÍN who created a motley mosaic of scenes from village life in stories inspired by the congenial humor and colorful speech of the Slovak peasants.

At the turn of the century, a group of critical realists, no longer content with Kukučín's idyllic realism, came to the fore. The novelist Timrava (pseud. of Božena Slančíková, 1867–1951) exposed the negative sides of village life. The stories of Jozef Gregor-Tajovský (1874–1940), a pioneer in the popular realist drama, were written in a similar spirit. Naturalism is first evident in the novels of city life by Jégé (pseud. of Ladislav Nádaši, 1866–1940), whose *Adam Šangala* (1923) rid Slovak historical fiction of its customary romantic emotionalism. Another critical realist was Janko JESENSKÝ, whose satirical tales ridicule the philistine manners of the rising bourgeoisie.

Jesenský's collection *Verše* (1905; Verses) marks the transition to the poetry of the Slovak modernists. They belonged for the most part to the liberal wing of the Slovak middle class and were grouped around the review *Hlas* (The Voice), which invoked the philosophic realism of Tomáš Garrigue MASARYK and formulated a pragmatic program that called for raising the economic and cultural level of the Slovak people. František Votruba (1880–1953) subjected the work of the realists to severe critical analysis and thus helped to lay the basis for the modernist, or "Moderna," movement, which drew inspiration from contemporary European trends, especially from symbolism. The leading personality among the modernists was the poet Ivan KRASKO whose literary output, although small, signified a qualitative break in the evolution of Slovak poetry, opened new horizons, and formatively influenced the younger poets who appeared after World War I. In the poetry of Krasko's contemporaries, Martin Rázus (1888–1937) and Janko Jesenský, nationalist motifs predominate, while the poetry of Vladimír Roy (1885–1936) is notable both for its melancholy and for its striving for absolutist symbols.

The creation of an independent Czechoslovak Republic in 1918 provided the basis for the normal development of cultural and literary life in Slovakia. Cultural and scholarly institutes were founded, such as the Slovak National Theater and Comenius University in Bratislava, while the Matica Slovenská began to publish again, along with newly founded publishing enterprises. Slovak writers were no longer restricted to functioning as defenders of national rights. Thus with truth the literary critic Štefan Krčméry (1892–1955) hailed the new literary generation as "writers with untied tongues." Slovak literary life grew more varied; writers gained acquaintance with foreign avant-garde trends, adapted them to Slovak conditions, and enriched Slovak literature with new themes and new formal and expressive means.

The literary ferment of this period—reflected in numerous Slovak literary journals—is evidence of the effort to overcome the cultural lag caused by the unfavorable conditions of the past. Some writers, such as Rázus and Jesenský, continued in the realist tradition, which Milo URBAN deepened through his development of psychological motivation. Jozef Ciger-Hronský (1896–1961), in his *Jozef Mak* (1933), created an impressionist type of novel; the impressionist trend was further developed in the tales of Ivan Horváth (1904–60). Erotic problems, heretofore taboo in Slovak fiction, were introduced in the works of the physician Gejza Vámoš (1901–56). The novels of Frano Král' (1903–55) and Peter JILEMNICKÝ are typical representatives of Slovak fiction that treats social problems.

Slovak poetry was dominated by the sensualism and vitalism of Ján SMREK, the Claudelian mysticism (*see* Paul CLAUDEL) of Emil Boleslav LUKÁČ, and the "poetism" or "pure poetry" of Valentín Beniak (1894–1973) and Laco NOVOMESKÝ. Novomeský, along with Ján Poničan (1902–), was also the founder of Slovak proletarian poetry. The leftist intellectuals published the journal *DAV* (1924–37), in which they sought to formulate a socialist literary theory. The Catholic poets Pavol Gašparovič-Hlbina (1908–) and Rudolf Dilong (1905–), although inspired by the disquisitions of Henri BREMOND on the essence of poetry, were differentiated from their contemporaries more by their political than by their aesthetic program. In 1935, Rudolf Fabry (1915–) published the first Slovak collection of surrealist essays, *Ut'até ruky* (Sundered Hands). The work of the Slovak surrealists, who invoked not only André BRETON but also the Slovak revolutionary romantic poet Janko Král', reached its zenith in the 1940s with verse collections by Štefan Záry (1918–), Vladimír Reisel (1919–), and Pavel Bunčák (1915–), and can be considered a form of intellectual resistance to the wartime fascist regime.

Only a small number of writers, such as Urban, Ciger-Hronský, Beniak, and Dilong, supported the ultranationalist line of the autonomous Slovak state (1939–45). While some, such as Margita Figuli (1910–), Dobroslav Chrobák (1907–51), and Ľudo Mistrík-Ondrejov (1901–62), drew inspiration from the village fiction of Jean GIONO and Charles-Ferdinand RAMUZ, most writers withdrew from the literary scene and devoted themselves to works that could appear only after the war.

A significant watershed in Slovak life and literature is marked by the national uprising in 1944 against Nazi domination. The uprising served both as a subject and an inspiration for such diverse writers as Dominik TATARKA, Alfonz Bednár (1914–), Ladislav MŇAČKO, and Vladimír Mináč (1922–).

In 1949, following the seizure of power by the Communist Party a year before, Slovak intellectuals formulated a manifesto of socialist humanism, one that demanded broad freedom for artistic and literary creation. Stalinist ideologists and politicians rejected these demands, however, and in 1951 they condemned the avantgarde trends of the 1930s and 1940s as "cosmopolitan." The writers Mináč and Tatarka, as well as the critics Alexander Matuška (1910–), Michal Chorváth (1910–), and the structuralist theoretician Mikuláš Bakoš (1914–), were also condemned. Creativity was limited by the prescriptive dogmas of socialist realism; poetry soon degenerated into verse sloganeering, as in the work of Milan Lajčiak (1926–); in fiction, realist techniques were combined with a socialist ideology, and problems were restricted to those of the collectivized, planned economy, industrialization, and class struggle, as in the novel *Drevená dedina* (1951; The Wooden Village) by František Hečko (1905–60).

After 1956, Slovak writers gradually reverted to the positions they had been forced to abandon, and the trends and authors condemned in the early 1950s returned. Continuity of development was again possible, while ideological rigor ceased to be the chief criterion for judging literary works. Slovak poetry abandoned cheap enthusiasm and found new strength in the power of simplified expression; it became the sensitive indicator of the feelings of 20th-century man, as can be seen in the collections by Pavel Horov (1914–), Vojtech Mihálik (1926–), and Milan Rúfus (1928–), and in the poems of Jozef Mihalkovič (1935–) and Ján Stacho (1936–), representatives of the younger generation.

The inevitable "positive hero" of the 1950s gave way to more diversified characters who encountered all the contradictions of modern reality; such characters can be found in Bednár's short stories in *Hodiny a minúty* (1956; Hours and Minutes) in Ladislav Mňačko's novel *Ako chuti moc* (1967; Eng. tr., *The Taste of Power*, 1967), and in the tales of Ladislav Ťažký (1924–) collected under the title *Kŕdeľ divých Adamov* (1966; A Crowd of Wild Adams). The playwright Peter Karvaš (1922–) dramatized conflicts of a new type in *Jazva* (1963; The Scar), a play that probes the differences between the ideal and the real. Literary criticism gave energetic support to this process of regeneration. The intimate life of young people growing up under socialism was explored by the writers born in the 1930s, such as Jaroslava Blazková (1932–), Anton Hykisch (1932–), and Ján Johanides (1934–), the last of whom attempted to create a "new" novel of the French type.

In 1968, Slovak literature experienced a new shock with the Soviet occupation of Czechoslovakia. A small but significant number of Slovak writers lost the right to publish (Tatarka, Ťažký, Karvaš, and Mňačko). Except for some notable verse, their contemporaries and younger colleagues have published almost nothing of significance. Thus Slovak literature, having finally caught up with its European counterparts, was again threatened with isolation and provincialism as well as ideological constraint.

See: S. Krčméry, "A Survey of Modern Slovak Literature," *SEER* 6 (1928): 160–70; P. Selver, "The Literature of the Slovaks," *SEER* 12 (1933–34); 691–703; A. Mráz, *Dejiny slovenskej literatúry* (1948); M. Bakoš, *Vývin slovenského verša od školy Štúrovej* (2d ed., 1949); A. Mráz, *O slovenských realistických prozaikoch* (1950); A. Matuška, *Pre a proti* (1956); B. Meriggi, *Storia della litteratura ceca a slovacca* (1958); M. Chorvath, *Cesty literatúry*, 2 vols. (1960); M. Pišút, *Dejiny slovenskej literatúry* (1962); J. Noge, *Aperçu de la littérature slovaque* (1968).   F.M.B.

Slovenian literature. Slovenian literature expresses the spiritual identity of the westernmost Slavic nation, which is deeply affected by Roman Catholicism and by its geographic and cultural symbiosis with the German and Latin civilizations. From the 7th to the 16th centuries, Slovenian literature was limited to religious writings. Existing alongside Church Latin and the feudal German tongue, Slovenian remained the language of a dependent province. In the 16th century, the Protestant Reformation brought about a revolutionary cultural upsurge that gave the Slovenes a wealth of printed books, including the complete Slovenian Bible (1584). Despite the Reformation, however, Roman Catholicism held Slovenia firmly within the framework of Tridentine dogma. On the cultural level, Catholicism was able to effect a more meaningful reaction only 100 years later with the baroque homiletics of the Capuchin monk Tobija Lionelli, better known as Janez Svetokriški (1647–1714), the author of five volumes of Slovenian sermons included in the work *Sacrum Promptuarium* (1691–1707; Holy Repository). Among the historians of this period who did not write in Slovenian, Baron Janez Vajkard Valvasor (1641–93) stands out. His ethnographically fascinating description of Slovenia, *Die Ehre des Herzogtums Krain* (1689; The Glory of the Duchy of Carniola), was written in German.

Literature as an artistic activity emerged in Slovenia only in the 18th century, with the intellectual spring of the European Enlightenment. The patron and guiding spirit of this period was Baron Žiga Zois (1747–1818), along with two mediocre but cultured authors, the poet Valentin Vodnik (1758–1819) and the dramatist Anton Tomaz Linhart (1756–95).

In the 19th century, romanticism was dominated by the lyrical genius of France Prešeren (1800–49), the creator of monumental, tragic sonnets, the author of the lyrical collection *Poezija* (1847; Poetry), and the chronicler of the era of Christianization in the epic *Krst pri Savici* (1836; The Baptism at the Savica). Prešeren's lofty emotions and Dantesque power of expression assure him a position of lasting primacy in Slovenian literature.

The middle of the 19th century saw the birth of Slovenian narrative prose. The most talented writer in this field was Josip Jurčič (1844–81), the author of the first Slovenian novel, *Deseti brat* (1866; The Tenth Brother). Janko Kersnik (1852–97) and Ivan Tavčar (1851–1923) continued Jurčič's work in a realistic vein. Literary criticism found eminent representatives during this period in the nationally oriented Fran Levstik (1831–87), who was the patriarchal stimulus to the national awakening, and in the cosmopolitan Josip Stritar (1836–1923). Toward the end of the century, the poet-priest Simon Gregorčič (1844–1906), the "nightingale from Gorica," won universal popularity among Slovenes with his melodious verse.

After Prešeren, Slovenian literature reached a new level of achievement in the first years of the 20th century, the so-called Moderna period, in which the rationalism of the European fin de siècle was grafted onto the Slovenian national sensibility. The star of the Slovenian Moderna was the novelist, dramatist, and essayist Ivan CANKAR, whose works are characterized by biblical zeal and the fusion of socialist Utopianism with a Christian eschatological vision. The poet Oton ŽUPANČIČ, an extraordinary master of language and unsurpassed Slovenian translator of William Shakespeare, ranks alongside Ivan Cankar. The quartet of important Moderna writers is completed by two lyrical poets, both of whom died young: Josip Murn-Aleksandrov (1879–1901) and Dragotin Kette (1876–99). This exceptionally creative period also produced the great critic Izidor Cankar (1889–1957), who blended a profound aesthetic sense with an equally profound intellectuality.

During the period between the two world wars, Slovenes attained political independence for the first time in history. The literary atmosphere of these years was at first influenced by expressionism. The 1920s were dominated by the volcanic figure of Srečko KOSOVEL, the seer of apocalyptic ecstasies and the herald of a redemptive eschatological revolution. Ivan PREGELJ was the outstanding prose writer of this period, combining a powerful Catholic confessional tendency with a fiery epic passion and a propensity for historical subjects. Fran Saleški Finžgar (1871–1962) and France Bevk (1890–1970) attained great popularity with their folk narratives. The lyrical poet and translator Alojz GRADNIK was a highly individual figure who stood apart from the fashionable currents of the time.

In the 1940s, the dogmatic artistic doctrine of socialist realism asserted itself. Its most meaningful and powerful representatives are the Marxist writers Lovro Kuhar, known under the name of Voranc PREŽIHOV, Miško Kranjec (1908–), and the less creative Ciril Kosmač (1910–). A symbolic tendency is represented on a high artistic and psychological level by Stanko Majcen (1888–1970), a master of the sketch and drama. Among 20th-century dramatists, noteworthy figures include the Freudian Slavko Grun (1901–49) and the socially engaged Bratko Kraft (1905–). Literary criticism reached a high level with Josip Vidmar (1895–), who concentrates on the artistic value of a given work.

The triple German-Italian-Hungarian occupation of Slovenia during World War II provoked a national resistance that was transformed into a Marxist revolution. The Partisan faction had its bard in Vladimir Pavšič, better known as Matej Bor (1911–), and its lyrical poet in Karl Destovnik-Kajuh (1922–44). The anti-Partisan side spoke out in the mystical zeal of France Balantič (1921–43), a master of the sonnet.

In the postwar period, Slovenian literature broke free of the stultifying mold of socialist realism, but only after the split between the Yugoslav Communist Party with the Cominform. During this period, some prewar poets blossomed into full artistic maturity, such as Božo Vodušek (1905–), an impetuous, Promethean writer and the translator of Johann Wolfgang von Goethe's *Faust*, and Anton Vodnik (1901–65), a refined master of spiritual moods. The humanistic and classical lyrical poetry of Cene Vipotnik (1914–72) and Jože Udovič (1912–) also attained their maturity.

The younger literary generation is passing through a number of ideational metamorphoses, reflecting influences ranging from Karl Marx to Jean-Paul SARTRE and Martin HEIDEGGER. Poetry, which has almost totally evaporated in modish experimentation, finds its principal spokesman in Danet Zajc (1929–), whose menacing metaphoric system conveys the sense of an almost ontological disintegration. The prose of Zdravko Slamin, better known as Pavle Zidar (1932–), reveals an exceptional mastery of emotion and imagery, while the dramas of Dominik Smole (1929–) exhibit his great virtuosity in treating the central questions of life.

The major figure of post–World War II Slovenian literature, both in terms of his artistic value and his ideological autonomy, is the poet, essayist, and prose writer Edvard KOCBEK, a Christian ally of the Communists during the revolution and a gadfly in the postwar atmosphere of uniformity. Outside Yugoslav Slovenia, the prose writer and essayists Boris Pahor (1913–) and Alojz Rebula (1924–) were active after the war within the Slovenian minority in Italy; the former holds lay, humanistic views, while the latter subscribes to a Christian position. The literature of the postwar political emigration, which is mainly concentrated in Argentina, is represented by the poets Vinko Beličič (1913–), Karel Vladimir Truhlar, and Vladimir Kos; Tine Debeljak (1903–), the critic and translator of Dante and Fierra; and the prosaists Zorko Simčič and Ruda Jurčec.

See: A. Barac, *A History of Yugoslav Literature* (1955, 1973); A. Slodnjak, *Geschichte der slowenischen Literatur* (1958); B. Meriggi, *Storia della letteratura slovena* (1961).   A.Re.

Slutsky, Boris Abramovich (1919–), Russian poet, born in Slavyansk, is an important representative of the post-World War II generation of poets that rejected the rhetoric of Stalinist verse. The son of a white-collar worker, Slutsky studied law in Moscow before World War II. During the war he served in the army and was severely wounded. In 1956, Ilya ERENBURG drew attention to Slutsky's verse, and a first volume, *Pamyat* (1957; Memory), finally appeared. It was followed by three others, from which Slutsky drew the poems for two volumes of selected works in 1965. Slutsky, who is of Jewish origin, edited a collection of Jewish poetry in 1963. Another four collections of his own verse appeared between 1969 and 1975. Like that of Yevgeny VINOKUROV, Slutsky's poetry returns repeatedly to the themes of war and a generation lost in World War II. The finality of death and its ubiquity in the 20th century have left their mark on his verse. Nor has he shrunk from dealing with the tensions manifest in his own society; in a famous poem, "Bog" (Eng. tr., "God" 1974), which for years circulated anonymously, he touched even upon the person of Stalin. Like others of his generation, Slutsky has developed a language largely stripped of poeticisms and ornamentation.

D.T.W.

Smrek, Ján, pseud. of Ján Čietek (1898–) Slovak poet, was born in Zemianske Lieskové in western Slovakia. He worked as a journalist, editor, and organizer of Slovak cultural life. His first verse collection, *Odsúdeny k večitej žízni* (1922; Condemned to Eternal Thirsting), reveals symbolist influence. In his subsequent books, *Cválajúce dni* (1925; The Galloping Days), *Božské uzly* (1929; Divine Knots), *Iba oči* (1933; Only Eyes), and *Básnik a žena* (1934; The Poet and the Woman), Smrek emerges as a sensualist and vitalist. His poetry is a torrent of optimism, a celebration of friendship, love, and eroticism. These themes, an obvious personal defense against the threat and actuality of war, also inform the collections *Hostina* (1944; The Feast) and *Studňa* (1945; The Well), although the latter does include some antiwar poems. Smrek's later works, such as *Obraz sveta* (1958; The Image of the World) and *Struny* (1962; Strings), fail to show any significant development in either ideas or poetical technique. He has also translated the works of François Villon, Aleksandr Pushkin, and the Hungarian poets Sándor Petőfi, Endre ADY, and Attila JÓZSEF into Slovak.

See: B. Kováč, *Poézia Jána Smreka* (1961).   F.M.B.

Snoek, Paul pseud. of Edmond Schietekat (1933–), Belgian (Flemish) poet, prose writer, and painter of Flemish extraction, was born in Saint-Nicolas. The early poetry volumes *Archipel* (1954; Archipelago), *Noodbrug* (1955; Emergency Bridge), *Tussen vel en vlees* (1956; Between Skin and Flesh), and *Aardrijkskunde* (1956; Geography), although finger exercises, illustrate Snoek's anthropomorphic conception of nature and the associative power of his water imagery. In *Ik root een vredespijp* (1957; I Smoke a Peace Pipe), it becomes clear that the poet's dreaminess calls forth a strictly personal, autonomous world picture; "for mine are the inventor's soft hands." *De heilige gedichten* (1959; The Holy Poems) come to terms with logic, with rationalism, with the army, and with any form of organized society; so also does *Solda-tenbrieven* (1961; Soldiers' Letters), a correspondence with Hugues C. PERNATH. *Hercules* (1960), *Richelieu* (1961), and *Nostradamus* (1963) introduce the poet as a clairvoyant and a prophet: "My place is among the gods!" These extremely apodictic verses leave little room for uncertainty or doubt and carry an occasional proverbial resonance. Self-mockery and a sense of relativity still prevail, although in a minor key in the more "humane" volume *De swarte muze* (1967; The Black Muse). *Ren-aissance* (1963) and *Gedichten 1954–1968* (1969; Poems 1954–1968) collect formerly published works. Snoek's more recent books of poems, *Gedrichten* (1971; Mon-stroems)—the title puns on *gedicht* (poem) and *gedrocht* (monster)—and *Frankenstein, nagelaten gedrichten* (1973; Frankenstein, Remaining Monstroems), are more concerned with topics of the hour and continue the cy-nicism of *De heilige gedichten*. The charm of this poet originates not so much in what he tells us, but rather in his refined skill in versification, as in, for example, *Ged-ichten voor Maria Magdalena* (1971; Poems for Mary Magdalene), a series of erotic poems. Snoek's prose works include *Reptielen en amfibieën* (1957; Reptiles and Amphibians), *Bultaco 250 cc* (1972), *Kwaak-en kruipdi-eren* (1972; Quacking and Creeping Animals), and *Een honsdolle tijd* (1978; Rabies Days). Recently, Snoek has concentrated on painting. His own gouaches illustrate his volume *Ik heb vannacht de liefde uitgevonden* (1973; I Invented Love Tonight). As a poet, Snoek has been awarded several prizes, including the Triennial State Prize for Poetry in 1968.

See: L. Scheer, *De poëtische wereld van Paul Snoek, proeve van close-reading* (1966); P. de Vree, *Paul Snoek* (1977). M.B.

Sodenkamp, Andrée (1906–), Belgian poet, was born in Brussels. She taught history and geography and later on became inspector of public libraries. Sodenkamp pub-lished *Sainte Terre* (Holy Land) in 1954, *Femmes des longs matins* (Women of the Long Mornings) in 1965, and *La Fête debout* (Upright Holiday) in 1973. Basically cen-tered on love and death, the three collections also have the richness of colors and sonorities in common; the verse is classical, perfectly cadenced, but in no way confined in the rigors of a blind prosody. If death occupies an important place in Sodenkamp's work, the frenzy of liv-ing, of exploiting the resources of each instant to the maximum, is set up against sterile despair as well as resignation. Although characterized by a calculated in-genuity and science of effect, Sodenkamp's poetry for-tunately escapes, thanks to its vigor, sentimentalism, and affectation.

See: R. Burniaux and R. Frickx, *La Littérature belge d'expression française* (1973); A. Jans, *Lettres vivantes, 1945–1975* (1975); R. Frickx and M. Joiret, *La poésie française de Belgique de 1880 à nos jours* (1976). R.F.

Söderberg, Hjalmar (1869–1941), Swedish short-story writer, novelist, and dramatist, was born in Stockholm, which is the setting of all his novels and most of his plays, and lived after 1908 in Copenhagen. His first novel, *Förvillelser* (1895; Aberrations), introduces the typical disillusioned, skeptical hero of most of Söderberg's books, the so-called flaneur. His masterpiece in depicting the flaneur is *Martin Bircks ungdom* (1901; Eng. tr., *Mar-tin Birck's Youth*, 1930), which is in part autobiographical. The main problem of the skeptical flaneur, living beside real life in his own melancholy fin-de-siècle mood, is the

problem of action: is it of any use to intervene in what must inevitably happen? The question of free will is cen-tral in Söderberg's most disputed novel, *Doktor Glas* (1905; Eng. tr., *Doctor Glas,* 1963), the theme of which is an ethically justified murder. The murder is a well-founded act, but it leads up to nothing; life goes on as usual, without anything having really changed. In most of Söderberg's novels, there are erotic themes, and his novel *Den allvarsamma leken* (1912; The Serious Game) has been ranked among the greatest Swedish novels about love. Love is perhaps the central value of life for Söderberg, and it must be taken seriously and without compromises. The deception of love gives a tragic note to *Den allvarsamma leken*. Much of the same autobio-graphical background recurs in the erotic motif in Söderberg's most frequently staged play, *Gertrud* (1906). Throughout his life, Söderberg wrote short stories, and many critics consider him at his best in this field. He published five collections of short stories, among others— the first *Historietter* (1898; Very Short Stories) and *Det mörknar öfver vägen* (1907; The Darkening Road). *Se-lected Short Stories,* translated by C. W. Stork, appeared in 1935. The stories are mostly very short, depicting a situation and concluding with an ironical twist. And they are all written in clear, witty, exact prose. Among his models were French authors like Guy de Maupassant and Anatole FRANCE. Söderberg's anticlerical attitude is often prominent and made him write three books, consisting partly of fiction and partly of research in the history of religion, to answer the question, How was it possible that the Christian religion could arise and reach its position of power? These books are *Jahves eld* (1918; The Fire of Jahve), *Jesus Barabbas* (1928), and *Den förvandlade Messias* (1932; The Transformed Messiah). Not until after his death was Söderberg looked upon as the first great name in 20th-century Swedish literature.

See: B. Bergman, *Hjalmar Söderberg* (1951); S. Rein, *Hjalmar Söderbergs Gertrud* (1962); B. Holmbäck, *Det lekfulla allvaret: en Hjalmar Söderbergstudie* (1969). G. Brandell, *Svensk litteratur 1870–1970*, vol. 1 (1974) pp. 314–20. N.Å.S.

Södergran, Edith (1892–1923), Finland-Swedish poet, was born in Petersburg, Russia. Her father, a mechanic and "engineer" (for, among others, Alfred Nobel), had mar-ried the daughter of a prosperous Finland-Swedish factory owner in the Russian capital. The father-in-law gave the couple a summer home at Raivola in Karelia, which, after Edith Södergran's death, became a place of pilgrimage for devotees of her poetry. The villa and its garden—both of which play a central role in Södergran's lyrics—were destroyed in the Winter War of 1939–40.

Södergran attended the German St. Petrischule. Here she began to write verse, mainly in the school's language of instruction and under the influence of Heinrich Heine and the "decadent" poets of Hans Benzmann's *Moderne deutsche Lyrik* (1904); but, in her "oilcloth notebook" (published in 1961 by Olof Enckell), she also tried poems in French, Russian, and, finally, Swedish, her native tongue. Coming down with the tuberculosis that had killed her father, she was an occasional patient (1909–11) at Nummela Sanatorium, near Helsinki (a circumstance bringing her into closer contact with the Finland-Swedish and Finnish worlds); then, from 1911 to 1914, she under-went treatment at Davos, enjoying the international clien-tele and reading Friedrich NIETZSCHE in one of his fa-vorite landscapes. In Karelia again, she had an affair with a Russian physician that inspired her *Dikter* (1916: Poems), composed in a style blending literary influences

(from Walt Whitman, Max Dauthendey, Alfred MOM-
BERT, Else LASKER-SCHÜLER, Maurice MAETERLINCK,
the Russian symbolists, and the Finland-Swedish classic,
Johan Ludvig Runeberg) with her own visionary naiveté.
The witticisms she was accorded in the press and unpleasant experiences during a trip to Helsinki (a body of legend
has formed around the visit, as around so much else in
her life) made her retreat to Raivola, where she and her
mother lived in poverty, once their resources had been
wiped out by the October Revolution of 1917. *Septem-
berlyran* (1918: September Lyre) reflected, in some of its
poems, the Finnish Civil War just ended and, in others,
revealed a prophetic gift; it led to her friendship with the
critic Hagar Olsson, a tie between "sisters" celebrated
in *Rosenaltaret* (1919: The Rose Alter), amid more general dithyrambs on life's Dionysian forces. (Södergran's
letters to Olsson were edited by the latter in 1955 as
Ediths brev; Edith's Letters.) A belief in a splendid human
race-to-be, posited in the aphorisms of *Brokiga iaktta-
gelser* (1919: Motley Observations), became more exalted
in *Framtidens skugga* (1920: The Future's Shadow), with
its roamings through space, its polymorphic and redemptive Eros, and its sensations of strength ("I am an eagle")
amidst hints of exhaustion ("My crown is too heavy").
A spiritual crisis brought Södergran to Rudolf Steiner's
anthroposophy, then to an elementary Christianity; in
these last years, she became an idol of the younger modernist poets in Swedish Finland and repaid them by trying
to arrange the publication of their (and her) work in German at her own expense—this although malnutrition was
hastening her end. She died on Midsummer Day, 1923.
Her final poems and other uncollected verses were issued
by Elmer DIKTONIUS as *Landet som icke är* (1925; The
Land Which Is Not), a title taken from the most moving
of them, in which the poet gives expression to her longing
for "the land which is not."

It is understandable that Södergran has inspired a cultic
admiration among her followers, and it is regrettable that
(despite the translation of the whole oeuvre into French
and—by Nelly SACHS—some poems into German) she
has not received the larger attention she desired and that
she deserves.

See: G. Tideström, *Edith Södergran* (1949); O. Enckell,
Esteticism och nietzscheanism i Edith Södergrans lyrik
(1949); L. de Fages, *Edith Södergran* (1970); S. Charters,
We Women: Selected Poems of Edith Södergran (1977);
K. R. Kern, *Edith Södergran: Feindliche sterne: Gesammelte Gedichte* (1977), rev. by G. Schoolfield in *SS* 5,
no. 3 (1979), pp. 319–25; L. Gustafson, *Forays into Swedish Poetry* (1978), pp. 99–106.   **G.C.S.**

Soldati, Mario (1906–), Italian short-story writer, novelist,
film director, and essayist, was born in Turin, where he
studied with the Jesuits and received a degree in letters.
He studied art history at the Istituto Superiore di Storia
dell'Arte in Rome and showed an early interest in both
art criticism and theater. In 1929, Soldati traveled to the
United States on a scholarship and remained there until
1931; his impressions are recorded in *America, primo
amore* (1935; America, First Love), which explores in
depth the myth of America among Europeans. His early
career was devoted almost exclusively to the film industry, in which he became a leading stylist. He collaborated
with the director Mario Camerini and wrote the script for
Gli uomini, che mascalzoni! (1932; Men, What Scoundrels!). Among the films he himself directed are *Piccolo
mondo antico* (1941; Little World of Old), *Eugenia Gran-
det* (1946), and *La provinciale* (1953; Girl from the Provinces).

Soldati's first literary success was his novel *Le lettere
da Capri* (1954; Eng. tr., *The Capri Letters*, 1955), a
psychological study of a troubled marriage in Allied-oc-
cupied Rome. Soldati's several novels and collections of
short stories are strongly autobiographical. His early
work in particular was influenced by his Jesuit education,
which, in such works as the novel *L'amico gesuita* (1943;
The Jesuit Friend), becomes a repressive force responsible for moral hypocrisy. His characters, especially the
males, are anxiety-ridden, tormented by their sexual
drives. Relationships with women, even wives, are distorted, as in the short stories of *Salmace* (1929). In *La
confessione* (1955; Eng. tr., *The Confession*, 1958), the
rigidly imposed restrictions of the Jesuits lead the young
protagonist from moral turmoil to homosexuality. Soldati
uses his writing to pose moral questions, yet he avoids
harsh judgments, preferring instead the concessionary attitude that characterizes much of Italian Catholicism.
Other works that have met with critical success are *A
cena col commendatore* (1952; Eng. tr., *Dinner with the
Commendatore*, 1953), a collection of three novellas that
deal with moral ambiguities; *Il vero Silvestri* (1957; Eng.
tr., *The Real Silvestri*, 1961), concerning the moral identity of the protagonist; *La busta arancione* (1966; Eng.
tr., *The Orange Envelope*, 1969), a psychological study
of the effects of religious education; *Lo smeraldo* (1974;
Eng. tr., *The Emerald*, 1977), a fantasy romance; *Da
spettatore* (1973; As a Spectator), a collection of essays
on film; and two diaries covering the years 1947–71, *Un
prato di papaveri* (1973; A Field of Poppies) and *Lo specchio inclinato* (1975; The Tilted Mirror). Soldati's work
is particularly effective in evoking picturesque local color,
especially of his native Piedmont, and in the incorporation
of certain cinematic techniques into his prose style.

See: D. Heiney, in *America in Modern Italian Literature* (1964), pp. 187–201; P. De Tommaso, in *Letteratura
italiana: i contemporanei*, vol. 3 (1975), pp. 495–513.

R.J.R.

Soler i Hubert, Frederic: *see* PITTARA, SERAFI.

Sollers, Philippe (1936–), French novelist, literary theorist, and editor of *Tel Quel*, was born in Talence. He wrote
his first two novels, *Le Défi* (1957; The Challenge) and
Une Curieuse Solitude (1958; A Strange Solitude), before
he was 21. Sollers later felt, however, that both books
were written less by him than through him; their "author"
was the upper social class to which his family belonged.
After that realization, he made a constant effort to increase the perceptiveness of the "writing subject" of his
novels in order to account, within the framework of history, both for his unconscious drives and for the forces
at work at all levels of society. This effort is evident in
the series of novels from *Le Parc* (1961; Eng. tr., *The
Park*, 1968), the first in which an awareness of the writing
process is clearly displayed, and *Drame* (1965), to
Nombres (1968; Numbers), *Lois* (1972; Laws), *H* (1973),
and *Paradis* (1978). *Nombres* deals in part with the subject's experience with language and the challenge presented by an alien linguistic system; *Lois* might be viewed
as a mock-epic of Western culture; *H* suggests an im-
mersion in history that is total, both communal and dissonant, lyrical and comical. These latter works balk at
any attempt to reinsert them into a tradition of French
(or Western) literature. They are "open" texts the reader
works himself into and experiences actively, transforming
them and being transformed by them.

Sollers's fiction and essays are interdependent. An
early volume, *L'Intermédiaire* (1963; The Intermediary),

had brought together brief works of fiction, essays, and criticism. Later, Sollers suggested that *Nombres* and *Logiques* (1968), a collection of theoretical essays, are to be read "simultaneously and dialectically." Indeed, *Logiques* provides a key to his theory and practice (making allowances for subsequent evolution); here he affirms some basic principles: "reality" is what the ideology of the dominant class imposes as such; traditional novels teach the ethics of bourgeois society and tell the reader how he or she must behave in order to be accepted in it; textual practice (the material act of writing) does not reflect reality, nor does it express a preexistent meaning inserted by a proprietary author—it is at once the production of new meaning and the destruction of the old. More important still are the texts Sollers has written since 1968, culminating in *Sur le matérialisme* (1974; On Materialism). They are, like *H*, emblematic of a refusal to consider literature as aseptically isolated from politics or from the movement of history. Dialectical materialism has become central to Sollers's writing, not as a foundation for dogma, but as an activating principle that enables one to rethink problems as changes occur.

The progression seen in Sollers's texts parallels that of *Tel Quel*. The first issue of the journal (Spring 1960) exuded ambiguity; the liminary "Declaration" stressed aesthetics and Paul VALÉRY, and the epigraph for the issue was from Friedrich NIETZSCHE. Eventually, the trend of the review was more in the direction connoted by Nietzsche's name, and a quotation from Karl Marx headed the 25th issue. The extent to which Sollers has been the prime mover in the group can be seen in the changing makeup of the editorial committee; none of the original five remained in 1967, and only two of the six then listed were still there in 1974. Among those who have served at one time or another are poets Michel Deguy and Denis ROCHE and novelists Jean-Louis Baudry, Jean Pierre FAYE, Jean RICARDOU, and Jean THIBAUDEAU; Marcelin Pleynet has been managing editor since 1963; Julia KRISTEVA joined in 1970. Contributors have included many outstanding contemporary writers. In 1965, *Tel Quel* sponsored Tzvetan Todorov's anthology of Russian formalism, which may have presented it with the structuralist temptation (*see* FRENCH LITERATURE)— but this was soon put aside. As Marxists, the *Tel Quel* group were tempted by the French Communist Party in 1967, but it too was rejected, and the journal assumed an antagonistic position in 1971. The Party's anti-Mao stand occasioned the break, but the essential point of contention was the Communists' dogmatic attitude and refusal to accept discoveries of psychoanalytic investigations. Impervious to blandishment or coercion on the part of any orthodoxy, *Tel Quel* pursues its own controversial, iconoclastic way to the extent of condemning nearly all Marxist ideologies and regimes—as opposed to principles set forth by Marx. Two discussions (originally radio broadcasts) shedding light on that position are Maurice Clavel's *Délivrance* (1977) and Edgar Faure's *Au-delà du dialogue* (1977; Beyond Dialogue).

See: "Writing Intransitively," *TLS* (Dec. 5, 1968); J. Derrida, *La Dissemination* (1972); special issue of *TelQ* 57 (1974); L. S. Roudiez, "Twelve Points from *Tel Quel*," *ECr* (1974); R. Barthes, *Sollers écrivain* (1979).

L.S.R.

Sologub, Fyodor, pseud. of Fyodor Kuzmich Teternikov (1863–1927), Russian poet, prose writer, and dramatist, was born in Petersburg. By profession a schoolteacher and later a school inspector, Sologub began publishing philosophical poetry in the 1880s. He developed into an astonishingly consistent representative of "true" decadence, combining the formal achievements of the French symbolists (Charles BAUDELAIRE and Paul VERLAINE) with elements of Russian romanticism. The years 1896 to 1908 marked the appearance of his best-known collections of poetry, in which he contrasted beauty in the forms of free imagination, nature, the spirit, the youthful body, and voluntary death, to ugliness in the forms of rigid natural law, old age, the laws of man, and political and social arbitrariness.

Sologub's greatest poetic achievement is the collection *Plamenny krug* (1908; Circle of Flame), which reflects his credo of radical solipsism and also contains a note of resignation concerning the miscarried 1905 Revolution, with which he sympathized. In his poems, Sologub conjures up a world that is at the mercy of evil, which has revealed itself in human as well as cosmic affairs. In his view, however, nature is not completely evil. Indeed, it was in the helpful magic of nature and in folklore that Sologub found his partially Utopian counterprinciple to the soulless phenomena of the workaday world. His language is always precise and transparent, although occasionally as rigid as a mathematical proof or an incantation.

Sologub's prose tales (written after 1896) portray the same world as his poetry. Their decadent note derives from Edgar Allan Poe, Joris Karl HUYSMANS, Georges RODENBACH, and Oscar Wilde. The tales often focus upon children who are haunted by abnormal psychic experiences and a longing for death. Among his greatest stories are "Teni" (1896; Shadows) and "Opechalennaya nevesta" (1908; The Sorrowing Bride). The story "V tolpe" (1907; In the Crowd), in which more than 1,000 persons, including many children, are trampled to death in a crowd at a public festival, was based on the historic catastrophe that occurred during the coronation of Nicholas II in 1896.

Sologub also wrote a series of symbolist dramas, among which *Pobeda smerti* (1908; The Victory of Death) is the most widely known. The play's characters appear detached from their environment, and inexorable fate itself assigns their roles to them.

Sologub's famous satirical novel *Melkiy bes* (1907; Eng. tr., *The Little Demon*, 1916), on which he had worked since 1892, contrasts the evil world of adults (provincial teachers and townspeople) to the more beautiful dream world of schoolchildren, who seek escape from somber reality. The anti-hero Peredonov, who can be traced back as a type to Nikolay Gogol, is the incarnation of all the petty, suspicious, superstitious, and sadistic traits of the Russian middle class. In this novel, Sologub, who himself came from the petite bourgeoisie, shows himself to be particularly sensitive to the social problems of his time. He was less successful in his satirical Utopian trilogy *Tvorimaya legenda* (1907–13; Eng. tr., *The Created Legend*, 1916), in which he never quite bridged the gap between lyrical imagination and destructive irony, between his omnipotent creative hero Trirodov and the absurdities of Russian reality. Even though *Tvorimaya legenda* is an important commentary upon Sologub's lyric poetry, its glorification of the satanic rites in honor of Lucifer, along with bitter political satire, fail to be entirely convincing.

See: J. Holthusen, *Fedor Sologubs Roman-Trilogie (Tvorimaja legenda): aus der Geschichte des russischen Symbolismus* (The Hague, 1960).   J.Ho.

Soloukhin, Vladimir Alekseyevich (1924–), Russian poet, journalist, essayist, story writer, and novelist, like his fellow "village writers, Fyodor ABRAMOV, Vasily BELOV, Yefim DOROSH, and Vasily SHUKSHIN, has become popular in post-Stalin Russia by seeking a positive and natural image of man in the return to Russian nature and Old Russian peasant traditions. Born in the central Russian village of Alepino, Soloukhin graduated from the Vladimir Technicum in 1942 and from the Gorky Institute of World Literature (Moscow) in 1951. He joined the Communist Party in 1952 and traveled frequently in Russia and abroad as a correspondant, especially for the magazine *Ogonyok*. Soloukhin's relative independence and his informal poetic style recall his younger, influential contemporary, Yevgeny YEVTUSHENKO. Folk devices such as repetition unify his verse, which avoids rhyme, metaphor, and regular meter.

Although he began his career as a poet, Soloukhin is known mainly for his prose. *Vladimirskiye prosyolki* (1957; Eng. tr., *A Walk in Rural Russia*, 1966), a mixture of travel sketch and lyrical diary, describes old-fashioned peasants whom he met one summer while he and his wife roamed his native district. Its sequel, the lyrical tale "Kaplya rosy" (1960; A Drop of Dew), focuses on Soloukhin's native village. In a 1958 article in *Literaturnaya gazeta*, Soloukhin attacked the patriotism of the western-oriented Yevtushenko. His second thoughts on this appear in a 1964 novel on a youth who, like Soloukhin, leaves the farm for the war, writes poetry at a literary institute in Moscow, and publicly attacks a friend to whom he is indebted. But Zolushkin (the hero's name is, significantly, a masculine form of "Cinderella") soon risks a run-in with the secret police. Returning to his old farm home, he comes to view Mother Russia, even there, as a stepmother. Hence the title of the novel, *Mat-machekha*, the Russian name for coltsfoot plant, which litcrally means mother-stepmother.

A nostalgiac lyricism infects the form as well as the mood and themes of Soloukhin's latest work. *Slavyanskaya tetrad* (1964; A Slavonic Notebook) is a collection of travel sketches of Bulgaria. *Pisma iz Russkogo muzeya* (1966; Letters from the [Leningrad] Russian Museum) praises the folk art and icons hidden in museum cellars and contrasts them to the mediocre art of socialist realism in Soviet exhibit halls. "Osenniye listya" (Autumn Leaves), which appeared in the Young Communist League journal *Molodaya gvardiya* in 1967–68, are notebook jottings on art, especially literature (Soloukhin became an editor of *Molodaya gvardiya* in 1967). *Chornye doski* (1969; Black Boards; Eng. tr., *Searching for Icons in Russia,* 1971) describes Soloukhin's growth from a fervent Pioneer (Soviet boy scout) to an icon collector and a pleader for salvaging medieval Russian art. The 14 short stories in his *Olepinskiye prudy* (1973; Olepino Ponds) argue for preserving the purity of the Russian countryside and reflect his delight in the colorful Russian personalities whom he meets in his travels.

Myod na khlebe (1978; Honey on Bread), a collection of five short stories and two short autobiographical novels, reveals the frustration of the village writer in the city. One story depicts a young man's pain when his Leningrad lady friend demands that he throw the beloved old-fashioned walking stick of the title ("Trost") into the Neva River. This capricious woman, who mouths chivalric clichés, represents the urban unconcern for plainer values from the past. Both novels, or rather lyrical diaries, *Prekrasnaya Adygene* (Beautiful Adygene) and *Prigovor* (Judgment), feature Vladimir Alekseyevich (Soloukhin) as narrator and central character. The first describes an ascent of Mount Adygene that enables Soloukhin to escape, if temporarily, the Moscow literary routine. The second, which is subtitled "Lyrical Reportage" and which contains some verse, grows from a series of medical observations into a complaint against the untimeliness of death. Implicit in the works of Soloukhin and other "village writers" is a note of the Christian and political protests that have been openly treated by Aleksandr SOLZHENITSYN, who shares many of their concerns.

H.A.G.

Solovyov, Vladimir Sergeyevich (1853–1900), Russian philosopher, theologian, critic, essayist, and poet, was born in Moscow, the son of a distinguished historian. Solovyov took his M.A. and Ph.D. degrees in philosophy (1874, 1880) and taught briefly at Moscow and Petersburg universities (1875–81), but spent his last two decades as a prolific free-lance writer and *Privatgelehrter*. Solovyov was polyglot, erudite, and versatile. In addition to important treaties (and dialogues) on speculative philosophy and theology, he wrote sensitive literary criticism and penetrating essays on current social, political, and ecclesiastical—including ecumenical—questions. His prose style is uniformly elegant and lucid, even when he is dealing with abstruse theoretical topics. His letters (collected in 4 vols., 1908–23) are second only to Aleksandr Pushkin's in brilliance and charm.

Solovyov wrote delightful light verse, humorous verse plays, and verse translations, as well as over 130 serious poems. In these poems—which at their best are subtle and delicate rather than powerful or original—he employed a traditional lexicon and classical meters, but showed a certain inventiveness in the use of slant and compound rhymes. The mystical image of the "Divine Sophia," which Solovyov articulated in theoretical concepts as well as in poetic symbols, strongly influenced the Russian symbolist poets—Andrey BELY, Aleksandr BLOK, and Vyacheslav IVANOV—despite the fact that Solovyov himself sometimes, as in the long poem *Tri svidaniya* (1898; Three Encounters), treated the sublime symbol of *Das Ewig-Weibliche* ironically or irreverently.

The 10-volume second edition of Solovyov's works, *Sobraniye sochineniy* (1911–14) was reprinted (Brussels, 1966), with two additional volumes (1969) of unpublished and uncollected articles, selected correspondence, and the complete poetry, including light verse. There is a virtually complete German edition of Solovyov's works, but only seven or eight of his dozen books have been published in English. Excerpts are in *A Solovyov Anthology*, comp. by S. L. Frank (1950) and *Russian Philosophy*, ed. J. M. Edie, et al. (1965), vol. 3, pp. 62–134.

See: K. Mochulsky, *Vladimir Solovyov: zhizn i ucheniye* (2d ed., 1951); V. V. Zenkovsky, *A History of Russian Philosophy*, vol. 2 (1953); pp. 469–531; F. Stepun, *Mystische Weltschau: fünf Gestalten des russischen Symbolismus* (1964), pp. 13–92; H. Urs von Balthasar, *Herrlichkeit: eine theologische Ästhetik*, vol. 2, pt. 2 (1964), pp. 645–716.   G.K.

Solzhenitsyn, Aleksandr Isayevich (1918–), Russian novelist and Nobel laureate (1970), was catapulted to fame with his first published work, *Odin den Ivana Denisovicha* (Eng. tr., *One Day in the Life of Ivan Denisovich,* 1963), which appeared in the November 1962 issue of the Moscow literary journal, *Novy mir*. Hailed in the Soviet press as a work of high literary distinction, it was also seen as constituting a social and political event, since it dealt with a hitherto taboo subject, life in Iosif Stalin's concentration camps. Premier Nikita Khrushchov, who was then pursuing his policy of destalinization, himself piloted a special resolution through the Communist Party Central Committee authorizing publication. In its January 1963 issue *Novy mir* published two of the author's short stories, "Sluchay na stantsii Krechetovka" (Eng. tr., "Incident at Krechetovka Station," 1963) and "Matryonin dvor" (Eng. tr., "Matryona's Home" 1963); one more, "Zakhar Kalita" (Eng. tr., "Zakhar the Pouch," 1969) appeared in the same journal in January 1966. A brief article on style, "Ne obychay dyogtem shchi belit, na to smetana" (It Is Not the Custom to Lighten Cabbage Soup with Tar, For That We Have Sour Cream), printed in the *Literary Gazette* on Nov. 4, 1965, completes the list of his publications in his homeland. *V kruge pervom* (1968; Eng. tr., *The First Circle*, 1968), a long novel portraying relatively privileged prisoners in a scientific research institute outside Moscow in the winter of 1949, was accepted by *Novy mir*, but never appeared; another, *Rakovy korpus* (1968; Eng. tr., *Cancer Ward*, 1968), was partially set in type when the secretariat of the Writers Union prohibited its publication. Solzhenitsyn had become a symbol in the struggle over domestic liberalization; by early 1966 mention of his name and works virtually ceased in the Soviet press. At the same time, works of his began finding their way abroad, and unauthorized publication in Western Europe of his prose miniatures, *Etyudy i krokhotnye rasskazy,* 1965; Eng. tr., "Prose Poems," 1965), followed by *The First Circle, Cancer Ward,* and a series of shorter writings, brought charges that he was defaming the Soviet Union and supporting its adversaries. In May 1967 he sent an unprecedented open letter to the Fourth Soviet Writers Congress urging an end to censorship, proposing that the Writers Union afford protection to its members, and detailing the persecutions to which he had recently been subjected. This letter, widely circulated at home and published abroad, was not discussed at the Congress. The campaign against Solzhenitsyn intensified, culminating in his expulsion from the Writers Union in November 1969. The following year he was awarded the Nobel Prize for Literature in recognition of "the ethical force with which he has pursued the indispensable traditions of Russian literature." In 1971 the first volume of a panoramic novel about Russia at the time of World War I appeared in Paris under the title, *Avgust chetyrnadtsatogo* (Eng. tr., *August 1914*, 1972), the first of his works to be published abroad with his permission. In 1973 state security organs confiscated the manuscript of *Arkhipelag GULAG* (3 vols., Paris, 1973–75; Eng. tr., *Gulag Archipelago*, 3 vols., 1974–78), an extraordinary memoir and study of the forced labor system in the USSR, subtitled "an experiment in artistic research," and Solzhenitsyn felt himself obliged to authorize its immediate publication in the West. As a result, the author was arrested and, on Feb. 13, 1974, abruptly deported to West Germany. He was at the same time stripped of his citizenship for "systematically performing actions incompatible with being a [Soviet] citizen." Soon after his expulsion he published a lengthy *Pismo vozhdyam Sovetskogo Soyuza* (1974; Eng. tr., *Letter to the Soviet Leaders*, 1974), a document with strong nationalist (some have said Slavophile) tendencies in which he urges the abandonment of Communist ideology, freedom of peripheral non-Russian nations to secede from the Soviet Union, and concentration on the sui generis development of Russia proper. A lengthy and circumstantial account of the author's vicissitudes and aspirations as a Soviet writer, *Bodalsya telyonok s dubom* (Eng. tr., *The Oak and the Calf,* 1980) appeared in Paris in 1975; labeled "Sketches of Literary Life," it consists of five sections (written between 1967 and 1974), and contains a series of documentary appendices. His *Lenin in Zurich* (1976; Russian ed., Paris, 1975), is a fictionalized portrait of the Bolshevik leader composed of an unpublished chapter from *August 1914,* as well as chap-

ters from its sequels, *October 1916* and *March 1917*. After his deportation Solzhenitsyn first resided in Switzerland. In 1976 he moved to the United States, and he now resides in Cavendish, Vermont.

Born in Kislovodsk in the Caucasus one year after the October Revolution, Solzhenitsyn belongs to the first entirely Soviet generation. A few days after his graduation from the Department of Physics and Mathematics of Rostov University, in June 1941, Russia was invaded; and in October Solzhenitsyn joined the army, serving from late 1942 until early 1945 as an artillery officer. Arrested in February 1945 for having made disparaging remarks about Stalin in letters to a friend, Solzhenitsyn was sentenced to eight years in the labor camps, following which he was sent into "perpetual exile" in Kazakhstan, where he taught mathematics and physics in a rural school and wrote in secret. Released from exile in 1956 and rehabilitated a year later, he moved to European Russia; there he continued to teach and to write—without hope of publication until, emboldened by the anti-Stalinism of the 22nd Party Congress in 1961, he submitted *One Day* to *Novy mir*.

All these experiences find expression in his work. Camp life is the subject of *One Day,* and of his play, *Olen' i shalashovka* (1968; The Tenderfoot and the Tramp; Eng. tr., *The Love Girl and the Innocent,* 1969), as well as of *The Gulag Archipelago*; the prison research center in which he served is the setting of *The First Circle; Cancer Ward* and the short story, "Pravaya kist" (1969; Eng. tr., "The Right Hand," 1969), are set in a central Asian hospital similar to the one in Tashkent, where the author was treated in 1954. Only after completing these was he able to take up the plan for "revolution," a novel-cycle (*August 1914* is the first section) which he had first conceived while a student in the 1930s.

Solzhenitsyn speaks in the afterword to *August 1914* of "resurrecting those years": the phrase applies equally to virtually all his writing. He seems committed to retracing, step by step, the path that led to present Soviet society, applying a strong moral imagination to the often-suppressed or distorted historical record. Truth is the recurrent watchword, along with justice and conscience. Solzhenitsyn is thus fundamentally in the 19th-century realist tradition; literature to him is at once testable against the records of the past and answerable to the experience of readers in the present (as he stressed in his Nobel lecture). Most of his works offer some example of triumphant moral selfhood, and all contain aphoristic passages that crystallize the informing ideas of the whole. His writing, which shows a growing religious orientation, is marked by high intelligence, high density of sharply observed detail, and exceptional linguistic vitality. Seldom solemn, it is permeated with high seriousness. Deeply concerned with Russia's destiny, Solzhenitsyn is an artist for whom faith in art arises from a faith in man. "The simple act of an ordinary brave man," he declares in the Nobel lecture, "is not to participate in lies. . . . But it is within the power of writers and artists to do much more: to defeat the lie!"

See: L. Labedz, ed., *Solzhenitsyn: A Documentary Record* (enlarged ed., 1973); J. B. Dunlop et al., eds., *Aleksandr Solzhenitsyn: Critical Essays and Documentary Materials* (1973); D. Fiene, comp., *Alexander Solzyhenitsyn: An International Bibliography of Writings by and about Him* (1973); K. Feuer, ed., *Solzyhenitsyn* (1976).

D.F.

Sønderby, Knud (1909–66), Danish novelist, was born in the western Jutland town of Esbjerg but grew up in Copenhagen. He received his law degree in 1935. His first novel, *Midt i en Jazztid* (1931; In the Middle of a Jazz Age), reveals his main theme: the young interwar generation and its problems. The cynicism of the characters—their denial of moral norms—depicted in a hard-boiled style influenced by Ernest Hemingway, proves to be a mask for an unexpressed longing for a realistic way of life independnet of all ideologies. *To Mennesker mødes* (1932; Two People Meet) is similarly built on the fear of the power of emotions, described in the tender but hopeless love story between two young people from different social levels. Another problem, the generation gap, is skillfully dealt with in *En Kvinde er overflødig* (1936, dramatized in 1942; Eng. tr., *A Woman Too Many*, 1955), neither generation wanting to accept the life-style of the other. *De kolde Flammer* (1940; The Cold Flames), a novel about marriage, and the prose sketches *Grønlandsk Sommer* (1941; Summer in Greenland) are inspired by a stay on Greenland. They illustrate the change to the descriptive essays of Sønderby's later years, in which his clear yet suggestive prose reached its full development.

See: P. Gadman, *Knud Sønderby's forfatterskab* (1976).

S.H.R.

Sonne, Jørgen (1925-), Danish poet, was born in Copenhagen. The recipient of a university degree in 1951, he is presently teaching in a Copenhagen college. Sonne's writing is steadily developing. His earlier form-bound poetry, collected in *Korte digte* (1950; Short Poems), *Delfiner i skoven* (1951; Dolphins in the Forest), and *I en levende tid* (1952; In a Living Time), is permeated by religious themes and by a belief in love and fertility. In *Italiensk suite* (1954; Italian Suite) these themes yield to moods of destruction and disintegration. An artistic maturing takes place in *Krese* (1963; Cycles), a process that also constitutes the collection's mental and poetical structure; the self is dissolved and disappears as a problem in the realization of the coherence of all things. As a poet, Sonne utilizes a linguistic ambiguity that is related to Gunnar EKELÖF's *Strountes* and Ezra Pound's *Cantos*. It is very characteristic of Sonne's poems in *Huset* (1976; The House), which employing a purely imagist technique, combine observations, reflections, and vision in an extensive associative journey into fantasy, memory, and history. Reversely, *Blå turist* (1971; Blue Tourist), an ironic travel book about a naïve photographer's confrontation with the realities of a developing country, is characterized by a minute and precise description of reality that is likewise to be found in the related poetry of *Thainoter* (1974; Thai Notes).

S.H.R.

Sonnevi, Göran (1939-), Swedish poet, was born in Jakobsberg. He is one of the most prominent of the younger Swedish poets who in the 1960s set out to tackle current political and social problems as directly as possible. Topical references and local situations provide the starting points of his poems, whose development is always hesitant, going from the concrete to the abstract to the concrete. In his avoidance of literary gesture, Sonnevi skirts the edge of banality and relies on his precise technique to retain his balance. Even his recurring images—vortices, mirrors, enclosing circles, white light, transparent skulls, and so on—are presented not as metaphors with literary resonance but like meticulously prepared specimens from which tentative conclusions may be evolved. At one level his work rigorously questions accepted ideas of poetry's role in society. At another, his work provokes more mundane questions: how far does it owe its reputation to current political trends in literary journalism, and how far

may it outlive these? Sonnevi's poems from the years 1959-68 are collected in *Det gäller oss* (1969; It Concerns Us), and more recent books are *Det måste gå* (1970; It Must Go), *Det oavslutade språket* (1972; The Unfinished Language), *Dikter 1959-1973* (1974; Poems), and *Det omöjliga* (1975; The Impossible). For a selection of Sonnevi's poems in English, see *Modern Swedish Poetry in Translation*, ed. by G. Harding and A. Hollo (1979), pp. 213-36.

See: A. Sjöbohm, "Den dubbla fånganskapen," *BLM* (1970); J. Stenkvist, *Svensk litteratur 1870-1970*, vol. 3 (1975), pp. 164-67, and "Göran Sonnevi och Noam Chomsky," in *Från Snoilsky till Sonnevi* (1976), pp. 206-18.

R.Fu.

Sorel, Georges (1847-1922), French social philosopher, was born in Cherbourg, of a typical bourgeois family. Sorel is generally recognized as the outstanding theoretician of revolutionary syndicalism. In 1865 he entered the Ecole Polytechnique and later became a highway engineer. In 1892, at the age of 45, he abruptly abandoned his profession in order to devote all his time to the study of social problems. His wife, who came from the working class, is said to have done much in bringing about this decision. When she died in 1897, Sorel retired to a modest villa at Boulogne-sur-Seine near Paris, to erect "a philosophical monument worthy of her memory."

By far Sorel's most famous book is his *Réflexions sur la violence* (1908; Eng. tr., *Reflections on Violence*, 1912)—a modified and enlarged version of several articles first published in the Italian *Divenire sociale* (1905) and in the *Mouvement socialiste* (1906-07). This work offers a curious mixture of Pierre-Joseph Proudhon's economic federalism, Karl Marx's "catastrophic" interpretation of history, Friedrich NIETZSCHE's hero worship, and Henri BERGSON's definition of movement as an "indivisible whole." Progress and revolution, according to Sorel, follow a subconscious pattern. Only in action, rebellion, and violence do men discover what they want and why they fight. It is unfair, therefore, to expect from militant syndicalism a precise exposition of its aims and purposes. Militant syndicalism is not rooted in ideas. It constitutes one tremendous intuitive force, a genuine élan vital of unpredicted and unpredictable consequences, a spontaneous surge that draws its strength from and finds its symbolic expression in "myths" and "images" such as that of the general strike. Through the incentive of the general strike, the workers' collective soul will rise to a "sublime" feeling truly consistent with the exalted mission of the proletariat. At the same time, the bourgeoisie, vitally threatened and aroused from its unwholesome lethargy, will resist the growing aggressiveness of labor and undergo in turn a process of rejuvenation.

The startling fact about *Réflexions sur la violence* is that it does not uphold a class theory. Sorel is much less preoccupied with the proletariat for its own sake than with the proletariat as the catalytic agent of a new social order to be brought about through a war of purification. Should labor weaken in its determination, the same end might still be sought and reached by means of the opposite policy—namely, by bolstering the fighting spirit of the bourgeoisie in order to rekindle the cooling ardor of the working classes. This willingness on Sorel's part to play one side against the other for what he sincerely considers the best interests of both explains to a large extent his many shifts and brazen contradictions. His early association with the parliamentary socialists did not survive the Dreyfus affair, the outcome of which, in his opinion as well as in that of Charles PÉGUY, was a "complete moral anarchy" and a drowning in politics of the mystical victory that had been won (see *La Décomposition du marxisme* [1908; The Decomposition of Marxism], *La Révolution dreyfusienne* [1909; The Dreyfus Revolution]). It was then (about 1898) that Sorel turned to the labor unions as the standard-bearers of pure, uncompromising socialism (many articles of this period were gathered later in his *Matériaux pour une théorie du prolétariat*, 1919). The gospel of "holy violence," however, did not have the desired effect upon the workers, who seemed more intent on obtaining the immediate satisfaction of higher wages and better living conditions. In 1910, Sorel was sympathetic to extreme conservatism in the person of Paul BOURGET, whose play *La Barricade* "transposed" the Sorelian creed for the benefit of the bourgeoisie. For several years he collaborated on the *Revue critique des idées et des livres* and on the short-lived *Indépendance* (1911-13), side by side with confirmed nationalists and royalists (Léon DAUDET, Charles MAURRAS, Georges Valois, Jean Variot). In the late stages of his career he lavished equal praise on Vladimir Lenin (see "Pour Lénine," appendix 3 to the 5th ed. of the *Réflexions sur la violence*, 1921) and on Benito Mussolini, whose blueprint of a corporate state was avowedly an extension of Sorelian syndicalism to all classes of society.

Throughout these metamorphoses, Sorel maintained the fierce antiintellectualistic attitude that, early in his crusade, inspired him to condemn Socrates' rationalism for having shaken the heroic traditions of Greece (*Le Procès de Socrate* [1889; The Trial of Socrates]). Plutodemocratic ideology, which tends to dissolve the class spirit, appeared to him equally vain and baneful (*Les Illusions du progrès*[1908; Eng. tr., *The Illusions of Progress*, 1969]). All told, his vision of the world of tomorrow was that of a technician and a moralist. Sorel the engineer, far from being the enemy of industry and production, counted on manmade instruments to free us some day from the deterministic yoke of nature (*Introduction à l'économie moderne* [1903; Introduction to Modern Economy] and "Les Préoccupations métaphysiques des physiciens modernes," *Revue de métaphysique et de morale* 13 (1905), reprinted in Charles Péguy's *Cahiers de la quinzaine*, 1907). Sorel the moralist—a moralist of almost puritanical mold—dreamed of injecting a high dose of spiritual energy into the material body of present-day civilization. How to moralize technology? That was the question. The multiplicity—or the debatability—of Sorel's answers should not hide from the historian's view the singleness of his purpose.

See: G. Pirou, *Georges Sorel* (1927); J. Rennes, *Georges Sorel et le syndicalisme révolutionnaire* (1936); V. Sartre, *Georges Sorel: Elites syndicalistes et révolution prolétarienne* (1937); R. Heyne, "Georges Sorel und der autoritäre Staat des 20. Jahrhunderts," *Archiv des öffentlichen Rechts*, Neue Folge, vol. 29 (1938), pp. 129-77, 257-309; P. Delesalle, "Bibliographie sorélienne," *IRHS* 4 (1939): 463-87; S. Malvigna, "Il pensiero politico di Sorel e il fascismo," *RIFD* 19 (1939): 69-106; F. Rossignol, *La Pensée de Georges Sorel* (1948); R. D. Humphrey, *Georges Sorel: Prophet without Honor: A Study in Anti-Intellectualism* (1951).

J.-A.B. rev. D.W.A.

Sørensen, Villy (1929-), Danish author and philosopher, was born in Copenhagen. He was coeditor from 1959 to 1963 of the magazine *Vindrosen*, the main organ of Danish modernism, which had its prose breakthrough in Sørensen's *Sære historier* (1953; Eng. tr., *Tiger in the Kitchen; and Other Strange Stories*, 1969) and *Ufarlige*

historier (1955; Safe Stories). The common theme of these books concerns the unliberated and unrealized part of ourselves and our attitude toward it. German modernism is Sørensen's philosophical base, whereas his poetic models are the works of Thomas MANN and Franz KAFKA. Mann's ironical rewriting of mythical tales forms the pattern for the legends that create a specific genre among Sørensen's short stories. Like Kafka's works, Sørensen's narrations are primarely existential interpretation. They take place either in an absurd or totally ironical world, most frequently in a Danish welfare milieu, expressing the opposition of the author to the creation of a barrier between intellect and emotion. Sørensen's third collection, *Formynderfortællinger* (1964; Tales of Guardianship), as bizarre and disquieting as his earlier works, poses the question, What is guardianship? Tyranny versus anarchy? These political perspectives form, in legends about Judas and Saint Paul, the starting point for a discussion of the free will versus determinism. Sørensen is a central figure in postwar Danish intellectual life. He has had extensive influence on the authors of his generation, less through his short stories than through his numerous aesthetic, philosophical, and political essays. He is also coauthor of *Oprør fra midten* (1978; Revolt from the Middle), a political vision of the future, which has given rise to fierce accusations that he advocates totalitarianism.

See: E. Sønderiis, *Villy Sørensen* (1972); J. Bonde Jensen, *Litterær arkaologi: studier i Villy Sørensens Formyndertortallinger* (1978).   S.H.R.

Soromenho, (Fernando Monteiro de) Castro (1910-68), Portuguese writer of prose fiction, essayist, journalist, and amateur ethnologist, was born of Portuguese parents in Vila de Chinde, Mozambique, but his name is inextricably linked with Angola, where his family moved in 1911. Despite nine years of schooling in Portugal, he spent most of his formative years, until the age of 27, in Angola. As the employee of a diamond-mining company, he traveled extensively in the northeastern area of the colony and there, in the Lunda bush country, became a student of indigenous cultures and their oral traditions. When he moved to Luanda, the capital of Angola, to work as a journalist, Soromenho was already laying the foundation for his success as a creative writer. In 1936 he published his first small collection of stories, *Lendas negras* (Black Legends). By the following year he had relocated in Lisbon, where he worked for newspapers and cemented his relationship with Portuguese neorealist writers, becoming one of the best of them. With his volume of stories *Nhari: O drama da gente negra* (1938; Nhari: The Drama of Black Folk), Soromenho's writing career began in earnest. Growing opposition to the Antonio de Olivera Salazar regime changed him from a contributor to the colonialist review *O Mundo Português* to an open critic of colonial policy. Deprived of his livelihood, he went as an exile first to Paris, then to the United States—where he taught briefly at the University of Wisconsin—and finally to São Paulo, Brazil, where he taught, suffered from disease and neglect, and died. Although his intellectual horizons were international, Soromenho's works deal exclusively with his beloved Angola.

Without abandoning the short story or the short journalistic sketch, Soromenho ushered in a second phase in his prose fiction with the novel *Noite de angústia* (1939; Night of Anguish). In the first phase he had recreated a pre-European Africa, earning for himself, mainly among Europeans, the reputation of a white man who understood the black man's soul. He may well have sympathized on a level of universal humanity with what he saw as the

African's perennial plight, but his acclaimed empathy was in essence nothing more than the paternalism of the colonialist. In *Nhari*, the prevailing theme is the hopeless, centuries-old ignorance and poverty of the "savage." But Soromenho was an enlightened colonialist, who, different from other white writers, had more than a superficial knowledge of traditional Angolan societies, although he may not have known as much about the African psyche as he thought he did. This awareness, coupled with his concern for human dignity and the epic sweep of his writing, translated into ever more sensitive stories and novels. Most critics concede that Soromenho went through a significant change; he purged the novels of his second phase of such pejorative words as *savage* and *simian* when describing the African. He stated in a magazine interview that because in his novels new social realities arose and presented themselves to him in their contradictions, it was incumbent upon him to adopt a new technique and a new literary style. This led to the stories collected later as *Histórias da terra negra* (2 vols., 1960; Stories of the Black Land) and to such works as *Terra morta* (1949; Dead Land), his most widely read novel, which was banned by the Portuguese authorities because of the unflattering way in which it depicted Portugal's colonial practice. He was at his artistic best when characterizing African societies in transition and in conflict with imposed European values, a theme that he developed further in his last novels, *Viragem* (1957; Turn) and *A chaga* (posthumously published 1970; The Wound).

Essentially, Soromenho's message was anticolonialist, and although his later writings brought him more suffering than fame, he has been vindicated by the disintegration of the Portuguese empire. He died just as his books were beginning to attract new readers.

See: R. Bastide, *L'Afrique dans l'œuvre de Castro Soromenho* (1960); G. Moser, "Castro Soromenho, an Angolan Realist," in his *Essays on Portuguese-African Literature* (1969), pp. 42–60; R. G. Hamilton, *Voices from an Empire* (1975), pp. 34–40.   R.G.H.

Sosnora, Viktor Aleksandrovich (1936–), Russian poet, born in Alyupka, is a writer whose avant-garde and futurist tendencies are combined with a Slavophilic attachment to Russian folklore and legend. As a child, Sosnora was in Leningrad during the World War II blockade and was later evacuated to the Kuban region, where he lived with a group of partisans. After serving in the army (1955–58), he worked in a metallurgical factory, at the same time pursuing his philological studies by correspondence. In 1958, Sosnora was discovered by Nikolay ASEYEV, the former futurist and colleague of Vladimir MAYAKOVSKY, who wrote the foreword to his first book of poems, *Yanvarskiy liven* (1962; January Shower). Richly metaphoric and euphonic, the poems in this early work have often been compared with those of Andrey VOZNESENSKY. His later collections, *Triptikh* (1965), *Vsadniki* (1969; Horsemen), and *Aist* (1972; The Stork), gave further evidence of his interest in Russian epic literature; the poems often place half-legendary, half-historical characters in everyday, frequently comic or ribald, human situations. Sometimes Sosnora's poetry is fancifully surrealistic, but often his animistic feeling for nature and his dedication to Slavic folk origins add an archetypal dimension to it.   D.T.W.

Soto, Vicente (1919–), Spanish novelist and short-story writer, was born in Valencia. After studying law he moved to Madrid and published *Vidas humildes, cuentos humildes* (1948; Humble Lives, Humble Stories). Since 1954 he has lived in London, where he works as a trans-

lator. Following his first publication, he did not appear on the Spanish literary scene until 1967, when he won the Nadal Prize for his novel *La zancada* (The Giant Step). The title refers to the transition from childhood to puberty, reconstructed by a nostalgic narrator living far from his native land. Soto's next two novels are set respectively in England and in Spain: *Bernard, uno que volaba* (1972; Bernard, a Fellow Who Flew) and *El gallo negro* (1972; The Black Rooster). Among his other works are: *Casicuentos de Londres* (1973; Semi-Stories of London), and *Cuentos del tiempo de nunca acabar* (1977; Stories of Endless Time). Soto's work is exceptional in the contemporary Spanish novel because his physical displacement has kept him independent of schools and fads, thus freeing him from the need to be true to anything but his inspiration and his own refined but profound literary art. In all of his books there is an exquisite sensibility. The author's constant humane interest in his characters leads him to treat them with tenderness, lyricism, humor, and restrained fantasy.

Soto's highly polished prose reveals, a stylistic concern perhaps strengthened by the pressure of living in an English language environment, some of whose characteristics he nevertheless attempts to assimilate into Spanish. A preoccupation with time provides the moving force behind this novelist's themes and structures.

See: A. Amorós et al., *Novela española actual* (1977), pp. 189–234.   D.V.

Soupault, Philippe (1897–), French poet, novelist, and critic, was born in Chaville. Collaborating with André BRETON, he provided the first major document of surrealism, *Les Champs magnétiques* (1920; The Magnetic Fields), an automatic text written at various, duly noted speeds, in which the two authors alternated their transcription. In 1926, Soupault was expelled from the surrealist group for refusing their new political orientation.

In the recently published collection of his poems (1975), one can clearly see an evolution, at the cost of a certain intensity, from an introverted lyric strain, almost sentimental and certainly self-concerned, to a greater involvement with the world outside. Soupault's early poems, published in *Aquarium* (1917) and *Rose des vents* (1920; Rose of the Winds), resemble those of Pierre REVERDY but show more vigor. *Westwego* (1922) and *Georgia* (1926) use the same settings and themes: cafés and travel, roads, colors, and motions.

In such early novels as *Le Grand Homme* (1925; The Great Man), Soupault eulogized energy and determination in the character of Putnam, a black singer turned businessman. His other novels include *Le Bon Apôtre* (1923; The Good Apostle), a sort of "Dialogues de Soupault, juge de Philippe"; *A la dérive* (1923; Adrift), the dream narrative of a restless, adventurous destiny; *En jouel* (1925; Aiming), an ironic satire of a shallow man of letters whose vain efforts at freeing himself lead to insanity; *Le Nègre* (1927; The Negro), which concerns the nightmarish pursuit of a freedom perpetually denied by ancestral shackles; and *Les Dernières Nuits de Paris* (1928; Eng. tr., Last Nights in Paris, 1929), a hallucination (resembling a detective story) whose villain and heroine is Paris herself.

Soupault has also studied other artists whose creative efforts were also directed toward absolute emancipation. His writings on these figures include *Henri Rousseau, le Douanier* (1927; Henri Rousseau, The Customs Man); *William Blake* (1928; Eng. tr., 1928); *Paolo Uccello* (1929; *Charlot* (1931), the lyric image of a true adventurer of the screen, Charlie Chaplin; *Baudelaire* (1931); *De-*

bussy (1932); and *Souvenirs de James Joyce* (1944; Memories of James Joyce). Above all, Soupault's writings are of interest in their reflections of changing epochs.

See: B. Crémieux, *Inquiétude et reconstruction* (1931), pp. 97–124; H. J. Dupuy, *Philippe Soupault* (1957); J. H. Matthews, *Surrealist Poetry in France* (1969), pp. 17–30.

C.L.B. rev. M.A.C.

Sova, Antonín (1864–1928), Czech poet and novelist, was born at Pacov in southern Bohemia, the son of a schoolteacher. He entered the service of the Prague Municipll Library, becoming director of the library late in his life. He died in his native town, after suffering long from a spinal affliction. Sova ranks after Josef Svatopluk MACHAR and Otokar BŘZINA as the most prominent poet of the generation that began writing in the 1890s and achieved fame and maturity in the early 20th century. He was an impressionist who, especially in his later work, used many of the techniques of symbolism. He started his writing career with realistic sketches in verse and with little landscapes, somewhat in the style of François Coppée but he soon turned to an introspective lyricism, in which he expressed the struggles, conflicts, and tragedies of his highly sensitive soul. Possibly his best work can be found in such collections of intimate lyrics as *Zlomená duše* (1896; A Broken Soul) and *Lyrika lásky a života* (1907; Lyrics of Love and Life), in which the poet hints at the tragedy of his unhappy married life. Many of the verses in these collections are songlike, full of sensitive observations and analyses, with only slight attempts at symbolic implications. This personal poetry, which continued as an undercurrent until Sova's death, was, at least in the public mind, overshadowed by his increasingly ambitious attempts at symbolist poetry, at grandiose visions and cosmic meditations, written in free verse in a style that resembles the hymns of Emile VERHAEREN. *Ještě jednou se vrátíme* (1900; We Shall Return Once More), especially the section entitled "Údolí nového království" (The Valley of the New Kingdom), expresses best the poet's generous hopes of a Utopian future for humanity. Other collections, notably *Krvácející bratrství* (1920; The Bleeding Brotherhood) voice his faith in democracy and universal socialism.

These visions dwindle imperceptibly into a considerable mass of political hymns and invectives. Best-known of these is "Theodoru Mommsenovi" (1897) Sova's sharp answer to the German historian Theodor Mommsen, who had recommended breaking the hard Czech skulls, but much of Sova's work on these themes is rhetorical and even dull. He also wrote distinguished ballads in the tradition of Czech folk poetry, collected in *Kniha baladická* (1915; A Book of Ballads) and a considerable body of prose, which suffers, however, from excessive lyricism and descriptiveness. Among his novels, *Ivův román* (1902; Ivo's Romance) is the study of an unhappy weakling; *Výpravy chudých* (1903; The Campaigns of the Poor) is a depiction of the struggles of Sova himself, in a slight fictional disguise, against poverty and indifference; and *Toma Bojar* (1910) is a slight novel about peasant life in his native district. Sova's finest prose work is found in the bitter short stories collected in *O milkování, lásce a zradě* (2 vols., 1909; Of Flirting, Love, and Betrayal).

Sova was primarily a man of feeling, a poet of the most delicate, evanescent shades of emotional conflicts, a sensitive painter of landscapes as states of his mind. He is at his best in traditional song forms, in melancholy meditations, in the "flowers of intimate moods," as he called one of his first collections, *Květy intimních nálad* (1891). Although the original enemy of Parnassian eloquence and bombast, Sova was seduced into attempting prophetic poetry, which turned all too frequently into blurred and even empty rhetorical exercises. But his mastery of nuance, the delicate melody of his early pieces, the sensitive impressionism of his landscapes, have inspired much later verse—like that of Stanislav Kostka NEUMANN—and constitute an important contribution to the body of Czech poetry.

See: F. X. Šalda, "Antonin Sova," in *Duše a dílo* (1913) and *A. Sova* (1924); L. N. Zverina, *A. Sova* (1918); J. Zika and J. Brabeck, *Antonín Sova* (1953). R.W.

Soya, Carl Erik Martin (1896–), Danish playwright, novelist, and short-story writer, was born in Copenhagen and grew up in an artistic home there. He made his literary debut in 1923 with a volume of fairy tales and has produced a long series of sharply focused and well-told short stories, the most representative selection being *Hvis Tilværelsen keder Dem* (1952; If Life Bores You). In *Sytten* (1953–54; eng. tr., *Seventeen*, 1969), a young man's problems of puberty are described very openly. Soya's most important prose work, *Min Farmors Hus* (1943; Eng. tr., *Farmor's House*, 1964) is regarded as one of the finest portrayals of childhood in Danish literature. His uneven output of plays includes more than 30 dramas, many of which have not been staged. His first play, *Parasitterne* (1929; The Parasites), is a naturalistic presentation of human meanness set in a petit bourgeois milieu. The comedy *Hvem er jeg?* (1932; Who Am I?), however, is written in an impressionistic style; it is a psychological analysis of the emotions of an ordinary human being, colored by a Freudian perspective. This comedy is the first in a series of dramatic experiments, influenced by Luigi PIRANDELLO and Kjeld ABELL, in which the author plays tricks with scenic illusions and time-dimension. *Umbabumba* (1935) is an absolutely realistic satire on Nazi Germany, whereas *Chas* (1938) is a denunciation of the sport obsession. In Soya's main dramatic work is a tetralogy consisting of *Brudstykker af et Mønster* (1940; Parts of a Pattern), *To Traade* (1943; Eng. tr., *Two Threads*, in *Contemporary Danish Plays*, 1955), *30 Aars Henstand* (1944; 30 Years' Reprieve), and *Frit Valg* (1948; Free Choice). All are tied together by means of speculations about the mingling of determinism and haphazardness and of fate and responsibility in life.

See: N. B. Wamberg, *Soya* (1966). S.H.R.

Spanish literature. Romanticism in Spain was brief and late; it did not involve a revolution or even a strong reaction in attitudes or techniques of literary composition comparable to what it caused in other countries. Although Gustavo Adolfo BÉCQUER, a late romantic of the second half of the 19th century, wrote a handful of poems and stories that reveal a delicate sensibility and an inclination to probe creativity in the literary work itself, this inclination neither then nor now characterizes Spanish lyric poetry.

In a parallel fashion and with obvious repercussions in the work of the romantics, the writers called *costumbristas* in their generally brief sketches strove to reflect modes and manners of collective life representative of well-differentiated social, regional, and local groups. Cecilia Böhl de Faber (pseud. Fernán Caballero, 1796–1877) included in her novels scenes of Andalusian life that enabled her to underscore the interest and the value of traditions and established customs that were being threatened by new and disruptive ideologies. The form taken by the *costumbrismo* of Fernán Caballero's novels inaugurated a genre that produced the realistic novels of José María PEREDA and Emilia PARDO BAZÁN in the last third of the 19th century. Benito PÉREZ GALDÓS and Leopoldo ALAS are nevertheless the most interesting figures of the realist group and, like Juan VALERA, the most resistant to any reductive classification. As Galdós recognized and declared, an emerging and soon to be dominant social class claimed its right to be novelized. Once converted into a subject for fiction, Spanish society demanded of the writer an attitude in which the will to create was merged with the need to investigate thoroughly the mechanisms of social reality and to make a more or less explicit moral declaration about it. It was necessary to be able to recognize in the imaginary world of the author both the configuration and the problematic of the referent. Because they heeded this call and were faithful to observed detail, these writers were called realistic. To deny this attitude and its results on the basis of either current or recent critical doctrines would be an anachronism. Like their descendants today, the realists of the 19th century felt an urgent need to comprehend themselves and their country. Galdós and his contemporaries had already realized that their country was undergoing a perpetual crisis and a spiritual poverty that cried out for instant correction. These preoccupations were not incompatible with a desire to do things in literature that had not been done before, such as venturing into the underside of reality as it surfaced in hallucinations, dreams, and neuroses and taking a close look at states that then as now were considered "abnormal" because they did not conform to norms of conduct acceptable to a given social group. As writers of fiction rather than lyric poets, they endowed their imaginary beings with a conscience that dramatized the anxieties and fantasies that both integrated and separated them from a world that was their own creation as well as their enemy. This explains why the main characters of many of the best novels of the period undergo a dual struggle with society, on the one hand, and with the hidden "I" that dwells within us, on the other. Isidora Rufete of Galdós's *La desheredada* (1880; Eng. tr., *The Disinherited Lady*, 1957) is a good example.

A city, a town, or an out-of-the-way village is a typical setting of realist novels featuring the middle and lower classes. *La Montálvez* (1900), by Pereda, and *Pequeñeces* (1891; Trivia), by the Jesuit Luis Coloma (1851–1915), are exceptions: their agonists are members of the aristocracy. In many cases, the ambience or milieu of the novel rivals the characters in importance. The milieu is not an illusion or a mere verbal construct but the center of conflicts that are experienced by the narrator, the characters, and ultimately by the reader, rather than simply described or shown. As novelistic material the middle class appeared richer in pretense than means. The cult of appearances did nothing to alleviate poverty; it merely plunged the middle classes into seeming to be what they were not. The political and commercial sectors ruled this class because they had the power. Women are portrayed as the backbone of the family and bulwarks of stability and order. In general the realists replaced the romantic archetypes of purity versus sensuality with a more varied feminine typology, thus creating more complex female characters. In probably the majority of 19th-century novels, women consequently held privileged positions. From *La gaviota* (1849; The Seagull), by Fernán Caballero, to *Misericordia* (1897; Eng. tr., *Compassion*, 1962), by Galdós, and including *Pepita Jiménez* (1874; Eng. tr., 1886) and *Juanita la larga* (1896), by Valera, certainly the most attractive fiction of the period has a woman as the center of interest. This is one unmistakable sign of social change and also of the fact that these novels were addressed to and written for a female reading public.

In the early realist novels, for example, the work of Fernán Caballero, ideologies are very visible. Even Galdós and Pereda wrote novels in which the thesis seems more important than the writing. In the best works of the period, however, ideology falls into place, functioning as one of the structural elements and obeying a conscious artistic purpose. Valera's exceptional case must be emphasized: remote heretical offspring of the doctrine of art for art's sake, he repeatedly declared that his purpose in writing novels was to amuse the reader and that for that reason he was able to free his novels of everything that did not fit his purpose of concentration on the essentials of personal relations, especially amorous ones. This attitude probably arose from his mild skepticism, which inclined him to view ideological struggles as products of an intransigent, partisan mentality very different from his own. Valera opted to separate his art from politics, never yielding to the temptation to use the novel as a weapon in the political, social, and even religious confrontations in which the writer as an individual and a citizen can be obliged to participate. Valera's case is unusual because he actually practiced the uninvolvement he preached in *Apuntes sobre el nuevo arte de escribir novelas* (1887; Notes on the New Art of Writing Novels).

Like Valera and Pardo Bazán, Leopoldo Alas was both an author of short and long fiction and a critic, and his militant stand and constant activity on the literary scene made him known as *the* critic of his time. Marcelino MENÉNDEZ PELAYO was the great scholar of the late 19th century, a historian of literally fabulous erudition, devoted not only to literature, but also to philosophy and the history of ideas. But as a critic of contemporary literature, no one could compete with Alas. Under the pseudonym Clarín he wrote hundreds of mostly satirical short articles which he called "hygienic" or "police work," as well as very perceptive long essays on authors and works he deemed worthy of careful study. Unfortunately, his critical activity and the animosity that it aroused blurred the fact that his short stories and novels were intensely dramatic, imaginative, and poetic.

Alas's are the only novels of 19th-century Spanish literature comparable with those of Galdós. This novelist has a unique place in the Spanish novel of the period. His modern techniques and themes are striking, as are the dramatic intensity and spatial scope of his work. Like Balzac and Dickens, whose work he translated, Galdós created an imaginary world very rich in characters and situations. The people of his novelistic world are able even now to emerge from it and break into ours in the strangest and most unexpected ways.

In 1885, Alas said that Spain had two and a half poets: Campoamor, Núñez de Arce, and Manuel del Palacio. Today this opinion seems optimistic, for one and a half have disappeared. Ramón de Campoamor (1817–1901) alone has survived. His tone is homey and confidential, and his imagination and poetic diction are nearly prosaic. Although his deliberate plainness smacks too often of triviality, it is still possible to read him for his tender humor and irony, which allow him to laugh at himself. Campoamor was the initiator of something resembling the so-called antipoetry of today.

Following romanticism and prior to the arrival of the modernists, Spanish poetry was left in a kind of limbo. It asserted itself only under the pressure of events that jarred the conscience of a great many Spaniards and awakened Spanish intellectual life. These events were the Spanish defeat in the war against the United States and the consequent loss of Cuba, Puerto Rico, and the Philippines; the culmination of domestic sociopolitical protest, notably in anarchist activities; and the fertilization of Spanish culture by renovative currents from Europe and Spanish-America. Modernism, for example, was brought by the Nicaraguan poet Rubén Darío (1867–1916).

At the turn of the century, the best Spanish theater also met with the greatest popular success. Although they were artistically unassuming, the *sainete* (one-act farce) and the so-called *género chico* (short musical) exuded wit and inventiveness. Amidst these very amusing, spontaneous works, the theater of José ECHEGARAY seemed like a military carrier surrounded by graceful sloops. Romantic in his gestures and vocabulary, Echegaray leaned toward rotundity and truculence and knew how to make an audience happy with his glibness. The same public that enjoyed the humorous little plays of the *género chico* also liked to be elevated to the heights of drama. It is not hard to understand the success of these pieces when one sees them performed. They are vigorously written, they have a passion that the actors' voices bring to life on the stage, and they end in a brilliant final coup. Echegaray's plays impress when staged and manage to seem more interesting than they are in print. Echegaray's exaggerated heroes contrast with the pretentious *señoritas,* the sassy young working women, and the good-natured craftsmen of the *sainete.* Critics like Bernard Shaw recognized and applauded Echegaray, and he shared the Nobel Prize for Literature in 1904. Perhaps it is better not to judge his works as they appear on the page. As literature, his plays seem to be alternately feverish or prosaic; his dialogues, for instance, oscillate between vulgarity and grandiloquence. When Echegaray won the Nobel Prize, a group of young writers signed a protest against him, which they used as a double-edged weapon, on the one hand directly (and perhaps unjustly) to deny the literary past and on the other hand to affirm the future, that is, their own future.

From time to time and mostly as a reflection of other writers' ideas, social problems emerge in Echegaray's drama, but it was in Joaquín DICENTA's work that class struggles and the proletarian hero first became central. Dicenta was a fighting journalist and onetime director of *Germinal* (1897–99), a meeting place for socially oriented writers who wanted to defend the humiliated and the offended. He put onto the Spanish stage figures not usually found there. He had strong but undisciplined talent and consequently encountered problems trying to adjust himself to the rules of the game. When he was able to do so, however, he had resounding success, as in *Juan José* (1895; Eng. tr., 1919).

Vicente BLASCO IBÁÑEZ shared certain social concerns with Dicenta. His literary beginning took place under the sign of naturalism. The short stories and novels of his first period are valuable for their narrative vigor, their detail, their descriptive dynamism, and the passionate voice that in some passages reaches a lyrical intensity. He did for the country and people of his native Valencia what Pardo Bazán did for Galicia and Alas for Asturias. Like them, he had an eye for detail, the ability to retain essentials, and a verbal facility that faithfully expressed emotions. Blasco took naturalism to an extreme, and neither his vision nor his prose failed when describing the precarious, hard life of poor country people. He tried not to refine the vulgar, but to capture the conditions of poverty. He had many literary followers, not all of whom are negligible. Several novels by Felipe TRIGO, cultivator of an experimental literature rich in erotic elements, and some pages by Eduardo ZAMACOIS, a late naturalist, are

still readable today. In these writers' novels, naturalism begins to connect with modernism: the erotic aspect of the former, for example, begins to associate itself with the refinements and follies of decadentism. Modernism did not bring modernity to Spain, but it did impose significant changes in literary attitudes and both verse and prose style. It was an intellectual and spiritual shock that almost coincided with the impact on Spanish intellectuals of Spain's surrender in the war against the United States.

Modernism inaugurated a historical period that begins at the turn of the century and extends to the outbreak of the Spanish Civil War in 1936. As in all historical periods, new and old ideologies converged. Modernism had vestiges of immediately prior tendencies like naturalism, which the new spirit opposed, as well as clear traces of more distant literary revolutions, like romanticism. The word modernism has been applied to different phenomena, but in general it can be said to connote a will to be up to date, whether in art, theology, dance, philosophy, or fashion. It was also an attempt to stand up to any and all orthodoxies—in sum, a radical nonconformism toward a society that the modernists hoped to renew, not to destroy. Rebels but unrevolutionary, their insurrection was nonviolent and took the form of wishful literary escapism, religious and political heterodoxy, and the exaltation of art to give life meaning.

José Martínez Ruiz (pseud. AZORÍN) wrote a semiautobiographical fictional trilogy in which the subdued, melancholy rebellion of the early modernists is reflected in a limpid, precise prose whose apparent lack of emotion enables the reader to identify with the characters. In *La voluntad* (1902: Will), Azorín tells the story of a failure; in *Antonio Azorín* (1903), tedium is conveyed by a lack of action; in *Las confesiones de un pequeño filósofo* (1904; Confessions of a Little Philosopher), he describes the protagonist's childhood and adolescence and the circumstances that explain his conduct as an adult. These three novels portray the pervasive passivity and despair of a country that was, as a politician of the times said, "pulseless." Pío BAROJA presented a similar disillusionment in his novel *Camino de perfección* (1902; The Way to Perfection). The protagonist totally lacks willpower. He travels through Spain and in the end unwittingly abandons his theoretical rebellion in favor of domesticity. In some of Miguel de Unamuno's short stories and Antonio Machado's poems this rebellion becomes an ironic stance when the writer understands that the power of the renovating impulses is diffused by the atmosphere of a country where nothing happens, where only time passes and life is a familiar continuation of deception, melancholy, and disenchantment in a reality that offers no hope. Even Juan Ramón JIMÉNEZ showed social concern in his early youth, as for example in his appropriately entitled poem "Las amantes del miserable" (The Underdog's Lovers).

The determining currents of the modernist period came partly from the German theologians and philosophers who aspired to moderate metaphysics by bringing it up to date. Miguel de UNAMUNO is the most distinguished representative of this tendency. A heretic among the orthodox, he saw some of his books included in the Catholic Index of forbidden works, but he denied his affiliation with modernism if it were understood as mere aestheticism. Perhaps no one expressed as intensely as he the anguish of modern man, deprived of all essence except his very existence and made to feel that life is a transitory, desperate waiting for death. A religious spirit, Unamuno was nevertheless incapable of accepting the dogmas on which the church is founded, and he brought to his work the sense of despair that this conflict produced in him.

The modernist epoch in the Spanish-speaking countries antedates and is different from Anglo-Saxon modernism as represented by such writers as James Joyce, Ezra Pound, and T. S. Eliot. Besides being an epoch, it is also a mood or state of mind not found in realism. Although opponents of modernism attempted to present it as a very limited poetic movement, characterizing it as a decadentism espoused by neurotics and aesthetes set against a vaguely melodic background of swans, dragon flies, princesses, and water lilies, it was apparent, even at a distance, that such a belittling picture was false. "Decadent" attitudes, insofar as they were signs of protest, were assumed during the first years of the period, but the pejorative use of this label is unfair when it connotes a taste for symbolism, a taste that in fact shocked and displeased those who tended to look for a more solid consistency in art. That solidity was offered by one of the two most obvious directions of modernism, French Parnassianism. The Parnassian poets stressed the importance of perfect, polished form. They wanted to give the stanza, and even the entire poem, the consistency of marble so as to ensure its durability. The modernists shared this desire, but they also wanted in their oscillation of purposes and achievements to make poetry ineffable. They wanted to express in words what cannot be said in words; they wanted, in short, to make words sound like music—heavenly if possible, and earthy if their verse could not reach such heights. Recent precedents were not lacking, but for Spaniards there was a more remote source in the "Noche oscura del alma" (Dark Night of the Soul) of Saint John of the Cross (1542–91). Modernist symbolism sprang from both far and near in time. A quarter of a century earlier, Gustavo Adolfo Bécquer and Rosalía de Castro (1837–85) had interiorized the poetry of their period and in intimacy a close relative of symbolism. From France, from Paul VERLAINE especially, similar resonances reached them. It would nevertheless be an error to divide the modernists into two groups, the Parnassians and the symbolists, for both tendencies sometimes operated in one poet, even in one poem, and were not felt to be incompatible at the time. Unamuno, Antonio MACHADO, and Juan Ramón Jiménez were the most distinguished representatives of the symbolist "tendency," while Antonio Zayas and Manuel MACHADO wrote admirable examples of Parnassian poetry.

To escape the confinement of the bourgeois society with which the realists had identified, the modernists sought in romanticism a precedent in the form of an alienation that included idealizing whatever was different or seemed to be most opposed to one's own world. Like the romantics, the modernists were attracted by the temporally or spatially distant. This explains why there are two parallel and complementary directions in their works: exoticism and indigenism (nativism). Exoticism is the attraction to faraway, faintly known, or unknown places. Mexico represented this for Ramón del VALLE-INCLÁN in his *Sonata de estío* (1903; Summer Sonata), as did New York and Boston for Juan Ramón Jiménez in his *Diario de un poeta recién casado* (1917; Diary of a Newly Married Poet). These were visions of other worlds that attracted them precisely because they were imprecise. When Jiménez wrote about blond-braided Puritan girls he had seen (or envisioned?) in New England as symbols of a land very different from his native Andalusia, he was yielding to recollections that were more literary than personal. Incompatible with, or at least uncomfortable in, their own milieu, Jiménez and other poets imagined that in faraway lands life and people might be more attractive, and they sometimes felt exiled within their own countries,

as Mariano José de Larra (1809–37) had felt during the Romantic period. The exotic Utopia they envisioned revealed itself in various fashions, including simple vignettes of beauty, as when Jiménez discovered Eurydice in a young black woman asleep in a New York subway with a rose in her hand, or in grand visions, such as Unamuno's dream of the splendid Argentina of the future. Indeed, Unamuno's admiration for Domingo Sarmiento, the Argentine writer and politician, stemmed partly from their mutually Utopian spirits. A certain strangeness and thematic uniqueness are good for literary creation. Imagining the unusual is easier if one conjures up a setting unlike one's familiar daily surroundings. Valle-Inclán indulged in his description of an incestuous love in Mexico because, although his own native Galicia would have permitted him to treat the same subject—Emilia Pardo Bazán presented incestuous love in her novel *La madre naturaleza* (1887; Mother Nature)—it would not have engendered the intense eroticism and cruelty that the tropical atmosphere allowed for. Valle-Inclán's taste for the Mexican milieu persisted until late in his life. Even in 1926, in *Tirano Banderas,* (Eng. tr., *The Tyrant*, 1929), he imagined a novelistic space full of Mexican resonances. In this novel about an archetypical Latin America dictatorship, he attempted to create an exotic language by concocting a hybrid of dialects from various Spanish-speaking countries of America.

Another way to create distance between oneself and one's society is through indigenism. This concept's roots extend beyond romanticism to its precursor, Jean Jacques Rousseau, and to the widespread belief in the essential goodness of man. If man is born good and society corrupts him, to recover his pristine purity requires that he go back to an age in which society has not yet perverted him. The noble savage, who ever since Chateaubriand's *Atala* (1801) had stood out as an exemplary figure in the minds of the disenchanted, reappears in Spanish American poetry with all the strength and authority of myth. Rubén Darío made of Caupolicán, the Araucanian chieftain who was tortured and executed by the Spaniards, a symbol of unconquerable heroism, nobility, and courage broken by disaster.

As Spaniards lacked Indians to idealize, indigenism in their work appeared in a slightly different guise. In their search for figures who could be idealized, they found the Arabs, defeated in the 8th century War of the Reconquest, but for eight centuries still the object of considerable emotional ambivalence. There were even interludes in which hostility gave way to mutual attraction. From their distance in time, the modernists could envision those eight centuries as they wished. Generally, they expressed compassion for the nobility of the vanquished, a compassion aroused not only by the Arabs' qualities but also by the persecutions to which they continued to be subjected after their final surrender in 1492. Although the novel that expresses these feelings most acutely was written by an Argentinian (Enrique Rodríguez Larreta's *La gloria de don Ramiro,* 1908), the author whose lyricism is most exalted was none other than an Andalusian who like many of his countrymen thought that the African heritage—so visible in southern Spain—was in his blood. In *El Alcázar de las perlas* (1911; The Castle of Pearls), Francisco VILLAESPESA expressed all of the extraordinary qualities that his reverie discovered in the Arabic-Andalusian world. Salvador RUEDA's best work also springs from a luminous, exalted vision of Andalusia.

Another, more profound form of Spanish indigenism attracted the most distinguished modernists. It was an exaltation of that almost mythical, mystified being designated by Unamuno as the "intrahistorical" man, the man who lives not in the mainstream or even on the sideline of history, but down below, on an unconscious level. The "intrahistorical" Spaniard works from sunrise to sunset, sleeps deeply, reproduces and dies in peace, and lets history pass him by without even noticing. Immovable, lodged in his home as if it were an extension of the womb, he is a figure around whom Unamuno built an entire theory. He dramatized the idea in his novel *Paz en la guerra* (1897; Peace in War), in which he presents a living creature suffering from a history that plagues and perhaps destroys him.

This indigenism, which was actually "Castilianism," exalted the virtues of the "race," that is, virtues that Spaniards liked to attribute to themselves or to those who seemed like typical Spaniards. In the atmosphere of sociopolitical corruption that threatened to destroy all Spaniards during those turn-of-the-century years, Azorín traveled all over Spain. In his book *Los pueblos* (1905; Towns), he recorded his admiration and sympathy for the poor, mistreated people he met. Antonio Machado did something similar in *Campos de Castilla* (1912; Fields of Castile), although several sections of the book contrast the idealization of rural life with its cruelty, showing that intrahistory is also the story of Cain and Abel.

This realistic tangent, which was also present in Unamuno, Azorín, and Baroja, is a peculiarity of Spanish modernism rarely found in the works of modernists from other Spanish-speaking countries. Baroja steeped himself in the traditions and atmosphere of the Basque country and in *Vidas sombrías* (1900; Somber Lives) presented a harsh image of the life and sufferings of intrahistorical characters. Valle-Inclán, in *Comedias bárbaras* (1907–08–22) and *Flor de santidad* (1904), similarly explores ancestral traditions and age-old superstitions of Galicia. The mist of the north seems to alter the perception of these writers when they talk about what is intrinsically theirs.

To journey into the depths of night, to cross the wall of shadow that held them back, was one of the modernists' most steadily sustained ambitions. Night is more than a theme in their poetry: it is an expression of their receptivity to obscure messages. The night, as Darío said, has a heart that beats in a language unknown to the waking world. Certain messages can be heard only at night, and underneath and beyond them circulate even deeper secrets that we suspect but cannot decipher. They are there, impregnable, untranslatable variations on an enigma like those of Edward Elgar's famous musical composition. That mystery of this kind could have a key or an order, however turbid, was made clear by Valle-Inclán in *Romance de lobos* (1908; Ballad of the Wolves). In this play, witches like those in *Macbeth* speak to the protagonist, who is forced to face his dark conscience in the shadows of the cave inhabited by "the other." The modernists' attraction to "mystery" is also evident in their selection of themes, motifs, and strange characters related to the occult. Satanic figures communicate with the dead (in novels like *El otro* [1910], by Eduardo Zamacois, a delirious example). As early as 1904, in *Jardines lejanos* (Distant Gardens) Juan Ramón Jiménez saw the self as split into several antagonistic or complementary selves. Analogous texts by Valle-Inclán are based on similar legendary beliefs and esoteric inclinations natural to the period that rediscovered Buddhism and Pythagoreanism and accepted Madame Blavatsky's vulgarized theosophy.

The modernist blend of exoticism and eroticism, spanning the extremes of Juan Ramón Jiménez's refinement and Zamacois's truculence, stems from cross-currents of naturalism, decadentism, and pre-Raphaelitism, to mention but a few. A passionate tremor runs through Spanish modernist literature: the image of the poet brandishing a bouquet of lilies before a naked girl is perhaps an emblem of the change from Bécquer to Jiménez or from Galdós to Valle-Inclán, who associates eroticism with the idea of sin to make it more exciting. How the opposites are bound together is hard to explain without reference to Eros and Thanatos, the two faces of human experience. When Unamuno wrote *Teresa* (1924), a novel in verse and prose, he presented the lovers on the bank of the river of death and also beyond it. Not even this austere philosopher could escape being conditioned by his context.

The modernists' aristocratic leanings—their hatred of the vulgar, an aversion to bourgeois bad taste—were not incompatible with their rebelliousness. Valle-Inclán was (or at least claimed to be) a traditionalist in politics without feeling alienated from the people. The target of his satire was rather the beneficiaries of power. Neither Azorín's red umbrella nor Jiménez's populist poems can deceive one: behind them one quickly discerns their wish to associate with the select few rather than the crowd. Unamuno's youthful socialism was short-lived, and his ferocious individualism soon showed, when he investigated something as remote from the average Spaniard's concerns as the complex issues of *El sentimiento trágico de la vida* (1913; Eng. tr., Tragic Sense of Life, 1921) and *La agonía del cristianismo* (1924).

The desire to explore the inner states of the human personality (the latter inevitably involving an analysis of one's country), is a sign of the predominant individualism. If a modernist like Baroja seems anarchistic, it is only because his extreme individualism made him see the state as the enemy and politicians as intruders on the sacred freedom of all. Angel GANIVET once stated that the ideal of all Spaniards was to carry a card authorizing them to do whatever they pleased. In literature this individualism led literally to subjectivism. In the novel, a genre usually conceived of as supremely impersonal, writers like Unamuno and Azorín infused their work with their authorial persona. The resulting tone of intimacy seems to be the most consistent characteristic of a long series of works spanning 30 years, from Azorín's *La voluntad* (1902) to Unamuno's *San Manuel bueno, mártir* (1933; Eng. tr., St. Emmanuel the Good, Martyr, 1956) and from Antonio Machado's *Soledades* (1902; Solitudes) to *Ríos que se van* (posthumous, 1975; Rivers That Pass), written by Jiménez in the last years of his exile.

The modernists successfully cultivated all literary genres, including the theater. Jacinto BENAVENTE, who won the Nobel Prize for Literature in 1922, wrote plays marked by their brilliant exoticism as well as rural dramas in which the interest in personal conflicts far exceeds any interest in social conflicts. He was especially successful in his satire of the bourgeoisie, delivered in over 50 comedies consisting largely of wit and conversation, but which lack passion and a traditional hero. Under Gregorio's name—and once in semisecret collaboration with Jiménez—María and Gregorio MARTÍNEZ SIERRA wrote fanciful plays that strike us today as somewhat dated. They, or rather Gregorio, also wrote the lyrics for several compositions by the musician Manuel de Falla (1876–1946). Martínez Sierra was more inclined to experiment as a director than as an author, and it was he who first produced and named a drama by Federico GARCÍA LORCA, *El maleficio de la mariposa* (1920; Eng. tr., The Butterfly's Evil Spell, 1953). Unamuno and Azorín both tried their hand at the theater with experimental plays not always understood by the audience. Some of them are as characteristically modernist as Unamuno's *El otro* (1932) and Azorín's trilogy, *Lo invisible* (1927), influenced by Maurice MAETERLINCK, whom Azorín had translated in his youth. Death enters the scene, and although she is invisible, becomes the protagonist.

Valle-Inclán's plays were pronounced unperformable in his own time. He is nevertheless the most interesting modernist playwright and also the one who drew the finest line between the dialogued novel and the drama. Several works that could be labeled novels he called comedies, although he qualified them as "barbarous." In fact, they are easy to stage. Although his early comedies are weakened by an excessive indulgence in ornamentation, Valle-Inclán evolved a genre in which the tragic mixes with the grotesque. He created a technique of expressionistic distortion that he called the *esperpento,* a form of distancing that allowed him to demonstrate more profound truths than are ordinarily revealed by more realist works.

No one wrote plays as original and exciting as Valle-Inclán's during the first 30 years of the century, but the Spanish scene was dominated by Benavente and other playwrights whose main concern was to please a very undemanding public. The brothers Serafín and Joaquín ÁLVAREZ QUINTERO and Pedro MUÑOZ SECA also produced many easily digestible works. The former were successful because of their sentimentalism and presentation of the then popular stereotyped images of Andalusia. Muñoz Seca created *astracanadas,* comical plays that did not exclude the absurd as long as it was funny. His *La venganza de don Mendo* (1918) has become a classic example of the comic parody. In inventing the "grotesque tragedy" that touched the very essence of the tiny dramas of daily life, Carlos ARNICHES went beyond his contemporaries. He knew how to dramatize minor incidents and characters whose insignificant and even ridiculous nature did not, however, mean that they were incapable of feeling and suffering. Some of his themes, such as the female essence defined as hope against all despair, were later treated by Federico García Lorca, and Arniches's version is not less sensitive than the Granadan poet's. When he overcame the *costumbrismo* of his early works and turned to sad or sentimental farce, Arniches was acclaimed by the best critics, especially by Ramón PÉREZ DE AYALA, who considered him superior to Benavente. All Madrid began to speak (and some Madrileños still do) a language that was as much an invention of the playwright as it was a reproduction of the characteristic neighborhood speech of the city.

Costumbrismo and intellectualism blended in the works of Pérez de Ayala, Gabriel MIRÓ, Manuel AZAÑA, and other novelists. Their works are characterized by stylization and the ideal of creating beautiful prose. Because it was sometimes too beautiful, however, the style interfered with the message and distracted the reader. Some pages by Miró and Ayala seem too heavily adorned, making the latter's work seem hermetic and the former's, as Ortega y Gasset observed, too dazzling. This group of novelists descends directly from Azorín, and its members can create memorable figures and even decisively change one's way of seeing literary types. Even the strongly characterized Don Juan figure in Ayala's hands—partly due to the influence of the physician-writer Gregorio MARAÑÓN—loses his traditional status as a prototype of satanism and masculinity and appears as an equivocal and hardly virile figure. The theme and character of Don Juan also appear in Unamuno, Azorín, and others, following

the same degrading trend. A contemporary of these writers was Eugenio D'ORS, a philosopher, historian of culture, and art critic, who acquainted Spain with the most interesting artists from Paul Cézanne onward.

The avant-garde began in Spain with Ramón GÓMEZ DE LA SERNA. A man of unbridled imagination, Ramón tirelessly produced prose of all sorts: essays, novels, countless articles, biographies, autobiographies, and theater. All his works have the imprint of his very personal style, called *ramonismo* and characterized by a cultivation of the outrageous for its own sake, ceaseless inventiveness, and an imagination that transforms everything it touches. The most pure and original of his inventions is what he called the *greguería,* a brief phrase offering to the reader in metaphorical form unexpected perceptions of objects. If the avant-garde is, above all, adventure, renewal, the desire to be ahead of the crowd and to alter the rules of the game by using subversive and disturbing techniques, few personify the concept more perfectly than Ramón. Nor was he free of that touch of extravagance that seemed to accompany the avant-garde explosion in Europe. He even lived in the turret of a house with a mannequin, the muse of the future.

Because of his own uncontrolled exuberance and almost excessive originality, however, Ramón could not be part of a group, let alone its head. One moment he would gravitate toward futurism, and the next moment he would repudiate it. Since it was pluralist, a succession of impulses toward change that circulated in different directions, the avant-garde in Spain had to await Vicente Huidobro's (1893–1948) arrival in Madrid to become an organized movement. The visit of this Chilean writer, who with Pierre REVERDY had founded creationism in France, encouraged poets of the stature of Juan LARREA and Gerardo DIEGO to join the avant-garde and stimulated in Madrid and Seville the development of ultraism, the only purely Spanish literary movement of this type. It was a curious individual whose literary origins were in modernism, Rafael CANSINOS ASSÉNS, who oriented the movement in its early phases. He was interested in all kinds of literary experimentation and, like Ramón Gómez de la Serna, tried his hand at almost every genre. He brought together a number of writers who wanted to do new things without knowing very well how to go about it. The word "ultra" declared their intention of going beyond the generally accepted literary conventions, but neither in the ultraist "Manifesto" written by Guillermo de TORRE nor in the works that he and others published was it apparent in what direction they were going. Ultraism will be remembered as an innovating force more than for the texts it left. Although Cansinos Asséns figures among its founders, as does the Argentinian Jorge Luis Borges (1899–), it would be inaccurate to call him an ultraist. His novel *El movimiento V.P.* (1921; The V.P. Movement) is clear evidence of his differences with the school that he himself helped to establish and with those who did not unconditionally accept his leadership.

Among the poets, José MORENO VILLA first followed the paths of the European avant-garde. When he presented *El pasajero* (1911; The Traveler), Ortega y Gasset praised its novelty. With his light and ingenious touch, Moreno Villa treated poetry like a complacent lover or made it into a dance. *Jacinta la pelirroja* (1929; Jacinta the Redhead) is a typically graceful work. His poems are lyrical games, admirable in their perfect phrasing and highly innovative. None of this is easy to find in Unamuno or in Machado, not even in Juan Ramón Jiménez who, like Moreno, and during the same years, lived in the

Residencia de Estudiantes in Madrid, where this and other cultural movements originated.

Futurism and dadaism did not put down roots in Spain and their impact was not great, whether they came directly from Russia, Italy, and Germany, or through the echoes of these movements in France. Surrealism, a later arrival, reached the editors of the *Gaceta de arte* in Tenerife and, in a much more diffuse way, was adopted by some of the poets of the Generation of 1927. One finds in this group's poetry nothing similar to the defense of automatism in literary expression or to the negation of rational control as proclaimed by André Breton. In Spain surrealism never became an orthodoxy or a discipline such as it was in France.

At the same time, the best of the Spanish avant-garde reflected the oneiric tendencies of surrealism and the desire to glimpse the underside of reality, which they hoped the subconscious would reveal. They searched there for clues absent in the light of consciousness. Freud's writings contributed to this interest, but they were not the sole determining force. Other major forces in shaping the poetry of the Generation of 1927 were the example of Juan Ramón Jiménez, who had entered his poetic vocation like a monk taking vows; the leadership of José ORTEGA Y GASSET; the rediscovery of Luis de Góngora's baroque poetry, culminating in Dámaso ALONSO's masterful commentary on the occasion of Góngora's tricentennial, in 1927; and later, the discovery of the great English and German poets, such as Gerard Manley Hopkins and Friedrich Hölderlin.

José Ortega y Gasset, director and founder of the *Revista de Occidente* (1923–36), welcomed these poets and published some of their most important books, as well as the prose of their most distinguished contemporaries. They appeared in the collection called *Nova Novorum,* which, along with the poetry series published by Juan Ramón Jiménez in the collection *Indice* and those that appeared as a supplement of the Málaga journal *Litoral* (1926–29), created the impression that something significant was happening in Spanish letters.

The prose writers of this period chose to follow diverse directions. In addition to Pedro SALINAS's Proustian *Vísperas del gozo* (1926; On the Eve of Joy) and the humorous and ironic inventions in *Pájaro pinto* (1927; Painted Bird) and *Luna de copas* (1929; Moon of Hearts) by Antonio ESPINA, there was Benjamín JARNÉS, perhaps the most personal among them, whose novel *El profesor inútil* (1926; The Useless Teacher), a small book of impressions, reduces the plot to practically nothing, replacing it with passages of delicate introspection. Ortega diagnosed this literature as "dehumanized," but a more accurate term would be "intellectualized." It was an intellectualization that excluded too much, but, in the case of Jarnés, it is clearly traceable to a current whose best-known representative was at that time Jean GIRAUDOUX.

Some younger dissidents like Carranque de Ríos (1902–36) were barely esteemed in their own day and are hardly remembered now, in spite of works like Carranque's *Cinematógrafo* (1936), which attempted the fusion of the Baroja novel with new narrative modes. In the years between the wars the novelists then called "social novelists" shared the limelight with the writers of erotic novels. The intellectualization of the "nova novorum" gave way in the socially oriented writers to a political motivation that they affirmed in public as well as in their work. Joaquín Arderíus (1890–1969) used the novel as a weapon in his fight to reform a corrupt society, and Ramón J. SENDER thought social criticism more important than imaginative invention. They considered aestheticism

to be unacceptable and incompatible with the moralism that attracted them.

The poets of the Generation of 1927, united by friendship and therefore sometimes clannish in their literary activities, must be seen for what they were: very different personalities with distinct poetic styles who appeared on the literary scene during the 1920s. Between 1923—when Pedro Salinas's *Presagios* was published—and the beginning of the Civil War in 1936, they presented a united front reinforced by what Albert Thibaudet called *de soutien* criticism. While this type of supportive criticism gave absolute praise to the members of the group, it often ignored the work of others. The case of Gerardo Diego's anthology *Poesía española contemporánea* (1932), limited to the group and to those they recognized as predecessors, is an extreme example of that tendency. Other poets active at that time, such as Antonio Espina and Juan José DOMENCHINA, were no less original, although perhaps less successful than the Generation of 1927. Acting as a group, under the intelligent direction of Salinas, the writers anthologized in 1932 chose their precursors well and gave Spain the poetry it needed, not in competition with but in consonance with Unamuno, Machado, and Jiménez. Friendship does not mean conformity, and while some of the group, like Federico García Lorca and Rafael ALBERTI, combined a popular taste with an inclination toward experimentation, others, like Vicente ALEIXANDRE and Luis CERNUDA, wrote fables of light and dark. Some, like Gerardo Diego, alternated inventiveness with traditional forms, while Jorge GUILLÉN engaged in the construction of one of the most extraordinary monuments of Spanish poetry of all time, an incredible undertaking in which the exaltation of life is accompanied by lamentation over the horrors of the contemporary world. If, on referring to the majority of these poets, the key words to describe their mood are anguish and despair, none would be better to synthesize Guillén's attitude than hope.

The prose writers did not present a united front as the poets did. Welcomed like the poets to *Revista de Occidente* and to *La gaceta literaria* (1927–32), a magazine founded by Ernesto Giménez Caballero (1899–) with Guillermo de Torre as secretary, they published there and in the newspapers successively under Ortega's influence, among them *El Sol, Crisol, Luz,* and *Diario de Madrid.* Ortega's journalistic and essayist activities were many, and he made a great contribution to the knowledge and diffusion of the works that marked the new literary direction within and outside of Spain. The essay and literary journalism reached their heights in this period, and from Unamuno and Ortega to the youngest of the avant-garde writers, few avoided the temptation to participate. Azorín, Jarnés, DÍEZ-CANEDO, and Salinas are known as much for their essays as for their creative works. The quality of some of their essays vies with that of their best work in other genres, and they were largely responsible for the revitalization of literary criticism. This criticism began, paradoxically enough, with a philosophical text, Ortega's *Meditaciones del Quijote* (1914).

Cultural activity was the first victim of the Spanish Civil War (1936–39). The division of the country into two halves that, at least for a moment, seemed to be identifiable as libertarianism and tradition, had its repercussions among the writers. There were not many who identified with Francisco Franco's cause, and there were more than a few who, in the course of the Civil War, opted for exile. After the war, the cultural life of the country slowly got back on its feet and, even more slowly, reincorporated the exiled writers. It became apparent very soon that, as

Unamuno had predicted, the conquered had not been convinced. First, a poetry of guarded protest emerged, then novels that implicitly contradicted official declarations and depicted a very different reality. Later, university groups and small theater companies staged the first plays of those playwrights "exiled" within the country, and, when censorship permitted it, something of what was then being done on European and North American stages. It was a slow process, a daily struggle to broaden the mental horizons of the Franco regime. While some poets grouped themselves around the name of the 16th-century poet Garcilaso de la Vega and wrote personal poetry in which collective problems were absent, others, above all in the provinces, came nearer to socially inspired creations that recorded their disagreement with, and, where possible, protest against the status quo.

Unamuno and Antonio Machado had died, victims of a conflict that had situated them, if only for a short while, in different camps. Like Salinas and Guillén, Jiménez was living and writing in the United States, welcomed by American universities. Mexico, Argentina, and other countries became the homes of Spanish exiles. Of the poets from the modernist period, Manuel Machado and Eduardo MARQUINA lived on in Spain, as did the old avant-gardists Diego, Aleixandre, and Alonso. Two books, *Sombra del paraíso* (1944; Shadow of Paradise) and *Hijos de la ira* (1947; Children of Rage) decisively influenced the younger poets. Aleixandre, author of the first, advised them and welcomed them to his home, which was frequented by many during the sad decade of the 1940s. Aleixandre set forth in that book a vision of the triumph of light, while Alonso, the author of the second, cried out in disgust and anger against the misfortune of being a man in a world full of misery.

Manuel Machado and the *Musa musae* academy he founded served to bring together writers who had been separated by politics. At the end of the Civil War, the young writers of 1936 emerged as the heirs of the exiles. Others joined them in the following year: in poetry, José HIERRO and José Luis HIDALGO, and in the novel, Carmen LAFORET and Camilo José CELA. Cela's *La familia de Pascual Duarte* (1942; Eng. tr., *Pascual Duarte's Family*, 1946) not only presented an image of reality that counterbalanced the official version; its harsh, direct style puts the reader in immediate communication with the writer. The words of the criminal protagonist represent a confession of actions that are understandable as effects of the atmosphere of cruelty and misery in which he was brought up. This work and *Nada* (1945; Nothing) by Carmen Laforet served as the bridgehead for the writers who during two decades were to evolve the so-called social novel as a means of bearing witness to events. The fiction written by exiles during the same period was also a testimonial. These books filtered into Spain and were greeted with great curiosity, as well as suspicion on the part of the establishment. Max AUB's *Campo cerrado* (Closed Field) was published in Mexico, in 1943. Francisco AYALA's *La cabeza del cordero* (1949; The Lamb's Head) and Arturo BAREA's *La forja de un rebelde* (1951; The Forging of a Rebel) both appeared in Argentina. Ayala's narratives surpass the testimonial and transcend the mire of political partisanship thanks to his commitment to good writing, something to which other writers, such as Barea, seemed indifferent.

The first indication that fantasy was again reclaiming its rights was Rafael SÁNCHEZ FERLOSIO's appearance on the literary scene with *Industrias y andanzas de Alfanhuí* (1951; The Labors and Fortunes of Alfanhuí), an enchanting little book that contrasted sharply with the predominant popularism. The novelist permitted himself the freedom of mixing the ordinary with the extraordinary, or, rather, that of erasing the frontiers between them, making the impossible seem not only possible but even natural and plausible. This is the moment of passage to new narrative dimensions, the point at which the novelist feels freer, untied from that fidelity to realism that marked and limited his predecessors. *Fiesta al noroeste* (1953; Festivity in the Northwest) by Ana María MATUTE is another example of inventive agility, of an imaginative stance, and of the creation, as in *Alfanhuí*, of a subject in which the referential element plays a secondary role. This tendency had a refreshing effect on the stifling atmosphere of a realism that was too limited to sociopolitical concerns.

The best poetry had been untouched from the beginning by this limitation. Neither those who directly fought or suffered in the War, like Leopoldo PANERO, Luis ROSALES, Gabriel CELAYA, and Ildefonso M. GIL, nor the victims of its aftermath, like Hierro, Blas de OTERO, and Hidalgo, maintained an attitude of total social commitment. Their poetry was always a creation of personal experiences that were not subordinated to their original context, although of course they did derive from it. There were those who, calling themselves "social poets," seemed to condemn out of hand whoever did not subscribe to their beliefs. And although, for obvious reasons, there can be no novel or poetry that is not in some sense social, that label was actually appropriate for characterizing the tendency toward political commitment in the first two decades of Franco's rule. León FELIPE said that when the exiles left, they took song with them. Be that as it may, it soon returned to speak of the pain of the poor and the rage of the oppressed, to talk of love, death, Spain, and God in accents that, though eternal, seemed new. The boy who "walked his sadness" in the jail where Hierro was confined; the old chestnut seller who heroically lived out her poverty in Panero's tender reflection; the house lit up by a love captured by Rosales's vision; the empty fields inhabited only by God, as Luis Felipe VIVANCO discovered; the dead who beckoned to Hidalgo from the shadows; the sad and beautiful country that Eugenio de Nora envisioned; emotions willing to name themselves in Gil's words; the special children who dream or are dreamt of in Julio Maruri's poetry; Vicente GAOS's somber archangels; and many more figures and inventions, bore witness to the fact that poetry was there, as certain of itself as the times were uncertain.

The decade of the 1950s brought together those who had stayed and those who had left. Jorge Guillén's and Luis Cernuda's presence began to be felt. In recent years Cernuda's work had become the embodiment of the rebellion against things Spanish. This found an echo in those who, for one reason or another, and sometimes without any reason, thought of themselves as victims of the oppression denounced by Cernuda. Suddenly Juan Ramón Jiménez's *Espacio* appeared, written in Coral Gables, Florida. Here poetry erases distance and annuls time, creating a poetic object that, like pure consciousness, is at once stillness and motion, perceptual intensity and discursive fluidity. During this period the journal *Insula* (1945 to the present) was the exiles' principal means of communication with the Spanish reader.

These, then, were the signs of change. Books of essays came from the outside, and some, like those of Américo CASTRO, imposed a revision of the habitual ways of approaching Spanish history. His studies represented a radical divergence from criteria and principles that had been perfunctorily accepted until then. In the 1960s it was clear that certain writers coming to the forefront were chronologically and spiritually removed from the Civil War and, perhaps more importantly, from the writing techniques of their predecessors. A discernible desire to become up-to-date runs through the novel, the theater, and literary criticism. The linguists "arrived," bringing the belief that their methods could contribute to the solution of some problems of literary criticism, which had always been frustrated by the difficulty, if not the impossibility, of achieving results of unquestioned validity and, therefore, of general acceptance. Ramón MENÉNDEZ PIDAL's group was followed by investigators who, though trained by their predecessor, also acquired other techniques and explored other possibilities. Fernando Lázaro Carreter (1924-), for example, moves freely from philology to poetics and from criticism to theory, following a tendency that is very generalized today.

The theater of Alfonso SASTRE and Antonio BUERO VALLEJO has, of course, political overtones, more muted in the latter's work. Miguel MIHURA's comedies of delicate humor and poetic fantasy were contemporary to that drama. By the 1960s, José RUIBAL had attempted to create a theater that cultivated paradox and the absurd. It has been staged less frequently than it deserves because of mental sloth rather than censorship. In the theater, as in the other genres, there has been a perceptible shift toward ever greater imaginative freedom. The novel has been perhaps the genre most affected by the change, with the "social" novels of the immediately previous period falling into excessive and unearned discredit. Novelists like Juan GOYTISOLO, José CABALLERO BONALD, and Antonio FERRES, who had by this time written works as acclaimed as *El circo* (1957; The Circus), *Dos días de setiembre* (1962; Two Days in September), and *Tierra de olivos* (1964; Land of Olive Trees), respectively, started on the route of experimentation. They now write from very different points of view.

One cannot categorize the present literary panorama without remembering that the precedents for the experimental novel are as clear as those of the social novel. The pendular movement never stops: when the pendulum is on one side, we can expect its natural motion to swing it to the other. Two novels, *El Jarama* (1956; Eng. tr., *One Day of the Week*, 1962) by Rafael SÁNCHEZ FERLOSIO, and *Tiempo de silencio* (1962; Eng. tr., *Time of Silence*, 1965) by Luis MARTÍN SANTOS, stand on the dividing line. The first is a lesson of coherence in the structural relation between language and plot, and the second presents an impressive thematic association between life in the modern city and the descent into hell, using the Orphic myths to show how and where the social cancer proliferates. Afterward, the pendulum swung closer to the experimental side, as is evidenced by a long series of works. While the latest novels of Miguel DELIBES are, of course, an obvious proof of this fact, Juan BENET has gone farthest toward perfecting an elusive and cryptic fictional style. The decade of the 1970s is Benet's, because of the considerable resonance of his words. In *Un viaje de invierno* (1972; A Winter Journey) the text achieves a mythopoetic intensity in which tensions shift from the character to the text. The result is an enigmatic and very exciting novel. Benet's work has found an echo in other writers who share the same lucid passion.

In these decades the poets had gone on ahead, as one would expect, loosening the bonds that they felt limited their creative freedom. Although politically committed, they wished to be artistically free. The best poetry of the first postwar decades had, as we saw, claimed this freedom. Claudio RODRÍGUEZ, José Angel VALENTE, and Angel GONZÁLEZ, among others, began writing poetry in the 1950s. In their separate and individual evolutions they share the demand that their work embody the irony, artistic grace, and hope necessary for the expression of their ideas. One of Rodríguez's books, *Alianza y condena* (1965), declares in the title itself what is surely the desire of many: condemnation of all that blocks the light and pollutes the air. Perhaps the most outstanding quality of these poets, now in the plenitude of their talent, is their moral dimension. As for Jiménez years before, ethics and aesthetics are for them inseparable. When he renounced his chair to protest the dismissal of three university professors in 1963, José María VALVERDE declared: "Without ethics there is no aesthetics."

It is not enough for these authors to write poetry: they must also question themselves incessantly about the what and the how of this exercise, the what pointing toward the reason for writing and the how toward the way to do it. Angel González indirectly suggested the answers to these questions in the titles of two of his books: *Sin esperanza, con convencimiento* (1961; Without Hope, Convinced) and *Palabra sobre palabra* (1968; Word Upon Word), his collected poems. These are key expressions, for by putting aside all grandiloquence they indicate an attitude and a mode of creation shared by his contemporaries. Writing is a question of conscience. One writes because a firm but disenchanted voice emerges from one's conscience with something to say. The poet who is a "tower of God"—a fabulator of shadows, a voice of his people, a bard, an entertainer—is a far cry from this. The task that awaits him now is just that, a task and not a mission: to construct a well-made object that concedes to form the value necessary for intuition to attain its full significance, without yielding in the process to the temptation of formalism.

See: S. H. Eoff, *The Modern Spanish Novel* (1961); A. del Río, *Historia de la literatura española,* vol. 2 (1963); G. de Torre, *Historia de las literaturas de vangardia* (1965); E. Díez-Canedo, *El teatro español de 1914 a 1936,* 4 vols. (1968); E. de Nora, *La novela española contemporánea* (1969); D. Alonso, *Poetas españoles contemporáneos* (1969); L. F. Vivanco, *Introducción a la poesía española contemporánea* (1971); R. Gullón, *Direcciones de modernismo* (1971); F. Ruiz Ramón, *Historia del teatro español,* vol. 2 (1971); E. de Zuleta, *Historia de la crítica española contemporánea* (1974); J. L. Cano, *Poesía española contemporánea: las generaciones de posguerra* (1974); G. Sobejano, *Novela española de nuestro tiempo* (1975).   R.G.

Spire, André (1868-1966), French poet and social reformer, was born in Nancy, the scion of a Lorraine industrialist. As a child, he roamed about the family factory and played with the children of the workers. At the age of 10, he entered the lycée, but by that time he had already learned two things: that life is unjust, and that one learns a great deal in a factory where the handling of tools is a precise thing that allows for no deception. Spire developed an upright and exacting nature. As a writer, his precise vocabulary was at odds with any image that was only approximate—thus his mistrust of the surrealists (*see* FRENCH LITERATURE). Regarding the inequality of social classes as unacceptable, he chose law as a career in the vain hope of cooperating in the establishment of equitable laws. He founded the Société des Visiteurs, not unlike the modern French Social Security System (except privately operated), and threw himself into the generous movement of the Universités Populaires.

Spire's enthusiasm for humanitarian activities and his subsequent bitterness and disappointment over their results were echoed in the poems of *Et vous riez* (1905; And So You Laugh), published in Charles PÉGUY's journal *Cahiers de la quinzaine*. After Lev TOLSTOY, Péguy exerted the most profound influence on him. Indeed, Spire hailed Péguy as "this conscience of the century." In *Et vous riez,* observed Edouard DUJARDIN, Spire found "his form, a nude and sober art, in which all is depth and concision." From the symbolists, Spire took on unrhymed free verse, but he found it spineless and sought a different poetic line, one that would be nonsyllabic but accented. His phonetic studies culminated in *Plaisir poétique et plaisir musculaire* (1949; Poetic Pleasure and Muscular Pleasure).

In 1902, the Office du Travail sent Spire to London to study the "sweating system." There he discovered the poorest of proletariats, the East European Jews. Yet in spite of the abject poverty, he noted, there was no illiteracy and the greatest respect for the things of the mind. Two years later, Spire discovered the work of the Jewish novelist Israel Zangwill. Already shaken by the Dreyfus Affair, Spire considered Zangwill a "revelation"; he thus became aware of his own identity as a Jew. In 1905, the year of the first Russian Revolution and the pogroms, Spire rallied to the aid of Zangwill's Jewish Territorial Organization, a group prepared to send Jews wherever they were welcome (thus differing from the Zionists, for whom Palestine was the only possible haven). Fighting with his pen, Spire composed his *Poèmes juifs* (1908; Jewish Poems, republished and enlarged in 1919 and 1959). This poetry was well received, and Guillaume APOLLINAIRE wrote: "It seems to us that your verse, whose disabused irony is so moving and so new, has the power to shake the foundations of empires." Spire subsequently published *Quelques Juifs* (1913; A Few Jews, republished in two volumes in 1928), *Les Juifs et la guerre* (1917; Jews and the War), and *Samaël* (1919). He became the principal promoter of Jewish literature in France. After the Balfour Declaration, Spire joined the Zionists and founded La Ligue des Amis du Sionisme (The League of the Friends of Zionism) and its organ, *Palestine nouvelle*. He later opposed the Nazis and the laws against Jews in France. In 1941 he became professor of the history of poetry at the New School for Social Research in New York. He published his last book, *Souvenirs à bâtons rompus* (Desultory Memories), in 1961. Spire's last years were spent in France; he died in Paris at the age of 98.

Spire's principal collections of poetry are *Vers les routes absurdes* (1911; Toward Absurd Roads), *Le Secret* (1919); *Poèmes de Loire* (1929), *Instants* (1936), *Poèmes d'ici et de là-bas* (1949; Poems from Here and Over There), and *Poèmes d'hier et d'aujourd'hui* (1953; Poems of Yesterday and Today).

See: S. Burnshaw, *André Spire and His Poetry* (1933); *Hommage à André Spire* (1939); P. Jamati, *André Spire* (1962).   T.S.

Spitteler, Carl (1845–1924), Swiss poet, novelist, and essayist, was born in Liestal, canton Basel-Land. Spitteler created an oeuvre that stands apart from the literature of his time. His preference for epic poetry was rooted in the extraordinary visual sense that retained his childhood experiences in bright, archetypal images vividly conveyed in *Meine frühesten Erlebnisse* (1914; My Earliest Experiences) and enabled him to depict inner life through action. Spitteler combined an idealistic belief in the individual with a pessimistic view of the world. In his epic poem *Prometheus und Epimetheus* (1881; Eng. tr., 1931) Prometheus is portrayed as an autonomous individual follow-

ing only his soul and opposing the world of King Epimetheus, who submits to empty conventional values. Much of the epic's power derives from Spitteler's combination of traditional myths with his own symbolism and from his use of uninterrupted iambs. His subsequent works, of a smaller scope, include: *Extramundana* (1883), a collection of legends about the world's origin; realistic prose, such as *Conrad der Leutnant* (1898; Conrad the Lieutenant) and *Die Mädchenfeinde* (1907; Eng. tr., *The Little Misogynists,* 1923); poetry and ballads. The epic poem *Olympischer Frühling* (1900–11; Olympian Spring), written in rhymed iambic hexameters, depicts the rise of new gods to consciousness and power and describes their carefree existence, set against a background of death and cruel fate. Spitteler's autobiographical novel, *Imago* (1906), concerns the friction between society and the uncompromising artist. The novel's blend of satirical description (of the Swiss bourgeoisie) and psychological insight fascinated Sigmund Freud and Carl Gustav Jung. Spitteler's last work, *Prometheus der Dulder* (1924; Prometheus the Long-Suffering), is a new, rhymed version of his first work; Prometheus is an artist whose sufferings teach him to abandon unrestrained subjectivism. Spitteler was awarded the 1919 Nobel Prize in Literature.

See: R. Faesi, *Spittelers Weg und Werk* (1933); J. F. Muirhead, "Spitteler and the New Epic," *TRSLUK* 10 (1931): 35–57; W. Stauffacher, *Carl Spitteler* (1973).
                                                M.Bu.

Šrámek, Fráňa (1877–1952), Czech fiction writer, poet, and playwright, was born in Sobotka in eastern Bohemia. Known principally as the leading Czech impressionist novelist, he was a master of describing and suggesting the most evanescent emotions and moods. Especially in his later work, he successfully evoked the atmosphere of adolescent sexuality, its joys and sorrows, exaltations and melancholy, when the whole of nature seems to be wrapped in a mist of complete animality. Šrámek's sheer joy in instinctive animal life appealed to the generation that had just endured the horrors of World War I and then discovered, somewhat naively, that life goes on and is worth living. The chief character of his best novel, *Tělo* (1919; The Body), is a girl of strong sexual instincts and the story is largely a sensitive chronicle of the meetings and partings, vacillations and temptations of lovers, set against a lightly sketched background of war. An earlier novel, *Stříbrný vítr* (1910; The Silver Wind), largely concerned with students and the problems of puberty, is also an attack on a society that hampers the free expression of instinct, and some of Šrámek's collections of short stories and sketches, such as *Žasnoucí voják* (1924; The Perplexed Soldier), are filled with an instinctive antimilitarism that condemns war as the enemy of love and life.

Šrámek was not, however, a writer concerned with ideas. He was, even in his prose, a lyrical poet. The quintessence of his mood is possibly found in his small collections of poetry, among which *Splav* (1916; The Weir) is the most memorable, and in his lyrical plays, where he depicts young people in the throes of sexual passion with delicacy and compassion. Two of his plays, *Léto* (1915; Summer) and *Měsíc nad řekou* (1922; The Moon above the River), were successfully produced on the stage. Šrámek was a specialist of narrow range, but he was also a genuine artist who failed only when, as in certain of his later books and plays, he grappled with contemporary problems and attempted ambitious, complex compositions.

See: J. Knap, ed., *Kniha o Šrámkovi* (1927); J. Durych in *Ejhle, člověk* (1928); F. X. Šalda in *Časové a nadčasové*

(1936); J. Knap, *Fráňa Šrámek* (1937); F. Buriánek, *Národní umělec Fráňa Šrámek* (1960). R.W.

Stadler, Ernst (1883-1914), German poet and scholar, was born in Colmar, Alsace. He studied Germanic literature in Munich and Strasbourg. With René SCHICKELE, he founded the periodical *Der Stürmer* in 1902. In 1903 he studied at Oxford, some years later began lecturing on Germanic literature at Strassbourg, and in 1910 was appointed professor at Brussels. He was killed in World War I.

Besides well-articulated articles on literature in 1910, he wrote two books of poems; the first, *Praeludien* (1904; Preludes), is not very important, but the other, *Der Aufbruch* (1915; The Uprising), is one of the most beautiful and disciplined examples of the early German expressionistic style. Although the work was influenced by Walt Whitman and Emile VERHAEREN, Stadler added to their *strömendes Weltgefühl* (streaming world-feeling) the deep mysticism of his homeland and an explosive, dynamic quality of his own. In contrast to most young expressionists, he never destroyed, but rather mastered, language with definite artistry. The visionary poem "Der Aufbruch," which gave the volume its title and in which he foresaw the war and his own death, was later regarded as symbolic of the emerging generation of expressionist poets.

See: H. Hestermann, *Ernst Stadler* (1929); H. Gier, *Die Entstehung des deutschen Expressionismus und die antisymbolistische Reaktion in Frankreich: die literarische Entwicklung Ernst Stadlers* (1977). K.Pi. rev. A.L.W.

Staff, Leopold (1878-1957), Polish poet, playwright, and translator, was born in Lvov, and died in Skarżysko-Kamienna. An outstanding representative of the "Młoda Polska" (Young Poland) tradition in his early creative period, he was infected by Friedrich NIETZSCHE's ideas about power and the special role of the outstanding individual, sometimes called "titanism," which is reflected in his first two collections of verse, *Sny o potędze* (1901; Dreams of Power), and *Dzień duszy* (1903; Day of the Soul), as well as in *Mistrz Twardowski* (1902; Master Twardowski), a verse tale. The theme of strength and self-assertion later gives way to the theme of tranquility and peace, which characterizes the greater number of poems and foreshadows the new outlook on life apparent in Staff's third collection, *Ptakom niebieskim* (1905; To the Birds of the Sky), whose title comes from Saint Francis of Assisi's sermon to the birds.

Such collections as *Gałąź kwitnąca* (1908; Blooming Branch), *Uśmiechy godzin* (1910; Smiles of the Hours), and *Łabędź i lira* (1914; The Swan and the Lyre), reflect the poet's moments of quiet joy in life, his view of life as a "pilgrimage," his varied experiences during his travels, particularly to Italy and Greece, and his fondness for antiquity. His great variety of themes found expression in a steadily improving poetic technique, which employed every possible poetic form, including the sonnet, the ballad, the elegy, and the verse tale.

After World War I, Staff continued translating from the great works of world literature, an activity he had started before the war, producing Polish versions of Greek and Latin writers, the Psalms, J. de Voragine's *Golden Legend,* the *Flowers* of Saint Francis, Michelangelo, Benvenuto Cellini, Leonardo da Vinci, Goethe, Friedrich Nietzsche, Thomas MANN, and others. He wrote dramas and again produced outstanding collections of verse, the best of which are *Wysokie drzewa* (1932; Tall Trees) and *Barwa miodu* (1936; The Color of Honey). Enjoyment of nature, pleasure in the simple tasks of everyday life, closeness to the earth, and a joyful, Franciscan acceptance of life in all its manifestations are characteristic features of Staff's poetic production.

Much of the anguish of World War II is expressed in Staff's *Martwa pogoda* (1946; A Time of Death). In his final two collections, *Wiklina* (1954; The Willow) and *Dziewięć Muz* (1958; Nine Muses), his poetic statement gains in simplicity and laconicism, concentrating its thought into a few lines, frequently no longer than four-line epigrams.

See: I. Maciejewska, *Leopold Staff*, part 1 (1965), part 2 (1973); *Słownik współczesnych pisarzy polskich,* vol. 3 (1964), pp. 192-207; J. Kwiatkowski, *U podstaw liryki Leopolda Staffa* (1966); J. T. Baer, "Friedrich Nietzsche in the Work of the Young Leopold Staff," *PolR* 15, no. 4 (1970): 64-85. J.T.B.

Staiger, Emil (1908-), Swiss literary critic and translator, was born in Kreuzlinger, canton Thurgau. For many years he was professor of German literature at the University of Zürich. Staiger gave new impulses to German literary criticism through comprehensive interpretations of individual works and a theoretical consideration of literature in connection with the existential philosophy of Martin HEIDEGGER. His book *Die Zeit als Einbildungskraft des Dichters* (1939; Time as Source for the Poetic Imagination) lays the groundwork for both concerns. Instead of relying solely on methods that are either too general (history of thought, psychology) or too restricted (positivistic biography), Staiger focuses on the text itself, although, in contrast to the New Criticism, he often uses "general" and "restrictive" methods to support his interpretations. To Staiger, close textual analysis, moving in the hermeneutic circle, leads to the comprehension of a text's specifically poetic and aesthetic features, which are ultimately rooted in time—the basic condition of human existence. In *Grundbegriffe der Poetik* (1946; Concepts of Poetics), Staiger poses an ontology of literature based on his conception of three genres (lyric, epic, dramatic) as the fundamental modes of human existence, determined by an individual's prevailing orientation toward the past, present, and future. Staiger's interpretation, as in *Die Kunst der Interpretation* (1955; The Art of Interpretation), transcends an individual work and includes more general perspectives, resulting in such separate monographs as *Goethe* (3 vols., 1952-59), *Schiller* (1967), and the historical study *Stilwandel* (1963; Change in Literary Style). In his critical prose as well as in his translations of classical Greek and Renaissance literature, Staiger presents a combination of knowledge, sensitivity, and lucid style.

See: A. Gelley, "Staiger, Heidegger, and the Task of Criticism," *MLQ* 23 (1962): 195-216; E. Jaeckle, *Der Zürcher Literaturschock* (1968); P. Salm, *Three Modes of Criticism* (1968), pp. 79-117. M.Bu.

Stancu, Zaharia (1902-74), Romanian novelist, poet, and journalist, was born in Salcia. In 1927 he founded the periodical *Azi.* Over the next 17 years, he published several volumes of verse: *Poeme Simple* (1927; Simple Poems), *Albe* (1937; Dawns), *Clopotol de aur* (1939; The Golden Bell), *Pomul roșu* (1940; The Red Tree), *Iarba fiarelor* (1941; The Magic Herb), and *Anii de fum* (1944; Years of Smoke). Stancu's translation of the Russian poet Sergey YESENIN, *Tălmăciri din Esenin* (1934; Translations from Sergei Yesenin), as well as his first novels, *Taifunul* (1937; The Typhoon) and *Tophat* (1941), also date from this period.

Stancu joined the Communist Party in the 1940s, serving as a deputy, as a member of the Central Committee and Council of State, as the general editor for literary journals, and as director of the National Theater. His anti-Fascist polemics and lampoons were collected in *Secolul omului de jos* (1946; Century of the Underdog), *Însemnările şi amintirile unui ziarist: sarea e dulce* (1955; Notes and Recollections of a Journalist: Salt Is Sweet), and *Cefe de taur* (1955; Bulls' Necks).

Stancu's major novel, *Desculţ* (1948; Eng. tr., *Barefoot*, 1951, 1971), set in early rural Romania, introduced the picaresque figure Darie, an alter ego for Stancu himself. This work won him an international reputation. From *Desculţ*, Stancu evolved an epic cycle tracing the adventures of Darie across the Balkans and into the present: *Dulăii* (1952; The Hounds), *Florile pămîntului* (1954; Flowers from the Earth), *Iarbă* (1957; Grass), *Rădăcinile sînt amare* (5 vols., 1958; Roots Are Bitter), *Clopote şi struguri* (1960; Bells and Grapes), *Printre stele* (1960; Among the Stars), *Carul de foc* (1960; Chariot of Fire), *Jocul cu moartea* (1962; Game with Death), and *Pădurea nebună* (1963; The Mad Woods). Other novels are *Ce mult te-am iubit* (1968; How Much I Loved You) and *Şatra* (1968; The Gypsy). Recent volumes of poetry are *Cîntec şoptit* (1970; Whispered Song), *Sabia timpului* (1972; The Sword of Time), and *Poeme cu lună* (1974; Poems by the Month). *Pentru oamenii acestui pămînt* (1971; To the Men of This Land) and *Triumful raţiunii* (1973; The Triumph of Reason) are collections of recent articles, essays, and reminiscences. His collected works have been published as *Scrieri* (6 vols., 1971–75). A selection of Stancu's poetry in English is available in R. MacGregor-Hastie, *Anthology of Contemporary Romanian Poetry* (1968).

Stancu's reputation as a poet rests upon his polish, as a novelist upon his mastery of new fictional techniques and effective prose rhythms. He was elected to the Romanian Academy in 1955 and was president of the Writers Union at the time of his death.

See: J. Steinberg, ed., *Introduction to Romanian Literature* (1966); A. Mitescu, "Zaharia Stancu," in *Revista de istorie şi teorie literară* (1973); V. Bugariu, *Zaharia Stancu* (1974).   T.A.P.

Stanković, Borisav (1875–1927), Serbian novelist, short-story writer, and dramatist, was born in Vranje and educated in Belgrade, where he studied law. Stanković spent most of his adult life in government service within the Serbian ministries of finance and education. In 1899 he published a collection of short stories, *Iz starog jevandjelja* (From the Old Gospel), which brought him instant recognition. He subsequently published two more collections of stories, *Stari dani* (1902; The Old Days) and *Božji ljudi* (1902; God's People), in which he clearly manifested his life-long interest in the semi-Oriental ambience of his native Vranje. His stories show how the clash of the new and old orders resulted in suffering, passion, and nostalgia for the old, patriarchal way of life, swept away by the steady pressure of social, economic, and cultural changes.

These motifs are even more apparent in Stanković's longer and more famous works, the play *Koštana* (1902) and the novel *Nečista krv* (1911; Tainted Blood). *Koštana* deals with the mesmeric influence of a young gypsy singer upon a whole group of men from Vranje, among whom the merchant Mitke stands out. Mitke, consumed by a melancholy pain over his lost youth, rebels not only against stifling social norms and customs but even against the very transience of life itself. *Nečista krv* presents the

material and moral decay of a once wealthy and powerful commercial family, now compelled to agree to the marriage of their only daughter to a mere boy from a clan of crude peasant upstarts. But the novel also concerns the spiritual conflict between legitimate personal aspirations and the social code, a struggle in which the young, beautiful Sofka is an innocent victim. Stanković was particularly successful in depicting secret human yearnings and passions, sensual weaknesses, and psychological whims. His characters are always on the verge of an emotional outburst, since they are constantly prevented by either custom or pride from reaching that which they crave.

Although Stanković is a realistic writer, his mode of expression is complex and emotionally charged, containing a wealth of romantic, symbolist, and naturalist characteristics.

See: J. Dučić, "Borisav Stanković," in *Srpski književni glasnik* 19 (1907): 26–33, 114–20; J. Skerlić, *Srpski književni glasnik* 24 (1910): 629–31; V. Gligorić, *Bora Stanković* (1936); B. Novaković, "Stanković u srpskoj umetničkoj prozi," *Susreti* (1959), pp. 77–107.   N.M.

Starobinski, Jean (1920–), Swiss literary critic, was born and educated in Geneva, where he completed studies in literature and medicine. Since 1958 he has taught at the University of Geneva. Like his masters Marcel Raymond and Georges Poulet, Starobinski interprets the act of literary creation as an existential project of self-discovery and self-realization, embodied in the dominant thematic patterns and motifs of an author's works. But his approach is more phenomenological and dialectical than that of the first-generation critics of consciousness. According to Starobinski, consciousness grows out of sense perception and the psychological interplay between the self and others. The tragedy of consciousness is that it remains unable to overcome the blindness inherent in its own subjectivity. The dominant motif and metaphor of Starobinski's critical studies (which have concentrated mainly on the 18th century) is that of the look or glance by means of which a writer, or his protagonist, seeks to pierce the veil of the subjectivity of consciousness, and to actualize the ideal relationship in which a true self and a true world become transparently open to one another. From *Montesquieu par lui-même* (1953; Montesquieu as He Saw Himself) and *Jean-Jacques Rousseau: la transparence et l'obstacle* (1957; Jean-Jacques Rousseau: Transparency and Obstacle), to *L'Oeil vivant* (1961; The Living Eye), and *L'Invention de la liberté, 1700–1789* (1961; Eng. tr., *Invention of Liberty*, 1964), he has probed the diverse forms this quest has taken and, conversely, the masks and other visual stratagems designed by the disillusioned hero to combat the hostile and potentially annihilating glance of others. In *La Relation critique: L'Oeil vivant II* (1970; The Critical Connections: Living Eye II), Starobinski pursues the search for a distortion-free and mutually illuminating interplay between critic and author, and advocates a mobile critical stance that can shift from close identification to objective distance.

See: S. Lawall, "Jean Starobinski," in *Critics of Consciousness* (1968), pp. 165–86.   G.R.Bl.

Stefánsson, Davíð (1895–1954), Icelandic novelist, playwright, and poet, was born in the Eyjafjörður district of northern Iceland. His parents were a prosperous farming couple—the father, a member of the Althing (Parliament); the mother, a clergyman's daughter—and his maternal uncle was a noted collector of folktales and poems, genres of literature Stefánsson was later to draw upon in regard to both motifs and verse forms.

Stefánsson was enrolled (1908-11) in a secondary school at Akureyri near his home, but illness caused a long interruption in his education; so he began to read literature on his own, including the the works of the Swedish poets Gustaf FRÖDING and Erik Axel KARL-FELDT. Later, he stayed in Copenhagen (1915-16), where he became acquainted with a number of young poets and also met Sigurður NORDAL, who encouraged him to write poetry and also arranged to have his first poems published in magazines in 1916. After returning to Iceland, Stefánsson enrolled at the Reykjavík gymnasium in 1916, and his first book of verse, *Svartar fjaðrir* (Black Feathers), appeared in 1919, the year he matriculated. With this work, Stefánsson, along with Stefán frá Hvítadal, who had published *Söngvar förumannsins* (1918; The Songs of the Vagabond), launched a new period in Icelandic verse writing.

Stefánsson's verse forms were lighter and freer than those of the earlier tradition, although he still maintained the time-honored alliteration and rhyme patterns. Rebelling against the puritanical mores of his elders, he preached erotic freedom and gave free rein to emotion in poetry that worshiped life, a marked departure from the chiefly intellectual outlook of such older poets as Einar BENEDIKTSSON and Stephan G. STEPHANSSON.

Following the publication of *Svartar fjaðrir*, Stefánsson spent considerable time in Denmark, Germany, and Italy; his second book, *Kvæði* (1922; Poems), contains several poems on themes related to his experiences during that overseas stay. Stefánsson took up residence in Akureyri in 1925 and worked there as a librarian for a long time. He lived in Akureyri until his death, although he made several more trips to foreign parts, including one to the Soviet Union in 1928, and until after 1930 radical views played some role in his poetry. In his works from this period, he attacks the church and clergy as well as social injustices; he is a spokesman for the weak and oppressed, yet makes clear his scorn for any appeal to mob psychology—and romantic hero worship can be detected on frequent occasions.

Stefánsson enjoyed enormous popularity throughout his career, no doubt because of his simple poetic forms and his choice of topics that appealed to the general public. His literary output is impressive: 10 books of verse by him were published from 1919 to 1966; he wrote four plays, the first two of which—*Munkarnir á Möðruvöllum* (1926; The Monks at Modruvellir) and *Gullna hliðið* (1941; Eng. tr., *The Golden Gate*, 1967)—are on folklore themes, whereas *Vopn guðanna* (1944; The Weapons of the Gods) has a biblical theme and *Landið gleymda* (1956; The Forgotten Land) deals with the return of Nordic men to Greenland.

His novel entitled *Sólon Islandus* (2 vols., 1940) portrays the life of an Icelandic drifter in the 19th century, a man of obvious artistic talent for which he has no outlet because of social circumstances; this protagonist hence seeks refuge in delusions of grandeur and achieves a degree of stature in spite of many humiliations.

Stefánsson's verse clearly shows the influence of Icelandic folk poems and, to an extent, also of Slavic folk poetry, which he knew through translations by Thor Lange. As for the impact of foreign literary figures on him, Gusta Fröding appears to be the most important, especially in regard to musical effects, although influences by neoromantic poets, such as Viggo STUCKENBERG and Sigbjörn OBSTFELDER, can also be detected.

Stefánsson's poetry is rich in contrasts: starkly drawn juxtapositions of joy and sorrow, pride and humility, the romantic life of the wandering minstrel and the farmer bonded to the soil. Above all else, however, his works are songs of praise to life and love, although philosophical and religious concerns became increasingly apparent in the later writings. Stefánsson's poetry is best described as a link between traditional Icelandic convention and the freer modernistic forms that came to predominate after 1940.

See: T. Guðmundsson, "Davíð Stefánsson, *Helgafell* (1955): 26-37; *Skáldið frá Fagraskógi* (1965). S.S.H.

Stefanyk, Vasyl (1871-1936), Ukrainian short-story writer, was born in the village of Rusiv. While studying medicine at Cracow University (1892-1900), Stefanyk met some Ukrainian and Polish modernist writers and began writing stories about peasant life, probing the agony beneath the grim reality of human existence. His style was innovative and his stories very short, often based on a dramatic dialogue and written with a strong admixture of local dialect. Stefanyk's works, such as "Maria" (1916) and "Syny" (1922; Eng. tr., "Sons," 1947), show strong national feeling. His best stories are in his first collections, *Synya knyzhechka* (1899; The Blue Book) and *Kaminny khrest* (1900; Eng. tr., *The Stone Cross*, 1971). The story "The Stone Cross" is a little masterpiece, and has been used for a film scenario. Later collections are *Doroha* (1901; The Path), *Moye slovo* (1905; My Word), and *Zemlya* (1926; The Earth). Stefanyk's radical political views rarely invaded his art. The current Soviet interpretation of his work is therefore not very satisfactory. Stefanyk was a highly original talent and the greatest modern Ukrainian writer of short stories, unique in their laconic, dramatic qualities. He had a strong impact on the younger generation of writers.

See: D. S. Struk, *A Study of Vasyl Stefanyk* (1973).
G.S.N.L.

Stehr, Hermann (1864-1940), German poet and novelist, was born in Habelschwerdt. He started with a number of tales, for example, *Der Graveur* (The Engraver) and *Meicke der Teufel* (Meicke the Devil), both 1898, and *Der Schindelmacher* (1899; The Shingle Maker), and was quickly labeled a naturalist. But even his earliest works reveal a much more intense reliance on the psychological qualities of his characters than on their physical environment. Any disturbance in emotional or intellectual balance seems to have attracted him more than social or political problems, perhaps because he felt his real strength lay in an almost pedantic but often penetrating power of psychological analysis. His favorite theme in these years concerned the explosion of pent-up emotions, usually revenge or hatred dating back to some gross injustice.

This pyschological naturalism was gradually superseded by the religious and mystic tradition of his native Silesian world. Although one would expect the experience of a mystic union with God to find its chief outlet in brief lyrical utterances, Stehr succeeded in permeating even long novels with his religious fervor. The irresistible growth of the divine spark in people, its flickering and extinction, or its triumphant expansion into heavenly light—these are the themes of Stehr's second period, in such novels as *Leonore Griebel* (1900), *Der begrabene Gott* (1905; The Buried God), *Drei Nächte* (1909; Three Nights), and *Geschichten aus dem Mandelhause* (1913; Stories from the House of Almonds). They all purport to show that a genuine desire to establish contact with God enriches even the most humble existence.

Der Heiligenhof (1918; The Court of Saints) marks the creation of at least one figure filled to the brim with divine powers. But the result is achieved at the expense of a normal human existence. Helen, the daughter of a wealthy farmer, attains an almost saintlike life. She is born blind and is, it first appears, beyond all medical help; shut off from the visible world, she turns inward to grasp and absorb God. Other characters around her, spurred on by her vision, catch an occasional glimpse of this higher world. Yet with all these honest efforts the novel ends on a tragic note; saintly Helen is rudely awakened into normal life through a sudden realization of her own erotic nature. As an immediate result of this, she gains her normal sight, only to lose her hold on the supernatural. Engrossed in desire, she finds that her only defense against such degradation is suicide. Stehr retold the same story from the viewpoint of the man who became chiefly responsible for Helen's downfall in *Peter Brindeisener* (1924). The conclusion remains the same; Peter, who once longed to be initiated through Helen into the mysteries of true existence, also ends by destroying himself.

Discovering that passive resignation is the result of religious intellectualism, of a tendency to experience religion in terms of philosophy instead of apprehending it by action, Stehr began to experiment with a new set of literary characters who, rather than speculating about religious matters, endeavor to incorporate them in the conduct of their daily lives. His popular violin maker stories, *Der Geigenmacher* (1926; The Violin Maker) and *Meister Cajetan* (1931), are attempts in this direction. The religious yearning of these craftsmen is no less intense, but its progress is no longer recorded in the form of philosophical definitions but of manual skill and production; the quality of the instruments created in the workshop is now made to reflect and measure the growth of inner perfection.

With his last significant novel, *Nathanael Maechler* (1929), Stehr came much closer to the real absorption of *vita contemplativa* in *vita activa;* in words reminiscent of Goethe's *Faust*, he voices his belief that God looks with favor on the incessant striving of people in the realm of human interests, provided it be directed toward the promotion of goodwill among human beings and filled with infinite gratitude toward God. A simple and, for that reason, perhaps all the more convincing enactment of mystic revelations in everyday life is found in *Gudnatz* (1921), a story that treats the conversion of a war profiteer into a fervent practical Christian.

Stehr's poems illustrate in briefer compass the same development of his novels. They likewise show his aversion to being satisfied with the impressionistic apprehension of the surface of things, his ability to fathom mystic experience and to create a language capable of expressing religious ecstasy, and his final conviction that religion is essentially a practical concern and a powerful incentive to social action.

See: W. A. Reichart, "Hermann Stehr and His Work," *PQ* 10 (1931): 47–61; G. Blanke, *Hermann Stehrs Menschengestaltung* (1939); K. S. Weimar, *The Concept of Love in the Works of Hermann Stehr* (1945); F. K. Richter, *Hermann Stehr* (1964).   H.Bo. rev. A.L.W.

Steiger, Anatoly Sergeyevich (1906–44), Russian émigré poet, was born into an aristocratic Russian-Swiss family. Although he lived outside Russia in difficult circumstances, he was proud of his lineage and his title—baron. Steiger was consumptive and died in a Swiss sanitarium for tuberculosis. He wrote four slender volumes of verse, the last published posthumously in 1950, *Dvazhdy dva chetyre* (Twice Two Is Four). It contains the best of his

life's work, barely 40 small pages of modest verse, expressing the simplest truths in the sparsest possible language. Encouraged by Georgy ADAMOVICH to write in this way, Steiger is possibly the poet most influenced by the former's poetic doctrine known as the "Parisian note." Steiger was capable, in his radically understated verse, of expressing the dull terror of the everyday, of loneliness and alienation in day-to-day reality. Often his brief poems turn on a single, telling word expressing a single understated irony. For all the restraint and sparseness of his very small number of poems, their quality provides assurance that Steiger will not be forgotten as a Russian poet, minor but genuine.   H.W.T.

Steinarr, Steinn, pseud. of Aðalsteinn Kristmundsson (1908–58), Icelandic poet, was born at Laugaland in northern Ísafjarðarsýsla, in northwestern Iceland, but was raised in the Dalasýsla district, where as a youth he had JÓHANNES ÚR KÖTLUM for a teacher. The son of destitute parents, Steinn Steinarr received little formal education, attending a folk high school for only one year. He was physically handicapped, too, and thus poorly suited for hard work. By 1930 he had moved to Reykjavík, which was then in the throes of an economic depression that had brought heavy unemployment and untold sufferings for working-class people.

These external circumstances, both his own and the disorder of the social scene that he witnessed, are strongly reflected in Steinn Steinarr's first book of verse, *Rauður loginn brann* (1934; The Red Flame Blazed). This book contained many poems sympathizing with the cause of proletarian laborers and bitterly attacking those in power. As for form, the poems are mostly traditional, although there are a few examples of free verse with concentrated images. Influences from both Jóhannes úr Kötlum and Tómas GUÐMUNDSSON are visible, for instance, in the frequent use of paradoxes. The satirical and cynical tone characterizing so many of the poems was to remain the hallmark of Steinn Steinarr's poetry until his death.

His second book, *Ljóð* (1937; Poems), marked the beginning of a new phase in his writing. The intense social criticism was giving way to a more introverted state of mind and a concern with philosophical issues and private psychological problems. With this book, Steinn Steinarr stated a definite view of the human condition, that life had no purpose. For him, the center of gravity had shifted from social reality to philosophical questions. The red flame of revolution conceived of earlier had yielded to a white fire of skepticism and a sense of futility—a stance that was symbolically reiterated in the very titles of Steinn Steinarr's next two volumes of verse: *Spor í sandi* (1940; Footprints in the Sand) and *Ferð án fyrirheits* (1942; Journey without a Promise).

Although most of the poems appearing in the two last-mentioned books had traditional form, Steinn Steinarr is, nevertheless, the most important of the pioneers who introduced modernistic verse in Iceland. His innovation is especially seen in his concentration of images, his crafting of a new poetic idiom, and his use of fresh symbols and nonlogical associations.

This development reached its highest point in *Tíminn og vatnið* (1948, Eng. tr., *Time and Water*, 1972), a lengthy cycle of poems written just after Steinn Steinarr had become acquainted with modern Swedish verse and had also grown especially fond of *The Waste Land* by T. S. Eliot. The imagery of this last work also shows a certain resemblance to the effects of modern abstract painting. Although its outward form is simplicity itself, *Tíminn og vatnið* is complex and difficult to fathom. It is built up from three thematic elements—the poet's ego, time, and water—but their symbolic values defy precise interpretation. There are also several mythological motifs. Taken as a whole, this cycle of poems, Steinn Steinarr's swan song, may be regarded as a sort of final settlement of accounts. The poet has in the end, through his art, made peace with the world of futility and thus united himself with eternity.

See: K. Karlsson, Introduction to S. Steinarr, *Kvæðasafn og greinar* (1964), pp. vii–xxvii; P. Carleton, "Tíminn og vatnið í nýju ljósi," *Tímarit Máls og menningar* (1964), pp. 179–91; P. M. Sørensen, "Bygging og tákn," *Skírnir* (1970): 129–52; S. S. Höskuldsson, "Þegar Tíminn og vatnið varð til," *Afmælisrit til Steingríms J. Þorsteinssonar* (1971), pp. 155–95.　　　S.S.H.

Stephansson, Stephan Guðmundsson (1854–1927), Icelandic-Canadian poet, was born at Kirkjuhóll in Skagafjöður, of poor but intellectually alert parents who tried to eke out a living in three different cottages in Iceland before they moved to the United States in 1873. Here Stephansson took land three times: in Wisconsin, in North Dakota, and finally in Alberta, Canada, near Markerville, where he lived as a hard-working farmer until his death in 1927. He married in 1878 and had eight children, losing two sons before he died. He never had any formal education, but as a boy in Iceland he had read the sagas, which he retained ever after in memory, as his poems show. From the 1890s onward his poems appeared in Icelandic periodicals and weeklies in Winnipeg. His first volume of poems was *Á ferð og flugi* (1900; On the Go), but most of his poems were gradually published in the collection *Andvökur* (6 vols., 1909–1938; Wakeful Nights), the name referring to the fact that he composed most of his poetry while others slept. Other publications were *Kolbeinslag* (1914; Lay of Kolbeinn), *Heimleiðis* (1917; Homeward Bound), about a trip to Iceland made on the invitation of grateful countrymen, and *Vígslóði* (1920; On the War Path), about World War I. His letters were published in Iceland.

Stephansson never assimilated the spirit of English literature, although he read it. He saw the New World from the point of view of the Icelander and of the pioneer. The attitude was, perhaps, one-sided, but certainly not a narrow one, and it was sustained by the unremitting idealism and manliness of the poet. He was an ardent liberal and a thoroughgoing individualist—a king in his farmer's realm. Related to this are his anticlericalism, even atheism, and his hatred of all capitalistic exploitation, whether it was that which he saw rampant in the United States or that in the imperialistic wars (notably the Boer War) of Great Britain. Nor had he any sympathy for either side in World War I, and he said so in terms that might have cost him dearly had his language been better understood by his ruling fellow Canadians.

But Stephansson was not only a prophet crying in the wilderness. He was also a poet sensitive to the shifting seasons and to the charms of nature even in his adopted land. He has described the prairie, the wide, checkered cornland of the Middle West, and the Canadian Rockies in magnificent poems.

Yet above all he was an Icelandic poet. His homeland is crystallized in beautiful visions in his poems, and figures from the old sagas and romances haunt his mind and take on new symbolic value in his poetry. These and the language had been the sole heritage of the boy when he left his fatherland. They were destined to bear fruit a thousandfold in his new environment. Stephansson is rec-

ognized as one of the greatest poets that Canada has fostered.　　　S.E.

Sternheim, Carl (1881–1943), German dramatist, social critic, and novelist, was born in Leipzig of a prominent family. Sternheim's comedies mercilessly satirize the philistinism of the German bourgeoisie before and after World War I. In an 11-play cycle entitled *Aus dem bürgerlichen Heldenleben* (From the Lives of Bourgeois Heroes), Sternheim presented a series of greedy, obsessed, and grotesque characters. In *Die Hose* (1911; Eng. tr., *The Underpants*) he created Theobald Maske, the first of his shallow, materialistic, and sexually preoccupied antiheroes. The other major plays in this series are *Die Kassette* (1912; Eng. tr., *The Strongbox*), *Bürger Schippel* (1913; Citizen Schippel), and *Der Snob* (1914).

In order to underline the grotesque quality of his characters, Sternhein created an almost cold-blooded language of staccato diction that approaches eccentricity. Often called the German Molière, Sternheim represents the high point of social satire in German theater during the first two decades of the 20th century. His works are part of dramatic expressionism but represent the more cynical phase of the movement, which has its visual counterpart in the paintings of George Grosz and Otto Dix.

Sternheim's language forms a link between the plays of Frank WEDEKIND and Bertolt BRECHT. More than any other German literary figure, Sternheim anticipated the type of mentality that, he felt, would propel Adolf Hitler into power. His essays and social commentary appeared in two volumes, *Tasso oder die Kunst des Juste Milieu* (1921; Tasso or the Art of the Juste Milieu) and *Berlin oder Juste Milieu* (1920; Berlin or Juste Milieu). His play *Die neue Sachlichkeit* (1926; The New Objectivity) provided the name for the "cool," detached spirit that became associated with the Weimar Republic. In 1930, Sternheim married Pamela Wedekind, the dramatist's daughter. He exiled himself from Nazi Germany and died in Belgium after wandering throughout Europe.

See: H. Karasek, *Carl Sternheim* (1965); R. Billetta, *Sternheim-Kompendium* (1975); W. Freund, *Die Bürgerkomödie Carl Sternheims* (1976).　　　S.G.

Stevo, Jean (1914–74), Belgian poet, essayist, art critic, and artist, was born in Brussels, where he spent most of his life. As early as 1931, Stevo became active in the literary and artistic circles of his city. He participated in the weekly and monthly meetings of such avant-garde groups as "Le Rouge et le noir," "La Tribune des Jeunes," and "La Revue Nationale." As a member of the Belgian underground during World War II, he was awarded the medal of "Resistant civil." A long-time friend of James Ensor, he published in 1946 *James Ensor*, the first substantial monograph on the painter, who was especially famous for his grotesque masks, often symbols of corruption and evil. Other monographs on Belgian artists followed—in 1962, on Marie Howet, and in 1968, on Paul Maas. Profoundly influenced by the surrealist movement, Stevo edited in 1968 a special issue of *L'Art belge* devoted to René Magritte. He also maintained a lengthy correspondence with the dramatist Michel de GHELDERODE. Stevo's study of Ghelderode's personality and work, *Office des Ténèbres pour Michel de Ghelderode* (1972; Requiem for Michel de Ghelderode), received the Leopold Rosy Prize of Belgium's Royal Academy of French Language and Literature in 1973. Stevo's poetic and graphic expressions are closely linked. Three volumes of poetry, *La Chanson Grise* (1962; The Gray Song), *La*

Nuit de Hollande (1967; The Dutch Night), and *America America* (1969) reveal a world of dream and sensitivity that is, in some respects, reminiscent of that of Jean COCTEAU, who prefaced *La Nuit de Hollande* with an ink drawing. But Stevo's sense of the color and power of words is all his own, and his feeling for the macabre and the bizarre unfolds in a collection of short stories, *Haute Solitude* (1967; Deep Solitude). His literary and artistic contribution has been best summed up by Philippe JONES: "When did he gather his first sea-shell which, in the words of Valéry, 'captivates one's gaze and lifts it to an undefinable perfect whirlpool'? If he found it on the beaches of Ensorian memory, the spiral sets him on the path to 'cosmogonies' wherein the rhythm of slack or taut strokes are the graphic expressions of the poems orbiting in his heart." Stevo's wide culture, his extensive travels, and his friendships with, among others, COLETTE, Curzio MALAPARTE, Jean Cocteau, and Paul Delvaux are reflected in numerous articles in French and Belgian periodicals and in his short films, notably the one about Edgard Tytgat, *Le Simple Bonheur d'Edgard Tytgat* (1952; The Simple and Happy Life of Edgard Tytgat), and the film about Paul Delvaux.

See: R. Merget, "Jean Stevo," *Revue Nationale* (1969); J. Vovelle, *Le Surréalisme en Belgique: histoire du mouvement surréaliste en Belgique* (1969).   O.F.

Stigen, Terje (1922-), Norwegian novelist and short-story writer, was born on the island Magerøy in northern Norway. When he was 10, he moved with his family south to Oslo, where he has lived since. Although his first novels reveal his ability to handle action deftly, there is little depth or psychological penetration to his character development. Yet strong lyrical overtones and a capacity to engage the reader in a good story are already apparent in these early novels. These qualities are the main ingredients in the book that was Stigen's breakthrough, *Vindstille underveis* (1956; Eng. tr., *An Interrupted Passage*, 1973), which is more a short-story collection in the tradition of Boccaccio than a novel. As they move by ship southward along the northern Norwegian coast, a group of people entertain each other with fantastic tales, stories that in the end turn out to be curiously connected.

In the more recent novels, *Stjernøy* (1960; Star Island) and *Det flyktige hjerte* (1967; The Fickle Heart), Stigen depicts the people of northern Norway through the eyes of history. In these novels, which are unconfined by modern realism, Stigen can give his fantasy free rein. But underneath his lyrical gaiety and vivid imagination lie the more serious themes of love—a saving, but also deformed and therefore destructive, force—and of man as a marionette in the hands of fate. A volume of Stigen's short stories, *Glasskulen* (1963), appeared in English as *The Crystal Ball* (1971).   K.A.F.

Stramm, August (1874-1915), German poet and dramatist, was born in Münster, Westphalia. He attended school at Eupen and at Aachen. His Catholic mother wanted him to study for the priesthood, but his Protestant father insisted on his entering the federal service. He enrolled at the universities of Berlin and Halle and in 1909 received a Ph.D. degree. He later held the position of postal inspector in Bremen and Berlin and still later was called into the national postal ministry. In 1914, as a captain in the reserve, he was called to duty and in 1915 died on the Russian Front.

For 20 years no publisher accepted his work. In 1913, however, a friend, Herwarth Walden, published the drama *Sancta Susanna* in *Der Sturm,* and Stramm became a leader in the "Sturmgruppe," a literary circle representing the extreme in expressionism. In the next year his love songs appeared, *Du* (You), and the dramas *Die Haidebraut* (Eng. tr., *The Bride of the Moor,* 1914), *Rudimentär,* and *Die Unfruchtbaren* (The Barren). Three more plays were published in 1915: *Erwachen* (Awakening), *Kräfte* (Powers), and *Geschehen* (Happenings). Stramm's war verses were published posthumously with the title *Tropfblut* (1919; Dripping Blood). His plays are so-called *Schreidramen,* consisting to a great extent of ecstatic ejaculations and outcries. His lyric poetry, too, often takes this bizarre form, usually in lines of one-syllable words. These expressionistic explosions are genuine poetic phenomena in literary history. A selection of his poems appeared in 1914 in English translation with the title *The Song of a May Night.*

See: H. Jansen, *Der Westfale August Stramm als Hauptvertreter des dichterischen Frühexpressionismus* (1928).   F.Sp. rev. A.L.W.

Strauss und Torney, Lulu von (1873-1956), German poet and prose writer, was born in Bückeburg. She was married to the publisher Eugen Diederichs in 1916. Like the great 19th-century poet Annette von Droste-Hülshoff, she was firmly rooted in the soil of her homeland. Her works are strangely unrevealing as to her emotional experiences and her inner life, and even her lyrics are likely to assume an objective, balladlike quality. In her narrative prose her heroes are sparing of words: a thought wells up, a long-harbored desire becomes a firm resolve, and its sole expression is a firmer setting of the lips while the averted eyes gaze off into the distance. An earthbound realism, which depicts every significant detail, is coupled with a visionary intensity that would pierce this earthly veil.

Her first published work of importance is a collection of peasant tales, *Bauernstolz: Dorfgeschichten aus dem Weserland* (1901; Peasant Pride: Village Tales from the Weserland). A second collection of short stories, *Sieger und Besiegte* (1909; Victors and Vanquished), contains her finest and most powerful novella, "Auge um Auge" (Eye for an Eye). A heroic and tragic touch characterizes her longer novels, the first of which is *Luzifer* (1907), in which a 13th-century heretic forsakes the trinitarian doctrine for a belief in four gods, the fourth of which is Lucifer, the innocent force of evil inherent in all life. Her next novel is *Judas* (1911), set in the Westphalian countryside in the days when the theories of the French Revolution stirred the peasantry to revolt. *Der jüngste Tag* (1921; Judgment Day), her masterpiece, has its setting in the same landscape in the days of the Anabaptists.

The verse of Lulu von Strauss und Torney ranks with her prose fiction. In her collected poems and ballads, one group bears the significant title "Mutter Erde" (Mother Earth). Earth is our mother, from whose womb we spring and to whose womb we return. The majestic song of the beeches in "Grüne Zeit" (Green Time) marks the pinnacle of her lyric art. Her ballads place her among the very first masters of this form. Many have a historical setting and deal with great heroic figures. The collected poems and ballads were published in 1919 in *Reif steht die Saat* (Ripe Stands the Grain). The final enlarged collection of her verse bears the title *Erde der Väter* (1936; Earth of Fathers).   F.Br. rev. A.L.W.

Streuvels, Stijn, pseud. of Frank Lateur (1871-1969), Belgian (Flemish) novelist and short-story writer, was born in Heule. His mother was the sister of the poet Guido

Gezelle. For 15 years, Streuvels was the Avelghem village baker. In 1906 he moved to Ingooigem, from then on devoting himself entirely to writing. In his novels, Streuvels depicted the life of the Flemish peasantry with the plastic power of a Bruegel. Although he participated in some of the activities of the "Van Nu en Straks" movement, Streuvels neither really belonged to any school nor did he proclaim any theory of art; he just wrote with enthusiasm for his native Flanders. Nature is the dominating power in all his stories. Everything that happens to his characters is predetermined by their subjection to that force. Hence Streuvels is a fatalist. Nature's dark, incalculable designs shape man's destinies, especially in Streuvels's earlier tales, *Lenteleven* (1899; Spring Life), *Zomerland* (1900; Summer Land), *Zonnetij* (1900: Sun Tide), *Doodendans* (1901; Dance of Death), and the novel *Langs de wegen* (1902; Eng. tr., *Old Jan,* 1936). The influence of August STRINDBERG and Fyodor DOSTOYEVSKY no doubt colored his pessimism. In later stories, however, a more serene mood prevails. In *Stille avonden* (1905; Quiet Evenings), the tone becomes more compassionate and tender. Disillusionment gives way to a contented acceptance of life, and although nature still dominates, it is no longer an inexorable nemesis. In the novel *De Vlaschaard* (1907; The Flax Field), the story unwinds with the rhythm of the seasons. Against the backdrop of the sky, the characters move charged with passions whose explosion is an intrinsic part of the cosmic drama. The work possesses a biblical grandeur. *De Vlaschaard* has been considered one of the great novels of the 20th century. Indeed, Streuvels is a great narrator, but only in his narrowly restricted genre.

Between 1926 and 1930, Streuvels experienced the second creative phase of his life. During that period, he wrote one of his best novels, *Het leven en de dood in den ast* (1926; Life and Death in den ast). The hallucinating story takes place in a chicory drying house where three men must keep a fire going for a whole night. Caught in a sphere where dream and reality intermingle, they stand as unconscious witnesses to the great tragedy that is life: while they are dreaming and watching, they do not realize that the tramp, who has sought refuge in their workshop, is about to die.

Streuvels is uniquely the epic poet of the Flemish soil. Yet within that range, he is also one of the most moving writers of his generation.

See: A. de Ridder, *Stijn Streuvels, zijn leven en zijn werk* (1908); A. Demedts, *Stijn Streuvels* (1955); R. van de Linde, *Het œuvre van Streuvels, sociaal document* (1958; 1964).   A.J.B. rev. M.-R.L.

Strindberg, August (1849–1912), Swedish dramatist, novelist, short-story writer, poet, social critic, essayist, pseudoscientist, and painter, was born in Stockholm. Long periods of his life were embittered by the hostility of his countrymen, which forced him to extended stays abroad. In his choice of subjects, however, he clearly favored his native country and its scenery, people, and history. Another of his subjects remained readily accessible and was kept under constant watch—himself. Few modern writers have been so persistently autobiographical as Strindberg, and few indeed have reached the same depth of self-analysis. (In this article, references will be made only to current translations of Strindberg's works.)

Strindberg's four-part autobiography, *Tjänstekvinnans son* (1886–87; Eng. tr. of pt. 1, *The Son of a Servant,* 1967), strongly emphasizes his father's economic difficulties and the social problems of a mésalliance. Yet research has shown that Strindberg's parental home was not poor in a strict sense and that in time it became affluent. Nevertheless, young Strindberg's hypersensitive personality may have been permanently marked by sibling rivalry and the premature death of his mother in 1862. The heavily patriarchal atmosphere of the home may, in combination with its hectic pietism, also have been detrimental to the formation of a balanced personality. Strindberg's education was typical of the Swedish upper middle class of the period. The major achievement of his early period was a powerful historical prose drama, *Mäster Olof* (1872; Eng. tr., *Master Olof,* 1959), about the venerable Swedish Protestant reformer Olaus Petri. He is already a typically Strindbergian divided soul, whose strength is sapped by introspection. Stylistically, the play marked a new departure in Swedish literature. A strong influence from Shakespeare as interpreted by Georg BRANDES, the Danish critic, can be felt. Thematically, Henrik IBSEN (*Brand*) and Henry Buckle, the historian, had produced powerful impulses.

Toward the middle of the 1870s, Strindberg gave up his more or less bohemian style of life and entered a professional career, becoming a librarian. In 1877 he married Baroness Siri von Essen. In *Le plaidoyer d'un fou,* written in French in 1887 and published in a pruned version (1895; Swed. tr., *En dåres försvarstal,* 1920; Eng. tr., *A Madman's Defense,* 1967), Strindberg set out to tell the story of his first marriage in a bitterly vindictive mood. Throughout a human document of obsesssive intensity, the novel presents a narrator thrown between extremes of feeling, adoration, and revulsion, an ambivalence from which there is no escape. *Röda rummet* (1879; Eng. tr., *The Red Room,* 1967), a loosely jointed novel, on which Strindberg's reputation was long to rest in Sweden, castigates the flaws of contemporary society. It is far from a simple work, balancing as it does social criticism and a concern for the development of its central character, the sensitive, high-minded Arvid Falk.

Upon publication of *Röda rummet,* Strindberg found himself the leader of a group of radical young writers. Before long he made contacts with leading Scandinavian writers and critics. More rewarding, perhaps, were his friendships with progressive artists and painters. The more conservative of the cultural establishment by now sensed in him a dangerous disciple of Emile ZOLA. But Strindberg was not yet profoundly touched by naturalism, as is evident in the allegorical fairy play *Lycko-Pers resa* (1882; Eng. tr., *Lucky-Per's Journey,* 1965) and the historical fantasy *Herr Bengts hustru* (1882; Sir Bengt's Wife), in spite of the latter's concern with current social issues, such as woman's role in marriage. A good many of Strindberg's convictions at this time derive ultimately from Jean Jacques Rousseau and even appear to be founded on some natural religion. The writers still most dear to him were characteristically Charles Dickens, Victor Hugo, and Hans Christian Andersen. *Det nya riket* (1882; The New Kingdom) is a pamphlet of breathtaking brilliance and recklessness. Nettled by adverse criticism of his popular social history of Sweden, *Svenska folket* (1881–82; The Swedish People), he made an all-out attack on sacred institutions of the nation along with easily identifiable living persons. Overnight the author had made a host of influential enemies. Feeling compelled to leave Sweden with his wife and children, he launched on a career as a free-spoken European writer. In spite of immense productivity, however, he soon ran into financial difficulties, and the situation was further worsened by growing marital stress.

The process of liberation thus begun was followed up during the next few years. *Utopier i verkligheten* (1884;

Utopias in Reality) reflects his newly found interest in practical socialism and pacifism. It also contains a remarkable study of a mental breakdown and subsequent reintegration. All these works made an impact, but the scenes of marital life presented in *Giftas* (1884–86; Eng. tr., *Getting Married*, 1973) made the author notorious and fair game for merciless attacks from outraged members of the Swedish establishment. Legal proceedings were taken against him for alleged blasphemy. Although acquitted and much against his will cast in the role of tribune, Strindberg suffered great strain during the Stockholm trial of 1884, which proved harmful to his mental equilibrium. An immediate result, according to the autobiography, was his conversion to atheism, but other effects were also evident. Expressions of embittered antifeminism became rife, and there were signs of uncontrollable paranoiac ideas and psychic rigidity. In judging Strindberg's experiments with attitudes, it should be noted that, even as a professed naturalist, he was primarily a man of imagination. He was also a man engaged in a never-ending struggle to keep himself and his family afloat. While battling with the dragons of the mind, he could not afford to refrain from turning even his most private, obsessive ideas to literary profit. The writing of *A Madman's Defense* is the signal instance, but similar processes can be studied in the composition of the dramas on which his international fame has long rested. With his plays *Fadren*, *Fröken Julie*, and *Fordringsägare* (1887–88; Eng. tr., *The Father*, *Miss Julia*, and *Creditors*, 1965), Strindberg took strides against that naturalism in the theater heralded some years earlier by Zola. Yet Strindberg's brand of naturalism failed to satisfy the master as, to him, it fell short of the ideal of objectivity. Strindberg's strength resided rather in his grasp of factors such as tempo, rhythm, dialogue, and the presentation—not of well-defined characters but—of suffering souls, self-reflecting egos caught in the torment of inner division. All three plays are tragedies with a marked concentration on one theme. In *The Father* doubts about his paternity drive a man to mental collapse. Here the unconscious agent is the wife bent on her maternal rights. In *Miss Julie* an aristocratic girl is forced to suicide after giving herself up to her father's valet, who proves the stronger person. In *Creditors* a sensitive artist is shattered by a merciless shredding of protective illusions, the agents in this instance being his wife and her ex-husband.

After completing *Miss Julie*, Strindberg wrote his famous Preface, which reads like a personal manifesto for the naturalist theater. Acting on his own recommendation, he proceeded to write a group of one act plays, *Paria* (1889; Eng. tr., *Pariah*, 1969), *Den starkare* (1889; Eng. tr., *The Stronger*, 1964), and *Samum* (1889; Eng. tr., *Simoon*, 1969). These plays were written with Antoine's Théâtre Libre, the Paris experimental stage, in mind. They involve two or three actors only; in the case of *The Stronger*, concentration is carried to extremes, one of its two roles being silent.

Strindberg's naturalistic fiction includes two novels set in the Stockholm archipelago, the Swedish scenery he knew and loved best. *Hemsöborna* (1887; Eng. tr., *The Natives of Hemsö*, 1965) is Strindberg's most popular work among his countrymen. His other novel, *I havsbandet* (1890; Eng. tr., *By the Open Sea*, 1913), is Strindberg's most ambitious attempt at naturalistic prose, at least on the level of description. With regard to plot and presentation of character it again reflects that perennial dilemma: the Strindbergian divided self. It may be argued that the analytic detachment aimed at in the style is not ideally suited to the tragic theme, the destruction of a

self-sufficient superman in isolation. As the most Nietzschean of Strindberg's works, the novel marks a turning point. There had already been signs that he was wearying of his naturalistic method. *Skärkarlsliv* (1888; Life in the Skerries), a collection of short stories, had contained an example of deliberate transcendence of dogmatic naturalism in "Den romantiske klockaren på Rånö" (The Romantic Sexton at Rånö).

Deprived of his children through his divorce from Siri von Essen in 1891, Strindberg soon found himself in unproductive isolation. Yet in *Bandet* (1892; Eng. tr., *The Bond*, 1963), he wrote a powerful play of a more conventional type, a courtroom drama moving over the painful ground of divorce proceedings. Other plays of the period, including the comedy *Leka med elden* (1892; Eng. tr., *Playing with Fire*, 1964), show a general decline in intensity. By the end of 1892, Strindberg had stopped writing for the theater. Instead he took up painting and gave his mind to the study of natural science, chemistry, and biology in particular. The same year he settled in Berlin, where, for a short time, he became the center of a group of artists and writers, among them Edvard Munch, the Norwegian painter, and Stanisław PRZYBYSZEWSKI, the Polish novelist and playwright. These Bohemian days and the early part of his subsequent marriage (1893–97) to the young Austrian journalist Frida Uhl, his second wife, form the subject matter of the autobiographical sketch *Klostret* (1966, Eng. tr., *The Cloister*, 1969).

Settling in Paris in 1894, Strindberg appears to have sought liberation from all emotional ties, his devotion to his chemical studies becoming by now obsessive. During the next few years, commonly referred to as his "*Inferno* crisis," he was often a victim of penury and sometimes of ill health, but he was not in a state of unrelieved misery. A legend that dies hard has it that he was positively insane. Instead it would be true to say that he was actively exploring new dimensions of experience and esoteric knowledge, including alchemy, occultism, speculative philosophy, and Catholicism.

Of great importance for Strindberg's spiritual reorientation, in some ways a return to the religious concepts of his childhood, was his discovery of Emanuel Swedenborg, the 18th-century mystic and visionary. The reintegration of his personality, partial though it may seem, which was completed by 1898, was reached only after severe attacks of anxiety and paranoiac episodes culminating in 1896. Even then Strindberg did not give up trying to grasp, record, and work through his experiences. Working from entries in his "Occult Diary" and from copies of letters, but relying chiefly on his memory, he reconstructed the course of the crisis in *Inferno*, again writing in French (rev. ed., Paris, 1966; Swed. tr., 1897; Eng. tr., *Inferno*, 1962) and its sequel *Légendes* (Paris 1967; Swed. tr., *Legender*, 1898). The moral and intellectual reorientation described in Strindberg's confessions also restored a productive trust in his imagination, so that once more he found himself carried on the crest of a wave of powerful inspiration. Innovations in dramatic technique and expression introduced to convey his new vision made him a forerunner of the expressionists and even of the absurdists.

The decisive step in this development was taken as early as 1898 with the first part of the *Till Damaskus* trilogy (1898–1901; Eng. tr., *To Damascus*, 1965). Using material from his second marriage, it reenacts a spiritual journey in dramatic form. Whereas earlier critics (for example, Martin Lamm) emphasized the autobiographical nature of the play, later opinion (for example, Gunnar Brandell) has stressed the symbolic elements of the action and explored their relation to the central character. With regard to form, the intense visuality of Strindberg's drama of conversion and its striking contrapuntal arrangement of scenes are distinctive innovations. Other plays in a similar vein are *Advent* (1898), a Swedenborgian fantasy, and *Påsk* (1900; Eng. tr., *Easter,* 1963), a mystery play with a contemporary, middle-class setting, bringing one of Strindberg's most imaginative evocations of character in the girl Eleonora. In *Kronbruden* (1901; The Bridal Crown) and *Svanevit* (1901; Eng. tr., *Swanwhite,* 1963), the lyrical and legendary inspiration is obvious. A connection with the drama of Maurice MAETERLINCK can also be observed.

In 1899, Strindberg settled again in his native Stockholm. Returning at the same time to historical themes, he launched on an enterprise comparable only to Shakespeare's pageant of English history. The highlights of the series, which ranges from the Middles Ages to the 18th century, are *Folkungasagan* (Eng. tr., *The Saga of the Folkungs,* 1959), *Gustav Vasa, Erik XIV* (1899), and *Kristina, Karl XII, Gustav III* (1899; Eng. tr. in *Historical Plays,* 5 vols. 1955–59).

Plays retaining traces of the realistic manner, though basically akin to the symbolic dramas, are *Brott och brott* (1899; Eng. tr., *Crime and Crime,* 1963) and *Dödsdansen I–II* (1900; Eng. tr., *The Dance of Death,* 1963). In this evocation of marital hell, Strindberg does not side with any one party but examines the condition of the love-hate relationship with compassion. Formally, the first part offers an example of the circular plot.

In what is often regarded as Strindberg's most original work, *Ett drömspel* (1901; Eng. tr., *A Dream Play,* 1965), the loosely constructed plot is a calculated strategy serving the central symbolism. The effect of the whole is to convey the fleetingness and insubstantiality of human existence.

The powerful inspiration behind the luminous Daughter of Indra of *A Dream Play* was the young actress Harriet Bosse, who became Strindberg's third wife in 1901. Paradoxically, she has also been divined behind the destructively capricious title part of *Queen Christina.* The disillusionment of this marriage was the cause of Strindberg's greatest suffering. An insight into the mind of the aging Strindberg is offered in *Ensam* (1903; Eng. tr., in *Inferno, Alone, and Other Writings,* 1968), a meditative book written when the marriage was already drawing to its close. With the publication of *Ur ockulta dagboken* (1963; Eng. tr., *From an Occult Diary,* 1965) and Strindberg's letters to Harriet Bosse, a strange private world was made available to readers of our days. Here the reader is brought into contact with a mind that transformed even daily routine and trivial occurrences into poetry.

The harsh reception given his satirical, even misanthropic novel *Götiska rummen* (1903; The Gothic Rooms) revived the iconoclast of former days. Strindberg once more turned upon the literary establishment, which was by now in part recruited from his former friends. *Svarta fanor* (written 1904, pub. 1907; Black Banners) is possibly his most devastating attack on live targets.

A similar acerbity is often sensed in what must be regarded as the major achievement of Strindberg's later years, the "Chamber Plays" written for his own Intimate Theater at Stockholm in 1907. In the memorandum addressed to its actors, *Öppna brev till Intima teatern* (1908; Eng. tr., *Open Letters to the Intimate Theater,* 1968), however, he appears as an open-minded, positive theorist of dramatic art.

Most effective among these concentrated plays and most often performed is *Spöksonaten* (1907; Eng. tr., *The* *Ghost Sonata,* 1964), the third in the series. It can be said to enact the Swedenborgian notion of the unmasking of the soul after death; only here the condition is death in life. The play has a Buddhist implication: life is illusion and death the only source of hope. The action comes to rest upon a projection of the Swiss painter Arnold Böcklin's *Toteninsel.* The most accessible of the chamber plays is *Oväder* (1907; Eng. tr., *The Storm,* 1964), comparable even to late Ibsen or Maeterlinck in its melancholy realism. *Brända tomten* (1907; Eng. tr., *The Burned House,* 1962) is again more misanthropic, and *Pelikanen* (1907; Eng. tr., *The Pelican,* 1962) offers a terrible study of cannibalistic motherhood and final purgation through fire. The dramatic epilogue, *Stora landsvägen* (1909; Eng. tr., *The Great Highway,* 1963) is Strindberg's final cathartic self-portrayal. Formally an allegory, it is not free from personal rancor but also allows one to overhear the voice of the dramatist in his moral struggle with himself until the end.

Prompted by a desire to clarify his intentions, Strindberg compiled over the last five years of his life a collection of aphoristic, meditative, and polemic prose. He called the collection *En blå bok* (4 vols., 1907–12; Eng. tr. of vol. 1, *Zones of the Spirit,* 1913). In a spate of newspaper articles, later collected in *Tal till svenska nationen* (1910; Speeches to the Swedish Nation), Strindberg took his final stand against the conservative establishment. The national division known as "the Strindberg Feud" and triggered by his "speeches" gives an idea of his impact on his countrymen (*see* SWEDISH LITERATURE). Both as a man and a writer Strindberg had too many sides, however, to be summed up in a formula. He stands for egocentric inwardness, the perilous search of a soul, and for social defiance, the breaking of images— a source of health in spite of all accusations of sickness.

Strindberg's influence abroad has for natural reasons been narrower, limited on the whole to the theater. Through the work of Max Reinhardt he became the chief inspirer of German dramatic expressionism. His importance to individual dramatists, such as Sean O'Casey, Eugene O'Neill, Tennessee Williams, Jean-Paul SARTRE, Eugène IONESCO, Harold Pinter, and Peter WEISS, has been more or less gratefully acknowledged. Recently his role as a "protagonist" in a wide psychological sense has been repeatedly emphasized, also by psychiatrists: a man often at odds with himself and his surroundings, but capable of self-analysis and able to communicate his existential situation and so to instruct. When the edition of *August Strindbergs brev,* ed. by T. Eklund (14 vols. to date, 1948–), is completed, his life will be made almost transparent. Strindberg the man comes alive in many forms, but nowhere with greater force and immediacy than in his letters. The standard edition of Strindberg's collected works is *Samlade skrifter,* ed. by J. Landquist 55 vols. (1912–20).

See: M. Lamm, *August Strindberg* (1948; Eng. tr. by H. G. Carlson, *August Strindberg,* 1971); G. Brandell, *Strindbergs Infernokris* (1950; Eng. tr. by B. Jacobs, *Strindberg in Inferno,* 1974); B. Steene, *The Greatest Fire* (1973); W. Johnson, *August Strindberg, TWAS* 410 (1976); H. Carlson, *Strindberg och myterna* (1979).

S.Å.B.

Strug, Andrzej, pseud. of Tadeusz Gałecki, (1871–1937), Polish novelist and short-story writer, was born in Lublin and died in Warsaw. Involved in clandestine patriotic and socialist activities since early youth, he was arrested several times by the Russians. In 1897 he was deported to Archangelsk for three years. After the 1905 Revolution, in which he was particularly active, Strug became closely associated with the political camp of Jozef Piłsudski. During World War I he took part in military and political combat against Russian and German occupants. While on a political mission in Russia he witnessed the Bolshevik coup. On his return home he took part in establishing Poland's first independent government. After Piłsudski's 1926 coup, Strug became one of his most outspoken critics and opponents.

Strug's most acclaimed works are based largely on his experience, activity, and intimate knowledge of the Polish socialist and liberation movement, as exemplified in his collections of short stories *Ludzie podziemni* (1908-09; Underground People), *Jutro* (1909; Tomorrow), and the novels *Dzieje jednego pocisku* (1910; A Story of One Bullet), *Odznaka za wierną służbę* (1921; The Badge of Faithful Service), and *Mogiła nieznanego żołnierza* (1922; The Tomb of the Unknown Soldier).

In the interwar period, Strug's work reflected his deep disillusionment and bitter criticism of the social reality of independent Poland. Among the novels of this period the most significant are *Pokolenie Marka Świdy* (1925; The Generation of Mark Świda) and *W Nienadybach byczo jest* (unfinished, written 1937, pub. 1968; In Nienadyby Everything is Fine and Dandy). Another series of novels and short stories deals with the crises of moral values and the social upheavals throughout the modern world. Strug denounced social and moral corruption and the exploitation and coercion of man, as well as fascism, militarism, and political oppression in the Western world and in Communist Russia: *Pieniądz* (1921; Money), *Klucz otchłani* (1929; The Key to the Abyss), *Żółty krzyż*, (1932-33; The Yellow Cross), and the unfinished *Miliardy* (2 vols., 1937-38; Billions).

See: J. Rohozinski, "Andrzej Strug," in *Obraz literatury polskiej XIX i XX wieku. Literatura okresu Młodej Polski*, vol. 3 (1973), pp. 181-222; S. Sandler, *Andrzej Strug wśród ludzi podziemnych* (1959).   S.S.

Strugatsky, Arkady Natanovych (1925-) and **Boris Natanovych** (1933-), Russian coauthors of science fiction, were born in Batum and Leningrad, respectively. They are extraordinarily popular in their native land. Their works often blend satire, detection, and adventure in a manner that Soviet critics find dangerous. Most of the Strugatskys' writings do indeed have a sociopolitical subtext that is not lost on the Soviet reader. *Trudno byt bogom* (1964; Eng. tr., *Hard to Be a God*, 1973) takes as its starting point the possibility that the Marxist theory of history is flawed. *Khishchnye veshchi veka* (1965; Eng. tr., *The Final Circle of Paradise*, 1976), an anti-Utopian novel of sorts, cautions against both a foolhardy commitment to science and the creation of a society in which everyone's material needs are satisfied. Drawing deeply on Russian folklore, *Ponedelnik nachinayetsya v subbotu* (1965; Eng. tr., *Monday Begins on Saturday*, 1977) provides a witty commentary on modern science. *Skazka o troyke* (1968; Eng. tr., *Tale of the Troika*, 1977) is a black comedy about bureaucracy. *Obitayemy ostrov* (1969; Eng. tr., *Prisoners of Power*, 1977) describes a society ruled by propaganda.   D.A.L.

Stryjkowski, Julian (1905-), Polish novelist and short-story writer, was born in Stryj. He studied Polish philology at the University of Lvov, where he received his doctorate. Stryjkowski began his literary career with the novel *Bieg do Fragalá* (1951; A Run to Fragala), devoted to the struggle of Italian peasants for their land. This view of Italy from the standpoint of social contrasts is contin-

ued in the collection of reportage and short stories *Pożegnanie z Italią* (1954; Farewell to Italy). In the novel *Głosy w ciemności* (1956; Voices in the Darkness) Stryjkowski presented a lifelike depiction of the Jewish world of a small Galician town, with its exotic folklore, language, customs, and social relations, by means of which—according to the author—he sought to "rescue from oblivion a world that had ceased to exist." In 1961 he published *Imię własne* (One's Own Name), a collection of short stories written with a highly complicated narrative structure. In 1962 there appeared *Czarna róża* (1962; The Black Rose), another novel of social customs. Stryjkowski then returned to the theme of Jewish life in his novel *Austeria* (1966; Eng. tr., *The Inn*, 1971), in which he again portrayed a small Jewish town during World War I, facing a pogrom by Cossack soldiers. This portrayal becomes a horrifying prediction of the wholesale extermination of the Jewish people during World War II. More recently, Stryjkowski has published *Na wierzbach . . . nasze skrzypce* (1974; Our Harps upon the Willows), a collection of short stories.   S.F.

Stuckenberg, Viggo (1863-1905), Danish poet, playwright, novelist, and short-story writer, was born in the Zealand City of Vridsløselille. He was a teacher in Copenhagen. Stuckenberg continued the radical trend of the breakthrough literature of the 1870s with his first work, *Digte* (1886; Poems), and two stories of disillusion and determinism. But he broke with naturalistic psychology in the lyrical drama *Den vilde Jager* (1894; The Wild Huntsman), which shows the influence of French symbolism (*see* FRENCH LITERATURE). The soul's longing to escape daily life is expressed in a series of vagabond novels and in the small philosophical tales in *Vejbred* (1899; Eng. tr., *By the Wayside*, 1917), written in beautiful rhythmic prose. Stuckenberg's own tragic marriage became the central and desperate background for the main theme of his writings: the joyfulness and final foundering of love, treated in the novel *Fagre Ord* (1895; Fair Words), in the collection of poems *Flyvende Sommer* (1898; Gossamer), and especially in his lyrical main work, *Sne* (1901; Snow), ranging from resigned everyday happiness and desperation to philosophical confession. These works illustrate Stuckenberg's final departure from the metaphysics of the 1890s. On the basis of a stoic philosophy of life, the objects around us and the self's spiritual world are accepted as the sole reality.

See: J. Andersen, *Viggo Stuckenberg og hans Samtid* (1944).   S.H.R.

Suarès, André (1868-1948), French poet, dramatist, critic, and essayist, was born in Marseille, of a family whose ancestry was probably Portuguese. A prolific writer, he was praised by such contemporaries as Paul CLAUDEL, André GIDE, and Romain ROLLAND and was awarded the Grand Prix de Literature by the Académie Française in 1935 and the Literature Prize by the City of Paris in 1948. Nevertheless, Suarès has not yet achieved the reputation he deserves. Quixotic, proud, gifted with a brilliant and encyclopedic mind, his poetic and, at times, elliptical style has remained inaccessible to the average reader. From his early youth, he was self-conscious of his Jewish origins and foreign ancestry, yet he was convinced of his own superiority and felt the compulsion to excel, envisioning grandiose plans that would make all culture and civilization his province. Later, Suarès—about whom specific biographical knowledge is still scanty—pretended, for similar reasons, to be of Celtic origins, hiding behind such pseudonyms as Scantrel, Caërdal, and André de Séipse.

With Romain Rolland, his close friend and confidant since their student days at the Ecole Normale Supérieure (1886–89), Suarès shared an interest in music. Indeed, music occupied a prominent place in his aesthetics throughout his life, as attested by his books *Wagner* (1899), *Debussy* (1922), and articles on Beethoven and others in the *Revue musicale* (1920–38). Music is also the necessary adjunct of poetry in the volumes *Avis* (1900), *Images de la grandeur* (1901; Images of Grandeur), and *Musique et poésie* (1928; Music and Poetry).

Suarès's early, unpublished notebooks give abundant evidence of his ambitions to be known as a dramatist. As a writer, he used his knowledge of Greek and Roman culture to depict mythological heroes as the embodiment of genius. His published plays, *La Tragédie d'Elektre et d'Oreste* (1905), *Cressida* (1913), and *Polyxène* (1925), lack action, consisting instead of poetic dialogues that reflect the inner turmoil of the human being and the heroic struggles in which the spiritual self rises to grandeur and inevitable solitude. In *Poète tragique* (1921), an apotheosis of Shakespeare as poet, Suarès explores the tragic mood—the very mood he had attempted to portray in his dramas.

His observations in *De Napoléon* (1912); *Trois Hommes: Pascal, Ibsen, Dostoïevski* (1913; Three Men: Pascal, IBSEN, DOSTOYEVSKY); and *Trois Grands Vivants: Cervantes, Tolstoï, Baudelaire* (1937; Three Great Living Men: Cervantes, Tolstoy, BAUDELAIRE) illustrate his originality as a literary critic. Like Montaigne, but in a more oblique manner, he studied himself as he identified psychologically with those who reflected his own thought, emotions, obsessions, and contradictions. His essays, published as *Voici l'homme* (1905; Here is Man), *Sur la vie* (3 vols., 1925–28; On Life), *Variables* (1929), and *Valeurs* (1936; Values), which present a composite of all his contradictions, may be characterized as prose poems. As a moralist, Suarès belongs to the tradition of Blaise Pascal and La Rochefoucauld, yet he differs from the latter in that his hatred of death and desperate love of life lead him to conceive of self-fulfillment on a truly heroic scale. His role as the knight-errant of Beauty, as in his *Voyage du condottiere* (1910, 1932), relates the drama of life to artistic creation.

In the final analysis, Suarès's vision of life represents a kind of preexistentialist "engagement" involving the values of mankind. His attack on anti-Dreyfusism and his *Vues sur l'Europe* (1939; Views on Europe), with their condemnation of the Hitlerian period, are its most eloquent expression.

See: M. Maurin, "André Suarès: esquisse de biographie," *Preuves* 2 (1952): 21–32; S. D. Braun, "André Suarès, Moralist," *PMLA* 70 (1955): 285–91, and "André Suarès' Unpublished Early Notebooks," *RR* 68 (1967): 254–70; G. Savet, *André Suarès, critique* (1959); M. Dietschy, *Le Cas André Suarès* (1967); F. Busi, *L'Esthétique d'André Suarès: étude thématique sur une vision de l'art* (1969).

S.D.B.

Sudermann, Hermann (1857–1928), German dramatist and novelist, was born in Matziken, close to the Russian border in East Prussia. He was the son of a brewer in a Mennonite family, originally from Holland; his mother belonged to a local family in his birthplace. Sudermann attended the University of Königsberg; then, at the age of 20, he went to the University of Berlin. Except for short travels, he never left that city.

Sudermann's development was somewhat influenced by the writer Hans Hopfen, into whose home he came as a teacher for Hopfen's children. After a lean beginning as an editor of a small political weekly, Sudermann began writing short stories, the first of which appeared in a collection in 1886 under the title *Im Zwielicht* (At Twilight). He then wrote two novels, *Frau Sorge* (1887; Eng. tr., *Dame Care*, 1891) and *Der Katzensteg* (1889; Eng. tr., *Regine*, 1894); neither won attention until the overwhelming success of his first play, *Die Ehre* (1889; Eng. tr., *Honor*, 1915).

From then on, one play after another came from his pen in rapid succession. The best known are *Sodoms Ende* (1891; Eng. tr., *The Man and His Picture*, 1903), *Heimat* (1893; Eng. tr., *Magda*, 1896), *Die Schmetterlingsschlacht* (1895; Eng. tr., *The Battle of the Butterflies*, 1914), *Das Glück im Winkel* (1895; Eng. tr., *The Vale of Content*, 1915), *Morituri* (1896; Eng. tr., 1910), *Johannes* (1898; Eng. tr., *John*, 1902), *Die drei Reiherfedern* (New York, 1898; Stuttgart, 1899; Eng. tr., *The Three Heron's Feathers*, 1900), *Johannesfeuer* (1900; Eng. tr., *St. John's Fire*, 1904), and *Es lebe das Leben* (1902; Eng. tr., *The Joy of Living*, 1902). With *Blumenboot* (1906; Flower Boat), he returned to a kind of social drama he had begun with *Sodoms Ende*. *Sturmgeselle Sokrates* (1903; Socrates, Companion in Storm) was meant to be a political comedy. *Stein unter Steinen* (1905; Stone among Stones) is an ex-convict drama. The novel *Das hohe Lied* (1908; Eng. tr., *The Song of Songs*, 1909) and the historical play *Strandkinder* (1909; Children of the Shore) mark the end of Sudermann's first period. Three plays he wrote before World War I, *Der Bettler von Syrakus* (1911; The Beggar from Syracuse), *Der gute Ruf* (1912; Eng. tr., *A Good Reputation*, 1915), and *Die Lobgesänge des Claudian* (1914; Claudian's Hymns), demonstrated somewhat new approaches to the dramatic field, but they were only mildly successful.

When Sudermann turned toward patriotic topics during and after World War I, as with *Das deutsche Schicksal* (1921; German Destiny), the public ignored his efforts. But at the same time he found a fertile field in the stories, legends, and beliefs of his East Prussian birthplace. His volume of prose *Litauische Geschichten* (1917; Eng. tr., *The Excursion to Tilsit*, 1930) is generally regarded as his best work. The autobiographical *Bilderbuch meiner Jugend* (1922; Eng. tr., *Book of My Youth*, 1923) leads to the third and last phase of his life, during which he produced three important novels, *Der tolle Professor* (1926; Eng. tr., *The Mad Professor*, 1928), *Die Frau des Steffen Tromholt* (1927; Eng. tr., *The Wife of Steffen Tromholt*, 1929), and *Purzelchen* (1928; Eng. tr., *The Dance of Youth*, 1930).

See: A. Kerr, *Das neue Drama*, vol. 1 (1917), pp. 219–84; K. Busse, *Hermann Sudermann, sein Werk und sein Wesen* (1927); T. Duqlor, ed., *Hermann Sudermann: ein Dichter an der Grenzscheide zweier Welten* (1958).

W.N. rev. A.L.W.

Sueiro, Daniel (1931–), Spanish journalist, novelist, short-story and script writer, was born in Ribasar, in the province of La Coruña. He successfully harmonizes the influence of the contemporary American novel and the Spanish realist tradition, especially Pío BAROJA. His realism has a social bent expressed by effective if not profoundly elaborated techniques. His objective of communicating directly with the reader and inspiring in him a rejection of social injustice is apparent in *La criba* (1961; The Sieve), an immature and schematic novel. A constant theme of Sueiro has been the violence of the so-called dark Spain, as evidenced in his documentary works, *El* arte de matar (1968; The Art of Killing) and *Los verdugos españoles* (1971; The Spanish Executioners), and in his two complementary novels, *Estos son tus hermanos* (1965; These Are Your Brothers) and *La noche más caliente* (1965; The Hottest Night). *Estos son tus hermanos* depicts the brutal hostility encountered by a former exile upon returning to his home town two decades after the Spanish Civil War, while *La noche más caliente* presents the moral confrontation of the two figures who have shared the power in a little town following the end of the Civil War in 1939. Since writing his short novel *Solo de moto* (1967; Motorbike Solo), Sueiro has experimented with themes of violence and social criticism in the science-fiction novel *Corte de corteza* (1969; Brain Transplant). He is also a first-rate short-story writer, as evidenced by such collections as *Los conspiradores* (1964), *Toda la semana* (1965; All Week), *El cuidado de las manos* (1974; Hand Care), and *Servicio de navaja* (1977; Shave).

See: A. M. Navales, *Cuatro novelistas españoles: Miguel Delibes, Ignacio Aldecoa, Daniel Sueiro, Francisco Umbral* (1974), pp. 151–212. D.V.

Sułkowski, Tadeusz (1907–60), Polish poet, was born in Skierniewice and died in London. He graduated from military college with the rank of lieutenant, and went on to study Polish literature at the University of Warsaw. Wounded in 1939, he spent the rest of the war in a prisoner-of-war camp in Murnau and then reached England via Italy. He lived in London, working as the caretaker of the Polish Writers Home in Finchley.

Sułkowsky wrote little, revised his poems endlessly, and was reluctant to publish: he brought out only one volume of poems during his lifetime, *List do dnia* (1933; Letter to the Day). His mature work, which revealed an authentic philosophical poet, is represented by a selection of lyrical poems in the anthology *Przypływ* (1946, Tide); the long, neoclassical poem *Tarcza* (1961, Shield), and the collection *Dom złoty* (1961, Golden Home). Treating the creation of harmonious forms as an ethical task, he "wanted to dissolve despair into its primary elements, and found in description an element of joy. . . ."

See: K. Sowiński and T. Terlecki, eds., *O Tadeuszu Sułkowskim* (1967). B.Cz.

Sully-Prudhomme, pseud. of René François Armand Prudhomme (1839–1907), French poet, was a Parisian by birth. He prepared for the Ecole Polytechnique, thought seriously of entering the Dominican order, worked for a time in the great Schneider factories at Le Creusot, studied law and philosophy, and finally, as a sequel to an unhappy love affair, became a poet. "Le Vase brisé" (in *Stances et poèmes,* 1865) revealed best his "blessure fine et profonde" and proved so popular that it is now a hackneyed piece. *Les Epreuves* (1866), *Les Solitudes* (1869), *Les Vaines Tendresses* (1875), and the posthumous *Epaves* (1907) belong to the same elegiac inspiration, tactfully confidential and equally removed from romantic emotionalism and Parnassian frigidity.

As early 1869, Sully-Prudhomme's translation of the first book of Lucretius, together with the accompanying preface, heralded a new trend. *Les Destins* (1872), *La Justice* (1886), and *Le Bonheur* (1888) were increasingly ambitious attempts to create the so-called scientific-philosophic poem envisioned by André Chénier a century earlier. However disputable the merits of the performance, it must be said for the author that he achieves on occasion a beautiful ethereal quality in his use of symbols and that he is besides the only poet of his time who gives an impression of solid competence in the fields of science and metaphysics. Here again Sully-Prudhomme, although usually classified with the Parnassians, stands athwart the line that divides them from the romanticists. No self-appointed messiah like Victor Hugo but no nihilist like Leconte de Lisle, he lifted poetry from some of the gloom into which positivistic pessimism had plunged it for a generation and taught his belief that the road to happiness lies through pain, self-sacrifice, and brotherly love. "Le Zénith," a poem of circumstance published in the *Revue des deux mondes* in 1876, commemorated the fatal ascent of three balloonists who anticipated present-day excursions into the stratosphere. This lofty composition, dedicated to man's intrepid quest for the truth, gives a cue to Sully-Prudhomme's own lifework and to the reasons why he, a member of the Académie Française since 1881, was deemed worthy of the Nobel Prize for Literature (1901).

See: C. Hémon, *La Philosophie de M. Sully-Prudhomme* (1907); E. Zyromsky, *Sully-Prudhomme* (1907); E. Estève, *Sully-Prudhomme, poëte sentimental et poëte philosophe* (1925); P. Flottes, *Sully-Prudhomme et sa pensée* (1930). J.-A.B. rev. D.W.A.

Sundberg, Kjell, (1934–1978), Swedish novelist and playwright, was born in Östersund. He made his debut with *Människors lek* (1958; People's Games), a novel dealing with some individuals living in the Swedish countryside, all of whom seek to avail themselves of deeper life values, which they badly miss and can only divine. With this work Sundberg had already struck the theme that would become the focal point of his entire literary output. In this volume are also manifestations of joy in narration and in blending the comic with the burlesque. The semi-autobiographical work *Hos de levande* (1960; Among the Living) portrays a boy who is a "stranger" within his own family and among his friends as well, yet in his alienation he is actually intimately attached to life. This theme is further developed in *Offret* (1962; The Victim or The Sacrifice), describing "Il Sacco di Roma," the ravaging of Rome (in May 1527) in the fight between pope and emperor.

Sundberg returned to the present with *Historierna* (1964; The Stories). As in all of his books, the mood shifts from festivity to absurdity, from humor to desperation. His portraits are sharply drawn and his satire is pungent. The theme again is alienation: a middle-aged traveling salesman searches for his estranged wife. Another theme is innocence and a concern with incomprehensible life values in an absurd existence, by which Sundberg is associated with the existentialist tradition of writers such as Fyodor DOSTOYEVSKY, Søren KIERKEGAARD, Franz KAFKA, and Albert CAMUS. The main ingredient of this picaresque novel is an intense variety of dread, also to be found in *Den förvirrade medborgaren* (1967; The Confused Citizen), in which the complex of problems has been transformed from the individual to the national level. In this work, Sundberg presents a series of pieces on Swedish consciousness (its moral tone, sensibility, and so on). Life in Stockholm—a mixture of everyday experience and science fiction elements—is rendered by means of such abstractions as guilt, responsibility, and security, made visible and vividly concrete.

The alleged schizophrenia of Sweden's welfare state is exposed, as the nation is depicted as an island of wealth in a world of strife and destitution. The protagonist, Mr. Virgin [sic!], takes his commission so seriously that he is unable to deny what he knows and feels and he becomes, by understatement, the confused citizen. Then society's welfare and eudaemonics are seen as a form of terror, and the book ends with an exasperated death warrant for traditional Western morality, which in today's world is merely "a rubbish heap of old worn-out thoughts and feelings."

In *Ja må han leva eller Häng dig om du kan* (1970; Many Happy Returns of the Day, or Hang Yourself If You Can), Sundberg continued his critique of society's deepest fundamentals: the feelings and morals that determine how man deals with life values. If there is a message in the novel, it is that no individual has intrinsic value alone; value is derived from others. That which makes us human and gives us a soul is to be found not *in* us but *among* us. We live in the space between our bodies.

This philosophical notion, according to the author, should be interpreted so literally that no individual can be viewed as more than a body. A true human being results from an interchange between people. This philosophy is realized in Sundberg's latest novel, *Seger* (1975; Victor or Victory), about a quest but a tale also of peace. The merits of characters such as Seger, Svenne, and Anna involve their attention to fellowship or communion.

Sundberg said that all human beings share something that only poetry and art can preserve. To assist this quality, to sustain and bolster it, is a supremely important task in this time of change. Sundberg here touches upon the fundamentals of the humanized socialism that he saw as an indispensable precondition for the survival of human beings in the forthcoming civilization.

See: K. E. Lagerlöff, "Inte oskuld men oskyidig," in *Strömkantringens år* (1975), pp. 106–12, and "Människors förnedrade oskuld, *DN* (Sept. 13, 1978); B. N. Sundberg, *Svarta krusbär* (1980).   L.S.

Sundman, Per Olof (1922–), Swedish novelist and short-story writer, was born in Vaxholm. He endeavors as a literary artist to make a clear distinction between what can and what cannot be known. He does not take his readers beyond "external events," nor does he delve into the psychology or "internal events" of his characters. In summary, Sundman has three rules: "Restrict the descriptions of your characters' emotions to those that you could have experienced yourself if the situation had occurred in real life;" "As soon as you clothe your thoughts in words, you have been witness to a very dubious metamorphosis. Later, when there is a question of the reader's 'interpretation' of your words, you cannot even be a witness, and you know nothing"; "There is actually no such creature as an 'isolated' individual. A person must be regarded in terms of his or her relationship to others and within the environment in which he or she has a position and a *Gestalt*."

Examples of this viewpoint can be found in *Jägarna* (The Hunters) and *Observatören* (The Observer), novellas of Sundman's belated literary debut in 1957. The Observer, in describing his own method, says: "Actually it is always necessary to adhere to observations and nothing else. Avoid conclusions, avoid evaluations, avoid judgments! This is my first instruction to my assistant observers." Here we have Sundman's technique in a nutshell.

In the novel *Undersökningen* (1958; The Investigation), about society's right to take sanctions against the alcoholic chief of a power plant, Sundman has refined his methods to inquire into reality. Complications in the investigator's "objective" approach provide ample opportunities to describe social realities in a time of change and expansion.

In terms of setting and technique, the novel *Skytten*

(1960; The Marksman) is akin to the two books mentioned previously. All three are concerned with sparsely populated areas in west central Sweden, but the novel *Expeditionen* (1962; Eng. tr., *The Expedition*) introduced new elements. For the setting, Sundman has used authentic material from Henry M. Stanley's *The Congo* and *In Darkest Africa*, which deal with the three-year expedition to rescue Emin Pasha. "My book does not, however, concern itself with this relief expedition," Sundman states in a note. He seeks to arrive at truth by various means and makes no attempt to induce his readers to accept it uncritically. He patiently guides them through the area of exploration and, so to speak, permits them to examine the research data independently so as to arrive at their own conclusions.

After a short-story collection, *Sökarna* (1963; The Seekers), Sundman published a novel, *Två dagar, två nätter* (1965; Eng. tr., *Two Days, Two Nights,* 1969), in which two friends, a policeman and a schoolteacher, pursue a young criminal. The former, essentially sympathetic, finds the chase abhorrent, whereas the latter, a smart aleck, must demonstrate his superiority at all times. The reader has the chance to observe a very interesting interplay between the two. The subject is the relationship between the two men (with their relationships to their wives in the background): how they affect each other's actions, attitudes, and even their habits of speech.

Sundman's greatest success came in 1967 with *Ingenjör Andrées luftfärd* (Eng. tr., *The Flight of the Eagle,* 1970). Whereas the setting of *The Expedition* is in the equatorial regions, the Andrée expedition actually headed for the North Pole. Instead of the 1,300 men (and no females!) in *The Expedition*, there are only three (male) characters in *The Flight of the Eagle*. Andrée's group set out for the North Pole on July 11, 1897, in a hydrogen gas balloon named *The Eagle*. The book has been called "a study in the principles of human failure." It has also been described as a novel of human relations and, "finally, aside from a precise portrayal of the unmerciful adventure of the polar night, it provides a chilling insight into loneliness which cannot be endured." Indeed, the plight of our entire culture comes to mind,

Sundman exploited his subject further in a separate book of documents, *Ingen fruktan, intet hopp. Ett collage om Salomon August Andrée, hans medresenärer och hans polarexpedition* (1968; No Fear, No Hope, A Collage on S. A. Andrée, His Fellow Travelers, and His Polar Expedition). It is, as it were, an updated version of *Med Örnen mot Polen* (Eng. tr., *Andrée's Story,* 1930) minus some hero worship of the time, plus an examination of the hindsight that Andrée may have been a madman. Although Sundman attempts to be an unbiased observer, he forces interpretations on his material in several instances. For example, the title itself, "No Fear, No Hope," is taken out of context and therefore becomes somewhat misleading. Sundman's *Berättelsen om Såm* (1977; The Story of Sam) is a modern "psychological" interpretation of the ancient Icelandic saga of Hrafnkel. Sundman became a member of the Swedish Academy in 1975.

See: N. G. Åsling, *Per Olof Sundman* (1970); L. Sjöberg, "Per Olof Sundman: The Writer as Reasonably Unbiased Observer," *BA* 2 (Spring 1973): 253–60; G. Tideström, "Ingenjör Andrées Luftfärd som dokumentärskildring och Litterärt konstverk," in *Från Snoilsky till Sonnevi* (1976), pp. 182–202.   L.S.

Supervielle, Jules (1884–1960), French poet, novelist, short-story writer, and dramatist, was born in Montevideo, Uruguay, into a French family originally from the town of Oloron-Sainte-Marie. At the age of eight months, he was taken to France. There, both his parents died when he was still an infant, and he was taken back to Uruguay, where he was brought up by the brother and sister of his parents. His life was divided between Uruguay and France. Studies in the law, political science, and modern languages seemed to be leading to a career in diplomacy. Then he married, dedicated himself to poetry, had six children.

Supervielle's first slender volumes, *Brumes du passé* (1900; Mists of the Past) and *Comme des voiliers* (1910; Like Sailing Ships) contained poems mainly imitating the Parnassian manner. His *Poèmes* (1919), which included *Les Poèmes de l'humour triste* (1919; Poems of Wistful Humor), and *Débarcadères* (1922; Landing Stations) contain admirable lines. *Gravitations* (1925) is a more mature volume in which the inner self fraternizes with the whole interstellar world. His subsequent works of poetry include *Le Forçat innocent* (1930; The Innocent Convict); *Les Amis inconnus* (1934; Unknown Friends); *La Fable du monde* (1938; The Story of the World), in which a God unable to help his Creation speaks with modesty and tenderness; and *Poèmes de la France malheureuse* (1941; Poems of Unhappy France), written in Uruguay and circulated in France during the Resistance.

After the poet's return to France, his volume *1939–1945* appeared in 1946, along with the *Poèmes de la France malheureuse* and other groups of poems, among them the poignant "Le Mort en peine" (The One Who Died and Lives). Other postwar volumes include *A la nuit* (1947; To the Night), whose lines have a controlled force reminiscent of the 16th-century poet Maurice Scève; *Oublieuse Mémoire* (1949; Forgetful Memory), whose title indicates the poet's preoccupation; *Naissances* (1951; Births), which contains Supervielle's statement on poetry, "En songeant à un art poétique" (Thinking of an *ars poetica*); and *L'Escalier* (1956; The Stairs), which included new poems as well as those of *A la nuit, Poèmes de l'humour triste,* and *Débarcadères*. His last book of poems was *Le Corps Tragique* (1959; The Tragic Body). In these last volumes, Supervielle developed his favorite themes: birth, memory, and those stairs about which he wrote: "It is often only a long time after something has happened that I hear the creaking of my own private stairs, my stairs for poems."

After several experiments in fiction—*L'Homme de la pampa* (1923; The Man from the Pampas), *Le Voleur d'enfants* (1926; Eng. tr., *The Colonel's Children,* 1950); and *Le Survivant* (1928; The Survivor)—Supervielle found the right formula in 1931 with his first short stories, *L'Enfant de la haute mer* (The Child of the High Seas). Other short-story collections followed: *L'Arche de Noé* (1938; Noah's Ark) and *Premiers Pas de l'univers* (1950; The First Steps of the World), which contains the tales he had published in Mexico as *Le Petit Bois* (1942; The Little Wood). Supervielle's stories give myths a new life, revealing a narrator whose tone is unique in French letters, a marvelous fusion of the tender and the burlesque, of grandeur and simplicity.

Supervielle also wrote plays, some in several versions: *La Belle au bois* (1932; 1953; Sleeping Beauty); *Bolivar* (1936); *La Première Famille* (1955; The Original Family); *Shéhérazade* (1948); a dramatization of his *Le Voleur d'enfants* (1949); and *Robinson* (1953). *Comme il vous plaira,* his adaptation of Shakespeare's *As You Like It,* was published in 1935. Among Supervielle's other writings are his autobiographical volume *Boire à la source: confidences de la mèmoire et du paysage* (1933; Drinking

at the Spring: Confessions of Memories and Places), a 1954 translation (based on the 1890 translation of Jean-Jacques Réthoré) of the Uruguayan epic *Tabaré* (1888) by Juan Zorrilla de San Martín, and *Le Jeune Homme du dimanche et des autres jours* (1955; The Young Man for Sunday and the Other Days), a novel of love, metamorphosis, and metempsychosis.

Supervielle lived mostly in a universe of myth and restless fancy, claiming that poetry was the rarely explored domain of the most recondite feelings. Nevertheless, he was not indifferent to historical realities. The Boer War, World War I, the Spanish Civil War, and the occupation of France during World War II all had echoes in his poetry. At the same time, he remained the poet concerned with the humblest objects as well as with the sweep of the planets through space, the poet of those feelings so basic that they are too often neglected. This most unassuming of men possessed a warmth and respectful generosity that, coupled with his talent, won him the admiration and the affection of many young writers after 1930. Testimonial numbers of the periodicals *L'Avant-Poste, Regains,* and *Gants du ciel* are evidence of the impression he made on them. Several of the poets who have written about him consider Supervielle a foil, or at least a complement, to Arthur RIMBAUD.

See: C. Sénéchal, *Jules Supervielle* (1939); L. Specker, *Jules Supervielle: eine Stilstudie* (1942); T. Greene, *Jules Supervielle* (1958); R. Etiemble, *Supervielle* (1960); D. S. Blair, *Jules Supervielle* (1960); J. A. Hiddleston, *L'Univers de Jules Supervielle* (1965); P. Viallaneix, *Le Hors-venu ou le personnage poétique de Supervielle* (1972); R. Vivier, *Lire Supervielle* (1972).   T.W.G.

Svensson, Jón (1857–1944), Icelandic novelist, was born at Möðruvellir, Hörgárdalur, north Iceland. As a boy he was offered free education in France by Catholic missionaries in Iceland, with a view to making a convert out of him. He became a Jesuit and a teacher in Denmark. Just before World War I he began to write down the memories of his youth that he had so often told to his pupils with marked success. The result was the book *Nonni* (1913; "Nonni" was his own pet name as a boy), the first in a long series of *Nonni* books that have become extremely popular reading among boys, especially Catholic boys, all over the world. Written originally in German, they have since been translated into many languages. Of the other books in the series, these may be mentioned: *Nonni und Manni* (1914), *Sonnentage* (1915), and *Die Stadt am Meer* (1922).

Svensson wrote with classic and telling simplicity of the adventures of his childhood, of his first trip to Denmark, of his early days in Copenhagen, of excursions about the smiling Danish islands. His subjects are often seemingly commonplace, but he holds the attention of both young and old as if he were telling an adventure story. He had two aims: to educate young readers in good Christian ways and to impart to them some of his own deep-felt love for his distant homeland. Svensson was an extremely popular lecturer in Catholic Europe and elsewhere. As an octogenarian he went on a lecture trip around the world, visiting the United States and Japan, where he was hailed by the youngsters as if he were a new Hans Christian Andersen. Returning to Europe just before the World War II, he died in Cologne on Nov. 1, 1944.   S.E.

Svetlov, Mikhail Arkadyevich (1903–64), Russian poet and dramatist, was born in Yekaterinoslav (now Dnepropetrovsk) and died in Moscow. In 1919 he joined the recently formed Komsomol (Communist Youth Organization) and in 1920 volunteered for the First Yekaterinoslav Territorial Regiment. In 1922 he moved to Moscow and published his first collection of poetry, *Relsy* (Rails), the following year. His last collection, *Okhotnichiy domik* (A Hunter's Cabin), came out in 1964, and his posthumous collection *Stikhy poslednikh let* (Poems of the Final Years) was awarded the Lenin Prize in 1967. In 1935 he wrote the first in a series of plays, which were more distinguished for their lyric atmosphere than for complexities of plot. Until the 1950s, Svetlov was especially known in the Soviet Union for two poems—"Grenada" (1926) and "Pesnya o Kakhovke" (1936; A Song about Kakhovka), which was set to music by I. Dunayevsky. Singing—as the expression of a mode of being—plays a distinctive role in Svetlov's poetry. Other characteristic concerns are the significance of being young, of dreams and fantasy, and the importance of retaining a sense of humor, especially about oneself.

See: Z. Paperny, *Chelovek, pokhozhiy na samogo sebya* (1967); W. Kasack, *Lexikon der russischen Literatur ab 1917* (1976), pp. 392–93.   V.L.

Svevo, Italo, pseud. of Ettore Schmitz (1861–1928), Italian novelist, was born in Trieste, then an active port of the Austro-Hungarian Empire, into a well-to-do Jewish family, his father being of German descent, his mother Italian. He coined the pen name "Italus the Swabian" to reflect his mixed ancestry and education. Having attended a private secondary school in Germany, he returned to Trieste for his advanced studies, but due to his father's bankruptcy he had to leave school and find employment as a bank clerk. After the death of his parents, Svevo married Livia Veneziani and became a partner in the Veneziani manufacturing firm, where he was to work all his life, becoming a rather wealthy businessman.

The desire to be a writer, which he had nourished since his adolescent years, was thwarted at first by economic necessity, then by the total unresponsiveness of contemporary critics to his first two novels, *Una vita* (1893; Eng. tr., *A Life*, 1963) and *Senilità* (1898; Eng. tr., *As a Man Grows Older*, 1932). For the next 25 years, embittered by lack of recognition and skeptical of the literary establishment, Svevo did not publish anything; yet during this time he never ceased to write fables, short stories, plays, and a diary, whose purpose was essentially self-analytical. In 1907, needing a knowledge of English for his business-related travels, Svevo met James Joyce, who was then relatively unknown as a writer and was making his living as an English teacher in Trieste. Years later, their friendship resulted in international literary success for Svevo when he published his third major work, *La coscienza di Zeno* (1923; Eng. tr., *The Confessions of Zeno*, 1930). Joyce, who greatly admired Svevo's writing, took it upon himself to make the novel known. It was translated and published in Paris by Joyce's friends Valery LARBAUD and Benjamin CRÉMIEUX, who hailed it as a masterpiece and dubbed its author "the Italian Proust." Svevo's extraordinary and sudden success in France soon reached Italy where a few critics, first among them Eugenio MONTALE in an article published in *L'esame* (1925), began to reevaluate his fiction and to appreciate its modern sensitivity and innovative complexity. During the last years of his life, encouraged by the long-awaited critical recognition, Svevo wrote many shorter pieces such as "Una burla riuscita" (1929; Eng. tr., *The Hoax,* 1929); "La novella del buon vecchio e della bella fanciulla" (1929; Eng. tr., *The Nice Old Man and the Pretty Girls and Other Stories,* 1930); "Corto viaggio sentimentale" (1949;

Eng. tr., *Short Sentimental Journey,* 1967), and a few chapters of a projected novel, "Il vecchione" (Eng. tr., "The Old Old Man," in *Further Confessions of Zeno,* 1969), which remained unfinished because of Svevo's death as a result of an automobile accident.

The belated, uneasy beginning of Svevo's fortune as Italy's greatest early-20th-century novelist stirred up what is commonly known as "the Svevo case," an ongoing and rather heated debate among Italian critics on the quality and literary status of his novels. Comparing him with his contemporary Gabriele D'ANNUNZIO, Svevo's adversaries lamented his "slipshod," dry prose style, which remained too close to the Triestine dialect and betrayed his formal training in the German language; the lack of organic novelistic form and of a sublime vision; and his choice of unattractive, weak, commonplace heroes. On the other hand, his supporters, whose numbers grew in time and spread beyond the boundaries of Italy, appreciated the subtle irony of his portrayal of the bourgeoisie; his keen sense of humor; his masterful handling of the subjective point of view, mainly through the technique of interior monologue; and his analytical excavation into the personality in search of inner reality. Svevo's fiction is often compared to that of Franz KAFKA, Robert MUSIL, Joyce, and Thomas MANN; his acknowledged masters were the naturalist novelists, Arthur Schopenhauer, and Sigmund Freud, whose theories Svevo had discovered around 1912 and had admittedly used in the writing of *Coscienza.* Svevo's complex, intriguingly ambivalent attitude toward psychoanalysis, undoubtedly dictated by the very unfavorable reception of the latter in Italy, is studied by Michel David in *La psicoanalisi nella cultura italiana* (1966; Psychoanalysis in Italian Culture).

Svevo's major narrative works are extraordinarily similar to one another in theme and structure. In large part autobiographical, they are each centered on an introspective, weak-willed antihero whose relationships with his parents or with parental figures and attempts to find love, self-determination, and identity form the unheroic, uneventful story line. The recurring Svevian themes are the dialectical interrelation of guilt and disease, and love and jealousy, in all-encompassing preoccupation with death and the passing of time (whence the insistent motif of old age), and the yearning for expression and creativity. Conscience and consciousness, the two meanings of the ambiguous title *La coscienza di Zeno,* are also the objects to be attained at the end of the hero's journey through the arc of the three novels. Their protagonists are but different images of a single experience seen from subsequent points in time along the path to self-discovery. As Zeno recounts his life—allegedly in an attempt to find the origin of his smoking habit, and thus a "cure," by means of psychoanalysis, to his innumerable psychosomatic diseases—he treads over the emotional footprints of his two predecessors, Alfonso Nitti in *Una vita,* a suicide at the age of 20, and Emilio Brentani, whose "senility" at 35 and self-contained, unfulfilled existence are witness to his failure and inability to live. But from the vantage point of his 57 years, Zeno reshapes events and characters, turning tables, settling accounts, and emerging the winner. Through Zeno, who lies and distorts, or fictionalizes, the story of his life, Svevo shows his belief in the power of language to transform and recreate experience. Ironically, although Svevo was once disparaged because of his style, his contemporary appeal is due largely to his total commitment to literary form and to symbolic discourse, which alone recapture and ultimately conquer time.

After Giovanni VERGA (whose great and truly innovative contribution to the language of fiction was also not recognized until after his death), Svevo is responsible for the second major shift in the direction of the Italian novel, influencing it from the early work of Alberto MORAVIA to the novels of the late 1960s. A bibliography up to 1969 and a survey of Svevo criticism by Bruno Maier are included in vol. 2 of Svevo, *Opera omnia* (1969).

T. de L.

Svobodová, Růžena (1868–1920), Czech novelist, was the leading woman fiction writer in Czechoslovakia during the early 20th century. She was born Růžena Čápová in Mikulovice, near Znojmo in southern Moravia, but spent most of her life in Prague. She married the novelist František Xaver Svoboda, who had a good reputation among the early Czech realists. Later she became the intimate friend of the critic František Xaver ŠALDA.

Svobodová began to write novels in the atmosphere of later 19th-century naturalism and feminism. Her early works, notably *Na písčité půdě* (1895; On Sandy Soil), are studies of sensitive, refined women who are crushed by the brutality of men and the stupidity of conventional society. The accusatory tone is strident, the style rhetorical. Later Svobodová changed both her outlook and technique very considerably, and her best work was done early in the 20th century. She became less pessimistic and feminist, less preoccupied with the problems of the "misunderstood" woman. Her themes widened, although she still liked to depict the tragedies and erotic disillusionments experienced by sensitive women. As a remedy, Svobodová advocated collective love and sacrifice. She analyzed the fatal consequences of hedonistic aestheticism—she herself never quite escaped its atmosphere—and even treated the metaphysical themes of death, nature, and immortality. Her technique became impressionistic: there is much visual metaphor, delicate observation, and evidence of a knowledge of the plastic arts and their influence. Her style became elaborately chiseled, ornate, and frequently precious. All Svobodová's novels suffer from her inability to depict male characters and to handle large themes. Even her most ambitious work, *Zahrada irémská* (1921; The Garden of Irem; in six parts, uncompleted), a symbolic picture of the whole of civilization, is lifeless and overburdened by unassimilated discussion. *Zamotaná vlákna* (1898; The Twisted Threads) and *Milenky* (1902; Sweethearts) are much better composed, but they have sensational, sentimental plots. Svobodová was at her best when writing short stories, particularly when she used forms derived from traditional folk art, such as fairy tales, ballads in prose, and legends. Her short-story collections include *Plameny a plaménky* (1905; Flames and Little Flames), *Marné lásky* (1907; Frustrated Loves), *Posvátné jaro* (1916; Sacred Spring), and *Po svatební hostině* (1916; After the Wedding Feast), all of which are surpassed by *Černí myslivci* (1908; Black Foresters), a collection that is unified by its finely described setting in the Bezkydy Mountains of Moravia. Svobodová's charming childhood reminiscences, *Ráj* (1920; Paradise), remain only a fragment.

Svobodová was a sensitive, self-conscious artist of great ambitions who unfortunately, in spite of her ethical and social feelings, never escaped the aestheticism of her youth. Her reputation rather passed into eclipse, partly because she had been extravagently overpraised by F. X. Šalda, partly because her problems and outlook (the misunderstood woman, admiration for the aristocracy) as well as her frequently affected style seemed remote to later generations.

See: F. X. Šalda in *Duše a dílo* (1913) and *In memoriam*

R. Svobodové (1921); M. Nováková, *Básnířka života a snu* (1940).

R.W.

Swedish literature. After a notable flourishing of romanticism during the early 19th century, Swedish literature began around 1830 to follow the general European tendency toward greater realism. One striking transition figure was C. J. L. Almqvist (1793–1866), once described as Sweden's most modern writer. He was deeply rooted in the romantic world view but was a prominent liberal in social questions; his discussion of marriage in particular insured him a wide audience, which grew quickly through the years. In the middle of the 19th century Viktor RYDBERG published a series of historical novels with markedly liberal tendencies. He argued in particular for religious freedom and, through his theoretical work *Bibelns lära om Kristus* (1862; The Doctrine of Christ in the Bible), he became the nation's foremost advocate of religious liberalism. He was also a journalist and a cultural historian and was strongly committed to linguistic reform—the pure Swedish he advocated was to be "Nordic," not "German" Swedish (a corresponding battle of language was raging in Norway at this time). Rydberg's most notable achievement was his poetry—a "problem lyric" that gave voice to an idealistic world view and a lively social conscience opposing the increasingly conspicuous materialism of his time. Rydberg's poem "Den nya grottesången" (1895; The New Song of Grotte) centers around the social problems of capitalism and industrialism. During the 1860s a literary society usually referred to as "The Signatures" was formed in Uppsala. Two of the most prominent members of this group were Carl Snoilsky and Carl David af Wirsén. Snoilsky (1841–1903), the foremost poet of the time other than Rydberg, produced poetry that was consummate in form and distinction. Snoilsky soon took on the poetic realism cultivated by "The Signatures" with the Finland-Swedish poet J. L. Runeberg (1804–77) as a model, but for a period he was also inspired by French Parnassian poetry and the notion of *l'art pour l'art*. As a young man Snoilsky celebrated in the liberal spirit the freedom movements of Europe; his mature poems such as *Svenska bilder* (1866; Swedish Pictures), were mainly concerned with national history and expressed disquiet in the face of social development. Wirsén (1842–1912) was relatively unimportant as a poet but quite significant as a critic.

The regeneration and radicalization of literature that occurred during the second half of the 19th century, primarily through French naturalism, appeared later in Sweden than in the other Scandinavian countries; what Georg BRANDES called "the modern breakthrough" took place almost a decade earlier in Denmark and Norway than in Sweden. This breakthrough period in Sweden is called the "Eighties" (*åttiotalet*). It was represented by a group of younger writers, including Gustaf af Geijerstam, Ola Hansson, and Oscar Levertin; but it came to be dominated in all essentials by a single writer, August STRINDBERG. The onset of the "Eighties" was marked by Strindberg's first great novel, *Röda rummet* (1879; Eng. tr., *The Red Room,* 1913, 1967), which was characterized by fresh realism as well as by high-spirited and bitter social criticism. "Put the question to a debate" was the watchword of the new literature. Authority of all kinds was attacked, and humbug was exposed in politics, business, culture, and religion. The foremost pamphlets were written by Strindberg. The women's issue was discussed, with Henrik IBSEN's *Et Dukkehjem* (1879; A Doll's House, Eng. tr., *Nora,* 1882) as the point of departure for a series of plays written by women authors. Strindberg soon came to take a position on this issue opposing the ideas of Ibsen, Brandes, and John Stuart Mill; his *Giftas* (1884–86; Eng. tr., *Married,* 1913, *Getting Married,* 1973) was accused of, and its earlier part marked by, misogyny. Strindberg, who began his writing career with historical dramas, wrote during the "Eighties" a series of naturalistic contemporary dramas, the best known of which are *Fadren* (1887; Eng. tr., *The Father,* 1899, 1965), and *Fröken Julie* (1888; Eng. tr., *Miss Julie,* 1911, 1965). Toward the end of the "Eighties," Strindberg's social criticism faded, and his last important work from this era is the novel *I havsbandet* (1890; Eng. tr., *By the Open Sea,* 1913), which was influenced by Friedrich NIETZSCHE's theories of the superman. Around the turn of the century Strindberg's writing changed direction and became marked by his renewed (and utterly personal) religious belief and by literary experimentation of a sort that had never before occurred in Swedish literature. During this time he wrote his "dream play" and "chamber plays," which were influential in European drama, particularly in expressionism, and possibly also in the theater of the absurd. The most memorable of the writers of the "Eighties" besides Strindberg were two who happily went their own way to one side of the literary party line: Victoria Benedictsson (1850–88), who wrote under the masculine pseudonym Ernst Ahlgren and discussed marriage and love problems from the background of her own poignant, tragic life, and Ola Hansson, who made his greatest contribution as a poet in a decade hostile to lyricism. Hansson did not reach the peak of his individual development until the last part of his life, which he spent in exile and thus was hardly able to affect literary history in his homeland.

Around 1890 the literary situation altered markedly with the dawn of a new literary period known as the "Nineties" (*nittiotalet*). In 1888, Verner von HEIDENSTAM had made his literary debut with a collection of poems, *Vallfart och vandringsår* (Pilgrimage and Wanderyears), in which carefree joie de vivre and colorful exoticism replaced serious social discussion and shortsighted realism. Together with Oscar Levertin (1882–1906), who had been a leading figure of the "Eighties," Heidenstam formulated the program for a new poetry and many new poets followed more or less publicly: Gustaf FRÖDING, Selma LAGERLÖF, Erik Axel KARLFELDT, and Per Hallström (1866–1960). The break with the previous decade was hardly as strong and marked as the program makers maintained, but nevertheless these writers of the "Nineties" formed a group united by certain similar qualities. Social discussion was not abolished (Lagerlöf, for example, wrote about socialism, the temperance movement, and the peace movement), but the accent had changed: arguments and agitation were replaced by an interest in the artist as protagonist. The role of imagination and emotion was emphasized; Heidenstam, for example, wanted to replace "shoemaker's realism" with "naturalism of the fantasy." Motifs from history or rural life were favored. Characters in novels were presented as "heroes," morally superior, more or less idealized, not as naturalistic case histories. Lyric poetry again became the most important form. Fröding and Karlfeldt were almost exclusively poets, and poetry constitutes a major portion of the work of Levertin and Heidenstam. Only one writer of this time devoted herself exclusively to prose—Selma Lagerlöf, possibly the finest narrator in Swedish literature. Heidenstam's interest in history was accompanied by an expression of national moods and marked patriotism. The "Nineties" took its rather special character from its use of national and provincial motifs, although Swedish literature was also influenced by the

shift away from naturalism that marked European literature at the close of the 19th century. Only Levertin among the poets of the "Nineties" took an interest in the poetry of symbolism. The decadent element often found in fin-de-siècle literature is seldom seen in the poets of the nineties, although there is a glimpse of the motif "death in beauty" in the work of Heidenstam.

In the shadow of the writers of the "Nineties" were a few authors who set their mark on the year 1900, especially Hjalmar SÖDERBERG and Bo Bergman (1869–1967). Although fin-de-siècle tendencies are visible in their work, bottomless pessimism is more characteristic than decadence. A feeling that it is futile to intervene in the course of events leads Söderberg's characters to adopt an attitude of observation rather than one of accomplishment; the protagonists in the novels *Martin Bircks ungdom* (1901; Eng. tr., *Martin Birck's Youth,* 1930) and *Doktor Glas* (1905; Eng. tr., *Doctor Glas,* 1963) all exemplify this attitude. Söderberg's greatest artistry is evident in the short story, a form in which he ranks with such masters as Guy de Maupassant, Alexander KIELLAND, and Anatole FRANCE. Bo Bergman, who was still writing at the age of 90, devoted his long artistic career principally to poetry; his verse approaches colloquial speech but is also softly musical. Both Bergman and Söderberg were expert portraitists of the scenes and moods of Stockholm.

In past centuries poetry had held a dominant place in Swedish literature, and the "Nineties" had amounted to a lyric renaissance. So, in the literature of the 20th century, the most remarkable achievements have been made in poetry. By 1907, Vilhelm EKELUND had already published seven poetry collections, including *Melodier i skymning* (1902; Melodies in Twilight) and *Dithyramber i aftonglans* (1906; Dithyrambs in Evening's Splendor). Ekelund was inspired mainly by French and German symbolism (Paul VERLAINE, Stefan GEORGE). For him lyric poetry was an explanation of life, a way of clarifying and interpreting human perception of, and relation to, life's most profound questions. After these collections, Ekelund turned to the aphorism and the short essay as his principal forms. Ekelund was born in Skåne, the southernmost of Sweden's provinces, and often took the motif of his poems from this landscape. Both as a symbolist and as a portraitist of Skåne, Ekelund was followed by Anders Österling (1884–). During World War I, Österling gave his poetry a realistic direction and sought beauty and security in simple everyday things. A third important poet who made his debut during the first year of the century was Bertil MALMBERG. His early work was marked by decadence and symbolism and was strongly influenced by German writers and thinkers, including Rainer Maria RILKE, Stefan George, and Oswald Spengler. Until the early 1940s he chose a traditional, classic form for his poetry, but during the last two decades of his life he gave up rhyme and meter and wrote a free modernist verse that presented a fresh view of reality, unmasked and without illusion, warmly welcomed by the youngest generation of writers during the 1940s.

The years between 1910 and 1912 marked one of the hottest battles in Swedish literature, the "Strindberg feud." The aging Strindberg attacked the writers of the "Nineties," particularly Heidenstam, and the entire Swedish press took sides. The result was a confrontation between the partisans of the "Nineties," aesthetic and romantic, and those of the "Eighties," more realistic and oriented toward contemporary society. At the same time (ca. 1910) many new writers who had just made their debut were strongly susceptible to impressions from fin-de-siècle pessimism and decadence, opposing a more positive portrayal of contemporary life and its economic and social aspects. The writers of the decade 1910-20 (*tiotalisterna*) included Sigfrid Siwertz (1882-1970), Gustaf Hellström (1882-1953), Sven Lidman (1882-1960), Elin Wägner (1882-1949), Ludvig Nordström (1882-1942) and, most important of all, Hjalmar BERGMAN. Through them the realistic novel, concerned with psychology and social analysis, finally arrived in Sweden. Writers in the decade 1910-20 provided Swedish counterparts to Thomas MANN's *Buddenbrooks,* John Galsworthy's and H. G. Wells's contemporary novels, and French works such as Roger MARTIN DU GARD's *Les Thibault.* Swedish settings attracted the interest of these new writers: Norrland (Nordström), Bergslagen (Bergman), Skåne (Hellström), and Stockholm (Siwertz, Lidman). New groups of professional women, such as office workers and journalists, were portrayed, especially by Elin Wägner, whose later works concerning women's role and duties, such as *Väckarklocka* (1941; The Alarm Clock) held much interest for the feminists who followed her. Hjalmar Bergman was the genius of these years; his works combine humor with images of reality, fantasy, and the grotesque to transcend the traditional boundaries of realism.

Nearly all of the writers mentioned thus far had had an academic education, and they had come from backgrounds of the middle class or the nobility. During the decade 1910-20, however, the first proletarian writers (*arbetardiktare*) appeared, writers of the working class who had gotten their education on their own. They brought new settings to literature and portrayed problems and conditions that earlier had either not reached literature at all or at most been described only by outsiders. To the first generation of proletarian writers belonged Gustav Hedenvind-Eriksson (1880-1967), a farmer's son, lumberjack, and railroad laborer, and Martin Koch (1882-1940), whose novel *Arbetare* (1912; Workers) is one of the first collective novels in Swedish (that is, a novel with a group as the protagonist), modeled on the works of Emile ZOLA, Jack London, and Upton Sinclair. Charcoal burner, seaman, and journalist, Dan ANDERSSON wrote prose but was primarily a poet whose work presents a complex of religious problems.

The intimacy with reality generally expressed by the proletarian writers as well as by the middle- and upper-class writers of this period was challenged by the time of World War I by representatives of an entirely different literary ideal, most accurately described as the Swedish counterpart to German expressionism and French modernism. An artistic constructivism was demanded in place of photographic representations of reality. The new "isms" of painting began to serve as signals for literature as well. The spokesman for this new literature was Pär LAGERKVIST, a central figure in 20th-century Swedish literature. His works until 1925 can best be characterized as expressionistic: stylized dramas that consciously follow the lead of Strindberg's dream-play technique; prose stories in which nightmare and reality are mixed or where the action is played out among the dead in eternal darkness; and poems that represent a completely inner reality—metaphysical terror and despair for humanity's fate in the age of war. His autobiographical novel *Gäst hos verkligheten* (1925; Eng. tr., *Guest of Reality,* 1936) is deliberately naive in style but realistically narrated. During the 1920s, Lagerkvist strove to develop a humanist philosophy, his famous "life-faith" (*livstro*), which, however, eventually became a faith in "humanity" rather than in "life." In 1933 he wrote the novel *Bödeln* (Eng. tr., *The Hangman,* 1936) as a reaction against fascism

and Hitlerism, a political stance in which he was joined by many other prominent Swedish writers. His most important novels are *Dvärgen* (1944; Eng. tr., *The Dwarf,* 1945) and *Barabbas* (1950; Eng. tr., 1951). Religious problems dominate *Barabbas* and his later novels: Lagerkvist called himself "a believer without belief, a religious atheist."

Lagerkvist's strong engagement in contemporary problems gave his work great representativity, but because of his profound originality he did not have many followers. Even the expressionistic breakthrough of his early writing inspired relatively few other writers. Modernism, primarily expressionistic, was more influential at this time in Swedish literature in Finland, where Edith SÖDERGRAN, whose first work was published in 1916, was followed by Elmer DIKTONIUS, Gunnar BJÖRLING, and Rabbe ENCKELL (*see* FINLAND-SWEDISH LITERATURE). This Finnish modernism was later of great significance for the development of poetry in Sweden, but in the 1920s Lagerkvist remained almost the lone expressionist writer in Sweden. There appeared at this time a group of "bourgeois intimates" (*borgerliga intimister*) who sang of workdays and idylls and whose cultural outlook was academic humanism. Independently of these writers, two balladeers gained great popularity: Evert Taube (1890-1976) made himself loved through a series of seaman's songs, and Birger SJÖBERG published *Fridas bok* (1922; Frida's Book), "small-town ballads about Frida and nature, death and the universe." *Fridas bok* unites fresh lyric feeling with delicate irony in a unique manner. With his third book, *Kriser och kransar* (1926; Crises and Laurels), Sjöberg established himself as a serious poet with an utterly personal style best described as expressionistic. The work of Karin BOYE was first published in 1922, the same year as that of Sjöberg. She wrote prose but is most important as a poet. Her poetry is intellectual and philosophical, similar in this way to that of Vilhelm Ekelund. Very much influenced by Freudian psychoanalysis, Boye was one of the first Swedish poets for whom the principles of psychoanalysis were a philosophy of life. A few years after Boye published her first work, Bo Johannes EDFELT and Hjalmar GULLBERG, both of whom wrote works more traditionally academic in form than hers, made their debut as poets. Edfelt especially is part of the German movement known as *die neue Sachlichkeit* (the new objectivity), represented by Bertolt BRECHT and Erich KÄSTNER. Edfelt's modern, matter-of-fact vocabulary combined with traditionally formed verse results in an ironic effect that shatters traditional boundaries of style. In his mature poems Edfelt replaced this manner with a rigid realism that represented his disillusionment with life: his themes were disintegration and death, torment and terror. Gullberg became the most prominent poet of the 1930s with his collections of poems *Andliga övningar* (1932; Spiritual Exercises), *Kärlek i tjugonde seklet* (1933; Love in the Twentieth Century), and *Att övervinna varlden* (1937; To Overcome the World). Contemporary satire and the image of an intellectual's uneasy searching characterize his work; religious features signal an inner mysticism. His last collection, *Ögon, läppar* (1959; Eyes, Lips), is his most poignant. Nils Ferlin (1898-1961), using folk songs as a backdrop, created during the 1930s a highly personal poetry, deeply pessimistic and in many ways compatible with his bohemian life-style.

With the conscious intention of regenerating Swedish literature five writers in 1929 published the anthology *Fem unga* (Five Young Men). In the midst of the academics and traditionalists, all five were autodidacts; many had done physical labor before taking up the pen. They aimed to attack academic skepticism and pessimism, including Lagerkvist's fighting humanism. Instead they expressed a youthful intoxication with life, a brutal and powerful feeling of primitive vitalism. Among the Five Young Men, Artur LUNDKVIST was most knowledgeable about theory. His own development as a writer was influenced by the new poetry he introduced: during the 1930s he was one of the first surrealists in Sweden. Of the remaining Five Young Men, Harry MARTINSON is especially notable. He had been a stoker at sea. Experiences of the sea and faraway lands are portrayed in Martinson's first prose works, *Resor utan mål* (1932; Travels without a Destination) and *Kap Farväl!* (1933; Eng. tr., *Cape Farewell*, 1934). In the autobiographical novels *Nässlorna blomma* (1935; Eng. tr., *Flowering Nettle*, 1936) and *Vägen ut* (1936; The Way Out), Martinson recounted his own difficult childhood with sharpness as well as a balanced spirit of conciliation. These books achieved a renewal of language because of Martinson's playful stylistic imagination. His interest in nature, in plants and insects, plays a large part in both his poetry and prose. The "space epic" *Aniara* (1956; Eng. tr., 1963) must be counted among his most remarkable accomplishments. It concerns a spaceship that goes off course while on the way from radiation-damaged earth to Mars and is headed for its destruction. *Aniara* is an ingenious poem about the fate of humanity in time and space. Martinson shared the Nobel Prize for Literature with Evynd JOHNSON in 1976.

A considerably more radical lyric modernism than that prevalent at the end of the 1920s was revealed in the collection of poems *Sent på jorden* (1932; Late on Earth) by Gunnar EKELÖF. At the time of its publication, *Sent på jorden* was called Sweden's first surrealistic poetry. Ekelöf's major themes are loneliness, the ego and its relation to the cosmos, death. These appear in many forms not only in his first book but also in his principal collections of poetry, *Färjesång* (1941; Ferry Song), *Non Serviam* (1945; I Will Not Serve), and *Om hösten* (1951; In Autumn). His greatest work is *En Mölna-elegi* (1960; Eng. tr., *A Mölna Elegy*, 1979), a poem about the moment embracing both past and future. Ekelöf's last three books together comprise an ingeniously composed lyric suite on suffering, love, and death into which are woven the central motifs from all of the poet's earlier work. These three works include *Dīwān över fursten av Emgión* (1965; Divan on the Prince of Emgión), *Sagan om Fatumeh* (1966; Eng. tr., *Selected Poems,* 1971), and *Vägvisare till underjorden* (1967; Eng. tr., *Guide to the Underworld*, 1980).

The development toward lyric modernism between the two world wars illustrated by the works of Karin Boye, Lundkvist, Martinson, and Ekelöf had no direct counterpart in prose during the same time. The novel often followed in the footsteps of realistic traditions, and the "new" was determined by new subjects or new concepts in psychological analysis. Agnes von Krusenstjerna (1894–1940), from an aristocratic background, portrayed a young noblewoman's growing up and rebelling against her milieu in two long novel series with strong autobiographical elements. Krusenstjerna's main work is the novel series *Fröknarna von Pahlen* (7 vols., 1930–35; The Misses von Pahlen), whose wide-ranging portrayal of life and manners includes descriptions of both normal and homosexual sexuality. From 1930 until his death (in 1974), Olle Hedberg published a novel every year. In clear, often ironic prose he scourged the bourgeois milieu he knew so well and portrayed characters endowed with numerous banal weaknesses. In many of his novels, Hedberg's mo-

rality is visible against an expressly religious background. Unconcerned with social or ethical purpose but possessed of an extraordinary narrative power, Fritjof NILSSON PIRATEN wrote humorous portraits of original characters from the Skåne countryside. The narratives are sometimes veritable grotesques in which the humor has a bitter aftertaste of grimness and suffering.

The most important achievement in prose writing between the two world wars was made by the proletarian writers. Their novels are usually traditionally realistic in form. In some of them political trends are important, but typically they are autobiographical at heart. It is even possible to maintain that, because of these writers, the autobiographical novel was the dominant prose genre during the 1930s. Vilhelm MOBERG was born in the countryside of Småland and became a journalist. Leaving Småland farm life for a new milieu is a dominant motif in his work, which encompasses drama as well as novels and journalism. This is the theme of his major work: the novel tetralogy on emigration from the poverty-stricken Småland to the new uncleared lands in North America during the 19th century, *Utvandrarna* (1949; Eng. tr., *The Emigrants*, 1951), *Invandrarna* (1952; Eng. tr., *Unto a Good Land*, 1954), *Nybyggarna* (1956), and *Sista brevet till Sverige* (1959; abridged Eng. tr., of *Nybyggarna* and *Sista brevet till Sverige, The Last Letter Home,* 1961). Ivar LO-JOHANSSON had a powerful political awareness. His most significant work is his portrait of Swedish sharecroppers, begun with the autobiographical *Godnatt, jord* (1933; Good Night, Earth). He later devoted several volumes of short stories to the portrayal of the farm worker collective, including *Statarna I-II* (1936, 1937; The Sharecroppers I-II). He consciously strove to give a collective portrayal of an entire social class; but the finest of his novels, *Bara en mor* (1939; Only a Mother), places the sharecropper woman Rya-Rya in its center, probably almost against the author's will. In novels and short stories, Lo-Johansson combined documentation of the sharecroppers' conditions with a political battle to get rid of the sharecropper system. Other social issues to which Lo-Johansson directed himself include the gypsy question and old-age homes. Lo-Johansson spent the decade of the 1950s on a series of autobiographical novels (1951–60). Like Lo-Johansson, Jan FRIDEGÅRD had come from the sharecropper class and had used sharecropping as a motif; but, in contrast to Lo-Johansson, he was more individualistic and less inclined to paint a collective portrait. His most important work is a series of autobiographical novels about Lars Hård, including *Jag, Lars Hård* (1935; I, Lars Hård), *Tack för himlastegen* (1936; Thanks for the Heavenly Ladder), and *Barmhärtighet* (1936; Charity); a fourth part was added later. Besides Lo-Johansson and Fridegård, the "sharecroppers' school" in literature included Moa MARTINSON. Like most of the proletarian writers, she wrote historical novels, but her most significant work is a series of autobiographical novels including *Mor gifter sig* (1936; Mother Gets Married). Of all the proletarian writers, she was probably the most gifted, with original narrative powers; she was also, however, the most undisciplined. The foremost prose author during the time between the two world wars was also a proletarian writer and an autodidact—Eyvind JOHNSON; born in Norrbotten, he lived for several years during the 1920s in Paris and Berlin. Although his early works are in the novel form typical of the decade 1910–20, he soon turned to other models. Johnson himself has called André GIDE, Marcel PROUST, and James Joyce the most important of these. His novel *Minnas* (1928; To Remember) is the first

Swedish novel to use the technique of the interior monologue. Johnson's political conscience was strongly evident from the very beginning. After a short interlude of sexual romanticism in the manner of D. H. Lawrence, he published (1934–37) his autobiographical novel *Romanen om Olof* (The Novel about Olof), in four parts: *Nu var det 1914* (1934; Eng. tr., *1914*, 1970); *Här har du dit liv* (1935; Here's Your Life); *Se dig inte om* (1936; Don't Look Back); and *Slutspel i ungdomen* (1937; Youth's Finale). *Romanen om Olof* is primarily about how Johnson experienced his youth and matured to face new challenges, but at the same time the novel shows the whole region's existence against the gloomy background of the war years. It is characteristic of Johnson that, even in his concentration on the individual, he never ceased seeing him in the larger context—in time, the environment, and international politics. The problems that faced democracy, such as fascism and Nazism, were taken up by Johnson in a series of novels published during the 1930s and 1940s. In his rich production after World War II there is a new tendency: in the tradition of Thomas MANN, he chose to penetrate contemporary problems by immersing himself in history or the mythical world of the poetic past. The novel *Strändernas svall* (1946; Eng. tr., *Return to Ithaca*, 1952) is a naturalistic prose adaptation of the *Odyssey*, but it is subtitled "a novel about the present." In the novel, Johnson discussed the return of humanity from World War II. Johnson's very best books, among them *Return to Ithaca*, belong to this historical category. Others that deserve mention include *Drömmar om rosor och eld* (1949; Dreams about Roses and Fire), in which the main character, the priest Grainier, provides a fine synthesis of Johnson's personal ideal; and particularly *Hans nådes tid* (1960; Eng. tr., *The Days of His Grace*, 1968), which portrays Charlemagne's subjugation of the Lombard kingdom. Johnson shared the Nobel Prize for literature with Harry Martinson in 1974.

Johnson's style, full of nuances and variations, made him nearly an alien to the modern novel, with its hard-boiled, tough style usually associated with Ernest Hemingway. Swedish novelists who followed in Hemingway's footsteps included Walter Ljungquist (1900–74), author of the short novel *Ombyte av tåg* (1933; Change of Trains), and the novelist and critic Thorsten Georg JONSSON, for a time a newspaper correspondent in New York. The most original prose writer of the 1930s was the Värmland author Tage Aurell (1895–1976), whose individual lapidary style originated in his oral narrative techniques.

The literature that appeared during World War II represented a more radical modernism than the expressionism of World War I, and it is usually called the literature of the "Forties." Wartime experiences of meaningless destruction and suffering nourished a pessimism akin to Franz KAFKA's portrayal of terror and Jean-Paul SARTRE's and Albert CAMUS's existentialism. The poets of the "Forties" produced substantial achievements in both prose and drama, but their revival of lyric poetry was of prime importance.

The central figure among the poets of the "Forties" was Erik LINDEGREN. During the first year of World War II, he wrote the collection of poems that established his reputation, *mannen utan väg* (1942; Eng. tr., *The Man Without a Way*, 1969). The uncertainty expressed by the title refers not only to the reality of war; it concerns a profound crisis caused by the questioning of all aesthetic, intellectual, moral, and religious values—including scientific ones. The collection contains 40 14-line poems, "exploded sonnets," which together build a sequence of surrealistically arranged metaphors. Lindegren's conscious effort to create an interplay between thought, metaphor, and feeling is probably his personal application of T. S. Eliot's theory of the objective correlative. In addition to influences from surrealism and Eliot a fleeting impression can be glimpsed of Stephen Spender and Rilke, who are discernible behind the thought of transforming life and the world, of reaching out to new prospects through defeat. These themes provide a brighter stripe in the metaphorical weave of *The Man without a Way*. In Lindegren's next collection, *Sviter* (1947; Suites), there is, even more than in the previous work, a conscious linking of poetry to music and techniques of musical composition. Lindegren's lyrical diction here achieves a harmony and beauty that have seldom been surpassed in Swedish poetry. *Vinteroffer* (1954; Winter Sacrifice) was Lindegren's last book; many of its poems take up Lindegren's central theme: life and death as destruction and renewal interwoven. Like Lindegren, Karl VENNBERG stands out as a significant poet of the "Forties." During a personal crisis in the middle of the 1930s, Vennberg had read the works of Kafka; and, largely because of Vennberg, existential search for truth in the spirit of Kafka became a central theme in the Swedish literature of the "Forties." In a 1945 statement on Kafka and other pessimists, Vennberg called analysis of "cowardice, fear, and powerlessness . . .the correct action." This revealing analysis characterizes a major part of the poems in Vennberg's first two collections published in the 1940s, *Halmfackla* (1944; Straw Torch) and *Tideräkning* (1945; Reckoning of Time), and can be said to be a concise statement of the principal concerns of Swedish literature of the "Forties." The constellation of religious and existential problems that recurs in all of Vennberg's work is especially tangible in the collection *Fiskefärd* (1949; Fishing Trip), in which bitter analysis is counterbalanced by a kind of ironically guarded repose in simple idyll. In Vennberg's later poetry metaphysical motifs are rather prominent. In addition to these two central figures, the "Forties" produced an exceptionally large number of prominent poets, among them Gösta Oswald (1926–50), Ragnar Thoursie (1919–), Elsa Grave (1918–), Sven Alfons (1918–), and Werner ASPENSTRÖM. Aspenström began his "Forties" poetry in a self-assured, revealing manner in the style of Vennberg. Of the great poets of the decade, he is perhaps the most easily accessible; other poets of the "Forties" have often been accused of being incomprehensible. Aspenström's work also includes drama, for example, *Det eviga* (1958; Eng. tr., *The Apes Shall Inherit the Earth*, 1961), and *Mattan* (1964; The Carpet).

In the work of the novelist and dramatist Stig DAGERMAN can be seen most of the threads of the "Forties'" intricate weave—pessimism, existentialism, Kafkaesque terror, inaccessibility, analysis of human conditions, and political radicalism. His first book, a novel entitled *Ormen* (1945; The Serpent), was a Kafkaesque study of terror that did not, however, actually use Kafka's style. His second book, *De dömdas ö* (1946; The Isle of the Damned) was called by Lindegren "a flying fortress of the 'Forties' problems." In fact, this book's incredible richness of symbol may be seen as a prose counterpart to Lindegren's *The Man Without a Way*. Nightmares pursue one another in a nearly surrealistic technique of composition. The analysis of anxiety threatens to result in complete defeat before life, but the book also offers a kind of paradoxical attempt at solution in the "total, clearly enlightened conscience." Among Dagerman's plays, *Den dödsdömde* (1947; *The Condemned,* 1951), a study of guilt, deserves particular mention. In Dagerman's last novels the earlier symbolic technique has yielded to a stronger link with reality, although this realism is never far from the bizarre and the fantastic.

The picture of prose writing during the "Forties" is perhaps more diversified than that of poetry. A radical revival of proletarian writing was attempted by Folke Fridell (1904–), and the Norrland portraitist Björn-Erik Höijer (1907–) also took as his point of departure the proletarian writing tradition of the "Thirties." Sivar Arnér (1909–) is a university man by education. His style is clear, direct, and to the point; many of his books have a realistic, scarcely modernistic quality. Nevertheless, the inner monologue is one of his earlier and most significant narrative techniques. In an early article he clearly rejected simple realism, as well as mere aesthetic observation: literature is to be judged as "an assertion about life." This implies that he gives his books an allegorical cast. In his first novel, *Plånbok borttappad* (1943; Lost Wallet), he let the story of an ordinary sausage dealer become a mirror of the battle between nations and ideologies. Arnér is almost a pacifist and commits himself to the "third standpoint" (*tredje ståndpunkten*), an attempt to choose neither East nor West in Cold War times. One of his themes is the question of whether one should become involved in or stand outside of the world and its strife—his problem of the will is linked to that of existentialism. In spite of his pessimistic viewpoint, he opposes a gloomy view of humanity such as that found, for example in Samuel BECKETT and absurdism. In many novels he seeks to balance his pessimistic view of life with a mystical kind of "unity experience." Arnér has also written plays for the stage and radio. Considerably more complex is the work of Lars AHLIN, possibly the foremost narrator of the generation of the "Forties." Even before publishing his first work, he had rejected the concept of what he called "novels of illusion," that is, the realistic and naturalistic novels that began with Gustave Flaubert. Instead, he referred to what he called the "real realism" or the "Christian realism" he found in Fyodor DOSTO-YEVSKY and Sigrid UNDSET. Ahlin's basic theme is equality. In his first book, *Tåbb med manifestet* (1943; Tåbb and the Manifesto), the protagonist learns that Marxism does not solve the problem of equality; elitist thinking has made inroads even in Marxism. Instead, he refers to Martin Luther's view of humanity: "simul justus et peccator" (righteous and sinning at the same time), a formula that breaks down all rank between individuals. Equality demands that men accept each other's differences. Ahlin has experimented in all of his work with a new novel form. Instead of following naturalistic representation, his novels are intended as a play on words, a game with the conventions of the language, a conspiracy between address and answer. In *Min död är min* (1945; My Death is Mine) there are some autobiographic aspects, but the realism breaks down into the grotesque and the fantastic. Ahlin's foremost novels include *Fromma mord* (1954; Pious Murder) and *Natt i marknadstältet* (1957; Night in the Booth). A novel that attempts to make precise the kernel of Ahlin's aesthetic speculation is *Bark och löv* (1961; Bark and Leaves). Outside the circle of the "Forties" writers but nevertheless expressing the decade's central themes is Ingmar BERGMAN, best known as a theater and film director. He has written the scripts for many of his films, and in 1942 he wrote the play *Kaspers död* (The Death of Casper). Disgust with life, fear of death, terror, and the moral problems of good and evil characterize his plays as well as his film scripts.

In spite of its many nuances, the decade of the "Forties" appears as an unusually unified literary period. The literature of the 1950s and 1960s hardly shows the same kind of unity. Sometimes certain isolated tendencies from the "Forties" have been followed, for example, allusion and metaphor technique on the one hand and political consciousness on the other. Sometimes writers have reacted against the complexity and inaccessibility of the modernism of the "Forties." Lyric poetry hardly plays the same dominant role, but it is still the most sensitive expression of new literary tendencies. Lars Forssell made his debut as a poet with *Ryttaren* (1949; The Rider). Although in his erudite sensibility he resembles the writers of the "Forties," he is more interested in Ezra Pound, whose works he has translated, than in Eliot. It is characteristic of him that he was later interested in songs, especially carbaret songs with a French flavor, such as "Snurra min jord och andra visor" (1958; Spin, My Earth, and New Ballads), and this simplicity makes itself felt in his other lyrics, and in the collection *Telegram* (1957). Forssell's songs often were politically topical; during the 1960s he followed the general politicization and radicalization of literature that accompanied the Vietnam War. His dramatic works are frequently staged; his first play, *Kröningen* (1956; Eng. tr., *The Coronation,* 1963), about Alcestis, has an antique motif. A central theme in Forssell's works is fear, as, for example in *The Coronation.* Östen SJÖSTRAND made his debut in the same year as Forssell, with the collection *Unio* (1949; Union). Sjöstrand is primarily a poet, but also a librettist and essayist. He has been a Catholic, and his poetic striving has a religious aspect. To him, words are inadequate as a mode of expression, but poetry reaches out to the ineffable. Strong religious aspects also are found in the work of Bo Setterlind (1923–). The foremost lyric poet to appear after the "Forties" is perhaps Tomas Tranströmer, who made his literary debut with *17 dikter* (1954; 17 Poems). Although he followed the traditions of the "Forties" as well as of surrealism, it was in his own strongly restrained form. Few poets build so entirely on metaphors as he; but at the same time his powerful, sensual concreteness results in an intense contact with reality. Out of his poems comes a vision of profound coherence, which sometimes takes on a religious, mystical character. One of his most noteworthy collections of poems is *Östersjöar* (1974; Eng. tr., *Baltics,* 1975), in which the experience of the moment is illuminated by a confrontation with the past. Göran PALM began his career as a literary critic, an extremely sensitive interpreter of the complex poetry of the "Forties," sometimes dissociating himself from every political judgment in the poem. Toward the close of the 1950s he turned away entirely from "difficult" modern literature and demanded from poetry a political commitment to the overthrow of the established society. In his own poetry collections, *Hundens besök* (1961; The Dog's Visit) and *Världen ser dig* (1964; The World Sees You), he rejects "the old metaphysical aristocratic modernism" and performs instead "experiments in simplicity." His use of everyday speech and aggressive political messages certainly fulfills the requirement of reaching out to the public, but Palm's "new and simple" (*nyenkel*) poetry seeks also to communicate a specific experience of reality, and this subtle message is not directly accessible. Palm is also part of the movement toward a more documentary approach, which is very important in the Swedish literature of the 1960s. Instead of literary criticism he writes personal social reportage, for example, *En orättvis betraktelse* (1966; Eng. tr., *As The World Sees Us,* 1968), an indictment of the outdated Western view of the Third World and *Indoktrineringen i Sverige* (1968; Indoctrination in Sweden), about how human beings' mode of observation is determined from childhood by the social and economic system. Other representatives of "new and simple" poetry are Björn Håkansson (1937–) and Sonja Åkesson (1926–77). The everyday motifs in Åkesson's poetry and prose are often pungently formulated social satire. Her poems about discrimination against women have had great impact, as, for example, in the collection *Husfrid* (1963; Domestic Peace). At about the same time as the "new and simple" poets turned to everyday speech and sought the widest possible comprehensibility, other poets appeared who leaned in exactly the opposite direction. These were "concretists," who disregard the conventional meaning of words and seek to build their work on the pattern of music and modern art by treating words as pure sound groups or as shapes on a page. Some of the concretists were originally artists, painters, or sculptors, as, for example, Öjvind Fahlström (1928–1976) and Carl Fredrik Reuterswärd (1934–). The foremost representative of concretism is Bengt Emil Johnson (1936–), who is also a musician. Certain of his poems consist of more or less meaningless words, whose placement on a page forms graphic patterns. Other poems begin with a strong group of words, which are then repeated, varied, or have their letters shuffled according to a purely musical pattern. In his more recent poetry, Johnson has begun to deal with the meaning of words—he is no longer a concretist although in his poetry he seeks to use certain of concretism's conquests of new territory. Extraordinarily productive as a critic, prose writer, and poet is Lars GUSTAFSSON. He is a philosopher by profession, having studied with Gilbert Ryle at Oxford. Despite his grounding in sober English antimetaphysical philosophy, he has a lively interest in the categories of the fantastic. The bondage of humanity to various types of order becomes an important motif in his poetry. Sudden awareness of the grotesque net in which humanity is caught, liberates, so to speak, the fantastic in his work. Often this antimetaphysician consciously brushes against mysticism. The work of another poet, Göran SONNEVI, has strong ties to modern linguistic philosophy. Sonnevi's starting point is that humanity is determined by language and its possibilities. His poem about the Vietnam War, printed in a magazine in 1965, took as its point of departure the problem of language and communication and derived its striking power largely from this.

Swedish prose writing after the 1940s exhibits to some extent the same tendencies as poetry. A modernist, experimental trend develops from the prose of the 1940s, particularly that of Ahlin; the religious novel makes an appearance; the affinity for the simple and ordinary finds a certain counterpart in a tendency to give documentation and facts almost literary formulation; and, naturally enough, the politicization and social direction of the 1960s are reflected in the novel. The most multifaceted and possibly the most significant prose writer is Lars GYLLENSTEN. He is a medical researcher with a large scientific output, a background basic to his fiction. His first literary work was a sort of parody of the poetry of the "Forties," but the body of his work is, nevertheless, a fulfillment of the experimental modernist trend of the "Forties." He tries new concepts from work to work. His first three prose works experiment with attitudes toward life in the manner of Søren KIRKEGAARD and form a trilogy as thesis, antithesis, and synthesis. Other works of his are dominated by a stream-of-consciousness technique, some by experiments with time in the style of Thomas Mann. Gyllensten has also constructed books

using Emanuel Swedenborg as a starting point, as well as writing frequent polemic articles in the daily press. A considerably smaller body of work has been produced by the Finnish writer Willy KYRKLUND. With a refined, ironic style, Kyrklund outlines the problems of human existence. Some of his books are virtually collections of short stories. In others, he gropes along his own highly unusual path, using as forms pastiche, parody, fairy tale, and a kind of philosophical travel description. He has few peers in his exact, precise prose style. The first books by Birgitta TROTZIG such as *Bilder* (1954; Pictures) possess a certain relationship to the visual arts. In a few historical novels with motifs from Skåne in the 15th and 17th centuries, she depicts human suffering with nearly unendurable intensity. Suffering and a search for God are central motifs in her work, which has its background in her Catholic faith and obviously is not uninfluenced by French Catholic writers. The first novel by Sara LIDMAN, *Tjärdalen* (1953; The Tar Well), took its motif from her Norrland home region in northern Sweden; in several other novels about Norrland, she portrays moral problems such as deceit and responsibility among people in an isolated rural area. After a sojourn in South Africa (1960–61), her work took a new direction, first seen in her novel *Jag och min son* (1961; I and My Son). Its set of moral problems is given political dimensions in the shadow of apartheid politics. Lidman is a central example of politicization and internationalization in Swedish literature of the 1960s. Her last books touched on the Vietnam War and the working conditions of the miners in northern Sweden. A trip to South Africa meant a conversion to reporting and to stronger political commitment also for Per WÄSTBERG. He nonetheless continues his richly varied novel writing, in which the milieu is often Stockholm and the discussion often centers on the problems of love. Jan Myrdal (1927–) has been strongly international and politically directed. In many novels written during the 1950s he satirized domestic phenomena. Lengthy foreign visits (for example, to Afghanistan and China) resulted in a new type of book, documented social reportage, of which the most important is *Rapport från kinesisk by* (1963; Eng. tr., *Report from a Chinese Village*, 1966). In his writings Myrdal continues to cultivate social criticism in almost journalistic form. Sven Lindqvist (1932–) began his career by writing personally felt aphorisms and essays, directed toward finding a valid philosophy of life. His reflections on life took the form of travel writing in *Hemmaresan* (1959; The Trip at Home). The tension between life and art is central in Lindqvist's most important work, *Myten om Wu Tao-tzu* (1967; The Myth about Wu Tao-Tzu), which also builds on travel experiences in India and China. His pointed political awareness has been expressed in large, politically analytical travel accounts from various parts of the world, including South America (*Slagskuggan*, 1969; The Cast Shadow). Dealing with many of the same problems as Lindqvist but always very much the novelist is Per Olov ENQUIST. The theme of his early novels is the writer and his possibility of discovering truth. Enquist takes a step over into the documentary novel with *Legionärerna* (1968; Eng. tr., *The Legionnaires*, 1973), concerning a historical occurrence right after the close of World War II, in which the Swedish government accommodated a Russian demand to surrender certain Baltic refugees. In its documentary approach the work is like a scientific inquiry without, however, ceasing to be a novel. A form of objectivity other than the documentary is to be found in the work of Per Olof SUNDMAN. His is a purely behavioristic viewpoint: people's inner life, their feelings and thoughts, are unobtainable information—only their speech and deeds can be recorded. Sundman makes this an aesthetic principle. In a dry, matter-of-fact style he records objective facts about the scene and characters. His technique can be seen as a variant of the French "new novel" of Alain ROBBE-GRILLET and Michel BUTOR, although Sundman is hardly directly influenced by them. Sundman is extremely interested in social interplay. His novel *Ingenjör Andrées luftfärd* (1967; Eng. tr., *The Flight of the Eagle,* 1970) is about a factual event, an attempt to reach the North Pole in a balloon in 1897, and it approaches in form a documentary novel. The first novels of Torsten Ekbom (1938-) are based on the techniques of the "new novel," and he has since continued to experiment, for example, with collage. In 1960 the physician Per Christian JERSILD published his first work, a collection of short stories. In a series of richly varied books, often playfully grotesque, he has revealed the seamy side of the welfare state. In *Calvinols resa genom världen* (1965; Calvinol's Journey through the World), he has satirized worldwide folly, from the medieval Children's Crusade to the recent Russian dictators. The most significant prose writer of the 1960s is Sven *Delblanc.* A literary historian by profession, he uses his knowledge of literary and historical milieus in his writing. His rich narrative powers enable him to use grotesques in the spirited manner of Rabelais or philosophical stories in the manner of Voltaire. He can write a contemporary diary and a picaresque travel novel with equal ease.

The interest in children's and young people's literature has been astonishing in the last decades. Around the turn of the century Sweden had an internationally renowned children's writer in Elsa Beskow (1874-1953), and the works of Astrid Lindgren (1907-) have awakened similar interest in every country. Lindgren's first popular book was *Pippi Långstrump* (1945; Eng. tr., *Pippi Longstocking,* 1950). Her humor and linguistic imagination, masterfully utilizing the possibilities of everyday language, raise her books above most other children's literature. At approximately the same time the Finnish writer Tove Jansson (1914-) appeared on the scene with children's books, which she herself illustrated. Jansson creates an imaginary world around the family of the "moomintrolls," whose fairy-tale community comes close to mirroring the warm relationships of the artistic-bohemian family in which the author grew up. In the intense debate of the 1960s on children's literature and its significance there was a demand from the radical Left for a consciously political children's literature.

Swedish literary criticism after Levertin has had significant representatives. Levertin's heir as leading critic was the literary scholar Fredrik Böök (1883-1961). He admired the writers of the "Nineties" and was an advocate of the sober, often realistic, realism that he rediscovered in the works of some of the writers around 1910. John Landquist (1881-1974) has generally been considered the foremost critic of these years. In a certain opposition to these middle-class critics were the critics of the working-class press, in particular, Bengt Lidforss (1868-1913) and Erik Hedén (1875-1925). Left-oriented criticism was continued by the literary historian Victor Svanberg (1896-) and the poet and art historian Erik Blomberg (1894-1965); the latter sought to adopt a Marxist viewpoint in his literary judgment. The most important critic of the 1930s was Knut Jaensson (1883-1958). He opposed conventional morality in criticism and demanded of a writer first and foremost truth and individuality. Artur Lundkvist's great contribution as a critic has been mentioned, as has that of the leading writers of the "Forties,"

Lindegren and Vennberg. Bengt Holmqvist (1924-) has shown profound understanding of the modernist tradition in Finland-Swedish literature and the writers of the "Forties." An erratic personal performance as a critic has marked the career of Olof Lagercrantz (1911-), from 1960 to 1975 editor in chief of Sweden's leading newspaper, *Dagens Nyheter.*

Literary criticism in the tradition of Hippolyte Taine was founded in Sweden at the close of the 19th century by Henrik Schück (1885-1947), who emphasized aspects of cultural and critical history. During the first years of the 20th century, comparative literature made great gains in Swedish criticism, primarily through the work of Martin Lamm (1880-1950) and Anton Blanck (1881-1951). Since then the comparative direction has been dominant in Swedish criticism. It has also been influential on researchers who sought other paths. Thus it was with Fredrik Böök, who early in his career opposed the domination of the historical and comparative viewpoint and attempted to reach a more profound literary understanding with *Geistesgeschichte* from Germany. Henry Olsson (1896-) is also essentially a comparatist (although he attempts psychological analysis of the type of Alfred Adler's individual psychology) as is Victor Svanberg, who shifted from comparative studies to the sociology of literature. Comparative literature had a coloration of history of ideas and aestheticism in the work of Albert Nilsson (1878-1936). Medieval ballads were researched by Sverker Ek (1887-) and Karl-Ivar Hildeman (1919-). Important contributions to the study of baroque literature were made by Carl Fehrman (1915-), Magnus von Platen (1920-), and Bernt Olsson (1929-). The study of aesthetics of the novel was introduced in Sweden by Staffan Björck (1915-). The comparatist Gunnar Tideström (1906-) sought regeneration with New Criticism, and one of the themes of his criticism has been the relationship between literature and other art forms. In the abundant scholarship on Strindberg, which was introduced in earnest by Martin Lamm, important contributions have been made by Gunnar Brandell (1916-) and Hans Lindström (1918-). Studies on drama have been made by Lennart Breitholtz (1909-) and Ingvar Holm (1923-). Peter Hallberg (1916-) has researched Icelandic literature, including the sagas and the works of Halldór LAXNESS.

See: A. Gustafson, *A History of Swedish Literature* (1961; includes a detailed bibliographical guide and a list of translations); E. Hj. Linder, *Fem decennier av nittonhundratalet,* vols. 1-2, (4th ed. 1965-66); G. Brandell, *Svensk litteratur 1900-1950,* (2d ed. 1967); *Ny illustrerad svensk litteraturhistoria,* ed. by E. N. Tigerstedt, vol. 4 (2d ed. 1967); *Svenskt litteraturlexikon,* (2d ed. 1970); *Epoker och diktare, 2. Allmän och svensk litteraturhistoria,* ed. by L. Breitholtz (1972); J. Stenkvist, *Den nyaste litteraturen,* vol. 3 in Brandell-Stenkvist, *Svensk litteratur 1870-1970* (1975).   N.Å.S.

Swiss literature. Switzerland has a rich literary tradition. In modern times both the German- and the French-speaking regions have produced important writers who left distinctive marks on the literature and culture of their time. The 18th century was a time of literary florescence in Switzerland. Important writers of that period include the Bernese patrician Albrecht von Haller (1708-77), whose long poem *Die Alpen* (1729; The Alps) extols the beauty and grandeur of nature; Johann Jokob Bodmer (1698-1783) and Johann Jakob Breitinger (1701-66) of Zürich, who helped free German literature from the confines of rigid rules; Jean-Jacques Rousseau (1712-78), "citizen of Geneva," whose epochal writings reflect the indelible impressions he received while growing up in Geneva and on the shores of Lake Leman; Benjamin Constant (1767–1830) and Madame de Staël (née Germaine Necker, 1766–1817), the brilliant, cosmopolitan couple from Coppet; and Johann Heinrich Pestalozzi (1746–1827), the Zürich humanitarian and pedagogue, whose didactic village novel *Lienhard und Gertrud* (1781) became a bible for educators while achieving great popularity among the common people for whom it was written.

Of the many writers Switzerland produced during the 19th century, three overshadow all others: Jeremias Gotthelf, pseud. of Albert Bitzius (1797–1854), Gottfried Keller (1819–90), and Conrad Ferdinand Meyer (1825–98). They are important in the history of German und European literature as well as in that of Switzerland. Gotthelf is internationally the least known largely because his writings, interspersed with difficult dialect passages, seem on the surface to be folkloristic village stories. Yet the patient reader can derive great satisfaction from Gotthelf's religious and political engagement, his faith in the good in man, and his ability to depict peasant life in the Bernese Emmental with sweep and power. *Uli der Knecht* (1841; Eng. tr., *Uli the Farm Servant*, 1888), *Anne Bäbi Jowäger* (1843–44), and *Geld und Geist* (1843–44; Eng. tr., *Wealth and Welfare*, 1866) are three of the dozen great novels that, together with his many short stories—notably "Die schwarze Spinne" (The Black Spider) and "Elsi die seltsame Magd" (Elsie the Strange Maid)—have established Gotthelf as "perhaps the greatest epic genius of the German tongue" (Werner Günther).

Keller and Meyer were both from Zürich, and both found their calling as writers relatively late in life. Keller's famous autobiographical novel *Der grüne Heinrich* (1854; Eng. tr., *Green Henry*, 1960), as well as his short stories and many of his poems, reflect his close ties to his native soil, sometimes expressed as exuberant love and pride, at other times as sustained social criticism. More reserved and detached, Meyer chose for his subject matter events and figures from the distant past. His only novel, *Jürg Jenatsch* (1876), focuses on the religious wars of the 17th century; his short stories are set in Renaissance Italy and France. These works, as well as many of his poems, are perfect in form and style.

The heights of achievement and recognition reached by Gotthelf, Keller, and Meyer were not to be approached by any other Swiss writer until Max FRISCH and Friedrich DÜRRENMATT began to attract international attention after World War II. And yet the writers after Keller and Meyer and before Frisch and Dürrenmatt, who published during the first half of the 20th century, were by no means insignificant. Among them were Charles-Ferdinand RAMUZ, the greatest of the French-Swiss writers, and Francesco CHIESA, the best of the Italian-Swiss. Important German-Swiss writers of that period include Carl SPITTELER, Jakob BOSSHART, Jakob SCHAFFNER, Robert WALSER, Meinrad INGLIN, and Albin ZOLLINGER.

Many Swiss writers struggle with the fateful fact that they are citizens of a small country. To begin with, this means that their works find a limited public at home and that, to get the desired artistic echo and necessary financial security, they must appeal to foreign readers. At another level, these writers may suffer the anxiety of belonging to a nation that seems stranded at a historical dead end. They view the political neutrality that kept Switzerland out of two world wars as an unheroic stance that condemned the Swiss to an existence without history (*Geschichtslosigkeit*), forcing them to be mere onlookers at the epochal events of their time. In consequence, a sense of unrest characteristically pervades much of 20th-century Swiss literature; it is reflected in the titles of novels such as Zollinger's *Die große Unruhe* (1939; The Great Restlessness), or in those of more recent works of criticism like Karl Schmid's (1907–74) *Unbehagen im Kleinstaat* (1963; Discomfort in the Small State), Paul Nizon's (1929–) *Diskurs in der Enge* (1970; Discussion under Constraint), and Dieter Fringeli's (1942–) *Dichter im Abseits* (1974; Writers on the Sideline).

This dissatisfaction with Switzerland led different writers to take different courses of action. Some, feeling neglected or alienated at home, left Switzerland in an attempt to break away from what they felt to be their country's stifling confines. But even though they might write their best works abroad or have their deepest experiences there, many returned to their homeland in the end. One who did not was Jakob Schaffner, who sought the fulfillment of his longing in the folkish movement of Hitler's Germany and died in a bombing attack on Strasberg in 1944. Schaffner's fellow countrymen never forgave him for his desertion; his name and works are still taboo, even though his prose writings are among the finest in 20th-century Swiss literature. Other members of the interwar "lost generation" fared better. The works of writers such as Walser, Zollinger, Inglin, Friedrich Glauser (1896–1938) and, among the French-Swiss, Blaise CENDRARS, have been republished in collected works, and the men themselves have become "textbook saints" and "instant classics" (D. Fringeli).

Discontented Swiss writers had recourse to two other remedies in addition to that of going abroad: either they took refuge in some kind of Utopia, or they became absorbed in the small world of their community and region. Carl Spitteler is the outstanding example of one who chose the former remedy. In his grandiose verse epics he created a world filled with gods and mythical heroes. Among those who immersed themselves in their immediate neighborhoods were the "fatherland poets" who wrote in a folkloristic genre and petty bourgeois mood about Switzerland. Other writers limited themselves to small geographic and social circles but filled them with real life, thus producing works of true excellence. Many French-Swiss writers and poets, solitary wanderers like Rousseau, chose a corner of their Romandie and transformed it in lasting works of art. Ramuz is the greatest of these, but others of importance are S. Corinna Bille (1912–79), Maurice Chappaz (1916–), and Yves Velan (1925–), who write of the Valais, and Jacques CHESSEX, who produces superb portraits of the Vaud and the Vaudois. Giuseppe ZOPPI from Ticino and Romansh writers from Canton Graubünden, such as Artur Caflisch (1893–1967) and Andri Peer (1921–) should also be mentioned.

The French- and Italian-Swiss writers suffer more than their German-speaking compatriots from being cut off from their natural language community by political boundaries. Ramuz's discouragement is revealed in his expressions of love-hatred for the Swiss confederation in general and his Alemannic compatriots in particular. Yet the belief in Switzerland and its political and cultural mission is rooted strongly among most of these writers. If only the obstacles *within* the country itself could be broken down! Chappaz and others have been calling for an intensified program of translating literary works from French into German and vice versa, and major concerted efforts in this direction are now under way. The six million inhabitants of Switzerland should be a sufficiently large public to sustain their authors, even though these write in four different languages. Of course, some critics feel that Switzerland is anything but a cultural entity.

Thus, an authoritative recent work on Swiss literature significantly is entitled *Die zeitgenössischen Literaturen der Schweiz* (1974; The Contemporary Literatures of Switzerland). Other critics, including the author of this article, have maintained that there is a specifically Swiss culture—not of the melting-pot variety—which is based on a community of will, a sense and knowledge of belonging to a historically grown organism the reality of which transcends linguistic barriers.

The German-Swiss writers have had still another difficulty to overcome: since their mother tongue is the dialect of the community and region in which they grow up, and since they have to learn the high-German language in school, they are bilingual within their own cultural province. Many writers have attempted to express themselves in their dialect, and some have achieved considerable distinction. Meinrad Lienert's (1865-1933) *Schwäbelpfyffli* (1913), written in Schwyz dialect, elevated the dialect poem from the level of children's verses and patriotic occasion pieces to that of a true art form. Rudolf von Tavel's (1866-1934) *Ring i der Chetti* (1931; Links in the Chain) is a powerful novel of his native Bern during the 15th-century Burgundian wars, even though it, like his other novels, is difficult for non-Bernese to read. Josef Reinhart (1875-1957) wrote poems and stories in the Solothurn dialect.

Dialect literature had its heyday during the 1930s, when a movement was under way to elevate "Alemannic" into one of the official administrative languages of Switzerland. One of the many manifestations of resistance to the folkish allurements of Nazi Germany, this movement never got anywhere, even though it gave important impulses to a more intensive linguistic analysis of the Swiss dialects. (The article "Swiss literature in Alamannic" in the first edition of the *Columbia Dictionary of Modern European Literature* is a historical document, reflecting the spirit of those years.) Contemporary Swiss writers continue to experiment with dialect forms. They consciously avoid, however, folkloristic, patriotic, and historic motives and instead use the dialect as an idiom to express modern thoughts and problems. The Bernese pastor Kurt Marti has been most successful in this genre, and his thin volume of poems, *rosa loui* (1967), has had a succès d'estime even in Germany.

The two decades from Hitler's accession to power in Germany to the end of the Korean War were difficult for Swiss writers. Their country was on the defensive throughout, seeking strength in an essentially conservative attitude toward outside forces and influences. All energies were concentrated on preserving the historic Swiss heritage and upholding traditional values. The Cold War prolonged this frozen state of affairs. Thus, much of the contemporary literary production in Switzerland must be understood as a reaction to what is still felt to have been a stifling confinement. The first writers to break out of it, to bring in a fresh breath of air and set the dialogue with the outside world going again, were Frisch and Dürrenmatt. For more than a decade they dominated the Swiss literary scene, mainly through an astonishing outpouring of excellent plays, but also through various prose works. For the educated public abroad they symbolize Swiss literature in the 20th century.

Since about 1960, however, the literary scene in Switzerland has changed drastically. Frisch and Dürrenmatt are still productive, but they are no longer the lone, towering giants. Many new talents have emerged and are freely competing with their famous compatriots for the attention of the public. Representative of this outburst of creative writing are Marti, Erika Burkart, Otto F. Walter, Jürg Federspiel, Adolf Muschg, Chessex, and Peter Bichsel. Examples of works by these and other writers can be found in two anthologies: *Bestand und Versuch: Schweizer Schrifttum der Gegenwart* (1964; Inventory and Experiment: Swiss Literature of Our Time), which includes works by 160 authors writing in five languages, if the various Alemannic dialects are counted as one separate tongue, and *Gut zum Druck: Literatur der deutschen Schweiz seit 1964* (1972; Fit to Print; Literature of German Switzerland since 1964), which contains samples of the works of 97 writers.

Many of the samples in these volumes, even the prose pieces, are complete literary works. This points to the fact that some of the best contemporary Swiss prose writers are literary miniaturists. They, including Max Frisch in his *Tagebuch 1966-1971* (1972; Eng. tr. *Sketchbook 1966-1971*, 1974), feel more comfortable with the short story, the aphorism, the reportage, the sketch. These forms express their restlessness, ideas, and poetic needs. Many of the younger authors also write scripts for radio and television and are involved in the remarkable renaissance of Swiss filmmaking. They contribute to a literary output of a richness and variety unprecedented in the history of Swiss literature.

This brief overview would be incomplete if no mention were made of a few of the outstanding scholars and essayists who have brought their intellectual resources and capacity for understanding to bear on the cultural and political aspects of Swiss life. *Bestand und Versuch* contains works by a number of these writers, including Gonzague de Reynold (1880-1970), the Fribourg artistocrat, founder of the New Helvetic Society and indefatigable promotor of Swiss values and traditions: Carl Jacob Burckhardt (1891-1974), the internationally famous Basel diplomat, historian, and essayist; Hans Zbinden (1893-1971), professor of the sociology and critique of culture at the University of Bern; Max Rychner (1897-1965), honored as the great mediator of European literature of the interwar years; Denis de Rougemont (1906-), from Neuchâtel, the ardent missionary of a united Europe; Emil Staiger, former professor at the University of Zürich and internationally recognized as an authority on Goethe and German literature; Werner Weber (1919-), the learned and incisive literary critic of the *Neue Zürcher Zeitung*, since 1973 professor at the University of Zürich; and Jean Starobinski, the Geneva scholar and expert on the Enlightenment and Rousseau. Again, these few prominent individuals stand for numerous others. All are an integral part of the rich and complex literary life of modern Switzerland.

See: W. Günther, *Dichter der neueren Schweiz*, 2 vols. (1963, 1968); G. Calgari, *Die vier Literaturen der Schweiz* (1966; original in Italian, 1958): K. Marti, *Die Schweiz und ihre Schriftsteller—die Schriftsteller und ihre Schweiz* (1966); E. Wilbert-Collins, *A Bibliography of Four Contemporary German-Swiss Authors* (1967; Dürrenmatt, Frisch, Walser, Zollinger); J. P. Monnier, *Littérature romande d'aujourd'hui* (1970); W. Bucher and G. Ammann, eds., *Schweizer Schriftsteller im Gespräch*, 2 vols. (1970, 1971); W. Sorell, *The Swiss: A Cultural Panorama of Switzerland* (1972); D. Fringeli, *Dichter im Abseits* (1974); M. Gsteiger, ed., *Die zeitgenössichen Literaturen der Schweiz* (1974); M. Gsteiger, *La nouvelle littérature romande* (1978; tr. of the part on French-Swiss literature in the preceding work); U. von Wiese, ed., *Schweiz/Suisse/Svizzera/Svizra: Schriftsteller der Gegenwart* (1978; lists 773 German-Swiss, 339 French-Swiss, 74 Italian-Swiss and 28 Romansh authors); D. Bachmann, ed., *Fortschreiben* (1977); E. Ammann and E. Faes, eds., *Literatur aus der Schweiz, Texte und Materialien* (1978).   H.K.M.

Symonenko, Vasyl (1935–63), Ukrainian poet and short-story writer. He was one of the so-called *shestydesyatnyky* (the Generation of the 1960s), who led a new wave of literary protest during that decade. In contrast to his contemporaries, Symonenko's poetry is more traditional than modernist in form. Some critics compare his simplicity, social satire, and national pathos to those of Taras Shevchenko (see UKRAINIAN LITERATURE). His collections of poetry are *Tysha i hrim* (1962; Silence and Thunder) and *Zemne tyazhinnya* (1964; Earth's Gravity). The short-story collection *Vyno z troyand* (Rose Wine) was published in 1965. Some hitherto unpublished poems and a diary appeared abroad under the title *Bereh chekan* (1965; Edge of Anticipation). English translations of some of his poems are available in *Four Ukrainian Poets* (1969). A selection of his poems has appeared in English under the title *Granite Obelisks* (1975).   G.S.N.L.

Szabó, Dezső (1879–1945), Hungarian novelist, essayist, and pamphleteer, was born in Kolozsvár (now Cluj-Napoca, Romania). He studied Hungarian and French philology at the University of Budapest. After graduation, he spent a year in Paris and later visited France on several occasions. Between 1906 and 1918, Szabó was a schoolteacher in various provincial towns; his first political involvement dates from this period, during which his views swung wildly from the extreme Right to the extreme Left. Szabó published essays on French literature as well as some early short stories in the journal *Nyugat*. These stories, collected in the volumes *Napló és elbeszélések* (1918; Diary and Stories) and *Mesék a kacagó emberről* (1919; Tales about the Laughing Man), were the first examples of expressionistic prose in Hungary.

Szabó's ideology was influenced by Friedrich NIETZSCHE, Maurice BARRÈS, positivism, and social Darwinism, yet his abhorrence of war, and revulsion over the profiteering and moral collapse of the bourgeoisie, led to a conscientious dilemma that he thought he could solve by relying on the myth of the vital forces of the peasantry and of the "pure Hungarian race." These concepts formed the basis of his major novel, *Az elsodort falu* (1919; The Village That Was Swept Away), which made an enormous impact on the average middle-class reader, impoverished by the war and frightened by revolution. In the years following the counterrevolution of 1919, the book became Hungary's greatest best-seller; its message was racist and xenophobic, and its anticapitalism based on populist delusions. The book's style, although dynamic, is also verbose and turgid. Szabó's later novels, *Csodálatos élet* (1921; Wondrous Life) and *Segítség!* (1925; Help!), are even less coherent and more widely melodramatic than *Az elsodort falu*, yet these later works are increasingly critical of the opportunism, dishonesty, and corruption of the "Christian and conservative" regime of Admiral Horthy. Although Szabó's ideas influenced the young "village-explorers" of the 1930s, he became more and more isolated both as a public figure and as a writer: the one-man periodicals he launched in rapid succession foundered on the rocks of public indifference. Furthermore, in the 1930s he became a passionate critic of German expansionist aspirations and attacked the pro-German Hungarian Fascists with his usual vehemence, unaware that his own myth of Hungarian ethnic purity was congruent with most rightist ideologies. Szabó was

an irascible and histrionic personality with a special gift for vituperative pamphleteering; this talent served him well in political and literary debates but was largely responsible for his failure as a creative writer. Of his entire output only two short novels—*Feltámadás Makucskán* (1932; Resurrection at Makucska) and *A kötél legendája* (1934; The Legend of the Rope)—are regarded as being of lasting literary value, while his posthumously published autobiography, *Életeim* (2 vols., My Lives), has both a documentary and a literary significance.

See: P. Nagy, *Szabó Dezső az ellenforradalomban* (1960); P. Nagy, *Szabó Dezső* (1964); J. Reményi, *Hungarian Writers and Literature* (1964), pp. 341–47; Gy. Gombos, *Szabó Dezső* (1966).   G.G.

Szabó, Lőrinc (1900–57), Hungarian poet and translator, was born in Miskolc. He was an outstanding representative of the second *Nyugat* generation (*see* HUNGARIAN LITERATURE). The son of a locomotive engineer, Szabó was drafted into the army, but he left it in the aftermath of the 1918 Hungarian revolution. He studied Hungarian, German, and Latin philology at the University of Budapest but did not take a degree; instead, he joined the staff of the liberal *Est* newspapers in 1921. His skill at poetic translation, already in evidence during his student days, attracted the attention of Mihály BABITS. Szabó, Babits, and Árpád TÓTH published a translation of Charles BAUDELAIRE's complete *Fleurs du mal* in 1923. Translation interested Szabó throughout his life, and he produced accomplished, often brilliant translations of English, French, German, and (after World War II) Russian poetry.

Szabó's first volume of poetry, *Föld, erdő, Isten* (1922; Earth, Wood, God), was influenced both by Stefan GEORGE's cult of nature and Hellenism and by Babits's clarity of expression. His next three books of poetry, however, beginning with *Kalibán* (1923; Caliban), rebelled against the aesthetic ideals of the intelligentsia and against society. His was a double act of rebellion. On the formal level he experimented with expressionism, often abandoning rhymes, while his language, especially in *A Sátán műremekei* (1926; The Devil's Masterpieces), was edging closer to everyday speech. On the ideological plane, he emerged as a radical anticapitalist, whose fury against a society ruled and structured by money was more anarchistic than socialist. István Sőtér observed that Szabó's early poetry expressed the predicament of "the intellectual proletarian of the twenties."

For the year 1927, Szabó edited the short-lived but ambitious literary review *Pandora*. After 1926 his poetry became more intellectual. The collection *Te meg a világ* (1932; You and the World) and especially *Különbéke* (1936; A Separate Peace) contain fine self-analytical and reflexive poems that reveal a broader field of vision and a deeper understanding of psychological realism. These two volumes also demonstrated a willingness to come to terms with an irrational and immoral (or amoral) world. Philosophically, Szabó's poems seem to oscillate between a crude biological determinism and, as in "Tao-te-king" (1931) and "Szu-Vu-Kung lázadása" (1935; The Revolt of Szu-Vu-Kung), a dialectical agnosticism gleaned from Oriental philosophies. His most famous love poem of the period, "Semmiért egészen" (1931; Completely—For Nothing), is a dramatic summary of the demands of tyrannical love. Before and during World War II, Szabó's admiration for power and for "strong individuals" turned him into a sympathizer of the Third Reich but, with the exception of some nationalistic verse, his personal views left no trace on his poetry. Shortly after the war he began work on a cycle of sonnets, *Tücsökzene* (1947; Cricket Music), which he developed into his lyrical autobiography. These "Shakespearean" sonnets are characterized by a distinctive tension, an extraordinary richness of sensuous detail, and skillful dramatic composition. Szabó's last major work, *A huszonhatodik év* (1957; The 26th Year), is another cycle of sonnets that recounts a long love affair while it explores the nature of sensual and spiritual love. Both cycles illustrate Szabó's innovative use of direct speech and enjambment within the sonnet form.

See: G. Halász, "Te meg a világ," *Nyugat* 26 (1933): 133–135; Gy. Illyés, Foreword to *Szabó Lőrinc: válogatott versei* (1956); Gy. Rónay, "Tücsökzene," *Irodalomtörténet* (1959): 296–301; L. Kabdebó, *Szabó Lőrinc lázadó évtizede* (1970); Gy. Rába, *Szabó Lőrinc* (1972).
G.G.

Szaniawski, Jerzy (1886–1970), Polish dramatist and prose writer, was born in Zegrzynek, near Warsaw, and died in Warsaw. In 1933 he was elected a member of the Polish Academy of Literature. His theater is poetic, although it uses a realistic setting. It focuses on the conflict between the ideals and dreams of the individual and the common sense of society regarding the affirmation of traditional values that are rejected in the contemporary world. Szaniawski uses undertones, allegory, poetic moods, and subtle intellectual irony and humor mixed with melancholy, to show the diversity in meaning of the moral motivation attributed to human deeds and their evaluation. He is occupied with the dichotomy of dream and reality in such plays as *Ptak* (staged in 1923; publ. in 1930; The Bird), *Żeglarz* (staged in 1925; publ. in 1930; The Sailor), *Adwokat i róże* (staged in 1929; publ. in 1930; The Lawyer and the Roses), *Most* (staged in 1933; publ. in 1947; The Bridge), *Kowal, pieniądze i gwiazdy* (staged in 1948; publ. in 1957; The Blacksmith, Money, and the Stars). In his best-known play, *Dwa teatry* (1946; Two Theaters), in which the confrontation of dreams with reality is based on the dramatic experience of the Warsaw uprising during World War II, Szaniawski turns toward symbolism, toward psychological analysis of the human subconscious, toward grotesque deformation. His most popular short stories, *Profesor Tutka i inne opowiadania* (1954; Professor Tutka and Other Stories), are written in the form of a tale in which the imaginary title character tells stories in an aphoristic and grotesque manner about the mysteries of human behavior.

See: *Słownik Współczesnych Pisarzy Polskich*, vol. 3 (1964), pp. 252–61; K. Nastulanka, *Jerzy Szaniawski* (1973).
A.W. with S.F.

Szelburg-Zarembina, Ewa (1899–), Polish novelist, short-story writer, and playwright, was born in Bronowice, near Puławy. She first established her literary reputation with a collection of short stories for children, *Wesołe historie* (1928; Eng. tr., *Who Can Tell*, 1959). Soon, however, she emerged as a major author of contemporary psychological novels, often with strong moral and social overtones and filled with lyricism and fantasy of folk origin, such as the cycle of novels later called *Rzeka kłamstwa* (The Stream of Lies), which consists of five parts: *Wędrówka Joanny* (1935; Joanna's Journey), *Ludzie z wosku* (1936; The Wax People), *Miasteczko aniołów* (1959; Little Town of Angels), *Iskry na wiatr* (1963; Sparks in the Wind), and *Gaudeamus* (1968; Let Us Rejoice). Her numerous collections of short stories, for example, *Legendy Warszawy* (1938; Legends of Warsaw) and *Ziarno gorczyczne* (1947;

Grain of Mustard), stories about Saint Francis and Saint Clara, her journalistic accounts, her numerous books for children, and so on, prove her one of the most prolific of Polish authors.

See: K. Kuliczkowska, *Droga twórcza Ewy Szelburg-Zarembiny* (1965).
J.R.K.

Szerb, Antal (1901–45), Hungarian novelist, critic, and literary historian, was born in Budapest. Having studied Hungarian, English, and German philology in Budapest and Graz, he traveled extensively throughout Western Europe and spent a year in England before settling down to teaching and writing in Hungary. His publications appeared in such reviews as *Széphalom, Minerva*, and *Nyugat*. Szerb's literary activity can be roughly divided into three groups. He was a conscientious philologist who could write with equal persuasiveness on such diverse subjects as the Hungarian preromantics, William Blake, Baldassare Castiglione, or Stefan George. He was also an erudite and sensitive critic and successful popularizer of modern Western literature, as in the essays in *Hétköznapok és csodák* (n.d., Weekdays and Miracles), and an entertaining, occasionally brilliant writer of fiction. Szerb's essays were published only after his death, the longer ones in *Gondolatok a könyvtárban* (1946; Reflections in the Library), the smaller articles in *A varázsló eltöri pálcáját* (1948; The Magician Breaks His Wand).

Szerb's fiction was influenced by Virginia Woolf and Aldous Huxley. His finest novel is *A Pendragon legenda* (1934; The Legend of Pendragon), a thriller, skillfully spun around the Rosicrucian legend, blending wit with irrational terror. Szerb's short stories, collected posthumously in *Madelon, az eb* (1947; Madelon: A Dog) and *Szerelem a palackban* (1963; Love in the Bottle), are slightly frivolous but eminently readable sketches set in London, Paris, Renaissance Italy, and the England of Arthurian legend. His attempt at a "serious" modern novel, *Utas és holdvilág* (1937; Wanderer and Moonlight), was not entirely successful. His next work, *A királyné nyaklánca* (1943; The Queen's Necklace), a study of pre-revolutionary France, is more the work of a writer of fiction. Szerb's conclusion that the ancien régime collapsed in 1789 because of internal corruption was interpreted by some critics as an indictment of pre-World War I Hungarian society as well.

Szerb is best remembered, however, for his two major books: *Magyar irodalomtörténet* (2 vols., 1934; History of Hungarian Literature), which opened a new chapter in the history of Hungarian letters, and *A világirodalom története* (3 vols., 1941; The History of World Literature). His method was basically an amalgam of Wilhelm Dilthey's cultural-psychological (*Geistesgeschichtlich*) approach and a literary-sociological approach, but the book's success was due above all to its lively, pithy, and elegant characterizations of important writers. Szerb's history of world literature, which shows the influence of Oswald Spengler's pessimistic ideas, is more open to criticism. Although Szerb was familiar with the literatures of the major European languages, he did not always do justice in this work to the smaller, less accessible literatures.

See: A. Schöpflin, "Szerb Antal: Magyar irodalomtörténete," *Nyugat* 27 (1934): 156–60; L. Kardos, *Vázlatok, esszék kritikák* (1959); Gy. Poszler, *Szerb Antal* (1973).
G.G.

Szymborska, Wisława (1923–), Polish poet and translator, was born in Bnin, near Poznań. She made her literary debut in 1945. Her early poems, collected in the volumes

Dlatego żyjemy (1952; That's Why We're Alive) and *Pytania zadawane sobie* (1954; Questions for Oneself), are highly political. With *Wołanie do Yeti* (1957; Calling to the Yeti), she turned to philosophical observations, seeking meaning for humanity in the history of evolution and exploring from a woman's perspective the poignancy of human isolation while celebrating as a poet the death-defying joy of creation. The development of these themes is continued in *Sól* (1962; Salt) and *Sto pociech* (1967; A Barrel of Laughs). Her style is concise and understated; urgent issues are raised in commonplace scenes described in colloquial language. Her tone is often ironic, the dry mocking humor effectively controlling the tragic undertones of the message.

See; J. Kwiatkowski, "Słowo wstępne," in W. Szymborska, *Poezje* (1970), pp. 5-16; *Słownik współczesnych pisarzy polskich,* series II, vol. 2 (1978), pp. 534-38.

M.G.L.

T

Tadijanović, Dragutin (1905-), Croatian poet, was born into a poor family in Rastušje, near Slavonski Brod. While he was still a youth, his father and a brother died of consumption. After completing secondary school in Slavonski Brod, he earned a master's degree in Slavic literatures at the University of Zagreb and was employed for years as a proofreader for a newspaper. In 1945 he became an editor in a publishing house and later served as the director of the Institute for Croatian Literature in Zagreb.

Tadijanović's poetry is closely linked with the events of his personal life; the members of his family, living and dead, and his small village with its vineyards are the usual subjects of his early poems. Tadijanović later published these poems, along with those written while he was working and studying in Zagreb, in the volumes *Lirika* (1931; Lyrics), *Sunce nad oranicama* (1933; Sun over the Fields), *Pepeo srca* (1936; The Heart's Ashes), and *Duni djetinjstva* (1937; Childhood Days). With the passing of time, his travels abroad, and his work on translations of foreign authors, Tadijanović's horizons broadened and his poetry developed thematically. Yet its basic characteristics remained the same in such later collections as *Tuga zemlje* (1942; Earth's Sorrow), *Pjesme* (1951; Songs), *Blagdan žetve* (1956; Harvest Feast), and *Prsten* (1963, 1965, 1967; The Ring). In his later verse, the poet questions the meaning of a life, filled with troubles and sorrows, which in the end leads only to the grave.

Few Croatian writers have been the subject of as many studies as has Tadijanović. Most of them stress the uniqueness of his style, the simplicity and purity of his language, and the musicality of his verse, while the less sophisticated complain that his poetry is on the border line of prose and is distressingly limited in its subject matter. All critics, however, emphasize that beneath Tadijanović's narrative approach there is hidden a special rhythm that, although apparently without any rhyme, appeals to listeners with a kind of primitive authenticity.

See: V. Nazor, "Primjer Tadijanovićeve versifikacije," in *Eseji* (1950), pp. 414-18; J. Kaštelan, "Vizija harmonije," *Kolo* 10 (1969): 942-60; A. Kadić, "Dragutin Tadijanović: Veličina neposrednosti," in *Zbornik hrvatske revije* (1976), pp. 615-33.

A.K.

Tamási, Áron (1877-1966), Hungarian novelist, was born in Farkaslaka (now in Romania) of Székely stock. Throughout his career, Tamási was concerned with the characteristic speech, behavior, and modes of thought of the Seklers. As a young man he studied in Székelyudvarhely (now Odorhei, Romania) and Kolozsvár (now Cluj, Romania). In 1923 he emigrated to the United States, returning home three years later. From 1944 until his death he lived in Budapest. In 1956 he was active in the writers' resistance to the restoration of Communist one-party rule in Hungary, and he composed a manifesto of the Hungarian Writers Association on this issue.

Tamási's first book of short stories, *Lélekindulás* (1925; The Soul's Trek), was the work of a mature writer. His narrative style is romantic and poetic, in the spirit of a folk ballad or a fairy tale, and, like everyday Székely speech, it is spiced with frequent jokes and puns. His heroes are simple mountaineers or farmers who usually outwit the powers that be. Tamási was aware of social conflicts, as evidenced by the short story "Rendes feltámadás" (1931; Eng. tr., "Orderly Resurrection," 1963) or the novel *Címeresek* (1931; The Titled Ones), which castigates the Transylvanian aristocracy. Yet he paid less attention to class controversies than to the individual's search for a place in the world.

Tamási's most popular novel, *Ábel a rengetegben* (1932; Abel in the Wilderness), concerns a poor Sekler youth who works as a forest guard. Abel, the narrator-hero, uses both physical skill and cunning to accomplish his often difficult tasks. Tamási describes these adventures in an effortlessly lyrical and humorous prose style. The great success of this book induced Tamási to continue Abel's story, but neither *Ábel az országban* (1933; Abel in the Country) nor *Ábel Amerikában* (1934; Abel in America) can compete with the first novel. At the end of the trilogy, Tamási's hero returns to his country, turning away from society and toward the solitude of the mountains.

In the field of politics, Tamási advocated democratic reforms. As chairman of the 1937 Vásárhely Convention (a conference of left-wing writers), he called for a Hungarian-Romanian understanding. Yet in his own writing he steered clear of social commitment. Despite their realistic evocations of Transylvanian village life, both *Jégtörő Mátyás* (1936; Matthias the Icebreaker) and its sequel, *Ragyog egy csillag* (1938; A Star Is Shining), are closer to myth than to reality. The hero of *Jégtörő Mátyás* is a wise wandering spirit who passes through a series of reincarnations, becoming a flea, an owl, other animals, and finally a newborn human baby. Reminiscence is also the key to *Szülőföldem* (1939; My Birthplace), Tamási's contribution to the then popular genre of village sociography. Joseph Reményi called this work, much praised for its authenticity and the beauty of its language, "the autobiography of a village using the writer as interpreter." Tamási's childhood and youth are also the subject of *Bölcső és bagoly* (1949; Cradle and Owl). On the other hand, *Hazai tükör* (1953; A Review of Our Country), although set in Transylvania, is a historical novel about the years prior to the Hungarian War of Independence of 1848-49.

Tamási was an accomplished writer of fiction, but he was less successful as a playwright. His best play is probably *Énekes madár* (1934; Song Bird), a Transylvanian "folk tale" about two young lovers who overcome all obstacles.

See: L. Németh, "Tamási Áron," *Nyugat* 24 (1931): 307–10; L. Bóka, "Tamási Áron novellái," *Magyar Csillag* 2 (1942): 237–40; M. Czine, "Tamási Áron ujabb műveiről," *Csillag* 8 (1954): 516–27; J. Reményi, *Hungarian Writers and Literature* (1964), pp. 424–36; Z. Szabó, "Rendkivüli ember," *Új Látóhatár* 4 (1967): 289–301; J. Izsák, *Tamási Áron* (1969). G.G.

Tammsaare, Anton Hansen, pseud. of Anton Hansen (1878–1940), Estonian novelist, was born in Albu. The most widely acclaimed Estonian novelist, he has been compared as a chronicler of peasant life with Władysław REYMONT and Frans Emil SILLANPÄÄ, but in his philosophical bent he has been thought to resemble Fyodor DOSTOYEVSKY. Tammsaare's fame rests on *Tõde ja õigus* (5 vols., 1926–36; Truth and Justice), a monumental novel that captures the essential Estonian experience during a crucial period: that of the movement from farm to city, as well as the evolution from tsarist province to independent state. (The novel has been translated into French and German but not English.) Although Tammsaare was a subtle psychological realist at heart, he also wrote in a neoromantic vein and authored some powerful allegorical texts, such as the novel *Põrgupõhja uus Vanapagan* (1939; The New Vanapagan of "Põrgupõhja"). The dramatic character of his narrative art also made his occasional ventures into writing plays, such as *Juudit* (1921; Judith), highly successful. His collected works, *Kogutud teosed* began to be published in 1978.

See: A. Mägi, *Estonian Literature* (1968); E. Nirk, *Estonian Literature* (1970); L. Siimisker and A. Palm, *A. H. Tammsaare* (1978). I.I.

Tarasov-Rodionov, Aleksandr Ignatiyevich (1885–1938), Russian novelist whose controversial novel *Shokolad* (1922; Eng. tr., *Chocolate,* 1932) prophesied the show trials of the 1930s, in which the author himself perished. Born in Astrakhan into the family of a surveyor, he studied law at Kazan University and joined the Communist Party in 1905. After the October Revolution (1917) he entered the Red Army. He worked as an investigator for the Communist courts and as an organizer of the proletarian literary group "October" (1922) and the Russian Association of Proletarian Writers (RAPP).

Shokolad concerns a loyal secret-police official who submits to execution for the crime of pardoning a class enemy, a prostitute who repaid his mercy with chocolates (symbolizing the allure of capitalist luxuries). Tarasov-Rodionov's second novel, *Linyov* (1924, 2d ed. retitled *Trava i krov*; Grass and Blood), attacks the cult of Vladimir Lenin by describing the power that the title-hero gains from his resemblance to Lenin. Tarasov-Rodionov published two volumes of *Tyazholye shagi* (Difficult Steps), an autobiographical trilogy on the Revolution: *Fevral* (1927; Eng. tr., *February 1917,* 1931) and *Iyul* (1930; July). He was expelled from the Union of Soviet Writers as an alleged Trotskyite in 1936, executed during the terror of 1938, and rehabilitated after Iosif Stalin's death. H.A.G.

Tardieu, Jean (1903–), French poet, playwright, and translator, was born in Saint-Germain-de-Joux (Jura) into a family of artists. He studied law and literature in Paris. His first poems were published in the *Nouvelle Revue française* in 1927. After World War I, Tardieu directed the famous "Club d'Essai" of the French Radio for 14 years, during which time he became very interested in the theater. His "pocket theater"—short experimental plays—heralded the "antitheater" of the 1950s. Tardieu's plays have been published in the volumes *Théâtre de chambre* (1955: Chamber Theater) and *Poèmes à jouer* (1969; Eng. tr., *The Underground Lovers and Other Experimental Plays,* 1968).

Most of Tardieu's nontheatrical works have been collected in two volumes, *Le Fleuve caché* (1968; The Hidden River) and *La Part de l'ombre* (1972; The Shadow's Share). He has also published *Les Portes de toile* (1969; Doors of Canvas), a collection of essays on such artists as Hartung, Vieira da Silva, Villon, and Albert Giacometti. *Obscurité du jour* (1974; Obscurity of the Day) is an elegant essay on the creative process. *Formeries* (1976) is Tardieu's most recent book of poetry. He has also translated works by Friedrich Hölderlin and Goethe.

As a playwright, Tardieu is obsessed with the problems of language. His motto is "Very few words, very few gestures." This is the key to his dramas, played out at the border of silence. He continually searches for new structures in which themes replace plots. Despite the seriousness of his pursuit, Tardieu possesses a delightful sense of humor that has been compared to that of the composer Eric Satie.

See: E. Noulet, *Jean Tardieu* (1964); *Littérature de notre temps,* vol. 3 (1971); G. E. Clancier, *La Poésie et ses environs* (1973). J.-C.M.

Tarkovsky, Arseny Aleksandrovich (1907–), Russian poet, was born in Yelizavetgrad (now Kirovograd). In 1925, while working for the newspaper *Gudok,* he began studying at the State School for Advanced Literary Studies, completing his course in 1929. Tarkovsky published few of his poems until 1962 when the first collection of his verse, *Pered snegom,* immediately brought him recognition as one of the best lyric poets in the country. Three collections then followed: *Zemle zemnoye* (1966; To Earth the Earthly), *Vestnik* (1969; The Herald), and *Stixotvorenija* (1974; Poems). Tarkovsky has published numerous reviews and critical articles, and he is well known for his translations of literature from a number of Oriental languages. He occupies a distinctive position in present-day Soviet Russian poetry by reason of his concern with the "Orphic" role of the poet and his insistence on the exemplary function of the "classical line" in Russian poetry (Pushkin, Baratynsky, Tyutchev, Fet).

See: A. Urban in *Kratkaya literaturnaya entsiklopediya,* vol. 7 (1972), pp. 392–93; W. Kasack, *Lexikon der russischen literatur ab 1917* (1976), p. 395; Interview with Tarkovsky, *VLit,* no. 6 (1979). V.L.

Tasis i Marca, Rafael (1906–67), Catalan novelist, critic, and historian, was born in Barcelona and died in Paris. The critic Joan Fuster considers him to be a representative of the petit bourgeoisie depicted in some of his narratives. At the age of 16 he was already adapting children's stories into Catalan and soon he began to contribute to Catalan newspapers and magazines. His first books were *El daltabaix* (1924; The Ups and Downs), *Vint anys* (1931; Twenty Years), and *Una visió de conjunt de la novel·la catalana* (1935; An Overview of the Catalonian Novel). During the Spanish Civil War he published *La revolució en els Ajuntaments* (1937), *La Literatura catalana moderna* (1937; Modern Catalonian Literature), and *Les pedres parlen* (1938; The Stones Speak). He went into exile in 1939. He worked for the French Radio in Paris, where he published *Tot l'any* (1943; All Year Long), *Històries de coneguts* (1945; Stories of Acquaintances), and *L'etudiant et la sorcière* (1947; The Sorcerer's Apprentice). On his return to Barcelona he published his novel *Sol ponent* (1953; Setting Sun) and the detective novels *La Biblia valenciana* (1955; The Valencian Bible), *Es hora de plegar* (1956; It's Time to Stop), and *Un crim al Paralelo* (1960). *Tres* (1962) is his most ambitious novel.

As a historian, he received the Aedos Prize in 1957 for his *Joan I, rei cacador i music* (1958; King Joan I, Hunter and Musician). Other works are *La vida del Rei en Pere III* (1961; The Life of King Pere III) and *Pere el Cerimoniós i els seus fills* (Pere the Ceremonious and His Sons). As a critic, he was actively involved in compiling, in collaboration with Joan Torrent, many anthologies and books about the Catalan novel and the Catalan press. His most outstanding theatrical works are *Gulliver i els gegants* (1952; Gulliver and the Giants); *Paralel 1934* (1953), coauthored by J. M. Poblet; *Un home entre herois* (A Man Among Heroes), which won the Guimera Prize in 1954; and *La maleta*. He received the Catalonia Prize for the Novel in 1953. Various books of his were published posthumously: *La Renaixença catalana* (1967; The Catalonian Renaissance), *El mon modern i nosaltres* (1967; We and the Modern World), *America del Nord, avui* (1967; North America, Now), and *Un segle de poesia catalana* (1967; A Century of Catalonian Poetry).

See: F. Sodevila, Prologue to R. Tasis i Marca, *La vida del rey en Pere III* (1961); J. M. Poblet, *Rafael Tasis, conducta i exemple* (1967).   J.F.C.

Tatarka, Dominik (1913–), Slovak novelist, was born in Drienové in central Slovakia. He has been professor and scenarist, and has also translated works of French literature into Slovak. His first two short novels, *V úzkosti hl'adania* (1942; The Anxiety of Searching) and *Panna zázračnica* (1945; The Miraculous Virgin), are unconventional novels that probe the problems of relations and communication between individuals. *Družné letá* (1954; Summers of Friendship) and *Radostník* (1954; The Wedding Cake), on the other hand, are products of socialist realism and therefore present idyllic pictures of the building of socialism. Tatarka's later works depict the lives of people living through a time of war; *Farská republika* (1948; The Parsons' Republic), the most significant Slovak work of fiction about the Fascist period (1939–45), describes the complex experience of a Slovak intellectual seeking to escape from fascism's stifling atmosphere. In *Prvý a druhý úder* (1950; The First and Second Blows), Tatarka attempts an unemotional survey of Slovak life during the national uprising of 1944 and the first years of liberation.

Tatarka's greatest works of fiction are *Rozhovory bez konce* (1959; Conversations without End), a volume of stories in which, among other things, he sensitively analyzes the relationship between a mother and son, and the novel *Prútené kreslá* (1962; The Wicker Chairs), the love story of a Slovak student in France at the time of the fall of Paris. His short novel *Démon súhlasu* (1963; The Demon of Compliance) is the first literary analysis of the moral and psychological distortions of personality under Stalinism. Tatarka has not been published since 1968, but to a great degree he has remained an influence on the younger generation of Slovak writers.

See: A. J. Liehm, *The Politics of Culture* (1970), pp. 251–75.   F.M.B.

Teffi, N. A., pseud. of Nadezhda Alekseyevna Buczyńska, née Lokhvitskaya (1875–1952), Russian humorist, feuilletonist, short-story writer, dramatist, and poet, was born in Petersburg. Her father, Aleksandr Lokhvitsky, was a famous lawyer and professor; her older sister Mirra twice won the coveted Pushkin Prize for poetry. Around 1900, Teffi began writing for various newspapers and magazines. Her first collection of prose, *Yumoristicheskiye rasskazy* (1910; Humorous Stories), which contains contributions to satirical journals, and one-act plays, established her reputation as a talented humorist (*see* RUSSIAN LITERATURE). Despite the fact that some of her very first published poems and stories had been serious in tone, often revealing the influence of the symbolists, Teffi's best collection of pre-Revolutionary stories, *Nezhivoy zver* (1916; The Unliving Animal), surprised her vast reading public by its predominant note of sadness. In 1920 she left Russia, finally settling in Paris. Her stories and feuilletons appeared in almost every émigré periodical.

Although Teffi's literary output was large and diverse (poetry, drama, a novel, memoirs, film scenarios, criticism, and songs), she is best known for her short stories, published in more than 40 volumes. Her stories include delicate miniatures of children, old people, and animals; pathetic vignettes and farcical sketches of émigré life; and purely humorous anecdotes. Among her important collections published in emigration are *Gorodok* (1927; The Little Town), *Vedma* (1935; The Witch), and *Zigzag* (1939).

See: O. Mikhailov, "O Teffi," in Teffi, *Rasskazy* (1971), pp. 3–16; E. Neatrour, "Miniatures of Russian Life at Home and in Emigration: The Works of N. A. Teffi," Ph.D. Dissertation, Indiana University (1973).   E.B.N.

Teilhard de Chardin, Pierre (1881–1955), French Jesuit paleontologist and philosopher, devoted his life to religious meditation and to scientific research. Teilhard taught geology and paleontology and traveled widely, mainly in Asia. After 1924, he directed excavations at Chou-ken-tien near Peking.

Although he was a scientist of international renown, he became famous as a mystical philosopher after the publication of *Le Phénomène humain* (1955; Eng. tr., *The Phenomenon of Man*, 1965). In this work, published almost 50 years after Henri BERGSON's *L'Evolution créatrice* (1907; Eng. tr., *Creative Evolution*, 1911), Teilhard proposed a new answer, both scientific and prophetic, to the problem of biological transformism. As a paleontologist, he developed his theory in terms of large synthetic movements covering billions of years. According to his view, the mystical experiences that have inspired religions and their revelations (although not their intellectual orthodoxies) have been anticipations of scientific experiments and laws. His intuition is thus Christocentric and evolutionist at the same time. Since the hydrogen atom, says Teilhard, the evolution of life has been nothing less than the history of successive Christic incarnations. At present, the human race is experiencing the passage from the biosphere to the noosphere, that is, the transition from biological individualities to personal unities, a state where consciousness and its reflective power will no longer be imprisoned within the narrow limits of pitiful, aggressive egos. Mystically speaking, this is also the first step on a long odyssey, a movement that will bring humanity back to the womb of infinite reality, to the Point Omega, as Teilhard calls it.

For Teilhard, progress is a sort of permanent fall-forward, by which he meant that a biological consciousness has been present in each form of life, from the first chemical units on. Each biological being, at its own level, expresses and sums up total reality. With the appearance of mankind, the unifying power of life has become reflective, and the acquisition of knowledge has become an increasingly absorbing activity. Teilhard foresaw a time when researchers would be the dominant members of human society. After human cultures have undergone their economic, military, and political phases, they will become gigantic research organizations in which the biological structure of the individual will at last disappear.

Teilhard's vision is based upon a simultaneous faith in the revealed truths of religion and in the experimental truths of science. Both, he thought, justified his optimism. Yet evil, or the Devil, is never far from Teilhard's universe. Under its scientific name—entropy—it permanently endangers the progress of life's fall-forward. Teilhard's other published writings include *Le Milieu divin* (1926–27; Eng. tr., *The Divine Milieu*, 1960), *Le Cœur de la matière* (1950; Eng. tr., *The Heart of the Matter*, 1979), and his important correspondence. E.M.-S.

Teirlinck, Herman (1879–1967), Belgian (Flemish) essayist, playwright, and novelist, was born in a suburb of Brussels. He attended school there, was employed for a time in the municipal department of fine arts, taught Dutch literature in various schools, became director of the Institute of Decorative Arts in Brussels, and was appointed by young King Albert to be his private counselor on matters of art and sciences. Teirlinck was the only son of the well-known linguist Isidoor Teirlinck (1851–1934), who conveyed to the young Herman his interest in folklore and his love for the countryside of Brabant and southeastern Flanders.

Teirlinck made his debut as a writer with *De wonderbare wereld* (1902; The Wondrous World), a collection of three stories in which he vividly describes the landscapes of Flanders and the life of the peasants. With *Mijnheer Serjanszoon* (1908) and *Het ivoren Aapje* (1909; The Ivory Monkey), Teirlinck won recognition not only in Belgium but also in Holland. In both novels, Teirlinck displays a sensitive, impressionistic style akin to that of the great Dutch writer Lodewijk van DEYSSEL. In *Serjanszoon*, Teirlinck evokes the life of an 18th-century lover of beauty whose hedonistic and narcissistic tendencies lead him to become a victim of his own behavior. Teirlinck's portrayal of Brussels life during the Belle Epoque in *Het ivoren Aapje* reveals the talent of a perceptive observer who is also a brilliant stylist. In 1917, Teirlinck published *Johan Doxa,* a tragic tale in which he combines gentle irony with emotion and charm. With his friend Karel van de WOESTIJNE, he wrote *Leemen torens* (1928; Loamy Towers), a literary account of Brussels and Ghent during World War I. During World War II, Teirlinck produced three novels concerning the lives of three sensual and strong women: *Maria Speermalie* (1940); *Griseldis* (1942), the retelling of a medieval tale; and *Rolande met de bles* (1944; Rolande with the Blaze), a fresco of sensuality and urban decadence.

Teirlinck wrote his best and most elaborate novels after World War II. *Het Gevecht met de Engel* (1952; The Fight with the Angel) is an epic account of the conflict between generations. The imposing decor of the forest of Zoniën plays a major role in this work. In *Zelfportret op het Galgemaal* (1956; Eng. tr., *The Man in the Mirror*, 1963), Teirlinck masterfully explored the memories and recollections of Henri, a middle-aged businessman driven by his selfish sensuality and lust. The interior monologue suggests the pathos and dynamism found in the works of Rembrandt, Vincent van Gogh, and James Ensor.

Teirlinck has also been widely acclaimed as an innovative playwright. He wrote several dramatic sketches, and shortly after World War I he became active in the theatrical circles of Brussels. Such three-act plays as *De vertraaagde film* (1922; The Slowed-Down Motion Picture) and *Ik Dien* (1923; I Serve) were especially well received. In those plays, Teirlinck shows his affiliation with earlier Flemish theater as well as with such writers as Maurice MAETERLINCK, August STRINDBERG, Fyodor DOSTOYEVSKY, and Fernand CROMMELYNCK. The entire second act of *De vertraagde film* takes place under water: two lovers, who sought to drown themselves and the little child whose birth brought disgrace upon them, relive their lives. Every flash of recollection contains a wide array of symbols. *Ik Dien* is a dramatization of the Beatrice legend, the story of a runaway nun who, after a life of debauchery, returns as a penitent to her convent, not knowing that the Virgin Mary had taken her place during her absence. Teirlinck's version of the medieval Miracle play brings to mind both the world of Pieter Bruegel and that of Vsevolod Meyerhold.

Teirlinck's play *De Man zonder Lijf* (1925; The Man without a Body) may be termed expressionistic, not only because of its great power to move audiences but also because of its great reliance upon technical methods. The composition of this work was patterned after Luigi PIRANDELLO as well as after Russian and French models. Teirlinck's expressionism is, however, stylistically restrained. His own experimentation with dramatic techniques at the Brussels Higher Institute for Architecture and the Applied Arts (La Cambre) played an important role in the growth of his theatrical insights. In this school, he experimented with the "climate" of a play and the lighting; he simplified decor and transformed the role of the actors. The impact of these techniques manifested itself in *Ave* (1928) and *De Stervende Boer* (1930; The Dying Farmer). His experimental work was also reflected in his adaptations of plays by Aeschylus and Sophocles, as well as of medieval farces. Teirlinck's own awareness of the struggle between elemental powers and modern technology emerges in a monumental dramatic atmosphere often influenced by Wagnerian concepts.

As a teacher at the Brussels Conservatory and, later, at the Studio for National Theater in Antwerp (founded in 1946), he underlined the importance of both craftsmanship and creativity. He analyzed acting and playing as elements of "improvisation," summarizing his ideas about dramatic art in *Dramatiek Peripatetikon* (1959). Teirlinck's importance and originality lie in his blending of varied systems and concepts of drama into a new theatrical unity. For him, the content of a play can be fully revealed only when the technical means are brought to perfection and when the actors reach a high level of craftsmanship. One of the most versatile and prolific of modern Flemish authors, Teirlinck also served, at the end of his life, as Dutch-language cultural advisor to King Baudouin.

See: W. Putman, *Van en Over Herman Teirlinck* (1954); M. Roelants, *Schrijvers, Wat is er van de mens?*, vol. 2 (1957); P. Brachin, *L'expressionisme dans le théâtre d'Herman Teirlinck* (1958); T. Oegema van der Wal, *Herman Teirlinck* (1965). J. van S.

Teixeira de Pascoaes, Joaquim: see PASCOAES, JOAQUIM TEIXEIRA DE.

Tendryakov, Vladimir Fyodorovich (1923–), Russian writer, was born near Vologda, the son of a government office employee. He graduated from the Gorky Literary Institute in Moscow and began to publish in 1953. He quickly acquired a reputation as a "new wave" writer rebelling against the dictates of socialist realism.

Between 1956 and 1965—the peak of post-Stalin liberalization in Soviet letters—Tendryakov published his best stories. *Ukhaby* (1956; Potholes) describes a motor accident, the fear and confusion of those involved in it, and the cold indifference of local authorities who leave a dying victim without medical help. In "Troyka, semyorka, tuz" (1960; Eng. tr., "Three, Seven, Ace," 1962) a former convict and cardsharp brings violence, anguish, and ruthless prosecution to a peaceful loggers' camp. *Sud* (1969; The Trial) reveals the inadequacy of the courts in clarifying the circumstances of a hunting accident. In *Chrezvychaynoye* (1961; An Extraordinary Affair) a confrontation takes place between two religious individuals and the atheist community of a small town. *Podyanka—vek korotkiy* (1965; Creature of a Day) portrays a decent, hard-working girl who tends pigs on a collective farm; the pressure to fulfill the farm's economic plan at any cost leads her to commit a crime.

Tendryakov's works deal with moral crises that arise out of conflicts between individuals and the establishment. Each conflict is a test of personal integrity and courage, and few are strong enough to pass it. Tendryakov is an excellent storyteller and master of suspense; in this respect he has been compared to Aleksandr Pushkin and Fyodor DOSTOYEVSKY. The novella (*povest*) is his forte. His longer novels, *Za begushchim dnyam* (1959; On the Heels of Time) and *Svidaniye s Nefertiti* (1964; A Rendezvous with Nefertiti), although raising interesting issues, are structurally weak.

See: M. Hayward, Foreword in Tendryakov, *"Three, Seven, Ace" and Other Stories* (1973).   I.H.C.

Tenreiro, Francisco José (1921–63), often called the most authentic *négritude* poet in the Portuguese language, was born of an African woman and a European agronomist on São Tomé Island in the Gulf of Guinea. Tenreiro was still a child when his father took him to Portugal, where he spent most of his life. By the time he had risen to a high position in Portugal's Overseas Ministry, Tenreiro had already distinguished himself as a geographer and teacher.

The gap between Tenreiro's public life and his poetic world might lead one to believe that he had a split personality, but perhaps no more so than Léopold SENGHOR and Aimé CÉSAIRE, those paragons of francophone *négritude*. What makes Tenreiro's situation curious is his tacit support of Portugal's colonial regime, which conflicted with his poetic and essayistic statements of black cultural nationalism. He sought to resolve the contradiction by adjusting his pan-Africanism to Portuguese "lusotropicalist" theory, *lusotropicology* being the quasi-scientific expression, coined by the Brazilian sociologist Gilberto Freyre, of the myths of multiracialism and acculturation. A Portuguese writer has cited Tenreiro's poem "Canção do mestiço" (Mestizo's Song) as an example of Afro-Portuguese *négritude*. In this poem the mulatto does not so much exult in his blackness as he does in his ability to move comfortably between the two races. Tenreiro did, however, possess a sense of black solidarity, which he expressed a number of times, for example, in his poem "Negro de todo o mundo" (Black Man of the Whole World). By turning the familiar into the alien, Tenreiro confronted Europe with his "heart in Africa," as he titled one of his most poignant pieces. In some of his long compositions, the mestizo views Europe with derisive scorn as he strolls along the Tagus River with a bebop rhythm on his lips. Passersby react variously, with curiosity, fear, or superiority, but he knows where his defiant heart belongs and who he is. By bridging the gap between Africa and Europe, Tenreiro, despite his

premature death, made a lasting contribution as a pioneer. He left one collection of poems, *Ilha de nome santo* (1942; Isle of a Holy Name), and these were included in the posthumous *Obra poética de Francisco José Tenreiro* (1967; Poetic Works of Francisco José Tenreiro). His short stories were collected in *Nós voltaremos juntos* (1942; Together We Shall Return). He lectured on black art, music, and literature and published essays in these fields—for example, an introduction to the anthology *Poesia negra de express ão portuguesa*, edited with Mário de Andrade (1953; Black Poetry in the Portuguese Language).

See: M. A. Fernandes de Oliveira, "Francisco José Tenreiro, poeta," in *Obra poética de Francisco José Tenreiro* (1967), pp. 21–31; R. G. Hamilton, in his *Voices from an Empire* (1975), pp. 381–88.   R.G.H.

Tertz, Abram: *see* SINYAVSKY, ANDREY DONATOVICH.

Testori, Giovanni (1923–), Italian novelist, poet, and playwright, was born in Novate, a suburb of Milan. As a novelist, he first experimented with Milanese dialect in *Il dio di Roserio* (1954; The Idol of Roserio), a vivid, introspective tale concerning a promising amateur cyclist who sacrifices his teammate in order to win a race. He soon set aside linguistic innovation in favor of a streamlined narrative sustained by a skillful, although on occasion excessive, use of interior monologue. His style is rendered bland by overreliance on a fluent, conversational language, sprinkled with ready-made phrases that are often coarse and sexually explicit.

The body of Testori's fiction is contained in the five-volume *I segreti di Milano* (1958–61; The Secrets of Milan), a *commedia lombarda* (as the author calls it) concerning subproletarian life in the sprawling suburbia of Milan. The first two volumes in this series, *Il ponte della Ghisolfa* (1958; The Bridge on the River Ghisolfa), which includes a shortened edition of *Il dio di Roserio* free of dialect, and *La Gilda del Mac Mahon* (1959; Gilda, the Streetwalker of Mac Mahon Avenue), are collections of short stories displaying a fresco of underworld and popular characters. Their exploits, painted with crude realism, exhibit a cynical disregard for moral values and usually concern physical violence, blackmail, male exploitation of women, and, all too often, the reduction of love to sensual gratification. In *Il fabbricone* (1961; Eng. tr., *The House in Milan*, 1962), the last volume of the series, a proletarian version of *Romeo and Juliet* is played out against the background of conflicting political ideologies and amid the frustrations of daily life in a tenement house.

Testori's plays are dominated by embittered, rebellious women who display an indomitable willpower in their struggle for self-determination. Thus the rivalry between two women to win a man ends in tragedy in *L'Arialda* (1960), and in victory for the stronger of the two in *La Maria Brasca* (1960). In *La monaca di Monza* (1967; The Nun of Monza), a sordid story of crime and lascivious passion, a historical nun—the same woman immortalized by Alessandro Manzoni in *I promessi sposi* (1840–42; Eng. tr., *The Betrothed*, 1951)—inveighs against parental authority and social codes to justify her conduct. *Erodiade* (1969; Herodias) is an overwrought monologue in the course of which Herod's wife lays bare her lustful attraction to John the Baptist. In *Ambleto* (1972), *Hamlet* is transposed to a rustic setting in Lombardy and cleverly refashioned with the aid of Milanese dialect and distorted forms of several languages, including Latin.

In his first three volumes of poetry, *I trionfi* (1965;

Triumphs), *Crocifissione* (1966; Crucifixion), and *L'amore* (1968; Love), Testori probes incessantly into the meaning and purpose of human existence; the result is tension, anguish, and despair. The same sentiments are echoed in *Per sempre* (1970; Forever), although in a milder form, attenuated by the presence of childhood memories and the comfort of loved ones. A later volume, *Nel tuo sangue* (1973; In Your Blood), is pervaded by an unrelenting quest for religious truth as embodied in the figure of Christ, a quest pursued with a fervor that becomes an obsession. The work's profane language borders on the obscene.

See: G. Mariani, in *La giovane narrativa italiana tra documento e poesia* (1962); P. de Tommaso, "Senso e coscienza in Giovanni Testori," *Letteratura* (March–April 1963); R. Barilli, in *La barriera del naturalismo* (1970).

A.Pal.

Tetmajer Przerwa, Kazimierz (1865–1940), Polish poet, novelist, short-story writer, and playwright, was born in Ludźmierz, at the foot of the Tatra Mountains, and died in Warsaw. After studying philosophy at the Jagiellonian University and in Heidelberg, he settled in Cracow; after World War I he moved to Warsaw. His poetic debut, the volume *Illa* (1886), still bears the mark of romantic influence, especially Słowacki, but in a short time he became one of the most outstanding and popular representatives of the new trend known as "Young Poland" (*see* POLISH LITERATURE) and a cofounder of the modernistic program in literature. In 1889 he published a kind of manifesto of this new trend, "Zamiast programu" (Instead of a Program). Closely connected with Bohemian circles, he was hailed as their poet idol. Aestheticism, pessimism, and an atmosphere of decadence dominate his lyrics. He published eight volumes under the same title: *Poezje* (Poems: 1891, 1894, 1898, to 1924). The second and third volumes are the most important in the development of his poetry. A sense of the uselessness and absurdity of existence often appears in Tetmajer's poetry, accompanied by the conviction that only art can give meaning to and justify existence. These ideas led to an emphasis on individualism and to a cult of art for art's sake. A desire to submerge oneself in nothingness or nirvana is also a frequent motif in his poetry. His passionate and sensual lyrics, permeated with eroticism, introduced a new feature into Polish love poetry. Nevertheless, only his Tatra poems, describing mountain landscapes and concretizing the atmosphere of a particular moment by means of an impressionistic technique, have stood the test of time.

Tetmajer began to write prose somewhat later than he did poetry and reached his highest artistic achievement in a series of collections of short stories written in mountaineers' dialect, *Na Skalnym Podhalu* (1903–10; In the Rocky Highlands). For these stories, he gathered and re-created legends and oral tales of the mountaineers, masterfully transforming his material and adding some epic elements. He presents the charm of highland life against the background of wild nature, the mountaineers' attachment to freedom, their sense of honor, their ability to experience strong passion, and their great sense of humor. The two-volume novel, *Legenda Tatr*, is connected with the same region. Part one, *Maryna z Hrubego* (1910), describes the revolt of Kostka Napierski, an historical figure; part two, *Janosik Nędza Litmanowski* (1911), is a narrative about a legendary mountain robber (a kind of Robin Hood). Tetmajer also wrote contemporary novels, such as *Anioł śmierci* (1898; Angel of Death); a historical novel in four volumes, *Koniec epopei* (1913–17; The End of an Epic); and a collection of short stories, *Ksiądz Piotr* (1896; Father Piotr), as well as dramas, such as *Zawisza*

Czarny (1901), *Rewolucja* (1906; The Revolution), and *Judasz* (1917; Judas). These works, however, are of lesser importance.

See: J. Błonski, "Kazimierz Tetmajer," in *Obraz literatury polskiej XIX i XX wieku. Literatura okresu Młodej Polski*, vol. 1 (1968), pp. 279–320.

A.Z.

Tevfik Fikret (1867–1915), Turkish poet, was born in Istanbul. He graduated from the Galatasaray Lycée, where he became proficient in French language and literature. He served as editor in chief of the literary magazine *Servet-i Fünun*, which played a major role in the Europeanization of Turkish poetry. For brief periods, he was a coeditor of the influential Istanbul daily *Tanin* and the director of the Galatasaray Lycée. From 1910 until his death in 1915, he taught Turkish literature at Robert College, the leading American college in Istanbul. His house just off the campus is now a museum.

Fikret's major collection of poems is *Rübab-ı Şikeste* (The Broken Lyre), published in 1900. *Halûk'un Defteri* (1911; Halûk's Notebook) contains poems of social concern and protest, in which the poet's young son is often presented as the symbol of the new Turkey. *Şermin*, published in 1914, is a collection of children's poems. Many of Fikret's poems were collected posthumously. His life and poetry have been the subject of hundreds of articles and dozens of books.

Starting out as a romantic lyricist par excellence who introduced numerous stanzaic and stylistic innovations, Fikret became a strong critic of the cultural values and the entrenched establishment of Ottoman society and functioned at the turn of the century as one of the sultan's most eloquent opponents.

See: S. Sertel, *Tevfik Fikret: Ideolojisi ve Felsefesi* (1946); K. Akyüz, *Tevfik Fikret* (1947); M. Kaplan, *Tevfik Fikret* (1971).

T.S.H.

Tharaud, Jérôme (1874–1953) and **Jean** (1877–1952), French novelists and journalists, were both born in Saint-Junien. The Tharauds, who collaborated on a number of books, belonged to the literary generation that came to maturity around 1895. The novel *Dingley l'illustre écrivain* (1906; Dingley the Illustrious Writer), which won the Goncourt Prize, established their reputation as professional writers. Both were elected to the Académie Française, Jérôme in 1939 and Jean in 1946. They continued writing until 1952, when they published their final work, *La Double Confidence* (The Double Confession). This book remains the most reliable index to their character and temperament, their work habits, and the peculiar nature of their collaboration, which they declared to be as mysterious to themselves as it was to everyone else: two minds were at all times indispensable to the creation of a single work, and one brother was helpless in the absence of the other.

Temperamentally, the Tharaud brothers remained forever fixed in that period of national rediscovery that characterized the final years of 19th-century French literature, a period dominated by the youthful idealism of Charles PÉGUY, Jacques MARITAIN, and Maurice BARRÈS. Exoticism is the keynote of the writings of the Tharauds. These works, substantially more reportorial than fictional, reflect their endless travels and their many-sided interests, as well as revealing the tendency of both men to find meaning in the fragmentary moment and to reject, in the fashion of romantic dreamers, the discipline of mature decision.

At the same time, the impressions that the Tharaud brothers synthesized from their collaboration served a fundamentally didactic purpose. Their propensity for universalizing their experiences stemmed from the influence of a sound classical education, which constantly influenced their writing and thinking. Disturbed by the materialism of an increasingly turbulent world, the Tharauds chose to retreat into an egocentric, antirational life of contemplation. The security they found in the "truth of the dream" and in the identification of the individual with the larger totality of national heritage was as romantic as it was inconclusive. Mystery, above all, satisfied their inveterately romantic temperaments and their taste for a kind of self-centered reverie.

As worshipers of tradition, the Tharauds avoided controversy. Even when they treated such matters as the ethics of imperialism, as in *Dingley, l'illustre écrivain,* the political and social role of the Jew in modern Europe, as in *Quand Israël est roi* (1921; When Israel Is King), or the genesis of religious fanaticism, as in *Quand Israël n'est plus roi* (1933; When Israel Is No Longer King), they remained curiously shy about reaching viable conclusions. Apparently, they could not satiate their thirst for beauty and mystery long enough to worry about conclusiveness. They preferred instead to idealize the past, developing an ideology based upon narrow nationalism, an oversimplification of the problems of history, and a penchant for fusing reality and illusion. P.A.M.

Theer, Otakar (1880–1917), Czech poet, was born in Czernowitz, Romania (now in the Ukrainian USSR), the son of an army officer. After studying languages at the University of Prague, he joined the staff of the university library.

Theer's first volume of poems, *Háje, kde se tančí* (1897; Groves Where There Is Dancing), expresses a rather crude pagan sensualism. But *Výpravy k Já* (1900; Expeditions to the Self) begins Theer's development of a poetry highly speculative and austere, yet revealing a fresh sensibility for metaphor. In *Úzkosti a naděje* (1911; Anxieties and Hopes) and especially in his last volume, *Všemu na vzdory* (1916; In Spite of Everything), Theer succeeded in evolving a new type of free verse, strictly and paradoxically designed to achieve classical and sculpturesque effects. In his thought, he leaned towards the titanic individualism of Friedrich NIETZSCHE and cultivated the heroic ideal in life and death. The heroic ideal is the theme of Theer's only play, the tragedy *Faëthón* (1917; Phaeton), a remarkably successful attempt to revive the form of the Aeschylean mythical drama and to give it a personal content of heroic frustrate ambition. Theer's early stories, decorative and romantic, were rejected by the mature artist. His criticism is valuable for a quality of sympathy—for example, with an advocate of heroism like Pierre Corneille—that was rare in Theer's time and place. The pagan sensualism, strong philosophical content, and striving for a severe classical form in free verse, make Theer's poetry original among modern Czech poets. But his art was too individual to find a wide audience or to exercise influence.

See: O. Fischer, A. Novák, O. Šimek, eds., *Na pamět Otakara Theera* (1920); A. M. Píša, *Otakar Theer,* 2 vols. (1928–33); B. Václavek in *Literarní studie a podobizny* (1962), pp. 224–27. R.W.

Thibaudeau, Jean (1935–), French novelist and essayist, was born at La Roche sur Yon. He grew up in Vendée and in Senegal. After a short career as a school teacher, Thibaudeau decided to devote himself entirely to writing. In 1960, he joined the group that had formed around the journal *Tel Quel* and published his first novel, *Cérémonie royale* (Royal Ceremony). Written in the style of the *nouveau roman, Cérémonie royale* earned him the Fénéon Prize. In subsequent novels, *Ouverture* (1966; Overture), *Imaginez la nuit, Ouverture II* (1968; Fancy the Night), and *Voilà les morts à notre tour d'en sortir* (1974; The Dead Are There, It is Our Turn to Move On), Thibaudeau has progressively moved away from the narrative techniques of the *nouveau roman.* Thibaudeau's novels are in part autobiographical: they explore the relationship between the unconscious and the real, between the individual and the community. Thibaudeau has described his narrative style as a "method of slow automatic writing" which, "has the effect of removing personal and cultural barriers." After the student revolt of May 1968, Thibaudeau wrote *Mai 1968—en France* (1968; May 1968 in France). The essay was prefaced by Philippe SOLLERS. Both writers expressed their disappointment with the turn of the events of May. They also criticized the French intellectuals for their apathy. From 1960 to 1971, Thibaudeau contributed regularly to *Tel Quel.* In 1971, he severed all ties with *Tel Quel* and became a member of the French Communist Party. The numerous essays he has published in such magazines as *Dialectiques, Europe, Digraphe,* and *Yale French Studies* reflect his questioning of the role of the intellectual in society as well as his interest in popular literature. In 1976, Thibaudeau founded his own magazine, *Les cahiers critiques de la littérature.* Profoundly influenced by Antonio GRAMSCI and Louis ALTHUSSER, about whom he has written penetrating studies, Jean Thibaudeau appears as one of the most sincere writers of his generation.

See: J.-F. Chevrier, "Actualité du roman, Voir-Ecrire-Parler, Jean Thibaudeau," *Crit* (1975); J. Thibaudeau, "Novels, Not Philosophy," *YFS* (1975), ed. by M.-R. Logan; J. Ristat, ed., "L'Amour de la Littérature," *Diagraphe* (special issue on Thibaudeau) (1978). M.-R.L.

Thibaudet, Albert (1874–1936), French literary critic, was born in Tournus (Burgundy). After obtaining a *licence* in philosophy from Dijon in 1894, he taught in several lycées. When school was out, he would hasten to the cafés where the symbolists discussed literature. Thibaudet entertained thoughts of writing himself and also of preparing for a doctorate in philosophy, but he momentarily succumbed to wanderlust and traveled to Greece (1902–03). Upon his return, he settled down to teaching and writing.

Thibaudet's principal work prior to World War I is the now classic *La Poésie de Stéphane Mallarmé* (1913; The Poetry of Stéphane MALLARMÉ). After the war, Thibaudet taught French at the University of Uppsala in Sweden. Although he was out of the country from 1919 to 1922, he maintained contact with the literary world of Paris through *La Nouvelle Revue française.* As literary critic for this prestigious magazine, Thibaudet became very well known. Returning to Paris, he continued to rise in reputation, writing numerous essays and studies and giving lectures. In 1924 he was invited to the University of Geneva; he was eventually appointed to the chair of French language and literature there, a post he held for the rest of his life. Albert Thibaudet is considered the best French literary critic of the period between the two world wars.

The philosophy of Henri BERGSON, one of Thibaudet's lycée teachers, must have been a formative influence on the critic's theory of "relativism." For Thibaudet, literature is a dynamic phenomenon constantly in movement, and the critic can grasp it only intuitively, through sympathetic understanding. Yet although Thibaudet was not very much concerned with value judgments, there is more than simple communion or communication in his criticism. In line with the university tradition of "scientific" classification, Thibaudet (like Bergson himself) organized, arranged, and classified—with due regard for facts and for clear exposition. His devotion to literature expressed itself in such a lively, picturesque way that this critic has been compared to a wine grower of Burgundy savoring the bouquet of his crop. The problem of classifying a literature constantly in movement led Thibaudet to the notion of literary generations, since developed by Henri Peyre and others. The essence of Thibaudet's critical thought may be found in *Physiologie de la critique* (1930) and in the volume of *Réflexions* (1939) devoted to criticism.

See: A. Glauser, *Albert Thibaudet ou la critique créatrice* (1952); J. C. Davies, *L'Œuvre critique d'Albert Thibaudet* (1955); M. Devaud, *Albert Thibaudet: critique de la poésie et des poètes* (1967).   L.LeS.

Thiry, Marcel (1897–1977), Belgian poet, novelist, short-story writer, and essayist, was born in Charleroi. He was a volunteer during World War I. This unforgettable war and travel experience furnished him major themes for *Toi qui pâlis au nom de Vancouver* (1924; You Who Turn Pale at the Name of Vancouver), his first important and, no doubt, most famous poetic work, as well as for *Plongeantes Proues* (1925; Diving Prows) and *L'Enfant prodigue* (1927; The Prodigal Child). After law studies, Thiry directed the family enterprise of forest cultivation. His poetic writing, notably *Statue de la fatigue* (1934; Statue of Weariness) and *La Mer de la tranquilité* (1938; The Sea of Tranquility), as well as a collection of short stories and poems, *Marchands* (1936; Merchants), evokes this gray life of a timberman, a life haunted by the presence of poetry and the nostalgia for happiness. Elected in 1939 to the Royal Academy of French Language and Literature of Belgium, Marcel Thiry became its permanent secretary in 1960. He was also a senator to the Walloon Assembly and a member of the European Parliament.

Along with external themes such as the fugacity of time, the fragility of happiness, the love and beauty of women, Thiry's poetry evokes the most modern aspects of a civilization whose movements and upheavals it espouses. It reveals the extraordinary and poetic importance of the automobile and telephone, of money and the airplane, of the bank and scientific discoveries. *Ages* (1950; Ages), which includes poems written between 1938 and 1950, and certain subsequent collections such as *Usine à penser des choses tristes* (1957; A Manufacture of Sad Things), *Vie Poésie* (1961; Life Poetry), or *Le Festin d'attente* (1963; At the Banquet of Anticipation) are especially representative of this poetry, at once contemporary and timeless. Thiry's verse is sometimes full and supple, as in the great prose works in verse of *Les Trois Longs Regrets du lis des champs* (1955; The Three Long Regrets of the Lilies in the Fields), sometimes extremely restrained and labored, especially in the last collections, *Songes et Spélonques* (1973; Dreams and Retreats) and *L'Encore* (1975; The Encore). Thiry was always enamored of the phenomenon of literary creation and the mysteries of poetic invention, as his essay *Le Poème et la Langue* (1967; The Poem and the Tongue) and the collection entitled *Attouchements des sonnets de Shakespeare* (1970; Trifling with Shakespeare's Sonnets) testify.

Nourished by the same themes more systematically exploited, Thiry's prose work displays an obsession with certain metaphysical problems. Haunted by the irreparable and irreversible nature of human time, by the death of loved ones, and by the feeling of wrongdoing, Thiry calls upon a more or less affirmed mysteriousness in order to imagine the return of persons who have disappeared

and the abolition of mistakes. Whereas the novel *Echec au temps* (1945; Checkmating Time) is a chronicle that transforms the Battle of Waterloo into a Napoleonic victory and the short story "Le Concerto pour Anne Queur" (1949; The Concerto for Anne Queur) proposes an anticipation in which one is witness to the resurrection of dead persons, in the short story "Distances" (1960; Distances) and the novels *Simul* (1963) and *Nondum jam non* (1966), the powers of love and friendship, of imagination and poetry are enough to transform society. *Juste ou la Quête d'Hélène* (1953; Juste or the Quest for Helen), which describes the quest that the son of Faust and Helen of Sparta made for his mother, gives evidence of the metaphysical obsession with whiteness, a synonym for absolute peace and purity.

Thiry's whole poetic output, accompanied by a bibliography, was republished in 1975 in a single volume by Edition Seghers (Paris) under the title *Toi qui pâlis au nom de Vancouver . . . œuvres poétiques (1924–1975)* (You Who Turn Pale at the Name of Vancouver . . . Poetic Works).

See: D. Bertin, "Juste ou la Quête d'Hélène de Marcel Thiry," *BARLLF* 50, nos. 3–4 (1972): 201–17.   D.Be.

Thomas, Henri (1912–), French poet and novelist, was born in Anglemont (Alsace). His works of poetry include the volumes *Travaux d'aveugle* (1941; Labors of a Blind Man), *Signe de vie* (1944; Sign of Life), *Le Monde absent* (1947; An Absent World), and *Nul désordre* (1950; No Disorder at All). He writes in a conventional meter and is occasionally reminiscent of Paul VERLAINE, but his poetry lacks true inspiration.

Thomas's novels are numerous, and several have won him distinction; *John Perkins,* published in 1960, earned him the Médicis Prize the same year, and *Le Promontoire* (1961; The Promontory) won the Femina Prize. His other novels include *Sous le lien du temps* (1963; Bound by Time), *Le Parjure* (1964; Perjury), *La Relique* (1969; The Relic), and *Tristan, le dépossédé* (1972; Tristan the Loser).

He has also written a critical essay, *Chasse aux trésors* (1961; Treasure Hunt), and translated works by Shakespeare, Goethe, Ernst JÜNGER, and Aleksandr Pushkin. For his work as a whole, Thomas received the Valery Larbaud Prize in 1970.   B.C.

Þórðarson, Þorbergur (1889–1975), Icelandic poet, essayist, and biographer, was born in the out-of-the-way parish of Suðursveit in southeastern Iceland. The son of a poor farm couple, he received little formal education as a youth, and he moved to Reykjavik at 17 to become a fisherman, a trade he was to work at for the next few years. In the winter of 1908, he attended evening school and, later, a teachers college (1909–10), but he dropped out. He held odd jobs as a laborer during the summers and attempted to enroll at a gymnasium, but abandoned the plan. He was, however, admitted as a special student by the University of Iceland, where he read Nordic philology and literature (1913–18), subsequently spending a number of years as a collector of folk idiom and as an instructor in Icelandic.

Þórðarson launched his literary career with *Hálfir skósólar* (1915; Half Soles), a verse collection soon to be followed by another, *Spaks manns spjarir* (1917; Wise Man's Garbs). The poems contained in both exhibit qualities that later became characteristic of his prose works, too: a rich and ever-alert sense of humor, coupled with his total lack of respect for pretension and accepted tradition. He early developed a strong interest in theosophy and spiritualism, writing essays on these subjects. An

Esperanto enthusiast, he authored a textbook of that language, and many of his essays written in Esperanto saw publication internationally. His preoccupation with the world scene also led him toward socialism. As a mature writer he was at once a theosophist, spiritualist, and dedicated socialist—apparently without having any difficulty whatever in distilling from these various systems of thought a personal philosophy of his own making.

Þórðarson's breakthrough work, *Bréf til Láru* (1924; A Letter to Laura), is a long essay or perhaps a series of essays on a great variety of subjects, including religion and philosophy but, above all, social issues and politics. As for the last topic, Þórðarson appeared as an ardent champion of socialism in Iceland. Written with tempestuous eloquence, animated style, and prophetic inspiration, *Bréf til Láru* aroused immediate and heated controversy. Its style was entirely fresh, freed from the lingering inhibitions that had survived from the 19th-century tradition. Because of both its style and its ideological content, this book was to exert influence on Halldór LAXNESS as well as on other young prose writers. *Bréf til Láru* marks the beginning of a period characterized by leftist-leaning literature focusing on social issues—the predominant school of writing in Iceland through the 1930s. At the same time, the book is autobiographical, as are all of Þórðarson's most significant works. The author himself occupies a central position, as a subject to be analyzed and expounded upon. The same is true of his more recent books like *Íslenzkur aðall* (1938; Eng. tr., *In Search of My Beloved,* 1967) and *Ofvitinn I–II* (1940–41; The All-Too-Wise). Besides their merits as autobiography, all these prose works present a believable and unforgettable account of the lives of young Icelandic writers and artists at the beginning of the 20th century. In addition to the above quasi-autobiographical writings, Þórðarson has published a four-volume story of his youth (1956–75). A prolific biographer, he has also written a number of lives, and his most ambitious project of this kind is *Æfisaga Árna prófasts Þórarinssonar I–VI* (1945–50; The Biography of the Rev. Árni Thórarinsson).

Þórðarson is a consummate master at writing about children, as is testified to by his *Viðfjarðarundrin* (1943; The Wonders at Vidfjördur) and even more so by *Sálmurinn um blómið I–II* (1954–55; The Hymn about the Flower); in the latter, the author employs childlike idiom and achieves, through his great skill, effects of extraordinary charm. Consistent with his interest in folk culture as well as spiritualism and other occult matters, he collected folk tales, publishing—in collaboration with Sigurður NORDAL—two volumes of such material: *Gráskinna* (1962; Book Bound in Gray) and *Gráskinna hin meiri* (1962; The Larger Book Bound in Gray).

Without doubt ranking among the greatest Icelandic stylists of all time, Þórðarson has his own idiosyncratic diction, which combines in a miraculous way richness and transparency. His attitude toward any subject is a paradoxical mixture of childlike simplicity and scientific concern for truth. Above all else, however, his works are always enlivened by wit, a fertile imagination, and prophetic eloquence, as well as by his indignation at that which he regards foolish and unjust in the world.

See: S. Einarsson, *Þórbergur Þórðarson fimmtugur* (1939); M. Jóhannessen, *I kompanii við allífið* (1959).

S.S.H.

Þorstein frá Hamri, pseud. of Þorsteinn Jónsson (1938–), Icelandic essayist, novelist and poet, and the son of a farm couple, was born in Borgarfjörður district in southwestern Iceland. After completing compulsory education, he enrolled at a teachers college and graduated in 1957, but he has supported himself exclusively by writing since then. His first collection of verse, *Í svörtum kufli* (In a Black Mantle), appeared in 1958, and he has subsequently published five other volumes of poetry.

Þorsteinn frá Hamri resembles Snorri HJARTARSON and Hannes PÉTURSSON in that he has attempted to follow a middle course between Icelandic verse tradition and European modernism. A salient feature of his poetry, especially noticeable in his first few books, is the close connection with Icelandic folktales and fairy tales. Archaic at the outset, his diction has increasingly approached everyday modern idiom. His style is typically marked by caution and often by understatement, a quality giving his poetry a modest, quiet tone. His poems are noted for their frequent allusions to Icelandic history and literature as well as for their extremely rich imagery. Although his typical subjects are derived from the life of the common people in Iceland, such topics are developed symbolically.

As a poet, Þorsteinn frá Hamri is both a philosopher and a social critic, and many of his poems deal with the problems facing Icelandic society in the modern world. His outlook is, at the same time, international and reflects his socialist convictions; he frequently expresses sympathy for the oppressed throughout the world. In general, his stance is that of opposition to the status quo, and his later works have become increasingly pessimistic as well as more revolutionary in tone. As is logical in view of such a position, the imagery abounds in descriptions of difficult journeys, hardships, wastelands, and winter landscapes, but the center of attention is always the brave individuals who never yield, human beings as a part of society, and the problems of that society.

In addition to his books of verse, Þorsteinn frá Hamri has published a collection of essays entitled *Skuldaskil* (1963; Settling of Accounts) and two novels: *Himingjargarsaga eða skógardraumur* (1969; Dream in a Forest), and *Möttull konungur eða Caterpillar* (1974; King Mantle or Caterpillar); in both of these novels, the author utilizes folktale or fairy-tale motifs to comment on modern problems.

See: J. Sigurdsson, "Minn trúnaður er ykkar trúnaður," in *Tímarit Máls og menningar* (1969), pp. 132–62, 300–26.

S.S.H.

Tierno Galván, Enrique (1918–), Spanish political scientist, sociologist, philosopher, essayist, and politician, was born in Madrid, where he earned doctorates in law and philosophy. He has been a professor of political science at the universities of Murcia (1948–53) and Salamanca (1953–65) and a visiting professor at the universities of Puerto Rico and Princeton and at Bryn Mawr College. In his formative years he eschewed post-Civil War philosophical currents. He was influenced by the linguistic philosophy of Gottlob Frege and, especially, Ludwig Wittgenstein, whose *Tractatus* helped him to resolve the problem of meaning and to surmount metaphysics. In 1959 he published his first major work, *La realidad como resultado* (Reality as Resultant), a treatise of some 200 aphorisms on the theory of meaning and social epistemology. This work became the foundation of the neopositivist or "operational" theory of social science that he expounded in *Conocimiento y ciencias sociales* (1966; Knowledge and the Social Sciences). In the major theoretical work that followed, *Razón mecánica y razón dialéctica* (1969; Mechanical Reason and Dialectical Reason), Tierno's thought assumes a decidedly Marxist orientation, which coincides with his political and moral concerns as leader of Spain's Social Democratic Party. As a philosopher of praxis, Tierno's long-standing objective has been to substitute for the metaphysical concerns prevalent in contemporary Spanish thought a positive, critical attitude and to replace notions of subjectivism and abstract discourse with a scientific and dialectical vocabulary capable of describing the structure of social reality. Implicit in his approach is an effort to draw attention to political problems and to provide a theory of action consonant with socialist values.

Tierno has also written a number of studies in the history of ideas, the most important of which are *Costa y el regeneracionismo* (1960), *Tradición y modernismo* (1962) and the highly impressionistic, but brilliant, *Acotaciones a la historia de la cultura universal en la edad moderna* (1964; Marginal Notes on the Cultural History of the West in the Modern Era).

Tierno's numerous essays deal essentially with social and cultural topics. They constitute a critique of traditional humanism. His style is terse, direct, and lucid. He creates rhetorical effects by the use of provocative antithesis and bold definitions rather than metaphor. Notable examples are *Desde el espectáculo a la trivialización* (1961; From Spectacle to Trivialization), *Humanismo y sociedad* (1964), *Diderot como pretexto* (1965; Diderot as Pretext), and *¿Qué es ser agnóstico?* (1975; What Is an Agnostic?), his briefest and most synthetic statement of his philosophical and moral position. The author defines the agnostic as a person who has transcended the traditional dualisms of Western thought and who experiences and accepts the finite dimension of existence, understanding reality only from within the boundaries of the world.

See: T. Mermall, *The Rhetoric of Humanism: Spanish Culture after Ortega y Gasset* (1976), pp. 85–107.

T.Me.

Tikhonov, Nikolay Semyonovich (1896–), Russian poet, prose writer, and Soviet literary official, was born in Petersburg and began his literary career in the early 1920s as an associate of Konstantin VAGINOV and a member of the Serapion Brotherhood (*see* RUSSIAN LITERATURE). A romantic by temperament, Tikhonov from the outset gave evidence of a genuine poetic talent, which reflected the influence in particular of the acmeists and of Boris PASTERNAK and Nikolay KHLEBNIKOV. The sprightly independence of outlook that he had shown during his association with the Serapion Brothers faded, however, with the passing years and the changing times. He became more and more involved in administrative work, serving on the presidium at the first congress of Soviet writers in 1934 and later as president of the Union of Soviet Writers, as a member of the Supreme Soviet, and as an active participant in the Soviet-sponsored world peace movement. With his growing commitment to official and administrative duties Tikhonov's literary work has tended to approach the level of literary journalism.

See: G. Struve, *Russian Literature under Lenin and Stalin 1917–1953* (1971), pp. 73–75, 188–91; M. Slonim, *Soviet Russian Literature* (1977), pp. 129–32; D. Brown, *Soviet Russian Literature since Stalin* (1978), pp. 31–32.

W.B.E.

Timmermans, Felix (1886–1947), Belgian (Flemish) novelist, was born in Lier. Timmermans's work is representative of a trend in Flemish literature during the first half of the 20th century. A born raconteur, Timmermans presented an idyllic and sympathetic view of rural and small-town life in Flanders. His love for archaic and folklore elements, which he very cleverly incorporated in such writings as *Het Kindeken Jezus in Vlaanderen* (1917; The Infant Jesus in Flanders) and *De Harp van St. Franciscus*

(1936; The Harp of Saint Francis), gives his books a Biedermeier atmosphere.

Timmermans's first literary success came with *Pallieter* (1916; Eng. tr., 1924), a series of sketches about a lyrical, slightly Rabelaisian figure who lives in a strongly idealized Flemish landscape. This aesthetic sensualist spends his time enjoying the physical world, adding to these pleasures the delight of well-chosen readings from poets and mystics. In one of his late books, *Boerenpsalm* (1935; Peasant Psalm), Timmermans almost completely abandoned conventional decorative writing and created a novel of peasant life surpassing his former works in depth and significance.

Timmermans enjoyed life and interpreted it with colorful simplicity and sly humor. In many instances, his books are literary transcriptions of the illuminations of medieval manuscripts and of the paintings of the masters of the Flemish school. *Pieter Brueghel* (1928; Eng. tr., *Droll Peter,* 1930), a lyrical account of the life of the great painter, is the most striking example of this quality of his writing. Timmermans's popularity exceeds the boundaries of the Dutch-speaking countries. Almost all of his work has been translated into German, and several of his books exist in English or American versions, including *Driekoningentryptiek* (1923; Eng. tr., *The Triptych of the Three Kings,* 1936). In 1941, he published a family chronicle, *De familie Hernat* (The Hernat Family). The verve of Timmermans's prose is, however, contrasted by the serenity and melancholy of his poetry, such as *Adagio* (1947).

See: E. van der Hallen, *Felix Timmermans* (1948); K. Goossens, *Timmermans en de mystieke blijdschap* (1951); J. de Ceulaer, *De mens in het werk van Felix Timmermans* (1957); J. de Ceulaer, *Felix Timmermans* (1961).

J.-A.G. rev. M.-R.L.

Tobino, Mario (1910–), Italian novelist, short-story writer, and poet, was born in Viareggio. He is a psychiatrist who has for many years been in charge of the women's ward of a mental hospital near Lucca, an experience he has written about in his novels *Le libere donne di Magliano* (1953; Eng. tr., *The Women of Magliano,* 1954) and *Per le antiche scale* (1972; Up the Ancient Staircase). Tobino's other works include *Il figlio del farmacista* (1942; The Pharmacist's Son), about his own youth in Viareggio; *Bandiera nera* (1950; Black Flag), a tale of university students under fascism; *Il deserto della Libia* (1952; Eng. tr., "The Deserts of Libia," in *The Lost Legions,* 1967), concerning the author's experiences in Africa during World War II; and *Il clandestino* (1962; Eng. tr., *The Underground,* 1966), which won the Strega Prize in 1962, an account of Tobino's participation in the Resistance upon his return from Africa to his native Viareggio. The history and inhabitants of this city, as well as its sea lore and yarns, are treated extensively in the short stories collected in *La gelosia del marinaio* (1942; The Sailor's Jealousy), *L'angelo del Liponard* (1951; The Angel of Liponard), *Sulla spiaggia e di là del molo* (1966; On the Beach and beyond the Breakwater), and *La bella degli specchi* (1976; The Beauty of the Mirrors), which won the Viareggio Prize in 1976. In *La brace dei Biassoli* (1956; The Embers of the Biassoli Family) and *Una giornata con Dufenne* (1968; A Day with Dufenne), however, Tobino returns to more frankly autobiographical subject matter of the sort that also dominates the poetry collected in *L'asso di picche* (1955; The Ace of Spades) and in *Veleno e amore secondo* (1974; Poison and Love the Second).

In his novels, short stories, and poems, as well as in his unconventional, fictionalized life of Dante, *Biondo era e bello* (1974; He Was Blond and Beautiful), Tobino embraces and celebrates life in its many manifestations. These include madness, as in his two books about the mental hospital; the imperious force of the sexual passions, as in *Due italiani a Parigi* (1954; Two Italians in Paris), *L'angelo del Liponard,* and other works; the exhilarating joy of armed political conflict, as in *Il clandestino*; and the calm, enduring force of filial affection, as in *La brace dei Biassoli.* All his works bear the stamp of his extremely forceful personality, and perhaps for this reason they tend to be confessional in nature, more semifictionalized diaries than conventional novels.

Tobino's energetic, idiosyncratic prose is known for its sometimes violent imagery and occasional disregard for the rules of formal grammar. By his own account, the marks of his works are "liberty and transfiguration," but to these must be added his extraordinary open-mindedness and compassion for human foibles and weaknesses.

See: F. Del Beccaro, *Tobino* (1967).   C.K.

Toller, Ernst (1893–1939), German writer notable chiefly for his expressionist dramas and his involvement in socialist politics, wrote 13 plays, 4 volumes of poetry, and 7 volumes of prose (speeches, autobiography, travel notes, and letters). Born into a middle-class Jewish family in Samotschin, Posen, he attended the University of Grenoble. At the outbreak of World War I he volunteered enthusiastically, but after witnessing the carnage in the trenches he became an ardent pacifist. When he received a medical discharge in 1916, Toller went to Munich, where he made contact both with literary circles and with those leaders of the working class who sought an early end to the war. A vivid and critical account of his prominent role in the short-lived Bavarian Soviet Republic of 1919 is incorporated into his autobiography, *Eine Jugend in Deutschland* (1933; Eng. tr., *I Was a German,* 1934). Convicted of treason, Toller served a five-year prison term. The works written, published, and produced during that period established his reputation.

In *Masse-Mensch* (1922; Eng. tr., *Masses and Man,* 1923), an expressionist masterpiece, Toller drew on his 1919 experiences. The play, set among striking workers, portrays the torment and death of the protagonist named "Woman." She advocates a general strike because to her, revolutionary violence—called for by the "Nameless One" who emerges as the voice of the masses—is irreconcilable with the vision of a more humane society. In *Die Maschinenstürmer* (1922; Eng. tr., *The Machine-Wreckers,* 1923) a prophetic leader rises among the English Luddites. To him the wrecking of the steam loom is "but a deed of slaves who mutiny"; the irate workers consider him a traitor and kill him just before their uprising is put down. While the humane protagonists of these plays fail to transform their sympathy for the rebellious masses into effective action, are rejected, and perish, their optimistic message about man's potential for brotherhood is clearly stated.

In contrast, complete disillusionment marks the tragedy *Hinkemann* (1924; Eng. tr., *Brokenbrow,* 1926). This work depicts the desolate existence of a veteran (a common topic at the time) unmanned by a bullet, mocked by his friends, brutalized by an employer in a fashion reminiscent of Georg Büchner's Woyzeck, and utterly victimized by his inability to trust in his wife's love.

Toller's best volume of poetry, *Das Schwalbenbuch* (1924; Eng. tr., *The Swallow Book,* 1924, 1937), tells of a prisoner to whom the swallows nesting in his cell are messengers and symbols of life. His *Briefe aus dem Gefängnis* (1935; Eng. tr., *Look through the Bars, Letters from Prison,* 1937) provides insight into the long struggle

of this unequivocally sincere man to maintain his humanist faith: "I believed in the saving power of socialism; that was perhaps the 'illusion of my life.'" Toller left Germany in 1933 and committed suicide in New York in 1939.

See: W. A. Willibrand, *Ernst Toller* (1941); J. M. Spalek, *Ernst Toller and His Critics* (1968).   W.H.

Tolstoy, Aleksey Nikolayevich (1883–1945), Russian novelist, dramatist, short-story writer, essayist, and publicist, was born at Nikolayevsk. Although a nobleman by birth, he became, toward the end of his life, the most authoritative apologist for the Stalin regime.

Tolstoy began his writing career as a modernist and neoromantic poet deeply influenced by the symbolists, but he soon turned to prose. During World War I, he was a war correspondent, and after the October Revolution went into voluntary exile in Berlin and Paris. When he returned to the Soviet Union in 1923, he brought with him the novel *Syostry* (1921; The Sisters), which was to be the first book of the trilogy *Khozhdeniye po mukam* (1921–40; Eng. tr., *Road to Calvary,* 1946; *Ordeal,* 1953), the novella *Detstvo Nikity* (1920; Nikita's Childhood), and the Utopian novel *Aelita* (1922; Eng. tr. 1958). In the mid-1920s Tolstoy continued to write novels of adventure, science fiction, and Utopian novels, but the growing interest in historical fiction in the Soviet Union prompted him to try his hand at this genre as well.

In his historical novel *Pyotr pervy* (1929–43; Eng. tr., *Peter the First,* 1959), Tolstoy finally found the medium that best suited his talents. No other Soviet historical novel has been the subject of so much controversy. Books 1 and 2 appeared at a time of turmoil and uncertainty in Soviet literature, when the Pokrovsky school of Soviet historiography, which denied the validity of great historical personalities, was still extremely influential. Despite the Pokrovsky school, however, Tolstoy's novel, which depicts Peter as a maker of history, remained virtually intact until 1944, when the author made a few changes that did not radically alter its concept. *Pyotr pervy* has survived precisely because it is apolitical and traditional. Tolstoy made no attempt to uncover some new "truth" about Peter the Great. He borrowed trite and traditional material from his predecessors: the novelists Dmitry MEREZHKOVSKY and Daniil Mordovtsev, and the historians Vasily Klyuchevsky and Vladimir SOLOVYOV. He utilized some of Walter Scott's techniques in making secondary, nonhistorical characters examples of the social and economic changes wrought by Peter. Critics and readers both within and outside the Soviet Union consider *Pyotr pervy* to be the best Soviet historical novel ever written. It is also the best novel on the theme of Peter the Great in all of Russian literature. New editions or printings are still being produced virtually every year.

Tolstoy was and still is a very popular writer, but he also did much to advance the cultural life of his country. He helped in the compilation and publication of histories of the literatures of the nationalities of the USSR, and did much to ensure the publication of Russian folklore. He was elected to the Academy of Sciences in 1939, and served as a journalist and propagandist during World War II. Death interrupted his work on Book 3 of *Pyotr pervy.*

See: A. V. Alpatov, *Aleksey Tolstoy—Master istoricheskogo romana* (Moscow, 1958); M. B. Charny, *Put Alekseya Tolstogo: ocherk tvorchestva* (Moscow, 1961).   L.T.

Tolstoy, Lev Nikolayevich (1828–1910), Russian novelist and religious and social thinker, produced two of the world's greatest novels and a host of shorter masterpieces, but in sheer drama none of his contributions to literature surpassed the story of his own life. At the age of 50, at the height of his creative powers, he was brought to the brink of suicide by a profound spiritual crisis that ultimately transformed his world outlook, his personal life, and his literary career. The result was that in addition to his worldwide literary audience he also attracted a worldwide following of seekers after moral and spiritual truth.

Tolstoy was born in the province of Tula at Yasnaya Polyana, the family estate where he lived out his long life, and which has since been turned into a national shrine. At the age of 16 he entered Kazan University, dropping out after three years of indifferent success as a student and of alternating debauchery, self-reproach, and attempts at self-discipline in his personal life. After trying his hand during the next four years at various endeavors on the family estate and in Moscow and Petersburg, he went to the Caucasus in 1851 along with his elder brother Nikolay, who was stationed there as an officer. It was during the nearly three years he spent in the Caucasus that Tolstoy began his career as a writer. His first published work was *Detstvo* (1852; Eng. tr., *Childhood,* 1862), part of a fictional trilogy in autobiographical form that includes *Otrochestvo* (1854; Eng. tr., *Boyhood,* 1886) and *Yunost* (1857; Eng. tr., *Youth,* 1886), and is written from the dual perspective of the narrator as a young boy experiencing the events of the story and as a mature man recollecting them. *Childhood* shows the conflict between the unspoiled child's fresh, authentic perception of reality and the distorted, artificial, and even hypocritical view of reality that is gradually imposed on children by society.

Another masterly product of Tolstoy's experience in the Caucasus is *Kazaki* (1863; Eng. tr., *The Cossacks,* 1872), which he began writing in 1852 but did not complete and publish until 11 years later. It is the gently humorous story of a young Russian who goes to the Caucasus with his head full of romantic dreams about a wild, free life among the natives, only to find himself disillusioned by reality, rejected by the Cossacks, and perhaps a little wiser and more sober when he goes back to his homeland.

A year after arriving in the Caucasus, Tolstoy joined the army as a cadet; and early in 1854, on the eve of the Crimean War, he won his commission as an officer. He took part in the ill-fated defense of Sevastopol, where he was under fire many times; and out of this experience he produced a masterpiece of fictionalized war reportage, *Sevastopolskiye rasskazy* (1855–56; Eng. tr., *Sebastopol,* 1887), which is one of the first works in European literature to present war stripped of all romantic glamour.

Returning home late in 1855 after the Russian defeat, Tolstoy found himself welcomed as a literary hero first in Petersburg and then in Moscow by the leading writers of the two capital cities. His triumph proved to be short-lived, however, partly because of his own cantankerous disposition at that time and partly because the works he wrote in the next few years did not for the most part fulfill the promise of *Childhood* and the *Sevastopol Tales.* "Dva gusara" (1856; Eng. tr., "Two Hussars," 1887) offers a highly amusing, if superficial, contrast between two generations in 19th-century Russia; but "Iz zapisok knyazya D. Nekhlyudova. Lyutsern" (1857; Eng. tr., "Lucerne," 1887) and "Albert" (1858; Eng. tr., 1887) are flawed stories interesting mainly as stages in Tolstoy's literary development. "Tri smerti" (1859; Eng. tr., "Three Deaths," 1887) is significant as an early treatment of one of the major themes running throughout Tolstoy's writings. The best work of this not very distinguished period is the short novel *Semeynoye schastye* (1859; Eng. tr., *Family Happiness,* 1888), and "Polikushka" (1863;

Eng. tr., 1886), a powerful and complex story of tragedy in the life of a serf.

The years from 1856 to 1862 were a difficult period in Tolstoy's life, full of restlessness and uncertainty about his future. His marriage in 1862 at the age of 34 to Sofya Bers, a young girl of 17, marked the beginning of the happiest and most productive period of his long life. Within a year after his marriage he plunged into the writing of his first masterpiece, *Voyna i mir* (1863–69; Eng. tr., *War and Peace,* 1886), which was to establish him along with Fyodor DOSTOYEVSKY as one of the two greatest novelists in Russian literature. A huge novel of more than 1,500 pages with well over 500 characters in all, *War and Peace* is a philosophical exploration of the meaning of life, shown dramatically through the intertwined fates of three families during a great national crisis in Russian history: the Napoleonic invasion of 1812. Despite the widespread destruction and loss of life during the war, and despite the death of Prince Andrey Bolkonsky, one of the two principal male characters along with Pierre Bezukhov, the total effect of the novel is a joyous affirmation of life. Natasha Rostova, who ultimately becomes Pierre's wife, is one of the most famous feminine characters in all Russian fiction.

During the 1870s, Tolstoy created his second masterpiece, *Anna Karenina* (1875–77; Eng. tr., 1886), a tragedy based on the old eternal triangle, but with social and spiritual dimensions that lift it far above the plane of the usual European novel of adultery. Into his account of the illicit love affair between Anna Karenina and the officer Aleksey Vronsky, which ends with her disintegration and suicide, Tolstoy interweaves a contrasting story of the love that culminates in marriage between Anna's sister-in-law Kitty and the brooding, independent-minded Levin, who is modeled in many ways on Tolstoy himself.

As he was writing the last chapters of *Anna Karenina,* Tolstoy found himself unable to evade any longer the great philosophical question that had been lurking in the back of his mind ever since his revered elder brother Nikolay had died in his arms of consumption in 1860: what meaning can life possibly have if nothing awaits us after death except—nothingness? This question forced Tolstoy to go through a long and painful process of inner turmoil and searching, which he subsequently described in *Ispoved* (written 1879, pub. Geneva, 1884; Eng. tr., *A Confession,* 1885), a little classic in European confessional literature.

Out of this spiritual travail Tolstoy finally arrived at a new religious philosophy that rested essentially on his belief—set forth in his essay *O zhizni* (printed 1888 but banned; pub. Geneva, 1891; Eng. trs., *Life,* 1888; *On Life,* 1902)—that our existence in this physical world has meaning only as part of a larger spiritual life before birth and after death, during which Tolstoy does not exclude the possibility of other physical existences, in keeping with the Buddhist idea of reincarnation. Within this spiritual context Tolstoy accepts Jesus' Sermon on the Mount as the fundamental law of life; and this leads him to a kind of religious anarchism involving the rejection of all violence and all institutions resting on violence, including armies, police, law courts, prisons, and even private property, money, and the state itself. He advocated a New Testament standard of personal conduct that included absolute truth, love of one's neighbor, the rejection of all exploitation of others, including the sexual exploitation of women, and—later in his life—abstinence from meat, alcohol, and tobacco. Along with *On Life,* the principal works in which he set forth these views are *V chom moya vera* (printed 1884 but banned; pub. Geneva, n.d., before 1888; Eng. tr., *What I Believe,* 1885) and

Tsarstvo Bozhiye vnutri vas (Berlin, 1894; Eng. tr., *The Kingdom of God Is Within You,* 1894).

Tolstoy's literary works after his spiritual revolution fall into two classes: (1) simple tales especially written for the peasants, which Tolstoy printed in a publishing house that he and his followers established for the express purpose of making good literature available to the masses in very cheap editions; and (2) literary works written in the spirit of his new convictions for members of his own social class. The best of these latter include the stories "Smert Ivana Ilyicha" (1886; Eng. tr., "The Death of Ivan Ilyich," 1887), "Khozyain i rabotnik" (1895; Eng. tr., "Master and Man," 1895), "Kreytserova sonata" (1891; Eng. tr., "The Kreutzer Sonata," 1890), and "Khadzhi Murat" (written 1904, pub. posthumously; Eng. tr., "Hadji Murad," 1911); and the heavily didactic but still impressive novel *Voskreseniye* (1899; Eng. tr., *Resurrection,* 1899), which Tolstoy completed and published in order to contribute the proceeds toward helping the much-oppressed religious sect of Dukhobors emigrate from Russia to a haven of freedom in Canada. In 1898, Tolstoy published *Chto takoye iskusstvo?* (Eng. tr., *What Is Art?,* 1898), in which he set forth his controversial but still highly stimulating theories on art.

Tolstoy's far-reaching impact on the rest of the world has been dual in nature. It is reflected in the literary works of numerous writers, among them Romain ROL-LAND in France, Benito PÉREZ GALDÓS and Miguel de UNAMUNO in Spain, William Dean Howells in the United States, and Mushakoji Saneatsu in Japan. As a religious and social prophet he influenced the personal lives of thousands of individuals around the world, including the great Indian leader Mohandas Gandhi, who as a young man corresponded with Tolstoy about nonviolence and looked on him as one of his spiritual mentors.

See: A. Maude, *The Life of Tolstoy,* 2 vols. (rev., 1930); B. Eykhenbaum, *Lev Tolstoy,* 2 vols. (1928, 1931); E. Simmons, *Leo Tolstoy* (1946); N. Weisbein, *L'Evolution religieuse de Tolstoï* (1960); B. Eykhenbaum, *Lev Tolstoy: semidesyatye gody* (1960); R. Christian, *Tolstoy: A Critical Introduction* (1969); E. Wasiolek, *Tolstoy's Major Fiction* (1978); R. Christian, *Tolstoy's Letters,* 2 vols. (1979).   W.B.E.

Tomasi di Lampedusa, Giuseppe (1896–1957), Italian novelist and short-story writer, was born in Palermo. He achieved posthumous fame with his first and only novel, *Il gattopardo* (1958; Eng. tr., *The Leopard,* 1960). Several factors contributed to turning the book into a literary phenomenon: the personality of the author, a Sicilian prince who had read and traveled widely but had shunned all public life during the Fascist era; the circumstances of publication (the book had been rejected by Elio VITTO-RINI, then of the Einaudi publishing firm, before being accepted by Giorgio BASSANI for Feltrinelli); critical discussions concerning the disappearance of the traditional, 19th-century type novel, which had become frequent and explosive in the wake of the introduction of the "new novel" (*see* FRENCH LITERATURE) in Italy; and the celebration of the anniversary of Italian unity, accompanied by controversial and divergent assessments of the national picture. The bibliography of secondary literature on the work for 1959–60 is particularly extensive. The book has been widely translated.

Except for three articles published in 1926–27, Lampedusa's extant works belong to the brief span of time from 1954, when he attended a literary conference with his cousin, the poet Lucio PICCOLO, until his death. Two of the short pieces collected in *Racconti* (1961; Eng. tr., *Two Stories and a Memory,* 1962) are related to the sub-ject matter of *Il gattopardo.* The third and best, "Lighea" (Eng. tr., "The Professor and the Mermaid"), belongs to the fiction of the supernatural and deals with a theme that is also prominent in *Il gattopardo*: the instability of earthly pleasures. Of fundamental importance for a full understanding of the novel is "Lezioni su Stendhal" (Lectures on Stendhal), published in *Paragone* (April 1959), lectures Lampedusa gave to a group of young friends. "Lezioni" contains an in-depth appreciation of Stendhal's work and an analysis of narrative technique that shows that, unlike most Italian critics, Lampedusa was well acquainted with the Jamesian tradition of novel criticism. *Il gattopardo* is not simply a historical novel but shares the characteristics, as defined in "Lezioni," of both Stendhal's *Le Rouge et le noir* and *La Chartreuse de Parme.*

In historico-political terms, the subject of *Il gattopardo* is the Risorgimento and its effects on Sicilian life. Giuseppe Garibaldi's liberation, or conquest, of Sicily is seen through the eyes of "the Leopard," Don Fabrizio, prince of Salina, who in May 1860, the opening date of the book, accepts the fact that Tancredi, his favorite nephew, is leaving to join the rebels. While on the one hand Lampedusa develops the plot of Tancredi's reaching for success, on the other he dwells on the reactions of Don Fabrizio. The prince sees the aristocracy of the old regime displaced by the inexorable rise of a grasping, unpolished middle class and observes a parallel decline in his own vitality as compared with the fresh will and passions of the younger generation. Introspection, analysis, and lyricism take precedence over narrative in *Il gattopardo*, as the subjective tone is increased by the obvious if ambiguous coinciding of the prince's consciousness with Lampedusa's. The present intrudes upon the past, and the omniscient narrator, not content with knowing everything there is to know about his characters, also hints at what will happen after the story is finished. Thus *Il gattopardo* ends not with the death of the title character nor yet with the final chapter, set in 1910, which rounds out a 50-year span and shows the decline of his once proud family and "the end of everything," but opens up into the world contemporary with the book's writing and publication. This variation on the classical form of the historical novel, which gives a strong sense of immediacy to the fictional world Lampedusa chronicles, is no doubt partly responsible for the heated ideological arguments that the novel occasioned.

In its narrative sweep and emotional impact, *Il gattopardo* has been compared to Margaret Mitchell's *Gone with the Wind.* Its metaphorical, rhetorical, and highly literary style, however, marks it as belonging to the art prose movement (*see* ITALIAN LITERATURE) of the 1930s.

See: O. Ragusa, "Stendhal, Tomasi di Lampedusa, and the Novel," *CLS* 10 (1973), pp. 195–228; S. Salvestroni, *Tomasi di Lampedusa* (1973).   O.R.

Tomizza, Fulvio (1935–), Italian novelist, was born in Materada di Umago in Istria. He comes from a rural background; his father was a landowner, though hardly wealthy. Tomizza has a double linguistic and cultural inheritance. After growing up in Istria during the difficult times of World War II and its aftermath, he spent two years in Yugoslavia, where he attended the Belgrade Academy of Dramatic Arts. Since 1955 he has lived in Trieste. His early works, *Materada* (1960), *La ragazza di Petrovia* (1963; The Girl from Petrovia), and *Il bosco di acacie* (1966; The Acacia Grove), all deal with the Istrian "exodus" of the mid-1950s when the province was assigned to Yugoslavia and those inhabitants who wished to retain Italian citizenship were obliged to emigrate. These works, republished as *Trilogia istriana* (1967; Istrian Trilogy), brought Tomizza into prominence among contemporary Italian writers. *La quinta stagione* (1965; The Fifth Season) might serve as an introduction to the *Trilogia*. It portrays the tormented life of the author's native province in the last years of World War II. This work has a perceptible autobiographical vein, as does *L'albero dei sogni* (1969; The Tree of Dreams), the story of a man torn between two cultures and ideologies. *La città di Miriam* (1972; Miriam's City) is a sensitive study of a woman, a marriage, and a culture.

Critics have found in Tomizza's works sundry affinities with other writers: the scene of his novels is the same as that exploited by Pier Antonio Quarantotti Gambini; his "lyric realism" bears a certain resemblance to Cesare PAVESE; his psychological perception suggests Italo SVEVO (and Fyodor DOSTOYEVSKY); and his quiet if unpolemical sympathy with the common folk, as well as his art in portraying "choral" scenes and emotions, is reminiscent of Giovanni VERGA. In this respect one might add that, as in the case of Verga, Tomizza's language, while always lucid and unpretentious, has undertones of dialect both in vocabulary and syntax. Whatever be his affinities, however, his art is as truly his own as his Istrian *piccolo mondo* is autonomous in Italian letters. Tomizza's strength derives from a serene objectivity. He writes of war without rancor, of sex without morbidity, and of death without rhetoric. In his pages there is room for animals, birds, and trees as well as for an appreciation of the human condition. He must be judged a major novelist of his generation. Other works include *La torre capovolta* (1971; The Tower Overthrown), *Dove tornare* (1973; Whither to Return), *La miglior vita* (1977; The Better Life), and the play *Vera Verk* (1963).

See: G. Pampaloni, *La fiera letteraria* (Nov. 16, 1967); Bruno Maier, in *Belfagor* (1968); M. Grillandi, in *Il ponte* (1972); R. Damiani, in *Letteratura italiana: i contemporanei,* vol. 6 (1974), pp. 1959–80.   T.G.B.

Topîrceanu, George (1886–1937), Romanian poet, was born in Bucharest. Until 1911 he held various office jobs. This experience with small-minded officials is reflected in his gently ironic poetry. In 1909 he began his collaboration with the journal *Viaţa românească,* and in 1916 his first volumes of poetry appeared: *Balade vesele* (Merry Ballads) and *Parodii originale* (Original Parodies). After spending two years as a prisoner of war, during World War I, Topîrceanu resumed his literary activity with several volumes of prose works: *Amintiri din luptele de la Turtucaia* (1918; Memories of the Struggles of Turtucaia), *Scrisori Turtucaia fără adresă* (1930; Turtucaian Letters Without Address), and *Pirin-Planina* (1936). In 1921 he translated Shakespeare's *A Midsummer Night's Dream* in an unequaled Romanian version. Another volume of poems, *Migdale amare* (Bitter Almonds), was published in 1928.

Topîrceanu created a new technique in poetry, notable for its natural tone and irony, and he used this irony to condemn successfully what is artificial and false in lyric art. Through his lyricism, he conveyed a feeling of solidarity with the common people and in many poems shows a bitter, but not insensitive, humor.

See: C. Ciopraga, *George Topîrceanu* (1966); G. Topîrceanu, *Scrieri alese* (1970).   P.G.T.

Torbado, Jesús (1943–), Spanish novelist, was born in León and lives primarily in Madrid. He studied journalism but never finished his degree. He spent some time hitchhiking through most of Western Europe, an experience reflected in his novels and in his travel books. He has also written radio and television scripts.

As a novelist, Torbado has sampled the various literary tendencies that have been in vogue in Spain during the last 20 years. *En el día de hoy* (1976; At the Present Time) is written in the vein of "objective realism," *Moira estuvo aquí* (1971; Moira Was Here) belongs to the "new novel," and *Las corrupciones* (1966) conforms to "eclectic realism." Chronologically he belongs to the group of writers who began to write after the crisis of objective realism, that is, after the appearance of Luis MARTÍN-SANTOS's novel *Tiempo de silencio* (1962).

The dominant theme of Torbado's novels is the double problem of personality and individuality. His characters often appear to be asphyxiated by modern civilization, crushed by obligations and necessities. Neither the values nor the beliefs they profess aid them in finding solace or happiness. This theme leads the author to populate his fictional world with marginal people. His fiction appears to mirror a real world he knows very well.

Torbado's best novel to date is probably *Las corrupciones,* for which he received the Alfaguara Prize. In the novel, Torbado utilizes various devices peculiar to eclectic realism (letters, notes, songs, the "objective" and the "subjective," the "interior" and the "exterior") to reveal the main character's personality and the meaning of his actions. The protagonist is presented at three successive stages of his life, always searching for some intimate security. During his search, he begins to lose faith in all that he has believed before. He discovers that God is nonexistent, that religion kills vitality, that money leads to baseness, and that love is an egotistical act. The only true and certain refuge that remains open to him is ultimately loneliness, as he has lost the meaning of life, hope, and solace.

Alain ROBBE-GRILLET's novel *Le voyeur* serves as the direct inspiration for Torbado's *Moira estuvo aquí.* There are obvious parallels between the atmosphere, the nature of the characters, and even some narrative situations in these two novels. The narrative process itself is characteristic of the "nouveau roman" (*see* FRENCH LITERATURE). This work is not as hermetic, however, as are most Spanish "new novels."

En el día de hoy springs from the stimulating hypothesis that the Republic won the Civil War in 1939, instead of the Nationalists. Despite the intrinsic interest of such a situation, this novel is his weakest effort to date. Of higher artistic caliber are *Profesor particular* (1966; Private Teacher), *La construcción del odio* (1968; The Construction of Hatred), and *Historias de amor* (1968).   P.G.C.

Torczyner, Harry (1910–), Belgian poet and essayist, was born in Antwerp and raised in The Hague, Antwerp, and Brussels. He received his higher education at the University of Brussels, the University of Heidelberg, and Columbia University. During World War II, Torczyner was a member of the Review Board of the Overseas Branch of the Office of War Information. Shortly thereafter, he became legal adviser to a number of artists and writers as well as to such countries as Argentina, Costa Rica, Ivory Coast, and Sierra Leone. In addition to his career in international law in the United States, he has pursued interests in poetry and the visual arts. Two volumes of his poetry have appeared: *Miettes* (1952; Crumbs), with a preface by Leon Kochnitzky, and *Un Coin de désert* (1958; A Corner of the Desert), with a preface by Marnix Gijsen and illustrations by Octave Landuyt. Through the often surprising juxtaposition of repeated sounds and of images from everyday life, Torczyner's brief poems offer a bemused, sometimes sharply ironical portrait of the human situation. It could also be said that, upon occasion, his verse, like that of the late Italian poet Giuseppe UNGARETTI, may be characterized by the sparing use of words and the power to create illuminating images. In all this there is a marked independence of mind and spirit. In the 1960s, with Louis Scutenaire, Marcel Lecomte, André PIEYRE DE MANDIARGUES, and René Magritte, among others, Torczyner contributed to the literary and artistic journal *Rhétorique*. Moreover, various poems of his have appeared in the periodical *Le Moi* and in Spanish in *Comentario*. In his *René Magritte: signes et images* (1977; Eng. tr., *Magritte: Ideas and Images*, 1977), Torczyner's commentaries on Magritte and his paintings and writings reflect in considerable degree Torczyner's own literary and aesthetic preoccupations, as well as those of the surrealist painter Magritte.   O.F.

Torga, Miguel, pseud. of Adolfo Correia da Rocha (1907–), Portuguese poet, playwright, and short-story writer, was born into a farming family in São Martinho da Anta, in the Trás-os-Montes province. He is a practicing physician in the university town of Coimbra, where he obtained his degree. He began his literary career in 1928, when, still using his legal name, he published a book of verse, *Ansiedade* (Anxiety). During those early years, he collaborated with other young poets in the literary journal *Presença* (*see* PORTUGUESE LITERATURE), but his independent character and preoccupation with metaphysical and social problems soon led to a break with his more aesthetic-minded companions. His love for the rough hill country of his native Trás-os-Montes prompted him to choose the *torga*—a hardy species of mountain heather—as an apt symbol for his own proud individualism. With the publication of his first major collection of poems, *O outro livro de Job* (1936; The Other Book of Job), the writer permanently adopted the name that has since become one of the most honored in contemporary Portuguese letters.

Torga's weltanschauung owes much to the existential angst as articulated by his fellow Iberian, Miguel de UNAMUNO, in the latter's *Del sentimiento trágico de la vida* (1912). Throughout the works of the Portuguese writers there appears the drama of the modern rationalist, unable to accept the Catholicism of his cultural tradition but haunted by a deep-rooted need for spiritual significance and the security of divine providence. Torga's predominant attitude is that of the defiant romantic, asserting his individuality against the threats of mass values, ideological totalitarianism, and philosophical nihilism.

Torga's poetry combines personal confession and humanistic concern with a great variety of moods and structures ranging from the sonnet to the most liberated form of free verse. Besides the tortured queries of a modern Job, there are examples of Nietzschean sarcasm and blasphemous rebellion (*see* Friedrich NIETZSCHE) in *Lamentação* (1943; Lamentation) and *Penas do Purgatório* (1954; Pains of Purgatory), moments of exultation in *Odes* (1946), and optimistic hope in man's eventual integration with a nature immune to Christian asceticism in *Cântico do homem* (1950; Canticle of Man). Except for an occasional lapse into declamation, the poet cultivates vigorous diction and decisive rhythms. As a critic, too, he is almost painfully sensitive to the technical demands of his craft.

A similar perspective characterizes *Portugal* (1950), a collection of 15 essays on as many regions and cities throughout his native land. For Torga, patriotism is at best a bittersweet emotion, ranging from pride and affection to admiration tempered by sharp criticism ("Coimbra") and melancholy and resignation ("Sagres"). Less poetic and more "public" is the tone of *Traço de união*

(1955; Hyphen), which comprises lectures, letters, and essays concerning Portugal's long and uneven cultural relationship with Brazil. The author's intensely personal point of view explains the autobiographical perspective of early prose works, such as *A criação do mundo, Os dois primeiros dias* (1937; The Creation of the World, The First Two Days), which closely mirrors his poor boyhood and emigration to Brazil, where he spent his teens. In 1941, with *Diário I* (Diary I), he abandoned even the pretense of fiction. The 11 volumes of *Diário*, which had appeared by 1977, comprise rich and varied memoirs in the form of introspective social and literary observations, travel, journals, and perhaps the best of Torga's poetry.

In several collections of short stories, colored by the writer's much-discussed telluric fixation with Trás-os-Montes, one finds mountain peasants courageously struggling against poverty, ignorance, official neglect, and a harsh nature. Vivid characterization and dialogue with all the flavor of the rural north help explain the perennial popularity of *Montanha* (1941; Mountains) and *Novos contos da montanha* (1944; New Tales from the Mountains). The author's ability to impart universal significance to individual suffering and his sympathy for the humble are especially apparent in *Bichos* (1940; Eng. tr., *Farrusco the Blackbird and Other Stories*, 1951). His admiration for the courage of Portugal's peasants and fishermen is no less evident in his two 1941 plays *Terra firme* (Mainland) and *Mar* (Sea). Other plays of his are *Sinfonia* (1947; Symphony) and *O Paraíso* (1949; Paradise). In the latter, Torga is at his sardonic best, lampooning political and social pretensions.

See: A. Casais Monteiro, *O romance e os seus problemas* (1950), pp. 238-51; E. Lourenço, *O desespero humanista de Miguel Torga e o das novas gerações* (1958); J. de Melo, *Miguel Torga* (1960); C. Crabbé Rocha, *O espago autobiográfico em Miguel Torga* (1977).

                                                                                R.A.P.-R.

Torre, Guillermo de (1900–76), Spanish literary and art critic, was born in Madrid and died in Buenos Aires, where he had resided since 1937. In the Hispanic world he was the most prominent specialist in the history of ideas and critical theory. He began his career within the ultraist group (1919–23). His sole book of poetry, *Hélices* (1923; *Rudders*), shows the influence of futurism, creationism, Guillaume APOLLINAIRE's cubism, and haiku. In 1925 he published *Literaturas europeas de vanguardia* which introduced in Spain the theories behind all the "isms." Torre cofounded *La Gaceta Literaria* (1927–31), then the most influential and best-informed Spanish journal on contemporary European letters. In Argentina he was editorial secretary of *Sur* and wrote countless articles and reviews for other prominent newspapers and literary journals. Most of his books are collections of these always polemical essays.

Torre was influenced by José ORTEGA Y GASSET in believing that criticism should be supportive and explicative, not negative. It should be especially alert to new tendencies, which should be interpreted within the ideological context of their times. Like Ortega, Torre constantly brought out common grounds between literature and painting, as in his *Guillermo Apollinaire y el cubismo* (1946). While he defends experimentation, he condemns exclusivism. In the 1950s, for example, he spoke against neorealism when it claimed to be the only viable solution to the problems of the novel. He also believed that while literature should be responsible, creativity should be free from ideological strictures.

Torre wrote pioneering studies on many modern Spanish writers. He was one of the first to reevaluate the novels of Benito PÉREZ GALDÓS, in articles written in *La Nación* and *Sur* in 1943. Three essays on Miguel de UNAMUNO, Federico GARCÍA LORCA, and Antonio MACHADO form his *Tríptico de sacrificio* (1948). He was also the first to edit the complete works of García Lorca in 11 volumes (1938), at a time when reliable texts were difficult to find. A representative collection of his essays is entitled *Doctrina y estética literaria* (1970). *Historia de las literaturas de vanguardia* (1965) is a considerably updated version of the 1925 study.

See: E. de Zuleta, *Guillermo de Torre* (1962). J.Cr.

Torrente Ballester, Gonzalo (1910–), Spanish novelist, playwright, journalist, and literary critic, was born in El Ferrol, in the province of Coruña. He studied law and philosophy and letters at the universities of Santiago and Madrid and has been a professor of history and literature. His *Panorama de la literatura española* has been published several times.

El viaje del joven Tobías (1935; The Journey of Young Tobías) is an avant-garde play written under the influence of Edgar Allan Poe and Stéphane MALLARMÉ. In 1943 he published the novel *Javier Mariño*, a human testimony to the moral and political conversion of Javier and Magdalena in Paris during the early 1930s. *El golpe de Estado de Guadalupe Limón* (1946; Guadalupe Limón's Coup d'Etat) is a novelistic farce set in an imaginary Latin American republic reminiscent of that of Ramón del VALLE-INCLÁN's *Tirano Banderas*.

The trilogy *Los gozos y las sombras* (Joys and Shadows)—*El señor llega* (1957; The Master Arrives), *Donde da la vuelta el aire* (1960; Where the Air Takes a Turn), and *La Pascua triste* (1962; The Sad Easter)—presents the symbolic confrontation of one man's spiritual apathy with the pragmatic materialism of another in an imaginary Galician setting prior to the Spanish Civil War. Torrente Ballester revealed his power as a writer in his psychological study of the characters and the community, as well as in his skillful use of narrative technique. In *Don Juan* (1963), by combining humor and imagination the novelist presented a new version of the Don Juan myth, and in *Off-Side* (1969) he depicted contemporary Spanish society through a number of humorous sketches.

La saga/fuga de J.B. (1972) is the mythical story of an imaginary Galician town as told by an ugly and intelligent dreamer. Technique, rather than plot, is the author's primary interest in this narrative. The novel's construction, inspired by the musical form of the fugue, is a parody of the highly structured novel. It is a satire of the collective legend of a people and their heroes. *Fragmentos de Apocalipsis* (1977; Fragments of Apocalypse) reaffirms Torrente Ballester's qualities as a novelist. In this work, theories on the creative process are combined with an investigation into language by means of a vivid, imaginative, and cultured prose. With his vigorous realism, linguistic invention, control of different novelistic techniques, and acute psychological study of characters—especially in works published in the 1970s—Torrente Ballester has become one of the leading narrators of our time.

See: G. Sobejano, *Novela española de nuestro tiempo* (1975), pp. 231–49; L. Suñén, "Gonzalo Torrente Ballester: El placer de escribir (y leer) una novela," *Insula* 376 (March 1978): 5. J.O.

Tóth, Árpád (1886–1928), Hungarian poet and translator was born in Debrecen. He studied philology at the University of Budapest but failed to graduate. Between 1909 and 1913 Tóth worked as a journalist in Debrecen, afterwards returning to Budapest where for a time he was employed by a wealthy family as a private tutor. In 1918 he was elected secretary of the Vörösmarty Academy, a body founded by progressive writers. Tóth wrote an ode in honor of the newly proclaimed Hungarian Soviet Republic (1919), because of which he suffered political attacks and economic hardship after the counterrevolution that same year. In 1921 he found employment with a liberal newspaper. His premature death was a result of tuberculosis.

Tóth is a representative poet of the first *Nyugat* generation (*see* HUNGARIAN LITERATURE). His early poetry, dominated by sadness and resignation, often culminates in an invocation of death. His language, influenced by Charles BAUDELAIRE and Albert Samain, is impressionistic. He used certain adjectives with great frequency and preferred the structure of the iambic line, particularly the dignified alexandrine. Around 1913, Tóth's poetry became less personal and more concerned with social and patriotic subjects. During World War I, he expressed his pacifistic sentiments in such poems as "Elégia egy rekettyebokorhoz" (1917; Elegy to a Thicket of Broom). In the 1919 Hungarian revolution he saw a fulfillment of his expectations, but it was his romantic anticapitalism rather than a genuine commitment to Marxism that made him write his controversial poem "Az új Isten (1919; The New God). Tóth's two postwar volumes of poetry, *Az öröm illan* (1922; Inconstant Joy) and *Lélektől lélekig* (1928; From Soul to Soul), marked a return to the themes of his early verse, although by now Tóth's sadness had lost its timeless character and his sighs of frustration had gained a new meaning. He also wrote some tender, beautifully structured love poems during the 1920s. Disenchanted with the present, Tóth hoped for a different, less hectic future that would appreciate his "gentle song." This desire is the subject of "Jó éjszakát!" (1928; Good Night!). During the last decade of his life, his poetry became more classical, although it never lost its mellow, nostalgic, slightly decadent undertones. Tóth's reputation as an outstanding translator of foreign poetry is based on his renderings of John Keats, Baudelaire, and Oscar Wilde. His translation of Percy Bysshe Shelley's "Ode to the West Wind" ranks among the most beautiful Hungarian poetic texts.

See: G. Oláh, "Tóth Árpád költészete," *Nyugat* 22 (1929): 398–405; L. Kardos, *Tóth Árpád* (1955); J. Reményi, *Hungarian Writers and Literature* (1964), pp. 292–97; A. Karátson, *Le Symbolisme en Hongrie* (1969), pp. 268–319. G.G.

Toulet, Paul-Jean (1867–1920), French poet and novelist, was born in Pau into a family of planters from the island of Mauritius. Brought up in Béarn, he attended various scholastic establishments, succeeded in getting a bachelor's degree, and then joined his father in the Ile-de-France, where he remained for three years. After working as a journalist in Algiers, he spent nine years (1889–98) in Mauritius, enjoying the idle existence of a young dandy, exclusively occupied with his personal pleasures.

In 1898, Toulet descended upon Paris, almost immediately publishing *Monsieur de Paur, homme public* (Mr. de Paur, Man of Importance), a strange novel influenced by the mysterious tales of the English writer Arthur Machen, whose *Great God Pan* Toulet translated in 1901. Toulet soon found himself following around in the shadow of Maurice Curnonsky, the future Prince of Gastronomers, with whom he wrote, under the pseudonym of Perdiccas, *Le Bréviaire des courtisans* (1899; The Breviary of the Courtiers), and *Le Métier d'amant* (1900; Lover's Trade)—frivolous novels that revive the atmosphere of the Belle Epoque. At the same time, Toulet contributed short stories, articles of criticism, and fantasies of all kinds to various periodicals, such as *La Vie parisienne*. In this journal he published *Les Tendres Ménages* (1904; Tender Couples), and the chapters of a charming turn-of-the-century story, *Mon Amie Nane* (1905; My Friend Nane).

After 1907, Toulet also wrote, completed, or retyped novels or parts of novels for Henri Gauthier-Villars, better known as Willy, the husband of COLETTE. The novels in which Toulet was involved include *La Tournée du petit duc* (1908; The Little Duke's Tour), *Les Amis de Siska* (1914; The Friends of Siska), *Lélie fumeuse d'opium* (Lélie the Opium Smoker), and *Maugis en ménage* (1910; Maugis Married). The short stories and tales to which he signed his own name, however, gave evidence of greater refinement. These include *Le Mariage de Don Quichotte* (1902; The Marriage of Don Quixote), *Comme une fantaisie* (1918; Like a Fantasy), and *Les Contes de Béhanzigue* (1920; Stories of Béhanzigue). *La Jeune Fille verte* (1920; The Little Green Girl), an evocation of the frolicking and hesitations of a young, middle-class girl from Béarn, is especially noteworthy.

But Toulet the poet is vastly superior to Toulet the novelist. The series of poems he published around 1910 in various periodicals immediately gained him a reputation. Toulet was hailed in the "Poètes fantaisistes" number of *Vers et prose* (1913) and in a special number of *Divan* (August 1914) devoted to him. Yet by this date, Toulet, his health and fortune in ruins, had retired to a family estate in the Bordelais, the chateau of La Rafette. Near the end of his life, he married a native of the Basque region and retired to Guéthary, where he died on September 6, 1920.

Just six months after his death, his first collection of verse appeared, *Les Contrerimes*. This volume had been announced since 1913, but Toulet spent his last years revising it. A perfect work, this collection is rooted in an epigrammatic tradition encompassing the "précieux" of the 17th century as well as the "fantaisistes" of the 20th (Francis CARCO, Tristan DERÈME, Jean Victor PELLERIN, Philippe Chabaneix), who moreover acknowledged Toulet as their leader. Toulet's customary form (which he invented) is the "contrerime" (a series of quatrains of the type 8a-6b-8b-6c). Its structure obligates the poet to condense and forbids outpourings of emotion. His themes are thus attuned to his memory rather than to his imagination; his poetry is filled with exotic scenes, both from Béarn and Paris, reminiscences of love and of travels, reflections of Bayonne and Pau, epitaphs, epigrams, and preposterous fantasies. A tone of Attic elegy unifies these diverse elements.　　　　　　　　　　　　　　　　　　　　　　P.-O.W

Tozzi, Federigo (1883–1920), Italian novelist, was born in Siena, the son of a well-to-do peasant and innkeeper. Tozzi's youth was an unhappy one. His mother, an epileptic, died when he was still a child. He did poorly at school and was constantly at odds with his father. In 1907 he left home and worked for the state railroads. He returned to Siena the following year on the death of his father. While trying to manage two farms, Tozzi began his writing career. In 1908 he married Emma Palagi. A few years later, they moved with their son to Rome. During World War I, Tozzi worked in the press office of the Red Cross. He died in 1920 after the publication of his first full-length novel.

Tozzi's life was one of constant frustration and misfortune. It is hardly surprising that his work, essentially autobiographical, is harsh and disillusioned, relieved—one might also say emphasized—by a strain of compassionate sensibility that is Dostoievskyan if not Christian. *Tre croci* (1920; Eng. tr., *Three Crosses*, 1921), which

many consider Tozzi's masterpiece, is the story of three brothers who inherit a bookshop and through irresponsibility, dishonesty, and ineptitude destroy the business and themselves as well. In *Il podere* (1921; The Farm) a son who has left home returns to take over a farm from his dying father. His struggles with jealous relatives, suspicious neighbors, and the hostile forces of nature lead to his defeat and ultimately his violent death. In both novels Siena and its countryside provide the background of the action, but the action is less impressive than the characterizations and much less memorable than the pervasive air of brooding tragedy. *Ricordi di un impiegato* (1920; Eng. tr., *Journal of a Clerk*, 1964) and *Con gli occhi chiusi* (1918; Blindfolded) are novels of scarcely veiled autobiographical content, and *Novale* (1925; Virgin Ground) contains many letters written by Tozzi to his wife before their marriage. The posthumous novel *Gli egoisti* (1923; The Egoists) deals again with the theme of the son's return. Tozzi is also the author of a number of powerful and moving short stories, published in *Bestie* (1917; Beasts) and *L'amore* (1920; Love), as well as a half dozen plays not highly esteemed by critics.

At the time of his death, Tozzi had won scant recognition. Although critics, notably Giuseppe BORGESE, praised his work, he remained largely ignored by the public for a generation. Recent years have brought about a favorable reappraisal of his contribution to Italian letters. The rough-grained vigor of his prose and, perhaps, the latently Marxist implications of his plots greatly appealed to writers of the post-Fascist period. In some ways his vision seems to anticipate the view of life set forth by Franz KAFKA or the existentialists. The themes of alienation, solitude, and the plight of the beleaguered individual in an indifferent or hostile society, so frequently exploited by writers of today, are central to Tozzi's inspiration. Alberto MORAVIA considers him the fourth great Italian novelist, after Alessandro Manzoni (1785–1873), Italo SVEVO, and Giovanni VERGA, with the last of whom Tozzi has recognizable affinities. Luigi Russo has some reservations about Tozzi's work, finding the novels lacking in cohesion. If the verdict of Moravia is destined to stand, it will signify the triumph of Tozzi's abrasive genius over the traditional Italian admiration for *il bello stile*.

See: G. Benedetti, "Federigo Tozzi: A Psychological Interpretation," in S. Pacifici, *From Verismo to Experimentalism* (1969); G. Tellini, *La tela di fumo* (1972); S. Pacifici, in *The Modern Italian Novel from Capuana to Tozzi* (1973); F. Ulivi, in *Letteratura italiana: i contemporanei*, vol. 1 (1975), pp. 469–91.　　　　　　　T.G.B.

Trakl, Georg (1887–1914), Austrian poet, was born in Salzburg. A leading lyrical talent of German preexpressionism, he was the son of a hardware dealer, studied in Vienna, and became a druggist in Salzburg, where he met his later friend and protector Ludwig Ficker, in whose magazine *Brenner* he published nearly all his poems. At the outbreak of World War I he went with an ambulance corps to the Galician Front but soon had to be taken to the military hospital at Cracow for medical treatment. There he died from an overdose of poison, which he apparently had taken to end his suffering.

Trakl was an exclusively lyrical writer, endowed with an almost morbid sensitiveness and an unusually fine feeling for rhythm and color. His first collection of poems, *Gedichte* (1913; Poems), shows influences of Fyodor DOSTOYEVSKY, François Villon, Stefan GEORGE, and Hugo von HOFMANNSTHAL. From Friedrich NIETZSCHE he inherited a deep cultural pessimism that caused him to interpret life in terms of sickness and decay. Unable to find a remedy for this cosmic evil, he indulged in an orgy of somber visions filled with pictures of putrefaction and death. The later poems, published under the title *Sebastian im Traum* (1915; Sebastian Dreaming), reveal a more wholesome, although by no means optimistic, concept of life. Under Friedrich Hölderlin's influence, Trakl found a pantheistic creed and established a spiritual community with mankind and nature, life and death. His language, less rigid than George's and less rhetorical than Hofmannsthal's, is free from expressionistic exaggerations. In the finest examples of this language there is reborn the solemn simplicity and nobleness of Hölderlin. English translations are found in *Selected Poems* (1968) and *Poems* (1973).

See: J. T. Casey, *Manshape That Shone* (1964); O. Basil, *Georg Trakl in Selbstzeugnissen und Bilddokumenten* (1966); W. Killy, *Über Georg Trakl* (1967); H. Lindenberger, *Georg Trakl* (1971); M. J. Kurrik, *Georg Trakl* (1974).   E.J. rev. A.L.W.

Tranströmer, Tomas (1931–), Swedish poet and psychologist at Roxtuna, a prison for young people, and from 1966 in Västerås, was born in Stockholm. He created something of a sensation with his first slim volume, *17 dikter* (1954; 17 Poems). Its perfect use of classical metrics, its density of acute images (written in a mild modernism more suggestive of Paul ELUARD and Dylan Thomas than of Erik LINDEGREN and Ragnar Thoursie, and its startling discoveries of Swedish land- and seascapes made Transtömer widely imitated in Sweden. The point of departure for his nature impressions was most often Runmarö, a small island in the Stockholm skerries, where he has spent his summers since childhood.

Whereas *17 dikter* was quite Swedish in theme, Transtömer's next book, *Hemligheter på vägen* (1958; Secrets on the Way) was more international and also more dependent on "crutches." This dependency can be seen in the poet's employment of themes from his travels, that is, the Balkans, Turkey, Italy, and Spain. The title of one of the poems, "Caprichios," is Spanish for "whims" or "fancies," but it also alludes to one of Francisco Goya's series of etchings. Among poems directly inspired by art works should be mentioned "A Man from Benin." The bronze relief it refers to can be seen at the Museum für Völkerkunde in Vienna, and "After an Attack" refers to a Vincent van Gogh painting.

Den halvfärdiga himlen (1962; The Half-Finished Heaven or The Half-Ready Sky), Transtömer's third book, presents further travel impressions from Italy, Greece, and Egypt. It also contains a few love poems. Transtömer's debt to music is noticeable in his work, even in his fourth book, *Klanger och spår* (1966; Echoes and Traces). Form is emphasized less than before. Instead of nature impromptus there are larger statements and greater cohesiveness. The surprising juxtapositions with a mystical isolation of phenomena, reminiscent of dream flight, are less frequent than in earlier collections, and the poet appears less anonymous. This volume also contains poems on Lisbon, Oklahoma, and Central Africa and a notable portrait of the composer Edvard Grieg, who urges himself to "simplify!"

Mörkerseende (1970; Eng. tr., *Night Vision*, 1971) shows great simplification in regard to form. The biographical element in these 10 poems is more pronounced than earlier. The poems are entirely documentary, almost confessional. *Seeing in the Dark*, as the Scottish poet R. Fulton called the book, (*Lines Review*, 35 December, 1970, pp. 37–54) reflects a serious crisis or perhaps a series of crises. It speaks of great and shattering changes in the poet's personal life, such as death and disease

among his kin, a sense of lost identity, worries about the war between technology and nature, and so on.

Stigar (1973; Paths) consists of Transtömer's translations of poems by Robert Bly and of poems by János PILINSZKY (tr. from the Hungarian, with G. Thinsz), for which he feels affinity; and 12 of his own poems, among which is "To Friends behind a Curtain," referring to a totalitarian state in which censorship is enforced and political oppression is at work.

Östersjöar (1974; Eng. tr., *Baltics*, 1975) consists of six long poems that, in a real sense, deal with a few of the poet's ancestors. Themes that hold the poems together are sailing, transience, and time. Transtömer's *Sanningsbarriären* (1978; The Truth Barrier) contains a remarkable suite, "Schubertiana." At the Poetry Center of America in New York in 1971, Transtömer disclosed that Walt Whitman had been important to him from early years, as had T. S. Eliot, Robert Lowell, Wallace Stevens, Robert Bly, Louis Simpson, Gary Snyder, and James Wright. Translations of Transtömer's poetry can be found in *Friends, You Drank Some Darkness*, tr. by R. Bly (1975), pp. 167–267, and in *Modern Swedish Poetry in Translation*, ed. by G. Harding and A. Hollo (1979), pp. 235–55.

See: B. Steene, "Vision and Reality in the Poetry of Tomas Transtömer," *SS* 37, no. 3 (1965): 236–44; E. Sellin, "Tomas Transtrsömer, Trafficker in Miracles," *BA* 46, no. 1: 44–47; L. Sjöberg, "The Poetry of Tomas Transtömer," *ASR* 49, no. 1 (1972): 37–42; and Introduction to T. Transtömer, *Windows and Stones*, tr. with May Swenson (1972), pp. xix–xxvi; L. Gustafson, *Forays into Swedish Poetry* (1978), pp. 33–38.   L.S.

Trausti, Jón, pseud. of Guðmundur Magnússon (1873–1918), Icelandic novelist and poet, was born at Rif, the northernmost farm in Iceland, on the shore of the Arctic. His parents were poor, and the famine of 1882 left indelible marks on the mind of the boy. He was, however, steeled by his experiences. In order to get books to read he learned the trade of printing, and he remained a printer to the end of his life. After an apprenticeship in Copenhagen he went to Reykjavik, living there until his death from influenza in the epidemic of 1918.

After two volumes of poetry and one historical play had appeared, Trausti finally found his place as an author in the broad social novel and the short story. In *Halla-Heiðarbýlið* (4 vols., 1906–11; Halla and Heath Cottage) he draws on a vast canvas the Icelandic rural scene as he had known it in his youth, teeming with characters, the figure of the poor cotter's wife, Halla, in the foreground gradually growing into heroic proportions. In *Leysing* (1907; Thaw) he uses economic changes, in *Borgir* (1910; Castles) the advent of new ideas in the church, as a background for his strong, conservative characters. Later he re-creates in *Sögur frá Skaftáreldi* (2 vols., 1912–13; Stories from the Eruption of Skaftá, 1783) the most crucial years in Icelandic history, when the nation almost perished in the terrible famine which was the aftermath of the eruption. After that he wrote a series of romantic novels based on the Icelandic middle ages (14th–16th centuries). As an apostle of progress and rugged individualism he reacted vigorously in *Bessi gamli* (1918; Old Bessi) against the coming socialistic tendencies. Though his style was uneven, Trausti's narrative talent was considerable, and his characters are always vibrantly alive.   S.E.

Trenyov, Konstantin Andreyevich (1876–1945), Russian playwright, was born in the province of Kharkov. He began writing fiction in 1898 but is remembered mainly for two post-Revolutionary plays, *Pugachovshchina* (1924; The Pugachyov Rebellion) and *Lyubov Yarovaya* (1926; Eng. tr., 1946). *Pugachovshchina*—about the 18th-century peasant rebel Yemelyan Pugachyov—was officially criticized for merely showing the personal tragedy of a crude, self-made leader, rather than dramatizing the Communist Party dictum that leaders are advanced by and accomplish what they do through the masses. In response, Trenyov rewrote the play twice, each time increasing the influence of the people and toning down the negative traits of his hero. *Lyubov Yarovaya* also aroused criticism; nevertheless, today in the USSR it is considered a gem of socialist realism. The play centers on the personal dilemma of Lyubov (intended as a model of the new Soviet woman), who, after siding with the Bolsheviks during the Russian Civil War, turns her White officer husband over to them for execution. Despite the play's longwindedness and episodic nature, it is theatrically effective. Particularly commendable are its character portrayals and vivid speech, something that can be said of Trenyov's plays in general.

See: R. Fainberg, *K. A. Trenyov: ocherki tvorchestva* (1962).　　　　　　　　　　　　　　　　　　S.E.R.

Triadú i Font, Joan (1921–), Catalan critic, was born in Ribes de Freser, received a degree in classical languages from the University of Barcelona, and was reader of Catalan language and literature in the University of Liverpool from 1948 to 1950. In 1950 he published *Endimió*. His later works are *Antologia de contistes catalans 1850–1950* (1950; Anthology of Catalan Tales), *Antologia de la poesía catalana* (1951), and the *Anthology of Catalan Lyric Poetry* (1953). *Panorama de la poesía catalana* and an edition of *Les Olímpiques* of Pindar also came out in 1953. In *La poesía segons Carles Riba* (1954), Triadú pays homage to the man who was his mentor and in *Narcís Oller* (1955) he presents a biography of the great Catalan novelist. Other works include *El collsacabra* (1956), *La literatura catalana i el poble* (1961; Catalonian Literature and the People), *Lectures escollides* (Selected Readings), coauthored by Eduard Artells, *Llegir com Viure* (1963; Reading like Living), *Prudenci Bertrana per ell mateix* (1967; Prudenci Bertrana by Himself), and *Una cultura sense llibertat* (1978; A Culture without Liberty). With F. P. Verrie and J. Molas he translated the sonnets of Shakespeare into Catalan verse.

His years of struggle in behalf of Catalan letters culminated in his election as president of the International Association for the Defense of Threatened Languages and Cultures at the meeting of the sixth congress of the association in Barcelona in July 1978. As a participant in this congress, Triadú, speaking about "Language and Nation," referred to the language, territory, history, proper culture, and will to exist as reasons that confirm the existence of the Catalan nation.

The most significant prizes he has received are: an award made in São Paulo in 1954 for an essay about the Ampurdan as seen by Catalan writers, a prize presented to him in Paris in 1959 for his translations of the sonnets of Shakespeare, and the 1960 Joseph Yxart Prize for *La literatura catalana i el poble*.

See: B. Pocel, "Joan Triadú o l'estat de lluita," *Serra d'Or*, no. 7 (July 1966): 31–37.　　　　　　J.F.C.

Trifonov, Yury Valentinovich (1925–), Russian writer, was born in Moscow. He is best known as a chronicler of the life of the intelligentsia. His Stalin Prize-winning first novel, *Studenty* (1950; Eng. tr., *Students,* 1953) is, predictably, his least interesting work, but it introduces the author's major themes: morality and interpersonal rela-

tionships in the peculiar circumstances of Soviet reality. His next novel, *Utoleniye zhazhdy* (1963; The Quenching of a Thirst), set during the period 1957–58, argues unambiguously for an end to Stalinist attitudes in all areas of Soviet life. Trifonov's more recent long novellas *Obmen* (1969; Eng. tr., *The Exchange,* 1977), *Predvaritelnye itogi* (1970; Eng. tr., *Taking Stock,* 1977), *Dolgoye proshchaniye* (1971; Eng. tr., *The Long Goodbye,* 1977), *Dom na naberezhnoy* (1976; The House on the Embankment), and *Drugaya zhizn* (1975; Another Life) are at once surprisingly frank treatments of the less attractive aspects of Soviet life and evidence of Trifonov's growing mastery of psychological portraiture. His other works include two collections of short stories and two historical novels, the more recent of which, *Neterpeniye* (1973; Impatience), is a nondidactic account of the assassination of Tsar Aleksandr II.　　　　　　　　　　　D.A.L.

Trigo, Felipe (1864–1916), Spanish novelist, was born in the province of Badajoz, to which he returned to practice medicine after studying in Madrid. It was there that he acquired the acquaintance with rural life later depicted in *El médico rural* (1912; The Country Doctor). He soon became an army doctor and was stationed in Seville, where he devoted himself to journalism and literature in addition to his military duties and published a book entitled *Etiología moral* (1891). He was ordered to the Philippine Islands and was badly wounded in an uprising of Tagal prisoners. On his return to Spain he continued his journalistic activities, writing a series of articles collected in *La campaña filipina: Impresiones de un soldado* (1897; The Philippine Campaign. A Soldier's Impressions). Discharged from the army for reasons of health, he resumed the practice of medicine in his native province and wrote his first novel, *Las ingenuas* (1901), a great success that launched his second career as a novelist in Madrid. Bestsellers like *La sed de amor* (1902, Thirst for Love) and *La bruta* (1904) followed, their popularity due to a frank eroticism and the bold handling of sexual matters. His fame as a pornographic writer was deserved, considering when and where he wrote, but he is not frivolous or immoral. Rather, he expressed a fierce faith in a new and freer morality as part of an anarchistic idealism that in combination with the scientific outlook of the medical profession found expression in his naturalistic concept of the novel. Trigo is arguably the best of the many late naturalist Spanish novelists, none of whom was an artist of the first rank. Like Emile ZOLA, he combined social denunciation with materialistic studies of the darker side of human nature. His artistic weaknesses are those of thematic overkill and a somewhat heavy and inflexible novelistic technique. *Jarrapellejos* (1914), perhaps his finest work, is a chilling portrait of rural vice (lust, betrayal, and murder) fostered by corrupt political bossism. Trigo, who died in Madrid by his own hand, may deserve a somewhat higher place in the annals of modern Spanish literature than he is often assigned.

See: R. Conte, "Prólogo," to F. Trigo, *Jarrapellejos* (1975).　　　　　　　　　　　F. de O. rev. H.L.B.

Triolet, Elsa, pseud. of Elsa Kagan (1896–1970), French novelist, short-story writer, translator, and critic of Russian origin, was born in Moscow. She was the wife of Louis ARAGON, who celebrated her in his verse, and the sister of Lilya Brik, the intimate friend of Vladimir MAYAKOVSKY, whose plays and poems Triolet introduced in France. Triolet had already written three books in Russian when she started her French literary career with *Bonsoir Thérèse* (1938; Goodnight Theresa). Echoes of World War II, during which she and Aragon were active resistants in occupied France, are found in *Mille Regrets* (1942; A Thousand Regrets), *Le Cheval blanc* (1943; Eng. tr., *The White Charger*, 1946), and *Le Premier Accroc coûte deux cent francs* (1945; Eng. tr., *A Fine of 200 Francs*, 1947). The difficult postwar period serves as backdrop for *Personne ne m'aime* (1946; Nobody Loves Me), *Les Fantômes armés* (1947; Armed Phantoms), and *L'Inspecteur des ruines* (1948; Eng. tr., *The Inspector of Ruins*, 1953), works in which Triolet combined a strong narrative line with vivid psychology. To her basic concern, the mystery of mankind and the search for self-fulfillment, Triolet brought a poetic fantasy and an interest in science fiction. In *Le Cheval roux* (1953; The Sorrel Horse), a survivor of atomic disaster encounters the future race, while the three-volume cycle *L'Age de nylon*— *Roses à crédit* (1959), *Luna Park* (1959), and *L'Ame* (1963; The Soul)—speculates on human destiny from the Stone Age to the era of cybernetics. Triolet's later work— *Le Grand Jamais* (1965; The Great Never), *Ecoutez voir* (1968; Just Listen), *La Mise en mots* (1969; Putting into Words), and *Le Rossignol se tait à l'aube* (1970; The Nightingale Becomes Silent at Dawn)—constitutes a free and brilliant meditation on the problems of historical truth, life, and death.

See: J. Madaule, *Ce que dit Elsa* (1961); *Europe*, special Triolet and Aragon number (Feb.–Mar. 1967), and special Triolet number (June 1971).   Y.G.

Trotzig, Birgitta (1929–), Swedish novelist, was born Birgitta Kjellén in Göteborg. Her first book, *Ur de älskandes liv* (1951; From the Lives of Lovers), is a collection of delicately impressionistic prose sketches dealing with lonely young girls, which reveals her rare sense of style but nothing of the dark strength of her mature writings. With the novels *De utsatta* (1957; The Outcasts) and *En berättelse från kusten* (1961; A Tale from the Coast), Trotzig came into her own. In both novels, the setting is historical; and the scenery the province of Skåne. A landscape of mud, clay, salty winds, and a leaden gray sky is the passive witness and silent accompaniment to tales of utter misery and degradation. In *De utsatta* Isak Graa (Isaac Gray) is a country parson who is driven to the extreme limits of human suffering by being confined to a madhouse where he is treated worse than a beast, yet retains within himself the image of God. That is what most of Birgitta Trotzig's work is about: the invisible presence of God even in the midst of unspeakable suffering and debasement, even though very little is ever said of this divine presence.

Sense impressions, particularly colors and smells and the details of carnal existence, are important features of Trotzig's style, but it is the spiritual condition of people that is her chief concern as a novelist. The influences of Fyodor DOSTOYEVSKY and such modern French Catholic novelists as François MAURIAC are noticeable, and she is generally considered a "Roman Catholic author" in spite of the fact that the world she pictures is a world without grace, at least without manifest grace. *Levande och döda* (1964; The Living and the Dead) contains three long stories on the common theme of love and lovelessness. *Sveket* (1966; The Betrayal) and *Sjukdomen* (1972; The Sickness) are both set in the author's recurrent gray southern Swedish landscape; the time is no longer historical but the present or the near past. The sickness of the second title refers explicitly to the mentally retarded hero's tragic development but implicitly also to the sickness of human existence in a world of cruel selfishness and brutal violence.

Language as a means of giving voice to suffering is a theme of a collection of prose sketches, *Ordgränser* (1968;

Word Limits), which reveals Trotzig's constant questioning of her own medium as a self-conscious artist. Another theme is "He who is a word against death," the motto of the book, referring to Christ the Word. Invaluable for an understanding of Trotzig's writing is her collection of essays, *Jaget och världen* (1977; The Ego and the World), discussing formative experiences in her life, also reflected in her novels and her short stories, *I kejsarens tid* (1975; In the Time of the Emperor) and *Berättelser* (1977; Tales).

See: B. Wigforss, "Brinnande enkelhet," in K. E. Lagerlöf, *Femtitalet i backspegeln* (1968), pp. 157–65; J. Stenkvist, *Svensk litteratur 1870–1970*, vol. 3 (1975); pp. 70–82.   G.B.

Troyat, Henri, pseud. of Lev Tarassov (1911–), French novelist and biographer, was born in Moscow, the son of a merchant. After his family emigrated from Russia during the Revolution of 1917, Troyat was educated in the French school system. Having completed his secondary schooling at the Lycée Pasteur in Neuilly-sur-Seine, he obtained his *licence en droit* and, from 1935 until 1941, he worked as an editorial staff member of the Prefecture of the Seine. Heartened by the success of his initial literary efforts, he decided to give up the security of the French civil service and to devote all his time and energies to a career as a writer.

Troyat was awarded the Populist Prize for his first novel, *Faux Jour* (1935; False Light), and his literary output has been voluminous ever since. His fourth novel, *L'Araignée* (1938; The Spider), won the much-coveted Goncourt Prize. It remains one of Troyat's most compelling works in its vivid depiction of a sickly and neurotic young man who tyrannizes his mother and sisters. Troyat's career as a novelist and a biographer has been a remarkably successful and prolific one, and his Russian background has provided much of the material that went into his work, both fiction and nonfiction. This is eminently the case in his novel trilogy, *Tant que la terre durera* (1947; Eng. trs., *While the Earth Endures*, 1951; *My Father's House*, 1952), *Le Sac et la cendre* (1948; Eng. trs., *Sackcloth and Ashes*, 1956, *The Red and the White*, 1956), and in *Etrangers sur la terre* (1950; Eng. trs., *Strangers in the Land*, 1958, *Strangers on Earth*, 1958), which presents the saga of prerevolutionary Russia and the aftermath of the struggle. Troyat's second and longest epic is *Les Semailles et les moissons* (1953–58; Eng. tr., *The Seed and the Fruit*, 1956–59). This five-volume, cyclic novel relates the story of two Limousin farmers who settle in Paris and open a café in Montmartre and of their daughter Elisabeth, her childhood, adolescence, marriage, and love life.

Troyat's aesthetic and technique as storyteller remain faithful to 19th-century narrative conventions and devices. He is generally considered a modern French novelist in the tradition of Honoré de Balzac and Emile ZOLA, if not in greatness and genius, at least in breadth of vision and inspiration. His work also shows the influence of such Russian authors as Lev TOLSTOY and Fyodor DOSTOYEVSKY, but while achieving for the most part a high degree of readability (the main reason for his lasting success with a large, loyal following), Troyat fails to match his French and Russian models. His literary style, while vivid and eminently serviceable, lacks originality, and his fictional techniques are too pat and predictable to place him on a par with the masters of the novelistic form. Neither has he participated in any way in the experiments practiced by the French writers of the "new novel" (*see* FRENCH LITERATURE).

In his popular biographies of Russian writers, notably his *Dostoïevsky: l'homme et son œuvre* (1940; Eng. tr.,

Firebrand: The Life of Dostoevsky, 1946), *Pouchkine* (1946; Eng. tr., *Pushkin,* 1970), *L'Etrange Destin de Lermontov* (1952; The Strange Fate of Lermontov), *Tolstoï* (1965; Eng. tr., *Tolstoy,* 1967), and *Gogol* (1971; Eng. tr., *Divided Soul: The Life of Gogol,* 1973), Troyat is consistent in showing that he is more adept at portraying the persona of his authors than at pondering their works. Troyat is, of course, a fine craftsman as a biographer, just as he is a consummate storyteller as a novelist; his technical expertise in unfolding a narrative serves him in good stead in both genres.

Throughout his long career, Troyat has been awarded numerous prizes and honors, including election to the Académie Française in 1959. He has steadily continued to write cyclic novels, notably a five-volume series entitled *La Lumière des justes* (1959–63; two vols. in Eng. tr., *The Light of the Just: The Barones,* 1961, *The Brotherhood of the Red Poppy,* 1961), as well as a trilogy, *Les Eygletière* (1965–67). He has also published collections of short stories, such as *La Fosse commune* (1937; The Common Grave), *Du philanthrope à la rouquine* (1945; From the Philanthropist to the Redhead), *Le Geste d'Eve* (1964; The Heroic Life of Eve), and *Les Ailes du diable* (1966; The Wings of the Devil), and he has tried his hand at travelogues—*Les Ponts de Paris* (1946; The Bridges of Paris), *La Case de l'Oncle Sam* (1948; Uncle Sam's Cabin), and *Du gratte-ciel en cocotier, à travers l'Amérique indienne* (1955; From the Skyscraper to the Coconut Tree, across America of the Indians). He has also written plays: *Les Vivants* (1946; The Living), *Sébastien* (1949), and *Madame d'Arches a dit peut-être* (1952; Madame d'Arches Said Maybe). One of his novels, *La Neige en deuil* (1952; Eng. tr., *The Mountain,* 1953), was adapted for the screen in 1956.

Troyat's productivity remains undiminished. A three-volume novel entitled *Le Moscovite* (1975) was followed by yet another work of fiction with a Russian theme, *Grimsbog* (1976). Not least among Troyat's attractions as a biographer and novelist is his exceptional ability to fuse into the canvas of his works the diverse strands of his Russian heritage and his French upbringing and culture.

G.M.

Tsvetayeva, Marina Ivanovna (1892–1941), Russian poet, playwright, and memoirist, was born in Moscow, the daughter of Ivan Tsvetayev, a professor of art history, and his second wife Mariya, née Meyn, who was half-German and half-Polish. Tsvetayeva began writing verse in early childhood and published her first collection of poems, *Vecherniy albom* (1910; Evening Album), at the age of 18. Privately published, the book was favorably reviewed by such leading literary figures as Nikolay GU-MILYOV. Her second collection, *Volshebny fonar* (1912; Magic Lantern) and a selection of poems from these two volumes, *Iz dvukh knig* (1913; From Two Books), soon followed. Tsvetayeva's early poetry displays impressive technical mastery, but it imitates the secondary 19th-century romantic poets and is frankly adolescent in its tone and themes.

In 1911, Tsvetayeva married Sergey Efron, the son of a prominent family of Moscow intellectuals. Her next collection, *Versty I* (1922; Versts I), reveals her growing awareness of the themes and techniques of the major symbolist and futurist poets, especially Aleksandr BLOK and Anna AKHMATOVA, her stylized use of folk song and folk lament diction, and her ever-growing metrical inventiveness and fluency. Separated from her husband for five years during the Civil War (he was fighting on the White side), Tsvetayeva turned to political and topical poetry in *Lebediny stan* (1917–22, pub. 1957; The Swans' Encamp-

ment), wrote a series of verse plays set mostly in the 18th century, and began her cycle of autobiographical narrative poems. In 1922, Tsvetayeva emigrated, first to Berlin, where she rejoined her husband, then to Prague, and finally to Paris. Within a two-year period she published five volumes of verse plus a number of narrative poems, plays, and essays, all at once becoming one of the foremost post-Revolutionary poets both in emigration and in the Soviet Union. Her literary art matured and was further perfected in her two collections published in the 1920s, *Remeslo* (1923; Craft) and *Posle Rossii* (1928; After Russia). Tsvetayeva's mature poetic manner organically blends an archaic diction derived from Orthodox prayers and 18th-century Russian poets, folklore elements, and an innovative modern idiom that parallels, without imitating, the futurist-influenced idioms of Vladimir MA-YAKOVSKY and Boris PASTERNAK. The modernity of her language and versification contrasts with the basically romantic orientation of her sensibility. Recurrent themes in her poetry are: the escape into another, better reality from the unbearable events of the 20th century; the refuge from the imperfection inherent in all interpersonal relationships sought in nature and art; the inability of humans to communicate with each other; and the idealization of the poet's favorite historical periods, the 18th century and the Russian romantic age.

Tsvetayeva's personal themes were also developed in her long narrative poems of the 1920s. Some of these are lyrical and autobiographical: "Na krasnom kone" (1920; On a Red Steed), "Poema gory" and "Poema kontsa" (both 1924; Poem of the Hill; Poem of the End), "S morya," "Popytka komnaty," and "Lestnitsa" (all 1926; From the Seacoast; Essay of the Room; The Staircase), and "Novogodneye" and "Poema vozdukha" (both 1927; New Year's Greetings; Poem of the Air). Others among these long poems are epics that project the poet's personal emotions and preoccupations into plots derived from Russian and German folklore: "Tsar-devitsa" (1920; The Tsar Maiden), "Pereulochki" (1922; Sidestreets), "Molodets" (1924; The Swain), and "Krysolov" (1925; The Pied Piper). "Perekop" (1929, pub. 1967) is a historical poem about the Russian Civil War. Tsvetayeva's narrative poems belong among the finest and most original such works written in this century.

By the 1930s, Tsvetayeva was no longer published in the USSR and felt more and more isolated among the émigrés. Turning to prose, she wrote an important series of personal and literary memoirs (about Valery BRYUSOV, Andrey BELY, Maksimilian VOLOSHIN, and Mikhail KUZ-MIN, *inter alios*) couched in a fresh, inventive, highly personal prose style. Tsvetayeva returned to the Soviet Union in 1939. Ostracized by the literary community, unable to write or publish, she committed suicide. Her work, banned till the mid-1950s, has enjoyed a tremendous revival in recent decades. For a selection of Tsvetayeva's poetry in English, see *Marina Tsvetayeva, Selected Poems,* tr. by E. Feinstein (London, 1971).

See: S. Karlinsky, *Marina Cvetaeva: Her Life and Art* (1966).

S.K.

Turkish literature. Modern Turkish literature is a microcosm of, and has acted as a major catalyst for, the vast transformation of Turkish society that has occurred since the middle of the 19th century. It embodies the themes and the tensions of the transition from the multiethnic Ottoman Empire to the Republic of Turkey, a homogeneous nation-state, which has replaced theocracy with a secular form of government, autocratic rule with parliamentary democracy, and an Islamic orientation with educational, legal, and cultural institutions adapted from

Western models. There is no Western genre or literary form that had not attained its maturity in Turkey by the 1980s.

The heritage that many modern Turkish authors have sought to supplant with European norms and values spans many centuries. Its earliest written specimens—excluding verse fragments and short lyrics, presumably dating from the second century B.C. to the sixth century A.D.—are the Orkhon Inscriptions of the early eighth century (discovered near ancient Karakorum), and two major works, both written around the year 1070—Mahmud of Kashghar's *Divan ü Lugat-it Türk,* a lexicon and compendium of Turkic lore, containing more than 200 verses in indigenous syllabic meters, and Yusuf Has Hacib's *Kutadgu Bilig* (Blissful Knowledge), a philosophical treatise of more than 6,500 couplets in *aruz* (the Arabo-Persian prosody), designed as a "mirror for princes" providing guidance on the precepts of ethics, justice, and good government.

The *Dede Korkut* tales, first recorded in book form in the 15th century although they were probably part of the oral tradition from the 11th or the 12th century, constitute the Turkish national epic. This narrative of 12 parts, with many passages in verse, depicts nomadic Turks moving westward from Central Asia and embracing Islam.

The new faith gave the Turks an impetus for political ascendancy and the urge to emulate the cultural achievement of the Arabs and the Persians. Their Anatolian Seljuk state (11th to 13th centuries) and their far-flung Ottoman Empire (from the late 13th century to the early 1920s) produced a vast corpus of literature. Three mainstreams evolved: *Divan,* the classical literature of the elite; *Halk,* the oral narratives and folk poetry of the countryside; *Tekke,* religious poetry, including a large body of mystical verse of the Islamic sects. The *Divan* tradition, heavily influenced by Arabo-Persian forms, vocabulary, and aesthetic values, stressed refinement of structure, effusive romanticism, eloquence of diction, elaborate euphony, and a system of stock metaphors. In its purity, classical verse gave expression to an intense spiritual fervor, and distilled its subjective themes into tidy abstractions. The *Halk* literature, employing native forms and meters, was—and remains—lyrical and sensuous, steeped in concrete images and local lore. *Tekke* verse, which made use of both *Divan* and *Halk* genres, oscillated between the didactic and the passionately mystical.

By the middle of the 19th century, these traditions seemed to have little vitality left, although the great classical figures (particularly Fuzuli and Baki of the 16th century, Nef'î of the 17th century, and Nedim and Şeyh Galib of the 18th century) were, and still are, read with reverence. In the countryside the love lyrics, hymns, and mystical verses of Yunus Emre (d. ca. 1321), who wrote humanistic lines calling for a united mankind, and the romantic poems of the 17th-century minstrel Karacaoğlan and many other folk poets continued to provide entertainment and enlightenment for rural communities.

As the Ottoman state declined inexorably, many prominent statesmen and intellectuals sought its salvation through technological and cultural westernization. A series of reforms ushered in by the Imperial Rescript of 1839 led to the emergence of *Tanzimat* (transformation) literature whose proponents—Şinasi (d. 1871), Namık Kemal (d. 1888), Ziya Pasha (d. 1880), and others—challenged the modes of the classical period (although they did not altogether break away from tradition), articulated a new cultural and political consciousness, and emphasized European-style progressive liberalism. They introduced new genres. Şinasi, a poet and lexicographer who

studied in Paris, pioneered translations of French poetry. He founded the daily *Tercüman-ı Ahval* (The Interpreter of Events) in 1860 and the *Tasvir-i Efkâr* (The Journal of Ideas) in 1862, becoming the first major Turkish journalistic essayist. He wrote the first native play for the legitimate stage, *Şair Evlenmesi* (Poet's Marriage), which incorporated some of the devices of the traditional *Karagöz* (shadow theater) and *Orta Ounu* (a theater-in-the-round), and satirized the antequated mores of Ottoman society. Namık Kemal, a patriotic poet and tireless critic of the established order as well as of conventional literature, wrote a major nationalistic play, *Vatan Yahut Silistre* (Fatherland or Silistria), about an incident during the Russo-Turkish War, and many articles calling for governmental reforms. The passions aroused by this play when it was produced in 1873 led to the playwright's banishment to the island of Cyprus.

The novel made its appearance on the Ottoman scene in the early 1870s. It was popularized by Ahmet Mithat (1844–1912), a prolific author who exposed some of the ills of his times in fiction written in simple language for the widest possible readership. Namık Kemal's historical and social novels also expanded the reading public as did scores of adaptations and translations from the French. Earlier periods of Turkish literature had included, in addition to the *Dede Korkut* epic, a large repertoire of folk narratives and dozens of classical romances in verse. The Ottoman elite had a decided preference for poetry over prose; few major prose works were produced, among them some interesting treatises, histories, and epistolographical monographs, the travelogues of Evliya Chelebi, a 17th-century cultural commentator, and the *Muhayyelat,* an interrelated series of stories, written in the late 18th century by Aziz Efendi. In the 20th century, fiction by Turkish and foreign authors became a dominant genre although poetry, the most prevalent art form among the Turks, was never relegated to a secondary place.

Progressively since the mid-19th century, westernization has held sway over urban life and literature. The phenomenon was articulated in the early 1910s by the influential writer Abdullah Cevdet in such terms as "There is only one civilization in the world, and that is Western civilization. We must embrace it with its roses and thorns." Since the 1840s, the focal problem of Turkish literature has been its thrust towards Europe and the United States versus its urge to come to terms with its own heritage.

Westernization spurred literary criticism in Ottoman Turkey, which had confined its critical assessments to superficial observations recorded in the *Tezkiret üş şüera* (Who's Who in Poetry) in the previous periods. Lively rhetorical arguments were advanced in the second half of the 19th century by Namık Kemal and Recaizade Ekrem (1847–1914), among others, who advocated European values, and Muallim Naci (1850–93) who upheld the classical tradition. In a spate of poetic satire, despite strong censorship, Ziya Pasha and Eşref (1846–1912) denounced the ruling establishment in vitriolic poems.

Abdülhak Hamit (1852–1937) was a leading modernist of the 19th century who wrote more than 20 plays and 15 books of poetry, making a synthesis of modified Ottoman forms and prosody, European sensibilities, historical and mythological themes, and metaphysical exploration. His verse plays, in the manner of Pierre Corneille and Jean Racine, with some Shakespearean influences, fired the public imagination and helped establish a penchant for European drama, including melodrama and light comedies.

Following French trends, Turkish fiction of the late 19th century produced works in the romantic, realist, and naturalist veins. Notable among them were *Sergüzeşt* (1889; The Adventure) by Samipaşazade Sezai (1860-1936); *Araba Sevdası* (1889; Carriage Craze) by Recaizade Ekrem, a satirical depiction of aristocrats torn between their Ottoman background and their European predilection; and *Kara Bibik* (1890), after Emile ZOLA, a short novel about the harsh realities of rural Anatolia, by Nabizade Nazım (1862-93).

The second major stage of modernization was the *Edebiyat-ı Cedide* (New Literature) movement, whose principal figure, TEVFIK FIKRET, under the influence of the French romantics and symbolists, introduced major innovations of style, theme, imagery, stanzaic structure (including the adoption of the sonnet), and rhythm, in his verse. Writing in the influential magazine, *Servet-i Fünun* (Wealth of Knowledge), he and his group, which included the genteel sentimental poet Cenab Şehabettin (1870-1934) paved the way for even bolder poetic innovations. Fikret also wrote vehement denunciations of the sultan, of malfeasance, and of reactionary dogma, becoming the most effective voice of intellectual opposition at the turn of the century. He called for positive rationalism as the basis of progress and made a plea for freedoms and humanism.

The towering figure in fiction at the start of the 20th century was Halit Ziya Uşaklıgil (1866-1945), sometimes referred to as "the Turkish Alphonse Daudet," whose masterful novels *Mai ve Siyah* (1897; The Blue and the Black), about a struggling writer and his sufferings, and *Aşk-ı Memnu* (1900; Forbidden Love), a vivid depiction of Istanbul's high society, and several other well-constructed works of fiction, constitute an impressive achievement. Other novelists who gained stature were Mehmet Rauf (1875-1931) for his *Eylül* (1900; September), a sentimental story of star-crossed lovers; Hüseyin Rahmi Gürpınar (1864-1944), who wrote many humorous novels about the colorful people of city neighborhoods; Ahmet Rasim (1864-1932), whose fiction treats the daily life of Istanbul residents; and Ebubekir Hazım Tepeyran (1864-1947), the author of the first realistic "village novel."

The 1908 Young Turk Revolution led to the emergence of several significant movements. *Fecr-i Ati* (Dawn of the Future), around which some of the best younger writers rallied, including AHMET HAŞIM, a major symbolist; Yakup Kadri KARAOSMANOĞLU, who was to become a prominent novelist; and Fuad Köprülü, the first scholar to systematize the study of Turkish literary history. They all attempted to forge a synthesis between valuable elements from the West and viable ingredients from the Turkish cultural legacy. *Millî Edebiyat* (National Literature), endorsed by the fervent nationalists Ahmet Hikmet Müftüoğlu (1870-1927) and Mehmet Emin Yurdakul (1869-1944), sought to create a patriotic consciousness and to simplify the literary language so that it could be used to enlighten the people and disseminate the themes of poverty and communal suffering. *Genç Kalemler* stressed realism, populism, and the simplest possible vernacular, principles-that found their most effective application in the short stories and novellas of ÖMER SEYFETTIN, who delineated the bitter and humorous aspects of Turkish life in a plain but compellingly vivid style. These movements, in the Young Turk era, underscored the emerging democratization of Turkish culture and the utilitarian function of literature. Ziya Gökalp (1876-1924), a social thinker and cultural historian, articulated the nationalistic imperative in simple verses designed to create the consciousness of Turkism among the Ottomans as well as Turks in many other countries. In the same closing years of the Ottoman state, Mehmet Akif ERSOY was endeavoring to revitalize the classical prosody with the pure diction of his day in giving new impetus to the moral and political force of Islam and blending it with nationalism.

In 1923, after an arduous war of independence, Turkey became a republic under the leadership of Mustafa Kemal Pasha (known more commonly as Kemal Atatürk since 1934). An ambitious series of reforms took place in the first 10 years: political, educational, and judicial institutions were westernized; Islam's hold on urban life was decreased; and progressive nationalism became the state ideology. Among the cataclysmic changes, perhaps the most significant for literature was the so-called language revolution of 1928, which brought about the abrupt adoption of the Latin alphabet to replace the Arabic script used by the Turks for nearly a thousand years and which, by the 1980s, succeeded in ridding Turkish of thousands of borrowings from the Arabic and Persian and in creating a large new vocabulary of revived words and neologisms.

The early years of the Republic witnessed, in addition to a profusion of patriotic verse, the emergence of groups of poets dedicated to the revitalization of the forms, meters, and the lucid style of folk poetry. These included the *Hececiler* (Syllabists), among them Enis Behiç Koryürek (d. 1949), Halit Fahri Ozansoy (d. 1971), Yusuf Ziya Ortaç (d. 1967), Orhan Seyfi Orhon (d. 1972), and the *Yedi Meş'ale* (The Seven Torches), among them Sabri Esat Siyavuşgil (d. 1968), who in 1942 made a Turkish version of *Cyrano de Bergerac* that is regarded as the best verse translation of a play into Turkish, and Yaşar Nabi Nayır (1908-), who later became the publisher of *Varlık*, Turkey's most influential literary magazine since 1933. Faruk Nafiz Çamlıbel (1898-1973) was the best craftsman of this movement: he produced in both syllabic and classical meters many well-wrought poems concerning love, Anatolia's beauty, and national pride. Syllabic verse was further refined by several highly accomplished poets writing in a neoromantic and occasionally philosophical vein—Ahmet Hamdi Tanpınar (1901-62), Necip Fazıl Kısakürek (1905-), Ahmet Kutsi Tecer (1901-67), Cahit Sıtkı Tarancı (1910-56), Ziya Osman Saba (1910-57), Ahmet Muhip Dıranas (1909-)—and still enjoys popularity not only among the folk poets (one of Turkey's most acclaimed poets was the minstrel, Âşık Veysel, who died in 1973) but also among urban poets.

Ahmet Haşim produced many striking poems in the manner of the French symbolists, blending vivid imagery with his melancholy moods, evoking a Utopia never to be reached.

Neoclassicism was the hallmark of Yahya Kemal BEYATLI who captured the aura and the eloquence of *Divan* verse and gave it new vigor in his meticulously crafted lyric poems of romantic love, Istanbul's sights and scenes, the Ottoman Empire's military and cultural triumphs, and quiet contemplation of life and death.

Turkish poetry was revolutionized in form and substance by the Marxist poet Nazım HIKMET who introduced free verse in the 1920s under Vladimir MAYAKOVSKY's incipient influence. His innovative style, structure, and rhythmic effects, and his relentless *cri de cœur* against imperialism and oppression have dominated Turkey's poetry of protest since the early 1920s. Having been translated into all major languages, Hikmet is Turkey's most famous poet internationally.

Fiction in the 1920s and 1930s concerned itself with themes related to the vast changes in Turkish society. HALIDE EDIB (ADIVAR) produced, in addition to novels and stories dealing with the Turkish war of independence, a number of psychological and sociological novels, the most interesting of which is *Sinekli Bakkal* (1936), which she originally wrote in English and published in 1935 in

England under the title *The Clown and His Daughter*. Reşat Nuri Güntekin (1889–1956), Refik Halit Karay (1888–1965), Mahmut Yesari (1895–1945), Sadri Ertem (1900–1943), and others wrote many widely read novels that exposed the superstitions and inequities of the old order at a time of revolutionary change in a poverty-stricken country that had yet to establish a system of social justice. The major novelist of the period was Yakup Kadri Karaosmanoğlu, who exposed the tragic life of the peasants in *Yaban* (1932; Stranger).

Since the 1940s, Turkish literature—spurred by a growing freedom of expression despite occasional repressive measures against writers—has feverishly sought new ideologies and a more effective voice in making the public aware of social problems. It has also been attuned to the main currents of the Western world. Having gone through Parnassian, symbolist, and neoclassical experiences, it embraced surrealism, the stream-of-consciousness technique, epic theater, socialist realism, obscurantist poetry, theater of the absurd, concrete and found poetry, and virtually all other new movements.

A new phase of poetic modernization was initiated by three young poets: Orhan Veli KANIK, Melih Cevdet ANDAY, and Oktay Rifat (1914–). In 1941 they published a manifesto calling for the elimination from poetry of all conventional elements and for a revamping of the language itself. Their work, which could be defined as "poetic realism," made the man in the street its hero, stressed the precision of the colloquial idiom, and valued the concrete image rather than the metaphor. Much of the poetry of the 1950s and 1960s, including the populist work of the poet-painter Bedri Rahmi Eyuboğlu (1908–73) and Ceyhun Atuf Kansu (1919–78) depicting the colorful and bittersweet life of the countryside in a vivid vernacular, as well as the satiric verses of Orhon Murat Arıburnu (1918–) and Nevzat Üstün (1924–79) owes a great deal to the innovations of Kanık, Anday, and Rifat.

After Kanık's death in 1950, İlhan Berk (1916–), whose credo may be summed up as "Art for innovation's sake," Metin Eloğlu (1927–), and several younger poets, notably Edip Cansever (1928–) and Cemal Süreya (1931–), challenged poetic realism and expanded the frontiers of surrealism beyond the pioneering earlier work of Ercüment Behzat Lav (1903–) and Asaf Halet Çelebi (1907–1958) into a brave new obscurantism that they called "The Second New," although they were not averse to their poetry being called "meaningless." The linguistic imagination and the metaphorical richness of "The Second New," accompanied by its captivating melodiousness, attracted wide attention. Even Anday and Oktay Rifat wrote poems in the same vein, but later, particularly in the 1970s, the first moved in the direction of an ambitious mythological synthesis and the latter towards a "supreme fiction" in the manner of Wallace Stevens. The leading poets of the 1960s and 1970s seemed committed to artistic individualism rather than to movements: Behçet NECATIGIL pursued a highly subjective, almost cubistic, arrangement of reality and language; Turgut Uyar (1926–) and Ülkü Tamer (1937–) stressed a comprehensive aesthetic strategy that used the most powerful resources of the language; Ece Ayhan (1931–) endeavored to force neosurrealism to its outer limits; Necati Cumalı (1921–) blended realism and romantic sensibilities; Attilâ İlhan (1925–), who is also a fine novelist and essayist, succeeded in laying the groundwork for a grand synthesis of many traditional modes and molds, including classical, folk and early 20th century elements.

After Nazım Hikmet's death in Moscow in 1963, Fazıl Hüsnü DAĞLARCA was generally recognized as Turkey's leading poet. His enormous output in the lyric, epic, metaphysical, political veins and his unique poetic personality gained admiration not only in Turkey but also abroad, winning him honors in the United States, Yugoslavia, Holland, and elsewhere.

Fiction since 1940 has been almost as versatile as it is in Europe and the United States. An early master of socialist realism was Sabahattin Ali (1906–48), who revealed, in story after story, the sufferings of the Anatolian peasants and made a scathing indictment of the Turkish bourgeoisie. A virtuoso of the short story, SAIT FAIK (ABASIYANIK) captured the pathos and the bathos of life in Istanbul, and using himself as the persona of his fiction shed light on human foibles. Several major novelists are credited for mastery of psychological exploration in works that, at the same time, succeed in conveying social reality: Abdülhak Şinasi Hisar (1888–1963); Peyami Safa (1899–1961); and Ahmet Hamdi Tanpınar, who was also a prominent literary historian.

At the middle of the century, the fiction of the proletariat burst upon the Turkish scene. Encouraged by Sabahattin Ali's popularity and the impact made by Dağlarca's *Toprak Ana* (Mother Earth) and Mahmut MAKAL's *Bizim Köy* (Our Village; translated into English as *A Village in Anatolia*), many writers, including some who were villagers themselves, started to produce a large body of fiction that has come to be known as "village fiction". The publication of *İnce Memed* (Memed, My Hawk) by Yashar KEMAL in 1955, not only catapulted its author to nationwide fame but also secured a permanent place for "village fiction." This gripping novel of a rural hero fighting oppressors and exploiters has been translated into many languages. Yashar Kemal's massive output, now available the world over, brought him very close to winning the Nobel Prize in the late 1970s. Also writing about the predicament of peasants are numerous major novelists: Samim Kocagöz (1916–), Kemal Bilbaşar (1910–), Mehmet Başaran (1926–), Talip Apaydın (1926–), and many others. Among the masterworks of "village fiction" is *Yılanların Öcü* (The Revenge of the Snakes) by a prolific author, Fakir Baykurt, who was born in a village in 1929 and had his education in a village teachers institute. A prominent figure of *lumpenproletariat* literature was ORHAN KEMAL.

KEMAL TAHIR, who also wrote a number of engrossing works about the poor classes, published several historical novels, notably a long romance about the early years of the Ottoman state, *Devlet Ana* (1967; Mother State). Other major fiction writers include the satirists Haldun Taner (1916–), Rifat Ilgaz (1911–), and HALIKARNAS BALIKÇISI, who chronicled the struggles of the fishermen along the Aegean coast. Orhan Hançerlioğlu (1916–) and Oktay Akbal (1923–) portray city people gripped by social and psychological crises. Stream of consciousness and the *nouveau roman* techniques, with hints of Joycean and Faulknerian style, have dominated the fiction of Feyyaz Kayacan (1919–), Nezihe Meriç (1925–), Bilge Karasu (1930–), Sevim Burak (1931–), Demir Özlü (1935–), Ferit Edgü (1936–), and others. In the 1970s several new novelists using many of the elements of contemporary American fiction have produced sophisticated novels that treat Turkish themes and characters with a truly universal novelistic approach. Among them are Adalet Ağaoğlu (1929–), Sevgi Soysal (1936–1977), Çetin Altan (1926–), who is also Turkey's best-known columnist, Oğuz Atay (1934–1978), Pınar Kür, Nazlı Eray, and Tomris Uyar.

Turkey's most effective satirist is Aziz NESIN, who pokes fun at all things sacred and governmental and lampoons human folly of all types. Many of his stories have become classics, and scores of his quips are proverbial among Turks.

Literary criticism assumed an important function in the latter part of the 19th century. Its cultural context was provided by the rhetorical essays of Namık Kemal, and, later, by the progressive articles of Ahmet Şuayip (1876–1910). Ziya Gökalp, author of several influential works on cultural nationalism, particularly *Türkçülüğün Esasları* (1923; Engl. tr., *The Foundations of Turkish Nationalism*, 1950), and Fuad Köprülü, the pioneer of Turkish literary history, established the critical principles that were to guide much of the intellectual activity and literary evaluation in the first two decades of Atatürk's Republic. The essays of two major poets—Beyatlı and Haşim—and the journalistic articles of Hüseyin Cahit Yalçın (1874–1957) and Falih Rıfkı Atay (1894–1971) helped expand the frontiers of literary as well as social criticism, which received a further impetus from the essays of the "humanists"—Hasan Âli Yücel (1897–61), who exerted an enduring impact as minister of education from 1938 to 1946, and Orhan Burian (1914–53). Humanism and many socialist precepts dominated the essays of Sabahattin Eyuboğlu (1908–73), Vedat Günyol (1912–), Melih Cevdet ANDAY, and Azra Erhat (1915–). A revival of interest in Ottoman literature was spurred by Ahmet Hamdi Tanpınar, who wrote an excellent history of 19th century literature and many fine essays on classical poetry, and Mehmet Kaplan (1915–) who produced several works of textual analysis. The critics who have exerted wide influence since the late 1940s include Nurullah Ataç (1898–1957), who wrote impressionistic evaluations of classical poetry and gave enthusiastic support to many young poets; Suut Kemal Yetkin (1903–) and Yaşar Nabi Nayır, who offer lucid views of literary developments; Asım Bezirci (1927–), Memet Fuat (1926–), Nermi Uygur (1925–), Cemal Süreya (1931–), Rauf Mutluay (1925–), Hilmi Yavuz (1936–), Mehmet Doğan (1931), among others, who provide, frequently with methodologies acquired from the West, critical commentary on literature at large as well as reviews of individual books.

Translation, particularly from French, English, and German, has become a fine art in modern Turkey. It gained momentum from a massive governmental project—nearly 1,000 volumes translated from mainly Western and some Eastern classics in the 1940s and 1950s. About 1,000 of the 6,000 to 7,000 titles published annually in Turkey in the 1970s were literary works, mostly in major European languages and English. The quality of many of the translations of fiction, poetry, and drama was extraordinarily high.

In the 20th century, traditional Turkish theater, consisting of *Karagöz* (the shadow play), *Orta Oyunu* (theater-in-the round comparable to commedia dell'arte), and one-man *Meddah* (storyteller) shows steadily declined and the legitimate theater gained ascendancy. The City Theater of Istanbul, founded in 1914, the People's Houses (community centers or town halls of the 1930s and 1940s), the State Theater of Ankara (established in the late 1940s and active in Istanbul and several other cities as well since the late 1960s), and a large group of independent theaters encouraged dramatic writing and translations. From the mid-1960s onwards, the Turkish theater was one of the liveliest in the world.

The early years of the Republic witnessed plays satirizing Ottoman life and administration by Musahipzade Celâl (1870–1959) and İbnürrefik Ahmet Nuri (1874–1935), patriotic plays about Turkish heroics in the pre-Islamic period and in modern times by Faruk Nafiz Çamlıbel, melodramas by Mahmut Yesari (1895–1945) and Reşat Nuri Güntekin. Nazım Hikmet's avant-garde plays, particularly *Kafatası* (The Skull) and *Unutulan Adam* (The Forgotten Man), stirred excitement in the

1930s as did *Bir Adam Yaratmak* (To Create A Man) by Necip Fazıl Kısakürek about a brilliant man's breakdown. Psychological dramas were also written by Vedat Nedim Tör (1897–), some of whose plays were also produced in Germany and France, and Ahmet Muhip Dıranas.

Some of the best dramatic writing has concerned itself with village life. Plays about peasants by Cahit Atay (1925–), Necati Cumalı, Hidayet Sayın (1929–), Güngör DILMEN, Recep Bilginer (1922–), and others have presented harsh realities by means of vivid episodes, authentic characters, and a language that blends forcefulness with an elegiac tone.

Ottoman history has provided themes and dramatis personae for several modern tragedies in the grand manner by Turan Oflazoğlu (1932–). Orhan Asena (1921–) has written notable plays based on the Gilgamesh Epic, early Turkish legends, Ottoman history, modern Turkey, and international themes, notably a trilogy on Chile in the 1970s. Güngör Dilmen is the most successful adaptor of ancient Near Eastern and classical Greek mythology to the Turkish stage.

Comedies, dramas of social criticism, and satirical plays flourish. Following the wide popularity of Cevat Fehmi Başkut (1905–71) in this genre, Haldun Taner, Orhan Kemal, Refik Erduran (1928–), Nazım Kurşunlu (1911–), and many others wrote a large number of vibrant plays poking fun at social imbalances and injustice. Aziz Nesin, Sabahattin Kudret Aksal (1920–), Oktay Rifat, Turgut Özakman (1930–), Adalet Ağaoğlu, Yıldırım Keskin (1932–), among others, are notable for their universal approach to drama. Brechtian drama served as the model for several major Turkish plays, most compellingly for *Keşanlı Ali Destanı* (The Ballad of Ali of Keshan), a play that was successfully produced in West Germany, Poland, and Czechoslovakia as well, by Haldun Taner, and *Ayak Bacak Fabrikası* (The Orthopedic Factory) by Sermet Çağan (1929–70). The 1970s witnessed the efflorescence of socialist realist drama.

By the early 1980s, Turkish literature had achieved a remarkable diversity of genres, forms, techniques, and cultural perspectives and begun to constitute a fertile synthesis of its own heritage and acquired elements.

See: E. J. W. Gibb, *A History of Ottoman Poetry*, 6 vols. (1901–09); D. Patmore, *The Star and the Crescent* (1946); N. Menemencioğlu, "Modern Turkish Poetry," *WR* 23 (1959); K. H. Karpat, "Social Themes in Contemporary Turkish Literature," *TMEJ* 14, nos. 1–2 (Winter, Spring 1960); *TLR* (Turkish issue) 4 (1960–61); M. And, *A History of Theater and Popular Entertainment in Turkey* (1963–64); T. S. Halman, "Turkish Poetry," in *Encyclopedia of Poetry and Poetics*, ed. by A. Preminger (1965); *MPT* (Turkish issue) 10 (1971); T. S. Halman, "Turkish Literature," in *Encyclopedia of World Literature in the 20th Century* (1971); "Poetry and Society: The Turkish Experience," *Modern Near East: Literature and Society*, ed. C. M. Kortepeter (1971); "Modern Turkish Literature: Disorientation and Reorientation," *BA* 46, no. 2 (Spring 1972); C. Rathbun, *The Village in the Turkish Novel and Short Story* (1972); *TLR* (Turkish Issue) 4 (Summer 1972); K. Burrill, "Modern Turkish Literature," *RNL* 4, no. 1 (Spring 1973); B. Turgay-Ahmad, "Modern Turkish Theater," *RNL* 4, no. 1 (Spring 1973); F. A. Stone, *The Rub of Cultures in Modern Turkey* (1973); *LE&W* (Turkish issue) 17, no. 1 (March 1973; actual publication date, August 1975); *CLIT* 22 (Fall 1975); B. Robson, *The Drum Beats Nightly: The Development of the Turkish Drama as a Vehicle for Social and Political Comment in the Post-Revolutionary Period, 1924 to The Present* (1976); W. G. Andrews, *An Introduction to Ottoman Poetry* (1976); T. S. Halman, *Modern Turkish*

Drama (1976); L. Hamalian and J. D. Yohannan, *New Writing from the Middle East* (1978); F. İz, *An Anthology of Modern Turkish Short Stories* (1978); N. Menemencioğlu, *The Penguin Book of Turkish Verse* (1978); T. S. Halman, *Contemporary Turkish Literature* (1980).

T.S.H.

Tuwim, Julian (1894–1953), Polish poet, satirist, editor, and translator, was born in Łódź of middle-class Jewish parents and died in Zakopane. He studied law and philosophy at the University of Warsaw. He was cofounder and one of the leading poets of the "Skamander" group. (*see* POLISH LITERATURE). Incited by Arthur RIMBAUD and Walt Whitman, he shocked the public while still a student with the poem "Wiosna" (Spring), proclaiming brutal urbanism. Although his early writing developed in opposition to the "Young Poland" tradition, his poetry revealed some ties with this period, mainly with the works of Leopold STAFF and Bolesław LEŚMIAN. In his first volume, *Czyhanie na Boga* (1918; Ambushing God), he called himself a futurist, alluding not to his diction but to his effort to blend idyllic literary tradition with modern industrial and technical progress. Among earlier Polish masters valued by him were Jan Kochanowski, Adam Mickiewicz, and Cyprian NORWID. He worshiped the outburst of elemental power, but he also hated tyranny and was a militant supporter of pacifism and the little, humble man. He glorified the magic of words, and he considered himself a verbal conjurer. His writings were prolific and amazingly versatile. In the interwar period he published nine volumes of poetry, including *Sokrates tańczący* (1920; Dancing Socrates), *Siódma jesień* (1922; The Seventh Autumn), *Wierszy tom czwarty* (1923; The Fourth Book of Poems), *Słowa we krwi* (1926; Words in Blood), *Rzecz czarnoleska* (1929; Czarnala's Speech), *Biblia cygańska* (1933; The Gypsy Bible), and *Treść gorejąca* (1936; The Burning Essence). He was a vigorous and witty satirist. His most virulent satirical poem is *Bal w operze* (written 1936; pub. 1946; The Ball at the Opera), which shows a corrupt society dancing under the patronage of Pantokrator, a fascist tyrant. He contributed to humorous periodicals and literary cabarets, and he also wrote fine verse for children, such as *Lokomotywa* (1938; Eng. tr., *The Locomotive,* 1938). As a translator he especially excelled in the poetry of Aleksandr Pushkin. He collected literary curiosities in such volumes as *Pegaz dęba* (1959; Pegasus Rearing). During World War II he escaped abroad and lived in Brazil and the United States. He returned to Warsaw in 1946. His narrative poem *Kwiaty polskie* (1949; Polish Flowers), written mostly during the war, abounded in nostalgic visions of interwar life. A volume of his poetry has been published in English translation, *The Dancing Socrates and Other Poems* (1969).

See: J. Stradecki, *Julian Tuwim: bibliografia* (1959); M. Głowiński, *Poetyka Tuwima a polska tradycja literacka* (1962); J. Sawicka, *Filozofia słowa Juliana Tuwima* (1975).

M.G.

Tvardovsky, Aleksandr Trifonovich (1910–71), Russian poet, was the moving spirit behind the Soviet literary renaissance of the 1960s. He was born at Zagorye in the province of Smolensk, the son of a village blacksmith who was deported as an alleged kulak during the Soviet collectivization of agriculture. Beginning with his first long poem, *Strana Muraviya* (1936; The Land of Muravia), Tvardovsky was recognized as one of those rare writers of the period who had a sense of the realities of peasant life. As editor of an army publication during World War II, he published bit by bit, from 1941 to 1945, "Kniga pro

boytsa" (A Book About the Fighting Man), a homespun epic about the ordinary foot soldier that, under the better-known title taken from the name of its protagonist, Vasily Tyorkin, achieved immense popularity overnight. While editor of the literary journal *Novy mir* (1950–54, 1958–70), Tvardovsky wrote two more long poems, *Za dalyu dal* (1960; Far, Far Away), about an actual journey from Moscow to the Pacific; and *Tyorkin na tom svete* (Tyorkin in the Next World), a satire on the Soviet bureaucracy that was published only in 1963 through the personal intervention of Nikita Khrushchov. Tvardovsky's last collections of verse, notably *Iz liriki etikh let* (1967; Lyric Poems of Recent Years), and, even more, "Po pravu pamyati" (By Rights of Memory; publication forbidden by the censorship in 1968), betray his apprehensions about a revival of Stalinism.

Whatever the importance of his poetic work, which is without any question the most popular in the Soviet Union, Tvardovsky will be remembered in history above all for his activity during the 16 years he edited *Novy mir*. Passionately devoted to literature, which he conceived of as a vehicle for ideas, Tvardovsky wished *Novy mir* to provide a platform for everyone who had something to say: experienced writers like Ilya ERENBURG, Valentin KATAYEV, Veniamin KAVERIN, or Konstantin PAUSTOVSKY; newcomers who were just getting started, such as Fyodor ABRAMOV, Olga BERGGOLTS, Viktor NEKRASOV, or Sergey ZALYGIN; novelists or poets of the other Soviet nationalities (the Kirghiz Chingiz AYTMATOV, the Avar Rasul Hamzatov, or the Lithuanian Eduardas Mieželaitis) as well as foreigners then still unpublished in Russian (such as Heinrich BÖLL, Albert CAMUS, Cesare PAVESE, Raymond QUENEAU, Nathalie SARRAUTE, and Jean-Paul SARTRE). He brought back into print writers who had been excluded from the official literature, notably Anna AKHMATOVA, Mikhail BULGAKOV, and Boris PASTERNAK. To him is also due the credit for discovering most of the best writers of his time: Vasily BELOV, Vasil BYKOV, Yury DOMBROVSKY, Yefim DOROSH, Boris MOZHAYEV, and—the greatest of them all—Aleksandr SOLZHENITSYN.

Abroad Tvardovsky has been labeled a "liberal," which is an oversimplification. And Solzhenitsyn's ambiguous portrait of him in *Bodalsya telyonok s dubom* (1975; Eng. tr., *The Oak and the Calf,* 1980) is distorted by the author's too egocentric point of view. In actual fact, Tvardovsky was a Communist persuaded of the need for "socialism with a human face," a socialism in which literature, freed of administrative tutelage, should play a liberating role. Once Khrushchov had disappeared from the political stage, the supporters of orthodoxy switched over to a counterattack. Even though he was a member of the Central Committee of the Communist Party, Tvardovsky was not allowed to participate in the work of the Party Congress in 1966. Every issue of *Novy mir* was mutilated by censorship. "Inspired" denunciations turned up everywhere in the press. The Union of Soviet Writers delivered the final blow by dismantling the editorial staff that Tvardovsky had built up. Forced to resign in January 1970, he was struck down by a cerebral hemorrhage shortly afterward and died in the following year. Thus came to an end one of the most brilliant periods in Soviet literature.

J.Ca.

Tvedt, Jens (1857–1935), Norwegian novelist, was born in Hardanger on the western coast of Norway. After graduating from a teachers college, he lived most of his life in Stavanger as a schoolmaster, journalist, and librarian. His main contribution to literature is a series of novels describing the life of the people of his home region. Indeed,

Tvedt is the outstanding representative of the Norwegian school of regionalists (see NORWEGIAN LITERATURE).

Tvedt's first books shocked readers with their unvarnished descriptions of life in the small farms along the narrow fjords of the west. But Tvedt's realism is never brutal or morbid. Behind his careful, veracious descriptions there is a strong optimism, a belief in the inherent health and vitality of the people. There is no psychological piquancy in his books, but one finds real life in them, sound feeling, and a natural harmony of subject and form; they are plastic in the classical sense. Noteworthy among his novels are *Vanheppa* (1891; Bad Luck) and *Madli und' apalen* (1900; Madli under the Apple Tree), stories of everyday endurance of hardship written, with sympathy and genial humor, in a firm *nynorsk* (see NORWEGIAN LITERATURE) close to the style of the folk narrators. Tvedt's later movement toward lyricism is conspicuous in the love story *Djup jord* (1904; Deep Soil), perhaps his most important novel.

See: H. Espeland, *Jens Tvedt* (1959).   S.Sk.

Tychyna, Pavlo (1891–1967), the greatest Ukrainian symbolist poet of the modern era, was born in Pisky. The son of a village deacon, he studied at a seminary. He started writing before the Revolution. His first collection of verse, *Sonyashni klyarnety* (1918; The Clarinets of the Sun), was also his best; in it, he displayed extraordinary poetic power in depicting the Ukrainian Revolution (1917) as a cosmic event. Tychyna's early work displays a concern with pantheism, but gradually his lyrical and philosophical poetry became permeated by social concerns. This progressive change in emphasis is visible in his other early collections: *Pluh* (1920; The Plough), *Viter z Ukrayiny* (1924; Wind from Ukraine), *Skovoroda* (1924), and *Chernihiv* (1931). The breaking point in Tychyna's outlook and style came in the early 1930s, when under pressure he adopted socialist realism. His subsequent decline as a poet may be seen in *Partiya vede* (1934; The Party Is Leading) and *Stal i nizhnist* (1941; Steel and Tenderness). During World War II, Tychyna occasionally rose to new heights as in "Pokhoron druha" (1943; Funeral of a Friend). After the war he remained faithful to Communist Party ideology and was rewarded with prizes and high office. Tychyna was a gifted translator from Russian and other languages.

See: L. Novychenko, *Poeziya i revolyutsiya* (1956).
                                                            G.S.N.L.

Tynyanov, Yury Nikolayevich (1894–1943), Russian literary scholar and fiction writer, was born in the town of Rezhitsa, in the province of Vitebsk, and studied at the University of Petersburg from 1912 to 1918. During the years 1921 to 1930 he lectured on Russian poetry at the Division of Literary History of the Petrograd State Institute of Art History. In 1918 he joined the Petrograd Society for the Study of Poetic Language (Opoyaz), the chief nucleus of the so-called formalist school in Russian literary scholarship, and soon became one of its most influential and articulate exponents. His magisterial studies on Aleksandr Pushkin, most notably "Arkhaisty i Pushkin" (1926; The Archaists and Pushkin), which present the great poet's achievement against the backdrop of the literary crosscurrents of his time, challenge the traditional notions about Pushkin's place in the history of Russian literature. His seminal *Dostoyevsky i Gogol* (1921; Dostoyevsky and Gogol), an amply documented reinterpretation of a Dostoyevsky novel as a parody of Nikolay Gogol's controversial moral tract, serves as a springboard for generalizations about the uses of parody. While most of Tynyanov's literary-historical studies have broad

methodological implications, some of his writings of the 1920s address themselves directly to problems of literary theory. The essays "Literaturny fakt" (1924; The Literary Fact) and "O literaturnoy evolyutsii" (1927; Eng. tr., "On Literary Evolution," 1971) probe the nature of the boundary between literature and life, and the mechanics of literary change. *Problema stikhotvornogo yazyka* (1924; The Problem of Verse Language) inquires into the "semantic dynamics of the poetic text" and remains one of the most authoritative treatments of the subject in the language.

As the Soviet intellectual climate grew increasingly hostile to the formalist brand of criticism, Tynyanov's considerable resources, especially his prodigious knowledge of the Pushkin era, were channeled into historical fiction. *Kyukhlya* (1925), a vivid and affectionate novel about Pushkin's friend and associate, the brave libertarian poet V. Küchelbecker, was followed by *Smert' Vazir Mukhtara* (1929; Eng. tr., *Death and Diplomacy in Persia*, 1938), a masterful re-creation of the tragic plight of A. S. Griboyedov, a brilliant playwright-poet turned diplomat. Both novels sound the topical theme of the creative intellectual's predicament under an autocratic regime. The wanton arbitrariness of tsarist bureaucracy is satirized in "Podporuchik Kizhe" (1927; Eng. tr., "Second Lieutenant Asfor," 1965), the first of Tynyanov's shorter historical narratives, which include "Voskovaya persona" (1930; The Wax Person) and "Maloletniy Vitushishnikov" (1933; The Minor Vitushishnikov). In the mid-1930s, Tynyanov began a voluminous novel about Pushkin. Protracted illness and premature death prevented him from completing this long-cherished project. *Pushkin* (1936–43), blends meticulous scholarship with narrative skill, but lacks the incisiveness of Tynyanov's earlier historical fiction.

See: A. Belinkov, *Yury Tynyanov* (2d ed., Moscow, 1965); V. Erlich, *Russian Formalism, History—Doctrine* (3d ed., The Hague, 1969).   V.E.

Tzara, Tristan, pseud. of Samuel Rosenstock (1896–1963), French poet, was born in Moineşti, Romania. Along with Hugo Ball, Tzara was the main founder of the Dada movement in Zurich in 1916–19. The movement's principles were exemplified in his *Sept Manifestes Dada* (1916–20; Seven Dada Manifestos). Greeted in Paris by those soon to be surrealists, Tzara took part in the provocative Dada manifestations but separated from André BRETON in 1921–22. For a time, he was again associated with surrealist action, but after 1935 he became more involved in political commitment. One of the major Dada-surrealist poets, he left some three dozen books of poetry, five plays, and a score of critical essays ranking among the best interpretations of modern art and poetry.

Tzara's literary terrorism was a revolt against the bourgeois ethics that he held responsible for World War I, and a radical rejection of bourgeois culture and stereotyped language. Breaking away from literary structures, his *Vingt-cinq poèmes* (1918; 25 Poems) and his *De nos oiseaux* (1923; Of Our Birds) try to recapture, through a distorted, chaotic language using meaningless sounds, the vivid strength of poetry: a primitive vitality, a complete freedom of the mind discovering its own interior necessity. With no less volcanic verbal power, a more sustained and clear lyricism gradually emerges in his masterpieces: *L'Homme approximatif* (1930; Eng. tr., *Approximate Man and Other Writings*, 1973), an interior epic pilgrimage; and the great prose poems of *L'Antitête* (1933; The Antihead), *Grains et issues* (1935; Grains and By-Products), and *Midis gagnés* (1939; Noontimes Gained). A tragic sense of man's fate of solitude and tedium prompts the poet's search for fullness and illumination through the reconciliation of dream and action. Among Tzara's theoretical texts, the *Essai sur la situation de la poésie* (1931; Essay on the Situation of Poetry) focuses on a distinction between poetry as a stereotyped means of expression and poetry as mental activity bringing liberation for the whole human race, a position in contrast to the early individualistic bias of dada. This revolutionary and humanistic

commitment was to be emphasized in Tzara's later poetry, *Terre sur terre* (1946; Earth upon Earth) and *La Face intérieure* (1953; The Inside Face). The standard edition of Tzara's works, now in the process of being published, is *Tristan Tzara: œuvres complètes,* ed. by H. Béhar (1975–).

See: M. A. Caws, *The Poetry of Dada and Surrealism* (1970); E. Peterson, *Tristan Tzara* (1971).   D.Ba.

U

Ujević, Tin (1891–1955), Croatian poet and essayist, was born in Vrgorac, Dalmatia. After living for a time in Makarska and then attending the classical gymnasium at Split, he moved to Zagreb in 1909 to study philosophy and literature, but soon became involved in politics. This political activity led to his arrest, but in 1913 he escaped from Split to France, where he was active in the propaganda struggle against Germany and Austria. Disappointed by the Serbian and other Yugoslav politicians and having encountered amorous and financial difficulties as well, Ujević withdrew completely from active life and became solitary, egocentric, disorderly, and alcoholic. Upon his return to Yugoslavia in 1919, he lived for 10 years in Belgrade, 7 years in Sarajevo, and 3 in Split, before settling in 1940 in Zagreb, where he remained until his death in 1955.

Ujević began publishing poetry at an early age, and by 1914 he had become well known through the inclusion of 10 of his poems in the anthology *Mlada hrvatska lirika* (Young Croatian Poetry). The impact of French literature is obvious on his later poetry, but many critics overlook the fact that Ujević's early work was strongly influenced by Antun Gustav MATOŠ and Silvije Strahimir KRANJČEVIĆ as well as by the Croatian poets of earlier centuries. A number of poems included in Ujević's first collections, *Lelek sebra* (1920; Serf's Lament) and *Kolajna* (1926; The Necklace), were written while he was living in France. Their classical structure is similar to that of his prewar verse, but in *Lelek sebra* there is a new pathos, the desperate cry of a human being wounded and bleeding, at the bottom of a dark pit. In *Kolajna,* Ujević created beautiful love songs in celebration of an idealized lady similar to Petrarch's Laura.

Inconsistency and paradox characterize Ujević's later works: *Auto na korzu* (1932; A Car on the Corso), *Ojadjeno Zvono* (1933; The Aggrieved Bell), and *Žedan kamen na studencu* (1954; A Thirsty Well-Stone). In these books, the poet is an egocentric who paradoxically stresses the solidarity of the human race; he addresses fervent prayers to the Christian God but is also a pantheist and an admirer of Buddha; he inextricably mixes hallucinations and reality; and he confidently, but not always successfully, plays with rhythm and rhyme. Even in his later period, however, Ujević occasionally wrote poems that are unique in their content and expression.

Ujević also wrote prose poems, first collected under the title *Mudre i lude djevice* (1957; Wise and Foolish Virgins), but they are more poetry than prose. The same may be said of his "confessions" and his travelogues, particularly when he writes about Makarska, and about Supetar, on the island of Brač, where he became "invigorated" by the unique Dalmatian maritime landscape.

In addition to his creative writing, Ujević wrote many reviews of and essays on works of Croatian, Serbian, and French literature. He was also highly regarded as a translator of several languages, particularly French. He possessed tremendous knowledge and good judgment, yet he

had no definite theory of literature, and his critical appraisals (like those of Matoš before him) tended to be subjective and impressionistic. Although a modernist himself, he did not appreciate the extreme positions of some contemporary trends.

See: V. Pavletić; "Kaos na pragu idealnoga," *Rep* 7–9 (1951): 640–52; A. Kadic, "Ispit savjesti Tina Ujevicá," *Hrvatska revija* 2–3 (1960): 187–92; N. Mihanović, "Tin Ujević i nadrealizam," *Književnik* 19 (1961): 29–37; M. Vaupotić, "Ujevicéva kritička proza," *Hrvatska književna kritika,* vol. 8 (1964), pp. 7–34; S. Vučetic, "Naša vertikala, Krleža i Ujević," *Rep* 7 (1968): 383–91.   A.K.

Ukrainian literature. Modern Ukrainian literature began at the end of the 19th century but developed slowly, coexisting for a long time with the earlier realistic and romantic literatures. Western European influences came to the Ukraine through Russia and Poland, and their new trends were considerably delayed and often diluted. These innovations have struggled against those romantic and realist traditions that have survived, in disguise, up to the present. The purely aesthetic concerns of 20th-century arts penetrated the Ukraine slowly, against the opposition of entrenched populist and socionational aspirations. The enormous influence of the greatest Ukrainian romantic poet, Taras Shevchenko (1814–61), was felt for decades after his death and blocked new literary currents. Throughout the 19th century, Ukrainian literature had been seriously threatened by oppressive tsarist policies, which culminated in the ban on printing in Ukrainian in 1876. Literature, therefore, was in the forefront of the struggle for national survival, and as a result little attention was paid to purely literary values. It was not until the 1905 Russian Revolution, which led to the partial abolition of police controls over Ukrainian culture, that there was a vigorous new revival, culminating in the literary and artistic flowering of the 1920s. Unfortunately, extreme political pressures have continued to influence the development of literature in the Ukraine.

Modernism, the new literary movement of the 1920s, had few theoreticians in the Ukraine. Two literary groups were leaders in this field: "Moloda muza" (The Young Muse) in Galicia and "Ukrayinska khata" (Ukrainian Home) in the eastern Ukraine. Their theoreticians, Ostap Lutsky and Mykola Vorony, were both severely criticized by the dean of Ukrainian letters, Ivan FRANKO, who, although politically a radical, remained aesthetically a conservative. "Moloda muza" produced little of lasting value. Among its members were the poets Petro Karmansky(1878–1956) and Vasyl Pachovsky (1878–1942), and the prose writers Osyp Turyansky (1890–1933) and Mykhaylo Yatskiv (1873–1961). A close associate was the poet, short-story writer, and, later, novelist Bohdan Lepky (1872–1941). Much more talented were some poets in the eastern Ukraine: Oleksander Oles, pseud. of Oleksander Kandyba (1878–1944), Mykola Vorony (1871–1942), and Hryhoriy Chuprynka (1879–1921), all of whom excelled in lyric verse. The best modernist literary criticism was published in *Ukrayinska khata*. A much more influential periodical, however, was *Literaturno-naukovy visnyk* (1898–1932; Literary and Scientific Herald), hardly modernist in its orientation.

The greatest Ukrainian modernist writers, Lesya UKRAYINKA, Mykhaylo KOTSYUBYNSKY, Volodymyr VYNNYCHENKO, and Vasyl STEFANYK, remained strictly outside the modernist coteries. Some of them began their writing in the realist tradition, but all went over to new forms and they each in their own way developed original styles consonant with the spirit of the age. Ukrayinka's finest achievements were her poetic dramas; Kotsyubynsky's, his impressionistic short stories; Vynnychenko's, his psychological, "decadent" tales, and Stefanyk's, his realistic, highly concentrated short stories. Stefanyk and Kotsyubynsky still often drew their themes from the life of the peasants and the intelligentsia, but Ukrayinka frequently also drew inspiration from foreign literature and history and Kotsyubynsky from exotic lands. All four immensely enriched Ukrainian literature by successfully bringing it into the mainstream of modern European literature. There were many other prominent writers who leaned towards modernism: Olha Kobylyanska (1865–1942), Stepan Vasylchenko, pseud. of Stepan Panasenko (1878–1932), and Ahatanhel Krymsky (1871–1942). Others continued to write in the traditions of realism and romanticism: Spyrydon Cherkasenko (1876–1939), Osyp Makovey (1867–1925), Les Martovych (1871–1916), and Marko Cheremshyna (1874–1927), the last two well known for their stories of peasant life.

The October Revolution (1917) in the Ukraine took on the character of a war for national and social liberation. Not until 1920 did the Bolsheviks succeed in destroying the strong movement for national independence, and even then they were forced to make considerable concessions to Ukrainian national aspirations, especially in the areas of education and culture. In 1922 the Ukraine became one of the republics of the Soviet Union, and Ukrainian Communist leaders such as Volodymyr Zatonsky, Vlas Chubar, Oleksander Shumsky, and Mykola Skrypnyk exercised a good deal of control over internal policies. The Revolution led to an upsurge of creativity in the field of literature that reached the proportions of a truly national artistic renaissance in just over a decade. Although the stimulus was provided by the revolution, the end product was apolitical, with Marxism as a minor influence.

The modernist trend in poetry found new expression in symbolism and futurism. The greatest individual achievement in this area was by the symbolist poet Pavlo TYCHYNA, whose collection *Sonyashni klyarnety* (1918; The Clarinets of the Sun) is a true landmark in modern Ukrainian poetry. Another symbolist of interest was Mykola Filyansky (1873–1945). The leader of the futurists was Mykhaylo Semenko (1892–1939), whose poetry was meant to startle and shock. In the 1920s, the futurists centered around the journal *Nova generatsiya* (The New Generation) and tried unsuccessfully to combine their futurist objectives with Marxism. A group of writers who expressly rejected politics and were concerned with literature per se was "Lanka" (The Link). Among its members was the gifted novelist Valeriyan PIDMOHYLNY, the highly original short-story writer Hryhoriy Kosynka (1899–1934), and the lyric poet Yevhen Pluzhnyk (1898–1936). Their works often dealt with the Revolution, but in personal terms. Another literary group, "Pluh" (The Plough), centering around the journal *Pluh*, united the peasant writers under the leadership of Serhiy Pylypenko (1891–1943). Far more significant in its influence was a small Kiev group of poets and literary critics who were

called the Neoclassic group. Their guiding light was Mykola ZEROV. The other members of this group were Maksym RYLSKY, Pavlo Fylypovych (1891–1937), Mykhaylo Dray-Khmara (1889–1938), and Osvald Burkhardt (1891–1947), who later emigrated and wrote under the pseudonym Yury Klen. A close associate was Viktor Petrov (1893–1969), a prominent scholar and author of several novels, which he published under the pen name Domontovych. In their poetry, the Neoclassic group often used the sonnet form and admired the French Parnassians. They attempted to emulate the classical heritage, which to them meant counterposing old European models against the official proletarian art. Although their styles differed widely, they were all still under the influence of symbolism. A much greater influence was exerted by the group of "proletarian" writers VAPLITE (Free Academy of Proletarian Literature), formed in 1925 in Kharkiv out of the remnants of the group "Hart" (Tempering) after the death of its leader, Vasyl Ellan Blakytny (1894–1925). The "Vaplitians," led by the colorful Mykola KHVYLOVY, had in their ranks such prominent writers as Mykola KULISH, Yuriy YANOVSKY, Oles Dosvitny (1891–1934), Oleska Slisarenko (1891–1937), Yury Smolych (1900–76), and Mayk Yohansen (1895–1937). These writers cultivated a variety of styles and were bent on maintaining high literary standards in literature and literary criticism. As open adherents of the regime, they gained the support of influential Ukrainian Communists such as Oleksander Shumsky, who were committed to the policy of "Ukrainization" (promotion of Ukrainian as the official language). Ideologically, therefore, they could be described as "national Communists." Their leader, Khvylovy, through a series of articles and pamphlets, initiated the so-called literary discussion (1925–28), pleading for the raising of literary standards, a break with the old *prosvita* (mass reading circles) mentality, and an orientation towards Western European, rather than Russian, literature. This debate, which was carried on the pages of the leading periodicals *Vaplite, Chervony shlyakh* (The Red Pathway), *Pluzhanyn* (Ploughman), and *Zhyttya i revolyutsiya* (Life and Revolution), revitalized Ukrainian literature and was the last free discussion of aesthetic and ideological issues in that country. While some Communist Party officials (notably Mykola Skrypnyk) encouraged this development, others under the influence of Moscow (like Lazar Kaganovich) viewed it with alarm. Finally, centralist policies prevailed with the onset of Stalinism in the early 1930s.

In the comparatively free atmosphere of the 1920s, literature and the arts reached a flowering unparalleled in the history of the Ukraine. The poetry of Tychyna, Rylsky, Zerov, and Mykola BAZHAN, the novels of Yanovsky and Pidmohylny, the stories of Khvylovy and Hryhoriy Kosynka, and the plays of Kulish raised Ukrainian literature to new levels. A similar development could be seen in the films of Oleksander Dovzhenko, the Berezil Theater, directed by Les Kurbas, the paintings of Mykhaylo Boychuk, and the music of Borys Lyatoshynsky. This revival was never narrowly nationalist, but, on the contrary, expressed a new, universal sensibility. Attempts to class the literary works of this period under one style are futile, but while it is true that there was a great deal of variety in Ukrainian letters, they were largely pervaded by what Khvylovy attempted to define as "vitaism,"—an awareness of the many-sidedness of life.

A new period in the cultural life of the country began with the introduction of the first Five-Year Plan (1928) and paved the way for Stalinism a few years later. Although political controls over literature were tightened, the spirit of the decade was not extinguished overnight.

After the dissolution of the VAPLITE group in 1928, Khvylovy and his friends continued their activities in the journal *Literaturny yarmarok* (1929; Literary Fair) and later, less successfully, in *Prolitfront*. In the early 1930s the security police intensified the drive against the alleged "nationalists" among Ukrainian intellectuals. In 1930 there was an open show trial of the secret society "Union for the Liberation of the Ukraine"; heavy sentences were imposed on the accused, among them the prominent literary scholars Serhiy Yefremov and Andriy Nikovsky. Gradually, police methods were used to destroy literary and scholarly organizations and to exterminate hundreds of writers and artists. The purges coincided with the forced collectivization and the ensuing famine in 1932–33. Some leading personalities, including Khvylovy and Skrypnyk, committed suicide as a protest against Iosif Stalin's genocidal policies. To be sure, purges were conducted on a wide scale throughout the Soviet Union, but in the Ukraine the charges of "bourgeois nationalism" were added to other "offenses" and therefore the devastation of Ukrainian culture was especially severe. In most instances the charges of "nationalism" were false, and many devoted Communists, as well as apolitical writers, perished in the holocaust. Those who escaped had to admit their alleged mistakes openly and prove their reliability by producing new works glorifying the Communist Party and the regime.

In 1932 all literary groups were disbanded in the Ukraine, as in the rest of the Soviet Union, and in 1934 a centrally controlled Soviet Writers Union was created. Its Ukrainian branch had practically no autonomy in important matters of literary policy. The new official literary method to which all writers had to subscribe was known as socialist realism. Stylistically, this often meant a return to the old realistic and pseudoromantic devices; thematically, socialist realism meant the glorification of the regime. The decade 1931–41 was thus one of rapid decline. A new brand of literary criticism—based on outright denunciation—gained ascendancy. Odes and panegyrics were written to Stalin by writers in order to avoid deportation to concentration camps. It is possible that the reign of terror brought about a genuine ideological change of heart in some writers, but on the whole it was too brutal to succeed in converting them.

Any account of Ukrainian literature in the period between the two world wars must include some mention of literary developments in Galicia and Volynia, the parts of the Ukraine that remained under Polish rule after the Treaty of Versailles, as well as of Ukrainian writers who lived as émigrés in Poland and Czechoslovakia. In Galicia, the most prominent group centered around the journal *Literaturno-naukovy visnyk* (1922–32), later called *Visnyk* (1933–39). This monthly was edited by the leading nationalist publicist, Dmytro Dontsov (1883–1973). Its contributors were mostly émigré writers: the poets Yevhen MALANYUK, Oleh Olzhych, pseud. of Oleh Kandyba (1909–44), Olena Teliha (1907–42), Oleksa Stefanovych (1900–70), Oksana Lyaturynska (1902–70), and Bohdan Kravtsiv (1904–75), Leonid Mosendz (1897–1948), poet and novelist, and Yuriy Lypa (1900–44), well known for his essays and short stories. Most of them admired heroic virtues and energy and were concerned with national destiny. Another group of writers, centered around the journal *Dzvony* (1930–39; The Bells), were Catholics. Among them was the greatest western Ukrainian poet, Bohdan Ihor ANTONYCH. Yet another group, centered around the journal *Nazustrich* (1934–39; Toward), numbered among its ranks the prominent critic Mykhaylo Rudnytsky (1889–1975), the poet Svyatoslav Hordynsky (1909–), and the talented short-story writer Yuriy Kosach (1909–). A So-

vietophile group of writers published *Novi shlyakhy* (1929–32; New Paths), while the followers of the nationalist leader Symon Petlyura (1879–1926) published the journal *My* (We) in Warsaw. The latter group included a talented publicist, Borys Olkhivsky (1908–44). The literary activity of all these groups came to an end in 1939 with the Soviet occupation of the western Ukraine.

Despite the ravages of the German invasion, World War II was a time of relaxed literary controls in the Ukraine. Some return to patriotic themes was allowed, and this led some writers, such as Oleksander KORNIYCHUK, to stress national sentiments. Immediately after the war, however, strict controls were reimposed, following the infamous speech in which Andrey Zhdanov proclaimed the new course of Soviet literature. In the Ukraine this meant a renewed attack on "bourgeois nationalism" (notably the condemnation of Volodymyr Sosyura's poem "Love the Ukraine" in 1951). Yet at that time Oles HONCHAR, a talented new prose writer, appeared on the scene. It was not until after Stalin's death in 1953 that a new, more promising spirit spread throughout Soviet literature. The so-called thaw came to the Ukraine a few years after it had arrived in Russia. Some older writers returned to personal themes, as did Oleksander Dovzhenko in his novel *Zacharovana Desna* (1954; The Enchanted Desna), or to lyrical poetry, as did Rylsky in *Troyandy i vynohrad* (1958; Roses and Grapes). Historical novels without ideological distortions, such as Oleksander Ilchenko's *Kozatskomu rodu nema perevodu* (1958; There Is No End to the Cossack Breed), became popular once more. Following Nikita Khrushchov's speech denouncing Iosif Stalin at the 20th Party Congress (1956), some writers who had fallen victim to the Stalinist terror were partially rehabilitated (Kulish, Hryhoriy Kosynka, Slisarenko, Zerov, Yevhen Pluzhnyk) while others were not (Khvylovy, Pidmohylny). Rehabilitation had a powerful impact on the younger generation. Only a few older writers—Leonid Pervomaysky (1908–73), Borys Antonenko-Davydovych (1899–)—were able to take advantage of the more liberal trend and produce some works of merit. In this respect, Pervomaysky's novel *Dyky med* (1963; Wild Honey) is noteworthy. Many members of the older generation viewed the new developments rather skeptically. It was, therefore, the younger writers who embarked on the new course in a spirit of hope and adventure. Most of them broke into print in the 1960s and were therefore known as *shestydesyatnyky* (the Generation of the 1960s). Among them were Lina Kostenko (1930–), Ivan DRACH, Vitaliy Korotych (1936–), Mykola Vinhranovsky (1936–), and Vasyl SYMONENKO. They reestablished the poem as the lyrical expression of an individual identity. Philosophical and social overtones were occasionally present, but poetry now stood on its artistic merit alone. After decades of stagnation, the rediscovery of this function of poetry was truly revolutionary. It found a warm response among the young prose writers Yevhen Hutsalo (1937–) and Valeriy Shevchuk (1939–) and literary critics such as Marharyta Malynovska (1941–), who tended to ignore politics and ideology in favor of literary concerns. But the new spirit did not last long, for after Khrushchov's fall in 1964 the Communist Party, already alarmed by this development, reimposed stricter controls. This has not resulted in a complete return to Stalinist methods, however, and bold experimentation has continued in the poetry of Borys Necherda (1939–) and in the prose writings of Yuriy Shcherbak (1934–) and Hryhir Tyutyunnyk (1931–).

A new development in Ukrainian literature began about 1964 with the start of Ukrainian *samvydav* (*samizdat*, "self-publishing," later published abroad). Although it represents a wide spectrum of political dissent, it is often led by writers and is literary in character. The first major collection of this type was Vyacheslav Chornovil's (1938-) *Lykho z rozumu* (Eng. tr., *The Chornovil Papers*, 1968), mostly documenting miscarriages in Soviet justice but also containing some poems by various dissenters. Three literary critics became prominent dissidents: Ivan DZYUBA, Yevhen Sverstyuk (1928-), and Ivan Svitlychny (1929-). Dzyuba is the author of *Internatsyonalizm chy rusyfikatsiya* (Eng. tr., *Internationalism or Russification*, 1968), a scholarly study of the misapplication of Vladimir Lenin's nationality policy in the Ukraine. Sverstyuk wrote *Sobor u ryshtovanni* (1970; Eng. tr., *Clandestine Essays*, 1976), a perceptive commentary on the novel *Sobor* (1968; The Cathedral) by Oles Honchar. The dissenter who has gained the widest acclaim both at home and abroad is Valentyn Moroz (1936-), the author of the truly Orwellian *Reportazh iz zapovidnyka im. Beriyi* (Eng. tr., *Report from the Beria Reservation*, 1974) and other essays. While other dissenters, such as Dzyuba, often adhere to Leninist doctrine, Moroz represents the nationalistic, radical wing of the movement. In 1979 Moroz was released and allowed to go to the United States, where he accepted a research appointment at Harvard. Several young poets, unable to publish their works, joined in the clandestine *samvydav*. The most talented were Vasyl Holoborodko (1942-), the author of *Letyuche vikontse* (1970; The Flying Window), and Ihor Kalynets (1939-), whose *Pidsumovuyuchy movchannya* (1971; Summary Silence) he called "a book of lyrics on contemporary themes." Equally promising are the poets Mykola Vorobyov and Hryhoriy Chubay. The only prose writers to appear in *samvydav* are Mykhaylo Osadchy (1936-), the author of an autobiographical novel of concentration-camp life, *Bilmo* (1971; Eng. tr., *Cataract*, 1976), and Oles Berdnyk (1927-). Early in 1972, after a new wave of arrests, most of the Ukrainian dissidents were jailed. Only one of them, Dzyuba, was released a year later after making an open admission of his "mistakes." The dissident movement defended national as well as civil rights. It has left a deep impression not so much on literature as on the intellectual atmosphere of the country. Above all, it has provided examples of literary excellence and civic courage that have helped to expose the hollowness of socialist realism and the impotence of political controls over literature.

See: G. S. N. Luckyj, *Literary Politics in the Soviet Ukraine: 1917-34* (1956), and "Literature," in *Ukraine: A Concise Encyclopaedia*, vol. 1 (1963); C. H. Andrusyshen and W. Kirkconnell, eds., *The Ukrainian Poets* (1963); I. Koshelivets, *Suchasna literaturea v URSR* (1964); *Istoriya ukrayinskoyi literatury*, vols. 5-8 (1968-71). G.S.N.L.

Ukrayinka, Lesya, pseud. of Larysa Kòsach-Kvitka, (1871-1913), Ukrainian poet, was born in Novohrad Volynsky (Novograd Volynsky). She was the daughter of the writer Olena Pchilka and niece of the prominent scholar Mykhaylo Drahomanov, both of whom greatly influenced her. Educated at home, she mastered several foreign languages. Ukrayinka suffered from tuberculosis all her life and sought a cure in the warm climates of the Crimea, Italy, and Egypt. Through her uncle's influence she was for a time attracted to socialism and Marxism and took an interest in the Social-Democratic Party. Furthermore she was, in the wider sense, a writer committed to revolutionary and Promethean ideals.

As a poet, Ukrayinka wrote some inspiring verse, such as "Contra spem spero" (1890; Against Hope I Hope), but did not reach the first rank of Ukrainian poets. Her collections of poetry include *Na krylakh pisen* (1893; On

the Wings of Songs), *Dumy i mriyi* (1899; Thoughts and Dreams), and *Vidhuky* (1902; Echoes). She also wrote longer poems, such as "Robert Bruce" (1894). Her greatest achievement, however, was in the field of poetic drama, and her modernist stage works are among the finest in any Slavic literature. Many of her plays were set in foreign lands or in periods of ancient history. They include *Vavylonsky polon* (1908; Babylonian Captivity), *Kassandra* (1908), *U pushchi* (1910; In the Wilderness), *Boyarynya* (1910; Noblewoman), *Rufin i Pristsilla* (1911), and *Kaminny hospodar* (1912; The Stone Host). Despite their locales, nearly all have clear allusions to the Ukraine. Her masterpiece is *Lisova pisnya* (1912; Eng. tr., *The Forest Song*, 1950), based on Ukrainian folklore.

See: P. Cundy, *Spirit of Flame* (1950); C. Bida, "Life and Work," in *Lesya Ukrainka* (1968). G.S.N.L.

Umbral, Francisco (1935-), Spanish journalist and fiction writer, was born in Madrid. He has achieved great success with his articles on social customs, later collected in such books as *Diario de un snob* (1973) and *Diario de un español cansado* (1975; Diary of a Tired Spaniard). Self-educated, Umbral sees himself as following in the footsteps of Mariano José de Larra and Ramón GÓMEZ DE LA SERNA. He has written essays on these writers, in 1965 and 1978, respectively, and on other men who influenced him: Federico GARCÍA LORCA (1968), Ramón del VALLE-INCLÁN (1968), and Miguel DELIBES (1970). Above all, he is a lyrical stylist. His short stories, collected in *Teoría de Lola* (1977; Lola's Theory), impart poetry to vulgar language and reflect in a lyrical fashion Umbral's view of the hopelessness of life. His novels are loosely structured and often made up of juxtaposed sketches, as in *Travesía de Madrid* (1966; Across Madrid) and *Las respetuosas* (1977; Respectful Women). Erotic themes are common, as in *Si hubiéramos sabido que el amor era eso* (1969; If We Had Only Known That That Was Love) and *El Giocondo* (1970)—while focuses on women are frequent.

Umbral's technique of fragmenting produces particularly brilliant results in the novelized memoirs and introspective sagas of a writer recreating his childhood and adolescence: *Balada de gamberros* (1965; Ballad of Punks), *Memorias de un niño de derechas* (1972; Memories of a Rightist Childhood), *Las ninfas* (1976), to which one might add *Retrato de un joven malvado* (1973; Portrait of a Young Delinquent), and *Mortal y rosa* (1975). *La noche que llegué al Café Gijón* (1977; My First Night at the Café Gijón) well illustrate Umbral's blending of autobiography and novel.

See: A. M. Navales, *Cuatro novelistas españolas: Miguel Delibes, Ignacio Aldecoa, Daniel Sueiro, Francisco Umbral* (1974), pp. 213-290. D.V.

Unamuno y Jugo, Miguel de (1864-1936), Spanish novelist, essayist, poet, playwright, and philosopher, was born in Bilbao. He is the most prominent personality of the Generation of 1898 and has a worldwide literary reputation. Unamuno attended school in his native city, where he spent his deeply religious early years. In 1880 he went to Madrid to study philosophy and letters. There he was an assiduous visitor at the Ateneo (the so-called blasphemy center of the city), especially its library, where he familiarized himself with the most liberal theories recently imported from elsewhere in Europe. After completing his doctorate in 1884, he returned to Bilbao, where he and some friends founded the weekly *La Lucha de Clases* (The Class Struggle), the first socialist journal to be published in that city. He married, and in 1891 he moved to Salamanca to assume the chair of Greek, which he had just won. Through the years he was several times rector of that famous university. He was also dismissed from the post more than once because of his public opposition to the established government, whether it was rightist or leftist. When the dictator Miguel Primo de Rivera exiled him in 1924, he lived quite unhappily in Paris, despite the efforts of French friends who helped him to turn his exile into an international scandal. Upon the dictator's death, Unamuno returned to Salamanca, where he died shortly after the outbreak of the Civil War.

In both content and style, Unamuno's work can be divided into two periods. In his series of essays entitled *En torno al casticismo* (1895; Concerning the Essence of Spain), he attempts to define Spain's character and its collective psychology by studying the "soul of Castile." His first novel, *Paz en la guerra* (1897; Peace in War), has a similar orientation. It is a populist work in which Unamuno, with rigorous historical objectivity, searches for the "true tradition," eternal and buried, which survives unaltered beneath the changing events of war. He called this tradition "intrahistory." His thought is here deeply rooted in German ideological romanticism—in Friedrich von Schelling, Georg Wilhelm Friedrich Hegel, Alexander von Humboldt, Friedrich and August von Schlegel, and *Völkerpsychologie*. At the same time it owes much to French naturalism and Hippolyte Taine.

The image of Unamuno is conditioned by the personality crisis he suffered in 1896–97, when he lost his religious faith. The loss was permanent, but he was never able to reconcile himself to it. From this time on, Unamuno's main concern was the individual person, his reality, and his fate. These are the themes underlying his great essays and his moving poems. He abandoned the pursuit of the unconscious and the nature in which it lodges, even though it is nature that makes peace possible in the midst of war. Unamuno's war moves into the heart of the individual himself. Personal struggle becomes the only path to self-awareness and a vision of truly human reality. His later novels no longer contain landscapes or descriptions of the natural world. In *Amor y pedagogía* (1904), a work already influenced by *Don Quijote* (Unamuno's *Vida de don Quijote y Sancho* appeared the following year), characters are presented as independent of milieu. In later novels they are completely autonomous, independent even of their author. Augusto Pérez, hero of the thematically and technically innovative novel *Niebla* (1914; Eng. tr., *Mist*, 1923), contests his own existence throughout, and in a final and justly famous scene, written long before Luigi PIRANDELLO's *Six Characters in Search of an Author*, confronts his own creator, Unamuno, with the knowledge that he too is but a shadow and a dream and destined to die. Unamuno's novels and numerous novellas portray increasingly interiorized dramas of the struggle to be. Perhaps the most impressive of these is the short novel *San Manuel Bueno, Mártir* (1933; Eng. tr., *St. Emmanuel the Good, Martyr*, 1956), Unamuno's spiritual testament in the form of the drama of a parish priest who cannot believe. This existential novel—antiintellectual, poetic, and disturbing—remains always open to new critical perspectives and unsuspected meanings.

A number of Unamuno's short works of fiction were rewritten in dramatic form and taken to the stage during their author's lifetime. His theater focuses exclusively on the inner spiritual struggles of the characters and shows no concern for theatrical conventions, traditional plot development, or the exterior world.

Unamuno's philosophy is contained in his monumental essay *Del sentimiento trágico de la vida en los hombres y en los pueblos* (1913; Eng. tr., *The Tragic Sense of Life in Men and Peoples,* 1921). In this work he undertakes a demolishing critique of philosophy and theology, showing that neither can offer a rational explanation of man, God, and the universe, as their proponents claim. On the contrary, philosophy and theology are nothing but formulas born of man's desire for immortality. Moreover, modern scientific knowledge is incompatible with a belief in God and immortality. This does not mean, however, that we are to resign ourselves to this loss, to give up what according to Baruch Spinoza is the very essence of being. Unamuno rejects resignation. Philosophy or religion may not give meaning to life, but neither does the nihilism that replaces shattered belief. The only road open, then, is to live according to human and religious values even though we know that they lack a rational basis. Reason combats faith, faith combats reason, and we must live in the midst of this struggle, vitalized by our own resultant agony. These views of Unamuno bring him close to the despairing souls of history (Blaise Pascal, Etienne de Sénancour, Søren KIERKEGAARD) and even closer to reformers like Martin Luther, while at the same time they point the way to such contemporary existentialists as Albert CAMUS and Jean-Paul SARTRE.

Unamuno's work is fundamentally poetic, despite its coherent, well-elaborated, rational structure. His insight into the unreality of transitory existence and the ultimate enigma of man and the universe is poetic, and although his poetry might be termed philosophical, it is never coldly intellectual. As he put it, "Let feeling think and thought feel." In *Poesías* (1907), rather than fin-de-siècle aestheticism or decadent musical preciosity, we find profound, direct expression. Juan Ramón JIMÉNEZ and Antonio MACHADO Y RUIZ were influenced by him, and through them he influenced later generations. In *Teresa* (1924), Unamuno returns in theme and style to a romantic world, in particular that of Gustavo BÉCQUER, whose influence is clear. Here the verse is more musical and more appealing to the senses. In the booklength poem *El Cristo de Velázquez* (1920; partial Eng. tr., *The Christ of Velazquez,* 1924), inspired by the great portrait's vision of serenity in the presence of death, Unamuno's poetic language becomes much richer and more symbolic without losing depth and directness. His numerous last poems, written between 1928 and 1936 and published posthumously in *Cancionero* (1953; Songbook), a kind of poetic diary, are highly concentrated and economical. His poetry, like his work in other genres, carries the imprint of a powerful personality. The essence of Unamuno's thought and feeling is present in every one of his works, be it essay, novel, play, or poem. In all of these genres he achieved a seldom-matched eminence.

Few modern European writers have had the erudition, the command of classical and modern languages, and the intellectual curiosity of Unamuno. His work reflects his broad knowledge of world literature, history, philosophy, and theology, Catholic and Protestant alike.

See: J. Ferrater Mora, *Unamuno, Philosopher of Tragedy,* tr. by P. Silver (1962); J. Marías, *Miguel de Unamuno,* tr. by F. López-Morillas (1966); M. Valdés, *Death in the Literature of Unamuno* (1966); E. Salcedo, *Vida de don Miguel* (1970). F F.-T.

Under, Marie (1883–), Estonian poet, was born in Tallinn. She is generally considered the greatest poet in her language. Under became famous as a member of the "Siuru" group of writers (*see* ESTONIAN LITERATURE) with her sensuous, colorful volume *Sonetid* (1917; Sonnets). Her production spans six decades and ranges from impressionist delicacy in her earliest collections through expressionist experiments in her middle phase to full maturity best characterized by the simultaneously composed volumes *Hääl varjust* (1927; Voice from the Shadows) and *Rõõm Ühest ilusast päevast* (1928; Delight in a Lovely Day). Under has been compared to both Goethe and Rainer Maria RILKE in terms of her expressive power, yet she is unmistakably her own when she creates visions that fuse metaphysical searching with an intense experience of life and nature perceived through keen senses. A selected volume of her verse is fittingly entitled *Ja liha sai sõnaks* (1936; And the Flesh Became Word). In 1944, Under went into exile in Sweden. Her later poetry reflects dramatically the plight of her people under the burdens of German and Soviet occupation, war, and exile. Her other works include *La Pierre ôtée du cœur* (1970), and, in English translation, *Child of Man* (1955). A selection of poetry in English can be found in *Anthology of Modern Estonian Poetry*, ed. by W. K. Matthews (1953).

See: I. Ivask, "The Main Tradition of Estonian Poetry," in *Estonian Poetry and Language*, ed. by V. Kõressaar and A. Rannit (1965), pp. 272–80; Marie Under, *La Pierre ôtée du cœur* (1970); A. Oras, "M. Under and Estonian Poetry," SR 78 (1970): 247–68; A. Adson, ed., *Marie Under eluraamst*, 2 vols. (1974).

I.I.

Undset, Sigrid (1882–1949), Norwegian novelist and essayist, is one of the most distinguished Norwegian writers of the 20th century. After her conversion to Roman Catholicism in the mid-1920s, Unset gained considerable attention throughout the rest of the Western world because of her espousal of the church's doctrines. She was born in Kallundborg, Denmark. In 1884, she moved with her family to Christiania (now Oslo), where she grew up under the most liberal and liberating circumstances. Undset was a precocious child, with a fabulous talent for observation not only of the physical world but also of the people who inhabited it, an ability repeatedly demonstrated throughout her works. She explored this early period of her life in a fascinating autobiographical novel, *Elleve år* (1934; Eng. tr., *The Longest Years*, 1935). Her father was a well-known archaeologist with a special interest in Scandinavian, and particularly Norwegian, antiquities. From him, Undset gained early insight into the culture of medieval Scandinavia. As she grew older, she continued to be interested in the medieval history of Scandinavia, England, and Germany, especially its literary expressions: its sagas, ballads, legends, and mythology. Her intelligent, somewhat impetuous Danish mother sought to develop in her daughter, at an early age, a critical, realistic attitude toward life in general and religion in particular. In this latter respect she became an important (perhaps subconscious) negative influence on her daughter, since most of Undset's works seem to represent a hegira from her mother's rationalism.

Undset's father died when she was 11 years old, and when she was 16 she had to seek employment to help her mother support the family. During her 10 years as an office worker, she learned to know women who slaved away for paltry wages, and when, in her middle twenties, she began writing her first novels, Undset drew on these experiences. *Fru Martha Oulie* (1907), *Jenny* (1911; Eng. tr., 1921), *Våren* (1914; Springtime), and the short-story collection *Fattige skjæbner* (1912; Humble Existences) all have as their principal characters women caught between their drive for independence and their desire for fulfillment in love and marriage. *Jenny*, the most important of these works, is filled with idealism and unrequited passion, reflecting Undset's own situation in this period. The novels and essays that in the next years led up to her great historical fiction reflect her own search for an ethical or religious component in her life, one that she at last

found in the Catholic church. At the time of her conversion in 1925, she had completed her main work set in the Norwegian Catholic Middle Ages, *Kristin Lavransdatter* (1920–22; Eng. tr., 1923–27). This work shows Undset's profound knowledge of medieval Norway–every detail attests to her painstaking research and intuitive historical insight—but the portrayal of the life of the passionate and proud Kirstin nevertheless echoes, both in its realism and in its themes, Undset's earlier novels of modern life. Undset's insights into and realistic depictions of erotic love, marriage, and family life in this novel of 14th-century Norway do reveal, however, new dimensions to her writing. Moreover, *Kristin Lavransdatter* is set in a moral universe in which God and the church rule; here the moral vacuum of the earlier novels is filled.

The conflict between the law of God and proud independence is even more pronounced in Undset's next great novels, *Olav Audunssøn i Hestviken* and *Olav Audunssøn og hans børn* (1925–27; Eng. tr., *The Master of Hestviken*, 1928–30, 1934). Set in 13th-century Norway, these novels pit the proud, unyielding Olav, with his old Norse sense of honor, against the church's demands for humility and atonement. After this novel, for which she was awarded the Nobel Prize for Literature in 1928, Undset moved into a phase in which her espousal of the Catholic faith threatened the vitality of her psychological portrayals. For example, both *Gymnadenia* (1929; Eng. tr., *The Wild Orchid*, 1931) and its sequel *Den brændende busk* (1930; Eng. tr., *the Burning Bush*, 1932) are marred by the author's insistence that human problems can be solved only through the Catholic faith. Undset's last novel, however, *Madame Dorothea* (1939; Eng. tr., 1940), is set in Norway around the year 1800, is a significant work in the tradition of historical realism.

Throughout her life, Undset was an alert observer of contemporary event. She published a number of essays, some of them collected in *Etapper I & II* (1929, 1933; Eng. tr., *Stages on the Road*, 1934), *Selvportretter og landskapsbilleder* (1938; Eng. tr., *Men, Women and Places*, 1939), and *Artikler og taler fra krigstiden* (1953; Wartime Articles and Speeches). She was one of the first to detect and fight the menace of Nazism. Her boundless contempt for the forces of fascism, expressed in essays and articles, forced her to leave Norway immediately after the German invasion. She spent the World War II years in the United States, demonstrating, in speeches and articles, her unflagging commitment to the ideals of humanism.

See: A. H. Winsnes, *Sigrid Undset* (1953); C. F. Bayerschmidt, *Sigrid Undset* (1970). S.A. with K.A.F.

Ungaretti, Giuseppe (1888–1970), Italian poet, essayist, educator, and translator, was born in Alexandria, Egypt, where his parents had immigrated from Lucca, in Tuscany. Not surprisingly for a man who spent the first 24 years of his life near the Sahara, the desert is a recurring theme in Ungaretti's poetry, embodying distance, freedom, light, sensuality, and, above all, the dreams and mirages of the nomad. The nomad becomes the metaphor for the poet himself in his perennial wanderings in search of innocence, happiness, and love. Ungaretti acknowledged the pervasive influence of those formative Egyptian years on numerous occasions, particularly in a collection of travel notes and reminiscences that he published toward the end of his life under the title *Il deserto e dopo* (1961; The Desert and Afterwards).

In 1912, Ungaretti left Alexandria for Paris to study at the Sorbonne. He attended the lectures of Joseph Bédier, Henri BERGSON, Gustave Lanson, and Fortunat Strowski and formed friendships with the leaders of the artistic and literary avant-garde: Georges Braque, Giorgio De Chirico, Fernand Léger, Amedeo Modigliani, Pablo Picasso, Guillaume APOLLINAIRE, Blaise CENDRARS, Max JACOB, and André SALMON.

With the outbreak of World War I, Ungaretti moved to Italy. In 1915 he volunteered as a private in the infantry. His first major poetry was born against the background of that wartime experience. In the trenches, during lulls between battles, or at night in his tent, Ungaretti kept a sort of intimate journal in verse form—poems, mostly short, focusing on the precariousness of life and on man's need for love and his search for identity. These were discovered by a literary-minded lieutenant, Ettore Serra, who published them at his own expense in an edition of 80 copies. That slender volume, *Il porto sepolto* (1916; The Buried Port), characterized by an unconventional, staccato style without punctuation or regular rhymes, was destined to have a deep, long-lasting impact on Italian poetry.

Il porto sepolto was followed by a book of poems in French, *La guerre* (1919; War). These two volumes were subsequently incorporated into a larger collection, *Allegria di naufragi* (1919; Joy of Shipwrecks), whose title, echoing the famous concluding line of Giacomo Leopardi's poem "L'infinito," offers the first indication that Ungaretti was by then seeking to enter the mainstream of the Italian lyric tradition. This gradual process, achieved in part through the personal rediscovery of the meters of the old masters, led to the publication of *Sentimento del tempo* (1933; Sentiment of Time), a book reflecting what Ungaretti called the "summer" of his life, a phase highlighted by love, sensuality, and at one point by a tormenting religious crisis. Next, Ungaretti planned a volume of poems depicting the "autumn" of his human experience, an autumn, he wrote, that bids farewell to the last signs of earthly youth, the last carnal appetites. But its publication was delayed by the death of his nine-year-old son in 1939 and by the long, dark years of World War II. These tragic events were responsible for the outpouring of *Il dolore* (1947; Grief), where some of the most striking lyrics in his entire output are to be found. Three years later, the "autumn" poems that had been put aside were finally published as *La terra promessa* (1950; The Promised Land).

During the last two decades of his life, Ungaretti brought out four additional volumes of verse: *Un grido e paesaggi* (1952; A Shout and Landscapes), which includes new poems for his dead son; *Il taccuino del vecchio* (1960; The Old Man's Notebook), a collection in the metaphysical vein of *La terra promessa; Morte delle stagioni* (1967; Death of the Seasons), which many thought was his swan song; and, in his 80th year, *Dialogo* (1968), a love dialogue dazzling for its verbal virtuosity and youthful confidence. The following year he supervised the publication of his complete poems in a single, annotated volume, *Vita d'un uomo: tutte le poesie* (1969; Life of a Man: Complete Poems). A comprehensive collection of his essays, articles, notes, and lectures appeared posthumously in a companion volume, *Vita d'un uomo: saggi e interventi* (1974; Life of a Man: Essays and Other Writings). Some of these selections, notably the studies on Dante, Petrarch, Giambattista Vico, and Leopardi, originated in courses Ungaretti taught at the University of São Paulo in Brazil (1936–42), the University of Rome (1942–63), and Columbia University (1964).

The leading role played by Ungaretti in the renewal of modern verse literature in Italy is today universally acknowledged. By daring to reexplore the hidden potentialities of the Italian language, he was the first to revitalize a lyric tradition that, after Giosuè Carducci (1835–1907), Giovanni PASCOLI, and Gabriele D'ANNUNZIO, had threatened to become stagnant. The impact of his poetry—his sparing use of words, his capacity to bring language to unusual heights of lyric tension, and his power to create illuminating images—ranks among the foremost literary accomplishments of the 20th century.

Ungaretti is also noted for distinguished translations of Shakespeare, William Blake, Luis de Góngora, Jean Racine, and Stéphane MALLARMÉ, among others. His own poetry has been translated into every major Western language. English versions of his poetry are available in Giuseppe Ungaretti, *Selected Poems,* tr. by Patrick Greagh (1971) and *Selected Poems of Giuseppe Ungaretti,* tr. by Allen Mandelbaum (1975).

See: L. Rebay, *Le origini della poesia di Giuseppe Ungaretti* (1962); J. Cary, *Three Modern Italian Poets: Saba, Ungaretti, Montale* (1969); C. Ossola, *Giuseppe Ungaretti* (1975); G. Cambon, *La poesia di Ungaretti* (1976).

L.R.

Uniłowski, Zbigniew (1909–37), Polish novelist and short-story writer, was born and died in Warsaw. He was associated with the vanguard group "Kwadryga" (Quadriga). Uniłowski started his literary career with short expressionistic stories, later collected in the volume *Człowiek w oknie* (1933; The Man in the Window). In his novel *Wspólny pokój* (1932; A Shared Room), he depicted vividly the life of young Warsaw bohemians. In 1934 appeared his short antimilitaristic story *Dzień rekruta* (One Day In the Life of a Conscript). In the unfinished autobiographical novel *Dwadzieścia lat życia* (1937; Twenty Years of Life), written in the form of memoirs, Uniłowski presents the life of a homeless young boy in the Warsaw proletarian milieu and the extreme poverty and sordidness of his living conditions. In his prose, which was rooted in his real-life experiences, Uniłowski applied the techniques of both naturalistic description and grotesque and distorted stylization. He visited settlements of Polish colonists in South America and published two volumes of travel impressions, *Żyto w dżungli* (1936; Rye in the Jungle) and *Pamiętnik morski* (1937; A Voyager's Diary).

See: B. Faron, "W kręgu autobiografizmu—Zbigniew Uniłowski," in *Prozaicy dwudziestolecia międzywojennego. Sylwetki,* ed. by B. Faron (1972), pp. 691–719.

S.S.

Unruh, Fritz von (1885–1970), German dramatist and poet, was born in Koblenz. Scion of a noble family, son of a Prussian general, he was educated for a military career at Plön and entered active service in the German army. The young officer pondered over the problem of the soldier, whose profession in times of peace is futile and in times of war seems nothing but subordination. From his musings came the drama *Offiziere* (1912; Officers), which Max Reinhardt produced with great success. Feeling that a military career was incompatible with the creative forces of a writer, Unruh resigned his commission and wrote the drama *Prinz Louis Ferdinand von Preussen* (1913), in which duty frustrates the hero's judgment and desire. In 1914, Unruh was called back to the colors and fought through World War I. His heart, however, battled for peace. The dramatic poem *Vor der Entscheidung* (written 1914, published 1919; Before the Decision) was one of the first antiwar tracts in Germany. In the narrative *Opfergang* (written 1916 at Verdun, pub. 1918; Eng. tr., *Way of Sacrifice,* 1928), a metaphysical reason for war was sought but sadly found wanting. The idea of war was pursued to its mythical depth in the tragedy *Ein Geschlecht* (1916; A Family). *Platz* (1920; Room), its sequel, showed that the revolution in Germany was a wrong solution. It did not bring forth the "new being," the dream of the expressionists.

Unruh tried a political career, became a member of the Reichstag, and gave a dithyrambic oration in memory of the murdered Walther Rathenau (1867–1922). When the idea of revenge threatened the understanding between nations, Unruh worked for greater amity by writing the travel book *Flügel der Nike* (1924: Wings of Nike), publishing his speeches in *Reden* (1924; Speeches), and giving the world the festival play *Heinrich von Andernach* (1925), a great plea for love among men. He foresaw in his drama *Bonaparte* (1927; Eng. tr., 1928) a coming dictatorship and appealed to his countrymen to be alert. The plays that followed, *Phaea* (1930), *Berlin in Monte Carlo* (1931), and *Zero* (1932), failed to make an impression. When Adolf Hitler gained control, Fritz von Unruh, winner of the Kleist and Schiller prizes, left Germany for Italy and France and finally found refuge in the United States. He returned to Germany and settled in Diez on the Lahn in 1952—after having delivered a moving *Rede an die Deutschen* in 1948 in the Paulskirche in Frankfurt am Main—but returned to the United States in 1955. When he lost his possessions in a flood in 1962, he returned to Diez, where he lived until his death.

In the years of his exile, Unruh turned principally to prose; although he did write dramas, they were not well received in Germany. His novel *Der nie verlor* (pub. Germany 1949, but first in English translation as *The End Is Not Yet* in 1947) was followed by *Die Heilige* (1952; Eng. tr., *The Saint*, 1950) and *Fürchtet nichts* (1952; Be Not Afraid). Other works include *Der Sohn des Generals* (1957; The General's Son), *Im Haus der Prinzen* (1967; In the House of Princes), and *Kaserne und Sphinx* (1969).

See: W. Geyer, *Fritz von Unruh* (1924); R. Meister, *Fritz von Unruh* (1925); A. Kronacher, *Fritz von Unruh* (1946). H.Bf. rev. A.L.W.

Uppdal, Kristofer (1878–1961), Norwegian poet and novelist, was born in Opdal in the district of Nord-Trøndelag. The son of a poor farmer and laborer, he had to work from an early age. After two years at a folk high school, he began his adult life as a mine worker and railroad builder. He was a union official and later a journalist for the labor press in Oslo, where from 1913 on he lived as a free-lance writer and author. Uppdal's first books, drawing upon his days as an itinerant worker, were combinations of harsh realism and idyll, prose and poetry. In 1910 he began the 10-volume work that, receiving its title from one of the volumes, became known as *Dansen gjenom skuggeheimen* (1910–24; The Dance through the Shadow Land). In this work, Uppdal attempted to create a unified history of the labor movement from the uprooting of the farming class to the present. Each of its 10 component novels is an autonomous work of art, yet they share common characters. This massive work combines raw realism, trivial details, and poetic visions into a rich saga about the emergence of the Norwegian industrial worker.

In addition to his novels, Uppdal produced collections of poetry, such as *Elskhug* (1919; Love) and *Alterelden* (1920; The Altar Fire), that are remarkable for their originality. Together with the Finnish-Swedish poets Edith SÖDERGRAN and Elmer DIKTONIUS, Uppdal was among the first to break away from the traditional aesthetic language of Scandinavian poetry and to combine the influences of the French symbolists with literary expressionism. Whether he was viewing contemporary situations or recreating universal myths, Uppdal demonstrated both a visionary power and the will and ability to create new poetic forms.

See: O. Solumsmoen, *Kristofer Uppdal* (1959), N. Ystad, *Kristofer Uppdals Lyrikk* (1978). K.A.F.

Urban, Milo (1904–), Slovak novelist, was born in Rabčica in northern Slovakia. He worked as a journalist and was involved in the Slovak nationalist movement, especially during World War II. His early work consists of collections of long tales, such as *Za vyšným mlynom* (1926; Behind the Upper Mill), in which he added new psychological dimensions to Slovak fiction. The publication of his first novel, *Živý bič* (1927; The Live Whip), which has been translated into several foreign languages, is a significant watershed in modern Slovak writing. In this picture of poverty in a Slovak village during World War I, Urban created a new type of Slovak fictional hero: Adam Hlavaj, a peasant torn by conflict, who awakens from passivity as a result of his wartime experiences and resolves to join in the struggle to build a better world. This novel, the next two, *Hmly na úsvite* (1930; Mists at Dawn) and *V osídlach* (1940; In the Snares), form a trilogy that richly documents Slovak life between the two world wars. Urban's last two novels, *Zhasnuté svetlá* (1957; The Light Went Out) and *Kto seje vietor* (1964; He Who Sows the Wind), evoke events from the time of the Munich Pact (1938) and the fall of Czechoslovakia to the Nazis (1939), but do not reach the level of his earlier work. F.M.B.

Urzidil, Johannes (1896–1970), German poet and novelist, was born in Prague, the son of a railroad official. He studied philology and art history at the University of Prague and served as a press attaché to the German embassy there. He befriended Franz KAFKA and Franz WERFEL. In 1939 he emigrated to England and in 1941 to the United States, settling in New York where he supported himself through newspaper work, leathercraft, and broadcasting (the "Voice of America"). He died while vacationing in Rome.

Urzidil's first volume of poetry appeared in 1919, followed by other works including novels, essays, short stories, and translations. By his own admission his work is not confined to any literary movement, although he may have been influenced by "Prague expressionism." He considered literature a "creative responsibility," and in his devotion to creation his writings are reminiscent of Adalbert Stifter's—classic in their humanity but receptive to the supernatural. In many of his stories, Urzidil returns to Prague, where he rebuilds the city with much the same perception as did Sherwood Anderson in *Winesburg, Ohio*.

In an age of total mobilization, Urzidil saw the poet not as the keeper of the "most sacred possessions" but as a craftsman who participates actively in the metamorphosis, creating that which is irretrievable. In *Da geht Kafka* (1965; Eng. tr., *There Goes Kafka*, 1968), Kafka appears as an 80-year-old gardener on Long Island, leading a simple life, far removed from all Kafka research. "One does not live with reality, not even with one's own, but only with imagination," Urzidil states in *Die erbeuteten Frauen* (1966; The Captive Women). Informative is the description of *Amerika und die Antike* (1964; America and Antiquity), dedicated to "the eagles over Delphi and their relatives over the Rockies."

See: G. Trapp, *Die Prosa Johannes Urzidils* (1967); K. H. Waggerl, *Blick in die Werkstatt* (1967). O.W.T.

V

Vaa, Aslaug (1889–1967), Norwegian poet and dramatist, was born and raised in the region of Telemark, in south-central Norway. By the time she published her first volume of poetry, *Nord i leite* (1934; Up North), at the age of 45, Vaa had amassed years of extensive reading and travel experience and had absorbed influences from sources as varied as William Blake and such movements as cubism, dadaism, and dramatic expressionism. On the one hand, her poetry is marked by Blakean innocence and simplicity of expression. This is especially true of her images from the folk life of Telemark, whose nature and rich cultural traditions she extolled in a lyrical verse reflecting the meter and rhythm of ballads and folk song stanzas (*stev*). On the other hand, she is a visionary poet of universal themes whose work is closely related to that of Olav AUKRUST and Olav NYGARD. Her later collections, particularly *Fotefar* (1947; Footprints), *Skjenkarsveinens visur* (1954; The Cupbearer's Songs), and *Bustader* (1963; Dwellings), reveal a searching, philosophical attitude. In these volumes, much more frequently than before, she focused on the fundamental questions of human life, seeking and seeming to find harmony in the acceptance of a divine order. Although in her later poetry she continued to use images from nature and everyday life, these elements were now subdued and integrated into a metaphysical structure.

As a dramatist, Vaa combined elements of realistic and expressionistic theater. Yet such plays as *Steinguden* (1938; The Stone God) and *Munkeklokka* (1950; The Monastery Bell) are, above all, noteworthy for their creation of lyrical moods.

See: L. Mæhle, *Frå bygda til verda* (1967), pp. 143–95.

K.A.F.

Vaculík, Ludvík (1926–), Czech novelist, was born in the town of Brumov in Moravian Slovakia. He first worked in a factory but later completed his education, becoming an editor and broadcaster. During the 1960s, as a member of the Communist Party, Vaculík was active in the struggle for liberalization, and he is the author of the celebrated "Two Thousand Words" manifesto of 1968, which called on the government and the Communist Party to end restrictions on individual liberty.

Vaculík has written two significant political novels. The first, *Sekyra* (1966; Eng. tr., *The Axe*, 1974), depicts the conflict between a father and his son, who gradually comes to realize that the father, a minor Communist Party functionary whom the boy had adored, has often acted unjustly in the struggle to collectivize the countryside. Since 1969, Vaculík has not been published in Czechoslovakia. His second novel, *Morčete* (Eng. tr., *The Guinea Pigs*, 1973), appeared only abroad. Totally different in style from its predecessor, it is a Kafkaesque (*see* Franz KAFKA) allegory of guinea pigs and their world; their arbitrary and sadistic treatment by their once-beneficient master serves as a metaphor for the totalitarian state and its treatment of its citizens.

In 1975, Vaculík broke his enforced silence by launching a series of feuilletons (short informal essays) that would embody a new spirit of freedom and a fresh creative spirit; these were circulated in Czechoslovakia in typescript. A number of prominent writers joined him in this effort; the collective product was published abroad as *Čára na zdi* (1977; Line on the Wall).

See: A. J. Liehm, *The Politics of Culture* (1970), pp. 181–201; W. E. Harkins, "The New Czechoslovak Feuil-

leton," *UB* 1, no. 2 (1979); W. E. Harkins and P. I. Trensky, eds., *Czech Literature since 1956: A Symposium* (1980).

W.E.H.

Vaginov, Konstantin Konstantinovich, pseud. of Konstantin Konstantinovich Vagingejm (1899–1934), Russian poet, was born in Petersburg and educated there from 1917 to 1921 at the University Faculty of Jurisprudence. His first collection of poems was *Puteshestviye v khaos* (1921; Journey into Chaos). He published two more collections in 1926, *Sikhotvoreniya* (Poems), and in 1931, *Opyty soyedineniya slov posredstvom ritma* (Experiments in the Union of Words through Rhyme). The cycle of poems written from 1930 to 1933, "Zvukopodobiye" (The Likeness of Sounds), remains unpublished. Vaginov also published prose fiction, including three novels: *Kozlinaya pesn* (1928; Goat Song), *Trudy i dni Svistonova* (1929; The Works and Days of Svistonov), and *Bambochada* (1931). When Daniil KHARMS, Aleksandr Vvedensky, Nikolay ZABOLOTSKY, and others formed the "Oberiu" group (1926–30), they invited Vaginov to participate (*see* RUSSIAN LITERATURE). Vaginov's poetry and prose have been undeservedly neglected. He is a genuine avant-garde writer, especially in his prose, which should be studied in contexts that include André GIDE's *Les Faux-Monnayeurs* and M. Bakhtin's conception of "carnivalized' literature. Some of his unpublished poems of the early 1930s have appeared in *Apollon 1977* (Paris).

See: T. L. Nikolskaya in *Kratkaya literaturnaya entsiklopediya*, vol. 9 (1978), p. 169; W. Kasack, *Lexikon der russischen Literatur ab 1917* (1976), pp. 415–16.

V.L.

Vailland, Roger (1907–65), French novelist, journalist, and essayist, was born in Acy-le-Multien (Aisne). He spent his life seeking a balance between a prickly individualism and a yearning for solidarity with his fellows. This duality expressed itself in experimentation with drugs, alcohol, and sex, service in the Resistance, and a passing infatuation with communism. Vailland's novels have achieved wide popularity. He is a master storyteller, with a knack for creating atmosphere, evoking character, and orchestrating suspense. His hard, concise, impersonal style mirrors the cold light in which he views society. *Drôle de jeu* (1945; Strange Game) poses a cold, objective look at the heroes of the Resistance; *Beau masque* (1954; Beautiful Mask) depicts the bitter struggle between a rising labor force and a decaying bourgeoisie; *325.000 francs* (1955) is a pessimistic representation of working-class conditions and carries the implicit lesson that individual happiness is impossible if divorced from social commitment. After Vailland's disenchantment with Stalinism in 1956, the Bolshevik hero in his novels is displaced by the figure of the libertine. Don Cesare in *La Loi* (1957, The Law), which won the Goncourt Prize, incarnates the "man of quality" whose dispassion and distance epitomizes the ideal of Vailland's later works.

See: J. Recanati, *Esquisse pour la psychanalyse d'un libertin* (1971); M. Picard, *Libertinage et tragique dans l'œuvre de Roger Vailland* (1972); J.-P. Tusseau, *Roger Vailland: un écrivain au service du peuple* (1976).

G.R.B.

Valente, José Angel (1929–), Spanish poet and critic born in Orense, has resided in Oxford, Geneva, and France since 1955. He is the most intellectual representative of a generation, sometimes called "the second promotion," which grew up in the post-Civil War years and engaged in social protest without relinquishing the ideal of original artistic expression. Valente's first book, *A modo de esperanza* (1955; In a Way of Hope), received the prestigious Adonais Prize. *Punto cero* (1972; Zero Degree) consists of seven books of poetry. He has continued to publish prose and poetry. His best-known collection of essays in literary criticism, *Las palabras de la tribu* (Words of the Tribe), appeared in 1971. Valente's approach to poetry, Spain, and human existence is critical. His intention is to unmask false values and appearances. The voice of doubt that often speaks from his lines relates him to earlier philosophically inclined poets like Antonio MACHADO and Francisco Quevedo. Like his contemporaries, he considers that the main function of poetry is to bear witness, to open channels of communication, and to lead to self-discovery. Pointing to César Vallejo and Luis CERNUDA as the decisive influences on his generation, he implies that commitment to one's fellowman need not preclude intimate lyricism. His verse is succinct and unadorned, and its power derives from its density and capacity for connotation. Its syncopated rhythm and elliptical structure allow for symbolic interpretation. The themes of death, exile, and solitude often recur. Spain is the pivotal point of Valente's meditations, while memory serves as both motif and device. Even poems consisting of seemingly journalistic "reports" have metaphysical implications. The ethical aspect is usually more important than the aesthetic. His last collections veer toward intexuality, their tone being less lyrical and the preoccupations more universal. Distancing has always been an essential procedure for Valente, as it paves the way to irony, objectification, and abstraction, even of himself. It also allows him to create masterful synthetic portraits of men, situations, and a whole country. Valente's art is low-keyed, with suggestive understatements made of few words and dense with ideas. He exploits the phonic and combinatory values of words to full capacity. His poetry offers no external brilliance, but it is not easily forgotten. More than one critic considers him to have the greatest stature of any member of his generation.

See: H. St. Martin, ed., *Roots and Wings: Poetry from Spain, 1900–1976: A Bilingual Anthology* (1976).   B.Ci.

Valera, Juan (1824–1905), Spanish novelist and critic, was born in Cabra, in the province of Córdoba. He spent his early years there and at Doña Mencía, where his mother, the Marquise de la Paniega, owned a large estate. After he completed his law studies, his family secured for young Valera an appointment as attaché to the Duke of Rivas, ambassador at Naples. During his stay there (1847–49), Valera studied Italian and Greek and greatly reinforced his native inclination toward the classical in art and literature. His subsequent diplomatic posts in Lisbon, Rio de Janeiro, Russia, Washington, Brussels, and Vienna, provided him with the opportunity further to cultivate his mind.

Valera's literary work, in 50 volumes, was, he would have us believe, but a parenthesis in his diplomatic career. This view may account for a certain lack of depth in his work as a whole. He began by writing poetry—*Ensayos poéticas* (1844; Poetic Beginnings) and *Poesías* (1858)—and found it difficult at first to write prose. It was not until his diplomatic career was interrupted in 1854 that he decided to try his hand at literary criticism. From then on he wrote innumerable articles for Spanish and later for Spanish American periodicals; they fill many volumes of his *Obras completas* (1905). These articles are delightful causeries that reveal broad learning and a detachment

rare in Spanish critics. In his reviews of contemporary works, however, Valera is too discreet to be direct. In addition to books on Spanish romanticism, Cervantes, and Goethe, he wrote many essays on political, historical, and philosophical themes.

Valera won early acclaim as a critic and a master of Spanish prose, but his audience was as yet restricted. It was not until 1874, when he wrote *Pepita Jiménez* (first Eng. tr., 1886), the novel on which his fame most solidly rests, that he became a popular author. He held consistently, from *De la naturaleza y carácter de la novela* (1860; On the Nature and Character of the Novel) to *Apuntes sobre el nuevo arte de escribir novelas* (1886–87; Notes on the New Art of Writing Novels), that a novel should be entertaining rather than instructive and that its only end as a form of art is to delight with the creation of beautiful form. His concept of "art for art's sake" was not very meaningful, however, as for him this was synonymous with avoiding contemporary problems and anything considered distasteful or morally suspect while entertaining and consoling the reader. He mistrusted progress and berated the sociological and scientific aims of the naturalistic novelists, finding their deterministic philosophy intolerable. In *Pepita Jiménez,* the hero, who is about to take holy orders, suddenly discovers his love for the attractive young widow, Pepita. Most of the novel is a subtle analysis of his inner conflict, which ends in his choosing marriage with Pepita over the religious life. The novel makes it clear that in any case he had only romantic notions about the latter. Valera's other novels, *El comendador Mendoza* (1877; Eng. tr., *Commander Mendoza,* 1893), *Doña Luz* (1879; Eng. tr., 1891), and the later works he dictated after he went blind, *Juanita la larga* (1895), *Genio y figura* (1897; Constancy), and *Morsamor* (1899), are all simple, loosely woven, idealized tales, in which the action takes place in the mind or conscience of the main characters.

In all of his work Valera struck a note—unusual in Spain—of tolerance, moderation, and harmony. Even in politics, as a member of the Cortes and later as senator for life, he always took a position midway between both extremes. He never joined a political party, as he was equally opposed to the neo-Catholic reactionaries and to the positivist progressives. Although he was not a great or original thinker, Valera was a writer of charm and stylistic elegance.

See: J. F. Montesinos, *Valera o la ficción libre* (1957); C. DeCoster, *Juan Valera* (1974).   E.F.H. rev. H.L.B.

Valeri, Diego (1887–1976), Italian poet, literary critic, essayist, and translator, was born in Pieve di Sacco, near Padua. He taught Italian, Latin, and French in schools and universities, but because of his opposition to the Fascist regime, he retired from teaching during World War II. From 1943 to 1945 he lived in exile in Switzerland; this experience is the subject of *Taccuino svizzero* (1946; Swiss Notebook). After his return to Italy, Valeri held the chair of modern French literature at the University of Padua until his retirement.

For over 40 years, Valeri lived in Venice, a city that he celebrated in verse and prose. In *Fantasie veneziane* (1934; Venetian Fantasies) and *Guida sentimentale di Venezia* (1942; Eng. tr., *A Sentimental Guide to Venice,* 1956), he excelled in capturing the genius loci through poetic and painterly evocations of his adopted city. The 1953 edition of *Fantasie veneziane* also includes *Città materna* (1944; Maternal City), about Padua, and *I Colli Euganei* (1932; The Euganean Hills).

Valeri's early volumes of verse, beginning with *Le gaie tristezze* (1913; The Gay Sadnesses), reflect the influence

of Giovanni PASCOLI and the *crepuscolari* (*see* ITALIAN
LITERATURE). *Poesie* (1962; Poems) includes almost all
his lyric poems written from 1910 to 1960. Together they
show that he achieved a personal tone of gentle but unmistakable irony and understatement to express the
themes of love, melancholy, and time. His style is natural,
simple, and free, and his pictorial and sensual images are
especially felicitous. Valeri also tried his hand at French
verse in the volume *Jeux de mots* (1956; Word Games).

Valeri was also a skillful, sensitive translator. His verse
translations include La Fontaine, *Quaranta favole* (1925;
40 Fables); Gabriella Mistral, *Mirella* (1930, 1944);
Goethe, *Cinquanta poesie* (1954; 50 Poems); and *Lirici
tedeschi* (1959; German Lyric Poets) and *Lirici francesi*
(1960; French Lyric Poets). Those in prose include Stendhal's *Il rosso e il nero* (1936; The Red and the Black)
and Gustave Flaubert's *La Signora Bovary* (1936, 1951;
Madame Bovary). In *Tempo e poesia* (1956; Time and
Poetry), which contains an essay on the translation of
verse, the poet and critic merge in a series of light yet
profound meditations on poetry.

As a literary critic, Valeri made a significant contribution to Franco-Italian studies. His writing is perceptive
and original and has a style of exceptional clarity and
grace. His critical works include *Montaigne* (1925), *Il
simbolismo francese de Nerval a De Régnier* (1954;
French Symbolism from Nerval to De Régnier), *Da Racine a Picasso: nuovi studi francesi* (1956; From Racine
to Picasso: New French Studies), and *Littérature
française* (rev. ed., 1949; French Literature). *Conversazioni italiane* (1968; Italian Conversations) is a collection
of articles and lectures on Italian literature reprinted by
his students and colleagues in honor of his 80th birthday.

See: V. Zambon, *La poesia di Diego Valeri* (1968); R.
Ribière, *Diego Valeri: essai* (1971).   S.Pa.

Valéry, Paul (1871–1945), French poet and essayist, was
born in Sète, where his father, a customs inspector from
Corsica, had married one of the daughters of the Genoese
Italian consul. Valéry always remained conscious of his
Mediterranean origins. He began his studies with the Do-
minicans but soon transferred to the municipal *collège;*
from there he went on to the lycée of Montpellier, the
city to which his father had meanwhile retired, and finished his studies in law in the same city, obtaining his
licence in 1892. Valéry had interrupted his education for
one year to do voluntary service in the infantry. Although
he had wanted to become a candidate for the Naval
School, he was prevented from doing so by his weakness
in mathematics, a subject that never ceased to fascinate
him and for which he dreamed of creating an equivalent
in reflective thought. Even poetry, in which he began to
find enjoyment after his 13th year, was, in his opinion,
only a particular application of those powers of the mind
whose secrets he wanted to formulate and utilize. Indeed,
although he was a mediocre student, Valéry was endowed
with a hypercritical mind and with an ambition as disinterested as it was superhuman. Skeptical of all opinions,
even his own, he was haunted by an ideal of methodical
rigor. One can well imagine the extraordinary attraction
he had for those who knew him near his 20th year. One
of them, Pierre LOUŸS, introduced him to André GIDE
who, by virtue of their very differences, was to become
Valéry's best friend. Louÿs also put him in touch with
the prestigious Stéphane MALLARMÉ, for whom Valéry
had a total devotion and an admiration almost as great as
for his true inspiration, Edgar Allan Poe.

Seeking employment, Valéry took up residence in
Paris. Here he became acquainted with the symbolist
poets, the impressionist painters, and other members of

the avant-garde. He met Joris-Karl HUYSMANS, who persuaded him to become a clerk at the Ministry of War,
where he remained for three years, and Edgar Degas,
who called him "Monsieur Angel." Degas refused the
dedication of Valéry's *La Soirée avec Monsieur Teste*
(1896; Eng. trs., *An Evening with Mr. Teste, 1925, Monsieur Teste,* 1947). Published in *Le Centaure,* this brief
portrait of a genius hidden in the secrecy of impeccable
speculation sprang from the plan to write the *Mémoires
du chevalier Dupin,* inspired by Poe. This work was reprinted by Paul FORT, in his periodical *Vers et prose,*
affording Valéry's small public an idea of his fundamental
exigencies, for which he had abandoned all plans to make
a name for himself in literature, even in poetry. As a poet,
he had already demonstrated his talent by publishing in
several little reviews, notably in *La Conque,* directed by
his friend Louÿs. Rarely did he come out of his silence
and then only when the temptation to express himself
was spurred on by others. For example, it was Léon
DAUDET who sought to procure for the *Nouvelle Revue
française* Valéry's *Introduction à la méthode de Léonard
de Vinci* (pub. separately 1919; Eng. tr., *Introduction to
the Method of Leonardo da Vinci,* 1929), in which he
sketched not just a portrait, but an ideal of rigor and
universality. Similar preoccupations are manifested in
other works of Valéry including *Le Paradoxe sur
l'architecte* (1891; The Paradox concerning the Architect), *La Conquête allemande* (The German Conquest),
and three articles on method in the *Mercure de France*
(1897–99). After 1900, Valéry published little. He married
a niece of Berthe Morisot and entered the service of
Edouard Lebey, the administrator of the Agence Havas
(a news agency) who was afflicted with paralysis agitans.
Although he now had much more leisure time, he devoted
it to his wife and three children and to the pursuit of his
thought. Meanwhile, two famous anthologies kept Valéry
in the limelight as a poet.

In 1892, in Genoa, during a stormy night that has been
compared to René Descartes's famous night of crisis,
Valéry underwent the experience that transformed him.
Torn between literary ambition and Platonic love for a
Catalonian girl he had only glimpsed at Montpellier,
young Valéry decided to oppose with all his strength
whatever appeared to interfere with his freedom of mind.
At that moment, he savagely demanded that independence that was to make him a lifelong adversary of sentiment. Later, Valéry recognized that besides the mind,
there was this indestructible, "deuced heart." This antagonism between mind and heart was to illuminate both
his new conception of poetry and his doctrinal positions.
Shortly after that night in Genoa, he began to write down
his reflections. The first notebook now extant dates from
1894, the 201st and last from 1945 (they were published
posthumously in several editions and have now become
the subject of extensive study).

One wonders whether Valéry would have ever left his
retreat but for World War I, which led him, with the
encouragement of Gide and the publisher Gallimard, to
bring together in one volume the production of his youth,
to polish up his published poems, and to attempt, in a
final piece of about 40 lines, a kind of adieu to poetry. As
he began this task, an intense patriotism inspired him to
undertake an homage to the French language that was to
become the 512 lines of *La Jeune Parque* (1917; The
Young Parca). Although hardly accessible (in both meanings of the word), this poem immediately made its author
famous. This evocation, in a Mediterranean setting, of
one night in the life of a conscience was the fruit of
intensive labor. *La Jeune Parque* echoed both Mallarmé
and Racine. From its style were born the few, fortunate

pieces that were to constitute the collection *Charmes* (1922). Everything in this volume was admirable, from the short pieces to the odes in the perfectionist tradition: "Aurore," "Palme," "La Pythie," "Ebauche d'un serpent" (Outline of a Serpent), and *Le Cimetière marin* (1920; Eng. tr., *The Graveyard by the Sea*, 1932), the most often quoted of his poems. Valéry added nothing important except some complements to his *Fragments d'un Narcisse*, to the general collection of his *Poésies* (1924), which included the *Album de vers anciens* (Album of Old Verse), published by Adrienne Monnier four years earlier.

Lebey's death in 1922 was capital in the destiny of the writer. Being without employment, Valéry was forced to live by his pen and his voice, with little time for "pure" poetry. He was helped in making a living by the sudden fame that led him quickly to the Académie Française (1925). Solicited on all sides, he responded to requests for lectures, prefaces to ancient and modern works, contributions to special numbers of periodicals, interviews, replies to numerous opinion polls; everyone took advantage of his complaisance. Although a profound skeptic, he seemed to have received a mandate from the French to represent them, whether to help celebrate Goethe or Voltaire at the Sorbonne, to participate in an international congress on philosophy or aesthetics, to inaugurate a monument to Emile VERHAEREN, to put a tablet on the house of Henri BRÉMOND, to preside over a surgical congress, or to discuss cinema before the alumni of the Ecole des Sciences Politiques. It was Valéry's policy to accept. He regarded his life as having been delivered over to chance and other people; to Valéry's great dismay, Gide considered it a learned game of chess.

Valéry was laden with honors; he became *chevalier* of the Legion of Honor in 1923 and ran through all the ranks up to *grand officer* in 1939, accumulated foreign decorations, received honorary doctorates, was appointed to presidencies of official commissions (Intellectual Cooperation of the League of Nations, International Exposition of Paris in 1937), and was a member of the council of the National Museums. Yet he derived financial profit from only two appointments, that of administrator of the Centre Universitaire Méditerranéen of Nice (1933) and that of professor of poetry at the Collège de France (1937), where he made his debut at retirement age. If one considers these appointments, an enforced social life, morning hours devoted to his *Cahiers*, an enormous correspondence, and the visits of people asking favors, one wonders how Valéry could have met the demands of a productivity so plentiful, even if it was sometimes permissible to dig into the reserve of the aforementioned *Cahiers*. Yet over a quarter of a century, he managed to produce the five volumes of *Variétés* (1924–44; Eng. tr., *Variety*, 1927, 1938), a collection of literary, philosophical, quasi-political, and aesthetic studies; his *Regards sur le monde actuel* (1931, 1945; Eng. tr., *Reflections on the World Today*, 1948); *Pièces sur l'art* (1934; Pieces on Art); and the delightful recollections of *Degas danse dessin* (1935; Eng. tr., *Degas Dance Drawing*, 1948). Then there were also the more confidential collections in which Valéry revealed himself to be a moralist (although he refused the appellation) in the line of La Rochefoucauld and La Bruyère, but with a strange admixture of modernist traditionalism; these works include the two volumes of *Tel Quel* (1941–43), the half-poetic, half-speculative volume entitled *Mélange* (1941), the paradoxical and provoking *Mauvaises Pensées et autres* (1942; Evil Thoughts and Others), and *Propos me concernant* (1944; Words Concerning Me).

Valéry had already revealed himself to be as great a prose writer as he was a poet in that mixture of analysis and poetry entitled *Eupalinos et l'architecte* (1921) and in *L'Ame et la danse* (1923; Eng. tr., *Dance and the Soul*, 1951), in which he renewed the Socratic dialogue and the dialogue of the dead. In *L'Idée fixe* (1932; Eng. tr., 1965), he modernized the dialogue genre with a Voltairean wit in the nervous exchange of ideas between an obliging doctor and a subtle, complex-ridden intellectual. The *Dialogue de l'arbre* (1933; Dialogue of the Tree), in which blank verse slips insidiously into his prose, reminds one of an eclogue, and indeed at that time Valéry was working on his translation of Vergil's *Bucolics* (1953). With his gift for dialogue, Valéry was tempted by the theater. But, as with everything else, he conceived of it in his own fashion, as a solemn ceremony. Hence the coldness of his "mélodrames" *Amphion* and *Sémiramis*, with music by Arthur Honegger, played at the Paris Opera in 1931 and 1934. He also wrote the libretto for Germaine Taillefer's *Cantate du Narcisse* (1939). His real success is the fragments of *Mon Faust* (1941; My Faust), devoted to the relationship of a traditional scholar with a devil and a seductive secretary full of tenderness (Lust) and this scholar's metaphysical encounter with a rebel fallen into savagery (Le Solitaire). The inventor of Monsieur Teste, a fictional character definitely assured of an afterlife, found amusement in providing his creation with a companion (*Lettre de Madame Emilie Teste*). In a similar vein, it has been possible to extract from the *Cahiers* the *Histoires brisées* (Broken Stories), in which some curious creatures are sketched.

Since the death of Valéry, his *Inédits* (Unpublished Works) have appeared, but it is his *Cahiers* that have particularly aroused curiosity. The Centre National de la Recherche Scientifique published a facsimile reprint of them in 29 volumes (1957–61), almost complete except for some passages temporarily omitted and one notebook that was overlooked. An extensive compilation of selections from the *Cahiers* in two large volumes, the first published in 1973, is presented under rubrics planned by Valéry himself; some are obvious (Language, Philosophy, Memory, Time, Attention), but others bear more distinctly his personal imprint (Ego; Ego scriptor; Somnia; Eros; Système; CEM=Corps, Esprit, Monde). Valéry's *Collected Works* (1956–) have been edited by Jackson Matthews.

See: G. Cohen, *Essai d'explication du Cimetière marin* (1933, 1958); E. Noulet, *Paul Valéry: études* (1938, 1951); J. Hytier, *The Poetics of Paul Valéry* (1966); C. Crow, *Paul Valéry: Consciousness and Nature* (1972); H. Laurenti, *Paul Valéry et le théâtre* (1973); J. R. Lawler, *The Poet as Analyst: Essays on Paul Valéry* (1974).   J.Hy.

Valle-Inclán, Ramón María del (1866–1936), Spanish novelist, playwright and poet, was born in Villanueva de Arosa in the province of Pontevedra, Galicia. He figures prominently among the writers of the Generation of 1898 who appeared on the national scene at the turn of the century to renovate Spain's consciousness of itself and to revitalize its literature with radical innovations in language, style, and philosophy. Valle-Inclán, however, rejected his contemporaries' propensity for critical introspection and instead followed the aesthetic orientation of Spanish-American modernism in which the dominant force was his close friend, the Nicaraguan poet Rubén Darío. Until relatively late in his career, Valle-Inclán considered literature a matter of artistic creation and the writer an artist and verbal craftsman rather than a philosopher or idealogue. He exploited the themes for aesthetic objectives, stripping them of their traditional meanings and converting them into vehicles for evocative impressions. Beneath this attitude of apparent evasion ran a vein of scorn and malicious irony that manifested itself in the deliberate subversion of the conventional values of the bourgeois society that for him incarnated the dismal Spanish present. The exuberant stylizations of his works had their counterpart in the figure of the man himself. Through his physical appearance he affected a persona of bizarre extravagance: flowing beard, long hair, purple cape, and thick-rimmed glasses. In combination with his temperamental nature and constant public disquisitions on any and all subjects, these affectations made him one of the most colorful figures on the literary scene. He became a legend in his own time, largely because of his calculated sense of theatricality.

Like most of the writers of his generation, Valle-Inclán cultivated a variety of genres with remarkable virtuosity. Although he began and ended his career as a writer of fiction, with major achievements as a novelist, the theater was his primary concern for the two decades between 1905 and 1926. In 1895 he published his first book, a collection of six short stories called *Femeninas* and marked by fin-de-siècle decadence (*see* SPANISH LITERATURE). Throughout the 1890s he wrote stories and articles, many of them destined to be reworked and republished or incorporated as segments into subsequent novels. In the period from 1902 to 1905 he produced his first masterworks as a prose writer. His native Galicia served him as a primary source of material. In numerous stories he sought out and expressed in symbolist fashion the poetic essence of that archaic province as manifested in its language and legends, its superstitions and echoes of a feudal past. A number of these stories were published in 1903 with the title *Jardín umbrío* (Shadowy Garden). In 1904 he published the short novel *Flor de santidad* (Flower of Sanctity), in which an ingenuous peasant girl who has been seduced by an unknown beggar believes herself impregnated by the Holy Spirit. The Marquis de Bradomín, the most famous of Valle-Inclán's characters and the one with whom he is most often identified, also originates from Galicia. Bradomín is the narrator of his own fictional memoirs, which take the form of four "sonatas," each corresponding to one of the seasons of the year. This tetralogy (1902–05; Eng. tr., *The Pleasant Memoirs of the Marquis de Bradomín*, 1924) definitively established Valle-Inclán as a master of evocative modernist prose, cynical irony, and antibourgeois iconoclasm. Bradomín is a decadent Don Juan whose traits run counter to the traditional image of the famous lover (he is "homely, Catholic, and sentimental") but who proceeds to remythify the legend by creating his own, in which a Spanish aristocrat displays the refined sensibility of an authentic decadent. Galicia is fundamental in still other works of this decade. The essence of the old province is the substance of his first volume of poetry, *Aromas de leyenda* (1907; The Aroma of Legends), and the background of his first major dramatic works, *Águila de blasón* (1907; Eagle of Heraldry) and *Romance de lobos* (1907; Ballad of the Wolves), which together form two parts of the epic trilogy about the Montenegro family, called the "Comedias bárbaras." The last novels of the period, the trilogy of "La guerra carlista" (1908–09; The Carlist Wars), are also rooted in Galicia, and Bradomín and the Montenegros reappear in them as characters. The persistent reappearance of characters in Valle-Inclán's Galician works gives the whole the aspect of a vast theatrical panorama.

Valle-Inclán's theater is a multifaceted phenomenon of some 23 works in a wide variety of genres, styles, and techniques that illustrate the playwright's unusual powers of invention. He conceives of theater as spectacle, in which the plasticity of the human figure and scenic diversity are indispensable factors. In terms of his inventiveness, notably in his early use of advanced techniques of cinematography, which posed serious obstacles for the resources of the orthodox stage, Valle-Inclán is an avant-garde unto himself. To communicate this complex visuality, he resorts to extensive stage directions, which at times are so meticulously composed as to give the impression, however erroneous, that a novelist is at work rather than a playwright. The problem of generic interpretation disappeared during the period of transition he entered just before World War I. Three of the five plays of this period are in verse, and two of these are farces in which satire, parody, and humor are added to irony as basic elements of his style: *La cabeza del dragón* (1910; Eng. tr., *The Dragon's Head,* 1918) and *La marquesa Rosalinda* (1912). In these plays the stylizations of the human figure are systematically slanted toward physical distortion, and Spanish institutions enter Valle-Inclán's repertory as explicit objects of ridicule. Both of these elements presage a new attitude of social commitment as well as a new aesthetic of critical deformation. The grotesque verses of *La pipa de Kif* (1919; The Hashish Pipe) are a further manifestation of change. This new orientation became definitive with the publication of four major plays in 1920: two satirical farces, a Galician tragicomedy entitled *Divinas palabras* (Eng. tr., *Divine Words,* 1968), and *Luces de Bohemia* (Eng. tr., *Bohemian Lights,* 1976), which is the first of a new genre baptized and expounded in this play by Valle-Inclán as the *esperpento.* Theoretically, the *esperpento* is based on the opinion that Spain is a grotesque deformation of European civilization, and that the tragic sense of such an anomaly can be communicated only by an aesthetic in which classic norms and heroes are systematically subjected to geometric distortions like those of a concave mirror. The result is a devastating attack on the country's institutions and contemporary history. Like Goya, Valle-Inclán reduces his victims to absurdity or to sordid grotesqueness. Three *esperpentos* follow *Luces de Bohemia,* notably *Los cuernos de don Friolera* (1921; The Cuckolding of Don Friolera). The aesthetic of *esperpentismo* conditions every play Valle-Inclán wrote in the 1920s, whatever its subject matter, and its influence is no less evident in the novels he began to write in the middle of that decade. *Tirano Banderas* (1926; Eng. tr., *The Tyrant,* 1929) is an awesome, grotesque depiction of an archetypal Spanish-American dictator beset by revolution in an imaginary American republic very suggestive of Mexico, a country Valle-Inclán knew firsthand. Similarly "esperpentized" are the historical novels *La corte de los milagros* (1927; The Court of Miracles) and *Viva mi dueño* (1928; Long Live My Master), the first of an unfinished cycle of masterful satires on the 19th-century reign of Isabel II entitled "El ruedo ibérico" (The Iberian Bullring). Valle-Inclán's impact on Hispanic letters still persists. *Tirano Banderas* is the prototype of subsequent depictions of the American dictator by Spanish-American novelists, and avant-garde playwrights in Spain today continue to pay him homage.

See: M. Fernández Almagro, *Vida y literatura de Valle-Inclán* (1966); Anthony Zahareas, ed., *Ramón del Valle-Inclán: An Appraisal of His Life and Works* (1968); S. M. Greenfield, *Valle-Inclán: anatomía de un teatro problemático* (1972). S.M.G.

Valverde, José María (1926–), Spanish poet and critic, was born in Valencia de Alcántara in the province of Cáceres. He began his literary career as a member of the group known as "Juventud Creadora." Although his first book, *Hombre de Dios* (1945; Man of God), followed the trend of the religious poetry abundantly written in Spain immediately after the Civil War (1936–39), it deserves special attention because of its aesthetic distinctiveness. As a critic and theorist of poetry, Valverde has excellent technical control over his poetic voice, which more often than not seems to be dominated by intellectual rationality and stylistic exactness rather than by lyrical impulses. *La espera* (1949; The Waiting), a book dealing with God and marital love, two well-accepted poetic themes during that period, received the José Primo de Rivera Poetry Prize. Later he changed his point of view from an individualistic one to a wider consideration of men in the socially unjust contemporary world. *Versos del domingo* (1954; Sunday Poems), for example, is clearly influenced by his critical studies of César Vallejo's poetry of human suffering and despair. This was in keeping with the main evolution of post-Civil War Spanish poetry toward an interest in man in society. Valverde's first approach to the subject of everyday life appears in *Voces y acompañamientos para San Mateo* (1959) Voices and Accompaniments for St. Matthew) and *La conquista de este mundo* (1960; The Conquest of This World). In 1972 he published *Enseñanzas de la edad* (Teachings of the Age), a coherent anthology that gives a definite structure to the poet's ideas about man's place in the world and his relationship with God.

Valverde has taught literature and aesthetics in Spain, Italy, the United States, and Canada. After a self-imposed exile of a little more than a decade, he is now again teaching at the University of Barcelona.

See: F. Lucio, "José María Valverde: una palabra poética actual," *Insula* 306 (1972): 15.   S.D.-T.

Vančura, Vladislav (1891–1942), Czech novelist, was the leading prose writer of Czech expressionism. He was born in Háj near Opava (then in Austrian Silesia). He served in the medical corps of the Austrian army during World War I, and after the war became a practicing physician. On June 1, 1942, he was executed by the Nazis, one victim of the "reprisal" for the assassination of the German *Reichsprotektor*, Reinhard Heydrich.

Vančura's writings are extremely varied both in form and subject matter. His first successful novel, *Pekař Jan Marhoul* (1924; The Baker John Marhoul), glorifies the "poor in spirit" as well as the poor in earthly goods, in a style influenced by Fyodor DOSTOYEVSKY. *Pole orná a válečná* (1925; Fields and Battlefields) is an antiwar novel of unsurpassed bitterness and horror. The following, much weaker work, *Poslední soud* (1929; The Last Judgment), returns to the theme of *Pekař Jan Marhoul*. It depicts a feeble-minded Ruthenian peasant transplanted to the puzzling and cruel urban civilization of Prague. *Markéta Lazarová* (1931) represents a complete change of style and subject matter—the social pathos and the glorification of the "idiot" have disappeared. *Markéta* is an exciting yarn about robbers and knights, rapes and elopements. Only the display of language and metaphor suggests that the author has ambitions beyond those of an adventure writer. In addition, the celebration of brute force and lust seems to represent a definite break with the past. *Útěk do Budína* (1932; The Flight to Budapest) is, however, a fairly traditional psychological novel about maritial difficulties, which attempts to expose the differences between the Czech and Slovak character in the attitudes of the Czech hero and the Slovak heroine. *Konec starých časů* (1934; Eng. tr., *The End of the Old Times*, 1965) is again completely different: it is a whimsical revival of the Münchhausen theme, with a grotesque setting and veritable fireworks of language and technique. Metaphors, slang, and archaic Czech are used with surprising effectiveness, and the author deliberately breaks any il-

lusion of reality by constant interference with and manipulation of his materials. In these books, Vančura shows himself to be a virtuoso of story-telling and linguistic inventiveness, but he seems to have given up any attempt at a unified outlook on life or even art. Nevertheless, the novel *Tři řeky* (1936; Three Rivers), although badly composed, is a return to the early themes. It attempts to depict the spiritual growth of its hero through World War I and the Russian Revolution (1917). An unfinished trilogy, *Koně a vůz* (Horses and a Carriage) is represented only by the first novel, *Rodina Horvatova* (1938; The Horvat Family). The planned trilogy would have traced the fortunes of a landowning family, thus illustrating the development of Czech society in village and city from the middle of the 19th century onwards.

It is difficult to find any unity in Vančura's artistic development: the interest of his work derives from the sheer virtuosity with which he managed the language and technique of storytelling. His most successful work is possibly the short-story collection *Luk královny Dorotky* (1932, The Bow of Queen Dorothy), for there he escaped his evident difficulties with large-scale composition and elaborate characterization. The onset of World War II induced Vančura to begin the unfinished *Obrazy z dějin národa českého* (1939–40; Scenes from the History of the Czech Nation), a series of ornate, nostalgic sketches that sought to give support to the national spirit in a difficult time. The theme of hatred for war and social oppression runs through all Vančura's work. He paid for his convictions with his life.

See: F. Götz in *Básnický dnešek* (1931); A. Vyskočil in *Básnikovo slovo* (1930), pp. 149–76; M. Kundera, *Uměni románu* (1960); L. Doležel, "Karel Čapek and Vladislav Vančura," in *Narrative Modes in Czech Literature* (1973), pp. 91–111.   R.W.

Vandeloo, Jos (1925–), Belgian (Flemish) prose writer, was born in Zonhoven. He treats the modern themes of anguish, solitude, alienation, and threatening absurdity, as in the short story "De muur" (1958; The Wall). In this story, the main character's horizon is limited to an office from where he sees nothing but a blank wall. In *Het Gevaar* (1960; The Danger), three men who are given deadly x-ray treatments are excluded from the world of healthy people. They try to escape and hope to be accepted, but their efforts are doomed to fail. Vandeloo's other works include *De croton* (1962; The Croton), *Het huis der onbekenden* (1963; The House of the Unknown Ones), and *De coladrinkers* (1963; The Coladrinkers).
                                                                                     P. van A.

Van Lerberghe, Charles: *see* LERBERGHE, CHARLES VAN.

Varnalis, Kostas (1883–1974), Greek poet, prose satirist, and critic, was born in Pyrgos, Bulgaria. He is Greece's greatest modern satirist and among the country's finest lyric poets. Varnalis's early work gives no indication of his future development as the champion of socialist ideas in modern Greek literature. In 1919, he went to Paris to study at the Sorbonne. Under the influence of the Russian Revolution (1917) and the antiwar mood that dominated Europe at the time, he turned suddenly and decisively to Marxism. In 1925 he was dismissed from a teaching post because of his left-wing views, and thereafter he earned his living as a journalist and translator. Varnalis was awarded the Lenin Peace Prize in 1958.

Varnalis began by writing romantic, patriotic poetry in the puristic language, but he turned to love poetry in the demotic mode (*see* GREEK LITERATURE) for his first collection, *Kerithres* (1905; Honeycombs). In Paris he wrote *To fos pou kaiei* (1922; The Light That Burns), containing poems and a play, and *Sklavoi poliorkimenoi* (1927; Slaves Besieged), a volume of poetry. *To fos pou kaiei* describes man's struggle for social justice from primitive times to the present, using Prometheus, Christ, and a modern proletarian leader as its symbols. *Sklavoi poliorkimenoi*—whose title is an inversion of *Free Besieged* (ca. 1830-44), a poem by Dionysios Solomos—attacks idealism for abetting man's intellectual enslavement, strips war of its heroic content, and calls upon the common people to break the bonds of superstition and to revolt. In the prose work *I alithini apologia tou Sokrati* (1931; Eng. tr., *The True Apology of Socrates,* 1955), Varnalis uses Socrates' trial in the slave-owning democracy of ancient Anthens to satirize contemporary bourgeois society, making Socrates renounce idealism and confess the damage his teaching has caused. In *Solomos horis metaphysiki* (1925; Solomos without Metaphysics), Varnalis introduced the sociohistorical method into Greek literary criticism. Among his other works the most important are: *To imerologio tis Penelopes* (1946; The Diary of Penelope), a prose satire on the morality of class society; *Eleftheros kosmos* (1965; Free World), a volume of poems satirizing the hypocrisy of the Western world's self-styled freedom; *Attalos o tritos* (1972; Attalos the Third), a historical drama about a slave revolt in ancient times, with obvious implications for the present; and *Orgi Laou* (1975; Wrath of the People), a collection of enraged, bitter, satirical poems written during the dictatorship of 1967-74.

Varnalis's work is characterized by a unique blend of merciless satire and passionate lyricism, acuteness of perception and fierce anger. He succeeds in expressing contemporary ideas by means of ancient symbols and traditional forms. Like Solomos and Kostis PALAMAS, Varnalis expressed his age and revealed new horizons, not in the sphere of aesthetics, as did George SEFERIS, but in the search for ideas. Three volumes of *Ta apanta tou Varnali* (Complete Works of Varnalis) have been published (1956-71).

See: K. Friar, ed., *Modern Greek Poetry* (1973).

C.A.

Vas, István (1910-), Hungarian poet and translator, was born in Budapest into a middle-class Jewish family. As a young man he studied business in Vienna. After a short period of youthful radicalism and association with Lajos KASSÁK's review *Munka,* Vas arrived at a critical, but more rational and dispassionate interpretation of social reality. This was, to some extent, connected with his failed revolutionary hopes and with the rise of Hitlerism. During the 1930s, Vas published frequently in *Nyugat* and was regarded as a representative poet of the third *Nyugat* generation (*see* HUNGARIAN LITERATURE).

Although thoroughly urban in his roots, Vas nevertheless emerged as a bucolic poet. He greatly admired Horace and his classicist leanings were recognizable in his first book of poetry, *Őszi rombolás* (1932; Destruction in Autumn), despite its debts to the best *Nyugat* poets. A predominantly elegiac tone and the recurrence of such age-old themes as nature or love make Vas's pre-World War II poetry fairly traditional. But in 1944, when the Germans occupied Hungary, the tone of Vas's poetry changed and his political inertia suddenly disappeared. He reacted to the event in sharply focused, ironical poems. Vas carried this new political commitment over into the postwar years, albeit in a more philosophical form. Vas's *Római pillanat* (1948; Moment in Rome) reflected both his pessimism about the future and his allegiance to both the European humanism and revolutionary

Marxism; "I am looking back at the old and the new," he wrote, "And I am both of them."

Between 1949 and 1953, Vas devoted himself to the translation of foreign classics, among them the English metaphysical poets. In his subsequent work, there was a noticeable shift from reflexive to "responsive" poetry in which the consideration of a situation taken from everyday life is brought to a "philosophical" or axiomatic conclusion. In the more liberal atmosphere of "the thaw," his book of poetry *A teremtett világ* (1956; The Creation) was well received and afforded proof of Vas's considerable poetic gifts. His most accomplished poems since 1956 grapple with the problems of old age and with the basic questions of life, death and loyalty, in a language that is clear and precise, yet rich in metaphor. His autobiography, *Nehéz szerelem* (2 vols., 1964, 1967; A Difficult Love), has won much critical acclaim in recent years. This unpretentious, intelligent work describes the young Vas's emotional and creative development and paints a vivid picture of literary Budapest in the 1920s and 1930s. His poems have been translated into English by W. J. Smith, Donald Davie, Edwin Morgan, and Clive Wilmer, among others.

See: G. Halász, "A század gyermekei," *Nyugat* 32 (1939): 108-12; E. Vajda, "A teremtett világ," *Dunántúl* 5 (1956): 153-57; Gy. Rónay, "Vas István lírája," *ÚÍ* 3 (1963): 886-90; G. Gömöri, "István Vas at Sixty," *BA* 45 (1971): 46-49.   G.G.

Vasconcelos, Mário Cesariny de (1923-), Portuguese poet, was born in Lisbon, where he studied fine arts for a time. In 1947 he was one of the founders of the first group in Portugal to develop an outspoken and aggressive practice of surrealism. Although the ideas and devices of this movement had been known, no formal group had ever gathered in Portugal before the revival that European surrealism experienced by the end of World War II. Later on, when the ephemeral group broke apart, Vasconcelos, more than anybody else, became the embodiment of orthodox surrealism, something of a Portuguese André BRETON. His poetry, which kept undertones of the social realism that had attracted him in his younger years, is intensely and sarcastically pitted against everything and even against itself, as if he were a kind of Álvaro de Campos (*see* Fernando PESSOA), who had gone through a real experience of Portuguese life and applied to it the corrosive acid of surrealist rebellion. Although always tending toward a kind of self-destruction, this poetry culminates, in its best moments, in admirable explosions of desperately erotic lyricism. Always divided between a repressed tenderness and a ferocious taste for the mere pun, that powerful poetry has been highly influential in the Portuguese literature of recent years because of its vigor and suggestiveness. *Poesia (1944-55)* collects the best of Vasconcelos's earlier and more influential poems. Of late the poet has become very successful as a painter. His polemical and highly personal account of the chronological evolution of Portuguese surrealism appeared in French translation in the review *Phases* (December 1973), pp. 58-67, summarizing his *Intervenção surrealista* (1966; The Surrealist Intervention).   J. de S.

Vauthier, Jean (1910-), French playwright, was born in Liège, Belgium, the son of a bridge engineer whose employment took the family to Russia, Portugal, and throughout France and Belgium. In 1920 the family settled in Bordeaux, Madame Vauthier's native city. Following study at the lycée, Jean soon began to write poetic essays, paint, and develop a love for the theater. In 1933, he enrolled at the Ecole des Beaux-Arts; five years later, he set out to earn his living as a journalist and illustrator. He devoted his spare time to painting and writing, and at night he worked at various jobs in the theater.

In 1951, Vauthier's play *L'Impromptu d'Arras* was produced by André Reybaz. In 1952, his *Capitaine Bada* was awarded the Ibsen Prize. Gérard Philippe directed and acted in *La Nouvelle Mandragore* (1953; The New Mandrake) and Jean-Louis BARRAULT appeared in *Le Personnage combattant* (1956; The Character against Himself). Vauthier's adaptation of Shakespeare's *Romeo and Juliet* was performed at the Festival of Blois, and his *Les Prodiges* (1957; The Prodigies) was staged at the Staatstheater in Kassel, Germany. His other works include the film scenario *Les Abysses* (1961) and such plays as *Le Rêveur* (1961; The Dreamer), *Le Sang* (1970; Blood), an adaptation of Christopher Marlowe's *The Massacre of Paris* (1972), and *Ton Nom dans le feu des nues* (1976; Your Name in the Fire of the Clouds).

Vauthier is primarily a poet who sees the theater as a vehicle for self-expression. His dark plays present tortured conflicts and extreme situations. Utilizing brilliant imagery with symbolic overtones and intricate rhythmic effects, Vauthier achieves compactness, momentum, and depth. His work has been influenced by earlier innovators, particularly Antonin ARTAUD. Like his predecessor, Vauthier assaults his audiences, trumpeting harsh animal sounds as well as screams, whines, laughter, and brutally exciting explosions. His frequently puppetlike characters, although wooden in their movements, gesticulate wildly; their violence and sadomasochism are far-reaching. As Artaud had suggested, Vauthier uses the stage as a vehicle for a total emotive experience. It is his intention to break down social man's customs and habits as well as the formal, traditional divisions separating actor and audience.

See: R. Abirached, *Jean Vauthier* (1973).   B.K.

Vaz de Soto, José María (1938-), Spanish novelist was born in Paymogo, in the province of Huelva. His first novel, *El infierno y la brisa* (1971; Hell and the Breeze), describes with expressive technique the repression in a Jesuit boarding school in the 1950s. Since then, with his *Diálogos del anochecer* (1972; Dialogues at Dusk) and *Fabián* (1977), the two published parts of his tetralogy *Diálogos de la vida y de la muerte* (Dialogues of Life and Death), which will be completed with *Sabas* and *Diálogos de la alta noche* (Late Night Dialogues), Vaz de Soto has developed into one of the most important talents in the Spanish novel. Countering the sterile experimentalism of other young novelists, he believes, in the words of one of his characters, that "the essence of the novel is still . . . narration." He juxtaposes subtle intellectual digressions with the narration through use of the "dramatic mode," that is, action conveyed entirely through dialogue. For example, during the brief encounter that will end in death, the two protagonists of the tetralogy, Sabas and Fabián, recall their respective childhoods and their shared university experience, discuss the history and the sociopolitical situation of their country, ponder point of view and other aspects of narrative art (in which area they recognize the mastery of Pío BAROJA), all the while inserting into their conversation verses and entire poems of Luis CERNUDA, whom they admire. Eventually they recognize their frustration as members of a lost generation, that of the university students born after the Civil War, a group whose youthful nonconformity has grown into nothing but a chilling existential nihilism.

See: F. Alvarez Palacios, *Novela y cultura española de postguerra* (1975), pp. 262-56.   D.V.

Vazov, Ivan (1850-1921), Bulgarian poet, novelist, essayist, dramatist, and prose writer, was born in Sopot. As a youth he read widely in Russian and French literature. He became active in the national revolutionary movement of the 1870s that culminated in the liberation of 1878. Then, as one of the few educated Bulgarians available, he was pressed into the official service of the newly autonomous state. He did not abandon his literary vocation, however, and during the 1880s he almost single-handedly began the task of creating a modern Bulgarian national literature.

Vazov's earliest works are in verse. One of his initial collections is *Izbavlenie* (1878; Liberation), which was followed by such volumes as *Gusla* (1881; title refers to the musical instrument of that name) and *Polya i gori* (1884; Fields and Forests). One of his major contributions to the stimulation of the Bulgarian national consciousness was the monumental cycle *Epopeya na zabravenite* (1880s; Epic of the Forgotten), in which he dedicated individual poems to the great historical and cultural heroes of the Bulgarian Renaissance, which began in the mid-18th century and culminated with the liberation in 1878.

Domestic political instability led to Vazov's exile in Russia during the late 1880s, and it was there that he wrote the classic Bulgarian novel *Pod igoto* (1893; Eng. tr., *Under the Yoke*, 1893). The novel describes the unsuccessful uprising of April 1876 against the Turks when, the author emphasizes, the entire nation, disregarding political and social differences, rose as one against its oppressors. *Pod igoto* was the first novel in a trilogy—the other two being *Nova zemya* (1896; New Land) and *Kazalarskata tsaritsa* (1903; The Tsarina of Kazalar)—in which Vazov brought his account of contemporary Bulgarian history up to the time of writing.

By the 1890s, however, Vazov, back in Bulgaria, was disenchanted with the spiritual pettiness exhibited by his liberated countrymen, and he turned his pen to satire, chiefly utilizing for this the short story and the drama, notably the play *Sluzhbogontsi* (1900; Jobseekers). But Vazov never ceased to seek the historic sources of Bulgarian greatness, and most of his plays written in the early 20th century—badly needed by the fledgling national theater—depict striking episodes of medieval Bulgarian history. During the same period he published a number of domestic travel sketches, which provide not only excellent nature descriptions of the countryside, but also historical ruminations designed to elevate the national morale. Vazov continued to write lyric poetry as well, some of it personal in nature, but for the most part nobly patriotic. He was also active in intellectual journalism.

During World War I the poet continued to give his pen over to the service of the national cause, suffering with his countrymen at Bulgaria's defeat in that conflict. In 1920 the government celebrated the 50th anniversary of Vazov's literary activity officially and extensively, even exempting him from income taxes. His funeral in 1921 was virtually a state occasion, with a cortege headed by the king. He now lies buried in the center of Bulgaria's capital, honored as the founder of modern Bulgarian literature in almost every important genre, the author of the classic Bulgarian novel, and still very much the national poet.

See: P. Christophorov, *Ivan Vazov: la formation d'un écrivain bulgare (1850-1921)* (1938); M. Arnaudov, *Ivan Vazov: zhivot i delo* (1944).   C.A.M.

Vázquez Azpiri, Héctor (1931-), Spanish novelist and essay writer, was born in Oviedo. He studied medicine at the University of Madrid but, abandoned it for a degree in philosophy. After the publication of his first novel, *Víbora*, (1956; Viper), he spent some time at sea, working on merchant vessels. Since 1961 he has made Madrid his permanent residence.

Chronologically, he is a member of the Generation of 1954. Within this group he may be counted as one of the writers who have stayed away from critical social realism, replacing it with thematic material of a more individualistic nature and psychological orientation, to which he frequently adds autobiographical elements. The style of Vázquez Azpiri's early novels is extremely baroque but shifts in later works to an unadorned realism.

In his novel *Fauna* (1968), which received the Alfaguara Prize, the reaction against the objective realism (that began in Spain in 1962) is carried to an extreme. This exceedingly hermetic work may well be termed the antithesis of a novel: there is no action and the passage of time is consciously negated. The story arises from a brief moment when five friends are having a drink and one of them says: "To fornicate or not to fornicate: that is the question." These unlikely words provoke the main character immediately to examine his conscience and explore his profound feeling of failure. The actual printed presentation reveals highly uncommon arrangements, such as the alternation of lines and columns throughout the text and the manner in which the words themselves appear to have been scattered about on the paper.

After the excessively baroque experimentation of *Fauna*, the author opted for a realistic novel reminiscent of those of Ignacio ALDECOA. Thus, the subject of *La arrancada* (1975; Sudden Start), as well as its theme, coincides with Aldecoa's *Gran Sol* (1957). P.G.C.

Vennberg, Karl (1910-), Swedish poet, critic, and journalist, was born on a farm in Blädinge, in the province of Småland. Vennberg's role in giving shape and profile to the literary 1940s in Sweden cannot be exaggerated. He edited, together with other outstanding poets, the anthology *40-talslyrik* (1946; Poetry, Anthology for the 1940s) and the programmatic collection of essays *Kritiskt 40-tal* (1948; Critical Essays, Anthology for the 1940s). He translated Franz KAFKA and T. S. Eliot, and their skepticism and feeling of loss became for Vennberg an experience of something positive. Coming from a puritan background, Vennberg had no nostalgia for inherited ideologies. Dread itself became the valued warrant against the foul temptation to erect new value scales. His skepticism and his admonition "to abandon the perspective toward the dead center" were readily appropriated by the World War II generation who learned by heart the poems in *Halmfackla* (1944; Straw Torch) and *Tideräkning* (1945; Reckoning of Time). His next collection, *Fiskefärd* (1949; Fishing Expedition), with its sensuality and stress on self-centered pleasure, came, therefore, as a surprise. It became an early signal of the poetry that would dominate the next decade. In Vennberg's work, however, that tone was soon gone, and instead he became the introducer of, and spokesman for, a political stance, "Tredje Ståndpunkten" (the third alternative), arguing that Sweden should not get involved in the Cold War on either side. It was a moral argument because, as Vennberg later reminisced: "We did not understand economics then and had to fall back on ethics." Politically, Vennberg sympathizes with the Left and has earned his keep by writing for socialist papers. In the early 1960s Vennberg again introduced a debate pleading for noncommitment (*trolöshetsdebatten*). During the turbulent and committed 1960s, Vennberg did not publish any poetry but, in 1971, produced *Sju ord på tunnelbanan* (Seven Words in the Subway), which begins with a sad, ironic self-portrait. In spite of his wish to write poetry in order to give voice to what others feel and in spite of his contempt for private "display of furniture," Vennberg's poetry is both complicated and subjective. Yet he fascinates because he has always been ahead. He was one of the first to understand the real meaning of pluralism and warned against the indoctrination in Sweden. Consistent with what he always has been pleading for, he says in a later book: "Repeat the words in the illegal language."

Other collections by Vennberg include: *Hymn och hunger* (1937; Hymn and Hunger), *Gatukorsning* (1952; Intersection), *Vårövning* (1953; Spring Exercise). *Synfält* (1954; Span of Vision), *Vid det röda trädet* (1955; At the Red Tree), and *Tillskrift* (1960; Addition). Vennberg's collection of poetry *Vägen till Spånga Folkan* (1976; The Road to Spånga Community Center)—his eleventh—reveals his increasing pessimism and feelings of alienation in a world beset with problems. It contains a noteworthy poem to the memory of Salvador Allende, which seems to sum up the poet's position.

See: G. Printz-Påhlson, *Solen i spegeln* (1958), pp. 185–217; E. Lagerlöf, *Den unge Karl Vennberg* (1967); M. L. Ramnefalk, *Tre lärodiktare* (1974). B.K.S.

Vercors, pseud. of Jean Bruller (1902-), French novelist and essayist, was born in Paris of parents who had immigrated from Hungary. After receiving his baccalaureate, he studied engineering to please his father, but he never engaged in this profession. Instead, following his artistic calling, he became a well-known engraver and illustrator and has remained active as such under his real name. He has published over a dozen albums of his drawings and has illustrated a number of books. From 1930 to 1938 he also regularly wrote essays on the graphic arts; he has continued to do so since, although less frequently. Thus, when in 1942 he published his first work of fiction, *Le Silence de la mer* (Eng. trs., *Put Out the Light*, 1944, *The Silence of the Sea*, 1944), Vercors was not a novice writer. This short novel appeared in the clandestine Editions de Minuit, which he had cofounded in occupied France with Pierre de Lescure in 1941.

Poignantly showing that collaboration was ethically impossible even with "good" Germans, *Le Silence de la mer* was an instant success. This profound work is still a widely read book in France and throughout the world, so that Vercors is all too often known only as the author of this masterpiece. Yet among the works of his first literary period, *La Marche à l'étoile* (1943; Eng. tr., *Guiding Star* in *Three Short Novels*, 1947) also enjoyed great popularity, as did *Les Armes de la nuit* (1946; The Weapons of the Night), *Les Yeux et la lumière* (1948; The Eyes and the Light), and *La Puissance du jour* (1951; The Power of the Day). In these novels, Vercors placed his characters in problematic situations created by the war. Like the characters of Antoine de SAINT-EXUPÉRY, Albert CAMUS, André MALRAUX, and Jean-Paul SARTRE, they find solutions based not on specific religious or political credos, but on transcending human values.

In such works of his second period as *Les Animaux dénaturés* (1952; Eng. tr., *You Shall Know Them*, 1953; partial Eng. tr., *The Murder of the Missing Link*, 1953), and in *Colères* (1956; Eng. tr., *The Insurgents*, 1956), Vercors broadened his scope to ponder human nature and the distinction between man and animals. In *Plus ou moins homme* (1950; More or Less Human), Vercors—like Camus—treats the theme of rebellion, but unlike Camus, he finds its optimal form in art. For Vercors, however, art is not merely a way to vanquish time, but the only means for the human spirit to create.

Although increasingly interested in developing his mastery of the art of the novel rather than his moralistic themes, Vercors's thought continues to be dominated by humanism. This is evident even in such uncommitted novels of his third period as his trilogy *Sur ce rivage* (On This Shore)—*Le Périple* (1958; The Long Journey), *Monsieur Prousthe* (1958; Eng. tr., 1961), and *La Liberté de décembre* (1960; Eng. trs., *Freedom in Decemher,* 1961, *Paths of Love,* 1961)—as well as in *Sylva* (1962; Eng. tr., 1962) and *Quota ou les Pléthoriens* (1966; Eng. tr., *Quota,* 1966).

Vercors has published two volumes of memoirs, *Pour prendre congé* (1960; Eng. tr., *For the Time Being,* 1960) and *La Bataille du silence* (1967; Eng. tr., *The Battle of Silence,* 1968). His more recent works include *Le Radeau de la Méduse* (1969; Eng. tr., *The Raft of the Medusa,* 1971), *Sillages* (1972; Seaways), *Sept sentiers du désert* (1972; Seven Paths in the Desert), an adaptation of Shakespeare's *Hamlet,* and several plays, essays, and children's books (which he also illustrated). Although a well-known writer whose works have been translated into English and into numerous other languages, Vercors has not yet received from the critics the recognition he deserves as a moralist and as literary artist.

See: R. D. Konstantinović, *Vercors: Writer and Illustrator* (1969).   J.-P.C.

Verdaguer i Santaló, Jacint (1845–1902), Catalan poet, prose writer, and mystic, was born in a small village in the district of Vich. His father was an obscure stonecutter. From his mother Verdaguer heard the stories and tales which village folk tell one another on long evenings before the fire. These humble circumstances gave birth to the greatest Catalonian poet of the 19th century and a major figure in the movement of cultural revival of Catalonia, Valencia, and the Balearic Islands known as the Renaixença.

While studying for the church, Verdaguer worked as a farmhand and as a teacher. In 1865 his poetic gifts received their first public acclaim at the recently revived "Jocs Florals," where he won two prizes. He became a priest and spent peaceful years among the 200 parishioners of the village of Vinyoles D'Oris in his native district. He also made several ocean trips, perhaps owing to delicate health, and was a chaplain on the ships of the Marqués de Comillas from 1873 to 1875. On the high seas he finished his famous epic poem, *La Atlàntida,* which was awarded a prize in the Jocs Florals of 1877. On the basis of this poem he became known throughout Europe, and his works began to be translated into various languages. He then abandoned his employment as a ship's chaplain and entered the home of the Comillas as an almoner. His *Idil·lis i cants mistics* (Idyls and Mystic Songs) was published in 1879. He was offically hailed as *mestre en gai saber* (master troubadour) in the year 1880. He continued to write important books: *Canigó* (1885); *Excursions i viatges* (1887; Excursions and Trips); *Lo somni de Sant Joan* (1887; The Dream of Saint John); *Dietari d'un pelegri a Terra Santa* (Diary of a Pilgrim to the Holy Land); and the trilogy dedicated to the child Jesus, *Natzareth* (1890; Nazareth), *Betlem* (1891; Bethlehem), and *La fugida d'Egipte* (1893; The Flight from Egypt).

A period of crisis and suffering then followed. Verdaguer became the victim of intrigues not yet thoroughly studied or understood. Works such as *En defensa propia* (1895; In Self-Defense) and *Flors del Calvari: llibre de consols* (1896; Flowers of Calvary: Book of Consolations) brought the personal drama of Verdaguer to the common people, who rose to support their great poet. Unfortunately, the strong feelings that had been stirred by his powerful personality persisted and even cast a sinister shadow over his deathbed.

See: M. Milá i Fontanals, Prologue, in J. Verdaguer, *Idil·lis i cants mistics;* A Vassal, *Mossèn Jacint Verdaguer: sa vie, ses œuvres, sa mort* (1903); V. Serra i Boldu, *Mossèn Jacint Verdaguer* (1915); J. Folguera, *Les noves valors de la poesia catalana* (1919); J. Amade, *Origines et premières manifestations de la renaissance littéraire en Catalogne* (1924).   F. de P.

Veresayev, Vikenty Vikentyevich, pseud. of Vikenty Smidovich ' (1867–1945), Russian fiction writer and social critic, was born in Tula of a Russian mother married to a highly respected physician of Polish origin. He followed his father in the medical profession but began publishing fiction even before he completed his medical education.

Veresayev's best-known works of fiction are a series of stories in which he chronicled some four decades in the history of the Russian intelligentsia, beginning with the crisis in the Populist movement and continuing with the conflict between Populism and Marxism, the crisis in Marxism between the revolutionaries and the revisionists, and the disillusionment that set in among Russian intellectuals after the abortive Revolution of 1905. Veresayev's best work of fiction, *V tupike* (1923; In a Blind Alley; Eng. tr., *The Deadlock,* 1928), is a remarkably honest and dispassionate account of the moral dilemmas confronting Communist and non-Communist intellectuals alike during the Civil War that followed the October Revolution of 1917. Almost as if he were conducting a laboratory experiment in politics and morality, Veresayev takes a cross section of the population of a Crimean resort town and studies their behavior first when the town is under the control of the White forces, then when it falls to the Communists, and finally after the Communists are driven out and the anti-Communist forces return. Widely printed and discussed in the 1920s, the work has apparently not been republished in the Soviet Union since 1931 and is seldom mentioned nowadays in Soviet publications. *Syostry* (1933; Eng. tr., *The Sisters,* 1936), completed Veresayev's chronicle of the intelligentsia with an account of two sisters' contrasting attempts to cope with the new sexual laxity and political rigidity during the turbulent period of the first Five-Year Plan. Apart from these two novels Veresayev devoted most of his time after the October Revolution to memoirs, translations from the Greek classics, and works of literary scholarship.

While not a towering figure in Russian literature, Veresayev was, like Vladimir KOROLENKO, a man of great moral ·integrity and admirable humanity, who used his modest talent well. His novel *V tupike* deserves wider recognition as a landmark in literary documentation about the October Revolution and Civil War.

See: W. B. Edgerton, "The Evolution of the Russian Intelligentsia as Reflected in the Works of V. V. Veresayev," Russian Institute Essay, Columbia University, (1949); G. Brovman, *V. V. Veresayev: zhizn i tvorchestvo* (1959).   W.B.E.

Verga, Giovanni (1840–1922), Italian novelist, short-story writer, and dramatist, was born in Catania. Before leaving his native city for Florence in 1865, he had written three historical novels. These works dealt with progressively more recent struggles for national self-determination: "Amore e patria" (unpublished; Love and Country) concerns an episode in the American Revolution; *I Carbonari della montagna* (1861–62; The Mountain Carbonári) is set in Calabria during the Napoleonic period; and *Sulle lagune* (1862–63; On the Lagoon) takes place in Venice in

1860-61, when the city was still under Austrian rule. All three reflect the influence of Victor Hugo, Alexandre Dumas *père,* Alessandro Manzoni (1785-1873), and especially contemporary Sicilian writers with whose work Verga was closely acquainted.

Verga's move to Florence, which had just become the provisional capital of the new nation, was motivated by his serious intention to make literature his career. The literary circles he frequented there had moderate socialist leanings and favored the new realism, which, in the wake of Alexandre Dumas *fils'* rehabilitation of the fallen woman in *La Dame aux camélias* (1848), was sweeping the last vestiges of romantic historical drama from the stage. Like his fellow Sicilian writer Luigi Capuana (*see* ITALIAN LITERATURE), who had preceded him to Florence, Verga was interested in the theater. Of the plays he wrote at the time, the only one to survive is *Rose caduche* (1928; Fading Roses), a reworking of the theme of his novel *Una peccatrice* (1866; A Sinner). The novel's heroine, a femme fatale, was described by Verga himself, referring to Dumas's work, as "a Marguerite of the aristocracy." While in Florence, Verga also published *Storia di una capinera* (1869; Eng. tr., *Story of a Blackcap,* 1888), an epistolary novel that, without the benefit of an omniscient narrator, tells the pathetic story of a young nun driven to insanity and death by unrequited love. Its gentle protagonist, a victim of social injustice, and its sympathetic portrayal of the simple pleasures of rural life (a favorite topic in the declining romantic literature of Lombardy and Venetia) made *Storia di una capinera* Verga's only popular work until Luigi Russo's *Giovanni Verga* (1919), the first of many extended critical studies devoted to the writer, called attention to other more important aspects of his work.

Verga's next novel, *Eva* (1873), also begun in Florence, was thoroughly revised after his move to Milan in 1872, when, having definitely opted for narrative as opposed to dramatic literature, he chose the publishing capital of Italy as the seat of his yearly sojourns in northern Italy. Together with *Tigre reale* (1873; Royal Tigress) and *Eros* (1875), *Eva* belongs to the disdained and long neglected novels of Verga's so-called mundane period. The setting of these novels—aristocratic and bohemian milieux—and their protagonists—dominated by unrealistic aspirations and unwholesome passions—have tended to blind critics to the fact that the same formal problems preoccupied Verga in these works as in the more typical ones dealing with life among the small-town and peasant Sicilian poor.

For Verga, as for Capuana, theorist of *verismo,* the Italian version of realism and naturalism (*see* ITALIAN LITERATURE), the novelist's basic objective is to contribute to the knowledge of man; hence the desire to examine the whole social spectrum, expressed emblematically in Verga's program for a series of novels that would cover all the classes of society from the fishermen, in *I Malavoglia* (1881; Eng. tr., *The House by the Medlar Tree,* 1890, 1953, and 1964), to the aesthetes, in a novel he never wrote but had planned to call "L'uomo di lusso" (The Man of Luxury). The organizing principle of *I vinti* (The Doomed), the collective title of this series of novels, differs noticeably from that of Emile ZOLA's family history, *Les Rougon-Macquart* (1871-93), in which positivism appears under the guise of biological rather than environmental determinism. The model of science also lies at the base of Verga's mature narrative method: the objectivity of the scientist becomes the impersonality, impassibility, or detachment of the writer. In the introductory paragraphs of the short story "L'amante di Gramigna" (1880; Eng. tr., "Gramigna's Mistress," 1893), Verga wrote that in storytelling, the hand of the artist should remain absolutely invisible and the work of art "appear to have produced itself." In order to achieve this effect, so that the reader might find himself "face to face with the bare straightforward fact without having to look for it through the lens of the writer," Verga experimented with abandoning such narrative techniques as framing devices, introductory descriptions of setting and characters, and indirect discourse. Instead, in order to create the illusion of absolute reality, he places the reader into direct contact with the characters as though "he had always known them and been born among them." He replaces "presentation" with "representation" ("scenes," as in drama, instead of "narrative summary") and with *style indirect libre* (in which the character can be said to describe himself through the author's reproduction of his precise mode of expression). That Capuana and Verga were aware that their innovations concerned technique rather than subject matter is borne out by their correspondence and by Capuana's reviews and articles.

Verga's "new manner" is usually said to begin with the Sicilian sketch *Nedda* (1874; Eng. tr., 1888), whose protagonist, a young olive picker occupying "the lowest rung on the social ladder," loses her mother and her lover, and is at the end grateful for the death of her baby, who is thus spared her own fate of deprivation and suffering. None of Verga's later technical innovations are exhibited in *Nedda,* but they are present in "Primavera" (1876; Spring), the story of a love affair (that seems to come straight out of Henri Murger's *Vie de Bohème*) between an aspiring musician who has come to try his luck in Milan and a local shopgirl. The urban setting, with its impoverished working classes, its starving music hall entertainers, its prostitutes, invalids, consumptives, and small-time criminals, recurs in *Per le vie* (1883; On the Streets), whose stories were conceived by Verga as a pendant to those of *Vita dei campi* (1880; Eng. tr., *Cavalleria Rusticana and Other Tales of Sicilian Peasant Life,* 1893; *Under the Shadow of Etna,* 1896). In 1875, Verga was already at work on a sketch of sea life, "Padron 'Ntoni," which became his masterpiece, *I Malavoglia.* The second novel of *I vinti, Mastro-don Gesualdo* (1888-89; Eng. trs., 1893, 1923), marked the end of Verga's period of exceptional productivity, which had also included the collection *Novelle rusticane* (1883; Eng. tr., *Little Novels of Sicily,* 1925); *Il marito d'Elena* (1882; Elena's Husband), a novel reminiscent of Gustave Flaubert's *Madame Bovary;* and the dramatization of some of his short stories (such as "Cavalleria rusticana," first performed as a one-act play in 1884 and then becoming world famous in the operatic version by Pietro Mascagni). The remaining collections of stories, *Vagabondaggio* (1887; Wandering), *I ricordi del Capitano d'Arce* (1891; The Recollections of Captain d'Arce), and *Don Candeloro e Cia* (1894; Don Candeloro and Company), reflect the same themes (country and city life, destructive passions and beneficial affections, the psychological problems of the privileged classes and the economic problems of the poor) and the same technical experimentation that one finds in the rest of his work. The stories concerning Don Candeloro, the provincial strolling puppeteer who helplessly witnesses the decline of his profession, are of special interest because they prefigure aspects of Luigi PIRANDELLO's involvement with the theater.

Verga's original conception of *I Malavoglia* as a short story influenced its style and structure. In contrast to the typical epic narrative manner of *Mastro-don Gesualdo,* *I Malavoglia* is lyrical in tone, fragmentary, allusive, and elliptical in plot construction. The impersonal narrator depends on the reader's full collaboration for achieving his effect. While the central characters are members of the family whose nickname gives the book its title, the whole village of Aci Trezza (on the eastern coast of Sicily not far from Verga's birthplace) is involved in experiences that are not individual, but collective and typical. Different destinies are worked out: young 'Ntoni, unable to attain the easier way of life that attracts him, is in the end forced to leave his village and his family forever; Alessi, who has inherited his father's and grandfather's capacity for hard work as well as their tenacious, unquestioning attachment to traditional values, succeeds in reestablishing the family home, which had been lost through a business venture gone wrong; Lia becomes a prostitute; Mena sacrifices her love for Alfio and devotes herself to raising the children of Alessi and his wife. The sense of fatality that hangs over the whole is expressed in the folk wisdom concentrated in the sayings and proverbs that abound in the dialogue of the characters and in the "narrated monologue" of the author. Cohesion of form and content is the great aesthetic achievement of the work, as it is also of Verga's best short stories, "La lupa" (The She-Wolf), "Jeli il pastore" (Jeli), "Rosso Malpelo," "La roba" (Property), "I galantuomini" (The Gentry), "Libertà" (Freedom), and "Cavalleria rusticana." *The She-Wolf and Other Stories* (1958, rev. ed., 1973) contains a selection of stories in English translation.

In spite of an undisputed succès d'estime outside of Italy and the championship of D. H. Lawrence, who translated him in the 1920s, Verga has never rated as high as Zola in worldwide reputation. Nor did his reserved, resigned Catholic Sicilian primitives have the impact of the violent and raucous Russian muzhiks familiar in 19th-century Russian novels. In Italy, however, Verga is considered the greatest prose writer after Manzoni and has served as a model of that *stile di cose* (factual style) proposed by Pirandello as a sharp corrective to the full-blown, ornate, decadent manner of Gabriele D'ANNUNZIO. In the post–World War II period, Marxist critics, while recognizing Verga's sympathy for the plight of the underprivileged, have expressed reservations with regard to the social and historical pessimism that made him seek a refuge in a world outside time from the restless quest for social and economic betterment engendered by material progress.

See: T. G. Bergin, *Giovanni Verga* (1931; rpt., 1969); O. Ragusa, "Narrative vs. Stylistic Structure in *I Malavoglia*," *RR* 62 (1971): 211–30; S. B. Chandler, "The Primitive World of Giovanni Verga," *Mosaic* 5, no. 3 (1972): 177–28; G. Raya, *Bibliografia verghiana* (1972).

O.R.

Verhaeren, Emile (1855–1916), Belgian poet, was born in Saint-Amand. He appears as the typical example of those poets of Flemish origin but French expression who dominated Belgian literature from 1880 to 1920. Born of a father from Brussels and a Flemish mother, he studied in French, first at the Collège Sainte-Barbe of Ghent, then at the University of Louvain. After receiving his law degree, he quickly abandoned the bar to devote himself to literature. Verhaeren is a poet of modern life, nearer René GHIL and Walt Whitman than Albert MOCKEL and Stéphane MALLARMÉ. His work is abundant: four plays, among which *Le Cloître* (1909; Eng. tr., *The Cloister*, 1915) will especially be remembered, and more than 20 collections of verse. After the pictorial and descriptive poetry of the first volumes—*Les Flamandes* (1883; Flemish Women) and *Les Moines* (1886; The Monks)—came, between 1887 and 1890, a symbolist trilogy dominated by neurosis and anguish: *Les Soirs* (Evenings), *Les Débâcles* (The Downfalls), and *Les Flambeaux noirs* (The Black Torches). Progressive use of free verse; rapid and nervous

rhythm; singular, heavy, and abrupt elocution; taste for excess and tendency toward hyperbole; frequent recourse to assonance and alliteration; language abounding in barbarisms, pleonastic turns, neologisms, adverbs in *ment*, substantive adjectives, and disconcerting metaphors—such are the formal dominating characteristics of these collections and the ones that, for the most part, remain present in the later works. About 1890, Verhaeren resolved his crisis. *Les Apparus dans mes chemins* (1891; Those Who Appeared on My Paths) celebrates regained health and confidence in the future. If, in *Les Campagnes hallucinées* (1893; The Hallucinated Countrysides) and *Les Villes tentaculaires* (1895; The Tentacular Cities), Verhaeren deplored the fascination exercised by the city on the inhabitants of the country and the painful rural exodus that empties the fields of their energies, he did not hesitate to exalt technical progress, scientific thought, and the industrial West, as well as work, fervor, fraternity, and joy. A noble socialism impregnates *Les Forces tumultueuses* (1902; The Tumultuous Forces), *La Multiple Splendeur* (1906; The Manifold Splendor), and *Les Rythmes souverains* (1910; The Supreme Rhythms). With this evolution toward optimism, Verhaeren's style becomes flexible; and his rhythm, less frantic. Beginning in 1902, a return to the use of stanza and regular verse becomes perceptible. From 1904 to 1911 he published *Toute la Flandre* (All of Flanders), a polyptych in five panels: *Les Tendresses premières* (The Manifestations of Affection), *La Guirlande des dunes* (The Garland of Dunes), *Les Héros* (Heroes), *Les Villes à pignons* (Cities with Gables), and *Les Plaines* (The Plains), in which, stirring up his memories again, he seems to give us the best of himself. In 1914 the poet was at the height of his glory; he was famous in Moscow, known even in Japan. World War I dealt him a terrible blow; his dream of friendship and universal fraternity crumbled brutally. Patriotism swept Verhaeren off on a political ideal, and he celebrated his bruised country in *Les Ailes rouges de la guerre* (1916; The Red Wings of War). In 1916, he died in an accident at the Rouen railroad station, crushed by the train he was about to board to return to Paris; he was buried at Saint-Amand, along the Escaut, as he had wished. His last collection, *Les Flammes hautes* (Tall Flames), appeared in 1917. To most people's minds, Verhaeren remains, above all else, the singer of energy, work, and modern life; but, rather than this typical aspect of his work, it is permissible to prefer the more discreet and nuanced vein of the trilogy of *Les Heures* (The Hours)— *Les Heures claires* (1896; Eng. tr., *The Sunlit Hours*, 1916), *Les Heures d'après-midi* (1905; Eng. tr., *Afternoon*, 1917), and *Les Heures du soir* (1911; Eng. tr., *The Evening Hours*, 1918)—in which Verhaeren's innate ardor is tempered with sweetness and serenity. Without question, it is unfortunate that, in this monumental work, the style does not always measure up to the inspiration. Verhaeren abuses expletives, repetitions, antithesis, and anastrophe. His language is exempt from neither impurities nor incorrectness. He was, however, the only Belgian poet not to limit himself to the traditional themes of contemporary poetry. His powerful lyricism, with its torrential rhythm, inspired, so it seems, by the cadence of marching, admirably expresses the fight of human beings against their destiny and excels at seizing life at its most vibrant.

See: S. Zweig, *Emile Verhaeren* (1910); A. Mockel, *Un poète de l'énergie, Emile Verhaeren: l'œuvre et l'homme* (1917); G. Doutrepont, *Les débuts littéraires d'Emile Verhaeren à Louvain* (1920); A. Mabille de Poncheville, *Verhaeren en Hainaut* (1920); *Documents inédits sur Verhaeren, deux maisons du poète* (1923); L. C. Baudouin,

Le symbole chez Verhaeren, Essai de psychanalyse de l'art (1924; Eng. tr., *Psychoanalysis and Aesthetics*); A. de Bersaucourt, *Emile Verhaeren, son œuvre* (1924); P. Mansell Jones, *Emile Verhaeren: A Study on the Development of His Art and Ideas* (1926; rpt., 1957); E. Starkie, *Les Sources du lyrisme dans la poésie d'Emile Verhaeren* (1927); E. Estève, *Un grand poète de la vie moderne, Emile Verhaeren* (1928); C. Brutsch, *Essai sur la poésie de Verhaeren* (1929); A. Fontaine, *Verhaeren et son oeuvre, suivi de la bibliographie des éditions originales et de la liste des publications signées ou anonymes parues dans les revues belges* (1929); R. T. Sussex, *L'Idée d'humanité chez Emile Verhaeren* (1938); H. Morier, *Le Rythme du vers libre symboliste: étudié chez Verhaeren, Henri de Régnier, Viélé-Griffin, et ses relations avec le sens* (1943); F. Olivero, *Il contrasto nella lirica di Emile Verhaeren* (1943); F. Hellens, *Verhaeren* (1952); A. Mabille de Poncheville, *Vie de Verhaeren* (1953); J.-M. Culot *Bibliographie d'Emile Verhaeren* (1954); L. Christophe, *Emile Verhaeren* (1955); H. Braet, *L'Accueil fait au symbolisme en Belgique (1885–1900)* (1967).   R.F.

Verlaine, Paul (1844–96), French poet, was born in Metz, where his father, an infantry captain from the Ardennes, happened to be stationed. An only child, he was spoiled by his parents and by Elisa Dehée, an orphan cousin six years his elder, who lived with the Verlaines and whom the young poet was later to love passionately. The family having moved to Paris in 1851, Verlaine was sent to the lycée, where he had a good record, contrary to the legend that he himself was responsible for spreading. At 14, he discovered Charles BAUDELAIRE's *Les Fleurs du mal* and decided to become a poet. Having received his bachelor's degree in 1862, he became a clerk at the City Hall and began to associate with the Parnassian poets, Leconte de Lisle, Théodore de Banville, Louis Xavier de Ricard, Catulle Mendès, and François Coppée. He frequented the literary salon of Nina de Villars and the mezzanine of the publisher Alphonse Lemerre. Verlaine also spent much time at the ale houses of the rue Soufflot where, with literary companions, he engaged in long discussions punctuated by numerous glasses of absinthe. From these sessions, Verlaine developed his passion for that drink, which transformed him into a brute and led him finally to a hospital bed. A man of homosexual tendencies, Verlaine had a penchant for reverie and a natural timidity in the presence of women. Physically he was very ugly, with a broad and bumpy forehead, a receding hairline, little oblique eyes, and a snub nose giving him a monkeylike appearance.

Verlaine's first collection of verse, *Poèmes saturniens* (Saturnian Poems), was published in 1866. Beneath the book's vast humanistic, classical, and modern cultural lore, one detects an original poet and a vibrant personality who has already been tested by life. His second collection, *Fêtes galantes* (1869; Eng. tr., *Gallant Parties*, 1912), published following the death of his beloved cousin Elisa, is, more than the first, situated outside reality. This dream of unrequited love revives visions of a time gone by, recalling the gallant, fascinating world of the 18th century as painted by Jean Antoine Watteau. In these poems, in which a Shakespearean grace mingles with the fantasy of Alfred de Musset, Verlaine attempted to cast into Parnassian form the expression of a wounded heart, the sublimation of an unconfessed passion.

Cured of his passion by this poetic expression, Verlaine nevertheless encountered love in the person of a 16-year-old girl, Mathilde Mauté de Fleurville, whom he married in 1870 after a two-year betrothal. During this period, he composed his third collection, *La Bonne Chanson* (1870;

The Good Song), consisting of a series of short poems offered to his fiancée with bouquets of flowers. Here Verlaine sings of his dreams of the future, of his anxieties, and of his hopes for happiness. Now isolated in his love, cut off from the literary circles that provided intellectual nourishment, the poet mired himself in reality and gave himself over to facile exercises in eloquence and rhetoric.

This phase of Verlaine's career, in which his genius was running the danger of foundering, came to an end with the arrival of Arthur RIMBAUD in Paris. For this extraordinary poet of 17, with his "face of an angel in exile," Verlaine left everything—his friends, his home, his wife, and his newborn son. For a year, Verlaine followed Rimbaud everywhere, even to Belgium and England, with no concern for social proprieties. Intoxicated by their liberty, the two poets went from city to city and from bar to bar, creating a scene wherever they stopped. Yet by coming into contact with Rimbaud's own prodigious poetic potential, Verlaine rediscovered his own inspiration and composed his greatest masterpiece, *Romances sans paroles* (1874; Eng. tr., *Romances without Words*, 1921). The title of this collection clearly indicates his new poetic orientation: verbal music would henceforth become the essential quality of his verse and would predominate over meaning. He focused on fresh sensations collected directly from nature and expressed immediately without stylization; his principal motifs became impressionistic Belgian scenes, London scenes mixed with fog and rain, melancholy memories, regrets over a torrid past, nostalgia for an impossible happiness, and songs so sad as to make one cry. *Romances sans paroles* illustrates the teachings of Verlaine's "Art poétique," a work he composed at this time but that was only published 10 years later in *Jadis et naguère* (1884; Formerly and Recently).

In 1873, Rimbaud decided to end their partnership, but Verlaine could not consent to a separation. On July 12, in Brussels, Verlaine fired two shots at the young poet, wounding him slightly in the elbow. Arrested by the Belgian police, Verlaine was sentenced for a crime of passion to two years in prison. Thus began the most somber period of his life. Yet a ray of divine light penetrated into Verlaine's cell and into his soul. In his solitude and sorrow he was converted; returning to the faith of his childhood, he composed the most beautiful poems of French Catholic literature, published under the title *Sagesse* (1881; Wisdom).

After his release from prison in January 1875, Verlaine spent several months in England as a French teacher and then returned to France to teach at the college of Rethel. This period in his life was one of moral solitude and poetic isolation, followed by decadence. In 1879 he gave up teaching, bought a farm at Juniville, went bankrupt, and then returned to Paris, forgotten and without employment. There he published a series of articles entitled "Les Poètes maudits" (The Accursed Poets), which directed the attention of the public to the new decadent-symbolist generation.

After a second attempt at living in the country at Coulommes (an experiment that also ended in bankruptcy), much wandering through the Ardennes, and another month in prison, Verlaine returned one last time to Paris. Poverty and misfortune pursued him relentlessly, and after 1886 illness confined him for long periods in public hospitals. Yet whenever he was released, it was only to lead, in the furnished rooms of the slums, a licentious life with those prostitutes of the Latin Quarter whose faded charms he sang in numerous poems of little value.

But poetic glory began to smile on him; his scandalous life was attracting admirers. One after the other he published collections of verse of lesser value—*Amour* (1888; Love), *Parallèlement* (1889; In Parallel), *Bonheur* (1891; Happiness)—in which religious inspiration alternates with the profane. Yet while his poetic inspiration was vanishing, Verlaine's first collections of poetry were rediscovered, and he was proclaimed one of the greatest poets of France. At the death of Leconte de Lisle in 1894, Verlaine was elected "Prince of Poets." He died two years later, at the age of 52, worn out by his excesses, leaving behind him poetry of delicate and disturbing beauty and of an incomparable musicality.

Verlaine's originality stems principally from the drama of his personal life. Yet being a romantic turned Parnassian, he was saved by a certain sense of modesty from dramatizing his feelings. The enemy of pomposity and eloquence, he is candidly naive in the expression of passion and sorrow. His themes, characterized by simplicity, gentleness, and lightness, are decanted into very small poems with a short meter. Verlaine's languishing rhythm does not proceed from strophe to strophe toward a greater precision, but instead loses its clarity and contour, becoming veiled in unreality and transformed into music. Although he respected the outward form of classical poetry and the poetic language of his day (to which his genius readily adapted), Verlaine dislocated the traditional rhythm of verse, employing uneven meters, internal rhymes, and rhymes of the same gender. In his poems, the meanings of words become more fluid and more volatile; the marvelous exactness of his ear enabled him to play with words as a musician does with sounds, to empty them, so to speak, of their intellectual content in order to place them like musical notes in the range of the verse. Verlaine's poetic practice opened the way for free verse and pure poetry.

See: P. Martino, *Verlaine* (1924; 1951); G. Zayed, *La Formation littéraire de Verlaine* (1962; 1970); E. Zimmerman, *Magies de Verlaine* (1967); A. E. Carter, *Verlaine: A Study in Parallels* (1969); J. Richardson, *Verlaine* (1971).   G.Z.

Vermeylen, August (1872–1945), Belgian (Flemish) essayist, novelist, literary critic, art historian, and politician, studied history and art history at the Free University of Brussels and continued his education in Berlin and Vienna. Although his family was Roman Catholic and of Flemish origin, as a student he moved mostly in the French-speaking and free-thinking circles of Brussels. He lost his faith early in life, but as early as 1889 gave proof of his sympathy for the Flemish movement, contributing to the reviews *Jong Vlaanderen* (1889–90), and *Ons Tooneel* (1890–91), and becoming a member of the literary society "De Distel" (The Thistle).

In 1893, Vermeylen was one of the founders of the literary and cultural review *Van Nu en Straks* (1893–94; 1896–1901) and soon emerged as the theoretical leader of the aesthetic movement of the same name. *Van Nu en Straks* became the vehicle for a Flemish literary revival that closely paralleled the Dutch revival of 1880 and the flowering of Belgian literature in French around *La Jeune Belgique*. As part of the Flemish movement, *Van Nu en Straks* was able to participate in the cultural, political, and social emancipation of the Flemish community. As a leading authority, Vermeylen never took a narrow view of either aesthetics or politics. He equally promoted the impressionist poetry of Karel van de WOESTIJNE and the naturalist novels of Cyriel BUYSSE and Stijn STREUVELS, accepting an art for art's sake view alongside his own more humanitarian stand. In two influential essays, *Kritiek der Vlaamsche Beweging* (1896; A Critique of the Flemish Movement) and *Vlaamsche en Europeesche*

Beweging (1900; Flemish and European Movement), he pointed to the flaws of folklore and narrow nationalism in the Flemish movement, broadened the aims of it into the social field, and put them in a European perspective. He continued to expound his ideas in *Vlaanderen* (1903–07; Flanders) and *Vandaag* (1929–30; Today), and shortly before his death planned *Diogenes*, which was to appear as *Nieuw Vlaams Tijdschrift* (from 1946 on; New Flemish Review).

Vermeylen's creative work consists mainly of prose. *Eene Jeugd* (1896; My Youth) is mostly autobiographical. *De Wandelende Jood* (1906; The Wandering Jew), by far his best work, is a short allegorical novel exposing the curious amalgam of humanism, anarchism, and individualism that was Vermeylen's own philosophy. The hero Ahasverus passes through religious and existential crises toward a humanism without God, in which personal and social aspirations are at one. Allegorical form and the use of symbols and moral intention are organically combined; he is a brilliant stylist. As to structure and scope (not breadth), *De Wandelende Jood* is akin to the "Johannes" cycle of the Dutch author F. W. van EEDEN. *Twee Vrienden* (1943; Two Friends) deals with familiar subject matter, yet without reaching the same aesthetic dimension.

Vermeylen taught art history and literature first at the Free University of Brussels (1901–23) and later on at the University of Ghent (1923–40), where he became the first president of the Flemish-speaking university (1930)–33). He produced valuable essays in his field, generally linking artistic creation to society.

As Vermeylen deserted more and more the anarchism of his younger years, his humanist and humanitarian streaks came to the forefront. From 1921 to 1945 he served as a socialist representative, steadily defending a nondogmatic and measured point of view. His refusal to promote the aims of the Flemish movement with the help of the German invaders (1914–18, 1940–44) greatly added to his national credibility and turned him into one of the most influential defenders of the Flemish political aims.

In 1945 the Vermeylen-Fonds (Vermeylen Foundation) was founded, aiming not only at making Vermeylen's work known but also at continuing his endeavor of promoting the Flemish movement through intellectual freedom and social justice.

See: R. Roemans, *Het werk van Prof. Dr. August Vermeylen* (1953); A. Westerlinck, *De wereldbeschouwing van August Vermeylen* (1953); J. Venstermans, *August Vermeylen* (1965); Vermeylen issue *Nieuw Vlaams Tijdschrift* (Vermeylen issue) 25, no. 3 (1972).
                                                                D. van B.

Verne, Jules (1828–1905), French novelist, was born in Nantes. Although Verne did not invent science fiction, he did the most to popularize it, and today he remains a classic of juvenile literature. Having moved to Paris, he spent some years in obscurity as a student of law before writing his first successful comedies. Verne soon envisioned a vast project, a "roman de la science," comparable to the "Comédie humaine" of Honoré de Balzac. Verne was encouraged in this effort by the first great success of *Cinq semaines en ballon* (1863; Eng. tr., *Five Weeks in a Balloon*, 1870) and by the shrewd publicity of his editor, Hetzel. Verne's formula proved simple and foolproof: a felicitous mixture of fiction and scientific verisimiltude. His production in that vein, entitled "Voyages extraordinaires dans les mondes connus et inconnus" (Extraordinary Voyages in Worlds Known and Unknown), comprises 60 volumes. Verne also wrote 10 volumes of short stories; 5 volumes of geographical works; 8 excellent, posthumously published novels; and 20 plays.

Ignored by the histories of literature, Verne belongs with the other giants of his century: Balzac, Victor Hugo, and Emile ZOLA. Indeed, his works seem to have regained their topicality, especially *De la terre à la lune: traget direct en 97 heures* (1865) and *Autour de la lune* (1869; both translated as *From the Earth to the Moon Direct in 97 Hours, 20 Minutes; and a Trip around It*, 1873), in which spaceships are launched from Florida; *Vingt mille lieues sous les mers* (1872; Eng. tr., *Twenty Thousand Leagues under the Seas*, 1873), considered his masterpiece; and *Le Tour du monde en quatre-vingt jours* (1873; Eng. tr., *Around the World in Eighty Days*, 1874). These works have not aged very much, even if their Victorian positivism seems a bit naive today.

In his later years, Verne became decidedly socialistic—to the horror of his conservative family. This side of Verne's personality appears in such nonscientific works as *Mathias Sandorf* (1885; Eng. tr., 1886), a novel concerning a social revolutionary, and in *Naufragés du Jonathan* (1909; The Shipwrecked People from the *Jonathan*), in which there appears a noble anarchist who seems to be based on Prince Pjotr Kropotkin, whom Verne admired. Although he acquired great honors and great wealth, Verne does not seem to have known great happiness; he was moody and often depressed, yet at times he was, like one of his characters, fabulously energetic, puritanical, introverted, and courageous—altogether more British than French.

With the advent of modern space flight, Verne has received a large amount of critical attention. While he exhibits enormous imaginative powers, his psychology is rather limited: there are few women in his works, and his Nietzschean characters (*see* Friedrich NIETZSCHE) at times foreshadow the *Superman* comic strip. Finally, it should be noted that in such little-known works as *Eternel Adam* (1910) and *L'Etonnante Aventure de la mission Barzac* (1920; The Astonishing Adventure of the Barzac Mission), Verne displayed a new pessimism concerning the perfectibility of human civilization.

See: M. More, *Le Très Curieux Jules Verne* (1960); B. Becker, *Jules Verne* (1966); I. O. Evans, *Jules Verne and His Works* (1966).   J.B.

Verwey, Albert (1865–1937), Dutch poet, critic, and literary historian, was born in Amsterdam. He started out in business, but soon gave this up for literature. He came under the literary guidance of Willem KLOOS, whom he admired, and whose enthusiasm for Jacques Perk, Percy Bysshe Shelley, and John Keats he shared. Verwey was one of the founders of *De Nieuwe Gids*. The feeling for nature that British poetry inspired in him is evident in *Persephone* (1883), which also reflects his study of the classics. This was included in *Persephone en andere gedichten* (1885; Persephone and Other Poems), which was partly republished, along with the poetry of the "Nieuwe Gids" movement, as *Verzamelde gedichten* (1889; Collected Poems). *Cor Cordium* (Heart of Hearts) shows him looking inward and turning away from Kloos. Verwey came to oppose the ideas of the "Eighties" (*see* DUTCH LITERATURE) and the cult of individualism, and he broke with Kloos in 1889. *Aarde* (1896) reveals his pantheism and the influence of Baruch Spinoza. He took up the study of history and of literature, but he always remained a leader, and in 1894, he and Lodewijk van DEYSSEL founded *Het Tweemaandelijksch Tijdschrift,* which he transformed into a monthly, *De XXste Eeuw,* in 1902. In the meantime, Verwey had formed a stimulating relation-

ship with the German poet Stefan GEORGE and his circle, a relationship of mutual influences, which lasted until the beginning of World War I. Differences developed between Verwey and van Deyssel, and in 1905, Verwey began publishing *De Beweging*, with himself as editor. Although the movement of the title was that of the "Eighties," the magazines was against individualism and preferred philosophical to sensuous poetry. Verwey, indeed, had become a poet of the idea. *De Beweging* survived until 1919, and Verwey regularly contributed essays on both Dutch and foreign literature, which were later collected in ten volumes as *Proza* (1905–19). His many volumes of poetry and three poetic dramas, *Johan van Oldenbarneveldt, Jacoba van Beieren,* and *Cola Rienzi,* appeared in three volumes of *Verzamelde gedichten* (1911–12; Collected Poems). In the 1920s he went over to a freer verse form but soon added rhyme to this. *De figuren van de sarkofaag* (1930; The Figures of the Sarcophagus) contains thoughts of death. All his poetry was published posthumously as *Oorspronkelijk dichtwerk* (Original Poetry).

Although Verwey's reputation as a poet may have lost some of its luster, his importance as a literary leader, critic, and scholar remains undiminished. He was professor of Dutch literature at the University of Leiden (1924–35) and produced excellent literary studies of Vondel, Potgieter, Spieghel, van der Noot, and a biography of Frederik van Eeden. He also translated Dante and other poets.

See: F. W van Heerikhuizen, *Albert Verwey* (1963); T. Weevers, *Mythe en vorm in de gedichten van Albert Verwey* (1965).   S.L.F.

Vesaas, Halldis Moren (1907–), Norwegian poet, was born in Trysil in southeastern Norway, the daughter of the regional writer Sven Moren (*see* NORWEGIAN LITERATURE). She graduated from a teachers college and worked in Oslo and Geneva before marrying the writer Tarjei VESAAS and settling in the rural region of Telemark.

Vesaas's early collections of poetry, such as *Harpe og dolk* (1929; Harp and Dagger) and *Morgonen* (1930; The Morning), were strongly influenced by the works of Edith SÖDERGRAN. They represent a new feminine assertion in modern Norwegian poetry. Vesaas's verse is imbued with a spontaneous, warm eroticism and faith in life. Her later collections are characterized by a quiet harmony and focus on the small, universal details of life. In *Tung tids tale* (1945; The Voice of Tragic Times) she writes of wartime Norway, brotherhood, and communion. In *Treet* (1947; The Tree) there looms the horror of nuclear war, but here, as in the more deeply probing *I ein annan skog* (1955; In a Different Forest), she retains her faith in the elemental forces of good. For Vesaas, nature becomes symbolic of the regenerating power of human life. Her poetic form is mostly traditional, but inspired by Södergran, she has continually experimented with it. In addition to her own poetry, Vesaas has also translated Racine and Shakespeare into Norwegian.   K.A.F.

Vesaas, Tarjei (1897–1970), Norwegian novelist and poet, was born and spent most of his life in the province of Telemark and was during the last 30 years of his life Norway's leading writer. Although writing in *nynorsk* (*see* NORWEGIAN LITERATURE), a language with strong roots in rural traditions, realistic prose and rhymed verse, Vesaas succeeded in creating his own distinctive nontraditional prose style and an expressive poetic form through which he offered his own highly personal, insightful interpretation of universal problems and human isolation and alienation.

Vesaas produced many novels and articles during the 1920s and 1930s. In his earliest writings, beginning with the novel *Menneskeborn* (1923; Children of Man), he was closely tied to the culturally and religiously conservative outlook of traditional *nynorsk* literature. During a series of stays abroad, primarily in Germany, during the latter half of the 1920s, he gradually freed himself from the restriction of this tradition as well as from the suicidal compulsions that nearly brought his life and career to a premature end. Although they are hinted at only indirectly in his articles and novels from the 1920s, Vesaas's fantasies of suicide by drowning appear prominently in a series of novels written during the 1930s: *Fars reise* (1930; Father's Journey), *Sigrid Stallbrokk* (1931), *Dei ukjende mennene* (1932; The Unknown Men), and *Hjarta høyrer sine heimlandstonar* (1938; The Heart Hears Its Native Music). Artistically weak, often repetitive and dull, these novels nevertheless occupy a crucial position in Vesaas's writing, for they document a young man's struggle to accept his role in life and the acceptance of other human beings for what they were. Two other novels, *Det Store spelet* (1934; Eng. tr., *The Great Cycle*, 1970) and *Kvinnor ropar heim* (1935; Women Call Come Home), reflect Vesaas's own experiences of marriage (to Halldis Moren VESAAS) and parenthood. *Det store spelet*, written during a surge of faith in life's regenerative processes, is one of his most successful books, even though it does not match the abstract beauty of his post-World War II works.

Vesaas's major artistic achievement was a series of novels that he wrote between 1940 and 1968. The first *Kimen* (1940; Eng. tr., *The Seed*, 1964), is a study of violence and irrationality inspired by the German invasion of Norway, while the last one *Båten om kvelden* (1968; Eng. tr., *The Boat in the Evening*, 1971), is a highly abstract, but moving portrait of Vesaas's own psychological development from his childhood realization of the individual's state of separateness to his final acceptance of the reality and necessity of death. Between these two works there appeared nine other novels, two collections of short stories, and five collections of poems. The central theme of all these writings is the danger of psychological isolation, which can be counterbalanced by the individual's ability to reach out and aid another person in distress. These novels encompass a variety of styles and techniques. *Huset i Mørkret* (1945; Eng. tr., *The House in the Dark*, 1976 is an allegorical depiction of Norway during World War II, *Fuglane* (1957; Eng. tr., *The Birds*, 1968) is a highly realistic, moving portrait of a mentally retarded man, while *Brannen* (1961; the Fire) is a surrealistic nightmare about man's quest for contact and purpose. *Båten om kvelden* provides an abstract vision of the human condition, communicated through a series of evocative images in both prose and poetry and without an overt unifying plot. Noteworthy among Vesaas's other mature novels are *Vårnatt* (1954; Eng. tr., *Spring Night*, 1964), *Isslottet* (1963; Eng. tr., *The Ice Palace*, 1966), and *Bruene* (1966; Eng. tr., *The Bridges*, 1969). In each of these books Vesaas treats young people at various stages of their development from child to adult. He displays great sensitivity toward the emotional conflicts of those years, evoking them in haunting images that reflect his deep contact with nature and his own personal struggle, documented in his early writings.

In poetry collections like *Løynde eldars land* (1853; Eng. tr., *Land of Hidden Fires*, 1973) and *Ver ny, vår draum* (1956; Live On, Our Dream), and in the short-story collections *Vindane* (1952; The Winds) and *Ein vakker dag* (1959; One Fine Day), Vesaas displays the same high quality of imagery and concentration found in the

best of his novels. Vesaas's last volume of poetry, *Liv ved straumen* (1970; Life by the River), contains some of his most striking images of life and death.

See: K. Chapman, *Tarjei Vesaas* (1969).   K.C.

Vestdijk, Simon (1898–1971), Dutch novelist, poet, and critic, was born in Harlingen. He studied medicine at Amsterdam, and after receiving his M.D. degree in 1927, he studied psychology and philosophy at Leiden. He practiced medicine for only five years and then devoted himself completely to a literary career. During World War II, he was interned by the Nazis for almost a year.

A prolific writer, Vestdijk published almost 100 books. He began by publishing poetry, but the long manuscript of his first novel was rejected and appeared only posthumously as *Kind tusschen vier vrouwen* (1972; A Child among Four Women). This manuscript, however, formed the basis of the eight novels in the Anton Wachter series; and the third one, *Terug tot Ina Damman* (1934; Back to Ina Damman), marked Vestdijk's first success as a novelist. *Ina Damman* is a poignant recollection, based on his own experiences, of unrequited adolescent love, of a boy growing up in school, and of his relationships with friends and family. The memory of this first love haunts the hero, Anton Wachter, and is a theme that returns again and again in other novels of the series. In *Else Böhler, Duitsch dienstmeisje* (1935), Vestdijk displayed his mastery of psychology in a compelling novel, based on contemporary historical events, in which the hero destroys himself through his love for the German maid, who is the heroine of the title. He combined his knowledge of depth psychology with James Joyce's stream of consciousness technique in *Meneer Visser's hellevaart* (1936; Mr. Visser's Descent into Hell), which is actually the first novel he ever wrote. *De koperen tuin* (1950; Eng. tr., *The Garden Where the Brass Band Played*, 1965), which Vestdijk considered his best novel, reveals in both background and structure its author's love of music. Again the theme is that of youthful and tragic love.

Vestdijk also wrote a number of historical novels, based on extensive research. In *Het vijfde zegel* (1936; The Fifth Seal), he portrayed the life of El Greco in Spain at the end of the 16th century. *Rumeiland* (1940) presents the life of the pirates on the island of Jamaica in the 18th century, and *Ierse Nachten* (1949; Irish Nights) is an account of the British oppression of the Irish in the middle of the 19th century. *Aktaion onder de sterren* (1941; Actaeon among the Stars) and *De verminkte Apollo* (1952; The Crippled Apollo) belong to the group sometimes described as Vestdijk's "Greek novels" and are based on the mythology, as well as the history, of ancient Greece.

In *De dokter en het lichte meisje* (1951; The Doctor and the Prostitute), Vestdijk draws upon the experiences of his brief medical career, when he served as a substitute for other physicians, and creates a novel filled with social criticism and psychological insight. Vestdijk disguised himself again, not only by using his initials in reverse, but by the skin disease from which the hero suffers in the Victor Slingeland trilogy: *Het glinsterend pantser: symfonie van Victor Slingeland I* (1956; The Shining Armor: Victor Slingeland's Symphony I), *Open boek: symfonie van Victor Slingeland II* (1957), and *De arme Heinrich: symfonie van Victor Slingeland III* (1958; Poor Henry). These novels are filled with the author's passion for music and also reflect his interest in the tension between the lowlands and the mountains. This tension appears again in his "Alpine novels," *Een alpenroman* (1961; A Novel of the Alps) and *Het genadeschot* (1964; The Coup de Grace). Vestdijk's study of philosophy and religion is woven into *De kelner en de levenden* (1952; The Waiter and the Living) and *Bericht uit het hiernamaals* (1964; Report from the Hereafter) and forms the basis of his volume of essays *De toekomst der religie* (1947; The Future of Religion). His importance as an essayist is also evident from such books as *Albert Verwey en de idee* (1940), *Muiterij tegen het etmaal*, vols 1, 2 (1942, 1947; Mutiny against the Day), *Essays in duodecimo* (1952), *Gestalten tegenover mij* (1961; Figures Facing Me), and *De leugen is onze moeder* (1965; The Lie Is Our Mother). In addition to his early *Verzen* (1932), his poetry includes *Mnemosyne in de bergen* (1946; Mnemosyne in the Mountains) and *Gestelsche liederen* (1949; Institutional Songs). Vestdijk was an editor of the literary magazines *Centaur* and *Podium* and was a literary and music critic for Dutch newspapers. He has been awarded literary prizes by the city of Amsterdam, the Dutch government, the Jan-Gampertstichting, and the Maatschappij der Nederlandsche Letterkunde; and he has also received the P. C. Hooft Prize and the Prize der Nederlandse Letteren. In 1964 the University of Groningen conferred on him an honorary doctor of letters degree.

See: M. Nord, ed., *Over Simon Vestdijk* (1948); T. Govaart, *Simon Vestdijk* (1960); H. S. Haasse, *Tweemaal Vestdijk* (1970). S.L.F.

Vian, Boris (1920–59), French novelist and playwright, died in a Parisian cinema at the age of 39 from a long-standing heart condition while watching a preview of the film *J'irai cracher sur vos tombes* (I Shall Spit on Your Graves), an unauthorized adaptation of the scandalous novel he published in 1946. Vian had pretended that the book, "translated from the American by Boris Vian," was the largely autobiographical story of an American black named Vernon Sullivan, who avenges the lynching of his younger brother by raping and killing white girls. Dashed off in two weeks, this combination of sex, sadism, and American racial attitudes became a best-seller and was banned.

Vian's last and most important play, *Les Bâtisseurs d'empire* (1959; The Empire Builders), was produced by the Théâtre National Populaire soon after his death. Despite its success, however, Vernon Sullivan's reputation continued to eclipse Boris Vian's. But from the mid-1960s on, reprints of his novels, beginning with *L'Ecume des jours* (1947; The Froth of Days), and almost everything else he wrote have flooded bookstores in France and elsewhere in Europe. Vian's posthumous climb to fame, especially among the young, has been one of the most phenomenal a French writer has ever known.

Vian's personality was multifaceted. An engineer by training, he was a jazz connoisseur and critic as well as Dixieland trumpeter, *chansonnier,* and author of more than 400 popular songs; he was also a poet, film writer and actor, journalist, translator, and "Transcendent Satrap" in the Collège de Pataphysique. Many young people have found in him someone whose nonconformist attitudes, nihilism, and opposition to most of society's standards of good taste and admissible behavior are echoed in their own ways of thought and life. His writings betray an astonishing facility and an original way of using language to create an unreal, blackly comical universe that, paradoxically, reveals the author's real thoughts and feelings as well as his preoccupation with a death he felt to be imminent and final.

See: D. Noakes, *Boris Vian* (1964); M. Rybalka, *Boris Vian* (1969); N. Arnaud, *Les Vies parallèles de Boris Vian* (1970). D.N.

Vida, Viktor (1913–60), Croatian poet, was born in Kotor.

After teaching Croatian and Italian at a Zagreb gymnasium, he went to Venice in 1942 and to Rome in 1943 as a journalist, living in Rome until his emigration to Argentina in 1948, after the establishment of Marshal Tito's Communist government in Yugoslavia. He held a minor government position in Buenas Aires until his suicide in 1960. During Vida's lifetime, two collections of his poems were published: *Svemir osobe* (1951; The Universe of the Individual) and *Sužanj vremena* (1956; The Slave of Time). His *Sabrane pjesme* (1962; Selected Poems) were edited by Vinko Nikolić, who also provided a solid commentary on Vida's life and work.

Vida began to write his poetry at an early age, and his pre–World War II poems were published in some of the better Croatian literary periodicals. During his stay in Italy (1942–47), he devoted himself mainly to translations, composing little original work. Upon settling in Argentina, he at first contributed to a Croatian religious monthly, *Glas svetog Antuna,* but from 1951 on, he wrote for Nikolić's newly founded literary quarterly, *Hrvatska revija.*

Vida is a lyricist in a direct line from such Croatian poets as Antun Gustav MATOŠ, Vladimir Vidrić, Tin UJEVIĆ, and Ljubo Wiesner (*see* CROATIAN LITERATURE). Vida's first collection of poems appearing in the early 1950s, was a refreshingly subdued expression of personal feelings, in contrast to the usual émigré laments. The predominant themes of his second collection are the unique Dalmatian landscape, God, and death. In this volume, the poet is puzzled by the mysterious ways in which the Lord governs this world; as regards death, there are times, he writes, when he would welcome it.

See: B. Kadić, in *Hrvatska revija* 3 (1951): 263–66, and 2 (1957): 165–69; I. Lendić, in *Hrvatska revija,* 4 (1960): 345–58; A. Kadić, "Victor Vida and his Poetry," *B-CR* 4, no. 10 (January 1977): 11–13. A.K.

Viebig, Clara (Clara Viebig Cohn) (1860–1952), German novelist, disciple of Emile ZOLA, outstanding woman novelist of the naturalistic school, was born in Trier. She first became famous by introducing into literature her native region, the bleak and volcanic uplands of the Eifel with its pine forests and its dangerous swamps. How perfectly people and landscape are blended may be seen in her story "Am Totenmaar" from *Kinder der Eifel* (1897; Children of the Eifel), where the austerity of the landscape mirrors the moral rigor of an old shepherd and where its desolation is a symbol of the utter loneliness of his abandoned child. Viebig's early novels could not escape the influence of Gabriele Reuter's courageous and widely discussed novel *Aus guter Familie* (1895; From a Good Family), the story of a sensitive girl of the upper middle class whose life is ruined by the conventional narrow-minded prudishness of her religious and social training, but Clara Viebig was more outspoken in her presentation of the erotic side of life, which, to cite an early example, is treated with fine humor in the novel *Das Weiberdorf* (1900; Village of Women). The masses, who act with collective instinct like one monstrous organism, are pictured here in a masterly fashion, as is the religious ecstasy of the pilgrims to the shrine at Echternach in the Eifel in *Das Kreuz im Venn* (1908; The Cross in Venn) or the suppressed hatred and secret patriotic longing of the servile Polish peasants under German domination, portrayed in *Das schlafende Heer* (1904; Eng. tr., *The Sleeping Army,* 1929). As a young girl, Viebig had lived in Düsseldorf, the scene of her historic novel *Die Wacht am Rhein* (1902; The Watch on the Rhine). Here the peaceful fusion by marriage of the old Prussian element with the population of the Rhineland is demonstrated in the history of a family through three generations. The novel ends in 1870. Modern Berlin, where Viebig spent her adult years, as the wife of the publisher Fritz Theodor Cohn, is the background of many of her social novels. Among these *Das tägliche Brot* (1900; Eng. tr., *Our Daily Bread*, 1908), depicting the life of a servant girl in the lower middle class, is an example of the author's intense human sympathy. Two other works, *Einer Mutter Sohn* (1907; Eng. tr., *The Son of His Mother*, 1913) and *Töchter der Hekuba* (1917; Eng. tr., *Daughters of Hecuba*, 1922), epitomize her visual style, a succession of pictures, vivid and concrete in every detail. Viebig was at her best when portraying characters governed by elemental needs and desires, especially women from the lower classes.

See: C. Scheuffler, *Clara Viebig* (1926).

E.Ho. rev. A.L.W.

Vieira, (José) Luandino, pseud. of José Mateus Vieira da Graça (1935-), Portuguese writer of short fiction, was born in Vila Nova de Ourém in central Portugal. Taken to Luanda as a child, he became the quintessential Angolan, so much so that *Luandino* (son of Luanda) identifies him better than his long Portuguese name. Even as a schoolboy, he had to work at a variety of mundane jobs. After working hours, he observed and shared the life of Luanda's black slums, the *musseques,* assimilating the cadences of speech flavored with African phrases. The first hesitant result was a collection of stories, *A cidade e a infância* (1962; City and Childhood). So intense was his participation that it led him to involvement in African nationalist politics and eventually to imprisonment for 11 long years. Between 1962 and 1964, writing in Luandan jails, he completed *Luuanda* (1964), three long short stories modeled on oral tales in the *musseques.* A controversy arose when the Portuguese Writers Society awarded *Luuanda* its grand prize for fiction in 1965 and the authorities protested, ostensibly because of the book's lack of artistic value and the author's status as a political prisoner. Literati sympathetic to the regime testified that, among other failings, *Luuanda*'s dialogues were dialectal contrivances of how colonialist whites think black Angolans speak Portuguese. In Vieira's case, however, even a casual reading reveals him to be a European who permitted himself to be so transformed by indigenous culture that he could recreate *musseque* speech with a poetic faithfulness to social realities. In the spring of 1972, the writer was released from the infamous Tarrafal prison camp in the Cape Verde Islands and assigned a fixed residence in Lisbon. The fall of the rightist regime in 1974 signaled his rebirth, and several stories, also written in prison, were almost immediately published as *Velhas estórias* (1974; Old Stories), a companion volume to the clandestine collection *Vidas novas* (n.d., New Lives). Also in 1974 appeared the collection *No antigamente na vida* (In the Long Ago of Life), which displayed a linguistic virtuosity akin to the experiments of the Brazilian J. Guimarães Rosa. Vieira was also able to publish the Portuguese original of *A vida verdadeira de Domingos Xavier* (1974; Domingos Xavier's Real Life), a novella first published in French (1971), and *Nós, os do Makulusu* (1974; Our Gang from Makulusu), another novella that is a moving, bitter lament for the youth killed on both sides of the Angolan war.

See: M. de Andrade, "Nouveau langage dans l'imaginaire angolais," in L. Vieira, *La vraie vie de Domingos Xavier* (1971), pp. 7-18; R. G. Hamilton, *Voices from an Empire* (1975), pp. 134- 40: M. Ferreira, Preface to L. Vieira, *A cidade e a infância* (new ed., 1978).

R.G.H.

Vielé-Griffin, Francis, pseud. of Egbert Ludovicus Viele (1864-1937), French poet, was born in Norfolk, Virginia. He moved to France in 1872, where he spent the rest of his life. Vielé-Griffin's first collection of poems, *Cueille d'avril* (1886; April's Harvest), depicts pastoral life in Touraine, a theme prevalent in much of his poetic creation. Under the acknowledged influence of Stéphane MALLARMÉ, Vielé-Griffin became an avid theoretician-poet of the symbolist movement. His theories on the vers libre form, published in the symbolist review *Les Entretiens politiques et littéraires* (1890-92), are put into practice in his poetry. Retaining rhyme, he breaks away from the rhythmic stringencies of traditional prosody. His poems exhibit an overwhelming optimism, a belief in the goodness of man and the bounty of nature, as seen in such titles as *Les Joies* (1888; The Joys) and *La Clarté de la vie* (1897; Life's Brightness). Ancient and medieval legend as well as Christian folklore provide the basis for many of Vielé-Griffin's more ambitious works: *La Chevauchée d'Yeldis* (1893; Yeldis's Ride), *Swanhilde* (1893), *La Légende ailée de Wieland le forgeron* (1900; The Winged Legend of Wieland the Blacksmith), and *Phocas le jardinier* (1898; Phocas the Gardener), the last a drama of early Christian martyrdom. A complete edition of his poems and plays is available in four volumes (1924-30). Judged by today's standards, Vielé-Griffin's poetry seems shallow and wordy. Nevertheless, his works possess a lyrical beauty that should ultimately allow them to withstand the test of time.

See: J. de Cours, *Francis Vielé-Griffin: son œuvre, sa pensée, son art* (1930).

D.C. and A.C.

Vilar, Jean (1912-71), French director and actor, was born and died in Séte. Trained as an actor in the school of Charles DULLIN, Vilar directed his first play in 1942 and founded his first company, La Compagnie des Sept, in 1943. The Festival of Avignon, which he created in 1947, was an immediate success. In 1951, the French government appointed Vilar director of the Chaillot Theater, the title of which he changed to Le Théâtre National Populaire (T.N.P.), a name once made famous by Firmin GÉMIER. Vilar gathered around him a remarkable crew of actors (Gérard Philippe, D. Sorano, Maria Casares, Jeanne Moreau), designers and musicians (Léon Gischia, Maurice Jarre), and technicians and administrators (Jean Rouvet) who, in a dozen years, put on more than 75 plays. Most of these were French and foreign classics (thoroughly rejuvenated) including plays by Sophocles, Corneille, Racine, Molière, Calderón, Georg Büchner, Heinrich von Kleist, Shakespeare, and Alfred de Musset, but they also encompassed great contemporary plays by T. S. Eliot and Bertolt BRECHT. In 1963, Vilar gave up the directorship of the T.N.P., but he continued to run the Avignon Festival and to "sign" numerous productions (*Les Noces de Figaro* and the *Macbeth* of Verdi at La Scala in Milan). Vilar accepted the responsibility of reorganizing the Paris Opera in 1967, but he gave up his assignment the following year and broke with the government of General Charles de Gaulle.

Of all modern stage directors, Vilar is the one who has most profoundly marked the French theater since 1945. This is in part due to the style that he inherited from Jacques COPEAU (elimination of the curtain, footlights, and set in favor of a more flexible use of lights and movable stage elements; respect for the texts and attention paid to their theatricality; bursting out of the stage in the Italian manner), but it is especially due to his conception of the theater as a "public service"—as an activity of the city, disengaged from the obsession of profit, open to all social classes by virtue of its repertory and its modest prices, and designed to educate its public. The success of the T.N.P. was a decisive element in the spread of state-subsidized "public theater" throughout France.

See: G. Leclerc, *Le T.N.P. de Jean Vilar* (1971).

R.A.

Vildrac, Charles, pseud. of Charles Messager (1882–1971), French essayist, critic, poet, dramatist, and writer of children's books, was born in Paris. He began his literary career with an article on versification entitled "Le Verslibrisme" (1901) and two collections of poems illustrating its poetic techniques: *Poèmes* (1905) and *Images et mirages* (1908). In 1906, he and some artistically inclined friends rented a house in Créteil, calling it L'Abbaye. The community they established there had a lasting effect on Vildrac, and the idealistic beliefs of L'Abbaye are frequently echoed in his later writings.

With his brother-in-law, Georges DUHAMEL, Vildrac composed *Notes sur la technique poétique* (1910; Notes on Poetic Technique). He published verse in accordance with its precepts in *Livre d'amour* (1910; Eng. tr., *A Book of Love*, 1923), containing poems on love, friendship, and communion with nature, and *Chants du désespéré* (1914–20; Songs of a Desperate Man), expressing anguish at war's horrors. The poetry of *Prolongements* (1927, rev. 1946; Extension) as well as three other collections of prose poems—*Decouvertes* (1912–31; Discoveries), *Vitrines* (1953; Show Windows), and *Le Vin de Paris* (1953; Parisian Wine)—all depict the virtues of living in harmony with one's fellow man and nature.

Although he worked in many genres, Vildrac is best known for his plays. In 1921, Jacques COPEAU produced his *Le Paquebot Tenacity* (1919; Eng. tr., *The Steamship Tenacity* 1921) at the Théâtre du Vieux-Colombier. This play is typical of Vildrac's earlier works in several respects: the main characters are members of the working class: the dialogue is simple and colloquial; the primary themes are friendship, love, and interpersonal relations; and the plot is a psychological drama, taking place at a moment of crisis. Other plays by Vildrac incorporating these characteristics are *Michel Auclair* (1921), *Le Pèlerin* (1921; The Pilgrim), *Madame Béliard* (1928), and *La Brouille* (1931; The Misunderstanding).

Vildrac's critical works, travel notes, memoirs, and stories for children all reveal a sensitive yet vigorous prose style, one that speaks directly to the reader without condescension or affectation.

See: G. Bouquet and P. Menanteau, *Charles Vildrac* (1959).

D.C. and A.C.

Vilhjálmsson, Thor (1925–), Icelandic essayist and novelist, was born in Edinburgh, Scotland, but was soon taken to Reykjavik, where his father served as the manager of Iceland's largest steamship company. Vilhjálmsson matriculated in Reykjavik in 1944 and then studied literature at the University of Iceland and subsequently in England and Paris.

Not surprisingly for a writer who had resided in Paris immediately after World War II. Vilhjálmsson evinces certain influences from French existentialism, although the source of this is more the works of Albert CAMUS than the theoretical formulations of Jean-Paul SARTRE. That aside, Vilhjálmsson has perhaps the most cosmopolitan outlook of all modern writers in Iceland. He is quite familiar, for instance, with the Russian 19th-century novelists, T. S. Eliot, and the French "new novel," but his work has also been enriched by effects coming from modern painting and film techniques. No living author in Iceland is better acquainted with trends in literature and art in the Latin region of Europe or more indebted to this cultural sphere than he.

Vilhjálmsson's first book, *Maðurinn er alltaf einn* (1950; Man Is Always Alone), is a collection of short stories and literary sketches, as are his next two works: *Dagar mannsins* (1954; The Days of Man) and *Andlit í spegli dropans* (1957; Eng. tr., *Faces Reflected in a Drop,* 1966).

A world traveler, Vilhjálmsson has written travelogues and other accounts of his overseas stays including *Undir gervitungli* (1959; Under a Satellite), describing a trip to the Soviet Union; *Regn á rykið* (1960; Rain on the Dust), and *Svipir dagsins og nótt* (1961; The Shades of the Day, and Night). The latter two are about his journeys in Western and Southern Europe. Vilhjálmsson has also published two collections of essays: *Hvað er San Marínó?* (1973; What Is San Marino?) and *Fiskur í sjó, fugl úr beini* (1974; Fish in the Sea, Bird Made from Bone). Through his travelogues and essays, Vilhjálmsson has done much to introduce contemporary European culture and literature to his countrymen; and being a disseminator of culture is indeed not a new role for him, because he was, from 1955 to 1968, on the editorial board of *Birtingur,* which was the organ of modernist writers in Iceland at that time.

Vilhjálmsson's first three works of fiction, mentioned above, marked a new epoch in Icelandic literature, for he made a clean break with the epic-naturalistic tradition of Icelandic prose, replacing it with timeless pictorial sketches of people today. These books are in a sense a cry of anguish over the atomic bomb, the Cold War, and the alienation of modern people—concerns emerging even more strongly in the longer prose works: *Fljótt, fljótt sagði fuglinn* (1968; Quickly, Quickly, Said the Bird), *Óp bjöllunnar* (1970; The Cry of the Beetle), and *Fuglaskottís* (1975; The Schottische of the Birds). All three of these books have their settings in Western and Southern Europe, and the general theme is humanity's fate in the modern world of rapid change. The narrative technique consists in suspending time, thus merging past and present, with the result that these books seem static to many readers.

In addition to his cosmopolitan vision, Vilhjálmsson is noted for his close examination of minute details that affect people in their environment—naturalistic observations through a microscope, as it were. His writing has a pictorial quality, often reminiscent of modern film-making techniques. His language is varied; his style, characterized by vigor and lively imagination. One feature recurring in all of his work is the use of allusions to European culture from any period—a sphere where the author feels he has a firm foothold, a vantage point from which he can observe how people today fearfully confronts their own rootlessness in a world of change.

See: S. S. Höskuldsson, "Thor Vilhjálmsson och modernismen i isländsk prosa," *Horisont* 5-6 (1970): 21–24; P. Hallberg, "Við vitum ekki hvort þau hafa andlit," *Tímarit Máls og menningar* (1972), pp. 119–34.

S.S.H.

Villaespesa, Francisco (1877–1936), minor Spanish poet and playwright, was born in the former mansion of Abén-Humeya in Laujar, Almería. All his life Villaespesa was a fervid admirer of Arab culture. After studying at the University of Granada, he went to Madrid in 1897 and plunged into the whirlwind of *modernista* life (*see* SPANISH LITERATURE). Energetic, restless, a "collector" of writers, an advocate of Latin American literature, a devotee of Moorish customs, Villaespesa seemed to represent for Antonio and Manuel MACHADO and Juan Ramón

JIMÉNEZ the great *modernista* writer. The promise was never fulfilled, however, and Villaespesa's flood of poems, plays, and novels has not managed to shake off the opprobium of their facile rhetoricism and superficiality.

La copa del rey de Thule (1900; The King of Thule's Goblet) registers typical *modernista* themes: slightly morbid sensuality ("lecherous bites," "the virgin dying from tenderness"), the proclamation that art is eternal, and the image of a world wrapped in "blue daydreams."

He wrote 23 plays, many of them in verse. *El alcázar de las perlas* (1911; The Castle of Pearls) exemplifies his fondness for Granada. Its tragic love story is based on Arab legends and also owes something to Washington Irving's *Tales of the Alhambra*. Like José Zorrilla, Villaespesa traveled widely in Latin America in order to promote his plays. He also wrote a score of novels, many of which are still in print.

See: J. Ramón Jiménez, "Recuerdo del primer Villaespesa," in *La corriente infinita* (1961); E. Cortés, *El teatro de Villaespesa* (1971).   H.T.Y.

Villalón Daoiz y Halcón, Fernando (1881–1930), Spanish poet, was born in Morón de la Frontera, in the province of Seville, of an affluent and aristocratic family. From his father he inherited the title of count of Miraflores de los Ángeles and a liking for books. A vigorous man, an excellent horseman, breeder of fine cattle, friend of bullfighters and of popular singers, he felt and captured all the color and power of his luminous region. An important figure in the literary journals of his country, he had a quiet inclination for poetry, a familiarity with the classics, and a broad acquaintance with other poets. At the age of 46 he published his first book, *Andalucía la Baja* (1927; Lower Andalusia). This was followed by *La Toriada* (1928; Epic of the Bulls) and *Romances del 800* (1929; 19th-Century Ballads).

Readers of Villalón will appreciate in his work the forms, color, and popular Andulusian concerns that find much more profound expression in the work of his great contemporary, Federico GARCÍA LORCA.

See: M. Halcón, *Recuerdos de Fernando Villalón* (1941); J. M. de Cossío, "Prólogo" to F. Villalón, *Poesías* (1944).   A.Id. rev. H.L.B.

Villalonga, Llorenç (1897–), Majorcan novelist and playwright, was born in Palma de Mallorca, the "Ciutat" of his narrations. He studied medicine and specialized in psychiatry, later becoming the director of the Mental Clinic of Jesus in his native city. He often wrote in collaboration with his now deceased brother Miguel. Under the pseudonym Dhey he wrote *Mort de Dama* (A Lady's Death), a caricature of Majorcan life that was published in 1931 although written 10 years earlier. Among his other works in Catalan are *Les temptacions* (1937), a new version of his earlier experimental novel *Mme. Dillon* (1937); *La novel.la de Palmira* (1952; Palmira's Novel), *El lledoner de la clastra* (1958; The Linden Tree in the Cloister), *L'Angel Rebel* (1960), *Aquil, les o l'impossible* (1964), *Desbarats* (1965; Nonsense), *Falses memòries de Salvador Orlan* (1967; The Spurious Memoirs of Salvador Orlan), and *Les Fures* (1967; The Vixens).

Villalonga's greatest book is *Bearn* (1961), in which, according to his own statement, he wanted to create a nostalgic "poem" or a "portrait" of postwar Majorca, to evoke a "paradise" that was fast disappearing before his very eyes. There followed *Desenllac a Montlleó* (1963; The Solution to Montlleó) and *L'Hereva de donya Obdulia* (1964; The Heiress of Donya Obdulia). His later

works include *La gran batuda* (1968; The Great Threshing), *La Virreyna* (1969), and *La Lulú* (1971).

The critic Joan Fuster has associated the names of Josep PLA and Salvador ESPRIU with Llorenç Villalonga, comparisons with which Joaquim Molas concurs, at the same time likening him to André GIDE and Albert CAMUS. Villalonga himself pays homage to Marcel PROUST. His "remembrance of things past" is the theme that unites his myth of Bearn.

Villalonga has also written plays: *Fedra*, in Castilian (pub. in Catalan in 1966), and *Faust* (1956), in Catalan. He received the National Prize for Literary Criticism in 1961 for *Bearn*, the City of Palma Prize in 1963, and the National Prize of Catalonian Literature Narcís Oller in 1970.

See: J. Marco, "Llorenç Villalonga i les seves 'Obres Completes,'" in *Sobre literatura catalana i altres assaigs* (1968); J. Molas, "El mite de Bearn en l'obra de Villalonga" in LL. Villalonga, *Obres Completes* (1966); B. Porcel, "Llorenç Villalonga, com el lluc," *Serra d'Or*, no. 127 (1970): 35–40.   J.F.C.

Vilmorin, Louise de (1902–69), French novelist and poet, was born in Verrières-le-Buisson. She published her first novel, *Sainte-Unefois* (Saint Onetime), in 1934. An essentially autobiographical narration, it reveals an intensely personal yearning for impossible love told in a charmingly naive and original manner. Vilmorin's earliest collection of verse, *Fiançailles pour rire* (1939; Betrothal in Jest), appeared shortly after her second and more successful marriage to Count Paul Palffy. Another volume of poems, *L'Alphabet des aveux* (1954; The Alphabet of Avowals), consists of several brilliantly executed semantic exercises, many of which are also deeply touching. Vilmorin is, however, far better known for her novels, a number of which have been made into films. Among the latter are *Le Lit à colonnes* (1941; Eng. tr., *The Tapestry Bed*, 1948), *Julietta* (1951), and *Madame de. . .* (1951). Her more popular novels include *La Fin des Villavide* (1937; Eng. tr., *The Last of the Villavides*, 1938), *La Lettre dans un taxi* (1958), and *Le Retour d'Erica* (1948; Erica's Return).

Vilmorin's style is light, elegant, and witty. Her cleverness with words is carried over into her intricate plots, in which entertainment, fantasy, and suspense are the key elements. The characters themselves are generally refined, superficial members of high society. These well-organized stories, drawn with deft touches of irony, typically relate a tale of illicit or despairing love set in the most luxurious of surroundings. Vilmorin received the Grand Prix Littéraire de Monaco in 1955.

See: A. de Vilmorin, *Louise de Vilmorin* (1972).

D.C. and A.C.

Vincenz, Stanisław (1888–1971), Polish folklorist and poetic prose writer, was born in Słoboda Rungurska in eastern Galicia and died in Lausanne, Switzerland. He received his doctorate from the University of Vienna. Between the two world wars he published *Na wysokiej połoninie. Obrazy, dumy i gawędy z Wierchowiny Huculskiej* (1936; abridged Eng. tr., *On the High Uplands: Sagas, Songs, Tales and Legends of the Carpathians*, 1955). A second volume, *Zwada* (The Rift) appeared in 1970. After World War II, Vincenz lived in France and published in émigré periodicals and presses. *Po stronie pamięci* (1965; On the Side of Memory) is a collection of essays in literary criticism; *Dialogi z Sowietami* (1966; Dialogues with the Soviets) are his memoirs of war and exile. *On the High Uplands* is Vincenz's principal work.

It is a fictionalized collection of tales, legends, and descriptions of the ways of living practiced by the Huculs in the Carpathians. The work defies genre boundaries; it creates some half-dozen characters who combine local color and psychological depth, and it contains passages of remarkable poetic prose. The book is interlaced with humor: particularly amusing are the religious discussions between mountaineers, Catholic and Orthodox priests, and Jews, with the old farmer Tarasenko serving as the catalyst.   E.M.T.

Vinokurov, Yevgeny Mikhaylovich (1925–), Russian poet, born in Bryansk, is one of a number of writers whose experiences of war seem to have precipitated a dissatisfaction with the inflated rhetoric and falsifying accounts of reality that were typical of Stalinist literature. Born into the family of a career soldier, he fought on the Ukrainian Front from adolescence to early manhood. After the war he entered the Gorky Literary Institute, where he himself began teaching in 1966. His first poems were published in 1948, followed by a volume, *Stikhi o dolge* (1951; Poems about Duty). His next book, *Sineva* (Blue) had to wait until 1956, but since then his poetry has appeared widely in periodicals, and he has published almost annually one or more slender collections, mostly with single word titles, such as *Slovo* (1962; Word), as well as larger collections, *Izbrannoye, Iz devyati knig* (1976; Selections. From Nine Books) and *Izbrannye proizvedeniya v dvukh tomakh* (1976; Selected Works in Two Volumes). A collection of his literary essays, *Poeziya i mysl* (Poetry and Thought), appeared in 1968. Vinokurov is currently poetry editor of the literary magazine *Novy mir,* which has published some of the best post-Stalinist literature. Although he has always avoided public appearances and has never concerned himself with topical or controversial themes, Vinokurov enjoys great popularity at home. His poetry, whose starting point was his war experiences, narrated starkly without false heroics, has ranged widely. Metrically and lexically no innovator, Vinokurov has deliberately chosen the path of prosaicism and understatement. The absence of heroics has its counterpart in a humanistic espousal of the cause of the "ordinary" individual, but he also makes effective use of paradox and exhibits a sense of historical perspective that seems to transcend the conventional Marxist dialectic.

D.T.W.

Virta, Nikolay Yevgenyvich (1906–), Russian novelist, was born in the province of Tambov, the son of a village priest. His first successful novel, *Odinochestvo* (1935; Eng. tr., *Alone,* 1958) concerns Antonov's kulak revolt (1920–21); it was adapted as a play, *Zemlya* (1937; Earth), and as an opera, *V buryu* (1939; Into the Storm), composed by T. N. Khrennikov. Virta's combat experience during World War II provided material for the novel *Soldaty Stalingrada* (1944; Soldiers of Stalingrad), filmed as *Stalingradskaya bitva* (1949; The Battle of Stalingrad). Virta was awarded the Order of Lenin and four Stalin prizes, proof of his responsiveness to Communist Party criticism. The strength of his work lies not in its content but in its rendering of observed wartime experience.

M.L.H.

Vitrac, Roger (1899–1952), French playwright, poet, essayist, was born in Puissac. He was an early adherent of the surrealist group (*see* FRENCH LITERATURE), from which he and Antonin ARTAUD were the first to be excluded. Vitrac founded the review *Aventure* with friends. He published several volumes of poetry, including *Le Faune noir* (1919; The Black Faun), a volume of poems

of symbolist inspiration; the surrealist *Humoristiques* (1927; Humorous Verses); *Cruautés de la nuit* (1927; Nocturnal Acts of Cruelty); and the essay *Connaissance de la mort* (1927; Acquaintance with Death). His poetry was collected posthumously as *Dés-lyre* (1964; Dice-Lyre-Delirium), whose untranslatable pun reflects his poetic temperament.

Vitrac's fame, however, rests on his plays, of which the earliest were a series of whimsical skits applying surrealist aesthetics to dramatic art. In such works as *Le Peintre* (1922; The Painter), *Mlle Piège* (1922; Miss Trap), *Entrée libre* (1922; Browse at Will), *L'Ephémère* (1922; The Mayfly) and *Poison* (1923), Vitrac attempted to express the anguish, eroticism, and hidden criminal thoughts of modern man, while closely associating the tragic with the ludicrous. In 1927, Vitrac, Robert Aron, and Artaud founded the avant-garde Théâtre Alfred Jarry and produced Vitrac's most truly surrealist play, the provocative and curious *Les Mystères de l'amour* (1924; The Mysteries of Love). This work and his following misunderstood efforts failed, but his masterpiece, *Victor, ou les enfants au pouvoir* (1929; Victor, or the Children in Power), was successfully revived in 1962 by Jean ANOUILH and is now a classic. On his ninth birthday, Victor, a six-foot wunderkind who is both holy terror and holy innocent, discovers and denounces in comically outrageous fashion the hypocrisy of adult middle-class society. A mysterious complicity draws him to the flatulent Ida Mortemart, who is death personified; during the course of his mad birthday party, she carries him off, resulting in the total collapse of a morally decaying society. With its energetic assault on language and on the formula of the commercial bedroom farce, *Victor* clearly foretells the black humor and comic violence of the playwrights of the 1950s and 1960s, notably Eugène IONESCO. Vitrac's later plays continue to depict a morally bankrupt society willfully living in a kind of Pirandellian dream-world of illusion (*see* Luigi PIRANDELLO). Although these plays hardly display the genius of *Victor,* they nonetheless deserve more attention than they have received. They include *Le Coup de Trafalgar* (1934; Unforseen Disaster), revived in 1972 with success; *Le Loup garou* (1935; The Werewolf); *Le Camelot* (1936; The Huckster); *Les Demoiselles du large* (1938; Maids on the Beach); *La Bagarre* (1938; The Scuffle); *Médor* (1939); *La Croisière oubliée* (1941; The Forgotten Cruise); *Le Sabre de mon père* (1950; My Father's Saber); and *Le Condamné* (1951; Condemned). All are collected in Vitrac's *Théâtre complet* (1964; Complete Plays).

Vitrac also composed revealing essays on the artists Giorgio Di Chirico (1925), Jacques Lipschitz (1929), and Max Ernst (1930).

See: H. Béhar, *Roger Vitrac, un réprouvé du surréalisme* (1966).   R.G.M.

Vittorini, Elio (1908–66), Italian translator, novelist, and critic, was born in Siracusa. At the age of 17, he ran away to join a road-building gang, and in 1929 he went to Florence, where he became a proofreader, journalist, and member of the *Solaria* group (*see* ITALIAN LITERATURE). He moved to Milan in 1936, where he worked as a translator and served as editor of major series for the publishing firms of Bompini, Einaudi, and Mondadori. Vittorini's importance is due as much to his cultural projects as to his fiction: his pre–World War II translations of and articles on American and British authors—Edgar Allan Poe, D. H. Lawrence, William Faulkner, T. F. Powys, John Steinbeck, William Saroyan, Daniel Defoe, Erskine Caldwell, and John Fante—did much to break the stuffy regional and academic traditions then current in Italian literature. After the war, he founded and directed two of the most interesting and controversial Italian periodicals: *Il politecnico* (1945–47) and *Il menabò* (1959–67). *Il politecnico* was a brilliantly conceived attempt to catch up in political, economic, and cultural fields after 20 years of Fascist censorship, a meeting place for the Sino-Soviet and Western points of view, and a cultural forum for workers and intellectuals. *Il menabò* was an avant-garde literary periodical that focused on presenting important problems by means of innovations in style and language. Vittorini also directed *I gettoni* (Telephone Tokens), an Einaudi series founded in 1951 to publish translations and the work of young Italian authors with a new approach or style (such as Italo CALVINO). He also directed the *Nuovi scrittori stranieri* (New Foreign Writers) series founded for Mondadori in 1964 as part of the battle against the recurrent tendency toward provincialism in postwar Italy, and *Nuovo politecnico*, another Einaudi series, founded in 1965, which published everything from Jan Myrdal's *Report from a Chinese Village* to Roland BARTHES's *Elements of Semiology*.

Vittorini was probably the most multifaceted, courageous, and open-minded Italian writer of his day; his influence played a major part in the development of Italian literature from the 1930s until his death, and his work can to some extent serve as a guide to it. He is still a controversial figure who has been called everything from an avant-garde innovator to a sentimental neoromantic. His first book, *Piccola borghesia* (1931; Petty Bourgeoisie), is a well-written series of ironic studies. *Nei Morlacchi— Viaggio in Sardegna* (written 1932, pub. 1936; In the Morlacchi—Voyage to Sardinia) is far more lyrical, a nostalgic hymn to the magic of childhood. The first part of the book is a poor prose poem, but the second recounts a trip through Sardinia in an impressionistic style that also possesses strong social overtones. *Il garofano rosso* (written 1933, pub. 1948; The Red Carnation) is a rather precious psychological novel of adolescence, sex, violence, and revolution that documents the attraction of fascism for Vittorini's generation. *Il garofano rosso* also reveals his growing sympathy for leftist social ideals. These exploded in his first major work, the unfinished *Erica e i suoi fratelli* (written 1936, pub. 1956 together with *La Garibaldina; Eng.* tr. of both works, *The Dark and the Light,* 1960). *Erica* is a Marxist affirmation that work and the basic human necessities are rights. Its protagonist is a child who clearly sees the basic injustice of the world and refuses to accept "charity." Here Vittorini succeeded in creating a fable that poetically fuses his myth of childhood as a time of innocence, vision, and vitality with the myth of the noble working class.

For many years, Vittorini sought a style that would give his writing greater immediacy, or "poetry," as he called it. *Conversazione in Sicilia* (written 1936–38, pub. 1941; Eng. tr., *In Sicily,* 1947), his best work, was the fruit of these experiments and of the tremendous emotional impact of his protest against fascism, precipitated by the Civil War in Spain. Its language is new and daring in its use of poetic repetition, musical rhythms, and paratactic syntax. Its allegorical statement of the necessity of reforming "the evil in the suffering world" caused it to become an almost mystical rallying point for anti-Fascist intellectuals. These factors, combined with Vittorini's generosity to young writers and his eclectic avant-gardism, catapulted him into a position of leadership among postwar writers.

While working for the Italian underground, he wrote a Resistance novel, *Uomini e no* (1945; Men and Non-Men). It became an example of neorealism, but it is really a bad pastiche of *Conversazione* and Ernest Hemingway. The very short *Il Sempione strizza l'occhio al Fréjus* (1947;

Eng. tr., *Tune for an Elephant,* 1955), is an intense, highly symbolic, allegorical work that states the necessity of the old civilization's giving way to the new. This moral is presented through the figure of a grandfather elephant, a useless old worker with a prodigious appetite who is advised to seek the elephants' traditional graveyard. Stylistically, it is Vittorini's most perfect work. *Le donne di Messina* (1949, rev. 1964; Eng. tr., *The Women of Messina,* 1974) is an epic novel of a commune's attempt to survive in spite of the unregenerate Fascist spirit of the surrounding towns and one of their own leaders' losing battle with the "fascism" (egoism) within him. The novel is set against the background of a whole people turned nomad by the war. Vittorini later rewrote the work to emphasize his belief in technological progress and to show that a solitary agricultural commune cannot really survive. *La Garabaldina* (1956) is a gay yet bitter comment on Sicily's insistence on living in a feudal past. After this work, Vittorini stopped publishing fiction. *Diario in pubblico* (1957; Public Diary) is an intellectual biography in the form of excerpts from his works of nonfiction, *Le due tensioni* (1967; The Two Tensions), an important collection of thoughts on life, language, and literature, was published posthumously, as was *Le città del mondo* (1969; The Cities of the World), fragments of three novels in one, which he had refused to publish. For a selection of his novels in English, see *The Twilight of the Elephant and Other Novels* (1974).

See: S. Pautasso, *Elio Vittorini* (1967); S. Briosi, *Elio Vittorini* (1970).   J.M.P.

Vivanco, Luis Felipe (1907–75), Spanish poet and critic, was born in San Lorenzo del Escorial near Madrid. He studied philosophy and letters but was by profession an architect. He was closely associated with the important literary journals *Cruz y Raya* and *Escorial*. The best-known of his several critical works is *Introducción a la poesía española contemporánea* (1957), which was awarded the Fastenrath Prize. This work contains studies of many of the poets of his own Generation of 1936, among them Luis ROSALES, Leopoldo PANERO, and Dionisio RIDRUEJO.

Vivanco's first book of poetry was *Cantos de primavera* (1936; Songs of Spring). It was followed by *Tiempo de dolor* (1940; Time of Grief), one of his best-known books, although the poet preferred his later "less baroque" work. Among the collections of his mature poetry are *Continuación de la vida* (1949) and *El descampado* (1957; Open Country), considered one of his best. *Los caminos (1945–1965)* (Roads) was reedited in 1974 in a volume that includes other earlier titles. Some of his work remains uncollected. Like other poets of his generation, Vivanco wrote poetry of classical forms and serenity with greater emphasis on words than on metaphor. His subject is a poeticized but everyday life; his themes are love, family, nature, and faith. Perhaps the most characteristic theme in Vivanco's work is that of God in the world, usually elaborated in the form of a religious contemplation of landscape. The poet himself called this a "pseudomysticism of things." *Luis Felipe Vivanco: antología poética* (1976), ed. by J. M. Valverde, was published in 1976.

                                                                                                   H.L.B.

Vivanti, Annie (1868–1942), Italian novelist and poet, was born in London of German-Italian parentage. Her early volume of poetry, *Lirica* (1890; Lyric), and the novel *Marion, artista da caffè concerto* (1891; Marion, Café Entertainer) were sponsored by Giosuè Carducci (1835–1907), dean of Italian poets, whose own late poetry was influenced by their friendship. Nevertheless, critics condemned Vivanti's immature productions. Her friendship with Carducci lasted until his death. In 1908, Vivanti married the Irish lawyer and patriot John Chartres and spent some time in the United States. In 1910 she published a novel in English, *The Devourers* (Ital. tr., *I divoratori*, 1911). Some 20 books followed: autobiographical and melodramatic novels, such as *Zingaresca* (1918; Gypsy Love) and *Naja Tripudians* (1921); volumes of short stories, such as *Perdonate Eglantina!* (1926; Forgive, Eglantina!); plays, such as *L'invasore* (1917; The Invader); and travel books, such as *Terra di Cleopatra* (1925; Cleopatra's Land).

See: B. Croce, *La letteratura della nuova Italia*, vol. 2 (1914); R. S. Phelps, *Italian Silhouettes* (1924); P. Pancrazi, *Un incontro amoroso della fine Ottocento* (1951).

B.Co.

Vivien, Renée, pseud. of Pauline M. Tarn (1877–1909), French poet, was born in London. She is best known as a follower of the cult of Sappho. Vivien's poetry bears testimony to a passion for perfectionism, and adhering to traditional rules of form while expressing deeply felt emotion. In her richly Hellenic verse, musicality and a dreamlike mysticism are united with sensuality. Lovely heroines, often in the image of Greek maidens, are limned with burning ardor. A hatred for contemporary civilization combines with yearning for an earlier Golden Age. Intense anguish, voluptuous languor, and a craving for death intertwine in images of exquisite, haunting exoticism.

Vivien spent many years traveling before settling permanently in Paris. Profoundly influenced by her visits to the East, she subsequently translated the ancient Greek writings of Sappho and other women poets of Lesbos. These translations, *Les Kitharèdes* (1904), may be considered a revealing expression of Vivien's own lesbian tendencies. Her early collections of verse have melancholy and expressive titles, such as *Cendres et poussières* (1902; Cinders and Dust), *Evocations* (1903), and *Les Flambeaux éteints* (1907; Extinguished Torches). Her *Poésies complètes* (1901–10; Complete Poetry), originally issued in 12 volumes, was published in two volumes in 1934. Vivien died at age 32 of self-imposed starvation.

See: Y. Le Dantec, *Renée Vivien: femme damnée, femme sauvée* (1930).   D.C. and A.C.

Vladimov, Georgy Nikolayevich (1931–), Russian novelist, born in Kharkov, has made his name, almost like a good socialist realist, through the portrayal of young people seeking the meaning of their life in the work situation. But there is always more psychological and social analysis than mythmaking in his work. In *Bolshaya ruda* (1961; Eng. tr., *The Great Ore*, 1965), for example, the record-breaking hero, Pronyakin, is depicted as an obsessive achiever and potential alcoholic, desperate for success, security, and love. *Tri minuty molchaniya* (1969; Three Minutes' Silence) extends the range of this kind of analysis in a long rendering of life in the far northern fishing fleets. *Verny Ruslan* (Faithful Ruslan, which circulated in the Soviet Union in *samizdat* for years before being revised and published in the West in 1975) examines the immediate post-Stalin years by recounting the dissolution of a labor camp through the eyes of a guard dog, Ruslan, who is in effect a parody of both the "positive hero" and the traditional socialist realist narrator. In October 1977, Vladimov resigned from the Union of Soviet Writers, calling it a "police apparatus," and became secretary of the Moscow branch of Amnesty International.

See: V. Chernavsky, "Gibel geroyev," *Grani*, no. 106 (1977): 204–28.   G.H.

Vogt, Nils Collett (1864–1937), Norwegian poet, was born in Christiania (now Oslo), the son of an engineer and a sensitive, artistic, although conservative, mother. He broke early with his bourgeois family to become a follower of Georg BRANDES and the liberal tradition in Scandinavia in the 1880s. He became acquainted with the works of Lord Byron, Percy Bysshe Shelley, and Holger DRACHMANN as well as with those of Bjørnstjerne BJØRNSON. He eventually adopted a moderate socialist view, which he held throughout his life and which is reflected in his entire literary production.

Although a minor poet, Vogt did attain considerable recognition; his poetry is reminiscent of the greater Norwegian poet of an earlier time, Henrik Wergeland (*see* NORWEGIAN LITERATURE). In his poetry, Vogt revealed himself as a warm, intense, committed human being, especially when he dealt with his impassioned youth, including relations with his family, the plight of the underprivileged, and the majestic nature of his homeland. Like Wergeland, Vogt was for the most part not a very "musical" poet, but the vigor of his language very often compensates for this deficiency. Many of Vogt's poems are a delight to read, several are superbly constructed, and two or three might well take their place among the great poems of all literatures. Although Vogt's first volume of poems, *Digte* (1887; Poems), was rather insubstantial, it was an early harbinger of the Norwegian neoromantic movement of the 1890s, among whose more notable practitioners were Knut HAMSUN and Sigbjørn OBSTFELDER. Vogt's poetic collections include *Fra vaar til høst* (1894; From Spring to Autumn), *Det dyre brød* (1900; The Costly Bread), *Septemberbrand* (1907; September Flame), and *Hjemkomst* (1917; Homecoming). He published more poems in 1925 and 1927. Vogt also wrote novels and plays; although of slight literary value, they nevertheless deal cogently with the "generation gap" and express sympathy for the underdog. His two volumes of memoirs, *Fra gutt til mann* (1932; From Boy to Man) and *Oplevelser* (1934; Experiences), contain delightful and moving accounts of a life that registered the changes of the times.

S.A.

Vogüé, Eugène-Melchior, vicomte de (1848–1910), French critic, novelist, historian, and travel writer, was born in Nice but grew up in his ancestral castle of Gourdan (Ardèche). He was wounded and taken prisoner in the War of 1870. Once freed, Vogüé began a career in diplomacy as secretary to his cousin, the ambassador to Turkey. During his Constantinople years he managed visits to the Near East, out of which came a superb travel book, *Syrie, Palestine, Mont Athos* (1876), and the start of his lifelong collaboration with the *Revue des deux mondes*. He was attached to the embassy at St. Petersburg from 1876 to 1882, a fruitful period during which he found the inspiration for his most famous book, *Le Roman russe* (1886; Eng. trs., *The Russian Novelists*, 1887; *The Russian Novel*, 1913). Having returned to France, Vogüé was elected to the Académie Française in 1889, served in the Chambre des Députés as a member from Ardèche (1893–98), and wrote some 20 volumes of literary criticism, polemics, history, and fiction, including the novels *Jean d'Agrève* (1897), *Les Morts qui parlent* (1899; The Dead Who Speak), and *Le Maître de la mer* (1903; The Master of the Sea).

An intellectual with a stoic aristocrat's sense of duty and service, Vogüé was proud, austere, and inwardly warm if diffident. His tastes were catholic, his erudition vast. His polished, poetic style was universally acclaimed. Although resigned to the Third Republic, this conservative Catholic preferred the ancien régime. A logical rationalist, he still demanded a place for intuition, faith, and mystery, thus his great quarrel with Emile ZOLA and the naturalists, writers who lacked the human sympathy of Russian realists like Fyodor DOSTOYEVSKY and Lev TOLSTOY. "Realism becomes odious as soon as it ceases to be charitable," wrote Vogüé in the preface to *The Russian Novel*. Indeed, he is considered a major contributor to the downfall of the French realistic-naturalistic movement and to the rebirth of fiction with a more Christian ethic and a renewed sense of mystery.

See: E. Gosse, *Portraits and Sketches* (1912); V. Giraud, *Les Maîtres de l'heure*, vol. 1 (1914).   A.E.S.

Voigt-Diederichs, Helene (1875–1961), German novelist and short-story writer, was born at Marienhoff, a famtly estate in Schleswig-Holstein, where she received her early education from tutors and lived until she was 14. After several years spent traveling she married the publisher Eugen Diederichs in 1898, then of Leipzig, who later moved to Jena. From 1911 on she lived in Brunswick, separated from her husband, but she returned to Jena in 1931.

Voigt-Diederichs's literary traits are North German: somber seriousness—relieved occasionally by touches of humor—restraint, and aversion to everything strident. The influence of the Danish novelist Jens Peter JACOBSEN is seen in her only volume of lyrics, *Unterstrom* (1901; Undercurrent). Her main works are confined to the real experiences of her own life, the rural community, marriage, and children, as in such novels as *Regine Vosgerau* (1901) and *Dreiviertel Stund vor Tag* (1905; Three-Quarters of an Hour before Daybreak). She described the life of her mother in *Auf Marienhoff: das Leben einer deutschen Mutter* (1925; Marienhoff: The Life of a German Mother). Problems of marriage are depicted in the stories of *Mann und Frau* (1921; Husband and Wife) and in the novel *Ring um Roderich* (1929; A Ring about Roderich). *Kinderland* (1907; The Land of Children) and *Der grüne Papagei* (1934; The Green Parrot) contain stories about children. The unassuming sobriety of her style is apparent in the travel books *Wandertage in England* (1912; Wandering in England) and *Gast in Siebenbürgen* (1936; Visitor in Siebenbürgen). She is also the author of the novels *Das Verlöbnis* (1942; The Engagement) and *Waage des Lebens* (1952; The Scale of Life), as well as of stories contained in *Der Zaubertrank* (1948; The Enchanted Drink) and *Die Bernsteinkette* (1951; The Amber Necklace).   W.R.G. rev. A.L.W.

Vojnović, Ivo (1857–1929), Croatian dramatist and fiction writers, was born in Dubrovnik. His father was a lawyer and later a professor at the University of Zagreb; his mother (whose maiden name was Serragli) had a deep influence on her son. After graduating with a degree in law, Vojnović entered government service, but for personal and political reasons his career was not smooth. In 1914 the Austrian authorities arrested him along with other supporters of a Yugoslav state but he was eventually released because of serious eye trouble. A jubilee performance of his play *Ekvinocij* (1895; The Equinox) in Zagreb on his 60th birthday in 1917 became the occasion for a spontaneous ovation in honor of his literary achievement and his political position. After 1918 he served for a while as Yugoslav consul in Nice, and spent his last years in Belgrade and Dubrovnik.

In his story "Geranium" (1880), written under the influence of Gustave Flaubert's "Un cœur simple," Vojnović attempted a symbolical comparison between a spinster and a geranium. His collection of short stories, *Perom i olovkom* (1884; With Pen and Pencil), deals with emi-

grants who moved in the aristocratic and artistic circles of Vienna, whereas his novella *Ksanta* (1886) describes the tragic destiny of some Dubrovnik sailors. Thus, in this novella, as later in his plays, Vojnović was mainly concerned either with the glorious past of his native city or with its current economic hardships. As a means of escape from the oncoming masses and their petit-bourgeois mentality, Vojnović tended to retreat into portrayals of a cosmopolitan elite. His works are often characterized by dramatic conflicts, unusual events, and lyricism.

Vojnović's plays can be divided into three categories: those with a cosmopolitan setting, such as *Psyche* (1899) and *Gospodja sa suncokretom* (1912; The Lady with a Sunflower); those with a strong political tendency and that show the influence of folk poetry, such as *Smrt majke Jugovića* (1907; The Death of the Jugović Mother) and *Lazarevo vaskresenje* (1913; The Resurrection of Lazarus); and finally those connected with Dubrovnik—*Ekvinocij* (1902); *Dubrovačka trilogija* (A Dubrovnik Trilogy), and *Maskerate ispod kuplja* (1922; Masquerades in an Attic). Although Vojnović's cosmopolitan and patriotic plays generally failed because his characters are unconvincing, overly melodramatic, or snobbish, he reached the summit of his artistry in depicting his beloved native city. *Equinox* is the tragic story of a father and son who intend to marry the same girl. The *Dubrovnik Trilogy* depicts the steady political, economic, and physical decline of the former Dubrovnik nobility. Even though Vojnović belonged to this class, he superbly portrayed the aristocrats as people doomed by their own folly. *Masquerade* is a light, lyrical epilogue to Vojnović's significant dramatic output.

See: M. Begović, "Konte Ivo," *Hrvatska revija* 10 (1929): 561–69; V. Pavletić, *Drame Ive Vojnovića* (1962); M. Matković, "Ivo Vojnović," *ForumZ* 12 (1964): 820–41; F. Čale, "Dante u djelima Ive Vojnovića," *Rep* 5 (1965): 195–97.   A.K.

Voloshin, Maksimilian Aleksandrovich, full name Maksimilian Aleksandrovich Kirienko-Voloshin (1877–1932), Russian poet, translator, critic, and painter, was born in Kiev and spent his youth partly at Feodosiya in the Crimea and partly in Paris. He entered Moscow University in 1897 and in 1910 was expelled for "student disorders" and exiled for six months to Tashkent. Voloshin traveled a great deal in Europe, often on foot, before settling at Koktebel in 1917. His outlook was cosmopolitan and aesthetic, his orientation was toward the Latin countries of the West, and he was essentially apolitical. These attitudes were not consonant with those prevalent after the October Revolution (1917); his last major publication was in 1919, *Demony Glukhonemye* (Deaf-mute Demons), which contains poetry of mystical, Utopian hope for his strife-torn country. From 1917 to the end of his life, Voloshin remained at Koktebel, at odds with the Communist regime and removed from literary developments; the poems from his last period deal with nature in the Crimea.

Voloshin's first serious publication of verse was in 1903, and his first published collection in 1910 assured his reputation. Some six volumes followed, for the most part quite brief, with the last in 1923, *Usobitsa* (Internal Strife). Among his translations, especially noteworthy are two volumes of Emile VERHAEREN, published in 1916 and 1919. Voloshin also wrote articles on art and French literature, some of which are printed in *Liki tvorčestva* (1914; Faces of Creativity). When the new journal *Apollon* was founded in 1909 in part as a reaction to the symbolist movement in poetry, Voloshin was one of its theoreticians, making an appeal for a "New Realism" (*neorealizm*).

Although Voloshin has been largely ignored since the early 1920s, there has lately been a renaissance of interest in this minor but far from insignificant poet. It is worth noting that Marina TSVETAYEVA's essay on Voloshin is one of the outstanding ones on modern Russian poetry.

See: M. Tsvetayeva, "Zhivoye o zhivom," in *Proza* (New York, 1953).   S.N.D.

Volponi, Paolo (1924-), Italian novelist and poet, was born in Urbino in rural central Italy, where he lived until he finished his law studies in 1947. From 1950 to 1955 he worked in various parts of Italy as a special social services consultant. From 1956 to 1971 he worked for Olivetti in Ivrea, where he became thoroughly acquainted with the structure and problems of a large modern company. He was also briefly associated with the Agnelli Foundation. At present he lives in Milan with his family.

Volponi began his literary career as a poet, with the collection *Il ramarro* (1948; The Green Lizard), followed by *L'antica moneta* (1955; The Ancient Coin) and *Le porte dell'Appennino* (1960; Eng. tr., *The Apennine Year*, 1961), which won the Viareggio Prize. But his reputation rests on his novels, *Memoriale* (1962; Eng. tr., *My Troubles Began*, 1964); *La macchina mondiale* (1965; Eng. tr., *The World-Wide Machine*, 1967), winner of the Strega Prize; *Corporale* (1974; Bodily); and *Il sipario ducale* (1975; The Duke's Curtain).

The two poles of Volponi's inspiration are the country, which he celebrates especially in his first, posthermetic poems, and the city (the industrial companies), which provides the background for his novels. These two poles contrast nature and history, irrationality and rationality, lyricism and objectivity. Volponi is one of the very few contemporary Italian writers who never let these two poles become a dichotomy. Instead, he uses them to represent the dialectical, problematic movements of all reality—perhaps in imitation of Elio VITTORINI's "affective" and "rational" tensions. The "alienated lyricism" of his "neurotic" protagonists Albino Saluggia, Anteo Crocioni, Gerolamo Aspri, and Gaspare Subissoni is the effective stylistic device he uses to provide a faithful portrait of contemporary man and society. Both theme and style confirm that Volponi follows the lead of Italo SVEVO and Luigi PIRANDELLO in judging the present negatively and in considering literature—specifically the novel—an act of knowledge.

See: G. C. Ferretti, *Volponi* (1972); R. Capozzi, "The Narrator-Protagonist and the Divided Self in Volponi's *Corporale*," *FI* 10 (1976): 203-17.   G.P.B.

Voronsky, Aleksandr Konstantinovich (1884-1943), Russian Marxist critic, aesthetician, and editor, was born into a family of priests in Tambov, but early became a revolutionary. In 1921, Vladimir Lenin appointed him editor of a new journal, *Krasnaya nov*, which was meant to boost the regime's prestige and attract fresh literary talent (*see* RUSSIAN LITERATURE). It soon became the center of the best writing of the 1920s. Gradually, however, Voronsky fell from favor; in 1927 he was dismissed from his post; finally he was arrested on charges of "Trotskyism."

As a prolific and highly influential critic, Voronsky covered the entire range of contemporary literature. To him what counted most in a writer was not ideological position, but rather an interest in Soviet society, a general sympathy for the aims of the October Revolution (1917), and, especially, high artistic standards. Hereby Voronsky virtually defined the so-called fellow travelers, who included most of the finest writers of the time. He was skeptical of the widely held assumption that a uniquely "proletarian" literature could develop, insisting instead

on continuity with the Russian classics, and advocating such supposedly "classical" qualities as large-scale works with complex characters. In his aesthetics he eventually arrived at a thesis that many of his contemporaries deemed un-Marxist: art's main function is to restore, through "immediate impressions," a lost harmony with a pristine and virtually changeless world of "objective beauty." Recently, Voronsky has been partially "rehabilitated" in the Soviet Union, and something of his importance is coming to be appreciated.

See: R. A. Maguire, *Red Virgin Soil: Soviet Literature in the 1920s* (1968).   R.A.M.

Voynovich, Vladimir Nikolaevich (1932-), Russian author of novellas, stories, and a satirical novel, was born in Stalinabad. He attained prominence in 1961 with the story "My zdes zhivyom" (We Live Here), which portrays life on a collective farm. This work appeared separately in book form in 1963 and was included in the collection *Povesti* (1972; Novellas) with two other long stories, "Dva tovarishcha" (1967; Two Comrades), a humorous, satirical, and deeply moral narrative about an adolescent boy reminiscent of J. D. Salinger's Holden Caulfield, and "Vladychitsa" (1969; Sovereign Mistress), a brilliant commentary on political power and authority in the form of a fable. His earlier stories include "Rasstoyaniye v polkilometra" (1963; Eng. tr., "A Distance of Half a Kilometer," 1978) and "Khochu byt chestnym (1963; Eng. tr., "I'd Be Honest If They'd Let Me," 1965), the latter portraying a construction foreman who places personal integrity above loyalty to the Communist Party. A later work is *Stepen doveriya* (1972; Degree of Trust), a fictionalized biography of the 19th-century revolutionary, Vera Figner.

Voynovich's more recent works, all published in the West, are the satirical novel *Zhizn i neobychaynye priklyucheniya soldata Ivana Chonkina* (parts 1 and 2, 1975; Eng. tr., *The Life and Extraordinary Adventures of Private Ivan Chonkin*, 1977); two satirical, nonfictional accounts of Voynovich's recent dealings with the Soviet bureaucracy: "Proisshestviye v 'Metropole'" (1975; Eng. tr., "Incident at the Metropole," 1977) and *Ivankiada* (1976; Eng. tr., *Ivankiad*, 1977); and a collection of stories, *Putyom vzaimnoy perepiski* (1979; Eng. tr., *In Plain Russian*, 1979).

Chonkin, a broadly comic satire on Soviet red tape, might have been publishable in the USSR if it had not also lampooned the Soviet army of 1941. For sending his manuscript to the West (where, in translation, it proved to be one of the more popular Russian works published abroad in the 1970s), Voynovich was dismissed from the Union of Soviet Writers. A writer of proletarian origins who 20 years ago composed the lyrics to the "Cosmonauts' Hymn," he now plays the ironical role of a nonchalantly fearless dissident who declines to take himself too seriously.

See: G. Hosking, "The Good Soldier Chonkin," *TLS* (Jan. 23, 1976), p. 92; and M. A. Szporluk, "Vladimir Voinovich: The Development of a New Satirical Voice," *RLT* 14 (1976): 99-121.   D.Fi.

Voznesensky, Andrey Andreyevich (1933-), Russian poet, was born in Moscow. He became prominent in the early 1960s, when a pleiade of young poets made its appearance in Moscow, illuminating the Russian literary scene—then just emerging from the long night of Stalinism—with its originality, boldness, and talent. In a poem dedicated to Bela Akhmadulina, "Nas mnogo. Nas mozhet byt chetvero," (1964; Eng. tr. in "We are Many, Four Perhaps, Altogether," 1967) Voznesensky restricts the number of new poetic stars to four, including, certainly, Akhmadulina, Yevgeny YEVTUSHENKO, and himself. In the poem, Voznesensky suggests that the poets, traveling as they do, at a reckless pace, are likely to come to a bad end. "To argue with a cop is a losing proposition," he writes. "He can't appreciate your lyric speech. . . . We were the first to crack the sound barrier. . . . Who cares if we're smashed to bits in the end?" (from *Antiworlds and the Fifth Ace*, by Andrei Voznesensky, edited by Patricia Blake and Max Hayward, © 1966, 1967 by Basic Books, © 1963 by Encounter). At least two members of the quartet did not emerge unscathed from the massive campaign against artistic experimentation initiated by Nikita Khrushchov in 1963 and the increasingly severe cultural controls imposed by Leonid Brezhnev. Only Voznesensky seems to have fulfilled, and even transcended, the promise of the early 1960s. He continues to write prolifically, without artistic or moral compromise, and to be published in the Soviet Union, albeit in the face of relentless criticism in the press by orthodox writers.

Voznesensky's great-grandfather was a Russian Orthodox priest, his paternal grandfather a doctor, and his father, Andrey, a professor of engineering and a well-known designer of hydroelectric stations. During World War II, young Andrey lived with his mother and younger sister in Kurgan, in the Ural Mountains, while his father was in Leningrad, engaged in evacuating factories from the beleaguered city. The family was reunited in Moscow after the war. Voznesensky started out as a painter and later studied architecture. Just before his graduation from the Moscow Architectural Institute in 1957, an event occurred that informs his amusing, ebullient poem "Pozhar v Arkhitekturnom Institute" (1958; Eng. tr., in *Fire in the Architectural Institute,* 1966). A fire swept through the place, consuming Voznesensky's elaborate design project. "I believe in symbols," he wrote. "I understood that architecture was burned out in *me* ; I became a poet." Voznesensky remains a secret painter, and his continuing interest in the visual arts and in architecture is manifest in the themes and symbols he chooses for his poetry.

Although isolated poems by Voznesensky began to appear in Soviet periodicals after 1957, the three volumes of his verse published in the Soviet Union between 1960 and 1963 served to make him famous. This was a time of mass poetry readings in sports stadiums. Voznesensky and Yevtushenko adopted a style of public reading pioneered by Vladimir MAYAKOVSKY, involving histrionic, full-voice delivery. Voznesensky has trained his powerful voice to display the assonances, rhythms, and modulations of pitch and intensity that abound in his poetry. His readings have mesmerized large audiences in the Soviet Union, as well as in Western Europe and the United States, where Voznesensky has frequently traveled. One of his American translators, Robert Bly, has described the spectacle:

Voznesensky has a curious look like a wood animal . . . . Waiting to read while the translation is being spoken, he sits with a blank expressionless face—like a pool unstirred by the wind—the hair falling over the pale forehead is like little birch branches swaying over the water. . . . He strolls slowly towards the microphone, his hands put in slit front pockets, the thumbs pointing towards each other. As he begins to read, his knees bent, the right hand swings back and forth like the Neanderthal man complimenting himself after having thrown the first stone. He looks straight forward, bending over slowly—a fantastic and resonant voice booms out, not angry, but sheer power, like

enormous dynamos, like immense waterfalls falling. . . . Then it drops suddenly into the most matter-of-fact tone, emotionless, muttering.

Voznesensky stands out among the other poets who emerged in the post-Stalin era for the resourcefulness with which he handles language. Together with the young Yevtushenko he pioneered the emancipation of Russian poetic language from the deadly restriction it had suffered. Apart from his superb mastery of contemporary Russian idiom, he also brings to his craft an impressive knowledge of his native poetic tradition. His own original manner is enhanced by a familiarity with Mayakovsky and Boris PASTERNAK, both of whom have influenced him, as well as with the classical Russian heritage.

Another of his translators, W. H. Auden, pointed to

the wide range of subject matter by which Mr. Voznesensky is imaginatively excited—he is equally interested in animals and airports, native and alien landscapes—and the variety of tones, elegiac, comic, grotesque, quiet, rebellious, etc. which he can command.

Robert Lowell welcomed him to New York in 1966 in these terms:

He comes to us with the careless gaiety of the Twenties and Apollinaire. Surrealism sprouts from his fingertips: birds with aluminum bodies and women's faces, houses losing their walls, men losing their skins, a girl who sees the past as the future, and noses that go on growing all night. . . . Every other poem is a love poem or about a woman. He is a difficult poet and the disciple of difficult poets, yet he moves large audiences, and I think this has encouraged him to give an immediate spoken vitality to his surprising thoughts and most ingenious images.

In the 1970s, partly because of restrictions placed on public readings and foreign travel, and partly as a result of his development as a poet, Voznesensky tended to reduce his public appearances to the relative privacy of the printed word. His recent production has also encompassed a broad range of subjects and tonalities. He has made a short-lived foray into concrete poetry. He composed a long, pessimistic poem, "Lyod-69" (1970; Ice-69) dedicated to a 20-year-old girl who froze to death on a skiing trip. The poem is the result of a letter the poet received from the girl's father, who told him that she had tried to keep alive by reciting his poems to herself. Voznesensky's comic gifts, with their usual sexual and political undertones, were deployed in a "Bill of Fare" splashed across an entire page of the magazine *Moskva* in 1973. This included such items as "one Fiat for 1,000 persons," "ear à la Van Gogh, 150,000 kroner," "sweets for authority, 30 pieces . . . ."

Such playful digs at the establishment have earned Voznesensky countless pompous articles in Soviet newspapers and periodicals accusing him of "sensational supermodernism" or unintelligibility. Nonetheless, between 1970 and 1974 three volumes of Voznesensky's verse passed the Soviet censorship: *Ten zvuka* (1970; Shadow of Sound), *Vzglyad* (1972; A Glance), and *Vypusti ptitsu* (1974; Set the Bird Free!). In the United States, his work has aroused more interest among distinguished poets than that of any other Russian of his generation. Among his translators are William Jay Smith, Louis Simpson, Richard Wilbur, and Jean Garrigue. The most complete collection of his work in English translation is *Antiworlds and The Fifth Ace* (1967), edited by Patricia Blake and Max Hayward, translated by W. H. Auden, and others. Stanley Kunitz has translated his long poem "Avos!" (1971; Perhaps!), published under the title *Story under Full Sail* (1974). P.Bl.

Vroman, Leo (1915–), Dutch poet and writer of prose fiction, was born in Gouda. He left the Netherlands as soon as the Nazi Occupation began and arrived in the Dutch East Indies, eventually living as a captive of the Japanese there and in Japan. On his way home via San Francisco at the end of the war, he decided to stay in the United States, where he now lives in New York. Vroman has earned a livelihood in physiology and studies of the blood, and in 1958 he received his doctorate in the natural sciences from the University of Utrecht. He has also attempted to write poetry in English, and his *Gedichten* (1946; Poems) and *Gedichten, vroegere en latere* (1949; Poems, Earlier and Later) were soon followed by *Poems in English* (1953). Vroman is an innovator in language, style, and technique. He does not hesitate to invent new words and sometimes doubles or even triples letters to lengthen the vowels of standard words. Vroman creates an intimate relationship with his readers, speaking directly to them in a conversational style. He mentions his wife, Tineke, his daughters, and other members of his family, assuming that his readers will know who they are. Although Vroman uses the first person singular in setting down his poems, the narrator who appears as *I* is not necessarily identical in personality with Vroman. His professional interest in science is evident in both the vocabulary and the ideas in his poetry. One of his poems, for example, is entitled "De reactic van plasma thromboplastin antecedent (PTA) met Hageman factor (HF)." *Manke vliegen* (1963; Crippled Flies) consists of quatrains followed by little pen-and-ink sketches (Vroman has also earned a living as an artist), with a final line. *Almanak* (1965) includes a group of 12 poems, one for each month, in which the first part, describing the American scene, is printed in Roman type, and the second half, recalling memories of the Netherlands, appears in italics. In addition to such volumes of prose fiction as *Tineke* (1948), *De adem van Mars* (1956; The Breath of Mars), *Snippers van Leo Vroman* (1958; Snippets of Leo Vroman), and *Leo Vromans Proza* (1960), he has also published the follow-ing volumes of poetry: *Inleiding tot een leegte* (1955; Introduction to a Void), *Uit slaapwandelen* (1957; Out Sleepwalking), *De ontvachting en andere gedichten* (1960; The Flaying and Other Poems), *Twee gedichten* (1961; Two Poems), *Fabels van Leo Vroman* (1962; Fables by Leo Vroman), *126 gedichten* (1964; 126 Poems), *God en godin* (1967; God and Goddess), and *114 gedichten* (1969; 114 Poems).

See: L. H. Pelzer, *Leo Vroman* (1965). S.L.F.

Vynnychenko, Volodymyr (1880–1941), Ukrainian playwright and novelist, was born of peasant stock in Kherson province. While studying at Kiev University, he became an ardent socialist. During the Revolution of 1917, his political activity led him to become one of the leaders of the Ukrainian national government, the Central Rada. After its collapse in 1919, Vynnychenko emigrated to Western Europe and settled in France, where he lived until his death. He left an account of the Revolution in his memoirs *Vidrodzhennya natsiyi* (1920; The Rebirth of a Nation).

Vynnychenko began writing in 1902, and his naturalistic short stories became very popular even though his iconoclasm, cynicism, and sharp social satire offended many readers. In 1914, Vladimir Lenin compared him in a pejorative way to Fyodor DOSTOYEVSKY. Vynnychenko's novel *Chesnist z soboyu* (1911; Honesty with Oneself) caused a great stir. His second creative period began in the 1920s when he wrote his Utopian novel *Sonyashna mashyna* (1921–24; The Sun Machine). His plays, written earlier, were published in foreign translation and successfully staged in Western Europe. These include *Chorna pantera i bily vedmid* (1911; The Black Panther and the White Bear), *Brekhnya* (1910; The Lie), *Hrikh* (1920; Sin), and *Zakon* (1923; The Law). The first of these was made into a German film. In his last period Vynnychenko wrote several novels and tracts based on his own Utopian philosophy of "concordism," including *Nova zapovid*. (1950; A New Commandment) and *Slovo za toboyu, Staline* (1971; Take the Floor, Stalin). Many of his works were collected in a multivolume edition in the Ukraine in the 1920s. In the 1930s they were withdrawn, and today this interesting writer is totally ignored in his homeland. G.S.N.L.

W

Waggerl, Karl Heinrich (1897–), German novelist, established his reputation with his first book *Brot* (1930; Eng. tr., *Bread*, 1931). He was born and grew up in Bad Gastein. The hardships of his youth and his captivity in Italy during World War I undermined his health and prevented him from resuming teaching, the profession for which he had studied. With a craftsman's knowledge, Waggerl wrote of the activities that make up village and farm life in the mountains. In *Das Jahr des Herrn* (1934; The Year of the Lord) worship and religious ministrations and festivals accompany, hallow, and round out the farmer's year. *Mütter* (1936; Mothers) celebrates motherhood.

Although Waggerl's people are simple folk, they are in some senses just as complex as their "betters" and just as prone to transgress. The totality of life, with the interrelationships between individuals and children, the problems of chance and character, is Waggerl's subject, which he treats with a delicate literary art. Poems are contained in his *Heiteres Herbarium* (1950; Cheerful Herbarium), and pleasant stories are found in *Die Pfingstreise* (1947;

The Trip at Pentecost), *Und es begab sich . . .* (1953; And It Happened . . .), and *Die grünen Freunde* (1955; The Green Friends). Further prose is represented in the impressionistic *Liebe Dinge* (1956; Nice Things) and in his autobiography *Wanderung und Heimkehr* (1957; Wandering and Homecoming). His works were collected in an edition published between 1948 and 1952.

See: R. Bayr, *Karl Heinrich Waggerl, der Dichter und sein Werk* (1947); L. Besch, ed., *Karl Heinrich Waggerl genauer betrachtet* (1967). J.F.G. rev. A.L.W.

Wagner, Richard (1813–83), German dramatic composer, was born in Leipzig, the ninth child of Friedrich Wagner, not, as some maintain, the natural son of the actor and painter Ludwig Geyer. His father died when Richard was six months old. Geyer married the widow and gave the family a new home in Dresden. After Geyer's death in 1821 the family returned to Leipzig, where Wagner in his 15th year heard Beethoven's music to Goethe's *Egmont* and was so impressed that he determined to compose music to his own first dramatic attempt, a blood-dripping tragedy, *Leubald und Adelaide* (1828). In school he had shown no musical talent; his tastes were solely literary, his chief interest the classics. Wagner's classical training and his later intensive study of Greek drama determined his subsequent epoch-making conception of the tone drama. His interest in music once aroused through literature, he set out to conquer composition by himself; but he found a teacher who in six months' instruction, based on an analysis of Mozart's and Beethoven's masterpieces, gave him the command of the musical idiom that he perfected in *Tristan* and the *Ring*. In 1833 he began his professional career as chorus master of the Würzburg opera company. Here he composed his first opera, *Die Feen* (1834; The Fairies). He drifted now from one bankrupt opera company to another. At Magdeburg his *Liebesverbot* (Love Forbidden), an immature work in the spirit of Das Junge Deutschland and patterned after *Measure for Measure*, was composed in 1836. In the hope of conquering the German stage via Paris and the Meyerbeerian grand opera, Wagner spent three years of deprivation and discouragement in the French capital. As there seemed no hope of placing his *Rienzi,* he abandoned the traditional opera and completed *Der fliegende Holländer* (1841; The Flying Dutchman) in six weeks. He recognized the novelty of his attempt to create a new art form in which music should not be primarily an entertainment but should derive from and interpret a true drama, and he wrote: "Here begins my career as poet; I cease to be a concocter of opera librettos."

Wagner returned to Dresden, where in 1842 *Rienzi* was produced with great success. Fame and fortune seemed assured. To the bitter disappointment of his wife, the actress Minna Planer, Wagner continued the reforms begun with the *Holländer*. The study of the literature of medieval Germany and his Parisian sojourn had convinced him that his nature was essentially German and that only Germanic sources could inspire him to supreme artistic creation. In *Tannhäuser* (1845) Wagner, on the background of the dull Wartburgkrieg and the Tannhäuser legend, created a powerful psychological love drama in which, as so often in his works, redemption is achieved through a woman's self-sacrificing love. *Lohengrin,* a modernization of the Zeus and Semele theme based on the medieval swan-knight legend, had its premiere under Franz Liszt at Weimar in 1850, after Wagner had fled from Dresden on account of his participation in the May revolution of 1849. In 1848 he had wavered between spoken drama with a historical theme, *Friedrich Barbarossa,* and a musical treatment of the Siegfried myth. He chose mythical rather than historical sources for his following works (with the exception of *Die Meistersinger,* produced in 1868) and documented this decision in a series of expository and propagandistic prose works to which the first years of his banishment at Zürich were devoted and which, especially his *Oper und Drama* (1851; Opera and the Drama), elaborate his theories of the new "tone drama." He hoped to create a drama in which, as in Attic tragedy, the separate arts should be united in an artistic whole. Unfortunately, Wagner's prose style, largely influenced by the philosopher Ludwig Feuerbach, is often nebulous or ponderous. Meanwhile the original *Siegfrieds Tod* (1848; The Death of Siegfried) was being expanded into the *Ring* tetralogy. Unlike Friedrich Hebbel, who in writing his drama used only the Middle High German Nibelungenlied, Wagner chose the Scandinavian Eddic poems and the Volsunga Saga and gave a mythical rather than a historical interpretation. The old world of Wotan and Valhalla must perish, a victim of its dishonest greed and lust for power. George Bernard Shaw could well call the *Ring* "the work of a social revolutionary." But exaggerated use of alliteration, verbosity, and inconsistencies would have prevented its success were it not for the power and wealth of the music. Here the leitmotif, Wagner's new type of musical pattern, is perfected and masterfully employed. By 1857, *Das Rheingold* (The Gold in the Rhine), *Die Walküre* (The Valkyries), and the first part of *Siegfried* were completed, but Wagner, abandoning hope of any performance of the stupendous cycle and convinced that a single opera might more easily be given a hearing, at the same time inspired by his love for Mathilde Wesendonk and engrossed in Arthur Schopenhauer's doctrine of renunciation, turned to the story of *Tristan und Isolde* (completed in 1859). In seeking the ethical kernel he transformed a medieval triangle narrative into a drama of ethical as well as musical sublimity.

The accession to the Bavarian throne of the youthful king Ludwig, who had been captivated by Wagner's music and ideas, inaugurated a new era for the composer, who now became the friend and guest of a monarch. In 1868, Wagner sat in the royal box with Ludwig to witness the premiere of *Die Meistersinger von Nürnberg* (The Master Singers of Nuremberg), that inspired study of renunciation combined with the symbolical depiction of the eternal conflict of genius and caviling pedantry. Court jealousies, Wagner's indiscretions, his liaison with Cosima, Hans von Bülow's wife (daughter of Liszt), necessitated his departure to Triebschen near Lucerne, where he resided until 1872. In that year Bayreuth became his permanent home, and in 1876 it was the scene of the festival performances of the entire *Ring des Nibelungen*. After the performance in 1882 of his last work, *Parsifal,* he went to Venice and there succumbed to a heart attack on Feb. 13, 1883.

Idolized by friends and bitterly attacked by hostile critics, Wagner was all artist, actuated by a demoniac creative urge brooking no opposition, unwilling to compromise with mediocrity, demanding surroundings sybaritic in their luxury, and subordinating everything to his single creative purpose. Not always of complete integrity in his private life, he presented in his tone dramas the highest ethical values, especially the themes of renunciation and of redemption. *Parsifal,* which embodies Wagner's conceptions of Christian and Buddhistic purity, represents Christlike redemption through self-sacrifice and understanding sympathy. This "sinking down at the foot of the Cross" was largely responsible for Friedrich NIETZSCHE's defection from his formerly beloved and admired master.

Wagner's operatic reforms include the requirement that the text be a consistent drama and form a perfect unity with the interpreting, not merely accompanying, orchestra and the stage picture. Poetic language should harmonize with the nature of the drama. Stylistic unity is attained by the skillful use of the leitmotif. All this was demonstrated in the model festival performances at Bayreuth. Their influence and that of Wagner's music and theories in general were enormous on all aspects of 19th-century culture. In France in particular, from Charles BAUDELAIRE, Wagner's first staunch advocate, to Paul CLAUDEL, writers as well as musicians have been affected. André GIDE, in describing one literary circle, said, "Wagner was their God." Romain ROLLAND and Marcel PROUST represent the height of this influence, which was potent with the prose writers as well as the lyric poets.

See: W. J. Henderson, *Richard Wagner: His Life and His Dramas* (2d ed., rev., 1923); E. Newman, *The Life of Richard Wagner* 4 vols. (1933–46); T. Mann, *Freud, Goethe, Wagner* (1937); R. W. Gutman, *Richard Wagner: The Man, His Mind, His Music* (1968); H. Mayer, *Portrait of Wagner* (1972). P.R.P. rev. A.L.W.

Walravens, Jan (1920–65), Belgian (Flemish) essayist, critic, and novelist, was born in Anderlecht, a suburb of Brussels. Walravens is best known as a defender of avant-garde art movements and as a promoter of postwar Sartrian existentialist philosophy (*see* Jean-Paul SARTRE). Walravens's numerous articles in literary magazines and newspapers established his reputation as a serious art critic who knew how to discover promising talents. He was also a novelist of reknown.

In 1951, Walravens published *Roerloos aan zee* (Motionless at Sea). The process at play in *Roerloos* may best be described as psychosociological and metaphysical: the main character, Herman Kempadel, is the archetype of the modern Catholic intellectual for whom the external signs and values of the faith have become meaningless but who cannot rid himself of his obsessions with God, of the certitude that his link with God will never enable him to be free and untroubled. He fights desperately against deep frustrations provoked by his relationship with a tyrannical father and by his own sexual experiences. He engages in a relationship with a sensual woman, Nana, whom he murders in order to come to terms with the discrepancies between his spiritual and physical tendencies. Kempadel's lawyer does not present him as an impulsive impassioned murderer, however, but as a witness and victim of our degenerate and amoral time. In many ways, *Negatief* (1958; Negative) supplements *Roerloos aan zee*. For the 60-year-old Pierre Esneux, God is dead. Esneux strives for the pure and true experience of nothingness. At the time of his death Walravens was working on a third novel, which was to be part of a trilogy. Walravens's novels are philosophical and, therefore, not entirely convincing. Yet they render subtly and accurately the intellectual climate of the 1950s.

Among Walravens's critical essays, *Phenomenologie van de moderne poëzie* (1950; Phenomenology of Modern Poetry) and *Opstand, verrukelijke arend* (1953; Revolution, That Splendid Eagle) deserved to be mentioned. The insightful introductions he wrote for two anthologies that he also edited, *Waar is de eerste morgen?* (1955; Where Is the First Sunrise?) and *Vijfde kolom* (1967; The Fifth Column), contributed to the furthering of experimental poetry and new prose in Flanders.

See: P. de Wispelaere, *Jan Walravens* (1974); R. van den Borre, *De romans van Walravens in existentialistisch perspectief* (1977).   P. van A.

Walschap, Gerard (1898–), Belgian (Flemish) novelist, short-story writer, and essayist, was born in Londerzeel. In the 1920s, Walschap published a series of poems in the humanitarian expressionist mode. A few plays and a novel, *Waldo* (1928), written in a similar vein, received little attention. As Walschap himself has written in *Voorpostgevechten* (1943; Outpost Flights), the 1930s brought about a new approach to the novel, affecting him as well as his contemporaries. They chose to describe the tragedy inherent in the life of the so-called simple Christian folk of Flanders through ordinary village stories. Such novels as *Volk* (1930; Village People), *De dood in het dorp* (1930; Death in the Village), and *De wereld van Soo Moereman* (1941; The World of Soo Moereman) undermine the idyllic world view of Flanders so dear to "folklore" writers. Walschap's characters are truly human, displaying both the good and the less worthy sides of their personalities.

Walschap, whose affiliation with Roman Catholicism was very strong in the beginning of his career, also confronts his readers in those early novels with a sharp criticism of the physical and moral degeneration of the society he describes. Moral depravation serves again as a backdrop in Walschap's great novels, *Adelaïde* (1929),

Eric (1931), and *Carla* (1933). Despite their deliberately moralistic tone, Walschap's first novels were fiercely attacked by Catholic authorities who objected to his portrayal of Christian upbringing and of prevalent morality. The critic Jean Weisgerber has pointed out that Walschap's characters "are neurotic, demential, doomed by heredity or sadistic and reveal the monstrous degenerations of souls caught in a dilemma between lust and conscience, between the attraction of evil and the anguish of sin." Weisgerber also notes that this degeneration is outweighed and overcome by nature, which in this context designates both the human instinct and the landscape. The positive influence of nature plays a significant role in the novel *Trouwen* (1933; Matrimony), in which the intellectual Rik engages in a relationship with the wholesome Mie Zaterdag. Their marriage leads to the moral rescue Rik has always sought. *Celibaat* (1934; Celibacy) and *Een mens van goede wil* (1936; A Man of Good Will) successfully deal with similar issues. On the other hand, such novels as *Sibylle* (1938), *Het kind* (1939; The Child), and *Bejegening van Christus* (1940; Treatment of Christ) reflect Walschap's conflict with the Catholic faith.

Walschap's best novel, *Houtekiet* (1939), presents a synthesis of all these themes. In *Houtekiet*, Walschap describes the foundation and the growth of a primitive, overtly pagan community. Its "patriarch," Jan Houtekiet, is a man who sets his drives, his instincts, and his natural needs up against the rigid laws and conventions of a so-called civilized society. Houtekiet's world view gives him the strength to rebel successfully against authority figures. When his settlement, Deps, becomes a little society of its own, elements from the once hated outside world begin to creep in, as for example the spiritual Apostle who introduces faith (and therefore tradition) and who gains control over the women. The real drama of this isolated microcosm takes place in the life and in the mind of the founder himself. Houtekiet, who has known many women, discovers, in the love of Iphigenie, spiritual values that form the base of human relationships and that outweigh the hazards of an instinctive existence. In this respect, *Houtekiet* constitutes a turning point in Walschap's spiritual evolution: in this novel, the author confronts his crisis of faith and his longing for a humanistic world view.

In *Zuster Virgilia* (1951; Virgilia the Nun), Walschap deals with similar issues. Whereas Houtekiet embodied the unconquerable power of life, Virgilia symbolizes an even more important aspect of life, the strive for spiritual perfection. Like *Zuster Virgilia*, such novels as *Denise* (1942) and *De Française* (1957; The French Woman) portray strong, convincing female characters. *Zwart en wit* (1948; Black and White), *Oproer in Congo* (1953; Revolution in the Congo), *De verloren zoon* (1958; The Prodigal Son), *De ongeloofelijke avonturen van Tilman Armenaas* (1960; The Incredible Adventures of Tilman Armenaas), and *Nieuw Deps* (1961; The New Village of Deps), a continuation of *Houtekiet*, reveal the versatility of Walschap's artistic temper. In the 1960s, he published a series of novels—*Alter Ego* (1964), *De Kaartridder* (1966; The Quartered Coat of Arms), and *De Gastmaal* (1966; The Feast)—in which introspection and an awareness of writing contrast with the behaviorism of the typical Walschap novels. Yet in *Het Oramproject* (1975; The Oram Project) and in *De heilige Jan Mus* (1979; Saintly Jan Mus), the author returns to his earlier narrative style. *Het Oramproject* recounts an expedition through the South American wilderness. *De heilige Jan Mus* is the story of a young man who feels called to become an apostle of peace; he fails and returns to bourgeois life.

Walschap's critical essays also constitute an important

part of his work. In *Voorpostgevechten,* he argues that a novel is a story and nothing more. Such essays as *Vaarwel dan!* (1940; So Long Then!), *Salut en Merci* (1955; Goodbye and Thank You), and *Muziek voor twee stemmen* (1963; Music for Two Voices) treat the themes central to his prose while dealing with the issues of faith and freethinking within the context of an outspoken Catholic and conservative Flanders. In this respect, the essays are polemical. *De culturele repressie* (1969; The Cultural Repression) is a completely different piece of work. Half pamphlet, half roman à clef. *De culturele repressie* describes Walschap's attitude toward the turbulent years of leather-jacket boys, cultural revolution, and literary engagement. Walschap's best essays were gathered in *Dossier Walschap* (1966; Documents on Walschap). His children's stories and animal tales, especially the beautiful Christmas story *De vierde koning* (1934; The Fourth King), also deserve to be mentioned.

See: B. F. van Vlierden, *Gerard Walschap* (1958); J. C. Brandt Corstius, *Gerard Walschap* (1960); A. Westerlinck, *Gesprekken met Walschap* (1969, 1970).

P. van A.

Walser, Martin (1927–), German novelist, playwright, and critic, born of middle-class parents at Wasserburg on Lake Constance, studied the humanities at the universities of Regensburg and Tübingen (1947 to 1951), and earned his Ph.D. with a dissertation on Franz KAFKA. After a few years as a radio program producer, he turned to writing, and a number of literary prizes won him early recognition. Married in 1950, he has lived at Nußdorf, since 1968.

Walser's early prose, stories published in *Ein Flugzeug über dem Haus* (1955; An Airplane above the House), was influenced by Franz KAFKA. Peaceful, banal lives are suddenly disrupted by physical malaise or hostile social forces beyond control. The narrator microscopically observes society and its games, but Walser, unlike Kafka, focuses on the grotesque and is more playful. Protagonists suffer but are potentially able to adjust or to withdraw.

Whereas Kafka's parables are not fixed in time or place, Walser deals directly with post-World War II Germany and its decadent affluent society, which forces the individual to submit to the arbitrary collective exigencies of a sick and lethargic environment as the only way to social success.

In Walser's first long prose work, *Ehen in Philippsburg* (1957; Eng. tr., *Marriage in Philippsburg,* 1961), the protagonist at first struggles but then gives up hope for any self-fulfillment, marries a rich girl, and joins the corrupt bourgeois society, where "everyone is either exploiter or victim." Philippsburg, the imaginary yet very real provincial town, is also the setting for three novels about Anselm Kristlein. In *Halbzeit* (1960; Half-Time), Kristlein is a traveling salesman, alienated from himself as he is torn between the lure of nature and the conquest of women and social recognition. In *Das Einhorn* (1966; Eng. tr., *The Unicorn,* 1971) Kristlein, now a writer, tries to experience and express love, but is able to record only the futile endeavor. In the third volume, *Der Sturz* (1973; The Fall), women and social success seem desirable up to the very end when, after terrible suffering, Kristlein finds the strength to renounce his ambitions and to withdraw. When he decides to drive over dangerous mountain roads in winter, presumably he seeks what Walser has called "the death that does not allow a coffin. Maybe the Alps . . .," a fitting end for the suffering "little Christ."

Walser's novel *Die Gallistl'sche Krankheit* (1972; The Gallistl Syndrome) again displays the author-narrator's exploration of his own consciousness. Josef Georg Gallistl

suffers from unhappiness with himself, his family, and German society at large, which he holds responsible for all misfortunes. But new friends initiate him into socialist collective action and give him hope for a more meaningful future.

Walser's theater also deals with contemporary problems. According to Günther Rühl, Walser was the first German playwright to come to grips with the stark realities of the 1960s. *Eiche und Angora* (1962; Oak and Angora) takes place in Philippsburg in 1945, 1950, and 1960, focusing on guilt, suffering, and commitment; the play puts Germany on trial. So do *Überlebensgroß Herr Krott* (1963; Herr Krott, Larger than Life), about a ruthless capitalist, and *Der schwarze Schwann* (1964; The Black Swan), a *Hamlet*-like play in which a son uncovers a father's guilt. An epitaph in the Kristlein trilogy, "War is the father of all things," might well apply to all of Walser's works, particularly to his theater. The war of the sexes, an inferno of lies and hostility matched only by August STRINDBERG and Edward Albee, is vividly portrayed in *Die Zimmerschlacht* (1967; Eng. tr., *Home Front,* 1972) and *Der Abstecher* (1967; The Side Trip). *Ein Kinderspiel* (1970; Child's Play) deals again with a guilty father whose children demand justice. Although primarily philosophical, Walser's plays have considerable impact on German audiences because of their timeliness.

It is his revelation of his time that assures Walser's place in contemporary German letters. Since his consciousness is rooted in the large sociohistorical context, he observes and formulates problems shared by society at large. When Kristlein says, "I am Don Quixote, after he has read what Cervantes wrote about him," he accurately states Walser's approach.

It was, for instance, from his writings that Walser deduced that his experiences tended toward socialism long before he made public his transition from phenomenology to Marxism. Walser's works are essentially confessional in spite of the wealth of information on postwar German society and, in his later works, experimentation with stylistic devices of fragmentation, quotation, intertextuality (reminiscent of some French new novelists). Within German letters, Walser also follows the general trend from the nonideological, generally humane tone of the early postwar years through the period of self-criticism of the 1960s to the politicization of the 1970s.

His experimental play, *Wir werden schon noch handeln* (1968; Eng. tr., *Acting is Our Business,* 1969), is in reality a critique of contemporary theatrical modes. His novel *Jenseits der Liebe* (1976; Beyond Love) launched him as a popular writer, which the best seller *Das fliehende Pferd* (1978; The Horse in Flight) proved him to be. The novel *Seelenarbeit* (1979; Soul Work) concerns a chauffeur who seeks to come to terms with his own circumstances, with his marriage, his fatherhood, his employment, and essentially with himself.

See: Thomas Beckermann, ed., *Über Martin Walser (1970);* W. J. Schwarz, *Der Erzähler Martin Walser* (1971).

A.P.O.

Walser, Robert Otto (1878–1956), Swiss feuilltonist, novelist, and short-story writer, was born in Biel, canton Bern, the seventh of eight children. He left school at the age of 14 and worked for most of his life as a clerk in such places as Zürich, Wädenswil, Thun, Solothurn, Basel, and Stuttgart. After Walser's first book, *Fritz Kochers Aufsätze* (1904; Fritz Kocher's Essays) was published, he lived for some years with his brother Karl in Berlin. Through Karl, a well-known book illustrator and stage designer, Walser met, among others, the publishers Bruno Cassirer and Samuel Fischer. While in Berlin, he wrote six novels, three of which were published in quick succession: *Geschwister Tanner* (1907; The Tanner Children), *Der Gehülfe* (1908; The Assistant), and *Jakob von Gunten* (1909; Eng. tr., 1969). Walser also wrote hundreds of short prose sketches, many of which were published in newspapers. Always a poor man, in 1920 he began working as a clerk again, first in Biel, later in Bern. In 1929, at the age of 51, Walser retreated from the world and was hospitalized in Waldau and subsequently in the asylum at Herisau. He died at the age of 78, having been a schizophrenic for many years.

During his lifetime, Walser's name was known to only a few; yet, today, some two decades since his death, there are strong signs of interest being shown by a growing reading public as well as by literary scholars. Walser's undeniable influence upon Franz KAFKA, perhaps first noted by Robert MUSIL, is certainly one factor in his growing popularity. Like Kafka, Walser was a master of parody and an acute observer of the minute. His prose sketches, each akin to a still life, reveal hidden perspectives in the most mundane objects and situations. Walser wrote with a sense of altered orientation that enabled him to penetrate below the surface of literary platitudes. His prose represents a private fantasy world, a labyrinthian structure that allows for a multiplicity of interpretations. Yet there is a unity of theme in his writings, no matter what his stylistic innovations might be: that of self-fulfillment through service to others.

See: C. Seelig, *Wanderungen mit Robert Walser* (1957); R. Mächler, *Das Leben Robert Walsers: eine dokumentarische Biographie* (1966); G. C. Avery, *Inquiry and Testament* (1968).   H.L.K.

Walter, Otto F. (1928-), Swiss novelist and playwright, was born in Rickenbach near Olten, canton Solothurn. After graduating from the gymnasium, he served as an apprentice to a bookseller and worked for a printing office in Cologne. In 1956 he took charge of the literary program of the Walter publishing house in Olten. Eleven years later, in 1967, he joined the firm of Luchterhand in Darmstadt in the same capacity.

Walter's first novel, *Der Stumme* (1959; Eng. tr., *The Mute*, 1962), like all of his works, is set in a fictitious town on the Aare River, called Jammers. (The word *Jammer* means lamentation, misery, wretchedness.) In *Herr Tourel* (1962), a photographer returns to Jammers, where he spent his childhood. There, in a boathouse inhabited by martens, he sets out to defend himself in writing against numerous accusations that have been directed at him. Although the episodes in this novel are entangled and unfold on different levels of time, the themes are simple and skillfully related to one another.

Encouraged by the drama critic Kurt Hirschfeld, Walter wrote the play *Elio oder: eine fröhliche Gesellschaft* (1963; Elio or A Merry Gathering). In the play, an escaped prisoner appears in the house of a middle-aged couple. Ella, the wife, calls him "Elio," the nickname she gave her husband 20 years before; and with the granting of that name, the hopes and anticipations of long-forgotten days come to life again. Coping with the past is also a theme in the play *Die Katze* (1967; Eng. tr., *The Cat*, 1970). Walter's novel *Die ersten Unruhen* (1972; The First Disturbances) again focuses on the progressive community of Jammers. Its citizens boast, "Together we know a whole lot"; their sources are statistics, communal ordinances, news reports, historical facts, and fictional texts. The short paragraphs attesting to this knowledge do not make up a continuous story, but a clear picture emerges: the prosperity and growth of Jammers are in sharp contrast to its increasing criminality and the lack of public

spirit and mutual trust of its inhabitants. In *Verwilderung* (1977; Return to a Primitive State) a disenchanted intellectual returns to Jammers and joins a group of people who live in a clay-pit where they search for new values. *Wie wird Beton zu Gras* (1979; How Concrete Turns to Grass) has as its theme a mass demonstration in opposition to the construction of an atomic energy plant. With this work Walter established himself in the forefront of those contemporary Swiss writers who are politically engaged.

See: W. Weber, "Otto F. Walter" in *Tagebuch eines Lesers* (1965), pp. 232–50; W. Bucher and G. Ammann, eds., *Schweizer Schriftsteller im Gespräch*, vol. 2 (1971), pp. 219–40.   R.A.Me.

Wańkowicz, Melchior (1892–1974), Polish fiction writer and journalist, was born at Kalużyce in Belorussia and died in Warsaw. He studied in Cracow in the School of Social Sciences and in the Department of Law at Jagiellonian University. He fought in World War I and in the war with the Soviet Union in 1920. During World War II, Wańkowicz went abroad, and the vicissitudes of war took him to Romania, the Middle East, and England. In 1943–46 he was a war correspondent and accompanied the Polish armed forces in Italy. In 1949 he settled in the United States, and in 1958 he returned to Poland. Wańkowicz originated a new form of Polish literary reportage, combining authenticity of detail with reminiscences and fictional elements. His rich picturesque language, jovial humor, and vivid colorful narrative link him with the old Polish spoken tale (*gawęda*) and Henryk SIENKIEWICZ's style of narration. In 1927 Wańkowicz published an account of his trip to Mexico, *W kościołach Meksyku* (In the Churches of Mexico); in 1934 about the Soviet Union, *Opierzona rewolucja* (The Full-Fledged Revolution); and in 1936 about Poles living in East Prussian Warmia and Mazuria, *Na tropach Smętka* (On the Trail of Sorrow). His two novels *Szczenięcę lata* (1934; Puppyhood) and *Ziele na kraterze* (1951; Herbs on the Crater) have an autobiographical character. In 1944 he wrote the novel *Dzieje rodziny Korzeniewskich* (Eng. tr., *Golgotha Road*, 1945). Wańkowicz depicts the feats of the Polish armed forces during World War II in *Bitwa o Monte Cassino* (1945–47; The Battle of Monte Cassino), a monumental account of the victory of Polish armed forces in the Battle of Monte Cassino; and in *Wrzesień żagwiący* (1947; September in Flames), which includes among others two well-known stories, *Westerplatte* and *Hubalczycy* (Hubal's Men). He wrote a big novel about the Polish emigration, *Panorama losu polskiego* (Panorama of Polish Fate), which consists of two volumes, *Tworzywo* (1954; Eng. tr., *Three Generations*, 1973) and *Drogą do Urzędowa* (1955; The Road to Urzędów).

His observations about the United States were included in the books *W ślady Kolumba* (In the Footsteps of Columbus), consisting of three parts: *Atlantyk–Pacyfik* (1967), *Królik i oceany* (1968; The Bunny and the Oceans), and *W pępku Ameryki* (1969; In the Hub of America). The last collection prepared by the writer is *Karafka La Fontaine'a* (1972; La Fontaine's Decanter).

See: M. Kurzyna, *O Melchiorze Wańkowiczu—nie wszystko* (1975).   A.Z.

Wassermann, Jakob (1873–1934), German novelist, was born in Fürth, Bavaria. His youth was spent in the milieu of small-town Jewish life. With the loss of his mother when he was nine, he retreated into a world of fantasy, which contributed to his gift as storyteller. When scarcely 13 years old, he published his first novel in a local newspaper. Apprenticed to an uncle's business in Vienna,

Wassermann soon ran away, only to begin a hand-to-mouth existence in Munich. His service in the army left him with memories of racial discrimination.

Wassermann's fortunes rose when his writings were accepted by the magazine *Simplicissimus*. His first important work, *Die Juden von Zirndorf* (1897; Eng. tr., *The Jews of Zirndorf*, 1933), contains themes that recur in later novels: social injustice, woman's role in society, malcontents and outsiders in a middle-class world, the conflict between father and son, and the isolation of the Jew in German life. *Caspar Hauser* (1908; Eng. tr., 1928) is one of Wasserman's most enduring works, having as its subject the indifference of the heart. The plot is based on an early 19th-century event concerning Caspar Hauser, who was alleged to be both a kidnapped prince and an imposter. Wassermann's interest focused on the various people who exploit the youth. *Das Gänsemännchen* (1915; Eng. tr., *The Goose Man*, 1922), a semiexpressionist novel, has maintained its popularity. It is the story of a composer so dedicated to his art that he becomes blind to life.

Christian Wahnschaffe (1919; Eng. tr., *The World's Illusion*, 1920), is an ambitious novel that became, like many of Wassermann's other works, an international best-seller. The influence of Lev TOLSTOY and Fyodor DOSTOYEVSKY is evident in this epic about a young man who renounces his wealth in the tradition of Saint Francis to minister to prostitutes and the poor. Prominent among Wassermann's many novels is *Der Fall Maurizius* (1928; Eng. tr., *The Maurizius Case*, 1929), the themes of which are justice, the letter of the law versus compassion, and the effect of imprisonment on the condemned as well as on those who condemn. It is Wassermann's most mature novel, free of the melodrama, sensationalism, and grotesque characterizations found in his earlier works.

Wassermann's usually unfavorable portrayal of Jews perplexed his readers. The writer's attitude toward Jews is explained in *Mein Weg als Deutscher und Jude* (1921; Eng. tr., *My Life as German and Jew*, 1934). This autobiographical account of his early years is the key to Wassermann's other works as well, for in it his concern with poverty, injustice, and anti-Semitism are dealt with at length. Wassermann admitted the impossibility of realizing his dream to live as a German and as a Jew accepted on equal terms. As a document of the position of the Jew in pre-Nazi Germany, this work earns itself a place alongside Wassermann's works of imagination.

See: J. C. Blankenagel, *The Writings of Jakob Wassermann* (1942); S. Liptzin, "Jacob Wassermann," in *Germany's Stepchildren* (1944); A. C. Hernberg, *The Humanism of Jacob Wassermann* (1953); W. Voegeli, *Jacob Wassermann und die Trägheit des Herzens* (1956); H. Miller, *Reflections on the Maurizius Case* (1974).

K.S.M.

Wästberg, Per (1933–) Swedish novelist, poet, essayist, and editor, was born in Stockholm of well-to-do parents. Wästberg has a B.A. degree (1955) from Harvard University and Ph.D. from Uppsala University. He is a professional author whose discipline and enormous working capacity have successfully brought him through varied assignments. He has edited anthologies and correspondences and has written introductions, reviews, and histories. He is also a prominent member of the international PEN Club. Wästberg has twice inspired a change in the Swedish literary climate; and through his passion for old Stockholm, with its surroundings lovingly described and documented, he has helped to turn the tide toward conservation. Wästberg began his career early with *Pojke med såpbubblor* (1949; Boy Blowing Soap Bubbles), and its merit is precisely its youth, which is not something remembered but registered with felicity of expression at a time close to the actual experience. Wästberg continued to register his learning experiences, well aware of his privileged and limited range. The titles *Halva kungariket* (1955; Half the Kingdom) and *Arvtagaren* (1958; The Heir) reflect his awareness. His method as a novelist was always to take stock from his own experiences and invent only a thin story line. In his later novels this method is unchanged; only in the later works there is more to what he has to say.

In the late 1950s, Wästberg accepted a Rotary grant to travel in Africa in order to check up on the enticing world of the adventure books of his youth. The outcome of his trip, however, was unexpected. Two books of straight reporting, *Förbjudet område* (1960; No Trespassing) and *På svarta listan* (1960; On the Black List), attracted great public attention and initiated an intense social debate that soon overshadowed the entire Swedish literary scene. With his African journey began Wästberg's collaboration with African writers, which has brought about several anthologies and also *Angola and Mozambique: The Case against Portugal* (1963; written with Anders Ehnmark). At this time Wästberg also began to publish poetry that expresses the conflict between the shortness of life and its richness both in terror and beauty as in *Tio Atmosfärer* (1963; The Pressure at Ten Atmospheres) and *Enkel resa* (1964; No Return Ticket). Wästberg pleads for time "to hear what my ears have heard and to see what my eyes have seen." In the late 1960s, Wästberg composed a trilogy about what had happened in Sweden during the previous two decades in terms of increased possibilities but also in terms of increased threats. The middle volume, *Luftburen* (1969; Eng. tr., *The Air Cage*, 1973), has been translated into English, whereas *Vattenslottet* (1968; The Castle in the Water) and *Jordmånen* (1972; The Soil) have not. It is only as a whole, seen as an attempt to describe both concretely and symbolically what modern freedom and modern bondage mean, that the work is impressive.

See: C. Mannheimer, "Adjö ungdom," in K. E. Lagerlöf, *Femtitalet i backspegeln* (1968) pp. 167–70; G. A. Mannberg, "Per Wästberg mitt i världen," in *Samtal med författare* (1971), pp. 111–18; *En bibliografi över Per Wästbergs skrifter 1943–1973, sammanställd av Anders Ryberg* (1974); J. Stenkvist, *Svensk litteratur 1870–1970*, vol. 3 (1975), pp. 67–70.

B.K.S.

Wat, Aleksander, pseud. of Aleksander Chwat (1900–67), Polish poet and essayist, was born in Warsaw and died in Paris. Around 1919 he was one of the initiators of the short-lived Polish futurist movement, which he himself defined later on as a brand of dadaism. That futurist phase found expression in his volume of poems *Ja z jednej strony i Ja z drugiej strony mego mopsożelaznego piecyka* (1920; I on One Side and I on the Other Side of my Pug-Iron Stove). In 1927 he published a collection of short stories—bizarre in their intellectual acrobatics—that are parables on the history of the 20th to 25th centuries; it was entitled *Bezrobotny Lucyfer* (1927; Lucifer Unemployed). Then Wat embraced Marxism and from 1929 to 1931 was the editor in chief of *Miesięcznik Literacki*, the most important Polish Communist periodical before World War II. After his escape from the Nazis in 1939 to the Soviet zone, Wat was soon arrested there and spent long periods in various prisons and in deportation in Soviet Asia, returning to Poland only in 1946. He showed his full stature as a poet in his late works, notably *Wiersze* (1957; Poems) and *Wiersze Śródziemnomorskie* (1962; Mediterranean Poems). His late poetry mixes an acute feeling of historical tragedy with self-irony and buffoonery. From the late 1950s on, he lived mostly in Italy and in France. He left valuable tape-recorded memoirs on literary life, politics, and the various prisons he had gone through—*Mój wiek. Pamiętnik mówiony* (1977; My Century: An Oral Diary), interviewer, Czesław Miłosz.

C.Mi.

Ważyk, Adam (1905–), Polish poet, novelist, short-story writer, literary critic, and translator, was born in Warsaw. He did not belong to any literary group, but he was closest to the "Second Vanguard." Ważyk's volumes of early poetry, *Semafory* (1924; Semaphores) and *Oczy i usta* (1926; Eyes and Lips), were in tune with Vanguard experimentation under the influence of the poetry of Guillaume APOLLINAIRE, Blaise CENDRARS, and the French cubist painters and poets. In the 1930s, Ważyk took up prose, publishing a collection of short stories, *Człowiek w burym ubraniu* (1930; Man in a Dark Gray Suit), and the novels *Latarnie świecą w Karpowie* (1933; Lamps are Lit in Karpów) and *Mity rodzinne* (1938; Family Myths). Ważyk returned to poetry during World War II, which he spent in the Soviet Union. A volume of his wartime poems devoted to contemporary political and social events, *Serce granatu* (1944; The Heart of a Grenade), is marked by an absence of formal experimentation and is written in traditional style. After publishing in 1955 a poem full of disillusionment and condemnation of the Stalin years in Poland, "Poemat dla dorosłych" (Poem for Adults), Ważyk returned to the experiences of his prewar poetry, to the antimetaphorical style, the technique of juxtaposition of separate elements, and images created on associative basis. These new features are clearly visible in his long poem *Labirynt* (1961; Labyrinth) and in his volume of poems *Wagon* (1963; The Car). Ważyk's concern with poetic technique and with 20th-century European literary trends is apparent in his many translations of Horace, French poetry, and Aleksandr Pushkin and in his critical writing, which includes *Mickiewicz i wersyfikacja narodowa* (1951; Mickiewicz and National Versification), *Od Rimbauda do Eluarda* (1965; From Rimbaud to Eluard), and *Dziwna historia awangardy* (1976; The Strange History of the Vanguard).

See: J. Trznadel, "Wątpiący i empiryczny," in *Róże trzecie* (1966), pp. 11–59. M.G.L.

Wedekind, Frank (Benjamin Franklin Wedekind) (1864–1918), German dramatist, was born in Hanover a few months after the return of his parents from the United States. His emotional intensity and his love of the exotic were a natural heritage: the wanderings of his physician father, a fierce democrat who worshiped George Washington and hated Otto von Bismarck, extended as widely as Turkey and California; it was in San Francisco that he married a young German actress half his age. Wedekind grew up in Switzerland but spent his mature years in Germany, where he was variously journalist, playwright, and actor. Political poems published in the satirical magazine *Simplicissimus* resulted in 1899 in his conviction and imprisonment for offenses against the sovereign power of the state.

The keystone of Wedekind's work is eroticism. His is not poetic dalliance, however, for he sees love as the elemental driving force to which human beings are enslaved. To cover up that slavery, people practice hypocrisies, and Wedekind, like Friedrich Schlegel in his *Lucinde* (1799), felt called on to attack this attitude. The Mephistophelean Wedekind cuts a queer figure among the moralists, but however paradoxical he and his works are, no one can doubt his serious intentions. In "Über die Erotik" (On Eroticism), a preface to his stories in *Feuerwerk* (1905; Fireworks), he sets forth the problem. "Der Brand von Egliswyl" (The Conflagration of Egliswyl) in this volume is an effective example of the power of love. *Frühlings Erwachen* (1891; Eng. tr., *The Awakening of Spring*, 1909), Wedekind's first success and one of his most poetic plays, arraigns the adult world for its misunderstanding and mismanagement of children at puberty. Karl Hetmann, in the drama of that name (1904; first called *Hidalla*), is a fantastic moralist bent on reforming society. Indeed, Wedekind's every work is a thrust at the shams of society, particularly its moral hypocrisy, as in *Totentanz* (1906; retitled *Tod und Teufel* in 1909; Eng. tr., *Death and Devil*, 1952).

Wedekind's most notorious creation is his appalling version of the eternal feminine whom he presents as the real earth spirit. She is generally known as Lulu, but she answers to any name of Eve's daughters. Through the two dramas *Der Erdgeist* (1895; Eng. tr., *Earth Spirit*, 1914) and *Die Büchse der Pandora* (1903; Eng. tr., *Pandora's Box*, 1918, both in *The Lulu Plays*, 1972), she runs her course, consuming one man after another until Jack the Ripper puts an end to her. This ageless, amoral incarnation of the sex urge lives in a seething mass of evil and gets down to the dregs of life, but she remains essentially natural and unchanged. The triumph of primitive nature over civilization is the formula for all of Wedekind's work. In *Schloß Wetterstein* (1910; Eng. tr., *Castle Wetterstein*, 1952) Effie, a lesser Lulu, also makes prostitution on a grand scale her career and dies at the hands of a pervert. Franziska, in the drama of that name (1912), is a variation of the type. She is a feminine Faust experimenting with love and life at their various levels and—a unique ending for Wedekind—finding happiness at last in simple domestic love. Wedekind calls this play a modern mystery.

Woman is not always the protagonist, nor is love the exclusive theme: Wedekind also had a predilection for men on the lunatic fringe who lead an existence that, in the eyes of society, is decidedly shady. They, too, are "naturals." The masterpiece in this vein is *Der Marquis von Keith* (1901). Here the hero, with his spurious title of nobility, is a soldier of fortune, a swindler whose calculations go awry and who at the last curtain, faced with the choice between a revolver and a monetary sop tossed him by his successful rival, grins and takes the money. Cold, calculating self-interest also inspire Gerardo in *Der Kammersänger* (1899; Eng. tr., *Heart of a Tenor*, 1913), a one-act tragicomedy and Wedekind's most effective and popular work; but, unlike Keith, this erstwhile paperhanger and now operatic tenor and slave to his art is overwhelmed by success. Wedekind erected a real monument to the tragedy of the artist in *König Nicolo, oder So ist das Leben* (1902; Eng. tr., *Such is Life*, 1912). The deposed king suffers many humiliations, even becoming his successor's court fool, but his kingship remains truly inalienable. The play was written in the depression following Wedekind's imprisonment and is perhaps the most heartfelt of all the dramatist's charges against his fellow man.

Wedekind stood alone in his time. He refused to associate with the naturalists, and his kind of romanticism had little in common with the prevailing brand. He was a forerunner of expressionism.

See: A. Kutscher, *Frank Wedekind*, 3 vols. (1922–31); G. Seehaus, *Frank Wedekind und das Theater* (1964); S. Gittleman *Frank Wedekind* (1969); G. Seehaus, *Frank Wedekind in Selbstzeugnissen und Bilddokumenten* (1974). H.W.P. rev. A.L.W.

Weil, Simone (1909–43), French philosopher and mystic, was born and educated in Paris. A brilliant student of ALAIN and René LE SENNE, she completed her studies at the Ecole Normale Supérieure. Weil empathized deeply with the millions who suffered as a result of the growing mechanization of labor and the political violence of the 1930s and 1940s. Soon the need to share their hardships propelled her life beyond the confines of a teaching career. Convinced that the intellectual life had to be reintegrated with manual labor and spiritual contemplation in order to be fruitful, she lived in poverty, sharing her salary with the unemployed. Weil worked for a time for the anarchist trade union movement La Révolution Prolétarienne, spent a year as a factory worker, worked as a farmhand, fought briefly with the Loyalist forces in the Spanish Civil War, and finally perished in exile in England from self-imposed privation and anorexia at the age of 34.

Weil's essay and journals, most of which were edited and published posthumously, constitute one of the most austere and inspired expressions of a contemporary Western spirituality that had turned away from the Judaeo-Christian tradition and found its roots in Greece and in the mysticism of the East. In her inquiries into the nature of man, God, the universe, and human society, a rigorous philosophic determinism, going back to Pythagorean, Stoic, and Neoplatonic doctrines, merges and at times conflicts with mystic intuitions of a predominantly Buddhist and Taoist character. She postulates a cosmos ruled by a wholly impersonal logos that no will, divine or human, can abrogate and that man confronts most directly in physical labor. "Necessity is everywhere, the good nowhere," she wrote. Echoing the Stoics, Weil defined human freedom as man's power to give free consent to necessity, without slavishness or illusion. The violation of this freedom by machine power as well as by today's political and economic power structures is the major concern of *La Condition ouvrière* (1951; The Working-Class Condition), *L'Enracinement* (1949; Eng. tr., *The Need for Roots*, 1952), and *Oppression et liberté* (1955; Eng. tr., *Oppression and Liberty*, 1958). Demythologizing the idol that the modern world has made of science, she stresses the need to make science compatible once again with spirituality, as it had been for the Greeks. The foremost task facing the technological era, she argues, must be to rectify the distorted relationships between man and machine, and between man and institutions, which have reduced entire populations to the affliction of slavery, that is, of knowing oneself subject, not to necessity, but to injustice. Her proposals for bringing industrial planning into closer conformity with the workers' need for self-respect, responsibility, community, and justice have gained wide assent.

The same fundamental themes of necessity and affliction form the cornerstones of the religious meditations and aphorisms of Weil's last years, which include *La Pesanteur et la grâce* (1947; Eng. tr., *Gravity and Grace*, 1952), *La Connaissance surnaturelle* (1950; Supernatural Knowledge), and *Attente de Dieu* (1950; Eng. tr., *Waiting on God*, 1951). Although deeply drawn to Christ, she held fast to her rejection of a personal god and individual redemption. According to the Weilian vision, God, in creating the universe, effaced himself from it and surrendered it to its own law of gravity, or necessity. In response, man must in turn "decreate" himself and, by emptying himself of the illusion of selfhood, return to God what divine love has relinquished. In this mathematically rigorous dialectical vision, the infinite separation between two poles, divine being and cosmic void, is seen as but a challenge by creator to creature. The Weilian ascetic ideal is to emulate the docility of inert matter in its obedience to necessity, to the point where, out of the depth of emptiness and pain, the truth of God's being is reborn and made manifest. In the transparency of the soul thus emptied, gravity is overcome; all becomes grace. Transient phenomena, no longer falsely perceived as ends and therefore idolized, reveal themselves as bridges to the eternal.

See: J. Cabaud, *Simone Weil* (1964).   G.R.Bl.

Weiner, Richard (1884–1937), Czech poet and short-story writer, was born in Písek in southern Bohemia. After studying to become a chemical engineer, he turned to literature, eventually settling in Paris, where he worked as a foreign correspondent for Czech newspapers. He returned to Prague shortly before his death.

Weiner is perhaps the most original representative of the Czech avant-garde of the 1920s and 1930s. He was preoccupied with problems of individual identity, guilt, and alienation, as well as with the irrationality of man's existence. As his poetry and prose became increasingly surrealistic, he turned to the subconscious and dreams. In Paris he became an active member of the surrealist circle known as "Le Grand Jeu." Weiner's early short-story collection, *Lítice* (1916; The Fury), depicts the irrationality of war and the problems of fate and guilt haunting the individuals involved in war. His next collection, *Škleb* (1919; The Grimace), and especially the long story, "Prazdná židle" (The Empty Chair), concern the metaphysical horror of an empty universe in which man disappears without a trace. Weiner's later prose became more and more difficult and esoteric, but his last book, *Hra doopravdy* (1937; A Play in Earnest), contains two "dramatic" novellas that embody the culmination of his existentialist and surrealist thinking: they indicate a belief in individual responsibility and in the possibility of a corresponding, if limited, individual well-being. Similar ideas are expressed in Weiner's poetry, contained in collections such as *Rozcestí* (1918; The Crossroads), *Mnoho nocí* (1928; Many Nights), and *Mezopotámie* (1930); in the last collection, a faith in a moral absolute gradually replaces the poet's earlier relativism. Weiner has been much neglected, but he was a leading influence on younger Czech poets and prose writers of the 1960s.

See: J. Chalupecky, *Richard Weiner* (1947).   W.E.H.

Weingarten, Romain (1926–), French poet, dramatist, and actor, was born in Paris. His name reflects his father's Alsatian roots. As a student at the Sorbonne, Weingarten wrote his first play, *Akara* (1948). Presented by Le Groupe de Théâtre Moderne de la Maison des Lettres at the Concours des Jeunes Compagnies, *Akara* created such a stir that the veteran dramatist Jacques AUDIBERTI nicknamed it "Hernani 48," alluding to the sensation caused by Victor Hugo's *Hernani*. Indeed, *Akara* is the first antiplay, preceding by two years Eugène IONESCO's *Le Cantatrice chauve*. Like all of Weingarten's poems and plays, *Akara* issues from the realm of the subconscious, the locus of dreams and fairy tales. The main character is Le Chat, an escapee from Lewis Carroll's *Alice in Wonderland,* one of Weingarten's favorite books. The role was played by the dramatist himself, a case of perfect casting since Weingarten looks like a lean, overgrown Baudelairean cat. Some of the other dramatis personae are Milord (played by the dramatist-actor Roland DUBILLARD), Milady, Le Comte, Le Juge, Marthe, and Marie. They play a hermetic word game, a variation on whist that reveals the author's fascination with language. Indeed, Weingarten's poetic explorations parallel the findings of the structuralists (*see* FRENCH LITERATURE).

While earning his livelihood with a picture-framing shop, Weingarten wrote *Les Nourrices* (1961; The Wet Nurses) and *L'Été* (1966; Summer). Although the first earned him a succès d'estime, the latter established his reputation. Both are haunted by a feeling of the presence of danger in everyday life, but also of mystery and the obsessive power of love. In his plays, love is both present and absent, elusive and all-important. Weingarten published a volume of *Poèmes* in 1968. His recent dramatic works include *Alice dans les jardins du Luxembourg* (1970; Alice in the Luxembourg Gardens) and *La Mandore* (1974; The Mandola). The first is an ingenuous vision of the apocalyptic end of our planet, the second a whirling dance of the living, the dying, and the dead. *Neige* (Snow) was first performed in 1979.

Together with Jean TARDIEU, Boris VIAN, Henri Pichette, and Jean VAUTHIER, Weingarten is the chief exponent of poetic theater in France. Rejecting psychological, realistic theater, he pursues an inner reality, one that is phantasmagoric and cruelly childlike. More than any other dramatist of the 20th century, Weingarten writes from within the universe beyond "the looking glass."

See: R. C. Lamont, "The Nouvelle Vague in French Theatre," *MR* 5, no. 2 (Winter 1964): 381–96; B. Knapp, "Alice in the Luxembourg Gardens: Structurally Speaking," *ASoc* (Fall-Winter 1972): 457–68, "Romain Weingarten's Stage Play *Akara* and the A-Temporal Realm," *MD* (December 1973): 355–67, and *Off-Stage Voices* (1975), pp. 146–159.   R.C.L.

Weinheber, Josef (1892–1945), Austrian poet, was born in Vienna, the son of a butcher. Losing both parents early in life, he spent six loveless years in an orphanage, portrayed in his autobiographic novel *Das Waisenhaus* (1925; The Orphanage), but he was then taken in by an aunt, in whose home his first poems were written, published in *Der einsame Mensch* (1920; The Lonely Person). In 1911 he obtained a position in the postal system, where he continued to earn his living for many years. To his profound disgust the poems in his volumes *Von beiden Ufern* (1923; From Both Shores) and *Boot in der Bucht* (1926; Boat in the Bay) were virtually ignored. At last the volume *Adel und Untergang* (1932; enlarged 1934; Nobility and Defeat) attracted critical attention; with the award of the Mozart Prize in 1935 he suddenly became famous, and critics vied with each other in praising him. With gentle irony he named the following book of poems *Späte Krone* (1936; Late Crown).

Weinheber's mastery of form is noted by all who mention him at all, and comparison with Friedrich Hölderlin has become almost a commonplace. He might be called a neoclassicist, provided the term is not taken to mean imitative dependence; it expresses rather his conscious espousal of formal perfection as one of the external manifestations of high artistry. Aside from this formal element, it seems hardly possible to reduce Wienheber's work to any common denominator. His utterance is impressive, often significant, always competent; his best poems achieve a rare beauty.

See: A. Luser, ed., *Josef Weinheber, Persönlichkeit und Schaffen* (1935); E. Finke, *Josef Weinheber* (1950); F. Feldner, *Josef Weinheber* (1965).

B.Q.M. rev. A.L.W.

Weiss, Peter (1916–), German dramatist and prose writer, was born in Nowawes near Berlin. Raised in Bremen and Berlin, he emigrated to London with his parents in 1934. From 1936 to 1938 he attended the Academy of Fine Arts in Prague. In 1939 he joined his family in Sweden, where he was active as a film director and painter. In 1945 he became a Swedish citizen, and since 1960 he has earned his living as a professional author in Stockholm.

Weiss, who initially devoted his creative energies to painting and experimental film, held his first exhibition of paintings in London in 1935. His first book-length publication was a volume of prose poems, *Från ö till ö* (1946; From Island to Island). His first play, *Der Turm* (1963; Eng. tr., *The Tower*, 1966) was broadcast by Radio Stockholm in 1949, but it was not performed in German until 1962. Weiss has received, among other prizes, the Charles Veillon Prize (1963), the Lessing Prize (1965), and the Heinrich Mann Prize (1966).

Weiss's personal existence is a constant component in his writings: a self-analytic confession, dominated by the problem of rebellion. The basic theme of his literary work can be understood from the perspective of the "suppressed son" who demands justice, not mercy. The basis of the philosophic confession of the *homme revolté* Sade in *Die Verfolgung und Ermordung Jean Paul Marats*[. . .] (1964; Eng. tr., *The Persecution and Assassination of Jean-Paul Marat* [. . .], 1965) lies in the experience of the absurdity and the material reality of the world and of its hellish character as described in Weiss's personal confessions *Abschied von den Eltern* (1961; Eng. tr., *Leavetaking*, 1966) and *Fluchtpunkt* (1962; Eng. tr., *Vanishing Point*, 1966) both in a volume entitled *Exiles*. In these two works Weiss discusses the influence of Franz KAFKA, Hermann HESSE, August STRINDBERG, the French surrealists, and others on his work and provides insight into the role they played in the development of his political activism. This same experience is also the deciding factor in his "micronovel" *Der Schatten des Körpers des Kutschers* (1960; Eng. tr., *The Shadow of the Coachman's Body*, 1969), in which he deliberately exaggerated the stylistic principle of naturalism.

The author's development leads from the parable *Der Turm* (still indebted to expressionism and existentialism) to an intermediate stage dominated by the surrealist-grotesque—*Die Versicherung* (1952, first published 1967; The Insurance), *Nacht mit Gästen* (1963; Eng. tr., *Night with Guests*, 1968), and *Wie dem Herrn Mockinpott das Leiden ausgetrieben wird* (1968; Eng. tr., *How Mister Mockinpott was Cured of His Suffering*, 1971)—to his documentary theater, made self-contradictory by its Marxist bias—*Die Ermittlung* (1965; Eng. tr., *The Investigation*, 1966), *Gesang vom Lusitanischen Popanz* (1967; Eng. tr., *Song of the Lusitanian Bogey*, 1970), *Viet Nam Diskurs über die Vorgeschichte und den Verlauf des lang andauernden Befreiungskriegs in Viet Nam*,[. . .] (1967; Eng. tr. *Discourse on the Progress of the Prolonged War of Liberation in Viet Nam* [. . .], 1970)—and finally to the revuelike martyr-plays *Trotzki im Exil* (1970; Eng. tr., *Trotsky in Exile*, 1972) and *Hölderlin* (1971).

The climax and turning point is reached in the grotesque "Moritat" *Marat/Sade*, which is composed of elements of the *Schaubude*, *Théatre de la Cruelté*, and the philosophical conversation play; the antitheses father/son and violation/salvation find their reconciliation in the Utopia of a postrevolutionary society, a society characterized by solidarity and identity. In his *Wunschbiographie* (his autobiography fictionalized as he would have it), *Die Ästhetik des Widerstands* (vol. 1, 1975; vol. 2, 1978; The Aesthetics of Resistance), the author blended a historical report with fictional narration and (according to surrealist principle) bonds political and aesthetic elements in a perspective of epiphany.

See: I. Hilton, *Peter Weiss* (1970); O. F. Best, *Peter Weiss* (1976). O.F.B.

Wellershoff, Dieter (1925-), German novelist, short-story writer, essayist, poet, and dramatist, was born in Neuss on the Rhine and spent his childhood in Grevenbroich. From 1943 to 1945 he was in the army, and in 1947 he entered the University of Bonn to study German literature psychology, and art history. In 1952 he received his Ph.D. with a thesis on Gottfried BENN, whose complete works he later edited. After leaving the university he worked as a free-lance writer for various newspapers and radio stations, and in 1959 he became an editor in the well-known German publishing house Kiepenheuer & Witsch.

Of Wellershoff's four novels, to date only one has been translated into English: *Ein schöner Tag* (1966; Eng. tr., *A Beautiful Day,* 1966). The other three novels are *Die Schattengrenze* (1969; The Edge of Shadow); *Einladung an alle* (1972; Invitation to Everyone), and *Die Schönheit des Schimpansen* (1977, The Beauty of the Chimpanzee). In his novels Wellershoff tries to create a new sense of reality that searches behind appearances for the complexity of life, a complexity lost in the routine of daily perceptions. Through the situations in his novels, Wellershoff wants to shock the reader back into a reality that makes moments of freedom and creativity possible. In addition to his numerous radio plays and television and film scripts, Wellershoff has made a major contribution to modern literature and culture through the intensity and insights presented in his collections of essays: *Literatur und Veränderung* (1969; Literature and Change), *Literatur und Lustprinzip* (1973; Literature and the Pleasure Principle), and *Die Auflösung des Kunstbegriffs* (1976; The Destruction of the Concept of Art). Wellershoff has been instrumental in redefining the social and cultural role of man in a society devoid of aesthetic and intellectual values.

See: "A Portrait of Wellershoff," *MArt* 9, no. 2 (1976); R. H. Thomas, *Der Schriftsteller Dieter Wellershoff* (1975). R.Sc.

Weöres, Sándor (1913-), Hungarian poet and translator, was born into a family of small landowners in Szombathely. At the University of Pécs, he studied various subjects, finally taking a doctorate in aesthetics. Between 1941 and 1950 he worked as a librarian in Pécs and Budapest. Since 1951 he has earned his living as a writer. In 1970 he was awarded the Kossuth Prize.

Weöres published his first book of poetry, *Hideg van* (1934; It Is Cold), before he was 20. At the time, he was already known to Mihály BABITS, who from 1932 onward had printed his poems in the literary review *Nyugat* (*see* HUNGARIAN LITERATURE). Weöres's unusual mimetic talent, readiness to absorb all styles, and great linguistic ingenuity in the use of different personae were apparent even in his early work. During the 1930s, Weöres traveled widely. In India he discovered Eastern philosophy under the guidance of Béla Hamvas and developed an interest in ancient religions: these influences gave a new, "cultural-anthropological" bent to his poetry. The poems of *A teremtés dícsérete* (1938; In Praise of Creation) and *Medúza* (1943; Medusa) barely identify the age and social system in which the poet lives, for his world revolves around the great myths of mankind—creation, cosmic destruction, individual resurrection. Like some of the German romanticists, Weöres suffers from "the metaphysical wound" (man's alienation from God). On the one hand he has tried to restore harmony through the magic of words, yet on the other he sees the actual world as a fragmented entity where reason is helpless against

the forces of unreason and naked self-interest. His pessimism about the state of human affairs is particularly striking in such poems as "De profundis" (1942) or the apocalyptic and courageously apolitical "XX. századi freskó" (1945; Eng. tr., "Mural of the 20th Century," 1967), where the Angel of Disgust advises people to stop "swaying banners" and trying to save the world with slogans of social activism.

Apart from writing philosophical poems and surrealistic grotesques, Weöres found an outlet for his creative gifts in songs, epigrams, and nursery-rhyme ditties. These were collected in *Bóbita* (1955; Tuft, a Fairy) and *Zimzizim* (1969). Because of their vivid imagery and unusual rhythmic patterns some of these poems became immensely popular among children. The composer András Hajdú pointed out that Weöres enriched Hungarian prosody with new rhythmic and musical elements. In the early 1950s, when socialist realism was the only approved creative method in Communist Hungary, Weöres was unable to publish anything but poems for children. This situation came to an end during the "thaw," when generous selections from Weöres's work were published under the title *A hallgatás tornya* (1956; The Tower of Silence). Once again he proved his amazing versatility: the book contains intricately composed long poems, such as "Az elveszett napernyő" (Eng. tr., "The Lost Sunshade," 1970), alternating with short, grotesque pieces and gnomic epigrams. His next collection, *Tüzkút* (1964; Well of Flames), includes an intriguing cycle of sonnets and some longer poems that reflect his continuous search for the adequate expression of spiritual and transcendant reality. The charming poem "Fairy Spring" (English title in original text), with its beautiful, outspoken accounts of physical love, upset some conservative readers.

Since 1963, Weöres has visited most European countries as well as the United States. His international reputation and the growing recognition at home made possible the publication of *Egybegyüjtött irások* (2 vols., 1970; Collected Writings), which, apart from poems, includes his much-maligned collection of philosophical gnomes and axioms, *A teljesség felé* (1945; Toward Completeness), as well as several plays in verse. Since then, Weöres's most interesting and controversial book has been *Psyché: egy hajdani költőnő irásai* (1972; Psyche: Writings of a Poetess of Yore), a skillful pastiche of early 19th-century poetry, written in the guise of an imaginary—and somewhat wild—woman poet. The feminine persona of these poems adds a new aspect to Weöres's delightful playacting. Although he may be criticized for the esoteric quality of much of his work, Weöres's alleged lack of concern for society is deceptive: his avowed aim is to shake up the reader. *A lélek idézése* (1958; Evocation of the Spirit) is a collection of his translations from several languages, including Chinese. Recently Weöres selected and edited a fascinating anthology, published in 1977, drawing on the hidden values and oddities of Hungarian poetry through the ages.

See: A. Hajdú, "A Bóbita ritmikája," *Csillag* 10 (1956): 768-78; M. Sükösd, "Weöres és világa," *Kortárs* 2 (1958): 93-102; I. Bori, "A látomások költészete," *Híd* 1-2 (1964): 909-43, 1215-34; G. Gömöri, "Sándor Weöres: Unity in Diversity," *BA* 43 (1969): 36-40; E. Morgan, Introduction to *Sándor Weöres: Selected Poems* (1970); A. Tamás, *Weöres, Sándor* (1970). G.G.

Werfel, Franz (1890-1945), Austrian poet, dramatist, and novelist, was born in Prague. While still a gymnasium student, he became friends with Max Brod and Franz KAFKA. During his early career, Werfel wrote outstanding expressionist poetry, *Der Weltfreund* (1911; Friend to the

World), *Wir sind* (1913; We Are), and *Einander* (1915; To One Another). The poet's identification with his fellow man, especially the outsider, is exemplified by the line "My only wish is to be related to you, O Man!"

Among Werfel's early work for the stage is his adaptation of Euripides' *The Trojan Women* (1916), followed by the "magic trilogy" *Spiegelmensch* (1920; Eng. tr., *Mirror Man*, n.d.), whose theme is the release of the alter ego. *Bocksgesang* (1921; Eng. tr., *Goat Song*, 1926) is a mythical drama of human social passions. *Juarez und Maximilian* (1924; Eng. tr., 1926), a drama about the Hapsburg emperor of Mexico, was an international success. *Paulus unter den Juden* (1926; Eng. tr., *Paul among the Jews*, 1928) depicts the moment in history when Christianity broke away from Judaism. Conscious of his Jewish heritage throughout his life, Werfel felt himself drawn to Christianity, although he never converted.

Today Werfel is chiefly remembered for his novels. Dominant influences in these works are Prague and the Czech environment, Catholicism, and music. *Verdi* (1924; Eng. tr., *Verdi: A Novel of the Opera*, 1947) deals with the artist's crisis when his creative powers fail. Other novels of this period include *Barbara oder die Frömmigkeit* (1929; Eng. tr., *The Pure in Heart*, 1931) and *Die Geschwister von Neapel* (1931; Eng. tr., *The Pascarella Family*, 1932). A trip to the Middle East inspired Werfel to write *Die vierzig Tage des Musa Dagh* (1933; Eng. tr., *The Forty Days of Musa Dagh*, 1934), an account of the Turkish persecution of the Armenians in 1915.

After World War I, Werfel lived in Vienna, where he married Alma Mahler, the widow of the composer Gustav Mahler. Following the *Anschluss* in 1938, the Werfels fled to France. When the Germans invaded that country, the couple took refuge in Lourdes, where the poet vowed to "sing the song" of Saint Bernadette. Werfel and his wife reached the United States by way of Spain and Portugal.

In California, Werfel wrote some of his most popular works, reflecting his experiences in France: *Das Lied von Bernadette* (1941; Eng. tr., *Song of Bernadette*, 1942), a novel of simple faith, and *Jakobowsky und der Oberst* (1944; Eng. tr., *Jakobowsky and the Colonel*, 1944), a "comedy of a tragedy" whose protagonists-antagonists are a quixotic Polish officer and a Jew with unshakable faith in reason and *Kultur*. Werfel completed his last novel, *Stern der Ungeborenen* (1946; Eng. tr., *Star of the Unborn*, 1946), a few days before his fatal heart attack. This visionary novel examines futuristic civilization of astromental man far in the future. Here the end of suffering has not brought about a new golden age but has cut off the chance of man's redemption. The book ends, however, on a note of faith.

See: L. B. Foltin, ed. *Franz Werfel 1890–1945* (1961) and *Franz Werfel* (1972).   K.S.M.

Weyrauch, Wolfgang (1907–), German poet, storyteller, and author of radio plays, was born in Königsberg, the son of a land surveyor. He spent his school years in Frankfurt am Main, where he attended an actors academy. He became an actor on the municipal stages of Münster and Bochum, later studying history, Romance languages, and German literature in Berlin, where he subsequently worked as a publisher's reader. He published his first book, *Der Main* (The Main River), a legend, in 1934 and the autobiographical, unpolitical novel *Strudel und Quell* (Whirlpool and Spring) in 1936. He was a soldier from 1940 to 1945 but was able to continue his writing. The tale *Eine Inselgeschichte* (1939; An Island Story) was followed in 1940 by a volume of stories, *Ein Band für die Nacht* (A Volume for the Night) and in 1942 by a

long story, *Das Liebespaar* (The Loving Couple). After captivity in the Soviet Union he published a long story, *Auf der bewegten Erde* (1946; On the Moving Earth), which has war experiences as its theme, as does the volume of poems *Von des Glückes Barmherzigheit* (1946; On the Mercy of Fortune), which was followed by a second collection of poems, *Lerche und Sperber* (Lark and Sparrow Hawk) in 1948. The story *Die Liebenden* (1948; The Lovers) was followed in the same year by an avant-garde programmatic tale, *Die Davids-Bündler* (The Members of the Covenant of David). In 1949, Weyrauch coined the term *Kahlschlag* (clear-cutting) in the afterword to an anthology of prose by 30 young writers, *Tausend Gramm* (A Thousand Grams), to indicate the sense of "starting over," after having wiped the language slate clean of besmirched Nazi jargon. In 1965 he edited yet another anthology of prose, *Alle diese Straßen* (All These Roads).

From 1946 to 1948, Weyrauch was an editor of the satiric periodical *Ulenspiegel* in Berlin, and in 1950 he worked in Worpswede and in Hamburg as an editorial reader for the Rowohlt publishing house until 1952. After 1959 he was a free-lance writer, living at first in Munich and then in Darmstadt. His anthology of contemporary lyric poets, *Expeditionen* (1959), collected poems written after 1945; the *Neue Expeditionen* (1975) brought the collection up to date with poems from 1960 to 1975. A pragmatist in his own poetry, a poet who believes that the thematics of poetry must involve people, the poet whose lyric contribution supplied the title of Hans BENDER'S anthology *Mein Gedicht ist mein Messer* (1955; My Poem Is My Blade), Weyrauch combines formalistic experimentation and moral commitment in his poems, as in the collections *An die Wand geschrieben* (1950; Written on the Wall). He wishes to create a feeling of disquiet in his readers, to communicate with them, to effect dialogue. Other collections of poetry, such as *Gesang um nicht zu sterben* (1956; Song so as not to Die), *Nie trifft das Finsternis* (1956; Darkness Never Strikes), and *Die Spur* (1963; The Track), continue the restless language, the constant questioning of Weyrauch.

In his radio plays, Weyrauch's anxiety in the new age, the age of the atom, is felt repeatedly in the collections *Dialog mit dem Unsichtbaren* (1962; Dialogue with the Unseen) and *Das grüne Zelt. Die japanischen Fischer* (1963; The Green Tent. The Japanese Fishermen). He received the prize of the German War Blind in 1961 for his radio play *Totentanz* (Dance of Death) and was one of the first to write plays for stereo broadcasts.

The collection of stories *Mein Schiff, das heißt Taifun* (1959; My Ship, with the Name Typhoon), thrust Weyrauch to the forefront among short prose writers, with fiction heavily laced with lyrical moments. His prose sketch *Etwas geschieht* (1966; Something's Happening) is typical for its experimental language and its spirit of engagement, here delineating the sequence of events leading to a protest action. *Unterhaltungen von Fußgängern* (1966; Conversations of Strollers) and *Geschichten zum Weiterschreiben* (1969; Stories to Write Further) continue his probing advancement of experiment. The prose work *Wie geht es Ihnen* (1971; How Are You) was followed by *Mit dem Kopf durch die Wand* (1972; Come Hell or High Water), a collection of miscellaneous stories, poems, essays, and a radio play. In 1974 appeared the stories collected in *Das Ende von Frankfurt am Main* (The End of Frankfurt am Main). An indefatigable and daring handler of words and skeptic of language, he produced the stories in *Beinahe täglich* (Almost Daily) in 1975.

A long poem, written for his teenage son, "Kein Nachtwächter, ein Tagwächter" ("Wide-Awake, Not

Half-Awake,'' 1974 in English in the magazine *Dimension*), appeared in 1975 under the title of *Lieber T* (a fairly obvious and awful, but appropriate, pun). Weyrauch's ever-present urge to experiment produced the volume *Hans Dumm, 111 Geschichten* (Hans Dumm, 111 Stories) in 1978, where each page contains a different ''story'' about Hans Dumm in a few lines. The example of Weyrauch, one of the first writers to voice his experiences after World War II and one devoted to involving readers with topics of the day, moral stands, and the possibilities of language, has kept him in the forefront of postwar German writing.   A.L.W.

Weyssenhoff, Józef (1860–1932), Polish novelist, was born in Kolano and died in Warsaw. After studying law at the University of Dorpat, Weyssenhoff became a landowner. He published poetry, short stories, and essays of his own as well as translations, particularly from Heinrich Heine.

In 1898, Weyssenhoff published the novel *Żywot i myśli Zygmunta Podfilipskiego* (The Life and Thoughts of Sigismund Podfilipski), which brought him immediate recognition and assured him an outstanding position in modern Polish literature. The novel portrays a representative of the Polish aristocratic milieu. What is supposedly a eulogy of a great personality, told by a gullible and simple-minded admirer and disciple, turns out to be an ironic and satirical exposure and mockery of aristocratic snobbery and parasitic existence, of sybaritism and moral wretchness, all eloquently disguised.

Weyssenhoff's later novels show a striking decline in standards of writing. They are obtrusively tendentious and made him a proponent of social conservatism, advocating the revival of the providential mission of the aristocracy to govern society. Some of the later novels, however, were acclaimed for their colorful depiction of the Lithuanian and east Polish landscape and nature, used by Weyssenhoff as the background for his portrayals of gentry life, notably in *Soból i panna* (1911; Eng. tr., *The Sable and the Girl*, 1929) and *Puszcza* (1915; The Virgin Forest).

See: M. Czermińska, ''Józef Weyssenhoff,'' in *Obraz literatury polskiej XIX i XX wieku. Literatura okresu Młodej Polski*, vol. 3, (1973), pp. 481–514.   S.S.

Wiechert, Ernst (1887–1950), German novelist, was the son of a forester in East Prussia. In *Wälder und Menschen* (1936; Forests and People) he tells about his own childhood spent in close contact with nature. These early impressions, together with his memories of an oversensitive, melancholy mother and the stories of the Bible as well as the weird tales and fantastic legends of the countryside, were to influence all his later writing. At the age of 11 he was sent to school in Königsberg, where he continued his academic studies and took his degree. Teaching in secondary schools left him dissatisfied. Preoccupation with outstanding Russian and Scandinavian writers increased his original leaning toward self-destructive criticism, and in his first novel, *Die Flucht* .(1916; Flight), the hero significantly takes his own life.

World War I did not brighten the young author's views. In his novel *Jedermann* (1931; Everyman) he expressed the enervating experience of endless, despairing waiting, of emptiness that scarred every soldier's mind. After the war he withdrew into the great woods of his homeland. His novels *Der Wald* (1922; The Forest) and *Der Totenwolf* (1924; The Death Wolf) reflect the chaotic violence of his reaction against postwar conditions and the spirit of the age. But he soon sought redemption in the universal suffering of man from which love is born. *Der Knecht Gottes Andreas Nyland* (1926; Andreas Nyland, The

Servant of God) tries to follow Christ's demands to the letter, the hero devoting himself, like Jakob Wassermann's *Christian Wahnschaffe* (1919), to all that is miserable and ugly in order to redeem it through love. However, the abundance of human suffering overwhelms his sensitive soul—he realizes the smallness of his attempts and seeks refuge in the woods from the curse of civilization.

Wiechert's foremost concern was to reconcile his deep love of nature, his faith in life close to the soil, with the demands of Christian ethics. Again and again the problem of struggle and conflict between human beings is contrasted with and overcome by the quiet forces of nature that are in league with God. Outstanding among his short stories are ''Tobias'' (1932), the story of a student who commits a political murder and of his final confession and atonement under the relentless silent accusation of the peaceful life in an old mill and of his grandmother's faith in the Bible; and *Hirtennovelle* (1935; Eng. tr., *The Shepherd's Novella* (1971), the tale of a boy-shepherd in a poor, remote village, who leads the villagers to safety at their enemies' approach but dies trying to save a stray lamb. These two stories show Wiechert at his best—his gift of imagery, his symbolic interpretation of reality, his intensity of mood and yet simplicity of expression.

Wiechert became best known through his novels *Die Magd des Jürgen Doscozil* (1932; Eng. tr., *The Girl and the Ferryman*, 1947), obviously influenced by Knut HAMSUN's *Growth of the Soil*, best in its descriptions of primitive living, less convincing in its somewhat sensational plot; and *Die Majorin* (1934; Eng. tr., *The Baroness*, 1936), psychologically more interesting, dealing with the fate of two people representative of the age: the major's widow, disillusioned and lonely yet bravely administering her estate, and Michael, the soldier, returned from years of war and imprisonment, bitter, burnt out, uprooted— the central problem of the novel is the woman's struggle to win this man back to life. Other works by Weichert include the tale *Die Gebärde* (1947; The Gesture) and the novels *Die Jeromin-Kinder* (1945; The Children of Jerome), *Das einfache Leben* (1946; Eng. tr., *The Simple Life*, 1954), and *Missa sine Nomine* (1950; Eng. tr., *Tidings*, 1959).

See: H. Ebeling, *Ernst Wiechert: der Weg eines Dichters* (1937); H. Ebeling, *Ernst Wiechert, das Werk eines Dichters* (1947).   E.M.F. rev. A.L.W.

Wied, Gustav (1858–1914), Danish short-story writer, novelist, and playwright, was born on the island of Lolland. Having failed as an actor, he had his breakthrough in a series of stories, *Silhuetter* (1891; Silhouettes) and *Barnlige Sjæle* (1893; Childish Souls), humorous portraits of country and small-town life that lead up to his major satirical works, *Livsens Ondskab* (1899; Life's Malice) and *Knagsted* (1902). These are precise but malicious caricatures of provincial types and milieus. Wied's redeeming humor is replaced by acrid pessimism in *Slægten* (1898; The Family) and *Fædrene æde Druer* (1908; The Fathers Eat Grapes). The naturalistic motifs— heredity and instincts—are here grotesquely changed into degeneration and perversion. In his dramatic works Wied's satire also swings between good-natured humor and loathing of the human animal. The former is found in *Skærmydsler* (1901; Skirmishes), an intimate portrayal of old people and Wied's greatest dramatic success, and the latter dominates his self-invented ''satyr plays.'' The best of these reading dramas are collected in *Adel, Gejstlighed, Borger, og Bonde* (1897; Nobility, Clergy, Bourgeoisie and Peasantry) and *Dansemus* (1905; Dancing Mice), masterpieces, in which the ironical stage directions increasingly encroach upon the dialogue and betray the author's tragic view of life, which eventually led to suicide.

See: K. Ahnlund, *Den unge Gustav Wied* (1964).

S.H.R.

Wierzyński, Kazimierz (1894–1969), Polish poet, short-story writer, essayist, and theater critic, was born in Drohobych and died in London. In his long creative career he published 22 volumes of poetry and 8 books of nonpoetic character. His development as a lyricist attests to an amazing ability for renewal and transformation.

At the dawn of Poland's second independence, Wierzyński, then a member of the "Skamander" group, gave the most exuberant, joyful, Dionysian expression to the common feelings in two volumes of poems, *Wiosna i wino* (1919; Spring and Wine) and *Wróble na dachu* (1921; Sparrows on the Roof). In 1927 he won the first prize in the literary contest of the ninth Olympic Games in Amsterdam for a collection of masterly Pindaric odes, *Laur olimpijski* (1927; Olympic Laurel), which was translated into many languages.

With time, Wierzyński's unconditional affirmation of life and humanity, with their beauty, richness, and inexhaustible potentialities, was overshadowed by concern with moral, social, and national issues, particularly in *Rozmowa z puszczą* (1929; Conversation with the Forest), *Pieśni fanatyczne* (1929; Fanatical Songs), and *Gorzki urodzaj* (1933; Bitter Harvest). In the volume *Gorzki urodzaj*, he was the first Polish poet who revealed to his readers modern America with all its complex implications. With the approach of war, his concern changed to anxiety, together with exhortations to heroism voiced in *Wolność tragiczna* (1936; Tragic Freedom), a tightly knit cycle of poems about Józef Piłsudski and the fight for national independence.

On the very eve of World War II Wierzyński, adopted the patriotic stance characteristic of Polish romanticism; he became a poet who shared with his nation all the vicissitudes of fate. At the same time he gave a deeper meaning to the heroic efforts and tragic experiences of his people, connecting them with the defense of universal cultural values. This phase is represented by six volumes, among which the most striking are *Ziemia wilczyca* (1941; Earth, the She-Wolf), containing the programmatic poem "Via Appia," and *Krzyże i miecze* (1946; Crosses and Swords).

After the end of the war, Wierzyński chose exile and settled in the United States, where he experienced an astounding resurgence of creative energy. The outcome was six substantial collections of poems: *Korzec maku* (1951; A Bushel of Poppy Seed), *Siedem podków* (1954; Seven Horseshoes), *Tkanka ziemi* (1960; Tissue of Earth), *Kufer na plecąch* (1964; With a Trunk on My Shoulder), *Czarny polonez* (1968; Black Polonaise), and *Sen-mara* (1969; Nightmare). This phase is marked by a decisive turn from heterotelic to autotelic poetry, encompassing a wide gamut of subjects, from nostalgia for the poet's mother country, through concern with the future of Atlantic civilization and the human race, to eschatological problems of death and its aftermath. Wierzyński's late poetry is also revealing in its texture and literary instrumentation. Until this late breakthrough, he represented predominantly the classicist approach and was a master of regular poetic form. The poetry of the last period opened the way for experimentation aiming at a more relaxed and, in all aspects, more daring, "organic" form—changeable, innovative, perfectly suited to the content.

Although he was mainly a lyric poet, Wierzyński left behind samples of by no means insignificant artistic prose. This medium, which he had practiced before World War II, underwent a total change thereafter, thanks to the sobering influence of American prose writing; his prose became disciplined, muscular, and purposeful. It is noticeable in his factographic book about the September campaign, *Pobojowisko* (1944; Eng. tr., *The Forgotten Battlefield*, 1944) and in *The Life and Death of Chopin* (1949), translated into many languages, as well as in a collection of essays and radio talks, *Moja prywatna Ameryka* (1966; My Private America). A volume of his poetry in English translation was published in 1959, *Selected Poems*, ed. by C. Mills and L. Krzyżanowski.

See: *Słownik współczesnych pisarzy polskich*, vol. 3 (1964), pp. 473–79; T. Terlecki, "Wierzyński czyli poeta," in *Przebity światłem* (1969), pp. 17–40; M. Dłuska, *Studia i rozprawy*, vol. 3 (devoted exclusively to Wierzyński) (1972).

T.T.

Wiktor, Jan (1890–1967), Polish novelist, short-story writer, and publicist, was born in Radomyśl, near Tarnobrzeg, and died in Cracow. After two years at the Academy of Medicine in Lvov he had to leave his studies because of tuberculosis. After that time he lived mostly in Cracow and Szczawnica. His early novels like *Zwariowane miasto* (1931; Crazy Town) and *Czarna Rózia* (1932; Black Rózia) express an idealization of village life and antiurban tendencies. His prose developed under the auspices of Stefan Żeromski and Władysław ORKAN. He first won recognition with the novel *Wierzby nad Sekwaną* (1933; Willows on the Banks of the Seine), describing the misery and struggles of the emigrant worker in France, as well as his next novel, *Orka na ugorze* (1935; Plowing Fallow Ground), where he depicted the social and economic situation in the village. After World War II he turned in his writing to the past: *Skrzydlaty mnich* (1947; The Winged Monk), *Papież i buntownik* (1953; The Pope and the Rebel). In later work he returned to his beloved region and wrote large monographs about it, notably *Pieniny i ziemia sądecka* (1956; The Pieniny Mountains and the Sącz Region).

See: J. Zając, "Społecznik i moralista—Jan Wiktor" in *Prozaicy dwudziestolecia międzywojennego*, ed. by B. Faron (1972), pp. 721–48.

A.Z.

Wildenvey, Herman (1886–1959), Norwegian poet, was born of farming stock in the community of Eiker. He is the troubadour of Norwegian verse, the tireless singer of youth, beauty, and summer. Wildenvey, whose real family name was Portaas, attended secondary school in Norway and then studied for a time at a theological seminary in the United States. His first mature collection of verse, *Nyinger* (1907; Bonfires), at once established him as a popular idol and the standard-bearer of a lyric revival in Norwegian letters. Disclaiming all social purpose, he declared that he was a pagan worshiper of life and beauty.

Building on the form and spirit of Knut HAMSON's poetry, Wildenvey developed an "ambling" verse line all his own, with an easy billowing cadence produced by the alternation of three- and four-syllable feet and by the enjambment of sentences over several lines. With this technique he was able to relieve Norwegian verse of its usual sobriety, giving it a new lightness that is sometimes merely frothy, but often ingratiatingly charming, as well as witty and daring. He enjoyed irritating the staid and the bourgeois, and he treated love with a flippancy that is reminiscent of Heinrich Heine—whose *Buch der Lieder* he translated in 1929—yet he lacks the German poet's tragic undertone. Widenvey's admiring public came to expect a colloquial, even slangy style, a sudden, teasing quip at the end, a glittering, summary love of nature, and a ready tenderness for children and the unhappy. Verse collections such as *Kjærtegn* (1916; Caresses), *Ildorkestret* (1923; The Orchestra of Fire), and *Høstens lyre* (1931; The Lyre of Autumn), to mention but a few of his many volumes, reveal a true poet, progressively deepening his formal mastery and the seriousness of his themes. Wildenvey's post-World War II collections of verse lack his earlier infatuating charm and grace, but they still demonstrate a marvelous vitality and an ability to create fresh, startling images of man face to face with nature and the cosmos.

See: J. Auslander, Introduction to H. Wildenvey, *Owls to Athens* (1934); K. Haave, *Herman Wildenvey* (1952).

E.H.

Wildgans, Anton (1881-1932), Austrian poet and dramatist, was born in Vienna, the son of a cabinet minister. He completed his law studies in 1908, but when the success of his first book of poems, *Herbstfrühling* (1909; Autumn-Spring) made him financially independent, he gave up a state position. For a time, 1921 to 1922 and 1930 to 1932, he was director of the famous Burgtheater, a leading German theater then as now, but he devoted himself mainly to writing. His lyric utterance is prominent; a posthumously published selection of his poems, *Späte Ernte* (1933; Late Harvest), reveals the fertility and power of his invention. His tragedy *Armut* (1914; Poverty) won acclaim such as Vienna had not granted a play for years. Only a little less applause greeted the tragedies *Liebe* (1916; Love) and *Dies irae* (1919).

Because his dramas are regarded as restatements of ideas set forth in the poems and because they show an eclecticism of structure rather than any one consistent pattern or trend, his strongest claim to lasting esteem will rest on his poetry, some of the best and most authentic of which is to be found in the *Sonette an Ead* (1912; Sonnets to Ead). Typically Viennese in softheartedness, fine sensitivity, and the mild humanity of his outlook, he avoided the effeminacy that sometimes characterizes Austrian Francophiles. He turned to the soil and its toilers and found his motifs in the fundamental experiences of human life—man and nature, man and woman, the urge to communal living, and the longing for solitude.

See: J. Soyka, ed., *Das Anton Wildgans Buch*(1932).

B.Q.M. rev. A.L.W.

Willems, Paul (1912-), Belgian novelist, essayist, and playwright, was born near Antwerp. He began his writing career as the author of poetic novels and essays: *Tout est réel ici* (1941; Everything Is Real Here), *L'Herbe qui tremble* (1942; Trembling Grass), *Blessures* (1945; Wounds), and *Cronique du cygne* (1949; Chronicle of the Swan). This was before he asserted himself as one of the masters of the poetic and fairy-tale theater, somewhat in the line of Jules SUPERVIELLE. After some highly colored, fantastic, too willingly vaudevillesque, and somewhat awkward stories—*Le Bon Vin de M. Nuche* (1949; Mr. Nuche's Good Wine), *Peau d'ours* (1951; Bearskin), *Off et la lune* (1958; Off and the Moon), and *La Plage aux anguilles* (1959; The Beach with Eels)—Willems found his style with *Il pleut dans ma maison* (1962; It's Raining in My House), in which the rejection of materialism dominates and the barriers between dream and reality collapse. A supple writing, the art of evoking the inexpressible, a mixture of tenderness and seriousness, of fairyland and sweetness—all these characterize Willems's theater. Dreaming makes itself nostalgic, and the rejection of reality becomes staggering with *Warna* (1963), in which, in an imaginary Middle Ages, a woman grown

old and forgotten by her lover wants to persist in believing that time has not passed—or again in *Ville à voile* (1966; Sailing City), in which maturity strives in vain to regain former youth and dreams. After *Le Soleil sur la mer* (1970; Sunlight on the Sea), a somewhat melodramatic denunciation of tyranny, Willems returns, with *Miroirs d'Ostende* (1974; Mirrors of Ostend), to his beloved theme, that of the pursuit of time and the authenticity of existence, not without melancholy; for the heroes fail to "invent their life," to give it those foundations of drama that an ineluctable reality ruins.

See: *Le Théâtre contemporain* (1969), pp. 112-17; J. Burniaux and R. Frickx, *La Littérature belge d'expression française* (1973), p. 103; A. Jans, *Lettres vivantes 1945-1975* (1975), pp. 317-18.

R.T.

Wispeleare, Paul de (1928-), Belgian (Flemish) prose writer and essayist, was born in Assebroek (Bruges). Throughout his creative and critical work, de Wispeleare questions the role of the writer as well as the various manifestations of the writing process. In the short story "Scherzando ma non troppo" (1959), and especially in such novels as *Een eiland worden* (1963; To Become an Island) and *Mijn levende schaduw* (1965; My Living Shadow), he deals with the issue of the writer as "I." Caught between writing and living, between being a writer and being an ordinary observer, de Wispeleare tries to resolve the discrepancy between reality and fiction. Clearly he opts for the latter—without, however, losing sight of the former. Hence, his essays and novels are to be considered as parts or fragments of a unique experience, as emanations of a writer's consciousness.

In *Paul-Tegenpaul* (1970; Paul Againstpaul) and *Een dag op het land* (1976; A Day on the Ground), de Wispeleare carries even further his exploration of the problematic "I." Indeed, if living and writing are two activities that complement each other, they are also presented in the two works mentioned above as polar opposites. The title *Paul-Tegenpaul* might thus be read as "Pole-Against-pole." In the space between these two poles there unfolds an authentic existence in which the writer engages his responsibility.

In his last autobiographical essays, de Wispeleare has tackled the problem of historical and social responsibility. In *Tussen tuin en wereld* (1979; Between Garden and World), for example, the indignation stemming from social injustice and corruption alternates with an awareness of impotence and a longing for idyllic noninvolvement. De Wispeleare is also the author of such noteworthy critical essays as *Het Perzische tapijt* (1966; The Persian Rug) and *Met kritisch oog* (1967; With a Critical Eye).

P. van A.

Witkiewicz, Stanisław Ignacy, pseud. Witkacy (1885-1939), Polish playwright, novelist, aesthetician, painter, and philosopher, was born in Warsaw, but grew up in Zakopane in the literary and artistic circle of "Young Poland." He was the son of the painter, critic, and writer Stanisław Witkiewicz. In 1904 and 1905, he studied in the Academy of Fine Arts in Cracow, and later he continued his studies in painting in Italy, France, and Germany. In 1914, Witkiewicz went with a friend, the anthropologist Bronisław Malinowski, on a scientific expedition to Australia, developing a lasting interest in non-Western cultures. Upon the outbreak of World War I, he went to Russia, where he served first as a tsarist officer, and later, during the Russian Revolution, he was elected political commissar by his regiment.

From 1918 until his death, Witkiewicz was active in Poland as an artist and writer, earning his living as a portrait painter. Between 1918 and 1922 he became one of the most active members of the "Vanguard" group of painters and poets called the formists. In an essay, *Nowe formy w malarstwie i wynikające stad nieporozumienia* (1919; New Forms in Painting and the Resulting Misunderstandings), Witkiewicz presented his own aesthetic theory as well as his philosophical views. In *Teatr. Wstęp do teorii czystej formy w teatrze* (1923; Theater. Introduction to the Theory of Pure Form in the Theater), he formulated a theory of nonrealistic theater designed to liberate drama from conventional psychology and storytelling and give it the formal possibilities of modern art and music. His aim was to "abandon lifelike logic in art by introducing a fantastic psychology and fantastic action in order to win the complete freedom of formal elements." In the face of an inexplicable universe, the theater should arouse bafflement in the audience over the "metaphysical feeling of the strangeness of existence."

In a period of 8 years, Witkiewicz wrote over 30 plays, many unpublished and unperformed in his lifetime. His 23 surviving dramas were published in 1962 and include such important works as *Nowe Wyzwolenie* (1922; Eng. tr., *The New Deliverance*, 1973), *Kurka wodna* (1962; Eng. tr., *The Water Hen*, 1968), *Mątwa* (1923; Eng. tr., *The Cuttlefish*, 1970), *Wariat i zakonnica* (1925; Eng. tr., *The Madman and the Nun*, 1968), *Matka* (1962; Eng. tr., *The Mother*, 1968), and *Szewcy* (1948; Eng. tr., *The Shoemakers*, 1968).

Characterized by grotesque humor, dreamlike illogicality, vivid color, and spectacular stage effects, his theater is at once both metaphysical and social, portraying what Witkiewicz called "the experiences of a group of degenerate ex-people in the face of the growing mechanization of life." With affinities to both expressionism and surrealism, Witkiewicz's "comedies with corpses" and "non-Euclidian dramas" remain unique in their personal and highly ironic visions of an insane world heading for disaster.

A lonely and misunderstood figure whose flamboyant life and intense individuality created an adverse legend, Witkiewicz was savagely attacked by critics and radically underestimated by his contemporaries, who treated him like a madman. He turned from playwriting to fiction, producing two major anti-Utopian novels that predict the collapse of Western civilization and the coming of totalitarianism, *Pożegnanie jesieni* (1927; Farewell to Autumn) and *Nienasycenie* (1930; Eng. tr., *Insatiability*, 1975). His autobiographical novel about a self-examination of his inner life as an artist, *622 upadki Bunga* (1972; 622 Downfalls of Bungo), was written between 1910 and 1919. He devoted his last years to philosophy, creating his own existential system in *Pojęcia i twierdzenia implikowane przez pojęcie istnienia* (1935; The Concepts and Principles Implied by the Concept of Existence).

In poor health and despairing over the fate of civilization, Witkiewicz committed suicide on Sept. 18, 1939, in Jeziora (Wolhynia), after first the Germans and then the Russians invaded Poland. Forgotten during the Stalin years, Witkiewicz was rediscovered in Poland after 1956, when his works played an influential part in freeing the arts from socialist realism and in the formation of a new Polish avant-garde theater. His dramas have been translated into 14 languages and played throughout the world, and Witkiewicz is now recognized as a major figure in modern European literature. His collected plays have been published, *Dramaty,* ed. by K. Puzyna, vols. 1 and 2 (1962), and collections in English translation have also appeared, *The Madman and the Nun and Other Plays* (1968) and *Tropical Madness* (1972).

See A. van Crugten, *S. I. Witkiewicz: aux sources d'un Théâtre Nouveau* (1971); *Studia o Stanisławie Ignacym Witkiewiczu* (1972); *PolR* 18, nos. 1–2 (special Witkiewicz issue) (1973); B. Danek-Wojnowska, *Stanisław Ignacy Witkiewicz a modernizm* (1976); M. Szpakowska, *Swiatopogląd Stanisława Ignacego Witkiewicza* (1976); D. Gerould, *Witkacy* (1979). D.C.G.

Wittlin, Józef (1896–1976), Polish poet, novelist, essayist and translator, was born in the manor of Dmytrów, near Radziechów, and died in New York. He studied philosophy at Vienna and Lvov universities. During World War I he served in the Austrian infantry. He was affiliated with the group of Polish expressionists known as "Zdrój." Wittlin "settled his accounts with war" first in the expressionistic collection of poems *Hymny* (1920; Hymns) and later in an antiwar novel, *Sól ziemi* (1936; Eng. tr., *The Salt of the Earth*, 1939), translated into many languages. Wittlin's *Hymny* appeals for peace and urges people to abandon their weapons. The tone of the hymns ranges from one of despair, rebellion, and blasphemy to that of psalmodic serenity and Christian humility. Following Jan Kasprowicz and Emile VERHAEREN, Wittlin used free verse in the *Hymny*. In them he combined archaic words and syntactic constructions with everyday and sometimes even vulgar words. The war experiences became the core of his novel *The Salt of the Earth*, which was designed to examine and destroy the war myth, to laugh it out of existence by turning it into absurdity. Irony linked with parody and the grotesque seems to predominate in the book for all its strong lyrical strain. Wittlin is also the author of a book of memoirs, *Mój Lwów* (1946; My Lvov); a collection of essays and other prose writings, *Orfeusz w piekle XX wieku* (1963; Orpheus in the Inferno of the 20th Century), and a translation of Homer's *Odyssey* (1924), later revised in 1935 and 1957. A collective volume of his poetry, *Poezje*, was published in 1978 and his *Sól ziemi* in 1979.

See: Z. Yurieff, *Joseph Wittlin* (1973); K. Jakowska, *Z dziejów ekspresjonizmu w Polsce. Wokół "Soli ziemi"* (1977). Z.Y.

Wivel, Ole (1921–), Danish poet, was born in Copenhagen. From 1945 to 1953 he was the owner of a publishing house, after which he was a teacher for a while, later again becoming a manager in the publishing business. Sentiments of catastrophe caused by World War II are described in his *Digte* (1943; Poems) in a form-bound style influenced by Rainer Maria RILKE. In *I Fiskens Tegn* (1948; In the Sign of the Fish), these sentiments are followed by an elegiac longing for a new God and a new human race. But the contact between men can only be established when the individual dares to accept his or her own life conditions as well as those of others. The breaking of the isolation is for Wivel a matter of grace. The confessional collections, *Jævndøgnselegier* (1949; Equinoctial Elegies) and *Maanen* (1952; The Moon), their form being inspired by T. S. Eliot, demonstrate that Wivel's dream of the medieval, universal culture also is nourished by a longing for the cosmic mysteries. In *Nike* (1958) and *Templet for Kybele* (1961; The Temple for Cybele), the atmosphere of longing is directed toward the present and toward action in a number of contemporary poems about the atomic threat and international political crises. This tendency is strengthened in the uneven collection *Gravskrifter* (1970; Epitaphs), also contemporary poems. The volume opens with a string of Vietnam poems, built up like reportage, and contains monologues confirming Wivel's political engagement and a new but now pessimistic belief in fate. S.H.R.

Woestijne, Karel van de (1879-1929), Belgian (Flemish) poet, was born in Ghent. He attended school there, studied Germanic philology at the State University of Ghent, and taught Dutch in various schools until he was appointed to the chair of Dutch literature at Ghent. He was associated with the literary movement *Van Nu en Straks*.

The decadent, fin-de-siècle mentality that prevailed during that period in European literature also played an important role in van de Woestijne's work. Van de Woestijne was a tormented person who on the one hand was weary of life and on the other hand longed for a full sensual and cerebral life. His poetry should be read as the expression of a "symbolized autobiography." The term "symbolism" is particularly appropriate in this case since van de Woestijne truly belonged to that artistic movement. Musicality, slow rhythm, and muted accents that render again and again a bursting sensuality are the main characteristics of van de Woestijne's languid and tormented poetry. *Het vaderhuis* (1903; The Father House), *De Boomgaard der vogelen en der vruchten* (1905; The Orchard of Birds and Fruit), and *De gulden schaduw* (1910; The Golden Shadow), three early collections of poems, contain some of van de Woestijne's greatest lyrical achievements. Later poems gathered in *De modderen man* (1920; The Man of Mud), *God aan Zee* (1926; God by the Sea) and *Het Bergmeer* (1928; The Mountain Lake) are also very moving. From the titles of these volumes, a reader might conclude that spirituality dominates, that earth-bound man has purified himself through his confrontation with the spiritual (God), with the pure (water), and with the lofty (mountain lake). There is, however, no absolute victory of the spiritual over the matter in van de Woestijne's work.

In his best short story, "De boer die sterft" (1918; The Dying Peasant), van de Woestijne shows that sensuality plays a positive role in his imagination. There is no trace of decadent aesthetics in this story, but rather an affirmation of life, symbolized by five women figures (the five senses) who convince the dying peasant that his life has been meaningful. When he finally accepts death and fathoms the last secret, he is grateful that, through their apology, he has come to an understanding of his situation. Van de Woestijne's poetry and prose are extremely sophisticated. His language is sometimes baroque, filled with neologisms and colorful, unique impressionistic words.

See: U. van de Voorde, *Essay over Karel van de Woestijne* (1934); M. Rutten, *De esthetische opvattingen van Karel van de Woestijne* (1943); A. Westerlinck, *De psychologische figuur van Karel van de Woestijne als dichter* (1952); J. Aerts, *Stijlgeheimen van Karel van de Woestijne* (1956).   P. van A.

Wohmann, Gabriele (1932-), German poet, novelist, and short-story writer, was born Gabriele Guyot in Darmstadt, where she now resides. She studied philosophy, music, and modern languages at the University of Frankfurt. Her short interlude as a teacher on a North Sea island is reflected in the anxiety she attributes to women teachers in her fiction, notably *Die grosse Liebe* (1966; True Love). Her marriage (1953) remains childless; her pessimism precludes biological hope. She is a member of the PEN Club (1960), "Gruppe 47" (1966), and the Academy of Arts in Berlin (1976), and the recipient of many literary prizes, including the Bremen Literary Prize (1971).

Wohmann's first short story, "Ein unwiderstehlicher Mann" (1956; An Irresistible Man), published in *Akzente*, earned immediate acclaim. Her early short fiction is superlative in its precise, analytical, ironic style; at the end of her stories an unexpected twist often surprises the reader. Recently, Wohmann has concentrated on socially committed poetry and novels that focus on a search for identity. She exposes with a sharp satirical pen the horror of everyday existence and the isolation of people within the family, as in *Die Bütows* (1967) and *Ländliches Fest* (1971; Country Party). Selfishness, lies, alcohol, drugs, reveries of real or imagined illnesses, and meditations on death, as in *Ernste Absicht* 1970; Serious Intention), are utilized as escapes from the banality and boredom of bourgeois life. But these endeavors merely betray helplessness and resignation.

Wohmann's characters do not find solace in nature or in other people, with whom they are incapable of communicating on any meaningful level, as in *Abschied für länger* (1965; A Farewell for a Long Time). Wohmann countered an accusation of banality with two collections of short fiction, provocatively entitled *Selbstverteidigung* (1971; Self-Defense), and *Gegenangriff* (1972; Counterattack). Her most recent works reveal a shift in emphasis. No longer do her artistic personae—Plath in *Schönes Gehege* (1975; Beautiful Enclosure) or Hubert in *Frühherbst in Badenweiler* (1978; Early Fall in Badenweiler)—feel compelled to dwell on the negative aspects of life. Likewise, *Ausflug mit der Mutter* (1976; Excursion with Mother), her warmest book, is burdened with none of her earlier sarcasm.

See: T. Scheuffleen, ed., *Materialienbuch* (1976); K. Wellner, *Leiden an der Familie, Zur sozialpathologischen Rollenanlayse im Werk Gabriele Wohmanns* (1976).
                                                                                    G.G.S.

Wolf, Christa (1929-), East German novelist and critic was born in Landsberg, Poland, and moved to Mecklenburg, East Germany, in 1945. From 1949 until 1953 she studied German literature at the universities in Jena and Leipzig. After completion of her studies she worked as an editor of the magazine *Neue Deutsche Literatur* and as a critic for the Mitteldeutscher Verlag and the Verlag Neues Leben. Much of her early essayistic work is devoted to contemporary socialist authors and to their place in the history of German literature.

Wolf turned to writing in 1959 and has been a major force in literature of the German Democratic Republic ever since the publication in 1961 of *Moskauer Novelle* (Tale of Moscow), a love story set against the background of war and its uncertain aftermath. Although she has written other short works of prose—*Unter den Linden* (1974)—and has continued to publish essays on literature—*Lesen und Schreiben* (1972; Eng. tr., The Reader and the Writer, 1978), *Fortgesetzter Versuch* (1979; Continued Attempt)—it is nonetheless as a novelist that she has gained her much deserved recognition.

Wolf's widely acclaimed novel *Der geteilte Himmel* (1963; Eng. tr., Divided Heaven, 1976), which was awarded the prestigious Heinrich Mann Prize, deals with the conflict between personal and communal goals in a socialist system; in emphasizing the individual sacrifice often necessary under socialism, Wolf fashions a heroine who finds the identity for which she is searching, precisely in becoming a meaningful part of the whole. Her novel *Nachdenken über Christa T.* (1968; Eng. tr., The Quest for Christa T., 1970) similarly reflects her strong concern for personal identity, although here the emphasis has shifted from the external world of social roles and ideological objectives to the inner world of memory. *Kindheitsmuster* (1977; Childhood Pattern) continues this progression and could easily bear the subtitle, "Remembrance of Things Past," for Wolf, like Marcel PROUST, similarly attempts to grasp—and to articulate—

the actuality of one's existence in a recollection of one's past; what comes to light is the inevitable discrepancy between lived and remembered experiences of a prewar Germany, which shaped her identity and that of all her contemporaries.

Her most recent work is the well-received story *Kein Ort. Nirgends* (1979, No Place. Anywhere), an articulate and at times highly lyrical look at the nature of artistic destiny. For the first time Wolf turns away from the problematics of contemporary life in the German Democratic Republic and chooses instead to focus her attention on the tragic fate of two 19th-century writers, Heinrich von Kleist and Karoline von Günderode. Other awards she has received are the Literary Prize of the City of Halle (1961) and the National Prize for Art and Literature of the GDR (1964).

See: C. Cosentino, "Eine Untersuchung des sozialistischen Realismus im Werke Christa Wolfs," *GQ*, 47, no. 2 (1974): 245–61; A. Stephan, "Christa Wolf," *Text & Kritik* (Special Issue, 1975): H 46; W. Cirker, "The Socialist Education of Rita Seidel: The Dialectics of Humanism and Authoritarianism in Christa Wolf's *Der geteilte Himmel*," *UDB* 13, no. 2 (Winter, 1978): 105–11.

T. Di. N.

Wolfskehl, Karl (1869–1948), German lyric poet, was born in Darmstadt into a wealthy Jewish patrician family. He studied German literature in Berlin, Leipzig, and Gießen, earning a Ph.D. At the turn of the century he became acquainted with Stefan GEORGE, having worked previously on the periodical *Blätter für die Kunst*. He lived in Munich in the artists' section, Schwabing, where his home was a gathering place for admireres of George. With the inauguration of the Nazi government in 1933 he went to Italy and to New Zealand in 1938, where he lived in Auckland until his death.

One of the many German writers living in exile during the Nazi years, Wolfskehl wrote mystical lyric poems that, like some by George, had a hymnlike character, often reaching into mythology for their thematic focus. Books of lyrics included *Der Umkreis* (1927; The Circumference), *Die Stimme spricht* (1934; The Voice Speaks), *An die Deutschen* (1947; To the Germans), *Sang aus dem Exil* (1950; Song from Exile), and *Hiob* (1950; Job). Wolfskehl was also the author of dramas such as *Saul* (1905), *Thors Hammer* (1908; The Hammer of Thor), and *Sanctus und Orpheus* (1909). A collection of letters from 10 years of exile appeared posthumously in 1959.

A.L.W.

Wolker, Jiří (1900–24), Czech poet, was the leading poet of the "proletarian" group that became prominent just after World War I. He was born in Prostějov, Moravia, of a good middle-class family. He came to Prague in 1919 to study law, but instead plunged into the literary life of the new capital city. He died of tuberculosis before he was 24, in his native town.

Wolker is the author of two popular collections of verse. The first, *Host do domu* (1921; The Guest in the House) is a collection of simple poems in which the poet dreams about the country world of his boyhood. Wolker obviously believed in the goodness of man and in the fundamental identity of all men, as preached by the French *unanimisme*. In the poem "Svatý Kopeček" (The Holy Hill), which can be compared with Guillaume APOLLINAIRE's "Zone," the earth melts into the sky, the shadow of death dissolves, silent matter comes alive— there is unity and continuity everywhere. Wolker's second collection, *Těžká hodina* (1922; The Grievous Hour), is very different. The poet had discovered the cause of the proletariat and communism, which he saw as an

earthly paradise, the fulfillment of his longing for identification with all humanity. In the second collection are effective social ballads, like "Balada o očích topičových" (Eyes of the Fireman), set in a power station, where the eyes of the fireman gradually change into lights of the city. Wolker rediscovered the style of the Czech folk ballad and its greatest master, Karel Jaromír Erben. A few poems, published after Wolker's death, give moving expression to his personal tragedy—dying in early youth and knowning all too clearly of his approaching doom. His tragic fate, his personal charm, and the popular tone of his lyrics have, however, elevated him to a position in recent Czech poetry that the actual substance of his work does not altogether support. The posthumous, overcomplete editions including even his earliest verse, some short plays, and some rather crude prose hardly enhance his reputation with critical readers. There is much adolescent naiveté and sentimentality in Wolker's work. But he had genuine talent, and his historical importance—his rediscovery of the style of the folk ballad, his ardent collectivist faith—cannot be overrated. There is a simple charm in his best verse that is beyond sophisticated criticism.

See: V. Nezval, *Wolker* (1925); Z. Kalista, *Kamarád Wolker* (1933); L. Kratochvíl, *Wolker a Nezval* (1936); A. C. Nor, *Jiří Wolker básník a člověk* (1947); F. Soldan, *Jiří Wolker* (1964); A. French, *The Poets of Prague* (1969).

R.W.

Wolkers, Jan (1925–), Dutch novelist, short-story writer, and dramatist, was born in Oegstgeest. After studying painting and sculpture with some success, he turned to writing, beginning his literary career with a volume of short stories, *Serpentina's Petticoat* (1961), for which he received the Amsterdam Literature Prize. His first novel, *Kort Amerikaans* (1962; Crew Cut) contained most of the themes—the father-son conflict, death, sex, loneliness, and alienation—that were to recur in his later work. Children and animals also occupy an important place in his fiction. Like much of his writing, his novel *Een roos van vlees* (1963; Eng. tr., *A Rose of Flesh*, 1967) is, to a large extent, autobiographical; and *Turks fruit* (1969; Eng. tr., *Turkish Delight*, 1974) reflects the breakup of his second marriage. *Terug naar Oegstgeest* (1965; Back to Oegstgeest) and *Horrible Tango* (1967; Eng. tr., *The Horrible Tango*, 1970) are both based on the events of his early life and the death of his brother. Although Wolkers's use of sex often seems pornographic, he believes that "eroticism is . . . tragically illuminated." In addition to the novels *De walgvogel* (1974; The Dodo) and *De kus* (1976; The Kiss) and the volumes of short stories *Gesponnen suiker* (1963; Cotton Candy) and *De hond met de blauwe tong* (1964; The Dog with the Blue Tongue), Wolkers has also published two plays, *Wegens sterfgeval gesloten* (1963; Closed on Account of Death) and *De Babel* (1963; Babel); a documentary on ecology, *Groeten van Rottumerplaat* (1971; Greetings from Rottumerplaat); and a photobiography, *Werkkleding* (1971; Work Clothes).

See: J. G. M. Weck, J. H. Caspers, M. J. C. M. Krekels, *In contact met het werk van moderne schrijvers, Deel 1: Jan Wolkers* (1974).

S.L.F.

Wyspiański, Stanisław (1869–1907), Polish dramatist, poet, painter, and reformer of the theater, was born and died in Cracow. He studied painting at the School of Fine Arts in Cracow and history, the history of art, and literature at the Jagiellonian University. Wyspiański was the most outstanding representative of the "Young Poland" movement. He intended to devote his life to the fine arts, but unexpectedly revealed a gift for poetry. It happened under the influence of Polish romantic poetry, Richard

WAGNER, and the atmosphere of symbolist Paris (he stayed for various lengths of time in that city, altogether some three and one-half years between 1890 and 1894). He never relinquished his interest in the arts, however, and they influenced his dramatic and scenic vision decisively and from its inception.

Wyspański's career as a dramatist began in his native city of Cracow in 1898 with *Warszawianka* (The Song of Warsaw), a one-act poetic drama of considerable originality. Thereafter, in less than one decade, racing with hectic haste against a premature death, he authored almost 20 dramas, a few lyric-epic poems ("rhapsodies"), some poignant lyrics, and some critical comments, in addition to his vast output in the field of the visual arts, which includes polychrome murals, stained-glass windows, innumerable pastels, innovations in typography, even architectonic projects and applied art (furniture design). Produced under such circumstances, the bulk of Wyspiański's dramatic creation can hardly be regarded as an organic development; it rather resembles a series of chain detonations. It may be arranged, according to the simplest principle of contents, into four groups: historical, contemporary, classically inspired, and mythological-metaphysical dramas. This very crude and approximate division at least indicates the scope of Wyspiański's creative power.

Warszawianka is the first of a cluster of historical plays pertaining to the unhappy November uprising against Russia (1830-31) and judges it with acute severity. This revisionist approach is also discernible in the rather weak *Lelewel* (1899), about a historian and leader, and in one of Wyspiański's masterpieces, *Noc listopadowa* (1904; November Night). The critical evaluation of the momentous historic episode was enlarged and encompassed the entire romantic movement in *Legion* (1900; The Legion); unique in its kind, it is a visionary, symbolic dramatic biography of Adam Mickiewicz, the towering figure of that era and the exponent of Polish messianism.

The group of contemporary dramas is heterogenous and overlaps on one side with the previous group and on the other with that of the classically inspired dramas. *Wesele* (1901; The Wedding), the unquestionable summit of Wyspiański's creative genius, is—at least in its genesis and on the surface—a topical drama. It was inspired by the marriage of the poet L. Rydel, a friend of Wyspiański, to a peasant girl. This event served as a springboard for a satirical, sublime, and pathetic evocation of the actual present, the heroic past, and the future of the Polish nation. Similarly, *Wyzwolenie* (1903; The Deliverance) is a pitiless reckoning with Poland, an outright condemnation of her petrified, crippling romantic leanings. *Klątwa* (1899; The Curse) and *Sędziowie* (1907; The Judges) were to all appearances a dramatic presentation of two *faits divers*, two fatal incidents: one in the vicarage of a village priest, the other in a Jewish country inn. But both assume the proportions of ancient tragedy, betray an underlying tragic vision of life, and strike the imagination with their monumental proportions.

The classically inspired dramas display a similarly mixed character. The two early ones, *Meleager* (1899; Eng. tr., 1933) and *Protesilas i Laodamia* (1899; Eng. tr., 1933), can be linked with the Parnassian and symbolist attraction to ancient Greece. Two others are *Achilleis* (1903), a most daring dramatization of the whole *Iliad*, raised to a synthesis of human existence, and *Powrót Odysa* (1907; The Return of Odysseus), which projects the end of Homer's second epic as a covertly personal drama of fate.

Most strongly heterogenous are the works belonging to the last group of mythological-metaphysical plays. The early *Legenda* (1898; The Legend) is relatively the least original, an attempt (obviously inspired by Wagner) to create a mythological music drama connected with Cracow and the river Vistula. The twin dramas *Bolesław Śmiały* (1903; Boleslaw the Bold) and *Skałka* (1907; The Little Rock), based on the history of the Polish Middle Ages, expose two concepts of man in a violently dramatic clash: the Nietzschean superman and the representative of Christian ethics. *Akropolis* (1904) is a work without precedence, which uses a free, dreamlike association of visions: its "action" takes place in the cathedral of Wawel, the Polish national Acropolis, and its "characters" are statues, figures from wall hangings, liturgical paraments. Its scope is very wide: it is best defined as the drama of Judeo-Greco-Roman-Christian culture and as a cosmic drama.

Seen from the formal standpoint, Wyspiański's dramatic creativity was a continuous experimentation, a probing of all the potentialities opened up by the symbolist movement. He tried them out, evaluated them critically, and finally transcended them. *Wesele*, the only example of symbolic satire, introduced an extremely rich language of multilevel theatrical metaphors. *Noc listopadowa* craftily interwove historical events with mythological motifs. *Wyzwolenie* enlarged to its ultimate limits the concept of "theater within the theater." For the first time in the history of modern stage, the scenic mechanism was stripped, laid bare, for the purpose of artistic effect. *Bolesław Śmiały* is a visualization of the future within a concrete historical actuality. *Akropolis* forestalled in the most daring way the poetics of surrealist dramas.

Wyspiański was an accomplished man of the theater, endowed with all its skills and crafts; he designed the settings for some of his own plays. He was the first producer (in 1901) of the complete version of Mickiewicz's *Dziady* (1823-32; Eng. tr., *Forefather's Eve*, 1968). His unique competence and achievement were confirmed by Gordon Craig, the father of the "great theatrical reform," who recognized in Wyspiański the first "artist of the theater." Lately, the thesis has been put forward that Wyspiański should be considered the most syncretic dramatist of the European symbolist movement.

See: C. Backvis, *Le Dramaturge Stanislas Wyspiański* (1952); S. Wyspiański, *Dzieła zebrane*, vols. 1-15, ed. by L. Płoszewski (1958-68); the last volume is split into four parts that include an exhaustive bibliography prepared by M. Stokowa); T. Terlecki, "Stanisław Wyspiański and the Poetics of Symbolist Drama," *PolR* 15, no. 4 (1970): 55-63, and "The Greatness and Ill Fortune of Stanislaw Wyspiański," *Antemurale*, 14 (1970): 259-77; A. Łempicka, *Wyspiański pisarz dramatyczny. Idee i formy* (1973).   T.T.

Wyzewa, Teodor de (1862-1917), French critic, was born on his grandmother's estate in the village of Kalusik, Russian Poland. His father was a physician. When the boy was 10 years old, his father decided to move the family to France so that his son could be educated in the French schools that he had learned to prize, having studied there himself while a political exile. The family settled in a village of Normandy, and the young Teodor was sent as a boarding student to the *collège* of Beauvais. Except for vacations, the next years of Wyzewa's life were spent, not happily, in the French schools for which he obtained scholarships. A year of teaching philosophy in the small provincial town of Châtellerault disgusted Wyzewa forever with pedagogy. Having returned to Paris and changed his name from Wyżewski to the more easily pronounced form Wyzewa, he undertook to make a living with his pen. The years of solitude and recollections of his Polish childhood had already taught Wyzewa to find, in dream, a refuge from drab reality.

In 1885 he and Edouard DUJARDIN founded the *Revue wagnérienne,* which was to play such an important part in the orientation and the expression of the symbolist movement. Wyzewa was then one of the most brilliant and certainly the most cosmopolitan of a group of young men who gathered every Tuesday at Stéphane MAL-LARMÉ's to discuss poetry, music, and philosophy. He knew many languages, had traveled extensively, and understood the most difficult poets and philosophers. His knowledge of German and of music was to make him the interpreter of Richard WAGNER to his contemporaries and one of the most important critics of his school. Consciously or not, Wyzewa attributed to Wagner many of his own ideas, and the series of articles on Wagnerian art published in the *Revue wagnérienne* (1885–86; later reprinted in *Nos Maîtres,* 1895) is one of the best expressions of symbolist aesthetics as conceived by a disciple of Mallarmé. The influence on that generation of this pseudo-Wagnerian philosophy, with its negation of the reality of the outside world ("Alone the 'I' exists and its eternal task is to create"), was heavy. The trilogy *Le Culte du moi* of Maurice BARRÈS is an example.

In the *Revue indépendante,* which in 1886 succeeded the *Revue wagnérienne* as a vehicle for symbolist doctrines, Wyzewa found the field in which he was to specialize, the criticism of foreign literature. Lev TOLSTOY was then superseding Richard Wagner as a model for the idealistically inclined. Wyzewa continued to conduct in the name of Tolstoy and with the label of "antiintellectualism" the propaganda he had begun in the name of Wagner and with the label of "idealism." His criticism was always propaganda against naturalism, against materialism, and against an undue faith in science. He wrote in *Vogue,* in the *Revue bleue,* and after 1891 in the *Revue des deux mondes,* to which he was called by Ferdinand BRUNETIÈRE. Wyzewa's evolution is a reflection of the evolution of the symbolist movement during these years, the end of which was, of course, for many a return to Christianity. The final stage marked by a new generation of poets, Paul CLAUDEL, Charles PÉGUY, Francis JAMMES, was reached by Wyzewa about 1900 (see *Contes chrétiens* [1901]). At that time, too, he was left a widower, after seven years of dreamlike happiness. Abandoning all worldly pursuits, he withdrew into almost complete seclusion, dividing his life between the work that provided his livelihood (articles for such publications as the *Revue des deux mondes* and *Temps* and translations, many of which were religious in character, such as *The Golden Legend* and Saint Francis of Assisi's *Fioretti*) and the music of Mozart, his only solace.

In 1916 he published (in collaboration with a friend, G. de St. Foix) an exhaustive study of Mozart's early works, *La Jeunesse de Mozart,* which had occupied his leisure for 10 years. When in 1917 a sudden illness took him away, his real spirit and all his ambition had long since departed this world.

See: E. L. Duval, *Teodor de Wyzewa: Critic without a Country* (1961); P. Delsemme, *Teodor de Wyzewa et le cosmopolitisme littéraire en France à l'époque du symbolisme,* 2 vols. (1967); N. di Girolamo, *Teodor de Wyzewa dal simbolismo al tradizionalismo: 1885–1887* (1969).   I. de W. rev. D.W.A.

Y

Yanovsky, Yuriy (1902–54), Ukrainian short-story writer and novelist, was born in Yelizavetgrad (now Kirovograd). The son of a clerk, he studied at the Kiev Polytechnic Institute and worked for a while in the film studios at Odessa. At first he wrote poetry, which was published later in the collection *Prekrasna Ut* (1929; The Most Beautiful Ut), but he gained prominence as a writer with his collections of short stories *Mamutovi byvni* (1925; Mammoth's Tusks) and *Krov zemlyi* (1927; The Blood of the Soil). In 1928, Yanovsky published a strikingly original novel about the film world, *Mayster korablya* (The Shipbuilder). His most notable achievement was the novel *Chotyry shablyi* (1930; Four Sabres), in which he depicted the 1917 Revolution and subsequent Civil War in the Ukraine in a series of heroic episodes. Permeated by historical references, this poetic novel is a powerful depiction of destruction during that period. The book was criticized for its "nationalism," however, and later banned. Yanovsky dealt with the same topic in his next novel, *Vershnyky* (1935; The Riders; French tr., *Les Cavaliers,* 1957). Louis ARAGON said of it that "we find ourselves transported further than Stendhal dared to envisage." Some of Yanovsky's plays, such as *Syn dynastiyi* (1942; The Son of the Dynasty) and *Dochka prokurora* (1953; The Daughter of the Procurator), reflect Communist ideology. His last notable work, *Zhyva voda* (1947; The Living Water), was a novel about post-World War II reconstruction. It was severely criticized and subsequently rewritten and published posthumously under the title *Myr* (1956; Peace).   G.S.N.L.

Yashin, Aleksandr Yakovlevich (1913–68), Russian poet and novelist, came to maturity, as he himself confessed, relatively late in life. Much of his early work belongs to the category of "varnishing reality" characteristic of post-World War II rural fiction and poetry. His mature style flowered in his unhurried accounts of walks through the countryside of his native Vologda province, describing plants, animals, buildings, and individuals, and real or legendary episodes connected with them. He continues the tradition of Mikhail PRISHVIN, whom he knew well. Much of the lyricism and irony of his work is concerned with the contrast between town and country, tradition and modernity. This is especially evident in his best-known work, *Vologodskaya svadba* (1962; Vologda Wedding), which was severely criticised in some Soviet journals for its bleak portrayal of village life and of the way young people no longer understand or value the morals and traditions of their parents.

See: A. Mikhaylov, *Aleksandr Yashin* (1975).   G.H.

Yavorov, Peyo, pseud. of Payo Kracholov (1878–1914), Bulgarian poet, playwright, and prose writer, was born in the small town of Chirpan. He submitted his first poems for publication in 1898 and in 1900 moved to Sofia to join the "Misul" (Thought) circle (*see* BULGARIAN LITERATURE). His direct involvement in the Macedonian revolutionary movement inspired him to write a biography of an old revolutionary comrade, *Gotse Delchev* (1904), and tautly composed memoirs of his guerrilla days, *Khaydushki kopneniya* (1908; Rebel Dreams). His modernist and decadent lyric poems appeared in such collections as *Bezsunitsi* (1907; Insomnias) and *Podir senkite na oblatsite* (1910; Following the Shadows of the Clouds). They display a fascination with the themes of love and death;

the poet's approach is for the most part darkly pessimistic and despairing.

Yavorov hoped for the advent of a new social order but was far from sure that it would bring him personal happiness, which he sought in love affairs of passionate intensity. His personal situation was reflected in the play *V polite na Vitosha* (1911; In the Foothills of Mount Vitosha), the finest psychological drama in Bulgarian literature. In the play an idealistic young man, active in politics, kills himself at the bedside of his beloved, who is dying after a suicide attempt brought on by her family's determination to prevent their marriage. A few years later this dramatic tragedy was closely reenacted in reality when Yavorov's wife killed herself in a jealous rage, and he eventually took his own life, in order to follow her in death.

See: E. Damiani, *Un poeta delle tenebre: P. K. Yavorov* (1940); M. Arnaudov, *Yavorov: lichnost—tvorchesto—sudba* (1961).   C.A.M.

Yelagin, Ivan, pseud. of Ivan Venediktovich Matveyev (1918–), Russian poet, was born in Vladivostok into a family of literati. His studies of medicine in Kiev were interrupted by World War II. Displaced to Germany, he published his first collections of poetry in Munich: *Po doroge ottuda* (1947; Coming from There) and *Ty moyo stoletiye* (1948; You My Century). After his immigration to the United States, Yelagin embarked upon an academic career. He holds a Ph.D. in Russian literature from New York University (1970) and has taught there and at the University of Pittsburgh. Further collections of his poetry include *Po doroge ottuda* (New York, 1953), *Politicheskiye felyetony v stikhakh* (Munich, 1959; Political Feuilletons in Verse), *Otsvety nochnye* (New York, 1963; Reflections of Night), *Kosoy polyot* (New York, 1967; Slanting Flight), and *Drakon na kryshe* (New York, 1974; Dragon on a Roof). They reflect successive stages in the life of a "displaced person": nostalgia, bewilderment, conflict, assimilation (Yelagin is fascinated by New York), and estrangement. Yelagin's language is modern, vigorous, often colloquial. In his satirical and grotesque verse, traditional forms and echoes of classical poetry contrast effectively with supermodern imagery.   V.T.

Yesenin, Sergey Aleksandrovich (1895–1925), Russian poet, was born in the village of Konstantinovo in Ryazan to a peasant family. He attended the village school from 1904 to 1909 and the church-run Spas-Klepiki pedagogical school from 1909 to 1912. On completion of school he left for Moscow, worked for a year in the Sytin Printing House, and became involved in the "Surikov" circle, a group of peasant and proletarian poets. He briefly attended lectures at the Shanyavsky People's University. His first poem was published in 1914 in the magazine *Mirok*.

In 1915, Yesenin moved to Petrograd. He soon became acquainted with the poets Aleksandr BLOK, Andrey BELY, Sergey GORODETSKY, and Nikolay KLYUYEV. While Klyuyev was also of peasant background and exerted a strong influence on Yesenin's early poetry, the two had a stormy relationship that lasted throughout Yesenin's life. Yesenin's first poetry collection, *Radunitsa* (Memorial Service), appeared in November 1915. It is dominated by folk motifs, images of nature, religious themes, and pictures of peasant village life.

In 1916, Yesenin served briefly in the army, and in 1917 he contracted a short-lived marriage with Z. N. Raykh. The long poems of his second collection *Goluben* (1918),—"Preobrazheniye" (Transfiguration), "Prishestviye" (The Coming), and "Inoniya"—were attempts to

accept and praise the October Revolution as a glorious cosmic upheaval leading to a resurrection of Russia and in particular of the village and peasantry. But by 1920 Yesenin understood that the world of the village was gone forever; "Ya posledniy poet derevni" (I am the last poet of the village), he wrote.

In 1919–21, Yesenin fell strongly under the influence of the imagist poets Anatoly Mariengof, Vadim Shershenevich, and Aleksandr Kusikov. He turned from poems of religion, Russia, and nature to a heavily ornamented style using images primarily designed to shock. He drank heavily and embarked on the many well-known debauches that led to the self-image described in "Ispoved khuligana" (1921; Confessions of a Hooligan). In 1922, Yesenin published the play *Pugachov,* perhaps the most imagist of all his works. In the same year he married the American dancer Isadora Duncan and from 1922 to 1923 they traveled through Europe and the United States. Yesenin wrote very little during this period. In 1924 he published *Moskva kabatskaya* (Tavern Moscow) reflecting his feelings on love and drinking and his disappointment with himself. His trips to the Crimea and Baku resulted in the *Persidskiye motivy* (1925; Persian Motifs). In his last works, Yesenin sought a clearer, almost Pushkinian style. He tried to write contemporary political poetry, as in the collection *Rus sovetskaya* (1925; Soviet Russia) and *Strana sovetskaya* (1925; Soviet country), which included "Lenin" as well as the lyrical "Pismo materi" (1925; Letter to My Mother). The poems of 1925 are full of lyric sadness for the lost world of the village and for the poet's unfulfilled hopes. The long poem *Anna Snegina* (1925) describes the fate of pre-Revolutionary people in post-Revolutionary Russia.

In 1925, Yesenin married Sofya Tolstaya, a granddaughter of Lev TOLSTOY. The marriage was unhappy and Yesenin's deteriorating health forced his hospitalization. In December 1925 he left his wife and went to Leningrad, where he hanged himself during the night of December 27 in the Hotel Angleterre.

In addition to his poetic output, Yesenin's works include three early prose fragments and two articles on poetry, "Klyuchi Marii" (1918; The Keys of Mary) and "Byt i iskusstvo" (1921; Everyday Life and Art), in which Yesenin links poetic images with folk art.

After Yesenin's death he fell into disrepute in the USSR and was out of favor until after World War II. During this period he was considered a hooligan and a political reactionary. At present, however, he is extremely popular in the USSR and has been fully rehabilitated.

See: F. de Graaff, *Sergej Esenin: A Biographical Sketch* (1966); C. Auras, *Sergej Esenin, Bilder- und Symbolwelt* (1965); E. Naumov, *Sergey Yesenin, lichnost, tvorchestvo, epokha* (1969); P. E. Yushin, *Sergey Yesenin, ideyno-tvorcheskaya evolyutsiya* (1969).   L.V.

Yevreinov, Nikolay Nikolayevich (1879–1953), Russian dramatist, theater director, theorist, and historian, conceived innovations central to 20th-century theater, although without fully realizing them. He early succeeded Vsevolod Meyerhold as director for the actress-manager Vera Komissarzhevskaya (1907) and produced with N. V. Drizen two seasons of "Starinny" (archaic) theater (1907–08, 1911–12), one of medieval French, one of Renaissance Spanish drama. In theory, Yevreinov sometimes presaged essential insights, such as the reaction against illusionism in favor of earlier naive modes and the abrogation of barriers between actor and audience. He exceeded even radical theory by his insistence that role-playing is a basic human impulse and all life is conscious acting, which he discussed in *Teatr kak takovoy* (1912;

Theater As Such) and *Teatr dlya sebya* (1915; Eng. tr., *The Theatre in Life,* 1927).

Yevreinov published in elitist periodicals, and for the Petersburg cabaret "Krivoye zerkalo" (The Crooked Mirror, 1908–13) he wrote and directed satiric sketches, such as his parody on four modes of directing *The Inspector General.* His monodrama *V kulisakh dushi* (1912; Eng. trs., *The Theatre of the Soul,* 1915, *Behind the Curtain of the Soul,* 1922, *The Back Stage of the Soul,* 1925), which has been translated into several languages, is an examplary expressionist work. Two years before Luigi PIRANDELLO, Yevreinov dramatized the Italian's recurrent theme, "What is truth, what is illusion?" in *Samoye glavnoye* (1921; Eng. tr., *The Chief Thing,* 1926). Yevreinov's emigration to France in the 1920s and his play *Shagi nemezidy* (1956; Advancing Nemesis), vividly documenting the Stalinist purges of the mid-1930s, explain his undeserved obscurity in the Soviet Union. His history of the Russian theater, first in French (1947), then in Russian (New York, 1955), reflects the participant rather than the uninvolved historian. A collection of his works, *Dramaticheskiye sochineniya,* 3 vols. (1908–23), has been published in Russian and a selection of his plays is available in English, *Life as Theater: Five Modern Plays,* ed. and tr. by C. Collins (1973).   M.L.H.

Yevtushenko, Yevgeny Aleksandrovich (1933–), Russian poet, is the best known of the "post-Stalin" generation of poets. He was born at the Zima (Winter) station on the trans-Siberian railroad near Irkutsk. His first volume of poetry, *Razvedchiki gryadushchego* (1952; Scouts of the Future) was published a year before Iosif Stalin's death while Yevtushenko was still a student at the Gorky Literary Institute, and it naturally suffered from the severe limitations of the period. Like many of his generation, Yevtushenko was deeply affected by the mood of disillusionment that set in after Stalin's death in 1953. In his *Avtobiografiya* (London, 1963; Eng. tr., *Precocious Autobiography,* 1963), which has never been published in the Soviet Union, he stated that his first rude awakening came at the funeral of Stalin, when he was trapped in the crowds and saw people trampled to death through the negligence of the authorities—as though by way of a final blood sacrifice to the dead leader. In the period after the 20th Party Congress (1956), at which Nikita Khrushchov revealed something of the enormity of Stalin's crimes, Yevtushenko achieved great renown both in the Soviet Union and the outside world as a spokesman for the momentarily ascendent "liberal" forces, and—perhaps more importantly—as the poet who first articulated the vast change of mood among his contemporaries. This change can be described as revulsion at the public values on which they had been reared and a turn towards a world of private feeling that had long been denied expression. Yevtushenko was soon joined by a number of other younger poets, notably Andrey VOZNESENSKY, who in a short time restored lyric poetry to its preeminent position in the esteem of the Soviet public.

Although much of Yevtushenko's verse is personal and intimate, often marked by a wistfulness and candor reminiscent of Sergey YESENIN, he is better known for his more combative, "civic" poems in which he sometimes was the first to break the conspiracy of silence about such issues as Soviet anti-Semitism, in "Babi Yar" (1961; Eng. tr. 1962), and the persistence of Stalinism as a social and political force, in "Nasledniki Stalina" (1962; Eng. tr., "The Heirs of Stalin," 1963). He has written several long poems, notably *Stantsiya Zima* (1956; Eng. tr., "Zima Junction," 1962), about his birthplace, and *Bratskaya GES* (1964–65; Eng. tr., *The Bratsk Station,* 1966), about

the construction of a giant hydroelectric plant in Siberia, which offers an excuse for suggestive excursions into Russia's past. Another long poem, *Kazanski universitet* (1970; Kazan University), was published on the occasion of the 100th anniversary of Vladimir Lenin's birth and exhibits a libertarian philosophy that is somewhat audacious in this context. An important aspect of Yevtushenko's work consists of the poems in which he gives his impressions of his numerous journeys to many parts of the world (including North and South America, Africa, and Australia): "Senegalskaya ballada" (1966; Eng. tr., "Black and White," 1971); "Monolog pestsa na alyaskinskoy zveroferme" (1967; Eng. tr., "Monologue of a Polar Fox on an Alaskan Fur Farm," 1971); and the long composite work "Pod kozhey Statui Svobody" (1972; Under the Skin of the Statue of Liberty), which contains significant reflections on the United States and other subjects. Several collections of Yevtushenko's work have appeared in the Soviet Union, including *Poyushchaya damba* (1972; The Singing Dam) and *Ottsovskiy slukh* (1975; Father's Hearing). Two important bilingual volumes—English translations, with the Russian texts—have appeared in the West: *The Poetry of Yevgeny Yevtushenko 1953 to 1965,* tr. by G. Reavey (1965), and *Stolen Apples,* with trs. by eight American poets (1971).   M.Ha.

Yiddish literature. Since the Middle Ages, Yiddish has been the spoken language of Ashkenazic Jews. Hebrew remained the dominant literary language. Yiddish literature, primarily verse epics, prose narratives and religious tracts, flourished in Central Europe in the 16th and 17th centuries but has declined steadily since then. In Eastern Europe, however, Yiddish literature witnessed an upsurge in the 19th century and, as East European Jews emigrated to France, England, North and South America, Australia, South Africa, and Israel, centers of Yiddish literary activity arose in their new homes. Nevertheless, writers never emancipated themselves from their East European origins and their works have dealt mainly with their experiences in the "Old Country."

The classical period of modern Yiddish literature comprises the generation before World War I. The three dominant figures of that generation—MENDELE MOCHER SFORIM, SHOLOM ALEICHEM, and Yitzkhok Leibush PERETZ—all died during World War I. This literature matured further in the period between the two world wars, but in the following decades more than half of the 10 million Yiddish-speaking Jews perished in the Nazi holocaust and the dictatorship of Iosif Stalin liquidated the foremost Yiddish Soviet writers. Yiddish literature has not completely recovered from these events.

Prior to the middle of the 19th century, Hebrew was the principal literary medium of Jews. The audience for Yiddish books consisted largely of women and of men less learned in Hebrew. With the appearance of the classical triumvirate and the rise to importance of the Yiddish theater and press, Yiddish was no longer deprecated as a jargon but became a linguistic medium for talented poets, serious dramatists, distinguished novelists, and scholars in every field.

The earliest of the classical masters was Mendele mocher sforim, pseud. of Sholem Yakob Abramowitz. Eschewing German, Polish, and Russian models, Mendele created realistic portrayals of Jewish life, the treasures of Jewish folklore, and the Messianic longing of the Jewish heart. He used mockery and grim irony as didactic instruments for inspiring readers to higher moral behavior. His satire, at first searing, later became milder and paved the way for Sholom Aleichem, who dubbed Mendele the "grandfather of Yiddish literature." Sholom Aleichem, pseud. of Sholom Rabinowitz, sought to bring gaiety and lightheartedness to the inhabitants of the Pale of Settlement, the Russian territory where Jews were permitted to live. He believed in the therapeutic value of laughter. His unheroic heroes have a shabby appearance, but their souls are colorful, good, and alert, optimistic despite penury, and lovable because of their mute idealism and quiet submission to God. The third classical Yiddish writer, Yitzkhok Leibush Peretz, was the awakener of Jewish youth. He was also the spokesman not only of the awakening Jewish working masses but also of the intellectuals, whom he weaned from subservience to alien ideals and to whom he preached self-emancipation, a return to ancestral roots, and a rejuvenation of Jewishness. Like Mendele and Sholom Aleichem, Peretz deals realistically with problems of average human beings. However, the incidents related in his narratives, poems, and dramas are irradiated by a romantic, mystical light that leads his characters from their drab existence to a realm beyond life. Peretz was the mentor of a galaxy of disciples whose careers he furthered and in whom he awakened a pride in their heritage. These followers included David Pinski (1872–1959); Hirsh David Nomberg (1874–1927); Abraham Reisen (1876–1953); Sholem ASCH; Isaac Meir Weissenberg (1881–1938); Peretz Hirshbein (1880–1948); Yehoash, pseud. of Solomon Bloomgarden (1870–1927); and Menachem Boraisha, pseud. of Menachem Goldberg (1888–1949).

David Pinski began his career as a member of the Warsaw circle of Peretz, writing realistic short stories. He then moved to Berlin, where he composed naturalistic tragedies of Jewish proletarian life. After emigrating to New York in 1899, Pinski completed his most popular comedy, *Der Oitzer* (1906; Eng. tr., *The Treasure*, 1915). His depiction of human folly involves laughter without malice and has a moral undertone. In his later historical and Messianic dramas, Pinski turned from realism to symbolism. In 1949 he settled in Haifa, and his home became a center for the writers of the group called "Young Israel," who sought his encouragement. Hirsh David Nomberg was at the height of his popularity in 1908 at the Czernowitz Language Conference, which undertook to work for the standardization of Yiddish spelling, grammar, and vocabulary. The conference proclaimed Yiddish to be *a* national language of the Jews, standing alongside Hebrew, *the* national language. Nomberg's novels and short stories are characterized by an acute skepticism and pessimism. His heroes are usually decadent intellectuals, and his heroines inhibited, overripe, self-centered, and embittered women. Abraham Reisen, Peretz's gentlest disciple, depicted in his short stories and poems defeated, rejected, colorless men and women who, despite their poverty, retain dignity and goodness. His lyrics are simple and unsophisticated, melancholic but not depressing. His narratives achieve intense dramatic effects with a minimum of words.

The most talented of Peretz's disciples was Sholem Asch. He was the first Yiddish writer to enjoy a worldwide vogue. It was Asch who made foreign readers aware that Yiddish literature harbored works of aesthetic beauty and moral grandeur.

Isaac Meir Weissenberg was a consistent exponent of pure naturalism. In contrast to the young Asch's romantic idealization of the Jewish shtetl, Weissenberg's tales emphasize its uglier aspects and revolutionary stirrings. Hirshbein was first a writer of naturalistic plays in Hebrew and was hailed as the poet of the cellar-dwellings. But he soon adopted symbolist techniques and began writing Yiddish dramas that sought to communicate moods rather than lucid visions of reality. He was then acclaimed as "the Yiddish Maeterlinck." In his later period, after making his home in the United States in 1915, Hirshbein wrote long, neorealistic novels.

Yehoash was the first important Yiddish nature poet. Arriving in New York in 1890, he opposed the dominant trend of socialist and anarchist lyricists. Writers such as David Edelstadt (1866–92), Joseph Bovshover (1873–1915), Morris Vinchevsky (1956–1933), and Morris Rosenfeld (1862–1923) had won the hearts of the immigrant masses with their impassioned, didactic lyrics of social protest. But for Yehoash, poetry was the imaginative expression of purely individual experiences and feelings. He was the singer of love's intensity and contradictions. His greatest achievement was his translation of the Bible, on which he worked for 30 years and for which he made use of the idiomatic treasures of many dialects and generations.

Menachem Boraisha was primarily a religious poet. After leaving Peretz's Warsaw circle for the United States in 1914, he participated on the American scene in many communal and publicistic activities. Yet he remained a lonely wayfarer, always in search of deeper insights and always dissatisfied with the fragmentary wisdom within his reach. His philosophic verse epic, *Der Geher* (1943; The Wayfarer), is a record of his adventures in the realm of ideas.

The writers discussed above came under the direct personal influence of Peretz, but almost all Yiddish writers of the period felt the impact of Peretz's literary innovations. The shtetl culture of that generation, however, was shattered beyond recovery by the Russian Revolution of October 1917, by the urbanization of the Jewish masses, and by the continuing flow of emigration to Western Europe and to non-European lands. Furthermore, after World War I, the unity of Yiddish literature was weakened by the increasing divergence of Soviet Yiddish literature from the mainstream, which was moving from Poland, Romania, and the Baltic states to the Americas.

Kiev was the center of Soviet Yiddish literature in the 1920s. During this decade, the Kiev group of Yiddish writers was organized around the leadership of David Bergelson (1884–1952) and Der Nister (1884–1950). Bergelson's earliest long novel, *Nokh Alemen* (1913; After All), was hailed as a tender masterpiece of impressionistic writing. In his pre-Revolutionary tales, Bergelson was the painter of twilight moods, autumnal landscapes, withering hopes, and chronic unhappiness. In his post-Revolutionary novels, he depicted the painful transition of the lethargic shtetls of the Ukraine to the new Soviet order. Despite his affirmation of Soviet reality, however, he retained a nostalgia for a world that was no more, the world of his childhood, with its unhurried pace, its shabby respectability, and its wasteful aimlessness. Der Nister (the Hebrew-Yiddish pseudonym of Pinchas Kagonovitch) may be translated as "the hidden one" or "the occult person." The term aptly characterizes this writer, who was the finest Yiddish symbolist novelist and poet. In 1907, Der Nister began writing prose poems, dream images in which he intermingled Jewish, Christian, and Olympian supernatural creatures. He went on to produce allegories and mystic visions, works intended to delight children, but that also hinted at meanings beyond their grasp. After the Russian Revolution (1917), Der Nister felt isolated as a romantic, nonpolitical writer. He remained mute as antiromanticism and socialist realism became the prescribed literary slogans. When the pressure upon him finally became too strong, he adopted the realistic style, producing his last and greatest prose epic, *Mishpokhe Mashber* (1939; Family Mashber).

The most talented disciple of Der Nister was Leib

Kvitko (1890–1952), who, together with David Hofstein (1889–1952), and Peretz Markish (1895–1952), formed the lyric triumvirate of the Kiev Group. These poets composed hymns of joy, celebrating the October Revolution as the hour of emancipation for Russia's Jews. They sang of the glory of Soviet achievements both in war and peace, and they envisaged a brotherhood of peoples, as prescribed by the Yevsektsiye, as the officially recognized leadership of the Jewish Communist movement was called. Despite their patriotic submission to every aspect of Soviet policy over the next 30 years, all three were imprisoned in 1948, together with Bergelson, Der Nister, and many Jewish intellectuals. All three were shot on Aug. 12, 1952, only to be rehabilitated later as victims of Stalin's so-called personality cult.

In the 1930s, Minsk, the large White Russian Yiddish center, replaced Kiev as the hub of Yiddish literary activity. The younger Minsk writers contrasted their own proletarian realism and Communist patriotism with the decadent symbolism and insufficient Communist fervor of the Kiev Yiddish writers, with the single exception of the Kiev poet Itzig Fefer (1900–52). The Minsk group was led by the poet Izzie Charik (1898–1937), editor of its literary organ *Shtern*, founded in 1925. The group included the expressionist poet and realistic novelist Moshe Kulbak (1896–1940), the literary historian Max Erik (1898–1937), and the poet Selig Axelrod (1904–41). After most of the Minsk writers were purged in 1937, and after Kiev had fallen to the Nazi invaders, Moscow became the principal center of Yiddish literary activity. In Moscow, the spokesman of the Communist Party line in literature had been Moshe Litvakov (1875–1938?), chief editor of *Emes*, the main organ of the Yiddish Communists since 1918. When Litvakov, too, was purged in 1937, Itzig Fefer dominated the Yiddish literary scene. Fefer celebrated Communist achievements with sonorous lyrics and trod the narrow path of strict conformity to the ever-changing Communist Party line. In 1943 he was sent to the United States, along with the Soviet Union's best Yiddish actor Shlomo Michoels (1890–1948), in order to win Jewish support for the Soviet struggle against the Nazis. It was then that Fefer penned his proud lyric affirming his joy in belonging to the Jewish people. For this affirmation, Fefer was eventually liquidated, together with both his friends and his foes. The purges of the late 1940s effectively destroyed the Yiddish literary elite in the Soviet capital. In 1948, 60 Yiddish books were published, but not a single volume appeared during the entire following decade. Only one monthly, *Sovetish Heimland*, has been permitted since 1962. Before the postwar purges, Moscow's distinguished Yiddish writers included the poets Aaron Kushnirov (1890–1949), Shmuel Halkin (1897–1960), and Ezra Fininberg (1899–1946), and the novelists Shmuel Persov (1890–1952) and Itzig Kipnis (1896–1974).

Across the border of Soviet Russia, Yiddish flourished in Poland, Lithuania, and Romania. Yiddish schools, academies, and ideologies raised the prestige of the language. The theories of diaspora nationalism propounded by Shimon Dubnow (1860–1941) sought to further the use of both Hebrew and Yiddish. While the Zionist movement gave priority to Hebrew, the Bundist movement gave priority to Yiddish. The philosopher of Yiddishism, Chaim Zhitlowsky (1865–1943), saw in the Yiddish language and literature the unifying factors that could ensure the survival of the widely dispersed Jewish people. Through the inspiration of Zhitlowsky and of the essayist Nathan Birnbaum (1864–1937), the Czernowitz Language Conference of 1908 was convened. But it was not until after the founding of the Yiddish Scientific Institute

(YIVO) in 1925 that the standardization of Yiddish was achieved on a large scale. For the next 50 years, YIVO forged ahead as the most important center for Yiddish research and scholarly publication, operating first in Vilna and later in New York.

In Poland, the death of Peretz in 1915 left a hiatus that was not easily filled. The naturalistic novelist Isaac Meir Weissenberg and his gifted followers Oizer Varshavsky (1893–1944) and Shimon Horonchek (1889–1939) only briefly excited the Warsaw literary scene. They were soon eclipsed by the neoromantic writers, including the folklorist S. Anski, pseud. of Solomon Zainwil Rapaport (1863–1920), whose mystic drama *Dybbuk* (1920; Eng. tr., 1926), held the stage for decades; Alter Kacyne (1885–1941), Anski's literary heir, the author of ballads, grotesques, poetic dramas, and tales blending reality and a ghostly surrealism; Yekhiel Yeshaia Trunk (1887–1961), a meticulous essayist and novelist who followed in the wake of Peretz's romanticism and who made his profoundest impact with the autobiographical, nostalgic prose epic, *Poiln* (1944–53; Poland); Israel Joshua Singer (1893–1944), author of the Hassidic novel *Yoshe Kalb* (1932; Eng. tr., *The Sinner*, 1953) and the prose epic *Brieder Ashkenazi* (1936; Eng. tr., *Brothers Ashkenazi*, 1936); and his brother Isaac Bashevis Singer (1904–) who, after emigrating to the United States, rose to fame with his tender, idyllic tales, his grotesque narratives emphasizing the lure of the flesh and the emergence from sin to holiness, and, above all, with his most ambitious novel, *Familie Mushkat* (1950; Eng. tr., *Family Moskat*, 1950). Isaac Bashevis Singer won the 1978 Nobel Prize for Literature.

Between the two world wars, there also flourished in Poland a galaxy of poets who enriched Yiddish with enduring lyrics. They included Aaron Zeitlin (1898–1973), a religious poet deeply steeped in Jewish mysticism and Messianic visions, which he incorporated in concrete images and rhythmic patterns; David Einhorn (1886–1973), who captured the rhythm of sad, still moments and converted reality into dreams; Zysman Segalowitch (1884–1949), whose early Byronic, sentimental lyrics, written for longing youths in the awakening shtetls, were followed, under the impact of the holocaust, by the heartrending elegy *Dorten* (1944; There); and Kadia Molodowsky (1894–1975), whose early lyrics and tales in verse were sung in Yiddish schools in Poland until these schools ceased to exist, and whose later lyrics and prose narratives alternated between tragic visions of children trapped in ghettos and idealized visions of the survivors, building in Israel a new holy abode for her people.

On the eve of World War II, "Young Vilna," a circle of Lithuanian writers, was the most promising Yiddish literary group. Most Vilna writers perished in the holocaust, including Hirsh Glik (1922–44), author of the "Partisanerlied" (1943; Song of the Partisans), which instantly won the hearts of the Resistance groups and which is still sung at memorial assemblies for Jewish Nazi victims. Of those survivors who fought with both guns and flaming verses, the most prominent were Schmerke Kaczerginski (1908–54), Chaim Grade (1910–), and Abraham Sutzkever (1913–). Grade matured in his later, American years, and in his novels he became the most profound interpreter of Jewish life in preholocaust Poland. In his dirges, he was the threnodist of the holocaust. Abraham Sutzkever, who penned memorable lyrics of his experience in the Vilna ghetto and as a partisan in Polish forests, continued his search for lyric perfection in Israel. There, the themes of the holocaust gradually gave way in Sutzkever's writing to Israeli themes based on his experiences in the Jewish homeland and in Israel's four wars for survival. He has been the editor of the literary quarterly *Di Goldene Keyt* since its founding in 1949, and has become the central figure in the Yiddish revival in Israel.

Among those writers who streamed to the state of Israel after its founding in 1948, the most profound impact was made by the religious poet Jacob Friedman (1906–72) and the narrative interpreters of the holocaust Isaiah Spiegel and Mendl Mann (1916–74). Israel was also the last asylum of Itzig Manger (1901–69), the errant troubadour of Romania, after his peregrinations in Warsaw, London, and New York. Israeli youth sang Manger's songs and flocked to his dramatic spectacles. In the 1970s, Soviet writers were permitted to leave for Israel and so they, too, enriched its literary scene. Although in the 1960s, Elie Wiesel had dubbed Soviet Jews "the Jews of silence," the emigrants of the 1970s demonstrated that some Jewish writers had indeed survived. The first Soviet writer to arrive was Joseph Kerler (1918–), who edited annual anthologies of works by the newcomers. The most talented of the Soviet immigrants was Elya Shechtman (1808–), author of *Erev* (1974; On the Eve).

The dispersion of Yiddish-speaking Jews from the East European heartland led to the rise of literary centers in Paris, London, Johannesburg, Melbourne, Buenos Aires, Mexico City, Montreal, Los Angeles, and above all New York. Since the 1880s, the New York Yiddish literary scene had been dominated by realistic, didactic social poets and novelists who expressed the sorrows and disillusionments of slum-dwellers and sweatshop workers. This literary style was challenged in 1907 by young, newly immigrated writers who gradually turned the tide toward impressionism and individualism. This group was known as "Die Yunge," a name derived from its organ, *Yugend* (Youth). Its earliest adherents were the dynamic novelist David Ignatoff (1885–1953); the colorful poet Moshe Leib Halpern (1886–1932); the restless romantic lyricist Mani Leib, pseud. of Mani Leib Brahinsky (1883–1953); the ironic poet and dramatist Zishe Landau (1889–1937); and the painter in verse Reuben Iceland (1884–1955). "Die Yunge" were later joined by Israel Jacob Schwartz (1885–1971), author of the verse epic *Kentucky* (1925); the controversial, pessimistic humorist in verse Moishe Nadir, pseud. of Isaac Reis (1885–1943); the cowboy-novelist Isaac Raboy (1882–1944); and Joseph Opatoshu (1886–1954), who began with realistic narratives of thieves, smugglers, and drunkards, and attained worldwide recognition with his long historical novels. Hard on the heels of "Die Yunge" the poets Ephraim Auerbach (1892–1973) and H. Leivick, pseud. of Leivick Halpern (1888–1962), came to the United States. Auerbach's poetry first sang of Bessarabian Jewry, and then, in optimistic tones, about his immigrant generation in New York. His verse comforted the survivors of the holocaust and hymned his people's return from exile to their old-new home, Israel, which was his own final home, as well. Leivick wrote his first lyrics and plays while in tsarist jails and Siberian exile, but it was on American soil that he created his social dramas, his biblical plays, his lyrics of the holocaust, and his compassionate visions of human suffering and Messianic redemption.

The reaction to the impressionism of "Die Yunge" came in 1919 when the introspectivist movement, insichism, was launched by three young poets, Aaron Glanz-Leyeles (1889–1966), Jacob Glatstein (1896–1971), and Nahum Baruch Minkoff (1898–1958). Insichism stressed that poetry was the expression of emotionalized thought or intellectualized emotion. It was inspired by the European expressionist movement and it in turn inspired the Warsaw literary group, "Khaliastre" (The Gang), led by Melech Ravitch (1893–1976), Uri Zvi Greenberg (1894–), and Peretz Markish (1895–1952), which adopted the innovations of German expressionism and Russian futurism. These movements, however, disintegrated as the poets matured. Glatstein was transformed from a cosmopolite, intoxicated with beauty, into a lyric poet of Jewish tragedy and rebirth. Minkoff, who stressed subjectivity in verse, became more influential as an objective literary critic and scholar. Ravitch abandoned expressionistic rebelliousness when he settled in Montreal. Markish left Warsaw for Kiev and composed hymns to communism, while Greenberg left for Israel and became a Hebrew poet of great distinction.

The Nazi holocaust, which destroyed a third of the Jewish people, became the main literary theme not only of the survivors but also of other writers on all continents. The lyrics written by the ghetto poets during their last days are immeasurably sad and yet irradiated by pride. Mordecai Gebirtig (1877–1942) continued to write folk songs in Cracow's ghetto until he was shot. Yitzkhak Katzenelson (1886–1944) wrote a most memorable lament for the slaughtered Jews shortly before he was deported from France to Auschwitz. Rachmil Bryks (1912–74), the poet of the Łódź ghetto, survived to pen realistic narratives interlaced with sardonic humor. Leib Rochman (1918–78), the sole survivor of a Polish-Jewish town whose painful dying he witnessed from his hiding place, recorded his experiences after the liberation when he was haunted by the ghosts of slaughtered Jews, in his Kafkaesque novel *Mit Blinde Trit iber der Erd* (1968; With Blind Steps over the Earth). Joseph Rubinstein (1900–78) composed a stirring poetic trilogy in which he recorded his flight before the Nazis, his wandering in Asiatic Russia, and his temporary havens before his exodus from Europe.

The grim impact upon writers of the greatest Jewish catastrophe of modern times was counterbalanced by the exhilaration of the rise of the Jewish state. Elegies of Auschwitz and Treblinka were succeeded by hymns to the heroic warriors and pioneering builders of a new society on Israel's resuscitated soil. Yiddish literature, silenced in Russia, dying in Poland, and aging in Romania, France, England, and the Americas, rose to new vitality and vigor in Israel, where writers, actors, and educators have gathered from many lands to enrich the Hebrew-speaking Jewish homeland with Yiddish cultural treasures.

See: *Leksikon fun der Nayer Yidisher Literatur* (7 vols. since 1956; final 2 vols. in preparation); C. A. Madison, *Yiddish Literature* (1968); S. Liptzin, *A History of Yiddish Literature* (1972).   S.L.

Yourcenar, Marguerite, pseud. of Marguerite de Crayencour (1903–), French novelist, essayist, poet, and translator, was born in Brussels. She has taught and now lives in the United States. A scholar and classicist, Yourcenar is steeped in the culture of Greece and Rome, and she has translated and written critical works on ancient and modern Greek writers. Yourcenar's cosmopolitan turn of mind led her to study Hindu mysticism, on which she has written in *Préface à la Gita-Gavinda* (1958), as well as black American poetry, as evidenced in *Fleuve profond, sombre rivière* (1964; Deep, Dark River), an anthology of spirituals. She has also translated novels by Virginia Woolf and Henry James from English into French. Her elegantly polished style, astute powers of psychological analysis, impressive erudition, and wide cultural interests make each of her novels and essays an enriching experience for the reader.

Yourcenar's best known novels are *Les Mémoires d'Hadrien* (1951; Eng. trs., *Memoirs of Hadrian*, 1954,

Hadrian's Memoirs, 1957, Memoirs of Hadrian, and Reflections on the Composition of Memoirs of Hadrian, 1963), which ensured her a place among the great French writers of her time, and *L'Œuvre au noir* (1968; Eng. tr., *The Abyss,* 1976). Yet all her writings are worthy of interest, including such works of fiction as *Alexis ou le traité du vain combat* (1929; Alexis or the Treaty of the Useless Combat), *La Nouvelle Eurydice* (1931; The New Eurydice), *La Mort conduit l'attelage* (1934; Death Leads the Team), *Nouvelles orientales* (1937; Oriental Stories), *Le Coup de grâce* (1939; Eng. tr., *Coup de Grâce,* 1957), and *Sans bénéfice d'inventaire* (1962; Without Benefit of Inventory), as well as her important essays *Pindare, Les Songes et les sorts* (Dreams and Spells), *Présentation critique de Constantin Cavafy* (1958; Critical Presentation of Constantine CAVAFY), and *Electre ou la chute des masques* (1954; Electra or the Masks Fall). In 1977 she published an introspective psychological autobiography, *Souvenirs pieux* (Pious Memories). Yourcenar is a writer whose appeal does not so much depend on the stories she tells as on her fascinating reconstruction of a period in history, the human complexity of her characters, and the consummate art that characterizes her style. In 1980 she became the first woman to be elected to the Académie Française.					D.Br.

Yovkov, Yordan (1880–1937), Bulgarian short-story writer, novelist, and playwright, was born in a Bulgarian village; as a young man he taught school for a time in the disputed region of Romania known as Dobruja. Although he wrote a number of poems and short stories before World War I, he attained prominence in the 1920s with his novella *Zhetvaryat* (1920; The Harvester) and the collections of short stories *Posledna radost* (1926; Last Joy), *Staroplaninski legendi* (1927; Balkan Legends), and *Vecheri v antimovskiya khan* (1927; Evenings at the Antimovo Inn). During the 1930s, as an established writer, he published four plays, including *Albena* (1928); a novel, *Chiflikut kray granitsata* (1934; The Farmstead at the Frontier); and several collections of short stories, including *Zhensko surtse* (1935; A Woman's Heart) and the animal stories collected in *Ako mozhekha da govoryat* (1936; If They Could Speak).

Yovkov was an introspective man who relived nostalgically his memories of a Dobruja lost to Romania after World War I. The prose poet of rural Bulgaria, he possessed a gentle disposition and was bent on resolving the most agonizing conflicts, even those described in his war stories. He believed in the reconciling power of beauty and harmony. One of his most characteristic figures is the dreamer who perishes because he cannot adjust to the real world. Yovkov's death in 1937 was an acute loss to Bulgarian letters, for he wrote the most compact and finely wrought prose in the history of Bulgarian literature, and he deserves to be better known beyond the borders of his homeland.

See: C. A. Moser, "The Visionary Realism of Jordan Jovkov," *SEEJ,* 11 (1967): 44–58; S. Sultanov, *Yovkov i negoviyat svyat* (1968).					C.A.M.

Yugoslav literature: *see* separate articles on CROATIAN LITERATURE; MACEDONIAN LITERATURE; SERBIAN LITERATURE; SLOVENIAN LITERATURE.

Z

Zabolotsky, Nikolay Alekseyevich (1903–1958), Russian poet, was born on a farm near Kazan into the family of an agronomist of peasant descent. After graduating from a teachers college in 1925, Zabolotsky lived in Leningrad in considerable poverty, supporting himself by writing stories and poetry for children's magazines. In the late 1920s he became one of the founding members of the literary group OBERIU, which experimented with alogical and absurdist imagery and was in some ways the Russian counterpart of the surrealists in the West (*see* RUSSIAN LITERATURE). Zabolotsky's first collection of verse, *Stolbtsy* (1929; Eng. tr., *Scrolls,* 1971), portrays life in Leningrad during the period of the New Economic Policy as a phantasmagoria; to achieve this effect the poet deployed fragments of everyday existence in deliberately incongruous juxtapositions, interspersed with passages that imitate ungrammatical and graphomaniac writing and with unexpected allusions to Russian classical poets such as Gavrila Derzhavin and Aleksandr Pushkin.

Stolbtsy was received by the press with hostility, which was further increased by the publication in 1933 of Zabolotsky's narrative poem about collectivization, "Torzhestvo zemledeliya" (Triumph of Agriculture). While ostensibly supporting the government's policies, the poem, inspired, like much of Zabolotsky's work, by the pantheistic and fatidic visions of Velimir KHLEBNIKOV, contrasts man's agricultural endeavors with the implacable and unchanging processes of nature and fate. Combined with Zabolotsky's typical fantastic and alogical touches, such a view of Soviet agriculture led the press to ignore the poem's unique beauty and originality and to launch a barrage of hostile and slanderous ad hominem attacks on the poet, which were further exacerbated with the appearance of his second narrative poem "Lodeynikov" (1933, rev. 1937). The denunciations prevented the publication of the poet's second collection in 1937 and led to his arrest in 1938.

Zabolotsky spent the years 1938 to 1946 at various labor camps in Siberia. Allowed to live near Moscow upon his release, he translated Georgian poets. In his own poetry he gave up his earlier style and manner and turned to the traditions of the 19th-century Russian poets, primarily Fyodor Tyutchev and Nikolay Nekrasov. Because of Zabolotsky's tremendous talent, many of his poems written from 1946 to 1958 possess considerable beauty and philosophical depth despite their self-imposed conformity and conventionality. Shortly before his death, the poet prepared a revised edition of his earlier work, eliminating its surrealist and modernist aspects. Zabolotsky has now come to be recognized as the most powerful and profound Russian poet to emerge in the Soviet period.

See: S. Karlinksy, "Surrealism in 20th Century Russian Poetry; Churilin, Zabolotskii, Poplavskii," *SlavR* 26, no. 4 (1967): 604–17; R. R. Milner-Gulland, "Zabolotsky: Philosopher Poet," *SovS* 22, no. 4 (1971): 598–608.					S.K.

Zaitsev, Boris Konstantinovich (1881–1972), Russian novelist, short-story writer, and biographer, was born at Orel and spent much of his childhood on the Kaluga estate of his father, a mining engineer. Zaitsev studied at Kaluga and Moscow, but left the university for Italy, returning to Russia in 1904. Zaitsev was never a true realist: his gift is essentially subjective and lyric. His pre-Revolutionary stories are delicately sketched impressions almost lacking in plot and sustained chiefly by a mystic atmosphere. Hostile to the Revolution, he left Russia in 1922 and settled in Paris. The stories included in *Ulitsa sv. Niko-laya* (1923; St. Nicholas Street) and *Strannoye putesh-estviye* (1927; A Strange Trip) show an advance in nar-rative technique, as well as firmer characterization. At the same time Zaitsev embarked on longer works, tem-pering his subjectivism by the requirements of the novel form. *Zolotoy uzor* (1926; The Golden Pattern) is cast in the form of the autobiography of a singer, but also gives a picture of life in Russia and abroad. *Anna* (1929; Eng. tr., *Anna,* 1937) is a compact narrative of tragic love, set against the background of the Revolution. *Dom v Passy* (1935; The House in Passy), a rambling novel of the Rus-sian émigrés in Paris, was a return to the earlier manner. The tetralogy *Puteshestviye Gleba* (Gleb's Journey), com-prising *Zarya* (1937; Dawn), *Tishina* (1948; Stillness), *Yu-nost* (1950; Youth), and *Drevo zhizni* (1953; The Tree of Life), an autobiographical narrative of broad sweep, is Zaitsev's major achievement in fiction. Zaitsev's miscel-laneous works reflect well his various interests. His ac-count of his visits to Mount Athos and Valaam, some of his stories, and *Prepodobny Sergy Radoneshsky* (1925; Saint Sergius of Radonezh) testify to his devotion to the Orthodox Church. The retrospective *Italiya* (1923; Italy) and *Moskva* (1939; Moscow) are autobiography as well as description. His *Zhizn Turgeneva* (1932; Life of Turge-nev), *Zhukovsky* (1951), and *Chekhov* (1954) are highly impressionistic biographies of writers with whom he felt a special kinship.

See: G. Struve, "Boris Zaytsev," *SR* 17 (1938–39): 445–51, and *Russkaya literatura v izgnanii* (1956), pp. 101–04, 262–66; N. Pervouchine, "La Place de B. Zaitsev dans la littérature russe du XXᵉ siècle," *ESl* 14 (1969): 121–28; P. Gribanovsky, "Boris Konstantinovich Zay-tsev," in *Russkaya literatura v emigratsii* (Pittsburgh, 1972), pp. 133–50.   P.A.P. rev. W.B.E.

Zalygin, Sergey Pavlovich (1913–), Russian novelist, is one of the older generation of Soviet prose writers dedicated to describing frankly and thus preserving for posterity the life of the peasants, "a thousand-year-old way of life out of which nearly all of us have grown," as he has put it. Born in the province of Ufa, he worked for many years as a hydraulic engineer on irrigation projects in Siberia. *Na Irtyshe* (1964; On the River Irtysh) was the first work to bring him international recognition, as well as some notoriety at home. The novel depicts fairly frankly the harshness with which the Soviet collectivization of agri-culture was implemented in the early 1930s; its main char-acter is a responsible, capable, and compassionate farmer whose very qualities bring him into conflict with the au-thorities and lead ultimately to his exile from his village. *Solyonaya Pad* (1968; Salt Hollow) portrays the tense relationship between a Civil War partisan leader and the political organisation man working for the Communist Party. The best of Zalygin's novels to date is *Komissiya* (1975; The Commission), in which a peasant community try to evolve their own forms of self-government in the spring and summer of 1918. In *Komissiya* Zalygin drew extensively upon chronicle and legend in his presentation of the peasant world, and also gave sympathetic attention to the peasants' religious beliefs. Zalygin has also written a number of novels and short stories on academic life, as well as works of literary criticism, notably on Anton CHEKHOV.

See: G. Kolesnikova, *Sergey Zalygin: tvorcheskaya biografiya* (1969).   G.H.

Zamacois, Eduardo (1873–1971), Spanish novelist, was born in Cuba of a Cuban mother and a Basque father. He arrived in Madrid at the age of 15, having divided his childhood almost equally among Cuba, Paris, and Seville. Throughout his life he traveled a great deal in Europe and North and South America. He left Spain permanently at the end of the Civil War in 1939, finally settling in Argen-tina, where he remained until his death. The last version of his autobiography, *Un hombre que se va . . .* (1964; A Man on His Way Out), is an uninhibited account of a colorful, Don Juanesque life.

Following the French model, Zamacois—along with Felipe Trigo—introduced the erotic novel into Spain. He founded the frivolous journal *Vida Galante,* which was intended, according to its creator, to "capture the bed-room aroma that perfumes French literature of the 18th century." He also founded and edited the widely read short novel collections *El Cuento Semanal* (1907) and *Los Contemporáneos* (1910).

Zamacois's playful early works are characterized by the mildly spiced amorous concerns of the bedroom novel. These are exemplified by *Loca de amor* (1902; Madly in Love) and *Memorias de una cortesana* (1903). Beginning with *El otro* (1910; The Other) and such other pieces as *La opinión ajena* (1913; Reputation), however, he leaves this tone and preoccupation behind, in literature if not in life. In his third and final phase, represented by the trilogy of *Las Raíces* (1927; Roots), *Los vivos muertos* (1929; The Living Dead), and *El delito de todos* (1933; Everyone's Crime), and the transition to serious, realistic works of naturalistic documentation of villages, slums, and prisons is complete.

Zamacois is a representative rather than an important novelist. His work created and continued to stimulate broad reader interest first in "literatura galante" and then in the naturalistic novel he inherited from the 19th cen-tury.

See: L. S. Granjel, "Vida y literatura en Eduardo Za-macois," *CHA* 311 (1976): 319–44.   H.L.B.

Zamfirescu, Duiliu (1858–1922), Romanian poet, novelist, and statesman. He was born at Plăineşti (now Dumbrăveni) and studied at Focşani and Bucharest, where he practiced law for a short period. Much of his life was devoted to journalism, politics, and diplomacy. He served as Romanian minister of foreign affairs im-mediately after World War I.

Encouraged by Alexandru MACEDONSKI, Zamfirescu published his early work in the journal *Literatorul.* His early poems are symbolist in character, but he experi-enced a shift in poetic values, and the subject matter of the later poems exalts national legends and history. Zam-firescu's early short stories are romantic, while the later ones hesitate between classicism and realism. Although he was considered to be the greatest Romanian poet after Mihail Eminescu (*see* ROMANIAN LITERATURE), Zamfi-rescu's importance is primarily due to his novels, notably *The Comăneşteni* (The Comanesteana Family), an epic in two cycles, the first describing the fight for Romania's political independence and the second, the reunification of the country. Mihail Comănesteanu is the hero of the first three novels: *Viaţa la ţară* 1894–95; Eng. tr., *Sasha,* 1926), *Tănase Scatiu* (1895–96), and *In război* (1897–98; At War). The second cycle began with *Îndrepteri* (1901–02; Improvements) and *Anna Anna sau Ceea ce nu sa-poate* (1906–10; Anna or The Impossible), but was never completed. The panoramic scope of this tremendously popular novel, with its similarities to Lev TOLSTOY and Honoré de Balzac, established Zamfirescu as the founder of the modern Romanian novel.

See: A. Sandulescu, *Duiliu Zamfirescu* (1970). S. Cio-culescu, *Istoria literaturii Române,* vol. 3. pp. 663–98 (1973).   V.A.

Zamyatin, Yevgeny Ivanovich (1884–1937), Russian novelist, critic, and playwright, was born in Lebedyan, Tambov province, the son of an Orthodox priest, and spent his early years in central Russia, graduating from the Voronezh gymnasium in 1902. His academic career at the Petersburg Polytechnic Institute was interrupted by arrest and exile for revolutionary activity in 1905, but upon graduating as a naval engineer in 1908 he was retained on the faculty of the Department of Naval Architecture. Exiled again in 1911, he satirized man's inhumanity in "Uyezdnoye" (1913; Eng. tr., "A Provincial Tale," 1966), which brought him widespread recognition. Amnestied in 1913, he drew close to the "Zavety" (Behests) group, which included the writers Aleksey REMIZOV, Mikhail PRISHVIN, Vyacheslav SHISHKOV, and the critic Ivanov-Razumnik. The negative depiction of Russian garrison life in "Na kulichkakh" (1914; Out in the Sticks) resulted in the tale's confiscation and a court trial. The ornamental prose of Zamyatin's early works was characterized by impressionistic animal imagery, a Gogolian predilection for the grotesque, and *skaz* narration in the tradition of Dal, Nikolay LESKOV, and Remizov. A decided primitivism was manifested in "Ihrevo" (1915; The Womb) and "Kryazhi" (1916; The Diehards).

During World War I, Zamyatin supervised the construction of Russian icebreakers in England. His stay inspired satirical tales on bourgeois conformity, "Ostrovityane" (1918; Eng. tr., *The Islanders*, 1972) and "Lovets chelovekov" (1922; The Fisher of Men). Returning to Russia in time to witness the October Revolution of 1917, Zamyatin played a vital role in the subsequent cultural and artistic upsurge, serving as editor and administrator in the Union of Practitioners of Imaginative Literature, House of Arts, World Literature Publishing House (where he edited Russian translations of Jack London, H. G. Wells, and Anatole France), All-Russian Union of Writers, and journals *Dom iskusstv* (House of Arts), *Sovremenny zapad* (The Contemporary West), and *Russkiy sovremennik* (The Russian Contemporary). He also lectured on writing techniques in literary studios, influencing many young writers including the Serapion Brothers (*see* RUSSIAN LITERATURE). Some of this material was published posthumously in the essays "Sovremennaya russkaya literatura" (1956; Eng. tr., "Contemporary Russian Literature," 1970), "Psikhologiya tvorchestva" (1956; Eng. tr., "The Psychology of Creative Work,", 1970), "O syuzhete i fabule" (1964; Eng. tr., "Theme and Plot," 1970), and "O yazyke" (1964; Eng. tr., "On Language," 1970).

The intensification and systematization of imagery, the development of a modernist color symbolism, and the shift to urban settings reached an apogee in Zamyatin's early post-Revolutionary prose, of which "Ostrovityane," "Lovets chelovekov," "Mamay" (1921; Eng. tr., 1933), "Peshchera" (1922; Eng. tr., "The Cave," 1923), and his single long novel *My* (written 1920–21; Eng. tr., *We*, 1924) are the best examples. His strong tendency toward primitivism, perhaps influenced by D. H. Lawrence and Knut HAMSUN, found eloquent expression in "Sever" (1922; Eng. tr., The North, 1966) and in the glorification of natural physical passion as a rebellion against the constraint of philistine society. Fyodor DOSTOEVSKY's Underground Man and Grand Inquisitor provided the philosophic antecedents for Zamyatin's anti-Utopian *My*, which anticipated Aldous Huxley's *Brave New World* by eight years and directly inspired George Orwell's *1984*, but has never been published in the USSR, where it is considered to be a "malicious slander on socialism." As a former Bolshevik, Zamyatin welcomed the Revolution but criticized the subsequent excesses, sycophancy, and repression both in political fables, *Bol-*

shim detyam skazki (1922; Fables for Grown-Up Children), and in literary essays that championed maximal personal and authorial freedom: "Ja boyus" (1921; Eng. tr., "I Am Afraid," 1970), "Ray" (1921; Eng. tr., "Paradise," 1970), "O literature, revolyutsii, entropii i o prochem" (1924; Eng. tr., "On Literature, Revolution and Entropy," 1962), and "O segodnyashnem i o sovremennom" (1924; Eng. tr., "The Day and the Age," 1970). Human frailties in adapting to the new Soviet environment were depicted in finely wrought novellas where literary parody often joined gentle irony: "Iks" (1926; Eng. tr., "X," 1966), "Slovo predostavlyaetsya tovarishchu Churyginu" (1927; Eng. tr., "Comrade Churygin Has the Floor," 1963), "Desyatiminutnaya drama" (1928; A Ten-Minute Drama), and "Mucheniki nauki" (written 1931; Eng. tr., "The Turning of Another Worm," 1931). In the late 1920s, Zamyatin developed a simple unobtrusive style based on the conversational literary language, with infrequent but audacious metaphors, which he used with consummate skill in creating two masterpieces of tragic passion, "Yola" (1928; The Yawl) and "Navodneniye" (1929; Engl. tr., "The Flood," 1966).

Of Zamyatin's eight plays, three were original works: *Ogni svyatogo Dominika* (1922; The Fires of Saint Dominic), which focuses on freedom and the fallibility of all monolithic truths; *Attila* (written 1925–27), a tragedy in verse on traditional themes of love, hate, vengeance, and betrayal; and *Afrikanskiy gost* (written 1929–30; The African Guest), a satire on superficial accommodation to Soviet ways. The best-known of his five stage adaptations were *Blokha* (1926; The Flea), a folk comedy based on Leskov's "Levsha" (Eng. tr., "The Steel Flea"), and *Obshchestvo pochotnykh zvonarey* (1926; The Society of Honorary Bellringers), based on his own "Ostrovityane."

In 1929, Zamyatin became the target of an intensive campaign of vilification; his plays were banned, his books were removed from circulation, and he was denied access to publication. He left the Soviet Union in 1931, and spent his last years in Paris working on *Bich Bozhiy* (1939; The Scourge of God), an unfinished novel on Attila, whose era he saw echoed in the present age. At his best, Zamyatin combines wit, imagination, and meticulous craftsmanship with a profound sense for the human condition, integrity of philosophy, and prophetic vision.

See: A. Shane, *The Life and Works of Evgenij Zamjatin* (1968); A. Voronsky, "Evgeny Zamyatin," *RLT* 3 (1972): 153–75; C. Collins, *Evgenij Zamjatin: An Interpretive Study* (1973). A.M.S.

Zanzotto, Andrea (1921–), Italian poet and critic, was born in Pieve di Soligo. He combines school teaching with work for various literary journals. With *Dietro il paesaggio* (1951; Behind the Landscape) he began to publish poetry based on contemplation of the natural phenomena lyrically exalted. His landscapes, however, possess a hyperliterary quality. Stylistic echoes and precise reminiscences of Petrarch, Friedrich Hölderlin, Paul ELUARD, and Giuseppe UNGARETTI, among others, mesh at surface level with his own inspired figures. The psychological pressures exercised by historical forces of dispersal upon the refuge of cultural life increase in the verse that followed during the 1950s. *Elegia e altri versi* (1954; Elegy and Other Verses) and *Vocativo* (1957; Vocative) are characterized by dislocations of syntax, crude onomatopoeia, and interruptions of the logical sequence of discourse.

With *IX Ecloghe* (1962; IX Eclogues), Zanzotto cast his net still wider, embracing a global vision of reality in all its cultural strata. Here he adds the language of everyday usage, dialect, technological jargon, Latin, and slang to a wide array of models as diverse as Vergil and Gabriele D'ANNUNZIO. So total is this experience that individual voice and language seem equated. In *La Beltà* (1968; Beauty) and *Pasque* (1974; Easters), fantastical self-governing sequences of words and sounds lead the reader to a sense of the primary, psychological power of language beyond any ideology or semantic field. Some of Zanzotto's poetry is available in English as *Selected Poetry of Andrea Zanzotto* (1976), ed. and tr. by R. Feldman and B. Swann.

See: S. Agosti, Preface to *Andrea Zanzotto: poesie* (1973).   M.G.

Zapolska, Gabriela, pseud. of Gabriela Korwin-Piotrowska (1857–1921), Polish novelist and playwright, was born in Podhajce, near Łuck in Volhynia, and died in Lvov. She was the daughter of Józefa Karska, a famous opera singer and beauty, and Wincenty Korwin-Piotrowski, a well-to-do landowner. Zapolska turned to the stage, where she made a name for herself in all the cities of Poland. Later, in 1881, she began to write, novels at first and then plays. Her first story, "Jeden dzień z życia róży" (A Day in the Life of a Rose), was published in the *Gazeta krakowska*. Most of her novels, however, appeared not in Cracow but in more liberal Warsaw, where the *Przegląd tygodniowy* of Wiślicki and Świętochowski was very friendly to her. In 1890, Zapolska left Poland for Paris, where for the ensuing five years she was a member of the famous Théâtre Libre of Antoine as well as other theaters. The training she received there stood her in good stead in her later years as the founder of the naturalist school of dramatic writing in Poland.

In 1896, Zapolska was back in Poland, there to make a name for herself as a veritable virtuoso of the theatrical art. Play after play flowed from her pen, the characters and situations of all of them being taken, as their creator declared, from scenes she herself witnessed "behind the window curtains" as she passed along the street. In *Kaśka Kariatyda* (1888), Zapolska made dramatic material out of the humble, "red-kneed" housemaid and with the two plays *Malka Szwarcenkopf* (1897) and *Jojne Firulkes* (1898) did the same for the Jew. The most popular of Zapolska's many dramas are *Moralność Pani Dulskiej* (1907; Eng. tr., *The Morals of Mrs. Dulska*, staged 1923), a "tragi-farce of bourgeois-dom," as Zapolska herself called it; *Skiz* (1909; Eng. tr., *The Secret of Skiz*, staged 1961); *Ich czworo* (1912; Four of Them); and *Panna Maliczewska* (1912; Miss Maliczewska). All these plays, though at first anathematized by the clergy and shunned by the more conservative elements, were frequently revived in Free Poland and always before a full house.

See: K. Wierzyński, *W garderobie duchów* (1938), pp. 83–86, 101–103; J. Czachowska, *Gabriela Zapolska. Monografia bio-bibliograficzna* (1966).   M.M.C.

Zardoya, Concha (1914–), Spanish poet and critic, was born in Valparaíso, Chile, but lived and studied in Spain before she came to the United States as a professor of Spanish literature, first at Tulane and then at the universities of California, Indiana, and Massachusetts. She now resides in Spain. Zardoya has been a prolific poet. Among her works are *Pájaros del Nuevo Mundo* (1945; Birds from the New World), *Dominio del llanto* (1948; Domain of Tears), *La hermosura sencilla* (1953; The Simple Beauty), *Los signos* (1955; Signs), *El desterrado ensueño* (1955; The Banished Illusion), *Debajo de la luz* (1955; Beneath the Light), for which she won the Boscán Prize, *Mirar al cielo es tu condena* (1957; You Are Condemned to Face the Sky), *Elegías* (1961), *Corral de vivos*

y muertos (1965; Gathering of the Living and the Dead), *Donde el tiempo resbala* (1966; Where Time Goes Astray), and *Hondo Sur* (1968; Deep South). The quality of her poetry, characterized by a simple but poignant lyricism, places her among the best 20th-century women poets in the Spanish language.

An excellent critic of poetry as well, Zardoya has published *Miguel Hernández: vida y obra* (1955), *Poesía española contemporánea* (1961), *Verdad, Belleza y Expresión* (1967; Truth, Beauty, and Expression), and *Poesía española del 98 y del 27* (1968; Spanish Poetry: The Generations of 1898 and 1927). She has also translated Walt Whitman.   E.I.F.

Zawieyski, Jerzy (1902–68), Polish novelist, dramatist, and essayist, was born in Radogoszcza, near Łódź, and died in Warsaw. He began his career in 1926 as an actor with the famed "Reduta" group, founded by Juliusz Osterwa. As a result of his work with this group, he developed a strong interest in the popular theater movement and accepted a post as cultural instructor among Polish emigrants in France (1929–32). He became involved politically after World War II with the Catholic movement in Poland.

A thoroughly educated man of letters, Zawieyski was preoccupied with moral problems and moral values, as well as with psychological and national problems. His writing was inspired by the Catholic philosophy of life. The publication in 1932 of his novel *Gdzie jesteś przyjacielu?* (Where are You, Friend?) marked his debut as a writer. A series of novels followed: *Daleko do rana* (1934; Far from Morning), *Droga do domu* (1946; The Way Home), *Noc Huberta* (1946; Hubert's Night), *Wawrzyny i cyprysy* (1966; Laurels and Cypresses), and *Konrad nie chce zejść ze sceny* (1966; Konrad Won't Leave the Stage), as well as two collections of short stories: *Pokój głębi* (1956; The Peace of the Depths) and *Romans z ojczyzną* (1963; Romance with Motherland). Zawieyski also published a number of plays—*Rozdroże miłości* (1947; Crossroads of Love), *Dzień Sądu* (1947; Judgment Day), *Ocalenie Jakuba* (1947; Jacob's Salvation), *Wysoka ściana* (1956; The High Wall), and others—and essays about philosophy, religion, and literature.

See: *Słownik współczesnych pisarzy polskich*, vol. 3 (1964), pp. 582–89.   E.J.C.

Zech, Paul, pseuds. Paul Robert, Timm Borah (1881–1946), German poet, novelist, and dramatist, was born in Briesen, Rheinland. His adventurous life was always the object of much mystery and controversy. The son of a teacher, he studied in Bonn, Heidelberg, and Zürich, and later he worked for a time in mines and factories. About 1910 he appeared in Berlin, where he published occasional issues of a luxuriously printed and illustrated periodical, *Das neue Pathos* (1913; 23). His own poetry is as eclectic as this periodical and is influenced by Rainer Maria RILKE, Emile VERHAEREN, Arthur RIMBAUD, and the poets of German expressionism. In his poetry he always insisted upon attention to form and mastery of language; he never indulged in the explosive words of the expressionists. Most of his early verses are recollections of his proletarian experience: *Schollenbruch* (1910; Stratum Cave In), *Die eiserne Brücke* (1912; The Iron Bridge), *Das schwarze Revier* (1913; The Black District). This is also true of the short stories published under the title *Der schwarze Baal* (1916; The Black Baal). *Das Grab der Welt* (1918; The Grave of the World) and *Golgotha* (1919) evoke memories of his participation in World War I. Later his poetry embraces larger issues and even strays into cosmic regions, as in: *Das Terzett der Sterne* (1919; The

Tercet of the Stars), *Die Ballade von mir* (1922; The Ballad of Myself), and *Die ewige Dreieinigkeit* (1924; The Eternal Trinity). Among his novels are *Die Reise um den Kummerberg* (1924; The Journey about the Kummerberg), *Das törichte Herz* (1925; The Foolish Heart), *Die Geschichte einer armen Johanna* (1925; The Story of Poor Joan), and *Ich bin du* (1926; I Am You). His most successful experiment in expressionism was the "scenic ballad" *Das trunkene Schiff* (1924; The Drunken Ship), a combination of music, drama, and film, dealing with a Negro revolt in Africa and a storm on the ocean and introducing aspects of Rimbaud's life. Other plays are *Steine* (1919; Stones), *Das Rad* (1924; The Wheel), *Der Turm* (1924; The Tower), *Erde* (1925; Earth), and *Triumph der Söhne* (1925; Triumph of the Sons). When Adolf Hitler came into power, Zech went voluntarily into exile and lived until his death in South America, where he published some volumes of poetry and an autobiographical novel, *Ich suchte Schmied und fand Malva* (1941; I Sought Schmied and Found Malva). Two posthumous works were *Kinder vom Paraná* (1952; Children of Paraná), a novel, and the collection of stories *Die grüne Flöte vom Rio Beni* (1955; The Green Flute of the Beni River).

See: W. B. Lewis, *Poetry and Exile: An Annotated Bibliography of Works and Criticism of Paul Zech* (1975).

K.Pi. rev. A.L.W.

Zegadłowicz, Emil (1888–1941), Polish poet, playwright, and novelist, was born in Bielsk and died in Sosnowiec. Zegadłowicz's literary work is diverse in style and genre and in the convictions it expresses. For many years an author of passionately religious poems and plays, he later turned against the Catholic Church and religion. Similarly, his political attitude underwent a change from that of a conservative to that of a radical leftist. This is reflected most conspicuously in his late novels and plays. Zegadłowicz's drama and poetry are also varied. He published dramatized ballads, imitations of classical drama and of medieval mystery plays, and plays directly reflecting contemporary political topics.

The most significant part of Zegadłowicz's literary work is poetry linked to the region of West Beskids, where he was brought up and where he lived for many years. He made the region the center of the literary group known as "Czartak," which advocated a return to cultural regionalism and folkloristic primitivism along with religious admiration of the native soil and primitive peasantry. These tendencies were reflected most fully in Zegadłowicz's collections of poetry, especially in the large volume of ballads *Dziewanny* (1927; Mullein).

Some of Zegadłowicz's late novels are largely autobiographical. Although not of significant literary merit, they caused much uproar and controversy, particularly *Zmory* (1935; Incubi) and *Motory* (1938; Motors) because of their daring eroticism. *Motory* was even confiscated by the authorities as pornography.

See: W. Studencki, *Twórczość dramatyczna Emila Zegadłowicza* (1962); E. Kozkowski, *Portret Zegadłowicza bez ramy* (1966).

S.S.

Żeleński, Tadeusz (pseud. Boy) (1874–1941), Polish critic, essayist, and translator, was born in Warsaw, the son of Władysław Żeleński, a noted composer. After studying medicine at the Jagiellonian University in Cracow, Boy went to Paris in 1895 and while there came under the influence of the brilliant fin-de-siècle literary movement. While completing his medical studies in Cracow, he found time to establish the soon famous literary cabaret "Zielony Balonik" (Little Green Balloon), an imitation of the Parisian "Chat Noir." For this he himself provided a stream of witty, satirical ditties, skits, and lampoons, which were later published in a series of volumes, among them *Piosenki i fraszki "Zielonego Balonika"* (1908; Ditties and Trifles from the Zielony Balonik) and *Słówka* (1913; Mere Words). Boy's contributions were welcomed by the rebellious "Young Poland" set of Cracow.

Boy did not practice medicine for long, but turned rather to translating, producing in the space of three decades some 120 volumes of translations from the French alone, *Biblioteka Boya* (Boy's Library). Besides rendering into flawless Polish all Molière and most of Honoré de Balzac, this tireless laborer translated also the works of such widely divergent authors as François Villon, Rabelais, Montaigne, René Descartes, Jean Racine, Marivaux, Voltaire, Beaumarchais, Chateaubriand, Stendhal, Paul VERLAINE, Marcel PROUST, and many others, prefacing his translation in each case with an illuminating essay on the author in question. The principal marks of these essays were keen psychological penetration, clever and telling use of anecdotes, and great skill in the evocation of personality. Boy's most notable long studies are his *Molière* (1924), *Pani Hańska* (1925), a lively portrait of Balzac's Evelina, and *Marysieńka Sobieska* (1937), a somewhat unorthodox interpretation of the French wife of the Polish national hero, King John III.

Boy was as deeply versed in Polish as in French literature and in this field as in the French often shattered time-honored interpretations. He did this by a process he himself christened "de-bronzing," which consisted of scraping ruthlessly away from the figures of the great the accumulated patina of tradition, thus exposing all the passions and foibles that lay underneath, as well as all the virtues and true greatness. A major literary tempest was stirred up in the early 1930s when Boy applied this process to Mickiewicz, the great 19th-century romantic poet and patriot, in *Brązownicy,* (1930; Those Who Bronze Over). When the storm had subsided, Boy proceeded to present fresh and revealing sidelights on another great literary figure from the past, namely the dramatist Aleksander Fredro, in *Obrachunki Fredrowskie,* (1934; Settling Scores with Fredro).

Boy was an outstanding dramatic critic. His articles in this field fill many volumes: *Flirt z Melpomeną,* and 7 more volumes under various titles, such as *Romanse cieniów,* (1935; Romances of the Shadows); *Murzyn zrobił . . .* (1939; A Hack's Work . . .). They are invaluable documents for the study of social trends.

A fearless crusader against hypocrisy whether in life or literature, Boy often aroused public sentiment pro and con by his espousal of advanced causes. In *Dziewice konsystorskie* (1929; Virgins before the Bar) he stated the case for divorce and for the marriage of the clergy. In *Piekło kobiet* (1929; Women's Hell) he made a plea for birth control and legalized abortion.

Boy refused to leave Poland when the Germans occupied Warsaw in 1939. He fled to Lvov, at first under Soviet occupation, and there continued to write and translate. With the German occupation of Lvov in 1941, he was arrested together with several other Polish professors and executed.

See: F. L. Schoell, "L'Enfant terrible de la Pologne," *La Pologne* (1931), pp. 580–600; B. Winklowa, *Tadeusz Żeleński (Boy). Twórczość i życie* (1967); S. Sterkowicz, *Tadeusz Boy-Żeleński. Lekarz-pisarz-społecznik* (1974).

H.C. rev. S.F.

Żeromski, Stefan (1864–1925), pseud. Maurycy Zych, Polish short-story writer, dramatist, and the most outstanding prose writer of the "Młoda Polska" period, was born in Strawczyn near Kielce and died in Warsaw. He was descended from an impoverished gentry family that kept alive the tradition of struggle for Poland's independence. He attended the gymnasium in Kielce, where he encountered the absolute Russification policies carried out by the tsarist authorities. Because of financial difficulties, he had to interrupt his studies at the Veterinary Institute in Warsaw. His first collections of short stories and sketches are: *Rozdziobią nas kruki, wrony* (1895; Ravens and Crows Will Pick Our Bones), *Opowiadania* (1895; Short Stories), and *Utwory powieściowe* (1898; Novelettes); they contain themes to which Żeromski returned throughout his literary career, such as the struggle for national independence, the tragic defeats of the national uprisings, a deeply felt sensitivity to social injustice both in the countryside and in the city, and a strong sense of responsibility for evil and injustice. The national question is the topic of Żeromski's autobiographical first novel: *Syzyfowe prace* (1898; Sisyphean Labors). The novel deals with the efforts of the school authorities to Russify students, but Żeromski's belief in the futility of such efforts is indicated in the novel's very title. At the same time, the novel is a penetrating psychological study of the intellectual and patriotic maturation of young people and the awakening of their first emotions. Characteristic features of Żeromski's style and outlook were immediately apparent in his early works: realism combined with naturalism and an expressive lyricism; and a distinctive moral viewpoint based upon strict ethical values, and a mingling of romantic ideals of freedom and romantic heroism with the social theories of positivism. Żeromski's next novel, *Ludzie bezdomni* (1900; Homeless People) crowns his early work; its appearance was both a great literary and national event. The novel's hero, Dr. Judym, feels responsible for poverty and injustice; he sacrifices personal happiness in order to devote himself completely to the struggle with social evil. Judym became the symbol of an uncompromising ethical attitude. The hero's tragic dilemma between his own personal desires and the obligations to the cause of justice forms the plot of the novel. At the same time, *Ludzie bezdomni* portrays various social milieus, such as the proletariat, the professional intelligentsia, and so on. Żeromski treats the subject of struggle for national independence and the participation of Poles in the Napoleonic campaigns in his three-volume historical novel, *Popioły* (1904; Eng. tr., *Ashes*, 1928). The novel opens at the end of the 18th century and closes in the year 1812. Against the background of separate and loosely connected scenes, appears a broad and colorful panorama of Polish life, as well as an immense gallery of characters. The novelist treats armed struggle as a turning point in the nation's consciousness as it rises from its ashes. In addition to its battle scenes portrayed in all the cruelty of naturalism, its portrayal of soldiers' misery, and especially the lot of the peasant whose situation of serfdom remains unchanged despite his heroism, *Popioły* also contains a love plot that is presented with unusual sensual vitality. The poetic nature descriptions in the novel are a feature typical of all Żeromski's work, in which nature often plays a symbolic role. A growing naturalism is evident in the novel's style, emotional lyricism, and poeticized language. Stylized language is particularly apparent in Żeromski's long poems in prose, historical and legendary, such as *Powieść o Udałym Walgierzu* (1905; The Story of Walgierz Udaly), *Duma o hetmanie* (1908; An Elegy on the Hetman). Elements of brutal naturalism appear in the novel *Dzieje grzechu* (1909; A Story of Sin). Żeromski portrays the awakening of the national consciousness in the hero of his novel *Uroda życia* (1912; The Glory of Life). The events of the national uprisings are the subject of the novel *Wierna rzeka* (1912; Eng. tr.,

The Faithful River, 1943), written on the 50th anniversary of the 1863 uprising. Here, against the background of the tragic love of a poor noblewoman for an aristocrat, Żeromski evaluates both the uprising and the social causes of its failure. During 1916 to 1919, Żeromski published his three-volume novel *Walka z szatanem* (Struggle against Satan), in which he returns to the subject of a lonely hero and social reformer who struggles against evil and ends in defeat. Żeromski's last novel is *Przedwiośnie* (1925; Before the Spring). Through a confrontation between the myth of "beautiful glass houses" and the different aspects of reality in the newly reborn state as experienced by the novel's hero, Cezary Baryka, Żeromski portrays the confrontation of a whole generation's dreams about a free and socially just Poland with the complex problems of rebuilding a nation. The novel proposes no solutions; rather, it focuses attention upon the need to search for solutions and warns against dangers which threaten Poland along the road from early spring to the real spring to come. *Wiatr od morza* (1922; Wind from the Sea), a collection of poetic scenes from the history of the Polish coastal lands, and *Puszcza jodłowa* (1925; Fir Forest), a prose poem about the Holy Cross Mountains, the writer's childhood home, are some of Żeromski's last works. Żeromski was also a dramatist; among his early plays are *Róża* (1909; Rose) and *Sułkowski* (1910). During the last years of his life, Żeromski wrote *Ponad śnieg bielszym się stanę* (1919; I'll be Whiter Than Snow), *Biała rękawiczka* (1921; The White Glove), *Turoń* (1923), and the most stageworthy of all his plays, *Uciekła mi przepióreczka* (1924; A Quail Escaped Me), in which Żeromski again presented a hero who devotes himself to social causes. Żeromski was considered the "conscience of Polish literature"; he was able to express burning social and national issues with extraordinary passion. His varied style, shaped by the literary period to which he belonged, is distinguished by great mastery and an unusually rich vocabulary.

See: S. Adamczewski, *Serce nienasycone* (1930); W. Borowy, *O Żeromskim* (1960); A. Hutnikiewicz, *Stefan Żeromski* (1967). S.F.

Zerov, Mykola (1890–1941), Ukrainian critic and poet, was born in Zinkiv and educated in Kiev. Zerov was an outstanding scholar, a professor of literature at Kiev University, and a literary historian, the author of *Nove ukrayinske pysmenstvo* (1924; Modern Ukrainian Literature). He was also a prominent theoretician. In *Do dzherel* (1926, To the Sources), Zerov defended the aesthetic principle of literature and called for an orientation toward Western European and classical literature. Himself an able translator from the Classics (Horace, Vergil, Catullus) as well as the French (Pierre de Ronsard, José Maria de HEREDIA), he valiantly fought against the official policy of promoting cheap literature for the masses. For a time he succeeded in gathering around him a group of kindred scholars and poets—Pavlo Fylypovych, Mykhaylo Dray-Khmara, Maksym RYLSKY, Osvald Burkhardt, and Viktor Petrov—who formed the so-called Neoclassicist group, as well as in attracting the support of some Communist writers of the VAPLITE group (*see* UKRAINIAN LITERATURE). Zerov died in a Soviet concentration camp. Three collections of his poetry were published posthumously in the West: *Sonnetarium* (1948), *Catalepton* (1952), and *Corollarium* (1958). He was partially rehabilitated in the late 1950s and a volume of his selected verse was published in Kiev in 1966. His lectures on the history of Ukrainian literature (in Ukrainian) were first published in Toronto in 1977. G.S.N.L.

Zīverts, Mārtiņš (1903–), Latvian playwright, was born in the district of Mežmuiža and began his career in the 1930s. He went to Sweden in 1944 to escape the Soviet occupation of Latvia; about half of his 50 titles were written abroad despite the limitations of the exile Latvian theater and his own determination to write exclusively for actual performance. Zīverts has directed some of his own plays and acted in many of them. His early comedies, *Āksts* (1938; The Jester), whose protagonist is Shakespeare, *Ķīnas vāze* (1940; The China Vase), and *Minhauzena precības* (1941; The Marriage of Münchhausen), based on an episode in the life of Baron Münchhausen, the famous German liar, have proved to be his most enduring works. *Vara* (1944; Power), dealing with the fall of Mindaugas, the first Lithuanian king, comes closest to being a classical tragedy.

The plays Zīverts wrote in exile have been of necessity adapted to limited facilities—small, ill-equipped, oftentimes rented stages, and a severely restricted number of actors. Among the exile plays, *Kāds, kuŗa nav* (1947; Someone Who Is Not), *Tvans* (1950; Carbon Monoxide), and *Fiasko* (1960; Clown Fiasco) are based on wartime situations; *Rūda* (1960; The Ore), develops an anecdote concerning the discovery of ore deposits in northern Sweden; and *Kurrpurrū* (1962) takes place in Australia, where many of Zīverts's plays have been performed and published. Zīverts classifies his dramas as either "synthetic" (or "scenic") or "analytic," giving preference to and achieving more striking results with the latter category. In the "synthetic" plays, dramatic action unfolds from scene to scene, whereas the "analytic" plays start with a basic situation or premise and proceed to "unravel" it. Most of the latter are one-act plays or extended one-act plays, tightly constructed and observing the classic unities. There is little stage action; conflict is created and tension maintained by the adroit use of dialogue that is terse, witty, and designed more to hide than to reveal.

Zīverts enjoys the unexpected, the paradoxical, even the grotesque. Although he professes to be a nonphilosopher, some of his plays have existentialist overtones. He is today the leading contemporary Latvian playwright both in exile and in Soviet Latvia, although only a few of his earlier plays have been performed there.   V.N.

Zola, Emile (1840–1902), French novelist, dramatist, and critic, was born in Paris, the son of a civil engineer of Italian origin. He spent most of his childhood and adolescence in Aix-en-Provence, but in 1847 he returned to Paris, which was to be his permanent residence. Zola's widowed mother had wanted him to follow in his father's footsteps, but his failure to obtain his baccalaureate made this impossible, freeing him to pursue his true vocation.

At first, Zola leaned heavily on the classics and on Victor Hugo, Jules Michelet, and other first-generation romantics. Their influence is evident in *Contes à Ninon* (1864; Eng. tr., *Stories for Ninon*, 1895) and *La Confession de Claude* (1865; Eng. tr., *Claude's Confession*, 1888). By his late twenties, however, Zola had developed an art, style, and theory of his own, combining elements derived from these older authors with other elements rooted in the avant-garde cultural life of the Second Empire. Guided by his liberal republication principles and his aesthetic conviction that there could be no great art that was not of its own time, he wholeheartedly identified himself with the new scientific, democratic society that he believed he could see emerging in the momentous changes and upheavals of his day. Zola wanted to serve and exalt the forces of progress. He could imagine no more poetic subject than, as he put it in one of his articles, "the immense and grandiose spectacle of this age that is surely in the process of giving birth to a new world." In an effort to reconcile his romantic individualism and idealism with his growing commitment to science-oriented realism, he developed his famous definition of a work of art as "a corner of nature seen through a temperament." Convinced, like many other mid-19th-century thinkers, that man's best hope for salvation lay in science, he arrived at the conception, central to his naturalism (the name he gave to the movement he headed), of the "experimental novelist." By this he meant a novelist who not only exploits science but actually participates in the scientific process, gathering and analyzing human documents, turning fiction into a kind of physiological or sociological laboratory.

In 1868, armed with these ideas, which he had tested in isolated novels such as *Les Mystères de Marseille* (1867; Eng. tr., *The Mysteries of Marseilles*, 1895), *Madeleine Férat* (1868), and *Thérèse Raquin* (1868; Eng. tr., 1886), Zola submitted to his publisher the outline for what would be his major life's work, a series of novels to be based on a physiological study of a large Second-Empire family group and a sociohistorical study of a large Second-Empire family group and a sociohistorical study of the Second Empire itself. Summing up his intentions, he wrote, "I want to portray, at the outset of a century of liberty and truth, a family that cannot restrain itself in its rush to possess all the good things that progress is making available and is derailed by its own momentum, precisely because of the troubled gleams of the moment, the fatal convulsions that accompany the birth of a new world." The series, *Les Rougon-Macquart*, was originally to consist of 10 volumes, but ultimately grew to 20. The first, tracing the family's origins and the repercussions in Provence of the coup d'etat that ushered in the Second Empire, was published in 1871 as *La Fortune des Rougon* (Eng. tr., *The Fortune of the Rougons*, 1886). Thereafter, Zola managed to turn out the remaining volumes at the rate of about one a year. After completing the conclusion, *le Docteur Pascal* (1893; Eng. tr., *Doctor Pascal, or, Life and Heredity*, 1893), he wrote a three-volume sequel, *Les Trois Villes* (The Three Cities)—*Lourdes* (1894; Eng. tr., 1894), *Rome* (1896; Eng. tr., 1896), and *Paris* (1898; Eng. tr., 1898)—concerning the spiritual odyssey of a troubled priest, Pierre Froment, who finally sheds his frock, marries, and is converted to the religion of science. In 1897, Zola began another sequel, a tetralogy, *Les Quatre Evangiles* (The Four Gospels), proclaiming his own "scientiste" gospel of fecundity, work, truth, and justice, while prophetically portraying the glorious 20th century of his dreams. Before he died, however, Zola was able to complete only the first three volumes, *Fécondité* (1899; Eng. tr., *Fruitfulness*, 1900). *Travail* (1901; Eng. tr., *Work*, 1901), and *Vérité* (1903; Eng. tr., *Truth*, 1903).

Zola's enduring power is due, above all, to his very real gifts as a sociologist and historian and to the more obviously artistic and poetic aspects of his genius. In his three series of novels, which together form what must be regarded as a single immense work, he portrays with Homeric vividness and sweep the battle between traditional culture and modern culture. In *La Terre* (1887; Eng. tr., *The Soil*, 1888) and *Le Rêve* (1888; Eng. tr., *The Dream*, 1893), he explored the world of the past as it still existed in his own day. In *La Conquête de Plassans* (1876; Eng. tr., *The Conquest of Plassans; or the Priest in the House*, 1887), he depicted the declining aristocracy and the Church struggling for survival; in *Nana* (1880; Eng. tr., 1880, Zola focused on the whole glittering, corrupt high society of his epoch. He takes his readers into the midst of earthshaking historical events—the rise and fall of regimes, the Franco-Prussian War, and the Paris Commune, as in *La Débâcle* (1892; Eng. tr., *The Downfall*, 1892). He shows the 20th century being born—the rise of modern big business, finance, and industry, in *La Curée* (1871; Eng. tr., *The Rush for the Spoil*, 1886), *Au bonheur des dames* (1883; Eng. tr., *The Ladies' Paradise*, 1883), and *L'Argent* (1891; Eng. tr., *Money*, 1894); the emergence of the modern proletariat, in "*L'Assommoir*" (1877; Eng. trs., *The "Assommoir,"* 1884; *The Dram-Shop*, 1897) and *Germinal* (1885; Eng. tr., *Germinal; or, Master and Man*, 1885); and the birth of modern art in *L'Œuvre* (1886; Eng. tr., *His Masterpiece*, 1886). But he also focuses on the impact of the revolutionary events he relates on the lives of the people caught up in them. He conveys to his readers the suffering of the victims of progress in *La Joie de vivre* (1884; Eng. tr., *How Jolly Life Is*, 1886), but he also depicts the exultation and satisfaction of those who benefited from change, as in *Le Ventre de Paris* (1874; Eng. tr., *Fat and Thin*, 1888) and *Son Excellence Eugène Rougon* (1876; Eng. tr., *His Excellency Eugène Rougon*, 1887). In such major works as *Germinal*, one of the world's great novels, the reader is especially struck not only by Zola's extraordinary dramatic skill, but also by his tendency to transform everything into symbol, his mythopoetic imagination nourished by the Bible and Greco-Roman mythology, his gift for strong, complex, geometrical construction reminiscent of the work of his friend the painter Paul Cézanne.

The better one knows Zola's fiction, furthermore, the more aware one becomes of the great extent to which it is the product of Zola's own social and religious thought. For example, the great emphasis he places on physiology and especially the science of heredity is due to his religious reverence for life (which he equated with God) and his desire to understand the process whereby life eternally renews itself, perpetuating the old forms and inventing new forms in pursuit of its far-off, mysterious goal. A modern Isaiah, he makes his readers see the violent historical occurrences through his own fiery, apocalyptic eyes. Pointing out the social problems that need attention, attacking the enemies of reform, arousing sympathy for the oppressed, combatting the fashionable pessimism of the fin de siècle, glorifying the heroes of progress (especially the scientist), he is as committed to the cause of progress as any of his contemporaries. At the same time—and this is the reason for the curiously unstable, incoherent, often contradictory philosophical and religious vision of reality that emerges from his works as a whole—he is as involved as any of his contemporaries in modern man's quest for faith. Striving endlessly (but never successfully) to combine his lifelong cults of nature, love, life, work, progress, power, and science into a single consistent religious system, Zola embodies better than any other creative writer of his time not only the spiritual and intellectual chaos of the modern age, but also its anguished efforts to work out a new harmony and order.

A tireless worker, he wrote 31 novels, 13 plays and opera librettos, nearly 100 short stories, and a great mass of journalistic articles, many of which still make absorbing reading. He was, among other things, a first-rate art critic, the first major champion of Edouard Manet and the Impressionists.

In 1897, just as the last volume of *Les Trois Villes* was appearing in serial form, Zola was persuaded by friends of Captain Dreyfus, then languishing on Devil's Island, to come to Dreyfus's defense. He fired off a series of articles culminating in a sensational open letter addressed to the President of the Republic and charging the whole War Department with having plotted the condemnation of an innocent man. Published on January 13, 1898, in Georges Clemenceau's newspaper, *L'Aurore*, under the

title "J'accuse" (I Accuse), it accomplished its purpose, which was to force the government to prosecute Zola, thus reopening the Dreyfus case. Zola was twice brought to trial. In July, 1898, in order to escape imprisonment and a fine and—what was more important—to keep the case open, Zola fled to England, where he remained for almost a year. Upon his return to France, he was hailed by Dreyfus's supporters as a hero.

On Sept. 28, 1902, Zola was asphyxiated in his sleep by fumes from a blocked chimney in the bedroom where he was sleeping. At his funeral, Anatole France called him "a moment of the human conscience," and the crowds passing by his coffin shouted "Germinal! Germinal!" In 1908, his remains were transferred to the Panthéon, where they lie next to those of Hugo, his first great literary idol.

See: E. M. Grant, *Emile Zola* (1966); F. J. Hemmings, *Emile Zola* (2d. ed., 1966); J.-A. Bédé, *Emile Zola* (1974).   P.D.W.

Zollinger, Albin (1895–1949), Swiss poet, novelist, and essayist, was born in Rüti, canton Zürich, where he spent his life as a schoolteacher. Zollinger is probably the greatest lyric poet in 20th-century Swiss-German literature. His poetical style shows a genuine relationship to the styles of Georg TRAKL, Gottfried BENN, Wilhelm LEHMANN, and Peter HUCHEL. *Gedichte*, his first volume of poems, was published in 1933, and it was followed by *Sternfrühe* (1936; Dawn of the Stars), *Stille des Herbstes* (1939; Silence of Autumn), and *Haus des Lebens* (1939; House of Life). Zollinger's poetic language stems predominantly from a transcendentalized nature imagery that has strong surrealistic features. He viewed the modest hills surrounding Zürich with great imagination, transforming them into fantastic landscapes in his poem "Die Zimmetinseln" (The Cinnamon Islands), transporting them to Homeric Greece in "Arkadischer Abend" (Arcadian Evening), and even transplanting them to a strange planet in "Die Kanalbauer im Mars" (The Canal Diggers on Mars). According to Max FRISCH, "He [Zollinger] opens windows of language, with views into the miracle of the unexpected, the land of origin of the poetic word." As a novelist, Zollinger sought to continue the tradition of Gottfried KELLER, Jakob SCHAFFNER, and Meinraid INGLIN. Two early works about artists, *Der halbe Mensch* (1929; Half a Man) and *Die große Unruhe* (1939; The Great Restlessness) were followed by Zollinger's most important novels, *Pfannenstiel, Geschichte eines Bildhauers* (1940; Pfannenstiel, The Story of a Sculptor) and *Bohnenblust oder Die Erzieher* (1942; Bohnenblust, or the Educators).

See: P. Häfliger, *Der Dichter Albin Zollinger* (1954); W. Günther, *Dichter der neuren Schweiz*, vol. 1 (1963), pp. 488–535; B. Albrecht, *Die Lyrik Albin Zollingers* (1964); T. Lengborn, *Schriftsteller und Gesellschaft in der Schweiz* (1972).   R.K.

Zoppi, Giuseppe (1896–1952), Swiss poet, short-story writer, novelist, and essayist, was born in Broglio, canton Ticino. Zoppi left his beloved mountains at the age of 11 to enter a religious school near Ascona. He later studied at the University of Fribourg, graduating in 1920 with a thesis on the poetry of Francesco CHIESA. After teaching at gymnasiums in places such as Saint Gallen, Lugano, and Locarno, Zoppi became professor of Italian literature at the Swiss Institute of Technology in Zürich in 1931.

Throughout much of his oeuvre, Zoppi celebrates the candor and simplicity of rustic mountain life. In his first and most successful collection of prose poems, *Il libro dell'Alpe* (1922; The Book of the Alps), set in the mountains where he spent his childhood, Zoppi evokes the desperate adventures and rough life of the shepherds. The idylls and perils of the Alps are also the subject of his only novel, *Dove nascono i fiumi* (1949; Where the Rivers Are Born). In the short stories collected in *Quando avevo le ali* (1925; When I Had Wings), he tells of the easier life down in the valleys. *Il libro dei gigli* (1924; The Lily Book), on the other hand, reflects his teaching experience in Lugano. A collection of short poems in prose, whose intonation recalls Edmondo De Amicis, *Il libro* reveals the poet's tender love for the young and his anxious desire for purity and innocence. The language of Zoppi's poetry is as lucid as that of his prose. His volumes of poetry include *Nuvola bianca* (1923; The White Cloud), *Azzurro sui monti* (1936; Azure on the Mountains), *Quartine dei fiori* (1953; Flower Quatrains), and *Le Alpe* (1957; The Alps). Zoppi was a strong fighter for the *italianità* of the Ticino; some of his writings, notably *Leggende del Ticino* (1928; Legends of Ticino), and *Presento il mio Ticino* (1939; My Ticino), are partly political in nature. He also published essays, an *Antologia della letteratura italiana* (1939–43; Anthology of Italian Literature), and translations of works by such writers as Charles-Ferdinand RAMUZ and Conrad Ferdinand Meyer.

See: G. Calgari, *Le quattro letterature della Svizzera* (1958).   H.W.H.

Zorin, Leonid Genrikovich (1924–), Russian dramatist, was born in Baku and studied literature at Azerbaijn University and the Gorky Literary Institute in Moscow. His early plays, written during the 1940s, were performed in Baku. Later works, notably *Molodost* (1949; Youth), *Otkrovenny razgovor* (1953; A Frank Conversation), *Chempiony* (1955; Champions) and almost a play a year thereafter were performed in Moscow. Typically, Zorin renders contemporary situations in rapid, laconic interchange; thus *Druzya i gody* (1961; Friends and Years) is a 30-year panorama of characters from school graduation (1934) through World War II and the postwar years. In *Dekabristy* (1967; The Decembrists), written to commemorate the 50th anniversary of the October Revolution, he underlined the conflict of conscience inherent in revolution, whereas in *Varshavskaya melodiya* (1971; Eng. tr., A Warsaw Melody, 1968), he dramatized the hardship of a Soviet citizen's inability to marry a foreigner. Their "problem" interest and their viability as vehicles for ideas have led to the frequent production of Zorin's plays on the Soviet stage.   M.L.H.

Zoshchenko, Mikhail Mikhaylovich (1895–1958), Russian humorist, was born in Poltava, in the Ukraine. His father, a Ukrainian nobleman, was a painter; his mother, née Surina, had been an actress. In 1904 the family moved to Petersburg, which became his permanent home. After finishing the gymnasium he matriculated in law at the university there, but World War I had begun and before completing the course he volunteered for military service. In 1915 he was commissioned and sent to the front. During two years of fighting he was decorated and also wounded and gassed, with permanent damage to his health. In 1917 he served briefly as commandant of the Petrograd post office. The next year he volunteered for the Red Army. Demobilized in 1919, he passed through a kaleidoscopic succession of diverse jobs.

Zoshchenko began writing stories in 1920, and his first book appeared in 1921. His stories were immensely successful with the reading public, and he became the most popular living writer next to Maksim GORKY. He associated himself with the Serapion Brothers (*see* RUSSIAN LITERATURE), a group of writers who tried to assert the

independence of art from politics, and remained loyal to that principle as long as he could. In his stories, Zoshchenko's skeptical and ironic view of human life, and especially of any regime's ability to transform human nature, is camouflaged by his use of interposed narrators, typically semieducated men in the street obviously not to be identified with the author. Zoshchenko's trademark genre was the short-short story deriving situational humor from the many incongruities of everyday Soviet life; his focus on mundane realities proved a refreshing antidote to Communist bombast. He also wrote several more conventionally literary novellas, of which the most substantial is *Michel Sinyagin* (1930; Eng. tr., 1961).

During the 1930s, Zoshchenko came under increasing pressure to write in a more "Soviet" spirit. His subsequent work divides into two classes; serious, ideologically "correct" works; and ambiguous ones in which he contrived to pursue his own artistic bents. Among the former are a story about the transformation in a labor camp of a criminal into a useful citizen; a satirical biography of Aleksandr Kerensky; and some saccharine children's stories about Vladimir Lenin. Much more interesting are the ambiguous works: *Vozvrashchonnaya molodost* (1933; Youth Restored) and *Golubaya kniga* (1935; The Blue Book), in which he sought to create a new literary form, presenting a theoretical argument in which fictional stories are introduced as illustrations. *Vozvrashchonnaya* is ostensibly a treatise on senescence, "illustrated" by a tale about an aging professor who runs off with his neighbor's young wife; *Golubaya kniga*, also "illustrated," is a discussion of the effect on history of such "forces" as money, love, and perfidy. There are clearly parodic elements in both works, but the line between seriousness and mockery is intentionally unclear. In 1943, Zoshchenko published the first part of another "research" work, *Pered voskhodom solntsa* (Eng. tr., *Before Sunrise*, 1974), a search for the causes of his own unhappiness. For such outrageous subjectivism in time of war, Zoshchenko was censured and publication of the work halted (the remainder appeared only in 1972).

In 1946, Zoshchenko was singled out, together with Anna AKHMATOVA, as sacrificial victims for demonstrating the new, toughened party line. Iosif Stalin's satrap Andrey Zhdanov delivered a vituperative attack on him, and he was expelled from the Union of Soviet Writers. Unable to publish original work, he lived thereafter by translating. After Stalin's death he was gradually rehabilitated. New editions of his stories were published, but he did not succeed in producing much significant new work. Besides his fiction, Zoshchenko also wrote plays, such as "Parusinovy portfel" (1944; The Canvas Briefcase), an adaptation of a famous short story; and film scenarios such as "Soldatskoye schastye" (1943; Soldier's Luck).

See: R. A. Domar, "The Tragedy of a Soviet Satirist," in *Through the Glass of Soviet Literature*, ed. by E. J. Simmons (New York, 1953), pp. 201–43; V. Von Wiren, "Zoshchenko in Retrospect," *RusR* (October 1962): 348–61; H. McLean, Introduction to M. Zoshchenko, *Nervous People* (New York, 1963).   H.McL.

Zuckmayer, Carl (1896–1977), German poet, novelist, and playwright, was born at Nackenheim on the Rhine, the son of a manufacturer. He attended school in Mainz until 1914 and spent four years serving with German troops in World War I, followed by study of the natural sciences at Heidelberg. A member of the young radical literati after the war, Zuckmayer devoted his formative years to writing. The German inflation of the 1920s forced him to try all kinds of work. After having been a play reader for the Reinhardt theaters he wrote the hilarious comedy *Der fröhliche Weinberg* (1925; The Merry Vineyard), which brought him the Kleist Prize and the dislike of the Nazi Party. Zuckmayer settled down to an industrious career, not far from Salzburg. A drama about Germany's famous outlaw *Schinderhannes* (1927) proved a literary success. German prewar militarism was satirized in *Der Hauptmann von Köpenick* (1931; Eng. tr., *The Captain of Köpenick*, 1932), which was filmed twice. His antiwar feelings were expressed in a number of adaptations: *Rivalen* (1929), from the American play *What Price Glory* by Maxwell Anderson and Laurence Stallings, and *Kat* (1931), a dramatization of Ernest Hemingway's novel *A Farewell to Arms*. Since Zuckmayer's plays abound in action, they found their way into films, and the dramatist had a number of successful movie scenarios to his credit. When the political flood reached his mountain home and Hitler overran Austria in 1938, Zuckmayer escaped via Switzerland and France to the United States.

Zuckmayer's prose works never attained the success of his plays: *Der Bauer aus dem Taunus* (1929; The Peasant from the Taunus), *Die Affenhochzeit* (1932; The Monkey Wedding), *Salvare oder die Magdalene von Bozen* (1936; Eng. tr., *The Moons Ride Over,* 1937), *Herr über Leben und Tod* (1928; Lord of Life and Death). Recollections in autobiographical form under the title *Second Wind* (1940; in English only) tell a vivid story of Zuckmayer's career and his finding a haven in the green hills of Vermont on Backwoods Farm near Barnard. The title was prophetic, for the dramatist soon produced new works, such as the world success *Des Teufels General* (1946; The Devil's General) about a recalcitrant Luftwaffe pilot. *Barbara Blomberg* (1948) was followed by *Der Gesang im Feuerofen* (1951; Song in the Fiery Furnace) and the drama on the building of the atomic bomb among the New Mexico hills in Los Alamos, *Das kalte Licht* (1955; The Cold Light). A comedy about circus life, *Katharina Knie* (1960), was followed by *Die Uhr schlägt eins* (1961; The Clock Strikes One). After 1951, Zuckmayer traveled repeatedly to Europe while still living in Vermont, until in 1958 he moved to Saas-Fee in the canton of Wallis in Switzerland. The drama *Das Leben des Horace A. W. Tabor* (1964; The Life of Horace A. W. Tabor) was followed by a play about the pied piper of Hamlin, *Der Rattenfänger* (1975; The Rat Catcher). Zuckmayer's autobiographical work *Als wär's ein Stück von mir* (1966; Eng. tr., *A Part of Myself*), a title from a line from a pacifist poem, is a poignant but proud record of a rich and dramatic life. His poems, little noticed, were collected in 1968.

See: R. Lange, *Carl Zuckmayer* (1969); A. Bauer, *Carl Zuckmayer* (1976); T. Ayck, *Carl Zuckmayer in Selbstzeugnissen und Bildokumenten* (1977).

H.Bf. rev. A.L.W.

Żukrowski, Wojciech (1916–), Polish novelist, short-story writer, and journalist, was born in Cracow. He studied Polish philology at the Jagiellonian University. During World War II, he took part in the September 1939 campaign in Poland and later, during the German occupation, he was involved in the underground movement. During the period 1953–60, Żukrowski spent a few years in Vietnam (as a war correspondent), in China, and in India (as a diplomat). In 1946 he published a collection of short stories, *Z kraju milczenia* (From the Land of Silence), containing realistic, vivid narratives about the September campaign and the German occupation. This theme returns in such later books as *Dni klęski* (1952; Days of Defeat) and *Skąpani w ogniu* (1961; Trial by Fire). *Porwanie w Tiutiurlistanie* (1946; Abduction in Tiutiurlistan) and

Piórkiem flaminga (1947; With a Flamingo Feather) are, however, written in a different style, that of the fantastic tale. Several collections of reportage and short stories resulted from his trips to Asia. These include *Wędrówki z moim Guru* (1960; Rambles with My Guru), *Ognisko w dżungli* (1955; Hearth in the Jungle), *Nieśmiały narzeczony* (1964; The Shy Fiancé), and *Szczęściarz* (1967; The Lucky Fellow). *Okruchy z weselnego tortu* (1958; Crumbs from a Wedding Cake) is a collection of short stories containing reminiscences from Żukrowski's childhood. The novel *Kamienne tablice* (1966; Stone Tablets) is set in the Hungarian embassy in India during the uprising in Hungary in 1956. In this work, Żukrowski presents the political and moral conflicts of both Poland and Hungary during that period.

See: *Słownik współczesnych pisarzy polskich*, vol. 3 (1964), pp. 635–40; Z. Lichniak, *Dokoła Wojtka. Rzecz o Wojciechu Żukrowskim* (1963). A.Z.

Zunzunegui, Juan Antonio (1901–), Spanish novelist and short-story writer, was born in Portugalete, in the province of Bilbao, and educated by the Jesuits at the Colegio de Orduña. He studied philosophy and letters and law in Deusto and Salamanca, where he was a pupil of Miguel de UNAMUNO, who encouraged his interest in Portuguese literature. In 1924 he pursued his studies in France and Italy. Zunzunegui was elected to the Royal Spanish Academy of the Language in 1957.

In 1926 he published his first work, *Vida y paisaje de Bilbao* (Life and Landscape of Bilbao), a series of sketches of the life of Bilbao. His first important novels, however, were *Chiripi* (1931; The Lucky One) and *El Chiplichandle* (1940; Ship Chandler). In the former he satirized the immoral social climate of Bilbao, and in the latter he projected his criticism onto Spanish society as a whole.

In his second phase, Zunzunegui's pessimism and sarcastic humor are directed against the corruption of Bilbao's oligarchy. The major works of this period are *¡Ay . . . estos hijos!* (1943; Oh, These Children), *El barco de la muerte* (1945; The Ship of Death), and *La quiebra* (1947; The Failure). *Las ratas del barco* (1950; The Ship Rats) deals with the crisis brought about by the Spanish Civil War. *El supremo bien* (1951; The Highest Good) recounts the history of the incorporation of a family of humble background into the bourgeoisie in the course of three generations, between 1880 and 1930. This novel is reminiscent of Benito PÉREZ GALDÓS in its detailed and scrupulous description of customs and the development of an individual destiny through different generations. *Esta oscura desbandada* (1952; This Dark Disorder) centers on the decadence and final dissolution of a middle-class family in the moral and economic crisis of the postwar years. *La vida como es* (1954; Life As It Is) is a portrait of Madrid's underworld. Unfortunately, Zunzunegui does not commit himself to the reality he describes, and his character development is thus rather shallow.

The rest of this prolific writer's production conforms to conventional realism. The prose is full of minutiae and digressions corresponding to a conservative and fatalistic attitude in which the author imposes his interpretation of reality in an antidialectical manner.

See: D. Carbonell Basset, *La novelística de Juan Antonio Zunzunegui* (1965). J.O.

Župančič, Oton (1878–1949), Slovenian poet, was born in the town of Vinica, which until 1918 was in Austria. Although he wrote in a language used by one of the smallest nations in Europe, he nevertheless won international attention and became the best-known figure of

20th-century Slovenian poetry. Župančič's parents were peasants of better than average means. After completing his gymnasium education in Ljubljana, the cultural center of Slovenia, he studied history and geography for four years at the University of Vienna and then continued these studies in Paris. In 1920 he was appointed to the important post of art director and manager of the National Dramatic Theater in Ljubljana. For many years he was also head of the Institute of French Studies in that city.

While still at the gymnasium, Župančič began to write little poems about childhood, full of simple charm and unusual insight into the innocently mischievous spirit of the very young. In 1900 he published a collection of these early poems entitled *Pisanice* (Easter Eggs). Ten years later, as a mature artist, he returned to this type of poetry, writing for and about his own children. In 1915 he published two collections of this verse—which may be read as pleasurably by adults as by children—*Ciciban in še kaj* (Ciciban and a Thing or Two Besides) and *Sto ugank* (100 Riddles).

Župančič's first book of poems, *Čaša opojnosti* (1899; Cup of Intoxication), was a derivative volume, betraying the influence of the symbolism and decadence of Central and Western European literature. But by 1910 he had begun to abandon exoticism and artificiality, achieving his poetic maturity through doubt, unhappiness, and self-examination. He began to confront his own personal problems and those of his hard-pressed nation with a strange sort of calmness that was much more stirring and stimulating to him than had been his former symbolic hints of doom. His thoughts became confident, almost optimistic; his passions, controlled. His poetic form achieved a firm lyricism that is a pleasure to read and that also provides the reader with a stimulating intellectual experience. Through his verse, Župančič became a moral force in the life of his people—a source of patriotic thought and feeling, a stabilizing, yet not conservative, influence. His vision of this as the role of the poet became especially clear in *V zarje Vidove* (1920; Toward the Dawn of Saint Vitus's Day).

In 1924, Župančič published his only play, *Veronika Deseniška* (Veronica of Desenice), a tragedy in verse that failed both as poetry and as drama and indicated that his creative talent lay largely in the short lyric. After this experiment, Župančič attempted no new genres. He revised his works, which began to appear in Ljubljana in a four-volume edition in 1935, and he translated into superb Slovenian all of the major Shakespeare plays, several novels by John Galsworthy, and other works from English and Russian literature.

As art director of the National Theater, Župančič insisted that actors speak naturally, in the manner of the plain people, even when portraying educated characters. This emphasis, coupled with the widespread reading of his own naturally idiomatic poetry, worked against the artificiality and affectation that were then all too common in the Slovenian speech of the educated classes. In other respects, too, Župančič's poetry has played an important role in Slovenian national life. Although most of his poetry was written many years before the outbreak of World War II, it nevertheless was an inspiration for the Slovenian Resistance movement. While Župančič himself did not participate actively in the Resistance, the poetry that he did write during the war makes it clear that his sympathies were totally on the side of the Partisans.

See: A. Cronia, *Ottone Župančič* (1928); J. Vidmar, *Oton Župančič* (1935); J. Mahnič, *Oton Župančič* (1955) and *Obdobji Moderne* (1964), pp. 148–201.

L.A. rev. W.B.E. and A.K.

Zweig, Arnold (1887–1968), German novelist and essayist, was born in Groß-Glogau, Silesia, of a Jewish middle-class family. Master of a superior-ironic style and of an apparently innocent approach to daring situations, he showed at first an interest in aesthetic mastery of the delicate and refined problems typical not of the great masses but of a thin layer of intellectuals. His initial success was *Novellen um Claudia* (1912; Eng. tr., *Claudia*, 1930), short stories that depict the suffering of a young woman from supersensitiveness and inhibitions and the final toilsome conquest of these through instinctive, natural forces. Zweig also showed a predilection for the experiences of young people, detached with an air of benevolent irony but obviously enamored of the world of youth.

World War I turned Zweig away from his preoccupation with the problems of modern intellectualism. It gave substance and ethos to his work and made him the author of one of the greatest war novels, *Der Streit um den Sergeanten Grischa* (1927; Eng. tr., *The Case of Sergeant Grischa*, 1927), published as the central panel of a projected "triptych" intended to give a broad picture and criticism of the war as it resulted from and reacted upon a class-torn, capitalistic society. The series included three additional novels: *Junge Frau von 1914* (1931; Eng. tr., *Young Woman of 1914*, 1932), *Erziehung vor Verdun* (1935; Eng. tr., *Education before Verdun*, 1936), and *Einsetzung eines Königs* (1937; Eng. tr., *The Crowning of a King*, 1938), in which the individual is always the center of interest; from him start all approaches to the problems raised by the war. Community values are recognized in terms of social class and a future socialist society, although references to racial affinities appear not infrequently. A transcendental law is conceived within the teachings of the Torah.

The story of the Russian sergeant, Grischa, who falls victim to a power-intoxicated Prussian war machine, is Zweig's best. While presenting a sequence of events in a well-knit plot, he depicts at the same time the social organism of the German army. Various classes and types appear, from the common man in the labor service to the commander-in-chief himself. The flight of a Russian prisoner, his adventures, recapture, trial, and death sentence as a result of mistaken identity, the establishment of his innocence, and his final judicial murder, make up the plot. It leads with inevitable logic through the various military strata, which thereby become the colorful milieu of a strong narrative.

Here as well as in other novels, Zweig's mastery of form controls his creative imagination. Freedom of poetic disposition is tempered by his knowledge of persons and situations. Genuine sympathy for suffering humanity is coupled with objective realism. His presentation has that degree of inner probability that reports, describes, and entertains and creates in the reader a true basis for a vicarious experience.

When Zweig was driven out of Germany, the manuscript of *Erziehung vor Verdun* was destroyed, and it had to be rewritten while he struggled against serious eye disease. After living in Palestine during the Hitler years, which is the setting of his novel *De Vriendt kehrt heim* (1933; Eng. tr., *De Vriendt Goes Home*, 1933), he returned to East Berlin in 1948. Successful also as an essayist and editor, Zweig was an active Zionist. An account of the Jewish contribution to modern German culture is given in *Bilanz der deutschen Judenheit 1933* (1934; Eng. tr., *Insulted and Exiled*, 1937). His novel *Das Beil von Wandsbeck* (1947; Eng. tr., *The Axe of Wandsbeck*, 1946), deals with the Third Reich and was published in English translation in England before it appeared in German. Four novels appeared after the war: *Verklungene Tage* (1950; Days Gone By), *Die Feuerpause* (1954; The Fire Pause), *Die Zeit ist reif* (1957; The Time Is Ripe), and *Traum ist teuer* (1962; Dream Is Expensive). Stories in *Spielzeug der Zeit* (1933; Eng. tr., *Playthings of Time*, 1935) were followed by others, some of which are collected in English translation in *A Bit of Blood and Other Stories* (1961).

See: E. Kaufmann, *Arnold Zweigs Weg zum Roman* (1967); E. Hilscher, *Arnold Zweig: Leben und Werk* (1968); G. Salamon, *Arnold Zweig* (1975).

W.K.P. rev. A.L.W.

Zweig, Stefan (1881–1942), Austrian biographer, dramatist, essayist, and story writer, was born in Vienna of a rich Jewish family. As a gymnasium student, Zweig absorbed the artistic and literary atmosphere of the metropolis, and he began gathering the autographs and manuscripts that grew into a world-famous collection. His earliest essays were accepted by the Zionist leader Theodor Herzl, literary editor of the *Neue Freie Presse*. Aside from his own works, Zweig established an international reputation as the translator of Paul VERLAINE, Charles BAUDELAIRE, and Emile VERHAEREN.

Zweig's pacifist philosophy was shared by Romain ROLLAND, with whom he envisioned a Europe united by humanitarian ideals. The antiwar drama *Jeremias* (1917; Eng. tr., *Jeremiah*, 1922) was written while Zweig was still in the army and brought a message of peace to a world wearied by war. A tireless traveler and lecturer, Zweig counted among his friends Maksim GORKY, Walther Rathenau, Rainer Maria RILKE, Auguste Rodin, Arturo Toscanini, and Sigmund Freud. The influence of the latter is evident in much of Zweig's writings.

In 1930, Zweig was considered the world's most translated author. Especially popular are the "historical miniatures" *Sternstunden der Menschheit* (1927; Eng. tr., *The Tide of Fortune*, 1955), which depicted critical moments that shaped history. His biographical studies of Stendhal, Honoré de Balzac, Charles Dickens, Friedrich Hölderlin, Heinrich von Kleist, Friedrich NIETZSCHE, Lev TOLSTOY, and others have been collected in *Baumeister der Welt* (1934; Eng. tr., *Master Builders*, 1939). Major biographies include *Marie Antoinette* (1932; Eng. tr., 1952), *Erasmus von Rotterdam* (1934; Eng. tr., *Right to Heresy*, 1951), and *Maria Stuart* (1935; Eng. tr., *The Queen of Scots*, 1950). Zweig's investigation into the lives of Franz Mesmer, Mary Baker Eddy, and Sigmund Freud is described in *Die Heilung durch den Geist* (1931; Eng. tr., *Mental Healers*, 1932). It is Zweig's vivid characterization of his subjects and their foibles, his probing of their minds with Freudian insight, that distinguishes him from other contemporary European writers.

On the stage, Zweig met success with his adaptation of Ben Jonson's plays *Volpone* (1925) and *Epicoene*, the libretto of which appeared as *Die schweigsame Frau* (1935; Eng. tr., *The Silent Woman*, n.d.), with music by Richard Strauss. The opera was banned by the Nazis after its premiere. Zweig was a master in the genre of the novella; his best stories appear in *Amok* (1922; Eng. tr., 1931) and *Verwirrung der Gefühle* (1927; Eng. tr., *Conflicts*, 1927). His last story, *Schachnovelle* (1942; Eng. tr., *The Royal Game*, 1945), analyzes the psychology of racial victimization.

Zweig's autobiography *Die Welt von gestern* (1944, first published in English as *The World of Yesterday*, 1943), written in his South American exile, is a work that will continue to be read for its elegiac longing for the Europe that was destroyed in 1914. His marriage to Friderike von Winternitz, a novelist in her own right, ended in divorce. Longing for the Europe to which he could never return, "exhausted by long years of homeless wanderings," and despairing over the fate of European Jewry, Zweig, with his second wife, Charlotte E. Altmann, committed suicide in Petropolis, Brazil.

See: R. J. Klawitzer, *Stefan Zweig: A Bibliography* (1965); E. Allday, *Stefan Zweig: A Critical Biography* (1972); D. A. Prater, *European of Yesterday: A Biography of Stefan Zweig* (1972).

K.S.M.